Contents at a Glance

Contents

About the Author

MICHAEL KOFLER EARNED HIS PH.D. in computer science at Graz Technical University. He has written a number of successful computer books on topics such as Visual Basic, Linux, Mathematica, and Maple. Kofler is also the author of *Definitive Guide to Excel VBA, Second Edition*, published by Apress.

About the Translator

DAVID KRAMER EARNED HIS PH.D. in mathematics at the University of Maryland, and his M.A. in music at Smith College. For many years he worked in academia, first as a professor of mathematics and computer science, and later as a director of academic computing. Over the past eight years he has edited hundreds of books in mathematics and the sciences, and has translated a number of books in a variety of fields, including *Definitive Guide to Excel VBA*, by Michael Kofler; *Enterprise JavaBeans 2.1*, by Stefan Denninger and Ingo Peters; and *Cryptography in C and C++*, by Michael Welschenbach, all published by Apress. Other translations include *The Game's Afoot! Game Theory in Myth and Paradox*, by Alexander Mehlmann; the children's musical *Red Riding! Red Riding!*, by Ernst Ekker with music by Sergei Dreznin; *In Quest of Tomorrow's Medicines*, by Jürgen Drews; and the novel *To Err Is Divine*, by Ágota Bozai, which will be published by Counterpoint Press in April 2004.

Preface

MYSQL IS THE MOST WIDELY used database system in the Open Source sector. There are many reasons why this is so:

- MySQL is fast.

- MySQL is stable.

- MySQL is easy to learn.

- MySQL runs on popular operating systems (Windows, Linux, Mac OS X, various flavors of Unix).

- MySQL applications can be created in a great variety of programming languages (such as C, C++, C#, Java, Perl, PHP, Python, VB, and VB.NET).

- MySQL is extensively documented on the Internet, and there are many books on the subject available.

- MySQL is available for many applications free of charge (GPL license).

- Since the licensing restrictions of GPL are unacceptable for many commercial applications, there are reasonably priced commercial licenses and optional support contracts.

MySQL is on the verge of repeating in the database market the success achieved by Linux in the operating system sector. In combination with PHP or Perl, MySQL is providing the database system for more and more web sites. (A favorite combination is Linux + Apache + MySQL + Perl or PHP. Such systems are called "LAMP systems" for short.) MySQL is not just for small web sites; it is used by large firms with huge amounts of data, such as Yahoo!, Slashdot, and Google.

What Does This Book Offer?

This book provides a complete application- and example-oriented introduction to the database system MySQL. No previous knowledge, either of SQL or database design, is assumed.

The introductory Part I of the book begins with an extensive introduction on installation under Windows and Linux. We also consider the installation of components that are used in combination with MySQL (Apache, PHP, phpMyAdmin, Perl, Connector/MyODBC). Building on this, our first example will show the basic use of MySQL and PHP.

Part II, "Fundamentals," provides a large amount of background material on the use of various user interfaces, on the database language SQL, on the proper design of databases, on the use of InnoDB tables, on the access system of MySQL, and on many other topics on administration (such as backups, logging, and replication).

In Part III, "Programming," we emphasize the language PHP: Three chapters cover basic techniques of programming and show how to construct two extensive examples (bookkeeping, a discussion forum). Most of the PHP examples can be tried out live on my web site. We deal with other programming languages, too, with chapters devoted to Perl, Java, C/C++, and VB/VB.NET/C#.

We end the main text with a reference section (Part IV) that provides an overview of the SQL commands of MySQL, the commands and options of the administrative tools, and the functions of important programming interfaces (PHP, Perl, C, Java).

Finally, there are several appendices, comprising (A) a glossary of terms, (B) breaking news on the forthcoming MySQL version 4.1, (C) information on the example files for this book (available at www.apress.com), and (D) a bibliography with suggestions for further reading.

In combination with the example databases and programs, this book should provide a good foundation for the development of your own database applications. In this I wish you much fun and success.

Michael Kofler, August 2003
<mysql@kofler.cc>
http://www.kofler.cc/mysql

What Is New in the Second Edition?

There is much that is new. This book has been completely revised, from the first page to the last. (It took as long to produce this second edition as to write the first edition from scratch!) The following list indicates the most important changes:

- **MySQL:** The book now covers MySQL 4.0 and to some extent MySQL 4.1. These changes appear throughout the entire book, from installation to the reference section to the appendixes.

- **User interface:** This book describes the new user interface MySQL Control Center and the latest version of phpMyAdmin.

- **SQL recipes:** There is a new chapter in the introduction on SQL that provides answers to frequently asked SQL questions: How can I process the first/last *n* data records? How can duplicate records be located? How are sub*SELECT* commands formed in MySQL 4.0 and 4.1? How can a full-text search be accomplished efficiently?

- **InnoDB tables, transactions, rules for integrity:** A new chapter is devoted to the InnoDB table format. InnoDB tables enable the execution of transactions with *row level locking* and the protection of the integrity of relations between tables (foreign key constraints).

- **Security, access rights:** Chapter 9 deals with all the innovations dealing with access rights (MySQL privileges). A new section gives a number of practical tips on solving problems with establishing connections.

- **Administration:** Everything related to administration is contained in a single clearly structured chapter. New sections deal with the administration of InnoDB tables and server tuning (including Query Cache).

- **PHP:** All PHP examples have been reworked in PHP 4.3. The HTML code generated from the PHP examples is now largely XHMTL compatible. The PHP text has been divided over four chapters and is now more clearly structured. In Chapter 11, on techniques of PHP programming, we now also deal with storing images (file upload/download).

- **Java:** A new chapter describes programming of Java and JSP applications on the basis of JDBC and Connector/JDBC.

- **C/C++:** A new chapter discusses the development of C and C++ programs.

- **VB6:** A new example program demonstrates the use of BLOBs.

- **VB.NET, C#:** A new section in Chapter 17 deals with the development of ADO.NET applications with the programming languages VB.NET and C#.

- **Reference:** The three reference chapters have been thoroughly brought up to date and expanded with new sections (C functions, JDBC classes).

- **MySQL 4.1:** Appendix B brings together all known changes in MySQL 4.1: improved character set support (including Unicode), the use of sub*SELECT*s, the management of geometric and geographic data (GIS), the use of precompiled commands (*prepared statements*), etc.

What Does This Book Not Offer?

Several chapters in this book deal with the programming of MySQL applications in a variety of programming languages, such as PHP, Perl, C, C++, Java, and Visual Basic. These chapters assume that the reader is familiar with the specific programming language. (There is simply no room in this book to offer an introduction to a number of programming languages.) In other words, you will profit from, say, the PHP chapter in this book only if you are already familiar with the programming language PHP.

Example Programs, Source Code

To the extent that we are dealing with web applications, almost all of the applications in this book can be tried out directly on my website (www.kofler.cc). The source code for all the examples is available at www.apress.com in the downloads section.

In the longer program listings in this book you will find at the beginning of the example a comment line that specifies the file name appearing in the example files on the web site, for example,

```
<!-- php-programming/simpleinput.php -->
```

To save space, sometimes only the most interesting passages in the program code are printed.

Versions

The functionality of MySQL and of the programs, programming languages, and libraries placed in its environment changes with every new version—which sometimes appear weekly. The following overview indicates which versions I have worked with (explanations of the various names will appear at appropriate places in the book):

- **Apache:** Versions 1.3.n and 2.0.n.

- **Connector/J:** Version 3.0.6.

- **Connector/ODBC (formerly MyODBC):** Version 3.51.06.

- **gcc:** Version 3.2

- **Java:** Version 1.4.1 (Windows) and 1.3.1 (Linux).

- **JSP:** see Tomcat.

- **Linux:** MySQL and other programs were tested for this book under Linux and Windows. Under Linux, the distributions Red Hat 8.0 and 9.0 (beta 3) and SuSE 8.1 and 8.2 (beta 5) were used.

- **MySQL:** Version 4.0.14. In most of the example programs, however, compatibility with MySQL 3.23.n was taken into account, since this version is still in use by many Internet service providers. On the other hand, the latest developments of MySQL 4.1 were tested with a development version (alpha version, from end of July 2003), as described in Appendix B.

- **Connector/C++:** Version 1.7.9.

- **Perl:** Versions 5.6 and 5.8.

- **PHP:** Versions 4.2 and 4.3. As file identifier, the suffix *.php is generally used.

- **phpMyAdmin:** Version 2.4.

- **Tomcat:** Version 4.0.4 (Java Servlet 2.2, Java Server 1.1).

- **Visual Basic, VBA, ADO:** Visual Basic programs were developed and tested with VB6 and VBA6 and ADO versions 2.1 and 2.7.

- **Visual Basic .NET, C#, ADO.NET, ASP.NET:** All of these are based on Visual Studio .NET 2002 (.NET Framework 1.0).

- **Windows:** All tests under Windows were carried out with Windows 2000. In principle, everything should be valid for Windows NT 4, Windows XP, and future versions of Windows.

Notation

- SQL commands and functions, as well as methods, classes, and key words in SQL, C, Java, PHP, Perl, VB, etc., generally appear in italic (e.g., *SELECT*, *mysql_query*). (Note, however, that when the background text is italic, as in the gray "Remark," "Tip," "Caution," and "Pointer" boxes and some section headings, *such commands and functions will appear in a* roman *font; e.g.*, SELECT.)

- Unix/Linux user names also appear in italic (e.g., *root*, *mysql*).

- MENU COMMANDS USE CAPS AND SMALL CAPS (e.g., FILE | OPEN).

- Keyboard shortcuts use a monospace font (e.g., Shift+Delete).

- File and directory names also use the monospace font (e.g., /usr/local or C:\Windows).

- Programs and programming commands are in the monospace font as well (e.g., mysql or cmd.exe).

- MySQL options and configuration parameters appear in regular roman type (e.g., default-charset).

- Program listings and command line input appear in a sans serif font.

SQL commands are generally written in UPPERCASE letters. This is not a syntactic necessity, but merely a convention. MySQL does not distinguish between uppercase and lowercase in interpreting SQL commands.

In specifying Windows directories, we will often not write out the absolute path, since it depends in any case on the particular installation. We observe the following conventions:

- \Windows\ means the Windows directory (e.g., C:\Windows or D:\WinNT4).

- Programs\ means the directory under Windows for program installation (e.g., C:\Programs or D:\Program Files).

- Mysql\ means the MySQL installation directory (e.g., C:\Mysql or D:\Program Files\Mysql).

Commands

Many commands will be presented in this book. We will be moving back and forth between the Unix/Linux and Windows conventions. The following two commands are equivalent:

```
root# mysqladmin -u root -h localhost password xxx
> mysqladmin -u root -h localhost password xxx
```

In each case we have given the system prompt (root# for Unix/Linux and > for Windows). You type in only what follows the prompt (here in **boldface type**). Under Unix/Linux it is possible to divide long inputs over several lines. The lines are separated by means of the backslash symbol \. We shall often use this convention in this book. The following command thus corresponds to the command above:

```
root#   mysqladmin -u root -h localhost \
        password xxx
```

In each case, *xxx* is to be replaced by the relevant text (in this example by your password). We have indicated that *xxx* is dummy text by the use of a slant font.

Abbreviations

I have attempted in this book to make as little use of abbreviations as possible. However, there are several abbreviations that will be used repeatedly without being introduced anew in each chapter:

ADO	Active Data Objects (Microsoft database library)
BLOB	Binary Large Object (binary data block)
GPL	GNU Public License (important license for Open Source software)
HTML	HyperText Markup Language (format for describing web documents)
InnoDB	Not an abbreviation, but the name of a company that has developed a special table format for MySQL (InnoDB tables)
ISP	Internet Service Provider
JSP	Java Server Pages
MySQL	The name of the company that developed the database system MySQL
ODBC	Open Database Connectivity (interface for database access, particularly popular under Windows)
PHP	PHP Hypertext Preprocessor (a scripting programming language for HTML pages)
RPM	Red Hat Packet Manager (a format for Linux software packages)
SQL	Structured Query Language (database programming language)
URL	Uniform Resource Locator (Internet address of the form http://www.company.com/page.html)
VB	Visual Basic (programming language)
VBA	Visual Basic for Applications (programming language within the Microsoft Office package)

Part I

Introduction

#### CHAPTER 1

What Is MySQL?

THIS CHAPTER BEGINS WITH AN overview of the most important concepts from the world of databases and then delves into the possibilities and limitations of MySQL. What is MySQL? What can it do, and what is it unable to do?

In addition to describing the central functions of MySQL, we shall also discuss fully the issue of licensing MySQL. When is one permitted to use MySQL without payment, and when is a license required?

Chapter Overview

What Is a Database?

Before we can answer the central question of this chapter, namely, *What is MySQL?* you and I must find a common language. Therefore, this section presents a rudimentary database glossary, without going into great detail. (If you have already had significant dealings with relational databases, you can skip the next couple of pages in good conscience.)

There is scarcely to be found a term that is less precise than *database*. A database can be a list of addresses residing in a spreadsheet program (such as Excel), or it can be the administration files of a telecommunications firm in which several million calls are registered daily, their charges accurately calculated, monthly bills computed, and warning letters sent to those who are in arrears. A simple database can be a stand-alone operation (residing locally on a computer for a single user), while others may be used simultaneously by thousands of users, with the data parceled out among several computers and dozens of hard drives. The size of a database can range from a few kilobytes into the terabytes.[1]

In ordinary usage, the word "database" is used to refer to the actual data, the resulting database files, the database system (such as MySQL or Oracle), or a database client (such as a PHP script or a program written in C++). Thus there arises a great potential for confusion as soon as two people begin to converse on the subject of databases.

Relations, Database Systems, Servers, and Clients

A *database* is an ordered collection of data, which is normally stored in one or more associated files. The data are structured as *tables*, where cross references among tables are possible. The existence of such *relations* among the tables leads to the database being called a *relational database*.

Let us clarify matters with an example. A database might consist of a table with data on a firm's customers (name, address, etc.), a table with data on the products the firm offers, and finally, a table containing the firm's orders. Through the table of orders it is possible to access the data in the other two tables (for example, via customer and product numbers).

MySQL, Oracle, the Microsoft SQL server, and IBM DB2 are examples of *relational database systems*. Such a system includes the programs for managing relational databases. Among the tasks of a relational database system are not only the secure storage of data, but also such jobs as the processing of commands for querying, analyzing, and sorting existing data and for storing new data. All of this should be able to take place not only on a single computer, but over a network as well. Instead of a *database system* we shall often speak of a *database server*.

Where there are servers, there are clients. Every program that is connected to the database system is called a *database client*. Database clients have the job of

---

[1]   It all started with the megabyte, which is about one million bytes. A terabyte is 1024 gigabytes, which in turn is approximately one thousand megabytes. The prefix "mega-" comes from the Greek for "great," or "large," while "giga-" is derived from the Greek word for "giant." In turn, "tera-" is from the Greek word for "monster." It would appear that numbers once regarded as large, gigantic, or even monstrously huge have become part of our everyday vocabulary.

simplifying the use of the database for the end user. No user of a database system in his or her right mind would wish to communicate directly with the database server. That is much too abstract and inconvenient. (Let programmers worry about such direct communication!) Instead, the user has a right to expect convenient tables, listboxes, and so on to enable the location of data or to input new data.

Database clients can assume a variety of forms, and indeed, they are often not recognized by the user as database programs at all. Some examples of this type of client are HTML pages for the display and input of messages in an on-line discussion group, a traditional program with several windows for managing addresses and appointments, and a Perl script for executing administrative tasks. There is thus wide scope for database programming.

Relational Versus Object-Oriented Database Systems

Relational databases have dominated the database world for decades, and they are particularly well suited for business data, which usually lend themselves to structuring in the form of tables. Except for the following two paragraphs, this entire book discusses only relational databases (though we shall not always stress this point).

Another kind of database is the *object-oriented database.* Such databases can store free-standing objects (without having to arrange them in tables). Although in recent years there has been a trend in the direction of object-oriented programming languages (such as Object-Store, O2, Caché), object-oriented databases have found only a small market niche.

Note that relational databases can be accessed by means of object-oriented programming languages. However, that does not turn a relational database into an object-oriented one. Object-oriented database systems enable direct access to objects defined in the programming language in question and the storage of such objects in the database without conversion (persistency). It is precisely this that is not possible with relational database systems, in which everything must be structured in tables.

Tables, Records, Fields, Queries, SQL, Index, Keys

We have already mentioned tables, which are the structures in which the actual data are located. Every line in such a table is called a *data record*, or simply *record*, where the structure of each record is determined by the definition of the table. For example, in a table of addresses every record might contain *fields* for family name, given name, street, and so on. For every field there are precise conditions on the type of information that can be stored (such as a number in a particular format, or a character string with a predetermined maximum number of characters).

NOTE *Sometimes, instead of data records with fields, we speak of rows and columns. The meaning is the same.*

The description of a database consisting of several tables with all of its fields, relations, and indexes (see below) is called a *database model*. This model defines the construction of the data structures and at the same time provides the format in which the actual data are to be stored.

Tables usually contain their data in no particular order (more precisely, the order is usually that in which the data have been entered or modified). However, for efficient use of the data it is necessary that from these unordered data a list can be created that is ordered according to one or more criteria. It is frequently useful for such a list to contain only a selection of the data in the table. For example, one could obtain a list of all of one's customers, ordered by ZIP code, who have ordered a rubber ducky within the past twelve months.

To create such a list, one formulates *queries*. The result of the query is again a table; however, it is one that exists in active memory (RAM) and not on the hard drive.

To formulate a query one uses SQL instructions, which are commands for selecting and extracting data. The abbreviation SQL stands for *Structured Query Language*, which has become a standard in the formulation of database queries. Needless to say, every producer of a database system offers certain extensions to this standard, which dilutes the goal of compatibility among various database systems.

When tables get large, the speed at which a query can be answered depends significantly on whether there is a suitable *index* giving the order of the data fields. An index is an auxiliary table that contains only information about the order of the records. An index is also called a *key*.

An index speeds up access to data, but it has disadvantages as well. First, every index increases the amount of storage on the hard drive necessary for the database file, and second, the index must be updated each time the data are altered, and this costs time. (Thus an index saves time in the reading of data, but it costs time in entering and altering data. It thus depends on the use to which the data are to be put whether an index is on the whole a net plus or minus in the quest for efficiency.)

A special case of an index is a *primary index*, or *primary key*, which is distinguished in that the primary index must ensure a *unique* reference to a record. Often, for this purpose one simply uses a running index number (ID number). Primary indexes play a significant role in relational databases, and they can speed up access to data considerably.

MySQL

MySQL is a relational database system. If you can believe many diehard MySQL fans, MySQL is faster, more reliable, and cheaper—or, simply put, better—than any other database system (including commercial systems such as Oracle and DB2). Many MySQL opponents continue to challenge this viewpoint, going even so far as to assert that MySQL is not even a relational database system. We can safely say that there is a large bandwidth of opinion.

- The fact is that there is an ever increasing number of MySQL users, and the overwhelming majority of them are quite satisfied with MySQL. Thus for these users we may say that MySQL is *good enough*.

- It is also the fact, however, that MySQL lacks a number of features that are taken for granted with other database systems. If you require such features, then MySQL is (at least for the present) not the database system for you. MySQL is not a panacea.

In this chapter we shall examine some of the possibilities and limitations of MySQL.

> **REMARK**   *In this book we are considering MySQL. Do not confuse MySQL with mSQL (MiniSQL). To be sure, MySQL and mSQL have similar programming interfaces (APIs), which merely facilitates the confusion between the two. However, the underlying database systems are completely different. More information on mSQL can be found at* http://www.hughes.com.au/

Features of MySQL

The following list shows the most important properties of MySQL. This section is directed to the reader who already has some knowledge of relational databases. We will use some terminology from the relational database world without defining our terms exactly. On the other hand, the explanations should make it possible for database novices to understand to some extent what we are talking about.

- **Relational Database System:** Like almost all other database systems on the market, MySQL is a relational database system.

- **Client/Server Architecture:** MySQL is a client/server system. There is a database server (MySQL) and arbitrarily many clients (application programs), which communicate with the server; that is, they query data, save changes, etc. The clients can run on the same computer as the server or on another computer (communication via a local network or the Internet).

  Almost all of the familiar large database systems (Oracle, Microsoft SQL Server, etc.) are client/server systems. These are in contrast to the *file-server systems*, which include Microsoft Access, dBase, and FoxPro. The decisive drawback to file-server systems is that when run over a network, they become extremely inefficient as the number of users grows.

- **SQL compatibility:** MySQL supports as its database language—as its name suggests—SQL (Structured Query Language). SQL is a standardized language for querying and updating data and for the administration of a database.

  There are several SQL dialects (about as many as there are database systems). MySQL adheres to the ANSI-SQL/92 standard, although with significant restrictions and many a number of extensions.

  This topic will be dealt with more extensively later. Beyond the ANSI-SQL/92 standard, MySQL supports, among other things, several additional data types, full-text indexes, and replication.

- **User Interface:** There are a number of convenient user interfaces for administering a MySQL server.

- **Full-text search:** Full-text search simplifies and accelerates the search for words that are located within a text field. If you employ MySQL for storing text (such as in an Internet discussion group), you can use full-text search to implement simply an efficient search function.

- **Replication:** Replication allows the contents of a database to be copied (replicated) onto a number of computers. In practice, this is done for two reasons: to increase protection against system failure (so that if one computer goes down, another can be put into service) and to improve the speed of database queries.

- **Transactions:** In the context of a database system, a transaction means the execution of several database operations as a block. The database system ensures that either all of the operations are correctly executed or none of them. This holds even if in the middle of a transaction there is a power failure, the computer crashes, or some other disaster occurs. Thus, for example, it cannot occur that a sum of money is withdrawn from account A but fails to be deposited in account B due to some type of system error.

  Transactions also give programmers the possibility of interrupting a series of already executed commands (a sort of revocation). In many situations this leads to a considerable simplification of the programming process.

  In spite of popular opinion, MySQL has supported transactions for a long time. One should note here that MySQL can store tables in a variety of formats. The default table format is called MyISAM, and this format does not support transactions. But there are a number of additional formats that do support transactions. The most popular of these is InnoDB, which will be described in its own chapter.

- **Foreign key constraints:** These are rules that ensure that there are no cross references in linked tables that lead to nowhere. MySQL supports foreign key constraints for InnoDB tables.

- **Programming languages:** There are quite a number of APIs (application programming interfaces) and libraries for the development of MySQL applications. For client programming you can use, among others, the languages C, C++, Java, Perl, PHP, Python, and Tcl.

- **ODBC:** MySQL supports the ODBC interface Connector/ODBC. This allows MySQL to be addressed by all the usual programming languages that run under Microsoft Windows (Delphi, Visual Basic, etc.). The ODBC interface can also be implemented under Unix, though that is seldom necessary.

  Windows programmers who have migrated to Microsoft's new .NET platform can, if they wish, use the ODBC provider or special MySQL providers for .NET.

- **Platform independence:** It is not only client applications that run under a variety of operating systems; MySQL itself (that is, the server) can be executed under a number of operating systems. The most important are Apple Macintosh OS X, Linux, Microsoft Windows, and the countless Unix variants, such as AIX, BSDI, FreeBSD, HP-UX, OpenBSD, Net BSD, SGI Iris, and Sun Solaris.

- **Speed:** MySQL is considered a very fast database program. This speed has been backed up by a large number of benchmark tests (though such tests—regardless of the source—should be considered with a good dose of skepticism).

Limitations of MySQL

Many of the shortcomings listed in this section can be found on the to-do list of the team of MySQL developers, or have already been implemented.

> **POINTER** *The documentation for MySQL is not at all silent on the subject of shortcomings or missing features. There is a quite readable section in the MySQL documentation on the topic "How standards-compatible is MySQL?" There you will find extensive information on the points at which MySQL fails to comply with current standards. Often, a reason for the shortcoming is provided, and sometimes as well some pointers on how to get around the difficulty:*
>
> http://www.mysql.com/doc/en/Compatibility.html
>
> *Note also that all of the shortcomings mentioned here are on the to-do list of the developers and will be alleviated in future versions of MySQL.*

ANSI-SQL/92 Limitations

ANSI SQL/92 is a standardized definition of the database query language SQL. Many commercial database systems are largely compatible with this standard and also offer many extensions.

MySQL is also conspicuous for its countless extensions, but unfortunately, the compatibility is not so extensive as is the case for other database systems. The points described in greater detail in what follows (sub*SELECT*s, views, triggers, stored procedures) are examples of the lack of ANSI-SQL/92 compatibility.

These limitations usually make it impossible (or merely very difficult) to adapt existing databases and the associated SQL code from other database systems into MySQL. Conversely, it is almost as difficult to transfer a MySQL solution to another database system if you have not scrupulously employed only the ANSI-SQL/92-conforming features of MySQL. (The temptation to use the useful proprietary features proves in most cases to be too great.)

- **Sub*SELECT*s:** MySQL is not capable of executing a query of the form

```
SELECT * FROM table1 WHERE x IN (SELECT y FROM table2)
```

This limitation can often be circumvented by *JOIN* operations or by setting up a temporary table. However, that is neither elegant nor particularly efficient. Sub*SELECT*s will soon be supported (from version 4.1; see Appendix B).

- **Views:** Simply put, with *views* we are dealing with an SQL query that is considered an independent database object and that permits a particular view into the database. MySQL currently does not support views (though we may expect this feature to be implemented shortly).

  Of course, with MySQL you can always execute those SQL commands that are defined as views in other databases. However, it is impossible to store these queries in objects in the database.

  Views assist in the administration of the database, since it is thereby relatively simple to control access to individual *parts* of the database. Views also help in avoiding redundancy in application development.

- **Stored Procedure:** When we speak of *stored procedures* we are referring to SQL code that is stored within a database system. Stored procedures (SPs for short) are usually employed to simplify certain steps in a procedure, such as inserting or deleting a record. For client programmers this has the advantage that these actions need not operate directly on the tables, but can rely on SPs. As with views, SPs also help in the administration of large database projects. Stored procedures can also increase efficiency in certain cases. Stored procedures are expected in MySQL 5.0.

- **Triggers:** A *trigger* is an SQL command that is automatically executed by the server during certain database operations. If a database is incapable on its own of ensuring referential integrity, then it is usually triggers that are brought into play to assist in this. For example, a trigger can be executed every time a record is to be deleted, which would test whether this operation is permissible and prohibit the action if need be.

The lack of sub*SELECT*s, views, SPs, and triggers does not greatly restrict the possibilities open to client programmers, but it does lead to a situation in which the program logic is transferred from the server level to the client level. The result is more complex or expensive client programming than would otherwise be the case, leading to redundancies in code and problems with maintenance and alteration of code.

Further Limitations

The following limitations actually have nothing to do with ANSI-SQL/92 but nonetheless play a significant role in practice.

- When MySQL is used with standard tables (table type MyISAM), then *locking*, that is, the temporary blocking of access to or alteration of database information, is in operation only for entire tables (*table locking*).

  You can circumvent the *table-locking* problem by implementing transaction-capable table formats, such as InnoDB, that support *row locking*.

- In using MyISAM tables, MySQL is not able to execute *hot backups*, which are backups during operation without blocking the tables with locks. Here again, the solution is InnoDB, though here the hot backup function is available only in the form of a commercial supplement.

- MySQL 4.0 supports a variety of character sets and the associated sort orders, but at present can have only a single *sort order* active at a time. If the sort order must be changed, MySQL has to be restarted. All table indexes must then be reset. This limitation has been removed in version 4.1.

- MySQL 4.0 is unable to deal with Unicode or other mutibyte character strings. (Of course, it is possible to treat such data as binary objects, but there are no functions for dealing with character strings, in particular, no usable sorting or comparison algorithms.) This limitation, too, has been removed in version 4.1.

MySQL Version Numbers

Even for connoisseurs of MySQL it is a bit of a challenge to keep track of which version of MySQL is current and which functions are contained in which versions. This section provides some information on MySQL numbering.

As of March 2002 there are four main versions being worked on by the MySQL development team:

- **MySQL 3.23.*n*:** The first version of this series, 3.23.0, was published in August 1999. Since 3.23.32 (January 2001) MySQL 3.23.*n* has been considered stable. The current version is 3.23.56.

  MySQL 3.23 is the version most in use among Internet providers, and is only gradually being displaced by version 4.0.*n*. There will be no further extensions to MySQL 3.23.*n*. New versions will only fix discovered errors or security holes.

- **MySQL 4.0.*n*:** The first version of this series, 4.0.0, was published in October 2001. Since 4.0.12 (March 2003) MySQL 4.0.*n* has been considered stable and is now recommended for production use. It is expected that in the coming months, a series of new versions of 4.0.*n* will appear to resolve errors that have been or are still being discovered. New functionality is not expected in this series.

- **MySQL 4.1.*n*:** The first version in this series was announced in January 2003, but it was not yet available for download as this book was being completed. (Developers can obtain daily updated code from the Internet. However, the MySQL server must itself be compiled from this code, which is no simple matter.) It is not clear when MySQL 4.1.*n* will be at a point where it can be recommended for production use, probably not before 2004.

- **MySQL 5.0.*n*:** The first published version in this series is expected in 2004. It is completely open as to when the first stable version will be ready. This version is currently of use only to developers who are working on functions that cannot be realized in MySQL 4.*n*.

Alpha, Beta, Gamma, Production

MySQL versions are identified by the attributes *alpha*, *beta*, *gamma*, and *production*:

- **Alpha** means that the version is in the throes of the development process and that new functions and even incompatible changes are to be expected. Although an alpha version is not published until it contains no known errors, it is highly probable that many undiscovered errors still lurk within. Loss of data during testing of an alpha version is quite possible!

- **Beta** means that this version is largely complete, but it has not been thoroughly tested. Major changes are not expected.

- **Gamma** means that the beta versions have become more or less stable. The goal now is discover errors and resolve them. Gamma versions are well suited to application developers who want to try out new functions on a test system.

- **Production** means that the MySQL development community has the impression that the version is mature and stable enough that it can be used for mission-critical purposes.

  According to the MySQL documentation, in production versions, only corrections, and no new functionality, are to be expected. However, this has not always held true in the past. Of particular note is the case of MySQL 3.23.*n*. After the version had been declared stable (3.23.32), there came general support for InnoDB and BDB tables (3.23.34), and later, integrity rules for InnoDB tables (3.23.44). Furthermore, many minor extensions were introduced. As a rule, MySQL developers are pleased with such extensions, but at the same time, compatibility problems among different production versions can arise.

In practice, this means that a new MySQL version (that is, *n.n.*0) always has the status *alpha*. With higher version numbers, the status rises to *beta*, *gamma*, and finally, *production*.

Normal MySQL users should use exclusively MySQL versions that have the status *production*. If you are developing web applications, you should find out which version your Internet service provider is using. (Since Internet service providers are concerned with maintenance and stability, they are not generally keen on using the latest version, preferring earlier versions, which may not contain many of the functions of the newer versions.)

> **TIP** *If you want to experiment with a development version that is not yet available in compiled format (and thus has not even reached alpha status), instructions on downloading and compiling the source code can be obtained at* `http://www.mysql.com/doc/en/Installing_source.html`

MySQL Functions Ordered by Version Number

It is not always the easiest thing in the world to determine which particular database function can be used with which version of MySQL. Of course, the version number often reveals when a function first became officially available, but it often happens that thereafter, significant changes to the function are made or bugs fixed, so that a stable implementation occurs only several versions later. Note as well that certain functions are available only for particular table formats.

Table 1-1 ventures a glance into the future. The entries are based on information contained in the MySQL documentation as of the end of July 2003, collected from the following web sites:

```
http://www.mysql.com/doc/en/TODO.html
http://www.mysql.com/doc/en/MySQL_4.0_In_A_Nutshell.html
http://www.mysql.com/doc/en/MySQL_4.1_In_A_Nutshell.html
http://www.mysql.com/doc/en/MySQL-PostgreSQL_features.html
http://www.mysql.com/doc/en/News.html
```

The projections into the future come, naturally, without warranty of any kind. In the past, it frequently occurred that particular functions became available earlier or later than originally projected.

Table 1-1. MySQL functions past and future

Function	Version
Replication	3.23
Full-text search in MyISAM tables	3.23
Transactions with BDB tables	3.23.34
Transactions with InnoDB tables	3.23.34
Referential integrity for InnoDB tables	3.23.44
DELETE across several tables	4.0
UPDATE across several tables	4.0
UNION (unite several *SELECT* results)	4.0
Query cache (speeds up repeated SQL commands)	4.0
Embedded MySQL library	4.0
Encrypted connections (Secure Socket Layer, SSL)	4.0
Hot backup for InnoDB (commercial add-on product)	4.0
Sub*SELECT*s	4.1
Unicode support (UTF8 and UCS2 = UTF16)	4.1
GIS support (*GEOMETRY* data type, R-tree index)	4.1
Prepared Statements (SQL commands with parameters)	4.1
ROLLUP extension for *GROUP BY*	4.1
Stored procedures (SPs)	probably 5.0
Trigger (automatic execution of SQL code)	probably 5.0
Referential integrity for MyISAM tables	probably 5.1
Fail-safe replication	probably 5.1
Hot backup for MyISAM tables	probably 5.1
Column-level constraints	probably 5.1
VIEWs	probably 5.1
XML data type	not currently planned
User-defined data types	not currently planned

MySQL Licensing

One of the most interesting features of MySQL is the license. MySQL is an open source project. That is, the complete source code of MySQL is freely available. Since June 2000 (that is, since version 3.23.19) the *GNU Public License* (GPL) is valid also for MySQL. It is thus ensured that MySQL will continue to be freely available in the sense of the open source idea. (For commercial applications of MySQL there is a second, commercial, license available in addition to GPL. More on this later.)

Rights and Duties with Respect to the GPL

Open source is often incorrectly interpreted to mean "without cost." It is indeed true that GPL software can be used without payment of fees, provided that one adheres to certain conditions. However, the open source idea goes much further:

- Since the source code is freely available, when there are problems, you are not at the mercy of a software vendor.

- When problems arise, you can perhaps attempt to repair the problem yourself or to implement features that are lacking. Furthermore, you can appeal to the developers' group for help.

- You can be certain that the program code has been read by many developers and does not contain any unsavory surprises (such as so-called back doors such as the database system Interbase had for many years, whereby access to every Interbase database was possible via a hard-coded password).

- You are permitted to alter GPL products, and indeed sell the resulting new programs.

At the end of this list of GPL merits there are a few demerits (for commercial applications). If you wish to use a GPL program as the basis for a commercial product, you must again make your own source code freely available, in the sense of GPL, with the changes made. This is seldom something that developers of commercial products wish to do.

In general, then, every program that is derived from GPL software exists under the terms of GPL. (GPL is, so to speak, contagious.)

> **POINTER** *Further information on the open source idea, the full text of GPL, and explanations can be found at the following addresses:*
>
> http://www.gnu.org/copyleft/gpl.html
> http://www.opensource.org/osd.html

Use of MySQL with an Open Source License

The following list collects the different situations in which one may freely use MySQL in the sense of GPL:

- MySQL can be used without cost if an application is locally developed and not used commercially. It is only when the resulting solution is to be sold to customers that the question of licensing comes into play. This rule is expressed on the MySQL home page as follows: *Free use for those who never copy, modify, or distribute.*

- MySQL can be used freely within a web site. If you also develop a PHP application and install it with your Internet service provider, you do not have to make your PHP code freely available in the sense of GPL.

- Likewise, an Internet service provider may make MySQL available to its customers without having to pay MySQL license fees. (Since MySQL is running exclusively on the ISP computer, this application is considered internal.)

- Finally, MySQL can be used free of charge for all projects that themselves run under the GPL or comparable free license. (If you have developed a new free e-mail client for Linux, say, and wish to store e-mails in a MySQL database, you may do so without further ado.)

Use of MySQL with a Commercial License

In the sense of GPL the following uses are prohibited:

- You may not change or extend MySQL (that is, the database server) or sell the new version or product thus created without simultaneously making the source code of your changes freely available. You are thus prohibited from developing a new database system based on MySQL if you are not prepared to make your extensions freely available to the MySQL community in the sense of GPL.

- It is forbidden to develop a commercial product, such as a bookkeeping program, that is geared toward MySQL as the database without making the code available in the open source sense.

If the limitations of the GPL are not acceptable to you as a commercial developer, then you may sell your product (program) together with a commercial MySQL license. This can prove worthwhile because MySQL remains available to you even if you are unable or unwilling to make your code available in the sense of GPL.

Commercial MySQL licensing fees are calculated based on the number of servers (where a server is considered to be a computer, regardless of the number of CPUs). There is no limitation on the number of clients that may access the server. The cost is quite reasonable in comparison to commercial database systems (currently $220 for a license without InnoDB support and $440 for a license with InnoDB support, with a significant reduction starting at ten licenses).

> **POINTER** *Read the licensing conditions presented in Appendix C! Further information on licensing MySQL can be found in the MySQL documentation, in the chapter "MySQL Licensing and Support," and at the following web sites:*
>
> ```
> http://www.mysql.com/support/arrangements.html
> https://order.mysql.com/
> ```

Commercial Licenses for Client Libraries (Connector/ODBC, Connector/J, etc.)

In addition to the actual MySQL server, the MySQL company offers client libraries that are necessary for the development of application programs:

C-API	*Application interface* for C programming
Connector/C++	Library for C++ programming
Connector/J	JDBC driver for Java programming
Connector/ODB	ODBC driver for all programming under Windows

Like MySQL, these drivers are available under GPL. Many MySQL client libraries, such as the JDBC driver Connector/J, used to be available in earlier versions under LGPL (lesser Gnu public license), which implies fewer restrictions for commercial applications. The situation has changed, however.

If you wish to use these drivers in commercial applications, the following rule is in force: If MySQL client programs access a MySQL-licensed server, then this server license is valid for the client libraries. It is thus usually unnecessary to obtain licenses for the use of client libraries, because the client libraries are automatically included with the server license.

However, if you develop and sell a commercial program but do not deliver it together with MySQL and leave the installation of the MySQL server and its licensing to the customer, then you must obtain licenses for the client libraries used in your program.

Explicit licensing of the client library is seen by the MySQL company as an exception, since as a rule, the server is licensed. Commercial licensing of the client library actually represents nothing other than a protection of the MySQL company's commercial interests. They want to avoid the situation in which commercial developers get around having to obtain a commercial license simply by not providing the MySQL server. The customer then loads the GPL version of the MySQL server from the Internet and believes that all is right with the world. In such a case the MySQL company would receive nothing for the development of a commercial MySQL product.

MySQL Version Names

Beginning with MySQL 4.0.5, the free (in the sense of GPL) and commercial versions have different names. Here they are:

Name	License	Functionality
MySQL Standard	GPL	All default functions that can be considered stable (including InnoDB)
MySQL Max	GPL	Same as MySQL Standard, but with the BDB table format as well as with additional functions that have not reached full maturity
MySQL Classic	commercial	Like MySQL Standard, but without InnoDB
MySQL Pro	commercial	Like MySQL Standard, but with InnoDB (thus with transactions)

For ordinary GPL applications, the use of the Standard version is recommended. The additional functions in the Max version are for use only in special applications. Currently (version 4.0.12), the Standard and Max versions differ in the support of BDB tables and the SSL encryption of client/server connections. These functions will be incorporated into the Standard and commercial versions only when they are considered sufficiently stable. You can determine which functions the running version of MySQL supports with the following SQL command:

```
mysql> SHOW VARIABLES LIKE 'have%';
```

Variable_name	Value
have_bdb	NO
have_crypt	NO
have_innodb	YES
have_isam	YES
have_raid	NO
have_symlink	YES
have_openssl	NO
have_query_cache	YES

In the case of commercial applications, the decision between Classic and Pro depends simply on whether InnoDB is needed. (The license for the Pro version is more expensive.) The Classic and Pro versions cannot be simply downloaded at www.mysql.com, but are provided only after a license has been issued.

If you wish to know which server version is being run, then execute the following SQL command:

```
mysql> SHOW VARIABLES LIKE 'version';
```

Variable_name	Value
version	4.0.12-nt-log

This output shows that the Standard version 4.0.12 is running under Windows NT/2000/XP and that logging is activated. There is no additional Max functionality and no license for commercial use.

Support Contracts

You may make a support contract with the MySQL company if you desire commercial support in the development of a MySQL application. You thereby simultaneously support the further development of MySQL.

> **POINTER** *Details on commercial MySQL licenses and paid support can be found at*
> `http://www.mysql.com/support/`
> *Links to various companies that offer commercial MySQL support can be found at*
> `http://www.mysql.com/information/partners.html`

Alternatives to MySQL

Of course, there are many alternatives to MySQL, particularly if you are prepared to pay (lots of) money for licenses and perhaps also for the requisite hardware. Among these are IBM DB2, Informix, Microsoft SQL Server, and Oracle.

If you are looking for a database in the open source realm, then PostgreSQL is currently perhaps the most interesting alternative. However, be warned: The discussion between advocates of MySQL and those of PostgreSQL usually resembles more a war of religions than what might be termed measured intellectual discourse. In any case, PostgreSQL offers many more functions than MySQL (even if MySQL is slowly catching up). At the same time, it is considered slower and less stable (even if in this regard the reputation of PostgreSQL has greatly improved).

Furthermore, there are several formerly commercial database systems that have been converted to open source. The two best known of these are Firebird (formerly Interbase from Inprise/Borland) and SAP DB.

> **POINTER** *Further information on PostgreSQL, Firebird, and SAP DB can be found on the Internet. The following web pages are a good starting point:*
>
> `http://www.postgresql.com/`
> `http://www.at.postgresql.org/`
> `http://openacs.org/`
> `http://firebird.sourceforge.net`
> `http://www.sapdb.org`

Summary

MySQL is a very capable relational client/server database system. It is sufficiently secure and stable for many applications, and it offers an excellent cost/benefit ratio (not only because MySQL is free itself, but also because it makes comparatively modest demands on hardware). MySQL has thus developed into a quasi standard in the realm of Internet databases.

Above all, in the Linux world, MySQL is used increasingly by applications as the background database engine, whether it be managing logging data more efficiently than previously or managing e-mail, MP3 files, addresses, or comparable data. MySQL is poised to play a similar role to that of the Jet Engine in the Microsoft operating system (where in many respects, MySQL offers a meaningfully better technical basis). Thanks to the ODBC interface, MySQL is now being used in the Windows world for such tasks.

Apart from technical data, MySQL has the advantage over other open source database systems in that it is by far the most widely used such system. It follows that MySQL has been more thoroughly tested and documented than other database systems and that it is relatively easy to find developers with MySQL experience.

However, MySQL cannot (yet) compete in every respect with the big boys of the commercial database system world. You are not likely to choose MySQL if you require functions that MySQL does not yet support.

#### CHAPTER 2

The Test Environment

IN THIS CHAPTER WE DISCUSS first of all how to set up the test environment for MySQL on a local computer. Since MySQL usually doesn't run all by itself, but in combination with other programs, this chapter also discusses Apache, PHP, Perl, Connector/ODBC, and phpMyAdmin. We consider installation under Windows and under Linux.

If MySQL has been made available by your Internet service provider (ISP) and you are not inclined to install MySQL on your own computer as well, the last section of this chapter gives a brief overview on how under these conditions you can quickly begin your first experiments.

This chapter is geared specifically to MySQL neophytes. If you already have access to a functioning MySQL system, you may feel free to skip it.

Chapter Overview

Windows or Unix/Linux?

The question of under which operating system to run MySQL can easily lead to fisticuffs, so strongly are opinions held. But we shall remain civil in this section, and perhaps for the entire book. The fact is that MySQL, as well as Apache, PHP, Perl, and most of the other programs that are usually run in conjunction with MySQL, were developed originally under Unix/Linux and only later ported to Windows.

MySQL in Practice (Public Internet Server)

In practice, that is, on a publicly available server on the Internet, the above-mentioned programs are run predominately under Unix/Linux. (There is scarcely an Internet service provider to be found that offers MySQL under Windows.) For this reason alone—the greater deployment in the world at large—the programs running under Unix/Linux have been better and more extensively tested. Possible errors or security holes in the Unix/Linux version of MySQL are thus more likely to be discovered and repaired quickly.

A further argument for deployment under Unix/Linux is that the programs function more efficiently as a rule. This has less to do with the view that Windows is generally slower than Unix/Linux (I have no desire to discuss that issue here), but with the fact that the process and thread models of these operating systems are quite different from each other. Programs such as Apache and MySQL are first and foremost optimized for the programming model of Unix/Linux, not for that of Windows, and this by itself often gives a significant speed advantage to Unix/Linux.

Therefore, the development communities of the programs mentioned above are unanimously in favor of having their programs run under Unix/Linux, and not under Windows. You would do well to take this opinion to heart.

> **REMARK** *When we speak of Windows, we generally mean Windows NT/2000. In principle, MySQL runs under Windows 9x/ME, but there it is impossible to provide reasonable security of the system against unauthorized access. In general, my tests were carried out under Windows 2000.*

Development Environment

Things look somewhat different if you are currently only developing a database application. During the development you will use a test environment that is usually accessible only to you or your team. Thus you have no reason to expect problems in security or in efficiency due to large numbers of accesses to the system. Since there is good compatibility between the Windows and Unix/Linux versions, there is little to be said against, for example, developing a discussion group first under Windows and then porting the completed solution to the Linux server of your ISP.

If you have at least two computers in your test environment, you can, of course, install MySQL, Apache, etc., on one computer under Linux, and carry out the actual development work (database design, creation of script files, etc., on the second computer under Windows (say, because your favorite editor runs under Windows).

To this extent, the entire discussion of Windows versus Unix/Linux doesn't amount to much, and for development you should use the operating system that you find more to your liking.

> **REMARK**   *Of course, there are also arguments against Windows even for the development of MySQL solutions. One is that by developing the entire project under Unix/Linux you gain considerable experience that will be valuable later during the process of bringing the project on line on a Unix/Linux server (specifically in reference to issues of access rights and security).*

> **REMARK**   *Another argument deals with the deployment of system functions that under Unix/Linux usually are available in a form different from that offered under Windows. For example, under Unix/Linux one can simply send an e-mail by program code (such as in a PHP or Perl script). Under Windows there are no standard interfaces for such tasks.*
>
> *A final argument is this: If you possess a typical Linux distribution (for example, SuSE or Red Hat) on CD-ROM, you also possess all the programs of the MySQL test environment. After the various packages have been installed, everything usually runs correctly at first go, without any further configuration nightmares. On the other hand, if you work with Windows, you must first obtain the individual programs from the Internet, install them, and then configure them in what often is painstaking, frustrating labor.*

MySQL (Server Installation)

MySQL is available over the Internet without cost, both as source code and in compiled form for most operating systems. Check out `http://www.mysql.com/downloads`.

This section describes the installation of the binary version of MySQL under Windows and under Linux.

> **REMARK**   *When one speaks of MySQL one is usually referring to the database server. A MySQL installation thus usually means the installation of the server, where usually all the client tools are installed at the same time, so that the server can be administered. This is the subject of the current section.*
>
> *If MySQL is already installed on another computer and you wish only to access that installation, then you need only the client tools. The next section discusses such a separate installation.*

> **TIP** *If you are developing a web application that is to be installed by an external Internet service provider, you should find out what version is being used. Many ISPs are reluctant (with good reason) to install the most recent version.*
>
> *If your ISP is using an older version of MySQL (for example, 3.23.n), then it is often a good idea to use the older version for your own development. In this way you avoid the situation in which you have used certain functions that will be unavailable on the system of your ISP.*

Installation Under Windows

MySQL for Windows is available as a WinZip archive. To install it, copy the contents of the archive to a temporary directory and there launch setup.exe. (With current versions of WinZip you can simply launch setup.exe. WinZip extracts the necessary files on its own into a directory and then deletes the archive when the installation is complete.)

The MySQL setup program assumes that under Windows, the Microsoft installer (MSI) is available. In current versions of Windows that is automatically the case. If you are using an older version of Windows, you can obtain MSI without charge at the following address:

```
http://support.microsoft.com/default.aspx?kbid=292539
```

The setup program itself offers no surprises. You may specify the installation location and select the components to be installed. If you stick with the default settings, then the database system, the documentation, and a default setting for access rights (the privileges database *mysql*) are installed into the directory C:\mysql. The space requirement is about 50 megabytes (where after the first launch an additional 20 megabytes for database files are needed). Optionally, you can also install files for benchmark tests as well as libraries and include files (if you wish to develop MySQL clients with C/C++).

> **WARNING** *The setup program takes no notice of any existing MySQL installations. If you wish to update an installation, you should first secure the existing databases, then deinstall the old version of MySQL, and then install the new version. This process is described more fully later.*

MySQL can be run as a freestanding program or as a *service*. The latter variant, however, can be used only under Windows NT/2000/XP.

> **REMARK**   *In this book it is generally assumed in descriptions of Windows NT/2000 that the installation of programs is executed by the* administrator *(or by a user with equivalent privileges) and that programs such as* WinMySQLadmin *are also executed by such a user.*
>
> *An installation without* administrator *privileges is usually impossible. Even with the use of programs without* administrator *privileges there can arise problems with access privileges, related to the manner in which access rights to files and processes are managed under Windows NT/2000. (A description of the access system of Windows NT/2000 is beyond the scope of this book.)*

Initial Configuration and Launch

For the initial launch of a MySQL server your best bet is to use the administration program mysql\bin\winmysqladmin.exe included with MySQL. (Simply launch the program in Windows Explorer with a double click.)

> **TIP**   WinMySQLadmin *was originally conceived as the user interface to MySQL. The program was never able to fulfill this task adequately. In the meantime, there have appeared many other programs that are better suited for this. Therefore, the further development of* WinMySQLadmin *was stopped. Nevertheless,* WinMySQLadmin *has a reason for being: The program is extremely practical for carrying out certain elementary administrative tasks:*
>
> - *starting and stopping the MySQL server*
> - *setting up the MySQL server (only under Windows NT/2000/XP)*
> - *setting up and editing a configuration file for the MySQL server*

On initial launch of WinMySQLadmin, the program asks for a user name and password. The program will use this information in the future in establishing a connection to the MySQL server. Since WinMySQLadmin, as mentioned, is seldom used as an administration program, an administration login is not required. Therefore, you should input any character string that you like in the dialog; WinMySQLadmin rewards this input by establishing the MySQL configuration file Windows\My.ini, which contains, in addition to the login information, other important information for launching MySQL.

> **WARNING** *Note that the user name and password are stored in plain text in the file* Windows\my.ini. *Therefore, be sure not to provide a password that might endanger the security of the system.*

The following lines of code show the MySQL configuration file windows\my.ini generated by WinMySQLadmin. Of greatest importance are the settings basedir and datadir. They specify the MySQL installation directory and the directory with the MySQL databases. This information is required if MySQL was installed in a directory other than c:\mysql:

```
# MySQL-configuration file Windows\My.ini
[mysqld]
basedir=C:/mysql410
datadir=C:/mysql410/data

[WinMySQLadmin]
Server=C:/mysql410/bin/mysqld-nt.exe
user=abc
password=efg
```

After the configuration file has been set, WinMySQLadmin establishes the MySQL server as a Windows service (Windows NT/2000/XP only) and starts the service (see Figure 2-1).

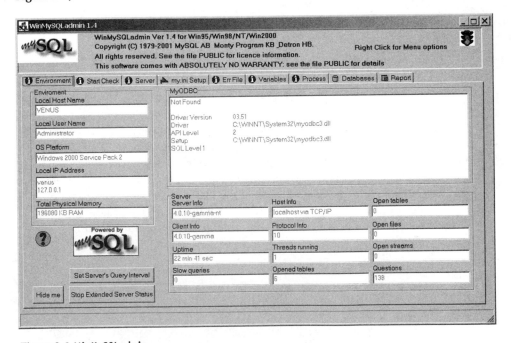

Figure 2-1. WinMySQLadmin

Then `WinMySQLadmin` establishes a start link in the `Autostart` directory so that the program will be launched automatically in the future. That is important especially under Windows 9x/ME: There the MySQL server cannot be started as a Windows service and therefore must be launched by `WinMySQLadmin`.

`WinMySQLadmin` minimizes itself directly after launch into a traffic-light-shaped icon in the task bar. The light gives the status of the MySQL server. (Green means that the server is running.) Using the light's context menu you can start or stop the server or open `WinMySQLadmin`'s window.

If there are problems at launch, then launch the user interface of `WinMySQLadmin` with the right mouse button using SHOW ME. The dialog form START CHECK provides information about possible causes of the launch failure. In the dialog MY.INI SETUP you can examine the file `Windows\My.ini`, make changes, and then save via SAVE. HIDE ME in the dialog sheet ENVIRONMENT minimizes `WinMySQLadmin` again into the traffic-light icon.

Starting and Stopping MySQL service under Windows NT/2000/XP

Once MySQL has been set up as a service, it will be started automatically each time the computer is booted up. If you wish to start or stop MySQL manually, you can use the Windows service manager instead of `WinMySQLadmin.exe`. To do this, execute SETTINGS | CONTROL PANEL | ADMINISTRATIVE TOOLS | SERVICES, select the service `mysql`, and then click on the desired button (START, STOP, etc.); see Figure 2-2.

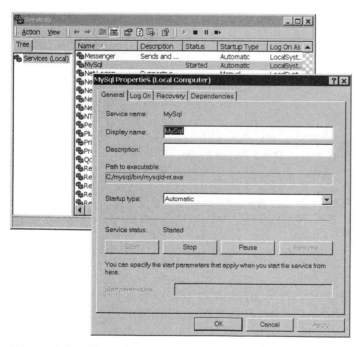

Figure 2-2. Starting and Stopping MySQL as a service

TIP *You are not dependent on* WinMySQLadmin *to set up your MySQL server as a service. If you want to do this task manually, then launch* mysql\bin\mysqld-nt.exe *in an input command window with the option* --install. *To deinstall the service, use the option* --remove.

POINTER *The configuration file* windows\My.ini *of course offers countless other configuration possibilities. Information on this can be found in Chapter 19. But first, it is important to get the MySQL server up and running.*

MySQL Server Variants Under Windows

Under Windows there is a selection of several variants of the MySQL server: mysqld-nt.exe, mysqld-max.exe, mysqld.exe, etc. The following table shows the differences among them:

Version	Debugging information	Additional functions (BDB tables, SSL, etc.)	Optimized for Windows
mysqld.exe	Yes	Yes	No
mysqld-opt.exe	No	No	No
mysqld-nt.exe	No	No	Yes
mysqld-max.exe	No	Yes	No
mysqld-max-nt.exe	No	Yes	Yes

The debugging information is relevant only if the MySQL server crashes (which has never happened to me with stable MySQL versions) and you wish to send the debugging information to the developer or use the debugger yourself to search for errors.

Additional functions are those that are rarely used or not yet mature. Currently (MySQL 4.0.12), this includes BDB tables and SSL encryption.

"Optimized for Windows NT/2000/XP" means that the server can be executed as a Windows service and that *named pipes* are available (these represent a seldom used form of communication between the server and Windows clients that run on the same computer).

Normally, you should use mysqld-opt.exe under Windows 9x/ME, and mysqld-nt.exe under Windows NT/2000/XP. The selection of the version of mysqld is most simply accomplished in WinMySQLadmin in the dialog sheet MY.INI SETUP.

Manually Installing and Deinstalling MySQL as a Windows Service

As we have described in some detail, the program WinMySQLadmin offers the simplest way of installing the MySQL server under Windows NT/2000/XP as a Windows service.

If the day were to come when this program was no longer provided with MySQL, then there would presumably be an improved setup program. In any case, it is good to know that you can easily install and deinstall Windows services manually.

Installation is accomplished by first opening an input command window and executing the following commands:

```
> cd mysql\bin
> mysqld-nt --install
```

With this, the program is installed as a Windows service with the name mysql, but not launched. In the future, the service mysql will be automatically launched at computer bootup, and terminated when the computer is shut down.

There are several installation variants:

- Instead of mysqld-nt, you can use one of the other mysqld variants mentioned earlier.

- If you do not want the service to start up automatically at system startup, then instead of --install, use the option --install-manual.

- If do not want to install the service under the name mysql, then with the --install option provide another name (--install *name*). This makes sense only in special cases, for example, with a parallel installation of several MySQL versions.

To start or stop the service manually, execute one of the following two commands:

```
> net start mysql
> net stop mysql
```

To stop the server, you can alternatively execute mysqladmin -u root -p shutdown, where you will have to provide the root password for the server.

To deinstall the service, use the option --remove:

```
> mysqld-nt --remove
```

> **TIP** *If you wish to start the MySQL server manually under Windows NT/2000/XP as a standalone program (not as a service), then execute the command* mysqld --standalone *or* mysqld --console. *In both cases the input window is blocked until the server is ended with* mysqladmin shutdown. *The difference between* --console *and* --standalone *is that in the former, the status information is displayed directly in the input window.*

Installation Under Linux

MySQL is included in most Linux distributions. The installation is here confined to installing the MySQL program package with the distribution's package manager. This is described below in detail for Red Hat and SuSE Linux.

Red Hat: Installation of the Included Version

Before MySQL is installed, some Perl packages must be installed, if they have not been installed already. All the packages are to be found on CD 2. The option --nodeps is necessary in the second rpm command, since on account of an error in Red Hat 9, the packages perl-DBD-MySQL and mysql are mutually dependent in that each package should be installed only after the other—a classic "Catch 22." The meaning of --nodeps is that package dependencies are to be ignored, which overcomes the dependency problem:

```
root# rpm -i /mnt/cdrom/RedHat/RPMS/perl-DBI-n.i386.rpm
root# rpm -i --nodeps /mnt/cdrom/RedHat/RPMS/perl-DBD-MySQL-n.i386.rpm
root# rpm -i /mnt/cdrom/RedHat/RPMS/perl-CGI-n.i386.rpm
```

MySQL 3.23.54 is included with Red Hat 9. MySQL is divided into four packages, whose RPM files are located on CD 2:

- mysql-version.rpm contains the client programs, including the *shared libraries*, which are used by many programs to access MySQL. The client programs (mysql, mysqladmin, etc.) aid in the administration of MySQL.

- mysql-server-version.rpm contains the actual MySQL server.

- mysql-devel-version.rpm contains the libraries and include files for program development in C.

Usually, only the first two of these packages need to be installed.

```
root# rpm -i /mnt/cdrom/RedHat/RPMS/mysql-n.i386.rpm
root# rpm -i /mnt/cdrom/RedHat/RPMS/mysql-server-n.i386.rpm
```

To determine whether MySQL is already installed on your computer (and if so, in which version), execute the following commands:

```
root# rpm -qa | grep -i mysql
mysql-3.23.54a-10
mysql-server-3.23.54a-10
perl-DBD-MySQL-2.1021-3
```

To try out your newly installed MySQL server, execute the following command:

```
root# /etc/init.d/mysqld start
```

If you want the MySQL server always to start automatically, you must add mysqld to the appropriate init-V run levels. The simplest way of proceeding is to make this setting with chkconfig:

```
root# chkconfig --level 235 mysqld on
```

As database directory, /var/lib/mysql is used.

SuSE: Installation of the Included Version

SuSE 8.2 is included with MySQL 3.23.55. To install it, launch the YaST2 module
INSTALL SOFTWARE, choose the filter SEARCH, and input `mysql`. Included in the search
result will be the following packages:

- `mysql` contains the actual MySQL server.

- `mysqlcc` contains the MySQL Control Center (a graphical user interface for administration).

- `mysql-client` contains the client programs (`mysql`, `mysqladmin`, etc.) for administration of MySQL.

- `mysql-shared` contains the *shared libraries*, which are used by many programs to access MySQL.

- `mysql-devel` contains libraries and include files for program development in C.

- `mysql-max` contains the Max version of the MySQL server, which, among other things, supports BDB tables.

As a rule, it suffices to install the three packages `mysql`, `mysql-client`, and
`mysql-shared`. If you want to try out the MySQL Control Center, then install `mysqlcc`
as well. The other packages are not of immediate interest. MySQL can be launched
manually after installation with the following command:

```
root# /etc/init.d/mysql start
```

To have MySQL launch automatically at startup, execute the following command:

```
root# insserv mysql
```

As database directory, `/var/lib/mysql` is used.

Installation of the MySQL Linux Package of mysql.com

Every Linux distribution comes with its own MySQL packages. Their installation
proceeds without difficulty (see the previous section), but the following two issues
should be taken into consideration:

- The included versions are often quite old. Update packages are produced generally only when serious security problems need to be fixed.

- In the past, the versions provided were generally unstable. For example, with both Red Hat 8 and SuSE 8.1 the included MySQL server would crash as soon as a MySQL client from another server attempted to make itself known. (The server is restarted automatically; the client receives an error message: *Lost connection to MySQL server during query*.) Both companies quickly provided updates to the server and affected libraries, but the problem caused a great deal of confusion and anger among MySQL beginners. (The versions provided with Red Hat 9 and SuSE 8.2 appear to be more stable.)

On the web site `mysql.com` it is therefore recommended that one use only MySQL packages from that site. It is with these packages only that one can be sure that they will be optimally compiled.

> **WARNING** *Alas, following this suggestion is problematic. Every Linux distributor has its own ideas of how the software packages and their dependencies should be managed, in which directories the files should be installed, how the programs should be executed on system startup, etc.*
>
> *For this reason, only experienced Linux users should install packages that are not explicitly prepared for the Linux distribution. It would also be good to have some MySQL experience in case the installation runs into difficulties.*
>
> *If the installation of new packages leads to a major change in the MySQL version (such as MySQL 3.23.n to 4.0.n, or from 4.0.n to 4.1.n), and you wish to transfer existing data, then you should read the sections on backup and data migration in Chapter 10.*

If you have not been frightened off by this warning and wish to try out the latest version of MySQL, then here are a few tips on installation. We begin with the assumption that you already have completed an installation of MySQL, Apache, PHP, Perl, etc., based on the packages included in the distribution. The goal now is to deinstall the existing version of MySQL and replace it with a more current version.

Organization of the `mysql.com` Packages (RPMs)

You will find at the download site `mysql.com` the following packages for the current version of MySQL in RPM format for Intel-compatible processors:

`mysql-server-n.rpm`	contains the MySQL server
`mysql-client-n.rpm`	contains client programs (`mysql`, `mysqladmin`, etc.)
`mysql-shared-n.rpm`	contains the *shared libraries* used by many programs to access MySQL
`mysql-devel-n.rpm`	contains libraries and include files for program development in C
`mysql-embedded-n.rpm`	contains a special version of the MySQL server that can be integrated into other programs (for C developers only)
`mysql-bench-n.rpm`	contains scripts with benchmark tests
`mysql-Max-n.rpm`	contains the Max version of the MySQL server, which supports BDB tables

Installation of `mysql.com` RPMs Under Red Hat 9

The following instructions are for MySQL 4.0.12 under Red Hat 9. With other versions of MySQL and Red Hat there might be variations. I have tested the installation as thoroughly as I could, but there is always the possibility that some problems could arise:

- Stop the server (/etc/init.d/mysqld stop).

- If you have changed the MySQL access privileges, then create a backup copy of the directory /var/lib/mysql/mysql with the database mysql.

- Create a backup of /etc/my.cnf.

- Create a backup copy of the library libmysqlclient.so.10. (This is a library that dynamically links MySQL programs used to access the MySQL server. Under Red Hat 9 this affects, for example, PHP and Perl.)

```
root# cd /usr/lib
root# cp -a mysql/ mysqlbak
```

- Deinstall the following packages (those that are installed): mysql, mysql-server, and mysql-devel:

```
root# rpm -e mysql-server
root# rpm -e --nodeps mysql
```

- Install the RPM package of mysql.com with the following commands:

```
root# rpm -i MySQL-server-n.rpm
root# rpm -i MySQL-client-n.rpm
root# rpm -i MySQL-shared-n.rpm
```

The newly installed server is launched at once. No configuration file /etc/my.cnf is installed (at least not with the version 4.0.12 tested). As before, /var/lib/mysql is used as data directory.

Make sure that the MySQL server will be launched automatically by each system startup:

```
root# chkconfig --level 235 mysql on
```

Note that the script for starting and stopping the server is now /etc/init.d/mysql (and no longer mysqld).

- Restore the libmyclient.so.10 libraries:

```
root# cd /usr/lib
root# rm -rf mysql
root# mv mysql-bak mysql
root# ldconfig
```

There are now two versions of libmyclient installed: libmyclient.so.10 in the directory /usr/lib/mysql, and libmyclient.so.12 in the directory /usr/lib. The older version is required for various Red Hat original packages (Perl, PHP, etc.), the new versions for MySQL client programs that use the new functions of the current version of MySQL.

- If necessary, restore the `mysql` database and `/etc/my.cnf`. After a significant version change you will have to execute the script `mysql_fix_privilege_tables` (see Chapter 10).

Installation of `mysql.com` RPMs Under SuSE 8.2

The following instructions are for the installation of MySQL 4.0.12 under SuSE 8.2. These can differ for other versions of MySQL and SuSE. I have tested the installation, but it is still possible for problems to arise.

- Stop the server (`/etc/init.d/mysqld stop`).

- If you have changed the MySQL access privileges, then create a backup copy of the directory `/var/lib/mysql/mysql` with the database `mysql`.

- Create a backup copy of `/etc/my.cnf`.

- Start YaST2, select the filter SEARCH, and search for currently installed `mysql` packages. Select the following packages for deinstallation (those that are installed): `mysql`, `mysql-bench`, `mysql-client`, `mysql-devel`, and `mysql-max`. Note that you may not deinstall `mysql-shared`!
  Click on the button CHECK DEPENDENCIES. A dialog appears in which YaST2 dependency conflicts are determined (that is, that other installed packages may no longer function if the MySQL packages are deinstalled). For solving conflicts choose the option IGNORE CONFLICT AND RISK SYSTEM INCONSISTENCIES. Deinstall the selected packages.

- Install the RPM packages of `mysql.com` with the following commands:

```
root# rpm -i MySQL-server-n.rpm
root# rpm -i MySQL-client-n.rpm
root# rpm -i MySQL-shared-n.rpm
```

  The newly installed server is launched at once. No configuration file `/etc/my.cnf` is installed (at least not with the version 4.0.12 tested). As before, `/var/lib/mysql` is used as data directory.
  Note that now two MySQL `shared` packages are installed simultaneously. One of them comes from SuSE and makes available the library `libmysqlclient.so.10`, which is needed by Perl or `mysqlcc`; the other package comes from `msql.com` and contains the new version `ysqlclient.so.12` for programs that wish to use the new MySQL functions.

- If necessary, restore the `mysql` database and `/etc/my.cnf`. After a major version change you must also execute the script `mysql_fix_privilege_tables` (see Chapter 10).

Incompatibilities After Installation

Red Hat: The Init-V script for starting the MySQL server now has the name `mysql` (instead of `mysqld`).

Both Distributions: A further difference affects the internal management of the package dependencies. If after the MySQL update you install other packages that require MySQL, it can happen that the distributions do not recognize that MySQL has already been installed. With Red Hat, in the installation of such packages you should use rpm with the option --nodeps (not redhat-config-packages). With SuSE you can specify in YaST2 that the package dependencies are to be ignored.

Finally, problems are also to expected in distribution updates. In an update to a new version of the Linux distribution, MySQL is probably left untouched and will not be updated automatically.

Testing the Installation

To test whether the MySQL server runs and whether you can use it, launch the program mysql. Under Linux you simply execute mysql in a shell window. Under Windows launch mysql/bin/mysql.exe with a double click in Explorer. In this program you execute the command status. Under Unix/Linux the result should look like what is pictured in Figure 2-3.

```
linux:~ # mysql
Welcome to the MySQL monitor.  Commands end with ; or \g.
Your MySQL connection id is 26 to server version: 4.0.12

Type 'help;' or '\h' for help. Type '\c' to clear the buffer.

mysql> status
--------------
mysql  Ver 12.18 Distrib 4.0.12, for pc-linux (i686)

Connection id:          26
Current database:
Current user:           root@localhost
SSL:                    Not in use
Current pager:          less
Using outfile:          ''
Server version:         4.0.12
Protocol version:       10
Connection:             Localhost via UNIX socket
Client characterset:    latin1
Server characterset:    latin1
UNIX socket:            /var/lib/mysql/mysql.sock
Uptime:                 7 days 23 hours 52 min 56 sec

Threads: 3  Questions: 421  Slow queries: 0  Opens: 39  Flush tables: 1  Open ta
bles: 22  Queries per second avg: 0.001
--------------

mysql> ▉
```

Figure 2-3. Testing the MySQL installation under Linux

If that doesn't work, check whether the MySQL server is running at all. Under Linux you would execute ps -ax. It is normal that mysqld appears several times in the resulting list. (The server was not started several times, but divided itself into several threads.)

```
root# ps -ax | grep mysqld
2725 pts/2    S      0:00 /bin/sh /usr/bin/safe_mysqld ...
 2756 pts/2    S      0:00 /usr/sbin/mysqld ...
 2757 pts/2    S      0:00 /usr/sbin/mysqld ...
 2758 pts/2    S      0:00 /usr/sbin/mysqld ...
 2799 pts/2    S      0:00 grep mysqld
```

Under Windows NT/2000, take a look at the task manager. There should be a process running called `mysqld*.exe`.

If the MySQL server is not running, you will probably have to start it manually. Under Linux you would use the init-V script `mysql[d] start`. Under Windows use instead the program `WinMySQLadmin`.

> **REMARK** *The name* `mysqld` *is short for the MySQL daemon. This is simply another name for the MySQL server.*
> *Under Unix/Linux it is usual to call auxiliary programs running in the background "daemons." (In Windows NT/2000 such programs are called "services.")*

Security

After a default installation, MySQL is insecure. Anyone can enter without a password as *root* and has unlimited privileges. (Under Windows the default installation is even more insecure, if that is possible.)

As long as you are not storing any critical data in MySQL, you can continue to use the database system unsecured (just be aware of the security risks, however). If you value security, then you will find in Chapter 9 an extensive description of the MySQL access system, including a step-by-step introduction to beginning to secure your system.

Updating MySQL

You will find the most recent versions of MySQL in various formats (ZIP, RPM) at `www.mysql.com`.

> **CAUTION** *In general, it is recommended that you back up all MySQL databases as well as the configuration files* `Window\my.ini` *and* `etc/my.cnf` *before undertaking a MySQL update.*
> *If you update MySQL within a main version, that is, a small version change such as 4.0.12 to 4.0.13, then you can use your database files without change. The backup is merely a security measure.*
> *In the case of a large version change (such as from 4.0.n to 4.1.n), it could happen that you will have to reconfigure the databases. (In the past, MySQL was always backward compatible, but that is no guarantee for the future.) Further information on making a backup and on migrating between databases of incompatible versions of MySQL, as well as general information on* `mysqldump`, *can be found in Chapter 10. This section assumes that a small version change is carried out and that therefore the database files can be used without alteration.*

Updating Under Windows

- Stop the server (for example, with WinMySQLadmin).

- By all means, execute a backup of the database mysql. This database is deleted by deinstallation of MySQL. It contains the settings of all access privileges. The simplest thing to do is to copy the directory Mysql/data/mysql to another location.

- Install the new version of MySQL in the same directory as before.

- Restore the backup copy of the mysql database. Also, copy the backed-up directory mysql into the MySQL data directory Mysql/data.

- Start the server.

Updating Under Linux

- Stop the server ((/etc/init.d/mysql[d]).

- Execute a backup of the database mysql and the file /etc/my.cnf.

- Deinstall the MySQL packages with rpm -e or another package management tool (SuSE: yast2).

- Install the updated MySQL packages.

- Restore the *mysql* database. (If the MySQL server was automatically launched after installation, you must first terminate it.)

- Launch the MySQL server.

MySQL (Client Installation)

All of the client programs are automatically installed with the MySQL installation described above. Often, however, the server runs on a different computer, and you require only the client tools to access the external server. In this case, a space-saving client installation is sufficient.

With a client installation, only various administration programs (mysql, mysqladmin, mysqldump, etc.) as well as the related libraries and character set files are installed. Then you can use these programs to create new databases on the external MySQL server, read existing data, execute SQL commands, and so on.

> **REMARK** *In some situations, you can dispense entirely with the installation of client tools on the local computer, namely, when an administration tool is installed on the MySQL computer that runs locally (for example, phpMyAdmin) and can be used over the Internet. If the MySQL server runs on the computer of an ISP, then that is the usual situation; see the last section of this chapter.*

Windows

The zip archive `Winclients-version.zip` with all the files for a client installation can be found at the following address:

```
http://www.mysql.com/downloads/os-win32.html
```

Unfortunately, the client installation files were completely outdated as this book was being written. For this reason, it is better to execute a complete server installation, even if the server itself is not even going to be used.

Unix/Linux

The most current Linux distributions provide packages for client installation. Simply install the packages `mysql-n.rpm` and `mysql-shared-n.rpm` (not `mysql-server-version.rpm`). You can find such RPM files for the client installation at the download site `www.mysql.com`, and, in contrast to the comparable Windows package, always in the latest version.

Apache

> **POINTER** *This section describes a basic installation of Apache and some elementary configuration steps. Detailed information on the countless configuration possibilities as well as security of the installation can be found in books on Apache and at the Apache documentation site:*
>
> ```
> http://www.apache.org/docs/
> ```

Apache 1.3 versus Apache 2.0

At present, there are two versions of Apache available: Apache 1.3.n and Apache 2.0.n. Both versions are considered basically stable. However, in comparison to Apache 1.3, version 2.0 offers extensive new developments. Many supplementary modules to Apache 2.0, however, are not as fully mature and well tested as those of version 1.3. This applies particularly to the frequently installed PHP module. (The combination Apache 2.n and PHP 4.3 was still in an experimental stage as the work on this book was being completed.)

For this reason, you will still see Apache 1.3 on many Internet servers (and thus with many Internet service providers) for a while to come. For the examples of this book it does not make a great deal of difference whether you use Apache 1.3 or 2.0. I have tested the PHP and Perl–CGI examples under both versions without encountering any difficulties. There are few differences between the two versions in their basic configurations.

If you are working under Linux, then you should install the default version of Apache that comes with your distribution. If you set up a test system under Windows, then the choice is yours. This book describes the installation of version 2.0. If you prefer to install version 1.3, you will encounter a few differences from what is presented here.

Apache 2: Installation Under Windows

Deinstalling IIS

If you are working with a Windows Server version, then you should first make sure that the Microsoft Internet Information Server (IIS for short) is not running. The standard installation of Apache (port 80) does not work if IIS is running in parallel (for which there is seldom a reason in any case).

For checking or deinstallation of IIS execute SETTINGS | CONTROL PANEL | ADD / REMOVE PROGRAMS | ADD / REMOVE WINDOWS COMPONENTS. If necessary, deactivate the option IIS in WINDOWS COMPONENTS WIZARD, upon which the program will be terminated and deinstalled.

Installing Apache

Apache is available at www.apache.org and at various mirror sites as an installation program for Windows. Download the file apache_2.n_xxx.msi to your computer and launch the installation program in Windows Explorer with a double click. A dialog box appears for the basic configuration (see Figure 2-4). You will have to give the domain name (e.g., sol) and server name (e.g., uranus.sol). This information is needed even if your computer runs as a standalone test computer. As a rule, give simply the domain or workgroup name as well as the computer name. If you do not know what these names are on your computer, you can find them in the dialog SETTINGS | CONTROL PANEL | SYSTEM | NETWORK IDENTIFICATION.

Then you should specify the e-mail address of the administrator of the web server (you!) and whether the web server should use port 80.

After installation, Apache will be set up automatically as a service and launched immediately. In the right part of the task bar a small icon will appear that shows the state of Apache (a green arrow if the program is running). This icon can be used for starting and stopping Apache.

> **WARNING** *Note that your web server is now accessible from the Internet if you are connected to it. This holds even if you are connected through a dial-up modem. The web server is not reachable through an easily guessed name like* http://www.kofler.cc, *but via the current IP number given by your Internet service provider (e.g.,* http://172.12.34.45). *You should make sure that no confidential information can leak out of your system, even in a test installation. The best security is a firewall that generally keeps out access from the outside.*

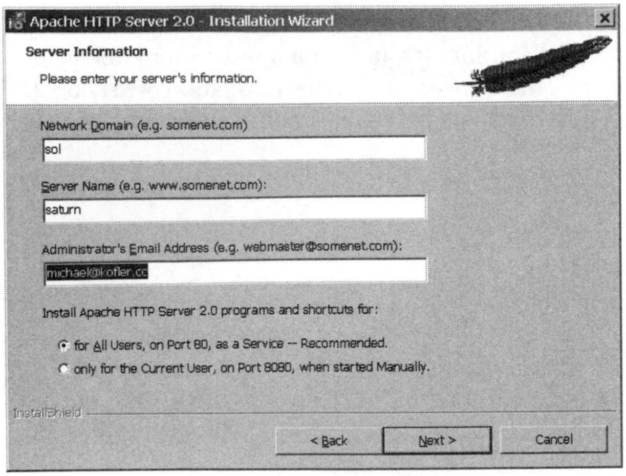

Figure 2-4. Apache basic configuration

Installation Under Linux

Apache is normally automatically installed under Linux. If that is not the case in your situation, you will have to install the relevant package (usually apache-*version*.rpm).

Red Hat

With Red Hat use the installation redhat-config-packages and choose the group *Webserver*. In addition to Apache 2, various associated programs are also installed.

SuSE

With SuSE launch the YaST2 module INSTALL SOFTWARE and install either the group SIMPLE WEBSERVER (Aache 1.31) or SIMPLE WEBSERVER WITH APACHE 2. Some additional packages will also be installed. The following description pertains to Apache 2.

Configuration and Start

Configuration File

Almost all Apache settings are managed via the configuration file httpd.conf. Important for the first startup is generally only the setting for *ServerName*. You should provide the network name of your computer, for example, the following:

```
# change in httpd.conf
ServerName saturn.sol # Here give the name of your computer
```

If the *ServerName* installation fails, Apache attempts to discover the computer name on its own. This works sometimes, but not always. Where `httpd.conf` is located depends on the operating system:

Windows	`Programs\Apache Group\Apache[2]\conf\httpd.conf`
Red Hat Linux	`/etc/httpd/conf/httpd.conf`
SuSE Linux	`/etc/apache2/httpd.conf`

Launching Apache

To launch the program after setting `httpd.conf`, the following commands are necessary:

Windows NT/2000/XP	Apache is executed by default as a service. You can check this in the dialog SETTINGS | CONTROL PANEL | ADMINISTRATIVE TOOLS | SERVICES.
Red Hat Linux	`root# /etc/init.d/httpd start`
SuSE Linux	`root# /etc/init.d/apache2 start`

To have Apache executed automatically under Linux at computer startup, execute the following commands:

Red Hat Linux	`root# chkconfig --level 35 httpd on`
SuSE Linux	`root# inssrv apache2`

Testing the Apache Installation

You can check with your web browser that everything is functioning correctly by calling up the page `http://localhost` or (following the example of this chapter) `http://saturn.sol`. This address leads to the start page of Apache, where temporarily only a single test page is displayed (see Figure 2-5).

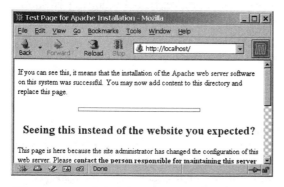

Figure 2-5. Apache's default start page

> **REMARK** *The name* localhost *is valid both under Windows and under Unix/Linux as the network name for the local computer. The address* http://localhost *therefore corresponds to* http://your.computer.name *(or whatever you have named your computer).*

Restarting Apache After Changing httpd.conf

After a change in httpd.conf, you must restart Apache so that the new configuration becomes effective. Depending on the operating system, the restart is carried out in one of several ways:

Windows First, execute START | PROGRAMS | APACHE | STOP APACHE; then START APACHE. You can also restart Apache 2 in the Apache Monitor (visible as an icon in the right part of the task bar). Under Windows NT/2000/XP there is a third variant: In SETTINGS | CONTROL PANEL | ADMINISTRATIVE TOOLS | SERVICES select the service Apache and click first on STOP in the SERVICES dialog, and then on START.

Red Hat Linux `root# /etc/init.d/httpd restart`

SuSE Linux `root# /etc/init.d/apache2 restart`

> **TIP** *If you encounter a (syntax) error in changing* httpd.conf, *the next Apache restart will fail. Information on the cause of the error can be found under Windows with* START | PROGRAMS | APACHE | CONFIGURE APACHE | TEST CONFIGURATION.

Creating an Alias (Virtual Directory)

In the default installation, Apache enables access to all files and subdirectories of a root directory. The path to this directory varies according to the operating system (in fact, according to the setting of DocumentRoot in httpd.conf). The following list shows the usual default settings:

Windows `Programs\Apache Group\Apache[2]\htdocs`

Red Hat Linux `/var/www/html`

SuSE Linux `/srv/www/htdocs`

With an alias it is possible to associate a virtual directory on the server with an arbitrary directory on the hard drive on the server. For example, via Apache, with the path http://computer.name/virtual you can access the actual directory e:\data\real or /usr/share/help. An alias is also helpful in simplifying access over the web server to directories located at various places on the hard drive.

To try out the PHP examples in this book you will not need an alias. You can simply copy the examples to the DocumentRoot directory. But if you would rather store the examples at a different location on your hard drive, you will have to add an alias line in httpd.conf according to the following template:

```
# in httpd.conf
Alias /mytest/ "E:/directory/subdirectory/"
```

In the definition of alias directories the following rules should be followed:

- All alias definitions usually occur in httpd.conf in a block that is introduced by *<IfModule mod_alias.c>* and ended with *</IfModule>*. In the Apache 2 default installation these tags are lacking, and the correct position can be recognized by the comment *#Aliases: Add here as many aliases as you need . . . .*

- Under Windows the directories must be indicated with a forward, not a backward, slash.

- Directories (e.g., e:/data/real/) must end with a forward slash.

- After the alias definition, the properties of the directory must be set with *<Directory "directory">*. A *<Directory>* block might look as follows:

```
<Directory "E:/dir/subdir/">
    Options Indexes MultiViews
    AllowOverride All
    Order allow,deny
    Allow from all
</Directory>
```

This means that when the directory does not contain the file *index.html* (option Indexes), a list of all files in this directory will be displayed; that the correct version of the files will automatically be used if there is a choice from among several languages (*MultiViews*); that .htaccess will be taken into account and all relevant options will be processed (*AllowOverride All*); and that everybody can access the directory (*Order* and *Allow*).

The option *Indexes* is useful for testing, but it should be eliminated in production, because it represents a security risk. (It is possible that a directory contains files that should not be visible to all. *Indexes* reveals the names of these files.)

For the change in httpd.conf to become effective, Apache must be restarted.

Access Protection for Individual Directories (.htaccess)

There are situations in which not all of the directories managed by Apache should be universally accessible. For example, if you install phpMyAdmin for administration of MySQL at an Internet service provider, these administrative tasks should be available to you alone, and not to every web surfer who happens by.

Password File

The simplest method of protecting individual directories is offered by the file
.htaccess, which is placed in the directory in question. However, it is first necessary
to set up a password file, which in the following example is named site.pwd. This file
can, in principle, be located just about anywhere, though for reasons of security it is
recommended to select a directory that is not accessible from without (that is, outside
of the directories reachable by Apache).

The password file is generated with the Apache auxiliary program htpasswd. (If
you are working under SuSE with Apache 2, the command is htpasswd2.) Choose the
option -c (*create*), and specify the name of the password file and a user name. The
program will ask you for the desired password, and then it generates the password file,
in which the user name appears in plain text, the password in encrypted form.

```
> htpasswd -c site.pwd myname
New password: **********
Re-type new password: **********
Adding password for user myname
```

To add an additional combination of user name and password to a preexisting
password file, execute htpasswd again, this time without the option -c:

```
> htpasswd site.pwd name2
New password: **********
Re-type new password: **********
Adding password for user name2
```

The resulting password file will look something like this:

```
myname:$apr1$gp1 .. ..$qljDszVJOSCS.oBoPJItS/
name2:$apr1$A22 .. ..$OVO1Nc1FcXgNsruT9c6Iq1
```

> **REMARK** *If you wish to execute* htpasswd.exe *under Windows, you have to open a
> command window (command prompt) and specify the complete path name inside
> quotation marks (usually* "Programs\Apache Group\Apache\bin\htpasswd.exe"*).*
>
> *If you want to create or enlarge the password file in a directory of an Internet
> service provider, then use* telnet *or* ssh *to access the computer of the ISP (in order to
> execute* htpasswd *there). Many ISPs make available other configuration aids.*

> **WARNING** .htaccess *files are effective only when allowed in the Apache configura-
> tion file* httpd.conf. *Sometimes, the Apache default configuration contains the entry*
> AllowOverride None, *and then the* .htaccess *files remain useless.*
>
> *For* .htaccess *files to be considered, the relevant directory (within a <Directory>
> group) must have specified the option* AllowOverride All *or* AllowOverride *with a
> combination of* AuthConfig, FileInfo, Limit, *and* Options.

> **REMARK**   *Under Windows, it is impossible with Windows Explorer to create a file with the name* .htaccess. *Explorer believes that this is an invalid name. Normally, this is no problem, since you can create* .htaccess *with the command* htaccess. *If for some reason you need to use Explorer, then first, name the file* htaccess.txt *and then, use an input window (DOS window) and rename the file with* RENAME htaccess.txt .htaccess

Building the .htaccess *File*

An .htaccess file protects the entire contents of a directory (including all subdirectories). The file normally consists of the following four lines. Here *AuthUserFile* specifies the complete file name of the password file:

```
AuthType Basic
AuthUserFile /www/username/htdocs/_private/site.pwd
AuthName "myrealm"
Require valid-user
```

AuthName denotes the *realm* within which access is valid. The point is that you do not have to execute a login every time want to access various directories protected by .htaccess. Once you have logged in with a particular *AuthName*, this login remains valid for all further directories with this *AuthName* indicator.

For .htaccess this means that you specify the same *AuthName* character string for directories with a common login. Conversely, for varying directories you may specify varying domain names, in which case a new login is required for each directory.

Require valid-user means that every valid combination of user name and password is allowed. Alternatively, you can specify here that a login is permitted only for particular users:

```
Require user myname name2 name3
```

Access to a Protected Directory

As soon as you attempt to read a file from a protected directory with a browser, the web browser presents a login dialog (see Figure 2-6).

> **POINTER**   *Further details on user authentication and* .htaccess *configuration can be found at the following web addresses:*
>
> ```
> http://apache-server.com/tutorials/ATusing-htaccess.html
> http://www.apacheweek.com/features/userauth
> ```

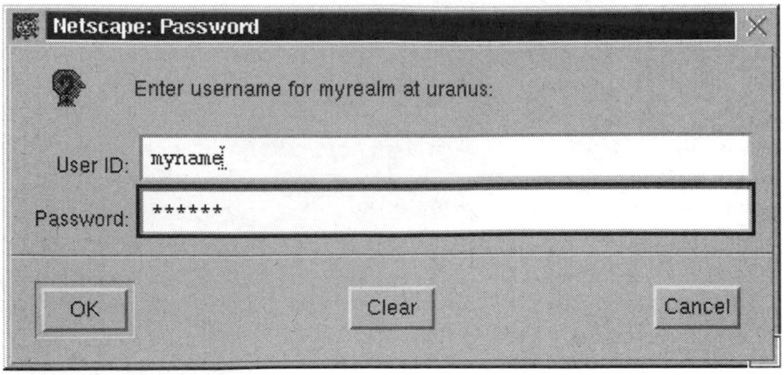

Figure 2-6. Access to a web directory protected by .htaccess

PHP

PHP stands for *PHP Hypertext Preprocessor* (which is to say that we are dealing with a recursive abbreviation, so beloved in the Unix community). PHP enables the insertion of script code into HTML files. It works like this: Every time a surfer requests a file with the identifier *.php, the web server (Apache, for example) transmits this file to the PHP interpreter. This, in turn, evaluates the PHP code and constructs the resulting HTML document, which is then returned to the web server. The web server then directs the file to the surfer. PHP thus offers a simple way of generating dynamic web pages. No assumptions need be made about the client.

The examples in this book were tested with the following versions of Apache and PHP:

- Windows 2000: Apache 1.3.n and Apache 2.n with PHP 4.3

- Red Hat 8.0: Apache 2.n with PHP 4.2

- Red Hat 9.0 beta 3: Apache 2.n with PHP 4.2

- SuSE 8.1: Apache 1.3.n with PHP 4.2

- SuSE 8.2 beta 5: Apache 2.n with PHP 4.3

REMARK *I would like to mention once again that as of March 2003 the combination of Apache 2 and PHP 4.2/4.3 still has the status* experimental *and is not to be recommended for use in production. No problems arose in my tests, but for web servers in production use the present recommendation is Apache 1.3.n.*

Perhaps the Apache/PHP combination will have matured by the time you are reading this book. With regard to the configuration possibilities described in this book, nothing changes in moving from Apache 1.3 to 2.0.

The CGI Version Versus the Apache Module

There are two basic ways that Apache can run the PHP interpreter: as a freestanding program and as a module.

- In the first variant, the PHP interpreter is executed as a *CGI program*. The program must be restarted for the translation of each *.php file, which is relatively inefficient. The advantage of the CGI variant is that installation and configuration are simpler.

- In the second variant, the PHP interpreter is run as an Apache module. The module is a sort of extension to the Apache program. It is loaded once and then remains in memory. The advantage of the module variant is that execution is considerably more efficient. Furthermore, some additional functions are available under PHP (for example, HTTP authentication functions).

  Under Windows, Apache has been extended to include the PHP module, using SAPI (Server Application Interface).

  Under Unix/Linux, on the other hand, the PHP module is usually included in the form of a *Dynamic Shared Object* (DSO). Both interfaces enable the subsequent addition or exchange of Apache modules without Apache itself having to be recompiled.

> **REMARK**   *You can easily configure Apache on your test system in such a way that it can deal with *.php, *.php3, and *.php4 files. However, on your ISP's system, that is not the case; that is, your ISP generally prescribes a particular file identifier (usually *.php). To avoid problems later with the installation of your PHP files on the ISP computer, you should use the same file identifier in your test environment as that of your ISP.*
>
> *In this book, we generally use the file identifier *.php. If your web server is configured in such a way that the file identifier *.php3 or *.php4 is prescribed, then you must make the appropriate changes. Furthermore, you must adapt all the links within HTML and PHP code (this affects particularly <a href= . . . > and <form action= . . . >).*

PHP4 Installation Under Windows

At the web site http://www.php.net/ you will find the most recent version of PHP in two variants: as a Zip archive (which can be opened with the free program WinZip) and as an installation program. Since the installation program is dependent on the Internet information server, while in this book Apache is used as the web server, you should choose the Zip variant.

Installation comprises the following steps:

- Simply copy all the files in the Zip archive into an arbitrary directory. (The following examples assume that the installation directory is C:\php-430.)

- Copy the file C:\php-430\php4ts.dll into the directory sapi in your PHP installation (C:\php-430\sapi).

- Insert the boldface lines below into the Apache configuration file httpd.conf.

```
# in httpd.conf for Apache 2
 ...
LoadModule php4_module c:/php-430/sapi/php4apache2.dll
AddType application/x-httpd-php .php .php3 .php4
 ...
```

If you are using Apache 1.3, the configuration looks like this:

```
# in httpd.conf for Apache 1.3
 ...
LoadModule php4_module c:/php-430/sapi/php4apache.dll
AddModule mod_php4.c
AddType application/x-httpd-php .php .php3 .php4
 ...
```

- Restart Apache. If a warning is displayed with Apache 1.3 that the mod_php4 module has already been loaded, delete the AddModule line from httpd.conf

PHP4 Installation Under Linux

PHP is included with all current Linux distributions and is generally included in an Apache installation. You can check this with the command rpm -qa | grep -i php.
Red Hat: If PHP is not yet installed, start the program redhat-config-packages. The packages are to be found in the group *Webserver*.

By default, the package *php-mysql*, which extends PHP with functions for communicating with MySQL, is not installed. Click on the button DETAILS in the group *Webserver* and select the package for installation.

Then Apache must be restarted.

```
root# /etc/init.d/httpd restart
```

SuSE: The two PHP packages mod_php4-core and apache2-mod_php4 are installed together with Apache 2. For PHP to function, the character string *php4* must be inserted into the declaration *APACHE_MODULES* in the file /etc/sysconfig/apache2. (Possibly, this change will not be required in the final version of SuSE 9 and is a problem only with the beta version.)

```
# in the file /etc/sysconfig/apache2
...
APACHE_MODULES="access actions alias auth auth_dbm autoindex cgi
  dir env expires include log_config mime negotiation php4
  setenvif status suexec userdir"
...
```

Then relaunch Apache:

```
root# /etc/init.d/apache2 restart
```

Testing the PHP Installation

Create a test file phptest.php according to the following template, and save the file in a location where Apache can access it (that is, in the htdocs directory or in an alias directory). The name of the file should not be test.php, since Apache is frequently configured, for reasons of security, in such a way that this file is not evaluated.

```
<?php phpinfo(); ?>
```

Now load this page with a web browser. Be sure that the page is not read directly from the file system but via Apache. (For example, you must use http://localhost/phptest.php as the address.) The result should look like Figure 2-7.

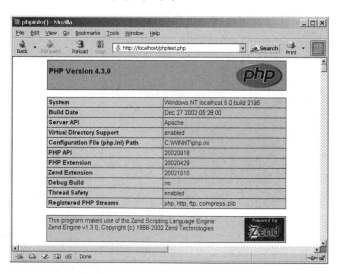

Figure 2-7. PHP 4 runs!

> **TIP** *If the test is unsuccessful, and instead of the table shown in Figure 2-7 you get only an empty page or a couple of lines of weird PHP code, the most probable cause of the trouble is that you are looking at the page directly and not via Apache. Please be sure that the path in the web browser contains* `http://localhost` *and not the direct file name, such as* `C:\path\phptest.php`. *Other possible causes of the error are Apache configuration problems. Have you restarted Apache after the change in the configuration file?*
>
> *If you see nothing at all, and instead, a download dialog appears, then the Apache configuration has failed. Apache does not recognize the file type* `*.php`, *and therefore does not know that it is supposed to execute the PHP file.*
>
> *If a download dialog continues to appear after a change in the configuration, then the web browser's cache might be at fault. In this regard, Mozilla seems especially guilty. Delete the cache to ensure that the problem is not caused by the web browser. (In Mozilla, execute* EDIT | PREFERENCES | ADVANCED | CACHE | CLEAR XXX CACHE.)

Testing PHP in Combination with MySQL

The following program (see Figure 2-8) provides a list of all MySQL databases. (Immediately after installation there are only two databases: *test* is empty, while *mysql* is responsible for the MySQL internal management of access privileges.) The variable *mysqlpasswd* can remain empty as long as MySQL access is not secured by a password.

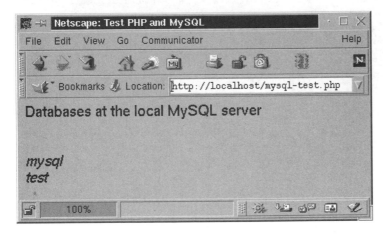

Figure 2-8. PHP can access MySQL.

```php
<?php // mysql-test.php ?>
<html><head>
<title>Test PHP and MySQL</title>
</head><body>
<?php
  $mysqluser="root";              // user name
  $mysqlpasswd="xxx";            // password
  $mysqlhost="localhost";    // computer name
```

```
   $connID = mysql_connect($mysqlhost, $mysqluser, $mysqlpasswd);
   $result=mysql_list_dbs();
   echo "<p>Databases at the local MySQL server<p>\n";
   echo "<p>";
   while($row = mysql_fetch_row($result)) {
     echo "<br><i>$row[0]</i>\n";}
   echo "<p>";
?>
</body></html>
```

> **TIP** *If access to a database fails, either because the MySQL server is not running or because the user name and password are invalid, a series of error messages should appear (e.g.,* Warning: mysql_connect(): Access denied for user: 'root@127.0.0.1' (Using password: NO). *In this case, set* mysqluser *and* mysqlpasswd *correctly.*
> *If nothing but an empty page appears, then an error has probably occurred, but it is not displayed. Alter* php.ini *so that* display_errors = On *is valid (details in the next section).*

PHP Configuration

Various configuration details of the PHP interpreter are controlled by the file php.ini. For this file to be recognized, under Unix/Linux it must be located in the directory /etc, while under Windows, in the PHP installation directory (e.g., c:\winnt\).

Under Linux, /etc/php.ini is usually preconfigured.

In the Windows installation of PHP, on the other hand, you will find in the PHP installation directory several options for php.ini:

- p.ini-recommended contains the settings recommended by the PHP developers, which are optimized for maximal security and speed.

- php.ini-dist contains settings that are compatible, as far as possible, with earlier versions of PHP; in many PHP installations these settings are used by default.

You should copy one of these options into the Windows directory and change its name to php.ini. (PHP will work entirely without php.ini: Then the PHP default settings are valid.)

> **WARNING** *If PHP fails to function as it ought, if it presents indecipherable error messages (or none at all), then frequently, the trouble is with* php.ini *(or possibly also with an old version of* php.ini *from an earlier version of PHP!). In such cases, you should first create a backup copy of the existing* php.ini *file and then install* php.ini-recommended *into the* etc *directory or in the Windows directory.*
> *Changes in* php.ini *become effective only after Apache has been restarted (if PHP is executed as an Apache module).*

PHP Extensions Under Windows (xtensions)

PHP extensions make possible the use of additional functions that are not directly integrated into PHP. Which functions are directly integrated into PHP and which are realized as *extensions* depends on how PHP is compiled. The MySQL functions are generally directly integrated into PHP; that is, they do not have to be loaded as extensions. With PHP 4.3, a glance into the directory `php-install-dir\extensions` provides a good overview of the selection of available extensions.

If you are using PHP under Windows and wish to use PHP extensions, then the variable *extension_dir* must be set so that it specifies the directory of the PHP installation:

```
extension_dir = "c:\php-430\extensions\"
```

Furthermore, you must specify in `php.ini` the desired extensions via *extension* settings. The line for the OpenSSL module, for example, looks like this:

```
extension=php_openssl.dll
```

php.ini *Settings for This Book*

For my tests under Linux, I have not changed the file `/etc/php.ini`. For tests under Windows I have used `php.ini-recommended` as a basis for `php.ini`, and made only the following changes:

- *display_errors = On*: this setting has the effect that error messages are displayed in the case of errors in PHP scripts. This is, of course, practical during program development. With servers deployed in the Internet, this setting should be *Off*, since error messages often give hints as to what is contained in the code and thus present a security problem. (If in developing a PHP page, instead of a result, only an empty page appears in the web browser, it is almost always the *display_errors* setting that is to blame.)

- *magic_quotes_gpc = On*: This setting has the effect that in transferring data between web sites (Get/Post/Cookie), special characters, such as ', ", \, and a zero byte, are replaced by \', \", \\, and \0. Details on *magic quotes* can be found in Chapter 11. The setting has been chosen to be *On*, because that is the case with almost all Internet service providers.

- **default_charset**: This option should either not be set at all (which is the case in the default setting), or set as *"iso-8859-1"*. The setting *default_charset* controls whether in the transfer of HTML documents, the PHP interpreter should specify that the pages should be coded according to a particular character set. If *default_charset* is not set, the the coding of HTML documents can be set by a *<meta>* tag between *<head>* and *</head>*:

```
<meta http-equiv="Content-Type"
      content="text/html; charset=iso-8859-1" />
```

The examples in this book generally use the ISO-8859-1 character set. This character set is also known as *latin1*, and it contains most of the characters used in Western European languages.

> **TIP** *If you change* php.ini, *then take care that you do not change merely the comments, but the actual option settings. Comments in* php.ini *are indicated by a semicolon. Everything after a semicolon in a line is ignored!*

phpMyAdmin

The best current tool for convenient administration of MySQL over an Internet connection is probably phpMyAdmin (Figure 2-9). The only condition for the use of phpMyAdmin is the installation of PHP on the computer on which the MySQL server is running. (Note that phpMyAdmin consists of numerous *.php files. Thus phpMyAdmin is not only a valuable tool, but at the same time an excellent example of MySQL programming with PHP.)

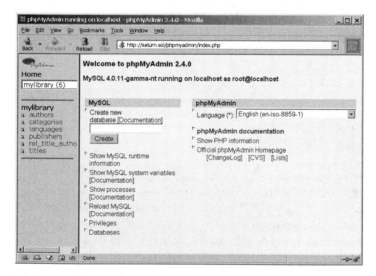

Figure 2-9. phpMyAdmin

> **POINTER** *This section describes only the installation of phpMyAdmin on a local test system. Further information on other installation variants (such as for administration of MySQL by an Internet service provider) as well as an extensive description of the application possibilities of phpMyAdmin can be found in Chapter 4.*

Installation

You can find phpMyAdmin at the web site http://www.phpmyadmin.net/ as a *tar.gz
or *.zip archive for downloading. All the files in this archive must be copied
into a subdirectory of the DocumentRoot directory of Apache. (Depending on the
operating system, the directory is called Programs\Apache Group\Apache[2]\htdocs,
/var/www/html, or /srv/www/htdocs.

Under Windows, you can use WinZip, for example, for expanding the archive.
Under Unix/Linux, on the other hand, you would use commands according to the
pattern below (adapt the archive name and target directory as required). This book
assumes that phpMyAdmin is installed in the directory phpmyadmin, but you can name
the directory as you like:

```
root# tar xzf phpMyAdmin-n-php.tar.gz -C /srv/www/htdocs/
root# mv /srv/www/htdocs/phpMyAdmin-n /srv/www/htdocs/phpmyadmin
```

The hard disk space needed for phpMyAdmin 2.4 is about 5.5 megabytes.

> **TIP** *With SuSE, phpMyAdmin is already included, and it can be installed with
> YaST. As installation location the directory* /srv/www/htdocs/phpMyAdmin *is used.*

Minimal Configuration for phpMyAdmin

Before you can use phpMyAdmin, you must first change some settings in the file
config.inc.php in the phpMyAdmin installation directory. The listing presented below
contains only the relevant lines for a minimal configuration. Normally, only the lines
in boldface need to be changed.

The address must be contained in *$cfg['PmaAbsoluteUri']*, by which the
phpMyAdmin files are reachable in the network (in my local testnetwork it is
uranus.sol). Here *localhost* is not allowable! Instead of *phpmyadmin*, the directory
under which phpMyAdmin is actually reachable in your installation must be given (in
correct upper- and lowercase letters, and terminated with a forward slash).

You could attempt simply to leave *$cfg['PmaAbsoluteUri']* empty; in many cases,
phpMyAdmin succeeds in determining the correct setting itself. However, if that does
not work, then in the use of phpMyAdmin, errors occur whose cause is difficult to
trace:

```
# changes in config.inc.php
...
# must contain the computer name and the phpMyAdmin installation directory:
$cfg['PmaAbsoluteUri'] = 'http://uranus.sol/phpmyadmin/';
...
```

The following parameters specify how phpMyAdmin creates the connection to
the MySQL server. If MySQL has not yet been secured with a password, then of course,
the password string should remain empty:

```
$cfg['Servers'][$i]['host']      = 'localhost';  // MySQL hostname
  ...
$cfg['Servers'][$i]['auth_type'] = 'config';     // must be 'config'
$cfg['Servers'][$i]['user']      = 'root';       // MySQL user
$cfg['Servers'][$i]['password']  = 'xxx';        // MySQL password
  ...
```

Then you can test phpMyAdmin by placing in your web browser the address `http://localhost/phpmyadmin/index.php` or `http://`*computername*`/phpmyadmin/index.php`. The start page should look somewhat like that depicted in Figure 2-9 (depending on which version of phpMyAdmin you have installed and what access rights phpMyAdmin has on the MySQL server).

Controlling Access to the phpMyAdmin Directory with a Password

With phpMyAdmin you are faced with a large security problem: Not only you, but every web surfer in the known universe can manipulate your databases with phpMyAdmin, or even delete them (if the surfer discovers the directory in which you have installed phpMyAdmin). You can prevent this by securing access to the phpMyAdmin directory with a password via an .htaccess file. (This is not a MySQL password, but one for Apache! The use of .htaccess has been described already in the section in this chapter on Apache.)

> **CAUTION** *A second security problem is presented by the file* config.inc.php, *which contains your MySQL password in plain text. Sometimes, the computer of the ISP is installed in such a way that web files can be accessed via FTP. then the protection offered by* .htaccess *is insufficient. Make sure that it is impossible to read* config.inc.php *by anonymous FTP.*

Perl

Perl is perhaps the best-loved scripting language running under Unix. It is used by system administrators and web programmers (for CGI scripts), among others. However, Perl is of interest to you even if you have no intention of programming in Perl. Namely, there is a host of scripts for various MySQL administrative tasks. (Some are provided with MySQL, while many others can be found on the Internet.) In order for these scripts to be usable, Perl must be installed on your computer.

> **REMARK** *The examples for this book were tested with Perl 5.6 and 5.8. However, they should work without problem with earlier versions of Perl.*

Installation

Perl Installation Under Windows

With its package ActivePerl, the company ActiveState offers the only current version of Perl for Windows. ActivePerl can be downloaded freely as an MSI file from `www.activestate.com`. (You will also find at that site a host of commercial Perl-related products.) With Windows ME or Windows 2000 you begin installation simply by double clicking on the MSI file. With older versions of Windows, you must first install the Windows installer (a download link can be found at `www.activestate.com`).

Perl Installation Under Linux

Perl is automatically installed with almost all Linux distributions, since countless administration tools require Perl. You can determine whether Perl is installed and, if so, what version, with the following command:

```
root# perl --version
This is perl, v5.8.0 built for i586-linux-thread-multi
```

If Perl happens not to have been installed, then you can install the Perl package with `rpm` or `redhat-config-packages` (Red Hat) or with YaST (SuSE).

Testing the Perl Installation

Create a test file with the name `test.pl` and the following contents:

```
#!/usr/bin/perl -w
print "Hello world!\n";
print "Please hit Return to end the program!";
$wait_for_return = <STDIN>;
```

Windows: Under Windows it should be possible to launch the file at once with a double click. The program prints "Hello world!" in a command window, waits for Return, and then terminates.

If a double click fails to bring about program execution, then open a command window and try the following command:

```
Q:\> perl Q:\directory_with_my_perl_files\test.pl
```

Linux: Under Unix/Linux you must first label `test.pl` as an executable file:

```
user$ chmod u+x test.pl
```

Now the program can be executed:

```
user$ ./test.pl
Hello World!
Please hit Return to end the program!<Return>
```

If this doesn't work, then perhaps the Perl interpreter has not been installed in the directory /usr/bin but in some other directory. Determine what directory this is, and make the necessary change in the file test.pl.

> **REMARK** *Under Unix/Linux it is not usual practice to give Perl files names of the form* *.pl *(even though it does no harm). Nonetheless, in this book we shall use this identifier to make it easier to exchange files between Windows and Unix/Linux.*

MySQL Support for Perl

The installation of Perl is not the end of the matter. Perl is not capable of communicating with MySQL all by itself. Perl must be extended with two auxiliary modules:

- **DBI:** *DBI* stands for *database interface*. With *DBI* modules we are dealing with a general interface for database programming.

- **DBD-Mysql:** *DBD* stands for *database driver*. This module contains the MySQL-specific extension to *DBI*.

> **WARNING** DBD-Mysql *assumes that the MySQL client libraries are installed on the computer (files* libmysqlclient *and* libmysql.dll*).*
>
> *For Windows the client library is not available separately. Therefore, it is simplest to install the complete package. It is important that the* PATH *variable contain the directory with the file* libmysql.dll *(usually,* C:\mysql\bin*).*

Installation of DBI and DBD-Mysql Under Windows

Extraordinarily frustrating was the attempt to install both packages under Windows (January 2003, ActivePerl 5.6.1 Build 633 and ActivePerl 5.8 Build 804). The installation takes place basically with the supplementary program ppm (*Perl package manager*), which is included with ActivePerl. The program can be started in a command window. It assumes a running Internet connection. The use of ppm follows from the following code lines (for ActivePerl 5.6.1):

```
C:> ppm
PPM interactive shell (2.1.6) - type \sqhelp\sq for available commands.
PPM> install dbi
Install package \sqdbi?\sq (y/N): y
Installing package \sqdbi\sq ...
Bytes transferred: 401795
Installing C:\Programs\perl\site\lib\auto\DBI\dbd_xsh.h
Installing C:\Programs\perl\site\lib\auto\DBI\DBI.bs
 ...
```

```
Writing C:\Programs\perl\site\lib\auto\DBI\.packlist

PPM> install DBD-Mysql
Install package \sqDBD-Mysql?\sq (y/N): y
Installing package \sqDBD-Mysql\sq ...
Error installing package \sqDBD-Mysql\sq: Could not locate a PPD file
for package DBD-Mysql
```

ActivePerl 5.8 contains a newer version of ppm. The command input is the same as with the previous version, though the displayed information looks a bit different.

> **TIP** *If your Internet connection is via an HTTP proxy, then before the* install *command, the following command must be executed, where* myproxy.com:8080 *should be replaced by the actual proxy address:*
>
> set http_proxy=http://myproxy.com:8080/
>
> *You can obtain the available packages with* search <pattern>. *For example,* search mysql *finds all supplementary Perl packages whose name contains* mysql *(regardless of where in the name the string is located).*

The problem here is that ppm does not find the package *dbd-mysql* either with ActivePerl 5.6.1 or ActivePerl 5.8 (see the error message at the end of the command install dbd-mysql). Here is a solution:

- If you are lucky, this problem will have been solved by the time this book has appeared in your hands. Then dbd-mysql should function as it did previously.

- If you are working with ActivePerl 5.6.1, you can use the following command for installation. Note the upper- and lowercase usage!

```
PPM> install http://www.activestate.com/PPMPackages/5.6/DBD-Mysql.ppd
Install package \sqhttp://www.activestate.com/PPMPackages/5.6/
  dbd-mysql.ppd?\sq (y/N): y
Installing package \sqdbd-mysql\sq ...
Bytes transferred: 104405
Installing C:\Programs\perl\site\lib\auto\DBD\mysql\mysql.bs
Installing C:\Programs\perl\site\lib\auto\DBD\mysql\mysql.dll
  ...
Writing C:\Programs\perl\site\lib\auto\DBD\Mysql\.packlist
```

Basically, the installation works. The problem is that in this manner you end up installing an ancient version of *dbd-mysql* from June 2000.

- If you are working with ActivePerl 5.8, then installation works with the following command (according to the discussion thread in the mailing list *mailing.database.msql-mysql-modules*; see http://www.mysqlforums.com/):

```
PPM> install http://theoryx5.uwinnipeg.ca/ppms/DBD-mysql.ppd
```

The problem this time is one of stability. Perl programs with MySQL access are executed, but at the program's end the Perl interpreter crashes or remains in an endless loop. (Hit `Control+C`!) It is not clear whether these problems are related to the particular version (4.0.*n*) of the MySQL server.

- With both ActivePerl versions, you can install the package *DBD-mysqlPP* instead of *DBD-Mysql*. This is a relatively new implementation of *DBD-Mysql*, which does not depend on the MySQL client library. Therefore, the package can be used even if the MySQL client library is not installed or (in the case of some operating systems) not even available.

  Unfortunately, *DBD-mysqlPP* is not fully mature and also not completely compatible with *DBD-Mysql*. Thus there are necessary code changes in Perl scripts that were originally planned for *DBD-Mysql*. Some *DBD-Mysql* functions are not implemented at all. Finally, *DBD-mysqlPP* is said to be slower than *DBD-Mysql* (which I have not checked).

  In short, *DBD-mysqlPP* is currently an imperfect substitute for *DBD-Mysql*.

In the end, I made my experiments under Windows with ActivePerl 5.6.1 and the old version of *DBD-mysql* for Perl 5.6.

Installation of DBI and DBD-Mysql Under Linux

Red Hat: With Red Hat 9.0, the packages `perl-DBI` and `perl-DBD-MySQL` are located on CD 2. The installation is accomplished most easily with `rpm -i` *package file name*.
SuSE: With SuSE you install the packages `perl-DBI` and `perl-Msql-MySQL-modules` with YaST2.

With both distributions you can check whether the packages are already installed with the command `rpm-qa | grep -i perl`.

Testing DBI and DBD-Mysql

The following Perl script shows all databases available to the MySQL server. Immediately after installation these are only *mysql* and *test*. The example will work only if the given user name and password permit access to this table. Change this information as need be. (The words in question are in slant script. If MySQL is still not password protected, then both character strings can be left empty. Information for setting MySQL access privileges can be found in Chapter 9.)

```perl
#!/usr/bin/perl -w
# Test file mysql-test.pl
use DBI();
# establish connection to database
$dbh = DBI->connect(
  "DBI:mysql:database=mysql;host=localhost",
  "user", "password", {'RaiseError' => 1});
# execute query
$sth = $dbh->prepare("SHOW DATABASES");
$sth->execute();
# show results
```

```
while(@ary = $sth->fetchrow_array()) {
  print join("\t", @ary), "\n";
}
$sth->finish();
```

The result of the script will look something like this (depending on how many databases have already been installed):

```
mysql
test
```

Apache Configuration for Perl and CGI

If you wish to use Perl via CGI for programming dynamic HTML pages, then you must store the Perl files in the directory `cgi-bin` of the Apache web server. The default location of this directory is system-dependent:

Windows	`Program Files/Apache Group/Apache/cgi-bin`
Red Hat Linux	`/var/www/cgi-bin`
SuSE Linux	`/srv/www/cgi-bin`

Furthermore, Apache must be so configured that Perl scripts are executed by the Perl interpreter. For this there are two possibilities: Either the Perl interpreter is restarted for every script, or the interpreter remains in memory. The second variant is much more efficient, but it assumes the Apache module *mod-perl*.

CGI on Windows Computers

For Apache actually to execute the page `http://www.meine-firma.com/cgi-bin/hello-cgi.pl`, the following setting within `httpd.conf` is necessary:

```
# in httpd.conf
ScriptAlias /cgi-bin/ "C:/Program Files/Apache Group/Apache/cgi-bin/"
<Directory "C:/Program Files/Apache Group/Apache/cgi-bin">
    AllowOverride None
    Options None
    ScriptInterpreterSource registry
</Directory>
```

The parts in slant font must, of course, be replaced by the directories that will actually be used on your computer.

REMARK *Pay particular attention to the* ScriptInterpreterSource *line, which is not always present by default. This line is necessary, because Apache normally evaluates the first line of a Perl script in order to search for the Perl interpreter. This line contains, as a rule, the text* #!/usr/bin/perl. *Under Unix/Linux the interpreter is located there, but not under Windows.*

With the ScriptInterpreterSource *line you obtain the result that Apache determines the location of the Perl interpreter, based on the file identifier of the script (which must now be* *.pl) and Windows registry. If you forget* ScriptInterpreterSource, *then you will generally get the error message* Internal Server Error.

Note also that apache must be restarted after a change in httpd.conf.

CGI on Unix/Linux Computers

With Red Hat and SuSE, httpd.conf is already correctly configured and does not need to be altered.

- **Special for Red Hat:** By default, all necessary modules are already installed.

- **SuSE:** To execute the example programs for this book you need the package perl-HTML-Parser, which in general you will have to install. All other Perl packages should be available by default.

- **Access privileges:** Note that the files in the cgi-bin directory are executable and that Apache (which usually is executed under a special account such as *apache* or *wwwrun*) is also allowed to read these files. Use chmod to set the appropriate access privileges.

TIP *Even if you move the CGI files via FTP into the* cgi-bin *directory of your ISP, you must set the access privileges. The FTP protocol provides for this possibility, and most FTP programs are capable of doing so. (With the program WS_FTP, which runs under Windows, you can click on the files with the right mouse button and execute the command* chmod.)

Testing CGI Scripts

To test whether CGI files are executed, create the file cgi-test.pl in the cgi-bin directory:

```
#!/usr/bin/perl -w
# Test file cgi-test.pl
use CGI qw(:standard);
use CGI::Carp qw(fatalsToBrowser);
print header(),
  start_html("Hello CGI"),
  p("Hello CGI"),
  end_html();
```

If you are working under Unix/Linux, then you must set the access privileges with chmod g+rx or chmod a+rx in such a way that Apache is able to access the files. Then open the following page with a web browser (see Figure 2-10). Instead of www.myserver.com, you must specify the network address of your computer or localhost:

http://*www.myserver.com*/cgi-bin/cgi-test.pl

Figure 2-10. CGI test page

Connector/ODBC

ODBC (Open Database Connectivity) is a popular mechanism, particularly under Windows, for uniform access to a wide variety of database systems. The only requirement is an ODBC driver for the database system, which creates the interface between the ODBC system and the database.

Connector/ODBC 3.51 (formerly MyODBC) is the ODBC driver for MySQL. The driver supports the functions defined in ODBC version 3.5.1 (according to the on-line handbook, *Complete Core API and Level 2 Features*). For installation you should obtain Connector/ODBC from the MySQL web server. Most recently, Connector/ODBC was to be found at the following address:

http://www.mysql.com/downloads/api-myodbc-3.51.html

There are two different download variants:

- Connector/ODBC with setup program (*driver installer*) for initial installation;

- Only the driver DLLs (*DLLs only*) for an update.

For initial installation use the setup program. If later you wish to update the installation, it suffices to replace the file myodbc3.dll in the Windows system directory (e.g., C:\Windows\System32). There is no provision for a deinstallation of MyODBC.

> **REMARK**   *ODBC is now also used under Unix. Thus there exists Connector/ODBC for Unix. However, in this book we treat only the Windows version of Connector/ODBC.*

Setup Program

> **REMARK**   *The MySQL documentation announces that the Connector/ODBC installation under Windows sometimes breaks down to the accompaniment of mysterious error messages (for example, that the file* Windows\System\Mfc30.dll *cannot be copied). It is recommended as a solution to this problem to start up Windows in* safe *mode. To activate this mode it is necessary at Windows startup to hold down the* F8 *key. This should lead to a successful installation. I must say that I have installed MyODBC successfully on a variety of computers without having to take this measure.*

Connector/ODBC Character Set

Connector/ODBC does not assume a MySQL client installation on the computer. If you use ODBC on a computer exclusively for access to a MySQL server running somewhere else, then the installation of Connector/ODBC alone suffices.

In Connector/ODBC, only the default character set of the client tools is included. (This includes *latin1*, *big5*, *euc_kr*, *gb2312*, *gbk*, *sjis*, *tis620*, and *ujis*. If the server uses a different character set (option default-character-set), then one receives the error message *Can't initialize character set n.*

The solution to this problem is simple: The directory c:\mysql\share\charsets must be created on the the ODBC computer. There, all MySQL character set files must be copied. (These files reside on the computer on which the MySQL server is running. If it is a Windows machine, the path is usually Program Files\mysql\share\charsets, while under Unix/Linux it might be /usr/local/mysql/share/mysql.)

Editors

To complete the testing environment you will need an editor for developing your MySQL programs. If you are developing web applications and are using, say, PHP or Perl, in principle you can use any editor you like, under Windows even notepad.exe. It is more convenient to work with an editor that understands HTML/PHP/Perl, etc., that displays your code in different colors, assists with the insertion of frequently used code blocks, and so on. Under Linux, the KDE standard editor kate is a good choice.

> **TIP**   *The choice of editor is, of course, primarily a matter of taste. But if you are looking for a good editor, the links at my web site,* www.kofler.cc/mysql, *might be of use. Popular editors include Quanta and Bluefish (Linux) and HTML-Kit (Windows).*

Emacs/XEmacs

The editors Emacs and XEmacs are considered by many Unix/Linux fans to be the measure of all things. Their use takes a bit of getting used to, but in exchange these editors are probably unsurpassed for their adaptability to your individual requirements, and they are more stable than most other editors. (X)Emacs is obtainable without charge for Unix/Linux and is also obtainable for Windows. (As the names suggest, these two editors have a common ancestor. They are relatively compatible one with the other and differ only a little in their use.)

```
http://www.gnu.org/software/emacs/emacs.html
http://www.xemacs.org/
```

Both Emacs and XEmacs work without problems with HTML files as well as with files of most programming languages (Perl, Java, C, etc.). They can highlight different code elements in color, help with compiling, etc. However, the situation with PHP support is less good. There is no PHP mode included with the current versions of Emacs and XEmacs. The simplest solution is to select C++ mode. (This, however, does not work properly with HTML code, as one would expect.) To make Emacs/XEmacs view a PHP file as a C++ file, add the following text to the first line:

```
<?php // -*- C++ -*- --
```

On the Internet one can find certain PHP extensions for Emacs. However, their installation requires a fundamental knowledge of the internal workings of Emacs. Links can be found at my web site.

vi/vim

Unix fans who dislike the editor (X)Emacs usually use vi or vim. This editor has similar functions and modes to those of (X)Emacs, but takes even more getting used to.

Using MySQL with an ISP

This book generally assumes that you have installed MySQL on your own computer. It is only in this way that you have the possibility of trying out MySQL in all of its many facets. Furthermore, it is helpful to develop MySQL solutions first on a test system and to port them to a web site only after sufficient testing.

However, in principle, it is also possible to do without one's own MySQL installation entirely. In this case you develop a dynamic web site based exclusively on the MySQL access that your Internet service provider makes available. Here we shall briefly describe the necessary course of action.

MySQL Administration at an ISP with phpMyAdmin

As a rule, ISPs permit only local MySQL access for reasons of security. You can thus register with MySQL only if you are working locally on a computer of the ISP. But generally, that is precisely what you are not allowed to do (it could also be that you have telnet/ssh access, but that is also seldom allowed due to security considerations).

To the extent that your ISP supports PHP, MySQL administration is still possible. The favored program for this purpose is the PHP script collection phpMyAdmin that we have already mentioned. These scripts fulfill the condition that they can be executed on the ISP computer, while on the other hand, phpMyAdmin can be conveniently used over the Internet (that is, for administration you simply use a browser that runs locally on your computer).

With a little luck, your ISP offers phpMyAdmin. If that is not the case, then you must install phpMyAdmin yourself. If you do not have telnet/ssh access, first unpack the phpMyAdmin archive on your local computer. Then set the access information in config.inc.php (ISP host name, user name, password). You should have obtained this information from your ISP.

Finally, use an FTP client (under Windows, for example, WS_FTP) to move all the phpMyAdmin files from your computer into a WWW directory (such as phpmyadmin) at your ISP.

If all has gone well, then you can now launch phpMyAdmin with a browser with the address www.mysite.com/phpmyadmin/index.php or -/index.php3. With phpMyAdmin you can now create and delete your own database tables, add data, etc. You may also in some circumstances be able to use phpMyAdmin for the purpose of creating new databases. That depends on the MySQL administration privileges granted you by your ISP. (Details on config.inc.php as well as further information on using phpMyAdmin can be found in Chapter 4.)

> **CAUTION** *Everyone who guesses the address of* phpmyadmin/index.php *can administer your database just as you can. It is thus absolutely essential that access to the directory* phpmyadmin *be secured via a* .htaccess *file. The method for doing this is described in the section on Apache in this chapter.*

Database Upload

> **POINTER** *If you develop MySQL solutions first locally and then port them to the computer of your ISP, it is necessary to create there a copy of your test database. Thus you must copy the locally created database (perhaps together with all its data) to the MySQL server of the ISP. This modus operandi is often called "database upload." Hints on how to carry out this upload can be found in the last section of Chapter 10.*

CHAPTER 3

Introductory Example (An Opinion Poll)

THE BEST WAY OF BECOMING familiar with a new database or development system is to work through a full-fledged example. Thus in this chapter our goal is to create a web site for the purpose of conducting an opinion poll.

To a certain extent this is a trivial example, and its results certainly could be accomplished without the use of MySQL. However, it brings into focus the interplay between MySQL and a script programming language (for this example we have used PHP). Moreover, our example casts light on the entire process of database design from first beginnings right up to the completed application.

Chapter Overview

Overview

Our opinion poll consists of two pages. The file vote.html contains a simple questionnaire with a single question: What is your favorite programming language for developing MySQL applications? The question is followed by a selection of choices for a response (see Figure 3-1). After one of the options is selected and OK is clicked, the result page results.php is displayed (see Figure 3-2).

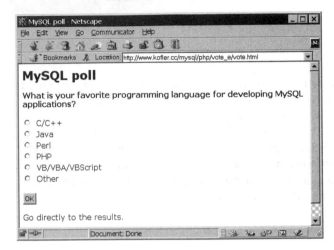

Figure 3-1. The questionnaire

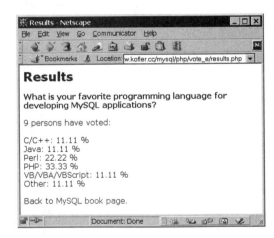

Figure 3-2. Results of the survey

Assumptions

You can try out this example on my web site (www.kofler.cc). However, from a pedagogical point of view it would be better for you to attempt to recreate this example for yourself. For this you will need a test environment consisting of Apache/MySQL/PHP that permits you the following:

- creation of a new MySQL database (that is, you need sufficient privileges to be able to execute *CREATE DATABASE*)

- moving files into a directory on the web server

- executing PHP script files

Information on setting up such a test environment on a local computer can be found in the previous chapter.

A complete understanding of our example requires some basic knowledge of databases. If you have never had much, if anything, to do with databases and as a consequence run into difficulties in understanding what is going on, please do not despair. Chapter 5 provides an introduction to relational database systems, while Chapter 6 explains how to use the database query language SQL.

In this example, the programming language PHP will be used. The code is rather straightforward; that is, you should have no difficulty in understanding it even you don't know a word of PHP. However, you should know in general how embedded script languages function in HTML. (The Active Server pages developed by Microsoft are based on the same idea.)

Database Development

To save the results of our questionnaire with MySQL, you must first set up a database and then place a table in that database. (Every MySQL database consists of tables. A particular feature of this example is that only a single table is required. As a rule, that is, when the requirements of the project are more complex, several linked tables will be used.)

Executing mysql

Both operations—generating a database and creating a new table—require that you communicate with MySQL. Under Unix/Linux you execute the command mysql. Under Windows you search in Explorer for the program mysql.exe and launch it with a double click. (The program should reside in the bin directory of the MySQL installation directory, that is, in C:\Programs\MySQL\bin.)

> **REMARK** *If* `mysql` *immediately terminates, possibly with an error message such as* Access denied for user xy, *then either access to MySQL is completely denied to user xy, or it is protected by a password. In either case you must invoke* `mysql` *with the options* `-u` name *and* `-p`:
>
> ```
> > mysql -u username -p
> Enter password: xxx
> ```
>
> *Furthermore,* `mysql` *has dozens of other options. The most important of these are described in Chapter 4, while all of them are collected in Chapter 19. Background information on the MySQL security system (access protection, passwords, privileges) can be found in Chapter 9.*

> **REMARK** *The distinction between MySQL and* `mysql` *is somewhat confusing. MySQL denotes the database server, which normally is launched automatically at system startup. The server runs continuously in the background. (This chapter assumes that the server is up and running.) The program name of the server is, depending on the operating system,* `mysqld` *(Unix/Linux) or* `mysqld.exe`, `mysqld-nt.exe`, *etc. (Windows).*
>
> *In contrast to these, we have the auxiliary programs* `mysql` *and* `mysql.exe`. *These programs come into play when administration or maintenance are to be carried out interactively. The program* `mysql` *has the task of transmitting interactive commands to the server and displaying the results of these commands on the monitor. The official name of* `mysql` *is MySQL Monitor, but the functionality and mode of action are more reminiscent of a command-line interpreter.*
>
> *Alternatives to* `mysql`, *such as the more convenient HTML interface phpMyAdmin, will be introduced in Chapter 4.*

In `mysql` you can now input commands that will be transmitted to the database server (see Figure 3-3). To test whether a connection can even be made, execute the command *STATUS*. The result should be the display of various pieces of status information about the database (such as the version number):

```
mysql> STATUS;
mysql Ver 12.18 Distrib 4.0.10-gamma, for Win95/Win98 (i32)
Connection id:          2
Current database:
Current user:           ODBC@localhost
SSL:                    Not in use
Server version:         4.0.10-gamma-nt
Protocol version:       10
Connection:             localhost via TCP/IP
Client characterset:    latin1
Server characterset:    latin1
TCP port:               3306
Uptime:                 12 days 1 hour 26 min 20 sec1
Threads: 2  Questions: 3099  Slow queries: 0  Opens: 6
Flush tables: 1 Open tables: 0  Queries per second avg: 0.003
```

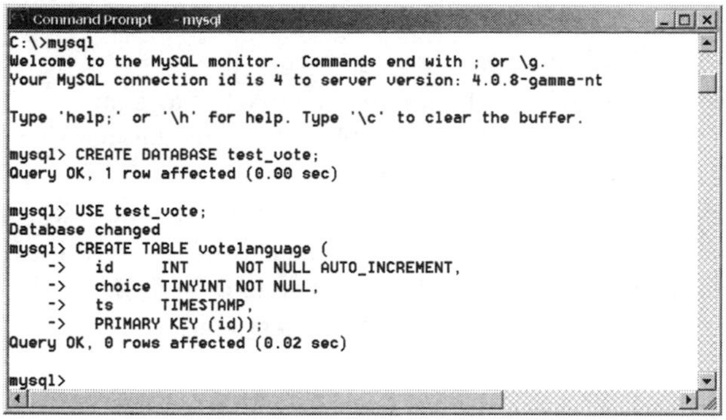

```
Command Prompt  - mysql                                    _ □ x
C:\>mysql
Welcome to the MySQL monitor.  Commands end with ; or \g.
Your MySQL connection id is 4 to server version: 4.0.8-gamma-nt

Type 'help;' or '\h' for help. Type '\c' to clear the buffer.

mysql> CREATE DATABASE test_vote;
Query OK, 1 row affected (0.00 sec)

mysql> USE test_vote;
Database changed
mysql> CREATE TABLE votelanguage (
    ->   id      INT     NOT NULL AUTO_INCREMENT,
    ->   choice  TINYINT NOT NULL,
    ->   ts      TIMESTAMP,
    ->   PRIMARY KEY (id));
Query OK, 0 rows affected (0.02 sec)

mysql>
```

Figure 3-3. The MySQL monitor

POINTER   *If problems arise in starting up* mysql *or in executing* status, *the most probable cause is that the database server hasn't even been started or that access has been denied to you. More information on installation can be found in Chapter 2, while information on access and security can be found in Chapter 9.*

Setting Up the Database

To set up the new database *test_vote*, in mysql execute the command *CREATE DATABASE*. Note that you must end the command with a semicolon. In the following two lines your input appears in boldface:

```
mysql> CREATE DATABASE test_vote;
Query OK, 1 row affected (0.01 sec)
```

The reply delivered by mysql may look a bit weird. The output 1 row affected indicates that in the list of all databases, which internally, of course, is in the form of a MySQL table, one row was changed. What is important here is only that the *CREATE DATABASE* command was executed correctly.

REMARK   *The database name* test_vote *was not chosen quite arbitrarily. In the default setting of MySQL access privileges, every user is permitted to create databases on a local computer that begin with the word "test." In particular, when you yourself are not the MySQL administrator (but rely on the help of a system administrator), a name of the form* test_xy *can save any number of e-mails or telephone calls.*

The drawback of the name test_xy *is that every user of the local computer can edit, or even delete, the database. This is no problem for this introductory example, but in the case of a real-life application you probably will want to give your database a bit more security. Necessary information on this can be found in Chapter 9.*

Creating Tables

The database *test_vote* has been created, but it is not yet possible to store any information. For this you need tables. To create a new table within the database *test_vote*, use the command *CREATE TABLE*.

Before you execute this command, however, you must specify the database into which the table is to be placed. The requisite command for this is *USE*. It determines the default database to which further commands are to be applied. (MySQL is managing other databases besides the newly created database *test_vote*.)

```
mysql> USE test_vote;
Database changed
mysql> CREATE TABLE votelanguage (
    -> id INT NOT NULL AUTO_INCREMENT,
    -> choice TINYINT NOT NULL,
    -> ts TIMESTAMP,
    -> PRIMARY KEY (id));
Query OK, 0 rows affected (0.01 sec)
```

The *CREATE TABLE* command may seem a bit strange at first. But just go ahead and input the boldface commands listed above line for line. (You can terminate each command with Return. The semicolon indicates to mysql that the end of a command has been reached.)

> **TIP** *If you should make a typing error during the input of a command, MySQL will usually inform you of this fact with an error message. You must now repeat the entire command. Using the cursor keys ↑ and ↓ you can recall and correct previously input lines.*
>
> *If MySQL has accepted* CREATE TABLE *in spite of a typographical error (because the command, though semantically not what you had in mind, is nonetheless syntactically correct), you can delete the incorrectly defined table with* DROP TABLE votelanguage;. *That accomplished, you can repeat the command* CREATE TABLE.
>
> *Instead of creating the table* votelanguage *via a* CREATE TABLE *command, you could, of course, use an administration tool such as MySQL ControlCenter or phpMyAdmin. This assumes, of course, that such a program is installed and that you have learned how to use it. The program* mysql *is not known for its ease of use, but it has the advantage of offering the best way of documenting the steps to be executed.*

Now let us explain what is actually going on. With *CREATE TABLE* you have brought into being a table with three columns, *id, choice*, and *ts*. Once the table is filled with data (namely, the results of the survey), the content of the table can be displayed something like this:

```
id  choice    ts
1   4         20030114154618
2   5         20030114154944
3   4         20030114154953
4   3         20030114154954
5   3         20030114154957
6   6         20030114155012
7   3         20030114155021
8   1         20030114155027
. . .
```

The interpretation of these data is that the first person to respond to the survey chose the programming language PHP, while the second chose VB, and the third selected PHP. The next respondents chose, in order, Perl, Other, Perl, and C. The column *id* thus contains a running identification number that identifies the lines (the data set). The column *choice* contains, in coded form, the selection made by the survey participant, where the numbers 1 through 6 correspond to the programming languages C, Java, Perl, PHP, VB, and Other. The column *ts* contains the time at which the query was executed. (For example, the first participant filled out vote.html on January 14, 2003, at 15:46:18.)

> **TIP** *Like any other specialized subject, the database world has its own argot. Database vocabulary includes the term* data record *for each line of the table above. Instead of* columns *(here* id *and* choice*) one often speaks of* fields.

In order to generate a table with the two columns *id* and *choice*, the following command would suffice:

```
CREATE TABLE votelanguage (id INT, choice TINYINT, ts TIMESTAMP);
```

The result is that the column *id* is declared with the data type *INT*, and *choice* is declared to be of data type *TINYINT*. This means that in theory, 2^{31} individuals (2,147,483,648, that is) could participate in our survey before the range for *id* was exhausted. (If *id* were declared as type *UNSIGNED INT*, then the number of potential participants would be doubled.) In *choice*, on the other hand, there are 2^{16} different values available. (The data types *INT* and *TINYINT* are discussed in Chapter 5 together with the other MySQL data types.)

By this point, you may be wondering why I have plagued you with such a complicated command as *CREATE TABLE* when there is a much easier way to achieve the same result. The difference between the complicated and simple variants is the difference between good and bad database creation. (And you wouldn't want me to be leading you astray on our very first example, would you?)

The attribute *AUTO_INCREMENT* for the column *id* has the effect that with each new record the appropriate value for *id* is automatically inserted. Thus when the results of the survey are saved, only *choice* has to be specified, since the database takes care of *id* on its own. This attribute ensures a consistent numbering of the data records, which is important for efficient management of the table.

The attribute *NOT NULL* ensures that actual values must be placed in both columns. It is not permitted to store the data record *NULL* or (in the case of *choice*) not to insert any value at all. Thus this attribute prevents invalid data records from being stored. (Go ahead and try to force MySQL to accept such a data record. It will refuse and present you with an error message.)

PRIMARY KEY (id) has the effect that the column *id* is used to identify the data records. That is the reason that the column was provided for in the first place, but MySQL is not so clever as to be able to read your mind, and it requires that it be informed precisely as to what your wishes are. (In this case, *id* will from now on be called a *primary key*.) The definition of a primary key has a decisive influence on the speed with which data records can be accessed. That holds especially for linked tables—but let us not get ahead of ourselves. We shall stick for the moment with simple tables, always define a single primary key (and do so, if possible, for an *INT* field with the attributes *NOT NULL* and *AUTO_INCREMENT*).

Why Make It Complicated, When It Could Be So Much Easier?

Perhaps it has occurred to you that we have presented a rather complex solution to an easy problem. It could done in a much simpler fashion. All we need to do is to control six counters, such as in a table of the following form:

id	counter
1	2
2	0
3	7
4	9
5	2
6	1

Such a display would mean that two participants expressed a preference for the C language, none for Java, seven for Perl, nine for PHP, and so on. Each time a preference is registered, the corresponding counter is incremented by 1. The database would consist altogether of six lines; one wouldn't have to worry about performance; memory requirements would be essentially zero—nothing but advantages! And all of this is aside from the fact that the six counters could be effortlessly stored in a small text file. In short, MySQL is totally unnecessary for this survey.

All right, then, you are correct! However, such an attitude is helpful only as long as we are dealing with a simple application. What happens when you would like to offer each participant the opportunity to make a comment? What if you allow the participants to fill out the questionnaire only after a login (to rule out the possibility of multiple voting)? What if you wish to record the time and IP address for each participant (again to secure against attempts at manipulating the survey)?

In all these cases, you would have to store the responses in a table like the one that we have presented. (The table would have merely to be enlarged by a column or two. The structure of the program can remain essentially the same.) So, if the conception of this example seems a bit overly complicated at first glance, the reason is that we are keeping open the possibility, even in this first example, of a later extension.

The Questionnaire

As we have mentioned already in the introduction, our entire project consists of two web pages. The first page (vote.html) contains the questionnaire. This is pure HTML code (without PHP). The second page (results.php) carries out two tasks: evaluating the questionnaire and displaying the results.

The HTML code of the questionnaire is given here, so that the code for evaluation in the next section will be understandable. Most important are the attributes *name* and *value* of the elements of the questionnaire. All of the radio buttons have the name *vote*, while *value* contains values between 1 and 6. The OK button has the name *submitbutton*, and as *value* the character string *"OK"* is used.

```
<!DOCTYPE HTML PUBLIC "-//W3C//DTD HTML 4.0//EN">
<!-- php/vote/vote.html -->
<html><head>
  <meta http-equiv="Content-Type"
        content="text/html; charset=iso-8859-1" />
  <title>MySQL-poll</title>
</head>
<body>
<h2>MySQL- poll </h2>
<p><b> What is your favorite
programming language for developing MySQL applications?</b>
<form method="POST" action="results.php">
  <p>
  <input type="radio" name="vote" value="1">C/C++
  <br><input type="radio" name="vote" value="2">Java
  <br><input type="radio" name="vote" value="3">Perl
  <br><input type="radio" name="vote" value="4">PHP
  <br><input type="radio" name="vote" value="5"> ASP[.NET] / C# / VB[.NET] / VBA
  <br><input type="radio" name="vote" value="6"> Other
  </p>
  <p><input type="submit" name="submitbutton" value="OK"/></p>
</form>
<p>Go directly to the <a href="./results.php">results</a>.</p>
<p>Back to the
<a href="../mysqlbook.html">MySQL book page</a>.
</body>
</html>
```

Questionnaire Evaluation and Displaying Results

One can call results.php either directly (for example, via a link) or using the data in the questionnaire. In one case, what is shown is only the current state of the questionnaire. In the other case, the data are also evaluated and stored in the database.

Establishing a Connection to the Database

The opening lines of results.php consist of HTML code. Then comes the first task within the PHP code, which is to create a link to MySQL. For this purpose, the PHP function *mysql_connect* is used, to which three pieces of information are passed:

- user name
- password
- computer name (host name)

If you have installed MySQL yourself on the local computer and have not yet secured it with a password, then you may simply pass empty character strings as parameters. The specification of the computer name is necessary only if the web server (that is, Apache) is running on a different computer from the one that is running MySQL.

The function mysql_connect returns an identification number that is stored in the variable *link*. In the present example, *link* is used only to identify possible problems in creating the link. In this case, an error message is displayed, and the PHP code is ended abruptly with *exit*. Otherwise, the active database is selected with *mysql_select_db*. (MySQL usually manages several databases, and the effect of *mysql_select_db* is that the following commands automatically refer to *test_vote*.)

Evaluating the Data and Storing Them in the Database

The next task in results.php consists in evaluating the data in the questionnaire and storing them in the database. The data are passed to the elements *submitbutton* and *vote* of the global field *$_POST*. (Compare the *name* and *value* attributes in vote.html.) The auxiliary function *array_item* is used to read out this field.

> **WARNING**   *If you try out this example with PHP 4.0 or an earlier version of PHP, you must comment out or delete the lines* $submitbutton = array_item(. . .) *and* $vote = array_item(. . .).
>
> *The field* $_POST *is not available in older versions of PHP. Instead, the variables* $submitbutton *and* $vote *are defined automatically. However, this behavior is relatively insecure and was therefore changed beginning with PHP 4.1.*

If results.php was called via the questionnaire of vote.html, then the variable *submitbutton* contains the character string *"OK"*.

For the sake of security, a validation test is also carried out for the variable *vote*. (For example, a participant may have forgotten to select one of the choices.) If *vote* contains a valid value, then this value is stored in the database. The SQL command to accomplish this will look something like the following:

```
INSERT INTO votelanguage (choice) VALUES (3)
```

What *INSERT INTO* accomplishes is to insert a new data record (a new row) into the table *votelanguage*. The expression *(choice)* specifies all of the fields of the data record for which values should be passed by means of the command *VALUES (. . .)*. Since MySQL takes responsibility on its own for the field *id* (attribute *AUTO_INCREMENT*; see above), in this example *choice* is the only field affected. Of course, instead of "3" the value of the variable *vote* will be placed, depending on which of the programming languages was selected in the questionnaire. The SQL command thus constructed is then passed along to MySQL with the PHP function *mysql_query*.

> **POINTER**   *If you have never had dealings with SQL and thus are unfamiliar with the syntax of SQL commands, fear not. In Chapter 6 you will find an extensive introduction to SQL. The two commands used in this chapter, namely,* INSERT *and* SELECT, *are presumably more or less self-explanatory.*
>
> *The columns* id *and* ts *of the* votelanguage *table are automatically filled in by MySQL:* id *with the unique running number, and* ts *with the current time.*

Displaying the Survey Results

Regardless of whether the questionnaire has just been evaluated, the previous results of the survey must be able to be displayed. (If a new vote has been cast, it will be taken into account.)

First a check must be made as to whether the *votelanguage* table contains any data at all. (When the questionnaire is first placed on the Internet, no votes have yet been cast.) The required SQL query looks like this:

```
SELECT COUNT(choice) FROM votelanguage
```

The SQL command is again executed with *mysql_query*. What is new this time is that a link to the result of the query is stored in the variable *result*. The result of a *SELECT* command is, in general, a table. However, in the above example this table consists of merely a single row and a single column. (Furthermore, *result* contains only an ID number, which is used as a parameter in various other *mysql_xxx* functions. It is the task of PHP to take care of the actual management of the result.)

To evaluate the result, the function *mysql_result($result, 0, 0)* is used, by which the element in the table from the first row and first column is read. (With MySQL functions, counting begins with 0.)

Provided that the *votelanguage* table is not empty, a loop is executed to report the percentage of votes cast for each programming language. The requisite SQL queries look similar to the one above, only now the number of data records that contain a particular value of *choice* (for example, 3) is counted:

```
SELECT COUNT(choice) FROM votelanguage WHERE choice = 3
```

For evaluation, *mysql_result* is used. Then a bit of calculation is necessary to round the percentages to two decimal places.

Program Code (results.php)

```php
<!DOCTYPE HTML PUBLIC "-//W3C//DTD HTML 4.0//EN">
<!-- php/vote/results.php-->
<html><head>
<meta http-equiv="Content-Type"
      content="text/html; charset=iso-8859-1" />
<title>Survey Result</title>
</head><body>
<h2> Survey Result </h2>
<?php
  $mysqlhost="localhost";
  $mysqluser="root";
  $mysqlpasswd="";
  $mysqldbname="test_vote";
  Create Link to Database
  $link =
    @mysql_connect($mysqlhost, $mysqluser, $mysqlpasswd);
  if ($link == FALSE) {
    echo "<p><b>Unfortunately, no link to the database
          can be made. Therefore, the results
          cannot be displayed at present. Please try
          again later.</b></p>
          </body></html>\n";
    exit();
  }
  mysql_select_db($mysqldbname);

  // if questionnaire data are available:
  // evaluate + store
  function array_item($ar, $key) {
    if(array_key_exists($key, $ar)) return(\ar[\key]);
    return(\sq\sq);  }

  $submitbutton = array_item($_POST, \sqsubmitbutton\sq);
  $vote = array_item($_POST, \sqvote\sq);
  if($submitbutton=="OK") {
    if($vote>=1 && $vote<=6) {
      mysql_query(
```

```
              "INSERT INTO votelanguage (choice) VALUES ($vote)");
      }
      else {
        echo "<p>Not a valid selection. Please vote
               again. Back to
               <a href=\" vote.html\">questionnaire</a>.</p>
               </body></html>\n";
        exit();
      }
  }

  // display results
  echo "<P><B> What is your favorite programming language
        for developing MySQL applications?</b></p>\n";

  // Number of votes cast
  $result =
    mysql_query("SELECT COUNT(choice) FROM votelanguage");
  $choice_count = mysql_result($result, 0, 0);

  // Percentages for the individual voting categories
  if($choice_count == 0) {
    echo "<p>No one has voted yet.</p>\n";
  }
else {
    echo "<p>$choice_count individuals have thus far taken part
           in this survey:</p>\n";
    $choicetext = array("", "C/C++", "Java", "Perl", "PHP",
                        "VB/VBA/VBScript", "Other");
    print("<p><table>\n");
    for($i=1; $i<=6; $i++) {
      $result = mysql_query(
          "SELECT COUNT(choice) FROM votelanguage " .
          "WHERE choice = $i");
      $choice[$i] = mysql_result($result, 0, 0);
      $percent = round($choice[$i]/$choice_count*10000)/100;
      print("<tr><td>$choicetext[$i]:</td>");
    } print("<td>$percent
    print("</table></p>\n");
  }
?>
</body>
</html>
```

The Resulting HTML Code

If you are relatively inexperienced with PHP, you might find it helpful to have a look at the resulting HTML code (that is, what the user finally sees in the browser, as depicted in Figure 3-2) as an aid to understanding the program presented above.

```
<!DOCTYPE HTML PUBLIC "-//W3C//DTD HTML 4.0//EN">
<!-- results.php -->
<html><head>
```

```
<meta http-equiv="Content-Type"
      content="text/html; charset=iso-8859-1" />
<title>Survey Results</title>
</head><body>
<h2>Survey Results</h2>
<p><b>What is your favorite programming language
        for the development of MySQL applications?</b></p>
<p>17 people have thus far taken part
          in this survey:</p>
<p><table>
<tr><td>C/C++:</td><td>17.65 %</td></tr>
<tr><td>Java:</td><td>11.76 %</td></tr>
<tr><td>Perl:</td><td>17.65 %</td></tr>
<tr><td>PHP:</td><td>41.18 %</td></tr>
<tr><td>ASP[.NET] / C# / VB[.NET] / VBA:</td><td>11.76 %</td></tr>
<tr><td>Other:</td><td>0 %</td></tr>
</table></p>
</body></html>
```

Ideas for Improvements

Layout

It may have occurred to you that I have not paid much attention to the appearance of things in this example. Naturally, the results of the survey could be presented in a colorful bar graph. However, that has nothing to do with the subject of this book, namely, MySQL. Introductions to the attractive presentation of HTML documents, to the PHP programming of graphics libraries, and the like can be found in quantity in a number of books on HTML and PHP (and, of course, on the Internet).

Questionnaire and Results on a Single Page

It is certainly possible to execute all the elements of our survey—questionnaire, evaluation, and presentation of results—with a single PHP script. However, as a rule, it is a good idea for the participants not to see the previous results before casting a vote.

Options

You could make the survey more interesting or more informative by offering additional opportunities for input. In our example, there could be a text field for the input of other programming languages or perhaps a text field for comments or for information about the professional background of the participants. However, you must consider that the more you ask, the more superfluous data you will collect. (If someone does not want to answer a required question, you may get a deliberately false response.)

Multiple Selection

In principle, you could construct the questionnaire in such a way that a participant could select more than one programming language. In the HTML form you would use check boxes instead of radio buttons. However, the necessary changes in the design of the database are somewhat more complicated. The table *votes* must now be able to store in each data record an arbitrary collection of programming languages. It would be easy, though inefficient, to reserve a separate column in the table for each programming language and then store the value 1 or 0 depending on whether or not the language was voted for. If you do not want the *votes* table to take up any more space in memory than necessary, then you could store a multiple selection as a combination of bits. For this purpose, MySQL offers the data type (*SET*). But this option would make the program code for the storage and evaluation of the survey results considerably more complicated.

Protection Against Manipulation

In most Internet surveys, the goal is not to obtain information but to promote interest, and thereby obtain a large number of accesses to one's web page. In such cases, there is not much point in protecting the survey against misuse. However, if you wish to provide such protection, you have a number of possibilities:

- You could place a "cookie" containing a random number on the participant's computer and store this same value in the database. In this way, an attempt to cast additional votes could be easily caught. (The disadvantage is that many Internet users are opposed to cookies and delete all cookies at startup or else prohibit their placement altogether.)

- You could require a login with e-mail address and password. Only those who have registered may vote. You store information in the database on who has already voted. (The disadvantage is that Internet users tend to have little patience for logins. Not many Internet users would give their e-mail address simply for the privilege of filling out your questionnaire.)

It is true, in general, that you cannot completely prevent such manipulation of a survey. That is, every system of security can be gotten around by someone who puts enough effort into the attempt.

> **POINTER** *There are many complete PHP solutions for questionnaires available, both with and without MySQL support. Before you set about reinventing the wheel, you might want to take a squint at some of the PHP sites on the Internet, for example the following:*
>
> http://www.hotscripts.com/PHP/

Part II

Fundamentals

CHAPTER 4

User Interfaces

THE END USER SHOULD NEVER see MySQL as a program. Instead, a convenient program or several web sites should be used to provide access to the database or assist in the input of new data.

Developers and database administrators, on the other hand, must frequently communicate directly with MySQL, for example, when new databases are created, existing databases enlarged, individual data records added, or queries tested. Such administrative tasks are simplified by user interfaces.

This chapter introduces the most important user interfaces for MySQL. The command program mysql (all operating systems), WinMySQLadmin (Windows), the MySQL Control Center (Windows/Linux), and the HTML interface phpMyAdmin for web administration.

Chapter Overview

Overview

For MySQL there is not merely one user interface, but a host of them. In this chapter we will look at only the most important of these. Here is a brief overview:

- The command `mysql` (`mysql.exe` under Windows) offers the least amount of convenience. It enables the input of text commands and returns results in text format. Nonetheless, this tool cannot be done without. It has the advantages that it is a fixed component of every MySQL installation, is available under all operating systems, makes little demand on hardware, and can be run via `telnet` or `ssh`.

- **WinMySQLadmin** is provided with the Windows version of MySQL. The program is of use most of all in the setup and configuration of the MySQL server under Windows. However, the program is not a complete user interface.

- The **MySQL Control Center** will probably soon become the official interface for MySQL. This program was still in beta version when this book went to press, but it already functions quite reliably. The program currently runs under Unix and Linux. See `http://www.mysql.com/products/mycc/`

- **phpMyAdmin** consists of a collection of PHP scripts. It is used via a web browser, and therefore phpMyAdmin is best suited for the administration of a MySQL server on a remote computer. See `tp://phpmyadmin.sourceforge.net/`

All of the above programs are available without charge. But do check the licensing agreement.

Brief Description of Some Other Programs

- **MysqlTool** is Perl's answer to phpMyAdmin. It is a collection of Perl CGI scripts that cover all the principal administrative tasks (generate and edit databases and tables, view and edit data, execute queries, set MySQL access privileges, manage MySQL processes, etc.). See `http://www.dajoba.com/projects/mysqltool/index.html`

- **SQLyog** is a compact and very fast Windows program that in addition to the usual administrative tasks, fulfills a host of additional functions: exportation and importation of databases, importation of ODBC data sources, synchronization of two MySQL databases, and so on. If you cannot get on friendly terms with the MySQL Control Center, then this program is perhaps the most attractive alternative. See `http://www.webyog.com/sqlyog/index.html`

- **DBtools** is another Windows program with interesting supplementary functions. Noteworthy are the importation function for Access databases, Excel tables, and ODBC data sources; the PHP script generator; and the support for integrity rules (*foreign key constraints*) for InnoDB tables. However, using DBtools is less intuitive than is the case for the other programs mentioned here. See `http://www.dbtools.com.br/EN/`

- **MySQL Navigator** is a compact and simple administration program that can be run under both Windows and Linux. See `http://sql.kldp.org/mysql/`

> **TIP** *Download links to many additional user interfaces (including commercial programs) can be found at my web site:* http://www.kofler.cc/mysql/

mysql

In the previous chapter you became acquainted with mysql as a simple command interpreter, with which you can execute SQL commands and view the resulting tables in text mode. This section gives some further tips for using mysql with MySQL. Please note that mysql is sometimes called "Monitor," in part to avoid confusion among MySQL in general, the MySQL server, and the program mysql.

> **POINTER** mysql *can also be used for a variety of administrative tasks in batch mode, such as for saving tables in ASCII, HTML, or XML files for saving or restoring previously backed-up databases. These possibilities for using* mysql *are presented in Chapter 10, where it is described how frequently used* mysql *options can be stored in configuration files.*
>
> *For more complex management tasks (backups, ASCII import and export, repairing table files, etc.) there are additional command tools provided with MySQL, such as* mysqladmin *and* myisamchk *(see also Chapter 10). A reference to all the options and functions of the command-oriented administration tools can be found in Chapter 19.*

Executing mysql and Other MySQL Commands

Unix/Linux: On Unix/Linux systems you simply specify mysql in a console window and press Return. The programs are normally installed in the directory /usr/bin, so that it is unnecessary to provide the name of the directory.

Windows: mysql and most other MySQL commands are generally stored in the directory C:\mysql\bin. Furthermore, C:\mysql\scripts contains several Perl script files (not all of which, however, can be used under Windows). Both directories are normally not a part of the *PATH* system variable, which contains all directories with executable programs. Therefore, there are the following possibilities for launching the programs:

- The simplest and most convenient approach is a double click in Windows Explorer. A disadvantage of this procedure is that no options can be passed to the program, yet in most cases it is necessary at the very least to provide the user name and password.
- Via START | RUN you can launch the program in a small dialog window. There you can also provide options. (You can most easily copy the command name together with all directories with Explorer's *Drag&Drop* in the start window.) This method is acceptable in isolated instances, but if the command is to be used frequently, this is much too inconvenient.

- You can open a command window (START | PROGRAMS | ACCESSORIES | COMMAND PROMPT) and there give the name of the program and the complete path. Again, you can save some typing and use Explorer with *Drag&Drop* to copy the name into the window. Alternatively, you can first use CD to move into the directory C:\mysql\bin.

- In the long run, it will prove most convenient to extend the system variable *PATH* to the MySQL tools. To do this execute START | SETTINGS | SYSTEM, click in the dialog sheet ADVANCED, select the system variable *PATH* with a double click, and enlarge the list of directories to include the MySQL bin directory and the MySQL script directory. Directories must be separated by semicolons. (Figure 4-1 shows the setting of the system variables in Windows 2000.)

  From now on, in every command window (regardless of the current directory or drive), input of the MySQL command name is sufficient to execute it.

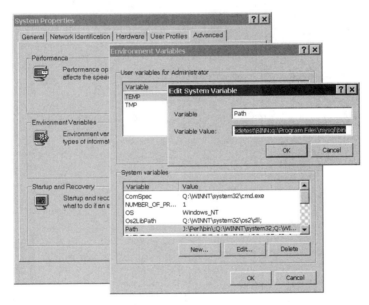

Figure 4-1. Setting the Windows system variables

Using MySQL Interactively

The program mysql is launched as usual with the options -u and -p. (One can do without the options if the login name is the same as the MySQL user name and MySQL has not been password protected and so a password is not required.)

Now SQL commands can be input. The commands can extend over several lines and must be terminated with a semicolon:

```
> mysql -u root -p
Enter password: xxx
Welcome to the MySQL monitor. Commands end with ; or \g.
Your MySQL connection id is 248 to server version: 3.23.24-beta
Type 'help;' or '\h' for help. Type '\c' to clear the buffer
mysql> USE books;
Database changed
mysql> SELECT * FROM title;
  titleID   title                                    publisherID   year
        1   Linux, 5th ed.                                     1   2000
        2   Definitive Guide to Excel VBA                      2   2000
        3   Client/Server Survival Guide                       1   1997
        4   Web Application Development with PHP 4.0            3   2000
        6   test                                               1   2000
        7   MySQL                                              1   2001
        9   MySQL & mSQL                                        4   1999
7 rows in set (0.01 sec)
```

> **CAUTION**   *You can do a great deal of damage with* mysql. *For example,* DELETE
> FROM tablename *deletes all data records from the table* tablename *without so much
> as a "by your leave." And what is more, there is no way of undoing the damage.
> If you would like to avoid such fatal errors, you should use* mysql *with the option*
> --i-am-a-dummy. *Then* mysql *permits the commands* UPDATE *and* DELETE *only if
> they are protected with the key word* WHERE *or* LIMIT. *There are some additional
> security limitations.*

In addition to the SQL commands, you can use some additional commands offered by mysql (for example, *source filename*). These commands do not need to be terminated with a semicolon. As with SQL commands, these are case-insensitive. Each of the commands exists in a two-character short form, such as \h for *help*. In the short form the commands can also be given at the end of a line; the only place they must be written out in full is at the beginning of a new line. Table 4-1 gives only the most important commands. A list of all the commands can be found in Chapter 19.

Simplifying Input

Terminating Input: It often occurs, particularly with multiline commands, that you note an error in a line above the one that you are typing and as a result wish to terminate the entire input (so that you can start all over again). To accomplish this, regardless of the cursor position, simply input \c and press Return. Note, however, that \c does not have this effect within a character string enclosed in single or double quotation marks.

History Function: mysql remembers the last commands that were input (even after program termination!). These commands can be recalled with the cursor keys ↑ and ↓.

Table 4-1. `mysql` *commands in interactive mode*

\c	`clear` breaks off input of a command.
\h	`help` displays the list of commands.
\q	`exit` or `quit` terminates `mysql`; under Unix/Linux this can also be done with Ctrl + D.
\s	`status` displays status information of the MySQL server.
\T [*f*]	`tee` [*filename*] logs all input and output in the specified file.
\t	`notee` ends tee; the logging can be resumed at any time with `tee` or \T; note that the file name must be given again.
\u *db*	`use` *database* makes the specified database the default.
\#	`rehash` creates an internal list of all `mysql` commands, the most important SQL key words, and all names of tables and columns of the current database; then it suffices to input only the initial letters; with Tab the initial letters are expanded into the complete key word. Unfortunately, this functions only under Unix/Linux, where `rehash` is executed automatically.
\. *fn*	`source` *filename* executes the SQL commands contained in the specified file; the commands must be separated by semicolons.

Tips for Using `mysql` Under Unix/Linux

Scroll Region: Under Unix/Linux, `mysql` is usually executed in a shell window. Every such program (`xterm` (Figure 4-2), `kvt`, `nxterm`, `gnome-terminal`, etc.) offers the possibility of setting the number of lines that are kept in temporary storage. If you provide a large enough value, then you can use a scroll bar to examine previously input commands and copy them with the mouse to the clipboard.

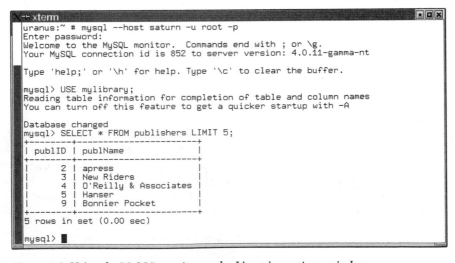

Figure 4-2. Using the MySQL monitor under Linux in an **xterm** *window*

Keyboard Shortcuts: Under most operating systems, mysql relies on the readline library. Therefore, the usual suspects in the lineup of Unix/Linux keyboard shortcuts are available for editing input (for example, Ctrl + K for deleting a line from the cursor location to the end, Ctrl + Y for restoring the most recently deleted text). Most of the keyboard shortcuts correspond to those under the editor Emacs. Furthermore, names of tables and columns can be automatically completed with Tab, after the initial letters have been input (see also rehash).

Private Configuration File: Frequently used settings or options (such as user name and password) can be stored under Unix/Linux in a user-specific configuration file with the name ˜/.my.cnf. Options related to all client tools are placed in the group [client], while those relating specifically to mysql go into the group [mysql]. The following lines provide an example. (Further details on creating configuration files can be found in Chapter 19.)

```
# Options for all MySQL tools
[client]
user=username
password=xxx
# Options for mysql
[mysql]
database=mydatabase
```

Since the file contains a password in plain text, it should be protected from prying eyes:

```
user$ chmod 600 ˜/.my.cnf
```

Tips for Using mysql Under Windows

mysql is executed in a command window. Many of the particulars of this program are configurable. You can access the configuration dialog by clicking on the title bar with the right mouse button (see Figure 4-3).

- **Color:** In the command window are usually displayed white characters on a black background. That is not particularly easy on the eyes. If your eyes would prefer a white background and black characters, then consult the COLORS dialog sheet to change the setting.

- **Window Size:** There is not much room in an 80×25 character display for representing the results of *SELECT*. The dialog sheet LAYOUT comes to your aid here, allowing you to change the window size.

- **Scroll Region:** A larger window does nothing to increase the number of lines displayed. This setting can be changed by enlarging the SCREEN BUFFER SIZE in the dialog sheet LAYOUT. This sets the virtual window size. In the window, a segment of the virtual window is visible, and you can use the scroll bar to see previous commands and results.

- **Clipboard:** The command window offers the not-well-known possibility of copying and pasting text to and from the clipboard. To copy, select a rectangular region with the mouse and simply hit Return. To paste, click anywhere in the window with the right mouse button. For these shortcuts to function you must have activated the option QUICKEDIT MODE in the OPTIONS dialog sheet.

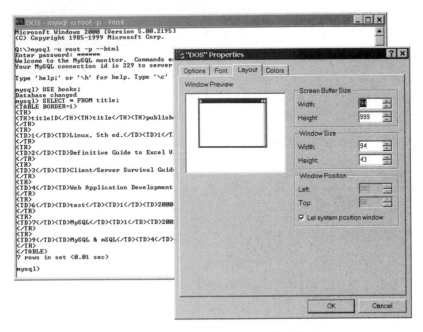

Figure 4-3. Configuration of the MySQL monitor under Windows

When you close the configuration dialog, you are asked whether the settings should hold only for the current window or whether they should be saved, with the result that the shortcut (link) to the input window will be changed. Choosing the second variant will ensure that in the future, the command window will have the properties described here.

CAUTION *In MySQL databases, the character set* latin1 *is used by default. In the command window, however, what is used is an older (DOS-compatible) character set. For this reason, various special characters (such as äåéèöüß) are incorrectly displayed in the command window. What is worse, the DOS character set is also used in data records that are stored using an* INSERT *or* UPDATE *command in the command window. If you then look at those data records with another program (for example, with phpMyAdmin), the special characters are seen to be incorrect.*

The solution is not to input data records containing such special characters in the command window with mysql. *Make such inputs either with another program or with* mysql *under another operating system (Unix/Linux). If this is impossible, write the input command with a text editor (such as Notepad) and paste it into the command window via the clipboard.*

Accessing an External Server with `mysql`

If on launching `mysql` you provide the option `--host` *computername*, then the program establishes a connection to the MySQL server running on *computername*. However, for this to function, certain conditions must be met:

- *computername* must be reachable over the network. This can be checked, for example, with the command `ping` *computername*.

- The TCP/IP port 3306 must be usable. If there is a firewall between your computer and the computer on which the MySQL server is running, it can happen that the firewall blocks communication over this port.

- The MySQL server must be so configured that it allows connections from your computer. This is not the case by default! Information on the correct configuration of access privileges is discussed in Chapter 9.

> **REMARK** *If you execute* `mysql` *under Unix/Linux, then the option* -h *has meaning when you establish a connection to a MySQL server on the local computer. If you specify* -h localhost *(or ignore the option entirely), then the connection is established over a so-called socket file. On the other hand, if you specify the name of the local computer or its IP number (*-h mycomputer*), then the connection is established via TCP/IP. Different access settings can hold for these two variants. See Chapter 9.*

Terminating `mysql`

You can terminate `mysql` with *exit* or *quit* or `\q` or `Ctrl+D` (the last of these only under Unix/Linux). Under Windows, you can also simply close the command window.

WinMySQLadmin (Windows)

WinMySQLadmin was originally conceived as a complete Windows interface for MySQL. However, the development of this program long ago came to a halt, and its development has been terminated. (In the meanwhile, a number of newer interfaces for Windows have been developed, which function considerably better.)

The program is included with the Windows version of MySQL and is automatically installed. Even though it does not offer a full-fledged user interface, it is nevertheless a useful tool. Namely, it helps in starting, stopping, and configuring the MySQL server.

> **REMARK** *If you wish to start or stop the MySQL server with WinMySQLadmin under Windows NT/2000, you must log into Windows as* Administrator *or as a user with* Administrator *privileges.*

After the first launch (which is done manually), the program registers itself in
START | PROGRAMS | STARTUP and in future will be launched automatically at startup.
WinMySQLadmin, for its part, automatically launches the MySQL server if it is not
already running. (This function is especially practical under Windows 9x/ME, where
the MySQL server cannot be executed as a Windows service.)

The program is usually visible as a small icon in the Windows task bar. It uses
a stoplight to indicate the state of the MySQL server (see Figure 4-4). A green lamp
indicates that the server is running, while red indicates that it is not.

Figure 4-4. WinMySQLadmin as an icon

Displaying WinMySQLadmin

After it has been launched, WinMySQLadmin shrinks to a stoplight icon. If you click
on this icon with the right mouse button, you can display WinMySQLadmin with
SHOW ME. The button HIDE ME in the dialog sheet Environment shrinks the window
again into an icon. In this dialog sheet you can also summon the on-line help for
WinMySQLadmin, which, unfortunately, is not much help at all.

Starting and Stopping the MySQL Server as a Service Under Windows NT/2000/XP

When WinMySQLadmin is executed under Windows NT/2000/XP, it automatically
registers the MySQL server as an operating system service and then launches this
service. Thereafter, you can use WinMySQLadmin to stop the service and to start
it again. You can also unregister the service with WinMySQLadmin, but at the next
startup of WinMySQLadmin, the service will be automatically registered again.

MySQL Configuration

At first launch, WinMySQLadmin creates the file Windows\my.ini if such a file does not
yet exist. This file can be viewed and edited in the dialog sheet MY.INI SETUP.

Sad to tell, the entire user interface in the dialog sheet (see Figure 4-5) is a bit
complicated and confusing. The following description explains the effect of the
individual dialog elements and how they are related to one another:

- **BASE DIR:** In this text field, the MySQL installation directory can be set (for
  example, C:\mysql or Program\mysql). You can then find in this directory the
  directories data, with the MySQL databases, and bin, with the MySQL programs
  and commands. A change in this directory is generally not necessary.

  The directory set here is used to determine the file names for the MySQL server
  (bin\mysqld.exe is simply added to the directory).

- **MYSQLD FILE:** With these options one can set which of the MySQL server variants should be launched. Normally, you should use `mysqld-opt.exe` under Windows 9x/ME, and `mysqld-nt.exe` under Windows NT/2000/XP. Details on the different versions can be found in Chapter 2.

  Which of these variants you want to use should be specified in MySQLadmin, in the dialog sheet MY.INI SETUP. Under windows 9x/ME, you then stop MySQL and restart the server. Under Windows NT/2000/XP, the process is somewhat more complex: You stop the server, deinstall the service (REMOVE SERVICE), reinstall the service, and then restart the server. All steps are carried within a context menu, obtained with a right mouse click.

- **PICK-UP AND EDIT MY.INI:** With this button, `Windows\my.ini` is read anew and displayed in the dialog. Any changes made in WinMySQLadmin will be lost.

- **SAVE MODIFICATIONS:** With this button, first the settings BASE DIR and MYSQLD FILE are evaluated and saved in the option `Server` of the group `[WinMySQLadmin]`. Then `Windows\my.ini` is saved.

- **CREATE SHORT CUT:** With this button, the entry PROGRAMS | STARTUP | WINMYSQLADMIN is generated in the Windows start menu (if it does not yet exist).

> **CAUTION** *For specifying path names in the configuration file, the forward slash / must be used, not the backslash \, as is usual under Windows.*

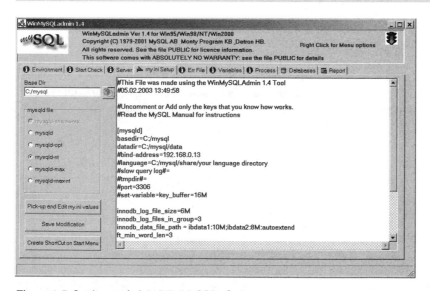

Figure 4-5. Setting `my.ini` *in WinMySQLadmin*

> **REMARK**   *Please note that there can be two additional configuration files for the MySQL server:* C:\my.cnf *and* DATADIR\my.cnf. *If there are several configuration files existing simultaneously, they are read in the following order:*
>
> C:\my.cnf → Windows\my.ini → DATADIR\my.cnf (only mysqld).
>
> *Settings in the last file to be read have priority. Using configuration files is discussed in detail in Chapter 19.*

Displaying Status and Database Structure Information

WinMySQLadmin provides much information in the dialog sheets ENVIRONMENT, SERVER, VARIABLES, and PROCESS about the state of the MySQL server: status information, the contents of the status and system variables, and a list of all running MySQL processes. Furthermore, the DATABASE dialog sheet gives a quick overview of the databases, rows, and columns managed by MySQL. Unfortunately, the database schema cannot be altered; nor can the content of tables be examined.

However, WinMySQLadmin can display this status information only if the MySQL server makes this program available. WinMySQLadmin must declare itself to the MySQL server just like any other client. The program uses the user name and password combination stored in Windows\my.ini. These two entries are set during the initial launch of WinMySQLadmin:

```
[WinMySQLadmin]
user=username
password=xxx
  ...
```

If these two lines are missing in my.ini, the program will attempt to register with the MySQL server without a password as *odbc@localhost*. This will work only if the access rules of the MySQL server allow registration without a password.

> **CAUTION**   *Since by default,* Windows\my.ini *can be read by every Windows user, you should not put the password for* root *access to the MySQL server into this file. That would be a tremendous security risk.*

Examining Error Logs and Creating Bug Reports

In the dialog sheet ERRFILE, the (most recent) lines of the file *hostname*.err should be displayed. However, this no longer functions in the most recent version of WinMySQLadmin.

The dialog sheet REPORT is provided for the purpose of preparing an error report, which can then be sent to the MySQL company or to a mailing list. The button CREATE REPORT collects all available status information about the MySQL server and places it in a text field. This text can be copied and inserted into an e-mail or word processing program.

MySQL Control Center (Windows, Linux)

The MySQL Control Center, or MyCC for short, is currently the most promising user interface, brought to you directly from the MySQL company. The program uses a general public license (GPL). Commercial use is without charge if one has a commercial license for MySQL.

The Control Center is available in the current version (0.8.10 beta) as pre-compiled code for Windows and Linux (glibc 2.2 and 2.3) at the following address: http://www.mysql.com/products/mysqlcc/index.html.

The Windows installation is carried out with a setup program. Under Linux, the tar.gz archive must be extracted with tar to the desired directory. Then a link to the file mysqlcc must be established from an arbitrary bin directory:

```
root# cd /usr/local
root# tar xzf mysqlcc-n.tar.gz
root# cd /usr/X11R6/bin
root# ln -s /usr/local/mysqlcc-n/mysqlcc mysqlcc
```

Those who use other Unix versions must compile the Control Center themselves. The program is based internally on the Qt library. (It is to be expected that the program will exist in several binary versions once it reaches the status *stable*. Even a version for Mac OS X is planned.)

Adding a Server

The Control Center allows for the administration of several MySQL servers (including those not running on the local computer). However, first, for each server, with FILE | NEW you must set up a dialog with all the connection parameters (Figure 4-6). If the server is running on the same computer as the Control Center, the correct setting for HOST NAME is simply *localhost*. As long as MySQL is not password secured, use *root* as user name and do not specify a password.

> **WARNING**   *If the MySQL server is already secured (see Chapter 9), the temptation is great to specify the password in the password dialog. This is, however, a great security risk, since it is stored in plain text in the configuration files (under Linux in the directory ~/*.mysqlcc/, *under Windows in the directory* Documents and settings\usernamme\.mysqlcc*).*

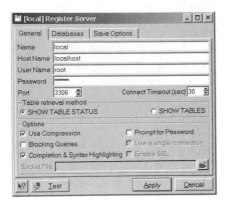

Figure 4-6. Setting up a new server

Using the Control Center

Using the MySQL Control Center is quite easy. In the window CONSOLE MANAGER a listbox in the form of a tree is displayed on the left, in which you can select from among all MySQL servers, their databases, and their tables (see Figure 4-7). A double click on a table displays the data contained within. All other operations are performed through either a context menu or the ACTION menu.

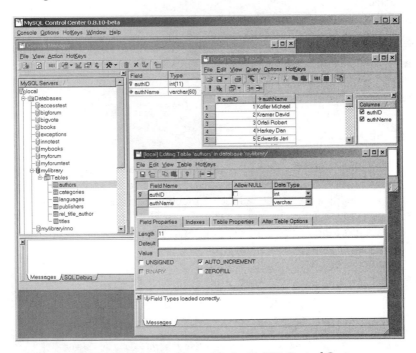

Figure 4-7. Database administration with the MySQL Control Center

Managing Databases and Tables

Using the context menus in the listbox, you can perform such tasks as creating new databases and tables, checking a table's integrity (CHECK TABLE), or displaying the *CREATE TABLE* command. In designing tables, a dialog is available to assist you (see Figure 4-7, lower right), in which you can name the individual columns, set their data type and additional attributes, define indexes, and change table properties (e.g., the type of table). With the same dialog you can also change existing tables.

In the windows that show the content of a table you can also alter existing data, insert new data records, and delete existing data records.

> **CAUTION** *The program deletes all records that are selected or in which the cursor is located. If you select entire rows by clicking on the row numbers, then the cursor remains where it was (by default on the first row). This leads to the possibility of deleting one data record too many unintentionally. The solution is to select the records to be deleted by selecting a range of cells inside the table with the mouse, not entire rows.*

BLOB fields with binary data can also be displayed with a double click in JPEG, PNG, and GIF format. (This functions only if bitmap data are available.)

Executing SQL Commands

In every table window a click on the button SQL makes a range of cells visible in which the underlying *SELECT* command is displayed. Here, you can input new SQL commands (where several commands are to be separated by a semicolon). To execute them, press **Ctrl+E** or click the button with the exclamation mark. In the SQL code, key words and character strings are shown in color, which simplifies the input process. (See Figure 4-8.)

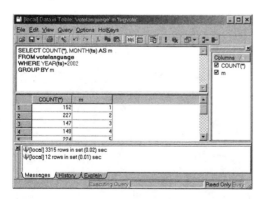

Figure 4-8. Executing SQL commands

> **TIP** *Unfortunately, the Control Center currently offers no import or export commands. However, you can always store the results of an SQL query or the contents of a table as a text file or load a text file with SQL commands. For this, you use the* FILE *command of the table window.*

Server Administration

In the listbox of the CONSOLE MANAGER, under the server's databases, there are two additional entries: SERVER ADMINISTRATION and USER ADMINISTRATION. A double click on SERVER ADMINISTRATION leads to a window that displays all MySQL processes, variables, and status information. Furthermore, via a context menu you can execute various *FLUSH* commands and even shut down the server with *SHUTDOWN*. However, the program offers no way of restarting the server; for that, you have to use WinMySQLadmin under Windows, and execute /etc/init.d/mysql[d] start under Unix/Linux.

User Administration

The entry USER ADMINISTRATION leads to a list of all users who can access the MySQL server. A double click on a user allows the alteration of that user's privileges. The dialog for this purpose is easy to use (see Figure 4-9), and of course, all of this assumes that you know and understand the access system for MySQL. (A detailed description appears in Chapter 9.)

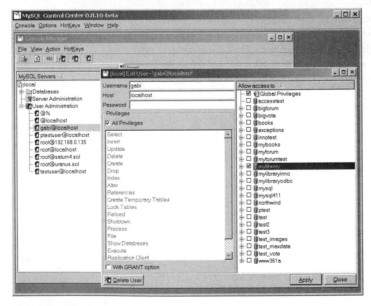

Figure 4-9. User administration with the MySQL Control Center.

phpMyAdmin (HTML)

phpMyAdmin consists of a number of PHP scripts that enable nearly all of the administration of MySQL. Thanks to the HTML interface the administration can be carried out with almost any web browser, independent of operating system, locally as well as over a network.

Overview of the User Interface

The user interface of phpMyAdmin consists principally of three HTML pages (based on various PHP scripts). If you work with phpMyAdmin, you will, of course, stumble on many pages, but the three discussed here (and we shall continually refer to them in this section) represent the starting point for all navigation with phpMyAdmin.

- **Start Page** (Figure 4-10): The initial page index.php3 enables the selection of desired MySQL servers (if phpMyAdmin was set up for the administration of several servers), the creation of a new database, and the execution of various administrative tasks related to the server. (Depending on the access rights phpMyAdmin has with the MySQL server, many links will be missing. For example, if you do not have the right to generate new databases, then phpMyAdmin does not even offer this command.) Using the listbox in the left area of the start page, you can select a database for further processing.

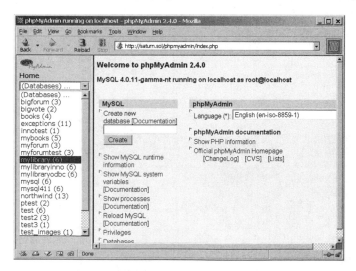

Figure 4-10. Start page of phpMyAdmin

- **Database View** (Figure 4-11): The database view provides an overview of all tables of the database and shows a collection of various functions for processing the entire database (generate and delete tables, execute SQL commands, export the database, etc.).

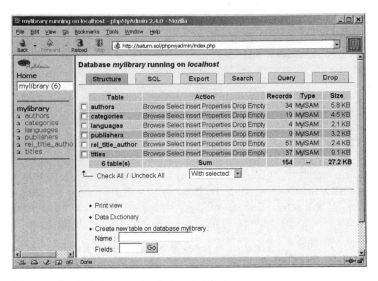

Figure 4-11. Database view of phpMyAdmin

- **Table View** (Figure 4-12): In table view, you see all the columns of the database with their properties. Here you can insert columns, edit or delete, and execute various administrative functions for individual tables (rename tables, copy, export, import ASCII files, etc.).

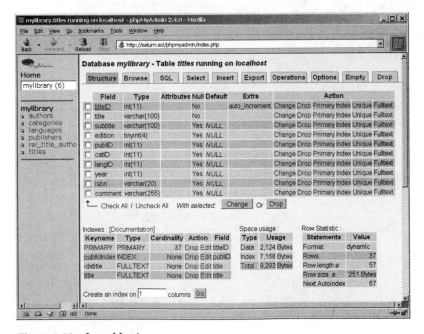

Figure 4-12. php table view

> **POINTER** *You can find extensive on-line help via the start page of phpMyAdmin by following the link* PHPMYADMIN DOCUMENTATION.

Installation and Configuration

Installation Variants

There are several possibilities for installing and using phpMyAdmin:

- In the simplest case, both phpMyAdmin and MySQL run on the same local computer (that is, Apache, PHP, MySQL, and the scripts for phpMyAdmin are all locally installed). This installation variant has already been described in Chapter 2.

- It is not much more complicated to install phpMyAdmin locally and thereby maintain a MySQL server that is running on another computer. The only difference is that config.inc.php must be set so that phpMyAdmin creates a connection to the external MySQL server. However, often, the problem arises that MySQL must be configured on the external computer in such a way that external administration is permitted. But for security reasons, ISPs in particular usually permit only local access to the server (that is, by *localhost*).

- For the administration of a MySQL server located at an ISP, it is worthwhile to install phpMyAdmin there. As a rule, only the script files of phpMyAdmin need to be transported into a directory of the web server. All other conditions (Apache, PHP) are automatically fulfilled by most ISPs. Even access to MySQL is now not a problem, since phpMyAdmin is now, from the point of view of MySQL, being executed locally.

> **CAUTION** *It happens frequently that phpMyAdmin is installed in such a way that it is accessible to all users over a local network or even over the Internet who know or can guess the network address of the start page. To avoid giving complete MySQL access to just anyone, the access and phpMyAdmin script files must be password protected. Usually, a* .htaccess *file is used. Introductory information on dealing with such files can be found in Chapter 2. Further information can be found in any half-decent book on Apache.*

Configuration of MySQL Access

The complete configuration of phpMyAdmin is accomplished in the file config.inc.php. In the simplest case, it suffices to set the following variables:

```
# configuration file config.inc.php
 ...
// must contain the web address of the phpMyAdmin directory
$cfg['PmaAbsoluteUri'] =
  'http://computer.name/phpmyadmin directory/';
 ...
$cfg['Servers'][$i]['host']       = 'computer.name'; // or 'localhost'
 ...
$cfg['Servers'][$i]['auth_type'] = 'config';         // must be 'config'
$cfg['Servers'][$i]['user']      = 'root';           // MySQL user
$cfg['Servers'][$i]['password']  = 'xxxx';           // MySQL password
 ...
```

If the MySQL server is running on the same computer as the web server that is executing the phpMyAdmin script files with PHP, then you give *localhost* as the computer name. Optionally, with $cfgServers[1]['port'] the TCP/IP port over which the link is established can be specified. That is necessary only if the default port 3306 is not the one to be used.

CAUTION   *The file* config.inc.php *contains the user name and password in plain text. That is always a security risk. Make sure that unauthorized access to this file, such as via anonymous FTP, is not possible.*

REMARK   *This section describes phpMyAdmin 2.4. If you update from an earlier version, you should not take the configuration file* config.inc.php *from the older installation (copy), but create a new file, because the syntax of this file has changed somewhat.*

REMARK   *The extent of the possibilities for administration with phpMyAdmin depends, of course, on the MySQL access rights possessed by the MySQL user whose name phpMyAdmin has used at login (that is,* $cfgServers[1] ['user']= ... *). Therefore, phpMyAdmin is not responsible for access protection, but rather the MySQL access system with the privilege database* mysql, *which is described fully in Chapter 9.*

Conversely, we see that if only some of the options for phpMyAdmin described below work for you, then it is not that phpMyAdmin is flawed, but that you have insufficient access rights to MySQL. In particular, if you use phpMyAdmin to manage a database located at an ISP, you will generally have access only to your own database. (Otherwise, your ISP would be guilty of a serious breach of administrative etiquette.)

Servicing Several MySQL Servers with phpMyAdmin

Host, user, and password entries for multiple MySQL servers are possible in config.inc.php. If you make such entries, then on the start page of MySQL there appears a listbox with the names of the computers whose MySQL servers can be managed. Selecting one of these names establishes a link to that server.

The variable *$cfg['ServerDefault']* determines the server that phpMyAdmin uses to establish a link at startup. If the variable is set to 0, then at startup phpMyAdmin initially sets no link, but merely presents a listbox with the selection of servers.

If you do not wish to have simply the computer name (array variable *host*) displayed in the listbox, then you can use *$cfg['Servers'][$i]['verbose']* to display a different character string.

Additional Configuration Possibilities

In addition to the MySQL access data in config.inc.php, you can also set various options. The following list describes only the most important of these, together with their associated variables:

- *$cfg['Confirm']* = *true/false:* This variable specifies whether a confirmation query should be displayed before data are deleted (default: true).

- *$cfg['MaxRows']* = *n:* Specifies how many data records should be displayed per page as the result of a query (default is 30).

- *$cfg['ExecTimeLimit']* = *n:* Specifies how long the execution of the PHP code will be allowed to run (default is 300 seconds). The time is relevant primarily for time-intensive import/export commands.

- *$cfg['ShowBlob']=true/false:* Specifies whether the contents of fields of type *xxxBLOB* are to be displayed (default: false).

- *$cfg['ProtectBinary']* = *false/'blob'/'all':* Specifies whether the contents of *BLOB* fields are to be write protected. By default (*'blob'*), *BLOB*s cannot be changed. The prohibition against change to any table content (regardless of data type) is effected by *'all'*, while *'false'* permits everything to be changed.

- *$cfg['LeftWidth']* = *n:* Specifies the width of the left column of the main window (by default, 150 pixels). In this column are displayed the listbox for database selection and the list of tables in the current database.

http and Cookie Authentication

The configuration described in the previous section with *$cfg['Servers'][$i]['auth_type']* = *'config'* is simple, but it is inflexible if various users wish to manage their own databases, and insecure because user names and passwords appear in plain text in config.inc.php. If you as an Internet service provider wish to allow many users uniform access to phpMyAdmin, you should consider the two configuration variants described here.

Assumptions

- This section assumes that you are familiar with MySQL and in particular, with its security system (see Chapter 9). If that is not yet the case, you should skip this section and stick with the standard configuration described above (which is sufficient for most purposes).

- You must have administrator privileges for the MySQL server. That is not the case for installing phpMyAdmin on an ISP's computer.

- It is assumed in *http* authentication that the PHP interpreter is executed as an Apache module (and not as a CGI program). This is generally the case with current versions of PHP (even under Windows).

- *cookie* authentication is designed for the case in which *http* authentication is not possible (for example, when the Microsoft Internet Information Server (IIS) is used as the web server). This form of authentication assumes that the user permits cookies from phpMyAdmin and that the PHP interpreter and the user's browser are in agreement on the management of cookies. The phpMyAdmin documentation discusses problems with Internet Explorer (through version 6) and with PHP 4.1.1.

Creating a MySQL User for phpMyAdmin

Before *http* or *cookie* authentication can be used, a MySQL user must be created that can read *mysql.user, mysql.db, and mysql.tables_priv* (that is, it must be provided with the *SELECT* privilege).

The MySQL administrator can create such a user with the following SQL commands. The name of this user is irrelevant. For the following example, the name *pmaUser* will be used:

```
GRANT USAGE ON mysql.* TO pmaUser@localhost
  IDENTIFIED BY 'xxxx'
GRANT SELECT (Host, User, Select_priv, Insert_priv, Update_priv,
    Delete_priv, Create_priv, Drop_priv, Reload_priv, Shutdown_priv,
    Process_priv, File_priv, Grant_priv, References_priv, Index_priv,
    Alter_priv)
  ON mysql.user TO pmaUser@localhost;
GRANT SELECT ON mysql.db TO pmaUser@localhost
GRANT SELECT (Host, Db, User, Table_name, Table_priv, Column_priv)
  ON mysql.tables_priv TO pmaUser@localhost
```

http *authentication*

In order to be able to use phpMyAdmin *http* authentication, make the changes shown in boldface to the file config.inc.php:

```
# in config.inc.php
$cfg['Servers'][$i]['controluser']  = 'pmaUser';  // Read-only-User
$cfg['Servers'][$i]['controlpass']  = 'xxx';      // password
$cfg['Servers'][$i]['auth_type']    = 'http';     // http authentication
$cfg['Servers'][$i]['user']         = '';         // empty!
$cfg['Servers'][$i]['password'] = '';             // empty!
```

Now, every time that you want to use phpMyAdmin, the web browser's login dialog appears (see Figure 4-13), in which you must give a MySQL user name and associated password. For further work in phpMyAdmin, you then have the privileges of this MySQL user.

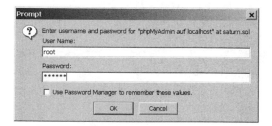

Figure 4-13. Login dialog for http *authentication*

As always, config.inc.php contains a user name and password (*pmaUser* and *xxx*). But now the security risk is much less, because this MySQL user can read only a few tables on the MySQL server and cannot change any of them.

> **REMARK**   *Due to an error in phpMyAdmin 2.4, it is impossible to log in twice consecutively with the same user name and password. To bypass this error, you have to quit the web browser and restart.*

cookie *Authentication*

For *cookie* authentication, you must change only the *auth_type* line in config.inc.php:

```
# in config.inc.php
$cfg['Servers'][$i]['controluser']  = 'pmaUser';  // Read-only-User
$cfg['Servers'][$i]['controlpass']  = 'xxx';      // password
$cfg['Servers'][$i]['auth_type']    = 'cookie';   // cookie authentication
$cfg['Servers'][$i]['user']         = '';         // empty!
$cfg['Servers'][$i]['password'] = '';             // empty!
```

Login errors are not shown within the phpMyAdmin start page (see Figure 4-14).

phpMyAdmin 2.4.0 - Mozilla
File Edit View Go Bookmarks Tools Window Help
Back Forward Reload Stop
http://localhost/phpmyadmin/
Welcome to phpMyAdmin 2.4.0 - Login
Language: English (en-iso-8859-1)
Go
Cookies must be enabled past this point.
Username: root
Password: ******
Login
Done

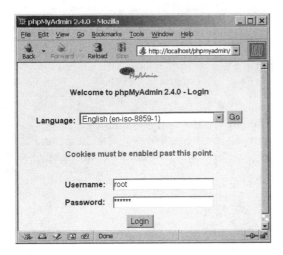

Figure 4-14. Login dialog for cookie *authentication*

Creating and Editing Databases

If your desires run in the direction of creating a new database, phpMyAdmin can save you the necessity of having to deal with many complex *CREATE TABLE* commands.

Creating a Database

The creation of a new database begins on the start page of phpMyAdmin, in which you provide the name of the new database. This database then becomes the active database. (If you wish to insert a table into a preexisting database, then click on that database in the list of databases.)

Creating a Table

On the table page you will find, among other things, CREATE NEW TABLE. There you give the desired name of the table and the number of columns (when in doubt, just give a number that is too large. You can always leave the extra columns empty). OK leads to the next form (see Figure 4-15), in which you can conveniently set the names and properties of the columns.

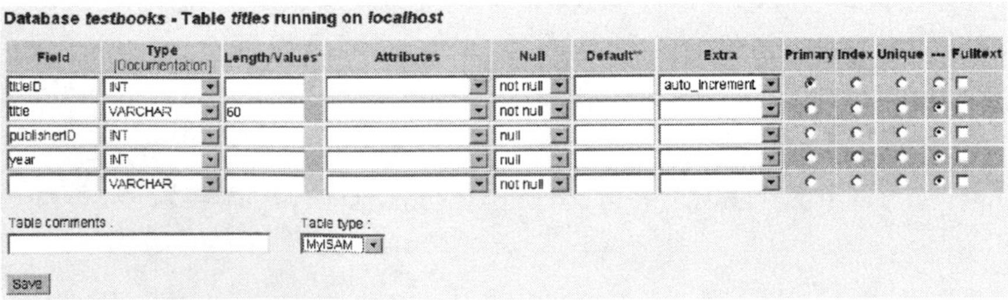

Database testbooks - Table titles running on localhost
Field
Type (Documentation)
Length/Values*
Attributes
Null
Default**
Extra
Primary
Index
Unique

Fulltext
titleID
INT
not null
auto_increment
title
VARCHAR
60
not null
publisherID
INT
null
year
INT
null
VARCHAR
not null
Table comments :
Table type :
MyISAM
Save

Figure 4-15. Design of the table titles *in phpMyAdmin*

The use of phpMyAdmin requires a bit of knowledge about the possible and necessary settings for the various data types. For example, you will get slapped with an error message if you attempt to declare a *VARCHAR* column without providing a length, or a *TEXT* column with a length (neither variant is provided for in MySQL). You may then, of course, correct your error.

Changing the Table Design

In the phpMyAdmin table view (Figure 4-16) you can equip each column with an index by a simple click of the mouse. It is just as simple to change the column attributes, such as the maximal length of character strings (link CHANGE). You can delete existing columns and insert new columns at any position (ADD NEW FIELD).

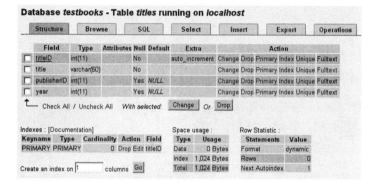

Figure 4-16. Table view with many options for changing the design

Inserting, Displaying, and Editing Table Data

Inserting Data into a Table

In the dialog sheet INSERT (Figure 4-17) you can insert individual data records into a table.

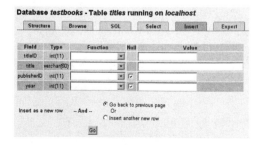

Figure 4-17. Adding a data record

This is a convenient way of proceeding for a few test records. However, only one data record can be edited (not several simultaneously), so this procedure is rather cumbersome for larger data sets.

- **Functions:** It is often the case in the input of a data record that an SQL function is to be inserted, such as *PASSWORD('xxx')* to store *xxx* in encrypted form. For this, phpMyAdmin offers several frequently used functions in the column FUNCTION, including *ASCII, CURTIME, NOW*. Figure 4-18 demonstrates the use of such functions.

| password | varchar(16) | PASSWORD ▾ | secret |

Figure 4-18. Adding a password

> **TIP** *It is relatively tedious to input several data records with phpMyAdmin. In many cases, it is more efficient to input the records and then import them with* INSERT TEXTFILE INTO TABLE *on the dialog sheet* STRUCTURE.

Displaying Table Contents

In both database view (see Figure 4-11) and table view (see Figure 4-16) the link BROWSE leads to a display of the contents of the table. For this, the command *SELECT * FROM table LIMIT 0, 30* is executed. You may then move backward and forward through the table.

> **TIP** *If you would like to sort a table according to a different criterion, simply click in the relevant column.*

Editing Existing Data

If you click on the link EDIT shown in Figure 4-19, you will land on a new page, in which the data record can be edited. This page looks as depicted in Figure 4-17, where in the column VALUE the previous contents of the record are displayed, where they can be easily edited.

> **REMARK** *A change in data is possible only if the table has a column identified as* PRIMARY KEY *(usually with* id *values that identify each record).*

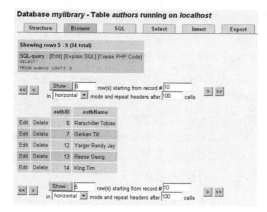

Figure 4-19. Page-by-page representation of data records

Server Administration

Executing SQL Commands

In the dialog sheet SQL, in table view (see Figure 4-11) you can input SQL commands. With OK, the command is then executed for the current database. The SQL command does not have to be terminated with a semicolon, as in mysql. However, a semicolon is necessary if several commands are to be executed simultaneously.

If the command involves *SELECT*, then the results are displayed page by page, like the contents of a table. However, the links EDIT and DELETE function only if the query results come from a single table (no *JOIN*s from several tables) and the *PRIMARY KEY* column of the table is a part of the query results.

Instead of inputting SQL commands, you can input instead the name of a file containing SQL commands. Then phpMyAdmin loads this file and executes the commands contained therein. This procedure can also be used to load a previously executed phpMyAdmin database backup.

> **REMARK**   *phpMyAdmin also offers a query editor. However, the interface is rather a disappointment, and it is difficult to use. Without a good fundamental knowledge of SQL it is practically impossible to link two tables. As a rule, it is easier just to type in the SQL code.*

Executing Backups, Saving the Database Structure

In both database and table views, one has available the dialog sheet EXPORT (see Figure 4-20). Here you can transform an entire database (or just the design or the data) or individual tables into a text file.

There are several options:

- STRUCTURE ONLY: phpMyAdmin generates SQL commands to generate new empty tables.

- STRUCTURE AND DATA: phpMyAdmin generates SQL commands to generate new tables and fill them with data (*INSERT* commands).

- DATA ONLY: phpMyAdmin generates only *INSERT* commands for restoring data.

- LATEX: phpMyAdmin generates a text file for representing data as a LaTeX table. (LaTeX is program available under Unix/Linux and other operating systems for typesetting scientific texts. This book was typeset in LaTeX.)

- CSV DATA: phpMyAdmin generates a text file that can be imported into Excel or another program. (CSV stands for comma-separated values.)

- XML: phpMyAdmin generates a text file in XML format.

- WITH DROP TABLE: Before every *CREATE TABLE* command a *DROP TABLE* command is inserted. If you later use the resulting file to recreate the table, then this file will first be deleted.

- COMPLETE INSERTs: For every INSERT command, phpMyAdmin also specifies the column name, for example, in the form *INSERT INTO author (authorID, author) VALUES ('1', 'name')*. Without this option, the *INSERT* command would be generated in a more compact form: *INSERT INTO author VALUES ('1', 'name')*.
  COMPLETE INSERTs are necessary if the data are to be inserted from one table into another that exhibits additional columns or whose arrangement of columns is different from that in the initial table.

- EXTENDED INSERTs: phpMyAdmin joins all *INSERT* commands into a single long command: *INSERT INTO author VALUES (1, 'name1'), (2, 'name2') . . . .*

- *Send*: phpMyAdmin does not display the resulting text file, but sends it to the user (as with a download). The data can optionally be compressed to lessen transmission time.

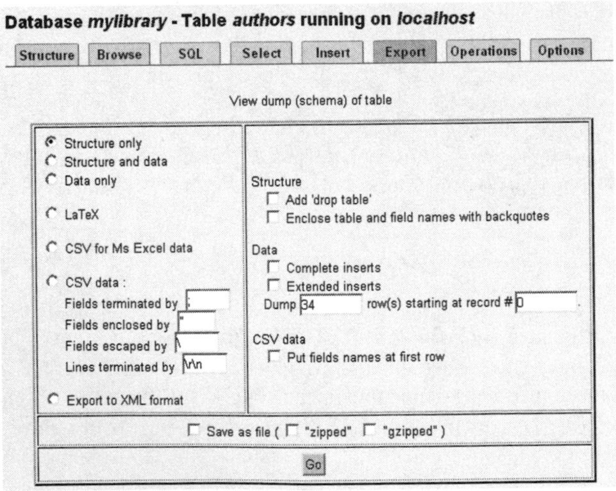

Figure 4-20. Executing a database backup

> **REMARK**   *The exportation of very large databases and tables is problematic, because a PHP script's maximal run time is limited. You can attempt to increase this time in* config.inc.php *($cfg['ExecTimeLimit'] = n), which does not always help (depending on how PHP itself is configured).*

Database Upload

To read in a database (database uploading), the database must first be created. Then in the dialog sheet SQL you use Browse to select the name of the SQL file and execute the SQL commands contained therein with OK.

> **REMARK**   *As with exporting databases, there can be problems in importing large databases or tables. In addition to the time limit, PHP also limits the size of upload files (setting* upload_max_filesize = 2M *in* php.ini*). When PHP is executed on your Internet service provider's computer, you have no influence over the file* php.ini*. (Of course, you can ask your ISP to change certain variables, but experience suggests that you will not meet with an enthusiastic response.) The only solution is usually to break the upload file into smaller units and read them in one at a time.*

Importing Text

What do you do when you have a text file with data (not SQL commands) that you would like to import into a table? Here, too, phpMyAdmin comes to your assistance. In the dialog sheet SQL of table view you will find the link INSERT TEXTFILES INTO TABLE. This link leads you to the dialog depicted in Figure 4-21. There you specify the name of the file. Moreover, you can set a number of options that format the text file.

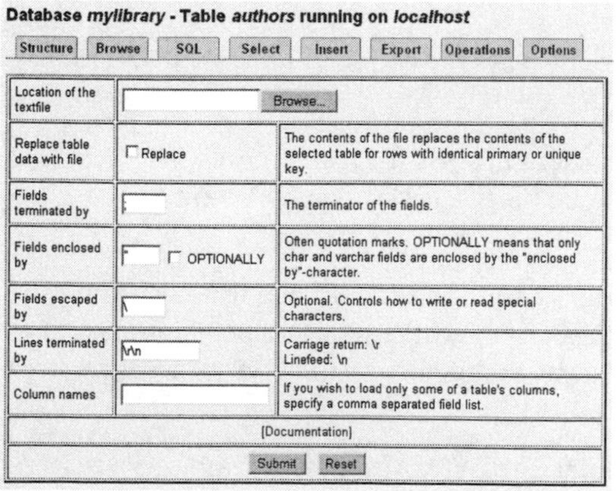

Figure 4-21. Text importation of table data

POINTER *The meaning of the various options is detailed in the description of the command* LOAD DATA *in Chapter 18. Examples of the application of* LOAD DATA, *which can also be used for importing with phpMyAdmin, can be found in Chapter 10.*

NULL *is usually represented in a text file as* \N *(with uppercase* N, *not* n).

Renaming and Copying Tables, Changing the Table Type

The dialog sheet OPERATIONS in table view contains commands for renaming and copying tables and transferring tables to another database.

If you wish to change the type of a table, you can do this in the dialog sheet OPTIONS.

Commands for deleting indexes or inserting new ones can be found in the dialog sheet STRUCTURE. However, phpMyAdmin 2.4 does not offer the possibility of defining integrity rules (*foreign key constraints*) for InnoDB tables.

At the bottom of the table view you will find the commands RENAME TABLE TO and COPY TABLE TO. With RENAME you can, as you might expect, give a table a new name. With COPY you make a duplicate table within the same database, where either just the table structure is created or the entire table with its contents. If you wish to copy a table into another database, you specify the new table name in the form *databasename.tablename.*

Other Administrative Tasks

If you click on HOME at the top of the database tree (left area of the window), you find yourself back at the phpMyAdmin start page. If you have sufficient phpMyAdmin login privileges, this page contains links for carrying out various administrative tasks:

- SHOW MYSQL RUNTIME INFORMATION displays the status of the MySQL server (corresponds to *SHOW STATUS*).

- SHOW MYSQL SYSTEM VARIABLES displays the content of the MySQL variables (corresponds to *SHOW VARIABLES*).

- SHOW PROCESSES displays the current process list (corresponds to *SHOW PROCESSLIST*). If you have sufficient privileges, you can also terminate a process.

- PRIVILEGES leads to a page that lists all MySQL users. From this page you can add new users, change the privileges of existing users, and delete users. This assumes, however, that you already are familiar with the MySQL access system (see Chapter 9).

- DATABASES leads to a list of all databases. With ACTIVATE DATABASE STATISTICS you can determine the sizes of all databases. Also practical is the link CHECK PRIVILEGES, which leads to a page that tells which MySQL users have access to a database.

Additional Functions

The program phpMyAdmin recognizes some additional functions that are available only when phpMyAdmin has been configured for their use and can store data in tables especially for such purposes. This section describes how you can use these additional functions. We assume that you are already familiar with MySQL and are capable of creating new databases and tables and executing SQL commands.

Creating a Database for phpMyAdmin

The program phpMyAdmin requires a database whose tables it is permitted to read and edit. If you have installed phpMyAdmin on your website, where the MySQL server is managed by your ISP, you are usually not permitted to create new databases. In this case, you simply use one of your existing databases. The name of this database is specified in the phpMyAdmin configuration file `config.inc.php`:

```
# in config.inc.php
$cfg['Servers'][$i]['pmadb'] = 'mydatabase';
```

If you are permitted to create new databases, then it is simpler to create a new database for storing phpMyAdmin administrative data. This database can have whatever name you choose to bestow on it. In the following, we will eschew our wildest flights of fancy and choose the name that appears in the phpMyAdmin documentation: *phpmyadmin.*

```
CREATE DATABASE phpmyadmin
# in config.inc.php
$cfg['Servers'][$i]['pmadb'] = 'phpmyadmin';
```

The MySQL login under which phpMyAdmin runs must have read and write privileges for this database. If you have set up phpMyAdmin for *http* or *cookie* authentication, as discussed previously, the phpMyAdmin *controluser* must have these privileges. For this, you execute the following command:

```
GRANT SELECT,INSERT,UPDATE,DELETE ON phpmyadmin.*
TO pmaUser@localhost
```

Saving SQL Queries (bookmarks)

If you frequently execute SQL commands in phpMyAdmin, it is burdensome to have to input the same command over and over. If you create the table *PMA_bookmark,* then in the future, you can give each of your SQL commands a name and store it. The table *PMA_bookmark* is generated by the following command (if you use your own database for storing the phpMyAdmin administrative data, then the command must be called *CREATE TABLE mydatabase.PMA_bookmark*):

```
CREATE TABLE phpmyadmin.pma_bookmark (
  id    INT NOT NULL AUTO_INCREMENT,
```

```
  dbase VARCHAR(255) NOT NULL,
  user  VARCHAR(255) NOT NULL,
  label VARCHAR(255) NOT NULL,
  query TEXT NOT NULL,
  PRIMARY KEY (id)
) TYPE=MyISAM COMMENT='Bookmarks'
```

The name of this database must be specified in config.inc.php.

```
# in config.inc.php
$cfg['Se vers'][$i]['bookmarktable'] = 'pma_bookmark';
```

From now on, after the execution of an SQL command, you can store the SQL code. For this purpose, the end of the result page contains a text field for the name of the query, as well as a button called SAVE SQL QUERY. Moreover, you can use the stored SQL code for constructing new SQL commands.

Saving Information About Relations

The program phpMyAdmin is not able to determine which fields are used to link two tables together (not even if integrity rules are defined for InnoDB tables; see Chapter 8). However, if you create the following two tables, then you can specify this information yourself:

```
CREATE TABLE phpmyadmin.pma_relation (
  master_db     VARCHAR(64) NOT NULL,
  master_table  VARCHAR(64) NOT NULL,
  master_field  VARCHAR(64) NOT NULL,
  foreign_db    VARCHAR(64) NOT NULL,
  foreign_table VARCHAR(64) NOT NULL,
  foreign_field VARCHAR(64) NOT NULL,
  PRIMARY KEY (master_db, master_table, master_field) ,
  KEY foreign_field(foreign_db, foreign_table)
) TYPE = MYISAM COMMENT = 'Relation table'
CREATE TABLE phpmyadmin.pma_table_info (
  db_name       VARCHAR(64) NOT NULL,
  table_name    VARCHAR(64) NOT NULL,
  display_field VARCHAR(64) NOT NULL,
  PRIMARY KEY (db_name, table_name)
) TYPE=MyISAM COMMENT='Table information for phpMyAdmin'
```

The name of this table must, in turn, be supplied to config.inc.php:

```
# in config.inc.php
$cfg['Servers'][$i]['relation']   = 'pma_relation';
$cfg['Servers'][$i]['table_info'] = 'pma_table_info';
```

> **REMARK** *Even after you have constructed both tables correctly, the* STRUCTURE *sheet still shows an error message:* The additional features for working with linked tables have been deactivated. *However, this error message means only that a* part *of these functions have been deactivated. (These additional functions will be described later.) However, the basic functions should be functioning correctly.*

Now in the STRUCTURE sheet of table view, via the link RELATION VIEW you can specify for each foreign key field (*foreign key column*) which field of another table it refers to. Furthermore, you can specify which columns of the table are displayed when another table refers to it.

This is perhaps most simply explained with an example. The fields *publID*, *catID*, and *langID* in the table *titles* from the example database *mylibrary* (see Chapter 5) refer to the tables *publishers*, *categories*, and *languages*. This information was depicted in Figure 4-22. If another table refers to the *titles* table, than the *titleID* number should not be displayed, but the book title (field *title*, Figure 4-22).

Figure 4-22. References by the table titles *to other tables in the database* mylibrary

The input of this additional information for all tables is, of course, a bit tiresome. In what follows, however, the processing of this database by phpMyAdmin will be significantly easier.

- When you look at the contents of a table, foreign key fields are executed as links. When you click on a link, the corresonding data record of the linked table is displayed.

- When you change a data record in a table or input a new one, you no longer have to specify an ID number in the foreign key fields. Instead, listboxes are displayed that enable you to select the linked fields (see Figure 4-23).

- The QUERY EDITOR now automatically recognizes links between tables and is much simpler to use.

- The link DATA DICTIONARY in the STRUCTURE page of table view now provides detailed information about the structure of the database and can be easily printed (as documentation about the database).

- Finally, you can generate a pdf file for documenting the table structure that contains all the relevant information.

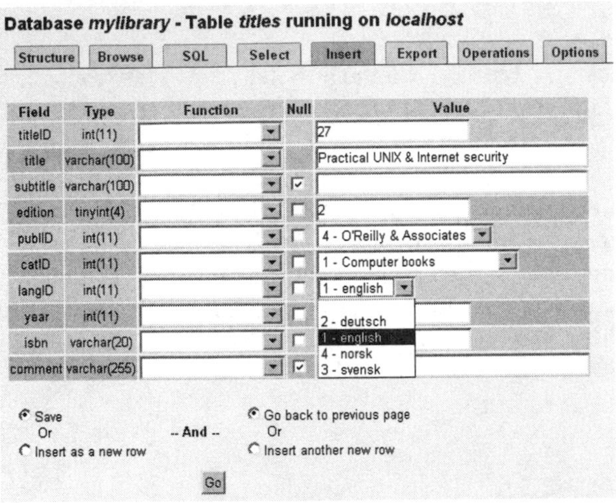

Figure 4-23. Listboxes simplify the input of foreign key fields.

Saving Column Comments

In version 4.0.*n*, MySQL allows the storing of comments for every table, but not does offer the option of storing comments on columns. If you wish to do this (for better documentation of your database), you need an additional table:

```
CREATE TABLE phpmyadmin.pma_column_comments (
  id int(5)   UNSIGNED NOT NULL AUTO_INCREMENT,
  db_name     VARCHAR(64) NOT NULL,
  table_name  VARCHAR(64) NOT NULL,
  column_name VARCHAR(64) NOT NULL,
  comment     VARCHAR(255) NOT NULL,
  PRIMARY KEY (id),
  UNIQUE KEY db_name (db_name, table_name, column_name)
) TYPE=MyISAM COMMENT='Comments for Columns'
```

The associated entry in `config.inc.php` looks like this:

```
$cfg['Servers'][$i]['column_comments'] = 'pma_column_comments';
```

The input of column comments in phpMyAdmin is accomplished in the same dialog as that for relations (link RELATION VIEW in the STRUCTURE page of table view).

Creating pdf Documents

The function introduced in phpMyAdmin 2.3 for creating pdf files to document table design seems a bit unripe. You need two additional tables to execute this function:

```
CREATE TABLE phpmyadmin.pma_table_coords (
        db_name        VARCHAR(64) NOT NULL,
        table_name     VARCHAR(64) NOT NULL,
        pdf_page_number INT NOT NULL,
        x
    FLOAT UNSIGNED NOT NULL,
        y
    FLOAT UNSIGNED NOT NULL,
        PRIMARY KEY (db_name, table_name, pdf_page_number)
) TYPE=MyISAM COMMENT='Table coordinates for phpMyAdmin PDF output'

CREATE TABLE phpmyadmin.pma_pdf_pages (
        db_name    VARCHAR(64) NOT NULL,
        page_nr    INT(10) UNSIGNED NOT NULL AUTO_INCREMENT,
        page_descr VARCHAR(50) NOT NULL,
        PRIMARY KEY (page_nr),
        KEY (db_name)
) TYPE=MyISAM COMMENT='PDF Relationpages for PMA'
```

Both tables must be entered in `config.inc.php`.

```
$cfg['Servers'][$i]['table_coords'] = 'pma_table_cords';
$cfg['Servers'][$i]['pdf_pages'] = 'pma_pdf_pages';
```

The creation of a pdf document is accomplished in several steps:

- The process begins in the STRUCTURE page of database view with the link EDIT PDF PAGES.

- Now you give a name to the pdf document that is to be created and select it for processing.

- Now you must select all the tables that are to be documented. (Surprisingly, all tables must be selected individually.)

- For the structure view in which the links between tables are represented, you must give the start coordinates for each table. The coordinate range is by default from 0 (left) to 300 (right) for the x-coordinate, and from 0 (above) to 200 (below) for the y-coordinate. However, phpMyAdmin automatically adjusts the coordinate range if you place a table outside this region.
  It is rather a bother to arrange tables nicely, and generally, one uses the method of trial and error. (You begin with some arbitrary values, look at the resulting pdf page, make an adjustment, try again, and so on.)

The remaining options specify features of the pdf document:

- SHOW GRID has the effect that the table schema is underlaid by coordinates and gridlines. This is helpful during the layout phase.

- SHOW COLOR relates to the color of the lines joining tables. (When colored lines are printed on a black-and-white printer, the results are not always lovely.)

- DISPLAY TABLE DIMENSIONS results in every table's size being specified in the coordinate system of the pdf document. This option is useful only during the layout phase.

- DISPLAY ALL TABLES WITH SAME WIDTH? relates to the width of tables in the pdf document. A uniform width is often easier to read.

- DATA DICTIONARY specifies whether in addition to the table structure, a detailed description of the properties of all tables should be integrated into the pdf document (one page per table).

An OK allows the pdf document to be generated and transmitted to the web browser. Depending on the browser's settings, you can display it at once with Adobe Acrobat, or else you have to save it first to a local file. Figure 4-24 shows the settings for the table structure of *mylibrary* (Figure 4-25).

Figure 4-24. Setting the layout of the pdf table schema

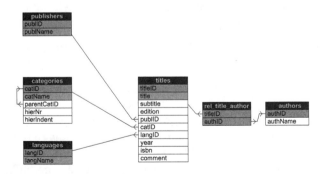

Figure 4-25. The resulting structure as a pdf document

#### CHAPTER 5

Database Design

THE FIRST STAGE IN ANY database application is the design of the database. The design will have a great influence on the efficiency of the application, the degree of simplicity or difficulty in programming and maintenance, and the flexibility in making changes in the design. Errors that occur in the design phase will come home to roost in the heartache of future efforts at correction.

This chapter discusses the fundamentals of relational databases, collects the varieties of data and tables available under MySQL, offers concrete examples of MySQL database structures, shows how indexes enable more efficient table access, and, finally, offers enlightenment on concrete ways that databases and tables can be generated.

Chapter Overview

Introduction

Database design is doubtless one of the greatest challenges in the development of complex database applications. This chapter attempts to provide a first introduction to the topic. But please don't expect any foolproof recipes. Many of the skills in database design are won by experience, and in a single chapter we can transmit only some of the basic principles.

To help in your orientation in this relatively long chapter, here is an overview:

- The following two sections provide basic information. We discuss how to divide data logically among several tables, where the primary goal is to avoid redundancy. The *normalization* process helps in this.

    We also present the data types belonging to MySQL. For example, we answer the question as to what data type should be used for storing amounts of money and for long and short character strings.

- We then go into some more advanced topics: How can searching and sorting tables be speeded up with the help of indexes? What types of tables does MySQL recognize, and which should be used when?

- How are databases and their tables actually generated? A separate section introduces various *CREATE* commands, which help in this. (However, it is considerably more convenient to create new tables using instead a user interface such as phpMyAdmin.)

- Theory is all well and good, but at some point we have to roll up our sleeves, put on an apron, and start cooking up some databases of our own. Therefore, the last sections of this chapter offer some concrete examples of the design of databases: for managing a small library, for running a discussion group, and for testing special cases.

> **POINTER** *In this chapter we cannot avoid using some SQL commands now and then, although SQL is actually introduced in detail only in the next chapter. (However, it is conversely also impossible to describe SQL without assuming a particular database layout.) You may find it necessary at times to flip back and forth between this chapter and the next.*

Further Reading

There are countless books that deal exclusively, independently of any specific database system, with database design and SQL. Needless to say, there is a variety of opinion as to which of these books are the good ones. Therefore, consider the following recommendations as my personal hit list:

1. Joe Celko: *SQL for Smarties*, Morgan Kaufmann Publishers, 1999. (This is not a book for SQL beginners. Many examples are currently not realizable in MySQL, because MySQL is not sufficiently compatible with ANSI-SQL/92. Nonetheless, it is a terrific example-oriented book on SQL.)

2. Judith S. Bowman et al.: *The Practical SQL Handbook*, Addison-Wesley, 2001.

3. Michael J. Hernandez: *Database Design for Mere Mortals*, Addison-Wesley, 2003. (The first half is somewhat long-winded, but the second half is excellent and very clearly written.)

4. The MySQL documentation recommends an additional book as an introduction to SQL, though I am not acquainted with it: Martin Gruber's *Mastering SQL*, Sybex, 2000.

5. Another book that is frequently recommended is Peter Gulutzan and Trudy Pelzer's *SQL-99 Complete, Really*, R&D Books, 1999.

> **POINTER** *If you are not quite ready to shell out your hard-earned (or perhaps even ill-gotten) cash for yet another book and you are interested for now in database design only, you may find the compact introduction on the design of relational databases by Fernando Lozano adequate to your needs. See* `http://www.edm2.com/0612/msql7.html`.

Database Theory

Why is that that authors of books think about nothing (well, almost nothing) but books? The author begs the indulgence of his readers in that the example in this section deals with books. The goal of the section is to create a small database in which data about books can be stored: book title, publisher, author(s), publication date, and so on.

Normal Forms

These data can, of course, be stored without a database, in a simple list in text format, for example, as appears in the Bibliography at the end of this book:

Michael Kofler: *Linux*. Addison-Wesley 2000.

Michael Kofler, David Kramer: *Definitive Guide to Excel VBA*, second edition. Apress 2003.

Robert Orfali, Dan Harkey, Jeri Edwards: *Client/Server Survival Guide*. Addison-Wesley 1997.

Tobias Ratschiller, Till Gerken: *Web Application Development with PHP 4.0*. New Riders 2000.

This is a nice and convenient list, containing all necessary information. Why bother with all the effort to transform this text (which perhaps exists as a document composed with some word-processing program) into a database?

Needless to say, the reasons are legion. Our list can be easily searched, but it is impossible to organize it in a different way, for example, to create a list of all books by author x or to create a new list ordered not by author, but by title.

Our First Attempt

Just think: Nothing is easier than to turn our list into a database table. (To save space we are going to abbreviate the book titles and names of authors.)

Table 5-1 immediately shows itself to be riddled with problems. A first glance reveals that limiting the number of authors to three was an arbitrary decision. What do you do with a book that has four or five authors? Do we just keep adding columns, up to *authorN*, painfully aware that those columns will be empty for most entries?

Table 5-1. A book database: first attempt.

title	publisher	year	author1	author2	author3
Linux	Addison-Wesley	2000	Kofler, M.		
Definitive . . .	Apress	2000	Kofler, M.	Kramer, D.	
Client . . .	Addison-Wesley	1997	Orfali, R.	Harkey, D.	Edwards, E.
Web . . .	New Riders	2000	Ratschiller, T.	Gerken, T.	

The First Normal Form

Database theorists have found, I am happy to report, a solution to such problems. Simply apply to your database, one after the other, the rules for the three *normal forms*. The rules for the first normal form are as follows (though for the benefit of the reader, they have been translated from the language of database theorists into what we might frivolously call "linguistic normal form," or, more simply, plain English):

- Columns with similar content must be eliminated.

- A table must be created for each group of associated data.

- Each data record must be identifiable by means of a *primary key*.

In our example, the first rule is clearly applicable to the *authorN* columns.

The second rule seems not to be applicable here, since in our example we are dealing exclusively with data that pertain specifically to the books in the database. Thus a single table would seem to suffice. (We will see, however, that this is not, in fact, the case.)

The third rule signifies in practice that a running index must be used that uniquely identifies each row of the table. (It is not strictly necessary that an integer be used as primary key. Formally, only the uniqueness is required. For reasons of efficiency the primary key should be as small as possible, and thus an integer is generally more suitable than a character string of variable length.)

A reconfiguration of our table after application of the first and third rules might look like that depicted in Table 5-2.

Clearly, the problem of multiple columns for multiple authors has been eliminated. Regardless of the number of authors, they can all be stored in our table. Of course, there is no free luncheon, and the price of a meal here is rather high: The contents of the columns *title*, *publisher*, and *year* are repeated for each author. There must be a better way!

Table 5-2. A book database: first normal form

id	title	publisher	year	author
1	Linux	Addison-Wesley	2000	Kofler, M.
2	Definitive Guide . . .	Apress	2000	Kofler, M.
3	Definitive Guide . . .	Apress	2000	Kramer, D.
4	Client/Server . . .	Addison-Wesley	1997	Orfali, R.
5	Client/Server . . .	Addison-Wesley	1997	Harkey, D.
6	Client/Server . . .	Addison-Wesley	1997	Edwards, E.
7	Web Application . . .	New Riders	2000	Ratschiller, T.
8	Web Application . . .	New Riders	2000	Gerken, T.

Second Normal Form

Here are the rules for the second normal form:

- Whenever the contents of columns repeat themselves, this means that the table must be divided into several subtables.

- These tables must be linked by *foreign keys*.

If you are new to the lingo of the database world, then the term *foreign key* probably seems a bit, well, foreign. A better word in everyday English would probably be *cross reference*, since a foreign key refers to a line in a different (hence foreign) table. For programmers, the word *pointer* would perhaps be more to the point, while in Internet jargon the term *link* would be appropriate.

In Table 5-2, we see that data are repeated in practically every column. The culprit of this redundancy is clearly the author column. Our first attempt to give the authors their very own table can be seen in Tables 5-3 and 5-4.

Table 5-3. title table: second normal form

titleID	title	publisher	year
1	Linux	Addison-Wesley	2000
2	Definitive Guide . . .	Apress	2000
3	Client/Server . . .	Addison-Wesley	1997
4	Web Application . . .	New Riders	2000

Table 5-4. author table: second normal form

authorID	titleID	author
1	1	Kofler, M.
2	2	Kofler, M.
3	2	Kramer, D.
4	3	Orfali, R.
5	3	Harkey, D.
6	3	Edwards, E.
7	4	Ratschiller, T.
8	4	Gerken, T.

In the *author* table, the first column, with its running *authorID* values, provides the primary key. The second column takes over the task of the foreign key. It points, or refers, to rows of the *title* table. For example, row 7 of the *author* table indicates that *Ratschiller, T.* is an author of the book with ID *titleID=4*, that is, the book *Web Application . . . .*

Second Normal Form, Second Attempt

Our result could hardly be called optimal. In the *author* table, the name *Kofler, M.* appears twice. As the number of books in this database increases, the amount of such redundancy will increase as well, whenever an author has worked on more than one book.

The only solution is to split the *authors* table again and live without the *titleID* column. The information as to which book belongs to which author must be specified in yet a third table. These three tables are shown in Tables 5-5 through 5-7.

Table 5-5. title *table: second normal form*

titleID	title	publisher	year
1	Linux	Addison-Wesley	2000
2	Definitive Guide . . .	Apress	2000
3	Client/Server . . .	Addison-Wesley	1997
4	Web Application . . .	New Riders	2000

Table 5-6. author *table: second normal form*

authorID	author
1	Kofler, M.
2	Kramer, D.
3	Orfali, R.
4	Harkey, D.
5	Edwards, E.
6	Ratschiller, T.
7	Gerken, T.

Table 5-7. rel_title_author *table: second normal form*

titleID	authorID
1	1
2	1
2	2
3	3
3	4
3	5
4	6
4	7

This is certainly the most difficult and abstract step, probably because a table of the form *rel_title_author* has no real-world content. Such a table would be completely unsuited for unautomated management. But then, computers are another matter altogether, being totally without consciousness, regardless of what the nuttier cognitive scientists have to say.

Once a computer has been provided with a suitable program, such as MySQL, it has no trouble at all processing such data. Suppose you would like to obtain a list of all authors of the book *Client/Server* . . . . MySQL would first look in the *title* table to find out what *titleID* number is associated with this book. Then it would search in the *rel_title_author* table for data records containing this number. The associated *authorID* numbers then lead to the names of the authors.

> **REMARK**   *It may have occurred to you to ask why in the* rel_title_author *table there is no* ID *column, say,* rel_title_author_ID. *Usually, such a column is omitted, since the combination of* titleID *and* authorID *is already an optimal primary key. (Relational database systems permit such primary keys, those made up of several columns.)*

Third Normal Form

The third normal form has a single rule, and here it is:

- Columns that are not directly related to the primary key must be eliminated (that is, transplanted into a table of their own).

In the example under consideration, the column *publisher* appears in the *title* table. The set of publishers and the set of book titles are independent of one another and therefore should be separated. Of course, it should be noted that each title must be related to the information as to the publisher of that title, but it is not necessary that the entire name of the publisher be given. A foreign key (that is, a reference, a pointer, a link) suffices. See Tables 5-8 and 5-9.

Table 5-8. title *table: third normal form*

titleID	title	publisherID	year
1	Linux	1	2000
2	Definitive Guide . . .	2	2000
3	Client/Server . . .	1	1997
4	Web Application . . .	3	2000

Table 5-9. publisher *table: third normal form*

publisherID	publisher
1	Addison-Wesley
2	Apress
3	New Riders

The *author* and *rel_title_author* tables remain the same in the third normal form. The completed book database now consists of four tables, as indicated in Figure 5-1.

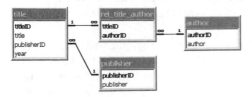

Figure 5-1. The structure of the database books

If we had paid closer attention to the rules for the first normal form (associated data belong together in a table), we could, of course, have saved some of our intermediate attempts. But that would have diminished the pedagogical value of our example. In fact, in practice, it often occurs that only when test data are inserted and redundancies are noticed does it become clear how the tables need to be subdivided.

The Bestowal of Names

In our example, we have attempted to leave the names of fields unaltered from the beginning (before normalization) right through to the end, so as not to cause more confusion than absolutely necessary. The result is not quite optimal, and it would be worth going back and looking at the complete table structure and reconsidering what names should be given to the various fields. The following points provide some tips on the naming of tables and their columns (fields).

- MySQL distinguishes between uppercase and lowercase in the naming of tables, but not in the naming of columns (see also Chapter 18). Thus it is important to pay attention to this case sensitivity at least in names of tables. (In the example databases in this book, we shall use only lowercase letters for the names of tables.)

- Of course, field and table names should be as clear as possible. Field names like *author* and *publisher* are not particularly good role models. First of all, they coincide with table names, which can cause confusion, and second, *name* or *authorsName* or *companyName* would have been more precise.

- A uniform pattern for naming fields will save many errors caused by haste. Whether you prefer *authors_name* or *authorsName*, choose one format and stick with it.

- Likewise, you should consider how to deal with singular and plural forms. In our example, I could have named the tables *title*, *author*, and *publisher* just as easily *titles*, *authors*, and *publishers*. There is no rule as to what is right or wrong here, but it is certainly confusing if half of your tables use the singular, and the other half, the plural.

- Finally, it is worth thinking about whether field names should provide information about the table. In our example there are fields called *titleID*, *publisherID*, and the like. Fields containing a primary key could as well be called *id*. This would satisfy the uniqueness criterion, since in *SELECT* queries that encompass several tables, the table name has often to be provided in any case. (SQL allows the format *tablename.fieldname.*) This could lead to confusing instructions like *WHERE publisher.publisherID = title.publisherID*.

On the other hand, many tables also contain foreign keys, and there the specification of the table name is unavoidable. (In the *title* table, for example, you could not have three columns all labeled *id*.) That would lead to *publisher.id = title.publisherID*, which is also not optimal. (You can see that there is no easy solution that works optimally for all cases.)

> **POINTER** *From* books *another example database was created called* mylibrary. *The design of that database is described later in this chapter. It is better than the* books *database in the sense of the bestowal of names. The database* mylibrary *serves as the basis for many examples in this book, while* books *exists only for the purpose of introducing a bit of database theory.*

More Theory . . .

The three normal forms for relational databases were first formulated by the researcher E. F. Codd. They continue to form the basis for a branch of research that is concerned with the formal description of mathematical sets in general and of relational databases in particular.

Depending on what you read, you may come across three additional normal forms, which, however, are of much less significance in practice. The normal forms and their rules are described much more precisely than we have done. However, such descriptions are so teeming with such exotica as *entities*, *attributes*, and their ilk that the connection with relational databases can easily be lost.

If you are interested in further details on this topic, then you are encouraged to look into a good book on the subject of database design (see also the suggestions at the beginning of this chapter).

Less Theory . . .

I have attempted to present the first three normal forms in as simple and example-oriented a way as possible, but perhaps even that was too theoretical. Actually, the normal forms are not necessarily helpful to database beginners, since the correct interpretation of the rules is often difficult. Here are some rules that will perhaps make those first baby steps less shaky:

- Give yourself sufficient time to develop the database. (If at a later date you have to alter the database design, when the database is already stuffed with real data and there is already client code in existence, changes will take a great deal of time and effort.)

- Avoid giving columns names with numbers, such as *name1*, *name2*, or *object1*, *object2*. There is almost certainly a better solution involving an additional table.

- Immediately supply your database with some test data. Attempt to include as many special cases as possible. If you encounter redundancies, that is, columns in which the same content appears several times, this is usually a hint that you should break your table into two (or more) new tables.

- Try to understand the ideas of relations (see the next section).

- A good database design cannot be obtained unless you have had some experience with SQL (see also next chapter). Only when you know and understand the range of SQL queries can you judge the consequences of the various ways of organizing your data.

- Orient yourself using an example database (from this book or from another book on databases).

TIP *A good example of normalizing a database can be found at the following Internet location:*

```
http://www.phpbuilder.com/columns/barry20000731.php3
```

Normal Forms: Pro and Con

Normal forms are a means to an end, nothing more and nothing less. Normal forms should be a help in the design of databases, but they cannot replace human reasoning. Furthermore, it is not always a good idea to follow the normal form thoughtlessly, that is, to eliminate every redundancy.

- **Con:** The input of new data, say, in a form on a web page, becomes more and more complex as the number of tables among which the data are distributed increases. This is true as much for the end user (who is led from one page to another) as for the programmer.

  Furthermore, for efficiency in queries, it is sometimes advantageous to allow for a bit of redundancy. Bringing together data from several tables is usually slower than reading data from a single table. This is true especially for databases that do not change much but that are frequently given complex queries to respond to. (In a special area of databases, the *data warehouses*, redundancy is often deliberately planned for in order to obtain better response times. The purpose of data warehouses is the analysis of complex data according to various criteria. However, MySQL is not a reasonable choice of database system for such tasks anyhow, and therefore, we shall not go more deeply into the particular features of this special application area.)

- **Pro:** Redundancy is generally a waste of storage space. You may hold the opinion that in the era of hundred-gigabyte hard drives this is not an issue, but a large database will inevitably become a slow database (at the latest, when the database size exceeds the amount of RAM).

  As a rule, databases in normal form offer more flexible query options. (Unfortunately, one usually notices this only when a new form of data query or grouping is required, which often occurs months after the database has become operational.)

Relations

If you want to transform a database into normal form, you have to link a number of tables. These links are called *relations* in database-speak. At bottom, there are three possible relations between two tables:

$1:1$
In a one-to-one relation between two tables, each data record of the first table corresponds to precisely one data record of the second table and vice versa. Such relations are rare, since in such a case the information in both tables could as easily be stored in a single table.

$1:n$
In a one-to-many relation, a single record in the first table can correspond to several records in the second table (for example, a vendor can be associated with many orders). The converse may be impossible: A single order cannot, say, be filled by many vendors. Occasionally, one hears of an n-to-1 relation, but this is merely a 1-to-n relation from the opposite point of view.

$n:m$
Here a data record in the first table can be linked to several records in the second table, and vice versa. (For example, several articles can be included in a single order, while the same article may be included in several different orders. Another example is books and their authors. Several authors may have written a single book, while one author may have written several books.)

$1:1$ Relations

A one-to-one relation typically comes into being when a table is divided into two tables that use the same primary key. This situation is most easily grasped with the aid of an example. A table containing a corporation's personnel records contains a great deal of information: name, department, date of birth, date of employment, and so on. This table could be split into two tables, called, say, *personnel* and *personnel_extra*, where *personnel* contains the frequently queried and generally accessible data, while *personnel_extra* contains additional, less used and more private, data.

There are two possible reasons for such a division. One is the security aspect: It is simple to protect the table *personnel_extra* from general access. (For MySQL, this argument is less important, since access privileges can in any case be set separately for each column of a table.)

The other reason is that of speed. If a table contains many columns, of which only a few are required by most queries, it is more efficient to keep the frequently used columns in a single table. (In the ideal situation, the first table would contain exclusively columns of a given size. Such tables are more efficient to manage than tables whose columns are of variable size. An overview of the types of tables supported by MySQL can be found later in this chapter.)

The significant disadvantage of such a separation of tables is the added overhead of ensuring that the tables remain synchronized.

$1:n$ *Relations*

One-to-many relations come into play whenever a particular field of a data record in a detail table can refer to various columns of another table (the master table).

The linkage takes place via key fields. The columns of the master table are identified by a primary key. The detail table contains a foreign key field, whose contents refer to the master table. Here are a few examples:

- The normalization example of the previous section (book database): Here there is a one-to-many relation between the *title* and *publisher* tables. The table *publisher* is the master table with the primary key *publisher.publisherID*. The title table is the detail table, with the foreign key *title.publisherID* (see Figure 5-1).

  Each publisher (1) can publish several books (n).

- A business application containing tables with orders: A detail table contains data on all processed orders. In this table, a foreign key field refers to the master table, with its list of all customers.

  Each customer (1) can execute many orders (n).

- Discussion groups containing tables with messages: A detail table contains data on every contribution to a discussion group in place on the web site (title, text, date, author, group, etc.). Two possible master tables are a group table with a list of all discussion groups, and an author table with a list of all members of the web site who are allowed to make contributions to a discussion.

  Each author (1) can contribute to arbitrarily many discussions (n). Each discussion group (1) can contain arbitrarily many contributions (n).

- A database containing tables of music CDs: A detail table contains data on every CD in the collection (title, performer, number of disks, etc.). Two possible master tables are a table containing a list of performers occurring in the database, and a recording label table with a list of recording companies.

  Each performer (1) can appear on arbitrarily many CDs (n). Each label (1) can market arbitrarily many CDs (n).

REMARK *Often during the creation of a database, one attempts to give the same name to fields of two tables that will later be linked by a relation. This contributes to clarity, but it is not required.*

The table diagrams in this book (such as shown in Figure 5-1) were created with Microsoft Access. For all of the technical drawbacks that Access offers on account of the file/server architecture vis-à-vis MySQL, the user interface is easy to use. There is hardly a program with which relation diagrams can be so quickly drawn. However, Access has the peculiarity of labeling $1:n$ diagrams with $1:\infty$. Here 1 denotes the master table (primary key), while infinitely many n stands for the detail table (foreign key). Often, an arrow is used instead of this nomenclature.

It is also possible for the primary and foreign keys to be located in the same table. Then a data record in such a table can refer to another record in the same table. This is useful if a hierarchy is to be represented. Here are a few examples:

- A table of personnel, in which each employee record (except for that of the top banana) refers to a field containing that individual's immediate supervisor.

- Discussion groups, with tables with messages, in which each message refers to a field containing the next-higher message in the hierarchy (that is, the one to which the current message is responding).

- A music database, containing tables with different types of music. Each style field refers to a field with the name of the genre of which the current style is a subset (for example, bebop within the category jazz, or string quartet within the category of chamber music; see http://www.mp3.com).

> **REMARK**   *Relations within a table indeed allow for a very simple way to store a hierarchy, but the evaluation of such data is more complicated. For example, the query command* SELECT *does not allow for recursion, which is often necessary for the analysis of hierarchical relations. Consider carefully the types of queries that will be applied to your database before you heedlessly implement complex hierarchies based on internal table references.*
>
> *The database* mylibrary *introduced later in this chapter provides a concrete example of the representation of hierarchies.*

$n : m$ Relations

For $n : m$ relations, it is necessary to add an auxiliary table to the two original tables so that the $n : m$ relation can be reduced to two $1 : n$ relations. Here are some examples:

- Normalization example (*books* database): Here we have an $n : m$ relation between book titles and authors. The relation is established by means of the *rel_title_author* table.

- Business application, tables with orders: To establish a relation between an order and the articles included in the order, the auxiliary table specifies how many of article x are included in order y.

- College administration, list of exams: To keep track of which student has passed which exam and when and with what grade, it is necessary to have a table that stands between the table of students and the table of exams.

Primary and Foreign Keys

Relations depend intimately on primary and foreign keys. This section provides a comprehensive explanation of these two topics and their application. Alas, we cannot avoid entirely a bit of an excursus into SQL commands, which are not formally introduced until the end of this chapter and the chapter following.

Primary Key

The job of the primary key is to locate, as fast as possible, a particular data record in a table (for example, to locate the record with *id=314159* from a table of a million records). This operation must be carried out whenever data from several tables are assembled—in short, very often indeed.

With most database systems, including MySQL, it is also permitted to have primary keys that are formed from several fields of a table. Whether it is a single field or several that serve as primary key, the following properties should be satisfied:

- The primary key must be unique. It is not permitted that two records have the same content in their primary key field.

- The primary key should be compact, and there are two reasons for this:
  First, for the primary key it is necessary to maintain an index (the primary index) to maximize the speed of search (e.g., for *id=314159*). The more compact the primary field key, the more efficient the management of this index. Therefore, an integer is more suitable than a character string of variable length for use as a primary key field.

  Second, the content of the primary key field is used as a foreign key in other tables, and there, as well, it is efficient to have the foreign key as compact as possible. (Relations between tables are established not least to avoid wasted space on account of redundancies. This makes sense only if the use of key fields doesn't take up even more space.)

With most database systems it has become standard practice to use a 32- or 64-bit integer as primary key field, generated automatically in sequence (1, 2, 3, . . .) by the database system. Thus neither the programmer nor the user need be concerned how a new and unique primary key value is to be found for each new record.

In MySQL such fields are declared as follows:

```
CREATE TABLE publisher
  (publisherID INT NOT NULL AUTO_INCREMENT,
  othercolumns ... ,
  PRIMARY KEY (publisherID))
```

If we translate from SQL into English, what we have is this: The field *publisherID* is not permitted to contain *NULL*. Its contents are generated by the database (unless another value is explicitly inserted there). The field functions as a primary key; that is, MySQL creates an auxiliary index file to enable rapid search. Simultaneously, it is thereby ensured that the *publisherID* value is unique when new records are input (even if a particular *publisherID* is specified in the *INSERT* command).

For tables in which one expects to make many new entries or changes, one should usually use *BIGINT* (64-bit integer) instead of *INT* (32 bits).

> **REMARK** *The name of the primary key field plays no role. In this book we usually use* id *or* tablenameID. *Often, you will see combinations with* no *or* nr *(for "number") as, for example, in* customerNr.

> **POINTER**   *To generate sequential numbers for primary keys automatically, in MySQL the column is usually created with the attribute* AUTO_INCREMENT. *Additional information on* AUTO_INCREMENT *can be found in the next section of this chapter.*

Foreign Key

The task of the foreign key field is to refer to a record in the detail table. However, this reference comes into being only when a database query is formulated, for example, in the following form:

```
SELECT title.title, publisher.publisher FROM title, publisher
WHERE title.publisherID = publisher.publisherID
ORDER BY title
```

With this, an alphabetical list of all book titles is generated, in which the second column gives the publisher of the book. The result would look something like this:

title	publisher
Client/Server ...	Addison-Wesley
Definitive Guide ...	Apress
Linux	Addison-Wesley
Web Application ...	New Riders

Decisive here is the clause *WHERE title.publisherID = publisher.publisherID*. It is here that the link between the tables is created.

On the other hand, in the declaration of a table the foreign key plays no particular role. For MySQL, a foreign key field is just another ordinary table field. There are no particular key words that must be employed. In particular, no index is necessary (there is practically never a search to find the contents of the foreign key). Of course, you would not be permitted to supply the attribute *AUTO_INCREMENT*. After all, you want to specify yourself the record to which the field refers. You need to take care, though, that the foreign key field is of the same data type as the type of the primary key field. Otherwise, the evaluation of the *WHERE* condition can be very slow.

```
CREATE TABLE title
  (othercolumns ... ,
  publisherID INT NOT NULL)
```

Whether you specify the attribute *NOT NULL* depends on the context. In most cases, *NOT NULL* is to be recommended in order to avoid at the outset the occurrence of incomplete data. However, if you wish to allow, for example, that in the book database a book could be entered that had no publisher, then you should do without *NOT NULL*.

Referential Integrity

If you delete the author *Kofler* from the *author* table in the example of the normalized database (see Tables 5-6 through 5-9 and Figure 5-1), you will encounter problems in many SQL queries that access the books *Linux* and *Definitive Guide*. The *authorID* number 1 specified in the *rel_title_author* table no longer exists in the *author* table. In database language, one would put it like this: The referential integrity of the database has been damaged.

As a database developer, it is your responsibility to see that such events cannot happen. Therefore, before deleting a data record you must always check whether there exists a reference to the record in question in another table.

Since one cannot always rely on programmers (and databases often must be altered by hand), many databases have rules for maintaining referential integrity. Such rules test at every change in the database whether any cross references between tables are affected. Depending on the declaration of the foreign key, there are then two possible consequences: Either the operation will simply not be executed (error message), or all affected records in dependent tables are deleted as well. Which modus operandi is to be preferred depends on the data themselves.

In MySQL 4.0, referential integrity can be automatically ensured only with InnoDB tables. Independent control of referential integrity for the more commonly deployed MyISAM tables is planned for MySQL 5.0.

With InnoDB tables, you can declare foreign key fields like this:

```
CREATE TABLE title
  (column1, column2,  ... ,
  publisherID INT,
  KEY (publisherID),
  FOREIGN KEY (publisherID) REFERENCES publisher (publisherID)
)
```

This means that *title.publisherID* is a foreign key that refers to the primary key *publisher.publisherID*. With options such as *ON DELETE*, *RESTRICT*, and *ON DELETE CASCADE*, one may further specify how the database system is to respond to potential damage to its referential integrity.

Moreover, this instruction will then be correctly executed even if the table driver does not support integrity rules. In this case, however, the *FOREIGN KEY* information is ignored, and currently, not even saved. (At least this latter should change in the future: Even if MySQL does not concern itself with maintaining referential integrity, the corresponding table declarations should be maintained. This would be particularly practical for programs for formulating SQL queries and for graphical user interfaces, which then would know how tables are linked with one another.)

POINTER   *In Chapter 8, SQL commands for declaring referential integrity for InnoDB tables will be discussed in detail.*

Other Indexes

> **POINTER** *The primary index, which is inseparably bound to the primary key, is a special case of an index. Indexes always have the task of speeding up searching and sorting in tables by particular columns. Other indexes supported by MySQL are introduced later in the chapter.*

MySQL Data Types

Now that we have dealt with the first issue in database design, dividing the data among several tables in the most sensible way, in this section we go a level deeper. Here you will find information about the data types that MySQL provides for every field (every column). Should a character string stored in a field be of fixed or variable length? Should currency amounts be stored as fixed-point or floating-point numbers? How are binary objects handled?

> **POINTER** *This section describes the data types, but not the* CREATE TABLE *command, with which tables are actually created. Information on how tables can be created, that is, how the database, having been designed, can actually be implemented, can be found later in this chapter.*

Default Values and NULL

Note that for each column, in addition to the data type, you can specify additional attributes. The following list names the three most important of these that are available for all data types:

- *NOT NULL:* The column may not contain the value *NULL.* This means that in saving a new data record an explicit value must be given (unless there is a default value for the column).

- *NULL:* The column is allowed to contain the value *NULL.* This is the default setting if when the table was created, neither *NOT NULL* nor *NULL* was specified.

- *DEFAULT n* or *DEFAULT 'abc':* If no value is specified for a data record, MySQL automatically provides the value *n* or the character string *'abc'.* (Here is a tip for advanced users: If you would like MySQL to insert the default value for an *INSERT* command, you must specify for the column either no value at all, or an empty character string. It is not permitted to supply the value *NULL.* In that case, MySQL stores *NULL* or returns an error message if *NULL* is not allowed.)

Even if you do not explicitly provide a default value, in many instances, MySQL will itself provide one: *NULL* if *NULL* is allowed, and otherwise, 0 for a numerical column, an empty character string for *VARCHAR*, the date 0000-00-00 in the case of dates, the year 0000 for *YEAR*, or the first element of an *ENUM* enumeration.

> **REMARK** *Unfortunately, MySQL does not allow a function as default value. Thus it is not possible to specify* DEFAULT RAND() *if you want a random number to be entered automatically in a column.*

Integers: xxxINT

TINYINT(M)	8-bit integer (1 byte, -128 to $+127$)
SMALLINT(M)	16- bit integer (2 bytes, $-32,769$ to $+32,767$)
MEDIUMINT	24- bit integer (3 bytes, $-8,388,608$ to $+8,388,607$)
INT, INTEGER(M)	32- bit integer (4 bytes, $-2,147,483,648$ to $+2,147,483,647$)
BIGINT(M)	64- bit integer (8 bytes, $\pm 9.22 \times 10^{18}$)

With the *INT* data type, both positive and negative numbers are generally allowed. With the attribute *UNSIGNED*, the range can be restricted to the positive integers. But note that then subtraction returns *UNSIGNED* integers, which can lead to deceptive and confusing results.

With *TINYINT*, numbers between -128 and $+127$ are allowed. With the attribute *UNSIGNED*, the range is 0 to 255. If one attempts to store a value above or below the given range, MySQL simply replaces the input with the largest or, respectively, smallest permissible value.

Optionally, in the definition of an integer field, the desired column width (number of digits) can be specified, such as, for example, *INT(4)*. This parameter is called *M* (for *maximum display size*) in the literature. It assists MySQL as well as various user interfaces in presenting query results in a readable format.

> **REMARK** *Note that with the* INT *data types, the M restricts neither the allowable range of numbers nor the possible number of digits. In spite of setting* INT(4), *for example, you can still store numbers greater than 9999. However, in certain rare cases (such as in complex queries for the evaluation of which MySQL constructs a temporary table), the numerical values in the temporary tables can be truncated, with incorrect results as a consequence.*

AUTO_INCREMENT *Integers*

With the optional attribute *AUTO_INCREMENT* you can achieve for integers that MySQL automatically inserts a number that is 1 larger than the currently largest value in the column when a new record is created for the field in question. *AUTO_INCREMENT* is generally used in the definition of fields that are to serve as the primary key for a table.

The following rules hold for *AUTO_INCREMENT*:

- This attribute is permitted only when one of the attributes *NOT NULL*, *PRIMARY KEY*, or *UNIQUE* is used as well.

- It is not permitted for a table to possess more than one *AUTO_INCREMENT* column.

- The automatic generation of an ID value functions only when in inserting a new data record with *INSERT*, a specific value or *NULL* is not specified. However, it is possible to generate a new data record with a specific ID value, provided that the value in question is not already in use.

- If you want to find out the *AUTO_INCREMENT* value that a newly inserted data record has received, after executing the *INSERT* command (but within the same connection or transaction), execute the command *SELECT LAST_INSERT_ID()*.

- If the *AUTO_INCREMENT* counter reaches its maximal value, based on the selected integer format, it will not be increased further. No more insert operations are possible. With tables that experience many insert and delete commands, it can happen that the 32-bit *INT* range will become used up, even though there are many fewer than two billion records in the table. In such a case, use a *BIGINT* column.

Floating-Point Numbers: FLOAT *and* DOUBLE

FLOAT(M, D)	floating-point number, 8-place precision (4 bytes)
DOUBLE(M, D)	floating-point number, 16-place precision (8 bytes)
REAL(M, D)	Synonym for *DOUBLE*

Since version 3.23 of MySQL, the types *FLOAT* and *DOUBLE* correspond to the IEEE numerical types for single and double precision that are available in many programming languages.

Optionally, the number of digits in *FLOAT* and *DOUBLE* values can be set with the two parameters M and D. In that case, M specifies the number of digits before the decimal point, while D gives the number of places after the decimal point.

The parameter *M* does no more than assist in the formatting of numbers; it does not limit the permissible range of numbers. On the other hand, *D* has the effect of rounding numbers when they are stored. For example, if you attempt to save the number 123456.789877 in a field with the attribute *DOUBLE(6,3)*, the number stored will, in fact, be 123456.790.

> **REMARK** *MySQL expects floating-point numbers in international notation, that is, with a decimal point, and not a comma (which is used in a number of European countries). Results of queries are always returned in this notation, and very large or very small values are expressed in scientific notation (e.g., 1.2345678901279e+017).*
>
> *If you have your heart set on formatting floating-point numbers differently, you will have either to employ the function FORMAT in your SQL queries (though this function is of use only in the thousands groupings) or to carry out your formatting in the client programming language (that is, in PHP, Perl, etc.).*

Fixed-Point Numbers: DECIMAL(P, S)

DECIMAL(p, s)	fixed-point number, saved as a character string; arbitrary number of digits (one byte per digit + 2 bytes overhead)
NUMERIC, DEC	synonym for *DECIMAL*

The integer type *DECIMAL* is recommended when rounding errors caused by the internal representation of numbers as *FLOAT* or *DOUBLE* are unacceptable, perhaps with currency values. Since the numbers are stored as character strings, the storage requirement is much greater. At the same time, the possible range of values is smaller, since exponential notation is ruled out.

The two parameters *P* and *S* specify the total number of digits (*precision*) and, respectively, the number of digits after the decimal point (*scale*). The range in the case of *DECIMAL(6,3)* is from 9999.999 to −999.999. This bizarre range results from the apparent fact that six places are reserved for the number plus an additional place for the minus sign. When the number is positive, the place for the minus sign can be commandeered to store another digit. If *P* and *S* are not specified, then MySQL automatically uses $(10, 0)$, with the result that positive integers with eleven digits and negative integers with ten digits can be stored.

Date and Time: DATE, TIME, *and* DATETIME

DATE	date in the form '2003-12-31', range 1000-01-01 to 9999-12-31 (3 bytes)
TIME	time in the form '23:59:59', range $\pm838 : 59 : 59$ (3 bytes)
DATETIME	combination of *DATE* and *TIME* in the form '2003-12-31 23:59:59' (8 bytes)
YEAR	year 1900–2155 (1 byte)

With the *DATE* and *DATETIME* data types, only a limited amount of type checking takes place. Values between 0 and 12 for months, and between 0 and 31 for days, are generally allowed. However, it is the responsibility of the client program to provide correct data. (For example, 0 is a permissible value for a month or day, in order to provide the possibility of storing incomplete or unknown data.) As for the question that may have occurred to you—Why is it that *DATETIME* requires eight bytes, while *DATE* and *TIME* each require only three bytes?—the answer is that I have no idea.

MySQL returns results of queries in the form 2003-12-31. However, with *INSERT* and *UPDATE* it manages to deal with other formats, provided that the order year/month/day is adhered to and the values are numeric. If the year is given as a two-digit number, then the following interpretation is made: 70–99 becomes 1970–1999, while 00–69 becomes 2000–2069.

If query results are to be specially formatted, there are several MySQL functions available for processing date and time values. The most flexible of these is *DATE_FORMAT*, whose application is demonstrated in the following example:

```
SELECT DATE_FORMAT(birthdate, '%Y %M %e') FROM students
2000   September 3
2000   October 25
  ...
```

Time of the Most Recent Change: TIMESTAMP(M)

TIMESTAMP	date and time in the form 20031231235959 for times between 1970 and 2038 (4 bytes)

Among the data types for date and time, *TIMESTAMP* plays a particular role. Fields of this type are automatically updated whenever the record is altered, thereby reflecting the time of the last change. Fields of type *TIMESTAMP* are therefore usually employed only for internal management, not for the storage of "real" data, though such is possible.

For the automatic *TIMESTAMP* updating to function properly, either no explicit value is assigned to the field, or else the value *NULL*. In both cases MySQL itself inserts the current time.

In the declaration of a *TIMESTAMP* column, the desired column width is specified. The *TIMESTAMP* values that then result from queries will be truncated. (In the case of $M = 8$, for example, the result will be a date without the time). Internally, however, the values continue to be stored in their complete form.

REMARK *Since version 4.1, MySQL automatically returns* TIMESTAMP *columns in the form* YYYY-MM-DD HH:MM:DD *(instead of the earlier* YYYYMMDDHHM-MDD*). This can result in incompatibilities in data processing. Append a zero if you wish to use the old form:* SELECT ts+0 FROM table.

WARNING *Do not use a* TIMESTAMP *column if you wish to store the date and time yourself. For that, one has the data type* DATETIME. *With* TIMESTAMP *columns the MySQL server automatically changes the content of the column every time a change is made. You can prevent this behavior only by explicitly giving the desired date and time with each* UPDATE *or* INSERT *command. (The following example assumes that the* TIMESTAMP *column is called* ts.)

```
UPDATE tablename SET col='new value', ts=ts;
```

Sooner or later, you will forget ts=ts *and will then have the incorrect date/time in your table.*

REMARK *Many database operations with particular client libraries (for example, with Connector/ODBC) function only when each table of the database displays a* TIMESTAMP *column. The time of the last update is often needed in the internal administration of data.*

Character Strings

CHAR(n)	character string with specified length, maximum 255 bytes
VARCHAR(n)	character string with variable length, maximum 255 bytes
TINYTEXT	character string with variable length, maximum 255 bytes
TEXT	character string with variable length, maximum $2^{16} - 1 = 65,535$ bytes
MEDIUMTEXT	character string with variable length, maximum $2^{24} - 1 = 16,777,215$ bytes
LONGTEXT	character string with variable length, maximum $2^{32} - 1 = 4,294,967,295$ bytes

With *CHAR*, the length of a character string is strictly specified. For example, *CHAR(20)* demands 20 bytes in each record, regardless of the length of the character string actually stored. (Blank characters at the beginning of a character string are eliminated before storage. Short character strings are extended with blanks. These blank characters are automatically deleted when the data are read out, with the result that it is impossible to store a character string that actually has blank characters at the end.)

In contrast, the length of a character string of type *VARCHAR* or one of the four *TEXT* types is variable. The storage requirement depends on the actual length of the character string.

> **REMARK** *MySQL 4.0 uses the character set* latin1 *by default for all databases, where there is the simple rule of one byte per character for storage.*
>
> *Since MySQL 4.1, on the other hand, each column of a table can have a particular character set assigned to it. This includes character sets for which the storage requirement varies according to the character, for example, Unicode UTF8. This has the consequence that in a* VARCHAR(50) *column with the UTF8 character set, you can store fifty ASCII characters (one byte per character), but only twenty-five special German characters (two bytes per character). Many Asian characters require even more bytes. Thus it is no longer possible to specify exactly how many characters can be stored in a column. It depends on the character set used.*

Although *VARCHAR* and *TINYTEXT*, both of which can accept a character string up to a length of 255 characters, at first glance seem equivalent, there are, in fact, several features that distinguish one from the other:

- The maximum number of characters in *VARCHAR* columns must be specified (in the range 0 to 255) when the table is declared. Character strings that are too long will be unceremoniously, without warning, truncated when they are stored.

  In contrast, with *xxxTEXT* columns one cannot specify a maximal length. (The only limit is the maximal length of the particular text type.)

- In *VARCHAR* columns, as with *CHAR* columns, blank characters are deleted from the beginning of a character string. (This behavior is ANSI compliant only for *CHAR* columns, not for *VARCHAR* columns. This behavior may change in future versions of MySQL.)

  With *xxxTEXT* columns, character strings are stored exactly as they are input.

Columns of type *CHAR* and *VARCHAR* can optionally be given the attribute *BINARY*. They then behave essentially like *BLOB* columns (see below). The attribute *BINARY* can be useful when you store text (and not binary objects): What you achieve is that in sorting, it is exclusively the binary code of the characters that is considered (and not a particular sorting table). Thus case distinction is made (which otherwise would not be the case). The internal management of binary character strings is simpler and therefore faster than is the case with garden-variety character strings.

> **REMARK** *As we have already mentioned, MySQL supports Unicode character strings, beginning with version 4.1. Of course, in version 4.0 as well you can store Unicode character strings in* TEXT *as well as* BLOB *fields. MySQL, however, is incapable of sorting such tables correctly, and there can be problems in searching and comparing as well.*

Binary Data (xxxBLOB)

TINYBLOB	binary data, variable length, max 255 bytes
BLOB	binary data, variable length, max $2^{16} - 1$ bytes (64 kilobytes)
MEDIUMBLOB	binary data, variable length, max $2^{24} - 1$ bytes (16 megabytes)
LONGBLOB	binary data, variable length, max $2^{32} - 1$ bytes (4 gigabytes)

For the storage of binary data there are four *BLOB* data types at your service, all of which display almost the same properties as the *TEXT* data types. (Recall that "BLOB" is an acronym for "binary large object.") The only difference is that text data are usually compared and sorted in text mode (case-insensitive), while binary data are sorted and compared according to their binary codes.

> **REMARK** *There is considerable disagreement as to whether large binary objects should even be stored in a database. The alternative would be to store the data (images, for example) in external files and provide links to these files in the database.*
>
> *The advantage to using BLOBs is the resulting integration into the database (more security, simpler backups). The drawback is the usually significant slowdown. It is particularly disadvantageous that large and small data elements—strings, integers, etc.—on the one hand and BLOBs and long texts on the other must be stored all mixed together in a table file. The result is a slowdown in access to all of the data records.*
>
> *Note as well that BLOBs in general can be read only as a whole. That is, it is impossible to read, say, the last 100 kilobytes of an 800 kilobyte BLOB. The entire BLOB must be transmitted.*

Enumerations: ENUM, SET

ENUM	selects one from at most 65,535 character strings (1 or 2 bytes)
SET	combines at most 64 character strings (1–8 bytes)

MySQL offers the two special enumeration types *ENUM* and *SET*. With *ENUM*, you can manage a list of up to 65,535 character strings, ordered by a running index. Then, in a field, one of these character strings can be selected.

In queries involving comparison of character strings there is no case distinction. In addition to the predefined character strings, an empty character string can also be stored in a field (as well as *NULL*, unless this has been excluded via *NOT NULL*).

Such a field is then handled like any other character string field. The following commands show how a table with an *ENUM* enumeration is generated and used. In the field *color* of the table *testenum*, one of five predefined colors can be stored:

```
CREATE TABLE testenum
  (color ENUM ('red', 'green', 'blue', 'black', 'white'))
INSERT testenum VALUES ('red')
SELECT * FROM testenum WHERE color='red'
```

SET uses a similar idea, though here arbitrary combinations are possible. Internally, the character strings are ordered by powers of 2 (1, 2, 4, 8, etc.), so that a bitwise combination is possible. The storage requirement is correspondingly larger (one bit per character string). At most 64 character strings can be combined (in which case the storage requirement is 8 bytes).

For a combination of several character strings to be stored in one field, these must be given separated by commas (and with no blank characters between strings). The order of the strings is irrelevant and is not considered. In query results, combinations are always specified in the order in which the set was defined:

```
CREATE TABLE testset
  (fontattr SET ('bold', 'italic', 'underlined'))
INSERT testset VALUES ('bold,italic')
```

In queries with the operator "=" an exact comparison is made of the entire combination. The result is that only those records are returned for which the combination corresponds exactly. Thus if in *testset* only the above-inserted record is stored with *'bold,italic'*, then the following query returns no result:

```
SELECT * FROM testset WHERE fontattr='italic'
```

In order to locate records in which an attribute has been set (regardless of its combination with other attributes), the MySQL function *FIND_IN_SET* can be used. This function returns the position of the sought character string within the set (in our example, 1 if *'bold'* is found, 2 for *'italic'*, etc.):

```
SELECT * FROM testset WHERE FIND_IN_SET('italic', fontattr)>0
```

> **TIP** ENUM *and* SET *values are represented internally as integers, not as character strings. If you wish to determine the internally stored value via a query, simply use* SELECT x+0 FROM table, *where* x *is the column name of the* ENUM *or* SET *column. It is also permitted to store numeric values with* INSERT *and* UPDATE *commands.*

> **REMARK** *The contents of* ENUM *and* SET *fields are not alphabetically sorted, but are maintained in the order in which the character strings for selection were defined. The reason for this is that MySQL works internally with numeric values associated with the character strings. If you would like an alphabetic sorting, you must transform the string explicitly into a character string, for example, via* SELECT CONCAT(x) AS xstr . . . ORDER BY xstr.

> **TIP** *If you would like to determine the list of all admissible character strings for an* ENUM *or* SET *field (in a client program, for example), you must summon* DESCRIBE tablename columnname *to your aid. This SQL command returns a table in which the field* columnname *is described. The column* Type *of this table contains the* ENUM *or* SET *definition. In Chapter 11 you will find an example for the evaluation of this information (in the programming language PHP).*

Indexes

If you are searching for a particular record in a table or would like to create a series of data records for an ordered table, MySQL must load *all* the records of the table. The following lines show some of the relevant *SELECT* commands (details to follow in the next chapter):

```
SELECT column1, column2 ... FROM table WHERE column3=12345
SELECT column1, column2 ... FROM table ORDER BY column3
SELECT column1, column2 ... FROM table WHERE column3 LIKE 'Smith%'
SELECT column1, column2 ... FROM table WHERE column3 > 2000
```

With large tables, performance will suffer under such everyday queries. Fortunately, there is a simple solution to cure our table's performance anxiety: Simply use an index for the affected column (in the example above, for *column3*).

An index is a special file or, in the case of InnoDB, a part of the tablespace, containing references to all the records of a table. (Thus a database index functions like the index in this book. The index saves you the trouble of reading the entire book from one end to the other if you simply want to find out where a particular topic is covered.)

In principle, an index can be created for each field of a table, up to a maximum of sixteen indexes per table. (MySQL also permits indexes for several fields simultaneously. That makes sense if sorting is frequently carried out according to a combination of fields, as in *WHERE country='Austria' AND city='Graz'*).

> **CAUTION** *Indexes are not a panacea! They speed up access to data, but they slow down each alteration in the database. Every time a data record in changed, the index must be updated. This drawback can be ameliorated to some extent with various SQL commands by means of the option* DELAY_KEY_WRITE. *The effect of this option is that the index is not updated with each new or changed record, but only now and then.* DELAY_KEY_WRITE *is useful, for example, when many new records are to be inserted in a table as quickly as possible.*
>
> *A further apparent disadvantage of indexes is that they take up additional space on the hard drive. (Internally, in addition, B trees are used for managing the index entries.)*
>
> *Therefore, use indexes only for those columns that will often be searched and sorted. Indexes remain largely useless when the column contains many identical entries. (In such cases, you might ask yourself whether the normalization of the database has been optimally carried out.)*

Types of Index

All indexes are not alike, and in this section we discuss the various types of indexes.

Ordinary Index

The only task of an ordinary index (defined via the key word *INDEX*) is to speed up access to data.

> **TIP** *Index only those columns that you require in conditions (WHERE column= . . .) or for sorting (ORDER BY column). Index, if possible, columns with compact data (for example, integers). Do not index columns that contain many identical values. (For example, it makes little sense to index a column with 0/1 or Y/N values.)*

Restrictions

MySQL cannot use indexes where inequality operators are used (*WHERE column !=* . . .). Likewise, indexes cannot be used for comparisons where the contents of the column are processed by a function (*WHERE DAY(column)=* . . .).

With *JOIN* operations (that is, in uniting data from various tables), indexes are of use only when primary and foreign keys refer to the same data type.

If the comparison operators *LIKE* and *REGEXP* are used, an index is of use only when there is no wild card at the beginning of the search pattern. With *LIKE 'abc%'* an index is of use, but with *LIKE '%abc'*, it is not.

Finally, indexes are used with *ORDER BY* operations only if the records do not have to be previously selected by other criteria. (Unfortunately, an index rarely helps to speed up *ORDER BY* with queries in which the records are taken from several tables.)

Unique Index

With an ordinary index it is allowed for several data records in the indexed field to refer to the same value. (In a table of personnel, for example, the same name can appear twice, even though it refers to two distinct individuals.)

When it is clear from context that a column contains unique values, you should then define an index with the key word *UNIQUE*. This has two consequences. One is that MySQL has an easier time managing the index; that is, the index is more efficient. The other is that MySQL ensures that no new record is added if there is already another record that refers to the same value in the indexed field. (Often, a *UNIQUE* index is defined for this reason alone, that is, not for access optimization, but to avoid duplication.)

Primary Index

The primary index mentioned again and again in this chapter is nothing more than an ordinary *UNIQUE* index. The only peculiarity is that the index has the name *PRIMARY*.

(You can tell that a primary index is an ordinary index because MySQL uses the first *UNIQUE* index of a table as a substitute for the missing primary index.)

Combined Indexes

An index can cover several columns, as in *INDEX(columnA, columnB)*. A peculiarity of such indexes is that MySQL can selectively use such an index. Thus when a query requires an index for *columnA* only, the combined index for *INDEX(columnA, columnB)* can be used. This holds, however, only for partial indexes at the beginning of the series. For instance, *INDEX(A, B, C)* can be used as index for *A* or *(A, B)*, but not as index for *B* or *C* or *(B,C)*.

Limits on the Index Length

In the definition of an index for *CHAR* and *VARCHAR* columns you can limit an index to a particular number of characters (which must be smaller than the maximum number of characters allowed in this field). The consequence is that the resulting index file is smaller and its evaluation quicker than otherwise. In most applications, that is, with character strings representing names, perhaps ten to fifteen characters altogether suffice to reduce the search set to a few data records.

With *BLOB* and *TEXT* columns you must institute this restriction, where MySQL permits a maximal index length of 255 characters.

Full-Text Index

An ordinary index for text fields helps only in the search for character strings that stand at the beginning of the field (that is, whose initial letters are known). On the other hand, if you store texts in fields that consist of several, or possibly very many, words, an ordinary index is useless. The search must be formulated in the form *LIKE '%word%'*, which for MySQL is rather complex and with large data sets leads to long response times.

In such cases it helps to use a full-text index. With this type of index, MySQL creates a list of all words that appear in the text. A full-text index can be created during the database design or afterwards:

```
ALTER TABLE tablename ADD FULLTEXT(column1, column2)
```

In *SELECT* queries, one can now search for records that contain one or more words. This is the query syntax:

```
SELECT * FROM tablename
WHERE MATCH(column1, column2) AGAINST('word1', 'word2', 'word3')
```

Then all records will be found for which the words *word1*, *word2*, and *word3* appear in the columns *column1* and *column2*.

POINTER *An extensive description of the SQL syntax for full-text search, together with a host of application examples, can be found in Chapter 7.*

Query and Index Optimization

Realistic performance estimates can be made only when the database has been filled with a sufficient quantity of test data. A test database with several hundred data records will usually be located entirely in RAM after the first three queries, and all queries will be answered quickly with or without an index. Things become interesting when tables contain well over 1000 records and when the entire size of the database is larger than the total RAM of the MySQL server.

In making the decision as to which columns should be provided with indexes, one may sometimes obtain some assistance from the command *EXPLAIN SELECT*. This is simply an ordinary *SELECT* command prefixed with the key word *EXPLAIN*. Instead of the *SELECT* being simply executed, MySQL places information in a table as to how the query was executed and which indexes (to the extent that they exist) came into play.

Here are some pointers for interpreting the table created by *EXPLAIN*. In the first column appear the names of the tables in the order in which they were read from the database. The column *type* specifies how the table is linked to the other tables (*JOIN*). This functions most efficiently (i.e., quickly) with the type *system*, while more costly are the types *const, eq_ref, ref, range, index*, and *ALL*. (*ALL* means that for each record in the next-higher table in the hierarchy, all records of this table must be read. That can usually be prevented with an index. Further information on all *JOIN* types can by found in the MySQL documentation.)

The column *possible_keys* specifies which indexes MySQL can access in the search for data records. The column *key* specifies which index MySQL has actually chosen. The length of the index in bytes is given by *key_len*. For example, with an index for an *INTEGER* column, the number of bytes is 4. Information on how many parts of a multipart index are used is also given by *key_len*. As a rule, the smaller *key_len* is, the better (that is, the faster).

The column *ref* specifies the column of a second table with which the linkage was made, while *rows* contains an estimate of how many records MySQL expects to read in order to execute the entire query. The product of all the numbers in the *rows* column allows one to draw a conclusion as to how many combinations arise from the query.

Finally, the column *extra* provides additional information on the *JOIN* operation, for example, *using temporary* when MySQL must create a temporary table in executing a query.

POINTER *Though the information proffered by* EXPLAIN *is often useful, the interpretation requires a certain amount of MySQL and database experience. You will find further information in the MySQL documentation:*

```
http://www.mysql.com/doc/en/Query_Speed.html
http://www.mysql.com/doc/en/EXPLAIN.html
```

Chapter 5

Example 1

This query produces an unordered list of all books with all their authors. All *ID* columns are equipped with primary indexes.

```
USE mylibrary
EXPLAIN SELECT * FROM titles, rel_title_author, authors
  WHERE rel_title_author.authID = authors.authID
  AND rel_title_author.titleID = titles.titleID
```

table	type	possible_key	key_len	ref	rows
titles	ALL	PRIMARY			23
rel_title_author	ref	PRIMARY PRIMARY	4	titles.titleID	1
authors	eq_ref	PRIMARY PRIMARY	4	rel_title_author.authID	1

This means that first all records from the *titles* table are read, without using an index. For *titles.titleID* there is, in fact, an index, but since the query considers all records in any case, the index is not used. Then with the help of the primary indexes of *rel_title_author* and *authors*, the links to the two other tables are made. The tables are thus optimally indexed, and for each part of the query there are indexes available.

Example 2

Here the query produces a list of all books (together with their authors) that have been published by a particular publisher. The list is ordered by book title. Again, all *ID* columns are equipped with indexes. Furthermore, in the *titles* table, *title* and *publID* are indexed:

```
EXPLAIN SELECT title, authName
FROM titles, rel_title_author, authors
WHERE titles.publID=1
  AND titles.titleID = rel_title_author.titleID
  AND authors.authID = rel_title_author.authID
ORDER BY title
```

table	type	key	key_len	ref	rows	Extra
titles	ref	publIDIndex	5	const	2	Using where; Using filesort
rel_title_author	ref	PRIMARY	4	titles.titleID	1	Using index
authors	eq_ref	PRIMARY	4	rel_title_author.authID	1	

To save space in this example, we have not shown the column *possible_keys*. The interpretation is this: The tables are optimally indexed; that is, for each part of the query there are indexes available. It is interesting that the title list (*ORDER BY title*) is apparently sorted externally, although there is an index for the *title* column as well. The reason for this is perhaps that the *title* records are first selected in accordance with the condition *publID=2*, and the *title* index can then no longer be applied.

Example 3

This example uses the same *SELECT* query as does Example 2, but it assumes that *titles.publID* does not have an index. The result is that now all 36 records of the *titles* table must be read, and no index can be used:

table	type	key	key_ len	ref	rows	Extra
titles	ALL				36	Using where; Using filesort
rel_title_ author	ref	PRIMARY	4	titles.titleID	1	Using index
authors	eq_ref	PRIMARY	4	rel_title_author. authID	1	

MySQL Table Types

Up till now, we have tacitly assumed that all tables have been set up as MyISAM tables. That has been the default behavior since MySQL 3.23, and it holds automatically if you do not explicitly demand a different type of table when the table is generated. This section provides a brief overview of the different types of table recognized by MySQL, their properties, and when they should be used. (The MySQL server can, however, be configured using the option `default-table-type` to make another table type valid.)

- **MyISAM—Static:** These tables are used when all columns of the table have fixed, predetermined size. Access in such tables is particularly efficient. This is true even if the table is frequently changed (that is, when there are many *INSERT*, *UPDATE*, and *DELETE* commands). Moreover, data security is quite high, since in the case of corrupted files or other problems, it is relatively easy to extract records.

- **MyISAM—Dynamic:** If in the declaration of a table there is also only a single *VARCHAR*, *xxxTEXT*, or *xxxBLOB* field, then MySQL automatically selects this table type. The significant advantage over the static MyISAM variant is that the space requirement is usually significantly less: Character strings and binary objects require space commensurate with their actual size (plus a few bytes overhead).

  However, it is a fact that data records are not all the same size. If records are later altered, then their location within the database file may have to change. In the old place there appears a hole in the database file. Moreover, it is possible that the fields of a record are not all stored within a contiguous block within the database file, but in various locations. All of this results in increasingly longer access times as the edited table becomes more and more fragmented, unless an *OPTIMIZE TABLE* or an optimization program is executed every now and then (myisamchk; see Chapter 10).

- **MyISAM—Compressed:** Both dynamic and static MyISAM tables can be compressed with the auxiliary program `myisamchk`. This usually results in a shrinkage of the storage requirement for the table to less than one-half the original amount (depending on the contents of the table). To be sure, thereafter, every data record must be decompressed when it is read, but it is still possible under some conditions that access to the table is nevertheless faster, particularly with a combination of a slow hard drive and fast processor. The decisive drawback of compressed MyISAM tables is that they cannot be changed (that is, they are read-only tables).

- **ISAM tables:** The ISAM table type is the precursor of MyISAM, and is supported only for reasons of compatibility. ISAM tables exhibit a host of disadvantages with respect to MyISAM tables. Perhaps the most significant of these is that the resulting files are not independent of the operating system. Thus in general, an ISAM table that was generated by MySQL under operating system x cannot be used under operating system y. (Instead, you must use `mysqldump` and `mysql` to transfer it to the new operating system.) In general, there is no longer any good reason to use ISAM tables (unless, perhaps, you are using an antiquated version of MySQL).

- **InnoDB tables:** The InnoDB table type is the most important alternative to the MyISAM tables. The use of such tables involves a number of different advantages and disadvantages.

  - Advantages vis-à-vis MyISAM: InnoDB tables support transactions, which ensures the integrity of multistep database operations. InnoDB tables also support functions for ensuring referential integrity.
  - Disadvantages vis-à-vis MyISAM: All InnoDB tables are stored in a single binary file, which is thus to some extent a black box. To move a single table or database from one server to another requires the use of `mysqldump`. (With MyISAM tables you can simply copy and transfer the file.) Moreover, InnoDB tables do not yet support a full-text index. The storage requirements on the hard disk are greater than those of comparable MyISAM tables.

    Elementary database operations are generally slower with InnoDB tables than with MyISAM tables. InnoDB tables can, however, greatly improve their performance speed if through the use of transactions one can do without *LOCK* commands.

  In general, many InnoDB functions are similar to those in Oracle tables. The InnoDB table type has been developed over a number of years and is used in a large number of database systems. You will find extensive information on InnoDB in Chapter 8.

- **BDB (Berkeley_DB):** BDB tables also support transactions. (It was the BDB table type that first made transactions possible under MySQL.) In comparison to InnoDB, the integration into MySQL is not as good, and the documentation in a number of details is rather vague. For these reasons, the BDB table driver is not integrated into the standard version of the MySQL server. As a rule, it is advisable to use InnoDB tables in preference to BDB tables.

- **Gemini:** In 2001, the Nusphere company made available its own version of MySQL, distinguished by the addition of the Gemini table type, which supports transactions. Unfortunately, a legal battle developed between Nusphere and the MySQL company, a battle over whether Nusphere had adhered to the rules of the MySQL license (GPL). The disagreement was settled in November 2002, with the result that the code for the Gemini table type was not added to the official MySQL code.

- **MERGE:** MERGE tables are essentially a virtual union of several existing MyISAM tables all of which exhibit identical column definitions. A MERGE table composed of several tables can have some advantages over a single, large, MyISAM table, such as a higher read speed (if the tables are distributed over several hard drives) or a circumvention of the maximum file size in a number of older operating systems (for example, 2 gigabytes for Linux; 2.2 for 32-bit processors). Among the disadvantages are that it is impossible to insert data records into MERGE tables (that is, *INSERT* does not function). Instead, *INSERT* must be applied to one of the subtables.

  In the meanwhile, since most modern operating systems support files of arbitrary size, as well as RAID (that is, the division of a file system on several hard disks), MERGE tables play a subordinate role in practice.

- **HEAP:** HEAP tables exist only in RAM (not on the hard drive). They use a *hash index*, which results in particularly fast access to individual data records.

  In comparison to normal tables, HEAP tables present a large number of functional restrictions, of which we mention here only the most important: No *xxxTEXT* or *xxxBLOB* data types can be used. Records can be searched only with = or <=> (and not with <, >, <=, >=). *AUTO_INCREMENT* is not supported. Indexes can be set up only for *NOT NULL* columns.

  HEAP tables should be used whenever relatively small data sets are to be managed with maximal speed. Since HEAP tables are stored exclusively in RAM, they disappear as soon as MySQL is terminated. The maximum size of a HEAP table is determined by the parameter `max_heap_table_size`, which can be set when MySQL is launched.

REMARK *From among the table types listed above, only the most important will be discussed in this book: MyISAM, InnoDB, and HEAP. Further information on the other table types can be found in the MySQL documentation:*

`http://www.mysql.com/doc/en/Table_types.html`

Temporary Tables

With most of the table types listed above there exists the possibility of creating a table on a temporary basis. Such tables are automatically deleted as soon as the link with MySQL is terminated. Furthermore, temporary tables are invisible to other MySQL links (so that it is possible for two users to employ temporary tables with the same name without running into trouble).

Temporary tables are not a separate table type unto themselves, but rather a variant of the types that we have been describing. Temporary tables are often created automatically by MySQL in order to assist in the execution of *SELECT* queries.

Temporary tables are not stored in the same directory as the other MySQL tables, but in a special temporary directory (under Windows it is usually called `C:\Windows\Temp`, while under Unix it is generally `/tmp` or `/var/tmp` or `/usr/tmp`). The directory can be set at MySQL launch.

> **REMARK** *Often, temporary tables are generated that are of type* HEAP. *However, this is not a necessary combination. Note, however, that nontemporary* HEAP *tables are visible to all MySQL users until they are deleted.*

Table Files

The location of database files can be set when MySQL is launched. (Under Unix/Linux, `/var/lib/mysql` is frequently used, while under Windows it is usually `C:\mysql\data`.) All further input is given relative to this directory.

Where MySQL tables are actually stored depends very much on the table type. Basically, the description of each table is stored in a `*.frm` file, and these `*.frm` files are organized in directories that correspond to the names of the databases:

```
data/dbname/tablename.frm
```

for the table structure (data type of the columns, indexes, etc.).

For each MyISAM table, two additional files are created:

```
data/dbname/table name.MYD
```

for the MyISAM table data, and

```
data/dbname/tablename.MYI
```

for the MyISAM table indexes (all the indexes of the table).

InnoDB tables, on the other hand, are stored together in a single file or in several associated files. These files form the so-called *tablespace*, a sort of virtual storage for all tables. The name and location of these files can be prescribed by configuration settings. By default,

```
data/ibdata1, 2, 3
```

hold the InnoDB tables (data and indexes), while

```
data/ib_logfile0, 1, 2
```

hold the InnodDB logging files.

Starting with MySQL 4.1, an additional file, `db.opt`, is stored in the database directory. It contains settings that hold for the entire database:

```
data/dbname/db.opt
```

Creating Databases, Tables, and Indexes

In the course of this chapter you have learned a great deal about database design. But building castles in the air is one thing, and assembling the plans and materials for real-world construction quite another. We now confront the question of how a database and its tables are actually built. As always, there are several ways of going about this task:

- Genuine SQL pros will not shrink before the prospect of doing things the old-fashioned way and typing in a host of *CREATE TABLE* commands in `mysql`. However, the complicated syntax of this command is not compatible with the creative character of the design process. Nonetheless, SQL commands are often the only way to achieve certain features of tables.

- For beginners in the wonderful world of database construction (and for all who do not enjoy making their lives more complicated than necessary), the graphical user interfaces offer more convenience in the development of a database. Some of these programs (for example, the MySQL Control Center and phpMyAdmin) have been introduced in the previous chapter.

In this chapter, only the *CREATE TABLE* variant is considered. All of our examples refer to the little book database *books*, which in the portion of this chapter dealing with theory was introduced for the purpose of demonstrating the normalization process.

REMARK *Regardless of the tool that you choose to work with, before you begin, the question of access rights must be clarified. If MySQL is securely configured and you do not happen to be the MySQL administrator, then you are not permitted to create a new database at all.*

The topics of access privileges and security are not dealt with until Chapter 9. If you are responsible for the security of MySQL, then you should probably concern yourself with this issue before you create your new database. If there is an administrator, then please ask him or her to set up an empty database for you and provide you with a user name and password.

POINTER *This section assumes that the new database will be created on the local computer, which is plausible if one is creating a new application. What happens, then, when a web application will run on the Internet service provider's computer? How do you transport the database from the local computer to that of the ISP? How can you, should the occasion arise, create a new database directly on the ISP's computer? Such questions will be discussed in their own section of Chapter 10.*

> **POINTER** *There is yet another path to a MySQL database: the conversion of an existing database from another system. Fortunately, there are quite a few converters available, and they can be found at the MySQL web site, which at last sighting was at the following addresses:*
>
> ```
> http://www.mysql.com/doc/en/Contrib.html
> http://www.mysql.com/portal/software/index.html
> ```
>
> *In this book only two variants will be considered, namely, conversion of databases in the format of Microsoft Access or of Microsoft SQL Server. This topic is dealt with in Chapter 17.*

Creating a Database (CREATE DATABASE)

Before you can create tables for your database, you must first create the database itself. The creation of a database results in an empty directory being created on the hard drive. The following *USE* command makes the new database the default database for all further SQL commands:

```
CREATE DATABASE books
USE books
```

> **REMARK** *The commands given here can be executed, for example, in the MySQL monitor* mysql. *(Please recall that in* mysql *you must follow each command with a semicolon.)*
> *A complete syntax reference for the SQL commands introduced here can be found in Chapter 18.*

Creating Tables (CREATE TABLE)

For the four tables of our example database, we require four *CREATE TABLE* commands. Each of these commands contains a list of all fields (columns) with the associated data type and attributes. The syntax should be immediately clear. The definition of the primary index is effected with *PRIMARY KEY*, where all columns that are to be included in the index are specified in parentheses. Of interest here is the table *rel_title_author*, in which the primary index spans both columns:

```
CREATE TABLE author (
    authorID      INT             NOT NULL    AUTO_INCREMENT,
    author        VARCHAR(60)     NOT NULL,
    PRIMARY KEY   (authorID))
CREATE TABLE publisher (
    publisherID   INT             NOT NULL    AUTO_INCREMENT,
    publisher     VARCHAR(60)     NOT NULL,
    PRIMARY KEY   (publisherID))
```

```
CREATE TABLE rel_title_author (
    titleID      INT                    NOT NULL,
    authorID     INT                    NOT NULL,
    PRIMARY KEY  (titleID, authorID))
CREATE TABLE title (
    titleID      INT                    NOT NULL   AUTO_INCREMENT,
    title        VARCHAR(120)           NOT NULL,
    publisherID  INT                    NOT NULL,
    year         INT                    NOT NULL,
    PRIMARY KEY  (titleID))
```

Editing a Table Design (ALTER TABLE)

It is fortunate indeed that you do not have to recreate your database from scratch every time you wish to modify its design, say to add a new column or change the data type or default value of a column. The command *ALTER TABLE* offers sufficient flexibility in most cases. It is also good to know that MySQL is capable in most cases of preserving existing data (even if the data type of a column is changed). Nevertheless, it is a good idea to maintain a backup copy of the table in question.

The following example shows how the maximal number of characters in the *title* column of the *title* table is reduced to 100 characters. (Titles longer than 100 characters will be truncated.) The first line of code shows how to make a backup of the original table (which is a good idea, since we might lose some data if titles are truncated):

```
CREATE TABLE titlebackup SELECT * FROM title
ALTER TABLE title CHANGE title title VARCHAR(100)
NOT NULL
```

Something that might be a bit confusing with our use of the *ALTER TABLE* command is the threefold appearance of the name *title*. The first usage refers to the table, while the second is the name of the column before the change, and the third the new, in this case unchanged, name of the column.

Inserting Data (INSERT)

Normally, data are inserted into the database via a client program (which, it is to be hoped, is convenient and easy to use). Since you, as developer, are responsible in most cases for the code of these programs, it would not hurt for us to take a peek at the *INSERT* command. (Additional commands for inserting, changing, and deleting data can be found in the next chapter.)

```
INSERT INTO author VALUES ( '1', 'Kofler M.')
INSERT INTO author VALUES ('2', 'Kramer D.')
 ...
INSERT INTO publisher VALUES ('1', 'Addison-Wesley')
INSERT INTO publisher VALUES ('2', 'Apress')
 ...
INSERT INTO title VALUES ('1', 'Linux', '1', '2000')
INSERT INTO title VALUES ('2', 'Definitive Guide to Excel VBA', '2', '2000')
```

```
   . . .
INSERT INTO rel_title_author VALUES ('1', '1')
INSERT INTO rel_title_author VALUES ('2', '1')
INSERT INTO rel_title_author VALUES ('2', '2')
   . . .
```

You can also edit several records at once:

```
INSERT INTO rel_title_author VALUES ('1', '1'), ('2', '1'), ('2', '2'), . . .
```

Creating Indexes (CREATE INDEX)

Indexes can be created via the *CREATE TABLE* command or else later with an *ALTER TABLE* or *CREATE INDEX* command. The syntax for describing the index is the same in all three cases. The following three commands show three variants for providing the *title* column of the *title* table with an index. The index received the name *idxtitle*. (Of course, only one of the three commands can be executed. If you try a second command, MySQL will inform you that an index already exists.)

```
CREATE TABLE title (
  titleID ... , title ... , publisherID ... , year ... , PRIMARY KEY ... ,
  INDEX idxtitle (title))
CREATE INDEX idxtitle ON title (title)
ALTER TABLE title ADD INDEX idxtitle (title)
```

   SHOW INDEX FROM tablename produces a list of all defined indexes. Existing indexes can be eliminated with *DROP INDEX indexname ON tablename*.
   If you wish to reduce the number of significant characters per index in the index to the first 16 characters, the syntax looks like this:

```
ALTER TABLE title ADD INDEX idxtitle (title(16))
```

Example *mylibrary* (Library)

Writers of books frequently not only write books, but read them as well (as do many other individuals who do not write books), and over time, many of these readers acquire a significant collection of books, sometimes so many that they lose track of what's what and what's where. After a hopeless effort at bringing order to the author's domestic library, he created the database *mylibrary*. See Figure 5-2 for an overview of the structure of the *mylibrary* database. The database *mylibrary* is an extended version of the database *books* that was introduced at the beginning of this chapter. Note that the names of individual tables and columns have been changed in the migration from *books* to *library*.
   The main purpose of this database is to store the titles of books together with their authors and publishers in a convenient format. The database will additionally offer the convenient feature of allowing books to be ordered in various categories.

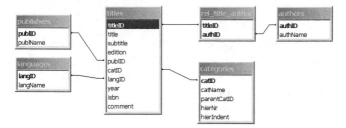

Figure 5-2. Structure of the mylibrary *database*

> **TIP** *If you happen to be a victim of the compulsion to collect something, you can use* mylibrary *as a basis for your own database. You should have little trouble in converting this database into one for CDs, MP3 files, stamps, scientific articles, postal and e-mail addresses, Barbie dolls, birthdays and other noteworthy dates, arachnids, and so on.*

> **REMARK** *The database* mylibrary *as well as its variants* mylibraryodbc *and* mylibraryinno, *are available at* www.apress.com.
> *For* mylibararyodbc, *all tables are equipped with an additional* timestamp *column. This column is necessary if the database is to be altered with ODBC programs (see Chapter 17).*
> *For* mylibraryinno, *all tables have been transformed into the InnoDB format. Furthermore, integrity rules (*foreign key constraints *have been defined.*

Basic Design

Titles, Authors, and Publishers

Just as in the *books* database, here there are three tables in which book titles, names of authors, and names of publishers are stored: *titles*, *authors*, and *publishers*.

The $n : m$ relation between *titles* and *authors* is created via the table *rel_title_author*. Here the sequence of authors for a given book can be specified in the field *authNr* (that is, the first, second, third, etc., author). This is practical above all if the database is to store the names of scientific publications, where it is not always a good idea to list the authors in alphabetical order. However, *authNr* can be left empty (that is, *NULL*) if you are not interested in such supplemental information.

In general, in the *library* database it is permitted to store the value *NULL* in many of the columns. Thus it is possible to store a book title quickly without bothering to specify the publisher or year of publication. Perfectionists in database design would, of course, frown on such practice, but on the other hand, too many restrictions often lead to the result that data simply do not get catalogued. From this point of view, it is practical to allow the publisher, say, to be indicated for some books without it being mandatory that it be given for all.

Categories and Languages

The table *categories* enables the construction of a hierarchical category list in which the books can be ordered. (Details on this table appear in the following section.) The table *languages* contains a list with the languages in which the books have appeared. Thus for each title, the language can be stored as well.

Dealing with (Author) Names

In *mylibrary*, names are generally stored in a field where the surname must be given first (to take a random example, *Kofler Michael*, and not *Michael Kofler*). This is the usual ordering for sorting by name.

A quite different approach would be to save surnames, given names, and even initials and titles, in separate fields (for example, *firstname*, *lastname*, and perhaps even *middlename*, etc.). Several fields are, of course, more trouble to manage than a single field, but in return, a greater flexibility is achieved as to how the name can be displayed. This is important, for example, if the data are to be used for personalizing letters or e-mail messages.

Independent of the internal storage, there is clearly a problem in that many people (myself included, alas) now and again input the surname and given name in the wrong order. One falsely input name will be practically untraceable in the database.

Therefore, it is important that the user interface always show and receive names in a uniform order and that the desired order—best indicated by an example—be shown in the input form. Be sure to label the input fields in a clear and unambiguous way (for example, use "family name" or "surname" and not "last name").

Data Types

All tables are provided with an *AUTO_INCREMENT* column, which also serves as the primary index. Most fields possess the attribute *NOT NULL*. Exceptions are those fields that describe the properties of the title. Thus *NULL* is allowed for *subtitle, edition, publID, catID, langID, year, isbn,* and *comment*.

Column name	Data type
All ID fields	INT
authors.authName	VARCHAR(60)
categories.catName	VARCHAR(60)
categories.hierNr	INT
categories.hierIndent	TINYINT
languages.langName	VARCHAR(40)
publishers.publName	VARCHAR(60)
titles.title and .subtitle	VARCHAR(100)
titles.year	INT
titles.edition	TINYINT
titles.isbn	VARCHAR(20)
titles.comment	VARCHAR(255)

Hierarchical Categorization of the Books

The table *categories* helps in ordering books into various categories (technical books, children's books, etc.). To make the *library* more interesting from the point of view of database design, the field *parentCatID* will be represented hierarchically. Here is an example: Figure 5-3 shows how the hierarchy represented in Table 5-10 can be depicted with respect to the database.

All books
    Children's books
    Computer books
        Databases
            Object-oriented databases
            Relational databases
            SQL
        Programming
            Perl
            PHP
    Literature and fiction

Figure 5-3. Example data for the categories *table*

Table 5-10. Database representation of the hierarchy in Figure 5-3

catID	catName	parentCatID
1	Computer books	11
2	Databases	1
3	Programming	1
4	Relational databases	2
5	Object-oriented databases	2
6	PHP	3
7	Perl	3
8	SQL	2
9	Children's books	11
10	Literature and fiction	11
11	All books	NULL

REMARK   *In the development of applications,* parentCatID=NULL *must be treated as a special case.*

Hierarchy Problems

Let me state at once that although the representation of such hierarchies looks simple and elegant at first glance, they cause many problems as well. (That this example nonetheless uses hierarchies has, of course, pedagogical purposes: It allows us to demonstrate interesting SQL programming techniques. Even though the representation of hierarchies in this example is somewhat artificial, there are many database applications where the use of hierarchies is unavoidable.)

> **POINTER** *In point of fact, this chapter is supposed to be dealing with database design and not with SQL, but these two topics cannot be cleanly separated. There is no point in creating a super database design if the capabilities of SQL do not suffice to extract the desired data from the database's tables.*
>
> *If you have no experience with SQL, you should dip into the following chapter a bit. Consider the following instructions as a sort of "advanced database design."*

Almost all problems with hierarchies have to do with the fact that SQL does not permit recursive queries:

- With individual queries it is impossible to find all categories lying above a given category in the hierarchy.
  Example: The root category is called *Relational databases* (*parentCatID=2*). You would like to create a list that contains *Computer books* → *Databases* → *Relational databases.*
  With *SELECT * FROM categories WHERE catID=2*, you indeed find *Databases*, but not *Computer books*, which lies two places up the hierarchy. For that, you must execute an additional query *SELECT * FROM categories WHERE catID=1*. Of course, this can be accomplished in a loop in the programming language of your choice (Perl, PHP, etc.), but not with a single SQL instruction.

- It is just as difficult to represent the entire table in hierarchical form (as a tree). Again, you must execute a number of queries.

- It is not possible without extra effort to search for all books in a higher category. Example: You would like to find all books in the category *Computer books*. With *SELECT * FROM titles WHERE catID=1* you find only those titles directly linked to the category *Computer books*, but not the titles in the categories *Databases, Relational databases, Object-oriented databases*, etc. The query must be the following: *SELECT * FROM titles WHERE catID IN (1, 2 . . .)*, where *1, 2 . . .* are the ID numbers of the subordinate categories. The actual problem is to determine these numbers.

- In the relatively simple representation that we have chosen, it is not possible to associate the same subcategory with two or more higher-ranking categories. Example: The programming language *SQL* is linked in the above hierarchy to the higher-ranking category *Databases*. It would be just as logical to have a link to *Programming*. Therefore, it would be optimal to have *SQL* appear as a subcategory of both *Databases* and *Programming*.

- There is the danger of circular references. Such references can, of course, appear only as a result of input error, but where there are human beings who input data (or who write programs), there are certain to be errors. If a circular reference is created, most database programs will find themselves in an infinite loop. The resolution of such problems can be difficult.

None of these problems is insuperable. However, hierarchies often lead to situations in which answering a relatively simple question involves executing a whole series of SQL queries, and that is often a slow process. Many problems can be avoided by doing without genuine hierarchies (for example, by allowing at most a two-stage hierarchy) or if supplementary information for a simpler resolution of hierarchies is provided in additional columns or tables (see the following section).

Optimization (Efficiency Versus Normalization)

If you have taken to heart the subject of normalization of databases as presented in this chapter, then you know that redundancy is bad. It leads to unnecessary usage of storage space, management issues when changes are made, etc.

Yet there are cases in which redundancy is quite consciously sought in order to increase the efficiency of an application. The *mylibrary* database contains many examples of this, which we shall discuss here rather fully.

This section should make clear that database design is a multifaceted subject. There are usually several ways that lead to the same goal, and each of these paths is, in fact, a compromise of one sort or another. Which compromise is best depends largely on the uses to which the database will be put: What types of queries will occur most frequently? Will data be frequently changed?

Authors' Names in the titles Table

The authors' names are stored in the *authors* table in normalized form. However, it will often happen that you wish to obtain a list of book titles, and with each book title you would like to list all of that book's authors, such as in the following form:

Client/Server Survival Guide by Robert Orfali, Dan Harkey, Jeri Edwards
Definitive Guide to Excel VBA by Michael Kofler, David Kramer
Linux by Michael Kofler
Web Application Development with PHP 4.0 by Tobias Ratschiller, Till Gerken

There are now two possible ways of proceeding:

- **Variant 1:** The simplest and thus most often chosen route is first to execute an SQL query to determine the desired list of titles, without the corresponding authors. Then for each title found, a further SQL query is formulated to determine all the authors of that title. Now, however, twenty-one SQL queries were necessary to obtain a list with twenty book titles. The following lines show the requisite pseudocode. The bits in pointy brackets cannot be executed in

SQL; they must be formulated in a client programming language (Perl, PHP, etc.).

```
SELECT titleID, title FROM titles WHERE ... ⟨for each titleID⟩
  SELECT authName FROM authors, rel_title_author
  WHERE rel_title_author.authID = authors.authID
  AND rel_title_author.titleID = ⟨titleID⟩
  ORDER BY authNR
```

- **Variant 2:** Another possibility is to include all the data in a single query:

```
SELECT titles.titleID, title, authName
FROM titles, rel_title_author, authors
WHERE rel_title_author.titleID = titles.titleID
AND rel_title_author.authID = authors.authID
ORDER BY title, rel_title_author.authNr, authName
```

You thereby obtain, however, a list in which each book title appears as many times as it has authors (see Table 5-11).

Table 5-11. Query result in the mylibrary *database*

titleID	title	authName
3	Client/Server Survival Guide	Edwards E.
3	Client/Server Survival Guide	Harkey D.
3	Client/Server Survival Guide	Orfali R.
2	Definitive Guide to Excel VBA	Kofler Michael
2	Definitive Guide to Excel VBA	Kramer David
1	Linux, 5th ed.	Kofler Michael
9	MySQL & mSQL	King T.
9	MySQL & mSQL	Reese G.
9	MySQL & mSQL	Yarger R.J.
4	Web Application Development with PHP 4.0	Gerken Till
4	Web Application Development with PHP 4.0	Ratschiller Tobias

At this point, you can use some client-side code to create the list of books by collecting authors' names for books with the same *titleID* number and displaying the book title only once.

The significant disadvantage of this modus operandi is that it is relatively difficult to represent the results in page format (for example, with twenty titles per page). Of course, you can limit the number of result records in the *SELECT* query with *LIMIT*, but you don't know in advance how many records will be required to obtain twenty titles (since it depends on the number of authors per title).

This problem can be circumvented if first a query is executed by which only the *titleID* values are determined. The second query then uses these *titleID* values. Unfortunately, MySQL 4.0 does not yet permit nested *SELECT* queries, and therefore either the *titleID* list must be processed by the client program in the second query (*WHERE titleID IN(x, y, . . .*), or a temporary table must be used. Beginning with MySQL 4.1, such queries can be formulated as sub*SELECT*s.

- **Solution:** From the standpoint of efficiency, the second variant is significantly better than the first, but even it is not wholly satisfying. The most efficient solution would be to provide a column *authorsList* in the *titles* table, in which the list of authors is stored for each title.

  Such a column is no substitute for the *authors* table, which will be used and reused (for example, to search for all books on which a particular author has worked, or to store additional information about an author). The column *authorsList* must be updated each time a new title is stored or an old one is changed. It is much more burdensome that now title records must also be updated when changes in the *authors* table are made (such as when a typo in an author's name is corrected): a classical redundancy problem.

  You thus have the choice between redundancy and efficiency. Which variant is better for your application depends on the size of the database, whether it will be used primarily in read-only mode for queries or frequently altered, what type of queries will be used most frequently, etc. (In our realization of *mylibrary*, we have done without *authorsList*.)

Hierarchical Order in the categories Table

The necessity will continually arise to display the *categories* table in hierarchical representation similar to that of Figure 5-3. As we have already mentioned, such processing of the data is connected either with countless SQL queries or complex client-side code. Both of these are unacceptable if the hierarchical representation is needed frequently (for example, for a listbox in a form).

A possible solution is provided by the two additional columns *hierNr* and *hierIndent*. The first of these gives the row number in which the record would be located in a hierarchical representation. (The assumption is that data records are sorted alphabetically by *catName* within a level of the hierarchy.) The second of these two columns determines the level of indentation. In Table 5-12 are displayed for both of these columns the values corresponding to the representation in Figure 5-3.

Table 5-12. categories *table with* hierNr *column*

catID	catName	parentCatID	hierNr	hierIndent
1	Computer books	11	2	1
2	Databases	1	3	2
3	Programming	1	7	2
4	Relational databases	2	5	3
5	Object-oriented databases	2	4	3
6	PHP	3	9	3
7	Perl	3	8	3
8	SQL	2	6	3
9	Children's books	11	1	1
10	Literature and fiction	11	10	1
11	All books	NULL	0	0

A simple query in mysql proves that this arrangement makes sense. Here are a few remarks on the SQL functions used: *CONCAT* joins two character strings. *SPACE* generates the specified number of blank characters. *AS* gives the entire expression the new Alias name *category*:

```
SELECT CONCAT(SPACE(hierIndent*2), catName) AS category
FROM categories ORDER BY hierNr
```

```
category
All books
  Children's books
  Computer books
    Databases
      Object-oriented databases
      Relational databases
      SQL
    Programming
      Perl
      PHP
  Literature and fiction
```

You may now ask how the numerical values *hierIndent* and *hierNr* actually come into existence. The following example-oriented instructions show how a new data record (the computer book category *Operating systems*) is inserted into the table:

1. The data of the higher-ranking initial record (that is, *Computer books*) are known: *catID=1, parentCatID=11, hierNr=1, hierIndent=1*.

2. (a) Now we search within the *Computer books* group for the first record that lies in the hierarchy immediately after the record to be newly inserted (here, this is *Programming*). See Figure 5-3. All that is of interest in this record is *hierNr*.

   Here is a brief explanation of the SQL command:

   WHERE parentCat_ID=1 finds all records that are immediately below *Computer books* in the hierarchy (that is, *Databases* and *Programming*). *catName>'Operating Systems'* restricts the list to those records that occur after the new record *Operating Systems*.

   ORDER BY catname sorts the records that are found.

   LIMIT 1 reduces the result to the first record.

```
SELECT hierNr FROM categories
WHERE parentCatID=1 AND catName>'Operating Systems'
ORDER BY catName
LIMIT 1
```

   The query just given returns the result *hierNr=7*. It is thereby clear that the new data record should receive this hierarchy number. First, however, all existing records with *hierNr>=7* should have their values of *hierNr* increased by 1.

(b) It can also happen that the query returns no result, namely, when there are no entries in the higher-ranking category or when all entries come before the new one in alphabetic order. (This would be the case if you wished to insert the new computer book category *Software engineering*.)

In that case, you must search for the next record whose *hierNr* is larger than *hierNr* for the initial record and whose *hierIndent* is less than or equal to *hierIndent* of the initial record. (In this way, the beginning of the next equal- or higher-ranking group in the hierarchy is sought.)

```
SELECT hierNr FROM categories
WHERE hierNr>1 AND hierIndent<=1
ORDER BY hierNr LIMIT 1
```

This query returns the result 10 (that is, *hierNr* for the record *Literature and fiction*). The new record will get this hierarchy number. All existing records with *hierNr>=10* must have their *hierNr* increased by 1.

(c) If this query also returns no result, then the new record must be inserted at the end of the hierarchy list. The current largest *hierNr* value can easily be determined:

```
SELECT MAX(hiernr) FROM categories
```

3. To increase the *hierNr* of the existing records, the following command is executed (for case 2a):

```
UPDATE categories SET hierNr=hierNr+1 WHERE hiernr>=7
```

4. Now the new record can be inserted. For *parentCatID*, the initial record *catID* will be used. Above, *hierNr=7* was determined. Here *hierIndent* must be larger by 1 than was the case with the initial record:

```
INSERT INTO categories (catName, parentCatID, hierNr, hierIndent)
VALUES ('Operating systems', 1, 7, 2)
```

The description of this algorithm proves that inserting a data record is a relatively complex and costly process. (A concrete realization of the algorithm can be found in the form of a PHP script in Chapter 12.) It is much more complicated to alter the hierarchy after the fact. Imagine that you wish to change the name of one of the categories in such a way as to change its place in the alphabetical order. This would affect not only the record itself, but many other records as well. For large sections of the table it will be necessary to determine *hierNr*. You see, therefore, that redundancy is bad.

Nevertheless, the advantages probably outweigh the drawbacks, above all because changes in the category list will be executed very infrequently (and thus the expenditure of time becomes insignificant), while queries to determine the hierarchical order, on the other hand, must be executed frequently.

Searching for Lower-Ranked Categories in the categories Table

Suppose you want to search for all *Databases* titles in the *titles* table. Then it would not suffice to search for all titles with *catId=2*, since you also want to see all the titles relating to *Relational databases*, *Object-oriented databases*, and *SQL* (that is, the titles with *catID* equal to 4, 5, and 8). The totality of all these categories will be described in the following search category group.

There are two problems to be solved: First, you must determine the list of the *catID* values for the search category group. For this a series of *SELECT* queries is needed, and we shall not go into that further here. Then you must determine from the *titles* table those records whose *catID* numbers agree with the values just found. Since MySQL, alas, does not support sub*SELECT*s, for the second step a temporary table will be necessary.

Thus in principle, the title search can be carried out, but the path is thorny, with the necessity of several SQL queries and client-side code.

The other solution consists in introducing a new (redundant) table, in which are stored all records lying above each of the *categories* records. This table could be called *rel_cat_parent*, and it would consist of two columns: *catID* and *parentID* (see Table 5-13). We see, then, for example, that the category *Relational databases (catID=4)* lies under the categories *All books*, *Computer books*, and *Databases (parentID=11, 1, 2)*.

Table 5-13. Some entries in the rel_cat_parent *table*

catID	parentID
1	11
2	1
2	11
3	1
3	11
4	1
4	2
4	11
. . .	. . .

The significant drawback of the *rel_cat_parent* table is that it must be synchronized with every change in the *categories* table. But that is relatively easy to take care of.

In exchange for that effort, now the question of all categories ranked below *Databases* is easily answered:

```
SELECT catID FROM rel_cat_parent
WHERE parentID=2
```

If you would like to determine all book titles that belong to the category *Databases* or its subcategories, the requisite query looks like the following. The key word *DISTINCT* is necessary here, since otherwise, the query would return many titles with multiplicity:

```
SELECT DISTINCT titles.title FROM titles, rel_cat_parent
WHERE (rel_cat_parent.parentID = 2 OR titles.catID = 2)
  AND titles.catID = rel_cat_parent.catID
```

We are once more caught on the horns of the efficiency versus normalization dilemma: The entire table *rel_cat_parent* contains nothing but data that can be determined directly from *categories*. In the concrete realization of the *mylibrary* database, we decided to do without *rel_cat_parent*, because the associated PHP example (see Chapter 12) in any case does not plan for category searches.

Searching for Higher-Ranked Categories in the categories Table

Here we confront the converse question to that posed in the last section: What are the higher-ranking categories above an initial, given, category? If the initial category is *Perl* (*catID=7*), then the higher-ranking categories are first *Programming*, then *Computer books*, and finally, *All books*.

When there is a table *rel_cat_parent* like that described above, then our question can be answered by a simple query:

```
SELECT CONCAT(SPACE(hierIndent*2), catName) AS category
FROM categories, rel_cat_parent
WHERE rel_cat_parent.catID = 7
  AND categories.catID = rel_cat_parent.parentID
ORDER BY hierNr
```

The result is seen in Figure 5-4.

```
category
All books
   Computer books
      Programming
```

Figure 5-4. Query result in search for higher-ranking categories

On the other hand, if *rel_cat_parent* is not available, then a series of *SELECT* instructions must be executed in a loop *categories.parentCatID* until this contains the value 0. This process is demonstrated in the PHP example program `categories.php` (see Chapter 12).

Indexes

All the *mylibrary* tables are supplied with a *PRIMARY* index for the *ID* column. Additionally, the following usual indexes are defined:

Table	Column	Purpose
authors	*author*	search/sort by author's name
categories	*catName*	search by category name
	hierNr	hierarchical sort of the category list
publishers	*publName*	search/sort by publisher's name
titles	*title*	search/sort by book title
	publID	search by titles from a particular publisher
	catID	search by titles from a particular category
	isbn	search by ISBN

Example *myforum* (Discussion Group)

Among the best-loved MySQL applications are guest books, discussion groups, and other web sites that offer users the possibility of creating a text and thereby adding their own voices to the web site. The database *myforum* creates the basis for a discussion group. The database consists of three tables:

- *forums* contains a list of the names of all discussion groups. Furthermore, each group can be assigned a particular language (English, German, Zemblan, etc.).

- *users* contains a list of all users registered in the database who are permitted to contribute to discussions. For each registered user, a login name, password, and e-mail address are stored. (One can imagine extending this to hold additional information.)

- *messages* contains all the stored contributions. These consist of a *Subject* row, the actual text, *forumID*, *userID*, and additional management information. This table is the most interesting of the three from the standpoint of database design.

The structure of the *myforum* database is depicted in Figure 5-5.

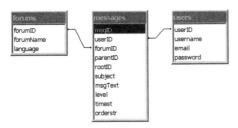

Figure 5-5. Structure of the myforum *database*

> **REMARK**   *Included in the code files for this book are two versions of the* myforum
> *database. The file* myforum.sql *contains the SQL instructions for creating a test
> version of* myforum *that contains only test contributions.*
>
>   *In contrast,* bigforum.sql *contains a larger version (18 forums, 1400
> contributions) that is the result of the discussion group on my web site. For this book,
> contributions have been made anonymous. (The* users *table contains only first
> names.) The database* bigforum *offers the possibility of trying out various MySQL
> operations (such as full-text search) on a database that is more than just a toy
> example.*
>
>   *The* bigforum *database contains messages in both English and German.
> However, the majority are in German. If you want to see only the English entries, you
> can build your queries thus:*

```
SELECT * FROM messages, forums
WHERE messages.forumID=forums.forumID AND forums.language="english"
```

Data Types

All three tables are equipped with *AUTO_INCREMENT* columns, which also serve as
primary index. In general, all fields have the attribute *NOT NULL*. Here we list the
column names and data types of the three tables:

Column name	Data type
All ID fields	*INT*
forums.forumname	*VARCHAR(80)*
forums.language	*ENUM('german', 'english', 'zemblan')*
messages.subject	*VARCHAR(80)*
messages.msgText	*TEXT*
messages.level	*INT*
messages.timest	*TIMESTAMP*
messages.orderstr	*VARCHAR(128), BINARY*
users.username	*VARCHAR(30)*
users.email	*VARCHAR(120)*
users.password	*VARCHAR(30)*

Hierarchies Among Messages

As we have already seen in the case of the *mylibrary* database, there is a battle in
myforum in dealing with hierarchies. A significant feature of discussion groups is that
the discussion thread is represented in a hierarchical list. The hierarchy is the result
of the fact that each contribution can elicit a response. A discussion among the five
participants Antony, Banquo, Coriolanus, Duncan, and Edmund (*A, B, C, D,* and *E* for
short) might look like that depicted in Figure 5-6.

A: How do I sort MySQL tables? (17.1.2003 12:00)
  B: first answer (1.17.2003 18:30)
    A: thanks (1.17.2003 19:45)
    C: better suggestion (1.19.2003 10:30)
  D: second answer (1.18.2003 3:45)
    A: I don't understand (1.18.2003 9:45)
    D: the same explanation, but more extensive (1.18.2003 22:05)
  E: third answer (1.18.2003 19:00)

Figure 5-6. A discussion thread

Here as illustration a description of the content is added to the title line (*subject*) of each contribution. In reality, the title line of a response is usually simply the letters *Re:* together with the original title line (e.g., *Re: How do I . . .*).

A representation in database format might look like that shown in Table 5-14. It is assumed here that the five participants *A* through *E* have *userID* numbers 201 through 205. The messages of the thread have *msgID* numbers that begin with 301. (In practice, it is natural to expect that a thread will not exhibit sequential *msgID* numbers. More likely, other threads will break into the sequence.) The table is sorted chronologically (that is, in the order in which the messages were posted).

Table 5-14. messages table with records of a discussion thread

msgID	userID	subject	parentID	timest
301	201	How do I . . .	0	2001-01-17 12:00
302	202	first answer	301	2001-01-17 18:30
303	201	thanks	302	2001-01-17 19:45
304	204	second answer	301	2001-01-18 3:45
305	201	I don't . . .	304	2001-01-18 9:45
306	205	third answer	301	2001-01-18 19:00
307	204	the same . . .	305	2001-01-18 22:05
308	203	better suggestion	302	2001-01-19 10:30

The hierarchy is expressed via the column *parentID*, which refers to the message up one level in the hierarchy. If *parentID* has the value 0, then the contribution is one that began a new thread.

Optimization

From the standpoint of normalization, *parentID* is sufficient to express the hierarchy. However, this slick table design makes some frequently occurring queries difficult to answer:

- What are all the messages in this discussion thread?

- How should the messages be sorted? (A glance at Table 5-14 shows that a chronological sorting is not our goal.)

- How far should each message be indented if the messages are to be represented hierarchically?

To answer the first question, it is necessary to search (in a recursive loop) through all *parentID/ msgID* pairs. With long threads, this will require a large number of *SELECT* queries. Of course, each of these queries can be quickly executed, but taken together, they represent a considerable degree of inefficiency.

Recursion also comes into play in the second question: A sorting by the time stored in *timest* leads to our goal, but the answers must be sorted by group for each branch of the hierarchical tree and inserted at the correct place in the list.

The answer to the third question is achieved by following the *parentID* pointer back to the start of the discussion thread.

To increase efficiency, we must back off from our wishful goal of zero redundancy. We shall add three new columns:

- *rootID* refers to the original message that begins the discussion thread and thus makes it possible to answer the first question easily.

- *orderstr* contains a binary concatenation of the *timest* times of all higher-ranking messages. As we shall soon see, this character string can be used for sorting messages within a thread.

- *level* specifies the level of the hierarchy and thus immediately answers the third question.

Having absorbed these new columns into our database, we have a new representation of our database, as depicted in Table 5-15. In comparison with Table 5-14, you can see in the column *timest* that now there are only three digits, which should correspond to the internal binary representation. (In fact, four bytes are used, which permits 256 different values. For greater clarity we have used three-digit numbers here.)

While the meaning of the contents of the columns *rootID* and *level* is clear, that of *orderstr* might be a bit more opaque. In this binary column is stored a binary sequence of *TIMESTAMP* values of all higher-ranking messages. This simple measure ensures that associated groups of messages are not separated during sorting.

Table 5-15. messages *table with records of a discussion thread*

msgID	userID	subject	parentID	timest	rootID	level	orderstr
301	201	How . . .	0	712	0	0	712
302	202	first . . .	301	718	301	1	712718
303	201	thanks	302	719	301	2	712718719
304	204	second . . .	301	803	301	1	712803
305	201	I don't . . .	304	809	301	2	712803809
306	205	third . . .	301	819	301	1	712819
307	204	the same	305	822	301	3	712803809822
		. . .					
308	203	better . . .	302	910	301	2	712718910

Pluses and Minuses

The obvious advantage of the three additional columns is the increased efficiency in displaying the messages. Since the reading operation occurs much more frequently than the writing operation in a discussion forum, reading efficiency has a correspondingly high status in the design of our database. (Furthermore, saving a new data record is efficient and not at all problematic. The values for the three supplementary columns can be easily determined for a response from the associated higher-ranking message. If the message begins a new thread, then *rootID* and *level* are 0, while *orderstr* contains the binary representation of the current time.)

The single drawback is the additional storage space required for the three columns. However, in comparison to the typical storage requirement of a message with several lines of text, this additional storage requirement can be considered negligible. (The maximum length of *orderstr* is limited to 128 characters. That is, at most 32 hierarchical levels can be represented.)

Due to the nature of discussion groups, the additional disadvantages due to redundancy, that is, the problems of subsequent changes in data, are insignificant. Changes in existing messages are not anticipated, and neither are additions and deletions after the fact, which would have the effect of changing the sequence of messages.

> **REMARK** *Please note that the* orderstr *character string is based on* TIMESTAMP *values, which change only once per second. If it should chance that two messages are received at the same second, the sort order could become confused.*

Indexes

All *myforum* tables are supplied with a *PRIMARY* index for the *ID* column. Furthermore, the following usual indexes are defined:

Table	Column	Purpose
users	*userName*	search for user name (at login)
messages	*orderStr*	sort messages in discussion order
	forumID	search for messages in a discussion group
	rootID	search for messages in a thread

The PHP example for *myforum* does not provide for searching for messages. For such a search, a full-text index covering the columns *subject* and *msgText* is recommended.

Example *exceptions* (Special Cases)

When you begin to develop an application with a new database, programming language, or API that is unfamiliar to you it is often practical to implement a simple test database for quickly testing various special cases. For the work on this book, as well as for testing various APIs and various import and export tests, the database *exceptions* was used. Among the tables of this database are the following:

- Columns with most data types supported by MySQL, including *xxxTEXT*, *xxxBLOB*, *SET*, and *ENUM*

- *NULL* values

- Texts and BLOBs with all possible special characters

- All 255 text characters (code 1 to 255)

The following paragraphs provide an overview of the tables and their contents. The column names indicate the data type (thus the column *a_blob* has data type *BLOB*). The *id* column is an *AUTO_INCREMENT* column (type *INT*). In all the columns except the *id* column the value *NULL* is allowed.

testall

This table contains columns with the most important MySQL data types (though not all types).

Columns: *id, a_char, a_text, a_blob, a_date, a_time, a_timestamp, a_float, a_decimal, a_enum, a_set*

text_text

With this table you can test the use of text.

Columns: *id, a_varchar* (maximum 100 characters), *a_text, a_tinytext, a_longtext*

test_blob

With the *test_blob* table you can test the use of binary data (import, export, reading and storing a client program, etc.).

Columns: *id, a_blob*.

Contents: A record (*id=1*) with a 512-byte binary block. The binary data represent byte for byte the codes 0, 1, 2, . . . , 255, 0, 1, . . . , 255.

test_date

With this table you can test the use of dates and times.

Columns: *id, a_date, a_time, a_datetime, a_timestamp*.

Content: A data record (*id=1*) with the values *2000-12-07, 09:06:29, 2000-12-07 09:06:29*, and *20001207090649*.

test_enum

With this table you can test the use of *SET* and *ENUM*.

Columns: *id, a_enum,* and *a_set* (with the character strings 'a', 'b', 'c', 'd', 'e').

Content:

id	a_enum	a_set
1	a	a
2	e	b,c,d
3		
4	NULL	NULL

test_null

With this table you can test whether *NULL* (first record) can be distinguished from an empty character string (second record).

Columns: *id, a_text.*

Content:

id	a_text
1	NULL
2	
3	'a text'

test_order_by

With this table you can test *ORDER BY* and the character set in use (including sort order). The table consists of two columns: *id* and *a_char*. The column *id* contains sequential numbers from 1 to 255, while *a_char* contains the associated character code. An index was deliberately not defined for the column *a_char*.

Content:

id	a_char
...	
65	'A'
66	'B'
...	

importtable1, importtable2, exporttable

These three tables contain test data for importation and exportation of text files. A description of the tables as well as numerous possibilities for import and export by MySQL can be found in Chapter 10.

#### CHAPTER 6

An Introduction to SQL

THIS CHAPTER PROVIDES AN INTRODUCTION to the database language *Structured Query Language,* or SQL for short. This language is used primarily to formulate instructions to a database system, including queries and commands to change or delete database objects. The most important of these commands are *SELECT, INSERT, UPDATE,* and *DELETE,* and these are the main attractions in this chapter, which aims to instruct in large part by presenting many examples.

Chapter Overview

> **POINTER** *The following chapter, as a sort of continuation of the present one, provides a selection of recipes for solving everyday SQL problems, such as how to deal with character strings and with dates and times, and how to formulate subSELECT instructions (that is, SELECT commands whose results depend on another SELECT command).*

Introduction

Prerequisites

All of the examples presented in this chapter are based on our example databases, and they use the database *mylibrary*, which was introduced in Chapter 5. If you wish to try out these databases for yourself, then you must download them to your own test environment.

> **TIP** *Which database is involved in a particular example will be clear from the line* USE databasename *that appears at the beginning of the example or the beginning of the section in question.*

The best way of testing simple SQL commands is to use the MySQL monitor mysql. This program can be launched under Unix/Linux with the command mysql. (Please note that you must terminate mysql commands with a semicolon. We shall not indicate the semicolon in this chapter, because it is not required by other client programs. That is, it is not part of the MySQL syntax. Additional information on the mysql monitor can be found in Chapter 4.)

When you get to the point of editing multiline SQL commands, you will find that the level of comfort and convenience afforded by mysql goes into a steep decline. A better alternative is to use one of the numerous MySQL interfaces (such as the MySQL Control Center). Such programs have the advantage that the results of a query are displayed in a reader-friendly tabular format.

> **POINTER** *In this book we generally write SQL commands and key words in uppercase letters, reserving lowercase for the names of databases, tables, and columns. Sometimes, we use a mixed format (e.g.,* columnName*). MySQL is largely case-insensitive. The exception is in the names of databases and tables, where case distinction is made. With names for such objects you must hew to the straight and narrow path of exactitude with regard to case. Details on naming rules can be found in Chapter 18.*

DML, DDL, and DCL

SQL commands can be divided into three groups:

- **Data Manipulation Language (DML):** *SELECT, INSERT, UPDATE*, and *DELETE*, and several additional commands, serve to read from the tables of a database and to store and update them. These commands form the centerpiece of this and the next chapter. Commands for controlling the transaction mechanism appear in Chapter 8.

- **Data Definition Language (DDL):** With *CREATE TABLE, ALTER TABLE*, and their ilk the design (schema) of a database can be changed. Some such commands were used as examples in the previous chapter.

- **Data Control Language (DCL):** *GRANT, REVOKE*, and several additional SQL commands help in setting the security mechansisms of MySQL. They will be presented in Chapter 10.

In Chapter 18 you will find an alpabetical reference to all SQL commands.

Simple Queries (*SELECT*)

Here is a simple database query: *SELECT * FROM tablename*. This query returns all data records of the table specified. The asterisk indicates that the query is to encompass all the columns of the table. (See Figure 6-1.)

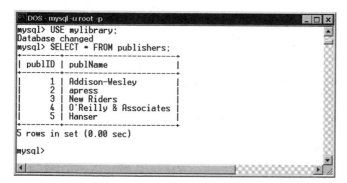

Figure 6-1. First SQL experiments in MySQL monitor mysql

```
USE mylibrary
SELECT * FROM publishers
 publID    publName
 1         Addison-Wesley
 2         Apress
 3         New Riders
 4         O'Reilly & Associates
 5         Hanser
```

REMARK SELECT *can be used without reference to a database or to tables, for example, in the form* SELECT 2*3, *in which case* SELECT *returns its result in the form of a small table (one column, one row). This is used relatively often to determine the content of MySQL variables or functions (as in, say,* SELECT NOW( )*, to determine the current time).*

Determining the Number of Data Records (Lines)

Perhaps you do not have a craving to view your data records in gruesome detail, but would like merely to determine how many records there are in one of your tables. For that, you can use the following query:

```
SELECT COUNT(publID) FROM publishers
```

COUNT(publID)
_____
5

In this query you could specify, instead of *publID*, any column of the table (or *
for all columns). In any case, MySQL optimizes the query and returns only the *number*
of records, without actually reading them.

Column Restriction

Often, you are not interested in all the columns of a table. In such a case you must specify the columns explicitly (instead of using the asterisk).

```
SELECT publName FROM publishers
```

publName
_____
Addison-Wesley
Apress
New Riders
O'Reilly & Associates
Hanser

TIP *If a query is going to return a large number of data records, you should get accustomed to the idea of specifying explicitly only those columns of interest (instead of taking the lazy person's route of simply typing an asterisk). The reason is that MySQL (unnecessary data extraction), the client program (memory usage), and the network (unnecessary data transfer) work significantly more efficiently if the data set to be processed is limited to the absolute minimum.*

Limiting the Number of Resulting Records (LIMIT)

You can limit not only the number of columns in a query result, but also the number of data records. Imagine that your *titles* table contains the names of 100,000 books, but you would like to access only the first ten of these (for example, to display in an HTML document). To query the remaining 99,990 records would be a gross squandering of CPU time, memory, and network capacity. To avoid such a scenario, you can limit the number of records returned with *LIMIT n*. The following command returns two records from the *titles* table:

```
SELECT title FROM titles LIMIT 2
```

title
Client/Server Survival Guide
Definitive Guide to Excel VBA

To return the next two records, execute a new query, but this time with *LIMIT offset, n*. Here *offset* specifies the number of the record at which access to the table is to begin. (Warning: The enumeration of data records begins with 0. An *offset* of n skips the first n records and, since counting begins with 0, starts processing at record number n.)

```
SELECT title FROM titles LIMIT 2, 2
```

title
Linux
Web Application Development with PHP 4.0

Determing the Number of Records Suppressed by LIMIT (SQL_CALC_FOUND_ROWS, FOUND_ROWS)

When you execute a *SELECT* query with *LIMIT*, you obtain only a partial result. Particularly in the page-by-page display of data, it would often be helpful to know exactly how many records are available altogether.

Beginning with MySQL 4.0, you can use in a *SELECT* query the additional option *SQL_CALC_FOUND_ROWS*. Then, in a second query you can evaluate the SQL function *FOUND_ROWS()*, which tells how many records the query would have returned without *LIMIT*.

The following query returns the three alphabetically first titles from the *titles* table. Then, with *FOUND_ROWS* it is determined how many records are available altogether:

```
USE mylibrary
SELECT SQL_CALC_FOUND_ROWS title FROM titles
ORDER BY title LIMIT 3
```

title
A Guide to the SQL Standard
Alltid den där Annette
Client/Server Survival Guide

```
SELECT FOUND_ROWS()
```

FOUND_ROWS()
26

The use of *CALC_FOUND_ROWS* and *FOUND_ROWS* is especially useful in complex queries in which a separate *SELECT* query for determing the number of records would be time intensive. Note, however, that the option *CALC_FOUND_ROWS* prevents certain kinds of optimization that MySQL carries out in *LIMIT* queries. Therefore, use *CALC_FOUND_ROWS* only when you then really wish to evaluate *FOUND_ROWS*.

Sorting Results (ORDER BY)

SELECT returns its results in no particular order. If you would like your list of results ordered, then you must request this explicitly via *ORDER BY column*. The following command returns an alphabetically ordered list of the authors in the *mylibrary* database.

```
SELECT authName FROM authors ORDER BY authName
```

authName
Bitsch Gerhard
Darween Hugh
Date Chris
DuBois Paul
Edwards E.
Garfinkel Simon
Gerken Till
Harkey D.
Holz Helmut
...

If you would like the reverse order, then you must add the key word *DESC* (for *descending*) to *ORDER BY*, as in, for example, *ORDER BY authName DESC.*

In sorting by character string, the order is determined by the character set chosen at the startup of MySQL. This is of particular importance when the character strings contain special characters outside of the ASCII character set. Information on selecting the character set for sorting can be found in Chapter 10.

> **REMARK**   *In point of fact, the sequence of* SELECT *results, even without* ORDER BY, *is not random, but it depends rather on the order in which the records are stored in the table. However, you probably have no influence on this order. Therefore, do not expect that* SELECT *results will have a particular order. In the case of new tables, query results usually are returned ordered by increasing* id *number (if* id *is an* AUTO_INCREMENT *field). But as soon as records are altered or deleted, the ordering is ruined. Do not rely on it!*

> **TIP**   *If you require your data records to be returned in a random order, then use* ORDER BY RAND(). *For example, to choose two records from a table at random, use* ORDER BY RAND() LIMIT 2.
>
> *Note, however, that* ORDER BY RAND() LIMIT n *without additional conditions is a very costly operation. For each record in the table, a random number must be generated. Then all the random numbers are sorted so that the first* n *records can be returned.*

Selecting Data Records by Conditions (WHERE, HAVING)

Often, it is not all of the records in a table that are of interest, but only those that satisfy one or more conditions. Such conditionals are introduced with *WHERE*. In our first example, we wish to display the names of only those authors whose surname starts with one of the letters L through Z:

```
SELECT authName FROM authors WHERE authName>='L'
```
author
Orfali R.
Pohl Peter
Ratschiller Tobias
Reese G.
...

In our second example, we employ the operator *LIKE* to compare character strings. The query determines all authors whose names contain the sequence of letters *er*. With the operator *LIKE*, the character % serves as a placeholder for an arbitrary character string.

```
SELECT authName FROM authors WHERE authName LIKE '%er%'
```
author
Bitsch Gerhard
Gerken Till
Kofler Michael
Kramer David
Pohl Peter
Ratschiller Tobias
Schmitt Bernd
Yarger R.J.

> **CAUTION** *Comparisons with* LIKE *can be very slow when they are applied to large tables. All the data records must be read and analyzed. It is impossible to use indexes to optimize such queries. A frequently used alternative to* LIKE *is the employment of a full-text index; see Chapter 7.*

Comparisons with a large number of values can be carried out easily with *IN*:

```
SELECT authID, authName FROM authors
WHERE authID IN (2, 7, 12)
```

authID	authName
2	Kramer David
7	Gerken Till
12	Yarger R.J.

> **REMARK** *Instead of formulating conditionals with* WHERE, *you could instead use* HAVING. *The* WHERE *conditionals are executed first, while* HAVING *conditionals are used only on intermediate results (returned by* WHERE*). The advantage of* HAVING *is that the conditions can also be applied to calculated fields (for example, to* SUM(columnXy) *in a* GROUP BY *query). An example appears in the section after next.*
>
> HAVING *conditionals are less easily optimized for MySQL than* WHERE *conditionals, and they should be avoided if an equivalent* WHERE *is possible.*

> **REMARK** *Please note that the conditional* colname = NULL *is not permitted. If you are searching for records that contain* NULL, *you must work with* ISNULL(colname).

Queries with Related Tables

Up to now, all of our examples with *SELECT* have been applied to the search for records from a single table. However, with relational databases we are usually dealing with a number of related tables. Therefore, we are usually interested in applying a *SELECT* command to combine data from several tables. For this we will use the *JOIN* syntax.

JOINs *Across Two Tables*

A first attempt to create a list of all book titles (column *title*) together with their publishers (column *publName*) from the tables *titles* and *publishers* is a colossal failure:

```
USE mylibrary
SELECT title, publName FROM titles, publishers
```

title	publName
Client/Server Survival Guide	Addison-Wesley
Definitive Guide to Excel VBA	Addison-Wesley
Linux	Addison-Wesley
Web Application Development with PHP 4.0	Addison-Wesley
Client/Server Survival Guide	Apress
Definitive Guide to Excel VBA	Apress
Linux	Apress
Web Application Development with PHP 4.0	Apress
Client/Server Survival Guide	New Riders
Definitive Guide to Excel VBA	New Riders
Linux	New Riders
Web Application Development with PHP 4.0	New Riders
...	

MySQL returns a list of all possible combinations of titles and publishers. In our relatively small database we can pick ourselves up from this minicatastrophe without too much damage. But imagine a database with 10,000 titles and 500 publishers, resulting in 5,000,000 combinations.

If queries spanning several tables are to return sensible results, precise information must be given as to how the data from the different tables are to be joined together. One possibility for formulating this connection is offered by *WHERE*. Since the linking field *publID* occurs in both tables, we must use the form *table.column* to indicate precisely which field is meant.

```
SELECT title, publName FROM titles, publishers
WHERE titles.publID = publishers.publID
```

title	publName
Linux, 5th ed.	Addison-Wesley
Definitive Guide to Excel VBA	Apress
Client/Server Survival Guide	Addison-Wesley
Web Application Development with PHP 4.0	New Riders
MySQL	New Riders
MySQL & mSQL	O'Reilly & Associates
...	

There are quite a few additional ways of arriving at the same result. One variant consists in creating the table list with *LEFT JOIN* and then forming the linking connection with *ON*:

```
SELECT title, publName
  FROM titles LEFT JOIN publishers
    ON titles.publID = publishers.publID
```

Another variant makes use of the key word *USING*, in which the common linking field is specified. However, this variant assumes that the linking field (in this case *publID*) has the same name in both tables. That is, of course, not always the case:

```
SELECT title, publName
  FROM titles LEFT JOIN publishers
USING (publID)
```

JOINs *Across Three or More Tables*

Things become a bit more confusing when the query must examine data from more than two tables. The following query returns a list of all book titles with all their authors. (Books with several authors occur in this list with multiplicity.)

```
SELECT title, authName
  FROM titles, rel_title_author, authors
WHERE titles.titleID = rel_title_author.titleID
  AND authors.authID = rel_title_author.authID
ORDER BY title
```

title	author
A Guide to the SQL Standard	Date Chris
A Guide to the SQL Standard	Darween Hugh
Alltid den där Annette	Pohl Peter
Client/Server Survival Guide	Orfali R.
Client/Server Survival Guide	Harkey D.
Client/Server Survival Guide	Edwards E.
Definitive Guide to Excel VBA	Kofler Michael
Definitive Guide to Excel VBA	Kramer David
Excel 2000 programmieren	Kofler Michael
Jag saknar dig, jag saknar dig	Pohl Peter
LaTeX	Kopka Helmut
Linux für Internet und Intranet	Holz Helmut
Linux für Internet und Intranet	Schmitt Bernd
Linux für Internet und Intranet	Tikart Andreas
Linux, 5th ed.	Kofler Michael
Maple	Kofler Michael
Maple	Komma Michael
Maple	Bitsch Gerhard
...	

Our next example is somewhat more complex: Here we generate a list of publishers and their authors. (Thus the query determines which authors write for which publishers.) The connection between publishers and authors is made via the tables *titles* and *rel_title_author*, so that altogether, four tables are brought into play.

New in this query is the SQL key word *DISTINCT*. It has the effect that equivalent data records are output only once. Since there are authors in the *mylibrary* database who have written several books (for the same publisher), the simple joining of these tables would result in many combinations in which an author and publisher combination occurred with multiplicity.

```
SELECT DISTINCT publName, authName
  FROM publishers, titles, rel_title_author, authors
WHERE titles.titleID = rel_title_author.titleID
  AND authors.authID = rel_title_author.authID
```

```
AND publishers.publID = titles.publID
ORDER BY publName, authName
```

publName	authName
Addison-Wesley	Bitsch Gerhard
Addison-Wesley	Darween Hugh
Addison-Wesley	Date Chris
Addison-Wesley	Edwards E.
Addison-Wesley	Harkey D.
. . .	
Apress	Kofler Michael
Apress	Kramer David
New Riders	DuBois Paul
New Riders	Gerken Till
New Riders	Ratschiller Tobias
. . .	

Syntax Variants

If you read about the details of *FROM* under the description of the *SELECT* syntax in the MySQL documentation, you may find your head spinning from the large number of (almost) identical variants. Here is a brief overview:

JOIN *without condition (combination of all possibilities)*

(1) *FROM table1, table2*

(2) *FROM table1 JOIN table2*

(3) *FROM table1 CROSS JOIN table2*

(4) *FROM table1 INNER JOIN table2*

(5) *FROM table1 STRAIGHT_JOIN table2*

In (1) through (4), MySQL tries on its own to find an optimal sequence for access to the data. Variant (5) is distinguished from the other four in that there, the order of data extraction from the tables is not optimized by MySQL. Option (5) is then to be recommended when you have doubts as to MySQL's ability to optimize its performance.

JOIN *(with condition)*

(1) *FROM table1, table2 WHERE table1.xyID = table2.xyID*

(2) *FROM table1 LEFT [OUTER] JOIN table2 ON table1.xyID = table2.xyID*

(3) *FROM table1 LEFT [OUTER] JOIN table2 USING (xyID)*

(4) *FROM table1 NATURAL [LEFT [OUTER]] JOIN table2*

(5) *FROM table2 RIGHT [OUTER] JOIN table1 ON table1.xyID = table2.xyID*

(6) *FROM table2 RIGHT [OUTER] JOIN table1 USING (xyID)*

With option (1), only those fields that are identical are considered in joining the two tables. With (2) and (4), on the other hand, for every record of the first (left) table a result record is generated, even when the linked field contains *NULL*. For example, if the *titles* table is used for *table1*, and the *publishers* table for *table2*, then *LEFT JOIN* will return even those titles for which no publisher name has been stored. (The key word *OUTER* is optional and has no effect on the function.)

Variants (5) and (6) correspond exactly to (2) and (3). Note, however, that *table1* and *table2* have been interchanged. *RIGHT JOIN* thus considers the query in a certain sense from the other direction. The MySQL documentation recommends not using *RIGHT JOIN* for improved compatibility with other databases, but instead using *LEFT JOIN* (with exchanged order of tables).

The variants with *USING* and *NATURAL* work only when the *ID* fields in both tables have the same name. In the case of *NATURAL*, like-named fields in both tables are used for joining. For *NATURAL* to work, the *ID* fields must have the same name and type. Furthermore, there must be no other like-named fields.

> **WARNING**   *Please note that with* LEFT JOIN *the order of the tables is significant.*
>
> - titles LEFT JOIN publishers *returns titles that have no publisher, but no publishers that have not published a single title.*
>
> - publishers LEFT JOIN titles *returns, contrariwise, publishers that have yet to publish a title, but no titles that do not have an associated publisher.*
>
> *In contrast to many other SQL dialects, MySQL recognizes no* FULL JOIN, *which would return all such combinations.*

Uniting Query Results

Starting with MySQL 4.0, with *UNION* you can unite two or more *SELECT* queries. You thereby obtain a table of results in which the results of the individual queries are arranged one after another:

```
SELECT command UNION [ALL] SELECT command ...
```

The following example shows how the results of two *SELECT* commands on the same table are united. (Of course, the queries could also be with regard to separate tables, but then you would have to be sure that the tables had the same number of columns. Furthermore, the columns should exhibit the same data type. If that is not the case, then MySQL attempts to fit the data to the data type of the first *SELECT* command.)

```
USE mylibrary
SELECT * FROM authors WHERE authName LIKE 'b%'
UNION
SELECT * FROM authors WHERE authName LIKE 'g%'
  authID authName
      22 Bitsch Gerhard
      26 Garfinkel Simon
       7 Gerken Till
```

Normally, duplicate records are automatically eliminated from the result. Only when you use *UNION ALL* does the result contain the duplicates.

You can also place the individual *SELECT* terms in parentheses. Then, for each part of the query, as well as for the complete result, you can use *LIMIT* and *ORDER* as you wish. The following query first selects at most ten records from the tables *tbl1* and *tbl2* and unites them. From these (at most twenty) records, only the five most recent are displayed:

```
(SELECT * FROM tbl1 ORDER BY colA LIMIT 10)
UNION
(SELECT * FROM tbl2 ORDER BY colA LIMIT 10)
ORDER BY colTimestamp LIMIT 5
```

> **REMARK**   *At present,* UNION *is the only set operator in MySQL. The key words* MINUS *and* INTERSECT, *available in many other database systems, are not availble in MySQL.*

Grouped Queries, Aggregate Functions

The data records for our books, stored in the *mylibrary* database, are assigned to various categories. If you require information as to which categories contain which books, then you will find the following query helpful. (Warning: Books that have not been assigned to a category will not appear at all. If you wish to see all books, then you must execute *FROM titles LEFT JOIN categories ON titles.catID = categories.catID.*)

```
USE mylibrary
SELECT catName, title FROM titles, categories
WHERE titles.catID = categories.catID
ORDER BY catName, title
```

catName	title
Children's books	Alltid den där Annette
Children's books	Jag saknar dig, jag saknar dig
Computer books	LaTeX
Computer books	Linux, 5th ed.
Computer books	Maple
Databases	Client/Server Survival Guide
Databases	Visual Basic Datenbankprogrammierung
Programming	Definitive Guide to Excel VBA
Programming	Visual Basic
SQL	A Guide to the SQL Standard

If you wish to determine only how many books there are in each category, you can put the fingers of both hands to work and begin counting in the list just produced: two children's books, three computer books not more precisely categorized, two books on databases, and so on.

It has probably crossed your mind that there may be a more automated way of doing this: *GROUP BY name* creates in the resulting list a group for each member of the specified column. With *GROUP BY catName* in the above query a single row is made out of the two entries with *catName='Children's books'*. Which title is shown depends on the sort order, if any.

We see that with *GROUP BY* alone we do not accomplish much (unless we merely wanted to generate a list of all the categories, but there are easier ways of accomplishing that). However, in connection with *GROUP BY*, SQL supports *aggregate functions*. This means that in the column list at the beginning of a *SELECT* you can use functions like *COUNT, SUM, MIN*, and *MAX*. It is when these functions are brought into play that *GROUP BY* finally becomes a useful tool, as is demonstrated by the following example: We shall count (*COUNT*) how many entries are associated with each category.

New here is also the use of the key word *AS*, whereby the second column in the query is given the name *nrOfItems*. Without *AS*, the column would have the name *'COUNT(itemID)'*, which not only would be a bit confusing, but would increase the amount of typing each time the column was referenced (e.g., in *ORDER BY*).

```
SELECT catName, COUNT(title) AS nrOfItems
FROM titles, categories
WHERE titles.catID = categories.catID
GROUP BY catname
ORDER BY catname
```

catName	nrOfItems
Children's books	2
Computer books	3
Databases	2
Programming	2
SQL	1

If you would like a list of *all* categories, even those for which at present there are no books, then you must make the connection between the two tables with *LEFT JOIN* (as described in the previous section). This time, the resulting list will be sorted so that the categories with the most books are displayed first.

```
SELECT catName, COUNT(title) AS nrOfItems
FROM categories textbfLEFT JOIN  titles ON titles.catid = categories.catid
GROUP BY catname
ORDER BY nrOfItems DESC
```

catName	nrOfItems
Computer books	5
MySQL	4
Programming	3
Children's books	3
PHP	2
Databases	2
Literature and fiction	2
LaTeX, TeX	1
SQL	1
Object-oriented databases	0
All books	0
Relational Databases	0
Perl	0

GROUP BY *for Several Columns*

GROUP BY can also be used for several columns. The following query provides information about the numbers of book titles in various languages and the categories in which they appear. Note that with this query, all titles are lost that are not assigned a language or category.

```
SELECT COUNT(*), langName, catName
FROM titles, languages, categories
WHERE titles.catID = categories.catID
  AND titles.langID = languages.langID
GROUP BY titles.langID, titles.catID
```

COUNT(*)	langName	catName
1	english	Computer books
1	english	PHP
1	english	SQL
2	english	MySQL
5	deutsch	Computer books
1	deutsch	Databases
3	deutsch	Programming
1	deutsch	Relational Databases
1	deutsch	PHP
1	deutsch	Children's books
1	deutsch	Literature and fiction
1	deutsch	MySQL
1	deutsch	LaTeX, TeX
2	svensk	Children's books
3	svensk	Literature and fiction
1	norsk	Literature and fiction

Altering Data (*INSERT, UPDATE,* and *DELETE*)

> **TIP**   *MySQL novices frequently change or delete more records than intended in applying* UPDATE *and* DELETE *commands, by applying them to the entire table. If you launch* mysql *with the option* --i-am-a-dummy, *then the risk of accidental damage is reduced considerably:* mysql *refuses to execute* UPDATE *and* DELETE *commands without a* WHERE.

Executing a Backup

Before you start playing around with your database, you should consider backing up individual tables or perhaps the whole database, so that after you make a mess of things, you can restore the database to its original pristine condition.

Creating Copies of a Table

The following instruction creates a new table with the name *newtable* and copies all the data records of *table* into the new table. The column definitions of the new table are identical to those of the old one, but there are some occasional differences. For example, the attribute *AUTO_INCREMENT* is lost. Moreover, in the new table, no indexes are created:

```
CREATE TABLE newtable SELECT * FROM table
```

Restoring Tables

With the given commands, first all data records of the original table *table* are deleted. Then the records that were saved into *newtable* are copied back into *table*. (The original *AUTO_INCREMENT* values remain untouched during the copying back and forth.)

```
DELETE FROM table
INSERT INTO table SELECT * FROM newtable
```

If you no longer require the backup data, you can simply delete *newtable*:

```
DROP TABLE newtable
```

Backing Up a Table

To the extent that you have access in MySQL to the file system (which depends on the security settings), you can back up a table very efficiently with *BACKUP TABLE*:

```
BACKUP TABLE table TO '/tmp/backups'
```

Instead of *'/tmp/backups'* you can specify an existing directory into which the files are to be copied. To recreate the table, execute *RESTORE TABLE*.

```
RESTORE TABLE table FROM '/tmp/backups'
```

BACKUP and *RESTORE* work only for MyISAM tables (not for InnoDB tables). Under Unix/Linux, the backup directory for the account under which MySQL is executed must be writable:

```
root# mkdir /tmp/backups
root# chown mysql /tmp/backups
```

Making a Backup of an Entire Database

With the program mysqldump (under Windows it is mysqldump.exe) you can create a backup file (in text format) of a complete database. Note, please, that you cannot execute mysqldump from within mysql, but rather, you must launch it as a freestanding program in a shell or command window. (The program will be described in detail in Chapter 10.)

```
user$ mysqldump -u loginame -p --opt dbname > backupfile
Enter password: xxx
```

Restoring a Database

There is no counterpart to mysqldump for reading in a saved database. Instead, you will have to rely on our old friend the SQL monitor mysql, where you give the backup file as input source. The database *dbname* must already exist.

```
user$ mysql -u loginname -p dbname < backupfile
Enter password: xxx
```

Of course, you can also recreate the database in interactive mode:

```
user$ mysql -u root -p
Enter password: xxx
Welcome to the MySQL monitor ...
mysql> CREATE DATABASE dbname; -- if dbname does not yet exist
mysql> USE dbname;
mysql> SOURCE backupfile;
```

Inserting Data Records (INSERT)

With *INSERT* you can add a new record to a table. After the name of the table there must appear first a list of the column names and then a list with the values to be inserted. (Columns with a default value, columns that can be *NULL*, and *AUTO_INCREMENT* columns do not have to be specified.)

In the following example, a new data record is saved in the table *titles* in the *mylibrary* database. Only two columns (*title* and *year*) will be specified. All remaining columns are taken care of by MySQL: A new *AUTO_INCREMENT* value is placed in *titleID*, and in the other columns, the requisite default value or *NULL*. (This process is allowed only because when the *titles* table was created, a default value was specifically provided for, and *NULL* was specified as a permissible value.)

```
USE mylibrary
INSERT INTO titles (title, year)
VALUES ('MySQL', 2001)
```

One may do without naming the columns if values for all columns (including default and *AUTO_INCREMENT* columns) are given and the order of the columns is followed exactly. In the case of *titles*, there are quite a few columns: *titleID, title, subtitle, edition, publID, catID, langID, year, isbn,* and *comment.*

For some columns, the value *NULL* is given. In most cases MySQL actually stores the value *NULL.* The only exception here is the column *titleID*, into which MySQL automatically places a new ID number. Instead of *NULL*, you can specify an explicit

ID number. However, this will result in an error if this number is already being used by another record. (There is one further column type in which MySQL places a value on its own if *NULL* is given: In *TIMESTAMP* columns, instead of *NULL*, the current date and time are stored.)

```
INSERT INTO titles
VALUES (NULL, 'deleteme', ' ', 1, NULL, NULL, NULL, 2001, NULL, NULL)
```

Another syntax variant enables several new records to be inserted with a single command:

```
INSERT INTO table (columnA, columnB, columnC)
VALUES ('a', 1, 2), ('b', 12, 13), ('c', 22, 33), ...
```

INSERT *with Related Tables*

If you are dealing with related tables, then normally, insertion of records is not accomplished with a single *INSERT* command. For example, to store a book record in the *mylibrary* database, new records must be stored in at least the tables *titles* and *rel_title_author*. If the new book was written by an author or authors whose names have not yet been stored in the database, or if it was published by a publisher that is currently unknown to the database, then new data records will also have to be added to the tables *publishers* and *authors* (see also Figure 5-2).

However, now we have the problem that not all the data for the insert command are known at the outset. To store a book published by a new publisher, the *publID* of the publisher must be given in the *titles* table. This is an *AUTO_INCREMENT* value, which is generated by MySQL only when the new publisher is stored in the database.

There must, then, be a way to access the last-generated *AUTO_INCREMENT* value. And indeed there is. The function for this is *LAST_INSERT_ID()*, which returns the *AUTO_INCREMENT* value of the last *INSERT* command. This function has effect only within the current connection. That is, *AUTO_INCREMENT* values that may have arisen through the *INSERT* commands of other database users are ignored.

The following lines show how a book with a good deal of new information (three new authors, a new publisher) is stored. The book in question is the following: Randy Yarger, George Reese, Tim King: *MySQL & mSQL*. O'Reilly 1999.

```
INSERT INTO publishers (publName) VALUES ('O''Reilly & Associates')
SELECT LAST_INSERT_ID()
    4 <--- publID for the publisher

INSERT INTO authors (authName) VALUES (('Yarger R.')
SELECT LAST_INSERT_ID()
    12 <--- authorID for the first author

INSERT INTO author (author) VALUES (('Reese G.')
SELECT LAST_INSERT_ID()
    13 <--- authorID for the second author

INSERT INTO author (author) VALUES (('King T.'')
SELECT LAST_INSERT_ID()
    14 <--- authorID for the third author
```

```
INSERT INTO titles (title, publID, year)
VALUES ('MySQL & mSQL', 4, 1999)
SELECT LAST_INSERT_ID()
     9 <--- titleID for the book
INSERT INTO rel_title_author
VALUES (9, 12), (9, 13), (9,14)
```

In practice, you will not, of course, input these commands manually. That would be terribly boring, and the probability of error would be high. Rather, the insertions will be made in program code by way of a user interface. The code will concern itself not only with the evaluation and reevaluation of the *ID* values, but will ensure that authors and publishers who already appear in the database are not stored again by mistake.

Altering Data Records (UPDATE)

With *UPDATE* you can change individual fields of an existing database. The usual syntax of this command is the following:

```
UPDATE tablename
SET column1=value1, column2=value2, ...
WHERE columnID=n
```

Thus individual fields of a record specified by its *ID* value are changed. In the following example we change the title of the Linux book (*titleID=1*):

```
USE mylibrary
UPDATE titles SET title='Linux, 5th ed.' WHERE titleID=1
```

If *UPDATE* is used without *WHERE*, then the change is instituted for all data records (so beware!). The following command, for example, would change the publication date of all books to the year 2003:

```
UPDATE titles SET year=2003
```

With certain restrictions, calculations are permissible in *UPDATE* commands. Let us suppose that the price of the book was stored in the *titles* table. Then it would be easy to increase all prices by five percent:

```
UPDATE title SET price=price*1.05
```

Editing Data Records in Sorted Lists (UPDATE *with* ORDER BY *and* LIMIT)

If you want to change the first or last *n* data records, with the *UPDATE* command you can also specify *ORDER BY* and *LIMIT*. Such a possbility has existed only since MySQL 4.0. The following command sets the field *mydata* to zero for the first ten data records (in alphabetical order) of the table *tablename*:

```
UPDATE tablename SET mydata=0 ORDER BY name LIMIT 10
```

Updating with Linked Tables

Furthermore, since MySQL 4.0 you can process the data from several tables with *UPDATE* commands. The following example changes the column *columnA* of *table1*, where the new data come from *table2.columnB*. The link between the two fields is established via the common ID field *table1ID* (a genuine example of a multitable *UPDATE* command is given in Chapter 7:

```
UPDATE table1, table1
SET table1.columnA = table.columnB
WHERE table1.table1ID = table2.table1ID
```

Deleting Data Records (DELETE)

There can be little doubt that the syntactically simplest command of this section is *DELETE*. All records selected with *WHERE* are simply deleted. Here it is not required to specify the columns (indeed, it is not possible), since in any case, the entire data record is made to disappear without a trace. The following instruction deletes a single record from the *titles* table:

```
USE mylibrary
DELETE FROM titles WHERE titleID=8
```

> **CAUTION** *If* DELETE *is executed without a* WHERE *condition, then all the records of the table will be deleted. There is no "undo" possibility.*
> *The table itself with its definition of columns, indexes, etc., remains intact. If you wish to delete the table itself, then you must execute the command* DROP TABLE.

Deleting Records from Linked Tables

In MySQL 3.23, the *DELETE* command can be used with reference to only a single table. Since MySQL 4.0, the following syntax is allowed:

```
DELETE t1, t2 FROM t1, t2, t3 WHERE condition1 AND condition2 ...
```

With this, all data records from tables *t1* and *t2* that satisfy the specified conditions are deleted. The conditions may contain arbitrary connections among the tables *t1*, *t2*, and *t3*. (To formulate it more generally, *DELETE* deletes records from only those tables that are given before *FROM*. In the conditions, records can be used from all tables that appear after *FROM*.)

The following example deletes from the *titles* table all book titles of the author *Kofler Michael*. To find the titles to be deleted, a link is created among the three tables *tltles*, *rel_title_author*, and *authors*:

```
USE mylibrary[1ex] DELETE titles FROM titles, rel_title_author, authors
WHERE titles.titleID=rel_title_author.titleID
  AND authors.authID=rel_title_author.authID
  AND authors.authName='Kofler Michael'
```

The following variant of the command given above deletes not only the titles, but *Kofler Michael* from the *authors* table, as well as all records from *rel_tltle_author* that create the link between the author *Kofler Michael* and his books (the difference here is that now all three tables are listed before *FROM*):

```
DELETE titles, rel_title_author, authors
  FROM titles, rel_title_author, authors
WHERE titles.titleID=rel_title_author.titleID
  AND authors.authID=rel_title_author.authID
   AND authors.authName='Kofler Michael'
```

The linkage between the tables can also be made via *JOIN* operators.

Deleting Data Records from Sorted Lists (DELETE with ORDER BY and LIMIT)

From version 4.0, *ORDER BY* can be used in *DELETE* commands. This makes sense only in combination with *LIMIT*. Now it is possible to delete the first or last n elements of a table based on an arbitrary sort criterion. The following command deletes the author with the highest *authID* number from the *authors* table:

```
DELETE FROM authors ORDER BY authID DESC LIMIT 1
```

Creating New Tables

You can store the result of a query directly in a new table. (In practice, this path is often followed in order to store the results of a complex query temporarily.) To do this, you simply specify the name of a new table with *CREATE TABLE* and insert an ordinary *SELECT* command at the end of the instruction. The following instruction copies all titles with *catID=1* (category *Computer books*) into the new table *computerbooks*.

```
USE mylibrary
CREATE TABLE computerbooks
SELECT * FROM titles WHERE catID=1
```

From then on, the new table is available. With *SELECT* you can convince yourself that indeed the desired data are in the table:

```
SELECT title FROM computerbooks
```

title
Linux, 5th ed.
LaTeX
Mathematica
Maple
Practical UNIX & Internet security

When the time comes that you no longer have any need of the table *computerbooks*, you can easily delete it:

```
DROP TABLE computerbooks
```

#### CHAPTER 7

SQL Recipes

THIS CHAPTER CONTAINS A COLLECTION of small SQL examples that go somewhat beyond the elementary level of the other examples in this chapter. The goal is to give you an idea of some of the possibilities that the world of SQL opens to you and to provide recipes for solving frequently occurring problems.

Most of these examples are based on the example databases introduced in chapter 5, and so you can easily try these commands out yourself. However, we will also introduce some techniques based on imaginary databases and tables.

> **POINTER** *Examples of SQL commands appear in Chapter 5 on the subject of database design. Furthermore, many further examples are contained in the code in the examples of Chapters 12 through 17.*

Chapter Overview

Character Strings

MySQL recognizes a large number of functions that allow for the processing of character strings in queries. The following examples introduce several of these functions. A reference for MySQL functions for processing character strings can be found in Chapter 18.

Basic Functions

Concatenating Character Strings

CONCAT(s1, s2, ...) concatenates the given character strings into a single string. This function is useful for joining together several columns (for example, when you have stored first and last names in different columns and now wish to put them together):

```
SELECT CONCAT(firstname, ' ', lastname) FROM addresses
```

Extracting Parts of Character Strings

SUBSTRING(s, pos, n) returns *n* characters of the character string *s* starting at position *pos*. (The first character is addressed at position *pos=1*, not at *pos=0*.) The following command returns the first ten characters of all book titles form the *mylibrary* database:

```
USE mylibrary
SELECT SUBSTR(title, 1, 10) FROM titles
```

Those familiar with the syntax of the programming language Basic can use *LEFT*, *RIGHT*, and *MID* instead of *SUBSTR* to read strings conveniently from the beginning or from the end. We will offer an example of this later.

Determining the Length of a Character String

LENGTH(s) returns the number of characters in a character string.

Shortening Strings to a Particular Length

The function *IF(a, b, c)* evaluates expression *a*. If the result is (*TRUE*), the function returns *b*; otherwise, *c*.

The goal of the following example is to shorten book titles to the form "beginning of title, ... , end of title," so that the entire length of the resulting character string is at most thirty characters. Titles with thirty characters or fewer are unchanged:

```
SELECT IF(LENGTH(title)>30,
          CONCAT (LEFT(title, 20), ' ... ', RIGHT(title, 5)),
          title)
FROM titles AS shorttitle
```

shorttitle

```
Linux für Internet u ... ranet
Mathematica
Practical UNIX & Int ... urity
Visual Basic Datenba ... erung
  ...
```

Pattern Matching

Pattern Matching with LIKE

The operator *LIKE* is suited for simple pattern matching. It supports two wild cards: _ for a single arbitrary character, and % for an arbitrary number (including 0) of characters. As with ordinary string comparison, *LIKE* does not distinguish between uppercase and lowercase. Here is an example:

```
SELECT 'MySQL' LIKE '%sql'
    1
```

The following *SELECT* command returns all book titles that contain the character string SQL:

```
USE mylibrary
SELECT title FROM titles WHERE title LIKE '%SQL%'
```

If the character _ or % is itself to be used in the pattern to be matched, then it must be preceded by a backslash, as in *'50%' LIKE '%\%'*, which returns 1. If you wish to use a character other than the backslash as the escape character, then you may specify such a character with *ESCAPE*: *'50%' LIKE '%&%' ESCAPE '&'*, which also returns 1.

> **REMARK** *Please note that doing pattern matching in large tables is very slow. This holds for* LIKE, *and even more so for* REGEXP. *In many cases it makes more sense to do a full-text search instead of pattern matching.*

Pattern Matching with REGEXP

The command *REGEXP* offers many more possibilities for formulating a pattern, as does the equivalent command *RLIKE*. As with *LIKE*, case distinction is not made. Here we give simply a few syntatic examples. A table with the most important elements of *REGEXP* pattern matching appears in Chapter 18.

In the simplest case, *expr REGEXP pattern* tests whether the character string *pattern* is contained in *expr*:

```
SELECT 'abcabc' REGEXP 'abc',    'abcabc' REGEXP 'cb'
    1, 0
```

The search pattern does not have to describe the entire character string, but only a part. If you wish to encompass the entire character string, you must use ^ and $ in the search:

```
SELECT 'abc' REGEXP '^abc$', 'abcabc' REGEXP '^abc$'
  1, 0
```

Square brackets indicate a selection from among several characters, where a-c indicates the inclusive range from a to b. The operator + indicates that at least one of the characters must appear at least once in the search expression:

```
SELECT 'cde' REGEXP '[a-c]+', 'fgh' REGEXP '[a-c]+'
  1, 0
```

Parentheses indicate an entire character string, and curly braces indicate how many times the character string must appear in succession:

```
SELECT 'xabcabcz' REGEXP '(abc){2}', 'xabcyabcz' REGEXP '(abc){2}'
  1, 0
```

Note that *REGEXP* is successful when the the search pattern is found at any location within the character string.

> **POINTER** *A large number of additional examples can be found in the appendix to the MySQL documentation:*
>
> ```
> http://www.mysql.com/doc/en/Regexp.html
> ```

Binary Character String Comparison

Character strings are generally compared without regard to case sensitivity. That is, 'a'='A' returns 1 as result. If you wish to execute a binary search, you must write *BINARY* in front of one of the operands. *BINARY* is a "cast" operator. That is, it changes the data type of an operand (thus changes a number or character string into a binary object). *BINARY* can be used for ordinary string comparison and also for pattern matching with *LIKE* and *REGEXP*:

```
SELECT 'a'='A', BINARY 'a' = 'A', 'a' = BINARY 'A'
  1, 0, 0
SELECT 'abcabc' REGEXP 'ABC', 'abcabc' REGEXP BINARY 'ABC'
  1, 0
```

Editing Character Strings

Naturally, you can also use string functions to alter text in MySQL tables. The following examples assume that there exists a table *messages* with the column *author*

(*VARCHAR(60)*), which contains a name, an e-mail address, or some other text. The goal is to free this list of special characters and to make it anonymous. Therefore, everything except the first part of each name is to be expunged. Thus *Peter Miller* will become *Peter*, while *paul.simon@garfunkel.net* will be reduced to *paul*. This may be a somewhat unusual task, but you will see that the techniques introduced here are useful for many other applications.

Before having at it, you should make a copy of the column that is to be processed. Then if things go awry, you can restore the original state of the data:

```
ALTER TABLE messages ADD COLUMN origauthor VARCHAR(60)
UPDATE messages SET origauthor = author
```

In what follows, only *author* will be processed. The following command removes the double quote character ". For this, the function *REPLACE* is used:

```
UPDATE messages SET author = REPLACE(author, '"', '')
```

Next, each of the characters - , . _ @ will be replaced by a space:

```
UPDATE messages SET author = REPLACE(author, '-', ' ')
UPDATE messages SET author = REPLACE(author, '_', ' ')
UPDATE messages SET author = REPLACE(author, '@', ' ')
UPDATE messages SET author = REPLACE(author, ',', ' ')
UPDATE messages SET author = REPLACE(author, '.', ' ')
```

Now spaces will be searched for. If such a character is found, then apparently, the string consists of several parts (words). The *UPDATE* command truncates these strings to the first word. New here is the function *LOCATE*, which returns the position of a search pattern within a character string:

```
UPDATE messages SET author = LEFT(author, LOCATE(" ", author)-1)
WHERE LOCATE(" ", author) > 1
```

With *SELECT* one can check whether everything functioned as intended. (For privacy protection, here the original names and e-mail addresses have been replaced by *xxx*.)

```
SELECT author, origauthor FROM messages LIMIT 10
```

author	origauthor
Michael	Michael xxxxxxx
cjadner	cjadner@xxxxxx.xx
Frauke	"Frauke xxxxxxxxx"
Bernd	Bernd xxxxx, xxx@xxxxxxx.xx
jan	jan_xxxxx
test	test
Michael	Michael.xxxxxx@xxxxxx.xx
Thomas	Thomas xxxxxxxxx
Tobias	Tobias xxxx
sw410003	sw410003@xxxxxx.xxx.xxx

And now the column *origauthor* can be deleted:

```
ALTER TABLE messages DROP origauthor
```

Date and Time

Basically, dates and times in SQL commands must be given as character strings, using a syntax that the MySQL server understands. The following three queries are equivalent, and work for both *DATETIME* and *TIMESTAMP* columns:

```
SELECT COUNT(*) FROM table
WHERE d BETWEEN '2001-05-16 08:34:07' AND '2002-02-11 00:15:44'

SELECT COUNT(*) FROM table
WHERE d BETWEEN '2001/05/16 08:34:07' AND '2002/02/11 00:15:44'

SELECT COUNT(*) FROM table
WHERE d BETWEEN '20010516083407' AND '20020211001544'
```

Note that *BETWEEN a AND b* means that the start and end times are included (that is, *d>=a AND d<=b*).

Determining the Number of Records by Day, Month, etc.

It happens quite often that you want to know how many records there are for a particular day or month. Of course, you can execute a number of queries with *BETWEEN start AND end*. But it is much simpler to format the data field with various functions and determine the number using *GROUP BY* and *COUNT*.

Our first example returns the number of votes by month for the year 2002 for the database *bigvote*. Month and year are determined by the MySQL functions *MONTH* and *YEAR*:

```
USE bigvote
SELECT COUNT(*), MONTH(ts) AS m
FROM votelanguage
WHERE YEAR(ts)=2002
GROUP BY m
```

COUNT(*)	m
152	1
227	2
. . .	. . .
58	12

If you want all results (not just for one year), then the expression for the grouping must contain both the year and the month. For this, you should use the *DATE_FORMAT* function (whose syntax is described in Chapter 18):

```
SELECT COUNT(*), DATE_FORMAT(ts, '%Y-%m') AS m_y
FROM votelanguage
GROUP by m_y
```

count(*)	m_y
214	2001-05
111	2001-06
226	2001-07
...	...
73	2003-01

Calculations with Date and Time

MySQL offers, alas, only a few SQL functions for dealing with date and time. Therefore, it is seldom possible to execute date and time calculations directly with SQL commands. Instead, it is frequently necessary to use a client program that first executes a *SELECT* query and then carries out the calculations.

As the following example demonstrates, there are exceptional cases in which success can be attained using SQL code. But for this you have to transform date and time into a purely numerical format. The basis for the following example is the table *workingtimes*, in which working hours can be recorded:

```
USE test
CREATE TABLE workingtimes (
  id INT AUTO_INCREMENT,
  begintime DATETIME,
  endtime DATETIME,
  PRIMARY KEY (id))
INSERT INTO workingtimes (begintime, endtime) VALUES
  ('2003-03-27 7:15', '2003-03-27 18:00'),
  ('2003-03-28 8:00', '2003-03-28 18:00'),
  ('2003-03-29 7:30', '2003-03-29 16:50'),
  ('2003-03-30 7:00', '2003-03-30 17:15')
```

The first attempt to calculate the working time for each workday fails miserably. The reason is that MySQL interprets the character strings for the subtraction *endtime - begintime* with time values simply as integers, for example, *'2003-03-27 7:15:00'* as *20030327071500*. MySQL can subtract these numbers, of course, but the result is pure nonsense, since time is not recorded in the decimal system, with seconds and minutes in the range 0 to 59 instead of 0 to 99:

```
SELECT DATE_FORMAT(begintime, '%Y-%m-%d'), endtime - begintime
FROM workingtimes
```

DATE_FORMAT(begintime, '%Y-%m-%d')	endtime-begintime
2003-03-27	108500
2003-03-28	100000
2003-03-29	92000
2003-03-30	101500

With *UNIX_TIMESTAMP* you can transform time data into Unix *timestamps*. These are 32-bit integers that give the number of seconds that have elapsed since January 1, 1970. (Such a transformation thus makes sense only for times within the range 1970 to 2038.

For times before 1970, Unix *timestamps* are undefined, and after 2038, overflow kicks in.) After this transformation, the work time can be calculated in seconds:

```
SELECT DATE_FORMAT(begintime, '%Y-%m-%d') AS dt,
UNIX_TIMESTAMP(endtime) - UNIX_TIMESTAMP(begintime) AS s
FROM workingtimes
```

dt	s
2003-03-27	38700
2003-03-28	36000
2003-03-29	33600
2003-03-30	36900

To make these values in seconds comprehensible to human understanding, you can use the function *SEC_TO_TIME*. It returns a time value, where seconds have been calculated from midnight. (Times longer than twenty-four hours also appear in the form *hhhh:mm:ss*. Days are not calculated.)

```
SELECT DATE_FORMAT(begintime, '%Y-%m-%d') AS dt,
SEC_TO_TIME(UNIX_TIMESTAMP(endtime) - UNIX_TIMESTAMP (begintime)) AS t
FROM workingtimes
```

dt	t
2003-03-27	10:45:00
2003-03-28	10:00:00
2003-03-29	09:20:00
2003-03-30	10:15:00

The total working time can be easily determined with *SUM*, for example, for all days in March 2003:

```
SELECT SEC_TO_TIME(SUM(UNIX_TIMESTAMP(endtime)-UNIX_TIMESTAMP(begintime))) AS sumtime
FROM workingtimes
WHERE begintime>='2003-03-01 00:00:00' AND
begintime<='2003-03-31 23:59:59'
```

sumtime
40:20:00

In only a few cases do the SQL functions *DATE_ADD* and *DATE_SUB* help in carrying out such calculations. However, only a multiple of a particular interval can be added or subtracted, not an arbitrary time. (Details on the syntactic variants of *DATE_ADD* and *DATE_SUB* can be found in Chapter 18.) The following query returns the number of workdays with ten or more hours:

```
SELECT COUNT(*) FROM workingtimes
WHERE endtime >= DATE_ADD(begintime, INTERVAL 10 HOUR)
```

COUNT(*)
3

Peculiarities of TIMESTAMP

Avoiding Changes to TIMESTAMP

If you have a table with a *TIMESTAMP* column and execute an *UPDATE* on that table, then the content of the *TIMESTAMP* columns changes as well. (After all, the purpose of a *TIMESTAMP* column is to log the time of creation and the most recent change.)

It can happen, however, that in correcting a record you wish to avoid changing the *TIMESTAMP* value. For this, you can deal with the *TIMESTAMP* column explicitly with *SET*, returning the column to its previous value. The following example assumes that the *TIMESTAMP* column has the name *ts*:

```
UPDATE table SET data='new text', ts=ts WHERE id=123
```

When a large number of changes are in play, it is safer first to create a new column *oldts* of the previous *TIMESTAMP* values and copy all the *TIMESTAMP* values into it:

```
ALTER TABLE table ADD oldts DATETIME
UPDATE table SET ts=ts, oldts=ts
```

Now you can carry out all the changes you want without worrying about the *ts* column. When you are done, you simply restore the *ts* column to its original condition and delete the *oldts* column:

```
UPDATE table SET ts=oldts
ALTER TABLE table DROP oldts
```

Variables and Conditionals (*IF, CASE*)

The SQL dialect of MySQL contains few constructs that enable programming in the sense of a standard programming language. (This should change in MySQL 5.0, in which MySQL will allow the programming of custom functions with *stored procedures*.) But even with the few functions available now, we can do a bit of programming.

Variables

MySQL offers the possibility of storing simple values (scalars, but not lists, as, for example, the results of a *SELECT* command) in variables. These variables maintain their validity until the end of the MySQL connection. Variables are indicated by a prefixed "@" sign.

There are two syntax variants for variable assignment. If you are storing the result of a simple calculation, then *SET* is what you need, where either = or := may serve as the assignment operator:

```
SET @var1 := 3*4
```

More flexible than *SET* is *SELECT*, since with the latter, the assignment may now also contain the result of a query. With *SELECT* you must use := as the assignment operator. The following example returns from the table *votelanguage* from the questionnaire database *test_vote* (see Chapter 3) the time at which the last vote was cast:

```
USE test_vote SELECT @var2 := MAX(ts) FROM votelanguage
```

@var2 := MAX(ts)
20030115163054

You can also use *SELECT* to evaluate the contents of variables. Here case distinction is important (size matters):

```
SELECT @var1, @var2, @VAR2
```

@var1	@var2	@VAR2
20	20030115163054	NULL

Of course, you can use variables in queries or in other SQL commands. Here, however, variables can be used only in expressions, not, for example, in table or column names:

```
SELECT * FROM votelanguage WHERE ts = @var2
```

id	choice	ts
13	5	20030115163054

With variables, you can also perform simple calculations. The following example shows how you can determine, for the *bigvote* database, the percentage of participants who voted a certain way:

```
USE bigvote SELECT @total := COUNT(*) FROM votelanguage
```

@total := COUNT(*)
3315

```
SELECT choice, COUNT(*) / @total * 100
FROM votelanguage
GROUP BY choice
```

choice	COUNT(*) / @total * 100
1	10.015082956259
2	11.070889894419
3	15.444947209653
4	49.502262443439
5	7.782805429864
6	6.184012066365

In practice, however, such calculations are seldom used. Instead, for programming of complex query or insertion operations you should use a programming language such as PHP or Perl that makes variables available and therefore makes the use of MySQL variables unnecessary (see also the introductory example in Chapter 3).

> **POINTER**   *MySQL also recognizes system variables on a global level and the level of the connection. The use of such variables is descibed briefly in Chapter 18.*

IF *Queries*

With the function *IF* introduced earlier in this chapter, you can return one of two different results, depending on the evaluation of a condition:

```
IF(condition, result1, result2)
```

Of course, you can also nest *IF* queries:

```
IF(condition1, result1, IF(condition2, result2a, result2b))
```

If you wish to test whether a column contains *NULL*, you may use the function *ISNULL (expr)*. In many cases, you can use *IFNULL* instead of a nesting of *IF* and *ISNULL*. The following expression returns *expr2* if *expr1* is *NULL*, and *expr1* otherwise:

```
IFNULL(expr1, expr2)
```

corresponds to

```
IF(ISNULL(expr1), expr2, expr1)
```

CASE *Branching*

The *CASE* construct has two syntactic variants. The first of these returns *result1* if *expr=val1*, *result2* if *expr=val2*, and so on:

```
CASE expr
  WHEN val1 THEN result1
  WHEN val2 THEN result2
  ...
  ELSE resultn
END
```

With the second variant, it is not a condition that is evaluated, but an arbitrary number of conditions. The result is *result1* if condition *cond1* holds, *result2* if condition *cond2* holds, and so on:

```
CASE
  WHEN cond1 THEN result1
  WHEN cond2 THEN result2
  ...
  ELSE resultn
END
```

The following example returns an alphabetical list of all English book titles (*langID=1*) from the *mylibrary* database. What is of interest here is that the articles *a*, *an*, and *the* are ignored in sorting. Thus *A Programmer's Introduction* will be found under the letter P, not A. To achieve this, sorting is not done directly by title, but using the *CASE* construct, which returns a truncated character string, with any article removed:

```
USE mylibrary
SELECT title FROM titles
WHERE langID=1
ORDER BY
  CASE
    WHEN LEFT(title,2)="A "    THEN MID(title,3)
    WHEN LEFT(title,3)="An "   THEN MID(title,4)
    WHEN LEFT(title,4)="The "  THEN MID(title,5)
    ELSE title
  END title
```

title
A Guide to the SQL Standard
MySQL
MySQL Cookbook
PHP and MySQL Web Development
Practical UNIX & Internet security
A Programmer's Introduction to PHP 4.0

In analogy to this example, you could do the same with articles in German (*der, die, das*), French (*le, la, les*), or Russian (just kidding, Russian has no articles). You could also filter out the www in web addresses or any other part of a character string.

> **REMARK**   *Please observe that such search criteria significantly slow the execution of SQL queries. MySQL must first create a list of all titles and then sort them. It is not possible to use the existing index of the* title *column.*

Copying Data from One Table to Another

Creating a New Table in Copying

With the command *CREATE TABLE newtable SELECT . . . FROM oldtable* you can create a new table and insert into it all the records selected with a *SELECT* command. MySQL automatically generates all the necessary columns in *newtable* corresponding to the data selected by *SELECT*:

```
CREATE DATABASE newvote

USE newvote
CREATE TABLE votelanguage SELECT * FROM test_vote.votelanguage
    Query OK, 3328 rows affected (0.01 sec)
    Records: 3328 Duplicates: 0 Warnings: 0
```

If you now look at the table definition with *SHOW CREATE TABLE oldtable* or *newtable*, you will discover that in the process of copying, the index and *AUTO_INCREMENT* attribute for the column *id* have gone missing:

```
SHOW CREATE TABLE test_vote.votelanguage -- (original)
    CREATE TABLE votelanguage (
        id      int(11) NOT NULL AUTO_INCREMENT,
        choice tinyint(4) NOT NULL default '0',
        ts      timestamp(14) NOT NULL,
        PRIMARY KEY  (id)
    ) TYPE=MyISAM

SHOW CREATE TABLE newvote.votelanguage -- (new)
    CREATE TABLE votelanguage (
        id      int(11) NOT NULL default '0',
        choice tinyint(4) NOT NULL default '0',
        ts      timestamp(14) NOT NULL
    ) TYPE=MyISAM
```

The changes in table layout as a result of *CREATE TABLE . . . SELECT . . .* are burdensome in practice. Indexes are missing, column attributes disappear, *VARCHAR* tables become *CHAR* tables, and so on. Therefore, it is often better first to create the new table just like the old one with a separate *CREATE TABLE* command and then use *INSERT INTO . . . SELECT . . .* to fill it with data. The syntax for the *CREATE TABLE* command can be determined with *SHOW CREATE TABLE oldtable*:

```
CREATE TABLE votelanguage2 (
    id      INT NOT NULL AUTO_INCREMENT,
    choice TINYINT NOT NULL,
    ts      TIMESTAMP NOT NULL,
    PRIMARY KEY (id)
) TYPE=MyISAM
INSERT INTO votelanguage2 SELECT * FROM test_vote.votelanguage
```

Starting with MySQL 4.1, you can create the new table more simply thus:

```
CREATE TABLE newtable LIKE oldtable
```

> **POINTER** *Tables can also be copied and moved with the MySQL import and export commands. These commands are described in Chapter 10 in the discussion of backups.*

Copying into Existing Tables

To copy data into an existing table, use the command *INSERT INTO . . . SELECT*. You must make sure that the number of columns and their types match and that they are given in the correct order. If the source table has fewer columns than the target table, you can simply specify *NULL* or a fixed value for a column in the *SELECT* part, for example, *SELECT NULL, id, choice, timest, 0, "abc"*:

```
INSERT INTO newvote.votelanguage
SELECT id, choice, ts FROM test_vote.votelanguage
```

The greatest source of problems with such commands is, yet again, *AUTO_INCREMENT* fields. If the source and target tables contain records with the same ID number, then an *INSERT* command results in an error (*Duplicate entry xy for key . . .*). There are several ways of getting around this problem:

- You can use *INSERT IGNORE INTO . . .* , which avoids the error message and leads to the affected records being simply not copied.

- You can use *REPLACE . . .* instead of *INSERT INTO . . .* , which results in the affected records being overwritten on copying.

- You can change the *id* column in copying so that no conflicts arise. (This variant is possible only if no other records are referred to or if the foreign key field is also changed accordingly.)

```
SELECT @maxid := MAX(id) FROM newvote.votelanguage;
```

```
INSERT INTO newvote.votelanguage
SELECT id+@maxid, choice, ts FROM test_vote.votelanguage
```

Pivot Tables

Pivot tables collect information from a data source and arrange it in groups. The simplest way to understand these tables is by way of an example: In the *mylibrary* table, for each book title there can be stored a publisher, a category, and a language. Suppose we wish to know how many titles there are for every combination of category and language. Pivot tables provide a simple statistical evaluation of table data.

Many database systems offer special OLAP commands for creating pivot tables. OLAP stands for *online analytical processing* and includes special methods for the management and evaluation of multidimensional data, where here "multidimensional" refers to the several characteristics by which the data can be grouped. OLAP-capable database systems are often called *data warehouses*.

Unfortunately, MySQL does not yet support such OLAP functions. (These are planned for version 5.0.) Therefore, you generally have to use external programs to create pivot tables. (Especially well suited for this task is Microsoft Excel; see also Figure 17-5.)

In simple cases, you can make use of SQL functions in MySQL. Of particular practical use is the function *SUM* in combination with *IF*. *SUM* allows for the return of the sum of a grouped column. With *IF*, the formation of the sum can be made dependent on a number of criteria. The following two examples show how to proceed.

The Pivot Tables titles, languages, categories

For our first example we use the *mylibrary* database. The goal is to return a table that tells how many titles there are in each combination of category and language (of course, only for those titles that have such information associated with them). The starting data look like this:

```
USE mylibrary

SELECT title, langname, catname
FROM titles, categories, languages
WHERE titles.catID = categories.catID
  AND titles.langID = languages.langID
```

title	langname	catname
A Guide to the SQL Standard	english	SQL
Practical UNIX & Internet security	english	Computer books
MySQL	english	MySQL
MySQL Cookbook	english	MySQL
PHP and MySQL Web Development	english	PHP
Visual Basic	deutsch	Programming
Excel 2000 programmieren	deutsch	Programming
LaTeX	deutsch	Computer books
Nennen wir ihn Anna	deutsch	Children's books
Mathematica	deutsch	Computer books
Maple	deutsch	Computer books
Visual Basic Datenbankprogrammierung	deutsch	Databases
MySQL	deutsch	MySQL
PHP 4	deutsch	PHP
Mit LaTeX ins Web	deutsch	LaTeX, TeX
PostgreSQL	deutsch	Relational Databases
Anklage Vatermord	deutsch	Literature and fiction
Linux, 6th ed	deutsch	Computer books
Mathematica	deutsch	Computer books
Java	deutsch	Programming
Jag saknar dig, jag saknar dig	svensk	Children's books
Alltid den där Annette	svensk	Children's books
Kärleken	svensk	Literature and fiction
Comédia Infantil	svensk	Literature and fiction
Hunderna i Riga	svensk	Literature and fiction
Ute av verden	norsk	Literature and fiction

We will now group this list by category (*GROUP BY*). For each category we will use *SUM(IF(titles.langID=n, 1, 0))* to count the titles that appear in a particular language. *COUNT(*)* counts the titles in the category (independent of the category):

```
SELECT catName,
       SUM(IF(titles.langID=1, 1, 0)) AS english,
       SUM(IF(titles.langID=2, 1, 0)) AS deutsch,
       SUM(IF(titles.langID=3, 1, 0)) AS svensk,
       SUM(IF(titles.langID=4, 1, 0)) AS norsk,
       COUNT(*)
FROM titles, categories, languages
```

```
WHERE titles.catID = categories.catID
  AND titles.langID = languages.langID
GROUP BY catName
```

catName	english	deutsch	svensk	norsk	COUNT(*)
Children's books	0	1	2	0	3
Computer books	1	5	0	0	6
Databases	0	1	0	0	1
LaTeX, TeX	0	1	0	0	1
Literature and fiction	0	1	3	1	5
MySQL	2	1	0	0	3
PHP	1	1	0	0	2
Programming	0	3	0	0	3
Relational Databases	0	1	0	0	1
SQL	1	0	0	0	1

There is an obvious problem with this query in the *SUM(. . .)* terms. What would happen if the *languages* column contained not four, but twenty or thirty languages? In such cases you would have to write the SQL code for the query in a client program (e.g., in a PHP script): First you would obtain a list of all languages, then for each language, add a *SUM(. . .)* term to the SQL query.

The total numbers of titles for each language could be obtained thus:

```
SELECT langName, COUNT(*)
FROM titles, categories, languages
WHERE titles.catID = categories.catID
  AND titles.langID = languages.langID
GROUP BY langName
```

langName	COUNT(*)
deutsch	15
english	5
norsk	1
svensk	5

Pivot Table Query Results by Month

Our second example evaluates the table *bigvote.votelanguage*, with query results of a simple poll (see Chapter 3). The goal is to display for each month the percentages of votes, in order to determine a change in opinion or to detect an attempt at manipulating the results. The starting data, about 3300 records, look like this:

```
USE bigvote SELECT * FROM votelanguage LIMIT 5
```

id	choice	ts
1	4	20010516083407
2	3	20010516083407
3	5	20010516083407
4	4	20010516083407
5	2	20010516083407

It is easy to determine the number of participants in the poll by month:

```
SELECT DATE_FORMAT(ts, '%Y-%m') AS mnth, COUNT(*)
FROM votelanguage
GROUP BY mnth
```

textitmnth	textitCOUNT(*)
2001-05	214
2001-06	111
...	...
2002-12	58
2003-01	73

The number of votes for each programming language is determined with *SUM(IF(...))*:

```
SELECT DATE_FORMAT(ts, '%Y-%m') AS mnth,
       SUM(IF(choice=1, 1, 0)) AS c,
       SUM(IF(choice=2, 1, 0)) AS java,
       SUM(IF(choice=3, 1, 0)) AS perl,
       SUM(IF(choice=4, 1, 0)) AS php,
       SUM(IF(choice=5, 1, 0)) AS vb,
       SUM(IF(choice=6, 1, 0)) AS other,
       COUNT(*)
FROM votelanguage
GROUP BY mnth
```

mnth	c	java	perl	php	vb	other	COUNT(*)
2001-05	20	24	30	110	16	14	214
2001-06	6	13	15	64	7	6	111
...							
2002-12	8	4	6	31	5	4	58
2003-01	7	14	13	24	10	5	73

If you now want to know the percentage distribution, you have to divide the *SUM* expressions by *COUNT(*)*. The results are then made readable by multiplying by 100 and using the *ROUND* function:

```
SELECT DATE_FORMAT(ts, '%Y-%m') AS mnth,
       ROUND(SUM(IF(choice=1, 1, 0)) * 100 / COUNT(*), 1) AS c,
       ROUND(SUM(IF(choice=2, 1, 0)) * 100 / COUNT(*), 1) AS java,
       ROUND(SUM(IF(choice=3, 1, 0)) * 100 / COUNT(*), 1) AS perl,
       ROUND(SUM(IF(choice=4, 1, 0)) * 100 / COUNT(*), 1) AS php,
       ROUND(SUM(IF(choice=5, 1, 0)) * 100 / COUNT(*), 1) AS vb,
       ROUND(SUM(IF(choice=6, 1, 0)) * 100 / COUNT(*), 1) AS other
FROM votelanguage
GROUP BY mnth
```

mnth	c	java	perl	php	vb	other
2001-05	9.3	11.2	14.0	51.4	7.5	6.5
2001-06	5.4	11.7	13.5	57.7	6.3	5.4
...						
2002-12	13.8	6.9	10.3	53.4	8.6	6.9
2003-01	9.6	19.2	17.8	32.9	13.7	6.8

Determining the Number of Authors (mylibrary)

In the *mylibrary* database the association between the tables *titles* and *authors* is effected by means of the table *rel_title_author*. Yet it can happen that no author is associated with individual entries in the *titles* table. The following query determines the number of authors associated with each of the *titles* entries. The key point here is the use of *LEFT JOIN* (instead of simply enumerating the tables with *FROM*). This ensures that the result list also contains titles that do not have authors. The result is sorted by the number of authors, so that books with many authors are named first.

```
USE mylibrary

SELECT title, COUNT (authID) AS authCount
FROM titles LEFT JOIN rel_title_author USING(titleID)
GROUP BY titles.titleID
ORDER BY authCount DESC, title
```

title	authCount
Client/Server Survival Guide	3
Maple	3
MySQL & mSQL	3
A Guide to the SQL Standard	2
Definitive Guide to Excel VBA	2
Practical UNIX & Internet security	2
...	

SubSELECTs

Most database systems recognize sub*SELECT*s, that is, some degree of nested *SELECT* queries. For example, to search for book titles whose *publID* refers to a nonexistent publisher, a query in the following form could be used:

```
USE mylibrary

SELECT * FROM titles
WHERE publID NOT IN
  (SELECT publID FROM publishers)
```

Such commands are not possible through and including version 4.0.n of MySQL, becoming available only with version 4.1. Until this version has trickled up to your Internet service provider, one must circumvent this restriction with well-designed *JOIN* operations or the use of temporary tables (even though such a modus operandi is not particularly intuitive). For example, the following command is equivalent to the one above:

```
SELECT titles.*
FROM titles LEFT JOIN publishers
ON titles.publID=publishers.publID
WHERE ISNULL(publishers.publID) AND NOT(ISNULL(titles.publID))
```

This section has two goals: to present application examples for the new sub*SELECT* syntax in MySQL 4.1 (see also Appendix B) and to show that one can produce the equivalent of a sub*SELECT* in MySQL 4.0 through a careful reformulation.

> **TIP** *Additional examples using sub*SELECT*s appear in the next section, which deals with searching for defective data records in tables.*

Simple subSELECTs

Example 1: The following query returns all book titles whose publisher's name begins with "O." Then, a list of *publID* values for the key word *IN* is returned with a separate *SELECT* query.

```
USE mylibrary
SELECT title FROM titles WHERE publID IN
  (SELECT publID FROM publishers WHERE publName LIKE 'O%')
```

title
MySQL & mSQL
Practical UNIX & Internet security
MySQL Cookbook
Comédia Infantil
Hunderna i Riga

MySQL 4.1 recognizes an additional syntactic form, one that is less intuitive but that leads to the same result. In the following example, the second *SELECT* command, the one in parentheses, is executed for every book title. A book title returned by the first *SELECT* command is considered only if this second command has a nonempty result. The condition *titles.publID = publishers.publID* creates the relation between the two *SELECT* queries:

```
SELECT title FROM titles WHERE EXISTS
  (SELECT * FROM publishers WHERE
    titles.publID = publishers.publID AND
    publName LIKE 'O%')
```

In MySQL 4.0 and earlier versions, the same result can be attained by means of a simple *JOIN* operation. The similarity of the syntax with the *EXISTS* variant is unmistakable:

```
SELECT title FROM titles, publishers
WHERE titles.publID = publishers.publID AND publName LIKE 'O%'
```

Example 2: In this example we wish to return the oldest entry from the forum database *bigforum*. The time of this entry will be returned by the second query. The result of this query is used in the *WHERE* condition of the first query:

```
USE bigforum
SELECT msgID, timeSt FROM messages
WHERE timeSt = (SELECT MIN(timeSt) FROM messages)
```

msgID	timeSt
1	2000-09-30 00:31:02

This enquiry can also be effortlessly carried out with MySQL 4.0. To return the earliest entry, all entries are sorted according to date. Then *LIMIT* is used to select the first entry:

```
SELECT msgID, timeSt FROM messages ORDER BY timeSt LIMIT 1
```

The Use of Temporary Tables

It is not always possible to replace sub*SELECT*s by *JOIN* operations, for example, when the resulting list of records is to be sorted in a way different from that used in the selection query.

In the following example we wish to create an alphabetic list of the contributors of the previous ten listings in the *bigforum* database. In MySQL 4.1, the query looks like this:

```
USE bigforum SELECT DISTINCT userName FROM users
WHERE userID IN
  (SELECT userID FROM messages
   ORDER BY timest DESC
   LIMIT 10)
ORDER BY username
```

userName
Cees
Graham
matadordb
...

With a direct linkage between *users* and *messages* you can achieve a similar result, but then one cannot have either a sort by *userName* or the elimination of duplicates with *DISTINCT*. You must sort according to *timest*, so that *LIMIT* has the desired effect, namely, the selection of the first entry:

```
SELECT userName, messages.timest FROM users, messages
WHERE users.userID = messages.userID
ORDER BY messages.timest DESC LIMIT 10
```

username	timest
test	20030207102132
Cees	20030124154825
matadordb	20030124132214
Michael	20030124092312
Witzer	20030124052830
Graham	20030123211616
Volkan	20030123155707
Michael	20030123083245
Peter	20030122175147
Paul	20030121220412

The only possible solution without sub*SELECT*s consists in using a temporary table to store intermediate results. As table type you would use *HEAP*. This has the effect of keeping the temporary table in RAM (not on the hard drive, that is), which speeds up the operation considerably:

```
CREATE TEMPORARY TABLE tmp TYPE=HEAP
SELECT userID, timest FROM messages
ORDER BY timest DESC
LIMIT 10
```

The contents of the temporary table are now linked with *users*:

```
SELECT DISTINCT userName FROM users, tmp
WHERE users.userID = tmp.UserID
ORDER BY username
```

username
Cees Graham
matadordb
...

The temporary table can now be deleted:

```
DROP TABLE tmp
```

Ensuring the Integrity of Data

During the creation of a database project (database design, development of program code, and so on), it often happens that test data sets are incompletely deleted and some references to tables lead nowhere. Of course, programming errors can also lead to such problems in the actual operation of a database system, which is always an indication that somewhere or other there is an error in the code.

Whatever the cause, one of the burdensome tasks of database administration is to manage the integrity of the data and correct errors as they are discovered. In the following, you will find some tips for such error management. All the examples refer to the database *mylibrary*.

Searching for Titles Without Authors

Every title in the *mylibrary* database is required to have at least one author. The relationship between the tables *titles* and *authors* is via the table *rel_title_author*. To determine the number of authors for each title, the following query evaluates the tables *titles* and *rel_title_author*. Crucial here is the use of *LEFT JOIN* (instead of simply enumerating *titles* and *rel_title_author* with *FROM*): This ensures that the resulting list will contain all titles that have no associated authors. The result is sorted according to the number of authors, with titles with more authors coming before those with fewer authors:

```
USE mylibrary

SELECT title, COUNT(authID) AS authCount
FROM titles LEFT JOIN rel_title_author USING(titleID)
GROUP BY titles.titleID
ORDER BY authCount DESC, title
```

title	authCount
Client/Server Survival Guide	3
Maple	3
MySQL & mSQL	3
A Guide to the SQL Standard	2
Definitive Guide to Excel VBA	2
Practical UNIX & Internet security	2

```
...
```

It is then just a small step from the above query to finding the titles for which no author has been stored. In this example there is only one title that appears to have slipped into the database during a test run:

```
USE mylibrary SELECT title, COUNT(authID) AS authCount
FROM titles LEFT JOIN rel_title_author USING(titleID)
GROUP BY titles.titleID
HAVING authCount=0
ORDER BY title
```

title
dummy

> **REMARK** *Be sure to note that we have used* HAVING *here (and not* WHERE*!).* WHERE *is only for conditions that affect the original data, while* authCount *appeared as the result of the evaluation of an aggregation function.*

Starting with MySQL 4.1 you can retrieve such titles with sub*SELECT* queries. The following query tests each title in *titles* to see whether there is an entry in *rel_title_author* with a corresponding *titleID* number. Only the titles that do not have such an entry are displayed (due to *NOT EXISTS*):

```
SELECT title FROM titles WHERE NOT EXISTS
  (SELECT * FROM rel_title_author
   WHERE titles.titleID = rel_title_author.titleID)
```

Searching for Invalid Publisher Links: Invalid Records in $1 : n$ Relations

In an ideal world, all the records in the *titles* table should refer with *publID* to a publisher, or else the relevant field should contain *NULL*. But what happens if a publisher is inadvertently deleted? Then there are *titles* records with *publID*s that refer to a no longer existing publisher. (Similar problems can arise with other relations between other tables, with the *titles* table and the *catID* and *langID* fields. The following query thus does not find all *titles* records with invalid cross references, but only those whose *publID* is screwed up. Thus we are merely giving an example of how to find such records.)

To simulate the problem, we shall insert a defective title into the *titles* table. The command assumes that there is no publisher with *publID=9999*:

```
INSERT INTO titles (title, publID) VALUES ('deleteme', 9999)
```

The following query links the tables *titles* and *publishers* via the linking field *publID*. With *LEFT JOIN*, all the titles are found that lead to no result via this link. This can be for one of two reasons: Either *titles.publID* has the value *NULL* (which is permitted), or for *titles.publID* there is no corresponding entry in the *publishers* table (and an error has been found). The two *ISNULL* conditions are necessary so that in the end, only those records are displayed that were found for the second reason.

The query finds in *titles* only a single record (which was added expressly for this purpose):

```
SELECT title, titles.publID, publishers.publID
FROM titles LEFT JOIN publishers
ON titles.publID=publishers.publID
WHERE ISNULL(publishers.publID)
  AND NOT(ISNULL(titles.publID))
```

title	publID	publID
deleteme	9999	NULL

Starting with MySQL 4.1, this query can be formulated as a sub*SELECT* command:

```
SELECT * FROM titles
WHERE publID NOT IN (SELECT publID FROM publishers)
```

There are two ways to correct such errors: You can simply delete any invalid titles (which in this case is the called-for solution), or you can associate the title with a publisher (which you will have to create if the publisher does not already appear in the list of publishers).

Searching for Invalid Authors and Titles ($n : m$ Relation)

Somewhat more complicated is the search for $n : m$ relations (such as in the title/author relationship). Now there are three sources of error:

- Titles that refer via *rel_title_author* to nonexistent authors;
- Authors that refer via *rel_title_author* to nonexistent titles;
- Entries in *rel_title_author* for which both *titleID* and *authID* refer to invalid records. (If the search for illegal records is based on existing authors or titles, then this third source of errors remains unexposed.)

To simulate the error situation, three invalid records will be inserted into *rel_title_author*, covering all three error sources. The following instruction assumes that there exists an author with *authID=1* and a title with *titleID=1*, but no author or title with ID number *9999*:

```
INSERT INTO rel_title_author (titleID, authID)
VALUES (1,9999), (9999,1), (9999, 9999)
```

The following query refers to the first error (title with author IDs that do not exist in the database). It is interesting in this query that the link between *titles* and *rel_title_author* is effected with an ordinary *JOIN*, while that between *rel_title_author* and *authors* is done with *LEFT JOIN* (otherwise, the missing authors would not be included and thus would not be not found). The result is not very surprising: The title *Linux* with *titleID=1* refers to an author with *authID=9999*, which doesn't exist.

```
SELECT title, rel_title_author.titleID, rel_title_author.authID
FROM titles, rel_title_author
LEFT JOIN authors
ON rel_title_author.authID=authors.authID
WHERE titles.titleID=rel_title_author.titleID
  AND ISNULL(authors.authID)
```

title	titleID	authID
Linux, 5th ed.	1	9999

The symmetric command for the second error case looks like this:

```
SELECT authName, rel_title_author.authID, rel_title_author.titleID
FROM authors, rel_title_author
LEFT JOIN titles
ON rel_title_author.titleID=titles.titleID
WHERE authors.authID=rel_title_author.authID
  AND ISNULL(titles.titleID)
```

authName	authID	titleID
Kofler Michael	1	9999

The query for the third error case consists of two *LEFT JOINs*, one from *rel_title_author* to *authors*, and the other from *rel_title_author* to *titles*.

```
SELECT rel_title_author.authID, rel_title_author.titleID
FROM rel_title_author
LEFT JOIN titles
    ON rel_title_author.titleID=titles.titleID
LEFT JOIN authors
    ON rel_title_author.authID=authors.authID
WHERE ISNULL(titles.titleID) AND ISNULL(authors.authID)
```

authID	titleID
9999	9999

Instead of the three queries just formulated, we can get by with only one. For this to work, all the data in all three tables must be considered. Furthermore, in the conditional we will need to use *AND* and *OR*. (In practice, it is often more useful to split the query into three parts, because then one can tailor the response to the different types of error.)

```
SELECT rel_title_author.authID, rel_title_author.titleID,
authName, title
FROM rel_title_author
LEFT JOIN titles
    ON rel_title_author.titleID=titles.titleID
LEFT JOIN authors
    ON rel_title_author.authID=authors.authID
WHERE ISNULL(titles.titleID) OR ISNULL(authors.authID)
```

authID	titleID	authName	title
9999	1	NULL	Linux, 5th ed.
1	9999	Kofler Michael	NULL
9999	9999	NULL	NULL

One of the most important results of this example should be your realization of the universal applicability of *JOIN* operations. In MySQL 4.1, you can simplify your life by formulating the query as a sub*SELECT* command:

```
SELECT titleID, authID FROM rel_title_author
WHERE authID NOT IN (SELECT authID FROM authors) OR
titleID NOT IN (SELECT titleID FROM titles)
```

authID	titleID
9999	1
1	9999
9999	9999

Correcting Data (*n : m relations*)

Of course, it helps in correcting data to be able to determine which data are corrupt. It would be even better if one could correct errors automatically as soon as they were found. Alas, as a rule, errors must be corrected manually. For example, if a book title refers to a nonexistent author because of an error in *rel_title_author*, then it will not do simply to delete this entry. It must first be determined whether the author list for the book is, in fact, in error. It may be that a new author (or only a new reference in *rel_title_author* to an existing author) has to be incorporated into the database.

Even with the best SQL command you cannot automate such tasks. However, SQL is a good aid in searching through the database for errors and listing them in a readable format as a basis for manual correction to follow.

When the problem is only the syntactic correctness of data (and you have no possibility of tracking the error to its source and then manually recreating the data), you can, of course, simply delete erroneous data (for example, all records in *rel_title_author* that refer to a nonexistent author or title).

Since MySQL 3.23.*n* and all earlier versions do not, unfortunately, offer the possibility of accessing data in several tables with *DELETE* commands (no sub*SELECT*s), you must carry out such tasks in an external programming language (in Perl, for example). There you first determine with *SELECT* the list of erroneous data records and then delete them with *DELETE* commands. An example of this technique can be found in Chapter 14.

In MySQL 4.0, the entire process is made easier in that now, data from several tables can be considered. The following command deletes all invalid records from the table *rel_title_author*:

```
DELETE rel_title_author
FROM rel_title_author
LEFT JOIN titles
     ON rel_title_author.titleID=titles.titleID
LEFT JOIN authors
     ON rel_title_author.authID=authors.authID
WHERE ISNULL(titles.titleID) OR ISNULL(authors.authID)
```

In MySQL 4.1, it is possible to combine *DELETE* with *SELECT*:

```
DELETE FROM rel_title_author
WHERE authID  NOT IN (SELECT authID FROM authors) OR
     titleID NOT IN (SELECT titleID FROM titles)
```

Tracking Down Duplicates

In database management, the problem repeatedly arises that data records are stored inadvertently in duplicate. As the following example involving the table *authors* and the database *mylibrary* shows, such records are easy to find. To this end, we form groups of identical author names and then display those groups with more than one member:

```
USE mylibrary

SELECT authName, COUNT(*) AS cnt
FROM authors
GROUP BY authName
HAVING cnt>1
```

In a second step, one could obtain all the *authID* numbers for these records. Then duplicate entries can be removed, and you should replace in the table *rel_title_author* the second *authID* number by the first, and then delete the second entry from the table *authors*.

For example, suppose that due to an input error the author Gary Cornell appears twice:

authID	authName
123	Cornell Gary
758	Cornell Gary

In the *titles* table there are two different books by Gary. The first of these, *The Sex Life of Unix*, is associated with *authID=123*, while the second book, *More Sex Life of Unix*, has *authID=758*. Gary has two *authID*s!

To alleviate this problem, we decide to use only *authID=123*, and so we change all *rel_title_author* entries with 758 to 123:

```
UPDATE rel_title_authors SET authID=123 WHERE authID=758
```

Now all of Gary's books have *authID=123*. Finally, we delete the obsolete entry in the *authors* table:

```
DELETE FROM authors WHERE authID=758
```

In the *titles* table it is permitted for several books to have the same title. Therefore, several columns must be considered:

```
SELECT title, subtitle, edition, COUNT(*)AS cnt
FROM titles
GROUP BY title, subtitle, edition
HAVING cnt>1
```

It is more difficult to track down duplicates that involve typographical errors. With English words one can use *SOUNDEX*. This function returns a character string that corresponds to the pronunciation of the text. However, the result must be manually examined. *SOUNDEX* does not find all similar records, and it considers as duplicates names that are really different. The following query uses *MIN(authName)* to return the alphabetically first of the similar-sounding names:

```
SELECT SOUNDEX(authName) AS snd,
       COUNT(*)AS cnt,
       MIN(authName) AS firstname
FROM authors
GROUP BY snd
HAVING cnt>1
```

Bringing a Table into Normal Form

In Chapter 5 we described in detail the first three normal forms, which are considered the starting point for good database design. In the best of all possible worlds, all design issues are dealt with at the outset, but in the world as we know it, it frequently happens that one comes to grips with these rules after it is too late.

But what does that mean, "too late"? The example of this section shows how you can move redundant information into a new table, thereby creating the third normal form after the fact.

The starting point for our example is the table *messages*, which contains a field *author* with the names of the contributors to an on-line discussion forum. Since many authors contribute multiple messages, their names appear repeatedly. This shortcoming will be corrected with the new table *users*, which is to contain a list of all the authors' names. In *messages*, the *author* column will be replaced by a *userID* column.

The first step is to create the new table *users*:

```
CREATE TABLE users (userID INT NOT NULL AUTO_INCREMENT,
                    username VARCHAR(60) NOT NULL,
                    PRIMARY KEY (userID))
```

With the command *INSERT INTO . . . SELECT* introduced earlier in this chapter, all names can be inserted into the new *users* table. *SELECT* must be executed with the option *DISTINCT*, so that each name is inserted only once. For the *userID* column, the value *NULL* is passed. This leads to MySQL placing *AUTO_INCREMENT* numbers in the column automatically:

```
INSERT INTO users SELECT DISTINCT NULL, author FROM messages
```

Now the original table *messages* must be expanded to contain the new *userID* column:

```
ALTER TABLE messages ADD userID INT
```

Next, the *userID* column should be filled with data in such a way that the numbers refer to the corresponding entries in the *user* columnn. Note, please, that the *UPDATE* command in this form is valid only starting with version 4.0. (MySQL 3.23 offers no support for *UPDATE* commands in which data from more than one table are to be processed.) Although *UPDATE* refers to both *messages* and *users*, it is only the former that is changed. (Only *messages.userID* is newly set by *SET.*)

```
UPDATE messages, users
SET messages.userID = users.userID
WHERE messages.author = users.username
```

A brief check shows that everything worked as planned:

```
SELECT messages.author, users.userName, users.userID
FROM messages, users
WHERE messages.userID = users.userID LIMIT 5
```

author	userName	userID
boehnke	boehnke	9
Michael	Michael	10
cjander	cjander	11
Frauke	Frauke	12
Bernd	Bernd	13

Now the column *messages.author* can be deleted; the information contained therein is recoverable via *messages.userID* and the new *users* table:

```
ALTER TABLE messages DROP author
```

Processing the First or Last *n* Records

All the examples of this section use the test database *bigforum*, a large version of *myforum*.

Searching Data (SELECT)

The question repeatedly arises how to construct a list of the "top ten," or, better, the top *n*, which means the *n* first, the best, the worst, the oldest, or the most pleasing records in a data set. This question is easily answered: Use a *SELECT* command in combination with *ORDER BY* and *LIMIT*.

With *ORDER BY* you have to give a sort criterion, for example, a date. If you want not the first, but the last results, then reverse the sort order with *DESC*. (For example, *ORDER BY date DESC*, and *LIMIT* restricts the number of results to a particular value.)

The following query returns the last five entries in the *bigforum* discussion groups. With *LEFT*, the *subject* text is reduced to twenty characters, to make the result easier to read:

```
USE bigforum SELECT LEFT(subject, 20) AS subj, forumID, timest
FROM messages ORDER BY timest DESC LIMIT 5
```

subj	forumID	timest
Re: Run-time error '	1001	20030124154825
Re: Re: Suche Erfahr	1	20030124132214
Re: Full text search	1006	20030124092312
Re: MySQL on ASP wit	1006	20030124052830
Full text searches	1006	20030123211616

Our second example searches not for arbitrary messages, but for those that start a new thread (*rootID=0*), and only for the forum 1006 (MySQL, English):

```
SELECT LEFT(subject, 20) AS subj, forumID, timest FROM messages
WHERE rootID=0 AND forumID=1006
ORDER BY timest DESC LIMIT 5
```

subj	forumID	timest
Full text searches	1006	20030123211616
MySQL and ASP	1006	20021021223216
where do I save this	1006	20021016013629
samples do not work	1006	20021014151020
ASP and MySQL	1006	20020730224220

In our next example, the five longest threads are found (that is, the threads that have the largest number of contributions). For this, *COUNT* and *GROUP BY* are used to return to number of messages that have the same *rootID* number. (The *rootID* number refers to the first message of the thread.) We must exclude *rootID=0*, since that indicates the beginning of a thread:

```
SELECT COUNT(*)AS answerCount, rootID FROM messages
WHERE rootID<>0 GROUP BY rootID ORDER BY answerCount DESC LIMIT 5
```

answerCount	rootID
11	767
9	1392
8	1134
7	495
7	748

Unfortunately, with this query it was impossible to display the *subject*. The reason is that *GROUP BY* groups all the messages of a thread, and with *COUNT* the number of messages can be determined. But there is no string function that distinguishes the first of several *subject* texts. (With numerical values, one could use *MIN* or *MAX*.) You must therefore work either with temporary tables or manually execute an additional query:

```
SELECT subject FROM messages WHERE msgID IN (767, 1392 ... )
```

Changing Records (UPDATE and DELETE)

Just as with *SELECT* you can select the first or last *n* records using *ORDER BY* and *LIMIT n*, you can as well change these records with *UPDATE* and *DELETE*.

The first of our two examples is rather trivial: To save space, *UPDATE* replaces the text of the oldest 100 messages with the bilingual notification *message no longer available/Nachricht steht nicht mehr zur Verfügung.* Important here is the instruction *timest=timest*, which ensures that *timest* is left unchanged. (Otherwise, the oldest 100 messages would suddenly seemingly become the newest.)

```
UPDATE messages
SET msgText="message no ... / Nachricht ... ", timest=timest
ORDER BY timest LIMIT 100
```

It is even easier to delete the last 100 messages:

```
DELETE messages ORDER BY timest LIMIT 100
```

Both commands are easily understood, but they have the disadvantage that they destroy the threads. It can also happen that the start message of a thread is overwritten or deleted, while (newer) replies remain. That is not, of course, what we had in mind.

Delete All Threads Except the Last 500

The following commands delete complete threads except for the most recent 500. Unfortunately, the process is somewhat complex. The first command returns the time at which the oldest of the five hundred most recent threads was begun. This time is stored in the user variable *@oldtime*:

```
SELECT @oldtime := timest FROM messages
WHERE rootID=0 ORDER BY timest DESC LIMIT 499,1
```

@oldtime := timest
20030911093909

The next command tests how many threads exist that are even older. This information is not necessary for further processing, but it constitutes a sort of plausibility control:

```
SELECT COUNT (*) FROM messages WHERE timest<@oldtime AND rootID=0
```

COUNT(*)
117

Now we need to return a list of *msgID* numbers of the start messages of the threads that are to be deleted. This is written to a temporary table *msgIDs* using *CREATE . . . SELECT*. This table will be stored in RAM for reasons of efficiency (*TYPE=HEAP*):

```
CREATE TEMPORARY TABLE msgIDs TYPE=HEAP
SELECT msgID FROM messages WHERE timest<@oldtime AND rootID=0
```

The table *msgIDs* is now used to delete the old messages, in fact, both the start messages (*messages.msgID = msgIDs.msgID*) and the replies (*messages.rootID = msgIDs.msgID*):

```
DELETE messages FROM messages, msgIDs
WHERE messages.rootID=msgIDs.msgID OR messages.msgID=msgIDs.msgID
```

Now the temporary table *msgIDs* can be deleted:

```
DROP TABLE msgIDs
```

Selecting Random Records

It is sometimes desirable to select data records at random, for example, to display images or advertisements on a web site.

Selection without a random Column

The easiest procedure is to obtain a random selection by selecting all records with *SELECT*, but executing *ORDER BY* with the addition of *RAND()*. This will yield a list sorted by random numbers. Then *LIMIT* can be used to select the first record.

The following example is based on a copy of the *titles* table from the *mylibrary* database. With two queries, two (possibly) different (randomly selected) titles are selected from the copy *titlescopy*:

```
USE mylibrary
CREATE TABLE titlescopy SELECT * FROM titles SELECT titleID, title FROM titlescopy
ORDER BY RAND() LIMIT 1
```

titleID	title
59	PHP and MySQL Web Development

```
SELECT titleID, title FROM titlescopy
ORDER BY RAND() LIMIT 1
```

titleID	title
2	Definitive Guide to Excel VBA

If you wish to select two or more records randomly with only one *SELECT* query, then specify *LIMIT n* instead of *LIMIT 1*.

Selection with a random Column

The process just described has an obvious drawback: With large tables, it is extremely inefficient. All the records must be read into active memory, and there sorted by random numbers, all in order to select a single record.

For large tables it is therefore a good idea to provide the table with a column of random numbers at the time that the table is declared. Of course, the *random* column can also be created after the fact, as the following lines prove: The first *ALTER TABLE* command adds the column, while the second equips the column with an index. *UPDATE* then stores a random value in the new column for each existing record. (When a new record is added, you must then supply a new random number for the *random* column. Unfortunately, at present, MySQL does not allow a function such as *RAND* to be specified as a default value.)

```
ALTER TABLE titlescopy ADD random DOUBLE
ALTER TABLE titlescopy ADD INDEX (random)
UPDATE titlescopy SET random = RAND()
```

Now, to select a random record, use the following command:

```
SELECT titleID, title FROM titlescopy
WHERE random > RAND() ORDER BY random LIMIT 1
```

At first glance, this does not seem any more efficient than the previous example. In fact, however, MySQL now has selected only a single record from the table that satisfies the condition *random > RAND()*. Since an index was constructed for the *random* column, access is very efficient.

Do not forget *ORDER BY*! Otherwise, MySQL chooses any old record that satisfies *random > RAND()*, and not necessarily the one whose value is closest to the random number. The selection of a record would then no longer be purely random, but would depend on how the records are stored in the table.

Of course, the variant with the *random* column is not without its own drawbacks:

- More space on the hard drive is required to store the table (additional column plus index).

- Every change in the table is slower than previously (index for the *random* column).

- It is possible to select only a single random record. (If you use *LIMIT 5*, then you obtain five records to be sure, but it is always the same package of five records.)

- On inserting new records, you must always assign a random number to the *random* column.

Selection on the Basis of an id Column

Perhaps both of the solutions that we have offered seem unnecessarily complicated. We have only to read the *n*th of *nmax* records, where *nmax* can be easily obtained with *SELECT COUNT(*) FROM table*. Unfortunately, there is no SQL command to read the *n*th data record. MySQL decides the order in which the records are stored (for example, the table driver), and this cannot be controlled from outside.

One solution would be to use an *AUTO_INCREMENT* column. If the table contains 1000 records, then the *id* column would have to contain the values from 1 to 1000, and the selection would be possible with *WHERE id = CEILING(RAND()*1000)*. The problem, however, is that you cannot rely on the *id* column being filled without gaps. As soon as you delete records from the table, gaps arise that are never filled upon the addition of new records to the table.

Full-Text Search

If you are using SQL to search for a word in a character string, the query is often posed in the following form:

```
SELECT * FROM tablename WHERE column LIKE '%word%'
```

This query indeed achieves its goal. The only question is, when? There are few queries that are more time-consuming for MySQL to answer than this. (What is worse is searching for several words, perhaps in several columns.) It is not only that all the records of the table must be read. Additionally, many character string comparisons must be made. A traditional index cannot help you here.

Unfortunately, what is most difficult for the computer is simple for the user, who has become accustomed to using an Internet search engine to input a number of search terms without having to deal with complex search criteria.

If you wish to be able to process such queries efficiently in MySQL, you need a *full-text index*. This is a particular type of index, one that creates a list of all words that appear in a column of a table. MySQL has supported this type of index since version 3.23.23.

Fundamentals

Creating a Full-Text Index

To provide an existing table with a full-text index, you should execute the following command. You may specify arbitrarily many *xxxTEXT* and *(VAR)CHAR* columns.

```
ALTER TABLE tablename ADD FULLTEXT (columnname1, columnname2)
```

Of course, new tables can also be generated at once with a full-text index:

```
CREATE TABLE tablename (id INT NOT NULL AUTO_INCREMENT,
                        column1 VARCHAR(50), column2 VARCHAR(100),
                        PRIMARY KEY (id), FULLTEXT (column1, column2))
```

Full-Text Search

For a full-text search, the SQL expression *MATCH AGAINST* is used:

```
SELECT * FROM tablename
WHERE MATCH (column1, column2) AGAINST ('word1 word2 word3') > 0.001
```

The result is that all data records are found in which at least one of the three words *word1*, *word2*, *word3* is contained. The list of columns in *MATCH* must correspond exactly to the one with which the index was generated. There is no case distinction in the search criteria in *AGAINST*. The order of search criteria is also irrelevant. Words with three or fewer letters are generally ignored.

MATCH returns as result a floating-point number whose magnitude reflects the relevance of the result. If no words are found or if the search criteria appear in very many records and are therefore ignored, then *MATCH* returns 0.

The expression *MATCH . . . > 0.001* excludes results for which *MATCH* returns very small values. (This gets rid of statistical outliers and inaccuracies due to floating-point representation.)

A *MATCH* expression can be used to order results. The following query returns the five best results. The condition must be formulated with *HAVING*, since *WHERE* does not accept the alias *mtch*:

```
SELECT *,
       MATCH(column1, column2) AGAINST('word1 word2 word3') AS mtch
FROM tablename
HAVING mtch > 0.001
ORDER BY mtch DESC
LIMIT 5
```

Boolean Search Expressions

By default, all search criteria specified in *AGAINST* are joined by a logical *OR*. Since MySQL 4.0.1, you can connect search criteria using a Boolean expression. For this, you must follow the search expression with *IN BOOLEAN MODE*. Furthermore, the special symbols shown in Table 7-1 can be used in the formulation of the expression:

*Table 7-1. Boolean search expressions (*IN BOOLEAN MODE*)*

+*word*	The word must be contained in the data record. Thus *AGAINST('+word1 +word2' IN BOOLEAN MODE)* corresponds to a Boolean *AND* in both search criteria.
-*word*	The word may not appear in the data record.
˜*word*	The word should not appear in the record. In contrast to -*word*, such records are not completely excluded, but are given a lesser value. Thus ˜*word* is suited to eliminate "noise words," that is, expressions that are more hindrance than help in a search.
<*word*	Gives the word a lesser standing.
>*word*	Gives the word a greater standing.
*word**	Searches for words that begin with *word* (e.g., *word*, *words*, *wordless*).
"*word1 word2*"	This exact word order should be searched. Case-insensitive.
( )	Parentheses can be used to group expressions. *AGAINST('+mysql +(buch book)' IN BOOLEAN MODE)* searches for data records that contain *mysql* and either *buch* or *book*.

A Boolean full-text search might look like this:

```
SELECT * FROM tablename
WHERE MATCH(column1, column2)
      AGAINST('+word1 +word2 -word3' IN BOOLEAN MODE)
```

A significant drawback to Boolean search is that *MATCH* returns only 1 or 0, according to whether the search criteria were fulfilled or not. There is no longer an evaluation of relevance.

> **REMARK**   *Note that in a full-text search, search patterns like* LIKE *are not allowed. The only exception is the variant* word*, *where the wild card* * *must be placed at the end of the word.*

Full-Text Search over Several Tables

A full-text search can be defined only for a single table. To search for data in linked tables, you will have to equip both tables with a full index. The resulting SQL search queries are, however, complicated to formulate and difficult to optimize for the server. (There is an example in the following section.)

Limitations

- In order for full-text search to function, there must be at least three records in the table. Experiments with tables that contain only one or two records have ended in failure. In general, *MATCH* functions better with larger tables than with smaller, for which it occasionally returns results that are difficult to understand.

- Full-text search is based on entire words. The slightest alteration (plurals, endings, etc.) is considered a different word. This makes searching at times more difficult.

  To find all relevant records, variants have to be given in *AGAINST* (for example, *AGAINST('book books')* or *AGAINST('book books bookcase bookend')* to obtain all records having to do with books. One way out is offered by the wild card ***, which, however, can be used only in Boolean mode (*AGAINST('book*' IN BOOLEAN MODE*).

  A word in the sense of full-text search is considered to be a character string composed of letters, numbers, and the characters ' and _. Fortunately, letters with diacritical marks like *üàé* are considered letters. Note, however, that expressions like C++ are not considered words and therefore cannot be searched for.

- Words must be at least four characters in length if they are to be considered. This makes the search for abbreviations like *SQL* impossible. (This limitation can be removed by a reconfiguration of the server; see below.)

- Full-text search is case-insensitive (which usually makes sense, but sometimes is a bother).

- Full-text search is currently available only for MyISAM tables (and not for InnoDB tables).

- The creation of a full-text index is relatively slow (but nonetheless, much faster than in MySQL 3.23.*n*). This affects not only the initial creation of an index, but all further changes in the table as well.

- In MySQL 4.1, full text searches are not possible if a Unicode character set is used.

Full-Text Search for Words of Three Letters

As we have already mentioned, full-text search operates by default only for words of four or more letters. The reason for this is to avoid inflating the index with words like *a, and, the*, and the like. However, that makes the search for terms like *ADO* and *PHP* impossible.

With the configuration parameter *ft_min_word_len (mysqld)*, you can set the minimum length of words for the full-text index. To do this, enter the parameter into the MySQL configuration file (/etc/my.cnf or Windows \my.ini) in the section [mysqld]. For the setting to take effect, you will have to restart the MySQL server and regenerate the full-text index (the easiest way to do this is with *REPAIR TABLE tablename QUICK*).

Book Search

For the following examples, the column *title* of the table *titles* from the *mylibrary* database is equipped with a full-text index. Then the best hits of the search for *excel* or *basic* are returned.

```
USE mylibrary
ALTER TABLE titles ADD FULLTEXT (title)
SELECT title, MATCH (title) AGAINST ('excel basic') AS fulltextmatch
FROM titles
HAVING fulltextmatch > 0.001
ORDER BY fulltextmatch DESC
```

title	fulltextmatch
Visual Basic	2.7978503848587
Visual Basic Datenbankprogrammierung	2.7667480431589
VBA-Programmierung mit Excel 7	2.3731654830885
Definitive Guide to Excel VBA	2.3467841568515
Excel 2000 programmieren	2.3467841568515

In the above query, the condition *fulltextmatch > 0.001* was formulated with *HAVING*, since *WHERE* does not recognize the alias column name (that is, *AS fulltextname*). The following variant is a bit more efficient, but is more work to type in:

```
SELECT title, MATCH(title) AGAINST('excel basic') AS fulltextmatch
FROM titles
WHERE MATCH(title) AGAINST('excel basic') > 0.001
ORDER BY fulltextmatch DESC
```

Search for Title and Author

A full-text index can be defined only for a single table. If you wish to search for author and title simultaneously (such as *excel* and *kofler*), then you must equip all the tables with a full-text index and then in the query specify *MATCH* expressions for each index. However, the resulting queries are relatively inefficient (especially with large data sets).

```
USE mylibrary
ALTER TABLE titles ADD FULLTEXT (title)
ALTER TABLE authors ADD FULLTEXT (authName)
SELECT title, authname FROM titles, authors, rel_title_author
WHERE titles.titleID = rel_title_author.titleID
  AND authors.authID = rel_title_author.authID
  AND MATCH (title) AGAINST ('excel kofler')
  AND MATCH (authName) AGAINST ('excel kofler')
```

title	authname
VBA-Programmierung mit Excel 7	Kofler Michael
Excel 2000 programmieren	Kofler Michael
Definitive Guide to Excel VBA	Kofler Michael

If *titles* contained, say, 100,000 titles, and *authors* as many author names, then the above query would be somewhat slow despite the full-text index. It would be more efficient to store the relevant data in a single table. In the following example *titles* must be expanded to include an *authors* column with author names. It is precisely this that was suggested in Chapter 5 as a possible change in database design.

Forum Search

The following examples relate to the table *messages* in the database *bigforum* (a variant of the *myforum* database with about 1300 contributions to a discussion forum). The full-text index was created with the following command:

```
USE bigforum ALTER TABLE messages ADD FULLTEXT(msgText, subject)
```

Altogether, there are over 200 contributions that deal with MySQL:

```
SELECT COUNT(*)FROM messages
WHERE MATCH(msgText, subject) AGAINST('mysql') > 0.001
```

COUNT(*)
219

MySQL believes that the following entries have the greatest relevance. This result should be taken with a grain of salt: The mechanism of full-text search is not blessed with clairvoyant insight, and the selection from among the many contributions is more or less random, reflecting generally the frequency with which the expression "MySQL" appears:

```
SELECT subject, msgID,
       MATCH(msgText, subject) AGAINST('mysql') AS mtch
FROM messages
ORDER BY mtch DESC
LIMIT 5
```

subject	msgID	mtch
help needed with figuring out error message	332	3.222867812652
Re: where is MySQL database?	359	3.1858990010743
Re: Re: Re: MYSQL Zugriff ...	357	3.0232702237961
Re: An update to the first edition of MySQL?	775	3.0158353640643
Re: Datenbankanbindung	1262	2.8449136579526

The search for the strings *mysql* and *odbc* returns only 22 hits:

```
SELECT COUNT(*)FROM messages
WHERE MATCH(msgText, subject)
AGAINST('+mysql +odbc' IN BOOLEAN MODE)
```

COUNT(*)
22

To obtain the five best hits, the query has to be changed a bit. As *WHERE* criterion we have the Boolean search expression *'+mysql +odbc'*, which, however, returns only the values 0 and 1. For sorting, we use instead the expression *'mysql odbc'*:

```
SELECT LEFT(subject, 40) AS subj,
       msgID,
       MATCH(msgText, subject) AGAINST('mysql odbc') AS mtch
FROM messages
WHERE MATCH(msgText, subject) AGAINST('+mysql +odbc' IN BOOLEAN MODE)
ORDER BY mtch DESC
LIMIT 5
```

subj	msgID	mtch
Wie werde ich das mySQL ODBC-Fenster los	728	6.770324495441
Re: Re: Re: Wie werde ich das mySQL ODBC	842	6.453936383473
Re: Re: Wie werde ich das mySQL ODBC-Fen	734	6.093977318182
Datentransfer zwischen Excel und MySQL	876	5.270302575910
Re: Re: Re: MYSQL Zugriff ...	357	5.251107031037

#### CHAPTER 8

InnoDB Tables
and Transactions

BY DEFAULT, MYSQL USES THE MyISAM table driver. As an alternative, since version 3.23.34 there has been available the considerably more modern InnoDB table driver. InnoDB tables offer, among other things, two functions that MyISAM tables do not (yet) have: *transactions* and *integrity rules* (foreign key constraints). The latter of these involves an automatic ensuring of referential integrity in linked tables.

This chapter offers a brief introduction to the world of InnoDB, and with its comparison of MyISAM and InnoDB tables offers a basis for choosing the optimal table type for a particular application. Then there follows an extensive description of transactions and foreign key constraints.

POINTER *Tips on the administration of InnoDB tables, for example, for the management of* tablespace *files and the InnoDB logging files, can be found in Chapter 10, the chapter on administration. A summary of InnoDB configuration parameters can be found in Chapter 19.*

Chapter Overview

Introduction

Since MySQL 3.23, the default table format has been MyISAM. This format is mature, stable, and fast, and completely satisfactory for many applications. In addition to the MyISAM format, since version 3.23.34, MySQL has supported another, less well known, table format, namely, InnoDB. This is a modern alternative to MyISAM, which is distinguished primarily in that it offers the following supplementary functions:

- Database operations in InnoDB tables can be executed as transactions. This allows you to execute several logically connected SQL commands as a single entity. If an error occurs during execution, then all of the commands (not only the one during which the error occurred) are nullified. In addition, transactions offer other advantages that improve the security of database applications.

  Transactions can be executed in all four isolation levels of the ANSI-SQL/92 standard (*READ UNCOMMITTED, READ COMMITTED, REPEATABLE READ, SERIALIZABLE*).

- In implementing transactions, the InnoDB table driver uses internal *row level locking*. This means that during a transaction, the entire table does not have to be blocked for access by other users (which would be the case for a MyISAM table during a *LOCK TABLE* command), but only the data records actually affected. If many users are simultaneously making changes on a large table, row level locking can bring about an enormous advantage in efficiency.

  The InnoDB table driver automatically recognizes *deadlocks* (that is, the condition in which two processes mutually block each other) and in such a case, terminates one of the two processes automatically.

- When you define relations between your tables, the InnoDB table driver automatically ensures that the referential integrity of the table is preserved after delete commands. Thus it is impossible, for example, for a record in table A to refer to a no longer existing table B. (In database lingo this function is called a *foreign key constraint.*)

- After a crash, InnoDB tables are automatically and very quickly returned to a consistent state (provided that the file system of the computer was not damaged). I have not tested this functionality.

- Many of the features of the table driver are quite similar to those of Oracle, which should be helpful in porting database applications.

The InnoDB table driver has been an integral component of MySQL since version 3.23.34. The development of the table driver and its commercial support come from the independent company Innobase (see http://www.innodb.com).

It is difficult to say how far InnoDB has met the hopes and expectations of its author. In any event, InnoDB was developed with great diligence and could well quickly become one of the most attractive table formats alongside MyISAM.

POINTER *The use of InnoDB tables is described rather extensively in the MySQL documentation, in the chapter "MySQL Table Types." Further information, including many technical details, can be found at the Innobase web site:*

```
http://www.mysql.com/doc/en/InnoDB.html
http://www.innodb.com/
```

Limitations and Drawbacks

- While with the MyISAM table driver, each table is stored in its own file, which grows or shrinks as required, the InnoDB table driver stores all data and indexes in a *tablespace*, comprising one or more files, that forms a sort of virtual file system. These files cannot later be made smaller. Nor is it possible to stop the MySQL server and then copy a table by simply copying its file. Therefore, in the administration of InnoDB tables, the command `mysqldump` must be employed more frequently than with MyISAM tables.

- The storage requirements for InnoDB tables are much greater than those for equivalent MyISAM tables (up to twice as big).

- For InnoDB tables one cannot use a full-text index.

- Indexes for *TEXT/BLOB* columns are not possible. (This deficiency is supposed to be eliminated soon.)

- InnoDB supports foreign key constraints, but these can be removed only since MySQL 4.0.13. In older versions, you have to recreate the table and copy all the data into the new table.

- On account of open transactions, it is relatively difficult for the InnoDB table driver to determine the number of records in a table. Therefore, executing a *SELECT COUNT(*) FROM TABLE* is much slower than with MyISAM tables. This limitation should be soon eliminated, perhaps before you have this book in your hands.

- The *mysql* tables for managing MySQL access privileges cannot be transformed into InnoDB tables. They must remain in MyISAM format.

- Since InnoDB uses its own locking algorithms in executing transactions, *LOCK TABLE* should not be used. This command is executed outside the control of the InnoDB table driver by MySQL. It can therefore screw up the locking regime and in the worst case, lead to deadlock (where individual processes wait for each other endlessly).

> **POINTER** *Further details on the limitations of InnoDB tables in relation to MyISAM tables can be found at the following address:*
>
> `http://www.innodb.com/ibman.html#InnoDB_restrictions`

MyISAM or InnoDB?

You can specify individually for each table in your database which table driver is to be used. That is, it is permitted within a single database to install both MyISAM and InnoDB tables. This allows you to choose the optimal table driver for each table, depending on its content and the application that will be accessing it.

MyISAM tables are to be recommended whenever you want to manage tables in the most space- and time-efficient way possible. InnoDB tables, on the other hand, take precedence when your application makes use of transactions, requires greater security, or is to be accessed by many users simultaneously for making changes.

There is no generally valid answer to the question of which table type offers faster response. In principle, since transactions take time and InnoDB tables take up more space on the hard drive, MyISAM should have the advantage. But with InnoDB tables you can avoid the use of *LOCK TABLE* commands, which offers an advantage to InnoDB, which is better optimized for certain applications.

Furthermore, the speed of an application depends heavily on hardware (particularly the amount of RAM), the settings in the MySQL configuration file, and other factors. Therefore, I can provide here only the following advice: In speed-critical applications, perform your own tests on both types of tables.

Alternatives to InnoDB (BDB, Gemini)

If your main interest is the support of transactions, then instead of InnoDB tables, you could use BDB tables. BDB stands for *Berkeley Databases*, an open source library for storing data in tables. BDB is not in itself a complete database system, but rather is to be used in combination with MySQL or another program that offers the basic database functions. From a historical point of view, BDB was the first transaction-capable MySQL table type. The first version of MySQL with BDB arrived in 2001.

BDB tables are available only in special compiled versions of MySQL (*MySQL Max* and *MySQL Pro*). The next section explains how you can tell whether your version of MySQL supports BDB. With a BDB-capable version of MySQL you can create and use BDB tables more or less as you would InnoDB tables. Note, however, that the BDB table driver manages transactions internally completely differently from the InnoDB table driver. For this reason, there are some significant differences in the behavior of transactions between the two drivers.

> **POINTER** *In contrast to the first edition of this book, this second edition does not go into detail on the subject of BDB tables, since their importance for MySQL has become greatly diminished since the integration of the InnoDB format. The use of BDB tables is described in the MySQL documentation in the chapter "MySQL Table Types." Further information on BDB (independent of MySQL) can be found on the web site of the company SleepyCat:*
>
> http://www.mysql.com/doc/en/BDB.html
> http://www.sleepycat.com/

In 2001, there appeared a third transactions-capable table type, in addition to BDB and InnoDB, namely, Gemini. The code for the Gemini table driver comes from the Nusphere company (http://www.nusphere.com). Unfortunately, a legal battle between the MySQL company and Nusphere arose over the question of whether Gemini extensions of MySQL were in accord with the MySQL license. In the meantime, the legal issues have been resolved, but with the result that the Gemini table driver vanished into oblivion, and is now to be found neither in the official MySQL code nor on the Nusphere web site.

Determining Which Table Types Your Version of MySQL Supports

To determine which table formats (and other supplementary functions) your version of MySQL supports, execute the following SQL command (for example, in the program mysql):

SHOW VARIABLES LIKE 'have%'

Variable_name	Value
have_bdb	NO
have_crypt	NO
have_innodb	YES
have_isam	YES
have_raid	NO
have_symlink	YES
have_openssl	NO
have_query_cache	YES

We see from this result that InnoDB tables are supported, but not BDB tables. If for *have_bdb* or *have_innodb* the value *DISABLED* is displayed, then the format is supported in principle, but there is a configuration error somewhere, for which reason the function was deactivated when the server was started. Information is generally available in the MySQL logging file (Unix/Linux: /var/lib/mysql/*hostname*.err, Windows: mysql\data*hostname*.err).

First Experiments with InnoDB Tables

As we have already mentioned, all InnoDB tables (regardless of database of origin) are stored in one large file, together with their indexes. This file represents a sort of virtual storage, which is managed by the InnoDB driver itself.

In earlier versions of MySQL with InnoDB support, an explicit configuration for the location and size of the InnoDB file was required. In current versions, however, this is taken care of automatically: When MySQL supports InnoDB, at initial launch the file ibdata1 is created in the data directory with size 10 megabytes. As soon as the InnoDB tables stored in this file require more space, the file is expanded in 8-megabyte quanta. In addition to ibdata1, the logging files ib_logfile0, ib_logfile1, and ib_arch_log_0000000000 are created. All four of these files exist in binary format and should not be changed "by hand."

If you are working with MySQL 3.23*n*, you will need to add the following lines in /etc/my.cnf or Windows\my.ini and then restart the server:

```
innodb_data_home_dir = /var/lib/mysql
innodb_data_file_path = ibdata1:20M
```

Under windows, instead of /var/lib/mysql you specify the MySQL data directory (usually c:/mysql/data). Beginning with MySQL 3.23.50, you can use with innodb_data_file_path the autoextend attribute, which allows the database file to grow automatically:

```
innodb_data_file_path = ibdata1:10M:autoextend
```

Note that the InnoDB functions are automatically deactivated when MySQL 3.23*n* is started unless this minimal configuration has been put in place. Only starting with MySQL 4.0 does InnoDB function without previous configuration. Further information on InnoDB administration can be found in Chapter 10.

Creating InnoDB Tables

From now on, you can generate as many InnoDB tables as you like, which can be placed in existing databases or in new ones. In the following example, a database is created, and within it a new InnoDB table:

```
CREATE DATABASE innotest
USE innotest
CREATE TABLE table1 (colA INT AUTO_INCREMENT, colB INT,
PRIMARY KEY (colA)) TYPE=InnoDB
INSERT INTO table1 (colB) VALUES (10)
```

The following commands provide an overview of the files that now exist. The actual data are located in testib. The file innotest/table1.frm contains merely the definition of the table layout (in the same format as for all other MySQL tables):

```
root# cd /var/lib/mysql
root# ls -l ib* testib
-rw-rw---- 1 mysql mysql 25088 ib_arch_log_0000000000
-rw-rw---- 1 mysql mysql 5242880 ib_logfile0
-rw-rw---- 1 mysql mysql 5242880 ib_logfile1
-rw-rw---- 1 mysql mysql 10485760 testib
root# ls -l innotest/
-rw-rw---- 1 mysql mysql 8578 table1.frm
```

The above commands were executed under Linux. Under Windows, exactly the same file is created. (The files are transferable among various MySQL installations. You can copy the entire MySQL data directory with all MyISAM and InnoDB tables from Windows to Linux or in the opposite direction.)

Changing a Table Type

You can easily change existing tables from MyISAM to InnoDB (and, of course, from InnoDB to MyISAM). To accomplish this, you use the command *ALTER TABLE*:

```
ALTER TABLE tblname TYPE=InnoDB
```

The alteration fails if the MyISAM table contains a full-text index. This must first be deleted:

```
ALTER TABLE tblname DROP INDEX indexname
```

If you wish to change a large number of tables, then you will want to use (under Unix/Linux) the script mysql_convert_table_format. If you do not specify a table name, then all tables of the database will be converted:

```
root# mysql_convert_table_format [opt] --type=InnoDB dbname [tablename]
```

> **CAUTION** *Do not change the table type of the the tables in the* mysql *database. These tables, which contain management information internal to MySQL (user and access privileges) should remain in MyISAM format.*

Transactions

Why Transactions?

Transactions can help in making the operation of a database system more efficient and secure:

- Transactions ensure that a group of SQL commands that begin with *BEGIN* and end with *COMMIT* are executed either as a unit or not at all. Even if the connection with the server is dropped during the transaction, power goes out, or the computer crashes, it cannot happen that only some of the commands are executed.

  Let us look at an example: You wish to transfer 100 dollars from account 123 to account 456. Therefore, you first execute

```
UPDATE tablename SET value=value-100 WHERE accountno=123
```

  and then

```
UPDATE tablename SET value=value+100 WHERE accountno=456
```

  If you are working without transactions and some misfortune occurs between the two commands, it can happen that 100 dollars was withdrawn from the first account but not deposited to the second. With transactions, that cannot occur: Either both commands are correctly executed, or neither of them.

- Transactions also ensure that data cannot be simultaneously changed by two users. With MyISAM tables, you can achieve this result with *LOCK TABLE*. But that has the effect of blocking access to the entire table for all clients. With InnoDB tables, in contrast, only the affected records are blocked.

- Transactions make for easier programming. A transaction can be aborted at any time, which makes protecting against errors much simpler.

ACID Rules

The database-theoretic answer as to why one should use transactions can be summed up in one word: *ACID*. We are not talking about controlled substances here, but an acronym: *Atomicity, Consistency, Isolation, Durability*. Thus ACID encompasses four concepts that are considered in database theory to be the basis of secure simultaneous use of a database by multiple users. MySQL in combination with the InnoDB table driver passes the ACID test, adhering to its rules and regulations, which can be described in somewhat greater detail as follows:

- **Atomicity** means that a transaction is indivisible. The database system must ensure that either all the commands of a transaction are correctly executed, or none of them. This holds even for such extreme cases as a crash during execution of the transaction.

- **Consistency** requires that at the end of the transaction the database be in a consistent state. If a transaction were to lead to a violation of validity rules, then it must be broken off and undone (*ROLLBACK*). Validity rules include foreign key constraints, which will be discussed in greater detail in the following section.

- **Isolation** means that several transactions can run independently and simultaneously without interfering with each other. Each transaction sees the entire database in the condition that it found it right up to the end of the transaction (other than those changes made by the transaction). If a transaction inserts, changes, or deletes records, a transaction running in parallel does not see this.

Complete fulfillment of the isolation requirement can be achieved only at great cost, and in practice, this means cost in speed. For this reason, the ANSI-92/SQL standard provides for four degrees of isolation, so that database programmers can decide on the appropriate level of security and the tradeoff against speed. The default isolation level depends on the database system, and for the InnoDB table driver it is *REPEATABLE READ*. We will have more to say later on isolation degree.

- **Durability** requires that a transaction itself be preserved even if right after the end of the transaction there is a crash or other comparable problem. (The InnoDB table driver therefore writes changes first in a logging file. If a crash occurs, that is, before the changes can actually be made to the database, the changes can be reconstructed after restart of the MySQL server and transferred to the database.

Many database systems make compromises in their durability requirements to achieve improvements in speed. In the case of the InnoDB table driver, most significant in this regard is the option innodb_flush_log_at_trx_commit, which controls when transactions can be stored in the logging file.

Controlling Transactions

By default, MySQL is in auto commit mode. This means that every SQL command is executed in a single, small transaction. This has no effect on the use of transaction-capable tables.

There are two ways of executing several SQL commands together as a transaction:

- You can start an ad hoc transaction with *BEGIN* and terminate it with *COMMIT* or *ROLLBACK*. *BEGIN* deactivates the auto commit mode for this one transaction. If you subsequently wish to begin a transaction, then you must begin with another *BEGIN*.

  Since MySQL 4.0.11 you can introduce an ad hoc transaction with *START TRANSACTION* (instead of with *BEGIN*). *START TRANSACTION* conforms to the ANSI standard, but otherwise, is no different from *BEGIN*.

- You can turn off auto commit mode. Then all the commands are considered together as a transaction until confirmed by *COMMIT* or aborted by *ROLLBACK*.

BEGIN, COMMIT, *and* ROLLBACK

BEGIN or (since MySQL 4.0.11) *START TRANSACTION* introduces a transaction, *COMMIT* ends it and stores all changes, and *ROLLBACK* aborts the transaction and stores no changes.

In InnoDB tables one may not have nested transactions. If you begin a new transaction with *BEGIN* while a previous transaction is still open, the open transaction is closed with *COMMIT*.

Transactions are managed by the client. If the connection is lost during a transaction, then all uncommitted changes are aborted (as with *ROLLBACK*).

Savepoints

Since MySQL 4.0.14, InnoDB has supported *savepoints*. This allows points within a transaction to be marked using *SAVEPOINT name*. Then *ROLLBACK TO SAVEPOINT name* ends the transaction, accepting all changes up to the savepoint and aborting all those that follow. Savepoints can be used only within a transaction, and at the end of the transaction, all savepoints are deleted.

Automatic Transaction Termination

Transactions are also concluded automatically by the following commands (as with *COMMIT*):

> *ALTER TABLE, CREATE INDEX, CREATE TABLE, DROP DATABASE,*
> *DROP TABLE, LOCK TABLES, RENAME TABLE, SET AUTOCOMMIT=1,*
> *TRUNCATE, UNLOCK TABLES*

On the other hand, transactions are not ended when an ordinary error occurs in the execution of an SQL command.

Setting Auto Commit Mode

The auto commit mode is deactivated with the SQL command *SET AUTOCOMMIT = 0*. Commands that relate to transaction-capable tables will now automatically be considered a transaction until they are ended with *COMMIT* or *ROLLBACK*. Then a new transaction begins automatically. (That is, you do not need to execute a *BEGIN*. Just this convenience is often reason enough to work with *SET AUTOCOMMIT = 0*.)

An important consequence of *AUTOCOMMIT = 0* is that if the connection is lost, whether or not intentionally, all SQL commands that have not been confirmed with a *COMMIT* are aborted.

Note also that *AUTOCOMMIT=0* can lead to very long transactions if you do not regularly execute *COMMIT* or *ROLLBACK*. The current state of auto commit can be determined with *SELECT @@autocommit*.

Controlling Transactions in Client Programming

Most libraries and APIs for MySQL programming (such as JDBC, ODBC, ADO, ADO.NET) provide special functions or methods for beginning and ending trans-actions. However, the InnoDB documentation suggests that you not rely on such functions but that you explicitly execute the commands *SET AUTOCOMMIT* and *BEGIN/COMMIT/ROLLBACK*. The reason is that with many APIs the use of transaction functions in combination with MySQL has not been sufficiently tested and does not always work as advertised.

Trying Out Transactions

To try out transactions, you must establish two connections to the database. The simplest way to do this is to execute the monitor mysql in two windows. Then execute commands first in one window and then in the other. The following examples assume that there is a (still empty) table *table1* in the database *innotest*. (In practice, of course, you will have several records, but for the purposes of this first demonstration, even a single record suffices.)

> **REMARK** *This example shows the effect that transactions can have when data in a table are changed nearly simultaneously by two users. The example is very simple, and the simultaneity takes place in slow motion. Nonetheless, it should make you aware that in real applications it can certainly happen that database commands from two users or programs can be woven together as in the following example. If such an effect on the end result is possible, then you must exclude the possibility by the use of transactions or (if you wish to stick with MyISAM tables) by executing LOCK TABLE.*

At time point 0, connection A begins a transaction (*BEGIN*) and changes, in the confines of this transaction, a record of the table *table1*.

At time point 1 (as indicated in the right-hand column of Table 8-1) the contents of *table1* look different to the two different connections. For connection A, the record with *colA=1* already has *colB=11*. Since this transaction has not actually been executed, connection B sees the original value *colB=10* for the same record.

At time point 2, B begins a transaction, in which *colB* of the data record with *colA=1* is to be increased by 3. The InnoDB table driver recognizes that it cannot execute this command at this time, and it blocks B, which then waits until A completes its transaction.

At time point 3, A completes its transaction with *COMMIT*, whereby *colB* attains the definitive value 11. And now B's *UPDATE* command can be completed.

At time point 4, A sees *colB=11*. For B things look as though *colB* already had the value 14.

Now B cancels its transaction. Then at time point 5 both A and B see the value actually stored, namely *colB=11*.

> **REMARK** *Of course, you can try out this example with BDB tables. The result of the commands will be the same (if you maintain the sequence of execution). However, it can happen that blocking comes at other places.*

Table 8-1. Coordinating transactions

Connection A	Connection B	Time point
USE innotest	USE innotest	
INSERT INTO table1 VALUES (1, 10)		
SELECT * FROM table1 *colA colB* 1 10		
BEGIN		0
UPDATE table1 SET colB=11 WHERE colA=1		
SELECT * FROM table1 *colA colB* 1 11	SELECT * FROM table1 *colA colB* 1 10	1
	BEGIN UPDATE table1 SET colB=colB+3 WHERE colA=1	2
COMMIT		3
SELECT * FROM table1 *colA colB* 1 11	SELECT * FROM table1 *colA colB* 1 14	4
	ROLLBACK	
SELECT * FROM table1 *colA colB* 1 11	SELECT * FROM table1 *colA colB* 1 11	5

Transactions and Locking

The InnoDB table driver generally takes care of all necessary locking operations on its own, as soon as you execute your transactions. However, there are cases where the default behavior of InnoDB is not optimal. In such cases, InnoDB offers several possibilities of having its locking behavior altered.

SELECT ... LOCK IN SHARE MODE

A peculiarity of the InnoDB table driver is that *SELECT* commands are immediately executed even on blocked records. The results returned do not consider the possibility of open transactions of other clients (see connection B at time point 1 in the example above), and thus return potentially outmoded data.

If you execute the *SELECT* with the key word *LOCK IN SHARE MODE* appended, then when the command is executed, it is held pending until all transactions already begun have been terminated (of course, only to the extent that these transactions affect result records of the *SELECT* command). Thus if in the above example B were to issue the command

```
SELECT * FROM table1 LOCK IN SHARE MODE
```

at time 1, then a result would be displayed only when the transaction begun by A had been completed (time point 3).

If *SELECT . . . LOCK IN SHARE MODE* is executed within a transaction, then additionally, all result records for all other clients will be locked until the end of the transaction. Such a lock is called a *shared lock*, whence the key word *SHARE*. With a shared lock you are assured that the records read during your transactions are not being changed or deleted by other clients.

With a shared lock, locked records can continue to be read by all clients, even if other clients are also using *SELECT LOCK IN SHARE MODE*. Any attempt by a client to change such records leads to the client being blocked until your transaction is completed.

SELECT ... FOR UPDATE

The key words *FOR UPDATE* also represent an extension of the normal *SELECT*. With this, all result records are provided an *exclusive lock*.

With an exclusive lock, locked records cannot be changed by other clients. They can continue to be read by all clients with a normal *SELECT* command, but not with *SELECT . . . LOCK IN SHARE MODE*. The difference between a shared lock and an exclusive lock therefore relates only to whether other clients can execute *SELECT . . . LOCK IN SHARE MODE*.

INSERT, UPDATE, DELETE

All three of these commands have the effect that changed records are locked by an exclusive lock until the end of the transaction.

If links between tables must be checked (foreign key constraints) during the execution of an *INSERT*, *UPDATE*, or *DELETE* command, then the affected records of the linked tables will be locked by an *exclusive lock*.

Gap and Next Key Locks

InnoDB uses by default *gap* and *next key locks* when open conditions are used with *SELECT . . . LOCK IN SHARE MODE*, *SELECT . . . FOR UPDATE*, *UPDATE*, or *DELETE* (e.g., *WHERE id>100* or *WHERE id BETWEEN 100 AND 200*). The result is that not only the records currently affected by the condition are blocked, but also records that do not yet even exist that might be inserted by another transaction.

Thus if you execute *SELECT . . . WHERE id>100 FOR UPDATE* in a transaction, then no other user can input new records with *id>100* for the duration of the transaction.

> **POINTER**   *Which commands have next key locks placed on them is also affected by the isolation degree. See the following section.*

Deadlocks

The InnoDB table driver automatically recognizes deadlock situations (that is, situations in which two or more processes block one another, each waiting for the other to finish, ad infinitum). In such situations an error occurs in the process that triggered the deadlock; SQL commands that are still open are aborted with a *ROLLBACK.*

> **CAUTION**   *In no case should you execute a* LOCK TABLE *for an InnoDB table. This command is executed at the MySQL level, without the InnoDB table driver hearing about it. The consequence can be a deadlock of which InnoDB never becomes aware.*
>
> *Deadlocks that InnoDB doesn't know about can also arise when SQL commands affect both InnoDB tables and other tables as well. In order for the clients not to have to wait forever in such cases, the configuration setting* innodb_lock_wait_timeout=n *determines the maximum wait time (by default, 50 seconds).*

Isolation Degree for Transactions

Before the start of a transaction, its isolation level can be defined:

```
SET [SESSION|GLOBAL] TRANSACTION ISOLATION LEVEL
   READ UNCOMMITTED | READ COMMITTED |
   REPEATABLE READ | SERIALIZABLE
```

SET can be executed in three different ways:

- *SET* without *SESSION* or *GLOBAL:* In this case, the selected setting holds only for the next transaction. Note, please, that this behavior is different from that of the usual *SET* syntax, where *SET* works without the specification of what is to be set, as in *SET SESSION.*

- *SET SESSION:* Here, the setting holds for the current connection until its termination or until another isolation degree is specified.

- *SET GLOBAL:* Here, the setting holds for all new connections to MySQL (but not for the current connection).

The isolation degree influences the manner in which commands are executed within a transaction. In the following list, the isolation degrees are ordered according to increasing exclusivity. This means that you achieve the greatest access speed with *READ UNCOMMITTED* (no mutual blocking), while with *SERIALIZABLE*, you obtain the greatest security against simultaneous changes of data by clients. We now describe the four isolation degrees:

- **READ UNCOMMITTED:** *SELECT* reads the current data and considers all changes arising from other running transactions. *SELECT* is therefore *not* isolated from other transactions. (The expression *read uncommitted* means that data of other transactions that are not yet completed with *COMMIT* can flow into the *SELECT* result.) If you execute the example from Table 8-1 in *READ UNCOMMITTED* mode, then at time point 1, transaction B sees *colA=1* and *colB=11*.

  Please note that while *READ UNCOMMITTED* does not ensure isolation for *SELECT*, it does so for *UPDATE*. Even in *READ UNCOMMITTED* mode, the *UPDATE* command of transaction B is blocked at time point 2 until transaction A is finished. *UPDATE* is therefore correctly executed in *READ UNCOMMITTED* mode.

- **READ COMMITTED:** *SELECT* takes into account changes by other transactions that have been confirmed with *COMMIT*. This means that one and the same *SELECT* command within a transaction can have different results if another transaction is closed in the intervening time. In comparison with *READ UNCOMMITTED*, the isolation for *SELECT* is somewhat better, but not perfect.

- **REPEATABLE READ:** *SELECT* takes into account no changes by other transactions, regardless of whether these transactions have been confirmed with *COMMIT*. Thus the ACID isolation requirement for *SELECT* is satisfied for this isolation degree. One and the same *SELECT* command always returns one and the same result (as long, of course, as the transaction does not itself change data).

- **SERIALIZABLE:** This mode functions much like *REPEATABLE READ*. The only difference is that ordinary *SELECT* commands are automatically executed as *SELECT . . . LOCK IN SHARE MODE*, and therefore supply all records with a shared lock.

By default, InnoDB uses the isolation level *REPEATABLE READ*. In most cases, this mode offers sufficient isolation for a variety of transactions without influencing transaction speed unduly. InnoDB is optimized for *REPEATABLE READ* mode and executes the required locks especially efficiently.

One can change the default setting in the MySQL configuration file with the option `transaction-isolation`. In setting the option, the names of the isolation levels consisting of more than one word must be separated by hyphens (thus, for example, `transaction-level = read-committed`).

You can determine the isolation level of a connection or of the server with the following command:

```
SELECT @@tx_isolation, @@global.tx_isolation
```

@@tx_isolation	@@global.tx_isolation
READ-UNCOMMITTED	REPEATABLE-READ

Isolation Level and Next Key Locks

As we have already mentioned, InnoDB supports gap and next key locks. This means that in open conditions (e.g., *WHERE id>100*), not only currently existing records are blocked, but also data that do not yet exist that would satisfy the condition.

InnoDB uses gap and next key locks only when open conditions appear in commands. Moreover, the locking is also dependent on the command being executed and on the isolation level. The following conditions hold in MySQL 4.0:

- ***READ COMMITTED*** and ***READ UNCOMMITTED:*** Gap and next key locks are used only for commands of the form *INSERT INTO . . . SELECT . . . FROM s . . . .*

- ***REPEATABLE READ*** and ***SERIALIZABLE:*** Gap and next key locks are used for the following commands: *INSERT INTO . . . SELECT . . . FROM s . . . , SELECT . . . LOCK IN SHARE MODE, SELECT . . . FOR UPDATE, UPDATE, DELETE.*
  Starting with MySQL 4.1, it is planned that no locking will take place with the command *INSERT INTO . . . SELECT . . . FROM s . . . .* Instead, the command will be considered a *consistent read* command. The table driver then ensures (depending on isolation level) that a repeated execution of the command leads to the same result.

Error Protection

When you use transactions, you increase the odds of receiving certain error messages from the server. You should therefore always check in your code, even with apparently noncritical commands (such as *SELECT*), whether errors have occurred during execution:

- While a transaction is open, another client cannot execute any operation that affects the records of the open transaction.
  Example: Client A executes *BEGIN* and then *INSERT INTO table VALUES (1, 2).* Client B attempts to execute *SELECT * FROM table.* This command is blocked until client A terminates its transaction with *COMMIT* or *ROLLBACK.*
  Many clients, such as mysql, will wait forever for an open transaction to be completed (there is no timeout). But other clients can experience a timeout or other error. In sum, close your transactions as soon as possible.

- Every transaction can be broken off due to a deadlock situation. (The InnoDB table driver automatically recognizes deadlock situations, that is, the situation in which two transactions mutually block each other. To avoid a permanent blocking of the server, one client's transaction will be terminated.)

Integrity Rules (Foreign Key Constraints)

InnoDB is the first MySQL table driver that is capable of ensuring the referential integrity of linked tables through integrity rules (foreign key constraints). For example, in the *mylibrary* database you can thereby make it impossible to delete a publisher from the *publishers* table as long as there is at least one book title in the *titles* table that was published by that publisher.

The following commands show how a foreign key constraint can be employed after the fact using *ADD FOREIGN KEY*. (The key here is the second command. The first command merely creates an ordinary index for the column *titles.publID*, which is a precondition for the following foreign key constraint.)

```
ALTER TABLE titles ADD INDEX (publID) ALTER TABLE titles ADD FOREIGN KEY (publID)
REFERENCES publishers (publID)
```

Of course, foreign key constraints can also be given when a table is created, using *CREATE TABLE*, as in the following:

```
CREATE TABLE titles (
  titleID int(11) NOT NULL AUTO_INCREMENT
  ...
  PRIMARY KEY (titleID),
  KEY (publID),
  FOREIGN KEY (publID) REFERENCES publishers (publID)
) TYPE=InnoDB
```

The creation of foreign key constraints has consequences for both tables:

- In *titles* you cannot insert a title with a *publID* number that does not exist in the *publishers* table. (Nor can you change an existing value of *publID* for a title in the *titles* table if there is no corresponding *publishers* record.)

- You may not delete a publisher from *publishers* that is referred to in the *titles* table. (This restriction holds as well for *UPDATE* commands.)

These conditions have consequences for the order of operations: If you wish to store a new title for a new publisher, you must first enter the publisher, and only then the title. (You have already done this, because you needed the ID number of the publisher.) If you later wish to delete the publisher and the title, you must first delete the title and then the publisher. (Deleting the publisher is possible only if there are no other titles for that publisher.)

Syntax

The general syntax for defining a foreign key constraint for a foreign key field *table1.column1* looks as follows:

```
FOREIGN KEY [name] (column1) REFERENCES table2 (column2)
  [ON DELETE {CASCADE | SET NULL | NO ACTION | RESTRICT}]
  [ON UPDATE {CASCADE | SET NULL | NO ACTION | RESTRICT}]
```

The foreign key constraint can be named with *name*. The foreign key is *table1.column1* for which the constraint is defined. The field of the second table to which the constraint refers is *table2.column2*. (In many cases, *column2* is the primary key of *table2*. This is not requisite, but *column2* must be equipped with an index.)

One may also have foreign key constraints in which *table1* and *table2* are the same table. This makes sense when a table possesses references to itself. This is the case, for example, with the *categories* table in *mylibrary*, where *parentCatID* refers to *CatID*, thus creating a hierarchical relationship among the categories.

> **REMARK** *The MySQL documentation provides the syntax* CREATE TABLE table1 (column1 datatype REFERENCES table2(column2) . . .) *for* CREATE TABLE. *This syntax is currently ignored, regardless of which table driver you are using.*

Actions When Integrity Is Damaged

The optional clause *ON DELETE* determines how the table driver should behave if a record that is referred to by *table1* is deleted from *table2*. There are four possibilities:

- *RESTRICT* is the default behavior. The *DELETE* command causes an error, and the record is not deleted. (An error does not necessarily mean the termination of a running transaction. The command is simply not executed. The transaction must, as usual, be terminated with a *COMMIT* or *ROLLBACK*.)

- *SET NULL* has the effect that the record from *table2* is allowed to be deleted. In *table1*, all records that refer to the deleted record will have *column1* set to *NULL*. This rule assumes that *NULL* is a permitted value for *table1.column1*. For the *titles/publisher* example, this means that if you remove publisher *x* from *publishers*, then all records in *titles* that were published by this publisher will have their *publID* set to *NULL*.

- *CASCADE* has the effect that the record from *table2* is allowed to be deleted. At the same time, however, all records from *table1* that refer to that record will be deleted.
  For the *titles/publishers* example, this means that if you delete publisher *x* from the *publishers* table, then all records in *titles* that were published by publisher *x* will be deleted from *titles*.

- *NO ACTION* has the effect that the loss of referential integrity is tolerated. This action seldom makes sense, since it is easier simply not to use a foreign key constraint.

These four actions can also be specified analogously for *ON UPDATE* (where by default, *RESTRICT* again holds). The *UPDATE* rules come into effect if in *table2*, the key field of an existing record is altered. In such a case, the effect of *RESTRICT*, *SET NULL*, and *NO ACTION* is the same as with *ON DELETE*.

On the other hand, the effect of *CASCADE* is a bit different: A change in the key field in *table2* is now also carried out in the foreign key field in *table1*. For the *titles/publishers* example, this means that if you change the *publID* field for publisher *x* in *publishers*, then the *publID* field will be updated for all affected records in *titles*.

> **REMARK**   *Integrity rules do not prevent you from deleting an entire table. For example, you can execute* DROP TABLE publishers, *even if this means damaging the referential integrity.*

Conditions for Setting Up Integrity Rules

Foreign key constraints can be used only if a set of preconditions is satisfied. If such conditions have not been satisfied, then the result is an error message, generally *Error 1005: Can't create table xxx (errno: 150)*, and the constraint is not stored. (The cause of the error can be quite trivial, such as a typo in the name of a column.)

- Each of *table1.column1* and *table2.column2* must be equipped with at least an ordinary index. This index is not created by *FOREIGN KEY*, and must therefore be explicitly provided for in *CREATE TABLE* or after the fact with *ALTER TABLE*. *table2.column2* is often the primary key field of *table2*, but that is not necessary. If you use keys across several fields (*INDEX(columnA, columnB)*), then the key field from the foreign key constraint must appear first. Otherwise, an additional separate index for the field must be created.

- The data types of *table1.column1* and *table2.column2* must agree to the extent that a direct comparison is possible without transformation of data types. Most efficient is if both fields are declared with *INT* or *BIGINT*. Both columns must be of the same sign type (*SIGNED* or *UNSIGNED*).

- If the optional rule *ON DELETE/UPDATE SET NULL* is defined, then the value *NULL* must be permitted in *table1.column1*.

- The foreign key constraint must be satisfied from the start: If the tables are already filled with data, it can happen that individual records do not conform to the integrity rules. In this case, an *ALTER TABLE* command results in error 1216 (*A foreign key constraint fails*). The records must be corrected before the constraint can be set up.

> **TIP**   *If an error occurs in setting up a foreign key constraint, you can obtain more precise information, since MySQL 4.0.13, about the cause of the error with* SHOW INNODB STATUS.

Finding Unsatisfied Integrity Rules

The obvious question upon receipt of error 1216 is, "How can the error-ridden records be found?" The solution to this conundrum lies in Chapter 7, where it was demonstrated on the *tltles/publishers* connection how a simple *SELECT* command determines all records in the *titles* table for which *titles.publID* contains a value for which there is no corresponding value in *publishers.publID*:

```
SELECT titleID, titles.publID, publishers.publID
FROM titles LEFT JOIN publishers
  ON titles.publID = publishers.publID
WHERE ISNULL(publishers.publID) AND NOT ISNULL(titles.publID)
```

titleID	publID	publishers.publID
66	99	NULL

The title with *titleID=66* thus refers to a publisher with *publID=99* in the *publishers* table, but there is no such ID number in that table. Now you must either insert the missing publisher or delete the title with ID equal to 66. (In the *titles* table you could also change erroneous *publID*s to *NULL*, though in practice, that is often not allowed in linked tables.)

Since MySQL 4.1 you can formulate the same query with a sub*SELECT*. The logic of the query is then easier to understand:

```
SELECT titleID, publID FROM titles
WHERE publID NOT IN (SELECT publID FROM publishers)
```

Deleting Foreign Key Constraints

In MySQL 4.0 it was possible already to define foreign key constraints for InnoDB tables, but through version 4.0.12 it was impossible to delete them. The only solution was to recreate the table. The necessary commands (here for the *titles* table) are shown below. The syntax for *CREATE TABLE* can be retrieved with *SHOW CREATE TABLE* *oldtitles*:

```
RENAME TABLE titles TO oldtitles CREATE TABLE titles (
  titleID INT NOT NULL AUTO_INCREMENT
  title VARCHAR(100) NOT NULL,
  ...
  comment VARCHAR(255),
  PRIMARY KEY (titleID)
) TYPE=InnoDB INSERT INTO titles SELECT * FROM oldtitles DROP TABLE oldtitles
```

Since MySQL 4.0.13 it has been easier to delete foreign key constraints. You can use the following command:

```
ALTER TABLE tablename DROP FOREIGN KEY foreign_key_id
```

You can determine the *foreign_key_id* of the index to be deleted with *SHOW CREATE TABLE*.

Deactivating Integrity Checks

With *SET foreign_key_checks=0* you can turn off the automatic checking of integrity rules. This can make sense, for example, to speed up the reading in of large backup tables.

Integrity Rules for the mylibrary Database

In the accompanying files for this book you will find a variant of the *mylibrary* database, namely, *mylibraryinno*. As revealed by its name, all the tables of this database are in InnoDB format. Moreover, the following foreign key constraints have been defined. (Before this conversion could be done, a large number of new indexes had to be created and a few invalid records corrected.)

Foreign key	Referential key
titles.publID	*publishers.publID*
titles.langID	*languages.langID*
titles.catID	*categories.catID*
categories.parentCatID	*categories.catID*
rel_title_author.titleID	*titles.titleID*
rel_title_author.authID	*authors.authID*

Security

IT IS A FACT OF life, or at least of human social organization, that not all information is intended to be made available to all individuals. Thus with MySQL, a database is generally set up in such a way that not everyone can see all of the data (let alone change or delete it). In order to protect data from prying eyes (or unauthorized tampering), MySQL provides a dual access system. The first level determines whether the user has the right to communicate with MySQL at all. The second level determines what actions (such as *SELECT*, *INSERT*, *DROP*) are permitted for which databases, tables, or columns.

This chapter describes rather extensively the access system of MySQL, both its internal management and the tools that can assist you in changing access privileges.

Chapter Overview

Introduction

Normally, it is undesirable to allow everyone to execute all database operations. To be sure, there must be one, or perhaps even several, administrators who have wide-ranging powers. However, it would be a great security risk to allow all users to act as they please in altering records or even deleting entire databases.

There can be many different degrees of access rights. In a company with an employee database, for example, it may make sense to allow all employees to read part of the database (for example, to find someone's telephone number), while other parts remain invisible (such as personnel records).

MySQL offers a finely meshed system for setting such access privileges. In the MySQL documentation this system is called the *access privilege system*, while the individual lists of the system are called *access control lists* (ACLs). The management of these lists is carried out internally in the tables of the *mysql* database, which will be described in detail.

Setting the Access Privileges

There are several ways to set access privileges:

- The simplest and most convenient way is to use an administration program with a graphical user interface. Some of these programs were described in Chapter 4. Note, however, that even the most convenient user interface is of little help if you do not understand the concepts of MySQL access.

- You can change *mysql* directly with *INSERT* and *UPDATE* commands.

- You can use the SQL commands *GRANT* and *REVOKE*, which offer greater convenience.

- You can use the Perl script mysql_setpermission.pl. This script is even easier to use than *GRANT* and *REVOKE*, though it assumes, of course, that you have a Perl installation up and running.

User Name, Password, and Host Name

MySQL's access system has two phases. In the first phase, the question is whether the user is permitted to make a connection to MySQL at all. (Such does not imply the right to read or alter any databases, but nevertheless, such access provides the capability to pass SQL commands to MySQL. Then MySQL decides, based on its security settings, whether this command should actually be executed.)

While you are probably accustomed to providing a user name and password to enter the operating system of a multiuser computing system, MySQL evaluates a third piece of information: the name of the computer (host name) from which you are accessing MySQL. Since MySQL's entire security system is based on this informational triple, it seems not inappropriate to take a few moments now to explain what is going on:

User Name: The user name is the name under which you announce your presence to MySQL. The management of MySQL user names has nothing to do with login names managed by the operating system. It is, of course, possible, and indeed, it is often advisable, to use the same name for both purposes, but management of each of these names is independent of the other. There is no mechanism to synchronize these operations (such that, for example, a new MySQL user name is generated when the operating system generates a new user name).

The user name can be up to sixteen characters in length, and it is case-sensitive. In principle, such names do not have to be composed exclusively of ASCII characters. But since different operating systems handle special characters differently, such characters often lead to problems and therefore should be avoided.

Password: What holds for user names holds for passwords as well. There is no relation between the MySQL password and that for the operating system, even if they are identical. (Within MySQL, passwords are stored in 16-bit encrypted form, which allows passwords to be checked, but does not allow reconstruction of a password. Even if an attacker should gain access to the *user* table of MySQL, there is no way for the villain to determine the passwords themselves. Since MySQL 4.1 a stronger form of encryption has been used, with a code length of 45 characters.)

Passwords, like user names, are case-sensitive, and they can be of arbitrary length. Special characters outside of the ASCII character set are possible, but are not recommended.

> **CAUTION** For security reasons do not use the same password for MySQL as for the operating system!
>
> *MySQL passwords must often be supplied in plain text in script files, configuration files, and programs. Thus they are in danger of being intercepted. If an attacker who acquires such a password were to gain access not only to your database, but also discovers that the same password allows entry into the operating system, the villain will be very happy indeed.*
>
> *This warning is directed particularly at Internet service providers that allow their clients direct access to the computer (FTP, Telnet, SSH) in addition to access to a MySQL database. Be sure to give different passwords for these two different forms of access!*

Host Name: In establishing a connection, you must normally specify the computer on which the MySQL server is running. This computer name is generally referred to as *hostname*. The host name can be given as an IP number (e.g., 192.168.23.45). You can omit specification of the host name only if the MySQL server is running on the same computer as your client program.

In access checking, MySQL evaluates the information as to where the access request is coming from, that is, from what host name:

- The MySQL server must be capable of resolving the computer name. In establishing a connection, the server first receives from the client its IP number. Then the server attempts to find the associated computer name (by contacting a *name server*). If that is unsuccessful, then the computer uses the IP number instead of the name for determining whether access should be allowed.

- Even if the name resolution succeeds (so that a local connection is established), there can be complications. If you are working under Unix/Linux, there are two variants of how communication proceeds between client and server:
  - Usually, for reasons of efficiency, a local connection between client and server takes place over a *socket file*. In this case, *localhost* (the usual name of the local computer in a network) is the host name.
  - Only when the connection takes place over TCP/IP is the actual computer name used. This holds especially for Java programs, whose database driver does not support socket files.

> **POINTER**   *Extensive background information on these special cases and various other problems with host names and generally in establishing connections can be found later in this chapter.*

Default Values: If no other parameters are given in establishing a MySQL connection, then under Unix/Linux the current login name is given as user name, while under Windows it is the character string *ODBC*. As password an empty character string is passed. The host name is *localhost*.

You can easily test this. Launch the program `mysql` and execute the command *status*. The current user name is displayed in the line *current user*. The following commands were executed under Linux:

```
kofler:~ > mysql -p
Enter password: xxx
Welcome to the MySQL monitor.
mysql> status
  ...
Current user:    kofler@localhost
Connection:      localhost via UNIX socket
  ...
```

If in establishing a connection you must provide a user name other than the login name, a host name, and a password, then the start of `mysql` looks something like this:

```
kofler:~ > mysql -u surveyadmin -h uranus.sol -p
Enter password: xxx
Welcome to the MySQL monitor.
mysql> status
  ...
Current user:        surveyadmin@saturn.sol
Connection:          uranus.sol via TCP/IP
  ...
```

Here we have a TCP/IP connection between the client (computer *saturn.sol*) and the server (computer name *uranus.sol*).

> **REMARK** *MySQL recognizes the term* anonymous user. *This expression comes into play when any user name is permitted in establishing a connection to MySQL. (In the Windows default configuration this is precisely what is allowed.) In this case,* status *shows as* current user *the user name used when the connection was established, but internally, an empty character string is used as user name. This is important primarily for the evaluation of additional access privileges. Further background information is contained later in this chapter, where the inner workings of the access system are discussed.*

When a PHP script establishes the connection to the database and no other user name is supplied within mysql_connect() (or mysql_pconnect()), then what is used as user name is the name of the account under which the PHP interpreter is executed. (As a rule, this is the same account under which Apache is also executed. Thus for security reasons, most Unix/Linux systems use an account that has few privileges, such as *apache* or *wwwrun*.)

Default Security Settings

If you have newly installed MySQL on a test system, then you are starting out with an immensely insecure default setting, one that is not password-protected. It is interesting to note that this default setting depends on the operating system. Under Windows, the setting is even more insecure than under Unix and Linux. Please note that the default privileges have changed repeatedly over time. The specifications here relate to version 4.0.12.

Unix/Linux: The user *root* on the local system (host name *localhost* or *computername*) has unlimited rights. Furthermore, all users on the local system are permitted to access MySQL without a password; in contrast to *root*, these users have no rights whatsoever (they can't even execute a *SELECT* command). Access from an external computer is by default not allowed.

Windows: The user *root* has, as under Unix/Linux, unlimited rights. However, the security dilemma under Windows is more aggravating, since *root* is allowed access not only from the local system, but from an external computer in the network.

Moreover, all users of the local system can obtain access under an arbitrary name and have extensive access privileges; for example, they can read all databases, as well as alter them and completely delete them. Finally, anyone can log in (any user name, any host name), although such users, at least in this case, have no rights, and thus can do little after establishing a connection.

> **CAUTION**   *To make things perfectly clear: According to the MySQL default installation,* root *is not protected by a password. Under Unix/Linux anyone with access to the local system can connect to MySQL as* root *and do whatever he or she wants with your databases. Under windows it is not even necessary to use the local computer: A connection as* root *is possible over a network. In the next section, on first aid, you will learn how with a little effort you can replace this default setting with something more restrictive.*

> **REMARK**   *For those with little experience with Unix/Linux,* root *under Unix/Linux plays somewhat the same role as* Administrator *under Windows, that is, a superuser with almost unrestricted privileges. However, be advised that user names under MySQL have no connection with the login names for the operating system. Thus* root *has so many privileges under MySQL because the MySQL default setting was chosen, not because under Unix/Linux* root *has such privileges. It would have been possible to choose a name other than* root *for the MySQL user with administrative access rights.*

You may perhaps be asking yourself where the default security settings come from. These settings are stored in the *mysql* database, which under Windows is created by the MySQL setup program setup.exe. Under Unix/Linux, the script mysql_install_db is executed during RPM installation, which creates and sets up the *mysql* database.

Under Unix/Linux one can execute *mysql_install_db* manually, for example, to re-create the *mysql* database. To do this, the MySQL server must first be stopped. The script must be executed under the same account that is used for executing the MySQL server (usually *mysql*). You can execute *mysql_install_db* also as *root*, in which case you must be the owner of the mysql database directory and change the following files contained therein:

```
root# mysql_install_db
root# chown mysql -R /var/lib/mysql/mysql
```

Test Databases

Regardless of the operating system under which MySQL is installed, any user who connects to MySQL can create test databases. The only condition is that the name of the database must begin with the letters *test* (with older MySQL installations under Unix/Linux it must begin with *test_*). Please note that not only can every MySQL user create such a database, in addition, every user can read, alter, and delete all data in such a database. In fact, anyone can delete the entire database. In short, the data in *test* databases are completely unprotected.

> **POINTER** *Tables 9-3, 9-4, and 9-6 depict this default setting. To understand these figures it is necessary that you understand the* mysql *table functions* user *and* db, *which are described in this chapter.*

First Aid

Perhaps you are not quite ready to immerse yourself in the depths of SQL access management. In that case, this section provides a bit of first aid advice.

The instructions assume that you communicate with the MySQL server with the commands `mysql` and `mysqladmin`. You can, of course, execute equivalent commands with a graphical user interface.

Protecting the MySQL Installation Under Unix/Linux

The following commands assume that MySQL has been freshly installed and that no changes have been made to the default access privileges.

root *Password for Local Access*

With the following two commands you can secure *root* access with a password *xxx*. (Instead of *xxx*, you should, of course, provide the password of your choice.)

```
root# mysqladmin -u root -h computername password xxx
root# mysqladmin -u root -h localhost password xxx
```

Instead of *computername* you should give the name of the local computer (which you can determine with the command `hostname`). As we have mentioned, the name *localhost* is valid when the local connection is effected over a socket file (which is the usual state of affairs). On the other hand, *computername* holds when the local connection is via TCP/IP (in particular, with Java programs).

No Local Access Without Password: Please note that in accordance with the MySQL default settings, a MySQL connection can be made from the local computer with any user name other than *root*. In contrast to the *root* connection, such connections are, to be sure, provided with no privileges, but nonetheless they represent a security risk. (For example, such users have unrestricted access to *test* databases.)

However, here simple password security with `mysqladmin` is impossible, since there is no user name to which the password can be assigned. However, you can delete the two relevant entries in the *user* table of the *mysql* database. (This has the further advantage that in the evaluation of access privileges an invalid entry will not accidentally be introduced.) The necessary commands look like this:

```
root# mysql -p
Enter password: xxx
Welcome to the MySQL monitor. ...
mysql> USE mysql;
Database changed
mysql> DELETE FROM user WHERE user='';
Query OK, 2 rows affected (0.00 sec)
mysql> FLUSH PRIVILEGES;
Query OK, 0 rows affected (0.01 sec)
mysql> exit
```

Please note that in the future you will have to provide the password that was defined with `mysqladmin` at the beginning of this section to execute `mysql` and `mysqladmin` (option -p). *FLUSH PRIVILEGES* is necessary so that the changes carried out directly in the *mysql* database become effective. (MySQL keeps a copy of the *mysql* database in RAM, for speed optimization, which is updated via *FLUSH PRIVILEGES*. Instead of executing *FLUSH PRIVILEGES*, you can exit `mysql` and instead execute `mysqladmin reload`.)

Result: After execution of the above commands, only *root* from the local computer can gain access, and it must use a password.

Protecting the MySQL Installation Under Windows

The way of proceeding under Windows is very similar to that under Unix/Linux. However, the default configuration under Windows is even more insecure, for which reason a bit more work is necessary.

Furthermore, using the commands `mysql` and `mysqladmin` is more complex (in particular, when you wish to pass parameters). The simplest way of proceeding is first to open a command window (START | PROGRAMS | ACCESSORIES | COMMAND PROMPT) and there use `cd` to make the `bin\` directory of the MySQL installation the current directory. (Hint: You will save some typing if you move the directory via *Drag&Drop* from Explorer into the command window.)

> **TIP** *In the following, for the sake of clarity, we shall always launch* `mysql` *anew in order to carry out the individual security measures. If you wish to execute all of the security measures at once, you will, of course, not have to quit* `mysql` *each time.*

root **Password for Local Access**: With the following command you can secure *root* for the local computer with a password (where instead of *xxx* you provide the password of your choice). This example assumes that MySQL was installed in the directory `Q:\Programs\mysql`.

```
Q:\> cd 'Q:\Program \mysql\bin'
Q:\ ... \bin> mysql -u root
Welcome to the MySQL monitor.
```

```
mysql> SET PASSWORD FOR root@localhost = PASSWORD('xxx');
Query OK, 0 row affected (0.00 sec)
mysql> FLUSH PRIVILEGES;
Query OK, 0 rows affected (0.01 sec)
```

Instead of executing *SET PASSWORD* in *mysql*, it must also be possible simply to execute the command `mysqladmin -u root -h localhost password xxx` in order to change the password for *root*. However, it appears that this command does not always function reliably under Windows, and often, instead of changing the *root* password for *localhost*, changes the *root* password for access by any number of other computers.

No *root* Access from External Computers: The following commands prevent *root* access from external computers.

```
Q:\ ... \bin> mysql -u root -p
Enter password: xxx

Welcome to the MySQL monitor.
mysql> USE mysql;
mysql> DELETE FROM user WHERE user='root' AND host='%';
Query OK, 1 row affected (0.00 sec)
mysql> FLUSH PRIVILEGES;
Query OK, 0 rows affected (0.01 sec)
```

Fewer Privileges for Local Users: In the default setting, local users have almost unrestricted rights, even if they do not register as *root*. The following command deletes all privileges for non*root* access.

```
mysql> REVOKE ALL ON *.* FROM ''@localhost;
Query OK, 1 row affected (0.00 sec)
mysql> REVOKE GRANT OPTION ON *.* FROM ''@localhost;
Query OK, 1 row affected (0.00 sec)
mysql> FLUSH PRIVILEGES;
Query OK, 0 rows affected (0.01 sec)
```

No Local Access Without a Password: Local users can still access universally visible databases (for example, those whose name begins with *test_*).

If it is not your wish that anyone with access to the local computer be able to register without a password, you can do without the above command and instead simply forbid local access without a password. There is another reason to recommend this course of action: The entry *User = ' '* and *Host = 'localhost'* is often unsuspectingly given preference to other entries in the user table (e.g., those with *User = 'a name'* and *User = 'a name'* and *Host = '%'*). By deleting the entry, you avoid possible confusion:

```
mysql> DELETE FROM user WHERE user='' AND host='localhost';
Query OK, 1 row affected (0.00 sec)
mysql> FLUSH PRIVILEGES;
Query OK, 0 rows affected (0.01 sec)
```

From now on, administrative tasks are possible only as *root* under *localhost*. Therefore, you must use the commands `mysql` and `mysqladmin` with the options `-u root` and `-p`.

No Access from External Computers Without a Password: In the default setting, anyone can register with MySQL from an external computer. This access comes with no privileges, but nonetheless it should be prevented. Here are the necessary commands:

```
mysql> DELETE FROM user WHERE host='%' AND user='';
Query OK, 1 row affected (0.00 sec)
mysql> FLUSH PRIVILEGES;
Query OK, 0 rows affected (0.01 sec)
```

WinMySQLadmin Users: If you specified a user name and password at the initial launch of WinMySQLadmin, then under some conditions, the program has an additional user with unrestricted privileges (like those of *root*). This is particularly the case for older versions of WinMySQLadmin. In the following it is assumed that the user name is *namexy*.

User *namexy* is secured by a password, but this password is stored in plain text in the file `Windows\my.ini`. Anyone who is permitted to work at the computer and knows a bit about MySQL can easily obtain unrestricted access to MySQL. You have three options for closing this security loophole:

- Delete the user *namexy*.

- Delete the password line in `Windows\my.ini`.

- Restrict the privileges of this user.

The first two of these options are not ideal, because the program WinMySQLadmin can then be used only with severe restrictions. A workable compromise consists in setting the privileges of *namexy* in such a way that the most important administrative tasks are possible, but alteration of data is forbidden.

```
mysql> REVOKE INSERT, UPDATE, DELETE, DROP, FILE, ALTER
    > ON *.* FROM namexy@localhost;
Query OK, 1 row affected (0.00 sec)
mysql> REVOKE GRANT OPTION ON *.* FROM namexy@localhost;
Query OK, 1 row affected (0.00 sec)
mysql> FLUSH PRIVILEGES;
Query OK, 0 rows affected (0.01 sec)
```

REMARK   *From this point on,* `mysql` *commands will be shown without the* `mysql>` *prompt.*

Setting Access Without a Password

Perhaps you were too restrictive in securing MySQL and now would like to provide general access on the local computer (and possibly to a set of particular other computers as well) without the necessity of providing a user name and password. Then simply execute in `mysql` the following command:

```
GRANT USAGE ON *.* TO ''@localhost
```

Perhaps you would like to give the users some more privileges. Then in the command given above replace *USAGE* by a list containing, for example, *SELECT, INSERT, UPDATE*, etc. (A list of all possible privileges that are available under MySQL appears in the next section.)

Creating a New Database and User

Among the bread-and-butter tasks of a database administrator is setting up a new database and making it available to a user (who then can insert tables and fill them with data).

This task is easily accomplished. You have merely to execute the following two commands with `mysql`. The result is the creation of the database *forum*, to which the user *forumadmin* has been granted unrestricted access. (If you execute the commands in `mysql`, do me and yourself a favor and do not forget to terminate the commands with a semicolon.)

```
CREATE DATABASE forum
GRANT ALL ON forum.* TO forumadmin@localhost IDENTIFIED BY 'xxx'
```

It is often useful to create a second access to the database, one with fewer privileges (and therefore with fewer security risks):

```
GRANT SELECT, INSERT, UPDATE, DELETE ON forum.*
  TO forumuser@localhost IDENTIFIED BY 'xxx'
```

Depending on the application, it can be a good idea to give ordinary users the ability to lock (*LOCK*) tables and create temporary tables. This is possible since MySQL 4.0. (In MySQL 3.23, every user who had the right to change tables could execute *LOCK*. Everyone could create temporary tables who had the right to create any tables at all.)

In the following command, the *IDENTIFIED* part is omitted. The password of *forumuser* is then left unchanged:

```
GRANT LOCK TABLES, CREATE TEMPORARY TABLES ON forum.*
TO forumuser@localhost
```

Creating New Users

After the database that we have just created, *forum*, has been in operation for a while, it turns out that another individual, operating from another computer, requires unrestricted access to this database. The following command gives user *forumadmin2* on computer *uranus.sol* full privileges:

```
GRANT ALL ON forum.* TO forumadmin2@uranus.sol IDENTIFIED BY 'xxx'
```

If you wish to allow *forumadmin2* to sign in from any computer, then the command looks like this:

```
GRANT ALL ON forum.* TO forumadmin2@'%' IDENTIFIED BY 'xxx'
```

If you wish to go so far as to allow *forumadmin2* access to all databases (and not just *forum*), the command is as follows:

```
GRANT ALL ON *.* TO forumadmin2@uranus.sol IDENTIFIED BY 'xxx'
```

In comparison to *root*, the only privilege that *forumadmin2* does not possess is the right to change access privileges. But a small change remedies the situation:

```
GRANT ALL ON *.* TO forumadmin2@uranus.sol
IDENTIFIED BY 'xxx' WITH GRANT OPTION
```

Granting the Right to Create One's Own Database

When there are many users each with his or her own databases (for example, on the system of an Internet service provider), it becomes increasingly burdensome for the administrator to create yet another database for a particular user. In such cases it would be a good idea to give this user the right to create databases. In order to prevent a jungle of databases from appearing with no clue as to which belongs to whom, it is usual practice to allow a user to create only databases that begin with that user's user name. That is, a user named, say, *kofler*, is allowed to create databases named, say, *kofler_test*, *kofler_forum*, *kofler1*, *koflerXy*, etc., but no databases whose names do not begin with *kofler*.

In the following, the way to proceed will be demonstrated for a user with the remarkable user name *username*. If this user is not yet known to MySQL, then first it must be created:

```
GRANT USAGE ON *.* TO username@localhost IDENTIFIED BY 'xxx'
```

Then, sad to tell, you must wrestle with an *INSERT* command, since the more convenient *GRANT* command does not, alas, permit wild cards in the specification of database names. Therefore, the necessary changes in the database *db* must be made directly:

```
INSERT INTO mysql.db (Host, Db, User, Select_priv, Insert_priv,
  Update_priv, Delete_priv, Create_priv, Drop_priv, Grant_priv,
  References_priv, Index_priv, Alter_priv, Create_tmp_table_priv,
  Lock_tables_priv)
VALUES ('localhost', 'username%', 'username', 'Y', 'Y', 'Y', 'Y',
'Y', 'Y', 'N', 'Y', 'Y',
'Y', 'Y', 'Y')
```

For these changes to become effective, *FLUSH PRIVILEGES* must finally be executed.

```
FLUSH PRIVILEGES
```

Honey, I Forgot the root Password!

What do you do if you have forgotten the *root* password for MySQL (and there is no other MySQL user with sufficient administrative privileges and a known password to restore the forgotten password)?

Fear not, for I bring you glad tidings. MySQL has thought about this possibility. The way to proceed is this: Terminate MySQL (that is, the MySQL server mysqld) and then restart it with the option --skip-grant-tables. The result is that the table with access privileges is not loaded. You can now delete the encrypted password for *root*, terminate MySQL, and then restart without the given option. Now you can give the *root* user a new password.

The following example is based on MySQL under Linux, although the same procedure is possible under other configurations (though with slight variations). In each case, we assume that you have system administrator privileges on the operating system under which MySQL is running.

The first step is to terminate MySQL:

```
root# /etc/rc.d/mysql stop
```

Under Windows you end MySQL in the Service Manager (CONTROL PANEL | ADMINISTRATIVE TOOLS | SERVICES).

In the second step you relaunch mysqld via safe_mysqld (a launch script for mysqld) with the option --skip-grant-tables. The option --user specifies the account under which mysqld should be executed. The option --datadir tells where the MySQL databases can be found. Here the same setting as with a normal MySQL launch should be used. (The precise instruction depends on the system configuration.)

```
root# startproc /usr/bin/_mysqld_safe --user=mysql \
        --datadir=/var/lib/mysql --skip-grant-tables
```

Under Windows, execute the following commands for a manual start:

```
C:\> cd mysql\bin
C:\mysql\bin> mysqld --skip-grant-tables
```

Now you can use mysql to reset the *root* password both for the host name *localhost* and the actual computer name. (Under Windows you must execute mysql in a second command window, since the first window is blocked by mysqld.)

```
root# mysql -u root
Welcome to MySQL monitor.
mysql> USE mysql;
Database changed.
mysql> UPDATE user SET password=PASSWORD('new password')
    > WHERE user='root' AND host='localhost';
Query OK, 1 row affected (0.00 sec)

mysql> UPDATE user SET password=PASSWORD('new password')
    > WHERE user='root' AND host='computername';
Query OK, 1 row affected (0.00 sec)
```

Then, you must restart MySQL so that the access database *mysql* can again be used. (As long as MySQL is running with --skip-grant-tables, anyone can establish a connection to the server with unlimited privileges!) Under Linux you execute the following commands:

```
root# /etc/init.d/mysql[d] start
root# /etc/init.d/mysql[d] start
```

Under Windows, you stop MySQL with the following command:

```
C:\mysql\bin> mysqladmin shutdown
```

For a subsequent restart, use either the SERVICES dialog (CONTROL PANEL | ADMINISTRATIVE TOOLS) or WinMySQLadmin.

> **CAUTION**   *The procedures described here can, of course, be used by an attacker who wishes to spy on your data or manipulate it somehow. The only (fortunately, not easily achieved) condition is to acquire Unix/Linux root access (or administrator rights under Windows). This shows how important it is not only to secure MySQL, but also the computer on which MySQL is running. (The topic of security under Unix/Linux and Windows is, like any number of other topics, beyond the scope of this book.)*

The Internal Workings of the Access System

You are perhaps, dear reader, sorely tempted to skip over this foundational section, especially since the management of access privileges is rather complicated. However, I strongly suggest that you gird up your loins and make the effort to read through the description of the *mysql* tables. Regardless of the means that you use for setting up security on your system, it is helpful first to understand the inner workings of the system itself. This holds even for the case that you yourself are not the manager of access privileges, but that they are managed by a system administrator. It is only when you understand how it all works that you will be able to tell your system administrator just what your needs are.

Two-Tiered Access Control

Access control for MySQL databases is managed in two tiers: In the first tier it is merely checked whether the user has the right to establish a connection to MySQL. This is accomplished by the evaluation of three pieces of information: user name, host name, and password.

Only if a connection can be established does the second level of access control come into play, which involves every single database command. For example, if a *SELECT* is executed, MySQL checks whether the user has access rights to the database, the table, and the column. If an *INSERT* is executed, then MySQL tests whether the user is permitted to alter the database, the table, and finally the column.

Privileges

How, then, does MySQL manage the information as to which commands can be executed? MySQL uses tables in which are stored *privileges*. If a user, let us call her *athena*, has a *SELECT* privilege for the database *owls*, then she is permitted to read all the data in *owls* (but not to change it). If *athena* has a global *SELECT* privilege, then it holds for all databases saved under MySQL.

The privileges recognized by MySQL are displayed in Table 9-1. Note that the names in the corresponding columns of *mysql* tables always end in *_priv*. The *Select* privilege is thus stored in the column *Select_priv*. In part, the column names are abbreviated (e.g., *Create_tmp_table* for the *Create-Temporary-Table* privilege).

Note also that there are quite a few new privileges in MySQL 4.0 that were not present in version 3.23 (e.g., *Create Temporary Table, Execute, Lock Tables, Show Databases, Replication Client, Replication Slave, Super*), and that many old favorites have been changed (*Process*).

In the MySQL documentation, you will encounter (for example, in the description of the *GRANT* command) the privileges *All* and *Usage*. *All* means that all privileges should be granted with the exception of *Grant*. *Usage* means that all privileges should be denied.

All and *Usage* are thus themselves not independent privileges, but an aid in avoiding a listing of privileges in executing the *GRANT* command.

The meaning of most of the privileges listed in Table 9-1 should be clear without further explanation. For the not-so-clear privileges there will be some explanation in the coming paragraphs. *Replication Client* and *Replication Slave* are described in Chapter 10 in the discussion of replication.

> **REMARK** *Privileges are given in this book with an intial capital letter followed by lowercase letters in order to distinguish them from their like-named SQL commands (*Select *privilege and* SELECT *command). MySQL couldn't care less how you distribute uppercase and lowercase letters.*

Table 9-1. MySQL privileges

For access to tables	
Select	may read data (*SELECT* command)
Insert	may insert new records (*INSERT*)
Update	may change existing records (*UPDATE*)
Delete	may delete existing records (*DELETE*)
Lock Tables	may block tables (*LOCK*)
Execute	may execute stored procedures (since MySQL 5.0)
For databases, tables, and indexes	
Create	may create new databases and tables
Create Temporary Table	may create temporary tables
Alter	may rename and change the structure of tables (*ALTER*)
Index	may create and delete indexes for tables
References	undocumented; perhaps in the future will allow one to create relations between tables
Drop	may delete existing tables and databases
For file access	
File	may read and change files in the local file system
For MySQL administration	
Grant Option	may give other users one's own privileges
Show Databases	may obtain a list of all databases (*SHOW DATABASES*)
Process	may list MySQL processes of other users (*SHOW PROCESSLIST*)
Super	may terminate processes of other users (*KILL*) and execute certain other administrative commands (*CHANGE/PURGE MASTER, SET GLOBAL*)
Reload	may execute various commands (*reload, refresh, flush-xxx*)
Replication Client	may obtain information about the participants in a replication system
Replication Slave	may read MySQL server data via replication
Shutdown	may terminate MySQL

The Grant Privilege

The *Grant* privilege indicates that a MySQL user can dispense access privileges. (This is most easily accomplished with the SQL command *GRANT*, whence the name of the privilege.) However, the ability to dispense privileges is limited to the privileges possessed by the grantor. That is, no user can give privileges to another that he or she does not already possess.

CAUTION *The* Grant Option *privilege is an often overlooked security risk. For example, a test database is created to which all members of a team have unrestricted access. To this end, all the privileges in the relevant entry in the* db *table are set to* Y *(the* db *table will be described a bit later).*

A perhaps unforeseen consequence is that everyone who has unrestricted access to this test table can give unrestricted access privileges (either to him- or herself or to other MySQL users) for other databases as well!

The File Privilege

MySQL users with the *File* privilege may use SQL commands for direct access to the file system of the computer on which the MySQL server is running, for example, with the command *SELECT . . . INTO OUTFILE name* or the command *LOAD DATA* or with the function *LOAD_FILE*.

In the case of file access, it is necessary, of course, to pay heed to the access privileges of the file system. (Under Unix/Linux the MySQL server normally runs under the *mysql* account. Therefore, only those files that are readable by the Unix/Linux user *mysql* can be read.) Nevertheless, the *File* privilege is often a considerable security risk.

The Privileges PROCESS and SUPER

The *Process* privilege gives the user the right to determine, using the command *SHOW PROCESSLIST*, a list of all processes (connections), including those of other users. (One may obtain a list of one's own processes without this privilege.)

The privilege *Super* permits the user to end both his own and others' processes with *KILL*. (If the *Super* privilege has not been granted, then only the current process can be ended.)

The *Super* privilege also permits the execution of some administrative commands: *CHANGE MASTER* for executing the client configuration of a replication system, *PURGE MASTER* to delete binary logging files, and *SET GLOBAL* for changing global MySQL variables.

Global Privileges Versus Object Privileges

In MySQL privileges can be chosen to be either global or related to a particular object. Global indicates that the privilege is valid for all MySQL objects (that is, for all databases, tables, and columns of a table).

The management of object-related privileges is somewhat more difficult, but it is also more secure. Only thus can you achieve, for example, that a particular MySQL user can alter a particular table, and not all tables managed under MySQL. An assumption in the use of object-related privileges is that the corresponding global privileges are not set. (What is globally allowed cannot be withheld at the object level.)

This hierarchical idea is maintained within the object privileges as well. First it is checked whether access to an entire database is allowed. Only if that is not allowed is it then checked whether access to the entire table named in the SQL command is allowed. Only if that is forbidden is it then checked whether perhaps access to individual columns of the table is allowed.

The mysql Database

It is not surprising that the management by MySQL of access privileges is carried out by means of a database. This database has the name *mysql*, and it consists of several tables, responsible for various aspects of access privileges.

> **REMARK**   *It is sometimes not entirely a simple matter to distinguish among the various uses to which the word "MySQL" is put. In this book we attempt to use different type styles to obtain some degree of clarity:*
>
> - *MySQL: the database system as a whole.*
> - `mysqld`: *the MySQL server (MySQL daemon).*
> - `mysql`: *the MySQL monitor (a type of command interpreter).*
> - *mysql: the database for managing MySQL access privileges.*

The Tables of the Database `mysql`

The database *mysql* contains six tables (five in earlier versions) of which five are for managing access privileges. These five tables are often referred to as *grant* tables. The following list provides an overview of the tasks of these six tables:

- *user* controls who (user name) can access MySQL from which computer (host name). This table also contains global privileges.
- *db* specifies which user can access which databases.
- *host* extends the *db* table with information on the permissible host names (those that are not present in *db*).
- *tables_priv* specifies who can access which tables of a database.
- *columns_priv* specifies who can access which columns of a table.
- *func* enables the management of UDFs (*user-defined functions*); this is still undocumented.

> **REMARK**   *When you newly install MySQL, the default values of* user *and* db *depend on the operating system. The contents of these two tables are displayed in Tables 9-3, 9-4, and 9-6, which appear later. The effect of these settings was discussed earlier. (The tables* host, tables_priv, *and* columns_priv *start off life empty.)*
>
> *In MySQL's two-tiered access system, the table* user *is solely responsible for the first level (that is, for the connection to MySQL). The* user *table contains all global privileges.*
>
> *For the second tier (that is, access to specific objects: databases, tables, and columns) it is the tables* db, host, tables_priv, *and* columns_priv *that are responsible, in addition to* user.
>
> *The tables* db, host, tables_priv, *and* columns_priv *come into play in this order when the privileges for their respective tiers are set to* N *(which stands for "No"). In other words, if the* SELECT *privilege is granted to a user in* user, *then the other four tables will not be consulted in checking the permissibility of a* SELECT *command executed by that user.*
>
> *The result is that if fine distinctions in access privileges are to be made, the global privileges in the* user *table must be set to* N.

An Example

Before we attempt to describe the individual tables in detail, we present an example: Let us suppose that a particular MySQL user, let us call him *zeus*, is to be allowed to read a particular column of a particular table, and nothing else. Then *zeus* (user name, host name, password) must be entered in the *user* table. There all of *zeus*'s global privileges will be set to *N*.

Furthermore, *zeus* (user name, host name) must be registered in the *columns_priv* table as well. There it must also be specified which column *zeus* is permitted to access (database name, table name, column name). Finally, there the *Select* privilege (and only this privilege) must be activated. In the tables *db*, *host*, and *tables_priv* no entries for *zeus* are necessary.

The Table user

Table 9-2. Structure of the user *table*

Field	Type	Null	Default
Host	char(60)	No	
User	char(16)	No	
Password	char(16) (char(45) since MySQL 4.1)	No	
Select_priv	enum('N', 'Y')	No	N
Insert_priv	enum('N', 'Y')	No	N
Update_priv	enum('N', 'Y')	No	N
Delete_priv	enum('N', 'Y')	No	N
Create_priv	enum('N', 'Y')	No	N
Drop_priv	enum('N', 'Y')	No	N
Reload_priv	enum('N', 'Y')	No	N
Shutdown_priv	enum('N', 'Y')	No	N
Process_priv	enum('N', 'Y')	No	N
File_priv	enum('N', 'Y')	No	N
Grant_priv	enum('N', 'Y')	No	N
References_priv	enum('N', 'Y')	No	N
Index_priv	enum('N', 'Y')	No	N
Alter_priv	enum('N', 'Y')	No	N
Show_db_priv	enum('N', 'Y')	No	N
Super_priv	enum('N', 'Y')	No	N
Create_tmp_table_priv	enum('N', 'Y')	No	N
Lock_tables_priv	enum('N', 'Y')	No	N
Execute_priv	enum('N', 'Y')	No	N
Repl_slave_priv	enum('N', 'Y')	No	N
Repl_client_priv	enum('N', 'Y')	No	N
ssl_type	enum('', 'ANY', 'X509', 'SPECIFIED')	No	0
ssl_cipher	blob	No	0
x509_issuer	blob	No	0
x509_subject	blob	No	0
max_questions	int	No	0
max_updates	int	No	0
max_connections	int	No	0

The *user* table (see Table 9-2) fulfills three tasks:

- This table alone regulates who has any access at all to MySQL.

- global privileges can be granted through this table. Note that the column names of the table differ somewhat from those of the privileges (e.g., the *Create_tmp_table* column for the *Create Temporary Table* privilege).

- Since MySQL 4.0 the table contains several new columns for encrypted access via SSL (secure socket layer), for identity control in accordance with the X509 standard and for managing such control, and for the number of database connections, that is, the maximal number of updates and queries permitted to be executed per hour.

Access Control (User, Host, and Password Columns)

For control over who can connect to MySQL there are three necessary identifiers—as we have mentioned already several times—that must be evaluated: user name, host name, and password. Here we shall say a few words about how this information is stored in the fields *User*, *Host*, and *Password*.

- **User Name:** Access control is case-sensitive. In the *User* field no wild cards are allowed. If the *User* field is empty, then any user name is permitted for accessing MySQL. Then the user is considered to be an anonymous user. This means that in the second tier of access control the actual user name is not used, but rather an empty character string.

- **Password:** The password must be stored in the column *Password* and there be encrypted with the SQL function *PASSWORD*. It is not possible to store a password in plain text. Furthermore, wild cards are not allowed. If the password field remains empty, then a connection can be made with no password whatsoever. (An empty password field thus does not mean that an arbitrary password can be given.)

  With MySQL 4.1 the encryption of the *Password* columns has changed. The encrypted code of the password has been increased from 16 to 45 characters. Be thou once more warned: For reasons of security you should never use as your MySQL password a password that you use to gain admittance to the operating system.

- **Host Name:** The host name can be given either as a name or as an IP number. Here the wild cards _ (an arbitrary character) or % (zero or more characters) are permitted, for example, *192.168.37.%* or *%.myfavoriteenterprise.com*. In the case of IP numbers, the forms (which are equivalent to those of the first example) *192.168.37.0/255.255.255.0* and *192.168.37.0/24* are permitted. If the host name is given simply as the character %, a connection can be made from any computer. To enable access to users on the local computer, specify the host name *localhost*. As with the user name, the host name is case-sensitive.

  To enable access on the local computer, give *localhost* as the host name. When Unix/Linux users wish to obtain local access via TCP/IP (important for Java applications), then the actual computer name must be used as the host name. If both forms of access are to be enabled, then the user must be defined twice, once with the host name *localhost*, and once with *computername*.

POINTER *Normally, the host name must be given together with the domain name. Thus if the computer* saturn.sol *wants to gain access from the network* *.sol, *the column* Host *in the* user *table must contain the character string* saturn.sol *and not just* saturn. *Depending on your network configuration and that of the existing domain name server, it could be that one has to specify the host name without the domain name. Further details on this and other picky details will be discussed further along in this chapter.*

The Order of Evaluation in the user Table

It often happens that in making a connection to MySQL several records match the given login data. If, for example, you log in as *root* from the local computer under the default settings of the *user* table for Windows, then all four entries would match. MySQL then decides in favor of the most nearly exact description (thus in this case for *root/localhost* and not for ' '/%).). The reason for this is that with an exact match in the login one can expect more in the way of access privileges.

In order to speed up the selection of the correct record, the *user* table is sorted internally by MySQL. Here the field *Host* serves as the first sort criterion, and *User* as the second. In sorting, those character strings without the wild cards _ and % are given priority. Empty character strings and the character string % come in last in the sort order. Tables 9-3 and 9-4 show the default settings for the *user* table in their respective internal sort orders.

CAUTION *The order in which the entries in the* user *table are evaluated often leads to unexpected problems. Suppose that the MySQL default settings hold for user privileges and that you add a new user with* Host = '%' *and* User = 'peter' *in the* user *table. If* peter *now attempts to register from the local computer (that is, from* localhost*), it is not the entry* %/'peter' *that comes into play, but the entry from the default setting* Host = 'localhost' *and* User = ' '. *The reason is that MySQL gives precedence to entries with a unique hostname (*Host = 'localhost'*) over those with a wild card (*Host='%'*). The easiest and surest way out of this difficulty is to delete the entry* Host = 'localhost' *and* User = ' ' *from the* user *table.*

Privileges

In addition to MySQL access control, the *user* table also has the responsibility for global privileges. To this end there are currently 21 fields that take part, which can be set to *Y* or *N*. Since *Y* stands for "yes," this setting means that the associated privilege is set globally for the MySQL user (for all databases, tables, and columns). Contrariwise, *N* means "no" (or *non* in French, *nein* in German, *nyet* in Russian; you get the idea), and so such a setting means that the operation in question is not allowed globally, and therefore the tables *db*, *host*, *tables_priv*, and *columns_priv* will be consulted for object-specific privileges.

SSL Encryption and X509 Identification

To make communication between client and server particularly secure, the X509 standard can be used for user identification, and data transfer can be effected with SSL (secure socket layer) encryption. This requires a special compiled version of the MySQL server such as *MySQL Max*. (The SSL functions are not currently integrated into *MySQL Standard.*) Whether your version of MySQL supports SSL can be determined with the SQL command *SHOW VARIABLES LIKE 'have_openssl'*.

Note that the encryption of data affects the speed of the MySQL server and makes sense only if data transfer is taking place over the Internet, that is, if the MySQL server and the client are running on different computers.

The encryption of a local connection (if, for example, PHP/Apache accesses a MySQL server that is running on the same computer) does not increase the security of the application. In this case, the security is much more greatly determined by how communication between Apache and the web user takes place (e.g., encryption via HTTPS).

> **POINTER** *This book does not go into details of the configuration and application of SSL and X509. More extensive information can be found in the MySQL book of Paul DuBois (second edition) and the MySQL documentation on the Internet:*
>
> `http://www.mysql.com/doc/en/Secure_connections.html`

Limitation of MySQL

With the three columns *max_questions, max_updates, max_connections* you can specify how many queries (*SELECT* commands) and data changes (*INSERT* and *UPDATE*) are permitted to be executed per hour or how many connections established. The default setting 0 means that there are no restrictions.

Default Setting

As we described in the introduction to this chapter, after installation of MySQL there are various default settings of the *user* table that depend on the particular operating system. Tables 9-3 and 9-4 give these settings (for MySQL version 4.0.*n*).

Table 9-3. Default setting for the user *table under Unix/Linux*

Host	User	Password	Select_priv to Alter_priv	Super_priv to Repl_client_priv	ssl_xxx, x509_xxx	max_xxx
localhost	root		Y	Y	NULL	0
computer name	root		Y	Y	NULL	0
localhost			N	N	NULL	0
computer name			N	N	NULL	0

Table 9-4. Default setting for the user *table under Windows*

Host	User	Password	Select_priv to Alter_priv	Super_priv to Repl_client_priv	ssl_xxx, x509_xxx	max_xxx
localhost	root		Y	Y	NULL	0
localhost			Y	N	NULL	0
%	root		Y	Y	NULL	0
%			N	N	NULL	0

The user.Host *Column*

As briefly mentioned in the previous section, the *Host* column of the *user* table specifies from which computer a particular user is to obtain access to the MySQL server. The computer name can be given with the wild card % or by an IP number.

What looks simple at first glance is, alas, in practice a source of numerous problems. Therefore, this section contains various pieces of background information and some tips for solving connection problems.

Host Name with or without Domain Name?

When you insert a new entry in the *user* table, the question arises whether the host name should appear with or without the domain name, that is, for example, *uranus* or *uranus.sol*. Unfortunately, there is no generally valid answer to this question. You must simply experiment and find out. However, I have made the discovery that the probability of success is higher if you include the domain name. (The resolution of network names depends on the network configuration and, to the extent available, the configuration of the domain name server, thus on factors that lie outside of MySQL.)

Based on the default configuration, under Unix/Linux the host name, that is, the column *user.Host*, is entered without domain name (see Table 9-3). This is due to the script mysql_install_db, which is executed during the installation of the MySQL server. If MySQL evaluates the complete network name in establishing a connection, then a local connection under TCP/IP is impossible. The problem is that mysql -u root is functioning, but mysql -u root -h *computername* is not.

In this case, you have to change the domain name explicitly. The necessary commands look like those below (of course, you will have to change *uranus.sol* and *uranus* to the names that apply in your situation):

```
root# mysql -u root
mysql> USE mysql;
mysql> UPDATE user SET host="uranus.sol" WHERE host="Uranus";
mysql> FLUSH PRIVILEGES;
```

computerame *Versus* localhost *Under Unix/Linux*

When the MySQL server is executed under Unix/Linux, the default security settings provide two entries for local access to the server: *localhost* and *computername* (see Table 9-3). The reason for this dualism is that connections between the client program and the MySQL server can take place in two ways (only when client and server run on the same computer): over a socket file or via the network protocol TCP/IP.

- **Socket file:** The use of a socket file avoids the overhead of TCP/IP. For this reason, most MySQL clients that access MySQL from the local computer use this variant. In checking access privileges, the entry *localhost* is used.

  The socket file generally has the name var/lib/mysql/mysql.sock. The name can be changed in /etc/my.cnf with the option socket.

- **TCP/IP:** However, there are clients that do not support sockets. (This holds in particular for all clients programmed in Java.) In this case, TCP/IP is used even for connections to a local server. In checking access privileges, now the entry *computername* is used. For this reason it is to be recommended that for every *localhost* user an equivalent user be created for whom the name of the local computer is specified as host name.

If you launch the program mysql on the same computer as the MySQL server, you can test both connection options: If you do not specify a host name or if you give *localhost* as host name, the connection succeeds over the socket file (first and second commands below). If, on the other hand, you specify the actual computer name or the IP address, the connection proceeds over TCP/IP (third through sixth commands). You can use the command *status* to determine how the connection actually is made:

```
linux:~ $ mysql                      -u root -p    (1) via Socket-Datei
linux:~ $ mysql -h localhost    -u root -p    (2) via Socket-Datei
linux:~ $ mysql -h uranus        -u root -p    (3) via TCP/IP
linux:~ $ mysql -h uranus.sol   -u root -p    (4) via TCP/IP
linux:~ $ mysql -h 127.0.0.1    -u root -p    (5) via TCP/IP
linux:~ $ mysql -h 192.168.0.2 -u root -p    (6) via TCP/IP
Welcome to the MySQL monitor. ...
mysql> status
 ...
Current user:
 root@uranus.sol
SSL:                    Not in use
Current pager:          less
Using outfile:          ' '
Server version:         4.0.4-beta-log
Protocol version:       10
Connection:
    uranus via TCP/IP
TCP port:
    3306
 ...
```

REMARK *When client and server run on different computers, the connection always runs via TCP/IP, and there is no issue of duality.*

Under Windows NT/2000/XP there are two possibilities for a local connection: Communication can take place over TCP/IP or over a named pipe *(*mysql *option* --pipe*). However, this works only if the MySQL server was compiled with* named pipe *support, which is not the default. In contrast to the situation under Unix/Linux, the same user entry in the* user *table is used. The host name* localhost *is used for all local connections, regardless of how the connection is made.*

localhost *Problems with Red Hat Linux*

With Red Hat Linux it can be necessary, depending on the configuration, to enter *localhost.localdomain* in the *Host* column for local TCP/IP connections (instead of the otherwise usual computer name). The reason is that with Red Hat, the IP address 127.0.0.1 is linked to the name *localhost.localdomain* (file /etc/hosts).

localhost *Problems with SuSE Linux*

With SuSE as well there can be problems with *localhost*. The reason is that after the execution of a network configuration, the line *127.0.0.2 computername* is entered in /etc/hosts. This line can cause confusion if *computername* is associated with a different IP address. Such problems generally occur only when a local TCP/IP connection is sought. There are several options for alleviating this problem:

- As a first attempt, you should try to specify the complete computer name (including domain name) in the *Host* table. At least in my configuration, this was sufficient for establishing a local TCP/IP connection in spite of the 127.0.0.2 line in /etc/hosts.

- If that doesn't work, you can enter the IP number 127.0.0.2 in the *Host* column instead of the computer name. This should usually work, but it actually only alleviates the symptom, and does not get at the cause.

- A third variant is to specify the complete computer name in the *Host* column and to comment out the 127.0.0.2 line in /etc/hosts (by prefixing a # sign). However, then you must also set the variable *CHECK_ETC_HOSTS* in /etc/sysconfig/suseconfig to *no*. Otherwise, YaST undoes your change in /etc/hosts at the next opportunity.

  Then you must restart the network and the MySQL server, so that the changes can take effect and so that the MySQL server will no longer use temporary storage for name resolution:

  ```
  root# /etc/init.d/network restart
  root# /etc/init.d/mysql stop
  root# /etc/init.d/mysql start
  ```

  The main disadvantage of this variant is that there can now be compatibility problems with other SuSE packages that may depend on the SuSE standard configuration.

Establishing the Host Name and IP Address Under Unix/Linux

You can determine the current computer name with the command hostname. If you then pass this computer name to the command host, the complete computer name (including domain name) and associated IP address will be returned. Conversely, host can return a computer name given an IP address:

```
linux:~ $ /hostname
uranus
linux:~ $ /host uranus
uranus.sol. has address 192.168.0.2 linux:~ $ /host uranus.sol
uranus.sol. has address 192.168.0.2 linux:~ $ /host 192.168.0.2
2.0.168.192.in-addr.arpa. domain name pointer uranus.sol.
```

In addition to host, you can also use the command resolveip, which is installed
with MySQL. The MySQL server uses the same algorithm as resolveip in resolving
network names and IP addresses. If resolveip and host give different results, there is a
problem in the configuration. The most likely source of error is the file /etc/hosts or
an incorrect configuration of the domain name server (DNS) if one is used in the local
network:

```
linux:~ $ /resolveip uranus
IP address of uranus is 192.168.0.2

linux:~ $ /resolveip uranus.sol
IP address of uranus is 192.168.0.2

linux:~ $ /resolveip 192.168.0.2
Host name of 192.168.0.2 is uranus.sol
```

> **TIP** *The MySQL server takes care by default of the ordering of IP numbers and host
> names (so that repeated accesses can take place as rapidly as possible). If you change
> the network configuration, you must delete this temporary storage:*
>
> ```
> root# mysqladmin flush-hosts
> ```

> **REMARK** *Under Windows, the commands* hosts *and* resolveip *are not available.
> However, you can determine the computer name as under Unix/Linux with the
> command* hostname.

Host Name or IP Address?

In principle, in the *Host* column you can specify the computer's IP address instead
of the computer name. The advantage of IP numbers is that the numerous sources
of error in name resolution no longer exist. However, this advantage is paid for
in the drawback that in many networks, IP numbers frequently change (in some
circumstances at each restart if the IP number is assigned dynamically by a DHCP
server). Therefore, controlling access on the basis of IP addresses can succeed only if
the management of IP addresses in your network is organized relatively strictly.

The db and host Tables

The db Table

The *db* table (see Table 9-5) contains information on which databases a particular user is permitted to read, edit, and delete. The function of this table is easy to understand: If user *u* located at computer *h* wishes to access database *d* by executing a *SELECT* command and does not possess a global *Select* privilege, then MySQL pores over the *db* table and looks for the first *User/Host/Db* entry for the triple *u/h/d*. (As we saw in the case of the *user* table, uniquely identifying entries take precedence over those with wild cards. The entries are case-sensitive.) If a matching entry is found, then all that must be checked is whether the column *Select_priv* contains the value *Y*.

Table 9-5. Structure of the db *table*

Field	Type	Null	Default
Host	char(60)	No	
Db	char(64)	No	
User	char(16)	No	
Select_priv	enum('N', 'Y')	No	N
Insert_priv	enum('N', 'Y')	No	N
Update_priv	enum('N', 'Y')	No	N
Delete_priv	enum('N', 'Y')	No	N
Create_priv	enum('N', 'Y')	No	N
Drop_priv	enum('N', 'Y')	No	N
Grant_priv	enum('N', 'Y')	No	N
References_priv	enum('N', 'Y')	No	N
Index_priv	enum('N', 'Y')	No	N
Alter_priv	enum('N', 'Y')	No	N
Create_tmp_table_priv	enum('N', 'Y')	No	N
Lock_tables_priv	enum('N', 'Y')	No	N

Practically the same rules as in the *user* table hold for the settings of *User* and *Host* in the *db* table. The only exception relates to the *Host* column: If this remains empty, then MySQL evaluates the *host* table as well (see the heading "The *host* Table").

Default Setting

After installation of MySQL, all users (those who are able to access MySQL) are permitted to set up, edit, and delete databases whose names begin with *test_*. (Under Windows, the underscore in the database name is not required.) This default setting is supposed to allow a nonbureaucratic testing of MySQL without the beleaguered system administrator having to set up such databases.

An obvious problem with this arrangement is that anyone with access to MySQL has the right to create a database and stuff it with data and then stuff it some more until the computer's hard drive is full.

Table 9-6 shows the default setting for the *db* table. Please note in particular that for *test* databases all privileges except for *Grant, Create Temporary Tables,* and *Lock Tables* are set. *Grant='n'* is important, so that privileges from the *test* databases cannot be transferred to other databases.

Table 9-6. Default setting of the db *table under Unix/Linux*

Host	Db	User	Select_priv, Insert_priv, etc.	Grant_priv, Create_tmp_table_priv, Lock_tables_priv
%	test_%	Y	Y	N

> **REMARK**   *Have you understood the privileges system of MySQL? Then see whether you can answer the following question:*
>   *Can a MySQL user create and edit a* test *database even if all global privileges are set to* N*?*
>   *The answer is yes, of course. If all the global privileges are set to N, then the object-specific privileges are consulted (where every database that begins with* test *is considered an object). This is precisely the concept of the privilege system of MySQL.*

The host Table

The *host* table (see Table 9-7) is an extension of the *db* table if the latter's *Host* field is empty. In this case, entries for the database in question are sought in the *host* table. If an entry that matches the computer name is found there, the privilege settings in *db* and *host* are joined with a logical *AND* (that is, privileges must be granted in both tables).

The *host* table is brought into play relatively rarely. (As a rule, the settings of the *db* table meet all requirements.) This is also expressed in the fact that the commands *GRANT* and *REVOKE*, introduced below, do not affect the *host* table. Thus the *host* table is empty in the default setting.

Table 9-7. Structure of the host *table*

Field	Type	Null	Default
Host	char(60)	No	
Db	char(64)	No	
Select_priv	enum('N', 'Y')	No	N
Insert_priv	enum('N', 'Y')	No	N
...			
Lock_tables_priv	enum('N', 'Y')	No	N

The tables_priv *and* columns_priv *Tables*

With the tables *tables_priv* (see Table 9-8) and *columns_priv* (see Table 9-9) privileges can be set for individual tables and columns. For *Host* and *User* the same rules hold as for the *user* table. In the fields *Db, Table_name*, and *Column_name*, on the other hand, no wild cards are permitted. All the fields except *Column_name* are case-sensitive.

Table 9-8. Structure of the tables_priv *table*

Field	Type	Null	Default
Host	char(60)	No	
Db	char(64)	No	
User	char(16)	No	
Table_name	char(64)	No	
Grantor	char(77)	No	
Timestamp	timestamp(14)	Yes	
Table_priv	set1	No	
Column_priv	set2	No	

Table 9-9. Structure of the columns_priv *table*

Field	Type	Null	Default
Host	char(60)	No	
Db	char(64)	No	
User	char(16)	No	
Table_name	char(64)	No	
Column_name	char(64)	No	
Timestamp	timestamp(14)	Yes	
Column_priv	set2	No	

In the undocumented column *Grantor* is stored information as to who has granted the access rights (for example, *root@localhost*).

Unlike the tables described above, these tables have their privileges managed by two sets. (Sets are a peculiarity of MySQL; see also Chapter 5. With sets an arbitrary combination of all character strings specified by set definitions can be stored.) The two sets for *tables_priv* and *columns_priv* look like this:

```
set1: SET('Select', 'Insert', 'Update', 'Delete', 'Create', 'Drop',
          'Grant', 'References', 'Index', 'Alter')
set2: SET('Select', 'Insert', 'Update', 'References')
```

Here *set2* contains only those privileges that hold for individual columns. (The *Delete* privilege is missing, because only an entire data record can be deleted, not an individual field of a record. This field can, of course, be set to *NULL*, 0, or ' ', but for that the *Update* privilege suffices.)

It is my sad duty to report that it is not documented as to when in the table *tables_priv* the field *Table_priv* is to be used and when the field *Column_priv*. If one considers how the fields are changed by the SQL command *GRANT*, one may venture the following hypothesis:

- Privileges that relate to the entire table are stored in the field *Table_priv*.

- Privileges that relate to individual columns are stored in the field *Column_priv*, as well as in the *tables_priv* and *columns_priv* tables. The *tables_priv* table is to a certain extent a conglomeration of all privileges for which there are additional details in the *columns_priv* table (perhaps divided over several data records). The reason for this is probably the idea that evaluating both tables leads to simplification or increased speed for MySQL.

If you are in doubt, use the commands *GRANT* and *REVOKE* for setting column privileges. Have a look at the MySQL documentation. Perhaps since this was written the *Columns_priv* field has received a better treatment.

The tables *tables_priv* and *columns_priv* are empty in the default setting.

Tools for Setting Access Privileges

One can edit the tables of a database (assuming, of course, that you have the appropriate access privileges) with the usual SQL commands *INSERT, UPDATE,* and *DELETE.* However, that is a tiring and error-prone occupation. It is much more convenient to use the commands *GRANT* and *REVOKE*, which are the centerpiece of this section. Further alternatives for particular tasks are the MySQL tool `mysqladmin` and the Perl script `mysql_setpermission`.

> **CAUTION** *MySQL maintains, for reasons of speed optimization, copies of the* mysql *tables in RAM. Direct changes to the tables are effective only if they are explicitly reread by MySQL via the SQL command* FLUSH PRIVILEGES *or the external program* mysqladmin reload. *(With* GRANT *and* REVOKE *this rereading takes place automatically.)*

Changing Access Privileges with GRANT *and* REVOKE

The syntax of the *GRANT* and *REVOKE* commands, in simplified form, is as follows:

```
GRANT privileges
ON [database.]table
TO user@host [IDENTIFIED BY 'password']
[WITH GRANT OPTION]
REVOKE privileges
ON [database.]table
FROM user@host
```

If you wish to change the access privileges for all the tables of a database, the correct form to use is *ON database.**. If you wish to alter global privileges, then specify *ON *.**. It is not allowed to use wild cards in database names.

For *user* you can specify `' '` to indicate all users on a particular computer (for example, `' '@computername`). On the other hand, for *host* you must use `'%'` (for example, *username@'%'*).

Depending on their function, these commands change the *mysql* tables *user*, *db*, *tables_priv*, and *columns_priv*. (The *host* table remains untouched.)

> **POINTER** *The complete syntax of* GRANT *and* REVOKE *is given in Chapter 18. However, you can get a fairly good feel for these commands from the following examples.*

Registering New Users

All users with the computer name **.myorganization.com* are permitted to link to MySQL if they know the password *xxx*. The privilege *USAGE* means that all global privileges have been set to *N*. The users thereby at first have no privileges whatsoever (to the extent that so far no individual databases, tables, or columns have been made accessible to all users who can log into MySQL):

```
GRANT USAGE ON *.* TO ''@'%.myorganization.com' IDENTIFIED BY 'xxx'
```

The following command gives the user *admin* on the local computer unrestricted privileges. All privileges (including *Grant*) are set:

```
GRANT ALL ON *.* TO admin@localhost IDENTIFIED BY 'xxx'
WITH GRANT OPTION
```

Enabling Access to a Database

The following command gives the user *peter* on the local computer the right to read and alter data in all tables of the database *mylibrary*. If *peter@localhost* is unknown to the *user* table of the *mysql* database, then this name is added without a password. (If there is already a *peter@localhost*, then the password is not changed.)

```
GRANT SELECT, INSERT, UPDATE, DELETE
ON library.* TO peter@localhost
```

If you wish to add to *peter*'s privileges the right to lock tables and create temporary tables (which is useful in many applications), the command looks like this:

```
GRANT SELECT, INSERT, UPDATE, DELETE, CREATE TEMPORARY TABLES, LOCK TABLES
ON library.* TO peter@localhost
```

Prohibiting Changes in a Database

The next command takes away from *peter* the right to make changes to *mylibrary*, but *peter* retains the right to read the database using *SELECT* (assuming that the command of the previous example was just executed).

```
REVOKE INSERT, UPDATE, DELETE
ON mylibrary.* FROM peter@localhost
```

Enabling Access to Tables

With the following command the user *kahlila* on the local computer is given the right to read data from the table *authors* in the database *mylibrary* (but not to alter it):

```
GRANT SELECT ON mylibrary.authors TO kahlila@localhost
```

Enabling Access to Individual Columns

The access privileges for *katherine* are more restrictive than those for *kahlila*: She is permitted only to read the columns *title* and *subtitle* of the table *books* in the database *mylibrary*.

```
GRANT SELECT(title, subtitle) ON mylibrary.books TO katherine@localhost
```

Granting Database Access to All Local Users

All users on the local computer can read and edit data in the *mp3* database:

```
GRANT SELECT, INSERT, DELETE, UPDATE ON mp3.* TO ''@localhost
```

> **POINTER** *An additional example for changing access privileges can be found in this chapter under the heading "First Aid."*

Viewing Access Privileges with SHOW GRANTS

If you have lost track of which privileges a particular user has, the command *SHOW GRANTS* is just what you need:

```
SHOW GRANTS FOR peter@localhost;
  Grants for peter@localhost:
  GRANT SELECT ON mylibrary.* TO 'peter'@'localhost'
1 row in set (0.00 sec)

SHOW GRANTS FOR testuser@localhost
  GRANT USAGE ON *.* TO 'testuser'@'localhost'
    IDENTIFIED BY PASSWORD '663c5dd53dae4ed0'
  GRANT SELECT, INSERT, UPDATE, DELETE,
    CREATE TEMPORARY TABLES, LOCK TABLES
    ON 'myforum'.* TO 'ptestuser'@'localhost'
```

Changing a Password with `mysqladmin`

The program `mysqladmin` carries out various administrative tasks (see also Chapter 10). Although this program does not offer any immediate assistance in managing access privileges, it does offer two applications that seem to fit into this chapter.

Changing a Password

You can use *GRANT* to change the password of a previously registered user. However, *GRANT* can be used only when at the same time access privileges are to be changed. If all you want to do is to change a password, then `mysqladmin` is a simpler alternative:

```
> mysqladmin -u peter -p password newPW
Enter password: oldPW
```

The above command changes the password for the user *peter* on the computer *localhost*. Please note that the new password is passed as a parameter, while the old password is entered on request. (This order, first the new and then the old, is rather unusual.)

> **CAUTION** *Under Windows,* `mysqladmin` *frequently causes problems, because it does not correctly interpret the local computer name* localhost. *Often, the result is the error message* Can't find any matching row in the user table *or* Access denied for user: 'some-user@unknown' to database 'mysql'.
>
> *It is even more dangerous if* `mysqladmin` *is executed without any error message, and insead of changing the passward for* username@localhost, *changes it for* username@'%'. *(This can happen only if there exists such a user.)*
>
> *The solution is to use the program* `mysql` *and change the password with the following command:*
>
> ```
> SET PASSWORD FOR username@localhost = PASSWORD('xxx')
> ```

Reading in New `mysql` Tables

For speed enhancement, MySQL loads *mysql* into RAM at startup. The disadvantage of this is the following: If you change *mysql* directly using the *INSERT, UPDATE,* or *DELETE* commands, MySQL simply ignores these changes until you execute either the SQL command *FLUSH PRIVILEGES* or mysqladmin reload:

```
> mysqladmin -u root -p reload
Enter password: xxx
```

It is not necessary to use mysqladmin reload if you wish to change access privileges with *GRANT* or *REVOKE*. In those cases the altered tables are automatically read into RAM.

Viewing Access Privileges with `mysqlaccess`

Here we note that mysqlaccess is a rather old Perl script (last change in December 2000) that summarizes the access privileges of MySQL users. Thus mysqlaccess has a function similar to that of *SHOW GRANTS*, but with more features. It gives information as to which entries in the *mysql* tables are used for access, and it indicates security loopholes. This script is therefore useful if you need to get an overview of MySQL access privileges.

> **REMARK** *Information on using* mysqlaccess *can be obtained by executing the script with the option* --help *or* --howto. *The script can be used only under Unix/Linux, because in addition to the Perl interpreter, Unix-specific programs such as* diff *are necessary.*

Our first example shows how *peter* is able to access the database *mylibrary*:

```
user@linux:~ > mysqlaccess peter library
Password for MySQL superuser root: xxx
```

Sele	Inse	Upda	Dele	...	Alte	Host,User,DB
Y	N	N	N	...	N	localhost,peter,library

In our second example it is determined who (user name *) is permitted to access the *mysql* database:

```
user@linux:~ > mysqlaccess '*' mysql
Password for MySQL superuser root: xxx
```

Sele	Inse	Upda	Dele	...	Alte	Host,User,DB
Y	Y	Y	Y	...	Y	localhost,root,mysql
N	N	N	N	...	N	localhost,peter,mysql
N	N	N	N	...	N	localhost,ANY_NEW_USER,mysql

Changing Access Privileges with `mysql_setpermission`

If you find the commands *GRANT* and *REVOKE* too burdensome for standard tasks (such as giving a user access to a database), you may instead use the Perl script `mysql_setpermission`. The script is very simple to use, though the number of possible operations is small. (In particular, it is not possible to restrict privileges that have already been granted.)

> **REMARK** *The script* `mysql_setpermission` *assumes that Perl is installed on your computer together with the DBI and MySQL modules. The Windows version of the program can be found after a complete installation of MySQL in the directory* `mysql\scripts`.

The following example shows how with `mysql_setpermission` the database *webforum* is set up for the user *forumadmin*. As always, inputs are shown in boldface.

```
user@linux:~ > mysql_setpermission -u root
Password for user root to connect to MySQL: xxxx
What would you like to do:
  1. Set password for a user.
  2. Add a database + user privilege for that database.
   - user can do all except all admin functions
  3. Add user privilege for an existing database.
   - user can do all except all admin functions
  4. Add user privilege for an existing database.
   - user can do all except all admin functions + no create/drop
  5. Add user privilege for an existing database.
   - user can do only selects (no update/delete/insert etc.)
  0. exit this program

Make your choice [1,2,3,4,5,0]: 2

Which database would you like to add: webforum
The new database webforum will be created
What user name is to be created: forumadmin
user name = forumadmin
Would you like to set a password for [y/n]: y
What password do you want to specify for: newPW
Type the password again: newPW
We now need to know from what host(s) the user will connect.
Keep in mind that % means 'from any host' ...
The host please: localhost
Would you like to add another host [yes/no]: n
Okay we keep it with this ...
The following host(s) will be used: localhost.

That was it ... here is an overview of what you gave to me:
The database name    : webforum
The user name        : forumadmin
The host(s)          : localhost
```

```
Are you pretty sure you would like to implement this [yes/no]: y
Okay ... let's go then ...
Everything is inserted and mysql privileges have been reloaded.
```

With `mysqlaccess` you can quickly check which privileges `mysql_setpermission` has granted (in our example, all except *Reload, Shutdown, Process,* and *File*). The output of `mysqlaccess` is here shown in greatly compressed form over three lines:

```
user@linux:˜ > mysqlaccess forumadmin webforum
Password for MySQL superuser root: xxx
```

Sele	Inse	Upda	Dele	Crea	Drop	Relo	Shut	Proc	File	Gran
Y	Y	Y	Y	Y	Y	N	N	N	N	Y

Refe	Inde	Alte	Show	Supe	Crea	Lock	Exec	RepS	RepC
Y	Y	Y	N	N	N	N	N	N	N

SslT	SslC	X509	X509	MaxQ	MaxU	MaxC	host	User	DB
?	?	?	?	0	0	0	localhost	forumadmin	webforum

Problems with Establishing a Connection

TIP *If you experience connection problems, regardless of what programming language you are using, you should first perform a test interactively with the program* mysql *to determine whether you can establish a connection. Only when that succeeds is it worthwhile pursuing a search for the cause of the error in the program that you are using or developing.*

WARNING *Changes to access privileges or to the* mysql *database become effective only after* FLUSH PRIVILEGES *is executed (or after a restart of the MySQL server). Many administration programs with dialogs for user management do not automatically execute* FLUSH PRIVILEGES.

Therefore, if you have changed access privileges but see no result, execute in mysql *as* root *the command* FLUSH PRIVILEGES *(or the equivalent* mysqladmin flush-privileges*).*

In the case of an existing connection, changes made may take effect in part only after a new login, despite the execution of FLUSH PRIVILEGES. *The following rules are in effect:*

- *Changed global privileges will go into effect only after a new connection is made.*

- *Changed database privileges go into effect only after the command* USE table *is executed.*

- *Changed table and column privileges go into effect at the next SQL command.*

The following list gives the typical causes of problems in establishing connections. Note that a particular error message can arise from one of several different causes.

- **The MySQL server does not run:** If you attempt a connection with mysql, you obtain error 2002 (*Can't connect to MySQL server on 'hostname'*) or error 2003 (*Can't connect to local MySQL server through socket /var/lib/mysql/mysql.sock*). Under Windows, you can tell whether the server is running by looking in the task manager, while under Unix you use the command ps | grep -i mysql. As result, a list of processes should appear (since the server divides itself into a number of processes for reasons of efficiency). If that does not occur, then the server must be started (under Linux with the command /etc/init.d/mysql[d] start).

- **The client program does not find the socket file:** Under Unix/Linux, communication takes place mostly over a socket file if server and client are running on the same computer. For this to function, both programs must agree on the location of this file. When problems arise, you should ensure that there is an entry socket=*filename* in the configuration file /etc/my.cnf in the section [client], where *filename* specifies the actual location of the socket file. Normally, this file has the name /var/lib/mysql/mysql.sock.

- **The network connection between client and server is broken:** If your program is running on a different computer from that of the MySQL server, execute on the client computer the command ping serverhostname to test whether a connection to the server computer exists. If that is not the case, you must first repair the network configuration.

- **MySQL accepts no connections over the network (over TCP/IP):** This can be achieved with the option *–skip-networking* or a corresponding setting in my.cnf. This setting is often chosen to give MySQL maximum security. A database connection is then available only from the local computer and only via a socket file.
  The problem is generally recognizable from error 2003 (*Can't connect to MySQL server*). A solution is to remove the option my.cnf from the start script.

- **MySQL accepts no connections from your computer:** This problem generally arises when the MySQL server is running on the computer of an Internet service provider. There the server is generally so configured that only connections from local computers (or a local network) are allowed. For administration you must therefore either create a telnet-/ssh connection or use a program that is executed locally on the server and is served via the internet (e.g., phpMyAdmin).

- **Name resolution of host names does not work correctly:** In establishing a connection over a network, error 1130 arises (*Host n.n.n.n' is not allowed to connect to this MySQL server*). The most likely cause of this error is either the incorrect specification of the host name in the *mysql.user* table or an incorrect name-server configuration. Depending on the network configuration, the host names must be given in the column *user.Host* with or (more seldom) without domain name.

A solution is to add domain names to the host names in the *mysql.user* table (*uranus* ↦ *uranus.sol*) or to remove this (*uranus.sol* ↦ *uranus*) and try again. (Do not forget *FLUSH PRIVILEGES.*)

If that does not work, you can test with the commands hostname, host, and resolveip whether there are problems with name resolution. An emergency solution that almost always works (but is inflexible) is to give the IP number instead of the host name in the *user.Host* column. There are many other suggestions about dealing with host-name problems earlier in this chapter.

- **User name or password are incorrect:** Watch out for typos! Note as well that not only user name and password must correspond, but the host name as well. (Thus a connection is usually possible only from certain specific computers.) Also, read the previous point relating to resolution of the host name; perhaps that is where the problem resides.

  Note that the *user.Password* column does not contain passwords in plain text, but in encrypted form. If you wish to change a password with SQL commands, you must use the function *PASSWORD("xxx").*

- **An incorrect entry was used in the *mysql.user* table:** When user *x* attempts to register with computer *y*, the MySQL server compares the entries in the *user* table in a particular order: First, entries are considered whose *Host* character string is unique, and only then *Host* entries with wild cards (% and _). Within these two groups, again unique *User* strings are preferred to those with wild cards.

  The result of this order of precedence is that user *abc* on the local computer (*localhost*) will be unable under certain circumstances to register, although in the *user* table there is an entry *Host='%' / User='abc'*. The reason is that in the default setting of access privileges there is also an entry *Host='localhost' / User=' '*. This entry is given precedence to the first one because there the host name is given explicitly.

  To solve the problem, either add a second entry *Host='localhost' / User='abc'* to the *user* table or delete the entry *Host='localhost' / User=' '*. I would recommend the second variant, since that entry represents a security risk.

- **No user name was specified:** If you do not specify a user name in your program for making a connection, then the login name of the account under which the program was launched is given automatically. In programs that are launched interactively, this is your login name.

  With programs that run over a web server (PHP or JSP scripts, Perl CGI files, etc.), the account name of the web server is used. For security reasons the web server usually runs not as *root* (Linux) or with *administrator* privileges (Windows), but in a separate account, such as *wwwrun* or *apache*. The problem is now that in the *mysql* access tables, the user *wwwrun* or *apache* is unknown. Therefore, access to the database is denied. Therefore, do not forget in script files to specify the user name for the connection to MySQL explicitly.

- **The connection succeeds, but access to the database is impossible:** This error occurs immediately if you specify the desired database during the establishment of the connection. However, the error cannot occur until you select the desired database (*USE dbname*). Error message 1045 is, for example, *Access denied for user . . . to database . . . .*

The most likely cause of the error is that the user in fact does not have access rights to the database. Perhaps in *GRANT* you have specified only the *Usage* privilege (which allows a login, but not the actual use of a database). Execute the command *GRANT SELECT, INSERT . . . ON dbname.* TO name@hostname* to allow database access to *dbname*.

If the MySQL server is running on the computer of an Internet service provider (ISP),then the server is generally so configured that only local access is possible. In other words, your PHP or Perl scripts run without problems (because they are executed on the same computer), but you cannot access your databases from home, say, with the MySQL Control Center.

Here the issue is the correct (because secure) setting of the access privileges. You will find scarcely an ISP that allows MySQL connections from an arbitrary computer on the Intenet. You must therefore use programs for administration that run locally on the computer of the ISP (e.g., phpMyAdmin).

- **It is impossible to create a local TCP/IP connection:** This problem usually occurs under Unix/Linux. A local connection succeeds only if with option -h no computer name or IP number is specified. The most likely cause is a problem with the resolution of the host name. As a rule, you must add the domain name in the column *user.Host*, and then it works. Another cause can be the local network configuration (file /etc/hosts). We have already given some tips in this chapter especially for Red Hat and SuSE Linux.

- **The local connection fails for Java programs:** This problem is usually connected with the previous point, since Java programs, in contrast to most other MySQL clients, generally use TCP/IP (and not a socket file). Have a look in Chapter 15, where there are some trouble-shooting tips.

  Another cause of error can be the incorrect installation of Connector/J (see Chapter 15), but then an error occurs in the attempt to use JDBC (*java.lang.ClassNotFoundException: com.mysql.jdbc.Driver*).

- **Port 3306 is blocked:** Between the MySQL server and your program there is a firewall that is blocking port 3306. This problem can occur only when your program and the MySQL server are running on different computers. If you manage the firewall yourself, you must clear port 3306; otherwise, you must ask the administrator to do so.

- **The MySQL server crashes at every attempt at a TCP/IP connection:** This problem occurred in the past with Linux distributions. Since the server was immediately restarted, the problem was not always correctly identified. (The error message is usually *Lost connection to MySQL server during query*.)

  A solution to this problem is frequently an update of the glib library or the installation of the MySQL package from www.mysql.com. (The MySQL packages included in the distributions are not always optimally configured. This has been particularly bad in the case of Red Hat 8.0 and SuSE 8.1. The MySQL documentation therefore recommends using only versions of MySQL compiled by the MySQL team, and after a number of negative experiences, I agree.)

- **An update of the MySQL server causes problems:** In MySQL 4.0 the security
system was greatly expanded. If you are moving your database system
from version 3.23.*n* to 4.*n*, you must be sure to bring the *mysql* tables into
conformity with the new security system. For this, there is provided the script
`mysql_fix_privilege_tables` (see also Chapter 10). This script creates new
columns (vis-à-vis MySQL 3.23) in the *mysql* tables, but leaves the settings of
these columns in the default setting *N*. You may need to take a close look at
the new access privileges and explicitly grant certain individual new privileges,
such as *Lock, Create_tmp_table* for normal users, and *Super* for administrators.

> **POINTER** *An additional list of possible causes of error and some*
> *tips for alleviating them can be found in the MySQL documentation:*
> `http://www.mysql.com/doc/en/Access_denied.html`

The Special Case of Named Pipes

Named pipes represent a mechanism by which two programs can communicate under
Windows NT/2000/XP. Data exchange follows the first-in-first-out (FIFO) principle.

MySQL supports named pipes only under Windows NT/2000/XP, and not under
Windows 9x/ME or under Unix/Linux. Named pipes can be used only when the server
is appropriately compiled (`mysqld-nt` and `mysqld-max`, but not `mysqld-opt`) and when
the configuration file `Windows\my.ini` contains the option `enable-named-pipe` in the
group `[mysqld]`. By default, this is not the case, since in the past, open named pipes to
the MySQL server caused problems in shutting down Windows.

If you wish to establish an explicit named-pipe connection, specify a period (.) as
host name or use the option `--pipe`. Even if you specify no options, a named pipe will
be used if the server permits it:

```
C:\> mysql -u name -p
C:\> mysql -h . -u name -p
C:\> mysql -h localhost --pipe -u name -p
```

If you wish to create a connection explicitly over TCP/IP, you must specify the
host name:

```
C:\> mysql -h computername -u name -p
C:\> mysql -h localhost -u name -p
```

Whether named pipes are permitted can be determined in the program `mysql`
with the command *status.*

Further Tips for Error-Checking

If you believe that your *mysql* database is properly configured, yet database access fails nonetheless, stop the MySQL server, add temporarily *skip-grant-tables* to the [mysql] section in my.cn or my.ini and restart the server. Now everyone has access to all data. If access now succeeds, you at least know with certainty that the problem resides in the *mysql* tables. Do not forget to remove *skip-grant-tables* from the configuration file.

MySQL manages temporary storage (cache) with a list of most recently used IP addresses and associated host names. This cache makes it possible for the usually time-consuming process of name resolution to proceed efficiently. However, if you change your network configuration without restarting the MySQL server, it can happen that this cache contains incorrect, that is, no longer valid, entries. To run the MySQL server without this cache, add skip-host-cache in the [mysql[section of my.cnf or my.ini and restart the server.

Unfortunately, there is no way to make the MySQL server save precise information as to why a login attempt failed. In the error log (file hostname.err; see Chapter 10) is mentioned only the IP address of the login attempt, but not the course of name resolution, which entries in the *mysql* tables were looked at, etc.

System Security

Up to this point we have dealt in this chapter with issues of security as they apply directly to MySQL. In reality, of course, your data within a MySQL database are only as secure as the underlying operating system. (It is assumed that MySQL is running under an operating system that is equipped with security mechanisms. Security under Windows 9x/ME is a contradiction in terms, and it is to be hoped that no one will get the wild idea of running a public MySQL server under Windows 9x/ME.)

To secure your MySQL database system you should begin by asking the following questions:

- Are there security loopholes that would place an attacker in a position to log in as *root* (Unix/Linux) or with administrator privileges (Windows NT/2000)?

- Are the logging files secured? There, for example, the passwords can be found in plain text.

- Are script files containing passwords in plain text adequately secured? (And if full-fledged security is impossible, is it ensured that the user name/password combination in these files is provided with minimal access privileges? Is it ensured that the given password can really be used only for this MySQL login, that for convenience the same password as for *root* was not used?)

An additional issue concerns the data within a database. You should prepare yourself for the worst-case scenario—the possibility that an attacker gains access to your data—by encrypting key information within the database:

- If you store login information in the database (for example, the login information for users of your web site), then do not store the passwords in plain text, but only as MD5 check sums. These check sums are sufficient to verify a password. (The drawback is that a forgotten password cannot be restored from the check sum.)

- If you store even more sensitive data (credit card information, say, to take a particularly relevant example), such data should be encrypted. You should ask whether MySQL is a suitable database system for managing such data. If you store such critical data, you should engage security experts to make your system as secure as possible. Anything less should be considered gross negligence.

Note that MySQL itself can present a security risk that can be used for access to the entire operating system. For example, a MySQL user with *File* privileges can read and alter files in the local file system. The extent of this ability depends on how the file system itself is secured (access privileges for directories and files) and under what account the MySQL server (and thus mysqld) is running.

In no case should the server be run as *root* under Unix/Linux or with administrator privileges under Windows, since then, every MySQL user with *File* privileges would have the run of the entire file system.

With all current Linux distributions MySQL is already correctly configured. You can check this with the following command:

```
root# ps au | grep mysqld
root    ... /bin/sh /usr/bin/mysqld_safe ...
mysql   ... /usr/sbin/mysqld ...
mysql   ... /usr/sbin/mysqld ...
 ...
```

This means that the script mysqld_safe is executed by *root*, but the various threads of the MySQL server mysqld by the user *mysql*. (The script mysqld_safe must be executed by *root*. It serves only to start mysqld. It runs until the MySQL server is explicitly shut down. The script restarts mysqld automatically if the server crashes.)

If mysqld is executed as *root*, the following entry in /etc/my.cnf can help:

```
# file /etc/my.cnf
[mysqld]
user = mysql
```

> **POINTER** *A nice example of what can happen when* mysqld *is executed as* root *is shown by the text located at*
>
> ```
> http://www.dataloss.net/papers/how.defaced.apache.org.txt
> ```
>
> *where it is described how the web server of* apache.org *was attacked in May 2000. The document is somewhat old now, but the principle described therein has not lost its validity.*

TIP *If you set up MySQL as a database server only within a local network (that is, so that it is inaccessible from outside) and you use an IP packet filter as a firewall, then as an additional security measure you should close the IP port 3306. The result is that the MySQL server cannot be addressed directly from outside the network.*

Internet access over dynamic web sites is still possible in spite of all security measures, since dynamic web sites are generated from the locally running web server (which in turn calls a script interpreter). The MySQL server is thus addressed locally, and external communication is accomplished not via port 3306, but via the HTTP protocol (normally port 80). If there is a security loophole there, then closing port 3306 will not be of any help.

POINTER *We may sum up by saying that one can achieve genuine security of MySQL only if one has a deep understanding of the operating system itself, and this cannot be discussed here, not least because I myself know too little about such issues, especially in regard to security mechanisms under Windows NT/2000.*

However, there are many books on operating systems—completely independent of MySQL—that deal with the topics of administration and security.

#### CHAPTER 10

Administration and Server Configuration

THIS CHAPTER DESCRIBES THE ADMINISTRATION and configuration of the MySQL server. Among the most important themes that we treat are backups, logging files, migration of databases from one computer to another (or from one version of MySQL to a newer one), and import/export of text files. This chapter also goes specifically into the maintenance of MyISAM and InnoDB tables (such as the maintenance of InnoDB *tablespace* files).

Some advanced topics are treated in this chapter: Whether you change the character set of the MySQL server, set up a replication system, or wish to achieve greater processing speed, this chapter gives the relevant introductions and tips.

Finally, this chapter goes into the painful question of the various options for administration of databases that are present at an Internet service provider. (The problem is that in such a case you are not the database administrator and thus have very limited access rights.)

Chapter Overview

Basic Administration

> **POINTER** *Some additional topics related to administration of MySQL are discussed in the following chapters:*
>
> - *Chapter 4: Use of user interfaces for administration (*mysql*, MySQL Control Center, phpMyAdmin, etc.)*
> - *Chapter 9: Access controls,* mysql *databases*
> - *Chapter 19: Reference to* mysqld, mysql, mysqladmin, *etc.*

This section collects information on the elementary aspects of administration and refers the reader to other places in this book where additional details are to be found.

Basic Server Configuration

Setting the root Password

A fresh installation leaves MySQL completely unprotected. As soon as you begin to use MySQL for storing data, you should secure MySQL with a password. Under Unix/Linux the following commands suffice. (As *computername* the complete network name of the computer must be given.)

```
root# mysqladmin -u root -h localhost password xxx
root# mysqladmin -u root -h computername password xxx
```

The process is somewhat more complicated under Windows, since the default configuration is even more insecure, and mysqladmin frequently does not function as it should.

> **POINTER** *The MySQL access system was described in detail in Chapter 9. In particular, in the section "First Aid" you will find a concrete introduction to securing MySQL under both Windows and Unix/Linux.*

Personalizing the MySQL Server

If you have followed the installation instructions presented in Chapter 2, then the MySQL server should be running mysqld and should be functioning without any problems for most applications. But if you have particular wishes, say you need a particular sort order or wish to optimize performance, then you can specify a number of options for mysqld. Some important options are described in the course of this chapter. A reference section appears in Chapter 19.

Configuration File for Setting Options

Both at launch of mysqld and during the execution of administrative tools it is tiresome always having to specify the same old options. Therefore, one may specify these options in a configuration file:

Validity	Windows	Unix/Linux
global options (for both mysqld and administrative tools)	C:\my.cnf, Windows\my.ini	/etc/my.cnf
user-specific options (only for administrative tools)		~/.my.cnf

The server-specific options in the configuration file begin with the line [mysqld]. The following options have the effect that in sorting tables, the German alphabetic sort order is to be used.

```
# Example of the server-specific part of
# /etc/my.conf and Windows\my.ini
[mysqld]
default-character-set = latin1-de
```

Restarting the MySQL Server

Changes in configuration files become effective only after a restart of the affected program. This holds, of course, for the MySQL server as well. Thus, if you change server-specific options, you must restart the server (which is to be avoided as much as possible with a running system).

Under Windows you execute the restart most simply via WinMySQLadmin. (If you are working under NT/2000, you can also use the system administration services dialog.)

Under Unix/Linux you can use the appropriate Init-V script for restarting, which you typically execute first with the parameter *stop* and then with the parameter *start*.

```
Red Hat:  root# /etc/init.d/mysql stop
          root# /etc/init.d/mysql start

SuSE:     root# /etc/init.d/mysql stop
          root# /etc/init.d/mysql start
```

Using Administrative Tools

With MySQL you get a number of administrative tools (such as mysqladmin and myisamchk), some of which are described in some detail in this chapter. A common feature of all these tools is that they are command-oriented programs. That is, there is no graphical user interface, and the tool is used with options and commands.

Under Unix/Linux the tools are executed in a shell window, while under Windows they are executed in a command window. (Chapter 4 contains tips on the optimal configuration of the command window as well as the proper setup of the Windows system variable *PATH*.)

Most of the administrative tools can be used with their full functionality only if you sign in as *root* and provide your password. To do this you specify the options -u and -p at launch of mysqld. For example, with the following command all active logging files are closed and reopened (with the result that in update protocols the sequential file ending is increased by 1).

```
root# mysqladmin -u root -p flush-logs
Enter password: ******
```

> **REMARK** *Some of the commands described in this chapter, generally those involving shell or Perl scripts, are available only under Unix and Linux, and not under Windows.*

Creating a Database Structure (`mysqlshow`)

The command mysqlshow helps in obtaining a quick overview of the databases, tables, and columns managed by MySQL. If the command is executed without parameters, it simply returns a list of all databases managed by MySQL. If a database is specified, then mysqlshow shows a list of the tables contained within that database. If a table is specified in addition to the database, then mysqlshow displays a list of the columns of that table, including its properties (data type, default value, etc.).

In the last parameter the wild cards _ and % can be used to filter the indicated data. The same information obtained with mysqlshow can also be obtained with various variants of the SQL command *SHOW*. The advantage of mysqlshow is that the program is well suited for the automation of administrative tasks.

```
> mysqlshow -u root -p
Enter password: xxx
Databases:
  books
  myforum
  mylibrary
  mysql
  test
    ... > mysqlshow -u root -p mysql
Enter password: xxx
Database: mysql
Tables:
  columns_priv
  db
  host
  tables_priv
  user
```

```
> mysqlshow -u root -p books author
Enter password: xxxxxx
Database: books Table: author Rows: 10
```

Field	Type	Null	Key	Default	Extra		Privileges
authorID	int(11)		PRI		auto_increment		select, ...
author	varchar(60)						select, ...

Executing Administrative Commands (mysqladmin)

As the name of the program implies, mysqladmin assists in the execution of a variety of administrative tasks:

- Create and delete databases

- Change a user's password

- Input again the privileges database *mysql*

- Update database and logging files (clear buffer or intermediate storage)

- Determine status information and variables of the MySQL server

- List and store MySQL Processes

- Test connection to MySQL server (*ping*)

- Shut down the MySQL server (*shutdown*)

The following examples demonstrate a few possible applications:

```
> mysqladmin -u root -p create newDatabaseName
Enter password: xxx

> mysqladmin -i 5 ping
mysqld is alive
mysqld is alive
 . . .
> mysqladmin status
 Uptime: 435152    Threads: 2      Questions: 26464    Slow queries: 3
 Opens: 140        Flush tables: 1  Open tables: 0     Queries per second avg: 0.061
> mysqladmin -u root -p processlist
Enter password: xxx
 Id     User   Host       db       Command   Time   State   Info
 1      ODBC   localhost  books3   Sleep     7
 196    root   localhost           Query     0              show processlist
 . . .
```

Each time mysqladmin is called, only one operation can be executed. Most mysqladmin operations can be carried out as well with SQL commands (for example, with mysql or with a client program). The advantage of mysqladmin is that the program is easily adapted to the automation of administrative tasks.

Backups

Backups are doubtless one of the most important tasks of a database administrator. MySQL offers a variety of methods for executing a backup.

- The classical way, so to speak, uses the command mysqldump. This command returns a file with SQL commands for generating the tables of the database and filling them anew with data. Backups using mysqldump are comparatively slow, but they offer maximal portability. Therefore, mysqldump is used for database migration (for example, to copy a database from one MySQL installation to another).

  The command mysql is used to recreate the database.

- Significantly faster is simply to copy the database directories at the system level. This is quite efficient and secure if the MySQL server is stopped for this purpose. However, if the server is to continue running, then it must be ensured that during the copying process no changes are allowed to be made in the database. This task is taken care of by the script mysqlhotcopy.

  To recreate the database it is necessary merely to copy the backed-up directory into the MySQL database directory.

  Note that this form of backup is possible only for MyISAM tables (and not for InnoDB tables).

- One can use logging files in combination with regular backup files for incremental backups. However, that is practicable only as long as the number of changes in the database is not too large. Backup strategies based on logging files are not handled in this section, but in the section on logging.

- Another variant of securing data is replication. This mechanism allows a database to be synchronized on two different computers. For databases that are changed frequently this can result in a high demand on communication between the computers. If you really want nothing more than to keep two copies of your database on two different hard drives, then it is more efficient to mirror a hard drive using RAID. Replication is not dealt with in this section, but in the section of this chapter on replication.

Hot Backups: Both the execution of mysqldump and the copying of database directories can take place while the database is in operation. However, the integrity of the backup is ensured only if *read lock* is executed during the backup for the affected tables.

The result is, on the one hand, that the backup can be executed only when the table is not blocked by a *write lock*. On the other hand, no client can access the tables during the execution of the backup. Since the backup of large databases can take a relatively long time (especially if you use mysqldump), blocking is quite burdensome.

To circumvent this problem, commercial database systems offer *hot backup* mechanisms that permit a backup while the system is running without the complete blocking of entire tables. For MyISAM tables, MySQL is unfortunately incapable of this (despite the promises of mysqlhotcopy). If you use InnoDB tables, however, you can execute hot backups with the supplementary program InnoDB Hot Backup (see http://www.innodb.com/hotbackup.html).

Securing Databases (mysqldump)

The command mysqldump returns a long list of SQL commands required for the exact recreation of a database. Normally, the program returns a *CREATE TABLE* command for each table in order to generate the table together with indexes, as well as numerous *INSERT* commands (one for each record). The following example shows the result of mysqldump for the *authors* table of the *mylibrary* database presented in Chapter 5. (Lines that begin with -- are considered comments in SQL.)

```
> mysqldump -u root -p mylibrary author
Enter password: xxx
-- MySQL dump 9.07
-- Host: localhost   Database: mylibrary
-- Server version    4.0.12-nt-log
-- Table structure for table 'authors'
CREATE TABLE authors (
  authID int(11) NOT NULL auto_increment,
  authName varchar(60) NOT NULL default '',
  PRIMARY KEY  (authID),
  KEY authName (authName),
  FULLTEXT KEY authName_2 (authName)
) TYPE=MyISAM;
--
-- Dumping data for table 'authors'
INSERT INTO authors VALUES (1,'Kofler Michael');
INSERT INTO authors VALUES (2,'Kramer David');
INSERT INTO authors VALUES (3,'Orfali Robert');
INSERT INTO authors VALUES (4,'Harkey Dan');
```

Provided that the option --tab is not used, mysqldump displays the list of commands on the monitor. Usually, however, it makes more sense to direct the output to a file using > filename.

CAUTION *When output is redirected to a file under Windows, one has the problem that the line* Enter password *will be entered into the target file. When the file is later read, a syntax error will occur, since* Enter password *is not an SQL command. This is not a pretty error. However, the data can be input without difficulties. If you wish to avoid the error message, you must either delete the line with a text editor after the file has been dumped, or else specify the password directly with the option* --password=xxx, *which is insecure.*

Under Unix/Linux this error does not occur, because a distinction is made between the channel for standard output and that for error messages. The line Enter password *is normally displayed via the error channel on the monitor, while the SQL commands are stored by the output channel in the file.*

Backup of All Databases

The following command creates a backup of all databases managed by MySQL (provided that the user has *root* access) and stores these in a single file. During the backup, the database is blocked for all write operations:

```
> mysqldump -u root --password=xxx --opt --all-databases > backup.sql
```

Syntax of mysqldump

The general syntax of mysqldump is the following:

```
mysqldump [options] dbname [tables] > backup.sql
```

If no tables are specified, then mysqldump writes all the tables of the database *dbname* into the file backup.sql. Optionally, the backup can be limited to specific tables. If you wish to back up more than one database or even all of them, then the following syntax variants are what you use:

```
mysqldump [options] --databases dbname1 dbname2 ...
mysqldump [options] --all-databases
```

The details of the backup can be controlled by a large number of options. An extensive description and reference to all the options appears in Chapter 19. To execute a simple backup, a single option usually suffices, --opt, which has the following effect:

- During the backup *read lock* is executed for all tables.

- The resulting backup file is as small as possible (one *INSERT* command for all records of the table).

- The resulting file contains *DROP TABLE* commands to delete existing tables when the database is restored.

- All features of the database are retained (including MySQL-specific features that could interfere with migration to a different database system).

On the other hand, `--opt` is not to be recommended if you use InnoDB tables or if the resulting files are to be backward compatible (such as moving a database from a MySQL server 4.0.*n* to an older server 3.23.*n*).

> **REMARK** *Perhaps you are aware that there is also a command* mysqldumpslow. *This command has nothing to do with* mysqldump, *but helps in the evaluation of a special logging file in which all SQL commands that took a particularly long time to execute are recorded.*

mybackup

The Perl script `mybackup` is currently not included with MySQL. However, you can find it on the Internet: `http://www.mswanson.com/mybackup/`

The script `mybackup` uses `mysqldump`. The advantage over `mysqldump` is that the backup files (one per database) are written into a specified directory and there immediately compressed with `gzip`.

*Restoring a Database (*mysql*)*

There is no direct inverse operator for `mysqldump`, simply because the old workhorse `mysql` is completely satisfactory for this purpose.

> **REMARK** *Tables are automatically recreated in the type that they previously possessed. Thus* mysqldump *and* mysql *are well suited as tools for securing data independent of table type (MyISAM, BDB, etc.).*
>
> *The re-creation of a database works even if you use a different (newer) version of MySQL or if MySQL is running on a different computer (under a different operating system).*

Restoring a Single Database

If `backup.sql` contains only a single database, then the restore command looks like this:

```
> mysql -u root -p databasename < backup.sql
Enter password: xxx
```

The database *databasename* must already exist. If that is not the case, then you can easily create it with `mysqladmin create databasename`.

Restoring Several Databases

If several databases were backed up with mysqldump, then backup.sql contains the requisite *CREATE DATABASE* commands for creating the databases anew if they do not yet exist. There is no necessity to create the databases first. You also do not need to specify a database when mysql is called.

```
root# mysql -u root -p < backup.sql
Enter password: xxx
```

Reading In Databases and Tables Interactively

You can read in *.sql files interactively in the program mysql, that is, without restarting this program each time. For this, you use the command *SOURCE* or its abbreviated form /. and specify the file name of the *.sql file. (Under Windows, directories can be separated with either / or \. The file name does not need to be placed in quotation marks.)

Now mysql executes every SQL command in the file. However, the many outputs to the monitor (*Query OK, 1 row affected*) that are normally displayed are burdensome. They can be prevented by launching mysql with the option --silent:

```
root# mysql -u root -p --silent
Enter password: xxx
mysql> USE dbname
mysql> \. /tmp/backup.sql
```

Speeding Up the Reading of Databases and Tables

With small data sets (up to a few megabytes), the reading in of data is so fast that you do not need to worry about speed optimization. However, if you are dealing with large data sets, then a few thoughts in the direction of optimization are in order:

- In executing backups with mysqldump you should use at least the following options:
  --add-drop-table (existing tables are deleted)
  --all (complete MySQL syntax)
  --extended-inserts (compact *INSERT* commands)
  --disable-keys (more efficient index management)

- In the case of InnoDB tables, you should consider some of the tips for optimization presented later in this chapter.

Restoring InnoDB Tables (Integrity Rules)

In reading in InnoDB tables for which there exist integrity rules (foreign key constraints), you must execute *SET foreign_key_checks=0* and then *SET foreign_key_checks=1* before reading in the tables. The reason is that a condition for these rules always being satisfied is that the records be inserted in the correct order. This is difficult, and often impossible, to ensure when data are reread in. Therefore, turning off these rules is a necessity if the tables are to be reread in without error.

Fast Backups (`mysqlhotcopy`)

For a considerable time, the Perl script `mysqlhotcopy` has been provided with the Unix/Linux version of MySQL. This script is supposed to help in improving the speed of backups executed with `mysqldump`. The basic idea of the program is first to execute a *read lock* for the specified databases and then with *FLUSH TABLES* to ensure that the database files are actually in their current versions. Then the database files are directly copied.

> **CAUTION** `mysqlhotcopy` *creates a direct copy of table files. Therefore, the command can be used only with MyISAM tables.*
> *If you use* `mysqlhotcopy` *on InnoDB tables, only the* `*.frm` *files will be copied, and there will be no error message.*

> **TIP** *The documentation to* `mysqlhotcopy` *is obtained with the following command. Instead of* `/usr/bin` *you may have to give another path:*
>
> ```
> user$ perldoc /usr/bin/mysqlhotcopy
> ```

Making a Backup

In the simplest case, the use of `mysqlhotcopy` is as follows:

```
root# mysqlhotcopy dbname1 dbname2 dbname3 backup/
```

With this the databases *dbname1, dbname2, dbname3* are copied into the specified backup directory. (This backup directory must already exist.) Each database is copied into a subdirectory named for the database.

Options

The following list gives merely the most important options. A full description of all the options can be found in the documentation:

- `--allowold` overwrites existing backup files.
- `--keepold` archives existing backup files into the directory dbname_old. If this directory already exists, then its contents are overwritten.

- `--flushlog` has the effect that MySQL changes made in the databases after the backup are written to a new logging file. This option makes sense only if the logging files are to be used for an incremental backup.

- `--noindices` copies for (My)ISAM tables only the actual data, not the index files. (More precisely, the first two kilobytes of the index files are copied. This makes possible an uncomplicated, though slow, restoration of the index files with `myisamchk -r`. But the backup can be executed more quickly, because fewer data must be copied.)

The options `-u`, `-p`, `-P`, and `-S`, as well as `--user=`, `--password=`, `--port=`, and `--socket=`, function as they do with all MySQL tools, but with one exception. In the case of `-p`, the password must be given here (while all other tools provide interactive password input, which is more secure).

Restoring a Database

To restore a database you simply copy the relevant database directory into MySQL's data directory. If you execute this operation as *root,* you must then specify the owner of the database files with `chown`. (The owner must have the same account under which `mysqld` is running, usually *mysql.*)

```
root# chown -R mysql.mysql /var/lib/mysql/dbname
```

> **CAUTION**   *If the database to be restored already exists, the files involved in an operational MySQL cannot simply be overwritten. First execute DROP DATABASE.*
> *It is possible to recreate data only if the version of MySQL that is running is compatible with the version under which the backup was executed. This is the case with the various MySQL versions 4.n. However, it is not guaranteed that a backup executed with MySQL 4.0 will be able to be restored with MySQL 4.n. (With each change in the main version number the format of database files can conceivably change.)*

Database Migration

The term "migration" applied to databases denotes the transport of a database from one system to another. There are many reasons that can account for the migratory instinct appearing in a database:

- installation of a new database server
- transfer of a development system (for example, on a local computer) to a production system (on the ISP's computer)
- a MySQL update (for example, from version 3.23 to 4.0)
- a change in database system (for example, from Microsoft SQL Server to MySQL)

Transfer of Databases Between MySQL Systems

Migration between MySQL systems is generally carried out with the backup tools mysqldump and mysql, which we have previously described.

If the tables are in MyISAM format and compatible versions of MySQL are running on both computers (say, 3.23n), then the migration can be effected by simply copying the database files. This holds beginning with version 3.23 even if MySQL is running under different operating systems.

The main advantage of direct copying of MyISAM tables as opposed to the use of mysqldump/mysql is, of course, the much greater speed. Note, however, that you must recreate all the indexes with myisamchk if MySQL on the other computer uses a different character set (that is, a different sort order).

MySQL guarantees compatibility of database files only within main versions (such as from 4.0.17 to 4.0.18), and not between major updates (such as from 3.22 to 3.23 or 3.23 to 4.0). In fact, even major updates generally cause few problems (see the next section).

> **TIP** *If you wish to change only the format of database files, say from MyISAM to InnoDB, then you do not need to go through the migration process. The command ALTER TABLE tblname TYPE=newtype will be adequate to meet your needs. If you wish to convert a large number of tables, then under Unix/Linux the Perl script* mysql_convert_table_format *will save you a great deal of effort. (The script assumes that a connection to the MySQL server can be established.)*

> **TIP** *If you carry out the migration with* mysqldump/mysql, *then you do not necessarily have to create (possibly enormous) files. You can pass the output of* mysqldump *directly to* mysql.
>
> *The following command demonstrates the usual way of proceeding. It assumes that the command is executed on the computer with the source database and that the data are transported to a second computer (hostname* destinationhost). *There the database in question must already exist, and the access privileges must allow access to the source computer.*
>
> *For space considerations the command is broken over two lines:*

```
root# mysqldump -u root --password=xxx --opt sourcedb | \
      mysql -u root --password=yyy -h destinationhost dbname
```

> **POINTER** *A special case of migration, namely, setting up a database on an ISP, is described toward the end of this chapter. The usual problem in doing this is the possession of inadequate access privileges to the ISP computer.*

> **POINTER** *If you copy databases from Windows to Unix/Linux, there can arise prob-*
> *lems with the case-sensitivity of file extensions. The Perl script* mysql_fix_extensions
> *solves this problem (see Chapter19).*

MySQL Update from Version 3.23 to Version 4.0

Usually, an update to the MySQL server (such as from 4.0.7 to 4.0.8) is done in such
a way that the server is stopped, the old version deinstalled, and the new version
installed.

For the database *mysql*, before deinstallation a backup with access privileges
must be carried out, since this database will be deleted and overwritten. (Your best
course is to rename the mysql database directory mysqlold before the deinstallation.)
Like the configuration file for the server, all other database files will be carried over
unchanged.

> **TIP** *Although an update usually causes no problems, it is highly recommended*
> *before any server update to create a complete backup with* mysqldump *of all databases.*
> *Better safe than sorry!*

This simple process is possible in updating from 3.23n to 4.0.n. However, there
are also some details to keep track of:

- **Configuration file:** Some of the configuration options for the MySQL server
  have new names or were deleted. Make sure that no such options appear in
  Windows\my.ini or /etc/my.cnf. Otherwise, the server cannot be started. The
  following options have had their names changed:

Old name	New name
enable-locking	external-locking
myisam_bulk_insert_tree_size	bulk_insert_buffer_size
query_cache_startup_type	query_cache_type
record_buffer	read_buffer_size
record_rnd_buffer	read_rnd_buffer_size
skip-locking	skip-external-locking
sort_buffer	sort_buffer_size
warnings	log-warnings

- *mysql* **database:** In MySQL 4.0, some tables of the *mysql* database were
  expanded by additional columns. (The *mysql* database serves, as described
  extensively in Chapter 9, for managing access privileges under MySQL.)

Under Unix/Linux you can simply update the database *mysql* restored from an earlier version using the script `mysql_fix_privilege_tables`. To execute the script, you must give the *root* password (unless the password is empty). Then you may have to set certain privileges by hand, so that existing programs continue to be executed correctly. (This affects particularly the new privileges *Create Temporary Table* and *Lock Tables*, which by default are usually not specified, but which are required by many programs.)

Under Windows, the further use of the *mysql* database is more complicated: Although the script `mysql_fix_privilege_tables` is included (directory `scripts`), its execution is impossible, due to the absence of a suitable shell interpreter. The best approach is to restore the old *mysql* database under another name (e.g., *mysqlold*) and then copy the entries into the new *mysql* tables using *INSERT INTO . . . SELECT*. The following commands show how to proceed for the *user* table:

```
USE mysql

DELETE FROM user

INSERT INTO user (Host, User, Password,
    Select_priv, Insert_priv, Update_priv, Delete_priv,
    Create_priv, Drop_priv, Reload_priv, Shutdown_priv,
    Process_priv, File_priv, Grant_priv, References_priv,
    Index_priv, Alter_priv)

SELECT * FROM mysqlold.user
```

You proceed analogously for the other *mysql* tables. With these commands, only the old privileges, of course, are copied. The new ones must be granted manually (this is not the case by default). In particular, *root* should have all privileges! Finally, you must execute *FLUSH PRIVILEGES* for the changes to take effect.

- If you have been working with ISAM tables, then a transfer to tables of type MyISAM is to be recommended. For conversion, execute *ALTER TABLE tblname TYPE=MYISAM* or use the Perl script `mysql_convert_table_format` (only under Unix/Linux). (The script assumes that a connection to the database can be established.)

The ISAM table format (the predecessor to MyISAM) is still supported in MySQL 4.0, but it is considered obsolete (*deprecated*). By version 5.0 at the latest, ISAM tables will finally cease to be able to be used.

POINTER   *A list of further details that distinguish MySQL 3.23 from 4.0 can be found in the MySQL documentation, in the section "Upgrading/Downgrading":*

```
http://www.mysql.com/doc/en/Upgrade.html
```

Updating MySQL from Version 4.0 to Version 4.1

In principle, updating is accomplished by deinstalling the old version of the server and installing the new one. Then you must change only the table *mysql.user*. Version 4.1 provides a new password column in this table, which is supposed to improve security. Under Unix/Linux you simply execute the script mysql_fix_privilege_tables to introduce this column. It is unclear how best to proceed under Windows.

> **REMARK**   *As this book was being completed, there was still no stable version of MySQL 4.1. Therefore, it could be that the update process will require additional modifications to databases or configuration files.*

Changing the Database System

For migrating to MySQL from another database system or vice versa there is no universal solution. Almost every database system offers a tool, comparable to mysqldump, that represents the contents of the database as an SQL file. The problem is that the resulting files are seldom precisely compatible (for example, due to different column types or lack of ANSI SQL/92 conformity). With *Find and Replace* you can solve some of these problems. Under Unix/Linux the tools awk and sed can be helpful.

You will find converters for migration to MySQL for some database systems at the following addresses:

```
http://www.mysql.com/portal/software/index.html
http://www.mysql.com/downloads/contrib.html
```

If you are working under Windows, then ODBC is often helpful. For example, you can use Access to import a database of an ODBC-compatible system and then export it to MySQL. Do not expect, however, that all the details of the definition of the columns will remain intact.

> **POINTER**   *Information on the use of Connector/ODBC, the ODBC driver for MySQL, can be found in Chapter 17. There you will also find a description of how to move databases between MySQL and Access and how to convert databases from the Microsoft SQL server to MySQL.*

Importing and Exporting Text Files

Sometimes, the contents of a table should be written as efficiently as possible into a text file or read from such a file. MySQL offers several ways of doing this:

- The SQL command *LOAD DATA* reads in a text file and transfers the contents into a table.

- With `mysqlimport` there is a command available that is equivalent to *LOAD DATA*. It is especially well suited for automating the importation of a script file.

- The SQL command *SELECT . . . INTO OUTFILE* writes the result of a query into a text file.

- If you wish to automate exportation with a script, then the command `mysqldump` is to be recommended. Its functionality is similar to that of *SELECT . . . INTO OUTFILE*.

- In many cases you can use the universal tool `mysql` for implementing text, HTML, or XML exportation.

If none of the above commands suits your needs, then you will have to write your own script to assist you in importing or exporting. The programming language Perl was made for such tasks.

Special Characters in the Imported or Exported File

A common feature of *LOAD DATA, SELECT . . . INTO OUTFILE*, `mysqlimport`, and `mysqldump` is the set of options for handling special characters in a text file. There are four options for this purpose, which as SQL commands look like this:

```
FIELDS TERMINATED BY 'fieldtermstring'
       ENCLOSED BY 'enclosechar'
       ESCAPED BY 'escchar'
LINES TERMINATED BY 'linetermstring'
```

- *fieldtermstring* specifies the character string that separates the columns within the row (for example, a tab character).

- *enclosechar* specifies a character that is permitted to appear in the text file before and after individual entries (usually a single or double quote character for character strings). If an entry begins with this character, then that character is deleted at the beginning and end. (The end of a column is recognized by *fieldtermstring*.)

- *escchar* specifies the escape character that is to be used to indicate special characters (the default is the backslash). This is necessary if special characters appear in character strings of the text file that are also used for separating rows or columns. Moreover, MySQL expects code 0 in the form \0 (where the backslash is to be replaced by *escchar*).

- *linetermstring* specifies the character string with which a row is terminated. With DOS/Windows text files the character string '\r\n' must be used.

Working with Character Strings, Numbers, Dates, and BLOBs

For all the commands introduced in this section there is a data format that must be followed exactly. In particular, for importation you must hold to the format expected by MySQL. For exportation you have somewhat more leeway, in that you can use SQL functions for formatting data in the *SELECT* command (such as *DATE_FORMAT* for formatting dates and times).

Moreover, there are four options that you can use to determine how rows and columns should be separated and how character strings and special characters should be indicated. (Details can be found in Chapter 18 under *LOAD DATA* and *SELECT . . . INTO OUTFILE.*)

- **Numbers:** For very large and very small numbers in the *FLOAT* and *SINGLE* formats one has the use of scientific notation in the form *-2.3e-037.*

- **Character Strings:** Strings are not changed in importation and exportation (ANSI format, one byte per character). Special characters contained in the character string are marked by default with the backslash in order to distinguish these from the characters used for separation (e.g., tab, *carriage return, linefeed*).

- **BLOBs:** Binary objects are treated byte for byte like character strings. Neither in importing nor exporting is there the possibility of using hexadecimal character strings (0x123412341234 . . .).

- **Date and Time:** Dates are treated as character strings of the form *2003-12-31,* and times as character strings of the form *23:59:59.* Timestamp values are considered integers of the form *20031231235959.*

- *NULL:* The treatment of *NULL* is problematic. The following text assumes that the backslash is used as the escape character for special characters and the double quote character for indicating a character string. If you use other characters (options *FIELDS ESCAPED BY '?' ENCLOSED BY '?'*), then you will have to reconfigure the following paragraphs.

  In exporting with escape characters, *NULL* is represented by \N. In exporting without escape characters *NULL* is simply represented by the four characters *NULL.* However, *NULL* or \N is placed between double quote characters (though not if they are in a text or BLOB field) and can therefore be distinguished from character strings.

  In importing with escape characters, MySQL accepts *NULL,* \N, and *"\N"* as *NULL.* However, *"NULL"* is interpreted as a character string (consisting of the four characters *NULL*).

> **CAUTION** *If you use neither escape characters for special characters nor "enclose" characters for character strings in importing and exporting, then the condition* NULL *cannot be distinguished from the character string* NULL.
>
> *In the character string* \N *the N must be uppercase. Note that* \n *is the newline character.*

Importing with LOAD DATA INFILE

The syntax of *LOAD DATA* is as follows:

```
LOAD DATA [loadoptions] INFILE 'filename.txt' [duplicateoptions]
  INTO TABLE tablename [importoptions] [IGNORE ignorenr LINES]
  [(columnlist)]
```

The result is that the file filename.txt is imported into the table *tablename*. There are various options (see the SQL reference in Chapter 18) that can be given, as well as the column names for the table. To execute the command you need the *File* privilege (so that files can be read).

Example 1

The table *importtable1* consists of five columns: one *AUTO_INCREMENT* column (*id*) and the columns *a_double*, *a_datetime*, *a_time*, and *a_text*.

The column name refers to its data type. The Windows text file import1.txt is to be imported into this table. (Here ↪ represents a tab character):

```
12.3       ↪   12/31/1999   ↪   17:30   ↪   text
-0.33e-2   ↪   2000/12/31   ↪   11:20   ↪   "text in quotes"
1,23       ↪   31.12.2001   ↪   0:13    ↪   "german text with äöü"
```

The import command looks like this:

```
USE exceptions
LOAD DATA INFILE 'c:\import1.txt'
INTO TABLE importtable1
FIELDS TERMINATED BY '\t'
     ENCLOSED BY '\"'
LINES TERMINATED BY '\r\n'
(a_number, a_date, a_time, a_string)

  Query OK, 3 rows affected (0.00 sec)
  Records: 3 Deleted: 0 Skipped: 0 Warnings: 2
```

A *SELECT* command demonstrates that the importation was only partially successful. In both the first and third lines, the date has been incorrectly interpreted. Moreover, in the third line the decimal number with the German comma for a decimal point has caused problems; namely, the part to the right of the decimal point has gone missing. In sum, take care to obey the MySQL formatting rules to the letter when preparing a file for importation:

```
SELECT * FROM importtable1
```

id	a_number	a_datetime		a_time	a_string
1	12.3	0000-00-00	00:00:00	17:30:00	text
2	-0.0033	2000-12-31	00:00:00	11:20:00	text in quotes
3	1	2031-12-20	01:00:00	00:13:00	german text with äöü

Example 2 (BLOB, NULL)

The starting point for our second example is the table *importtable2* with columns *id* and *a_blob*. The second column is allowed to contain *NULL*.

The following Unix text file is to be imported into this table (again, ↪ represents a tab character):

```
1  ↪  NULL
2  ↪  "NULL"
3  ↪  \N
4  ↪  "\N"
5  ↪  \n
6  ↪  "\n"
7  ↪  0x414243
8  ↪  "0x414243"
9  ↪  blob blob
10 ↪  "blob blob"
```

The text file is imported with the following command. (By default, the backslash serves as escape character, and the tab sign as column separator.) *REPLACE* means that existing data records are to be replaced.

```
USE exceptions
TRUNCATE importtable2
LOAD DATA INFILE '/tmp/import2.txt' REPLACE
INTO TABLE importtable2
FIELDS ENCLOSED BY '\"'
  Query OK, 12 rows affected (0.00 sec)
  Records: 10 Deleted: 2 Skipped: 0 Warnings: 0
```

In order to analyze the result of the importation in more detail, we shall use *SELECT* * and add the additional columns *LENGTH(a_blob)* and *ISNULL*. This enables us to distinguish the state *NULL* (length *NULL*) from the character string *NULL* (length 4):

```
SELECT *, LENGTH(a_blob) FROM importtable2
```

id	a_blob	LENGTH(a_blob)	ISNULL(a_blob)
1	NULL	NULL	1
2	NULL	4	0
3	NULL	NULL	1
4	NULL	NULL	1
5		1	0
6		1	0
7	0x414243	8	0
8	0x414243	8	0
9	blob blob	9	0
10	blob blob	9	0

We see that in the first six records, *NULL* was treated correctly in only the first, third, and fourth records. In the second record, the character string *"NULL"* was stored, while in the fifth and sixth records a newline character was stored.

The attempt to read in a hexadecimal number as a binary object fails. Both times, 0x414243 is interpreted as the character string "0x414243" (and not, as intended in record 7, as hex code for the character string "ABC").

CSV Import

Sometimes, one wishes to import data into MySQL from a spreadsheet program like Excel. Such programs generally offer the possibility to store tables in CSV (comma-separated values) format. In principle, the importation of such files proceeds effortlessly. For files that were created with Excel under Windows, suitable import options look like this:

```
FIELDS TERMINATED BY ',' ENCLOSED BY '\"'
LINES TERMINATED BY '\r\n'
```

In practice, importation usually runs into trouble with the formatting of dates (usually in the form 12/31/2003, about which MySQL is clueless). In particular, with Microsoft software, the automatic country-specific formatting of numbers can cause problems when, for example, Excel suddenly represents a decimal number with a comma instead of a period for the decimal point. In such cases one can get help from a special import script for MySQL (or else you can program your own export filters for Excel).

Error Search

As the previous examples have shown, importing text is often problematic. Unfortunately, *LOAD DATA* returns in MySQL 4.0 merely a brief status output, which gives, among other things, the number of warnings:

```
Query OK, 15 rows affected (0.00 sec)
Records: 10 Deleted: 5 Skipped: 0 Warnings: 2
```

This result means that ten records were read in. Five existing records were replaced by new records (thus *15 rows affected*). There were problems with two records (rows) detected by *LOAD DATA* (*2 warnings*). The nature of the problems, and which rows of the file were affected, remains a mystery.

Paul DuBois, author of several books on MySQL, has created a Perl script for such cases that copies text files line by line into a temporary file and reads them in with *LOAD DATA*. This is slow, but it provides the opportunity to identify defective rows exactly and to obtain information about possible sources of error. The script is described in *MySQL Cookbook*, Chapter 10, and at the Internet address `http://www.kitebird.com/mysql-cookbook/examples-ld.php`.

Starting with MySQL 4.1, error searching should be easier: With the commands *SHOW WARNINGS* and *SHOW ERRORS* all problems that arose with the execution of the last command are listed.

Importing with `mysqlimport`

If you wish to execute *LOAD DATA* not as an SQL command but through an external program, then MySQL offers the tool `mysqlimport`. (It relies on *LOAD DATA*.)

```
mysqlimport databasename tablename.txt
```

The command reads the specified file into a like-named table of the database *databasename*. (The table name is thus taken from the file name, with the file identifier being eliminated. Thus `mysqlimport db1 authors.txt` imports the data into the table *authors* of the database *db1*.)

Please note that the file normally is read from the file system of the MySQL server. If you are working at another computer and wish to read a file that is located there, you must use the option `--local`. The options `--fields-terminated-by`, `--fields-enclosed-by`, `--fields-escaped-by`, and `--lines-terminated-by` correspond to the SQL options described at the beginning of this section. These options should be placed in quotation marks, for example, `"--fields-enclosed-by=+"`.

To carry out the importation demonstrated in the previous section (example 2) with `mysqlimport`, the file to be imported must first be renamed to correspond with the table name in `importtable2.txt`. Then the following command is necessary:

```
root# mysqlimport --local "--fields-enclosed-by=\"" \ exceptions /tmp/importtable2.txt
```

Under Windows (that is, for importing a Windows text file), the command would look like this (broken into two lines here for reasons of space):

```
> mysqlimport --local "--fields-enclosed-by=\"" "--lines-terminated-by=\r\n"
    exceptions c:\importtable2.txt
```

Exporting with `SELECT ... INTO OUTFILE`

With the command *SELECT... INTO OUTFILE* we are dealing with a garden-variety *SELECT*, where before the *FROM* part, *INTO OUTFILE* is used to specify a file name and several possible options:

```
SELECT [selectoptions] columnlist
INTO OUTFILE 'filename.txt' exportoptions
FROM ... WHERE ... GROUP BY ... HAVING ... ORDER BY ... LIMIT ...
```

The result of the query is thus stored in the file `filename.txt`. With *exportoptions* various options can be specified for dealing with special characters (see the SQL reference in Chapter 18).

Example

The following example assumes that there exists a table *exporttable* in the current database that has the following contents (note in particular the field *a_char* in the second data record):

`SELECT * FROM exporttable`

id	a_char	a_text	a_blob	a_date	a_time	...
1	char char	text text	blob blob	2001-12-31	12:30:00	
2	' " \ ; +	adsf	NULL	2000-11-17	16:54:54	

...	a_timestamp	a_float	a_decimal	a_enum	a_set
	20001117164643	3.14159	0.012	b	e,g
	20001117165454	-2.3e-037	12.345	b	f,g

The data types of the columns are taken from the column names. The following lines show the result of an *OUTFILE* exportation without special options. The tab character is again indicated by a hooked arrow. The resulting file has two lines, which for reasons of space are here distributed over five lines:

```
SELECT * INTO OUTFILE '/tmp/testfile.txt'
FROM exporttable
1 ↪ char char ↪ text text
  ↪ blob blob ↪ 2001-12-31 ↪ 12:30:00 ↪ 20001117164643 ↪ 3.14159 ↪ 0.012
  ↪ b ↪ e,g
2 ↪ ' " \\ ; + ↪ adsf ↪ \N ↪ 2000-11-17 ↪ 16:54:54 ↪ 20001117165454
  ↪ -2.3e-037 ↪ 12.345 ↪ b ↪ f,g
```

In the second attempt a semicolon is used as column separator. All fields are enclosed at beginning and end with a double quote character. As escape character the backslash is used (the default setting). Of particular interest is the behavior in the field *a_char*:

```
' " \ ; +
```

becomes

```
"' \" \\ ; +"
```

The semicolon within the character string remains untouched, since it is clear on account of the double quote character where *a_char* ends. However, the double quote becomes a backslash to ensure that the character is not misinterpreted at the end of the character string.

Please note also that *NULL* is represented as *N*, and in fact, without being enclosed in double quotes.

```
SELECT * INTO OUTFILE '/tmp/testfile.txt'
FIELDS TERMINATED BY ';' ENCLOSED BY '\"'
FROM exporttable

1;"char char";"text text";"blob blob";"2001-12-31";"12:30:00";
20001117164643;3.14159;0.012;"b";"e,g"

2;"' \" \\ ; +"; "adsf";\N;"2000-11-17";"16:54:54";
20001117165454;-2.3e-037;12.345;"b";"f,g"
```

In our third attempt, a semicolon is again used as a column separator. The plus sign (+) is used as optional field identifier (that is, only with character strings, dates, times, and BLOBs, and not with numbers). Finally, the exclamation mark (!) is used as escape character. Again the most interesting feature is the transformation of *a_char*:

```
' " \ ; +
```

becomes

```
+' " \ ; !++
```

```
SELECT * INTO OUTFILE '/tmp/testfile.txt'
FIELDS TERMINATED BY ':' OPTIONALLY ENCLOSED BY'+' ESCAPED BY '!'
FROM exporttable
```

Now *NULL* becomes *!N* (that is, for *NULL*, too, the changed escape character is used).

```
1;+char char+;+text text+;+blob blob+;+2001-12-31+;+12:30:00+; 20001117164643;
    3.14159;0.012;+b+;+e,g+

2;+' " \ ; !++;+adsf+;!N;+2000-11-17+;+16:54:54+; 20001117165454;
    -2.3e-037;12.345;+b+;+f,g+
```

Basically, the data stored in a text file with *LOAD DATA* can be read again into a table unchanged if the same options are used as with *SELECT . . . INTO OUTFILE*.

Exporting with `mysqldump`

As an alternative to *SELECT . . . INTO OUTFILE* there is the auxiliary program `mysqldump`. This program is actually primarily a backup program (see also earlier in this chapter and the references in Chapter 18).

The program `mysqldump` always stores entire tables (and not the result of a particular *SELECT* query). A further difference is that `mysqldump` normally does not return a text file with the raw data, but entire *INSERT* commands. The resulting file can then later be read in with `mysql`. To use `mysqldump` for text exportation you must specify the option `--tab`:

```
mysqldump --tab=verz [options] databasename tablename
```

With `--tab` a directory is specified. In this directory `mysqldump` stores two files for each table: `tablename.txt` and `tablename.sql`. The `*.txt` file contains the same data as after *SELECT . . . INTO OUTFILE*. The `*.sql` file contains a *CREATE TABLE* command, which allows the table to be re-created.

As with `mysqlimport`, the representation of special characters can be controlled with four options: `--fields-terminated-by`, `--fields-enclosed-by`, `--fields-escaped-by`, and `--lines-terminated-by`. These options are analogous to the SQL options described at the beginning of this section. They should be set in quotation marks (for example, `"--fields-enclosed-by=+"`):

```
C:\> mysqldump -u root -p --tab=c:\tmp "--fields-enclosed-by=\"" exceptions exporttable
Enter password: ******
```

XML Exporting with `mysqldump`

If you execute `mysqldump` with the option `--xml`, you obtain as result an XML file (where, however, characters outside the 7-bit ASCII character set are not represented by Unicode, but by the *latin1* character set):

```
root# mysqldump -u root -p --xml mylibrary > /tmp/mylibrary.xml
Enter password: ******
```

Exporting with `mysql` *in Batch Mode*

The universal tool `mysql` can be used to execute SQL commands in batch mode and store the results in a text file. In contrast to `mysqldump`, `mysql` is distinguished in that the resulting file is actually more or less readable—for human beings, that is. (However, there is no attempt to make the file suitable for a later reexportation.)

```
> mysql -u root --password=xxx --batch "--execute=SELECT * FROM TITLE;"
         databasename > output.txt
```

The SQL command is passed with the option --execute, where the entire option must be placed in quotation marks. In the resulting text file output.txt the columns are separated by tab characters. The first line contains the column headings.

Exchanging Rows and Columns

If a table has many columns, then mysql returns very long rows, which can be difficult to interpret. In this case, instead of --batch you can use the option --vertical. Then each record is divided over several lines, where in each row only one data item is given (this command must be typed on one line).

```
> mysql -u root --password=xxx --vertical
      "--execute=SELECT * FROM titles;" mylibrary > c:\tmp\test.txt
```

The resulting file looks like this:

```
*************************** 1. row ***************************
 titleID: 1
   title: Linux, 5th ed.
subtitle: NULL
 edition: NULL
  publID: 1
   catID: 1
  langID: NULL
    year: 2000
    isbn: NULL
 comment: NULL
*************************** 2. row ***************************
 titleID: 2
   title: Definitive Guide to Excel VBA
subtitle: NULL
 edition: NULL
  ...
```

Generating HTML Tables

If instead of --batch the option --html is used, then mysql generates an HTML table with column headers (see Figure 10-1). However, the resulting file does not contain any HTML headers. Note as well that mysql does not deal with coding of characters outside of the 7-bit ASCII character set:

```
> mysql -u root --password=xxx --html
      "--execute=SELECT * FROM titles;" mylibrary > c:\\test.html
```

XML Exporting with `mysql`

Like `mysqldump`, `mysql` is also capable of creating XML files. The XML file contains no character set information, although one supposes that the *latin1* character set is used (alas, not Unicode). The following command must be input in a single line:

```
> mysql -u root --password=saturn --xml
   "--execute=SELECT * FROM titles;" mylibrary > c:\test.xml
```

Astonishingly, the format of the resulting XML file is different from that of the file obtained by `mysqldump`; that is, it is apparently stored internally using a different conversion code.

International Customization, Character Sets

In the default setting of the binary distribution of MySQL (which is included in most Linux distributions), MySQL delivers error messages in English, uses the *latin1* character set (ISO-8859-1), and sorts texts according to the Swedish rules. For applications in the English-speaking world this default setting is as it should be. (The peculiarities of the Swedish sorting rules have to do with characters outside of the 7-bit ASCII character set and do not affect the sorting of normal English text.)

> **REMARK** *The information in this section relates to MySQL 4.0. It is in particular with respect to character sets that MySQL 4.1 is to differ significantly: Instead of a character set for the entire server, each table, each column of each table, can be assigned its own character set. Furthermore, MySQL 4.1 offers (finally) support for the Unicode character set. Further information on the new character set functions of MySQL 4.1 can be found in Appendix B of this book.*

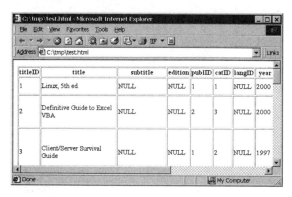

Figure 10-1. A table generated with `mysql`

Error Messages in Other Languages

If you wish to have your MySQL server deliver its error messages in a language other than English, say German or French, then you have merely to set the option `language` in one of the configuration files. The language selected is also used for entries in the error logging file `hostname.err`.

MySQL currently supports about twenty languages. A glance at the directory `mysql\share\` (Windows) or `/usr/share/mysql` (Linux) will tell you their names. If, for example, you find German error messages more to your liking than the English ones, then make the following change in the MySQL configuration file:

```
# in windows\my.ini or /etc/my.cnf
[mysqld]
language = german
```

> **TIP** *Do not forget that you must restart the server for the changes to take effect. If MySQL does not find the file with the error messages, you can also give the entire path name with* `language`, *as, for example (under Windows),* `D:\Program Files\mysql\share\german`

Selecting the Character Set and Sort Order

In MySQL the character set is selected with the option `default-character-set`, which is set in the MySQL configuration file. If this setting is missing, then the default is *latin1* (ISO-8859-1).

Which character set is active and which character sets are otherwise available can be determined from the variables *character_set* and *character_sets*:

```
SHOW VARIABLES LIKE '%char%'
```

Variable_name	Value
character_set	latin1
character_sets	latin1 big5 czech euc_kr gb2312 gbk latin1_de sjis tis620 ujis dec8 dos german1 hp8 koi8_ru latin2 swe7 usa7 cp1251 danish hebrew win1251 estonia hungarian koi8_ukr win1251ukr greek win1250 croat cp1257 latin5 convert_character_set

Default Sort Order

Just to make matters confusing, with MySQL the choice of character set also influences the sort order. And since MySQL comes from Sweden, with *latin1* the sort order is Swedish! Other SQL functions as well that are case-sensitive are influenced by the character set.

It is aggravating that the MySQL documentation offers no description of the available character sets. Their names are not always helpful, since they sometimes refer to the characters, sometimes to the sort order, and sometimes to both. (For example, *german1* denotes the character set *latin1* with German sort order, but *latin1_de* denotes the character set *latin1*, this time with the somewhat different German telephone directory order.)

Changing the Character Set and Sort Order

If you prefer a different sort order, you must change the option `default-character-set` in the MySQL configuration file (in the following example this is done for the German sort order). You will find a `*.conf` file for each supported character set in the directory `mysql/share/charsets` or `/usr/share/mysql/charsets`. If MySQL cannot find this directory, you must specify the location with the option `character-sets-dir`.

```
# in windows\my.ini or /etc/my.cnf
[mysqld]
character-sets-dir = Q:/mysql/share/charsets
default-character-set = german1
```

For the settings to become effective, the server must be restarted.

> **REMARK**   *In MySQL 4.0, the setting of the character set holds for all tables and all clients. It is impossible to set the sort order for each table (or database). In particular, you as MySQL user have no say in the sort order: Only the MySQL administrator can change it. (In other words, if MySQL is running at the site of an ISP, you will have to make do with the sort order in force there.) The situation will become more flexible with MySQL 4.1; see Appendix B.*

Resetting Indexes

After a change in the character set, you must reset all the table indexes. If you are using MyISAM tables, this is no problem. With `myisamchk` the indexes can be rather quickly regenerated. The required command looks like this:

```
root# myisamchk --recover --quick --set-character-set=german1 \
        mysqlpath/data/*/*.MYI
```

You must, of course, adapt the desired character set and the path to the database files to your own circumstances. On my test system the complete command looks like this:

```
root# myisamchk --recover --quick --set-character-set=german1 \
        /var/lib/mysql/*/*.MYI
```

> **POINTER** *While* myisamchk *is being executed, the server must not make any changes in the database. (The easiest way to ensure this condition is to stop the server.) Further information on* myisamchk *is to be found later in this chapter.*

It is somewhat more difficult to reset the indexes for InnoDB tables. Here you must delete the affected indexes with *ALTER TABLE name DROP KEY* and then replace them with *ALTER TABLE name ADD KEY (column)*.

Client Configuration

The MySQL server informs its clients as to which character set it is using. However, the problem sometimes occurs that the client (e.g., mysql) needs the character set table but cannot find it. In most cases, the problem can be solved with the correct setting of character-sets-dir in the mysql group of the MySQL configuration file:

```
# in Windows\my.ini or /etc/my.cnf
[mysql]
character-sets-dir = Q:/mysql/share/charsets
```

If you are working under Windows with Connector/ODBC, you must copy the character set files into the directory C:\mysql\share\charsets. (You may need to create this directory.) Connector/ODBC is not capable of evaluating the MySQL configuration files, and therefore always looks in this predefined place for the character set files.)

Tests with Some Character Sets

This section shows the results of some tests with various character sets. If you are working under Windows, you must execute the SQL commands in a program that uses the Windows character set (such as the MySQL Control Center). The program mysql, on the other hand, will not do, since the command window uses a DOS character set for compatibility reasons.

Default Character Set latin1 with Swedish Sort Order

That Swedish sort order is used becomes apparent when you sort records alphabetically. The table *test_order_by* in the test database *exceptions* contains 255 records, where *id* contains the code, and *a_char* the symbol for the corresponding code. (The result of the following query is displayed, exceptionally, not by columns, but by rows, with entries separated by commas. Various special symbols and unrepresentable symbols were deleted from the result.)

Note that certain variants of the letter A are arrayed between A and B, while the letters Å, Ä, and Ö appear after Z (gotta love that Swedish sort order!):

```
USE exceptions
SELECT a_char FROM test_order_by
WHERE id>31
ORDER BY a_char
!, ", #, $, %, &, ', (, ), *, +, ,, -, ., /, 0, 1, 2, 3, 4, 5, 6, 7,
8, 9, :, ;, <, =, >, ?, @,
A, a, À, Á, Â, Ã, Å, á, â, ã, B, b, C, c, Ç, ç, D, d, …, …, E, e, È,
É, Ê, Ë, è, é, ê, ë, F, f, G, g, H, h, I, i, Ì, Í, Î, Ï, ì, í, î, ï,
J, j, K, k, L, l, M, m, N, n, Ñ, ñ, O, o, Ò, Ó, Ô, Õ, ò, ó, ô, õ, P,
p, Q, q, R, r, S, s, T, t, U, u, Ù, Ú, Û, ù, ú, û, V, v, W, w, X, x,
Y, y, Ü, Ý, ü, ý, Z, z, [, Å, å, \, Ä, Æ, ä, æ, ], Ö, ö, …,
ƒ, …, Š, …, Ž, …, š, …, ž, Ÿ, …, …, …, ÿ, …
```

The character set influences how MySQL deals with character strings. Compare the result of the following command with the result using the character set *german1*, shown a few lines later:

```
SELECT 'a'='A', 'a'='ä'
```

'a'='A'	'a'='ä'
1	0

The consequence for sorting is that *a* and *A* are viewed as equivalent for sorting purposes, while *a* and *ä* are not. In fact, the Swedish town of Rämmen comes alphabetically after Rzeszów, in Poland.

Tests with `default-character-set=german1`

In what follows, the SQL test commands will be executed once again. We see that *a* and *ä* are viewed as equivalent for the purpose of sorting. Furthermore, the sort position of some letters has been changed:

```
!, ", #, $, %, &, ', (, ), *, +, ,, -, ., /, 0, 1, 2, 3, 4, 5, 6, 7, 8,
9, :, ;, <, =, >, ?, @,
A, a, À, Á, Â, Ã, Ä, Å, Æ, à, á, â, ã, ä, å, æ, B, b, C, c, Ç, ç, D, d, E, e,
È, É, Ê, Ë, è, é, ê, ë, F, f, G, g, H, h, I, i, Ì, Í, Î, Ï, ì, í, î, ï, J, j,
K, k, L, l, M, m, N, n, Ñ, ñ, O, o, Ò, Ó, Ô, Õ, Ö, Ø, ò, ó, ô, õ, ö, ø, P, p, Q, q,
R, r, S, s, …, T, t, U, u, Ù, Ú, Û, Ü, ù, ú, û, ü, V, v, W, w, X, x, Y, y, …, …, Z, z,
Š, …, š, …, ž, Ÿ, ÿ
```

```
SELECT 'a'='A', 'a'='ä'
```

'a'='A'	'a'='ä'
1	1

Logging

The term "logging" generally denotes the recording of each change in a database. (As you will see in the course of this section, there are other items that can be recorded as well.) Thus, if a MySQL client program executes the command

```
INSERT INTO mydatabase.mytable (col1, col2) VALUES (1, 'xy')
```

then MySQL changes the table *mydatabase.mytable* accordingly. If logging is activated, then the command itself is also saved in the logging file.

> **POINTER** *In the MySQL documentation you will find information on the subject of logging:*
>
> http://www.mysql.com/doc/en/Log_Files.html

Why Logging?

There are various goals that can be achieved through logging:

- **Security:** It is not possible to execute backups uninterruptedly. Thus, for example, if you make a backup every night, and then the next day your hard drive crashes, all that day's changes would be lost. If you have a logging file (naturally, on a different hard drive), then you can recreate the lost data. Logging files also help in determining who has used the database when, at what times an unusually large number of failed attempts to access MySQL were made, etc.

- **Monitoring:** Normally, you know only the current state of the data. If your tables contain *TIMESTAMP* columns, then the time of the last change can easily be determined. But it is impossible to determine who made this change. If such information is important for your system, if it should be possible to find out who changed what data when, then you can activate an expanded logging protocol that will capture this additional information.

- **Optimization:** Often, it is difficult to determine which queries are most burdensome to a database system. Therefore, MySQL offers the possibility to log all queries whose execution takes a particularly long time.

- **Replication:** Replication denotes the process of synchronizing databases on several computers. For replication it is required that logging be carried out on the *master* computer. (Details on replication follow in the next section of this chapter.)

- **Transactions:** Logging is also carried out with transaction-capable tables (such as InnoDB). In this case, logging files ensure that completed transactions can be executed even after a crash of the database. (Details on transaction logging for InnoDB tables appear later in this chapter.)

Based on the various purposes that it fulfills, MySQL supports various types of logging, which are presented in this section. As long as logging is activated, the logging files are stored in the same directory in which the directories of the various MySQL databases are located. (There is, however, the possibility of using various options to change the location. If you value maximum speed, the logging files should reside on a different hard drive from that on which the database files are located.)

Drawbacks

In the default setting almost all logging variants are deactivated. (The only exception is the logging of errors.) The main reason for this deactivation is speed: Logging slows down the operation of MySQL considerably (only, of course, if data are altered frequently).

The second drawback is the tendency of logging files rapidly to consume more and more space on your hard drive. In particular, with database systems in which data are frequently altered, logging files often require significantly more space than the actual database.

Logging Changes

The logging of changes to a database can be carried out in two ways in MySQL: in text form (log-update) or in binary format (log-bin). The binary format has a number of advantages:

- The logging file contains more information, such as the time of each change and the client thread ID number. (If you wish to know the users behind the ID numbers, you must activate an additional logging file with the option log, in which each login to the MySQL server is recorded.)

- Transactions are handled correctly. (The commands of a transaction are recorded only after a *COMMIT.*)

- The logging files are significantly smaller.

- Writing the logging files is more efficient.

- The logging files can be used as the basis for replication.

The only drawback to binary logging is that the logging files cannot be viewed with an ordinary text editor; however, they can be viewed with the auxiliary program mysqlbinlog.

Since the MySQL documentation considers text logging as obsolete and no longer recommends its use, this section concentrates on binary logging.

> **REMARK** *In principle, it is possible to use* log-bin *and* log-update *simultaneously. Then logging will take place simultaneously in text and binary modes. Of course, this will slow things down considerably.*

Activating Binary Update Logging

Binary logging is activated by the line log-bin in the configuration file. MySQL must then be restarted so that the change can become effective.

```
# in /etc/my.cnf or Windows\my.ini
[mysqld]
log-bin
```

MySQL now generates two new files, *hostname*-bin.001 and *hostname*-bin.index, in the directory in which the database directories are located. (Instead of *hostname*, the name of the computer is used.) The file *hostname*-bin.index contains merely a directory of all logging files. (At each server start a new logging file is begun.)

MySQL also logs in *hostname*-bin.*n* all changes to the contents and structure of all databases (thus, for example, the generation of a new table, adding a new column).

MySQL logs only actual changes. *SELECT* and *UPDATE* commands that leave the data unchanged will not be logged.

> **CAUTION** *In the case of text importation of data with* LOAD DATA *only the command itself is logged, not the changes to the database. The logging file can therefore be used for a backup only if the underlying import file is still available.*

The logging files can be viewed with mysqlbinlog; they look somewhat like the following example (where we have broken long lines and provided some comments):

```
> mysqlbinlog saturn-bin.002
# at 4
#030318 17:29:14 server id 1  log_pos 4
# Start: binlog v 3, server v 4.0.12-nt-log created 030318 17:29:14
# at 79
#030318 17:32:50 server id 1  log_pos 79 Intvar
SET INSERT_ID=61;
# at 107
#030318 17:32:50 server id 1  log_pos 107 Query
# thread_id=1 exec_time=0 error_code=0
USE mylibrary;
SET TIMESTAMP=1048005170;
INSERT INTO authors (authName) VALUES ('Hesse Hermann');
# at 202
#030318 17:47:00 server id 1  log_pos 202 Query
# thread_id=3 exec_time=0 error_code=0
USE myforum;
SET TIMESTAMP=1048006020;
UPDATE 'users'
SET 'email'='testaccount@dummy.com'
WHERE 'userID'=8;
```

Starting New Logging Files

When you stop and restart the MySQL server, the server automatically begins to fill the next logging file with data (*hostname*-bin.002, .003, etc.). A change in the logging file can, of course, be effected without a server restart, and in fact, with the SQL command *FLUSH LOGS* or with mysqladmin flush-logs. Furthermore, MySQL automatically begins a new logging file when the current file exceeds size max_binlog_size (1 gigabyte by default).

A suitable time to begin filling new logging files is after the execution of a complete backup. (The new logging file can help later to reconstruct all changes that occurred after the backup.)

Logging files that are no longer needed should be deleted with *PURGE MASTER LOGS TO*. This command is described later in this chapter when we discuss replication.

Restoring a Database on the Basis of a Logging File

If, perish the thought, misfortune should visit you, then the reconstruction of your database begins with the last full backup to restore the database. Then you employ all your logging files made since the last backup. The SQL commands contained therein are simply executed with mysql. (Be careful to follow the correct order. The oldest logging file must be executed first.)

```
root# mysqlbinlog hostname-bin.031 | mysql -u root -p
root# mysqlbinlog hostname-bin.032 | mysql -u root -p
root# mysqlbinlog hostname-bin.033 | mysql -u root -p
```

Determining the Location of the Logging File

You can determine the location of the logging file yourself. (For reasons of security and speed the logging files should be located on a different hard drive from that on which the database resides.) For this you specify the file name with the option log-bin. MySQL extends the file name with .*nnn* (that is, with a three-digit running integer).

Please make sure that the MySQL server, which under Unix/Linux is usually executed as user *mysql*, has writing privileges in the specified directory (here /var/log/mysql):

```
# in /etc/my.cnf or Windows\my.ini
[mysqld]
log-bin = /var/log/mysql/updates
```

Logging and Transactions

If you employ a table type that supports transactions, you must use binary logging. With traditional logging you will find *BEGIN*, *COMMIT*, and *ROLLBACK* simply ignored (that is, not logged). All other SQL commands will be logged at once. Therefore, even those SQL commands withdrawn by *ROLLBACK* will remain in the log.

On the other hand, with binary logging, changes will be logged only when the transaction has been completed with *COMMIT*.

Logging Files for Various Table Types

The logging procedure described in this section works for all table types (it is independent of type). However, some table types require their own logging files. Information on logging files for InnoDB appears later in this chapter.

Errors, Logins, and Slow Queries

Logging Errors

MySQL automatically logs each launch and shutdown of the MySQL server as well as all server error messages in the file *hostname*.err in the database directory. (Instead of *hostname*, the actual computer name is used.) Unfortunately, server start problems are not logged if they result from invalid configuration settings in my.ini or my.cnf.

There is no option whereby this error logging can be prevented. With the option log-error, however, you can set the name and location of the file:

```
# in /etc/my.cnf or Windows\my.ini
[mysqld]
log-error=/var/log/mysql/mysqlerrorlog
```

Logging Logins and Operations (General Query Log)

With the option log you can enable the logging of each connection to MySQL as well as every command. If you do not specify a file name, then MySQL creates the file hostname.log in the database directory, where instead of *hostname*, the actual computer name is used. The resulting file is not for the purpose of restoring data but for keeping track of which users are looking at and changing what data, etc.

```
# in /etc/my.cnf or Windows\my.ini
[mysqld]
log
```

The following lines show a small section of such a log:

```
MySql, Version: 4.0.12-nt-log, started with:
TCP Port: 3306, Named Pipe: MySQL
```

Time	Id	Command	Argument
030318 16:15:33	1	Connect	root@127.0.0.1 on
	1	Init DB	mylibrary
030318 16:15:38	1	Query	select * from authors
030318 16:16:01	2	Connect	root@127.0.0.1 on
	2	Init DB	mylibraryodbc
	2	Query	SHOW TABLE STATUS FROM 'mylibraryodbc'
030318 16:16:03	2	Init DB	mylibraryinno
	2	Query	SHOW TABLE STATUS FROM 'mylibraryinno'
030318 16:16:06	2	Query	SHOW COLUMNS FROM 'mylibraryinno'.'authors'
	3	Connect	root@127.0.0.1 on
	3	Query	SET SQL_SELECT_LIMIT=DEFAULT
	3	Init DB	mylibraryinno
	3	Query	SHOW TABLES
	3	Query	SHOW FIELDS FROM 'authors'

In comparison to *update logging*, here all commands are logged immediately, as soon as they are passed to the server. This holds as well for transactions, indpendent of whether they are later completed with a *COMMIT*. In contrast to *update logging*, all commands are actually logged, even those that do not alter any data.

Logging Slow Queries

If MySQL is becoming painfully slow due to the burden of complex queries, it is often useful to undertake an analysis to find out which *SELECT* queries are actually causing the greatest delays. To do this, use the option log-slow-queries. Then MySQL will create a logging file with the name *hostname*-slow.log.

All queries whose execution takes longer than ten seconds will be logged. You can change this default time limit by setting the variable long_query_time. By setting the option log-long-format you can have all queries logged, even those that must be carried out without the use of an index (e.g., *SELECT* * . . . *WHERE txtcolumn LIKE '%abc%'*):

```
# in /etc/my.cnf or Windows\my.ini
[mysqld]
log-slow-queries
long_query_time=5
log-long-format
```

Administration of Logging files

Logging files are like children: It is easier to create them than to take care of them, and furthermore, they grow on you. And just as children will take over your life if you aren't careful, your logging files will very quickly fill even the largest hard drive if you don't take prophylactic measures. So here is a bit of advice:

- Do not log more than is absolutely necessary.
- Use binary format if possible for update logs.

Update Logs

With `mysqladmin flush-logs` or the SQL command *FLUSH LOGS*, MySQL closes the currently active logging file and begins a new update logging file (with a new running number).

You have unrestricted access to all update logging files with the exception of the currently active file. You can thus move these files to another directory, compress them, and even delete them (for example, if they exceed a certain age or if they are older than the last complete backup). Under Unix/Linux you can develop a cron job to automate this task.

Logins and Slow Queries

With logging files for logins and operations (option `log`) and for slow queries (option `log-slow-queries`) there is a problem in that there is only one file, which gradually grows larger and larger. The MySQL documentation recommends that you simply rename these files while MySQL is running and then execute `mysqladmin flush-logs` or *FLUSH LOGS*:

```
root# cd logpath
root# mv hostname.log hostname.log.old
root# mv hostname-slow.log hostname-slow.old
root# mysqladmin flush-logs
```

The `*.old` files can now be compressed and eventually deleted.

Error Logging

Alas, neither `mysqladmin flush-logs` nor *FLUSH LOGS* has any effect on the logging file for error messages (`hostname.err`). Therefore, it is impossible to manipulate this file while MySQL is running. If this file becomes too large (which is seldom the case), you must stop MySQL, rename the file, and then restart MySQL.

Replication

Replication makes it possible to synchronize two or more MySQL servers running on different computers.

Different database systems employ differing methods of establishing replication. If you are familiar with replication from another database system, you should not expect MySQL to exhibit the exact same properties.

MySQL currently supports master/slave replication exclusively. There is one master system (*read/write*). This system is responsible for all changes to data. Additionally, there are one or more slave systems (*read-only*) on which, perhaps after a brief delay, exactly the same data are available as on the master system.

The exchange of data between the master and slaves is accomplished via binary logging files belonging to the master. The slaves remain in contact with the master and synchronize their databases by taking the requisite SQL commands from the logging files.

Replication functions even when the computers are running under different operating systems. (For example, the master can be running under Linux and a slave under Windows.)

> **POINTER** *In addition to the information of this section, in Chapter 18 you will find a reference to all SQL commands for running replication (Chapter 18 provides an overview), and in Chapter 19 there is a reference to all* mysqld *options related to replication.*
>
> *Further information can be found in the MySQL documentation, the section "Replication in MySQL":*
>
> http://www.mysql.com/doc/en/Replication.html

Why Replication?

There are two reasons that argue in favor of setting up a replication system: security and speed.

Security

Thanks to replication, your database is available on several computers. If a slave computer goes off line, the entire system can continue to run without interruption. (A new slave system can later synchronize itself.)

If the master computer goes off line, then the preservation of the data can be taken over by a slave computer. Alternatively, the entire system can be reconfigured so that a slave computer takes over the role of the master. In either case, though, the entire system is available as *read-only*.

If you are considering replication for reasons of security only, you should also consider a RAID system, whereby the contents of two (or more) hard drives are synchronized. A RAID system, however, protects only against a hard-drive crash, and not against an operating system crash, power outage, or the like.

Note that replication can also be used as a substitute for conventional backups. (Thanks to replication, the backup is always current. If you also require a conventional backup, you can execute it on the slave computer without involving the master computer.)

Speed

If the speed of a database system is limited primarily by many read-only queries (and not by a large number of alterations to the data), then a replication system can gain you great savings in time: The expensive queries are divided among several slave systems, while the master system is used exclusively or primarily for updates. (Of course, part of the theoretical increase in speed is lost due to the increased communication overhead.)

Please note that you can gain speed only if the programming of the client is compatible with your system. The client programs must divide your queries according to a load-balancing procedure (or simply at random) among all available slave systems. MySQL itself provides no mechanism for this purpose.

If your interest in replication is motivated by performance problems, you should consider alternative performance-enhancing measures, in particular, better hardware (in the following order: more RAM, faster hard drive, a RAID system, a multiprocessor system).

Limitations

- MySQL currently supports replication only in the form of a master/slave system (*one-way replication*). All changes in data must be carried out on a single master system. The slave systems can be used only for database queries (*read-only*).

  It is not currently possible for a slave system to take over the role of the master automatically if it should go out of service (*fail-safe replication*). Thus replication can produce a system that is secure against breakdowns for database queries, but not for alterations to the data. Fail-safe replication is planned for MySQL 5.0.

  It is also impossible to synchronize changes to several systems (*multiple-master replication*). That would lead to problems with *AUTO_INCREMENT* values. It is therefore impossible, for example, to execute changes in a MySQL database on a notebook computer and later bring these into balance with the master system on another computer.

- The replication system does not work properly with several SQL commands:

  o *RAND:* In MySQL 3.23, random numbers generated with *RAND* cannot be replicated. Every copy of the data contains a different value.
     To circumvent this problem, you may use *RAND(n)*, where *n* is a pseudorandom parameter of the current timestamp value of your client program. Starting with MySQL 4.0, replication works with *RAND()* even without a parameter.

  o *User variables:* In MySQL 4.0, SQL commands that contain their own variables (*@varname*) are not correctly replicated. This restriction will be removed with version 4.1.

  o *LOAD DATA INFILE:* Data balancing works only if the imported file on the server is available during replication.

- It is desirable that the same MySQL version be running on both master and slave computers. Replication generally functions correctly when the version number of the slave is higher than that of the client.

- On master and slave systems the same character set should be used (setting `default-character-set`).

Setting Up the Replication Master System

This section describes the preparatory work for setting up a replication system on the master computer. Note, please, that this introduction does not show the only way to proceed. There are even several ways for transferring the start data to the slave. (One variant will be shown a bit later in this chapter.)

This section and the next assume that the database *mysql*, too, is to be replicated with its access privileges. This is usually a good idea, so that all users who are permitted to read data from the master system will be able to read data from the slaves with the same access information.

This method of proceeding is, however, burdened with some drawbacks. Everyone who is permitted to change the master is now permitted to do the same to the slaves. However, changes to data should fundamentally be made to the master, for otherwise, replication falls apart. If you thus wish to exclude data alteration on the slaves, you (as database administrator) must exclude the *mysql* database from replication (`binlog-ignore-db=mysql`), and instead, manage the *mysql* databases separately for the master and all of the slaves. However, that causes synchronization problems. For example, if a user obtains a new password on the master, the changed password must be entered on all the slaves.

Setting Up the Replication User

The first step consists in setting up a new user on the master system that is responsible for communication between master and client. The user name is irrelevant, and in this section we will use the name *replicuser*.

This user requires the *Replication Slave* privilege for access to the binary logging files. Instead of *slavehostname*, specify the complete computer name or IP number of the slave computer. For security reasons you should use as password a combination of characters that is in use neither in the operating system nor in the database:

```
GRANT REPLICATION SLAVE ON *.* TO replicuser@slavehostname IDENTIFIED BY 'xxx'
```

If you have in mind to use the commands *LOAD TABLE FROM MASTER* and *LOAD DATA FROM MASTER*, then you must also grant *replicuser* the privileges *Select, Reload,* and *Super*. These commands are conceived primarily as aids for the MySQL developer and experts; they can help in setting up and managing a replication system.

If the replication system is to have several slaves, then you must execute *GRANT* for all the slave computers. Alternatively, you can permit access for all computers in the local system (e.g., *replicuser@'%.netname'*). This can simplify administration, though at the cost of introducing an unnecessary security risk.

On the slave system, test whether it is possible to establish a connection. (This has only the effect of ruling out possible errors that have nothing to do with replication.)

Shutdown

In setting up the slave (see the next section) you must specify the position in the logging files at which the slave is to begin reading. You can determine this position with the following command:

```
FLUSH TABLES WITH READ LOCK
SHOW MASTER STATUS
```

File	Position	Binlog_do_db	Binlog_ignore_db
saturn-bin.005	79		

You must note the information from the first two columns (*file* and *position*). If *SHOW MASTER STATUS* returns no result (*empty set*), then binary logging is not yet activated.

Next, the MySQL server must be shut down, for example, with `mysqladmin shutdown` or `/etc/init.d/mysql stop`), or under Windows, WinMySQLadmin.

Creating a Snapshot

Now you create a copy (called a *snapshot*) of all the databases. You will need this snapshot for the installation of the initial state of all the databases on the slave computers.

Under Windows use WinZip or another compression program; under Unix/Linux your best bet is to use `tar`. (If you have enough space on your hard drive, you may simply copy the database directory to another location.)

```
root# cd mysql-data-dir
root# tar czf snapshot.tgz database1/ database2/ database3/
```

With `tar` you cannot, unfortunately, use * to include all databases, because in the MySQL database directory there are usually many logging files that should not be installed on the slave system.

Server Configuration

In order for the MySQL server to be able to function as a replication master, you must associate a unique ID number with the server, using the option `server-id`. (Every computer in the replication system must be so designated.) Moreover, you must activate binary logging with the option `log-bin` if that has not yet been accomplished:

```
# master configuration
# in /etc/my.cnf or windows\my.ini
[mysqld]
log-bin
server-id=1
```

Then restart the server. (You can again use the server in normal fashion. All changes to the database will now be recorded in the binary logging file. As soon as a slave system goes on line, it will automatically synchronize its database based on the logging files.)

> **TIP** *A brief description of additional master options can be found in the* mysqld *reference in Chapter 19. For example, you can restrict the replication to individual databases (option* binlog-do-db) *or exclude several databases from the replication (*binlog-ignore-db).

Setting Up the Replication Slave System

Setting Up the Databases (Snapshot)

If the MySQL server is already using replication that is no longer to be used but is to be replaced by a new configuration, then execute *RESET SLAVE*. With this, the server forgets the old replication configuration.

Now stop the slave server. If there were already databases there, move their files into a backup directory (better safe than sorry).

Then copy the database files of the snapshot into the database directory with WinZip or tar xzf). Make sure that the files can be read and written by the MySQL server. Under Unix/Linux you do this by executing chown -R mysql.mysql (Red Hat) or chown -R mysql.daemon (SuSE).

Configuration File

With the slave system as well, the configuration file must be changed a bit. With server-id each slave system also obtains a unique identification number. With master-host, master-user, and master-password you specify how the slave system is related to the master:

```
# slave configuration
# in /etc/my.cnf or windows\my.ini
[mysqld]
server-id=2
default-character-set = <as for the master>
innodb_xxx = <as for the master>
```

Now the slave system can be brought on line. Start the server. If problems arise, look at the error log (file *hostname*.err).

> **REMARK** *Please be sure that the same character set is specified in the configuration files of all the slaves (option* default-character-set*) as for the master.*
>   *If InnoDB files were in the snapshot, then the configuration file of the slave must have exactly the same InnoDB options as that of the master so that the InnoDB tablespace files can be correctly recognized when the server is started.*
>   *The logging of all changes (i.e., update logging) is not necessary for the slaves and should be deactivated for speed optimization.*
>   *A short description of additional slave options can be found in the* mysqld *option reference in Chapter 19.*

Starting Replication

To start replication between slave and master, execute the following command. The slanted text should be replaced by the configuration data of the master:

```
CHANGE MASTER TO
  MASTER_HOST =       'master_hostname',
  MASTER_USER =       'replication user name',
  MASTER_PASSWORD = 'replication password',
  MASTER_LOG_FILE = 'log file name',
  MASTER_LOG_POS = log_offset
```

If the master is running on the computer *saturn.log* and all other specifications are the same as those of the previous section, then the command would look like this:

```
CHANGE MASTER TO
  MASTER_HOST =       'saturn.sol',
  MASTER_USER =       'replicuser',
  MASTER_PASSWORD = 'xxx',
  MASTER_LOG_FILE = 'saturn-bin.005',
  MASTER_LOG_POS = 79
```

If binary logging was not instituted before replication was set up, then specify *MASTER_LOG_FILE = ' '* and *MASTER_LOG_POS = 4*.

First Test

With mysql create a connection to the master system and add a new data record to the table of your choice. Then use mysql to establish a connection to a slave system and test whether the new record appears there. If that is the case, then rejoice, for your replication system is working already. (Of course, you could also generate and then delete new tables and even entire databases. The slave system understands and carries out these commands as well.)

Take a look, too, into the logging file *hostname*.err on the slave system. There you should see entries on the status of the replication, for example in the following form:

```
030319 14:11:57  Slave I/O thread: connected to master
  'replicuser@saturn.sol:3306',  replication started in log
'saturn-bin.005' at position 79
```

As a further test you can shut down the slave system, make changes in the master system, and then start up the slave system again. The databases on the slave system should be automatically synchronized within a couple of seconds.

Setting Up a Replication System with LOAD DATA

A replication system can be set up much more easily if one makes use of the command *LOAD DATA FROM MASTER*. A couple of conditions must be satisfied first:

- On the master, MyISAM tables must be used exclusively. (In MySQL 4.0.12, *LOAD DATA* does not work with InnoDB tables. This should change in future versions, but there is no concrete information in the MySQL documentation as to when that might be.)

- The *mysql* database should not be replicated. (*LOAD DATA* ignores the *mysql* database. Therefore, this database must already exist on the slave system.)

- The MySQL configuration file of the master should contain log-bin and a unique server-id setting.

- The MySQL configuration file of the slave should also contain log-bin and a unique server-id setting.

Master: If these conditions are satisfied, then setting up the replication system is child's play. You set up the replication user on the master, to which you grant the privileges *Select, Reload,* and *Super*:

```
GRANT SELECT, RELOAD, SUPER, REPLICATION SLAVE ON *.*
  TO replicuser@slavehostname IDENTIFIED BY 'xxx'
```

If the databases on the master are already filled in, then the variables *net_read_timeout* and *net_write_timeout* should have their values increased. (The default value is 20. The variables should be reset to the default after the replication system has been set up.)

```
SET GLOBAL net_read_timeout=600
SET GLOBAL net_write_timeout=600
```

Slave: On the slave, set the host name and user name and password for the replication process:

```
CHANGE MASTER TO
  MASTER_HOST =      'saturn.sol',
  MASTER_USER =      'replicuser',
  MASTER_PASSWORD = 'xxx'
```

On the slave as well, *net_read_timeout* and *net_write_timeout* should be increased:

```
SET net_read_timeout=600
SET net_write_timeout=600
```

The following command transfers all the databases and tables from master to slave and starts the replication system:

```
LOAD DATA FROM MASTER
```

If an error occurs in executing this command, then life becomes complicated: You must stop the slave server, delete all (partially) transferred database directories, and then begin again. Possible sources of the problem are too-small values of *net_read_timeout* and *net_write_timeout* (from master and/or slave) as well as the presence of InnoDB tables. *LOAD DATA FROM MASTER* looks at the configuration settings replicate_ignore_xxx, with which individual tables or entire databases can be excluded from replication (see Chapter 19).

Replication Viewed from Inside

The master.info *file*

At the initial startup of replication, the slave system will have the file master.in added to its database directory. In this file MySQL keeps track of which binary logging file is currently being used, to what point this file has been evaluated, how the master can be contacted (host name, user name, password), etc. This file is absolutely necessary for the operation of replication. The MySQL documentation naturally emphatically recommends that you not mess around with this file:

```
saturn-bin.007
265
saturn.sol
replicuser
saturn
3306
60
```

> **REMARK**   *The content of* master.info *can also be determined with the SQL command* SHOW SLAVE STATUS. *Changes can be carried out with* CHANGE MASTER TO. *Both of these commands will be described in the SQL reference in Chapter 18.*

relay *Files (Slave)*

Once replication is running on the slave computer, the files relay-log.info, *hostname*-relay-bin.index, and *hostname*-relay-bin.*nnn* appear in the data directory. These files are created by a separate IO thread (subprocess) on the slave server, using a copy of the binary logging files on the master. The sole task of the IO thread is to copy these data from master to slave. A second SQL thread then executes the SQL commands contained in the logging files.

Excluding Databases and Tables from Replication

If you do not want all of the databases or tables of the master replicated, there are two ways of excluding some of them: You can exclude databases from logging in the master configuration file (binlog-ignore-db), or you can exclude databases and tables from replication in the slave configuration file (replicate-ignore-table, replicate-wild-ignore-table, replication-ignore-db).

Excluding Replication Temporarily (Master)

If you wish to execute an SQL command on the master that is not to be replicated on the slave, then first execute the command *SQL_LOG_BIN=0* and then the command *SET SQL_LOG_BIN=1*. (For this, the *Super* privilege is necessary.)

Ending the Master and Slave Servers

Master and slave servers run independently of each other, and they can be stopped and restarted independently and in either order without loss of data. If the slave is unable to make a connection to the master, or to reconnect, then it attempts a connection every sixty seconds. As soon as the connection is reestablished, all outstanding changes are read from the binary logging files and executed on the slave. This works even if the slave was down for a long time and has a great deal of catching up to do.

Several Slaves, Replication Chains

One may have an arbitrary number of slaves, all accessing the same master. From the master's point of view, nothing is different (except for the additional burden of accesses).

In addition, MySQL offers the possibility of creating replication chains of the form $A \rightarrow B \rightarrow C$. Here B would be a slave with respect to A, but a master with respect to C. This generally increases the overhead and is therefore not worthwhile. However, a possible scenario is a slow network connection between A and B (say, one server is in Europe and the other in the USA) and a fast connection between B and C. On computer B, the configuration log-slave-updates must be used.

Replication and Transactions

Transactions are not executed on the slave systems until they have been terminated on the master by *COMMIT*. On the other hand, if a transaction on the master is terminated by *ROLLBACK*, then the affeced SQL commands are neither logged in the logging files nor executed on the slave system.

It is even possible to use a transaction-capable table format (InnoDB) on the master system, while using an ordinary MyISAM table on the slave. Since transaction management takes place entirely on the master, it is unnecessary to have slave support on the slave. However, it is necessary to have the slave properly set up before replication begins. (If the tables in the start state come from a file snapshot, then they are in the same format as those of the master and must be explicitly transformed on the slave to MyISAM tables. Note that changes in the format of a table are replicated from master to slaves.)

> **REMARK** *The seldom used commands* LOAD TABLE/DATA FROM MASTER *function only for MyISAM tables. It may be necessary for you to transform InnoDB tables on the master beforehand into this format.*

Client Programming

If the goal of a replication system is to ensure against system failure or to increase speed by dividing up the queries among several systems, then changes are necessary to the client as well.

In establishing the connection, a distinction must be made as to whether data are going to queried only or whether changes are required as well. If *INSERT, UPDATE,* or *DELETE* commands are to be executed, then a connection to the master system must be made.

On the other hand, if data are to be queried only, then the connection should be made to the server that is currently the least burdened. Since the client program as a rule has no way of determining this, the *Connect* function should randomly select a computer from a predetermined list of computer names or IP numbers and attempt to make a connection. If this does not succeed (because this server is currently unreachable), then *Connect* should make an attempt to connect to another server.

Random Server Selection

The following example in the programming language PHP assumes that you wish to read (and not alter) data and to select the server randomly to improve efficiency. To do this you define in *mysqlhosts[ ]* an array of all the server names (or IP addresses) and use *rand(min, max)* to select an element of the array.

After the connection has been established, the single query mysql_list_dbs is executed (corresponding to the SQL command *SHOW DATABASES*):

```
<html><head><title>test</title></head><body>
<?php
  $mysqlhosts[0]="venus.sol"; // list of all servers of the
  $mysqlhosts[1]="mars.sol";// replication system
  $mysqlhost=$mysqlhosts[rand(0,1)]; // select server randomly
  $mysqluser="user"; // user name
  $mysqlpasswd="xxx";// password
  $connID=mysql_connect($mysqlhost, $mysqluser, $mysqlpasswd);
  $result=mysql_list_dbs();
  echo "<p>Databases at $mysqlhost<p>\n";
  while($row = mysql_fetch_row($result)) {
    echo "<br /><i>$row[0]</i>\n"; }
?>
</body></html>
```

Crashproof Server Selection

The starting point for our second example is similar. However, now our goal is to make the connection process immune to a connection failure. The following lines demonstrate a possible procedure whereby at most ten connection attempts are made.

```
$tries=0;
while($tries<10 && !$connID) {
  $mysqlhost=$mysqlhosts[rand(0,1)];
  $connID = @mysqld endedysqluser, $mysqlpasswd);
  $tries++;
}
if(!$connID) {
  echo "<p>Sorry, no database server found.\n";
  echo "</body></html>";
  exit();
}
```

Maintenance of MyISAM Tables

As we have already mentioned in Chapter 5, MyISAM tables are stored in the files `dbname/tablename.MYD` (data) and `dbname/tablename.MYI` (indexes). This allows the simple copying and moving of tables and databases. However, such operations are allowed only if the server is not using the databases (the best procedure is to stop the server for this purpose).

In rare cases, it may be necessary to work with the MyISAM table files directly, such as to restore indexes or repair damaged files. This section offers the tools that you will need.

myisamchk

The command `myisamchk` is, in a sense, a universal tool for the maintenance of MyISAM tables. With this command you can accomplish the following:

- Check the integrity of MyISAM tables.

- Repair damaged MyISAM table files (e.g., after a power outage).

- Release unused storage space in MyISAM files.

- Recreate the index to MyISAM tables (for example, after a change in the sort order of the MySQL server).

Instead of `myisamchk`, you can also use the following SQL commands:

- *ANALYZE TABLE* provides information about internal index management.

- *CHECK TABLE* tests the table file for errors in consistency.

- *OPTIMIZE TABLE* optimizes the use of storage space in tables.

- *REPAIR TABLE* attempts to repair defective tables.

These commands currently work only for MyISAM tables. However, it is possible that their effectiveness will someday extend to other types of tables. The advantage of the SQL commands over myisamchk is that you do not need to worry about the MySQL server and myisamchk interfering with each other. The disadvantage is that the MySQL server must be running (which may be problematic after a crash), that under some circumstances not all errors can be corrected, that there are fewer options for control of the process, and that the SQL commands are somewhat slower in their execution.

An extension to myisamchk is the command myisampack, with which MyISAM tables can be compressed. In this way, a great deal of space can be saved. However, only read access to such tables is then possible. At the end of this section we shall have more to say about myisampack.

> **POINTER**   *A reference to all options of* myisamchk *and* myisampack *can be found in Chapter 19. Further information on the use of* myisamchk, *particularly for the repair of defective table files, can be found in the MySQL documentation:*
>
> ```
> http://www.mysql.com/doc/en/Table_maintenance.html
> ```

Using myisamchk

The syntax of the myisamchk command is as follows:

```
myisamchk [options] tablename1 tablename2 ...
```

The table names are given as complete file names, either with or without the ending *.MYI (but, surprisingly, not with *.MYD). Depending on the options specified, however, both MyISAM files, that is, name.MYD (data) and name.MYI (indexes), are analyzed or changed.

To check on the integrity of all tables in the database *mydatabase* you should execute the following command. (You must, of course, replace /var/lib/mysql with your actual database directory.)

```
root# myisamchk /var/lib/mysql/mydatabase/*.MYI
```

You can use myisamchk independently of the MySQL server (the server may be running, but it does not have to be). If the server is running, then mysqladmin flush-tables or the SQL command *FLUSH TABLES* must be executed first.

> **CAUTION**   *If* myisamchk *actually changes MyISAM files and not just checks them, it must be ensured that the MySQL server does not change any data during this time.*
> *Therefore, you must execute if necessary the SQL command* LOCK TABLES *with* mysql, *followed by* myisamchk, *and then, finally,* UNLOCK TABLES. *You must not leave* mysql *during this time, since otherwise, the LOCKs would end.*

Speed Optimization, Memory Usage

In the case of large tables, the analysis, and even more the repair, of tables is a very costly operation. The speed of myisamchk depends greatly on the amount of available RAM.

The memory usage of myisamchk is set by four variables. In the default setting, myisamchk requires about 3 megabytes of RAM. If you have more memory to squander, then you should raise the values of the appropriate variables, since then myisamchk will execute much more quickly for large tables. The MySQL documentation recommends the following values:

```
root# myisamchk -O sort=16M -O key=16M -O read=1M -O write=1M
 ...
```

Here *x* should represent about one-fourth of available RAM (e.g., 64 MB on a 256-MB computer).

Furthermore, for repairing database files myisamchk requires a huge amount of space on the hard drive (among other reasons, because a copy of the database file is first made). A copy of the file is placed in the directory specified by the environment variable TMPDIR. You can also specify this directory via --tmpdir.

Shrinking and Optimizing MyISAM Tables

The MyISAM table driver attempts, normally, to keep table files as small as possible. However, if you delete a large number of records from your tables or if you often carry out changes to records with columns of variable size (*VARCHAR, xxxTEXT, xxxBLOB*), then the optimization algorithm runs up against its limit. In the worst case, the database files are significantly larger than necessary. Moreover, the data are scattered throughout the file, which slows down access to the database.

The following command provides some assistance. It regenerates the database file and optimizes the index file in view of providing the speediest access to the database. With the option --set-character-set the character set is specified for the sort order. (You must be dealing with the same character set with which the MySQL server is running.) The effect of --check-only-changed is that only those tables are processed that were changed since the last processing by myisamchk. (For space reasons, the command has been split using a backslash over two lines.)

```
root# myisamchk --recover --check-only-changed --sort-index \
        --analyze --set-character-set=xxx databasepath/*.MYI
```

> **TIP** *If* myisamchk *is unable to find the character set files, you must specify it explicitly with* --character-set-dir. *Under Windows, the files can be found under a standard installation in* C:\mysql\share\charsets.

> **TIP** *If you would like to check the performance of* myisamchk, *create a test database and then delete at random about half of the data records:* `DELETE FROM testtable WHERE RAND()>0.5`

Repairing MyISAM Tables

For me, this section is largely of a theoretical nature, because fortunately, I have thus far had no problems with corrupt MyISAM tables. Corrupted files can arise when the database is stopped by a power failure, when MySQL or the operating system crashes, or if MySQL or the MyISAM table driver contains errors (which is rather unlikely, however).

Damaged MyISAM files make themselves known in MySQL service by error messages like *Index-file/Record-file/Table is crashed* or *No more room in index/record file*. In such a case, myisamchk will not, of course, be able to work a miracle. Data that for some reason are no longer available or have been overwritten cannot be restored. However, myisamchk can repair the database to the extent that at least all other records can again be read:

```
root# myisamchk --recover --set-character-set=xxx databasepath/*.MYI
```

If you suspect that only the index file has been affected, then execute myisamchk with the additional option --quick (which is considerably faster). In this case myisamchk regenerates the index file.

In particularly difficult cases, that is, when myisamchk --recover fails, you can attempt recovery with --safe-recover. However, that will take much longer than --recover.

If MySQL is running with a character set other than the standard *latin1*, you must specify the character set for sorting with the option --character-sets-dir.

Restoring or Creating a New MyISAM Index

If you change the character set of the MySQL server (for which a restart is necessary), then you must generate new indexes for all your tables. The command for doing so looks like this:

```
root# myisamchk --recover --quick --set-character-set=xxx databasepath/*.MYI
```

Compressing MyISAM Tables (myisampack)

If you exclusively read (but do not change) large tables, then it is a good idea to compress your files. Not only does this save space, but in general, it speeds up access (since larger portions of the table can reside in the file buffer of the operating system):

```
root# myisampack databasepath/*.MYI
```

Although with `myisampack` the identifier `*.MYI` is specified for the index file, the command changes only the data file `*.MYD`. To uncompress compressed table files, you should execute `myisamchk` with the option `--unpack`.

Administration of InnoDB Tables

As we have described extensively in Chapter 8, InnoDB tables offer, in comparison to MyISAM tables, a number of additional functions (in particular, transactions and integrity rules). However, the use of InnoDB tables makes the administration of MySQL a bit more complex. This section provides some tips for managing InnoDB tables and for the optimal configuration of the MySQL server.

> **POINTER** *A quick overview of the most important InnoDB parameters can be obtained with the command* SHOW VARIABLES LIKE 'innodb%'. *A summary of the InnoDB configuration parameters for the MySQL server can be found in Chapter 19.*

tablespace *Administration*

While MyISAM files and indexes are stored in their own files within a directory with the name of the database (e.g., `data/dbname/tablename.myd`), all InnoDB tables and indexes are stored in a virtual file system, which in the InnoDB documentation is called the *tablespace*. The *tablespace* itself can be composed of a number of files.

You can use InnoDB tables without any particular configuration settings, in which case at the first start of the MySQL server the file `ibdata1`, of size 10 megabytes, is created for the *tablespace* and can be enlarged repeatedly by 8 megabytes as required.

Determining the Space Requirements of InnoDB Tables

The *tablespace* is more or less a black box that you cannot see into. For example, there is no command to return any sort of directory of the *tablespace*. The command *SHOW TABLE STATUS* does give information about how much space the individual InnoDB tables and their indexes require within the *tablespace* and how much space is available before the *tablespace* will have to be enlarged.

In what follows, only the relevant columns of the *SHOW* command are displayed. The storage of tables and indexes is managed in 16-kilobyte blocks, which is why *SHOW* always returns integer multiples of 16,384:

`SHOW TABLE STATUS FROM` mylibraryinno

Name	Type	Data_Length	Index_Length	Comment
authors	InnoDB	16384	16384	InnoDB free: 3072 kB ...
categories	InnoDB	16384	49152	InnoDB free: 3072 kB ...
...				

Configuration of the tablespace *Files*

Where and in what size *tablespace* files are created is determined by the configuration parameters innodb_data_home and innodb_data_file_path. The former specifies the directory in which all InnoDb files are stored (by default the MySQL data directory), and the latter contains the names and sizes of the *tablespace* files. A possible setting in the MySQL configuration file is the following:

```
# in /etc/my.cnf bzw. Windows\my.ini
[myslqd]
innodb_data_home = D:/data
innodb_data_file_path = ibdata1:1G;ibdata2:1G:autoextend:max:2G
```

This means that the *tablespace* consists of the files D:\data\ibdata1 and D:\data\ibdata2. If these files do not exist, they will be created, of size 1 gigabyte each. If the InnoDB tables require more space while the server is running, then ibdata2 will be enlarged automatically in 8-megabyte increments (to a maximum of 2 gigabytes).

> **REMARK**   *The* autoextend *attribute has been available since MySQL 4.0.2 and 3.23.50. In MySQL 3.23.n, the configuration of* innodb_data_home *and* innodb_data_file_path *is absolutely required, while since 4.0.0 it has been optional.*

In the management of the *tablespace* files you should observe the following:

- The MySQL server requires write privileges for the innodb_data_home directory so that it can create and alter the *tablespace* files.

- As administrator you must enlarge the *tablespace* in good time (that is, before reaching the limits of a *tablespace* file). If the InnoDB driver determines in a transaction that the *tablespace* is full and cannot be enlarged any further, the transaction will be aborted with *ROLLBACK*.

Using Hard Drive Partitions Directly

InnoDB also offers the option of using an entire hard drive partition directly (that is, without a file system managed by the operating system). For this, instead of specifying the file name, you give the device name of the partition and append the exact size specification (newraw). The partition size must be an integer multiple of 1 megabyte. (The following example uses the Linux device notation.)

```
innodb_data_home_dir=
innodb_data_file_path=/dev/hdb1:61440Mnewraw
```

After the partition has been initialized by MySQL, you must stop the MySQL server and replace newraw by raw. (The former is necessary only if you are adding a new partition.)

```
innodb_data_file_path=/dev/hdb1:61440Mraw
```

The InnoDB documentation unfortunately contains no information about whether better performance can be obtained by the direct use of hard drive partitions (one suspects that it can) and if so, how much. I have been able to obtain little concrete information from the MySQL mailing list.

Enlarging the tablespace

In principle, one cannot enlarge individual *tablespace* files. (The one exception is the autoextend attribute, which, however, can be specified only for the last *tablespace* file.) To enlarge the *tablespace*, you must therefore add an additional file to innodb_data_file_path. The process looks in detail like this:

- Stop the MySQL server.

- If the size of the last *tablespace* file was variable due to autoextend, you must determine its actual size in megabytes (the number of bytes according to DIR or ls divided by 1,048,576). The resulting size must be specified in the innodb_data_file_path setting.
  If innodb_data_file_path does not yet exist in the configuration file, then previously, ibdata was used as the default file, and you must determine and specify its size.

- Add one or more new files to innodb_data_file_path.
  All files must be located in the one directory (or in directories relative to it). If you wish to divide the *tablespace* files among several partitions, hard drives, etc., then you must specify an empty character string for innodb_data_home, and in innodb_data_file_path you must use absolute file names.
  Note that the order of the files specified up to now in innodb_data_file_path cannot be changed (and that of course, none of the previous files may be missing).

- Restart the MySQL server. If the server does not detect an erroneous configuration, it will generate the new *tablespace* files. This process will also log any errors in the file *hostname*.err.

Let us suppose that the previous setting looks like the following and that ibdata2 has current size of 1904 megabytes:

```
innodb_data_file_path = ibdata1:1G;ibdata2:1G:autoextend
```

You now want to increase the size of the *tablespace* to 4 gigabytes. The new setting must look like the following:

```
innodb_data_file_path = ibdata1:1G;ibdata2:1904M;ibdata3:1100MB:autoextend
```

Shrinking the Size of the `tablespace`

It is, unfortunately, impossible to make the *tablespace* smaller. If you delete large InnoDB tables or change them into another table format, the space within the *tablespace* is freed up, but the *tablespace* files cannot be made smaller. The only way to shrink them is by the following process:

- Make a backup of all InnoDB tables with `mysqldump`.

- Delete all InnoDB tables (*DROP TABLE . . .*).

- Stop the MySQL server (`mysqladmin shutdown`).

- Delete the current *tablespace* files (`ibdata . . .`). If you have enough space, it is, of course, more secure first to move the files into another directory.

- Change `innodb_data_file_path` in the MySQL configuration file.

- Restart the MySQL server. New *tablespace* files corresponding to the `innodb_data_file_path` setting will be created.

- Recreate all your InnoDB tables from your backup files.

> **TIP** *Unfortunately, there is no way of obtaining a list of all InnoDB tables. If you are managing a large number of databases, you must search through the backup for each database for InnoDB tables. It is simpler to make a backup of* all *databases. The re-creation of the databases is also easier. But this way of proceeding makes sense only if the MyISAM tables constitute a small portion of the data or when you are going to make a complete backup anyhow.*
>
> *An alternative is to transform the InnoDB tables temporarily into MyISAM tables. This is easy to do, but involves a great deal of internal processing, and therefore, it is particularly slow for large tables. Furthermore, problems can arise if the tables use InnoDB-specific properties (such as foreign key constraints).*
>
> *Some tips for maximizing efficiency in large block operations such as inserting tables will be given later in this chapter.*

Copying, Deleting, and Moving InnoDB Tables

From your experience with MyISAM tables you are accustomed to the fact that (after a server shutdown) you can simply copy or move all files `dbname.tablename`. The MySQL server recognizes at restart which tables are to be found where. This is very practical for backups or making a copy of a table or database.

If you use InnoDB tables, none of this is possible. If you wish to copy a table, you must either create a new table and copy the data with *INSERT . . . SELECT*, or you must make a backup of the table (`mysqldump`) and then create the table under another name.

Furthermore, caution is necessary with the `*.frm` files. These files give the structure of a table and are located in the relevant database directory (even with InnoDB tables!). The `*.frm` files and associated tables stored in *tablespace* must always be synchronized. You must not simply delete *.frm files. If you wish to delete a table, execute *DROP TABLE*; then the *.frm file will be deleted.

Making a Backup

There are several ways of making a backup of InnoDB tables:

- The most elegant way is to use *InnoDB Hot Backup*. This auxiliary program makes the backup while the server is running, without blocking tables. However, *InnoDB Hot Backup* is a commercial program and is not to be had for free; see http://www.innodb.com/hotbackup.html.

- Of course, you can always use mysqldump. However, the results are consistent only if the tables are not changed during the execution of the command.

- If you are prepared to stop the MySQL server, you can simply copy the *tablespace* files. Note, though, that you must use the exact same innodb_data_file_path setting as well as all *.frm files. On the other hand, you do not require the transaction logging files. If the server was properly shut down, these files no longer contain any relevant data.

Moving the tablespace

According to the MySQL documentation, the *tablespace* files are independent of the operating system. Only the CPU's floating-point representation must be correct. If those conditions are satisfied, then the *tablespace* files can be moved without problem between, say, Windows and Linux. Of course, you must take care here, too, that the innodb_data_file_path setting is correct and that all *.frm files are moved as well. (In practice, it will usually be the case that both MyISAM and InnoDB tables are to be copied. For this, all database directories and all *tablespace* files are simply copied.

The InnoDB documentation contains no information as to whether the *tablespace* file format is dependent in any way on the version. Heikki Tuuri, the developer of the InnoDB table driver, has promised forward compatibility for all present and future versions. (It has always been a tradition with MySQL that database files be able to be moved without difficulty to a new version.)

Within MySQL 4.0.*n* I experience no problems with changing among numerous versions; however, I have not checked backward compatibility to earlier versions. In general, an occasional backup with mysqldump is a good idea. The backup file then exists in text format, which is immune against possible compatibility problems.

Logging Files

Transaction Logging

InnoDB logs all changes in logging files with the names ib_logfile0, ib_logfile1, etc. The purpose of these logging files is to make large transactions possible as well as to restore InnoDB data after a crash.

If MySQL is properly configured and there is sufficient memory, then most of the currently needed data should reside in RAM. To improve speed, changes to data are first made only in RAM, and not in the actual data files (that is, in the case of InnoDB, in the *tablespace*).

Only when a transaction is completed with *COMMIT* are the changes in data actually stored on the hard drive, and then first in the InnoDB logging files ib_logfile0, ib_logfile1, etc. The changed parts of the *tablespace* are only gradually transferred to the hard drive, all this for reasons of efficiency. If a crash occurs during these proceedings, then the *tablespace* can be restored with the help of the logging files.

The logging files ib_logfile0, etc., have two purposes. On the one hand, they satisfy the ACID condition of durability, so that transactions that have been carried out are not endangered even if there is a crash immediately after the transaction has been completed. On the other hand, the logging files enable transactions of almost unlimited size, even those for which it is not possible to hold all pending (but not yet confirmed) changes in RAM.

The InnoDB logging files are filled in order. When the last file is full, the InnoDB table driver begins writing data to the first logging file. Therefore, the entire size of all logging files limits the quantity of *tablespace* changes that can be temporarily stored before a *COMMIT*. The maximum size of all logging files is currently (MySQL 4.0.9) limited to 4 gigabytes.

The transaction logging files are necessary only while the MySQL server is running. As soon as the MySQL server has been properly shut down, these files are no longer needed. For example, if you make a backup with ibdata files, you do not need to copy the logging files.

Size and Location of the Logging Files

The proper dimensioning of the logging files has a great influence on the speed of MySQL/InnoDB. The location, size, and number of logging files are determined by the configuration parameters innodb_log_group_home, innodb_log_files_in_group, and innodb_log_file_size. By default, two logging files of size 5 megabytes each are created in MySQL's data directory.

The InnoDB documentation recommends that the total size of the logging files be about the size of the buffer (parameter innodb_buffer_pool_size, which is 8 megabytes by default). If the buffer is larger than the logging files, then it can happen that the InnoDB table driver will have to make a so-called *checkpoint*, involving temporary storage of uncommitted changes.

If you wish to change the location, size, or number of logging files, you must stop the MySQL server. Now delete the existing logging files ib_logfile*n* (only when you are sure that shutdown took place without error) and change /etc/my.cnf or Windows\my.ini. New logging files will be created at the subsequent restart of the MySQL server.

TIP *If you value maximal speed, then you should have the logging files stored on a different hard drive from that on which the* tablespace *files reside.*

> **REMARK**   *If the MySQL server finds logging files when it is started up that do not correspond to the* innodb_log_ *parameters, then the startup process is broken off. You will find error messages in the error logging file* hostname.err. *The creation of new logging files (even if there is no error) is also logged in* hostname.err.

Logging Synchronization

The configuration parameters innodb_flush_log_at_trx_commit and innodb_flush_method tell when (how often) and how logging files are synchronized. For innodb_log_at_trx_commit there are three settings, which allow one to make tradeoffs between speed and security:

- The default setting is 0. The data are written about once per second into the current logging file, and then the file is synchronized. (Writing means here that the data are passed to an I/O function of the operating system. Synchronization means that changes are actually physically written to the hard drive.)

  If there is a crash during the time between the *COMMIT* and the synchronization of the logging file, the transaction is lost and cannot be reconstructed at a later restart. Therefore, innodb_flush_log_at_trx_commit=0 is a strike against the ACID durability condition.

- More secure is the setting 1. Now writing and synchronization take place with each *COMMIT*. The drawback is that if you make mostly small transactions, then the hard drive limits the number of possible transactions per second. (For a hard drive with 7200 revolutions per minute, that is, 120 per second, at most 120 transactions can be executed per second, a theoretical limit that is never reached in practice.)

- The setting 2 is a good compromise. Here the writing takes place at each *COMMIT*, but the synchronization only about once per second. If the MySQL server crashes, then immediately terminated transactions are not lost (since the synchronization can take place after a crash). However, if the operating system crashes (power outage, for example), then transactions are lost as with setting 0.

The parameter innodb_flush_method determines whether the operating system function *fsync* (the default) or *O_SYNC* (setting O_DSYNC) is used for synchronizing the logging files. With many Unix versions, *O_SYNC* is faster.

Archive Logging

The transaction logging files are conceived only for internal data management, not for backups. If you require a record of all changes to data since a particular time (since the last complete backup), then you must use MySQL binary logging, which functions entirely independently of the InnoDB table driver. (See the discussion earlier in this chapter.)

InnoDB can, in principle, also carry out such logging. This type of logging is called *archive logging* in the InnoDB documentation. However, *archive logging* makes sense only if InnoDB is used independently of MySQL. The files ib_arch_log_*n* that appear in the data directory are a result of such *archive logging*. In them are logged, at the start of the MySQL server, the creation of new *tablespace* or transaction logging files. Then, however, *archive logging* is automatically shut off.

Should you wish for some reason to use *archive logging*, it can be activated with innodb_log_archive.

Tips for Speed Optimization

This section offers some tips for speed optimization. The information here is relevant only if you are using primarily InnoDB tables and are working with large data sets.

> **POINTER**   *Look at the section "Performance Tuning Tips" in the InnoDB documentation. In optimizing for speed there is also useful information in the InnoDB status information, which can be retrieved with* SHOW INNODB STATUS.

Buffer Settings

Perhaps the most important parameter for influencing the speed of the InnoDB table driver is innodb_buffer_pool_size. This parameter specifies how much RAM should be used for temporary storage of InnoDB tables and indexes. The more such data is available in RAM, the less often access must be made to the hard drive in *SELECT* commands. By default, the InnoDB table driver reserves only 8 megabytes as a buffer. Larger values (the InnoDB documentation recommends up to 80 percent of main memory for a dedicated database server) can dramatically increase the speed of *SELECT* queries. (The total size of the transaction logging files should be as large as the buffer storage.)

Depending on the application, two additional parameters influence what data are stored temporarily in RAM: innodb_log_buffer_size sets the size of the buffer for transaction logging, while innodb_additonal_mem_pool_size determines how much space in RAM is reserved for various other information such as metadata on open tables. This buffer (by default 1 megabyte) should be enlarged if you are dealing with a large number of InnoDB tables.

Block Operations

If you are carrying out extensive block operations (such as importing a table with a million data records or changing from MyISAM to InnoDB format), you can speed up the process with a few tricks:

- Use the setting *SET unique_checks=0*. Then no check is made whether the data of a *UNIQUE* column or the primary index column are actually unique. Of course, you should use this setting only if you are absolutely sure that there are, in fact, no duplicates!

- Use the setting *SET foreign_key_checks=0*. With this setting you achieve that the integrity conditions are not checked. Of course, here, too, this setting should be used only if you are convinced of the integrity of your data (e.g., in restoring backup data).

- Execute all the *INSERT* commands for a table as a single transaction. Usually, importation consists of countless *INSERT* commands, which by default (*auto commit*) are all carried out in separate transactions. With *SET AUTOCOMMIT=0*, all *INSERT* commands are collected into a single transaction. Keep in mind that this transaction must be confirmed with a *COMMIT*.

    This technique works only if the transaction logging files are large enough. Note that with large transactions, a *ROLLBACK* can be unusually long, even taking hours. Note as well that *CREATE TABLE* has the effect of *COMMIT*. Therefore, it is impossible to read in several tables in a single transaction.

Logging Settings

In the previous section we made reference to the possible settings of the logging parameters. Here is a brief summary:

- `innodb_flush_log_at_trx_commit=2` is useful is you wish to execute as many (small) transactions per second as possible and are prepared to lose the last few seconds of data in case of a crash.

- Ideally, the logging files should be located on a different hard disk from those of the *tablespace* files.

- Depending on the operating system, `innodb_flush_method=O_DSYNC` may speed up logging.

Server Tuning

Server tuning refers to the optimal configuration of the MySQL server so that it uses hardware as efficiently as possible and executes SQL commands with maximum efficiency.

Server tuning is worthwhile, as a rule, only if very large databases are involved (in the gigabyte range), many queries per second are to be processed, and the computer is serving primarily as a database server.

This section provides merely a first introduction to this topic and is restricted primarily to the correct configuration of the buffer storage and the use of the query cache. Note, however, that server tuning is only a component of the larger topic that perhaps might be called optimization of database applications. On this theme one could easily write an entire book, which would, among other things, answer the following questions:

- What possibilities are there to optimize the database design in such a way that the most frequently used commands are executed with maximum efficiency? Were the optimal indexes set up? The correct database design is assuredly the most important and undervalued component of speed optimization. Fine tuning the server for a poorly designed database is like hitching a racehorse to a carriage with square wheels. (See also Chapter 5.)

- What is the best hardware for the task (within a given price range)?

- What is the best operating system (if there is a choice)?

- What is the optimal table format (see also Chapter 8 on InnoDB).

- Can the burden of many *SELECT* queries be divided among a number of computers?

POINTER   *Many questions will go here unanswered, not least because I myself have too little experience with very large database applications. Further information can be found in the MySQL documentation:*

http://www.mysql.com/doc/en/MySQL_Optimisation.html

A wealth of tuning information is contained in the web sites, news, and mailing list contributions of the MySQL guru Jeremy Zawodny. Do a Google search or have a look at the following site:

http://jeremy.zawodny.com/mysql/

Optimal Memory Management

MySQL reserves at startup a portion of main memory for certain tasks, such as a cache for data records and a location for sorting data. The size of this buffer is controlled by options in the configuration file and generally cannot be altered while the server is in operation. It can happen that MySQL leaves a great deal of RAM unused, even though there was sufficient memory available and MySQL could make use of it.

The setting of the parameters takes place in the `mysqld` section of the MySQL configuration file. Memory sizes can be abbreviated by K (kilobytes), M (megabytes), and G (gigabytes). The following lines clarify the syntax. (In MySQL 3.23 the syntax is `set-variable = ` *varname=n*. This syntax is still allowed, but it is no longer necessary.)

```
# in /etc/my.cnf bzw. Windows\my.ini
[myslqd]
key_buffer_size = 32M
```

In the following, various important configuration parameters will be introduced (though not all of them by a long shot). Unfortunately, one cannot say which parameter settings should be changed and to what, it all depends heavily on the specific application. However, first attempts should include `key_buffer_size` and `table_cache`:

- The parameter `key_buffer_size` (default 8M) tells how much storage is to be reserved for index blocks. The higher the value, the more rapid is table access to columns for which there is an index. On dedicated database servers it can make sense to increase `key_buffer_size` up to one-fourth of the available RAM.

- The parameter `table_cache` (default 64) specifies how many tables can be open at one time. The opening and closing of table files costs time, and so a larger value of the parameter can increase parallel access to many tables. On the other hand, open tables cost RAM, and the number is also limited by the operating system. The number of tables open in MySQL can be determined with *SHOW STATUS* (variable *open_tables*).

- The parameter `sort_buffer` (default 2M) specifies the size of the sorting buffer. This buffer is used in *SELECT* commands with *ORDER BY* or *GROUP BY* if there is no index available. If the buffer is too small, then a temporary file must be used, which is, of course, slow. The default value of 2 megabytes should suffice for many purposes.

- The parameter `read_buffer_size` (formerly `record_buffer`, default 128K) specifies how much memory each thread reserves for reading sequential data from tables. The parameter should not be unnecessarily large, since this memory is required for each new MySQL connection (thus for each MySQL thread, not only once for the entire server). It is best to increase the parameter only when it is needed for a particular session with *SET SESSION read_buffer_size=n.*

- The parameter `read_rnd_buffer_size` (default 256K) has an effect similar to that of `read_buffer_size`, except that it is valid for the case in which the records are to be read out in a particular order (as with *ORDER BY*). A larger value can avoid search operations on the hard disk, which can slow things down considerably with large tables. As with `read_buffer_size`, `read_rnd_buffer_size` should be increased only as needed with *SET SESSION*.

- The parameter `bulk_insert_buffer_size` (default 8M) specifies how much memory is reserved for the execution of *INSERT* commands in which many records are to be inserted simultaneously (such as *INSERT . . . SELECT . . .*). This parameter can also be changed for individual connections with *SET SESSION*.

- The parameter `join_buffer_size` (default 128K) specifies how much memory is to be used for *JOIN* operations when there is no index for the *JOIN* columns. (For tables that are frequently linked there should definitely by an index for the linking field. This will contribute more to speed efficiency than increasing this parameter.)

- The parameter `tmp_table_size` (default 32M) specifies how large temporary *HEAP* tables can get. If this size is exceeded, then the tables are transformed into MyISAM tables and stored in a temporary file.

- The parameter `max_connections` (default 100) gives the maximum number of database connections that can be open at one time. The value should not be unnecessarily high, since each connection requires memory and a file descriptor. On the other hand, persistent connections profit from a larger number of allowed connections, since then it is less frequent that a connection is closed and a new one has to be opened. (With *SHOW STATUS* you can determine `max_used_connections`. This is the maximum number of connections that were open simultaneously up to a particular time.)

> **TIP** *You can get a look at the most important current settings with the command* SHOW VARIABLES LIKE '%size%.

> **POINTER** *If you use InnoDB tables, you should definitely look also at the InnoDB options; see the previous section of this chapter.*
> *A brief description of all available parameters of the MySQL server can be obtained by launching* mysqld *with the option* --help. *A more complete description is given in the MySQL documentation:*
>
> http://www.mysql.com/doc/en/SHOW_VARIABLES.html

Query Cache

The query cache is a new function in MySQL 4.0. The basic idea is to store the results of SQL queries. If later this exact same query is to be executed, then the stored result can be used instead of having to search through all the affected tables.

The query cache is no panacea, though, for speed optimization. In particular, queries must be deleted from the query cache as soon as the underlying tables are altered:

- The query cache is therefore useful only if the data change relatively seldom (thus many *SELECT* commands in relation to the number of *UPDATE, INSERT,* and *DELETE* commands), and it is expected that particular queries will be freqently repeated (which is frequently the case with web applications).

- The *SELECT* commands must be exactly the same (including spaces and case), so that the query cache knows that they are, in fact, the same.

- The *SELECT* commands cannot contain user-defined variables and cannot use certain functions, the most significant of which are *RAND, NOW, CURTIME, CURDATE, LAST_INSERT_ID, HOST.*

If these conditions are not satisfied, then the query cache *SELECT* queries will, in the worst case, slow the system down somewhat (due to the management overhead).

Activating the Query Cache

By default, the query cache is deactivated (due to the default setting query_cache_size=0). To activate the query cache, execute the following changes to the MySQL configuration file:

```
# in /etc/my.cnf or Windows\my.ini
[myslqd]
query_cache_size = 32M
query_cache_type = 1      # 0=Off, 1=On, 2=Demand
query_cache_limit = 50K
```

Now 32 megabytes of RAM is reserved for the query cache. In the cache are stored only *SELECT* results that require less than 50 kilobytes. (This avoids the situation in which a few large query results force all other results out of the cache.)

After a server restart, the cache is automatically active. For MySQL applications nothing changes (except that the reaction time to repeated queries is less).

Demand Mode

The query cache can also be run in demand mode. In this case, only those *SELECT* queries are considered that are executed with the option *SQL_CACHE*, as in *SELECT SQL_CACHE * FROM authors*. This mode is useful if you wish to control which commands use the cache.

No Temporary Storage of SQL Query Results

If you wish to prevent a *SELECT* command from using the active query cache (query_cache_type=1), then simply add the option *SQL_NO_CACHE*. This makes sense with commands about which one is certain that they will not soon be repeated and would therefore take up space unnecessarily in the query cache.

Turning the Query Cache On and Off for a Connection

You can change the mode of the query cache for a particular connection. Just execute *SET query_cache_type = 0/1/2/OFF/ON/DEMAND*.

Determining the Status of the Query Cache

If you wish to know how well the query cache is functioning, whether its size is well chosen, etc., then execute the command *SHOW STATUS LIKE 'qcache%'*. As result you receive a list of status variables, whose meaning is briefly described in Table 10-1.

With *FLUSH QUERY CACHE* you can defragment the cache (which, the MySQL documentation states, makes possible improved memory usage, but it does not empty the cache). *RESET QUERY CACHE* deletes all entries from the cache.

ISP Database Administration

Up to now we have assumed that you have installed MySQL on your own computer and have unrestricted access to the server. And indeed, this is the usual starting point for every database administrator.

However, with MySQL the situation can be a bit different. Often, your database is located on the computer of an Internet service provider. There you have almost no administrative privileges. That is, the ISP administers MySQL on its own. (If you have a responsible ISP, it will automatically carry out backups of your databases, but don't count on it.) Nonetheless, you will have to carry out certain administrative tasks:

- Create new databases (provided that the ISP permits this).

- Execute backups. (Even if your ISP does this regularly, it is good to be able to be responsible for your own data.)

- Execute a database upload. (For example, you have developed a database application on your own computer and now wish to transfer the completed database to the ISP computer.)

Working via `telnet/ssh`

Administration is at its simplest when your ISP provides you with `telnet` access (or `ssh` access, which would be more secure). Then you can log into the ISP's computer and use all of the commands introduced in this chapter. Needless to say, with commands such as `mysqldump` you can access only your own databases. But that should suffice. For moving files between your local computer and that of the ISP, you can use `ftp`.

Unfortunately, not all ISPs offer their clients access via `telnet` or `ssh` (or only for a large additional fee), since this means extra work for the ISP and greater security risks.

Working via `phpMyAdmin`

Probably the most popular solution to this administrative problem is offered by phpMyAdmin, a collection of PHP scripts installed in a www directory on the ISP's computer. In principle, phpMyAdmin is suited for all the administrative tasks mentioned above. In practice, however, there is usually a problem.

For the execution of PHP scripts—and thus for phpMyAdmin as well—there is a time limit. If the execution of a script exceeds the allotted time, the script is automatically terminated. In most cases this limit represents a sensible protective measure against programmer error (such as infinite loops), but unfortunately, it makes the backup of a large database impossible.

Table 10-1. Query cache status variables

Variable name	Description
Qcache_queries_in_cache	Tells how many queries have results in the cache.
Qcache_inserts	Tells how many queries have been cached up to now. This value is generally greater than *Qcache_queries_in_cache*, since results are removed from the cache due to lack of space or changes to tables.
Qcache_hits	Tells how often a query was able to be answered directly from the cache.
Qcache_lowmem_prunes	Tells how many results were deleted from the cache because it was full. (If this value is high, that is an indication that the cache size is too small.)
Qcache_not_cached	Tells how many queries were not accepted into the cache (e.g., because a function like *RAND* or *NOW* or the option *SQL_NO_CACHE* was used).
Qcache_free_memory	Tells how much memory is currently free in the cache.

> **POINTER** *The installation of phpMyAdmin on an ISP computer is discussed in Chapter 2, while the details of using it appear in Chapter 4.*

Implementing Custom PHP Scripts for Administration

Instead of working with phpMyAdmin, you can, of course, program your own PHP scripts for administration and store them in a directory on your web site. For example, you can execute a backup of a database with a PHP file of the following design:

```
<?php system("/usr/bin/mysqldump --host=hostname --user=username " .
             "--password=xxx dbname > backup.sql"); ?>
```

Instead of /usr/bin you may have to specify a different path (for example, /usr/local/bin). In some circumstances things will work without a path name being specified. As *hostname* you can use *localhost* if the web server and MySQL are running on the same computer.

After you have loaded the page via your web browser (and thereby executed the script), you can transfer the file backup.sql, which is located in the same directory as the script, to your computer, again via the web browser or FTP.

> **REMARK** *With an ISP the web server (and thus the PHP script as well) is usually executed under the account* nobody *or* apache. *This user usually has writing privileges in your directories.*
>
> mysqldump *works only if you have granted extensive write privileges for the directory in which the PHP script is located. For this the command* chmod a+w directory *would be necessary, but you might not be able to execute it without* telnet/ssh. *Instead, use your FTP client to set the directory's access privileges.*

Conversely, for an upload you first transfer via FTP the file upload.sql generated on your computer into the directory in which your PHP administration scripts are located. Then you execute a script via your web browser according to the following pattern:

```
<?php system("/usr/bin/mysql --host=hostname --user=username " .
             "--password=xxx dbname < upload.sql"); ?>
```

For the upload to succeed, the specified database must already exist. If that is not the case, you can first create the database with mysqladmin (which you also execute in the PHP script via *system*).

If you have previously created upload.sql with mysqldump, then the database at the ISP may not contain the tables defined in upload.sql. If necessary, you must insert some *DROP TABLE IF EXISTS* commands in upload.sql.

In comparison to phpMyAdmin, the advantage of this way of proceeding is that no time is lost in the transfer of the database files over the Internet. Instead, the upload file is read from the local computer, or the download file is written there. However, this does not change anything in regard to the time limit for PHP scripts. Of course, you can transport somewhat larger databases with the method presented here than with phpMyAdmin, but sooner or later you will find yourself nose to nose with the PHP time limit.

> **POINTER** *Do not forget to secure access to the directory with your administrative scripts with* .htaccess. *The use of* .htaccess *is described in Chapter 2.*

Custom Perl Scripts for Administration

What works with PHP works also, of course, with Perl, and often better. The advantage of Perl is that in the execution of CGI scripts there is often no time limit. (But this depends on the provider.)

In Perl, too, there is a *system* function for calling external commands. In the lines below there is also code added that evaluates and displays the return value of this function. The mysqldump and mysql commands look exactly the same in the PHP scripts presented above. Even the preparatory work is identical:

```
#!/usr/bin/perl -w
use CGI qw(:standard);
use CGI::Carp qw(fatalsToBrowser);
print header(), start_html("Backup");
if(system("/usr/bin/mysqldump --host=hostname --user=username " .
          "--password=xxx dbname > backup.sql")) {
  print p(), "failed", end_html(); }
else {
  print p(), "done", end_html(); }
```

Part III

Programming

#### CHAPTER 11

PHP: Fundamentals and Programming Techniques

THE LETTERS PHP STAND FOR *PHP Hypertext Preprocessor* (a recursive abbreviation typical of Unix-world shenanigans). PHP is a script programming language for HTML pages. The code embedded in an HTML file is executed by the server. (The *Active Server Pages* of Microsoft also follow this plan.)

When a programming language is brought into play with MySQL, that language is almost always PHP. The reason for this is that MySQL offers almost ideal conditions for building dynamic web sites: simple deployment, high speed, unbeatable price (free).

This chapter provides general programming techniques. The following two chapters demonstrate two rather long application examples. (The examples can be tested on line at `www.kofler.cc`.)

Chapter Overview

Introduction

This chapter assumes that MySQL and PHP are correctly installed on your test system and that everything functions as it should. (Chapter 2 discusses installation.)

POINTER   *All the example programs for this chapter are available for download at* www.apress.com *in the downloads section.*
    A compact reference to all MySQL functions in PHP can be found in Chapter 20.

PHP Compatibility Problems

The examples in this book were tested with PHP versions 4.2 and 4.3. Most of the examples should work with PHP 4.1 as well.

However, if you use PHP 4.0 or an earlier version, you will have difficulties with all the examples that use the *superglobal* fields *$GLOBALS, $_GET, $_PUT, $_COOKIE, $_SESSION*, etc. (The term superglobal means that the variables are available in called functions and do not have to be passed as parameters.) The content of these fields is explained in Table 11-1.

Table 11-1. Superglobal fields (available since PHP 4.1)

Variable	Content
$GLOBALS	Contains the names of all variables that are currently globally valid.
$_SERVER	Contains variables of the HTTP server (generally from Apache).
$_GET	Contains variables that were passed with HTTP-GET. (This includes variables that are declared in the web address, e.g., http://my.firm/script.php?variable=123.)
$_POST	Contains variables arising from a form that were passed with HTTP-POST.
$_COOKIE	Contains cookie variables.
$_FILES	Contains variables that were passed with HTTP-POST that have information about files.
$_ENV	Contains environmental variables of the operating system.
$_REQUEST	Contains all variables from *$_GET, $_POST, $_COOKIE* as well as variables that were passed via URL character strings (that is, all variables that can be manipulated by the user and are considered insecure).
$_SESSION	Contains session variables (*$_SESSION* is available only after a call from *start_session* or *session_register*).

Access to the data of superglobal fields takes place in the example programs of this book in a code block of the following pattern. The function *array_item* that we have defined serves to initialize variables without an error message even if no data were passed. (A PHP page for the evaluation of a form can be called by another page, so that the form data are then lacking.)

```
function array_item($ar, $key) {
  if(array_key_exists($key, $ar)) return($ar[$key]); }
$sqlType         = array_item($_REQUEST, 'sqlType');
$authID          = array_item($_REQUEST, 'authID');
$formSearch      = array_item($_POST,    'formSearch');
$formSubmitTitle = array_item($_POST, 'formSubmitTitle');
```

For these examples to work in PHP 3.*n* or 4.0, you must comment out these instructions. Variables like *sqlType* and *authID* are then automatically initialized if corresponding data are passed.

This type of data transfer often represents a security risk, for which reason since PHP 4.1 it has been available only in a particular configuration (variable *register_globals* in php.ini). Since PHP 4.2 this direct passing of global variables is deactivated by default (*register_globals=Off*).

> **POINTER** *Further information on security in PHP applications and the use of superglobal fields can be found at the following addresses:*
>
> http://www.zend.com/zend/art/art-oertli.php
> http://www.php.net/manual/en/reserved.variables.php
> http://www.php.net/manual/en/language.variables.external.php
> http://www.php.net/manual/en/security.registerglobals.php
> http://www.php.net/manual/en/security.variables.php

PEAR

Direct access to MySQL by PHP can take place in two different ways:

- by functions directly integrated into PHP, all of which begin with *mysql_*

- by functions from the *PHP Extension and Add-on Repository* (*PEAR* for short)

This book considers only the *mysql_* functions. PEAR offers better portability if the database system is later changed, but is not yet very widespread. (The PEAR database functions are comparable to DBI for Perl.)

> **POINTER** *Further information on the use of the PEAR database functions can be found at the following addresses:*
>
> http://pear.php.net/
> http://pear.php.net/manual/en/core.db.php
> http://www.phpbuilder.com/columns/allan20010115.php3

Establishing a Connection to the Database

The Connection

To create a connection, one usually uses the PHP function *mysql_connect*, to which three parameters are passed: the computer name (host name) of the MySQL server, the MySQL user name, and the password. If MySQL is running on the same computer as the PHP script (that is, on *localhost*), then the computer name does not have to be given:

```
$connId = mysql_connect("localhost", "username", "xxx");
```

This function returns an identification number for the connection. This number will be needed in the future only if you have more than one connection to MySQL open. (As long as there is only one connection to MySQL, this is the default connection. The ID number thus does not have to be given in calling various *mysql_xxx* functions.)

Optional Parameters

Beginning with PHP 4.1, you can specify with a fourth parameter whether in multiple execution of *mysql_connect* with the same connection data, simply a link to the existing connection should be passed (*false*, default behavior) or a new connection should be established (*true*). The form *mysql_connect($host, $name, $pw, true)* is required if you maintain several separate connections.

Beginning with PHP 4.2, you can pass client flags in a fifth parameter. A possible constant is *MYSQL_CLIENT_COMPRESS* (if the data exchange is to take place in compressed form):

```
$connId = mysql_connect("localhost", "username", "xxx",
  new_link, client_flags);
```

Problems with Establishing the Connection

If problems occur in establishing the connection, the variable *connId* will contain the value *FALSE*. Moreover, *mysql_connect* sends an error message to the web server, so that in the resulting HTML document a rather unattractive error message appears for you to behold. To avoid this error message it is necessary to place the @ character before *mysql_connect*. (In general, this character prevents error messages from being displayed in calls to PHP functions.)

If you would like to supply the PHP code for the connection with a readable error message, you might write code something like the following:

```
$connId = @mysql_connect("localhost", "username", "xxx");
if ($connID == FALSE) {
  echo "<p><b>I regret to inform you that a connection to the database
    cannot be established at this time.
    Please try again later. Perhaps you will have better luck.</b></p> \n";
  echo "</body></html>\n"; // close HTML Document!
  exit(); // end PHP Script
}
```

Selecting the Default Database

As soon as a connection is established, you can use various *mysql_xxx* functions to execute SQL commands and do a lot of other neat stuff as well. To avoid having to specify the desired database over and over, you can use *mysql_select_db* to select the default database (*mysql_select_db* corresponds to the SQL command *USE databasename*):

```
mysql_select_db("mylibrary");
```

Specifying the MySQL user Name and Password in an Include File

You should always avoid storing a user name and password in plain text in a file that is accessible over the web. Of course, visitors to your site should in principle never obtain a glimpse of the source text of PHP files, since the PHP code is evaluated by the web server and is no longer visible in the resulting HTML document. But configuration errors have been known to occur by which the PHP file in raw form is revealed to a web surfer.

An additional security risk is that the file might be read not via HTTP but via anonymous FTP. (That would also be the result of a configuration error. The directory for anonymous FTP should be completely separate from that with HTML files. Yet such configuration errors occur rather frequently.)

Thus to avoid allowing strangers to tumble onto your MySQL password too easily (but also so as not to have to write this information in every PHP script, which would entail a great deal of work if the MySQL password were to change), the MySQL login information is usually stored in its own file. For the examples of this section the password file has the name mylibraryconnect.inc.php, and it looks like this:

```php
<?php
  // file general/mylibraryconnect.inc.php
    $mysqluser="user";        // user name for MySQL access
    $mysqlpasswd="xxx";       // password
    $mysqlhost="localhost";   // name of the computer on which MySQL is running
?>
```

The best place to store this file depends on the configuration of the web server. On my web site I have created a directory htdocs/_private/. The directory _private is secured by .htaccess. Therefore, loading the file directly with http://www.kofler.cc/_private/mylibraryconnect.inc.php is possible only if the HTTP user name given in .htaccess and the associated encrypted password stored in the authentication file are given.

In order to discover my MySQL password, the PHP configuration of the ISP of my web site would have to be defective. Furthermore, you would have to guess the name of the directory _private and break the password protection via .htaccess. It is rather unlikely that all of these conditions could be satisfied.

CAUTION *Be absolutely certain that the include file cannot be accessed by anonymous FTP.*

Be sure as well that all include files end with *.php. *Thus do not use, say,* name.inc, *but* name.inc.php. *This ensures that the file will be executed by the PHP interpreter during an HTTP access in every case (for example, if an attacker guesses the* .htaccess *user name and associated password).*

Be sure that it is impossible via anonymous FTP to display a PHP file on your web server in such a way that this file can then be read over the web server. If there is an FTP directory called incoming, *then this directory must also not be accessible over the web server (for example, as* http://www.mysite.com/ftp/incoming). *If that were the case, then an attacker could write a simple PHP script that reads your include file and reads out the contents of the variables. (To do this, the attacker would have to know the name of the include file and names of the variables, but they just might be guessed. Often, examples are taken directly from various books.)*

We return now to the PHP file in which the connection to MySQL is to be established. There an *include* must be used to load the file with the password information. If you assume, for example, that the files intro.php and mylibrary-connect.inc.php are located in the directories

```
/www/user1234/htdocs/php-examples/general/intro.php
/www/user1234/htdocs/_private/mylibraryconnect.inc.php
```

then the *include* instruction in intro.php must look as follows:

```
// file intro.php
include("../../_private/mylibraryconnect.inc.php");
$connID = @mysql_connect($mysqlhost, $mysqluser, $mysqlpasswd);
```

Depending on how the directories containing the PHP scripts and the include file are located relative to each other, you will have to change the path information in the *include* command. The two periods (..) indicate that a subdirectory of the current directory is to be used.

REMARK *In the example files to this book, the include file is located in the same directory as the script files. The* include *instruction therefore contains only the file name (that is,* include("mylibraryconnect.inc.php")). *If you wish to secure the example files, you must move the file* mylibraryconnect.inc.php *into a secure directory and then alter the* include *instruction.*

Building the Connection in the Include File

If an include file is used, then one should make full use of its advantages. If you wish to create a connection to MySQL from several different PHP files, it makes sense to store all of the code for creating the connection together with error checking in the include file.

The following model assumes that the function *mylibrary_connect* is executed before any HTML headers or the like are created in the PHP script file. Of course, other ways of proceeding are possible, but take care that the resulting HTML document is complete (that is, inclusive of HTML header and with closure of all open HTML tags):

```php
<?php
// file general/mylibrary-connect.inc.php

function connect_to_mylibrary() {
  $mysqluser="useruser"; // user name
  $mysqlpasswd="xxx"; // password
  $mysqlhost="localhost"; // name of the computer of which MySQL is running
  $connID = @mysql_connect($mysqlhost, $mysqluser, $mysqlpasswd);
  if ($connID) {
    mysql_select_db("mylibrary"); // set default database
    return $connID;
  }
  else {
    echo "<!DOCTYPE HTML PUBLIC \"-//W3C//DTD HTML 4.0//EN\">
      <html><head>
      <title>Sorry, no connection ... </title>
      <body><p>Sorry, no connection to database ... </p>
      </head></html>\n";
    exit(); // terminate PHP interpreter
    }
  }
?>
```

Example

The following miniscript (see also Figure 11-1) makes use of the function called *connect_to_mylibrary* introduced above to establish a connection to MySQL, and it then determines the number of data records stored in the table *titles*. (The two functions *mysql_query* and *mysql_result* are introduced in the following sections.)

Figure 11-1. A simple PHP example

```
<!-- php  /file general/intro.php -->
<?php
  include("mylibraryconnect.inc.php");
  $connID = connect_to_mylibrary();
?>
<!DOCTYPE HTML PUBLIC "-//W3C//DTD HTML 4.0//EN">
<html><head><title>PHP Programming, intro sample</title>
</head><body>
<?php
  $result = mysql_query("SELECT COUNT(*) FROM titles");
  echo "<p>Table <i>titles</i> contains ",
    mysql_result($result, 0, 0),
    " records.</p>\n";
?>
</body></html>
```

Persistent Database Connections

PHP provides two functions for creating a connection to MySQL. One is the function *mysql_connect*, which we have already discussed, and the other is the function *mysql_pconnect*. The advantage of *mysql_pconnect* is that an attempt is made to reactivate an earlier connection with the same host name, user name, and password. This proceeds more quickly than establishing a completely new connection. In such a case, the connection is called *persistent*. (Establishing a connection to MySQL usually is rapid in any case, and thus the time savings resulting from a persistent connection are not enormous. On the other hand, with other database systems a persistent connection is absolutely necessary.)

Persistent connections are possible only if PHP is used as a module of the web server (and not in the CGI versions).

Persistent connections are managed by a thread. They are reused when the combination of host name, user name, and password coincides with an existing (but not currently in use) connection.

Regardless of how your web server is configured, you can always use *mysql_pconnect*. If recycling a connection is impossible, then a new connection is established. (Note that the ability to use persistent connections can be stopped in php.ini with the variable *mysql.allow_persistent*.)

> **CAUTION**   *The term "persistent" might lead one to think that the MySQL connection remains established when a PHP script is changed. That is not the case. In fact, it is quite the opposite.*
>
> *As a rule, after a change from one PHP page to another, a different MySQL connection is used (which has opened another script).*
>
> *Therefore, you may not depend on any connection-specific information (such as the current database) surviving a page change. In particular, you cannot execute SQL transactions over several pages.*

Disadvantages of Persistent Connections

The small speed advantage achieved by persistent connections is alas paid for with some drawbacks:

- On a heavily visited web server, *mysql_pconnect* leads to very many connections being opened to MySQL and then not being closed (so that they can be used again). This state of affairs consumes considerable memory; the number of connections is limited by `max_connections` (default setting is 100).

  Before you change `max_connections` in the MySQL configuration file, you should read about tuning. For example, with `max_connections` the number of file descriptors that `mysqld` needs increases. (The MySQL variable *max_used_connections* informs you about the maximum number of simultaneous connections that have occurred thus far. The content of the variable can be retrieved with *SHOW STATUS*.)

- All settings that were carried out in a persistent connection hold for the next page that this connection uses. This can cause unwanted side effects.

- If the PHP code of a page is aborted on account of an error, then temporary tables remain; already started transactions remain uncompleted (until they are either confirmed or rolled back by additional SQL commands, which might belong to an entirely different context); tables locked by *LOCK* remain locked.

- Do not rely on temporary tables being automatically deleted at the end of a script. Temporary tables are automatically deleted at the end of a connection to MySQL, but the life of a persistent connection is of uncertain length, and as a rule, is much longer than the time during which a script is executed. Delete your temporary tables explicitly at the end of a script with *DROP TABLE*.

> **POINTER**   *An extensive discussion of the advantages and drawbacks of persistent connections can be found at the following address:*
>
> http://www.mysql.com/newsletter/2002-11/

Executing SQL Commands

To execute an SQL command you pass it as a character string to the function *mysql_query*. If the command is not to be applied to the current database, then you can use *mysql_db_query* to provide the name of the intended database. With each of these functions the ID number of the connection (that is, the return value of *mysql_connect*) can be passed as the optional last parameter if there is more than one connection to MySQL:

```
$result = mysql_query("SELECT COUNT(*) FROM titles");
$result = mysql_db_query("mylibrary", "SELECT COUNT(*) FROM titles");
```

With *mysql_query*, any type of SQL command can be executed: queries with *SELECT*; changes to data with *INSERT*, *UPDATE*, and *DELETE*; changes to the database structure with *CREATE TABLE*; and so on.

> **REMARK**   *An SQL command may not be terminated with a semicolon. It is not possible to give several commands at once. If you wish to execute several commands, then you must execute* mysql_query *once for each command.*

Return Value ($result)

If an SQL command can be correctly executed, then *mysql_query* returns a nonzero value. If a query was involved, then, the return value of *mysql_query* is a reference to a PHP resource (for example, a character string of the form *"Resource id #2"*. This return value can then be inserted into various other functions (for example, *mysql_fetch_row*) to evaluate the individual fields of a table. In the examples of this chapter the return value is usually stored in a variable with the name *result*. (Working with *SELECT* results will be described in detail in the next section.)

On the other hand, if an SQL command cannot be executed, then *mysql_query* returns the result *FALSE* (i.e., 0). Moreover, an error message is displayed, which you may suppress by executing *mysql_query* with the @ prefixed. (The cause of the error can be determined by evaluating *mysql_errno* and *mysql_error*. Further information on error evaluation can be found further below.)

Metainformation on Query Results

After *INSERT*, *UPDATE*, and *DELETE* commands (and all other commands that change data records), you can determine with *mysql_affected_rows* how many records were changed. This function is also helpful after *CREATE TABLE . . . SELECT . . .* for determining how many records were inserted into the new table.

Moreover, you can determine with *mysql_insert_id* after an *INSERT* command which *AUTO_INCREMENT* value was used for inserting the last new record:

```
$n = mysql_affected_rows(); // number of changed records
$new_id = mysql_insert_id(); // ID number of the last AUTO_INCREMENT record
```

On the other hand, if you have executed a *SELECT* query with *mysql_query*, you can use the functions *mysql_num_rows* and *mysql_num_fields* to determine the number of resulting data records and columns, respectively:

```
$rows = mysql_num_rows($result); // number of records
$cols = mysql_num_fields($result); // number of columns
```

> **REMARK**   *Please note the various parameters that the functions we have been discussing take:*
>
> - *In the case of* mysql_affected_rows *and* mysql_insert_id *no parameter should be given. (Optionally, the ID number of the MySQL connection can be given, that is,* $connID, *if you follow the nomenclature of the examples of this chapter.)*
>
> - *On the other hand,* mysql_num_rows *and* mysql_num_fields *expect as parameter the ID number of the query (that is,* $result).

Releasing Query Results

PHP stores query results until the end of the script. If you wish to release these results sooner (for example, because you wish to execute a large number of queries in a script and do not wish to use more memory than necessary), you can release the query result early with *mysql_free_result*. This is particularly to be recommended when there is a loop in your script that executes SQL queries:

```
mysql_free_result($result);
```

SELECT Queries

Evaluation of SELECT Queries

If you execute a *SELECT* query with *mysql_query*, then as result you obtain a reference to a table with *rows* rows and *cols* columns:

```
$result = mysql_query("SELECT * FROM titles");
$rows = mysql_num_rows($result);
$cols = mysql_num_fields($result);
```

This holds as well for two special cases:

- If the query returns only a single value (for example, *SELECT COUNT(*) FROM table*), then the table has only one row and one column.

- If the query does not return any result at all (for example, if there are no records that correspond to a *WHERE* condition), then the table has zero rows. This case can be identified only by evaluating *mysql_num_rows*.

Only if the SQL query was syntactically incorrect or there was a problem with communication with MySQL will you receive no result at all (that is, the return value of *mysql_query* is *FALSE*).

Access to Individual Table Fields

The simplest, but also the slowest, access to individual fields of a table is offered by *mysql_result*. You simply provide the desired row and column numbers in two parameters. (Numbering begins with 0, as with all PHP MySQL functions.) Instead of the column number, you can give the column name (or the alias name if in the SQL query you have worked with *AS alias*):

```
$item = mysql_result($result, $row, $col);
```

It is considerably more efficient to evaluate the result by rows. There are four functions for this:

```
$row = mysql_fetch_row($result);
$row = mysql_fetch_array($result);
$row = mysql_fetch_assoc($result);  // since PHP 4.0.3
$row = mysql_fetch_object($result);
```

- *mysql_fetch_row* returns the record in the form of a simple array. Access to the columns is accomplished with *$row[$n]*.

- *mysql_fetch_array* returns the record in the form of an associative array. Access to the columns is accomplished with *$row[$n]* or *$row[$colname]* (thus, for example, *$row[3]* or *$row["publName"]*). The column name must be given in case-sensitive form.

- *mysql_fetch_arraymysql_fetch_assoc* (available since PHP 4.0.3) also returns an associative field, which can be read out in the form *$row[$colname]*. In contrast to *mysql_fetch_array*, here it is not allowed to pass the column number as parameter.

- *mysql_fetch_object* returns the record as an object. Access to the columns is accomplished with *$row->colname*.

A feature that all of these functions have in common is that with each call, the next record is automatically returned (or *FALSE* if the end of the list of records has been reached). If this given order is to be altered, then the currently active data record can be changed with *mysql_data_seek*:

```
mysql_data_seek($result, $rownr);
```

Column Names and Other Metainformation

If you have processed valid queries and wish to display the results, what you need are not only the data themselves, but also metainformation about the nature of the data: the names of the columns, their data types, and so on.

The function *mysql_field_name* returns the name of the specified column. The function *mysql_field_table* tells in addition from what table the data come (this is important in queries that collect data from several tables). The function *mysql_field_type* gives the data type of the column in the form of a character string (for example, *"BLOB"*). The function *mysql_field_len* gives the maximum length of a column (especially of interest with the data types *CHAR* and *VARCHAR*):

```
$colname = mysql_field_name($result, $n);
$tblname = mysql_field_table($result, $n);
$typename = mysql_field_type($result, $n);
$collength = mysql_field_len($result, $n);
```

Yet more detailed information about a column is given by *mysql_field_flags* and *mysql_fetch_field*: The function *mysql_field_flags* returns a character string in which the most important attributes of the column are given (for example, *"not_null primary_key"*). The properties are separated by a space. Evaluation proceeds most simply with the function *explode*.

On the other hand, *mysql_fetch_field* returns an object that partially provides the same information as the character string of *mysql_field_flags*. Evaluation proceeds in the form *colinfo->name, colinfo->blob*, etc. (A complete table of all object properties can be found in the API reference in Chapter 20.)

```
$colflags = mysql_field_flags($result, $n);
$colinfo = mysql_fetch_field($result, $n);
```

Displaying SELECT *Results as a Table*

The following example (see also Figure 11-2) shows how the result of a simple query (*SELECT * FROM titles*) can be displayed in an HTML table. The code for table output resides in the function *show_table*, which is defined in the file mylibraryconnect.inc.php. Note in particular that all character strings are translated into correct HTML code by the PHP function *htmlentities*. This function ensures that even character strings with HTML special characters like < and > are correctly represented.

The resulting table has the absolute minimum of bells and whistles. To be sure, background color and the like could yield a more cogent presentation, but that is not the theme of this book. (Any book on HTML will inform you of the necessary HTML tags that you would have to add to the code.)

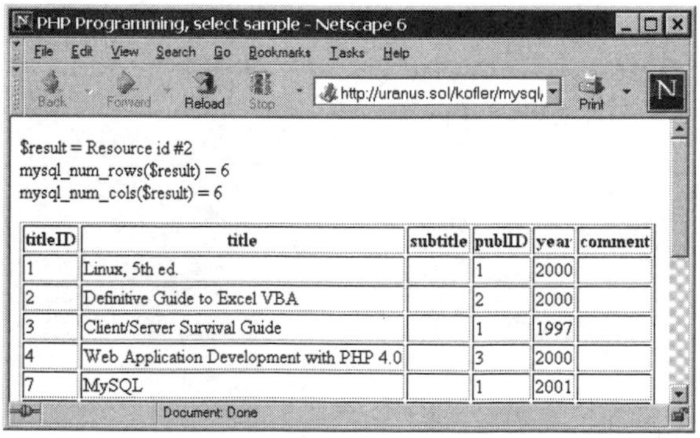

Figure 11-2. The result of a simple query displayed as a table

> **TIP** *Independent of questions of layout, you should take one further detail into consideration: In the display of numbers, right justification often gives a clearer presentation than left justification. You can determine the data type of each column and set the justification accordingly.*

```
// file general/mylibraryconnect.inc.php
// displays the result of a query as an HTML table
function show_table($result)
{
  if(!$result) {
    echo "<p>Error in SQL statement.\n"; return;
  }
  $rows = mysql_num_rows($result);
  $cols = mysql_num_fields($result);
  if($rows>0) {
    echo "<table border=1>";
    echo "<tr>";
    // column headings
    for($i=0; $i<$cols; $i++) {
      echo "<th>", htmlentities(mysql_field_name($result, $i)),
        "</th>";
    }
    echo "</tr>";
    // table content
    while($row = mysql_fetch_row($result)) {
      echo "<tr>";
      for($i=0; $i<$cols; $i++) {
        echo "<td>", htmlentities($row[$i]), "</td>";
      }
      echo "</tr>\n";
    }
    echo "</table>";
  }
}
?>
```

The function *show_table* is activated by the PHP script *select.php*. There a simple SQL query is executed and the result variable *result* passed to *show_table*:

```
<!DOCTYPE HTML PUBLIC "-//W3C//DTD HTML 4.0//EN">
<?php  // file general/select.php
  include("mylibraryconnect.inc.php");
  $connID = connect_to_mylibrary();
?>
<html><head>
<meta http-equiv="Content-Type"
      content="text/html; charset=iso-8859-1" />
<title>PHP Programming, SELECT sample</title>
</head><body>
```

```php
<?php
  // execute SQL query
  $result = mysql_query("SELECT * FROM titles");

  // display metainformation
  $rows = mysql_num_rows($result);
  $cols = mysql_num_fields($result);
  echo "<p>\$result = $result\n",
    "<br />mysql_num_rows(\$result) = $rows\n",
    "<br />mysql_num_cols(\$result) = $cols</p>\n";

  // display HTML table with result
  echo "<p>\n";
  show_table($result);
  echo "</p>\n";
?>
</body></html>
```

POINTER *When a query returns many results, it is not a good idea simply to display all the results. It is better to divide the results over several pages. Furthermore, the user should be given the option of jumping from one page to the next (and back again). An example of a pagewise representation of* SELECT *queries can be found in Chapter 12.*

SELECT *Queries with* `mysql_unbuffered_query`

Since PHP 4.0.6 you can execute *SELECT* queries with *mysql_unbuffered_query* (instead of with *mysql_buffered_query*). This has the effect that the query result is not immediately moved into the PHP interpreter's memory, but only when needed (that is, when individual result records are to be output). This yields the following consequences:

- The data remain on the server until they are fetched by the PHP script. This means that during this time, resources on the MySQL server are blocked. (In exchange, the PHP interpreter needs to reserve only a small amount of memory for intermediate storage.)

- You must read in the found records one at a time (*forward only*) with *mysql_fetch_row, mysql_fetch_object, mysql_fetch_assoc, mysql_fetch_array*. The functions *mysql_fetch_result* and *mysql_data_seek*, on the other hand, are not available. Already read records cannot be read a second time, since only a single record is ever located in the PHP interpreter's memory.

- You may not execute a new SQL command for the current MySQL connection until you have read all the records of the *SELECT* result. If you do not wish to do this, either you will need a second connection to the MySQL server or you will have to release the *SELECT* result explicitly with *mysql_free_result($result)*.

- You can determine the number of found records only by running through all the result records. You cannot use *mysql_num_rows*.

- *mysql_unbuffered_query* is designed only for *SELECT* queries (and not for commands that do not return results, such as *INSERT* and *DELETE*).

mysql_unbuffered_query is especially suited for cases in which large *SELECT* results are to be processed record by record, without the reservation of much client memory for the purpose. Since it is in the nature of PHP pages generally to process small quantities of data, and since the execution time of PHP code is limited (setting *max_execution_time* in php.ini), there are only a few situations in which the function offers real advantages over *mysql_query*.

Changes to Data (*INSERT, UPDATE, DELETE*)

There are no MySQL functions included in PHP for changing data. All alterations must be made with *mysql_query* in the form of SQL commands (*INSERT, UPDATE, DELETE*, etc.). This means as well that all data (BLOBs included) must be transmitted as character strings.

Inserting Linked Data Records

If you insert records into tables with *AUTO_INCREMENT*, you can determine the last *AUTO_INCREMENT* value generated by MySQL with the function *mysql_insert_id*, which we have already mentioned.

The following lines show how a new book title, together with its two authors, can be stored in the *mylibrary* database. Please note that three *ID* values must be temporarily stored, which then must be inserted together in the *rel_title_author* table. It is assumed that the publisher of this book (here Addison-Wesley) is already stored in the database with *publID=1*.

```
mysql_query("INSERT INTO titles (title, publID, year)
    VALUES ('A Guide to the SQL Standard', 1, 1997)");
$titleID = mysql_insert_id();
mysql_query("INSERT INTO authors (authName)
    VALUES ('Date Chris')");
$author1ID = mysql_insert_id();
mysql_query("INSERT INTO authors (authName)
    VALUES ('Darween Hugh')");
$author2ID = mysql_insert_id();
mysql_query("INSERT INTO rel_title_author (titleID, authID, authNr)
    VALUES ($titleID, $author1ID, 1),
      ($titleID, $author2ID, 2)");
```

> **POINTER**   *In practice, that is, when data are input interactively, the storing of new input is somewhat more complicated. For example, it must be checked whether an author already exists. If so, the ID of that author must be stored in* rel_title_author. *If not, a new author must be inserted. (Or was there perhaps a typo? To minimize this possibility, similar names in sound or appearance are displayed and offered as alternatives.) An extensive example will be presented in the next chapter.*

Determining the Number of Changed Records after INSERT, UPDATE, and DELETE

The function *mysql_affected_rows* that we have already mentioned returns the number of records that were changed by an *INSERT, UPDATE,* or *DELETE* command.

> **REMARK**   mysql_affected_rows *returns 0 if all records of a table were deleted with a* DELETE *command without a* WHERE *clause.*
> mysql_affected_rows *returns with an* UPDATE *command only the number of records that were actually changed. Records that were considered, say, with a* WHERE *clause but whose data agreed with the existing data are not counted.*
> mysql_affected_rows *is not designed for* SELECT *commands and returns 0 in such a case.*

Obtaining Status Information After Changes

Due to the limitations of *mysql_affected_rows*, since PHP 4.3 there has been the function *mysql_info*. This function returns, after the following commands, a character string with status information on the MySQL server:

ALTER TABLE

CREATE TABLE . . . SELECT

INSERT INTO

LOAD DATA

UPDATE

The character string contains, for example, information about duplicates and warnings. This is the same string that is displayed in mysql after the execution of the above-mentioned commands. The form of the string depends on the particular command (and could change with new versions of the MySQL server).

If, for example, you execute the command *CREATE TABLE backup SELECT * FROM table*, then *mysql_info* returns a string of the form *"Records: 27 Duplicates: 0 Warnings: 0"*.

Character Strings, BLOBs, DATEs, SETs, ENUMs, and *NULL*

This section describes how to deal with various data types that in practice present a number of difficulties. Coping with *NULL* will also be covered. This section deals separately with storing, altering, and output of data.

Altering Data

To alter data in a database the corresponding SQL commands must be passed as character strings to *mysql_query*. In constructing such character strings, the rules are the same as for MySQL (see Chapter 18). That is, dates and times must be passed in the syntax prescribed by MySQL.

The starting point for the following discussion of various data types is the variable *data*, which contains the data to be stored. The contents of this variable should be formed into an *INSERT* command, which is stored temporarily in the variable *sql*. In the simplest case it works like this:

```
$sql = "INSERT INTO tablename VALUES('$data1', '$data2', ... );
```

Of course, you can put *sql* together piece by piece:

```
$sql = "INSERT INTO tablename VALUES(";
$sql .= "'$data1', ";
$sql .= "'$data2', ";
 ...
$sql .= ")";
```

- **Dates and Times:** To format a date or time in accordance with the MySQL rules, you can summon to your aid the PHP functions *date* and *strftime*. If data are the result of user input, you should carry out the usual validation tests. (MySQL carries out only very superficial validation and is perfectly happy to store data that cannot possibly refer to a real date or time.)

- **Timestamps:** PHP and MySQL timestamps are really the same thing, but they are formatted differently. In the case of PHP timestamps we are dealing simply with a 32-bit integer that gives the number of seconds since 1/1/1970. MySQL, on the other hand, expects timestamps in the form *yyyyddmmhhmmss* or *yyyy-dd-mm hh:mm:ss*.

  As a rule, timestamps are used to indicate the time of the last change. In this case you simply pass *NULL*, and MySQL takes care of the correct storage automatically:

  ```
  $sql .= "NULL";
  ```

  On the other hand, if you wish to store a PHP timestamp as a MySQL timestamp, then you should rely on MySQL *FROM_UNIXTIME* in the *INSERT* or *UPDATE* command:

  ```
  $data = time(); // data contains the current time as a Unix timestamp
  $sql .= "FROM_UNIXTIME(" . $data . ")";
  ```

- **Character Strings and BLOBs:** If BLOBs or special characters appear in a character string, then there are frequently problems with quotation marks. SQL requires that the characters ', ", \, and the zero byte be prefixed by a backslash.

The usual way of quoting character strings that may contain special characters is via the PHP function *addslashes*. This function replaces the character with code 0 by \0 and prefixes the characters ', ", \, with a backslash. Please do not forget to place the result inside single quotation marks, so that SQL realizes that it is dealing with a character string:

```
$sql .= "'" . addslashes($data) . "'";
```

Instead of *addslashes*, you can also use, since PHP 4.0.3, the function *mysql_escape_string*, and, since PHP 4.3, the function *mysql_real_escape_string*:

- *mysql_escape_string* functions like *addslashes*, but it also replaces the characters *carriage return*, *line feed*, and Ctrl Z with the strings \n, \r, and \z. The SQL syntax of MySQL does not require these additional replacements, but the MySQL logging files are thereby made easier to read.
- *mysql_real_escape_string* functions like *mysql_escape_string*, but it also takes into account the character set of the MySQL connection. Neither the MySQL documentation (on the like-named C-API function) nor the PHP documentation gives any information on what influence the character set actually has. I have tested the MySQL server with the *usa7* character set. The special characters used in German, though no longer representable, remained unchanged by *mysql_real_escape_string*.

An additional alternative is to transmit such data in hexadecimal form. PHP offers the convenient function *bin2hex*, which transforms character strings of arbitrary length into hexadecimal. The hexadecimal character string must not be placed within single quotes.

```
$sql .= "0x" . bin2hex($data);
```

There is a drawback to this, however: For each byte of data, two bytes are transmitted to MySQL by PHP, thus almost double the number of bytes that are absolutely necessary.

REMARK *If the data to be stored come from an HTML form and the PHP configuration variable* magic_quotes_gpc *is set to* on *(which is usual), then the data are already quoted. In this case there should be no additional quotation. Further information on* magic quotes *appears later in this chapter.*

- *NULL:* If *data* contains no data (*isset($data)==FALSE*) and this condition is to be stored in the database as *NULL*, then the following is recommended:

```
$sql .= isset($data) ? "'$data'" : "NULL";
```

Please note that within the SQL character command you do not set *NULL* in single quotes as if it were a character string.

Reading Data

The starting point of this section is again the variable *data*, which contains a data field that results from a query. For example, *data* could be filled as follows:

```
$result = mysql_query("SELECT ... ");
$row = mysql_fetch_row($result);
$data = $row[0];
```

Timestamps: The variable *data* contains timestamps as a character string of the form 20001231235959. In PHP you cannot get very far with this. If you wish to work further with a timestamp value in PHP, you should employ the MySQL function *UNIX_TIMESTAMP* and formulate the *SELECT* query accordingly. Then *data* contains (for the above data) the value 978303599:

```
SELECT ... , UNIX_TIMESTAMP(a_timestamp) FROM ...
```

Date: In a *DATETIME* column, *data* contains a character string of the form 2000-12-31 23:59:59. In a *DATE* column, the time specification is lacking. In many instances it is most practical for the further processing of dates in PHP to use the function *UNIX_TIMESTAMP* here as well. You can achieve a desired format with the MySQL function *DATE_FORMAT*. With the following instruction, *data* receives a character string of the form *'December 31 2003'*:

```
SELECT ... , DATE_FORMAT(a_date, '%M %d %Y')
```

Time: In a *TIME* variable, *data* contains a character string of the form 23:59:59. If you do not wish to extract hours, minutes, and seconds from this character string, then you might use the MySQL function *TIME_TO_SEC*, which returns the number of seconds since 00:00:00. You can also use any of a number of additional MySQL functions for processing times. Caution: *UNIX_TIMESTAMP* does not work for *TIME* columns.

> **POINTER**   *You will find an overview of the functions provided by MySQL for processing dates and times in Chapter 18.*

Character Strings and BLOBs: PHP fortunately has (in contrast to C) no problems with truly binary data. That is, even 0-bytes within a character string are readily processed. Thus *data* truly contains all the data from the database in one-to-one correspondence.

> **CAUTION**   *Do not forget that in general, you cannot output character strings directly with* echo *into an HTML document. If the character string contains special characters like* <, >, ', ", *or characters outside of the 7-bit ASCII character set, you must replace these characters by the corresponding HTML code via the function* htmlentities.

NULL: When a data field contains *NULL,* then *isset($data)* returns the value *FALSE.* Similar tests could be carried out, depending on the data type, with *is_numeric, is_string,* etc. Please note, however, that tests on character strings with the function *empty* do not lead to correct results: With *NULL* as well as with an empty character string, *empty* returns the result *TRUE.*

Determining the Elements of an ENUM/SET

Working with *ENUM*s and *SET*s causes no difficulties: The values are passed in both directions as simple character strings. Note that with *ENUM*s, no additional spaces are allowed between comma-separated character strings.

Often, one wishes to display in an HTML input form all character strings of an *ENUM* or *SET* from which a selection is to be made (in a listbox, for example). To do this, you must determine with the SQL command *DESCRIBE tablename columnname* the definition of this field:

```
DESCRIBE test_enum a_enum
```

Field	Type	Null	Key	...
a_enum	enum('a','b','c','d','e')	YES		...

The column *Type* of the result table contains the required information. In the following code lines the character strings *enum('a','b','c')* and *set('a','b','c')* will be abbreviated via *ereg* to *'a','b','c'.* The function *str_replace* removes the single quotation marks, and then *explode* forms *a,b,c* into an array, which is stored in the variable *fieldvalues.* Then the *while* loop displays the values in the HTML document. You can use similar code to create an HTML form with radio buttons or a listbox using *SET* or *ENUM*:

```php
$result = mysql_query("DESCRIBE test_enum a_set");
$row = mysql_fetch_object($result);
$fieldtype = $row->Type;              // enum( ... ) or set( ... )
ereg("\\((.*)\\)", $row->Type, $tmp);   // xyz('a','b','c')
                                      // --> 'a','b','c'
$tmp = str_replace("'", "", $tmp[1]); // 'a','b','c' --> a,b,c
$fieldvalues = explode(",", $tmp);

// a, b, c display in rows
while($i = each($fieldvalues)) {
echo "<br />", htmlentities($i[1]), "\n";
}
```

> **POINTER** *The code directly above assumes that no commas appear within the* SET *and* ENUM *character strings. If there are commas, then the decomposition (pedagogically less intuitive, but syntactically more stable) can be expressed as follows:*
>
> ```php
> ereg("('(.*)')", $row->Type, $tmp);
> $fieldvalues = explode("','", $tmp[2]);
> ```

Processing Form Data (Magic Quotes)

This is not a book on PHP. However, the correct processing of form data and the storage of such data in a MySQL database leads so often to problems that it seems a good idea to discuss here some HTML and PHP basics.

Forms for Beginners

There are various ways of representing forms in HTML code. In the examples of this book, forms are generally sent with *POST*, and old tags (which almost every browser understands) are used for the representation of buttons. Then the construction of a simple form that consists of two text fields (*type="text"*) and an OK button *type="submit"*) looks like this:

```
<form method="POST" action="process.php">
  <p><input type="text" name="name1" size="30" maxlength="30" /></p>
  <p><input type="text" name="name2" size="30" maxlength="30" /></p>
  <p><input type="submit" name="submitbutton" value="OK" /></p>
</form>
```

> **POINTER** *Further information on the construction of forms is given in every HTML book.*

Evaluation of Forms

When the user clicks the OK button, the page process.php is called (*action* attribute of the *form* tag). In the PHP code you can output, since PHP 4.1, the content of both text fields with *$_POST['name1']* and *$_POST['name2']*. To avoid error messages, you should check with *if(array_key_exists('name1', $_POST))* whether the field *$_POST* has an entry with this key. This task is taken over in my examples by the function *array_item*:

```
function array_item($ar, $key) {
    if(array_key_exists($key, $ar)) return($ar[$key]); }
// copy form data in the variables
$submitbutton = array_item($_POST, 'submitbutton');
$name1 = array_item($_POST, 'name1');
$name2 = array_item($_POST, 'name2');

// display form data, process, etc.
echo "<p>name1 = ", htmlentities($name1), "</p>\n";
echo "<p>name2 = ", htmlentities($name2), "</p>\n";
```

With PHP 4.0 and earlier versions you can do without these instructions; the form data are available at once in the variables *$name1*, *$name2*, and *$submitbutton*. (This has been shown to be insecure, for which reason this has not been the default since PHP 4.2.)

Note that the representation of the form and the processing of the form data can take place from the same PHP page. Simply test at the start of the PHP code whether form data were passed. If that is the case, then begin to evaluate the data; otherwise, display the empty form. (To determine for the above form whether data were passed, simply test the content of *$submitbutton*. If the variable contains *"OK"*, then the PHP page was called for the evaluation of form data.)

```
if($submitbutton == "OK") {
  // evaluate form data
}
else {
  // display empty form
}
```

Placing Form Data in the Form

In practice, a PHP page often has a third task in addition to the representation and evaluation of forms, namely, the checking whether the input is error-free. If that is not the case, then the form together with an error message is displayed, where existing form data are replaced (so that the user does not have to input everything anew).

The code for inserting already known form data into a form usually looks like the following. (The PHP code within the HTML code appears in boldface.)

```
<form method="POST" action="magictest.php">
<p><input type="text" name="name1" size="30" maxlength="30"
    value="<?php echo $name1; ?>" /></p>
<p><input type="text" name="name2" size="30" maxlength="30"
    value="<?php echo $name2; ?>" /></p>
<p><input type="submit" name="submitbutton" value="OK" /></p>
</form>
```

By this step it is seen that working with forms becomes complicated:

- Because of *magic quotes*, it can happen that *$name1* does not contain exactly the same text as what the user originally provided. (More later on *magic quotes*.)

- You must consider what happens if the user inputs special characters in the form such as quotation marks or HTML tags.

Let us assume that in the first text field of the form the text *Hotel "Golden Coyote"* is input. Then *$name1* contains this character string. (We will not consider magic quotes just yet in order not to complicate the issue.) If you simply place the content of *$name1* in the form, then the following HTML code results, which the web browser sees:

```
<p><input type="text" name="name1" size="30" maxlength="30"
    value="hotel "Golden Coyote"" /></p>
```

It is not difficult to see where the syntax error is located. What the web browser makes of it depends on its implementation, but as a rule, in the first input field only *Hotel* is displayed, and the rest simply disappears. It should be clear that (perhaps with evil intent) HTML tags input into the text field can make the situation even more complex.

The usual solution to this problem consists in changing the content of form variables before replacing it in the form using *htmlspecialchars*. This function replaces the special characters ", &, <, and > as follows:

"   "
&   &
<   <
>   >

The code for representing the form looks like this:

```
<form method="POST" action="magictest.php">
  <p><input type="text" name="name1" size="30" maxlength="30"
      value="<?php echo htmlspecialchars($name1); ?>" /></p>
  <p><input type="text" name="name2" size="30" maxlength="30"
      value="<?<?php echo htmlspecialchars($name2); ?>" /></p>
  <p><input type="submit" name="submitbutton" value="OK" /></p>
</form>
```

Magic Quotes

The significance of *magic quotes* is that the PHP interpreter alters character strings that are read in from an external data source.

The special characters ', ", \, and the 0-byte are replaced by \', \", \\, and \0, respectively. (This operation can be carried out manually with the PHP function *addslashes*.)

In general, magic quotes have to do with data that come from outside, for example, from *GET/POST* forms, cookies, and SQL queries. In many cases this automatic alteration simplifies the further processing of character strings, but often it leads to confusion and chaos.

PHP recognizes three *magic quote* modes, which are set in `php.ini`.

- *magic_quotes_gpc*: GPC stands for get/post/cookie. That is, when a variable is set, data from these three sources are changed. Note that this affects all data in a form that are processed in PHP scripts.

- *magic_quotes_run-time*: When this variable is set, PHP in most cases quotes those character strings that come from external data sources (for example, from MySQL).

- *magic_quotes_sybase*: The character ' is quoted by doubling it (that is, by '' instead of by \'). However, this holds only when one of the other two *magic_quote* configuration variables is set.

Magic Quote Default Setting

In the default setting of PHP 4.0 to 4.3, *magic_quotes_gpc* is set to *On*, while the two other modes are *Off*. You will find this setting at most ISPs. It has the following consequences for programming:

- Data transmitted from forms can be used in *INSERT* commands without alteration. The critical characters ', ", and \ are already quoted:

  ```
  $sql = "INSERT ... VALUES('$formVar')";
  ```

- If you compare data in a form with data from an SQL query, you must first free the form data from backslash characters with the PHP function *stripslashes( )*:

  ```
  if(stripslashes($formVar) == $sql_result_row[0]) ...
  ```

  On the other hand, if you make the comparison not in PHP, but with MySQL (as part of a *WHERE* conditional), then no extra measures are required:

  ```
  $sql = "SELECT ... WHERE authorsName = '$formVar'";
  ```

- If you wish to display the form data in an HTML document (or in a new form, say to allow corrections to be made), then you must first delete the quotation marks with *stripslashes* and then quote anew (and differently!) all HTML-specific special characters with *htmlentities*:

  ```
  echo htmlentities(stripslashes($formVariable));
  ```

> **WARNING** *In* php.ini.recommended *(see Chapter 2), all three modes are switched to* Off *for reasons of speed optimization.*
>
> *Before you begin developing your own code, you should certainly determine* which *magic quote settings hold on your ISP's server.*

Determining and Changing Magic Quote Modes in a PHP Script

To some extent, you can determine or change the three configuration variables in the code of your PHP script:

- ***magic_quotes_gpc:*** *get_magic_quotes_gpc( )* determines the current status. A change cannot be made.

- ***magic_quotes_run-time***: *get_magic_quotes_runtime( )* determines the current status; *set_magic_quotes_runtime( )* changes it.

- ***magic_quotes_sybase:*** The status can be neither determined nor altered.

Removing Magic Quotes

Without doubt, magic quotes were created with the intention of simplifying the lives of programmers. In practice, alas, the opposite is often the case. When you develop code in which a large amount of data is read from forms and is later replaced in the same or another form, the automatic quoting of special characters often causes more problems than it solves.

If you are working with PHP 4.1 or higher, you can turn off the quoting by calling the following function:

```
function no_magic() {  // PHP >= 4.1
  if (get_magic_quotes_gpc()) {
    foreach($_GET as $k=>$v)      $_GET["$k"] = stripslashes($v);
    foreach($_POST as $k=>$v)     $_POST["$k"] = stripslashes($v);
    foreach($_COOKIE as $k=>$v) $_COOKIE["$k"] = stripslashes($v);
  }
}
```

Through and including PHP 4.0 you can instead use the following code (the code cannot, however, be placed in a function, since the fields *$HTTP_xxx_VARS* are not superglobal):

```
if (get_magic_quotes_gpc()) {  // PHP < 4.1
  foreach($HTTP_GET_VARS as $k=>$v)
    $HTTP_GET_VARS[$k] = stripslashes($v);
  foreach($HTTP_POST_VARS as $k=>$v)
    $HTTP_POST_VARS[$k] = stripslashes($v);
  foreach($HTTP_COOKIE_VARS as $k=>$v)
    $HTTP_COOKIE_VARS[$k] = stripslashes($v);
}
```

Then, you must read out the form variables with *$HTTP_POST_VARS['name']*.

Experimenting with Forms and Magic Quotes

If you do not yet have much experience with forms or magic quotes, I would heartily recommend to you to experiment a bit with them. The following PHP script testmagic.php consists of a simple form allowing for input into two text fields (*name1* and *name2*). If you click on OK, then the form data are passed to the same file, displayed with and without magic quotes, and then replaced in the form fields, so that they can be further edited.

Now try to input special characters like *ä, é, ü, ô, \, ', <, >,* or entire HTML tags. There should be no problems; that is, the special characters are displayed correctly. Now see what happens if you do without the functions *no_magic* and/or *htmlentities* (see Figure 11-3). Look at the HTML source code. (Most web browsers offer this possibility, Mozilla, for example, with Ctrl+U.)

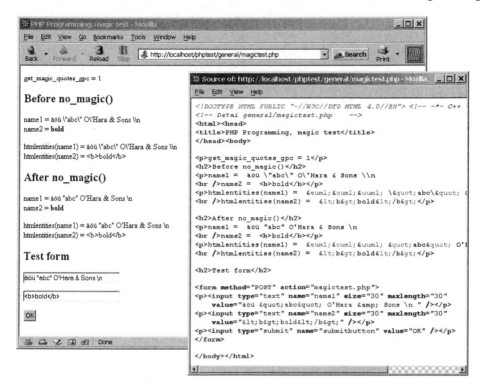

Figure 11-3. Testing magic quotes

```php
<!-- file general/magictest.php    -->
<html><head>
  <meta http-equiv="Content-Type"
        content="text/html; charset=iso-8859-1" />
  <title>PHP Programming, magic test</title>
</head><body>

<?php {

  function array_item($ar, $key) {
    if(array_key_exists($key, $ar))
      return($ar[$key]); }

  function no_magic() {  // needs PHP >= 4.1
    if (get_magic_quotes_gpc()) {
      foreach($_GET as $k=>$v)    $_GET["$k"] = stripslashes($v);
      foreach($_POST as $k=>$v)   $_POST["$k"] = stripslashes($v);
      foreach($_COOKIE as $k=>$v) $_COOKIE["$k"] = stripslashes($v);
    }
  }

  // magic_quotes_gpc show statius
  echo "<p>get_magic_quotes_gpc = ", get_magic_quotes_gpc(), "</p>\n";
```

```
    // copy form input into variables
    $submitbutton = array_item($_POST, 'submitbutton');
    $name1 = array_item($_POST, 'name1');
    $name2 = array_item($_POST, 'name2');

    // Is there any form input at all?
    if($submitbutton == "OK") {
      // disply input with magic quotes
      echo "<h2>Before no_magic()</h2>\n";
      echo "<p>name1 =  ", $name1, "\n";
      echo "<br />name2 =  ", $name2, "</p>\n";
      echo "<p>htmlentities(name1) =  ", htmlentities($name1), "\n";
      echo "<br />htmlentities(name2) =  ", htmlentities($name2),
         "</p>\n\n";

      // display input without magic quotes
      no_magic();
      echo "<h2>After no_magic()</h2>\n";
      $name1 = array_item($_POST, 'name1');
      $name2 = array_item($_POST, 'name2');
      echo "<p>name1 =  ", $name1, "\n";
      echo "<br />name2 =  ", $name2, "</p>\n";
      echo "<p>htmlentities(name1) =  ", htmlentities($name1), "\n";
      echo "<br />htmlentities(name2) =  ", htmlentities($name2), "</p>\n";
    }
} ?>

<h2>Test form</h2>

<form method="POST" action="magictest.php">
<p><input type="text" name="name1" size="30" maxlength="30"
    value="<?php echo htmlspecialchars($name1); ?>" /></p>
<p><input type="text" name="name2" size="30" maxlength="30"
    value="<?php echo htmlspecialchars($name2); ?>" /></p>
<p><input type="submit" name="submitbutton" value="OK" /></p>
</form>
</body></html>
```

Summary

In processing form data, you should take the following into consideration:

- Before further processing of form data, turn off, if necessary, magic quotes. The additional backspace characters will otherwise interfere with further processing.

- When you replace form input back into a form, use the function *htmlspecialchars*. You thereby avoid the invalid HTML code caused by the characters ", &, <, >.

- If you wish to represent form data in an HTML document (not within the input field of the form), then use the function *htmlentities*. With this, you achieve that all special characters (not only ", &, <, *and* <) are represented by the correct HTML code.

- If you wish to store form data in a MySQL database, then use the function *addslashes* (or *mysql_escape_string* or *mysql_real_escape_string*). You thereby prevent any input single quotes, double quotes, or backspaces from causing syntax errors in the SQL character strings.

Error Checking

All *mysql_xxx* functions return *FALSE* if an error occurs during execution. You obtain information as to the type of error by evaluating the functions *mysql_errno* (returns the error number) and *mysql_error* (error message):

```
$result=mysql_query($sql);
if(!$result) {
  echo "<P>error: ", mysql_errno(),
  ": " . htmlentities(mysql_error()), ".</p>\n";
}
```

One always must reckon with the reality of errors, and in particular in the execution of SQL commands that alter data. One possible source of error is in the connection to the MySQL server.

In the development of PHP scripts the function *mysql_query_test* is often very useful in searching for the cause of the error. It is meant as a replacement for *mysql_query*, displaying every executed SQL command in blue. If an error occurs, then an error message will be displayed as well:

```
// example file general/mylibraryconnect.inc.php
function mysql_query_test($sql) {
  echo '<p><font color="#0000ff"> SQL:', htmlentities($sql),
    "</font></p>\n";
  $result = mysql_query($sql);
  if($result) return($result);
  echo '<p><font color="#ff0000">Error: ',
    htmlentities(mysql_error()),
      "</font></p>\n";
  die();
}
```

> **POINTER** *A list of all error messages can be found in the files* errmsg.h *and* mysqld_error.h. *Both files are part of the source-code package for MySQL.*

Error Search

I am constantly receiving e-mail, and there appear contributions in discussion lists, about my book (see http://www.kofler.cc) with the question, What is one to do when an example from the book does not function properly? The error message (if indeed there is one) often gives no clear idea as to the cause of the problem, instead giving a cryptic message like *Supplied argument is not a valid MySQL result resource*. This means that you are attempting to evaluate a query result (in the examples of this book generally in the variable *$result*) that contains no data due to the error that has occurred.

The cause of the problem is almost always access to the database: The PHP script is unable or is forbidden to read the data from the database and therefore returns an incorrect result or no result at all. There are many reasons why this can happen, but it almost always has to do with access privileges: incorrect password, no password (although one was required). This topic is dealt with extensively in Chapter 9. Only when MySQL is completely unsecured does the combination *name = "root"* and *password = ""* work with accesses by the local computer.

The best remedy for determining the cause of the error is the function *mysql_query_test* introduced above. Simply replace all *mysql_query* functions with *mysql_query_test( )* and test the page again. Then you will at least know *what* is not working.

Storing and Displaying Images

A frequently posed question in PHP and MySQL newsgroups and discussion forums is this: How can I give visitors to my web site a way to upload their own images and then display them? This section answers this question with an example project (see Figure 11-4) that demonstrates the required programming techniques.

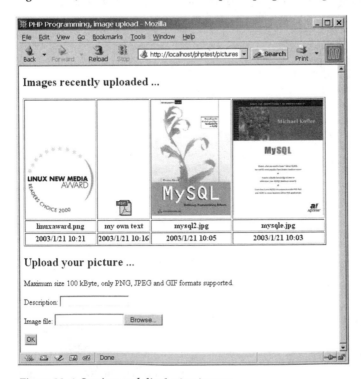

Figure 11-4. Storing and displaying images

Fundamentals and Programming Techniques

Database Design

The starting point for our example is the database *test_images* with the table *images*. This database and the table can be created with the following commands:

```
CREATE DATABASE test_images
USE test_images
CREATE TABLE images (
  id    BIGINT NOT NULL AUTO_INCREMENT,
  name  VARCHAR(100) NOT NULL,
  type  VARCHAR(100) NOT NULL,
  image MEDIUMBLOB NOT NULL,
  ts    TIMESTAMP(14) NOT NULL,
  PRIMARY KEY (id))
```

The *images* table contains, in addition to the usual primary index *id*, the column *name* to describe the image, *type* to store the image format (e.g., *"JPEG IMAGE"*), *image* to store the image data (where images have maximum size 16 megabytes), and *ts* to log the time of saving.

> **WARNING**   *From the standpoint of efficiency, it is not a good idea to store images or other large binary files in a database. For that, a traditional file system is more suitable. Databases with many BLOBs suffer in the area of speed above all because it is difficult for the database system to store frequently needed data and indexes in RAM. It would therefore make more sense to store images as ordinary files and enter only the file name in the database.*
>
> *In practice, however, the storage of binary data in BLOBs occurs frequently, and for two reasons: First, it is easier to deal with data (e.g., backup, server migration) if all data are stored in a central location, and second, many ISPs will not allow you to create and then read out local files in PHP scripts or other code.*

HTML Form for File Transfer

If you wish to offer the possibility on an HTML page for file transfer to the web server, then you will require a form with a particular structure. It is crucial that the attributes *method* and *enctype* be correctly set. The input field for the file name (to which the browser automatically adds the button BROWSE) is formed with an *<input>* tag with the attribute *type = "file"*. If you wish to place a limit on the file size, you can do that with a hidden field with the attribute *name = "MAX_FILE_SIZE"*. The following lines show the code for the upload form in Figure 11-4, where the file size is limited to 100 kilobytes:

```
<form method="post" action="pictures.php"
     enctype="multipart/form-data">
  <p>Description: <input name="descr" type="text" /></p>
  <p>Image file:  <input name="imgfile" type="file" /></p>
  <p><input type="submit" value="OK" name="submitbtn" /></p>
  <input type="hidden" value="102400" name="MAX_FILE_SIZE" />
</form>
```

PHP Evaluation of the $_FILES Field

The PHP script that is called with the form data contains the usual form fields as usual in the *$_POST* field (that is, *$_POST['descr']*) with a description of the image as well as *$_POST['submitbtn']* with the character string *"OK"*. The information on the transferred file is found in the *$_FILES* field. Access follows according to the above example form via the key *'imgfile'* (see the *name* attribute for *<input type="file">*) and again returns a field. Its elements give information about the transferred file:

```
$imgfile = $_FILES['imgfile'];
$name    = $imgfile['name'];     // file name (without drive/path)
$type    = $imgfile['type'];     // file type, e.g., "image/gif"
$size    = $imgfile['size'];     // file size in bytes
$uperr   = $imgfile['error'];    // error number (0 = no error)
$tmpfile = $imgfile['tmp_name']; // name of the local temporary file
```

> **REMARK** $imgfile['error'] *has been available only since PHP 4.2, and* $_FILES *only since PHP 4.1. With older versions of PHP (4.0 and earlier), you can read the information directly from the variables* $imgfile *(local file name, corresponds to* $tmpfile*),* $imgfile_name, $imgfile_type, *and* $imgfile_size.

The transferred file is stored temporarily by the web server in a temporary file (file name *$tmpfile*). This file can be read by the PHP script, for example, with the functions *fopen* and *fread*. Note that the file is automatically deleted after the execution of the PHP script.

From the point of view of security, file transfer is a dangerous operation. Therefore, it is recommended to secure the code for further processing of the file. The following query tests whether *$tmpfile* is empty, whether a transfer error has occurred, or whether the given file is not a transferred file (*is_uploaded_file*) but a local file. This security is important, so that an attacker cannot attempt to evaluate a local system file (e.g., the Unix/Linux password file /ect/passwd). Such cases are known to have occurred:

```
if(!$tmpfile or $uperr or !is_uploaded_file($tmpfile))
  echo "<p>error ... </p>\n";
else {
  ... // read and process the temporary file
}
```

Optionally, you can also evaluate the file type and size in the security query.

Storing a Transferred File in the MySQL Database

To store the transferred file in the MySQL database, read the entire file into a variable and execute an *INSERT* command. In the simplest case, the code looks like this:

```
$file = fopen($tmpfile, "rb");  // file open (read-only, binary)
$imgdata = fread($file, $size); // read file
fclose($file);
mysql_query("INSERT INTO images (image) " .
            "VALUES ('" . addslashes($imgdata) . "')");
```

In the code of our example program, the *INSERT* command is somewhat more complex, since in addition to the MIME type of the image (e.g., *"GIF image"*), its name or a description will be stored.

Displaying Images from the MySQL Database

It is somewhat more complicated to read an image out of the MySQL database and display it within an HTML document. It is fundamentally impossible within a single PHP script to create an HTML document (which is the usual task of a PHP script) and at the same time to generate the data for the representation of an image. The two tasks must be divided between two PHP scripts.

The first (usual) script creates the HTML page, including the *<img>* tag for the image. In this tag, however, instead of the usual name of a local image file, the name of the second PHP script is specified together with the ID number of the image:

```
// PHP-Script pictures.php
echo "<img src=\"showpic.php?id=$id\" />";
```

The browser sees, for example, the tag *<img src="showpic.php?id=3" />*, and now calls the second script showpic.php?id=3. Its code, somewhat simplified, looks like this:

```
// PHP-Script showpic.php
$result = @mysql_query(
  "SELECT image FROM images WHERE id = $id");
$row = @mysql_fetch_object($result);
header("GIF image");  // file type
echo $row->image;
```

In fact, a bit more code is required to create the database connection, to determine *$id*, and secure the script against possible errors. If the image database contains not only GIF images, but also bitmaps in other formats, then the file type set with *header* must also be retrieved from the database. At this place it is crucial that the second PHP script not generate an HTML file and in general, not perform any tasks with *echo* before the *header* function is called. This function instructs the PHP interpreter to create not, as usual, an HTML file, but an image file.

Processing Large Files

If you wish to allow the transfer of very large files, you must note a few things:

- The limit for the maximal size of files to be transferred must be set sufficiently high. The limit is set in php.ini with the variable *upload_max_file_size* (default value 2 megabytes).

- The limit for the *POST* transfer must also be high enough (php.ini, variable *post_max_size*, default value 8 megabytes).

- The PHP interpreter must be capable of reserving enough memory to process files of the maximal size that has been set (php.ini, variable *memory_limit*, default value 8 megabytes).

- The PHP interpreter must give the script sufficient time for processing the data (php.ini, variable *max_execution_time*). The default value of 30 seconds is generally too small for large files.

  You may also need to increase the variable *max_input_time* (default value 60 seconds). This variable specifies how long a wait will be permitted for transfer of data over the Internet.

- For the transfer of the image between the PHP script and the MySQL server to succeed, the maximal packet size (which, for example, the *INSERT* command limits) must be sufficiently large. The MySQL variable *max_allowed_packet* can be changed either in my.cnf or with the SQL command *SET max_allowed_packet=n*. The default value is only one megabyte.

Program Code

The entire code of the example project is contained in three files, which are located with the PHP example files in the directory pictures:

connect.inc.php	Makes available the functions *connect_to_picdb* and *array_item*.
pictures.php	Displays a table with the most recent ten images and a form for the transfer of additional images. The script contains as well the code for form evaluation.
showpic.php	Displays a single image.

The File connect.inc.php

This file contains two functions: *connect_to_picdb* creates a connection to the MySQL database *test_pictures*, while *array_item* reads an element from a PHP field (if such exists):

```php
<?php    //  -*- C++ -*-
// file pictures/connect.inc.php
function connect_to_picdb() {
  $mysqluser="root";       // username
  $mysqlpasswd="xxx";      // password
  $mysqlhost="localhost"; // name of computer MySQL is running
  $connID = @mysql_connect($mysqlhost, $mysqluser, $mysqlpasswd);
  if ($connID) {
    mysql_select_db("test_images");  // default database
    return $connID;
  }
  else {
    echo " ... error ... ";
    exit();
  }
}
function array_item($ar, $key) {
  if(array_key_exists($key, $ar))
    return($ar[$key]); }
?>
```

The File pictures.php

The code in pictures.php consists of three parts. The first part is responsible for the processing of form data. If a file is transferred without error, then its content is stored in the table *images*.

The *switch* construction evaluates the type of transferred file and from this makes a new MIME character string. (MIME stands for *Multipurpose Internet Mail Extensions*. Originally, MIME was used only for e-mail attachments, but in the meanwhile, MIME has come to control how a web browser should deal with various file types.) The MIME type must be specified when an image is displayed and is therefore stored together with each image in the *images* table. Unfortunately, the *type* information does not correspond to MIME, but rather uses different character strings (which on top of everything, depend on the web browser):

```php
<!DOCTYPE HTML PUBLIC "-//W3C//DTD HTML 4.0//EN">

<?php {  // file pictures/pictures.php
  include("connect.inc.php");
  $connID = connect_to_picdb();
} ?>

<html><head>
<meta http-equiv="Content-Type"
      content="text/html; charset=iso-8859-1" />
<title>PHP Programming, image upload</title>
</head><body>
```

```php
<?php {
  // part 1: form evaluation, store image in MySQL database
  $submitbtn = array_item($_POST, 'submitbtn');
  $descr =    array_item($_POST, 'descr');
  $imgfile =  array_item($_FILES, 'imgfile');
  // is there form data to process?
  if($submitbtn == 'OK' and is_array($imgfile)) {
    $name    = $imgfile['name'];
    $type    = $imgfile['type'];
    $size    = $imgfile['size'];
    $uperr   = array_item($imgfile, 'error'); // PHP >= 4.2.0
    $tmpfile = $imgfile['tmp_name'];
    if(!$descr) $descr = $name;

    switch ($type) {
    case "image/gif":
      $mime = "GIF Image";  break;
    case "image/jpeg":
    case "image/pjpeg":
      $mime = "JPEG Image"; break;
    case "image/png":
    case "image/x-png":
      $mime = "PNG Image";  break;
    default:
      $mime = "unknown";
    }

    // security test
    if(!$tmpfile or $uperr or $mime == "unknown" or
      !is_uploaded_file($tmpfile))
      echo "<p>An error occured when processing the form data:
              Perhaps you forgot to specify an
              image file or the file is too large
              or the image type is unknown.</p>\n";
    else {
      // read the transferred file and store it in the database
      $file = fopen($tmpfile, "rb");
      $imgdata = fread($file, $size);
      fclose($file);
      mysql_query(
        "INSERT INTO images (name, type, image) " .
        "VALUES ('" . addslashes($descr) . "', " .
        "        '$mime', " .
        "        '" . addslashes($imgdata) . "')");

    }
  }
}
```

The second code segment in pictures.php serves to read the last ten images from the database and display them in a table. As we have already described, the actual display of the images is delegated to the script showpic.php:

```
// part 2: display the last ten images as a table
echo "<h2>Images recently uploaded ... </h2>\n";
$result = mysql_query(
  "SELECT id, name, " .
  "DATE_FORMAT(ts, '%Y/%c/%e %k:%i') " .
  "FROM images ORDER BY ts DESC LIMIT 10");
$rows = mysql_num_rows($result);
$cols = mysql_num_fields($result);
if($rows==0)
  echo "<p>No images in database ... </p>\n";
else {
  echo "<table border=1>\n<tr>";
  for($i=0; $i < $rows; $i++)  // images
    echo "<th valign=\"bottom\"><img src=\"showpic.php?id=" .
      mysql_result($result, $i, 0) . "\" /></th>";
  echo "</tr>\n<tr>";
  for($i=0; $i < $rows; $i++)  // imagename/description
    echo "<th>" . htmlentities(mysql_result($result, $i, 1)) .
        "</th>";
  echo "</tr>\n<tr>";
  for($i=0; $i < $rows; $i++)  // date and time
    echo "<th>" . mysql_result($result, $i, 2) . "</th>";
  echo "</tr>\n</table>\n";
  }
} ?>
```

If the images are to be displayed underneath one another instead of side by side, then the code for generating the table can be simplified a bit:

```
echo "<table border=1>\n";
while($row = mysql_fetch_object($result)) {
  echo "<tr>";
  echo "<th>" . htmlentities($row->name) . "</th>";
  echo "<th>$row->ts</th>";
  echo "<th><img src=\"showpic.php?id=$row->id\" /></th>";
  echo "</tr>\n";
  }
echo "</table>\n";
```

The third part of pictures.php contains the HTML code for the form for transferring additional pictures:

```
<h2>Upload your picture ... </h2>

<p>Maximum size 100 kByte, only PNG, JPEG and GIF formats supported.</p>

<form method="post" action="pictures.php" enctype="multipart/form-data">
  <input type="hidden" value="10240000" name="MAX_FILE_SIZE" />
  <p>Description: <input name="descr" type="text" /></p>
  <p>Image file:  <input name="imgfile" type="file" /></p>
  <p><input type="submit" value="OK" name="submitbtn" /></p>
</form>
</body></html>
```

The Script showpic.php

The script showpic.php displays a single image, whose ID number is passed as parameter in the address. The code has already been described, and is here simply extended with a few security queries:

```php
<?php {  // file pictures/showpic.php?id=n
  include("connect.inc.php");

  // evaluate id parameter; exit, if no id
  $id = array_item($_GET, 'id');
  if(!$id) exit;

  // load image from the database
  $connID = connect_to_picdb();
  $result = @mysql_query(
    "SELECT image, type FROM images WHERE id = $id");
  if(!$result) exit;

  // display the image
  $row = @mysql_fetch_object($result);
  if(!$row) exit;
  header($row->type);
  echo $row->image;
} ?>
```

> **TIP** *If an error occurs in* showpic.php, *it is difficult to locate, since* showpic.php *is not normally displayed as an independent HTML document (and therefore, no error messages are displayed). However, for error searching you can try out* showpic.php *independently of* pictures.php *by specifying in your web browser the address* http://servername/pictures/showpic.php?id=123, *for example.*

#### CHAPTER 12

PHP: Library Management

THIS CHAPTER DESCRIBES A RELATIVELY large PHP example program that allows for querying the *mylibrary* database and adding new titles to it. After the relatively brief examples of the previous chapter, which demonstrated the most important programming techniques, the *mylibrary* project shows the complexity of managing PHP projects in practice.

Chapter Overview

Introduction

The example of this section is based on the database *mylibrary*, which was introduced in Chapter 5. It shows how a few PHP pages can be used to input book information into a database and then to search the database. Our example consists of the following files:

mylibrarypassword.inc.php	MySQL logging information (*$mysqluser, -password, -host, -dbname*)
mylibraryconnect.inc.php	various auxiliary functions (including database login)
find.php	search for authors/titles
simpleinput.php	input of new book titles
input.php	convienient input of new book titles
categories.php	management of the hierarchical category list

   The script files are independent of one another. Within each script the transmittal of session information is carried out as necessary via URL variables (that is, *name.php?variable=xxx*) or by formula fields (URL stands for *Uniform Resource Locator* and denotes addresses like http://www.company.com/page.html).

> **REMARK**   *The examples of this chapter assume at least PHP 4.1. Versions that will run under PHP 4.0 can be found at my web site* http://www.kofler.cc *in the PHP example files for the first edition of this book.*

Auxiliary Functions (*mylibraryconnect.inc.php*)

The file mylibraryconnect.inc.php contains several auxiliary functions that in part have already been introduced in the previous chapter. The following list gives a brief description:

- *connect_to_mylibrary( )* creates the connection to MySQL. If the connection cannot be made, an error message is displayed. Before the function is called, no HTML code is to be generated, since the error message represents a complete HTML page (including the HTML header).

- The function *array_item($ar, $key)* returns the element *$ar[$key]*, assuming that the field *$ar* contains an element with the key *$key*.

- *build_href($url, $query, $name)* creates an HTML link of the form *<a href="$url?$query">htmlentities($name)</a>*.

- *mysql_query_test($sql)* displays an SQL command, executes it, and displays an error message if necessary. This function returns the query result, and thus can be implemented like *mysql_query*, and moreover, it greatly simplifies debugging.

The following lines show the most important parts of mylibraryconnect.inc.php:

```
<?php    // mylibrary/mylibraryconnect.inc.php
// creates the connection to the database
function connect_to_mylibrary() {

  // definiert $mysqluser, -password, -host and -dbname
  include("mylibrarypassword.inc.php");

  $connID = @mysql_connect($mysqlhost, $mysqluser, $mysqlpasswd);
  if ($connID) {
    mysql_select_db($mysqldbname);  // default database
    return $connID; }
  else {
    echo " ... error message ... ";
    exit(); }
}

// reads an element from a PHP field
function array_item($ar, $key) {
  if(array_key_exists($key, $ar))
    return($ar[$key]); }

// returns <a href=$url?$query>$name</a>
function build_href($url, $query, $name) {
  if($query)
    return "<a href=\"$url?" . $query . "\">" .
           htmlentities($name) . "</a>";
  else
    return "<a href=\"$url\">" . htmlentities($name) . "</a>";
}
?>
```

Securing the mylibrary Project

The script mylibraryconnect.inc.php loads via *include* the file
mylibrarypassword.inc.php, whose few lines of code define the four variables
$mysqluser, -password, -host, -dbname:

```
<?php    // file mylibrary/mylibrarypassword.inc.php
  $mysqluser   = "root";      // MySQL user name
  $mysqlpasswd = "xxx";       // passwork
  $mysqlhost   = "localhost"; // computer name for the MySQL server
  $mysqldbname = "mylibrary"; // database name
?>
```

When you install the *mylibrary* project, you must first adapt the login and
password information to your MySQL installation. If you wish to provide better
security for the project, it is recommended to move mylibrarypassword.inc.php into
another directory, one that is secured with .htaccess and whose files are therefore
not accessible over the Internet. Of course, you must then correspondingly alter the
include instruction in mylibraryconnect.inc.php.

Book Search (*find.php*)

The file find.php helps in locating authors and books in the *mylibrary* database. To do this, the initial letters of the title or of the author are entered into the search form (see Figure 12-1).

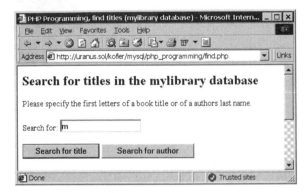

Figure 12-1. The search form

In the search results (see Figures 12-2 and 12-3), authors and publishers are executed as links, so that it is quite simple to find all the books of a given author or all books put out by a particular publisher.

If search results do not fit on a page, then one can leaf page by page through the results. (The number of titles per page is set in the program by the variable *$pagesize* to 5. This value can easily be increased.)

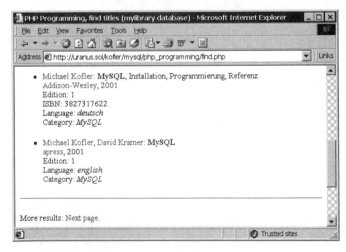

Figure 12-2. Results of a search for book titles beginning with the letter M

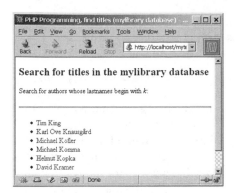

Figure 12-3. Results of a search for authors whose last name begins with K

Problems of Efficiency in the Representation of Search Results

The file find.php divides long lists of book titles into several pages. To this end, *SELECT* is called with *LIMIT pagesize * (pagenr-1), pagesize*. Unfortunately, there are two factors that make the paged representation of *SELECT* results inefficient:

- Generally, on each page of the results, you would like to report the number of additional pages. But to do this you need to know how many records the query returns. This can be easily determined via *SELECT COUNT(. . .)*, but if your query is complex, then the twofold execution—once with *SELECT COUNT* for the number and then with *SELECT LIMIT* for the results of the current page—is very inefficient.

  There is, alas, no optimal solution to this problem. One approach would be always to search for *pagesize+1* results. If *pagesize+1* results are actually found, it is then clear that there are more results (at least one, perhaps more). The program then displays *pagesize* results together with a MORE button, which indicates that there are additional results, but without telling how many. This is efficient, but not very elegant (find.php follows this strategy).

  Another possibility is to execute *SELECT* for the first page without *COUNT* and without *LIMIT* (or at least with a relatively high *LIMIT* value). The advantage is that with a single query you determine both the number of all data records (via *mysql_num_rows*) and the desired result records. The disadvantage is that if the query returns a large number of results, then all the records are transmitted from MySQL to PHP, even though relatively few records are actually to be displayed. This is probably even less efficient than two *SELECT* queries.

  Since MySQL 4.0 there has been a better variant: Execute the first *SELECT* command with *LIMIT* and the option *SQL_CALC_FOUND_ROW*. You obtain now, to be sure, only n records, but you can determine with the command *SELECT FOUND_ROWS( )* how many records there are altogether.

417

If you decide to determine the number of result records (by whatever means), then you should do this only for the first result page. For all further pages you should store this information in a session or transmit it as part of the link.

- The second problem is that for each page, the entire *SELECT* query with somewhat altered *LIMIT* parameters must be executed anew. Of course, the *LIMIT* clause prevents all the result records from being transmitted each time from MySQL to PHP, but depending on the query type, the cost is the same at least for MySQL. (This holds especially for queries that join information from several tables with *JOIN*, that sort or group the results, or that contain complex *WHERE* conditionals that cannot be resolved directly with the help of an index.)

Again, there is no perfect solution. Many programming languages offer the possibility of temporarily storing intermediate results, but not PHP. (Theoretically, you can store the query results in a new table, but then how and when will this table be deleted? Perhaps the user will be satisfied with the first search results anyhow, and then it would be excessively costly to construct a new table.)

The only generally valid recommendation is this: Display as many results per page as possible and thus avoid the user having to do too much paging. (If your main goal is to achieve the maximum number of page accesses, then of course, this is not the optimal recipe. In find.php the number of titles per page is limited for a different reason to five: The example database contains relatively few titles, and with *pagesize=25* you would scarcely have the chance to formulate a query that would yield that many results.)

Program Structure

The starting point for the program is the search form displayed in Figure 12-1. To evaluate the form's input we again call find.php. The search results and the page references again refer to find.php. In this case information such as the search item and the current page number are passed as part of the link (find.php?sqlType=author& ...).

In find.php, therefore, we must first analyze how the script was called: If no data are transferred, then find.php simply displays the empty form. But if there are predefined variables, then the program forms a corresponding SQL query and then displays the result of the search.

Code Outline

The following lines give an overview of the code in find.php, which should help in understanding the following extensive description:

```
<!-- php/mylibrary/find.php -->
<?php

// insert auxiliary functions
include("mylibraryconnect.inc.php");
```

```php
// read form and URL variables
// (necessary only with PHP >= 4.1)
$sqlType          = array_item($_REQUEST, 'sqlType');
$authID           = array_item($_REQUEST, 'authID');
$publID           = array_item($_REQUEST, 'publID');
$search           = array_item($_REQUEST, 'search');
$page             = array_item($_REQUEST, 'page');
$formSearch       = array_item($_POST,    'formSearch');
$formSubmitTitle  = array_item($_POST,    'formSubmitTitle');
$formSubmitAuthor = array_item($_POST,    'formSubmitAuthor');

// cancel URL encoding
$search = urldecode($search);

// slashes (eliminate magic quotes)
if(get_magic_quotes_gpc()) {
  $search = stripslashes($search);
  $formSearch = stripslashes($formSearch); }

// define additional auxiliary functions (see description
// in the next section)
function last_name_last($x) { ... }

// establish link to the database
$connID = connect_to_mylibrary();
?>

<!-- start of the HTML document -->
<!DOCTYPE HTML PUBLIC "-//W3C//DTD HTML 4.0//EN">
<html><head>
<html><head>
  <meta http-equiv="Content-Type"
        content="text/html; charset=iso-8859-1" />
<title>PHP Programming, find titles (mylibrary database)</title>
</head><body>
<h2>Search for titles in the mylibrary database</h2>

<?php
  // Main-Code
  //initialize $pagesize, validate $page
  // if called without parameters:
  //   display form
  // initialize $sql, $sqlcreate, $sqllimit
  // if there are form variables:
  //   form SQL query corresponding to form input (--> $sql)
  // if there are URL variables:
  //   form SQL query corresponding to the URL variables(--> $sql)
  // if the variable $sql is not empty
  //   execute SQL query
  //   display results
  //   if $page>1 or if there are additional results
  //     display links to other pages with search results
?>

</body></html>
```

> **POINTER** *The function* last_name_last *moves the first word in a character string to the end of the string. This turns the database-specific* "Kennedy John F." *into the more readable* "John F. Kennedy". *The code for this function and for the inverse function* last_name_first *appears in the next section.*

Form Variables

- *formSearch* contains the search character string (that is, the initial letters of the author or title sought).

- *formSubmitTitle* contains *"Search for title"* if the user clicks on the button for title search.

- *formSubmitAuthor* contains *"Search for author"* if the user clicks on the button for author search.

URL Variables

- *sqlType* contains *"title"* if the HTTP address contains further variables for the display of search results for a title search.

- *authID* contains the *ID* number of an author if a title by this author is to be displayed.

- *publID* contains the *ID* Number of a publisher if a title put out by that publisher is to be displayed.

- *search* contains the search character string if the title with these initial letters is to be displayed. Note that the search string in *search* is encoded with *urlencode* and must be decoded with *urldecode*. Moreover, the string can contain backslashes (magic quotes), which must be removed.

- *page* contains the page to be displayed. (The program code ensures that values less than zero and larger than 100 cannot be passed.)

Displaying the Form

If *sqlType* is empty (that is, if data were not passed via the HTTP address) and if either no form data or impermissible form data are at hand (that is, an empty search string), then the form is displayed:

```
if(empty($sqlType) and empty($formSearch)) {
?>
<form method="post" action="find.php">
<p>Please specify the first letters of a book title or
   of an authors last name.</p>
```

```
<p>Search for:
<input name="formSearch" size="20" maxlength="20" /></p>
<p>
<input type="submit" value="Search for title"
      name="formSubmitTitle" />
<input type="submit" value="Search for author"
      name="formSubmitAuthor" /></p>
</form>
<?php
  } // end of if ( ... )
```

Forming the SQL Command for Title or Author Search

In the following, our task is to formulate an SQL command for a search for a book title or author. Regardless of the database to which this query will be referred, several variables must be initialized.

The variable *pagesize* specifies how many titles can be displayed per page. If the variable *page* contains a value, this value specifies which page will be the next to be displayed. This variable is imported via the HTTP address and contains within it the risk of misuse. (Even if an evil-minded user specifies input.php?page=10000000000 as HTTP address, the program should react in a reasonable manner and not display links to the previous 9999999999 pages.) The permissible range for *page* will therefore be limited to the range 1–100.

```
// number of titles per page
$pagesize = 5;

// validate page variable
if($page>100)
  $page=100;
elseif($page<1)
  $page=1;
elseif(!is_numeric($page))
  unset($page);
```

The *SELECT* command for the title or author search is formed in the variable *sql*. If a title is the search object, then a title search takes place in five steps:

- The database *tmpTitleIDs* is deleted if it already exists (for example, because the script was broken off during its previous execution due to an error and was not executed to the end).

- With a *SELECT* query, the *titleID* numbers of the sought titles (only for the page to be displayed) are returned. These results are stored in the temporary table *tmpTitleIDs*.

- In a second query, the detailed information (that is, book title, subtitle, category, etc.) for each *titleID* number is determined from the tables *titles*, *categories*, *languages*, etc.

- In a third query, the tables *titles, rel_title,* and *authors* are consulted to determine the authors for each title.

- After the evaluation of all these data, the temporary table *tmpTitleIDs* is deleted.

At first, a title query proceeds only to the second step. In *sql,* therefore, only the command for the generation of the *tmpTitleIDs* table is temporarily stored. The beginning and end of this command are the same: It is the part of the command for the generation of the temporary table (*CREATE TEMPORARY . . .*) and the part for limiting the search results to one page (*LIMIT . . .*). To avoid redundant code, these parts of the SQL command are placed in advance in the variables *sqlcreate* and *sqllimit*:

> **POINTER** *The reason for working here with a temporary table and thereby determining title and author details separately is discussed in Chapter 5.*
>
> *The temporary table is very small: It contains at most* pagesize *ID numbers. To optimize speed, the table type* HEAP *is chosen. This ensures that the table is generated exclusively in the MySQL server's RAM, not on the hard disk.*

```
// predefine variables
$sql = "";
$sqlcreate = "CREATE TEMPORARY TABLE tmpTitleIDs TYPE=HEAP ";

if(isset($page))
  $sqllimit = "LIMIT " . (($page-1) * $pagesize) . "," .
    ($pagesize + 1);
else
  $sqllimit = "LIMIT " . ($pagesize + 1);
```

Creating SQL Queries from Form Data

If form data are available, then the following lines create the SQL command on that basis. First, the user input is separated from the PHP magic quotes. Then the special characters <, >, ", %, *, _, and \ are eliminated. The one remaining problematic special character, namely, the apostrophe, is permissible, since it can appear in names (e.g., *O'Reilly*):

```
// formulate SQL command from form data
if(isset(isset($formSearch)) {
  //remove < > " % _ * \ from $formSearch
  $search = trim(stripslashes($formSearch));
  $remove = "<>\"_%*\\";
  for($i=0; $i<strlen($remove); $i++)
    $search = str_replace(substr($remove, $i, 1), "", $search);
```

Depending on whether the search is for an author or a title, the program displays a brief text about the content of the search and then constructs *sql* according to one of the two following patterns. Note, please, that in the case of an author search a relatively high limit (not *pagesize*) is used. This is because the program anticipates more than one page in the search result only in the case of a title search.

```
SELECT authName, authID FROM authors
WHERE authName LIKE 'abc%'
ORDER BY authName LIMIT 100

CREATE TEMPORARY TABLE tmpTitleIDs TYPE=HEAP
SELECT titleID FROM titles " .
WHERE title LIKE 'abc%'
ORDER BY title LIMIT 21
```

Here is the PHP code for assigning this command to the variable *sql*:

```
if($search=="")
  unset($search);
else {
  // search for authors
  if($formSubmitAuthor) {
    echo "<p>Search for authors whose family names begin with <i>",
      htmlentities($search), "</i>:</p>\n";
    $sqlType = "author";
    $sql =
      "SELECT authName, authID FROM authors " .
      "WHERE authName LIKE '" . addslashes($search) . "%' " .
      "ORDER BY authName LIMIT 100";
  }
  // search for titles
  else {
    echo "<p>Search for titles beginning with <i>",
      htmlentities($search), "</i>:\n</p>";
    $sqlType = "title";
    $sql = $sqlcreate .
      "SELECT titleID FROM titles " .
      "WHERE title LIKE '" . addslashes($search) . "%' " .
      "ORDER BY title " . $sqllimit;
  }
}
}
```

Creating SQL Queries from URL Variables

One can deduce the existence of URL variables from the variable *sqlType*. In the current form, *sqlType=title* is specified exclusively in the HTTP address, but perhaps in an extension of find.php another search would be possible.

Three possible search criteria can be passed in the form of URL variables: *authID* (title by a particular author), *publID* (title from a particular publisher), or *search* (title with particular initial letters).

In the search for titles by a particular author, a query first determines and then displays the name of the author. This query also serves for validation of *authID*. If the query returns no result (or more than one), then there is something other than a unique valid ID value to be dealt with. In this case, a brief error message is displayed. Otherwise, the name of the author is displayed in the "usual" way of writing it (given name followed by family name), and an SQL command is created according to the following format:

```
CREATE TEMPORARY TABLE tmpTitleIDs TYPE=HEAP
SELECT titles.titleID
FROM titles, rel_title_author
WHERE rel_title_author.authID = '$authID'
  AND titles.titleID = rel_title_author.titleID
ORDER BY title LIMIT 21
```

The search for titles of a particular publisher is accomplished with almost the same pattern, but now no *JOIN* is necessary. The search for titles with particular initial letters proceeds as in the similar case involving form data:

```
elseif($sqlType=="title") {// else to: if( ... ) {sql form data }
  // authID contains a value: Search for titles by this author
  if($authID) {
    $result =
      mysql_query("SELECT authName FROM authors " .
                  "WHERE authID='$authID' LIMIT 2");
    if(mysql_num_rows($result)!=1)
      echo "<p>Sorry, ID number for author seems to be invalid.</p>\n";
    else {
      echo "<p>Titles written by <i>",
        htmlentities(last_name_last(mysql_result($result, 0, 0))),
        "</i>:\n";
      $sql = $sqlcreate .
        "SELECT titles.titleID " .
        "FROM titles JOIN rel_title_author " .
        "WHERE rel_title_author.authID = '$authID' " .
        " AND titles.titleID = rel_title_author.titleID " .
        "ORDER BY title " . $sqllimit;
    }
    mysql_free_result($result);
  }
  // publID contains a value: search for titles of this publisher
  elseif($publID) {
    $result =
      mysql_query("SELECT publName FROM publishers " .
                  "WHERE publID='$publID' LIMIT 2");
    if(mysql_num_rows($result)!=1)
      echo "<p>Sorry, ID number for publisher seems to be ",
          "invalid.</p>\n";
    else {
      echo "<p>Titles published by <i>",
        mysql_result($result, 0, 0), "</i>:</p>\n";
      $sql = $sqlcreate .
        "SELECT titleID FROM titles " .
        "WHERE publID = '$publID' " .
        "ORDER BY title " . $sqllimit;
    }
```

```
    mysql_free_result($result);
  }
  // search contains search character string: search for titles with these
  // initial letters
  elseif($search) {
    echo "<p>Titles beginning with <i>",
      htmlentities($search), "</i>:</p>\n";
    $sql = $sqlcreate .
      "SELECT titleID FROM titles " .
      "WHERE title LIKE '" . addslashes($search) . "%' " .
      "ORDER BY title " . $sqllimit;
  }
  if($page>1)
    echo "Page $page</p>\n";
} // end of elseif($sqlType=="title")
```

Displaying Results of an Author Search

The last part of find.php is responsible for executing the command stored in *sql* and displaying the result. This is relatively uncomplicated when the search is for authors. The names are transformed with *last_name_last* into a more readable format. Furthermore, *build_href* is used to represent the name as an HTTP link. Here, *sqlType= title* and *authID=n* are passed as search strings.

```
if(!empty($sql)) {
  if($sqlType=="author") {
    // display results for author search
    $result = mysql_query($sql);
    if(!$result or !mysql_num_rows($result))
      echo "<p>No results.</p>\n";
    else {
      echo "<hr /><ul>\n";
      while($row = mysql_fetch_object($result)) {
        echo "<li>",
          build_href("./find.php",
                     "sqlType=title&authID=$row->authID",
                     last_name_last($row->authName)),
          "</li>\n";
      }
      echo "</ul>\n";
    }
  }
}
```

Displaying Results of a Title Search

From the point of view of database programming, the code for the representation of book titles is much more interesting. With *DROP TABLE*, the table *tmpTitleIDs* is deleted (which can exist only if the script was previously executed and did not terminate due to an error). Then the table is rebuilt with the command contained in *sql*. If the query contained in *sql* has returned results, two additional queries are executed. The first determines the detailed information for each title:

```
SELECT titles.titleID AS titleID, titles.title AS title,
    titles.subtitle AS subtitle, titles.edition AS edition,
    titles.year, titles.isbn, titles.comment,
    publishers.publName AS publisher, publishers.publID,
    categories.catName AS category, languages.langName AS language
FROM titles JOIN tmpTitleIDs
LEFT JOIN categories ON titles.catID = categories.catID
LEFT JOIN languages ON titles.langID = languages.langID
LEFT JOIN publishers ON titles.publID = publishers.publID
WHERE titles.titleID = tmpTitleIDs.titleID
```

A result is the unification of data from five tables. In three cases, a *LEFT JOIN* is used, so that title records are created even if one of more of the fields *catID*, *langID*, and *publID* contain the value *NULL*.

```
elseif($sqlType=="title") {
  // there should not be any tmpTitleIDs---but let's be certain
  mysql_query("DROP TABLE IF EXISTS tmpTitleIDs");
  // create temporary table tmpTitleIDs
  mysql_query($sql);
  if(!mysql_affected_rows()) {
    echo "<p>No results.</p>\n";
  }
  else {
    // query for the detailed title data
    $result1 = mysql_query
      ("SELECT titles.titleID AS titleID, " .
      ... (see above)
      "WHERE titles.titleID = tmpTitleIDs.titleID");
```

The second query determines a list of all *titleID* values and the associated author names. Please observe that this list can contain several entries for each *titleID* value (since there can be several authors for a given title):

```
SELECT tmpTitleIDs.titleID, rel_title_author.authID,
    authName AS author
FROM authors, rel_title_author, tmpTitleIDs
WHERE authors.authID = rel_title_author.authID
  AND rel_title_author.titleID = tmpTitleIDs.titleID
ORDER BY rel_title_author.authNr, authName
```

In the query, an $n : m$ relation is created between the *titleID* in the *tmpTitleIDs* table and the *authID* values in the *author* table. The entries are sorted by *authNr* and *authName*. Thereby it is achieved that in the latter formation of the author list, the first author is indeed given first for each title. Only if no differentiation is possible based on *authNr* (because, for example, the field contains *NULL*) is an alphabetical order imposed:

```
// query for authors
$result2 = mysql_query
    ("SELECT tmpTitleIDs.titleID, rel_title_author.authID, " .
    ... (see above)
    "ORDER BY rel_title_author.authNr");
```

The results contained in *result2* are now brought into an array, where *titleID* is used as key. If there are several authors for a *titleID*, then the names are separated by commas. The author names are formatted with *build_href* as HTTP links, which later provide the user with a convenient way to search for all the titles of this author:

```
// enter author names in the field authors[]
while($row = mysql_fetch_object($result2)) {
    // separate authors by commas
    if($authors[$row->titleID])
        $authors[$row->titleID] .= ", ";
    $tmp = build_href("./find.php",
                      "sqlType=title&authID=$row->authID",
                      last_name_last($row->author));
    $authors[$row->titleID] .= $tmp;
}
```

After all data have been collected and the author list has been prepared, we may begin with the output of titles. In *publref* a publisher name is formatted as an HTTP link (similar to what was just done with author names). Then comes an almost interminable *echo* command, which looks quite complicated, because most of the title fields can be empty. Therefore, the PHP construction *condition ? result1 : result2* is used several times. The expression returns *result1* if *condition* is satisfied (is not 0); otherwise, *result2*.

```
// display title
echo "<hr /><ul>\n";
$titlecount=0;
while($row = mysql_fetch_object($result1)) {
    $titlecount++;
    if($titlecount<=$pagesize) {
        if($row->publisher)
            $publref = build_href("./find.php",
                      "sqlType=title&publID=$row->publID",
                      $row->publisher);
        echo "<p><li>", $authors[$row->titleID], ": ",
            "<b>", htmlentities($row->title), "</b>",
            $row->subtitle ?
              ", " . htmlentities($row->subtitle) . " " : "",
            $row->publisher || $row->year ? "<br />" : "",
            $row->publisher ? $publref : "",
            $row->year ? ", " . htmlentities($row->year) . " " : "",
            $row->edition ?
              "<br />Edition: " . htmlentities($row->edition) .
              " " : "",
```

```
        $row->isbn ?
          "<br />ISBN: " . htmlentities($row->isbn) . " " : "",
        $row->language ?
          "<br />Language: <i>" . htmlentities($row->language) .
          "</i> " : "",
        $row->category ?
          "<br />Category: <i>" . htmlentities($row->category) .
          "</i> " : "",
        $row->comment ?
          "<br />Comment: <i>" . htmlentities($row->comment) .
          "</i> " : "",
        "</li></p>\n";
    }
  }
  echo "</ul>\n";
```

All that remains is to delete the temporary table *tmpTitleIDs*:

```
} // end of the else block to if(!mysql_affected_rows())
// delete temporary table
mysql_query("DROP TABLE IF EXISTS tmpTitleIDs");
```

Links to Previous Pages and to the Next Page

If the displayed page number is greater than 1 or if more titles were found than were displayed (*$titlecount>$pagesize*), then a row with links to additional pages with search results is displayed (see Figure 12-4).

Figure 12-4. Links to additional pages with search results

Since for reasons of efficiency the total number of search results is not determined, near the top, only a link to the next page (*$page+1*) is displayed. Near the bottom, links to pages 1 through (*$page-1*) are displayed. Since the page *$page* is currently being shown, it does not make sense to display a link to this page. This number of pages is placed in parentheses for clarity. In addition to the page numbers, the two links PREVIOUS PAGE and NEXT PAGE are displayed.

Note that the PHP function *urlencode* is used in generating the page link for the part *search=searchpattern*, so that any blank or special characters contained in the search string will not cause problems:

```
    // display links to additional search results
    echo "<hr />\n";
    if(isset($page) or $titlecount>$pagesize) {
      $query = "sqlType=title";
      $query .= isset($authID) ? "&authID=$authID" : "";
      $query .= isset($publID) ? "&publID=$publID" : "";
      $query .= isset($search) ?
          "&search=" . urlencode($search) : "";
      echo "<p>More results: ";
      // links to previous pages
      if(isset($page) and $page>1) {
        echo build_href("find.php",
                        $query . "&page=" . ($page-1),
                        "Previous page");
        echo " / Page ";
        for($i=1; $i<$page; $i++) {
          if($i>1) echo " ";
          echo " ",
              build_href("find.php", $query . "&page=" . $i, $i);
        }
      }
      // place current page in parentheses
      if($page>1) echo " ";
      else       echo "Page ";
      echo "<b>($page)</b> ";
      // links to the next page
      if($titlecount>$pagesize) {
        if(isset($page)) echo " ";
        else             $page=1;
        echo build_href("find.php",
                        $query . "&page=" . ($page+1),
                        ($page+1)), " / ";
        echo build_href("./find.php",
                        $query . "&page=" . ($page+1),
                        "Next page");
      }
      echo "</p>\n";
    }
  }
}
```

Ideas for Improvements

The search options in this example are rather limited. The following list contains some ideas for improvements:

- **Search criteria:** Search for all books from publisher *x* that appeared between *year1* and *year2*. Limit the search results to books in a particular language.

- **Category search:** Search for all books in a given category and all subcategories.

- **Sort possibility:** Sort by year of publication, category, publisher, etc. (In find.php sorting is always by title.)

- **Full-text search:** Search by words that appear in the title, subtitle, commentary, or list of authors.

Simple Input of New Books (`simpleinput.php`)

This section shows a minimalist input form for new books (see Figure 12-5). A new book title together with a list of authors can be specified in only two input fields. Then the script tests whether any of the authors input are already stored in the database. All as yet unknown authors are inserted with *INSERT*. Then the new title is stored, as well as the required entries in *rel_title_author* for linking a title and its authors.

Figure 12-5. Simple book title input

The script `simpleinput.php` does not enable input of subtitles, publishers, category, and so on, and it is as good as useless in support of input error correction. The input of special characters can lead to problems. Boy, are we in trouble! Therefore, in the next section, where we introduce the script `input.php`, we will add all of these missing features as well as increase the convenience factor in input and allow for error correction.

The great advantage of `simpleinput.php` vis-à-vis `input.php` is its simplicity. The code is readable and easy to understand. Once you have understood `simpleinput.php`, you have a good foundation for what lies ahead, namely, wading through the much more extensive and sinuous highways and byways of `input.php`.

Program Structure, Code Outline

The structure of the script `simpleinput.php` is relatively simple. First some auxiliary functions are loaded from `mylibraryconnect.inc.php`, and the connection to the database is established. The next lines begin the resulting HTML document.

The script is responsible for both the display of the form and the evaluation of the form data. Therefore, the section *Main-Code* begins with the evaluation of several form variables. If these variables are empty, then all that happens is that the next form is displayed. If the input is incomplete, an error message is dispatched, and the form is displayed again so that input can be completed. If correct input is offered, then the data are stored in the database. In this case, too, an empty form is again displayed, so that additional data can be input.

```php
<?php  // file mylibrary/simpleinput.php
  include("private/mylibraryconnect.inc.php");
  // read form variables (necessary only with PHP >= 4.1)
  $formSubmit  = array_item($_POST, 'formSubmit');
  $formTitle   = array_item($_POST, 'formTitle');
  $formAuthors = array_item($_POST, 'formAuthors');
  // connection to database
  $connID = connect_to_mylibrary();
?>
<!DOCTYPE HTML PUBLIC "-//W3C//DTD HTML 4.0//EN">
<html><head>
  <meta http-equiv="Content-Type"
        content="text/html; charset=iso-8859-1" />
<title>PHP Programming: Input new titles (mylibrary database)</title>
</head><body>
<h2>Input a new title for the mylibrary database</h2>
<?php
  // Main-Code
  //evaluation of the form, store new record if any
   ...
?>
<!-- Form -->
<form method="post" action="simpleinput.php">
<p>Title:
  <br />
  <input name="formTitle" size=60 maxlength=80
         value="<?php echo htmlspecialchars($formTitle); ?>" /></p>
  <p>Authors:
  <br /><input name="formAuthors" size=60 maxlength=100
              value="<?php echo htmlspecialchars($formAuthors); ?>" />
  <br />(Last name first! If you want to specify more than one
         author, use ; to seperate them!)</p>
  <p><input type="submit" value="OK" name="formSubmit" /></p>
</form>
</body></html>
```

Form Variables

When the script for the evaluation of the form input is invoked, three variables receive the contents of the form fields:

- *formSubmit* contains *"OK"*.

1

- *formTitle* contains the title of the book to be stored.

- *formAuthors* contains the semicolon-separated list of authors.

Store a Title

The code for evaluating the form is executed only if the form variables contain data. In this case, it is first checked whether the input is complete, that is, whether both a title and author(s) were input. If that is not the case, then a brief error message is displayed and the form is again displayed with the partial data. The variables *formTitle* and *formAuthors* are then freed of any magic quote characters, so that the form is ready for additional input:

```
if($formSubmit) {
  // check for completeness of the form
  if(empty($formTitle) or empty($formAuthors)) {
    echo "<p>Please specify title and at least one author.</p>\n";
    // remove magic quotes
    if(get_magic_quotes_gpc()) {
      $formTitle = stripslashes($formTitle);
      $formAuthors = stripslashes($formAuthors);
    } }
```

The rest of the code, for storing the new record, is contained in the ensuing *else* block. The author character string is transformed by *explode* into an array, which then is run through a loop. For each author name a check is made as to whether that author already appears in the database. If that is the case, then the ID number is stored in the array *authIDs*. Otherwise, the new author is inserted into the database with *INSERT*. The ID number of the author is then determined with the function *mysql_insert_id*:

```
  else {
    $authCount=0;
    $authorsArray = explode(";", $formAuthors);
    // loop over all authors
    while($i = each($authorsArray)) {
      $author = trim($i[1]);
      if($author) {
        // is the author already known to the database?
        $result =
          mysql_query("SELECT authID FROM authors " .
                      "WHERE authName = '$author'");
        if(mysql_num_rows($result))
          $authIDs[$authCount++] = mysql_result($result, 0, 0);
        // author is not known --> insert author
        else {
          mysql_query("INSERT INTO authors (authName) " .
                      "VALUES('$author')");
          $authIDs[$authCount++] = mysql_insert_id();
        } } } // end of the author loop
```

A further *INSERT* command is then invoked to store the title. The resulting ID number is then used in constructing the SQL command by which the relation between the book title and its authors is established.

```
// store title
mysql_query("INSERT INTO titles (title) VALUES ('" .
            trim($formTitle) . "')");
$titleID=mysql_insert_id();
// establish title/author relation
$sql = "INSERT INTO rel_title_author " .
  "(titleID, authID, authNr) VALUES ";
for($i=0; $i<$authCount; $i++) {
  if($i!=0) $sql .= ",";
  $sql .= "($titleID, $authIDs[$i], $i)";
}
mysql_query($sql);
```

The SQL command has the following form:

```
INSERT INTO rel_title_author (titleID, authID, authNr)
VALUES (titleID, authorID1, 1), (titleID, authorID2, 2) ...
```

To finish, a message is displayed (in a very sloppy manner, without checking the return value *mysql_query*) that the data were stored and that input of the next data record may now begin. The input just carried out can be checked thanks to a link to find.php. (There, all titles whose names begin like that of the just-stored book are displayed.) In order that an empty form be displayed for the next input, the variables *formTitle* and *formAuthors* are cleared:

```
    echo "<p>Your last input has been saved and can be seen ",
      build_href("find.php",
                "sqlType=title&search=" . trim($formTitle),
                "here"),
      ".\n",
<br />You may now continue with the next title.</p>\n";
    $formTitle = $formAuthors = "";
  } // end of the else block for storing data
} // end of the if block for form evaluation
```

Convenient Input of New Book Data (input.php)

The input form introduced in the last section was a minimalist enterprise in every sense. (If it were music, it would be by Philip Glass.) The script input.php offers more in the way of input possibilities, more convenience, and more data security. The price for all of these added features is rather more complex code, that is, code that is closer to a real-world application than was our previous example simpleinput.php.

Operating Instructions

Title input takes place in two phases. In the first phase, only the initial letters of the author and publisher names may be input (see Figure 12-6).

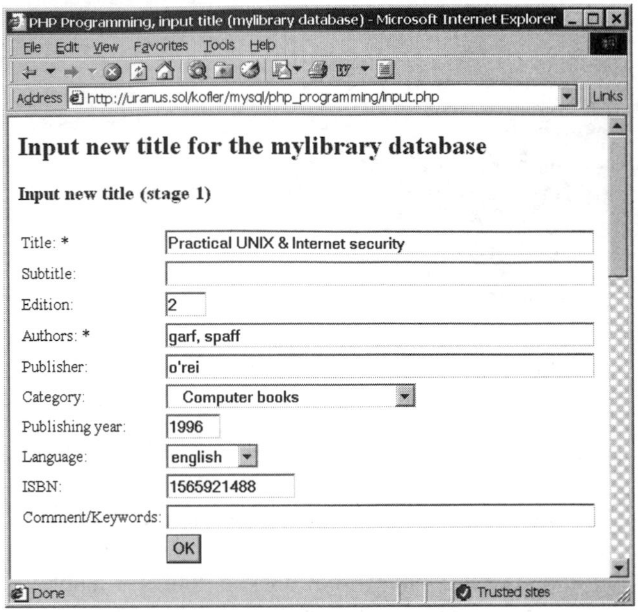

Figure 12-6. Input of a new book title (phase 1)

The script `input.php` searches the database for similar names and then in the second phase presents them as suggestions (see Figure 12-7). This can save the user a bit of typing, but the true benefit is the possible prevention of adding misspelled names to the database.

The script `input.php` expects author names in the customary (unless you are Hungarian, Chinese, . . .) order of given name followed by family name, and then it takes care of storing it in the form specific to the database, namely, family name, then given name.

The script recognizes existing authors even if the name is input in the incorrect order. Thus, for example, if you input (horror of horrors!) *King Stephen* instead of *Stephen King* and this particular author happens to be in the database already, then the program recognizes the existing name and does not store the "new" name, this time in the incorrect order. Needless to say, this technique of error correction does not work with new names. If the given and family names of an author are incorrectly input in reverse order, that author will always be displayed incorrectly in the future. (Nonetheless, the name is false in a consistent way, and can easily be corrected. There are no duplicates in the sense that the name is stored twice, once as *"Stephen King"*, and once as *"King Stephen"*.)

From the data input in Figure 12-6, the script has correctly recognized the first author (*Simon Garfinkel*) and the publisher from the initial letters. The second author (*Gene Spafford*) was not found in the database, and so this name must be input in full.

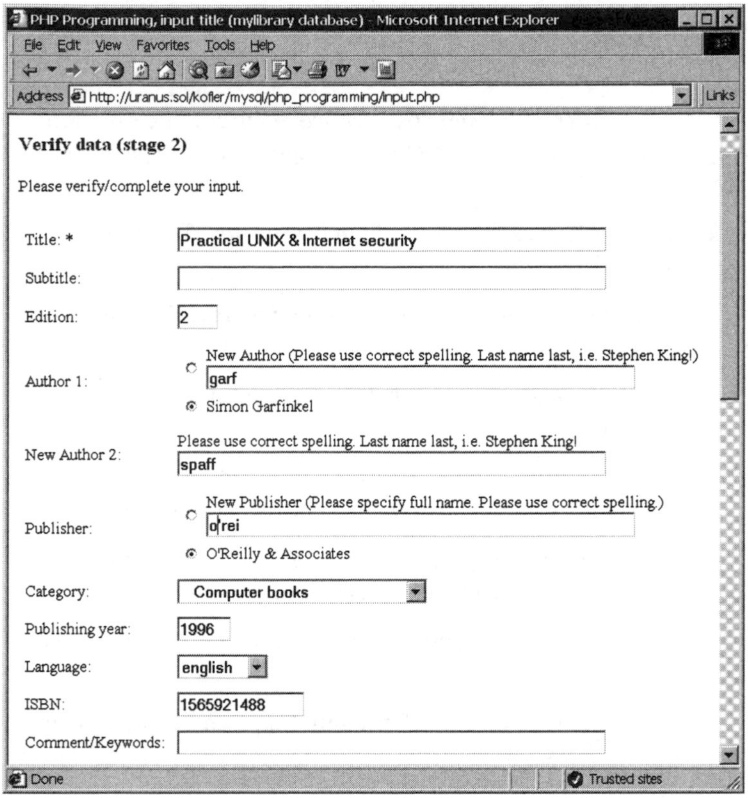

Figure 12-7. Checking the input (phase 2)

In addition, the first validation of the input now takes place. Was an integer greater than zero given as edition number? Is the year of publication believable (that is, not greater than the current year plus 1)? If input errors are suspected, the HTML document displays red warnings, such as, for example "Publishing year needs to be either empty or a 4-digit integer number not larger than 2002."

The validation process is repeated in connection with phase 2. Furthermore, it is checked whether an option was selected in the case that the user had a choice in the selection of the publisher or author names. If errors are detected, then an error message is displayed and the form is displayed again so that corrections can be entered.

Program Structure

The script input.php includes about one thousand lines of code. The first two-thirds of this code contains definitions of numerous functions that are called in the last third (*main code*). The code of most of the functions is described in this section. But first let us have a bit of an overview to orient ourselves:

- *sql_str* prepares a character string for use in an SQL command (*addslashes*, within single quotation marks).

- *str_or_null* returns *NULL* or an SQL-suitable character string (*sql_str($x)*).

- *num_or_null* returns *NULL* or an integer.

- *last_name_first("John F. Kennedy")* returns *"Kennedy John F."*. The function transforms a name from given name first format to the database-specific format of given name last.

- *last_name_last("Kennedy John F.")* returns *"John F. Kennedy"*. This represents the inverse function to *last_name_first*.

- *build_select_list* generates a selection list (*<select>*) for an HTML form from an SQL query.

- *build_categories_select* generates a hierarchical selection list for an HTML form from the *categories* table.

- *show_publisher_options* evaluates the publisher name and displays a list of similar names in the form. The function is called between input phases 1 and 2.

- *restore_publisher_options* again displays the publisher list. The function called in input phase 2 must be repeated due to input errors.

- *show_authors_options* and *restore_authors_options* fulfill the analogous tasks for the author names.

- *validate_stage1* and *validate_stage2* check the input data and display error messages as required.

- *save_data* stores the input data in the database.

Code Outline

The main code begins with an evaluation of the form data (if such are available). Depending on the result, these data are again displayed (for completion or correction), or the data are stored and a new form is displayed for input of the next data record:

```php
<!-->php/mylibrary/input.php
<?php

// read in auxiliary functions
include("../../_private/mylibraryconnect.inc.php");

// define new functions
function sql_str($x) { ... }
function str_or_null($x) { ... }
function num_or_null($x) { ... }
function last_name_first($x) { ... }
function last_name_last($x) { ... }
function build_select_list($formname, $sql, $defaultitem) { ... }
function build_categories_select($defaultitem) { ... }
function show_publisher_options($publname) { ... }
function restore_publisher_options($formvars) { ... }
function show_authors_options($formAuthors) { ... }
function restore_authors_options($formvars) { ... }
```

```php
function validate_stage1($formvars) { ... }
function validate_stage2($formvars) { ... }
function save_data($formvars) { ... }
// establish connection to the database
$connID = connect_to_mylibrary();
?>

<!-- HTML-Header -->
<!DOCTYPE HTML PUBLIC "-//W3C//DTD HTML 4.0//EN">
<html><head>
<title>PHP Programming, input title (mylibrary database)</title>
</head><body>
<h2>Input new title for the mylibrary database</h2>

<?php
// outline of the program structure
//eliminate \', \", \\ and \0 from form variables
// $stage=1;
// if there are form data from phase 1:
// validate data;
// $stage=2; (--> Phase 2)
// if there are form data from phase 2:
// validate data;
// if OK: store data; $stage=1; (--> next input)
// otherwise: display error message, $stage=2; (--> correction)
// if $stage==1:
// display form phase 1
// otherwise
// display form phase 2
?>
```

Form Variables: Phase 1

If the script is called with form data from phase 1, then the following variables are assigned values:

- *formSubmit1* contains *"OK"*.

- *formTitle* and *formSubtitle* contain book title and subtitle.

- *formAuthors* contains a comma- or semicolon-separated list of author names.

- *formEdition* contains the edition number.

- *formCategory* contains the ID number of the selected category.

- *formYear* contains the publication year of the book.

- *formLanguage* contains the ID number of the language of the book.

- *formISBN* contains the ISBN number.

- *formComment* contains a comment or key words.

All variables except for *formAuthors* and *formTitle* may be empty.

Form Variables: Phase 2

- *formSubmit2* contains *"OK"*.

- *formTitle, formSubtitle, formEdition, formCategory, formYear, formLanguage, formISBN, formComment* have the same meaning as above.

- *formAuthorsCount* specifies the number of authors displayed.

- *formAuthorType<n>* specifies how author *n* was handled: 1 means that the author is already known; 2 means that the author is unknown and no similar author names were found; 3 means that the author was not found exactly, but one or more authors with the same initial letters were found. These authors are displayed as options.

- *formAuthor<n>* contains the input name of *n*.

- *formAuthorRadio<n>* contains either *"new"*, if the radio button by the text field was clicked, or the ID number of an existing author if the option for that author was clicked (only for the case *formAuthorType<n>=3*).

- *formAuthorNames<n>* contains a semicolon-separated list of all authors found (only in the case *formAuthorType<n>=3*).

- *formAuthorIDs<n>* contains a semicolon-separated list of all found authors (only in the case *formAuthorType<n>=3*).

- *formPublType* tells whether a publisher was specified and whether this publisher is already known: 0 means no publisher; 1 means known publisher; 2 means unknown publisher; 3 means a list of publishers.

- *formPublisher* contains the name of the publisher.

- *formPublRadio* contains either *"new"* or the ID number of an existing publisher (only in the case *formAuthorType<n>=3*).

- *formPublNames* and *formPublIDs* have the same meaning as *formAuthorNames* and *IDs*.

Using Form Variables

The backslashes before single and double quotation marks that are usually inserted by PHP have proved to be troublesome in this program. For the time-consuming evaluation of a form and generation of new forms, it is burdensome always to be thinking about *stripslashes*. Therefore, the following loop at the start of code execution (*main code*) removes magic quotes from all form variables:

```
if(get_magic_quotes_gpc()) {
  while($i = each($_POST)) {
    $_POST[$i[0]] = stripslashes($i[1]);
  }
}
```

Then all form data are read form the *$_POST* field and stored in variables. The function *item_array*, described already several times in this book, is defined in mylibraryconnect.inc.php:

```
$formSubmit1      = array_item($_POST, 'formSubmit1');
$formTitle        = array_item($_POST, 'formTitle');
// etc. fÿr $formSubtitle, $formAuthors, $formEdition, $formCategory,
// $formYear, $formLanguage, $formISBN, $formComment, $formSubmit2,
// $formAuthorsCount, $formPublisher, $formPublType, $formPublRadio
// $formPublNames and $formPublIDs
```

The form data for authors requires special treatment, since their number is variable. You could actually encounter a book in the form that was written by ten authors. In such a case there are the variables *formAuthor1*, *formAuthor2*, through *formAuthor10*. Reading into these variables is done in a loop in which the variable names are created dynamically using an instruction of the form *${'name' . $n}*, where *$n* contains a number:

```
for($authCount=1; $authCount<=$formAuthorsCount; $authCount++) {
  ${'formAuthorType' . $authCount} =
    array_item($_POST, 'formAuthorType' . $authCount);
  ${'formAuthor' . $authCount} =
    array_item($_POST, 'formAuthor' . $authCount);
  ${'formAuthorRadio' . $authCount} =
    array_item($_POST, 'formAuthorRadio' . $authCount);
  ${'formAuthorNames' . $authCount} =
    array_item($_POST, 'formAuthorNames' . $authCount);
  ${'formAuthorIDs' . $authCount} =
    array_item($_POST, 'formAuthorIDs' . $authCount);
}
```

Special Features of PHP

The two PHP functions *htmlentities* and *htmlspecialchars* help in representing special characters correctly. *htmlspecialchars* changes only the characters ", &, <, >, while *htmlentities* also changes a number of other characters, such as *ü,é, à.*

- In input.php, *htmlspecialchars* is always used if existing data is to be reinserted into a text field of a form. (In this case, *htmlentities* is unsuitable, since then constructions like *ä* appear in character strings that are to be stored later in the database).

- *htmlentities*, on the other hand, is used when data are to be displayed unaltered (thus not within text input fields in a form). In fact, *htmlentities* should be superfluous, since in any case, ISO-8559-1 is used as the character set for the HTML file (that is, the *latin1* character set, which handles a number of European special characters). *htmlentities*, however, increases the probability that special characters will be displayed correctly, independent of the version and configuration of the web browser and of the PHP configuration (php.ini).

With the PHP command *echo*, character strings can be placed within single or double quotation marks. Each of these variants has its advantages, and both are frequently used. If *$variable* has the value 123, then the following hold:

- *echo "xy='$variable' \n"* outputs the character string *xy='123'* followed by a line break character. Thus *echo "..."* supports the automatic placing of variable contents, the output of the character ', and the output of special characters such as \n and \t. The double quote character can be represented by \", as in *echo "x=\"abc\""*.

- *echo 'xy="$variable"\n'* outputs the string *xy="$variable"\n*; thus *echo '...'* enables the direct output of the character " needed in HTML code. In general, everything is output unchanged in single quotation marks (no variable substitution, no support of special characters like \n).

In the code of input.php, the '...' and ... parts are often run together, for example thus:

```
echo '<input type="hidden" ', "name=$typename ", 'value="2" />', "\n";
```

Data Validation, Changeover for Input Phases 1 and 2

Depending on whether form data are present from phase 1 or phase 2, a more or less thorough validation of the data and their eventual storage takes place. The result of the validation process determines the content of the variable *stage*. This variable then determines in the rest of the program how the formula is displayed.

If data from phase 1 are present, then it is ensured that at least the author field has been filled in. If that is the case, then a changeover to phase 2 takes place. Otherwise, the input form for phase 1 is displayed anew:

```
// if $formSubmit1 and $formSubmit2 are empty
$stage=1;
// evaluation of form data from phase 1
if($formSubmit1) {
  // in the author list replace, by ;
  $formAuthors = str_replace(",", ";", $formAuthors);
  // check whether formAuthor contains data (other than ";" and " "):
  // if formAuthor is empty, remain at phase 2
  if(!trim(str_replace(";", "", $formAuthors))) {
    echo '<p><font color="#ff0000">You must specify ',
      "<i>authors</i> in stage 1.</font></p>\n";
    $stage=1;
  }
  // otherwise, change over to phase 2
  // possible display of error messages via validate_stage1()
  else {
    validate_stage1();
    $stage=2;
  }
}
```

If the form data come from phase 2, then the function *validate_stage2* is summoned. If no errors occur, then the data are stored with *save_data*. Then all of the input variables are reset. First *stage* is reset to 1; that is, an empty form is displayed for input of the next book title. If errors occurred in the validation process, then it remains at *stage=2*; that is, the form is displayed again in its current state.

```
// evaluation of form data from phase 2
if($formSubmit2) {
  // basic validation; then store data
  // or display input form again for corrections
  if(validate_stage2($HTTP_POST_VARS)) {
    save_data($HTTP_POST_VARS);
    echo "<p>Last input has been saved.\n";
    // input of next record
    $stage=1;
    // reset form variables
    $formTitle = $formSubtitle = $formYear = $formISBN="";
    $formAuthors = $formPublisher = $formCategory = "";
    $formComment = $formLanguage = $formEdition = "";
  } else
    // display form again for corrections
    $stage=2;
}
```

Validating Data (`validate_stage1` *and* `validate_stage2`)

In *validate_stage1* it is ensured that a title is specified, that the input field for the query either is empty or contains a number greater than 0, and that the input field for the publication year either is empty or contains a number that is not greater than one plus the current year. (It is typical for a book that appears in the last three months of the year to bear the next year as publication date.)

The function *validate_stage2* relies on *validate_stage1*. Moreover, the function checks the input for author and publisher names. It must be ensured that either a string was specified or an option selected. To save space, here we present only the code of *validate_stage1*:

> **REMARK**   *No parameters are passed to the functions* validate_stage1 *and* validate_stage2. *Instead, at the beginning of these functions the necessary variables are declared as* global, *so that they can be accessed. In* validate_stage2, *this is a bit more complicated in that depending on the number of authors, there can be a variable number of* formAuthorXxx *variables:*
>
> ```
> for($authCount=1; $authCount<=$formAuthorsCount; $authCount++)
>   global ${'formAuthorType' . $authCount},
>     ${'formAuthor' . $authCount},
>     ${'formAuthorRadio' . $authCount},
>     ${'formAuthorNames' . $authCount},
>     ${'formAuthorIDs' . $authCount};
> ```

```php
function validate_stage1() {
global $formTitle, $formEdition, $formYear;

  $errstart = '<br /><font color="#ff0000">';
  $errend = "</font>\n";
  $errors = 0;
  echo "<p>";

  // check title
  if(!trim($formTitle)) {
    echo $errstart, "Please enter an <i>title</i>.\n", $errend;
    $errors++;
  }

  // check publisher
  if($formEdition and
     (!is_numeric($formEdition) or intval($formEdition)<1)) {
    echo $errstart, "<i>Edition</i> needs to be either empty or an  ",
      "integer greater than or equal to 1.", $errend;
    $errors++;
  }

  // check year of publication; may not be greater
  // than the current year + 1
  // (31536000 is the number of seconds in a year)
  if($formYear and
     (!is_numeric($formYear) or
      intval($formYear) > date("Y", time()+31536000))) {
    echo $errstart, "<i>Publishing year</i> needs to be either ",
      "empty or a 4-digit integer number not larger than ",
      date("Y", time()+31536000), ".", $errend;
    $errors++;
  }
  echo "</p>\n";
  return($errors);
}
```

Displaying Forms

Displaying the Form for Input Phase 1

The HTML code for the form is given directly, for the most part. There are only a few embedded PHP functions for displaying the content of variables and creating the hierarchical category listbox (function *build_categories_select*) and the language listbox (function *build_select_list*). The code of both these functions will appear later.

Within the form, a table is used to achieve a somewhat pleasing appearance. In the following, only the more interesting code lines are given, where the PHP code embedded in the HTML code is printed in boldface:

```
if($stage==1) {
?>

<h3>Input new title (stage 1)</h3>
<form method="POST" action="input.php">
<table>
<tr><td>Title: *</td>
    <td><input name="formTitle" size="60" maxlength="80"
            value="<?php echo htmlspecialchars($formTitle); ?>" />
</td></tr>
<tr><td>Subtitle: ... (as above)
<tr><td>Edition: ...
<tr><td>Authors: *</td>
    <td><input name="formAuthors" size="60" maxlength="100"
            value="<?php echo htmlspecialchars($formAuthors); ?>" />
</td></tr>
<tr><td>Publisher:</td>
    <td><input name="formPublisher" size="60" maxlength="100"
            value="<?php echo htmlspecialchars($formPublisher); ?>" />
</td></tr>
<tr><td>Category:</td>
    <td><?php build_categories_select($formCategory); ?></td></tr>
<tr><td>Publishing year: ...
<tr><td>Language:</td>
    <td><?php build_select_list("formLanguage",
            "SELECT langID, langName FROM languages " .
            "ORDER BY langName", $formLanguage); ?></td></tr>
<tr><td>ISBN: ...
<tr><td>Comment/Keywords: ...
<tr><td>
    <td><input type="submit" value="OK" name="formSubmit1"></tr>
</table>
</form>
```

Displaying the Form for Input Phase 2

For most of the input fields the code for input phase 2 is simply a repetition of that for phase 1. What is new is the processing of authors and publisher. If a form from phase 1 was just displayed (that is, *if($formSubmit1)*), then the input is evaluated with *show_authors_options* or *show_publisher_options*. Similar names in the database are then displayed in the form in radio button fields.

If just previously, a form in phase 2 was displayed (during the evaluation of which input errors were detected that now must be corrected), then the radio button fields from the form just displayed must be restored. The functions *restore_authors_options* and *restore_publishers_options* access the data that have been stored in hidden fields of the form:

```php
<?php
if($stage==2) {
?>
<h3>Verify data (stage 2)</h3>
<form method="post" action="input.php">
<table cellpadding="5">
<tr><td>Title: *</td>
    <td><input name="formTitle" size="60" maxlength="80"
                value="<?php echo htmlspecialchars($formTitle); ?>" />
</td></tr>
<tr><td>Subtitle:
<tr><td>Edition:
<?php
if($formSubmit1)
  show_authors_options($formAuthors);
else
  restore_authors_options();
if($formSubmit1)
  show_publisher_options($formPublisher);
else
  restore_publisher_options();
?>

<tr><td>Category:
<tr><td>Publishing year:
<tr><td>Language:
<tr><td>ISBN:  ...
<tr><td>Comment/Keywords: ...
<tr><td>
    <td><input type="submit" value="OK" name="formSubmit2"></tr>
</table>
</form>
```

Auxiliary Functions

SQL Auxiliary Functions (sql_str, str_or_null, num_or_null)

In formulating SQL commands, character strings must always be given in single quotation marks. Special characters must be preceded by a backslash. Distinction must be made between a number or character string and *NULL* according to whether or not a PHP variable is empty. The following three functions are helpful in this regard:

```php
//mark ', ", and \, place character strings in '
function sql_str($x) {
  return "'" . addslashes($x) . "'";
}
// returns SQL-suitable character string or NULL
function str_or_null($x) {
  if(trim($x)=="")
    return("NULL");
```

```
  else
    return(sql_str(trim($x)));
}
// returns integer or NULL
function num_or_null($x) {
  if(empty($x))
    return("NULL");
  else
    return($x);
}
```

Functions for Name Processing (last_name_first, last_name_last)

In databases, names must generally be stored with family name first so that searching and sorting by family name can proceed in as simple a manner as possible. However, people are not, at least the last time we checked, computers. In many cultures they are accustomed to writing given name first, and they are inclined to write the name in that order.

The function *last_name_first* assumes that the character string passed as parameter contains a name in the given-name-first format. This function places the family name (the part of the character string after the last space character) at the beginning of the string. The string is unchanged if it consists of a single word or if it ends with a period. (Since usually, only given names are abbreviated with a period, in this case the assumption is made that the character string already appears in the form suitable for storage in the database. This safety measure is designed to recognize names that are input in the form in the incorrect order.)

```
// "John F. Kennedy" --> "Kennedy John F."
function last_name_first($x) {
  $x = trim($x);
  // no change if ends with a period
  if(substr($x, -1) == ".") return($x);
  // no change if there is no space character
  if(!$pos = strrpos($x, " ")) return($x);
  // place last word at the head of the character string
  return(trim(substr($x, $pos+1) . " " . substr($x, 0, $pos)));
}
```

The function *last_name_last* is more or less the inverse function. As parameter is passed a character string in the database-specific ordering (with family name at the head). The first word is then placed at the end of the string.

```
function last_name_last($x) {
  $x = trim($x);
  // no change if there is no space character
  if(!$pos = strpos($x, " ")) return($x);
  // place first word at the end of the string
  return(trim(substr($x, $pos+1) . " " . substr($x, 0, $pos)));
}
```

build_select_list

The function *build_select_list* expects as its first parameter the name of the listbox, and as the second parameter it wants an SQL query, while for the third parameter the ID number of the default entry for the listbox is required. The result of the SQL query must contain the ID value in the first column, and in the second, a character string from the table (here, for example, the name of the language). From this information the function creates the HTML code for the listbox (see Figure 12-8). The following lines show how the function is called:

```
build_select_list("formLanguage",
  "SELECT langID, langName FROM languages " .
  "ORDER BY langName", "");
```

The resulting HTML code looks as follows. Please note especially that although the character strings are displayed (in Figure 12-8 the names of languages), it is their ID numbers that are stored with *value=* .... . The ID numbers are much better suited than character strings for further processing of the selection:

Figure 12-8. Listbox for languages

```
<select name="formLanguage" size="1">
<option value="none">(choose)</option>
<option value="2"> deutsch</option>
<option value="1"> english</option>
<option value="4"> norsk</option>
<option value="3"> svensk</option>
</select>
function build_categories_select($defaultitem) {
  $result =
    mysql_query("SELECT catID, catName, hierIndent " .
                "FROM categories " .
                "ORDER BY hierNr");
  echo '<select name="formCategory" size="1">', "\n";
  echo '<option value="none">(choose)</option>', "\n";
  while($row=mysql_fetch_object($result)) {
    echo "<option ";
    if($defaultitem==$row->catID) echo 'selected="selected" ';
    echo "value=\"$row->catID\">",
      $row->hierIndent>0 ?
        str_repeat("   ", $row->hierIndent) : "",
      htmlentities($row->catName), "</option>\n";
  }
  echo "</select>\n";
  mysql_free_result($result);
}
```

Creating a Hierarchical Listbox (build_categories_select)

The function *build_categories_select* is related to the function just introduced, though it is less broadly applicable. The function evaluates the *categories* table and then creates a hierarchical listbox (that is, the list entries are indented according to their place in the hierarchy; see Figure 12-9). For indentation, nonbreaking space characters are used (HTML code). As a single parameter, the ID number of a default category can be passed to the function:

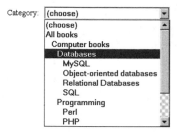

Figure 12-9. Hierarchical listbox for selecting the book category

```
function build_categories_select($defaultitem) {
  $result =
    mysql_query("SELECT catID, catName, hierIndent " .
                "FROM categories " .
                "ORDER BY hierNr");
  echo '<select name="formCategory" size="1">', "\n";
  echo '<option value="none">(choose)</option>', "\n";
  while($row=mysql_fetch_object($result)) {
    echo "<option ";
    if($defaultitem==$row->catID) echo 'selected="selected" ';
    echo "value=\"$row->catID\">",
      $row->hierIndent>0 ?
        str_repeat("   ", $row->hierIndent) : "",
      htmlentities($row->catName), "</option>\n";
  }
  echo "</select>\n";
  mysql_free_result($result);
}
```

Publisher Name (show_publisher_options)

The function *show_publisher_options* is invoked to display the input fields for the publisher name in the second form. The parameter *publname* contains the publisher name provided in the first form. Now an attempt is made to find the name that was input in the *publishers* table. If this does not succeed, then a list of similar names is sought. For this purpose the character string is reduced to at most six characters. Then a *SELECT* query is used to find all publisher names that begin with these letters:

```
function show_publisher_options($publname) {
  // if no name was given thus far, display an empty input field
  $publname=trim($publname);
  if($publname=="") {
    echo '<tr><td>Publisher:</td>', "\n",
      '<td><input name="formPublisher" size="60" maxlength="100" ',
      'value="" /></td></tr>', "\n",
      '<input type="hidden" name="formPublType" value="0" />', "\n";
    return;
  }
  // is this publisher known?
  $result = mysql_query("SELECT publName FROM publishers " .
                      "WHERE publName = " . sql_str($publname) . " LIMIT 2");
  if(mysql_num_rows($result)==1) {
    $known_publisher = 1;
    $publname = mysql_result($result, 0, 0);
    mysql_free_result($result);
  }
  // search for similar names
  else {
    if(strlen($publname<7))
      $publpattern = $publname . '%';
    else
      $publpattern = substr($publname, 0, 6) . '%';
    $result =
      mysql_query("SELECT publID, publName FROM publishers " .
                  "WHERE publName LIKE " . sql_str($publpattern) .
                  " ORDER BY publName LIMIT 20");
  }
```

The result is displayed for this analytical phase. There are three variants:

- The publisher was found. The name is displayed in an input field titled *Known publisher*.

- The publisher was not found, and there were no similar names found as well. Apparently, we are dealing with a new publisher. The name is again shown in an input field, but this time the title is *New publisher*. Furthermore, a message is displayed to the effect that input must be in the correct format.

- The publisher was not found, but there were found publishers with the same initial letters. In this case both an input field and radio button list with all publishers found are displayed. (The length of this list is limited by *LIMIT 20* in the *SELECT* query.) The user now has the opportunity to specify a new publisher name in detail or to select one of the options offered (see Figure 12-10). To keep the form readable, in this case the options are displayed as a table:

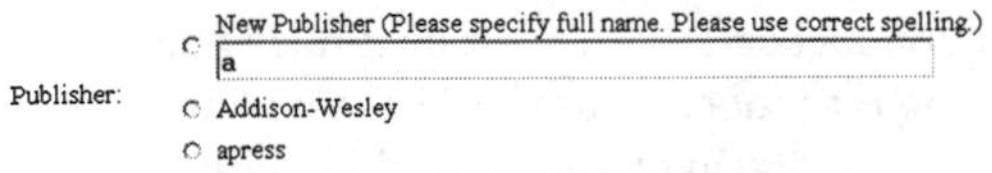

Figure 12-10. Selection or new input of a publisher name in the second input phase

```php
// display input field/radio-button options in form
// case 1: publisher is known
if(isset($known_publisher)) {
  echo "<tr><td>Known Publisher:</td>\n",
    '<td><input name="formPublisher" size="60" maxlength="100" ',
    'value="', htmlspecialchars($publname), '" />',
    "\n</td></tr>\n",
    '<input type="hidden" name="formPublType" value="1" />', "\n";
}
else {
  // case 2: publisher unknown, no similar publishers found
  if(!mysql_num_rows($result)) {
    echo "<tr><td>New Publisher:</td>\n",
      "<td>Please specify full name. Please use ",
      "correct spelling.\n",
      '<br /><input name="formPublisher" size="60" ',
      ' maxlength="100" value="', htmlspecialchars($publname),
      '" />', "\n</td></tr>\n",
      '<input type="hidden" name="formPublType" value="2" />', "\n";
  }
  // case 3: publisher unknown, but similar publishers found
  else {
    echo "<tr><td>Publisher:</td>\n",
      "<td><table cellpadding="2">\n";
    echo '<tr><td><input type="radio" name="formPublRadio" ',
      'value="new" /></td>',
      '<td>New Publisher (Please specify full name. Please use ',
      'correct spelling.)', "\n",
      '<input name="formPublisher" size="60" maxlength="100" ',
      'value="', htmlspecialchars($publname),
      '" /></td></tr>', "\n";
    // display list of similar publishers
    $publNames="";
    $publIDs="";
    while($row=mysql_fetch_object($result)) {
      echo '<tr><td><input type="radio" name="formPublRadio" ',
        mysql_num_rows($result)==1 ? 'checked="checked" ' : '',
        'value="', $row->publID, '" /></td>',
        '<td>', $row->publName, "</td></tr>\n";
      $publNames .= ";" . $row->publName;
      $publIDs .= ";" . $row->publID;
    }
    echo "</table></td>\n</tr>\n";
    // place information about input fields in hidden form fields
    echo '<input type="hidden" name="formPublType" value="3" />',
      "\n";
    echo '<input type="hidden" name="formPublNames" value="',
      htmlspecialchars(substr($publNames, 1)), '" />', "\n";
    echo '<input type="hidden" name="formPublIDs" value="',
      substr($publIDs, 1), '" />', "\n";
  }
  mysql_free_result($result);  }  }
```

At the end of the input, options information is stored in three hidden form fields as to whether the input name is known (*formPublType*). If options with similar publisher names were displayed, then a list of these names and ID numbers is stored. In this way the input form can be re-created if necessary with *restore_publisher_options*. (This will be necessary if the phase 2 form must be displayed again due to an input error having been discovered in one or another field.) The following lines show the HTML code corresponding to Figure 12-10, including the hidden fields:

```
<tr><td>Publisher:</td>
    <td>
    <table cellpadding="2">
    <tr>
    <td><input type="radio" name="formPublRadio" value="new" /></td>
        <td>New Publisher (Please specify full name. Please use
            correct spelling.)
        <input name="formPublisher" size=60 maxlength=100 value="a" />
    </td>
    </tr>
    <tr><td><input type="radio" name="formPublRadio" value="1" /></td>
        <td>Addison-Wesley</td></tr>
    <tr><td><input type=radio name="formPublRadio" value="2" /></td>
        <td>apress</td></tr>
    </table>
</td></tr>
<input type="hidden" name="formPublType" value="3" />
<input type="hidden" name="formPublNames"
        value="Addison-Wesley;apress" />
<input type=hidden name="formPublIDs" value="1;2" />
```

Restoring the Publisher Selection Fields (restore_publisher_options)

The function *restore_publisher_options* is called if the form displayed in phase 2 of the input process must be shown again (due to the discovery of an input error). The form variables *formPublisher* (from the input field) and *formPublRadio* (selected options), as well as *formPublType*, *formPublNames*, and *formPublIDs* (hidden fields), are used to restore the form to its last displayed condition.

From the point of view of database programming, the code is not particularly interesting, for which reason we shall refrain from presenting it.

Author Input (show_authors_options and restore_authors_options)

The functions *show_authors_options* and *restore_authors_options* take on the same tasks as the *publisher* functions that we have just described, although this time it is for the input of author names. There are two significant differences:

- In the input form in phase 1, several authors can be input. Therefore, *show_authors_options* decomposes the character string *formAuthors* into its components and then treats each author separately.

- With all the author names, the order of names is reversed. (The program expects input in the form *Stephen King,* and then it searches the database for *King Stephen.*) Just to be on the safe side, the author table searches for names in both forms, so that the author will be found even if the input was in the incorrect order:

```
function show_authors_options($formAuthors) {
  // decompose formAuthors into individual author names
  $authArray = explode(";", $formAuthors);
  $authCount = 0;
  // loop over all the authors
  while($i = each($authArray)) {
    $known_author = 0;
    $author = trim($i[1]);
    if($author) {
      $authCount++;
      // author perhaps has the given name first
      // but authorDB is in database format
      $authorDB = last_name_first($author);
      // search for names (with authorDB)
      $result1 =
        mysql_query("SELECT authName FROM authors " .
                    "WHERE authName = " . sql_str($authorDB) .
                    " LIMIT 2");
      if(mysql_num_rows($result1)==1) {
        $known_author=1;
        $authorDB = mysql_result($result1, 0, 0);
        $author = last_name_last($authorDB);
      }
      // search again for names (with author)
      else {
        $result2 =
          mysql_query("SELECT authName FROM authors " .
                      "WHERE authName = " . sql_str($author) .
                      " LIMIT 2");
    ...
```

The rest of the code for *show_authors_options* is very similar to that of *show_publisher_options,* for which reason we do not show it here. The same holds for *restore_authors_options.*

Storing Data

From the database programming viewpoint we are again in interesting territory with the function *save_data.* The data input in the form should now be stored in the database.

In the first step it is checked whether the input publisher already appears in the database. If this is the case, then the ID number of the record is temporarily stored in *publID.* (The ID number will be needed later to store the *title* data record.) If the publisher is as yet unknown, then an *INSERT* command is employed to insert it into the table. Now *publID* is determined via *mysql_insert_id*. Things are simpler if the user has clicked on one of the radio buttons. Then the form variable *formPublRadio* already contains the ID number. Finally, there is the possibility that no publisher was specified in the form. In that case, *publID* is deleted with *unset*. (The *titles* table allows the storage of records without a publisher. Likewise, most of the other columns of the *titles* table are optional, and may contain *NULL*.)

```php
function save_data() {
  global $formTitle, $formSubtitle, $formEdition,
    $formCategory, $formYear, $formLanguage, $formISBN,
    $formComment, $formAuthorsCount, $formPublisher, $formPublType,
    $formPublRadio, $formPublNames, $formPublIDs;
  for($authCount=1; $authCount<=$formAuthorsCount; $authCount++)
    global ${'formAuthorType' . $authCount},
      ${'formAuthor' . $authCount},
      ${'formAuthorRadio' . $authCount},
      ${'formAuthorNames' . $authCount},
      ${'formAuthorIDs' . $authCount};
  // search for or store publisher
  $formPublisher = trim($formPublisher);
  if(($formPublType<3 or
      ($formPublType==3 and $formPublRadio=="new"))
    and !empty($formPublisher)) {
    // is the publisher already known to the database?
    $result =
      mysql_query("SELECT publID FROM publishers " .
                  "WHERE publName = " . sql_str($formPublisher));
    if(mysql_num_rows($result))
      $publID = mysql_result($result, 0, 0);
    // publisher is not yet known; store it
    else {
      mysql_query("INSERT INTO publishers (publName) " .
                  "VALUES(" . sql_str($formPublisher) . ")");
      $publID = mysql_insert_id();
    }
    mysql_free_result($result);
  }
  // radio button with known publisher was selected
  elseif($formPublType==3 and $formPublRadio!="new") {
    $publID = $formPublRadio;
  }
  // no publisher was specified
  else
  ($publID = "";
```

A similar process is repeated for each of the authors. Since the relevant information is specified in variables such as *formAuthor1* and *formAuthor2*, in the author loop first the values must be extracted from these variable (!) variable names. To this end, the PHP syntax *${' name'}* is employed to determine the content of the specified variables in the nested parentheses:

```
// loop over all authors
$authCount=0;
for($i=1; $i<=$formAuthorsCount; $i++) {
  $newID = "none";
  // extract form variables
  $author = ${'formAuthor' . $i};
  $authorRadio = ${'formAuthorRadio' . $i};
  $authorType =${'formAuthorType' . $i};
  $author = trim($author);
  // author name in database-specific format
  $authorDB = last_name_first($author);
```

In the following lines, the ID number of the author is determined (variable *newID*). To accomplish this, the author is searched for in the database in both formats (given name followed by family name and conversely). If the name is not found, then it is inserted into the database as a new author with *INSERT*:

```
// author from text field
if($author and $authorType<3 or $authorRadio=="new") {
  // is the author already known to the database?
  $result =
    mysql_query("SELECT authID FROM authors " .
                "WHERE authName = " . sql_str($authorDB) .
                " OR authName = " . sql_str($author));
  if(mysql_num_rows($result))
    $newID = mysql_result($result, 0, 0);
  // the author is unknown: insert into database
  else {
    mysql_query("INSERT INTO authors (authName) " .
                "VALUES('" . sql_str($authorDB) . ")");
    $newID = mysql_insert_id();
  }
  mysql_free_result($result);
}
// radio button with known author was chosen
elseif ($authorRadio!="new")
  $newID = $authorRadio;
```

The variable *newID* is inserted into the field *authIDs*, which contains all the authors of the new book title. Here it must be ensured that the same author is not inserted twice due to improper input:

```
// each author must be inserted only once into the authIDs
for($j=0; $j<sizeof($authIDs); $j++)
  if($authIDs[$j]==$newID) {
    $newID="none"; break;
  }
```

```
      // insert newID in authIDs
      if($newID!="none") {
        $authIDs[$authCount]=$newID;
        $authCount++;
      }
    } // end of the loop over author names
```

Only one *INSERT* command is required in order to enter the new book into the *titles* table, but because of the numerous columns, it is rather substantial. To create the command, the functions *str_or_null* and *num_or_null* are called on, which return the content of the respective variable or else *NULL* if the variable is empty:

```
    // store book title
    if($formCategory=="none") $formCategory = "";
    if($formLanguage=="none") $formLanguage = "";
    mysql_query("INSERT INTO titles (title, subtitle, " .
                  " edition, publID, catID, langID, year, " .
                  " isbn, comment) VALUES (" .
                  sql_str(trim($formTitle)) . ", " .
                  str_or_null($formSubtitle) . ", " .
                  num_or_null($formEdition) . ", " .
                  num_or_null($publID) . ", " .
                  num_or_null($formCategory) . ", " .
                  num_or_null($formLanguage) . ", " .
                  num_or_null($formYear) . ", " .
                  str_or_null($formISBN) . ", " .
                  str_or_null($formComment) . ")");
    $titleID = mysql_insert_id();
```

Finally, the relation between the book title and the authors must be created. For this, the *INSERT* command is assembled in the variable *sql*:

```
    // store entries in rel_title_author
    $sql = "INSERT INTO rel_title_author " .
      "(titleID, authID, authNr) VALUES ";
    for($i=0; $i<$authCount; $i++) {
      if($i!=0) $sql .= ",";
      $sql .= "($titleID, $authIDs[$i], $i)";
    }
    mysql_query($sql);
  }
```

Room for Improvement

The script input.php does quite a bit, yet one can think of a number of ways in which it could be improved.

- The program does not check whether the book title that is input perhaps already exists in the database. Such a control is not trivial to implement, because a comparison of titles alone is not sufficient. For example, there might certainly be more than one book with the title *MySQL*. Thus all additional information such as subtitle, publisher, edition, authors, all of which are subject to error, must be taken into consideration. A possible solution would be to display a list of all books with the same or similar title in the second input phase to lessen the danger of a duplicate being inserted. (If all titles were consistently accompanied by their ISBN numbers, then a test for uniqueness would be easy. But in our program such input is optional.)

- In comparing author names, one can use the function *SOUNDEX*. This MySQL function returns the same value for similar-sounding English words (e.g., *Green* and *Greene*). In this way, possible typographical errors in author input can be repaired before it is too late. However, there is an assumption that the *authors* table is equipped with an additional *soundex* column in which all like-sounding names have been stored for existing authors. (It would be too costly to execute the *SOUNDEX* for all existing authors each time a comparison needs to be made.)

- There should be better protection of *save_data* against errors. It is relatively unlikely, based on the prior validation, that a problem will occur in storing a name, but an error can be caused externally, for example, from a locking problem. In general, after every call to *mysql_query* a check against possible errors should be carried out.

- A relatively obvious lack in the input form is that the number of authors is fixed in the first phase and cannot be changed in the second phase.

- There is an inconsistency in that with input.php there is the possibility of storing new titles, authors, publishers, etc., but these data cannot be changed.

- Data validation can be handled more easily with JavaScript. I am no great friend of JavaScript, preferring web pages that function without it. But no doubt, here at least one could well imagine a JavaScript option.

All of these goals are realizable, but they would make the code even more complex than it is already and begin to make this less of a demonstration example and more of a real-world application.

Managing the Book Categories (*categories.php*)

Each title in *mylibrary* can be associated with a category of books. This section is devoted to introducing a PHP page for managing these categories. With this page you will be able to create new categories and delete existing ones.

From the user's point of view, this management takes place over two pages: The initial page (see Figure 12-11) shows a hierarchical list of all the categories. You can select a category in order to insert subcategories (INSERT link) or delete one (DELETE link). If a category is deleted, then all of its subcategories are automatically deleted as well. Deletion is possible only if there is no book in the database that is associated with the category in question. Warning: Deletion takes place with no warning and no "undo" option.

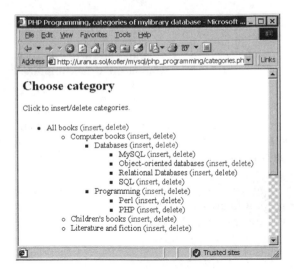

Figure 12-11. Select or delete a category

The form for input of a new category appears in Figure 12-12. Only the part of the hierarchy that applies to the selected entry (shown in boldface) is displayed. It is possible to input several new subcategories at one time (separated by a semicolon).

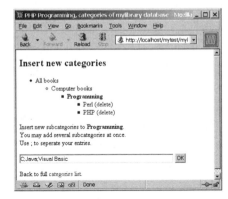

Figure 12-12. Adding the category Visual Basic *in the group* All books | Computer books | Programming

Code Outline

The script categories.php begins with two auxiliary functions: *insert_new_category* stores a new category in the database; *delete_category* deletes a category and all of its subcategories. These two functions are described at the end of this section.

We now present the code for representing the hierarchical list of all categories as well as the representation and evaluation of a form for input of new categories. The following outline should provide orientation inside of categories.php:

```php
<?php  file  mylibrary/categories.php
  // read in auxiliary functions
  include("private/mylibraryconnect.inc.php");

  // read form and URL variables
  $submitbutton  = array_item($_POST, 'submitbutton');
  $subcategories = array_item($_POST, 'subcategories');
  $catID         = array_item($_REQUEST, 'catID');
  $deleteID      = array_item($_REQUEST, 'deleteID');

  // ensure that magic quotes are present
  if(!get_magic_quotes_gpc())
    $subcategories = addslashes($subcategory);

  // define new functions
  function insert_new_category($catID, $newcatName) { ... }
  function delete_category($catID) { ... }

  // establish connection to database
  $connID = connect_to_mylibrary();
?>
<!DOCTYPE HTML PUBLIC "-//W3C//DTD HTML 4.0//EN">
<html><head>
  <meta http-equiv="Content-Type"
        content="text/html; charset=iso-8859-1" />
  <title>PHP Programming, categories of mylibrary database</title>
</head><body>
<?php
  // Main Code
  // if deleteID==n: delete category
  // if isempty(catID): display hierarchical list of all categories
  // else: - evaluate form data, insert new categories
  //       - display hierarchical list of the selected category
  //       - display form for input of a new category
php?>
</body></html>
```

URL Parameters

There are at most two variables that can be passed to the page as part of the address:

- *catID* contains the ID number of the selected category (into which the new subcategory is to be inserted).

- *deleteID* contains the ID number of the category that is to be deleted.

Form Variables

If the page used to evaluate form results is to be called, then two more variables are added to this list:

- *submitbutton* contains *"OK"*.

- *subcategories* contains a character string with the new category to be added.

The rest of the code relies on the special characters in *subcategories* being prefixed by backslashes (magic quotes). To ensure that this is the case, *addslashes* is executed if *get_magic_quotes_gpc* returns the result *false*.

Main Code

The code for the PHP page begins with a test of both parameters that may have been passed: *deleteID* and *catID*. If *deleteID* is the ID number of exactly one record in *categories*, then *delete_category* is called to delete this category. (The test should ensure that no wild cards are smuggled in as *deleteID* so that more will be deleted than was intended.)

A similar test is carried out for *catID*. If this test is passed successfully, then the variable *validCatID* is set to *TRUE*.

```
// test whether deleteID refers to exactly one categories record
if($deleteID) {
  $result = mysql_query("SELECT catID FROM categories " .
                        "WHERE catID='$deleteID'");
  // delete category
  if(mysql_num_rows($result)==1)
    delete_category($deleteID);
}
// test whether catID refers to an existing record
if($catID) {
  $result =
    mysql_query("SELECT catID FROM categories WHERE catID='$catID'");
  if(mysql_num_rows($result))
    $validCatID=TRUE;
}
```

Display Hierarchical List of All Categories

If *catID* is invalid or was not even passed, then a hierarchical list of all categories is displayed. For indenting the list the HTML tag *<ul>* is used. For each category the contents of the variable *lastIndent* is compared to the value of *hierIndent* from the database. If the indentation depth has changed, then the corresponding number of *<ul>* or *</ul>* tags are output.

For each category, a link to the insertion of a new record (with *?catID=n*) or to the deletion of the category is displayed (with *?deleteID=n*). These links are assembled via the auxiliary function *build_href*:

```
if(!$validCatID) {
  echo "<h2>Choose category</h2>\n";
  echo "<p>Click to insert/delete categories.</p>\n";
  // query over all categories
  $result = mysql_query("SELECT catName, catID, hierIndent " .
                        "FROM categories ORDER BY hierNr");
  // evaluate query result
  echo "<p>\n";
```

```
$lastIndent=-1;
while($row=mysql_fetch_object($result)) {
  // <ul>'s for the next hierarchy level
  if($row->hierIndent > $lastIndent)
    echo "<ul>\n";
  // </ul>'s, to get out of the last valid hierarchy level
  if($row->hierIndent < $lastIndent)
    for($i=$row->hierIndent; $i<$lastIndent; $i++)
      echo "</ul>\n";
  $lastIndent = $row->hierIndent;
  // display category names as well as insert and delete links
  echo "<li>",
    htmlentities($row->catName), " (",
    build_href("categories.php", "catID=$row->catID", "insert"),
    ", ",
    build_href("categories.php", "deleteID=$row->catID",
               "delete"),
    ")",
    "</li>\n";
}
// close all <ul>'s still open
for($i=-1; $i<=lastIndent; $i++)
  echo "</ul>\n";
echo "</p>\n";
}
```

Inserting New Categories

The *else* that begins here runs almost to the end of the PHP file. It is not the entire category list that should be displayed, but only one particular category into which new subcategories may be added (see Figure 12-12).

However, this code segment is executed only if form results are to be evaluated. To accomplish this, the variable *subcategories* is decomposed into an array containing all the new categories to be inserted. They are inserted into the database with *insert_new_category*. The variable *count* keeps track of how often this is successfully accomplished. A brief message reports on the result:

```
else {// to if(!validCatID)
  echo "<h2>Insert new categories</h2>\n";
  // evaluate form data (insert new subcategories)
  if($subcategories){
    $subcatarray = explode(";", $subcategories);
    $count=0;
    while($i = each($subcatarray)) {
      $newcatname = trim($i[1]);
      $count += insert_new_category($catID, $newcatname);
    }
    if($count)
      echo "<p>$count new categories have been inserted ",
        "into the categories table.\n";
  }
```

Representing a Branch of the Hierarchical Tree

The following lines of code have the purpose of displaying the category described by *catID* together with its super- and subcategories (see Figure 12-12). The purpose, then, is to display a small segment of the entire hierarchical tree.

In the first step, three arrays (*catNames, catIDs, parentCatIDs*) are constructed, which contain the higher levels of the hierarchy (*catNames[0]*, i.e., *all books*; *catNames[1]*, e.g., *Computer books*; *catNames[2]*, e.g., *Programming*, etc.); see Figure 12-12. The arrays are then filled with the data of the current record described by *catID*. Thereafter, a loop follows *parentCatIDs* back to the root of the hierarchy.

After these data have been determined, they are displayed in a loop (indented as required by means of <*ul*>). The current category is treated in the same manner, except that it is displayed in boldface type:

```
// determine data of the current category (catID)
$result =
  mysql_query("SELECT * FROM categories WHERE catID='$catID'");
$row = mysql_fetch_object($result);
$maxIndent = $row->hierIndent;
$catNames[$maxIndent] = $row->catName;
$catIDs[$maxIndent] = $row->catID;
$parentCatIDs[$maxIndent] = $row->parentCatID;

// loop to determine the data of the next higher category
for($i=$maxIndent-1; $i>=0; $i--) {
  $result = mysql_query("SELECT * FROM categories " .
                    "WHERE catID='" . $parentCatIDs[$i+1] . "'");
  $row = mysql_fetch_object($result);
  $catNames[$i] = $row->catName;
  $catIDs[$i] = $row->catID;
  $parentCatIDs[$i] = $row->parentCatID;
}

// display next higher category
for($i=0; $i<$maxIndent; $i++) {
  echo "<ul><li>", htmlentities($catNames[$i]), "</li>\n";
}
// display current category
echo "<ul><li><b>", htmlentities($catNames[$maxIndent]),
  "</b></li>\n";
```

To give a view as to which subcategories already exist, all existing subcategories of *catID* are determined and displayed. The categories are supplied with a DELETE link, so that incorrectly inserted categories can be deleted:

```
// display all subcategories of catID together with a delete link
$result =
  mysql_query("SELECT catName, catID FROM categories " .
                "WHERE parentCatID='$catID' ORDER BY catName");
```

```
      echo "<ul>\n";
      if(mysql_num_rows($result)) {
        while($row=mysql_fetch_object($result)) {
          echo "<li>", htmlentities($row->catName), " (",
            build_href("categories.php",
                       "catID=$catID&deleteID=$row->catID",
                       "delete") .
            ")</li>\n";
      }}
      else {
        echo "(No subcategories yet.)\n";
      }
      echo "</ul>\n";
```

Finally, all open *<ul>* tags must be closed:

```
// close hierarchical category list
for($i=0; $i<=$maxIndent; $i++) {
  echo "</ul>\n";
}
```

Input Form for New Categories

The input form for new categories consists merely of a text field (*subcategories*) and a "submit" button. The *action* link refers again to categories.php, where additionally, the current *catID* number is transmitted. This has the effect that as a result of the input, the reduced hierarchical tree and the form are shown. Thus the result of the input is immediately visible (in the form of additional subcategories). Moreover, additional categories can be immediately input:

```
  echo '<form method="post" action="categories.php?catID="',
    $catID, '">', "\n";
  echo "<p>Insert new sub-categories to ",
    "<b>$catNames[$maxIndent]</b>. <br />You may add several ",
    "subcategories at once. <br />Use ; to seperate ",
    "your entries.</p>\n";
  echo '<p><input name="subcategories" size="60" maxlength="80" />',
    "\n";
  echo '<input type="submit" value="OK" name="submitbutton" /></p>',
    "\n";
echo "</form>\n";
```

The PHP code ends with a link that leads back to the complete category list. The closing curly brace ends the long *else* block following *if(!validCatID)*:

```
  // link back to complete category list
  echo "<p>Back to full ",
    build_href("./categories.php", "", "categories list") . ".\n";
}
```

Function to Save a New Category

The function *insert_new_category* adds a new category to the table *categories*. The ID number (*catID*) of the category to which the new category (*newcatName*) is to be subordinated must be passed as parameter.

The function assumes that *catID* is valid. With *newcatName*, a test is made as to whether the character string is empty or whether perhaps the new category already exists as a subcategory of *catID*. If either case obtains, the function is immediately terminated:

```
function insert_new_category($catID, $newcatName) {
  // $catID: category into which the new subcategory is to be inserted
  // $newcatName: name of the new subcategory

  // terminate if newcatName is empty
  if(!$newcatName) return(0);

  // test whether the category already exists
  $result = mysql_query("SELECT catID FROM categories " .
                "WHERE parentCatID=$catID " .
                " AND catName='$newcatName'");
  if(mysql_num_rows($result)) return(0);
  mysql_free_result($result);
```

Now comes the actualization of the insertion algorithm that was explained in detail in Chapter 5. Briefly, the position of the new category within the hierarchical category list is found (that is, the *hierNr* value for the new category).

Note that *LOCK TABLE categories WRITE* should be executed before *SELECT*, *INSERT*, and *UPDATE* commands. This ensures that during a change in the *categories* table, no other program can make changes to that table. (Of course, that is an extremely unlikely scenario in this example, but it is theoretically possible.) At the end of the algorithm, the blocking must be lifted with *UNLOCK TABLES*. The *LOCK/UNLOCK* commands have been commented out in the code, because many database users do not have the *lock table* privilege in MySQL by default. Change the code and experiment for yourself.

> **TIP** *If you are working with InnoDB tables, it is more efficient to execute the entire algorithm as a transaction, rather than using* LOCK/UNLOCK *commands. Instead of* LOCK, *execute* SET AUTOCOMMIT = 0 *and* BEGIN, *and instead of* UNLOCK, *execute* COMMIT *and* SET AUTOCOMMIT=1.

```
  // protect table categories against external changes
  // mysql_query_test("LOCK TABLE categories WRITE");

  // (1) get information on the higher-ranking category
  $result =
    mysql_query("SELECT * FROM categories WHERE catID='$catID'");
  $base=mysql_fetch_object($result);
  mysql_free_result($result);
```

```
// (2a) search for the category below $newcatName
$result =
  mysql_query("SELECT hierNr FROM categories " .
              "WHERE parentCatID='$base->catID' " .
              "" AND catName>'$newcatName' " .
              "ORDER BY catName LIMIT 1");
if(mysql_num_rows($result)) {
  $newhierNr = mysql_result($result, 0, 0);
  mysql_free_result($result);
}
// (2b) search for the start of the next category group
else {
  $result =
    mysql_query("SELECT hierNr FROM categories " .
                "WHERE hierNr>'$base->hierNr' " .
                " AND hierIndent<='$base->hierIndent' " .
                "ORDER BY hierNr LIMIT 1");
if(mysql_num_rows($result)) {
    $newhierNr = mysql_result($result, 0, 0);
    mysql_free_result($result);
  }
  // (2c) search for the maximal hierNr in the table
  else {
    $result =
      mysql_query("SELECT MAX(hierNr) FROM categories");
    $newhierNr = mysql_result($result, 0, 0)+1;
    mysql_free_result($result);
  }
}
```

Once *hierNr* has been determined, this value is increased by 1 for all existing records with the same or higher *hierNr*, so as to make room for the new record. Then the new record is inserted:

```
// (3) increase hierNr for all categories below $newcatName
mysql_query("UPDATE categories SET hierNr=hierNr+1 " .
            "WHERE hiernr>=$newhierNr");

// (4) insert new category
mysql_query("INSERT INTO categories " .
            " (catName, parentCatID, hierNr, hierIndent) " .
            "VALUES ('$newcatName', $catID, $newhierNr, " .
                ($base->hierIndent+1) . ")");

// remove the LOCK
// mysql_query_test("UNLOCK TABLES");
return(1); }
```

A Function to Delete an Existing Category

As parameter to the function *delete_category* the ID number of the category to be deleted is passed. Within the function it is determined whether there are any subcategories to this category. If that is the case, then *delete_category* is called recursively to delete these subcategories. During this process a running total of return values is calculated, where 1 indicates that the category was able to be deleted, and 0 that it could not be. This allows a simple determination to be made as to whether all the subcategories were deleted. If that is not the case, then the function is terminated:

```
function delete_category($catID) {
  // search for subcategories of catID
  // and delete them with recursive calls to delete_category
  $result =
    mysql_query("SELECT catID FROM categories " .
                "WHERE parentCatID='$catID'");
  $rows = mysql_num_rows($result);
  $deletedRows = 0;
  while($row=mysql_fetch_row($result)) {
    $deletedRows += delete_category($row[0]);
  }
  mysql_free_result($result);

  // if not all subcategories could be deleted,
  // then the category catID cannot be deleted
  if($deletedRows != $rows)
    return(0);
```

Then a test is made as to whether there are book titles that belong to the category that is to be deleted. In such a case, the category cannot be deleted. If there are such titles, an error message is output that gives the name of the category and the number of associated titles.

```
  // are there titles that belong to catID?
  $result = mysql_query("SELECT COUNT(titleID) FROM titles " .
                "WHERE catID='$catID'");
  // yes, the category may not be deleted;
  // display error message
  if($nrOfTitles = mysql_result($result, 0, 0)) {
    mysql_free_result($result);
    $result = mysql_query("SELECT catName FROM categories " .
                "WHERE catID='$catID'");
```

```
  $catName = mysql_result($result, 0, 0);
  mysql_free_result($result);
  echo "<br />Category <b>$catName</b> is used in $nrOfTitles ",
    "titles. You cannot delete it and its parents.\n";
  return(0);
}
```

Otherwise, there is nothing to stop the hand of destruction: The category can now be deleted.

```
  // delete category
  mysql_query("DELETE FROM categories WHERE catID='$catID'");
  return(1);
}
```

> **REMARK**   *Deleting categories can result in holes in the sequence of* hierNr *values in the* categories *table. Thus you may not assume that the difference of two* hierNr *values represents the number of categories of intermediate records.*

Ideas for Improvements and Extensions

The three PHP pages displayed do not, unfortunately, represent a complete user interface to the *mylibrary* database. The following list presents some of the most pressing improvements that might be made:

- Altering existing records (for example, to correct typographical errors in title, author, or publisher names; change the association title ↔ publisher or title ↔ category).

- Delete existing records (title, author, publisher, etc.), with queries that ensure that no empty cross references remain.

- Unification of duplicates (for example, if an author has been stored two or three times due to a typographical error).

- Management of the table *languages*.

None of these points represents a difficult problem, but the amount of programming required is rather large. To keep the code readable, the various auxiliary functions should be organized on a modular plan.

However, one may ask the question whether such an HTML-based user interface is worth the effort. If the user interface were to be developed with a freestanding programming language (Java, Visual Basic, Delphi, for example), then the amount of work would not be much greater, but one could achieve greater ease of use and perhaps even greater speed.

#### CHAPTER 13

PHP: Discussion Forum

THE EXAMPLE OF THIS SECTION shows how a discussion forum managed by its users can be realized with several PHP script files and the database *myforum* introduced in Chapter 5.

> **POINTER** *As with all the examples in this book, we are interested more in explicating programming techniques than in producing a polished application. If your ambitions range in the direction of creating a web discussion forum, it would be worthwhile looking into the numerous off-the-shelf solutions available. The two currently most popular PHP scripts for discussion forums (or "fora" for all you Latinate purists out there) can be found at the following addresses:*
>
> http://www.phorum.org/
> http://www.phpbb.com/

Chapter Overview

How to Run It

From the user's viewpoint, the portals leading to the discussion forum are opened by a login dialog (see Figure 13-1).

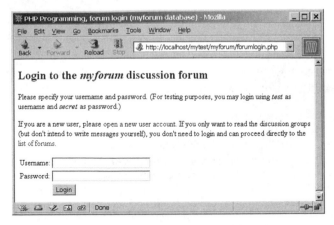

Figure 13-1. Login dialog for the myforum *discussion forum*

One need not log in if one wishes only to read the postings. For this purpose a direct link to all forums is offered. A login is, however, required for those wishing to post messages. But first it is necessary to establish a *myforum* account (see Figure 13-2).

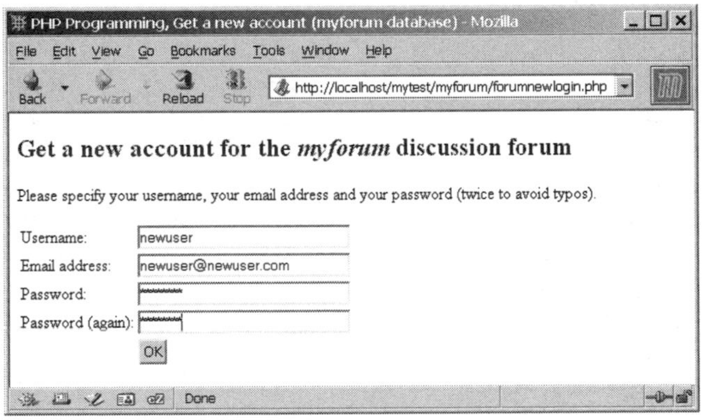

Figure 13-2. Establishing a new myforum *account*

(If you would like to try out the example on my web site, you can save yourself the trouble of establishing an account by logging in under the name *test* with the password *secret.*)

With or without registration you arrive at the page forumlist.php, in which all discussion forums are listed for your perusal (each with the language of the forum indicated). At the start of the page is displayed the user name of the current login (or *anonymous*). See Figure 13-3.

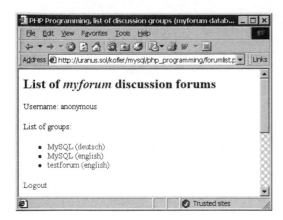

Figure 13-3. List of all discussion forums

On the page forumread.php (see Figure 13-4) the last fifty messages to have been posted are displayed. The most current discussion threads are displayed at the start of the page. Within the thread appears the place in the sequence in which each article was posted (oldest article first). To make clear which contributions belong to which threads, the background color changes for each thread. If there are more than fifty articles, then at the end of the page there appear links to the older contributions.

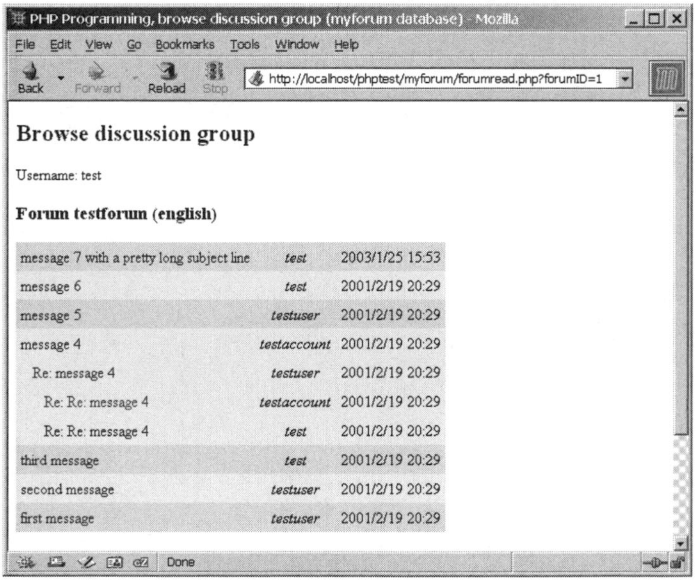

Figure 13-4. List of all postings to testforum

Individual messages are displayed by means of the script forummessage.php (see Figure 13-5). If there are several replies to a given message, then the entire thread (a list of all messages together with their texts) can be displayed on a single page with forumthread.php (see Figure 13-6).

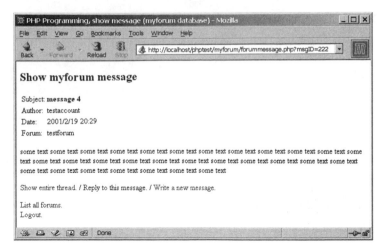

Figure 13-5. A single posting

Figure 13-6. An entire discussion thread

The script forumwrite.php (see Figure 13-7) assists in composing a new message or responding to an existing one.

Figure 13-7. Form for composing a message

Overview of the Program Code

Our example consists of the following files:

myforumconnect.inc.php	auxiliary functions (including database login)
myforumpassword.inc.php	login information and password
forumlogin.php	login to the forum
forumnewlogin.php	new registration
forumlist.php	display list of all discussion groups
forumread.php	display list of titles of all messages
forumthread.php	display discussion thread
forummessage.php	display discussion message
forumwrite.php	compose message
forumlogout.php	unregister

> **REMARK** *The example files assume at least PHP 4.1. A version of the entire example compatible with PHP 4.0 can be found at my web site (http://www.kofler.cc) among the PHP example files for the first edition of this book.*

The File myforumconnect.inc.php

The file myforumconnect.inc.php contains several auxiliary functions. The most important of these is *connect_to_myforum*, which establishes the connection to MySQL. These functions are nearly identical to those of mylibraryconnect.inc.php (see Chapter 12), and so we will not describe them here.

Managing a Session

> **POINTER**   *If you have never worked with PHP sessions, you should do some reading in this important area. Every book on PHP deals with this topic (in some, exhaustively to the point of exhaustion). The problem with many PHP books, however, is that they consider only PHP 4.0. Much has changed since then. Therefore, have a look at the official PHP documentation at the following address:*
>
> http://www.php.net/manual/en/ref.session.php

Passing information about who has registered between the script files is managed by means of a PHP session (variables *sesUserID* and *sesUserName*). Otherwise, the passing of information between the script files is carried out with URL parameters.

Since the required code for managing the session variables is in more or less the same form in all the script files, it is described here in one place. At the beginning of each script the function *session_start* is executed in order to activate the session support. Access to session variables is now accomplished through *$_SESSION['name']*. The following lines provide an example:

```
session_start();
if(empty($_SESSION['sesUserID'])) {
  $_SESSION['sesUserName'] = "anonymous";
}
```

With many web browsers there is a problem in connection with sessions: In the attempt to return to an already visited form using the BACK button, all input to the form is deleted. At times, this can increase the security of the application, but often, it is simply a pain in the neck for the user if there are corrections to be made in the previous input. If you want the BACK button to function as it should, then you should execute the following line immediately after *session_start*:

```
header("Cache-control: private"); // allow backspace in forms
```

Sessions Without Cookies

If the client permits cookies (that is, in the user's browser), then all of this happens automatically; that is, the content of the session variables continues to be available when a switch is made to a new page.

On the other hand, if cookies are not allowed, then a session identification number (SID) must be passed as part of the URL at each page change. If the PHP interpreter is appropriately compiled (option --enable-trans-sid) and configured (variable *session.use_trans_sid* in php.ini), then the SID will be automatically built into every URL. But do not rely on this! This automation is deactivated by default.

In order to ensure that management of the session functions dependably in all circumstances, the evaluation of the constant *SID* and a bit of hand operation are necessary. The constant *SID* contains a character string of the form *PHPSESSID=3ff5* . . . . This character string must be specified as a URL parameter at each change between PHP scripts. To avoid constant queries of the form *if(SID)* . . . , the two variables *sid1* and *sid2* are defined on the basis of *SID*.

```
if(SID) {
  $sid1 = "?" . SID;
  $sid2 = "&" . SID; }
```

In what follows, *sid1* (first URL parameter) or *sid2* (additional URL parameter) can simply be attached to URL character strings, for example, as follows:

```
// page change to forumlist.php
header("Location: ./forumlist.php$sid1");

// write link to page forumwrite.php in the HTML document
$query = "forumID=$row->forumID&msgID=$row->msgID" . $sid2;
echo "<p>",
  build_href("./forumwrite.php", $query, "Reply to this message"),
  ".</p>\n";
```

Registration (forumlogin.php)

The script forumlogin.php displays a simple form in which a login name and password can be given (see Figure 13-1). The evaluation of the form variables *formUser* and *formPassword* also takes place in this script:

```
<?php // php/myforum/forumlogin.php

// read in standard functions
include("myforumconnect.inc.php");

// Form variables
$formSubmit   = array_item($_POST, 'formSubmit');
$formPassword = array_item($_POST, 'formPassword');
$formUser     = array_item($_POST, 'formUser');

// ensure that special characters are marked by \
if(!get_magic_quotes_gpc()) {
  $formPassword = addslashes($formPassword);
  $formUser     = addslashes($formUser); }

// session management
session_start();
header("Cache-control: private"); // backspace in forms
$_SESSION['sesUserID']   = '';   // delete any existing
$_SESSION['sesUserName'] = '';   // data

// sid1/-2 help in generating URLs to other pages
// if the user prohibits cookies
if(SID) {
  $sid1 = "?" . SID;
  $sid2 = "&" . SID; }
```

```
else {
  $sid1=""; $sid2=""; }
// create connection to the database
$connID = connect_to_myforum();
```

If the *users* database contains the character string pair specified in the form (*username* and *password*), then the sessions variables *sesUserID* and *sesUserName* are initialized. Then the PHP function *header* is used to effect a change to the page forumlist.php. (In order for *header* to work, no HTML output can occur before this function. For this reason, the HTML header is output relatively late in forumlogin.php.)

```
// evaluate form data
if($formSubmit) {
  $result =
    mysql_query("SELECT userID, userName FROM users " .
                "WHERE userName = '$formUser' " .
                " AND password = PASSWORD('$formPassword')");
  // ok, user recognized
  if(mysql_num_rows($result)==1) {
    $_SESSION['sesUserID']   = mysql_result($result, 0, 0);
    $_SESSION['sesUserName'] = mysql_result($result, 0, 1);
    // change to page forumlist.php
    header("Location: ./forumlist.php$sid1");
    exit;
  }
}
?>
```

The remainder of the code serves to display the input form and some links and additional information:

```
<!DOCTYPE HTML PUBLIC "-//W3C//DTD HTML 4.0//EN">
<html><head>
  <meta http-equiv="Content-Type"
        content="text/html; charset=iso-8859-1" />
<title>PHP Programming, forum login (myforum database)</title>
</head><body>
<h2>Login to the <i>myforum</i> discussion forum</h2>
<?php

// error message if the login attempt fails
if($formSubmit and empty($userID))
  echo '<p><font color="#ff0000">Username or password ',
    "are invalid. Please try again.</font></p>\n";

?>

<p> ... some text ... </p>

<form method="post" action="forumlogin.php">
<p><table>
<tr><td>User name:</td>
    <td><input name="formUser" size="30" maxlength="30" /></td>
<tr><td>Password:</td>
```

```
    <td><input type="password" name="formPassword" size="30" maxlength="30" /></td>
<tr><td></td>
    <td><input type="submit" value="Login" name="formSubmit" /></td>
</table></p>
</form>

</body></html>
```

Defining a New User (forumnewlogin.php)

A new user for *myforum* can be defined in the form forumnewlogin.php (see
Figure 13-2). A user name, e-mail address, and (twice to avoid typos) password are
required:

```
<?php // php/myforum/forumnewlogin.php
// initialization code similar to that in forumlogin.php

// Form variables
$formSubmit    = array_item($_POST, 'formSubmit');
$formPassword1 = array_item($_POST, 'formPassword1');
$formPassword2 = array_item($_POST, 'formPassword2');
$formUser      = array_item($_POST, 'formUser');
$formEMail     = array_item($_POST, 'formEMail');

// no magic quotes
if(get_magic_quotes_gpc()) {
  $formPassword1 = stripslashes($formPassword1);
  $formPassword2 = stripslashes($formPassword2);
  $formUser      = stripslashes($formUser);
  $formEMail = stripslashes($formEMail); }
```

The actual program code begins with the evaluation of the form variables
formUser, *formEMail*, *formPassword1*, and *formPassword2*. The first thing to occur is
a check as to whether the name is already in use. If that is the case, then the variable
wrongName is set to 1 (for the purpose of a later error message to be displayed).
Additionally, a test is made as to whether an e-mail address was given (without
verifying its format) and whether the two passwords are identical:

```
// evaluate form variables
if($formSubmit=="OK") {
  $formUser = trim($formUser);
  $formEMail = trim($formEMail);
  $formPassword1 = trim($formPassword1);
  $formPassword2 = trim($formPassword2);
  // is the user name available?
  if($formUser) {
    $result =
      mysql_query("SELECT userID, userName FROM users " .
                  "WHERE userName = '" . addslashes($formUser) . "' ");
    if(mysql_num_rows($result)==1)
      $wrongName = 1; // name is in use
  }
```

475

```
else
  $wrongName = 1;// no name was given whatsoever
// was an e-mail address given?
if(!$formEMail)
  $wrongEMail=1;
// do the passwords agree?
if($formPassword1=="" or $formPassword1!=$formPassword2)
  $wrongPassword=1;
```

If no formal errors are detected, then the new user is stored in the *user* database with an *INSERT*. Then the session variables *sesUserID* and *sesUserName* are initialized and the page forumlist.php displayed:

```
// ok?
if(!($wrongName || $wrongPassword || $wrongEMail)) {
  // store user name and password, determine ID,
  mysql_query("INSERT INTO users (userName, email, password) " .
              "VALUES ('" . addslashes($formUser) . "', '" .
              addslashes($formEMail) . "', " .
              "   PASSWORD('" . addslashes($formPassword1) .
              "'))");
  $sesUserID = mysql_insert_id();
  $sesUserName = stripslashes($formUser);
  // page change to forumlist.php
  header("Location: ./forumlist.php$sid1");
  exit;
  }
}
?>
```

The remaining code serves to display the form and any error messages that might be required:

```
<!DOCTYPE HTML PUBLIC "-//W3C//DTD HTML 4.0//EN">
<html><head>
  <meta http-equiv="Content-Type"
        content="text/html; charset=iso-8859-1" />
<title>PHP Programming, Get a new account (myforum database)</title>
</head><body>
<h2>Get a new account for the <i>myforum</i> discussion forum</h2>

<p>Please specify your user name ...

<?php

// display error messages
if($wrongName) echo " ... ";
if($wrongEMail) echo " ... ";
if($wrongPassword) echo " ... ";

?>

<form method="post" action="forumnewlogin.php<?php echo $sid1;?>">
<p><table>
<tr><td>User name:</td>
```

```
    <td><input name="formUser" size="30" maxlength="30"
        value="<?php echo htmlspecialchars($formUser); ?>" /></td>
<tr><td>Email address:</td>
    <td><input name="formEMail" size="30" maxlength="30"
        value="<?php echo htmlspecialchars($formEMail); ?>" /></td>
<tr><td>Password: </td>
    <td><input type="password" name="formPassword1"
        size="30" maxlength="30"
        value="<?php echo htmlspecialchars($formPassword1); ?>" />
    </td>
<tr><td>Password (again): </td>
    <td><input type="password" name="formPassword2"
        size="30" maxlength="30"
        value="<?php echo htmlspecialchars($formPassword2); ?>" />
    </td>
<tr><td></td>
    <td><input type="submit" value="OK" name="formSubmit" /></td>
</table></p>
</form> </body></html>
```

Possibilities for Expansion

Verifying an e-mail address: The easiest improvement to implement is to send an initial access code to the specified e-mail address (optimally in the form of an HTTP link). You could use a random number, for example, that is generated at the time of registration and stored in the user table until the user first accesses the account.

Display List of All Discussion Groups (forumlist.php)

The script forumlist.php displays a list of all discussion groups defined in the table *forums* (see Figure 13-3). The list is determined by means of a simple *SELECT* instruction and represented in the form of links that refer to the script forumread.php:

```
<?php // php/myforum/forumlist.php

include("myforumconnect.inc.php");
session_start();
if(empty($_SESSION['sesUserID'])) {
  $_SESSION['sesUserName'] = "anonymous"; }
if(SID) { ... }   // code as in forumlogin.php
?>
<!DOCTYPE HTML PUBLIC "-//W3C//DTD HTML 4.0//EN">
<html><head>
  <meta http-equiv="Content-Type"
        content="text/html; charset=iso-8859-1" />
<title>PHP Programming, list of discussion groups
     (myforum database)</title>
</head><body>
<h2>List of <i>myforum</i> discussion forums</h2>
```

```php
<?php
echo "<p>Username: ", htmlentities($_SESSION['sesUserName']),
"</p>\n";

// display list of all discussion groups
echo "<p>List of groups:</p>\n";
echo "<ul>\n";
$result =
  mysql_query("SELECT forumID, forumName, language FROM forums " .
              "ORDER BY forumName, language ");
while($row=mysql_fetch_object($result)) {
  echo "<li>",
    build_href("forumread.php",
              "forumID=$row->forumID" . $sid2,
              "$row->forumName ($row ->language)"), "\n"; }
echo "</ul>\n";

// link to the logout script
echo "<p><a href=\"forumlogout.php$sid1\">Logout</a>\n";

?>

</body></html>
```

Message List of a Discussion Group (forumread.php)

From the viewpoint of database programming, the script forumread.php must be considered one of the most interesting modules of this example. Its task consists in displaying the fifty most recent messages of a discussion group (see Figure 13-4). If the discussion group contains more than that number of messages, then forumread.php enables the user to leaf pagewise through the messages.

Various Representations of Hierarchical Lists

The problem in representing the list of messages is that the pagewise division of the list results in the separation of discussion threads. (A recent message can arise as the reaction to a much older thread.)

To clarify the situation, we present Figure 13-8, which shows three discussion threads with seventeen messages altogether from users A through G. The threads are ordered chronologically (the newest thread first), and within the threads the messages are ordered hierarchically based on who was responding to whom.

Many discussion forums simply do not display the message hierarchy with the pagewise display of messages. The advantage of this is that such a solution is easy to implement, and the messages can be ordered according to their creation dates. However, the flow of the discussion is lost (see Figure 13-9 with the ten most current messages from Figure 13-8 ordered by creation time).

In Figure 13-10, on the other hand, an attempt is made to retain the hierarchy. In the most current thread this effort has brought success. In the two older threads the messages are properly indented, but the flow of the discussion is incomplete due to missing messages. The order of messages still corresponds to the thread structure, but the result is confusing.

Thread 3	G	*18.1.2003 21:00*
Re: Thread 3	B	*19.1.2003 15:30*
Re: Re: Thread 3	A	*19.1.2003 16:45*
Re: Re: Thread 3	C	*19.1.2003 17:30*
Re: Thread 3	E	*19.1.2003 19:00*
Thread 2	E	*17.1.2003 18:00*
Re: Thread 2	A	*18.1.2003 10:45*
Re: Re: Thread 2	B	*18.1.2003 10:55*
Re: Re: Re: Thread 2	F	*20.1.2003 22:05*
Re: Thread 2	C	*18.1.2003 19:00*
Thread 1	A	*17.1.2003 12:00*
Re: Thread 1	B	*17.1.2003 18:30*
Re: Re: Thread 1	A	*17.1.2003 19:45*
Re: Re: Thread 1	C	*19.1.2003 10:30*
Re: Thread 1	D	*18.1.2003 3:45*
Re: Re: Thread 1	A	*18.1.2003 9:45*
Re: Re: Re: Thread 1	D	*18.1.2003 22:05*

Figure 13-8. Hierarchical representation of three threads (ordered by flow of the discussion)

Re: Re: Re: Thread 2	F	*20.1.2003 22:05*
Re: Thread 3	E	*19.1.2003 19:00*
Re: Re: Thread 3	C	*19.1.2003 17:30*
Re: Re: Thread 3	A	*19.1.2003 16:45*
Re: Thread 3	B	*19.1.2003 15:30*
Re: Re: Thread 1	C	*19.1.2003 10:30*
Re: Re: Re: Thread 1	D	*18.1.2003 22:05*
Thread 3	G	*18.1.2003 21:00*
Re: Thread 2	C	*18.1.2003 19:00*
Re: Re: Thread 2	B	*18.1.2003 10:55*

Figure 13-9. Flat representation of the ten most recent messages from Figure 13-8 (ordered by time of creation)

Nonetheless, we have chosen this solution for forumread.php, because it seemed a reasonable compromise. (The number of messages per page is 50, and this number can be reset if it is so desired. Of course, the larger this value, the less often will there be dangling threads.) For threads whose starting message cannot be completely displayed on a page, the link *(show entire thread)* is displayed, which leads to the script forumthread.php. There the entire thread is displayed regardless of its length.

Thread 3	G	18.1.2003 21:00
Re: Thread 3	B	19.1.2003 15:30
Re: Re: Thread 3	A	19.1.2003 16:45
Re: Re: Thread 3	C	19.1.2003 17:30
Re: Thread 3	E	19.1.2003 19:00
(show entire thread)		
Re: Re: Thread 2	B	18.1.2003 10:55
Re: Re: Re: Thread 2	F	20.1.2003 22:05
Re: Thread 2	C	18.1.2003 19:00
(show entire thread)		
Re: Re: Thread 1	C	19.1.2003 10:30
Re: Re: Re: Thread 1	D	18.1.2003 22:05

Figure 13-10. Hierarchical representation of the most recent ten messages (ordered according to the discussion flow)

> **REMARK**   *Some discussion forums offer the possibility of expanding and contracting threads dynamically. This would be the most elegant solution, of course. However, in practice, the entire page must be reloaded every time the level of the representation is changed, which leads to annoying delays.*
>
> *Another solution consists in displaying on a page only the title of the first message, as a thread overview, so to speak. Only when the thread title is clicked on does a list appear with all the messages in this thread. I have chosen this method for the discussion forum on my web site* www.kofler.cc. *This variant is easy to read, but at first glance, it is difficult to see which messages arrived most recently and which threads are likely to be of interest.*
>
> *There is probably no truly perfect solution for HTML-based discussion forums. Forums that are very active are better off being organized as news groups, for which there are programs for reading threads.*

Program Structure

URL Variables

Two URL variables can be passed to forumread.php:

- *forumID* determines the forum whose messages are to be displayed.

- *page* specifies the page that is to be displayed.

Program Code

The program code begins with the by now well-known initialization instructions. If *forumID* is empty, the script is terminated, and instead, forumlist.php is displayed:

```php
<?php // php/myforum/\{forumread.php}

// read in standard functions,
include("myforumconnect.inc.php");

// read URL variables
$forumID = array_item($_REQUEST, 'forumID');
$page    = array_item($_REQUEST, 'page');

// session management
session_start();
if(empty($_SESSION['sesUserID'])) {
  $_SESSION['sesUserName'] = "anonymous"; }
if(SID) { ... }    // Code wie in forumlogin.php
if(empty($forumID)) {
  header("Location: forumlist.php$sid1");
  exit; }

?>
```

Validating ForumID

The following lines contain the HTML header. Then a *SELECT* query checks whether *forumID* refers to an existing discussion forum. In the *SELECT* query, *LIMIT* is used to ensure that no wild cards are passed in *forumID*. If *forumID* is valid, then the name of the forum is displayed:

```php
<!DOCTYPE HTML PUBLIC "-//W3C//DTD HTML 4.0//EN">
<html><head>
  <meta http-equiv="Content-Type"
        content="text/html; charset=iso-8859-1" />
<title>PHP Programming, browse discussion group (myforum database)</title>
</head><body>
<h2>Browse discussion group</h2>

<?php
echo "<p>Username: ", htmlentities($_SESSION['sesUserName']), "</p>\n";

// links forumID to a discussion group
$forumID = trim($forumID);
$result = mysql_query("SELECT forumName, language FROM forums " .
                      "WHERE forumID='$forumID' LIMIT 2");
if(!$result or mysql_num_rows($result)!=1) {
  echo '<p><font color="#ff0000">ID number of forum seems ',
    "to be invalid.</font> Please choose a forum in the ",
    "<a href=\"forumlist.php$sid1\">forum list</a>.</p>\n";
  echo "</body></html>\n";
  exit;
}

// display name of the forum
$row = mysql_fetch_object($result);
echo "<h3>Forum ", htmlentities($row->forumName),
  " (", htmlentities($row->language),  ")</h3>\n";
mysql_free_result($result);
```

Determining the Message Text

The page size is determined by the variable with the unsurprising name *pagesize*. If a valid page number was not specified, then the page number is set to 1:

```
$pagesize = 50;
if(!$page or !(is_numeric($page)) or $page<0 or $page>100)
  $page=1;
```

In the following, the list of message titles to be displayed is determined. To effect this, first the temporary table *tmpMsgIDs* with the *msgID* numbers of the desired page is generated. The variable *moremessages* is later evaluated to build into the HTML page a link to the next page with additional messages:

```
mysql_query("DROP TABLE IF EXISTS tmpMsgIDs");
mysql_query("CREATE TEMPORARY TABLE tmpMsgIDs TYPE = HEAP " .
            "SELECT msgID FROM messages " .
            "WHERE forumID = $forumID " .
            "ORDER BY timest DESC " .
            "LIMIT " . ($pagesize*($page-1)) . ", " . ($pagesize+1));
if(mysql_affected_rows() > $pagesize)
$moremessages=1;
```

In a second query, the data *msgID*, *subject*, *level*, *rootID*, *timest*, and *username* are determined for all messages contained in *tmpMsgIDs*. What is rather unconventional is the sorting of the messages: With *ORDER BY LEFT(orderstr, 4) DESC* we achieve that the creation time of the thread is used as the first sort criterion. New threads are displayed at the head of the list. As a second sort criterion, *orderstr* is used. This results in the messages being sorted hierarchically based on the flow of the discussion (see also Chapter 5, where the design of the *myforum* database is discussed):

```
$result =
  mysql_query("SELECT messages.msgID, subject, level, rootID, " .
              " DATE_FORMAT(timest, '%Y/%c/%e %k:%i') AS timest, " .
              " username " .
              "FROM messages, users, tmpMsgIDs " .
              "WHERE messages.msgID = tmpMsgIDs.msgID " .
              " AND messages.userID = users.userID " .
              "ORDER BY LEFT(orderstr, 4) DESC, orderstr");
// delete temporary table
mysql_query("DROP TABLE tmpMsgIDs");
```

Display Message List

The following loop displays the results of the above query. Each message is represented as an HTML link on the page forummessage.php. If the first message of the thread cannot be displayed, then instead, a link to forumthread.php is inserted, so that the entire thread can be displayed. This special case is shown in Figure 13-11 (*message 4*).

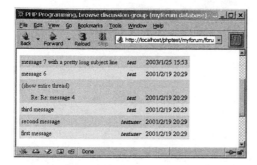

Figure 13-11. Representation of messages via forumread.php

The threads are indicated alternately with two different shades of gray, so that it is immediately clear which message belongs to which thread. For this, the variable *threadcounter* in increased by 1 at the start of each new thread. According to whether *threadcounter* is even or odd (test using the modulo operator %), the variable *color* is initialized with a lighter or darker shade of gray:

```php
}// display list with subject text, author name, and date
$oldthreadID = 0;
$threadCounter = 0;
if(mysql_num_rows($result)) {
  echo '<table border="0" cellpadding="5" cellspacing="0">', "\n";
while($row=mysql_fetch_object($result)) {

  // change background for a new thread
  if($row->rootID!=$oldthreadID) $threadCounter++;
  if($threadCounter % 2)
    $color = '"#eeeeee"';
  else
    $color = '"#dddddd"';

  // display link to entire thread if there are no messages
  if($row->rootID!=0 and $row->rootID!=$oldthreadID) {
    $query = "rootID=$row->rootID" . $sid2;
    echo "<tr bgcolor=$color><td>",
      build_href("forumthread.php", $query, "(show entire thread)"),
      "</td><td></td><td></td>\n";
  }

  // display subject, name, and date
  $query = "msgID=$row->msgID" . $sid2;
  $shortSubj = substr($row->subject, 0, 55);
  if(strlen($row->subject)>55)
    $shortSubj .= " ... ";
  echo "<tr bgcolor=$color><td>",
    $row->level ?
      str_repeat("   ", $row->level) : "",
    build_href("forummessage.php", $query, $shortSubj), "</td>",
    "<td align=\"center\"><i>", htmlentities($row->username),
    "</i>", "</td>",
    "<td align=\"right\"> $row->timest </td>\n";
```

```
      // update oldthreadID (to recognize new threads)
      if($row->rootID==0)
        $oldthreadID=$row->msgID;
      else
        $oldthreadID=$row->rootID;
    }
    echo "</table>\n";
}
```

Links to Other Pages

The program code ends with the output of links to later and earlier messages and to the form for input of a new message:

```
echo "<p><hr />\n";

// Are there new mesages?
if($page>1) {
  $query = "forumID=$forumID&page=" . ($page-1) . $sid2;
  echo build_href("forumread.php", $query, "Show newer messages.");
  if($moremessages) echo " / ";
}
// Are there older messages?
if($moremessages) {
  $query = "forumID=$forumID&page=" . ($page+1) . $sid2;
  echo build_href("forumread.php", $query, "Show older messages.");
}
echo "</p>\n";

// link to write a new message
if($page>1 or $moremessages)
  echo " / ";
$query = "forumID=$forumID" . $sid2;
echo build_href("forumwrite.php", $query, "Write a new message"),
  ".\n";

// links to the list of all forums
echo "<p>", build_href("forumlist.php", SID, "List of all forums"), ".</p>\n"; ?>

</body></html>
```

Representation of Message Text (forummessage.php)

In forumread.php the title of each message is linked to forummessage.php. This script displays not only the message text, but also links for creating a reply and for the display of the complete thread (see Figure 13-5). The message to be displayed is passed to the script via the URL variable *msgID*.

Once again, the program code begins with our tried and true initialization. If *msgID* is empty, then the script is terminated, and instead, forumlist.php is displayed:

```
<?php // php/myforum/forummessage.php

// read URL variable
$msgID = array_item($_REQUEST, 'msgID');

// the rest of the initialization is shown in the other
// forum examples
// if $msgID empty, display forumlist.php
if(empty($msgID)) {
  header("Location: ./forumlist.php$sid1");
exit; }

?>

<!DOCTYPE HTML PUBLIC "-//W3C//DTD HTML 4.0//EN">
<html><head>
  <meta http-equiv="Content-Type"
        content="text/html; charset=iso-8859-1" />
<title>PHP Programming, show message (myforum database)</title>
</head><body>
<h2>Show myforum message</h2>
```

The heart of the code begins with a test as to whether *msgID* actually refers to a message. If the *SELECT* is successful, then all the data are retrieved that will need to be displayed (*subject, msgText,* etc.):

```
<?php
$msgID = trim($msgID);
$result =
  mysql_query("SELECT msgID, rootID, subject, msgText, " .
                " username, forumName, messages.forumID, " .
                " DATE_FORMAT(timest, '%Y/%c/%e %k:%i') AS timest " .
                "FROM messages, users, forums " .
                "WHERE msgID='$msgID' " .
                " AND messages.userID = users.userID " .
                " AND messages.forumID = forums.forumID " .
                "LIMIT 2");
if(!$result or mysql_num_rows($result)!=1) {
  echo '<p><font color="#ff0000">ID number of message seems ',
    "to be invalid.</font> Please choose a forum in the ",
    "<a href=\"forumlist.php$sid1\">forum list</a>.</p>\n";
  show_copyright();
  echo "</body></html>\n";
  exit;
}
```

If all goes well, then first the message header (author, date, etc.) is displayed as a table, followed by the message itself. Please note in particular how the PHP function *nl2br* transforms line breaks in the message text into HTML line breaks and how *str_replace* replaces sequences of blank characters by nonbreaking HTML spaces with the code * * (important for the representation of indented program code!):

```
// show message
$fnt1s = '<font color="#b02020">';   // font 1 start
$fnt1e = '</font>';                   // font 1 end
$fnt2s = '<font color="#303030">';   // font 2 start
$fnt2e = '</font>';                   // font 2 end
$row = mysql_fetch_object($result);
echo "<table>\n";
echo "<tr><td>$fnt1s Subject:$fnt1e</td><td><b>", $fnt2s,
  htmlentities($row->subject), $fnt2e, "</td></b>\n";
echo "<tr><td>$fnt1s Author:$fnt1e</td><td>", $fnt2s,
  htmlentities($row->username), $fnt2e, "</td>\n";
echo "<tr><td>$fnt1s Date:$fnt1e</td><td>",
  "$fnt2s$row->timest$fnt2e</td>\n";
echo "<tr><td>$fnt1s Forum:$fnt1e</td><td>", $fnt2s,
  htmlentities($row->forumName), $fnt2e, "</td>\n"; echo "</table>\n";
$msg = nl2br(htmlentities($row->msgText));
$msg = str_replace(" ", "  ", $msg);
echo "<p>$msg</p>\n";
```

Links to forumthread.php and forumwrite.php are displayed at the bottom of the page:

```
// link to forumthread.php (display entire thread)
if($row->rootID)
  $query = "rootID=$row->rootID" . $sid2;
else
  $query = "rootID=$row->msgID" . $sid2;
echo "<p>",
  build_href("./forumthread.php", $query, "Show entire thread"),
  ".\n";
// link to forumwrite.php (reply to message)
$query = "forumID=$row->forumID&msgID=$row->msgID" . $sid2;
echo " / ",
  build_href("./forumwrite.php", $query, "Reply to this message"),
  ".\n";
// link to forumwrite.php (compose new message)
$query = "forumID=$row->forumID" .$sid2;
echo " / ",
  build_href("./forumwrite.php", $query, "Write a new message"),
  ".</p>\n";
?>
</body></html>
```

Displaying a Thread (forumthread.php)

The script forumthread.php is to some extent a combination of forumread.php and forummessage.php: With it, all messages of a thread—first the titles and then the actual text—are displayed on a single HTML page. This makes it possible to read the entire thread without having to jump back and forth between pages.

The URL variable *rootID* is passed to the script. After a brief test as to whether this variable contains reasonable data, a *SELECT* query is employed to read all the messages of the thread:

```php
<?php // php/myforum/forumthread.php
  . . .
$result =
  mysql_query("SELECT messages.msgID, subject, msgText, " .
              " level, rootID, username, forumName, " .
              " DATE_FORMAT(timest, '%Y/%c/%e %k:%i') AS timest " .
              "FROM messages, users, forums " .
              "WHERE (messages.rootID = '$rootID' " .
              " OR messages.msgID = '$rootID') " .
              " AND messages.userID = users.userID " .
              " AND messages.forumID = forums.forumID " .
              "ORDER BY orderstr");
  . . .
```

Otherwise, the script contains no code that is not similar to code that we have already described elsewhere. Therefore, we shall not include it here.

Contributing to a Discussion (forumwrite.php)

The script forumwrite.php enables the user to compose a new message in a discussion group or to reply to an existing message (see Figure 13-7). The program code is responsible both for the display of the form and for the evaluation of the form data.

Program Structure

Variables

The script expects two URL variables as parameters:

- *forumID* contains the ID number of the discussion forum.

- *msgID* contains the ID number of the message that is to be replied to. If *msgID* is absent, the script assumes that a new message is being composed (that is, a new thread is to be created).

The form data are read from the following variables:

- *formForumID* and *formMsgID* contain the ID numbers of the forum and the message that is to be replied to. (Both variables are represented in the form with *<input type="hidden" . . . >*.)

- *formSubject* contains the title of the message.

- *formText* contains the message text.

Initialization

The code begins as usual with the initialization of the passed variables:

```php
<?php // php/myforum/forumwrite.php
include("myforumconnect.inc.php");

// URL variables:  forumID, msgID (optional)
// form variables: formForumID, formMsgID, formText, formSubject, formSubmit
$forumID     = array_item($_REQUEST, 'forumID');
$msgID       = array_item($_REQUEST, 'msgID');
$formSubmit  = array_item($_POST,    'formSubmit');
$formForumID = array_item($_POST,    'formForumID');
$formMsgID   = array_item($_POST,    'formMsgID');
$formText    = array_item($_POST,    'formText');
$formSubject = array_item($_POST,    'formSubject');

// remove magic quotes \ from form variables
if(get_magic_quotes_gpc()) {
  $formText    = stripslashes($formText);
  $formSubject = stripslashes($formSubject); }

// session management
session_start();
header("Cache-control: private"); // \ in forms
$sesUserID   = array_item($_SESSION, 'sesUserID');
$sesUserName = array_item($_SESSION, 'sesUserName');
if(SID) { ... } // as in forumlogin.php
```

Storing a Message (insert_new_message)

In order to store the new message in the *messages* table, the following parameters are passed to the function *insert_new_message*: the ID number of the original message (or 0), the ID number of the forum, the ID number of the user, the message header, and the actual message text.

If 0 was not passed in *parentID*, then the function first returns information about the original message, which it stores in the variables *orderstr*, *level*, and *rootID*. Of particular interest is *orderstr*, which with the help of the PHP function *bin2hex* is transformed into hexadecimal format:

```php
// auxiliary function for storing a message
function insert_new_message($parentID, $forumID, $userID,
                    $msgSubject, $msgText) {
  if($parentID) {
    $result = mysql_query("SELECT * FROM messages WHERE msgID=$parentID");
    $row = mysql_fetch_object($result);
    $level = $row->level+1;
    $orderstr = bin2hex($row->orderstr);
    $rootID = $row->rootID;
    if(!$rootID) // if rootID=0, use msgID as rootID for new message
      $rootID = $row->msgID;
  }
```

```
else {
  $level=0; // new message: level=rootID=parentID=0
  $rootID=0;
  $parentID=0;
}
```

If the maximal hierarchical level within a thread has not been reached, then the character string *orderstr* is now extended by the hexadecimal code of the current timestamp value:

```
// create orderstr character string (append hex code of the current timestamp);
maximum level = 31
if($level<=31) {
  $tmp = dechex(time());
  if(strlen($tmp)<8)
    $tmp = str_repeat(" ", 8-strlen($tmp));
  $orderstr = "0x" . $orderstr . $tmp;
}
else {
  $level=31;
  $orderstr = "0x" . $orderstr; }
```

The data, after having been thus prepared, must now be stored:

```
mysql_query("INSERT INTO messages (forumID, parentID, rootID, " .
            "userID, subject, msgText, level, orderstr) " .
            "VALUES($forumID, $parentID, $rootID, $userID, " .
            " '" . addslashes($msgSubject) . "', " .
            " '" . addslashes($msgText) . "', " .
            " $level, $orderstr)");
}
```

Calling `insert_new_message`

When the script for evaluating form data is called, first a test is made as to whether *formMsgID* actually refers to an existing message. If that is the case, then the message is stored with the function *insert_new_message*, which was described above. Then a shift to page forumread.php is carried out, where the new message is to be displayed.

```
if($formSubmit=="OK" and $formSubject
   and $formText and $formForumID
   and $sesUserID) {
// is formMsgID (if specified) a valid ID number?
$invalidMsgID=0;
if($formMsgID) {
  $result = mysql_query("SELECT msgID FROM messages" .
                        "WHERE msgID = '$formMsgID' " .
                        "LIMIT 2");
  if(!$result or mysql_num_rows($result)!=1)
    $invalidMsgID=1;
}
```

```
  // store message
  if(!$invalidMsgID)
    insert_new_message($formMsgID, $formForumID, $sesUserID,
                       trim(stripslashes($formSubject)),
                       trim(stripslashes($formText)));
  // display new message in forumread.php
  header("Location: ./forumread.php?forumID=$formForumID$sid2");
  exit;
}
?>
```

Displaying the Form

The remaining code is responsible for displaying the form. First, however, some tests
are necessary: Does *sesUserID* contain an ID number? If not, the user is taken to the
login form.

Is *msgID* correct? If so, then the subject and text of the message for which an
answer is to be written are determined. (The message text is displayed before the
input form so that the author of the new message can refer to it and perhaps copy
and insert parts of it. If everything is all right to this point, the query results are stored
temporarily so that later, the form controls can be initialized.

Is *forumID* correct? If not, then an error message is displayed:

```
<!DOCTYPE HTML PUBLIC "-//W3C//DTD HTML 4.0//EN">
<html><head>
  <meta http-equiv="Content-Type"
        content="text/html; charset=iso-8859-1" />
<title>PHP Programming, new message (myforum database)</title>
</head><body>
<h2>myforum: New message</h2>

<?php

// does sesUserID contain a value?
if(empty($sesUserID)) ... display error message --> forumlogin.php
// copy form variables in forumID and msgID
if($formForumID) {
  $forumID = $formForumID;
  $msgID = $formMsgID;
}

// determine original message
if($msgID) {
  $result =
    mysql_query("SELECT msgID, msgText, subject, level, rootID, " .
                " DATE_FORMAT(timest,'%Y/%c/%e %k:%i') AS timest," .
                " forumID, username " .
                "FROM messages, users " .
                "WHERE msgID = '$msgID' " .
                " AND messages.userID = users.userID " .
                "LIMIT 2");
```

```
  // was msgID invalid?
  if(!$result or mysql_num_rows($result)!=1) {
    .. display error message, exit
  }
  // store query result
  $row = mysql_fetch_object($result);
  $forumID = $row->forumID;
  $oldMsg = $row->msgText;
  $oldSubject = $row->subject;
  $oldLevel = $row->level;
  $oldRoot = $row->rootID;
  $oldOrderstr = $row->orderstr;
  $oldAuthor = $row->username;
  $oldDate = $row->timest;
}
// determine name of the forum
$result = mysql_query("SELECT forumID, forumName FROM forums " .
                      "WHERE forumID = '$forumID' " .
                      "LIMIT 2");
// was forumID invalid?
if(!$result or mysql_num_rows($result)!=1) {
  ... display error message, exit
}
$forumID = mysql_result($result, 0, 0);
$forumName = mysql_result($result, 0, 1);
```

With this, all data are obtained for displaying the original message and then display the form:

```
// form header
if($msgID) {
  $fntBlue = '<font color="#0000ff">';
  echo "<p>$fntBlue", "Reply to message <i>",
    htmlentities($oldSubject), "</i></font></p>\n";
  echo "<p>$fntBlue", "Original message text:</font></p>\n";
  echo "<p>$fntBlue<i>",
    str_replace(" ", "  ", nl2br(htmlentities($oldMsg))),
    "</i></font></p>\n";
}
else
  echo "<p>New message for forum <i>", htmlentities($forumName),
"</i></p>\n";

// auxiliary variables for displaying the form
$actionscript = "forumwrite.php$sid1";

// message title
$newsubject = "";
if($formSubmit)
  $newsubject = htmlentities(stripslashes($formSubject));
```

```
elseif($msgID) {
  $newsubject = "Re: " . $oldSubject;
  if(strlen($newsubject)>78)
    $newsubject = substr($newsubject, 0, 78);
}
// message text
$newtext="";
if($formSubmit)
  $newtext = $formText;

// display form
?>
<form method="post" action="<?php echo $actionscript;?>">
<table>
<tr><td>Author:</td>
    <td> <?php echo htmlentities($sesUserName); ?></td>
<tr><td>Subject:</td>
    <td> <input name="formSubject" size="60" maxlength="78"
         value="<?php echo htmlspecialchars($newsubject); ?>" /></td>
<tr><td>Message:</td>
    <td><textarea name="formText" rows="12" cols="50"><?php
        echo htmlspecialchars($newtext); ?></textarea></td>
<tr><td></td>
    <td><input type="submit" value="OK" name="formSubmit" /></td>
<input type="hidden" name="formForumID"
       value="<?php echo $forumID;?>" />
<input type="hidden" name="formMsgID" value="<?php echo $msgID;?>" />
</table></form> </body></html>
```

Leaving the Forum (forumlogout.php)

The logout script has the sole task of deleting the session variables. Then the login page forumlogin.php is again displayed:

```
session_start();
unset($_SESSION['sesUserID']);
unset($_SESSION['$sesUserName']);
header("Location: ./forumlogin.php");
exit; ?>
```

Possibilities for Extension

In addition to the suggestions for detailed improvements and extensions mentioned as the individual script files were presented, there are, needless to say, a number of major features that could be added or improved:

- **Administrative tasks:** For the administrator of the forum there should be the simple option of generating new discussion groups or terminating existing ones, deleting individual messages, and so on. At present this is possible only via directly accessing the *myforum* database.

- **Moderated forum:** Experience has shown that open discussion groups with a great deal of activity tend to have a small number of relevant messages littered with a large quantity of garbage. A moderated forum can rescue the situation: Every message must be approved by the moderator before it is posted. Moderation requires a password-protected site, over which the moderator can publish or delete new contributions.

- **E-mail notification of replies:** An individual who posts a message to a forum is usually interested in the reactions to that posting. Instead of having to check daily (or even more often for the nervous Nellies and Nelsons among us) to see whether any responses have been posted, the poster of the original message might enjoy receiving notification by e-mail of any replies. This would enable the poster to fire off a rapid (but not, please, rabid) reply.

- **Multilingual guidance:** In the *forums* table a language is specified for each discussion group. However, all the instructions for all of the forums are in English. Wouldn't it be nice if all of the links, form titles, and so on, appeared in the language of the discussion?

- **Search option:** Currently, the forum offers no possibility of searching. It would be desirable to have a key-word search (full-text search) either for *Subject* lines only or for the full text of the message, as well as a search for authors (for example, display all messages posted by a particular author).

- **Personalization:** In addition to the name of the user, other information could be stored, for example, a default discussion group, desired parameters (such as the number of messages to be displayed per page), and so on. It would be more complicated to implement an option whereby messages that had been read could be marked as such or marked not to be displayed again.

TIP *Let us end by repeating the little tip with which we began this chapter: There is plenty to invent besides the wheel, which has already been invented, and reinvented. If you would like to practice your PHP and MySQL, then implementing all of these features would be a good exercise. However, if your goal is to create a stable and reliable discussion forum as quickly as possible, then your time might be better spent in seeking out tested solutions:*

```
http://www.phorum.org/
http://www.phpbb.com
```

Perl

FOR MANY YEARS, PERL HAS been the best-beloved scripting language in the Unix/Linux universe. Moreover, Perl continues to play an important role as a programming language for CGI scripts, by which dynamic web sites can be realized. This chapter gives a brief introduction to MySQL database access with Perl and shows, by means of a few examples, the large bandwidth of possible applications.

Chapter Overview

Programming Techniques

POINTER *This chapter assumes that Perl and the modules* DBI *and* DBD::mysql *are installed on your computer and that they are functioning properly. An introduction to the installation procedure can be found in Chapter 2.*

Further information on both Perl modules can be found in the official MySQL documentation (the chapter "MySQL APIs"). Furthermore, the command perldoc *nets you extensive on-line help:*

```
perldoc DBI
perldoc DBI::FAQ
perldoc DBD::mysql
```

HTML versions of these three help pages can be found at, for example, http://www.perldoc.com/. *Links to additional Internet pages with information on database programming with Perl and DBI can be found at my home page:* http://www.kofler.cc/mysql.

Finally, a compact reference to DBI functions and methods can be found in Chapter 20.

The Modules DBI *and* DBD::mysql

Access to MySQL is carried out in Perl via the modules *DBI* and *DBD::mysql*. (The abbreviation "DBI" stands for *database interface*, while "DBD" stands for *database driver*.) *DBI* is a general interface for database programming, independent of particular database systems. Thus DBI can be used for database programming with Oracle, DB/2, etc. Ideally, the code is the same in every case; that is, you can switch database systems without changing the Perl code (with the exception of *datasource* character strings for establishing the connection).

DBD::mysql is used by *DBI* to communicate with MySQL. (There exist comparable driver modules for a host of other database systems.) Which driver module *DBI* must use is determined by the character string specified when the connection is established (method *connect*). Therefore, the instruction *use DBI* at the beginning of the Perl script suffices for incorporating the DBI module.

Although *DBI* actually follows a process that is independent of the database, *DBD:: mysql* makes available a number of MySQL-specific functions. The reason for this is that DBI constitutes the greatest common denominator of all database systems, and thus is relatively small. The use of MySQL-specific functions simplifies MySQL programming with Perl considerably, but leads, of course, to the result that the code can be ported to another database system only with difficulty.

DBI and *DBD* are object-oriented modules. For this reason, most of their functions are available in the form of methods, which are applied to objects (which in Perl are represented by *handles*). For example, *DBI->connect* returns a handle to a *database* object (which is usually stored in the variable *$dbh*). Various functions that affect the database can now be executed as methods of this object, for example, *$dbh->do("INSERT . . . ")*, for executing an SQL command.

Establishing a Connection to the Database

The connection is established with the DBI method *connect*. The first parameter to this method is a character string specifying the type of the database and the name of the computer (or *localhost*). The syntax of the character string can be deduced from the following example. The next two parameters must contain the user name and password.

A fourth, optional, parameter can be used to specify numerous attributes. For example, *'RaiseError'=>1* has the effect that the Perl script is broken off with an error message if the connection to the database cannot be established. (A list of the possible attributes can be found in Chapter 20. Further information on error-handling can be found in this chapter.)

```
use DBI;
$datasource = "DBI:mysql:database=mylibrary;host=localhost";
$user = "root";
$passw = "xxx";
$dbh = DBI->connect($datasource, $user, $passw,
  {'RaiseError' => 1});
```

Specifying the Configuration File

In the *datasource* character string you may also specify the name of a configuration file in which the user name, password, and possible additional connection options are specified. This is particularly practical under Unix/Linux if such configuration files are stored in the home directories of the users. (Information on creating configuration files can be found in Chapter 19.)

In the following example, the option *mysql_read_default_file* specifies the location of the configuration file (relative to the home directory from the environment variable *HOME*).

The option *mysql_read_default_group* specifies the group *[mygroup]* within the configuration file. If this option is not used, then *connect* automatically evaluates the group *[client]*. The second and third parameters to the method *connect* are both specified as *undef*, to make it clear that the user name and password are specified in another location:

```
$datasource = "DBI:mysql:database=mylibrary;" .
  "mysql_read_default_file=$ENV{HOME}/.my.cnf;" .
  "mysql_read_default_group=mygroup";
$dbh = DBI->connect($datasource, undef, undef, {'RaiseError' => 1});
```

The associated configuration file ~/.my.cnf might look like the following:

```
[mygroup]
user=root
password=xxx
host=uranus.sol
```

Please note that access rights to this file are set in such a way that only the user is allowed to read it.

> **REMARK**   *Under Windows, I was unable to evaluate a configuration file with* DBI->connect(). *Perhaps this function is available only under Unix/Linux (though such is not explicitly documented).*

Terminating the Connection

All accesses to the database are attained via the variable *$dbh* (or from variables derived from it). When the connection to the database is no longer needed, it should be closed with *disconnect*:

```
$dbh->disconnect();
```

Persistent Connections

Unlike the case of MySQL functions for PHP, in the case of the Perl DBI module there is no possibility of making use of persistent connections in order to minimize the time for repeated establishment of a connection to the database.

If you execute CGI Perl scripts via the Apache module *mod_perl* (which is recommended for reasons of efficiency), you achieve by use of the Perl module *Apache::DBI* that MySQL connections remain after the script has ended and are reused when another script requires the same type of MySQL connection. To use the module you have merely to insert *use Apache::DBI* before all *use DBI* commands in your script. No other changes are necessary. (*Apache::DBI* replaces the *connect* method of *DBI* with its own version.) Additional information on *Apache::DBI* can be found at the following location: http://www.perldoc.com/cpan/Apache/DBI.html.

Executing SQL Commands

SQL Commands Without Record List as Result

SQL commands that do not return a list of records are generally executed by means of *do*:

```
$n = $dbh->do("INSERT INTO authors (authName) " . "VALUES ('New author')");
```

Normally, *do* returns the number of altered data records. Other possible return values are as follows:

- *"0E0"* means that no record has been changed. This character string can be changed into a number by means of an arithmetic operation (i.e., *$n+=0*).

- −1 means that the number of changed records is unknown.

- *undef* means that an error has occurred.

Determining `AUTO_INCREMENT` *Values*

After *INSERT* commands it is frequently necessary to determine the *AUTO_INCREMENT* value of the newly inserted data record. For this task, the attribute *mysql_insertid* of *DBD::mysql* is helpful:

```
$id = $dbh->{'mysql_insertid'};
```

> **REMARK**   *The attribute* mysql_insertid *is not portable; that is, it is available only for MySQL databases. In porting the code to another database system you will have to find another way of proceeding.*

SELECT *Queries*

SQL commands that return a list of records (typically *SELECT* commands) cannot be executed with *do*. Instead, the query must first be prepared with *prepare*. (Many database servers will compile the query or execute other operations. However, with MySQL that is not the case.)

The return value of *prepare* is a *statement handle*, which must be used for all further operations with the query, even for the method *execute*, in order actually to execute the query. (If an error occurs in the execution of the query, the return value is *undef*.)

```
$sth = $dbh->prepare("SELECT * FROM titles LIMIT 5");
$sth->execute();
```

Then the resulting records can be output with *$sth*, about which we shall have more to say in the next section. When the evaluation is complete, the resources bound to *$sth* should be released with *finish*:

```
$sth->finish();# delete query object
```

SQL *Queries with Wild Cards for Parameters*

It often happens that the same type of query needs to be executed over and over with varying parameters (*WHERE id=1, WHERE id=3*, etc.). In such cases, *DBI* offers the possibility of replacing the parameters in *prepare* by a question mark, which serves as a wild card. Each question mark corresponds to a parameter, whose value must subsequently be specified with *execute*. Note that in *execute*, the correct order of the parameters must be adhered to. The following lines demonstrate how to proceed:

```
$sth = $dbh->prepare("SELECT * FROM titles " . "WHERE catID=? AND publID=?");
$sth->execute(1, 1);     # title with catID=1 and publID=2
  ...                    # evaluate results
$sth->execute(1, 2); # title with catID=1 and publID=2
  ...                    # evaluate results
$sth->finish();          # delete query object
```

In working with wild cards a few points should be noted: First of all, wild cards must be given in SQL commands unquoted (even if it is a character string). Secondly, the value passed to *execute* by the *DBI* module is dealt with automatically with *quote*, which places character strings in single quotation marks and prefixes a backslash to the apostrophe and backslash characters. If you wish to pass *NULL* to an SQL command, you must specify the value *undef*, which *quote* turns into *NULL*.

If you execute the commands

```
$sth = $dbh->prepare("INSERT INTO publishers (publName)" .
                     "VALUES (?)");
$sth->execute("O'Reilly");
```

with Perl, then it is the following SQL command that is actually executed in MySQL:

```
INSERT INTO publishers (publName) VALUES ('O\'Reilly')
```

This example shows that *prepare* and *execute* are suitable not only for *SELECT* queries, but also for all SQL queries that need to be executed a number of times.

> **REMARK**   *This procedure is not only elegant, but with many database servers it is also efficient. Namely, the command is temporarily stored on the server with* prepare. *Thereafter, only the parameters need to be transmitted to the server. However, MySQL does not implement this type of optimization.*

> **TIP**   *Wild cards can also be used when SQL commands are executed with* do. *This does not contribute to increased speed, but it does generally improve readability, since* DBI *takes care of both single quotation marks and* quote:

```
$dbh->do("INSERT INTO table (cola, colb) VALUES (?, ?),
   undef, ($data1, $data2)");
```

Evaluating SELECT *Queries*

Provided that no error occurs in a query (test by *if(defined($sth))*), the resulting records can be read via the *statement handle* (i.e., *$sth*). There are several different methods for accomplishing this.

Reading Data Records with fetch *alias* fetchrow_array

The two equivalent methods *fetch* and *fetchrow_array* return an array with the values of the next record. Within the array, the value *NULL* is expressed by *undef*. When the end of the record list is reached or if an error occurs, the array is empty. (To distinguish between these two cases, *$sth->err()* must be evaluated.) The following lines execute a query and display the results line by line. Here *NULL* is represented as a character string *<NULL>*:

```
$sth = $dbh->prepare("SELECT * FROM titles LIMIT 5");
$sth->execute();
while(@row = $sth->fetchrow_array()) {# process all records
  foreach $field (@row) {# each field
    if(defined($field)) {# test for NULL
      print "$field\t";
    } else {
      print "<NULL>\t";
    }
  }
  print "\n";
}
$sth->finish();
```

The evaluation of the columns in a *foreach* loop is rather the exception. To be sure, the individual columns could also be selected in the form *$row[n]*, where *n=0* must be specified for the first column. A further variant consists in assigning all the columns at once to the variables in question. Then, of course, the correct order of the variables must be heeded:

```
($titleID, $title, ... ) = @row;
```

Selecting Individual Values

It is often clear from the outset that a query will return only a single value (e.g., *SELECT COUNT(*) FROM ...*). In this case, neither a loop over all records nor an evaluation of all elements of an array is necessary. Instead, simply assign *fetchrow_array* to a scalar variable:

```
$sth = $dbh->prepare("SELECT COUNT(*) FROM titles");
$sth->execute();
$result = $sth->fetchrow_array();
print "$result\n";
$sth->finish();
```

> **CAUTION** *According to the DBI documentation, in the scalar context (e.g., $field = $sth->fetchrow_array()), fetchrow_array should return the contents of the first column. However, tests with the available version have revealed that $field contains, to the contrary, the value of the last column. There should be no problem when there is only one column.*
>
> *But in addition, the scalar evaluation of fetchrow_array is not quite unproblematic. There are now three reasons for which $field can contain the value undef: The column contains NULL in the record in question, the last record was reached, or an error has occurred.*

Instead of the code given above, you could use the following shorthand version:

```
$result = $dbh->selectrow_array("SELECT COUNT(*) ... ");
```

Binding Columns to Variables

In processing a *SELECT* command, instead of transmitting every data record manually in variables, you can automate this step and at the same time increase the efficiency and readability of your program a bit. To do this you bind the column of the query with *bind_col* to individual variables. Each time that *fetchrow_array* is executed, the associated variables contain the value of the new record. It is necessary that *bind_col* be executed after *execute*. The return value of *bind_col* is *false* if an error occurs. Please note that column numbering begins with 1 (not, as is usual in Perl, with 0):

```
$sth = $dbh->prepare("SELECT titleID, title FROM titles");
$sth->execute();
$sth->bind_col(1, \$titleID);
$sth->bind_col(2, \$title);
while($sth->fetchrow_array()) {
  print "$title $titleID\n";
}
$sth->finish();
$dbh->disconnect();
```

Instead of binding the variables individually, you can do this for all columns at once with *bind_columns*. Please observe the correct sequence and number of variables:

```
$sth->bind_columns(\$titleID, \$title);
```

Determining the Number of Data Records

The *DBI* module provides no possibility of determining the number of records returned by a *SELECT* command. (This has to do with the fact that with many database servers the records are transmitted to the module only when they are needed.) If you wish to know how many resulting records there are, you have the following options:

- You can count during the evaluation. (This variant is ruled out if you wish to know the number of records in advance.)

- You can execute the second query with *SELECT COUNT(*)* .... Depending on the application, this can be relatively costly.

- You may use the *DBI* method *fetchall_arrayref* (see below). Thereby all resulting records are transmitted together into a local array, so that the number can easily be determined.

- You may use the method *$sth->rows()*. This method can be evaluated after *execute()*. At first glance, this seems the obvious solution, but it has, in fact, a number of drawbacks:

  First, the method is not portable. (According to the *DBI* documentation, *rows* may be used to determine the altered records, say after *UPDATE* or *DELETE*, but not for investigating records read with *SELECT*.)

  Second, the method is itself available in conjunction with the *DBD::mysql* driver only when queries are evaluated without the attribute *mysql_use_result*. That is indeed the default setting, but it is not always particularly efficient.

Determining Column Names and Other Metainformation

If you wish to program a generally valid function for representing tables, you need not only the data themselves, but also metainformation about the data (column names, data types, etc.). This information is made available by *DBI* via various attributes of *$sth*:

- *$sth->{'NUM_OF_FIELDS'}* returns the number of columns.

- *$sth->{'NAME'}* returns a pointer to an array with the names of all columns. The same holds for *$sth->{'NAME_lc'}* and *$sth->{'NAME_uc'}*, but with the names all in lowercase or uppercase, respectively.

- *$sth->{'NULLABLE'}* returns a pointer to an array whose values tell whether a column can contain *NULL*.

- *$sth->{'PRECISION'}* and $sth->{'SCALE'} return pointers to arrays with the maximum number of characters and the number of decimal places, respectively.

- *$sth->{'TYPE'}* returns a pointer to an array with numerical values that permit one to determine the data types of the columns.

The following loop demonstrates the evaluation of this information:

```
$sth = $dbh->prepare("SELECT * FROM testall");
$sth->execute();
for($i=0; $i < $sth->{'NUM_OF_FIELDS'}; $i++) {
  print @{$sth->{'NAME'}}[$i] . " " .
        @{$sth->{'TYPE'}}[$i] . "\n";
}
```

POINTER DBD::mysql *makes available some additional attributes with MySQL-specific information. These attributes are presented in their own subsection of this chapter, together with other MySQL-specific (and therefore nonportable) extensions of the* DBI *module.*

Reading Data Records with `fetchrow_arrayref`

The functioning of *fetchrow_arrayref* is similar to that of *fetchrow_array*. The sole difference is that now pointers (references) to arrays instead of the arrays themselves are returned. This method returns *undef* if the end of the data list is reached or an error has occurred.

```
while(my $arrayref = $sth->fetchrow_arrayref()) {
  foreach $field (@{$arrayref}) {
     ... as before
}
```

Reading Data Records with `fetchrow_hashref`

The method *fetchrow_hashref* returns an associative array (*hash*) with the values of the next data record. It returns *undef* if the end of the record list has been reached or an error has occurred.

Access to the individual columns is effected with *$row->{'columnname'}*. In providing the *columnname*, attention must be paid to case-sensitivity. The following lines demonstrate its application:

```
$sth = $dbh->prepare("SELECT title, titleID FROM titles LIMIT 5");
$sth->execute();
while($row = $sth->fetchrow_hashref()) {
  print "$row->{'title'}, $row->{'titleID'}\n";
}
$sth->finish();
$dbh->disconnect();
```

If *fetchrow_hashref* is called with the optional parameter *"NAME_lc"* or *"NAME_uc"*, then all the hash keys are transformed into lowercase or uppercase, respectively.

Reading All Data Records with `fetchall_arrayref`

A drawback to all the access methods described above is that the data records must be read sequentially, and thereafter, they are no longer available. It is thus impossible to move about to your heart's content in the list of data records. (Depending on the database system, this has at least the advantage that it is miserly with resources. Under MySQL, *fetchall_arrayref* does not exhibit this advantage because by default, all records that are found are immediately transmitted to the client. This can be avoided only by using the attribute *mysql_use_result*. More about *mysql_use_result* can be found further along in this section.)

If you wish to access all records in an arbitrary order and to do so multiple times, you could output the entire result of the query *fetchall_arrayref*. As result you obtain an array with pointers to the individual records, which themselves are arrays. Access to an individual element is then accomplished via *$result->[$row][$col]*, where the indices begin with 0:

```
$sth = $dbh->prepare("SELECT titleID, title FROM titles");
$sth->execute();
$result = $sth->fetchall_arrayref();
print "$result->[2][5]\n"; # third record, sixth column
$sth->finish();
$dbh->disconnect();
```

The number of records and columns can be determined as follows:

```
$rows = @{$result};
$cols = @{$result->[0]};
```

An optional parameter can be passed to *fetchall_arrayref*, which influences both the columns to be read and the organization of the data. The following command reads only the first, fourth, and last columns:

```
$result = $sth->fetchall_arrayref([0,3,-1]);
```

The following command reads all columns, but returns a pointer to an array that contains pointers to hashes. Access to individual elements is via *$result->[$row]->{'columnname'}*, as in, for example, *$result->[3]->{'titleID'}*:

```
$result = $sth->fetchall_arrayref({});
```

Our last example again returns hashes, but this time only for columns with the names *titleID* and *title*:

```
$result = $sth->fetchall_arrayref({titleID=>1, title=>1});
```

In general, it makes better sense to limit the number of columns in the *SELECT* command, instead of waiting until *fetchall_arrayref* to do so, after all the data have been extracted from the database. The method *fetchall_arrayref* can be executed only once per query. If you would like to execute the method more than once, you must execute *execute* before each call.

If the query has returned no result, then *fetchall_arrayref* returns a pointer to an empty array. If an error occurs during data selection, then *$result* contains all data read to that point. If in any event you are working without *'RaiseError' => 1*, then after *fetchall_arrayref*, you should see to it that *$sth->err()* is evaluated.

> **TIP**   *Instead of the three methods* prepare, execute, fetchall_arrayref, *you can also use the shorthand form* $dbh->selectall_arrayref($sql).

Character Strings, BLOBs, DATEs, SETs, ENUMs, and NULL

Altering Data

To alter data records in your database you must transmit the relevant SQL commands as character strings to *do*. The structure of this character string must conform to the syntax of MySQL (see Chapter 18).

The starting point for the following discussion of the various data types is the variable *data*, which contains the data to be stored. The contents of this variable should be placed in an *INSERT* command, which is stored temporarily in the variable *sql*. In the simplest case, it goes like this:

```
$sql = "INSERT INTO tablename VALUES('$data1', '$data2', ... );
```

- **Dates and times:** To format a date or time according to the MySQL official regulations, you must use the corresponding Perl function or module (for example, *gmtime( )* or *TIME::Local*).

- **Timestamps:** Perl and MySQL timestamps have the same meaning, but different formats. A Perl timestamp (function *time( )*) is simply a 32-bit integer that gives the number of seconds since 1/1/1970. MySQL, on the other hand, expects a timestamp in the form *yyyyddmmhhmmss* or *yyyy-dd-mm hh:mm:ss*. As a rule, timestamps are used to mark the time of the most recent change. In such a case, you simply pass *NULL*, and MySQL automatically takes care of proper storage:

  ```
  $sql .= "NULL";
  ```

  On the other hand, if you would like to store a Perl timestamp as a MySQL timestamp, then you should use the MySQL function *FROM_UNIXTIME* in your *INSERT* or *UPDATE* command:

  ```
  $data = time(); // data contains the current time as a Unix timestamp
  $sql .= "FROM_UNIXTIME(" . $data . ")";
  ```

- **Character strings and BLOBs:** If special characters occur in a character string or BLOB, then there are frequently problems with quotation. SQL requires that the single-quote, double-quote, 0-byte, and backslash characters be prefixed by a backslash.

  If you place value on the portability of your Perl code, then you should use the method *$dbh->quote( )* for quoting character strings. This method not only adds \ or \0 to the character string, but also encloses the character string in single quotation marks. Thus *$dbh->quote(''ab'c'')* returns *'ab\'c'*. (If you execute an SQL command with wild cards, *quote( )* will be used automatically.)

  ```
  $sql .= $dbh->quote($data);
  ```

In putting together SQL commands, the Perl construct *qq{}*, which returns the specified character string, is often useful. Within *qq{}*, variables are replaced by their contents (but not quoted). The advantage of *qq{}* over a direct concatenation of character strings with *$sql="INSERT . . . "* is that within *qq{}* the single- and double-quote characters may be used:

```
$data = $dbh->quote($data);
$sql = qq{INSERT INTO table (col1, col2, col3)
          VALUES ($data, 'abc', PASSWORD("abc"))};
```

- **NULL:** I am pleased to be able to inform you, dear reader, that *$dbh->quote()* also treats the value *undef* correctly, and in this case returns *NULL* (without a single quote):

```
$sql .= $dbh->quote($data);
```

  If you do not wish to use *quote()*, then you might try the following:

```
$sql .= defined($data) ? "'$data'" : "NULL";
```

  Please note that within an SQL character command you do not place *NULL* in quotation marks as if it were a character string.

Reading Data

The starting point for the following considerations is the variable *$data*, which contains a data field. For example, *$data* can be initialized as follows:

```
$sth = $dbh->prepare("SELECT * FROM titles");
$sth->execute();
@row = $sth->fetchrow_array();
$data = $row(0);
```

- **Timestamps:** Timestamps in the form of a character string of the form 20031231235959 are contained in *data*. This won't get you very far in Perl. If you want to work with the timestamp value in Perl, then use the MySQL function *UNIX_TIMESTAMP* and formulate the corresponding *SELECT* query. Then for the above date *data* contains the value 1072911599:

```
SELECT ... , UNIX_TIMESTAMP(a_timestamp) FROM ...
```

- **Date:** For a *DATETIME* column, *data* contains a character string of the form 2003-12-31 23:59:59. For *DATE* columns, the time information is lacking. For the further processing of dates in Perl, it is practical in many cases here, too, to use the function *UNIX_TIMESTAMP*. You can obtain any format you like with the MySQL format *DATE_FORMAT*. The following instruction results in *data* containing a character string of the form *'December 31 2003'*.

```
SELECT ... , DATE_FORMAT(a_date, '%M %d %Y')
```

- **Time:** For a *TIME* column, *data* contains a character string of the form 23:59:59. If you do not wish to extract hours, minutes, and seconds from this character string, then the MySQL function *TIME_TO_SEC* can be used to return the number of seconds since 00:00:00. Additionally, you can, of course, use any of the numerous MySQL functions for processing times. Warning: *UNIX_TIMESTAMP* does not work for *TIME* columns.

> **POINTER** *In Chapter 18 you will find an overview of the MySQL functions for processing and converting dates and times.*

- *NULL:* Since *$data* is as yet undefined, it contains *undef.* Whether *$data* contains *NULL* can most easily be determined with the Perl function *defined($data).* (Do not compare *$data* with " " or *0* to detect *NULL.* Both comparisons return *True,* though preceded by a Perl warning.)

- **Character strings and BLOBs:** Perl, in contrast to C, has no difficulties with binary data; that is, even zero-bytes within a character string are correctly handled. Thus *data* truly contains the exact data from the database.

> **TIP** *If you wish to output character strings read from tables into HTML documents, as a rule you must use the function* encode_entities *from the module* HTML::Entities. *The function* escapeHTML *from the module* CGI *can be used only if you are certain that the database contains no characters other than those of the 7-bit ASCII character set.*

> **REMARK** *If problems arise in reading large BLOBs because the maximum amount of data per field is limited, then this limit can be set (before* execute*) with* $dbh->{'LongReadLen'}=n. *The value* n *specifies the maximum number of bytes.*
> *Warning: 0 means that long fields will not be read at all. In this case,* $data *contains the value* undef, *which cannot be distinguished from* NULL.

Determining Elements of an ENUM or SET

The use of *ENUM*s and *SET*s presents no problems in and of itself: The values are passed in both directions as simple character strings. Note that with *ENUM*s no empty spaces are permitted between the comma-separated items.

When in a Perl program you wish to display the character strings of an *ENUM* or *SET* for selection (in an HTML listbox, for example), you must determine the definition of this field with the SQL command *DESCRIBE tablename columnname*:

```
USE exceptions
DESCRIBE test_enum a_enum
```

Field	Type	Null	Key	...
a_enum	enum('a','b','c','d', 'e')	YES		...

The column *Type* of the result table contains the required information. In the following lines of code, the character string *enum('a', 'b', 'c')* will first be decomposed step by step and then displayed line by line. (The algorithm assumes that the *SET* or *ENUM* character string contains no commas.)

```perl
$sth = $dbh->prepare("DESCRIBE test_enum a_set");
$sth->execute();
$row = $sth->fetchrow_hashref();
$tmp = $row->{'Type'};              # enum( ... ) or set( ... )
($tmp) = $tmp =~ m/\((.*)\)/;       # xyz('a','b','c') --> 'a','b','c'
$tmp =~ tr/'//d;                    # 'a','b','c' --> a,b,c
@enums = split(/,/, $tmp);          # @enums[0]=a, @enums[1]=b ...
foreach $enum (@enums) {            # output all values
  print "$enum\n";
}
```

DBD::mysql-*specific Methods and Attributes*

Whereas the *DBI* module represents the greatest common denominator of all database APIs, *DBD::mysql* contains as well various MySQL-specific functions. Their application leads to Perl code that can be transferred to other database systems only with difficulty. However, such code is often more efficient.

> **POINTER**   *This section introduces only the most important MySQL-specific methods and attributes. Chapter 20 contains a complete reference of* DBD::mysql *extensions.*

Using rows *to Determine the Number of Records Found with* SELECT

The method *$sth->rows()*, which was mentioned previously, is, in fact, not MySQL-specific. But only with the *DBD::mysql* driver does this method return, after *execute*, the number of records found. This holds only if queries are executed without the attribute *mysql_use_result*.

Determining the AUTO_INCREMENT *Value*

The *$dbh* attribute *mysql_insertid* has also been mentioned. It enables you to determine the *AUTO_INCREMENT* value of the most recently inserted data record after an *INSERT* command:

```perl
$id = $dbh->{'mysql_insertid'};
```

Determining Additional Column Information

DBI makes a number of *$sth* attributes available that make it possible to determine information about the columns of a *SELECT* result (for example, *$sth-> {'NAME'}*). *DBD::mysql* adds some additional attributes, such as *'MYSQL_IS_BLOB'*, to establish whether a column contains *BLOB*s; or *'MYSQL_TYPE_NAME'*, to determine the name of the data type of the column.

mysql_store_result *Versus* mysql_use_result

If a *SELECT* command is executed with *prepare* and *execute*, then usually, *DBD::mysql* calls the C function *mysql_store_result*. This means that all the data records found have been transmitted at once to the client and retained there in memory until *$sth->finish()* is executed.

If between *prepare* and *execute* you set the attribute *mysql_use_result* to 1, then *DBD::mysql* uses the C function *mysql_use_result* for transmitting the records. This means that records are brought from the server to the client only when they are needed. In particular, in processing large amounts of data the RAM requirement can be greatly lowered on the client side. (This advantage is lost if you use *fetchall_arrayref*.)

```
$sth = $dbh->prepare("SELECT * FROM table");
$sth->{'mysql_use_result'}=1;
$sth->execute();
```

	mysql_store_result (default)	mysql_use_result
$sth->rows();	This function returns the number of records found.	This function returns 0 or the number of records transmitted thus far.
Locking	The *READ-LOCK* time is minimal.	If locking is used, the table is blocked until the last record is read.
Client Memory Requirement	All found records are stored at the client.	Only one record is stored at the client at one time.
Speed	Access to the first record is comparatively slow (since all records are transmitted to the client); it is very fast thereafter.	Access to the first record is very rapid; further access is slower than with *mysql_store_result*.

Error-Handling

There are several possibilities for Perl-script error-handling. The most convenient way (especially during program development) is to specify the option *{'RaiseError'=>1}* in establishing the connection. The result is that an error message is automatically displayed at each error. Additionally, the Perl program is terminated immediately. (This holds not only for errors during the connection, but also for all additional errors that occur in the execution of DBI methods.)

For many administrative tasks this sort of error-handling is sufficient. However, once you employ Perl for programming dynamic web pages, the termination of a script (and perhaps the display of a cryptic error message) is quite the opposite of what one might call user-friendly.

You can achieve more refined error-handling by turning off *DBI*'s automatic response to errors and executing *connect()* with *{'PrintError'=>0}*. Now you must consistently evaluate the two DBI methods *err()* and *errstr()*. The first of these contains the error number, or 0 if no error has occurred, while *errstr()* contains the error text corresponding to the last error to have occurred.

> **REMARK**   *DBI methods return* undef *if an error has occurred. However, individual DBI methods sometimes also return* undef *in the course of their normal operation (such as when a data field contains* NULL*). For this reason, a simple evaluation of the return value is usually insufficient.*

The methods *err()* and *errstr()* can also be applied to the DBI handles *$dbh* and *$sth* (depending on the context in which the method that caused the error was executed). Immediately after the connection has been established, *err()* or *errstr()* must be applied to *DBI* (since *$dbh* cannot be used after an unsuccessful connection attempt).

Example

The following lines show error-handling for Perl DBI code. In this example, the reaction to an error is always that the script is terminated, but of course, you can execute other instructions. Note particularly how *err()* and *errstr()* are applied to the objects *DBI*, *$dbh*, and *$sth*.

The code contains something particular to MySQL: With the *SELECT* command, error-handling occurs only after *execute*. With many other database systems an error can be recognized after *prepare* (but not with MySQL):

```
$datasource = "DBI:mysql:database=exceptions;host=localhost;";
$user = "root";
$passw = "xxx";
$dbh = DBI->connect($datasource, $user, $passw,
  {'PrintError' => 0});
if(DBI->err()) {
  print "error with connection: " . DBI->errstr() . "\n";
  exit(); }

$dbh->do("INSERT INTO neu.autotest (data) VALUES (1)");
if($dbh->err()) {
  print "error with INSERT command: " . $dbh->errstr() . "\n";
  exit(); }

$sth = $dbh->prepare("SELECT * FROM test_blob");
$sth->execute();
if($sth->err()) {
  print "error with SELECT execute: " . $sth->errstr() . "\n";
  exit(); }
```

```
while(my $hashref = $sth->fetchrow_hashref()) {
  if($sth->err()) {
    print "error with SELECT fetch: " . $sth->errstr() . "\n";
    exit(); }
  print length($hashref->{'a_blob'}) . "\n";
}
$sth->finish();
$dbh->disconnect();
```

Logging (trace)

If you suspect that the cause of an error is not in your code, but in MySQL, *DBI*, or *DBD::mysql* (or if you have no idea as to the cause of the error), it can help to display internal DBI logging information or to write it to a file. This is enabled by *trace()*, which, like *err()* and *errstr()*, can be applied to all *DBI* objects (including *DBI* itself).

Expected as parameters are the desired logging level (0 = none, 9 = maximal logging) and an optional file name. Without a file name, the logging data are sent to *STDERR* (under Windows, to the standard output *STDOUT*):

```
DBI->trace(2); # activate logging globally for the DBI module
$sth->trace(3, 'c:/dbi-trace.txt'); # logging only for $sth methods
```

Example: Deleting Invalid Data Records (*mylibrary*)

After months-long experiments with the database *mylibrary*, a variety of invalid records have accumulated. This is a scenario well known to most database developers, and one often forgets to clean house after the testing is complete.

In the case of the *mylibrary* database, the script delete-invalid-entries.pl offers help in most cases. It takes care of the following cases:

- For book titles whose *publID* refers to a nonexistent publisher, *publID* is set to *NULL.*

- For book titles whose *catID* refers to a nonexistent category, *catID* is set to *NULL.*

- In the table *rel_title_author* all entries that refer to nonexistent book titles or authors are deleted. (This can result in titles without authors or authors without titles remaining. Such records are not deleted by the script.)

Of course, the script could be enlarged to include other tests, such as for checking the hierarchy within the *categories* table or for searching for invalid *langID* entries in the *titles* table.

> **POINTER** *The SQL commands that appear in the script for searching for incorrect data are described extensively in Chapter 7.*

Program Code

The script begins as usual with establishing a connection to the database. If an error occurs (then or later), the script, on account of *{' RaiseError' => 1}*, is simply terminated with an error message:

```perl
#!/usr/bin/perl -w
# delete-invalid-entries.pl
use strict;
use DBI;

# declare variables
my($datasource, $user, $passw, $dbh, $sth, $row);

# establish connection to the database
$datasource = "DBI:mysql:database=mylibrary;host=localhost;";
$user = "root";
$passw = "xxx";
$dbh = DBI->connect($datasource, $user, $passw,
  {'RaiseError' => 1});
```

The *SELECT* query finds all titles for which *publID* contains an invalid value (that is, a value that does not exist in the *publishers* table). In the following loop, *publID* is set to *NULL* with *UPDATE* for all of the defective records found:

```perl
# (1a) search for invalid publID entries in the titles table
$sth =
  $dbh->prepare("SELECT title, titleID " .
                "FROM titles LEFT JOIN publishers " .
                " ON titles.publID=publishers.publID " .
                "WHERE ISNULL(publishers.publID) " .
                " AND NOT(ISNULL(titles.publID))");
$sth->execute();
# set publID of the affected records to NULL
while($row = $sth->fetchrow_hashref()) {
  print "set publID=NULL for title: $row->{'title'}\n";
  $dbh->do("UPDATE titles SET publID=NULL " .
           "WHERE titleID=$row->{'titleID'}");
}
$sth->finish();
# (1b) search for invalid catID entries in the titles table
# ... code analogous to (1a)
```

A little more complex is the query for searching for invalid entries in the *rel_title_author* table. Such entries are simply deleted in the following loop. The *print* commands display the affected data records on the computer monitor, where the operator *?* is used to replace *undef* by *NULL*.

> **REMARK** *The following code is compatible with MySQL 3.23. Starting with MySQL 4.0, the invalid records from* rel_title_author *can be deleted with a single* DELETE *command (see Chapter 7).*

```
# (2) search for invalid authID or titleID entries in the
# rel_title_author table
$sth =
  $dbh->prepare("SELECT authName, title, rel_title_author.authID, " .
                " rel_title_author.titleID " .
                "FROM rel_title_author " .
                "LEFT JOIN titles " .
                " ON rel_title_author.titleID=titles.titleID " .
                "LEFT JOIN authors " .
                " ON rel_title_author.authID=authors.authID " .
                "WHERE ISNULL(titles.titleID) " .
                " OR ISNULL(authors.authID)");
$sth->execute();

# delete the affected entries in the rel_title_author table

while($row = $sth->fetchrow_hashref()) {
  print "delete rel_title_author entry:\n";
  print " title = ",
    defined($row->{'title'}) ? $row->{'title'} : "NULL", "\n";
  print " author = ",
    defined($row->{'authName'}) ? $row->{'authName'} : "NULL", "\n";
  $dbh->do("DELETE FROM rel_title_author " .
           "WHERE authID=$row->{'authID'} " .
           " AND titleID=$row->{'titleID'}");
}
$sth->finish();

# Program end
$dbh->disconnect();
```

CGI Example: Library Management (*mylibrary*)

Access to the database looks the same in CGI scripts as it does in Perl programs, which for administrative purposes are usually executed as *stand alone*. One must, however, note in the output of data from the database that special characters in character strings are coded with *encode_entities* according to the HTML syntax.

This section introduces two small Perl programs that access the *mylibrary* database:

- mylibrary-simpleinput.pl enables the input of new book titles.

- mylibrary-find.pl enables the search for book titles.

POINTER   *An interesting tool for Perl CGI programmers is* mysqltool. *This is a collection of CGI scripts for the administration of MySQL databases (comparable with phpMyAdmin). It can be found at the following address:*

```
http://www.dajoba.com/projects/mysqltool/
```

Book Search (`mylibrary-find.pl`)

The script `mylibrary-find.pl` assists in locating books in the *mylibrary* database. The initial letters of the title are given in the search form. Clicking the OK button leads to an alphabetical list of all titles found, together with their authors, publisher, and year of publication (see Figure 14-1).

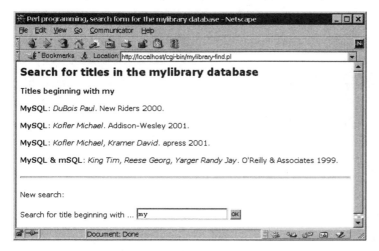

Figure 14-1. Searching for book titles

Program Structure

The script `mylibrary-find.pl` looks after the display of a simple form as well as the evaluation of that form (including the display of search results). The method *param()* of *CGI* is used to evaluate the form variable *formSearch*.

Program Code

The code begins with the declaration of modules and variables. The combination of *strict* and *my* helps in discovering typographical errors in variable names; *DBI* enables access to the database; *CGI* assists in the output of HTML structures; *CGI::Carp* displays error messages in the resulting HTML document, which is especially practical in searching for errors; *HTML::Entities* contains the function *encode_entities*, with which special characters are translated into HTML syntax:

```
#!/usr/bin/perl -w
# mylibrary-find.pl
use strict;
use DBI;
use CGI qw(:standard);
use CGI::Carp qw(fatalsToBrowser);
use HTML::Entities;

# declaration of variables
my($datasource, $user, $passw, $dbh, $search, $sql, $sth, $result,
  $rows, $i, $row, $authors);
```

Establishing the connection to the database offers nothing new over our previous examples in this chapter. If an error occurs, an error message (in the form of an HTML document) is displayed, and the script is terminated. If the connection succeeds, then the HTML document is opened with several methods from the *CGI* module:

```
# establish connection to the database
$datasource = "DBI:mysql:database=mylibrary;host=localhost;";
$user = "root";
$passw = "xxx";
$dbh = DBI->connect($datasource, $user, $passw,
  {'PrintError' => 0});

# display error message if required and terminate the script
if(DBI->err()) {
  print header(),
    start_html("Sorry, no database connection"),
    p("Sorry, no database connection"), end_html();
  exit();
}

# open HTML Document
print header(),
    start_html("Perl programming, search form for the ",
               "mylibrary database"), "\n",
    h2("Search for titles in the mylibrary database"), "\n";
```

Evaluate Form, Display Search Results

If the script is called with form data, then the form variable *formSearch* is evaluated with *param*. The special characters _ and % are removed from the character string. If the variable *search* is not empty, then in *sql* an extensive *SELECT* command is assembled and executed. The results are transmitted with *fetchall_arrayref* into a two-dimensional array:

```
# process form data
$search = param('formSearch');
# remove characters _ and %
$search =~ tr/%_//d;
if($search) {
  print p(), b("Titles beginning with ", encode_entities($search));
```

```perl
# title search
$sql = "SELECT titles.titleID, titles.title, titles.year, " .
       " publishers.publName, authors.authName " .
       "FROM titles, authors, rel_title_author " .
       "LEFT JOIN publishers " .
       " ON titles.publID = publishers.publID " .
       "WHERE titles.titleID = rel_title_author.titleID " .
       " AND authors.authID = rel_title_author.authID " .
       " AND title LIKE '$search%' " .
       "ORDER BY title, titleID, authName " .
       "LIMIT 100";
$sth = $dbh->prepare($sql);
$sth->execute();
$result = $sth->fetchall_arrayref({});
$sth->finish();
```

The evaluation of the array begins with a test as to whether any book titles were found at all. The following loop is somewhat complicated by the fact that book titles with several authors should be displayed only once, with all of the authors. Therefore, in *authors* a character string of all the authors is assembled. When the last record in *result* is reached or if the next record refers to a *titleID* other than the current record, then the book title is displayed:

```perl
# were any titles found?
$rows = @{$result};
if($rows==0) {
  print p(), "Sorry, no titles found."; }
# display titles
else {
  # loop over all records
  for($i=0; $i<$rows; $i++) {
    $row = $result->[$i];
    # create author list
    if($authors) {$authors .= ", ";}
    $authors .= $row->{'authName'};
    # output title if arrived at the last record
    # in result or if titleID for the next record refers to
    # another value
    if($i==$rows-1 ||
        $row->{'titleID'} != $result->[$i+1]->{'titleID'}) {
        print p(),
          b(encode_entities($row->{'title'})), ": ",
          i(encode_entities($authors)), ". ",
          encode_entities($row->{'publName'}), " ",
          $row->{'year'}, ".";
        $authors = "";
    }
  }
  print p(), hr(), p(), "New search:", p();
}
}
```

Display Form

```
# display form
print start_form(),
    p(), "Search for title beginning with ... ",
    textfield({-name => 'formSearch', -size => 20,
              -maxlength => 20}), " ",
    submit({-name => 'formSubmit', -value => 'OK'}),
    end_form();
print end_html();

# end of program
$dbh->disconnect();
```

Ideas for Improvements

The code as it stands permits only a search based on the initial letters of a title. It would be desirable, of course, to allow a search by author(s), categories, and so on, ideally in the form of a full-text search. (A somewhat more refined example of book search in *mylibrary* was presented in Chapter 12, where PHP was used as the programming language. That program offers pagewise representation of the search results as well as cross references between results, for example to display all titles written by a particular author.)

Simple Input of New Books (mylibrary-simpleinput.pl)

This section presents a minimalist input form for new books (see Figure 14-2). In two input fields are placed the new book title and a list of authors. The script then tests which if any of the authors are already stored in the database. All as yet unknown authors are added with *INSERT*. Then the new title is stored as well as the requisite entries in *rel_title_author* for relating title and authors.

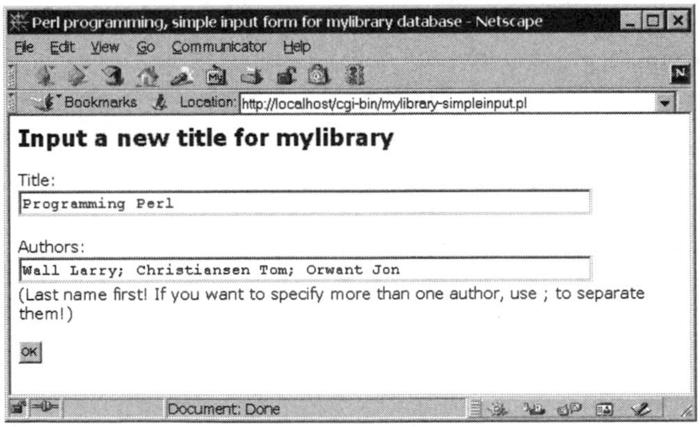

Figure 14-2. Simple book title input

Program Structure

The script `mylibrary-simpleinput.pl` displays a simple form and then evaluates it when OK is clicked. The method *param()* of the *CGI* module is used to transmit the two form variables: *formTitle* with the title, and *formAuthors* with the list of authors.

Program Code

As with `mylibrary-find.pl`, the code begins with the declaration of modules and variables:

```
#!/usr/bin/perl -w
# mylibrary-simpleinput.pl
use strict;
use DBI;
use CGI qw(:standard);
use CGI::Carp qw(fatalsToBrowser);
# Declaration of variables
my($datasource, $user, $passw, $dbh, @row,
  $formTitle, $formAuthors, $titleID, $authID, $author);
```

The next lines of code are similar to those of the script `mylibrary-find.pl`, which we have just seen, and so we do not reproduce the code:

```
# establish connection to the database
 ... as in mylibrary-find.pl
# if an error occurs, display error message and terminate script
 ... as in mylibrary-find.pl
# begin HTML document
 ... as in mylibrary-find.pl
```

Storing a Book Title and Its Authors

If the script is called with form data (these are located in *param()*), there follows a quick test as to whether a title and author list have been specified. If that is not the case, then an error message is displayed. The program is continued below with the redisplay of the form:

```
# evaluate form data
if(param()) {
  $formTitle = param('formTitle');
  $formAuthors = param('formAuthors');

  # title and authors were specified
  if($formTitle eq "" || $formAuthors eq "") {
    print p(), b("Please specify title and at least one author!"); }
```

For storing the book title in the *titles* table, the *INSERT* command with one parameter is passed to *do*. As parameter, *$formTitle* is passed. The effect of this way of proceeding is that *$formTitle* (with a minimal amount of typing) is placed in single quotation marks, and all special characters are handled correctly:

```
# form data are correct; store them
else {
  # store title
  $dbh->do("INSERT INTO titles (title) VALUES (?)",
           undef, ($formTitle));
  $titleID = $dbh->{'mysql_insertid'};
```

The list of authors is processed in a *foreach* loop. For each author, a test is made as to whether the author already resides in the *authors* table. If that is indeed the case, then *authID* is read from the *authors* table. Otherwise, the new author is stored, and the new *authID* value is determined with *mysql_insertid*. Finally, the combination of *titleID* and *authID* must be stored in the table *rel_title_author*:

```
# store authors
foreach $author (split(/;/, $formAuthors)) {
  # does the author already exist?
  @row = $dbh->selectrow_array("SELECT authID FROM authors " .
                "WHERE authName = " .
                $dbh->quote($author));
  # yes: determine existing authID
  if(@row) {
    $authID = $row[0]; }
  # no: store new author and determine new authID
  else {
    $dbh->do("INSERT INTO authors (authName) VALUES (?)",
             undef, ($author));
    $authID = $dbh->{'mysql_insertid'};
  }
  # store entry in rel_title_author table
  $dbh->do("INSERT INTO rel_title_author (titleID, authID) " .
           "VALUES ($titleID, $authID)");
}
```

In the HTML document a brief announcement is made that the new title was successfully stored. Then the form variables are deleted so that the next title can be input in the form:

```
# feedback
print p(), "Your last input has been saved.";
print br(), "You may now continue with the next title.";
# delete form variables (to prepare for the next input)
param(-name=>'formTitle', -value=>'');
param(-name=>'formAuthors', -value=>'');
  }
}
```

Displaying the Form

The remaining lines of code serve to display the form and close the HTML document:

```perl
print start_form(),
    p(), "Title:",
    br(), textfield({-name => 'formTitle', -size => 60,
                        -maxlength => 80}),
    p(), "Authors:",
    br(), textfield({-name => 'formAuthors', -size => 60,
                        -maxlength => 100}),
    br(), "(Last name first! If you want to specify more ",
          "than one author, use ; to separate them!)",
    p(), submit({-name => 'formSubmit', -value => 'OK'}),
    end_form();
print end_html();

# end of program
$dbh->disconnect();
```

Ideas for Improvements

The script mylibrary-simpleinput.pl does not permit one to specify subtitle, publisher, category, etc. Furthermore, it is as good as completely unprotected against input errors. It is impossible to make changes to titles already stored. Thus there is enormous potential to improve this script! (A much more satisfactory input form was presented in Chapter 12. There, to be sure, the programming language PHP was used. Nonetheless, many of the techniques employed there could easily be ported to Perl.)

#### CHAPTER 15

Java, JSP, JDBC

THIS CHAPTER DESCRIBES THE DEVELOPMENT of MySQL applications with the programming language Java and with Java Server Pages (JSP). As an interface to MySQL we will use JDBC (*Java Database Connectivity*) in combination with the driver *Connector/J*.

Chapter Overview

Introduction

REMARK   *All the tests for this chapter were carried out under Windows 2000 (with Sun JDK 1.4.1) and under SuSE Linux 8.1 (with Sun JDK 1.3.1, package* java2-1.3.1*). The connection to MySQL was made in each case with Connector/J 3.0.3. JSP was tested only under SuSE Linux, with Tomcat 4.0.4 (Java Servlet 2.3, JSP 1.2, Apache 1.3.n).*

The Java Installation

To develop your own Java programs you need the Java Software Development Kit (Java SDK, or simply JDK). The most widely distributed JDK is from Sun (the creator of Java); however, there are Java implementations available from other developers, such as IBM. This chapter focuses primarily on the Sun implementation.

JDK is bundled with many Linux implementations and can be simply installed with the package manager. For Linux distributions without Java, or for working under Windows, you can download the JDK without charge from java.sun.com/downloads (about 40 megabytes). The official name is *Java 2 Platform Standard Edition n SDK* (or J2SE *n* SDK for short), where *n* is the current version number.

After installation you have to complete the environment variable *PATH* to the bin directory of the Java installation. To do this, modify the file autoexec.bat under Windows 9x/ME. Under Windows NT/2000/XP, open the dialog CONTROL PANEL|SYSTEM (see Figure 4-1). The components of *PATH* are separated by semicolons. On my Windows test computer I have installed JDK in the directory c:\jdk1.4:

```
C:\> PATH
PATH=C:\WINNT\system32;C:\WINNT;C:\WINNT\System32\Wbem;
  C:\WINNT\Microsoft.NET\Framework\v1.0.3705;
  C:\Programs\SharpDevelop\bin;c:\mysql\bin;c:\jdk1.4\bin
```

With SuSE Linux 8.1, Java is located in the directory /usr/lib/SunJava2-1.3.1, where additionally, there is a link from /usr/lib/java to this directory. *PATH* is correctly set during the installation of the Java package and looks like this:

```
linux:~ $ echo $PATH
  /usr/local/bin:/usr/bin:/usr/X11R6/bin:/bin:/usr/games:
  /opt/kde3/bin:/usr/lib/java/bin:.
```

After installation, under Windows you can test in the command window, or under Linux in a console window, whether everything proceeded properly:

```
C:\> java Đversion
java version "1.4.1_01"
Java(TM) 2 Runtime Environment, Standard Edition (build 1.4.1_01-b01)
Java HotSpot(TM) Client VM (build 1.4.1_01-b01, mixed mode)

linux:~ # java Đversion
java version "1.3.1_04"
Java(TM) 2 Runtime Environment, Standard Edition (build 1.3.1_04-b02)
Java HotSpot(TM) Client VM (build 1.3.1_04-b02, mixed mode)
```

Hello, World!

To try out the Java compiler, create the following file Hellow.java. Note that the file name must match that of the class defined in the code exactly, including case distinction:

```
/* example file Hellow.java */
public class Hellow
{
  public static void main(String[] args)
  {
    System.out.println("Hello, world!");
  }
}
```

To compile, change to the directory of the file Hellow.java and execute the following command:

```
> javac Hellow.java
```

As result, you obtain the file Hellow.class. This program is executed as follows:

```
> java Hellow
Hello World!
```

Connector/J Installation

Connector/J is a JDBC driver for MySQL. (JDBC stands for *Java Database Connectivity.*) JDBC is a collection of classes that help in the programming of database applications with Java. JDBC is independent of specific database systems. Therefore, to create a connection to a database system via JDBC, a driver specific to the database must be used. For MySQL database systems this driver is Connector/J.

Connector/J is a so-called type-4 driver, which means that it is implemented completely in Java. The version 3 of Connector/J described here assumes JDBC 2.0 (that is, at least Java 2, version 1.2). Connector/J is compatible with MySQL 3.23.n and 4.0.n. (For MySQL 4.1, Connector/J3 is currently in development.)

> **REMARK**   *Earler versions of Connector/J had the name MM.MySQL. After the programmer Mark Matthews moved over to the MySQL team, the driver was called Connector/J and is now officially supported by MySQL.*
>
> *Connector/J is available under the GPL. If you wish to use Connector/J in commercial applications, the MySQL server used must be properly licensed. Alternatively, you can take out a separate client license for Connector/J (see Chapter 1).*
>
> *There are other JDBC drivers for MySQL besides Connector/J, for example, for Resin (a servlet and JSP environment):*
>
> `http://www.caucho.com/projects/jdbc-mysql/index.xtp`

> **POINTER**   *The documentation to Connector/J is currently rather thin, consisting only of a* Readme *file that is installed together with Connector/J. However, you can consult any book on Java that discusses JDBC programming for the fundamentals. With Connector/J there are few MySQL-specific differences from general JDBC programming aspects. Note, however, that Connector/J does not support some methods provided by JDBC, primarily because MySQL does not yet have the corresponding functions.*

Installation

Connector/J is available for download at `www.mysql.com` as a `*.zip` (Windows) or `*.tar.gz` file. Both Archives contain exactly the same files. (Java is platform-independent.) To install, unpack the contents of the archive into the directory of your choice. Under Windows, use the program Winzip, and under Linux the following command:

```
linux:~ # tar -xzf mysql-connector-java-n.tar.gz
```

Here is a list of the most important files and directories of the archive:

`mysql-connector-java-n/`	Directory with the actual library files; the rest of the entries in this list refer to this directory.
`README`	The documentation to Connector/J.
`/mysql-connector-java-n.jar`	All Java Classes of the driver as a Java archive file; this file is the actual driver.
`/com/*`	All Java classes of the driver as individual files.
`/org/*`	The driver's Java start class under the old driver name (`org.gjt.mm.mysql.Driver`).

The crucial point here is that the Java runtime environment should be able to find the new library when executing programs. To ensure this state of affairs, there are several possibilities:

- The simplest solution is generally to copy the file `mysql-connector-java-n.jar` into the directory *java-installation-directory*\jre\lib\ext, which is automatically checked during the execution of Java programs.

- Alternatively, you can set the environment variable *CLASSPATH*. This variable specifies all directories in which there are classes that should be taken into account when Java programs are executed. So that Connector/J will be considered, you must add the directory in which `mysql-connector-java-n.jar` is located to *CLASSPATH*. Note that for the execution of Java programs from the current directory, *CLASSPATH* must also contain the path "." (that is, a period, which denotes the current directory).

  Under Windows, you can set *CLASSPATH* temporarily with the DOS command *SET var=xxx*. To set it permanently, use the dialog CONTROL PANEL | SYSTEM under Windows NT/2000/XP (see Figure 4-1), or under Windows 9x/ME, the file `autoexec.bat`. Components of *CLASSPATH* are separated by semicolons.

  Under Linux, you can set *CLASSPATH* with the command *export var=xxx* or permanently in /etc/profile. The specified directories in *Classpath* are separated with colons.

- For initial testing there is also the option of copying the `com` and `org` directories from Connector/J into the local directory (that is, into the directory in which the program that you have developed resides).

You can test whether the installation of Connector/J was successful with the following miniprogram. It should run without reporting any errors:

```
/* example file HelloMySQL.java */
import java.sql.*;
public class HelloMySQL {
  public static void main(String[] args) {
    try {
      Driver d = (Driver)
        Class.forName("com.mysql.jdbc.Driver").newInstance();
      System.out.println("OK"); }
    catch(Exception e) {
      System.out.println("Error: " + e.toString()); }
  }
}
```

And If It Doesn't Work?

If something goes wrong, then the usual suspect is that the Connector/J classes have not been found. The error message usually looks something like this: *java.lang.ClassNotFoundException: com.mysql.jdbc.Driver*. Here are some of the possible sources of error:

- If you have copied `mysql-connector-java-3.0.n.jar` into the directory `jre\lib\ext`, then it is possible that more than one Java interpreter resides on the computer. (It is also possible that a run-time version and a development version have been installed in parallel.) You have apparently copied `mysql-connector-java-3.0.n.jar` into the directory of an interpreter that is not the active one.

  Under Linux you can determine the correct directory easily with `which java`. Unfortunately, there is not a comparable option under Windows, since the relevant settings are located in the somewhat opaque registration database. However, you can determine with START | SETTINGS | CONTROL PANEL | ADD / REMOVE HARDWARE which Java versions are already installed and when installation took place.

- If you have edited *CLASSPATH*, then perhaps Java is having no trouble locating Connector/J's classes, but is unable to locate the classes of your own program (error message *java.lang.NoClassDefFoundError*). If *CLASSPATH* is defined, then it must also point to the current directory.

  Under Windows, you can determine the contents of *CLASSPATH* in a command window with *%CLASSPATH%*, and under Linux in a console window with *$CLASSPATH*. Under Windows, the components of *CLASSPATH* are separated with semicolons, while under Linux it is colons that do the separation. The following commands show possible settings (where of course, you must adapt the configuration to your own installation):

```
> ECHO %CLASSPATH%
.;C:\Programs\mysql-connector-java-3.0.3-beta

linux:~ # echo $CLASSPATH
.:/usr/local/mysql-connector-java-3.0.3-beta/
```

Programming Techniques

The following examples assume that Java SDK and Connector/J have been correctly installed. All example programs run only in text mode. Of course, Java programs with an AWT or Swing interface will look more attractive, but for demonstrating programming techniques, text mode is completely satisfactory and offers the advantage that the code remains compact and easy to read.

> **POINTER** *This section provides only a first introduction to JDBC programming. More advanced information is to be found in books on Java that discuss JDBC.*

A First Example

The following example offers a first impression of the construction of a JDBC program. The use of *import java.sql* facilitates access to the JDBC interfaces and classes. The

Connector/J driver is loaded with *Class.forName(" . . . ").newInstance().* (This must take place before a connection is established.)

The connection is established with the method *DriverManager.getConnection,* where the most important parameters (driver name, host name, and database name) are passed in the form of a URL; details to follow.

Before you can execute an SQL command, a *Statement* object must be created, whose method *executeQuery* returns a *ResultSet* object, which contains the result of the query. In the following lines, all data records are read through (method *next*), selectively chosen (*getInt, getString,* etc.), and output to the console window:

```java
/* example SampleIntro.java */

import java.sql.*;

public class SampleIntro
{
  public static void main(String[] args)
  {
    try {
      Connection conn;
      Statement stmt;

      ResultSet res;        // load Connector/J driver
      Class.forName("com.mysql.jdbc.Driver").newInstance();

      // establish connection to MySQL
      conn = DriverManager.getConnection(
        "jdbc:mysql://uranus/mylibrary", "username", "xxx");

      // execute SELECT query
      stmt = conn.createStatement();
      res = stmt.executeQuery(
        "SELECT publID, publName FROM publishers " +
        "ORDER BY publName");

      // process results
      while (res.next()) {
        int id = res.getInt("publID");
        String name = res.getString("publName");
        System.out.println("ID: " + id + "  Name: " + name);
      }
      res.close();
    }
    catch(Exception e) {
      System.out.println("Error: " + e.toString() );
    } } }
```

Upon execution, the program returns the following result:

```
ID: 1  Name: Addison-Wesley
ID: 2  Name: apress
ID: 9  Name: Bonnier Pocket
ID: 5  Name: Hanser
ID: 3  Name: New Riders
ID: 4  Name: O'Reilly & Associates
```

Establishing the Connection

Establishing the Connection with DriverManager.getConnection

As already mentioned in our introductory example, the Connector/J driver must be loaded before the connection is established. For this, execute the method *Class.forName* and pass the name of the driver. The method returns a *Driver* object, which you generally will not need. More to the point is that Connector/J is registered as a result of this call as a JDBC driver, which now can be used:

```
// SampleConnection1.java
// load the Connector/J driver
Class.forName("com.mysql.jdbc.Driver").newInstance();
```

For further programming, what is much more important is the *Connection* object that you create with the method *DriverManager.getConnection*. To this method you usually pass three character strings, containing the basic information about the database, as a URL (uniform resource locator), the user name, and the password:

```
// connection to MySQL
Connection conn = DriverManager.getConnection(
  "jdbc:mysql://uranus/mylibrary", "username", "password");
```

The construction of the URL looks like this (here split into two lines):

```
jdbc:mysql://[host1][,host2 ... ][:port]/
  [dbname][?para1=val1][&para2=val2][&para3=val3] ...
```

Tables 15-1 and 15-2 describe the components of the connection URL and the most important optional connection parameters. A complete list of parameters can be found in the Connector/J Readme file.

Table 15-1. Components of the connection URL

Component	Function
jdbc:mysql	Selects the driver.
host1	Specifies the host name (*localhost* if a server on the local computer is to be accessed).
host2, host3	Specifies additional (optional) host names, to be used only if the connection to host1 is unsuccessful.
port	Specifies the port number (by default, 3306).
dbname	Specifies the default database.
para=value	Specifies optional parameters (see Table 15-2).

All further database operations proceed from the *Connection* object. If you wish to close the connection at the end of the program, simply use the method *close* on the *Connection* object.

Table 15-2. Optional parameters in the connection URL (with default settings)

Parameter	Function
connectTimeout=0	Specifies in milliseconds the wait time for a connection to be established. A setting of 0 means that no timeout is used. This setting functions only since Java 2, version 1.4.
autoreconnect=false	Specifies whether the driver should attempt on its own to reconnect if the connection is broken.
maxReconnects=3	Specifies the maximum number of reconnects.
initialTimeout=2	Specifies in seconds the time between attempts at reestablishing a broken connection. This time does not hold for the first connection.
useUnicode=true	Specifies whether Connector/J should convert the character set valid in MySQL to Unicode (Java). The setting *false* deactivates string conversion.
characterset=none	Specifies which character set should be used for Unicode conversion. This setting is seldom necessary, since Connector/J generally recognizes the correct character set on its own.
	You must specify the character set explicitly if you want a different character set from that valid under MySQL to be used, or if you are running MySQL with a custom-developed character set. This setting is considered only if *useUnicode=true* holds.
relaxAutoCommit=false	Specifies whether the driver is to accept *COMMIT* and *ROLLBACK* commands without reporting an error even if MySQL supports no transactions for the affected tables (for example, because the tables are in MyISAM format).
useTimezone=false	Specifies whether times should be converted between the client and server time zones.
serverTimezone=null	Specifies the time zone of the server via a time zone ID.

Establishing the Connection with `DataSource.getConnection`

Since Java 2, version 1.4, in addition to the method *DriverManager.getConnection*, which we have already described, there is an alternative way to establish a database connection: the *DataSource* class (package *javax.sql*). The JDBC documentation recommends this way, because it allows for the use of advanced functions, such as connection pooling and the execution of distributed transactions (that is, database operations that process data from several databases).

The following lines do not go into these additional possibilities, but simply show the principles of establishing the connection. To do this, you generate an object of the class *com.mysql.jdbc.jdbc2.optional.MysqlDataSource* and with the methods *setServerName* and *setDatabaseName*, set the host and database names. The actual connection is then established with *getConnection*, where you have to pass only the user name and password. This method returns a *Connection* object, which in the *DriverManager* variant is the starting point for all further database operations.

If you wish to set additional connection parameters, you can use the method *setURL* (the format of the URL, as described previously) or pass a *Properties* field to *getConnection*:

```
// SampleConnection2.java

import java.sql.*;
import javax.sql.*; // for DataSource

public class SampleConnection2
{
  public static void main(String[] args)
  {
    try {
      com.mysql.jdbc.jdbc2.optional.MysqlDataSource ds;
      Connection conn2;

      // establish connection with a DataSource object
      ds = new com.mysql.jdbc.jdbc2.optional.MysqlDataSource();
      ds.setServerName("uranus");
      ds.setDatabaseName("mylibrary");
      conn2 = ds.getConnection("root", "xxxx");

      // proceed as previously ...

    }
    catch(Exception e) {
      System.out.println("Error: " + e.toString() );
    }
  }
}
```

POINTER *If you wish to use more advanced JDBC functions, you should look at the Connector/J driver directory* com\mysql\jdbc\jdbc2\optional. *There you will find, for example, the Java source texts for the Connector/J classes* MysqlPooledConnection *and* MySQLConnectionPoolDataSource.

Problems in Establishing a Connection

Normally, the connection between a client program and the MySQL server is established via TCP/IP when the programs are running on different computers. On the other hand, if both programs are running on the same computer and a Linux/Unix system is being used, then the connection is established over a socket file, which is more efficient than TCP/IP.

However, Java does not support sockets, and so the connection is always over TCP/IP. The importance here is that in MySQL access control, the name *localhost* is not used as host name, but instead, the actual name of the computer. This state of affairs frequently leads to difficulties, with an error message that usually looks something like this:

```
linux:~/ java SampleConnection1
Error: java.sql.SQLException: Server configuration denies access to data source
```

What is particularly irritating is that a local connection using the same access information (e.g., with mysql -h localhost -u name -p) works just fine. The reason is that mysql deals with local access by default over socket files, but Java does not.

The following points should help you in solving such problems. The starting point for our example is a MySQL server that is running on the computer *uranus.sol* with IP number 192.168.0.2. The Java program is to run on the same computer.

- It can be that for security reasons, every network connection to the MySQL server is forbidden. (For this, at server start the option --skip-networking must be passed, or else this option must be entered in my.cnf.) Whether such is the case can be determined with the following command:

```
linux~/$ mysql -h uranus.sol -u name -p databasename
Enter password: xxxxx
ERROR 2003: Can't connect to MySQL server
```

  The only solution is to remove this option.

- It can also be the case that network access is indeed allowed, but the table *mysql.user*, which is responsible for access control, contains an invalid entry in the column *hostname*. This case can also be recognized with mysql. (Note that this time, the error message is different.)

```
linux~/$mysql -h uranus.sol -u name -p databasename
Enter password: xxxxx
ERROR 1130: Host '192.168.0.2' is not allowed to connect to this MySQL server
```

  With the command resolveip 192.168.0.2 you can determine which host name is expected by MySQL for this address. (On my computer, the command returns the result *uranus.sol.*) Then you can check whether the table *mysql.user* contains a corresponding entry (and not, say, simply *uranus*).

- Another possible cause is that there is a correct entry in *mysql.user*, but the specified user name and password do not match. Note that this time, the error message looks different:

```
linux~/$ mysql -h uranus.sol -u name -p databasename
Enter password: xxxxx
ERROR 1045: Access denied for user: 'root@192.168.0.2'
(Using password: YES)
```

Once you have succeeded in gaining access to the MySQL server with the program mysql by giving the computer name, the Java program should generally run if the same user name and password are used.

POINTER *Further tips on solving access problems (independent of Java) can be found in Chapter 9.*

Executing SQL Commands

Before you can execute SQL commands, you need a *Statement* object. You obtain it with *conn.createStatement*:

```
Statement stmt = conn.createStatement();
```

> **POINTER**   *If you have in mind executing* SELECT *queries, then you can use two optional parameters to select the cursor type and specify whether the data resulting from* SELECT *are able to be changed:*
>
> ```
> stmt = conn.createStatement(resultcursortype, resultconcurrency);
> ```
>
> *By default, the cursor type is* forward only, *and the data are* read only. *Additional details to follow.*

The *Statement* class now offers a selection of various *execute* methods:

- *executeUpdate* for *INSERT, UPDATE,* and *DELETE* commands;

- *executeQuery* for *SELECT* queries;

- *executeBatch* for executing several commands that have been previously specified with *addBatch* as a block (which can increase efficiency);

- *execute* to execute an arbitrary SQL command (where it is not known in advance what sort of command it will be).

In the following pages we shall look more closely at the variants *executeUpdate, executeQuery,* and *executeBatch.*

Executing INSERT, UPDATE, and DELETE Commands

The execution of an *INSERT, UPDATE,* or *DELETE* command is quite simple: You simply pass the SQL command as a character string to the method *executeUpdate*:

```
stmt.executeUpdate(
  "INSERT INTO publishers (publName) VALUES ('new publisher')");
```

The method *executeUpdate* returns an *int* value that specifies how many records were changed by the command.

> **POINTER**   *If you wish to pass strings to the SQL command that contain special characters like* ', ", \, *and so on, you should use* prepared statements, *which will be discussed shortly.*

Determining ID Numbers from a New Data Record (AUTO_INCREMENT)

There are several ways of determining the *AUTO_INCREMENT* number of newly created records. Which variant is to be preferred depends on the version of Java that you are using.

Variant 1: Starting with Java 1.4, the method *getGeneratedKeys* has been available. If you are working with a current version of Java, then *getGeneratedKeys* represents the best, most efficient, and most portable option. The method returns a *ResultSet* object (which will be described later when we discuss the evaluation of *SELECT* queries).

If there is precisely one new record, then the *ResultSet* object contains only one record with the sought ID number. To evaluate, execute first the method *next* (to address the first record of the *ResultSet* object) and then read the ID number with the method *getInt(1)* (the index 1 denotes the column of the record):

```
// SampleGetID1
stmt.executeUpdate("INSERT ... ");
ResultSet newid = stmt.getGeneratedKeys();
newid.next();
int id = newid.getInt(1);
```

According to the JDBC documentation, *getGeneratedKeys* should also return a list of new ID numbers when *INSERT* commands were executed that generate several new data records. In order for JDBC to take note of new ID numbers, the optional parameter *Statement.RETURN_GENERATED_KEYS* must be passed to *executeUpdate*. However, a subsequent evaluation of *ResultSets* returns only a single ID number (that of the first inserted record). The reason for this lies not with Connector/J, but in the fact that in this situation, the MySQL server is unable to make the ID information available:

```
stmt.executeUpdate(
  "INSERT INTO publishers (publName) VALUES ('publisher1'), (' publisher2')",
  Statement.RETURN_GENERATED_KEYS);
ResultSet newids = stmt.getGeneratedKeys();
while(newids.next()) {   // returns only the ID of publisher1!
  System.out.println("ID: " + newids.getInt(1));
}
```

Variant 2: If you are working with an older version of Java, you can use the method *getLastInsertID* of the *Statement* object to obtain the last *AUTO_INCREMENT* value. However, this method is defined specifically only for the *Statement* class of Connector/J, not for the *Statement* interface from *java.sql*. Therefore, you must transform the *Statement* object, via a cast operation, into an object of the class *com.mysql.jdbc.Statement* before you can use the method. (This works for *PreparedStatement* objects as well, which will be described further on.)

The principal disadvantage of *getLastInsertID* is that the resulting code is not portable, functioning only for MySQL in combination with the Connector/J driver:

```
// SampleGetID2.java
Statement stmt = conn.createStatement();
stmt.executeUpdate(
  "INSERT INTO publishers (publName) VALUES ('new publisher')");
long id = ((com.mysql.jdbc.Statement)stmt).getLastInsertID();
```

Variant 3: A third possibility (the slowest!) is to execute the additional SQL command *SELECT LAST_INSERT_ID( )* after the *INSERT* command. However, you must see to it that this command is executed in the same MySQL connection *and* within a transaction. If you are working with InnoDB tables, you must set *conn.setAutoCommit(false)* and close the transaction with *conn.commit( )*:

```
// SampleGetID3.java
conn.setAutoCommit(false);
stmt.executeUpdate(
  "INSERT INTO publishers (publName) VALUES ('new publisher')");
ResultSet newid = stmt.executeQuery("SELECT LAST_INSERT_ID()");
if(newid.next()) {
  id = newid.getInt(1);
  System.out.println("new ID = " + id); }
conn.commit();
```

Evaluating SELECT *Queries*

In order to be able to evaluate the results of a *SELECT* query, you must execute the SQL command with *executeQuery*. This method returns a *ResultSet* object:

```
Statement stmt = conn.createStatement();
ResultSet res = stmt.executeQuery(
  "SELECT publID, publName FROM publishers " +
  "WHERE publID < 10 ORDER BY publName");
```

> **WARNING**   *If you have already developed JDBC programs with database drivers other than Connector/J, you should take note of the default properties of* ResultSet *objects:*
>
> *By default, the* ResultSet *object cannot be edited (read only).*
>
> *By default, the* ResultSet *object supports free navigation. This has the consequence that all data are immediately transferred from MySQL server to client, even with large query results. This behavior differs from that of many other JDBC drivers, for which the* ResultSet *is forward only by default and is transferred only as required.*
>
> *If you wish to have* ResultSet *properties that differ from the default behavior, then you must specify this in the creation of* Statement *objects for the query. More details to follow (see the headings* Forward-only ResultSets *and* Variable ResultSets*).*

To begin, that is, immediately after the execution of *executeQuery*, no record is active. To address the first record, the method *res.next()* must be executed. All further records will be run through with *next()* until this method returns the result *false*.

For the currently active record, the individual columns can be selected with the methods *getInt, getString*, etc. Optionally, this method can be passed the column number (e.g., *res.getInt(1)* for the first column) or the column name (e.g., *res.getInt("publID")*. The latter variant leads to more readable code, but is slower.

The following loop selects all found records from the previously given *SELECT* query and displays them in the console window:

```
while (res.next()) {
  int id = res.getInt("publID");
  String name = res.getString("publName");
  System.out.println("ID: " + id + "  Name: " + name);
}
```

Invalid and Empty Queries

If the syntax of an SQL command is invalid, then the execution of *executeQuery* throws an *SQLException* exception.

If the query returns no result (zero records), then *executeQuery* returns simply an empty *ResultSet* object (not *NULL*). The only way to determine whether a *SELECT* query has returned results is by executing *res.next()*. Once this method has returned the value *false*, the *ResultSet* object is empty.

Checking for NULL

Methods such as *getInt* and *getFloat* that return elementary Java data types are incapable of differentiating 0 and *NULL*. To determine whether the last selected data field contained *NULL*, one has the method *wasNull*:

```
int n = res.getInt(1);
if(res.wasNull)
  System.out.println("n = [NULL]");
else
  System.out.println("n = " + n);
```

> **TIP** *With character strings, the use of* wasNull *is unnecessary, since in* String *variables, the state* null *can be stored. You can therefore execute* String s = res.getString(. . .) *and then test whether* s == null.

Navigating in the ResultSet

In addition to the method *next*, there are several additional methods for selecting the currently active data record: *previous* activates the previous record, while *first* and *last* activate the records that their names imply. With these methods, the data record pointer is directed to the place before the first or after the last record. You can test with *isFirst* and *isLast* whether the beginning or end of the record list has been reached. The method *getRow* returns the number of the current record (1 for the first); *absolute* activates a record that is specified by its number.

Determining the Number of Found Records

Since Connector/J returns by default navigable *ResultSet*s, it is rather simple to determine the number of records: With *last*, the last record is activated, and then with *getRow* its number is determined:

```
res.last();
int n = res.getRow();
```

If you then wish to run a loop over all records, you must set the record pointer to the beginning:

```
res.beforeFirst();
while(res.next()) ...
```

If you also want to determine the number of columns, you need a *ResultSetMetaData* object, which we discuss next.

Determining Metadata About the ResultSet

If you do not know in advance which data your *SELECT* query returns (for example, if you wish to write a program that can work with arbitrary tables), you can employ the class *ResultSetMetaData* to return all relevant information about the *SELECT* result: the number of columns (*getColumnCount*), their names (*getColumnName*), their data types (*getColumnType* and *getColumnTypeName*), and the number of decimal places (*getPrecision, getScale*). With methods such as *isNullable, isAutoIncrement*, and *isSigned*, you can find out additional properties of each column. All of these methods require as parameter the column number about which you want information.

You obtain a *ResultSetMetaData* object with the method *getMetaData*, which is applied to a *ResultSet* object. The following lines show a simple application of *ResultSetMetaData*:

```
int i, n;
ResultSetMetaData meta = res.getMetaData();
n = meta.getColumnCount();
System.out.println("number of columns: " + meta.getColumnCount());
for(i=1; i<=n; i++) {
  System.out.println("column " + i + ": " +
    " name: " + meta.getColumnName(i) +
    " data type: " + meta.getColumnTypeName(i));
}
```

Forward-Only ResultSets

By default, *ResultSet*s are freely navigable; that is, you can change the currently active record at will using *previous, next,* etc. This is convenient, but it has the drawback that when you execute *executeQuery*, all data records that are found must be transferred from the MySQL server to the Java program. This can involve not only large data sets, but also the need for the Java program to reserve a large amount of memory. When you are processing numerous data sequentially, this is not the optimal way to proceed.

If you wish to transfer the records individually, you must define the *Statement* object for your *SELECT* query as follows. (*Integer.MIN_VALUE* is the smallest representable integer. Connector/J requires that exactly this value be passed.)

```
Statement stmt = conn.createStatement(
  java.sql.ResultSet.TYPE_FORWARD_ONLY,
  java.sql.ResultSet.CONCUR_READ_ONLY);
stmt.setFetchSize(Integer.MIN_VALUE);
ResultSet res = stmt.executeQuery("SELECT ... ");
```

WARNING *Note that you can use only* next() *for navigation in the* ResultSet *(that is, navigation is* forward-only*). Note as well that you can execute a further SQL command for the existing connection (*Connection *object) only when you have completely run through the* ResultSet *or have closed the connection with* close. *(You may, of course, have a second connection open.)*

Variable ResultSets

If you want to edit the data in a table, you generally execute *INSERT, UPDATE,* and *DELETE* commands. However, JDBC offers another possibility: You can insert, edit, and delete data records directly in a *ResultSet* object; these changes are then executed in the underlying table. However, for this to function, certain conditions must be satisfied:

- The *Statement* object must be opened with the additional parameter *ResultSet.CONCUR_UPDATABLE*.

- The *SELECT* query can encompass only one table (no *JOINs*), may not use any *GROUP* functions, and must include the primary index.

If these conditions are satisfied, you can delete the current record from the *ResultSet* and the database with *deleteRow*.

To edit the current record, execute the methods *updateInt(n, 123), updateString(n, "new text"),* etc. You must then confirm these changes with *updateRow*.

To insert a new record, first execute *moveToInsertRow.* Now specify the value to be stored with *updateXxx* methods and confirm the insertion operation with *insertRow*.

If you wish to know the ID number of the new record (*AUTO_INCREMENT*), execute *last.* This ensures that the new record is also the active record. You can then select the ID column with *getInt(n)*.

The following program first selects all records from the *publisher* table of the *mylibrary* database. Then a new record is inserted, after which it is edited and then deleted.

> **REMARK**   *Records inserted into a* ResultSet *can no longer be edited. Therefore, in our example program, the* ResultSet *is first input afresh.*

```
// SampleChangeResultSet.java
stmt = conn.createStatement(ResultSet.TYPE_SCROLL_SENSITIVE,
ResultSet.CONCUR_UPDATABLE);

// insert new publisher, then display all publishers
res = stmt.executeQuery(
  "SELECT publID, publName FROM publishers ORDER BY publID");
res.moveToInsertRow();
res.updateString(2, "New publisher");
res.insertRow();
res.last();
int newid = res.getInt(1);
res.beforeFirst();
while (res.next())
  System.out.println(res.getString(1) + " " + res.getString(2));
res.close();
```

```
// edit the previously inserted new publisher
res = stmt.executeQuery(
  "SELECT publID, publName FROM publishers WHERE publID = " + newid);
res.next();
res.updateString(2, "new with another name");
res.updateRow();

// ... and delete
res.last();
res.deleteRow();
res.close();
```

Closing a `ResultSet` *Object*

If you no longer need a *ResultSet* object, you should close it explicitly with *close.* This allows reserved memory to be returned earlier than otherwise. In the case of incompletely run-through forward-only *ResultSet*s, the result is the release of resources blocked by the MySQL server.

Prepared Statements

Prepared statements make it possible to formulate an SQL command with placeholders. Before the execution of the command, the placeholders must be passed. The advantage of this way of proceeding is that JDBC looks after the transformation of character strings and binary data into a MySQL-compatible syntax. This includes both the addition of quotation marks at the beginning and end of strings and the transformation of special characters such as ' into \' and \ into \\.

With many database systems, prepared statements can offer an advantage in speed, since the SQL code must be transferred only once to the database server. However, this is not yet the case with MySQL 4.0. It is only starting with version 4.1 that MySQL is better optimized in this way (where the advantages are realized only if a suitable Connector/J version is used with MySQL 4.1).

The starting point for prepared statements is a *PreparedStatment* object, which is generated with the method *prepareStatment.* Note that character-string parameters may not be enclosed in quotation marks, which is usually the case with strings (that is, *VALUES (?)* and not *VALUES(' ?')*).

To pass parameters, use methods such as *setString, setInt, setNull, setDate,* and *setBinaryStream.* (A complete reference is given in the class description of *PreparedStatement.*)

To execute the SQL command, use, depending on the type of command, the familiar methods of the *Statement* class, for example, *executeUpdate, executeQuery, addBatch,* and *executeBatch.* What is new is that you can no longer pass parameters to these methods: The SQL command was already defined in *prepareStatement,* and the parameters are set with *setXxx* methods.

In the following example, two new publishers are inserted into the *publisher* table of the *mylibrary* database:

```
// SamplePreparedStatement.java
PreparedStatement pstmt = conn.prepareStatement(
  "INSERT INTO publishers (publName) VALUES (?)");
pstmt.setString(1, "O'Reilly");    // inserts O'Reilly
pstmt.executeUpdate();
pstmt.setString(1, "\\abc\"efg");  // inserts \abc"efg
pstmt.executeUpdate();
```

Unicode

Internally, all character strings in Java are stored in Unicode format, that is, using a character set that contains more than 65,000 characters. MySQL 4.0 is unfortunately not yet Unicode compatible. (Unicode support will come only with version 4.1. However, it is unclear how the Java support for this will look. Work is now proceeding on a new version of Connector/J.)

Transforming Unicode Character Strings into the Character Set of the MySQL server

By default, Connector/J transforms all Java character strings that become components of SQL commands from Unicode into the character set that the MySQL server uses (by default, *latin1*; see Chapter 10). Conversely, strings read from MySQL are transformed into Unicode.

> **REMARK** *As the basis for character set transformation, Connector/J attempts to recognize the character set of the MySQL server at the time of creation of the connection. This has functioned reliably since Connector/J 3.0.3. With earlier versions or if for some reason you wish to use a different character set, at connection time you must use a URL of the following pattern. (The string is divided here into two pieces.)*
>
> ```
> jdbc:mysql://hostname/databasename?useUnicode=true&
>     characterEncoding=ISO-8859-15
> ```
>
> *A list of character sets supported by Java can be found in the Java documentation, for version 1.4.1, for example, at the address below. In establishing the connection, the character set name of the second column must be specified* (Canonical name for java.io and java.lang API):
>
> ```
> http://java.sun.com/j2se/1.4.1/docs/guide/intl/encoding.doc.html
> ```

The automatic adaptation of the character set has the drawback that all characters that cannot be represented in the character set of the MySQL server are replaced by question marks.

In the following example, three records are stored in the table *test_text*:

```
// example SampleUnicode.java
Statement stmt = conn.createStatement();
stmt.executeUpdate(
  "INSERT INTO test_text (a_varchar) VALUES ('ÄÖÜ')");
stmt.executeUpdate(
  "INSERT INTO test_text (a_varchar) VALUES ('EURO \u20ac EURO')");
stmt.executeUpdate(
  "INSERT INTO test_text (a_varchar) VALUES ('Smiley \u263A')");
```

The table then contains three new records, whose *a_varchar* column contains the following strings. Note that in the MySQL's *latin1* character set, the unrepresentable characters for the smiley face and the euro symbol were automatically represented by the character ?. The characters ÄÖÜ, on the other hand, were represented correctly:

```
'ÄÖÜ', 'EURO ? EURO', 'Smiley ?'
```

You obtain exactly the same result if you generate the new records with a *PreparedStatment*:

```
PreparedStatement pstmt = conn.prepareStatement(
  "INSERT INTO test_text (a_varchar) VALUES (?)");
pstmt.setString(1, "ÄÖÜ");
pstmt.executeUpdate();
pstmt.setString(1, "EURO \u20ac EURO");
pstmt.executeUpdate();
pstmt.setString(1, "Smiley \u263A");
pstmt.executeUpdate();
```

Storing Unicode Character Strings Unchanged

If you wish to overcome the restrictions of the MySQL server's character set and store all Unicode characters unchanged (without running the risk of of losing individual characters), then at the establishment of the connection, you can specify the Unicode character set explicitly, e.g., UTF8.

The main disadvantage of this is that the MySQL server now has no practicable way of sorting or indexing data. Even such comparisons as *SELECT . . . WHERE x LIKE '%xy%'* are condemned to failure:

```
// example SampleUnicode.java
Connection conn2 = DriverManager.getConnection(
  "jdbc:mysql://uranus/exceptions?" +
  "useUnicode=true&characterEncoding=UTF8", "root", "uranus");
Statement stmt = conn2.createStatement();
stmt.executeUpdate(
  "INSERT INTO test_text (a_varchar) VALUES ('^…†')");
stmt.executeUpdate(
  "INSERT INTO test_text (a_varchar) VALUES ('EURO \u20ac EURO')");
stmt.executeUpdate(
  "INSERT INTO test_text (a_varchar) VALUES ('Smiley \u263A')");
```

Transactions

JDBC supports transactions via the *Connection* object. Of course, transactions are possible only if your MySQL tables are in a format that supports transactions (generally InnoDB).

By default, JDBC is in *AutoCommit* mode; that is, every SQL command is considered a separate transaction and is executed immediately. You can determine the mode with *getAutoCommit* and change it with *setAutoCommit*. At the same time, the starting point for the first transaction is specified by *setAutoCommit(false)*, which you can either confirm with *commit* or abort with *rollback*. These two commands simultaneously start the next transaction.

The following lines show a simple application. Several *INSERT* commands are executed within a *try* block. If an error occurs, the entire transaction is aborted:

```
// no AutoCommit after each command
conn.setAutoCommit(false);

// execute several commands
try {
  stmt.executeUpdate("INSERT INTO table1 ... ");
  stmt.executeUpdate("INSERT INTO table2 ... ");
  conn.commit();
}
catch(Exception e) {
  conn.rollback();
}
```

> **REMARK**   *The InnoDB documentation recommends that in client programming you generally not rely on the transaction methods of the library or API, and instead, that you execute the SQL commands* SET AUTOCOMMIT= ...   *and* BEGIN/COMMIT/ROLLBACK *explicitly. The reason is that with many libraries, the transaction functions in combination with MySQL have not been adequately tested.*

Batch Commands

JDBC offers the possibility of executing several SQL commands as a block. Such command blocks are called *batches* in the database community. The advantage over the individual execution of SQL commands is somewhat greater efficiency (depending on the application).

> **REMARK** *Do not confuse batches with transactions. Batches are appropriate only if you do not need to read in your altered data in the confines of the batch. Thus you can execute a series of* INSERT *or* UPDATE *commands within a batch only if you do not determine any* AUTO_INCREMENT *values or execute any* SELECT *queries in between. Moreover, batches offer no mechanism for error handling. If an error occurs within a batch, then all SQL commands executed to that point remain valid, while all further commands will be rejected.*
>
> *Batches are thus a simple aid in executing a large number of* INSERT *or* UPDATE *commands efficiently. The goal of a transaction, on the other hand, is to obtain greater data security. For example, transactions ensure that either all commands of a transaction are correctly executed, or none of them.*
>
> *Of course, a batch can be executed within a transaction.*

Batch commands are formed in two parts: First, all commands to be executed are passed with *addBatch* to a *Statement* or *PreparedStatment* command. Then the commands thus collected are executed with *executeBatch*.

The method *executeBatch* returns an *int* field, which for each SQL command specifies how many records were changed (a number greater than or equal to 0). If this number could not be determined, but the command was executed without error, then the return value is *SUCCESS_NO_INFO*. If an error did occur, then the return value is *EXECUTE_FAILED*. (Note, however, that with syntax errors, the execution of the batch command is broken off with an exception.)

The following lines show the execution of a simple batch command:

```
int i;
stmt = conn.createStatement();
stmt.addBatch("INSERT INTO publishers (publName) VALUES ('publ1')");
stmt.addBatch("INSERT INTO publishers (publName) VALUES ('publ2')");
stmt.addBatch("INSERT INTO publishers (publName) VALUES " +
            "('publ3'), ('publ4')");
int[] n = stmt.executeBatch();
for(i=0; i < n.length; i++)
  System.out.println(
    "Recordsets changed by batch command no " + (i+1) + ": " + n[i]);
```

If no errors occur during execution, the following text appears in the console window:

```
Recordsets changed by batch command no 1: 1
Recordsets changed by batch command no 2: 1
Recordsets changed by batch command no 3: 2
```

Working with Binary Data (BLOBs)

JDBC offers several ways of dealing with binary data:

- When the task at hand is to read data from a file or to store data to a file, the methods *ResultSet.getBinaryStream* and *PreparedStatement.setBinaryStream* are to be recommended. In the first case, you can read the binary data from the database with the aid of an *InputStream*. In the second case, you pass an existing *InputStream* object (e.g., that of a file) to transfer its data into a parameter of an SQL command.

- With BLOBs that contain Unicode text you will find *getCharacterStream* and *setCharacterStream* helpful. You can use *java.io.Reader* objects with them to select text at the character level.

- If you wish to process data as a *byte* array, you can use the methods *getBytes* and *setBytes*.

- Finally, JDBC offers the interfaces *Blob* and *Clob* (character large object): With *Blob* objects you can conveniently read and edit data byte by byte with the methods *getBytes* and *setBytes*. *Clob* objects offer a character-oriented approach with methods such as *getAsciiStream* and *getCharacterStream*. The passing of *Blob/Clob* objects takes place with the methods *getClob*, *setBlob*, *setClob*, and *getBlob*.

An Example

The following example shows the application of the methods *getBinaryStream* and *setBinaryStream*. The program loads the content of the file test.jpg, stores it in a new record in the database exceptions (table *a_blob*), reads it from there, and stores the data thus obtained in the new file test-copy.jpg. Then the new record in *a_blob* is deleted.

The SQL commands are executed with *PreparedStatement* objects that are created at the beginning of the program excerpt reproduced here. For transferring the file into the *a_blob* table, a *FileInputStream* object with *setBinaryStream* as parameter is simply passed to the first *PreparedStatement* object.

It is somewhat more complicated to read the data from the *a_blob* table and store it in a file. The *BinaryStream* object obtained from the *ResultSet* object via *getBinaryStream* must be read in a loop and copied with the help of a buffer into a *fileOutputStream* object:

```
// example SampleBlob.java
import java.sql.*;
import java.io.*;
 ...

// establish the connection
Connection conn = DriverManager.getConnection(
  "jdbc:mysql://uranus/exceptions", "root", "uranus");
```

```
// create three PreparedStatement objects
PreparedStatement pstmt1, pstmt2, pstmt3;
pstmt1 = conn.prepareStatement(
  "INSERT INTO test_blob (a_blob) VALUES(?)");
pstmt2 = conn.prepareStatement(
  "SELECT a_blob FROM test_blob WHERE id=?");
pstmt3 = conn.prepareStatement(
  "DELETE FROM test_blob WHERE id=?");

// read file test.jpg and store it in a BLOB field
File readfile = new File("test.jpg");
FileInputStream fis = new FileInputStream(readfile);
pstmt1.setBinaryStream(1, fis, (int)readfile.length());
pstmt1.executeUpdate();
fis.close();

// determine the ID of the new record
long id = ((com.mysql.jdbc.Statement)pstmt1).getLastInsertID();

// create new, empty, file copy-test.jpg
File writefile = new File("copy-test.jpg");
if(writefile.exists()) {
  writefile.delete();
  writefile.createNewFile(); }
FileOutputStream fos = new FileOutputStream(writefile);

// read BLOB field from the database
pstmt2.setLong(1, id);
ResultSet res = pstmt2.executeQuery();
res.next();
InputStream is = res.getBinaryStream(1);

// store binary data in the new file
final int BSIZE = 2^15;
int n;
byte[] buffer = new byte[BSIZE];
while((n=is.read(buffer, 0, BSIZE))>0)
  fos.write(buffer, 0, n);

// close open objects
is.close();
fos.close();
res.close();

// delete the new record
pstmt3.setLong(1, id);
pstmt3.executeUpdate();
```

Peculiarities of Large BLOBs

BLOBs are always transferred in their entirety between MySQL and the Java program. Connector/J is incapable of piecewise transfer. For this reason, the Java virtual machine (JVM) must be so configured that it can reserve enough space to hold the entire BLOB in local memory.

Moreover, the MySQL server must allow the transfer of large data packets (variable *max_allowed_packet*; see Chapter 19). If necessary, you can increase the value of the variable on the client side by executing the following command:

```
SET max_allowed_packet=16000000
```

Java Server Pages (JSP)

Tomcat Installation

Tomcat is a JSP-savvy web server. This section presents some tips for the installation and use of Tomcat 4.0.4 in combination with Apache 1.3.*n* under SuSE Linux 8.1.

> **POINTER** *There is not sufficient space here to describe all possible combinations and versions of Tomcat and Apache for various Linux distributions. If you are using other Tomcat, Apache, or Linux versions, you should look at the following web sites for the documentation relating to your particular distribution:*
>
> http://jakarta.apache.org/
> http://java.sun.com/products/jsp/
> http://java.sun.com/products/servlet/

The basic assumption is that in addition to Java SDK, the packages apache and jakarta-tomcat have been installed. So that Tomcat can be integrated into Apache (so that Apache knows how it is to deal with JSPs), the following line must be added to /etc/sysconfig/apache. (In principle, it is also possible to use Tomcat as an independent web server, that is, without Apache; however, we will not deal with that case here.)

```
HTTPD_SEC_MOD_TOMCAT=yes
```

Furthermore, it must be ensured that both Apache and Tomcat can actually be executed:

```
root# /etc/init.d/apache start
root# /etc/init.d/tomcat start
```

To make Apache and Tomcat start automatically when the computer is started, execute the following commands:

```
root# insserv apache
root# insserv tomcat
```

You can check with a web browser to see whether everything is functioning as it should by looking at the local page `http://localhost:8080`. You should see the Tomcat default start page.

By default, Tomcat in the SuSE configuration uses the directory `/opt/jakarta/tomcat/webapps`. We should look at several examples.

Hello, JSP World!

The Java servlet specification describes, since version 2.3, exactly how a directory with JSP and servlet applications should look. There is insufficient space here to discuss this concept in detail (and furthermore, this topic has nothing to do with MySQL). The following paragraphs describe only the steps necessary for carrying out initial tests with your own JSP files. For the development of real-world JSP applications, additional configuration is necessary, affecting particularly the directory `WEB-INF` and the file `WEB-INF/web.xml`.

> **POINTER** *Information on how to assemble and configure your JSP projects can be found in any current JSP book or, for example, at the following address:*
>
> `http://jakarta.apache.org/tomcat/tomcat-4.0-doc/appdev/deployment.html`

The first step in creating your own examples consists in creating a subdirectory in the webapps directory for your project:

```
root# cd /opt/jakarta/tomcat/webapps
root# mkdir mytest
root# cd mytest
```

To make Tomcat accept the directory mytest as a web application, the subdirectory `WEB-INF` must be created. This directory can contain various configuration files for the project as well as additional files that should not be publicly accessible over the web server. But even if `WEB-INF` is empty, as in this example, the directory must exist! Note also the correct spelling (including the uppercase letters).

```
root# mkdir WEB-INF
```

In order for Tomcat to become aware of the new project directory, the program has to be restarted:

```
root# /etc/init.d/tomcat restart
```

Now create a first JSP file with the name test.jsp, for example, according to the following design:

```
<!-- test.jsp -->
<html>
<head><title>Hello JSP</title></head>
<body>
<h2>
  <p>Hello JSP World!</p>
  <p>Date: <%= new java.util.Date() %></p>
</h2>
</body></html>
```

To check whether the JSP code is being executed by the web server, give the following address to the web browser. The result should look like that depicted in Figure 15-1:

```
http://localhost:8080/mytest/test.jsp
```

Figure 15-1. A first JSP example

Connector/J Installation

If you wish to access MySQL in JSP code, then Connector/J must be installed as with every Java program. For this there are several possibilities:

- Install the Connector/J *.jar file in the Java interpreter directory *installation_directory*\jre\lib\ext. Now Connector/J is available to all Java and JSP projects.

- Install the *.jar file in the Tomcat directory lib or common/lib. Now Connector/J is available to all JSP projects (in common/lib, to all except for Tomcat itself).

- Install the *.jar file in the JSP project directory webapps/jspproject/WEB-INF/lib. Now Connector/J is available only to the project jspproject. This variant is particularly attractive if your project runs on an ISP that does not wish to change its Java installation with global additional libraries.

The *CLASSPATH* variant discussed in the last section is not a possibility here, since Tomcat ignores this variable.

JSTL Installation

As will be described later, in JSP files you have the option of using conventional Java code or *tags* (such as *<sql:query ..>SELECT * FROM TABLE</sql:query>*). If you decide on the second option, you must install JSTL (JSP Standard Tag Library). This library is not a component of Tomcat. An archive with the JSTL for download is available at the following address:

```
http://jakarta.apache.org/taglibs/doc/standard-doc/intro.html
```

After you have downloaded the current version, you can unpack it into the directory of your choice with the following command:

```
root# tar xzf jakarta-taglibs-standard-n.tar.gz
```

As result, you obtain two directories: lib/, with *.jar files, and tld/, with *.tld files. Now you must copy those *.jar and *.tld files that you wish to deploy into the directories WEB-INF/lib or WEB-INF/. (For the examples of this chapter you will need jstl.jar and standard.jar, as well as c.tdl and sql.tdl.)

The last step requires you to add *<taglib>* entries to WEB-INF/web.xml, the configuration file for your JSP project. If you do not yet have a web.xml file (which is possible only with very simple JSP projects), the following lines give a minimal version of web.xml:

```
<?xml version="1.0" encoding="ISO-8859-1"?>
<!DOCTYPE web-app
    PUBLIC "-//Sun Microsystems, Inc.//DTD Web Application 2.3//EN"
    "http://java.sun.com/dtd/web-app_2_3.dtd">
<web-app>
  <taglib>
    <taglib-uri>http://java.sun.com/jstl/core</taglib-uri>
    <taglib-location>/WEB-INF/c.tld</taglib-location>
  </taglib>
  <taglib>
    <taglib-uri>http://java.sun.com/jstl/sql</taglib-uri>
    <taglib-location>/WEB-INF/sql.tld</taglib-location>
  </taglib>
</web-app>
```

Programming Techniques

JSP files are HTML documents with embedded Java code. There are two basic ways of specifying Java code:

- You can place traditional Java code between <% and %>. this code is executed when the page is displayed. All output carried out with *system.out* appears in the resulting HTML page. (This variant corresponds exactly to the way that PHP and ASP work.)

In addition to *<% xxx %>*, there are some further variants: *<%= xxx %>* for the direct output of the result of a Java expression, *<%! xxx%>* for the declaration of variables that maintain their value between several page calls, and *<%@ xxx%>* for the definition of attributes that hold for the entire page.

- You can also specify Java code in the form of tags, which take, for example, the form *<sql:query . . . >SELECT * FROM TABLE</sql:query>*. These tags are given directly in HTML code and make possible much more compact code. However, such a programmed JSP page has little to do with a traditional Java program. For XML fans, on the other hand, the syntax is rather intuitive.

Example with Traditional Java Code

If you specify traditional Java code between <% and %>, then all the programming techniques for JSP programming introduced in the previous section apply. The following JSP example file page1.jsp displays all the publishers in the *publisher* table of *mylibrary*. The code corresponds almost exactly to the introductory example of the previous sections. The only difference is the output, which now takes place over the variable *out*, predefined in the JSP environment, and contains HTML tags. Note as well the use of the method *encodeHTML*. This method is necessary so that any special characters <, >, & in names of *publishers* are translated into correct HTML code. See Figure 15-2:

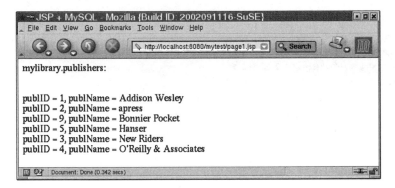

Figure 15-2. JSP example with traditional Java code

```
<!-- page1.jsp -->
<%@ page import="java.sql.*" %>
<%@ page contentType="text/html;charset=ISO-8859-1" %>

<html><head><title>JSP + MySQL</title></head>
<body>

<%!
    public String encodeHTML(String s) {
      StringBuffer sb = new StringBuffer();
      int slen = s.length();
      for(int i = 0; i < slen; i++) {
        char c = s.charAt(i);
```

```
      switch(c) {
        case '<': sb.append("&lt;");  break;
        case '>': sb.append("&gt;");  break;
        case '&': sb.append("&amp;"); break;
        default:  sb.append(c); }
    }
    return sb.toString();
  }
%>
<%
  // main code
  try {
    res;

    // establish the connection
    Class.forName("com.mysql.jdbc.Driver").newInstance();
    Connection conn = DriverManager.getConnection(
      "jdbc:mysql://uranus/mylibrary", "username", "password");

    // obtain publisher list ...
    Statement stmt = conn.createStatement();
    ResultSet res = stmt.executeQuery(
      "SELECT publID, publName FROM publishers " +
      "ORDER BY publName");

    // ... and display
    out.println("<p>mylibrary.publishers:</p><p>");
    while (res.next()) {
      int id = res.getInt("publID");
      String name = res.getString("publName");
      out.println("<br />publID = " + id + ",   name = "
        + encodeHTML(name));
    }
    res.close();
    out.println("</p>");

  }
  catch(Exception e) {
    out.println("<p>Error: " + e.toString() + "</p>");
  }
%>
</body></html>
```

Example with JSTL Tags

If you use tags from the JSTL, then the program just given can be formulated much more simply. (The resulting web page looks exactly like that in Figure 15-2.)

To make the program understandable, we give a brief description of the tags used: *<sql:setDataSource>* creates the connection to the databse. As with traditional Java code, the connection information is stored as a *Connection* object in the variable *conn*.

The tag *<sql:query>* executes an SQL query and stores the result in the variable *res*. In the loop *<c:forEach>*, the loop variable *row* runs through all records of the result of the SQL query (*res.rows*). Access to the individual columns takes place by their names (e.g., *row.publID*). The output is accomplished via *<c:out>*. Note that the function *encodeHTML* used earlier is no longer required, since *<c:out>* takes care of the HTML-compatible coding on its own:

```
<!-- page2.jsp -->
<%@ page contentType="text/html;charset=ISO-8859-1" %>
<%@ taglib uri="http://java.sun.com/jstl/core" prefix="c" %>
<%@ taglib uri="http://java.sun.com/jstl/sql"  prefix="sql" %>

<html><head><title>JSP + MySQL</title></head>
<body>
<sql:setDataSource var="conn" driver="com.mysql.jdbc.Driver"
  url="jdbc:mysql://uranus/mylibrary" user="username"
  password="password" />

<sql:query var="res" dataSource="${conn}">
  SELECT publID, publName
  FROM publishers
  ORDER BY publName
</sql:query>

<p>mylibrary.publishers:</p>
<p>
<c:forEach var="row" items="${res.rows}">
  <br />publID = <c:out value="${row.publID}" />,
      publName = <c:out value="${row.publName}" />
</c:forEach>

</body></html>
```

For the example to function, the Tomcat directory webapps/mytest must contain the following files:

```
uranus:~ # cd /opt/jakarta/tomcat/webapps/mytest/
uranus:/opt/jakarta/tomcat/webapps/mytest # ls ÐlR
.:
drwxr-xr-x    3 root     root          4096 Jan  8 16:58 WEB-INF
-rw-r--r--    1 root     root          1510 Jan  8 11:02 page1.jsp
-rw-r--r--    1 root     root           711 Jan  8 18:32 page2.jsp
-rw-r--r--    1 root     root           147 Jan  7 15:12 test.jsp

./WEB-INF:
-rw-r--r--    1 root     root         11310 Jan  8 16:54 c.tld
drwxr-xr-x    2 root     root          4096 Jan  8 16:54 lib
-rw-r--r--    1 root     root          6127 Jan  8 16:54 sql.tld
-rw-r--r--    1 root     root           561 Jan  8 17:14 web.xml

./WEB-INF/lib:
-rw-r--r--    1 root     root         20962 Jan  8 16:54 jstl.jar
-rw-r--r-- 1 root root 516487 Jan 8 16:54 standard.jar
```

POINTER *A brief description of JSTL <sql> tags can be found in the syntax reference of Chapter 20.*

#### CHAPTER 16

C and C++

THIS CHAPTER GIVES A FIRST introduction to programming MySQL applications with the programming languages C and C++. In particular, we will introduce the client libraries for C and C++, that is, `libmysqlclient` and Connector/C++ (formerly known as MySQL++). This chapter considers programming only under Unix/Linux, and not under Windows.

Chapter Overview

The C Application Programming Interface

The C application programming interface (API) is the most elementary interface to MySQL. All other APIs, such as those for PHP, Perl, and C++, are based on the C API. Thus a knowledge of the C API will facilitate learning about the other APIs. The API functions constitute a component of the library `libmysqlclient`. Every C program that wishes to use MySQL functions must therefore have access to this library.

Please note that there are several versions of `libmysqlclient` in use: version 10 for MySQL 3.23.*n*, version 11 for the alpha and beta versions of MySQL 4.0.*n*, version 12 for the stable versions of MySQL 4.0.*n*, and finally, version 14 for MySQL 4.1.*n*. These libraries are largely compatible. Version 12 differs from version 10 only by some extensions that allow the new features of MySQL 4.0 to be used. This chapter is based on version 12, but because of the narrow range of difference, most of the information is valid for version 10 as well.

Assumptions

For developing C programs under Linux or a comparable Unix system, you will need, of course, the usual equipment, in particular, a C compiler (generally gcc) and the program make. Furthermore, all the necessary include and library files for compiling and linking must be installed. With many distributions (such as SuSE), certain packages must be installed as well, ending with -devel (e.g., `glicb-devel`). It might be a good idea to test out your installation by translating a very simple C program.

For the development of MySQL programs you will need, in addition, the MySQL developer files, consisting of include files and libraries. These files usually are located in the package `MySQL-Devel-n`. This chapter assumes that the developer files are located in the following places:

Include files	`/usr/include/mysql`
Libraries	`/usr/lib/mysql`

If these files are located elsewhere on your system, then the compile and link options will have to be changed accordingly.

Hello World

Perhaps a little program will help develop some intuition in the direction of MySQL programming with C. The following example assumes that the database *mylibrary* has been installed on the local computer (see Chapter 5). Furthermore, in the code you must change, in the function call *mysql_real_connect*, the user name (*"root"*) and password (*"XXX"*). The code is documented to the extent that it should give at least some idea of what is going on. Details on the use of MySQL functions appear later, in the section on programming techniques.

Program Code

```c
// example file hellow/main.c
#include <stdio.h>
#include <mysql.h> // functions from libmysqlclient
int main(int argc, char *argv[])
{
  int i;
  MYSQL *conn;         // connection
  MYSQL_RES *result;   // result of the SELECT query
  MYSQL_ROW row;       // a record form the SELECT query
  // create connection to MySQL
  conn = mysql_init(NULL);
  if(mysql_real_connect(
        conn, "localhost", "root", "XXX",
        "mylibrary", 0, NULL, 0) == NULL) {
      fprintf(stderr, "sorry, no database connection ... \n");
      return 1;
    }
  // create list of all publishers and determine number
  // of published titles
  const char *sql="SELECT COUNT(titleID), publName \
                  FROM publishers, titles \
                  WHERE publishers.publID = titles.publID \
                  GROUP BY publishers.publID \
                  ORDER BY publName";
  if(mysql_query(conn, sql)) {
    fprintf(stderr, "%s\n", mysql_error(conn));
    fprintf(stderr, "%s\n", sql);
    return 1;
  }
  // process result
  result = mysql_store_result(conn);
  if(result==NULL) {
    if(mysql_error(conn))
      fprintf(stderr, "%s\n", mysql_error(conn));
    else
      fprintf(stderr, "%s\n", "unknown error\n");
    return 1;
  }
  printf("%i records found\n", (int)mysql_num_rows(result));
  // loop over all data records
  while((row = mysql_fetch_row(result)) != NULL) {
    for(i=0; i < mysql_num_fields(result); i++) {
      if(row[i] == NULL)
        printf("[NULL]\t");
      else
        printf("%s\t", row[i]);
    }
    printf("\n");
  }
```

```
// release memory, break connection
mysql_free_result(result);
mysql_close(conn);
return 0;
}
```

If you execute the program, you should get the following result:

```
uranus:~/hellow-c $ ./hellow
6 records found
11      Addison-Wesley
2       apress
1       Bonnier Pocket
1       Hanser
2       New Riders
2       O'Reilly & Associates
```

Compiling and Linking C Programs

To compile and link the example program just presented under Linux or comparable Unix system, execute the following command:

```
$ gcc -o hellow -I/usr/include/mysql -lmysqlclient main.c
```

The following table explains the components of the command:

gcc	The GNU C and C++ compiler
-o hellow	the name of the executable code
-I/usr/include/mysql	the location of the MySQL include files (in particular, mysql.h)
-lmysqlclient	links the executable with the MySQL client library
main.c	the code file

Depending on the system configuration, the location of the MySQL include files can be different from those presented here (e.g., /usr/local/include/mysql).

Makefile

Assembling the input for the command for compiling and linking a program is generally rather labor-intensive (especially when a project consists of several files). Therefore, it is a good idea to create a file with the name Makefile that contains all necessary instructions in the syntax of the make command. To compile, you simply input make, which decides on its own which parts of the program need to be recompiled.

As starting point for creating your own projects, you can use the following example. Note that the make syntax for the indendation requires tabs (not spaces):

```
# example file hellow/Makefile
CC = gcc
INCLUDES = -I/usr/include/mysql
LIBS = -lmysqlclient

all:hellow

main.o: main.c
        $(CC) -c $(INCLUDES) main.c

hellow: main.o
        $(CC) -o hellow main.o $(LIBS)

clean:
        rm -f hellow main.o
```

Program Development with KDevelop

If you wish to create MySQL C programs using the development environent KDevelop, you must make the following settings in the dialog PROJECT | OPTIONS:

- COMPILER OPTIONS | FLAGS AND WARNINGS,
  Textbox C COMPILER FLAGS: -I/usr/include/mysql

- COMPILER OPTIONS | LINKER FLAGS,
  Textbox ADDITIONAL FLAGS: -lmysqlclient -lz

Static Binding of MySQL Functions

With the Makefile presented here, the library libmysqlclient is linked to the program dynamically if the *shared* library libmysqlclient.so can be found in one of the usual places (under Linux in the directory /lib or /usr/lib).

If this fails (because the library was not found) or if you wish that all MySQL API functions should be integrated directly into the executable (static instead of dynamic binding), you must specify the location of the static library variant libmysqlclient.a. This is generally in the directory /usr/lib/mysql.

Furthermore, you must now specify the additional option -lz. This permits the library libz to be consulted during linking. It contains functions accessed by libmyssqlclient for compressing data exchange between client and server (when that is desired):

```
$ gcc main.c -I/usr/include/mysql -L/usr/lib/mysql -lmysqlclient -lz -o hellow
```

If you are using make, you need to change only the *LIBS* variable:

```
LIBS = -L/usr/lib/mysql -lmysqlclient -lz
```

It can happen (depending on the Unix system and on which libmysqlclient functions you use) that in addition to libz, you will require other libraries. The following table summarizes the options that might be necessary:

-L/usr/lib/mysql	the location of the static MySQL libraries (libmysqlclient.a)
-lc	base library with basic functions (libc)
-lcrypt	library with cryptographic functions (libcrypt)
-lm	library with mathematical functions (libm)
-lnsl	library with *Name Service* functions (libnsl)
-lnss_files and -lnss_dns	library with *Name Service Switch* functions; further information in man nsswitch.conf
-lz	library with compression functions (libz)

The static variant has the advantage that all libmysqlclient functions that the program uses are compiled directly into the executable. This allows the program to run on a computer that does not have the libmysqlclient library installed.

However, this advantage is paid for by a larger executable than that in the dynamic version. The difference in size depends on how many functions you use from libmysqlclient. In our "Hello World" program, the dynamic executable is only 13 kilobytes, while the static variant weighs in at 175 kilobytes. (Note that only the MySQL functions are statically bound, not all functions from all other libraries.)

You can easily determine which dynamic libraries a program must access during execution with the command ldd. In the static variant of the "Hello World" program, the result looked as follows on my test system:

```
$ ldd hellow
      libz.so.1 => /lib/libz.so.1 (0x40020000)
      libc.so.6 => /lib/libc.so.6 (0x4002f000)
      /lib/ld-linux.so.2 => /lib/ld-linux.so.2 (0x40000000)
```

In the dynamic variant, the list of libraries is much longer. It contains, in addition to libmysqlclient, all libraries that are accessed by libmysqlclient:

```
$ ldd hellow
      libmysqlclient.so.11 => /usr/lib/libmysqlclient.so.11
         (0x40020000)
      libc.so.6 => /lib/libc.so.6 (0x40057000)
      libz.so.1 => /lib/libz.so.1 (0x40175000)
      libcrypt.so.1 => /lib/libcrypt.so.1 (0x40184000)
      libnsl.so.1 => /lib/libnsl.so.1 (0x401b5000)
      libm.so.6 => /lib/libm.so.6 (0x401ca000)
      libnss_files.so.2 => /lib/libnss_files.so.2 (0x401ee000)
      libnss_dns.so.2 => /lib/libnss_dns.so.2 (0x401f8000)
      libresolv.so.2 => /lib/libresolv.so.2 (0x401fc000)
      /lib/ld-linux.so.2 => /lib/ld-linux.so.2 (0x40000000)
```

Programming Techniques

An extensive syntax reference for the data structures and functions from the library libmysqlclient mentioned in this section can be found in Chapter 20.

Establishing the Connection

Before establishing a connection, you must initialize a data structure of type *MYSQL* with *mysql_init*. The connection is then established with *mysql_real_connect*, where as parameter, a pointer to the *MYSQL* structure as well as the usual connection data must be specified: the host name (or *"localhost"*) or the IP number of the server, the user name, password, name of the default database, the socket number (or 0 for the default value), the name of the socket file (or *NULL* for the default socket file), as well as certain flags that describe particular properties of the connection. (A list of all possible constants can be found in Chapter 20.)

```
MYSQL *conn;
conn = mysql_init(NULL);
if(mysql_real_connect(conn, "hostname", "username", "password",
                      "databasename", 0, NULL, 0) == NULL) {
    fprintf(stderr, "error message ... \n");
}
```

Once the connection is no longer needed, it should be closed with *mysql_close*:

```
mysql_close(conn);
```

Evaluation of the Configuration File my.cnf

If in establishing the connection you wish to have the settings in the configuration file my.cnf automatically evaluated (e.g., connecting over a nonstandard port number or socket file), then add a call to the function *mysql_options* between *mysql_init* and *mysql_real_connect*. The following instruction yields the result that all configuration settings of the group *[client]* are considered, to the extent that *NULL* or 0 is passed for the corresponding parameters in the following *mysql_real_connect* call. (This holds for user name and password as well.)

```
conn = mysql_init(NULL);
mysql_options(conn, MYSQL_READ_DEFAULT_GROUP, "");
mysql_real_connect( ... );
```

If in addition to the *[client]* options, you also want a further options group to be considered, then you should give its name in the last parameter of *mysql_options*:

```
mysql_options(conn, MYSQL_READ_DEFAULT_GROUP, "mygroup");
```

Evaluation of Options in the Command Line

With many standard MySQL programs (such as mysql, mysqladmin, mysqldump), you can send a connection parameter in a uniform format in the command line, for example, -hname or --host==name. An evaluation of this command parameter is especially sensible if you are developing administration programs in C that are to be applied to arbitrary databases. Unfortunately, the MySQL library does not offer a convenient means of doing so like *mysql_options*. Instead, it must be done by hand. The following points sketch the way to proceed:

- Instead of *mysql_options*, you call the unfortunately undocumented MySQL function *load_defaults* to read the settings from my.cnf and to copy them into the field of the command parameters (*argc* and *argv* of *main*). This has the advantage that all settings, whether they come from my.cnf or were passed as parameters, can be processed uniformly. Also, the string field *groups* specifies which options groups from my.cnf should be read and copied into *argv*:

```
const char *groups[] = {"mygroup", "client", NULL};
load_defaults("my", groups, &argc, &argv);
```

- Now create a loop and evaluate, with the standard function *getopt_long* (include file getopt.h), all parameters from *argv* and initialize variables for the host name, user name, etc. If a password is to be passed in the command line, you should overwrite it with blank characters for reasons of security. For interactive input of a password you can use the function *get_tty_password*.

- Finally, pass the values thus determined to *mysql_real_connect*.

> **POINTER** *This way of proceeding is described in full in the chapter "The MySQL C API" in the book* MySQL *by Paul DuBois. This chapter can also be found as a sample chapter on the author's web site, most recently at the following address:*
>
> http://www.kitebird.com/mysql-book/

Executing SQL Commands

To execute an SQL command, pass it as a character string to the function *mysql_query*. The string must contain only one SQL command, and it may not end with a semicolon. The function returns 0 if the SQL command was accepted by the server. (The return value allows one to draw conclusions only about whether the command was syntactically correct, not about whether the command changed data or whether, say, a *SELECT* command returned results.)

After *DELETE, INSERT,* or *UPDATE* commands, you can use *mysql_affected_rows* to determine how many records were changed as a result of the command. The result has the data type *my_ulonglong*. This data type is defined in the MySQL library; it describes a 64-bit unsigned integer.

If you have inserted a new record—perhaps with *INSERT*—into a table with an *AUTO_INCREMENT* column, you can determine the value of the *AUTO_INCREMENT* field with the function *mysql_insert_id*. This function also returns a result in the form of a *my_ulonglong* integer:

```
mysql_query(conn, "INSERT INTO publishers (publName) VALUES ('publisher')");
printf("publID = %i\n", (int)mysql_insert_id(conn));
```

Evaluating SELECT Results

After a *SELECT* command executed with *mysql_query*, you can process the expected results with either *mysql_store_result* or *mysql_use_result*. Both functions return a *MYSQL_RES* structure, from which you will be able to read out all the records with *mysql_fetch_row* one after another. The following lines show the general way of proceeding:

```
MYSQL_RES *result;  // result of a SELECT query
MYSQL_ROW row;      // a record of the result
  ...
result = mysql_store_result(conn);
if(result==NULL)
  fprintf(stderr, "%fehler ... \n");
else {
  while((row = mysql_fetch_row(result)) != NULL) {
    // process each record
  }
  mysql_free_result(result);  // release result
}
```

The *MYSQL_RES* structure for the results should then be released as soon as possible with *mysql_free_result* in order to keep memory requirements in the client (*mysql_store_result*) and resource demands on the server (*mysql_use_result*) as small as possible.

As the following table shows, *mysql_store_result* and *mysql_use_result* differ fundamentally internally:

mysql_store_result	**mysql_use_result**
All found records are immediately transmitted to client memory. With large record lists, this can result in large memory requirements for the client.	At first, no records are transmitted; that is, the data remain on the server. This means that the server is responsible for record management. Until this process is complete, resources on the server are occupied.
The records can be addressed in any order and as often as desired (function *mysql_data_seek*).	The records must be processed one at a time, and can be read only once.
The number of records found by *SELECT* can be determined immediately with *mysql_num_rows*.	The number of found records is known only after all records have been run through with *mysql_fetch_row*.

If you expect smaller rather than larger *SELECT* results, then *mysql_store_result* is the better choice. It makes less of a demand on the server and offers more convenience for client programming. Only when you expect large quantities of data (in the megabyte quantity) should you consider *mysql_use_result*.

Once you have read a record with *mysql_fetch_row* into a *MYSQL_ROW* structure, you can access the individual fields (columns) easily with *row[n]*. All results are passed as 0-terminated strings (including numbers, dates, *TIMESTAMP*s, etc.). For fields that are empty in the database (*NULL*), *row[n]* also contains *NULL*. One must be careful in the evaluation of binary data, as we shall discuss a bit later.

The following loop runs through all records and outputs the individual columns, separated by tab characters, in the console window:

```
int i;
while((row = mysql_fetch_row(result)) != NULL) {
  for(i=0; i < mysql_num_fields(result); i++) {
    if(row[i] == NULL)
      printf("[NULL]\t");
    else
      printf("%s\t", row[i]);
  }
  printf("\n");
}
```

If you are developing a program to read arbitrary tables, that is, if you do not know in advance how many columns the result will include and what data types were originally in the MySQL database, you can use *mysql_num_fields* to determine the number of columns, and *mysql_fetch_fields* to get metainformation about each column (data type, maximum number of characters and digits, etc.). These functions are described in greater detail in Chapter 20.

Error-Handling

Most MySQL functions return an error number, or 0 if no error has occurred. With some functions that are supposed to return data structures (e.g., *mysql_store_result*, *mysql_fetch_row*), the situation is reversed: Here the return value *NULL* means that there were problems during execution.

If you have discovered an error in this way, you can use the functions *mysql_errno* and *mysql_error* to determine the associated MySQL error number or error message as a character string. The functions return 0 or an empty string (*""*) if no error occurred:

```
if(mysql_query(conn, sql)) {
  fprintf(stderr, "%s\n", mysql_error(conn));
  fprintf(stderr, "error number %i\n", mysql_errno(conn));
  ...
}
```

Working with Binary Data and Special Characters

Particular care needs to be taken in executing SQL commnds that contain zero bytes or special characters (such as the processing of BLOBs) or in situations in which you expect such data as the result of a *SELECT* query.

The function *mysql_real_escape_string* serves to mark problematic characters with a backslash (\0, \b, \t, \", \', etc.). This is accomplished by copying the starting character string into a new string, for which sufficient memory must be reserved in advance:

```
// char *s1          target string
// char *s2          start string (may contain zero bytes)
```

```
// unsigned long len2  the length of s2
mysql_real_escape_string(conn, s1, s2, len2);
```

The function *mysql_real_escape_string* should be used in assembling SQL commands when individual strings can contain special characters. The following lines give an example of how an *INSERT* command can be correctly assembled. (The resulting command looks like this: *INTO publishers(publName) VALUES ('O\'Reilly').*)

The example also shows the use of the auxiliary function *strmov*, which is also available from the MySQL library. It does the same thing as *strcpy*, but it returns a pointer that points to the end of the copied character string. Thus *strmov* is particularly well suited for assembling strings piece by piece (which under C is a particularly tiresome chore). To use *strmov*, it is necessary that *include* instructions for my_global.h and m_string.h be added (and in fact, in the order given below).

If you alter the code given below, you should ensure that the string buffer *tmp* is large enough for your requirements. Insert the requisite checks:

```
#include <my_global.h>  // necessary so that strmov works
#include <m_string.h>   // necessary so that strmov works
#include <mysql.h>
 . . .
char tmp[1000], *tmppos;
char *publname = "O'Reilly";

tmppos = strmov(tmp, "INSERT INTO publishers (publName) VALUES ('");
tmppos += mysql_real_escape_string(
  conn, tmppos, publname, strlen(publname));
tmppos = strmov(tmppos, "')");
*tmppos++ = (char)0;
mysql_query(conn, tmp);
```

To execute SQL commands that contain zero bytes, instead of *mysql_query*, you must use the function *mysql_real_query*. The difference is that the length of the SQL string is no longer determined by the first zero byte, but is given explicitly:

```
// sql points to the string with the SQL command
// n specifies the length of the string
mysql_real_query(conn, sql, n);
```

The reading of binary data also poses problems, since the string functions usually used assume that the data in *row[i]* end with the first zero byte. If it is not certain that such is the case with your data, then you must determine the actual size of the data with a call to the function *mysql_fetch_lengths*. This function returns an *unsigned long* field whose values specify the size for every column of the current record. The following example shows how the function is used.

Storing Binary Data in a Database and Reading It

With the following lines, the content of the file test.jpg from the current directory is stored in the table *test_blob* of the database *exception* (see Chapter 5). Then this record is read from the table and the result stored in a new file, test-copy.jpg. The new record can now be deleted. (Note that for the sake of simplicity, the program uses a fixed buffer of 512 kilobytes for transferring data to the database. There is no check whether test.jpg is smaller than this buffer. In a real application, you should, of course, adapt the memory size dynamically.)

```c
// example file blob/main.c
#include <stdio.h>
#include <my_global.h>  // for strmov
#include <m_string.h>   // for strmov
#include <mysql.h>
int main(int argc, char *argv[])
{
  int id;
  FILE *f;
  MYSQL *conn;        // connectionto MySQL
  MYSQL_RES *result;  // SELECT result
  MYSQL_ROW row;      // a record of the SELECT result
  size_t fsize;
  char fbuffer[512 * 1024];  // file size maximum 512 kilobytes
  char tmp[1024 * 1024], *tmppos;
  unsigned long *lengths;

  // establish the connection
  conn = mysql_init(NULL);
  if(mysql_real_connect(
        conn, "localhost", "root", "uranus",
        "exceptions", 0, NULL, 0) == NULL) {
      fprintf(stderr, "sorry, no database connection ... \n");
      return 1;
    }
  // read file test.jpg store in exceptions.test_blob
  f = fopen("test.jpg", "r");
  fsize = fread(fbuffer, 1, sizeof(fbuffer), f);
  fclose(f);
  tmppos = strmov(tmp, "INSERT INTO test_blob (a_blob) VALUES ('");
  tmppos += mysql_real_escape_string(
    conn, tmppos, fbuffer, fsize);
  tmppos = strmov(tmppos, "')");
  *tmppos++ = (char)0;
  mysql_query(conn, tmp);
  id = (int)mysql_insert_id(conn);

  // read the new record and store the new record
  // in the new file test-copy.jpg
  f = fopen("test-copy.jpg", "w");
  sprintf(tmp, "SELECT a_blob FROM test_blob WHERE id = %i", id);
  mysql_query(conn, tmp);
  result = mysql_store_result(conn);
  row = mysql_fetch_row(result);
  lengths = mysql_fetch_lengths(result);
  fwrite(row[0], 1, lengths[0], f);
  fclose(f);
```

```
  // delete the new record
  sprintf(tmp, "DELETE FROM test_blob WHERE id = %i", id);
  mysql_query(conn, tmp);

  // free resources
  mysql_free_result(result);
  mysql_close(conn);
  return 0;
}
```

Connector/C++ (MySQL++)

For friends of object-oriented programming, there is also an application programming interface (API) for C++ with Connector/C++ (formerly MySQL++). However, those who expect that this will make programming easier are likely to be disappointed. This is due primarily to the size of the API, which currently (version 1.7.9) consists of over sixty structures and classes with innumerable public methods. The result is that for every operation there are at least a dozen ways of performing it. (I admit that I am exaggerating a bit.) As a result, this section can offer only a couple of examples that constitute considerably less than a systematic description. For that, I would have had to write a hundred-page chapter, and for that, there is alas no room in this book.

The second great shortcoming in Connector/C++ is that although the documentation on the MySQL server www.mysql.com is extensive and conveniently example-oriented, there is no proper reference on classes, their methods, and, above all, the logic of their organization. (There is, in fact, a reference, but it seems to have been generated some time ago automatically from the header files; the reference is not complete, and it fails to provide a good understanding of the classes and their methods.)

In spite of these shortcomings, Connector/C++ is an interesting library for programmers who produce large quantities of C++ code. For such individuals, the steep learning curve is paid off with relatively elegant and, with some effort, quite readable code. However, those who write C++ code only occasionally would probably be better served by the C API described in the previous section (which is, of course, usable under C++).

> **POINTER** *Connector/C++ is the official MySQL-supported API for C++ programming:*
>
> http://www.mysql.com/products/mysql++/index.html
>
> *In addition, however, there are several alternative C++ APIs. Links to those can be found at the following addresses:*
>
> http://www.mysql.com/doc/en/Contrib.html
> http://www.mysql.com/portal/software/

POINTER
A further variant to Connector/C++ can be found at the following address. This API is derived from Connector/C++, but it is distinguished by a somewhat clearer programming style (with fewer syntax variants and alternative expressions). Unfortunately, there is no documentation whatsoever:

```
http://mysqlcppapi.sourceforge.net/
```

If you develop KDE or QT programs, the QT library offers, since version 3, classes for database access. In such cases it is useful to use these classes instead of Connector/C++. (However, the simultaneous use of QT and Connector/C++ is problematic due to name conflicts and conflicting modes of access.)

```
http://doc.trolltech.com/3.1/designer-manual-8.html
```

Assumptions

Connector/C++ is available for download on the MySQL server www.mysql.com for the current versions of Red Hat and SuSE Linux as a precompiled RPM package. To install it, you need only execute rpm -i *packagename*.rpm. The RPM packages use the following directories during installation:

Include files: /usr/include/sqlplus

Libraries: /usr/lib/libsqlplus.*

Documentation: /usr/share/doc/[packages/]Connector/C++

In addition to the Connector/C++ package, the libraries and include files from libmysqlclient must be installed; these were presented in the previous section. Both are components of the package MySQL-devel. The include files are usually found in the directory /usr/lib/mysql, and the libraries in /usr/lib/mysql.

The tested version 1.7.9 assumes libmysqlclient.so.10 (that is, the libmysqlclient version for MySQL 3.23.*n*). But it is expected that by the time this book appears, there will be precompiled packages that are compatible with libmysqlclient.so.12 (thus with MySQL 4.0).

If you are using a different operating system, then for you there exists Connector/C++ as a source-text package that you can compile yourself. If you are using gcc 3.2 as your compiler, you must first patch the code (an appropriate package is available for download). However, I have not tested this procedure, instead having tested complete RPMs under Red Hat 8.0 and SuSE 8.1.

Hello World in C++

As a first step into Connector/C++ programming, let us write a small program. It assumes that the database *mylibrary* is installed on the local computer (see Chapter 5). Furthermore, you must change the user name (*"username"*) and password (*"xxx"*) in the code for calling *conn.connect*. The code is documented to the extent that one can understand in principle what is going on. Details on the use of MySQL functions follow in the section on programming techniques:

```cpp
// example file hellow/main.cpp
#include <iostream>
#include <sqlplus.hh> // Connector/C++ API

using namespace std;

int main(int argc, char *argv[])
{
  Connection conn(use_exceptions);
  try {
    // create connection to the MySQL server
    conn.connect("mylibrary", "localhost", "username", "xxx");

    // execute SELECT query
    Query  query = conn.query();
    query << "SELECT publID, publName \
              FROM publishers \
              ORDER BY publName";

    // store results
    Result result = query.store();
    cout << result.size() << " records found:" << endl << endl;

    // loop over all result records
    Row row;
    Result::iterator it;
    for(it = result.begin(); it != result.end(); it++) {
      row = *it;
      cout << "publId=" << row["publId"] << "  "
           << "publName=" << row["publName"] << endl; }

    return 0;

  } // displays an error message if there were
    // problems with the connection or with the SELECT query
    catch(BadQuery er) {
    cerr << "connection or query exception: " << er.error << endl;
    return 1;
  }
}
```

Upon execution, the program yields the following result:

```
$ ./hellow
6 records found:

publId=1  publName=Addison-Wesley
publId=2  publName=apress
publId=9  publName=Bonnier Pocket
publId=5  publName=Hanser
publId=3  publName=New Riders
publId=4 publName=O'Reilly & Associates
```

Compiling and Linking Connector/C++ Programs

To compile and link the above introductory example under Linux or comparable Unix system, execute the following command. (The locations of the include files can be different, of course, on different systems.)

```
$ g++ -I/usr/include/mysql -I/usr/include/sqlplus \
    -l sqlplu -lmysqlclient -o hellow main.cpp
```

As with C projects, it can happen that you will have to specify some additional link options for the libraries `libz`, `libnsl`, etc. With the additional option `-Wno-deprecated` you stop the C++ compiler from complaining about the obsolete (according to the current C++ standard) use of header files within the include files of Connector/C++.

If you wish to use `make`, the following `Makefile` provides a simple formula:

```
# example file hellow-c++/Makefile
CPP = g++
INCLUDES = -I/usr/include/sqlplus -I/usr/include/mysql
LIBS = -lsqlplus -lmysqlclient -lz
OPTS = -Wno-deprecated

all:hellow

main.o: main.cpp
        $(CPP) -c $(OPTS) $(INCLUDES) main.cpp

hellow: main.o
        $(CPP) -o hellow main.o $(LIBS)

clean:
        rm -f hellow main.o
```

Program Development with KDevelop

The development of Connector/C++ programs with KDevelop breaks down at two points:

- KDevelop deactivates C++ exceptions by default. However, Connector/C++ makes extensive use of them.

- KDevelop uses the options `-pedantic` and `-ansi` during compilation. The Connector/C++ include files cannot be thus compiled without errors.

Although the activation of exceptions is relatively simple (through the use of *CXXFLAGS="$CXXFLAGS $USE_EXCEPTIONS"* in `configure.in.in`; see the FAQs to KDevelop under `http://www.kdevelop.org`), the deactivation of the options `-pedantic` and `-ansi` requires deeper penetration into the nested configuration files of the automake system used by KDevelop.

Programming Techniques

Establishing the Connection

The connection to the MySQL server is established through a *Connection* object. If errors are to be trapped while the connection is being established, the object must be created with the constructor *Connection(use_exceptions)*. If the connection fails to be established, then a *BadQuery* exception is triggered.

The actual connection is established with the method *connect*, to which up to four parameters may be passed: the database name, host name, user name, and password. Unspecified parameters are automatically read from my.cnf (*[client]* section). If no information is to be found at that location, then default values are used, namely, *localhost* as host name and the current login name as user name:

```
Connection conn(use_exceptions);
try {
  conn.connect("databasename", "hostname", "username", "password");
} // if an error occurs
catch(BadQuery er) {
  cerr << "error is establishing the connection: " << er.error << endl;
  return 1;
}
```

Instead of using *connect*, you can create a connection with *real_connect*. The advantage is that *real_connect* supports some additional parameters (such as for the port number and timeout period).

Once the connection has been established, you can use the methods of the *Connection* object to create additonal objects (such as the *Query* object, to be defined shortly), determine various properties of the current connection with *server_info*, *client_info*, etc., execute SQL commands with *exec*, shut down the server with *shutdown*, etc.

To break the connection prematurely, execute the *close* method. (The connection is broken automatically at the end of the program.)

```
conn.close();
```

Executing Queries

To execute a query without results (thus not *SELECT*), you can simply pass the SQL character string to the method *exec* of the *Connection* object. If you are sending an *INSERT* command, you can also determine the ID number of the new data record with *insert_id*:

```
conn.exec("INSERT INTO publishers (publName) VALUES ('test')");
int newid = conn.insert_id();
```

Evaluating SELECT Queries

If you execute a *SELECT* command and wish to evaluate its result, then you should use objects of the classes *Query*, *Result*, and *Row*:

```
Query  query = conn.query();   // generae Query object
query << "SELECT ... ";         // execute SQL command
Result result = query.store(); // store results
```

Once a *Result* object is at hand, you can determine the number of records returned by the *SELECT* command with one of the (equivalent) methods *size* or *rows*:

```
size_type rows = result.size();
```

If you wish to loop through all result records, then the *Result* object can provide an iterator. The following code lines show its use:

```
// loop over all result records
Row row;
Result::iterator it;
for(it = result.begin(); it != result.end(); it++) {
  row = *it;
  // evaluate row
}
```

> **REMARK**   *Instead of* Result, *you can also use the class* ResUse:
>
> ```
> ResUse resuse = query.use();
> ```
>
> *The main difference here is that all the data are not immediately transferred to the client program; instead, they must be read one at a time in predetermined order via* resuse.fetch_row(). *(Functionally, the classes* Result *and* ResUse *correspond to the functions* mysql_store_result *and* mysql_use_result *of the C API.)*
> *Within Connector/C++, the class* Result *is derived from* ResUse. Result *offers some additional methods that enable, for example, navigation among the records held in memory.*

You can determine the number of columns with the method *size* of the *Row* object. Access to the individual data fields is accomplished with *row[0]*, *row[1]*, etc., or in the more readable, but decidedly less efficient, manner *row["column_name"]*.

Worthy of note is the return data type of *row[...]*: It involves objects of the class *RowData*, which can be conveniently transformed by cast operations into the basic data types of C++ (for example, *int, double, Date*). On this point, Connector/C++ offers fundamental advantages over the C API, which always returns only character strings.

Thus, if the first column of a *SELECT* result has the data type *DATE* or *TIMESTAMP*, then you can assign the contents of this column to the variable *mydate*:

```
Date mydate = (Date)row[0];
```

Please note, however, that this transformation functions only if suitable data are available. (Thus you cannot change a *Double* into a date.)

Moreover, you should first test using *row[. . .].is_null()* whether the field contains *NULL*. In such a case, the transformation can result in an error. (In some cases, *NULL* is simply transformed to 0 or 0000-00-00. But even in such cases, a *NULL* test should be made to distinguish 0 from *NULL*.)

If you no longer require a *Result* or *ResUse* object, you should release it with a call to *purge*. In particular, if you are working with *ResUse* objects, then the execution of *purge* is often explicitly required before the next SQL command can be executed. (Otherwise, an error occurs: *commands out of sync*.)

Using Binary Data

If you wish to store binary data in a MySQL table or to read stored data from a table, Connector/C++ offers special manipulators and methods. First, for storing data, thus for formulating an SQL command in which all special characters and zero bytes are coded with backslash combinations, you use the manipulator *escape* for an arbitrary *iostream* object. This has the effect that special characters in the immediately following data element are coded in accord with *MySQL* format. *escape* is particularly well suited if you are passing a query with << to a *Query* object or are composing an SQL command with << in an *ostrstream* object:

```
query << "INSERT ... VALUES('" << escape << binarydata << "')";
```

In reading data, you do not access binary data with a *Row* object (i.e., with *row[column]*), but instead, you use the method *row.raw_data (column)*. You must first determine with the method *fetch_lengths* the extent of the data. This method returns a field with elements for all columns of the current record. *fetch_lengths* is available for objects of the classes *Result* and *ResUse*:

```
unsigned long *lengths;
lengths = result.fetch_lengths();
```

BLOB Example Program

The following example program stores the contents of the local file test.jpg in the table *exceptions.test_blob* (see Chapter 5). From there, the data are read and stored in the new file test-copy.jpg. Finally, the new record is deleted.

The transmission of data from the file to the database is somewhat complex, since the file first has to be read into a **char* buffer and then copied into a *string* buffer; this *string* buffer is finally used to compose the SQL command in an *ostrstream* buffer. Nevertheless, the reading of data with *raw_data* is accomplished significantly more elegantly than with C code:

```cpp
// example file blob/main.cpp
#include <iostream>
#include <fstream>
#include <sqlplus.hh>
using namespace std;
int main(int argc, char *argv[])
{
  Connection conn(use_exceptions);
  try {
    conn.connect("exceptions", "localhost", "username", "xxx");
    // first place binary data in a *char buffer and then
    // in a string buffer
    ifstream infile("test.jpg", ios::in | ios::binary | ios::ate);
    long size = infile.tellg();
    char *buffer = new char[size];
    infile.seekg(0, ios::beg);      // read from beginning of file
    infile.read(buffer, size);      // file --> *char
    string sbuffer(buffer, size);   // *char --> string
    infile.close();
    // store string buffer in the database
    ostrstream strbuf1;
    strbuf1 << "INSERT INTO test_blob (a_blob) VALUES ('"
        << escape << sbuffer << "')" << ends;
    conn.exec(strbuf1.str());
    // read BLOB field from the database
    int id = conn.insert_id();      // AUTO_INCREMENT id
    Query  query = conn.query();
    query << "SELECT a_blob FROM test_blob WHERE id=" << id;
    Result result = query.store();
    Row row = result.fetch_row();
    unsigned long *lengths;
    lengths = result.fetch_lengths();
    // store data in a new file
    ofstream outfile("test-copy.jpg", ios::out | ios::binary);
    outfile.write(row.raw_data(0), lengths[0]);
    outfile.close();
    //release Result object, delete temporary table
    result.purge();
    ostrstream strbuf2;
    strbuf2 << "DELETE FROM test_blob WHERE id=" << id << ends;
    conn.exec(strbuf2.str());
    // close connection
    conn.close();
    return 0;
  } // catch exceptions
    catch(BadQuery er) {
    cerr << "error: " << er.error << endl;
    return 1;
  }
}
```

Error-Handling

As we have already mentioned in our description of the *Connection* class at the beginning of this section, error-handling in Connector/C++ is based on *exceptions*. For this type of error-handling to be activated, the first *Connection* object must be generated with the constructor *Connection(use_exceptions)*. The result is that *exceptions* will be triggered that result from objects that are derived from this start object.

The most important exceptions that are triggered by operations within Connector/C++ are *BadQuery* (error in establishing the connection or in the execution of an SQL command), *BadConversion* (error in data type transformation), and *BadNullConversion* (error in data transformation due to data containing *NULL*). The following lines offer a simple plan for minimal error-handling in an entire Connector/C++ program:

```
int main(int argc, char *argv[])
{
  Connection conn(use_exceptions);
  try {
    ... all the code
  }
  catch(BadQuery er)          { ... error-handling }
  catch(BadConversion er)     { ... error-handling }
  catch(BadNullConversion er) { ... error-handling }
}
```

Specialized SQL Structures (SSQL)

In the previous examples, the individual columns were addressed with *row[n]* or *row["name"]*. Connector/C++ offers yet another possibility, using various *sql_create* macros, to create a structure at the start whose elements correspond to the columns of the query result. This has the advantage that the data appear immediately in the correct format, and so no *cast* operations are necessary.

The starting point for our first SSQL experiments is to consider the macros *sql_create_basic_<n>*, where *n* specifies the number of parameters. The macro call *sql_create_basic_2* defines the structure for the following example program (two columns: *publID* and *publName*):

```
sql_create_basic_2(publisher,     // Name of the structure
                   0,             // number of columns to compare
                   0,             // number of columns to initialize
                   int, publId,   // column publID
                   string, publName);// column publName
```

With this macro call, *publisher* specifies the name of the structure being defined. The second parameter tells how many columns should be considered in making comparisons between objects of the structure. The third parameter specifies how many columns can be initialized by the constructor of the structure. The remaining parameters specify the data types and names of the the columns. As data type one may use MySQL-specific types that are known to Connector/C++ (such as *Date, Time,* and *DateTime*).

The following program returns, like the "Hello World" example of this section, an alphabetic list of all publishers with their *publID* numbers. New here is the *Result* method *storein*, with which the found records are copied into a vector of the structure *publisher*. Within the loop over elements of the vector, the individual column elements can now be conveniently and efficiently addressed in the manner *in->name*:

```
// example file ssql/main.cpp
#include <iostream>
#include <vector>
#include <sqlplus.hh>
#include <custom.hh>

using namespace std;

sql_create_basic_2(publisher ... ); // defines the structure publisher;
                                     // for details, see above

int main(int argc, char *argv[])
{
  Connection conn(use_exceptions);
  try {
    // create connection to MySQL
    conn.connect("mylibrary", "localhost", "root", "");

    // process SELECT query
    Query  query = conn.query();
    query << "SELECT publID, publName \
             FROM publishers \
             ORDER BY publName";

    // copy result in vector of the the data type publisher
    vector <publisher> result;
    query.storein(result);

    // loop over all data records
    vector <publisher>::iterator it;
    for(it=result.begin(); it!=result.end(); it++) {
      cout << "publID=" << it->publId << "  "
           << "publName=" << it->publName
           << endl;
    }
  } // error-handling
    catch(BadQuery er) {
    cerr << "error: " << er.error << endl;
    return 1;
  }
}
```

POINTER *The Connector/C++ documentation describes a host of additional syntax variants and application options beyond this simple example. However, there is no room here to discuss them.*

#### CHAPTER 17

Visual Basic, C#, ODBC

ODBC (OPEN DATABASE CONNECTIVITY) IS above all a widely used interface in the world of Windows for accessing database systems. Thanks to the driver Connector/ODBC, MySQL can be accessed via ODBC.

This chapter begins with some background information about ODBC and the setting up of *data source names* (DSNs), which simplify access to ODBC data sources (for example, a MySQL database). The following two sections show how you can now use Access and Excel for processing and analyzing MySQL databases.

The main part of this chapter concerns itself with the programming of MySQL applications on the basis of the database libraries ADO and ADO.NET. This will also involve the programming languages VB (Visual Basic), VBA, VB.NET, and C#. (Under Visual Basic 6, you can use the library MyVbQL.dll instead of ADO and ODBC, which is more efficient in many cases. This special case will be handled as well.)

For those whom this chapter has convinced of the advantages of MySQSL, the last section describes the program `mssql2mysql`, a database converter that transfers databases from the Microsoft SQL server to MySQL.

Chapter Overview

Fundamentals

ODBC (Open Database Connectivity) is a popular mechanism under Windows for standardized access to a great variety of database systems. The only condition on ODBC for it to be used to access MySQL is the installation of Connector/ODBC, the ODBC driver for MySQL.

> **POINTER** *This chapter is based on the assumption that you have installed Connector/ODBC as described in Chapter 2. There is extensive documentation for Connector/ODBC, but it is scattered over three separate places, not all of which are up to date. Basic information is available in the MySQL documentation. There is also an extensive "frequently asked questions" (FAQs) section, as well as a technical reference. These documents were last available at*
>
> ```
> http://www.mysql.com/doc/en/ODBC.html
> http://www.mysql.com/products/myodbc/faq_toc.html
> http://www.mysql.com/products/myodbc/manual_toc.html
> ```
>
> *There is also a Connector/ODBC mailing list, which can be found at*
> ```
> http://lists.mysql.com/.
> ```

Determining the Connector/ODBC Version Number

To determine whether Connector/ODBC is installed on your computer (and in what version), execute START | SETTINGS | CONTROL PANEL | ADMINISTRATIVE TOOLS | DATA SOURCES (ODBC) and search in the DRIVERS dialog sheet of the ODBC dialog for the Connector/ODBC driver (see Figure 17-1).

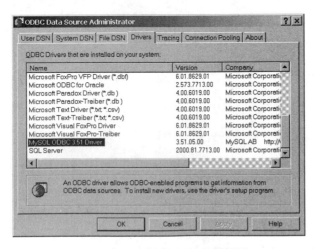

Figure 17-1. Determining the Connector/ODBC version number

REMARK *Note that this entire chapter is based on Connector/ODBC 3.51.n. (I ran my tests using versions 3.51.05 and 3.51.06.) Version 3.51.n offers a number of substantial improvements over the previous version 2.50.n. Make sure that you are not inadvertently working with an obsolete version.*

A Small Glossary from the World of Microsoft Databases

If you are new to the world of Microsoft databases, then ODBC is not the only abbreviation that is going to confuse you. Here is a brief overview:

- **ODBC (Open Database Connectivity):** ODBC is a popular, primarily Windows, mechanism for integrated access to a variety of database systems. ODBC is rather old, but it is supported by countless old and new database systems and libraries and will therefore likely be the most important producer-independent standard for communication and programming with database systems under Windows for a long time to come. ODBC is also available under Unix, but is seldom used in that context.

- **OLE-DB:** OLE-DB is the successor to ODBC, thus again an interface for providing unified access to various database systems. For MySQL there is at present, sad to say, no mature OLE-DB driver. However, there is an ODBC interface for OLE-DB, by means of which all ODBC-compatible databases without their own OLE-DB drivers can be addressed. As a MySQL programmer you generally have nothing to do directly with OLE-DB, since you use ADO for the actual programming.

- **ADO (ActiveX Data Objects):** ADO is a collection of objects that are used in the programming languages Visual Basic, VBA, Delphi, etc., for creating database programs. ADO stands between the programming language and OLE-DB. For programmers, the object-oriented ADO library offers much more convenience than direct access to the database via OLE-DB functions. Later in the chapter, we provide information on ADO programming with Visual Basic for accessing MySQL databases.

- **ADO.NET:** ADO.NET is the database interface of the new Microsoft .NET Framework. (This framework is an enormous class library that can be used only by .NET-compatible programming languages such as Visual Basic .NET and C#.) ADO.NET has a name similar to that of ADO, but internally it has little in common with it; the two are completely incompatible.

- **MDAC (Microsoft Data Access Components):** MDAC is the general term for the countless Microsoft database components and libraries (including ADO and OLE-DB). Various MDAC versions are installed as parts of Windows, Office, Internet Explorer, etc. The most current versions can be found (at no cost) at the following address:

```
http://www.microsoft.com/data/download.htm
```

- **DAO, RDO:** DAO and RDO are similar to the ADO libraries for database programming. These are precursors to ADO and are now supported by Microsoft only half-heartedly. DAO and RDO are not discussed further in this book.

- **DSN (Data Source Name):** With many programs with an ODBC interface (e.g., Access, Excel) you cannot directly select a database. Instead, you must have previously defined a DSN for the database in the ODBC manager. Access to the database then proceeds via the DSN. (If you access MySQL via a programming language, you can create the database access without a DSN as well. Later on, we will show both variants, that is, access with and without a DSN.)

Setting Up a DSN for a MySQL Database

DSNs are usually set up in the ODBC administrator dialog. (Many Windows programs themselves provide dialogs for this purpose, but they are no improvement.) You launch the ODBC administrator dialog in the system control, under Windows 2000, for example, with START | SETTINGS | CONTROL PANEL | ADMINISTRATIVE TOOLS | DATA SOURCES (ODBC). There you have the choice among three DSN types: user, system, and file DSNs.

- **User DSNs:** These are available only to the user who has defined the DSN. (During Connector/ODBC installation a user DSN with the name *sample-MySQL* is automatically set up.) However, with this DSN the correct database name must first be employed before the DSN can be used.

- **System DSNs:** These DSNs are available to all users of the computer. With both user and system DSNs the settings are managed internally by ODBC.

- **File DSNs:** Here we are dealing with individual files with the identifier *.dsn, in which all setting data are stored in text format. These files are usually stored in the directory Program Files\Common Files\ODBC\Data Sources. File DSNs are more transparent to some extent, because it is clear what information is stored where.

> **TIP** *If you wish to access more than one MySQL database, you must make use of the corresponding number of DSNs.*

The definition of a new DSN begins with clicking on the ADD button in the User DSN or System DSN dialog sheet. There appears a dialog in which you can choose from among various ODBC drivers.

The correct choice in our case is, of course, MySQL. A double click now leads into a dialog (see Figure 17-2), in which you must make the following settings:

- **Data Source Name:** Here is where you specify the name of the DSN (that is, under what name the data source can be addressed by ODBC programs). Select a name that is connected to the database name and the use to which the DSN is to be put.

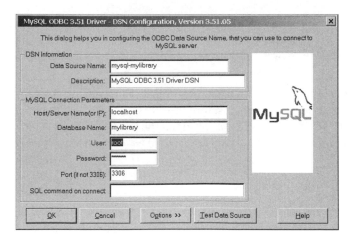

Figure 17-2. Basic Connector/ODBC setting

- **Host/Server Name (or IP):** Here you give the name or IP number of the computer on which MySQL (i.e., the server) is running. If it is the local computer, then give *localhost*.

- **Database Name:** Here you give the name of the MySQL database (for example, *mylibrary*, if you wish to access the database used for many examples in this book).

- *User* **and** *Password***:** Of course, the access system described in Chapter 9 holds for Connector/ODBC as well. (If you have begun to read the book at this point and are unable to achieve a Connector/ODBC connection, then inadequate access privileges is the most likely cause of the difficulty.)

  In the fields *User* and *Password* you can input the user name and password for access to the database. However, whether you should actually do this is another question entirely. First, you provide access to the database to anyone who can use the DSN. Second, the password is not encrypted and can therefore easily be discovered.

  To circumvent this security risk, you can leave both fields empty. Then every time you or someone else wishes to use this DSN to obtain a connection to MySQL, the dialog pictured in Figure 17-2 appears. While this is very practical, in that name and password can be input, it is very confusing for the average user. It is not clear that user name and password are indeed to be entered, and it is possible that the poor user will stumble around in the other input fields of this dialog, which can lead to errors that will be difficult to unravel.

- **Port:** Here is where the IP port can be specified, in case it should be other than 3306. In most cases this field is left empty.

  If MySQL is running on a computer other than the one on which Connector/ODBC is running and there is a firewall between the two computers, then port 3306 must be opened. Otherwise, no communication between MySQL and Connector/ODBC will be possible.

- **SQL Command on Connect:** Here an SQL command can be given that is to be executed immediately upon establishment of the connection. In rare cases this can be used to create a temporary table or set a variable (*SET*). As a rule, this field is left empty.

With the button TEST DATA SOURCE you can quickly check whether a connection to the MySQL server succeeds with the current settings.

If you later change the settings of a DSN, simply open the ODBC administration dialog. A double click on the DSN (or the button CONFIGURE) leads again to the dialog shown in Figure 17-2.

Connector/ODBC Options

The button OPTIONS leads to a second dialog box with a number of options (see Figure 17-3). The following list describes the most important options, where the order reflects that in the OPTIONS dialog box. The number in parentheses represents the numerical value of the option, which is important if you wish to set the options in program code (as we shall do in the upcoming ADO example).

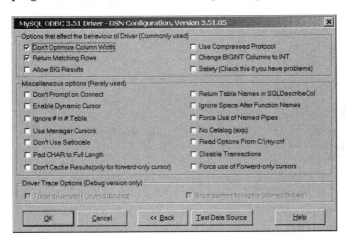

Figure 17-3. Connector/ODBC Options

- **Don't Optimize Column Width (1):** If the query *SELECT col FROM table* returns character strings with a maximal length of n characters, and n is smaller than the maximal string length for this column, then Connector/ODBC returns n as the optimal column width. The option *Don't Optimize Column Width* avoids such problems.

- **Return Matching Rows (2):** With many commands (e.g., *UPDATE*), the MySQL server can return the number of affected data records (*affected rows*). However, many ODBC clients are incapable of interpreting this information correctly. If this option is used, Connector/ODBC returns *found rows* instead of *affected rows* (thus 0 in the case of *UPDATE* commands). This option must be set for Connector/ODBC to be able to function in combination with a number of programs (including Microsoft Access and Visual Basic/VBA with ADO).

- **Allow Big Results (8):** With this option, the size of packets that are transmitted between an ODBC program and the server is unlimited. This option must be used if large *SELECT* commands are anticipated or large BLOB fields are to be processed.

- **Use Compressed Protocol (2048):** Data transmission between the ODBC program and MySQL is in compressed form, thus reducing the amount of network traffic. However, the cost is more CPU time on both client and server, since all data must be compressed and decompressed.

- **Change *BIGINT* Columns to *INT* (16384):** Most Microsoft libraries are unable to deal with 64-bit integers. This option has the effect that MySQL *BIGINT* fields are automatically reduced to 32 bits upon transmittal. This option is necessary in particular for ADO programming with Visual Basic/VBA. Be thou warned, however: The most-significant 32 bits will be lost.

- **Safety (131072):** This option has the effect that Connector/ODBC makes some additional checks. This option should be used when an ODBC client experiences problems in the processing of MySQL data. (The documentation does not offer a more precise description.)

- **Don't Prompt on Connect (16):** This option prevents the dialog displayed in Figure 17-2 from being displayed during the establishment of a connection due to the lack of relevant information. (Even if this option is activated, the dialog will appear if the database login is unsuccessful on account of an incorrect or missing user name or password.)

- **Enable Dynamic Cursor (32):** With this option, Connector/ODBC supports the cursor type *Dynamic*. The cursor is made available by the ODBC driver, not directly by the MySQL server (which currently supports no cursors at all). By default, the *Dynamic* option is deactivated for the sake of efficiency. Note that this option works only since Connector/ODBC 3.52.06 and is not available in versions 2.50.n.

- **Don't Cache Results (1048576):** Normally, all results of a *SELECT* command are transmitted as a block from server to client. This option prevents that. It makes sense only when huge (millions of records) *SELECT* results are being processed. This option takes effect only if in ADO programming a *forward only* cursor is used.

- **Force Use of Named Pipes (8192):** This option results in *named pipes* (instead of TCP/IP) being used in communication between client and server. This is possible only under Windows NT/2000/XP, and only if you use a MySQL server that was compiled with *named pipes* support (which is not the default behavior).

In many cases, it suffices to activate only the options *Don't Optimize Column Width* and *Return Matching Rows*.

POINTER *Further information on Connector/ODBC can be found at* `http://www.mysql.com/products/myodbc/faq_3.html`.

Access

Introduction

Access and MySQL are two programs that are fundamentally different from each other. Access has a very well developed user interface, which simplifies the design of databases as well as the development of database programs. Unfortunately, Access is as slow as molasses outdoors in Moscow in winter if more than three or four users wish to access the database simultaneously. Furthermore, Access is extremely unsuited for Internet applications.

In comparison, MySQL is incomparably more efficient and secure in multiuser operation. Here the problem is in using the darn thing: Although there exists a variety of user interfaces to MySQL, at present, none of these offers the convenience of Access.

Taking all of this into consideration, it seems a good idea to try to combine the best of both worlds. Even though there are many restrictions and limitations, the potential applications of Access in combination with MySQL are quite numerous:

- Access tables can be exported to MySQL and there processed further.

- MySQL tables can be imported to Access or a link to the tables can be created and the data further processed.

- Data from Access and MySQL databases can be combined.

- You can develop the design of a new database in Access and then export the entire database to MySQL.

- You can use Access as an interface for changing the contents of MySQL tables.

- You can develop complex queries in Access and then place the SQL code in your scripts.

- You can create and print database reports.

- You can develop VBA code in Access for automatically processing data from MySQL databases in Access.

- You can create diagrams of database structures. (All such diagrams in this book were created in this manner.)

> **REMARK** *This section assumes that you are familiar with Access. An introduction to Access would be beyond the scope of this book. All procedures described in this section were tested with Access 2000.*

Problems

Don't let your hopes soar too high. Access was never conceived as an interface to MySQL and will never become one. Thus it is not surprising that a number of difficulties exist in stretching Access on the Procrustean bed of an interface to MySQL:

- There are several data types that are available either only in Access or only in MySQL. In import/export such data types can create trouble. For example, MySQL *ENUM*s and *SET*s are turned into simple text fields upon importation. There are also problems to be had with single-precision *FLOAT*s. In general, you should use *DOUBLE* floating-point numbers if you plan on working with Access.

  You should generally count on having to change various attributes of a MySQL table as a result of importing it into Access and later exporting it back to MySQL.

- MySQL presently offers a way of creating links between tables only for the InnoDB format. Relations (including rules for ensuring referential integrity) that are easily constructed in Access are lost upon exportation to MySQL.

- The SQL dialect of MySQL and that of Access are not quite identical. Thus it can happen that SQL queries developed in Access will function in MySQL only after some minor adjustments.

Assumptions

- If you wish to change data from linked MySQL tables in Access, the option *Return Matching Rows* must be set in the definition of the DSN. If you are working with Access 2.0, you will also need the option *Simulate ODBC 1.0*.

- Furthermore, all linked MySQL tables must be equipped with a *TIMESTAMP* field so that data can be altered. (You don't need to concern yourself with the care and feeding of this field, since both MySQL and Access automatically store the time of the last change. Access requires this information to distinguish altered data from unaltered data.)

- All MySQL tables must be equipped with a primary index (usually an *INT* field with the property *AUTO_INCREMENT*).

- A significant source of problems is the existence of incompatible data types:
  - MySQL tables use *DOUBLE* instead of *FLOAT* and *DATETIME* instead of *DATE*.
  - Avoid *BIGINT*, *SET*, and *ENUM*.
  - Access has occasional problems with *BLOB*s and believes that it is dealing with OLE objects. It is usually better to represent such columns in MySQL as *BLOB*s.

TIP *If you develop queries in Access and then wish to use the SQL code in MySQL, you will frequently find yourself in a compatibility quagmire. (The SQL dialect of Access is different from that in MySQL.) Here is how you can solve this problem: Work with linked tables, and in Access execute the following command (while the window for query formulation is open):* QUERY | SQL SPECIFIC | PASS-THROUGH. *You thereby let Access know in no uncertain terms that the program should hold more rigorously to SQL standards.*

> **TIP** *If you are working in Access with linked tables and if after an alteration in a data record you see #deleted displayed, then one of the above conditions has not been satisfied.*

Importing and Exporting Tables

Imported Tables Versus Linked Tables

If you wish to process MySQL data in Access, then you have two possibilities: You can first import the table(s) into Access and then do the processing, or else you can merely create a link between Access and the MySQL tables.

- With linked tables you can insert or alter data, although the table will then be managed by MySQL. Here Access serves simply as the interface. A change in the table's properties (insertion or deletion of a column, for example) is not possible with linked tables. The principal advantages are that the creation of links proceeds very quickly (independent of the size of the tables) and the data remain with MySQL (where they are well cared for).

- There are no restrictions on imported tables as they pertain to changes in the table design. Since the tables are now stored in an Access database file, you can carry out all the operations provided by Access. However, there can be problems if you later attempt to return the table(s) to MySQL, since not all of the Access data types can be transformed to MySQL data types without further ado.

Importing MySQL Tables into Access

The first step is either to open an existing Access database or to create a new (empty) database. Then you execute FILE | GET EXTERNAL DATA | IMPORT and in the file selection dialog you choose ODBC as file type. As if by magic, the dialog SELECT DATASOURCE appears. In the dialog sheet MACHINE DATA SOURCES, all the user and system DSNs are enumerated. Select the DSN of your choice. As a rule, there will now appear the dialog shown in Figure 17-2, in which you have merely to provide the user name and password.

If the connection to MySQL can be established, then the next dialog (see Figure 17-4) shows a list of all tables in the database specified by the DSN. There you can mark several tables at once (mouse button and Ctrl). The importation is initiated with OK, which can take a bit of time if the tables are large. (Access creates a local copy of the tables and stores them in an Access database file.)

Note that on being imported, many column attributes (e.g., *AUTO_INCREMENT*) are lost, and that the forms of indexes are frequently changed (so that a MySQL *UNIQUE* index in Access becomes an index that allows duplicates).

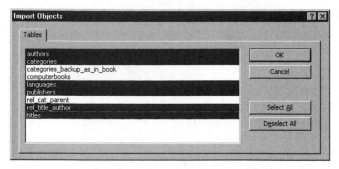

Figure 17-4. Selection of the tables to be imported into Access

Creating Links to MySQL Tables

The way to create a database link is the same as with the importation of a MySQL table. The only difference is that this time, you begin with the Access menu command FILE | GET EXTERNAL DATA | IMPORT | LINK TABLES.

> **CAUTION**   *If you change the properties of a table in MySQL (for example, if you add a new column), then you must update the connection to this table in Access. To do this, execute* TOOLS | DATABASE UTILITIES | LINKED TABLE MANAGER *and select the table to be updated.*

Exporting Access Tables to MySQL

If you have imported a table from MySQL to Access and then changed it, or if you have developed an entire database in Access and then wish to transport it to MySQL, then you have to go in the opposite direction.

To do this, you mark the table in the Access database window, execute the command FILE | EXPORT, and choose the file type ODBC. In the EXPORT dialog you can specify the name of the table under MySQL. (As a rule, you can use the name being used under Access simply with an OK.) Now comes the familiar selection of the DSN. And that does it!

In principle, exportation functions acceptably well, but usually there is some additional manual work required. The following list gives some of the basic problems with exportation:

- All indexes defined in Access are lost (including the primary index).

- The Access column property *Required* is not translated into the MySQL attribute *NOT NULL*.

- The Access column property *Autonumber* is not translated into the MySQL attribute *AUTO_INCREMENT*.

- The translation of data types is not always optimal. For example, *Currency* is translated to *DOUBLE* (MySQL). Here *DECIMAL* would be preferable. In general, you should check your MySQL tables carefully for such losses in translation.

Unfortunately, there is no possibility in Access to export several tables simultaneously. Thus if you wish to export an entire database, you must repeat the steps outlined above for each table.

Converter: Access → MySQL (exportsql.txt)

Due to the problems enumerated in the previous section that arise in the export of individual tables from Access to MySQL, Pedro Freire has programmed a converter that writes an entire Access database to a file *.sql, which then can be input with mysql. The quality of this converter is considerably better than ODBC Export, which is integrated into Access. This free program, exportSQL.txt, can be obtained at the following address:

http://www.cynergi.net/exportsql/

The method for exporting is documented in the program code. Here is a summary:

- Load the database to be exported into Access.

- With Alt+F11 switch into the VBA editor, there insert a new module (INSERT I MODULE), and copy the entire file exportsql.txt into the module (see the link above).
  You can work in the VBA editor only if you are working with an Access 2000 database. If the database was created with an earlier version of Access, then you must open a new module in the database window and insert the code into this module.

- Change the export options in the program code. This involves a block of constants (*Private Const name = ...*) that control certain parameters of the exportation process. As a rule, you will have to change only the two constants *ADD_SQL_FILE* and *DEL_SQL_FILE*, which specify the names of the file into which the export files are to be written.

- Begin exporting with F5. (In the macro dialog you must select the procedure *exportSQL.*)

- During the exportation process you may see displayed some warning messages relating to incompatibilities between Access and MySQL data types, which you must approve by clicking OK. The warnings will appear as well in the resulting files. (The affected lines begin with *#Warning.*)

- In MySQL generate an empty new database (with *CREATE DATABASE*).

- Execute the SQL command specified in esql_add.txt. You can best accomplish this with mysql:

```
> mysql -u root -p databasename < q:\tmp\esql_add.txt
Enter password: xxxxx
```

If errors occur, you may have to alter esql_add.txt in a text editor. In some situations some small changes in the program code of the converter may be necessary.

Before making a new attempt, you must delete any existing data. For this, the second file esql_del.txt will be of help:

```
> mysql -u root -p databasename < q:\tmp\esql_del.txt
Enter password: xxxxx
```

Problems

- Access permits a number of special characters in table and column names that MySQL does not allow. The following changes in the program code (indicated in boldface) will permit exportSQL.txt to replace these characters automatically with an underscore (_):

```
Private Function conv_name(strname As String) As String
  ...
  Select Case Mid$(str, I, 1)
    Case " ", Chr$(9), Chr$(10), Chr$(13), "-", ")", "("
  ...
```

- In those countries where floating-point numbers are formatted with a comma for the decimal point (MySQL is clueless about this), the following remedy is available:

```
Sub exportSQL()
  ...
  Select Case crs.Fields(cfieldix).Type
  ...
  Case Else
    sqlcode = sqlcode & conv_str(str(crs.Fields(cfieldix).Value))
```

- *PRIMARY KEY* columns must have the attribute *NOT NULL* in MySQL. However, exportsql.txt does not guarantee this condition, and that can lead to problems. The solution is to edit the column definitions of the export file esql_add.txt in a text editor.

Other Converters Between MySQL and Access

In addition to exportsql.txt, there are many other converters between MySQL and Access (in both directions) that I have not tested in detail, such as importsql and MyAccess. Many of these tools are freely available, while others are commercial programs. An overview of such programs is available at

```
http://www.mysql.com/portal/software/
http://www.mysql.com/doc/en/Contrib.html
```

Data Analysis with Excel

Excel is of interest to users of MySQL primarily as a tool for data analysis. Thanks to Connector/ODBC, you can import MySQL data into an Excel worksheet and there perform analyses, create graphics, and so on. In Figure 17-5 you can see, as an example, a pivot table that for the *mylibrary* database tells which publisher has published how many books in a given category. (Because of the relatively small number of data records the result is, of course, not very informative. But if *mylibrary* contained a large number of books, then this table would allow you to determine easily which publishers specialize in which subjects.)

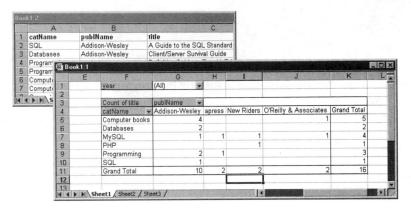

Figure 17-5. Excel pivot table

> **POINTER** *If you use the macro programming language VBA, which is included in Excel, then a broader range of options is open to you, particularly if your goal is to automate or simplify the steps discussed here. A brief introduction to database access via VBA (or Visual Basic) will be given later in the chapter.*

Importing Data with MS Query

Whether you wish to insert MySQL data directly into an Excel worksheet (command DATA | GET EXTERNAL DATA | NEW DATABASE QUERY) or to create a pivot table or chart based on external data, Excel will launch the auxiliary program MS Query. This program functions as the interface between Excel and an external database, and it assists in the setting of import and query parameters.

In this program you select the DSN in the dialog CHOOSE DATA SOURCE. At that point, the QUERY WIZARD appears, which assists in the creation of a database query. In the first step you select the required tables or table fields (see Figure 17-6). In the next two steps you can specify the filter criteria (corresponding to *WHERE* conditions) and the sort order.

If these specifications suffice for executing the query, you can now terminate MS Query with FINISH. Usually, however, it is preferable first to click on the option VIEW

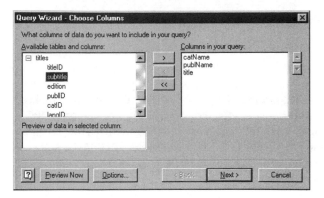

Figure 17-6. Selecting the desired columns in MS Query

DATA OR EDIT QUERY. In this case, the query is displayed by MS Query in development mode, where it can be optimized (see Figure 17-7). In particular, any relations between the tables that MS Query has not recognized on its own can be established. To accomplish this you simply *Drag&Drop* the ID fields from one table to the other. A dialog appears in which you can set the relational properties.

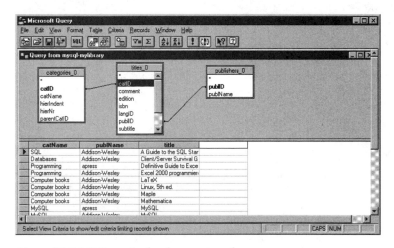

Figure 17-7. MS Query in development mode

TIP *Excel frequently has difficulties with the importation of information about data. You can solve some of these problems with the help of the SQL function* CONCAT. *To format a column with this function, open the dialog* EDIT COLUMN *in MS Query with a double click on the column in question. In the input field* FIELD *you set the expression present there in* CONCAT(...). *For example, from* table.birthdate *you would produce* CONCAT(table.birthdate).

ADO Programming and Visual Basic/VBA

Introduction

In this section we describe access to MySQL databases via program code, where we use Visual Basic or VBA as our programming language. We use ADO as our database library. The actual access to the database is effected by means of Connector/ODBC, where between ADO and Connector/ODBC we have OLE-DB and the ODBC driver for OLE-DB. Thus communication takes place in the following way: VB/VBA → ADO → OLE-DB → ODBC driver for OLE-DB → Connector/ODBC → MySQL.

If MySQL is running on a computer as a Visual Basic program, then the first five stages of this communication chain take place on the client computer. It is Connector/ODBC that first communicates over the network with the MySQL server.

> **POINTER** *In this book we are assuming that the reader has basic knowledge of ADO. If you know nothing much about ADO, do not know what* Connection *and* Recordset *objects are or the purpose of bound controls, then you should consult the literature on ADO programming before you read further, since we are not making much ado about nothing.*
>
> *The code presented here was developed with Connector/ODBC 3.51.05, Visual Basic 6, and ADO 2.5. The code should function as well with VBA 6 and ADO 2.1 (Office 2000), except as it involves ADO controls.*
>
> *Of course, you can also work with a scripting variant of Visual Basic, for example, if you wish to develop Active Server Pages (ASP) or programs for the Windows Scripting Host (WSH). In that case you must leave out* As typename *in the variable declaration and create ADO objects according to* Set conn = CreateObject("ADODB.Connection"). *There are several good articles specifically on ASP/MySQL programming available on the Internet, including the following:*
>
> ```
> http://www.devarticles.com/art/1/50
> http://www.dwam.net/mysql/asp_myodbc.asp
> ```

> **POINTER** *There is also an OLE-DB driver for MySQL (MyOLEDB). However, according to information on the Internet, the currently available version, 3.0, is not really ready for use, and moreover, further development has been halted. I have not tested this driver. If you wish to experiment with MyOLEDB, further information can be found on the Internet, in particular at the following location:*
>
> ```
> http://www.mysql.com/portal/sites/index.html
> ```

POINTER *Please note as well that MySQL may not be deployed in all circumstances without cost, despite popular opinion to the contrary. Free use is permitted only for open-source projects and for databases on dynamic web sites. If, on the other hand, you wish to develop, say, a commercial bookkeeping program based on MySQL, you must purchase a MySQL license for your customers. This issue is discussed in Chapter 1 and on the Internet, at*

```
http://www.mysql.com/doc/L/i/Licensing_and_Support.html
```

Assumptions and Limitations

- **MySQL tables:** Tables that you wish to alter via ADO *Recordset*s or in bound controls (*Insert, Update, Delete*) must have a primary index and a *TIMESTAMP* column.

- **Connector/ODBC options:** In the configuration of a DSN, the options *Don't optimize column width, Return matching rows*, and *Change BIGINT into INT* must be selected. If the connection is made without a DSN, then instead, the equivalent setting *Options=16387 (1 + 2 + 16384)* must be specified. If you wish to use a dynamic server cursor in your ADO program (*CursorType=adOpenDynamic, CursorLocation=adUseServer*), then the correct *Options* setting is *16419 (1 + 2 + 32 + 16384)*.

- **Changing data with *Recordset*s and bound controls:** If the above conditions have been satisfied, you can use *Recordset*s and bound controls to read, display, and alter data.

  This last point can often cause problems. Storing altered data (whether via a *Recordset* object or a bound control) functions properly in many simple cases, but in more complex applications it often leads to problems that are difficult to resolve. These problems do not always have to do with MySQL or Connector/ODBC, but with the vagaries of OLE-DB/ADO. Many experienced ADO programmers therefore do without bound controls, even if a Microsoft database system is used as the data source.

  For this reason you will continually find in MySQL newsgroups and mailing lists the recommendation to use *Recordset*s and bound controls exclusively for reading or displaying data. If you wish to alter data, then you should formulate a traditional SQL command (*UPDATE . . .*) and execute it with *conn.Execute*. Even if I have demonstrated both methods in this chapter (both the convenient editing of data with a *Recordset* object and the variant with SQL commands), I recommend the second variant.

- **Speed:** Because of the many layers and libraries between Visual Basic and MySQL, and also because of the lower speed in the processing of character strings with Visual Basic, solutions using Visual Basic and MySQL tend to be comparatively slow. Better performance is promised by the *MyVbQL* library, which establishes a direct connection between Visual Basic and MySQL (without ODBC).

Example Programs

As with the other chapters in this book, there are extensive examples available at www.apress.com. These examples assume that you have Visual Basic 6. Most of the examples also assume previous installation of the *mylibraryodbc* database (this database corresponds to the *mylibrary* database used throughout this book, except that in this version, all tables have been equipped with an additional *timestamp* column).

Note that at the beginning of the program (usually in *Form_Load*), you must set the connection parameters (computer name, user name, password) in accord with the settings of your system. In the example programs, the computer name is *localhost*, the user name is *root*, and the password is *saturn*.

Establishing the Connection

Establishing the Connection with a DSN

The following lines show a code outline for establishing a connection to MySQL based on a DSN and for executing a simple *SELECT* query. The resulting record list can then be processed with the properties and methods of the *rec* object:

```
Dim conn As Connection
Dim rec As Recordset
Set conn = New Connection
conn.ConnectionString = "DSN=mysql-mylibrary"
conn.Open
Set rec = New Recordset
rec.CursorLocation=adUseClient
rec.Open "SELECT * FROM tablename", conn
   ...    'process record list
rec.Close 'close record list
conn.Close 'terminate connection
```

The only really interesting code line is the one for setting the *ConnectionString* property. In the simplest case you specify the DSN. Optionally, you can also specify the user name and password. These parameters must be separated by semicolons. The *ConnectionString* character string looks like this:

```
conn.ConnectionString = "DSN=mysql-mylibrary;UID=root;PWD=xxx"
```

The *UID* and *PWD* settings have precedence over the DSN settings.

Here are the *ConnectionString* parameters for establishing a connection with a DSN:

DSN=name	DSN
UID=name	user name for the MySQL connection
PWD=password	password for the MySQL connection

Establishing a Connection Without a DSN

With Visual Basic you can also establish a connection to a MySQL database without previously having defined a DSN. (This is particularly practical if you wish to develop a program to access an arbitrary MySQL database.) The *ConnectionString* character string looks like this:

```
conn.ConnectionString = "Provider=MSDASQL;" + _
  "DRIVER=MySQL ODBC 3.51 Driver;" + _
  "Server=localhost;UID=username;PWD=xxx;" + _
  "database=databasename;Option=16387"
```

Here are the *ConnectionString* parameters for establishing a connection without a DSN:

Provider=MSDASQL	name of the ODBC driver for OLE-DB (Microsoft Data Access SQL)
Driver={MySQL ODBC 3.51 Driver}	name of the MySQL ODBC driver
Server=name	name or IP address of the computer on which MySQL is running
Port=n	IP port of the MySQL server (default 3306)
UID=name	user name for the MySQL connection
PWD=password	password for the MySQL connection
Database=name	name of the database
Prompt=noprompt/complete	display Connector/ODBC dialog if connection fails
Option=n	Connector/ODBC options

Prompt=complete leads to the program automatically displaying the dialog depicted in Figure 17-2. This dialog can be used, for example, to provide a missing or incorrect password. Moreover, an arbitrary character string must be specified in the field WINDOWS DSN NAME so that the dialog can be exited.

Since the dialog is not particularly user-friendly (the many choices are more confusing than helpful), it is better to do without *Prompt=complete*. (The default setting is *noprompt*.)

Instead, execute *On Error Resume Next* before establishing the connection and test after establishing the connection whether an error has occurred. If this is the case, display your own dialog, in which the user can input other connection parameters as necessary and from which the program can then construct a new *ConnectionString* character string.

Options enables the setting of a number of Connector/ODBC connection options. The required value is determined from the sum of the values of the individual options. For Visual Basic/ADO programs, the value *16387 = 1 + 2 + 16384* must generally be specified, corresponding to the options *Don't optimize column width*, *Return matching rows*, and *Change BIGINT into INT*. If you wish to use dynamic cursors in your ADO program, the correct *Options* setting is *16419 = 1 + 2 + 32 + 16384*.

> **REMARK** *If you are working with the old Connector/ODBC version 2.50.n (and not with the current version 3.51.n), you must use the setting* Driver=MySQL *in* ConnectionString. *Note, though, that a number of functions are unavailable in version 2.50.n.*

Establishing the Connection with DataEnvironment

If you are working with Visual Basic Professional or Enterprise version 6, then you have *DataEnvironment* available for setting connection properties.

In the properties dialog for the *Connection* object, in the dialog sheet PROVIDER, the entry MICROSOFT OLE-DB PROVIDER FOR ODBC DRIVERS. You can then choose, in the dialog sheet CONNECTION (see Figure 17-8), an already defined DSN or assemble an equivalent character string with the required connection properties with the button BUILD. (This button leads to the familiar ODBC dialogs and finally to the Connector/ODBC dialog depicted in Figure 17-2. However, the result of the setting is copied as a character string into the *DataEnvironment* dialog, where it can be edited as necessary.)

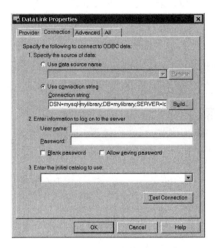

Figure 17-8. DataEnvironment *dialog for setting the connection properties*

In the further program code you can now access the *Connection* object. (The following lines assume that the *DataEnvironment* object has the name *DE* and the *Connection* the name *Conn*.)

```
Dim rec As Recordset
Set rec = New Recordset
If DE.Conn.State = adStateClosed Then
  DE.Conn.Open
End If
rec.CursorLocation=adUseClient
rec.Open "SELECT * FROM database", DE.Conn
  ...
```

The *DataEnvironment* helps not only in setting the connection data, but also in the development of SQL queries. With the SQL generator you have a convenient tool for this purpose. You can then access the query in code via the *Command* object.

Connection Properties

The *ConnectionString* parameters described in this section represent only a small part of the available parameters. For those parameters that are not specified, ADO/ODBC simply uses various default settings.

Sometimes, it is useful to know how these parameters are set. The property *ConnectionString*, which is changed in establishing the connection (and then no longer contains the character string originally set), provides our first overview. Here most of the parameters are collected into a sort of superparameter called *Extended Properties*:

```
conn.ConnectionString = "Provider=MSDASQL;Driver=MySQL;Server= ... "
conn.Open
Debug.Print conn.ConnectionString
  Provider=MSDASQL.1;Extended Properties=
   "DRIVER={MySQL ODBC 3.51 Driver};DESC=;DATABASE=mylibraryodbc;
   SERVER=localhost;UID=root;PASSWORD=saturn;PORT=;
   OPTION=16387;STMT=;"
```

Considerably more information is provided by the *Properties* enumeration of the *Connection* object. Moreover, the values saved there can be more easily extracted:

```
Debug.Print conn.Properties("Max Columns in Index")
  32
```

A complete list of all properties and their values can be obtained with the following loop:

```
Dim p As Property
For Each p In conn.Properties
  Debug.Print p.Name & " = " & p.Value
Next
```

And here is the output (squeezed into two columns to save space and sorted for easier reference):

```
Accessible Procedures = False        Catalog Usage = 29
Accessible Tables = True             Column Definition = 1
Active Sessions = 0                  Connect Timeout = 15
Active Statements = 0                Connection Status = 1
Asynchable Abort = False             Current Catalog = mylibraryodbc
Asynchable Commit = False            Data Source =
Autocommit Isolation Levels          Data Source Name =
= 4096                               Data Source Object Threading
Catalog Location = 1                 Model = 1
Catalog Term = database              DBMS Name = MySQL
```

```
DBMS Version = 4.0.10-gamma-nt        Open Rowset Support = 0
Driver Name = myodbc3.dll             ORDER BY Columns in Select
Driver ODBC Version = 03.51           List = True
Driver Version = 03.51.05             Outer Join Capabilities = 123
Extended Properties = DRIVER=         Outer Joins = Y
{MySQL ODBC 3.51 Driver};             Output Parameter Availability = 4
DESC=;DATABASE=mylibraryodbc;         Pass By Ref Accessors = True
SERVER=localhost;UID=root;            Password =
PASSWORD=saturn;PORT=;OPTION=16387;STMT=; Persist Security Info =
File Usage = 0                        Persistent ID Type = 4
General Timeout =                     Prepare Abort Behavior = 2
GROUP BY Support = 3                  Prepare Commit Behavior = 2
Heterogeneous Table Support = 0       Procedure Term =
Identifier Case Sensitivity = 8       Prompt = 4
Initial Catalog =                     Provider Friendly Name =
Integrity Enhancement Facility        Microsoft OLE DB Provider
= False                               for ODBC Drivers
Isolation Levels = 1118464            Provider Name = MSDASQL.DLL
Isolation Retention = 0               Provider Version = 02.70.7713.0
Like Escape Clause = Y                Quoted Identifier Sensitivity = 4
Locale Identifier = 1031              Read-Only Data Source = False
Location =                            Reset Datasource =
Max Columns in Group By = 0           Rowset Conversions on Command
Max Columns in Index = 32             = True
Max Columns in Order By = 0           Schema Term =
Max Columns in Select = 0             Schema Usage = 0
Max Columns in Table = 0              Server Name = localhost
Maximum Index Size = 500              via TCP/IP
Maximum Row Size = 0                  Special Characters =
Maximum Row Size Includes             ÇüáâåçêëèïîìÄ
BLOB = True                           SQL Grammar Support = 1
Maximum Tables in SELECT = 31         SQL Support = 259
Mode =                                Stored Procedures = False
Multiple Parameter Sets = True        String Functions = 491519
Multiple Results = 1                  Structured Storage = 1
Multiple Storage Objects = False      Subquery Support = 0
Multi-Table Update = False            System Functions = 7
NULL Collation Order = 8              Table Term = table
NULL Concatenation Behavior = 0       Time/Date Functions = 106495
Numeric Functions = 16777215          Transaction DDL = 2
OLE DB Services = -7                  User ID =
OLE DB Version = 02.00                User Name = root
OLE Object Support = 1                Window Handle =
```

ADO Programming Techniques

Recordsets *with Client-Side Cursors*

Recordset objects are opened on the basis of an existing *Connection* object (see the
previous section). In all the examples in this chapter the variable name for this object
is *conn*.

Since ADO provides a server-side cursor as the default cursor position, a client-side cursor must be set before the *Open* method. The following lines demonstrate how this is done:

```
Dim rec As Recordset
rec.CursorLocation = adUseClient 'client-side cursor
rec.Open "SELECT ... FROM ... WHERE ... ", _
        conn, adOpenStatic, adLockReadOnly
```

We note the following about the parameters of *Open*: In the first parameter, the SQL code is expected; in the second, the *Connection* variable. The third parameter describes the desired cursor type. Since for client-side cursors only the type *adOpenStatic* is supported, it doesn't matter what is given here. The fourth parameter specifies whether the data in the *Recordset* are read-only (*adLockReadOnly*) or whether changes are permitted (*adLockOptimistic*). ADO provides the locking types *adLockPessimistic* and *adLockBatchOptimistic* as well, which, however, I have not tested.

With the *Open* method, all the data encompassed by the SQL query are transmitted to the program. (This can take considerable time with large data sets.) You can then apply all *Recordset* properties and methods to run through the data (*MoveNext*, etc.), to search (*Find*), to sort locally (*Sort*), to change (*column="new value": rec.Update*), etc.

Recordset *with Server-Side Cursor*

You can open a *Recordset* with a server-side cursor with the property *CursorType = adForwardOnly*. You can thereby move through and read all the records of the query with *MoveNext*, and also change them (unless you are operating with *LockType = adLockReadOnly*):

```
Dim rec As Recordset
rec.CursorLocation = adUseServer
rec.Open "SELECT ... FROM ... WHERE ... ", _
        conn, adOpenForwardOnly, adLockOptimistic
```

The only navigation method allowed is *MoveNext*. You cannot use *Bookmarks*. You cannot determine the number of records without running through all of them. (You would do better to use a separate query with *SELECT COUNT(*) FROM . . . .*)

In spite of all these restrictions, in a few cases it can make sense to use a server-side cursor, namely, when large quantities of data are to be read sequentially. The drawbacks of the client-side cursor are thereby avoided (namely, that all the records are transmitted at once to the client).

Possible Recordset Properties

ADO provides for an almost endless number of combinations of properties of a *Recordset*. But the *Recordset* does not always contain the properties requested by *Open*. If a given driver does not support a particular cursor type, then ADO automatically chooses another.

As a way of testing which properties a *Recordset* actually possesses, you can use the program `Cursortypes.vbp` (see Figure 17-9). With a click of the mouse you can set the desired properties. The program then opens the *Recordset*, determines the actual properties, and then displays them. (Note, please, that the results of the program are not always correct for a server-side cursor. In particular, the *Recordset* method *Supports(. . .)* sometimes returns completely incorrect results.)

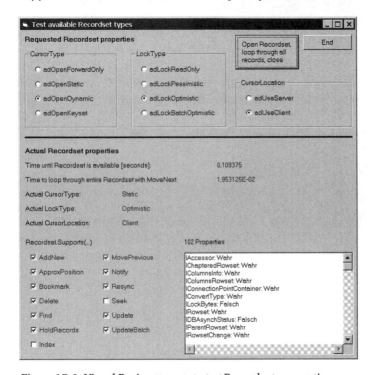

Figure 17-9. Visual Basic program to test Recordset *properties*

In sum, ADO + Connector/ODBC supports the following cursor combinations:

> *CursorLocation = Client*
> *CursorType = Static*
> *LockType = ReadOnly or Optimistic or BatchOptimistic*
> *CursorLocation = Server*
> *CursorType = ForwardOnly/Static/Dynamic*
> *LockType = all*

In the case of *CursorLocation=Server*, the ODBC option *Enable dynamic cursor (32)* determines whether you obtain a dynamic or static cursor.

Behavior of Recordsets *with* Null, Dates and Times, *and* Suchlike

The following list describes how various MySQL data types are represented in ADO
*Recordset*s:

- **Null:** The value *Null* in a column of a *Recordset* can be determined with
  IsNull(rec!column).

- **Date/Time:** Columns in the MySQL formats *DATE, TIME, DATETIME,* and
  TIMESTAMP are automatically transformed into the Visual Basic data type
  Date. Please exercise caution with *TIME* values: These values are supplemented
  with the current date. (For example, from 9:00 you may get 2003/3/17 9:00.)

- **BLOB:** *BLOB*s are transformed into *Byte* arrays. Access to individual bytes is
  effected in the manner *rec!a_blob(n)*, where *n=0* addresses the first byte.
  A *Byte* array can be interpreted by Visual Basic as a character string. However,
  again caution is advised: Since internally, Visual Basic works with Unicode, a
  BLOB with 512 bytes corresponds in Visual Basic to a character string with 256
  Unicode characters. For bytewise evaluation of the character string, the Visual
  Basic functions *AscB, ChrB, LenB, MidB, LeftB, RightB, InStrB,* etc., must be
  used.

- **Decimal:** Columns in the MySQL format *DECIMAL* are metamorphosed into
  the Visual Basic data type *Decimal*, which is not to be confused with *Currency*.
  It is to be thought of more as a subtype of *Variant*.

- **Sets/Enums:** Columns in the MySQL formats *SET* and *ENUM* are transformed
  into garden-variety character strings.

- **Character strings:** MySQL-specific special characters in strings (\, ', ", and
  0-byte) are correctly handled automatically.

*Unicode Character Strings and Binary Data (*AppendChunk, GetChunk*)*

Within Visual Basic, character strings are represented with Unicode. In storing a
string, an attempt is automatically made to transform it into the character set of the
MySQL server (generally *latin1*). If the attempt fails, then error 80040E21 is triggered.
In loading a string, the characters are interpreted according to the character set of the
server.

Thanks to this automatic character adaptation, the euro symbol can be stored
and then loaded when the server uses the *latin1* character set. In the MySQL table, the
character has code 128, while in Visual Basic, the code is 8364 (*AscW*).

If you wish to store Unicode character strings as such (without character
adaptation), then you must use *BLOB* columns in the MySQL table. You can use the
method *AppendChunk* to store a character string:

```
Dim rec As New Recordset
rec.CursorLocation = adUseClient
rec.Open "SELECT * FROM test LIMIT 1", conn, adOpenStatic, _
  adLockPessimistic
```

```
rec.AddNew
rec!blobcolumn.AppendChunk s
rec.Update
```

With *GetChunk* you can read your string. You have to use *ActualSize* to determine the size of the data:

```
x = rec!blobcolumn.GetChunk(rec!blobcolumn.ActualSize)
```

With *AppendChunk* and *GetChunk* you can process all types of binary data. (The data type of the *AppendChunk* parameter and *GetChunk* return value is *Variant*.) You can also transmit the data piecewise (by executing *AppendChunk* and *GetChunk* repeatedly). This is of particular utility in managing large data sets.

> **REMARK**   AppendChunk *and* GetChunk *function only if you use a client-side cursor. Note that Visual Basic strings are coded in* Unicode Transformation Format 16 *(UTF16 for short), and not UTF8, which is more prevalent under Unix. This has the consequence that ASCII characters so coded have every second byte equal to zero. Many MySQL programs have problems with such data. Visual Basic, ADO, and Connector/ODBC do not, unfortunately, offer the option of transforming strings into UTF8.*

Storing Files in a Database as BLOBs and Then Reading Them

You could also use *AppendChunk* and *Get Chunk* to store files in a MySQL database and then read them. However, the *Stream* class from the ADO library (version 2.5 and higher) offers a more elegant alternative: The following lines show how you can open a file with *LoadFromFile* as a binary stream and store it in the field *rec!pic* (*rec* is a *Recordset* object, and *pic* is a *BLOB* column of the previously executed *SELECT* query):

```
Dim st As New Stream
st.Type = adTypeBinary
st.Open
st.LoadFromFile "C:\test1.gif"
rec!pic = st.Read
```

Conversely, you can read a *BLOB* field from the table and store it in a file with *SaveToFile*:

```
Dim st As New Stream
st.Type = adTypeBinary
st.Open
st.Write rec!pic
st.SaveToFile "C:\test2.gif", adSaveCreateOverWrite
```

A complete example showing the use of these methods appears later in this chapter.

Determining the `AUTO_INCREMENT` Number After the Insertion of a Data Record

It often occurs that after the insertion of a new data record into a table, you require the ID number of that record (that is, the value of the *AUTO_INCREMENT* column for the primary index). Unfortunately, this cannot be read from the *Recordset* with which the record was inserted. The solution to this conundrum is to determine the ID number via *SELECT LAST_INSERT_ID()*. To accomplish this, you would do well to add the following function to your program:

```
Private Function LastInsertedID() As Long
  Dim rec As New Recordset
  rec.CursorLocation = adUseClient
  rec.Open "SELECT LAST_INSERT_ID()", conn
  LastInsertedID = rec.Fields(0)
End Function
```

Bound Database Controls

Visual Basic offers several controls that can be bound directly to database queries (to *Recordset* objects). Within the control, the contents of the *Recordset* (or perhaps only of the currently active data record) are displayed. Such controls offer a great savings in effort in the representation of database queries. Some controls even offer the possibility of altering data directly. In the ideal case, one can program a database interface with a minimal amount of code (see Figure 17-10).

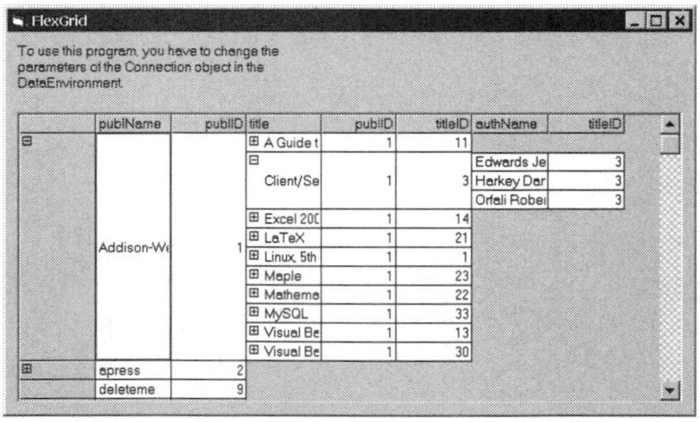

Figure 17-10. Visual Basic example program with the MSHFlexGrid *for representing data from the* mylibrary *database*

In reality, things do not always go so smoothly. In general, you must take care in your work with Connector/ODBC that for bound controls, too, you work with a client-side cursor. Furthermore, the alteration of data does not always function reliably, so that (except in well-tested special cases) one is advised not to use this feature.

Apart from that, the use of bound controls is independent of whether you use a Microsoft database system or MySQL as the data source. Additional information on using bound controls can be found in any book on database programming with Visual Basic.

Executing SQL Commands Directly

ADO *Recordset*s can simplify your dealings with query results, but it is often necessary to execute SQL commands directly. To do this, use the *Execute* method of the *Connection* object:

```
conn.Execute "INSERT INTO table (a, b) VALUES ('x', 'y')"
```

As with other programming languages, with Visual Basic you also run into the problem that you have to format various data in conformity with the rules of MySQL. In the following, you will find some auxiliary functions to help you in this task:

- **Floating-Point Numbers:** With floating-point numbers you must take into account that Visual Basic normally formats such numbers according to the country for which the language has been customized (for example, in Germany one has 3,14159265 instead of 3.14159265). If your program is to function equally well everywhere in the known universe, you should transform your floating-point numbers into character strings with the Visual Basic function *Str*.

- **Date:** The following *Format* instruction formats the date contained in *x* in accord with MySQL conventions:

```
Format(x, "'yyyy-mm-dd Hh:Nn:Ss'")
```

- **Character Strings:** *Quote* places a backslash character before the backslash and before the single- and double-quote characters, and it replaces the byte code 0 with \0:

```
Function Quote(tmp)
  tmp = Replace(tmp, "\", "\\")
  tmp = Replace(tmp, """", "\""")
  tmp = Replace(tmp, "'", "\'")
  Quote = Replace(tmp, Chr(0), "\0")
End Function
```

- **Binary Data:** *HexCode* transforms a byte array of arbitrary length into a hexadecimal character string of the form *0x0102031232*:

```
Function HexCode$(bytedata() As Byte)
  Dim i&
  Dim tmp$
  tmp = ""
  For i = LBound(bytedata) To UBound(bytedata)
    If bytedata(i) <= 15 Then
      tmp = tmp + "0" + Hex(bytedata(i))
    Else
      tmp = tmp + Hex(bytedata(i))
    End If
  Next
  HexCode = "0x" + tmp
End Function
```

You might use this function in the following way:

```
conn.Execute "INSERT INTO table (col) VALUES (" + HexCode( ... ) + ")"
```

HexCodeStr functions in principle like *Hexcode*, except that it expects data bytewise in a character string. Therefore, you can also store Unicode character strings with *HexCodeStr*:

```
s = "Unicode character string ... "
conn.Execute "INSERT INTO table (col) VALUES (" + HexCode(s) + ")"
```

Note, however, that Visual Basic character strings are UTF16 encoded, and not in the form UTF8, which is more usual under Unix:

```
Function HexCodeStr$(bytedata$)
  Dim i&, b&
  Dim tmp$
  tmp = ""
  For i = 1 To LenB(bytedata)
    b = AscB(MidB(bytedata, i, 1))
    If b <= 15 Then
      tmp = tmp + "0" + Hex(b)
    Else
      tmp = tmp + Hex(b)
    End If
  Next
  HexCodeStr = "0x" + tmp
End Function
```

Example: authors Column for the titles Table

In Chapter 5 we described a possible extension for the *titles* table of the *mylibrary* database, whereby the table would be equipped with an additional *authors* column in which the authors' names would be stored. To be sure, this is redundant, but it will speed up read access to the database.

Figure 17-11. Visual Basic example program for changing the titles *table*

The example program presented here (see Figure 17-11) shows how the *authors* column can be filled with data. For this, we simply run through all the *titles* records, determine the authors for each book, combine the authors into a character string, and store them.

> **REMARK** *Our program assumes that the* titles *table has been enlarged to include an (as of yet empty)* authors *column of type* VARCHAR(255)*:*
>
> ```
> ALTER TABLE titles ADD authors VARCHAR(255)
> ```

Variant 1: Changing Data with Read/Write Recordsets

All of the code is contained in the event procedure *Command2a_Click*. This procedure assumes that the global variable *conn* creates the connection to the database (*Connection* object).

In the program, two *Recordsets* are opened. One of them, *titles*, refers directly to the like-named table and enables changes to it (*LockingType=adLockOptimistic*). The second, *authors*, contains a list of all *titleID* values and their authors. The *Recordset* is sorted locally after being read in (property *Sort*), and apart from the database, in order not to put unnecessary demands on resources.

The following loop runs through all the *titleID* values of the *titles Recordset*. With *Find*, the associated authors in the *authors Recordset* are determined and joined into the character string *authors_str*. This character string is then stored:

```vb
' example vb6 \authors_for_titles\form1.frm
Private Sub Command2a_Click()
  Dim authors_str As String
  Dim titles As New Recordset
  Dim authors As New Recordset
  ' titles Recordset: read/write
  titles.CursorLocation = adUseClient
  titles.Open "SELECT titleID, authors FROM titles", _
              conn, adOpenStatic, adLockOptimistic
  ' authors Recordset: readonly, disconnected
  authors.CursorLocation = adUseClient
  authors.Open "SELECT titleID, authname " _
              "FROM authors, rel_title_author " & _
              "WHERE authors.authID=rel_title_author.authID", _
              conn, adOpenStatic, adLockReadOnly
  authors.Sort = "titleID, authname"
  Set authors.ActiveConnection = Nothing
  ' loop over all titles
  While Not titles.EOF
    authors_str = ""
    ' loop over all authors of this title
    authors.MoveFirst
    authors.Find "titleID=" & titles!titleID
    While Not authors.EOF
      If authors_str <> "" Then authors_str = authors_str + "; "
      authors_str = authors_str & authors!authName
      authors.MoveNext
      authors.Find "titleID=" & titles!titleID
    Wend
```

```
    ' store author list
    If authors_str <> "" Then
      titles!authors = authors_str
      titles.Update
    End If
    titles.MoveNext
  Wend
End Sub
```

Variant 2: Changing Data with conn.Execute

In our second variant, the *authors Recordset* is opened just as in variant 1. The structure of the loop is a bit different in how it finds all the authors of the current *titleID* value. The authors are stored temporarily in the variable *authors_str*.

What is new in comparison to variant 1 is the instruction *conn.Execute*, with which the list of authors is stored in the *titles* table with the help of an *UPDATE* command. The function *Quote* is necessary to ensure that the SQL command is correct even when the author name has special characters such as ':

```
Private Sub Command2b_Click()
  Dim authors_str, titleID
  Dim authors As New Recordset

  ' authors Recordset: client-side, readonly, disconnected
  authors.CursorLocation = adUseClient
  authors.Open "SELECT titleID, authname " & _
               "FROM authors, rel_title_author " & _
               "WHERE authors.authID=rel_title_author.authID " & _
               "ORDER BY titleID, authName", _
               conn, adOpenStatic, adLockReadOnly
  authors.Sort = "titleID, authname"
  Set authors.ActiveConnection = Nothing

  ' loop over all titles (titleID)
  While Not authors.EOF
    titleID = authors!titleID
    authors_str = ""
    ' search for all authors of the current titleID value
    authors_str = ""
    Do While Not authors.EOF
      ' at the next titleID jump out of the inner loop
      If authors!titleID <> titleID Then
        Exit Do
      End If
      ' add the author name to authors_str
      If Not IsNull(authors!authName) Then
        If authors_str <> "" Then authors_str = authors_str + "; "
        authors_str = authors_str & authors!authName
      End If
      authors.MoveNext
    Loop
```

```
  ' store author list
  If authors_str <> "" Then
    conn.Execute "UPDATE titles " & _
                 "SET authors = '" & Quote(authors_str) & "'" & _
                 "WHERE titleID=" & titleID
  End If
 Wend
End Sub
' place \ before ', ", and \ , replace Chr(0) by \0
Private Function Quote(tmp)
  tmp = Replace(tmp, "\", "\\")
  tmp = Replace(tmp, """", "\""")
  tmp = Replace(tmp, "'", "\'")
  Quote = Replace(tmp, Chr(0), "\0")
End Function
```

Example: Adding a New Book Title

With the following example program you can store a new book title in the *mylibrary* database. The book title consists of the title itself, one or more authors, and a publisher (see Figure 17-12). The program does not test whether the authors or publisher already exists in the database. The goal of this program is simply to demonstrate the principal methods of inserting data into linked tables.

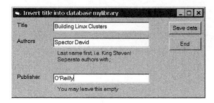

Figure 17-12. Visual Basic example program for inserting a new book title

Variant 1: Changing Data with Read/Write Recordsets

At the beginning of the procedure, four *Recordset* objects are opened, with whose help the data are to be stored. Without *LIMIT 1*, the *SELECT* statement would retrieve all matching *Recordset*s. But we are not interested in these (we want only to change data here), so this would be a waste of time. What we want is an ADO object pointing to this table, and to get one, we have to execute a *SELECT* statement. The use of *LIMIT 1* thus speeds things up for us. (If you would like to improve the efficiency of the code, you should define the four *Recordset* variables globally and open them in *Form_Load*. You thereby avoid the *Recordset*s having to be opened for each storage event.)

The commands for storing the data from the three text fields *txtPublisher*, *txtTitle*, and *txtAuthors* are easy to understand. Worthy of note is the use of the auxiliary function *LastInsertedID( )*, described above, for determining the most recently added *AUTO_INCREMENT* value:

```vb6
' example vb6 \insert_new_title\form1.frm
Private Sub SaveData_WithRecordsets()
  Dim i&, titleID&, authID&, publID&
  Dim authors_array
  Dim authors As New Recordset, titles As New Recordset
  Dim publishers As New Recordset, rel_title_author As New Recordset
  ' open Recordsets
  authors.CursorLocation = adUseClient
  titles.CursorLocation = adUseClient
  publishers.CursorLocation = adUseClient
  rel_title_author.CursorLocation = adUseClient
  authors.Open "SELECT * FROM authors LIMIT 1", _
    conn, adOpenStatic, adLockOptimistic
  titles.Open "SELECT * FROM titles LIMIT 1", _
    conn, adOpenStatic, adLockOptimistic
  publishers.Open "SELECT * FROM publishers LIMIT 1", _
    conn, adOpenStatic, adLockOptimistic
  rel_title_author.Open "SELECT * FROM rel_title_author LIMIT 1", _
    conn, adOpenStatic, adLockOptimistic

  ' store publisher (if given)
  If Trim(txtPublisher) <> "" Then
    publishers.AddNew
    publishers!publName = Trim(txtPublisher)
    publishers.Update
    publID = LastInsertedID()
  End If

  ' store book title (with publID reference as needed)
  titles.AddNew
  titles!Title = Trim(txtTitle)
  If publID <> 0 Then titles!publID = publID
  titles.Update
  titleID = LastInsertedID()

  ' store authors and make entries in rel_title_author
  authors_array = Split(txtAuthor, ";")
  For i = LBound(authors_array) To UBound(authors_array)
    authors.AddNew
    authors!authName = Trim(authors_array(i))
    authors.Update
    authID = LastInsertedID()
    rel_title_author.AddNew
    rel_title_author!titleID = titleID
    rel_title_author!authID = authID
    rel_title_author.Update
  Next
End Sub

Private Function LastInsertedID() ... see the heading "ADO Programming Techniques"
```

Variant 2: Changing Data with `conn.Execute`

In our second variant, the code is more like that to which you are accustomed in MySQL programming with languages such as PHP or Perl: You need to cobble together the SQL commands painstakingly, taking care to treat special characters correctly. (For this, the auxiliary function *Quote* will be used.) The structure of the code is otherwise like that of the first variant:

```
Private Sub SaveData_WithSQLCommands()
  Dim i&, titleID&, authID&, publID&
  Dim authors_array
  ' store publisher (if given)
  If Trim(txtPublisher) <> "" Then
    conn.Execute "INSERT INTO publishers (publName) " & _
                 "VALUES ('" & Quote(Trim(txtPublisher)) & "')"
    publID = LastInsertedID()
  End If

  ' store book title (with publID as needed)
  conn.Execute "INSERT INTO titles (title, publID) " & _
               "VALUES ('" & Quote(Trim(txtTitle)) & "', " & _
                      IIf(publID <> 0, publID, "NULL") & ")"
  titleID = LastInsertedID()
  ' store authors and add entries to rel_title_author
  authors_array = Split(txtAuthor, ";")
  For i = LBound(authors_array) To UBound(authors_array)
    conn.Execute "INSERT INTO authors (authName) " & _
                 "VALUES ('" & Quote(Trim(authors_array(i))) & "')"
    authID = LastInsertedID()
    conn.Execute "INSERT INTO rel_title_author " & _
                 " (titleID, authID) " & _
                 "VALUES (" & titleID & ", " & authID & ")"
  Next
End Sub

Private Function Quote(tmp) ... see heading "ADO Programming Techniques"
```

Example: Storing an Image File in BLOB Format and then Reading It

The following example program reads the file test.jpg from the current directory and stores it in a table (*Command2_Click*). In a second step, the binary data are read from the table and stored in the file test1.jpg (*Command3_Click*). As a visual check whether everything worked as it should have, the new file will be displayed in a *Picture* control (see Figure 17-13). For storing the image, at the beginning of the program a table is created in the following way and then deleted at the end of the program:

```
CREATE TABLE IF NOT EXISTS testpic
  (id INT NOT NULL AUTO_INCREMENT, pic BLOB, PRIMARY KEY (id))
```

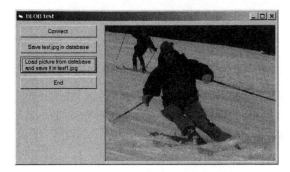

Figure 17-13. The photograph is loaded from a BLOB field and displayed

Here is the code:

```
' Example vb6\blob\form1.frm
Option Explicit
Dim conn As Connection
Dim id As Long

' create connection to MySQL
Private Sub Command1_Click()
  Set conn = New Connection
  'Options: 16395 = 16384 + 8 + 2 + 1
  '  Don't Optimize Column Width + Return Matching Rows +
  '  Allow Big Results + Change BIGINT Columns to INT
  conn.ConnectionString = "Provider=MSDASQL;" + _
    "DRIVER={MySQL ODBC 3.51 Driver};" + _
    "Server=localhost;UID=root;PWD=saturn;" + _
    "database=mylibraryodbc;Option=16395"
  conn.Open

  ' create table
  conn.Execute "CREATE TABLE IF NOT EXISTS testpic " + _
      "(id INT NOT NULL AUTO_INCREMENT, pic BLOB, PRIMARY KEY (id))"
  Command2.Enabled = True
End Sub

' read file into a Stream object and
' store it in the table testpic
Private Sub Command2_Click()
  Dim rec As New Recordset
  Dim fname As String
  Dim st As New Stream

  ' open file
  fname = App.Path + "\test.jpg"
  st.Type = adTypeBinary
  st.Open
  st.LoadFromFile fname

  ' store the file in the table
  rec.CursorLocation = adUseClient
  rec.Open "SELECT * FROM testpic LIMIT 1", conn, adOpenKeyset, adLockOptimistic
```

```
    rec.AddNew
    rec!pic = st.Read
    rec.Update
    rec.Close
    st.Close

    ' note id (AUTO_INCREMENT number)
    id = LastInsertedID()
    Command3.Enabled = True
End Sub

' read the BLOB from the table testpic and store it in a new file
Private Sub Command3_Click()
    Dim rec As New Recordset
    Dim fname As String
    Dim st As New Stream

    ' Stream object for the new file
    fname = App.Path + "\test1.jpg"
    st.Type = adTypeBinary
    st.Open

    ' read the BLOB into the Stream object
    rec.CursorLocation = adUseClient
    rec.Open "SELECT pic FROM testpic WHERE id = " & id, conn, _
      adOpenKeyset, adLockReadOnly
    st.Write rec!pic
    rec.Close

    'store the Stream in the file
    st.SaveToFile fname, adSaveCreateOverWrite
    st.Close

    ' display the file in a Picture control
    Picture1.Picture = LoadPicture(fname)
End Sub
```

MyVbQL (Visual Basic Programming Without ADO/ODBC)

The ADO programming based on Connector/ODBC introduced in the previous
section works, but it is not particularly efficient. This section offers as an alternative
the object library *MyVbQL*. This library, developed in Visual Basic, offers Visual
Basic programmers more direct access to MySQL. To this end, the *MyVbQL* objects
MYSQL_CONNECTION, MYSQL_RS, MYSQL_FIELD, and *MYSQL_ERR* display
functionality similar to that of the ADO objects *Connection, Recordset, Field*, and *Error*,
without, however, being compatible with them.

    MyVbQL is available without charge. The *GNU Library General Public License* is
used. This means that libraries may also be used in commercial applications (see also
http://www.gnu.org/copyleft/library.html).

    For this book, *MyVbQL 2* was tested.

    The DLL and underlying Visual Basic code can be found on the Internet:

http://www.icarz.com/mysql/

MyVbQL builds on the MySQL client library `libmySQL.dll`. Access to MySQL via *MyVbQL* takes place according to the following scheme: Visual Basic → MyVbQL Object library → `libmySQL.dll` → MySQL.

In comparison to ADO + Connector/ODBC, *MyVbQL* code is generally faster. A further considerable advantage is that *MyVbQL* is much less complex than ADO + Connector/ODBC. In other words, there are fewer functions, and they are generally less likely to cause errors. It is also quite practical that in distributing *MyVbQL* programs, one does not have to include ADO libraries, which inflate the setup files considerably. Unfortunately, there are some drawbacks as well:

- The time for establishing the connection is somewhat longer (particularly if MySQL is running on another computer under another operating system).

- *MyVbQL* currently does not support BLOBs.

- *MyVbQL* is not ADO-compatible. It therefore takes some effort to convert existing ADO code to *MyVbQL*.

- The *MYSQL_RS* object cannot be used as the data basis for bound database controls, which makes the use of ADO database controls in combination with *MyVbQL* impossible.

- The included documentation for *MyVbQL* is in the nature of a simple reference. The use of *MyVbQL* therefore assumes some background in Visual Basic and databases.

- *MyVbQL* will presumably not be developed further. (The tested version 2 dates from January 2001 and has not been changed since then.)

Installation

In order for *MyVbQL* to be able to be used, the two DLLs `MyVbQL.dll` and `libmysql.dll` must be installed on the computer. Both files are located in `MyVbQL.zip` on the web site `http://www.icarz.com/mysql/`.

With `MyVbQL.dll` we are dealing with an ActiveX DLL. This file may be copied into the directory of your choice (e.g., the Windows system directory). Furthermore, the file must be registered in the Windows registration database. This takes place automatically as soon as the library is transformed for the first time via PROJECT | REFERENCES into a Visual Basic project.

The file `libmysql.dll` is a traditional DLL. During program development, it must be located in the directory of the Visual Basic development environment (e.g., `C:\Programs\Visual Basic 6`). Once your Visual Basic program is complete and compiled, then `libmysql.dll` must be copied into the directory of the compiled Visual Basic program.

> **CAUTION** *Note that with every new MySQL installation, a (more current) version of* libmysql.dll *is installed, usually in the directory* C:\mysql\bin.
>
> *It is difficult to say whether* MyVbQL *should be used with the included (old) version of* libmysql.dll, *or with the more current one from the MySQL installation. On the one hand, in the current version, various errors have been corrected that still exist in the version provided with* MyVbQL. *On the other hand, the new version could have some incompatibilities.*
>
> *In no case should you copy the version from* MyVbQL *into the Windows system directory (or to another place where the file might be used by programs other than* MyVbQL). *The reason is that in addition to* MyVbQL, *there are other programs and libraries that depend on* libmysql.dll, *and these programs generally expect the most current version.*

Application

In order to use *MyVbQL* in your own Visual Basic project you must simply create a reference to the library. As soon as the library is registered, you will find it under the name *MySQL Visual Basic API* in the dialog PROJECT | REFERENCES. If the library has not yet been registered, then use the button BROWSE in order to load the DLL. You can then use the four *MYSQL_xxx* objects as you would normal Visual Basic objects.

Example

Again we shall use as an example the program that stores a character string with all the authors belonging to a given book title in the *authors* column of the *titles* table.

For establishing the connection you create an object of type *MYSQL_CONNECTION* and pass the computer name, user name, password, and database name to the method *OpenConnection*:

```
' authors_for_titles_myvbql\form1.frm
' establish connection to MySQL
Dim conn As New MYSQL_CONNECTION
Private Sub Command1_Click()
  conn.OpenConnection "localhost", "root", "xxx", "mylibraryodbc"
  Command2.Enabled = True
End Sub
```

MYSQL_RS objects are derived with the method *Execute* from the *MYSQL_CONNECTION* object. Access to individual fields of the current record is effected with *rs.Fields("columnName").Value* (instead of *rs!columnName*, as with ADO).

To alter data in *MYSQL_RS* objects, simply assign a new value to the *Value* property of the affected column and store the changes with the *Update* method. (You can also insert a new record with *AddNew* or delete one with *Delete*, but these are not demonstrated in our example.)

> **CAUTION** *Be sure to close every* MYSQL_RS *object explicitly with* Close *after you are through with it. If you forget this, then the piece of memory for storing the object will never be released. (This is due to a known, but not fixed, error in the* MyVbQL *library.)*

```vb
' change titles table
Private Sub Command2_Click()
  Dim authors_str, titleID
  Dim titles As MYSQL_RS
  Dim authors As MYSQL_RS

  ' titles Recordset for a loop over all titles
  ' and for altering the authors column
  Set titles = conn.Execute( _
    "SELECT titleID, authors FROM titles")

  ' loop over all book titles
  While Not titles.EOF
    titleID = titles.Fields("titleID").Value
    ' authors Recordset to read the authors of a title
    Set authors = conn.Execute( _
      "SELECT authname FROM authors, rel_title_author " & _
      "WHERE authors.authID=rel_title_author.authID " & _
      " AND rel_title_author.titleID = " & titleID & " " & _
      "ORDER BY authName")

    ' loop over all authors
    authors_str = ""
    Do While Not authors.EOF
      ' assemble string with author names
      If Not IsNull(authors.Fields("authName").Value) Then
        If authors_str <> "" Then authors_str = authors_str + "; "
        authors_str = authors_str & authors.Fields("authName").Value
      End If
      authors.MoveNext
    Loop
    authors.CloseRecordset

    ' save authors field in titles Recordset object
    If Len(authors_str) > 254 Then _
      authors_str = Left(authors_str, 254)
    titles.Fields("authors").Value = authors_str
    titles.Update
    titles.MoveNext
  Wend
  titles.CloseRecordset
End Sub
```

ADO.NET (Visual Basic .NET, C#)

The ADO library is also available for the programming languages Visual Basic .NET and C#. You can therefore create database applications like those that we have introduced. However, ADO in combination with VB.NET or C# is not very popular, for several reasons:

- In VB.NET/C#, the library ADO.NET is available, which offers numerous advantages in comparison to ADO. The abbreviation ADO.NET stands for *ActiveX Data Objects .NET*, but internally, ADO.NET has nothing to do with ADO. It is rather a .NET-conforming new implementation in the name space *System.Data*.

- ADO can be executed in VB.NET/C# only over the COM compatibility layer. This is considered inefficient (although the speed differences with most database applications are scarcely noticeable any longer). Furthermore, many advantages of pure .NET applications are lost (the .NET security system, the relatively simple transfer without DLL version problems, etc.).

In short, those who use VB.NET/C# generally also use ADO.NET. This section gives an overview of the available variants and discusses some of the basic concepts.

Note, please, that the classes and methods of ADO.NET are completely incompatible with those of ADO. Microsoft has not simply made an existing library .NET compatible, but has completely rethought its structure, and has realized a host of new concepts and approaches.

> **REMARK** *The examples presented in this chapter use, with few exceptions, VB.NET as the programming language. Friends of C# will find equivalent C# projects to most of these examples in the source code (www.apress.com).*
>
> *All examples were developed with the VS.NET development environment; that is, we have used the usual default settings for libraries and imports.*

> **REMARK** *It is basically true that MySQL programming with ADO.NET is not particularly MySQL-specific. Once the connection has been made, the rest is like any other ADO.NET program. The only major difference is that instead of the classes OleDbXxx and SqlXxx described in all the ADO.NET books, the largely equivalent classes OdbcXxx and MySQLXxx must be used.*
>
> *Due to space limitations, it is not possible in this book to give an introduction to ADO.NET. I therefore must assume that you are familiar with the basics of ADO.NET. If that is not the case, then before reading this section, you should get yourself a book on ADO.NET.*

Communication Between ADO.NET and MySQL

Many roads lead from ADO.NET to MySQL, regardless of whether you prefer to work with C# or VB.NET. The following list gives an overview:

- **Connector/ODBC + ODBC data provider:** In this variant, communication takes place via ODBC. The interface between MySQL and ODBC is provided by Connector/ODBC. As data provider for ADO.NET, the ODBC data provider (name space *Microsoft.Data.Odbd*) is used. This data provider is not provided with .NET 1.0 and must be installed separately. The ODBC provider will be an integral component of ADO.NET beginning with .NET 1.1:

  VB.NET/C# → ADO.NET → ODBC data provider → Connector/ODBC → MySQL

- **Connector/ODBC + OLEDB data provider:** In this variant as well, communication takes place via ODBC. However, the access route to MySQL is now extended by an additional component, the OLEDB provider for ODBC:

  VB.NET/C# → ADO.NET → OLEDB data provider → OLEDB provider for ODBC → Connector/ODBC → MySQL

- **Managed data provider for ADO.NET:** For efficient communication between ADO.NET and MySQL, it is best to use a special provider for ADO.NET:

  VB.NET/C# → ADO.NET → MySQL data provider → MySQL

The obvious advantage of such a provider is that the communication path is the shortest. This represents fewer compatibility problems between the individual layers and greater efficiency. Moreover, specially tailored providers for MySQL can provide MySQL-specific functions (such as support of the compressed communication protocol). These additional functions can be useful, but they have the drawback of making difficult a later change of provider (or even the database system).

Fortnately, there is now a host of such providers. In February 2003 I found the following drivers on the Internet:

- *ByteFX.Data,* **alias MySQLNet (Open Source, LGPL):** This open-source driver was still in beta test stage in February 2003, but it made a very good impression. Unfortunately, there is no documentation at all. The driver also contains classes for programming of database applications with PostgresSQL:

  http://sourceforge.net/projects/mysqlnet/

- *MySQLDriverCS* **(Open Source, GPL):** This open-source driver is, according to its developers, fully mature. However, the driver currently provides only a fraction of the usual .NET driver classes. (For example, *MySQLDataAdapter*, *MySQLParameter*, and *MySQLCommandBuilder* are lacking.)

  http://sourceforge.net/projects/mysqldrivercs/

- *dbProvider* **from eInfoDesign:** According to its creators, this commercial driver completely implements the .NET data interface. The reduced-functionality *Personal Edition* (no support for transactions, only *latin1* allowed as character set) is available free of charge:

  http://www.einfodesigns.com/dbProvider_info.aspx

- ***MySQLDirect .NET* from CoreLab:** This is yet another commercial driver. It is based on the MySQL client library `libmysql.dll` (which is included and can be installed directly into the directory `Windows\Systems32`). There is a free test version available. A particular advantage of this driver is its extensive documentation (`*.chm` help file).

It was, of course, impossible to test all the variants introduced here. I have tried out connections with the combination *Connector/ODBC + ODBC provider* as well as with the providers *ByteFX*, *dbProvider*, and *MySQLDirect .NET*. However, all further tests were made exclusively with *Connector/ODBC + ODBC provider*.

The ODBC example should function with the three MySQL providers without noteworthy changes if you change the lines for establishing the connection and replace *OdbcXxx* by *MySQLXxx* or *MySqlXxx*. (The use of upper- and lowercase in the name *MySQL* differs among the three providers. In my experiments it was sometimes necessary to use cast operations. There are also some small syntactic variants in the initialization of objects.)

Establishing the Connection with the ODBC Data Provider

Assumptions

Before you start programming, three conditions must be satisfied:

- **ODBC data provider:** The library *Microsoft.Data.Odbc* has been included with the .NET Framework only since version 1.1. If you are working with version 1.0, you must download the `*.msi` file from the address below. A double click installs the provider in the *global assembly cache* of the .NET Framework, making it available to all .NET programs:

  ```
  http://www.microsoft.com/downloads/release.asp?ReleaseID=35715
  ```

  A reference to this library must now be established for each project. To save typing, one should include the instruction *Imports Microsoft.Data.Odbc* or *using Microsoft.Data.Odbc* at the beginning of the code.

- **Connector/ODBC:** The second requirement for access to MySQL is Connector/ODBC, whose installation we have described in Chapter 2.

- **MDAC update:** The third condition is to install an update (bug fix) to the Microsoft database components (MDAC 2.7). An error in the ODBC driver manager leads to the exception *SQL_NO_DATA* being triggered in ODBC.NET programs when an empty string is read via ODBC. The update can be found at

  ```
  http://support.microsoft.com/default.aspx?scid=kb;EN-US;q319243
  ```

Establishing the Connection

The connection looks very much as it did with ADO. The main difference is that now
an *OdbcConnection* object is used, and the connection string can be passed to the
constructor. The connection string is exactly the same as with ADO. As a rule, the
Options setting should be 3. (This corresponds to the options *Don't optimize column
width* (1) and *Return matching rows* (2). The option *Change BIGINT into INT (16384)*
is not required with ADO.NET.)

```
' VB.NET
Dim odbcconn As New Microsoft.Data.Odbc.OdbcConnection( _
  "Driver={MySQL ODBC 3.51 Driver};Server=localhost;" + _
  "Database=mylibraryodbc;UID=root;PWD=saturn;Options=3")
odbcconn.Open()
```

```
// C#
OdbcConnection odbcconn = new OdbcConnection(
  "Driver={MySQL ODBC 3.51 Driver};Server=localhost;" +
  "Database=mylibraryodbc;UID=root;PWD=saturn;Options=3");
odbcconn.Open();
```

VB.NET Example

The following small program displays an alphabetic list of all publishers in
mylibraryodbc.publishers in a console window. After the connection is established
with *OdbcCommand*, a *SELECT* query is executed. The result is evaluated with an
OdbdDataReader object in a loop:

```
' example vbnet/odbc_connect/module1.vb
Option Strict On
Imports System.Data
Imports Microsoft.Data.Odbc
Module Module1
  Dim odbcconn As OdbcConnection

  Sub Main()
    odbcconn = New OdbcConnection( _
      "Driver=MySQL ODBC 3.51 Driver;Server=localhost;" + _
      "Database=mylibraryodbc;UID=root;PWD=saturn;Options=16387")
    odbcconn.Open()
    read_publishers_datareader()
    odbcconn.Close()
  End Sub

  ' example for OdbcDataReader
  Sub read_publishers_datareader()
    Dim com As OdbcCommand
    Dim dr As OdbcDataReader
    com = New OdbcCommand( _
      "SELECT publID, publName FROM publishers ORDER BY publName", _
      odbcconn)
    dr = com.ExecuteReader()
```

```
      While dr.Read()
        Console.WriteLine("id: {0} name: {1}", dr!publID, dr!publName)
      End While
      dr.Close()
    End Sub
End Module
```

C# Example

The equivalent C# code looks like this:

```
// example csharp\odbc_connect\Class1.cs
using System;
using Microsoft.Data.Odbc;

namespace odbc_connect {
  class mainclass          {
    [STAThread]
    static void Main(string[] args) {
      Odbctest tst = new Odbctest();
      tst.ReadPublishersDataset();
      Console.WriteLine("Return drŸcken");
      Console.ReadLine();
    }
  }

  class Odbctest {
    OdbcConnection odbcconn;

    public Odbctest() {      // use constructor to connect
      odbcconn = new OdbcConnection(
        "Driver={MySQL ODBC 3.51 Driver};Server=localhost;" +
        "Database=mylibraryodbc;UID=root;PWD=saturn;Options=16387");
      odbcconn.Open();
    }

    public void ReadPublishersDataset() {
      OdbcCommand com = new OdbcCommand(
        "SELECT publID, publName FROM publishers ORDER BY publName",
        odbcconn);
      OdbcDataReader dr = com.ExecuteReader();
      while(dr.Read()) {
        Console.WriteLine("id: {0} name: {1}",
          dr["publID"], dr["publName"]);
      }
      dr.Close();
    }
  }
}
```

Establishing the Connection with the ByteFX.Data Provider

Assumptions

The ByteFX.Data provider is available at http://sourceforge.net/projects/mysqlnet/ as a simple ZIP file. It contains two files: ByteFX.Data.dll and SharpZipLib.dll. Both files must be copied either into the *global assembly cache* (GAC) or into the project directory. Then you must place a reference to both files in your new project (ByteFX.Data contains the actual ADO classes, while SharpZipLib.dll has the compression functions).

To avoid having to specify *ByteFX.Data.MySQLClient.xxx* repeatedly, you should place an *Imports* or *using* instruction at the beginning of your code:

```
Imports ByteFX.Data.MySQLClient  '  VB.NET
using ByteFX.Data.MySQLClient; // C#
```

The information in this section is based on the tested version 0.65.

Establishing the Connection

The connection is now made with a *MySQLConnection* object. The string with connection data is made up of the following pieces:

Data Source	host name or IP address of the MySQL server
Initial Catalog	name of the database
User ID	user name
Password	password
Use Compression	compress communication between client and server? (True/False)

```
Dim myconn As New MySQLConnection( _
  "Data Source=localhost;Initial Catalog=mylibraryodbc;" + _
  "User ID=root;PWD=saturn;Use Compression=true")
myconn.Open()
```

In contrast to the other providers that we have discussed, *ByteFX* supports compressed data exchange to the server (connection parameter *Use Compression*). Whether compression is being used can be determined from the property *UseCompression.*

The source code for this book includes examples in VB.NET and C#. After the connection is established, an alphabetic list of all publishers is displayed in a console window.

Establishing the Connection with dbProvider (eInfoDesign)

Assumptions

The freely available *Personal Edition* of *dbProvider* from eInfoDesign is available at `http://www.einfodesigns.com/dbProvider_info.aspx` as a *.msi file. You must register before downloading the file.

Installation of the file `dbProvider.dll` is by default into the directory `Programs\eInfoDesigns\dbProvider Personal Edition`. You should copy the *.dll file either into the *global assembly cache* or into your project directory. Then you must set up a reference in your new project to the *.dll file.

To avoid having to specify the name space of the *dbProvider* classes repeatedly in your code, you should place an *Imports* or *using* instruction at the beginning of your code:

```
Imports eInfoDesigns.dbProvider.MySqlClient   '  VB.NET
using eInfoDesigns.dbProvider.MySqlClient; // C#
```

The information in this section is based on the *Personal Edition*, version 1.6.977 (version number according to DLL properties).

Establishing the Connection

The character string with the connection data for the *MySQLConnection* object consists of the following pieces:

Data Source	host name or IP address of the MySQL server
Database	name of the database
User ID	user name
Password	password
COMMAND LOGGING	command logging? (true/false)
POOLING	use connection pooling? (true/false)

```
myconn = New MySqlConnection( _
  "Data Source=localhost;Database=mylibraryodbc;" + _
  "User ID=root;Password=saturn")
myconn.Open()
```

The source code for this book includes examples in VB.NET and C#. After the connection is established, an alphabetic list of all publishers is displayed in a console window.

Establishing the Connection with MySQLDirect .NET (CoreLab)

Assumptions

The test version of *MySQLDirect .NET* can be downloaded from the site
http://crlab.com/download.html. The installation program (*.msi) installs two
*.dll files into the *global assembly cache*. Furthermore, after asking, it copies
libmysql.dll into the Windows system directory. (If you have a newer version of this
client library from a MySQL installation, you should use it. Copy the file if necessary
from C:\mysql\bin into the Windows system directory.)

Add a reference in your new project to the library *CoreLab.MySQL*. To save typing,
add the following *Imports/using* instruction:

```
Imports CoreLab.MySql  ' VB.NET
using CoreLab.MySql; // C#
```

MySQLDirect .NET was the only one of the providers tested that had
acceptable on-line documentation. (However, help must be invoked with
START | PROGRAMS | CORELAB. The shortcut F1 does not work in the develoment
environment.) The version tested was 1.21.6.

Establishing the Connection

The string with connection data for the *MySqlConnection* object can be assembled
from the following parts:

Data Source or *Host* or *Server*	host name or IP Address of the MySQL server
Database or *Initial Catalog*	name of the database
User or *User ID*	user name
Password or *PWD*	password
Port	IP port (default 3306)
Connection Timeout	maximum wait for connection (default 15 seconds)

```
Dim myconn As New MySqlConnection( _
  "Host=localhost;Database=mylibraryodbc;" + _
  "User=root;Password=saturn;Connection Timeout=30")
myconn.Open()
```

For the *MySqlDirect .NET* provider as well there is a C# example in the source
code for this book.

Programming Techniques

> **REMARK**   *As we have already mentioned, the remaining sections relate exclusively to Connector/ODBC in combination with the ODBC data provider (though we may occasionally make reference to other providers).*
>
> *If you are not keen on using ODBC, but rather one of the other providers that we have described, you must establish a reference to the appropriate library, change the* Imports/using *instruction, replace* OdbcXxx *by* MySqlXxx, *and adapt the connection string according to the provider's required syntax. Depending on the provider, you may also have to make minor changes in the code (e.g., cast operators, parameter syntax in SQL commands).*

All the examples assume that *odbcconn* is an open *OdbcConnection* object that refers to a suitable MySQL database.

Executing SQL Commands (OdbcCommand)

To execute SQL commands, you need an *OdbcCommand* object. The basic *OdbcConnection* object and the SQL command can be passed to the constructor or handled separately. (The latter is especially useful if you wish to execute several SQL commands with a single *OdbcCommand* object.)

There are three ways to execute SQL commands:

- *ExecuteNonQuery* is used for all commands that do not immediately return a result (e.g., *UPDATE, INSERT, DELETE*):

```
Dim com As New OdbcCommand()
com.Connection = odbcconn
com.CommandText = "INSERT INTO table (colname) VALUES ('abc')"
com.ExecuteNonQuery()
```

- *ExecuteReader* is used if you wish to execute a *SELECT* query and read the result with *OdbcDataReader* (see the example somewhat later in this chapter).

- *ExecuteScalar* is used when the command returns a single value (e.g., *SELECT COUNT(*) FROM table*); an example follows shortly.

If an error occurs during the execution of an SQL command, an *OdbcException* occurs, which can be caught with *Try/Catch*:

```
Try
  com.ExecuteNonQuery()
Catch e As OdbcException
  MsgBox(e.Message)
  Stop
End Try
```

In formulating an SQL command, you must heed the usual MySQL peculiarities: In character strings, the characters ', ", \, and the zero-byte must be indicated by \', \", \\, and \0. Dates must also be correctly formatted (*2003-12-31 23:59:59*). You can save effort with *INSERT* and *DELETE* commands by using commands with parameters, which we now discuss.

Commands with Parameters (ODBC Parameters)

Parameters in SQL commands are indicated by *?*. Then, for each parameter, you use *Parameters.Add* to specify the name and data type. Make sure that you present the parameters in the correct order:

```
Dim com As New OdbcCommand()
com.Connection = odbcconn
com.CommandText = _
  "INSERT INTO tablename (a_date, a_text, a_blob) VALUES(?, ?, ?)"
com.Parameters.Add("pdate", OdbcType.DateTime)
com.Parameters.Add("ptext", OdbcType.Text)
com.Parameters.Add("pblob", OdbcType.Binary)
```

Whenever you wish to execute an *INSERT* command, you must now pass the appropriate data to the parameters, which could look like this:

```
Dim bin(49) As Byte   '50 Bytes
...
com.Parameters!pdate.Value = Now
com.Parameters!ptext.Value = "O'Hara"
com.Parameters!pblob.Value = bin
com.ExecuteNonQuery()
```

> **TIP** *The definition of a parameter and specification of the parameter value for the first call can be squeezed into a single line:*
>
> ```
> com.Parameters.Add("ptext", OdbcType.Text).Value = "O'Hara"
> ```

The equivalent C# code looks like this:

```
OdbcCommand com = new OdbcCommand();
com.Connection = odbcconn;
com.CommandText =
  "INSERT INTO tablename (a_date, a_text, a_blob) VALUES(?, ?, ?)";
com.Parameters.Add("pdate", OdbcType.DateTime);
com.Parameters.Add("ptext", OdbcType.Text);
com.Parameters.Add("pblob", OdbcType.Binary);
byte[] bin = new byte[50];
...
```

```
com.Parameters["pdate"].Value = DateTime.Now;
com.Parameters["ptext"].Value = "O'Hara";
com.Parameters["pblob"].Value = bin;
com.ExecuteNonQuery();
```

Parameters with MySQL Providers

In the use of parameters, there are considerable differences between the ODBC provider and the various MySQL providers. There, you must pass the parameters in the form *@parametername*. (This has the advantage that the parameters cannot be confused among one another, and thus the order of *Parameters.Add* instructions is arbitrary.) The following lines were tested with the *ByteFX* provider:

```
Dim com As New MySQLCommand()
com.Connection = myconn
com.CommandText = _
  "INSERT INTO tablename (a_date, a_text) VALUES(@p1, @p2)"
com.Parameters.Add("@p1", MySQLDbType.Datetime)
com.Parameters.Add("@p2", MySQLDbType.String)
com.Parameters("@p1").Value = Now
com.Parameters("@p2").Value = "O'Hara"
com.ExecuteNonQuery()
```

Reading SELECT Results (OdbcDataReader)

The *OdbcDataReader* class offers the simplest way of reading *SELECT* results. The *OdbcDataReader* does not support free navigation in the result list (hence only *forward only*). Nor are changes possible. In return, *OdbcDataReader* is frugal with resources and offers the most efficient path to *SELECT* results.

You obtain an *OdbcDataReader* when you execute an SQL command with the method *ExecuteReader*. *Read* reads the first, or next, record, and returns *True* or *False* depending on whether a record was found. The *OdbcDataReader* object should be explicitly closed with *Close* as soon as it is no longer needed. (Otherwise, it holds onto ODBC resources.)

The following lines show how all records can be run through in a loop:

```
Dim com As New OdbcCommand( _
  "SELECT publID, publName FROM publishers", odbcconn)
Dim dr As OdbcDataReader = com.ExecuteReader()
While dr.Read()
  Console.WriteLine("id: {0} name: {1}", dr!publID, dr!publName)
End While
dr.Close()
```

The *OdbcDataReader* offers no way of determining the number of records in advance. Thus you must count along as you read all the records, or else execute a *SELECT COUNT(*)* . . . query.

Access to data fields: In VB.NET, access to data fields takes place in the form *dr!columnname*. In C#, you must instead write *dr["columnname"]*. In each case, you obtain as result an object of the interface *IDataRecord*, which you must explicitly transform when saving into another data type.

As an alternative, you can read data with *GetByte(n)*, *GetDateTime(n)*, *GetInt32(n)*, etc., where *n* is the column number (0 for the first column).

NULL: Data fields that in the database contain *NULL* have in ADO.NET the value *System.DBNull*. A *NULL* test can be caried out with the method *Convert.IsDBNull*:

```
If Convert.IsDBNull(dr!column) Then ...
```

In saving *SELECT* results (e.g., *stringvar = CStr(dr!textcolumn)*), you must always consider the case that the data field contains *NULL:* Then the VB.NET method *CStr* or the C# cast operator (*string*) leads to an error.

If you wish to save the value *NULL*, you can prefix the parameter *DBNull.Value*:

```
com.Parameters(0).Value = DBNull.Value
```

Dates: Dates (*DATE*, *TIMESTAMP*) are automatically transformed in ADO.NET into *Date* objects.

Times: Times (*TIME*) are transformed in ADO.NET into *TimeSpan* objects.

Fixed-point numbers: Fixed-point numbers (*DECIMAL*) are represented in ADO.NET by *Decimal* objects.

BIGINTs: In contrast to ADO, ADO.NET has no problems with 64-bit integers (*BIGINT*). Such numbers are represented in ADO.NET as *Long* numbers.

BLOBs: Binary data are represented in ADO.NET by *Byte* fields.

Character strings: In VB.NET and C#, character strings are coded in UTF16. In transfer between ADO.NET and MySQL, a transformation takes place automatically into the character set of the MySQL server (generally *latin1*). Unrepresentable characters are replaced by question marks without an error message.

If you wish to save Unicode strings as such in MySQL, you must use a *BLOB* field. To transform a .NET *String*, say *s*, into a UTF8 *Byte* field, use *Text.Encoding.UTF8.GetBytes(s)*. To transform in the opposite direction, use *Text.Encoding.UTF8.GetString(bytes)*. The following lines show how a Unicode string is stored and then read:

```
com.CommandText = "INSERT INTO table (a_blob) VALUES (?)"
com.Parameters.Add("blob", OdbcType.Binary)
com.Parameters!blob.Value = _
  Text.Encoding.UTF8.GetBytes("Smiley: " + ChrW(9786))
com.ExecuteNonQuery()
```

```
com.CommandText = "SELECT * FROM table"
Dim dr As OdbcDataReader = com.ExecuteReader()
dr.Read()
Dim s As String = _
  Text.Encoding.UTF8.GetString(CType(dr!a_blob, Byte()))
```

Evaluating SELECT *Scalars* (OdbcCommand.ExecuteScalar)

Queries such as *SELECT COUNT(*) FROM . . .* represent a special case. They return a single record with a single column. In this case, you can do without a *DataReader*. Instead, execute the SQL command (*OdbcCommand* object) with the method *ExecuteScalar*, which returns the result as an *Object*. With *CInt* (C# cast operator *int*), you obtain the corresponding *Integer*:

```
Dim n As Integer
Dim com As New OdbcCommand("SELECT COUNT(*) FROM table", odbcconn)
n = CInt(com.ExecuteScalar())
```

AUTO_INCREMENT *Columns* (LAST_INSERT_ID)

The ID number of the last data record inserted with *INSERT* can be determined with the command *SELECT LAST_INSERT_ID()*. The method *ExecuteScalar*, just described, returns the ID number as a *long* integer:

```
Dim n As Long
Dim com As New OdbcCommand()
com.Connection = odbcconn
com.CommandText = "INSERT INTO table (columns ... ) VALUES (ldots)"
com.ExecuteNonQuery()
com.CommandText = "SELECT LAST_INSERT_ID()"
n = CLng(com.ExecuteScalar())
```

DataSet, DataTable, OdbcDataAdapter

If you wish to navigate at will (backward as well as forward) through *SELECT* results and alter, delete, or insert new records, then you need a *DataSet* object and at least one *DataTable* contained therein. (A *DataSet* helps in managing one or more *DataTable*s. A *DataTable* is simply a table with data, usually the result of *SELECT* queries. *DataSet* and *DataTable* are general ADO.NET classes, and are independent of the provider. For this reason, there are no independent *OdbcDataSet*s, *MySqlDataSet*s, etc. However, for communication between the *DataSet* and the provider, an *OdbcDataAdapter* or *MySqlDataApapter* is necessary.)

All the data contained in a *DataSet* are located in the memory of the ADO.NET program. When a *DataTable* contained in a *DataSet* is created on the basis of a *SELECT* query, all resulting records from the query are transmitted to the ADO.NET program. From this point on, you are processing the local copy of the data. The data stored on the MySQL server are updated only when the *Update* method for the *OdbcDataAdapter* is executed.

The following commands show how to fill a *DataTable* with the results of a *SELECT* query. As usual, you first create an *OdbcCommand* object for your SQL command. This object will be passed to an *OdbcDataAdapter*. The *SELECT* query is executed by the method *Fill* of the *OdbcDataAdapter*. The results are stored in the *DataSet*. For this, a new *DataTable* is created in the *DataSet*, which in this example is given the name *"test"*. You can now access this *DataTable* via *ds.Tables("name")*:

```
Dim com As New OdbcCommand("SELECT * FROM testall", odbcconn)
Dim da As New OdbcDataAdapter(com)
Dim ds As New DataSet()              'preveiously empty DataSet ds
da.Fill(ds, "test")                  'creates DataTable "test" in ds
Dim dt As DataTable = ds.Tables("test") 'access to the DataTable
```

You can now access the data of the *DataTable* in the form of *dt.Row(rowno)!columnname*. Here, *Row(n)* return a single record (class *DataRow*), and *Rows.Count* gives the number of records. A loop over all records can be formulated thus:

```
Dim row As DataRow
For Each row In dt.Rows  'loop over all records
  row!columnname = ...    'change data
Next
```

With *datarow.Delete* you can delete individual records. It is somewhat more complex to insert new records. For that, you first create a new record with *datatable.NewRow*, change its contents, and finally add it with *datatable.Rows.Add* to the *DataTable*:

```
Dim newrow As DataRow
newrow = dt.NewRow()
newrow!a_big_int = 12345
dt.Rows.Add(newrow)
```

As already mentioned, all changes in the *DataSet* are valid initially only locally (that is, in memory of the ADO.NET program). For the changes to be carried out in the MySQL database, you must execute the method *Update* for the *OdbcDataAdapter*. The update is carried out in a series of *INSERT*, *UPDATE*, and *DELETE* commands, which the *OdbcDataAdapter* sends to MySQL. However, the *OdbcDataAdapter* is not able to generate these commands. Therefore, first, before the *Update* method, an *OdbcCommandBuilder* object must be generated to take over this task. The following lines demonstrate how that is done:

```
' ... Code to alter data in dt
Dim cb As New OdbcCommandBuilder(da)
Try
  da.Update(ds, "test")
Catch e As Exception
  Stop
End Try
```

If you wish to know which *UPDATE, INSERT*, and *DELETE* commands are being executed, you can find this out with *cb.GetInsert/Update/DeleteCommand()*. (These commands depend heavily on the provider being used.)

What looks great in theory, is in practice hemmed in with many limitations:

- Changes can be stored only if the *DataTables* contained in the *DataSet* come directly form a MySQL table. *DataTable*s based on *SELECT* commands that include several tables (*JOIN*) or use aggregating functions (*GROUP BY*) cannot be updated. In this case, the *OdbcCommandBuilder* is incapable of determining the appropriate SQL commands. (This limitation is not one of ADO.NET, but has to do with the fact that changes in such tables can often be interpreted in more than one way, and ADO.NET and the *CommandBuilder* are not clairvoyant.)

- In general, the change in a *DataSet* is strongly provider-dependent. My worst experiences were (not surprisingly) with the ODBC provider. The MySQL providers, on the other hand, are better adapted to the peculiarities of MySQL. For example, after the insertion of a new record, the *ByteFX* provider automatically determines the ID number of the new record (*AUTO_INCREMENT* column) and updates the row in the *DataTable* accordingly. The ODBC variant is incapable of doing this, which makes the insertion of linked records into several tables of a *DataSet* impossible from the outset.

   The strong provider-dependence also means that you cannot count on your code functioning after a change of provider.

- Aside from these limitations, in my experiments with *DataSet* updating, various other problems and errors arose, whose cause was not always completely discernible. (The generally cryptic error messages were not very helpful. Some of the errors perhaps have to do with incorrect handling of MySQL-specific data types.)

In sum, not everything that looks technologically appealing is ready to be used in the real world. I recommend that you use *DataSets* in general only for reading data. If you wish to alter data, you should create the necessary SQL commands yourself and execute them with *OdbcCommand*s (preferably using parameters).

Windows.Forms and ASP.NET Controls

The .NET Framework offers a great number of controls for Windows and Internet applications (ASP.NET) that can be bound to *DataSet*s. This simplifies the representation and processing of lists and tables on the basis of query results.

A basic rule is that as long as you display only data with the controls, and don't try to alter the data, you may expect few problems. However, if you permit data updating, then you should test extensively what is possible. (Internally, data bound controls use *DataSet*s almost exclusively, and I have already referred to their *Update* problems.)

Space here does not suffice to introduce data bound controls and go into the details of their deployment. The following example program should at least provide a first impression of what can be done with them. The program contains a listbox with all publishers. When one is selected, a table field displays that publisher's titles (see Figure 17-14):

Figure 17-14. ADO.NET example program

```
' example program vbnet\datacontrols
Imports Microsoft.Data.Odbc
Public Class Form1
  Inherits System.Windows.Forms.Form
  ' Windows Forms Designer generated code ...

  Dim odbcconn As OdbcConnection
  Dim titlecommand As OdbcCommand

  ' initialization tasks
  Private Sub Form1_Load( _
    ByVal sender As System.Object, _
    ByVal e As System.EventArgs) Handles MyBase.Load

    ' establish connection to the database
    odbcconn = New OdbcConnection( _
      "Driver={MySQL ODBC 3.51 Driver};Server=localhost;" + _
      "Database=mylibraryodbc;UID=root;PWD=saturn;Options=3")
    odbcconn.Open()

    'prepare OdbcCommand for titles
    titlecommand = New OdbcCommand( _
      "SELECT title, subtitle, langName FROM titles, languages " + _
      "WHERE publID = ? AND titles.langID = languages.langID " + _
      "ORDER BY title", _
      odbcconn)
    titlecommand.Parameters.Add("publID", OdbcType.Int)

    'fill the listbox for publishers
    Dim com As New OdbcCommand( _
      "SELECT publID, publName FROM publishers ORDER BY publName", _
      odbcconn)
    Dim da As New OdbcDataAdapter(com)
    Dim ds As New DataSet()
    da.Fill(ds, "publishers")
    ComboBox1.DisplayMember = "publName"
    ComboBox1.ValueMember = "publID"
    ComboBox1.DataSource = ds.Tables("publishers")
  End Sub

  ' update table fields for each selection in the listbox
  Private Sub ComboBox1_SelectedIndexChanged( _
    ByVal sender As System.Object, _
    ByVal e As System.EventArgs) _
    Handles ComboBox1.SelectedIndexChanged
```

```
      titlecommand.Parameters("publID").Value = ComboBox1.SelectedValue
      Dim ds As New DataSet()
      Dim da As New OdbcDataAdapter(titlecommand)
      da.Fill(ds, "titles")
      DataGrid1.DataSource = ds.Tables("titles")
   End Sub
End Class
```

Transactions

At the beginning of a transaction, execute the method *BeginTransaction* for the object *OdbcConnection* object. As result, you obtain an *OdbcTransaction* object, with whose method *Commit* or *Rollback* you can end the transaction. For all commands that are executed within the confines of the transaction, the *Transaction* property must be set, either through the third parameter of the *OdbcCommand* constructor or through an explicit allocation of the *Transaction* property. The following lines show the usual way of proceeding:

```
Dim tr As OdbcTransaction
tr = odbcconn.BeginTransaction()
Dim com As New OdbcCommand("UPDATE ... ", odbcconn, tr)
com.ExecuteNonQuery()
' ... further commands of the transaction
tr.Commit()
```

> **REMARK** *The InnoDB documentation recommends in client programming not to rely in general on the transaction methods of the particular library or API, and instead, to execute the SQL commands* SET AUTOCOMMIT= ... *and* BEGIN/COMMIT/ROLLBACK *explicitly. The reason is that with many libraries, the transaction functions have not been sufficiently tested in combination with MySQL. In my experience, I can say at least that with ADO.NET in combination with the ODBC driver, everything seems to work without any problems.*

Example: Storing New Titles in `mylibraryodbc`

The example program of this section consists of a simple input mask in which you can input new book titles together with their authors and publishers. In the author field you may input more than one name, separated by semicolons. The publisher field is allowed to remain empty (in which case, the title is stored without a publisher). (See Figure 17-15.) In storing a new title, a check is made whether the authors and publisher are already known to the database, in which case the records already stored are used. There are no other plausibility checks or error-checking.

The program code is broken into two procdures. In *Form1_Load*, a number of *OdbcCommand* objects are initialized with *INSERT* and *SELECT* commands. These commands are then used when the procedure *btnSave_Click* is called for storing input:

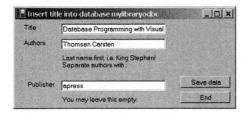

Figure 17-15. Form for storing a new book title

```vbnet
' example vbnet\newtitleform
Option Strict On
Imports Microsoft.Data.Odbc

Public Class Form1
  Inherits System.Windows.Forms.Form
  ' Windows Forms Designer generated code ...
  Dim odbcConn As OdbcConnection
  Dim insertPublisherCom, insertAuthorCom, _
      insertTitleCom, insertRelAuthTitleCom, _
      selectPublisherCom, selectAuthorCom, _
      lastIDCom As OdbcCommand

  Private Sub Form1_Load( ... ) Handles MyBase.Load
    ' establish connection to the database
    odbcconn = New OdbcConnection( _
      "Driver={MySQL ODBC 3.51 Driver};Server=localhost;" + _
      "Database=mylibraryodbc;UID=root;PWD=saturn;Options=3")
    odbcconn.Open()

    'prepare various INSERT and SELECT commands
    insertAuthorCom = New OdbcCommand( _
      "INSERT INTO authors (authName) VALUES (?)", odbcConn)
    insertAuthorCom.Parameters.Add("name", OdbcType.Text)

    selectAuthorCom = New OdbcCommand( _
      "SELECT authID FROM authors WHERE authName = ? LIMIT 1", _
      odbcConn)
    selectAuthorCom.Parameters.Add("name", OdbcType.Text)

    insertTitleCom = New OdbcCommand( _
      "INSERT INTO titles (title, publID) VALUES (?, ?)", _
      odbcConn)
    insertTitleCom.Parameters.Add("title", OdbcType.Text)
    insertTitleCom.Parameters.Add("publID", OdbcType.Int)

    insertPublisherCom = New OdbcCommand( _
      "INSERT INTO publishers (publName) VALUES (?)", odbcConn)
    insertPublisherCom.Parameters.Add("name", OdbcType.Text)

    selectPublisherCom = New OdbcCommand( _
      "SELECT publID FROM publishers WHERE publName = ? LIMIT 1", _
      odbcConn)
    selectPublisherCom.Parameters.Add("name", OdbcType.Text)
```

```
    insertRelAuthTitleCom = New OdbcCommand( _
      "INSERT INTO rel_title_author (titleID, authID) " + _
      " VALUES (?, ?)", odbcConn)
    insertRelAuthTitleCom.Parameters.Add("titleID", OdbcType.Int)
    insertRelAuthTitleCom.Parameters.Add("authID", OdbcType.Int)

    lastIDCom = New OdbcCommand( _
      "SELECT LAST_INSERT_ID()", odbcConn)
  End Sub
  Private Sub btnSave_Click( ... ) Handles btnSave.Click
    Dim publID, titleID As Integer
    Dim result As Object
    Dim author, authors() As String
    txtTitle.Text = Trim(txtTitle.Text)
    txtAuthors.Text = Trim(txtAuthors.Text)
    txtPublisher.Text = Trim(txtPublisher.Text)
    If txtTitle.Text = "" Or txtAuthors.Text = "" Then
      MsgBox("Please specify title and authors!")
      Exit Sub
    End If

    'search for and store publisher in publisher table
    If txtPublisher.Text <> "" Then
      ' does the publisher already exist?
      selectPublisherCom.Parameters(0).Value = txtPublisher.Text
      result = selectPublisherCom.ExecuteScalar()
      If result Is Nothing Then
        ' no: store
        insertPublisherCom.Parameters(0).Value = txtPublisher.Text
        insertPublisherCom.ExecuteNonQuery()
        publID = CInt(lastIDCom.ExecuteScalar())
      Else
        publID = CInt(result)
      End If
    End If

    ' store title
    insertTitleCom.Parameters(0).Value = txtTitle.Text
    If publID > 0 Then
      insertTitleCom.Parameters(1).Value = publID
    Else
      insertTitleCom.Parameters(1).Value = DBNull.Value
    End If
    insertTitleCom.ExecuteNonQuery()
    titleID = CInt(lastIDCom.ExecuteScalar())

    ' store authors
    authors = Split(txtAuthors.Text, ";")
    insertRelAuthTitleCom.Parameters(0).Value = titleID
    For Each author In authors
      'does the author already exist?
      selectAuthorCom.Parameters(0).Value = author
      result = selectAuthorCom.ExecuteScalar()
      If result Is Nothing Then
        ' no, store new author
```

```
      insertAuthorCom.Parameters(0).Value = author
      insertAuthorCom.ExecuteNonQuery()
      insertRelAuthTitleCom.Parameters(1).Value = _
        CInt(lastIDCom.ExecuteScalar())
    Else
      insertRelAuthTitleCom.Parameters(1).Value = _
        CInt(result)
    End If
    ' store link title/authors
    insertRelAuthTitleCom.ExecuteNonQuery()
  Next

  MsgBox("Your input has been saved")
  txtTitle.Text = ""
  txtAuthors.Text = ""
  txtPublisher.Text = ""
End Sub
```

Converter: Microsoft SQL Server → MySQL

If up to now you have managed a database with the Microsoft SQL Server (or the MSDE, that is, the Microsoft Data Engine) and are considering porting it to MySQL, there are two main ways of bringing your data into a MySQL database.

- Summon Access to your assistance. First, import the table into an empty Access database, and then export it to MySQL.

- Use the VBA/Visual Basic script mssql2mysql (developed in its first version by me). The program should generally enable a more exact copy of the database structure, since there is no intermediate Access step. The remainder of this section is related to this program. The program can also be seen as a further example of ADO database programming with MySQL, although for reasons of space we omit the source code.

> **POINTER**   *Converters, both commercial and free of charge, between MySQL and a number of other databases (dBase, FoxPro, mSQL) can be found at the following addresses:*
>
> http://www.mysql.com/portal/software/index.html
> http://www.mysql.com/doc/en/Contrib.html

Properties of mssql2mysql

- freely obtainable (GPL)

- copies an entire database, that is, all user-defined tables (structure, indexes, data)

- automatically changes the name of a table or column if the name is not allowable in MySQL (for example, *My table* becomes *My_table*)

- changes Unicode character strings into ANSI character strings or BLOBs

- generates either a text file with SQL commands or executes the required commands directly on the MySQL server

Assumptions

- To execute the script, either a more or less current VBA interpreter (e.g., in all components of Microsoft Office since Office 2000) or the programming language Visual Basic 6 must be available.

- The program requires the libraries ADO and SQLDMO. (SQLDMO allows the control of the Microsoft SQL server. The library is installed together with the SQL server.)

- If the converted database is not to be written into a text file (*.sql), but transmitted directly to a running MySQL server, then Connector/ODBC must also be installed.

The converter was tested with SQL Server 7 and 2000, MySQL 3.23 and 4.0, ADO 2.5 and 2.7, and Connector/ODBC 2.50 and 3.51.*n*.

Restrictions

- In MySQL, currently unavailable or incompatible (with the SQL server) database attributes are not supported (views, stored procedures, user-defined data type, access privileges, etc.).

- MySQL allows only one *AUTO_INCREMENT* column per table, and that column must be defined as *PRIMARY KEY*. The converter does not check this condition. You must therefore change your SQL server as necessary before starting the script.

- SQL server *TIMESTAMP*s are incompatible with MySQL *TIMESTAMP*s and are therefore transformed into *TINYBLOB*s.

- Integrity rules (foreign key constraints) are not supported by the script.

How to Use It

The text file mssql2mysql is available over the Internet:

http://www.kofler.cc/mysql/mssql2mysql.html

To execute the code, use either Visual Basic 6 or a program with VBA 6 support (for example, Excel 2000, Word 2000, Access 2000).

- **Visual Basic 6:** If you are working with Visual Basic 6, begin a new standard project and insert the entire code into the code window of a form. Then start the program with F5.

- **VBA:** If you are working with a VBA 6 compatible program, switch with Alt+F11 into the VBA development environment, insert a new, empty, module, and copy the code into this module. Then with F5 open the dialog for macro execution and execute the procedure *main*.

Setting Parameters

All the parameters of the conversion process are controlled by a number of constants, which can be found at the beginning of the code. The first five constants describe the database on the Microsoft SQL server. The login to the database can be effected either via the security system integrated into Windows NT/2000/XP or by the explicit specification of user name and password:

```
Const MSSQL_SECURE_LOGIN = True   'login type (True for NT Security)
Const MSSQL_LOGIN_NAME = ""       'username ("" for NT Security)
Const MSSQL_PASSWORD = ""         'password (""for NT Security)
Const MSSQL_HOST = "mars"         'computer ("(local)" for localhost)
Const MSSQL_DB_NAME = "pubs"      'database name
```

OUTPUT_TO_FILE specifies whether the program should generate a text file with SQL commands or whether the commands should be executed at once. The first variant has the advantage that if problems arise, the text file can be directly edited:

```
Const OUTPUT_TO_FILE = 0     '1 write file,
                             '0 execute SQL commands at once
```

If you have decided for *OUTPUT_TO_FILE=1*, you must specify the name of the resulting file in *OUTPUT_FILENAME*:

```
Const OUTPUT_FILENAME = "c:\export.sql"
```

With *OUTPUT_TO_FILE=0* you must specify all parameters so that a connection to MySQL can be created. For this there must be sufficient access privileges so that *CREATE DATABASE*, etc., can be executed:

```
Const MYSQL_USER_NAME = "root"       'username
Const MYSQL_PASSWORD = "uranus"      'password
Const MYSQL_HOST = "localhost"       'computer name or "localhost"
Const MYSQL_PORT = 3306              'MySQL port
```

Which of the following two commands is necessary depends on whether you are using Connector/ODBC 3.51 or 2.51:

```
Const MyODBCVersion = "MySQL ODBC 3.51 Driver"
Const MyODBCVersion = "MySQL" 'for 2.50.n
```

Finally, we mention a few conversion options:

- *NEW_DB_NAME* enables the name of the new MySQL database to be given. If the constant remains empty, the new database keeps the same name as the SQL server database.

- *UNICODE_TO_BLOB* specifies whether *UNICODE* character strings should be transformed into *BLOB*s (*True*) or ANSI character strings (*False*). The second variant makes sense if Unicode data types were used in the SQL server database, but within them no special characters were used outside of the ANSI character set.

- *DROP_DATABASE* specifies whether at the beginning of the conversion any existing MySQL database with the same name should be deleted.

- *MAX_RECORDS* specifies how many records per table should be converted. Here 0 means that all data records should be converted. This option is practical for first carrying out a quick test and, for example, converting only ten records per table. Only after it has been verified that all is well is the entire database converted:

```
Const NEW_DB_NAME = ""          'MySQL database name
Const UNICODE_TO_BLOB = False   'Unicode --> BLOBs?
Const DROP_DATABASE = True      'begin with DROP database?
Const MAX_RECORDS = 0           '0: convert all data
```

Graphical User Interface for `mssql2mysql`

If you have VB6, you can also use a graphical user interface to `mssql2mysql`, developed by Roberto Alicata based on the script version 0.06 (see Figure 17-16). This version exhibits no new functions, but it is intuitively easy to use.

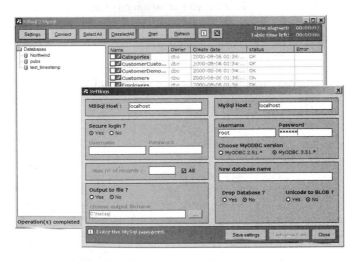

Figure 17-16. Graphical user interface for `mssql2mysql`

Part IV

Reference

SQL Reference

THIS CHAPTER GIVES AN OVERVIEW of the SQL operators, functions, and commands available under MySQL. My goal in organizing the information in this chapter was to give you, dear reader, a compact overview of the most important and useful syntactic variants.

Please note that MySQL boasts countless extensions as well as, alas, certain shortcomings with respect to the ANSI-SQL/92 standard.

This chapter is based on MySQL 4.0. To the extent that they are known, new syntactic features of MySQL 4.1 are also described. (We will always make clear what information relates specifically to version 4.1.) Appendix B contains a summary of what is new in MySQL 4.1.

Chapter Overview

Syntax

We begin with a brief section describing the syntax of object names, character strings, dates and times, and binary data.

Object Names

Names of objects—databases, tables, columns, etc.—can be at most 64 characters in length. Permitted characters are all the alphanumeric characters of the character set used by MySQL as well as the characters _ and $. There are two reasons for this:

- The coding of special characters depends on the character set in force in MySQL and the client program. If these settings are changed, then access to objects might become problematic.

- The names of databases and tables can be stored in files, and it is not MySQL, but the operating system that is responsible for the naming rules for files. This can be yet another source of conflict (especially if databases must be exchanged among various operating systems).

For reasons of practicality, it is a good idea to limit oneself to the alphanumeric ASCII characters and the underscore, and generally to avoid the use of special characters.

Table names that do not refer to the current database must have the database name prefixed to them. Likewise, the name of a column must be extended by the name of the table and that of the database if the column name alone fails to provide a unique identification (such as in queries in which several like-named columns in different tables appear):

- **Table names:** *tablename* or *db.tablename*

- **Column names:** *colname* or *tblname.colname* or *dbname.tblname.colname*

Case Sensitivity

The following objects are listed according to whether they exhibit case sensitivity:

- **Case Sensitivity:** Database names, table names, alias names, variable names

- **No Case Sensitivity:** SQL commands and functions, column names, index names

Under Windows, MySQL is flexible with respect to case in the naming of databases and tables. The reason is that the operating system does not distinguish case in the naming of directories and files. Note, however, that case must be consistent within an SQL command. The following command will not function properly: *SELECT * FROM authors WHERE Authors.authName = "xxx"*.

Since MySQL 4.0.2 and 4.1.1, MySQL under Windows uses exclusively lowercase names in the creation of new databases and tables (regardless of how it is written in the *CREATE* command). This should simplify the migration of databases from

Windows to Unix/Linux. This automatic transformation is the result of the option `lower_case_table_names`, which is set to 1 under Windows by default.

Character Strings in MySQL 3.23 and 4.0

MySQL 4.0 offers good support for 8-bit character sets. Multibyte character sets like Unicode will be correctly supported only starting with MySQL 4.1; see the next section. Character strings can be enclosed in single or double quotes. The following two expressions are equivalent in MySQL (though only the single-quote variant conforms to the ANSI-SQL/92 standard):

```
'character string'
"character string"
```

If a quotation mark should happen to be part of the character string, then there are various ways of expressing this:

```
"abc'abc"     means    abc'abc
"abc""abc"    means    abc"abc
"abc\'abc"    means    abc'abc
"abc\"abc"    means    abc"abc
'abc"abc'     means    abc"abc
'abc''abc'    means    abc'abc
'abc\"abc'    means    abc"abc
'abc\'abc'    means    abc'abc
```

Within a character string, the special characters provided by the prevailing character set are allowed, for example, äöüßàáéő if you are working with the default character set ISO-8859-1 (*latin1*). However, some special characters must be specially coded:

Quoting of Special Characters Within a Character String

`\0` 0 character (code 0)
`\b` backspace character (code 8)
`\t` tab character (code 9)
`\n` newline character (code 10)
`\r` carriage return character (code 13)
`\"` double quote character (code 34)
`\'` single quote character (code 39)
`\\` backslash (code 92)

If x is not one of the above-mentioned special characters, then $\x$ simply returns the character x. Even if a character string is to be stored as a BLOB (binary object), then the 0 character as well as the single quote, double quote, and backslash must be given in the form \0, \', \", and \\.

Instead of indicating special characters in character strings or BLOBs by the backslash escape character, it is often easier simply to specify the entire object using hexadecimal notation. MySQL accepts hex codes of arbitrary length in SQL commands in the following form: 0x4142434445464748494a.

However, MySQL is incapable of returning the result of a query in this form. (If you are working with PHP, then that programming language offers a convenient function for this purpose: *bin2hex.*)

> **POINTER** *If two character strings are to be concatenated, then you must use the function* CONCAT. *(The operator + will not serve the purpose.) In general, MySQL provides a broad range of functions for working with character strings.*

Character Strings in MySQL 4.1

Starting with MySQL 4.1, three things will change with respect to character strings:

- The character string and sort order (*collation*) will be set independently of each other.

- Each table, and indeed each column within a table, can have its own character set and its own sort order.

- Unicode is now a possible choice for the character set (in formats UTF8 and UCS2 = UTF16).

This has consequences, of course, for the use of character strings in SQL commands. One can specify the character set for every string. For this, you can use the function *CONVERT* or the cast operator *_characterset*. Here are two equivalent examples, demonstrating the internal Unicode encoding in the format UTF8:

```
SELECT HEX(CONVERT('ABCäöü' USING utf8))
  414243C3A4C3B6C3BC
SELECT HEX(_utf8 'ABCäöü ')
  414243C3A4C3B6C3BC
```

In many cases, it can be necessary to specify the sort order as well as the character set. (This determines which characters are considered equivalent and how character strings are to be sorted.) For this, one has the syntax *_characterset 'abc' COLLATE collname*. Here is an example:

```
SELECT _latin1 'a' = _latin1 'ä'
  0
SELECT _latin1 'a' COLLATE german1 = _latin1 'ä' COLLATE german1
  1
```

> **POINTER** *Further details on string management in MySQL 4.1 and other innovations in this version can be found in Appendix B.*

Numbers

Decimal numbers are written with a period for the decimal point and without a thousands separator (thus 27345 or 2.71828). One may also use scientific notation (6.0225e23 or 6.626e-34) for very large or very small numbers.

MySQL can also interpret hexadecimal numbers prefixed by 0x. Depending on the context, the number is interpreted as a character string or as a 64-bit integer:

```
SELECT 0x4142434445464748494a
       ABCDEFGHIJ
SELECT 0x41 + 0
       66
```

Automatic Transformation of Numbers and Character Strings

In carrying out an operation on two different data types, MySQL makes every attempt to find a compatible data type. Integers are automatically changed into floating-point numbers if one of the operators is a floating-point number. Character strings are automatically changed into numbers if the operation involves a calculation. (If the beginning of the character string cannot be interpreted as a number, then MySQL calculates with 0.)

```
SELECT  '3.14abc' + 1
        4.14
```

Date and Time

MySQL represents dates as character strings of the form *2003-12-31*, and times in the form *23:59:59*. With the data type *DATETIME* both formats are simply concatenated, yielding, for example, *2003-12-31 23:59:59*. In dealing with values in *TIMESTAMP* columns, MySQL leaves out all spaces, hyphens, and colons. In our example, we would have *20031231235959*:

```
USE exceptions
SELECT * FROM test_date
```

id	a_date	a_time	a_datetime	a_timestamp
1	2003-12-07	09:06:29	2003-12-07 09:06:29	20031207090649

> **CAUTION** *The default setting of* TIMESTAMP *has changed in MySQL 4.1. It is now returned from the server in the format* YYYY-MM-DD HH:MM:DD, *that is, like* DATETIME *values. Add a zero if you wish to use the old format (*SELECT ts+0 FROM table*).*

In storing dates, MySQL is quite flexible: Both numbers (e.g., *20031231*) and character strings are accepted. Hyphens are allowed in character strings, or they can simply be done without. If a year is given but no century is specified, then MySQL automatically uses the range 1970–2069. Therefore, MySQL accepts the following character strings for a *DATETIME* column: '*2003 12 31*', '*20031231*', '*2003.12.31*', and '*2003&12&31*'.

> **REMARK** *In storing dates, MySQL carries out only an incomplete check as to whether the date is a possible one. Thus, for example, it is possible to store '2003-2-29' in a date field, even though 2003 was not a leap year.*
>
> *The date '0000-00-00' has a special meaning. This value is officially allowed as a date in MySQL. MySQL uses this value itself when it recognizes a date as patently incorrect (e.g., '2003-2-32').*

Binary Data

Binary data that are to be stored in *BLOB* fields are dealt with in SQL commands like character strings; see above. (However, there are differences in sorting.)

Comments

There are three ways of supplying comments in SQL commands:

```
SELECT 1 # comment
SELECT 1 /* comment */
SELECT 1 -- comment since MySQL 3.23
```

Comments that begin with # or with -- (there must be a space after the --) hold until the end of the line. Comments between /* and */ can extend over several lines, as in C. Nesting is not allowed.

If you wish to write SQL code that makes use of some of the peculiarities of MySQL yet remains compatible as much as possible with other dialects, a particular variant of the comment is often useful:

```
SELECT /*! STRAIGHT_JOIN */ col FROM table ...
```

With the MySQL-specific *SELECT* extension, *STRAIGHT_JOIN* will be executed only by MySQL; all other SQL dialects will consider this a comment.

A variant of this enables differentiation among various MySQL dialects:

```
CREATE /*!32302 TEMPORARY */ TABLE ...
```

In this case, the key word *TEMPORARY* is processed only if the command is executed by MySQL 3.23.02 or a more recent version.

Semicolons at the End of SQL Commands

> **CAUTION** *Be careful with semicolons! On the basis of your experience with the MySQL monitor (that is, the program* mysql*), you have probably become accustomed to placing a semicolon at the end of SQL commands. Even phpMyAdmin deals properly with such semicolons (in particular, to separate several SQL commands from each other). However, the following must be observed:* Neither ANSI-SQL nor the SQL dialect of MySQL allows semicolons at the end of an instruction or for separating commands!

Semicolons are thus merely a peculiarity of mysql and phpMyAdmin. If you send SQL commands to MySQL in other programs (or in program code), they must appear without semicolons. Likewise, it is generally not permitted to send several commands at once. If you wish to execute several commands, you must send them one at a time (e.g., in a loop).

Operators

MySQL Operators

	Arithmetic Operators
+, -, *, /	basic arithmetic
%	mod (remainder of integer division)
DIV	alternative division operator (since MySQL 4.1)
MOD	alternative modulo operator (since MySQL 4.1)
	Bit Operators
|	binary OR
&	binary AND
~	binary negation (inverts all bits)
<<	shift bits left (multiplication by 2^n)
>>	shift bits right (division by 2^n)
	Comparison Operators
=	equality operator
<=>	equality operator, permitting comparison with *NULL*
!=, <>	inequality operator
<, >, <=, >=	comparison operators
IS [NOT] NULL	*NULL* comparison
BETWEEN	range membership (e.g., *x BETWEEN 1 AND 3*)
IN	set membership (e.g., *x IN (1, 2, 3)* or *x IN ('a', 'b', 'c')*)
NOT IN	set membership (e.g., *x NOT IN ('a', 'b', 'c')*)
	Pattern Matching
[NOT] LIKE	simple pattern matching (e.g., *x LIKE 'm%'*)
[NOT] REGEXP	extended pattern matching (e.g., *x REGEXP '.*x$'*)
SOUNDS LIKE	corresponds to *SOUNDEX(a) = SOUNDEX(b)*, since MySQL 4.1

	Binary Comparison
BINARY	identifies operand as binary (e.g., *BINARY x = y*)

	Logical Operators
!, NOT	negation
||, OR	logical OR
&&, AND	logical AND
XOR	logical exclusive OR (new in MySQL 4.0)

	Cast Operator (since MySQL 4.1)
_charset 'abc'	for the string 'abc' the character set *charset* is valid
_chs 'abc' COLLATE coll	string 'abc' has character set *charset* and sort order *coll*

Arithmetic Operators, Bit Operators

Arithmetic operators for which one of the operands is *NULL* generally return *NULL* as result. In MySQL, a division by zero also returns the result *NULL*.

Comparison Operators

Comparison operators normally return 1 (corresponding to *TRUE*) or 0 (*FALSE*). Comparisons with *NULL* return *NULL*. The two exceptions are the operators <=> and *IS NULL*, which even in comparison with *NULL* return 0 or 1:

```
SELECT NULL=NULL, NULL=0
  NULL, NULL
SELECT NULL<=>NULL, NULL<=>0
  1, 0
SELECT NULL IS NULL, NULL IS 0
  1, 0
```

In comparing character strings with <, <=, >, >=, as well as with *BETWEEN* (and, of course, with all sorting operations), the character set in force when MySQL was launched plays a decisive role. In the default setting, the character set is *latin1* (ISO-8859-1) with Swedish sort order.

The following examples show that the default behavior of MySQL is not always what you would expect. Thus, for example, *UCASE* (for changing characters to uppercase) does not apply to all special characters. Character comparison, however, works much better:

```
SELECT UCASE('abc äöüÿ åêõ')
  ABC Äöüÿ Åêõ
SELECT 'a'='A', 'a'='ä', 'ä'='Ä', 'ö'='Ö', 'ü'='Ü'
```

'a'='A'	'a'='ä'	'ä'='Ä'	'ö'='Ö'	'ü'='Ü'
1	0	1	1	1

In sorting, Swedish rules are in effect. Here we do not display the result of the query by columns in order to save space. Various special characters and unrepresentable characters have been omitted from the result (and replaced by ...):

```
USE exceptions
SELECT a_char FROM test_order_by
WHERE id>31
ORDER BY a_char
!, ", #, $, %, &, ', (, ), *, +, ,, -, ., /, 0, 1, 2, 3, 4, 5, 6, 7, 8, 9, :, ;, <,
=, >, ?, @, A, a, À, Á, Â, Ã, à, á, â, ã, B, b, C, c, Ç, ç, D, d, …, E, e, È, É,
Ê, Ë, è, é, ê, ë, F, f, G, g, H, h, I, i, Ì, Í, Î, Ï, ì, í, î, ï, J, j, K, k, L, l,
M, m, N, n, Ñ, ñ, O, o, Ò, Ó, Ô, Õ, ò, ó, ô, õ, P, p, Q, q, R, r, S, s, T,
t, U, u, Ù, Ú, Û, ù, ú, û, V, v, W, w, X, x, Y, y, Ü, Ý, ü, ý, Z, z, [, Å,
å, \, Ä, Æ, ä, æ, ], Ö, ö, ^, _, `, {, |, }, ~, …, •, …, ƒ, … ,Š, ‹, Œ,
…, ž, … ,', ', ", ", …, š, ›, œ, …, ž, Ÿ, …, £, …, ß, …, ÿ, …
```

If you need to store and sort characters outside of the ASCII character set, see Chapter 10, in which the setting of the character set at launch of MySQL is discussed.

> **CAUTION** *If you are using the monitor* mysql.exe *under Windows, it runs in a DOS-like environment, which has its own character set, which is not compatible with that of MySQL. For this reason, SQL commands with special characters seem to be executed incorrectly in* mysql.exe. *In reality, MySQL is working correctly, but because of the DOS character set—which is valid for* mysql.exe—*incorrect character codes for such special characters as* åäê *are transmitted to the MySQL server.*

Pattern Matching with LIKE

MySQL offers two operators for pattern matching. The simpler, and ANSI-compatible, of these is *LIKE*. As with normal character string comparison, there is no case distinction. In addition, there are two wild cards:

_	an arbitrary character
%	arbitrarily many (even 0) characters (but not for *NULL*)
_	the character _
\%	the character %

```
SELECT 'MySQL' LIKE '%sql'
    1
```

Pattern Matching with REGEXP

Considerably wider scope in the formulation of a pattern is offered by *REGEXP* and the equivalent command *RLIKE*. The relatively complicated syntax for the pattern corresponds to the Unix commands grep and sed.

REGEXP *Search Patterns*

Pattern Definition

abc	character string *abc*
(abc)	character string *abc* (made into a group)
[abc]	one of the characters *a, b, c*
[a-z]	one of the characters *a–z*
[^abc]	none of these characters (any others)
.	any character

Pattern Appearance

x	expression *x* must appear once
x | y	expression *x* or *y* must appear once
x?	expression *x* may appear at most once
x*	expression *x* may appear arbitrarily often (including not at all)
x+	expression *x* may appear arbitrarily often (but at least once)
x{n}	expression *x* must appear exactly *n* times
x{,n}	expression *x* may appear at most *n* times
x{n,}	expression *x* must appear at least *n* times
x{n,m}	expression *x* must appear at least *n* and at most *m* times
^	wild card for the beginning of a character string
$	wild card for the end of a character string
x	special character *x* (e.g., \\$ for $)

As with *LIKE*, there is no case distinction. Please note that *REGEXP* is successful when the search pattern is found somewhere within the character string. The search pattern is thus not required to describe the entire character string, but only a part of it. If you wish to encompass the entire character string, then you must use ^ and $ in the search pattern.

> **POINTER** *The above table contains only the most important elements of* REGEXP *patterns. A complete description can be obtained under Unix/Linux with* man 7 regex. *This can also be found on the Internet, for example, at* http://linux.ctyme.com/man/alpha7.htm

Binary Character String Comparison

Character strings are normally compared without case being taken into consideration. Thus 'a' = 'A' returns 1 (true). If you wish to execute a binary comparison, then you must place *BINARY* in front of one of the operands. *BINARY* is a *cast* operator; that is, it alters the data type of one of the operands (in this case it changes a number or character string into a binary object). *BINARY* can be used both for ordinary character string comparison and for pattern matching with *LIKE* and *REGEXP*:

```
SELECT 'a'='A', BINARY 'a' = 'A', 'a' = BINARY 'A'
     1, 0, 0
```

Logical Operators

Logical operators likewise return 0 or 1, or *NULL* if one of the operands is *NULL*. This holds also for *NOT*; that is, *NOT NULL* again returns *NULL*.

Variables and Constants

MySQL supports two types of variables: user variables (*@name*) and system variables *@@name*. Furthermore, there are many special cases that arise from the MySQL syntax. Note that MySQL is case-sensitive in the naming of variables.

User Variables (@name)

As the following examples demonstrate, you can assign your own variables in SQL commands:

```
SET @varname = 3
SELECT @varname := 3
SELECT @varname = MIN(birthdate) FROM table
```

These variables can be used in other SQL commands. Their contents disappear at the end of the connection.

System Variables (@@name)

Various pieces of status information are accessible over the MySQL server as variables. There are two ways of looking at these variables: *SHOW VARIABLES* and *SELECT*.

SHOW VARIABLES can display an entire list of variables:

```
SHOW VARIABLES LIKE 'b%'
```

Variable_name	Value
back_log	50
basedir	C:\mysql\
binlog_cache_size	32768
bulk_insert_buffer_size	8388608

> **REMARK** *Please note that for some strange reason,* SHOW *ignores a number of variables (e.g.,* autocommit*). For such variables, you must use* SELECT.

With *SELECT*, the variable name must be given exactly, prefixed by two @ signs:

```
SELECT @@binlog_cache_size
```

@@binlog_cache_size
32768

Global System Variables Versus System Variables at the Connection Level

In its system variables, MySQL distinguishes between *SESSION* and *GLOBAL* variables. *SESSION* variables are valid only for the current session (connection), while *GLOBAL* variables hold for the entire server:

```
SELECT @@wait_timeout              -- Session (connection level)
SELECT @@session.wait_timeout      -- Session (connection level)
SELECT @@global.wait_timeout       -- Global
```

System variables can also be changed. According to whether the change is only for the current connection or should be valid globally, the following syntax variants are available. Note that with *SET*, you may omit the two @ symbols. One cannot change system variables with *SELECT*:

```
SET @@wait_timeout = 10000              -- Session (connection level)
SET @@session.wait_timeout = 10000     -- Session (connection level)
SET SESSION @@wait_timeout = 10000     -- Session (connection level)
SET @@global.wait_timeout = 10000      -- Global
SET GLOBAL @@wait_timeout = 10000       -- Global
```

Variables at the global level can be changed by users possessing the *Super* privilege. When a global variable is changed, the new value holds for all new connections, but not for those already in existence.

Changes in *SESSION* variables, on the other hand, hold only until the end of the current connection. When a new connection is made, the global default value again holds.

> **POINTER** *This book does not contain a complete description of all MySQL system variables. In the description of the command* SET *later in this chapter, only the most important variables are described.*
>
> *A complete list of* GLOBAL *and* SESSION *variables can be found in the MySQL documentation:*
>
> http://www.mysql.com/doc/en/System_Variables.html
>
> *You may end up at the key word* LOCAL, *which has the same meaning in this context as* SESSION.
>
> *Enlightenment on the contents of the variables can be found in the MySQL documentation at the following pages:*
>
> http://www.mysql.com/doc/en/Server_parameters.html
> http://www.mysql.com/doc/en/SET_OPTION.html
> http://www.mysql.com/doc/en/SHOW_VARIABLES.html

Special Cases (Options, Passwords)

The command *SET* can also be used to change some of the MySQL options and the connection passwords. These options look like variables, but they cannot be read with *SELECT* or *SHOW VARIABLES*. The following list names the most frequently used special forms. A complete list can be found later in the chapter, when the syntax of *SET* is elucidated:

```
SET AUTOCOMMIT = 0 | 1
SET LAST_INSERT_ID = #
SET PASSWORD = PASSWORD('xxx')
SET PASSWORD FOR user@hostname = PASSWORD('xxx')
SET QUERY_CACHE_TYPE = 0 | 1 | 2
SET QUERY_CACHE_TYPE = OFF | ON | DEMAND
SET SQL_SAFE_UPDATES = 0 | 1
SET SQL_SELECT_LIMIT = value | DEFAULT
SET TIMESTAMP = timestamp_value | DEFAULT
```

Constants

Starting with version 4.1, MySQL recognizes the constants *TRUE* (1) and *FALSE* (0).

MySQL Data Types

	Integers
TINYINT(m)	8-bit integer (1 byte); the optional value *m* specifies the desired column width in *SELECT* results (*maximum display width*), and has no influence on the allowable range of numbers
SMALLINT(m)	16-bit integer (2 bytes)
MEDIUMINT(m)	24-bit integer (3 bytes)
INT(m), INTEGER(m)	32-bit integer (4 bytes)
BIGINT(m)	64-bit integer (8 bytes)
	Floating-Point Number
FLOAT(m, d)	floating-point number, 8-place precision (4 bytes); the optional values *m* and *d* specify the desired number of places before and after the decimal point in *SELECT* results; the values have no influence over the way the number is stored
DOUBLE(m, d)	floating-point number, 16-place precision (8 bytes)
REAL(m, d)	synonym for *DOUBLE*
DECIMAL(p, s)	fixed-point number, stored as string; arbitrary number of places (1 byte per digit + 2 bytes overhead); *p* specifies the entire number of places, where *s* is the number of places after the decimal point; default is *DECIMAL(10,0)*
NUMERIC, DEC	synonyms for *DECIMAL*

Date, Time

DATE	date in the form '2003-12-31', range 1000-01-01 to 9999-12-31 (3 bytes)
TIME	time in the form '23:59:59', range ±838:59:59 (3 bytes)
DATETIME	combination of *DATE* and *TIME* in the form '2003-12-31 23:59:59' (8 bytes)
YEAR	year 1900–2155 (1 byte)
TIMESTAMP(m)	date and time in the form 20031231235959 for times between 1970 and 2038 (4 bytes); the optional value *m* specifies the number of places in *SELECT* results; *m=8*, for example, has the effect that only year, month, and day are displayed

Character Strings (ANSI)

CHAR(n)	string with preset length, max 255 characters (*n* bytes)
VARCHAR(n)	string with variable length, max *n* bytes ($n < 256$) memory requirement for *latin1* characters: 1 byte per character (actual length) + 1
NCHAR(n)	Unicode character string (corresponds to *CHAR(n) CHARSET utf8*)
NCHAR VARCHAR(n)	Unicode character string with variable length (corresponds to *VARCHAR(n) CHARSET utf8*)
TINYTEXT	string with variable length, max 255 bytes
TEXT	string with variable length, max $2^{16} - 1$ bytes
MEDIUMTEXT	string with variable length, max $2^{24} - 1$ bytes
LONGTEXT	string with variable length, max $2^{32} - 1$ bytes

Binary Data

TINYBLOB	binary data with variable length, max 255 bytes
BLOB	binary data with variable length, max $2^{16} - 1$ bytes
MEDIUMBLOB	binary data with variable length, max $2^{24} - 1$ bytes
LONGBLOB	binary data with variable length, max $2^{32} - 1$ bytes

Geometric Data (since MySQL 4.1)

GEOMETRY	a general geometric object

Other

ENUM	enumeration of max 65535 character strings (1 or 2 bytes)
SET	enumeration of max 255 character strings (1–8 bytes)

Options for MySQL Data Types

In the definition of columns (*CREATE TABLE, ALTER TABLE*), each column can be assigned different options. The following table summarizes these options. Note that not all options are applicable to all data types:

NULL	specifies that the column may contain the value *NULL*; this setting holds by default
NOT NULL	forbids the value *NULL*
DEFAULT 'xxx'	specifies the default value *xxx* to be used if no other input value is specified
PRIMARY KEY	defines the primary key column
AUTO_INCREMENT	results in an automatically increasing number being inserted in the column; it can be used for only one column, with integer values; moreover, the options *NOT NULL* and *PRIMARY KEY* must be specified (instead of *PRIMARY KEY*, the column can be given a *UNIQUE* index)
UNSIGNED	integers are stored without a sign; note that calculations are also made without signs
ZEROFILL	integers in *SELECT* results are padded with zeros (e.g., five-digit numbers 00123, 01234)
BINARY	with *CHAR* and *VARCHAR* columns, comparison and sort operations are executed in binary; uppercase letters are ordered before lowercase; this is more efficient, but generally impractical when sorted results are to be displayed

Starting with MySQL 4.1, the character set and sort order can be set for text columns. This is the syntax: *[DEFAULT] CHARACTER SET csname [COLLATE collname]*.

Command Overview (Thematic)

In the following section, SQL commands will be listed in alphabetical order. As a supplementary aid to orientation, we provide here a systematic overview:

Database Queries, Data Manipulation

SELECT	queries existing data records (data search)
INSERT	inserts a new record
REPLACE	replaces an existing record
UPDATE	changes an existing record
DELETE	deletes selected records
TRUNCATE TABLE	deletes all records
LOAD DATA	inserts records from a text file
HANDLER	reads records more efficiently than *SELECT* (since MySQL 4.0)

Transactions (Only for Some Table Types)

BEGIN	begins a group of SQL commands
COMMIT	confirms all executed commands
ROLLBACK	cancels all executed commands

Generate Databases/Tables, Change Database Design

ALTER DATABASE	makes changes to the database (since MySQL 4.1)
ALTER TABLE	changes individual columns of a table, adds indexes, etc.
CREATE DATABASE	creates a new database
CREATE FUNCTION	includes a function programmed in C/C++ into MySQL
CREATE INDEX	creates a new index for a table
CREATE TABLE	creates a new table
DROP DATABASE	deletes an entire database
DROP INDEX	deletes an index
DROP TABLE	deletes an entire table
RENAME TABLE	renames a table

Table Management (General)

FLUSH TABLES	closes all table files and then reopens them
LOCK TABLE	blocks tables for (write) access by other users
UNLOCK TABLES	releases a table that has been locked with *LOCK*

Management of MyISAM Tables

ANALYZE TABLE	returns information about internal index management
BACKUP TABLE	copies table files into a backup directory
CHECK TABLE	tests the table file for consistency
OPTIMIZE TABLE	optimizes memory usage in tables
REPAIR TABLE	attempts to repair errors in table files
RESTORE TABLE	restores a table that has been backed up with *BACKUP*

Information on the Database Structure, Other Management Information

DESCRIBE	corresponds to *SHOW COLUMNS*
EXPLAIN	explains how a *SELECT* command is executed internally
SHOW	gives information on databases, tables, fields, etc.

Administration, Access Privileges, etc.

FLUSH	empties MySQL intermediate storage or inputs it anew
GRANT	grants additional access privileges
KILL	terminates a process
REVOKE	restricts access privileges
RESET QUERY CACHE	deletes the query cache
SET	changes the contents of MySQL system variables
SHOW	shows the MySQL status, system variables, processes, etc.
USE	changes the active database

Replication (Master)

PURGE MASTER LOGS	deletes old logging files
RESET MASTER	deletes all logging files
SET SQL_LOG_BIN=0/1	deactivates/activates binary logging
SHOW BINLOG EVENTS	returns a list of entries from the active logging file (since MySQL 4.0)
SHOW MASTER LOGS	returns a list of all binary files
SHOW MASTER STATUS	gives the current logging file
SHOW SLAVE HOSTS	returns a list of all registered slaves (from MySQL 4.0)

Replication (Slave)

CHANGE MASTER TO	changes replication settings in `master.info`
LOAD DATA FROM	copies all tables from master to slave (since MySQL 4.0)
LOAD TABLE FROM	copies a table from master to slave
RESET SLAVE	reinitializes `master.info`
SHOW SLAVE STATUS	displays the contents of `master.info`
SLAVE START/STOP	starts or ends replication

Command Reference (Alphabetical)

In the following reference section, the following syntax is in force:

- Optional parts of a command are written in square brackets (*[option]*).

- Alternatives are separated by a vertical bar (*variant1* | *variant2* | *variant3*).

ALTER DATABASE dbname *actions*

Since MySQL 4.1, with *ALTER DATABASE* you can change global database attributes. The settings are stored in the file *dbname*/db.opt.

- *actions:* In MySQL 4.1 alpha, only an *action* command has been implemented. *CHARACTER SET charset [COLLATE collname]* specifies which character set the database should use by default and what sort order should be used with it. Without this setting, the database will use the default character set of the MySQL server. Moreover, with *CREATE TABLE*, a different character set can be chosen for the table or for individual columns.

ALTER TABLE *tblname tbloptions*

ALTER TABLE can be used to change various details of the structure of a table. In the following, we present an overview of the syntactic variants.

In the syntactically simplest form that we shall show here, *ALTER TABLE* changes the table options. The possible options are described in *CREATE TABLE*. The command can be used, for example, to change the type of a table (e.g., from MyISAM to InnoDB).

Note that with many *ALTER TABLE* variants, the table must be re-created. To do this, MySQL creates a new table *X* with the new table properties, and then copies all the records into this new table. Then the existing table is renamed *Y*, and table *X* is renamed *tblname*. Finally, *Y* is deleted. On large tables, this can take considerable time and temporarily use a great deal of hard-disk space.

ALTER TABLE *tblname* **ADD** *newcolname coltype coloptions*
[FIRST | AFTER existingcolumn]

This command adds a new column to a table. The definition of the new column takes place as with *CREATE TABLE*. If the position of the new column is not specified with *FIRST* or *AFTER*, then the new column will be the last column of the table.

The following example adds a new column *ts* with data type *TIMESTAMP* to the *authors* table:

```
ALTER TABLE authors ADD ts TIMESTAMP
```

ALTER TABLE *tblname* **ADD INDEX** *[indexname] (indexcols . . .)*
ALTER TABLE *tblname* **ADD FULLTEXT** *[indexname] (indexcols . . .)*
ALTER [IGNORE] TABLE *tblname* **ADD UNIQUE** *[indexname] (indexcols . . .)*
ALTER [IGNORE] TABLE *tblname* **ADD PRIMARY KEY** *(indexcols . . .)*
ALTER TABLE *tblname* **ADD SPATIAL INDEX** *(indexcol)*

These commands create a new index for a table. If no *indexname* is specified, then MySQL simply uses the name of the indexed column.

The optional key word *IGNORE* comes into play if several identical fields are discovered in the creation of a *UNIQUE* or primary index. Without *IGNORE*, the command will be terminated with an error, and the index will not be generated. With *IGNORE*, such duplicate records are simply deleted.

A spatial index for geometric data can be created starting with MySQL 4.1. The column *indexcol* must have data type *GEOMETRY* and the attribute *NOT NULL*.

ALTER TABLE *tblname* **ADD FOREIGN KEY** *[name]*
(column1) **REFERENCES** *table2 (column2)*
[ON DELETE {CASCADE | SET NULL | NO ACTION | RESTRICT}]
[ON UPDATE {CASCADE | SET NULL | NO ACTION | RESTRICT}]

This command defines a foreign key constraint. This means that the foreign key *tblname.column1* refers to *table2.column2*, and the table driver should ensure that no references point to nowhere.

The optional *ON DELETE* and *ON UPDATE* clauses specify how the table driver is to react to damage to integrity on *DELETE* and *UPDATE* commands (see Chapter 8 for details). By default, the condition is *STRICT*, meaning that potential damage to integrity results in the command not being issued and an error message being triggered.

Currently (MySQL 4.0.*n*), foreign key constraints can be applied only to InnoDB tables. Both *column1* and *column2* must be given indexes and must be of the same data type.

ALTER TABLE *tblname* **ALTER** *colname* **SET DEFAULT** *value*
ALTER TABLE *tblname* **ALTER** *colname* **DROP DEFAULT**

This command changes the default value for a column or table or deletes an existing default value.

ALTER TABLE *tblname* **CHANGE** *oldcolname newcolname coltype coloptions*

This command changes the default value for a column in a table or deletes an existing default value. The description of the column proceeds as with *CREATE TABLE*, which you may refer to. If the column name is to remain unchanged, then it must be given twice (that is, *oldcolname* and *newcolname* are identical). Even if *ALTER TABLE* is used only to change the name of a column, both *coltype* and *coloptions* must be completely specified.

ALTER TABLE *tblname* **DISABLE KEYS**
ALTER TABLE *tblname* **ENABLE KEYS**

Since MySQL 4.0, *ALTER TABLE . . . DISABLE KEYS* has the effect that all *nonunique* indexes are no longer automatically updated with *INSERT, UPDATE,* and *DELETE* commands. *ALTER TABLE . . . ENABLE KEYS* restores activation and updating of indexes.

The two commands should be used for carrying out extensive revisions to tables in the most efficient manner possible. (The reconstruction of indexes with *ENABLE KEYS* costs considerably less time than the constant updating with each altered record.)

ALTER TABLE *tblname* ***DROP*** *colname*
ALTER TABLE *tblname* ***DROP INDEX*** *indexname*
ALTER TABLE *tblname* ***DROP PRIMARY KEY***
ALTER TABLE *tblname* ***DROP FOREIGN KEY*** *foreign_key_id*

The first three commands delete a column, an index, or the primary index. The fourth command, since MySQL 4.0.13, deletes the specified foreign key constraint. You must first determine with *SHOW CREATE TABLE* the *foreign_key_id* of the index to be deleted.

ALTER TABLE *tblname* ***MODIFY*** *colname coltype coloptions*

This command functions like *ALTER TABLE . . . CHANGE* (see above). The only difference is that the column cannot be changed, and thus the name needs to be given only once.

ALTER TABLE *tblname* ***RENAME AS*** *newtblname*

This command renames a table. See also *RENAME TABLE*.

ALTER TABLE *tblname* ***TYPE*** *typename*

This command changes the type of the table (the table driver). Allowable table types are *InnoDB* and *MyISAM*. Note that a type change is possible only if the new table driver supports all the properties of the table. For example, the InnoDB table driver currently does not support a full-text index. If you wish to change a MyISAM table to InnoDB, you must first remove any full-text index (*ALTER TABLE tblname DROP indexname*).

ANALYZE TABLE *tablename1, tablename2, . . .*

ANALYZE TABLE performs an analysis of the indexed values of a column. The results are stored, and in the future, this speeds up index access to data records a bit.

   ANALYZE TABLE can be used only with tables of type *MyISAM*. Instead of this command, the external program `myisamchk -a tblfile` can be used.

BACKUP TABLE *tblname* ***TO*** *'/backup/directory'*

BACKUP TABLE copies the files for the specified MyISAM table into a backup directory. The table can be re-created with *RESTORE TABLE*.

   Under Unix/Linux, the backup directory for the account under which MySQL is executed must be writable. *BACKUP* and *RESTORE* do not work for InnoDB tables.

BEGIN

If you are working with transaction-capable tables, then *BEGIN* introduces a new transaction. The following SQL commands can then be confirmed with *COMMIT* or revoked with *ROLLBACK*. (All changes to tables are executed only via *COMMIT*.)

Further information and examples on the topic of transactions can be found in Chapter 8.

Since MySQL 4.0.11, you can use the ANSI-conforming command *START TRANSACTION* instead of *BEGIN*.

CHANGE MASTER TO *variable1=value1, variable2=value2, . . .*

With this command, the replication settings for slave are carried out. The settings are stored in the file master.info. The command can be used only for slave computers in a replication system, and it requires the *Super* privilege. It recognizes the following variable names:

MASTER_HOST	specifies the hostname or IP number of the master computer
MASTER_USER	specifies the username used for communication with the master computer
MASTER_PASSWORD	specifies the associated password
MASTER_PORT	specifies the port number of the master computer (normally 3306)
MASTER_LOG_FILE	specifies the current logging file on the master computer
MASTER_LOG_POS	specifies the current read position within the logging file on the master computer

---

CHECK TABLE *tablename1, tablename2 . . . [TYPE=QUICK]*

CHECK TABLE tests the internal integrity of the database file for the specified table. Any errors that are discovered are not corrected.

With MyISAM tables, instead of this command, the external program myisamchk -m tblfile can be used.

COMMIT

COMMIT ends a transaction and stores all changes in the database. (Instead of executing *COMMIT*, you can cancel the pending changes with *ROLLBACK*.) *BEGIN/COMMIT/ROLLBACK* function only if you are working with transaction-capable tables. Further information and examples on transactions can be found in Chapter 8.

CREATE DATABASE *dbname [options]*

CREATE DATABASE generates the specified database. (More precisely, an empty directory is created in which tables belonging to the new database can be stored.) Note that database names are case-sensitive. This command can be executed only if the user has sufficient access privileges to create new databases.

- *options:* Since MySQL 4.1, you can specify the default character set for a table: *[DEFAULT] CHARACTER SET charset [COLLATE collname]*. The optional key word *DEFAULT* has no function (that is, it does not matter whether you specify it or not). With *COLLATE* you can select the sort order if there is more than one for the character set in question. If you do not specify the *CHARACTER SET*, then the default character set of the server is used.

CREATE FUNCTION *fnname RETURNS datatype SONAME libraryname*

CREATE FUNCTION makes it possible to bring a function in an external library into MySQL. Such functions are called *user-defined functions*, or UDFs for short.

If you believe that this means that you can simply equip MySQL with a variety of new functions, you are sadly mistaken: The syntax of *CREATE FUNCTION* is simple, but the problem is that first the code for the function must be written in C or C++ and then compiled into a library. This requires a degree of background knowledge about how functions work in MySQL (and, of course, the requisite tools, like compilers). Further information on creating MySQL functions can be found in the MySQL documentation:

```
http://www.mysql.com/doc/en/Extending_MySQL.html
```

It is planned for MySQL 5.0 that in addition to UDFs, there will be the possibility of realizing custom SQL functions and commands in the form of stored procedures (SPs). Stored procedures are simpler to program, but not as efficient as UDFs.

CREATE *[UNIQUE|FULLTEXT]* **INDEX** *indexname ON tablename (indexcols . . .)*

CREATE INDEX enlarges an existing database to include an index. As *indexname*, the name of the column is generally used. *CREATE INDEX* is not a freestanding command, but merely an alternative form of *ALTER TABLE ADD INDEX/UNIQUE*, which you should see for details.

CREATE *[TEMPORARY]* **TABLE** *[IF NOT EXISTS] tblname*
(colname1 coltype coloptions reference,
colname2 coltype coloptions reference . . .
[, index1, index2 . . .]
)
[tbloptions]

CREATE TABLE generates a new table in the current database. If a database other than the current one is to be used, the table name can be specified in the form *dbname.tblname*. If the table already exists, an error message results. There is no error message if *IF NOT EXISTS* is used, but in this case, the existing table is not affected, and no new table is created.

If the key word *TEMPORARY* is used (as of version 3.23), then the table that is created is a temporary one. If a temporary table is created and a like-named, but nontemporary, table already exists, the temporary table is created without an error message. The old table is preserved, but it is masked by the temporary table. If you want your temporary table to exist only in RAM (for increased speed), you must also specify *TYPE = HEAP*.

The creation of regular tables requires the *Create* privilege. Since version 4.0, the creation of temporary tables requires the *Create Temporary Table* privilege.

- *colname:* Name of the column.

- *coltype:* Data type of the column. A list of all MySQL data types (*INT, TEXT,* etc.) appears in Chapter 18.

- *coloptions:* Here, several attributes (options) can be specified:

  - *NOT NULL | NULL: NOT NULL* indicates that no *NULL* values may be stored in the column, and thus the column may not have empty cells. (By default, columns are created with the attribute *NULL.*)
  - *DEFAULT defaultval: DEFAULT* specifies a default value that is then stored if no value is specified.
  - *AUTO_INCREMENT | IDENTITY: AUTO_INCREMENT* indicates that MySQL inserts a unique numerical value for each new record (ideal for primary key fields).
  - *PRIMARY KEY: PRIMARY KEY* signifies that the field is to be used as a primary key. (MySQL creates a *UNIQUE* index for the field. The field must have the attribute *NOT NULL.*)
  - *CHARACTER SET charset [COLLATE collname]:* Since MySQL 4.1, with *CHARACTER SET,* you can specify a separate character set for each table column. *COLLATE* determines the sort order if for the given character set there is more than one from which to choose.
  - *COMMENT:* With *COMMENT* you can also, since MySQL 4.1, save a brief comment about the meaning of the column.

- *reference:* MySQL provides various key words for the declaration of foreign keys in keeping track of referential integrity, e.g., *REFERENCES tblname (idcolumn).* These key words are currently ignored, however (and with no error message). Even if you use InnoDB tables, the foreign key constraints for such tables must be specified within the confines of the index definition.

- *index: KEY* or *INDEX* defines a usual index spanning one or more columns. *UNIQUE* defines a unique index (that is, in the column or columns, no identical values or groups of values can be stored). With both variants an arbitrary index name may be given for the internal management of the index. *PRIMARY KEY* likewise defines a *UNIQUE* index. Here, however, the index name is predefined: It is, not surprisingly, *PRIMARY.* With *FULLTEXT,* an index is declared for full-text search (in MySQL 4.0, only with MyISAM tables). Since MySQL 4.1, an index for *GEOMETRY* data can be created with *SPATIAL INDEX; indexcol* must be defined with the attribute *NOT NULL.*

  - *KEY | INDEX [indexname] (indexcols . . .)*
  - *UNIQUE [INDEX] [indexname] (indexcols . . .)*
  - *PRIMARY KEY (indexcols . . .)*
  - *FULLTEXT [indexname] (indexcols . . .)*
  - *SPATIAL INDEX [indexname] (indexcol)*

Foreign key constraints: If you are using InnoDB tables, here you can formulate foreign key constraints. The syntax is as follows:

FOREIGN KEY [name] (column1) REFERENCES table2 (column2)
[ON DELETE {CASCADE | SET NULL | NO ACTION | RESTRICT}]
[ON UPDATE {CASCADE | SET NULL | NO ACTION | RESTRICT}]

This means that *tblname.column1* is a foreign key that refers to *table2.column2*. The table driver ensures that no references can point to nowhere (to nonexistent values in *table2.column2*).

With the optional *ON DELETE* and *ON UPDATE* clauses, you can specify how the table driver should react to damage to integrity on *UPDATE* and *DELETE* commands (for details, see Chapter 8). By default, *RESTRICT* is in force; that is, if integrity is to be damaged, the command in question is not executed, and an error is triggered.

- *tbloptions:* Here various table options can be specified, though here we shall exhibit only the most important of them. Not all options are possible with every table type. Information on the different table types and their variants (MyISAM static, dynamic, or compressed) can be found in Chapter 5. InnoDB tables were described in Chapter 8.

  o *TYPE = ISAM | MYISAM | HEAP | BDB | MERGE | INNODB.*
  o *ROW_FORMAT= default | dynamic | static | compressed.*
  o *AUTO_INCREMENT = n: AUTO_INCREMENT* gives the initial value for the counter of an *AUTO_INCREMENT* column (e.g., 100000 if you wish to have six-digit integers).
  o *CHECKSUM = 0 | 1: CHECK_SUM=1* has the effect that a check sum is stored for each data record, which helps in reconstruction if the database is damaged.
  o *PACK_KEYS = 0 | 1: PACK_KEYS=1* results in a smaller index file. This speeds up read access, but slows down changes.
  o *DELAY_KEY_WRITE = 0 | 1: DELAY_KEY_WRITE = 1* results in indexes not being updated each time a change to a record is made. Rather, they are updated every now and then.
  o With *COMMENT* you can save a brief text, for example, to describe the purpose of the table. The comment can be read with *SHOW CREATE DATABASE dbname*: *COMMENT= 'comment'*.
  o Since MySQL 4.1, you can specify the character set and sort order for a table. (You can also set these parameters for a single column.) If no character set is specified, then the default character set for the table or that of the MySQL server is used: *[DEFAULT] CHARACTER SET charset [COLLATE collname]*.

The *CREATE TABLE* syntax contains some duplication. For example, a primary index can be declared in two different ways, either as an attribute of a column (*coloptions*) or as an independent index (*index*). The result is, of course, the same. It is up to you to decide which form you prefer. Here is an example:

```
CREATE TABLE test    (id INT NOT NULL AUTO_INCREMENT,
                     data INT NOT NULL,
                     txt VARCHAR(60),
                     PRIMARY KEY (id))
```

Additional examples can be found in Chapter 5, under the topic database design.

CREATE *[TEMPORARY]* ***TABLE*** *[IF NOT EXISTS] tblname*
[(newcolname1 coltype coloptions reference,
newcolname2 coltype coloptions reference . . .
[, key1, key2 . . .]
)]
[tbloptions]
*[IGNORE | REPLACE]**SELECT* . . .

With this variant of the *CREATE TABLE* command, a table is filled with the result of a *SELECT* command. The individual columns of the new table take their types from the data types of the *SELECT* command and thus do not have to be (and may not be!) declared explicitly.

Unfortunately, neither indexes nor attributes such as *AUTO_INCREMENT* are carried over from the old table. There can also be changes in column types, such as *VARCHAR* columns turning into *CHAR*.

If an index is to be created in the new table for individual columns (e.g., *PRIMARY KEY (id)*), then this can be specified. Moreover, there is the option of defining new columns (e.g., an *AUTO INCREMENT* column). On the other hand, if you want an *AUTO INCREMENT* in the old table to become again an *AUTO INCREMENT* column in the new table, then you must execute an *ALTER TABLE CHANGE* command after the *CREATE* command.

The key words *IGNORE* and *REPLACE* specify how MySQL should behave if several records with the same value are placed by the command into a *UNIQUE* column. With *IGNORE*, the existing record is retained, and new records are ignored. With *REPLACE* existing records are replaced by the new ones. If neither option is used, an error message results.

Examples

This command provides a simple mechanism in MySQL for copying complete tables:

```
CREATE TABLE backuptable SELECT * FROM table
```

However, you may also copy only parts of a table into a temporary table:

```
CREATE TEMPORARY TABLE tmp
  SELECT id, authname FROM authors WHERE id<20
```

If the specification of the new table is to meet that of the old table exactly, then frequently, a great deal of cleanup work is necessary, as indicated by the following commands:

```
CREATE TABLE table2 SELECT * FROM table1
ALTER TABLE table2 ADD PRIMARY KEY(id)
ALTER TABLE table2 CHANGE titleID titleID INT AUTO_INCREMENT
ALTER TABLE table2 CHANGE title title VARCHAR(100)
```

If a table is to be copied exactly, it is better to create a new table with a *CREATE TABLE* command and then copy the data with *INSERT INTO table2 SELECT * FROM table1*. Since MySQL 4.1 there is the convenient command *CREATE TABLE table2 LIKE table1*.

CREATE *[TEMPORARY]* **TABLE** *[IF NOT EXISTS] newtable* **LIKE** *oldtable*

This command creates a new, empty, table *newtable* corresponding to the declaration of the existing table *oldtable*. This *CREATE TABLE* variant is available since version 4.1.

DELETE *[deleteoptions]* **FROM** *tablename*
[WHERE condition]
[ORDER BY ordercolumn [DESC]]
[LIMIT maxrecords]

DELETE deletes the records in a table encompassed by *condition*.

- *deleteoptions:* The *LOW_PRIORITY* option has the effect that the data records are deleted only when all read operations are complete. (The goal of this option is to avoid having *SELECT* queries unnecessarily delayed due to *DELETE* operations.)
  The option *QUICK* has the effect that during deletion, an existing index is not optimized. This speeds up the *DELETE* command, but it can lead to a somewhat inefficient index.

- *condition:* This condition specifies which records are to be deleted. For the syntax of *condition*, see *SELECT*.

- *ordercolumn:* With *ORDER BY* you can first sort the data to be deleted. This makes sense only in combination with *LIMIT*, in order, for example, to delete the first or last ten records (according to some sort criterion).

- *maxrecords:* With *LIMIT*, the maximum number of records that may be deleted is specified.

If *DELETE* is executed without conditions, then all records of the table are deleted (so be careful!). *DELETE* without conditions cannot be part of a transaction. If a transaction is open, it is closed with *COMMIT* before the *DELETE* command is executed. If you wish to delete large tables completely, it is more efficient to use the command *TRUNCATE*.

DELETE *[deleteoptions] table1, table2, . . .*
FROM *table1, table2, table3, . . .*
[USING columns]
WHERE *conditions*

This variant of *DELETE* (available since version 4.0) deletes records from tables *table1*, *table2*, etc., where the data of additional tables (*table3*, etc.) are considered in the search criteria.

After *DELETE*, all tables from which data are to be deleted must be specified. After *FROM*, all *DELETE* tables must appear, as well as any additional tables that serve only in formulating the search criteria.

- *deleteoptions:* Here you can specify options as in a usual *DELETE* command.

- *columns:* Here fields that link the tables can be specified (see also *SELECT*). This assumes that the linking field has the same name in both tables.

- *conditions:* In addition to the usual delete criteria, here one may specify linking conditions (e.g., *WHERE table1.id = table2.forgeinID*).

DESCRIBE *tablename [columnname]*

DESCRIBE returns information about the specified table in the current database (or about a particular column of this table). Instead of *columnname*, a pattern with the wild cards _ and % can be given. In this case, *DESCRIBE* displays information about those columns matching the pattern. *DESCRIBE* returns the same information as *EXPLAIN* or *SHOW TABLE* or *SHOW COLUMN*.

DO *selectcommand*

DO is a variant of *SELECT* and has basically the same syntax. The difference between the two is that *DO* returns no results. For example, *DO* can be used for variable assignment, for which it is somewhat faster than *SELECT* (thus, for example, *DO @var:=3*).

DROP DATABASE *[IF EXISTS] dbname*

DROP DATABASE deletes an existing database with all of its data. This cannot be undone, so be careful! If the database does not exist, then an error is reported. This error can be avoided with an *IF EXISTS*.

In the execution of this command, all files in the directory dbname with the following endings are deleted, among others: .BAK, .DAT, .HSH, .ISD, .ISM, .MRG, .MYD, .MYI, .db, .frm.

DROP FUNCTION *fnname*

DROP FUNCTION deactivates an auxiliary function that was made available to MySQL earlier with *CREATE FUNCTION*.

DROP INDEX *indexname ON tablename*

DROP INDEX removes an index from the specified table. Usually, *indexname* is the name of the indexed column, or else *PRIMARY* for the primary index.

DROP TABLE *[IF EXISTS] tablename1, tablename2, . . .*

DROP TABLE deletes the specified tables irrevocably. The option *IF EXISTS* avoids an error message if the tables do not exist.

Note that until MySQL 4.0, *DROP TABLE* automatically ends a running transaction (*COMMIT*). This holds even in the case of a temporary table. Since MySQL 4.1 the behavior has changed somewhat: *DROP TABLE* ends a transaction only for regular tables, not for temporary ones.

EXPLAIN *tablename*

EXPLAIN returns a table with information about all the columns of a table (field name, field type, index, default value, etc.). The same information can be determined as well with *SHOW COLUMNS* or *DESCRIBE*, or via an external program such as mysqlshow.

EXPLAIN SELECT *selectcommand*

EXPLAIN SELECT returns a table with information about how the specified *SELECT* command was executed. These data can help in speed optimization of queries, and in particular in deciding which columns of a table should be indexed. (The syntax of *selectcommand* was described under *SELECT*. An example of the use of *EXPLAIN SELECT* and a brief description of the resulting table can be found in Chapter 5.)

FLUSH *flushoptions*

FLUSH empties the MySQL internal intermediate storage. Any information not stored already is thereby stored in the database. The execution of *FLUSH* requires the *RELOAD* privilege.

- *flushoptions:* Here one may specify which cache(s) should be emptied. Multiple options should be separated by commas.
  - *DES_KEY_FILE*: Reloads the key files for the functions *DES_ENCRYPT* and *DES_DECRYPT*.
  - *HOSTS:* Empties the host cache table. This is necessary especially if in the local network the arrangement of IP numbers has changed.
  - *LOGS:* Closes all logging files and then reopens them. In the case of update logs, a new logging file is created, whereby the number of the file ending is increased by 1 (*file.003* → *file.004*).
  - *QUERY CACHE:* Defragments the query cache so that it can use its memory more efficiently. The cache is not emptied.
  - *PRIVILEGES:* Reloads the privileges database *mysql* (corresponds to mysqladmin reload).
  - *STATUS:* Sets most status variables to 0.
  - *TABLES:* Closes all open tables.
  - *TABLE[S] tblname1, tblname2, . . . :* Closes the specified tables.
  - *TABLES WITH READ LOCK:* As above, except that additionally, *LOCK* is executed for all tables, which remains in force until the advent of a corresponding *UNLOCK table*.
  - *USER_RESOURCES:* Resets the counters for *MAX_QUERIES_PER_HOUR*, *MAX_UPDATES_PER_HOUR*, and *MAX_CONNECTIONS_PER_HOUR* (see *maxlimits* under *GRANT*).

Most *FLUSH* operations can also be executed through the auxiliary program mysqladmin.

GRANT *privileges ON objects*
TO users [IDENTIFIED BY 'password']
[REQUIRE ssloptions]
[WITH GRANT OPTION | maxlimits]

GRANT helps in the allocation of access privileges to database objects.

- *privileges:* Several privileges may be specified (separated by commas):

    ALTER, CREATE, DELETE, DROP, FILE, INDEX, PROCESS, REFERENCES, RELOAD, SELECT, SHUTDOWN, UPDATE.

    If you wish to set all (or no) privileges, then specify *ALL* (or *USAGE*). (The second variant is useful if you wish to create a new MySQL user to whom as of yet no privileges have been granted.) The *Grant* privilege can be set only via *WITH GRANT OPTION*; that is, *ALL* does not include the *Grant* privilege.

    If the privileges are to hold only for certain columns of a table, then specify the columns in parentheses. For example, you may specify *GRANT SELECT(columnA, columnB)*.

- *objects:* Here databases and tables are specified. The following syntactic variants are available:

databasename.tablename	only this table in this database
databasename.*	all tables in this database
tablename	only this table in the current database
*	all tables of the current database
.	global privileges

    Wild cards may not be used in the database names.

- *users:* Here one or more (comma-separated) users may be specified. If these users are not yet known to the *user* table, they are created. The following variants are allowed:

username@hostname	only this user at *hostname*
'username' @'hostname'	as above, with wild cards
username	this user on all computers
'' @hostname	all users on *hostname*
''	all users on all computers

- *password:* Optionally, with *IDENTIFIED BY*, a password in plain text can be specified. *GRANT* encrypts this password with the function *PASSWORD* before it is entered in the *user* table. If more than one user is specified, then more than one password may be given:
    TO user1 IDENTIFIED BY 'pw1', user2 IDENTIFIED BY 'pw2',...

- *ssloptions:* If access to MySQL is to be SSL encrypted or if user identification is to take place with X509, you can specify the required information for establishing the connection here. The syntax is as follows:

REQUIRE SSL | X509 [ISSUER 'iss'] [SUBJECT 'subj'] [CIPHER 'ciph']

REQUIRE SSL means that the connection must be SSL encrypted (thus a normal connection is not permitted). *REQUIRE X509* means that the user must possess a valid certificate for identification that meets the X509 standard.

ISSUER specifies the required issuer of the certificate. (Without *ISSUER*, the origin of the certificate is not considered.)

SUBJECT specifies the required content of the certificate's *subject* field. (Without *SUBJECT*, the content is not considered.)

CIPHER specifies the required SSL encryption algorithm. (SSL supports various algorithms. Without this specification, all algorithms are allowed, including older ones that may have security loopholes.)

- *maxlimits:* Here you can specify how many connections per hour the user is allowed to establish, as well as the number of *SELECT* and *INSERT/UPDATE/DELETE* commands. The default setting for all three values is 0 (no limit):

MAX_QUERIES_PER_HOUR n
MAX_UPDATES_PER_HOUR n
MAX_CONNECTIONS_PER_HOUR n

If the specified user does not yet exist and *GRANT* is executed without *IDENTIFIED BY*, then the new user has no password (which represents a security risk). On the other hand, if the user already exists, then *GRANT* without *IDENTIFIED BY* does not alter the password. (There is thus no danger that a password can be accidentally deleted by *GRANT*.)

It is impossible with *GRANT* to delete privileges that have already been granted (for example, by executing the command again with a smaller list of privileges). If you wish to take away privileges, you must use *REVOKE*.

GRANT may be used only by users with the *Grant* privilege. The user that executes *GRANT* may bestow only those privileges that he himself possesses. If the MySQL server is started with the option safe-user-create, then to create a new user, a user needs the *Insert* privilege for the table *mysql.user* in addition to the *Grant* privilege.

HANDLER *tablename* **OPEN** *[AS aliasname]*
HANDLER *tablename* **READ** *FIRST\NEXT [WHERE condition LIMIT n, m]*
HANDLER *tablename* **READ** *indexname FIRST\NEXT\PREV\LAST [WHERE . . .*
     LIMIT . . .]
HANDLER *tablename* **CLOSE**

Since MySQL 4.0, *HANDLER* enables direct access to MyISAM tables, and since MySQL 4.0.3, to InnoDB tables as well. This command can be used as a more efficient substitute for simple *SELECT* commands. This is particularly true if records are to be processed one at a time or in small groups.

The command is easy to use: First, access to a table is achieved with *HANDLER OPEN*. Then, *HANDLER READ* may be executed as often as you like, generally the first time with *FIRST*, and thereafter with *NEXT*, until no further results are forthcoming. The command returns results as with *SELECT* * (that is, all columns). *HANDLER CLOSE* terminates access.

HANDLER tablename READ reads the records in the order in which they were stored. On the other hand, the variant *HANDLER tablename READ indexname* uses the specified index. In my experiments, however, it has been impossible to use the *primary* index for this purpose, though it works with other indexes.

HANDLER was not conceived for use with typical MySQL applications, if for no other reason than that the code would be completely incompatible with every other database server. *HANDLER* is suitable for programming low-level tools (e.g., backup tools or drivers that simulate simple data access with a cursor). Note that *HANDLER* does not block tables (no *locking*), and therefore, the table can change while its data are being read.

HELP *function*

Since MySQL 4.1, *HELP* returns a brief help text for the specified *function*.

INSERT *[insertoptions] [INTO] tablename [(columnlist)]***VALUES** *(valuelist1), (. . .)*

 . . .

INSERT *[insertoptions] [INTO] tablename* **SET** *column1=value1, column2=value2*

 . . .

INSERT *[insertoptions] [INTO] tablename [(columnlist)]* **SELECT** . . .

The *INSERT* command has the job of inserting new records into an existing table. There are three main syntax variants. In the first (and most frequently used) of these, new data records are specified in parentheses. Thus a typical *INSERT* command looks like this:

```
INSERT INTO tablename (columnA, columnB, columnC)
VALUES ('a', 1, 2), ('b', 7, 5)
```

The result is the insertion of two new records into the table. Columns that are allowed to be *NULL*, for which there is a default value, or which are automatically filled in by MySQL via *AUTO_IN* do not have to be specified. If the column names (i.e., in *columnlist*) are not given, then in *VALUES* all values must be given in the order of the columns.

With the second variant, only one record can be changed (not several simultaneously). Such a command looks like this:

```
INSERT INTO tablename SET columnA='a', columnB=1, columnC=2
```

For the third variant, the data come from a *SELECT* instruction.

- *insertoptions:* The behavior of this command can be controlled with a number of global options:
  - *IGNORE* has the effect that the insertion of records with existing values is simply ignored for *UNIQUE KEY* columns. (Without this option, the result would be an error message.)
  - *LOW_PRIORITY | DELAYED* have influence over when the insertion operation is carried out. In both cases, MySQL delays its storage operation until there are no pending read accesses to the table. The

advantage of *DELAYED* is that MySQL returns OK at once, and the client does not need to wait for the end of the saving operation. However, *DELAYED* cannot be used if then an *AUTO_INCREMENT* value with *LAST_INSERT_ID()* is to be determined. *DELAYED* should also not be used if a *LOCK* was placed on the table. (The reason is this: For executing *INSERT DELAYED*, a new MySQL thread is started, and table locking uses threads in its operation.)

The records to be inserted are stored in RAM until the insertion operation has actually been carried out. If MySQL should be terminated for some reason (crash, power outage), then the data are lost.

Please note that in using default values, there are special rules for *TIMESTAMP* and *AUTO_INCREMENT* values. (These rules hold for *UPDATE* commands as well.)

- **Columns with default values:** If you want MySQL to use the default value for a column, then either do not specify this column in your *INSERT* command, or pass an empty character string (not *NULL*) as the value:

```
INSERT INTO table (col1, col2_with_default_value) VALUES ('abc', '')
```

- *TIMESTAMP* **columns:** If you want MySQL to insert the current time in the column, then either omit this column in your *INSERT* command, or pass the value *NULL* (not an empty character string). It is also allowed to pass a character string with a timestamp value if you wish to store a particular value.

- *AUTO_INCREMENT* **columns:** Here as well, either you don't pass the column, or you pass the value *NULL* if MySQL is to determine the *AUTO_INCREMENT* value itself. You may pass any other value that is not otherwise in use.

JOIN

JOIN is not actually an SQL command. This key word is mostly used as part of a *SELECT* command, to link data from several tables. *JOIN* will be described under *SELECT*.

KILL *threadid*

This command terminates a specified thread (subprocess) of the MySQL server. It is allowed only to those users who possess the *Super* privilege. A list of running threads can be obtained via *SHOW PROCESSLIST* (where again, this command assumes the *Process* privilege). Threads can also be terminated via the external program `mysqladmin`.

LOAD DATA *[loadoptions]* INFILE *'filename' [duplicateoptions]*
    INTO TABLE *tablename*
    [importoptions]
    [IGNORE ignorenr LINES]
    [(columnlist)]

LOAD DATA reads a text file and inserts the data contained therein line by line into a table as data records. *LOAD DATA* is significantly faster then inserting data by multiple *INSERT* commands.

Normally, the file *filename* is read from the server's file system, on which MySQL is running. (For this, the *FILE* privilege is required. For security reasons, the file must either be located in the directory of the database or be readable by all users of the computer.)

- *loadoptions: LOCAL* has the effect that the file *filename* on the local client computer is read (that is, the computer on which the command *LOAD DATA* is executed, not on the server computer). For this, no *FILE* privilege is necessary. (The *FILE* privilege relates only to the file system of the MySQL server computer.) Note that *LOAD DATA LOCAL* can be deactivated, depending on how the MySQL server was compiled and configured (option local-infile). *LOW PRIORITY* has the effect that the data are inserted into the table only if no other user is reading the table.

- *filename:* If a file name is given without the path, then MySQL searches for this file in the directory of the current database (e.g., '*bulk.txt*').

  If the file name is given with a relative path, then the path is interpreted by MySQL relative to the data directory (e.g., '*mydir/bulk.txt*').

  File names with absolute path are taken without alteration (for example, '*/tmp/mydir/bulk.txt*').

- *duplicateoptions: IGNORE | REPLACE* determine the behavior of MySQL when a new data record has the same *UNIQUE* or *PRIMARY KEY* value as an existing record. With *IGNORE*, the existing record is preserved, and the new records are ignored. With *REPLACE*, existing records are replaced by the new ones. If neither of these options is used, then the result is an error message.

- *importoptions:* Here is specified how the data should be formatted in the file to be imported. The entire *importoptions* block looks like this:

  [FIELDS
    *[TERMINATED BY '*fieldtermstring*']*
    *[ENCLOSED BY '*enclosechar*']*
    *[ESCAPED BY '*escchar*']]*
  *[LINES TERMINATED BY '*linetermstring*']*

  - *fieldtermstring* specifies the character string that separates the individual columns within the row (e.g., a tab character).
  - *enclosechar* specifies the character that should stand before and after individual entries in the text file (usually the single or double quote character for character strings). If an entry begins with this character, then that character is removed from the beginning and end. Entries that do not begin with the *enclosechar* character will still be accepted. The use of the character in the text file is thus to some extent optional.
  - *escchar* specifies which character is to be used to mark special characters (usually the backslash). This is necessary if special characters appear in character strings in the text file that are also used to separate columns or

rows. Furthermore, MySQL expects the zero-byte in the form \0, where the backslash is to be replaced as necessary by *escchar* if a character has been specified for *escchar*).

    o *linetermstring* specifies the character string with which rows are to be terminated. With DOS/Windows text files this must be the character string ' \r\n'.

In these four character strings, the following special characters can be specified:

\0	code 0	\t	tab	
\b	backspace	\'	singe quote	
\n	newline	\"	double quote	
\r	carriage return	\\	backslash	
\s	blank character			

Furthermore, the character strings can be given in hexadecimal form (e.g., *0x22* instead of ' \"').

If no character strings are given, then the following is the default setting:

FIELDS TERMINATED BY ' \t' ENCLOSED BY '' ESCAPED BY ' \\'
LINES TERMINATED BY ' \n'

- *ignorenr:* This value specifies how many lines should be ignored at the beginning of the text file. This is particularly useful if the first lines contain table headings.

- *columnlist:* If the order of the columns in the text file does not exactly correspond to that in the table, then here one may specify which file columns correspond with which table columns. The list of columns must be set in parentheses: for example, *(firstname, lastname, birthdate)*.

If *TIMESTAMP* columns are not considered during importation or if *NULL* is inserted, then MySQL inserts the actual time. MySQL exhibits analogous behavior with *AUTO_INCREMENT* columns.

LOAD DATA displays as result, among other things, an integer representing the number of warnings. Unfortunately, in MySQL 4.0 there is no way of determining the cause of the warnings (or at least the records or rows that caused the warnings). A typical cause is too many or too few columns in the file to be imported. Excess columns are simply ignored; for missing columns, either 0 or an empty character string is inserted. (An incorrect number of columns can also signify that MySQL was unable to locate the exact column boundaries.)

It looks as though starting with MySQL 4.1 you will be able to display all warnings and errors caused by *LOAD DATA* with the commands *SHOW WARNINGS* and *SHOW ERRORS*

Instead of *LOAD DATA*, you can also use the program mysqlimport. This program creates a link to MySQL and then uses *LOAD DATA*. The inverse of *LOAD DATA* is the command *SELECT . . . INTO OUTFILE*. With it you can export a table into an text file. Further information and concrete examples can be found in Chapter 10.

LOAD DATA FROM MASTER

This command (available since MySQL 4.0) copies all MyISAM tables from master to slave of a replication system. The tables of the *mysql* database are not copied. After copying, replication is begun on the slave (that is, the variables *MASTER_LOG_FILE* and *MASTER_LOG_POS* are set, which normally must be set with *CHANGE MASTER TO*).

This command can be used in many cases, in particular when no InnoDB tables are being used, for a convenient setting up of a replication system. It assumes that the replication user possesses the privileges *Select, Reload*, and *Super*.

LOAD TABLE dbname.tablename FROM MASTER

This command copies a table in a replication system from master to slave, if the table does not yet exist there. The purpose of the command is actually to simplify debugging for MySQL developers. However, the command can possibly also be used for repairing a replication system after errors have been detected. The execution of the command requires that the replication user possess the privileges *Select, Reload*, and *Super*. *LOAD TABLE* works only for MyISAM tables.

LOCK TABLE tablename1 [AS aliasname] locktype, table1 [AS alias2] locktype, . . .

LOCK TABLE prevents other MySQL users from executing write or read operations on the specified tables. If a table is already blocked by another user, then the command waits (unfortunately, without a timeout value, thus theoretically forever) until that block is released.

Table *LOCK*s ensure that during the execution of several commands no data are changed by other users. Typically, *LOCK*s are necessary when first a *SELECT* query is executed and then tables are changed with *UPDATE*, where the results of the previous query are used. (For a single *UPDATE* command, on the other hand, no *LOCK* is necessary. Individual *UPDATE* commands are always completely executed by the MySQL server without giving other users the opportunity to change data.)

LOCK TABLE should not be used on InnoDB tables, for which you can achieve much more efficient locking using transactions and with the commands *SELECT . . . IN SHARE MODE* and *SELECT . . . FOR UPDATE*.

- *locktype:* Here one of four possible locking types must be specified.
  - **READ:** All MySQL users may read the table, but no one may change anything (including the user who executed the *LOCK* command). A *READ LOCK* is allocated only when the table is not blocked by other *WRITE LOCK*s. (Existing *READ LOCK*s, on the other hand, are no hindrance for new *READ LOCK*s. It is thus possible for several users to have simultaneous *READ LOCK*s on the same table.)
  - **READ LOCAL:** Like READ, except that *INSERT*s are allowed if they do not change existing data records.

       o *WRITE:* The current user may read and change the table. All other users are completely blocked. They may neither change data in the blocked table nor read it. A *WRITE LOCK* is allocated only if the table is not blocked by other *LOCK*s (*READ* or *WRITE*). Until the *WRITE LOCK* is lifted, other users can obtain neither a *READ LOCK* nor a *WRITE LOCK.*

       o *LOW PRIORITY WRITE:* Like WRITE, except that during the waiting time (that is, until all other *READ* and *WRITE LOCK*s have been ended) other users may obtain on demand a new *READ LOCK.* However, this means as well that the *LOCK* will be allocated only when there is no other user who wishes a *READ LOCK.*

Table *LOCK*s can increase the speed with which several database commands can be executed one after the other (of course, at the cost that other users are blocked during this time).

MySQL manages table *LOCK*s by means of a thread, where each connection is associated with its own thread. Only one *LOCK* command is considered per thread. (But several tables may be included.) As soon as *UNLOCK TABLES* or *LOCK* is executed for any other table, then all previous locks become invalid.

For reasons of efficiency, it should definitely be attempted to keep *LOCK*s as brief as possible and to end them as quickly as possible by *UNLOCK. LOCK*s end automatically when the current process ends (that is, for example, when the connection between server and client is broken).

OPTIMIZE TABLE *tablename*

OPTIMIZE TABLE removes unused storage space from a table file and ensures that associated data in a data record are stored together. Currently (version 4.0.*n*), this functions only for MyISAM tables.

OPTIMIZE TABLE should be regularly executed for tables whose contents are continually being changed (many *UPDATE* and *DELETE* commands). Not only is the file made smaller, but access is speeded up. (Alternatively, the program `myisamchk` can be executed.)

PROCEDURE *procname*

MySQL can be extended with procedures. However, their code must be formulated in the C++ programming language. To use such functions in *SELECT* commands, the key word *PROCEDURE* must be used.

As an example of such a procedure, the MySQL program code contains the function *ANALYSE*. This procedure can be used to analyze the contents of a table in the hope of determining a better table definition. The function is called thus:

```
SELECT * FROM tablename PROCEDURE ANALYSE()
```

As with the creation of user-defined functions (UDFs; see *CREATE FUNCTION*), the programming of procedures requires a great deal of MySQL background knowledge. Further information can be found in the MySQL documentation:

http://www.mysql.com/doc/en/Extending_MySQL.html

MySQL 5.0 plans on offering, in addition to UDFs, the possibility of creating one's own SQL functions and commands in the form of stored procedures (SPs). SPs are easier to program, but not as efficient as UDFs.

PURGE MASTER LOGS TO '*hostname-bin.n*'

This command deletes all binary logging files that are older than the file specified. Execute this command only when you are sure that the logging files are no longer needed, that is, when all slave computers have synchronized their databases. This command can be executed only on the master computer of a replication system, and only if the *Super* privilege has been granted. See also *RESET MASTER*.

RENAME TABLE oldtablename *TO* newtablename

RENAME TABLE gives a new name to an existing table. It is also possible to rename several tables, e.g., *a TO b, c TO d*, etc.

In older versions of MySQL, *RENAME TABLE* is not available as a freestanding command. There you must use *ALTER TABLE . . . RENAME AS*.

There is no command for giving a new name to an entire database. If you are using MyISAM tables, then to do so, you can stop the MySQL server, rename the database directory (mysql/data/*dbname*), and then restart the server. Note that you may have to change access privileges in the *mysql* database. With InnoDB tables, you must make a backup (mysqldump) and then import the tables into a new database.

REPAIR TABLE tablename1, tablename2, . . . *[TYPE = QUICK]*

REPAIR TABLE attempts to repair a defective table file. With the option *TYPE = QUICK* only the index is re-created.

REPAIR TABLE can currently (version 4.0.*n*) be used only with MyISAM tables. Instead of this command, you may also use the external program myisamchk -r tblfile. (If *REPAIR TABLE* does not return OK as result, then you might try myisamchk -o. This program offers more repair possibilities than *REPAIR TABLE*.)

REPLACE [INTO] see *INSERT*

REPLACE is a variant of *INSERT*. The only difference relates to new records whose key word is the same as that of an existing record. In this case, the existing record is deleted and the new one stored in the table. Since the behavior with duplicates is so clearly defined, *REPLACE* does not have the *IGNORE* option possessed by the *INSERT* command.

RESET MASTER

This command deletes all binary logging files including the index file hostname-bin.index. With this command, replication can be restarted at a particular time. For this, *RESET SLAVE* must be executed on all slave systems. Before the command is executed it must be ensured that the databases on all slave systems are identical to those of the master system. This command assumes the *reload* privilege.

If you wish to delete only old (no longer needed) logging files, then use *PURGE MASTER LOGS*.

RESET QUERY CACHE

This command deletes all entries from the query cache. It assumes the *reload* privilege.

RESET SLAVE

This command reinitializes the slave system. The contents of master.info (and with it the current logging file and its position) are deleted. The command assumes the *reload* privilege.

This command makes sense only if after some problems the databases are to be set up on the slave based on previous snapshots so that the slave system then can synchronize itself by replication, or when *RESET MASTER* was executed on the master system (so that all logging files are deleted there). In this case, first *SLAVE STOP* and then *SLAVE START* should be executed on the slave system.

RESTORE TABLE *tblname* FROM '*/backup/directory*'

RESTORE TABLE copies the files of the specified table from a backup directory into the data directory of the current database. *RESTORE TABLE* is the inverse of *BACKUP TABLE*.

REVOKE *privileges* ON *objects* FROM *users*

REVOKE is the inverse of *GRANT*. With this command you can remove individual privileges previously granted. The syntax for the parameters *privileges*, *objects*, and *users* can be read about under the *GRANT* command. The only difference relates to the *Grant* privilege: To revoke this privilege from a user, *REVOKE* can be used in the following form: *REVOKE GRANT OPTION ON . . . FROM . . .* .

Although *GRANT* inserts new users into the *mysql.user* table, *REVOKE* is incapable of deleting this user. You can remove all privileges from this user with *REVOKE*, but you cannot prevent this user from establishing a connection to MySQL. (If you wish to take that capability away as well, you must explicitly remove the entries from the *user* database with the *DELETE* command.)

Please note that in the MySQL access system you cannot forbid what is allowed at a higher level. If you allow x access to database d, then you cannot exclude table $d.t$ with *REVOKE*. If you wish to allow x access to all tables of the database d with the exception of table t, then you must forbid access to the entire database and then allow access to individual tables of the database (with exception of d). *REVOKE* is not smart enough to carry out such operations on its own.

ROLLBACK

ROLLBACK undoes the most recent transaction. (Instead of *ROLLBACK*, you can confirm the pending changes with *COMMIT* and thereby finalize their execution.)

BEGIN/COMMIT/ROLLBACK work only if you are working with transaction-capable tables. Further information and examples on transactions can be found in Chapter 8.

SELECT *[selectoptions] column1 [AS alias1], column2 [AS alias2] . . .*
   [FROM tablelist]
   [WHERE condition]
   [GROUP BY groupfield [ASC | DESC]]
   [HAVING condition]
   [ORDER BY ordercolumn1 [DESC], ordercolumn2 [DESC] . . .]
   [LIMIT [offset,] rows]
   [PROCEDURE procname]
   [LOCK IN SHARE MODE | FOR UPDATE]

SELECT serves to formulate database queries. It returns the query result in tabular form. *SELECT* is usually implemented in the following form:

```
SELECT column1, column2, column3 FROM table ORDER BY column1
```

However, there are countless syntactic variants, thanks to which *SELECT* can be used also, for example, for processing simple expressions.

```
SELECT HOUR(NOW())
```

Note that the various parts of the *SELECT* command must be given in the order presented here.

- *selectoptions:* The behavior of this command can be controlled by a number of options:
    - *DISTINCT | ALL* specify how MySQL should behave when a query returns several identical records. *DISTINCT* means that identical result records should be displayed only once. *ALL* means that all records should be displayed (the default setting).
    Since MySQL 4.1, the sort order can also be specified for *DISTINCT* (which is also the basis for determining equivalence of character strings): The syntax is *DISTINCT column COLLATE collname*.
    - *HIGH_PRIORITY* has the effect that a query with higher priority than change or insert commands will be executed. *HIGH_PRIORITY* should be used only for queries that need to be executed very quickly.
    - *SQL_BUFFER_RESULT* has the effect that the result of a query is stored in a temporary table. This option should be used when the evaluation of the query is expected to range over a long period of time and locking problems are to be avoided during this period.
    - *SQL_CACHE* and *SQL_NO_CACHE* specify whether the results of the *SELECT* command should be stored in the query cache or whether such storage should be prevented. By default, *SQL_CACHE* usually holds, unless the query cache is executed in demand mode (*QUERY_CACHE_TYPE=2*).
    - *SQL_CALC_FOUND_ROWS* has the effect that MySQL determines the total number of found records even if you limit the result with *LIMIT*.

The number can then be determined with a second query *SELECT FOUND_ROWS()*.

- ○ *SQL_SMALL_RESULT* | *SQL_BIG_RESULT* specify whether a large or small record list is expected as result, and they help MySQL in optimization. Both options are useful only with *GROUP BY* and *DISTINCT* queries.
- ○ *STRAIGHT_JOIN* has the effect that data collected from queries extending over more than one table should be joined in the order of the *FROM* expression. (Without *STRAIGHT_JOIN*, MySQL attempts to find the optimal order on its own. *STRAIGHT_JOIN* bypasses this optimization algorithm.)

- *column:* Here column names are normally given. If the query encompasses several tables, then the format is *table.column*. If a query is to encompass all the columns of the tables specified by *FROM*, then you can save yourself some typing and simply specify *. (Note, however, that this is inefficient in execution if you do not need all the columns.)

  However, instead of column names, you may also use general expressions or functions, e.g., for formatting a column (*DATE_FORMAT(. . .)*) or for calculating an expression (*COUNT(. . .)*).

  With *AS*, a column can be given a new name. This is practical in using functions such as *HOUR(column) AS hr*.

  Such an alias name can then be used in most of the rest of the *SELECT* command (e.g., *ORDER BY hr*). The alias name cannot, however, be placed in a *WHERE* clause.

  Since MySQL 4.1, the desired sort order can be specified with *COLLATE* (e.g., *column COLLATE german1 AS alias*).

- *tablelist:* In the simplest case, there is simply a list (separated by commas) of all tables that are to be considered in the query. If no relational conditions (further below with *WHERE*) are formulated, then MySQL returns a list of all possible combinations of data records of all affected tables.

  There is the possibility of specifying here a condition for linking the tables, for example in the following forms:

      table1 LEFT [OUTER] JOIN table2 ON table1.xyID = table2.xyID
      table1 LEFT [OUTER] JOIN table2 USING (xyID)
      table1 NATURAL [LEFT [OUTER]] JOIN

  An extensive list of the many syntactic synonyms can be found in Chapter 6, where the topic of links among several tables is covered in great detail.

- *condition:* Here is where conditions that the query results must fulfill can be formulated. Conditions can contain comparisons (*column1>10* or *column1=column2*) or pattern expressions (*column LIKE ' %xy '*), for example. Several conditions can be joined with *AND*, *OR*, and *NOT*.

  MySQL allows selection conditions with *IN*:

  WHERE id IN(1, 2, 3) corresponds to *WHERE id=1 OR id=2 OR id=3*.
  WHERE id NOT IN (1,2) corresponds to *WHERE NOT (id=1 OR id=2)*.

Sub*SELECT*s: Beginning with version 4.1, MySQL supports sub*SELECT*s. This means that the results of one query can become part of the conditions of another. There are several syntactic variants:

SELECT . . . WHERE col = (SELECT . . .)

SELECT . . . WHERE col [NOT] IN (SELECT . . .)

SELECT . . . WHERE [NOT] EXISTS (SELECT . . .)

With the first variant, the second *SELECT* command must return a single value (e.g., *SELECT MAX(col) FROM . . .*); with the other variants, a list of values is possible. Examples of the use of sub*SELECT*s can be found in Chapter 7 and Appendix B.

Full-text search: Conditions can also be formulated with *MATCH(col1, col2) AGAINST(' word1 word2 word3')*. Thereby a full-text search is carried out in the columns *col1* and *col2* for the words *word1*, *word2*, and *word3*. (This assumes that a full-text index for the columns *col1* and *col2* has been created.)

AGAINST also supports Boolean search expressions, for example, in the form *AGAINST(' +word1 +word2 -word3' IN BOOLEAN MODE)*. Here the plus sign represents a logical AND operation, while the minus sign means that the specified word may not appear in the record. The full syntax for search expressions can be found in Chapter 7.

***WHERE* versus *HAVING*:** Conditions can be formulated with *WHERE* or *HAVING*. *WHERE* conditions are applied directly to the columns of the tables named in *FROM*.

HAVING conditions, on the other hand, are applied only after the *WHERE* conditions to the intermediate result of the query. The advantage of *HAVING* is that conditions can also be specified for function results (for example, *SUM(column1)* in a *GROUP BY* query). Alias names can be used in *HAVING* conditions (*AS xxx*), which is not possible in *WHERE*.

Conditions that can be equally well formulated with *WHERE* or *HAVING* should be expressed with *WHERE*, because in that case, better optimization is possible.

- *groupfield:* With *GROUP BY*, you can specify a group column. If the query returns several records with the same values for the group column, then these records are collected into a single new record. Along with *GROUP BY*, in the *column* part of the query so-called aggregate functions are usually placed, with which calculations can be made over grouped fields (e.g., *COUNT, SUM, MIN, MAX*).

  By default, grouped results are sorted as though *ORDER BY* had been specified for the columns. Optionally, the sort order can be determined with *ASC* or *DESC*.

  Since MySQL 4.1, the desired sort order can be given with *COLLATE* (e.g., *GROUP BY column COLLATE german1*).

- *ordercolumn:* With *ORDER BY* several columns or expressions can be specified according to which the query result should be sorted. Sorting normally proceeds in increasing order (A, B, C, . . . or 1, 2, 3, . . .). With the option *DESC* (for *descending*) you have decreasing order.

- *[offset,] row:* With *LIMIT* the query results can be reduced to an arbitrary selection. This is to be recommended especially when the results are to be displayed pagewise or when the number of result records is to be limited. The position at which the results are to begin is given by *offset* (0 for the first data record), while *row* determines the maximum number of result records.

- *procname:* This enables the call of a user-defined procedure (see the description of *PROCEDURE*).

If you use transactions, then the addition of *LOCK IN SHARE MODE* has the effect that all records found by the *SELECT* command will be blocked by a *shared lock* until the end of the transaction. This has two consequences: First, your *SELECT* query will not be executed until there is no running transaction that could change the result. Second, the affected records cannot now be changed by other connections (though they can be read with *SELECT*) until your transaction has ended.

FOR UPDATE is even more restrictive, blocking the found records with an *exclusive lock*. In contrast to a *shared lock*, other connections that execute *SELECT...* *LOCK IN SHARE MODE* must now wait until the end of your transaction (of course, only if the same records are affected by *SELECT* queries).

MySQL does not currently support the formulation *SELECT... INTO table*, known in many other SQL dialects. In most cases, you can use *INSERT INTO...* *SELECT* or *CREATE TABLE tablename... SELECT....*

ROLLBACK TO SAVEPOINT *name*

ROLLBACK ends the current transaction, aborting all SQL commands that were executed after the specified *SAVEPOINT*. Commands up through *SAVEPOINT* are accepted. This command has been available since version 4.0.14.

SAVEPOINT *name*

Since MySQL 4.0.14, this command places a marker in a running transaction. With *ROLLBACK TO SAVEPOINT*, the transaction can be recalled up to this point. *SAVEPOINT*s are valid only within a transaction, and they are deleted at the end of the transaction.

SELECT *[selectoptions] columnlist*
INTO OUTFILE *'filename' exportoptions*
[FROM... WHERE... GROUP BY... HAVING... ORDER BY... LIMIT...]

With this variant of the *SELECT* command, the records are written into a text file. Here we describe only those options that are specific to this variant. All other points of syntax can be found under *SELECT*.

- *filename:* The file is generated in the file system of the MySQL server. For security reasons, the file should not already exist. Moreover, you must have the *FILE* privilege to be able to execute this *SELECT* variant.

- *exportoptions:* Here it is specified how the text file is formatted. The entire option block looks like this:

  [FIELDS
    [TERMINATED BY 'fieldtermstring']
    [[OPTIONALLY] ENCLOSED BY 'enclosechar']
    [ESCAPED BY 'escchar']]
  [LINES TERMINATED BY 'linetermstring']

  - *fieldtermstring* specifies the character string that separates columns within a line (e.g., a tab character).
  - *enclosechar* specifies a character that is placed before and after every entry, e.g., '123' with *ENCLOSED BY ' \' '*. With *OPTIONALLY*, the character is used only on *CHAR, VARCHAR, TEXT, BLOB, TIME, DATE, SET*, and *ENUM* columns (and not for every number format, such as *TIMESTAMP*).
  - *escchar* specifies the character to be used to mark special characters (usually the backslash). This is especially necessary when in character strings of a text file special characters appear that are also used for separating data elements.

    If *escchar* is specified, then the escape character is always used for itself (\\) as well as for ASCII code 0 (\0). If *enclosechar* is empty, then the escape character is also used as identifier of the first character of *fieldtermstring* and *linetermstring* (e.g., \t and \n). On the other hand, if *enclosechar* is not empty, then *escchar* is used only for *enclosechar* (e.g., \"), and not for *fieldtermstring* and *linetermstring*. (This is no longer necessary, since the end of the character string is uniquely identifiable due to *enclosechar*.)
  - *linetermstring* specifies the character string with which lines are to be terminated. With DOS/Windows text files this must be the character string ' \r\n '.

In the four character strings, special characters can be specified, for example, \b for backspace. The list of permissible special characters can be found at the command *LOAD DATA*. Moreover, character strings can be given in hexadecimal notation (such as *0x22* instead of ' \' ').

As with *LOAD DATA* the following is the default setting:

FIELDS TERMINATED BY ' \t' ENCLOSED BY ' ' ESCAPED BY ' \\'
LINES TERMINATED BY ' \n'

If you wish to input files generated with *SELECT . . . INTO OUTFILE* again into a table, then use *LOAD DATA*. This command is the inverse of *SELECT . . . INTO OUTFILE*. Further information and concrete application examples for both commands can be found in Chapter 10.

SELECT *[selectoptions] column*
INTO DUMPFILE *'filename'*
[FROM . . . WHERE . . . GROUP BY . . . HAVING . . . ORDER BY . . . LIMIT . . .]

SELECT . . . INTO DUMPFILE has, in principle, the same function as *SELECT . . . INTO OUTFILE* (see above). The difference is that here data are stored without any characters to indicate column or row division.

SELECT . . . INTO DUMPFILE is designed for saving a single BLOB object into a file. The *SELECT* query should therefore return precisely one column and one row as result. Should that not be the case, that is, if the query returns more than one data element, then usually (and for some strange reason not always) one receives an error message: *ERROR 1172: Result consisted of more than one row.*

(SELECT selectoptions) UNION [ALL] (SELECT selectoptions) unionoptions

Since MySQL 4.0 you can use *UNION* to unite the results of two or more *SELECT* queries. You thereby obtain a result table in which the results of the individual queries are simply strung together. The individual queries can affect different tables, though you must ensure that the number of columns and their data types are the same.

The optional key word *ALL* has the effect that duplicates (that is, results that arise in more than one *SELECT* query) appear in the end result with their corresponding multiplicity. Without *ALL*, duplicates are eliminated (as with *DISTINCT* in *SELECT*).

With *SELECT* commands, all options described earlier for selecting columns, setting sort order, etc., are permitted. With *unionoptions* you can also specify how the final result is to be sorted (*ORDER BY*) and reduced (*LIMIT*).

SET @variable = expression

MySQL permits the management of one's own user variables. These variables are indicated by the @ symbol before the name. These variables are managed separately for each client connection, so that no naming conflicts can arise among clients. The content of such variables is lost at the end of the connection.

Instead of *SET*, one may also use *SELECT* for the assignment of user variables. The syntax is *SELECT @variable:=expression* (note that := must be used instead of =).

SET [options] [@@]systemvariable = expression

If the variable name has either no @ prefixed or two of them (@@), then *SET* is setting system variables.

- *options:* MySQL distinguishes two levels of validity among system variables: *GLOBAL* (valid for the entire MySQL server) and *SESSION* (valid only for the current connection). The default setting is *SESSION*.

Variables at the global level can be changed only by users with the *Super* privilege. Global changes are valid only for new connections, not those already in existence.

***SET [OPTION]** option=value*

SET can also used to modify certain MySQL options as well as the password. Although the syntax looks the same as that for variable assignment, here we are not dealing with system variables that can be evaluated with *SELECT @@name* or *SHOW VARIABLES*.

For example, with

```
SET SQL_LOW_PRIORITY_UPDATES = 0 / 1
```

it is possible to determine the order in which MySQL executes queries and change commands. The default behavior (1) gives priority to change commands. (This has the effect that a lengthy *SELECT* command will not block change commands, which are usually executed quickly.) With the setting 0, on the other hand, changes are executed only when no *SELECT* command is waiting to be executed.

SET PASSWORD also offers a convenient way of changing one's password (and saves the relatively more cumbersome manipulation of the access table of the *mysql* database:

```
SET PASSWORD = PASSWORD('some password')
```

If you have sufficient privileges, you can use *SET* to set the password of another user:

```
SET PASSWORD FOR username@hostname = PASSWORD('newPassword')
```

SET AUTOCOMMIT = 0 or *1* switches the autocommit mode for transactions off or on. Autocommit mode holds only for transaction-capable tables (see Chapter 8).

If you use replication, you can temporarily interrupt binary logging on the master system with *SET SQL_LOG_BIN =0* in order to make manual changes that should not be replicated. *SET SQL_LOG_BIN=1* resumes logging.

SET SQL_QUERY_CACHE = 0|1|2|ON|OFF|DEMAND sets the mode of the query cache (see Chapter 10).

SET TRANSACTION ISOLATION LEVEL sets the isolation level for transactions. The setting holds for transaction-capable tables. Here is the syntax:

```
SET [SESSION|GLOBAL] TRANSACTION ISOLATION LEVEL
  READ UNCOMMITTED | READ COMMITTED |
  REPEATABLE READ | SERIALIZABLE
```

SET SESSION changes the transaction degree for the current connection, and *SET GLOBAL* for all future connections (but not the current one). If neither *SESSION* nor *GLOBAL* is specified, then the setting is valid only for the coming transaction. (Note that *SESSION* and *GLOBAL* in *SET TRANSACTION* have a somewhat different effect from that of *SET [@@]systemvariable*.)

The four isolation degrees are described in Chapter 8. With InnoDB tables, the default is *REPEATABLE READ*. The isolation degree can also be read from the variable *@@[global.]tx_isolation*.

Additional *SET* options: The following list presents all the options that can be changed with *SET*:

```
SET BIG_TABLES = 0 | 1
SET CHARACTER SET character_set_name | DEFAULT
SET INSERT_ID = #
SET LAST_INSERT_ID = #
SET LOW_PRIORITY_UPDATES = 0 | 1
SET MAX_JOIN_SIZE = value | DEFAULT
SET QUERY_CACHE_TYPE = 0 | 1 | 2
SET QUERY_CACHE_TYPE = OFF | ON | DEMAND
SET SQL_AUTO_IS_NULL = 0 | 1
SET SQL_BIG_SELECTS = 0 | 1
SET SQL_BUFFER_RESULT = 0 | 1
SET SQL_LOG_OFF = 0 | 1
SET SQL_LOG_UPDATE = 0 | 1
SET SQL_QUOTE_SHOW_CREATE = 0 | 1
SET SQL_SAFE_UPDATES = 0 | 1
SET SQL_SELECT_LIMIT = value | DEFAULT
SET TIMESTAMP = timestamp_value | DEFAULT
```

A description of these (mostly seldom used) setting options can be found in the MySQL documentation in the description of the *SET* command:

```
http://www.mysql.com/doc/en/SET_OPTION.html
```

SHOW BINLOG EVENTS *[IN logname] [FROM pos] [LIMIT offset, rows]*

If this command is executed without options, then it returns the complete contents of the currently active binary logging file. The options allow for the specification of other logging files or for limiting the output. Note that this command can also be used to read the logging file of an external MySQL server.

SHOW CHARACTER SET *[LIKE pattern]*

Since MySQL 4.1, *SHOW CHARACTER SET* returns a list of all available character sets and their default sort orders.

SHOW COLLATION *[LIKE pattern]*

Since MySQL 4.1, *SHOW COLLATION* returns a list of all available sort orders.

SHOW COLUMN TYPES

Since MySQL 4.1, *SHOW COLUMN TYPES* returns a list of all data types available for column definition. (In the tested alpha version this did not yet work.)

One may store results of queries in user variables. However, the storage of several values is not possible:

```
SELECT @a:=SUM(colA) FROM table1
```

User variables can be placed, for example, into *WHERE* conditionals:

```
SELECT * FROM table2 WHERE colA>@a
```

SHOW [FULL] COLUMNS FROM tablename *[FROM databasename] [LIKE pattern]*

SHOW COLUMNS returns a table with information on all columns of a table (field name, field type, index, default value, etc.). With *LIKE* the list of columns can be filtered with a search pattern with the wild cards _ and %. The optional key word *FULL* has the effect that the access privileges of the current user are also displayed on the columns. The same information can be obtained with *SHOW FIELDS FROM tablename, EXPLAIN tablename*, or *DESCRIBE tablename*, as well as with the external program mysqlshow.

SHOW CREATE DATABASE tablename

Since MySQL 4.1, *SHOW CREATE DATABASE* displays the SQL command with which the specified database can be re-created.

SHOW CREATE TABLE tablename

SHOW CREATE TABLE displays the SQL command with which the specified table can be re-created.

SHOW DATABASES [LIKE pattern]

SHOW DATABASES returns a list of all databases that the user can access. The list can be filtered with a search pattern with the wild cards _ and %. The same information can also be obtained with the external program mysqlshow.

For users possessing the *Show Databases* privilege, *SHOW DATABASES* returns a list of all databases, including those to which the user does not have access.

SHOW [COUNT(*)] ERRORS

Since MySQL 4.1, *SHOW ERRORS* returns a list of errors that were triggered by the execution of the most recent command.

SHOW FIELDS see *SHOW COLUMNS*

SHOW GRANTS *FOR user@host*

SHOW GRANTS displays a list of all access privileges for a particular user. It is necessary that *user* and *host* be specified exactly as these character strings are stored in the various *mysql* access tables. Wild cards are not permitted.

SHOW INDEX *FROM table*

SHOW INDEX returns a table with information about all indexes of the given table.

SHOW INNODB STATUS

SHOW INNODB STATUS returns information about various internal workings of the InnoDB table driver. The data can be used for speed optimization (see the section *Performance Tuning Tips* in the InnoDB documentation).

SHOW KEYS see SHOW INDEX

SHOW LOGS

This command shows which BDB logging files are currently being used. (If you are not using BDB tables, the command returns no result.)

SHOW MASTER LOGS

This command returns a list of all binary logging files. It can be executed only on the master computer of a replication system.

SHOW MASTER STATUS

This command shows which logging file is the current one, as well as the current position in this file and which databases are excepted from logging (configuration settings `binlog-do-db` and `binlog-ignore-db`). This command can be used only on the master computer of a replication system.

SHOW PRIVILEGES

Since MySQL 4.1, this command returns a list of all available privileges with a brief description.

SHOW [FULL] PROCESSLIST

This command returns a list of all running threads (subprocesses) of the MySQL server. If the *PROCESS* privilege has been granted, then all threads are shown. Otherwise, only the user's threads are displayed.

The option *FULL* has the effect that for each thread, the complete text of the most recently executed command is displayed. Without this option, only the first 100 characters are shown.

The process list can also be determined with the external command `mysqladmin`.

SHOW SLAVE HOSTS

This command returns a list of all slaves that replicate the master's databases. The command can be used only by the master computer of a replication system. It functions only for slaves for which the host name is specified in the configuration file explicitly in the form `report-host=`*hostname*.

SHOW SLAVE STATUS

This command provides information on the state of replication, including the display of all information about the file `master.info`. This command can be executed only on a slave computer in a replication system.

SHOW STATUS

This command returns a list of various MySQL variables that provide information on the current state of MySQL (for example, *Connections*, *Open_files*, *Uptime*). This same information can also be determined with the external program `mysqladmin`. A description of all variables can be found in the MySQL documentation under the command *SHOW STATUS*:

```
http://www.mysql.com/doc/en/SHOW_STATUS.html
```

SHOW TABLE STATUS *[FROM database] [LIKE pattern]*

SHOW TABLE STATUS returns information about all tables of the currently active or specified database: table type, number of records, average record length, *Create_time*, *Update_time*, etc. The same information can also be determined with the external program `mysqlshow`. With *pattern* the list of tables can be limited; the SQL wild cards % and _ are permitted in *pattern*.

SHOW TABLE TYPES

Since MySQL 4.1, *SHOW TABLE TYPES* returns a list of all available table types (MyISAM, HEAP, InnoDB, etc.).

SHOW TABLES *[FROM database] [LIKE pattern]*

SHOW TABLES returns a list of all tables of the current (or specified) database. Optionally, the list of all tables can be reduced to those matching the search pattern *pattern* (where the SQL wild cards % and _ are allowed). More information on the construction of individual tables can be obtained with *DESCRIBE TABLE* and *SHOW COLUMNS*. The list of tables can also be retrieved with the external program `mysqlshow`.

SHOW *[options]* **VARIABLES** *[LIKE pattern]*

This command returns a seemingly endless list of all system variables defined by MySQL together with their values (e.g., *ansi_mode, sort_buffer, tmpdir, wait_timeout*, to name but a very few). To limit the list, a pattern can be given (e.g., *LIKE 'char%'*).

Many of these variables can be set at launch of MySQL or afterwards with *SET*. The list of variables can also be recovered with the external command mysqladmin.

- *options:* Here you can specify *GLOBAL* or *SESSION*. *GLOBAL* has the effect that the default values valid at the global level are displayed. *SESSION*, on the other hand, results in the values being displayed that are valid for the current connection. The default is *SESSION*.

An extensive description of the variables can be found in the MySQL documentation:

```
http://www.mysql.com/doc/en/SHOW_VARIABLES.html
```

SHOW *[COUNT(*)]* **WARNINGS**

Since MySQL 4.1, this command returns a list of all warnings that arose from the execution of the most recent command.

SLAVE START/STOP *[IO_THREAD | SQL_THREAD]*

These commands start and stop replication (we leave it to the reader to determine which is which). They can be executed only on the slave computer of a replication system.

By default, two threads are started for replication: the IO thread (copies the binary logging data from the master to the slave) and the SQL thread (executes the logging file's SQL command). With the optional specification of *IO_THREAD* or *SQL_THREAD*, these two threads can be started or stopped independently (which makes sense only for debugging).

START TRANSACTION

If you are working with transaction-capable tables, *START TRANSACTION* initiates a new transaction. The command is ANSI-99 conforming, but it has been available only since MySQL 4.0.11. In earlier versions, you must use the equivalent command *BEGIN*.

TRUNCATE TABLE *tablename*

TRUNCATE has the same functionality as *DELETE* without a *WHERE* condition; that is, the effect is that all records in the table are deleted. This is accomplished by deleting the entire table and then recreating it. (This is considerably faster than deleting each record individually.)

TRUNCATE cannot be part of a transaction. *TRUNCATE* functions like *COMMIT*; that is, all pending changes are first executed. *TRUNCATE* can also be undone with *ROLLBACK*.

UNION see **SELECT UNION**

With *UNION*, you can assemble the results of several *SELECT* queries.

UNLOCK TABLES

UNLOCK TABLES removes all of the user's *LOCK*s. This command holds for all databases (that is, it doesn't matter which database is the current one).

UPDATE *[updateoptions] tablename* **SET** *col1=value1, col2=value2, . . .*
[WHERE condition]
[ORDER BY columns]
[LIMIT maxrecords]

UPDATE changes individual fields of the table records specified by *WHERE*. Those fields not specified by *SET* remain unchanged. In *value* one can refer to existing fields. For example, an *UPDATE* command may be of the following form:

```
UPDATE products SET price = price + 5 WHERE productID=3
```

Warning: Without a *WHERE* condition, all data records in the table will be changed. (In the above example, the prices of all products would be increased by 5.)

- *updateoptions:* Here the options *LOW PRIORITY* and *IGNORE* may be given. The effect is the same as with *INSERT*.

- *condition:* This condition specifies which records are affected by the change. For the syntax of *condition* see *SELECT*.

- *columns:* With *ORDER BY*, you can sort the record list before making changes. This makes sense only in combination with *LIMIT*, for example, to change the first or last ten records (ordered according to some criterion). This possibility has existed since MySQL 4.0.

- *maxrecords:* With *LIMIT*, the maximum number of records that may be changed is specified.

UPDATE *[updateoptions] table1, table2, table3*
SET *table1.col1=table2.col2 . . .*
    [WHERE condition] [ORDER BY columns] [LIMIT maxrecords]

Since MySQL 4.0, *UPDATE* commands can include more than one table. All tables included in the query must be specified after *UPDATE*. The only tables that are changed are those whose fields were specified by *SET*. The link between the tables must be set with *WHERE* conditions.

USE *databasename*

USE turns the specified database into the default database for the current connection to MySQL. Until the end of the connection (or until the next *USE* command), all table names are automatically assigned to the database *databasename*.

Function Reference

The functions described here can be used in *SELECT* queries are well as in other SQL commands. We begin with a few examples. In our first example, we shall join two table columns with *CONCAT* to create a new character string. In the second example, the function *PASSWORD* will be used to store an encrypted password in a column. In the third example, the function *DATE_FORMAT* will be summoned to help us format a date:

```
SELECT CONCAT(firstname, ' ', lastname) FROM users

  Peter Smith

  ...

INSERT INTO logins (username, userpassword)
VALUES ('smith', PASSWORD('xxx'))

SELECT DATE_FORMAT(a_date, '%Y %M %e')
FROM exceptions.test_date
    2003 December 7
```

> **POINTER** *This section aims to provide only a compact overview of the functions available. Extensive information on these functions can be found in the MySQL documentation. Some of these functions have been introduced at various places in this book by way of example. See the Index for page numbers.*

Arithmetic Functions

ABS(x)	calculates the absolute value (nonnegative number)
ACOS(x), ASIN(x)	calculates the arcsin and arccos
ATAN(x), ATAN2(x, y)	calculates the arctangent
CEILING(x)	rounds up to the least integer greater than or equal to x
COS(x)	calculates the cosine; x is given in radians
COT(x)	calculates the cotangent
DEGREES(x)	converts radians to degrees (multiplication by $180/\pi$)
EXP(x)	returns e^x
FLOOR(x)	rounds down to the greatest integer less than or equal to x
LOG(x)	returns the natural logarithm (i.e., to base e)
LOG10(x)	returns the logarithm to base 10
MOD(x, y)	returns the mod function, equivalent to $x \% y$
PI()	returns 3.1415927
POW(x, y)	returns x^y
POWER(x, y)	corresponds to *POW(x, y)*
RADIANS(x)	converts degrees into radians (multiplication by $\pi/180$)
RAND()	returns a random number between 0.0 and 1.0
RAND(n)	returns a reproducible (thus not quite random) number
ROUND(x)	rounds to the nearest integer
ROUND(x, y)	rounds to y decimal places
SIGN(x)	returns -1, 0, or 1 depending on the sign of x
SIN(x)	calculates the sine
SQRT(x)	calculates the square root
TAN(x)	calculates the tangent
TRUNCATE(x)	removes digits after the decimal point
TRUNCATE(x, y)	retains y digits after the decimal point (thus *TRUNCATE(1.236439, 2)* returns 1.23)

In general, all functions return *NULL* if provided with invalid parameters (e.g., *SQRT(-1)*).

Comparison Functions, Tests, Branching

Comparison Functions

COALESCE(x, y, z . . .)	returns the first parameter that is not *NULL*
GREATEST(x, y, z, . . .)	returns the greatest value or greatest character string
IF(expr, val1, val2)	returns *val1* if *expr* is true; otherwise, *val2*
IFNULL(expr1, expr2)	returns *expr2* if *expr1* is *NULL*; otherwise, *expr1*
INTERVAL(x, n1, n2, . . .)	returns 0 if $x < n1$; 1 if $x < n2$, etc.; all parameters must be integers, and $n1 < n2 < \cdots$ must hold
ISNULL(x)	returns 1 or 0, according to whether *x IS NULL* holds
LEAST(x, y, z, . . .)	returns the smallest value or smallest character string
STRCMP(s1, s2)	returns 0 if $s1 = s2$ in sort order, -1 if $s1 < s2$, 1 if $s1 > s2$.

Tests, Branching

IF(expr, result1, result2)	returns *result1* if *expr* is true; otherwise, *result2*
CASE expr *WHEN val1 THEN result1* *WHEN val2 THEN result2* *ELSE resultn* *END*	returns *result1* if *expr=val1*, returns *result2* if *expr=val2*, etc. If no condition is satisfied, then the result is *resultn*
CASE *WHEN cond1 THEN result1* *WHEN cond2 THEN result2* *ELSE resultn* *END*	returns *result1* if condition *cond1* is true, etc.

Type Conversion (CAST)

CAST(x AS type)	transforms *x* into the specified *type*; *CAST* can deal with the following types: *BINARY, CHAR, DATE, DATETIME, SIGNED [INTEGER], TIME, UNSIGNED [INTEGER]*
CONVERT(x, type)	equivalent to *CAST(x AS type)*
CONVERT(s USING cs)	represents the string *s* in the character set *cs* (since MySQL 4.1)

String Processing

Most character string functions can also be used for processing binary data. Since MySQL 4.1 (with Unicode support), the position and length specification functions such as *LEFT* and *MID* apply to characters, not bytes. *MID(column, 3, 1)* thus returns the third character, regardless of the character set that is defined for *column*.

Processing Character Strings

CHAR_LENGTH(s)	returns the number of characters in *s*; *CHAR_LENGTH* works also for multibyte character sets (e.g., Unicode)
CONCAT(s1, s2, s3, . . .)	concatenates the strings
CONCAT_WS(x, s1, s2, . . .)	functions like *CONCAT*, except that *x* is inserted between each string; *CONCAT_WS(', ', 'a', 'b', 'c')* returns *'a, b, c'*
ELT(n, s1, s2, . . .)	returns the *n*th string; *ELT(2, 'a', 'b', 'c')* returns *'b'*
EXPORT_SET(x, s1, s2)	creates a string from *s1* and *s2* based on the bit coding of *x*; *x* is interpreted as a 64-bit integer
FIELD(s, s1, s2, . . .)	compares *s* with strings *s1, s2* and returns the index of the first matching string; *FIELD('b', 'a', 'b', 'c')* returns 2
FIND_IN_SET(s1, s2)	searches for *s1* in *s2*; *s2* contains a comma-separated list of strings; *FIND_IN_SET('b', 'a,b,c')* returns 2
INSERT(s1, pos, 0, s2) *INSERT('ABCDEF', 3, 0, 'abc')*	inserts *s2* into position *pos* in *s1*; returns *'ABabcDEF'*

INSERT(s1, pos, len, s2)	inserts *s2* at position *pos* in *s1* and replaces *len* characters of *s2* with the new characters; INSERT(' ABCDEF', 3, 2, ' abc') returns ' ABabcEF'
INSTR(s, sub)	returns the position of *sub* in *s*;
INSTR(' abcde', 'bc')	returns 2
LCASE(s)	changes uppercase characters to lowercase
LEFT(s, n)	returns the first *n* characters of *s*
LENGTH(s)	returns the number of bytes necessary to store the string *s*; if multibyte character sets are used (e.g., Unicode), then *CHAR_LENGTH* must be used to determine the number of characters
LOCATE(sub, s)	returns the position of *sub* in *s*; LOCATE(' bc', 'abcde') returns 2
LOCATE(sub, s, n)	as above, but the search for *sub* begins only at the *n*th character of *s*
LOWER(s)	transforms uppercase characters to lowercase
LPAD(s, len, fill)	inserts the fill character *fill* into *s*, so that *s* ends up with length *len*; LPAD(' ab', 5, '*') returns '***ab'
LTRIM(s)	removes spaces at the beginning of *s*
MAKE_SET(x, s1, s2 . . .)	forms a new string in which all strings *sn* appear for which in *x* the bit *n* is set; MAKE_SET(1+2+8, 'a', 'b', 'c', 'd') returns 'a,b,d'
MID(s, pos, len)	reads *len* characters from position *pos* from the string *s*; MID(' abcde', 3, 2) returns 'cd'
POSITION(sub IN s)	equivalent to *LOCATE(sub, s)*
QUOTE(s)	since MySQL 4.0, returns a string suitable for SQL commands; special characters such as ', ", \ are prefixed with a backspace
REPEAT(s, n)	joins *s* to itself *n* times; REPEAT(' ab', 3) returns 'ababab'
REPLACE(s, fnd, rpl)	replaces in *s* all *fnd* strings by *rpl*; REPLACE(' abcde', 'b', 'xy') returns 'axycde'
REVERSE(s)	reverses the string
RIGHT(s, n)	returns the last *n* characters of *s*
RPAD(s, len, fill)	inserts the fill character *fill* at the end of *s*, so that *s* has length *len*; RPAD(' ab', 5, '*') returns 'ab***'
RTRIM(s)	removes spaces from the end of *s*
SPACE(n)	returns *n* space characters
SUBSTRING(s, pos)	returns the right part of *s* from position *pos*
SUBSTRING(s, pos, len)	as above, but only *len* characters (equivalent to *MID(s, pos, len)*)
SUBSTRING_INDEX(s, f, n)	searches for the *n*th appearance of *f* in *s* and returns the left part of the string up to this position (exclusive); for negative *n*, the search begins at the end of the string, and the right part of the string is returned; SUBSTRING_INDEX(' abcabc', 'b', 2) returns 'abca' SUBSTRING_INDEX(' abcabc', 'b', -2) returns 'cabc'
TRIM(s)	removes spaces from the beginning and end of *s*
TRIM(f FROM s)	removes the character *f* from the beginning and end of *s*
UCASE(s) / UPPER(s)	transforms lowercase characters to uppercase

Converting Numbers and Character Strings

ASCII(s)	returns the byte code of the first character of *s*: thus *ASCII('A')* returns 65; see also *ORD*
BIN(x)	returns the binary code of *x*; *BIN(12)* returns '*1010*'
CHAR(x, y, z, ...)	returns the string formed from the code *x, y, . . . ; CHAR(65, 66)* returns '*AB*'
CHARSET(s)	since MySQL 4.1, returns the name of the character set in which *s* is represented
CONV(x, from, to)	transforms *x* from number base *from* to base *to*; *CONV(25, 10, 16)* returns the hexadecimal '*19*'
CONVERT(s USING cs)	since MySQL 4.1, represents the string *s* in the character set *cs*
FORMAT(x, n)	formats *x* with commas for thousands separation and *n* decimal places; *FORMAT(12345.678, 2)* returns '*12,345.68*'
HEX(x)	returns the hexadecimal code for *x*; *x* can be a 64-bit integer or (since MySQL 4.0) a character string; in the second case, each character is transformed into an 8-bit hex code; *HEX('abc')* returns '*414243*'
INET_NTOA(n)	transforms *n* into an IP address with at least four groups; *INET_NTOA(1852797041)* returns '*110.111.112.113*' *INET_ATON(ipadr)* transforms an IP address into the corresponding 32- or 64-bit integer; *INET_ATON('110.111.112.113')* returns 1852797041
OCT(x)	returns the octal code of *x*
ORD(s)	like *ASCII(s)*, returns the code of the first character, but functions also for multibyte character sets
SOUNDEX(s)	returns a string that should match similar-sounding English words; *SOUNDEX('hat')* and *SOUNDEX('head')* both return '*H300*'; extensive information on the SOUNDEX algorithm can be found in the book *SQL for Smarties* by Joe Celko

Check Sums

CRC32(s)	since MySQL 4.1, computes a check (cyclic redundancy check value) for the string *s*
MD5(str)	computes the MD5 check sum for the string *str*
SHA(str), SHA1(str)	since MySQL 4.0, computes a 160-bit check sum using the SHA1 algorithm (defined in RFC 3174). SHA is considered more secure than MD5. The result is returned as a string containing a 40-digit hexadecimal code; SHA and SHA1 are synonyms.

Encryption of Character Strings and Password Management

AES_DECRYPT(crypt, key)	decrypts *crypt* since MySQL 4.0 with the AES algorithm (Rijndael) and uses *key* for decryption
AES_ENCRYPT(str, key)	encrypts *str* using *key* for encryption
DES_DECRYPT(crypt [, keyno | keystr])	decrypts *crypt* using the DES algorithm; available since MySQL 4.0 and only when MySQL is compiled with SSL functions; without the optional second parameter, the first key form the DES key file is used for encryption; optionally, the number or name of the key can be specified
DES_ENCRYPT(str [, keyno | keystr])	encrypts *str* using the DES algorithm
DECODE(crypt, pw)	decrypts *crypt* using the password *pw*
ENCODE(str, pw)	encrypts *str* using *pw* as password; the result is a binary object that can be decrypted with *DECODE*
ENCRYPT(pw)	encrypts the password with the UNIX *crypt* function; if this function is unavailable, returns *ENCRYPT NULL*
PASSWORD(pw)	encrypts the password with the algorithm that was used for storing passwords in the *USER* table; the result is a 16-character string; note that since MySQL 4.1, *PASSWORD* uses stronger encryption and returns a string of 45 characters
OLD_PASSWORD(pw)	encrypts the password as for *PASSWORD* under MySQL 3.23.*n* and 4.0.*n*; available since MySQL 4.1

Date and Time

There are various synonyms for the functions in the following table, *CUR-RENT_TIMESTAMP*, for example, as an alternative to *NOW()*, which have not been listed. The functions for dealing with dates and times generally assume that the initial data are correct. Thus do not expect a sensible result if you provide the date '*2003-02-31*'.

With all functions that return a time or date (or both), the format of the result depends on the context. Normally, the result is a character string (e.g., '*2003-12-31 23:59:59*'). However, if the function is used in a numerical computation, such as *NOW() + 0*, then the result is an integer of the form *20031231235959*.

Several of the functions listed in the table process Unix timestamps, and there is a MySQL data type for such timestamps. What, then, is a timestamp?

In Unix, time is counted for timestamps from 1 January 1970. Each second since then is counted. Since the (signed) integer used for this number was declared as a 32-bit integer, it will overflow in the year 2038. For the time period from 1970 to 2038, then, a timestamp is a practical affair: compact and simple to use. But then what?

First of all, there is still one bit in reserve if the timestamp is viewed as an unsigned integer. On this assumption we have until the beginning of the twenty-second century until overflow occurs. But on the other hand, it is expected that in the next few years, Unix/Linux will obtain a 64-bit timestamp. At that point, presumably, MySQL will be reconfigured. Because of the increased memory requirement (eight bytes instead of four), all tables will have to migrate to the new format. Presumably, there will be no problems with this, and the year 2000 problem will not repeat itself in 2038 (at least with respect to MySQL).

Using Dates and Times

CURDATE()	returns the current date in the form *'2003-12-31'*
CURTIME()	returns the current time either as a string or number, depending on context; e.g., *'23:59:59'* or 235959 (integer)
DATE_ADD(. . .)	adds a time interval to a starting time; see below
DATE_FORMAT(d, form)	formats *d* according to formatting string *f*; see below
DATE_SUB(. . .)	subtracts a time interval from the start time; see below
DAYNAME(date)	returns *'Monday'*, *'Tuesday'*, etc.
DAYOFMONTH(date)	returns the day of the month (1–31)
DAYOFWEEK(date)	returns the day of the week (1 = Sunday through 7 = Saturday)
DAYOFYEAR(date)	returns the day in the year (1–366)
EXTRACT(i FROM date)	returns a number for the desired interval
EXTRACT(YEAR FROM '2003-12-31')	returns 2003
FROM_DAYS(n)	returns the date *n* days after the year 0
FROM_DAYS(3660)	returns *'0010-01-08'*
FROM_UNIXTIME(t)	transforms the Unix timestamp number *t* into a date
FROM_UNIXTIME(0)	returns *'1970-01-01 01:00:00'*
FROM_UNIXTIME(t, f)	as above, but with formatting as in *DATE_FORMAT*
HOUR(time)	returns the hour (0–23)
MINUTE(time)	returns the minute (0–59)
MONTH(date)	returns the month (1–12)
MONTHNAME(date)	returns the name of the month (*'January'*, etc.)
NOW()	returns the current time in the form *'2003-12-31 23:59:59'*
QUARTER(date)	returns the quarter (1–4)
SECOND(time)	returns the second (0–59)
SEC_TO_TIME(n)	returns the time *n* seconds after midnight
SEC_TO_TIME(3603)	returns *'01:00:03'*
TIME_FORMAT(time, f)	like *DATE_FORMAT*, but for times only
TIME_TO_SEC(time)	returns the seconds since midnight
TO_DAYS(date)	returns the number of days since the year 0
UNIX_TIMESTAMP()	returns the current time as a Unix timestamp number
UNIX_TIMESTAMP(d)	returns the timestamp number for the given date
WEEK(date)	returns week number (1 for the week beginning with the first Sunday in the year)
WEEK(date, day)	as above, but specifies with *day* the day on which the week should begin (0 = Sunday, 1 = Monday, etc.)
WEEKDAY(date)	returns the day of the week (0 = Monday, 1 = Tuesday, etc.)
YEAR(date)	returns the year

Calculating with Dates

DATE_ADD(date, INTERVAL n i) adds *n* times the interval *i* to the starting date *date*. Our first example shows how intelligently the function deals with ends of months (31.12 or 28.2):

> *DATE_ADD('2003-12-31', INTERVAL 2 month)* returns *'2004-02-28'*
> *DATE_ADD('2003-12-31', INTERVAL '3:30' HOUR_MINUTE)* returns *'2003-12-31 03:30:00'*

Intervals for DATE_ADD, DATE_SUB, EXTRACT

SECOND	*n*
MINUTE	*n*
HOUR	*n*
DAY	*n*
MONTH	*n*
YEAR	*n*
HOUR_MINUTE	*'hh:mm'*
HOUR_SECOND	*'hh:mm:ss'*
MINUTE_SECOND	*'mm:ss'*
DAY_HOUR	*'dd hh'*
DAY_MINUTE	*'dd hh:mm'*
DAY_SECOND	*'dd hh:mm:ss'*
YEAR_MONTH	*'yy-mm'*

Formatting Dates and Times

DATE_FORMAT(date, format) helps in representing dates and times in other formats than the usual MySQL format. Two examples illustrate the syntax:

> *DATE_FORMAT('2003-12-31', '%M %d %Y')* returns *'December 31 2003'*
> *DATE_FORMAT('2003-12-31', '%D of %M')* returns *'31st of December'*

Names of days of the week, months, etc., are always given in English, regardless of the MySQL language setting (*language* option).

Time Symbols in DATE_FORMAT, TIME_FORMAT, and FROM_UNIXTIME

%S, %s	seconds, two-digit	00–59
%i	minutes, two-digit	00–59
%k	hours (24-hour clock)	0–23
%H	hours, two-digit, 0 to 23 o'clock	00–23
%l	hours (12-hour clock)	1–12
%h, %I	hours, two-digit, to 12 o'clock	01–12
%T	24-hour clock	00:00:00 to 23:59:59
%r	12-hour clock	12:00:00 AM to 11:59:59 PM
%p	AM or PM	AM, PM

Date Symbols in DATE_FORMAT, TIME_FORMAT, FROM_UNIXTIME

%W	day of week	Monday to Sunday
%a	day of week abbreviated	Mon to Sun
%e	day of month	1–31
%d	day of month two-digit	01–31
%D	day of month with ending	1st, 2nd, 3rd, 4th . . .
%w	day of week as number	0 (Sunday)–6 (Saturday)
%j	day in year, three-digit	001–366
%U	week number, two-digit (Sunday)	00–52
%u	week number, two-digit (Monday)	00–52
%M	name of month	January–December
%b	name of month abbreviated	Jan–Dec
%c	month number	1–12
%m	month number, two-digit	01–12
%Y	year, four-digit	2002, 2003, . . .
%y	year, two-digit	00, 01, . . .
%%	the symbol %	%

A few remarks about the week number are in order: *%U* returns 0 for the days from before the first Sunday in the year. From the first Sunday until the following Saturday, it returns 1, then 2, etc. With *%u* you get the same thing, with the first Sunday replaced by the first Monday.

GROUP BY *Functions*

The following functions can be used in *SELECT* queries (frequently in combination with *GROUP BY*):

```
USE mylibrary
SELECT catName, COUNT(titleID) FROM titles, categories
WHERE titles.catID=categories.catID
GROUP BY catName
ORDER BY catName
```

catName	COUNT(titleID)
Children's books	3
Computer books	5
Databases	2
. . .	

Since MySQL 4.1, the desired sort order can be specified in some aggregate functions, as in *MAX(column COLLATE collname)*.

Aggregate Functions

AVG(expr)	computes the average of *expr*
BIT_AND(expr)	performs a bitwise AND of *expr*
BIT_OR(expr)	performs a bitwise OR of *expr*
COUNT(expr)	returns the number of *expr*
COUNT(DISTINCT expr)	returns the number of different *expr* expressions
MAX(expr)	returns the maximum of *expr*
MIN(expr)	returns the minimum of *expr*
STD(expr)	computes the standard deviation of *expr*
STDDEV(expr)	like *STD(expr)*
SUM(expr)	computes the sum of *expr*
VARIANCE(expr)	computes the variance of *expr* (since MySQL 4.1)

Additional Functions

Administrative Functions

BENCHMARK(n, expr)	executes *expr* a total of *n* times and measures the time elapsed
CONNECTION_ID()	returns the ID number of the current database connection
CURRENT_USER()	returns the name of the current user in the form in which authentication takes place (that is, with the IP number instead of the host name, e.g., *"radha@127.0.0.1"*)
DATABASE()	returns the name of the current database
FOUND_ROWS()	returns since MySQL 4.0 the number of records found by a *SELECT LIMIT* query if in the *SELECT* command, the option *SQL_CALC_FOUND_ROWS* was used
GET_LOCK(name, time)	defines a lock with the name *name* for the time *time* (in seconds); usually executed with *DO*, as in *DO GET_LOCK('abc', 10)*
IDENTITY()	since MySQL 4.0 equivalent to *LAST_INSERT_ID()*
IS_FREE_LOCK(name)	tests whether the lock *name* is available; returns 0 if the lock is currently in use (thus before *GET_LOCK* was executed), otherwise, 1
LAST_INSERT_ID()	returns the *AUTO_INCREMENT* number most recently generated within the current connection to the database
RELEASE_LOCK(name)	releases the lock *name*
SESSION_USER()	equivalent to *USER()*
SYSTEM_USER()	equivalent to *USER()*
USER()	returns the name of the current user and associated host name (e.g., *"root@localhost"*)
VERSION()	returns the MySQL version number as a string

Miscellaneous

BIT_COUNT(x)	returns the number of set bits
COALESCE(list)	returns the first element of the list that is not *NULL*
LOAD_FILE(filename)	loads a file from the local file system

The two functions *GET_LOCK* and *RELEASE_LOCK* do not execute a lock; that is, neither MySQL nor a database is blocked. These functions serve, rather, for communication between processes. As long as a process has a lock with a particular name defined, no other process can obtain a lock with the same name. The second process in this case receives, with *GET_LOCK*, the return value 0 and therefore knows that currently another process has obtained a lock. (As a rule, the second process must just wait a bit and then try again.)

#### CHAPTER 19

MySQL Tools

THIS CHAPTER IS A REFERENCE for the options and functions of the most important MySQL tools. We discuss the server mysqld, the monitor mysql, and the administration tools mysqladmin, myisamchk, etc.

These tools have a number of common options, and they evaluate configuration files in the same manner. For this reason, the chapter begins with a section describing these common properties.

Chapter Overview

Overview

The common feature exhibited by the commands introduced in this section is that they are launched as external programs in a command window (Windows) or in a command shell (Unix/Linux). The entire operation of these programs is carried out in text mode and is therefore not what one would term excessively convenient. However, these commands are very well suited for execution in scripts in the automation of administrative tasks.

The following list provides an overview of the commands discussed in this section.

MySQL Server and Included Administration Tools

`mysqld*`	starts the MySQL server, known under Unix/Linux as the MySQL daemon (whence the letter "d"); under Windows, there are several variants (`mysqld`, `mysqld-nt`, `mysqld-opt`); see Chapter 2
`mysqld_safe`	should be used under Unix/Linux for a secure server launch
`mysql`	enables interactive execution of SQL commands
`mysqladmin`	assists in various administrative tasks (display status, reinput privileges, execute shutdown, etc.)
`mysqldump`	saves contents of a MySQL database in a text file
`mysqlimport`	inputs a table from a text file
`mysqlshow`	displays information on databases, tables, and columns
`mysqlbug`	sends (via e-mail) an error message (Unix/Linux only)
`myisamchk`	checks the integrity of MyISAM table files and repairs them as necessary
`myisampack`	compresses MyISAM table files for more efficient read-only access

POINTER *The two Perl scripts* `mysqlaccess` *and* `mysql_setpermission` *assist in the administration of MySQL access privileges. These scripts were described in Chapter 9, in the discussion of managing access privileges.*

There are several additional scripts and programs for special tasks, and these were presented in Chapter 10 (e.g., `mysqlhotcopy`*). However, some of these programs are available only under Unix/Linux.*

REMARK *Most of the commands presented here are compiled programs (*`*.exe` *under Windows). However, others are in script form and can be executed only if a suitable script interpreter is installed. This is usually the case under Unix/Linux. Under Windows, it may be that you have to install Perl yourself (see Chapter 2).*

Common Options and Configuration Files

A common feature of the programs described in this chapter is that there are certain options that can be used by almost all of the commands, and these options can be preset in a common configuration file, so as to save typing when the commands are invoked.

Common Options

Various options can be passed to all commands when they are executed. As is usual with Unix/Linux, commands can be prefixed with a hyphen (short form) or two hyphens (full option name). Please note that the short forms of options are case-sensitive.

Common Options of `mysql`, `mysqladmin`, `mysqld`, `mysqldump`, `mysqlimport`, `myisamchk`, `myisampack`

`--help`	displays a brief operation introduction
`--print-defaults`	displays default values for options; default values can come from configuration files or system variables
`--nodefaults`	causes no configuration files to be read at startup
`--defaults-file=`*filename*	causes only this configuration file to be read at startup
`--defaults-extra-file=`*filename*	first the global configuration file is read, and then *filename*, and finally (only under Unix/Linux), the user-specific configuration file
`--port=`*n*	specifies the TCP/IP port over which communication takes place (usually 3306)
`--socket=filename`	specifies which socket file should be used for local communication between client and server (only under Unix/Linux; by default usually `/var/lib/mysql/mysql.sock`)
`--version`	displays the version number of the program

Common Options of the MySQL Client Tools

-u *un*	--user=*username*	determines the username for registration with MySQL
-p	--password	asks for input of password immediately after start of the command
-p*xxx*	--password=*xxx*	passes the password directly; in contrast to other options, there can be no space after -p; this is more convenient than interactive input of the password, but it can represent a considerable security risk and thus should generally be avoided; under some operating systems, any user can see the password by looking at the process list
h *emphhn*	--host=*hostname*	gives the name of the computer on which the server is running (assumed by default to be *localhost*, that is, the local computer)
-W	--pipe	uses a *named pipe* for communication with the MySQL server. Named pipes are available only for local connections under Windows NT/2000/XP and only if MySQL was appropriately compiled (which is not the default)
-C	--compress	minimizes the data flow between client and server by making use of data compression

TIP *For a connection to the MySQL server to be at all possible, the following two options must generally be used at the start of each client command:*

```
> mysql -u username -p
Enter Password: xxxxxx
```

If MySQL is not yet password-secured, then this will work, of course, without a password being specified. Information on user and privilege management in MySQL can be found in Chapter 9.

CAUTION *If you execute MySQL commands under Windows and create a directory with options, then instead of the backslash you should use the forward slash (/). If the file name contains space characters, then put the entire path in quotation marks, as in the following example:*

```
--character-sets-dir="Q:/Program Files/mysql/share/charsets"
```

Setting Options in Configuration Files

If you observe that you are using particular options over and over, you can save these in options files for many of the commands covered in this section. The options are used by mysql, mysqladmin, mysqld, mysqldump, mysqlimport, myisamchk, myisampack, and mysqld_safe.

The following list collects the locations where the options files must be stored. At startup, all options files—those that exist already—are read in the order in which they are listed below. In the case of contradictory settings, the most recently read options file takes precedence. (Whether and what configuration files will be read depends on the options --no-defaults, --defaults-file, and --defaults-extra-file; see above.)

Where Options Files Are Stored

Validity	Windows	Unix/Linux
global options	C:\my.cnf, Windows\my.ini	/etc/my.cnf
user-specific options (no evaluation by mysqld)		~/.my.cnf
server-specifc options (for mysqld only)	DATADIR\my.cnf	DATADIR/my.cnf

The directory DATADIR is the default directory, which during compilation of MySQL is provided as data directory. Under Windows, this is normally C:\mysql\data, while under Unix/Linux, it is generally /var/lib/mysql. Note that DATADIR need not be the directory in which MySQL actually stores the database files. This directory is usually set when the MySQL server is launched with the option --datadir. However, access to the configuration file takes place before this option is evaluated.

The syntax of the file is based on the following pattern:

```
# comment
[programname]
option1  # equivalent to --option1
option2=abc  # equivalent to --option2=abc
```

These options are divided into groups for each program. Instead of *programname*, you should specify the name of the program:

- Settings that are to be used by all programs other than mysqld are assigned to the group [client].

- Settings that relate only to the server are assigned to the group [mysqld]. (The group [server] is also used by mysqld.)

- Settings special to the program *xyz* are assigned to the group [*xyz*].

Here, option is the option name in long form, but without hyphens. (So, for example, the option --host in the configuration file becomes simply host.) If options expect parameters, then these are specified with =.

> **REMARK** *In MySQL 3.23, there was a distinction between options and variables in the configuration settings. Variables had to be set with* set-variable varname=value. *Beginning with MySQL 4.0, the intuitive short form* varname=value *is permitted, regardless of whether a configuration key word is considered an option or a variable. (The old form continues to be accepted.)*

Let us see, finally, a concrete example of a configuration file:

```
# configuration file /etc/my.cnf or Windows\my.ini
# options for all MySQL tools
[client]
user=username
password=xxx
host=uranus.sol
# options for mysqldump
[mysqldump]
force
# options for mysql (monitor)
[mysql]
safe-updates
select_limit=100
```

> **TIP** *Changes to configuration files are effective only after a restart of the program in question. This holds in particular for the MySQL server (thus for options in the group* [mysqld]*).*

> **CAUTION** *Please be sure that the options specified in the* [client] *section are truly supported by all MySQL tools. If a MySQL tool finds an unknown option in the* [client] *section, then the command is terminated with an error message.*

> **CAUTION** *If you wish under Unix/Linux to execute user-specific options settings in* ~/.my.cnf *and possibly specify passwords there, then ensure that no other users are able to read this file.*
>
> user$ **chmod 600 ~/.my.cnf**

> **CAUTION** *If you specify Windows paths or directories in a configuration file, then you must use / or \\ instead of the backslash \. (In the Windows version of MySQL, the backslash is used as escape character.)*
>
> *Furthermore, paths cannot be placed in quotation marks within a configuration file (even if the path contains space characters).*
>
> *Please note that these rules are different from those that obtain for a direct setting of options with --option = ...*

> **TIP** *Under Unix/Linux, you can use the program* my_print_defaults *grp to determine the options set for* [grp] *in the configuration file. The program is particularly suited for use in custom scripts.*

Memory Specifications

For options and variables that expect a memory specification, the letters K, M, G may be used to denote kilobytes (1024 bytes), megabytes, and gigabytes. Thus the settings key_buffer_size=16M, key_buffer_size=16384K, and key_buffer_size=16777216 are equivalent.

Options in Environment Variables (aka System Variables)

An additional possibility for specifying options are environment variables at the level of the operating system. (Under Windows, these variables are usually known as system variables.)

The following list names the most important of these variables. To set such variables under Windows, you use the dialog for system control (see Figure 4-1). Under Linux you can define such variables in script files (e.g., in /etc/profile or ~/.profile) with export. Depending on which shell you use, you may use the command declare -x or setenv instead of export.

Import and Environment Variables for mysql, mysqladmin, mysqld, mysqldump, ...

MYSQL_TCP_PORT	specifies the port number for the TCP/IP connection to MySQL (generally 3306)
MYSQL_UNIX_PORT	specifies the socket file for local communication under Linux/Unix (e.g., /var/mysql.lock)
TMPDIR	specifies the directory to be used for temporary files; this directory is also used for temporary tables
USER	specifies the user name

Precedence

Option settings are read in the following order: environment variables, configuration files, options at program startup.

In the case of contradictory settings, the last setting read takes precedence. For example, options at program startup supersede settings in environment variables.

New in MySQL 4.0

There are many changes relating to options and configuration settings beginning with MySQL 4.0.2:

- As already mentioned, variables can now be specified directly (thus `--variable=123` instead of `--setvariable variable=123`). This holds as well for settings in configuration files.

- A hyphen may replace an underscore in variable names (thus `--variable-name=123` instead of `--variable_name=123`).

- Options that activate a particular function were previously used simply in the form `--option`. Now, with many such options, several forms are permitted for activating or deactivating a function:

`--option`	activates the function (as previously)
`--option=1`	activates the function
`--enable-option`	activates the function
`--option=0`	deactivates the function
`--disable-option`	deactivates the function
`--skip-option`	deactivates the function

  Note, however, that there are options like `--skip-grant-tables` for which `skip` is an integral part of the operator name. In this case, `--enable-grant-tables` and `-grant-tables=0` do not function.

- There are MySQL server variables that can be changed by the user at run time specifically for the currently active connection. To do this, the user simply executes an SQL command like *SET read_buffer_size=16M*. For such variables, an upper bound can be set at server start by prefixing `--maximum`, as in `--maximum-read_buffer_size=32M`.

- Every new version of MySQL offers new options. If you are writing a script and do not wish to prescribe a particular version of MySQL, you may use the new option `--loose` as a prefix (e.g., `--loose-`*optionname*`=3`). If the option exists, it will be properly set. On the other hand, if the program does not recognize the option, then the setting is ignored without an error message.

Since the syntax of MySQL 3.23 is still allowed for compatibility, there are often various ways of making a particular configuration setting. This situation makes a complete and standardized documentation difficult.

mysqld (Server)

The following lists, organized by topic, summarize the most-used mysqld options.

> **POINTER** *A complete reference to the long list of* mysqld *options can be obtained in* mysqld --help. *In the MySQL documentation there is unfortunately no unified description of all options. Instead, it is distributed among a number of sections (e.g., replication options, InnoDB options). The following addresses will lead you to the most important of these:*
>
> http://www.mysql.com/doc/en/Command-line_options.html
> http://www.mysql.com/doc/en/Privileges_options.html
> http://www.mysql.com/doc/en/Replication_Options.html
> http://www.mysql.com/doc/en/InnoDB_start.html

The MySQL server is generally started as a service (Windows NT/2000/XP) or via the script mysqld_safe (Unix/Linux). In such a case, it is impossible to specify options directly. Therefore, mysqld options are specified almost exclusively in configuration files. For this reason, in the following tables, the options are given in the manner in which they would appear in a configuration file (that is, without the prefixed --).

Two exceptions are the options --defaults-extra-file and --user:

- With --defaults-extra-file=*filename*, an additional configuration file can be specified that is read after all other configuration files.

- user=*name* specifies the Unix/Linux account under which mysqld is to be executed. For a change of account to take place at the start of MySQL, mysqld must be started by *root*. Normally, mysqld is started by the script mysqld_safe with --user =mysql.

Both options must be passed directly to mysqld or to the start script mysqld_safe. They cannot be specified in a configuration file.

Basic Settings

mysqld *Language Setting*

default-characterset=*name*	specifies the character set to be used (for sorting, comparison, etc.)
language=*name*	specifies the language in which error messages, etc., are to be output

`mysqld` *Directories and Files*

basedir=path	uses the given directory as base directory (installation directory)
character-sets-dir=*path*	specifies the directory for the character set files
datadir=*path*	reads database files from the specified directory
pid-file= *filename*	specifies the file in which the process ID number should be stored (under Unix/Linux only); the file is evaluated by the init-V script to terminate `mysqld`
socket=*filename*	specifies the file name `mysql.sock` (only Unix/Linux, by default generally /var/lib/mysql/mysql.sock)
lower_case_table_names=1/0	specifies whether in the creation of new directories and tables, lowercase should be used exclusively; under Windows, since MySQL 4.0.2 and 4.1.1 default is 1

`mysqld` *Security, Network Access*

enable-named-pipes	enables a connection under Windows NT/2000/XP between client and server with named pipes; this option has effect only if the MySQL server was compiled to support named pipes
local-infile[=0]	activates/deactivates the ability to process local files with *LOAD DATA LOCAL*
myisam-recover[=opt1, opt2, ...]	has the effect that at startup, all damaged MyISAM tables are automatically restored; the possible options are *DEFAULT*, *BACKUP*, *QUICK*, and *FORCE*; they correspond to the `myisamchk` options
old-passwords	passwords in the *mysql* database in MySQL 4.1 are encrypted as in MySQL 3.23 and 4.0 (by default, a new, more secure, encryption is used); this option is available since MySQL 4.1
safe-user-create	a user can create a new user with *GRANT* only if he has the *Insert* privilege for the table *mysql.user*; this is a supplementary security mechanism (the user also needs the *Grant* privilege to be able to execute *GRANT*
skip-grant-tables	omits input of *mysql* database with access information; (caution: anyone can change any database!)
skip-host-cache	a cache is not used to store the association between computer names and IP numbers
skip-name-resolve	suppresses the resolution of IP numbers into the corresponding host names, resulting in access control (table *mysql.user*) exclusively via IP numbers
skip-networking	permits only local connections over a socket file (Unix/Linux) or over named pipes (Windows), not over TCP/IP; this increases security but excludes external connections over a network and excludes all Java clients (which use TCP/IP even in a local connection)
user=*name*	specifies the Unix/Linux account under which `mysqld` is to be executed; for the switch to work after startup, `mysqld` must be started up from *root*; normally, `mysqld` is started via the script `mysqld_safe` with user=*mysql*

mysqld: *Memory Usage, Tuning, Query Cache*

bulk_insert_buffer_size=*n*	specifies how much memory is allocated for executing *INSERT* commands in which many records are simultaneously inserted (default 8 megabytes)
key_buffer_size=*n*	specifies how much RAM is reserved for index blocks (default 8 megabytes).
join_buffer_size=*n*	specifies how much memory is to be allocated for *JOIN* operations when there is no index for the *JOIN* columns (default 128 kilobytes)
max_heap_table_size=*n*	specifies the maximum size of *HEAP* tables (default 16 megabytes); if this size is exceeded, the table is stored in a temporary file instead of in RAM
max_connections=*n*	specifies the maximum number of simultaneous database connections (default 100)
query_cache_limit=*n*	specifies the maximum size of a query result to be stored in the query cache (default 1 megabyte)
query_cache_size=*n*	specifies the size of the query cache (by default 0, meaning that the query cache is inactive)
query_cache_type=0/1/2	specifies the mode in which query cache runs: 0: query cache is off 1: query cache is on (default mode) 2: demand mode only for *SELECT SQL_CACHE*
read_buffer_size=*n*	specifies how much memory is reserved for each thread for reading sequential data from tables (default 128 kilobytes); the parameter can be set as needed with *SET SESSION read_buffer_size=n*
read_rnd_buffer_size=*n*	similar to read_buffer_size, but holds for the case that the records are to be output in a particular order, e.g., with *ORDER BY* (default 256 kilobytes)
sort_buffer=*n*	specifies the size of the buffer for sorting (default 2 megabytes); if the buffer is too small, a temporary file must be used
table_cache=*n*	specifies the maximum number of open tables (default 64)
tmp_table_size=*n*	specifies the maximum size of temporary *HEAP* tables (default 32 megabytes); if this size is exceeded, the tables are transformed to MyISAM tables and stored in a temporary file

Logging, Replication

mysqld Logging

log[=*file*]	logs every connection as well as all SQL commands (general query log); if no file name is specified, then MySQL uses the file name *hostname.log* in the database directory
log-slow-queries[=*file*]	logs queries whose execution takes longer than the time specified in the variable *long_query_time* (slow query log)
long_query_time=*n*	specifies the time limit for slow queries (default 10 seconds)
log-long-format	logs not only slow queries, but also all queries that are carried out without the use of an index (holds for log-slow-queries)
log-bin[=*filename*]	logs all SQL commands that make a change in the data, in particular, all *INSERT, UPDATE,* and *DELETE* commands; a binary format is used (binary update log); as file name, file.*n* or the default *hostname*.n is used, where *n* is a three-digit integer (the logging files are sequentially numbered)
log-bin-index=*filename*	specifies the file name for the index file for binary logging
max_binlog_size=*n*	specifies the maximal size of a binary logging file (default 1 gigabyte)
binlog-do-db=*dbname*	limits binary logging to the specified database; changes in other databases are not logged; to specify more than one database, the option must be repeated in the configuration file, one database in each line
binlog-ignore-db=*dbname*	excludes the database from binary logging; changes in this database are not logged
log-update[=*file]*	has the same function as log-bin, but the logging is in text format (text update log); use the more efficient binary logging if you can
log-error=*file*	specifies the file name for the error logging file (error log); this logging variant cannot be deactivated; if the option is not specified, MySQL uses the file name *hostname*.err

mysqld Replication (Master)

server-id=*n*	assigns the server a unique ID number; *n* can be between 1 and 2^{31}
log-bin	activates binary logging
binlog-do/ignore-db=*dbname*	logs only the specified databases or ignores the specified databases in logging

mysqld *Replication (Slave)*

server-id=*n*	assigns a unique ID number to the server
log-slave-updates	executes logging on the slave so that the computer can be used to continue a replication chain ($A \rightarrow B \rightarrow C$)
master-host=*hostname*	specifies the host name or IP address of the replication master; this setting is ignored once replication is set up if the file master.info exists
master-user=*replicusername*	specifies the user name for replication communication; ignored once master.info exists
master-password=*pword*	specifies the associated password; ignored if master.info exists
master-port=*n*	specifies the port number of the master server (default 3306); ignored if master.info exists
master-connect-retry=*n*	specifies after how many seconds an attempt to reestablish a broken connection to the master can be made (default 60); ignored if master.info exists
master-ssl-*xxx*=*xxx*	enables the configuration of SSL communication between master and slave; according to the MySQL documentation (as of version 4.0.12), it has not been adequately tested
replicate-do-table =*dbname.tablename*	replicates only this table; to specify more than one table, the option must be repeated (each table requires its own line in the configuration file)
replicate-wild-do-table =*dbname.tablename*	functions like replicate-do-table except that the wild card % is allowed to form a pattern (e.g., test%.% to replicate all tables of all databases whose name begins with test)
replicate-do-db=*dbname*	replicates only this database
replicate-ignore-table =*dbname.tablename*	excludes this table from replication
replicate-wild-ignore-table =*dbn.tablen*	excludes these tables from replication
replicate-do-db=*dbname*	excludes this database from replication
replicate-rewrite-db =*db1name->db2name*	replicates the database db1name on the master under the name db2name on the slave
report-host=*hostname*	specifies the host name of the slave; this information is relevant only for the command *SHOW SLAVE HOSTS*, which allows on the master system the creation of a list of all slaves
slave_compressed_protocol=1	enables compressed communication between master and slave if both servers are capable of it
slave-skip-errors=*n1,n2, ...* or all	continues replication even if errors *n1*, *n2*, etc., have occurred, or (with all) regardless of any errors being triggered; under a correct configuration, no errors should occur on the slave due to SQL commands being executed (if an error occurs on the master, the command is not replicated); without slave-skip-errors, replication is stopped by an error and must be manually resumed

InnoDB Configuration

mysqld *InnoDB: General Settings,* Tablespace Files

`skip-innodb`	specifies that the InnoDB table driver should not be loaded; useful to save memory when no InnoDB tables are to be used
`innodb_data_home_dir=`*p*	specifies the InnoDB directory; all additional directory or file specifications are relative to the path p; by default, the InnoDB driver uses the MySQL data directory
`innodb_data_file_path=`*ts*	specifies the tablespace for all InnoDB tables; can involve more than one file; the size of each file must be specified in bytes, megabytes (M), or gigabytes (G); the names of the tablespace files are separated by semi-colons; for the last of the tablespace files, the attribute autoextend and a maximal size (`max:n`) can be specified (e.g., `ibdata1:1G;ibdata2:1G:autoextend:max:2G`, by which `ibdata1` has size 1 gigabyte, `ibdata2` is set up with the same size and can grow as large as 2 gigabytes); instead of a file, the device name of a hard-drive partition can be given; in this case, the key word `newraw` must follow the exact size for initialization, and for further use, the key word `raw` (e.g., `/dev/hdb1:20Gnewraw` or `/dev/hdb1:20Graw`); the default setting since MySQL 4.0 is `ibdata1:10M:autoextend`
`innodb_lock_wait_timeout=`*n*	specifies how long (in seconds) should be waited for the release of locks; after this time, the transaction is broken off with *ROLLBACK*; the setting is especially important when deadlocks develop that the InnoDB driver does not recognize; the default value is 50 seconds
`innodb_fast_shutdown=On/Off`	specifies whether InnoDB should shut down as quickly as possible; in the default setting On, InnoDB does not transfer the *INSERT* buffer into the tables; this process is repeated at the next start of the MySQL server (the setting On does not represent a risk, since the *INSERT* buffer is a component of the tablespace; thus no data can be lost; the setting Off is more dangerous, since in a computer shutdown it could happen that InnoDB would not have enough time for its synchronization work and would be stopped in its tracks by the operating system)

mysqld *Options: InnoDB Tables*

mysqld *InnoDB: Logging*

innodb_log_group_home_dir=*lp*	specifies the directory for InnoDB logging files (ib_logfile0, 1, etc.); by default, the InnoDB driver uses the MySQL data directory
innodb_log_files_in_group=*n*	specifies how many logging files should be used (default is 2); the InnoDB table driver fills these files sequentially; when all files are full, the first is overwritten with data, etc.
innodb_log_file_size=*n*	specifies how large each logging file should be (default 5 megabytes); the size specification uses M for megabytes and G for gigabytes
innodb_flush_log_at_trx_commit=0/1/2	determines when data should be written to the logging file and when these files should be synchronized (that is, when changes should be physically stored to the hard disk); the default setting 0 means that the data are written and synchronized about once per second; the setting 1 is more secure (save and synchronize after each *COMMIT*); a compromise is the setting 2, with writing after *COMMIT* and synchronization only about once per second
innodb_flush_method=*x*	under Unix/Linux, specifies how logging files are synchronized (i.e., how they are stored on the hard drive); choices are fdatasync: synchronization with *fsync()* (default) and O_DSYNC: update with *O_SYNC()*
innodb_log_archive=1	activates archive logging in the files ib_arch_log_*n*; this type of logging does not make sense when InnoDB is used together with MySQL (instead, use binary logging of the MySQL server); archive logging is therefore by default deactivated immediately after the start of the MySQL server (only the creation of the new tablespace or transaction logging files are logged)

mysqld *InnoDB: Buffer Settings and Tuning*

innodb_buffer_pool_size=*n*	specifies how much RAM should be used for table data and indexes (default 8 megabytes); this parameter has considerable influence on speed and should be up to 80% of available RAM on computers used exclusively as MySQL/InnoDB database servers
innodb_log_buffer_size=*n*	specifies how much RAM should be used for writing the transaction logging files (default 1 megabyte)
innodb_additional_mem_pool_size=*n*	specifies how much RAM should be used for various internal management structures (default 1 megabyte)
innodb_file_io_threads=*n*	specifies how many threads for I/O operations, that is, for access to the hard drive, should be used (default 4)
innodb_thread_concurrency=*n*	specifies how many threads InnoDB should use altogether (default 8)

mysqld *Miscellaneous*

bind-address=ipadr	specifies the IP address that MySQL should use; this option is important if the computer is so configured that it uses several IP addresses
default-table-type=type	specifies the table type that new tables are to use if the type is not explicitly given (default is *MyISAM*)
ft_min_word_len=n	specifies the minimal word length for a full-text index; in the default setting 4, words with three or fewer letters are not included
max-allowed-packet=n	specifies the maximum packet size for data exchange between client and server; max-allowed-packet must be at least as large as the largest *BLOB* to be processed by client programs; default is 1 megabyte
new	makes MySQL 4.0 behave is some ways like MySQL 4.1; this enables uncomplicated testing of many changes; at the moment, all that is affected is the representation of *TIMESTAMP*s in the new form *YYYY-MM-DD HH:MM:DD*
port=n	specifies the IP port that the server should use (default 3306)

> **CAUTION** *If you specify an option in a configuration file that* mysqld *does not know about (for example, due to a silly typo), then the server cannot start up. So watch out!*

mysqld_safe (Server Start)

Under Unix/Linux, the MySQL server is usually started by an Init-V script (e.g., /etc/init.d/mysql or /etc/init.d/mysql). This script is automatically executed at the startup of the operating system. It does not directly launch the server, but instead, executes the script mysqld_safe. It is this script that starts the MySQL server. (In MySQL 3.23, the script is called safe_mysqld.)

The script mysqld_safe is started with *root* privileges. The MySQL server, on the other hand, is started with the privileges of a user designed for this purpose (normally with the name *mysql*).

After the start of the MySQL server, mysqld_safe continues to run until it is explicitly ended (e.g., with mysqladmin shutdown). If the MySQL server is ended unexpectedly due to a crash, then it is immediately restarted by mysqld_safe.

Usually, only a few options are passed to mysqld_safe (e.g., --data-dir and --pid-file), which transmit the script to the MySQL server mysqld. There are also some options specifically for mysqld_safe.

mysqld_safe *Options*

--core-file-size=*n*	limits the size of the core file, which contains an image of the server after a crash and makes debugging possible; *n* must be given in bytes
--ledir=*dirname*	specifies the directory in which the MySQL server is located (by default /usr/sbin)
--mysqld=*filename*	specifies the name of the MySQL server that is to be started (default mysqld)
--mysqld-version=*suffix*	specifies an extension to the server name (e.g., max if mysqld-max should be started instead of mysqld)

mysql_install_db (New Installation of *mysql* Database)

Under Unix/Linux, the *mysql* database can be freshly installed with the script mysql_install_db. For this, the server must be stopped. (The script starts the server itself with the option --bootstrap.)

Among other things, the script must be executed in the same account as is used for executing the MySQL server (usually *mysql*). You can also execute mysql_install_db as *root*, in which case you must subsequently change the owner of the database directory mysql and the files contained therein:

```
root#mysql_install_db
root# chown mysql -R /var/lib/mysql/mysql
```

The script is generally executed automatically as a component of a new MySQL installation. The script is also suited to recreating the default state of the *mysql* database.

> **CAUTION** *In a test, the script used* uranus *as the local host name, although the complete computer name is* uranus.sol. *The use of an abbreviated computer name can lead to login problems. It may be necessary to place the complete computer name manually in the* mysql.user *table (see also Chapter 9).*

Although mysql_install_db is available under Windows (directory scripts), execution of it fails for the lack of a suitable shell interpreter.

mysql_fix_privileges (Updating the *mysql* Database)

The *mysql* database for managing MySQL access privileges is being continually extended and improved. If you carry out a MySQL update and use the *mysql* database from a previous installation (see Chapter 10), you should execute the script mysql_fix_privileges, which updates the database, inserts new columns as necessary, etc. The single parameter that must be passed to the script is the MySQL *root* password.

After the script has been executed, there is generally some work that has to be done by hand, because the script does not always know whether certain new privileges should be set. In case of doubt, the script elects not to set, which is more secure, but for some MySQL users, it reduces their privileges with respect to previous versions of MySQL.

Although the script is available under Windows (directory `scripts`) as well as under Unix/Linux, execution under Windows fails for the lack of a suitable shell interpreter.

mysql_fix_extensions (Renaming MyISAM Files)

In transferring database directories with MyISAM tables from Windows to Unix/Linux, the problem sometimes occurs that the case (upper/lower) of the file identifier is incorrect. (Unix/Linux is case-sensitive, while Windows could use some case-sensitivity training.) MySQL expects, for example, *.frm, but *.MYI and *.MYD.

The Perl script `mysql_fix_extensions` solves this problem. For some strange reason, in MySQL 4.0, the script is included only with the Windows version of MySQL (directory `scripts`), although it is usually used under Unix/Linux after table files have been copied onto a Unix/Linux computer. (With MySQL 4.1, the script is also installed with the Linux version.)

The single parameter passed to the script is the name of the MySQL data directory. There are no options.

mysql (SQL Command Interpreter)

The monitor `mysql` allows interactive execution of SQL commands. This program can also be run in batch mode for many administrative tasks, including the generation of HTML tables. The commands are input from a file with `< file`. All SQL commands can be used in this file. The commands must be followed by a semicolon. Comments are introduced with the character #. (All additional characters to the end of the line are then ignored.)

At the launch of `mysql`, numerous options can be specified. Furthermore, an optional database name can be given, in which case this database becomes the default database (corresponds to the command *USE databasename*).

mysql: *Syntax*

```
mysql [options] [databasename] [ < commands.sql]
```

mysql: *General Options*

-e *cmd*	--execute=*cmd*	executes the given command(s); commands must be separated by semicolons and placed in quotation marks;
-i	--ignore-space	recognizes functions even if there are spaces between function names and their parameters; with -i, for example, *SUM (price)* is allowed, while without the option it must be written *SUM(price)*
-L	--skip-line-numbers	displays error messages without line numbers; the line numbers otherwise displayed refer to the location at which the faulty SQL command is located in a batch file and is generally an aid in debugging
-U	--i-am-a-dummy or --safe-updates	permits *UPDATE* and *DELETE* commands only if the effective range is limited with *WHERE* or *LIMIT*; furthermore, there is a maximum number of query results from *SELECT* commands as well as a maximum number of *JOIN*s
-V	--version	displays the version of mysql; mysql is then terminated
	--tee=*filename*	copies all input and output into the specified logging file; this option is allowed only if mysql is used in interactive mode (not in batch mode)
	--no-tee	does not use logging (the default)

mysql: *Formatting and Output Options*

-B	--batch	separates columns in tables by tab characters (instead of by spaces and lines); moreover, only results of queries are displayed, and no status information
-E	--vertical	lists the results of queries with columns displayed horizontally, one below the next (instead of with vertical columns, one next to the other); this option is particularly to be recommended if a query returns many columns but few rows (ideally only one); as with --batch, only results of queries are shown, and no status information
-H	--html	formats the results of queries as HTML tables; as with --batch, only results of queries are shown, and no status information
-N	--skip-column-names	leaves off column titles in the output of tables
-r	--raw	in query results, outputs the characters zero-byte, tab, newline, and \ unchanged (normally, these characters are output as \0, \t, \n, and \\); this option is effective only in combination with --batch
-s	--silent	displays less status information than in normal mode; does not use costly table formatting
-t	--table	formats tables with lines and spaces (default setting)
-v	--verbose	displays extensive status information, more than in normal mode
-X	--xml	formats the results of queries as an XML document

`mysql:` *Commands for Interactive Mode*

\c	clear	interrupts input of a command; \c can be given at the end of a command and leads to the entire input being simply ignored
\e	edit	calls the external editor named in the environment variable *EDITOR* and there enables a change in the command; this works only under Unix/Linux; after the return to mysql, the command given in the editor is not displayed in mysql, which makes this option somewhat confusing to use
\g	go	executes the command (equivalent to ; and Return)
\h	help	displays a list of commands
\p	print	displays the entire current command on the screen
\q	exit or quit	terminates mysql (under Unix/Linux, this works also with Ctrl+D)
\r	connect	terminates the current connection to MySQL and creates a new connection; optionally, a database name and host name of the MySQL server can be given (in that order)
\s	status	displays status information about the MySQL server
\T [*fn*]	tee [*filename*]	logs all input and output into the specified file; if no file name is given, then the file name used in the previous tee command is used; if the file already exists, then the input and output are appended to the end of the file
\t	notee	ends tee; logging can be resumed at any time with tee or \T
\u *db*	use *database*	makes the given database the default database
\#	rehash	creates (only under Unix/Linux) an internal list of all mysql commands, the most important SQL key words, and all table and column names of the current database; in the sequel, the input of the initial letters suffices; with Tab the abbreviation is extended to the full key word
\. *fn*	source *filename*	executes the SQL commands contained in the file; the commands must be separated by semicolons

mysqladmin (Administration)

Various administrative tasks can be accomplished with mysqladmin, such as creating new databases and changing passwords. There are several commands that can be passed to mysqladmin, which are then executed sequentially.

> **TIP** *The names of* mysqladmin *commands can be abbreviated to the point where the name remains unique (e.g.,* flush-l *instead of* flush-logs, *or* k *instead of* kill*).*
> *Most* mysqladmin *commands can also be executed as SQL commands, for example, by* CREATE DATABASE, DROP DATABASE, FLUSH, KILL, SHOW.
> *These commands are given in parentheses in the lists below. There is additional information in the SQL reference in Chapter 18.*

mysqladmin: *Syntax*

```
mysqladmin [options] command1 command2 ...
```

mysqladmin: *Options*

-f	--force	no warnings are displayed (e.g., with drop database); further commands are executed even after errors
-i *n*	--sleep=*n*	repeats the command every *n* seconds (for example, for regular display of status or for ping); mysqladmin now runs endlessly; under Unix/Linux, it can be terminated with Ctrl + C, under Windows, only by closing the command window
-r	--relative	displays, in combination with -i and the command extended-status, a change in the previous status
-E	--vertical	has the same effect as --relative, but changes are displayed in a single, very long, line
-t *n*	--timeout=*n*	sets the timeout time for establishing a connection to the server; if after *n* seconds no connection has been established, then mysqladmin is terminated
-w *n*	--wait=n	attempts *n* times to establish a connection to the MySQL server

mysqladmin: *Commands*

create *dbname*	generates a new database (corresponds to *CREATE DATABASE*)
drop *dbname*	deletes an existing database irrevocably (corresponds to *DROP DATABASE*)
extended-status	displays countless status variables of the server (*SHOW STATUS*)
flush-hosts	empties the host cache table (*FLUSH HOSTS*)
flush-logs	closes all logging files and then reopens them (*FLUSH LOGS*); with update logs, a new file is created, where the number of the file terminator is increased by 1 (e.g., *file.003* → *file.004*)
flush-status	resets many status variables to 0 (*FLUSH STATUS*)
flush-tables	closes all open tables (*FLUSH TABLES*)
flush-threads	empties the thread cache
flush-privileges	reinputs the privileges database *mysql* (*FLUSH PRIVILEGES*)
kill *id1*, *id2*, ...	terminates the specified threads (*KILL*)
password *newpassw*	changes the password of the current user; under Windows, this command often causes problems; one could use instead the SQL command *SET PASSWORD* (see Chapter 9)
ping	tests whether a connection to the server can be established
processlist	displays all threads (*SHOW THREADS*)
reload	reinputs the privileges database *mysql*
refresh	closes all tables and log files and then reopens them
shutdown	terminates the SQL server
start-slave / stop-slave	starts/stops a slave process for replication
status	displays some server status variables
variables	displays the system variables of the SQL server (*SHOW VARIABLES*)
version	determines the version of the MySQL server

mysqldump (Backup/Export)

With mysqldump, you get a long list of all SQL commands that are necessary to re-create a database exactly as it was. There are three syntax variants of mysqldump, depending on whether a database, several enumerated databases, or all databases managed by MySQL are to be stored. Only with the first variant can the output be limited to particular tables.

mysqldump: *Syntax*

```
mysqldump [options] dbname [tables]
mysqldump [options] --databases [moreoptions] dbname1 [dbname2 ... ]
mysqldump [options] --all-databases [moreoptions]
```

mysqldump: *Options*

	--add-drop-table	inserts a *DROP TABLE* command before every *CREATE TABLE*; when tables are read in, existing tables are deleted
	--add-locks	inserts *LOCK TABLE* before the first *INSERT* command and *UNLOCK* after the last *INSERT* command; generally speeds up reading in a database; the option should not be used with InnoDB tables
	--all	specifies all MySQL-specific options in the *CREATE TABLE* command
-A	--all-databases	saves all databases managed by MySQL; *CREATE DATABASE* and *USE* are placed in the backup file
-B	--databases	stores several databases
	--complete-inserts	generates for each data record a separate *INSERT* command; this is the default setting; use --extended-insert to minimize the size of the backup file
	--delayed-inserts	creates *INSERT* commands with the option *DELAYED*
-K	--disable-keys	inserts *ALTER TABLE ... DISABLE KEYS* or ... *ENABLE KEYS* before or after *INSERT* commands; indexes are thereby not updated until the end of the insertion process, which is faster
-e	--extended-insert	generates few *INSERT* commands with which several records can be inserted simultaneously (more efficient and reduces the size of the backup file)
-F	--flush-logs	updates the logging files before the backup is begun
-f	--force	continues even after errors
	--no-create-db	does not generate *CREATE TABLE* commands (only *INSERT*s)
	--no-data	generates no INSERT commands (only *CREATE TABLE* commands to re-create the structure of the database)

-l	--lock-tables	executes a *LOCK TABLE READ* for all tables before the data are read; this ensures that no data can be changed while mysqldump is running; the obvious drawback is that all write processes are blocked until mysqldump is done, which can take a while with large databases (with InnoDB tables, you should use --single-transaction instead of --lock-tables)
	--opt	shorthand for the following options: --add-drop-table, --add-locks --quick --all --extended-insert --lock-tables (in most cases, this is an optimal setting, though not when you use InnoDB tables, on account of --lock-tables)
-q	--quick	outputs results record by record without internal intermediate storage; without this option, first the entire table is moved into RAM and then output; the advantage of --quick is the lower memory requirement; the disadvantage is that the MySQL server is generally blocked for a longer period of time; --quick should definitely be used for very large tables (when the entire table cannot be held in RAM of the local computer)
-Q	--quote-names	encloses table and column names in single quotes (e.g., 'name')
	--single-transaction	results in all tables being read within a single transaction; this makes sense only when InnoDB tables are used, in which case this option ensures that no data are changed during output (with MyISAM tables, you should instead use --lock-tables)
-T *dir*	--tab=*dir*	writes the result directly into the specified directory, whereby for each table two files are created, one with the table structure (*.sql) and the second with the stored data in the format of the command *SELECT . . . INTO OUTFILE* (*.txt)
-w *cnd*	--where=*condition*	considers only data records that satisfy the *WHERE* condition *cnd* or *condition*; the entire option must be placed in quotation marks, e.g., " -wprice>5 " or " --where=ID=3 "
-X	--xml	creates an XML file with the contents of the table (without information on the table structure)

mysqldump: *Formatting Options (only in combination with --tab)*

--fields-terminated-by	see Chapter 18: *SELECT . . . INTO OUTFILE*
--fields-enclosed-by	
--fields-optionally-enclosed-by	
--fields-escaped-by	
--lines-terminated-by	

If you are using --tab, then the second file (tablename.txt) contains the contents of the table directly (that is, not in the form of *INSERT* commands). This has several advantages: The resulting file is somewhat more compact, and a later importation can be executed significantly more quickly. (However, the operation is more complex, and only a single table can be handled.)

The options --fields and --lines should each be set in quotation marks. The following example shows how you can pass the double quote itself as a character to the option:

```
> mysqldump -u root -p --tab /tmp "--fields-enclosed-by=\"" ...
```

To reinput the file thus generated (*.txt) with mysqldump, you can use either the program mysqlimport, discussed in the following section, or the SQL command *LOAD DATA*.

mysqlimport (Text Import, Bulk Import)

With mysqlimport, it is possible to import specially formatted text files into MySQL tables. Here, mysqlimport represents merely an interface to the command *LOAD DATA*, described in detail in Chapter 10.

mysqlimport: *Syntax*

```
mysqlimport [options] databasename filename
```

mysqlimport: *Options*

-d	--delete	deletes all existing records in the table before importation
-i	--ignore	ignores new records with an existing value for a *UNIQUE* or *PRIMARY KEY* column
-L	--local	reads the file from the local file system (not from that of the MySQL server)
-l	--lock-tables	blocks the tables for all other clients during importation
-r	--replace	overwrites existing records with the same value in a *UNIQUE* or *PRIMARY KEY* column
	--fields-terminated-by --fields-enclosed-by --fields-optionally-enclosed-by --fields-escaped-by --lines-terminated-by	affects special characters; see *LOAD DATA* in Chapter 18

mysqlshow (Displaying Information)

With `mysqlshow`, you can quickly obtain an overview of the databases, tables, and columns managed by MySQL. Without parameters, the command returns a list of all databases managed by MySQL. With parameters, the command displays information on the specified database, table, or column.

mysqlshow: *Syntax*

```
mysqlshow [options] [databasename [tablename [columnname]]]
```

mysqlshow: *Options*

-i	--status	displays additional status for tables (table type, average record length, etc.)

mysqlbug (Sending Error Notification)

The script `mysqlbug` helps in composing error messages to `mysql@lists.mysql.com`. The script is available only under Unix/Linux. It collects the most important information about the MySQL version installed on the system (version number of the server, options used at compilation, version number of the libraries, version number of Perl, etc.) and then displays a text template using the editor specified by *$VISUAL*.

You can now report information on your problems or errors at the locations provided for. As soon as you leave the editor, you have the possibility of terminating the error report, sending it, or editing it.

> **TIP** *Under Windows, you can create error reports with the dialog sheet* REPORT *of the program WinMySQLadmin, instead of with* `mysqlbug`.
> *Errors can also be reported in the error database of the MySQL web site:*
>
> ```
> http://bugs.mysql.com/
> ```

myisamchk (Repairing MyISAM Files)

With myisamchk you can check the integrity of MyISAM database files (name.MYD and name.MYI). Damaged files and indexes can be repaired as required. Re-creation of the index is necessary as well if the sort order of the server was changed.

The parameters of myisamchk are tables names. Here the complete file name is given (either without ending or with the ending *.MYI). Depending on the options specified, however, both MyISAM files, that is, name.MYD and name.MYI, are analyzed or changed.

Please note that with myisamchk there are several options whose significance depends on whether the program is used simply for checking (without -r, -o, --recover, --saferecover) or for changing table files (with one of these options).

If you are still working with ISAM tables (usually with older versions of MySQL), you can repair their files with isamchk. However, the options here are somewhat different from those of myisamchk.

myisamchk: Syntax

```
myisamchk [options] tablename1 tablename2 ...
```

myisamchk: Options (Analyze Table File without -r or -o)

-c	--check	checks the integrity of the table files; -c is the default option if no options are specified
-e	--extend-check	checks most thoroughly (and slowly)
-F	--fast	checks only tables whose files were not properly closed
-C	--check-only-changed	checks only tables that were changed since the last check
-f	--force	restarts myisamchk with the option -r if errors are discovered
-i	--information	displays statistical information about the tables
-m	--medium-check	checks more thoroughly (and slowly) than with -c
-U	--update-state	marks a file as damaged if errors are discovered
-T	--read-only	does not change the file

myisamchk: *Options (Repair and Change Table File with -r or -o)*

-B	--backup	creates the backup file name.bak for name.myi
-e	--extend-check	attempts to re-create every data record; however, this usually leads to many records with incorrect or deleted data; moreover, the repair takes a long time; this option should be used seldom
-f	--force	overwrites temporary files
-l	--no-symlinks	follows no symbolic links (that is, only those files are repaired that are found under the actual file name; available only under Unix/Linux)
-o	--safe-recover	like -r, but a different algorithm is used
-q	--quick	only an index file is repaired; the actual file is left untouched
-q -q		has almost the same effect as -q, but the data file is unchanged if key fields are not unique
-r	--recover	attempts to re-create defective files
-t *p*	--tmpdir=*path*	uses the specified directory for temporary files
-u	--unpack	decompresses table files that were compressed with myisampack
	--character-sets-dir=*dir*	reads character set data from the specified directory
	--set-character-set=*name*	uses the specified character set for recreating indexes

myisamchk: *Other Options*

-a	--analyze	analyzes and stores the distribution of key fields in the indexes; this can speed up table access somewhat
-A *n*	--set-auto-increment[=n]	uses as start value for *AUTO-INCREMENT* a number that is one greater than the highest value used so far, or else *n* (whichever is greater)
-d	--description	displays various information about the table (record format and length, character set, indexes, etc.)
-R	--sort-records=*idxnr*	sorts the records in the table file according to the specified index; the index is specified as a number (where this number can be determined first with -d); then nearby records in the index are located near each other in the table file as well; this can speed up access if records are frequently read in the order defined by the index
-S	--sort-index	sorts the blocks of the index file

myisamchk: *Variables for Memory Management*

-O key_buffer_size=*n*	specifies the size of the key buffer (default 512 K)
-O read_buffer_size=*n*	specifies the size of the read buffer (default 256 K)
-O sort_buffer_size=*n*	specifies the size of the sort buffer (default 2 MB)
-O write_buffer_size=*n*	specifies the size of the write buffer (default 256 K)

myisampack (Compressing MyISAM Files)

MyISAM database files (name.MYD) are compressed with myisampack. Thereby one can achieve drastic reductions in storage requirements for tables (often considerably more than one-half) and under some circumstances increased access speed to the data. However, the data can now no longer be changed.

myisampack: *Syntax*

```
myisampack [options] tablename1 tablename2 ...
```

myisampack: *Options*

-b	--backup	creates a backup name.old of the table file
-f	--force	executes the operation even if the resulting file is bigger than the original
-j	--join='*new_table_name*'	unites all tables specified into a single, large, file; the tables must all have exactly the same column definitions
-t	--test	executes myisampack provisionally without actually changing any data
-T *p*	--tmpdir=*path*	uses the specified directory for temporary files

CHAPTER 20

API Reference

THIS CHAPTER CONTAINS A REFERENCE to the APIs (application interfaces) that were introduced in this book for the programming languages PHP, Perl, Java, and C.

Chapter Overview

PHP API

This reference gives a compact overview of the PHP functions and their parameters for access to MySQL databases. First a few formal remarks:

- Square brackets in the left column indicate optional parameters.

- For all functions for which there is an enumeration over an index n, this index is in the range 0 to $nmax - 1$.

- Examples of the application of these functions can be found particularly in Chapters 3 and 11 through 13. Further references can be found in the Index.

Most of the functions presented here have been available since PHP 3, while some appeared in the course of development of PHP 4.n. All functions that came after PHP 4.0 are explicitly so designated.

Connection and Administration

$id =**mysql_connect**($host, $user, $pw);	establishes a connection
$id = mysql_connect($host, $user, $pw, $new_link, $client_flags);	as above, except that new_link specifies whether a new connection should be made if a similar connection already exists (default false); client_flags specifies whether particular connection properties should be used (e.g., *MYSQL_CLIENT_COMPRESS*); these two optional parameters have been available only since PHP 4.3
$id=**mysql_pconnect**($host, $user, $pw); [, $new_link [, $client_flags]]);	establishes a persistent connection or attempts to reuse a still open connection of another PHP page
***mysql_change_user**($newuser, $passw);*	changes the user name for the connection
***mysql_select_db**($dbname);*	determines the default database
***mysql_close**([$id]);*	closes the connection

Generally, the specification *id* can be omitted as long as there is only one connection to MySQL and thus no possibility of confusion.

Administration

$result = **mysql_list_dbs**([$id]);	determines a list of all known databases; the evaluation is like that of *SELECT* queries
$result = **mysql_list_tables**($dbname [,$id]);	determines a list of all tables of the database; evaluation like that of *SELECT* queries
$result = **mysql_list_fields**($dbn, $tbln [,$id]);	determines a list of all fields of the table; evaluation like that of *SELECT* queries
***mysql_create_db**($dbname [,$id]);*	creates a new database
***mysql_drop_db**($dbname [,$id]);*	deletes a database

Error Evaluation

$n = **mysql_errno**([$id]);	determines the number of the most recent error
$txt = **mysql_error**([$id]);	determines the error message

Information Functions

$txt = mysql_client_encoding([$id]);	since PHP 4.3 returns the name of the MySQL character set (e.g., *"latin1"*)
$txt = mysql_get_client_info([$id]);	since PHP 4.0.5 returns a character string with the version number of the client library
$txt = mysql_get_host_info([$id]);	since PHP 4.0.5 returns a character string that describes the connection with the server (including host name, e.g., *"localhost via TCP/IP"*)
$n = mysql_get_proto_info([$id]);	since PHP 4.0.5 returns an integer with the number of the communication protocol in use (e.g., 10)
$txt = mysql_get_server_info([$id]);	since PHP 4.0.5 returns a character string with the version number of the server (e.g., *"4.0.12-nt"*)
$n = mysql_thread_id([$id]);	since PHP 4.3 returns an integer with the thread number of the given connection
$txt = mysql_stat([$id]);	since PHP 4.3 returns a character string with a brief status report on the server (e.g., *"Uptime: 24763 Threads: 1 Questions: 65 . . . "*)

Executing SQL Commands

[$result =] **mysql_query**($sql [, $id])	executes an SQL command for the default database; if it is a *SELECT* command, the found records can be evaluated with *$result*
*[$result =] **mysql_db_query**($db, $sql [, $id]);*	executes a command for the database *db* (which becomes the default database for all further queries)
$result = mysql_unbuffered_query($sql [, $id]);	functions in principle like *mysql_query*, but is designed only for *SELECT* queries; the difference between this and *mysql_query* is that found records remain at first on the server and are transferred only as needed; the number of found records can be determined only by running through all of them; *mysql_num_rows* cannot be used
$sql = addslashes($s);	replaces zero-bytes and the characters ', ", and \ in *$s* with the strings \0, \', \", and \\
$sql = mysql_escape_string($s);	since PHP 4.0.3 functions like *addslashes*, but also replaces carriage return, line feed, and CTRL Z with the strings \n, \r, and \z
$sql = mysql_real_escape_string($s [,$id]);	since PHP 4.3 functions like *mysql_escape_string*, but also considers the character set of the MySQL connection

Output of SELECT Query Results

***mysql_data_seek**($result, $rownr);*	determines the active data record within the result
$row = **mysql_fetch_array**($result);	returns the next record of the result (or *false*); access to individual fields takes place with *row[n]* or *row['fieldname']*, where case sensitivity is in force
$row = mysql_fetch_assoc($result);	functions like *mysql_fetch_array*, except that field access must be by column name; *row[n]* is not permitted
$row = **mysql_fetch_row**($result);	returns the next record of the result (or *false*); access to individual fields is via *row[n]*
$row = **mysql_fetch_object**($result);	returns the next record of the result (or *false*); access to individual fields is via *row->fieldname*
$data = **mysql_result**($result, $rownr, $colnr);	returns the contents of the field in row *rownr* and column *colnr*; this function is slower than the other functions in this list and should therefore be used only in particular cases (such as to read a single value, e.g., *SELECT COUNT(*)*)
mysql_free_result($result);	frees the query result immediately (otherwise, not till the end of the script)

Here *result* is a value that enables access to the list of data records from a *SELECT* query. In evaluation by the functions in the following list there is always one record in the list that is active. Usually, all records are output one after the other with *mysql_fetch_array*, *mysql_fetch_row*, or *mysql_fetch_object*. The next record then automatically becomes the active one. The active record can also be set with *mysql_data_seek*

The three functions *mysql_fetch_array*, *mysql_fetch_row*, and *mysql_fetch_object* differ only in the way in which individual fields of a record are accessed: *row['fieldname']*, *row[n]*, or *row->fieldname*. Of the three functions, *mysql_fetch_row* is the most efficient, but the difference in speed is very small.

Metainformation on Query Results

$n = **mysql_num_rows**($result);	determines the number of result records (*SELECT*)
$n = **mysql_num_fields**($result);	determines the number of result columns (*SELECT*)
$n = **mysql_affected_rows**([$id]);	determines the number of records that were changed by the last SQL command (*INSERT, UPDATE, DELETE, CREATE, ... , SELECT*)
$autoid = **mysql_insert_id**([$id]);	determines the *AUTO_INCREMENT* value generated by the last *INSERT* command
$txt = mysql_info([$id]);	since PHP 4.3 returns status information on the last command, e.g., *"Rows matched: 65 Changed: 65 Warnings: 0"*; *mysql_info* is designed only for commands that usually affect large numbers of records (*INSERT INTO, UPDATE, ALTER TABLE*, etc.)

Metainformation on the Fields (Columns) of Query Results

*$fname =* **mysql_field_name**($result, $n);	returns the field name of column *n*
*$tblname =* **mysql_field_table**($result, $n);	returns the table name for column *n*
*$typename =* **mysql_field_type**($result, $n);	returns the data type of column *n* (e.g., *"TINYINT"*)
*$length =* **mysql_field_len**($result, $n);	returns the maximum length of the column
*$lengths =* **mysql_fetch_length**($result);	returns a field with length information for all fields of the last-read data record (access with *lengths[n]*)
*$flags =* **mysql_field_flags**($result, $n);	returns the attribute properties of a column as a character string (e.g., *"not_null primary_key"*); the properties are separated by spaces; evaluation is done most easily with *explode*
*$info =* **mysql_fetch_field**($result, $n);	returns information on column *n* as an object; evaluation proceeds with *info->name* (see the list below); note that *info* may contain, in part, properties other than *flags*

Attributes of mysql_field_flags

auto_increment	attribute *AUTO_INCREMENT*
binary	attribute *BINARY*
blob	data type *BLOB, TINYBLOB*, etc.
enum	data type *ENUM*
multiple_key	field is part of a nonunique index
not_null	attribute *NOT NULL*
primary_key	attribute *PRIMARY KEY*
timestamp	attribute *TIMESTAMP*
unique_key	attribute *UNIQUE*
unsigned	attribute *UNSIGNED*
zerofill	attribute *ZEROFILL*

Field Information for mysql_fetch_field

info->name	column name (field name)
info->table	name of the table from which the field comes
info->max_length	maximum length of the field
info->type	name of the data type of the field (e.g., *"TINYINT"*)
info->numeric	1 or 0, depending on whether the field contains numeric data

info->blob, not_null, multiple_key,
  primary_key, unique_key, unsigned,
  zerofill
	1 or 0; see list above for interpretation

Perl DBI

The following lines shown the principles for building a Perl script file:

```
#!/usr/bin/perl -w
use DBI;                            # database access
use CGI qw(:standard);              # necessary only with CGI scripts
use CGI::Carp qw(fatalsToBrowser);  # only with CGI scripts
use HTML::Entities;                 # only with CGI scripts
 ...                                # the actual code follows
```

Common Variable Names

The Perl *DBI* module is object-oriented. Thus the key words introduced in this section relate in part to methods that can be applied to specific objects (which in Perl are generally called *Handles*). In this reference the following variable names will be used for such objects:

Common Variable Names for DBI Handles

$dbh	(*database handle*)	represents the connection to the database
$sth	(*statement handle*)	enables evaluation of query results (with *SELECT* queries)
$h	(*handle*)	general handles, used in this section with methods that are available to *$dbh*, *$sth*, and *DBI*
$drh	(*driver handle*)	enables access to many administrative functions

Establishing the Connection

The Connection

use DBI();	activates the DBI module
$datasource = "DBI:mysql:dbname;" . "host=hostname";	specifies database names and computer names; the database name may be omitted, but then at least the colon must be given
$dbh = DBI->**connect**(*$datasource, $username, $password [, %attributes]);*	creates the connection to the database

Within the *datasource* character string, further parameters—separated by semicolons—may be given. (Information on setting up MySQL configuration files can be found in Chapter 19.)

Optional Parameters in the datasource Character String

host=hostname	specifies the name of the computer with the MySQL server (default *localhost*)
port=n	specifies the IP port (default 3306)
mysql_compression=0/1	compresses communication (default 0)
mysql_read_default_file=filename	specifies the file name of the MySQL configuration file
mysql_read_default_group=mygroup	reads the group *[mygroup]* within the configuration (default group *[client]*)

A list with attributes can be passed as an optional fourth parameter of *connect*. You can supply these attributes either directly or in the form of an array variable:

```
$dbh = DBI->connect($source, $user, $pw, Attr1=>val1, Attr2=>val2);
%attr = (Attr1=>val1, Attr2=>val2);
$dbh = DBI->connect($source, $user, $pw, \%attr);
```

To a great extent, these attributes can be read and changed with *$dbh* after the connection has been established:

```
$dbh->'LongReadLen' = 1000000;
```

The following table describes the most important *connect* attributes.

Optional connect *Attributes ($dbh Attributes)*

RaiseError=>0/1	displays an error message and ends the program if the connection is not properly established (default 0)
PrintError=>0/1	displays an error message but continues execution if the connection is not properly established (default 1)
LongReadLen=>n	determines the maximum size of an individual data field in bytes (0: do not even read long fields)
LongTruncOK=>0/1	specifies whether data fields that are too long should be truncated (1) or whether an error should be triggered (0)

Terminate Connection

*$dbh->**disconnect**();*	terminate connection to the database

Executing SQL Commands, Evaluating SELECT Queries

Execute Queries Without Return of Data Records

*$n = $dbh->**do**("INSERT ...");*	executes an SQL query without returning records; *$n* contains the number of records that were changed, or *0E0* if no records were changed, or *−1* if the number is unknown, or *undef* if an error has occurred
$n = $dbh->**do**($sql, \%attr, @values);	executes a parameterized query; *@values* contains values for the wild card expressed in the SQL command by *?*; these values are handled automatically with *quote()*; *%attr* can contain optional attributes (otherwise, specify *undef*)
*$id = $dbh->{'**mysql_insertid**'};*	returns the *AUTO_INCREMENT* value of the last record to be inserted (caution: the attribute *mysql_insertid* is MySQL-specific)

Execute Queries with Return of Data Records

*$sth = $dbh->**prepare**("SELECT ... ");*	prepares an SQL query (generally *SELECT* queries); all further operations proceed with the help of the *statement handle*
*$sth->**execute**();*	executes the query
*$sth->**execute**(@values);*	executes a parameterized query; *@values* contains values for the wild card expressed in the SQL command by *?*;
*$sth->**fetchxxx**();*	evaluates the results (see below)
*$sth->**finish**();*	releases the resources of the *statement handle*

If a query was executed with *prepare* and *execute* and a list of records was returned as result, then this list can be evaluated with a number of *fetch* methods.

Evaluate List of Data Records

*@row = $sth->**fetchrow_array**();*	reads the next record into the array *@row*; if the end of the list is reached or if an error occurs, then *@row* contains an empty array; access to individual elements proceeds with *$row[n]* (where for the first column, *n=0*)
*@row = $sth->**fetch**();*	equivalent to *fetchrow_array()*
*$rowptr = $sth->**fetchrow_arrayref**();*	equivalent to *fetchrow_array()*, but returns pointers to arrays (or *undef* if the end of the list of records is reached or an error occurs)
*$row = $sth->**fetchrow_hashref**();*	reads the next record into the associated array *$row*; if the end of the list of records is reached or if an error occurs, then *$row* contains the value *undef*; access to individual elements proceeds with *$row->{'columnname'}*, where case sensitivity is in force
*$result = $sth->**fetchall_arrayref**();*	reads all records and returns a pointer to an array of pointers to the individual records; access to individual elements proceeds with *$result->[$row][$col]*
*$result = $sth->**fetchall_arrayref**();*	as above, but the records are now associative arrays; access is via *$result->[$row]->'columnname'*

Bind Variables to Columns (for fetchrow_array)

$sth->**bind_col**($n, \$var);	binds the column *n* to the variable *$var* (where for the first column we have, exceptionally, *n=1*); the variable is automatically updated when the next record is read; *bind_col* must be executed after *execute*; the function returns *false* if an error occurs
*$sth->**bind_columns**(\$var1, \$var2, . . .);*	equivalent to *bind_col*, except that variables are assigned to all columns of the query; make sure you have the correct number of variables

Metainformation on SQL Commands

*$n = $sth->{'**NUM_OF_FIELDS**'};*	returns the number of result columns (after *SELECT*)
*$n = $sth->{'**NUM_OF_PARAMS**'};*	returns the number of parameters in queries with wild cards
*$sql = $sth->{'**Statement**'};*	returns the underlying SQL command

Determine Column Names, Data Types, etc., of SELECT Results

$array_ref = $sth->{'**NAME**'};	returns a pointer to an array with the names of all columns; evaluation takes place with @$array_ref[$n], where *n* ranges from 0 to $sth->{'NUM_OF_FIELDS'}-1
$array_ref = $sth->{'**NAME_lc**'};	as above, but names in lowercase
$array_ref = $sth->{'**NAME_uc**'};	as above, but names in uppercase
$array_ref = $sth->{'**NULLABLE**'};	specifies for each column whether *NULL* may be stored there (1) or not (0); if this information cannot be determined, then the array contains the value 2 for this column
$array_ref = $sth->{'**PRECISION**'};	specifies the precision in the sense of ODBC (here is meant the maximum column width)
$array_ref = $sth->{'**SCALE**'};	specifies the number of decimal places for floating-point numbers
$array_ref = $sth->{'**TYPE**'};	specifies the data type of all columns in the form of numerical values; the values relate to the ODBC standard; tests determined the following values: *CHAR: 12, INT: 4, TEXT/BLOB: −1, DATE: 9, TIME: 10, TIMESTAMP: 11, FLOAT: 7, DECIMAL: 3, ENUM/SET: 1*

Shorthand Notation

@row = $dbh->**selectrow_array**($sql);	corresponds to a combination of *prepare*, *execute*, and *fetchrow_array*; the result is an array of the first result data record; access to further records is not possible
$result = $dbh->**selectrow_array**($sql);	as above, but *$result* contains the value of the first column of the first result record
$result = $dbh->**selectall_arrayref**($sql);	corresponds to *prepare*, *execute*, and *fetchall_arrayref*; for evaluation of *$result*, see *fetchall_arrayref*

Marking Special Characters in Character Strings and BLOBs with the Backslash

$dbh->quote($data);	prefixes the contents of *$data* between single quotes, prefixes \ and ' with \, and replaces zero-bytes by \0; if *$data* is empty (*undef*), then *quote()* returns the character string *NULL*

Error Handling

Methods for Error Handling

*$h->**err**();*	returns the error number of the last error (0: no error)
*$h->**errstr**();*	describes the last error (empty character string: no error)
$h->**trace**($n [, $filename]);	logs all internal MySQL data accesses and redirects output to *STDERR* or the given file; *n* specifies the degree of detail to be logged (0 deactivates logging, 9 logs everything)

Auxiliary Functions

DBI Functions

@bool *= DBI::**looks_like_a_number**(@data);*	tests for each element in the array *@data* whether it is a number and returns *true* or *undef* in the result array
$result = DBI::**neat**($data [, $maxlen]);	formats the character string contained in *$data* in a form suitable for output; character strings are placed in single quotes; non-ASCII characters are replaced by a period; if the character string is longer than *$maxlen* characters (default 400), then it is truncated and terminated with ...
*$result = DBI::**neat_list**(\@listref, $maxlen, $sep);*	as above, but for an entire array of data; the individual elements are separated by *$sep* (default ",")

$dbh Methods

*$ok = $dbh->**ping**();*	tests whether the connection to MySQL still exists and returns *true* or *false* accordingly

MySQL-Specific Extension of the DBD::mysql Driver

If you use the *DBI* module for access to MySQL databases, then there are some supplementary functions available via *DBI* methods and attributes, of which we shall now describe some of the most important. The use of these functions can simplify programming and can make Perl programs more efficient. However, the code will no longer be portable; that is, a later change to another database system will require additional work.

Administrative Functions Based on a Separated Connection

$drh = DBI->install_driver('mysql');	returns a *driver handle*
*$drh->func('**createdb**', $database, $host, $user, $password, 'admin');*	creates a new database; a new connection is used for this
*$drh->func('**dropdb**', $database, $host, $user, $password, 'admin');*	deletes a database
*$drh->func('**shutdown**', $host, $user, $password, 'admin');*	shuts down the MySQL server
*$drh->func('**reload**', $host, $user, $password, 'admin');*	reinputs all MySQL tables (including the *mysql* tables with privilege management)

Administrative Functions Within the Current Connection

*$dbh->func('**createdb**', $database, 'admin');*	creates a new database
*$dbh->func('**dropdb**', $database, 'admin');*	deletes a database
*$dbh->func('**shutdown**', 'admin');*	shuts down the MySQL server
*$dbh->func('**reload**', 'admin');*	reinputs all MySQL tables

$dbh Attributes

*$id = $dbh->'**mysql_insertid**';*	returns the *AUTO_INCREMENT* value of the most recently inserted data record
*$info = $dbh->'**info**';*	after certain special SQL commands is supposed to return a character string with information about the command (e.g., after an *UPDATE* command: *Rows matched: 13 Changed: 13 Warnings: 0*); however, several tests of this attribute were unsuccessful
*$threadid = $dhb->'**thread_id**';*	returns the thread ID number of the current connection to MySQL

$sth Methods and Attributes

*$sth->**rows**();*	returns after *SELECT* queries the number of data records found by *SELECT*; caution: this does not work if *$sth->'mysql_use_result'* =1 holds
*$sth->'**mysql_store_result**' =1;*	activates *mysql_store_result*, so that with *SELECT* queries all results are stored temporarily on the client computer (default setting)
*$sth->'**mysql_use_result**' =1;*	activates *mysql_use_result*, so that with *SELECT* queries only a single record is stored temporarily on the client

$sth *Attributes for Determining Metadata on* SELECT *Results*

*$ar_ref = $sth->'**MYSQL_IS_BLOB**';*	returns a pointer to an array whose values specify whether the column contains *BLOBs*; evaluation with @$ar_ref[$n], where *n* ranges from 0 to *$sth->'NUM_OF_FIELDS' -1*
*$ar_ref = $sth->'**MYSQL_IS_KEY**';*	specifies whether the columns are indexed
*$ar_ref = $sth->'**MYSQL_IS_NOT_NULL**';*	specifies whether the attribute *NOT NULL* holds for the columns
*$ar_ref = $sth->'**MYSQL_IS_NUM**';*	specifies whether numerical data are stored in the columns
*$ar_ref = $sth->'**MYSQL_IS_PRI_KEY**';*	specifies which columns are part of the primary index
*$ar_ref = $sth->'**MYSQL_MAX_LENGTH**';*	specifies the maximum column width of the query results
*$ar_ref = $sth->'**MYSQL_TABLE**';*	specifies the underlying table names for all columns
*$ar_ref = $sth->'**MYSQL_TYPE_NAME**';*	specifies the names of the data types for all columns

JDBC (Connector/J)

In order to be able to access MySQL under Java, a JDBC driver for MySQL must be installed. This book assumes that you are using Connector/J version 3.*n*. If this assumption is satisfied, you can use numerous classes and methods of JDBC (Java Database Connectivity) with the names *java.sql.** and *javax.sql.**. The following tables assemble only the most important classes and methods of JDBC. There is simply no room for a complete reference to this complex library for database programming.

Establishing a Connection

Connection with DriverManager

import java.sql.;*	enables direct access to the JDBC base classes
Class.forName("com.mysql.jdbc.Driver"). newInstance();	loads and registers Connector/J, the MySQL driver for JDBC
Connection conn = DriverManager.getConnection("jdbc:mysql://hostname/dbname", "username", "password");	creates a connection to the database *dbname* on the computer *hostname*; in the connection string, a large number of additional optional parameters may be passed, the most important of which appear in a table of Chapter 15

Connection with DataSource (since Java 2, Version 1.4)

import java.sql.*; *import javax.sql.*;*	enables direct access to the JDBC base and extension classes

com.mysql.jdbc.jdbc2.optional.
  MysqlDataSource ds =
  new com.mysql.jdbc.jdbc2.optional.
  MysqlDataSource();
ds.setServerName("hostname");
ds.setDatabaseName("dbname");
Connection conn =
  ds.getConnection(
  "username", "password");
	creates an object of the class *com.-mysql.jdbc.jdbc2.optional.MysqlDataSource*, sets the host and database names, and finally establishes the connection;

ds.setUrl(" . . . ");	to be used instead of *setServerName* and *setDatabaseName* for setting various connection parameters; the syntax of the connection string (URL) is the same as for *DriverManager.getConnection*

Transactions

conn.setAutoCommit(false);	enables transactions (only, of course, if the MySQL tables are transaction-capable)
conn.commit();	confirms all SQL commands executed in the last transaction and starts the next transaction
conn.rollback();	aborts the commands of the last transaction and begins a new transaction

Executing SQL Commands

SQL Commands (Statement)

Statement stmt = *conn.**createStatement**( );*	creates a statement object, necessary to execute an SQL command
Statement stmt = *conn.createStatement(* *java.sql.ResultSet.* *TYPE_FORWARD_ONLY,* *java.sql.ResultSet.* *CONCUR_READ_ONLY);* *stmt.setFetchSize(* *Integer.MIN_VALUE);*	defines a statment object for *forward only* *ResultSets*
Statement stmt = *conn.createStatement(* *java.sql.ResultSet.* *TYPE_SCROLL_SENSITIVE,* *java.sql.ResultSet.* *CONCUR_UPDATABLE);*	defines a statement object for a variable *ResultSet*
int n = stmt.executeUpdate(*"INSERT . . . ");*	executes *INSERT, UPDATE,* and *DELETE* commands; the return value specifies the number of changed data records
ResultSet res = *stmt.executeQuery("SELECT . . . ");*	executes a *SELECT* query and returns as result a *ResultSet* object
stmt.addBatch("INSERT . . . "); *stmt.addBatch("INSERT . . . ");* *int[ ] n = stm.executeBatch( );*	collects a number of SQL commands and executes them as a group; *executeBatch* returns an *int* field that specifies the number of changed records

Determining AUTO_INCREMENT IDs After INSERT Commands

*stmt.**executeUpdate**("INSERT . . . ");*	the starting point for the following three variants

ResultSet newid =
  *stmt.**getGeneratedKeys**();*
if(newid.next()) {
  int id = newid.getInt(1); }
	getGeneratedKeys returns a *ResultSet* object with the most recently generated ID number(s); normally, that is, after a usual *INSERT* command, *res* contains exactly one ID number that is read with *next()* and *getInt(1)*; *getGeneratedKeys* is available since Java 2, version 1.4

long id = ((com.mysql.jdbc. *Statement)stmt).**getLastInsertID**();*	*getLastInsertID* also returns the ID number; however, the method is Connector/J-specific and not portable

ResultSet newid =
  stmt.executeQuery(
   "SELECT LAST_INSERT_ID()");
	Here the ID number is returned with a separate SQL command; note that the command is executed in the same transaction

if(newid.next()) { *id = newid.getInt(1); }*	

Executing PreparedStatments

PreparedStatement pstmt =
  *conn.**prepareStatement**(*
   "INSERT . . . (?, ?)");
	declares an SQL command with two parameters indicated by question marks

*pstmt.**setString**(1, "O'Reilly");* *pstmt.**setInt**(2, 7878);*	passes the parameter; there are numerous methods in addition to *setString* and *setInt*, e.g., *setNull, setDate, setTime, setFloat, setBinaryStream*; to these methods are passed the parameter number (beginning with 1) and the actual data
*int n = pstmt.**executeUpdate**();* *ResultSet res = pstmt.**executeQuery**();* *pstmt.**addBatch**();* *int n pstm.**executeBatch**();*	executes the command(s); the methods have the same meaning as for the *Statement* class

Changing ResultSets

*res.**deleteRow**();*	deletes the active record
*res.**updateXxx**(n, data);* *res.**updateRow**();*	first changes the specified columns of the active record and then stores the changes
*res.**moveToInsertRow**();* *res.**updateXxx**(n, data);* *res.**insertRow**();*	inserts a new record, changes its columns, and then stores the changes

Evaluating SELECT Queries

Evaluating ResultSet

res.**getInt**(n); res.**getString**(n); res.**getBytes**(n); . . .	returns the data field of column *n* of the currently active record; instead of the column number (1 for the first column), the name of the column may be specified, e.g., *getDate("birthdate")*
res.**wasNull**();	tests whether the most recently read data field was *NULL*; this test is necessary with elementary Java data types that cannot store the value *NULL* and instead contain 0; *wasNull* offers the only way of distinguishing between 0 and *NULL*
res.**getBinaryStream**(n);	returns an *InputStream* object for bytewise reading of binary data
res.**getCharacterStream**(n);	returns a *Reader* object for character-wise reading of binary data
res.**getBlob/getClob**(n);	returns a *Blob* or *Clob* object for reading binary data

ResultSet Navigation

res.**next**();	makes the next record in *ResultSet* the active record; the method returns *false* if there are no more records
res.**first**();	activates the first record; the method returns *false* if the *ResultSet* contains no records
res.**previous**();	activates the previous record
res.**last**();	activates the last record
res.**beforeFirst**();	places the record cursor before the first record; the *ResultSet* object is thereby in the same condition as immediately after *executeQuery*; now the first record can be activated with *next*
res.**afterLast**();	places the record cursor after the last record; *previous* activates the last record
res.**isFirst**(); res.**isLast**();	tests whether the current record is the first/last
int n = res.**getRow**(); res.**isLast**();	returns the number of the active record (1 for the first record)
res.**absolute**(n);	activates record *n*

Metadata on ResultSet

ResultSetMetaData meta = res.getMetaData();	returns a *ResultSetMetaData* object that gives information about the *SELECT* result
meta.getColumnCount();	returns the number of columns
meta.getColumnName(i);	returns the name (*String*) of column *i*
meta.getColumnType(i);	returns the data type of column *i*; the result is an *int* with one of the constants from *java.sql.Types*
meta.getColumnTypeName(i);	returns the name (*String*) of the data type of column *i*
meta.IsNullable(i);	tells whether the column may contain *NULL*
meta.IsAutoIncrement(i);	tells whether it is an *AUTO_INCREMENT* column

<sql:xxx> Tags for Database Access in JSP Projects

Establishing the Connection

<%@ taglib uri="http://java.sun.com/jstl/sql" prefix="sql" %>	tells that SQL tags are used in the JSP file (for this to work, the relevant parts of the JSTL must be correctly installed in the project directory; see Chapter 15)
<sql:setDataSource *var="conn" driver="com.mysql.jdbc.Driver" url="jdbc:mysql://hostname/dbname" user="username" password="password" />*	creates the connection to the database *db-name* on computer *hostname* and stores the connection information in the variable *conn*

Executing SQL Commands

<sql:query *var="res" dataSource="${conn}"* *[startRow ="n" maxRows="m"] >* *SELECT . . .* **</sql:query>**	for the database connection *conn*, executes the specified *SELECT* query and stores the result in the variable *res*; optionally, the result list can be limited via *startRow* and *maxRows*; in the query, parameters are denoted by ?; these parameters must then be specified by *<sql:param>* or *<sql:dataParam>*
<sql:update *var="count" dataSource="${conn}" >* *UPDATE/INSERT/DELETE . . .* **</sql:update>**	executes an *UPDATE, INSERT,* or *DELETE* command and stores the number of changed records in the variable *count*; JSTL appears to offer no mechanism to determine the *AUTO_INCREMENT* number of the last-inserted record (at least I have not found one); you must therefore execute a separate query *SELECT LAST_INSERT_ID()*; if you are working with InnoDB, then the *INSERT* and *SELECT* commands must be executed within a transaction
<sql:param *value="${var}" />*	passes to a parameter the content of the variable *var*; *<sql:param>* must be placed within *<sql:query>* or *<sql:update>*, where the order of the ? signs in the SQL command must be adhered to; Example: **<sql:update** *dataSource="${conn}" >* *DELETE FROM x WHERE a=? AND b=?* **<sql:param** *value="${varA}" />* **<sql:param** *value="${varB}" />* **</sql:update>**
<sql:dataParam *value="${var}"* *type="date" / "time" / "timestamp" />*	specifies a parameter for the date (*type="date"*, time (*"time"*), or both (*"timestamp"*)
<sql:transaction> *<sql:query . . . > . . . </sql:query>* *<sql:update . . . > . . . </sql:update>* *<sql:update . . . > . . . </sql:update>* **</sql:transaction>**	executes several SQL commands within a transaction

Evaluating SELECT Results

`<c:forEach`
  `var="row"`
  `items="${res.rows}" >`
  `<c:out value="${row.colname}" />`
 	
  `. . .`
`</c:forEach>`
	using `<c:forEach>`, the variable *row* runs through all rows of the result *res*; *row.columnname* gives access to a single column of the current record

`<c:forEach`
  `var="row"`
  `items="${res.rowsByIndex}" >`
  `<c:out value="${row[0]}" />`
 	
  `. . .`
`</c:forEach>`
	as above, but access to the columns is now via index numbers (0 for the first column)

`${res.rowCount}`	returns the number of found data records

C API

The following tables assemble the most important functions and structures of the C API.

Data Structures

Basic Structures

MYSQL *conn;	structure with connection data
MYSQL_RES *result;	structure with the results of a *SELECT* query
MYSQL_ROW row;	pointer to the results of a row (i.e., of a data record)
MYSQL_ROW_OFFSET roffset;	pointer to a record within the result list
MYSQL_FIELD *field;	structure for describing a column (column name, data type, number of digits, etc.); details in the next table
MYSQL_FIELD_OFFSET foffset;	offset within a record (0 for the first column, 1 for the second, etc.)
my_ulonglong n;	64-bit integer; some of the MySQL functions described below return results of this data type

In all further syntax tables, the variables *conn, result, row, field, roffset,* and *foffset* will be used as if declared in the above table. Note that *MYSQL_ROW* is already a pointer and is therefore declared without *.

Elements of the `MYSQL_FIELD` *Structure*

char *name;	name of the column
char *table;	name of the table from which the column comes; if the column was computed or an *ALIAS* was used, then *table* points to a character string with the formula or the *ALIAS* name
char *def;	default value of the column or *NULL*
enum enum_field_types type;	data type of the column; these are the choices: *FIELD_TYPE_BLOB*, *FIELD_TYPE_CHAR*, *FIELD_TYPE_DATE*, *FIELD_TYPE_DATETIME*, *FIELD_TYPE_DECIMAL*, *FIELD_TYPE_DOUBLE*, *FIELD_TYPE_ENUM*, *FIELD_TYPE_FLOAT*, *FIELD_TYPE_INT24*, *FIELD_TYPE_LONG*, *FIELD_TYPE_LONGLONG*, *FIELD_TYPE_NULL*, *FIELD_TYPE_SET*, *FIELD_TYPE_SHORT*, *FIELD_TYPE_STRING*, *FIELD_TYPE_TIME*, *FIELD_TYPE_TIMESTAMP*, *FIELD_TYPE_TINY*, *FIELD_TYPE_YEAR*
unsigned int length;	length of the column according to the column definition
unsigned int max_length;	maximal length of a column within the query result; the value is always 0 if you use *mysql_use_result()*
unsigned int flags;	additional information for describing the column: *AUTO_INCREMENT_FLAG*, *BINARY_FLAG*, *MULTIPLE_KEY_FLAG*, *NOT_NULL_FLAG*, *PRI_KEY_FLAG*, *UNIQUE_KEY_FLAG*, *UNSIGNED_FLAG*, *ZEROFILL_FLAG*
unsigned int decimals;	number of places after the decimal point in *DECIMAL* columns (e.g., 5 for *DECIMAL(10,5)*)

Connection and Administration

Establishing a Connection

MYSQL *conn; *conn = mysql_init(NULL);*	initializes the *MYSQL* data structure
mysql_options(conn, option, "value");	sets additonal options for the connection; an option with one of the following values must be passed: *MYSQL_OPT_CONNECT_TIMEOUT,* *MYSQL_OPT_LOCAL_INFILE,* *MYSQL_OPT_NAMED_PIPE,* *MYSQL_INIT_COMMAND,* *MYSQL_READ_DEFAULT_FILE,* *MYSQL_READ_DEFAULT_GROUP;* with some of these options, *"value"* can be used to specify the desired value; for setting several options, the function must be called repeatedly; *mysql_options* must be exectued before *mysql_real_connect*
mysql_real_connect(conn, "hostname", *"username", "password", "dbname",* *portnum, "socketname", flags);*	makes a connection to the database and returns *NULL* in case of error; *flags* can contain a combination of the following values: *CLIENT_COMPRESS,* *CLIENT_FOUND_ROWS,* *CLIENT_IGNORE_SPACE,* *CLIENT_INTERACTIVE,* *CLIENT_NO_SCHEMA,* *CLIENT_ODBC,* *CLIENT_SSL*
mysql_change_user(conn, "username", *"password", "dbname");*	changes the user and the default database for an existing connection
mysql_change_db(conn, "dbname");	changes the default database; the function assumes that the user has access to the database
mysql_ping(conn);	tests whether the connection still exists; if not, the connection is recreated; returns 0 as result if an active connection exists
mysql_close(conn);	closes the connection

Acquiring Information on the Current Connection

mysql_characterset_name(conn);	returns a character string with the default character set of the connection
mysql_get_client_info();	returns a character string with information on the version of the client library in use (e.g., *"4.0.12"*)
mysql_get_server_info(conn);	returns a string with information on the version of the server (e.g., *"4.0.12"*)
mysql_get_host_info(conn);	returns a string with information on the connection to the server (e.g., *"localhost via UNIX socket"*)
mysql_get_proto_info(conn);	returns the version number (*unsigned int*) of the connection protocol, e.g., 10 or 11
mysql_info(conn);	returns a string with information on the execution of the last *INSERT, UPDATE, LOAD DATA,* or *ALTER TABLE* command (e.g., *"Rows matched: 3 Changed: 3 Warnings: 0"*)
mysql_stat(conn);	returns a string with the server status (number of threads, number of open tables, etc.)
mysql_thread_id(conn);	returns the number (*unsigned long*) of the thread that the current connection is processing on the server

Adminstrative Functions

mysql_kill(conn, n);	ends the thread specified by *n* (requires the *Process* privilege)
mysql_shutdown(conn);	shuts down the server (execution requires the *Shutdown* privilege)

Error-Handling

mysql_errno(conn);	returns the error number (*unsigned int*) for the most recently executed command (or 0 if there was no error)
mysql_error(conn);	returns a string with the error message (or an empty string *""* if there was no error)

Executing and Evaluating SQL Commands

Execution of SQL Commands

mysql_query(conn, "SELECT . . . ");	executes the specified command and returns 0 if the server accepts the command without triggering an error
mysql_real_query(conn, "SELECT . . . ", len);	like *mysql_query*, except that the SQL command may now contain the zero-byte (e.g., to store *BLOB*s); for this, the length of the string must be specified explicitly
mysql_affected_rows(conn);	returns the number (data type *my_ulonglong*) of changed records after a *DELETE*, *INSERT*, or *UPDATE* command; the function does not return the number of results of a *SELECT* command
mysql_insert_id(conn);	returns the *AUTO_INCREMENT* value (data type *my_ulonglong*) of the last record created via *INSERT*

Processing SELECT Results

result = mysql_store_result(conn);	transfers all results from the server to the client and stores then in the *MYSQL_RES* structure
result = mysql_use_result(conn);	represents an alternative to *mysql_store_result*; the transfer of individual records is only prepared; no data are actually transferred
mysql_num_fields(result);	returns the number of columns of the result
row = mysql_fetch_row(result);	transfers the next record to a *MYSQL_ROW* structure; the function returns *NULL* if there are no further records available, i.e., if all records have already been processed
row[n];	returns a 0-terminated string with the content of column *n* of the current record; note that *row[n]* can contain *NULL*; if you are processing binary data with zero-bytes, you must make the call with *mysql_fetch_lengths* to determine the size of the data field
mysql_free_result(result);	releases the result structure; if you are working with *mysql_use_result*, the result is only now released by the server

Processing SELECT *Results: Metainformation on Columns and Fields*

mysql_fetch_lengths(result);	returns for the current record an *unsigned long* field with the length of the result string in *row[n]*
field = mysql_fetch_field(result);	returns a description (*MYSQL_FIELD* structure) of the data type of a column; the first call returns the data for the first column, the next for the second column, etc.; the function returns *NULL* after all columns have been run through; the elements of the *MYSQL_FIELD* structure were described previously
field = mysql_fetch_field_direct(result, n);	returns a description of column *n* (0 for the first column, etc.)
mysql_fetch_fields(result);	returns a description of all columns as a *MYSQL_FIELD* field

The following functions can be used only if you are using *mysql_store_result* (and are not working with *mysql_use_result*).

Processing SELECT *Results: Additional Functions for* mysql_store_result

mysql_num_rows(result);	returns the number of found records
mysql_data_seek(result, n);	moves the row cursor to record *n* (0 for the first record); then *mysql_fetch_row* must be executed to reinput data
roffset = mysql_row_tell(result);	returns a pointer (a sort of bookmark) to the current record
mysql_row_seek(result, roffset);	moves the row cursor to a particular location within the result list; then *mysql_fetch_row* must be executed to reinput data; *roffset* must be determined earlier with *mysql_row_tell*

Auxiliary Functions

n = mysql_real_escape_string(*conn, dest, src, srclen);*	copies the string *src* into the string *dest* while replacing the special characters with \ character combinations (\0, \b, \t, \", \', etc.); *dest* is terminated with a zero-byte; *srclen* specifies the number of characters in *src*; *dest* must be previously initialized with a string of the appropriate length; to be able to copy a string full of special characters without error, *dest* must offer place for *srclen*2+1* characters; the function returns the number of characters in *dest* (without the zero-byte). If *"O'Reilly"* is copied, then afterward, *src* contains the string *O\'Reilly*, and *n* the value 9
destpt = strmov(dest, src);	like *strcpy*, copies the string *src* to the string *dest*; the difference is in the return value, which points to the end of the string in *dest*; this makes it easy to construct a string from several pieces; to be able to use *strmov*, the files my_global.h and m_string.h must be included before mysql.h

Part V

Appendices

APPENDIX A

Glossary

THIS APPENDIX CONTAINS A BRIEF description of the most important notions from the world of databases and related areas.

Character Set: A character set is a specification that tells which characters are represented by which code. Among the oldest character sets is the ASCII (American Standard Code for Information Interchange) character set, in which the letter A is coded by the integer 65.

Client: A client is a program that accesses a central service. In connection with databases, a client denotes a program that accesses a central database. The database is managed by another program, the database server.

Client/Server Architecture: Most modern database systems are based on a server that manages the data and executes SQL commands, and an arbitrary number of clients that access the server over a network. This concept is called client/server architecture. Alternatives to this model are file-server databases such as dBase and Access, in which all clients access the database file directly through a common file system. (This is quite inefficient when many users are trying to edit data simultaneously.)

Database: Generally speaking, a database is an ordered collection of data. In connection with MySQL, a database consists of a number of tables. In common usage, a database can also refer to an entire database system, that is, the program that manages the data. In MySQL, this program is called the database server (MySQL server).

Database Server: A database server is a program that permits access to databases over a network. The server is responsible for the management of the data and for the execution of SQL commands.

Data Record: A data record, or simply *record*, is a row of a table.

Domain Name: The domain name denotes an entire network. A local network might consist of computers with the names *mars.sol*, *uranus.sol*, and *jupiter.sol*, in which case *mars*, *uranus*, and *jupiter* are computer names (*hostnames*), and *sol* is the domain name.

Domain Name Server (DNS): Internally, communication within a network takes place on the basis of IP numbers (e.g., 192.168.0.27). Since mere mortals do not keep track of such numbers very well, each computer also has a computer name, composed of host name and domain name (e.g., *uranus.sol*).

Whenever such a name is used, the running program must determine the associated IP number. Sometimes, the converse case arises, and for a given IP number, the computer name is required. In both situations, the domain name server provides the answer. (Small networks can get by without a DNS. In that case, the association between IP numbers and computer names is determined from static tables, under Unix/Linux in the file /etc/hosts.)

Foreign Key: A foreign key is a unique value (usually an integer) that refers to a particular column of another table. A foreign key thus creates a link (relation) between two tables.

Full-Text Index: A full-text index enables the search for several words in arbitrary order within a text. To make full-text search efficient, a special index is required, known as a full-text index.

Global Assembly Cache (GAC): This notion is specific to Microsoft. It describes a central directory of all *.dll files for .NET programs. In contrast to the Windows system directory, in the GAC, several different versions of a library can be installed simultaneously without leading to a conflict.

Host Name: The host name is the name of a computer valid over a network. If the complete name of the computer is *jupiter.sol*, then *jupiter* is the host name and *sol* the domain name.

Hot Backup: What makes a hot backup hot is that during the backup process, the database server can continue to run almost completely undisturbed. (During a normal backup, on the other hand, no changes in the data may be made.) Hot backups can currently be made in MySQL only with a commercial auxiliary program that works only for InnoDB tables.

Include File: An include file is a part of program code. It is read by the compiler (e.g., C) or during code execution (e.g., PHP).

Index: In database-speak, an index, or its synonym *key*, is an ordered list of the content of a table. An index serves primarily to speed up access to individual records: Instead of searching through all records, it suffices to search the index. Then, the desired record can be read directly. The use of an index is comparable to that of an index in a book.

InnoDB Tables: In MySQL, tables can be stored on the hard drive in more than one format, including MyISAM and InnoDB. InnoDB tables possess some additional functionality over MyISAM tables, such as transactions and foreign key constraints. The name InnoDB is derived from the name of the company Innobase, with DB being short for *database*.

Internet Service Provider (ISP): An ISP is a company that provides technical support and hosting of web sites. ISPs are used by commercial enterprises and private individuals who wish to maintain web sites on the Internet but do not themselves possess a permanent or sufficiently high-speed Internet connection. Be careful in your choice of ISP that it supports the programs presented in this book (Apache, PHP, MySQL, etc.). There are, of course, ISPs that offer Microsoft products instead.

Key: A key is an ordered index of a table. See also the entry of the synonym *Index*.

Logging: Logging refers to the recording of SQL commands in a file. The motivation for logging is usually to have available all the changes to the database made since the last backup so that the database can be recreated in the event of disaster. With MySQL, logging is also a prerequisite for replication.

MyISAM Tables: The MySQL server can store tables in various formats. The most important such format is called MyISAM, which stands for *indexed sequential access method*, referring to the method of access to data records within a file with the aid of an index. An alternative to MyISAM tables is InnoDB tables.

Named Pipes: Named pipes represent a mechanism whereby two programs can communicate under Windows NT/2000/XP. Data exchange takes place according to the principle of first in, first out (FIFO).

Normal Form: A database generally consists of a number of tables. A goal in the design of tables is to avoid redundancy. This goal is supported by particular rules. When the first *n* such rules are adhered to, the database is said to be in *n*th normal form.

Normalization: This term refers to the optimization of the database design to avoid redundancy. The goal is generally to achieve third normal form.

PHP: PHP is a script language for programming dynamic web sites. The program code is located in *.php files. These files are executed by the PHP interpreter at each access over the web server. The resulting HTML document is passed on to the web server.

Port: Network packets that are sent using the TCP/IP protocol are always addressed to a particular port. The port number is thus part of the address to which the packet is sent. Ports help in categorizing network traffic. For example, for data exchange between web browsers and web servers, port 80 is used. MySQL uses port 3306 by default.

Primary Index (Primary Key): The primary index identifies each record of a table uniquely. Normally, the primary key field is an integer column. Whenever a new record is inserted, the database server determines a new, unique, value for this column.

Privilege: In MySQL nomenclature, a privilege is a right to execute particular database operations (e.g., read or change data in a particular table).

Query: In database language, a query is generally a *SELECT* command. The syntax of this command is part of the language SQL (structured query language). SQL specifies how commands to the database server must be structured.

Query Cache: In many database applications, it happens that the same queries must be executed over and over. To speed up such queries, MySQL possesses, since version 4.0, a query cache, that is, temporary storage in which queries and their results can be stored. Queries thus stored can be answered much more rapidly than otherwise. However, this temporary storage must be deleted at each change in the underlying table.

Referential Integrity: Referential integrity holds if between linked tables, no reference points to nowhere. (For example, if referential integrity is satisfied for a library database, then there cannot exist a book title whose associated publisher does not exist in the database. On the other hand, if referential integrity has been damaged, then there might well be a publisher number in the titles table that does not exist in the publisher table.)

Many database systems can automatically check referential integrity when changes to a database are made. This requires the setting up of foreign key constraints, otherwise known as integrity rules. MySQL currently supports foreign key constraints only for InnoDB tables.

Relations: The most characteristic feature of relational databases is that a number of tables in a database can be linked based on their contents. These links are also called *relations*. The links are referenced in SQL commands by the *JOIN* operator or with *WHERE* conditions.

Replication: Through the process of replication, all changes to a database are carried out not on one, but on several database servers. Thus the same database exists on several servers. The advantages are increased security (if one server goes down) and greater speed (all servers can answer SQL queries, even if only one can make changes).

Schema: The schema (or *database schema*) describes the layout of a database, that is, the tables, their columns and data types, indexes, links between tables, etc.

Server: A server is a central program that provides services or data to other programs (called *clients*). Examples of servers are the MySQL server (a database server) and Apache (a web server).

Socket File: A socket file enables communication under Unix/Linux between two programs. A socket file is not a real file, in that it contains no data and has length zero.

Local connections between a MySQL client and the MySQL server generally take place under Unix/Linux over a socket file, since this type of communication is more efficient than the network protocol TCP/IP. (An exception is Java clients, which do not support socket files.) The usual file name is /var/lib/mysql/mysql.sock. This file name can be set via the configuration file /etc/my.cnf.

Stored Procedures: A stored procedure is program code that is executed directly by the database server. Often, stored procedures are formulated in a programming language that extends SQL through the use of control structures (loops, branching, etc.). MySQL currently does not support stored procedures.

Tables: A table is a part of a database. The properties of a table are determined by its columns or fields (name and data type) and indexes. The rows of a table are also called data records. The MySQL server can store tables in several formats (e.g., MyISAM, InnoDB).

Timestamps: The data type *TIMESTAMP* is characterized by the fact that columns of this type store the current date and time each time a change is made.

Transaction: A transaction is a group of logically related SQL commands. Transaction-capable database systems are able to confirm all the commands of a transaction together or to abort them as a group. That is, a transaction is never only partially completed. Transactions thereby contribute to data security.

Transactions can also improve efficiency in that there is no longer the need to lock entire tables with *LOCK* during the execution of several SQL commands.

MySQL currently supports transactions only for particular table formats, such as InnoDB.

Trigger: This term refers to SQL code (stored procedures) that is automatically executed as a result of particular actions (e.g., upon an *UPDATE* or *INSERT* command). Triggers can be used, for example, to ensure that certain rules are followed in changing data. MySQL currently does not support triggers.

Unicode: Unicode is a character set in which every character is represented by a 16-bit integer. Thus almost all the special characters of the world's languages can be represented in this character set. MySQL supports the storage of Unicode character sets since version 4.1.

Within Unicode, there are various formats that specify the byte order of the 16-bit integer. Common formats are UTF8 (1 to 3 bytes, depending on the character code, avoids code 0) and UTF16 (2 bytes for each character code).

Uniform Resource Locator (URL): This unwieldy term denotes Internet addresses (e.g., `http://www.kofler.cc/mysql/` or `ftp://ftp.mysql.com`). Additional information can be provided in a URL, such as in `http://my.company/page.html?var=123` or `ftp://username.company/directory`.

Views: A view is an SQL query that enables a special view of several tables of a database. Views are used, for example, to enable simple access to particular parts of a table (e.g., for reasons of security if only part of a table is to be processed). Currently, MySQL does not support views.

Web Server: A web server is a program that makes HTML pages available over the Internet. The most popular web server today (current market share about sixty percent) is Apache.

MySQL 4.1

MYSQL 4.1 WAS OFFICIALLY INTRODUCED IN January 2003. As I was completing this appendix in July 2003, an alpha version of MySQL 4.1.0 had been available for several months on the MySQL web site. In order to be able to present the most current information possible, I downloaded the developer's version of the source code (as of 28 July 2003) and compiled it under Red Hat Linux 9. The information in this appendix is thus based on a version that lies somewhere between 4.1.0 and 4.1.1.

The first stable MySQL 4.1.n will probably not appear until 2004. By then, there are likely to be considerable changes from what appears here.

SubSELECTs

The improvement desired most by many MySQL users relates to the *SELECT* command. MySQL finally supports the syntax for formulating nested *SELECT* commands. There are three syntactic variants:

- *SELECT . . . WHERE col = (SELECT . . .)*
  In this variant, the second *SELECT* query must return a single value (one row, one column). This value is used for the comparison *col = ...* (Other comparison operators are permitted, such as *col> . . . , col <= . . . , col <> . . . .*)

- *SELECT . . . WHERE col IN (SELECT . . .)*
  In this variant, the second *SELECT* query may return a list of individual values. This list is then processed in the form *SELECT . . . WHERE col IN (n1, n2, n3)*. Instead of *IN*, one may also use *NOT IN*.

- *SELECT . . . WHERE EXISTS (SELECT . . .)*
  In this variant, the second query is executed for each found record from the first *SELECT* query. A record from the first *SELECT* query remains in the result list only if the second query returns a result (at least one record). In this variant as well, the negation operator *NOT* may be used.
  EXISTS constructions are generally useful only when the two *SELECT* commands are linked by a *WHERE* condition (as with a *JOIN* operation). We will give an example shortly.

SELECT commands can also be used in the *WHERE* condition of *UPDATE* and *DELETE* commands to determine what records have been altered or deleted.

Examples: The following examples are based on the database *mylibrary*. The first command determines the number of titles published by *Addison-Wesley*:

```
USE mylibrary
SELECT COUNT(*) FROM titles WHERE publID =
  (SELECT publID FROM publishers WHERE publName = "Addison-Wesley")
```

The next command searches for titles for which no author has been stored:

```
SELECT title FROM titles
WHERE titleID NOT IN (SELECT titleID FROM rel_title_author)
```

The following command is equivalent to the one above:

```
SELECT title FROM titles WHERE NOT EXISTS
  (SELECT * FROM rel_title_author
    WHERE titles.titleID = rel_title_author.titleID)
```

The following command deletes all entries from the table *rel_title_author* that do not refer to existing records in *authors* or *titles*:

```
DELETE FROM rel_title_author
WHERE authID NOT IN (SELECT authID FROM authors) OR
      titleID NOT IN (SELECT titleID FROM titles)
```

> **POINTER**   *Additional subSELECT examples appear in Chapter 7. There, it is shown how equivalent queries can be composed in MySQL 4.0. (SubSELECTs simplify the construction of many commands. In most cases, however, it is possible to create equivalent commands using JOIN operations. This holds as well for the commands just presented.)*

Limitations: The version of MySQL that I tested was incapable of evaluating *LIMIT* in sub*SELECT* commands (e.g., *SELECT . . . WHERE . . . IN (SELECT . . . LIMIT 10)*).

Working with Character Strings

The management of character sets has fundamentally changed in MySQL 4.1. The following list summarizes the most important changes:

- While MySQL 4.0 uses a single character set for the entire server (that is, for all databases), now a separate character set can be used for each database, indeed, for each table and each column within a table.

- The character set and sort order (*collation*) have been separated. With many character sets, one may now choose between two or more sort orders.

The character set is responsible only for the encoding of characters, for changing between uppercase and lowercase (*UCASE, LCASE*), and transformation into Unicode. Furthermore, the character set determines the type of a character (e.g., number, letter, or white space).

The sort order influences comparison operations like =, <, and >, which also appear in *ORDER BY, GROUP BY, DISTINCT, MIN, MAX*, etc.

- MySQL now supports Unicode, and in fact, in two formats: UTF8 and UCS2. In both cases, a 16-bit code is assigned to each character. The formats vary in how these codes are stored.

  With UCS2, 2 bytes are always used. The higher-valued byte is stored first. The character A, with code 65, is thus stored with 2 bytes with values 0 and 65. Thus each character requires exactly 2 bytes. The result is that with ASCII text, every second byte is a zero-byte. (UCS2 is also a synonym for UTF16; both denote the same Unicode format.)

  With UTF8, the number of bytes used for a character depends on the code. ASCII characters (code less than 128) are stored with a single byte, while other characters use 2 to 3 bytes. UTF8 has two advantages: First, problems with the zero-byte are avoided (important for programming in C, which assumes that character strings end with the zero-byte). Second, the storage of English text is much more compact.

The default character set in MySQL remains *latin1* with sort order *latin1_swedish_ci*. If the new string functions are not used, then nothing should change in MySQL's sorting behavior.

> **WARNING**   *For text columns declared with* VARCHAR(n) *or* CHAR(n), *currently* n *specifies the number of bytes. However, depending on the character set, you may only be able to store many fewer than* n *characters. With UCS2 the number is simply* n/2, *while with UTF8, the number varies, since different characters are coded with different numbers of bytes. It is possible that the column length in future versions of MySQL will be oriented to the character set, so that with* CHAR(10) CHARSET utf8, *a column with thirty bytes is reserved, so that in the worst case, ten UTF8 characters will have sufficient space.*
>
> *String functions like* LEFT, MID, *and their kin function without problems with Unicode.* MID(column, 3, 1) *thus returns the third character (not the third byte). However, caution is called for in determining the length of a character string:* LENGTH(column) *returns the number of bytes, while* CHAR_LENGTH(col) *returns the number of characters.*

Determining the available character sets and sort orders: The new command *SHOW CHARACTER SET* returns a list of all character sets and their default sort orders. The column *Maxlen* gives the maximum number of bytes required to store a character. The following table gives the sorted result of the command *SHOW CHARACTER SET*:

SHOW CHARACTER SET

Charset	Description	Default collation	Maxlen
armscii8	ARMSCII-8 Armenian	armscii8_general_ci	1
ascii	US ASCII	ascii_general_ci	1
big5	Big5 Traditional Chinese	big5_chinese_ci	2
binary	Binary pseudo charset	binary	1
cp1250	Windows Central European	cp1250_general_ci	1
cp1251	Windows Cyrillic	cp1251_general_ci	1
cp1256	Windows Arabic	cp1256_general_ci	1
cp1257	Windows Baltic	cp1257_general_ci	1
cp850	DOS West European	cp850_general_ci	1
cp852	DOS Central European	cp852_general_ci	1
cp866	DOS Russian	cp866_general_ci	1
dec8	DEC West European	dec8_swedish_ci	1
euckr	EUC-KR Korean	euckr_korean_ci	2
gb2312	GB2312 Simplified Chinese	gb2312_chinese_ci	2
gbk	GBK Simplified Chinese	gbk_chinese_ci	2
greek	ISO 8859-7 Greek	greek_general_ci	1
hebrew	ISO 8859-8 Hebrew	hebrew_general_ci	1
hp8	HP West European	hp8_english_ci	1
keybcs2	DOS Kamenicky Czech-Slovak	keybcs2_general_ci	1
koi8r	KOI8-R Relcom Russian	koi8r_general_ci	1
koi8u	KOI8-U Ukrainian	koi8u_general_ci	1
latin1	ISO 8859-1 West European	latin1_swedish_ci	1
latin2	ISO 8859-2 Central European	latin2_general_ci	1
latin5	ISO 8859-9 Turkish	latin5_turkish_ci	1
latin7	ISO 8859-13 Baltic	latin7_general_ci	1
macce	Mac Central European	macce_general_ci	1
macroman	Mac West European	macroman_general_ci	1
sjis	Shift-JIS Japanese	sjis_japanese_ci	2
swe7	7bit Swedish	swe7_swedish_ci	1
tis620	TIS620 Thai	tis620_thai_ci	1
ucs2	UCS-2 Unicode	ucs2_general_ci	2
ujis	EUC-JP Japanese	ujis_japanese_ci	3
utf8	UTF-8 Unicode	utf8_general_ci	3

The command *SHOW COLLATION LIKE 'name%'* returns a list of all sort orders that begin with *name*. The following table shows the sort orders available for the *latin1* character set:

SHOW COLLATION LIKE 'latin1%'

Collation	Charset	Id	Default	Compiled	Sortlen
latin1_bin	latin1	47		Yes	0
latin1_danish_ci	latin1	15			0
latin1_general_ci	latin1	48			0
latin1_general_cs	latin1	49			0
latin1_german1_ci	latin1	5			0
latin1_german2_ci	latin1	31		Yes	2
latin1_swedish_ci	latin1	8	Yes	Yes	0

From the table, one can see what the naming convention is: The name of the sort order begins with the name of the character set. The abbreviations *_bin*, *_ci*, and *_cs* at the end of the name stand for *binary*, *case insensitive*, and *case sensitive*. With *binary* sorting, only the codes of characters are compared. The other variants take conventions of the language in question into account. The *ci* variant considers upper- and lowercase letters to be equivalent.

The sorting behavior of both *german* variants is defined by the German Industrial Standard (Deutsche Industrienorm, or DIN). Thus *german1* considers *ä, ö, ü*, and *ß* as equivalent to *a, o, u*, and *s*, while *german2* considers *ä, ö, ü*, and *ß* as equivalent to *ae, oe, ue*, and *ss*.

SQL commands and syntax: To control the character-set functions, there are many new SQL commands and syntactic extensions:

- The commands *CREATE/ALTER DATABASE* and *CREATE/ALTER TABLE* have been extended so that the character set and sort order can be specified for each database, table, and individual text columns (see the command reference in Chapter 18). Here is the syntax for specifying the character set:

```
CHARACTER SET csname [COLLATE colname]
```

In addition, there are several syntactic variants, such as *CHARSET* as an abbreviation for *CHARACTER SET* and the form *CHARACTER SET = csname* (in the form of an assignment). The following command creates a new table in which Unicode character strings can be stored in all text columns:

```
CREATE TABLE test (id INT NOT NULL AUTO_INCREMENT,
                   data1 VARCHAR(30),
                   ... ,
                   PRIMARY KEY(id))
    CHARSET utf8
```

- With *CONVERT(s USING charset)*, the string *s* is transformed into the desired character set. *SELECT HEX(CONVERT('ABCäöü' USING utf8))* returns, for example, the hexadecimal code *414243C3A4C3B6C3BC*. For the character set *ucs2*, the result is *00410042004300E400F600FC*.

- In the specification of character strings, the name of the character set can be prefixed with *_*, e.g., *_latin1 "abcäöü"* or *_utf8 "abc"*.
  If the sort order is to be specified in comparisons, this can be given with *COLLATE*. For example, the following query without *COLLATE* returns 0 (*FALSE*), while with *COLLATE* the result is 1 (*TRUE*). The same holds as well for comparisons with *WHERE* and with *HAVING*:

```
SELECT _latin1 "a" COLLATE latin1_german1_ci =
       _latin1 "ä" COLLATE german1_latin1_ci
```

COLLATE leads to an error if the desired sort order is unavailable for the given character set.

- *COLLATE* can also be used with a variety of other SQL commands:

```
SELECT column COLLATE colname [AS aliasname]
ORDER BY column COLLATE colname
GROUP BY column COLLATE colname
DISTINCT column COLLATE colname
```

- *COLLATE* can also be used in aggregation functions (e.g., *SELECT MAX(column COLLATE colname)* . . .).

- The new data type *NCHAR* (for *national character*) corresponds to *CHAR CHARSET utf8*. (If you wish to define a UTF8 column, then with *NCHAR* you avoid having to specify the character set.)

  UTF8 columns of variable length can be declared with *NCHAR VARCHAR(n)*. (The key word *NVARCAHR* does not exist.)

> **POINTER**   *There is much more information on character set management in a new chapter of the MySQL documentation:*
>
> http://www.mysql.com/doc/en/Charset.html

A Unicode Example

The following commands show how one can begin experimenting with the new functions. We create a table with two columns, one in the character set *latin1*, the other in the character set *utf8*:

```
USE test
CREATE TABLE t1
  (col1 VARCHAR(50) CHARACTER SET latin1,
  col2 VARCHAR(50) CHARACTER SET utf8)
INSERT INTO t1 (col1) VALUES
  ('abc'), ('Abc'), ('ABC'), ('bar'), ('Barenboim'),
  ('Bär'), ('Bären'), ('bärtig'), ('Ärger')
UPDATE t1 SET col2 = CONVERT(col1 USING utf8)
SELECT *, LENGTH(col2), CHAR_LENGTH(col2) FROM t1
```

col1	col2	LENGTH(col2)	CHAR_LENGTH(col2)
abc	abc	3	3
Abc	Abc	3	3
ABC	ABC	3	3
bar	bar	3	3
Barenboim	Barenboim	9	9
Bär	Bär	4	3
Bären	Bären	6	5
bärtig	bärtig	7	6
Ärger	Ärger	6	5

By default, column *col1* uses Swedish sort order:

```
SELECT col1 FROM t1 ORDER BY col1
```

col1
abc
Abc
ABC
bar
Barenboim
Bär
Bären
bärtig
Ärger

However, one could just as well use the *german1* sort order:

```
SELECT col1 FROM t1 ORDER BY col1 COLLATE latin1_german1_ci
```

col1
abc
Abc
ABC
Ärger
bar
Bär
Bären
Barenboim
bärtig

For *col2*, there are currently no available country-specific sort orders.

Managing Geometric and Geographic Data (OpenGIS)

Traditional tables and indexes are not very suitable for storing geometric and geographic data. For MySQL to be usable with geographic information systems (GIS for short), MySQL 4.1 has been extended with various new data types and a special R-tree index. The implementation adheres largely to the OpenGIS standard:

```
http://www.mysql.com/doc/en/Spatial_extensions_in_MySQL.html
http://www.opengis.org/
```

There is insufficient space here for a complete description of the possibilities opened up by these new developments. The following overview will have to serve as a brief introduction.

SQL commands and syntax: The commands *CREATE* and *ALTER TABLE* have been extended so that columns of data type *GEOMETRY* and spatial indexes (*SPATIAL INDEX*) can be defined:

```
CREATE TABLE t (id INT NOT NULL AUTO_INCREMENT,
                g GEOMETRY NOT NULL,
                PRIMARY KEY (id),
                SPATIAL INDEX (g))
```

The spatial index is based internally on R-trees. The basic idea is that for all geometric objects, a minimal *bounding box* is determined. Then, for the index, groups of neighboring objects are collected within a large rectangle. The result is a treelike index whose root node encompasses all the objects. The smaller rectangles contained within the larger one encompass smaller subsets of the geometric objects. A geometric search for objects can be speeded up considerably by such a structure, because one must search only those rectangles that overlap the search area.

Instead of *GEOMETRY*, the terms *POINT, MULTIPOINT, LINESTRING, MULTI-LINESTRING, POLYGON, MULTIPOLYGON*, and *GEOMETRYCOLLECTION* can be used. In each case, the column has type *GEOMETRY*. (In MySQL, in contrast to the OpenGIS specification, there do not exist different geometric data types, but only the all-inclusive type *GEOMETRY*, in which all possible geometric objects can be stored.)

To insert data into a *GEOMETRY* column, one can use the new functions *GeomFromText* and *GeomFromWBK*. The function *GeomFromText* expects as argument a character string, while *GeomFromWBK* expects a binary object that conforms to the WBK specification of OpenGIS. (WBK stands for *well-known binary representations*; it is a format for the binary representation of geometric objects.)

```
INSERT INTO t (g) VALUES(
  GeomFromText('POINT(10 10)'))
INSERT INTO t (g) VALUES(
  GeomFromText('LINESTRING(0 0, 10 10, 0 20)'))
INSERT INTO t (g) VALUES(
  GeomFromText('POLYGON((30 30, 30 40, 40 40, 40 30, 30 30))'))
```

To indicate geometric objects with *SELECT*, you must use the function *AsText*. If you require binary representation, then instead, use the function *AsBinary*:

```
SELECT id, AsText(g) FROM t
```

id	AsText(g)
1	POINT(10 10)
3	LINESTRING(0 0,10 10,0 20)
4	POLYGON((30 30,30 40,40 40,40 30,30 30))

If you wish to select all objects within a particular geometric region, then you can formulate your *WHERE* condition using the new function *WITHIN*:

```
SELECT id, AsText(g) FROM t
WHERE Within(g, textbfGeomFromText('POLYGON((5 5, 5 15, 15 15, 15 5, 5 5))'))
```

id	AsText(g)
1	POINT(10 10)

There are many additional functions for processing geometric objects, and here we can mention only a few representative examples to give you a taste of what is available:

- *GeometryType(geom)* determines the type of a *GEOMETRY* object (e.g., *POINT* or *LINESTRING*).

- *X(point)* and *Y(point)* determine the *X* and *Y* coordinates of a point.

- *Envelope(geom)* determines the bounding box, that is, the minimal circumscribing rectangle for the object. The result is a rectangular *POLYGON* object.

- *Area(polyg)* calculates the area of a polygon.

- *Intersects(g1, g2)* tests whether two geometric objects overlap.

Here is an example:

```
SELECT id, GeometryType(g), AsText(Envelope(g)) FROM t
```

id	GeometryType(g)	AsText(Envelope(g))
1	POINT	POLYGON((10 10,10 10,10 10,10 10 10))
3	LINESTRING	POLYGON((0 0,10 0,10 20,0 20,0 0))
4	POLYGON	POLYGON((30 30,40 30,40 40,30 40,30 30))

Limitations: There are some restrictions to be aware of in the use of OpenGIS functions:

- GIS data can be stored only in MyISAM tables.

- Only two-dimensional objects can be managed.

- Various functions were not yet implemented in the alpha version tested. It is to be expected that many tests will have to be made before one can consider the OpenGIS functions in MySQL to be mature and stable.

Precompiled SQL Commands (Prepared Statements)

The MySQL server and its client library are now capable of first sending an SQL command and then executing it repeatedly with various parameters. At the moment, it is only C programmers who can profit from this capability, but one may expect that the APIs for PHP, Perl, etc., will soon offer equivalent commands.

This type of command execution is useful whenever the identical command (generally *INSERT* or *UPDATE*) is to be executed repeatedly with differing parameters. Precompiled commands should be more efficient in such a case, since there would be less data traffic between client and server and since the server can optimize the execution of the command.

It remains, however, to see how noticeable this speed improvement will be in practice. I have not made any speed tests, but I suspect that the difference will be small. I see the principal advantage in the fact that in many cases, more readable program code will be achievable. In particular, as a programmer, you need no longer consider whether special characters appear in character strings or how numbers in strings are transformed.

Let us consider an example. The command *INSERT INTO titles (title, subtitle, langID) VALUES (?, ?, ?)* will be sent to the server with *mysql_prepare*. Then, three parameters (two strings and an integer) will be declared in a *MYSQL_BIND* field and added to the command with *mysql_bind_param*. With the strings, a buffer will be used for data transfer; with the integer, on the other hand, a direct connection to a variable (here *langID*) will be made.

The command can now be executed as often as you like with *mysql_execute* after the parameters have been set:

```c
// example c/prepare/main.c
#include <stdio.h>
#include <mysql.h>

int {main}(int argc, char *argv[])
{
  MYSQL *conn;        // connection to MySQL server
  MYSQL_STMT *stmt;   // prepared statement
  MYSQL_BIND bind[3]; // parameters

  char *insert =
    "INSERT INTO titles (title, subtitle, langID) VALUES (?, ?, ?)";
  char titlebuf[256], subtitlebuf[256];
  int langID;

  // establish connection to MySQL
  conn = mysql_init(NULL);
  ...

  // prepare SQL command with three parameters
  stmt = mysql_prepare(conn, insert, strlen(insert));
  bind[0].buffer_type = FIELD_TYPE_STRING;
  bind[0].buffer = titlebuf;
  bind[0].buffer_length = 256;

  bind[1].buffer_type = FIELD_TYPE_STRING;
  bind[1].buffer = subtitlebuf;
  bind[1].buffer_length = 256;

  bind[2].buffer_type = FIELD_TYPE_LONG;
  bind[2].buffer = (gptr) &langID;
  mysql_bind_param(stmt, bind);

  // execute SQL command
  strcpy(titlebuf, "title1");
  strcpy(subtitlebuf, "subtitle1");
  langID=999;
  mysql_execute(stmt);

  // execute SQL command again with other parameters
  strcpy(titlebuf, "title2");
  strcpy(subtitlebuf, "subtitle2");
  langID++;
  mysql_execute(stmt);

  // close connection
  mysql_close(conn);
  return 0;
}
```

More New Stuff

Operators: There are three new operators: *DIV* for integer division, *MOD* for the modulus function (the remainder upon integer division), and *SOUNDS LIKE* for text comparison. *WHERE SOUNDEX(a) = SOUNDEX(b)* is equivalent to *WHERE a SOUNDS LIKE b*.

ROLLUP: With *GROUP BY* queries, the new extension *WITH ROLLUP* results in a partial sum being created for each group, as well as a total sum for all the results. The following example determines how many discussion contributions there are in the individual discussion groups of *bigforum* and in which years they were written. The *NULL* rows contain the partial sums and complete sum:

```
USE bigforum

SELECT forumID, YEAR(timest) AS year, COUNT(*)
FROM messages
WHERE forumID<=3
GROUP BY forumID, year
WITH ROLLUP
```

forumID	year	COUNT(*)
1	2000	11
1	2001	101
1	2002 7	158
1	2003	16
1	[NULL]	286
2	2000	7
2	2001	64
2	2002	27
2	2003	2
2	[NULL]	100
3	2000	2
3	2001	31
3	2002	46
3	2003	2
3	[NULL]	81
[NULL]	[NULL]	467

Compression functions: *COMPRESS(string)* compresses the passed character string and returns as result a binary object that can be stored space-efficiently in a *BLOB* column. *UNCOMPRESS(binarydata)* undoes the compression. *UN-COMPRESSED_LENGTH(binarydata)* returns the length of the original character string.

Warnings and errors: With *SHOW WARNINGS* and *SHOW ERRORS* one can determine the warnings and errors triggered by the last-executed command. The variant forms *SHOW COUNT(*) WARNINGS/ERRORS* return the number of warnings/errors. Access to warnings is especially practical for the importation of text files with *LOAD DATA*.

Help: The new command *HELP* returns a brief help text to the specified functions. However, this command did not function in the version tested, so I cannot offer an example here.

Database directory: The new file db.opt, containing database options, is stored within database directories. (In the tested version, all that was in the file was the setting for the default character set for the database.)

Creating tables with identical layout: A new variant of *CREATE TABLE* simplifies the creation of new tables that are defined exactly like an existing table. (The new table is empty.)

```
CREATE TABLEnewtable LIKE oldtable
```

MySQL monitor: The program mysql recognizes two new options: --reconnect makes the program automatically attempt to recreate a broken connection; --disable-connect turns off this behavior. (The default is --reconnect.)

Client Programming

The libraries for client programming (C-API, PHP-API, Connector/ODBC, Connector/J) must be adapted for multibyte character sets. New versions of these APIs are already in development, but there was no documentation available at the time this book was completed. It is thus unclear, for example, how in the future a Unicode character string can be most easily stored by Perl, Java, VB, etc., in a MySQL table and then read out.

In the case of PHP, full support for the new MySQL functions is not expected until PHP 5, which was in beta testing as this text was written. However, some details are known. PHP will offer two MySQL APIs:

- One of these APIs should be 100 percent compatible with the API of PHP 4.*n* described in this book.

- However, the new MySQL functions will be supported only by the second MySQL API. Of course, many functions of this API can be used more or less as before, but there are many changes. The most apparent difference is that the function names begin with *mysqli_* (instead of *mysql_*).

Incompatibilities

As far as I know, MySQL 4.1 is incompatible with MySQL 4.0 in at least two points:

- *PASSWORD* returns longer and more robust encrypted character strings than previously. To encrypt strings as before, you must use *OLD_PASSWORD*. The stronger encryption of passwords affects the table *mysql.user*, in which access information for all MySQL users is stored. When the *mysql* database is taken over from an older MySQL version, the *mysql* database must be adapted with the script mysql_fix_privilege_tables. The column *user.password* will thereby be increased to 45 characters. New or changed passwords will automatically be encrypted with *PASSWORD*, while old passwords (with only 16 characters) will continue to be recognized and accepted.

- Values from *TIMESTAMP* columns will now be formatted like *DATETIME* values, that is, by *YYYY-MM-DD HH:MM:DD* (instead of by *YYYYMMDDHHMMDD*).

If your program makes use of the old form, then simply add 0 to *TIMESTAMP* values (thus *SELECT ts+0 FROM table*).

It remains to be seen how much in the way of changes to client programming will be required as a result of the new character-set functions.

Overview of New and Changed Commands

The following list summarizes all SQL commands that are either completely new or whose syntax has been significantly altered or extended:

ALTER DATABASE (character set)
ALTER TABLE (character set)
CREATE DATABASE (character set)
CREATE TABLE (character set)
CREATE TABLE newtable LIKE existingtable
DELETE (sub*SELECT*s)
GROUP BY . . . WITH ROLLUP
HELP
SELECT (sub*SELECT*s)
SHOW CHARACTER SET
SHOW COLLATION
SHOW COLUMN TYPES
SHOW CREATE DATABASE
SHOW ERRORS, SHOW COUNT(*) ERRORS
SHOW PRIVILEGES
SHOW TABLE TYPES
SHOW WARNINGS, SHOW COUNT(*) WARNINGS
UPDATE (sub*SELECT*s)

Additionally, there are many new or changed functions, of which we mention here only the most important. (In this list are missing, among others, countless new GIS functions.)

CHARSET
COMPRESS, UNCOMPRESS, UNCOMPRESSED_LENGTH
CONVERT(s USING charset)
CRC32
PASSWORD (stronger encryption)
OLD_PASSWORD (encryption as before)
VARIANCE

Moreover, there are new data types *GEOMETRY* and *NCHAR*, the index type *SPATIAL INDEX*, the constants *TRUE* and *FALSE*, and the operators *MOD, DIV*, and *SOUNDS LIKE*.

APPENDIX C

Example Files

THE EXAMPLE FILES FOR THIS book are available as compressed files for download at the web site www.apress.com. To decompress them under Windows, you can use, for example, WinZip (http://www.winzip.com/), while under Unix/Linux, you use the command unzip.

Trying Out the Example Programs

REMARK *All the example programs will work only if the databases described in this book are made available and if you change the user names and passwords in the code so that they are accepted by your MySQL installation.*

Some of the examples assume at least MySQL 4.0.n, while most are compatible with MySQL 3.23.n.

PHP examples: All the PHP files assume at least PHP 4.1. Better would be PHP 4.2 or 4.3. You must change the login name and password in the code! This affects the following files:

```
general/*.php
myforum/myforumpassword.inc.php
mylibrary/mylibrarypassword.inc.php
pictures/connect.inc.php
vote_xxx/results.php
```

If you have problems in executing the example programs, please read the section "Error Checking" of Chapter 11.

Updates, Errata, Links, Discussion Forum

A collection of MySQL links, a discussion forum for this book, and any updates and errata that come to my attention can be found at my web site: http://www.kofler.cc.

APPENDIX D
Bibliography

1. Sharon Bjeletich et al. *Microsoft SQL Server 7.0 Unleashed*. SAMS, 1999.

2. Rich Bowen et al. *Apache Server Unleashed*. SAMS, 2000.

3. Chris Date, Hugh Darwen. *A Guide to the SQL Standard*. Addison-Wesley Longman, 1998.

4. Paul DuBois. *MySQL*, second edition. Sams, 2003.

5. Paul DuBois. *MySQL Cookbook*. O'Reilly, 2002.

6. W. J. Gilmore. *A Programmer's Introduction to PHP 4.0*. Apress, 2001.

7. Cay S. Horstmann, Gary Cornell. *Core Java 2*, volume 2. Sun Microsystems Press/Prentice Hall, 1997.

8. Michael Kofler. *Definitive Guide to Excel VBA*, second edition. Apress, 2003.

9. Michael Kofler. *Linux: Installation, Configuration, and Use*, second edition. Addison-Wesley, 1999.

10. Michael Kofler. *Visual Basic Database Programming*. Addison-Wesley, 2001.

11. Laura Lemay. *Teach Yourself Perl in 21 Days*, third edition. SAMS, 1999.

12. Robert Orfali, Dan Harkey, Jeri Edwards. *Client/Server Survival Guide*, third edition. John Wiley & Sons, 1999.

13. Tobias Ratschiller, Till Gerken. *Web Application Development with PHP 4.0*. New Riders, 2000.

14. David Sceppa. *Microsoft ADO.NET (Core Reference)*. Microsoft Press, 2002.

15. David Solomon et al. *Microsoft SQL Server 6.5 Unleashed*. SAMS, 1996.

16. Carsten Thomsen. *Database Programming with Visual Basic .NET*. Apress, 2002.

17. Luke Welling, Laura Thomson. *PHP and MySQL Web Development*. SAMS, 2001.

18. Randy Yarger, George Reese, Tim King. *MySQL & mSQL*. O'Reilly, 1999.

Index

3ds Max® 2012 Bible

Kelly L. Murdock

WILEY

John Wiley & Sons, Inc.

3ds Max® 2012 Bible

Published by
John Wiley & Sons, Inc.
10475 Crosspoint Boulevard
Indianapolis, IN 46256
www.wiley.com

For general information on our other products and services or to obtain technical support, please contact our Customer Care Department within the U.S. at (877) 762-2974, outside the U.S. at (317) 572-3993 or fax (317) 572-4002.

Wiley also publishes its books in a variety of electronic formats. Some content that appears in print may not be available in electronic books.

Library of Congress Control Number: 2011932100

How can one tell if a marriage will thrive?
It has to be more than just learning to survive.
A marriage isn't just to keep and protect,
but will succeed if built on love and respect,
where two lives together are never apart.
and their souls are united and they love with one heart.
Each spouse must learn to forgive and forget,
and work together to overcome every threat.
A successful marriage weathers storms that descend,
and always finds a way to help each other transcend.
Each must be willing to shed and share tears,
and help one another to silence all fears.
An enduring marriage has smiles and laughter,
and shares the promise of love ever after.
A lasting marriage is one to which I aspire
having seen it in my parents whom I greatly admire.

To Mom and Dad, on the year of their 50th wedding
anniversary, 2012.

About the Author

Kelly Murdock has been authoring computer books for many years now and still gets immense enjoyment from the completed work. His book credits include various 3D, graphics, multimedia, and Web titles, including ten previous editions of this book, *3ds Max Bible*. Other major accomplishments include *Google SketchUp Bible, Edgeloop Character Modeling for 3D Professionals Only, Maya 6 and 7 Revealed, LightWave 3D 8 Revealed, The Official Guide to Anime Studio, Poser 6, 7, and 8 Revealed, 3D Game Animation For Dummies, gmax Bible, Adobe Atmosphere Bible, Master VISUALLY HTML and XHTML, JavaScript Visual Blueprint,* and co-authoring duties on two editions of the *Illustrator Bible* (for versions 9 and 10) and five editions of the *Adobe Creative Suite Bible*.

With a background in engineering and computer graphics, Kelly has been all over the 3D industry and still finds it fascinating. He's used high-level CAD workstations for product design and analysis, completed several large-scale visualization projects, created 3D models for feature films and games, worked as a freelance 3D artist, and even did some 3D programming. Kelly's been using 3D Studio since version 3 for DOS. Kelly has also branched into training others in 3D technologies. He currently works as a production manager for an upcoming game company.

In his spare time, Kelly enjoys playing basketball and collecting video games.

Credits

Senior Acquisitions Editor
Stephanie McComb

Project Editor
Martin V. Minner

Technical Editor
Chris Murdock

Copy Editor
Gwenette Gaddis

Editorial Director
Robyn Siesky

Business Manager
Amy Knies

Senior Marketing Manager
Sandy Smith

Vice President and Executive Group Publisher
Richard Swadley

Vice President and Executive Publisher
Barry Pruett

Project Coordinator
Patrick Redmond

Graphics and Production Specialists
Timothy C. Detrick
Joyce Haughey

Quality Control Technician
Lindsay Amones

Proofreading and Indexing
ConText Editorial Services, Inc.
BIM Indexing & Proofreading Services

Vertical Websites Project Manager
Laura Moss-Hollister

Vertical Websites Assistant Project Manager
Jenny Swisher

Vertical Websites Associate Producer
Doug Kuhn

Contents at a Glance

Contents

Contents

Contents

Contents

Contents

Contents

Contents

Contents

Contents

Contents

Contents

Contents

Contents

Contents

Contents

Contents

Contents

Contents

Contents

Preface

Every time I enter the computer room (which my wife calls the dungeon), my wife still says that I am off to my "fun and games." I, as always, flatly deny this accusation, saying that it is serious work that I am involved in. But later, when I emerge with a twinkle in my eye and excitedly ask her to take a look at my latest rendering, I know that she is right. Working with 3D graphics is pure "fun and games."

My goal in writing this book was to take all my fun years of playing and working in 3D and boil them down into something that's worthwhile for you, the reader. This goal was compounded by the fact that all you Max-heads out there are at different levels. Luckily, this book is thick enough to include a little something for everyone.

The audience level for the book ranges from beginning to intermediate, with a smattering of advanced topics for the seasoned user. If you're new to Max, then you'll want to start at the beginning and move methodically through the book. If you're relatively comfortable making your way around Max, then review the Table of Contents for sections that can enhance your fundamental base. If you're a seasoned pro, then you'll want to watch for coverage of the features new to Release 2012.

Another goal of this book is to make it a complete reference for Max. To achieve this goal, I've gone into painstaking detail to cover almost every feature in Max, including coverage of every primitive, material and map type, modifier, and controller.

As this book has come together, I've tried to write the type of book that I'd like to read. I've tried to include a variety of scenes that are infused with creativity. It is my hope that these examples will not only teach you how to use the software but also provide a creative springboard for you in your own projects. After all, that's what turns 3D graphics from work into "fun and games."

Who Is Max?

Before you go any further, I should explain my naming convention. The official name of the product in this release is 3ds Max 2012, but I simply refer to it as Max. This reference is a nickname given to a piece of software that has become more familiar to me than the family pets (whose names are Fuzzy, Snickers, and Pooky). Note: I have not been successful in training Max to come when I call or to sit on command, but it will on occasion play dead.

One way we humans develop our personalities is to incorporate desirable personality traits from those around us. Max's personality is developing as well: Every new release has incorporated a plethora of desirable new features. Many of these features come from the many additional plug-ins being developed to enhance Max. With each new release, Max has adopted many features that were available as plug-ins for previous releases. Several new features have been magically assimilated into the core product, such as the Character Studio and the Hair and Fur system. These additions make Max's personality much more likable, like a human developing a sense of humor.

Other personality traits are gained by stretching in new directions. Max and its developers have accomplished this feat as well. Many of the new features are completely new, not only to Max, but also to the industry. As Max grows up, it will continue to mature by adopting new features and inventing others. I just hope Max doesn't experience a midlife crisis in the next version.

Along with adopted features and new developments, the development teams at Autodesk have sought feedback from Max users. This feedback has resulted in many small tweaks to the package that enable scenes to be created more quickly and easily.

Some additional factors have appeared in Max's house that certainly affect Max's development. First is the appearance of Max's adopted brother, Maya. There are other siblings in the Autodesk household (including MotionBuilder and AutoCAD), but Maya is closest in age to Max, and its personality likely will rub off in different ways.

The second big factor is that Max has developed an alter ego that imagines it is a superhero. The 3ds Max installation discs ship with both 32-bit and 64-bit versions. The 64-bit version overcomes the 2GB hardware restriction and lets users work with huge datasets. This represents a huge leap forward in the scale of models that you can work with. In time, I see Max assuming this superhero persona permanently.

Max also has a split personality with two different versions. The standard 3ds Max 2012 is intended for the entertainment markets, and the new 3ds Max 2012 Design package is intended for visualization and architecture users. The differences between these two versions are subtle, but I'm glad to report that both versions are covered.

About This Book

Let me paint a picture of the writing process. It starts with years of experience, which are followed by months of painstaking research. There were system crashes and personal catastrophes and the always-present, ever-looming deadlines. I wrote into the early hours of the morning and during the late hours of the night—burning the candle at both ends and in the middle all at the same time. It was grueling and difficult, and spending all this time staring at the Max interface made me feel like . . . well . . . like an animator.

Sound familiar? This process actually isn't much different from what 3D artists, modelers, and animators do on a daily basis, and, like you, I find satisfaction in the finished product.

Tutorials aplenty

I've always been a very visual learner—the easiest way for me to gain knowledge is by doing things for myself while exploring at the same time. Other people learn by reading and comprehending ideas. In this book, I've tried to present information in a number of ways to make the information usable for all types of learners. That is why you see detailed discussions of the various features along with tutorials that show these concepts in action.

The tutorials appear throughout the book and are clearly marked with the "Tutorial" label in front of the title. They always include a series of logical steps, typically ending with a figure for you to study and compare. These tutorial examples are provided on the book's CD to give you a firsthand look and a chance to get some hands-on experience.

I've attempted to "laser focus" all the tutorials down to one or two key concepts. All tutorials are designed to be completed in 10 steps or less. This means that you probably will not want to place the results in your portfolio. For example, many of the early tutorials don't have any materials applied because I felt that using materials before they've been explained would only confuse you.

I've attempted to think of and use examples that are diverse, unique, and interesting, while striving to make them simple, light, and easy to follow. I'm happy to report that every example in the book is included on the CD along with the models and textures required to complete the tutorial.

The tutorials often don't start from scratch but instead give you a starting point. This approach lets me "laser focus" the tutorials even more, and with fewer, more relevant steps, you can learn and experience the concepts without the complexity. On the book's CD, you will find the Max files that are referenced in Step 1 of most tutorials.

In addition to the starting-point files, every tutorial has been saved at the completion of the tutorial steps. These files are marked with the word *final* at the end of the filename. If you get stuck in a tutorial, simply open the final example and compare the settings.

I've put lots of effort into this book, and I hope it helps you in your efforts. I present this book as a starting point. In each tutorial, I've purposely left out most of the creative spice, leaving room for you to put it in—you're the one with the vision.

Eleventh time around

This book is now in its 11th edition, and the editors have requested some fanfare. We considered including a slice of celebration cake with the book, but someone in marketing decided that a CD full of good stuff would be better (if you look closely, you can find a tutorial that features doughnuts). This edition is packed with the maximum number of pages that can be bound into a paperback book, so if you're planning on taking a book to read on a subway ride, take this book and leave all the others behind. I'd hate to think that I caused some loyal readers back pain.

Several changes have been made in this edition. Many of the older tutorials have been retired to make room for the new features. I've also included a new Quick Start. And I've made room for new sections throughout the book covering the new features.

Although I've strived to make the book comprehensive, some features have fallen by the wayside and remain in the software only for backward compatibility. The Dynamics utility, for example, has been replaced with the much more agile reactor system. These deprecated features are mentioned but not covered in depth. If you need to learn about these features, I suggest you look for a previous edition of the *3ds Max Bible* where these older features were covered.

Designed for educators

Since I've begun teaching at the local university, I've begun to rethink how the book is organized. Previous editions presented all the information on specific topics like animation together. This is a fine approach for experienced users who are getting up to speed with Max, but for students just starting out, this comprehensive approach easily overloads beginners before they even get out of the starting gate.

The new approach splits the book into beginning-level topics that cover modeling, animation, and rendering before moving on to the advanced features in each topic. This allows the first half of the book to be used for beginning students as an introduction to the software without digging too deep into the advanced, trickier features.

How this book is organized

Many different aspects of 3D graphics exist, and in some larger production houses, you might be focused on only one specific area. However, for smaller organizations or the general hobbyist, you end up wearing all the hats—from modeler and lighting director to animator and post-production compositor. This book is organized to cover all the various aspects of 3D graphics, regardless of the hat on your head.

If you're so excited to be working with Max that you can't decide where to start, then head straight for the Quick Start. The Quick Start is a single chapter-long tutorial that takes you through the creation and animation of an entire scene. This Quick Start was included in response to some feedback from readers of the first edition who complained that they didn't know where to start. For those of you who were too anxious to wade through a mountain of material before you could create something, this Quick Start is for you.

The book is divided into the following parts:

- **Quick Start**—This single chapter (which is actually a chapter in Part I) is an entire animation project presented in several focused tutorials. It is designed to whet your appetite and get you up to speed and producing animations immediately.

- **Part I: Getting Started with 3ds Max**—Whether it's understanding the interface, working with the viewports, dealing with files, or customizing the interface, the chapters in this part get you comfortable with the interface so you won't get lost moving about this mammoth package.

- **Part II: Working with Objects**—Max objects can include meshes, cameras, lights, Space Warps, and anything that can be viewed in a viewport. This part starts by introducing the various primitive objects and also includes chapters on how to reference, select, clone, group, link, transform, and modify these various objects.

- **Part III: Modeling Basics**—Max includes several different ways to model objects. This part includes chapters covering the basic modeling methods and constructs including working with spline shapes, meshes, and polys. It also introduces modifiers and the Modifier Stack.

- **Part IV: Materials, Cameras, and Lighting Basics**—This part shows how to apply basic materials to objects including maps. It then delves into using cameras and lights, but it focuses on the basics of these topics while avoiding the advanced features.

- **Part V: Animation and Rendering Basics**—The simplest animation features include keyframing, constraints, and controllers. With these topics, you'll be able to animate scenes. This part also covers the basics of rendering scenes.

- **Part VI: Advanced Modeling**—This part continues the modeling features with coverage of XRefs, the Schematic View, mesh modifiers, compound objects, NURBS, patches, hair, fur, and cloth.

- **Part VII: Advanced Materials**—The Advanced Materials part includes coverage of unwrapping, UV coordinates, pelt mapping, the Render to Texture interface, and Normal maps.

- **Part VIII: Advanced Animation Techniques**—After users are comfortable with the basics of animation, they can move on to advanced techniques, including animation modifiers, the expression controller, wiring parameters, the Track View, and the Motion Mixer.
- **Part IX: Working with Characters**—This part covers creating and working with bipeds, bone systems, rigging, skinning, and character crowds. It also provides coverage of the various inverse kinematics methods.
- **Part X: Dynamic Animation**—This part covers creating animation sequences using physics calculations. It includes coverage of particles, Space Warps, the cool features of reactor, and using forces to animate hair and cloth.
- **Part XI: Advanced Lighting and Rendering**—Advanced lighting concepts include using the Light Tracer and Radiosity, and the advanced rendering topics include Atmospheric and Render Effects, network rendering, raytracing, and mental ray.
- **Appendixes**—At the very end of this book, you'll find two appendixes that cover the new features of Max 2012 and the contents of the book's CD.

Using the book's icons

The following margin icons are used to help you get the most out of this book:

Note
Notes highlight useful information that you should take into consideration. ∎

Tip
Tips provide additional bits of advice that make particular features quicker or easier to use. ∎

Caution
Cautions warn you of potential problems before you make a mistake. ∎

New Feature
The New Feature icon highlights features that are new to the 2012 release. ∎

Cross-Reference
Watch for the Cross-Reference icon to learn where in another chapter you can go to find more information on a particular feature. ∎

On the CD-ROM
This icon points you toward related material on the book's CD. ∎

The book's CD

Computer-book CD-ROMs are sometimes just an afterthought that includes a handful of examples and product demos. This book's CD, however, includes a diverse selection of 3D models that you can use in your projects if you choose. Many of these models are used in the tutorials. The CD also includes the Max files for every tutorial.

Because we have more information that can be contained within a mere 1,200 pages, we've moved some material to the CD as bonus chapters, so if you feel cheated because something isn't covered, take a close look at the bonus chapters.

Since the second edition, I've been including Quick Start chapters in every new edition and over time they have been quietly improving with age. For this edition, I've dusted them off and included the Quick Start chapters from all the previous editions on the book's CD.

Color insert pages

The possibilities of Max are endless, but many individuals and groups have pushed the software a long way. As a sampling of the finished work that can be created, I've included a set of color insert pages that showcase some amazing work done with Max. The 3D artists represented in these pages give you some idea of what is possible.

Acknowledgments

I have a host of people to thank for their involvement in this major work. The order in which they are mentioned doesn't necessarily represent the amount of work they did.

Thanks as always to my dear wife, Angela, and my sons, Eric and Thomas, without whose support I wouldn't get very far. They are my QA team and my brainstorming team who always provide honest feedback on my latest example. We have had many family sessions to think of good tutorial examples, and I'm always amazed with what they come up with. One of my favorites that hasn't been implemented yet is a tutorial of a group of bicycles chasing an ice cream truck.

In the first edition, the task at hand was too big for just me, so I shared the pain with two co-authors—Dave Brueck and Sanford Kennedy (both of whom have gone on to write books of their own). I still thank them for their work, which, although overhauled, retains their spirits. In a later edition, I again asked for help, a request that was answered by Sue Blackman. Sue provided several excellent examples that show off the power of the Track View interface. Thanks for your help, Sue.

Major thanks to the editors and personnel at Wiley. I'd like to specifically thank Stephanie McComb, who has stepped into an established team and done a great job. Her encouragement, dedication, and positive attitude have made a big difference as I've faced some tough deadlines. Huge thanks to Marty Minner (the double M), who has once again managed the entire editing process, and to Gwenette Gaddis for her excellent copyediting input. Marty's comments during the review cycle always crack me up.

I'd also like to thank Chris Murdock for taking on the technical editing in a crunched schedule. Additional thanks go out to Jenny Swisher and her co-workers in the Media Development department for chasing down the required permissions and for compiling the resources for the DVD, and finally, to the entire staff at Wiley who helped me on this journey. Of particular note are the cover designers who have been delightfully stuck on reptiles and amphibians for the covers to the last several editions. I'm starting to refer to the titles by their cover creature; that is, "hand me the frog book next to the lizard book."

The various people who work in the graphics industry are amazing in their willingness to help and support. I'd like to thank first of all Rob Hoffman, Brittany Bonhomme, and the entire Autodesk team for their timely support and help. I'd also like to thank the talented people at Zygote Media, Curious Labs, and Viewpoint Digital Media for many of their models, which make the examples much more interesting. (You can only do so much with the teapot after all.) Thanks to Michael Valentine at Zygote Media and Tom Avikigos at Digimation for help in securing a new set of Viewpoint models. Additional thanks go out to David Mathis, Sue Blackman, and Chris Murdock for completing models used in some of the tutorials.

Finally, I'd like to thank the many artists who contributed images for the color insert pages for sharing their talent, knowledge, and vision with us. They are an inspiration to me.

Part I

Getting Started with 3ds Max

Laying Siege to the Castle Wall

W hen you first got your hands on 3ds Max, you were probably focused on one goal—creating cool 3D images and animations. I know that many of you bought Max to make money, claim a tax write-off, earn a way to Hollywood, or impress your girlfriend or boyfriend, but I'll just ignore those reasons for now. The goal is to create something cool.

If you've perused this book's Table of Contents or thumbed through its many pages, you've seen sections on modeling, materials, dynamics, and other topics. But if you're like me, you don't want to wade through tons of material before you have something to show off to Mom. (Actually, if you're like me, you opened straight to the special effects section, in which case you won't be reading this.)

The purpose of this Quick Start is to give you a taste of what Max can do. This soaring view of the software from 20,000 feet is intended to show you the big picture before you delve into the details. It exposes you to some of the most common features and, I hope, whets your appetite for the more in-depth chapters to follow.

This part of the book is intended for those new to the software. If you're an experienced user, then your mom no doubt is already impressed with your work, so you can happily advance to whichever chapter appeals to you. (Forgive me for catering to the newbie, but we were all beginners once.)

IN THIS CHAPTER

Planning the production

Gathering models

Applying materials

Adding a Sun & Sky system

Animating a CAT rig

Rendering the final animation

Breaking the Walls—Planning the Production

For this Quick Start, you use lots of primitives to create a fortress wall and then you use the new MassFX physics engine to break it all down. This gives you a chance to set up a scene, create a wall of primitives, apply materials to it, and work with MassFX system to animate the destruction.

The first thing to consider is setting up the scene. For this sequence, we need lots of blocks that are easy to create using primitives, and with the Array system, we can quickly build them into a solid wall. But a wall by itself is somewhat boring, so we dress up the scene with some palm trees and maybe a turret or two. Building walls from primitives is easy, but palm trees and turrets can take some time, so we're going to cheat. Yes, that is allowed, because it saves us some time. If you can locate some models that fit your needs without having to model them, you're ahead of the game. The book's CD includes a large number of models created by professionals to get you started, including conveniently a turret and some palm trees. Finally, we need a large cannonball to throw at the wall.

After the models are in place, we can use the new Substance textures to add variety and details to the objects without lots of overhead.

We also want a background and a ground plane for this scene. For the background, we use a Daylight system, which not only gives us nice outdoor lighting but also a horizon effect that works for this scene. For the ground plane, we use a flat plane object with a noise modifier applied to it to give it some subtle hills. Because both of these scene elements are generated by Max, we don't need to locate a background texture.

For the animation phase, we define all the bricks and the cannonball as rigid body objects, give the cannonball some initial velocity, and let the MassFX system do its magic.

On the CD-ROM

After each of the following tutorials, I saved the scene file. You can find these files in the Quick Start directory on the book's CD. ■

Setting Up the Scene

This section on setting up is divided into several simple tutorials. The first step in the production is to pull in all the models we need. Then we can position them where we need them, with the cannonball initially off-screen. We also want to position our camera in a good spot.

After the models are in place, we can create the ground plane, and then we're ready to add some materials and lights.

Tutorial: Building a wall

Your first step begins with the task of building a wall. Because this is the main element of the scene, we want it to be added to the scene first.

To build a wall, follow these steps:

1. Reset the interface with the Application Button ⇨ Reset menu command. Answer Yes in the warning box that appears.

2. In the Command Panel, click the Box button and drag in the Front viewport to create a rectangular block.

Note

This chapter uses Generic Units. You can change the units using the Units Setup dialog box, which you open using the Customize ⇨ Units Setup menu command. ∎

3. Press and hold the Shift key and drag the block in the Front viewport to create another block that is positioned on top of the first and offset half the width of the first block.

4. Drag over both blocks to select them, and choose the Tools ⇨ Array menu. In the Array dialog box that opens, set the 1D Count to **24** and the 2D Count to **8**. Then enable the Preview button to see the changes, and drag the spinner next to the Incremental X value until the blocks are horizontally positioned next to each other. Then do the same for the Incremental Row Z value, and click OK.

The castle wall is complete and ready to go, as shown in Figure QS.1.

FIGURE QS.1

The wall was quickly created using the Array dialog box.

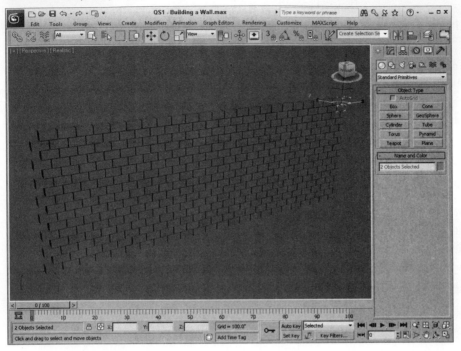

Tutorial: Gathering models

The wall looks great, but we need to dress up the scene a little. Using the Merge command, we can pull some models into the current scene. This also involves scaling them so they are the right size relative to each other.

To load the models, follow these steps:

1. Use the Application Button ➪ Import ➪ Merge menu command, and locate the Turret and trees.max file from the Quick Start directory on the CD. In the Merge dialog box, select the All button and click OK.

2. The turret model is loaded right in the middle of the scene and consists of a single part. We need to scale the turret and move it to the side of the wall.

3. Click the turret to select it, and then select the Scale tool. Then drag the top handle only to scale it in the Z-direction. Then move it in the Front viewport using the Move tool so it lines up with the left side of the wall and its base it even with the base of the wall. Then move it in the Left viewport until it is centered and overlaps the wall.

4. With the turret still selected, press and hold the Shift key and drag the turret to the right to create another turret positioned at the right edge of the wall. In the Clone Options dialog box, select the Copy option and click OK.

5. Select the Create ⇨ AEC Objects ⇨ Foliage menu command, and click the Foliage button. Then select the Generic Palm, and click in the Top viewport to create four trees. Use the Scale tool to increase their size along the Z-axis.

Turrets now stand on either side of the wall, and some trees add to the scene, as shown in Figure QS.2.

FIGURE QS.2

The loaded turrets make the wall seem stronger.

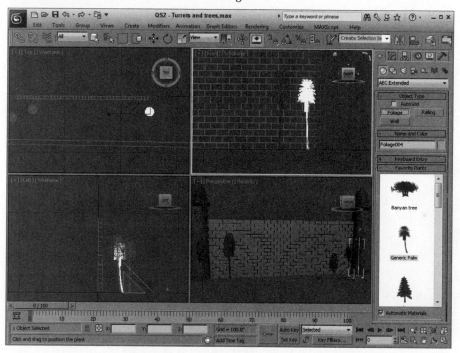

Tutorial: Adding a ground plane

With the turret model loaded, we next add a ground plane to the scene. This can be a simple plane object, and we want to apply a Noise modifier to give it some bumps.

To add a ground plane, follow these steps:

1. Click the Top viewport, and zoom out. Select the Plane button in the Command Panel to the right, and drag from the upper-left corner to the lower-right corner in the Top viewport to create a large plane object.

2. In the Create panel, set the Length Segs and Width Segs to **30** to increase the plane's polygon density.

3. With the plane object still selected, choose the Modifiers ➪ Parametric Deformers ➪ Noise menu command to apply a Noise modifier to the plane object. In the Parameters rollout, set the Scale value to **100** and the Z Strength value to **200**.

The ground plane with a Noise modifier creates a nice landscape of rolling hills, as shown in Figure QS.3.

FIGURE QS.3

The scene now has a ground plane of rolling hills.

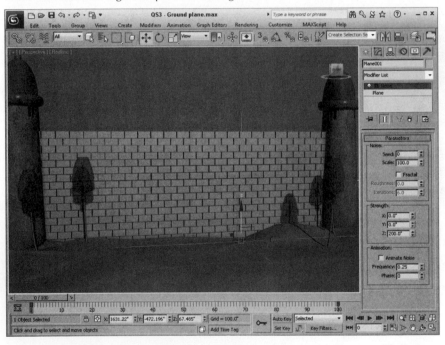

Adding Materials and Lights

The modeling phase, which usually is quite time-consuming, went really quickly when we used the Array dialog box and existing models. The next phase is to add materials to the models and lights to the scene. Because some of the models have applied materials already, this phase also goes pretty quickly.

Tutorial: Adding materials

After the modeling is complete, you can add materials to the objects to improve their look. Materials are added using the Material Editor, which is opened using the Rendering ⇨ Material Editor ⇨ Slate Material Editor menu command or by pressing the M keyboard shortcut.

Max 2012 includes a special set of procedural materials called Substance materials that are created using small bits of code instead of bitmaps.

To add materials to the wall and ground plane, follow these steps:

1. Select the Rendering ⇨ Material Editor ⇨ Slate Material Editor menu command (or press the M key) to open the Material Editor. Locate and double-click the Standard material in the Material/Map Browser and also the Substance map in the Maps category.

2. Double-click the Substance node, and click the Load Substance button in the Substance Package Browser rollout of the Material Editor. In the textures folder, locate and load the Desert Sand 01 texture, and connect the Diffuse and Bump channels of the Substance node to the Standard node.

3. With the ground plane selected in the viewports and the Standard material node selected in the Material Editor, click the Assign Material to Selection button in the toolbar of the Material Editor. This applies the material to the selected object.

4. Click the Select by Name button on the main toolbar. Press and hold the Shift key, and click the first and last Box objects to select all the block objects in the scene.

5. Repeat Steps 2 and 3 in the Material Editor, and apply the Rock 02 Substance texture to the scene blocks.

The rest of the models have materials already, so we can move on to lights. Figure QS.4 shows the Slate Material Editor.

FIGURE QS.4

The Material Editor lets you configure and apply materials to scene objects.

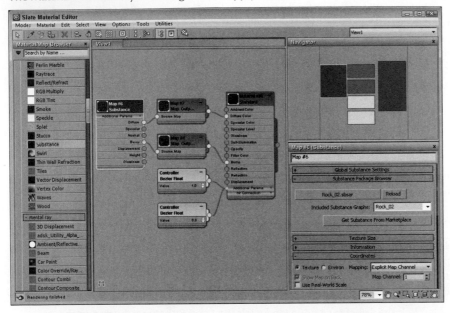

Tutorial: Adding a Sun & Sky system

One benefit of having the mental ray renderer enabled is that you also can use the Sun & Sky system. This system simulates outdoor lighting from a distant source like the sun and generates a sky for the background.

To add a Sun & Sky system to the scene, follow these steps:

1. Select the Rendering ⇨ Render Setup menu command (or press F10) to open the Render Setup dialog box. At the very bottom of the Common panel is the Assign Renderer rollout. Within this rollout, click the button to the right of the Production Renderer and double-click the mental ray Renderer option in the Choose Renderer dialog box that opens. Then close the Render Setup dialog box.

2. Select the Create ⇨ Lights ⇨ Daylight System menu command, and drag in the Top viewport to add a compass helper to the scene. Click Ok to the request to enable the Exposure Control warning dialog box. Then click and drag to position the Sun light icon in the Top viewport.

Note

When the Daylight system is applied, a dialog box automatically appears recommending that you use the Logarithmic Exposure Control and asking whether you want to make this change. Click Yes to continue. ∎

3. Select the Rendering ⇨ Environment menu command (or press the 8 key) to open the Environment and Effects dialog box. Click the Environment Map button, and select the mr Physical Sky map from the Maps/mental ray folder in the Material/Map Browser. Then enable the Use Map option, and close the Environment dialog box.

4. Choose the Views ⇨ Viewport Background ⇨ Viewport Background menu command (or press Alt+B) to open the Viewport Background dialog box. Select the Perspective viewport, enable the Use Environment Background and the Display Background options, and close the dialog box.

5. Click the Maximize Viewport button in the lower-right corner of the interface (or press Alt+W) to make the Perspective viewport full-sized.

6. With the daylight light selected, click the Setup button in the Daylight Parameters rollout found in the Modify panel. Then set the Time Hours to **11**. This sets the time of day to late afternoon.

7. To see the lights and shadows in the viewport, click the viewport shading label in the upper-left corner of the viewport and select the Lighting and Shadows ⇨ Illuminate with Scene Lights menu command (or press Shift+F3). Then turn on Shadows and Ambient Occlusion in the same Lighting and Shadows menu.

The viewport now shows the scene with a background sky, as shown in Figure QS.5.

FIGURE QS.5

The sky background is visible within the viewport.

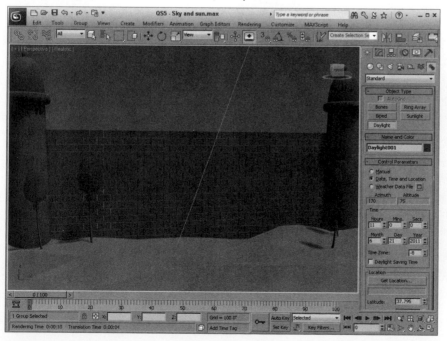

Tutorial: Rendering a preview

Before moving to animation, you can render the scene now that lights have been added. Rendering is configured using the Render Scene dialog box.

To render a preview of the castle wall scene, follow these steps:

1. Select the Rendering⇨Render menu command (or press the F10 key), and open the Indirect Illumination panel. Turn on the Enable Final Gather option, and set the Preset to Medium. This computes a global illumination model by determining how light rays bounce about the scene.

2. Back in the Common panel of the Render Scene dialog box, select the image size in the Common Parameters rollout and click the Render button. The active viewport is rendered and displayed in the Render Frame Window.

Tip

This scene is fairly simply and renders quickly, but if you need the test render to be even faster, you can enable the Quicksilver Hardware Renderer instead of the mental ray. ■

The rendered image, as shown in Figure QS.6, includes all the materials and lighting effects.

FIGURE QS.6

The rendered image of the scene includes the lighting effects.

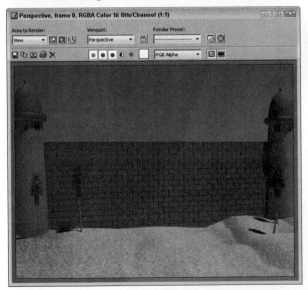

Creating a Dynamic Animation with MassFX

With the test render complete and the scene looking good, we can move to the animation phase. This phase relies on the MassFX tools to create a dynamic animation.

Tutorial: Running a simulation

The first step in creating a dynamic animation with MassFX is to select and define all the pieces that will be included in the simulation; then we can run the simulation and see how it looks.

To set up the simulation using MassFX, follow these steps:

1. We still need a projectile, so create a simple sphere object and position it about mid-wall height and set its color to black to look like a cannonball.

2. Open the MassFX toolbar by right-clicking the main toolbar and selecting MassFX from the pop-up menu.

3. Use the Select by Name button on the main toolbar to select all the blocks and the sphere object, and then click the Set Selected as Dynamic Rigid Body button in the MassFX toolbar.

4. Select and zoom in on the cannonball in the Left viewport. In the Modify panel, expand the MassFX Rigid Body modifier and select the Initial Velocity option. In the Advanced rollout, set the Speed value to **5000** and X value of Initial Velocity to **-180**. Also in the Physical Material rollout, set the Density of the cannonball to **5.5**.

Tip

If you find that the cannonball moves parallel to or away from the wall, adjust the Initial Velocity for another axis and try again. ■

5. Press the Start Simulation button on the MassFX toolbar, and the cannonball crashes into the wall causing the blocks to fall.

6. Click the Time Configuration button below the Play button, and set the End Time value to **350**. This gives the scene more frames for the simulation.

7. Select all the blocks and the sphere, and in the MassFX Tools dialog box, click the Bake Selected button to create animation keys for the most recent simulation.

Figure QS.7 shows the castle wall after the cannonball has crashed through.

FIGURE QS.7

The broken wall after the cannonball has crashed through

Tutorial: Rendering the final animation

After the simulation looks good in the viewport, you are ready to render the final animation. This is a process that you can start by specifying the animation format. Once started, Max automatically proceeds through all the frames of the animation and notifies you when it is completed.

To render the final animation, follow these steps:

1. Select the Rendering ⇨ Render Setup menu command to open the Render Setup dialog box.

2. At the top of the dialog box, enable the Active Time Segment so that all 350 frames of the animation will be rendered. Then set the Output Size to 640x480.

3. In the Render Output section, click the Files button to open a File dialog box. Set the format as AVI, give the file a name such as Crashing Wall, and click the Save button. In the AVI Compression Setup dialog box that appears, simply select the default and click OK.

4. At the very bottom of the Render Setup dialog box, make sure the Perspective view is selected and click the Render button.

Max then renders each frame of the animation and shows its progress in a dialog box. When completed, the final animation file is saved with the filename you entered. You then can locate and play it. Figure QS.8 shows a frame of the final animation.

The final animation includes rendered results of each frame.

Summary

I hope you're happy with your first footsteps into Max. This chapter exposed you to a number of important aspects of Max, including the following:

- Setting up a scene
- Using the Array dialog box
- Applying materials to scene objects
- Enabling mental ray
- Using the Sun & Sky system, and enabling lights and shadows in the viewport
- Running dynamic simulations using MassFX
- Rendering the final animation

But hold onto your seats, because so much of the software lies ahead. In Chapter 1, you start easily with an in-depth look at the Max interface. If you feel ready for more advanced challenges, review the Table of Contents and dive into any topic that looks good.

Exploring the Max Interface

Well, here we are again with a new version of Max, and the first question on the minds of existing users is, "Did the interface change?" The answer is a happy "very little." Most serious users would rather go through root canal surgery than have their user interface (UI) change, and Autodesk has learned and respected this valued opinion by keeping the interface changes to a minimum.

As you look around the new interface, you'll see that everything is still there, but that Max has a few new additions. You may find yourself saying, as you navigate the interface, "Where did that come from?" But, just like encountering a new house in your neighborhood, over time you'll become accustomed to the addition and may even meet some new friends.

Why is the software interface so important? Well, consider this: The interface is the set of controls that enable you to access the program's features. Without a good interface, you may never use many of the best features of the software or may spend a frustrating bit of time locating those features. A piece of software can have all the greatest features, but if the user can't find or access them, then the software won't be used to its full potential. Max is a powerful piece of software with some amazing features, and luckily the interface makes these amazing features easy to find and use.

The interface's purpose is to make the software features accessible, and in Max you have many different ways to access the features. Some of these access methods are faster than others. This design is intentional because it gives beginning users an intuitive command and advanced users direct access. For example, to undo a command, you can choose Edit ➪ Undo (requiring two mouse clicks), but as you gain more experience, you can simply click the Undo icon on the toolbar (only one click); an expert with his hands on the keyboard can press Ctrl+Z without having to reach for the mouse at all. All three of these methods have the same result, but you can use the one that is easiest for you.

Has the Max interface succeeded? Yes, to a degree, but like most interfaces, it always has room for improvement, and we hope that each new version takes us closer to the perfect interface (but I'm still looking for the "read my thoughts" feature). Autodesk has built a loophole into the program to cover anyone who complains about the interface—customization. If you don't like the current interface, you can change it to be exactly what you want.

Cross-Reference

Customizing the Max interface is covered in Chapter 4, "Customizing the Max Interface and Setting Preferences." ■

This chapter examines the latest incarnation of the Max interface and presents some tips that make the interface feel comfortable, not cumbersome.

New Feature

If you've used Max before, then you'll notice that the default color scheme has changed with this version. Many Max users claim that the dark gray color scheme is easier on your eyes in low light. The Customize menu includes options to change the color scheme back to light gray if you prefer that scheme. ■

Note

When Max starts, the default color scheme uses dark gray colors with white text. Although this scheme works great for artists who stare at a computer monitor for long periods of time with little or no background light, it isn't the ideal setting for printing. All the figures in this book use the alternate lighter gray color scheme. You can easily switch between the different color schemes using the Customize⇨Custom UI and Defaults Switch menu command. ■

Learning the Interface Elements

If you're new to the Max interface, the first order of business is to take a stroll around the block and meet the neighbors. The Max interface has a number of interface elements that neatly group all the similar commands together. For example, all the commands for controlling the viewports are grouped together in the Viewport Navigation Controls found in the lower-right corner of the interface.

Note

If all the details of every interface command were covered in this chapter, it would be an awfully long chapter. So for those commands that are covered in more detail elsewhere, I include a cross-reference to the chapter where you can find their coverage. ■

The entire interface can be divided into six easy elements. Each of these interface elements, in turn, has groupings of sub-elements. The six main interface elements are listed here and shown separated in Figure 1.1:

- **Title Bar and Menus:** This is the default source for most commands, but also one of the most time-consuming interface methods. The title bar and menus are found along the top edge of the Max window.
- **Toolbars:** Max includes several toolbars of icon buttons that provide single-click access to features. These toolbars can float independently or can be docked to an interface edge. The main toolbar is the only toolbar that is visible by default.

- **Modeling Ribbon:** Configurable tabs and panels provide quick access to modeling features, including the Graphite Modeling Tools.
- **Viewports:** Four separate views into the scene show the Top, Front, Left, and Perspective viewpoints.

FIGURE 1.1

Max includes six main interface elements.

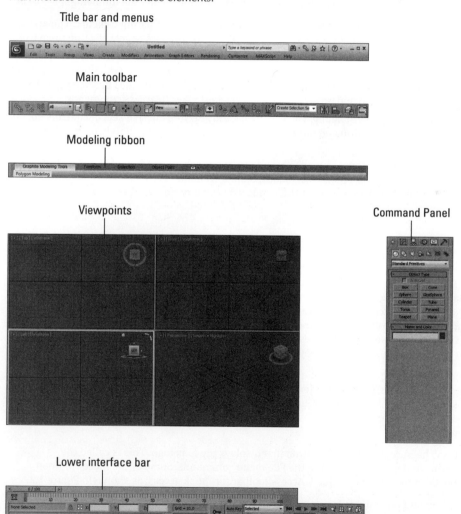

Title bar and menus

Main toolbar

Modeling ribbon

Viewpoints

Command Panel

Lower interface bar

- **Command Panel:** The major control panel located to the right of the four viewports, it has six tabbed icons at its top that you can click to open the various panels. Each panel includes rollouts containing parameters and settings. These rollouts change, depending on the object and tab that is selected.

- **Lower Interface Bar:** Along the bottom edge of the interface window is a collection of miscellaneous controls.

In addition to these default elements are several additional interface elements that aren't initially visible when Max is first loaded. These additional interface elements include the following:

- **Floating toolbars:** Several additional toolbars are available as floating toolbars. You access them by choosing Customize ⇨ Show UI ⇨ Show Floating Toolbars or by selecting them from the toolbar's right-click pop-up menu.

- **Quadmenus:** Right-clicking the active viewport reveals a pop-up menu with up to four panes, referred to as a quadmenu. *Quadmenus* offer context-sensitive commands based on the object or location being clicked and provide one of the quickest ways to access commands.

- **Caddy Settings:** When modeling, you can open Caddy Settings. These sets of controls float above the current selection and offer several settings that are immediately updated in the viewport.

- **Dialog boxes and editors:** Some commands open a separate window of controls. These dialog boxes may contain their own menus, toolbars, and interface elements. A good example of this interface element type is the Rendered Frame Window, which has enough controls to keep you busy for a while.

Using the Menus

The pull-down menus at the top of the Max interface include most of the features available in Max and are a great place for beginners to start. Several of the menu commands have corresponding toolbar buttons and keyboard shortcuts. To execute a menu command, you can choose it from the menu with the mouse cursor, click its corresponding toolbar button if it has one, or press its keyboard shortcut. You also can select menu commands by pressing the Alt key and using the keyboard arrows. After you select a menu command, press the Enter key to execute it.

The main menu includes the following options: Application Button, Edit, Tools, Group, Views, Create, Modifiers, Animation, Graph Editors, Rendering, Customize, MAXScript, and Help. If you're using 3ds Max 2010 Design, then you'll find one additional menu item: Lighting Analysis. Unlike some other programs, these menu options do not disappear if not needed. The list is set, and they are always there when you need them.

The File menu has been replaced with a button that displays the Max logo. This is called the Application Button, and it includes most of the File menu commands. Some of the more common commands have been located on the Quick Access toolbar for quick access, as shown in Figure 1.2.

If a keyboard command is available for a menu command, it is shown to the right of the menu item. If an ellipsis (three dots) appears after a menu item, that menu command causes a separate dialog box to open. A small black arrow to the right of a menu item indicates that a submenu exists. Clicking the menu item or holding the mouse over the top of a menu item makes the submenu appear. Toggle menu options (such as Views⇨Show Ghosting) change state each time they are selected. If a toggle menu option is enabled, a small check mark appears to its left; if disabled, no check mark appears.

FIGURE 1.2

The Max title bar includes the Application Button, the Quick Access toolbar, and the InfoCenter toolbar.

Application Button

Quick Access toolbar   InfoCenter toolbar

On the CD-ROM

A complete list of keyboard shortcuts can be found in Bonus Chapter 2, "3ds Max 2012 Keyboard Shortcuts," on the CD. ∎

You also can navigate the menus using the keyboard by pressing the Alt key by itself. Doing so selects the Edit menu, and then you can use the arrow keys to move up and down and between menus. With a menu selected, you can press the keyboard letter that is underlined to select and execute a menu command. For example, pressing and holding down the Alt and then E (for Edit) and then pressing U (for Undo) executes the Edit⇨Undo command; or you can press Alt, use the down arrow to select the Undo command, and press the Enter key.

Tip

By learning the underlined letters in the menu, you can use the keyboard to quickly access menu commands, even if the menu command doesn't have an assigned keyboard shortcut. And because you don't need to stretch for the Y key while holding down the Ctrl key, underlined menu letters can be faster. For example, by pressing Alt, G, and U successively, you can access the Group⇨Ungroup menu command. The keyboard buffer remembers the order of the letters you type regardless of how fast you key them, making it possible to quickly access menu commands using the keyboard. Over time, you can learn patterns to help you remember how to access certain menu commands, such as Alt, C, H, E for creating an ellipse. ∎

Not all menu commands are available at all times. If a menu command is unavailable, then it is grayed out, as shown in Figure 1.3, and you cannot select it. For example, the Clone command is available only when an object is selected, so if no objects are selected, the Clone command is grayed out and unavailable. After you select an object, this command becomes available.

Tip

If you right-click the menu bar, you can access a pop-up command to hide the menu bar. If you accidentally dismiss the menu bar, you can recover it using the Show Menu Bar command in the Quick Access toolbar menu. ∎

FIGURE 1.3

All menus feature visual clues.

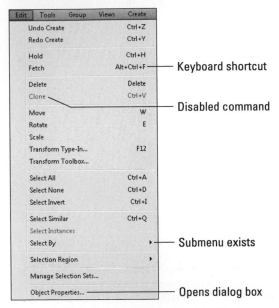

Keyboard shortcut

Disabled command

Submenu exists

Opens dialog box

Using the Toolbars

Now that you've learned the menu two-step, it is time for the toolbar one-step. The main toolbar appears by default directly under the menus at the top of the Max window. Using toolbars is one of the most convenient ways to execute commands because most commands require only a single click.

Docking and floating toolbars

By default, the main toolbar is docked along the top edge of the interface above the viewports, but you can make any docked toolbar (including the main toolbar) a floating toolbar by clicking and dragging the two vertical lines on the left (or top) end of the toolbar away from the interface edge. After you separate it from the window, you can resize the floating toolbar by dragging on its edges or corners. You can then drag and dock it to any of the window edges or double-click the toolbar title bar to automatically dock the toolbar to its latest docked location. Figure 1.4 shows the main toolbar as a floating panel.

If you right-click any floating toolbar away from the buttons, you can access a pop-up menu that includes options to dock or float the current toolbar, access the Customize UI window, or show or hide any of the toolbars or the Command Panel. The main toolbar can be hidden and made visible again with the Alt+6 keyboard shortcut toggle.

Cross-Reference

You can customize the buttons that appear on any of the toolbars. See Chapter 4, "Customizing the Max Interface and Setting Preferences." ■

FIGURE 1.4

The main toolbar includes buttons and drop-down lists for controlling many of the most popular Max functions.

If you select the Customize ⇨ Show UI ⇨ Show Floating Toolbars menu command, several additional toolbars appear. These are floating toolbars. You also can make them appear by selecting them individually from the toolbar right-click pop-up menu. These floating toolbars include Axis Constraints, Layers, Extras, Render Shortcuts, Snaps, Animation Layers, Containers, MassFX toolbar, and Brush Presets.

The InfoCenter toolbar is permanently attached to the title bar. Using the InfoCenter toolbar is covered later in this chapter.

Using tooltips and flyouts

All icon buttons (including those found in toolbars, the Command Panel, and other dialog boxes and windows) include tooltips, which are identifying text labels. If you hold the mouse cursor over an icon button, the tooltip label appears. This feature is useful for identifying buttons. If you can't remember what a specific button does, hold the cursor over the top of it and the tooltip gives you its name.

All toolbar buttons with a small triangle in the lower-right corner are flyouts. A *flyout* is a single toolbar button that expands to reveal additional buttons. Click and hold on the flyout to reveal the additional icons, and drag to select one. Figure 1.5 shows the flyout for the Align button on the main toolbar.

FIGURE 1.5

Flyout menus bundle several toolbar buttons together.

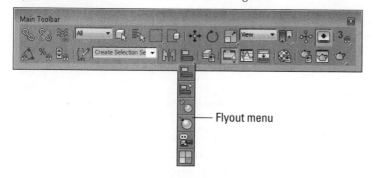

Flyout menu

Note

The General panel of the Preference Settings dialog box contains an option for setting the number of milliseconds to wait before the flyout appears. ∎

Using the Quick Access toolbar

Located next to the Application Button on the title bar is the Quick Access toolbar. This mini toolbar includes icons for the following commands: New Scene, Open File, Save File, Undo, Redo, and Set Project Folder. If you click the down-arrow icon on the right end of the toolbar, you can access a menu with options to hide any one of the icons or the entire toolbar. You can also select to show the toolbar beneath the Ribbon.

Learning the main toolbar

On smaller-resolution screens, the main toolbar is too long to be entirely visible. To see the entire main toolbar, you need to set your monitor resolution to be at least 1280 pixels wide. To scroll the toolbar to see the end, position the cursor on the toolbar away from the buttons, such as below one of the drop-down lists (the cursor changes to a hand); then click and drag the toolbar in either direction. Using the hand cursor to scroll also works in the Command Panel, Material Editor, and any other place where the panel exceeds the given space.

Tip

The easiest way to scroll the main toolbar is to drag with the middle mouse button. ■

Toolbar buttons that open dialog boxes such as the Layer Manager, Material Editor, and Render Setup buttons are toggle buttons. When the dialog box is open, the button is highlighted in light gray, indicating that the dialog box is open. Clicking a highlighted toggle button closes the dialog box. Corresponding menus (and keyboard shortcuts) work the same way, with a small check mark appearing to the left of the menu command when a dialog box is opened.

Table 1.1 lists the controls found in the main toolbar. Buttons with flyouts are separated with commas.

TABLE 1.1

Main Toolbar Buttons

Toolbar Button	Name	Description
	Select and Link	Establishes links between objects.
	Unlink Selection	Breaks links between objects.
	Bind to Space Warp	Assigns objects to be modified by a space warp.
All ▼	Selection Filter drop-down list	Limits the type of objects that can be selected.
	Select Object (Q)	Chooses an object.
	Select by Name (H)	Opens a dialog box for selecting objects by name.

Toolbar Button	Name	Description
	Rectangular Selection Region, Circular Selection Region, Fence Selection Region, Lasso Selection Region, Paint Selection Region (Ctrl+F to cycle)	Determines the shape used for selecting objects with the mouse.
	Window/Crossing Toggle	Specifies whether an object must be crossed or windowed to be selected.
	Select and Move (W)	Selects an object and allows positional translations.
	Select and Rotate (E)	Selects an object and allows rotational transforms.
	Select and Uniform Scale, Select and Non-Uniform Scale, Select and Squash (R to cycle)	Selects an object and allows scaling transforms using different methods.
View	Reference Coordinate System drop-down list	Specifies the coordinate system used for transforms.
	Use Pivot Point Center, Use Selection Center, Use Transform Coordinate Center	Specifies the center about which rotations are completed.
	Select and Manipulate	Selects an object and allows parameter manipulation via a manipulator.
	Keyboard Shortcut Override Toggle	Allows keyboard shortcuts for the main interface and the active dialog box or feature set to be used when enabled. Only main interface shortcuts are available when disabled.
	Snap Toggle 2D, Snap Toggle 2.5D, Snap Toggle 3D (S)	Specifies the snap mode. 2D snaps only to the active construction grid, 2.5D snaps to the construction grid or to geometry projected from the grid, and 3D snaps to anywhere in 3D space.
	Angle Snap Toggle (A)	Causes rotations to snap to specified angles.
	Percent Snap (Shift+Ctrl+P)	Causes scaling to snap to specified percentages.
	Spinner Snap Toggle	Determines the amount a spinner value changes with each click.
	Edit Named Selection Sets	Opens a dialog box for creating and managing selection sets.
New Set	Named Selection Sets drop-down list	Lists and allows you to select a set of named objects.

continued

TABLE 1.1 *(continued)*

Toolbar Button	Name	Description
	Align (Alt+A), Quick Align, Normal Align (Alt+N), Place Highlight (Ctrl+H), Align to Camera, Align to View	Opens the alignment dialog box for positioning objects, allows objects to be aligned by their normals, determines the location of highlights, and aligns objects to a camera or view.
	Manage Layers	Opens the Layer Manager interface where you can work with layers.
	Graphite Modeling Tools	Opens the Graphite Modeling Tools panel.
	Open Curve Editor	Opens the Function Curves Editor.
	Open Schematic View	Opens the Schematic View window.
	Compact Material Editor (M), Slate Material Editor (M)	Opens either the compact Material Editor window or the Slate Material Editor window.
	Render Setup (F10)	Opens the Render Setup dialog box for setting rendering options.
	Rendered Frame Window	Opens the Rendered Frame Window.
	Quick Render (Production), Render Iterative, Quick Render (ActiveShade)	Produces a quick test rendering of the current viewport without opening the Render Setup dialog box using the production settings, the iterative render mode, or the ActiveShade window.

Using the Ribbon

The Ribbon interface is a deluxe toolbar with many different tool sections. It currently is populated with a variety of modeling tools that are collectively called the Graphite Modeling Tools. You can turn the Ribbon on and off using the Graphite Modeling Tools button on the main toolbar. When enabled, tabs for the Graphite Modeling Tools, Freeform, Selection, and Object Paint are displayed.

Cross-Reference

Most Ribbon buttons are visible only when an Editable Poly object is selected. You can learn more about Editable Poly objects and the Graphite Modeling Tools in Chapter 13, "Modeling with Polygons," and Chapter 14, "Using the Graphite Modeling Tools and Painting with Objects." ∎

Using the Minimize button at the right end of the Ribbon, you can switch the display mode to minimize to only the tabs, only the panel titles, or only the panel buttons, or to enable the Minimize button to cycle through each of the modes. You can also double-click the Ribbon tabs to minimize the Ribbon or to cycle through the minimized modes.

Right-click the Ribbon title bar to access menu options to show or hide specific tabs or panels, customize the ribbon, save or load a custom ribbon configuration, switch between horizontal and vertical orientations, reset the ribbon to its default, or enable tooltips. Figure 1.6 shows the different Ribbon display modes.

Cross-Reference

The Ribbon customization features are covered in Chapter 4, "Customizing the Max Interface and Setting Preferences." ■

FIGURE 1.6

The Ribbon can be set to be displayed using several different modes.

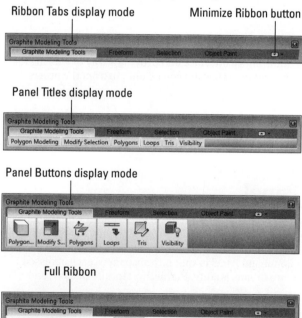

The entire Ribbon, as well as each individual panel of buttons, can be made into a floating control by dragging the Ribbon title bar or the lower panel bar away from the rest of the buttons. When a panel is made into a floating panel, like the one in Figure 1.7, the icons in the upper right of the floating panel let you return the panel to the Ribbon or toggle the orientation between vertical and horizontal. You also can move the floating panel about by dragging on the gray bar on either side of the panel.

FIGURE 1.7

Ribbon panels can float independent of each other.

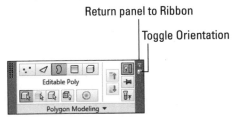

Using the Viewports

The four viewports make up the largest area of the entire interface and provide a way of viewing the objects within the scene. Each of the viewports is configurable and can be unique from the others.

Cross-Reference

Understanding how to work with the viewports is vital to accomplishing tasks with Max, so viewports have an entire chapter dedicated just to them—Chapter 2, "Controlling and Configuring the Viewports." ■

Using the Command Panel

If there is one place in Max, besides the viewports, where you'll spend all your time, it's the Command Panel (at least until you're comfortable enough with the quadmenus). The Command Panel is located to the right of the viewports along the right edge of the interface. This is where all the specific parameters, settings, and controls are located. The Command Panel is split into six panels, each accessed via a tab icon located at its top. These six tabs are Create, Modify, Hierarchy, Motion, Display, and Utilities.

You can pull away the Command Panel from the right window edge as a floating dialog box, as shown in Figure 1.8, by clicking the open space to the right of the tabbed icons at the top of the Command Panel and dragging away from the interface edge. You also can dock it to the left window edge, which is really handy if you're left-handed. While it's a floating panel, you can resize the Command Panel by dragging on its edges or corners (but its width remains constant).

After you've pulled the Command Panel or any of the toolbars away from the interface, you can red-ock them to their last position by double-clicking their title bar. You also can right-click the title bar to access the pop-up menu of floating toolbars, but the pop-up menu also includes options to Dock (either Left or Right for the Command Panel or Left, Right, Top, or Bottom for toolbars), Float, and Minimize.

The right-click pop-up menu for the Command Panel also includes a Minimize command. If enabled, the Command Panel collapses to the edge of the interface, but moving the mouse near the interface where the Command Panel is minimized expands the Command Panel again. Moving the mouse away from the Command Panel makes it collapse to the interface edge again. You can take the Command Panel out of Minimize mode by selecting one of the Dock commands.

FIGURE 1.8

The Command Panel includes six separate panels accessed via tab icons.

Hierarchy   Motion

Modify   Display

Create   Utilities

Working with rollouts

Most of the controls, buttons, and parameters in the Command Panel are contained within sections called rollouts. A *rollout* is a grouping of controls positioned under a gray, boxed title, as shown in Figure 1.9. Each rollout title bar includes a plus or minus sign (a minus sign indicates that the rollout is open; a plus sign shows closed rollouts). Clicking the rollout title opens or closes the rollout. You also can reposition the order of the rollouts by dragging the rollout title and dropping it above or below the other rollouts.

Note

You cannot reposition some of the rollouts, such as the Object Type and the Name and Color rollouts, found in the Create panel. ■

Right-clicking away from the buttons in a rollout presents a pop-up menu where you can select to close the rollout you've clicked in, Close All, Open All, or Reset Rollout Order. The pop-up menu also lists all available rollouts within the current panel with a check mark next to the ones that are open.

Expanding all the rollouts often exceeds the screen space allotted to the Command Panel. If the rollouts exceed the given space, then a small vertical scroll bar appears at the right edge of the Command Panel. You can drag this scroll bar to access the rollouts at the bottom of the Command Panel, or you can click away from the controls when a hand cursor appears. With the hand cursor, click and drag in either direction to scroll the Command Panel. You also can scroll the Command Panel with the scroll wheel on the mouse.

FIGURE 1.9

Open and close rollouts by clicking the rollout title.

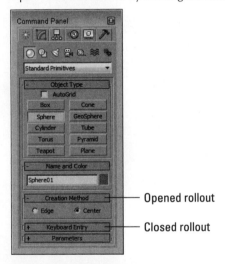

Opened rollout
Closed rollout

Cross-Reference

You can customize the Command Panel like the other toolbars. Customizing the Command Panel is covered in Chapter 4, "Customizing the Max Interface and Setting Preferences." ■

Increasing the Command Panel's width

The Command Panel can be doubled or tripled (or any multiple, as long as you have room) in width by dragging its left edge toward the center of the interface. The width of the Command Panel is increased at the expense of the viewports. Figure 1.10 shows the Command Panel double its normal size.

FIGURE 1.10

Increase the width of the Command Panel by dragging its left edge.

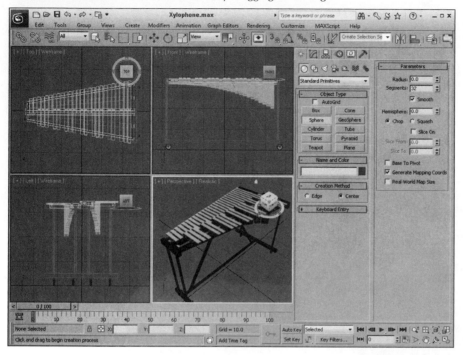

Tutorial: Rearranging the interface for lefties

I used to work for a company that required that all computers have the mouse to the left of the keyboard. We swapped computers often, and the boss hated having to move the mouse to the other side of the keyboard (and you thought your work environment was weird). The reality is that some people like it on the left and others prefer it on the right, and Max can accommodate both.

With the Command Panel on the right side of the interface, the default Max interface obviously favors right-handers, but with the docking panels, you can quickly change it to be friendly to lefties.

To rearrange the interface for lefties, follow these steps:

1. Click the Command Panel on the empty space to the right of the Utilities tab, and drag toward the center of the interface. As you drag the Command Panel away from the right edge, the cursor changes.

2. Continue to drag the Command Panel to the left edge, and the cursor changes again to indicate that it will be docked when released. Release the mouse button, and the Command Panel docks to the left side.

3. For an even easier method, you can right-click the Command Panel's title bar and select Dock ⇨ Left from the pop-up menu.

Figure 1.11 shows the rearranged interface ready for all you southpaws.

Tip

To save the interface changes, use the Customize ➪ Save Custom UI Scheme menu. The maxstart.cui file is loaded by default when Max is started. ■

Using the Lower Interface Bar Controls

The last major interface element isn't really an interface element but just a collection of several sets of controls located along the bottom edge of the interface window. These controls cannot be pulled away from the interface like the main toolbar, but you can hide them using Expert Mode (Ctrl+X). These controls, shown in Figure 1.12, include the following, from left to right:

- **Time Slider:** The Time Slider, located under the viewports, enables you to quickly locate a specific animation frame. It spans the number of frames included in the current animation. Dragging the Time Slider moves you quickly between frames. Clicking the arrow buttons on either side of the Time Slider moves to the previous or next frame (or key).

FIGURE 1.11

Left-handed users can move the Command Panel to the left side.

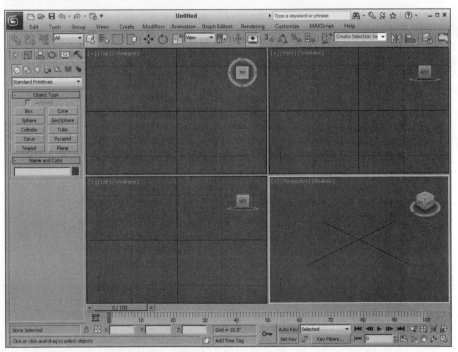

- **Track Bar:** The Track Bar displays animation keys as color-coded rectangles with red for positional keys, green for rotational keys, and blue for scale keys. Parameter change keys are denoted by gray rectangles. Using the Track Bar, you can select, move, and delete animation keys. The button at the left end of the Track Bar is the Open Mini Curve Editor button. It provides access to the animation function curves.

- **Status Bar:** The Status Bar is below the Track Bar. It provides valuable information, such as the number and type of objects selected, transformation values, and grid size. It also includes the Selection Lock Toggle, Transform Type-In fields, and the value of the current Grid size.

- **Prompt Line:** The Prompt Line is text located at the bottom of the window. If you're stuck as to what to do next, look at the Prompt Line for information on what Max expects. The Prompt Line also includes buttons for enabling Adaptive Degradation and adding and editing Time Tags, which are used to name specific animation frames.

- **Key Controls:** These controls are for creating animation keys and include two different modes—Auto Key (keyboard shortcut, N) and Set Key (keyboard shortcut, '). Auto Key mode sets keys for any changes made to the scene objects. Set Key mode gives you more precise control and sets keys for the selected filters only when you click the Set Keys button (keyboard shortcut, K).

- **Time Controls:** Resembling the controls on an audio or video device, the Time Controls offer an easy way to move through the various animation frames and keys. Based on the selected mode (keys or frames), the Time Controls can move among the first, previous, next, and last frames or keys.

- **Viewport Navigation Controls:** In the lower-right corner of the interface are the controls for manipulating the viewports. They enable you to zoom, pan, and rotate the active viewport's view.

Cross-Reference

Most of the controls on the lower interface bar—including the Time Slider, the Track Bar, and the Key and Time Controls—deal with animation. You can learn more about these controls in Chapter 21, "Understanding Animation and Keyframes." The Viewport Navigation Controls are covered in Chapter 2, "Controlling and Configuring the Viewports." ■

FIGURE 1.12

The Lower Interface Bar includes several sets of controls.

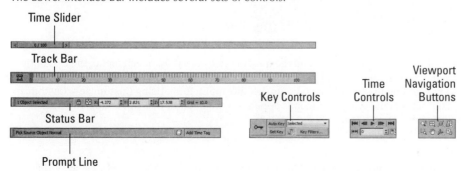

Time Slider

Track Bar

Status Bar

Prompt Line

Key Controls

Time Controls

Viewport Navigation Buttons

Interacting with the Interface

Knowing where all the interface elements are located is only the start. Max includes several interactive features that make the interface work. Learning these features makes the difference between an interface that works for you and one that doesn't.

Gaining quick access with the right-click quadmenus

Quadmenus are pop-up menus with up to four separate sections that surround the cursor, as shown in Figure 1.13. Right-clicking in the active viewport opens these quadmenus. The contents of the menus depend on the object selected.

Tip

Many of the real pros use quadmenus extensively. One reason is that they can access the commands from the mouse's current location using a couple of clicks without having to go all the way to the Command Panel to click a button. ∎

FIGURE 1.13

Quadmenus contain a host of commands in an easily accessible location.

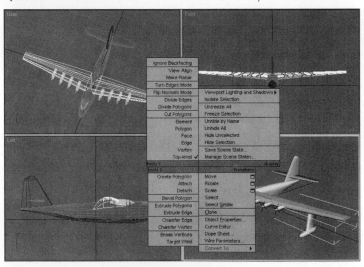

Clicking with the left mouse button away from the quadmenu closes it. For each menu, the text of the last menu item selected is displayed in blue. To quickly access the blue menu item again, simply click the gray-shaded bar for the quadrant that contains the blue menu item. Using Customize ⇨ Customize User Interface, you can specify which commands appear on the quadmenus, but the default options have just about everything you need.

Cross-Reference

You can learn more about customizing the interface in Chapter 4, "Customizing the Max Interface and Setting Preferences." ∎

If you press and hold the Alt, Ctrl, and Shift keys while right-clicking in the active viewport, you can access specific sets of commands; Shift+right-click opens the Snap options, Alt+right-click opens Animation commands, Ctrl+right-click opens a menu of primitives, Shift+Alt+right-click opens a menu of reactor commands, and Ctrl+Alt+right-click opens a menu of rendering commands.

Using Caddy controls

Quadmenus are great for accessing specific commands, but changing the settings for the various features still requires that you visit the Command Panel. This is where the Caddy controls help. Certain modeling features such as Bevel and Extrude let you open a select set of controls, known as a Caddy, overlaid over the selected object, as shown in Figure 1.14. Changing any of these settings updates the selection and lets you see if the change is what you want. If you're happy with the setting, you can accept the change and dismiss the Caddy control.

A key benefit of the Caddy controls is that they stay near the selected subobject even if you change the viewport. In addition to several settings that are updated immediately, there are buttons to accept and commit the current change, to apply the change and continue to work with the tool, or to cancel. Using the Apply and Continue button keeps the tool around for more work.

FIGURE 1.14

Caddy controls appear above the selection and let you try several different settings.

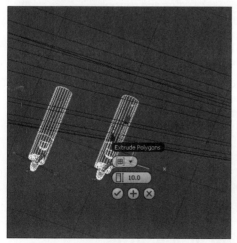

Understanding the button color cues

Max's interface uses color cues to help remind you of the current mode. When a button is yellow, it warns that it has control of the interface. For example, if one of the subobject buttons in the Command Panel is selected, it turns yellow, and the ability to select another object is disabled until this subobject mode is turned off. Knowing what the current mode is at all times can keep you out of trouble.

Another common button color is red. When either the Auto Key or Set Key buttons is depressed, it turns red. The edge of the active viewport being animated along with the Time Slider also turns red. This reminds you that any modifications will be saved as a key.

Toggle buttons can be turned on and off. Example toggle buttons include the Snap buttons. When a toggle button is enabled, it also turns light gray. Toggle buttons highlighted in blue are nonexclusive, but they notify you of a mode that is enabled, such as the Key Mode Toggle or the Affect Pivot Only button.

Cross-Reference

All interface colors can be customized using the Customize User Interface dialog box, which is discussed in Chapter 4, "Customizing the Max Interface and Setting Preferences." ■

Using drag-and-drop features

Dialog boxes that work with files benefit greatly from Max's drag-and-drop features. The Material Editor, Background Image, View File, and Environmental Settings dialog boxes all use drag and drop. These dialog boxes let you select a file or a material and drag it on top of where you want to apply it. For example, with the Maps rollout in the Material Editor open, you can drag a texture image filename from Windows Explorer or the Asset Manager and drop it on the Map button. You can even drag and drop Max files from Windows Explorer into the Max interface to open them.

Controlling spinners

Spinners are those little controls throughout the interface with a value field and two small arrows to its right. As you would expect, clicking the up arrow increases the value and clicking the down arrow decreases the value. The amount of the increase or decrease depends on the setting in the General tab of the Preference Settings dialog box. Right-clicking the spinner resets the value to its lowest acceptable value. Another way to control the spinner value is to click the arrows and drag with the mouse. Dragging up increases the value, and dragging down decreases it.

The effect of the spinner drag is shown in the viewport if the Update During Spinner Drag menu option is enabled in the Views menu. If the cursor is located within a spinner, you can press Ctrl+N to open the Numeric Expression Evaluator, which lets you set the value using an expression. For example, you can set a spinner value by adding numbers together as you would if using a calculator. An expression of 30+40+35 sets the value to 105.

Cross-Reference

Chapter 36, "Animating with the Expression Controller and Wiring Parameters," covers the Numeric Expression Evaluator in more detail. ■

Understanding modeless and persistent dialog boxes

Many dialog boxes in Max are *modeless,* which means that the dialog box doesn't need to be closed before you can work with objects in the background viewports. The Material Editor is an example of a modeless dialog box. With the Material Editor open, you can create, select, and transform objects in the background. Other modeless dialog boxes include the Material/Map Browser, the Render Scene dialog box, Caddy controls, the Video Post dialog box, the Transform Type-In dialog box, the Display and Selection Floaters, and the various graph editors. Pressing the Ctrl+~ keyboard shortcut closes all open dialog boxes. Pressing the same keyboard shortcut again reopens the dialog boxes that were previously closed.

Another feature of many, but not all, dialog boxes is *persistence,* which means that values added to a dialog box remain set when the dialog box is reopened. This feature applies only within a given Max session. Choosing the File➪Reset command button or exiting and restarting Max resets all the dialog boxes.

Getting Help

If you get stuck, Max won't leave you stranded. You can turn to several places in Max to get help. The Help menu is a valuable resource that provides access to references and tutorials. The 3ds Max Help and MAXScript Help are comprehensive help systems. They are HTML pages that are accessible through the Autodesk.com website. Selecting the Autodesk 3ds Max Help menu from the Help menu opens a web browser and loads the help files. This ensures that the latest and most up-to-date help files are available. Additional Help presents help systems for any external plug-ins that are loaded. The Tutorials command loads the tutorials, which offer a chance to gain valuable experience.

New Feature

Accessing help files from the Autodesk.com website is a new feature in 3ds Max 2012. ■

If you are working with Max offline, you can download and access a local copy of the help files. The Help panel in the Preference Settings dialog box, shown in Figure 1.15, lets you specify whether to use the online or the local help files.

FIGURE 1.15

The Help panel includes buttons for downloading the latest help files.

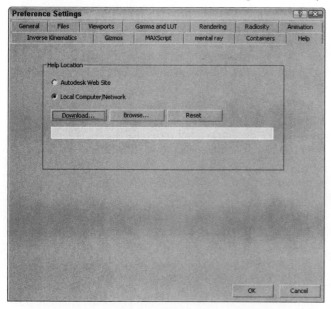

Using the InfoCenter toolbar

With all the various help files, it can be tough to know exactly which one to look in for the information you need sometimes. To help with this, 3ds Max includes an InfoCenter toolbar located at the right end of the title bar.

When you enter a keyword in the InfoCenter toolbar, Max performs a search and presents a list of information on where the keyword is found in all the various help files, including Max documentation and online resources, as shown in Figure 1.16.

FIGURE 1.16

The InfoCenter toolbar lets you search multiple help files at once.

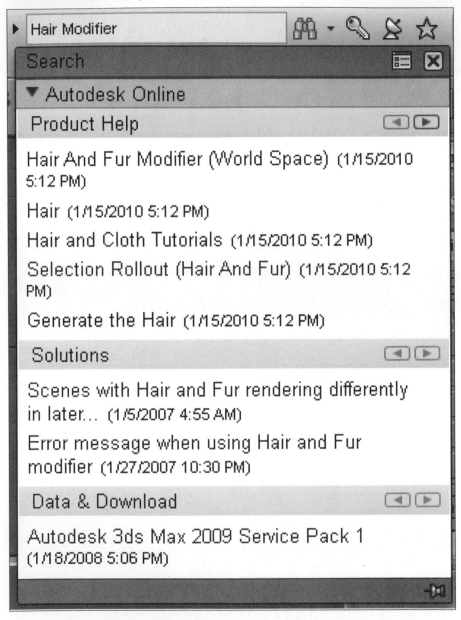

Tip

You can use wildcards when searching for keywords. The asterisk (*) replaces one or more characters, the question mark (?) replaces a single character, and the tilde (~) looks for prefixes and/or suffixes added to the word. For example, con* finds controller, construct, and contour; sta? finds star and stat; ~lit finds prelit and relit; and limit~ finds limited and limitless. ■

Clicking the Search icon located to the right of the search text field (which looks like a tiny pair of binoculars) starts the search. The InfoCenter toolbar also includes buttons for accessing Subscription Center, Communication Center, and Favorites. For each of these buttons, a pop-up dialog box appears that includes icon buttons in the upper right for closing the dialog box and for opening the InfoCenter Settings dialog box, shown in Figure 1.17. The InfoCenter Settings dialog box includes settings for configuring the Communication Center, which is a resource for getting information and announcements from Autodesk. You can configure the Communication Center to inform you when updates are available, display product support issues, and even include RSS feeds from Autodesk.

Tip

Within the InfoCenter Settings dialog box is an option to disable those annoying balloon notifications that frequently pop up, or you can make them semitransparent. ■

FIGURE 1.17

The InfoCenter Settings dialog box lets you specify which items are searchable.

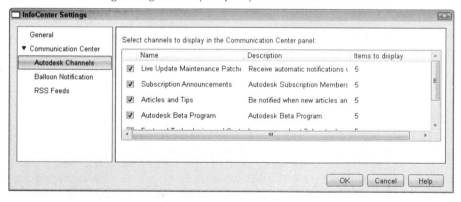

Viewing the Essential Skills Movies

When Max first loads, users are greeted with a Welcome to 3ds Max dialog box, shown in Figure 1.18, that includes several Essential Skills Movies. These simple movies explain the basics of working with Max.

The Welcome to 3ds Max dialog box also includes links to What's New and to Learning Channel, which are pages where you can find more tutorials and resources. After viewing the Essential Skills Movies, you can disable the Show this dialog at startup option to prevent this dialog box from appearing the next time you start Max. You can access the Learning Movies dialog box at any time using the Help menu.

Note
The Essential Skills Movies require an installation of Flash. ■

FIGURE 1.18

The Welcome to 3ds Max dialog box includes video clips showing the basic skills you need for working with Max.

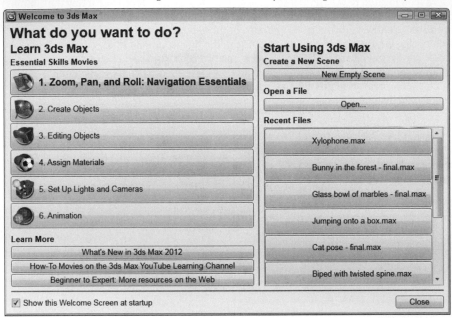

Using the online reference guides

The Autodesk 3ds Max Help, What's New, MAXScript Help, and Tutorials are all loaded within a Web browser. An organized list of topics is available in the left navigation pane, as shown in Figure 1.19, and the right includes a pane where the details on the selected topic are displayed. Across the top are several toolbar buttons used to control the interface. The Show in Contents button opens the selected help page in the Contents navigation list. The Add to Favorites button adds the current help page to the Favorites drop-down list accessible in the InfoCenter toolbar at the top of the interface. The Home button returns to the first page of the Help file. The Back, Up, and Forward buttons move to the last, above, or previous page in the navigation.

Tip
You also can use the web browser buttons to move back and forth between the last-visited and next-visited pages. ■

Above the left navigation pane are four tabs that open separate panels when selected. The Contents panel displays a list of topics; the Index panel lists all topics alphabetically, the Search panel includes a text field where you can search for specific keywords, and the Favorites panel keeps a list of book-marks to topics you add to the list.

FIGURE 1.19

The 3ds Max Reference includes panels for viewing the index of commands and searching the reference.

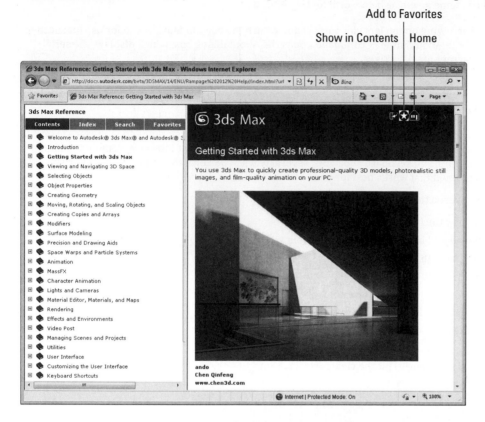

Throughout the textual descriptions, keywords linked to other related topics are highlighted in blue and underlined.

Using the rest of the Help menu

The Keyboard Shortcut Map displays an interactive interface for learning all the keyboard shortcuts. The Help ⇨ Data Exchange Solutions menu opens a web page that explains how to use the FBX format to exchange files with other software packages. The Customer Involvement Program provides an interface where you can send feedback to Autodesk regarding 3ds Max. The program lets you send feedback anonymously or you can include your e-mail. If you notice a problem with the software, you can report it with the Report a Problem feature.

The 3ds Max on the Web options (The Area, Online Support, Updates, Resources, Partners, Training, and so on) automatically open a web browser and load the Autodesk Support web pages or look for updates. The Area website is another excellent resource for help. It is the community site for 3ds Max users.

Tip

If you need help from something more personable than a Help file, the Area website is a Max community sponsored by Autodesk. It has some awesome help worth looking into. ■

The License Borrowing option lets you borrow and return the current Max license for use on another computer; and the About 3ds Max command opens the About dialog box, which displays the serial number and current display driver.

Summary

You should now be familiar with the interface elements for Max. Understanding the interface is one of the keys to success in using 3ds Max. Max includes a variety of different interface elements. Among the menus, toolbars, and keyboard shortcuts, several ways to perform the same command exist. Discover the method that works best for you.

This chapter covered the following topics:

- Learning the interface elements
- Viewing and using the pull-down menus
- Working with toolbars
- Accessing the Command Panel
- Learning the lower interface controls
- Interacting with the Max interface
- Getting additional help

In this chapter, I've skirted about the viewports covering all the other interface elements, but in the next chapter, you're going to hit the viewports head-on.

Controlling and Configuring the Viewports

A lthough Max consists of many different interface elements, such as panels, dialog boxes, and menus, the viewports are the main areas that will catch your attention. The four main viewports make up the bulk of the interface. You can think of the viewports as looking at the television screen instead of the remote. Learning to control and use the viewports can make a huge difference in your comfort level with Max. Nothing is more frustrating than not being able to rotate, pan, and zoom the view.

The viewports have numerous settings and controls that you can use to provide thousands of different ways to look at your scene, and beginners can feel frustrated at not being able to control what they see. Max includes several handy little gizmos that make navigating the viewports much easier. This chapter includes all the details you need to make the viewports reveal their secrets.

Understanding 3D Space

It seems silly to be talking about 3D space because we live and move in 3D space. If we stop and think about it, 3D space is natural to us. For example, consider trying to locate your kids at the swimming pool. If you're standing poolside, the kids could be to your left or right, in front of you or behind you, or in the water below you or on the high dive above you. Each of these sets of directions represents a dimension in 3D space.

Now imagine that you're drawing a map that pinpoints the kid's location at the swimming pool. Using the drawing (which is 2D), you can describe the kid's position on the map as left, right, top, or bottom, but the descriptions of above and below have been lost. By moving from a 3D reference to a 2D one, the number of dimensions has decreased.

The conundrum that 3D computer artists face is, how do you represent 3D objects on a 2D device such as a computer screen? The answer that 3ds Max provides is to present several views, called *viewports*, of the scene. A viewport is a small window that displays the scene from one perspective. These viewports are the windows into Max's 3D world. Each viewport has numerous settings and viewing options.

Learning Axonometric versus Perspective

When it comes to views in the 3D world, two different types exist—Axonometric and Perspective. Axonometric views are common in the CAD world where the viewer is set at an infinite distance from the object such that all parallel lines remain parallel. A Perspective view simulates how our eyes actually work and converges all points to a single location off in the distance.

You can see the difference between these two types of views clearly if you look at a long line of objects. For example, if you were to look down a long row of trees lining a road, the trees would eventually merge on the horizon. In Axonometric views, lines stay parallel as they recede into the distance. Figure 2.1 shows this example with the Axonometric view on the left and the Perspective view on the right.

FIGURE 2.1

Axonometric and Perspective views

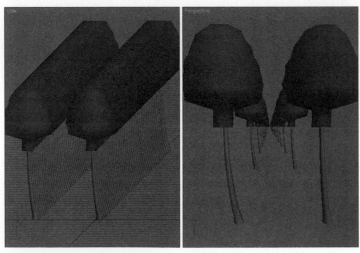

Learning Orthographic and Isometric views

If you dig a little deeper into Axonometric views, you find two different types: Orthographic and Isometric. Orthographic views are displayed from the perspective of looking straight down an axis at an object. This reveals a view in only one plane. Because orthographic viewports are constrained to one plane, they show the actual height and width of the object, which is why the CAD world uses orthographic views extensively. Isometric views are not constrained to a single axis and can view the scene from any location, but all dimensions are still maintained.

Discovering the viewports in Max

Available orthographic viewports in Max include Front, Back, Top, Bottom, Left, and Right. Max starts up with the Top, Front, and Left orthographic viewports visible. The top-left corner of the viewport displays the viewport name. The fourth default viewport is a Perspective view. Only one viewport, known as the *active viewport*, is enabled at a time. A yellow border highlights the active viewport.

Figure 2.2 shows the viewports with a Viewpoint model of a PT-328 U.S. Torpedo boat. You can see the model from a different direction in each viewport. If you want to measure the boat's length from aft to stern, you could get an accurate measurement using the Top or Left viewport, whereas you can use the Front and Left viewports to measure its precise height. So, using these different viewports, you can accurately work with all object dimensions.

FIGURE 2.2

The Max interface includes four viewports, each with a different view.

Isometric views in Max are called Orthographic viewports. You can create an Orthographic viewport by rotating any of the default non-perspective views.

Tip

Max includes several keyboard shortcuts for quickly changing the view in the active viewport including T (Top view), B (Bottom view), F (Front view), L (Left view), C (Camera view), $ (Spotlight view), P (Perspective view), and U (Orthographic User view). Pressing the V key opens a quadmenu that lets you select a new view. ■

Using the Navigation Gizmos

One of the key advantages of working in 3D is that you can view your models from an endless number of viewpoints, but you won't be able to switch to these endless viewpoints until you learn to navigate the viewports. Being able to quickly navigate the viewports is essential to working in Max and one of the first skills you should master.

To make the process of navigating within the viewports and switching among the various views easier, Max has some navigation gizmos that make this chore easy. These semitransparent gizmos hover in the upper-right corner of each viewport and provide a way to change the view without having to access a tool, select a menu, or even use a keyboard shortcut.

Working with the ViewCube

The ViewCube consists of a 3D cube that is labeled on each side and centered in a ring located on the ground plane. Its purpose is to show the current orientation of the viewport, but it is also interactive and provides a way to quickly move among the different views.

If you drag the cursor over the top of the ViewCube, shown in Figure 2.3, you'll notice that the cube's faces, corners, and edges are highlighted as the cursor moves over them. If you click when any of the cube's parts are highlighted, the viewport is animated and moves to the new view so it's positioned as if it's pointing at the selected part. By slowly animating the transition to the new view, you get a better idea of the size and shape of the model. It also makes it easy to reorient the model if it gets twisted around to an odd angle. For example, if you click the cube's face labeled Top, then the view moves from its current view until the Top view is assumed.

FIGURE 2.3

The ViewCube lets you quickly change the current view.

Go to home view

The ViewCube also lets you click and drag on the cube to rotate the view around. You can also click and drag on the base ring to spin the model about its current orientation. Above the ViewCube is a small house icon. Clicking this icon changes the view to the defined home view. You can set the Home view by right-clicking the ViewCube and selecting the Set Current View as Home option from the pop-up menu. These same menu options are also available in the Views ➪ ViewCube menu. If the ViewCube isn't visible, you can enable it using the Views ➪ ViewCube ➪ Show For Active View. There is also an option to Show For All Views.

Other pop-up menu options let you switch the view between Orthographic and Perspective views. You can also set the current view as Front, reset the Front view, and open the ViewCube panel that is located in the Viewport Configuration dialog box, as shown in Figure 2.4.

The ViewCube panel in the Viewport Configuration dialog box lets you control where and how the ViewCube appears.

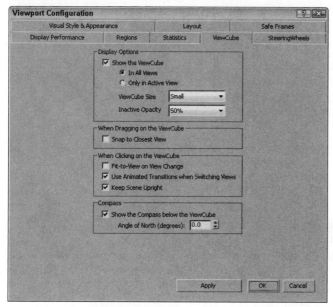

The ViewCube panel in the Viewport Configuration dialog box includes settings for turning the ViewCube on and off for All Views or for Only the Active View. You can also set the ViewCube size and its inactive opacity.

Tip

If you like the ViewCube but you feel that it takes up too much of the viewport, then you can change its size to Small or Tiny or you can set its inactive opacity to 0. When its inactive opacity is set to 0, the ViewCube isn't visible at all until you move the cursor over its location, causing it to appear. ■

You also have options to control what happens when you click or drag the ViewCube. You can snap to the closest view when dragging the ViewCube and options to automatically make the models fit to the view when the view changes, to use animated transitions, and to keep the scene upright. If you find that the view keeps ending up at odd angles when you drag the ViewCube, try enabling the Keep Scene Upright option. Finally, you have an option to display the compass under the ViewCube and a setting for the Angle of North so you can change the compass' orientation. The compass is helpful in being able to spin the model around, but if your model is something like a planet that doesn't have a top or bottom, disabling the compass makes sense.

Using the SteeringWheels

The ViewCube is great for switching between the default views and for rotating the current view, but there are many additional navigation tools that aren't covered with the ViewCube. To handle many of these other navigation tools, such as zooming and panning, Max includes the SteeringWheels, another gizmo for navigating the viewports.

When Max is first started, the SteeringWheels are turned off, but you can enable this gizmo with the Views ➪ SteeringWheels ➪ Toggle SteeringWheels menu or by pressing the Shift+W shortcut. Once enabled, different parts of the wheel are highlighted when you move over them. The full navigation wheel, shown in Figure 2.5, includes the following modes:

FIGURE 2.5

The SteeringWheel gizmo includes several different ways to navigate the viewports.

- **Zoom:** Causes the view to zoom in and out of the scene about the pivot. The pivot is set by holding down the Ctrl key while clicking.
- **Orbit:** Causes the view to orbit about the pivot. The pivot is set by holding down the Ctrl key while clicking.
- **Pan:** Causes the view to pan in the direction that you drag the cursor.
- **Rewind:** As you change the scene, Max remembers each view where you stop and keeps these views in a buffer. The Rewind mode displays these views as small thumbnails, as shown in Figure 2.6, and lets you move through them by dragging the mouse. This allows you to rewind back and move forward through the buffered views.

Tip

Moving between the buffered thumbnail views with the Rewind feature gradually animates the transition between adjacent thumbnails and allows you to click to change the view to one that is between two buffered views. ■

- **Center:** Lets you click an object to be the pivot center for zooming and orbiting.
- **Walk:** Moves you forward through the scene as if you were walking through it. Holding down the Shift key lets you move up and down.
- **Look:** Causes the camera to rotate side to side as if looking to the side.
- **Up/Down:** Moves the view up and down from the current location.

FIGURE 2.6

Rewind mode lets you move back and forth through recent views.

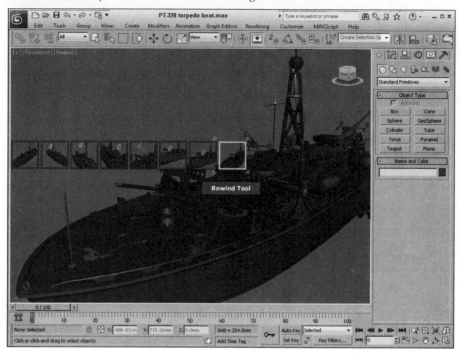

Note

It is covered later in the chapter, but you can maximize the active viewport by clicking the Maximize Viewport Toggle button (the button in the lower-left corner of the interface) or by pressing Alt+W. ■

In the upper-right corner of the wheel is a small X icon. This icon is used to close the SteeringWheel gizmo. In the lower-right corner of the wheel is a small down arrow. This icon opens a pop-up menu. Using the pop-up menu, you can select a different wheel type, go to the home view as defined by the ViewCube, increase or decrease the walk speed, restore the original center, or open the SteeringWheels panel in the Viewport Configuration dialog box, as shown in Figure 2.7. These same options are also available in the Views ⇨ SteeringWheels menu, along with an option to Toggle the SteeringWheels on and off (Shift+W).

Using the SteeringWheels panel in the Viewport Configuration dialog box, you can set the size and opacity of the SteeringWheels. There are also settings for controlling many of the different modes.

FIGURE 2.7

The SteeringWheels panel in the Viewport Configuration dialog box includes settings for the various wheels.

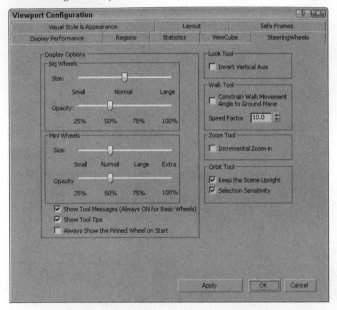

Tutorial: Navigating the active viewport

Over time, navigating the viewports becomes second nature to you, but you need to practice to get to that point. In this tutorial, you get a chance to take the viewports for a spin—literally.

To practice navigating a viewport, follow these steps:

1. Open the Bruce the dog.max file from the Chap 02 directory on the CD.

   This file includes a model of a dog (affectionately named Bruce) created by Viewpoint. It provides a reference as you navigate the viewport. The active viewport is the Perspective viewport.

2. Click the Maximize Viewport Toggle button (or press Alt+W) to make the Perspective viewport fill the space of all four viewports.

3. Click the Front face in the ViewCube to transition the view to the front view. Then move the cursor over the upper-right corner of the ViewCube and click to set the view to a perspective view.

4. Select the Views ⇨ SteeringWheels ⇨ Toggle SteeringWheels (or press Shift+W); then hold down the Ctrl key and click Bruce's head to set the pivot. Then move the cursor over the Zoom button and drag until Bruce's head fills the viewport.

5. With the Steering Wheel still active, move the cursor over the Pan button and drag the window until Bruce's head is centered evenly in the viewport, as shown in Figure 2.8. Right-click in the viewport to toggle the SteeringWheel gizmo off.

FIGURE 2.8

The Perspective viewport is zoomed in on the dog's head using the Zoom and Pan controls.

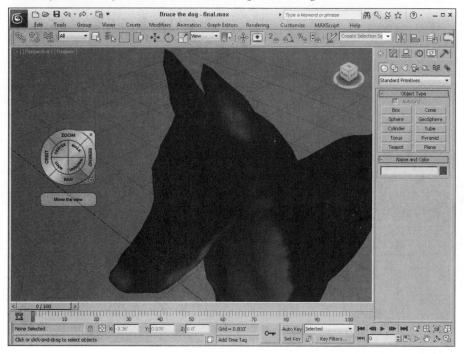

Controlling Viewports with a Scroll Wheel Mouse

Now that I've explained the viewport navigation gizmos, I'll explain another easy way to control the viewports. Often, the quickest way to control the viewports is with the mouse. To really get the benefit of the mouse, you need to use a mouse with a scroll wheel (which also acts as a middle mouse button).

Rolling the scroll wheel in the active viewport zooms in to and out of the viewport by steps just like the bracket keys ([and]). You can zoom precisely by holding down the Ctrl and Alt keys while dragging the scroll wheel.

Clicking and dragging the scroll wheel button pans the active viewport. Clicking and dragging with the Alt button held down rotates the active viewport. If the scroll wheel isn't working, check the Viewports panel in the Preference Settings dialog box. You can select to use the scroll wheel control to pan and zoom in the viewports or to define and use Strokes.

Caution

Be careful when zooming in with the scroll wheel. If you zoom in too far, the internal field of width approaches its minimum value and zooming becomes unstable. If this happens, you can select the Views ⇨ Undo View Change (Shift+Z) menu command to undo the zoom or use the Zoom Extents button. ∎

Cross-Reference

Strokes are covered in Chapter 4, "Customizing the Max Interface and Setting Preferences." ∎

Using the Viewport Navigation Controls

Although the ViewCube, the SteeringWheels, and the scroll wheel make navigating the viewports easy, you can still use the standard navigation tools located in the bottom-right corner of the interface. The standard viewports show you several different views of your current project, but within each viewport you can zoom in on certain objects, pan the view, or rotate about the center of the viewport. Clicking a viewport with any of the Viewport Navigation Controls automatically makes the selected viewport the active viewport. In Table 2.1, the keyboard shortcut for each button is listed in parentheses next to its name.

TABLE 2.1

Viewport Navigation Controls

Toolbar Button	Name	Description
	Zoom (Alt+Z or [or])	Moves closer to or farther from the objects in the active viewport by dragging the mouse or zooming by steps with the bracket keys.
	Zoom All	Zooms into or out of all the viewports simultaneously by dragging the mouse.
	Zoom Extents (Ctrl+Alt+Z), Zoom Extents Selected	Zooms in on all objects or just the selected object until it fills the active viewport.
	Zoom Extents All (Ctrl+Shift+Z), Zoom Extents All Selected (Z)	Zooms in on all objects or just the selected object until it fills all the viewports.
	Field of View, Region Zoom (Ctrl+W)	The Field of View button (available only in the Perspective view) controls the width of the view. The Region Zoom button zooms in to the region selected by dragging the mouse.
	Pan (Ctrl+P or I), Walk Through	Moves the view to the left, to the right, up, or down by dragging the mouse or by moving the mouse while holding down the I key. The Walk Through feature moves through the scene using the arrow keys or a mouse like a first-person video game.
	Orbit (Ctrl+R), Orbit Selected, Orbit SubObject	Rotates the view around the global axis, selected object, or subobject by dragging the mouse.
	Maximize Viewport Toggle (Alt+W)	Makes the active viewport fill the screen, replacing the four separate viewports. Clicking this button a second time shows all four viewports again.

Caution

When one of the Viewport Navigation buttons is selected, it is highlighted yellow. You cannot select, create, or transform objects while one of these buttons is highlighted. Right-clicking in the active viewpoint or clicking the Select Objects tool reverts to select object mode. ∎

Zooming a view

You can zoom into and out of the scene in several ways. Clicking the Zoom (Alt+Z) button enters zoom mode where you can zoom into and out of a viewport by dragging the mouse. This works in which-ever viewport you drag in. To the right of the Zoom button is the Zoom All button, which does the same thing as the Zoom button, only to all four viewports at once. If you hold down the Ctrl key while dragging in Zoom mode, the zoom action happens more quickly, requiring only a small mouse move-ment to get a large zoom amount. Holding down the Alt key while dragging in Zoom mode has the opposite effect; the zoom happens much more slowly, and a large mouse move is required for a small zoom amount. This is helpful for fine-tuning the zoom.

The Zoom Extents (Ctrl+Alt+Z) button zooms the active viewport so that all objects (or the selected objects with the Zoom Extents Selected button) are visible in the viewport. A Zoom Extents All (Ctrl+Shift+Z) button is available for zooming in all viewports to all objects' extents; the most popular zoom command (and the easiest to remember) is Zoom Extents All Selected (Z), which is for zooming into the extents of the selected objects in all viewports.

You can use the brackets keys to zoom in ([) and out (]) by steps. Each key press zooms in (or out) another step. The Region Zoom (Ctrl+W) button lets you drag over the region that you want to zoom in on. If you select a non-orthogonal view, such as the Perspective view, the Region Zoom button has a flyout called the Field of View. Using this button, you can control how wide or narrow the view is. This is like using a wide angle or telephoto lens on your camera. This feature is different from zoom in that the perspective is distorted as the Field of View is increased.

Cross-Reference

Field of View is covered in more detail in Chapter 19, "Configuring and Aiming Cameras." ∎

Panning a view

The Viewport Navigation Controls also offer two ways to pan in a viewport. In Pan mode (Ctrl+P), dragging in a viewport pans the view. Note that this doesn't move the objects, only the view. The sec-ond way to pan is to hold down the I key while moving the mouse. This is known as an *interactive* pan. In addition, the Ctrl and Alt keys can be held down to speed or slow the panning motions.

Walking through a view

The Walk Through button, found as a flyout button under the Pan button, allows you to move through the scene in the Perspective or Camera viewport using the arrow keys or the mouse just as you would if you were playing a first-person computer game. When this button is active, the cursor changes to a small circle with an arrow inside it that points in the direction you are moving. You need to first click in the viewport before you can use the arrow keys.

Caution

The Pan button is a flyout only if the Perspective view or a Camera view is selected. ∎

The Walk Through feature includes several keystrokes for controlling the camera's movement. The arrow keys move the camera forward, left, back, and right (or you can use the W, A, S, and D keys). You can change the speed of the motion with the Q (accelerate) and Z (decelerate) keys or with the [(decrease step size) and] (increase step size) keys. The E and C keys (or the Shift+up or Shift+down arrows) are used to move up and down in the scene. The Shift+spacebar key causes the camera to be set level. Dragging the mouse while the camera is moving changes the direction in which the camera points.

A handy alternative to Walk Through mode is the Walkthrough Assistant, which is found on the Animation menu. This utility opens a dialog box that includes buttons for creating and adding a camera to a path. It also has controls from turning the view side to side as the camera moves along the path.

Cross-Reference
The Walkthrough Assistant is covered in more detail in Chapter 22, "Animating with Constraints and Simple Controllers." ∎

Rotating a view

Rotating the view can be the most revealing of all the view changes. When the Orbit (Ctrl+R) button is selected, a rotation guide appears in the active viewport, as shown in Figure 2.9. This rotation guide is a circle with a square located at each quadrant. Clicking and dragging the left or right squares rotates the view side to side; the same action with the top and bottom squares rotates the view up and down. Clicking within the circle and dragging rotates within a single plane, and clicking and dragging out side of the circle rotates the view about the circle's center either clockwise or counterclockwise. If you get confused, look at the cursor, which changes depending on the type of rotation. The Ctrl and Alt keys also can speed and slow the rotating view.

FIGURE 2.9

The rotation guide appears whenever the Orbit button is selected.

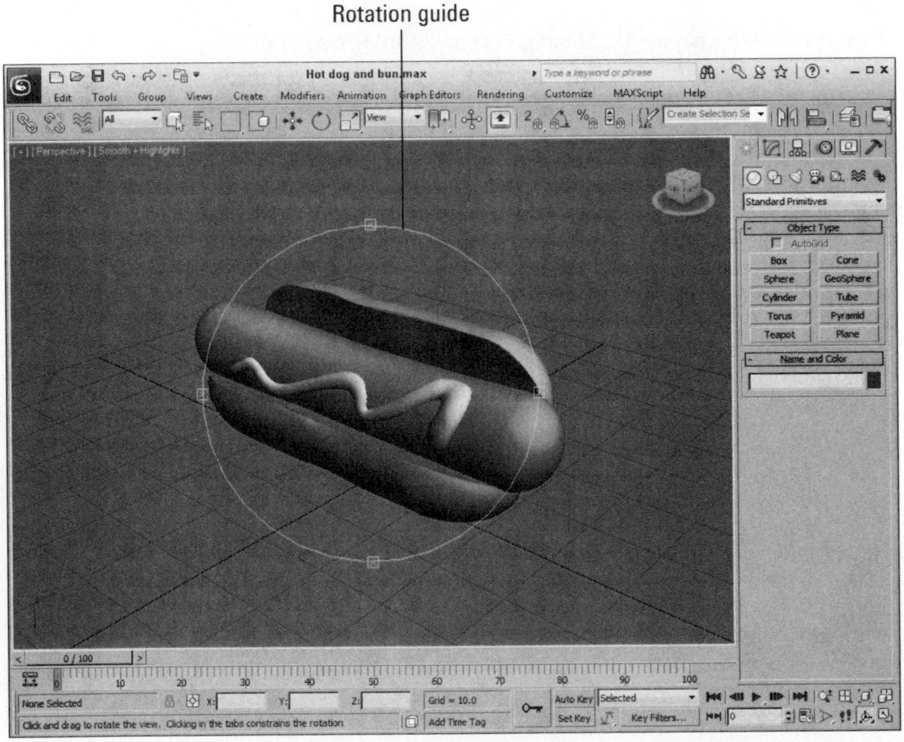

Rotation guide

Note

If you rotate one of the default non-perspective views, it automatically becomes an Orthographic view, but you can undo the change using the Views ⇨ Undo View Change command or the Shift+Z shortcut. ∎

Maximizing the active viewport

Sooner or later, the viewports will feel too small. When this happens, you have several ways to increase the size of your viewports. The first trick to try is to change the viewport sizes by clicking and dragging any of the viewport borders. Dragging on the intersection of the viewports resizes all the viewports. Figure 2.10 shows the viewports after being dynamically resized.

Tip

You can return to the original layout by right-clicking any of the viewport borders and selecting Reset Layout from the pop-up menu. ∎

FIGURE 2.10

You can dynamically resize viewports by dragging their borders.

The second trick is to use the Maximize Viewport Toggle (Alt+W) to expand the active viewport to fill the space reserved for all four viewports. Clicking the Maximize Viewport Toggle (or pressing Alt+W) a second time returns to the defined layout.

Maximizing the viewport helps temporarily, but you can take another step before convincing your boss that you need a larger monitor. You can enter Expert Mode by choosing Views ⇨ Expert Mode (Ctrl+X). It maximizes the viewport space by removing the main toolbar, the Command Panel, and most of the Lower Interface Bar.

With most of the interface elements gone, you'll need to rely on the menus, keyboard shortcuts, and quadmenus to execute commands. To reenable the default interface, click the Cancel Expert Mode button in the lower right of the Max window (or press Ctrl+X again). Figure 2.11 shows the interface in Expert Mode.

FIGURE 2.11

Expert Mode maximizes the viewports by eliminating most of the interface elements.

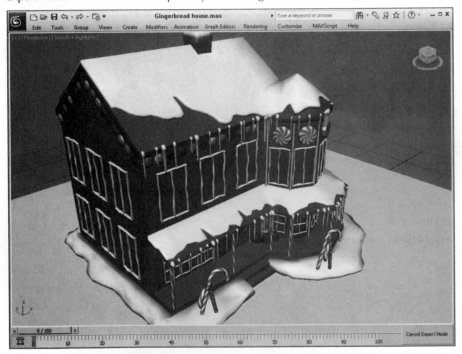

Controlling camera and spotlight views

You can set any viewport to be a Camera view (C) or a Spotlight view ($) if a camera or a spotlight exists in the scene. When either of these views is active, the Viewport Navigation Control buttons change. In Camera view, controls for dolly, roll, truck, pan, orbit, and field of view become active. A light view includes controls for falloff and hotspots.

Cross-Reference

Chapter 19, "Configuring and Aiming Cameras," and Chapter 20, "Using Lights and Basic Lighting Techniques," cover these changes in more detail. ■

Changing the Viewport Display

Although the Viewport Navigation Controls are focused on controlling what is visible in the viewports, there are also a number of useful commands in the Views menu and in the viewport labels at the top-left corner of each viewport that directly affect the viewports. The three viewport labels include the General viewport label (which is a simple plus sign), the Point-of-View viewport label, and the Shading viewport label. The last two labels show the current setting.

Undoing and saving viewport changes

If you get lost in your view, you can undo and redo viewport changes with Views ⇨ Undo View Change (Shift+Z) and Views ⇨ Redo View Change (Shift+Y). These commands are different from the Edit ⇨ Undo and Edit ⇨ Redo commands, which can undo or redo geometry changes.

You can save changes made to a viewport by using the Views ⇨ Save Active Viewport menu command. This command saves the Viewport Navigation settings for recall. To restore these settings, use Views ⇨ Restore Active Viewport.

Note

The Save and Restore Active Viewport commands do not save any viewport configuration settings, just the navigated view. Saving an active view uses a buffer, so it remembers only one view for each viewport. ■

Disabling and refreshing viewports

If your scene gets too complicated, you can experience some slow-down waiting for each viewport to be updated with changes, but fear not, because several options will come to your rescue. The first option to try is to disable a viewport.

You can disable a viewport by right-clicking the general viewport label and selecting the Disable View menu command from the pop-up menu, or you can press the keyboard shortcut, D. When a disabled viewport is active, it is updated as normal; when it is inactive, the viewport is not updated at all until it becomes active again. Disabled viewports are identified by the word "Disabled," which appears next to the viewport's labels in the upper-left corner.

Another trick to increase the viewport update speed is to disable the Views ⇨ Update During Spinner Drag menu option. Changing parameter spinners can cause a slowdown by requiring every viewport to update as the spinner changes. If the spinner is changing rapidly, it can really slow even a powerful system. Disabling this option causes the viewport to wait for the spinner to stop changing before updating.

Sometimes when changes are made, the viewports aren't completely refreshed. This typically happens when dialog boxes from other programs are moved in front of the viewports or as objects get moved around, because they often mask one another and lines disappear. If this happens, you can force Max to refresh all the viewports with the Views ⇨ Redraw All Views (keyboard shortcut, `) menu command. The Redraw All Views command refreshes each viewport and makes everything visible again.

Viewing materials in the viewports

The Views menu also includes several commands for making scene details such as materials, lighting, and shadows visible in the viewports. Each of these options can slow down the refresh rate, but they provide immediate feedback, which is often helpful.

Texture maps can also take up lots of memory. The Views ⇨ Show Materials in Viewport As ⇨ Shaded Materials with Maps command shows all applied texture maps in the viewports. If you don't need to see the texture maps, then switching to Views⇨Show Materials in Viewport As⇨Shaded Materials without Maps will speed up the display. There is also an option to use Realistic Materials without Maps and Realistic Materials with Maps that uses the video card's memory to display the applied textures.

The Views⇨Show Materials in Viewport As menu also includes a toggle to Enable Transparency in the viewport.

Tip
The options for enabling materials in the viewports are also available as a submenu under the Shading viewport label menu. ■

Cross-Reference
More on applying texture maps is covered in Chapter 17, "Adding Material Details with Maps." ■

Displaying lights and shadows in the viewports

Options for enabling lighting and shadow effects within the viewports are located in the Shading viewport label menu. By default, both shadows and ambient occlusion are enabled when the Realistic shading mode is selected, but you can disable them using the toggle menu options under the Lighting and Shadows menu. There is also an option to Illuminate the scene using Scene Lights or Default Lights. Figure 2.12 shows an example of viewport shadows and Ambient Occlusion.

FIGURE 2.12

Viewport Shading shown with shadows enabled

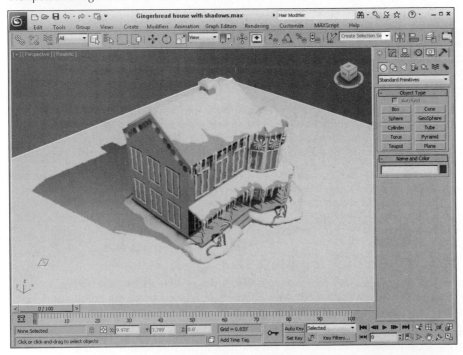

Ambient Occlusion is a lighting effect that adds to the realism of a scene by making objects cast shadows on surrounding objects based on how they block the light. Objects that are close to one another spread a soft shadow onto nearby objects. Figure 2.13 gives a good example. Notice how the columns cast a light shadow onto the walls and onto the areas around the column caps.

FIGURE 2.13

Ambient Occlusion can often be used as an alternative to full shadows

Caution

Displaying shadows in the viewport requires Direct3D 9.0 to be installed on your system, and your video card must support Shader Model 2.0 or Shader Model 3.0. If your computer doesn't support either of these Shader models, then the options will be disabled in the viewport shading label menu and in the Viewport Configuration dialog box. You can check the capabilities of your video card using the Help ⇨ Diagnose Video Hardware command. ∎

Configuring viewport lighting and shadows

The Viewport Configuration dialog box includes a number of settings for the viewport lighting and shadows in the Visual Style & Appearance panel, shown in Figure 2.14. This panel includes options to illuminate the scene with Default lights (either one or two) or with Scene lights, just like the viewport Shading label menu. The one-light option creates a single light positioned behind the viewer and at an angle to the scene. Scenes with one light update more quickly than scenes with two lights.

The Default Lighting toggle deactivates your current lights and uses the default lights. This option can be helpful when you're trying to view objects in a dark setting because the default lighting illuminates the entire scene without requiring you to remove or turn off lights. This dialog box also includes options for enabling Highlights and displaying light from the selected lights.

FIGURE 2.14

The Lighting and Shadows panel includes default settings for displaying interactive lights and shadows in the viewport.

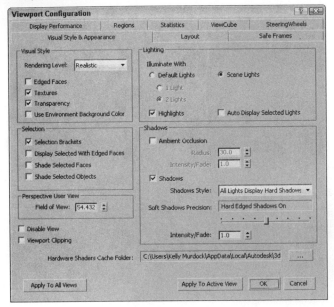

Note
If you are not using the Nitrous display drivers, then the configuration options for lighting and shadows are different. ■

The Lighting and Shadows Quality slider lets you select from several different quality settings by dragging the slider. The options range from Point Lights/Hard Shadows and Point Lights/Soft-Edge Shadows on the left through 0.125X-Very Low to 16X-Very High Quality on the right. The rightmost options can take longer to render and use area lights to improve the quality.

Beneath the Quality slider are options to enable or disable Shadows and Ambient Occlusion. You also have options to adjust the Intensity/Fade value for shadows and the Radius and Intensity/Fade amount of the Ambient Occlusion effect. These values are used to override the Viewport Shadow Intensity to dim the shadows if they are too dark. The Radius value sets how close objects need to be in order to be included in the ambient occlusion solution.

New Feature
Using and configuring viewport lighting options have been simplified in 3ds Max 2012. You no longer need to enable Hardware Rendering to see viewport shadows. ■

To enable and configure lighting and shadows in the viewports, follow these steps:

1. Open the Foot bones.max file from the Chap 02 directory on the CD.

   This file includes a set of foot bones created by Viewpoint Datalabs. There is also an Omni light added to the scene.

2. Click in the viewport Shading label, and select the Lighting and Shadows ⇨ Shadows option. Then select the Configure option from the same menu to access the Visual Style & Appearance panel in the Viewport Configuration dialog box.

Caution

If you don't see the Visual Style & Appearance panel in the Viewport Configuration dialog box, then you probably have a different display driver enabled. ∎

   Select the Enable Ambient Occlusion setting with the Radius of 10 and an Intensity/Fade value of 1. Select the Point Lights/Soft-Edged Shadows option in the Lighting and Shadows Quality slider. Then click the OK button.

3. Click the Select and Move toolbar button, and drag the light object about the scene.

   The shadows under the foot bones are automatically updated as the light is moved, as shown in Figure 2.15. Notice how the shadows are soft.

FIGURE 2.15

Lights and shadows are updated in real time when the light is moved about the scene.

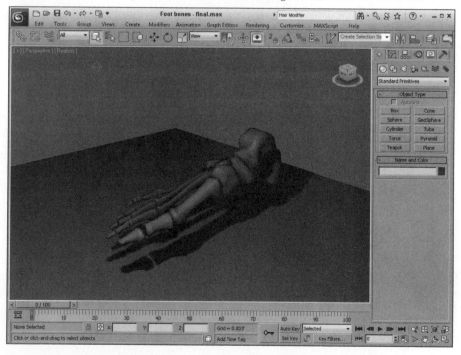

Another option available in the Visual Style & Appearance panel is the Auto Display Selected Lights. This option also is available in the Views⟹ Viewport Lighting and Shadows menu. It is helpful when you're placing and aiming lights in the scene. It causes the selected light to be displayed in the shaded viewport automatically. The Views⟹ Viewport Lighting and Shadows menu also includes options for locking and unlocking selected lights.

Locating mesh problems with xView

When modeling or importing mesh objects, a number of problems with the geometry could cause rendering artifacts such as flipped normals, overlapping faces, and open edges. Locating these problem areas can be tricky, requiring multiple renders to get it right. Within the viewports is a powerful analysis feature for locating a number of specific problem areas. This feature is called xView, and you can access it from the Views menu.

The xView analysis tool can locate and highlight the following anomalies:

- **Show Statistics (7):** Displays the number of Polys, Tris, Edges, Verts, and FPS for the entire scene and for the selected object.
- **Face Orientation:** Highlights the back side of the faces in the current selection to quickly identify faces with flipped normals.
- **Overlapping Faces:** Highlights any faces that are stacked on top of each other, which can cause render problems.
- **Open Edges:** Identifies unwanted holes in the geometry.
- **Multiple Edges:** Checks for edges that are stacked on each other. Each edge should be connected to only two faces.
- **Isolated Vertices:** Highlights vertices that aren't connected to anything. These vertices just take up space.
- **Overlapping Vertices:** Flags vertices that are within a given tolerance.
- **T-Vertices:** Highlights vertices where three edges meet. This can terminate an edge loop.
- **Missing UVW Coordinates:** Shows any faces that have no UVW coordinates for applying textures.
- **Flipped UVW Faces:** Highlights any faces that are flipped with opposite-pointing normals.
- **Overlapping UVW Faces:** Displays any faces where the textures are overlapping.

Whichever option is selected is listed at the bottom of the viewport in green along with the number of offending subobjects, such as Isolated Vertices: 12 Vertices. The menu also includes options to Select the Results, which provides to a way to quickly select and delete problem subobjects like isolated vertices. If the selected option has a setting such as the Tolerance of overlapping edges, you can select the Configure option to set this setting or click the Click Here to Configure text at the bottom of the viewport. There are also menu options to See Through the model, Auto Update the results, and display the results at the top of the viewport.

Tip

If any xView data is displayed in the viewport, you can click it to select another data option. This lets you quickly view all the potential problems with the current object. ∎

Configuring the Viewports

If the Viewport Navigation Controls help define what you see, then the Viewport Configuration dialog box helps define how you see objects in the viewports. You can configure each viewport using this dialog box. To open this dialog box, choose the Views ⇨ Viewport Configuration menu command. You can also open this dialog box by right-clicking the viewport's general label located in the upper-left corner of each viewport and choosing Configure from the pop-up menu.

The viewport labels are divided into a General menu (shown as a plus sign), a point of view label, and a shading method label. The various pop-up menus for these labels also include many of the settings found in the Viewport Configuration dialog box, but the dialog box lets you alter several settings at once. You can also make this dialog box appear for the active viewport by right-clicking any of the Viewport Navigation Control buttons in the lower-right corner.

The Viewport Configuration dialog box contains several panels, including Visual Style & Appearance, Layout, Safe Frames, Display Performance, Regions, Statistics, ViewCube, and SteeringWheels. The Preference Settings dialog box also includes many settings for controlling the behavior and look of the viewports.

New Feature

Several Viewport Configuration panels have been simplified in 3ds Max 2012. Two panels were combined into the Visual Style & Appearance panel, and the Display Performance panel also has been greatly simplified. ■

Cross-Reference

See Chapter 4, "Customizing the Max Interface and Setting Preferences," for more on the Preference Settings dialog box and all its options. ■

Setting the viewport visual style

Complex scenes take longer to display and render. The renderer used for the viewports is highly optimized to be very quick, but if you're working on a huge model with lots of complex textures and every viewport is set to display the highest quality view, then updating each viewport can slow the program to a crawl. The Viewport Configuration dialog box's Visual Style & Appearance panel, shown earlier in Figure 2.13, lets you set the visual style settings for the current viewport.

Tip

If you ever get stuck waiting for Max to complete a task, such as redrawing the viewports, you can always press the Escape key to suspend any task immediately and return control to the interface. ■

Note

These settings have no effect on the final rendering specified using the Rendering menu. They affect only the display in the viewport. ■

Rendering levels

The Rendering Level options, from slowest to fastest, include the following:

- **Realistic:** Shows smooth surfaces with lighting highlights
- **Shaded:** Shows smooth surfaces without any lighting effects
- **Consistent Colors:** Shows the entire object with minimal lighting
- **Hidden Line:** Shows only polygon edges facing the camera
- **Wireframe:** Shows all polygon edges only
- **Bounding Box:** Shows a box that would enclose the object

New Feature

Most of the rendering levels in 3ds Max 2012 have been renamed, and a few have gone away, simplifying the list. ■

Cross-Reference

Within the Rendering Level drop-down list are several Stylized options, including Graphite, Color Pencil, Ink, Color Ink, Acrylic, Pastel, and Tech. These non-photorealistic rendering methods also can be rendered and are covered in Chapter 24, "Rendering Non-Photorealistic Effects." ■

Although it really isn't a rendering method, the Edged Faces option shows the edges for each face when a shaded rendering method is selected. You can enable and disable this option with the F4 keyboard shortcut. Figure 2.16 shows, side by side, all the various viewport rendering methods applied to a simple sphere.

FIGURE 2.16

The viewport rendering methods are shown from left to right. First Row: Realistic, Shaded, Consistent Colors, Hidden Line, and Wireframe. Second Row: Bounding Box, and Edged Faces applied to Shaded.

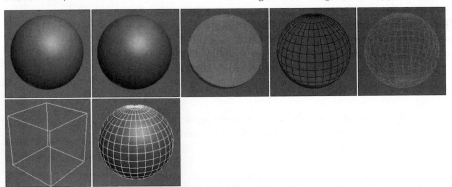

The Realistic shading method uses any applied textures and high-quality lighting and shadows. The Shaded method is similar, but it uses a quick shading method called Phong shading. The Consistent Color method displays the entire object using a single color without any shading. The simplest rendering setting that represents the shape of the object is Wireframe. It gives a good representation of the object while redrawing very quickly. By default, the Top, Front, and Left viewports are set to

Wireframe, and the Perspective viewport is set to Realistic. The Bounding Box method shows only the limits of the object as a rectangular shaped box.

Note

Many material effects, such as bump and displacement maps, cannot be seen in the viewport and show up only in the final render. ■

Viewing transparency

In addition to these shading types, you also can set the viewport to display objects that contain transparency (which is set in the Material Editor dialog box). The Transparency option is located under the viewport Shading label in the Material submenu. The Enable Transparency option also is located in the Visual Style & Appearance panel of the Viewport Configuration dialog box and in the Views ⇨ Show Materials in Viewport As menu. Figure 2.17 shows the transparency option disabled and enabled with the help of a hungry little animated creature and his ghostly rival.

New Feature

Previous versions of Max included options for making transparency appear as None, Simple, and Best, but improvements in the way transparency is displayed made these different options unnecessary. ■

FIGURE 2.17

Transparency in the viewport can be enabled using the Views ⇨ Show Materials in Viewport As menu.

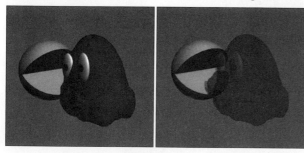

Other rendering options

The other rendering options, such as Disable View (D), Viewport Clipping, and an option to turn Textures on and off also are available. These options can help speed up viewport updates or increase the visual detail of the objects in the viewport.

Tip

At any time during a viewport update, you can click the mouse or press a key to cancel the redraw. Max doesn't make you wait for a screen redraw to be able to execute commands with the mouse or keyboard shortcuts. ■

Within the Selection section are several options that make it easier to see the selected object and/or subobjects. The Selection Brackets option displays white corners around the current selection. Selection brackets are useful for helping you see the entire size of a grouped object, but can be annoying if left on with many objects selected. Uncheck this option (or press the J key) to make these brackets disappear. The option to Display Selected with Edged Faces helps to highlight the selected object. If this option is enabled, then the edges of the current selection are displayed regardless of whether the Edged Faces check box is enabled. Figure 2.18 shows the grips of an M-203 rifle that was created by Viewpoint Datalabs selected with the Display Selected with Edged Faces and the Use Selection Brackets options enabled. These options make the current selection easy to see.

FIGURE 2.18

The Display Selected with Edged Faces and Use Selection Brackets options make identifying the current selection easy.

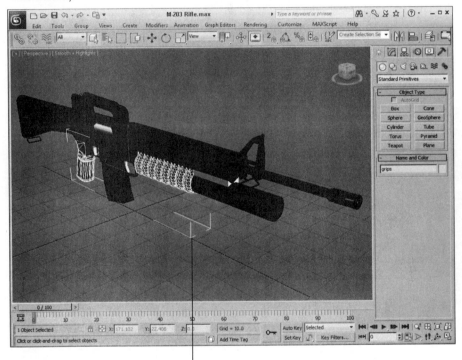

Selection brackets

You use Shade Selected Faces (F2) to shade selected subobject faces in red, making them easy to see. The Shade Selected Objects option causes the selected object to be shaded. This is noticeable only if the render level is set to Wireframe or Hidden Line. It causes the selected object to be shaded.

Note

The Shade Selected Faces (F2) option, which shades selected subobject faces, is different from the Views ⇨ Shade Selected menu command, which turns on shading for the selected object in all viewports. ■

Using clipping planes

Clipping planes define an invisible barrier beyond which all objects are invisible. For example, if you have a scene with many detailed mountain objects in the background, working with an object in the front of the scene can be difficult. By setting the clipping plane between the two, you can work on the front objects without having to redraw the mountain objects every time you update the scene. This affects only the viewport, not the rendered output.

Enabling the Viewport Clipping option in the viewport point-of-view label menu places a yellow line with two arrows on the right side of the viewport, as shown in Figure 2.19. The top arrow represents the back clipping plane, and the bottom arrow is the front clipping plane. Drag the arrows up and down to set the clipping planes.

FIGURE 2.19

The clipping planes can be used to show the interior of this car model.

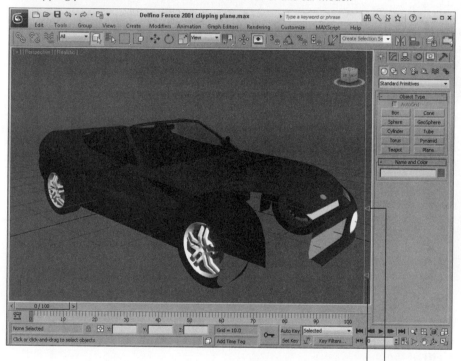

Near Clipping Plane marker

Far Clipping Plane marker

Tutorial: Viewing the interior of a heart with Clipping Planes

You can use the Viewport Clipping setting in the viewport point-of-view label to view the interior of a model such as this heart model created by Viewpoint.

To view the interior of a heart model, follow these steps:

1. Open the Heart interior.max file from the Chap 02 directory on the CD.
2. Choose Views ⇨ Viewport Configuration to open the Viewport Configuration dialog box. Enable the Viewport Clipping option, and then close the dialog box.
3. The Clipping Plane markers appear to the right of the viewport. The top marker controls the back clipping plane, and the bottom marker controls the front clipping plane. Drag the bottom clipping plane marker upward to slice through the heart model to reveal its interior, as shown in Figure 2.20.

FIGURE 2.20

By using Clipping Planes, you can reveal the interior of a model.

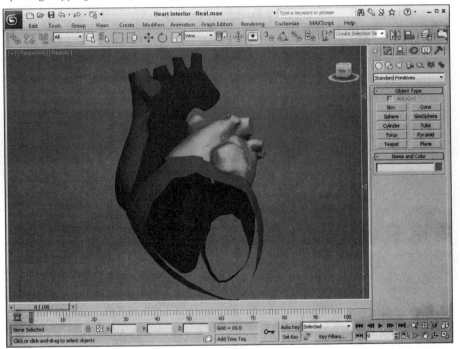

Setting the Field of View

You can also alter the Field of View (FOV) for the Perspective view in the Viewport Configuration dialog box. To create a fish-eye view, increase the FOV setting to 10 or less. The maximum FOV value is 180, and the default value is 45. You can also change the Field of View using the Field of View button in the Viewport Navigation Controls. The Viewport Configuration dialog box, however, lets you enter precise values.

Cross-Reference

See Chapter 19, "Configuring and Aiming Cameras," for more coverage on Field of View. ■

Grabbing a viewport image

It's not rendering, but you can grab an image of the active viewport using Tools ⇨ Views - Grab Viewport. Before grabbing the image, a simple dialog box appears asking you to add a label to the grabbed image. The image is loaded into the Rendered Frame Window, and its label appears in the lower-right corner of the image, as shown in Figure 2.21. The Tools ⇨ Grab Viewport menu also includes options for creating, viewing, and renaming animated sequence files, which provides a quick way to create animation previews.

Tip

If you want to save the image loaded in the Rendered Frame Window, simply click the Save Image button. You also can copy, clone, and print from this same window. ■

Cross-Reference

More on working with animation previews is covered in Chapter 21, "Understanding Animation and Keyframes." ■

FIGURE 2.21

A viewport image can be grabbed using a menu command found in the Tools menu.

Altering the viewport layout

Now that you've started to figure out the viewports, you may want to change the number and size of viewports displayed. The Layout panel, shown in Figure 2.22, in the Viewpoint Configuration dialog box, offers several layouts as alternatives to the default layout (not that there is anything wrong with the default and its four equally sized viewports).

The Layout panel offers many layout options.

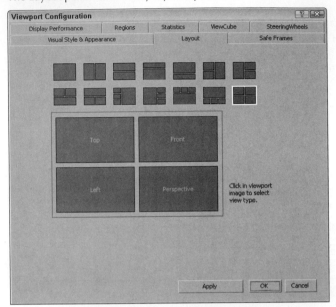

After selecting a layout from the options at the top of the panel, you can assign each individual view-port a different view by clicking each viewport in the Layout panel and choosing a view from the pop-up menu. The view options include Perspective, Orthographic, Front, Back, Top, Bottom, Left, Right, ActiveShade, Track, Grid (Front, Back, Top, Bottom, Left, Right, Display Planes), Scene Explorer, Extended (Biped Animation WorkBench, Motion Mixer, Material Explorer, MAXScript Listener), and Shape. These view options are also available by right-clicking the viewport Point-of-View label in the upper-left corner of the viewport. Figure 2.23 shows a viewport layout with the Track view, Schematic view, Asset Browser, and Perspective views open.

Views can also be set to Camera and Spotlight if they exist in the scene. Each camera and light that exists is listed by name at the top of the pop-up menu.

Using Safe Frames

Completing an animation and converting it to some broadcast medium, only to see that the whole left side of the animation is being cut off in the final screening, can be discouraging. If you rely on the size of the active viewport to show the edges of the final output, you could be way off. Using the Safe Frames feature, you can display some guides within the viewport that show where the content must be to avoid such problems.

FIGURE 2.23

Other interfaces such as the Track view, Schematic view, and Scene Explorer can be opened within a viewport.

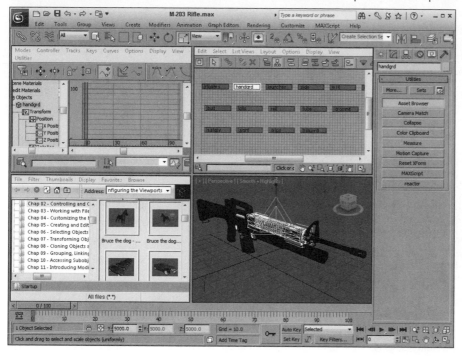

The Safe Frames panel of the Viewport Configuration dialog box lets you define several safe frame options, as shown in Figure 2.24, including the following:

- **Live Area:** Marks the area that will be rendered, shown as yellow lines. If a background image is added to the viewport and the Match Rendering Output option is selected, then the background image will fit within the Live Area.

- **Action Safe:** The area ensured to be visible in the final rendered file, marked with light blue lines; objects outside this area will be at the edge of the monitor and could be distorted.

- **Title Safe:** The area where the title can safely appear without distortion or bleeding, marked with orange lines.

- **User Safe:** The output area defined by the user, marked with magenta lines.

- **12-Field Grid:** Displays a grid in the viewport, marked with a pink grid.

FIGURE 2.24

The Safe Frames panel lets you specify areas to render.

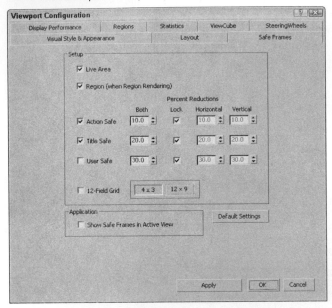

For each type of safe frame, you can set the percent reduction by entering values in the Horizontal, Vertical, or Both fields. The 12-Field Grid option offers 4×3 and 12×9 aspect ratios.

The Show Safe Frames in Active View option displays the Safe Frame borders in the active viewport. You can quickly enable or disable Safe Frames by right-clicking the viewport Point-of-View label and choosing Show Safe Frame in the pop-up menu (or you can use the Shift+F keyboard shortcut).

Figure 2.25 shows an elongated Perspective viewport with all the safe frame guides enabled. The Safe Frames show that the top and bottom of my dinosaur will be cut off when rendered.

Setting Display Performance

Within the Display Performance panel, shown in Figure 2.26, are a couple of simple settings. The Improve Quality Progressively setting causes a rough approximation of the viewport update to be rendered immediately, and gradually the details are added to improve the displayed results as time progresses. This progressive update doesn't slow you down but provides more detail if there is time to add it before the next update.

New Feature

Because of the speed of newer processors and improvements in the rendering algorithms, the complex Adaptive Degradation system found in previous versions has been replaced with this simplified version that is new to 3ds Max 2012. ∎

FIGURE 2.25

Safe frames provide guides that help you see when the scene objects are out of bounds.

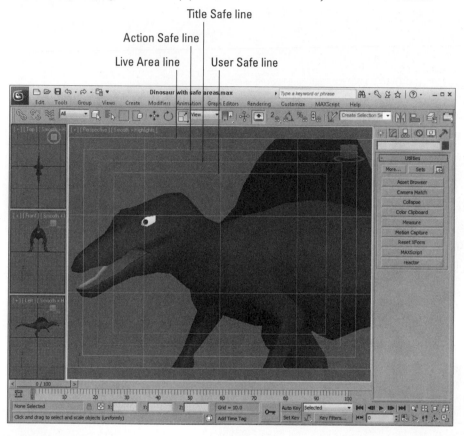

Title Safe line

Action Safe line

Live Area line   User Safe line

Note

If the Nitrous display driver is not enabled, then the Adaptive Degradation panel is available in the Viewport Configuration dialog box.

You also can set the display resolution used on procedural maps. Higher resolution values have more detail, and lower resolution maps render and are updated more quickly.

 You can enable Progressive Display option using the Views ➪ Progressive Display menu command (or by pressing the O key). You also can turn Adaptive Degradation on and off with a button located at the bottom of the interface between the Prompt Bar and the Add Time Tag. The Progressive Display button looks like a simple cube.

73

FIGURE 2.26

The Display Performance panel offers only a few simple settings.

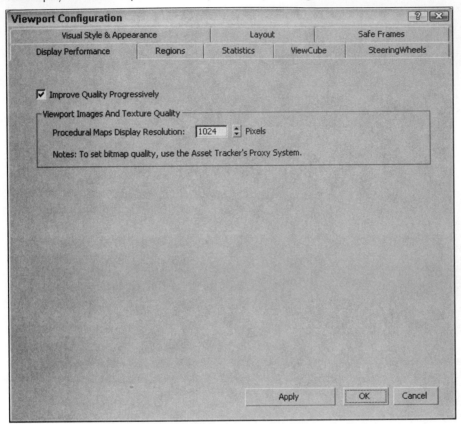

Tip

Right-clicking the Progressive Display button opens the Display Performance panel in the Viewport Configuration dialog box. ■

Defining regions

The Regions panel enables you to define regions and focus your rendering energies on a smaller area. Complex scenes can take considerable time and machine power to render. Sometimes, you want to test render only a portion of a viewport to check material assignment, texture map placement, or lighting.

You can define the size of the various Regions in the Regions panel of the Viewport Configuration dialog box, shown in Figure 2.27.

FIGURE 2.27

The Regions panel enables you to work with smaller regions within your scene.

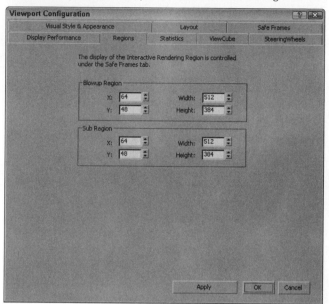

After you've specified a Blowup Region or a Sub Region, you can select to render using these regions by selecting Region or Blowup from the Render Frame Window and clicking the Render button. If you click the Edit Region button, the specified region is displayed as an outline in the viewport. You can move this outline to reposition it, or drag its edge or corner handles to resize the region. The new position and dimension values are updated in the Regions panel for next time. Click the Render button to begin the rendering process.

The difference between these two regions is that the Sub Region displays the Rendered Frame Window in black, except for the specified sub-region. The Blowup Region fills the entire Rendered Frame Window, as shown in Figure 2.28.

FIGURE 2.28

The image on the left was rendered using the Sub Region option; the right image used the Blowup Region.

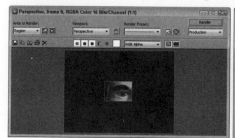 

Cross-Reference

You can learn more about Render Types and the Rendered Frame Window in Chapter 23, "Rendering a Scene and Enabling Quicksilver." ∎

Viewing statistics

The Statistics panel, shown in Figure 2.29, lets you display valuable statistics in the viewport window. These statistics can include Polygon Count, Triangle Count, Edge Count, Vertex Count, and Frames Per Second. You can also select to view these statistics for all the objects in the scene (Total), for just the selected object, or for both. You can toggle statistics on and off for the active viewport using the Views ⇨ xView ⇨ Show Statistics menu command or the 7 key.

FIGURE 2.29

The Statistics panel lets you display polygon count and frames per second in the viewport.

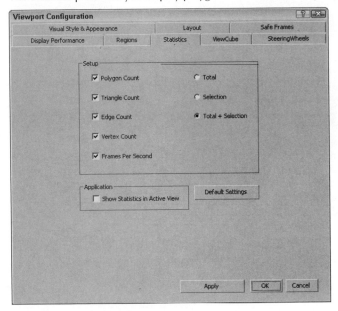

By enabling the Show Statistics in Active View option, the selected statistics are overlaid on the active viewport, as shown in Figure 2.30.

FIGURE 2.30

The active viewport can be set to display the selected statistics.

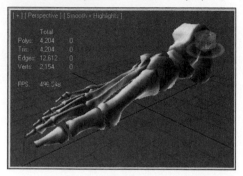

Working with Viewport Backgrounds

Remember in grade school when you realized that you could immediately draw really well using tracing paper (where all you needed to do was follow the lines)? Well, it's not quite tracing paper, but you can load background images into a viewport that can help as you create and position your objects.

Loading viewport background images

The Views ➪ Viewport Background ➪ Viewport Background menu command (Alt+B) opens a dialog box, shown in Figure 2.31, in which you can select an image or animation to appear behind a viewport. Each viewport can have a different background image. The displayed background image is helpful for aligning objects in a scene, but it is for display purposes only and will not be rendered. To create a background image to be rendered, you need to specify the background in the Environment dialog box, opened using the Rendering ➪ Environment (keyboard shortcut, 8) menu command.

If the background image changes, you can update the viewport using the Views ➪ Viewport Background ➪ Update Background Image menu command (Alt+Shift+Ctrl+B). This is helpful if you have the background image opened in Photoshop at the same time. You can update the background image, save it, and then immediately update the image in Max. The Views Viewport Background ➪ Reset Background Transform menu command automatically rescales and recenters the background image to fit the viewport. You should use this if you've changed the viewport size or changed the background's size.

The Files button in the Viewport Background dialog box opens the Select Background Image dialog box, where you can select the image to load. The Devices button lets you obtain a background from a device such as a Video Recorder. If an environment map is already loaded into the Environment dialog box, you can simply click the Use Environment Background option. Keep in mind that the background image will not be rendered unless it is made into an Environment map.

FIGURE 2.31

The Viewport Background dialog box lets you select a background source image or animation.

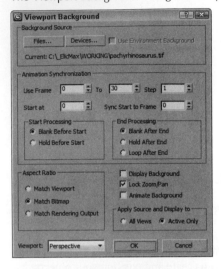

Cross-Reference

Environment maps are covered in Chapter 23, "Rendering a Scene and Enabling Quicksilver." ■

Loading viewport background animations

The Animation Synchronization section of the Viewport Background dialog box lets you set which frames of a background animation sequence are displayed. The Use Frame and To values determine which frames of the loaded animation are used. The Step value trims the number of frames that are to be used by selecting every Nth frame. For example, a Step value of 4 would use every fourth frame.

Tip

Loading an animation sequence as a viewport background can really help as you begin to animate complex motions, like a running horse. By stepping through the frames of the animation, you can line up your model with the background image for realistic animations. ■

The Start At value is the frame in the current scene where this background animation would first appear. The Sync Start to Frame value is the frame of the background animation that should appear first. The Start and End Processing options let you determine what appears before the Start and End frames. Options include displaying a blank, holding the current frame, and looping.

If you select an animation as the background, make sure that the Animate Background option is selected. Also note that the viewport background is not visible if the Display Background option is not selected.

The Aspect Ratio section offers options for setting the size of the background image. You can select to Match Viewport, Match Bitmap, or Match Rendering Output.

The Lock Zoom/Pan option is available if either the Match Bitmap option or the Match Rendering Output option is selected. This option locks the background image to the geometry so that when the objects in the scene are zoomed or panned, the background image follows. If the background gets out of line, you can reset its position with the Views ⇨ Viewport Background ⇨ Reset Background Transform command.

Caution

When the Lock Zoom/Pan option is selected, the background image is resized when you zoom in on an object. Resizing the background image fills the virtual memory, and if you zoom in too far, the background image could exceed your virtual memory. If this happens, a dialog box appears to inform you of the problem and gives you the option of not displaying the background image. ■

You can set the Apply Source and Display to option to display the background in All Views or in the active viewport only.

Tutorial: Loading reference images for modeling

When modeling a physical object, you can get a jump on the project by taking pictures with a digital camera of the front, top, and left views of the object and then load them as background images in the respective viewports. The background images can then be a reference for your work. This is especially helpful with models that need to be precise. You can even work from CAD drawings.

To load the background images of a brass swan, follow these steps:

1. Choose File ⇨ New (or press Ctrl+N) to open a blank scene file.
2. Right-click the Front viewport to make it the active viewport, and choose Views ⇨ Viewport Background (or press Alt+B).

   The Viewport Background dialog box opens.
3. Click the Files button, and in the File dialog box that opens, select the Brass swan-front view. jpg image from the Chap 02 directory on the CD.
4. Select the Match Bitmap, Display Background, Lock Zoom/Pan, and Active Only options, and click OK to close the dialog box.

   The image now appears in the background of the Front viewport.
5. Repeat Steps 2 through 4 for the Top and Left viewports.

Figure 2.32 shows the Max interface with background images loaded in the Front, Top, and Left viewports.

FIGURE 2.32

Adding a background image to a viewport can help as you begin to model objects.

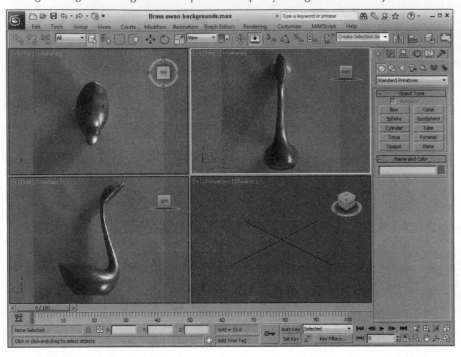

Summary

Viewports are the window into the Max world. Remember that if you can't see it, you can't work with it, so you need to learn to use the viewports. You can also configure viewports to display just the way you desire.

This chapter covered the following topics:

- Understanding 3D space and the various viewport points-of-view
- Navigating with the ViewCube, the SteeringWheels, and the scroll wheel
- Using the various Viewport Navigation Control buttons
- Changing the Visual Style & Appearance options in the Viewport Configuration dialog box
- Discovering the other panels of the Viewport Configuration dialog box that allow you to change the layout, safe frames, regions, and statistics
- Finding out how to use Progressive Display to speed up viewport updates
- Working with viewport background images

In the next chapter, you find out all the details about working with files, including loading, saving, and merging scene files. The next chapter also covers import and export options for interfacing with other software packages.

Working with Files, Importing, and Exporting

Complex scenes can end up being a collection of hundreds of files, and misplacing any of them will affect the final output, so learning to work with files is critical. This chapter focuses on working with files, whether they are object files, texture images, or background images. Files enable you to move scene pieces into and out of Max. You also can export and import files to and from other packages.

This chapter also includes perhaps the most important feature in Max, the Save feature, which I suggest you use often. Remember the mantra: Save Early, Save Often.

Working with Max Scene Files

Of all the different file types and formats, you probably will work with one type of file more than any other—the Max format. Max has its own proprietary format for its scene files. These files have the .max extension and allow you to save your work as a file and return to it at a later time. Max also supports files saved with the .chr extension used for character files.

Using the Application Button

All the various file commands are located by clicking the 3ds Max logo in the upper-left corner. This logo is called the Application Button. The Application Button menu, shown in Figure 3.1, presents its menu options as icons. Several shortcuts also are presented on the Quick Access toolbar located to the right of the Application Button.

FIGURE 3.1

The Application Button holds all the various file commands.

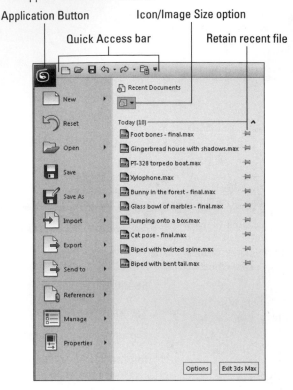

The right half of the Application Button menu displays an extensive list of recently opened Max files. This list fills the given space with the most recently accessed files, but clicking the pushpin icon to the right of the filename causes the selected file to remain on the list.

The icon button at the top of the list lets you change the size of the display icons. The options include Small Icons, Large Icons, Small Images, and Large Images.

Tip

The image options display a thumbnail of the Max file. ■

To the right of the Application Button is the Quick Access toolbar, shown in Figure 3.2. This bar contains icons for the following commands: New, Open, Save, Undo, Redo, and Set Project Folder. The arrows to the right of the Undo and Redo icons present a list of buffered commands, and you can select one to undo or redo all commands up to the selected one. Clicking the small arrow icon at the right end of the toolbar presents a menu where you can toggle the visibility of each icon. Additional options allow you to hide the menu bar and to move the Quick Access toolbar below the Ribbon.

FIGURE 3.2

The Quick Access toolbar offers quick access for opening and saving files. It also holds the Undo and Redo buttons.

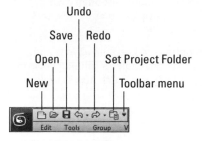

Using the Welcome Screen

When Max first starts, the Welcome Screen appears, as shown in Figure 3.3. The Welcome Screen includes Essential Skill Movies that show the basics of Max. It also includes buttons to create a new scene, open an existing scene, and open a recently opened scene.

New Feature

The options to create a new scene, open a file, and open a recent file are all new to the Welcome Screen in 3ds Max 2012. ■

FIGURE 3.3

The Welcome Screen includes buttons for opening files and creating new scene files.

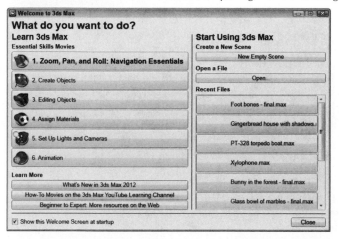

If the Show This Welcome Screen at Startup option is disabled, the Welcome Screen won't appear when Max starts, but you can access it at any time using the Help ➪ Essential Skills Movies menu command.

Starting new

When Max starts, a new scene opens. You can start a new scene at any time with the button on the Quick Access toolbar or with the Application Button ⇨ New (Ctrl+N) command. Although each instance of Max can have only one scene open at a time, you can open multiple copies of Max, each with its own scene instance, if you have enough memory.

Starting a new scene deletes the current scene, but Max gives you options to keep the objects and hierarchy, keep the objects, or make everything new. These options are available as submenu options if you use the Application Button or as a dialog box, shown in Figure 3.4, if the Quick Access toolbar icon or the keyboard shortcut is used.

FIGURE 3.4

When creating a new scene, you can keep the current objects or select New All.

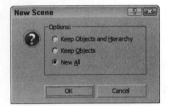

Starting a new scene maintains all the current interface settings, including the viewport configurations, any interface changes, viewport backgrounds, and any changes to the Command Panel. To reset the interface, choose Application Button ⇨ Reset. When reset, all interface settings return to their default states, but interface changes aren't affected.

Saving files

After you start up Max, the first thing you should learn is how to save your work. After a scene has changed, you can save it as a file. Before a file is saved, the word "Untitled" appears in the title bar; after you save the file, its filename appears in the title bar. Choose the Save icon on the Quick Access toolbar or Application Button ⇨ Save (Ctrl+S) to save the scene. If the scene hasn't been saved yet, then a Save File As dialog box appears, as shown in Figure 3.5. You also can make this dialog box appear using the Application Button ⇨ Save As command. After a file has been saved, using the Save command saves the file without opening the File dialog box. Pretty simple—just don't forget to do it often.

Within the Save File As dialog box is an option in the Save as Type field to save the file as a 3ds Max file, a 3ds Max 2010 file, or a 3ds Max 2011 file. Files saved using a format for a previous version of Max can be opened only within the designated version or any version newer than that version. Be aware that any new features included in Max 2012 are not included in the saved file using an older format. For example, if the current file uses a newer feature, and you save the file to an older format, then support for the new feature is lost.

Caution

Be aware that Max files beyond 3ds Max 2010 are not backward-compatible. A .max file saved using 3ds Max 2012 cannot be opened in an earlier version of 3ds Max. The solution to compatibility issues is to export the file using the FBX format and then import it in the older version of Max. ■

FIGURE 3.5

Use the Save File As dialog box to save a scene as a file.

The Application Button ⇨ Save As submenu includes options to Save As, Save Copy As, Save Selected, and Archive. The Save File As dialog box keeps a history list of the last several directories that you've opened. You can select these directories from the History drop-down list at the top of the dialog box. The buttons in this dialog box are the standard Windows file dialog box buttons used to go to the last folder visited, go up one directory, create a new folder, and to view a pop-up menu of file view options.

Note

If you try to save a scene over the top of an existing scene, Max presents a dialog box confirming this action. ∎

 Clicking the button with a plus sign to the right of the Save button automatically appends a number onto the end of the current filename and saves the file. For example, if you select the myScene.max file and click the plus button, a file named myScene01.max is saved.

Tip

Use the auto increment file number and Save button to save progressive versions of a scene. This is an easy version control system. If you need to backtrack to an earlier version, you can. ∎

The Application Button ⇨ Save As ⇨ Save Copy As menu command lets you save the current scene to a different name without changing its current name. The Application Button ⇨ Save As ⇨ Save Selected option saves the current selected objects to a separate scene file. If you create a single object that you might use again, select the object and use the Save Selected option to save it to a directory of models.

Tip

Another useful feature for saving files is to enable the Auto Backup feature in the Files panel of the Preference Settings dialog box. This dialog box can be accessed with the Customize ⇨ Preferences menu command, which is covered later in this chapter. ∎

Archiving files

By archiving a Max scene along with its reference bitmaps, you can ensure that the file includes all the necessary files. This is especially useful if you need to send the project to your cousin to show off or to your boss and you don't want to miss any ancillary files. Choose Application Button ⇨ Save As ⇨ Archive to save all scene files as a compressed archive. The default archive format is .zip (but you can change it in the Files panel of the Preference Settings dialog box to use whatever archive format you want).

Saving an archive as a ZIP file compiles all external files, such as bitmaps, into a single compressed file. Along with all the scene files, a text file is automatically created that lists all the files and their paths.

Opening files

When you want to open a file you've saved, you may do so by choosing the Open icon on the Quick Access toolbar or Application Button ⇨ Open (Ctrl+O), which opens a file dialog box that is similar to the one used to save files. Max can open files saved with the .max and .chr extensions. Max also can open VIZ Render files that have the .drf extension. Selecting a file and clicking the plus button opens a copy of the selected file with a new version number appended to its name.

Cross-Reference

The Application Button ⇨ Open menu also includes commands for opening files from Vault. Vault is a version control system for Max resources. It is covered in more detail in Bonus Chapter 4, "Using Asset Tracking." ■

If Max cannot locate resources used within a scene (such as maps) when you open a Max file, then the Missing External Files dialog box, shown in Figure 3.6, appears, enabling you to Continue without the file or to Browse for the missing files. If you click the Browse button, the Configure External File Paths dialog box opens, where you can add a path to the missing files.

FIGURE 3.6

The Missing External Files dialog box identifies files for the current scene that are missing.

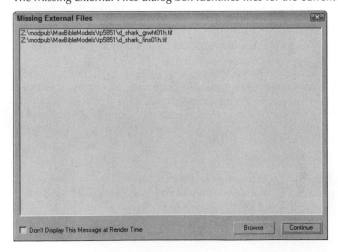

Note

If Max cannot locate missing files, a similar warning dialog box also appears when you try to render the scene with missing files. ■

If you open a file saved using a previous version of Max that includes features that have changed since the previous version, then Max presents an obsolete data format warning statement. Resaving the file can fix this problem. However, if you save a file created with a previous version of Max as a Max 2012 scene file, then you won't be able to open the file again in the previous versions of Max.

Tip

You can disable the Obsolete File Message in the Files panel of the Preference Settings dialog box. ■

Note

You can also open files from the command line by placing the filename after the executable name, as in 3dsmax. exe myFile.max. You can also use the –L switch after the executable name to open the last file that was opened. ■

Setting a Project Folder

By default, Max's Open File dialog box opens to the Scenes directory where Max is installed, but you can set a Project Folder that may be located anywhere on your local hard drive or on the network. All file dialog boxes will then open to the new project folder automatically. The Set Project Folder icon on the Quick Access toolbar or the Application Button ⇨ Manage ⇨ Set Project Folder menu opens a dialog box where you can select a project folder. After a project folder is selected, the folder is automatically populated with a series of resource folders.

Within the project folder's root is a file with the .mxp extension named the same as the project folder. This file is a simple text file that can be opened within a text editor. Editing this file lets you define which subfolders are created within the project folder. The defined project folder also is visible within the title bar.

Merging and replacing objects

If you happen to create the perfect prop in one scene and want to integrate the prop into another scene, you can use the Merge menu command. Choose Application Button ⇨ Import ⇨ Merge to load objects from another scene into the current scene. Using this menu command opens a file dialog box that is exactly like the Open File dialog box, but after you select a scene and click the Open button, the Merge dialog box, shown in Figure 3.7, appears. This dialog box displays all the objects found in the selected scene file. It also has options for sorting the objects and filtering certain types of objects. Selecting an object and clicking OK loads the object into the current scene.

If you ever get involved in a modeling duel, then you'll probably be using the Application Button ⇨ Import ⇨ Replace menu command at some time. A modeling duel is when two modelers work on the same rough model of named objects and the animator (or boss) gets to choose which object to use. With the Replace command, you can replace a named object with an object of the same name in a different scene. The objects are selected using the same dialog box, but only the objects with identical names in both scene files display. If no objects with the same name appear in both scene files, a warning box is displayed.

FIGURE 3.7

The Merge dialog box lists all the objects from a merging scene.

Tip

When working with a team, one person, such as an environment modeler, can add a dummy object to the scene that shares the name of a more detailed model, such as "furniture." When the detailed model is completed, the Replace command adds the detailed model to the scene. This lets the environment modeler work, even though the detailed models aren't completed yet. ■

Getting out

As you can probably guess, you use the Application Button ⇨ Exit 3ds Max command in the lower-right corner to exit the program, but only after it gives you a chance to save your work. Clicking the window icon with an X on it in the upper right has the same effect (but I'm sure you knew that).

Setting File Preferences

The Files panel of the Preference Settings dialog box holds the controls for backing up, archiving, and logging Max files. You can open this dialog box using the Options button in the lower-right corner of the Application Button panel or with the Customize ⇨ Preferences menu command. Figure 3.8 shows this panel.

Handling files

The Files panel includes several options that define how to handle files. The first option is to Convert file paths to UNC (Universal Naming Convention). This option displays file paths using the UNC for any files accessed over a mapped drive. The Convert local file paths to Relative option causes all paths to be saved internally as relative paths to the project folder. This is useful if all files you access are in the same folder, but if you use files such as bitmaps from a different folder, then be sure to disable this option.

FIGURE 3.8

The Files panel includes an Auto Backup feature.

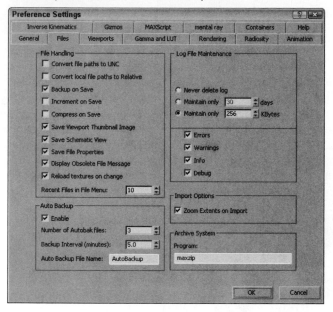

The next option is Backup on Save. When you save a file using the Application Button ⇨ Save (Ctrl+S) menu command, the existing file is overwritten. The Backup on Save option causes the current scene file to be saved as a backup (with the name MaxBack.bak in the 3dsmax\autobak directory) before saving the new file. If the changes you made were a mistake, you can recover the file before the last changes by renaming the MaxBack.bak file to MaxBack.max and reopening it in Max.

Another option to prevent overwriting your changes is the Increment on Save option. This option adds an incremented number to the end of the existing filename every time it is saved (the same as when clicking the plus button in the Save As dialog box). This retains multiple copies of the file and is an easy version-control method for your scene files. This way, you can always go back to an earlier file when the client changes his mind. With this option enabled, the MaxBack.bak file isn't used.

The Compress on Save option compresses the file automatically when it is saved. Compressed files require less file space but take longer to load. If you're running low on hard drive space, then you'll want to enable this option.

Tip

Another reason to enable the Compress on Save option is that large files (100MB or greater) load into the Network Queue Manager much more quickly when compressed for network rendering. ∎

The Save Viewport Thumbnail Image option saves a 64 × 64-pixel thumbnail of the active viewport along with the file. This thumbnail is displayed in the Open dialog box and can also be seen from Windows Explorer on Windows XP, as shown in Figure 3.9. Saving a thumbnail with a scene adds about 9K to the file size.

Caution

Although thumbnails appear when viewed from within Windows XP, they do not appear in Windows Vista or Windows 7. ∎

Tip

The Save Viewport Thumbnail Image option is another good option to keep enabled. Thumbnails help you to find scene files later, and nothing is more frustrating than seeing a scene's filename without a thumbnail. ∎

FIGURE 3.9

Max files with thumbnails show up in Windows Explorer on Windows XP.

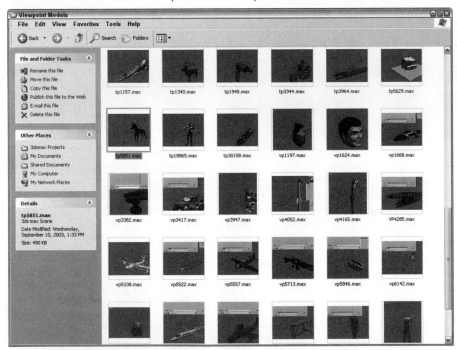

In addition to a thumbnail, Max also offers an option to save the Schematic View with the file. Although Max can generate a new Schematic View from an existing file, saving the Schematic View with the file is quicker if you work with this view often. Saving File Properties with the file is also helpful, but be warned that saving this extra info with the file increases its file size slightly. Still, doing so is worth the effort because you can easily locate and understand the scene file later on.

Cross-Reference

More details on using Schematic View are covered in Chapter 25, "Building Complex Scenes with Containers, XRefs, and the Schematic View." ■

When a Max file created in a previous version of Max is opened, a warning dialog box appears that says, "Obsolete data format found—Please resave file." To eliminate this warning, disable the Display Obsolete File Message option. The warning dialog box also includes an option to Don't Display Again that enables this option when selected.

When textures are updated, the Reload textures on change option forces the textures to be reloaded when they are altered. This slows your system while Max waits for the textures to reload but offers the latest look immediately.

The Recent Files in File Menu option determines the number of recently opened files that appear in the Application Button ⇨ Recent Documents menu. The maximum value is 50.

Backing up files

The Auto Backup feature in Max can save you from the nightmare of losing all your work because of a system crash. With Auto Backup enabled, you can select the number of Autobak files to keep around and how often the files are backed up. The backup files are saved to the directory specified by the Configure Paths dialog box. The default is to save these backups to the 3dsmax\autoback directory. You can also select a name for the backup files.

Note

Even if you have this feature enabled, you should still save your file often. ■

This is how it works: If you've set the number of backup files to two, the interval to five minutes, and the backup name to MyBackup, then after five minutes the current file is saved as MyBackup1.max. After another five minutes, another file named MyBackup2.max is saved, and then after another five minutes, the MyBackup1.max file is overwritten with the latest changes.

If you lose your work as a result of a power failure or by having your toddler accidentally pull out the plug, you can recover your work by locating the Autobak file with the latest date and reloading it into Max. This file won't include all the latest changes; it updates only to the last backup save.

Tip

I highly recommend that you keep the Auto Backup option enabled. This feature has saved my bacon more than once. Also, if you enter a different autoback name for different projects, then you won't accidentally overwrite a backed-up project. ■

Tutorial: Setting up Auto Backup

Now that I have stressed that setting up Auto Backup is an important step to do, here's exactly how to set it up.

To set up the Auto Backup feature, follow these steps:

1. Open the Preference Settings dialog box by choosing Customize ➪ Preferences, and click the Files panel.
2. Turn on Auto Backup by selecting the Enable option in the Auto Backup section.
3. Set the number of Autobak files to **5**.

Note

To maintain version control of your Max scenes, use the Increment on Save feature instead of increasing the Number of Autobak Files. ■

4. Set the Backup Interval to the amount of time to wait between backups.

   The Backup Interval should be set to the maximum amount of work that you are willing to redo. (I keep my settings at 15 minutes.) You can also give the Auto Backup file a name.
5. Auto Backup saves the files in the directory specified by the Auto Backup path. To view where this path is located, choose Customize ➪ Configure User Paths.

Maintaining log files

You can also use the Files panel to control log files. Log files keep track of any errors and warnings, general command info, and any debugging information. You can set log files to never be deleted, expire after so many days, or keep a specified file size with the latest information. If your system is having trouble, checking the error log gives you some idea as to what the problem is. Logs are essential if you plan on developing any custom scripts or plug-ins. You can select that the log contain all Errors, Warnings, Info, and Debug statements.

Each entry in the log file includes a date-time stamp and a three-letter designation of the type of message with DBG for debug, INF for info, WRN for warning, and ERR for error messages, followed by the message. The name of the log file is Max.log.

Configuring Paths

When strolling through a park, chances are good that you'll see several different paths. One might take you to the lake and another to the playground. Knowing where the various paths lead can help you as you navigate around the park. Paths in Max lead, or point, to various resources, either locally or across the network.

All paths can be configured using two distinct Configure Paths dialog boxes found in the Customize menu: Configure User Paths and Configure System Paths. The Configure User Paths dialog box is used to specify where to look for scene resource files such as scenes, animations, and textures. The Configure System Paths dialog box is used to specify where the system looks to load files that Max uses, such as fonts, scripts, and plug-ins.

Configuring user paths

The Configure User Paths dialog box, shown in Figure 3.10, holds the path definitions to all the various resource folders. The dialog box includes three panels: File I/O, External Files, and XRefs.

FIGURE 3.10

The Configure User Paths dialog box specifies where to look for various resources.

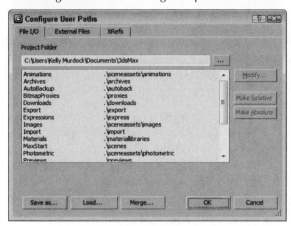

The main panel in the Configure User Paths dialog box is the File I/O panel. The Project Folder is listed at the top of the dialog box and can be changed in this dialog box or with the Application Button ⇨ Manage ⇨ Set Project Folder menu. This panel includes entries for Animations, Archives, Auto Backup, Bitmap Proxies, Downloads, Export, Expressions, Images, Import, Materials, Max Start, Photometric, Previews, Render Assets, Render Output, Render Presets, Scenes, Sounds, and Video Post. If you select any of these entries, you can click the Modify button to change its path. All paths are set by default to folders contained within the designated Project Folder, but you can change them to whatever you want. The Make Relative and Make Absolute buttons cause the selected entry to be displayed as a relative path based on the Project Folder or an absolute path.

Tip

Personally, I like to keep all my content in a separate directory from where the application is installed. That way, new installs or upgrades don't risk overwriting my files. To do this, simply change the Project Folder to a location separate from the 3ds Max installation directory. ∎

Under the External Files and XRefs panels, you can add and delete paths that specify where Max looks to find specific files. All paths specified in both these panels are searched in the order they are listed when you're looking for resources such as plug-ins, but file dialog boxes open only to the first path. Use the Move Up and Move Down buttons to realign path entries.

Caution

Using the Customize ⇨ Revert to Startup UI Layout command does not reset path configuration changes. ∎

At the bottom of the Configure User Paths dialog box are buttons for saving, loading, and merging the defined configuration paths into a separate file. These files are saved using the .mxp format. This file can be found in the root of the Project Folder.

Tip

Setting up a Project Folder on the network gives every team member access to all the project files and synchronizes all the paths for a project. ∎

Configuring system paths

Max default paths are listed in the Configure System Paths dialog box, shown in Figure 3.11. When Max is installed, all the paths are set to point to the default subdirectories where Max was installed. To modify a path, select the path and click the Modify button. A file dialog box lets you locate the new directory.

The Configure System Paths dialog box also includes the 3rd Party Plug-Ins panel where you can add directories for Max to search when looking for plug-ins.

FIGURE 3.11

The Configure System Paths dialog box specifies additional paths.

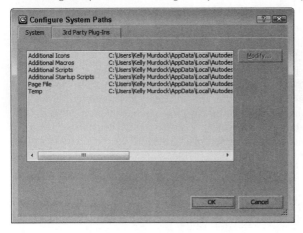

Importing and Exporting

If you haven't noticed, Max isn't the only game in town. A number of different 3D packages exist, and exchanging files between them is where the importing and exporting menu commands come in. You can find both of these commands in the Application Button menu.

Importing supported formats

Choose Application Button ⇨ Import ⇨ Import to open the Import dialog box. This dialog box looks like a typical Windows file dialog box. The real power comes with the various Import Settings dialog boxes that are available for each format. These dialog boxes appear after you select a file to import. The settings in the Import Settings dialog box are different for the various format types.

Max can import several different formats. All acceptable files are automatically displayed in the file dialog box, or you can filter for a specific format using the Files of Type drop-down list at the bottom of the file dialog box. The available import formats include the following:

- Autodesk (FBX)
- 3D Studio Mesh, Projects, and Shapes (3DS, PRJ, SHP)
- Adobe Illustrator (AI)
- Autodesk Alias/Showcase (APF, WIRE)
- Collada (DAE)
- LandXML/DEM/DDF
- AutoCAD and Legacy AutoCAD (DWG, DXF)
- Flight Studio OpenFlight (FLT)
- Motion Analysis (HTR, TRC)
- Initial Graphics Exchange Standard (IGE, IGS, IGES)
- Autodesk Inventor (IPT, IAM)
- Lightscape (LS, VW, LP)
- OBJ Material and Object (OBJ)
- ACIS SAT (SAT)
- Google SketchUp (SKP)
- StereoLitho (STL)
- VIZ Material XML Import (XML)

New Feature

The ability to import and work with Alias Wire files is new to 3ds Max 2012. ■

Cross-Reference

More on import and export SAT files is covered in Chapter 28, "Working with Solids and Body Objects." ■

Note

Be aware that these formats are used for different types of data. For example, Adobe Illustrator files typically hold only 2D data, and Motion Analysis files hold motion capture data for animations. ■

Import preference

The Files panel of the Preference Settings dialog box has a single option dealing with importing— Zoom Extents on Import. When this option is enabled, it automatically zooms all viewports to the extent of the imported objects. Imported objects can often be scaled so small that they aren't even visible. This option helps you to locate an object when imported.

Exporting supported formats

In addition to importing, you'll sometimes want to export Max objects for use in other programs. You access the Export command by choosing Application Button ➪ Export ➪ Export. You also have the option to Export Selected (available only if an object is selected) and Export to DWF.

Max can export to several different formats, including the following:

- Autodesk (FBX)
- 3D Studio (3DS)

- Adobe Illustrator (AI)
- ASCII Scene Export (ASE)
- AutoCAD (DWG, DXF)
- Collada (DAE)
- Initial Graphics Exchange Standard (IGS)
- Flight Studio OpenFlight (FLT)
- JSR-184 (M3G)
- Lightscape Material, Blocks, Parameters, Layers, Preparations, and Views (ATR, BLK, DF, LAY, LP, VW)
- Motion Analysis (HTR)
- Publish to DWF (DWF)
- OBJ Material and Object (OBJ)
- ACIS SAT (SAT)
- StereoLithography (STL)
- VRML97 (WRL)

Moving files to Softimage, MotionBuilder, and Mudbox

3ds Max is available as a standalone product, but it also ships within a Creative Suite of applications offered by Autodesk. These suites can include Softimage, MotionBuilder, and Mudbox, and you can easily move the current Max scene file to one of these other applications using the Application Button ⇨ Send To menu. For each application, you can choose to send the scene as a New Scene, Update the Current Scene, Add to the Current Scene, or Select the Previously Sent Objects.

New Feature

The ability to move the current Max scene to Softimage, MotionBuilder, or Mudbox is new to 3ds Max 2012. ■

Moving files to and from Maya

Maya is Autodesk's sister to Max, so you may find yourself having to move scene files between Max and Maya at some time. The best format to transport files between Max and Maya is the FBX format. Autodesk controls this format and has endowed it with the ability to seamlessly transport files among these packages.

Tip

The FBX format also is the format to choose when transferring files back and forth with Max files in older versions of 3ds Max. ■

The FBX format includes support for all the scene constructs, including animation, bone systems, morph targets, and animation cache files. It has an option to embed textures with the export file or to convert them to the TIF format. Other import and export settings deal with the system units and world coordinate orientation. You also have the ability to filter specific objects. The FBX Export dialog box is shown in Figure 3.12.

FIGURE 3.12

The FBX Export dialog box provides the best way of transferring among Max, Maya, and MotionBuilder.

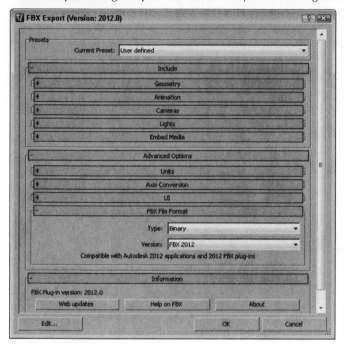

The FBX import and export dialog boxes include the ability to save and load configuration presets. This is helpful because once you figure out the correct settings to get models in and out of Max, you can save the preset and instantly select it the next time you need to move a file. The Web updates button lets you check for updates to the FBX format online.

Tip

When exporting a file for use in Maya, be sure to set the Up Axis to Y-up, or the models will show up rotated. ■

When exporting the file to FBX format, you have a Type option that you can use to export the file as an ASCII text file or as a Binary file. Binary files are typically smaller, but ASCII files can be edited in a text editor.

The FBX format is being continually updated, but the FBX Export dialog box lets you select which FBX version to use. If you need to export a Max file for use on an older version of Max, be sure to select an older FBX version in the FBX Version drop-down list.

Using the OBJ format

The OBJ format is a text-based format that has been around since the early days of Wavefront, an early 3D package. It is a common format and used to exchange 3D data with a variety of programs, including Poser and ZBrush.

One aspect of the OBJ format is that it separates the model data and the texture data into two different files. The OBJ file holds the geometry data, and the MTL file holds the texture data. Previous versions of Max required that you import each of these data files separately, but the latest OBJ workflow imports these two data files together. The new OBJ workflow is a plug-in developed by GuruWare.

The new OBJ import and export workflow is much smoother and automatically gets the right materials and textures for the object. The dialog box for importing OBJ files is shown in Figure 3.13. Notice how each of the individual objects is recognized and displayed in a list. This gives you the option of importing only specific objects. You also have control over how normals are handled, the ability to convert units, and several options for dealing with materials. The small green and red lights to the left of some options indicate whether the option is in the OBJ file. Green indicates that it exists, and red means it doesn't exist.

FIGURE 3.13

The OBJ Import dialog box provides another excellent choice for transporting files from other packages.

Not included in OBJ file (red)

Included in OBJ file (green)

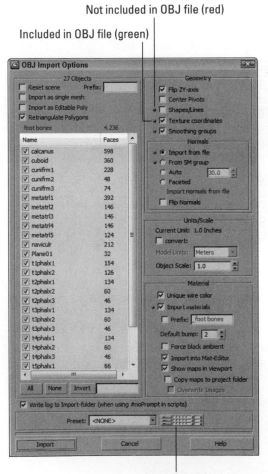

Presets button

A similar dialog box of settings appears when exporting a scene to the OBJ format, as shown in Figure 3.14.

The OBJ Export dialog box lets you export Max scenes to other packages.

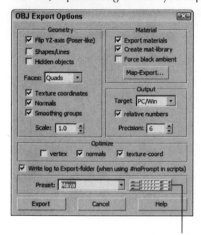

Presets button

The OBJ Export dialog box includes presets for most common 3D apps including Amapi Pro, Blender, Bryce, Carrara, Cinema-4D, DAZ Studio, Deep Paint, Hexagon, Lightwave, Maya, Modo, Motion Builder, Mudbox, Poser, Realflow, Rhino, Silo, Softimage XSI, UV Mapper, VUE, Worldbuilder, and ZBrush.

Clicking the Map Export button lets you specify the export map path where the textures for the scene are saved. You also can automatically convert the maps to a specific size or format. For each map format, you can configure the bits per pixel and any compression settings.

If you click the Presets button in the OBJ Export dialog box, then the export options for each format are shown in a table, like the one in Figure 3.15. Each of these settings can be quickly altered using this dialog box.

The Edit OBJ-Export Presets dialog box lets you change the settings for multiple formats quickly.

Exporting to the JSR-184 (M3G) format

The JSR-184 export option lets you save a scene to a format that can be viewed on mobile devices that support the Java 2 Micro Edition standard interface, such as mobile phones and PDA devices.

Because wireless devices have such a limited bandwidth, the JSR-184 Exporter dialog box, shown in Figure 3.16, includes several options for optimizing the exported scene. This dialog box lists the Max scene hierarchy, the JSR-184 scene hierarchy, and the parameters for the selected scene object. Using the toolbar buttons at the top of the dialog box, you can change the hierarchy that is to be exported.

The JSR-184 Export dialog box lets you choose which resources to export.

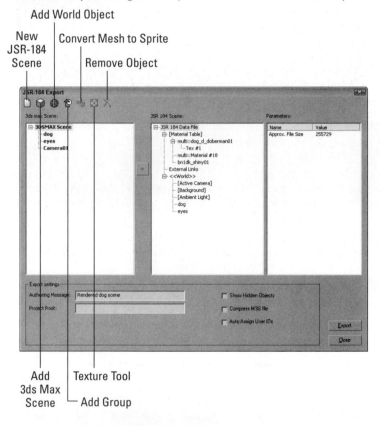

Before a scene can be exported, the Max scene must include a camera, and you must specify an Active Camera in the JSR-184 Exported dialog box. When a material map is selected from the JSR-184 hierarchy list, the Texture Tool icon on the toolbar becomes active. Clicking this button opens the Texture Tool dialog box, shown in Figure 3.17, where you can precisely control the size and format of the exported maps.

FIGURE 3.17

The Texture Tool lets you specify the exact size of texture maps to be exported for mobile devices.

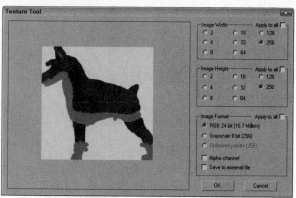

To view the exported M3G files, the default installation of Max includes an M3G Player, which can be found along with the other Max programs in Start ⇨ Programs ⇨ Autodesk ⇨ 3ds Max 2012 ⇨ JSR Viewer. To use this player, the Java Runtime Environment needs to be installed. You can install it from the Max setup disc.

Note

The JSR Viewer application is built using Java. If you're having trouble with the viewer, try installing the latest Java version from the installation DVD. ■

Exporting to the DWF format

The Design Web Format (DWF) is an ideal format for displaying your textured models to others via the Web. It creates relatively small files that can be attached easily to an e-mail. You can use the Application Button ⇨ Export ⇨ Export to DWF menu command to export the current scene to this format. This command opens a dialog box of options, shown in Figure 3.18, that specify to Group by Object or Group by Layer. You also can choose to publish the Object Properties, Materials, Selected Objects Only, or Hidden Objects. Another option is to Rescale Bitmaps to a size entered in pixels.

Saved files can be viewed in the Autodesk DWF Viewer, shown in Figure 3.19. The Autodesk DWF Viewer can be downloaded for free from the Autodesk website. This provides a way for users without Max installed to view models.

If you want to view the exported files in the viewer, simply enable the Show DWF in Viewer option in the DWF Publish Options dialog box. The viewer includes controls for transforming the model, changing its shading and view, and printing the current view.

FIGURE 3.18

The DWF Publish Options dialog box lets you set the options for the exported DWF file.

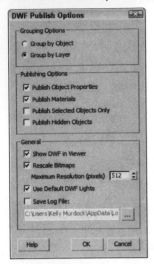

FIGURE 3.19

The Autodesk DWF Viewer is used to view files exported using the DWF format.

Copy to Clipboard

Print | Orbit

Open | Pan Zoom tools

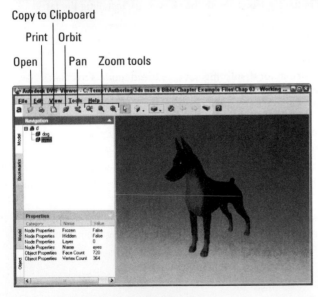

Exporting utilities

In addition to the menu commands found in the File menu, Max includes a couple of utilities that export specific information: the Lighting Data Export Utility and the Material XML Exporter Utility.

You can access these utilities from the Utilities panel in the Command Panel by clicking the More button and selecting them from the pop-up list that appears.

Lighting Data Export Utility

The Lighting Data Export Utility exports exposure control data for a scene's Illuminance and Luminance values. These files can be saved as PIC or TIF files, which you can select in the 2D Lighting Data Exporter rollout. You also can set an image's Width and Height dimensions.

Caution

Exposure Control must be enabled for this utility to be enabled. You can learn about exposure control in Chapter 46, "Using Atmospheric and Render Effects." ∎

Material XML Exporter Utility

The Material XML Exporter Utility exports a selected material to an XML file format, where it can be easily shared with other users. After you select this utility, the Parameters rollout offers four options for selecting the material to export: the Material/Map Browser, the Object List, Pick Object in Scene, and All Objects in Scene.

The utility also offers several export options including Native XML, export to an Autodesk Tool Catalog, and using an XSLT template. You also can select to export the material with a thumbnail and along with its mapping modifiers.

Panorama Exporter Utility

The Panorama Exporter Utility exports a scene into a format that allows all 360 degrees of the scene to be viewed. Using this utility, you can open the Render parameters for rendering a panoramic scene or accessing a viewer for viewing rendered panoramic scenes.

Cross-Reference

More on creating panoramic scenes is covered in Chapter 23, "Rendering a Scene and Enabling Quicksilver." ∎

Tutorial: Importing vector drawings from Illustrator

Before leaving this section, let's look at an example of importing a file for use in Max.

In most companies, a professional creative team uses an advanced vector drawing tool such as Illustrator to design the company logo. If you need to work with such a logo, learning how to import the externally created file gives you a jumpstart on your project.

Note

When importing vector-based files into Max, only the lines are imported. Max cannot import fills, blends, or other specialized vector effects. All imported lines are automatically converted to Bézier splines in Max. ∎

Although Max can draw and work with splines, Max's spline features take a backseat to the vector functions available in Adobe Illustrator. If you have an Illustrator (AI) file, you can import it directly into Max.

To import Adobe Illustrator files into Max, follow these steps:

1. Within Illustrator, save your file as **Box It Up Co logo** using the .ai file format by choosing Application Button ⇨ Save As. This file is also saved on the book's CD if you don't have Illustrator.

Note

When saving the Illustrator file, don't use the latest file format. For this example, I've saved the file using the Illustrator 8 format instead of one of the latest Illustrator CS formats. ∎

Figure 3.20 shows a logo created using Illustrator.

A company logo created in Illustrator and ready to save and import into Max

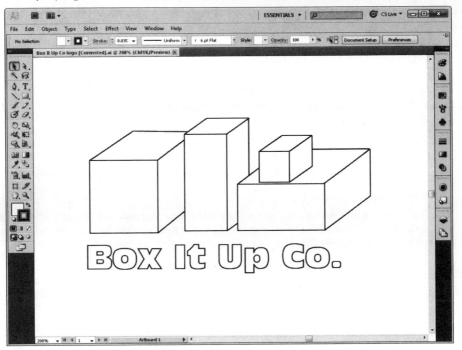

2. Open Max, and choose Application Button ⇨ Import ⇨ Import.

   A file dialog box opens.

3. Select Adobe Illustrator (AI) as the File Type. Locate the file to import, and click OK.

   The AI Import dialog box asks whether you want to merge the objects with the current scene or replace the current scene.

4. For your purposes, select the replace the current scene option and click OK.

5. The Shape Import dialog box asks whether you want to import the shapes as single or multiple objects. Select multiple, and click OK.

Figure 3.21 shows the logo after it has been imported into Max. Notice that all the fills are missing.

FIGURE 3.21

A company logo created in Illustrator and imported into Max

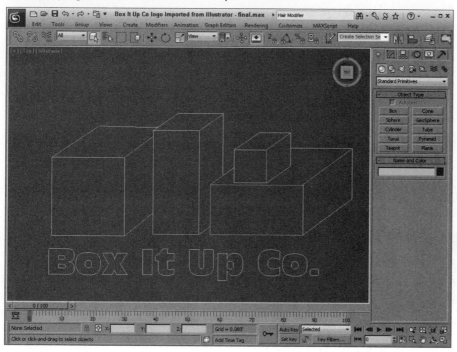

Cross-Reference

Spline objects that are imported from Illustrator appear in Max as Editable Spline objects. You can learn more about Editable Splines in Chapter 12, "Drawing and Editing 2D Splines and Shapes." ■

Using the File Utilities

With all these various files floating around, Max has included several utilities that make working with them easier. The Utilities panel of the Command Panel includes several useful utilities for working with files. You can access these utilities by opening the Utilities panel and clicking the More button to see a list of available utilities.

Using the Asset Browser utility

The Asset Browser utility is the first default button in the Utility panel. Clicking this button opens the Asset Browser window. The Asset Browser resembles Windows Explorer, except that it displays thumbnail images of all the supported formats contained within the current directory. Using this window, shown in Figure 3.22, you can browse through directory files and see thumbnails of images and scenes.

Note

Even though thumbnails aren't visible in Windows Explorer on Vista or Windows 7, thumbnails are visible when you use Asset Browser. ■

FIGURE 3.22

The Asset Browser window displays thumbnails of the files in the current directory.

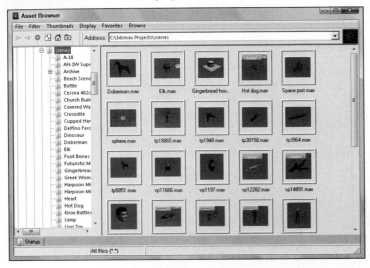

The supported file types include AVI, BMP, CIN, CEL, DDS, GIF, HDRI, IFL, IPP, JPEG, MPEG, PNG, PSD, MOV, RGB, RLA, RPF, VST, TIF, and YUV. These types are the same ones that the Application Button ⇨ View Image File command can open. All files with these extensions are viewable within the Asset Browser. You can select to view only a certain type of file using the Filter menu. You also can view and filter MAXScript and AutoCAD DWG files.

Tip

Open and display the Asset Manager within a viewport by right-clicking the viewport Point-of-View label and choosing Extended ⇨ Asset Manager from the pop-up menu. ■

You also can drag and drop files from the Asset Browser window to Max. Drag a scene file, and drop it on Max's title bar to open the scene file within Max. You can drop image files onto the map buttons in the Material Editor window or drop an image file onto a viewport to make a dialog box appear, which lets you apply the image as an Environment Map or as a Viewport Background, respectively.

The Asset Browser window is modeless, so you can work with the Max interface while the Asset Browser window is open. Double-clicking an image opens it full size in the Rendered Frame window.

The Asset Browser also can act as a Web browser to look at content online. When the Asset Browser first opens, a dialog box reminds you that online content may be copyrighted and cannot be used without consent from the owner.

The Display menu includes three panes that you can select. The Thumbnail pane shows the files as thumbnails. You can change the size of these thumbnails using the Thumbnails menu. The Explorer pane displays the files as icons the same as you would see in Windows Explorer. The Web pane displays the web page for the site listed in the Address field.

To view websites, you need to be connected to the Internet. The Asset Browser can remember your favorite websites using the Favorites menu. The Asset Browser window also includes the standard web browser navigation buttons, such as Back, Forward, Home, Refresh, and Stop. You also can find these commands in the Browse menu.

Max keeps thumbnails of all the images you access in its cache. The *cache* is a directory that holds thumbnails of all the recently accessed images. Each thumbnail image points to the actual directory where the image is located. Choose Application Button ⇨ Preferences to open the Preferences dialog box, in which you can specify where you want the cache directory to be located. To view the cached files, choose Filter ⇨ All in Cache. The Preferences dialog box also includes options to define how to handle dropped files. The options include Always Merge or Import, Always XRef, or Ask Each Time.

Choose File ⇨ Print to print the file view or web window.

Finding files with the Max File Finder utility

Another useful utility for locating files is the Max File Finder utility, which you get to by using the More button in the Utilities panel of the Command Panel. When you select this utility, a rollout with a Start button appears in the Utilities panel. Clicking this button opens the MAXFinder dialog box. Using MAXFinder, you can search for scene files by any of the information listed in the File Properties dialog box.

Tip
You also can access the MAXFinder dialog box using the MaxFind icon located in the same folder where 3ds Max is installed. ■

You can use the Browse button to specify the root directory to search. You can select to have the search also examine any subfolders. Figure 3.23 shows the MAXFinder dialog box locating all the scene files that include the word *blue*.

FIGURE 3.23

You can use the MAXFinder utility to search for scene files by property.

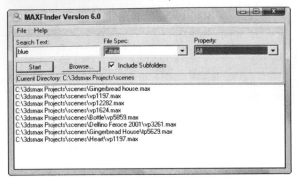

Collecting files with the Resource Collector utility

When a scene is created, image and object files can be pulled from several different locations. The Resource Collector utility helps you consolidate all these files into one location. The settings for this utility appear in the Parameters rollout in the Utility panel of the Command Panel, as shown in Figure 3.24. The Output Path is the location where the files are collected. You can change this location using the Browse button.

FIGURE 3.24

The Resource Collector utility can compile all referenced files into a single location.

The utility includes options to Collect Bitmaps, to include the Max scene file, and to compress the files into a compressed WinZip file. The Copy option makes copies of the files, and the Move option moves the actual file into the directory specified in the Output Path field. The Update Materials option updates all material paths in the Material Editor. When you're comfortable with the settings, click the Begin button to start the collecting.

Using the File Link Manager utility

The File Link Manager utility (which also can be accessed using the Application Button ⇨ References ⇨ File Link Manager menu) lets you use external AutoCAD and Revit files in the same way that you use Max's XRef features. By creating links between the current Max scene and an external AutoCAD or Revit file, you can reload the linked file when the external AutoCAD or Revit file has been updated and see the updates within Max.

Cross-Reference

XRefs are covered in Chapter 25, "Building Complex Scenes with Containers, XRefs, and the Schematic View." ■

This utility is divided into three panels: Attach, Files, and Presets. The Attach panel includes a File button to select and open a DWG or DXF file. The Attach panel also includes options to rescale the file units, a button to select which layers to include, and a button to attach the file. The Files panel displays each linked AutoCAD file along with icons to show if the linked file has changed. A Reload button allows you to click to reload the linked file within Max. The Preset panel lets you define file linking presets.

Using i-drop

To make accessing needed files from the Web even easier, Autodesk has created a technology known as i-drop that lets you drag files from i-drop–supported web pages and drop them directly into Max. With i-drop, you can drag and drop Max-created light fixture models, textures, or any other Max-supported file from a light manufacturer's website into your scene without importing and positioning a file. This format allows you to add geometry, photometric data, and materials.

Accessing File Information

As you work with files, several dialog boxes in Max supply you with extra information about your scene. You can use this information to keep track of files and record valuable statistics about a scene.

Displaying scene information

If you like to keep statistics on your files (to see whether you've broken the company record for the model with the greatest number of faces), you'll find the Summary Info dialog box useful. Use the Application Button ⇨ Properties ⇨ Summary Info menu command to open a dialog box that displays all the relevant details about the current scene, such as the number of objects, lights, and cameras; the total number of vertices and faces; and various model settings, as well as a Description field where you can describe the scene. Figure 3.25 shows the Summary Info dialog box.

The Plug-In Info button on the Summary Info dialog box displays a list of all the plug-ins currently installed on your system. Even without any external plug-ins installed, the list is fairly long because many of the core features in Max are implemented as plug-ins. The Summary Info dialog box also includes a Save to File button for saving the scene summary information as a text file.

FIGURE 3.25

The Summary Info dialog box shows all the basic information about the current scene.

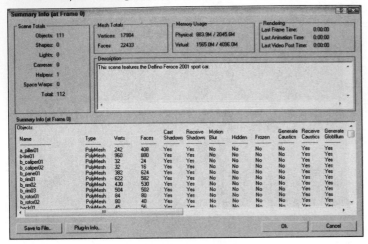

Viewing file properties

As the number of files on your system increases, you'll be wishing you had a card catalog to keep track of them all. Max has an interface that you can use to attach keywords and other descriptive information about the scene to the file. The Application Button ⇨ Properties ⇨ File Properties menu command opens the File Properties dialog box. This dialog box, shown in Figure 3.23, includes three panels: Summary, Contents, and Custom. The Summary panel holds information such as the Title, Subject, and Author of the Max file and can be useful for managing a collaborative project. The Contents panel holds information about the scene, such as the total number of objects and much more. Much of this information also is found in the Summary Info dialog box. The Custom panel, also shown in Figure 3.26, includes a way to enter a custom list of properties such as client information, language, and so on.

Note

You also can view the File Properties dialog box information while working in Windows Explorer by right-clicking the file and selecting Properties. Three unique tabs are visible: Summary, Contents, and Custom. The Summary tab holds the file identification information, including the Title, Subject, Author, Category, Keywords, and Comments. ■

Viewing files

Sometimes looking at the thumbnail of an image isn't enough to help you decide whether you have the right image. For these cases, you can quickly load the image in question into a viewer to look at it closely. The Rendering ⇨ View Image File menu command opens the View File dialog box shown in Figure 3.27. This dialog box lets you load and view graphic and animation files using the Rendered Frame Window or the default Media Player for your system.

FIGURE 3.26

The File Properties dialog box contains workflow information such as the scene author, comments, and revision dates.

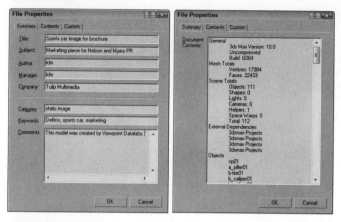

FIGURE 3.27

The View File dialog box can open an assortment of image and animation formats.

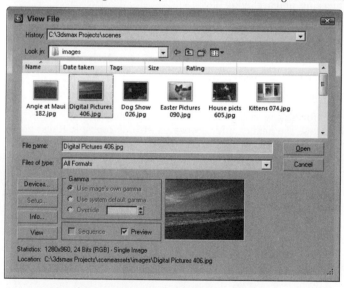

Cross-Reference

The Rendered Frame Window is discussed in more detail in Chapter 23, "Rendering a Scene and Enabling Quicksilver." ∎

The View File dialog box includes several controls for viewing files. The Devices and Setup buttons let you set up and view a file using external devices such as video recorders. The Info button lets you view detailed information about the selected file. The View button opens the file for viewing while leaving the View File dialog box open. The Open button opens the selected file and closes the dialog box. At the bottom of the View File dialog box, the statistics and path of the current file are displayed.

The View File dialog box can open many types of files, including Microsoft videos (AVI), MPEG files, bitmap images (BMP), Kodak Cineon images (CIN), Combustion files (CWS), Graphics Image Format images (GIF), Radiance HDRI image files (HDR), Image File List files (IFL), JPEG images (JPG), OpenEXR image files (EXR), Portable Network Graphics images (PNG), Adobe Photoshop images (PSD), QuickTime movies (MOV), SGI images (RGB), RLA images, RPF images, Targa images (TGA, VST), Tagged Image File Format images (TIF), Abekas Digital Disk images (YUV), and DirectDraw Surface (DDS) images.

You use the Gamma area on the View File dialog box to specify whether an image uses its own gamma settings or the system's default setting, or whether an override value should be used.

Summary

Working with files lets you save your work, share it with others, and reload it for more work. This chapter covered the following topics:

- Creating, saving, opening, merging, and archiving files
- Changing file preferences and configuring paths
- Understanding the various import and export types
- Importing models from other programs, such as Illustrator, Maya, and MotionBuilder
- Working with the file utilities, such as the Asset Browser
- Using the Summary Info and File Properties dialog boxes to keep track of scene files

By now, you should be feeling more comfortable with the user interface and using files, but if you want to make some changes to the interface, the next chapter covers how to customize it. It also covers the available preference settings.

Changing Interface Units and Setting Preferences

One of the first things you'll want to set before beginning a project is the scene units. Units can be as small as millimeters or as large as kilometers, or they could be generic, which means they have meaning only relative to the other parts of the scene. Max offers a large array of available units, or you can even define your own.

Max also has a rather bulky set of preferences that you can use to set almost every aspect of the program. This chapter also covers various ways to make the Max interface more comfortable for you.

Selecting System Units

One of the first tasks you need to complete before you can begin modeling is to set the system units. The system units have a direct impact on modeling and define the units that are represented by the coordinate values. Units directly relate to parameters entered with the keyboard. For example, with the units set to meters, a sphere created with the radius parameter of 2 would be 4 meters across.

Max supports several different measurement systems, including Metric and U.S. Standard units. You also can define a Custom units system. (I suggest parsecs if you're working on a space scene.) Working with a units system enables you to work with precision and accuracy using realistic values.

Tip
Most game engines work with meters, so if you're building assets for a game, set the units to meters. ■

To specify a units system, choose Customize ⇨ Units Setup to display the Units Setup dialog box, shown in Figure 4.1. For the Metric system, options include Millimeters, Centimeters, Meters, and Kilometers. The U.S. Standard units system can be set to the default units of Feet or Inches displayed as decimals or fractional units. You also can select to display feet with fractional inches or feet with decimal inches. Fractional values can be divided from $1/1$ to $1/100$ increments.

FIGURE 4.1

The Units Setup dialog box lets you choose which units system to use. Options include Metric, U.S. Standard, Custom, and Generic.

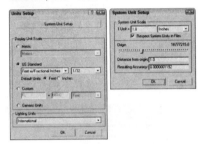

Using Custom and Generic units

To define a Custom units system, modify the fields under the Custom option, including a units label and its equivalence to known units. The final option is to use the default Generic units. Generic units relate distances to each other, but the numbers themselves are irrelevant. You also can set lighting units to use American or International standards. Lighting units are used to define Photometric lights.

At the top of the Units Setup dialog box is the System Unit Setup button. This button opens the System Unit Scale dialog box, also shown in Figure 4.1. This dialog box enables you to define the measurement system used by Max. Options include Inches, Feet, Miles, Millimeters, Centimeters, Meters, and Kilometers.

For example, when using Max to create models that are to be used in the Unreal game editor, you can use the Custom option to define a unit called the Unreal Foot unit that sets 1 Uft equal to 16 units, which matches the units in the Unreal editor just fine.

A multiplier field allows you to alter the value of each unit. The Respect System Units in Files toggle presents a dialog box whenever a file with a different system units setting is encountered. If this option is disabled, all new objects are automatically converted to the current units system.

The Origin control helps you determine the accuracy of an object as it is moved away from the scene origin. If you know how far objects will be located from the origin, then entering that value tells you the Resulting Accuracy. You can use this feature to determine the accuracy of your parameters. Objects farther from the origin have a lower accuracy.

Caution

Be cautious when working with objects that are positioned a long way from the scene origin. The farther an object is from the origin, the lower its accuracy and the less precisely you can move it. If you are having trouble precisely positioning an object (in particular, an object that has been imported from an external file), check the object's distance from the origin. Moving it closer to the origin should help resolve the problem. ∎

Handling mismatched units

Imagine designing a new ski resort layout. For such a project, you'd want to probably use kilometers as the file units. If your next project is to design a custom body design on a race car, then you'll want to use meters as the new units. If you need to reopen the ski resort project while your units are set to meters, then you'll get a File Load: Units Mismatch dialog box, shown in Figure 4.2.

This dialog box reminds you that the units specified in the file that you are opening don't match the current units setting. This also can happen when trying to merge in an object with a different units setting. The dialog box lists the units used in both the file and the system and offers two options. The Rescale the File Objects to the System Unit Scale option changes the units in the file to match the current system units setting. The second option changes the system units to match the file unit settings.

Tip

If you rescale the file object to match the system file units setting, then the objects will either appear tiny or huge in the current scene. Use the Zoom Extents All button to see the rescaled objects in the viewport. ■

FIGURE 4.2

The Units Mismatch dialog box lets you synch up units between the current file and the system settings.

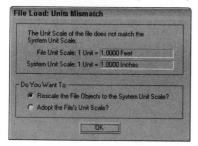

Rescaling world units

If you discover halfway through your scene that you're working with the wrong units, you can use the Rescale World Units utility to scale up the entire scene or just selected objects. To access this utility, click the Utilities panel and then the More button. In the utilities list, select the Rescale World Units utility and click OK.

The Rescale World Units dialog box has a Scale Factor value, which is the value by which the scene or objects are increased or decreased. If your world was created using millimeter units and you need to work in meters, then increasing by a Scale Factor of 1000 will set the world right.

Setting Preferences

The Preference Settings dialog box lets you configure Max so it works in a way that is most comfortable for you. You open it by choosing Customize ⇨ Preferences. The dialog box includes several panels: General, Files, Viewports, Gamma and LUT, Rendering, Radiosity, Animation, Inverse Kinematics, Gizmos, MAXScript, mental ray, Containers, and Help.

New Feature

The Help panel in the Preference Settings dialog box is new to 3ds Max 2012. ∎

Tip

The quickest way I've found to open the Preference Settings dialog box is to right-click the Spinner Snap Toggle button on the main toolbar. ∎

General preferences

The first panel in the Preference Settings dialog box is for General settings, as shown in Figure 4.3. The General panel includes many global settings that affect the entire interface.

FIGURE 4.3

The General panel lets you change many UI settings.

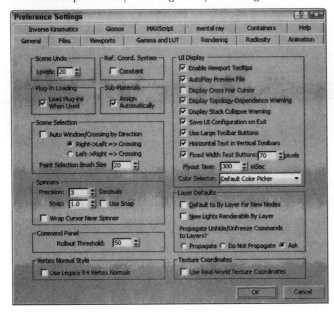

Undo Levels and the Reference Coordinate System

The Scene Undo spinner sets the number of commands that can be kept in a buffer for undoing. A smaller number frees up memory, but does not let you backtrack as far through your work. The default Undo Levels is 20.

Tip

Although it takes up some valuable memory, I've found that increasing the number of Undos is very helpful. When working on a model, it takes almost no time to do 20 commands. ∎

The Reference Coordinate System setting makes all transform tools use the same coordinate system and transform center when the Constant option is enabled. If disabled, each transform (move, scale, and rotate) uses the coordinate system last selected.

Loading Plug-Ins and Sub-Material settings

The Load Plug-Ins When Used option keeps plug-ins out of memory until they are accessed. This saves valuable memory and still makes the plug-ins accessible.

The Automatic Sub-Material Assignment option, when checked, enables materials to be dragged and dropped directly onto a subobject selection. This applies the Multi/Sub-Object material to the object with the dropped material corresponding with the subobject selection's Material ID. If you regularly use the Multi/Sub-Object material, enabling this option can be a great timesaver, but if you aren't familiar with the Multi/Sub-Object material, this option can lead to confusion, making it difficult to locate applied materials.

Scene Selection settings

The Auto Window/Crossing by Direction option lets you select scene objects using the windowing method (the entire object must be within the selected windowed area to be selected) and the crossing method (which selects objects if their borders are crossed with the mouse) at the same time, depending on the direction that the mouse is dragged. If you select the first option, then the Crossing method is used when the mouse is dragged from right to left, and the Window method is used when the mouse is dragged from left to right.

Tip

I like to keep the Auto Window/Crossing by Direction option disabled. I use the Crossing selection method and find that I don't always start my selection from the same side. ∎

The Paint Selection Brush Size value sets the default size of the Paint Selection Brush. In the default interface, this size is set to 20. If you find yourself changing the brush size every time you use this tool, then you can alter its default size with this setting.

Spinner, Rollout, and Vertex Normal settings

Spinners are interface controls that enable you to enter values or interactively increase or decrease the value by clicking the arrows on the right. The Preference Settings dialog box includes settings for changing the number of decimals displayed in spinners and the increment or decrement value for clicking an arrow. The Use Spinner Snap option enables the snap mode.

 You also can enable the snap mode using the Spinner Snap button on the main toolbar.

Tip

Right-click a spinner to automatically set its value to 0 or its lowest threshold. ∎

You also can change the values in the spinner by clicking the spinner and dragging up to increase the value or down to decrease it. The Wrap Cursor Near Spinner option keeps the cursor close to the spinner when you change values by dragging with the mouse, so you can drag the mouse continuously without worrying about hitting the top or bottom of the screen.

The Rollout Threshold value sets how many pixels can be scrolled before the rollup shifts to another column. This is used only if you've made the Command Panel wider or floating.

The Use Legacy R4 Vertex Normals option computes vertex normals based on the Max version 4 instead of the newer method. The newer method is more accurate but may affect smoothing groups. Enable this setting only if you plan on using any models created using Max R4 or earlier.

Interface Display settings

The options in the UI Display section control additional aspects of the interface. The Enable Viewport Tooltips option can toggle tooltips on or off. Tooltips are helpful when you're first learning the Max interface, but they quickly become annoying, and you'll want to turn them off.

The AutoPlay Preview File setting automatically plays Preview Files in the default media player when they are finished rendering. If this option is disabled, you need to play the previews with the Tools ➪ Grab Viewport ➪ View Animated Sequence File menu command. The Display Cross Hair Cursor option changes the cursor from the Windows default arrow to a crosshair cursor similar to the one used in AutoCAD.

For some actions, such as non-uniform scaling, Max displays a warning dialog box asking whether you are sure of the action. To disable these warnings, uncheck this option (or you could check the Disable this Warning box in the dialog box). Actions with warnings include topology-dependence and collapsing the Modifier Stack.

The Save UI Configuration on Exit switch automatically saves any interface configuration changes when you exit Max. You can deselect the Use Large Toolbar Buttons option, enabling the use of smaller toolbar buttons and icons, which reclaims valuable screen real estate.

The Horizontal Text in Vertical Toolbars option fixes the problem of text buttons that take up too much space, especially when printed horizontally on a vertical toolbar. You also can specify a width for text buttons. Any text larger than this value is clipped off at the edges of the button.

The Flyout Time spinner adjusts the time the system waits before displaying flyout buttons. The Color Selection drop-down list lets you choose which color selector interface Max uses.

Layer settings

If you select an object and open its Properties dialog box, the Display Properties, Rendering Control, and Motion Blur sections each have a button that can toggle between ByLayer and ByObject. If ByObject is selected, then the options are enabled and you can set them for the object in the Properties dialog box, but if the ByLayer option is selected, then the settings are determined by the setting defined for all objects in the layer in the Layer Manager.

The settings in the Preference Settings dialog box set the ByLayer option as the default for new objects and new lights. You also have an option to propagate all unhide and unfreeze commands to the layer. You can select Propagate, Do Not Propagate, or Ask.

Real-World Texture Coordinates setting

The Use Real-World Texture Coordinates setting causes the Real-World Scale or the Real-World Map Size option in the Coordinates rollout to be enabled. This setting is off by default, but it can be enabled to be the default by using this setting.

Cross-Reference

Real-World Texture Coordinates is a mapping method explained in more detail in Chapter 17, "Adding Material Details with Maps." ■

Files panel preferences

The Files panel holds the controls for backing up, archiving, and logging Max files. You can set files to be backed up, saved incrementally, or compressed when saved.

Cross-Reference

The Files panel is covered in Chapter 3, "Working with Files, Importing, and Exporting." ■

Viewport preferences

The viewports are your window into the scene. The Viewports panel, shown in Figure 4.4, contains many options for controlling these viewports.

FIGURE 4.4

The Viewports panel contains several viewport parameter settings.

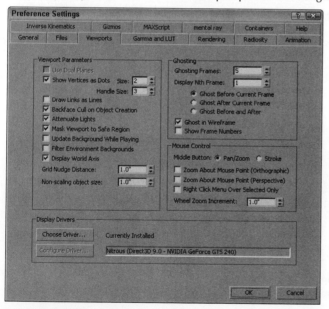

Cross-Reference

Although the viewports are the major topic in Chapter 2, "Controlling and Configuring the Viewports," the viewport preference settings are covered here. ■

Viewport parameter options

The Use Dual Planes option enables a method designed to speed up viewport redraws. Objects close to the scene are included in a front plane, and objects farther back are included in a back plane. When this option is enabled, only the objects on the front plane are redrawn.

In subobject mode, the default is to display vertices as small plus signs. The Show Vertices as Dots option displays vertices as either Small or Large dots. The Draw Links as Lines option shows all displayed links as lines that connect the two linked objects.

Caution

I've found that keeping the Draw Links as Lines option turned on can make it confusing to see objects clearly, so I tend to keep it turned off, but it is occasionally useful when trying to determine which objects are linked and to which other object. ■

When the Backface Cull on Object Creation option is enabled, the backside of an object in wireframe mode is not displayed. If disabled, you can see the wireframe lines that make up the backside of the object. The Backface Cull option setting is determined when the object is created, so some objects in your scene may be backface culled and others may not be. Figure 4.5 includes a sphere and a cube on the left that are backface culled and a sphere and cube on the right that are not.

Note

The Object Properties dialog box also contains a Backface Cull option. ■

FIGURE 4.5

Backface culling simplifies objects by hiding their backsides.

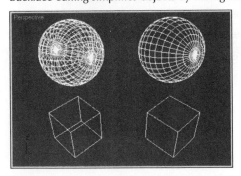

The Attenuate Lights option causes objects farther back in a viewport to appear darker. Attenuation is the property that causes lights to diminish over distance.

In the Viewport Configuration dialog box, you can set Safe Regions, which are borders that the renderer includes. The Mask Viewport to Safe Region option causes the objects beyond the Safe Region border to be invisible.

The Update Background While Playing option causes viewport background bitmaps to be updated while an animation sequence plays. Viewport backgrounds can be filtered if the Filter Environment

Background option is enabled, but this slows the update time. If this option is disabled, the background image appears aliased and pixelated.

The Display World Axis option displays the axes in the lower-left corner of each viewport. This can be helpful as you learn to navigate in 3D space. The Grid Nudge Distance is the distance that an object moves when Grid Nudge (+ and – on the numeric keypad) keys are used. Objects without scale, such as lights and cameras, appear in the scene according to the Non-Scaling Object Size value. Making this value large makes lights and camera objects very obvious.

Enabling ghosting

Ghosting is similar to the use of "onion skins" in traditional animation, causing an object's prior position and next position to be displayed. When producing animation, knowing where you're going and where you've come from is helpful.

Max offers several ghosting options. You can set whether a ghost appears before the current frame, after the current frame, or both before and after the current frame. You can set the total number of ghosting frames and how often they should appear. You also can set an option to show the frame numbers.

Cross-Reference

For a more detailed discussion of ghosting, see Chapter 21, "Understanding Animation and Keyframes." ■

Using the middle mouse button

If you're using a mouse that includes a middle button (this includes a mouse with a scrolling wheel), then you can define how the middle button is used. The two options are Pan/Zoom and Stroke.

Panning, rotating, and zooming with the middle mouse button

The Pan/Zoom option pans the active viewport if the middle button is held down, zooms in and out by steps if you move the scrolling wheel, rotates the view if you hold down the Alt key while dragging, and zooms smoothly if you drag the middle mouse button with the Ctrl and Alt keys held down. You also can zoom in quickly using the scroll wheel with the Ctrl button held down, or more slowly with the Alt key held down. You can select options to zoom about the mouse point in the Orthographic and Perspective viewports. If disabled, you'll zoom about the center of the viewport. The Right Click Menu Over Selected Only option causes the quadmenus to appear only if you right-click on top of the selected object. This is a bad idea if you use the quadmenus frequently.

Tip

I've found that using the middle mouse button along with the Alt key for rotating is the simplest and easiest way to navigate the viewport, so although Strokes is a clever idea, I always set the middle mouse button to Pan/Zoom. ■

Using strokes

The Stroke option lets you execute commands by dragging a predefined stroke in a viewport. With the Stroke option selected, close the Preference Settings dialog box and drag with the middle mouse button held down in one of the viewports. A simple dialog box identifies the stroke and executes the command associated with it. If no command is associated, then a simple dialog box appears that lets you Continue (do nothing) or Define the stroke.

Another way to work with strokes is to enable the Strokes Utility. This is done by selecting the Utility panel, clicking the More button, and selecting Strokes from the pop-up list of utilities. This utility makes a Draw Strokes button active. When the button is enabled, it turns yellow and you can draw strokes with the left mouse button and access defined strokes with the middle mouse button.

If you select to define the stroke, the Define Stroke dialog box, shown in Figure 4.6, is opened. You also can open this dialog box directly by holding down the Ctrl key while dragging a stroke with the middle mouse button. In the upper-left corner of this dialog box is a grid. Strokes are identified by the lines they cross on this grid as they are drawn. For example, an "HK" stroke would be a vertical line dragged from the top of the viewport straight down to the bottom.

FIGURE 4.6

The Define Stroke dialog box lets you define specific command strokes that are executed by drawing the stroke with the middle mouse button.

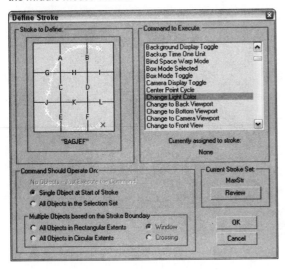

With a stroke identified, you can select a command in the upper-right pane. This is the command that executes when you drag the stroke with the middle mouse button in the viewport. For each command, you can set the options found below the stroke grid. These options define what the command is executed on.

All defined strokes are saved in a set, and you can review the current set of defined strokes with the Review button. Clicking this button opens the Review Strokes dialog box where all defined strokes and their commands are displayed, as shown in Figure 4.7.

One of the commands available in the list of commands is Stroke Preferences. Using this command opens the Stroke Preferences dialog box, also shown in Figure 4.7, where you can save and delete different stroke sets, specify to list commands or strokes in the Review Strokes dialog box, set how long the stroke grid and extents appear, and set the Stroke Point Size.

FIGURE 4.7

The Review Strokes and Stroke Preferences dialog boxes list all defined strokes and their respective commands.

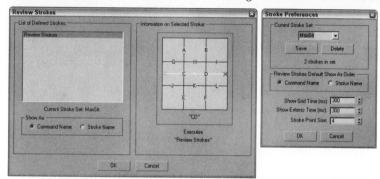

Choosing and configuring display drivers

When Max is installed, it loads the latest custom driver called Nitrous and sets the display to use that driver, but you can change the display driver to Direct3D, OpenGL, or to Software if your video card doesn't support the needed drivers.

New Feature

The new Nitrous display driver allows fast, realistic rendering within the viewport. It also lets you render out non-realistic styles. This display driver and its features are new to 3ds Max 2012. ■

The Display Drivers section in the Viewports panel of the Preference Settings dialog box lists the currently installed driver. Clicking the Configure Driver button opens a dialog box of settings for the current driver. Clicking the Choose Driver button opens the Display Driver Selection dialog box, shown in Figure 4.8. This dialog box lets you change the display driver to Direct3D, OpenGL, or some custom driver, but unless you have a reason to change it, keep it set to Nitrous or you'll disable some features. If you change the display driver, you need to restart Max.

Caution

The Display Driver Selection dialog box displays the options only for the drivers that it finds on your system, but just because an option exists doesn't mean it works correctly. If a driver hangs your system, you can restart it from a command line with the –h flag after 3dsmax.exe to force Max to present the Graphics Driver Setup dialog box again or use the Start ➪ Programs ➪ Autodesk ➪ 3ds Max 2012 ➪ Change Graphics Mode program icon to restart the program. ■

The Configure Driver option opens a dialog box of configurations for the driver that is currently installed. The various configuration dialog boxes include options such as specifying the Texture Size, which is the size of the bitmap used to texture map an object. Larger maps have better image quality but can slow down your display.

All the display driver configuration settings present tradeoffs between image quality and speed of display. By tweaking the configuration settings, you can optimize these settings to suit your needs. In general, the more memory available on your video card, the better the results.

FIGURE 4.8

You use the Display Driver Selection dialog box to select a different display driver.

On the CD-ROM

You can learn more about the various display drivers in Bonus Chapter 1, "Installing and Configuring 3ds Max 2012," on the CD. ■

Gamma preferences

The Gamma and LUT panel, shown in Figure 4.9, controls the gamma correction for the display and for bitmap files. It also includes a Browse button for loading an Autodesk Look-up Table (LUT) file. A Look-up Table is a file that holds all the color calibration settings that can be shared across different types of software and hardware within a studio to maintain consistency.

FIGURE 4.9

Enabling gamma correction makes colors consistent regardless of the monitor.

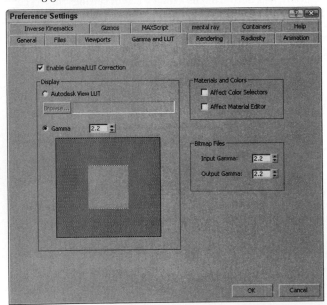

Setting screen gamma

Have you ever noticed in an electronics store that television-screen displays vary in color? Colors on monitor screens may be fairly consistent for related models but may vary across brands. *Gamma settings* are a means by which colors can be consistently represented regardless of the monitor that is being used.

Gamma value regulates the contrast of an image. It is a numerical offset required by an individual monitor in order to be consistent with a standard. To enable gamma correction for Max, open the Gamma and LUT panel in the Preference Settings dialog box and click the Enable Gamma/LUT Correction option. To determine the gamma value, use the spinner or adjust the Gamma value until the gray square blends in unnoticeably with the background.

Note

3ds Max cannot create LUT files, but it can use existing LUT files created in other software packages, such as Combustion. ■

Propagating gamma settings

Although gamma settings have a direct impact on the viewports, they do not affect the colors found in the Color Selector or in the Material Editor. Using the Affect Color Selectors and Affect Material Editor options, you can propagate the gamma settings to these other interfaces also.

Setting bitmap gamma

Many bitmap formats, such as TGA, contain their own gamma settings. The Input Gamma setting for Bitmap files sets the gamma for bitmaps that don't have a gamma setting. The Output Gamma setting is the value set for bitmaps being output from Max.

Note

Match the Input Gamma value to the Display Gamma value so that bitmaps loaded for textures are displayed correctly. ■

Other preference panels

The remaining preference panels, including Rendering, Animation, Inverse Kinematics, Gizmos, MAXScript, Radiosity, mental ray, and Containers, are covered in the related chapters.

Cross-Reference

The details of the Rendering Preferences panel are covered in Chapter 23, "Rendering a Scene and Enabling Quicksilver." The Animation Preferences panel is covered in Chapter 21, "Understanding Animation and Keyframes." To learn more about Applied IK and Interactive IK, see Chapter 38, "Understanding Rigging, Kinematics, and Working with Bones." See Chapter 7, "Transforming Objects, Pivoting, Aligning, and Snapping" for more detail on Gizmo preferences. Check out Bonus Chapter 21, "Automating with MAXScript" for more on MAXScript commands and preferences. Swing over to Chapter 45, "Working with Advanced Lighting, Light Tracing, and Radiosity," for greater detail on Radiosity preferences. Look to Chapter 47, "Rendering with mental ray and iray," for more detail on the mental ray renderer. Chapter 9, "Grouping, Linking, and Parenting Objects," covers the container preferences. ■

Summary

You can customize the Max interface in many ways. Most of these customization options are included under the Customize menu. In this chapter, you learned how to use this menu and its commands to customize many aspects of the interface. Customizing makes the Max interface more efficient and comfortable for you.

Specifically, this chapter covered the following topics:

- Handling system units
- Setting general preferences
- Changing viewport and gamma preferences

Part II, "Working with Objects," is next. The first chapter covers the primitive objects and gets some objects into a scene for you to work with.

Part II

Working with Objects

Creating and Editing Primitive Objects

So what exactly did the Romans use to build their civilization? The answer is lots and lots of basic blocks. The basic building blocks in Max are called *primitives*. You can use these primitives to start any modeling job. After you create a primitive, you can then bend it, stretch it, smash it, or cut it to create new objects, but for now, you'll focus on using primitives in their default shape.

This chapter covers the basics of primitive object types and introduces the various primitive objects, including how to accurately create and configure them. You also use these base objects in the coming chapters to learn about selecting, cloning, grouping, and transforming.

Modeling is covered in depth in Part III, but first you need to learn how to create some basic blocks and move them around. Later, you can work on building a civilization. I'm sure workers in Rome would be jealous.

IN THIS CHAPTER

Creating primitive objects

Naming objects and setting object colors

Using creation methods

Setting object parameters

Exploring the various primitive types

Using the AEC Objects

Creating Primitive Objects

Max is all about creating objects and scenes, so it's appropriate that one of the first things to learn is how to create objects. Although you can create complex models and objects, Max includes many simple, default geometric objects, called *primitives*, that you can use as a starting point. Creating these primitive objects can be as easy as clicking and dragging in a viewport.

Using the Create menu

The Create menu offers quick access to the buttons in the Create panel. All the objects that you can create using the Create panel you can access using the Create menu. Selecting an object from the Create menu automatically opens the Create panel in the Command Panel and selects the correct category, sub-category, and button needed to create the object. After selecting the menu option, you simply need to click in one of the viewports to create the object.

Using the Create panel

The creation of all default Max objects, such as primitive spheres, shapes, lights, and cameras, starts with the Create panel (or the Create menu, which leads to the Create panel). This panel is the first in the Command Panel, indicated by a star icon.

Of all the panels in the Command Panel, only the Create panel—shown in Figure 5.1—includes both categories and subcategories. After you click the Create tab, seven category icons are displayed. From left to right, they are Geometry, Shapes, Lights, Cameras, Helpers, Space Warps, and Systems.

The Create panel is the place you go to create objects for the scene. These objects could be geometric objects such as spheres, cones, and boxes or other objects such as lights, cameras, or Space Warps. The Create panel contains a huge variety of objects. To create an object, you simply need to find the button for the object that you want to create, click it, click in one of the viewports, and *voilà*—instant object.

 After you select the Geometry category icon (which has an icon of a sphere on it), a drop-down list with several subcategories appears directly below the category icons. The first available subcategory is Standard Primitives. After you select this subcategory, several text buttons appear that enable you to create some simple primitive objects.

Note

The second subcategory is called Extended Primitives. It also includes primitive objects. The Extended Primitives are more specialized and aren't used as often. ■

FIGURE 5.1

The Create panel includes categories and subcategories.

Create panel

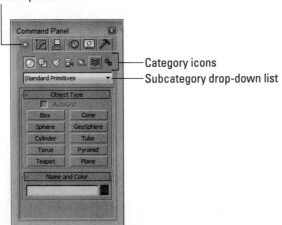

As an example, click the button labeled Sphere (not to be confused with the Geometry category, which has a sphere icon). Several rollouts appear at the bottom of the Command Panel: These rollouts for the Sphere primitive object include Name and Color, Creation Method, Keyboard Entry, and

Parameters. The rollouts for each primitive are slightly different, as well as the parameters within each rollout.

If you want to ignore these rollouts and just create a sphere, simply click and drag within one of the viewports, and a sphere object appears. The size of the sphere is determined by how far you drag the mouse before releasing the mouse button. Figure 5.2 shows the new sphere and its parameters.

You can create primitive spheres easily by dragging in a viewport.

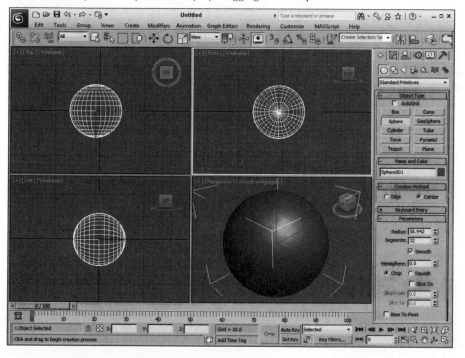

When an object button, such as the Sphere button, is selected, it turns dark gray. This color change reminds you that you are in creation mode. Clicking and dragging within any viewport creates an additional sphere. While in creation mode, you can create many spheres by clicking and dragging several times in one of the viewports. To get out of creation mode, right-click in the active viewport, or click the Select Object button or one of the transform buttons on the main toolbar.

After you select a primitive button, several additional rollouts magically appear. These new rollouts hold the parameters for the selected object and are displayed in the Create panel below the Name and Color rollout. Altering these parameters changes the most recently created object.

Naming and renaming objects

Every object in the scene can have both a name and a color assigned to it. Each object is given a default name and random color when first created. The default name is the type of object followed by a number. For example, when you create a sphere object, Max labels it "Sphere01." These default names aren't very exciting and can be confusing if you have many objects. You can change the object's name at any time by modifying the Name field in the Name and Color rollout of the Command Panel.

Note

Max gives each newly created object a unique name. Max is smart enough to give each new object a different name by adding a sequential number to the end of the name. ■

Caution

Be aware that Max allows you to give two different objects the same name. ■

Cross-Reference

Names and colors are useful for locating and selecting objects, as you find out in Chapter 6, "Selecting Objects and Setting Object Properties." ■

The Tools ⇨ Rename Objects menu command opens a dialog box that lets you change the object name of several objects at once. The Rename Objects dialog box, shown in Figure 5.3, lets you set the Base Name along with a Prefix, a Suffix, or a number. These new names can be applied to the selected objects or to the specific objects that you pick from the Select Objects dialog box.

FIGURE 5.3

The Rename Objects dialog box can rename several objects at once.

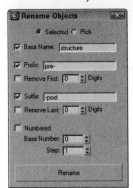

Assigning colors

The object color is shown in the color swatch to the right of the object name. This color is the color that is used to display the object within the viewports and to render the object if a material isn't applied. To change an object's color, just click the color swatch next to the Name field to make the Object Color dialog box appear. This dialog box, shown in Figure 5.4, lets you select a different color or pick a custom color.

FIGURE 5.4

You use the Object Color dialog box to define the color of objects displayed in the viewports.

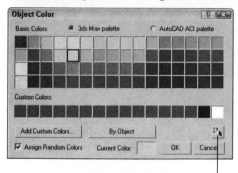

Select by Color button

The Object Color dialog box includes the standard 3ds Max palette and the AutoCAD ACI palette. The AutoCAD palette has many more colors than the Max palette, but the Max palette allows a row of custom colors. Above the Cancel button is the Select by Color button. Click this button to open the Select Objects dialog box, where you can select all the objects that have a certain color.

With the Object Color dialog box, if the Assign Random Colors option is selected, then a random color from the palette is chosen every time a new object is created. If this option is not selected, the color of all new objects is the same until you choose a different object color. Making objects different colors allows you to more easily distinguish between two objects for selection and transformation.

The Object Color dialog box also includes a button that toggles between By Layer and By Object, which appears only when an object is selected. Using this button, you can cause objects to accept color according to their object definition or based on the layer of which they are a part.

You can select custom colors by clicking the Add Custom Colors button. This button opens a Color Selector dialog box, shown in Figure 5.5. Selecting a color and clicking the Add Color button adds the selected color to the row of Custom Colors in the Object Color palette. You can also open the Color Selector by clicking on the Current Color swatch. The current color can then be dragged to the row of Custom Colors.

Tip

You can fill the entire row of Custom Colors by clicking repeatedly on the Add Color button. ■

The Color Selector dialog box defines colors using the RGB (red, green, and blue) and HSV (hue, saturation, and value) color systems. Another way to select colors is to drag the cursor around the rainbow palette on the left. After you find the perfect custom color to add to the Object Color dialog box, click the Add Color button. This custom color is then available wherever the Object Color dialog box is opened.

Object colors are also important because you can use them to select and filter objects. For example, use the Edit ➪ Select by ➪ Color menu (or click the Select by Color button in the Object Color dialog box) to select only objects that match a selected color.

FIGURE 5.5

The Color Selector dialog box lets you choose new custom colors.

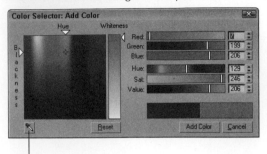

Sample screen color

Note

You can set objects to display an object's default color or its Material Color. These options are in the Display Color rollout under the Display panel (the fifth tab from the left in the Command Panel with an icon of a monitor). You can set them differently for Wireframe and Shaded views. ■

The Sample Screen Color tool, located at the bottom of the Color Selector dialog box, lets you select colors from any open Max window, including the Rendered Scene window. This gives you the ability to sample colors directly from a rendered image. To use this tool, simply click it and drag around the screen. The cursor changes to an eyedropper. If you click and drag around the window, the color is instantly updated in the Color Selector dialog box. If you hold down the Shift key while dragging, then the selected colors are blended together to create a summed color.

Note

The Sample Screen Color tool works only within Max windows. ■

Using the Color Clipboard

The object color is one of the first places where colors are encountered, but it certainly won't be the last. If you find a specific color that you like and want to use elsewhere, you can use the Color Clipboard utility to carry colors to other interfaces. You can access this utility using the Tools ⇨ Color Clipboard menu command, which opens the Utilities panel, as shown in Figure 5.6.

FIGURE 5.6

The Color Clipboard utility offers a way to transport colors.

When selected, the Color Clipboard appears as a rollout in the Utilities panel and includes four color swatches. These color swatches can be dragged to other interfaces such as the Material Editor. Clicking on any of these swatches launches the Color Selector. The New Floater button opens a floatable Color Clipboard that holds 12 colors, shown in Figure 5.7. Right-clicking the color swatches opens a pop-up menu with Copy and Paste options. Using this clipboard, you can open and save color configurations. The files are saved as Color Clipboard files with the .ccb extension.

FIGURE 5.7

The Color Clipboard floating palette can hold 12 colors.

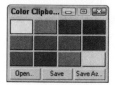

Using different creation methods

You actually have a couple of ways to create primitive objects by dragging in a viewport. With the first method, the first place you click sets the object's initial position. You then need to drag the mouse to define the object's first dimension and then click again to set each additional dimension, if needed. Primitive objects with a different number of dimensions require a different number of clicks and drags.

For example, a sphere is one of the simplest objects to create. To create a sphere, click in a viewport to set the location of the sphere's center, drag the mouse to the desired radius, and release the mouse button to complete. A Box object, on the other hand, requires a click-and-drag move to define the base (width and depth), and another drag-and-click move to set the height. If you ever get lost when defining these dimensions, check the Prompt Line to see what dimension the interface expects next.

When you click a primitive object button, the Creation Method rollout appears and offers different methods for creating the primitives. For example, click the Sphere button, and the Creation Method rollout displays two options: Edge and Center. When you choose the Edge method, the first viewport click sets one edge of the sphere, and dragging and clicking again sets the diameter of the sphere. The default Center creation method defines the sphere's center location; dragging sets the sphere's radius. The creation method for each primitive can be different. For example, the Box primitive object has a creation method for creating perfect cubes, which require only a single click and drag. Table 5.1 shows the number of clicks required to create an object and the creation methods for each primitive object.

Tip

If you're dragging to create a primitive object and halfway through its creation you change your mind, you can right-click to eliminate the creation of the object. ■

TABLE 5.1

Primitive Object Creation Methods

Primitive Object	Primitive Object Name	Number of Viewport Clicks to Create	Default Creation Method	Other Creation Method
	Box	2	Box	Cube
	Cone	3	Center	Edge
	Sphere	1	Center	Edge
	GeoSphere	1	Center	Diameter
	Cylinder	2	Center	Edge
	Tube	3	Center	Edge
	Torus	2	Center	Edge
	Pyramid	2	Base/Apex	Center
	Teapot	1	Center	Edge
	Plane	1	Rectangular	Square
	Hedra	1	-	-
	Torus Knot	2	Radius	Diameter
	ChamferBox	3	Box	Cube
	ChamferCyl	3	Center	Edge
	OilTank	3	Center	Edge
	Capsule	2	Center	Edge
	Spindle	3	Center	Edge
	L-Ext	3	Corners	Center

Primitive Object	Primitive Object Name	Number of Viewport Clicks to Create	Default Creation Method	Other Creation Method
	Gengon	3	Center	Edge
	C-Ext	3	Corners	Center
	RingWave	2	-	-
	Hose	2	-	-
	Prism	3	Base/Apex	Isosceles

Note

Some primitive objects, such as the Hedra, RingWave, and Hose, don't have any creation methods. ■

Using the Keyboard Entry rollout for precise dimensions

When creating a primitive object, you can define its location and dimensions by clicking in a viewport and dragging, or you can enter precise values in the Keyboard Entry rollout, located in the Create panel. Within this rollout, you can enter the offset XYZ values for positioning the origin of the primitive and the dimensions of the object. The offset values are defined relative to the active construction plane that is usually the Home Grid.

When all the dimension fields are set, click the Create button to create the actual primitive. You can create multiple objects by clicking the Create button several times. After a primitive is created, altering the fields in the Keyboard Entry rollout has no effect on the current object, but you can always use the Undo feature to try again.

Altering object parameters

The final rollout for all primitive objects is the Parameters rollout. This rollout holds all the various settings for the object. Compared to the Keyboard Entry rollout, which you can use only when creating the primitive, you can use the Parameters rollout to alter the primitive's parameters before or after the creation of the object. For example, increasing the Radius value after creating an object makes an existing sphere larger. This works only while the primitive mode is still enabled.

The parameters are different for each primitive object, but you can generally use them to control the dimensions, the number of segments that make up the object, and whether the object is sliced into sections. You can also select the Generate Mapping Coordinates option (which automatically creates material mapping coordinates that are used to position texture maps) and the Real-World Map Size option (which lets you define a texture's dimensions that are maintained regardless of the object size).

Note

After you deselect an object, the Parameters rollout disappears from the Create tab and moves to the Modify tab. You can make future parameter adjustments by selecting an object and clicking the Modify tab. ■

Recovering from mistakes and deleting objects

Before going any further, you need to be reminded how to undo the last action with the Undo menu command. The Undo (Ctrl+Z) menu command will undo the last action, whether it's creating an object or changing a parameter. The Redo (Ctrl+Y) menu command lets you redo an action that was undone.

Note

A separate undo feature for undoing a view change is available in the Views menu. The Views ➪ Undo View Change (Shift+Z) applies to any viewport changes like zooming, panning, and rotating the view. ■

You can set the levels of undo in the General panel of the Preference Settings dialog box. If you click on the small arrow to the left of either the Undo button or the Redo button on the Quick Access toolbar, a list of recent actions is displayed. You can select any action from this list to be undone.

Tip

Another way to experiment with objects is with the Hold (Ctrl+H) and Fetch (Alt+Ctrl+F) features, also found in the Edit menu. The Hold command holds the entire scene, including any viewport configurations, in a temporary buffer. You can recall a held scene at any time using the Fetch command. This is a quick alternative to saving a file. ■

The Edit ➪ Delete menu command removes the selected object (or objects) from the scene. (The keyboard shortcut for this command is, luckily, the Delete key, because anything else would be confusing.)

Tutorial: Exploring the Platonic solids

Among the many discoveries of Plato, an ancient Greek mathematician and philosopher, were the mathematical formulas that defined perfect geometric solids. A perfect geometric solid is one that is made up of polygon faces that are consistent throughout the object. The five solids that meet these criteria have come to be known as the Platonic solids.

Using Max, you can create and explore these interesting geometric shapes. Each of these shapes is available as a primitive object using the Hedra primitive object. The Hedra primitive object is one of the Extended Primitives.

To create the five Platonic solids as primitive objects, follow these steps:

1. Open the Create panel, click the Geometry category button, and select Extended Primitives from the subcategory drop-down list. Click the Hedra button to enter Hedra creation mode, or select the Create ➪ Extended Primitives ➪ Hedra menu command.

2. Click in the Top viewport, and drag to the left to create a simple Tetrahedron object.

   After the object is created, you can adjust its settings by altering the settings in the Parameters rollout.

Caution

Primitive parameters are available in the Create panel only while the new object is selected. If you deselect the new object, then the parameters are no longer visible in the Create panel, but you can access the object's parameters in the Modify panel. ■

3. Select the Tetra option in the Parameters rollout, set the P value in the Family Parameters section to **1.0**, and enter a value of **50** for the Radius. Be sure to press the Enter key after entering a value to update the object. Enter the name **Tetrahedron** in the Object Name field.

4. Click and drag again in the Top viewport to create another Hedra object. In the Parameters rollout, select the Cube/Octa option, and enter a value of **1.0** in the Family Parameter's P field and a value of **50** in the Radius field. Name this object **Octagon**.

5. Drag in the Top viewport to create another object. The Cube/Octa option is still selected. Enter a value of **1.0** in the Family Parameter's Q field this time, and set the Radius to **50**. Name this object **Cube**.

6. Drag in the Top viewport again to create the fourth Hedra object. In the Parameters rollout, select the Dodec/Icos option, enter a value of **1.0** in the P field, and set the Radius value to **50**. Name the object **Icosahedron**.

7. Drag in the Top viewport to create the final object. With the Dodec/Icos option set, enter **1.0** for the Q value, and set the Radius to **50**. Name this object **Dodecahedron**.

8. To get a good look at the objects, click the Perspective viewport, press the Zoom Extents button, and maximize the viewport by clicking the Min/Max Toggle (or press Alt+W) in the lower-right corner of the window.

Figure 5.8 shows the five perfect solid primitive objects. Using the Modify panel, you can return to these objects and change their parameters to learn the relationships among them. Later in this chapter, you can read about the Hedra primitive in greater detail.

FIGURE 5.8

The octagon, cube, tetrahedron, icosahedron, and dodecahedron objects; Plato would be amazed.

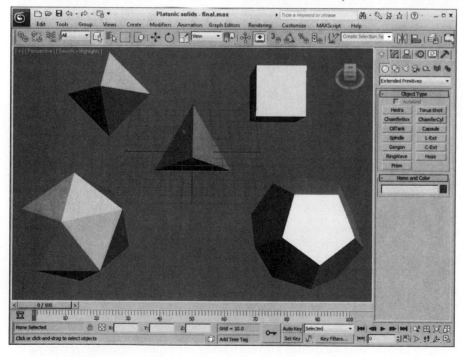

Exploring the Primitive Object Types

In the Create panel are actually two different subcategories of geometric primitives: Standard Primitives and Extended Primitives. These primitives include a diverse range of objects, from simple boxes and spheres to complex torus knots. You can create all these primitives from the Create panel.

Starting with the Standard Primitives

The Standard Primitives include many of the most basic and most used objects, including boxes, spheres, and cylinders. Figure 5.9 shows all the Standard Primitives.

FIGURE 5.9

The Standard Primitives: Box, Sphere, Cylinder, Torus, Teapot, Cone, GeoSphere, Tube, Pyramid, and Plane

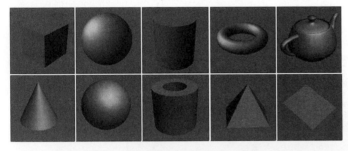

Box

You can use the Box primitive to create regular cubes and boxes of any width, length, and height. Holding down the Ctrl key while dragging the box base creates a perfect square for the base. To create a cube, select the Cube option in the Creation Method rollout. A single click and drag completes the cube.

The Length, Width, and Height Segment values indicate how many polygons make up each dimension. The default is only one segment.

Sphere

Spheres appear everywhere from sports balls to planets in space. Spheres are also among the easiest primitives to create. After clicking the Sphere button, simply click and drag in a viewport.

In the Parameters rollout, the Segments value specifies the number of polygons that make up the sphere. The higher the number of segments, the smoother the sphere is. The default value of 32 produces a smooth sphere, and a value of 4 actually produces a diamond-shaped object. The Smooth option lets you make the sphere smooth or faceted. Faceted spheres are useful for identifying faces for modifications. Figure 5.10 shows five spheres. The one on the left has 32 Segments and the Smooth option turned on. The remaining spheres have the Smooth option disabled with Segment values of 32, 16, 8, and 4.

The Parameters rollout also lets you create hemispheres. The hemisphere shape is set by the Hemisphere value, which can range from 0.0 to 1.0, with 0 being a full sphere and 1 being nothing at all. (A value of 0.5 would be a perfect hemisphere.) With the Hemisphere value specified, you now have two options with which to deal with the unused polygons that make up the originating sphere: the Chop option, which removes the unused polygons, and the Squash option, which retains the polygons but "squashes" them to fit in the hemisphere shape.

FIGURE 5.10

Sphere primitives of various Segment values with the Smooth option turned on and off

Figure 5.11 shows two hemispheres with Hemisphere values of 0.5. The Edged Faces option was enabled so you can see the polygon faces. The left hemisphere was created using the Chop option, and the right hemisphere was created with the Squash option. Notice how many extra polygons are included in the right hemisphere.

FIGURE 5.11

Creating hemispheres with the Chop and Squash options

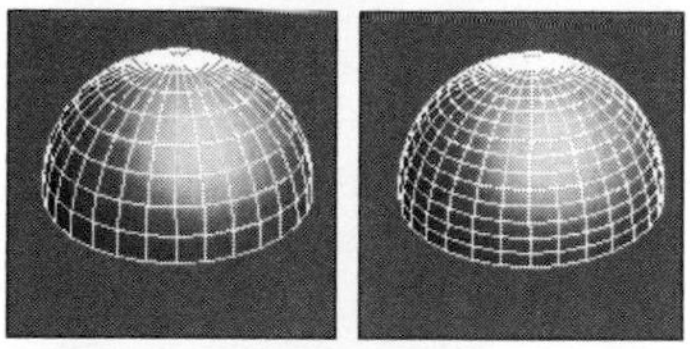

The Slice option enables you to dissect the sphere into slices (like segmenting an orange). The Slice From and Slice To fields accept values ranging from 0 to 360 degrees. Figure 5.12 shows four spheres that have been sliced. Notice that because the Segments value hasn't changed, all slices have the same number of faces.

Note

You can use the Slice feature on several primitives, including the sphere, cylinder, torus, cone, tube, oiltank, spindle, chamfercyl, and capsule. ■

FIGURE 5.12

Using the Slice option to create sphere slices

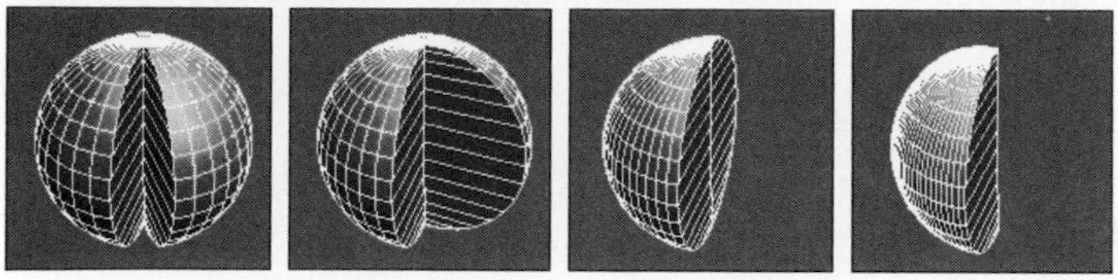

The Base to Pivot parameter determines whether the position of the pivot point (or the point about which the object rotates) is at the bottom of the sphere or at the center. The default (with the Base to Pivot setting not enabled) sets the pivot point for the sphere at the center of the sphere.

Cylinder

You can use a cylinder in many places—for example, as a pillar in front of a home or as a car driveshaft. To create one, first specify a base circle and then a height. The default number of sides is 18, which produces a smooth cylinder. Height and Cap Segments values define the number of polygons that make up the cylinder sides and caps. The Smooth and Slice options work the same as they do with a sphere (see the preceding section).

Tip

If you don't plan on modifying the ends of the cylinder, make the Cap Segments equal to 1 to keep the model complexity down. ■

Torus

A *torus* (which is the mathematical name for a "doughnut") is a ring with a circular cross section. To create a torus, you need to specify two radii values. The first is the value from the center of the torus to the center of the ring; the second is the radius of the circular cross section. The default settings create a torus with 24 segments and 12 sides. The Rotation and Twist options cause the sides to twist a specified value as the ring is circumnavigated.

Figure 5.13 shows some sample toruses with a Smooth setting of None. The first three have Segments values of 24, 12, and 6. The last two have Twist values of 90 and 360. The higher the number of segments, the rounder the torus looks when viewed from above. The default of 24 is sufficient to create a smooth torus. The number of sides defines the circular smoothness of the cross section.

FIGURE 5.13

Using the Segments and Twist options on a torus

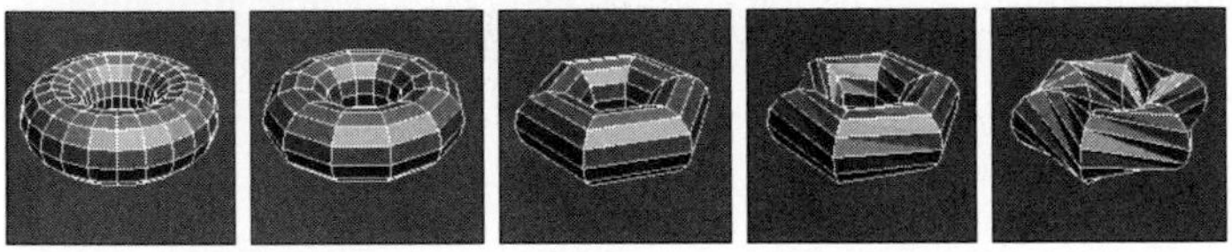

The Parameters rollout includes settings for four different Smooth options. The All option smoothes all edges, and the None option displays all polygons as faceted. The Sides option smoothes edges between sides, resulting in a torus with banded sides. The Segment option smoothes between segment edges, resulting in separate smooth sections around the torus.

The Slice options work with a torus the same way as they do with the sphere and cylinder objects; see the "Sphere" section earlier in this chapter.

Teapot

Okay, let's all sing together, "I'm a little teapot, short and stout. . . ." The teapot is another object that, like the sphere, is easy to create. Within the Parameters rollout, you can specify the number of

Segments, whether the surface is smooth or faceted, and which parts to display, including Body, Handle, Spout, and Lid.

Note

You may recognize most of these primitives as standard shapes, with the exception of the teapot. The teapot has a special place in computer graphics. In early computer graphics development labs, the teapot was chosen as the test model for many early algorithms. It is still included as a valuable benchmark for computer graphics programmers. ■

Cone

The Cone object, whether used to create ice cream cones or megaphones, is created exactly like the cylinder object except that the second cap can have a radius different from that of the first. You create it by clicking and dragging to specify the base circle, dragging to specify the cone's height, and then dragging again for the second cap to create a Cone.

In addition to the two cap radii and the Height, parameter options include the number of Height and Cap Segments, the number of Sides, and the Smooth and Slice options.

GeoSphere

The GeoSphere object is a sphere created by using fewer polygon faces than the standard Sphere object. This type of sphere spreads the polygon faces, which are all roughly equal in size, around the object, instead of concentrating them on either end like the normal Sphere object. This makes the GeoSphere a better choice for surface modeling because its polygon resolution is consistent. Geospheres also render more quickly and have faster transformation times than normal spheres. One reason for this is that a GeoSphere uses triangle faces instead of square faces.

In the Parameters rollout are several Geodesic Base Type options, including Tetra, Octa, and Icosa. The Tetra type is based on a four-sided tetrahedron, the Octa type is based on an eight-sided Octahedron, and the Icosa type is based on the 20-sided Icosahedron. Setting the Segment value to 1 produces each of these Hedra shapes. Each type aligns the triangle faces differently.

GeoSpheres also have the same Smooth, Hemisphere, and Base to Pivot options as the Sphere primitive. Selecting the Hemisphere option changes the GeoSphere into a hemisphere, but you have no additional options like Chop and Squash. GeoSphere primitives do not include an option to be sliced.

Tutorial: Comparing Spheres and GeoSpheres

To prove that GeoSpheres are more efficient than Sphere objects, follow these steps:

1. Create a normal Sphere, and set its Segment value to **4**.
2. Next to the Sphere object, create a GeoSphere object with a Tetra Base Type and the number of Segments set to **4**.
3. Create another GeoSphere object with the Octa Base Type and **4** Segments.
4. Finally, create a GeoSphere with the Icosa Base Type and **4** Segments.

Figure 5.14 shows these spheres as a comparison. The normal sphere, shown to the left, looks like a diamond, but the GeoSpheres still resemble spheres. Notice that the Icosa type GeoSphere, shown on the right, produces the smoothest sphere.

FIGURE 5.14

Even with a similar number of segments, GeoSpheres are much more spherical.

Tube

The Tube primitive is useful any time you need a pipe object. You can also use it to create ring-shaped objects that have rectangular cross sections. Creating a Tube object is very similar to the Cylinder and Cone objects. Tube parameters include two radii for the inner and outer tube walls. Tubes also have the Smooth and Slice options.

Pyramid

Pyramid primitives are constructed with a rectangular base and triangles at each edge that rise to meet at the top, just like the ones in Egypt, only easier to build. Two different creation methods are used to create the base rectangle. With the Base/Apex method, you create the base by dragging corner to corner, and with the Center method, you drag from the base center to a corner.

The Width and Depth parameters define the base dimensions, and the Height value determines how tall the pyramid is. You can also specify the number of segments for each dimension.

Plane

The Plane object enables you to model the Great Plains (good pun, eh?). The Plane primitive creates a simple plane that looks like a rectangle, but it includes Multiplier parameters that let you specify the size of the plane at render time. This feature makes working in a viewport convenient because you don't have to worry about creating a huge plane object representing the ground plane that makes all other scene objects really small in comparison.

Tip

Dense plane objects can be made into a terrain by randomly altering the height of each interior vertex with a Noise modifier. ■

The Plane primitive includes two creation methods: Rectangle and Square. The Square method creates a perfect square in the viewport when dragged. Holding down the Ctrl key while creating a Plane object also creates a perfect square. You can also define the Length and Width Segments, but the real benefits of the Plane object are derived from the use of the Render Multipliers.

The Scale Multiplier value determines how many times larger the plane should be at render time. Both Length and Width are multiplied by equal values. The Density Multiplier specifies the number of segments to produce at render time. The Total Faces value lets you know how many polygons are added to the scene using the specified Density Multiplier value.

Using these multipliers, you can create a small Plane object in the scene that automatically increases to the size and density it needs to be when rendered. This allows you to use the Zoom Extents button to see all objects without having a huge Plane object define the extents.

Extended Primitives

You access the Extended Primitives by selecting Extended Primitives in the subcategory drop-down list in the Create panel. These primitives aren't as generic as the Standard Primitives, but are equally useful, as shown in Figure 5.15.

FIGURE 5.15

The Extended Primitives: Hedra, ChamferBox, OilTank, Spindle, Gengon, RingWave, Hose, Torus Knot, ChamferCyl, Capsule, L-Ext, C-Ext, and Prism

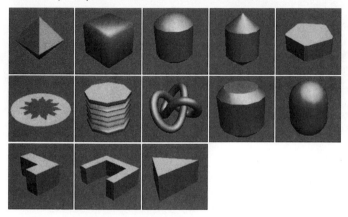

Hedra

Hedras, or Polyhedra, form the basis for a class of geometry defined by fundamental mathematical principles. In addition to Plato, Johannes Kepler used these Polyhedra as the basis for his famous "Harmony of the Spheres" theory. The Hedra primitives available in Max are Tetrahedron, Cube/Octahedron, Dodecahedron/Icosahedron, and two Star types called Star1 and Star2. From these basic Polyhedra, you can create many different variations.

The Family section options determine the shape of the Hedra. Each member of a Hedra pair is mathematically related to the other member. The Family Parameters include P and Q values. These values change the Hedra between the two shapes that make up the pair. For example, if the Family option is set to Cube/Octa, then a P value of 1 displays an Octagon, and a Q value of 1 displays a Cube. When both P and Q values are set to 0, the shape becomes an intermediate shape somewhere between a Cube and an Octagon. Because the values are interrelated, only one shape of the pair can have a value of 1 at any given time. Both P and Q cannot be set to 1 at the same time.

Figure 5.16 shows each of the basic Hedra Families in columns from left to right: Tetra, Cube/Octa, Dodec/Icos, Star1, and Star2. The top row has a P value of 1 and a Q value of 0, the middle row has both P and Q set to 0, and the bottom row sets P to 0 and Q to 1. Notice that the middle row shapes are a combination of the top and bottom rows.

The relationship between P and Q can be described in this manner: When the P value is set to 1 and the Q value is set to 0, one shape of the pair is displayed. As the P value decreases, each vertex becomes a separate face. The edges of these new faces increase as the value is decreased down to 0. The same holds true for the Q value.

FIGURE 5.16

The Hedra Families with the standard shapes in the top and bottom rows and the intermediate shapes in the middle row

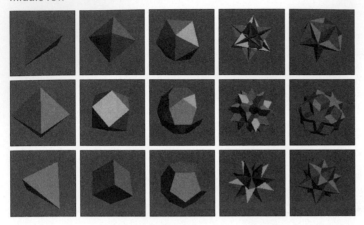

Tip

Altering the P and Q parameters can create many unique shapes. For each Hedra, try the following combinations: P = 0, Q = 0; P = 1, Q = 0; P = 0, Q = 1; P = 0.5, Q = 0.5; P = 0.5, Q = 0; P = 0, Q = 0.5. These represent the main intermediate objects. ■

As the geometry of the objects changes, the Hedra can have as many as three different types of polygons making up the faces. These polygons are represented by the P, Q, and R Axis Scaling values. Each type of face can be scaled, creating sharp points extending from each face. If only one unique polygon is used for the faces, then only one Axis Scaling parameter is active. The Reset button simply returns the Axis Scaling value to its default at 100. For example, using the R Axis Scaling value, pyramid shapes can be extended from each face of a cube.

Figure 5.17 shows some results of using the Axis Scaling options. One of each family type has been created and displayed in the top row for reference. The bottom row has had an axis scaled to a value of 170. This setting causes one type of polygon face to be extended, thereby producing a new shape.

FIGURE 5.17

Hedras with extended faces, compliments of the Axis Scaling option

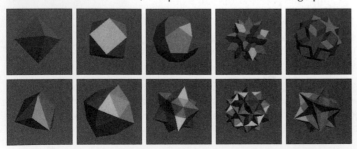

The Vertices parameter options add more vertices and edges to the center of each extended polygon. The three options are Basic, which is the default and doesn't add any new information to the Hedra; Center, which adds vertices to the center of each extended polygon; and Center and Sides, which add both center vertices and connecting edges for each face that is extended using the Axis Scaling options. With these options set, you can extend the polygon faces at your own discretion.

Way at the bottom of the Parameters rollout is the Radius value, which generally sets the size of the hedra object.

ChamferBox

A *chamfered* object is one whose edges have been smoothed out, so a ChamferBox primitive is a box with beveled edges. The parameter that determines the amount of roundness applied to an edge is *Fillet.* In many ways, this object is just a simple extension of the Box primitive.

The only additions in the Parameters rollout are two fields for controlling the Fillet dimension and the Fillet Segments. Figure 5.18 shows a ChamferBox with Fillet values of 0, 5, 10, 20, and 30 and the Smooth option turned on.

FIGURE 5.18

A ChamferBox with progressively increasing Fillet values

Cylindrical Extended Primitives

The Extended Primitives include several objects based on the Cylinder primitive that are very similar. The only real difference is the shape of the caps at either end. These four similar objects include the OilTank, Spindle, ChamferCyl, and Capsule. Figure 5.19 shows these similar objects side by side.

FIGURE 5.19

Several different cylindrical Extended Primitive objects exist, including OilTank, Spindle, ChamferCyl, and Capsule.

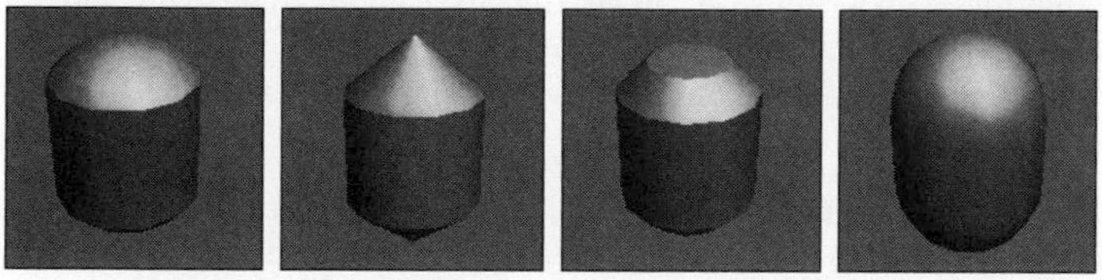

OilTank

OilTank seems like a strange name for a primitive. This object is essentially the Cylinder primitive with dome caps like you would see on a diesel truck transporting oil. The Parameters rollout includes an additional option for specifying the Cap Height. The Height value can be set to indicate the entire height of the object with the Overall option or the height to the edge of the domes using the Centers option. The only other new option is Blend, which smoothes the edges between the cylinder and the caps. All cylindrical primitives can also be sliced just like the sphere object.

Spindle

The Spindle primitive is the same as the OilTank primitive, except that the dome caps are replaced with conical caps. All other options in the Parameters rollout are identical to the OilTank primitive.

ChamferCyl

The ChamferCyl primitive is very similar to the ChamferBox primitive, but is applied to a cylinder instead of a box. The Parameters rollout includes some additional fields for handling the Fillet values.

Capsule

The Capsule primitive is yet another primitive based on the cylinder, but this time with hemispherical caps. This object resembles the OilTank primitive very closely. The only noticeable difference is in the border between the cylinder and caps.

Gengon

The Gengon primitive creates and extrudes regular polygons such as triangles, squares, and pentagons. There is even an option to Fillet (or smooth) the edges. To specify which polygon to use, enter a value in the Sides field.

Figure 5.20 shows five simple Gengons with different numbers of edges.

FIGURE 5.20

Gengon primitives are actually just extruded regular polygons.

RingWave

The RingWave primitive is a specialized primitive that you can use to create a simple gear or a sparkling sun. It consists of two circles that make up a ring. You can set the circle edges to be wavy and even fluctuate over time. You can also use RingWaves to simulate rapidly expanding gases that would result from a planetary explosion. If you're considering a Shockwave effect, then you should look into using a RingWave primitive.

The Radius setting defines the outer edge of the RingWave, and the Ring Width defines the inner edge. This ring can also have a Height. The Radial and Height Segments and the number of Sides determine the complexity of the object.

The RingWave Timing controls set the expansion values. The Start Time is the frame where the ring begins at zero, the Grow Time is the number of frames required to reach its full size, and the End Time is the frame where the RingWave object stops expanding. The No Growth option prevents the object from expanding, and it remains the same size from the Start frame to the End frame. The Grow and Stay option causes the RingWave to expand from the Start Time until the Grow Time frame is reached and remains full grown until the End Time. The Cyclic Growth begins expanding the objects until the Grow Time is reached. It then starts again from zero and expands repeatedly until the End Time is reached.

The last two sections of the Parameters rollout define how the inner and outer edges look and are animated. If the Edge Breakup option is on, then the rest of the settings are enabled. These additional settings control the number of Major and Minor Cycles, the Width Flux for these cycles, and the Crawl Time, which is the number of frames to animate.

The Surface Parameters section includes an option for creating Texture Coordinates, which are the same as mapping coordinates for applying textures. There is also an option to Smooth the surface of the object.

Figure 5.21 shows five animated frames of a RingWave object with both Inner and Outer Edge Breakup settings. Notice that the edges change over the different frames.

FIGURE 5.21

Five frames of a rapidly expanding and turbulent RingWave object

Tutorial: Creating a pie

This tutorial provides a very different recipe for creating a pie using a RingWave object. Although the RingWave object can be animated, you also can use it to create static objects such as this pie, or moving objects such as a set of gears.

To create a pie using the RingWave object, follow these steps:

1. Select Create ⇨ Extended Primitives ⇨ RingWave, and drag in the Top viewport to create a RingWave object.

2. In the Parameters rollout, set the Radius to **115**, the Ring Width to **90**, and the Height to **30**.

3. In the RingWave Timing section, select the No Growth option. Then enable the Outer Edge Breakup option, set the Major Cycles to **25**, the Width Flux to **4.0**, and the Minor Cycles to **0**.

4. Enable the Inner Edge Breakup option. Set the Major Cycles to **6**, the Width Flux to **15**, and the Minor Cycles to **25** with a Width Flux of **10**.

Figure 5.22 shows a nice pie object as good as Grandmother made. You can take this pie one step further by selecting Modifiers ⇨ Parametric Deformers ⇨ Taper to apply the Taper modifier and set the Amount to 0.1.

FIGURE 5.22

This pie object was created using the RingWave object.

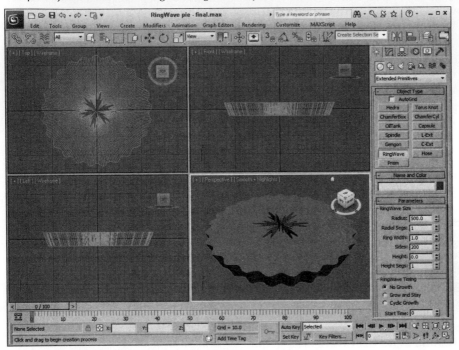

Prism

The Prism primitive is essentially an extruded triangle. If you select the Base/Apex creation method, then each of the sides of the base triangle can have a different length. With this creation method, the first click in the viewport sets one edge of the base triangle, the second click sets the opposite corner of the triangle that affects the other two edges, and the final click sets the height of the object.

The other creation method is Isosceles, which doesn't let you skew the triangle before setting the height.

Torus Knot

A Torus Knot is similar to the Torus covered earlier, except that the circular cross section follows a 3D curve instead of a simple circle. The method for creating the Torus Knot primitive is the same as that for creating the Torus. The Parameters rollout even lets you specify the base curve to be a circle instead of a knot. A knot is a standard, mathematically defined 3D curve.

Below the Radius and Segment parameters are the P and Q values. These values can be used to create wildly variant Torus Knots. The P value is a mathematical factor for computing how the knot winds about its vertical axis. The maximum value is 25, which makes the knot resemble a tightly wound spool. The Q value causes the knot to wind horizontally. It also has a maximum value of 25. Setting both values to the same number results in a simple circular ring.

Figure 5.23 shows some of the beautiful shapes that are possible by altering the P and Q values of a Torus Knot. These Torus Knots have these values: the first has P = 3, Q = 2; the second has P = 1, Q = 3; the third has P = 10, Q = 15; the fourth has P = 15, Q = 20; and the fifth has P = 25, Q = 25.

FIGURE 5.23

Various Torus Knots display the beauty of mathematics.

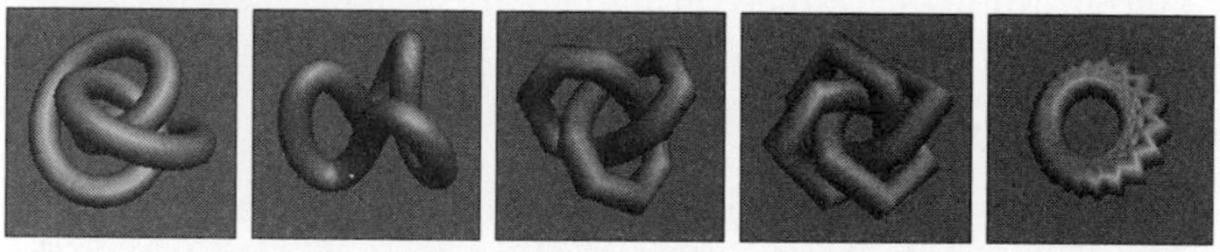

When the Base Curve is set to Circle, like those in Figure 5.23, the P and Q values become disabled, and the Warp Count and Warp Height fields become active. These fields control the number of ripples in the ring and their height. Figure 5.24 shows several possibilities. From left to right, the settings are Warp Count = 5, Warp Height = 0.5; Warp Count = 10, Warp Height = 0.5; Warp Count = 20, Warp Height = 0.5; Warp Count = 50, Warp Height = 0.5; and Warp Count = 100, Warp Height = 0.75.

FIGURE 5.24

Torus Knots with a Circle Base Curve are useful for creating impressive rings.

In addition to the Base Curve settings, you can also control several settings for the Cross Section. The Radius and Sides values determine the size of the circular cross section and the number of segments used to create the cross section. The Eccentricity value makes the circular cross section elliptical by stretching it along one of its axes. The Twist value rotates each successive cross section relative to the previous one creating a twisting look along the object. The Lumps value sets the number of lumps that appear in the Torus Knot, and the Lump Height and Offset values set the height and starting point of these lumps.

The Smooth options work just like those for the Torus object by smoothing the entire object, just the sides, or none. You can also set the U and V axis Offset and Tiling values for the mapping coordinates.

L-Ext

The L-Ext primitive stands for L-Extension. You can think of it as two rectangular boxes connected at right angles to each other. To create an L-Ext object, you need to first drag to create a rectangle that defines the overall area of the object. Next, you drag to define the Height of the object, and finally, you drag to define the width of each leg.

The Parameters rollout includes dimensions for Side and Front Lengths, Side and Front Widths, and the Height. You can also define the number of Segments for each dimension.

C-Ext

The C-Ext primitive is the same as the L-Ext primitive with an extra rectangular box. The C shape connects three rectangular boxes at right angles to each other.

The Parameters rollout includes dimensions for Side, Front, and Back Lengths and Widths, and the Height. You can also define the number of Segments for each dimension. These primitives are great if your name is Clive Logan or Carrie Lincoln. No, actually, these primitives are used to create architectural beams.

Hose

The Hose primitive is a flexible connector that can be positioned between two other objects. It acts much like a spring but has no dynamic properties. In the Hose Parameters rollout, you can specify the Hose as a Free Hose or Bound to Object Pivots. If the Free Hose option is selected, you can set the Hose Height. If the Bound to Object Pivots option is selected, then two Pick Object buttons appear for the Top and Bottom objects. Once bound to two objects, the hose stretches between the two objects when either is moved. You can also set the Tension for each bound object.

For either the Bound Hose or Free Hose, you can set the number of Segments that make up the hose; whether the flexible section is enabled; to smooth along the Sides, Segments, neither, or all; whether the hose is Renderable; and to Generate Mapping Coordinates for applying texture maps. If the flexible section is enabled, then you can set where the flexible section Starts and Ends, the number of Cycles, and its Diameter.

You can also set the Hose Shape to Round, Rectangular, or D-Section. Figure 5.25 shows a flexible hose object bound to two sphere objects.

FIGURE 5.25

The Hose object flexes between its two bound objects.

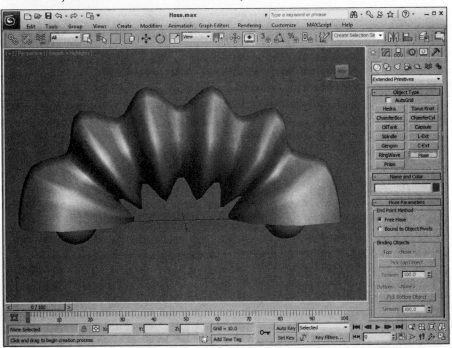

Tutorial: Creating a bendable straw

If you've ever found yourself modeling a juice box (or drinking from a juice box and wondering, "How would I model this bendable straw?"), then this tutorial is for you. The nice part about the Hose primitive is that once you've created the model, you can reposition the straw, and the bend changes as needed, just like a real straw.

To create a bendable straw, follow these steps:

1. Open the Bendable straw.max file from the Chap 05 directory on the CD.

   This file includes two Tube primitives to represent the top and bottom portions of a straw. I've oriented their pivot points so the Z-axis points toward where the Hose primitive will go.

2. Select Create ⇨ Extended Primitives ⇨ Hose, and drag in the Top viewport close to where the two straws meet. Select the Bound to Object Pivots option, click on the Pick Top Object button, and select the top Tube object. Then click on the Pick Bottom Object button, and select the bottom Tube object. This step positions the Hose object between the two Tube pieces.

3. In the Hose Parameters rollout, set the Tension for the Top object to **35** and the Tension for the bottom object to **10.0**. Set the Segments to **40**, the Starts value to **0**, the Ends value to **100**, the Cycles to **10**, and the Diameter to **24**. Make sure that the Renderable option is enabled, and enable the Round Hose option with a Diameter of **20.0**.

Figure 5.26 shows the completed bendable straw created using a Hose primitive.

FIGURE 5.26

Use the Hose primitive to connect two objects.

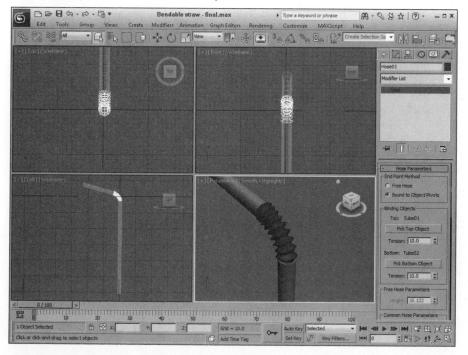

Modifying object parameters

Primitive objects provide a good starting point for many of the other modeling types. They also provide a good way to show off parameter-based modeling.

All objects have parameters. These parameters help define how the object looks. For example, consider the primitive objects. The primitive objects contained in Max are parametric. Parametric objects are mathematically defined, and you can change them by modifying their parameters. The easiest object modifications to make are simply changing these parameters. For example, a sphere with a radius of 4 can be made into a sphere with a radius of 10 by simply typing a 10 in the Radius field. The viewports display these changes automatically when you press the Enter key.

Note

When an object is first created, its parameters are displayed in the Parameters rollout of the Create panel. As long as the object remains the current object, you can modify its parameters using this rollout. After you select a different tool or object, the Parameters rollout is no longer accessible from the Create panel, but if you select the object and open the Modify panel, all the parameters can be changed for the selected object. ■

Tutorial: Filling a treasure chest with gems

I haven't found many treasure chests lately, but if I remember correctly, they are normally filled with bright, sparkling gems. In this tutorial, you'll fill the chest with a number of Hedra primitives and alter the object properties in the Modify panel to create a diverse offering of gems.

To create a treasure chest with many unique gems, follow these steps:

1. Open the Treasure chest of gems.max file from the Chap 05 directory on the CD.

   This file includes a simple treasure chest model.

2. Select Create ⇨ Extended Primitives ⇨ Hedra to open the Extended Primitives subcategory in the Create panel. At the top of the Object Type rollout, enable the AutoGrid option and select the Hedra button.

   The AutoGrid option creates all new objects on the surface of other objects.

3. Create several Hedra objects.

   The size of the objects doesn't matter at this time.

4. Open the Modify panel, and select one of the Hedra objects.

5. Alter the values in the Parameters rollout to produce a nice gem.

6. Repeat Step 5 for all Hedra objects in the chest.

Figure 5.27 shows the resulting chest with a variety of gems.

FIGURE 5.27

A treasure chest full of gems quickly created by altering object parameters

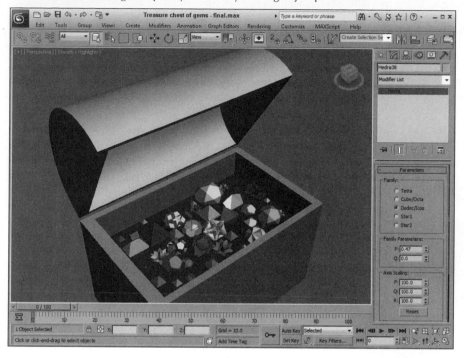

Using Architecture Primitives

If you wander about the various departments at Autodesk, you run into several groups that deal with products for visualizing architecture, including the well-known product AutoCAD. This product is used by a vast number of engineers and architects to design the layouts for building physical structures.

Along with AutoCAD is Revit, another very popular package that would be considered a close sibling to Max. AutoCAD Revit is used to create visualizations of AutoCAD data and, like Max, deals with modeling, rendering, and shading 3D objects. In fact, many of the new features found in Max were originally developed for Revit.

Using AEC Objects

Included in the features that have migrated over from the AutoCAD world are all the various architectural objects commonly found in buildings. These objects can all be found in the Create ➪ AEC Objects menu. The AEC Objects menu includes many different architecture primitives: Foliage, Railings, Walls, Doors, Stairs, and Windows.

Foliage

The Foliage category includes several different plants, all listed in the Favorite Plants rollout and shown in Figure 5.28. The available plants include a Banyan tree, Generic Palm, Scotch Pine, Yucca, Blue Spruce, American Elm, Weeping Willow, Euphorbia, Society Garlic, Big Yucca, Japanese Flowering Cherry, and Generic Oak.

Caution

The various foliage objects are large models that can quickly slow down the scene if multiple copies are added to a scene. For example, a single Banyan tree has more than 100,000 polygons. Adding several such trees to your scene can make it quite slow. ■

FIGURE 5.28

The Favorite Plants rollout shows thumbnails of the various plants.

At the bottom of the Favorite Plants rollout is a button called Plant Library that opens a dialog box where you can see the details of all the plants, including the total number of faces. The winner is the Banyan tree with 100,000 faces. Using the Parameters rollout, you can set the Height, Density, and Pruning values for each of these plants. Also, depending on the tree type, you can select to show the Leaves, Trunk, Fruit, Branches, Flowers, and Roots, and you can set the Level of Detail to Low, Medium, or High.

Tip

After some time, the Foliage set starts to feel rather limited. You can use the Help ⇨ 3ds Max on the Web ⇨ Download Vegetation menu to access the Autodesk Seek website. This site holds a repository of architecturally related objects, including a huge selection of plants and trees. ■

Railings

The Railings option lets you pick a path that the railing will follow. You can then select the number of Segments to use to create the railing. For the Top Rail, you can select to use No Railing or a Round or Square Profile and set its Depth, Width, and Height. You can also set parameters for the Lower Rails, Posts (which appear at either end), and Fencing (which are the vertical slats that support the railing).

The Lower Rails, Posts, and Fencing sections feature an icon that can be used to set the Spacing of these elements. The Spacing dialog box that opens looks like the same dialog box that is used for the Spacing Tool, where you can specify a Count, Spacing value, and Offsets.

Walls

Walls are simple, with parameters for Width and Height. You can also set the Justification to Left, Center, or Right. The nice part about creating wall objects is that you can connect several walls together just like the Line tool. For example, creating a single wall in the Top viewport extends a connected wall from the last point where you clicked that is connected to the previous wall. Right-click to exit wall creation mode. Figure 5.29 shows a room of walls created simply by clicking at the intersection points in the Top view.

FIGURE 5.29

Rooms of walls can be created simply by clicking where the corners are located.

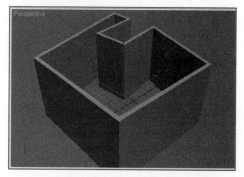

Doors

The Doors category includes three types of doors: Pivot, Sliding, and BiFold. Each of these types has its own parameters that you can set, but for each of these door types you can set its Height, Width, and Depth dimensions and the amount the door is Open.

Be aware when creating doors that Doors have two different Creation Methods—Width/Depth/Height and Width/Height/Depth. The first is the default, and it requires that the first click sets the Width, the second click sets the Depth, and the third click sets the Height. The Parameters rollout includes options to flip the direction in which the door opens. This is very handy if you position your door incorrectly.

Stairs

The Stairs category includes four types of stairs: LType, Spiral, Straight, and UType. For each type, you can select Open (single slats with no vertical backing behind the stairs), Closed (each stair includes a horizontal and vertical portion), or Box (the entire staircase is one solid object). For each type, you also can control the parameters for the Carriage (the center support that holds the stairs together), Stringers (the base boards that run along the sides of the stairs), and Railings.

The Rise section determines the overall height of the staircase. It can be set by an Overall height value, a Riser Height value (the height of each individual stair), or by a Riser Count (the total number of stairs). You also can specify the Thickness and Depth of the stairs.

Windows

The Windows category includes six types of windows: Awning, Casement, Fixed, Pivoted, Projected, and Sliding. As with doors, you can choose from two different Creation Methods. The default Creation Method creates windows with Width, then Depth, and then Height. Parameters include the Window and Frame dimensions, the Thickness of the Glazing, and Rails and Panels. You can also open all windows, except for the Fixed Window type.

Tutorial: Adding stairs to a clock tower building

I'll leave the architectural design to the architects, but for this example, you'll create a simple staircase and add it to the front of a clock tower building.

To add stairs to a building, follow these steps.

1. Open the Clock tower building.max file from the Chap 05 directory on the CD. This file includes a building with a clock tower extending from its center, but the main entrance is empty.
2. Select Create ⇨ AEC Objects ⇨ Straight Stair. Click and drag in the Top viewport from the location where the lower-left corner of the stair is located and drag to the upper-left corner of the stairs where the stairs meet the entryway into the building to set the stair's length. Then drag across to set the stairs' width and click at the opposite side of the entryway. Then drag downward in the Left viewport to set the stairs' height and click. Then right-click in the Top viewport to exit Stairs creation mode.
3. With the stairs selected, click the Select and Move (W) button in the main toolbar and drag the stairs in the Front viewport until they align with the front of one side of the entryway.
4. Open the Modify panel, and select the Box option in the Parameters rollout. Then adjust the Overall Rise value so it matches the entryway.
5. Select Tools ⇨ Mirror, and select the Copy option with an Offset of around **–140** about the X-Axis. Click OK.

Figure 5.30 shows the clock tower building with stairs.

FIGURE 5.30

The AEC Objects category makes adding structural objects like stairs easy.

Summary

Primitives are the most basic shapes and often provide a starting point for more ambitious modeling projects. The two classes of primitives—Standard and Extended—provide a host of possible objects. This chapter covered the following topics:

- The basics of creating primitives by both dragging and entering keyboard values
- How to name objects and set and change the object color
- The various creation methods for all the primitive objects
- The various primitives in both the Standard and Extended subcategories
- The possible parameters for each of the primitive objects
- Creating AEC Objects, including plants, railings, doors, and windows

Now that you know how to create objects, you can focus on selecting them after they're created, which is what the next chapter covers. You can select objects in numerous ways. Layers and setting object properties are also discussed.

Selecting Objects and Setting Object Properties

Now that you've learned how to create objects and had some practice, you've probably created more than you really need. To eliminate, move, or change the look of any objects, you first have to know how to select the object. Doing so can be tricky if the viewports are all full of objects lying on top of one another. Luckily, Max offers several selection features that make looking for a needle in a haystack easier.

Max offers many different ways to select objects. You can select by name, color, type, and even material. You also can use selection filters to make only certain types of objects selectable. And after you've found all the objects you need, you can make a selection set, which will allow you to quickly select a set of objects by name. Now where is that needle?

All objects have properties that define their physical characteristics, such as shape, radius, and smoothness, but objects also have properties that control where they are located in the scene, how they are displayed and rendered, and what their parent object is. These properties have a major impact on how you work with objects; understanding them can make objects in a scene easier to work with.

Selecting Objects

Max includes several methods for selecting objects—the easiest being simply clicking the object or dragging over it in one of the viewports. Selected objects turn white and are enclosed in brackets called *selection brackets*.

In addition to turning white and displaying selection brackets, several options allow you to mark selected objects. You can find these options in the Viewport Configuration dialog box (which you access with the

IN THIS CHAPTER

Selecting objects using toolbars and menus

Using named selection sets

Setting object properties

Hiding and freezing objects

Working with layers

Exploring the Scene Explorer

Views ⇨ Viewport Configuration menu command); they include selection brackets (keyboard short-cut, J) and edged faces (F4). Either or both of these options can be enabled, as shown in Figure 6.1. Another way to detect the selected object is that the object's axes appear at the object's pivot point. The Views ⇨ Shade Selected command turns on shading for the selected object in all viewports.

Caution

The Viewport Configuration dialog box also includes an option to Shade Selected Faces (F2), but this option shades only selected subobject faces. ■

FIGURE 6.1

Selected objects can be highlighted with selection brackets (left), edged faces (middle), or both (right).

With many objects in a scene, clicking directly on a single object, free from the others, can be difficult, but persistence can pay off. If you continue to click an object that is already selected, then the object directly behind the object you clicked is selected. For example, if you have a row of spheres lined up, you can select the third sphere by clicking three times on the first object.

Tip

In complicated scenes, finding an object is often much easier if it has a relevant name. Be sure to name your new objects using the Name and Color rollout. If a single object is selected, its name appears in the Name and Color rollout. ■

Selection filters

Before examining the selection commands in the Edit menu, I need to tell you about Selection Filters. With a complex scene that includes geometry, lights, cameras, shapes, and so on, selecting the exact object that you want can be difficult. Selection filters can simplify this task.

A selection filter specifies which types of objects can be selected. The Selection Filter drop-down list is located on the main toolbar to the left of the Select Object button. Selecting Shapes, for example, makes only shape objects available for selection. Clicking a geometry object with the Shape Selection Filter enabled does nothing.

The available filters include All, Geometry, Shapes, Lights, Cameras, Helpers, and Space Warps. If you're using Inverse Kinematics, you also can filter by Bone, IK Chain Object, and Point.

The Combos option opens the Filter Combinations dialog box, shown in Figure 6.2. From this dialog box, you can select combinations of objects to filter. These new filter combinations are added to the drop-down list. For example, to create a filter combination for lights and cameras, open the Filter Combinations dialog box, select Lights and Cameras, and click Add. The combination is listed as LC in the Current Combinations section, and the LC option is added to the drop-down list.

FIGURE 6.2

The Filter Combinations dialog box enables you to create a custom selection filter.

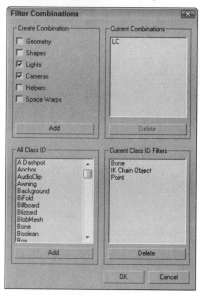

The Filter Combinations dialog box also includes a list of additional objects. Using this list, you can filter very specific object types, such as a Boolean object or a Box primitive. In fact, the Bone, IK Chain Object, and Point filters that appear in the default main toolbar drop-down list all come from this additional list.

Select buttons

On the main toolbar are several buttons used to select objects, shown in Table 6.1. The Select Object button looks like the arrow cursor. The other three buttons select and transform objects. They are Select and Move (W), Select and Rotate (E), and Select and Scale (R). These commands also are available on the quadmenu. The final selection button is the Select and Manipulate button. With this button, you can select and use special helpers such as sliders.

TABLE 6.1	

Select Buttons

Button	Description
	Select Object (Q)
	Select and Move (W)
	Select and Rotate (E)
	Select and Scale (R)
	Select and Manipulate

Cross-Reference

See Chapter 7, "Transforming Objects, Pivoting, Aligning, and Snapping," for more details on the Select and Transform buttons. ■

Selecting with the Edit menu

The Edit menu includes several convenient selection commands. The Edit ⇨ Select All (Ctrl+A) menu command does just what you would think it does: It selects all unfrozen and unhidden objects in the current scene of the type defined by the selection filter. The Edit ⇨ Select None (Ctrl+D) menu command deselects all objects. You also can simulate this command by clicking in any viewport away from all objects. The Edit ⇨ Select Invert (Ctrl+I) menu command selects all objects defined by the selection filter that are currently not selected and deselects all currently selected objects.

The Edit ⇨ Select Similar (Ctrl+Q) command selects all objects that are similar to the current selection. If multiple objects are selected, the Select Similar command selects the objects that meet the criteria for being similar to each of the selected objects. Objects are similar if they meet one of the following criteria:

- Same object type such as lights, helpers, or Space Warps
- Same primitive object such as Sphere, Box, or Hedra
- Same modeling type such as Editable Spline, Editable Poly, or Editable Patch
- Imported objects from an AutoCAD DWG file that have the same style applied
- Same applied material
- Objects existing on the same layer

Figure 6.3 shows a treasure chest of Hedra gems created in Chapter 5. With a single object selected, choosing Edit ⇨ Select Similar (Ctrl+Q) causes all Hedra primitive objects to be selected.

FIGURE 6.3

The Select Similar command selects all Hedra objects.

Select by Name

Choosing Edit ⇨ Select by ⇨ Name opens the Select From Scene dialog box, which is a version of the Scene Explorer dialog box, except that you can't change any parameters. Clicking the Select by Name button on the main toolbar, positioned to the right of the Select Object button, or pressing the keyboard shortcut, H, also opens this dialog box.

Cross-Reference

The Scene Explorer dialog box is covered in detail later in this chapter. ■

You select objects by clicking their names in the list and then clicking OK, or by simply double-clicking a single item. To pick and choose several objects, hold down the Ctrl key while selecting. Holding down the Shift key selects a range of objects.

Select by Layer

The Layer Manager lets you separate all scene objects into layers for easy selection. The Edit ⇨ Select by ⇨ Layer command opens a simple dialog box listing the defined layers and lets you select a layer. All objects in the selected layer are then selected. The Layer Manager is covered in detail later in this chapter.

Select by Color

Choosing Edit ⇨ Select by ⇨ Color lets you click a single object in any of the viewports. All objects with the same color as the one you selected are selected. Even if you already have an object of that color selected, you still must select an object of the desired color. Be aware that this is the object color, not the applied material color. This command, of course, does not work on any objects without an associated color, such as Space Warps.

Select by Region

The Edit ⇨ Selection Region command lets you select from one of two different methods for selecting objects in the viewport using the mouse. First, make sure that you're in select mode, and then click away from any of the objects and drag over the objects to select. The first method for selecting objects is Window Selection. This method selects all objects that are contained completely within the dragged outline. The Crossing Selection method selects any objects that are inside or overlapping the dragged outline. You also can access these two selection methods via the Window Selection buttons on the main toolbar—Window and Crossing, shown in Table 6.2.

Tip

If you can't decide whether to use the Crossing or Window selection method, you can select to use both. The General panel of the Preference Settings dialog box provides an option to enable Auto Window/Crossing by Direction. When this option is enabled, you can select a direction, and the Crossing selection method is used for all selections that move from that direction. The Window selection method is used for all selections that move from the opposite direction. For example, if you select Left to Right for the Crossing selection method, then moving from Left to Right uses the Crossing selection method, and selecting from Right to Left uses the Window selection method. ■

TABLE 6.2

Window Selection Buttons

Button	Description
	Window
	Crossing

You also can change the shape of the selection outline. The Selection Region button on the main toolbar to the left of the Selection Filter drop-down list includes flyout buttons for Rectangular, Circular, Fence, Lasso, and Paint Selection Regions, shown in Table 6.3.

The Rectangular selection method lets you select objects by dragging a rectangular section (from corner to corner) over a viewport. The Circular selection method selects objects within a circle that grows from the center outward. The Fence method lets you draw a polygon-shaped selection area by clicking at each corner. Simply double-click to finish the fenced selection. The Lasso method lets you draw by freehand the selection area. The Paint method lets you choose objects by painting an area. All objects covered by the paint brush area are selected.

TABLE 6.3

Shape-Shifting Selection Region Buttons

Button	Description
	Rectangular
	Circular
	Fence
	Lasso
	Paint

Pressing the Q keyboard shortcut selects the Select Object mode in the main toolbar, but repeated pressing of the Q keyboard shortcut cycles through the selection methods. Figure 6.4 shows each of the selection methods.

FIGURE 6.4

The drill's front is selected using the Rectangular, Circular, Fence, and Lasso selection methods.

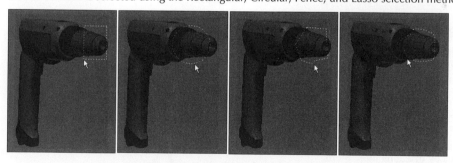

Selecting multiple objects

As you work with objects in Max, you'll sometimes want to apply a modification or transform to several objects at once. You can select multiple objects in several ways. Using the Edit ⇨ Select by ⇨ Name command, the Select by Name main toolbar button, or by pressing the H key, you can open the Select

From Scene dialog box. With the Select From Scene dialog box open, you can choose several objects from the list using the standard Ctrl and Shift keys. Holding down the Ctrl key selects or deselects multiple list items, but holding down the Shift key selects all consecutive list items between the first selected and the second selected items.

The Ctrl key also works when selecting objects in the viewport using one of the main toolbar Select buttons. You can tell whether you're in select mode by looking for a button that's highlighted yellow. If you hold down the Ctrl key and click an object, then the object is added to the current selection set. If you drag over multiple objects while holding down the Ctrl key, then all items in the dragged selection are added to the current selection set.

The Alt key deselects objects from the current selection set, which is opposite of what the Ctrl key does.

If you drag over several objects while holding down the Shift key, then the selection set is inverted. Each item that was selected is deselected, and vice versa.

Object hierarchies are established using the Link button on the main toolbar. You can select an entire hierarchy of objects by double-clicking its parent object. You also can select multiple objects within the hierarchy. When you double-click an object, any children of that object are also selected. When an object with a hierarchy is selected, the Page Up and Page Down keys select the next object up or down the hierarchy.

Another way to select multiple objects is by dragging within the viewport using the Window and Crossing Selection methods discussed previously in the "Select by Region" section.

Caution

Although the Move, Rotate, and Scale buttons may also be used to select objects, they can cause problems when selecting multiple objects. If you are selecting multiple objects with the Select and Move tool and you accidentally drag the mouse while moving to the next item, then the entire selection is moved out of place. You can use the Undo feature to return it to its original position. To prevent this from happening, use the Select Tool when selecting multiple objects. ■

Using the Paint Selection Region tool

The Paint Selection Region tool is the last flyout button under the Rectangle Selection Region button. Using this tool, you can drag a circular paint brush area over the viewports, and all objects or subobjects underneath the brush are selected.

The size of the Selection Paint brush is shown as a circle when the tool is selected and may be changed using the Paint Selection Brush Size field in the General panel of the Preference Settings dialog box. Right-clicking the Paint Selection Region button on the main toolbar automatically opens the Preference Settings dialog box. Figure 6.5 shows how the Paint Selection Region may be used to select several spheres by dragging over them.

FIGURE 6.5

The Paint Selection Region tool makes it easy to select spheres by dragging.

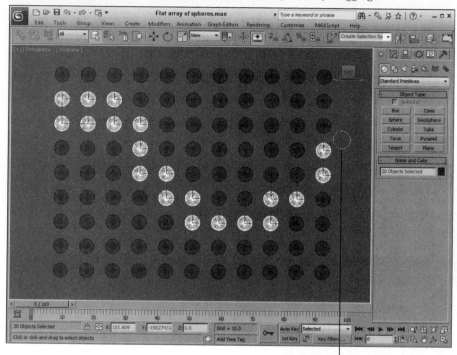

Paint Selection brush

Tutorial: Selecting objects

To practice selecting objects, you'll work with a simple model of the lion toy. When you're finished, you can throw this model to your dog for a chew toy.

To select objects, follow these steps:

1. Open the Lion toy.max scene, which you can find in the Chap 06 directory on the CD.
2. Click the Select Object button (or press the Q key), and click the lion's body in one of the viewports.

   In the Command Panel, the name for this object, lion, is displayed in the Name and Color rollout.
3. Click the Select and Move button (or press the W key), click the lion's body, and drag in the Perspective viewport to the right.

   As you can see, the lion's head and body form an object independent of the other parts of the lion object. Moving it separates it from the rest of the model's parts.
4. Choose Edit ⇨ Undo Move (or press Ctrl+Z) to piece the lion back together.

5. With the Select and Move tool still selected, drag an outline around the entire lion in the Top view to select all the lion parts, and then click and drag the entire lion again.

This time, the entire lion moves as one entity, and the name field displays Multiple Selected.

6. Open the Select Objects dialog box by clicking the Select by Name button on the main toolbar (or by pressing the H key).

All the individual parts that make up this model are listed.

7. Double-click the nose object listed in the dialog box.

The Select Objects dialog box automatically closes, and the nose object becomes selected in the viewports.

Figure 6.6 shows our lion friend with just its nose object selected. Notice that the name of the selected object in the Name and Color rollout says "nose."

FIGURE 6.6

A lion cartoon character with its white selected nose

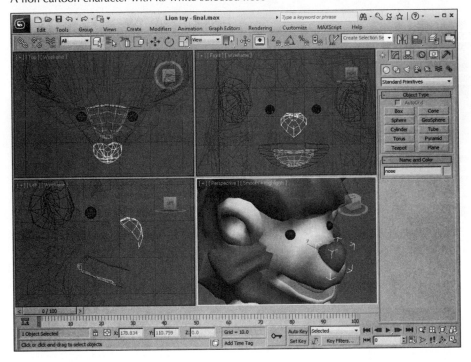

Locking selection sets

If you've finally selected the exact objects that you want to work with, you can disable any other selections using the Selection Lock toggle button on the Status Bar. (It looks like a lock.) When this button is enabled, it is colored yellow, and clicking objects in the viewports won't have any effect on the current selection. The keyboard shortcut toggle for this command is the spacebar.

Caution

In Photoshop and Illustrator, the spacebar is the keyboard shortcut to pan, but in Max it locks the current selection. If you accidentally lock the current selection, then you can't select any other objects until the lock is removed. ∎

Using named selection sets

With a group of selected objects, you can establish a selection set. Once it's established as a selection set, you can recall this group of selected objects at any time by selecting its name from the Named Selection Set drop-down list on the main toolbar or by opening the Named Selection Sets dialog box, shown in Figure 6.7.

 You can access this dialog box using the Edit Named Selection Sets button on the main toolbar or by selecting the Edit ⇨ Manage Selection Sets menu command. To establish a selection set, type a name in the Named Selection Set drop-down list toward the right end of the main toolbar or use the dialog box.

FIGURE 6.7

The Edit Named Selections dialog box lets you view and manage selection sets.

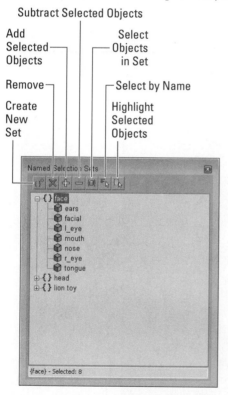

You also can create named selection sets for subobject selections. Be aware that these subobject selection sets are available only when you're in subobject edit mode and only for the currently selected object.

Editing named selections

After you've created several named selection sets, you can use the Named Selections Sets dialog box to manage the selection sets. The buttons at the top let you create and delete sets, add or remove objects from a set, and select and highlight set objects. You also can move an object between sets by dragging its name to the set name to which you want to add it. Dragging one set name onto another set name combines all the objects from both sets under the second set name. Double-clicking a set name selects all the objects in the set.

Isolating the current selection

The Tools ⇨ Isolate Selection (Alt+Q) menu command hides all objects except for the selected object. It also zooms to extents on the object in the active viewport. And it opens a simple dialog box with an Exit Isolation button in it. Clicking this button or selecting the Isolate command again exits isolation mode and displays all the objects again.

Isolate Selection mode is very convenient for working on a certain area. Figure 6.8 shows the Isolate Selection mode for a selection set that includes all elements of the lion toy's face.

FIGURE 6.8

Isolated Selection mode lets you focus on the details of the selected object.

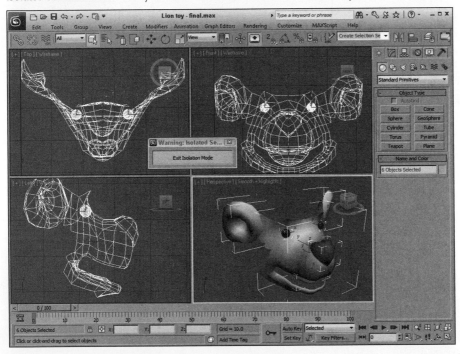

Selecting objects in other interfaces

In addition to selecting objects in the viewports, you can use many of the other interfaces and dialog boxes to select objects. For example, the Material Editor includes a button that selects all objects in a scene with the same material applied.

 The Select by Material button opens the Select Object dialog box with all objects that use the selected material highlighted.

Another way to select objects is in the Track View, which can be opened using the Graph Editors ⇨ New Track View menu command. To view all the objects, click the + sign that precedes the Objects track. You can identify the Objects track by a small, yellow cube. A hierarchy of all the objects in a scene is displayed. At the bottom left of the Track View window is the Select by Name text field. Typing an object name in this field automatically selects the object's track in the editor's window, but not in the viewport. Clicking the yellow cube icon selects the object in the viewport.

A third interface that you can use to select objects is the Schematic View, which is opened using the Graph Editors ⇨ New Schematic View menu command. It offers a hierarchical look at your scene and displays all links and relationships between objects. Each object in the Schematic View is displayed as a rectangular node.

To select an object in the viewport, find its rectangular representation in the Schematic View and simply click it. To select multiple objects in the Schematic View, you need to enable Sync Selection mode with the Select ⇨ Sync Selection command in the Schematic View menu and then drag an outline over all the rectangular nodes that you want to select.

The Schematic View also includes the Select by Name text field, just like the Curve Editor, for selecting an object by typing its name.

Cross-Reference

The Material Editor is covered in detail in Chapter 15, "Using the Slate Material Editor"; the Track View is covered in Chapter 36, "Working with the F-Curve Editor in the Track View"; and the Schematic View interface is covered in Chapter 25, "Building Complex Scenes with Containers, XRefs, and the Schematic View." ■

Setting Object Properties

After you select an object or multiple objects, you can view their object properties by choosing Edit ⇨ Object Properties. Alternatively, you can right-click the object and select Properties from the pop-up menu. Figure 6.9 shows the Object Properties dialog box. This dialog box includes four panels—General, Advanced Lighting, mental ray, and User Defined.

Viewing object information

For a single object, the General panel of the Object Properties dialog box lists details about the object in the Object Information section. These details include the object's name; color; extent distances from the origin along the X-, Y-, and Z-axes; number of vertices and faces; the object's parent; the object's Material Name; the number of children attached to the object; the object's group name if it's part of a group; and the layer on which the object can be found. All this information (except for its name and color) is for display only and cannot be changed.

FIGURE 6.9

The Object Properties dialog box displays valuable information about a selected object.

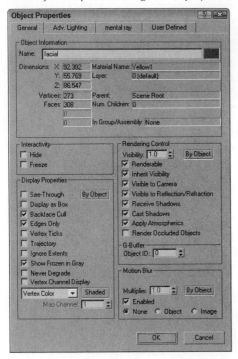

Note

The two fields under the Vertices and Faces are used only when the properties for a Shape are being displayed. These fields show the number of Shape Vertices and Shape Curves. ∎

If the properties for multiple objects are to be displayed, the Object Properties dialog box places the text "Multiple Selected" in the Name field. The properties that are in common between all these objects are displayed. With multiple objects selected, you can set their display and rendering properties all at once.

The Object Properties dialog box can be displayed for all geometric objects and shapes, as well as for lights, cameras, helpers, and Space Warps. Not all properties are available for all objects.

Cross-Reference

The Hide and Freeze options included in the Interactivity section are covered later in this chapter in the "Hiding and Freezing Objects" section. ∎

Setting display properties

Display properties don't affect how an object is rendered, only how it is displayed in the viewports. In this section, along with the Rendering Control and Motion Blur sections, are three By Object/By Layer toggle buttons. If the By Object button is displayed, then options can be set for the selected object, but if the By Layer option is enabled, then all options become disabled and the object gets its display properties from the layer settings found in the Layer Manager.

Note

You also can find and set the same Display Properties that are listed in the Object Properties dialog box in the Display Properties rollout of the Display panel in the Command Panel and in the Display Floater. ∎

The See-Through option causes shaded objects to appear transparent. This option is similar to the Visibility setting in the Rendering Control section, except that it doesn't affect the rendered image. It is only for displaying objects in the viewports. This option really doesn't help in wireframe viewports. Figure 6.10 shows the lion toy model with spheres behind it with and without this option selected.

FIGURE 6.10

The See-Through display property can make objects transparent in the viewports.

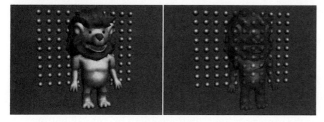

Many of these display properties can speed up or slow down the viewport refresh rates. For example, Display as Box increases the viewport update rate dramatically for complex scenes, but at the expense of any detail. This setting can be useful to see how the objects generally fit in comparison to one another. This option also can be accessed from the Viewport Configuration dialog box or from the Viewport name right-click pop-up menu, but the Object Properties dialog box lets you set this option for a single object instead of for the entire viewport.

When the Backface Cull option is enabled, it causes the faces on the backside of the object to not be displayed. Max considers the direction that each normal is pointing and doesn't display a face if its normal points away from the view. A *normal* is a vector that extends perpendicular to the face and is used to determine the orientation of individual faces. This option produces the same result of the Force 2-Sided option in the Viewport Configuration dialog box, except that it can be applied to a single object and not the entire viewport. This display option works only in wireframe viewports.

The Edges Only option displays only the edges of each object when the viewport is set to Wireframe mode. When Edges Only is not selected, a dashed line indicates the junction of individual faces.

When the Vertex subobject mode is selected for an object, all vertices for the selected object appear as blue + signs. The Vertex Ticks option displays all object vertices in this same way without requiring the Vertex subobject mode. Figure 6.11 shows the lion toy mesh with this option enabled. The Trajectory option displays the animation path that the object follows. You also can make the trajectory of the selected object appear without enabling the Trajectory option by selecting the Trajectories button in the Motion panel.

FIGURE 6.11

The Vertex Ticks option displays all vertices as small, blue tick marks.

The Trajectory option displays any animated motions as a spline path.

Cross-Reference

To learn more about using animated motion paths, see Chapter 21, "Understanding Animation and Keyframes." ■

The Ignore Extents option causes an object to be ignored when you are using the Zoom Extents button in the Viewport Navigation controls. For example, if you have a camera or light positioned at a distance from the objects in the scene, then anytime you use the Zoom Extents All button, the center objects are so small that you cannot see them because the Zoom Extents needs to include the distance light. If you set the Ignore Extent option for the camera or light, then the Zoom Extents All button zooms in on just the geometry objects.

When objects are frozen, they appear dark gray, but if the Show Frozen in Gray option is disabled, then the object appears as it normally does in the viewport. The Never Degrade option causes the object to be removed from the Adaptive Degradation settings used to maintain a given frame rate to get the animation timing right.

The Vertex Channel Display option displays the colors of any object vertices that have been assigned colors. You can select to use Vertex Color, Vertex Illumination, Vertex Alpha, Map Channel Color, or Soft Selection Color. The Shaded button causes the meshes to be shaded by the vertex colors. If the Shaded button is disabled, the object is unshaded. You can assign vertex colors only to editable meshes, editable polys, and editable patches. If the Map Channel Color option is selected, you can specify the Map Channel.

Cross-Reference

For more information about vertex colors, check out Chapter 34, "Creating Baked Textures and Normal Maps." ■

Setting rendering controls

In the Object Properties dialog box, the Rendering Controls section includes options that affect how an object is rendered.

The Visibility spinner defines a value for how opaque (nontransparent) an object is. A value of 1 makes the object completely visible. A setting of 0.1 makes the object almost transparent. The Inherit Visibility option causes an object to adopt the same visibility setting as its parent.

Tip

The Visibility option also can be animated for making objects slowly disappear. ■

The Renderable option determines whether the object is rendered. If this option isn't selected, then the rest of the options are disabled because they don't have any effect if the object isn't rendered. The Renderable option is useful if you have a complex object that takes a while to render. You can disable the renderability of the single object to quickly render the other objects in the scene.

You can use the Visible to Camera and Visible to Reflection/Refraction options to make objects invisible to the camera or to any reflections or refractions. This feature can be useful when you are test-rendering scene elements and raytraced objects.

Tip

If an object has the Visible to Camera option disabled and the Cast Shadows option enabled, then the object isn't rendered, but its shadows are. ■

The Receive Shadows and Cast Shadows options control how shadows are rendered for the selected object. The Apply Atmospherics options enable or disable rendering atmospherics. Atmospheric effects can increase the rendering time by a factor of 10, in some cases.

Cross-Reference

Atmospheric and render effects are covered in Chapter 46, "Using Atmospheric and Render Effects." ■

The Render Occluded Objects option causes the rendering engine to render all objects that are hidden behind the selected object. The hidden or occluded objects can have glows or other effects applied to them that would show up if rendered.

You use the G-Buffer Object Channel value to apply Render or Video Post effects to an object. By matching the Object Channel value to an effect ID, you can make an object receive an effect. A *g-buffer* is a temporary bit of memory used to process an image that isn't interrupted by transferring the data to the hard disk.

Cross-Reference

The Video Post interface is covered in Chapter 49, "Compositing with Render Elements and the Video Post Interface." ■

Enabling Motion Blur

You also can set Motion Blur from within the Object Properties dialog box. The Motion Blur effect causes objects that move fast (such as the Road Runner) to be blurred (which is useful in portraying speed). The render engine accomplishes this effect by rendering multiple copies of the object or image.

Cross-Reference

More information on these blur options is in Chapter 23, "Rendering a Scene and Enabling Quicksilver." ■

The Object Properties dialog box can set two different types of Motion Blur: Object and Image. Object motion blur affects only the object and is not affected by the camera movement. Image motion blur applies the effect to the entire image and is applied after rendering.

Cross-Reference

A third type of Motion Blur is called Scene Motion Blur and is available in the Video Post interface. See Chapter 49, "Compositing with Render Elements and the Video Post Interface," for information on using Scene Motion Blur. ∎

You can turn the Enabled option on and off as an animation progresses, allowing you to motion blur select sections of your animation sequence. The Multiplier value is enabled only for the Image Motion Blur type. It is used to set the length of the blur effect. The higher the Multiplier value, the longer the blurring streaks. The Motion Blur settings found in the Object Properties dialog box can be overridden by the settings in the Render Scene dialog box.

Caution

If the Motion Blur option in the Object Properties dialog box is enabled but the Motion Blur option in the Renderer panel of the Render Scene dialog box is disabled, then motion blur will not be included in the final rendered image. ∎

Using the Advanced Lighting and mental ray panels

The second and third panels in the Object Properties dialog box contain object settings for working with Advanced Lighting and the mental ray renderer. Using the settings in the Advanced Lighting panel, you can exclude an object from any Advanced Lighting calculations, set an object to cast shadows and receive illumination, and set the number of refine iterations to complete.

The mental ray panel includes options for making an object generate and/or receive caustics and global illumination.

Cross-Reference

Advanced Lighting is covered in Chapter 45, "Working with Advanced Lighting, Light Tracing, and Radiosity," and the mental ray renderer is covered in Chapter 47, "Rendering with mental ray and iray." ∎

Using the User-Defined panel

The User-Defined panel contains a simple text window. In this window, you can type any sort of information. This information is saved with the scene and can be referred to as notes about an object.

Hiding and Freezing Objects

Hidden and frozen objects cannot be selected, and as such they cannot be moved from their existing positions. This becomes convenient when you move objects around in the scene. If you have an object in a correct position, you can freeze it to prevent it from being moved accidentally or you can hide it from the viewports completely. A key difference between these modes is that frozen objects are still rendered, but hidden objects are not.

You can hide and freeze objects in several ways. You can hide or freeze objects in a scene by selecting the Hide or Freeze options in the Object Properties dialog box. You also can hide and freeze objects using the Display Floater dialog box, which you access by choosing Tools ⇨ Display Floater.

Tip

Several keyboard shortcuts can be used to hide specific objects. These shortcuts are toggles, so one press makes the objects disappear and another press makes them reappear. Object types that can be hidden with these short-cuts include cameras (Shift+C), geometry (Shift+G), grids (G), helpers (Shift+H), lights (Shift+L), particle systems (Shift+P), shapes (Shift+S), and Space Warps (Shift+W). ■

The Hide option makes the selected object in the scene invisible, and the Freeze option turns the selected object dark gray (if the Show Frozen in Gray option in the Object Properties dialog box is enabled) and doesn't allow it to be transformed or selected. You cannot select hidden objects by clicking in the viewport.

Note

When you use the Zoom Extents button to resize the viewports around the current objects, hidden objects aren't included. ■

Using the Display Floater dialog box

The Display Floater dialog box includes two tabs: Hide/Freeze and Object Level. The Hide/Freeze tab splits the dialog box into two columns, one for Hide and one for Freeze. Both columns have similar buttons that let you hide or freeze Selected or Unselected objects, By Name or By Hit. The By Name button opens the Select Objects dialog box (which is labeled Hide or Freeze Objects). The By Hit option lets you click in one of the viewports to select an object to hide or freeze. Each column also has additional buttons to unhide or unfreeze All objects, By Name, or in the case of Freeze, By Hit. You also can select an option to Hide Frozen Objects.

Note

Other places to find the same buttons found in the Display Floater are the Hide and Freeze rollouts of the Display panel of the Command Panel and in the right-click quadmenu. ■

The Object Level panel of the Display Floater lets you hide objects by category such as All Lights or Cameras. You also can view and change many of the Display Properties that are listed in the Object Properties dialog box.

Figure 6.12 shows the Hide/Freeze and Object Level panels of the Display Floater dialog box.

Using the Display panel

If you took many of the features of the Display Floater and the Object Properties dialog box and mixed them together, the result would be the Display panel. You access this panel by clicking the fifth icon from the left in the Command Panel (the icon that looks like a monitor screen).

The first rollout in the Display panel, shown in Figure 6.13, is the Display Color rollout. This rollout includes options for setting whether Wireframe and Shaded objects in the viewports are displayed using the Object Color or the Material Color.

FIGURE 6.12

The Display Floater dialog box includes two panels: Hide/Freeze and Object Level.

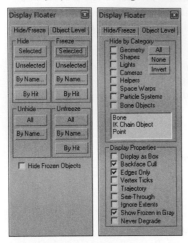

FIGURE 6.13

The Display panel includes many of the same features as the Display Floater and the Object Properties dialog box.

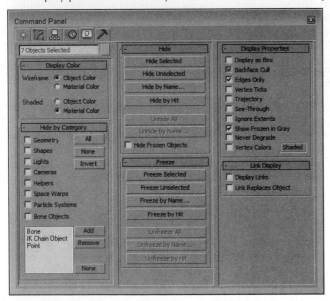

The panel also includes a Hide by Category rollout. Using this rollout, you can add new categories that will appear in the Object Level panel of the Display Floater. To add a new category, click the Add button of the Hide by Category rollout. The Add Display Filter list appears, as shown in Figure 6.14. From this list, you can choose specific object categories to add to the Hide by Category list.

FIGURE 6.14

From this dialog box, you can add new categories to the Hide by Category list.

The Display panel also includes Hide and Freeze rollouts that include the same buttons and features as the Hide/Freeze panel of the Display Floater. You also find a Display Properties rollout that is the same as the list found in the Display Floater's Object Level panel and the Object Properties dialog box.

The Link Display rollout at the bottom of the Display panel includes options for displaying links in the viewports. Links are displayed as lines that extend from the child to its parent object. Using the Link Replaces Object option, you can hide the objects in the viewport and see only the links.

Tutorial: Hidden toothbrushes

In this example, I've hidden several toothbrushes in the scene, and your task is to find them. To find the hidden objects, follow these steps:

1. Open the Toothbrushes.max scene file.

   This file appears to contain only a single toothbrush, but it really contains more. Can you find them? The toothbrush model was created by Viewpoint Datalabs. You can find it in the Chap 06 directory on the CD.

2. Locate the hidden object in the scene by opening the Display Floater (choose Tools ⇨ Display Floater).

3. In the Display Floater, select the Hide/Freeze tab. In the Unhide section, click the Name button.

   The Unhide Objects dialog box appears, which lists all the hidden objects in the scene.

4. Select the green toothbrush object from the list, and click the Unhide button.

   The Unhide Objects dialog box closes, and the hidden objects become visible again.

Note

Notice that the Display Floater is still open. That's because it's modeless. You don't need to close it to keep working. ■

5. To see all the remaining objects, click the All button in the Unhide column of the Display Floater.

Figure 6.15 shows the finished scene with all toothbrushes visible.

FIGURE 6.15

Here are toothbrushes for the whole family; just remember which color is yours.

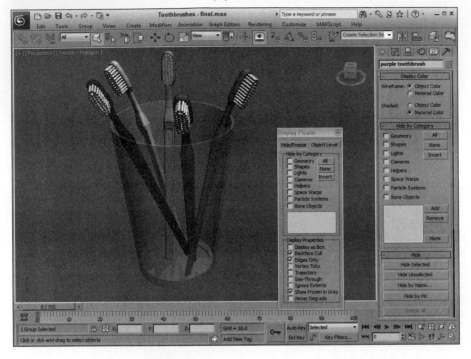

Using Layers

So what does 3ds Max have in common with a wedding cake? The answer is layers. Layers provide a way to separate scene objects into easy-to-select and easy-to-work-with groupings. These individual layers have properties that can then be turned on and off.

Cross-Reference

Animation sequences also can be split into layers using the Animation Layers. You can learn more about these layers in Chapter 35, "Using Animation Layers, Modifiers, and Complex Controllers." ■

Using the Layer Manager

You create, access, and manage layers through the Layer Manager dialog box, shown in Figure 6.16. This dialog box is a floater that can remain open as you work with objects in the viewports. You can access the Layer Manager using the Tools ⇨ Manage Layers menu command, by clicking the Layer Manager button on the main toolbar, or by clicking the same button in the Layers toolbar.

Cross-Reference

These layers are different from Animation Layers that are used to break an animation sequence into several different parts that can be blended together. Animation Layers are covered in Chapter 35, "Using Animation Layers, Modifiers, and Complex Controllers." ■

FIGURE 6.16

The Layer Manager lists all the layers and the objects contained within each layer.

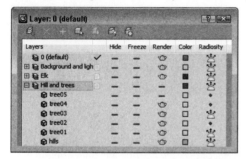

After you've set up your layers, you can control them using the Layers toolbar, shown in Figure 6.17, rather than having the Layer Manager open. You can access the Layers toolbar by right-clicking the main toolbar away from the buttons and selecting the Layers toolbar from the pop-up menu or by selecting the Customize ⇨ Show UI ⇨ Floating Toolbars menu command.

FIGURE 6.17

Use the Layers toolbar to set the active layer.

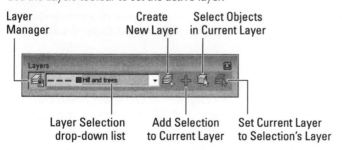

Table 6.4 lists the buttons found in the Layer Manager.

TABLE 6.4

Layer Manager Buttons

Button Icon	Name	Description
	Create New Layer	Creates a new layer that includes the selected objects
	Delete Highlighted Empty Layers	Deletes a layer if the layer is highlighted and empty
	Add Selected Objects to Highlighted Layer	Adds any selected objects to the current highlighted layer
	Select Highlighted Objects and Layers	Selects in the viewports any highlighted layers or objects
	Highlight Selected Object's Layers	Highlights the layer of the viewport's selected object in the Layer Manager
	Hide/Unhide All Layers	Toggles between hiding and unhiding all layers
	Freeze/Unfreeze All Layers	Toggles between freezing and unfreezing all layers

With the Layer Manager open, you can create new layers by clicking the Create New Layer button. This adds a new layer to the manager, names it "Layer01," and includes any selected objects as part of the layer. If you click the layer's name, you can rename it. Layer 0 is the default layer to which all objects are added, if other layers don't exist. Layer 0 cannot be renamed.

Note

Although you can rename layers in the Layer Manager, you cannot use the Layer Manager to rename objects. To rename an object from the Layer Manager, simply click the object's icon to open the Object Properties dialog box, where you can change the object's name. ■

Creating a new layer automatically makes the new layer the current layer as denoted by the check mark in the first column of the Layer Manager. All new objects that are created are automatically added to the current layer. Only one layer can be current at a time, but several layers or objects can be highlighted. To highlight a layer, click it in the Layer Manager. Highlighted layers are highlighted in yellow.

A highlighted layer can be deleted with the Delete Highlighted Empty Layer button, but only if it is not the current layer and it doesn't contain any objects.

Newly created objects are added to the current layer (the one marked with a check mark in the first column of the Layer Manager). If you forget to select the correct layer for the new objects, you can select the objects in the viewports, highlight the correct layer, and use the Add Selected Objects to Highlighted Layer button to add the objects to the correct layer.

Note

Every object can be added only to a single layer. You cannot add the same object to multiple layers. ■

The Select Highlighted Objects and Layers button selects the highlighted layers (and objects) in the viewports. This provides a way to select all the objects on a given layer. If an object in the viewports is selected, you can quickly see which layer it belongs to with the Highlight Selected Object's Layers button.

If you expand the layer name in the Layer Manager, you see a list of all the objects contained within the layer. If you click the Layer icon (to the left of the layer's name), the Layer Properties dialog box, shown in Figure 6.18, opens. Clicking the Object icon opens the Object Properties dialog box. You also can open either of these dialog boxes by right-clicking the layer name and selecting either from the pop-up menu.

FIGURE 6.18

The Layer Properties dialog box is similar to the Object Properties dialog box, but it applies to the entire layer.

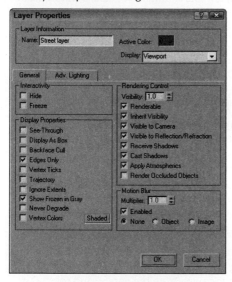

Using the layer list

The main section of the Layer Manager (and repeated in the Layers toolbar) is the layer list and its columns, which allow you to turn certain properties on and off. The properties in the columns include Hide, Freeze, Render, Color, and Radiosity. If a property is enabled, a simple icon is displayed; if disabled, a dash is displayed. If an object is set to get its property from the layer (by clicking the ByLayer button in the Object Properties dialog box), then a dot icon is displayed. Individual objects within a layer can have different properties. You can sort the column properties by clicking the column head.

You can toggle these properties on and off by clicking them. You also can set these properties in the Layers toolbar. The Hide toggle determines whether the layer's objects are visible in the viewports. The Freeze toggle makes objects on a layer unselectable. The Render toggle enables the layer's objects to be rendered. The Color toggle sets the layer color. Layer 0 is set to assign random colors and cannot be changed. The Radiosity toggle includes the layer's objects in the radiosity calculations.

The Layer Manager also includes a right-click pop-up menu that includes many of the same commands found as buttons, but a unique set of commands found in the right-click pop-up menu are the Cut and Paste commands. With these commands, you can select objects in one layer to cut and paste into another layer.

Caution

If multiple objects are selected within the Layer Manager, then right-clicking an object's name deselects all the selected objects. To maintain the current selection, right-click within the Layer Manager, away from the Layers column. ■

Tutorial: Dividing a scene into layers

As a scene begins to come together, you'll start to find that it is difficult to keep track of all the different pieces. This is where the layers interface can really help. In this example, you take a simple scene and divide it into several layers.

To divide a scene into layers, follow these steps:

1. Open the Elk on hill layers.max scene file.

   You can find it in the Chap 06 directory on the CD. This file includes an Elk model created by Viewpoint Datalabs.

2. Select Tools ⇨ Manage Layers to open the Layer Manager.

3. With no objects selected, click the Create New Layer button and name the layer **Hill and trees**. Click the Create New Layer button again, and name this layer **Elk**. Click the Create New Layer button again, and create a layer named **Background and light**. The Layer Manager now includes four layers, including layer 0.

4. In the Layer Manager, click the first column for the Elk layer to make it the current layer. With the Edit ⇨ Select All (Ctrl+A) menu command, select all objects in the scene and click the Add Selected Objects to Highlighted Layer button in the Layer Manager.

5. Expand the Elk layer by clicking the + icon to the left of its name.

   This displays all the objects within this layer.

6. Select all the trees and the hill objects by holding down the Ctrl key and clicking each object's name in the Layer Manager. Then right-click away from the names, and select Cut from the pop-up menu. Then select the Hill and trees layer, and select Paste from the right-click pop-up menu.

7. Select the background and light objects from within the Elk layer, and click the Select Highlighted Objects and Layers button. Then select the Background and light layer, and click the Add Selected Objects to Highlighted Layer button to move the background and light objects to the correct layer.

You can now switch between the layers, depending on which one you want to add objects to or work on, and you can change properties as needed. For example, to focus on the deer object, you can quickly hide the other layers using the Layer Manager.

Using the Scene Explorer

The Scene Explorer is a one-stop shop for all scene objects and display properties. It displays all the objects in the scene in a hierarchical list along with various display properties. It allows you to filter the display so you can see just what you want and customize the display so only those properties you want to see are visible. The Scene Explorer also lets you select, rename, hide, sort, freeze, link, and delete objects and change the object color.

A Scene Explorer dialog box, shown in Figure 6.19, is opened using the Tools ⇨ New Scene Explorer menu command (Alt+Ctrl+O). Each subsequent Scene Explorer view is numbered, but these individual views also can be named using the View field at the top of each Scene Explorer window. Each new or named view can be recalled with the Tools ⇨ Saved Scene Explorers menu, and the Tools ⇨ Manage Scene Explorers opens a simple dialog box where you can Load, Save, Delete, and Rename the saved views.

Note

Scene Explorer views are automatically saved and reloaded with the Max file. ∎

FIGURE 6.19

The Scene Explorer dialog box displays all scene objects and their display properties.

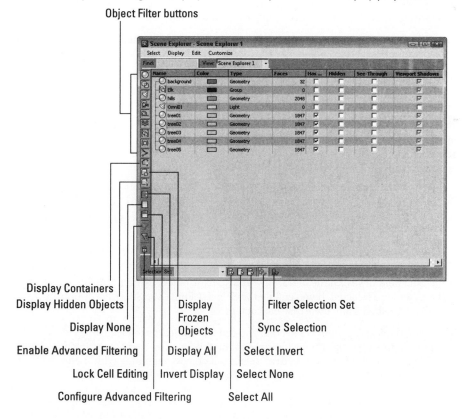

All scene objects in the Scene Explorer are listed in hierarchical order with children objects indented under their parent objects. You can expand or contract children objects by clicking the plus (+) or minus (–) icon to the left of the parent object.

Selecting and filtering objects

If you click an object in the Scene Explorer dialog box, the object row is highlighted. Holding down the Ctrl key lets you click to select multiple objects, or you can use the Shift key to select a range of adjacent objects. Selected objects also can be removed from the current selection with the Ctrl key held down.

The Select menu also includes options for selecting objects. The All (Ctrl+A), None (Ctrl+D), and Invert (Ctrl+I) menu commands work as expected, selecting all objects, deselecting all objects, and selecting the inverse of the current selection. You also can access these commands using the buttons at the bottom of the dialog box.

The Select Children (Ctrl+C) option causes all children objects to automatically be selected when the parent is selected. The Select Influences option selects all influence objects that are attached to the selected objects. An influence object is an object that controls or shapes another object. For example, when a sphere is constrained to follow an animation path, the path is an influence object to the sphere. Another example is a skin mesh being influenced by a biped rig. The Select Dependencies option selects any objects that are dependent on the selected object, such as an instance and reference.

When the Select ⇨ Sync Selection option is enabled, any objects selected in the Scene Explorer dialog box are automatically selected in the viewports also. This also works in reverse, causing any objects selected in the viewport to be selected in the Scene Explorer dialog box.

The Scene Explorer recognizes any defined Selection Sets and lets you select these sets from the drop-down list at the bottom of the interface.

The Display toolbar includes several object type icons. The yellow icons are selected and allowed to be viewed in the Scene Explorer. To filter out a specific object type, disable its icon, and then all objects of that type are no longer displayed in the list. These same commands are available in the Display ⇨ Object Types menu.

The Display menu includes some additional commands for displaying children, influences, and dependencies. You also have an option to Display in Track View. This option opens the Track View with the selected object's tracks visible.

Cross-Reference

The Track View interface is covered in more detail in Chapter 36, "Working with the F-Curve Editor in the Track View." ∎

Finding objects

You also can use the Find field to search the hierarchy for a specific object by name. All objects that match the typed characters are selected. If you enable the Select ⇨ Find Case Sensitive option, upper-case characters are distinguished from lowercase characters.

If the Select ⇨ Find Using Wildcards option is selected, you can use wildcards to locate objects. Acceptable wildcards include an asterisk (*) for multiple characters in a row and a question mark (?) for single characters. For example, an entry of **hedra*** selects all objects beginning with "hedra," regardless of the ending and **hedra?1** finds "hedra01" and "hedra11" but not "hedra02" or "hedra0001."

The Select ⇨ Find Using Regular Expressions option provides yet another way to search for specific objects. Regular expressions are commonly used in various scripting languages and require specific syntax in order to locate objects. Table 6.5 lists some common regular expression characters.

TABLE 6.5

Common Regular Expression Syntax

Character	Description	Example
[htk]	Used to define a group of search characters	Matches all objects beginning with the letters h, t, and k
Eye|light|key	Used to separate words to search for	Matches all objects beginning with eye, light, or key
\w	Used to identify any letter or number, just like the ? wildcard	Matches any number or letter
\s	Used to identify any white space	Matches any space between words, no matter the length
\d	Used to identify any single digit number	Matches any single-digit number, 0 through 9
[^geft]	Used to match all objects except for the ones inside the brackets	Matches all objects except for those that begin with g, e, f, or t
t.*1	Used to match multiple letters in between two specified characters	Matches all objects that begin with the letter t and end with the number 1

If regular expressions seem confusing, you also can search using the Advanced Search dialog box, shown in Figure 6.20. This dialog box is opened using the Select ⇨ Search or by clicking the Configure Advanced Filter button. In the Property field, you can search by Name, Type, Color, Faces, or any of the other available columns. In the Condition, the options include Starts With, Does Not Start With, Contains String, Does Not Contain String, Regular Expression Matches, and Inverse Regular Expression Matches. Multiple criteria can be added to the search list.

Editing in the Scene Explorer

Any of the display properties listed in the Scene Explorer can be enabled by simply clicking the check box to enable the property. If multiple objects are selected when a property is enabled or disabled, the same property is enabled or disabled for all the selected objects at the same time.

Note

If the Lock Cell Editing button is enabled, none of the properties can be changed. ∎

If you click the column name, you can sort all the listed objects either in descending or ascending order. Click the column name once to sort in ascending order and again to sort in descending order. You also can right-click and select the sorting order from the pop-up menu. For example, if you click the Faces column, all the objects are sorted so the objects with the smallest number of faces are listed at the top of the interface and the objects with the most faces are listed at the bottom.

FIGURE 6.20

The Advanced Search dialog box lets you select search criteria using drop-down lists.

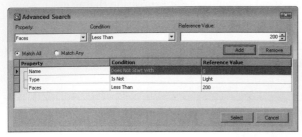

You also can rearrange the columns by dragging and dropping them to a new location. Selecting the Customize ➪ Configure Columns menu opens the Configure Columns dialog box, shown in Figure 6.21. This dialog box lists all the available remaining display property columns. To add one to the Scene Explorer, simply select it from the Configure Columns dialog box and drop it where you want it.

The Configure Columns dialog box includes a large number of properties that can be added as columns to the Scene Explorer including Revit Category, Revit Family, Revit Level, Revit Type, and Application Origin.

Tip

The width of each column can be altered by dragging on either side. To reset all column widths, right-click a column name and choose Best Fit (all columns) from the pop-up menu. ■

FIGURE 6.21

The Configure Columns dialog box holds all the display properties not currently available in the Scene Explorer.

Using the Edit menu, you also can cut, copy, and paste selected objects, called nodes. Pasting objects opens the Clone Options dialog box. The Customize menu also includes options to hide various toolbars and a choice to lay out the window using horizontal or vertical icons.

Summary

Selecting objects enables you to work with them, and Max includes many different ways to select objects. In this chapter, you've done the following:

- Learned how to use selection filters
- Selected objects with the Edit menu by Name, Layer, Color, and Region
- Selected multiple objects and used a named selection set to find the set easily
- Selected objects using other interfaces
- Accessed the Object Properties dialog box to set Display and Rendering settings for an object
- Learned how to hide and freeze objects
- Separated objects using layers
- Used the Scene Explorer dialog box

Now that you've learned how to select objects, you're ready to move them about using the transform tools, which are covered in the next chapter.

Transforming Objects, Pivoting, Aligning, and Snapping

Although a *transformation* sounds like something that would happen during the climax of a superhero film, transformation is simply the process of "repositioning" or changing an object's position, rotation, or scale. So moving an object from here to there is a transformation. Superman would be so envious.

Max includes several tools to help in the transformation of objects, including the Transform Gizmos, the Transform Type-In dialog box, and the Transform Managers.

This chapter covers each of these tools and several others that make transformations more automatic, such as the alignment, grid, and snap features.

Translating, Rotating, and Scaling Objects

So you have an object created, and it's just sitting there—sitting and waiting. Waiting for what? Waiting to be transformed. To be moved a little to the left or rotated around to show its good side or scaled down a little smaller. These actions are called transformations because they transform the object to a different state. Transformations are different from modifications. Modifications change the object's geometry, but transformations do not affect the object's geometry at all.

The three different types of transformations are translation (which is a fancy word for moving objects), rotation, and scaling.

Translating objects

The first transformation type is *translation*, or moving objects. This is identified in the various transform interfaces as the object's Position. You can move objects along any of the three axes or within the three planes. You can move objects to an absolute coordinate location or move them to a certain offset distance from their current location.

 To move objects, click the Select and Move button on the main toolbar (or press the W key), select the object to move, and drag the object in the viewport to the desired location. Translations are measured in the defined system units for the scene, which may be inches, centimeters, meters, and so on.

Rotating objects

 Rotation is the process of spinning the object about its Transform Center point. To rotate objects, click the Select and Rotate button on the main toolbar (or press the E key), select an object to rotate, and drag it in a viewport. Rotations are measured in degrees, where 360 degrees is a full rotation.

Scaling objects

Scaling increases or decreases the overall size of an object. Most scaling operations are uniform, or equal in all directions. All Scaling is done about the Transform Center point.

 To scale objects uniformly, click the Select and Uniform Scale button on the main toolbar (or press the R key), select an object to scale, and drag it in a viewport. Scalings are measured as a percentage of the original. For example, a cube scaled to a value of 200 percent is twice as big as the original.

Non-uniform scaling

 The Select and Scale button includes two flyout buttons for scaling objects non-uniformly, allowing objects to be scaled unequally in different dimensions. The two additional tools are Select and Non-Uniform Scale, and Select and Squash, shown in Table 7.1. Resizing a basketball with the Select and Non-Uniform Scale tool could result in a ball that is oblong and taller than it is wide. Scaling is done about whatever axes have been constrained (or limited) using the Restrict Axes buttons on the Axis Constraints toolbar.

Squashing objects

 The Squash option is a specialized type of non-uniform scaling. This scaling causes the constrained axis to be scaled at the same time that the opposite axes are scaled in the opposite direction. For example, if you push down on the top of a basketball by scaling the Z-axis, the sides, or the X- and Y-axes, it bulges outward. This simulates the actual results of such materials as rubber and plastic.

Tip
You can cycle through the different Scaling tools by repeatedly pressing the R key. ■

Figure 7.1 shows a basketball that has been scaled using uniform scaling, non-uniform scaling, and squash modes.

Note
It is also important to be aware of the order of things. Transformations typically happen at the top of the stack after all object properties and modifiers are applied. More on the stack is covered in Chapter 11, "Introducing Modifiers and Using the Modifier Stack." ■

These basketballs have been scaled using uniform, non-uniform, and squash modes.

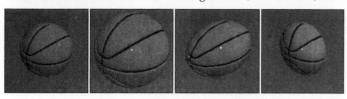

Using the transform buttons

The three transform buttons located on the main toolbar are Select and Move, Select and Rotate, and Select and Uniform Scale, as shown in Table 7.1. Using these buttons, you can select objects and transform them by dragging in one of the viewports with the mouse. You can access these buttons using three of the big four keyboard shortcuts: Q for Select Objects, W for Select and Move, E for Select and Rotate, and R for Select and Uniform Scale.

Transform Buttons

Toolbar Button	Name	Description
	Select and Move (W)	Enters move mode where clicking and dragging an object moves it.
	Select and Rotate (E)	Enters rotate mode where clicking and dragging an object rotates it.
	Select and Uniform Scale (R), Select and Non-Uniform Scale, Select and Squash	Enters scale mode where clicking and dragging an object scales it.

Working with the Transformation Tools

To help you in your transformations, you can use several tools to transform objects (and you don't even need a phone booth). These tools include the Transform Gizmos, the Transform Type-In dialog box (F12), Status Bar transform fields, and the Transform Managers.

Working with the Transform Gizmos

The Transform Gizmos appear at the center of the selected object (actually at the object's pivot point) when you click one of the transform buttons. The type of gizmo that appears depends on the transformation mode that is selected. You can choose from three different gizmos, one for each transformation type. Each gizmo includes three color-coded arrows, circles, and lines representing the X-, Y-, and Z-axes. The X-axis is colored red, the Y-axis is colored green, and the Z-axis is colored blue. Figure 7.2 shows the gizmos for each of the transformation types—move, rotate, and scale.

If the Transform Gizmo is not visible, you can enable it by choosing Views ➪ Show Transform Gizmo or by pressing the X key to toggle it on and off. You can use the – (minus) and = (equal) keys to decrease or increase the gizmo's size.

FIGURE 7.2

The Transform Gizmos let you constrain a transformation to a single axis or a plane.

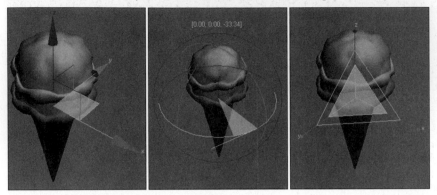

Using the interactive gizmos

Moving the cursor over the top of one of the Transform Gizmo's axes in the active viewport selects the axis, which changes to yellow. Dragging the selected axis restricts the transformation to that axis only. For example, selecting the red X-axis on the Move Gizmo and dragging moves the selected object along only the X-axis.

Note

The transformation gizmos provide an alternate (and visual) method for constraining transformations along an axis or plane. This reduces the need for the Axis Constraint buttons, which have been removed to a separate floating toolbar. Learning to use these gizmos is well worth the time. ■

The Move Gizmo

In addition to the arrows for each axis, in each corner of the Move Gizmo are two perpendicular lines for each plane. These lines let you transform along two axes simultaneously. The colors of these lines match the various colors used for the axes. For example, in the Perspective view, dragging on a red and blue corner would constrain the movement to the XZ plane. Selecting one of these lines highlights it. At the center of the Move Gizmo is a Center Box that marks the pivot point's origin.

The Rotate Gizmo

The Rotate Gizmo surrounds the selected object in a sphere. A colored line for each axis circles the surrounding sphere. As you select an axis and drag, an arc is highlighted that shows the distance of the rotation along that axis and the offset value is displayed in text above the object. Clicking the sphere away from the axes lets you rotate the selected object in all directions. Dragging on the outer gray circle causes the selected object to spin about its center.

The Scale Gizmo

The Scale Gizmo consists of two triangles and a line for each axis. Selecting and dragging the center triangle uniformly scales the entire object. Selecting a slice of the outer triangle scales the object along the adjacent two axes, and dragging on the axis lines scales the object in a non-uniform manner along a single axis.

Tip

To keep the various gizmo colors straight, simply remember that RGB = XYZ. ■

Setting gizmo preferences

For each of these gizmos, you can set the preferences using the Gizmos panel in the Preference Settings dialog box, shown in Figure 7.3, which is accessed from the Customize menu. In this panel for all gizmos, you can turn the gizmos on or off, set to Show Axis Labels, Allow Multiple Gizmos, and set the Size of the gizmo's axes. The Allow Multiple Gizmos option enables a separate gizmo for each selection set object. The Labels option labels each axis with an X, Y, or Z.

FIGURE 7.3

The Gizmos panel in the Preference Settings dialog box lets you control how the Transform Gizmos look.

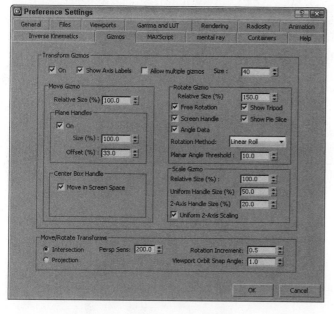

For the Move Gizmo section, you can set the Relative Size of the gizmo, which is relative to the top Size value, so a setting of 100 percent makes the size of the gizmo a full 30, and a setting of 50 percent makes it 15, or half the full Size value. You also can select to turn the plane handles on or off and set their Size and Offset values, which determine how large the highlighted planes are and where they are located relative to the center of the gizmo. A Size value of 100 percent extends the plane handles to be as long as the axis handles. You also can enable the Center Box Handle for moving in all three axes.

The Rotate Gizmo preferences also include a Relative Size value. The Free Rotation option enables you to click and drag between the axes to rotate the object freely along all axes. The Show Tripod option displays the axes tripod at the center of the object. The Screen Handle option displays an additional gray circle that surrounds all the axes. Dragging on this handle spins the object about the viewport's center. The Show Pie Slice highlights a slice along the selected axis that is as big as the offset distance. The Angle Data option displays the rotation values above the gizmo as it's being rotated.

The Gizmos panel offers three Rotation Methods: Linear Roll, Circular Crank, and Legacy R4. The Linear Roll method displays a tangent line at the source point where the rotation starts. The Circular Crank method rotates using the gizmo axes that surround the object. The Legacy R4 method uses a gizmo that looks just like the Move Gizmo that was available in the previous Max version. The Planar Angle Threshold value determines the minimum value to rotate within a plane.

The Scale Gizmo section also can set a Relative Size of the gizmo. The Uniform Handle Size value sets the size of the inner triangle, and the 2-Axis Handle Size value sets the size of the outer triangle. The Uniform 2-Axis Scaling option makes scaling with the outer triangle uniform along both axes.

The Move/Rotate Transforms section has some additional settings that control how objects move in the Perspective viewport. The Intersection and Projection options are for two different modes. The Intersection mode moves objects faster the farther they get from the center. In Projection mode, the Perspective Sensitivity value is used to set the mouse movements to the distance of the transformation. Small values result in small transformations for large mouse drags. The Rotation Increment value sets the amount of rotation that occurs for a given mouse drag distance, and the Viewport Arc Rotate Snap Angle sets where the arc snaps to.

Using the Transform Toolbox

The Transform Toolbox, shown in Figure 7.4, is a pop-up panel that offers quick access to the most common transformation operations. You can open this panel using the Edit⇨ Transform Toolbox menu command. The panel can be docked to the side of the interface by dragging it near the window border.

FIGURE 7.4

The Transform Toolbox provides quick access to the most common transformation operation.

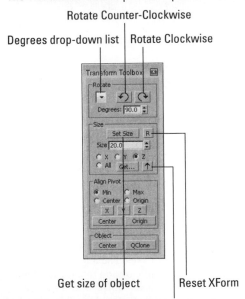

Rotate Counter-Clockwise

Degrees drop-down list | Rotate Clockwise

Get size of object   Reset XForm

Put current size in spinner

The Transform Toolbox is divided into four sections—Rotate, Size, Align Pivot, and Object. The Rotate section includes buttons for rotating the current selection by a set number of degrees in a clockwise or counterclockwise direction based on the current view. The drop-down list includes rotation values ranging from 1, 5, and 10 up to 180 and 240.

The Size section includes controls for scaling objects. The Set Size button scales the current object to the Size value along the specified axis or uniformly if the All option is selected. The R button resets the object transform by automatically applying the XForm modifier and then collapsing the stack to its base object. The Get button opens a small pop-up panel that lists the scale values for each of the axes and the Put Size button places the scale value for the selected object in the Size field for the specified axis.

The Align Pivot section changes the location of the selected object's pivot without having to open the Hierarchy panel. Using the Min, Max, Center, and Origin options, you can move the pivot's origin for the X, Y, or Z axes or you can use the Center and Origin buttons to move it for all three axes.

The Object section includes only two buttons. The Center button moves the entire object to the world's origin. The QClone button, which stands for Quick Clone, creates a duplicate object and moves it to the side of the original object.

Cross-Reference

More information on the Quick Clone feature is available in Chapter 8, "Cloning Objects and Creating Object Arrays." ■

Using the Transform Type-In dialog box

The Transform Type-In dialog box (F12) lets you input precise values for moving, rotating, and scaling objects. This command provides more exact control over the placement of objects than dragging with the mouse.

The Transform Type-In dialog box allows you to enter numerical coordinates or offsets that can be used for precise transformations. Open this dialog box by choosing Edit ⇨ Transform Type-In or by pressing the F12 key.

Tip

Right-clicking any of the transform buttons opens the Transform Type-In dialog box for the transform button that is clicked on. ■

The Transform Type-In dialog box is modeless and allows you to select new objects as needed or to switch between the various transforms. When the dialog box appears, it displays the coordinate locations for the pivot point of the current selection in the Absolute: World column.

Within the Transform Type-In dialog box are two columns. The first column displays the current Absolute coordinates. Updating these coordinates transforms the selected object in the viewport. The second column displays the Offset values. These values are all set to 0.0 when the dialog box is first opened, but changing these values transforms the object along the designated axis by the entered value. Figure 7.5 shows the Transform Type-In dialog box for the Move Transform.

Note

The name of this dialog box changes depending on the type of transformation taking place and the coordinate system. If the Select and Move button is selected along with the world coordinate system, the Transform Type-In dialog box is labeled Move Transform Type-In, and the column titles indicate the coordinate system. ■

FIGURE 7.5

The Transform Type-In dialog box displays the current Absolute coordinates and Offset values.

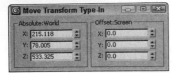

Using the status bar Type-In fields

The status bar includes three fields labeled X, Y, and Z for displaying transformation coordinates. When you move, rotate, or scale an object, the X, Y, and Z offset values appear in these fields. The values depend on the type of transformation taking place. Translation shows the unit distances, rotation displays the angle in degrees, and scaling shows a percentage value of the original size.

When you click the Select Objects button, these fields show the absolute position of the cursor in world coordinates based on the active viewport.

You also can use these fields to enter values, as with the Transform Type-In dialog box. The type of transform depends on which transform button you select. The values that you enter can be either absolute coordinates or offset values, depending on the setting of the Transform Type-In toggle button that appears to the left of the transform fields. This toggle button lets you switch between Absolute and Offset modes, as shown in Table 7.2.

Tip

If you right-click any of these fields, a pop-up menu appears where you can cut, copy, or paste the current value. ■

TABLE 7.2

Absolute/Offset Buttons

Button	Description
⊕	Absolute
⊗	Offset

Understanding the Transform Managers

To keep track of the position of every object in a scene, internally Max records the position of the object's vertices in reference to a Universal Coordinate System (UCS). This coordinate system defines vertex position using the X, Y, and Z coordinates from the scene's origin.

However, even though Max uses the UCS to internally keep track of all the points, this isn't always the easiest way to reference the position of an object. Imagine a train with several cars. For each individual train car, it is often easier to describe its position as an offset from the car in front of it.

The Transform Managers are three types of controls that help you define the system about which objects are transformed. These controls, found on the main toolbar and on the Axis Constraints toolbar, directly affect your transformations. They include the following:

- **Reference Coordinate System:** Defines the coordinate system about which the transformations take place.

- **Transform Center settings:** The Pivot Point Center, the Selection Center, and the Transform Coordinate Center. These settings specify the center about which the transformations take place.

- **Axis Constraint settings:** Allow the transformation to happen using only one axis or plane. These buttons are on the Axis Constraints toolbar.

Understanding reference coordinate systems

Max supports several reference coordinate systems based on the UCS, and knowing which reference coordinate system you are working with as you transform an object is important. Using the wrong reference coordinate system can produce unexpected transformations.

Within the viewports, the UCS coordinates are displayed as a set of coordinates in the lower-left corner of the viewport, and the Transform Gizmo is oriented with respect to the reference coordinate system.

To understand the concept of reference coordinate systems, imagine that you're visiting the Grand Canyon and are standing precariously on the edge of a lookout. To nervous onlookers calling the park rangers, the description of your position varies from viewpoint to viewpoint. A person standing by you would say you are next to him. A person on the other side of the canyon would say that you're across from her. A person at the floor of the canyon would say you're above him. And a person in an airplane would describe you as being on the east side of the canyon. Each person has a different viewpoint of you (the object), even though you have not moved.

Max recognizes the following reference coordinate systems:

- **View Coordinate System:** A reference coordinate system based on the viewports; X points right, Y points up, and Z points out of the screen (toward you). The views are fixed, making this perhaps the most intuitive coordinate system to work with.

- **Screen Coordinate System:** Identical to the View Coordinate System, except the active viewport determines the coordinate system axes, whereas the inactive viewports show the axes as defined by the active viewport.

- **World Coordinate System:** Specifies X pointing to the right, Z pointing up, and Y pointing into the screen (away from you). The coordinate axes remain fixed regardless of any transformations applied to an object. For Max, this system matches the UCS.

- **Parent Coordinate System:** Uses the reference coordinate system applied to a linked object's parent and maintains consistency between hierarchical transformations. If an object doesn't have a parent, then the world is its parent and the system works the same as the World Coordinate System.

- **Local Coordinate System:** Sets the coordinate system based on the selected object. The axes are located at the pivot point for the object. You can reorient and move the pivot point using the Pivot button in the Hierarchy panel.

- **Gimbal Coordinate System:** Provides interactive feedback for objects using the Euler XYZ controller. If the object doesn't use the Euler XYZ controller, then this coordinate system works just like the World Coordinate System.

- **Grid Coordinate System:** Uses the coordinate system for the active grid.
- **Working Coordinate System:** Lets you transform the selected object about the scene's Working Pivot as defined in the Hierarchy panel.
- **Pick Coordinate System:** Lets you select an object about which to transform. The Coordinate System list keeps the last four picked objects as coordinate system options.

All transforms occur relative to the current reference coordinate system as selected in the Referenced Coordinate System drop-down list found on the main toolbar.

Each of the three basic transforms can have a different coordinate system specified, or you can set it to change uniformly when a new coordinate system is selected. To do this, open the General panel in the Preference Settings dialog box and select the Constant option in the Reference Coordinate System section.

Using a transform center

All transforms are done about a center point. When transforming an object, you must understand what the object's current center point is, as well as the coordinate system in which you're working.

The Transform Center flyout consists of three buttons: Use Pivot Point Center, Use Selection Center, and Use Transform Coordinate Center, which are shown in Table 7.3. Each of these buttons alters how the transformations are done. The origin of the Transform Gizmo is always positioned at the center point specified by these buttons.

TABLE 7.3

Transform Center Buttons

Button	Description
	Use Pivot Point Center
	Use Selection Center
	Use Transform Coordinate Center

Pivot Point Center

Pivot points are typically set to the center of an object when the object is first created, but they can be relocated anywhere within the scene including outside of the object. Relocating the pivot point allows you to change the point about which objects are rotated. For example, if you have a car model that you want to position along an incline, moving the pivot point to the bottom of one of the tires allows you to easily line up the car with the incline.

If you select the Use Pivot Point Center button, then the Select and Rotate tool rotates about the pivot point for the selected object, which can be located anywhere in the scene.

Note
Pivot points are discussed in detail in the next section. ∎

Selection Center

The Use Selection Center button sets the transform center to the center of the selected object or objects regardless of the individual object's pivot point. If multiple objects are selected, then the center is computed to be in the middle of a bounding box that surrounds all the objects.

Transform Coordinate Center

The Transform Coordinate Center button uses the center of the Local Coordinate System. If the View Coordinate System is selected, then all objects are transformed about the center of the viewport grid. If an object is selected as the coordinate system using the Pick option, then all transformations are transformed about that object's center.

When you select the Local Coordinate System, the Use Transform Center button is ignored and objects are transformed about their local axes. If you select multiple objects, then they all transform individually about their local axes. Grouped objects transform about the group axes.

For example, the default pivot point for a Cylinder object is in the middle of the cylinder's base, so if the Transform Center is set to the Use Pivot Point option, then the cylinder rotates about its base pivot point. If the Use Selection Center option is selected, then the cylinder rotates about its center point. If the Use Transform Coordinate Center option is selected for the View Coordinate System, then the cylinder is rotated about the grid origin.

Figure 7.6 shows a simple cylinder object in the Left viewport using the different transform center modes. The left image shows the Pivot Point Center mode, the middle image shows the Selection Center mode with both objects selected, and the right image shows the Transform Coordinate Center mode. For each mode, notice that the Rotate Gizmo is located at different locations.

FIGURE 7.6

The Rotate Gizmo is located in different places, depending on the selected Transform Center mode.

Selecting Axis Constraints

Three-dimensional space consists of three basic directions defined by three axes: X, Y, and Z. If you were to stand on each axis and look at a scene, you would see three separate planes: the XY plane, the YZ plane, and the ZX plane. These planes show only two dimensions at a time and restrict any transformations to the two axes. These planes are visible from the Top, Left, and Front viewports.

By default, the Top, Left, and Front viewports show only a single plane and thereby restrict transformations to that single plane. The Top view constrains movement to the XY plane, the Left or Right side view constrains movement to the YZ plane, and the Front view constrains movement to the ZX plane. This setting is adequate for most modeling purposes, but sometimes you might need to limit the transformations in all the viewports to a single plane. In Max, you can restrict movement to specific transform axes using the Restrict Axes buttons in the Axis Constraints toolbar. You access this toolbar, shown in Figure 7.7, by right-clicking the main toolbar (away from the buttons) and selecting Axis Constraints options from the pop-up menu.

FIGURE 7.7

The Axis Constraints toolbar includes buttons for restricting transformations to a single axis or plane.

The first four buttons on this toolbar are Restrict axes buttons: Restrict to X (F5); Restrict to Y (F6); Restrict to Z (F7); and the flyout buttons, Restrict to XY, YZ, and ZX Plane (F8). The last button is the Snaps Use Axis Constraints toggle button. The effect of selecting one of the Restrict axes buttons is based on the selected coordinate system. For example, if you click the Restrict to X button and the reference coordinate system is set to View, then the object always transforms to the right because, in the View Coordinate System, the X-axis is always to the right. If you click the Restrict to X button and the coordinate system is set to Local, the axes are attached to the object, so transformations along the X-axis are consistent in all viewports (with this setting, the object does not move in the Left view because it shows only the YZ plane).

Caution

If the axis constraints don't seem to be working, check the Preference Settings dialog box and look at the General panel to make sure that the Reference Coordinate System option is set to Constant. ■

Additionally, you can restrict movement to a single plane with the Restrict to Plane flyouts consisting of Restrict to XY, Restrict to YZ, and Restrict to ZX. (Use the F8 key to cycle quickly through the various planes.)

Note

If the Transform Gizmo is enabled, then the axis or plane that is selected in the Axis Constraints toolbar initially is displayed in yellow. If you transform an object using a Transform Gizmo, then the respective Axis Constraints toolbar button is selected after you complete the transform. ■

Locking axes transformations

To lock an object's transformation axes on a more permanent basis, go to the Command Panel and select the Hierarchy tab. Click the Link Info button to open the Locks rollout, shown in Figure 7.8. The rollout displays each axis for the three types of transformations: Move, Rotate, and Scale. Make sure that the object is selected, and then click the transformation axes that you want to lock. Be aware that if all Move axes are selected, you won't be able to move the object until you deselect the axes.

Note

Another option is to use the Display floater to freeze the object. ■

Locking axes is helpful if you want to prevent accidental scaling of an object or restrict a vehicle's movement to a plane that makes up a road.

FIGURE 7.8

The Locks rollout can prevent any transforms along an axis.

The Locks rollout displays unselected X, Y, and Z check boxes for the Move, Rotate, and Scale transformations. By selecting the check boxes, you limit the axes about which the object can be transformed. For example, if you check the X and Y boxes under the Move transformation, the object can move only in the Z direction of the Local Coordinate System.

Note

These locks work regardless of the axis constraint settings. ∎

Tutorial: Landing a spaceship in port

Transformations are the most basic object manipulation that you will do and probably the most common. This tutorial includes a spaceship object and a spaceport. The goal is to position the spaceship on the landing pad of the spaceport, but it is too big and in the wrong spot. With a few clever transformations, you'll be set.

To transform a spaceship to land in a spaceport, follow these steps:

1. Open the Transforming spaceship.max file from the Chap 07 directory on the CD.
2. To prevent any extraneous movements of the spaceport, select the spaceport by clicking it. Open the Hierarchy panel, and click the Link Info button. Then in the Locks rollout, select all nine boxes to restrict all transformations so that that spaceport won't be accidentally moved.
3. To position the spaceship over the landing platform, select the spaceship object and click the Select and Move button in the main toolbar (or press the W key). The Move Gizmo appears in the center of the spaceship object. If you don't see the Move Gizmo, press the X key. Make sure that the Reference Coordinate System is set to View and that the Use Selection Center option is enabled. Right-click the Left viewport to make it active, select the red X-axis line of the gizmo, and drag to the right until the center of the spaceship is over the landing pad.
4. Right-click the Front viewport, and drag the red X-axis gizmo line to the left to line up the spaceship with the center of the landing pad.
5. Click the Select and Uniform Scale button (or press the R key). Place the cursor over the center gizmo triangle, and drag downward until the spaceship fits within the landing pad.

6. Click the Select and Move button again (or press the W key), and drag the green Y-axis gizmo line downward in the Front viewport to move the spaceship toward the landing pad.

7. Click the Select and Rotate button (or press the E key). Right-click the Top viewport, and drag the blue Z-axis gizmo circle downward to rotate the spaceship clockwise so that its front end points away from the buildings.

Figure 7.9 shows the spaceship correctly positioned.

FIGURE 7.9

Transformation buttons and the Transform Gizmos were used to position this spaceship.

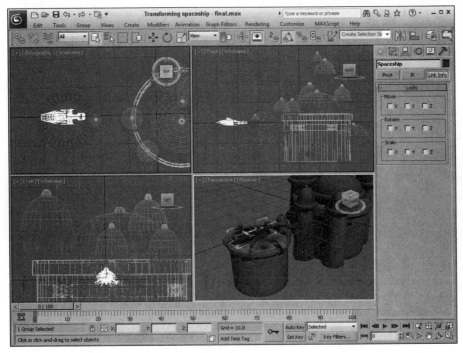

Using Pivot Points

An object's pivot point is the center about which the object is rotated and scaled and about which most modifiers are applied. Pivot points are created by default when an object is created and are usually created at the center or base of an object. You can move and orient a pivot point in any direction, but repositioning the pivot cannot be animated. Pivot points exist for all objects, whether or not they are part of a hierarchy.

Caution
Try to set your pivot points before animating any objects in your scene. If you relocate the pivot point after animation keys have been placed, all transformations are modified to use the new pivot point. ■

Positioning pivot points

To move and orient a pivot point, open the Hierarchy panel in the Command Panel and click the Pivot button. At the top of the Adjust Pivot rollout are three buttons; each button represents a different mode. The Affect Pivot Only mode makes the transformation buttons affect only the pivot point of the current selection. The object does not move. The Affect Object Only mode causes the object to be transformed, but not the pivot point. The Affect Hierarchy Only mode allows an object's links to be moved.

The pivot point is easily identified as the place where the Transform Gizmo is located when the object is selected, as shown in Figure 7.10.

FIGURE 7.10

The Transform Gizmo is located at the object's pivot point.

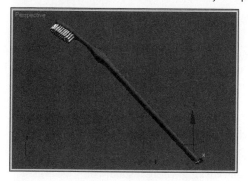

Note

Using the Scale transformation while one of these modes is selected alters the selected object but has no effect on the pivot point or the link. ■

Aligning pivot points

Below the mode buttons are three more buttons that are used to align the pivot points. These buttons are active only when a mode is selected. These buttons are Center to Object/Pivot, Align to Object/Pivot, and Align to World. The first two buttons switch between Object and Pivot, depending on the mode selected. You may select only one mode at a time. The button turns light blue when selected.

The Center to Object button moves the pivot point so that it is aligned with the object center, and the Center to Pivot button moves the object so it is centered on its own pivot point. The Align to Object/Pivot button rotates the object or pivot point until the object's Local Coordinate System and the pivot point are aligned. The Align to World button rotates either the object or the pivot to the World Coordinate System. For example, if the Affect Object Only mode is selected and the object is separated from the pivot point, clicking the Center to Pivot button moves the object so that its center is on the pivot point.

Under these three alignment buttons is another button labeled Reset Pivot, which you use to reset the pivot point to its original location.

Using the Working Pivot

Underneath the Adjust Pivot rollout is the Working Pivot rollout. Working Pivots are handy if you want to position an object using a temporary pivot without having to change the default object pivot. To position a Working Pivot, click the Edit Working Pivot button. This enters a mode just like the Affect Pivot Only button described previously, except it works with the working pivot.

After the Working Pivot is in place, you can select to use it instead of the object pivot by clicking the Use Working Pivot button. The Working Pivot stays active until you disable it in the Hierarchy panel. The Working Pivot works for all objects in the scene. When the Working Pivot is active, reminder text "USE WP" appears in all the viewports under the viewport name; when the Edit Working Pivot mode is enabled, this text reads, "EDIT WP."

Tip

You can quickly enable the Working Pivot by selecting the Working option from the Reference Coordinate System drop-down list in the main toolbar. ■

The Working Pivot rollout includes several buttons to help position the Working Pivot. The Align to View button reorients the Working Pivot to the current view. The Reset button moves the Working Pivot to the object pivot location of the selected object or to the view center if no object is selected.

Note

There is only one working pivot that you can use, but it can be used by any selected object. ■

The View button enters a mode identified by "EDIT WP" in the viewports that lets you place the Working Pivot anywhere in the current viewport by simply clicking where it should be. This is great for visually eyeballing the Working Pivots location. The Surface button (also identified by the EDIT WP text in the viewport) enters a mode where you can position the Working Pivot on the surface of an object by interactively dragging the cursor over the object surface. The cursor automatically reorients itself to be aligned with the surface normal. If the Align to View option is selected, then the Working Pivot is automatically aligned to the current view.

Transform adjustments

The Hierarchy panel of the Command Panel includes another useful rollout labeled Adjust Transform. This rollout includes another mode that you can use with hierarchies of objects. Clicking the Don't Affect Children button places you in a mode where any transformations of a linked hierarchy don't affect the children. Typically, transformations are applied to all linked children of a hierarchy, but this mode disables that.

The Adjust Transform rollout also includes two buttons that allow you to reset the Local Coordinate System and scale percentage. These buttons set the current orientation of an object as the World coordinate or as the 100 percent standard. For example, if you select an object, move it 30 units to the left, and scale it to 200 percent, these values are displayed in the coordinate fields on the status bar. Clicking the Reset Transform and Reset Scale buttons resets these values to 0 and 100 percent.

You use the Reset Scale button to reset the scale values for an object that has been scaled using non-uniform scaling. Non-uniform scaling can cause problems for child objects that inherit this type of scaling, such as shortening the links. The Reset Scale button can remedy these problems by resetting the parent's scaling values. When the scale is reset, you won't see a visible change to the object, but if you open the Scale Transform Type-In dialog box while the scale is being reset, you see the absolute local values being set back to 100 each.

Tip

If you are using an object that has been non-uniformly scaled, using Reset Scale before the item is linked saves you some headaches if you plan on using modifiers. ■

Using the Reset XForm utility

You also can reset transform values using the Reset XForm utility. To use this utility, open the Utility panel and click the Reset XForm button, which is one of the default buttons. The benefit of this utility is that you can reset the transform values for multiple objects simultaneously. This happens by applying the XForm modifier to the objects. The rollout for this utility includes only a single button labeled Reset Selected.

Tutorial: A bee buzzing about a flower

By adjusting an object's pivot point, you can control how the object is transformed about the scene. In this example, you animate a bee's flapping wings by repositioning the wings' pivot points. You then reposition the pivot point for the entire bee so it can rotate about the flower object.

To control how a bee rotates about a flower, follow these steps:

1. Open the Buzzing bee.max file from the Chap 07 directory on the CD.

   This file includes a bee created from primitives and a flower model created by Zygote Media.

2. Click the bee object to select it, and press Z to zoom in on it in all viewports. Click the right wing, open the Hierarchy panel, and click the Affect Pivot Only button. This displays the pivot point in the center of the wing oriented to the wing surface. Select the Local coordinate system from the list in the main toolbar. This orients the Transform Gizmo to match the pivot's orientation. Drag the wing's pivot point along its X-axis to the place where the wing contacts the body object. Then disable the Affect Pivot Only button. Then select and repeat this step for the left wing.

3. Click the Auto Key button (or press N) to enable animate mode, and drag the Time Slider to frame 1. Then, with the Select and Rotate button (E), rotate the wing about its Z-axis until it is almost vertical in the Front viewport. Notice how the wing rotates about its new pivot point. Then drag the Time Slider to frame 2, and rotate the wing back to its original position. Click the Auto Key button again (N) to disable key mode.

4. If you want to make these rotations repeat throughout the animation using the Track View, right-click the wing object and select Curve Editor in the pop-up quadmenu that appears. This opens a Track View with the Rotation tracks selected. In the Track View, select Controller ⇨ Out-of-Range Types to open the Param Out-of-Range Types dialog box, select the Loop option, and click OK. Then close the Track View.

Cross-Reference

Working with the Track View is beyond the scope of this chapter, but you can find more information on the Track View in Chapter 37, "Working with the F-Curve Editor in the Track View." ■

5. Repeat Steps 3 and 4 for the second wing object. Press the Play Animation button to see both wings flap for the entire animation.

6. Select all parts that make up the bee in the Top viewport, select Group ⇨ Group, and name the object **bee**. Then select the bee and the flower in the Left viewport, and press Z to zoom in on them.

7. With the bee group selected, click the Affect Pivot Only button in the Hierarchy panel and move the pivot point to the center of the flower in the Front viewport. Click the Affect Pivot Only button again to disable it.

Note

If you don't want to move the object pivot in Step 7, you can use the Working Pivot to rotate the bee around the flower, or you could select the Pick coordinate system and select the flower. ■

8. Enable the Auto Key button (N) again, and drag to frame 35. With the Select and Rotate button (E), rotate the bee in the Top viewport a third of the way around the flower. Drag the Time Slider to frame 70, and rotate the bee another third of the way. With the Time Slider at frame 100, complete the rotation. Click the Auto Key button again to display key mode.

9. Click the Play button (/) to see the final rotating bee.

Figure 7.11 shows the bee as it moves around the flower where its pivot point is located.

FIGURE 7.11

By moving the pivot point of the bee, you can control how it spins about the flower.

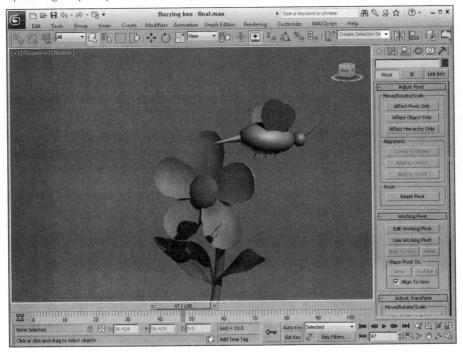

Using the Align Commands

The Align commands are an easy way to automatically transform objects. You can use these commands to line up object centers or edges, align normals and highlights, align to views and grids, and even line up cameras.

Aligning objects

Any object that you can transform, you can align, including lights, cameras, and Space Warps. After selecting the object to be aligned, click the Align flyout button on the main toolbar or choose Tools ⇨ Align ⇨ Align (or press Alt+A). The cursor changes to the Align icon. Now, click a target object with which you want to align all the selected objects. Clicking the target object opens the Align Selection dialog box with the target object's name displayed in the dialog box's title, as shown in Figure 7.12.

FIGURE 7.12

The Align Selection dialog box can align objects along any axes by their Minimum, Center, Pivot, or Maximum points.

The Align Selection dialog box includes settings for the X, Y, and Z positions to line up the Minimum, Center, Pivot Point, or Maximum dimensions for the selected or target object's bounding box. As you change the settings in the dialog box, the objects reposition themselves, but the actual transformations don't take place until you click Apply or OK.

Cross-Reference

Another way to align objects is with the Clone and Align tool, which is covered in Chapter 8, "Cloning Objects and Creating Object Arrays." ∎

Using the Quick Align tool

The first flyout tool under the Align tool in the main toolbar (and in the Tools menu) is the Quick Align tool (Shift+A). This tool aligns the pivot points of the selected object with the object that you click without opening a separate dialog box. This is much more helpful than the Align tool, which causes a separate dialog box to open.

Aligning normals

You can use the Normal Align command to line up points of the surface of two objects. A Normal vector is a projected line that extends from the center of a polygon face exactly perpendicular to the surface. When two Normal vectors are aligned, the objects are perfectly adjacent to one another. If the two objects are spheres, then they touch at only one point.

To align normals, you need to first select the object to move (this is the source object). Then choose Tools ⇨ Align ⇨ Normal Align or click the Normal Align flyout button under the Align button on the main toolbar (or press Alt+N). The cursor changes to the Normal Align icon. Drag the cursor across the surface of the source object, and a blue arrow pointing out from the face center appears. Release the mouse when you've correctly pinpointed the position to align.

Next, click the target object, and drag the mouse to locate the target object's align point. This is displayed as a green arrow. When you release the mouse, the source object moves to align the two points and the Normal Align dialog box appears, as shown in Figure 7.13.

FIGURE 7.13

The Normal Align dialog box allows you to define offset values when aligning normals.

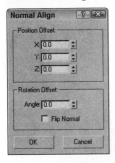

When the objects are aligned, the two points match up exactly. The Normal Align dialog box lets you specify offset values that you can use to keep a distance between the two objects. You also can specify an Angle Offset, which is used to deviate the parallelism of the normals. The Flip Normal option aligns the objects so that their selected normals point in the same direction.

Objects without any faces, like Point Helper objects and Space Warps, use a vector between the origin and the Z-axis for normal alignment.

Tutorial: Aligning a kissing couple

Aligning normals positions two object faces directly opposite one another, so what better way to practice this tool than to align two faces?

To connect the kissing couple using the Normal Align command, follow these steps:

1. Open the Kissing couple.max file from the Chap 07 directory on the CD.

   This file includes two extruded shapes of a boy and a girl. The extruded shapes give you flat faces that are easy to align.

2. Select the girl shape, and choose the Tools ⇨ Align ⇨ Normal Align menu command (or press Alt+N). Then click and drag the cursor over the extruded shape until the blue vector points out from the front of the lips, as shown in Figure 7.14.

3. Then click and drag the cursor over the boy shape until the green vector points out from the front of the lips. This vector pointing out from the face is the surface normal. Then click and release the mouse, and the Normal Align dialog box appears. Enter a value of **5** in the Z-Axis Offset field, and click OK.

Figure 7.14 shows the resulting couple with normal aligned faces.

FIGURE 7.14

Using the Normal Align feature, you can align object faces.

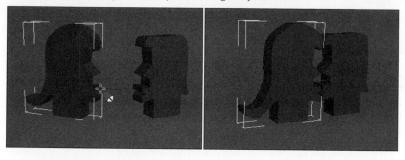

Cross-Reference

In the Align button flyout are two other common ways to align objects: Align Camera and Place Highlight (Ctrl+H). To learn about these features, see Chapter 19, "Configuring and Aiming Cameras," and Chapter 20, "Using Lights and Basic Lighting Techniques," respectively. ■

Aligning to a view

The Align to View command provides an easy and quick way to reposition objects to one of the axes. To use this command, select an object and choose Tools ⇨ Align ⇨ Align to View. The Align to View dialog box appears, as shown in Figure 7.15. Changing the settings in this dialog box displays the results in the viewports. You can use the Flip command for altering the direction of the object points. If no object is selected, then the Align to View command cannot be used.

FIGURE 7.15

The Align to View dialog box is a quick way to line up objects with the axes.

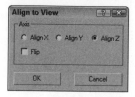

The Align to View command is especially useful for fixing the orientation of objects when you create them in the wrong view. All alignments are completed relative to the object's Local Coordinate System. If several objects are selected, each object is reoriented according to its Local Coordinate System.

Note

Using the Align to View command on symmetrical objects like spheres doesn't produce any noticeable difference in the viewports. ■

Using Grids

When Max is started, the one element that is visible is the Home Grid. This grid is there to give you a reference point for creating objects in 3D space. At the center of each grid are two darker lines. These lines meet at the origin point for the World Coordinate System where the coordinates for X, Y, and Z are all 0.0. This point is where all objects are placed by default.

In addition to the Home Grid, you can create and place new grids in the scene. These grids are not rendered, but you can use them to help you locate and align objects in 3D space.

The Home Grid

You can turn the Home Grid on and off by choosing Tools ➪ Grid and Snaps ➪ Show Home Grid. (You also can turn the Home Grid on and off for the active viewport using the G key.) If the Home Grid is the only grid in the scene, then by default it is also the construction grid where new objects are positioned when created.

You can access the Home Grid parameters (shown in Figure 7.16) by choosing Tools ➪ Grid and Snaps ➪ Grid and Snap Settings. You also can access this dialog box by right-clicking the Snap, Angle Snap, or Percent Snap toggle buttons located on the main toolbar.

In the Home Grid panel of the Grid and Snap Settings dialog box, you can set how often Major Lines appear, as well as Grid Spacing. (The Spacing value for the active grid is displayed on the status bar.) You also can specify to dynamically update the grid view in all viewports or just in the active one.

The User Grids panel lets you activate any new grids when created.

FIGURE 7.16

The Home Grid and User Grids panels of the Grid and Snap Settings dialog box let you define the grid spacing.

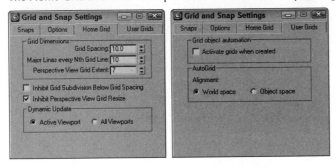

Creating and activating new grids

In addition to the Home Grid, you can create new grids. To create a new Grid object, select the Create ➪ Helpers ➪ Grid menu command, or open the Create panel, select the Helpers category, and click the Grid button. In the Parameters rollout are settings for specifying the new grid object's dimensions, spacing, and color, as well as which coordinate plane to display (XY, YZ, or ZX).

You can designate any newly created grid as the default active grid. To activate a grid, make sure that it is selected and choose Tools ➪ Grid and Snaps ➪ Activate Grid Object. Keep in mind that only one grid may be active at a time and that the default Home Grid cannot be selected. You also can activate a grid by right-clicking the grid object and selecting Activate Grid from the pop-up menu. To deactivate the new grid and reactivate the Home Grid, choose Tools ⇨ Grid and Snaps ⇨ Activate Home Grid, or right-click the grid object and choose Activate Grid ⇨ Home Grid from the pop-up quadmenu.

You can find further grid settings for new grids in the Grid and Snap Settings dialog box on the User Grids panel. The settings include automatically activating the grid when created and an option for aligning an AutoGrid using World space or Object space coordinates.

Using AutoGrid

You can use the AutoGrid feature to create a new construction plane perpendicular to a face normal. This feature provides an easy way to create and align objects directly next to one another without manually lining them up or using the Align features.

The AutoGrid feature shows up as a check box at the top of the Object Type rollout for every category in the Create panel. It becomes active only when you're in Create Object mode.

To use AutoGrid, click the AutoGrid option after selecting an object type to create. If no objects are in the scene, then the object is created as usual. If an object is in the scene, then the cursor moves around on the surface of the object with its coordinate axes perpendicular to the surface that the cursor is over. Clicking and dragging creates the new object based on the precise location of the object under the mouse.

The AutoGrid option stays active for all new objects that you create until you turn it off by unchecking the box.

Tip

Holding down the Alt key before creating the object makes the new construction grid visible, disables the AutoGrid option, and causes all new objects to use the new active construction grid. You can disable this active construction grid by enabling the AutoGrid option again. ∎

Tutorial: Creating a spyglass

As you begin to build objects for an existing scene, you find that working away from the scene origin is much easier if you enable the AutoGrid feature for the new objects you create. This feature enables you to position the new objects on (or close to) the surfaces of the nearby objects. It works best with objects that have pivot points located at their edges, such as Box and Cylinder objects.

In this example, you quickly create a spyglass object using the AutoGrid without needing to perform additional moves.

To create a spyglass using the AutoGrid and Snap features, follow these steps:

1. Before starting, click the Left viewport and zoom way out so you can see the height of the spyglass pieces.
2. Select Create ⇨ Standard Primitives ⇨ Cylinder, and drag from the origin in the Top viewport to create a Cylinder object. Set the Radius value to **40** and the Height value to **200**. Then enable the AutoGrid option in the Object Type rollout.
3. Drag from the origin again in the Top viewport to create another Cylinder object. Set its Radius to **35** and its Height to **200**. Repeat this step three times, reducing the Radius by 5 each time.

Figure 7.17 shows the resulting spyglass object.

FIGURE 7.17

This spyglass object was created quickly and easily using the AutoGrid option.

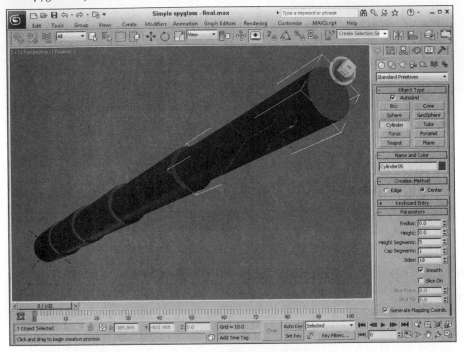

Using Snap Options

Often, when an object is being transformed, you know exactly where you want to put it. The Snap feature can be the means whereby objects get to the precise place they should be. For example, if you are constructing a set of stairs from box primitives, you can enable the Edge Snap feature to make each adjacent step align precisely along the edge of the previous step. With the Snap feature enabled, an object automatically moves (or snaps) to the specified snap position when you place it close enough. If you enable the Snap features, they affect any transformations that you make in a scene.

Snap points are defined in the Grid and Snap Settings dialog box that you can open by choosing Tools ⇨ Grid and Snaps ⇨ Grid and Snap Settings or by right-clicking any of the first three Snap buttons on the main toolbar. (These Snap buttons have a small magnet icon in them.) Figure 7.18 shows the Snaps panel of the Grid and Snap Settings dialog box for Standard and Body objects. An option for configuring NURBS snapping also is available. NURBS stands for Non-Uniform Rational B-Splines. They are a special type of object created from spline curves.

Cross-Reference
For more information on NURBS, see Bonus Chapter 5 on the CD, "Working with NURBS." ∎

After snap points have been defined, the Snap buttons on the main toolbar activate the Snap feature, or you can press the S key. The first Snaps button consists of a flyout with three buttons: 3D Snap toggle,

2.5D Snap toggle, and 2D Snap toggle. The 2D Snap toggle button limits all snaps to the active construction grid. The 2.5D Snap toggle button snaps to points on the construction grid as well as projected points from objects in the scene. The 3D Snap toggle button can snap to any points in 3D space.

The Snaps panel includes many different points to snap to depending on the object type.

When snapping is enabled, a small circle appears at the center of the pivot point. This circle is a visual reminder that snapping is enabled. When you move an object while snapping is enabled, you can either drag the small circle to move the object freely between snapping points or drag the Move tool's controls to constrain the object's movement.

As you drag an object, the starting position is marked and a line is drawn between this starting point and the destination point. Available snapping points are marked with a set of cross-hairs. If you release the object, it snaps to the highlighted set of cross-hairs. The line connecting the starting and end points and the snapping point cross-hairs are colored green when the object is over an available snapping point and yellow when not.

In addition to the small circle icon and the Move tool controls, you can move the mouse over the object and any available snapping points on the object are highlighted. For example, if the Vertex option in the Grid and Snap Settings dialog box is enabled, moving the mouse over one of a box object's corners highlights the corner with a set of yellow cross-hairs. Dragging while a vertex's cross-hair is highlighted lets you snap the selected corner to another position.

Tutorial: Creating a 2D outline of an object

The 2.5D snap can be confusing. It limits snapping to the active construction grid, but within the active grid, it can snap to 3D points that are projected onto the active grid. You can create a 2D representation of a 3D object by snapping to the vertices of the suspended object.

To create a 2D outline of a cylinder object, follow these steps:

1. Select the Create ⇨ Standard Primitives ⇨ Cylinder menu to create a simple cylinder object.
2. Select and rotate the cylinder so it is suspended and rotated at an angle above the construction grid.
3. Click and hold the Snap toggle button, and select the 2.5D Snap flyout option. Then right-click the Snap toggle and select only the Vertex option in the Snaps panel. Then close the Grid and Snap Settings dialog box.
4. Choose the Create ⇨ Shapes ⇨ Line menu and create a line in the Top viewport by snapping to the points that make the outline of the cylinder.

Figure 7.19 shows the projected outline.

FIGURE 7.19

The 2.5D snap feature snaps to vertices of 3D objects projected onto the active grid.

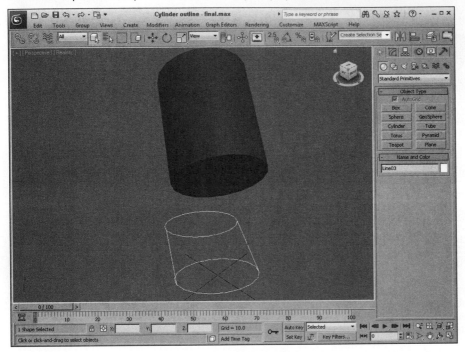

Tip

Right-clicking the Snap toggle opens the Grid and Snap Settings dialog box, except for the Spinner Snap toggle, which opens the Preference Settings dialog box. ∎

These Snap buttons control the snapping for translations. To the right are two other buttons: Angle Snap toggle and Percent Snap. These buttons control the snapping of rotations and scalings.

Note

The keyboard shortcut for turning the Snap feature on and off is the S key. ∎

Setting snap points

The Snaps tab in the Grid and Snap Settings dialog box has many points that can be snapped to in two categories: Standard and NURBS. The Standard snap points (previously shown in Figure 7.18) include the following:

- **Grid Points:** Snaps to the Grid intersection points
- **Grid Lines:** Snaps only to positions located on the Grid lines

- **Pivot:** Snaps to an object's pivot point
- **Bounding Box:** Snaps to one of the corners of a bounding box
- **Perpendicular:** Snaps to a spline's next perpendicular point
- **Tangent:** Snaps to a spline's next tangent point
- **Vertex:** Snaps to polygon vertices
- **Endpoint:** Snaps to a spline's end point or the end of a polygon edge
- **Edge/Segment:** Snaps to positions only on an edge
- **Midpoint:** Snaps to a spline's midpoint or the middle of a polygon edge
- **Face:** Snaps to any point on the surface of a face
- **Center Face:** Snaps to the center of a face

Several snap points specific to NURBS objects, such as NURBS points and curves, are also shown in Figure 7.18. These points include:

- **CV:** Snaps to any NURBS Control Vertex subobject
- **Point:** Snaps to a NURBS point
- **Curve Center:** Snaps to the center of the NURBS curve
- **Curve Normal:** Snaps to a point that is normal to a NURBS curve
- **Curve Tangent:** Snaps to a point that is tangent to a NURBS curve
- **Curve Edge:** Snaps to the edge of a NURBS curve
- **Curve End:** Snaps to the end of a NURBS curve
- **Surf Center:** Snaps to the center of a NURBS surface
- **Surf Normal:** Snaps to a point that is normal to a NURBS surface
- **Surf Edge:** Snaps to the edge of a NURBS surface

Setting snap options

The Grid and Snap Settings dialog box holds a panel of Options, shown in Figure 7.20, in which you can set the marker size and whether they display. The Snap Preview Radius defines the radial distance from the snap point required before the object that is being moved is displayed at the target snap point as a preview. This value can be larger than the actual Snap Radius and is meant to provide visual feedback on the snap operation. The Snap Radius setting determines how close the cursor must be to a snap point before it snaps to it.

The Angle and Percent values are the strengths for any Rotate and Scale transformations, respectively. The Snap to Frozen Objects lets you control whether frozen items can be snapped to. You also can cause translations to be affected by the designated axis constraints with the Use Axis Constraints option. The Display Rubber Band option draws a line from the object's starting location to its snapping location.

Within any viewpoint, holding down the Shift key and right-clicking in the viewport can access a pop-up menu of grid points and options. This pop-up quadmenu lets you quickly add or reset all the current snap points and change snap options, such as Transformed Constraints and Snap to Frozen.

FIGURE 7.20

The Options panel includes settings for marker size and color and the Snap Strength value.

Using the Snaps toolbar

As a shortcut to enabling the various snapping categories, you can access the Snaps toolbar by right-clicking the main toolbar away from the buttons and selecting Snaps from the popup menu. The Snaps toolbar, shown in Figure 7.21, can have several toggle buttons enabled at a time. Each enabled button is highlighted in yellow.

FIGURE 7.21

The Snaps toolbar provides a quick way to access several snap settings.

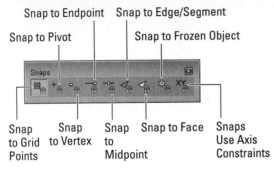

Tutorial: Creating a lattice for a methane molecule

Many molecules are represented by a lattice of spheres. Trying to line up the exact positions of the spheres by hand could be extremely frustrating, but using the Snap feature makes this challenge . . . well . . . a snap.

One of the simpler molecules is methane, which is composed of one carbon atom surrounded by four smaller hydrogen atoms. To reproduce this molecule as a lattice, you first need to create a tetrahedron primitive and snap spheres to each of its corners.

To create a lattice of the methane molecule, follow these steps:

1. Right-click the Snap toggle button in the main toolbar to open the Grid and Snap Settings, and enable the Grid Points and Vertex options. Then click the Snap toggle button (or press the S key) to enable 3D Snap mode.

2. Select the Create ⇨ Extended Primitives ⇨ Hedra menu command, set the P Family Parameter to **1.0**, and drag in the Top viewport from the center of the Home Grid to the first grid point to the right to create a Tetrahedron shape.

3. Click and hold the Snap toggle button, and select the 3D Snap flyout option. Select the Create ⇨ Standard Primitives ⇨ Sphere menu command. Right-click in the Left viewport, and drag from the top-left vertex to create a sphere. Set the sphere's Radius to **25**.

4. Create three more sphere objects with Radius values of 25 that are snapped to the vertices of the Tetrahedron object.

5. Finally, create a sphere in the Top viewport using the same snap point as the initial tetrahedron. Set its Radius to **80**.

Figure 7.22 shows the finished methane molecule.

FIGURE 7.22

A methane molecule lattice drawn with the help of the Snap feature

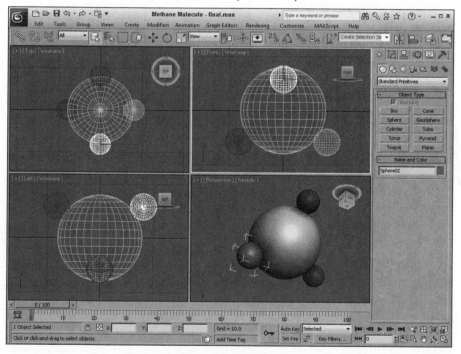

Summary

Transforming objects in Max is one of the fundamental actions you can perform. The three basic ways to transform objects are moving, rotating, and scaling. Max includes many helpful features to enable these transformations to take place quickly and easily. In this chapter, you learned these features:

- Using the Move, Rotate, and Scale buttons and the Transform Gizmos
- Transforming objects precisely with the Transform Type-In dialog box and status bar fields
- Using Transform Managers to change coordinate systems and lock axes
- Aligning objects with the align tool, aligning normals, and aligning to views
- Manipulating pivot points and using a Working Pivot
- Working with grids
- Setting up snap points
- Snapping objects to snap points

In the next chapter, you work more with multiple objects by learning how to clone objects. Using these techniques, you could very quickly have too many objects (and you were worried that there weren't enough objects).

8

Cloning Objects and Creating Object Arrays

T he only thing better than one perfect object is two perfect objects. Cloning objects is the process of creating copies of objects. These copies can maintain an internal connection (called an instance or a reference) to the original object that allows them to be modified along with the original object. For example, if you create a school desk and clone it multiple times as an instance to fill a room, then changing the parameter of one of the desks automatically changes it for all the other desks also.

An *array* is a discrete set of regularly ordered objects. So creating an array of objects involves cloning several copies of an object in a pattern, such as in rows and columns or in a circle.

I'm sure you have the concept for that perfect object in your little bag of tricks, and this chapter lets you copy it over and over after you get it out.

Cloning Objects

You can clone objects in Max in a couple of ways (and cloning luckily has nothing to do with DNA or gene splices). One method is to use the Edit ⇨ Clone (Ctrl+V) menu command, and another method is to transform an object while holding down the Shift key. You won't need to worry about these clones attacking anyone (unlike *Star Wars: Episode II*).

Using the Clone command

You can create a duplicate object by choosing the Edit ⇨ Clone (Ctrl+V) menu command. You must select an object before the Clone command becomes active, and you must not be in a Create mode. Selecting this command opens the Clone Options dialog box, shown in Figure 8.1, where you can give the clone a name and specify it as a Copy, Instance, or Reference. You can also copy any controllers associated with the object as a Copy or an Instance.

Caution

The Edit menu doesn't include the common Windows cut, copy, and paste commands because many objects and subobjects cannot be easily pasted into a different place. However, you will find a Clone (Ctrl+V) command, which can duplicate a selected object. ■

The Clone Options dialog box defines the new object as a Copy, Instance, or Reference.

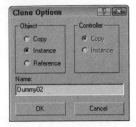

Note

The difference between Copy, Instance, and Reference is discussed in the "Understanding Cloning Options" section in this chapter. ■

When a clone is created with the Clone menu, it is positioned directly on top of the original, which makes distinguishing it from the original difficult. To verify that a clone has been created, open the Select by Name dialog box by pressing H and look for the cloned object (it has the same name, but an incremented number has been added). To see both objects, click the Select and Move button on the main toolbar and move one of the objects away from the other.

Using the Shift-clone method

An easier way to create clones is with the Shift key. You can use the Shift key when objects are transformed using the Select and Move, Select and Rotate, and Select and Scale commands. Holding down the Shift key while you use any of these commands on an object clones the object and opens the Clone Options dialog box. This Clone Options dialog box is identical to the dialog box previously shown, except it includes a spinner to specify the number of copies.

Performing a transformation with the Shift key held down defines an offset that is applied repeatedly to each copy. For example, holding down the Shift key while moving an object 5 units to the left (with the Number of Copies set to 5) places the first cloned object 5 units away from the original, the second cloned object 10 units away from the original object, and so on.

Tutorial: Cloning dinosaurs

The story behind *Jurassic Park* is pretty exciting, but in Max you can clone dinosaurs without their DNA.

To investigate cloning objects, follow these steps:

1. Open the Cloning dinosaurs.max file found in the Chap 08 directory of the CD.
2. Select the dinosaur object by clicking it in one of the viewports.

3. With the dinosaur model selected, choose Edit ⇨ Clone (or press Ctrl+V).

    The Clone Options dialog box appears.

4. Name the clone **First clone**, select the Copy option, and click OK.

5. Click the Select and Move button (or press the W key) on the main toolbar. Then in the Top viewport, click and drag the dinosaur model to the right.

    As you move the model, the original model beneath it is revealed.

6. Select each model in turn, and notice the name change in the Create panel's Name field. Notice that the clone is even the same object color as the original.

7. With the Select and Move button still active, hold down the Shift key, click the cloned dinosaur in the Top viewport, and move it to the right again. In the Clone Options dialog box that appears, select the Copy option, set the Number of Copies to **3**, and click OK.

8. Click the Zoom Extents All button (or press Shift+Ctrl+Z) in the lower-right corner to view all the new dinosaurs.

    Three additional dinosaurs have appeared, equally spaced from each other. The spacing was determined by the distance that you moved the second clone before releasing the mouse. Figure 8.2 shows the results of our dinosaur cloning experiment. (Now you'll need to build a really strong fence.)

FIGURE 8.2

Cloning multiple objects is easy with the Shift-clone feature.

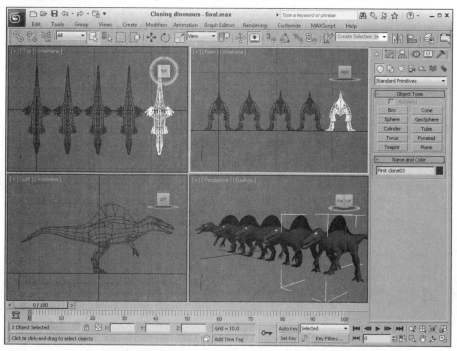

Using Quick Clone

Within the Transform Toolbox is a QClone button. This Quick Clone button creates a clone of the selected object and places it to the side of the selected object. The placement is exactly half the width of the selected object so the cloned object just touches the original. Holding down the Shift key creates an Instanced copy, and holding down the Alt key creates two copies. This provides a quick and easy way to clone and move the object at the same time.

Understanding Cloning Options

When cloning in Max, you're offered the option to create the clone as a copy, an instance, or a reference. This is true not only for objects but for materials, modifiers, and controllers as well.

Working with copies, instances, and references

When an object is cloned, the Clone Options dialog box appears. This dialog box enables you to select to make a copy, an instance, or a reference of the original object. Each of these clone types is unique and offers different capabilities.

A copy is just what it sounds like—an exact replica of the original object. The new copy maintains no ties to the original object and is a unique object in its own right. Any changes to the copy do not affect the original object, and vice versa.

Instances are different from copies in that they maintain strong ties to the original object. All instances of an object are interconnected, so that any geometry modifications (done with modifiers or object parameters) to any single instance changes all instances. For example, if you create several instances of a mailbox and then use a modifier on one of them, all instances are also modified.

Note
Instances and references can have different object colors, materials, transformations (moving, rotating, or scaling), and object properties. ∎

References are objects that inherit modifier changes from their parent objects but do not affect the parent when modified. Referenced objects get all the modifiers applied to the parent and can have their own modifiers as well. For example, suppose that you have an apple object and a whole bunch of references to that apple. Applying a modifier to the base apple changes all the remaining apples, but you can also apply a modifier to any of the references without affecting the rest of the bunch.

Cross-Reference
Instances and references are tied to the applied object modifiers, which are covered in more detail in Chapter 11, "Introducing Modifiers and Using the Modifier Stack." ∎

 At any time, you can break the tie between objects with the Make Unique button in the Modifier Stack. The Views ⇨ Show Dependencies command shows in magenta any objects that are instanced or referenced when the Modify panel is opened. This means that you can easily see which objects are instanced or referenced from the current selection.

Tutorial: Creating instanced doughnuts

Learning how the different clone options work will save you lots of future modifications. To investigate these options, you'll take a quick trip to the local doughnut shop.

To clone some doughnuts, follow these steps:

1. Create a doughnut using the Torus primitive by selecting Create ⇨ Standard Primitives ⇨ Torus, and then dragging and clicking twice in the Top viewport to create a torus object.

2. Click the torus object in the Top viewport to select it.

3. With the doughnut model selected, click the Select and Move button (or press the W key). Hold down the Shift key, and in the Top viewport, move the doughnut upward. In the Clone Options dialog box, select the Instance option, set the Number of Copies to **5**, and click OK. Click the Zoom Extents All (or press the Shift+Ctrl+Z key) button to widen your view.

4. Select all objects with the Edit ⇨ Select All (Ctrl+A) command, and then Shift+drag the doughnuts in the Top viewport to the right. In the Clone Options dialog box, select the Instance option again, set **3** for the Number of Copies, and click OK. This creates a nice array of two dozen doughnuts. Click the Zoom Extents All button (or press the Ctrl+Shift+Z key) to see all the doughnuts.

5. Select a single doughnut, and in the Parameters rollout of the Modify panel, set Radius1 to **20** and Radius2 to **10**.

   This makes a nice doughnut and changes all doughnuts at once.

6. Select the Modifiers ⇨ Parametric Deformers ⇨ Bend command. Then in the Parameters rollout of the Command Panel, enter **25** in the Angle field and select the X Bend Axis.

   This adds a slight bend to the doughnuts.

Cross-Reference

You can use modifiers to alter geometry. You can learn about using modifiers in Chapter 11, "Introducing Modifiers and Using the Modifier Stack." ∎

Figure 8.3 shows the doughnuts all changed exactly the same. You can imagine the amount of time it would take to change each doughnut individually. Using instances made these changes easy.

Tutorial: Working with referenced apples

Now that you have filled our bellies with doughnuts, you need some healthful food for balance. What better way to add balance than to have an apple or two to keep the doctor away?

To create some apples using referenced clones, follow these steps:

1. Open the Referenced Apples.max file from the Chap 08 directory on the CD.

2. Select the apple, and Shift+drag with the Select and Move (W) tool in the Top viewport to create a cloned reference. Select the Reference option in the Clone Options dialog box. Then close the Clone Options dialog box.

3. Select the original apple again, and repeat Step 2 until several referenced apples surround the original apple.

4. Select the original apple in the middle again, and choose the Modifiers ⇨ Subdivision Surfaces ⇨ MeshSmooth command. In the Subdivision Amount rollout, set the number of Iterations to **2**.

   This smoothes all the apples.

5. Select one of the surrounding apples, and apply the Modifiers ⇨ Parametric Deformers ⇨ Taper command. Set the Amount value to **0.5** about the Z-axis.

6. Select another of the surrounding apples, and apply the Modifiers ⇨ Parametric Deformers ⇨ Squeeze command. Set the Axial Bulge Amount value to **0.3**.

7. Select another of the surrounding apples, and apply the Modifiers ⇨ Parametric Deformers ⇨ Squeeze command. Set the Radial Squeeze Amount value to **0.2**.

8. Select another of the surrounding apples, and apply the Modifiers ⇨ Parametric Deformers ⇨ Bend command. Set the Angle value to **20** about the Z axis.

Note

As you apply modifiers to a referenced object, notice the thick, gray bar in the Modifier Stack. This bar, called the Derived Object Line, separates which modifiers get applied to all referenced objects (below the line) and which modifiers get applied to only the selected object (above the line). If you drag a modifier from above the gray bar to below the gray bar, then that modifier is applied to all references. ∎

Using referenced objects, you can apply the major changes to similar objects but still make minor changes to objects to make them a little different. Figure 8.4 shows the apples. Notice that they are not all exactly the same.

FIGURE 8.3

Two dozen doughnut instances ready for glaze

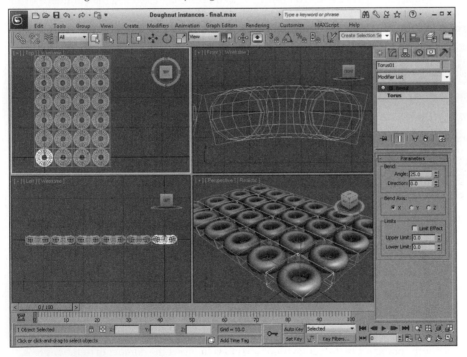

FIGURE 8.4

Even apples from the same tree should be slightly different.

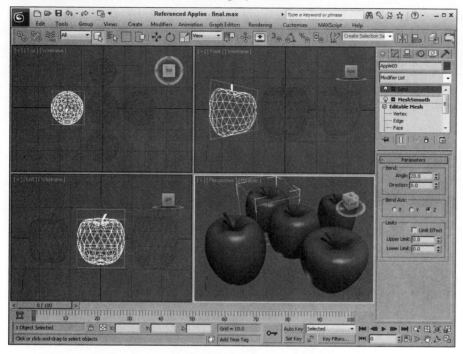

Mirroring Objects

Have you ever held the edge of a mirror up to your face to see half of your head in the mirror? Many objects have a natural symmetry that you can exploit to require that only half an object be modeled. The human face is a good example. You can clone symmetrical parts using the Mirror command.

Using the Mirror command

The Mirror command creates a clone (or No Clone, if you so choose) of the selected object about the current coordinate system. To open the Mirror dialog box, shown in Figure 8.5, choose Tools ⇨ Mirror, or click the Mirror button located on the main toolbar. You can access the Mirror dialog box only if an object is selected.

Within the Mirror dialog box, you can specify an axis or plane about which to mirror the selected object. You can also define an Offset value. As with the other clone commands, you can specify whether the clone is to be a Copy, an Instance, or a Reference, or you can choose No Clone, which flips the object around the axis you specify. The dialog box also lets you mirror IK (inverse kinematics) Limits, which reduces the number of IK parameters that need to be set.

Cross-Reference

Learn more about inverse kinematics in Chapter 38, "Understanding Rigging, Kinematics, and Working with Bones." ■

229

FIGURE 8.5

The Mirror dialog box can create an inverted clone of an object.

Tutorial: Mirroring a robot's leg

Many characters have symmetry that you can use to your advantage, but to use symmetry, you can't just clone one half. Consider the position of a character's right ear relative to its right eye. If you clone the ear, then the position of each ear will be identical, with the ear to the right of the eye, which would make for a strange-looking creature. What you need to use is the Mirror command, which clones the object and rotates it about a selected axis.

In this example, you have a complex mechanical robot with one of its legs created. Using Mirror, you can quickly clone and position its second leg.

To mirror a robot's leg, follow these steps:

1. Open the Robot mech.max file from the Chap 08 directory on the CD.

   This file includes a robot with one of its legs deleted.

2. Select all objects that make up the robot's leg in the Left viewport, and open the Mirror dialog box with the Tools ⇨ Mirror menu command.

3. In the Mirror dialog box, select X as the Mirror Axis and Instance as the Clone Selection. Change the Offset value until the cloned leg is in position, which should be at around **–2.55**.

Note

The mirror axis depends on the viewport, so make sure that the Left viewport is selected. ∎

Any changes made to the dialog box are immediately shown in the viewports.

4. Click OK to close the dialog box.

Note

By making the clone selection an instance, you can ensure that any future modifications to the right half of the figure are automatically applied to the left half. ∎

Figure 8.6 shows the resulting robot, which won't be falling over now.

FIGURE 8.6

A perfectly symmetrical robot, compliments of the Mirror tool

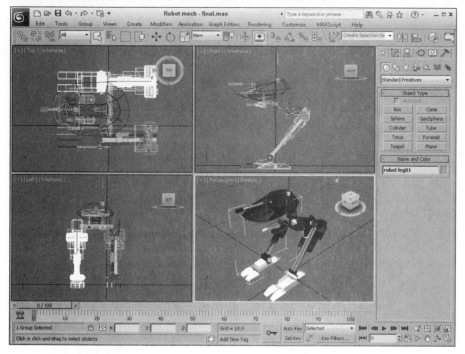

Cloning over Time

Another useful way to create multiple copies of an object is to have an object be created based on its position during a specific frame of an animation. This cloning at specific times is accomplished with the Snapshot feature.

Using the Snapshot command

The Snapshot command creates static copies, instances, references, or even meshes of a selected object as it moves along an animation path. For example, you could create a series of footprints by animating a set of footprints moving across the screen from frame 1 to frame 100, and then choose Tools ➪ Snapshot and enter the number of steps to appear over this range of frames in the Snapshot dialog box. The designated number of steps is created at regular intervals for the animation range. Be aware that the Snapshot command works only with objects that have an animation path defined.

 You can open the Snapshot dialog box by choosing Tools ➪ Snapshot or by clicking the Snapshot button (under the Array flyout on the Extras toolbar). Snapshot is the second button in the flyout. In the Snapshot dialog box, shown in Figure 8.7, you can choose to produce a single clone or a range of clones over a given number of frames. Selecting Single creates a single clone at the current frame.

Note

When you enter the number of Copies in the Snapshot dialog box, a copy is placed at both the beginning and end of the specified range, so if your animation path is a closed path, two objects are stacked on top of each other. For example, if you have a square animation path and you want to place a copy at each corner, you need to enter a value of 5. ■

FIGURE 8.7

The Snapshot dialog box lets you clone a Copy, Instance, Reference, or Mesh.

Tip

The Snapshot tool can also be used with particle systems. ■

Tutorial: Creating a path through a maze

The Snapshot tool can be used to create objects as a model is moved along an animated path. In this example, you create a series of footsteps through a maze.

To create a set of footprints through a maze with the Snapshot tool, follow these steps:

1. Open the Path through a maze.max file from the Chap 08 directory on the CD. This file includes a set of animated footprints that travel to the exit of a maze.
2. Select both footprint objects at the entrance to the maze.
3. Choose the Tools ⇨ Snapshot menu to open the Snapshot dialog box. Select the Range option, set the number of Copies to **20**, and select the Instance option. Then click OK.

Figure 8.8 shows the path of footsteps leading the way through the maze, which are easier to follow than breadcrumbs.

The Snapshot tool helps to build a set of footprints through a maze.

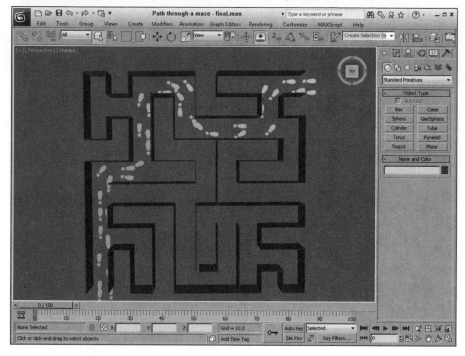

Spacing Cloned Objects

The Snapshot tool offers a convenient way to clone objects along an animation path, but what if you want to clone objects along a path that isn't animated? The answer is the Spacing tool. The Spacing tool can position clones at regular intervals along a path by either selecting a path and the number of cloned objects or by picking two points in the viewport.

Using the Spacing tool

 You access the Spacing tool by clicking on a button in the flyout under the Array button on the Extras toolbar (the Extras toolbar can be made visible by right-clicking on the main toolbar away from the buttons). You can also access it using the Tools ➪ Align ➪ Spacing Tool (Shift+I) menu command. When accessed, it opens the Spacing Tool dialog box, shown in Figure 8.9. At the top of this dialog box are two buttons: Pick Path and Pick Points. If a path is selected, its name appears on the Pick Path button.

FIGURE 8.9

The Spacing Tool dialog box lets you select how to position clones along a path.

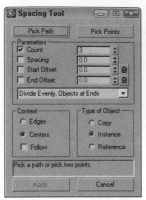

You can also specify Count, Spacing, Start Offset, and End Offset values. The drop-down list offers several preset options, including Divide Evenly, Free Center, End Offset, and more. These values and preset options are used to define the number and spacing of the objects. The spacing and position of the objects depend on the values that are included. For example, if you include only a Count value, then the objects are evenly spaced along the path including an object at each end. If an offset value is included, then the first or last item is moved away from the end by the offset value. If a Spacing value is included, then the number of objects required to meet this value is included automatically.

The Lock icons next to the Start and End Offset values force the Start or End Offset values to be the same as the Spacing value. This has the effect of pushing the objects away from their end points.

Before you can use either the Pick Path or Pick Points buttons, you must select the object to be cloned. Using the Pick Path button, you can select a spline path in the scene, and cloned objects are regularly spaced according to the values you selected. The Pick Points method lets you click to select the Start point and click again to select an end point. The cloned objects are spaced in a straight line between the two points.

The two options for determining the spacing width are Edges and Centers. The Edges option spaces objects from the edge of its bounding box to the edge of the adjacent bounding box, and the Centers option spaces objects based on their centers. The Follow option aligns the object with the path if the path is selected. Each object can be a copy, instance, or reference of the original. The text field at the bottom of the dialog box displays for your information the number of objects and the spacing value between each.

Tip

Lining up objects to correctly follow the path can be tricky. If the objects are misaligned, you can change the object's pivot point so it matches the viewport coordinates. This makes the object follow the path with the correct position. ■

You can continue to modify the Spacing Tool dialog box's values while the dialog box is open, but the objects are not added to the scene until you click the Apply button. The Cancel button closes the dialog box.

Tutorial: Stacking a row of dominoes

A good example of using the Spacing tool to accomplish something that is difficult in real life is to stack a row of dominoes. It is really a snap in Max, regardless of the path.

To stack a row of dominoes using the Spacing tool, follow these steps:

1. Open the Row of dominoes.max file from the Chap 08 directory on the CD.

   This file includes a single domino and a wavy spline path.

2. Select the domino object, and open the Spacing tool by selecting the flyout button under the Array button on the Extras toolbar (or by pressing Shift+I).

3. In the Spacing Tool dialog box, click the Pick Path button and select the wavy path.

   The path name appears on the Pick Path button.

4. From the drop-down list in the Parameters section of the Spacing Tool dialog box, select the Count option with a value of **35**.

   This is the same as the Divide Evenly, Objects at Ends option in the drop-down list.

5. Select the Edges context option, check the Follow check box, and make all clones Instances. Click Apply when the result looks right, and close the Spacing Tool dialog box.

Figure 8.10 shows the simple results. The Spacing Tool dialog box remains open until you click the Cancel button.

FIGURE 8.10

These dominoes were much easier to stack than the set in my living room.

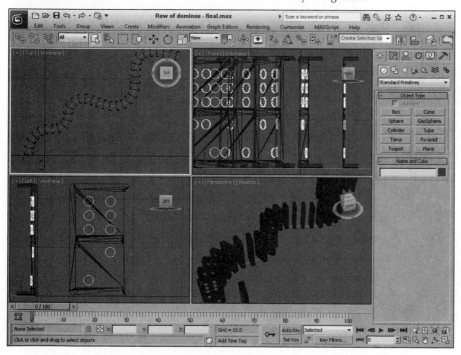

Using the Clone and Align Tool

Imagine you're working on a production team and the modeler assigned to the project says he needs some more time to make the building columns "something special." Just as you prepare to give him the "deadlines don't die" speech, you remember the Clone and Align tool. Using this tool, you can place proxy objects where the detailed ones are supposed to go. Then, when the detailed object is ready, the Clone and Align tool lets you clone the detailed object and place it where all the proxies are positioned. This, of course, makes the modeler happy and doesn't disrupt your workflow. Another production team victory.

Aligning source objects to destination objects

Before selecting the Tools ➪ Align ➪ Clone and Align tool, you need to select the detailed object that you want to place. This object is referred to as the *source object*. Selecting the Clone and Align tool opens a dialog box, shown in Figure 8.11. From this dialog box, you can pick the proxy objects that are positioned where the source objects are supposed to go. These proxy objects are referred to as *destination objects*. The dialog box shows the number of source and destination objects that are selected.

Cross-Reference

The Align tool is covered in Chapter 7, "Transforming Objects, Pivoting, Aligning, and Snapping." ■

The Clone and Align dialog box also lets you select whether source objects are cloned as copies, instances, or references. In the Align Parameters rollout, you can specify the object's position and orientation using the same controls that are used to align objects, including any Offset values.

As you make changes in the Clone and Align dialog box, the objects are updated in the viewports, but these changes don't become permanent until you click the Apply button. The Clone and Align dialog box is *persistent*, meaning that, after being applied, the settings remain until they are changed.

Tutorial: Cloning and aligning trees on a beach

To practice using the Clone and Align tool, you'll open a beach scene with a single set of grouped trees. Several other box objects have been positioned and rotated about the scene. The trees will be the source object and the box objects will be the destinations.

To position and orient several high-res trees using the Clone and Align tool, follow these steps:

1. Open the Trees on beach.max file from the Chap 08 directory on the CD.

   This file includes a beach scene created by Viewpoint Datalabs.

2. Select the tree objects that have been grouped together, and open the Clone and Align dialog box by selecting the Tools ➪ Align ➪ Clone and Align menu command.

FIGURE 8.11

The Clone and Align dialog box lets you choose which objects mark the place where the source object should go.

Note

The Clone and Align dialog box remembers the last settings used, which may be different from what you want. You can reset all the settings with the Reset All Parameters button at the bottom of the dialog box. ■

3. In the Clone and Align dialog box, click the Pick button and select each of the box objects in the scene.

4. In the Align Parameters rollout, enable the X and Y axes for the Positions and the X, Y, and Z axes for the Orientation. Then click the Apply button.

Figure 8.12 shows the simple results. Notice that the destination objects have not been replaced and are still there.

FIGURE 8.12

Using the Clone and Align dialog box, you can place these trees to match the stand-in objects' position and orientation.

Creating Arrays of Objects

Now that you've probably figured out how to create arrays of objects by hand with the Shift-clone method, the Array command multiplies the fun by making it easy to create many copies instantaneously. The Array dialog box lets you specify the array dimensions, offsets, and transformation values. These parameters enable you to create an array of objects easily.

 Access the Array dialog box by selecting an object and choosing Tools ⇨ Array or by clicking the Array button on the Extras toolbar. Figure 8.13 shows the Array dialog box. The top of the Array dialog box displays the coordinate system and the center about which the transformations are performed.

The Array dialog box is also *persistent*. You can reset all the values at once by clicking the Reset All Parameters button. You can also preview the current array settings without actually creating an array of objects using the Preview button. The Display as Box option lets you see the array as a bounding box to give you an idea of how large the array will be.

Linear arrays

Linear arrays are arrays in which the objects form straight lines, such as rows and columns. Using the Array dialog box, you can specify an offset along the X-, Y-, and Z-axes at the top of the dialog box and define this offset as an incremental amount or as a total amount. To change between incremental values and total values, click the arrows to the left and right of the Move, Rotate, and Scale labels. For example, an array with 10 elements and an incremental value of 5 will position each successive object a distance of 5 units from the previous one. An array with 10 elements and a total value of 100 will position each element a distance of 10 units apart by dividing the total value by the number of clones.

FIGURE 8.13

The Array dialog box defines the number of elements and transformation offsets in an array.

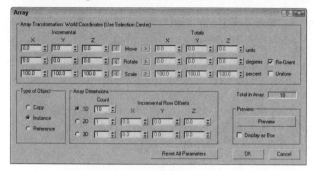

The Move row values represent units as specified in the Units Setup dialog box. The Rotate row values represent degrees, and the Scale row values are a percentage of the selected object. All values can be either positive or negative values.

Clicking the Re-Orient check box causes the coordinate system to be reoriented after each rotation is made. If this check box isn't enabled, then the objects in the array do not successively rotate. Clicking the Uniform check box to the right of the Scale row values disables the Y and Z Scale value columns and forces the scaling transformations to be uniform. To perform non-uniform scaling, simply deselect the Uniform check box.

The Type of Object section lets you define whether the new objects are copies, instances, or references, but unlike the other cloning tools, the Array tool defaults to Instance. If you plan on modeling all the objects in a similar manner, then you will want to select the Instance or Reference options.

In the Array Dimensions section, you can specify the number of objects to copy along three different dimensions. You can also define incremental offsets for each individual row.

Caution

You can use the Array dialog box to create a large number of objects. If your array of objects is too large, your system may crash. ■

Tutorial: Building a white picket fence

To start with a simple example, you'll create a white picket fence. Because a fence repeats, you need only to create a single slat; then you'll use the Array command to duplicate it consistently.

To create a picket fence, follow these steps:

1. Open the White picket fence.max file from the Chap 08 directory on the CD.
2. With the single fence board selected, choose Tools ⇨ Array or click on the Array button on the Extras toolbar to open the Array dialog box.

3. In the Array dialog box, click the Reset All Parameters button to start with a clean slate. Then enter a value of **50** in the X column's Move row under the Incremental section. (This is the incremental value for spacing each successive picket.) Next, enter **20** in the Array Dimensions section next to the 1D radio button. (This is the number of objects to include in the array.) Click OK to create the objects.

Tip

The Preview button lets you see the resulting array before it is created. Don't worry if you don't get the values right the first time. The most recent values you entered into the Array dialog box stay around until you exit Max. ■

4. Click the Zoom Extents All button (or press Shift+Ctrl+Z) in the lower-right corner of the Max window to see the entire fence in the viewports.

Figure 8.14 shows the completed fence.

FIGURE 8.14

Tom Sawyer would be pleased to see this white picket fence, created easily with the Array dialog box.

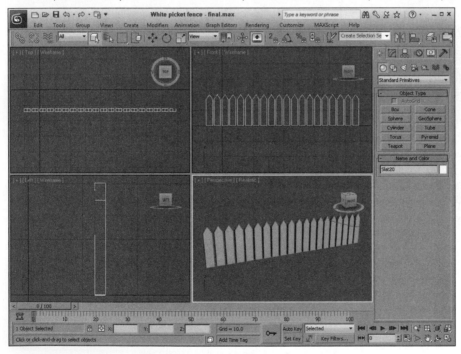

Circular arrays

 You can use the Array dialog box for creating more than just linear arrays. All transformations are done relative to a center point. You can change the center point about which transformations are performed using the Use Selection Center button on the main toolbar. The three flyout options are Use Pivot Point Center, Use Selection Center, and Use Transform Coordinate Center.

Cross-Reference

For more about how these settings affect transformations, see Chapter 7, "Transforming Objects, Pivoting, Aligning, and Snapping." ∎

Tutorial: Building a Ferris wheel

Ferris wheels, like most of the rides at the fair, entertain by going around and around, with the riders seated in chairs spaced around the Ferris wheel's central point. The Array dialog box can also create objects around a central point.

 In this example, you use the Rotate transformation along with the Use Transform Coordinate Center button to create a circular array.

To create a circular array, follow these steps:

1. Open the Ferris wheel.max file from the Chap 08 directory on the CD.

    This file has the Front viewport maximized to show the profile of the Ferris wheel.

2. Click the Use Pivot Point Center button on the main toolbar, and drag down to the last icon, which is the Use Transform Coordinate Center button.

    The Use Transform Coordinate Center button becomes active. This button causes all transformations to take place about the axis in the center of the screen.

3. Select the light blue chair object, and open the Array dialog box by choosing Tools ⇨ Array or by clicking the Array button on the Extras toolbar. Before entering any values into the Array dialog box, click the Reset All Parameters button.

4. Between the Incremental and Totals sections are the labels Move, Rotate, and Scale. Click the arrow button to the right of the Rotate label. Set the Z column value of the Rotate row to **360** degrees, and make sure that the Re-Orient option is disabled.

    A value of 360 degrees defines one complete revolution. Disabling the Re-Orient option keeps each chair object from gradually turning upside down.

5. In the Array Dimensions section, set the 1D spinner Count value to **8 and** click OK to create the array.

6. Next select the green strut, and open the Array dialog box again with the Tools ⇨ Array command. Select the Re-Orient option, and leave the rest of the settings as they are. Click OK to create the array.

Figure 8.15 shows the resulting Ferris wheel. You can click the Min/Max toggle in the lower-right corner to view all four viewports again.

Working with a ring array

You can find the Ring Array system by opening the Create panel and selecting the Systems category. Clicking the Ring Array button opens a Parameters rollout. In this rollout are parameters for the ring's Radius, Amplitude, Cycles, Phase, and the Number of elements to include.

You create the actual array by clicking and dragging in one of the viewports. Initially, all elements are simple box objects surrounding a green dummy object.

The Amplitude, Cycles, and Phase values define the sinusoidal nature of the circle. The Amplitude is the maximum distance that you can position the objects from the horizontal plane. If the Amplitude is set to 0, then all objects lie in the same horizontal plane. The Cycles value is the number of waves that occur around the entire circle. The Phase determines which position along the circle starts in the up position.

FIGURE 8.15

A circular array created by rotating objects about the Transform Coordinate Center

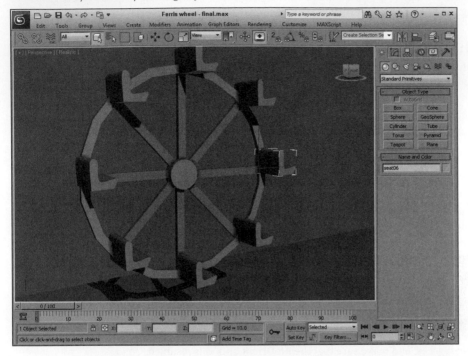

Tutorial: Using Ring Array to create a carousel

Continuing with the theme park attractions motif, this example creates a carousel. The horse model comes from Poser but was simplified using the MultiRes modifier.

To use a Ring Array system to create a carousel, follow these steps:

1. Open the Carousel.max file from the Chap 08 directory on the CD.

   This file includes a carousel structure made from primitives along with a carousel horse.

2. Open the Create panel, select the Systems category, and click the Ring Array button. Drag in the Top viewport from the center of the carousel to create a ring array. Then enter a Radius value of **250**, an Amplitude of **20**, a Cycles value of **3**, and a Number value of **6**. Then right-click in the active viewport to deselect the Ring Array tool.

Note

If the Ring Array object gets deselected, you can access its parameters in the Motion panel, not in the Modify panel. ∎

3. Select the Ring Array's Dummy object in the Left viewport, select the Tools ⇨ Align ⇨ Align menu command and then click on the center cylinder. The Align Selection dialog box opens. Enable the X, Y, and Z Position options, choose the Center options for both the Current and Target objects, and click the Apply button. This aligns the ring array to the center of the carousel.

4. Select the horse object, and choose the Tools ⇨ Align ⇨ Clone and Align menu command. In the Clone and Align dialog box that opens, select the Instance options along with the X, Y, and Z Position and Orientation options. Then click the Pick button and click on each of the boxes in the ring array. Set the Offset values for the X and Y Orientation values to **90** to fix the orientation of the placed horses. Then click the Apply button and close the Clone and Align dialog box.

Figure 8.16 shows the finished carousel. Notice that each horse is at a different height. Once the horses are placed, you can delete or hide the Ring Array object.

The horses in the carousel were created using a Ring Array system.

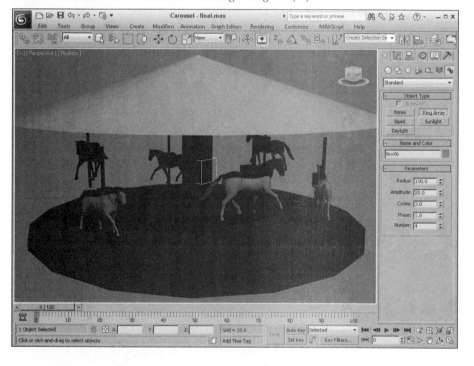

Summary

Many ways to clone an object are available. You can use the Clone command under the Edit menu or the Shift-clone feature for quickly creating numerous clones. Clones can be copies, instances, or references. Each differs in how it retains links to the original object. You can also clone using the Mirror, Snapshot, and Spacing tools.

Arrays are another means of cloning. You can use the Array dialog box to produce clones in three different dimensions, and you can specify the offset transformations.

This chapter covered the following cloning topics:

- Cloning objects and Shift-cloning
- Understanding copies, instances, and references
- Using the Mirror, Snapshot, Spacing, and Clone and Align tools
- Building linear, circular, and spiral arrays of objects
- Using the Ring Array system

In the next chapter, you learn to group objects and link them into hierarchies. Then you'll be able to organize into structures all the objects that you've learned to create.

Grouping, Linking, and Parenting Objects

N ow that you've learned how to select and clone objects, you'll want to learn how to group objects in an easily accessible form, especially as a scene becomes more complex. Max's grouping and container features enable you to organize all the objects that you're dealing with, thereby making your workflow more efficient.

Another way of organizing objects is to build a linked hierarchy. A *linked hierarchy* attaches, or links, one object to another and makes it possible to transform the attached object by moving the object to which it is linked. The arm is a classic example of a linked hierarchy: When the shoulder rotates, so do the elbow, wrist, and fingers. Establishing linked hierarchies can make moving, positioning, and animating many objects easy.

Working with Groups

Grouping objects organizes them and makes them easier to select and transform. Groups are different from selection sets in that groups exist like one object. Selecting any object in the group selects the entire group, whereas selecting an object in a selection set selects only that object and not the selection set. You can open groups to add, delete, or reposition objects within the group. Groups can also contain other groups. This is called *nesting groups*.

Creating groups

The Group command enables you to create a group. To do so, simply select the desired objects and choose Group ➪ Group. A simple Name Group dialog box opens and enables you to give the group a name. The newly created group displays a new bounding box that encompasses all the objects in the group.

Tip

You can easily identify groups in the Select from Scene dialog box by using the Groups display toggle. Groups appear in bold in the Name and Color rollout of the Command Panel. ■

Ungrouping objects

The Ungroup command enables you to break up a group (kind of like a poor music album). To do so, simply select the desired group and choose Group ⇨ Ungroup. This menu command dissolves the group, and all the objects within the group revert to separate objects. The Ungroup command breaks up only the currently selected group. All nested groups within a group stay intact.

Caution

If you animate a group and then later use the ungroup command, then all the keys created for the whole group are lost when you ungroup. ■

The easiest way to dissolve an entire group, including any nested groups, is with the Explode command. This command eliminates the group and the groups within the group and makes each object separate.

Opening and closing groups

The Open command enables you to access the objects within a group. Grouped objects move, scale, and rotate as a unit when transformed, but individual objects within a group can be transformed independently after you open a group with the Open command.

To move an individual object in a group, select the group and choose Group ⇨ Open. The white bounding box changes to a pink box. Then select an object within the group, and move it with the Select and Move button (keyboard shortcut, W). Choose Group ⇨ Close to reinstate the group.

Attaching and detaching objects

The Attach and Detach commands enable you to insert or remove objects from an opened group without dissolving the group. To attach objects to an existing group, you select an object, select the Attach menu command, and then click on the group to which you want to add the object. To detach an object from a group, you need to open the group and select the Detach menu command. Remember to close the group when finished.

Cross-Reference

Editable objects, like the Editable Poly, also can make use of an Attach feature, but attaching objects to an editable object permanently combines the objects together. You can learn more about the Editable Poly objects in Chapter 13, "Modeling with Polygons." ■

Cross-Reference

Another convenient way to make a set of objects portable is to combine them into a Container. Containers are discussed in Chapter 25, "Building Complex Scenes with Containers, XRefs, and the Schematic View." ■

Tutorial: Grouping a plane's parts together

Positioning objects relative to one another takes careful and precise work. After spending the time to place the wings, tail, and prop on a plane exactly where they need to be, transforming each object by itself can misalign all the parts. By grouping all the objects together, you can move all the objects at once.

For this tutorial, you can get some practice grouping all the parts of an airplane together. Follow these steps:

1. Open the T-28 Trojan plane.max file from the Chap 09 directory on the CD. This file includes a model created by Viewpoint Datalabs.

2. Click the Select by Name button on the main toolbar (or press the H key) to open the Select from Scene dialog box. In this dialog box, notice all the different plane parts. Click the Select All button to select all the separate objects, and click OK to close the dialog box.

3. With all the objects selected, choose Group ⇨ Group to open the Group dialog box. Give the group the name **Plane**, and click OK.

4. Click the Select and Move button (or press W), and click and drag the plane.

   The entire group now moves together.

Figure 9.1 shows the plane grouped as one unit. Notice how only one set of brackets surrounds the plane in the Perspective viewport. The group name is displayed in the Name field of the Command Panel instead of listing the number of objects selected.

FIGURE 9.1

The plane moves as one unit after its objects are grouped.

Building assemblies

At the bottom of the Group menu is a menu item called Assembly with a submenu that looks fright-fully similar to the Group menu. The difference between a group and an assembly is that an assembly can include a light object with a Luminaire helper object as its head. This enables you to build light fixtures where the light is actually grouped (or assembled) with the light stand objects. Once built, you can control the light by selecting and moving the light assembly.

After you've created the geometry for a light assembly, you can create an assembly with the Group ⇨ Assembly ⇨ Assemble menu command. This opens the Create Assembly dialog box, where you can name the assembly and add a Luminaire object as the head object. Because the Luminaire object is the head object, you can see its parameters in the Modify panel whenever the assembly is selected. Its parameters include a Dimmer value and a Filter Color. These parameters are used only if they are wired to an actual light object included in the assembly.

Luminaire objects can be confusing because they don't actually add light to an assembly. If you're curious about the Luminaire objects, you can find them in the Assembly Heads subcategory of the Helper category.

The benefit of the Luminaire helper object is that it can add to an assembly some simple parameters that are accessible whenever the assembly is selected. These parameters work only if you wire them to the parameters of the light object included in the assembly.

Cross-Reference

You can learn more about wiring parameters in Chapter 21, "Understanding Animation and Keyframes." ∎

To wire Luminaire parameters to the light object's parameters, select the assembly and open the Parameter Wiring dialog box with the Animation ⇨ Wire Parameters ⇨ Parameter Wiring Dialog menu command (or press the Alt+5 shortcut). In the left pane, locate and select the Dimmer parame-ter under the Object (Luminaire) track. Locate and select the Multiplier parameter under the Object (Light) track, which is under the Assembly01 track in the right pane. Click the one-way connection button in the center of the dialog box that links the Dimmer to the Multiplier parameters, and click the Connect button. Next, wire the FilterColor parameter to the light's Color parameter.

After the assembly light is wired to the Luminaire parameters, you can use the Dimmer and Filter Color parameters in the Modify panel whenever the assembly is selected.

Understanding Parent, Child, and Root Relationships

Max uses several terms to describe the relationships between objects. A *parent object* is an object that controls any secondary, or child, objects linked to it. A *child object* is an object that is linked to and controlled by a parent. A parent object can have many children, but a child can have only one parent. Additionally, an object can be both a parent and a child at the same time. Another way to say this is:

- Child objects are linked to parent objects.
- Moving a parent object moves its children with it.
- Child objects can move independently of their parents.

A hierarchy is the complete set of linked objects that includes these types of relationships. Ancestors are all the parents above a child object. Descendants are all the children below a parent object. The root object is the top parent object that has no parent and controls the entire hierarchy.

Each hierarchy can have several branches or subtrees. Any parent with two or more children represents the start of a new branch.

Cross-Reference

The default hierarchies established using the Link tool are referred to as forward-kinematics systems, in which control moves forward down the hierarchy from parent to child. In forward-kinematics systems, the child has no control over the parent. An inverse kinematics system (covered in Chapter 38, "Understanding Rigging, Kinematics, and Working with Bones") enables child objects to control their parents. ■

All objects in a scene, whether linked or not, belong to a hierarchy. Objects that aren't linked to any other objects are, by default, children of the *world object*, which is an imaginary object that holds all objects.

Note

You can view the world object, labeled Objects, in the Track View. Individual objects are listed under the Objects track by their object name. ■

You have several ways to establish hierarchies using Max. The simplest method is to use the Link and Unlink buttons found on the main toolbar. You can also find these buttons in the Schematic View window. The Hierarchy panel in the Command Panel provides access to valuable controls and information about established hierarchies. When creating complex hierarchies, a bones system can help.

Cross-Reference

The Schematic View window is covered in Chapter 25, "Building Complex Scenes with Containers, XRefs, and the Schematic View," and bone systems are covered in Chapter 38, "Understanding Rigging, Kinematics, and Working with Bones." ■

Building Links between Objects

The main toolbar includes two buttons that you can use to build a hierarchy: Link and Unlink. The order of selection defines which object becomes the parent and which becomes the child.

Linking objects

 The Link button always links children to the parents. To remind you of this order, remember that a parent can have many children, but a child can have only one parent.

To link two objects, click the Link button. This places you in Link mode, which continues until you turn it off by selecting another button, such as the Select button or one of the Transform buttons. When you're in Link mode, the Link button is highlighted in dark yellow.

With the Link button highlighted, click an object, which will be the child, and drag a line to the target parent object. The cursor arrow changes to the link icon when it is over a potential parent. When you release the mouse button, the parent object flashes once and the link is established. If you drag the same child object to a different parent, the link to the previous parent is replaced by the link to the new parent.

Once linked, all transformations applied to the parent are applied equally to its children about the parent's pivot point. A *pivot point* is the center about which the object rotates.

Unlinking objects

 The Unlink button is used to destroy links, but only to the parent. For example, if a selected object has both children and a parent, clicking the Unlink button destroys the link to the parent of the selected object but not the links to its children.

To eliminate all links for an entire hierarchy, double-click an object to select its entire hierarchy and click the Unlink button.

Tutorial: Linking a family of ducks

What better way to show off parent-child relationships than with a family? I could have modeled my own family, but for some reason, my little ducks don't always like to follow me around.

To create a linked family of ducks, follow these steps:

1. Open the Linked duck family.max file from the Chap 09 directory on the CD. This file includes several simple ducks lined up in a row.
2. Click the Select and Link button in the main toolbar, and drag a line from the last duck to the one just in front of it.

Tip
You can link several objects at once by highlighting all the objects you want to link and dragging the selected objects to the parent object. This procedure creates a link between the parent object and each selected object. ■

3. Continue to connect each duck to the one in front of it.
4. Click the Select and Move button (or press the W key), and move the Mommy duck. Notice how all the children move with her.

Figure 9.2 shows the duck family as they move forward in a line. The Link button made it possible to move all the ducks simply by moving the parent duck.

FIGURE 9.2

Linked child ducks inherit transformations from their parent duck.

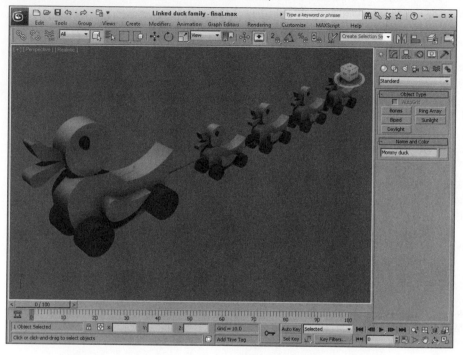

Displaying Links and Hierarchies

The Display panel includes a rollout that lets you display all the links in the viewports.

After links have been established, you can see linked objects listed as a hierarchy in several places. The Select Objects dialog box, opened with the Select by Name button (or with the H key), can display objects in this manner, as well as the Schematic and Track Views.

Displaying links in the viewport

You can choose to see the links between the selected objects in the viewports by selecting the Display Links option in the Link Display rollout of the Display panel. The Display Links option shows links as lines that run between the pivot points of the objects with a diamond-shaped marker at the end of each line; these lines and markers are the same color as the object.

Note

The Display Links option can be enabled or disabled for each object in the scene. To display the links for all objects, use the Edit ⇨ Select All (Ctrl+A) command and then enable the Display Links option. ∎

The Link Display rollout also offers the Link Replaces Object option, which removes the objects and displays only the link structure. This feature removes the complexity of the objects from the viewports and lets you work with the links directly. Although the objects disappear, you can still transform the objects using the link markers.

Viewing hierarchies

The Select From Scene dialog box (also called the Scene Explorer) and the Schematic and Track Views can display the hierarchy of objects in a scene as an ordered list, with child objects indented under parent objects.

Clicking the Select by Name button (H) on the main toolbar opens the Scene Explorer dialog box; select the Display ⇨ Display Children menu to see all the children under the selected object. Figure 9.3 shows the Select From Scene dialog box with the Display Children menu enabled.

Cross-Reference

You can learn more about the Scene Explorer in Chapter 6, "Selecting Objects and Setting Object Properties." ∎

FIGURE 9.3

The Select From Scene dialog box indents all child objects under their parent.

The Schematic View (opened with the Graph Editors ⇨ New Schematic View menu command) presents a graph in which objects are represented by rectangle nodes with their hierarchical links drawn as lines running between them.

Cross-Reference

For more information on using the Schematic View, see Chapter 25, "Building Complex Scenes with Containers, XRefs, and the Schematic View." ∎

The Track View (opened with the Graph Editors ⇨ New Track View menu command) displays lots of scene details in addition to the object hierarchy. In the Track View, you can easily expand and contract the hierarchy to focus on just the section you want to see or select.

Cross-Reference

For more information on using the Track View, see Chapter 37, "Working with the F-Curve Editor in the Track View." ∎

Working with Linked Objects

If you link some objects together and set some animation keys, and the magical Play button starts sending objects hurtling off into space, chances are good that you have a linked object that you didn't know about. Understanding object hierarchies and being able to transform those hierarchies are the keys to efficient animation sequences.

All transformations are done about an object's pivot point. You can move and reorient these pivot points as needed by clicking the Pivot button under the Hierarchy panel.

Several additional settings for controlling links are available under the Hierarchy panel of the Command Panel (the Hierarchy panel tab looks like a mini-organizational chart). Just click the Link Info button. This button opens two rollouts if a linked object is selected. You can use the Locks and Inherit rollouts to limit an object's transformations and specify the transformations that it inherits.

Cross-Reference

I present more information on object transformations in Chapter 7, "Transforming Objects, Pivoting, Aligning, and Snapping." ∎

Locking inheriting transformations

The Inherit rollout, like the Locks rollout, includes check boxes for each axis and each transformation, except that here, all the transformations are selected by default. By deselecting a check box, you specify which transformations an object does not inherit from its parent. The Inherit rollout appears only if the selected object is part of a hierarchy.

For example, suppose that a child object is created and linked to a parent and the X Move Inherit check box is deselected. As the parent is moved in the Y or Z directions, the child follows, but if the parent is moved in the X direction, the child does not follow. If a parent doesn't inherit a transformation, then its children don't, either.

Using the Link Inheritance utility

The Link Inheritance utility works in the same way as the Inherit rollout of the Hierarchy panel, except that you can apply it to multiple objects at the same time. To use this utility, open the Utility panel and click the More button. In the Utilities dialog box, select the Link Inheritance utility and click OK. The rollout for this utility is identical to the Inherit rollout discussed in the previous section.

Selecting hierarchies

You need to select a hierarchy before you can transform it, and you have several ways to do so. The easiest method is to simply double-click an object. Double-clicking the root object selects the entire hierarchy, and double-clicking an object within the hierarchy selects it and all of its children.

After you select an object in a hierarchy, pressing the Page Up or Page Down keyboard shortcut selects its parent or child objects. For example, if you select the Mommy duck object and press Page Down, the first baby duck object is selected and the Mommy duck object is deselected. Selecting any of the baby duck objects and pressing Page Up selects the duck object in front of it.

Linking to dummies

Dummy objects are useful as root objects for controlling the motion of hierarchies. By linking the parent object of a hierarchy to a dummy object, you can control all the objects by moving the dummy.

To create a dummy object, select Create ⇨ Helpers ⇨ Dummy, or open the Create panel, click the Helpers category button (this button looks like a small tape measure), and select the Standard category. Within the Object Type rollout is the Dummy button; click it, and then click in the viewport where you want the dummy object to be positioned. Dummy objects look like wireframe box objects in the viewports, but dummy objects are not rendered.

Tutorial: Circling the globe

When you work with complex models with lots of parts, you can control the object more easily if you link it to a Dummy object and then animate the dummy object instead of the entire model. To practice doing this, you'll create a simple animation of an airplane flying around the globe. To perform this feat, you create a dummy object in the center of a sphere, link the airplane model to it, and rotate the dummy object. This tutorial involves transforming and animating objects, which are covered in other chapters.

Cross-Reference
Rotating objects is covered in Chapter 7, "Transforming Objects, Pivoting, Aligning, and Snapping," and the basics of animation are covered in Chapter 21, "Understanding Animation and Keyframes." ∎

To link and rotate objects using a dummy object, follow these steps:

1. Open the Circling the globe.max file found in the Chap 09 directory on the CD.

   This file includes a texture mapped sphere with an airplane model positioned above it. The airplane model was created by Viewpoint Datalabs.

2. Select Create ⇨ Helpers ⇨ Dummy, and then drag in the center of the Sphere to create a Dummy object. With the Dummy object selected, choose the Tools ⇨ Align menu command (or press the Alt+A shortcut) and click on the globe. In the Align Selection dialog box, enable the X, Y, and Z Position options along with the Center options and click OK to align the centers of the dummy and globe objects.

3. Because the dummy object is inside the sphere, creating the link between the airplane and the dummy object can be difficult. To simplify this process, select and right-click the sphere object, and then select Hide Selection from the pop-up menu.

This hides the sphere so that you can create a link between the airplane and the dummy object.

4. Click the Select and Link button on the main toolbar, and drag a line from the airplane to the dummy object.

5. Click the Auto Key button (or press N) to enable animation key mode, and drag the Time Slider to frame 100. Then click the Select and Rotate button on the main toolbar (or press E), and select the dummy object. Then rotate the dummy object about its X-axis, and notice how the linked airplane also rotates over the surface of the sphere.

6. Select the dummy object and right-click to access the pop-up quadmenu. Then select the Unhide All menu command to make the sphere visible again.

By linking the airplane to a dummy object, you don't have to worry about moving the airplane's pivot point to get the correct motion. Figure 9.4 shows a frame from the final scene.

FIGURE 9.4

With a link to a dummy object, making the airplane circle the globe is easy.

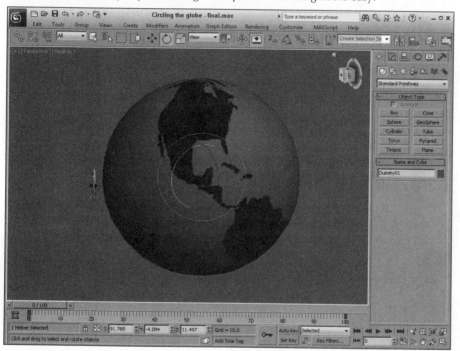

Summary

As scenes become more complex, the name of the game is organization. You can organize objects within the scene in several ways, including grouping, linking, and building hierarchies.

In this chapter, you've done the following:

- Grouped objects using the Group menu and learned to work with groups
- Learned about parent, child, and root relationships
- Created a hierarchy of objects using the Link and Unlink features
- Viewed links in the viewport
- Learned how to create and use dummy objects

In the next chapter, you jump headfirst into modeling by covering the basics of modeling and working with subobjects and helper objects.

Part III

Modeling Basics

Accessing Subobjects and Using Modeling Helpers

Modeling is the process of pure creation. Whether it is sculpting, building with blocks, construction work, carving, architecture, or advanced injection molding, many different ways exist for creating objects. Max includes many different model types and even more ways to work with them.

This chapter introduces the various modeling methods in Max. It also explains the common modeling components, including normals and subobjects. The chapter also covers many utilities and helpers that, well, help as you begin to model objects. The purpose of this chapter is to whet your whistle for modeling and to cover some of the general concepts that apply to all models. More specific details on the various modeling types are presented in the subsequent chapters, so onward into the realm of creation.

Exploring the Model Types

You can climb a mountain in many ways, and you can model one in many ways. You can make a mountain model out of primitive objects like blocks, cubes, and spheres, or you can create one as a polygon mesh. As your experience grows, you'll discover that some objects are easier to model using one method, and some are easier using another. Max offers several different modeling types to handle various modeling situations.

Parametric objects versus editable objects

All geometric objects in Max can be divided into two general categories—parametric objects and editable objects. *Parametric* means that the geometry of the object is controlled by variables called parameters. Modifying these parameters modifies the geometry of the object. This powerful concept gives parametric objects lots of flexibility. For example, the sphere object has a parameter called Radius. Changing this parameter changes the size of the sphere. Parametric objects in Max include all the objects found in the Create menu.

Editable objects do not have this flexibility of parameters, but they deal with subobjects and editing functions. The editable objects include Editable Spline, Mesh, Poly, Patch, and NURBS (Non-Uniform Rational B-Splines). Editable objects are listed in the Modifier Stack with the word *Editable* in front of their base object (except for NURBS objects, which are simply called NURBS Surfaces). For example, an editable mesh object is listed as Editable Mesh in the Modifier Stack.

Note

Actually, NURBS objects are a different beast altogether. When created using the Create menu, they are parametric objects, but after you select the Modify panel, they are editable objects with a host of subobject modes and editing functions. ■

Editable objects aren't created; instead, they are converted or modified from another object. When a primitive object is converted to a different object type like an Editable Mesh or a NURBS object, it loses its parametric nature and can no longer be changed by altering its base parameters. Editable objects do have their advantages, though. You can edit subobjects such as vertices, edges, and faces of meshes—all things that you cannot edit for a parametric object. Each editable object type has a host of functions that are specific to its type. These functions are discussed in the coming chapters.

Note

Several modifiers enable you to edit subobjects while maintaining the parametric nature of an object. These include Edit Patch, Edit Mesh, Edit Poly, and Edit Spline. ■

Max includes the following model types:

- **Primitives:** Basic parametric objects such as cubes, spheres, and pyramids. The primitives are divided into two groups consisting of Standard and Extended Primitives. The AEC Objects are also considered primitive objects. A complete list of primitives is covered in Chapter 5, "Creating and Editing Primitive Objects."

- **Shapes and splines:** Simple vector shapes such as circles, stars, arcs, and text, and splines such as the Helix. These objects are fully renderable. The Create menu includes many parametric shapes and splines. These parametric objects can be converted to Editable Spline objects for more editing. These are covered in Chapter 12, "Drawing and Editing 2D Splines and Shapes."

- **Meshes:** Complex models created from many polygon faces that are smoothed together when the object is rendered. These objects are available only as Editable Mesh objects. Meshes are covered in Chapter 13, "Modeling with Polygons."

- **Polys:** Objects composed of polygon faces, similar to mesh objects, but with unique features. These objects also are available only as Editable Poly objects. Poly objects are covered in Chapter 13, "Modeling with Polygons." The Graphite Modeling Tools are designed to work on Editable Poly objects. These tools are covered in Chapter 14, "Using the Graphite Modeling Tools and Painting with Objects."

- **Patches:** Based on spline curves; patches can be modified using control points. The Create menu includes two parametric Patch objects, but most objects can also be converted to Editable Patch objects. Bonus Chapter 5 on the CD, "Working with NURBS," covers patches in detail.

- **NURBS:** Stands for Non-Uniform Rational B-Splines. NURBS are similar to patches in that they also have control points. These control points define how a surface spreads over curves. NURBS are covered in Bonus Chapter 5 on the CD, "Working with NURBS."

- **Compound objects:** A miscellaneous group of model types, including Booleans, loft objects, and scatter objects. Other compound objects are good at modeling one specialized type of object such as Terrain or BlobMesh objects. All the Compound objects are covered in Chapter 27, "Working with Compound Objects."

- **Body objects:** Solid objects that are imported from an SAT file produced by a solid modeling application like Revit have the concept of volume. Max mesh objects typically only deal with surfaces but can be converted to a Body object. All the information on Body objects is covered in Chapter 28, "Working with Solids and Body Objects."

- **Particle systems:** Systems of small objects that work together as a single group. They are useful for creating effects such as rain, snow, and sparks. Particles are covered along with the Particle Flow interface in Chapter 41, "Creating Particles and Particle Flow."

- **Hair and fur:** Modeling hundreds of thousands of cylinder objects to create believable hair would quickly bog down any system, so hair is modeled using a separate system that represents each hair as a spline. The Hair and Fur modifiers are covered in Chapter 29, "Adding and Styling Hair and Fur, and Using Cloth."

- **Cloth systems:** Cloth—with its waving, free-flowing nature—behaves like water in some cases and like a solid in others. Max includes a specialized set of modifiers for handling cloth systems. Creating and using a cloth system is discussed in Chapter 29, "Adding and Styling Hair and Fur, and Using Cloth."

Note

Hair, fur, and cloth are often considered effects or dynamic simulations instead of modeling constructs, so their inclusion on this list should be considered a stretch. ■

With all these options, modeling in Max can be intimidating, but you learn how to use each of these types the more you work with Max. For starters, begin with primitive or imported objects and then branch out by converting to editable objects. A single Max scene can include multiple object types.

Converting to editable objects

Of all the commands found in the Create menu and in the Create panel, you won't find any menus or subcategories for creating editable objects.

To create an editable object, you need to import it or convert it from another object type. You can convert objects by right-clicking on the object in the viewport and selecting the Convert To submenu from the pop-up quadmenu, or by right-clicking on the base object in the Modifier Stack and selecting the object type to convert to in the pop-up menu.

Once converted, all the editing features of the selected type are available in the Modify panel, but the object is no longer parametric and loses access to its common parameters such as Radius and Segments. However, Max also includes specialized modifiers such as the Edit Poly modifier that maintain the parametric nature of primitive objects while giving you access to the editing features of the Editable object. More on these modifiers is presented in the later modeling chapters.

Caution

If a modifier has been applied to an object, the Convert To menu option in the Modifier Stack pop-up menu is not available until you use the Collapse All command. ■

The pop-up menu includes options to convert to editable mesh, editable poly, editable patch, and NURBS. If a shape or spline object is selected, then the object can also be converted to an editable spline. Using any of the Convert To menu options collapses the Modifier Stack.

Note

Objects can be converted between the different types several times, but each conversion may subdivide the object. Therefore, multiple conversions are not recommended. ∎

Converting between object types is done automatically using Max's best guess, but if you apply one of the Conversion modifiers to an object, several parameters are displayed that let you define how the object is converted. For example, the Turn to Mesh modifier includes an option to Use Invisible Edges, which divides polygons using invisible edges. If this option is disabled, then the entire object is triangulated. The Turn to Patch modifier includes an option to make quads into quad patches. If this option is disabled, all quads are triangulated.

The Turn to Poly modifier includes options to Keep Polygons Convex, Limit Polygon Size, Require Planar Polygons, and Remove Mid-Edge Vertices. The Keep Polygons Convex option divides any polygon that is concave, if enabled. The Limit Polygon Size option lets you specify the maximum allowable polygon size. This can be used to eliminate any pentagons and hexagons from the mesh. The Require Planar Polygons option keeps adjacent polygons as triangles if the angle between them is greater than the specified Threshold value. The Remove Mid-Edge Vertices option removes any vertices caused by intersections with invisible edges.

All Conversion modifiers also include options to preserve the current subobject selection (including any soft selection) and to specify the Selection Level. The From Pipeline option uses the current subobject selection that is selected on the given object. After a Conversion modifier is applied to an object, you must collapse the Modifier Stack in order to complete the conversion.

Understanding Normals

Before moving on to the various subobjects, you need to understand what a normal is and how it is used to tell which way the surface is facing. *Normals* are vectors that extend outward perpendicular to the surface of an object. These vectors aren't rendered and are used only to tell which way the surface face is pointing. If the normal vector points toward the camera, then the polygon is visible, but if it points away from the camera, then you are looking at its backside, which is visible only if the Backface Cull option in the Object Properties dialog box is disabled.

Several other properties also use the normal vector to determine how the polygon face is shaded, smoothed, and lighted. Normals are also used in dynamic simulations to determine collisions between objects.

Viewing normals

In all mesh subobject modes except for Edge, you can select the Show Normals option to see any object's normals and set a Scale value. Figure 10.1 shows a Plane, a Box, and a Sphere object. Each object has been converted to an Editable Mesh with all faces selected in Face subobject mode and with the Show Normals option selected.

Tutorial: Cleaning up imported meshes

Many 3D formats are mesh-based, and importing mesh objects sometimes can create problems. By collapsing an imported model to an Editable Mesh, you can take advantage of several of the editable mesh features to clean up these problems.

FIGURE 10.1

The Show Normals option shows the normal vectors for each face in a Plane, a Box, and a Sphere.

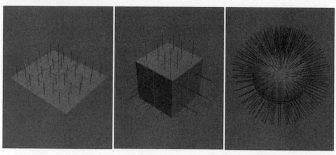

Cross-Reference

The Modifier menu includes two modifiers that you can use to work with normals. The Normals and Edit Normals modifiers are covered in Chapter 26, "Deforming Surfaces and Using the Mesh Modifiers." ∎

Figure 10.2 shows a model that was exported from Poser using the 3ds format. Notice that the model's waist is black. It appears this way because I've turned off the Backface Cull option in the Object Properties dialog box. If it were turned on, his waist would be invisible. The problem here is that the normals for this object are pointing in the wrong direction. This problem is common for imported meshes, and you'll fix it in this tutorial.

To fix the normals on an imported mesh model, follow these steps:

1. Open the Hailing taxi man with incorrect normals.max file from the Chap 10 directory on the CD.

2. Select the problem object—the waist on the right mesh. Open the object hierarchy by clicking the plus sign to the left of the Editable Mesh object in the Modifier Stack, and then select Element subobject mode and click on the waist area.

3. In the Selection rollout, select the Show Normals option and set the Scale value to a small number such as **0.1**.

   The normals are now visible. Notice that some of them point outward, and some of them point inward.

4. With the element subobject still selected, click the Unify button in the Surface Properties rollout and then click the Flip button until all normals are pointing outward.

This problem is fixed, and the waist object is now a visible part of the mesh. The fixed mesh on the right looks just like the original mesh on the left without the ugly black shorts, as shown in Figure 10.2.

FIGURE 10.2

This mesh suffers from objects with flipped normals, which makes them invisible.

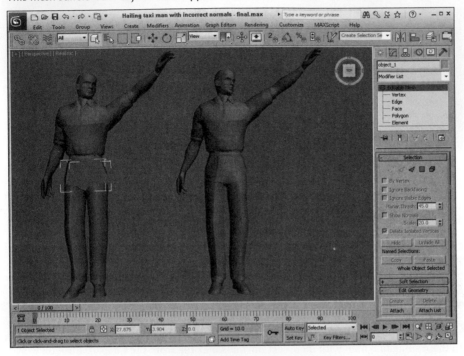

Working with Subobjects

All the editable modeling types offer the ability to work with subobjects. Subobjects are the elements that make up the model and can include vertices, edges, faces, polygons, and elements. These individual subobjects can be selected and transformed just like normal objects using the transformation tools located on the main toolbar. But, before you can transform these subobjects, you need to select them. You can select subobjects only when you're in a particular subobject mode. Each editable object type has a different set of subobjects.

If you expand the object's hierarchy in the Modifier Stack (by clicking the small plus sign to the left of the object's name), all subobjects for an object are displayed, as shown in Figure 10.3. Selecting a subobject in the Modifier Stack places you in subobject mode for that subobject type. You can also enter subobject mode by clicking on the subobject icons located at the top of the Selection rollout or by pressing the 1 through 5 keys on the keyboard. When you're in subobject mode, the subobject title and the icon in the Selection rollout are highlighted yellow. You can work with the selected subobjects only while in subobject mode. To transform the entire object again, you need to exit subobject mode, which you can do by clicking either the subobject title or the subobject icon, or by pressing one of the keyboard shortcuts, 1–5.

Tip

You can also access the subobject modes using the right-click quadmenu. To exit a subobject mode, select Top Level in the quadmenu. ■

FIGURE 10.3

Expanding an editable object in the Modifier Stack reveals its subobjects.

Subobjects icons

Subobject selections can be locked with the Selection Lock Toggle (spacebar) and be made into a Selection Set by typing a name into the Named Selection Set drop-down list on the main toolbar. After a Selection Set is created, you can recall it any time you are in that same subobject mode. Named Selection Sets can then be copied and pasted between objects using the Copy and Paste buttons found in the Selection rollout for most editable objects.

Using Soft Selection

When working with editable mesh, poly, patches, or splines, the Soft Selection rollout, shown in Figure 10.4, becomes available in subobject mode. Soft Selection selects all the subobjects surrounding the current selection and applies transformations to them to a lesser extent. For example, if a face is selected and moved a distance of 2, then with linear Soft Selection, the neighboring faces within the soft selection range move a distance of 1. The overall effect is a smoother transition.

Note

The Soft Selection options are different for the various modeling types. For example, the Editable Mesh includes a standard set of options like those in Figure 10.4, but the Editable Poly object has more options, including a Paint Soft Selection mode. ∎

The Use Soft Selection parameter enables or disables the Soft Selection feature. The Edge Distance option sets the range (the number of edges from the current selection) that the Soft Selection will affect. If disabled, the distance is determined by the Falloff amount. The Affect Backfacing option applies the Soft Selection to selected subobjects on the backside of an object. For example, if you are selecting vertices on the front of a sphere object and the Affect Backfacing option is enabled, then vertices on the opposite side of the sphere are also selected.

FIGURE 10.4

The Soft Selection rollout is available only in subobject mode.

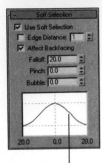

Soft Selection curve

The Soft Selection curve shows a graphical representation of how the Soft Selection is applied. The Falloff value defines the spherical region where the Soft Selection has an effect. The Pinch button sharpens the point at the top of the curve. The Bubble button has an opposite effect and widens the curve. Figure 10.5 shows several sample values and the resulting curve.

The Customize User Interface dialog box recognizes a mode to Edit Soft Selection if you select one of the modeling types in the Group drop-down list, which you can assign to a keyboard shortcut. You can toggle this mode on and off for the Edit Mesh modifier using the keyboard shortcut 7, but for Edit Poly, you'll need to set it yourself.

Cross-Reference

The Customize User Interface and assigning keyboard shortcuts are covered in Chapter 4, "Changing Interface Units and Setting Preferences." ∎

Once the Edit Soft Selection mode is enabled, the cursor changes to a custom cursor. When this cursor appears, you can drag to change the Soft Selection's falloff value. If you click, the cursor changes and lets you drag to change the Pinch value. One more click and you can edit the Bubble value and another click returns you to the falloff edit mode. Pressing the keyboard shortcut again exits Edit Soft Selection mode.

For Editable Poly objects, the bottom of the Soft Selection rollout includes a Paint Soft Selection section. You can use these controls to paint the soft selection weights that subobjects receive.

Cross-Reference

For more information on the paint interface and these controls, see Chapter 26, "Deforming Surfaces and Using the Mesh Modifiers." ∎

FIGURE 10.5

The Soft Selection curve is affected by the Falloff, Pinch, and Bubble values.

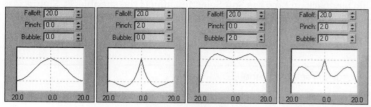

Tutorial: Soft selecting a heart shape from a plane

Soft Selection enables a smooth transition between subobjects, but sometimes you want the abrupt edge. This tutorial looks at moving some subobject vertices in a plane object with and without Soft Selection enabled.

To move subobject vertices with and without Soft Selection, follow these steps:

1. Open the Soft selection heart.max file from the Chap 10 directory on the CD.

   This file contains two simple plane objects that have been converted to Editable Mesh objects. Several vertices in the shape of a heart are selected.

2. The vertices on the first plane object are already selected; in Vertex subobject mode, click the Select and Move button (or press the W key), move the cursor over the selected vertices, and drag upward in the Left viewport away from the plane.

3. Exit subobject mode, select the second plane object, and enter Vertex subobject mode. The same vertices are again selected. Open the Soft Selection rollout, enable the Use Soft Selection option, and set the Falloff value to **40**.

4. Click the Select and Move button (or press the W key), and move the selected vertices upward. Notice the difference that Soft Selection makes.

Figure 10.6 shows the two resulting plane objects with the heart selections.

FIGURE 10.6

Soft Selection makes a smooth transition between the subobjects that are moved and those that are not.

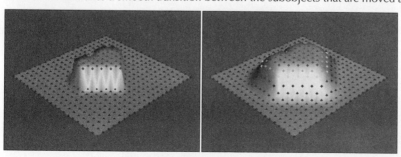

When you select subobjects, they turn red. Non-selected subobjects are blue, and soft selected subobjects are a gradient from orange to yellow, depending on their distance from the selected subobjects. This visual clue provides valuable feedback on how the Soft Selection affects the subobjects. Figure 10.7 shows the selected vertices from the preceding tutorial with Falloff values of 0, 20, 40, 60, and 80.

FIGURE 10.7

A gradient of colors shows the transition zone for soft selected subobjects.

For the Editable Poly and Editable Patch objects, the Soft Selection rollout includes a Shaded Face Toggle button below its curve. This button shades the surface using the soft selection gradient colors, as shown in Figure 10.8. This shaded surface is displayed in any shaded viewports. The cooler colors have less of an impact over the transform.

FIGURE 10.8

The Shaded Face Toggle shades the surface using the soft selection gradient colors.

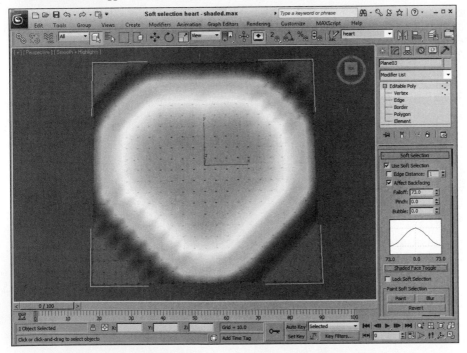

Applying modifiers to subobject selections

The preceding chapter introduced modifiers and showed how they can be applied to entire objects. But you can also apply modifiers to subobjects. If the modifier isn't available for subobjects, it is excluded from the Modifier List or disabled in the Modifiers menu.

If your object isn't an editable object with available subobjects, you can still apply a modifier using one of the specialized Select modifiers. These modifiers let you select a subobject and apply a modifier to it without having to convert it to a non-parametric object. These Select modifiers include Mesh Select, Poly Select, Patch Select, Spline Select, Volume Select, FFD (Free Form Deformers) Select, and Select by Channel. You can find all these modifiers in the Modifiers ⇨ Selection submenu.

After you apply a Select modifier to an object, you can select subobjects in the normal manner using the hierarchy in the Modifier Stack or the subobject icons in the Parameters rollout. Any modifiers that you apply after the Select modifier (they appear above the Select modifier in the Modifier Stack) affect only the subobject selection.

Using Modeling Helpers

In the Create panel (and the Create menu) is a category of miscellaneous objects called *helpers* (the icon looks like a tape measure). These objects are useful in positioning objects and measuring dimensions. The buttons in the Helper category include Dummy, Container, Crowd, Delegate, ExposeTM, Grid, Point, Tape, Protractor, and Compass.

Cross-Reference

The Container helper is covered in Chapter 9, "Grouping, Linking, and Parenting Objects." Crowd and Delegate helpers are discussed in Chapter 39, "Animating Characters with CAT," and the Expose Transform helper object is covered in Chapter 35, "Using Animation Layers, Modifiers and Complex Controllers." ■

Using Dummy and Point objects

The Dummy object is a useful object for controlling complex object hierarchies. A Dummy object appears in the viewports as a simple cube with a pivot point at its center, but the object will not be rendered and has no parameters. It is used only as an object about which to transform objects. For example, you could create a Dummy object that the camera could follow through an animation sequence. Dummy objects are used in many examples throughout the remainder of the book.

The Point object is very similar to the Dummy object in that it also is not rendered and has minimal parameters. A Point object defines a point in space and is identified as an X, an Axis Tripod, or a simple Box. The Center Marker option places an X at the center of the Point object (so X really does mark the spot). The Axis Tripod option displays the X-, Y-, and Z-axes, the Cross option extends the length of the marker along each axis, and the Box option displays the Point object as a Box. The Size value determines how big the Point object is.

Tip

The Size parameter actually makes Point helpers preferable over Dummy helpers because you can parametrically change their size. ■

The Constant Screen Size option keeps the size of the Point object constant, regardless of how much you zoom in or out of the scene. The Draw on Top option draws the Point object above all other scene objects, making it easy to locate. The main purpose for the Point object is to mark positions within the scene.

Caution

Point objects are difficult to see and easy to lose. If you use a point object, be sure to name it so you can find it easily in the Select from Scene dialog box. ■

Measuring coordinate distances

The Helpers category also includes several handy utilities for measuring dimensions and directions. These are the Tape, Protractor, and Compass objects. The units are all based on the current selected system units.

Using the Measure Distance tool

In the Tools menu is a command to Measure Distance. This tool is easy to use. Just select it and click at the starting point and again at the ending point; the distance between the two clicks is shown in the Status Bar at the bottom of the interface. Measure Distance also reports the Delta values in the X, Y, and Z directions. You can use this tool with the Snap feature enabled for accurate measurements.

Using the Tape helper

You use the Tape object to measure distances. To use it, simply drag the distance that you would like to measure and view the resulting dimension in the Parameters rollout. You can also set the length of the Tape object using the Specify Length option. You can move and reposition the end points of the Tape object with the Select and Move button, but the Rotate and Scale buttons have no effect.

Using the Protractor helper

The Protractor object works in a manner similar to the Tape object, but it measures the angle between two objects. To use the Protractor object, click in a viewport to position the Protractor object. (The Protractor object looks like two pyramids aligned point to point and represents the origin of the angle.) Then click the Pick Object 1 button, and select an object in the scene. A line is drawn from the Protractor object to the selected object. Next, click the Pick Object 2 button. The angle-formed objects and the Protractor object are displayed in the Parameters rollout. The value changes when either of the selected objects or the Protractor is moved.

Note

All measurement values are presented in gray fields within the Parameters rollout. This gray field indicates that the value cannot be modified. ■

Using the Compass helper

The Compass object identifies North, East, West, and South positions on a planar star-shaped object. You can drag the Compass object to increase its size.

Cross-Reference

The Grid helper object is discussed along with grids in Chapter 7, "Transforming Objects, Pivoting, Aligning, and Snapping." The Compass object is mainly used in conjunction with the Sunlight System, which you can learn about in Chapter 20, "Using Lights and Basic Lighting Techniques." ■

Using the Measure utility

In the Utilities panel is another useful tool for getting the scoop on the current selected object: the Measure utility. You can open the Measure utility as a floater dialog box, shown in Figure 10.9. This dialog box displays the object's name along with its Surface Area, Volume, Center of Mass, Length (for shapes), and Dimensions. It also includes an option to lock the current selection.

FIGURE 10.9

The Measure utility dialog box displays some useful information.

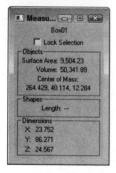

Using the Level of Detail utility

As a scene is animated, some objects are close to the camera, and others are far from it. Rendering a complex object that is far from the camera doesn't make much sense. Using the Level of Detail (LOD) utility, you can have Max render a simpler version of a model when it is farther from the camera and a more complex version when it is close to the camera.

Cross-Reference

The MultiRes modifier can also create real-time level of detail updates. It is covered in Chapter 26, "Deforming Surfaces and Using the Mesh Modifiers." ■

To open the utility, click the More button in the Utility panel and select the Level of Detail utility. A single rollout is loaded into the Utility panel, as shown in Figure 10.10. To use this utility, you need to create several versions of an object and group them together. The Create New Set button lets you pick an object group from the viewports. The objects within the group are individually listed in the rollout pane.

If you select a listed object, you can specify the Threshold Units in pixels or as a percentage of the target image. For each listed item, you can specify minimum and maximum thresholds. The Image Output Size values are used to specify the size of the output image, and the different models used are based on the size of the object in the final image. The Display in Viewports check box causes the appropriate LOD model to appear in the viewport.

FIGURE 10.10

The Level of Detail utility (split into two parts) can specify how objects are viewed, based on given thresholds.

Summary

Understanding the basics of modeling helps you as you build scenes. In this chapter, you've seen several different object types that are available in Max. Many of these types have similar features such as Soft Selection. Several helper objects can assist as well. This chapter covered the following topics:

- Understanding parametric objects and the various modeling types
- Viewing normals
- Using subobjects and soft selections
- Using helper objects and utilities

In the next chapter, you learn another excellent tool for deforming mesh objects. Modifiers allow specific types of deformation to be applied to an object such as bending, twisting, or rippling a surface.

Introducing Modifiers and Using the Modifier Stack

Think for a moment of a woodshop with all its various (and expensive) tools and machines. Some tools, like a screwdriver or a sander, are simple, and others, like a lathe or router, are more complex, but they all change the wood (or models) in different ways. In some ways, you can think of modifiers as the tools and machines that work on 3D objects.

Each woodshop tool has different parameters that control how it works, such as how hard you turn the screwdriver or the coarseness of the sandpaper. Likewise, each modifier has parameters that you can set that determine how it affects the 3D object.

Modifiers can be used in a number of different ways to reshape objects, apply material mappings, deform an object's surface, and perform many other actions. Many different types of modifiers exist. This chapter introduces you to the concept of modifiers and explains the basics on how to use them. The chapter concludes by exploring two different categories of modifiers that are used to deform geometry objects: Parametric Deformers and Free Form Deformers (FFD).

Exploring the Modifier Stack

All modifiers applied to an object are listed together in a single location known as the *Modifier Stack*. This Stack is the manager for all modifiers applied to an object and can be found at the top of the Modify panel in the Command Panel. You can also use the Stack to apply and delete modifiers; cut, copy, and paste modifiers between objects; and reorder them.

Understanding Base Objects

The first entry in the Modifier Stack isn't a modifier at all; it is the Base Object. The Base Object is the original object type. The Base Object for a primitive is listed as its object type, such as Sphere or Torus. Editable meshes, polys, patches, and splines can also be Base Objects. NURBS Surfaces and NURBS Curves are also Base Objects.

You can also see the Base Objects using the Schematic View window if you enable the Base Objects option in the Display floater.

Applying modifiers

An object can have several modifiers applied to it. Modifiers can be applied using the Modifiers menu or by selecting the modifier from the Modifier List drop-down list located at the top of the Modify panel directly under the object name. Selecting a modifier in the Modifiers menu or from the Modifier List applies the modifier to the current selected object. Modifiers can be applied to multiple objects if several objects are selected.

Tip

You can quickly jump to a specific modifier in the Modifier List by pressing the first letter of the modifier that you want to select. For example, pressing the T key when the Modifier List is open immediately selects the Taper modifier. ■

Note

Some modifiers aren't available for some types of objects. For example, the Extrude and Lathe modifiers are enabled only when a spline or shape is selected. ■

Other Modifier Stack entities

Most modifiers are Object-Space modifiers, but another category called World-Space modifiers also exists. World-Space modifiers are similar to Object-Space modifiers, except they are applied using a global coordinate system instead of a coordinate system that is local to the object. More on World-Space modifiers is presented later in this chapter, but you should be aware that World-Space modifiers (identified with the initials WSM) appear at the top of the Modifier Stack and are applied to the object after all Object-Space modifiers.

In addition to World-Space modifiers, Space Warp bindings also appear at the top of the Modifier Stack.

Cross-Reference

Space Warps are covered in Chapter 42, "Using Space Warps." ■

Using the Modifier Stack

After a modifier is applied, its parameters appear in rollouts within the Command Panel. The Modifier Stack rollout, shown in Figure 11.1, lists the base object and all the modifiers that have been applied to an object. Any new modifiers applied to an object are placed at the top of the stack. By selecting a modifier from the list in the Modifier Stack, all the parameters for that specific modifier are displayed in rollouts.

The Modifier Stack rollout displays all modifiers applied to an object.

Tip

You can increase or decrease the size of the Modifier Stack by dragging the horizontal bar that appears beneath the Modifier Stack buttons. ■

Beneath the Modifier Stack are five buttons that affect the selected modifier. They are as described in Table 11.1.

TABLE 11.1		
Modifier Stack Buttons		
Button	**Name**	**Description**
	Pin Stack	Makes the parameters for the selected modifier available for editing even if another object is selected (like taking a physical pin and sticking it into the screen so it won't move).
	Show End Result On/Off Toggle	Shows the end results of all the modifiers in the entire Stack when enabled and only the modifiers up to the current selected modifier if disabled.
	Make Unique	Used to break any instance or reference links to the selected object. After you click this button, an object will no longer be modified along with the other objects for which it was an instance or reference. Works for Base Object and modifiers.
	Remove Modifier from the Stack	Used to delete a modifier from the Stack or unbind a Space Warp if one is selected. Deleting a modifier restores it to the same state it was in before the modifier was applied.
	Configure Modifier Sets	Opens a pop-up menu where you can select to show a set of modifiers as buttons above the Modifier Stack. You can also select which modifier set appears at the top of the list of modifiers. The pop-up menu also includes an option to configure and define the various sets of modifiers.

Cross-Reference

For more information on configuring modifier sets, see Chapter 4, "Changing Interface Units and Setting Preferences." ■

If you right-click on a modifier, a pop-up menu appears. This pop-up menu includes commands to rename the selected modifier, which you might want to do if the same modifier is applied to the same object multiple times. This pop-up menu also includes an option to delete the selected modifier among other commands.

Copying and pasting modifiers

The pop-up menu also includes options to cut, copy, paste, and paste instance modifiers. The Cut command deletes the modifier from the current object but makes it available for pasting onto other objects. The Copy command retains the modifier for the current object and makes it available to paste onto another object. After you use the Cut or Copy command, you can use the Paste command to apply the modifier to another object. The Paste Instance command retains a link between the original modifier and the instanced modifier, so that any changes to either modifier affect the other instances.

You can also apply modifiers for the current object onto other objects by dragging the modifier from the Modifier Stack and dropping it on the other object in a viewport. Holding down the Ctrl key while dropping a modifier onto an object in a viewport applies the modifier as an instance (like the Paste Instanced command). Holding down the Shift key while dragging and dropping a modifier on an object in the viewport removes the modifier from the current object and applies it to the object on which it is dropped (like the Cut and Paste commands).

Cross-Reference

You can also cut, copy, and paste modifiers using the Schematic View window. See Chapter 25, "Building Complex Scenes with Containers, XRefs, and the Schematic View," for more details. ■

Using instanced modifiers

When you apply a single modifier to several objects at the same time, the modifier shows up in the Modifier Stack for each object. These are *instanced modifiers* that maintain a connection to each other. If one of these instanced modifiers is changed, the change is propagated to all other instances. This feature is very helpful for modifying large groups of objects.

When a modifier is copied between different objects, you can select to make the copy an instance.

To see all the objects that are linked to a particular modifier, select an object in the viewport and choose Views ⇨ Show Dependencies. All objects with instanced modifiers that are connected to the current selection appear in bright pink. At any time, you can break the link between a particular instanced modifier and the rest of the objects using the Make Unique button in the Modifier Stack rollout.

Identifying instances and references in the Modifier Stack

If you look closely at the Modifier Stack, you will notice that it includes some visual clues that help you identify instances and references. Regular object and modifier copies appear in normal text, but instances appear in bold. This applies to both objects and modifiers. If a modifier is applied to two or more objects, then it appears in italic.

Referenced objects and modifiers can be identified by a Reference Object Bar that splits the Modifier Stack into two categories—ones that are unique to the referenced object (above the bar) and ones that are shared with the other references (below the bar).

Figure 11.2 shows each of these cases in the Modifier Stack.

Disabling and removing modifiers

Clicking the light bulb icon to the left of the modifier name toggles the modifier on and off. The right-click pop-up menu also offers options to turn the modifier off in the viewport or off for the renderer.

To remove a modifier from the Modifier Stack, just select the modifier and press the Remove Modifier button below the stack. This button removes the selected modifier only. You can select multiple modifiers at once by holding down the Ctrl key while clicking individually on the modifiers or by holding down the Shift key and clicking on the first and last modifiers in a range.

Reordering the Stack

Modifiers are listed in the Modifier Stack with the first applied ones on the bottom and the newest applied ones on the top. The Stack order is important and can change the appearance of the object. Max applies the modifiers starting with the lowest one in the Stack first and the topmost modifier last. You can change the order of the modifiers in the Stack by selecting a modifier and dragging it above or below the other modifiers. You cannot drag it below the object type or above any World-Space modifiers or Space Warp bindings.

FIGURE 11.2

The Modifier Stack changes the text style to identify instances and references.

Referenced modifier applied to two or more objects

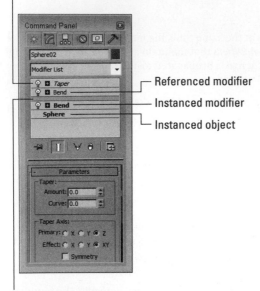

Reference object bar

Tutorial: Creating a molecular chain

Whether you're working with DNA splices or creating an animation to show how molecular chains are formed, you can use the Lattice and Twist modifiers to quickly create a molecular chain. Using these chains shows how reordering the Modifier Stack can change the outcome.

To create a molecular chain using modifiers, follow these steps:

1. Select Create ➪ Standard Primitives ➪ Plane, and drag in the Top viewport to create a Plane object. Set its Length to **300**, its Width to **60**, its Length Segments to **11**, and its Width Segments to **1**.

2. With the Plane object selected, select Modifiers ➪ Parametric Deformers ➪ Lattice to apply the Lattice modifier. Enable the Apply to Entire Object option. Then set the Struts Radius value to **1.0** with **12** sides and the Joints Base Type to **Icosa** with a Radius of **6.0** and a Segments value of **6**.

3. Select Modifiers ➪ Parametric Deformers ➪ Twist, and set the Twist Angle to **360** about the Y-axis.

4. Notice that the Sphere objects have been twisted along with the Plane object. You can fix this by switching the modifier order in the Modifier Stack. Select the Lattice modifier, and drag and drop it above the Twist modifier in the stack.

   This step corrects the elongated spheres.

Figure 11.3 shows the corrected molecular chain.

FIGURE 11.3

Changing the order of the modifiers in the Stack can affect the end result.

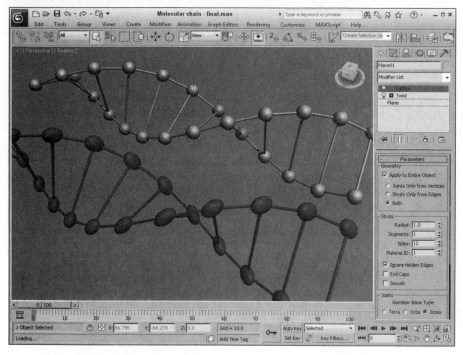

Holding and fetching a scene

Before going any further, you need to know about an important feature in Max that allows you to set a stopping point for the current scene. The Edit⮡ Hold command saves the scene into a temporary buffer for easy recovery. After a scene is set with the Hold command (Ctrl+H), you can bring it back instantly with the Edit⮡ Fetch command (Alt+Ctrl+F). These commands provide a quick way to backtrack on modifications to a scene or project without having to save and reload the project. If you use these commands before applying or deleting modifiers, you can avoid some potential headaches.

Tip

Along with saving your file often, using the Hold command before applying any complex modifier to an object is a good idea. ∎

Collapsing the Stack

Collapsing the Stack removes all its modifiers by permanently applying them to the object. It also resets the modification history to a baseline. All the individual modifiers in the Stack are combined into one single modification. This feature eliminates the ability to change any modifier parameters, but it simplifies the object. The right-click pop-up menu offers options to Collapse To and Collapse All. You can collapse the entire Stack with the Collapse All command, or you can collapse to the current selected modifier with the Collapse To command. Collapsed objects typically become Editable Mesh objects.

Tip

Another huge advantage of collapsing the Modifier Stack is that it conserves memory and results in smaller file sizes, which makes larger scenes load much quicker. Collapsing the Modifier Stack also speeds up rendering because Max doesn't need to calculate the stack results before rendering. ■

When you apply a collapse command, a warning dialog box appears, shown in Figure 11.4, notifying you that this action will delete all the creation parameters. Click Yes to continue with the collapse.

Note

In addition to the Yes and No buttons, the warning dialog box includes a Hold/Yes button. This button saves the current state of the object to the Hold buffer and then applies the Collapse All function. If you have any problems, you can retrieve the object's previous state before the collapse was applied by choosing Edit⇨Fetch (Alt+Ctrl+F). ■

FIGURE 11.4

Because the Collapse operation cannot be undone, this warning dialog box offers a chance to Hold the scene.

Using the Collapse utility

You can also use the Collapse utility found on the Utility panel to collapse the Modifier Stack. This utility enables you to collapse an object or several objects to a Modifier Stack Result or to a Mesh object. Collapsing to a Modifier Stack Result doesn't necessarily produce a mesh but collapses the object to its base object state, which is displayed at the bottom of the Stack hierarchy. Depending on the Stack, this could result in a mesh, patch, spline, or other object type. You can also collapse to a Single Object or to Multiple Objects.

If the Mesh and Single Object options are selected, you can also select to perform a Boolean operation. The Boolean operations are available if you are collapsing several overlapping objects into one. The options are Union (which combines geometries together), Intersection (which combines only the overlapping geometries), and Subtraction (which subtracts one geometry from another).

Cross-Reference

Boolean operations can also be performed using the Boolean compound object. See Chapter 27, "Working with Compound Objects," for details on this object type. ■

If multiple objects are selected, then a Boolean Intersection results in only the sections of the objects that are intersected by all objects; if no objects overlap, all objects disappear.

If you use the Boolean Subtraction option, you can specify which object is the base object from which the other objects are subtracted. To do so, select that object first and then select the other objects by holding down the Ctrl key and clicking them. Figure 11.5 shows an example of each of the Boolean operations.

FIGURE 11.5

Using the Collapse utility, you can select the following Boolean operations (shown from left to right): Union, Intersection, and Subtraction.

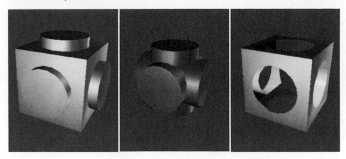

Using gizmo subobjects

As you've worked with modifiers, you've probably noticed the orange wireframe box that surrounds the object in the viewports when you apply the modifier. These boxes are called *modifier gizmos*, and they provide a visual control for how the modifier changes the geometry. If you want, you can work directly with these gizmos to affect the modifier.

Clicking the plus sign to the left of the modifier name reveals any subobjects associated with the modifier. To select the modifier subobjects, simply click the subobject name. The subobject name is highlighted in yellow when selected. Many modifiers create *gizmo subobjects*. Gizmos have an icon usually in the shape of a box that can be transformed and controlled like regular objects using the transformation buttons on the main toolbar. Another common modifier subobject is Center, which controls the point about which the gizmo is transformed.

Tutorial: Squeezing a plastic bottle

To get a feel for how the modifier gizmo and its center affect an object, this tutorial applies the Squeeze modifier to a plastic bottle; by moving its center, you can change the shape of the object.

To change a modifier's characteristics by moving its center, follow these steps:

1. Open the Plastic bottle.max file from the Chap 11 directory on the CD.

   This file includes a plastic squirt bottle with all the parts attached into a single mesh object.

2. With the bottle selected, choose the Modifiers ⇨ Parametric Deformers ⇨ Squeeze menu command to apply the Squeeze modifier to the bottle. Set the Radial Squeeze Amount value to **1**.

3. In the Modifier Stack, click the plus sign to the left of the Squeeze modifier to see the modifier's subobjects. Select the Center subobject.

   The selected subobject is highlighted in yellow.

4. Click the Select and Move (W) button on the main toolbar, and drag the center point in the Perspective viewport upward.

   Notice how the bottle's shape changes.

Figure 11.6 shows several different bottle shapes created by moving the modifier's center point.

FIGURE 11.6

By changing the modifier's center point, the bottle's shape changes.

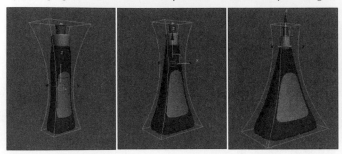

Modifying subobjects

In addition to being applied to complete objects, modifiers can also be applied and used to modify *subobjects*. A subobject is defined as a collection of object parts, such as vertices, edges, faces, or elements.

Cross-Reference

To learn more about applying modifiers to subobject selections, see Chapter 10, "Accessing Subobjects and Using Modeling Helpers." ■

To work in subobject selection mode, click the plus sign to the left of the object name to see the subobjects. Several modifiers, including Mesh Select, Spline Select, and Volume Select, can select subobject areas for passing these selections up to the next modifier in the Stack. For example, you can use the Mesh Select modifier to select several faces on the front of a sphere and then apply the Face Extrude modifier to extrude just those faces.

Topology dependency

When you attempt to modify the parameters of a Base Object that has a modifier applied, you sometimes get a warning dialog box that tells you that the modifier depends on topology that may change. Max is telling you that the surface of the object with that particular modifier is dependent on the subobjects that are selected and if you change the underlying subobjects, you may change the resulting topology. For example, the CrossSection and Surface modifiers build the surface using a set of splines, but if you change the original spline, you can destroy the resulting surfaced object. You can eliminate this problem by collapsing the Modifier Stack.

You can disable the warning by selecting the "Do not show this message again" option on the dialog box or by opening the Preference Settings dialog box and turning off the Display Topology-Dependence Warning option in the General panel of the Preference Settings dialog box. Disabling the warning does not make the potential problem go away; it only prevents the warning dialog box from appearing.

Exploring Modifier Types

To keep all the various modifiers organized, Max has grouped them into several distinct modifier sets. The modifier sets, as listed in the Modifier menu, include those listed in Table 11.2.

TABLE 11.2	

Modifiers Menu Items

Menu	Submenu Items
Selection Modifiers	FFD Select, Mesh Select, Patch Select, Poly Select, Select by Channel, Spline Select, Volume Select
Patch/Spline Editing	Cross Section, Delete Patch, Delete Spline, Edit Patch, Edit Spline, Fillet/ Chamfer, Lathe, Normalize Spline, Renderable Spline Modifier, Surface, Sweep, Trim/Extend
Mesh Editing	Cap Holes, Delete Mesh, Edit Mesh, Edit Normals, Edit Poly, Extrude, Face Extrude, MultiRes, Normal Modifier, Optimize, ProOptimizer, Quadify Mesh, Smooth, STL Check, Symmetry, Tessellate, Vertex Paint, Vertex Weld
Conversion	Turn to Mesh, Turn to Patch, Turn to Poly
Animation Modifiers	Attribute Holder, Flex, Linked XForm, Melt, Morpher, PatchDeform, PatchDeform (WSM), PathDeform, PathDeform (WSM), Skin, Skin Morph, Skin Wrap, Skin Wrap Patch, SplineIk Control, SurfDeform, SurfDeform (WSM)
Cloth	Cloth, Garment Maker, Welder
Hair and Fur	Hair and Fur (WSM)
UV Coordinates	Camera Map, Camera Map (WSM), MapScaler (WSM), Projection, Unwrap UVW, UVW Map, UVW Mapping Add, UVW Mapping Clear, UVW XForm
Cache Tools	Point Cache, Point Cache (WSM)
Subdivision Surfaces	HSDS Modifier, MeshSmooth, TurboSmooth
Free Form Deformers	FFD 2x2x2, FFD 3x3x3, FFD 4x4x4, FFD Box, FFD Cylinder
Parametric Deformers	Affect Region, Bend, Displace, Lattice, Mirror, Noise, Physique, Push, Preserve, Relax, Ripple, Shell, Slice, Skew, Stretch, Spherify, Squeeze, Twist, Taper, Substitute, XForm, Wave
Surface	Disp Approx, Displace Mesh (WSM), Material, Material By Element
NURBS Editing	Disp Approx, Surf Deform, Surface Select
Radiosity	Subdivide, Subdivide (WSM)
Cameras	Camera Correction

You can find roughly these same sets if you click the Configure Modifier Sets button in the Modifier Stack. Within this list is a single selected set. The selected set is marked with an arrow to the left of its name. The modifiers contained within the selected set appear at the very top of the Modifier List.

Cross-Reference

Covering all the modifiers together would result in a very long chapter. Instead, I decided to cover most of the modifiers in their respective chapters. For example, you can learn about the Mesh Editing modifiers in Chapter 26, "Deforming Surfaces and Using the Mesh Modifiers"; animation modifiers in Chapter 35, "Using Animation Layers, Modifiers, and Complex Controllers"; the UV Coordinates modifiers in Chapter 33, "Unwrapping UVs and Mapping Textures"; and so on. This chapter covers the Selection modifiers, Parametric Deformers, and FFD modifiers. ■

Object-Space versus World-Space modifiers

If you view the modifiers listed in the Modifier List, they are divided into two categories: Object-Space and World-Space modifiers (except for the selected set of modifiers that appear at the very top for quick access). Object-Space modifiers are more numerous than World-Space modifiers. For most World-Space modifiers, there is also an Object-Space version. World-Space modifiers are all identified with the abbreviation *WSM*, which appears next to the modifier's name.

Object-Space modifiers are modifiers that are applied to individual objects and that use the object's Local Coordinate System, so as the object is moved, the modifier goes with it.

World-Space modifiers are based on World-Space coordinates instead of on an object's Local Coordinate System, so after a World-Space modifier is applied, it stays put, no matter where the object with which it is associated moves.

Another key difference is that World-Space modifiers appear above all Object-Space modifiers in the Modifier Stack, so they affect the object only after all the other modifiers are applied.

Cross-Reference

All Space Warps are also applied using World-Space coordinates, so they also have the WSM letters next to their name. You can get more information on Space Warps in Chapter 42, "Using Space Warps." ■

Selection modifiers

The first modifiers available in the Modifiers menu are the Selection modifiers. You can use these modifiers to select subobjects for the various object types. You can then apply other modifiers to these subobject selections. Any modifiers that appear above a Selection modifier in the Modifier Stack are applied to the subobject selection.

Selection modifiers are available for every modeling type, including Mesh Select, Poly Select, Patch Select, Spline Select, Volume Select, FFD Select, and Select by Channel. There is also a Surface Select in the NURBS Editing category. You can apply the Mesh Select, Poly Select, Patch Select, and Volume Select modifiers to any 3D object, but you can apply the Spline Select modifier only to spline and shape objects, the FFD Select modifier only to the FFD Space Warps objects, and the NURBS Surface Select modifier (found in the NURBS Editing submenu) only to NURBS objects. Any modifiers that appear above one of these Selection modifiers in the Modifier Stack are applied only to the selected subobjects.

Cross-Reference

Each of the Selection modifiers is covered for the various modeling types in its respective chapter. For example, to learn about the Patch Select modifier, see Bonus Chapter 5 on the CD, "Working with NURBS." ■

When a Selection modifier is applied to an object, the transform buttons on the main toolbar become inactive. If you want to transform the subobject selection, you can do so with the XForm modifier.

Volume Select modifier

Among the Selection modifiers, the Volume Select modifier is unique. It selects subobjects based on the area defined by the modifier's gizmo. The Volume Select modifier selects all subobjects within the volume from a single object or from multiple objects. One of the benefits of using this modifier is that the subobjects within the volume can change as the object is moved during an animation sequence. It also can work with several objects at once.

In the Parameters rollout for the Volume Select modifier, you can specify whether subobjects selected within a given volume should be Object, Vertex, or Face subobjects. Any new selection can Replace, be Added to, or be Subtracted from the current selection. You can use the Invert option to select the subobjects outside of the current volume. You can also choose either a Window or Crossing Selection Type.

The actual shape of the gizmo can be a Box, Sphere, Cylinder, or Mesh Object. To use a Mesh Object, click the button beneath the Mesh Object option and then click the object to use in a viewport. In addition to selecting by a gizmo-defined volume, you can also select subobjects based on certain surface characteristics, such as Material IDs, Smoothing Groups, or a Texture Map including Mapping Channel or Vertex Color. This makes it possible to quickly select all vertices that have a Vertex Color assigned to them.

The Alignment options can Fit or Center the gizmo on the current subobject selection. The Reset button moves the gizmo to its original position and orientation, which typically is the bounding box of the object. The Auto Fit option automatically changes the size and orientation of the gizmo as the object it encompasses changes.

Note

The Volume Select modifier also includes a Soft Selection rollout. Soft Selection lets you select adjacent subobjects to a lesser extent. The result is a smoother selection over a broader surface area. The Soft Selection options are explained in Chapter 10, "Accessing Subobjects and Using Modeling Helpers." ■

Tutorial: Applying damage to a car

In this tutorial, you use the Volume Select modifier to select the front corner of a car and then apply Noise and XForm modifiers to make the corner look like it's been damaged in a collision.

To use modifiers to make a section of a car appear damaged, follow these steps:

1. Open the Damaged car.max file from the Chap 11 directory on the CD.

   This file includes a car model created by Viewpoint Datalabs.

2. With the front end of the car selected, choose the Modifiers ➪ Selection Modifiers ➪ Volume Select menu command.

   This command applies the Volume Select modifier to the group.

3. In the Modifier Stack, click the plus icon to the left of the modifier name and select the Gizmo subobject. Move the gizmo in the Top viewport so only the front corner of the car is selected. In the Parameters rollout, select the Vertex option.

4. Choose the Modifiers ➪ Parametric Deformers ➪ Noise menu command to apply the Noise modifier to the selected volume. In the Parameters rollout, enable the Fractal option and set the X, Y, and Z Strength values to **30**.

5. Choose Modifiers ➪ Parametric Deformers ➪ XForm to apply the XForm modifier, and use its gizmo to push the selected area up and to the left in the Top viewport. This step makes the section look dented.

Figure 11.7 shows the resulting damaged car. Notice that the rest of the object is fine and only the selected volume area is damaged.

Cross-Reference

You can see another example of how a Selection modifier can be used to select and apply a modifier to a subobject selection in Chapter 10, "Accessing Subobjects and Using Modeling Helpers." ■

FIGURE 11.7

The Noise and XForm modifiers are applied to just the subobject selection.

Parametric Deformer modifiers

Perhaps the most representative group of modifiers are the Parametric Deformers. These modifiers affect the geometry of objects by pulling, pushing, and stretching them. They all can be applied to any of the modeling types, including primitive objects.

Note

In the upcoming examples, you might start to get sick of seeing the hammer model used over and over, but using the same model enables you to more easily compare the effects of the various modifiers, and it's more interesting to look at than a simple box. ∎

Affect Region modifier

The Affect Region modifier can cause a local surface region to bubble up or be indented. Affect Region parameters include Falloff, Pinch, and Bubble values. The Falloff value sets the size of the affected area. The Pinch value makes the region tall and thin, and the Bubble value rounds the affected region.

You also can select the Ignore Back Facing option. Figure 11.8 shows the Affect Region modifier applied to a Quad Patch with a Falloff value of 80 on the left and with a Bubble value of 1.0 on the right. The height and direction of the region are determined by the position of the modifier gizmo, which is a line connected by two points.

Note

The Affect Region modifier accomplishes the same effect as the Soft Selection feature, but Affect Region applies the effect as a modifier, making it easier to discard. ■

FIGURE 11.8

The Affect Region modifier can raise or lower the surface region of an object.

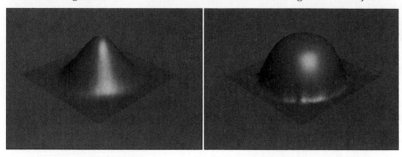

Bend modifier

The Bend modifier can bend an object along any axis. Bend parameters include the Bend Angle and Direction, Bend Axis, and Limits. The Bend Angle defines the bend in the vertical direction, and the Direction value defines the bend in the horizontal direction.

Limit settings are the boundaries beyond which the modifier has no effect. You can set Upper and Lower Limits relative to the object's center, which is placed at the object's pivot point. Limits are useful if you want the modifier applied to only one half of the object. The Upper and Lower Limits are visible as a simple plane on the modifier gizmo. For example, if you want to bend a tall cylinder object and have the top half remain straight, you can simply set an Upper Limit for the cylinder at the location where you want it to stay linear.

Note

Several modifiers have the option to impose limits on the modifier, including Upper and Lower Limit values. ■

The hammer in Figure 11.9 shows several bending options. The left hammer shows a Bend value of 75 degrees around the Z-axis, the middle hammer also has a Direction value of 60, and the right hammer has an Upper Limit of 8.

FIGURE 11.9

The Bend modifier can bend objects about any axis.

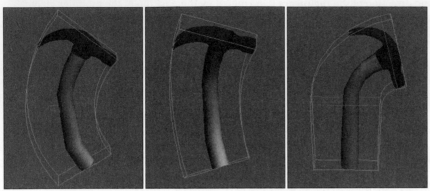

Tutorial: Bending a tree

If you have a tree model that you want to bend as if the wind were blowing, you can apply the Bend modifier. The tree then bends about its Pivot Point. Luckily, all the trees and plants found in the AEC Objects category have their Pivot Points set about their base, so bending a tree is really easy.

To bend a tree using the Bend modifier, follow these steps:

1. Select the Create ➪ AEC Objects ➪ Foliage menu command to access the available trees. Select a long, thin tree like the Yucca, and click in the Top viewport to add it to the scene.
2. With the tree selected, select the Modifiers ➪ Parametric Deformers ➪ Bend menu command to apply the Bend modifier to the tree.
3. In the Parameters rollout found in the Modify panel, set the Bend Axis to **Z** and the Bend Angle to **60**.

   The tree bends as desired.

Figure 11.10 shows the bending Yucca plant. To animate this tree bending back and forth, just set keys for the Angle parameter.

Displace modifier

The Displace modifier offers two unique sets of features. It can alter an object's geometry by displacing elements using a gizmo, or it can change the object's surface using a grayscale bitmap image. The Displace gizmo can have one of four different shapes: Planar, Cylindrical, Spherical, or Shrink Wrap. This gizmo can be placed exterior to an object or inside an object to push it from the inside.

Caution

In order for the Displace modifier to work, the surface requires a dense mesh, which can lead to very high polygon counts. ■

FIGURE 11.10

The Bend modifier can be used to bend trees.

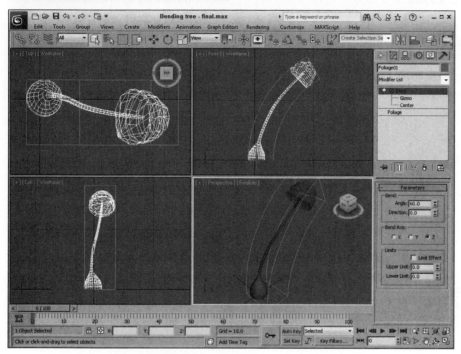

The Displace modifier parameters include Strength and Decay values. You can also specify the dimensions of the gizmo. A cylindrical-shaped gizmo can be capped or uncapped. The alignment parameters let you align the gizmo to the X-axis, Y-axis, or Z-axis, or you can align it to the current view. The rest of the parameters deal with displacing the surface using a bitmap image. Figure 11.11 shows a Quad Patch with the Plane-shaped gizmo applied with a Strength value of 25. To the right is a Quad Patch with the Sphere-shaped gizmo.

FIGURE 11.11

You can use the Displace modifier's gizmo as a modeling tool to change the surface of an object.

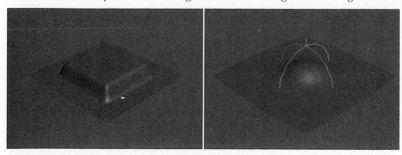

Cross-Reference

The Displace modifier can also alter an object's geometry using a grayscale bitmap image. This is similar to a Displacement map, which is covered in Chapter 17, "Adding Material Details with Maps." In many ways, the Displace gizmo works like the Conform compound object. You can learn about the Conform compound object in Chapter 27, "Working with Compound Objects." ■

Lattice modifier

The Lattice modifier changes an object into a lattice by creating struts where all the edges are located or by replacing each joint with an object. The Lattice modifier considers all edges as struts and all vertices as joints.

The parameters for this modifier include several options to determine how to apply the effect. These options include Apply to Entire Object, to Joints Only, to Struts Only, or Both (Struts and Joints). If the Apply to Entire Object option isn't selected, then the modifier is applied to the current subobject.

For struts, you can specify Radius, Segments, Sides, and Material ID values. You can also specify to Ignore Hidden Edges, to create End Caps, and to Smooth the Struts.

For joints, you can select Tetra, Octa, or Icosa types with Radius, Segments, and Material ID values. There are also controls for Mapping Coordinates.

Note

Although the joints settings enable you to select only one of three different types, you can use the Scatter compound object to place any type of object instead of the three defaults. To do this, apply the Lattice modifier and then select the Distribute Using All Vertices option in the Scatter Objects rollout. ■

Figure 11.12 shows the effect of the Lattice modifier. The left hammer has only joints applied, the middle hammer has only struts applied, and the right hammer has both applied.

FIGURE 11.12

The Lattice modifier divides an object into struts, joints, or both.

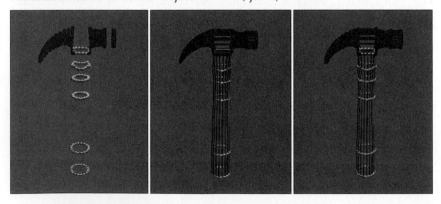

Mirror modifier

You can use the Mirror modifier to create a mirrored copy of an object or subobject. The Parameters rollout lets you pick a mirror axis or plane and an Offset value. The Copy option creates a copy of the mirrored object and retains the original selection.

Note

The Mirror modifier works the same as the Mirror command found in the Tools menu, but the modifier is handy if you want to be able to quickly discard the mirroring changes. ■

Noise modifier

The Noise modifier randomly varies the position of object vertices in the direction of the selected axes. Noise parameters include Seed and Scale values, a Fractal option with Roughness and Iterations settings, Strength about each axis, and Animation settings.

The Seed value sets the randomness of the noise. If two identical objects have the same settings and the same Seed value, they look exactly the same even though a random noise has been applied to them. If you alter the Seed value for one of them, then they will look dramatically different.

The Scale value determines the size of the position changes, so larger Scale values result in a smoother, less rough shape. The Fractal option enables fractal iterations, which result in more jagged surfaces. If Fractal is enabled, Roughness and Iterations become active. The Roughness value sets the amount of variation, and the Iterations value defines the number of times to complete the fractal computations. More iterations yield a wilder or chaotic surface but require more computation time.

If the Animate Noise option is selected, the vertices positions will modulate for the duration of frames. The Frequency value determines how quickly the object's noise changes, and the Phase setting determines where the noise wave starts and ends.

Figure 11.13 shows the Noise modifier applied to several sphere objects. These spheres make the Noise modifier easier to see than on the hammer object. The left sphere has Seed, Scale, and Strength values along all three axes set to 1.0, the middle sphere has increased the Strength values to 2.0, and the right sphere has the Fractal option enabled with a Roughness value of 1.0 and an Iterations value of 6.0.

FIGURE 11.13

The Noise modifier can apply a smooth or wild look to your objects.

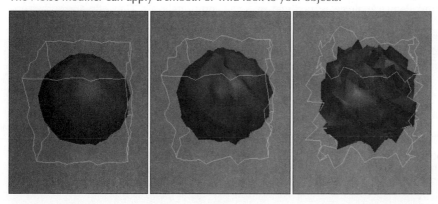

Cross-Reference

The Physique modifier is one of the original Character Studio tools. Although both modifiers still exist, the Skin modifier is preferred. It is covered in Chapter 40, "Skinning Characters." ■

Push modifier

The Push modifier pushes an object's vertices inward or outward as if they were being filled with air. The Push modifier also has one parameter: the Push value. This value is the distance to move with respect to the object's center.

The positive Push value pushes the vertices outward away from the center, and a negative Push value pulls the vertices in toward the center. The Push modifier can increase the size of characters or make an object thinner by pulling its vertices in. Figure 11.14 shows the hammer pushed with 0.05, 0.1, and 0.15 values.

FIGURE 11.14

The Push modifier can increase the volume of an object.

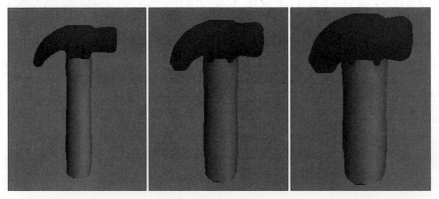

Preserve modifier

The Preserve modifier works to maintain Edge Lengths, Face Angles, and Volume as an object is deformed and edited. Before an object is modified, make an additional copy. Then edit one of the copies. To apply the Preserve modifier, click the Pick Original button; then click the unmodified object, and finally click the modified object. The object is modified to preserve the Edge Lengths, Face Angles, and Volume as defined in the Weight values. This helps prevent the topology of the modified object from becoming too irregular.

Note

In order for the Preserve modifier to keep objects and modifiers in check, it must be placed above the objects and modifiers it is watching. ■

The Iterations option determines the number of times the process is applied. You can also specify to apply to the Whole Mesh, to Selected Vertices Only, or to an Inverted Selection.

Relax modifier

The Relax modifier tends to smooth the overall geometry by separating vertices that lie closer than an average distance. Parameters include a Relax Value, which is the percentage of the distance that the vertices move. Values can range between 1.0 and –1.0. A value of 0 has no effect on the object. Negative values have the opposite effect, causing an object to become tighter and more distorted.

Tip

As you model, it is common for meshes to have sections that are too tight, which are dense locations in the mesh where a large concentration of vertices are close together. The Relax modifier can be used to cause the areas that are too tight to be relaxed. ■

The Iterations value determines how many times this calculation is computed. The Keep Boundary Points Fixed option removes any points that are next to an open hole. Save Outer Corners maintains the vertex position of corners of an object.

Ripple modifier

The Ripple modifier creates ripples across the surface of an object. This modifier is best used on a single object; if several objects need a ripple effect, use the Ripple Space Warp. The ripple is applied via a gizmo that you can control. Parameters for this modifier include two Amplitude values and values for the Wave Length, Phase, and Decay of the ripple.

The two amplitude values cause an increase in the height of the ripples opposite one another. Figure 11.15 shows the Ripple modifier applied to a simple Quad Patch with values of 10 for Amplitude 1 and a Wave Length value of 50. The right Quad Patch also has an Amplitude 2 value of 20.

FIGURE 11.15

The Ripple modifier can make small waves appear over the surface of an object.

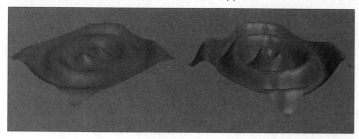

Shell modifier

When a mesh subobject is deleted, it leaves a hole in the surface that allows the inside of the object to be seen. This inside section doesn't have normals pointing the right direction, so the object appears blank unless the Force 2-Sided option in the Viewport Configuration dialog box is selected. The Shell modifier makes an object into a shell with a surface on the inside and outside of the object.

For the Shell modifier, you can specify Inner and Outer Amount values. This is the distance from the original position that the inner or outer surfaces are moved. These values together determine how thick the shell is. The Bevel Edges and Bevel Spline options let you bevel the edges of the shell. By clicking on the Bevel Spline button, you can select a spline to define the bevel shape.

For each Material ID, you can use the Material ID for the inner section or the outer section. The Auto Smooth Edge lets you smooth the edge for all edges that are within the Angle threshold. The edges can also be mapped using the Edge Mapping options. The options include Copy, None, Strip, and Interpolate. The Copy option uses the same mapping as the original face, None assigns new mapping coordinates, Strip maps the edges as one complete strip, and Interpolate interpolates the mapping between the inner and outer mapping.

The last options make selecting the edges, the inner faces, or the outer faces easy. The Straighten Corners option moves the vertices so the edges are straight.

Tutorial: Making a character from a sphere

Creating a little game character from a sphere is a good example of how the Shell modifier can be used.

To use the Shell modifier to create a character, follow these steps:

1. Open the Gobbleman shell.max file from the Chap 11 directory on the CD.

   This file includes a simple sphere object that has had several faces deleted.

2. With the sphere object selected, select Modifiers ⇨ Parametric Deformers ⇨ Shell to apply the Shell modifier. Set the Outer Amount to **5.0**.

   This makes the hollow sphere into a thin shell. Notice that the lighting inside the sphere is now correct.

Figure 11.16 shows the resulting shell.

FIGURE 11.16

The Shell modifier can add an inside to hollow objects.

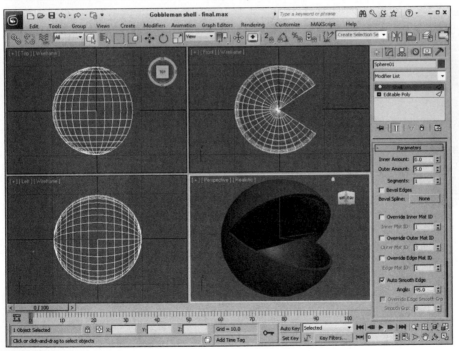

Slice modifier

You can use the Slice modifier to divide an object into two separate objects. Applying the Slice modifier creates a Slice gizmo. This gizmo looks like a simple plane and can be transformed and positioned to define the slice location. To transform the gizmo, you need to select it from the Stack hierarchy.

Note
You can use the Slice modifier to make objects slowly disappear a layer at a time. ■

The Slice parameters include four slice type options. Refine Mesh simply adds new vertices and edges where the gizmo intersects the object. The Split Mesh option creates two separate objects. The Remove Top and Remove Bottom options delete all faces and vertices above or below the gizmo intersection plane.

Using Triangular or Polygonal faces, you can also specify whether the faces are divided. Figure 11.17 shows the top and bottom halves of a hammer object. The right hammer is sliced at an angle.

The Slice modifier can cut objects into two separate pieces.

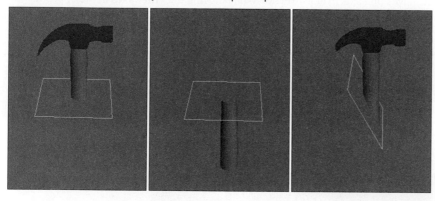

Note
Editable meshes also have a Slice tool that can produce similar results. The difference is that the Slice modifier can work on any type of object, not only on meshes. ■

Skew modifier

The Skew modifier changes the tilt of an object by moving its top portion while keeping the bottom half fixed. Skew parameters include Amount and Direction values, a Skew Axis, and Limits. Figure 11.18 shows the hammer on the left with a Skew value of 2.0, in the middle with a Skew value of 5, and on the right with an Upper Limit of 8.

FIGURE 11.18

You can use the Skew modifier to tilt objects.

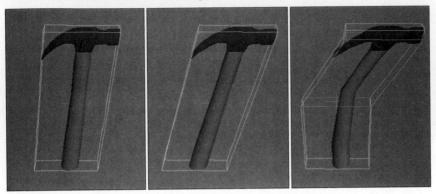

Stretch modifier

The Stretch modifier moves one axis in one direction while moving the other axes in the opposite direction, like pushing in on opposite sides of a balloon. Stretch parameters include Stretch and Amplify values, a Stretch Axis, and Limits.

The Stretch value equates the distance the object is pulled, and the Amplify value is a multiplier for the Stretch value. Positive values multiply the effect, and negative values reduce the stretch effect.

Figure 11.19 shows a Stretch value of 0.2 about the Z-axis applied to the hammer; the middle hammer also has an Amplify value of 2.0; and the right hammer has an Upper Limit value of 8.

FIGURE 11.19

The Stretch modifier pulls along one axis while pushing the other two.

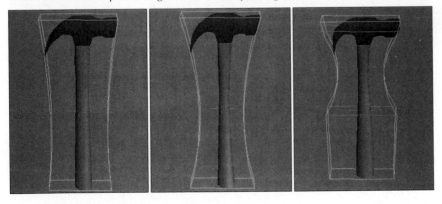

Spherify modifier

The Spherify modifier distorts an object into a spherical shape. The single Spherify parameter is the percent of the effect to apply. Figure 11.20 shows the hammer with Spherify values of 10, 20, and 30 percent.

The Spherify modifier is different from the Push modifier. Although they both are applied to the entire object, the Push modifier forces all vertices continuously outward, and the Spherify modifier uses a sphere shape as a limiting boundary. The visible difference is that the Spherify modifier creates a bulging effect.

FIGURE 11.20

The Spherify modifier pushes all vertices outward like a sphere.

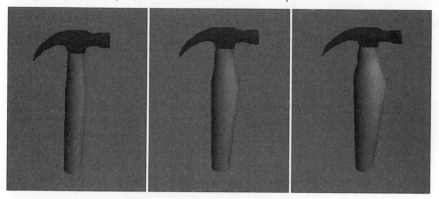

Tutorial: Making a fat crocodile

A good way to use the Spherify modifier is to add bulges to an object. For example, in this tutorial, you make a plump crocodile even fatter by applying the Spherify modifier.

To fatten up a crocodile character with the Spherify modifier, follow these steps:

1. Open the Fat crocodile.max file from the Chap 11 directory on the CD.

   This file includes a crocodile model created by Viewpoint Datalabs.

2. With the crocodile selected, select the Modifiers ⇨ Parametric Deformers ⇨ Spherify menu command to apply the Spherify modifier to the crocodile.

   The bulge appears around the object's pivot point.

3. In the Parameters rollout, set the Percent value to **15**.

Figure 11.21 shows the plump crocodile.

Note

The drawback of the Spherify modifier is that you have no control over its placement because there isn't a gizmo that you can position. One way around this problem is to use the Volume Select modifier to select a specific volume that is passed up the stack to the Spherify modifier. ■

FIGURE 11.21

The Spherify modifier can fatten up a crocodile.

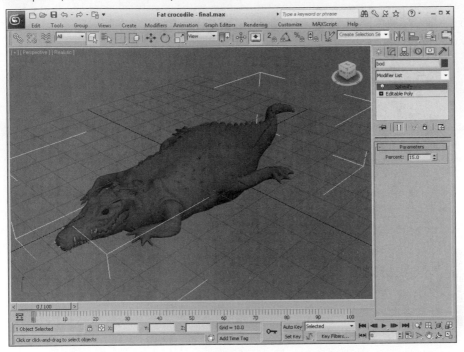

Squeeze modifier

The Squeeze modifier takes the points close to one axis and moves them away from the center of the object while it moves other points toward the center to create a bulging effect. Squeeze parameters include Amount and Curve values for Axial Bulge and Radial Squeeze, and Limits and Effect Balance settings.

The Effect Balance settings include a Bias value, which changes the object between the maximum Axial Bulge or the maximum Radial Squeeze. The Volume setting increases or decreases the volume of the object within the modifier's gizmo.

Axial Bulge is enabled with an Amount value of 0.2 and a Curve value of 2.0 in the left hammer in Figure 11.22; the middle hammer has also added Radial Squeeze values of 0.4 and 2.0; and the right hammer has an Upper Limit value of 8.

Twist modifier

The Twist modifier deforms an object by rotating one end of an axis in one direction and the other end in the opposite direction. Twist parameters include Angle and Bias values, a Twist Axis, and Limits.

The Angle value is the amount of twist in degrees that is applied to the object. The Bias value causes the twists to bunch up near the Pivot Point (for negative values) or away from the Pivot Point (for positive values).

FIGURE 11.22

The Squeeze modifier can bulge or squeeze along two different axes.

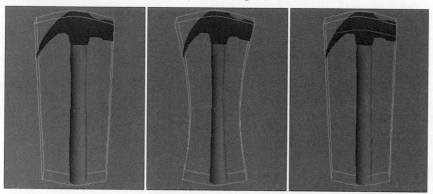

The left hammer in Figure 11.23 shows a twist angle of 120 about the Z-axis, the middle hammer shows a Bias value of 20, and the right hammer has an Upper Limit value of 8.

FIGURE 11.23

The Twist modifiers can twist an object about an axis.

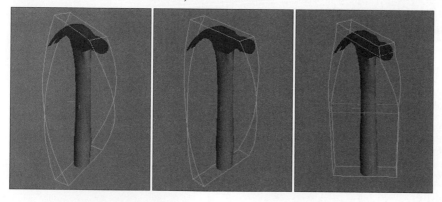

Taper modifier

The Taper modifier scales one end of an object. The tapered end is the end opposite the Pivot Point. Taper parameters include the Amount and Curve, Primary and Effect Axes, and Limits. The Amount value defines the amount of taper applied to the affected end. The Curve value bends the taper inward (for negative values) or outward (for positive values). You can see the curve clearly if you look at the modifier's gizmo. For example, you can create a simple vase or a bongo drum with the Taper modifier and a positive Curve value.

The Primary Axis defines the axis about which the taper is applied. The Effect axis can be a single axis or a plane, and the options change depending on your Primary Axis. This defines the axis or plane along which the object's end is scaled. For example, if the Z-axis is selected as the Primary Axis, then selecting the XY Effect plane scales the object equally along both the X-axis and the Y-axis. Selecting the Y Effect axis scales the end only along the Y-axis. You can also select a Symmetry option to taper both ends equally. Taper limits work just like the Bend modifier.

The left hammer in Figure 11.24 shows a taper of 1.0 about the Z-axis; the middle hammer has a Curve value of –2; and the right hammer has the Symmetry option selected.

FIGURE 11.24

The Taper modifier can proportionally scale one end of an object.

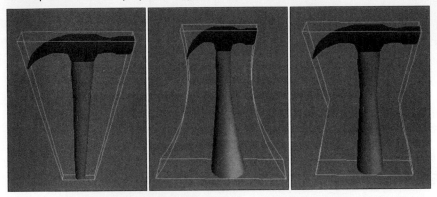

Tutorial: Creating a yo-yo

The Taper modifier can be used to create a variety of simple objects quickly, such as a yo-yo.

To create a yo-yo using the Taper modifier, follow these steps:

1. Select Create ⇨ Standard Primitives ⇨ Sphere, and drag in the Front viewport to create a sphere object.
2. With the sphere object selected, choose Modifiers ⇨ Parametric Deformers ⇨ Taper to apply the Taper modifier. Set the Taper Amount to **4.0** about the Primary Z-Axis and **XY** as the Effect plane, and enable the Symmetry option.

Figure 11.25 shows the resulting yo-yo; just add a string.

Substitute modifier

The Substitute modifier lets you place an object in the scene and substitute it with a higher-resolution object during render time. The substitute object may come from the scene or from an XRef file. To remove the substitute object, simply remove the Substitute modifier from the stack.

XForm modifier

The XForm modifier enables you to apply transforms such as Move, Rotate, and Scale to objects and/or subobjects. This modifier is applied by means of a gizmo that can be transformed using the transform buttons on the main toolbar. The XForm modifier has no parameters.

The XForm modifier solves a tricky problem that occurs during modeling. The problem happens when you scale, link, and animate objects in the scene, only to notice that the objects distort as they move. The distortion is caused because the transforms are the last action in the stack to be performed. So, when the object was first scaled and modifiers were applied, if you used the XForm modifier to do the scale transformation in the stack before the modifiers were applied, then the object's children won't inherit the scale transformation.

Note

XForm is short for the word transform. ∎

FIGURE 11.25

The Taper modifier can be used to create a simple yo-yo.

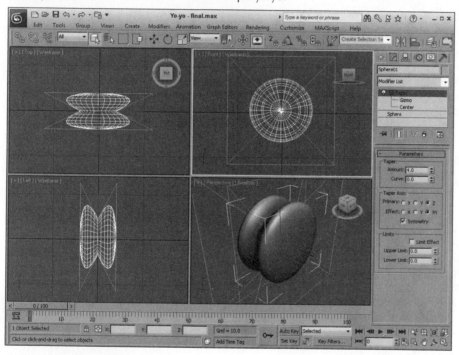

Wave modifier

The Wave modifier produces a wavelike effect across the surface of the object. All the parameters of the Wave Parameter are identical to the Ripple modifier parameters. The difference is that the waves produced by the Wave modifier are parallel, and they propagate in a straight line. Figure 11.26 shows the Wave modifier applied to a simple Quad Patch with values of 5 for Amplitude 1 and a Wave Length value of 50. The right Quad Patch also has an Amplitude 2 value of 20.

FIGURE 11.26

The Wave modifier produces parallel waves across the surface of an object.

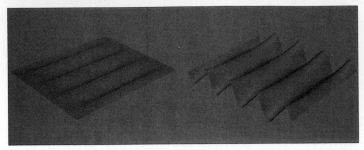

Tutorial: Waving a flag

The Wave modifier can add a gentle wave to an object such as a flag. If you animate the Phase value, you can show a flag unfurling in the breeze.

Cross-Reference

For a more realistic-looking flag, you can apply a Cloth modifier. See Chapter 29, "Adding and Styling Hair and Fur, and Using Cloth," for more information on the Cloth modifier. ■

To animate a flag waving with the Wave modifier, follow these steps:

1. Open the Waving US flag.max file from the Chap 11 directory on the CD.

   This file includes a simple flag and flagpole made from primitive objects.

2. With the flag selected, select the Modifiers ➪ Parametric Deformers ➪ Wave menu command to apply the Wave modifier to the flag.

3. Notice how the waves run from the top of the flag to the bottom. You can change this by rotating the gizmo. Click the plus sign to the left of the Wave modifier in the Modifier Stack and select the Gizmo subobject. With the Select and Rotate tool (E), rotate the gizmo 90 degrees and then scale the gizmo with the Select and Scale tool (R) so it covers the flag object. Click the Gizmo subobject again to deselect gizmo subobject mode.

4. Set Amplitude 1 to **25**, Amplitude 2 to **0**, and the Wave Length to **50**. Then click the Auto Key button (N), drag the Time Slider to frame 100, and set the Phase value to **4**. Click the Auto Key button (N) again to exit key mode.

Figure 11.27 shows the waving flag.

FIGURE 11.27

The Wave modifier can gently wave a flag.

Free Form Deformer modifiers

The Free Form Deformers category of modifiers causes a lattice to appear around an object. This lattice is bound to the object, and you can alter the object's surface by moving the lattice control points. Modifiers include FFD (Free Form Deformation) and FFD (Box/Cyl).

FFD (Free Form Deformation) modifier

The Free Form Deformation modifiers create a lattice of control points around the object. The object's surface can deform the object when you move the control points. The object is deformed only if it is within the volume of the FFD lattice. The three different resolutions of FFDs are 2 × 2, 3 × 3, and 4 × 4.

You can also select to display the lattice or the source volume, or both. If the Lattice option is disabled, only the control points are visible. The Source Volume option shows the original lattice before any vertices were moved.

The two deform options are Only In Volume and All Vertices. The Only In Volume option limits the vertices that can be moved to the interior vertices only. If the All Vertices option is selected, the Falloff value determines the point at which vertices are no longer affected by the FFD. Falloff values can range between 0 and 1. The Tension and Continuity values control how tight the lines of the lattice are when moved.

The three buttons at the bottom of the FFD Parameters rollout help in the selection of control points. If the All X button is selected, then when a single control point is selected, all the adjacent control points along the X-axis are also selected. This feature makes selecting an entire line of control points easier. The All Y and All Z buttons work in a similar manner in the other dimensions.

Use the Reset button to return the volume to its original shape if you make a mistake. The Conform to Shape button sets the offset of the Control Points with Inside Points, Outside Points, and Offset options.

To move the control points, select the Control Points subobject. This enables you to alter the control points individually.

FFD (Box/Cyl) modifiers

The FFD (Box) and FFD (Cyl) modifiers can create a box-shaped or cylinder-shaped lattice of control points for deforming objects. The Set Number of Points button enables you to specify the number of points to be included in the FFD lattice. Figure 11.28 shows how you can use the FFD modifier to distort the hammer by selecting the Control Point's subobjects. The left hammer is distorted using a $2 \times 2 \times 2$ FFD, the middle hammer has a $4 \times 4 \times 4$ FFD, and the right hammer is surrounded with an FFD (Cyl) modifier.

FIGURE 11.28

The FFD modifier changes the shape of an object by moving the lattice of Control Points that surround it.

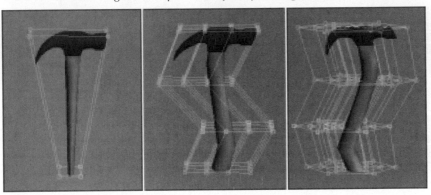

Cross-Reference

The FFD (Box) and FFD (Cyl) lattices are also available as Space Warps. To learn more about Space Warps, see Chapter 42, "Using Space Warps." ■

Tutorial: Modeling a tire striking a curb

The FFD modifiers are great for changing the shape of a soft-body object being struck by a solid object. Soft-body objects deform around the rigid object when they make contact. In this tutorial, you deform a tire hitting a curb.

To deform a tire striking a curb using an FFD modifier, follow these steps:

1. Open the Tire hitting a curb.max file from the Chap 11 directory on the CD.
   This file includes a simple tube object and a curb.
2. With the tire selected, choose the Modifiers ⇨ Free Form Deformers ⇨ FFD Cyl menu option.
   A cylinder gizmo appears around the tire.
3. Click the FFD name in the Modifier Stack, and select the Control Points subobject from the hierarchy list. Then select all the center control points in the Left viewport, and scale the control points outward with the Select and Scale tool (R) to add some roundness to the tire.
4. Then select all the control points in the lower-left corner of the Front viewport, and move these points diagonally up and to the right until the tire's edge lines up with the curb.

Figure 11.29 shows the tire as it strikes the hard curb.

FIGURE 11.29

This tire is being deformed via an FFD modifier.

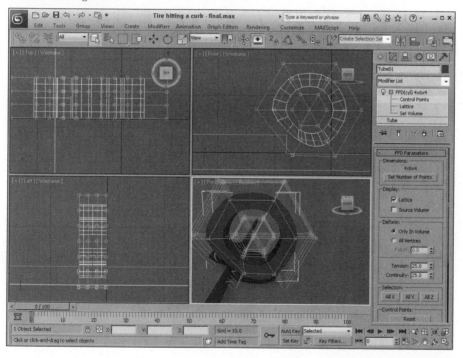

Summary

With the modifiers contained in the Modify panel, you can alter objects in a vast number of ways. Modifiers can work with every aspect of an object, including geometric deformations, materials, and general object maintenance. In this chapter, you looked at the Modifier Stack and how modifiers are applied and examined several useful modifier sets. These topics were covered in this chapter:

- Working with the Modifier Stack to apply, reorder, and collapse modifiers
- Exploring the Selection modifiers
- Using the Parametric Deformer and FFD modifiers

Now that you have the basics covered, you're ready to dive into the various modeling types. The first modeling type on the list is splines and shapes, which is covered in the next chapter.

Drawing and Editing 2D Splines and Shapes

Many modeling projects start from the ground up, and you can't get much lower to the ground than 2D. But this book is on 3D, you say? What place is there for 2D shapes? Within the 3D world, you frequently encounter flat surfaces—the side of a building, the top of a table, a billboard, and so on. All these objects have flat 2D surfaces. Understanding how objects are composed of 2D surfaces will help as you start to build objects in 3D. This chapter examines the 2D elements of 3D objects and covers the tools needed to work with them.

Working in 2D in Max, you use two general objects: splines and shapes. A *spline* is a special type of line that curves according to mathematical principles. In Max, splines are used to create all sorts of shapes such as circles, ellipses, and rectangles.

You can create splines and shapes using the Create ⇨ Shapes menu, which opens the Shapes category on the Create panel. Just as with the other categories, several spline-based shape primitives are available. Spline shapes can be rendered, but they are normally used to create more advanced 3D geometric objects by extruding or lathing the spline. You can even find a whole group of modifiers that apply to splines. You can use splines to create animation paths as well as Loft and NURBS (Non-Uniform Rational B-Splines) objects, and you will find that splines and shapes, although they are only 2D, are used frequently in Max.

> **IN THIS CHAPTER**
>
> **Working with shape primitives**
>
> **Editing splines and shapes**
>
> **Working with spline subobjects**
>
> **Using spline modifiers**

Drawing in 2D

Shapes in Max are unique from other objects because they are drawn in 2D, which confines them to a single plane. That plane is defined by the viewport used to create the shape. For example, drawing a shape in the Top view constrains the shape to the XY plane, whereas drawing the shape in the Front view constrains it to the ZX plane. Even shapes drawn in the Perspective view are constrained to a plane such as the Home Grid.

You usually produce 2D shapes in a drawing package such as Adobe Illustrator (AI) or CorelDRAW. Max supports importing line drawings using the AI format.

Cross-Reference

See Chapter 3, "Working with Files, Importing, and Exporting," to learn about importing AI files. ∎

Whereas newly created or imported shapes are 2D and are confined to a single plane, splines can exist in 3D space. The Helix spline, for example, exists in 3D, having height as well as width values. Animation paths in particular typically move into 3D space.

Working with shape primitives

The shape primitive buttons are displayed in the Object Type rollout of the Create panel when either the Create ➪ Shapes or the Create ➪ Extended Shapes menu is selected. The Shapes category include many basic shapes, including Line, Circle, Arc, NGon (a polygon where you can set the number of sides), Text, Section, Rectangle, Ellipse, Donut, Star, and Helix, as shown in Figure 12.1. The Extended Shapes category includes several shapes that are useful to architects, including WRectangle, Channel, Angle, Tee, and Wide Flange, as shown in Figure 12.2. Clicking any of these shape buttons lets you create the shape by dragging in one of the viewports. After a shape is created, several new rollouts appear.

FIGURE 12.1

The shape primitives in all their 2D glory: Line, Circle, Arc, NGon, Text, Section, Rectangle, Ellipse, Donut, Star, and Helix

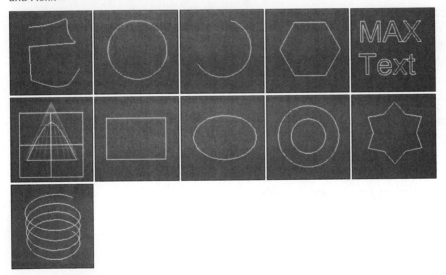

Above the Shape buttons are two check boxes: AutoGrid and Start New Shape. AutoGrid creates a temporary grid, which you can use to align the shape with the surface of the nearest object under the mouse at the time of creation. This feature is helpful for starting a new spline on the surface of an object.

FIGURE 12.2

The extended shape primitives: WRectangle, Channel, Angle, Tee, and Wide Flange

Cross-Reference

For more details on AutoGrid, see Chapter 7, "Transforming Objects, Pivoting, Aligning, and Snapping." ■

The Start New Shape option creates a new object with every new shape drawn in a viewport. Leaving this option unchecked lets you create compound shapes, which consist of several shapes used to create one object. Because compound shapes consist of several shapes, the shapes are automatically converted to be an Editable Spline object and you cannot edit them using the Parameters rollout. For example, if you want to create a target from several concentric circles, keep the Start New Shape option unselected to make all the circles part of the same object.

Just as with the Geometric primitives, every shape that is created is given a name and a color. You can change either of these in the Name and Color rollout.

Most of the shape primitives have several common rollouts: Rendering, Interpolation, Creation Method, Keyboard Entry, and Parameters, as shown in Figure 12.3. I cover these rollouts initially and then present the individual shape primitives.

FIGURE 12.3

These rollouts are common for most of the shape primitives.

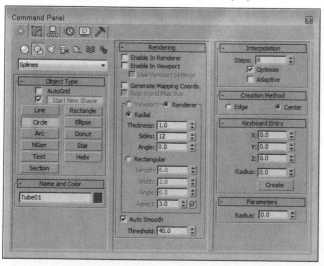

Rendering rollout

The Rendering rollout includes options for making a spline a renderable object. Making a spline a renderable object converts the spline into a 3D object that is visible when you render the scene. For renderable objects, you can choose to make the spline Radial or Rectangular. For the Radial option, you can specify a Thickness, the number of Sides, and the Angle values; for the Rectangular option, you can specify Length, Width, Angle, and Aspect values.

The Radial Thickness is the diameter of the renderable spline. The number of Sides sets the number of sides that make up the cross section of the renderable spline. The lowest value possible is 3, which creates a triangle cross section. The Length and Width values set the size along the Y-axis and the X-axis, respectively, of the rectangular sides. The Angle value determines where the corners of the cross section sides start, so you can set a three-sided spline to have a corner or an edge pointing upward. The Aspect value sets the ratio of the Length per Width. If the Lock icon to the right of the Aspect value is enabled, then the aspect ratio is locked, and changing one value affects the other.

Note

By default, a renderable spline has a 12-sided circle as its cross section. ■

You can choose different rendering values for the viewport and for the renderer using the Viewport and Renderer options above the Radial option. Each of these settings can be enabled or disabled using the Enable in Renderer and Enable in Viewport options at the top of the Rendering rollout. Renderable splines appear as normal splines in the viewport unless the Enable in Viewport option is selected. The Use Viewport Settings option gives the option of setting the spline render properties different in the viewport and the renderer.

The Auto Smooth option and Threshold value offer a way to smooth edges on the renderable spline. If the angle between two adjacent polygons is less than the Threshold value, then the edge between them is smoothed. If it is greater than the Threshold value, then the hard edge is preserved.

The Generate Mapping Coordinates option automatically generates mapping coordinates that are used to mark where a material map is placed, and the Real-World Map Size option allows real-world scaling to be used when mapping a texture onto the renderable spline.

Cross-Reference

To learn more about mapping coordinates and real-world scaling, see Chapter 17, "Adding Material Details with Maps." ■

Interpolation rollout

In the Interpolation rollout, you can define the number of interpolation steps or segments that make up the shape. The Steps value determines the number of segments to include between adjacent vertices. For example, a circle shape with a Steps value of 0 has only 4 segments and looks like a diamond. Increasing the Steps value to 1 makes a circle out of 8 segments. For shapes composed of straight lines (like the Rectangle and simple NGons) the Steps value is set to 0, but for a shape with many sides (like a Circle or Ellipse) the Steps value can have a big effect. Larger step values result in smoother curves.

The Adaptive option automatically sets the number of steps to produce a smooth curve by adding more interpolation points to the spline based on the spline's curvature. When the Adaptive option is enabled, the Steps and Optimize options become disabled. The Optimize option attempts to reduce the number of steps to produce a simpler spline by eliminating all the extra segments associated with the shape.

Note

The Section and Helix shape primitives have no Interpolation rollout. ∎

Figure 12.4 shows the number 5 drawn with the Line primitive in the Front viewport. The line has been made renderable so that you can see the cross sections. The images from left to right show the line with Steps values of 0, 1, and 3. The fourth image has the Optimize option enabled. Notice that it uses only one segment for the straight edges. The fifth image has the Adaptive option enabled.

FIGURE 12.4

Using the Interpolation rollout, you can control the number of segments that make up a line.

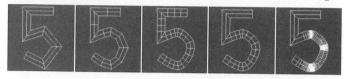

Creation Method and Keyboard Entry rollouts

Most shape primitives also include Creation Method and Keyboard Entry rollouts (Text, Section, and Star are the exceptions). The Creation Method rollout offers options for specifying different ways to create the spline by dragging in a viewport, such as from edge to edge or from the center out. Table 12.1 lists the various creation method options for each of the shapes and each of the extended shapes.

TABLE 12.1

Shape Primitive Creation Methods

Primitive Object	Primitive Object Name	Number of Viewport Clicks to Create	Default Creation Method	Other Creation Method
	Line	2 to Infinite	Corner Initial, Bézier Drag	Smooth, Initial, Corner, or Smooth Drag
	Circle	1	Center	Edge
	Arc	2	End-End-Middle	Center-End-End
	NGon	1	Center	Edge
	Text	1	none	none
	Section	1	none	none
	Rectangle	1	Edge	Center

continued

TABLE 12.1 (continued)

Primitive Object	Primitive Object Name	Number of Viewport Clicks to Create	Default Creation Method	Other Creation Method
⬖	Ellipse	1	Edge	Center
◎	Donut	2	Center	Edge
☆	Star	2	none	none
🌀	Helix	3	Center	Edge
-	WRectangle	2	Edge	Center
-	Channel	2	Edge	Center
-	Angle	2	Edge	Center
-	Tee	2	Edge	Center
-	Wide Flange	2	Edge	Center

Some shape primitives such as Star, Text, and Section don't have any creation methods because Max offers only a single way to create these shapes.

The Keyboard Entry rollout offers a way to enter exact position and dimension values. After you enter the values, click the Create button to create the spline or shape in the active viewport. The settings are different for each shape.

The Parameters rollout includes such basic settings for the primitive as Radius, Length, and Width. You can alter these settings immediately after an object is created. However, after you deselect an object, the Parameters rollout moves to the Modify panel, and you must do any alterations to the shape there.

Line

The Line primitive includes several creation method settings, enabling you to create hard, sharp corners or smooth corners. You can set the Initial Type option to either Corner or Smooth to create a sharp or smooth corner for the first point created.

After clicking where the initial point is located, you can add points by clicking in the viewport. Dragging while creating a new point can make a point a Corner, Smooth, or Bézier based on the Drag Type option selected in the Creation Method rollout. The curvature created by the Smooth option is determined by the distance between adjacent vertices, whereas you can control the curvature created by the Bézier option by dragging with the mouse a desired distance after the point is created. Bézier corners have control handles associated with them, enabling you to change their curvature.

Tip

Holding down the Shift key while clicking creates points that are constrained vertically or horizontally. This makes it easy to create straight lines that are at right angles to each other. Holding down the Ctrl key snaps new points at an angle from the last segment, as determined by the Angle Snap setting. ■

After creating all the points, you exit line mode by clicking the right mouse button. If the last point is on top of the first point, then a dialog box asks whether you want to close the spline. Click Yes to create a closed spline or No to continue adding points. Even after creating a closed spline, you can add more points to the current selection to create a compound shape if the Start New Shape option isn't selected. If the first and last points don't correspond, then an open spline is created.

Figure 12.5 shows several splines created using the various creation method settings. The left spline was created with all the options set to Corner, and the second spline with all the options set to Smooth. The third spline uses the Corner Initial type and shows where dragging has smoothed many of the points. The last spline was created using the Bézier option.

FIGURE 12.5

The Line shape can create various combinations of shapes with smooth and sharp corners.

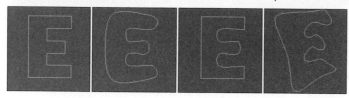

In the Keyboard Entry rollout, you can add points by entering their X, Y, and Z dimensions and clicking the Add Point button. You can close the spline at any time by clicking the Close button or keep it open by clicking the Finish button.

Rectangle

The Rectangle shape produces simple rectangles. In the Parameters rollout, you can specify the Length and Width and also a Corner Radius. Holding down the Ctrl key while dragging creates a perfect square shape.

Circle

The Circle button creates—you guessed it—circles. The only adjustable parameter in the Parameters rollout is the Radius. All other rollouts are the same, as explained earlier. Circles created with the Circle button have only four vertices.

Ellipse

Ellipses are simple variations of the Circle shape. You define them by Length and Width values. Holding down the Ctrl key while dragging creates a perfect circle (or you can use the Circle shape).

Arc

The Arc primitive has two creation methods. Use the End-End-Middle method to create an arc shape by clicking and dragging to specify the two end points and then dragging to complete the shape. Use the Center-End-End method to create an arc shape by clicking and dragging from the center to one of the end points and then dragging the arc length to the second end point.

Other parameters include the Radius and the From and To settings, where you can enter the value in degrees for the start and end of the arc. The Pie Slice option connects the end points of the arc to its center to create a pie-sliced shape, as shown in Figure 12.6. The Reverse option lets you reverse the arc's direction.

FIGURE 12.6

Enabling the Pie Slice option connects the arc ends with the center of the circle.

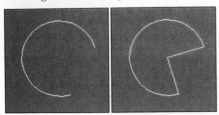

Donut

As another variation of the Circle shape, the Donut shape consists of two concentric circles; you can create it by dragging once to specify the outer circle and again to specify the inner circle. The parameters for this object are simply two radii.

NGon

The NGon shape lets you create regular polygons by specifying the Number of Sides and the Corner Radius. You can also specify whether the NGon is Inscribed or Circumscribed, as shown in Figure 12.7. Inscribed polygons are positioned within a circle that touches all the outer polygon's vertices. Circumscribed polygons are positioned outside of a circle that touches the midpoint of each polygon edge. The Circular option changes the polygon to a circle that inscribes the polygon.

FIGURE 12.7

An inscribed pentagon and a circumscribed pentagon

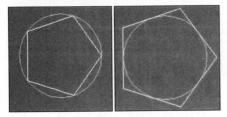

Star

The Star shape also includes two radii values—the larger Radius value defines the distance of the outer points of the Star shape from its center, and the smaller Radius value is the distance from the center of the star to the inner points. The Point setting indicates the number of points. This value can range from 3 to 100. The Distortion value causes the inner points to rotate relative to the outer points and can be used to create some interesting new star types. The Fillet Radius 1 and Fillet Radius 2 values adjust the Fillet for the inner and outer points. Figure 12.8 shows a sampling of what is possible with the Star shapes.

Text

You can use the Text primitive to add outlined text to the scene. In the Parameters rollout, you can specify a Font by choosing one from the drop-down list at the top of the Parameters rollout. Under the Font drop-down list are six icons, shown in Table 12.2. The left two icons are for the Italic and

Underline styles. Selecting either of these styles applies the style to all the text. The right four icons are for aligning the text to the left, centered, right, or justified.

The Star primitive can be changed to create some amazing shapes.

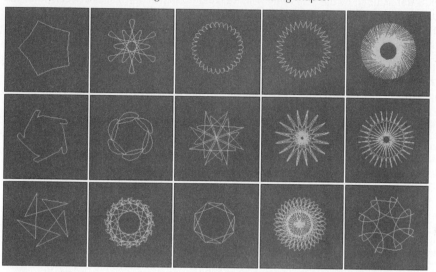

Text Font Attributes

Icon	Description
I	Italic
U	Underline
☰	Left
☰	Centered
☰	Right
☰	Justified

Note

The list of available fonts includes only the Windows TrueType fonts and Type 1 PostScript fonts installed on your system and any extra fonts located in the font path listed in the Configure Paths dialog box. You need to restart Max before the fonts in the font path are recognized. ■

The size of the text is determined by the Size value. The Kerning (which is the space between adjacent characters) and Leading (which is the space between adjacent lines of text) values can actually be negative. Setting the Kerning value to a large negative number actually displays the text backward. Figure 12.9 shows an example of some text and an example of Kerning values in the Max interface.

You can type the text to be created in the text area. You can cut, copy, and paste text into this text area from an external application if you right-click on the text area. After setting the parameters and typing the text, the text appears as soon as you click in one of the viewports. The text is updated automatically when any of the parameters (including the text) are changed. To turn off automatic updating, select the Manual Update toggle. You can then update with the Update button.

If you open the Character Map application, you can see a complete list of special characters. The Character Map application, shown in Figure 12.10, can be opened in Windows by selecting Start ⇨ All Programs ⇨ Accessories ⇨ System Tools ⇨ Character Map. To enter special characters into the text area in Max, choose the special character by clicking on it in the Character Map dialog box and click the Select button. Then click the Copy button to copy the character to the Windows clipboard and in Max, use the Ctrl+V paste command to add it to the text area.

FIGURE 12.9

The Text shape lets you control the space between letters, known as kerning.

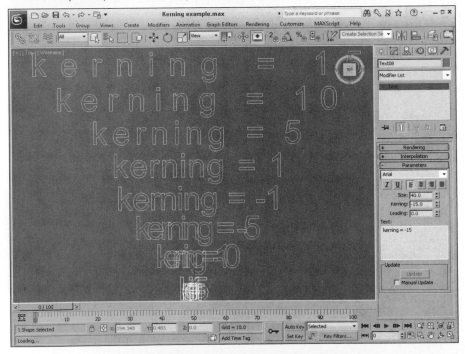

FIGURE 12.10

The Character Map application shows all the special characters that are available.

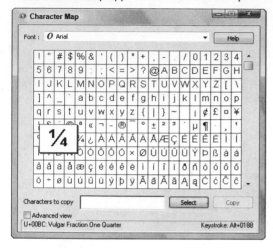

Helix

A Helix is like a spring coil shape, and it is the one shape of all the Shape primitives that exists in 3D. Helix parameters include two radii for specifying the inner and outer radius. These two values can be equal to create a coil or unequal to create a spiral. Parameters also exist for the Height and number of Turns. The Bias parameter causes the Helix turns to be gathered all together at the top or bottom of the shape. The CW and CCW options let you specify whether the Helix turns clockwise or counter-clockwise.

Figure 12.11 shows a sampling of Helix shapes: The first Helix has equal radii values, the second one has a smaller second radius, the third Helix spirals to a second radius value of 0, and the last two Helix objects have Bias values of 0.8 and –0.8.

FIGURE 12.11

The Helix shape can be straight or spiral shaped.

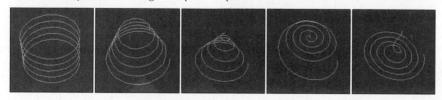

Section

Section stands for cross section. The Section shape is a cross section of the edges of any 3D object through which the Section's cutting plane passes. The process consists of dragging in the viewport to create a cross-sectioning plane. You can then move, rotate, or scale the cross-sectioning plane to obtain the desired cross section. In the Section Parameters rollout is a Create Shape button. Clicking this button opens a dialog box where you can name the new shape. You can use one Section object to create multiple shapes.

Note

You can make sections only from intersecting a 3D object. If the cross-sectioning plane doesn't intersect the 3D object, then it won't create a shape. You cannot use the Section primitive on shapes, even if it is a renderable spline. ■

The Parameters rollout includes settings for updating the Section shape. You can update it when the Section plane moves, when the Section is selected, or Manually (using the Update Section button). You can also set the Section Extents to Infinite, Section Boundary, or Off. The Infinite setting creates the cross-section spline as if the cross-sectioning plane were of infinite size, whereas the Section Boundary limits the plane's extents to the boundaries of the visible plane. The color swatch determines the color of the intersecting shape.

To give you an idea of what the Section shape can produce, Figure 12.12 shows the shapes resulting from sectioning two Cone objects, including a circle, an ellipse, a parabola, and a hyperbola. The shapes have been moved to the sides to be more visible.

FIGURE 12.12

You can use the Section shape primitive to create the conic sections (circle, ellipse, parabola, hyperbola) from a set of 3D cones.

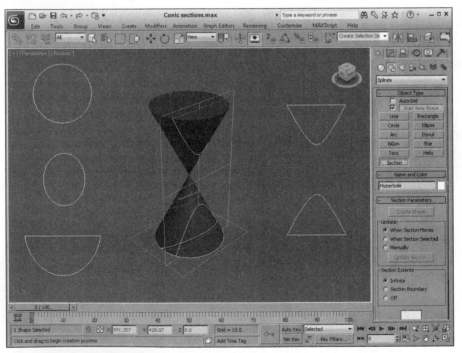

Tutorial: Drawing a company logo

One of the early uses for 3D graphics was to animate corporate logos, and although Max can still do this without any problems, it now has capabilities far beyond those available in the early days. The Shape tools can even be used to design the logo. In this example, you'll design and create a simple logo using the Shape tools for the fictitious company named Expeditions South.

To use the Shape tools to design and create a company logo, follow these steps:

1. Create a four-pointed star by clicking the Star button and dragging in the Top view to create a shape. Change the parameters for this star as follows: Radius1 = **60**, Radius2 = **20**, and Points = **4**.
2. Select and move the star shape to the left side of the viewport.
3. Now click the Text button, and change the font to **Impact** and the Size to **50**. In the Text area, type **Expeditions South** and include a line return and several spaces between the two words so they are offset. Click in the Top viewport to place the text.
4. Use the Select and Move button (W) to reposition the text next to the Star shape.
5. Click the Line button, and create several short highlighting lines around the bottom point of the star.

The finished logo is now ready to extrude and animate. Figure 12.13 shows the results.

FIGURE 12.13

A company logo created entirely in Max using shapes

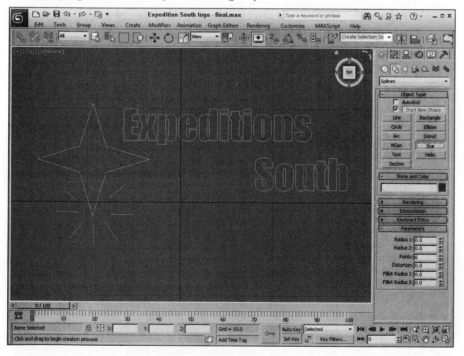

Tutorial: Viewing the interior of a heart

As an example of the Section primitive, you'll explore a section of a Heart model. The model was created by Viewpoint Datalabs and is very realistic—so realistic, in fact, that it could be used to teach medical students the inner workings of the heart.

To create a spline from the cross section of the heart, follow these steps:

1. Open the Heart section.max file from the Chap 12 directory on the CD.

   This file includes a physical model of a heart created by Viewpoint Datalabs.

2. Select Create ⇨ Shapes ⇨ Section, and drag a plane in the Front viewport that is large enough to cover the heart.

   This plane is your cross-sectioning plane.

3. Select the Select and Rotate button on the main toolbar (or press the E key), and rotate the cross-sectioning plane to cross the heart at the desired angle.

4. In the Parameters rollout of the Modify panel, click the Create Shape button and give the new shape the name **Heart Section**.

5. From the Select by Name dialog box (opened with the H key), select the section by name, separate it from the model, and reposition it to be visible.

Figure 12.14 shows the resulting model and section.

FIGURE 12.14

You can use the Section shape to view the interior area of the heart.

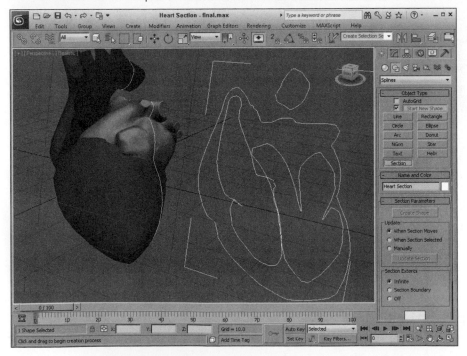

Editing Splines

After you create a shape primitive, you can edit it by modifying its parameters, but the parameters for shapes are fairly limited. For example, the only parameter for the Circle shape is Radius. All shapes can be converted to Editable Splines, or they can have the Edit Spline modifier applied to them. Doing either enables a host of editing features. Before you can use these editing features, you must convert the shape primitive to an Editable Spline (except for the Line shape). You can do so by right-clicking the spline shape in the viewport and choosing Convert to ⇨ Convert to Editable Spline from the pop-up quadmenu or by right-clicking on the Circle base object in the Modifier Stack and selecting Convert to Editable Spline in the pop-up menu. Another way to enable these features is to apply the Edit Spline modifier.

Editable Splines versus the Edit Spline modifier

After you convert the spline to an Editable Spline, you can edit individual subobjects within the spline, including Vertices, Segments, and Splines. There is a subtle difference between applying the Edit Spline modifier and converting the shape to an Editable Spline. Applying the Edit Spline modifier maintains the shape parameters and enables the editing features found in the Geometry rollout. However, an Editable Spline loses the ability to be able to change the base parameters associated with the spline shape.

Note

When you create an object that contains two or more splines (such as when you create splines with the Start New Shape option disabled), all the splines in the object are automatically converted into Editable Splines. ■

Another difference is that the shape primitive base name is listed along with the Edit Spline modifier in the Modifier Stack. Selecting the shape primitive name makes the Rendering, Interpolation, and Parameters rollouts visible, and the Selection, Soft Selection, and Geometry rollouts are made visible when you select the Edit Spline modifier in the Modifier Stack. For Editable Splines, only a single base object name is visible in the Modifier Stack, and all rollouts are accessible under it.

Note

Another key difference is that subobjects for the Edit Spline modifier cannot be animated. ■

Making splines renderable

Splines normally do not show up in a rendered image, but using the Renderable option in the Rendering rollout and assigning a thickness to the splines makes them appear in the rendered image. Figure 12.15 shows a rendered image of the Expeditions South logo after all shapes have been made renderable and assigned a Thickness of 3.0.

Note

The settings in the Rendering and Interpolation rollouts are the same as those used for newly created shapes, which were covered earlier in the chapter. ■

FIGURE 12.15

Using renderable splines with a Thickness of 3.0, the logo can be rendered.

Selecting spline subobjects

When editing splines, you must choose the subobject level to work on. For example, when editing splines, you can work with Vertex (1), Segment (2), or Spline (3) subobjects. Before you can edit spline subobjects, you must select them. To select the subobject type, click the small plus sign icon to the left of the Editable Spline object in the Modifier Stack. This lists all the subobjects available for this object. Click the subobject in the Modifier Stack to select it. Alternatively, you can click the red-colored icons under the Selection rollout, shown in Figure 12.16. You can also select the different sub-object modes using the 1, 2, and 3 keyboard shortcuts. When you select a subobject, the selection in the Modifier Stack and the associated icon in the Selection rollout turn yellow.

Note

The Sub-Object button turns yellow when selected to remind you that you are in subobject edit mode. Remember, you must exit this mode before you can select another object. ∎

You can select many subobjects at once by dragging an outline over them in the viewports. You can also select and deselect vertices by holding down the Ctrl key while clicking them. Holding down the Alt key removes any selected vertices from the selection set.

After selecting several vertices, you can create a named selection set by typing a name in the Name Selection Sets drop-down list in the main toolbar. You can then copy and paste these selection sets onto other shapes using the buttons in the Selection rollout.

The Lock Handles option allows you to move the handles of all selected vertices together when enabled, but each handle moves by itself when disabled. With the Lock Handles and the All options selected, all selected handles move together. The Alike option causes all handles on one side to move together.

FIGURE 12.16

The Selection rollout provides icons for entering the various subobject modes.

Spline subobject mode

Segment subobject mode

Vertex subobject mode

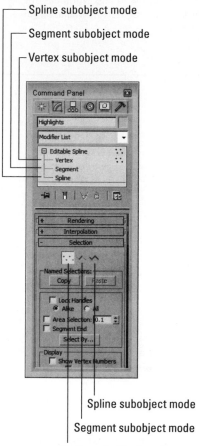

Spline subobject mode

Segment subobject mode

Vertex subobject mode

The Area Selection option selects all the vertices within a defined radius of where you click. The Segment End option, when enabled, allows you to select a vertex by clicking the segment. The closest vertex to the segment that you clicked is selected. This feature is useful when you are trying to select a vertex that lies near other vertices. The Select By button opens a dialog box with Segment and Spline buttons on it. These buttons allow you to select all the vertices on either a spline or segment that you choose.

The Selection rollout also has the Show Vertex Numbers option to display all the vertex numbers of a spline or to show the numbers of only the selected vertices. This can be convenient for understanding how a spline is put together and to help you find noncritical vertices. The Selected Only option displays the Vertex Numbers only for the selected subobjects when enabled.

Note

The vertex order is critical in determining the direction in which cross sections are swept when using the Loft and Sweep commands. You always can identify the first vertex in a spline because it is yellow. ∎

Figure 12.17 shows a simple star shape that was converted to an Editable Spline. The left image shows the spline in Vertex subobject mode. All the vertices are marked with small plus signs, and the starting point is marked with a small square. The middle image has the Show Vertex Numbers option enabled. For the right image, the vertex numbers are shown after the Reverse button was used (in Spline subobject mode).

FIGURE 12.17

Several spline shapes displayed with vertex numbering turned on

Spline end point

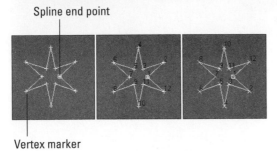

Vertex marker

At the bottom of the Selection rollout, the Selection Information is displayed. This information tells you the number of the spline (or segment) and vertex selected, or the number of selected items and whether a spline is closed.

Note

The Soft Selection rollout allows you to alter adjacent nonselected subobjects (to a lesser extent) when selected subobjects are moved, creating a smooth transition. See Chapter 10, "Accessing Subobjects and Using Modeling Helpers," for the details on this rollout. ■

Controlling spline geometry

Much of the power of editing splines is contained within the Geometry rollout, shown in Figure 12.18, including the ability to add new splines, attach objects to the spline, weld vertices, use Boolean operations such as Trim and Extend, and many more. Some Geometry buttons may be disabled, depending on the subobject type that you've selected. Many of the features in the Geometry rollout can be used in all subobject modes. Some of these features do not even require that you be in a subobject mode. These features are covered first.

Tip

The quadmenu provides quick access to the main features for each subobject mode. After you are familiar with the various features, you can quickly access them through the quadmenu by simply right-clicking in the viewport. ■

Create line

While editing splines, you can add new lines to a spline by clicking the Create Line button and then clicking in one of the viewports. You can add several lines at the same time, and all these new splines are part of the same object. Right-click in the viewport to exit this mode. Any new lines are their own spline, but you can weld them to the existing splines.

FIGURE 12.18

For Editable Splines, the Geometry rollout holds most of the features.

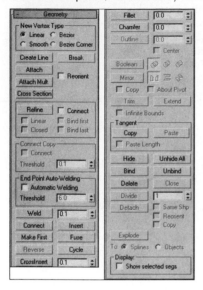

Break

Selecting a vertex and clicking the Break button in Vertex subobject mode breaks the segment at the selected vertex by creating two separate end points. You also can use the Break button in Segment subobject mode by clicking anywhere along the segment to add two separated vertices on the segment, thereby breaking the segment into two. You can also use the Break button in Vertex and Segment subobject modes.

Attach and Attach Multiple

The Attach button lets you attach any existing splines to the currently selected spline. The cursor changes when you're over the top of a spline that can be attached. Clicking an unselected object makes it part of the current object. The Reorient option aligns the coordinate system of the spline being attached with the selected spline's coordinate system.

For example, using the Boolean button requires that objects be part of the same object. You can use the Attach button to attach several splines into the same object.

The Attach Mult. button enables several splines to be attached at once. When you click the Attach Mult. button, the Attach Multiple dialog box (which looks much like the Select by Name dialog box) opens. Use this dialog box to select the objects you want to attach to the current selection. Click the Attach button in the dialog box when you're finished. You can use both the Attach and Attach Mult. buttons in all three subobject modes.

Note

If the spline object that is being attached has a material applied to it, then a dialog box appears that gives you options for handling the materials. These options include Match Material IDs to Material, Match Material to Material IDs, or Do Not Modify Material IDs or Material. Applying materials is covered in Chapter 15, "Using the Slate Material Editor." ∎

Cross Section

The Cross Section button works just like the Cross Section modifier by creating splines that run from one cross-section shape to another. For example, imagine creating a baseball bat by positioning circular cross sections for each diameter change and connecting each cross section from one end to the other. All the cross sections need to be part of the same Editable Spline object, and then using the Cross Section button, you can click from one cross section to another. The cursor changes when the mouse is over a shape that can be used. When you're finished selecting cross-section shapes, you can right-click to exit Cross Section mode.

The type of vertex used to create the new splines that run between the different cross sections is the type specified in the New Vertex Type section at the top of the Geometry rollout.

Caution

Although the splines that connect the cross sections are positioned alongside the cross section shape, they are not connected. ■

After the splines are created, you can use the Surface modifier to turn the splines into a 3D surface.

Auto Welding end points

To work with surfaces, you typically need a closed spline. When you enable the Automatic Welding option in the End Point Auto-Welding section and specify a Threshold, all end points within the threshold value are welded together, thus making a closed spline.

Insert

The Insert button adds vertices to a selected spline. Click the Insert button, and then click the spline to place the new vertex. At this point, you can reposition the new vertex and its attached segments—click again to set it in place. A single click adds a Corner type vertex, and a click-and-drag adds a Bézier type vertex.

After positioning the new vertex, you can add another vertex next to the first vertex by dragging the mouse and clicking. To add vertices to a different segment, right-click to release the currently selected segment, but stay in Insert mode. To exit Insert mode, right-click in the viewport again or click the Insert button to deselect it.

Tutorial: Working with cross sections to create a doorknob

You can work with cross sections in several ways. You can use the Cross Section feature for Editable Splines, the Cross Section modifier, or the Loft compound object. All these methods have advantages, but the first is probably the easiest and most forgiving method.

To create a simple doorknob using the Editable Spline Cross Section button, follow these steps:

1. Right-click any of the Snap toggle buttons on the main toolbar, and select Grid Points in the Grid and Snap Settings dialog box. Then click the Snap toggle button on the main toolbar (or press the S key) to enable grid snapping.

2. Select the Create ⇨ Shapes ⇨ Circle menu command, and drag from the center grid point in the Top viewport to create a small circle. Repeat this step to create two more circles: one the same size and one much larger.

3. Select the Create ⇨ Shapes ⇨ Rectangle menu command, and hold down the Ctrl key while dragging in the Top viewport to create a square that is smaller than the first circle. Repeat this step to create another square the same size. Aligning the squares is easier if you select the Center option in the Creation Method rollout.

4. Click the Select and Move (W) button on the main toolbar, and drag the shapes in the Left viewport upward in this order: square, square, small circle, large circle, small circle. Separate the squares by a distance equal to the width of a door, and spread the circles out to be the width of a doorknob.

5. Select the bottom-most square shape, and then right-click and select Convert To ⇨ Editable Spline in the pop-up quadmenu.

6. In the Geometry rollout, click the Attach button and then select the other shapes to add them to the selected Editable Spline object.

7. Rotate the Perspective viewport until all shapes are visible and easily selectable. Then select each and rotate each of the cross sections in the Top viewport so their first vertices are aligned. This helps prevent any twisting that may occur when the cross sections try to align the first vertices.

8. Select the Linear option in the New Vertex Type section in the Geometry rollout, and then click the Cross Section button. Click the lowest square shape in the Perspective viewport, followed by the higher square shape, and then the lower small circle. This creates a spline that runs linearly between these lowest three cross-section shapes. Right-click in the Perspective viewport to exit Cross Section mode.

9. Select the Bezier option in the New Vertex Type section, and then click the Cross Section button again. Click the lowest circle shape in the Perspective viewport, followed by the larger circle shape, and then the higher small circle. This creates a spline that runs smoothly between the last three cross-section shapes. Right-click in the Perspective viewport to exit Cross Section mode.

Tip

Once a spline outline is constructed, you can use the Surface modifier to add a surface to the object. ■

Figure 12.19 shows the splines running between the different cross sections. A key benefit to the Editable Spline approach is that you don't need to order the cross-section shapes exactly. You just need to click on them in the order that you want.

Editing vertices

To edit a vertex, click the Vertex subobject in the Modifier Stack or select the vertex icon from the Selection rollout (keyboard shortcut, 1). After the Vertex subobject type is selected, you can use the transform buttons on the main toolbar to move, rotate, and scale the selected vertex or vertices. Moving a vertex around causes the associated spline segments to follow.

With a vertex selected, you can change its type from Corner, Smooth, Bézier, or Bézier Corner by right-clicking and selecting the type from the pop-up quadmenu.

Caution

The New Vertex Type section in the top of the Geometry sets only the vertex type for new vertices created when you Shift-copy segments and splines or new vertices created with the Cross Section button. These options cannot be used to change vertex type for existing vertices. ■

Selecting the Bézier or Bézier Corner type vertex reveals green-colored handles on either side of the vertex. Dragging these handles away from the vertex alters the curvature of the segment. Bézier type vertices have both handles in the same line, but Corner Bézier type vertices do not. This allows them to create sharp angles.

FIGURE 12.19

The Cross Section feature of Editable Splines can create splines that run between several cross-section shapes.

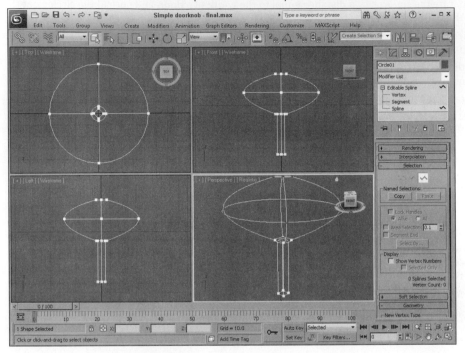

Note

Holding down the Shift key while clicking and dragging on a handle causes the handle to move independently of the other handle, turning it into a Bézier Corner type vertex instead of a plain Bézier. You can use it to create sharp corner points. ∎

Figure 12.20 shows how the Bézier and Bézier Corner handles work. The first image shows all vertices of a circle selected where you can see the handles protruding from both sides of each vertex. The second image shows what happens to the circle when one of the handles is moved. The handles for Bézier vertices move together, so moving one upward causes the other to move downward. The third image shows a Bézier Corner vertex where the handles can move independently to create sharp points. The fourth image shows two Bézier Corner vertices moved with the Lock Handles and Alike options enabled. This causes the handles to the left of the vertices to move together. The final image has the Lock Handles and All options selected, causing the handles of all selected vertices to move together.

The pop-up quadmenu also includes a command to Reset Tangents. This option makes the tangents revert to their original orientation before the handles were moved.

FIGURE 12.20

Moving the vertex handles alters the spline around the vertex.

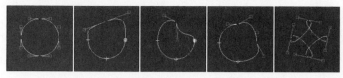

Refine

The Refine button lets you add vertices to a spline without changing the curvature, giving you more control over the details of the spline. With the Refine button selected, just click on a spline where you want the new vertex, and one is added.

The Connect option adds a new segment that connects each two successive points added with the Refine tool. These segments don't actually appear until the Refine button is disabled. This provides a method for copying part of an existing spline. When the Connect option is enabled, then the Linear, Closed, Bind First, and Bind Last options become enabled. The Linear option creates Corner type vertices, resulting in linear segments. The Closed option closes the spline by connecting the first and last vertices. The Bind First and Bind Last options bind the first and last vertices to the center of the selected segment. Refine is available only for Vertex and Segment subobject modes.

Weld and Fuse

When two end point vertices are selected and are within the specified Weld Threshold, they can be welded into one vertex and moved to a position that is the average of the welded points using the Weld button. Several vertices can be welded simultaneously. Another way to weld vertices is to move one vertex on top of another. If they are within the threshold distance, a dialog box asks whether you want them to be welded. Click the Yes button to weld them.

Caution

The Weld button can be used only to weld spline end points. ■

The Fuse button is similar to the Weld command, except that it doesn't delete any vertices. It just positions the two vertices on top of one another at a position that is the average of the selected vertices.

In Figure 12.21, the left image shows a star shape with all its lower vertices selected. The middle image is the same star shape after the selected vertices have been welded together, and the right image shows the star shape with the selected vertices fused. The Selection rollout shows five selected vertices for the fused version.

You can use the Fuse button to move the selected vertices to a single location. This is accomplished by selecting all the vertices to relocate and clicking the Fuse button. The average point between all the selected vertices becomes the new location. You can combine these vertices into one after they've been fused by clicking the Weld button.

FIGURE 12.21

Using the Fuse and Weld buttons, several vertices in the star shape have been combined.

Connect

The Connect button lets you connect end vertices to one another to create a new line. This works only on end vertices, not on connected points within a spline. To connect the ends, click the Connect button and drag the cursor from one end point to another (the cursor changes to a plus sign when it is over a valid end point) and release it. The first image in Figure 12.22 shows an incomplete star drawn with the Line primitive, the middle image shows a line being drawn between the end points (notice the cursor), and the third image is the resulting star.

FIGURE 12.22

You can use the Connect button to connect end points of shapes.

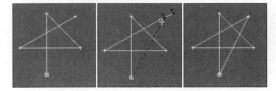

Make First

The Show Vertex Numbers option in the Selection rollout displays the number of each vertex. The first vertex is identified by the yellow color. The Make First button lets you change which vertex you want to be the first vertex in the spline. To do this, select a single vertex and click the Make First button. If more than one vertex is selected, Max ignores the command. If the selected spline is an open spline, again Max ignores the command; an end point must be selected.

Note

The vertex number is important because it determines the first key for path animations and where Loft objects start. ∎

Cycle

If a single vertex is selected, the Cycle button causes the next vertex in the Vertex Number order to be selected. The Cycle button can be used on open and closed splines and can be repeated around the spline. The exact vertex number is shown at the bottom of the Selection rollout. This is very useful for locating individual vertices in groups that are close together, such as groups that have been fused.

CrossInsert

If two splines that are part of the same object overlap, you can use the CrossInsert button to create a vertex on each spline at the location where they intersect. The distance between the two splines must be closer than the Threshold value for this to work. Note that this button does not join the two splines; it only creates a vertex on each spline. Use the Weld button to join the splines. Figure 12.23 shows how you can use the CrossInsert button to add vertices at the intersection points of two elliptical splines. Notice that each ellipse now has eight vertices.

FIGURE 12.23

The CrossInsert button can add vertices to any overlapping splines of the same object.

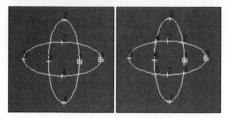

Fillet

The Fillet button is used to round the corners of a spline where two edges meet. To use the Fillet command, click the Fillet button and then drag on a corner vertex in the viewport. The more you drag, the larger the Fillet. You can also enter a Fillet value in the Fillet spinner for the vertices that are selected. The Fillet has a maximum value based on the geometry of the spline. Figure 12.24 shows the Fillet command applied to an 8-pointed star with values of 10, 15, and 20. Notice that each selected vertex has split into two.

Caution

Be careful not to apply the fillet command multiple times to the selected vertices. If the new vertices cross over each other, then the normals will be misaligned, which will cause problems when you use modifiers. ■

Note

You can fillet several vertices at once by selecting them and then clicking the Fillet button and dragging the Fillet distance. ■

FIGURE 12.24

The Fillet button can round the corners of a shape.

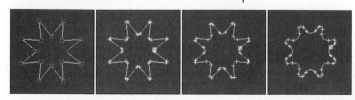

Chamfer

The Chamfer button works much like the Fillet button, except that the corners are replaced with straight-line segments instead of smooth curves. This keeps the resulting shape simpler and maintains hard corners. To use the Chamfer command, click the Chamfer button and drag on a vertex to create the Chamfer. You can also enter a Chamfer value in the rollout. Figure 12.25 shows chamfers applied to the same 8-pointed shape with the same values of 10, 15, and 20.

FIGURE 12.25

Chamfers alter the look of spline corners.

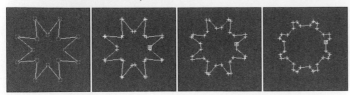

Tangent Copy and Tangent Paste

If you spend considerable time positioning the handles for the Bézier or Bézier Corner vertices just right, it can be tricky to repeat these precise positions again for other handles. Using the Tangent Copy and Tangent Paste buttons, you can copy the handle positions between different handles. To do so, simply select a handle that you wish to copy and click the Copy button, and then select the vertex to which you want to copy the handle and press the Paste button. The Paste Length button copies the handle length along with its orientation, if enabled.

Hide/Unhide All

The Hide and Unhide All buttons hide and unhide spline subobjects. They can be used in any subobject mode. To hide a subobject, select the subobject and click the Hide button. To unhide the hidden subobjects, click the Unhide All button.

Bind/Unbind

The Bind button attaches an end vertex to a segment. The bound vertex then cannot be moved independently, but only as part of the bound segment. The Unbind button removes the binding on the vertex and lets it move independently again. To bind a vertex, click the Bind button and then drag from the vertex to the segment to bind to. To exit Bind mode, right-click in the viewport or click the Bind button again.

For Figure 12.26, a circle shape is created and converted to an Editable Spline object. The right vertex is selected and then separated from the circle with the Break button. Then by clicking the Bind button and dragging the vertex to the opposite line segment, the vertex is bound to the segment. Any movement of the spline keeps this vertex bound to the segment.

FIGURE 12.26

The Bind button attaches one end of the circle shape to a segment.

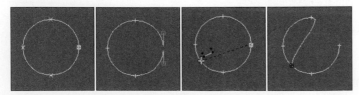

Delete

The Delete button deletes the selected subobject. You can use it to delete vertices, segments, or splines. This button is available in all subobject modes. Pressing the Delete key when the subobject is selected has the same effect.

Show Selected Segments

The Show Selected Segs option causes any selected segments to continue to be highlighted in Vertex subobject mode as well as Segment subobject mode. This feature helps you keep track of the segments that you are working on when moving vertices.

Tutorial: Making a ninja star

If you're involved with fighting games, either creating or playing them, then chances are good that when you look at the Star primitive, you think, "Wow, this is perfect for creating a ninja star weapon." If not, then just pretend.

To create a ninja star using splines, follow these steps:

1. Right-click any of the Snap toggle buttons on the main toolbar, and select Grid Points in the Grid and Snap Settings dialog box. Then click the Snap toggle button (or press the S key) on the main toolbar to enable grid snapping.

2. Select the Create ⇨ Shapes ⇨ Circle menu command, and drag from the center grid point in the Top viewport to create a circle.

3. Select the Create ⇨ Shapes ⇨ Star menu command, and drag again from the center of the Top viewport to center align the star with the circle. Make the star shape about three times the size of the circle, and set the number of Points to **10**.

4. With the star shape selected, right-click in the Top viewport and select Convert To ⇨ Editable Spline. In the Modify panel, click the Attach button, and click the circle shape. Then click the Vertex icon in the Selection rollout (or press 1) to enter Vertex subobject mode.

5. Click the Create Line button in the Geometry rollout; then click the circle's top vertex and bottom vertex, then right-click to end the line, and right-click again to exit Create Line mode.

6. Select the top vertex of the line that you just created (be careful not to select the circle's top vertex; you can use the Cycle button to find the correct vertex). Right-click the vertex, and select the Bézier vertex type from the quadmenu. Then drag its lower handle until it is on top of the circle's left vertex. Repeat this step for the bottom vertex, and drag its handle to the circle's right vertex to create a yin-yang symbol in the center of the ninja star.

7. While holding down the Ctrl key, click on all the inner vertices of the star shape. Click the Chamfer button, and change the value until the chamfer looks like that in Figure 12.27, and click the Chamfer key again to deselect it.

Figure 12.27 shows the resulting ninja star.

FIGURE 12.27

The completed ninja star, ready for action (or extruding)

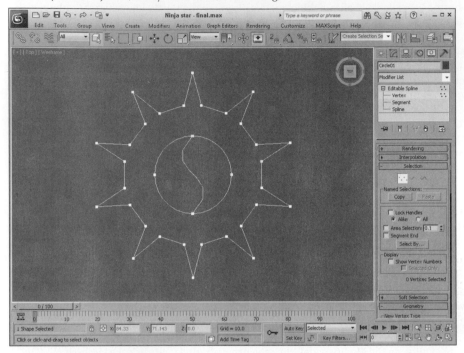

Editing segments

To edit a segment, click the Segment subobject in the Modifier Stack or select the segment icon from the Selection rollout to enter segment subobject mode. Clicking again on either exits this mode. *Segments* are the lines or edges that run between two vertices. Many of the editing options work in the same way as when you're editing Vertex subobjects. You can select multiple segments by holding down the Ctrl key while clicking the segments, or you can hold down the Alt key to remove selected segments from the selection set. You can also copy segments when they're being transformed by holding down the Shift key. The cloned segments break away from the original spline, but are still a part of the Editable Spline object.

You can change segments from straight lines to curves by right-clicking the segment and selecting Line or Curve from the pop-up quadmenu. Line segments created with the Corner type vertex option cannot be changed to Curves, but lines created with Smooth and Bézier type vertex options can be switched back and forth.

Several Geometry rollout buttons work on more than one subobject type.

Connect Copy

When you create a copy of a segment by moving a segment with the Shift key held down, you can enable the Connect Copy option to make segments that join the copied segment with its original. For example, if you have a single straight horizontal line segment, dragging it upward with the Copy

Connect option enabled creates a copy that is joined to the original, resulting in a rectangle. Be aware that the vertices that connect to the original segment are not welded to the original segment.

Divide

When you select a segment, the Divide button becomes active. This button adds the number of vertices specified to the selected segment or segments. These new vertices are positioned based on the curvature of the segment with more vertices being added to the areas of greater curvature. Figure 12.28 shows the diamond shape (second row, second from right) after all four segments were selected, a value of 1 was entered into the spinner, and the Divide button was clicked.

FIGURE 12.28

The Divide button adds segments to the spline.

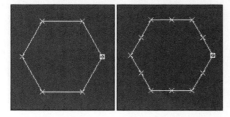

Detach

The Detach button separates the selected subobjects from the rest of the object (opposite of the Attach button). When you click this button, the Detach dialog box opens, enabling you to name the new detached subobject. When segments are detached, you can select the Same Shape option to keep them part of the original object. The Reorient option realigns the new detached subobject to match the position and orientation of the current active grid. The Copy option creates a new copy of the detached subobject.

You can use Detach on either selected Spline or Segment subobjects.

Tutorial: Using Connect Copy to create a simple flower

Connect Copy is one of the features that you'll use and wonder how you ever got along without it. For this tutorial, you create a simple flower from a circle shape using the Connect Copy feature.

To create a simple flower using the Connect Copy feature, follow these steps:

1. Select Create ⇨ Shapes ⇨ Circle, and drag in the Top viewport to create a simple circle shape.
2. Right-click on the circle, and select Convert to ⇨ Editable Spline to convert the shape.
3. In the Modifier Stack, select the Segment subobject mode (keyboard shortcut, 2) and enable the Connect option in the Connect Copy section.
4. Select one of the circle segments, and with the Shift key held down, drag it outward away from the circle. Then repeat this step for each segment.

Figure 12.29 shows the results. With the Connect Copy option, you don't need to worry about the connecting lines.

FIGURE 12.29

The Connect Copy feature joins newly copied segments to the original.

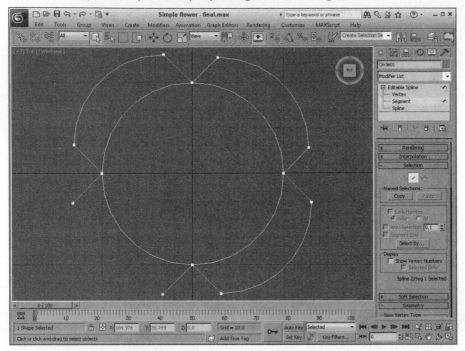

Surface Properties

For segment and spline subobjects, you can access a Surface Properties rollout that lets you assign a Material ID to the subobject. These Material IDs are used with the Multi/Sub-object Material available in the Material Editor. For example, suppose you've created a road from a bunch of splines that are part of the same object. You can assign one Material ID for the lines at the edge of the road that will be the curb and a different Material ID for the yellow lines running down the middle of the road. Separate materials then can be applied to each of the parts using the matching Material IDs.

Cross-Reference

You can find information on Material IDs in Chapter 16, "Creating and Applying Standard Materials." ∎

Using the Select ID button and drop-down list, you can locate and select all subobjects that have a certain Material ID. Simply select the Material ID that you are looking for and click the Select ID button, and all segments (or splines) with that Material ID are selected. Beneath the Select ID button is another drop-down list that lets you select segments by material name. The Clear Selection option clears all selections when the Select ID button is clicked. If disabled, then all new selections are added to the current selection set.

Editing Spline subobjects

To edit a spline, click the Spline subobject in the Modifier Stack or select the spline icon from the Selection rollout. Transforming a spline object containing only one spline works the same way in subobject mode as it does in a normal transformation. Working in spline subobject mode lets you move splines relative to one another. Right-clicking a spline in subobject mode opens a pop-up quadmenu that lets you convert it between Curve and Line types. The Curve type option changes all vertices to Bézier type, and the Line type option makes all vertices Corner type. Spline subobject mode includes many of the buttons previously discussed as well as some new ones in the Geometry rollout.

Reverse

The Reverse button is available only for Spline subobjects. It reverses the order of the vertex numbers. For example, a circle that is numbered clockwise from 1 to 4 is numbered counterclockwise after using the Reverse button. The vertex order is important for splines that are used for animation paths or loft compound objects.

Outline

The Outline button creates a spline that is identical to the one selected and offset by an amount specified by dragging or specified in the Offset value. The Center option creates an outline on either side of the selected spline, centered on the original spline. When the Center option is not selected, then an outline is created by offsetting a duplicate of the spline on only one side of the original spline. To exit Outline mode, click the Outline button again or right-click in the viewport. Figure 12.30 shows an arc that has had the Outline feature applied. In the right image, the Center option is enabled.

FIGURE 12.30

The Outline button creates a duplicate copy of the original spline and offsets it.

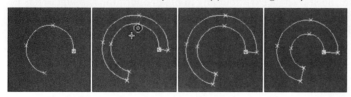

Boolean

Boolean operations work with two or more splines that overlap one another. There are three different operations that can happen: You can combine the splines to create a single spline (union), you can subtract the overlapping area from one of the splines (subtract), or you can throw away everything except the overlapping area (intersection).

Cross-Reference

You can also use Booleans to combine or subtract 3D volumes, which are covered in Chapter 27, "Working with Compound Objects." ∎

The Boolean button works on overlapping closed splines and has three different options—Union, Subtraction, and Intersection—shown in Table 12.3. The splines must all be part of the same object. The Union option combines the areas of both splines, the Subtraction option removes the second spline's area from the first, and the Intersection option keeps only the areas that overlap.

TABLE 12.3

Boolean Button Options

Button	Description
	Union
	Subtraction
	Intersection

To use the Boolean feature, select one of the splines and select one of the Boolean operation options. Then click the Boolean button, and select the second spline. Depending on which Boolean operation you chose, the overlapping area is deleted, the second spline acts to cut away the overlapping area on the first, or only the overlapping area remains. To exit Boolean mode, right-click in the viewport.

Note

Boolean operations can be performed only on closed splines that exist within a 2D plane. ■

Figure 12.31 shows the results of applying the Spline Boolean operators on a circle and star shape. The first image consists of the circle and star shapes without any Boolean operations applied. The second image shows the result of the Union feature; the third (circle selected first) and fourth (star selected first) use the Subtraction feature; and the fifth image uses the Intersection feature.

FIGURE 12.31

Using the Boolean operations on two overlapping shapes

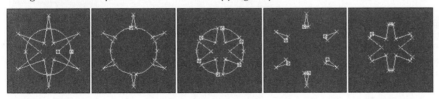

Mirror

You can use the Mirror button to mirror a spline object horizontally, vertically, or along both axes. To use this feature, select a spline object to mirror and then locate the Mirror button. To the right of the Mirror button are three smaller buttons, each of which indicates a direction—Mirror Horizontally, Mirror Vertically, and Mirror Both—shown in Table 12.4. Select a direction, and then click the Mirror button. If the Copy option is selected, a new spline is created and mirrored. The About Pivot option causes the mirroring to be completed about the pivot point axes.

TABLE 12.4

Mirror Button Options

Button	Description
	Mirror Horizontally
	Mirror Vertically
	Mirror Both

Figure 12.32 shows a little critter that has been mirrored horizontally, vertically, and both. The right image was horizontally mirrored with the About Pivot option disabled. Notice that the eye spline was mirrored about its own pivot.

FIGURE 12.32

Mirroring a shape is as simple as selecting a direction and clicking the Mirror button.

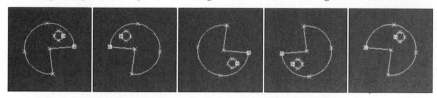

Trim and Extend

The Trim button cuts off any extending portion between two overlapping splines. The splines must be part of the same object. To use the Trim feature, select the spline that you want to keep, click the Trim button, and then click the segment to trim. The spline you click is trimmed back to the nearest inter-secting point of the selected object. This button works only in Spline subobject mode. The trimming command is dependent on the viewport that is active. When the Perspective or a Camera view is active, this command uses the Top viewport to trim.

Figure 12.33 shows a circle intersected by two ellipse shapes. The Trim button was used to cut the center sections of the ellipse shapes away.

FIGURE 12.33

You can use the Trim button to cut away the excess of a spline.

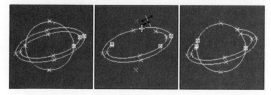

The Extend button works in the reverse manner compared to the Trim button. The Extend button lengthens the end of a spline until it encounters an intersection. (There must be a spline segment to intersect.) To use the Extend command, click the Extend button and then click the segment to extend. The spline you click is extended. To exit Extend mode, right-click in the viewport or click the Extend button again.

The Infinite Bounds option works for both the Trim and Extend buttons. When enabled, it treats all open splines as if they were infinite for the purpose of locating an intersecting point. The Extend command, like Trim, is dependent on the active viewport.

Close

The Close button completes an open spline and creates a closed spline by attaching a segment between the first and last vertices. You can check which vertex is first by enabling the Show Vertex Numbers in the Selection rollout. This is similar to the Connect feature (accessible in Vertex subobject mode), but the Connect feature can connect the end point of one spline to the end point of another as long as they are part of the same Editable Spline object. The Close feature works only in Spline subobject mode and connects only the end points of each given spline.

Explode

The Explode button performs the Detach command on all subobject splines at once. It separates each segment into a separate spline. You can select to explode all spline objects to separate Splines or Objects. If you select to explode to Objects, then a dialog box appears asking you for a name. Each spline uses the name you enter with a two-digit number appended to distinguish between the different splines.

Tutorial: Spinning a spider's web

Now that you're familiar with the many aspects of editing splines, you'll try to mimic one of the best spline producers in the world—the spider. The spider is an expert at connecting lines together to create an intricate pattern. (Luckily, unlike the spider that depends on its web for food, you won't go hungry if this example fails.)

To create a spider web from splines, follow these steps:

1. Select Create ➪ Shapes ➪ Circle, and drag in the Front viewport to create a large circle for the perimeter of the web (pretend that the spider is building this web inside a tire swing). Right-click on the circle, and select Convert To ➪ Editable Spline to convert the circle shape.

2. Select the Spline subobject in the Modifier Stack (or press the 3 key) to enter Spline subobject mode.

3. Click the Create Line button in the Geometry rollout, and click in the center of the circle and again outside the circle to create a line. Then right-click to end the line. Repeat this step until 12 or so radial lines extend from the center of the circle outward.

4. Select and right-click on the 2D Snaps Toggle in the main toolbar. In the Grid and Snap Settings dialog box, enable the Vertex and Edge/Segment options and close the dialog box. While you're still in Create Line mode, click on the circle's center and create lines in a spiral pattern by clicking on each radial line that you intersect. Right-click to end the line when you finally reach the edge of the circle. Then right-click again to exit Create Line mode.

5. Select the circle shape, and click the Trim button. Then click on each line segment on the portion that extends beyond the circle. This trims the radial lines to the edge of the circle. Click the Trim button again when you are finished to exit Trim mode.

6. Change to Vertex subobject mode by clicking Vertex in the Modifier Stack (or by pressing 1). Turn off the Snap toggle and then select all the vertices in the center of the circle, and click the Fuse button.

Figure 12.34 shows the finished spider web. (I have a new respect for spiders.)

FIGURE 12.34

A spider web made from Editable Splines

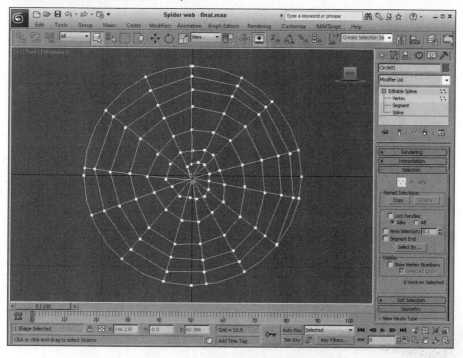

Using Spline Modifiers

In the Modifiers menu is a whole submenu of modifiers that apply strictly to splines. You can find these modifiers in the Modifiers ➪ Patch/Spline Editing menu.

Spline-specific modifiers

Of the modifiers that work only on splines, several of these duplicate functionality that is available for Editable Splines, such as the Fillet/Chamfer modifier. Applying these features as modifiers gives you better control over the results because you can remove them using the Modifier Stack at any time.

Edit Spline modifier

The Modifiers ➪ Patch/Spline Editing ➪ Edit Spline modifier (mentioned at the start of the chapter) makes spline objects so they can be edited. It has all the same features as the Editable Spline object. The Edit Spline modifier isn't really a modifier, but an Object type. It shows up in the Modifier Stack above the base object. The key benefit of the Edit Spline modifier is that it enables you to edit spline subobjects while maintaining the parametric nature of the primitive object.

Spline Select modifier

This modifier enables you to select spline subobjects, including Vertex, Segment, and Spline. You can copy and paste named selection sets. The selection can then be passed up the Stack to the next modifier. The Spline Select modifier provides a way to apply a modifier to a subobject selection.

The Modifiers ⇨ Selection Modifiers ⇨ Spline Select modifier lets you select objects from any of the subobject modes available in the Editable Spline object. It also includes buttons for selecting subobjects based on the other subobject modes. For example, if you select Vertex subobject mode, then two buttons available in the Select Vertex rollout are Get Segment Selection and Get Spline Selection. Clicking either of these buttons gets all the vertices that are part of the other subobject mode.

You can also Copy and Paste selection sets using the Copy and Paste buttons.

Delete Spline modifier

You can use the Delete Spline modifier to delete spline subobjects. This is helpful if you want to remove a spline from an object so it doesn't render without destroying the curvature of the other splines in the object. To do this, simply select the splines to remove from the object in Spline subobject mode and then apply the Delete Spline modifier. The selection will be passed up the stack.

Normalize Spline modifier

The Normalize Spline modifier adds new points to the spline. These points are spaced regularly based on the Segment Length value. Figure 12.35 shows a simple flower shape with the Spline Select modifier applied so you can see the vertices. The Normalize Spline modifier was then applied with Segment Length values of 1, 5, 10, and 15. Notice that the shape is changing with fewer vertices.

FIGURE 12.35

The Normalize Spline modifier relaxes the shape by removing vertices.

Fillet/Chamfer modifier

You can use the Fillet/Chamfer modifier to Fillet or Chamfer the corners of shapes. Fillet creates smooth corners, and Chamfer adds another segment where two edges meet. Parameters include the Fillet Radius and the Chamfer Distance. Both include an Apply button. The results of this modifier are the same as if you were to use the Fillet or Chamfer features of an Editable Spline.

Renderable Spline modifier

The Renderable Spline modifier lets you make any selected spline renderable. The Parameters rollout includes the same controls that are available for Editable Splines including Thickness, Sides, and Angle values.

Sweep modifier

The Sweep modifier works just like the loft compound object, letting you follow a spline path with a defined cross section, except that the Sweep modifier is a modifier, making it easier to apply and remove from splines and shapes. Another benefit of the Sweep modifier is that it has several Built-In Sections available that you can choose or you can pick your own. The built-in sections include many that are useful for architectural structures including Angle, Bar, Channel, Cylinder, Half Round, Pipe, Quarter Round, Tee, Tube, and Wide Flange.

Using the Merge From File button, you can choose a shape from another file. You can also set the number of interpolation steps. The Sweep Parameters rollout includes options for mirroring, offsetting, smoothing, aligning, and banking the generated sweep. The Union Intersecting option causes self-intersecting portions of the path to be combined using a union Boolean command. You also can select to have mapping coordinates generated on the sweep object.

Tutorial: Plumbing with pipes

If you want to create a shape that renders in the scene, you can use the Renderable Spline option or you can apply the Sweep modifier. In this example, you apply the Sweep modifier to a line that defines the path of a bathroom sink drain.

To create a pipe that follows a spline, follow these steps:

1. Open the Bathroom sink.max file from the Chap 12 directory on the CD.

   This file includes a simple bathroom sink and a line that defines its drain path.

2. With the spline selected, choose the Modifiers ➪ Patch/Spline Editing ➪ Sweep menu command to apply the Sweep modifier.

3. In the Section Type rollout, choose the Cylinder option from the Built-In Section drop-down list. Then set the Radius value to **10** in the Parameters rollout.

Figure 12.36 shows the resulting sink complete with a drain created using a cylinder cross section.

Trim/Extend modifier

The Trim/Extend modifier lets you trim the extending end of a spline or extend a spline until it meets another spline at a vertex. The Pick Locations button turns on Pick mode, where the cursor changes when it is over a valid point. Operations include Auto, Trim Only, and Extend Only with an option to compute Infinite Boundaries. You can also set the Intersection Projection to View, Construction Plane, or None.

Using the Shape Check utility

The Shape Check utility is helpful in verifying that a shape doesn't intersect itself. Shapes that have this problem cannot be extruded, lofted, or lathed without problems. To use this utility, open the Utilities panel (the icon for the Utilities panel looks like a hammer) and click the More button. Select Shape Check from the Utilities dialog box list, and click OK.

Note

The Shape Check utility is found in the Utilities panel and not in the Modifiers menu. ∎

The Shape Check rollout includes only two buttons: Pick Object and Close. Click the Pick Object button, and click the shape you want to check. Any intersection points are displayed as red squares, as shown in Figure 12.37, and the response field displays "Shape Self-Intersects." If the shape doesn't have any intersections, then the response field reports "Shape OK."

FIGURE 12.36

The resulting drain pipe was created using the Sweep modifier.

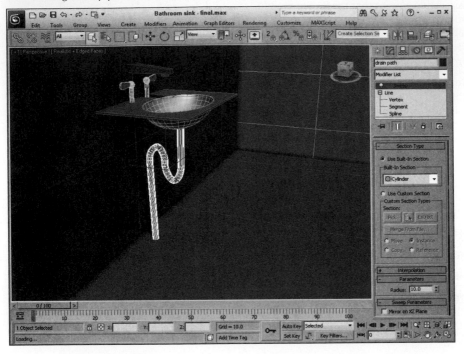

Note
You can use the Shape Check utility on normal splines and on NURBS splines. ■

Moving splines to 3D

Although splines can be rendered, the real benefit of splines in Max is to use them to create 3D objects and for animation paths. You can use splines in several ways as you model 3D objects, including Loft objects and modifiers. One way to use splines to make 3D objects is with modifiers.

Note
As you build splines that will be used to create mesh objects, remember that the number of vertices in a spline determines the number of segments in the final mesh. For example, if you have a spline with 10 points that is extruded 5 times, then you'll end up with more than 50 polygons, but the same spline with 80 points would have more than 400 polygons. ■

Cross-Reference
Using splines to create an animation path is covered in Chapter 21, "Understanding Animation and Keyframes," and Loft objects are covered in Chapter 27, "Working with Compound Objects." General information on working with modifiers is covered in Chapter 11, "Introducing Modifiers and Using the Modifier Stack." ■

FIGURE 12.37

The Shape Check utility can identify spline intersections.

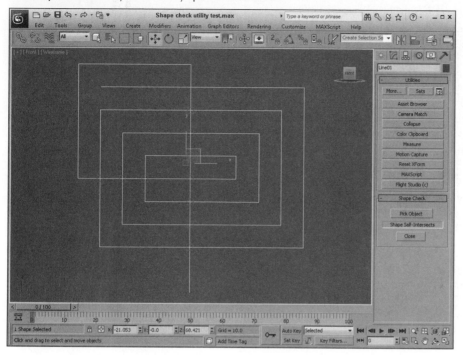

Extruding splines

Because splines are drawn in a 2D plane, they already include two of the three dimensions. By adding a Height value to the shape, you can create a simple 3D object. The process of adding Height to a shape is called *extruding*.

To extrude a shape, you need to apply the Extrude modifier. To do so, select a spline object and choose Modifiers ⇨ Mesh Editing ⇨ Extrude, or select the Extrude modifier from the Modifier Stack drop-down list. In the Parameters rollout, you can specify an Amount, which is the height value of the extrusion; the number of Segments; and the Capping options (caps fill in the surface at each end of the Extruded shape). You can also specify the final Output to be a Patch, Mesh, or NURBS object. Figure 12.38 shows capital *E*s that model the various vertex types extruded to a depth of 10.0.

FIGURE 12.38

Extruding simple shapes adds depth to the spline.

Tutorial: Routing a custom shelf

In Woodshop 101, you use a router to add a designer edge to doorframes, window frames, and shelving of all sorts. In Woodshop 3D, the Boolean tools work nicely as you customize a bookshelf.

To create a custom bookshelf using spline Boolean operations, follow these steps:

1. Open the Bookshelf.max file from the Chap 12 directory on the CD.

   This file includes a triangle shape drawn with the Line primitive that is overlapped by three circles. All these shapes have been converted and combined into a single Editable Spline object.

2. Select the shape, open the Modify panel, and select the Spline subobject mode (or press the 3 key) and select the triangle shape.

3. Select the Subtraction Boolean operation (the middle icon) in the Geometry rollout, and click the Boolean button. Then select each of the circles and right-click to exit Boolean mode. Then click Spline in the Modifier Stack again to exit subobject mode.

4. Back in the Modify panel, select the Extrude modifier from the Modifier drop-down list and enter an Amount of **1000**. Select Zoom Extents All to resize your viewports, switch to the Perspective viewport, and view your bookshelf.

Figure 12.39 shows the finished bookshelf in the Perspective viewport ready to hang on the wall.

FIGURE 12.39

The finished bookshelf created with spline Boolean operations and the Extrude modifier

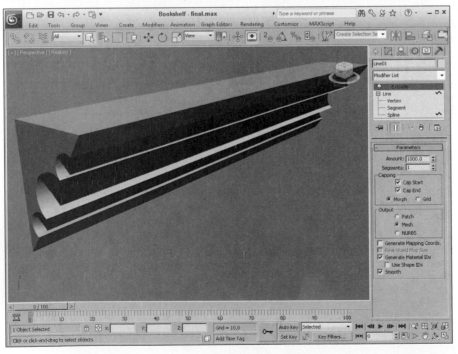

Lathing splines

Another useful modifier for 2D splines is the Lathe. This modifier rotates the spline about an axis to create an object with a circular cross section (such as a baseball bat). In the Parameters rollout, you can specify the Degrees to rotate (a value of 360 makes a full rotation) and Cappings, which add ends to the resulting mesh. Additional options include Weld Core, which causes all vertices at the center of the lathe to be welded together, and Flip Normals, which realigns all the normals.

The Direction option determines the axis about which the rotation takes place. The rotation takes place about the object's pivot point.

Caution

If your shape is created in the Top view, then lathing about the screen Z-axis produces a thin disc without any depth. ■

Tutorial: Lathing a crucible

As an example of the Lathe modifier, you create a simple crucible, although you could produce any object that has a circular cross section. A *crucible* is a thick porcelain cup used to melt chemicals. I chose this as an example because it is simple (and saying "crucible" sounds much more scientific than "cup").

To create a crucible using the Lathe modifier, follow these steps:

1. Open the Crucible.max file from the Chap 12 directory on the CD.

   This file includes a rough profile cross-section line of the crucible that has been converted to an Editable Spline.

2. Select the line, and select the Modifiers ⇨ Patch/Spline Editing ⇨ Lathe menu command. Set the Degrees value in the Parameters rollout to **360**. Because you'll lathe a full revolution, you don't need to check the Cap options. In the Direction section, select the Y button (the Y-axis), and you're finished.

Figure 12.40 shows the finished product. You can easily make this into a coffee mug by adding a handle. To make a handle, simply loft an ellipse along a curved path.

Bevel and Bevel Profile modifiers

Another common set of modifiers that can be used with splines and shapes are the Bevel and Bevel Profile modifiers.

Note

Neither the Bevel nor Bevel Profile modifiers are found in the Modifiers menu. To apply them, use the Modifier List found in the Modifier Stack. They are among the Object-Space modifiers. ■

Using the Bevel modifier, you can extrude and outline (scale) the shape in one operation. With the Bevel modifier, you can set the Height and Outline values for up to three different bevel levels. The Capping options let you select to cap either end of the beveled shape. The Cap Type can be either Morph or Grid. The Morph type is for objects that will be morphed. You can specify that the Surface use Linear or Curved Sides with a given number of segments. You can also select to Smooth Across Levels automatically. The Keep Lines from Crossing option avoids problems that may result from crossing lines.

The Bevel Profile modifier lets you select a spline to use for the bevel profile.

FIGURE 12.40

Lathing a simple profile can create a circular object.

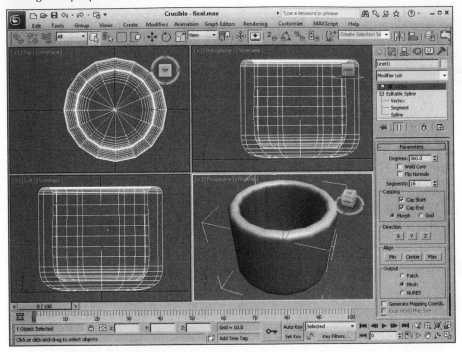

Tutorial: Modeling unique rings

You can create a simple ring using a Tube or Torus primitive object (or with an extruded donut shape), but if you want the ring to have a unique profile, then the Bevel and Bevel Profile modifiers are what you need.

To create a couple of unique rings with the Bevel and Bevel Profile modifiers, follow these steps:

1. Select Create ➪ Shapes ➪ Donut, and drag in the Top viewport to create two donut objects that are positioned side by side. Set the Radius 1 value to **80** and the Radius 2 value to **75** for both rings.

2. Select the ring on the left in the Top viewport, open the Modify panel, and select the Bevel modifier from the Modifier List drop-down list in the Modifier Stack. In the Bevel Values rollout, set the Start Outline to **0**, the Height values for Levels 1, 2, and 3 to **20**, the Outline for Level 1 to **15**, and the Outline value for Level 3 to **−15**. Then enable the Smooth Across Levels option.

3. Select Create ➪ Shapes ➪ Line, and draw a profile curve in the Front viewport from bottom to top that is about the same height as the first ring. This curve doesn't have to be a closed spline.

4. Select the donut shape on the right, open the Modify panel, and choose the Bevel Profile modifier from the Modifier List in the Modifier Stack. In the Parameters rollout, click the Pick Profile button and select the profile curve.

Figure 12.41 shows the finished rings.

FIGURE 12.41

Bevels applied to a shape can give a unique profile edge.

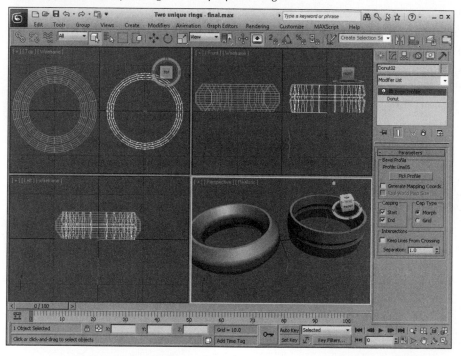

CrossSection modifier

The CrossSection modifier is one of two modifiers that collectively are referred to as the *surface tools*. The surface tools provide a way to cover a series of connected cross sections with a surface. The CrossSection modifier connects the vertices of several cross-sectional splines together with additional splines in preparation for the Surface modifier. These cross-sectional splines can have different numbers of vertices. Parameters include different spline types such as Linear, Smooth, Bézier, and Bézier Corner.

Cross-Reference

The second half of the surface tools is the Surface modifier. You can find this modifier and an example in Bonus Chapter 5 on the CD, "Working with NURBS." The surface tools are similar in many ways to the Loft compound object, which is covered in Chapter 27, "Working with Compound Objects." ∎

Summary

As this chapter has shown, there is much more to splines than just points, lines, and control handles. Splines in Max are one of the fundamental building blocks and the pathway to advanced modeling skills using NURBS.

This chapter covered the following spline topics:

- Understanding the various shape primitives
- Editing splines
- Working with the various spline subobjects
- Applying modifiers to splines

The next chapter continues your voyage down the modeling pathway with perhaps the most common modeling types—meshes and polys.

Modeling with Polygons

Meshes (or, more specifically, polygon meshes) are perhaps the most popular and the default model type for most 3D programs. You create them by placing polygonal faces next to one another so the edges are joined. The polygons can then be smoothed from face to face during the rendering process. Using meshes, you can create almost any 3D object, including simple primitives such as a cube or a realistic dinosaur.

Meshes have lots of advantages. They are common, intuitive to work with, and supported by a large number of 3D software packages. In this chapter, you learn how to create and edit mesh and poly objects.

Understanding Poly Objects

Before continuing, you need to understand exactly what a Poly object is, how it differs from a regular mesh object, and why it is the featured modeling type in Max. To understand these issues, you'll need a quick history lesson. Initially, Max supported only mesh objects, and all mesh objects had to be broken down into triangular faces. Subdividing the mesh into triangular faces ensured that all faces in the mesh object were coplanar, which prevented any hiccups with the rendering engine.

Over time, the rendering engines have been modified and upgraded to handle polygons that weren't subdivided (or whose subdivision was invisible to the user), and doing such actually makes the model more efficient by eliminating all the extra edges required to triangulate the mesh. Also, users can work with polygon objects more easily than individual faces. To take advantage of these new features, the Editable Poly object was added to Max.

As development has continued, many new features have been added to the Editable Poly object while the Editable Mesh remained mainly for backward compatibility. The one advantage that the Editable Mesh object had over the Editable Poly was that the Edit Mesh modifier could be applied, but as of version 7, Max has an Edit Poly modifier, which lets you make changes to an object as a modifier that can easily be removed.

Even with the addition of the Edit Poly modifier, the Editable Mesh object type still exists, and there are times when you'll want to use each type, shown in Figure 13.1. Editable Mesh objects split all polygons into triangular faces, but the Editable Poly object maintains four-sided (or more) polygon faces. Another key difference is found in the subobjects. Editable Meshes can work with Vertex, Edge, Face, Polygon, and Element subobjects; and Editable Poly objects can work with Vertex, Edge, Border, Polygon, and Element subobjects.

FIGURE 13.1

Editable Mesh objects have triangular faces; the Editable Poly object uses faces with four or more vertices.

Editable Mesh object   Editable Poly object

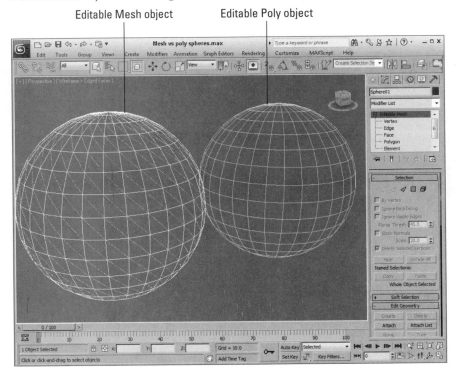

Some game engines still require that all faces be coplanar, and for such conditions you'll want to continue to use the Editable Mesh object. Another case where the Editable Mesh object is helpful is in performing certain face-oriented operations. In addition, normal meshes have a smaller memory footprint, which enables them to render more quickly, especially if you have many of them. Regardless, Max lets you convert seamlessly between these two modeling types.

Although many of the same features are available for both object types, the advance features available for the Editable Poly object make it the preferred object type to use for mesh modeling. This chapter focuses on working with Editable Poly objects. Although the specific features of the Editable Mesh object aren't covered, most of these same commands apply equally to the Editable Mesh object. However, the Graphite Modeling tools can be used only on Editable Poly objects.

Creating Editable Poly Objects

The Create panel has no method for making mesh objects—mesh objects must be converted from another object type or produced as the result of a modifier. Object types that you can convert include shapes, primitives, Booleans, patches, and NURBS. Many models that are imported appear as mesh objects. Most 3D formats, including 3DS and DXF, import as mesh objects.

Note
You can even convert spline shapes to Editable Poly objects, whether they are open or closed. Closed splines are filled with a polygon, whereas open splines are only a single edge and can be hard to see. ∎

Before you can use many of the mesh editing functions discussed in this chapter, you need to convert the object to an Editable Poly object, collapse an object with modifiers applied, or apply the Edit Poly modifier.

Converting objects

To convert an object into an Editable Poly object, right-click the object and choose Convert To ⇨ Convert to Editable Poly from the pop-up quadmenu. You can also convert an object by right-clicking the object within the Modifier Stack and selecting one of the convert options from the pop-up menu.

Collapsing to a mesh object

When an object is collapsed, it loses its parametric nature and the parameters associated with any applied modifiers. Only objects that have had modifiers applied to them can be collapsed. Objects are made into an Editable Poly object when you use the Collapse To option available from the right-click pop-up menu in the Modifier Stack or when you use the Collapse utility.

Tip
You can also collapse objects using the Collapse utility found in the Utilities panel. ∎

Most objects collapse to Editable Poly objects, but some objects, such as the compound objects, give you an option of which structure to collapse to.

Applying the Edit Poly modifier

Another way to enable the mesh editing features is to apply the Edit Poly modifier to an object. You apply this modifier by selecting the object and choosing Modifiers ⇨ Mesh Editing ⇨ Edit Poly, or selecting Edit Poly from the Modifier drop-down list in the Modify panel.

The Edit Poly modifier is different from the Editable Poly object in that, as an applied modifier, it maintains the parametric nature of the original object. For example, you cannot change the Radius value of a sphere object that has been converted to an Editable Poly, but you could if the Edit Poly modifier were applied.

Editing Poly Objects

After an object has been converted to an Editable Poly, you can alter its shape by applying modifiers, or you can work with the mesh subobjects. You can find the editing features for these objects in the Modify panel, but the better place to look for the Editable Poly features is in the Graphite Modeling tools.

Cross-Reference

This chapter presents many of the editing features found in the Modify panel. These same features are available in the Graphite Modeling Tool's Ribbon, which is covered in Chapter 14, "Using the Graphite Modeling Tools and Painting with Objects." ∎

Cross-Reference

The mesh-related modifiers are covered in Chapter 26, "Deforming Surfaces and Using the Mesh Modifiers." ∎

Editable Poly subobject modes

Before you can edit poly subobjects, you must select them. To select a subobject mode, select Editable Poly in the Modifier Stack, click the small plus sign to its left to display a hierarchy of subobjects, and then click the subobject type with which you want to work. Another way to select a subobject type is to click on the appropriate subobject button in the Selection rollout. The subobject button in the Selection rollout and the subobject listed in the Modifier Stack both turn bright yellow when selected. You can also type a number from 1 to 5 to enter subobject mode with 1 for Vertex, 2 for Edge, 3 for Border, 4 for Polygon, and 5 for Element.

The Vertex subobject mode lets you select and work with all vertices in the object. Edge subobject mode makes all edges that run between two vertices available for selection. The Border subobject mode lets you select all edges that run around an opening in the object such as a hole. The Polygon subobject mode lets you work with individual polygon faces, and the Element subobject mode picks individual objects if the object includes several different elements.

To exit subobject edit mode, click the subobject button (displayed in yellow) again. Remember, you must exit this mode before you can select another object.

Note

Selected subobject edges appear in the viewports in red to distinguish them from edges of the selected object, which appear white when displayed as wireframes. ∎

After you're in a subobject mode, you can click on a subobject (or drag over an area to select multiple subobjects) to select it and edit the subobject using the transformation buttons on the main toolbar. You can transform subobjects just like other objects.

Cross-Reference

For more information on transforming objects, see Chapter 7, "Transforming Objects, Pivoting, Aligning, and Snapping." ∎

When working with Editable Poly objects in subobject mode, you can use Press and Release keyboard shortcuts. These shortcuts are identified in bold in the Editable Poly group of the Keyboard panel of the Customize User Interface dialog box. When using these keyboard shortcuts, you can access a different editing mode without having to exit subobject mode. For example, if you press and hold Alt+C while in Polygon subobject mode, you can make a cut with the Cut tool, and when you release the keyboard keys you'll return to Polygon subobject mode.

Cross-Reference

You can learn more about the Customize User Interface dialog box in Chapter 4, "Changing Interface Units and Setting Preferences." ∎

You can select multiple subobjects at the same time by dragging an outline over them. You can also select multiple subobjects by holding down the Ctrl key while clicking them. The Ctrl key can also deselect selected subobjects while maintaining the rest of the selection. Holding down the Alt key removes any selected vertices from the current selection set.

With one of the transform buttons selected, hold down the Shift key while clicking and dragging on a subobject to clone it. During cloning, the Clone Part of Mesh dialog box appears, enabling you to Clone to Object or Clone to Element. Using the Clone to Object option makes the selection an entirely new object, and you are able to give the new object a name. If the Clone to Element option is selected, the clone remains part of the existing object but is a new element within that object.

If you hold down the Ctrl key while choosing a different subobject mode, the current selection is maintained for the new subobject type. For example, if you select all the polygons in the top half of a model using the Polygon subobject mode and click the Vertex subobject mode while holding down the Ctrl key, all vertices in the top half of the model are selected. This works only for the applicable subobjects. If the selection of polygons doesn't have any borders, then holding down the Ctrl key while clicking the Border subobject mode selects nothing.

You also can hold down the Shift key to select only those subobjects that lie on the borders of the current selection. For example, selecting all the polygons in the top half of a model using the Polygon subobject mode and clicking the Vertex subobject mode with the Shift key held down selects only those vertices that surround the selection and not the interior vertices.

Subobject selection

The Selection rollout, shown in Figure 13.2, includes options for selecting subobjects. The By Vertex option is available in all but the Vertex subobject mode. It requires that you click a vertex in order to select an edge, border, polygon, or element. It selects all edges and borders that are connected to a vertex when the vertex is selected. The Ignore Backfacing option selects only those subobjects with normals pointing toward the current viewport. For example, if you are trying to select some faces on a sphere, only the faces on the side closest to you are selected. If this option is off, then faces on both sides of the sphere are selected. This option is helpful if many subobjects are on top of one another in the viewport.

Tip

The select commands in the Edit menu also work with subobjects. For example, in Vertex subobject mode, you can select Edit⇨Select All (or press Ctrl+A) to select all vertices. ■

The By Angle option selects adjacent polygons that are within the specified threshold. The threshold value is defined as the angle between the normals of adjacent polygons. For example, if you have a terrain mesh with a smooth, flat lake area in its middle, you can select the entire lake area if you set the Planar Threshold to 0 and click the lake.

The Selection rollout also includes four buttons. These buttons include Shrink, Grow, Ring, and Loop. Use the Grow button to increase the current selection around the perimeter of the current selection, as shown in Figure 13.3. Click the Shrink button to do the opposite.

The Ring and Loop buttons are available only in Edge and Border subobject modes. Use Ring and Loop to select all adjacent subobjects horizontally and vertically around the entire object. Ring selection looks for parallel edges, and Loop selection looks for all edges around an object that are aligned the same as the initial selection. For example, if you select a single edge of a sphere, the Ring button selects all edges going around the sphere, and the Loop button selects all edges in a line from the top to the bottom of the sphere.

FIGURE 13.2

The Selection rollout includes options for determining which subobjects are selected.

Vertex subobject mode

Edge subobject mode

Border subobject mode

Polygon subobject mode

Element subobject mode

FIGURE 13.3

Using the Grow button, you can increase the subobject selection.

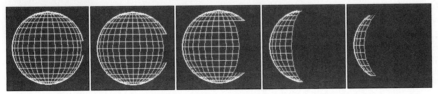

Next to the Ring and Loop buttons is a set of up/down arrows. These arrows are used to shift the current ring and/or loop selection left and right for the Ring selection, or up and down for the Loop selection. Holding down the Ctrl key adds the adjacent ring or loop to the current selection, and holding down the Alt key removes the adjacent selection. Figure 13-4 shows how the Ring and Loop buttons work. The first sphere shows a selection made using the Ring button; the second sphere has increased this selection by holding down the Ctrl key while clicking the up arrow next to the Loop button. The third sphere shows a selection made using the Loop button; the fourth sphere has increased this selection by holding down the Ctrl key while clicking the up arrow next to the Ring button.

Note

For Editable Poly objects, the Hide Selected, Unhide All, Copy, and Paste buttons are located at the bottom of the Edit Geometry rollout. ■

FIGURE 13.4

The Ring and Loop buttons can select an entire row and/or column of edges.

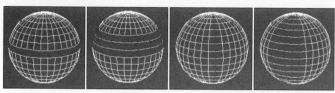

Cross-Reference

The Soft Selection rollout allows you to alter adjacent nonselected subobjects when selected subobjects are moved, creating a smooth transition. For the details on this rollout, see Chapter 10, "Accessing Subobjects and Using Modeling Helpers." ■

Tutorial: Modeling a clown head

Now that you know how to select subobjects, you can use the transform tools to move them. In this example, you'll quickly deform a sphere to create a clown face by selecting, moving, and working with some vertices.

To create a clown head by moving vertices, follow these steps:

1. Select Create ⇨ Standard Primitives ⇨ Sphere, and drag in the Front viewport to create a sphere object. Then right-click the sphere and select Convert To ⇨ Editable Poly in the pop-up quadmenu.

2. Open the Modify panel. Now make a long, pointy nose by pulling a vertex outward from the sphere object. Click the small plus sign to the left of the Editable Poly object in the Modifier Stack, and select Vertex in the hierarchy (or press the 1 key). This activates the Vertex sub-object mode. Enable the Ignore Backfacing option in the Selection rollout, and select the single vertex in the center of the Front viewport. Make sure that the Select and Move button (W) is selected, and in the Left viewport, drag the vertex along the Z-axis until it projects from the sphere.

3. Next, create the mouth by selecting and indenting a row of vertices in the Front viewport below the protruding nose. Holding down the Ctrl key makes selecting multiple vertices easy. Below the nose, select several vertices in a circular arc that make a smile. Then move the selected vertices along the negative Z-axis in the Left viewport.

4. For the eyes, select Create ⇨ Standard Primitives ⇨ Sphere and enable the AutoGrid option. Then drag in the Front viewport to create two eyes above the nose.

This clown head is just a simple example of what is possible by editing subobjects. Figure 13.5 shows the clown head in a shaded view.

FIGURE 13.5

A clown head created from an editable poly by selecting and moving vertices

Editing geometry

Much of the power of editing meshes is contained within the Edit Geometry rollout, shown in Figure 13.6. Features contained here include, among many others, the ability to create new subobjects, attach subobjects to the mesh, weld vertices, chamfer vertices, slice, explode, and align. Some Edit Geometry buttons are disabled depending on the subobject mode that you select. The features detailed in this section are enabled for the Editable Poly object before you enter a subobject mode.

Many of the buttons for the Editable Poly include a small icon to the right of the button that opens a settings caddy. These caddy interfaces appear around the selected subobject and allow you to change the settings and immediately see the results in the viewports. The OK button (a check mark icon) applies the settings and closes the dialog box, and the Apply button (a plus sign icon) applies the settings and leaves the dialog box open. These caddy interfaces are included next to the buttons such as Extrude, Bevel, Outline, and Inset.

Editable Poly objects include all their common buttons in the Edit Geometry rollout and all subobject-specific buttons is a separate rollout named after the subobject mode, such as Edit Vertices or Edit Edges.

Repeat Last

The first button in the Edit Geometry rollout is the Repeat Last button. This button repeats the last subobject command. This button does not work on all features, but it's very convenient for certain actions.

FIGURE 13.6

The Edit Geometry rollout includes many general-purpose editing features.

Tip

The tooltip for this button displays the last repeatable command. ∎

Enabling constraints

The Constraints options limit the movement of subobjects to a specified subobject. The available constraints are None, Edge, Face, and Normal. For example, if you select and move a vertex with the Edge constraint enabled, then the movement is constrained to the adjacent edges.

Tutorial: Creating a roof truss

When creating houses, modeling the roof can be tricky, but using an edge constraint makes it much easier.

To create a triangular roof truss, follow these steps:

1. Select Create ⇨ Standard Primitives ⇨ Box, and drag in the Top viewport to create a Box object centered over the Y-axis.
2. Right-click the box object and select Convert To ⇨ Editable Poly in the pop-up quadmenu.
3. Open the Modify panel, and choose the Vertex subobject mode. In the Constraints drop-down list of the Edit Geometry panel, select the Edge option.
4. With the Select and Move tool, drag over the top-left corners and drag them to the Y-axis; then repeat for the top-right corners.

Notice that the points are constrained to the top edge as they are dragged. Moving both sets of points results in a simple perfect triangle.

Tip

An even easier way to create such a triangle would be to use the Gengon primitive found among the Extended Primitives. ■

Preserve UVs

UV coordinates define how a texture map is applied to an object's surface. These UV coordinates are tied closely to the surface subobject positions, so moving a subobject after a texture is applied moves the texture also. This could cause discontinuities to the texture map. The Preserve UVs option lets you make subobject changes without altering the UV coordinates for an existing texture.

The Settings dialog box for the Preserve UVs option lets you select a Vertex Color and Texture Channel to preserve. Figure 13.7 shows two block objects with a brick texture map applied. The inner vertices on the left block were scaled outward without the Preserve UVs option selected; the right block had this option enabled.

FIGURE 13.7

The Preserve UVs option lets you make subobject changes after texture maps have been applied.

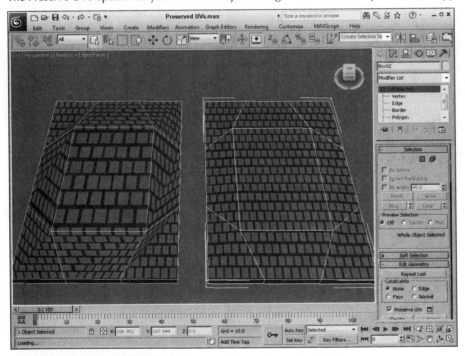

Create

The Create button lets you create new subobjects, specifically polygons, by connecting isolated vertices and border vertices. When the cursor is over a valid vertex, it changes to a crosshair, and you can click to create a polygon edge from the last clicked point. If no vertices are available, you can Shift-click to create one. This creates a vertex where you click. Be aware that creating a vertex doesn't add it to any of the edges, but the Create button in Edge subobject mode can connect edges to these isolated vertices.

Tip

As you create new polygons, the normal is determined by the direction in which you create the polygon using the right-hand rule. If you bend the fingers of your right hand in the direction (clockwise or counterclockwise) that the vertices are clicked, then your thumb will point in the direction of the normal. If the normal is pointing away from you, then the backside of the polygon will be visible and the lighting could be off. ∎

You can use the Create button to create new polygons based on new or existing vertices. To create a new face, click the Create button, which highlights all vertices in the selected mesh. Next, click a vertex to start the polygon; after you click two more vertices, a new face is created. You can also create a new vertex not based on any existing vertices by holding down the Shift key while clicking.

Polygons aren't limited to three vertices. You can click as many times as you want to add additional vertices to the polygon. Click the first vertex, or double-click to complete the polygon.

Collapse

The Collapse button is used to collapse all the selected subobjects to a single subobject located at the averaged center of the selection. This button is similar to the Weld button, except that the selected vertices don't need to be within a Threshold value to be combined. This button works in all subobject modes.

Attach and Detach

The Attach button is available with all subobject modes, even when you are not in subobject mode. Use the Attach button to add objects to the current Editable Poly object. You can add primitives, splines, patch objects, and other mesh objects. Any object attached to a mesh object is automatically converted into an editable poly and inherits the object color of the object to which it is attached. Any objects added to a poly object can be selected individually using the Element subobject mode.

Caution

If you attach an object that is smoothed using NURMS, the NURMS are lost when the object is attached. ∎

To use this feature, select the main object and click the Attach button. Move the mouse over the object to be attached; the cursor changes over acceptable objects. Click the object to select it. Click the Attach button again or right-click in the viewport to exit Attach mode.

Note

If the object that you click to attach already has a material applied that is different from the current Editable Poly object, then a dialog box appears giving you options to Match Material IDs to Material, Match Material to Material IDs, or Do Not Modify Material IDs or Material. Materials and Material IDs are discussed in more detail in Chapter 15, "Using the Slate Material Editor." ∎

Clicking the Attach List button opens the Attach List dialog box (which looks just like the Select Objects [H] dialog box) where you can select from a list of all the objects to attach. The list contains only objects that you can attach.

Note

When you enter a subobject mode, the Attach List button changes to a Detach button for poly objects. ∎

Attaching objects is different from grouping objects because all attached objects act as a single object with the same object color, name, and transforms. You can access individual attached objects using the Element subobject mode.

Use the Detach button to separate the selected subobjects from the rest of the object. To use this button, select the subobject and click the Detach button. The Detach dialog box opens, enabling you to name the new detached subobject. You also have the options to Detach to Element or to Detach as Clone. All subobject modes except Edge have a Detach option. This button appears in place of the Attach List button in all subobject modes.

Slicing and cutting options

The Slice Plane button lets you split the poly object along a plane. When you click the Slice Plane button, a yellow slice plane gizmo appears on the selected object. You can move, rotate, and scale this gizmo using the transform buttons. After you properly position the plane and set all options, click the Slice button to finish slicing the mesh. All intersected faces split in two, and new vertices and edges are added to the mesh where the Slice Plane intersects the original mesh.

The Slice Plane mode stays active until you deselect the Slice Plane button or until you right-click in the viewport; this feature enables you to make several slices in one session. The Slice Plane button is enabled for all subobject modes. For the Editable Poly object, a Reset Plane button is located next to the Slice Plane button. Use this button to reset the slice plane to its original location. You use the Split option to double the number of vertices and edges along the Slice Plane, so each side can be separated from the other. When used in Element mode, the Split option breaks the sliced object into two separate elements.

The QuickSlice button lets you click anywhere on an Editable Poly object where you want a slicing line to be located. You can then move the mouse, and the QuickSlice line rotates about the point you clicked on. When you click the mouse again, a new vertex is added at every place where the QuickSlice line intersects an object edge. This is a very convenient tool for slicing objects because the slice line follows the surface of the object, so you can see exactly where the slice will take place.

For the QuickSlice and Cut tools, you can enable the Full Interactivity option (located near the bottom of the Edit Geometry rollout). With this option enabled, the slice lines are shown as you move the mouse about the surface. With Full Interactivity disabled, the resulting lines are shown only when the mouse is clicked.

For Editable Poly objects, the Cut button is interactive. If you click a polygon corner, the cut edge snaps to the corner, and a new edge extends from the corner to a nearby corner. As you move the mouse around, the edge moves until you click where the edge should end. If you click in the middle of an edge or face, then new edges appear to the nearest corner.

Tutorial: Combining, cutting, and separating a car model

When dealing with a model that includes interior parts, you may want to slice the object and separate a portion to reveal the interior. Although this can be accomplished using a camera clipping plane, which is explained in Chapter 19, "Configuring and Aiming Cameras," a more permanent solution uses the QuickSlice and Detach operations.

To combine, slice, and detach a car model, follow these steps:

1. Open the Sliced car.max file from the Chap 13 directory on the CD.
2. Before you can slice the car, you'll need to combine the entire car into a single Editable Poly object. Select one of the body parts, right-click on it, and select the Convert To ⇨ Editable Poly in the pop-up quadmenu.

3. Open the Modify panel, and click on the dialog box icon next to the Attach button in the Edit Geometry rollout.

4. In the Attach List dialog box that opens, click the Select All button (or use the Ctrl+A shortcut) and select the Attach button. In the Attach Options dialog box that appears, select the Match Material IDs to Material option, you can leave the Condense Materials and IDs option checked, and then click OK.

    All objects are now combined into a single Editable Poly object.

5. Click the QuickSlice button, which is also in the Edit Geometry rollout, and click in the Top viewport at the point where you want to slice the car. Then drag to align the slicing plane, and click again to make the slice. Click on the QuickSlice button again to exit QuickSlice mode.

6. Select the Polygon subobject mode, and drag over all the polygons below the slice line in the Top viewport. Then click the Detach button in the Edit Geometry rollout. In the Detach dialog box, enter the name **Car Front** and click OK.

7. Disable Polygon subobject mode, and use the Select and Move tool to separate the car front from the rest of the car.

Figure 13.8 shows the separated car front.

FIGURE 13.8

Using the Attach, QuickSlice, and Detach features, you can slice and separate mode parts.

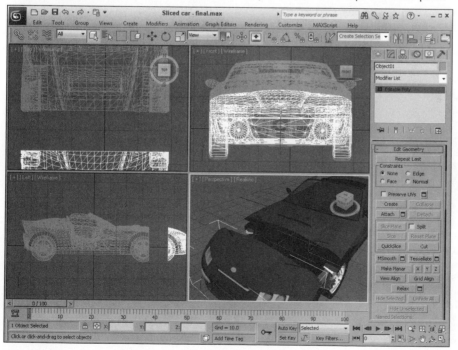

MSmooth

Both the MSmooth and Tessellate buttons include new caddy interfaces, as shown in Figure 13.9. The MSmooth setting for Smoothness rounds all the sharp edges of an object. Tessellation can be done using Edges or Faces, and the Tension setting controls how tight the adjacent faces are.

FIGURE 13.9

The Caddy interfaces for the MSmooth and Tessellate buttons let you interactively set the Smoothness and Tension values.

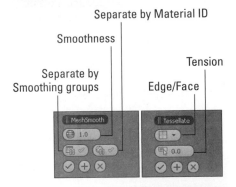

The MSmooth button can be used to smooth the selected subobjects in the same way as the MeshSmooth modifier. This button can be used several times. The Smoothness value determines which vertices are used to smooth the object. The higher the value, the more vertices are included and the smoother the result. You can also select that the smoothing is separated by Smoothing Groups or by Materials.

Figure 13.10 shows a simple diamond-shaped hedra that has been MeshSmoothed using the MSmooth button and then tessellated three consecutive times.

FIGURE 13.10

Using MSmooth reduces the sharp edges, and tessellating adds more editable faces.

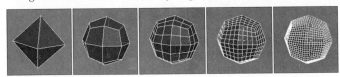

Tessellate

Tessellation is used to increase the density of the faces or edges. When modeling, you may want more details in a select area. This is where the tessellation command comes in. Tessellation can be applied to individual selected subobjects or to the entire object.

You can use the Tessellate button to increase the resolution of a mesh by splitting a face or polygon into several faces or polygons. You have two options to do this: Edge and Face.

The Edge method splits each edge at its midpoint. For example, a triangular face would be split into three smaller triangles. The Tension spinner to the right of the Tessellate button specifies a value that is used to make the tessellated face concave or convex.

The Face option creates a vertex in the center of the face and also creates three new edges, which extend from the center vertex to each original vertex. For a square polygon, this option would create six new triangular faces. (Remember, a square polygon is actually composed of two triangular faces.)

Figure 13.11 shows the faces of a cube that has been tessellated once using the Edge option and then again using the Face-Center option.

FIGURE 13.11

A cube tessellated twice, using each option once

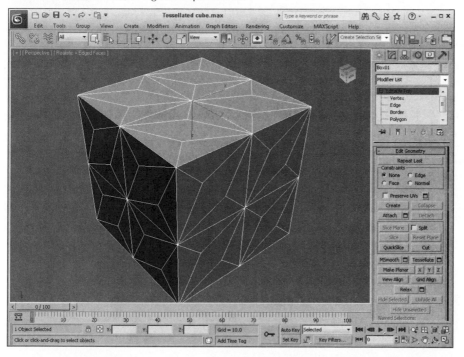

Make Planar

A single vertex or two vertices don't define a plane, but three or more vertices do. If three or more vertices are selected, you can use the Make Planar button to make these vertices coplanar (which means that all vertices are on the same plane). Doing so positions the selected vertices so that they lie in the same plane. This is helpful if you want to build a new polygon face. Polygonal faces need to be coplanar. This button works in all subobject modes. The X, Y, and Z buttons let you collapse the current object or subobject selection to a single plane lying on the specified axis.

View and Grid Align

The View and Grid Align buttons move and orient all selected vertices to the current active viewport or to the current construction grid. These buttons can also be used in all subobject modes. This causes all the selected face normals to point directly at the grid or view.

Relax

The Relax button works just like the Relax modifier by moving vertices so they are as far as possible from their adjacent vertices according to the Amount value listed in the Settings dialog box. The Settings dialog box also includes an Iterations value, which determines the number of times the operation is performed. You can also select to hold all Boundary and Outer points from being moved.

Hide, Copy, and Paste

The Hide button hides the selected subobjects. You can make hidden objects visible again with the Unhide All button.

After selecting several subobjects, you can create a named selection set by typing a name in the Name Selection Sets drop-down list in the main toolbar. You can then copy and paste these selection sets onto other shapes.

At the bottom of the Selection rollout is the Selection Information, which is a text line that automatically displays the number and subobject type of selected items.

Editing Vertex subobjects

When working with the Editable Poly objects, after you select a Vertex subobject mode (keyboard shortcut, 1) and select vertices, you can transform them using the transform buttons on the main toolbar. All vertex-specific commands are found within the Edit Vertices rollout, shown in Figure 13.12.

FIGURE 13.12

When the Vertex subobject mode is selected, these vertex commands become available.

Remove

The Remove button lets you delete the selected vertices. The Remove button automatically adjusts the surrounding subobjects to maintain the mesh integrity.

Note

You can also delete Editable Poly subobjects using the Delete key. ■

Figure 13.13 shows a sphere object with several vertex subobjects selected. The middle image is an Editable Mesh that used the Delete feature, and the right image is an Editable Poly that used the Remove feature.

The Remove button also is available in Edge subobject mode. If you hold down the Ctrl key when clicking the Remove button when an edge is selected, vertices at either end of the deleted edge are also removed.

FIGURE 13.13

Deleting vertices also deletes the adjoining faces and edges, but Remove maintains the mesh.

Break

You use the Break button to create a separate vertex for adjoining faces that are connected by a single vertex.

In a normal mesh, faces are all connected by vertices: Moving one vertex changes the position of all adjoining faces. The Break button enables you to move the vertex associated with each face independent of the others. The button is available only in Vertex subobject mode.

Figure 13.14 shows a hedra object. The Break button was used to separate the center vertex into separate vertices for each face. The face vertices can be manipulated independently, as the figure shows.

FIGURE 13.14

You can use the Break button to give each face its own vertex.

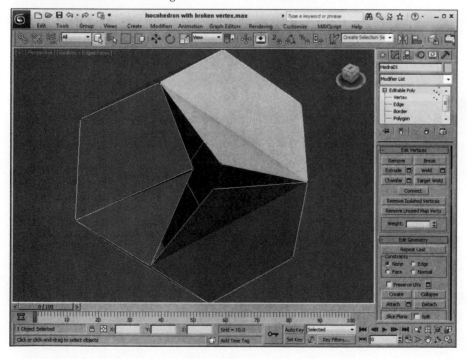

Extrude

The Extrude button copies and moves the selected subobject perpendicular a given distance and connects the new copy with the original one. For example, four edges forming a square extruded would form a box with no lid. To use this feature, select an edge or edges, click the Extrude button, and then drag in a viewport. The edges interactively show the extrude depth. Release the button when you've reached the desired distance.

Alternatively, you can set an extrude depth in the Extrusion spinner. The Group option extrudes all selected edges in the direction of the average of all the normals for the group (the normal runs perpendicular to the face) and the Normal Local option moves each individual edge along its local normal. For polygons, you can extrude By Polygons, which extrudes each individual polygon along its normal as a separate extrusion. To exit Extrude mode, click the Extrude button again or right-click in the viewport.

The Extrude button is enabled for Face, Polygon, and Element subobject modes for the Editable Poly object. Figure 13.15 shows a GeoSphere object with all edges selected and extruded. The Group Normal option averages all the normals and extrudes the edges in the averaged direction. The Local Normal option extrudes each edge along its own normal.

The Extrude settings dialog box includes options for setting the Extrusion Height and the Extrusion Base Width.

FIGURE 13.15

Subobjects can be extruded along an averaged normal or locally.

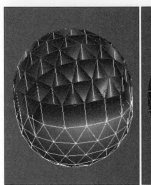
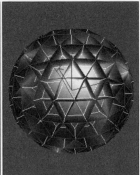

Weld and Chamfer

Vertices and edges that are close or on top of one another can be combined together into one using the Weld command. The Weld and Chamfer buttons include settings dialog boxes that let you interactively see the results of different settings. The Weld settings dialog box includes a weld Threshold value and displays the number of vertices before and after the welding process, which is very useful to check whether a weld was successful.

Tip

If you run into trouble with the Weld button and its Threshold value, try using the Collapse button. ■

The Target Weld button lets you click on a single vertex and move the cursor over an adjacent vertex. A rubber band line stretches from the first selected vertex to the target weld vertex and the cursor changes to indicate that the vertex under the cursor may be selected. Clicking on the target vertex welds the two vertices together.

Note

When two vertices are welded, the new vertex is positioned at a location that is halfway between both vertices, but when Target Weld is used, the first vertex is moved to the location of the second. ■

The Chamfer button—which is enabled in Vertex, Edge, and Border subobject modes—lets you cut the edge off a corner and replace it with a face. Using the settings dialog box, you can interactively specify a Chamfer Amount and the number of segments. The settings dialog box also includes an Open option, which cuts a hole in the polygon face instead of replacing it with a new polygon. Figure 13.16 shows two plane objects that have been chamfered with the Open option enabled. The left plane had all its interior vertices selected, and the right plane had a selection of interior edges selected.

FIGURE 13.16

Enabling the Open option in the Chamfer settings dialog box removes a polygon instead of replacing it.

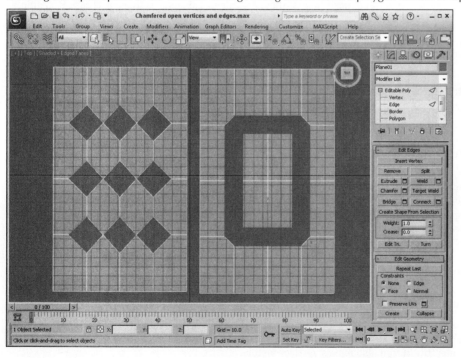

Connect

The Connect button can be used to add new edges to subobjects. In Vertex subobject mode, the button connects vertices on the opposite side of a face. In Edge and Border subobject mode, the button makes a settings dialog box available, which includes the Connect Edge Segments setting. This value is the number of edge segments to add between the selected edges or borders. It also includes Pinch and Slide values. The Pinch value moves the segments closer or farther away from each other; the Slide value moves the segments along the original edge.

Remove Isolated and Unused Map Vertices

The Remove Isolated Vertices button deletes all isolated vertices. Vertices become isolated by some operations and add unneeded data to your file. You can search and delete them quickly with this button. Good examples of isolated vertices are those created using the Create button but never attached to an edge.

The Remove Unused Map Vertices button removes any leftover mapping vertices from the object.

Weight and Crease

The Weight settings control the amount of pull that a vertex has when NURMS subdivision or a MeshSmooth modifier is used. The higher the Weight value, the more resistant a vertex is to smoothing. For edge and border subobjects, the Weight value is followed by a Crease value that determines how visible the edge is when the mesh is smoothed. A value of 1.0 ensures that the crease is visible.

Note

The Crease value is available only in Edge and Border subobject modes. ∎

Editing Edge subobjects

Edges are the lines that run between two vertices. Edges can be *closed*, which means that each side of the edge is connected to a face, or *open*, which means that only one face connects to the edge. When a hole exists in a mesh, all edges that are adjacent to the hole are open edges. Mesh edges, such as those in the interior of a shape that has been converted to a mesh, can also be *invisible*. These invisible edges appear as dotted lines that run across the face of the polygon.

You can select multiple edges by holding down either the Ctrl key while clicking the edges or the Alt key to remove selected edges from the selection set. You can also copy edges using the Shift key while transforming the edge. The cloned edge maintains connections to its vertices by creating new edges.

Many of the Edge subobject options work in the same way as the Vertex subobject options. Figure 13.17 shows the Edit Edges rollout.

Split and Insert Vertex

The Split button adds a new vertex at the middle of the edge and splits the edge into two equal sections. This button is handy when you need to increase the resolution of a section quickly.

The Insert Vertex button lets you add a new vertex anywhere along an edge. The cursor changes to crosshairs when it is over an edge. Click to create a vertex. When in Edge, Border, Polygon, or Element subobject mode, this button also makes vertices visible.

Bridge Edges

The Bridge button for edges allows you to create a new set of polygons that connect the selected edges. If two edges are selected when the Bridge button is pressed, then they are automatically connected with a new polygon. If no edges are selected, then you can click the edges to bridge after clicking the Bridge button. The selected edges on either side of the bridge can be different in number.

FIGURE 13.17

All the Edge specific commands are available when the Edge subobject mode is enabled.

You also can access the settings dialog box using a Caddy interface for the Bridge feature. This caddy offers the options to Use Specific Edges or to Use Edge Selection. The Use Specific Edges option has two buttons for each edge. If you click one of these buttons, you can select an edge in the viewport. The Use Edge Selection option lets you drag a marquee in the viewport to select the edges. The Bridge Edges dialog box also includes options for setting the number of Segments, the Smooth value, and a Bridge Adjacent value, which increases the triangulation for angles above the given threshold. There is also a Reverse Triangulation option.

Figure 13.18 shows a simple example of some edges that have been bridged. The letters before bridging are on the top and after bridging on the bottom.

FIGURE 13.18

Selecting two opposite edges and clicking the Bridge button in Edge subobject mode creates new connecting polygons.

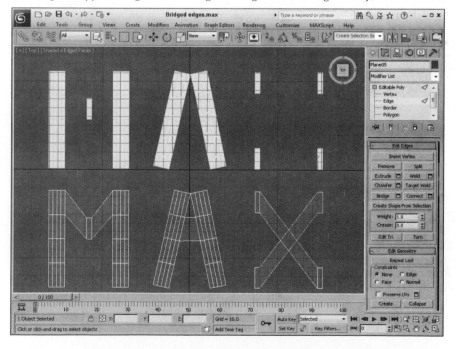

Create Shape from Selection

The Create Shape from Selection button creates a new spline shape from selected edges. The Create Shape dialog box appears, shown in Figure 13.19, enabling you to give the new shape a name. You can also select options for Smooth or Linear shape types.

FIGURE 13.19

The Create Shape dialog box lets you name shapes created from selected edge subobjects.

Edit Triangulation

For the Editable Poly object, the Edge, Border, Polygon, and Element subobjects include the Edit Triangulation button. The Edit Triangulation button lets you change the internal edges of the polygon by dragging from one vertex to another. When this button is clicked, all hidden edges appear. To edit the hidden edges, just click a vertex and then click again where you want the hidden edge to go. If you're dealing with multiple four-sided polygons, then the Turn button is quicker.

Turn

The Turn button rotates the hidden edges that break up the polygon into triangles (all polygonal faces include these hidden edges). For example, if a quadrilateral (four-sided) face has a hidden edge that runs between vertices 1 and 3, then the Turn button changes this hidden edge to run between vertices 2 and 4. This affects how the surface is smoothed when the polygon is not coplanar.

This button is available for all subobject modes except Vertex. When enabled, all subobjects that you click on are turned until the button is disabled again. Figure 13.20 shows the top face of a Box object with a hidden edge across it diagonally. The Turn button was used to turn this hidden edge.

Tip

Surfaces can deform only along places where there are edges, so as you create your models be aware of where you place edges and how the edges flow into one another. When building characters, it is important to have the edges follow the muscle flow to deform properly. ■

FIGURE 13.20

The Turn feature is used to change the direction of edges.

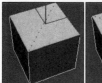

Editing Border subobjects

Editable Poly objects do not need the Face subobject that is found in the Editable Mesh objects because they support polygon faces. Instead, they have a Border subobject. Border subobjects are polygons with no faces that are actually holes within the geometry. The Border rollout is shown in Figure 13.21.

FIGURE 13.21

Many of the Border subobject commands are the same as those for Edges.

Cap

The Cap button causes the existing border selection to be filled in with a single coplanar polygon. After using this feature, the Border subobject is no longer identified as a Border subobject.

Bridge

The Bridge feature joins two selected Border subobjects with a tube of polygons that connect the two borders. The two selected borders must be part of the same object and need not have an equal number of segments.

The Bridge dialog box, shown in Figure 13.22, lets you specify twist values for each edge, the number of segments, and the Taper, Bias, and Smooth values.

FIGURE 13.22

The Bridge dialog box lets you specify options such as the number of segments, the Taper, and whether the bridge twists.

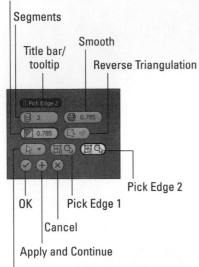

Bridge Adjacent

Segments

Title bar/
tooltip

Smooth

Reverse Triangulation

Pick Edge 2

OK

Pick Edge 1

Cancel

Apply and Continue

Use Specific Edges/Use Selected Edges

Tutorial: Bridging a forearm

The Bridge tool is great for working with two border selections, allowing you to create a smooth set of polygons that flow between them. For this example, you'll create a forearm by bridging a hi–res hand model with a simple cylinder. The polygons of the hand and the cylinder that are to be joined have already been removed.

To create a forearm object by bridging a cylinder with a hand model, follow these steps:

1. Open the Forearm bridge.max file from the Chap 13 directory on the CD.
2. With the body parts selected, open the Modify panel, and select the Border subobject mode. Then press and hold the Ctrl key, and click on the borders for the hand and cylinder objects.
3. With both facing Border subobjects selected, click the dialog box icon next to the Bridge button in the Edit Borders rollout.
4. In the Bridge caddy, select the Use Border Selection option and set the Segments value to **6**. Then click OK.

Figure 13.23 shows the resulting forearm object.

FIGURE 13.23

The Bridge feature can be used to quickly connect body parts such as this forearm.

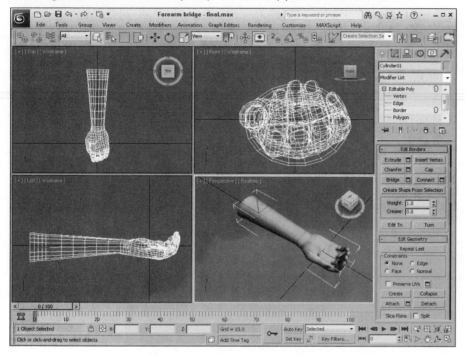

Editing Polygon and Element subobjects

Like the other subobject modes, Editable Polys can be edited at the polygon and element subobject level. The buttons for these modes are found in the Edit Polygons and Edit Elements rollouts. Figure 13.24 shows the Polygon rollout.

FIGURE 13.24

The Polygon subobjects commands are found in the Polygons rollout.

Outline and Inset

The Outline button offsets the selected polygon a specified amount. This increases the size of the selected polygon or element. The Inset button creates another polygon set within the selected polygon and connects their edges. For both these buttons, a Settings dialog box is available that includes the Outline or Inset Amount values.

Bevel

The Bevel button extrudes the Polygon subobject selection and then lets you bevel the edges. To use this feature, select a polygon, click the Bevel button, drag up or down in a viewport to the Extrusion depth, and release the button. Drag again to specify the Bevel amount. The Bevel amount determines the relative size of the extruded face.

Figure 13.25 displays a poly dodecahedron. Each face has been locally extruded with a value of 20 and then locally beveled with a value of –10.

FIGURE 13.25

The top faces of this dodecahedron have been individually extruded and beveled.

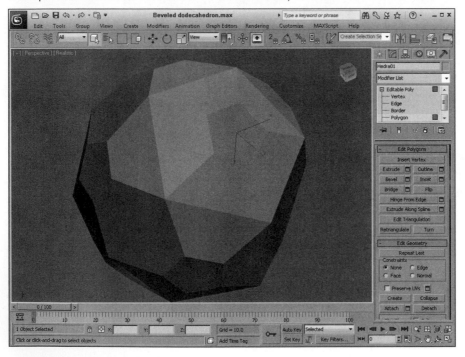

Flip

The Flip button flips the normal vectors for the selected subobjects. The Flip button is available only in Polygon and Element subobject modes.

Retriangulate

The Retriangulate button automatically computes all the internal edges for you for the selected subobjects.

Hinge From Edge

The Hinge From Edge button rotates a selected polygon as if one of its edges were a hinge. The angle of the hinge depends on the distance that you drag with the mouse, or you can use the available settings dialog box. In the settings dialog box, shown in Figure 13.26, you can specify an Angle value and the number of segments to use for the hinged section.

The Hinge Polygons From Edge dialog box lets you select a hinge.

Pick Hinge

Segment

Angle

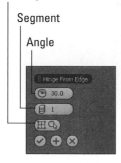

By default, one of the polygon's edges will be used as the hinge about which the section rotates, but in the settings dialog box, you can click the Pick Hinge button and select an edge (which doesn't need to be attached to the polygon). Figure 13.27 shows a sphere primitive with four polygon faces that have been hinged around an edge at the sphere's center.

Extrude Along Spline

The Extrude Along Spline button can be used to extrude a selected polygon along the spline path. The settings dialog box, shown in Figure 13.28, includes a Pick Spline button that you can use to select the spline to use. You can also specify the number of segments, the Taper Amount and Curve, and a Twist value. You also have an option to Align the extrusion to the face normal or to rotate about the normal.

FIGURE 13.27

Several polygon faces in the sphere have been extruded along a hinge.

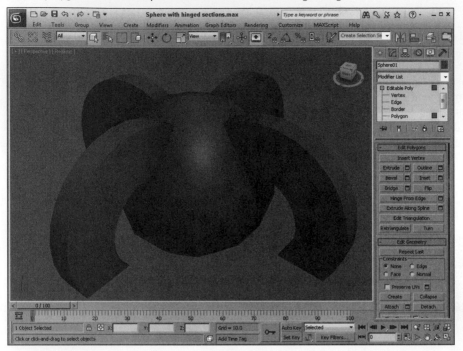

FIGURE 13.28

The Extrude Polygons Along Spline settings dialog box

Taper Curve

Segments   Taper amount

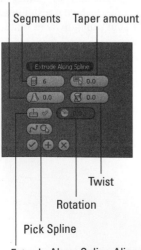

Twist

Rotation

Pick Spline

Extrude Along Spline Align

Tutorial: Building an octopus

The one thing about an octopus that makes it unique is the fact that it has eight tentacles. Creating these tentacles can be easily accomplished with the Extrude Along Spline feature.

To create an octopus using the Extrude Along Spline feature, follow these steps:

1. Open the Octopus.max file from the Chap 13 directory on the CD.

   This file includes the base of an octopus created from a squashed sphere primitive that has been converted to an Editable Poly. Eight splines surround the object.

2. Select the octopus object to automatically open the Modify panel. In the Selection rollout, click the Polygon subobject button (keyboard shortcut, 4) and enable the Ignore Backfacing option in the Selection rollout.

3. Right-click the Shading viewport label, and select the Edged Faces option from the pop-up menu (or press the F4 key).

   This makes the polygons easier to see.

4. Click a single face object at the base of the sphere object, and click the Extrude Along Spline settings dialog box button to open the Extrude Polygons Along Spline dialog box.

5. Click the Pick Spline button, and select the spline to the side of the face. Set the Segments to **6** and the Taper Amount to **–1.0**, and click OK. Make sure that the Align to Face Normal option isn't selected.

6. Repeat Steps 4 and 5 for each spline surrounding the octopus.

7. In the Subdivisions Surface rollout, enable the Use NURMS Subdivision option and set the Display Iterations value to **2** to smooth the entire octopus.

Figure 13.29 shows the resulting octopus.

Cross-Reference

You can find more information on vertex colors in Chapter 32, "Painting in the Viewport Canvas and Rendering Surface Maps." ∎

Polygon and Element Surface properties

For Polygon and Element subobjects, the rollouts shown in Figure 13.30 include Material IDs and Smoothing Groups options. The Material IDs option settings are used by the Multi/Sub-Object material type to apply different materials to faces or polygons within an object. By selecting a polygon subobject, you can use these option settings to apply a unique material to the selected polygon. The Select ID button selects all subobjects that have the designated Material ID, or you can select subobjects using a material name in the drop-down list under the Select ID button.

Cross-Reference

You can find more information on the Multi/Sub-Object material type in Chapter 16, "Creating and Applying Standard Materials." ∎

FIGURE 13.29

The tentacles of this octopus were created easily with the Extrude Along Spline feature.

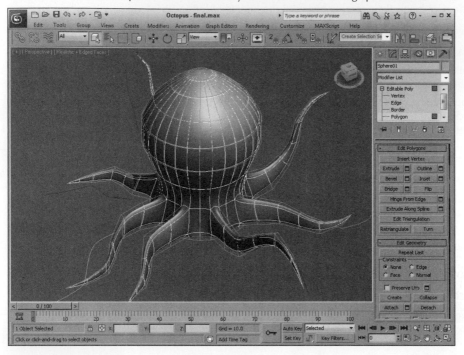

FIGURE 13.30

The Polygon Properties rollout includes settings for Material IDs, Smoothing Groups, and Vertex Colors.

You use the Smoothing Groups option to assign a subobject to a unique smoothing group. To do this, select a subobject and click a Smoothing Groups number. The Select By SG button, like the Select By ID button, opens a dialog box where you can enter a Smoothing Groups number, and all subobjects with that number are selected. The Clear All button clears all Smoothing Groups number assignments, and the Auto Smooth button automatically assigns Smoothing Groups numbers based on the angle between faces as set by the value to the right of the Auto Smooth button.

The Polygon Properties rollout also includes options for setting vertex Color, Illumination, and Alpha values.

Subdivision Surface

Editable Poly objects include an extra rollout called Subdivision Surface that automatically smoothes the object when enabled. The Subdivision Surface rollout, shown in Figure 13.31, applies a smoothing algorithm known as NURMS, which stands for Non-Uniform Rational MeshSmooth. It produces similar results to the MSmooth button but offers control over how aggressively the smoothing is applied; the settings can be different for the viewports and the renderer.

FIGURE 13.31

The Subdivision Surface rollout includes controls for NURMS subdivision.

Cage Selection color

Cage color

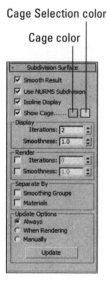

To enable NURMS subdivision, you need to enable the Use NURMS Subdivision option. The Smooth Result option places all polygons into the same smoothing group and applies the MeshSmooth to the entire object. Applying NURMS with a high Iterations value results in a very dense mesh, but the Isoline Display option displays a simplified number of edges, making the object easier to work with. The process of smoothing adds many edges to the object, and the Isoline Display option displays only the isolines. The Show Cage option makes the surrounding cage visible or invisible. The two color swatches to the right of the Show Cage option let you set the color of the cage and the selection.

The Iterations value determines how aggressive the smoothing is. The higher the Iterations value, the more time it takes to compute and the more complex the resulting object. The Smoothness value determines how sharp a corner must be before adding extra faces to smooth it. A value of 0 does not smooth any corners, and a maximum value of 1.0 smoothes all polygons.

Caution

Each smoothing iteration quadruples the number of faces. If you raise the number of Iterations too high, the system can become unstable quickly. ■

The two check boxes in the Render section can be used to set the values differently for the Display and Render sections. If disabled, then both the viewports and the renderer use the same settings. The smoothing algorithm can be set to ignore smoothing across Smoothing Groups and Materials.

If the Show Cage option is enabled (at the bottom of the Edit Geometry rollout), an orange cage surrounds the NURMS object and shows the position of the polygon faces that exist if NURMS is disabled. This cage makes selecting the polygon faces easier.

Tutorial: Modeling a tooth

If you've ever had a root canal, then you know how much pain dental work can cause. Luckily, modeling a tooth isn't painful at all, as you'll see in this example.

To model a tooth using NURMS, follow these steps:

1. Select Create ⇨ Standard Primitives ⇨ Box, and drag in the Top viewport to create a Box object. Set its dimensions to **140 × 180 × 110** with Segments of **1 × 1 × 1**. Then right-click, and select Convert To ⇨ Editable Poly from the pop-up quadmenu.

2. Click the Polygon icon in the Selection rollout to enable Polygon subobject mode. Then select the Top viewport, and press B to change it to the Bottom viewport. Then click the box's bottom polygon in the Bottom viewport.

3. Click the Select and Scale button (R), and scale the bottom polygon 10 percent.

4. Drag over the entire object to select all polygons, and click the Tessellate button in the Edit Geometry rollout once to divide the polygon into more polygons. Then select Edit ⇨ Region ⇨ Window (or click the Window/Crossing button in the main toolbar) to enable the Window selection method, and drag over the bottom of the Box object in the Left viewport to select just the bottom polygons. Click the Tessellate button again.

5. Select the Vertex subobject mode in the Selection rollout, press and hold the Ctrl key, and select the vertices at the center of each quadrant. Then move these vertices downward in the Left viewport a distance about equal to the height of the Box.

6. Select the Bottom viewport again, and press T to change it back to the Top viewport. Select the single vertex in the center of the polygon with the Ignore Backfacing option enabled in the Selection rollout, and drag it slightly downward in the Left viewport.

7. Disable the Ignore Backfacing option in the Selection rollout, and select the entire second row of vertices in the Left viewport. With the Select and Scale tool, scale these vertices toward the center in the polygon in the Top viewport.

8. In the Subdivision Surface rollout, enable the Use NURMS Subdivision option and set the Iterations value to **2**.

Figure 13.32 shows the completed tooth.

FIGURE 13.32

The organic look for this tooth is accomplished with NURMS.

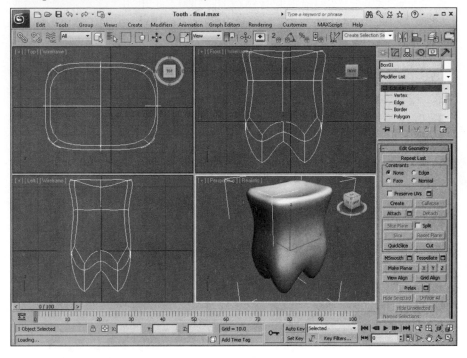

Summary

Meshes are probably the most common 3D modeling types. You can create them by converting objects to Editable Meshes or Editable Poly objects or by collapsing the Stack. Editable Poly objects in Max have a host of features for editing meshes, as you learned in this chapter. More specifically, this chapter covered the following topics:

- Creating Editable Poly objects by converting other objects or applying the Edit Poly modifier
- The features for editing Editable Poly objects
- How to select and use the various mesh subobject modes
- Editing mesh objects using the various features found in the Edit Geometry rollout
- Changing surface properties using features like NURMS

This chapter provided an introduction to mesh, polygon, and path objects, but the next chapter steps it up with coverage of the Graphite Modeling tools, which work with Editable Poly objects.

Using the Graphite Modeling Tools and Painting with Objects

The previous chapter covered everything you need to know about modeling with polygons, but the problem with the polygon workflow is the ping-pong effect of moving back and forth between the current model and the Command Panel. Although you can float the Command Panel or even use the quad menus to access most of these commands, the Max developers have presented an entirely new workflow based on the new Ribbon interface.

The Ribbon sits conveniently above the viewports, but you can pull off and float any of the individual panels as needed. The Ribbon panels are dynamic, so only those tools that work with the current selection are presented. This places the tools you need right in front of you when you need them.

The Ribbon is populated with all the features for working with Editable Poly objects that are found in the Command Panel. It also includes a large number of brand-new tools for selecting and working with polygon objects. These tools collectively are called the Graphite Modeling tools.

The Ribbon also is home to several additional panels of tools that allow you to paint deformations into your models, make unique selections, and select and paint with objects using brushes. The best part of these new tools is that they all eliminate the ping-pong effect. Our necks thank you, Autodesk.

Working with the Graphite Modeling Tools

 The Ribbon interface, shown in Figure 14.1, can be turned on and off using a button on the main toolbar or using the Customize ➪ Show UI ➪ Show Ribbon menu. When enabled, the button turns yellow and the Ribbon appears in the same state it was in the last time it was opened. By double-clicking the Ribbon title bar, you can switch among displaying just the top tabs; just the tabs and panel titles; just the tabs, panel titles, and panel buttons; or the entire panel. This is great if you want to keep the Ribbon around but hide most of the buttons.

Cross-Reference

You can learn more details on working with the Ribbon interface in Chapter 1, "Exploring the Max Interface." ∎

When expanded, the Graphic Modeling Tools tab shows several panels of tools. Each of these panels can be separated from the Ribbon and floated independently. You also can rearrange the panels by dragging them to a new position. If the icons displayed within a panel don't fit, a small downward-pointing arrow offers access to the additional tools.

All the panels and tools that make up the Ribbon are adaptable and change depending on the subobject mode you select. Only the relevant tools are visible, which saves space and makes it easier to locate the tool you want to use.

On the CD-ROM

If you don't like the layout of the tools in the Ribbon, you can customize your own panels of tools, which is covered in Bonus Chapter 22, "Customizing the Max Interface." ∎

FIGURE 14.1

The Ribbon holds several panels of modeling tools.

If you right-click the Ribbon's title bar, you can access a pop-up menu of options to hide and show different tabs and panels. There is also a Ribbon Configuration that includes options for customizing the Ribbon, loading and saving custom configurations, and switching to a vertically oriented Ribbon.

Using the Polygon Modeling panel

The Graphite Modeling tools are exclusive to Editable Poly objects or objects with the Edit Poly modifier applied. If you select any other type of object with the Ribbon open, all the buttons are disabled. However, two options are available in the Polygon Modeling panel of the Graphite Modeling Tools tab. These options are to Convert to Poly and Apply Edit Poly Mod. These commands convert the selected object to an Editable Poly object or apply an Edit Poly modifier and automatically open the Modify panel.

After an Editable Poly object or an object with the Edit Poly modifier applied is selected, the subobject modes can be selected from the top of the Graphite Modeling Tools panel. The Polygon Modeling panel, shown in Figure 14.2, includes options that work with the Modifier Stack including collapsing the stack, pinning the stack, and moving up and down between modifiers. The Show End Result button lets you see the object with all stack modifiers applied and options that apply to all subobject modes. A button in this panel lets you toggle the Command Panel off.

FIGURE 14.2

The Ribbon's Polygon Modeling panel includes options for determining which subobjects are selected.

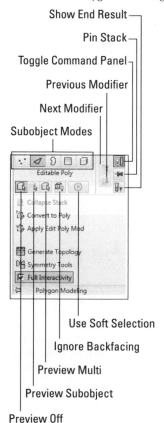

- Show End Result
- Pin Stack
- Toggle Command Panel
- Previous Modifier
- Next Modifier
- Subobject Modes
- Use Soft Selection
- Ignore Backfacing
- Preview Multi
- Preview Subobject
- Preview Off

The Polygon Modeling panel also includes buttons for turning on and off subobject selection preview and for ignoring backfacing. The Use Soft Selection button enables you to select a feathered group of subobjects. When enabled, the Soft panel appears, as shown in Figure 14.3.

Using the Soft panel, you can enable Edit mode, which lets you interactively change the Falloff, Pinch, and Bubble settings. When the Edit button is enabled, the cursor looks like two circles. This is Falloff mode, and dragging the mouse changes the amount of falloff for the soft selection. If you click in the viewport, the cursor changes to a peak indicating Pinch edit mode. Click again to access Bubble edit mode, which looks like an upside-down letter U. Continue to click to cycle through these edit modes. These values also can be set in the Soft panel using the various spinner controls.

Cross-Reference

Using the Soft Selection features is covered in Chapter 10, "Accessing Subobjects and Using Modeling Helpers." ∎

The Paint button in the Soft panel opens the PaintSS panel, also shown in Figure 14.3, with buttons for blurring, reverting, and opening the Painter Options dialog box, which holds the brush settings. You also can set the Value, Size, and Strength of the soft selection brush.

The Use Edge Distance option lets you select adjacent edges to the current selection rather than using a falloff amount.

FIGURE 14.3

The Soft and PaintSS panels let you control how soft selections are made.

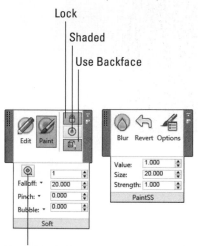

Lock

Shaded

Use Backface

Use Edge Distance

Generate Topology

Located at the bottom of the Ribbon's Polygon Modeling panel is an option to Generate Topology. This option opens the Topology pop-up panel, shown in Figure 14.4, showing several patterns. Selecting a pattern applies the selected pattern to the selected object or to the object's subobject selection if you hold down the Shift key.

The Topology pop-up panel lets you choose a pattern to apply to the object.

The Size, Iterations, and Smooth values let you configure the selected pattern. The ScrapVerts button removes any vertices with two edges going to it. The Plane button creates a simple plane object where the S value sets the resolution. Figure 14.5 shows four planes with different topologies applied.

Changing a plane's topology gives a unique set of faces to work with.

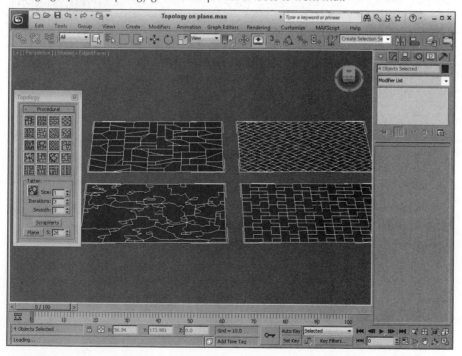

Using the Symmetry tools

The Polygon Modeling panel also holds a link for accessing the Symmetry tools. This command opens the Symmetry Tools dialog box, shown in Figure 14.6. Using this dialog box, you can select an object with the top button and automatically copy the changes on either side of any axis to the opposite side with the + to − and − to + buttons. You also can use the Flip Symmetry button to switch the moved subobjects to the opposite side of the model.

The Copy Selected button lets you copy the position of an entire object or of just the selected vertices and paste them onto another object with the same number of vertices.

FIGURE 14.6

The Symmetry Tools dialog box lets you mirror subobject movements across an axis.

Tutorial: Building a Skateboard wheel

Starting with a simple sphere, you can quickly create a symmetrical skateboard wheel using the Symmetry tools.

To create a skateboard wheel, follow these steps:

1. Use the Create ⇨ Standard Primitives ⇨ Sphere menu and drag in the Front viewport to create a sphere object.
2. Open the Graphite Modeling Tools by clicking its button in the main toolbar. Then select the Convert to Poly option from the Polygon Modeling panel in the Ribbon.
3. Select the Symmetry Tools option in the Polygon Modeling panel, click the top button in the Symmetry Tools dialog box, and pick the sphere object.
4. Select the Vertex subobject mode in the Polygon Modeling panel and drag over the top four rows of vertices in the Top viewport. Then drag with the Move tool downward in the Top viewport.
5. Back in the Symmetry Tools dialog box, enable the Z Axis and click the − to + button to symmetrically copy the moved vertices, as shown in Figure 14.7.

FIGURE 14.7

The skateboard wheel is symmetrical and ready to roll.

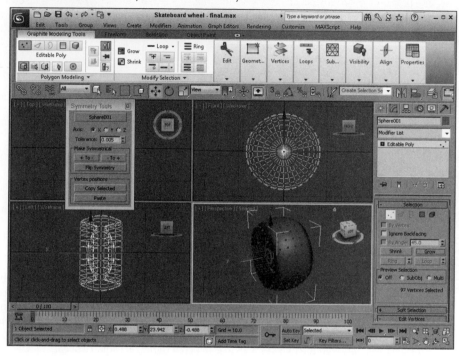

Using the Modify Selection panel

The Ribbon also holds tools for making Loop and Ring selections. These tools are found in the Modify Selection panel, shown in Figure 14.8. When a loop or ring is selected, there are also buttons for growing and shrinking the adjacent rows or columns. There are also tools called Loop Mode and Ring Mode that cause the entire edge loop or edge ring to be automatically selected when a single edge is picked when enabled. A text label appears in the viewport when LoopMode is enabled. Tools called Dot Loop and Dot Ring let an edge loop and edge ring with gaps be selected. The Ribbon's Loop and Ring tools also allow you to select rows and columns of vertices and faces.

Note

The Modify Selection panel is only visible when a subobject mode is enabled. ■

FIGURE 14.8

The Ribbon's Modify Selection panel includes tools for working with loops and rings.

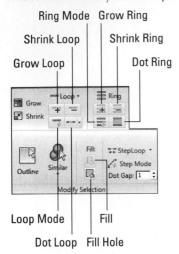

The Modify Selection panel also includes these tools: Outline, which selects all subobjects surrounding the current selection; Similar, which selects all subobjects that are similar to the current selection, including Edge Count, Edge Length, Face Count, Face Areas, and Normal Direction; and Fill, which selects all subobjects that are within the selected subobjects or within the current outlined selection. The Fill option lets you pick two vertices that are diagonally across from each other, and then all interior vertices between the two vertices are selected to make a square area.

The StepLoop option lets you select two subobjects within the same loop, and then all subobjects between the two are selected. When Step Mode is enabled, you can pick two subobjects in the same loop and all subobjects between the two are selected. This continues for all additional selections within the same loop until Step Mode is disabled again.

Tip

Using the Shift key, you can select loops of subobjects even more quickly. If you select a single vertex, edge, or polygon, and then hold down the Shift key and click on an adjacent subobject, the entire loop or ring of subobjects is automatically selected. ∎

Editing geometry

When no subobject modes are selected, several Ribbon panels are available, as shown in Figure 14.9. These panels contain many of the same features that are found in the Edit Geometry rollout in the Command Panel. Features contained here include, among many others, the ability to create new subobjects, attach subobjects to the mesh, weld vertices, chamfer vertices, slice, explode, and align. These panels are available regardless of the subobject mode that is selected, but some of these tools are disabled depending on the subobject mode that you select.

FIGURE 14.9

The Ribbon includes many general-purpose editing features that are always available.

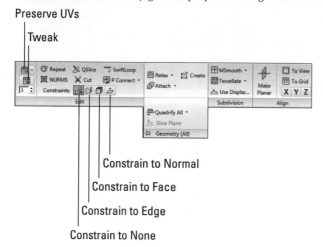

Preserve UVs

Tweak

Constrain to Normal

Constrain to Face

Constrain to Edge

Constrain to None

Many of the tools, such as Relax, MSmooth, Tessellate, PConnect, and Quadrify All, include options for accessing settings by clicking the small arrow to the right of the button. These options open up a caddy of settings that are located in the viewport right next to the selected subobject. These caddies allow you to change the settings and immediately see the results in the viewports. The OK (check mark icon) button applies the settings and closes the dialog box, and the Apply (plus sign icon) button applies the settings and leaves the dialog box open. Similar caddies are available for other subobject-specific buttons such as Extrude, Bevel, Outline, and Inset.

Preserve UVs

UV coordinates define how a texture map is applied to an object's surface. These UV coordinates are tied closely to the surface subobject positions, so moving a subobject after a texture is applied moves the texture also. This could cause discontinuities to the texture map. The Preserve UVs option lets you make subobject changes without altering the UV coordinates for an existing texture.

The caddy for the Preserve UVs option lets you select a Vertex Color and Texture Channel to preserve. Beneath the Preserve UVs button in the Edit panel is a Tweak button. This button lets you move the UVs for the given object. The value beneath this button is the map channel that you can adjust.

Repeat Last

The Repeat button in the Edit panel repeats the last subobject command. This button does not work on all features, but it's very convenient for certain actions.

Enabling constraints

The Constraints options limit the movement of subobjects to a specified subobject. The available constraints are None, Edge, Face, and Normal. For example, if you select and move a vertex with the Edge constraint enabled, the movement is constrained to the adjacent edges.

Slicing and cutting options

The QSlice button lets you click anywhere on an Editable Poly object where you want a slicing line to be located. You can then move the mouse, and the QuickSlice line rotates about the point you clicked. When you click the mouse again, a new vertex is added at every place where the QuickSlice line intersects an object edge. This is a very convenient tool for slicing objects because the slice line follows the surface of the object, so you can see exactly where the slice will take place.

For the QuickSlice and Cut tools, you can enable the Full Interactivity option (located near the bottom of the Polygon Modeling panel). With this option enabled, the slice lines are shown as you move the mouse about the surface. With Full Interactivity disabled, the resulting lines are shown only when the mouse is clicked.

Beneath the QSlice tool is the Cut tool. The Cut button is interactive. If you click a polygon corner, the cut edge snaps to the corner, and a new edge extends from the corner to a nearby corner. As you move the mouse around, the edge moves until you click where the edge should end. If you click in the middle of an edge or face, new edges appear to the nearest corner.

Another way to slice an object is with the SwiftLoop button. This button lets you click any open space between edges to add a loop between the adjacent edges. Once placed, you can drag to slide the loop to its actual location.

Another handy Ribbon tool for cutting holes is PConnect, which stands for Paint Connect. This tool lets you paint the location of a hole on the surface. As you paint, every edge that you cross is marked, and new edges are created between adjacent marks. By holding down the Shift key, you can make the connections happen in the middle of each edge. Holding down the Ctrl key lets you paint new edges between adjacent vertices. Clicking on a vertex with the Alt key held down removes the vertex, and the Ctrl+Alt keys together removes an edge. The Ctrl+Shift key is used to remove an entire edge loop, and the Shift+Alt keys are used to paint two parallel lines between edges.

Tip

Help videos are available for some tools, such as PConnect. These videos are located in the tooltips for the tool and appear when you hold the mouse over the tool. ■

NURMS

The Edit panel also includes a NURMS button. NURMS stands for Non-Uniform Rational MeshSmooth. It produces similar results to the MSmooth button, but offers control over how aggressively the smoothing is applied; the settings can be different for the viewports and the renderer. When NURMS is enabled, the Use NURMS panel, shown in Figure 14.10, appears.

To enable NURMS subdivision, you need to enable the Use NURMS Subdivision option. The Smooth Result option places all polygons into the same smoothing group and applies the MeshSmooth to the entire object. Applying NURMS with a high Iterations value results in a very dense mesh, but the Isoline Display option displays a simplified number of edges, making the object easier to work with. The process of smoothing adds many edges to the object, and the Isoline Display option displays only the isolines. The Show Cage option makes the surrounding cage visible or invisible. The two color swatches to the right of the Show Cage option let you set the color of the cage and the selection.

The Iterations value determines how aggressive the smoothing is. The higher the Iterations value, the more time it takes to compute and the more complex the resulting object. The Smoothness value determines how sharp a corner must be before adding extra faces to smooth it. A value of 0 does not smooth any corners, and a maximum value of 1.0 smoothes all polygons.

FIGURE 14.10

The Ribbon's Use NURMS panel includes controls for NURMS subdivision.

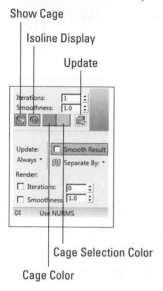

Show Cage

Isoline Display

Update

Cage Selection Color

Cage Color

Caution

Each smoothing iteration quadruples the number of faces. If you raise the number of Iterations too high, the system can become unstable quickly. ■

The two check boxes in the Render section can be used to set the values differently for the Display and Render sections. If disabled, then both the viewports and the renderer use the same settings. The smoothing algorithm can be set to ignore smoothing across Smoothing Groups and Materials.

If the Show Cage option is enabled (at the bottom of the Use NURMS panel), an orange cage surrounds the NURMS object and shows the position of the polygon faces that exist if NURMS is disabled. This cage makes selecting the polygon faces easier.

Tutorial: Smoothing an Ice Cube

NURMS can give a general smoothing to an object, which is just what we need to build an ice cube.

To create an ice cube, follow these steps:

1. Use the Create ⇨ Standard Primitives ⇨ Box menu and drag in the viewport to create a rectangular-shaped box object.
2. Open the Graphite Modeling Tools by clicking its button in the main toolbar. Then select the Convert to Poly option from the Polygon Modeling panel in the Ribbon.

3. Select the Vertex subobject mode and drag over the lower four vertices. Then drag inward with the Scale tool to make the base of the box smaller than the top.

4. Select the Edges subobject mode and drag over all the edges of the box object, and then Shift+click on the Chamfer button in the Edges panel to open the Chamfer caddy. Enter the value of **1** for the Chamfer Amount and the Edge Segments, and click the Ok button to apply the settings.

5. In the Edit panel, click the NURMS button and set the Iterations value in the Use NURMS panel to 1. This smoothes all the selected edges, as shown in Figure 14.11.

FIGURE 14.11

A simple ice cube made smooth with the NURMS feature.

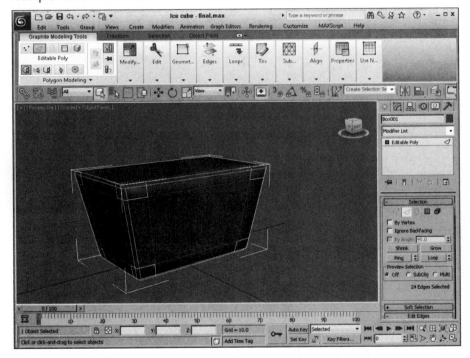

Relax

The Relax button works just like the Relax modifier by moving vertices so they are as far as possible from their adjacent vertices according to the Amount value listed in the pop-up caddy. The caddy also includes an Iterations value, which determines the number of times the operation is performed. You also can select to hold all Boundary and Outer points from being moved.

Create

The Create button lets you create new subobjects, specifically polygons, by connecting isolated vertices and border vertices. When the cursor is over a valid vertex, it changes to a cross-hair, and you can click to create a polygon edge from the last clicked point. If no vertices are available, you can Shift-click to create one. This creates a vertex where you click. Be aware that creating a vertex doesn't add it to any of the edges, but the Create button in Edge subobject mode can connect edges to these isolated vertices.

Tip

As you create new polygons, the normal is determined by the direction in which you create the polygon using the right-hand rule. If you bend the fingers of your right hand in the direction (clockwise or counterclockwise) that the vertices are clicked, then your thumb will point in the direction of the normal. If the normal is pointing away from you, then the backside of the polygon will be visible and the lighting could be off. ∎

You can use the Create button to create new polygons based on new or existing vertices. To create a new face, click the Create button, which highlights all vertices in the selected mesh. Next, click a vertex to start the polygon; after you click two more vertices, a new face is created. You can also create a new vertex not based on any existing vertices by holding down the Shift key while clicking.

Polygons aren't limited to three vertices. You can click as many times as you want to add additional vertices to the polygon. Click the first vertex, or double-click to complete the polygon.

Attach

The Attach button is available with all subobject modes, even when you are not in subobject mode. Use the Attach button to add objects to the current Editable Poly object. You can add primitives, splines, patch objects, and other mesh objects. Any object attached to a mesh object is automatically converted into an editable poly and inherits the object color of the object to which it is attached. Any objects added to a poly object can be selected individually using the Element subobject mode.

Caution

If you attach an object that is smoothed using NURMS, the NURMS are lost when the object is attached. ∎

To use this feature, select the main object and click the Attach button. Move the mouse over the object to be attached; the cursor changes over acceptable objects. Click the object to select it. Click the Attach button again or right-click in the viewport to exit Attach mode.

Note

If the object that you click to attach already has a material applied that is different from the current Editable Poly object, then a dialog box appears giving you options to Match Material IDs to Material, Match Material to Material IDs, or Do Not Modify Material IDs or Material. Materials and Material IDs are discussed in more detail in Chapter 15, "Using the Slate Material Editor." ∎

Selecting the Attach From List option opens the Attach List dialog box (which looks just like the Select Objects [H] dialog box) where you can select from a list of all the objects to attach. The list contains only objects that you can attach.

Note

When you enter a subobject mode, the Attach List button changes to a Detach button for poly objects. ∎

Attaching objects is different from grouping objects because all attached objects act as a single object with the same object color, name, and transforms. You can access individual attached objects using the Element subobject mode.

Quadrify All

The Ribbon's Geometry (All) panel also includes a Quadrify All tool in the pop-up section of the panel, for converting triangles to quads. You have options to Quadrify All, Quadrify Selection, Select Edges from All, and Select Edges from Selection. This is an awesome tool if you like to work with edge loops and edge rings.

Figure 14.12 shows a face model that has been built using triangular faces on the left. Using the Quadrify All command, the face on the right is aligned to much neater rows and columns of four-sided polys. This allows the edge loop features to be used.

FIGURE 14.12

The Quadrify All command greatly simplifies this model, making it easier to work with.

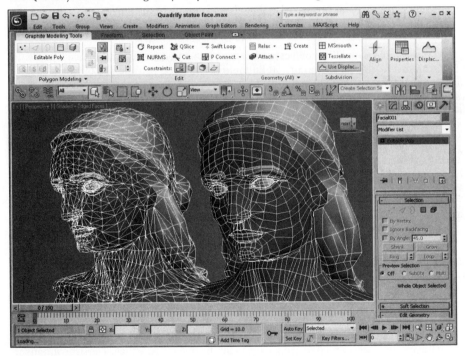

MSmooth and Tessellate Within the Subdivision panel are buttons for smoothing and tessellating the object. Both the MSmooth and Tessellate buttons include caddies, as shown in Figure 14.13. The MSmooth setting for Smoothness rounds all the sharp edges of an object. Tessellation can be done using Edges or Faces, and the Tension setting controls how tight the adjacent faces are.

FIGURE 14.13

The caddies for the MSmooth and Tessellate buttons let you interactively set the Smoothness and Tension values.

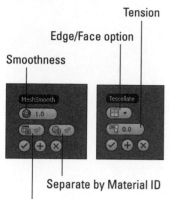

The MSmooth button can be used to smooth the selected subobjects in the same way as the MeshSmooth modifier. This button can be used several times. The Smoothness value determines which vertices are used to smooth the object. The higher the value, the more vertices are included and the smoother the result. You can also select that the smoothing is separated by Smoothing Groups or by Materials.

Tessellation is used to increase the density of the faces or edges. When modeling, you may want more details in a select area. This is where the tessellation command comes in. Tessellation can be applied to individual selected subobjects or to the entire object.

You can use the Tessellate button to increase the resolution of a mesh by splitting a face or polygon into several faces or polygons. You have two options to do this: Edge and Face.

The Edge method splits each edge at its midpoint. For example, a triangular face would be split into three smaller triangles. The Tension spinner to the right of the Tessellate button specifies a value that is used to make the tessellated face concave or convex.

The Face option creates a vertex in the center of the face and also creates three new edges, which extend from the center vertex to each original vertex. For a square polygon, this option would create six new triangular faces. (Remember, a square polygon is actually composed of two triangular faces.)

Use Displacement

The Use Displacement tool opens the Subdivision panel, shown in Figure 14.14, when enabled. Using this panel, you can specify the subdivision method that is used and the settings for the displacement.

Cross-Reference

You can learn more about using displacement maps in Chapter 18, "Creating Compound Materials and Using Material Modifiers." ■

FIGURE 14.14

The Subdivision panel includes all the subdivision settings.

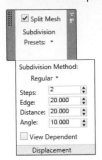

Alignment options

A single vertex or two vertices don't define a plane, but three or more vertices do. If three or more vertices are selected, you can use the Make Planar button to make these vertices coplanar (which means that all vertices are on the same plane). Doing so positions the selected vertices so that they lie in the same plane. This is helpful if you want to build a new polygon face. Polygonal faces need to be coplanar. This button works in all subobject modes. The X, Y, and Z buttons let you collapse the current object or subobject selection to a single plane lying on the specified axis.

The View and Grid Align buttons move and orient all selected vertices to the current active viewport or to the current construction grid. These buttons can also be used in all subobject modes. This causes all the selected face normals to point directly at the grid or view.

Editing Vertex subobjects

When working with the Editable Poly objects, after you select a Vertex subobject mode (keyboard shortcut, 1) and select vertices, you can transform them using the transform buttons on the main toolbar. All vertex-specific commands are found within the Vertices panel, shown in Figure 14.15, but some new tools also appear in the Geometry (All) panel including Collapse, Detach, and Cap Poly.

FIGURE 14.15

When the Vertex subobject mode is selected, these vertex commands become available.

Collapse

The Collapse button is used to collapse all the selected subobjects to a single subobject located at the averaged center of the selection. This button is similar to the Weld button, except that the selected vertices don't need to be within a Threshold value to be combined. This button works in all subobject modes.

Detach

Use the Detach button to separate the selected subobjects from the rest of the object. To use this button, select the subobject and click the Detach button. The Detach dialog box opens, enabling you to name the new detached subobject. You also have the options to Detach to Element or to Detach as Clone. All subobject modes except Edge have a Detach option.

Extrude

The Extrude button copies and moves the selected subobject perpendicular a given distance and connects the new copy with the original one. For example, four edges forming a square extruded would form a box with no lid. To use this feature, select an edge or edges, click the Extrude button, and then drag in a viewport. The edges interactively show the extrude depth. Release the button when you've reached the desired distance.

Alternatively, you can set an extrude depth in the Extrusion spinner in the caddy. The Group option extrudes all selected edges in the direction of the average of all the normals for the group (the normal runs perpendicular to the face), and the Normal Local option moves each individual edge along its local normal. For polygons, you can extrude By Polygons, which extrudes each individual polygon along its normal as a separate extrusion. To exit Extrude mode, click the Extrude button again or right-click in the viewport.

The Extrude button is enabled for Face, Polygon, and Element subobject modes for the Editable Poly object. The Local Normal option extrudes each edge along its own normal.

The Extrude settings caddy includes options for setting the Extrusion Height and the Extrusion Base Width.

Remove

The Remove button lets you delete the selected vertices. The Remove button automatically adjusts the surrounding subobjects to maintain the mesh integrity.

Note

You can also delete Editable Poly subobjects using the Delete key. ∎

The Remove button also is available in Edge subobject mode. If you hold down the Ctrl key when clicking the Remove button when an edge is selected, vertices at either end of the deleted edge are also removed.

Break

You use the Break button to create a separate vertex for adjoining faces that are connected by a single vertex.

In a normal mesh, faces are all connected by vertices: Moving one vertex changes the position of all adjoining faces. The Break button enables you to move the vertex associated with each face independent of the others. The button is available only in Vertex subobject mode.

Chamfer and Weld

The Chamfer button—which is enabled in Vertex, Edge, and Border subobject modes—lets you cut the edge off a corner and replace it with a face. Using the Chamfer caddy, you can interactively specify a Chamfer Amount and the number of segments. The caddy also includes an Open option, which cuts a hole in the polygon face instead of replacing it with a new polygon.

Vertices and edges that are close or on top of one another can be combined together into one using the Weld command. The Weld and Chamfer buttons include caddies that let you interactively see the results of different settings. The Weld caddy includes a weld Threshold value and displays the number of vertices before and after the welding process, which is very useful to check whether a weld was successful.

The Target button lets you click a single vertex and move the cursor over an adjacent vertex. A rubber band line stretches from the first selected vertex to the target weld vertex, and the cursor changes to indicate that the vertex under the cursor may be selected. Clicking the target vertex welds the two vertices together.

Note
When two vertices are welded, the new vertex is positioned at a location that is halfway between both vertices, but when Target Weld is used, the first vertex is moved to the location of the second. ■

Weight and Crease

The Weight settings control the amount of pull that a vertex has when NURMS subdivision or a MeshSmooth modifier is used. The higher the Weight value, the more resistant a vertex is to smoothing. For edge and border subobjects, the Weight value is followed by a Crease value that determines how visible the edge is when the mesh is smoothed. A value of 1.0 ensures that the crease is visible.

Remove Isolated and Unused Map Vertices

The Remove Isolated Vertices button deletes all isolated vertices. Vertices become isolated by some operations and add unneeded data to your file. You can search and delete them quickly with this button. Good examples of isolated vertices are those created using the Create button but never attached to an edge.

The Remove Unused Map Vertices button removes any leftover mapping vertices from the object.

Editing Edge and Border subobjects

All the edge editing tools are located in the Edges and Borders panels, shown in Figure 14.16. Many of the Edge subobject options work in the same way as the Vertex subobject options.

FIGURE 14.16

All the Edge specific commands are available when the Edge subobject mode is enabled. Many of the Border subobject commands are the same as those for Edges.

Insert Vertices

Bridge Edges

The Bridge button for edges allows you to create a new set of polygons that connect the selected edges. If two edges are selected when the Bridge button is pressed, then they are automatically connected with a new polygon. If no edges are selected, then you can click the edges to bridge after clicking the Bridge button. The selected edges on either side of the bridge can be different in number.

You also can access the caddy for the Bridge feature. This caddy offers the options to Bridge Specific Edges or to Use Edge Selection. The Bridge Specific Edges option has two buttons for each edge. If you click one of these buttons, you can select an edge in the viewport. The Use Edge Selection option lets you drag a marquee in the viewport to select the edges. The Bridge Edges caddy also includes options for setting the number of Segments, the Smooth value, and a Bridge Adjacent value, which increases the triangulation for angles above the given threshold.

Split and Insert Vertex

The Split button adds a new vertex at the middle of the edge and splits the edge into two equal sections. This button is handy when you need to increase the resolution of a section quickly.

The Insert Vertex button lets you add a new vertex anywhere along an edge. The cursor changes to cross-hairs when it is over an edge. Click to create a vertex. When in Edge, Border, Polygon, or Element subobject mode, this button also makes vertices visible. Within the Ribbon's Edges pane, you can set the number of vertices to be placed evenly along the selected edges using the number spinner next to the Insert Vertices tool.

Create Shape from Selection

The Create Shape from Selection button creates a new spline shape from selected edges. You can also select options for Smooth or Linear shape types.

Spin

The Spin button rotates the hidden edges that break up the polygon into triangles (all polygonal faces include these hidden edges). For example, if a quadrilateral (four-sided) face has a hidden edge that runs between vertices 1 and 3, then the Spin button changes this hidden edge to run between vertices 2 and 4. This affects how the surface is smoothed when the polygon is not coplanar.

Cap Poly

The Cap Poly button that appears in the Geometry (All) panel causes the existing border selection to be filled in with a single coplanar polygon. After using this feature, the Border subobject is no longer identified as a Border subobject.

Bridge

The Bridge feature joins two selected Border subobjects with a tube of polygons that connect the two borders. The two selected borders must be part of the same object and need not have an equal number of segments.

Editing Polygon and Element subobjects

Like the other subobject modes, Editable Polys can be edited at the polygon and element subobject level. The buttons for these modes are found in the Polygons and Elements panels. Figure 14.17 shows the Ribbon's Polygons and Elements panels.

FIGURE 14.17

The Polygon and Element subobjects commands are found in the Polygons and Elements panels.

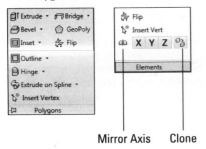

Mirror Axis   Clone

Bevel

The Bevel button extrudes the Polygon subobject selection and then lets you bevel the edges. To use this feature, select a polygon, click the Bevel button, drag up or down in a viewport to the Extrusion depth, and release the button. Drag again to specify the Bevel amount. The Bevel amount determines the relative size of the extruded face.

GeoPoly

The GeoPoly button moves the vertices of the selected polygon to make a regular polygon whose vertices are all equally spaced. The shape of the resulting polygon depends on the number of vertices included in the polygon face.

Inset and Outline

The Outline button offsets the selected polygon a specified amount. This increases the size of the selected polygon or element. The Inset button creates another polygon set within the selected polygon and connects their edges. For both these buttons, a caddy is available that includes the Outline or Inset Amount values.

Flip

The Flip button flips the normal vectors for the selected subobjects. The Flip button is available only in Polygon and Element subobject modes.

Hinge

The Hinge button rotates a selected polygon as if one of its edges were a hinge. The angle of the hinge depends on the distance that you drag with the mouse, or you can use the available caddy. By default, one of the polygon's edges will be used as the hinge about which the section rotates, but in the caddy, you can click the Pick Hinge button and select an edge (which doesn't need to be attached to the polygon).

Extrude Along Spline

The Extrude on Spline button can be used to extrude a selected polygon along the spline path. The caddy includes a Pick Spline button that you can use to select the spline to use. You can also specify the number of segments, the Taper Amount and Curve, and a Twist value. You also have an option to Align the extrusion to the face normal or to rotate about the normal.

Tutorial: Adding a handle to a mug

Creating a cup is fairly easy using the Lathe modifier, but adding the handle is another story. It could be created as half a torus and Boolean connected to the cup, but this example shows how to use the poly modeling features to hinge the handle on.

To add a handle to a mug, follow these steps:

1. Open the Mug.max file from the Chap 14 directory on the CD.

   This file includes a simple cup created using the Lathe modifier, and it has been converted to an Editable Poly object. Open the Graphite Modeling Tools by clicking on its button in the main toolbar.

2. Select the QSlice button Edit panel and click in the Front viewport about one-third up from the bottom of the cup, then orient the line to be horizontal and click again.

3. Click on the Cut button in the Edit panel and cut edges into each corner of one of the polygon faces near the bottom of the cup. Then cut another horizontal edge in the middle of the cup. Right-click in the viewport to exit the Cut tool.

4. Select the Polygon subobject mode in the Polygon Modeling panel and click on the interior of the cut polygon just created. Shift-click on the Hinge button in the Polygons panel. In the Hinge From Edge caddy, click the Pick Hinge button and click on the midline edge that was cut, set the Segments to 10, and the Angle to 185, then click on the Ok button.

Figure 14.18 shows the resulting handle on the mug. You can add a NURMS command to smooth the mug handle.

Mirroring elements

Within the Elements panel are commands for mirroring the current selection about the X, Y, or Z axes. These commands move the element to the opposite side, but clicking the Clone button creates a clone of the selected element.

FIGURE 14.18

The handle for this mug was created with the Hinge feature.

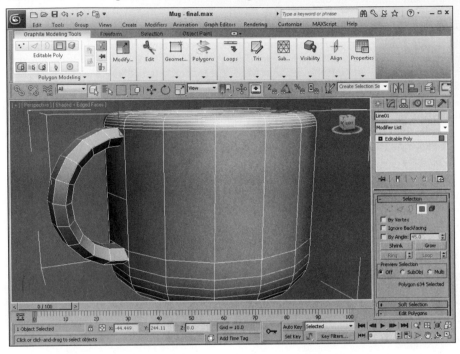

Surface properties

In the Properties panel are several settings for additional properties such as vertex colors, material IDs, and Smoothing Groups.

Vertex Surface properties

The Vertex Properties panel in Vertex subobject mode lets you define the Color, Illumination, and Alpha value of object vertices. The color swatches enable you to select Color and Illumination colors for the selected vertices. The Alpha value sets the amount of transparency for the vertices. After you assign colors, you can then recall vertices with the same color by selecting a color (or illumination color) in the Select Vertices By section and clicking the Select button. The RGB (red, green, and blue) values match all colors within the Range defined by these values.

Cross-Reference

You can find more information on vertex colors in Chapter 32, "Painting in the Viewport Canvas and Rendering Surface Maps." ∎

Polygon and Element Surface properties

For Polygon and Element subobjects, the Properties panel, shown in Figure 14.19, includes Material IDs and Smoothing Groups options. The Material IDs option settings are used by the Multi/Sub-Object material type to apply different materials to faces or polygons within an object. By selecting a polygon subobject, you can use these option settings to apply a unique material to the selected polygon. The Select ID button selects all subobjects that have the designated Material ID, or you can select subobjects using a material name in the drop-down list under the Select ID button.

Cross-Reference

You can find more information on the Multi/Sub-Object material type in Chapter 16, "Creating and Applying Standard Materials." ∎

FIGURE 14.19

The Properties panel includes settings for Material IDs, Smoothing Groups, and Vertex Colors.

You use the Smoothing Groups option to assign a subobject to a unique smoothing group. To do this, select a subobject and click a Smoothing Groups number. The Select By SG button, like the Select By ID button, opens a dialog box where you can enter a Smoothing Groups number, and all subobjects with that number are selected. The Clear All button clears all Smoothing Groups number assignments, and the Auto Smooth button automatically assigns Smoothing Groups numbers based on the angle between faces as set by the value to the right of the Auto Smooth button.

The Properties panel also includes options for setting vertex Color, Illumination, and Alpha values.

Using the Freeform Tools

The middle tab in the Graphite Modeling tools includes an assortment of Freeform tools for sculpting and modeling surfaces as if working with clay. These tools are divided into three panels—PolyDraw, Paint Deform, and Defaults. The PolyDraw panel is shown in Figure 14.20.

FIGURE 14.20

The Freeform tools let you model by sculpting.

Conform Move   Conform Rotate

Conform Scale   Conform Relax

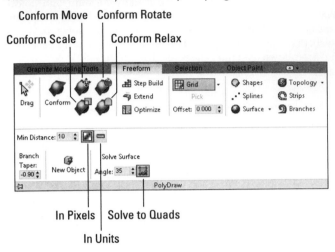

In Pixels | Solve to Quads

In Units

Using the PolyDraw tools

The various PolyDraw tools let you create and extend the surface subobjects using tools that work like a common drawing program.

Drag

The Drag tool lets you move selected subobjects around by simply dragging them with the mouse. Clicking a subobject automatically selects it and lets you drag it to a new position. Holding down the Shift key or the Ctrl key lets you drag edges or polygons regardless of the subobject mode that is selected. Pressing Shift+Ctrl keys together lets you drag entire edge loops, and the Alt key lets you move the subobject in a direction that is perpendicular to the view axis, which is great for dragging subobjects off to the side of an object.

Conform

The Conform brushes let you push all the vertices of the selected object toward a selected underlying object. When the Freeform panel is first accessed, you can select the Draw On: Surface option to the right of the Step Build button. When Surface is selected, the Pick button becomes active. Using this button, you can select the object to which you want the selected object to be conformed.

New Feature

The Conform brushes are new to 3ds Max 2012. ■

With the object to conform to selected, you can select the Conform button and change the options for this brush using the Conform panel, shown in Figure 14.21. Within the Conform panel, you can set the Strength, Falloff, and Conform values. The Conform value sets the rate at which the vertices move toward the conform object. Higher values make the vertices move immediately, and smaller values, such as 0.1, cause the movement to be gradual.

FIGURE 14.21

The Conform panel holds the options for using the Conform brushes.

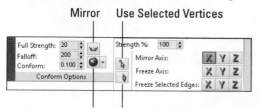

Mirror   Use Selected Vertices

Vertex Normals   Ignore Backfacing

The Mirror option causes the vertices' movement to be applied equally on either side of the mirror axis. The Vertex Normals/View drop-down list lets you control how the vertices move. The View option causes the vertices to move toward the target into the current view, and the Vertex Normals option moves the vertices along their normals toward the conform object. You also have options to move only the selected vertices, to Ignore Backfacing vertices, to select the mirror and freeze axes, and to freeze specific selected edges so no movement happens.

Within the PolyDraw panel are four brushes for defining how the vertices are transformed. The Conform Move brush moves vertices under its brush range. Vertices also can be rotated and scaled using the Conform Rotate and Conform Scale brushes, and the Conform Relax brush smoothes the moved vertices by moving them gradually toward their original position.

Tutorial: Matching a road to a rolling terrain

If you've created a rough rolling landscape using a Plane object and the Noise modifier, matching a road running across the surface can be tricky if you have to select and move each individual vertex. Instead, you can use the Conform brushes to move the vertices so they match the underlying hills.

To conform a road to an underlying terrain, follow these steps:

1. Open the Conforming road.max file from the Chap 14 directory on the CD.
2. With the road selected, click the Graphite Modeling Tools button on the main toolbar to make the Ribbon appear, and select the Freeform tab.
3. Select the Draw On: Surface option from the drop-down list to the right of the Step Build button, click the Pick button, and click the hilly object. Then select the straight road object, and click the Conform button.
4. In the Conform panel, select the View option and change the viewport to the Top view.
5. Select the Conform Move brush, and click and slowly rotate the brush in small circles over the road object to move its vertices to conform to the hilly landscape, as shown in Figure 14.22.

FIGURE 14.22

The Conform Move brush is used to make the road match the underlying terrain.

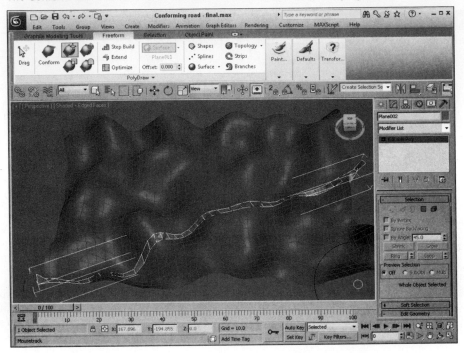

Step Build

The Step Build tool lets you click to place new vertices on the surface of the object. The location of these new vertices depends on the current Grid, on the current object's Surface, or within the Selection using the On selections located to the right of the Step Build button. If you select the On: Surface option, then you can use the Pick button to select the object whose surface you want to create vertices on. After freestanding vertices are created, you can hold down the Shift key and drag over these new vertices to create a polygon. The Ctrl key lets you remove polygons, and the Alt key lets you remove vertices. With these controls, you can quickly remove and rebuild polygons to create new shapes.

Extend

The Extend tool works on border subobjects and lets you add new polygons to fill the hole by dragging on the border vertices. If you press and hold the Shift key while dragging an edge, you can pull the edge away to create a new polygon. Dragging with the Shift+Ctrl keys lets you drag two adjacent edges out. The Ctrl key and a click deletes the polygon, and dragging with the Alt key held down moves the polygon perpendicular to the view axis.

Optimize

The Optimize tool quickly collapses subobjects. Click an edge with this tool to remove it and to combine its two end points into one. The Shift key is used to target weld two vertices into a single one, and the Alt key removes vertices. The Shift+Ctrl key combo can remove an entire edge loop at once.

Tutorial: Opening a diamond

Ever wonder what was inside a diamond? This example uses some of the PolyDraw tools to open up a diamond. Maybe there is treasure inside!

To edit a diamond-shaped object, follow these steps:

1. Select Create ➪ Standard Primitives ➪ Sphere, and drag in the Top viewport to create a Sphere object. Set its Segments value to **6**. Then right-click, and select Convert To ➪ Editable Poly from the pop-up quadmenu.

2. Open the Graphite Modeling tools, click the Freeform tab, select the Step Build tool, press and hold the Ctrl key, and click the center polygon to delete the polygon. Then click within the center polygon to create four vertices in the shape of a square. Then press and hold the Shift key, and drag near these vertices to create a polygon.

3. Select the Drag tool, and drag the new vertices until they are aligned with each other to form a square.

4. Select the Extend tool, and with the Shift key pressed, drag the edge on the left side of the open polygon toward the middle to create a new extended polygon. Then repeat for the left side.

Figure 14.23 shows the resulting diamond.

FIGURE 14.23

The PolyDraw tools let you work quickly to add, remove, and rebuild polygons.

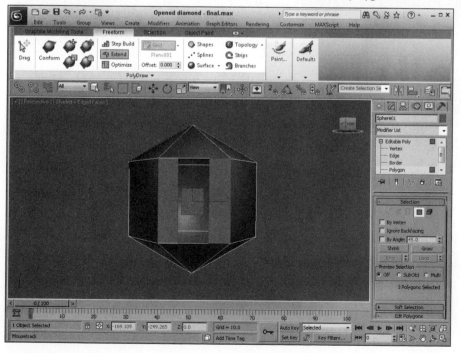

Draw On and Pick

The Draw On drop-down list gives you three options for specifying the object that is drawn on: Grid, Surface, and Selection. If Surface is selected, you can use the Pick button to choose the surface object. You also can set an Offset, which is the distance above the surface on which the drawn objects appear.

Tip

It is best to keep a non-zero offset value when drawing on the surface of an object, especially if the drawn object overlaps an edge. This keeps the surfaces from interpenetrating. ■

Shapes and Solve Surface

The Shapes tool lets you draw polygonal shapes directly on the surface of an object. Figure 14.24 shows three polygons drawn on the surface of a torus. You also can delete drawn polygons with the Ctrl key. The completed polygons likely will have multiple vertices, but you can reduce the polygons to tris and quads using the Solve Surface button.

FIGURE 14.24

Using the Shapes tool, you can draw polygons that conform to the surface of the underlying object.

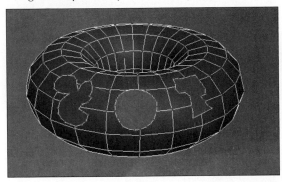

Splines

The Splines tool lets you draw spline objects that follow the surface of the underlying object. The Ctrl key can be used to delete drawn splines.

Surface, Topology, Strips, and Branches

The Surface tool covers the object with a mesh of quads by painting over the object. You can delete any polygon by clicking it with Ctrl key held down. The Topology tool lets you draw a series of parallel lines followed by a set of perpendicular lines to form quads. The Auto Weld option automatically welds vertices together to form a mesh. The Ctrl key extends a line from the nearest end point.

The Strips tool draws a consecutive row of quads that flow across the surface of the object. The Shift key extends the strip from the nearest edge. The Branches tool extends a tapered branch from a single polygon. For the branches, you can set a Taper amount; the Minimum Distance value sets the distance between the segments. This is useful for creating tentacles, as shown in Figure 14.25.

FIGURE 14.25

Using the Branches tool, you can drag out extending arms from polygons.

Using the Paint Deform tools

The Paint Deform tools let you sculpt the surface of an object by pushing, pulling, and modeling the object in organic ways like it was clay. Whenever any of the tools on the Paint Deform panel, shown in Figure 14.26, are selected, its settings for the brush's Size and Strength (and sometimes Offset, depending on the tool) appear in the Paint Options panel to the side of the Paint Deform panel.

FIGURE 14.26

The Paint Deform tools are used to sculpt an object's surface with gradual changes.

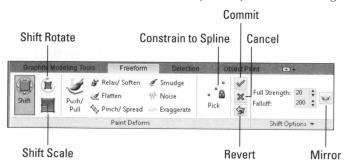

Shift/Shift Rotate/Shift Scale

The Shift tool lets you drag all subobjects within the brush radius, and all subobjects within the falloff radius are moved to a less extent. You can control the brush size and falloff in the Options panel, or you can press and hold the Ctrl key and drag to alter the brush's radius. The Shift+drag changes the brush's falloff indicated by the inner white circle.

The Shift Rotate and Shift Scale brushes are used to rotate and/or scale all the vertices within the brush's range.

New Feature

The Shift Rotate and Shift Scale brushes are new to 3ds Max 2012. ■

Push/Pull

The Push/Pull tool also has Size and Strength values, but it is different in that the brush follows the surface of the object. Dragging over an area pulls the vertices within the brush's radius outward, and holding down the Ctrl key pushes the vertices inward. The Shift key relaxes the area under the brush.

Relax/Soften

The Relax/Soften brush removes any extreme changes in the surface such as hard edges of a cube. The Alt key lets you relax the surface without changing its volume, and the Ctrl key causes the surface to revert to its previous state.

Flatten and Pinch/Spread

The Flatten brush pulls any bends out of the mesh causing the object to be working into a flat plane. The Ctrl key causes the object to revert to its previous state, and the Shift key accesses the Relax/Soften brush. The Pinch/Spread tool causes vertices to be pulled in closer to each other, and holding down the Alt key has the opposite effect and pushes them away.

Smudge, Noise, and Exaggerate

The Smudge tool pushes the surrounding vertices away from the center of the brush. Dragging over the same vertices multiple times moves them each time. Holding down the Alt key causes the vertices to be moved only along the surface and not to be moved along the normal. The Noise tool randomly moves the vertices about to create a random noise pattern. The Exaggerate tool pushes vertices farther in the current direction to emphasize the details.

Constrain to Spline

If you want more control over the precise surface area that is changed using the Paint Deform tools, you can select the Constrain to Spline option and use the Pick button to select a spline near the surface area to change.

New Feature

The Constrain to Spline feature is new to 3ds Max 2012. ■

Revert

At any point, you can use the Revert tool to gradually change the object back to its last saved point. You can set a save point by clicking the Commit button, which looks like a green check mark. The Cancel button (a red X) removes the recent changes from the object.

Using the Selection Tools

The next tab offers several additional Selection tools. These tools make it possible to locate specific subobjects by looking for certain criteria such as concavity, normals, and symmetry. Figure 14.27 shows the panels for this tab.

FIGURE 14.27

The Selection tab includes panels for selecting specific subobject selections.

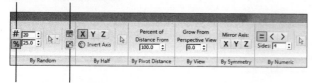

Selecting Tops, Open, and Non-Quads

The first three tools in the Selection tab are the Tops, Open, and Non-Quads tools. The Tops tool selects all vertices resulting from the extruded sections. This quickly lets you grab all extended sections and extend or reduce them as needed. The Open tool selects all open borders, and the Non-Quads tool finds all polygons that consist of trios or more than four corners. This is a valuable tool when working with edge loops.

Note

The Non-Quads option is only available when the Polygon or Element subobject mode is selected. ■

Copying and pasting selections

The Stored Selection panel lets you copy a selection of subobjects into two available stores. These copied selections can be restored at any time by clicking the Paste button. Additional buttons let you combine the two selection stores, subtracting one from another and getting only the intersecting selection between the two. The Clear button removes the selection from the store.

The Copy and Paste Sets buttons let you copy a selection set from the main toolbar and paste it as needed.

Selecting by criteria

The remaining selection criteria let you locate subobjects using a variety of different methods.

By Surface, Normal, and Perspective

The By Surface panel lets you specify a degree of concavity, and the tool locates all the concave areas in the current object. Negative values also can be used to find convex regions. Figure 14.28 shows the selected concave regions.

FIGURE 14.28

The By Surface tool can be used to find the concave regions of an object.

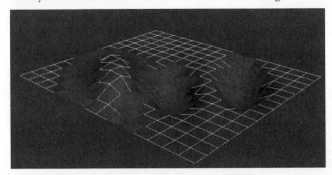

The By Normal panel lets you choose an axis and a value, and all subobjects within the Angle value for the selected axis are selected. This is a great way to quickly determine which polygons are facing away from the current view. The Invert button can find all normals pointing toward the negative axis side.

The By Perspective panel selects those polygons that are within the Angle value to the view axis. If the Outline button is enabled, then only the outer borders of polygons are selected. Click the Select button to see all the selected polygons meeting the criteria.

By Random, Half, and Pivot Distance

The By Random panel lets you randomly select polygons within the current object. You can set to randomly select a given number or a percentage of the total. The Select button makes the random selection, or you can randomly select within the current selection. Additional buttons grow or shrink the selection. Figure 14.29 shows a random selection.

The By Half panel lets you quickly choose half of the available polygons as determined by axis. The Invert Axis button lets you choose the negative side of the axis. The By Pivot Distance chooses those polygons that are farthest away from the current pivot point, creating a circular selection area. Reducing the distance value creeps the selection closer to the pivot's location.

FIGURE 14.29

The By Random tool can be used to make a random selection of polygons.

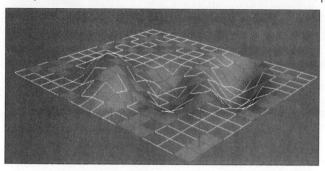

By View, Symmetry, and Numeric

The By View panel selects those polygons closest to the current view camera. Increasing this value extends the selection farther into the scene, as shown in Figure 14.30.

FIGURE 14.30

The By View tool is used to select those polygons closest to the current view.

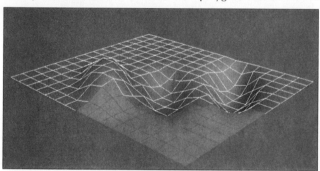

Regardless of the current selection, you can make it symmetrical about any of the three axes using the By Symmetry panel. The By Numeric panel, which is only available in Vertex and Polygon modes, lets you select all vertices that have a given number of edges or polygons that have a given number of sides. The Equal, Less Than, and Greater Than buttons are used to mathematically determine those subobjects.

By Color

The By Color panel, available in Vertex mode, lets you locate any vertices that have a given color or Illuminate vertex color setting according to the specified RGB values.

Using the Object Paint Tools

The last tab is the Object Paint tab. This tab includes tools that let you select and paint with a specific object. This is great for spreading objects around a scene. The tab also includes several options for randomizing the size, orientation, and placement of the painted objects.

Selecting an object to paint with

Within the Paint Objects panel, shown in Figure 14.31, are two paint modes for painting and filling. Each of these buttons is a toggle and turns the paint mode on and off. While each mode is active, you can switch between objects and subobjects as needed.

FIGURE 14.31

The Paint Objects panel lets you paint or fill with objects.

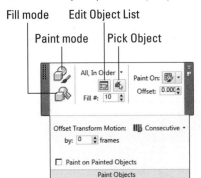

Before you can begin painting with an object, you need to select an object using the Pick Object button. Simply click the Pick Object button and select an object in the scene. The selected object is highlighted and added to the list of paint objects. If you select the Pick Object button again, you can add another object to the list of paint objects. Clicking the Edit Object List button opens the list of current paint objects, as shown in Figure 14.32. Using this list, you can change the order of the items, pick new items, add items using the Select Objects dialog box, add the selected scene object, or remove the selected item from the list.

FIGURE 14.32

The Paint Objects list lets you manage the objects that you're painting with.

Note

Edits to the Paint Objects list can be made only while the Paint and Fill modes are disabled. ■

Painting with objects

After a paint object is selected, you can click the Paint button to enable paint mode and then drag in the viewport, as shown in Figure 14.33. Each stroke drawn with the brush lays down a new curve. The Undo command can be used to remove the last stroke, but all strokes are not added to the scene until the Commit button in the Brush Settings panel is clicked. The Cancel button removes all strokes drawn since the last commit.

Caution

Painting with objects dramatically increases the overall polygon count of the scene, especially if you are painting with a complex object. Try to keep the paint object as simple as possible to avoid unwieldy scenes. ■

FIGURE 14.33

After an object is selected, simply drag in the viewport to paint with the selected object.

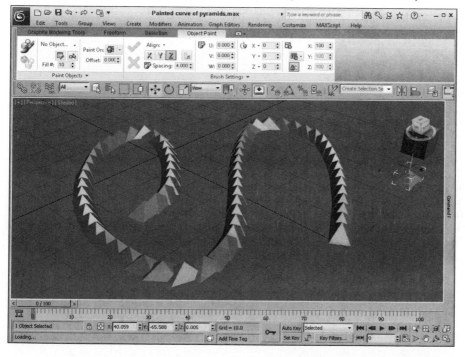

Before a painted set of objects is committed to the scene, you can use the settings in the Brush Settings panel, shown in Figure 14.34, to change the alignment, spacing, rotation, and scale of the objects. You have several options for randomly scattering the objects. The default alignment for the painted objects is to match the picked object, or you can align the object to the X, Y, or Z axis or flip it about the specified axis with the Flip Axis button.

FIGURE 14.34

The Brush Settings panel lets you change the position, rotation, and scale of the painted objects.

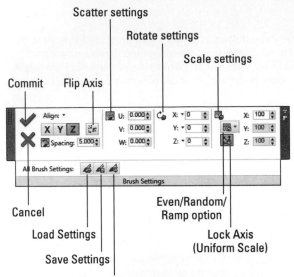

The Spacing value lets you change how far away each object is from its neighbor. The Scatter settings let you move the objects in the U, V, or W directions. The Rotation setting uniformly rotates all the objects together, or you can allow random rotations by clicking the small arrow to the right of each axis and enabling the Random option.

For the Scale settings, you can enable the Lock Axis (Uniform Scaling) option to scale all objects evenly or you can enable the Random option to randomly scale the objects within a set range of values. The Ramp option scales the objects gradually from the start of the stroke to the end of the stroke to a given size. Figure 14.35 shows several lines of pyramids with different settings. The top line is the default. The second line has an altered spacing value, the third line is oriented about the Y axis, and the final line uses a ramp scaling.

FIGURE 14.35

Painted objects can be altered by spacing, orientation, and scaling.

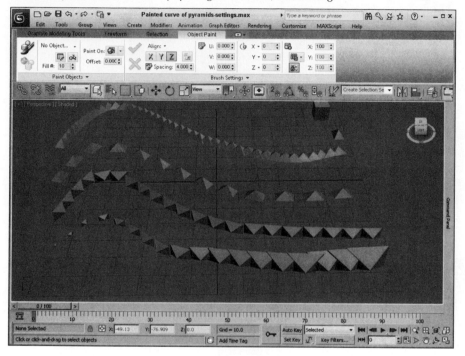

Painting with multiple objects

If you have multiple objects in the Paint Objects list, you can choose which objects to paint with using the option in the Paint Objects panel. The first option is to paint with just the most recently picked object. The second option is to paint with all objects in order, and the last option is to randomly paint with all objects. Figure 14.36 shows each of these options.

FIGURE 14.36

When painting with multiple objects, you can choose to paint the objects in order or randomly.

Painting on objects

The Object Paint feature lets you paint on the default construction grid, on the selected object or on the entire scene. These options are available in the Paint Objects panel. Figure 14.37 shows painting some cones on a simple sphere. The cones are aligned by default to the surface normals of the sphere.

When the Scene option is selected, the painted objects are placed on the default grid unless a scene object is encountered, and then it is placed on top of the scene object. The Offset value can be used to move the painted objects into or off of the surface of the underlying object.

FIGURE 14.37

Objects also can be painted on the surface of another object in the scene.

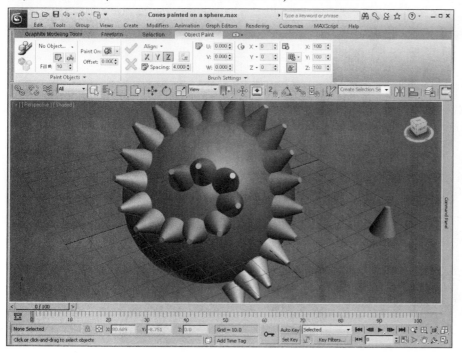

Using the Paint Fill mode

The Paint Fill mode allows you to place the paint object at regular intervals along a selected edge. Before the Paint Fill mode is enabled, you need to have a paint object selected and an edge or an edge loop selected. Once selected, the Paint Fill button simply places the paint object along the edge. The Fill Number value determines the number of objects that are placed along the selected edge loop. Figure 14.38 shows a sphere filled with several cone objects using this mode.

FIGURE 14.38

The Paint Fill mode places objects along a selected edge loop.

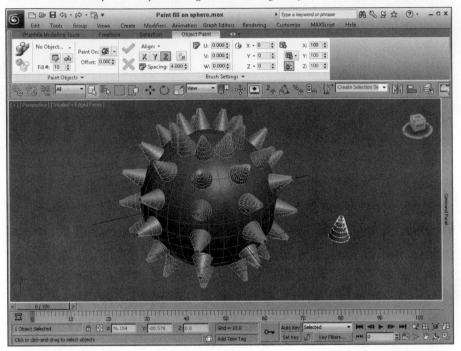

Painting with animated objects

If the object that you are painting with has some animation associated with it, then you can specify an offset for the motion of the object. The options for how the animated object plays are in the Paint Objects panel and include Consecutive, which plays the animation on each painted object in order offset by the By # Frames value. For example, if you have a box that spins and you set the By # Frames value to 2, then the first box in the painted line will start spinning at frame 0 and the second will start at frame 2, and so on. The other Offset Transform Motion option is Random, which randomly starts the animation for each object.

Tutorial: Painting a scar

Although medical companies are searching for an easy way to remove scars, we're going to use the Object Paint feature to add one to our character.

To add a character scar using the Object Paint feature, follow these steps:

1. Open the Futureman with scar.max file from the Chap 14 directory on the CD.
2. Click the Graphite Modeling Tools button on the main toolbar to make the Ribbon appear, and select the Object Paint tab.

3. Click the Pick Object button in the Paint Objects panel, and then click the scar object. Select the Paint On option, and select the futureman's face object.

4. Click the Paint button, and drag across futureman's face to place the scar.

5. In the Brush Settings panel, enable the Lock Axis (Uniform Scale) button, set the Scale X value to **17**, and drag the Spacing value until the scar is equally spaced out at a value around 11.5. Figure 14.39 shows the applied scar.

6. Click the Commit button in the Brush Settings panel to apply the scar to the face.

FIGURE 14.39

Applying scars on the surface of a character is easy with the Object Paint feature.

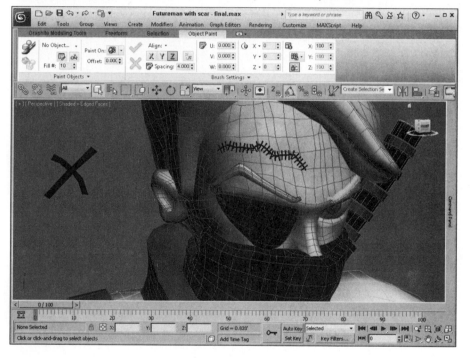

Summary

When modeling with polygons, the Graphite Modeling tools become your best friends. With all the tools at your fingertips, you can model faster and with greater ease. In addition to the base modeling features, the Freeform modeling tools, the Selection tools, and the Object Paint features make modeling a delight. More specifically, this chapter covered the following topics:

- Accessing and using the Graphite Modeling tools
- Modeling in the various subobject modes

- Using the Freeform tools to sculpt surfaces
- Making specific selections with the Selection tools
- Painting with objects and filling edges with the Paint Object panel

This chapter concludes Part III, "Modeling Basics." You're now ready to learn about dressing up objects with materials, cameras, and lights. The next chapter covers the basics of applying materials.

Part IV

Materials, Cameras, and Lighting Basics

Using the Slate Material Editor

Materials are used to dress, color, and paint objects. Just as materials in real life can be described as scaly, soft, smooth, opaque, or blue, materials applied to 3D objects can mimic properties such as color, texture, transparency, shininess, and so on. In this chapter, you learn the basics of working with materials and all the features of the Slate Material Editor and the Material Explorer.

Understanding Material Properties

Before jumping into the Material Editor, let's take a close look at the type of material properties that you will deal with. Understanding these properties will help you as you begin to create new materials.

Up until now, the only material property that has been applied to an object has been the default object color, randomly assigned by Max. The Material Editor can add a whole new level of realism using materials that simulate many different types of physical properties.

Note
Many of these material properties are not visible until the scene is rendered. ∎

Colors

Color is probably the simplest material property and the easiest to identify. However, unlike the object color defined in the Create and Modify panels, there isn't a single color swatch that controls an object's color.

Consider a basket of shiny, red apples. When you shine a bright blue spotlight on them, all the apples turn purple because the blue highlights from the light mix with the red of the apple's surface. So, even if the apples are assigned a red material, the final color in the image might be very different because the light makes the color change.

Within the Material Editor are several different color swatches that control different aspects of the object's color. The following list describes the types of color swatches that are available for various materials:

- **Ambient:** Defines an overall background lighting that affects all objects in the scene, including the color of the object when it is in the shadows. This color is locked to the Diffuse color by default so that they are changed together.
- **Diffuse:** The surface color of the object in normal, full, white light. The normal color of an object is typically defined by its Diffuse color.
- **Specular:** The color of the highlights where the light is focused on the surface of a shiny material.
- **Self-Illumination:** The color that the object glows from within. This color takes over any shadows on the object.
- **Filter:** The transmitted color caused by light shining through a transparent object.
- **Reflect:** The color reflected by a raytrace material to other objects in the scene.
- **Luminosity:** Causes an object to glow with the defined color. It is similar to Self-Illumination color but can be independent of the Diffuse color.

Note

Standard materials don't have Reflectivity and Luminosity color swatches, but these swatches are part of the raytrace material. ■

If you ask someone the color of an object, he or she would respond by identifying the Diffuse color, but all these properties play an important part in bringing a sense of realism to the material. Try applying very different, bright materials to each of these color swatches and notice the results. This gives a sense of the contribution of each color.

Tip

For realistic materials, your choice of colors depends greatly on the scene lights. Indoor lights have a result different from an outdoor light like the sun. You can simulate objects in direct sunlight by giving their Specular color a yellow tint and their Ambient color a complementary, dark, almost black or purple color. For indoor objects, make the Specular color bright white and use an Ambient color that is the same as the Diffuse color, only much darker. Another option is to change the light colors instead of changing the specular colors. ■

Opacity and transparency

Opaque objects are objects that you cannot see through, such as rocks and trees. Transparent objects, on the other hand, are objects that you can see through, such as glass and clear plastic. Max's materials include several controls for adjusting these properties, including Opacity and several Transparency controls.

Opacity is the amount that an object refuses to allow light to pass through it. It is the opposite of transparency and is typically measured as a percentage. An object with 0 percent opacity is completely transparent, and an object with 100 percent opacity doesn't let any light through.

Transparency is the amount of light that is allowed to pass through an object. Because this is the opposite of opacity, transparency can be defined by the opacity value. Several options enable you to control transparency, including Falloff, Amount, and Type. These options are discussed later in this chapter.

Reflection and refraction

A *reflection* is what you see when you look in the mirror. Shiny objects reflect their surroundings. By defining a material's reflection values, you can control how much it reflects its surroundings. A mirror, for example, reflects everything, but a rock won't reflect at all.

Reflection Dimming controls how much of the original reflection is lost as the surroundings are reflected within the scene.

Refraction is the bending of light as it moves through a transparent material. The amount of refraction that a material produces is expressed as a value called the Index of Refraction. The *Index of Refraction* is the amount that light bends as it goes through a transparent object. For example, a diamond bends light more than a glass of water, so it has a higher Index of Refraction value. The default Index of Refraction value is 1.0 for objects that don't bend light at all. Water has a value of 1.3, glass a value of around 1.5, and solid crystal a value of around 2.0.

Shininess and specular highlights

Shiny objects, such as polished metal or clean windows, include highlights where the lights reflect off their surfaces. These highlights are called *specular highlights* and are determined by the Specular settings. These settings include Specular Level, Glossiness, and Soften values.

The Specular Level is a setting for the intensity of the highlight. The Glossiness determines the size of the highlight: Higher Glossiness values result in a smaller highlight. The Soften value thins the highlight by lowering its intensity and increasing its size.

A rough material has the opposite properties of a shiny material and almost no highlights. The Roughness property sets how quickly the Diffuse color blends with the Ambient color. Cloth and fabric materials have a high Roughness value; plastic and metal Roughness values are low.

Note

Specularity is one of the most important properties that we sense to determine what kind of material the object is made from. For example, metallic objects have a specular color that is the same as their diffuse color. If the colors are different, then the objects look like plastic instead of metal. ■

Other properties

Max uses several miscellaneous properties to help define standard materials, including Diffuse Level and Metalness.

The Diffuse Level property controls the brightness of the Diffuse color. Decreasing this value darkens the material without affecting the specular highlights. The Metalness property controls the metallic look of the material. Some properties are available only for certain material types.

Note

Before proceeding, you need to understand the difference between a material and a map. A material is an effect that permeates the 3D object, but most maps are 2D images (although procedural 3D maps also exist) that can be wrapped on top of the object. Materials can contain maps, and maps can be made up of several materials. In the Material Editor, materials appear as blue nodes, and maps appear as green nodes in the View pane. Usually, you can tell whether you're working with a material or a map by looking at the default name. Maps show up in the name drop-down list as Map and a number (Map #1), and materials are named a number and Default (7- Default). ■

Working with the Slate Material Editor

The Material Editor is the interface with which you define, create, and apply materials. You can access the Material Editor by choosing Rendering ⇨ Material Editor ⇨ Slate Material Editor, clicking the Material Editor button on the main toolbar, or using the M keyboard shortcut.

The Material Editor comes in two flavors: regular and extra strength. The Material Editor from previous versions of Max is still there, but now it is called the Compact Material Editor, and the new Material Editor interface is called the Slate interface. You can choose either from the Rendering ⇨ Material Editor menu or switch between them using the Modes menu in the Material Editor.

Note

Although the Slate Editor and the Compact Material Editor share most controls, the Slate Material Editor has more features and is the focus of our discussion. The Compact Material Editor is maintained for backward compatibility and is easier to use for existing users. ■

Note

You can find coverage of the Compact Material Editor as a bonus chapter on the book's CD. ■

Using the Slate Material Editor controls

The Slate Material Editor, shown in Figure 15.1, consists of four panels: the Material/Map Browser panel, the Material Node View panel, the Navigator panel, and the Parameter Editor panel. Of these panels, only the Material View panel is open at all times. The others can be closed and reopened using the Tools menu. If you drag the panel title away from the interface, the panel floats independently. If you drag a floating panel over the interface, several arrow icons appear. Dropping a panel on one of these arrows positions the floating panel to the side of the panel in the direction of the arrow. This interface gives you the power to set up the Slate Material Editor just as you want.

Tip

You also can use a keyboard shortcut to show or hide the various panels: O for the Material/Map Browser, P for the Parameter Editor, and N for the Navigator panel. ■

At the top of the default Slate Material Editor window is a menu of options. The menu commands found in these menus offer most of the same functionality as the toolbar buttons, but the menus are often easier to find than the buttons with which you are unfamiliar.

Below the menus are several toolbar buttons. These buttons are defined in Table 15.1.

FIGURE 15.1

The Slate Material Editor has four unique panels.

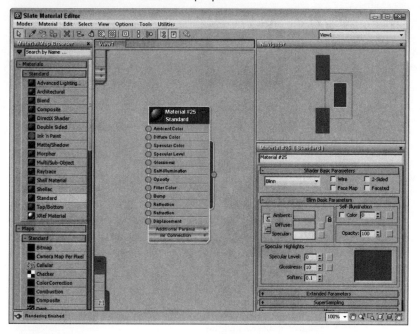

TABLE 15.1

Slate Material Editor Buttons

Toolbar Button	Name	Description
	Select Tool	Enables a tool for selecting, moving, and working with material trees and nodes.
	Pick Material From Object	Enables you to select a material from an object in the scene and load the material into the Node View panel.
	Put Material to Scene	If a new material is created with the same name as an applied material, then this command replaces the applied material with the new one.
	Assign Material to Selection	Applies the selected object with the selected material.
	Delete Selection	Removes any modified properties and resets the material properties to their defaults. The selected node is also deleted from the Node View panel.
	Move Children	Locks the position of the children nodes so they move with the material block. If disabled, the children nodes remain in place as the material block moves.

continued

TABLE 15.1	(continued)	
Toolbar Button	**Name**	**Description**
	Hide Unused Nodeslots	Condenses the material block so that only the nodes that are being used are visible.
	Show Map in Viewport, Show Hardware Map in Viewport	Displays 2D material maps and hardware maps on objects in the viewports.
	Show Background in Preview	Displays a checkered background image (or a custom background) behind the material, which is helpful when displaying a transparent material.
	Material ID Channel	Sets the Material ID for the selected material.
	Layout All - Vertical, Layout All - Horizontal	Aligns and places all material blocks in a vertical column or a horizontal row.
	Layout Children	Moves and orients all children nodes to be next to their respective material blocks.
	Material/Map Navigator	Opens the Material/Map Navigator dialog box, which displays a tree of all the levels for the current material.
	Parameter Editor	Toggles the Parameter Editor panel on and off.
	Select by Material	Selects all objects using the current material and opens the Select Objects dialog box with those objects selected.

Loading the Material Node View panel

When the Slate Material Editor is first opened, the Node View panel is blank. You can add material nodes to the node view by double-clicking them in the Material/Map Browser or by dragging them from the Material/Map Browser onto the Node View panel. This loads the selected node into the Node View.

If your scene has some objects with materials already applied, you can use the Material ➪ Pick from Object menu or select the eyedropper tool on the toolbar and click an object in the viewport. The applied material for that object is loaded in the Node View. If the selected object doesn't have an applied material, then nothing is loaded.

You can also get all the applied materials in the current scene using the Material ➪ Get All Scene Materials menu. This loads all applied materials. If all the scene materials make it tough to find what you are looking for, you can use the Edit ➪ Clear View menu to clear the Node View panel. This doesn't remove any assigned materials; it only clears the Node View panel.

Navigating the Material Node View panel

All current materials for the open scene are displayed as material node blocks in the Material Node View panel of the Slate Material Editor. At the top of each material node block are the material name and type. You can change the material name using the Name field at the top of the Parameter Editor or by right-clicking the material name and selecting Rename from the pop-up menu. Beneath the material name are all the parameters that are available for this material. Each of these parameters has a corresponding parameter in the Parameter Editor panel.

If you drag the material title (where the name is located), you can move the material node block around. You also can reduce the size of the material block by clicking the Hide Unused Nodeslots button. If multiple material blocks are present, you can use the Layout All buttons to align them in a column or a row. Figure 15.2 shows some material node blocks.

FIGURE 15.2

The Material View panel can hold multiple material blocks.

Material node output socket

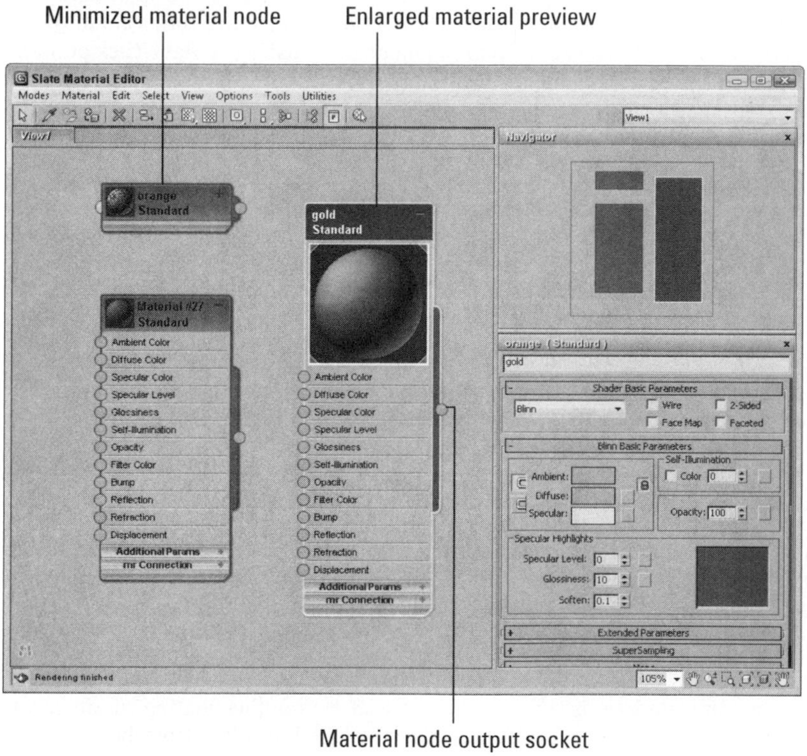

The Navigator panel shows all the material blocks and provides a way to quickly drag to view other sets of nodes. The red outline corresponds to the viewable area in the Material Node View panel. Navigating the Material Node View panel is accomplished using the navigation tools at the lower-right corner of the Slate Material Editor. These tools include a Zoom value list, and Pan, Zoom, Zoom Region, Zoom Extents, Zoom Extents Selected, and Pan to Selected tools.

Tip
You also can pan the view by dragging with the middle mouse button and zoom by scrubbing the mouse scroll wheel, just like you can in the viewports. ■

In addition to the navigation tools in the lower-right corner of the Material Editor, the View menu includes several options for navigating the Material Node View panel, including options to Show/Hide the Grid (G), show scrollbars, and options to lay out all nodes (L).

If you right-click the Node View tab, you can access a menu to rename or delete the current view. You can also create a new view. This new view appears as another tab at the top of the Material Editor. The new view is navigated independently of the other views and can hold a completely different set of materials. With several views created, you can drag the tabs to reorder the panels as desired.

Selecting and applying materials

A material node block can be selected by simply clicking its title. When selected, the title bar turns dark blue in both the Material Node View and Navigator panels. Selected materials are applied to the object selected in the viewport using the Assign Material to Selection button in the Material Editor toolbar, using the Material ⇨ Assign Material to Selection (A) menu or by using the right-click pop-up menu. You can also apply a material to a scene object by dragging on the material node's output socket and dropping the material on a viewport object whether it is selected or not.

Tip

Although they aren't listed in the menu options, you can use the Undo (Ctrl+Z) and Redo (Ctrl+Y) commands to undo and redo actions done in the Slate Material Editor.

Holding down the Ctrl key while clicking material node blocks lets you select multiple nodes at once. Pressing the Delete key deletes the selected material node.

The Material Node View panel is a temporary placeholder for materials and maps. An actual scene can have hundreds of materials. By loading a material into a material node, you can change its parameters, apply it to other objects, or save it to a library for use in other scenes. When a file is saved, all materials in the Material Editor are saved with the file.

Changing the material preview

Next to the material name is a preview of the material. If you double-click the preview, the preview is enlarged to show more detail. You can change the Sample Type object displayed in the material block to be a sphere, cylinder, or box using the Preview Object Type menu in the right-click pop-up menu.

The right-click pop-up menu also includes options to show the background in the preview, to show a backlight, and to change the preview tiling for applied maps. The Open Preview Window option opens the material preview in a separate window, as shown in Figure 15.3. Within this floating window, you can resize the preview to be larger, revealing more details. The Show End Result button shows the material with all materials and maps applied.

Tip

The Material Preview panel also can be docked to the Material Editor. ∎

When you assign a material to an object in the scene, the material becomes "hot." A *hot material* is automatically updated in the scene when the material parameters change. Hot materials have white corner brackets displayed around their material preview. You can "cool" a material by making a copy of its material block. To copy a material block, simply drag it with the Shift key held down. This detaches the material node from the object in the scene to which it is applied, so that any changes to the material aren't applied to the object.

FIGURE 15.3

Material previews can be opened in a floating window.

Show End Result

Whenever a material is applied to an object in the scene, the material is added to a special library of materials that get saved with the scene. Materials do not need to be seen in the Material Node View panel to be in the scene library. You can see all the materials included in the scene library in the Material/Map Browser by selecting the Scene Materials rollout.

Selecting objects by material

If you want to select all the objects in your scene with a specific material applied (like the shiny, gold material), then select the material in the View pane and click on the Select by Material button in the toolbar or use the Utilities ⇨ Select Objects by Material menu. This command opens the Select Objects dialog box with all the objects that have the selected material applied. Clicking the Select button selects these objects in the viewport.

Setting Slate Material Editor preferences

You open the Slate Material Editor Options dialog box, shown in Figure 15.4, by selecting the Options ⇨ Preferences menu. The top option lets you choose how the nodes are oriented. You also can select to hide the Additional Parameters and mr Connection set of parameters, use anti-aliased fonts, and set the number of default materials in a multi-subobject material and the grid spacing. The Bitmap Path Editor lets you set where to look for maps. By default, this is set to the maps directory where Max is installed, but you can change it to your current project folder.

FIGURE 15.4

The Slate Material Editor Options dialog box offers many options for controlling the Slate Material Editor window.

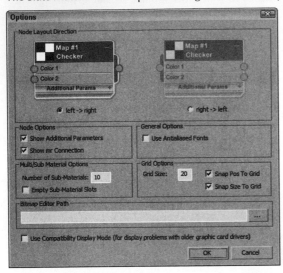

Removing materials and maps

If you accidentally apply an unwanted material to an object, you can replace the material with another material by applying a new material onto the object. If you want to view the object color within the viewport, then open the Display panel, and in the Display Color rollout, select the Object color option for Wireframe and Shaded. The Material Color options display the material color in the viewports.

If you apply a material or map to an object that doesn't look just right and tweaking it won't help, you can always return to square one by removing the material or any mappings that have been applied to the object. The tool to remove materials and maps is the UVW Remove utility. You can access this utility by clicking the More button in the Utility panel and selecting UVW Remove from the list of utilities.

This utility includes a single rollout that lists the number of objects selected. It also includes two buttons. The UVW button removes any mapping coordinates from the selected objects, and the Materials button removes any materials from the selected objects. This button restores the original object color to the selected objects. Alternatively, you can select the Set Gray option, which makes the selected object gray when the materials are removed.

Using utilities

Within the Utilities menu are several additional commands. The Render Map command lets you render out the selected map node. Once rendered, you can save the results to a file. The Render Map dialog box also lets you render out animated maps.

New Feature

The Utilities menu was previously only available in the Compact Material Editor, but in 3ds Max 2012, it is also in the Slate Material Editor. ∎

The Clean MultiMaterial utility removes any unused maps from the material tree and the Instance Duplicate Map identifies and uses instances of duplicate maps throughout the scene.

Cross-Reference

More information on using the Clean MultiMaterial utility is covered in Chapter 18, "Creating Compound Materials and Using Material Modifiers." The Instance Duplicate Map utility is presented in Chapter 17, "Adding Material Details with Maps." ∎

Using the Fix Ambient utility

Standard material types always have their Ambient and Diffuse colors locked together. If you have older files with unlocked Diffuse and Ambient colors, the Fix Ambient utility can be used to locate and fix all materials in the scene with this condition. To access this utility, open the Utilities panel, click the More button, and select the Fix Ambient utility. Clicking the Find All button opens a dialog box that lists all materials in the scene with unlocked Diffuse and Ambient colors.

Tutorial: Coloring Easter eggs

Everyone loves spring with its bright colors and newness of life. One of the highlights of the season is the tradition of coloring Easter eggs. In this tutorial, you use virtual eggs—no messy dyes and no egg salad sandwiches for the next two weeks.

To create your virtual Easter eggs and apply different colors to them, follow these steps:

1. Open the Easter eggs.max file from the Chap 15 directory on the CD.

   This file contains several egg-shaped objects.

2. Open the Slate Material Editor by choosing Rendering ⇨ Material Editor ⇨ Slate Material Editor (or press the M key).

3. Double-click the Standard material in the Material/Map Browser. Select the material node in the Node View, and click the Diffuse color swatch in the Parameter Editor panel. From the Color Selector that appears, drag the cursor around the color palette until you find the color you want and then click Close.

4. In any viewport, select an egg and then click the Assign Material to Selection button in the Material Editor, or you can simply drag from the material node's output socket to the viewport object.

5. Repeat Steps 4 and 5 for all the eggs.

Figure 15.5 shows the assortment of eggs that we just created.

FIGURE 15.5

These eggs have been assigned materials with different Diffuse colors.

Using the Material/Map Browser

Now that you know how to apply materials to objects, the easiest way to get materials is from the Material/Map Browser. Max ships with several libraries of materials that you can access. If you open the Material/Map Browser with the Tools ➪ Material/Map Browser menu, the Material/Map Browser panel appears, as shown in Figure 15.6.

Note

The Material/Map Browser can be docked to the left edge of the Slate Material Editor or pulled away from the interface as a floating dialog box. Double-click the title bar to re-dock it back to the interface.

The Material/Map Browser is the place where all your materials are stored. They are stored in sets called libraries. These libraries are saved along with the scene file or they can be saved as a separate file if you want to load and access them within a different scene. Within the Material/Map Browser, each library is contained with a separate rollout. These rollouts, called groups, hold any loaded material libraries, the available default Material and Map types, Controllers, Scene Materials, and Sample Slots, which hold the temporary material slots used by the Compact Material Editor.

FIGURE 15.6

The Material/Map Browser lets you select new materials from a library of materials.

Browser options

The text field directly above the material sample slot in the Material/Map Browser is a Search by Name field. By typing a name in this field, you can search and select materials.

Tip

When browsing materials in the Material/Map Browser, you can use the keyboard to move up and down the material list. The left and right keyboard keys are used to open and close rollouts and the Enter key adds the selected material to the View pane. ∎

Working with libraries

Any time you adjust a material or a map parameter, a new material is created and the material's sample slot is updated. Although newly created materials are saved along with the scene file, you can make them available for reuse by including them in a library.

As more and more libraries get added to the Material/Map Browser, it can be difficult to locate the specific library that you want to use. To help with this problem, you can right-click the library title and choose the Edit Color Group option. This opens a Color Selector where you can pick a color for the library rollout. There are also options for changing how the materials in the library are displayed. The options include Small, Medium and Large Icons, Icons and Text, or just Text.

The right-click pop-up menu also offers an option to create a new library. New Libraries can be saved and loaded also using the right-click pop-up menu.

Note

Max ships with several different material libraries and several architecture material sets. You can find all these libraries in the matlibs directory. Some libraries are only available when the mental ray renderer is enabled. ■

Save a layout with the current materials using the Material/Map Browser Options ⇨ Additional Options ⇨ Save Layout As. These files are saved as files with the .mpl extension.

Tip

Although materials can be saved out as libraries, perhaps the easiest ways to share materials between applications are using the Material XML Export utility or the Material ⇨ Export As XMSL File command. ■

Tutorial: Loading a custom material library

To practice loading a material library, I've created a custom library of materials using various textures created with Kai's Power Tools.

To load a custom material library into the Slate Material Editor, follow these steps:

1. Choose Rendering ⇨ Material Editor (or press the M key) to open the Material Editor. Then make sure the Material/Map Browser is active or select the Tools ⇨ Material/Map Browser menu to open the Material/Map Browser.
2. Click the small down arrow icon to the left of the Search field at the top of the Material/Map Browser and select Open Material Library from the pop-up menu.
3. Select and open the KPT samples.mat file from the Chap 15 directory on the CD.
   The library loads into the Material/Map Browser.
4. In the Search field (above the sample slot), type **Bug** to locate and select the bug eyes material.

Figure 15.7 shows the Material/Map Browser with the custom material library open.

FIGURE 15.7

The Material/Map Browser also lets you work with saved custom material libraries.

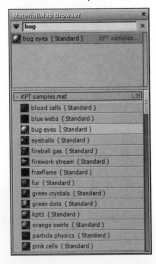

Using the Material Explorer

The Scene Explorer has been well received and has made working with scene objects much easier. So easy in fact that the Max team has looked for other places where a similar interface can be used, and the first stop is with materials. The result is the Material Explorer.

The Material Explorer, shown in Figure 15.8, lets you quickly view all the scene materials along with their hierarchies and all their properties in a single interface. It also lets you sort the materials by their various properties and even make changes to multiple materials at once. You can access the Material Explorer with the Rendering⇨ Material Explorer command.

FIGURE 15.8

The Material Explorer shows the layered material as a hierarchy.

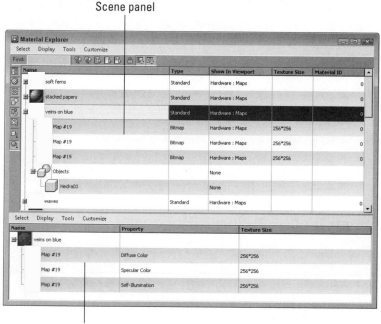

The Material Explorer works exactly like the Scene Explorer and has configurable columns. It is divided into two panels. The top panel shows all the materials in the current scene; the bottom panel shows the hierarchy of the selected material or submaterial.

In addition to the menus, several toolbar buttons run horizontally under the menus and several display buttons run vertically down the left side of the interface. These buttons are described in Tables 15.2 and 15.3.

Cross-Reference

To learn more about the Scene Explorer interface, see Chapter 6, "Selecting Objects and Setting Object Properties." ∎

TABLE 15.2

Material Explorer Display Buttons—Vertical

Toolbar Button	Name	Description
	Display Thumbnails	Displays thumbnails of the various material components as displayed in the material preview
	Display Materials	Includes materials within the hierarchy
	Display Maps	Includes maps within the material hierarchy
	Display Objects	Includes the applied object in the material hierarchy
	Display Sub-Materials/Maps	Includes any applied submaterials/ maps within the material hierarchy
	Display Unused Map Channels	Includes all unused map channels as part of the hierarchy
	Sort by Object	Sorts the materials based on the objects they are applied to and lists the materials underneath
	Sort by Material	Sorts the materials and lists the objects underneath

TABLE 15.3

Material Explorer Toolbar Buttons—Horizontal

Toolbar Button	Name	Description
Find	Find text field	Allows searching for specific named materials and maps
	Select All Materials	Selects all materials in the scene
	Select All Maps	Selects all maps in the scene
	Select All	Selects all entries in the list
	Select None	Deselects all entries in the list
	Select Invert	Inverts the current selection

Toolbar Button	Name	Description
	Lock Cell Editing	Locks all cells so they cannot be edited
	Sync to Material Explorer	Causes the material selected in the top panel to be visible in the lower panel
	Sync to Material Level	Displays the entire hierarchy for the selected material in the lower panel when enabled

The Material Explorer lets you apply materials directly to scene objects by simply dragging and dropping the material thumbnail onto the object. You also can drag and drop maps onto other materials and channels. The Material Explorer also works with the Material Browser; for example, you can drag the material type and drop it on the Type column in the Material Explorer to change a material type.

Summary

Materials can add much to the realism of your models. Learning to use the Material Editor, the Material/Map Browser, and the Material/Map Navigator enables you to work with materials. This chapter covered the following topics:

- Understanding various material properties
- Working with the Material Editor buttons and material nodes
- Using the Material/Map Browser and material libraries
- Using the Material Explorer to quickly see all materials in a scene

The next chapter delves more into the topic of material, including the standard material and all its settings.

Creating and Applying Standard Materials

N ow that you've learned the basic material properties and acquainted yourself with the Material Editor and the Material/Map Browser, this chapter gives you a chance to create some simple original materials and apply them to objects in the scene. The simplest material is based on the Standard material type, which is the default material type.

Using the Standard Material

Standard materials are the default Max material type. They provide a single, uniform color determined by the Ambient, Diffuse, Specular, and Filter color swatches. Standard materials can use any one of several different shaders. *Shaders* are algorithms used to compute how the material should look, given its parameters.

Standard materials have parameters for controlling highlights, opacity, and self-illumination. They also include many other parameters sprinkled throughout many different rollouts. With all the various rollouts, even a standard material has an infinite number of possibilities.

Using Shading Types

Max includes several different shader types. These shaders are all available in a drop-down list in the Shader Basic Parameters rollout at the top of the Parameter Editor panel in the Slate Material Editor. The Slate Material Editor is opened using the Rendering ⇨ Material Editor ⇨ Slate Material Editor menu command or by pressing the M key. Each shader type displays different options in its respective Basic Parameters rollout. Figure 16.1

shows the basic parameters for the Blinn shader. Other available shaders include Anisotropic, Metal, Multi-Layer, Oren-Nayar-Blinn, Phong, Strauss, and Translucent Shader.

Cross-Reference

The Material/Map Browser holds all the various material types. The other material types are covered in Chapter 18, "Creating Compound Materials and Using Material Modifiers," and Chapter 30, "Using Specialized Material Types." ■

The Shader Basic Parameters rollout also includes several options for shading the material, including Wire, 2-Sided, Face Map, and Faceted, as shown in Figure 16.1. Wire mode causes the model to appear as a wireframe model. The 2-Sided option makes the material appear on both sides of the face and is typically used in conjunction with the Wire option or with transparent materials. The Face Map mode applies maps to each single face on the object. Faceted ignores the smoothing between faces.

Note

Using the Wire option or the 2-Sided option is different from the wireframe display option in the viewports. The Wire and 2-Sided options define how the object looks when rendered. ■

FIGURE 16.1

Basic parameter options include (from left to right) Wire, 2-Sided, Face Map, and Faceted.

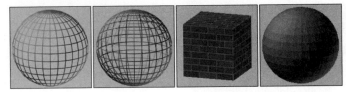

Blinn shader

This shader is the default. It renders simple circular highlights and smoothes adjacent faces.

The Blinn shader includes color swatches for setting Ambient, Diffuse, Specular, and Self-Illumination colors. To change the color, click the color swatch and select a new color in the Color Selector dialog box.

Note

You can drag colors among the various color swatches. When you do so, the Copy or Swap Colors dialog box appears, which enables you to copy or swap the colors. ■

You can use the Lock buttons to the left of the color swatches to lock the colors together so that both colors are identical and a change to one automatically changes the other. You can lock Ambient to Diffuse and Diffuse to Specular.

The small, square buttons to the right of the Ambient, Diffuse, Specular, Self-Illumination, Opacity, Specular Level, and Glossiness controls are shortcut buttons for adding a map in place of the respective parameter. Clicking these buttons opens the Material/Map Browser, where you can select the map type. You can also lock the Ambient and Diffuse maps together with the lock icon to the right of the map buttons. The Ambient and Diffuse colors are locked together by default.

When a map is loaded and active, it appears in the Maps rollout, and an uppercase letter *M* appears on its button. When a map is loaded but inactive, a lowercase *m* appears. After you apply a map, these buttons open to make the map the active level and display its parameters in the rollouts. Figure 16.2 shows these map buttons.

Cross-Reference

For more on maps and the various map types, see Chapter 17, "Adding Material Details with Maps." ■

FIGURE 16.2

The Blinn Basic Parameters rollout lets you select and control properties for the Blinn shader.

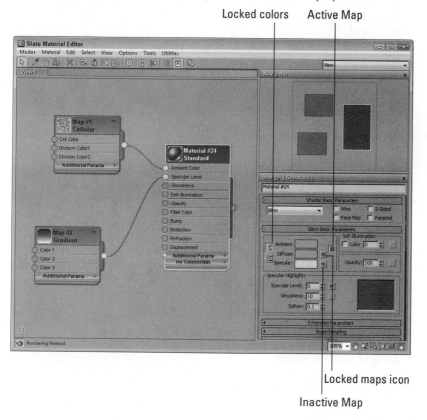

Locked colors   Active Map

Locked maps icon

Inactive Map

Self-Illumination can use a color if the Color option is enabled. If this option is disabled, a spinner appears that enables you to adjust the amount of default color used for illumination. Materials with a Self-Illumination value of 100 or a bright color like white lose all shadows and appear to glow from within. This happens because the self-illumination color replaces the ambient color, but a material with self-illumination can still have specular highlights. To remove the effect of Self-Illumination, set the spinner to 0 or the color to black. Figure 16.3 shows a sphere with Self-Illumination values (from left to right) of 0, 25, 50, 75, and 100.

Increasing the Self-Illumination value reduces the shadows in an object.

The Opacity spinner sets the level of transparency of an object. A value of 100 makes a material completely opaque, while a value of 0 makes the material completely transparent. Use the Background button (located on the upper-right side of the Material Editor) to enable a patterned background image to make it easier to view the effects of the Opacity setting. Figure 16.4 shows materials with Opacity values of 10, 25, 50, 75, and 90.

The Opacity value sets how transparent a material is.

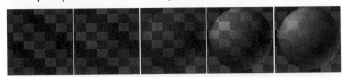

Specular highlights are the bright points on the surface where the light is reflected at a maximum value. The Specular Level value determines how bright the highlight is. Its values can range from 0, where there is no highlight, to 100, where the highlight is at a maximum. The graph to the right of the values displays the intensity per distance for a cross section of the highlight. The Specular Level defines the height of the curve or the value at the center of the highlight where it is the brightest. This value can be overloaded to accept numbers greater than 100. Overloaded values create a larger, wider highlight.

The Glossiness value determines the size of the highlight. A value of 100 produces a pinpoint highlight, and a value of 0 increases the highlight to the edges of the graph. The Soften value doesn't affect the graph, but it spreads the highlight across the area defined by the Glossiness value. It can range from 0 (wider) to 1 (thinner). Figure 16.5 shows a sampling of materials with specular highlights. The left image has a Specular Level of 20 and a Glossiness of 10, the second image has the Specular Level increased to 80, the third image has the Specular Level overloaded with a value of 150, and the last two images have the Glossiness value increased to 50 and 80, respectively.

You can control specular highlights by altering brightness and size.

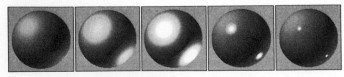

Phong shader

The Phong shader creates smooth surfaces like Blinn without the quality highlights, but it renders more quickly than the Blinn shader does. The parameters for the Phong shader are identical to those for the Blinn shader. The differences between Blinn and Phong are very subtle, but Blinn can produce highlights for lights at low angles to the surface, and its highlights are generally softer.

Tip

The Blinn shader is typically used to simulate softer materials like rubber, but the Phong shader is better for hard materials like plastic. ■

Anisotropic shader

The Anisotropic shader is characterized by noncircular highlights. The Anisotropy value is the difference between the two axes that make up the highlight. A value of 0 is circular, but higher values increase the difference between the axes, and the highlights are more elliptical.

Most of the parameters for this shader are the same as those for the Blinn shader, but several parameters of the Anisotropic type are unique. The Diffuse Level value determines how bright the Diffuse color appears. This is similar to Self-Illumination, but it doesn't affect the specular highlights or the shadows. Values can range from 0 to 400.

Compared with the Blinn shader, the Specular Highlight graph looks very different. That is because it displays two highlight components that intersect at the middle. The Specular Level value still controls the height of the curve, and the Glossiness still controls the width, but the Anisotropy value changes the width of one axis relative to the other, creating elliptical highlights. The Orientation value rotates the highlight. Figure 16.6 compares the Specular Highlight graphs for the Blinn and Anisotropic shaders.

Tip

Because the Anisotropy shader can produce elliptical highlights, it is often used on surfaces with strong grooves and strands, like fabrics and stainless steel objects. ■

FIGURE 16.6

The Specular Highlight graph for the Blinn and Anisotropic shaders

Figure 16.7 shows several materials with the Anisotropic shader applied. The first three images have Anisotropic values of 30, 60, and 90, and the last two images have Orientation values of 30 and 60.

FIGURE 16.7

Materials with the Anisotropic shader applied have elliptical highlights.

Multi-Layer shader

The Multi-Layer shader includes two Anisotropic highlights. Each of these highlights can have a different color. All parameters for this shader are the same as the Anisotropic shader described previously, except that there are two Specular Layers and one additional parameter: Roughness. The Roughness parameter defines how well the Diffuse color blends into the Ambient color. When Roughness is set to a value of 0, an object appears the same as with the Blinn shader, but with higher values, up to 100, the material grows darker.

Figure 16.8 shows several materials with a Multi-Layer shader applied. The first two images have two specular highlights, each with an Orientation value of 60 and Anisotropy values of 60 and 90. The third image has an increased Specular Level of 110 and a decrease in the Glossiness to 10. The fourth image has a change in the Orientation value for one of the highlights to 20, and the final image has a drop in the Anisotropy value to 10.

Tip

The Multi-Layer shader is useful to give a material a sense of surface depth. For example, it can give the illusion of a layer of shellac on wood or a layer of wax on tile. ■

FIGURE 16.8

Materials with a Multi-Layer shader applied can have two crossing highlights.

Oren-Nayar-Blinn shader

The Oren-Nayar-Blinn shader is useful for creating materials for matte surfaces such as cloth and fabric. The parameters are identical to the Blinn shader, with the addition of the Diffuse Level and Roughness values.

Metal shader

The Metal shader simulates the luster of metallic surfaces. The Highlight curve has a shape that is different from that of the other shaders. It is rounder at the top and doesn't include a Soften value. It can also accept a much higher Specular Level value (up to 999) than the other shaders. Also, you cannot specify a Specular color. All other parameters are similar to those of the Blinn shader. Figure 16.9 shows several materials with the Metal shader applied. These materials differ in Specular Level values, which are (from left to right) 50, 100, 200, 400, and 800.

Note

For the Metal shader, the specular color is always the same as the material's diffuse color. ■

FIGURE 16.9

A material with a Metal shader applied generates its own highlights.

Strauss shader

The Strauss shader provides another alternative for creating metal materials. This shader has only four parameters: Color, Glossiness, Metalness, and Opacity. Glossiness controls the entire highlight shape. The Metalness value makes the material appear more metal-like by affecting the primary and secondary highlights. Both of these values can range between 0 and 100.

Tip

The Strauss shader is often better at making metal than the Metal shader because of its smoothness value and the ability to mix colors with the Metalness property. ■

Translucent shader

The Translucent shader allows light to easily pass through an object. It is intended to be used on thin, flat plane objects, such as a bedsheet used for displaying shadow puppets. Most of the settings for this shader are the same as the others, except that it includes a Translucent color. This color is the color that the light becomes as it passes through an object with this material applied. This shader also includes a Filter color and an option for disabling the specular highlights on the backside of the object.

Tutorial: Making curtains translucent

The Translucent shader can be used to create an interesting effect. Not only does light shine through an object with this shader applied, but shadows also are visible.

To make window curtains translucent, follow these steps:

1. Open the Translucent curtains.max file from the Chap 16 directory on the CD.

   This file contains a simple scene of a tree positioned outside a window.

2. Open the Material Editor by choosing Rendering ⇨ Material Editor ⇨ Slate Material Editor, by clicking the Material Editor button on the main toolbar, or by pressing the M key.

3. In the Material/Map Browser panel of the Material Editor, double-click on the Standard material, then select the material block node, and in the Name field, name the material **Curtains**. Select the Translucent Shader from the Shader Basic Parameters rollout. Click the Diffuse color swatch, and select a light blue color. Click the Close button to exit the Color Selector.

4. Click the Translucent Color swatch, change its color to a light gray, and set the Opacity to **75**.

5. Drag the Curtains material's output node socket onto the curtain object in the Left viewport or select the curtains in the viewport and use the Assign Material to Selection button in the toolbar.

Figure 16.10 shows the resulting image. Notice that the tree's shadow is cast on the curtains.

FIGURE 16.10

These translucent window curtains show shadows.

Accessing Other Parameters

In addition to the basic shader parameters, several other rollouts of options can add to the look of a material.

Extended Parameters rollout

The Material Editor includes several settings, in addition to the basic parameters, that are common for most shaders. The Extended Parameters rollout, shown in Figure 16.11, includes Advanced Transparency, Reflection Dimming, and Wire controls. All shaders include these parameters.

You can use the Advanced Transparency controls to set the Falloff to be In, Out, or a specified Amount. The In option increases the transparency as you get farther inside the object, and the Out option does the opposite. The Amount value sets the transparency for the inner or outer edge. Figure 16.12 shows two materials that use the Transparency Falloff options on a gray background and on a patterned background. The two materials on the left use the In option, and the two on the right use the Out option. Both are set at Amount values of 100.

FIGURE 16.11

The Extended Parameters rollout includes Advanced Transparency, Reflection Dimming, and Wire settings.

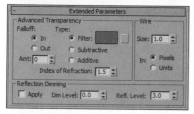

Tip

If you look closely at a glass sphere, you'll notice that the glass is thicker when you look through the edge of the sphere than through the sphere's center. This can be created using the In option in the Advanced Transparency section. ∎

FIGURE 16.12

Materials with the In and Out Falloff options applied

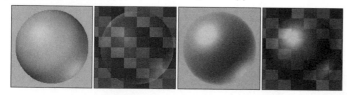

The three transparency types are Filter, Subtractive, and Additive. The Filter type multiplies the Filter color with any color surface that appears behind the transparent object. With this option, you can select a Filter color to use. The Subtractive and Additive types subtract from or add to the color behind the transparent object.

The Index of Refraction is a measure of the amount of distortion caused by light passing through a transparent object. Different physical materials have different Index of Refraction values. The amount of distortion also depends on the thickness of the transparent object. The Index of Refraction for water is 1.33 and for glass is 1.5. The default of 1.0 has no effect.

The Wire section lets you specify a wire size or thickness. Use this setting if the Wire option or the 2-Sided option is enabled in the Shaders Basic Parameters rollout. The size can be measured in either Pixels or Units. Figure 16.13 shows materials with different Wire values from 1 to 5 pixels.

FIGURE 16.13

Three materials with Wire values of (from left to right) 1, 2, 3, 4, and 5 pixels

Reflection Dimming controls how intense a reflection is. You enable it by using the Apply option. The Dim Level setting controls the intensity of the reflection within a shadow, and the Refl Level sets the intensity for all reflections not in the shadow.

SuperSampling rollout

Pixels are small square dots that collectively make up the entire screen. At the edges of objects where the material color changes from the object to the background, these square pixels can cause jagged edges to appear. These edges are called *artifacts* and can ruin an image. *Anti-aliasing* is the process through which these artifacts are removed by softening the transition between colors.

Max includes anti-aliasing filters as part of the rendering process. SuperSampling is an additional anti-aliasing pass that can improve image quality that is applied at the material level. You have several SuperSampling methods from which to choose. The SuperSampling method can be defined in the Material Editor, or you can choose the settings in the Default Scanline Renderer rollout of the Render Scene dialog box by enabling the Use Global Settings option.

Note

Anti-aliasing happens before raytracing when rendering, so even if the anti-aliasing option is enabled, the reflections and/or refractions will still be aliased. ■

Cross-Reference

For more about the various anti-aliasing filters, see Chapter 23, "Rendering a Scene and Enabling Quicksilver." ■

SuperSampling is calculated only if the Anti-Aliasing option in the Render Scene dialog box is enabled. The raytrace material type has its own SuperSampling pass that is required in order to get clean reflections.

Note

Using SuperSampling can greatly increase the time it takes to render an image. ■

In a SuperSampling pass, the colors at different points around the center of a pixel are sampled. These samples are then used to compute the final color of each pixel. The SuperSampling settings can be set globally in the Render Setup dialog box or for each material individually by disabling the Use Global Settings option. These four SuperSampling methods are available:

- **Adaptive Halton:** Takes semirandom samples along both the pixel's X-axis and Y-axis. It takes from 4 to 40 samples.
- **Adaptive Uniform:** Takes samples at regular intervals around the pixel's center. It takes from 4 to 26 samples.

- **Hammersley:** Takes samples at regular intervals along the X-axis, but takes random samples along the Y-axis. It takes from 4 to 40 samples.
- **Max 2.5 Star:** Takes four samples along each axis.

The first three methods enable you to select a Quality setting. This setting specifies the number of samples to be taken. The more samples taken, the higher the resolution, but the longer it takes to render. The two Adaptive methods (Adaptive Halton and Adaptive Uniform) offer an Adaptive option with a Threshold spinner. This option takes more samples if the change in color is within the Threshold value. The SuperSample Texture option includes maps in the SuperSampling process along with materials.

Tip

To get good reflections and refractions, enable SuperSampling for final renders. ■

Maps rollout

A *map* is a bitmap image that is wrapped about an object. The Maps rollout includes a list of the maps that you can apply to an object. Using this rollout, you can enable or disable maps, specify the intensity of the map in the Amount field, and load maps. Clicking the Map buttons opens the Material/Map Browser where you can select the map type.

Cross-Reference

Find out more about maps in Chapter 17, "Adding Material Details with Maps." ■

Caution

These dynamic properties are used only with the Dynamic utility. reactor is a more versatile and robust dynamics solution, making these properties obsolete; they are included only for backward compatibility. ■

DirectX Manager rollout

The DirectX Manager rollout lets you display the current material in the viewport as a DirectX shader when the DX Display of Standard Material option is enabled. The current material also can be saved as an .fx material file. Many game engines render using DirectX, so this option lets you view your materials in the viewport as they will appear within the game.

Caution

The DirectX Manager rollout isn't available by default. It appears only when the Direct3D display driver is selected. ■

At the bottom of the DirectX Manager rollout is a drop-down list for selecting to use the available DirectX shaders. The two available DirectX shaders are LightMap and Metal Bump 9. These shaders are generic, so they can be used on many different types of objects. The Light Map shader includes a parameter for loading a custom light map, and the Metal Bump 9 shader includes parameters for specifying two texture maps; specularity; and normal, bump, and reflection maps.

mental ray connection rollout

The mental ray connection rollout includes options for enabling different properties that are used by the mental ray rendering engine. The properties include Surface and Shadow Shaders, Photon and Photon Volume, and Extended Shaders and Advanced Shaders, including Contour and Light Map.

Cross-Reference

The mental ray rendering engine and its properties are covered in Chapter 47, "Rendering with mental ray and iray." ■

Tutorial: Coloring a dolphin

As a quick example of applying materials, you'll take a dolphin model created by Zygote Media and position it over a watery plane. You then apply custom materials to both objects.

To add materials to a dolphin, follow these steps:

1. Open the Dolphin.max file from the Chap 16 directory on the CD.

   This file contains a simple plane object and a dolphin mesh.

2. Open the Material Editor by choosing Rendering ⇨ Material Editor ⇨ Slate Material Editor, clicking the Material Editor button on the main toolbar, or pressing the M key.

3. In the Material/Map Browser panel, double-click on the Standard material; select the standard material block and, in the Name field in the Parameter Editor panel, rename the material **Dolphin Skin**. Click the Diffuse color swatch, and select a light gray color. Then click the Specular color swatch, and select a light yellow color. Click the Close button to exit the Color Selector. In the Specular Highlights section, increase the Specular Level to **45**.

4. Double-click on the Standard material in the Material/Map Browser again and name it **Ocean Surface**. Click the Diffuse color swatch, and select a light blue color. Set the Specular Level and Opacity values to **80**. In the Maps rollout, click the None button to the right of the Bump selection. In the Material/Map Browser that opens, double-click the Noise selection in the Maps rollout. Click on the Noise map button to access the Noise parameters, and then enable the Fractal option and set the Size value to **15** in the Noise Parameters rollout.

5. Select the dolphin body in the viewport and, with the Dolphin Skin material selected in the Material Editor, click the Assign Material to Selection button in the Material Editor toolbar. Then do the same for the ocean surface.

Note

This model also includes separate objects for the eyes, mouth, and tongue. These objects could have different materials applied to them, but they are so small in this image that you won't worry about them. ■

6. Choose Rendering ⇨ Environment (keyboard shortcut, 8), click the Background Color swatch, and change it to a light sky blue.

Figure 16.14 shows the resulting image.

A dolphin over the water with applied materials

Summary

This chapter presented the Standard material and gave you a chance to create some simple original materials.

In this chapter, you did the following:

- Learned about various material types
- Discovered and learned to use the various material parameters
- Discovered the basics of using standard materials
- Learned how to use the various shaders
- Explored the other Material rollouts
- Learned to apply materials to a model

This chapter should have been enough to whet your appetite for materials, and yet it really covered only one part of the equation. The other critical piece for materials is maps, and you'll dive into those in the next chapter.

Adding Material Details with Maps

In addition to using materials, another way to enhance an object is to use a map—but not a roadmap. In Max, maps are bitmaps, with patterns that can be applied to the surface of an object. Some maps wrap an image onto objects, but others, such as displacement and bump maps, modify the surface based on the map's intensity. For example, you can use a diffuse map to add a label to a soup can, or a bump map to add some texture to the surface of an orange.

Several external tools can be very helpful when you create texture maps. These tools include an image-editing package such as Photoshop, a digital camera, and a scanner. With these tools, you can create and capture bitmap images that can be applied as materials to the surface of the object.

Understanding Maps

To understand a material map, think of this example. Cut the label off of a soup can, scan it into the computer, and save the image as a bitmap. You can then create a cylinder with roughly the same dimensions as the can, load the scanned label image as a material map, and apply it to the cylinder object to simulate the original soup can.

Different map types

Different types of maps exist. Some maps wrap images about objects, while others define areas to be modified by comparing the intensity of the pixels in the map. An example of this is a *bump map*. A standard bump map would be a grayscale image—when mapped onto an object, lighter-colored sections would be raised to a maximum of pure white; darker sections would be those regions where a minimal bump or no bump is applied. This enables you to easily create surface textures, such as the rivets on the side of machine, without having to model them.

IN THIS CHAPTER

Understanding mapping

Connecting maps to material nodes

Exploring all the map types including 2D and 3D maps, compositors, color modifiers, and others

Applying maps to material properties using the Maps rollout

Using the Bitmap Path Editor

Creating textures with Photoshop

Still other uses for maps include background images called *environment* maps and *projection* maps that are used with lights.

Cross-Reference

For information on environment maps, see Chapter 23, "Rendering a Scene and Enabling Quicksilver." Chapter 20, "Using Lights and Basic Lighting Techniques," covers projection maps. ■

Maps that are used to create materials are all applied using the Material Editor. The Material/Map Browser provides access to all the available maps. These maps have many common features.

Enabling the global viewport rendering setting

To see applied maps in the viewports, select the Show Standard Map in Viewport button in the Material Editor or enable all scene maps with the Views ⇨ Show Materials in Viewport As ⇨ Shaded Display with Maps menu command.

For more accurate maps that show highlights, you can enable the Views ⇨ Show Materials in Viewport As ⇨ Hardware Display with Maps option. This is especially helpful when the scene objects use the Arch & Design materials. Hardware rendering in the viewport is available only when the Direct3D display driver is being used and if you are using a video card that supports hardware rendering.

Using Real-World maps

When maps are applied to scene objects, they are applied based on the object's UV coordinates, which control the size of the applied map. But, each bitmap can be sized along each axis to stretch the map over the surface. Another way to stretch a texture map is to resize the geometric object that the map is applied to. This is the default behavior of maps, but another option is available.

When a geometric object is created, you can enable the Real-World Map Size, which is generally next to the Generate Mapping Coords option. This option is also available when the UVW Mapping modifier is applied to an object. When enabled, this option lets you specify the size of the applied texture using scene units. When this option is enabled, it causes the texture maps to maintain their sizes as geometry objects are resized. Set the dimensions of applied texture maps in the Coordinates rollout.

Tip

You can select to have Real-World mapping enabled for all new objects by default by enabling the Use Real-World Texture Coordinates option in the General panel of the Preference Settings dialog box. ■

Working with Maps

Maps are typically used along with materials. You can open most material maps from the Material/Map Browser. To open the Material/Map Browser if it isn't visible in the Slate Material Editor, select the Tools ⇨ Material/Map Browser menu or press the O key in the Slate Material Editor. You also can open the Material/Map Browser by clicking any of the map buttons found throughout the Parameter Editor panel, including those found in the Maps rollout. Figure 17.1 shows this browser with its available maps.

In the Material/Map Browser all available maps are displayed by default in the Maps/Standard rollout, but if you have the Quicksilver Hardware or the mental ray renderer enabled, rollouts for mental ray maps and MetaSL maps are also displayed. If you right-click within the Material/Map Browser away from any rollouts and choose the Show Incompatible option from the pop-up menu, all map rollouts including mental ray maps are displayed even if the mental ray renderer isn't enabled.

FIGURE 17.1

Use the Material/Map Browser to list all the maps available for assigning to materials.

To load a map node into the Node View panel of the Slate Material Editor, simply double-click on it or drag the material from the Material/Map Browser to the Node View panel. All map nodes are easily identified by their green title bars in the Node View and Navigator panels.

Connecting maps to materials

A map by itself in the Node View panel cannot be applied to objects in the scene. To add a map to a material it must be connected to one of the material properties. This is done by dragging on the map node's output socket and dropping the connecting line on the input socket for the material property where the map is being applied. For example, Figure 17.2 shows a connection between the Checker map node and the Standard material node's Diffuse Color. Once a connection is made, the material preview is updated to show that the applied map and the sockets at either end of the connection are highlighted green.

Tip

If you drag from a map node's output socket and drop anywhere on the blank Node View, a pop-up menu lets you choose to select and create a material, map, controller, or sample slot material node. ∎

FIGURE 17.2

Map nodes need to be connected to material properties in order to show up in the material.

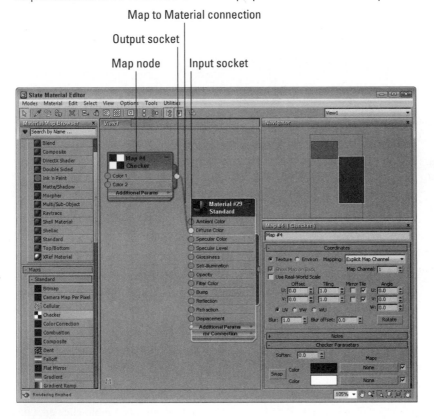

Note

When some maps are connected to a material node, a Controller node also appears. This controller node provides a way to animate the material's parameters. More on animating materials is covered in Chapter 21, "Understanding Animation and Keyframes." ∎

Double-clicking the map node's title opens the map's parameters in the Parameter Editor. Maps also can be applied by clicking on a map button in the Parameter Editor and selecting a map type from the Material/Map Browser that opens.

A single map node can be connected to several different material parameters on the same or on different nodes. Map nodes can also be connected to other map nodes. For example, Figure 17.3 shows a Marble and a Noise map connected to a Checker map node, which is connected to a standard material node.

FIGURE 17.3

Map nodes also can be connected to other map nodes.

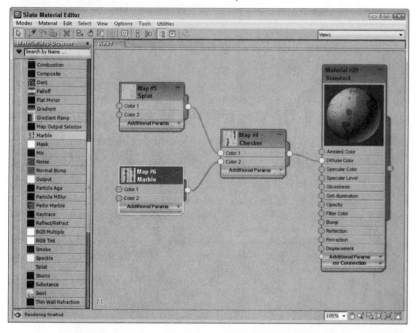

To disconnect a map from a material node, simply select the connection line and press the Delete key. This removes the connection but leaves both the map and material nodes in place.

Understanding Map Types

Within the Material/Map Browser is a wide variety of different map types. Understanding these maps and their parameters enables you to create lots of different materials.

Note

In previous versions of Max, the maps were divided into several different groups including 2D Maps, 3D Maps, Compositors, Color Mods, and Other, but now all maps are in the same group within the Material/Maps Browser. ■

2D maps

A two-dimensional map can be wrapped onto the surface of an object or used as an environment map for a scene's background image. Because they have no depth, 2D maps appear only on the surface. The Bitmap map is perhaps the most common 2D map. It enables you to load any image, which can be wrapped around an object's surface in a number of different ways.

Many maps have several rollouts in common. These include Coordinates, Noise, and Time. In addition to these rollouts, each individual map type has its own parameters rollout.

The Coordinates rollout

Every map that is applied to an object needs to have mapping coordinates that define how the map lines up with the object. For example, with the soup can label example mentioned earlier, you probably would want to align the top edge of the label with the top edge of the can, but you could position the top edge of the map at the middle of the can. Mapping coordinates define where the map's upper-right corner is located on the object.

All map coordinates are based on a UVW coordinate system that equates to the familiar XYZ coordinate system, except that it is named uniquely so as not to be confused with transformation coordinates. For UVW coordinates, U represents the horizontal coordinate, V is the vertical coordinate, and W is along the surface normal. To keep them straight, remember that the UVW coordinate system applies to surfaces and that the XYZ coordinate system applies to spatial objects. These coordinates are required for every object to which a map is applied. In most cases, you can generate these coordinates automatically when you create an object by selecting the Generate Mapping Coordinates option in the object's Parameter rollout.

Note

Editable meshes don't have any default mapping coordinates, but you can generate mapping coordinates using the UVW Map modifier. ■

In the Coordinates rollout for 2D Maps, shown in Figure 17.4, you can specify whether the map will be a texture map or an environment map. The Texture option applies the map to the surface of an object as a texture. This texture moves with the object as the object moves. The Environ option creates an environment map. Environment maps are locked to the world and not to an object. This causes the texture to change as the object is moved. Moving an object with an environment map applied to it scrolls the map across the surface of the object.

FIGURE 17.4

The Coordinates rollout lets you offset and tile a map.

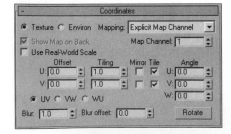

Different mapping types are available for both the Texture and Environ options. Mapping types for the Texture option include Explicit Map Channel, Vertex Color Channel, Planar from Object XYZ, and Planar from World XYZ. The Explicit Map Channel option is the default. It applies the map using the designated Map Channel. The Vertex Color Channel uses specified vertex colors as its channel. The two planar mapping types place the map in a plane based on the Local or World coordinate systems.

The Environ option includes Spherical Environment, Cylindrical Environment, Shrink-Wrap Environment, and Screen mapping types. The Spherical Environment mapping type is applied as if the entire scene were contained within a giant sphere. The same applies for the Cylindrical Environment mapping type, except that the shape is a cylinder. The Shrink-Wrap Environment plasters the map directly on the scene as if it were covering it like a blanket. All four corners of the bitmap are pulled together to the back of the wrapped object. The Screen mapping type just projects the map flatly on the background.

The Show Map on Back option causes planar maps to project through the object and be rendered on the object's back.

The U and V coordinates define the X and Y positions for the map. For each coordinate, you can specify an Offset value, which is the distance from the origin. The Tiling value is the number of times to repeat the image and is used only if the Tile option is selected. If the Use Real-World Scale option is selected, then the Offset fields change to Height and Width and the Tiling fields change to Size. The Mirror option inverts the map. The UV, VW, and WU options apply the map onto different planes.

Tiling is the process of placing a copy of the applied map next to the current one and so on until the entire surface is covered with the map placed edge to edge. You will often want to use tiled images that are seamless or that repeat from edge to edge.

Tip

Tiling can be enabled within the material itself or in the UVW Map modifier. ■

Figure 17.5 shows an image tile that is seamless. Notice how the horizontal and vertical seams line up. This figure shows three tiles positioned side by side, but because the opposite edges line up, the seams between the tiles aren't evident.

The Material Editor includes a button that you can use to check the Tiling and Mirror settings. The Sample UV Tiling button (fourth from the top) is a flyout button that you can switch to 2×2, 3×3, or 4×4.

FIGURE 17.5

Seamless image tiles are a useful way to cover an entire surface with a small map.

467

You can also rotate the map about each of the U, V, and W axes by entering values in the respective fields, or by clicking the Rotate button, which opens the Rotate Mapping Coordinates dialog box, shown in Figure 17.6. Using this dialog box, you can drag the mouse to rotate the mapping coordinates. Dragging within the circle rotates about all three coordinates, and dragging outside the circle rotates the mapping coordinates about their center point.

The Rotate Mapping Coordinates dialog box appears when you click the Rotate button in the Coordinates rollout.

The Blur and Blur Offset values affect the blurriness of the image. The Blur value blurs the image based on its distance from the view, whereas the Blur Offset value blurs the image regardless of its distance.

Tip

You can use the Blur setting to help make tile seams less noticeable. ■

The Noise rollout

You can use the Noise rollout to randomly alter the map settings in a predefined manner. Noise can be thought of as static that you see on the television added to a bitmap. This feature is helpful for making textures more grainy, which is useful for certain materials.

The Amount value is the strength of the noise function applied; the value ranges from 0 for no noise through 100 for maximum noise. You can disable this noise function at any time, using the On option.

The Levels value defines the number of times the noise function is applied. The Size value determines the extent of the noise function based on the geometry. You can also Animate the noise. The Phase value controls how quickly the noise changes over time.

The Time rollout

Maps, such as bitmaps, that can load animations also include a Time rollout for controlling animation files. In this rollout, you can choose a Start Frame and the Playback Rate. The default Playback Rate is 1.0; higher values run the animation faster, and lower values run it slower. You also can set the animation to Loop, Ping-Pong, or Hold on the last frame.

The Output rollout

The Output rollout includes settings for controlling the final look of the map. The Invert option creates a negative version of the bitmap. The Clamp option prevents any colors from exceeding a value of 1.0 and prevents maps from becoming self-illuminating if the brightness is increased.

The Alpha From RGB Intensity option generates an alpha channel based on the intensity of the map. Black areas become transparent and white areas opaque.

Note

For materials that don't include an Output rollout, you can apply an Output map, which accepts a submaterial. ∎

The Output Amount value controls how much of the map should be mixed when it is part of a composite material. You use the RGB Offset value to increase or decrease the map's tonal values. Use the RGB Level value to increase or decrease the saturation level of the map. The Bump Amount value is used only if the map is being used as a bump map—it determines the height of the bumps.

The Enable Color Map option enables the Color Map graph at the bottom of the Output rollout. This graph displays the tonal range of the map. Adjusting this graph affects the highlights, midtones, and shadows of the map. Figure 17.7 shows a Color Map graph.

FIGURE 17.7

The Color Map graph enables you to adjust the highlights, midtones, and shadows of a map.

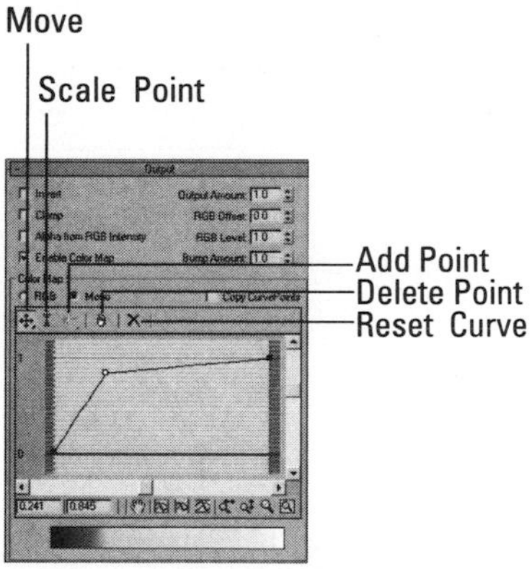

The left end of the graph equates to the shadows, and the right end is for the highlights. The RGB and Mono options let you display the graphs as independent red, green, and blue curves or as a single mono-color curve. The Copy CurvePoints option copies any existing points from Mono mode over to RGB mode, and vice versa. The buttons across the top of the graph are used to manage the graph points.

The buttons above the graph include Move (with flyout buttons for Move Horizontally and Move Vertically), Scale Point, Add Point (with a flyout button for adding a point with handles), Delete Point, and Reset Curves. Along the bottom of the graph are buttons for managing the graph view. The two fields at the bottom left contain the horizontal and vertical values for the current selected point. The other buttons are to Pan and Zoom the graph.

Bitmap map

Selecting the Bitmap map from the Material/Map Browser opens the Select Bitmap Image File dialog box, shown in Figure 17.8, where you can locate an image file. Various image and animation formats are supported, including AVI, MPEG, BMP, CIN, CWS, DDF, EXR, GIF, HDRI, IFL, IPP, FLC, JPEG, MOV, PNG, PSD, RGB, RLA, RPF, TGA, TIF, and YUV.

469

Note

Video sequences saved in the AVI, MPEG, and MOV formats can be loaded as a map. ∎

FIGURE 17.8

The Select Bitmap Image File dialog box lets you preview images before opening them.

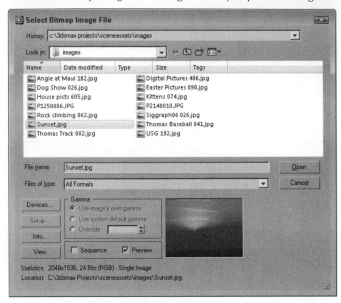

The name of the current bitmap file is displayed on the button in the Bitmap Parameters rollout, shown in Figure 17.9. If you need to change the bitmap file, click the Bitmap button and select the new file. Use the Reload button to update the bitmap if you've made changes to the bitmap image by an external program.

FIGURE 17.9

The Bitmap Parameters rollout offers several settings for controlling a bitmap map.

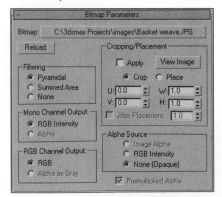

The Bitmap Parameters rollout includes three Filtering options: Pyramidal, Summed Area, and None. These methods perform a pixel-averaging operation to anti-alias the image. The Summed Area option requires more memory but produces better results.

You can also specify the output for a mono channel or for an RGB channel. For maps that use only the monochrome information in the image (such as an opacity map), the Mono Channel as RGB Intensity or Alpha option can be used. For maps that use color information (for example, a diffuse map), the RGB Channel can be RGB (full color) or Alpha as Gray.

The Cropping/Placement controls enable you to crop or place the image. *Cropping* is the process of cutting out a portion of the image, and *placing* is resizing the image while maintaining the entire image and positioning it. The View Image button opens the image in a Cropping/Placement dialog box, shown in Figure 17.10. The rectangle is available within the image when Crop mode is selected. You can move the handles of this rectangle to specify the crop region.

FIGURE 17.10

Viewing an image in the Cropping/Placement dialog box enables you to set the crop marks.

Cropping/Placement controls

Note

When the Crop option is selected, a UV button is displayed in the upper right of the Cropping/Placement dialog box. Clicking this button changes the U and V values to X and Y pixels. ∎

You can also adjust the U and V parameters, which define the upper-left corner of the cropping rectangle, and the W and H parameters, which define the crop or placement width and height. The Jitter Placement option works with the Place option to randomly place and size the image.

Note

The U and V values are a percentage of the total image. For example, a U value of 0.25 positions the image's left edge at a location that is 25 percent of the distance of the total width from the left edge of the original image. ∎

If the bitmap has an alpha channel, you can specify whether it is to be used with the Image Alpha option, or you can define the alpha values as RGB Intensity or as None. You can also select to use Premultiplied Alphas. Premultiplied Alphas are images that use the transparency information stored in the image.

Checker map

The Checker map creates a checkerboard image with two colors. The Checker Parameters rollout includes two color swatches for changing the checker colors. You can also load maps in place of each color. Use the Swap button to switch the position of the two colors and the Soften value to blur the edges between the two colors.

Figure 17.11 shows three Checker maps with Tiling values of 2 for the U and V directions and Soften values of (from left to right) 0, 0.2, and 0.5.

The Checker map can be softened as these three maps are with Soften values of 0, 0.2, and 0.5.

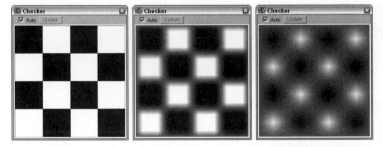

Combustion map

This map works with Autodesk's Combustion package, which is used for post-processing compositing. The Combustion map enables you to include Combustion-produced effects as a material map.

The Project button lets you load a file to paint on. These files are limited to the types that Combustion supports. Use the Edit button to load the Combustion interface.

In the Live Edit section, the Unwrap button places markings on the bitmap image to show where the mapping coordinates are located. The UV button lets you change from among UV, VW, and UW coordinate systems. The Track Time button lets you change the current frame, which enables you to paint materials that change over time. The Paint button changes the viewport cursor to enable you to paint interactively in the viewport. The Operator button lets you select a composition operator from within Combustion.

The Combustion map also includes information about current project settings for specifying a custom resolution. You can also control the Start Frame and Duration of an animation sequence. The Filtering options are Pyramidal, Summed Area, or None, and the End Conditions can be set to Loop, Ping Pong (which moves back and forth between the start and end positions), or Hold.

Caution

To use this map type, you must have the Combustion program. If the program isn't installed, the text "Error: Combustion Engine DLL Not Found" displays at the top of the Combustion Parameters rollout. ■

Gradient map

The Gradient map creates a gradient image using three colors. The Gradient Parameters rollout includes a color swatch and map button for each color. You can position the center color at any location between the two ends using the Color 2 Position value spinner. The value can range from 0 through 1. The rollout lets you choose between Linear and Radial gradient types.

The Noise Amount adds noise to the gradient if its value is nonzero. The Size value scales the noise effect, and the Phase controls how quickly the noise changes over time. The three types of noise that you can select are Regular, Fractal, and Turbulence. The Levels value determines how many times the noise function is applied. The High and Low Threshold and Smooth values set the limits of the noise function to eliminate discontinuities.

Figure 17.12 shows linear and radial Gradient maps.

FIGURE 17.12

A Gradient map can be linear (left) or radial (right).

Gradient Ramp map

This advanced version of the Gradient map can use many different colors. The Gradient Ramp Parameters rollout, shown in Figure 17.13, includes a color bar with several flags along its bottom edge. You can add flags by simply clicking along the bottom edge. You can also drag flags to reposition them or delete the interior flags by dragging them all the way to either end until they turn red.

To define the color for each flag, right-click the flag and then select Edit Properties from the pop-up menu. The Flag Properties dialog box, also shown in Figure 17.13, opens so you can select a color or texture to use.

The Gradient Type drop-down in the Gradient Ramp Parameters rollout offers various Gradient Types, including 4 Corner, Box, Diagonal, Lighting, Linear, Mapped, Normal, Pong, Radial, Spiral, Sweep, and Tartan. You can also select from several Interpolation types, including Custom, Ease In, Ease In Out, Ease Out, Linear, and Solid.

FIGURE 17.13

The Flag Properties dialog box enables you to specify a color and its position to use in the Gradient Ramp.

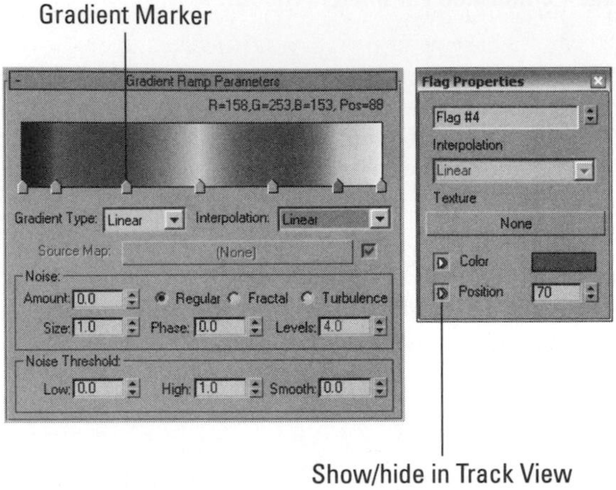

Gradient Marker

Show/hide in Track View

Figure 17.14 shows several of the gradient types available for the Gradient Ramp map.

FIGURE 17.14

The Gradient Ramp map offers several different gradient types, including (from top left to bottom right) Box, Diagonal, Normal, Pong, Spiral, and Tartan.

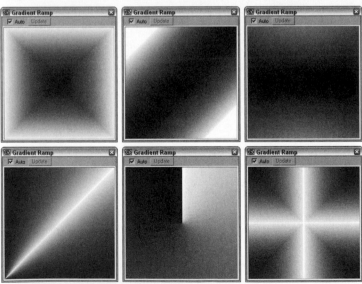

Swirl map

The Swirl map creates a swirled image of two colors: Base and Swirl. The Swirl Parameters rollout includes two color swatches and map buttons to specify these colors. The Swap button switches the two colors. Other options include Color Contrast, which controls the contrast between the two colors; Swirl Intensity, which defines the strength of the swirl color; and Swirl Amount, which is how much of the Swirl color gets mixed into the Base color.

Note

All maps that use two colors include a Swap button for switching between the colors. ■

The Twist value sets the number of swirls. Negative values cause the swirl to change direction. The Constant Detail value determines how much detail is included in the swirl.

With the Swirl Location X and Y values, you can move the center of the swirl. As the center is moved far from the materials center, the swirl rings become tighter. The Lock button causes both values to change equally. If the lock is disabled, then the values can be changed independently.

The Random Seed sets the randomness of the swirl effect.

Figure 17.15 shows the Swirl map with three different Twist values. From left to right, the Twist values are 1, 5, and 10.

FIGURE 17.15

The Swirl map combines two colors in a swirling pattern.

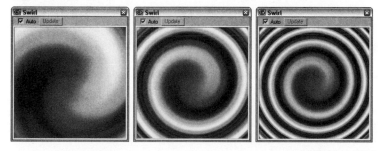

Tiles map

The Tiles map creates brick patterns. The Standard Controls rollout contains a Preset Type drop-down list with a list of preset tile patterns. These patterns are popular tile patterns including Running Bond, Common Flemish Bond, English Bond, $^1/_2$ Running Bond, Stack Bond, Fine Running Bond, and Fine Stack Bond.

In the Advanced Controls rollout under both the Tile and Grout Setup sections, you can use a custom texture map and color. You can specify the Horizontal and Vertical Count of the Tiles and the Grout's Horizontal and Vertical Gaps, as well as Color and Fade Variance values for both. The Horizontal and Vertical Gaps can be locked to always be equal. For Grout, you can also define the Percentage of Holes. Holes are where tiles have been left out. A Rough value controls the roughness of the mortar.

The Random Seed value controls the randomness of the patterns, and the Swap Texture Entries option exchanges the tile texture with the grout texture.

In the Stacking Layout section, the Line Shift and Random Shift values are used to move each row of tiles a defined or random distance.

The Row and Column Editing section offers options that let you change the number of tiles Per Row or Column and the Change (or leftover) in each row or column.

Figure 17.16 shows three different Tile map styles.

FIGURE 17.16

From the Standard Controls rollout, you can select from several preset Tile styles, including Running Bond, English Bond, and Fine Running Bond.

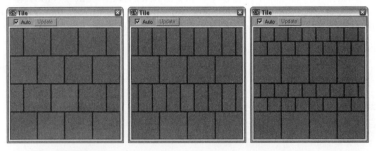

3D maps

3D maps are procedurally created, which means that these maps are more than just a grouping of pixels; they are actually created using a mathematical algorithm. This algorithm defines the map in three dimensions, so that if a portion of the object were to be cut away, the map would line up along each edge.

The Coordinates rollout for 3D maps is similar to the Coordinates rollout for 2D maps with a few exceptions; differences include Coordinate Source options of Object XYZ, World XYZ, Explicit Map Channel, and Vertex Color Channel. There are also Offset, Tiling, and Angle values for the X-, Y-, and Z-axes as well as Blur and Blur offset options.

Cellular map

The Cellular 3D map creates patterns of small objects referred to as *cells*. In the Cell Color section of the Cellular Parameters rollout, you can specify the color for the individual cells or apply a map. Setting the Variation value can vary the cell color.

In the Division Colors section, two color swatches are used to define the colors that appear between the cells. This space is a gradient between the two colors.

In the Cell Characteristics section, you can control the shape of the cells by selecting Circular or Chips, a Size, and how the cells are Spread. The Bump Smoothing value smoothes the jaggedness of the cells. The Fractal option causes the cells to be generated using a fractal algorithm. The Iterations value determines the number of times that the algorithm is applied. The Adaptive option determines automatically the number of iterations to complete. The Roughness setting determines how rough the surfaces of the cells are.

The Size value affects the overall scale of the map, while the Threshold values specify the specific size of the individual cells. Settings include Low, Mid, and High.

Figure 17.17 shows three Cellular maps: the first with Circular cells and a Size value of 20, the second with Chips cells, and the final one with the Fractal option enabled.

FIGURE 17.17

The Cellular map creates small, regular-shaped cells.

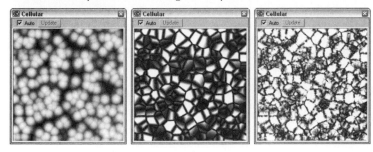

Dent map

The Dent 3D map works as a bump map to create indentations across the surface of an object. In the Dent Parameters rollout, the Size value sets the overall size of the dents. The Strength value determines how deep the dents are, and the Iterations value sets how many times the algorithm is to be computed. You can also specify the colors for the Dent map. The default colors are black and white. Black defines the areas that are indented.

Figure 17.18 shows three spheres with the Dent map applied as bump mapping. The three spheres, from left to right, have Size values of 500, 1000, and 2000.

FIGURE 17.18

The Dent map causes dents in the object when applied as bump mapping.

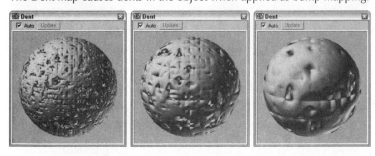

Falloff map

The Falloff 3D map creates a grayscale image based on the direction of the surface normals. Areas with normals that are parallel to the view are black, and areas whose normals are perpendicular to the view are white. This map is usually applied as an opacity map, giving you greater control over the opacity of the object.

Tip

The Falloff map is also useful for creating a Fresnel effect on a glazed surface through its reflections. ∎

The Falloff Parameters rollout includes two color swatches, a Strength value of each, and an optional map. There are also drop-down lists for setting the Falloff Type and the Falloff Direction. Falloff Types include Perpendicular/Parallel, Towards/Away, Fresnel, Shadow/Light, and Distance Blend. The Falloff Direction options include Viewing Direction (Camera Z axis); Camera X Axis; Camera Y Axis; Object; Local X, Y, and Z Axis; and World X, Y, and Z Axis.

In the Mode Specific Parameters section, several parameters are based on the Falloff Type and Direction. If Object is selected as the Falloff Direction, then a button that lets you select the object becomes active. The Fresnel Falloff Type is based on the Index of Refraction and provides an option to override the material's Index of Refraction value. The Distance Blend Falloff Type offers values for Near and Far distances.

The Falloff map also includes a Mix Curve graph and rollout that give you precise control over the fall-off gradient. Points at the top of the graph have a value of 1 and represent the white areas of falloff. Points at the bottom of the graph have a value of 0 and are black.

Marble map

The Marble 3D map creates a marbled material with random colored veins. The Marble Parameters rollout includes two color swatches: Color #1 is the vein color and Color #2 is the base color. You also have the option of loading maps for each color. The Swap button switches the two colors. The Size value determines how far the veins are from each other, and the Vein Width defines the vein thickness.

Figure 17.19 shows three Marble maps with Vein Width values of (from left to right) 0.01, 0.025, and 0.05.

FIGURE 17.19

The Marble map creates a marbled surface.

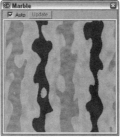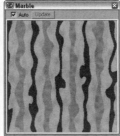

Noise map

The Noise 3D map randomly alters the surface of an object using two colors. The Noise Parameters rollout offers three Noise types: Regular, Fractal, and Turbulence. Each type uses a different algorithm for computing noise. The two color swatches let you alter the colors used to represent the noise. You also have the option of loading maps for each color. The Size value scales the noise effect. To prevent discontinuities, the High and Low Noise Threshold can be used to set noise limits.

Figure 17.20 shows Noise maps with the (from left to right) Regular, Fractal, and Turbulence options enabled.

FIGURE 17.20

The Noise map produces a random noise pattern on the surface of the object.

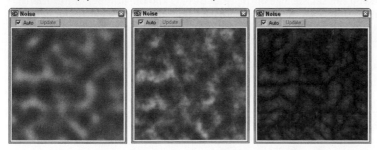

Particle Age map

The Particle Age map is used with particle systems to change the color of particles over their lifetime. The Particle Age Parameters rollout includes three different color swatches and age values.

Particle MBlur map

The Particle MBlur map is also used with particle systems. This map is used to blur particles as they increase in velocity. The Particle Motion Blur Parameters rollout includes two colors: The first color is the one used for the slower portions of the particle, and the second color is used for the fast portions. When you apply this map as an opacity map, the particles are blurred. The Sharpness value determines the amount of blur.

Cross-Reference

For more on both the Particle Age and Particle MBlur maps, see Chapter 41, "Creating Particles and Particle Flow." ■

Perlin Marble map

This map creates marble textures using a different algorithm. Perlin Marble is more chaotic and random than the Marble map. The Perlin Marble Parameters rollout includes a Size parameter, which adjusts the size of the marble pattern, and a Levels parameter, which determines how many times the algorithm is applied. The two color swatches determine the base and vein colors, or you can assign a map. There are also values for the Saturation of the colors.

Figure 17.21 shows the Perlin Marble map Size values of (from left to right) 50, 100, and 200.

FIGURE 17.21

The Perlin Marble map creates a marble pattern with random veins.

Smoke map

The Smoke map can create random fractal-based patterns such as those you would see in smoke. In the Smoke Parameters rollout, you can set the Size of the smoke areas and the number of Iterations (how many times the fractal algorithm is computed). The Phase value shifts the smoke about, and the Exponent value produces thin, wispy lines of smoke. The rollout also includes two colors for the smoke particles and the area between the smoke particles, or you can load maps instead.

Figure 17.22 shows the Smoke map with Size values of (from left to right) 40, 80, and 200.

FIGURE 17.22

The Smoke map simulates the look of smoke when applied as opacity mapping.

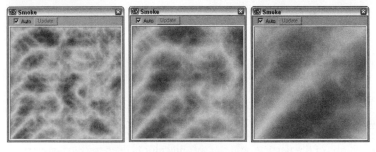

Speckle map

The Speckle map produces small, randomly positioned specks. The Speckle Parameters rollout lets you control the Size and color of the specks. Two color swatches are for the base and speck colors.

Figure 17.23 shows the Speckle map with Size values of (from left to right) 100, 200, and 400.

FIGURE 17.23

The Speckle map paints small, random specks on the surface of an object.

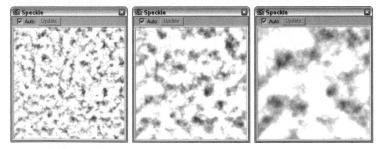

Splat map

The Splat map can create the look of covering an object with splattered paint. In the Splat Parameters rollout, you can set the Size of the splattered areas and the number of Iterations, which is how many times the fractal algorithm is computed. For each additional Iteration, a smaller set of spatters appears. The Threshold value determines how much of each color to mix. The rollout also includes two colors for the splattered sections, or you can load maps instead.

Figure 17.24 shows the Splat map with a Size value of 60, 6 Iterations, and Threshold values of (from left to right) 0.2, 0.3, and 0.4.

FIGURE 17.24

The Splat map splatters paint randomly across the surface of an object.

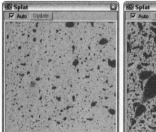 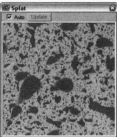 

Stucco map

The Stucco map generates random patches of gradients that create the look of a stucco surface if applied as a bump map. In the Stucco Parameters rollout, the Size value determines the size of these areas. The Thickness value determines how blurry the patches are, which changes the sharpness of the bumps for a bump map. The Threshold value determines how much of each color to mix. The rollout also includes two colors for the patchy sections, or you can load maps instead.

Figure 17.25 shows the Stucco map with a Threshold value of 0.5, Thickness of 0.02, and Size values of (from left to right) 10, 20, and 40.

FIGURE 17.25

The Stucco map creates soft indentations when applied as bump mapping.

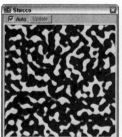 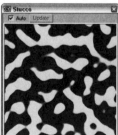 

Cross-Reference

Procedural textures are created with the Substance map, which is covered in Chapter 31, "Working with Procedural Substance Textures." ∎

Waves map

This map creates wavy, watery-looking maps and can be used as both a diffuse map and a bump map to create a water surface. You can use several values to set the wave characteristics in the Water

Parameters rollout, including the number of Wave Sets, the Wave Radius, the minimum and maximum Wave Length, the Amplitude, and the Phase. You can also Distribute the waves as 2D or 3D, and a Random Seed value is available.

Figure 17.26 shows the Water map with the Num Wave Sets value set to (from left to right) 1, 3, and 9.

FIGURE 17.26

You can use the Water map to create watery surfaces.

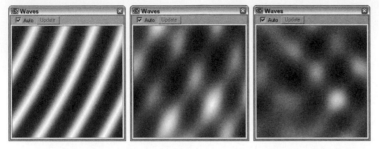

Wood map

The Wood map produces a two-color wood grain. The Wood Parameters rollout options include Grain Thickness, Radial, and Axial Noise. You can select the two colors to use for the wood grain.

Figure 17.27 shows the Wood map with Grain Thickness values of (from left to right) 8, 16, and 30.

FIGURE 17.27

The Wood map creates a map with a wood grain.

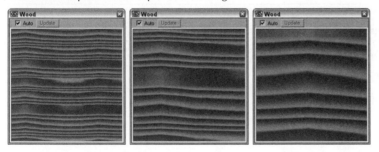

Compositor maps

Compositor maps are made by combining several maps into one. Compositor map types include Composite, Mask, Mix, and RGB Multiply.

Composite map

Composite maps combine a specified number of maps into a single map using the alpha channel. Each separate map is listed on a separate layer, and the layers are composited from the top layer down.

The Composite Parameters rollout lists the number of layers and includes a button for adding a new layer, as shown in Figure 17.28.

Each layer has preview swatches for specifying a texture and a mask. To the side of these preview swatches are buttons for hiding the layer or mask and for color correcting each. There are also buttons for deleting, renaming, and duplicating each layer.

FIGURE 17.28

The Composite Layers rollout lists each composite map as a separate layer.

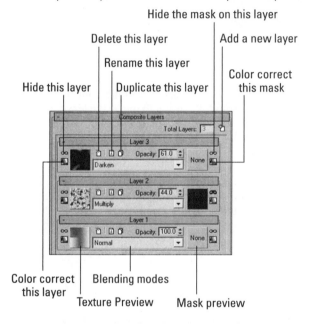

The Opacity value sets how transparent the layer is, and you can also change the blending mode using the drop-down list at the bottom of each layer. The blending mode defines how the texture on the current layer is combined with the layers below it. The available blending modes include Normal, Average, Addition, Subtract, Darken, Multiply, Color Burn, Linear Burn, Lighten, Screen, Color Dodge, Linear Dodge, Spotlight, Spotlight Blend, Overlay, Soft Light, Hard Light, Pinlight, Hard Mix, Difference, Exclusion, Hue, Saturation, Color, and Value.

Note

Composite maps and blending modes in 3ds Max 2009 work similar to layers in Photoshop. ∎

Figure 17.29 shows three different uses for the Composite map. The left image combines a Checker map with a Gradient map. The last two images combine a Swirl map with Checker and Cellular maps.

FIGURE 17.29

The Composite map can use multiple maps.

Mask map

In the Mask Parameters rollout, you can select one map to use as a Mask and another one to display through the holes in the mask simply called Map. You also have an option to Invert the Mask. The black areas of the masking map are the areas that hide the underlying map. The white areas allow the underlying map to show through. The result of the Mask map is visible only when rendered.

Mix map

You can use the Mix map to combine two maps or colors. It is similar to the Composite map, except that it uses a Mix Amount value to combine the two colors or maps instead of using the alpha channel. In the Mix Parameters rollout, the Mix Amount value of 0 includes only Color #1, and a value of 100 includes only Color #2. You can also use a Mixing Curve to define how the colors are mixed. The curve shape is controlled by altering its Upper and Lower values.

Figure 17.30 shows the Mix map with Perlin Marble and Checker maps applied as sub-maps and Mix values of (from left to right) 25, 50, and 75.

FIGURE 17.30

The Mix map lets you combine two maps and define the Mix Amount.

RGB Multiply map

The RGB Multiply map multiplies the RGB values for two separate maps and combines them to create a single map. Did you notice in the preceding figure that the Mix map fades both maps? The RGB Multiply map keeps the saturation of the individual maps by using each map's alpha channel to combine the maps.

The RGB Multiply Parameters rollout includes an option to use the Alpha from either Map #1 or Map #2 or to Multiply the Alphas.

Figure 17.31 shows three samples of the RGB Multiply map. Each of these images combines a Wood map with (from left to right) a Checker map, a Gradient map, and a Stucco map. Notice that the colors aren't faded for this map type.

FIGURE 17.31

The RGB Multiply map combines maps at full saturation using alpha channels.

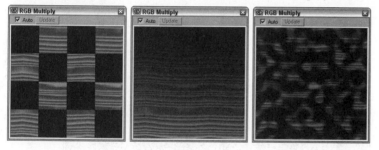

Color Modifier maps

You can use this group of maps to change the color of different materials. Color Modifier map types include Output, RGB Tint, and Vertex Color.

Color Correction map

The Color Correction map lets you change the colors of a texture. The corrections are applied using a stack approach. The Color Correction map includes four rollouts: Basic Parameters, Channels, Color, and Lightness, as shown in Figure 17.32, and each of these settings is in order starting from the top rollout.

The Basic Parameters rollout includes a color swatch and a map button that you can use to specify the color to affect the map. In the Channels rollout, you can select to make the map Normal, Monochrome, Invert, or Custom. If Custom is selected, then you can specify a specific color for each of the RGB and alpha channels. The available channel options are Red, Green, Blue, Alpha, the inverse for each, Monochrome, One, and Zero.

In the Color rollout, you can adjust the Hue Shift, Saturation, Hue Tint, and Strength for the map, and the Lightness rollout gives you two options: Standard and Advanced. In Standard mode, you can adjust the Brightness and Contrast using simple sliders, but Advanced mode gives you control over the Gain, F-Stops, and Printer Lights settings for each channel.

FIGURE 17.32

The Color Correction map lets you work with textures as if you had a photo lab.

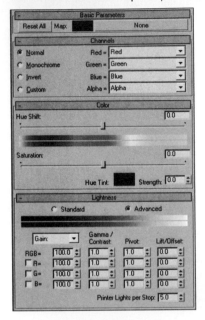

Output map

The Output map provides a way to add the functions of the Output rollout to maps that don't include an output rollout. Details on this map type are presented in the earlier section that covers the Output rollout.

RGB Tint map

The RGB Tint map includes color swatches for the red, green, and blue channel values. Adjusting these colors alters the amount of tint in the map. For example, setting the red color swatch in the RGB Tint Parameters rollout to white and the green and blue color swatches to black creates a map with a heavy red tint. You can also load maps in place of the colors.

Vertex Color map

The Vertex Color map makes the vertex colors assigned to an Editable Mesh, Poly, or Patch object visible when the object is rendered. When an Editable Mesh, Poly, or Patch object is in Vertex subobject mode, you can assign the selected vertices a Color, an Illumination color, and an Alpha value. These settings are in the Surface Properties rollout. You can also assign vertex colors using the Assign Vertex Colors utility. Use this utility to assign color to the current object or to assign material colors to the object's vertices using the given lights. A third way to assign vertex colors is with the Vertex Paint modifier, which you access using the Modifiers ⇨ Mesh Editing ⇨ Vertex Paint menu command. This modifier lets you color vertices by painting directly on an object.

Cross-Reference

For more detail on the Vertex Paint modifier, see Chapter 18, "Creating Compound Materials and Using Material Modifiers." ∎

After vertex colors are assigned, you need to apply the Vertex Color map to the diffuse color in the Material Editor and apply it to the object for the object to render the vertex colors. This map doesn't have any settings.

Miscellaneous maps

These maps are actually grouped into a category called *Other,* but they mostly deal with reflection and refraction effects. Maps in this category include Camera Map Per Pixel, Flat Mirror, Normal Bump, Raytrace, Reflect/Refract, and Thin Wall Refraction.

Camera Map Per Pixel map

The Camera Map Per Pixel map lets you project a map from the location of a camera. You use this map by rendering the scene, editing the rendered image in an image-editing program, and projecting the image back onto the scene.

The Camera Map Parameters rollout includes buttons that let you select the Camera, Texture, ZBuffer Mask, and Mask.

Flat Mirror map

The Flat Mirror map reflects the surroundings using a coplanar group of faces. In the Flat Mirror Parameters rollout, you can select a Blur amount to apply. You can specify whether to Render the First Frame Only or Every Nth Frame. You also have an option to Use the Environment Map or to apply to Faces with a given ID.

Note

Flat Mirror maps are applied only to selected coplanar faces using the material ID. ∎

The Distortion options include None, Use Bump Map, and Use Built-In Noise. If the Bump Map option is selected, you can define a Distortion Amount. If the Noise option is selected, you can choose Regular, Fractal, or Turbulence noise types with Phase, Size, and Levels values.

Tutorial: Creating a mirrored surface

Mirror, mirror on the wall, who's the best modeler of them all? Using the Flat Mirror map, you can create, believe it or not, mirrors. To create and configure a flat mirror map, follow these steps:

1. Open the Reflection in mirror.max file from the Chap 17 directory on the CD.

    This file includes a mesh of a man standing in front of a mirror. The mirror subobject faces have been selected and applied a material ID of 1.

2. Choose Rendering ⇨ Material Editor ⇨ Slate Material Editor (or press the M key) to open the Material Editor.

3. Locate and double-click the Flat Mirror option in the Material/Map Browser to add a node to the Node View. Drag a connection wire from the output socket, drop it anywhere on the Node View, and then select the Materials/Standard material from the pop-up menu and the Reflection channel from the parameters pop-up menu. This adds a standard material node to the Node View and connects the Flat Mirror node to the material's Reflection parameter.

Note

If the Flat Mirror map isn't available, select the Map radio button in the Show section. ∎

4. Double-click the Flat Mirror node to make its parameters appear in the Parameter Editor. In the Flat Mirror Parameters rollout, deselect the Apply Blur and Use Environment Map options and select the Apply to Faces with ID option. Then set the ID value to 1.

5. Drag the material node's output socket to the mirror object in the viewport to apply the material to the mirror.

Figure 17.33 shows a model being reflected off a simple patch object with a Flat Mirror map applied to it. The reflection is visible only in the final rendered image.

FIGURE 17.33

A Flat Mirror map causes the object to reflect its surroundings.

Normal Bump map

The Normal Bump map lets you alter the appearance of the details on the surface using a Normal map. Normal maps can be created using the Render to Texture dialog box. The Parameters rollout for this map type lets you specify a normal map along with another additional bump map. You also can set the amount each map is displaced. Additional options let you flip and swap the red and green channel directions, which define the X and Y axes.

Cross-Reference

The Render to Texture dialog box and Normal maps are covered in more detail in Chapter 34, "Creating Baked Textures and Normal Maps." ■

Raytrace map

The Raytrace map is an alternative to the raytrace material and, as a map, can be used in places where the raytrace material cannot.

Cross-Reference

Check out Chapter 47, "Rendering with mental ray and iray," for more on the Raytrace materials and maps. ∎

Reflect/Refract map

Reflect/Refract maps are yet another way to create reflections and refractions on objects. These maps work by producing a rendering from each axis of the object, like one for each face of a cube. These rendered images, called *cubic maps*, are then projected onto the object.

These rendered images can be created automatically or loaded from pre-rendered images using the Reflect/Refract Parameters rollout. Using automatic cubic maps is easier, but they take considerably more time. If you select the Automatic option, you can select to render the First Frame Only or Every Nth Frame. If you select the From File option, then you are offered six buttons that can load cubic maps for each of the different directions.

In the Reflect/Refract Parameters rollout, you can also specify the Blur settings and the Atmospheric Ranges.

Thin Wall Refraction map

The Thin Wall Refraction map simulates the refraction caused by a piece of glass, such as a magnifying glass. The same result is possible with the Reflect/Refract map, but the Thin Wall Refraction map achieves this result in a fraction of the time.

The Thin Wall Refraction Parameters rollout includes options for setting the Blur, the frames to render, and Refraction values. The Thickness Offset determines the amount of offset and can range from 0 through 10. The Bump Map Effect value changes the refraction based on the presence of a bump map.

Tutorial: Creating a magnifying glass effect

Another common property of glass besides reflection is refraction. Refraction can enlarge items when the glass is thick, such as when you look at the other side of the room through a glass of water. Using the Thin Wall Refraction map, you can simulate the effects of a magnifying glass.

To create a magnifying glass effect, follow these steps:

1. Open the Magnifying glass.max file from the Chap 17 directory on the CD.

   This file includes a simple sphere with a Perlin Marble map applied to it and a magnifying glass modeled from primitive objects.

2. Choose Rendering ⇨ Material Editor ⇨ Slate Material Editor (or press the M key) to open the Material Editor.

3. Locate and double-click the Thin Wall Refraction option in the Material/Map Browser to add a node to the Node View. Drag a connection wire from the output socket, drop it anywhere on the Node View, and then select the Materials/Standard material from the pop-up menu and the Refraction channel from the parameters pop-up menu. This adds a standard material node to the Node View and connects the Thin Wall Refraction node to the material's Reflection parameter.

4. Double-click the Thin Wall Refraction node to open its parameters in the Parameter Editor. In the Thin Wall Refraction Parameters rollout, set the Thickness Offset to **10** to increase the amount of magnification.

5. Drag the output socket for the material node and drop it on the magnifying glass object in the viewport to apply the material to the object.

Figure 17.34 shows the resulting rendered image. Notice that the texture in the magnifying glass appears magnified.

FIGURE 17.34

The Thin Wall Refraction map is applied to a magnifying glass.

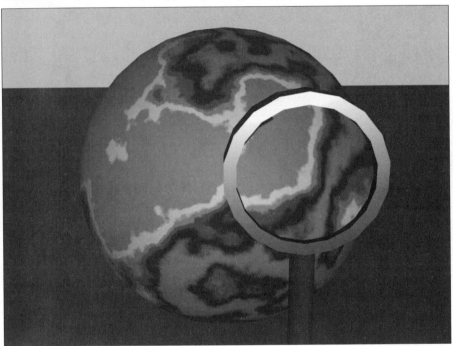

Using the Maps Rollout

Now that you've seen the different types of maps, we'll revisit the Maps rollout (introduced in Chapter 15), shown in Figure 17.35, and cover it in more detail.

The Maps rollout is where you apply maps to the various materials. To use a map, click the Map button; this opens the Material/Map Browser where you can select the map to use. The Amount spinner sets the intensity of the map, and an option to enable or disable the map is available. For example, a white diffuse color with a red Diffuse map set at 50 percent Intensity results in a pink material.

The available maps in the Maps rollout depend on the type of material and the Shader that you are using. Raytrace materials have many more available maps than the standard material. Some of the common mapping types found in the Maps rollout are discussed in Table 17.1.

FIGURE 17.35

The Maps rollout can turn maps on or off.

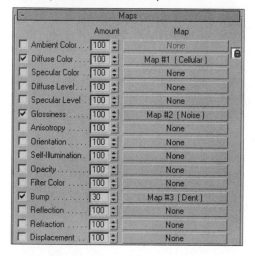

TABLE 17.1

Material Properties for Maps

Material Property	Description
Ambient Color	Replaces the ambient color component of the base material. You can use this feature to make an object's shadow appear as a map. Diffuse mapping (discussed next) also affects the Ambient color. A lock button in the Maps rollout enables you to lock these two mappings together.
Diffuse Color	Replaces the diffuse color component of the base material. This is the main color used for the object. When you select a map such as Wood, the object appears to be created out of wood. As mentioned previously, diffuse mapping also can affect the Ambient color if the lock button is selected.
Diffuse Level	Changes the diffuse color level from 0, where the map is black, to a maximum, where the map is white. This mapping is available only with the Anisotropic, Oren-Nayar-Blinn, and Multi-Level Shaders.
Diffuse Roughness	Sets the roughness value of the material from 0, where the map is black, to a maximum, where the map is white. This mapping is available only with the Oren-Nayar-Blinn and Multi-Layer Shaders.

continued

TABLE 17.1 *(continued)*	
Material Property	**Description**
Specular Level	Controls the intensity of the specular highlights from 0, where the map is black, to 1, where the map is white. For the best effect, apply this mapping along with the Glossiness mapping.
Glossiness	Defines where the specular highlights will appear. You can use this option to make an object appear older by diminishing certain areas. Black areas on the map show the non-glossy areas, and white areas are where the glossiness is at a maximum.
Opacity	Determines which areas are visible and which are transparent. Black areas for this map are transparent, and white areas are opaque. This mapping works in conjunction with the Opacity value in the Basic Parameters rollout. Transparent areas, even if perfectly transparent, still receive specular highlights.
Filter Color	Colors transparent areas for creating materials such as colored glass. White light that is cast through an object using filter color mapping is colored with the filter color.
Anisotropy	Controls the shape of an anisotropy highlight. This mapping is available only with the Anisotropic and Multi-Layer Shaders.
Orientation	Controls an anisotropic highlight's position. Anisotropic highlights are elliptical, and this mapping can position them at a different angle. Orientation mapping is available only with the Anisotropic and Multi-Layer Shaders.
Metalness	Controls how metallic an area looks. It specifies metalness values from 0, where the map is black, to a maximum, where the map is white. This mapping is available only with the Strauss Shader.
Bump	Uses the intensity of the bitmap to raise or indent the surface of an object. The white areas of the map are raised, and darker areas are lowered. Although bump mapping appears to alter the geometry, it actually doesn't affect the surface geometry.
Reflection	Reflects images off the surface as a mirror does. The three types of Reflection mapping are Basic, Automatic, and Flat Mirror. Basic reflection mapping simulates the reflection of an object's surroundings. Automatic reflection mapping projects the map outward from the center of the object. Flat-Mirror reflection mapping reflects a mirror image off a series of coplanar faces. Reflection mapping doesn't need mapping coordinates because the coordinates are based on world coordinates and not on object coordinates. Therefore, the map appears different if the object is moved, which is how reflections work in the real world.
Refraction	Bends light and displays images through a transparent object, in the same way a room appears through a glass of water. The amount of this effect is controlled by a value called the Index of Refraction. This value is set in the parent material's Extended Parameters rollout.
Displacement	Changes the geometry of an object. The white areas of the map are pushed outward, and the dark areas are pushed in. The amount of the surface displaced is based on a percentage of the diagonal that makes up the bounding box of the object. Displacement mapping isn't visible in the viewports unless the Displace NURBS (for NURBS, or Non-Uniform Rational B-Splines, objects) or the Displace Mesh (for Editable Meshes) modifiers have been applied.

Tutorial: Aging objects for realism

I don't know whether your toolbox is well worn like mine—it must be the hostile environment that it is always in (or all the things I keep dropping in and on it). Rendering a toolbox with nice specular highlights just doesn't feel right. This tutorial shows a few ways to age an object so that it looks older and worn.

To add maps to make an object look old, follow these steps:

1. Open the Toolbox.max file from the Chap 17 directory on the CD.

   This file contains a simple toolbox mesh created using extruded splines.

2. Press the M key to open the Slate Material Editor. Locate and double-click the Standard material in the Material/Map Browser, and then select the Metal shader from the drop-down list in the Shader Basic Parameters rollout. In the Metal Basic Parameters rollout, set the Diffuse color to a nice, shiny red and increase the Specular Level to **97** and the Glossiness value to **59**. Name the material **Toolbox**.

3. In the Maps rollout of the Material/Map Browser, double-click the option for the Splat map and connect this node to the Glossiness parameter. In the Splat Parameters rollout, set the Size value to **100** and change Color #1 to a rust color and Color #2 to white.

4. Double-click the Dent option in the Material/Map Browser and connect its node to the Bump parameter. Select the Dent map node and in the Dent Parameters rollout, set the Size value to **200**, Color #1 to black, and Color #2 to white.

5. Create another standard material node and name it **Hinge**. Select the Metal shader from the Shader Basic Parameters rollout for this material also, and increase the Specular Level in the Metal Basic Parameters rollout to **26** and the Glossiness value to **71**. Also change the Diffuse color to a light gray. Click the map button next to the Glossiness value, and double-click the Noise map in the Material/Map Browser. In the Noise Parameters rollout, set the Noise map to Fractal with a Size of **10**.

6. Drag the output socket for the "Toolbox" material to the toolbox object and the "Hinge" material to the hinge and the handle.

Note

Bump and glossiness mappings are not visible until the scene is rendered. To see the material's results, choose Rendering ⇨ Render and click the Render button. ■

Figure 17.36 shows the well-used toolbox.

FIGURE 17.36

This toolbox shows its age with Glossiness and Bump mappings.

Using the Map Path Utility

After you have all your maps in place, losing them can really make life troublesome. However, Max includes a utility that helps you determine which maps are missing and lets you edit the path to them to quickly and easily locate them. The Bitmap/Photometric Path Editor utility is available in the Utility panel. To find it, click the More button and select Bitmap/Photometric Path Editor from the list of utilities.

Cross-Reference

This utility is used for bitmaps as well as photometric lights. You can learn about photometric lights in Chapter 20, "Using Lights and Basic Lighting Techniques." ∎

When opened, the Path Editor rollout includes the Edit Resources button that opens the Bitmap/Photometric Path Editor window, shown in Figure 17.37. The rollout also includes two options for displaying the Materials Editor and Material Library bitmap paths. The Close button closes the rollout.

The Info button in the Bitmap/Photometric Path Editor dialog box lists all the nodes that use the selected map. The Copy Files button opens a File dialog box in which you can select a location to which to copy the selected map. The Select Missing Files button selects any maps in the list that can't be located. The Find Files button lists the maps in the current selection that can be located and the number that are missing. Stripping paths removes the path information and leaves only the map name. The New Path field lets you enter the path information to apply to the selected maps. The button with three dots to the right of the New Path field lets you browse for a path, and the Set Path button applies the path designated in the New Path field to the selected maps.

FIGURE 17.37

The Bitmap/Photometric Path Editor window lets you alter map paths.

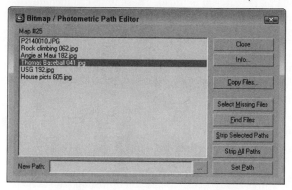

Using Map Instances

Using the same bitmap for many different map channels is common. For example, you may use the same bitmap for the Diffuse and Bump map channels. If a file includes the same bitmaps over and over, the file size can increase, and replacing a bitmap when you make changes can become difficult. This potential problem can be fixed easily by making the maps into instances instead of copies. If you have an existing Max file, you can use the Instance Duplicate Maps utility to find all the common maps and make them instances automatically.

Access this utility from the Utilities menu in the Material Editor or from the Utilities panel. Both commands open the same dialog box, shown in Figure 17.38. From this dialog box, you can select which maps to make instances or click Instance All to consolidate all the found maps into instances.

FIGURE 17.38

The Instance Duplicate Maps dialog box lets you consolidate maps into a single instance.

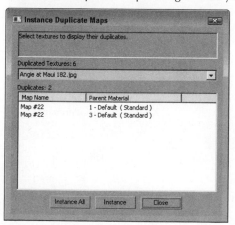

Creating Textures with External Tools

Several external tools can be valuable when you create material textures. These tools can include an image-editing program like Photoshop, a digital camera or camcorder, and a scanner. With these tools, you can create or capture images that can be applied as maps to a material using the map channels.

After the image is created or captured, you can apply it to a material by clicking a map shortcut button or by selecting a map in the Maps rollout. This opens the Material/Map Browser, where you can select the Bitmap map type and load the image file from the File dialog box that appears.

Creating material textures using Photoshop

When you begin creating texture images, Photoshop becomes your best friend. Using Photoshop's filters enables you to quickly create a huge variety of textures that add life and realism to your textures.

Table 17.2 is a recipe book of several common textures that you can create in Photoshop. The table provides only a quick sampling of some simple textures. Many other features and effects are possible with Photoshop.

TABLE 17.2

Photoshop Texture Recipes

Texture	Technique	Create in Photoshop	Apply in Max as
	Faded color	Decrease the image saturation value (Image ➪ Adjustments ➪ Hue/Saturation) by 20 to 30%.	Diffuse map
	Surface scratches	Apply the Chalk & Charcoal filter (Filter ➪ Sketch ➪ Chalk & Charcoal) with a Stroke Pressure of 2, to a blank white image, and then apply the Film Grain (Filter ➪ Artistic ➪ Film Grain) filter with maximum Grain and Intensity.	Bump map
	Stains on fabric	Use the Dodge and Burn tools to add stains to a fabric bitmap.	Diffuse map
	Surface relief texture	Apply Dark Strokes filter (Filter ➪ Brush Strokes ➪ Dark Strokes) to a texture bitmap, and save the image as a separate bump image.	Diffuse map (original texture), Bump map (Dark Strokes version)
	Planar hair	Apply the Fibers filter (Filter ➪ Render ➪ Fibers).	Diffuse, Bump, and Specular maps
	Clouds or fog background	Apply the Clouds filter (Filter ➪ Render ➪ Clouds).	Diffuse map

Texture	Technique	Create in Photoshop	Apply in Max as
	Nebula or plasma cloud	Apply the Difference Clouds filter (Filter ⇨ Render ⇨ Difference Clouds). Then switch black and white color positions, and apply the Difference Clouds filter again.	Diffuse map
	Rock wall	Apply the Clouds filter (Filter ⇨ Render ⇨ Clouds), and then apply the Bas Relief (Filter ⇨ Sketch ⇨ Bas Relief) filter.	Diffuse and Bump maps
	Burlap sack	Apply the Add Noise filter (Filter ⇨ Noise ⇨ Add Noise), followed by the Texturizer filter (Filter ⇨ Texture ⇨ Texturizer) with the Burlap setting.	Diffuse and Bump maps
	Tile floor	Apply the Add Noise filter (Filter ⇨ Noise ⇨ Add Noise), followed by the Stained Glass filter (Filter ⇨ Texture ⇨ Stained Glass).	Diffuse map
	Brushed metal	Apply the Add Noise filter (Filter ⇨ Noise ⇨ Add Noise), followed by the Angled Strokes filter (Filter ⇨ Brush Strokes ⇨ Angled Strokes).	Diffuse and Bump maps
	Frosted glass	Apply the Clouds filter (Filter ⇨ Render ⇨ Clouds), and then apply the Glass (Filter ⇨ Distort ⇨ Glass) filter and select the Frosted option.	Diffuse map
	Pumice stone	Apply the Add Noise filter (Filter ⇨ Noise ⇨ Add Noise), followed by the Chalk & Charcoal filter (Filter ⇨ Sketch ⇨ Chalk & Charcoal).	Diffuse and Bump maps
	Planet islands	Apply the Difference Clouds filter (Filter ⇨ Render ⇨ Difference Clouds), and then apply the Note Paper (Filter ⇨ Sketch ⇨ Note Paper) filter.	Diffuse and Shininess maps
	Netting	Apply the Mosaic Tiles filter (Filter ⇨ Texture ⇨ Mosaic Tiles), followed by the Stamp (Filter ⇨ Sketch ⇨ Stamp) filter.	Diffuse and Opacity maps
	Leopard skin	Apply the Grain filter (Filter ⇨ Texture ⇨ Grain) with the Clumped option, followed by the Poster Edges (Filter ⇨ Artistic ⇨ Poster Edges) filter applied twice.	Diffuse and Opacity maps

Capturing digital images

Digital cameras and camcorders are inexpensive enough that they really are necessary items when creating material textures. Although Photoshop can be used to create many unique and interesting textures, a digital image of riverbed stones is much more realistic than anything that can be created with Photoshop. The world is full of interesting textures that can be used when creating images.

Avoiding specular highlights

Nothing can ruin a good texture taken with a digital camera faster than the camera's flash. Taking a picture of a highly reflective surface like the surface of a table can reflect back to the camera, thereby ruining the texture.

You can counter this several ways. One technique is to block the flash and make sure that you have enough ambient light to capture the texture. Taking pictures outside can help with this because they don't need the flash. Another technique is to take the image at an angle, but this might skew the texture. A third technique is to take the image and then crop away the unwanted highlights.

Tip

The best time to take outdoor photos that are to be used for materials is on an overcast day. This eliminates the direct shadows from the sun, which are very difficult to remove. It also makes the light gradient across the surface much cleaner for tiling the photo. ■

Adjusting brightness

Digital images that are taken with a digital camera are typically pre-lit, meaning that they already have a light source lighting them. When these pre-lit images are added to a Max scene that includes lights, the image gets a double dose of light that typically washes out the images.

You can remedy this problem by adjusting the brightness of the image prior to loading it into Max. For images taken in normal indoor light, you'll want to decrease the brightness value by 10 to 20 percent. For outdoor scenes in full sunlight, you may want to decrease the brightness even more.

You can find the Brightness/Contrast control in Photoshop in the Image ⇨ Adjustments ⇨ Brightness/Contrast menu.

Scanning images

In addition to taking digital images with a digital camera, you can scan images from other sources. For example, the maple leaf modeled using patches in Chapter 13, "Modeling with Polygons," was scanned from a real leaf found in my yard.

When scanning images, use the scanner's descreen option to remove any dithering from the printed image. If you place the image on a piece of matte black construction paper, then the internal glare from the scanning bulb gets a more uniform light distribution.

Caution

Most magazine and book images are copyrighted and cannot be scanned and used without permission. ∎

Tutorial: Creating a fishing net

Some modeling tasks can be solved more easily with a material than with geometry changes. A fishing net is a good example. Using geometry to create the holes in the net would be tricky, but a simple Opacity map makes this complex modeling task easy.

To create a fishing net, follow these steps:

1. Before working in Max, create the needed texture in Photoshop. In Photoshop, select File ⇨ New, enter the dimensions of 512 pixels × 512 pixels in the New dialog box, and click OK to create a new image file.

2. Select the Filter ⇨ Texture ⇨ Mosaic Tiles menu command to apply the Mosaic Tiles filter. Set the Tile Size to **30** and the Grout Width to **3**, and click OK. Then select the Filter ⇨ Sketch ⇨ Stamp menu command to apply the Stamp filter with a Light/Dark Balance value of **49** and a Smooth value of **50**.

3. Choose File ⇨ Save As, and save the file as **Netting.tif**.

    A copy of this file is available in the Chap 17 directory on the CD.

4. Open the Fish net.max file from the Chap 17 directory on the CD.

    This file includes a fishing net model created by stretching half a sphere with the Shell modifier applied.

5. Select the Rendering ⇨ Material Editor ⇨ Slate Material Editor menu command (or press the M key) to open the Material Editor. Double-click the Standard option in the Material/Map Browser to create a material node. Name the material **net**.

6. Locate and double-click the Bitmap option in the Material/Map Browser to add a node to the Node View. In the File dialog box that opens, locate and select the netting.tif image file. Drag a connection wire from the output socket of the Bitmap node and drop it on the input node of the Opacity parameter of the material node. Then drag the output socket for the material node and drop it on the net object in the viewports.

7. If you were to render the viewport, the net would look rather funny because the black lines are transparent instead of the white spaces. To fix this, select the Bitmap node, open the Output rollout, and enable the Invert option. This inverts the texture image.

Note

Although you can enable the Show Map in Viewport button in the Material Editor, the transparency is not displayed until you render the scene. ∎

Figure 17.39 shows the rendered net.

FIGURE 17.39

A fishing net, completed easily with the net texture applied as an Opacity map

Summary

We've covered lots of ground in this chapter because Max has lots of different maps. Learning to use these maps will make a big difference in the realism of your materials.

In this chapter, you learned about the following:

- Connecting map nodes in the Slate Material Editor to material nodes.
- All the different map types in several different categories, including 2D, 3D, Compositors, Color Mods, and Reflection/Refraction
- The various mapping possibilities provided in the Maps rollout
- Using the Bitmap Path Editor to change map paths
- Using the Duplicate Map Instances utility
- How to create materials using external tools such as Photoshop and a digital camera

By combining materials and maps, you can create an infinite number of material combinations, but Max has even more ways to build and apply materials. In the next chapter, you learn how complex materials and material modifiers are used.

Creating Compound Materials and Using Material Modifiers

Now that you've learned to create materials using the Standard material type, you get a chance to see the variety of material types that you can create in Max. You can select all the various Max materials from the Material/Map Browser. Open this browser automatically by selecting Rendering ⇨ Material/Map Browser.

Although many of these materials are called compound materials, they are really just collections of materials that work together as one. Just like a mesh object can include multiple elements, materials also can be made up of several materials. Using material IDs, you can apply multiple materials to the subobject selections of a single mesh object. The chapter concludes with a quick look at the various modifiers that are applied to materials.

Using Compound Materials

Compound materials combine several different materials into one. You select a compound object type by double-clicking the material type from the Material/Map Browser. Most of the entries in the Material/Map Browser are compound objects.

Compound materials usually include several different levels. For example, a Top/Bottom material includes a separate material for the top and the bottom. Each of these submaterials can then include another Top/Bottom material, and so on. The links between these different submaterials are clearly visible in the View Node panel.

Each compound material includes a customized rollout in the Parameter Editor for specifying the submaterials associated with the compound material.

Cross-Reference

Some of the material types work closely with specific objects and other Max features. These materials are covered in their respective chapters. The Advanced Lighting Override and Lightscape materials are presented in Chapter 45, "Working with Advanced Lighting, Light Tracing, and Radiosity"; the raytracing and various mental ray material settings are covered in detail in Chapter 47, "Rendering with mental ray and iray"; and the XRef material is covered in Chapter 25, "Building Complex Scenes with Containers, XRefs, and the Schematic View." ■

Blend

The Blend material blends two separate materials on a surface. The Blend Basic Parameters rollout, shown in Figure 18.1, includes separate nodes for each of the two submaterials. The check boxes to the right of these buttons enable or disable each submaterial. The Interactive option enables you to select one of the submaterials to be viewed in the viewports.

The Mask button (which appears below the two submaterial buttons) lets you load a map to specify how the submaterials are mixed. Gray areas on the map are well blended, white areas show Material 1, and black areas show Material 2. As an alternative to a mask, the Mix Amount determines how much of each submaterial to display. A value of 0 displays only Material 1, and a value of 100 displays only Material 2. This value can be animated, allowing an object to gradually change between materials.

FIGURE 18.1

The Blend material can include a mask to define the areas that are blended.

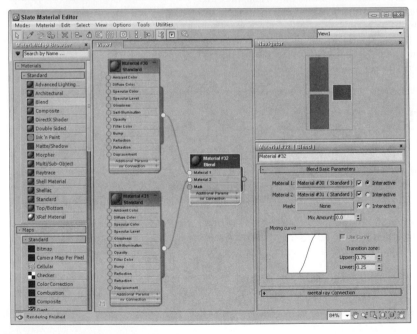

The Mixing curve defines the transition between edges of the two materials. The Upper and Lower spinners help you control the curve.

Composite

The Composite material mixes up to ten different materials by adding, subtracting, or mixing the opacity. The Composite Basic Parameters rollout, shown in Figure 18.2, includes buttons for the base material and nine additional materials that can be composited on top of the base material. The materials are applied from top to bottom.

FIGURE 18.2

Composite materials are applied from top to bottom, with the last layer placed on top of the rest.

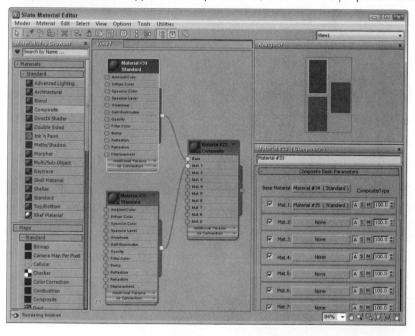

You enable or disable each material using the check box to its left. The buttons labeled with the letters A, S, and M specify the opacity type: Additive, Subtractive, or Mix. The Additive option brightens the material by adding the background colors to the current material. The Subtractive option has the opposite effect and subtracts the background colors from the current material. The Mix option blends the materials based on their Amount values.

To the right of the A, S, and M buttons is the Mix amount. This value can range from 0 to 200. At 0, none of the materials below it will be visible. At 100, full compositing occurs. Values greater than 100 cause transparent regions to become more opaque.

Cross-Reference

You can learn more about compositing and the Video Post interface in Chapter 49, "Compositing with Render Elements and the Video Post Interface." ∎

Double Sided

The Double Sided material specifies different materials for the front and back of object faces. You also have an option to make the material translucent. This material is for objects that have holes in their surface. Typically, objects with surface holes do not appear correctly because only the surfaces with normals pointing outward are visible. Applying the Double Sided material shows the interior and exterior of such an object.

The Double Sided Basic Parameters rollout includes two buttons, one for the Facing material and one for the Back material. The Translucency value sets how much of one material shows through the other.

Multi/Sub-Object

You can use the Multi/Sub-Object material to assign several different materials to a single object via the material IDs. You can use the Mesh or Poly Select modifier to select each subobject area to receive the different materials.

At the top of the Multi/Sub-Object Basic Parameters rollout, shown in Figure 18.3, is a Set Number button that lets you select the number of subobject materials to include. This number is displayed in a text field to the left of the button. Each submaterial is displayed as a separate area on the sample object in the sample slots. Using the Add and Delete buttons, you can selectively add or delete submaterials from the list.

FIGURE 18.3

The Multi/Sub-Object material defines materials according to material IDs.

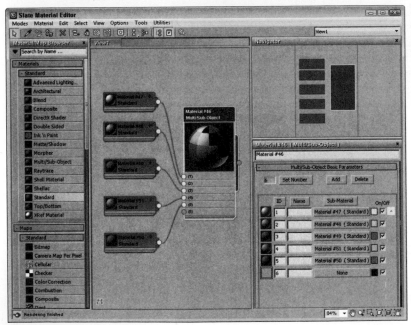

Tip

You can set the number of materials that are included by default in the Multi/Sub-Object material using the Options ⇨ Preferences dialog box. Nodes for each material are also included by default when a Multi/Sub-Object material node is created, but you can ensure that no extra material nodes are included by enabling the Empty Sub-Material Slots option in the Preferences dialog box. ∎

Each submaterial includes a sample preview of the submaterial and an index number listed to the left, a Name field where you can type the name of the submaterial, a button for selecting the material, a color swatch for creating solid color materials, and a check box for enabling or disabling the submaterial. You can sort the submaterials by clicking the ID, Name, or Sub-Material buttons at the top of each column.

After you apply a Multi/Sub-Object material to an object, convert the object to an Editable Mesh or Poly, or use the Mesh or Poly Select modifier to make a subobject selection and match the Material IDs in the Surface Properties rollout to the material for the subobject selection. In the Material section for this subobject selection, choose a material ID to associate with a submaterial ID or select the material by name from the drop-down list.

Tutorial: Creating a patchwork quilt

When I think of patches, I think of a 3D Max object type, but for many people "patches" instead bring to mind small scraps of cloth used to make a quilt. Because they share the same name, this example uses Max patches to create a quilt. You can then use the Multi/Sub-Object material to color the various patches appropriately.

Cross-Reference

You can learn more about modeling with patches in Chapter 13, "Modeling with Polygons." ∎

To create a quilt using patches, follow these steps:

1. Open the Patch quilt.max file from the Chap 18 directory on the DVD.

   This file contains a quilt made of patch objects that have been combined into one object.

2. Open the Material Editor by choosing Rendering ⇨ Material Editor ⇨ Slate Material Editor (or press M), and double-click on the Multi/Sub-Object material in the Material/Map Browser panel.

   The Multi/Sub-Object material node loads into the Node View, double-click the new node to make the Multi/Sub-Object Basic Parameters rollout appear in the Parameter Editor panel. Click the Set Number button and enter the value of **10**.

3. Double-click the Standard material in the Material/Map Browser to create a separate node for each materials included in the Multi/Sub-Object material. Then drag from the output socket of each Standard material node to the input socket in the Multi/Sub-Object node for each of the sub-materials.

4. In the Multi/Sub-Object Basic Parameters rollout, click the color swatches to the right of the Material button to open the Color Selector. Select different colors for each of the first ten material ID slots.

5. Drag the Multi/Sub-Object material node's output socket and drop it onto the patch object in the viewports. Close the Material Editor.

6. In the Modify panel, select the Patch subobject and scroll to the bottom of the Modify panel to the Surface Properties rollout.

7. Assign each patch a separate material ID by clicking a patch and changing the ID number in the rollout field.

Figure 18.4 shows the finished quilt. Because it's a patch, you can drape it over objects easily.

FIGURE 18.4

A quilt composed of patches and colored using the Multi/Sub-Object material

Morpher

The Morpher material type works with the Morpher modifier to change materials as an object morphs. For example, you can associate a blushing effect with light red applied to the cheeks of a facial expression to show embarrassment. You can use this material only on an object that has the Morpher modifier in its Stack. The Morpher modifier includes a button called Assign New Material in the Global Parameters rollout for loading the Material Editor with the Morpher material type.

Cross-Reference

Discover more about the Morpher modifier in Chapter 35, "Using Animation Layers, Modifiers, and Complex Controllers." ■

For the Morpher material, the Choose Morph Object button in the Morpher Basic Parameters rollout lets you pick a morpher object in the viewports and then open a dialog box used to bind the Morpher material to an object with the Morpher modifier applied. The Refresh button updates all the channels. The base material is the material used before any channel effects are used.

The Morpher material includes 100 channels that correlate to the channels included in the Morpher modifier. Each channel can be turned on and off. At the bottom of the parameters rollout are three Mixing Calculation options that can be used to determine how often the blending is calculated. The Always setting can consume lots of memory and can slow down the system. Other options are When Rendering and Never Calculate.

Shell

The Shell Material consists of an original material and a baked material. For each of these materials, you can specify which appear in the viewport and which are rendered.

Cross-Reference

More on baked materials is found in Chapter 34, "Creating Baked Textures and Normal Maps." ∎

Shellac

The Shellac material is added on top of the Base material. The Shellac Basic Parameters rollout includes only two buttons for each material, along with a Color Blend value. The Blend value has no upper limit.

Top/Bottom

The Top/Bottom material assigns different materials to the top and bottom of an object. The Top and Bottom areas are determined by the direction in which the face normals point. These normals can be according to the World or Local Coordinate System. You also can blend the two materials.

The Top/Bottom Basic Parameters rollout includes two buttons for loading the Top and Bottom materials. You can use the Swap button to switch the two materials. Using World coordinates enables you to rotate the object without changing the material positions. Local coordinates tie the material to the object.

The Blend value can range from 0 to 100, with 0 being a hard edge and 100 being a smooth transition. The Position value sets the location where the two materials meet. A value of 0 represents the bottom of the object and displays only the top material. A value of 100 represents the top of the object, and only the Bottom material is displayed.

Tutorial: Surfing the waves

There's nothing like hitting the surf early in the morning, unless you consider hitting the virtual surf early in the morning. As an example of a compound material, you apply the Top/Bottom material to a surfboard.

To apply a Top/Bottom compound material to a surfboard, follow these steps:

1. Open the Surfboard.max file from the Chap 18 directory on the DVD.

   This file contains a surfboard model and an infinite plane to represent the ocean.

2. Apply the Ocean Surface material, which is already created in the Material Editor, to the plane object by dragging the material node's output socket from the Material Editor to the Plane object.

3. In the Material Editor, select and double-click the Top/Bottom material to create a new material node.

4. Select the new material node and name it **Surfboard**. Then click the Top Material node, name the material **Surfboard Top**, and change the Diffuse color to White. In the material drop-down list, select Surfboard and then click the Bottom Material node. Give this material the name **Surfboard Bottom**, and change the Diffuse color to Black.

5. Then drag this material node's output socket to the surfboard object.

Figure 18.5 shows the resulting image.

FIGURE 18.5

A rendered image of a surfboard with the Top/Bottom compound material applied

Applying Multiple Materials

Most complex models are divided into multiple parts, each distinguished by the material type that is applied to it. For example, a car model would be separated into windows, tires, and the body, so that each part can have a unique material applied to it.

Using material IDs

Sometimes you may want to apply multiple materials to a single part. Selecting subobject areas and using material IDs can help you accomplish this task.

Many of the standard primitives have material IDs automatically assigned: Spheres get a single material ID, boxes get six (one for each side), and cylinders get three (one for the cylinder and one for each end cap). In addition to the standard primitives, you can assign material IDs to Editable Mesh objects. You also can assign these material IDs to any object or subobject using the Material modifier. These material IDs correspond to the various materials specified in the Multi/Sub-Object material.

Note

Don't confuse these material IDs with the material effect IDs, which are selected using the Material Effect flyout buttons under the sample slots. Material IDs are used only with the Multi/Sub-Object material type, whereas the effect IDs are used with the Render Effects and Video Post dialog boxes for adding effects such as glows to a material. ■

Tutorial: Mapping die faces

As an example of mapping multiple materials to a single object, consider a die. Splitting the cube object that makes up the die into several different parts wouldn't make sense, so you'll use the Multi/Sub-Object material instead.

To create a die model, follow these steps:

1. Open the Pair of dice.max file from the Chap 18 directory on the DVD.

    This file contains two simple cube primitives that represent a pair of dice. I also used Adobe Photoshop and created six images with the dots of a die on them. All of these images are the same size.

2. Open the Material Editor and double-click on the Multi/Sub-Object material from the Material/Map Browser. Then select the material node and name the material **Die Faces**.

3. In the Multi/Sub-Object Basic Parameters rollout, click the Set Number button and enter a value of **6**.

4. Name the first material **face 1**, and click the material button to the right that is currently labeled None to open the Material/Map Browser. Select the Standard material type and click OK. Then click the material button again to view the material parameter rollouts for the first material. Then click the map button to the right of the Diffuse color swatch to open the Material/Map Browser again, and double-click the Bitmap map type. In the Select Bitmap Image File dialog box, choose the dieface1.tif image from the Chap 18 directory on the DVD and click Open.

5. Back in the Material Editor, return to the Multi/Sub-Object Basic Parameters rollout and repeat Step 4 for each of the die faces.

6. When the Multi/Sub-Object material is defined, select the cube object and click the Assign Material to Selection button.

Note

Because the cube object used in this example is a box primitive, you didn't need to assign the material IDs to different subobject selections. The box primitive automatically assigned a different material ID to each face of the cube. When material IDs do need to be assigned, you can specify them in the Surface Properties rollout for editable meshes. ■

Figure 18.6 shows a rendered image of two dice being rolled.

Tip

If you enable the Views ➪ Show Materials in Viewports As ➪ Standard Display with Maps menu command, then the subobject materials are visible. ■

FIGURE 18.6

These dice have different bitmaps applied to each face.

Using the Clean MultiMaterial utility

All compound materials have submaterials that are used to add layers of detail to the material, but if these submaterials aren't used, they can take up memory and disk space. For example, if you have a Multi/Sub-Object material with 10 materials and the scene only uses 3 of the materials, then the other 7 materials aren't needed and can be eliminated.

You can locate and eliminate unused submaterials in the scene using the Clean MultiMaterial utility. This utility can be accessed from the Utility panel in the Command Panel by clicking the More button or from the Utilities menu in the Material Editor.

Clicking the Find All button finds all submaterials that aren't used and presents them in a list where you can select the ones to clean.

Material Modifiers

Of the many available modifiers, most modifiers change the geometry of an object, but several work specifically with materials and maps, including the Material, MaterialByElement, Disp Approx, and Displace Mesh (WSM) modifiers in the Surface category, and the Vertex Paint modifier in the Mesh Editing category. In this section, you get a chance to use several material-specific modifiers.

Material modifier

The Material modifier lets you change the material ID of an object. The only parameter for this modifier is the Material ID. When you select a subobject and apply this modifier, the material ID is applied only to the subobject selection. This modifier is used in conjunction with the Multi/Sub-Object Material type to create a single object with multiple materials.

MaterialByElement modifier

The MaterialByElement modifier enables you to change material IDs randomly. You can apply this modifier to an object with several elements. The object needs to have the Multi/Sub-Object material applied to it.

The parameters for this modifier can be set to assign material IDs randomly with the Random Distribution option or according to a desired Frequency. The ID Count is the minimum number of material IDs to use. You can specify the percentage of each ID to use in the fields under the List Frequency option. The Seed option alters the randomness of the materials.

Tutorial: Creating random marquee lights with the MaterialByElement modifier

The MaterialByElement modifier enables you to change material IDs randomly. In this tutorial, you reproduce the effect of lights randomly turning a marquee on and off by using the Multi/Sub-Object material together with the MaterialByElement modifier.

To create a randomly lighted marquee, follow these steps:

1. Open the Marquee Lights.max file from the Chap 18 directory on the DVD.

    This file includes some text displayed on a rectangular object surrounded by spheres that represent lights.

2. Open the Material Editor and double-click the Multi/Sub-Object material from the Material/Map Browser. Give the material the name **Random Lights**.

3. Double-click the Multi/Sub-Object material node and in the Multi/Sub-Object Basic Parameters rollout, click the Set Number button, and change its value to **2**. Then click the Material 1 button and select the Standard material type, and in the Material name field give the material the name **Light On**. Select the material button in the Multi/Sub-Object Basic Parameters rollout and set the Diffuse color to yellow and Self-Illumination to yellow. Then double-click again on the main material node.

4. Name the second material **Light Off**, and click the material button to right of the name field and select the Standard material type. Then click the material button again and select a gray Diffuse color. Then click the Multi/Sub-Object material node.

5. Select all the spheres, and click the Assign Material to Selection button to assign the material to the spheres.

6. With all the spheres selected, open the Modify panel and select the MaterialByElement modifier from the Modifier List drop-down list. In the Parameters rollout, select the Random Distribution option and set the ID Count to **2**.

Figure 18.7 shows the marquee with its random lights. (I've always wanted to see my name in lights!)

Tip

If you want to have the lights randomly flash, then simply animate the changing Seed value. ∎

FIGURE 18.7

This marquee is randomly lighted, thanks to the MaterialByElement modifier.

Disp Approx and Displace Mesh modifiers

You can change the geometry of an object in several ways using a bitmap. One way is to use the Displace modifier (found in the Modifiers ⇨ Parametric Deformers menu). The Displace modifier lets you specify a bitmap and a map to use to alter the object's geometry. Black areas on the bitmap are left unmoved, gray areas are indented, and white areas are indented a greater distance. Several controls are available for specifying how the image is mapped to the object and how it tiles, and buttons are available for setting its alignment, including Fit, Center, Bitmap Fit, Normal Align, View Align, Region Fit, Reset, and Acquire.

Note

Max also supports Vector Displacement maps, which are found in the Maps category of the Material/Map Browser. Vector Displacement maps require the mental ray renderer and they allow displacement in any direction and not just along surface normals like other displacement methods. Autodesk's Mudbox provides a good way to create this type of map saved using the EXR file format. ∎

Another way to displace geometry with a bitmap is to use a displacement map. Displacement maps can be applied directly to Editable Poly and Mesh, NURBS, and Patch objects. If you want to apply a displacement map to another object type, such as a primitive, you first need to apply the Modifiers ⇨ Surface ⇨ Disp Approx modifier, which is short for Displacement Approximation. This modifier includes three default presets for Low, Medium, and High that make it easy to use.

Cross-Reference

More details on working with maps are covered in Chapter 17, "Adding Material Details with Maps." ■

One drawback to using displacement maps is that you cannot see their result in the viewport, but if you apply the Modifiers ⇨ Surface ⇨ Displace Mesh (WSM) modifier, then the displacement map becomes visible in the viewports. If you change any of the displacement map settings, you can update the results by clicking the Update Mesh button in the Displacement Approx rollout.

Note

The Displace modifier requires a dense mesh in order to see the results of the displacement map, but the Disp Approx modifier creates the required density at render time. ■

Tutorial: Displacing geometry with a bitmap

When faced with how to displace an object using a bitmap, Max once again comes through with several ways to accomplish the task. The method you choose depends on the pipeline. You can choose to keep the displacement in the Modifier Stack or on the material level. This simple tutorial compares using both of these methods.

To compare the Displace modifier with a displacement map, follow these steps:

1. Create two square-shaped plane objects side by side in the Top viewport using the Create ⇨ Standard Primitives ⇨ Plane menu command. Then set the Length and Width Segments to **150** for the left plane object and to **20** for the right plane object.

Tip

When displacing geometry using a bitmap, make sure the object faces that will be displaced have sufficient resolution to represent the displacement. ■

2. Select the first plane object and apply the Displace modifier with the Modifiers ⇨ Parametric Deformers ⇨ Displace menu command. In the Parameters rollout, set the Strength value to **2** and click the Bitmap button. In the Select Displacement Image dialog box, select the Tulip logo.tif file from the Chap 18 directory on the DVD.

3. Select the second plane object and open the Material Editor by pressing the M key. In the Material Editor, open the Maps rollout, set the Displacement Map Amount value to **10**, and click the Displacement map button. Then double-click the Bitmap option in the Material/Map Browser, and load the same Tulip logo.tif file from the Chap 18 directory on the DVD. Then apply the material to the second plane object by pressing the Assign Material to Selection button, and close the Material Editor.

4. With the second plane still selected, choose the Modifiers ⇨ Surface ⇨ Displace Mesh (WSM) menu command. In the Displacement Approx. rollout, enable the Custom Settings option and click the High subdivision preset.

Figure 18.8 shows the resulting displacement on both plane objects.

Objects can be displaced using the Displace modifier or a displacement map.

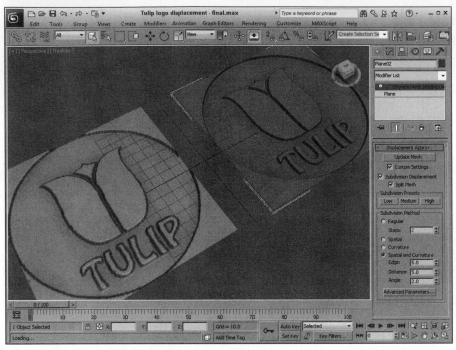

Summary

This chapter introduced several compound materials that you can create in Max. The chapter presented various material types, including compound and Multi/Sub-Object materials. The chapter also showed off a number of key material modifiers including the Displace Mesh and Vertex Paint modifiers.

The following topics were covered in this chapter:

- Various compound material types
- Applying multiple materials to an object with material IDs
- Exploring several material modifiers, including the Material and MaterialByElement
- Comparing the different displacement methods

In the next chapter, you gain some experience with using cameras to create and capture a unique view into the scene.

Configuring and Aiming Cameras

Do you remember as a kid when you first got your own camera? After taking the usual pictures of your dog and the neighbor's fence, you quickly learned how much fun you could have with camera placement, such as a picture of a flagpole from the top of the flagpole or your mom's timeless expression when she found you inside the dryer. Cameras in Max can also offer all kinds of amusing views of your scene.

The benefit of cameras is that you can position them anywhere within a scene to offer a custom view. Camera views let you see the scene from a different position such as from the top, front, or left. You can open camera views in a viewport, and you can also use them to render images or animated sequences. Cameras in Max can also be animated (without damaging the camera, even if your mischievous older brother turns on the dryer).

In the Camera Parameters rollout is a section for enabling multi-pass camera effects. These effects include Motion Blur and Depth of Field. Essentially, these effects are accomplished by taking several rendered images of a scene and combining them with some processing.

Learning to Work with Cameras

If you're a photography hobbyist or like to take your video camera out and shoot your own footage, then many of the terms in this section will be familiar to you. The cameras used in Max to get custom views of a scene behave in many respects just like real-world cameras.

Max and real-world cameras both work with different lens settings, which are measured and defined in millimeters. You can select from a variety of preset stock lenses, including 35mm, 80mm, and even 200mm. Max cameras also offer complete control over the camera's focal length, field of view, and perspective for wide-angle or telephoto shots. The big difference is that you never have to worry about setting flashes, replacing batteries, or loading film.

Light coming into a camera is bent through the camera lens and focused on the film, where the image is captured. The distance between the film and the lens is known as the *focal length*. This distance is measured in millimeters, and you can change it by switching to a different lens. On a camera that shoots 35mm film, a lens with a focal length of 50mm produces a view similar to what your eyes would see. A lens with a focal length less than 50mm is known as a wide-angle lens because it displays a wider view of the scene. A lens longer than 50mm is called a telephoto lens because it has the ability to give a closer view of objects for more detail, as a telescope does.

Field of view is directly related to focal length and is a measurement of how much of the scene is visible. It is measured in degrees. The shorter the focal length, the wider the field of view.

When you look at a scene, objects appear larger if they are up close than they would be lying at a farther distance. This effect is referred to as *perspective* and helps you interpret distances. As mentioned, a 50mm lens gives a perspective similar to what your eyes give. Images taken with a wide field of view look distorted because the effect of perspective is increased.

Creating a camera object

To create a camera object, you can use the Create ⇨ Cameras menu, or you can open the familiar Create panel and click the Cameras category button. The two types of cameras that you can create are a Free camera and a Target camera.

Camera objects are visible as icons in the viewports, but they aren't rendered. The camera icon looks like a box with a smaller box in front of it, which represents the lens or front end of the camera. Both the Free and Target camera types include a rectangular cone that shows where the camera is pointing.

Free camera

The Free camera object offers a view of the area that is directly in front of the camera and is the better choice if the camera will be animated. When a Free camera is initially created, it points at the negative Z-axis of the active viewport.

Target camera

A Target camera always points at a controllable target point some distance in front of the camera. Target cameras are easy to aim and are useful for situations where the camera won't move. To create this type of camera, click a viewport to position the camera and drag to the location of its target. The target can be named along with the camera. When a target is created, Max automatically names the target by attaching ".target" to the end of the camera name. You can change this default name by typing a different name in the Name field. Both the target and the camera can be selected and transformed independently of each other.

Creating a camera view

You can change any viewport to show a camera's viewpoint. To do so, right-click the viewport's title, and select View and the camera's name from the pop-up menu. Any movements done to the camera are reflected immediately in the viewport.

Another way to select a camera for a viewport is to press the C key. This keyboard shortcut makes the active viewport into a camera view. If several cameras exist in a scene, then the Select Camera dialog box appears, from which you can select a camera to use. You also can select a camera and choose the Set View to Selected Camera from the right-click pop-up menu. Figure 19.1 shows two Target cameras pointing at a car. The two viewports on the right are the views from these cameras.

FIGURE 19.1

A car as seen by two different cameras

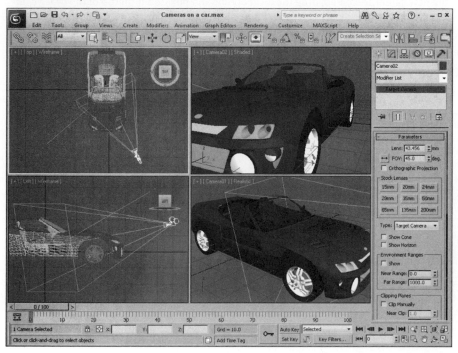

You can turn off the camera object icons using the Display panel. In the Display panel, under the Hide by Category rollout, select the Cameras option. When selected, the camera icons are not visible in the viewports.

Note

Cameras are usually positioned at some distance away from the rest of the scene. Their distant position can make scene objects appear very small when the Zoom Extents button is used. If the visibility of the camera icons is turned off, Zoom Extents does not include them in the zoom. You can also enable the Ignore Extents option in the camera's Object Properties dialog box. ■

Tutorial: Setting up an opponent's view

There is no limit to the number of cameras that you can place in a scene. Placing two cameras in a scene showing a game of checkers lets you see the game from the perspective of either player.

To create a new aligned view from the opponent's perspective, follow these steps:

1. Open the Checkers game.max file from the Chap 19 directory on the DVD.
2. Select Create ➪ Cameras ➪ Target Camera, and drag in the Top viewport to create the camera. Then give the new camera the name **Opponents Camera**.

3. Position the new target camera behind the opponent's pieces roughly symmetrical to the other camera by dragging the camera upward in the Front view.

4. With the new camera selected, drag the target point and position it on top of the other camera's target point somewhere below the center of the board.

To see the new camera view, right-click the Perspective viewport title and choose View ⇨ Black Camera (or select the camera and the Perspective viewport, and press the C key). Figure 19.2 shows the view from this camera.

FIGURE 19.2

Positioning an additional camera behind the Black player's pieces offers the opponent's view.

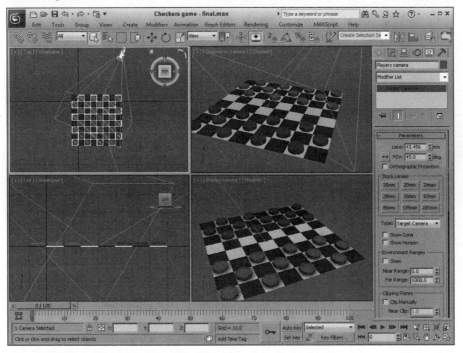

Tip

Because viewports can be resized, the view you see in the viewport isn't necessarily the view that will be rendered. Using the Safe Frames feature found in the Safe Frames panel of the Viewport Configuration dialog box, you can see a border around exactly what will be rendered. ∎

Controlling a camera

I was once on a ride at Disneyland when a person behind me decided to blatantly disregard the signs not to take photographs. As he leaned over to snap another picture, I heard a fumbling noise, a faint, "Oh no," and then the distinct sound of his camera falling into the depths of the ride. (That was actually more enjoyable than the ride. It served him right.) As this example shows, controlling a camera can be difficult. This chapter offers many tips and tricks for dealing with the cameras in Max, and you won't have to worry about dropping them.

You control the camera view in a viewport by means of the Camera Navigation controls located in the lower-right corner of the screen. These controls replace the viewport controls when a camera view is selected and are different from the normal Viewport Navigation controls. The Camera Navigation controls are identified and defined in Table 19.1.

Note

Many of these controls are identical to the controls for lights. ∎

You can constrain the movements to a single axis by holding down the Shift key. The Ctrl key causes the movements to increase rapidly. For example, holding down the Ctrl key while dragging the Perspective tool magnifies the amount of perspective applied to the viewport.

You can undo changes in the normal viewports using the Views⇨ Undo (Shift+Z) command, but you undo camera viewport changes with the regular Edit⇨ Undo command because it involves the movement of an object.

TABLE 19.1

Camera Navigation Control Buttons

Control Button	Name	Description
	Dolly Camera, Dolly Target, Dolly Camera + Target	Moves the camera, its target, or both the camera and its target closer to or farther away from the scene in the direction it is pointing.
	Perspective	Increases or decreases the viewport's perspective by dollying the camera and altering its field of view.
	Roll Camera	Spins the camera about its local Z-axis.
	Zoom Extents All, Zoom Extents All Selected	Zooms in on all objects or the selected objects by reducing the field of view until the objects fill the viewport.
	Field of View	Changes the width of the view, similar to changing the camera lens or zooming without moving the camera.
	Truck Camera, Walk Through	The Truck Camera button moves the camera perpendicular to the line of sight, and the Walk Through button enables a mode in which you can control the camera using the arrow keys and the mouse.
	Orbit, Pan Camera	The Orbit button rotates the camera around the target, and the Pan button rotates the target around the camera.
	Min/Max Toggle	Makes the current viewport fill the screen. Clicking this button a second time returns the display to several viewports.

Note

If a Free camera is selected, then the Dolly Target and Dolly Camera + Target buttons are not available. ∎

Aiming a camera

In addition to the Camera Navigation buttons, you can use the Transformation buttons on the main toolbar to reposition the camera object. To move a camera, select the camera object and click the Select and Move button (W). Then drag in the viewports to move the camera.

Using the Select and Rotate (E) button changes the direction in which a camera points, but only Free cameras rotate in all directions. When applied to a Target camera, the rotate transformation spins only the camera about the axis pointing to the target. You aim Target cameras by moving their targets.

Caution

Don't try to rotate a Target camera so that it is pointing directly up or down, or the camera will flip. ∎

Select the target for a Target camera by selecting its camera object, right-clicking to open the pop-up menu, and selecting Select Camera Target.

Tutorial: Watching a rocket

Because cameras can be transformed like any other geometry, they can also be set to watch the movements of any other geometry. In this tutorial, you aim a camera at a distant rocket and watch it as it flies past us and on into the sky. Zygote Media created the rocket model used in this tutorial.

To aim a camera at a rocket as it hurtles into the sky, follow these steps:

1. Open the Following a rocket.max file from the Chap 19 directory on the DVD.
   This file includes a rocket mesh.

2. Select Create ➪ Cameras ➪ Target Camera, and drag in the Front viewport from the top to the bottom of the viewport to create a camera. Set the Field of View value to **2.0** degrees. The corresponding Lens value is around 1031mm.

3. Select the camera target, click the Select and Link button in the main toolbar, and drag from the target to the rocket object.

4. To view the scene from the camera's viewpoint, right-click the Perspective viewport title and choose Views ➪ Camera01 from the pop-up menu (or press the C button). Then click the Play Animation button to see how well the camera follows the target.

Figure 19.3 shows some frames from this animation.

FIGURE 19.3

Positioning the camera's target on the rocket enables the camera to follow the rocket's ascent.

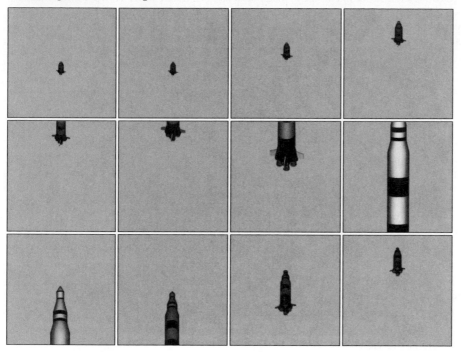

Aligning cameras

 Another way to aim a camera is with the Tools ⇨ Align ⇨ Align Camera menu command or by clicking the Align Camera button on the main toolbar (under the Align flyout). After selecting this command, click an object face and hold down the mouse button; the normal to the object face that is currently under the cursor icon is displayed as a blue arrow. When you've located the point at which you want the camera to point, release the mouse button. The camera is repositioned to point directly at the selected point on the selected face along the normal. The Align Camera command requires that a camera be selected before the command is used.

Cross-Reference

The Align Camera command does the same thing for cameras that the Place Highlight command does for lights. A discussion of the Place Highlight command appears in Chapter 20, "Using Lights and Basic Lighting Techniques." ■

Cameras can be positioned automatically to match any view that a viewport can display, including lights and the Perspective view. The Views ⇨ Create Camera From View (Ctrl+C) menu command creates a new Free camera if one doesn't already exist, matches the current active viewport, and makes the active viewport a camera view. This provides you with the ability to position the view using the Viewport Navigation Controls, and it automatically makes a camera that shows that view. If a camera already exists in the scene and is selected, this command uses the selected camera for the view.

Caution

If you use the Match Camera to View command while a camera view is the active viewport, the two cameras are positioned on top of each other. ■

Tutorial: Seeing the dinosaur's good side

Using the Align Camera tool, you can place a camera so that it points directly at an item or the face of an object, such as the dinosaur's good side (if a dinosaur has a good side). To align a camera with an object point, follow these steps:

1. Open the Dinosaur.max file from the Chap 19 directory on the DVD.

    This file includes a dinosaur model created by Viewpoint Datalabs.

2. Select Create ⇨ Cameras ⇨ Free Camera, and click in the Top viewport to create a new Free camera in the scene.

3. With the camera selected, choose Tools ⇨ Align ⇨ Align Camera or click the Align Camera flyout button on the main toolbar.

    The cursor changes to a small camera icon.

4. Select the Perspective viewport and click the cursor on the dinosaur's face just under its eye in the Perspective viewport.

    This point is where the camera will point.

5. To see the new camera view, right-click the viewport title and choose Views ⇨ Camera01 (or press C).

    Although the camera is pointing at the selected point, you may need to change the field of view or dolly the camera to correct the zoom ratios.

Figure 19.4 shows your dinosaur from the newly aligned camera.

The Align Camera command points a camera at an object only for the current frame. It does not follow an object if it moves during an animation. To have a camera follow an object, you need to use the Look At Constraint, which is covered in Chapter 22, "Animating with Constraints and Simple Controllers."

FIGURE 19.4

This new camera view of the dinosaur shows his best side.

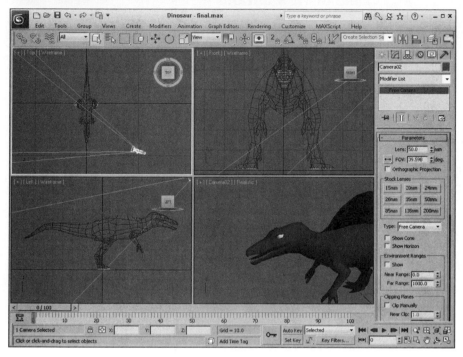

Setting Camera Parameters

When a camera is first created, you can modify the camera parameters directly in the Create panel as long as the new camera is selected. After the camera object has been deselected, you can make modifications in the Modify panel's Parameters rollout for the camera.

Lens settings and field of view

The first parameter in the Parameters rollout sets the Lens value or, more simply, the camera's focal length in millimeters.

The second parameter, FOV (which stands for Field of View), sets the width of the area that the camera displays. The value is specified in degrees and can be set to represent a Horizontal, Vertical, or Diagonal distance using the flyout button to its left, as shown in Table 19.2.

TABLE 19.2

Field of View Buttons

Button	Description
↔	Horizontal distance
↕	Vertical distance
⤢	Diagonal distance

The Orthographic Projection option displays the camera view in a manner similar to any of the orthographic viewports such as Top, Left, or Front. This eliminates any perspective distortion of objects farther back in the scene and displays true dimensions for all edges in the scene. This type of view is used heavily in architecture.

Professional photographers and film crews use standard stock lenses in the course of their work. These lenses can be simulated in Max by clicking one of the Stock Lens buttons. Preset stock lenses include 15, 20, 24, 28, 35, 50, 85, 135, and 200mm lengths. The Lens and FOV fields are automatically updated on stock lens selection.

Tip
On cameras that use 35mm film, the typical default lens is 50mm. ■

Camera type and display options

The Type option enables you to change a Free camera to a Target camera and then change back at any time.

The Show Cone option enables you to display the camera's cone, showing the boundaries of the camera view when the camera isn't selected. (The camera cone is always visible when a camera is selected.) The Show Horizon option sets a horizon line within the camera view, which is a dark gray line where the horizon is located.

Environment ranges and clipping planes

You use the Near and Far Range values to specify the volume within which atmospheric effects like fog and volume lights are to be contained. The Show option causes these limits to be displayed as yellow rectangles within the camera's cone.

You use clipping planes to designate the closest and farthest object that the camera can see. In Max, they are displayed as red rectangles with crossing diagonals in the camera cone. If the Clip Manually option is disabled, then the clipping planes are set automatically with the Near Clip Plane set to 3 units. Figure 19.5 shows a camera with Clipping Planes specified. The front Clipping Plane intersects the car and chops off its front end. The far Clipping Plane is far behind the car.

Tip
Clipping planes can be used to create a cutaway view of your model. ■

FIGURE 19.5

A camera cone displaying Clipping Planes

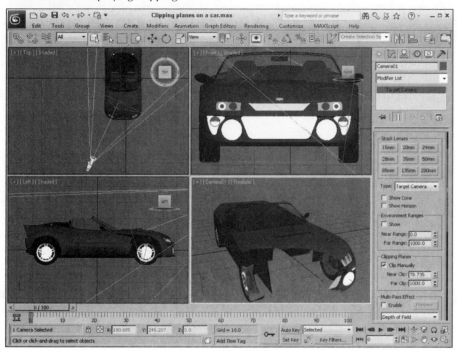

Camera Correction modifier

To understand the Camera Correction modifier, you first need to understand what two-point perspective is. Default cameras in Max use three-point perspective, which causes all lines to converge to a vanishing point off in the distance, but two-point perspective causes all vertical lines to remain vertical.

The visual effect of this modifier is that extra-tall objects appear to bend toward the camera when corrected. For example, if you have a camera pointed at a skyscraper, then correcting the camera with the Camera Correction modifier makes the top of the building appear closer rather than having it recede away.

The Camera Correction modifier has an Amount value that lets you specify how much correction to apply and a Direction value that orients the angle of vertical lines in the scene. There is also a Guess button, which automatically sets the correction values for you based on the Z-axis vertical.

Caution

The Camera Correction modifier doesn't appear in the Modifier List in the Modifier Stack, but you can select it from the Modifiers ➪ Cameras menu. ■

Creating multi-pass camera effects

All cameras have the option to enable them to become multi-pass cameras. You can find these settings in the Parameters rollout when a camera object is selected. Multi-pass cameras are created by checking the Enable button and selecting the effect from the drop-down list. The current available effects include Depth of Field (mental ray), Depth of Field, and Motion Blur. For each, an associated rollout of parameters opens.

Caution

Preview of the multi-pass camera effects in the viewport does not work when the Nitrous display drivers are enabled. ■

Note

The Depth of Field multi-pass effect is used with the default Scanline renderer, but the drop-down list also includes an option for enabling this effect for the mental ray or iray renderers. ■

The Multi-Pass Effect section of the Parameters rollout also includes a Preview button. This button makes the effect visible in the viewports for the current frame. This feature can save you a significant amount of time that normally would be spent test-rendering the scene. The Preview button is worth its weight in render speed. Using this button, you can preview the effect without having to render the entire sequence.

Caution

The Preview button does not work unless the Camera view is the active viewport. ■

The Render Effect Per Pass option causes any applied Render Effect to be applied at each pass. If disabled, then any applied Render Effect is applied after the passes are completed.

Cross-Reference

You can also apply these multi-pass effects as Render Effects. See Chapter 46, "Using Atmospheric and Render Effects." ■

Using the Depth of Field effect

The Depth of Field Parameters rollout, shown in Figure 19.6, appears when the Depth of Field option is selected in the Multi-Pass Effect section of the Parameters rollout. It includes settings for controlling the Depth of Field multi-pass effect.

You can select to use the Target Distance (which is the distance to the camera's target), or you can specify a separate Focal Depth distance. This location is the point where the camera is in focus. All scene objects closer and farther from this location are blurred to an extent, depending on their distance from the focal point.

Note

Even Free cameras have a Target Distance. This distance is displayed at the bottom of the Parameters rollout. ■

Within the Depth of Field Parameters rollout, you also have the option to display each separate pass in the Rendered Frame Window with the Display Passes option and to use the camera's original location for the first rendering pass by enabling the Use Original Location option.

FIGURE 19.6

Use the Depth of Field Parameters rollout to set the number of passes.

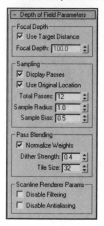

The Total Passes is the number of times the scene is rendered to produce the effect, and the Sample Radius is the potential distance that the scene can move during the passes. By moving the scene about the radius value and re-rendering a pass, the object becomes blurred more away from the focal distance. If you have a fairly tight scene, the default Radius value does not produce very visible results. Try increasing the Sample Radius value and re-rendering. Figure 19.7 shows a scene with Sample Radius values of 1 and 5.

FIGURE 19.7

Changing the Sample Radius value changes the amount of blur added to the scene.

Note

The Depth of Field effect is applied only to rendered scene objects. It is not applied to any background images. ∎

The Sample Bias value moves the blurring closer to the focal point (for higher values) or away from the focal point (for lower values). If you want to highlight the focal point and radically blur the other objects in the scene, set the Sample Bias to 1.0. A Sample Bias setting of 0 results in a more even blurring.

The Normalize Weights option allows you to control how the various passes are blended. When enabled, you can avoid streaking along the object edges. The Dither Strength value controls the amount of dither taking place. Higher Dither Strength values make the image grainier. The Tile Size value also controls dither by specifying the dither pattern size.

With lots of passes specified, the render time can be fairly steep. To lower the overall rendering time, you can disable the Anti-alias and filtering computations. These speed up the rendering time at the cost of image quality.

Tutorial: Applying a Depth of Field effect to a row of windmills

In the dry plains of Southwest America, the wind blows fiercely. Rows of windmills are lined up in an effort to harness this energy. For this example, you use the Depth of Field effect to display the windmills.

To apply a Depth of Field effect to a row of windmills, follow these steps:

1. Open the Depth of field windmills.max file from the Chap 19 directory on the DVD.

    This file includes a windmill object (created by Viewpoint Datalabs) duplicated multiple times and positioned in a row.

2. Select Create ➪ Cameras ➪ Target Camera, and drag in the Top viewport from the lower-left corner to the center of the windmills. In the Left vewpoint, select the camera and move it upward, and then select the Camera Target and also move it upward to the upper third of the windmill's height, so the entire row of windmills can be seen. If the windmills don't fill the camera view, adjust the Field of View (FOV) setting.

Tip
You can select both the camera and its target by clicking on the line that connects them. ∎

3. Select the Perspective viewport, right-click on the viewport title, and select Views ➪ Camera01 (or just press the C key) to make this viewport the Camera view.

4. With the Camera selected, open the Modify panel, enable the Multi-Pass Effect option, and then select Depth of Field in the drop-down list.

5. In the Depth of Field Parameters rollout, enable the Use Target Distance option and set the Total Passes to **15**, the Sample Radius to **3.0**, and the Sample Bias to **1.0**.

6. Select the Camera viewport, and click the Preview button in the Parameters rollout.

    This shows the Depth of Field effect in the viewport.

Figure 19.8 shows the resulting Depth of Field effect in the viewport for the row of windmills.

FIGURE 19.8

Multi-pass camera effects can be viewed in the viewport using the Preview button.

Using the Motion Blur effect

Motion Blur is an effect that shows motion by blurring objects that are moving. If a stationary object is surrounded by several moving objects, the Motion Blur effect blurs the moving objects and the stationary object remains in clear view, regardless of its position in the scene. The faster an object moves, the more blurry it becomes.

This blurring is accomplished in several ways, but with a multi-pass camera, the camera renders subsequent frames of an animation and then blurs the images together.

The Motion Blur Parameters rollout, shown in Figure 19.9, appears when the Motion Blur option is selected in the Multi-Pass Effect section of the Parameters rollout. Many of its parameters work the same as the Depth of Field effect.

FIGURE 19.9

For the Motion Blur effect, you can set the number of frames to include.

The Display Passes option displays the different frames as they are being rendered, and Total Passes is the number of frames that are included in the averaging. You can also select the Duration, which is the number of frames to include in the effect. The Bias option weights the averaging toward the current frame. Higher Bias values weight the average more toward the latter frames, and lower values lean toward the earlier frames.

The remaining options all work the same as for the Depth of Field effect.

Tutorial: Using a Motion Blur multi-pass camera effect

The Motion Blur effect works only on objects that are moving. Applying this effect to a stationary 2D shape does not produce any noticeable results. For this tutorial, you apply this effect to a speeding car model created by Viewpoint Datalabs.

To apply a Motion Blur multi-pass effect to the camera looking at a car mesh, follow these steps:

1. Open the Car at a stop sign.max file from the Chap 19 directory on the DVD.

   This file includes a car mesh (created by Viewpoint Datalabs), a camera, and a simple stop sign made of primitives. The car is animated.

2. Click the Select by Name button on the main toolbar to open the Select by Name dialog box (or press the H key). Double-click the Camera01 object to select it.

3. With the camera object selected, open the Modify panel. In the Multi-Pass Effect section of the Parameters rollout, click the Enable check box and select the Motion Blur effect from the drop-down list.

4. In the Motion Blur Parameters rollout, set the Total Passes to **10**, the Duration to **1.0**, and the Bias to **0.9**.

5. Drag the Time Slider to frame 57. This is the location where the car just passes the stop sign.

6. With the Camera selected in the active viewport, click the Modify tab in the Command Panel to reveal the Camera's Parameters rollout. Click the Preview button under Multi-pass effects.

Figure 19.10 shows the results of the Motion Blur effect. This effect has been exaggerated to show its result. Notice that the stop sign isn't blurred. The only problem with this example is that, with the Motion Blur effect enabled, you can't make out the license plate number, so you can't send this speeder a ticket.

FIGURE 19.10

Using the Motion Blur multi-pass effect for a camera, you can blur objects moving in the scene.

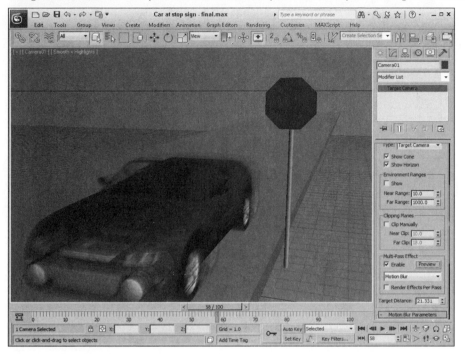

Summary

Cameras can offer a unique look at your scene. You can position and move them anywhere. In this chapter, you discovered how cameras work and how to control and aim them at objects. With multi-pass camera effects, you can add Depth of Field and Motion Blur effects.

In this chapter, you've accomplished the following:

- Learned the basics of cameras
- Created a camera object and view
- Discovered how to control a camera
- Aimed a camera at objects
- Changed camera parameters
- Learned to correct camera perspective with the Camera Correction modifier
- Used a multi-pass camera to create a Depth of Field effect
- Used a multi-pass camera to create a Motion Blur effect

Although the director typically says, "Lights, camera, action," you've switched the order to be cameras and then lights (action comes with animation later in the book). You just finished cameras, so next you move on to lights.

Using Lights and Basic Lighting Techniques

Lights play an important part in the visual process. Have you ever looked at a blank page and been told it was a picture of a polar bear in a blizzard or looked at a completely black image and been told it was a rendering of a black spider crawling down a chimney covered in soot? The point of these two examples is that with too much or too little light, you really can't see anything.

Light in the 3D world figures into every rendering calculation, and 3D artists often struggle with the same problem of too much or too little light. This chapter covers creating and controlling lights in your scene.

Understanding the Basics of Lighting

Lighting plays a critical part of any Max scene. Understanding the basics of lighting can make a big difference in the overall feeling and mood of your rendered scenes. Most Max scenes typically use one of two types of lighting: natural light or artificial light. *Natural light* is used for outside scenes and uses the sun and moon for its light source. *Artificial light* is usually reserved for indoor scenes where light bulbs provide the light. However, when working with lights, you'll sometimes use natural light indoors, such as sunlight streaming through a window, or artificial light outdoors, such as a streetlight.

Natural and artificial light

Natural light is best created using lights that have parallel light rays coming from a single direction: You can create this type of light using a Direct Light. The intensity of natural light is also dependent on the time, date, and location of the sun: You can control this intensity precisely using Max's Sunlight or Daylight systems.

The weather can also make a difference in the light color. In clear weather, the color of sunlight is pale yellow; in clouds, sunlight has a blue tint; and in dark, stormy weather, sunlight is dark gray. The colors of light at sunrise and sunset are more orange and red. Moonlight is typically white.

Artificial light is typically produced with multiple lights of lower intensity. The Omni light is usually a good choice for indoor lighting because it casts light rays in all directions from a single source. Standard white fluorescent lights usually have a light green or light blue tint.

A standard lighting method

When lighting a scene, not relying on a single light is best. A good lighting method includes one key light and several secondary lights.

A spotlight is good to use for the main key light. It should be positioned in front of and slightly above the subject, and it should usually be set to cast shadows, because it will be the main shadow-casting light in the scene.

The secondary lights fill in the lighting gaps and holes. You can position these at floor level on either side of the subject, with the intensity set at considerably less than the key light and set to cast no shadows. You can place one additional light behind the scene to backlight the subjects. This light should be very dim and also cast no shadows. From the user's perspective, all the objects in the scene will be illuminated, but the casual user will identify only the main spotlight as the light source because it casts shadows.

Figure 20.1 shows the position of the lights on an elk model that are included in the standard lighting model using a key light, two secondary lights, and a backlight. This model works for most standard scenes, but if you want to highlight a specific object, additional lights are needed.

Figure 20.2 shows an elk model that was rendered using different levels of the standard lighting model. The upper-left image uses the default lighting with no lights. The upper-right image uses only the key light. This makes a shadow visible, but the details around the head are hard to define. The lower-left image includes the secondary lights, making the head details more easily visible and adding some highlights to the antlers. The bottom-right image includes the backlight, which highlights the back end of the model and casts a halo around the edges if viewed from the front.

The final type of light to keep in mind is *ambient light*. Ambient light is not from a direct source, but is created by light that is deflected off walls and objects. It provides overall lighting to the entire scene and keeps shadows from becoming completely black. Global Lighting (including ambient light) is set in the Environment panel.

FIGURE 20.1

A standard lighting model includes a key light, two secondary lights, and a backlight.

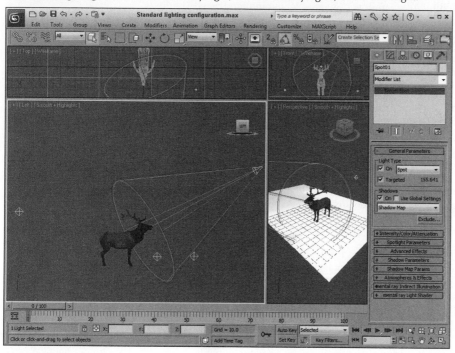

FIGURE 20.2

An elk model rendered using default lighting, a single key light, two secondary lights, and a backlight

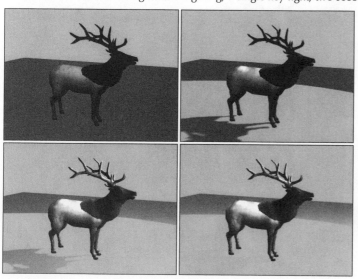

Shadows

Shadows are the areas behind an object where the light is obscured. Max supports several types of shadows, including Area Shadows, Shadow Maps, and Raytraced Shadows.

Area Shadows create shadows based on an area that casts a light. It doesn't require lots of memory and results in a soft shadow that is created from multiple light rays that blur the shadows. Shadow maps are actual bitmaps that the renderer produces and combines with the finished scene to produce an image. These maps can have different resolutions, but higher resolutions require more memory. Shadow maps typically create fairly realistic, softer shadows, but they don't support transparency.

Max calculates raytraced shadows by following the path of every light ray striking a scene. This process takes a significant amount of processing cycles, but can produce very accurate, hard-edged shadows. Raytracing enables you to create shadows for objects that shadow maps can't, such as transparent glass. The Shadows drop-down list also includes an option called Advanced Raytraced Shadows, which uses memory more efficiently than the standard Raytraced Shadows. Another option is the mental ray Shadow Map.

Cross-Reference

You can learn more about raytracing and mental ray in Chapter 47, "Rendering with mental ray and iray." ∎

Figure 20.3 shows several images rendered with the different shadow types. The image in the upper left includes no shadows. The upper-right image uses Area Shadows. The lower-left image uses a Shadow Map, and the lower-right image uses Advanced Raytraced Shadows. The last two images took considerably longer to create. Viewpoint Datalabs created the elk model shown in this figure.

FIGURE 20.3

Images rendered with different shadow types, including no shadow (upper left), Area Shadows (upper right), a Shadow Map (lower left), and Advanced Raytraced Shadows (lower right)

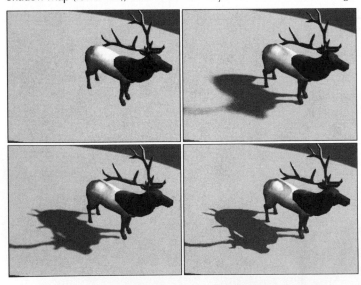

Getting to Know the Light Types

Max includes several different types of lights. The main difference in these types is how the light rays are cast into the scene. Light can come from the default lights that are present when no other user-created lights have been added to the scene. Light can also come from ambient light, which is light that bounces off other objects. Max includes several standard light objects that can be added where needed to a scene, including Omni, Direct, Spot, and skylights, each having its own characteristics. Max also includes a category of Photometric lights, which are based on real-world lights. Understanding these sources of light will help you know where to look to control the lighting.

Default lighting

So you get Max installed, and you eagerly start the application, throw some objects in a scene, and render it . . . and you'll be disappointed in the output, because you forgot to put lights in the scene. Right? Wrong! Max is smart enough to place default lighting in the scene that does not have any light.

The default lighting disappears as soon as a light is created in a scene (even if the light is turned off). When all the lights in a scene are deleted, default lighting magically reappears. So you can always be sure that your objects are rendered using some sort of lighting. Default lighting actually consists of two lights: The first light, the key light, is positioned above and to the left, and the bottom light, the fill light, is positioned below and to the right.

The Visual Style & Appearance panel of the Viewport Configuration dialog box has an option to enable default lighting for any viewport or set the default lighting to use only one light, the key light. You can open this dialog box by choosing Views ⇨ Viewport Configuration or by clicking on the plus sign viewport label and selecting Configuration from the pop-up menu.

If you want to access the default lights in your scene, you can use the Create ⇨ Lights ⇨ Standard Lights ⇨ Add Default Lights to Scene command to convert the default lights into actual light objects that you can control and reposition. This command opens a simple dialog box where you can select which lights to add to the scene and set the Distance Scaling value. This feature lets you start with the default lights and modify them as needed.

Caution

The Create ⇨ Lights ⇨ Standard Lights ⇨ Add Default Lights to Scene menu command is enabled only if the Default Lighting and 2 Lights options are selected in the Viewport Configuration dialog box. ■

Ambient light

Ambient light is general lighting that uniformly illuminates the entire scene. It is caused by light that bounces off other objects. Using the Environment dialog box, you can set the ambient light color. You can also set the default ambient light color in the Rendering panel of the Preference Settings dialog box. This is the darkest color that can appear in the scene, generally in the shadows.

In addition to these global ambient settings, each material can have an ambient color selected in the Material Editor.

Caution

Don't rely on ambient light to fill in unlit sections of your scene. If you use a heavy dose of ambient light instead of placing secondary lights, your scene objects appear flat, and you won't get the needed contrast to make your objects stand out. ■

Standard lights

Within the Create panel, the available lights are split into two subcategories: Standard and Photometric. Each subcategory has its own unique set of properties. The Standard light types include Omni, Spot (Target and Free) and Direct (Target and Free), Skylight, and two area lights (Spot and Omni) that work with mental ray.

Omni light

The Omni light is like a light bulb: It casts light rays in all directions. The two default lights are Omni lights.

Spotlight

Spotlights are directional: They can be pointed and sized. The two spotlights available in Max are a Target Spot and a Free Spot. A Target Spot light consists of a light object and a target marker at which the spotlight points. A Free Spot light has no target, which enables it to be rotated in any direction using the Select and Rotate transform button. Spotlights always are displayed in the viewport as a cone with the light positioned at the cone apex.

Cross-Reference

Both Target Spot and Target Direct lights are very similar in functionality to the Target Camera object, which you learn about in Chapter 19, "Configuring and Aiming Cameras." ■

Direct light

Direct lights cast parallel light rays in a single direction, like the sun. Just like spotlights, direct lights come in two types: a Target Direct light and a Free Direct light. The position of the Target Direct light always points toward the target, which you can move within the scene using the Select and Move button. A Free Direct light can be rotated to determine where it points. Direct lights are always displayed in the viewport as cylinders.

Skylight

The Skylight is like a controllable ambient light. You can move it about the scene just like the other lights, and you can select to use the Scene Environment settings or select a Sky Color.

Area Omni and Area Spot

The Area lights project light from a defined area instead of from a single point. This has the effect of casting light along a wider area with more cumulative intensity than a point light source. Area lights are supported only by the mental ray renderer. If you use the Scanline renderer, these lights behave like simple point lights.

The Area Omni light lets you set its shape as a Sphere or a Cylinder in the Area Light Parameters rollout. Area Spot lights can be set to be either Rectangular or Disc-shaped. Be aware that area lights can take significantly longer to render than point lights.

Cross-Reference

For more details on the mental ray renderer, see Chapter 47, "Rendering with mental ray and iray." ■

Photometric lights

The standard Max lights rely on parameters like Multiplier, Decay, and Attenuation, but the last time I was in the hardware store looking for a light bulb with a 2.5 Multiplier value, I was disappointed. Lights in the real world have their own set of measurements that define the type of light that is produced. Photometric lights are lights that are based on real-world light measurement values such as Intensity in Lumens and temperatures in degrees Kelvin.

If you select the Lights menu or the Lights category in the Create panel, you'll notice another subcategory called Photometric. Photometric lights are based on photometric values, which are the values of light energy. The lights found in this subcategory include Free and Target lights.

Cross-Reference

The Photometric category also includes a mr Sky Portal option that is used to focus lights coming in from an external source. This feature is covered in Chapter 47, "Rendering with mental ray and iray." ■

To make choosing the right light easier, Max includes a Templates rollout for photometric lights that lets you set the configuration for a number of different common real-world lights, including 40, 60, 75, and 100W light bulbs, a number of Halogen spotlights, recessed lights, fluorescent lights, and even street and stadium lights.

Note

Whenever a photometric light is created, a warning dialog box appears, informing you that it is recommended that the Logarithmic Exposure Control be enabled. It also offers you an option to enable this setting. You can learn more about this feature in Chapter 46, "Using Atmospheric and Render Effects." ■

Creating and Positioning Light Objects

Max, in its default setup, can create many different types of light. Each has different properties and features. To create a light, just select Create ➪ Lights and choose the lights type or click the Lights category button in the Create panel. Then click the button for the type of light you want to create and drag in a viewport to create it. Most light types are created with a single click, but you create Target lights by clicking at the light's position and dragging to the position of the target.

Transforming lights

Lights can be transformed just like other geometric objects. To transform a light, click one of the transformation buttons and then select and drag the light.

Target lights can have the light and the target transformed independently, or you can select both the light and target by clicking the line that connects them. Target lights can be rotated around the X and Y axes only if the light and target are selected together. A target light can spin about its local Z-axis even if the target isn't selected. Scaling a target light increases its cone or cylinder. Scaling a Target Direct light with only the light selected increases the diameter of the light's beam, but if the light and target are selected, then the diameter and distance are scaled.

An easy way to select or deselect the target is to right-click the light and choose Select Target from the pop-up menu. All transformations work on free lights.

Viewing lights and shadows in the viewport

Lights and shadows can be displayed in the viewports if you are using the Nitrous or the Direct3D display driver. You can check to see if your video card supports interactive lights and shadows using the Help ⇨ Diagnose Video Hardware menu command. This command runs a script and returns the results to the MAXScript Listener window.

If your graphics card supports viewport shadows, you can enable them using the Lighting and Shadows submenu under the viewport Shading label or in the Visual Style & Appearance panel of the Viewport Configuration dialog box. If you're using the Nitrous display driver, then the same menu also includes an option for enabling Ambient Occlusion.

The Viewport Lighting and Shadows quadmenu and the Views menu also include options to lock and unlock the selected light, and to display the effects of the selected light. Figure 20.4 shows a snowman with shadows enabled in the viewport.

FIGURE 20.4

By enabling viewport shadows, you can view shadows in real time.

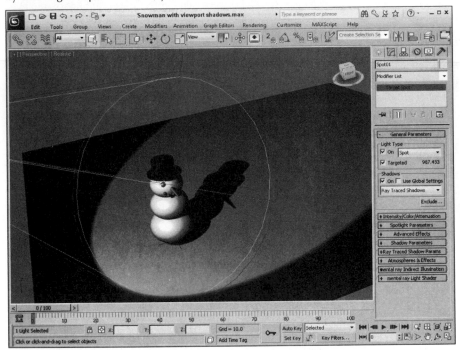

Listing lights

The Tools ⇨ Light Lister menu command opens the Light Lister dialog box, shown in Figure 20.5, where you can see at a quick glance all the details for all the lights in the scene. This dialog box also lets you change the light settings. It includes two rollouts: Configuration, which lets you select to see All Lights, the Selected Lights, or the General Settings that apply to all lights; and Lights, which holds details on each individual light.

FIGURE 20.5

The Light Lister dialog box includes a comprehensive list of light settings in one place.

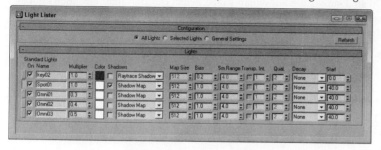

If the General Settings option is selected, then a separate rollout opens with all the typical settings, including Multiplier, Color, Shadows, Map Size, and so on. You can apply these changes to the Selected Lights or to All Lights. The Light Lister provides an easy way to change the parameters of many lights at once.

If either the All Lights option or the Selected Lights option is selected, then the parameters are listed in the Lights rollout. Using this rollout, you can change the settings for any of the listed lights that affect all lights. The Refresh button updates the Light Lister dialog box if a new light has been added to the scene or if any parameters have been altered in the Modify panel.

Note

If several lights are instanced, then only one of the instanced lights appears in the Light Lister dialog box, but each of the instanced lights can be selected from a drop-down list. ■

Placing highlights

The Place Highlight feature enables you to control the position and orientation of a light in order to achieve a highlight in a precise location. To use this feature, you must select a light object in the scene and then choose Tools ➪ Align ➪ Place Highlight, or click the Place Highlight flyout button on the toolbar. The cursor changes to the Place Highlight icon. Click a point on the object in the scene where you want the highlight to be positioned, and the selected light repositions itself to create a specular highlight at the exact location where you clicked. The light's position is determined by the Angle of Incidence between the highlight point and the light.

Tip

If you click and drag on the object surface, then a small blue vector points from the surface of the object. The light is positioned inline with this vector when the mouse button is released. This is helpful when trying to precisely place a light. ■

Tutorial: Lighting the snowman's face

You can use the Place Highlight feature to position a light for our snowman. To place a highlight, follow these steps:

1. Open the Snowman.max file from the Chap 20 directory on the CD.

    This file contains a simple snowman created using primitive objects.

2. Select the Create ▷ Lights ▷ Standard Lights ▷ Target Spotlight menu command, and position the spot light below and to the left of the Snowman model.

3. To place the highlight so it shows the Snowman's face, select the spot light and then choose Tools ▷ Align ▷ Place Highlight. Then click and drag on the Snowman's face where the highlight should be located, just above his right eye.

Figure 20.6 shows the results.

FIGURE 20.6

The snowman, after the lights have been automatically repositioned using the Place Highlights command

Note
The effect of lights can be fully seen in the viewport if the Best or Good shading option is enabled. ∎

Viewing a Scene from a Light

You can configure viewports to display the view from any light, with the exception of an Omni light. To do so, click the viewport Point-of-View label and then select Lights and the light name at the top of the pop-up menu.

Note

The keyboard shortcut for making the active viewport a Light view is the $ (the dollar sign that appears above the 4) key. If more than one light exists, then the Select Light dialog box appears and lets you select which light to use. This can be used only on spot and direct lights. ■

Light viewport controls

When a viewport is changed to show a light view, the Viewport Navigation buttons in the lower-right corner of the screen change into Light Navigation controls. Table 20.1 describes these controls.

Note

Many of these controls are identical for viewports displaying lights or cameras. ■

TABLE 20.1

Light Navigation Control Buttons

Toolbar Button	Name	Description
	Dolly, Target, Both	Moves the light, its target, or both the light and its target closer to or farther away from the scene in the direction it is pointing.
	Light Hotspot	Adjusts the angle of the light's hotspot, which is displayed as a blue cone.
	Roll Light	Spins the light about its local Z-axis.
	Zoom Extents All, Zoom Extents All Selected	Zooms in on all objects or the selected objects until they fill the viewport.
	Light Falloff	Changes the angle of the light's falloff cone.
	Truck Light	Moves the light perpendicular to the line of sight.
	Orbit, Pan Light	The Orbit button rotates the light around the target, whereas the Pan Light button rotates the target around the light.
	Min/Max Toggle	Makes the current viewport fill the screen. Clicking this button a second time returns the display to several viewports.

If you hold down the Ctrl key while using the Light Hotspot or Falloff buttons, Max maintains the distance between the hotspot and falloff cones. Holding down the Alt key causes the size to change at a much slower rate. The Hotspot cone cannot grow any larger than the Falloff cone, but if you hold down the Shift key, then trying to make the size of the hotspot larger than the falloff causes both to increase, and vice versa.

You can constrain any light movements to a single axis by holding down the Shift key. The Ctrl key causes the movements to increase rapidly.

For Free lights, an invisible target is determined by the distance computed from the other light properties. You can use the Shift key to constrain rotations to be vertical or horizontal.

Note
You can undo changes in the normal viewports using the Views ⇨ Undo command, but you undo light viewport changes with the regular Edit ⇨ Undo command. ∎

Tutorial: Lighting a lamp

To practice using lights, you'll try to get a lamp model to work as it should.

To add a light to a lamp model, follow these steps:

1. Open the Lamp.max file from the Chap 20 directory on the CD.

    This file includes a lamp mesh surrounded by some plane objects used to create the walls and floor. The lamp model was created by Zygote Media. It looks like a standard living room lamp that you could buy in any department store.

2. Select the Create ⇨ Lights ⇨ Standard Lights ⇨ Omni menu command, and click in any viewport.

3. Use the Select and Move transform button (W) to position the light object inside the lamp's light bulb.

The resulting image is shown in Figure 20.7. Notice that the light intensity is greater at places closer to the light.

FIGURE 20.7

The rendered lighted-lamp image

Altering Light Parameters

Lights affect every object in a scene and can really make or break a rendered image, so it shouldn't be surprising that each light comes with many controls and parameters. Several different rollouts work with lights.

If you're looking for a light switch to turn lights on and off, look no further than the Modify panel. When a light is selected, several different rollouts appear. The options contained in these rollouts enable you to turn the lights on and off, select a light color and intensity, and determine how a light affects object surfaces.

General parameters

The Light Type drop-down list in the General Parameters rollout lets you change the type of light instantly, so that you can switch from Omni light to Spotlight with little effort. You can also switch between targeted and untargeted lights. To the right of the Targeted option is the distance in scene units between the light and the target. This feature provides an easy way to look at the results of using a different type of light. When you change the type of light, you lose the settings for the previous light.

The General Parameters rollout also includes some settings for shadows. Shadows can be easily turned on or off. In this rollout, you can defer to the global settings by selecting the Use Global Settings option. This option helps to maintain consistent settings across several lights. It applies the same settings to all lights, so that changing the value for one light changes that same value for all lights that have this option selected.

You can also select from a drop-down list whether the shadows are created using Area Shadows, a Shadow Map, regular or advanced raytraced shadows, or a mental ray shadow map. A new rollout appears, depending on the selection that you make.

The Exclude button opens the Exclude/Include dialog box, where you can select objects to be included or excluded from illumination and/or shadows. The pane on the left includes a list of all the current objects in the scene. To exclude objects from being lit, select the Exclude option, select the objects to be excluded from the pane on the left, and click the double-arrow icon pointing to the right to move the objects to the pane on the right.

Figure 20.8 shows the Exclude/Include dialog box. This dialog box also recognizes any Selection Sets that you've previously defined. You select them from the Selection Sets drop-down list.

As an example of the Exclude/Include feature, Figure 20.9 shows the elk model with the antlers (left) and its body (right) excluded from the shadows pass.

FIGURE 20.8

The Exclude/Include dialog box lets you set which objects are excluded or included from being illuminated.

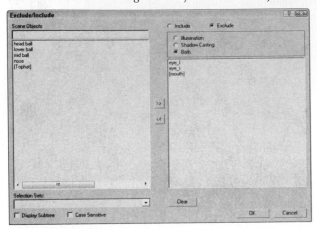

FIGURE 20.9

Using the Exclude/Include dialog box, you can exclude objects from casting shadows.

The Intensity/Color/Attenuation rollout

In the Intensity/Color/Attenuation rollout, the Multiplier value controls the light intensity. A light with a Multiplier set to 2 is twice as bright as a light with its Multiplier set to 1. Higher Multiplier values make a light appear white regardless of the light color. The Multiplier value can also be negative. A negative value can be used to pull light from a scene but should be used with caution.

Tip

Adding and positioning another light typically is better than increasing the multiplier. ∎

To the right of the Multiplier value is a color swatch. Clicking the color swatch opens a color selector where you can choose a new light color.

Attenuation is a property that determines how light fades over distance. An example of this is a candle set in a room. The farther you get from the candle, the less the light shines.

You use three basic parameters to simulate realistic attenuation. Near Attenuation sets the distance at which the light begins to fade, and Far Attenuation sets the distance at which the light falls to 0. Both these properties are ranges that include Start and End values. The third parameter sets the Decay value, which simulates attenuation using a mathematical formula to compute the drop in light intensity over time.

Selecting the Use option enables the Near and Far Attenuation values; both have Start and End values that set the range for these attenuation types. The Show option makes the attenuation distances and decay values visible in the viewports. The three types of decay from which you can choose are None, Inverse, and Inverse Square. The Inverse type decays linearly with the distance away from the light. The Inverse Square type decays exponentially with distance.

Note

The Inverse Square type approximates real lights the best, but it is often too dim for computer graphic images. You can compensate for this by increasing the Multiplier value. ∎

Spotlight and directional light parameters

The Spotlight Parameters rollout includes values to set the angular distance of both the Hot Spot and Falloff cones. The Show Cone option makes the Hotspot and Falloff cones visible in the viewport when the light is not selected. The Overshoot option makes the light shine in all directions like an Omni light, but projections and shadows occur only within the Falloff cone. You can also set the light shape to be circular or rectangular. For a rectangular-shaped spotlight, you can control the aspect ratio. You can use the Bitmap Fit button to make the aspect ratio match a particular bitmap.

The Directional Light Parameters rollout, which appears for Direct light types, is identical to the Spotlight Parameters rollout and also includes settings for the Hot Spot and Falloff values.

Advanced Effects

Options in the Affect Surface section of the Advanced Effects rollout control how light interacts with an object's surface. The Contrast value alters the contrast between the diffuse and the ambient surface areas. The Soften Diffuse Edge value blurs the edges between the diffuse and ambient areas of a surface. The Diffuse and Specular options let you disable these properties of an object's surface. When the Ambient Only option is turned on, the light affects only the ambient properties of the surface.

Cross-Reference

Find more detail on the Diffuse, Specular, and Ambient properties in Chapter 15, "Using the Slate Material Editor." ∎

You can use any light as a projector; you find this option in the Advanced Effects rollouts. Selecting the Map option enables you to use the light as a projector. You can select a map to project by clicking the button to the right of the map option. You can drag a material map directly from the Material/Map Browser onto the Projector Map button.

Shadow parameters

All light types have a Shadow Parameters rollout that you can use to select a shadow color by clicking the color swatch. The default color is black. The Dens setting stands for "Density" and controls how dark the shadow appears. Lower values produce light shadows, and higher values produce dark shadows. This value can also be negative.

The Map option, like the Projection Map, can be used to project a map along with the shadow color. The Light Affects Shadow Color option alters the Shadow Color by blending it with the light color if selected.

In the Atmosphere Shadows section, the On button lets you determine whether atmospheric effects, such as fog, can cast shadows. You can also control the Opacity and the degree to which atmospheric colors blend with the Shadow Color.

When you select a light and open the Modify panel, one additional rollout is available: the Atmospheres and Effects rollout. This rollout is a shortcut to the Environment dialog box, where you can specify atmospheric effects such as fog and volume lights.

Note
The only effects that can be used with lights are Volume Light and Lens Effects. ∎

Cross-Reference
Chapter 46, "Using Atmospheric and Render Effects," covers atmospheric effects. ∎

If the Area Shadows option is selected in the General Parameters rollout, then the Area Shadows roll-out appears, which includes several settings for controlling this shadow type. In the drop-down list at the top of the rollout, you can select from several Basic Options, including Simple, Rectangle Light, Disc Light, Box Light, and Sphere Light. You can select dimensions depending on which option is selected. You can also set the Integrity, Quality, Spread, Bias, and Jitter amounts.

For the Shadow Map option, the Shadow Map Params rollout includes values for the Bias, Size, and Sample Range. The Sample Range value softens the shadow edges. You can also select to use an Absolute Map Bias and 2 Sided Shadows.

If the Ray Traced Shadows option is selected in the Shadow Parameters rollout, the Ray Traced Shadows Parameters rollout appears below it. This simple rollout includes only two values: Bias and Max Quadtree Depth. The Bias settings cause the shadow to move toward or away from the object that casts the shadow. The Max Quadtree Depth determines the accuracy of the shadows by controlling how long the ray paths are followed. There is also an option to enable 2 Sided Shadows, which enables both sides of a face to cast shadows, including backfacing objects.

For the Advanced Raytraced Shadows options, the rollout includes many more options, including Simple, 1-Pass, or 2-Pass Anti-aliasing. This rollout also includes the same quality values found in the Area Shadows rollout.

Note
Depending on the number of objects in your scene, shadows can take a long time to render. Enabling raytraced shadows for a complex scene can greatly increase the render time. ∎

Optimizing lights
If you select either the Area Shadows type or the Advanced Raytracing Shadows type, then a separate Optimizations rollout appears. This rollout includes settings that help speed up the shadow rendering process. Using this rollout, you can enable Transparent Shadows. You can also specify a color that is used at the Anti-aliasing Threshold. You can also turn off anti-aliasing for materials that have

SuperSampling or Reflection/Refraction enabled. Or you can have the shadow renderer skip coplanar faces with a given threshold.

Manipulating Hotspot and Falloff cones

When the Select and Manipulate mode is enabled on the main toolbar, the end of the Hotspot and Falloff cones appear green for a selected spotlight. When you move the mouse over these lines, the lines turn red, allowing you to drag the lines and make the Hotspot and/or Falloff angle values greater. These manipulators provide visual feedback as you resize the spotlight cone.

Photometric light parameters

Several of the light rollouts for photometric lights are the same as those for the standard lights, but several key parameters are unique for photometric lights, such as the ability to choose a light distribution model and a shape type.

Distribution options

The Distribution options are listed in a drop-down list in the General rollout. Both Free and Target photometric lights can be set to one of four distribution types. Each of these types appears as a different icon in the viewports:

- **Uniform Spherical:** This distribution type emanates light equally in all directions from a central point, like the standard Omni light.

- **Uniform Diffuse:** This distribution type spreads light equally in all directions for only one hemisphere, such as when a light is positioned against a wall.

- **Spotlight:** This distribution type spreads the light in a cone shape, like a flashlight or a car's headlight.

- **Photometric Web:** This distribution type can be any arbitrary 3D representation and is defined in a separate file that can be obtained from the light manufacturer and loaded into the light object. Once loaded, the distribution graph is visible in the Distribution rollout.

The Uniform Spherical option distributes light equally in all directions. The Uniform Diffuse option has its greatest distribution at right angles to the surface it is emitted from and gradually decreases in intensity at increasing angles from the normal. For both options, the light gradually becomes weaker as the distance from the light increases.

The Spotlight option concentrates the light energy into a cone that emits from the light. This cone of light energy is directional and can be controlled with the Hotspot and Falloff values.

The Photometric Web option is a custom option that lets you open a separate file describing the light's emission pattern. These files have the .ies, .cibse, or .ltli extensions. Light manufacturers have this data for the various real-world lights that they sell. You load these files using the Choose Photometric File button found in the Distribution (Photometric Web) rollout. You can also specify the X-, Y-, and Z-axis rotation values.

Color options

The Color section of the Intensity/Color/Attenuation rollout, shown in Figure 20.10, includes two ways to specify a light's color. The first is a drop-down list of options. The options found in the list include standard real-world light types such as Cool White, Mercury, and Halogen. Table 20.2 lists each of these types and its approximate color.

FIGURE 20.10

The Intensity/Color/Attenuation rollout for photometric lights uses real-world intensity values.

TABLE 20.2

Photometric Light Colors

Light Type	Color
Cool White	Yellow-white
Custom	Any color
D65White	White
Daylight Fluorescent	Mostly white with a slight gray tint
Fluorescent	Yellow-white
Halogen	Beige-white
High-Pressure Sodium	Tan
Incandescent	Beige-white
Low Pressure Sodium	Light orange
Mercury	Green-white
Metal Halide	Yellow-white
Phosphor Mercury	Light green
Quartz	Yellow-white
White Fluorescent	Yellow-white
Xenon	White

In addition to a list of available light types, you can specify a color based on temperature expressed in degrees Kelvin. Temperature-based colors run from a cool 1,000 degrees, which is a mauve-pink color, through light yellow and white (at 6,000 degrees Kelvin) to a hot light blue at 20,000 degrees

Kelvin. Typical indoor lighting is fairly low on the Kelvin scale at around 3,300 degrees K. Direct sunlight is around 5,500 degrees K. Thunderbolts, arc welders, and electric bolts run much hotter, from 10,000 to 20,000 degrees Kelvin.

You also can set a Filter Color using the color swatch found in this section. The Filter Color simulates the color caused by colored cellophane placed in front of the light.

Intensity and Attenuation options

The Intensity options can be specified in Lumens, Candelas, or Lux at a given distance. Light manufacturers have this information available. You also can specify a Multiplier value, which determines how effective the light is. There is also a setting for specifying the intensity due to a dimming effect, and the Incandescent lamp color shift when dimming option causes the light from an incandescent light to turn more yellow as it is dimmed. This effect is common as you get farther from a light bulb.

All real-world lights have attenuation, and Far attenuation values also can be set for photometric lights. This helps to speed up rendering times for scenes with lots of lights by limiting the extent of the cast light rays.

Light shapes

In addition to the distribution type, you can also select the light shape, which has an impact on how shadows are cast in the scene. Selecting a different-shaped light causes the light to be spread over a wider area, so in most cases the Point light results in the brightest intensity with sharper shadows, and lights covering a larger area are less intense and have softer shadows. The available photometric light shapes include the following:

- **Point:** This shape emits light from a single point like a light bulb.
- **Line:** This shape emits light from a straight line like a fluorescent tube.
- **Rectangle:** This shape emits light from an area like a bank of fluorescent lights.
- **Disc:** This shape emits light from a circular area like the light out of the top of a shaded lamp.
- **Sphere:** This shape emits light from a spherical shape like a Chinese lantern.
- **Cylinder:** This shape emits light from a cylindrical shape like some kinds of track lighting.

For each shape you can set the shape's dimensions in the Shape/Area Shadows rollout. The rollout also lets you switch between the different shapes. If you need to see the actual light shape, then you can enable the Light Shape Visible in Rendering option in the Shape/Area Shadows rollout.

Using the Sunlight and Daylight Systems

The Sunlight and Daylight systems, accessed through the Systems category of the Create panel, create a light that simulates the sun for a specific geographic location, date, time, and compass direction. You can also create them using the Create ⇨ Lights ⇨ Daylight System menu command.

Note

The Daylight system can be created using the Create ⇨ Lights menu or the Create ⇨ Systems menu, but the Sunlight system cannot be created using a menu. ■

To create either of these systems, open the Create panel and click the Systems category button. Then click the Sunlight (or Daylight) button, and drag the mouse in a viewport. A Compass helper object appears. Click again to create a Direct light (or Skylight) representing the sun. Figure 20.11 shows the Compass helper created as part of the Sunlight system. The main difference between these two systems is that the Sunlight system uses a Directional light and the Daylight system uses the IES Sun and Sky lights.

Note

When you first create a Daylight system, a warning dialog box appears giving you the option to enable the Logarithmic Exposure Control for external light. Clicking the Yes button makes this change for you automatically. ■

Note

The Compass helper object's orientation aligns with the ViewCube's directions. ■

Tip

The best results for the Daylight system are realized when you use the mr Sun and mr Sky options. Using the Daylight system with these options also enables the mr Physical Sky environment settings. More on this system is covered in Chapter 47, "Rendering with mental ray and iray." ■

FIGURE 20.11

The Compass helper provides an orientation for positioning the sun in a Sunlight system.

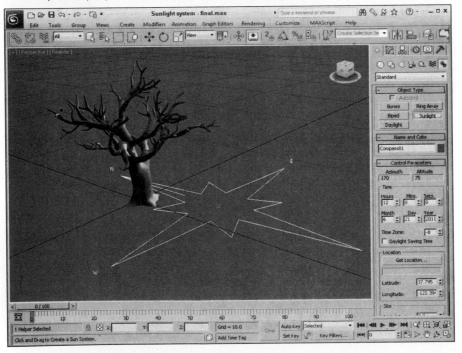

Using the Compass helper

The Compass helper is useful when working with a Sunlight system. It can be used to define the map directions of North, East, South, and West. The Sunlight system uses these directions to orient the system light. This helper is not renderable and is created automatically when you define a sunlight object. The Compass helper object is found in the Create ➪ Helpers menu.

After you create a Sunlight system, you can alter the point that the sun is pointing at by transforming the Compass helper. Doing so causes the direct light object to move appropriately. The light's position in the sky is controlled by the Time, Date, and Location parameters, but if you want to move the light independent of these parameters, you can select the Manual option and move the light using the transform tools.

Note

You can change the settings for the light that is the sun by selecting the light from the Select by Name dialog box and opening the Modify panel. The sunlight object uses raytraced shadows by default. ∎

Once created, the light parameters for the Daylight system, including light intensity and shadows, are located in the Modify panel, but the Date, Time, and Location parameters are in the Motion panel when the light object is selected. You can access the Motion panel parameters by clicking the Setup button in the Daylight Parameters rollout.

Understanding Azimuth and Altitude

Azimuth and Altitude are two values that help define the location of the sun in the sky. Both are measured in degrees. *Azimuth* refers to the compass direction and can range from 0 to 360, with 0 degrees being North, 90 degrees being East, 180 degrees being South, and 270 degrees being West. *Altitude* is the angle in degrees between the sun and the horizon. This value ranges typically between 0 and 90, with 0 degrees being either sunrise or sunset and 90 degrees when the sun is directly overhead.

Specifying date and time

The Time section of the Control Parameters rollout lets you define a time and date. The Time Zone value is the number of offset hours for your current time zone. You can also set the time to be converted for Daylight Saving Time.

Specifying location

Clicking the Get Location button in the Control Parameters rollout opens the Geographic Location dialog box, shown in Figure 20.12, which displays a map or a list of cities. Selecting a location using this dialog box automatically updates the Latitude and Longitude values. In addition to the Get Location button, you can enter Latitude and Longitude values directly in the Control Parameters rollout.

The Daylight system also includes an option to set the Sky value from Clear to Partly Cloudy to Cloudy.

FIGURE 20.12

The Geographic Location dialog box lets you specify where you want to use the Sunlight system. You have many different cities to choose from.

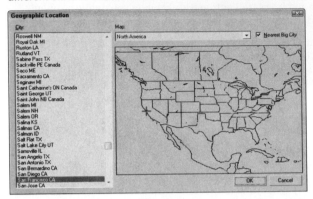

Tutorial: Animating a day in 20 seconds

You can animate the Sunlight system to show an entire day from sunrise to sundown in a short number of frames. In this tutorial, you focus on an old tree positioned somewhere in Phoenix, Arizona, on Christmas. The tree certainly won't move, but watch its shadows.

To use the Sunlight system to animate shadows, follow these steps:

1. Open the Sunlight system.max file from the Chap 20 directory on the CD.

   This file includes a tree mesh created by Zygote.

2. Add a Sunlight System by selecting the Systems category in the Create panel and clicking the Sunlight button. Then drag in the Top view to create the Compass helper, and click again to create the light. In the Control Parameters rollout (found in the Motion panel), enter **12/25** and the current year for the Date and an early morning hour for the Time.

3. Click the Get Location button, locate Phoenix in the Cities list, and click OK. Rotate the compass helper in the Top view so that north is pointing toward the top of the viewport.

4. Click the Auto Key button (or press the N key), and move the Time slider to frame 100.

5. In the Control Parameters rollout, change the Time value to an evening hour. Then click the Auto Key button (N) again to disable animation mode.

Note

You can tell when the sun comes up and goes down by looking at the Altitude value for each hour. A negative Altitude value indicates that the sun is below the horizon. ■

Figure 20.13 shows a snapshot of this quick day. The upper-left image shows the animation at frame 20, the upper-right image shows it at frame 40, the lower-left image shows it at frame 60, and the final image shows it at frame 80.

FIGURE 20.13

Several frames of an animation showing a tree scene from sunrise to sunset

Using Volume Lights

When light shines through fog, smoke, or dust, the beam of the light becomes visible. The effect is known as a *Volume Light*. To add a Volume Light to a scene, choose Rendering ⇨ Environment (or press the 8 key) to open the Environment dialog box. Then click the Add button in the Atmosphere rollout to open the Add Atmospheric Effect dialog box, and select Volume Light. The parameters for the volume light are presented in the Volume Light Parameters rollout.

You can also access the Volume Light effect from the Atmospheres and Effects rollout in the Modify panel when a light is selected.

Cross-Reference

Chapter 46, "Using Atmospheric and Render Effects," covers the other atmospheric effects. ∎

Volume light parameters

At the top of the Volume Light Parameters rollout, shown in Figure 20.14, is a Pick Light button, which enables you to select a light to apply the effect to. You can select several lights, which then appear in a drop-down list. You can remove lights from this list with the Remove Light button.

FIGURE 20.14

The Volume Light Parameters rollout in the Environment dialog box lets you choose which lights to include in the effect.

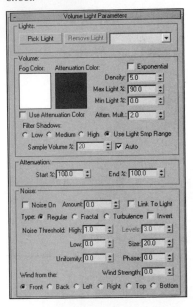

In the Volume section, the Fog Color swatch lets you select a color for the fog that is seen within the light. This color is combined with the color of the light. The Attenuation Color is the color the fog appears to have at a distance far from the light source. This color also combines with the Fog Color and is best set to a dark color.

The Density value determines the thickness of the fog. The Exponential option causes the density to increase exponentially with the distance. The Max and Min Light Percentage values determine the amount of glow that the volume light causes, and the Attenuation Multiplier controls the strength of the attenuation color.

You have four options for filtering shadows: Low, Medium, High, and Use Light Smp Range. The Low option renders shadows quickly but isn't very accurate. The High option takes a while but produces the best quality. The Use Light Smp Range option bases the filtering on the Sample Volume value and can be set to Auto. The Sample Volume can range from 1 to 10,000. The Low option has a Sample Volume value of 8; Medium, 25; and High, 50.

Note

Only Shadow Map type shadows cast shadows through volume fog. ■

The Start and End Attenuation values are percentages of the Start and End range values for the light's attenuation. These values have an impact only if attenuation is turned on for the light.

The Noise settings help to determine the randomness of Volume Light. Noise effects can be turned on and given an Amount. You can also Link the noise to the light instead of using world coordinates.

Noise types include Regular, Fractal, and Turbulence. Another option inverts the noise pattern. The Noise Threshold limits the effect of noise. Wind settings affect how the light moves as determined by the wind's direction, Wind Strength, and Phase.

Figure 20.15 shows several volume light possibilities. The left image includes the Volume Light effect, the middle image enables shadows, and the right image includes some Turbulent Noise.

FIGURE 20.15

The Volume Light effect makes the light visible.

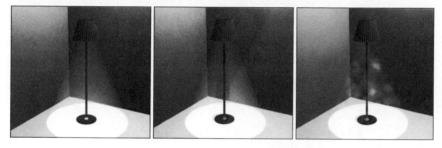

Tutorial: Showing car headlights

One popular way to use volume lights is to display the headlights of cars. For this tutorial, you're going to use the Delfino Feroce 2001 car model created by Viewpoint Datalabs.

To display the headlights of a car, follow these steps:

1. Open the Car headlights.max file from the Chap 20 directory on the CD.

   This file includes a model of a car.

2. Select the Create ⇨ Lights ⇨ Standard Lights ⇨ Target Spotlight menu command, and drag in the Left viewport to create a spotlight object. Select and move the spotlight and the target to be positioned to look as if a light is shining out from the left headlight.

3. Open the Modify panel, and in the Spotlight Parameters rollout, set the Hotspot value to **20** and the Falloff to **25**, and in the Intensity/Color/Attenuation rollout, set the Decay setting to Inverse Square with a Start value of **3.0**. In the Atmospheres and Effects rollout, click the Add button, select Volume Light from the Add Atmosphere or Effect dialog box that appears, and click OK.

Note

When a light is added to the scene, the default lights are automatically turned off. To provide any additional lighting, add some Omni lights above the car. ∎

4. Select the Volume Light effect in the list within the Atmospheres and Effects rollout, and click the Setup button. The Environment dialog box opens, in which you can edit the Volume Light parameters for the newly created light. Set the Density value to **100**.

5. Now create three more headlights. To do this, select both the first spotlight object and its target, and create a cloned copy by holding down the Shift key while moving it toward the right headlight. Position the other spotlights so that they shine outward from the other headlights.

Figure 20.16 shows the resulting car with its headlights illuminated.

FIGURE 20.16

The car now has headlights, thanks to spotlights and the Volume Light effect.

Tutorial: Creating laser beams

Laser beams are extremely useful lights. From your CD-ROM drive to your laser printer, lasers are found throughout a modern-day office. They also are great to use in fantasy and science fiction images. You can easily create laser beams using direct lights and the Volume Light effect. In this tutorial, you'll add some lasers to the spaceship model created by Viewpoint Datalabs.

To add some laser beams to a scene, follow these steps:

1. Open the Spaceship laser.max file from the Chap 20 directory on the CD.

    This file includes a spaceship model.

2. Select the Create ⇨ Lights ⇨ Standard Lights ⇨ Directional menu command, and add a Free Direct light to the end of one of the laser guns in the Front viewport. Scale the light down until the cylinder is the size of the desired laser beam and rotate it so it points away from the laser beam.

3. With the light selected, open the Modify panel. In the Atmospheres and Effects rollout, click the Add button and double-click the Volume Light selection. Then select the Volume Light option in the list, and click the Setup button to open the Environment dialog box. Change the Fog Color to red and the Density value to 50, and make sure that the Use Attenuation Color is disabled.

4. With the direct lights added to the scene, the default lights are deactivated, so you need to add some Omni lights above the spaceship to illuminate it. To do this, select the Create ⇨ Lights ⇨ Standard Lights ⇨ Omni menu command, and click above the spaceship in the Front view three times to create three lights. Set the Multiplier on the first light to **1.0**, and

position it directly above the spaceship. Set the other two lights to **0.5**, and position them on either side of the spaceship and lower than the first light.

Figure 20.17 shows the resulting laser beams shooting forth from the spaceship.

FIGURE 20.17

You can create laser beams using direct lights and the Volume Light effect.

Using projector maps and raytraced shadows

If a map is added to a light in the Parameters rollout, the light becomes a projector. Projector maps can be simple images, animated images, or black-and-white masks to cast shadows. To load a projector map, select a light and open the Modify panel. Under the Spotlight Parameters rollout, click the Projector Map button and select the map to use from the Material/Map Browser.

Raytraced shadows take longer to render than the Shadow Maps or Area Shadows option, but the shadows always have a hard edge and are an accurate representation of the object.

Note

You can create shadows for wireframe objects with transparency only by using raytraced shadows. ■

In the Shadow Parameters rollout, you can select whether shadows are computed using shadow maps or raytraced shadows. Using the latter selection lets you project a transparent object's color onto the shadow.

Tutorial: Projecting a trumpet image on a scene

As an example of a projector light, you create a musical scene with several musical notes and project the image of a trumpet on them.

To project an image onto a rendered scene, follow these steps:

1. Open the Trumpet mask.max file from the Chap 20 directory on the CD.

   This file includes a trumpet model shown in the maximized Left viewport. This file is used to generate a project map.

2. Choose Rendering ⇨ Render (or press the F10 key) to open the Render dialog box; set the resolution to 640×480, and select the Left viewport. Then select the Render Elements tab and click the Add button. Select Alpha from the Render Elements dialog box, click OK, and then click the Render button. The side view of the trumpet in the Rendered Frame Window renders along with an alpha channel rendering of the trumpet. When the rendering completes, click the Save File button in the Rendered Frame Window for the alpha channel and save the file as **trumpet mask.tif**.

3. Open the Musical notes.max file from the Chap 20 directory on the CD.

   This file contains several musical notes created from primitive objects.

4. Select the Create ⇨ Lights ⇨ Standard Lights ⇨ Target Spotlight menu command, and drag to create two lights in the Top viewport. Position the first spotlight to be perpendicular to the scene and to shine down on it from above.

5. Open the Modify panel; in the Advanced Effects rollout, click the Projector Map button and double-click Bitmap from the Material/Map Browser. Locate and select the Trumpet Mask. tif file, and click Open. This projects a silhouette of a trumpet onto the scene. Use the second spotlight to light the music notes.

Figure 20.18 shows the musical notes with the trumpet projection map.

FIGURE 20.18

You can use projection maps to project an image in the scene, like this trumpet.

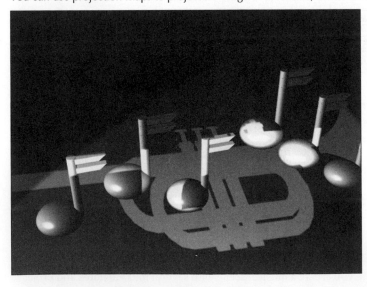

Tutorial: Creating a stained-glass window

When a light that uses raytraced shadows shines through an object with transparent materials, the Filter color of the material is projected onto objects behind. In this tutorial, you create a stained-glass window and shine a light through it using raytraced shadows.

To create a stained-glass window, follow these steps:

1. Open the Stained glass window.max file from the Chap 20 directory on the CD.

   This file includes a stained-glass window for a fish market. (Don't ask me why a fish market has a stained-glass window.)

2. Select the Create ⇨ Lights ⇨ Standard Lights ⇨ Target Spotlight menu command, and drag in the Left view from a position to the right and above the window to the window.

   This creates a target spotlight that shines through the stained-glass window onto the floor behind it.

3. In the General Parameters rollout, make sure that the On option is enabled in the Shadows section and select Ray Traced Shadows from the drop-down list.

Figure 20.19 shows the stained-glass window with the colored shadow cast on the scene floor.

FIGURE 20.19

A stained-glass window effect created with raytraced shadows

Summary

I hope you have found this chapter enlightening. (Sorry about the bad pun, but I need to work them in where I can.) Max has many different lights, each with plenty of controls. Learning to master these controls can take you a long way toward increasing the realism of the scene. In this chapter, you've accomplished the following:

- Learned the basics of lighting
- Discovered Max's standard and photometric light types
- Created and positioned light objects
- Learned to change the viewport view to a light
- Used the Sunlight and Daylight systems
- Used the Volume Light atmospheric effect
- Added projection maps to lights
- Used raytraced shadows to create a stained-glass window

In the next chapter you finally start animating objects, beginning with the basics, including keyframing.

Part V

Animation and Rendering Basics

Understanding Animation and Keyframes

M ax can be used to create some really amazing images, but I bet more of you go to the movies than go to see images in a museum. The difference is in seeing moving images versus static images.

In this chapter, I start discussing what is probably one of the main reasons you decided to learn 3ds Max in the first place—animation. Max includes many different features to create animations. This chapter covers the easiest and most basic of these features—keyframe animation.

Along the way, you'll examine all the various controls that are used to create, edit, and control animation keys, including the Time Controls, the Track Bar, and the Motion panel. Keyframes can be used to animate object transformations, but they also can be used to animate other parameters such as materials. If you get finished with this chapter in time, you may have time to watch a movie.

Using the Time Controls

Before jumping into animation, you need to understand the controls that make it possible. These controls collectively are called the Time Controls and can be found on the lower interface bar between the key controls and the Viewport Navigation Controls. The Time Controls also include the Time Slider found directly under the viewports.

The Time Slider provides an easy way to move through the frames of an animation. To do this, just drag the Time Slider button in either direction. The Time Slider button is labeled with the current frame number and the total number of frames. The arrow buttons on either side of this button work the same as the Previous and Next Frame (Key) buttons.

The Time Control buttons include buttons to jump to the Start or End of the animation, or to step forward or back by a single frame. You can also jump to an exact frame by entering the frame number in the frame number field. The Time Controls are presented in Table 21.1.

TABLE 21.1

Time Controls

Toolbar Button	Name	Description
	Go to Start	Sets the time to frame 1.
	Previous Frame/Key	Decreases the time by one frame or selects the previous key.
	Play Animation, Play Selected	Cycles through the frames; this button becomes a Stop button when an animation is playing.
	Next Frame/Key	Advances the time by one frame or selects the next key.
	Go to End	Sets the time to the final frame.
	Key Mode Toggle	Toggles between key and frame modes; with Key Mode on, the icon turns light blue and the Previous Frame and Next Frame buttons change to Previous Key and Next Key.
0	Current Frame field	Indicates the current frame; a frame number can be typed in this field for more exact control than the Time Slider.
	Time Configuration	Opens the Time Configuration dialog box where settings like frame rate, time display, and animation length can be set.

The default scene starts with 100 frames, but this is seldom what you actually need. You can change the number of frames at any time by clicking the Time Configuration button, which is to the right of the frame number field. Clicking this button opens the Time Configuration dialog box, shown in Figure 21.1. You can also access this dialog box by right-clicking any of the Time Control buttons.

Setting frame rate

Within this dialog box, you can set several options, including the Frame Rate. *Frame rate* provides the connection between the number of frames and time. It is measured in frames per second. The options include standard frame rates such as NTSC (National Television Standards Committee, around 30 frames per second), Film (around 24 frames per second), and PAL (Phase Alternate Line, used by European countries, around 25 frames per second), or you can select Custom and enter your own frame rate.

The Time Display section lets you set how time is displayed on the Time Slider. The options include Frames, SMPTE (Society of Motion Picture Technical Engineers), Frame:Ticks, or MM:SS:Ticks (Minutes and Seconds). *SMPTE* is a standard time measurement used in video and television. A *Tick* is $1/4800$ of a second.

FIGURE 21.1

The Time Configuration dialog box lets you set the number of frames to include in a scene.

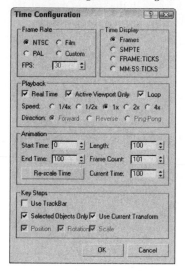

Setting speed and direction

The Playback section sets options for how the animation sequence is played back. The Real Time option skips frames to maintain the specified frame rate. The Active Viewport Only option causes the animation to play only in a single viewport, which speeds up the animation. The Loop option repeats the animation over and over. The Loop option is available only if the Real Time option is disabled. If the Loop option is set, then you can specify the Direction as Forward, Reverse, or Ping-Pong (which repeats, playing forward and then reverse). The Speed setting can be $^1/_4$, $^1/_2$, 1, 2, or 4 times normal.

The Time Configuration dialog box also lets you specify the Start Time, End Time, Length, and Current Time values. These values are all interrelated, so setting the Length and the Start Time, for example, automatically changes the End Time. These values can be changed at any time without destroying any keys. For example, if you have an animation of 500 frames and you set the Start and End Time to 30 and 50, the Time Slider controls only those 21 frames. Keys before or after this time are still available and can be accessed by resetting the Start and End Time values to 0 and 500.

The Re-scale Time button fits all the keys into the active time segment by stretching or shrinking the number of frames between keys. You can use this feature to resize the animation to the number of frames defined by Start and End Time values.

The Key Steps group lets you set which key objects are navigated using key mode. If you select Use Track Bar, key mode moves through only the keys on the Track Bar. If you select the Selected Objects Only option, key mode jumps only to the keys for the currently selected object. You can also filter to move between Position, Rotation, and Scale keys. The Use Current Transform option locates only those keys that are the same as the current selected transform button.

Using Time Tags

To the right of the Prompt Line is a field marked Add Time Tag. Clicking this field pops up a menu with options to Add or Edit a Time Tag. Time Tags can be set for each frame in the scene. Once set, the Time Tags are visible in the Time Tag field whenever that time is selected.

Working with Keys

It isn't just a coincidence that the largest button in the entire Max interface has a key on it. Creating and working with keys is how animations are accomplished. Keys define a particular state of an object at a particular time. Animations are created as the object moves or changes between two different key states. Complex animations can be generated with only a handful of keys.

You can create keys in numerous ways, but the easiest is with the Key Controls found on the lower interface bar. These controls are located to the left of the Time Controls. Table 21.2 displays and explains all these controls. Closely related to the Key Controls is the Track Bar, which is located under the Time Slider.

TABLE 21.2

Key Controls

Toolbar Button	Name	Description
⊶	Set Key (K)	Creates animation keys in Set Key mode.
Auto Key	Toggle Auto Key Mode (N)	Sets keys automatically for the selected object when enabled.
Set Key	Toggle Set Key Mode (')	Sets keys as specified by the key filters for the selected object when enabled.
Selected ▼	Selection Set drop-down list	Specifies a selection set to use for the given keys.
⟋	Default In/Out Tangents for New Keys	Assigns the default tangents that are used on all new keys.
Key Filters...	Open Filters Dialog box	Contains pop-up options for the filtering keys.

Max includes two animation modes: Auto Key (N) and Set Key ('). You can select either of these modes by clicking the respective buttons at the bottom of the interface. When active, the button turns bright red, and the border around the active viewport also turns red to remind you that you are in animate mode. Red also appears around a spinner for any animated parameters.

Auto Key mode

With the Auto Key button enabled, every transformation or parameter change creates a key that defines where and how an object should look at that specific frame.

To create a key, drag the Time Slider to a frame where you want to create a key and then move the selected object or change the parameter, and a key is automatically created. When the first key is created, Max automatically goes back and creates a key for frame 0 that holds the object's original position or parameter. Upon setting the key, Max then interpolates all the positions and changes between the keys. The keys are displayed in the Track Bar.

Each frame can hold several different keys, but only one for each type of transform and each parameter. For example, if you move, rotate, scale, and change the Radius parameter for a sphere object with the Auto Key mode enabled, then separate keys are created for position, rotation, scaling, and a parameter change.

Set Key mode

The Set Key button (') offers more control over key creation and sets keys only when you click the Set Key button (K). It also creates keys only for the key types enabled in the Key Filters dialog box. You can open the Key Filters dialog box, shown in Figure 21.2, by clicking the Key Filters button. Available key types include All, Position, Rotation, Scale, IK Parameters, Object Parameters, Custom Attributes, Modifiers, Materials, and Other (which allows keys to be set for manipulator values).

FIGURE 21.2

Use the Set Key Filters dialog box to specify the types of keys to create.

Tutorial: Rotating a windmill's blades

The best way to learn is to practice, and there's no better time to practice than now. For this quick example, you animate a set of blades on a windmill.

To animate a set of windmill blades rotating, follow these steps:

1. Open the Rotating windmill blades.max file from the Chap 21 directory on the CD.

   This file includes a windmill model created by Viewpoint Datalabs.

2. Click the Auto Key button (or press the N key) at the bottom of the Max window, and drag the Time Slider to frame 50.

3. Select the "prop" object at the top of the windmill in the Front viewport. The blades are attached to the center prop and rotate about its Pivot Point. Then click the Select and Rotate button on the main toolbar (or press E key), and rotate the "prop" object about its Y-axis.

4. Click the Auto Key button (or press the N key) again to disable animation mode. Select the key in the Track Bar located at frame 1, hold down the Shift key, and drag the key to frame 100 (or press the End key).

This step copies the key from frame 1 to frame 100. Doing so ensures a smooth looping animation (even though it spins the prop forward and then backward; I guess it must be a strange wind that's blowing).

5. Click the Play Animation button in the Time Controls to see the animation.

Figure 21.3 shows frame 50 of this simple animation.

FIGURE 21.3

Frame 50 of this simple windmill animation

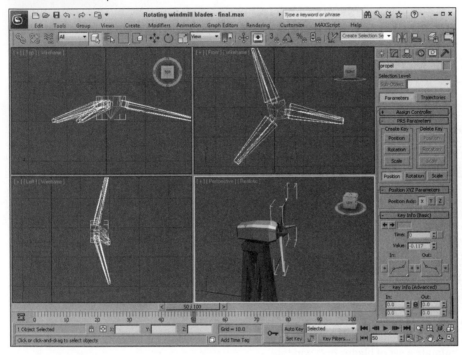

Another way to create keys is to select the object to be animated and right-click the Time Slider button. This opens the Create Key dialog box, shown in Figure 21.4, where you can set Position, Rotation, and Scale keys for the currently selected object. You can use this method only to create transform keys.

FIGURE 21.4

The Create Key dialog box enables you to create a Position, Rotation, or Scale key quickly.

If a key already exists, you can clone it by dragging the selected key with the Shift key held down. Dragging the Track Bar with the Ctrl and Alt keys held down changes the active time segment.

Copying parameter animation keys

If a parameter is changed while the Auto Key mode is enabled, then keys are set for that parameter. You can tell when a parameter has a key set because the arrows to the right of its spinner are outlined in red when the Time Slider is on the frame where the key is set. If you change the parameter value when the spinner is highlighted red, then the key value is changed (and the Auto Key mode doesn't need to be enabled).

If you highlight and right-click the parameter value, a pop-up menu of options appears. Using this pop-up menu, you can Cut, Copy, Paste, and Delete the parameter value. You can also select Copy Animation, which copies all the keys associated with this parameter and lets you paste them to another parameter. Pasting the animation keys can be done as a Copy, an Instance, or a Wire. A Copy is independent; an Instance ties the animation keys to the original copy so that they both are changed when either changes; and a Wire lets one parameter control some other parameter.

Caution

To copy a parameter value, be sure to select and right-click the value. If you right-click the parameter's spinner, the value is set to 0. ∎

The right-click pop-up menu also includes commands to let you Edit a wired parameter, show the parameter in the Track View, or show the parameter in the Parameter Wire dialog box.

Cross-Reference

Parameter wiring and the Parameter Wire dialog box are discussed in more detail in Chapter 35, "Using Animation Layers, Modifiers, and Complex Controllers." ∎

Deleting all object animation keys

Individual keys can be selected and deleted using the Track Bar or the right-click pop-up menu, but if an object has many keys, this can be time consuming. To delete all animation keys for the selected object quickly, choose the Animation ➪ Delete Selected Animation menu command.

Using the Track Bar

The Max interface includes a simple way to work with keys: with the Track Bar, which is situated directly under the Time Slider. The Track Bar displays a rectangular marker for every key for the selected object. These markers are color-coded, depending on the type of key. Position keys are red, rotation keys are green, scale keys are blue, and parameter keys are dark gray.

Caution

In the Track View—Dope Sheet interface, position, rotation, and scale keys are red, green, and blue, but parameter keys are yellow. ∎

The current frame also appears in the Track Bar as a light blue, transparent rectangle, as shown in Figure 21.5. The icon at the left end of the Track Bar is the Open Mini Curve Editor button, which opens a mini Track View.

Cross-Reference

For more on the Track View interface, see Chapter 37, "Working with the F-Curve Editor in the Track View." ∎

FIGURE 21.5

The Track Bar displays all keys for the selected object.

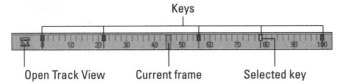

Using the Track Bar, you can move, copy, and delete keys. The Track Bar shows key markers only for the currently selected object or objects, and each marker can represent several different keys. When the mouse is moved over the top of these markers, the cursor changes to a plus sign, and you can select a marker by clicking it (selected markers turn white). Using the Ctrl key, you can select multiple keys at the same time. You can also select multiple key markers by clicking an area of the Track Bar that contains no keys and then dragging an outline over all the keys you want to select. If you move the cursor over the top of a selected key, the cursor is displayed as a set of arrows enabling you to drag the selected key to the left or right. Holding down the Shift key while dragging a key creates a copy of the key. Pressing the Delete key deletes the selected key.

Tip

If you drag a key off the end of the Track Bar, the frame number is displayed on the Prompt Line at the bottom of the interface and the key is not included in the current time range. If you ever want to hide a key without deleting it, you can drag it off the end of the Track Bar and recover it by resetting the time in the Time Configuration dialog box. ∎

Because each marker can represent several keys, you can view all the keys associated with the marker in a pop-up menu by right-clicking the marker.

Note

In the pop-up menu, a check mark next to a key indicates that the key is shared with another instance. ∎

The marker pop-up menu also offers options for deleting selected keys or filtering the keys. In addition, there is a Goto Time command, which automatically moves the Time Slider to the key's location when selected.

To delete a key marker with all of its keys, right-click to open the pop-up menu and choose Delete Key ⇨ All, or select the key marker and press the Delete key.

Viewing and Editing Key Values

At the top of the marker's right-click pop-up menu is a list of current keys for the selected object (or if there are too many keys for a marker, they are placed under the Key Properties menu). When you select one of these keys, a key information dialog box opens. This dialog box displays different controls, depending on the type of key selected. Figure 21.6 shows the dialog box for the Position key. There are slight variations in this dialog box, depending on the key type.

FIGURE 21.6

Key dialog boxes enable you to change the key parameters.

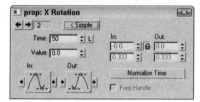

Note

You can also access key-specific dialog boxes in the Motion panel for a selected object by clicking the Parameters button. ∎

Within each of these key dialog boxes is a Time value that shows the current frame. Next to the Time value are two arrows that enable you to move easily to the other keys in the scene. The dialog box also includes several text fields, where you can change the key parameters.

Most of the key dialog boxes also include flyout buttons for selecting Key Tangents. Key Tangents determine how the animation moves into and out of the key. For example, if the In Key Tangent is set to Slow, and the Out Key Tangent is set to Fast, the object approaches the key position in a slow manner but accelerates as it leaves the key position. The arrow buttons on either side of the Key Tangent buttons can copy the current Key Tangent selection to the previous or next key.

The available types of Tangents are detailed in Table 21.3.

TABLE 21.3

Key Tangents

Toolbar Button	Name	Description
	Smooth	Produces straight, smooth motion; this is the default type.
	Linear	Moves at a constant rate between keys.
	Step	Causes discontinuous motion between keys; it occurs only between matching In-Out pairs.

continued

TABLE 21.3 (continued)		
Toolbar Button	Name	Description
	Slow	Decelerates as you approach the key.
	Fast	Accelerates as you approach the key.
	Custom	Lets you control the Tangent handles in function curves mode.
	Custom – Locked Handles	Lets you control the Tangent handles in function curves mode with the handles locked.

Using the Motion Panel

You have yet another way to create keys: by using the Motion panel. The Motion panel in the Command Panel includes settings and controls for animating objects. At the top of the Motion panel are two buttons: Parameters and Trajectories.

Setting parameters

The Parameters button on the Motion panel lets you assign controllers and create and delete keys. *Controllers* are custom key-creating algorithms that can be defined through the Parameters rollout, shown in Figure 21.7. You assign these controllers by selecting the position, rotation, or scaling track and clicking the Assign Controller button to open a list of applicable controllers that you can select.

FIGURE 21.7

The Parameters section of the Motion panel lets you assign controllers and create keys.

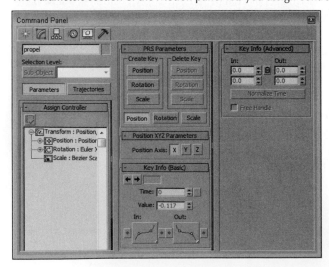

Cross-Reference

For more information on controllers, see Chapter 22, "Animating with Constraints and Simple Controllers." ■

When a keyable object is selected, below the Assign Controller rollout is the PRS Parameters rollout where you can create and delete Position, Rotation, and Scale keys. You can use this rollout to create Position, Rotation, and Scale keys whether or not the Auto Key or Set Key buttons are enabled. Additional rollouts may be available, depending upon the selected controller.

Below the PRS Parameters rollout are two Key Info rollouts: Basic and Advanced. These rollouts include the same key-specific information that you can access using the right-click pop-up menu found in the Track Bar.

Using trajectories

A *trajectory* is the actual path that the animation follows. When you click the Trajectories button in the Motion panel, the animation trajectory is shown as a spline with each key displayed as a node and each frame shown as a white dot. You can then edit the trajectory and its nodes by clicking the Sub-Object button at the top of the Motion panel, shown in Figure 21.8. The only subobject available is Keys. With the Sub-Object button enabled, you can use the transform buttons to move and reposition the trajectory nodes. You can also add and delete keys with the Add Key and Delete Key buttons.

FIGURE 21.8

The Trajectories rollout in the Motion panel enables you to see the animation path as a spline.

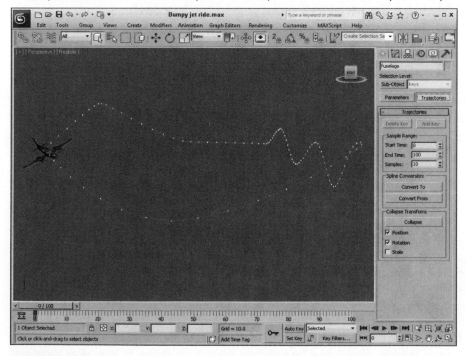

For more control over the trajectory path, you can convert the trajectory path to a normal editable spline with the Convert To button. You can also convert an existing spline into a trajectory with the Convert From button.

To use the Convert From button, select an object, click the Convert From button, and then click a spline path in the scene. This creates a new trajectory path for the selected object. The first key of this path is placed at the spline's first vertex, and the final key is placed as the spline's final vertex position. Additional keys are spaced out along the spline based on the spline's curvature as determined by the Samples value listed in the Sample Range group. All these new keys are roughly spaced between the Start and End times, but smaller Bézier handles result in more closely packed keys.

Click the Collapse button at the bottom of the Trajectories rollout to reduce all transform keys into a single editable path. You can select which transformations to collapse, including Position, Rotation, and Scale, using the options under the Collapse button. For example, an object with several Controllers assigned can be collapsed, thereby reducing the complexity of all the keys.

Note

If you collapse all keys, you cannot alter their parameters via the controller rollouts. ■

The Views menu includes an option to Show Key Times. The Show Key Times command displays frame numbers along the trajectory path where every animation key is located. Enabling this option displays the frame numbers next to any key along a trajectory path. You can make the trajectory visible for any object by enabling the Trajectory option in the Object Properties dialog box.

Tutorial: Making an airplane follow a looping path

Airplanes that perform aerobatic stunts often follow paths that are smooth. You can see this clearly when watching a sky writer. In this example, I've created a simple looping path using the Line spline primitive, and you'll use this path to make a plane complete a loop.

To make an airplane follow a looping path, follow these steps:

1. Open the Looping airplane.max file from the Chap 21 directory on the CD.

   This file includes a simple looping spline path and an airplane created by Viewpoint Datalabs.

2. With the airplane selected, open the Motion panel and click the Trajectories button. Then click the Convert From button in the Trajectories rollout, and select the path in the Front viewport.

3. If you drag the Time Slider, you'll notice that the plane moves along the path, but it doesn't rotate with the path. To fix this, click the Key Mode Toggle button in the Time Controls to easily move from key to key. Click the Key Filters button, select only Rotation, and then click the Set Key button (or press the ' key) to enter Set Key mode.

4. Before moving the Time Slider, click the Set Keys button to create a rotation key at frame 0. Then click the Select and Rotate button, click the Next Key button, rotate the plane in the Front viewport to match the path, and click the large Set Keys button (or press the K key) to create a rotation key. Click the Next Key button to move to the next key, and repeat this step until rotation keys have been set for the entire path.

5. Drag the Time Slider, and watch the airplane circle about the loop.

Cross-Reference

Max provides an easier way to make the plane follow the path using the Path constraint. To learn more about constraints, see Chapter 22, "Animating with Constraints and Simple Controllers." ■

Figure 21.9 shows the plane's trajectory.

When you use a spline path, the position keys are automatically set for this plane.

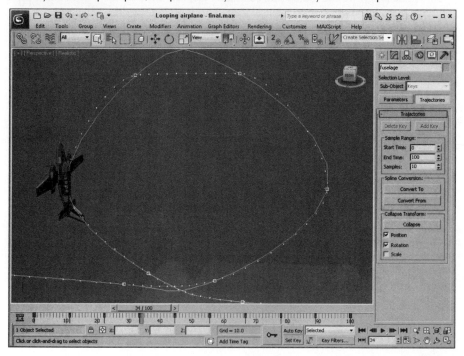

Using the Follow/Bank utility

When an object travels along a path that defines its trajectory, it maintains its same orientation without rotating. Imagine a roller coaster car; it rotates and banks as it moves around the track. This rotation and banking motion can be added to an object following a path using the Follow/Bank utility. You can access this utility by opening the Utilities panel and clicking the More button. Double-click the Follow/Bank utility to load it into the Utilities panel.

Caution

The Follow/Bank utility aligns the local X-axis of the object with the local Z-axis of the spline when the utility is applied, so you need to correctly orient the object's pivot point before applying the utility. If you don't, the object will be aligned at right angles to the path. ■

The Follow/Bank utility lets you enable a Bank option and set its Amount and Smoothness. Another option allows the object to turn upside down (not recommended for a traditional roller coaster car). Click the Apply Follow button to add the keys to cause the object to follow and bank. The Samples section determines how many keys are created.

Using Ghosting

As you're trying to animate objects, using the ghosting feature can be very helpful. This feature displays a copy of the object being animated before and after its current position. To enable ghosting, choose Views ➪ Show Ghosting. The Show Ghosting command displays the position of the selected object in the previous several frames, the next several frames, or both. This command uses the options set in the Preference Settings dialog box. Access this dialog box by choosing Customize ➪ Preferences. In the Viewports panel of this dialog box is a Ghosting section.

You use this Ghosting section to set how many ghosted objects are to appear; whether the ghosted objects appear before, after, or both before and after the current frame; and whether frame numbers should be shown. You can also specify every Nth frame to be displayed. You also have an option to display the ghost object in wireframe (it is displayed as shaded if this option is not enabled) and an option to Show Frame Numbers. Objects before the current frame are colored yellow, and objects after are colored light blue.

Figure 21.10 shows a lion toy object that is animated to travel in a bumpy circle with ghosting enabled. The Preference settings are set to show three ghosting frames at every other frame before and after the current frame.

FIGURE 21.10

Enabling ghosting lets you know where an object is and where it's going.

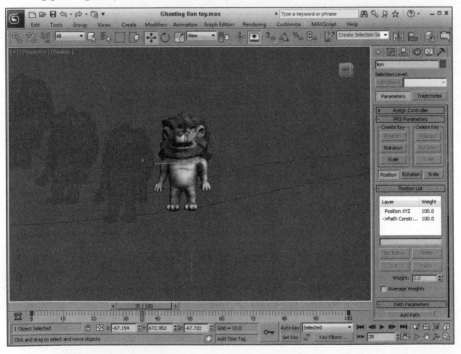

Animation Preferences

The Animation panel of the Preference Settings dialog box, shown in Figure 21.11, contains several preference options dealing with animations. When a specific frame is selected, all objects with keys for that frame are surrounded with white brackets. The Animation panel offers options that specify which objects get these brackets. Options include All Objects, Selected Objects, and None. You also can limit the brackets to only those objects with certain transform keys.

Tip

The Key Bracket Display option is helpful when you need to locate specific keys. When the selected object for the given frame has a key, the object is surrounded with brackets. ■

FIGURE 21.11

The Animation panel includes settings for displaying Key Brackets.

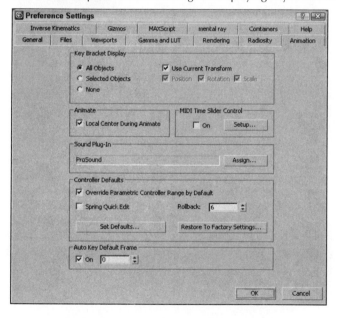

The Local Center During Animate option causes all objects to be animated about their local centers. Turning this option off enables animations about other centers (such as screen and world).

The MIDI Time Slider Controls include an On option and a Setup button. The Setup button opens the MIDI Time Slider Control Setup dialog box shown in Figure 21.12. After this control is set up, you can control an animation using a MIDI device.

FIGURE 21.12

The MIDI Time Slider Control Setup dialog box lets you set up specific notes to start, stop, and step through an animation.

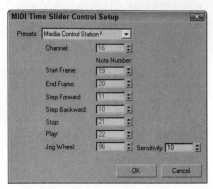

You can use the Animation panel to assign a new Sound Plug-In to use, as well as to set the default values of all animation controllers. The Override Parametric Controller Range by Default option causes controllers to be active for the entire animation sequence instead of just their designated range. The Spring Quick Edit option lets you change the accuracy of all Spring controllers in the entire scene in one place. The Rollback setting is the number of frames that the Spring controller uses to return to its original position.

Clicking the Set Defaults button opens the Set Controller Defaults dialog box. This dialog box includes a list of all the controllers and a Set button. When you select a controller and click the Set button, another dialog box appears with all the values for that controller.

When you first start up Max, the default first frame on the Timeline is frame 0, but if you enable the Auto Key Default Frame option, you can set the first frame to be any frame you want. This is convenient if you like to use some frames to set up a shot or if the starting frame of the shot is not at frame 0.

Cross-Reference

You can learn more about specific controllers in Chapter 22, "Animating with Constraints and Simple Controllers." ■

Animating Objects

Many different objects in Max can be animated, including geometric objects, cameras, lights, and materials. In this section, you'll look at several types of objects and parameters that can be animated.

Animating cameras

You can animate cameras using the standard transform buttons found on the main toolbar. When animating a camera that actually moves in the scene, using a Free camera is best. A Target camera can be pointed by moving its target, but you risk it being flipped over if the target is ever directly above the camera. If you want to use a Target camera, attach both the camera and its target to a Dummy object using the Link button and move the Dummy object.

Two useful constraints when animating cameras are the Path constraint and the Look At constraint. You can find both of these in the Animation ⇨ Constraints menu. The Path constraint can make a camera follow a spline path, and the Look At constraint can direct the focus of a camera to follow an object as the camera or the object moves through the scene.

Cross-Reference

For more on constraints, including these two, see Chapter 22, "Animating with Constraints and Simple Controllers." ∎

Tutorial: Animating darts hitting a dartboard

As a simple example of animating objects using the Auto Key button, you'll animate several darts hitting a dartboard.

To animate darts hitting a dartboard, follow these steps:

1. Open the Dart and dartboard.max file from the Chap 21 directory on the CD.

   This file includes a dart and dartboard objects created by Zygote Media.

2. Click the Auto Key button (or press the N key) to enable animation mode. Drag the Time Slider to frame 25, and click the Select and Move button on the main toolbar (or press the W key).

3. Select the first dart in the Left viewport, and drag it to the left until its tip just touches the dartboard.

   This step creates a key in the Track Bar for frames 0 and 25.

4. Click the Select and Rotate button on the main toolbar, set the reference coordinate system to Local, and constrain the rotation to the Y-axis. Then drag the selected dart in the Front viewport to rotate it about its local Y-axis.

   This step also sets a key in the Track Bar.

5. Select the second dart, and click the Select and Move button again. Right-click the Time Slider to make the Create Key dialog box appear. Make sure that the check boxes for Position and Rotation are selected, and click OK.

   This step creates a key that keeps the second dart from moving before it's ready.

6. With the second dart still selected, drag the Time Slider to frame 50 and move the dart to the dartboard as shown in Step 3. Then repeat Step 4 to set the rotation key for the second dart.

7. Repeat Steps 3, 4, and 5 for the last two darts.

8. Click the Auto Key button (or press the N key) again to disable animation mode, maximize the Perspective viewport, and click the Play Animation button to see the animation. Figure 21.13 shows the darts as they're flying toward the dartboard.

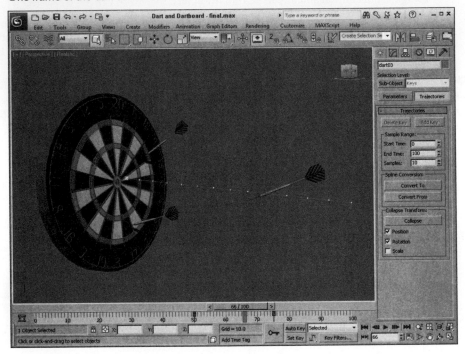

FIGURE 21.13

One frame of the dart animation

Animating lights

The process for animating lights includes many of the same techniques as those for animating cameras. For moving lights, use a Free Spot light or attach a Target Spot light to a Dummy object. You can also use the Look At and Path controllers with lights.

Cross-Reference

If you need to animate the Sun at different times in the day, use the Daylight or Sunlight systems, which are discussed in Chapter 20, "Using Lights and Basic Lighting Techniques." ■

To flash lights on and off, enable and disable the On parameter at different frames and assign a Step Tangent. To dim lights, just alter the Multiplier value over several frames.

Animating materials

Materials can be animated if their properties are altered while the Auto Key button is active. Max interpolates between the values as the animation progresses. The material must be consistent for the entire animation: You cannot change materials at different keys; you can only alter the existing material parameters.

If you want to change materials as the animation progresses, you can use a material that combines multiple materials, such as the Blend material. This material includes a Mix Amount value that can change at different keyframes. The next tutorial shows how to use the Blend material in this manner.

Several maps include a Phase value, including all maps that have a Noise rollout. This value provides the means to animate the map. For example, using a Noise map and changing the Phase value over many keys animates the noise effect.

Note

Another common way to animate materials is with the Controller nodes that are applied in the Slate Material Editor. Using these Controller nodes, you can alter material parameters for different frames and even access the Curve Editor for these controllers. ■

A useful way to view animated materials is to click the Make Preview button (the sixth button from the top) in the Compact Material Editor to open the Create Material Preview dialog box, shown in Figure 21.14. Select the Active Time Segment option, and click OK. The material renders every frame and automatically opens and plays the material preview.

FIGURE 21.14

The Create Material Preview dialog box can render the entire range of frames or a select number of frames.

Creating Image File Lists

Anywhere you can load a bitmap map, you can also load an animation file such as a Microsoft Video (AVI) or a QuickTime (MOV) file. Another way to create animated material is with an Image File List, which is a text file that lists each separate image file contained in an animation. Max supports two different image file formats—Autodesk ME Image Sequence File (IMSQ) and 3ds Max Image File List (IFL) files.

IMSQ and IFL files are text files that list which images should appear and for which frames. You save them with the .imsq or .ifl extension and load them using the Bitmap map. Image file lists can be created during the render process by selecting the Put Image File List in Output Path option in the Common Parameter rollout of the Render Scene dialog box. There is also a Create Now button to create an image file list at any time.

To manually create an IMSQ or IFL file, open a text editor and type the name of the image followed by the number of frames for which it should appear. Be sure to include a space between the name and the number of frames. The images are displayed in the order they are listed and repeated until all frames have been displayed. Once applied, the image file list is visible in the sample slot if you drag the Time slider, or you can create a material preview.

Note

You can also use the * and ? wildcard characters within an IFL file. For example, flyby* includes any image file that begins with "flyby," and flyby? includes any image file that begins with "flyby" and has one additional character. ∎

Generating IFL files with the IFL Manager Utility

If you don't want to create text files by yourself, you can use the IFL Manager Utility to generate IFL files for you. To use this utility, open the Utilities panel and click the More button. Then select the IFL Manager Utility, and click OK.

In the IFL Manager rollout, shown in Figure 21.15, the Select button opens a File dialog box where you can select a sequential list of images to include in an IFL file. After you select a list of images, you can specify the Start and End images. You can cause the images to be displayed in reverse by placing a greater number in the Start field than is in the End field. The Every Nth field can specify to use every Nth image. You use the Multiplier field to specify in how many frames each image should appear.

FIGURE 21.15

IFL Manager Utility can help to create IFL files.

The Create button opens a File dialog box where you can save the IFL file. The Edit button opens an IFL text file in the system's default text editor for editing.

Tutorial: What's on TV?

Animated files such as AVI and MOV can be opened and mapped to an object to animate the texture, but you can also use IFL files.

To create an IFL file that will be mapped on the front of a television model, follow these steps:

1. Open the Windows standard Notepad text editor, and type the following:

```
; these frames will be positioned on a television screen.
static.tif 20
Exploding planet - frame 10.tif 2
Exploding planet - frame 15.tif 2
Exploding planet - frame 20.tif 2
Exploding planet - frame 25.tif 2
Exploding planet - frame 30.tif 2
Exploding planet - frame 35.tif 2
Exploding planet - frame 40.tif 2
Exploding planet - frame 45.tif 2
Exploding planet - frame 50.tif 2
Exploding planet - frame 55.tif 2
static.tif 60
```

Note

The first line of text is referred to as a comment line. You enter comments into the IFL file by starting the line with a semicolon (;) character. ■

2. Save the file as **tv.ifl**. Make sure that your text editor doesn't add the extension .txt on the end of the file.

   You can check your file with the one I created, which you can find in the Chap 21 directory on the CD.

Note

The IFL file, as described earlier, looks for the image files in the same directory as the IFL file. Make sure that the images are included in this directory. ■

3. Open the Television—IFL File.max file from the Chap 21 directory on the CD.

   This file includes a television model created by Zygote Media.

4. Select the television front screen object, open the Material Editor, and double-click on the Standard material in the Material/Map Browser. Name the material **Television Screen**. Then create a Bitmap map node, locate the tv.ifl file, and connect it to the Diffuse color swatch. Then click the Assign Material to Selection button to apply the material to the screen.

Tip

To see the map in the viewport, click the Show Map in Viewport button. This button makes the frames of the IFL file visible in the viewport. ■

5. Because the screen object is a mesh object, you need to use the UVW Map modifier to create some mapping coordinates for the map. Open the Modify panel, and select the UVW Map modifier. Set the mapping option to Planar. Then select the Gizmo subobject mode and transform the planar gizmo until it covers the screen.

6. Click the Play button (/) to see the final animation.

Figure 21.16 shows one rendered frame of the television with the IFL file applied.

FIGURE 21.16

IFL files are commonly used to animate materials via a list of images such as the image on the front of this television.

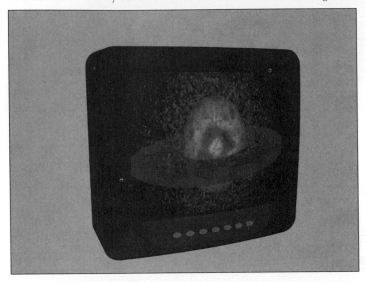

Working with Previews

More than likely, your final output will be rendered using the highest-quality settings with all effects enabled, and you can count on this taking a fair amount of time. After waiting several days for a sequence to render is a terrible time to find out that your animation keys are off. Even viewing animation sequences in the viewports with the Play Animation button cannot catch all problems.

One way to catch potential problems is to create a sample preview animation. Previews are test animation sequences that render quickly to give you an idea of the final output. The Tools ➪ Grab Viewport menu includes several commands for creating, renaming, and viewing previews. The rendering options available for previews are the same as the shading options available in the viewports.

Creating previews

You create previews by choosing Tools ➪ View: Grab Viewport ➪ Create Animated Sequence File to open the Make Preview dialog box, shown in Figure 21.17. You can also access this command from the viewport General label in the upper-left corner of the viewport.

In the Make Preview dialog box, you can specify what frames to include using the Active Time Segment or Custom Range options. You can also choose Every Nth Frame or select a specific frame rate in the Playback FPS field. The image size is determined by the Percent of Output value, which is a percentage of the final output size. The resolution is also displayed.

The Display Filter section offers a variety of options to include in the preview. These options include Geometry, Shapes, Lights, Cameras, Helpers, Space Warps, Particle Systems, Bone Objects, and Active Grid. Because the preview output is rendered like the viewports, certain selected objects such as Lights and Cameras actually display their icons as part of the file. The Overlay options prints the safe frame borders, frame number and the camera/view name in the upper-left corner of each frame. This is a nice feature that helps in identifying the results.

FIGURE 21.17

The Make Preview dialog box lets you specify the range, size, and output of a preview file.

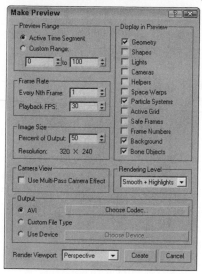

The Rendering Level drop-down list includes the same shading options used to display objects in the viewports, including Realistic, Shaded, Consistent Colors, Hidden Line, Wireframe, and Bounding Box. It also includes the various Stylized render options including Ink, Color Ink, Acrylic, Tech, Graphite, Color Pencil, and Pastel. There are also options to toggle on or off Edged Faces, Textures, Highlights, and the Background.

New Feature

The ability to render out previews to one of the Stylized options is new to 3ds Max 2012. ■

If the Camera View uses one of the multi-pass camera effects such as depth-of-field or motion blur, you can enable these effects for the preview also.

Output options include the default AVI option; a Custom File Type option, which enables you to choose your own format. For the AVI option, you can select a CODEC, which is used to compress the resulting file. Options include Cinepak Codec by Radius, Logitech Video (1420), Intel IYUV, Microsoft Video 1, Intel Indeo Video 4.5, DivX 5.0.5, and Full Frames (uncompressed), depending on the CODECs that are installed on your system.

At the bottom of the dialog box is a Render Viewport drop-down list, where you can select which viewport to use to create your preview file. The Create button starts the rendering process. When a preview is being rendered, the viewports are replaced with a single image of the current render frame, and the Status bar is replaced by a Progress bar and a Cancel button.

Tip

You can use the Esc key on your keyboard to cancel a rendering job. ■

If you cancel the rendering, the Make Preview alert box offers the options Stop and Play; Stop and Don't Play; and Don't Stop.

Viewing previews

When a preview file is finished rendering, the default Media Player for your system loads and displays the preview file. You can disable this autoplay feature using the Autoplay Preview File option in the General panel of the Preference Settings dialog box.

At any time, you can replay the preview file using the Tools ⇨ Views: Grab Viewport ⇨ View Animated Sequence File menu command. This command loads the latest preview file and displays it in the Media Player.

Renaming previews

The preview file is actually saved as a file named scene.avi and is saved by default in the previews subdirectory. Be aware that this file is automatically overwritten when a new preview is created. To save a preview file by renaming it, choose Tools ⇨ Views: Grab Viewport ⇨ Rename Animated Sequence File. This command opens the Save Preview As dialog box, where you can give the preview file a name.

Summary

This chapter covered the basics of animating objects in Max, including working with time and keys. You also learned about the two key creation modes and editing keys. Several animation helps are available, such as trajectories and ghosting. This chapter also discussed how to animate materials and how to create preview animations. In this chapter, you learned how to do the following:

- Control time and work with keys
- Use the two key creation modes
- Work with the Track Bar and the Motion panel
- View and edit key values
- Use trajectories and ghosting
- Animate materials and use IFL files
- Create preview animations

The next chapter shows how to automate the creation of animation keys with constraints and controllers.

Animating with Constraints and Simple Controllers

W hen you first begin animating and working with keys, having Max figure out all the frames between the start and end keys seems amazing, especially if you've ever animated in 2D by drawing every frame. But soon you realize that animating with keys can be time-consuming for complex realistic motions, and again, Max comes to the rescue. You can use animation constraints and controllers to automate the creation of keys for certain types of motions.

Constraints and controllers store and manage the key values for all animations in Max. When you animate an object using the Auto Key button, the default controller is automatically assigned. You can change the assigned controller or alter its parameters using the Motion panel or the Track View.

This chapter explains how to work with constraints and some simple controllers. For example, you can use the Noise controller to add random motion to a flag blowing in the wind or use the Surface constraint to keep a bumper car moving over the surface.

Restricting Movement with Constraints

The trick of animating an object is to make it go where you want it to go. Animating objects deals not only with controlling the motion of the object but also with controlling its lack of motion. Constraints are a type of animation controller that you can use to restrict the motion of an object.

Using these constraints, you can force objects to stay attached to another object or follow a path. For example, the Attachment constraint can be used to make a robot's feet stay connected to a ground plane as it moves. The purpose of these constraints is to make animating your objects easier.

Using constraints

You can apply constraints to selected objects using the Animation ⇨ Constraints menu. The constraints contained within this menu include Attachment, Surface, Path, Position, Link, LookAt, and Orientation.

 All constraints have the same controller icon displayed in the Motion panel or the Track View.

After you select one of the constraints from the Animation ⇨ Constraints menu, a dotted link line extends from the current selected object to the mouse cursor. You can select a target object in any of the viewports to apply the constraint. The cursor changes to a plus sign when it is over a target object that can be selected. Selecting a constraint from the Constraints menu also opens the Motion panel, where the settings of the constraint can be modified.

 You also can apply constraints using the Assign Controller button found in the Motion panel and in the Track View window.

Cross-Reference

Find out more about the Track View window in Chapter 37, "Working with the F-Curve Editor in the Track View." ∎

Working with the constraints

Each constraint is slightly different, but learning how to use these constraints will help you control the animated objects within a scene. You can apply several constraints to a single object. All constraints that are applied to an object are displayed in a list found in the Motion panel. From this list, you can select which constraint to make active and which to delete. You also can cut and paste constraints between objects.

Attachment constraint

The Attachment constraint determines an object's position by attaching it to the face of another object. This constraint lets you attach an object to the surface of another object. For example, you could animate the launch of a rocket ship with booster rockets that are attached with the Attachment constraint. The booster rockets would move along with the ship until the time when they are jettisoned.

The pivot point of the object that the constraint is applied to is attached to the target object. At the top of the Attachment Parameters rollout is a Pick Object button for selecting the target object to attach to. You can use this button to change the target object or to select the target object if the Animation ⇨ Constraints menu wasn't used. There is also an option to align the object to the surface. The Update section enables you to manually or automatically update the attachment values.

Note

The Attachment constraint shows up in the Position track of the Assign Controller rollout as the Position List controller. To minimize the effect of other controllers, set their Weight values in the Position List rollout to 0. ∎

The Key Info section of the Attachment Parameters rollout displays the key number and lets you move between the various keys. The Time value is the current key value. In the Face field, you can specify the exact number of the face to attach to. To set this face, click the Set Position button and drag over the target object. The A and B values represent Barycentric coordinates for defining how the object lies on the face. You can change these coordinate values by entering values or by dragging the red cross-hairs in the box below the A and B values. The easiest way to position an object is to use the Set Position button to place the object and then to enhance its position with the A and B values. The Set Position button stays active until you click it again.

The TCB section sets the Tension, Continuity, and Bias values for the constraint. You also can set the Ease To and Ease From values.

Tutorial: Attaching eyes to a melting snowman

When part of a model is deformed, such as applying the Melt modifier to a snowman's body, smaller parts like the eyes either get left behind or get the full weight of the modifier applied to them. If the Melt modifier weren't applied to these items, they would stay floating in the air while the rest of the snowman melted about them. This problem can be fixed with the Attachment constraint, which causes the eyes to remain attached to the snowball as it melts.

Cross-Reference
The tutorial where the Melt modifier is applied to the snowman is included in Chapter 35, "Using Animation Layers, Modifiers, and Complex Controllers." ■

To constrain the solid objects to a melting snowman, follow these steps:

1. Open the Melting snowman.max file from the Chap 22 directory on the CD.

   This file includes the melting snowman file from the previous chapter with the Melt modifier applied to all objects.

2. Select the left eye object in the scene. In the Modifier Stack, select the Melt modifier and click the Remove Modifier button to throw that modifier away.

3. With the left eye still selected, select Animation ⇨ Constraints ⇨ Attachment Constraint. A connecting line appears in the active viewport. Click the top snowball to select it as the attachment object. This moves the eye object to the top of the snowball where the snowball's first face is located.

4. In the Attachment Parameters rollout, change the Face value until the eye is positioned where it should be. This should be around face 315. Then change the A and B values (or drag in the Position graph) to position the eye where it looks good.

5. Repeat Step 5 for the right eye and for any other objects in the scene that you want to attach.

6. Click the Play button (/) and notice that the snow melts, but the eye objects stay the same size.

Figure 22.1 shows the resulting melted snowman.

Surface constraint

The Surface constraint moves an object so that it is on the surface of another object. The object with Surface constraint applied to it is positioned so that its pivot point is on the surface of the target object. You can use this constraint only on certain objects, including Spheres, Cones, Cylinders, Toruses, Quad Patches, Loft objects, and NURBS objects.

FIGURE 22.1

The Attachment constraint sticks one object to the surface of another.

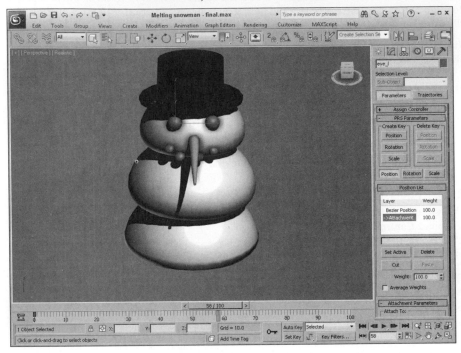

Caution

Because the Surface Constraint works using the parametric nature of the attached surface, only certain object types can be used with the surface constraint, including primitive objects like a sphere, cone, cylinder, patch, and NURBS objects. ■

In the Surface Controller Parameters rollout is the name of the target object that was selected after the menu command. The Pick Surface button enables you to select a different surface to attach to. You also can select specific U and V Position values. Alignment options include No Alignment, Align to U, Align to V, and a Flip toggle.

Note

Don't be confused because the rollout is named Surface Controller Parameters instead of Surface Constraint Parameters. The developers at Autodesk must have missed this one. ■

Tutorial: Rolling a tire down a hill with the Surface constraint

Moving a vehicle across a landscape can be a difficult procedure if you need to place every rotation and position key, but with the Surface constraint, it becomes easy. In this tutorial, you use the Surface constraint to roll a tire down a hill.

To roll a tire down a hill with the Surface constraint, follow these steps:

1. Open the Tire rolling on a hill.max file from the Chap 22 directory on the CD.

   This file includes a patch grid hill and a wheel object made from primitives.

2. Create a dummy object from the Helpers category, and link the tire object to it as a child. This causes the tire to move along with the dummy object. Position the dummy object's pivot point at the bottom of the tire and the top of the hill. The pivot point can be moved using the Affect Pivot Only button in the Hierarchy panel.

3. Select the dummy object, choose Animation ⇨ Constraints ⇨ Surface Constraint, and select the hill object.

4. In the Surface Controller Parameters rollout, select the Align to V and Flip options to position the dummy and tire objects at the top of the hill. Set the V Position value to **50** to move the tire down the hill.

5. Click the Auto Key button (or press the N key), drag the Time Slider to frame 100, and change the U Position to **100**. Click the Animate button again to deactivate it, and click the Play Animation button to see the tire move down the hill.

Figure 22.2 shows the tire as it moves down the hill. In the Top view, you can see the function curves for this motion.

FIGURE 22.2

The Surface constraint can animate one object moving across the surface of another.

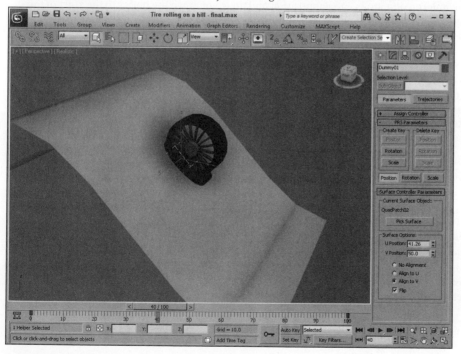

Path constraint

The Path constraint lets you select a spline path for the object to follow. The object is locked to the path and follows it even if the spline is changed. This is one of the most useful constraints because you can control the exact motion of an object using a spline. With Max's spline features, you can control very precisely the motions of objects that are constrained with the Path constraint. A good example of this constraint is an animated train following a track. Using a spline to create the train tracks, you can easily animate the train using the Path constraint.

When you choose the Animation ⇨ Constraints ⇨ Path Constraint menu command, you can select a single path for the object to follow. This path is added to a list of paths in the Path Parameters rollout.

The Path Parameters rollout also includes Add and Delete Path buttons for adding and deleting paths to and from the list. If two paths are added to the list, then the object follows the position centered between these two paths. By adjusting the Weight value for each path, you can make the object favor a specific path.

The Path Options include a % Along Path value for defining the object's position along the path. This value ranges from 0 at one end to 100 at the other end. The Follow option causes the object to be aligned with the path as it moves, and the Bank option causes the object to rotate to simulate a banking motion.

The Bank Amount value sets the depth of the bank, and the Smoothness value determines how smooth the bank is. The Allow Upside Down option lets the object spin completely about the axis, and the Constant Velocity option keeps the speed regular. The Loop option returns the object to its original position for the last frame of the animation, setting up a looping animation sequence. The Relative option lets the object maintain its current position and does not move the object to the start of the path. From its original position, it follows the path from its relative position. At the bottom of the Path Parameters rollout, you can select the axis to use.

Tutorial: Creating a spaceship flight path

Another way to use splines is to create animation paths. As an example, you use a Line spline to create an animation path. You can use splines for animation paths in two ways. One way is to create a spline and have an object follow it using either the Path constraint or the Path Follow Space Warp. The first vertex of the spline marks the first frame of the animation. The other way is to animate an object and then edit the Trajectory path.

In this tutorial, you use a simple path and attach it to a spaceship model. Viewpoint Datalabs provided the spaceship model.

To attach an object to a spline path, follow these steps:

1. Open the Spaceship and asteroids.max file from the Chap 22 directory on the CD.

   This file contains the spaceship model and several asteroid objects.

2. Select Create ⇨ Shapes ⇨ Line, and click and drag in the Top viewport to create an animation path that moves the spaceship through the asteroids. Right-click when the path is complete. Then select the Modify panel, click the Vertex button in the Selection rollout to enable Vertex subobject mode, and edit several vertices in the Front viewport. Then right-click to exit vertex subobject mode.

3. With the spaceship selected, choose Animation ⇨ Constraints ⇨ Path Constraint. Then click the animation path to select it as the path to follow. Select the Follow option in the Path Parameters rollout, and choose the Y-Axis option.

4. Click the Play Animation button in the Time Controls to see the spaceship follow the path.

Figure 22.3 shows the spaceship as it moves between the asteroids.

FIGURE 22.3

The spaceship object has been attached to a spline path that it follows.

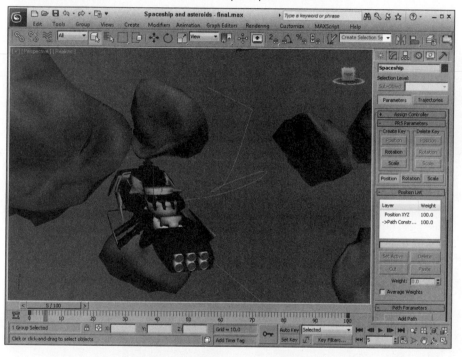

Position constraint

You can use the Position constraint to tie the position of an object to the weighted position of several target objects. For example, you could animate a formation of fighter jets by animating one of the jets and using Position constraints on all adjacent jets.

The Position constraint menu option lets you select a single target object, enabling you to place the pivot points of the two objects on top of one another. To add another target object, click the Add Position Target button in the Position Constraint rollout in the Motion panel. This button enables you to select another target object in the viewports; the target name appears within the target list in the rollout.

If you select a target name in the target list, you can assign a weight to the target. The constrained object is positioned close to the object with the higher weighted value. The Weight value provides a way to center objects between several other objects. The Keep Initial Offset option lets the object stay in its current location, but centers it relative to this position.

Figure 22.4 shows a sled positioned between four tree objects using the Position constraint. Notice how the weight of the downhill tree object is weighted higher than the other targets and the sled is close to it.

FIGURE 22.4

You can use the Position constraint to control the position of an object in relation to its targets.

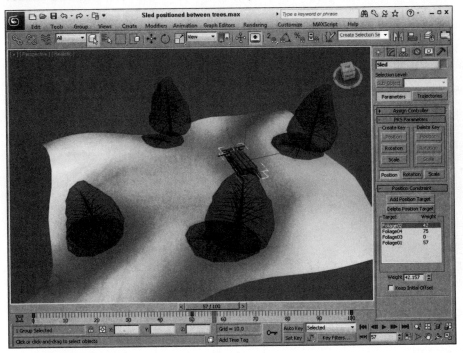

Link constraint

The Link constraint can transfer hierarchical links between objects. This constraint can cause a child's link to be switched during an animation. Any time you animate a complex model with a dummy object, the Link constraint makes it possible to switch control from one dummy object to another during the animation sequence. This keeps the motions of the dummy objects simple.

The Link Params rollout includes Add Link and Delete Link buttons, a list of linked objects, and the Start Time field. To switch the link of an object, enter for the Start Time the frame where you want the link to switch, or drag the Time Slider and click the Add Link button. Then select the new parent object. The Delete key becomes active when you select a link in the list.

Note

If you create a link using the Link constraint, the object is not recognized as a child in any hierarchies. ∎

All links are kept in a list in the Link Params rollout. You can add links to this list with the Add Link button, create a link to the world with the Link to World button, or delete links with the Delete Link button. The Start Time field specifies when the selected object takes control of the link. The object listed in the list is the parent object, so the Start Time setting determines when each parent object takes control.

The Key Mode section lets you choose a No Key option. This option does not write any keyframes for the object. If you want to set keys, you can choose the Key Nodes options and set keys for the object itself (Child option) or for the entire hierarchy (Parent option). The Key Entire Hierarchy sets keys for the object and its parents (Child option) or for the object and its targets and their hierarchies (Parent option).

This constraint also includes the PRS Parameters and Key Info rollouts.

Caution

You cannot use Link constraints with Inverse Kinematics systems. ∎

Tutorial: Skating a figure eight

For an animated object to switch its link from one parent to another halfway through an animation, you need to use the Link constraint. Rotating an object about a static point is easy enough: Simply link the object to a dummy object, and rotate the dummy object. The figure-eight motion is more complex, but you can do it with the Link constraint.

To move an object in a figure eight, follow these steps:

1. Open the Figure skater skating a figure eight.max file from the Chap 22 directory on the CD.

    This file includes a figure skater model imported from Poser and two dummy objects. The figure skater is linked to the first dummy object (the one initially closest to the skater).

2. Click the Auto Key button (or press the N key), drag the Time Slider to frame 100, and rotate the first dummy object two full revolutions in the Top viewport.

3. Select the second dummy object, and rotate it two full revolutions in the opposite direction. Click the Auto Key button again to deactivate it.

Tip

If you enable the Angle Snap Toggle button on the main toolbar, then it is easier to rotate objects exactly two revolutions. ∎

4. With the figure skater selected, choose Animation ➪ Constraints ➪ Link Constraint. Then click the first dummy object (the top one in the Top viewport).

    The Link constraint is assigned to the figure skater.

5. In the Link Params rollout, click the Add Link button. With the first dummy object selected in the viewport, set the Start Time value to **0**. Then click the second dummy object, and set the Start Time to **25** in the Link Params rollout. Finally, click the first dummy object again, and set the Start Time to **75**.

6. Click the Play Animation button (or press the / key) to see the animation play.

Tip

Another way to accomplish this same motion is to create a spline of a figure eight and use the Path constraint. ■

Figure 22.5 shows the skater as she makes her path around the two dummy objects.

FIGURE 22.5

With the Link constraint, the figure skater can move in a figure eight by rotating about two dummy objects.

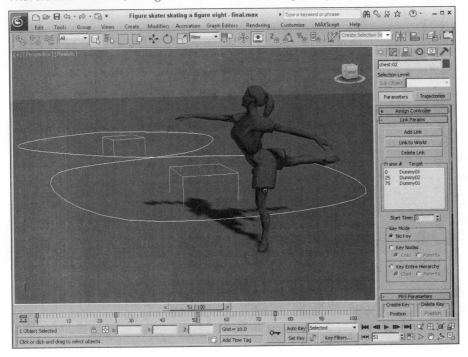

LookAt constraint

The LookAt constraint won't move an object, but it rotates the object so it is always orientated toward the target object. For example, you could use the LookAt constraint to animate a character's head that is watching a flying bumblebee. It is also very useful to apply to camera objects that follow a specific object throughout the animation.

After you select a target object, a single line extends from the object and points at the target object. This line, called the Viewline, is visible only within the viewports.

The LookAt Constraint rollout, like many of the other constraints, includes a list of targets. With the Add and Delete LookAt Target buttons, you can add and remove targets from the list. If several targets are on the list, the object is centered on a location between them. Using the Weight value, you can cause the various targets to have more of an influence over the orientation of the object. The Keep Initial Offset option prevents the object from reorienting itself when the constraint is applied. Any movement is relative to its original position.

You can set the Viewline length, which is the distance that the Viewline extends from the object. The Viewline Length Absolute option draws the Viewline from the object to its target, ignoring the length value.

The Set Orientation button lets you change the offset orientation of the object using the Select and Rotation button on the main toolbar. If you get lost, the Reset Orientation button returns the orientation to its original position. You can select which local axis points at the target object.

The Upnode is an object that defines the up direction. If the LookAt axis ever lines up with the Upnode axis, then the object flips upside-down. To prevent this, you can select which local axis is used as the LookAt axis and which axis points at the Upnode. The World is the default Upnode object, but you can select any object as the Upnode object by deselecting the World object and clicking the button to its right.

To control the Upnode, you can select the LookAt option or the Axis Alignment option, which enables the Align to Upnode Axis option. Using this option, you can specify which axis points toward the Upnode.

Caution

The object using the LookAt constraint flips when the target point is positioned directly above or below the object's pivot point. ■

When you assign the LookAt constraint, the Create Key button for rotation changes to Roll. This is because the camera is locked to point at the assigned object and cannot rotate; rather, it can only roll about the axis.

You can use the LookAt constraint to let cameras follow objects as they move around a scene. It is the default transform controller for Target camera objects.

Orientation constraint

You can use the Orientation constraint to lock the rotation of an object to another object. You can move and scale the objects independently, but the constrained object rotates along with the target object. A good example of an animation that uses this type of constraint is a satellite that orbits the Earth. You can offset the satellite and still constrain it to the Earth's surface. Then, as the Earth moves, the satellite follows.

In the Orientation Constraint rollout, you can select several orientation targets and weight them in the same manner as with the Position constraint. The target with the greatest weight value has the most influence over the object's orientation. You also can constrain an object to the World object. The Keep Initial Offset option maintains the object's original orientation and rotates it relative to this original orientation. The Transform Rule setting determines whether the object rotates using the Local or World Coordinate Systems.

Using the Walkthrough Assistant

One alternative to using the Path and LookAt constraint is to use the Walkthrough Assistant. This tool is accessed from the Animation menu. It opens up a utility panel with several rollouts, as shown in Figure 22.6. Using this panel, you can create a new camera, select a path, and set the viewport to use the created camera. You can then use the View Controls rollout to cause the view to tilt to the left or right as you move through the path. This automates the process of getting a camera to follow a path.

FIGURE 22.6

The Walkthrough Assistant automates several constraints into a single interface.

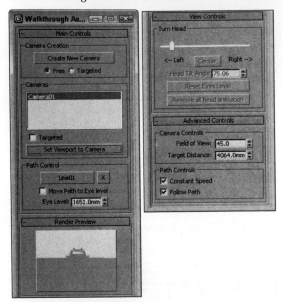

The Walkthrough Assistant also includes a Render Preview that you use to see the results. If you drag the Time Slider to a different frame and click the Render Preview pane, the preview is updated. At specific frames, you can drag the Turn Head slider to change where the camera is looking. You can even tilt the camera up and down as well as side to side.

In the Advanced Controls rollout (which appears only after a camera has been created) are options for changing the Field of View and the Target Distance, which is useful if you're using a Depth of Field effect. You also can set the camera to move at a constant speed and an option to cause the camera to follow the path.

Understanding Controller Types

Controllers are used to set the keys for animation sequences. Every object and parameter that is animated has a controller assigned, and almost every controller has parameters that you can alter to change its functionality. Some controllers present these parameters as rollouts in the Motion panel, and others use a Properties dialog box.

Max has five basic controller types that work with only a single parameter or track and one specialized controller type that manages several tracks at once (the Transform controllers). The type depends on the type of values the controller works with. The types include the following:

- **Transform controllers:** A special controller type that applies to all transforms (position, rotation, and scale) at the same time, such as the Position, Rotation, Scale (PRS) controllers
- **Position controllers:** Control the position coordinates for objects, consisting of X, Y, and Z values

- **Rotation controllers:** Control the rotation values for objects along all three axes
- **Scale controllers:** Control the scale values for objects as percentages for each axis
- **Float controllers:** Used for all parameters with a single numeric value, such as Wind Strength and Sphere Radius
- **Point3 controllers:** Consist of color components for red, green, and blue, such as Diffuse and Background colors

Note

Understanding the different controller types is important. When you copy and paste controller parameters between different tracks, both tracks must have the same controller type. ■

Float controllers work with parameters that use float numbers, such as a sphere's Radius or a plane object's Scale Multiplier value. Float values are numbers with a decimal value, such as 2.3 or 10.99. A Float controller is assigned to any parameter that is animated. After it is assigned, you can access the function curves and keys for this controller in the Track View and in the Track Bar. Because Float and Point3 controllers are assigned to parameters and not to objects, they don't appear in the Animation menu.

Assigning Controllers

Any object or parameter that is animated is automatically assigned a controller. The controller that is assigned is the default controller. The Animation panel in the Preference Settings dialog box lists the default controllers and lets you change them. You can change this automatic default controller using the Track View window or the transformation tracks located in the Motion panel.

Automatically assigned controllers

The default controllers are automatically assigned for an object's transformation tracks when the object is created. For example, if you create a simple sphere and then open the Motion panel (which has the icon that looks like a wheel), you can find the transformation tracks in the Assign Controller rollout. The default Position controller is Position XYZ, the default Rotation controller is Euler XYZ, and the default Scale controller is the Bézier Scale controller.

The default controller depends on the type of object. For example, the Barycentric Morph controller is automatically assigned when you create a morph compound object, and the Master Point controller is automatically assigned to any vertices or control points subobjects that are animated.

Note

Because controllers are automatically assigned to animation tracks, they cannot be removed; they can only be changed to a different controller. There is no function to delete controllers. ■

Assigning controllers with the Animation menu

The easiest way to assign a controller to an object is with the Animation menu. Located under the Animation menu are four controller submenus consisting of Transform, Position, Rotation, and Scale.

Note

Although constraints are contained within a separate menu, they control the animating of keys just like controllers. ■

When a controller is assigned to an object using the Animation menu, the existing controller is not removed, but the new controller is added as part of a list along with the other controllers. You can see all these controllers in the Motion panel.

For example, Figure 22.7 shows the Motion panel for a sphere object that has the default Position XYZ controller assigned to the Position track. If you choose Animation ⇨ Position Controllers ⇨ Noise, then the Position List controller is added to the Position track, of which Position XYZ and Noise are two available controllers. This lets you animate multiple motions such as the shimmy of a car with a bad carburetor as it moves down the road.

FIGURE 22.7

The Motion panel displays all transform controllers applied to an object.

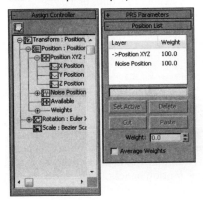

The List controller makes it possible to add several controllers to a single track. It also allows you to set Weights for each of its controllers. Using the Position List rollout, you can set the active controller and delete controllers from the list. You also can Cut and Paste controllers to other tracks.

Assigning controllers in the Motion panel

The top of the Motion panel includes two buttons: Parameters and Trajectories. Clicking the Parameters button makes the Assign Controller rollout available.

 To change a transformation track's controller, select the track and click the Assign Controller button positioned directly above the list. An Assign Controller dialog box opens that is specific to the track you selected.

Cross-Reference

For more about the Trajectories button, see Chapter 21, "Understanding Animation and Keyframes." ∎

For example, Figure 22.8 shows the Assign Position Controller dialog box for selecting a controller for the Position track. The arrow mark (>) shows the current selected controller. At the bottom of the dialog box, the default controller type is listed. Select a new controller from the list, and click OK. This new controller now is listed in the track, and the controller's rollouts appear beneath the Assign Controller rollout.

FIGURE 22.8

The Assign Position Controller dialog box lets you select a controller to assign.

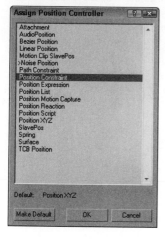

Note

Transformation controllers can be applied in the Motion panel, but the Track View can be used to apply controllers to all parameters including transforms. ■

Assigning controllers in the Track View

 You also can use the Track View to assign controllers. To do this, locate and select the track to apply a controller to, and then click the Assign Controller button on the Controllers toolbar, choose the Controller ➪ Assign (keyboard shortcut, C if the Keyboard Shortcut Override Toggle on the main toolbar is enabled) menu command, or right-click the track and select Assign Controller from the pop-up menu. An Assign Controller dialog box opens in which you can select the controller to use.

Cross-Reference

Chapter 37, "Working with the F-Curve Editor in the Track View," covers the details of the Track View. ■

You also can use the Controller toolbar to copy and paste controllers between tracks, but you can paste controllers only to similar types of tracks. When you paste controllers, the Paste dialog box lets you choose to paste the controller as a copy or as an instance. Changing an instanced controller's parameters changes the parameters for all instances. The Paste dialog box also includes an option to replace all instances. This option replaces all instances of the controller, whether or not they are selected.

Setting default controllers

When you assign controllers using the Track View, the Assign Controller dialog box includes the option Make Default. With this option, the selected controller becomes the default for the selected track.

You also can set the global default controller for each type of track by choosing Customize ⇨ Preferences, selecting the Animation panel, and then clicking the Set Defaults button. The Set Controller Defaults dialog box opens, in which you can set the default parameter settings, such as the In and Out curves for the controller. To set the default controller, select a controller from the list and click the Set Defaults button to open a controller–specific dialog box where you can adjust the controller parameters. The Animation panel also includes a button to revert to the original settings.

Note

Changing a default controller does not change any currently assigned controllers. ∎

Examining Some Simple Controllers

Now that you've learned how to assign controllers, let's look at some simple controllers.

Cross-Reference

Many more controllers are available. You can learn about these controllers in Chapter 35, "Using Animation Layers, Modifiers, and Complex Controllers." ∎

Earlier in the chapter, I mentioned six specific controller types. These types define the type of data that the controller works with. This section covers the various controllers according to the types of tracks with which they work.

Note

Looking at the function curves for a controller provides a good idea of how you can control it, so many of the figures that follow show the various function curves for the different controllers. ∎

Each of these controllers has a unique icon to represent it in the Track View. This makes them easy to identify.

Bézier controller

 The Bézier controller is the default controller for many parameters. It enables you to interpolate between values using an adjustable Bézier spline. By dragging its tangent vertex handles, you can control the spline's curvature. Tangent handles produce a smooth transition when they lie on the same line, or you can create an angle between them for a sharp point. Figure 22.9 shows the Bézier controller assigned to a Position track.

The Bézier controller parameters are displayed in the Motion panel under two rollouts: Key Info (Basic) and Key Info (Advanced).

At the top of the Key Info (Basic) rollout are two arrows and a field that shows the key number. The arrows let you move between the Previous and Next keys. Each vertex shown in the function curve represents a key. The Time field displays the frame number where the key is located. The Time Lock button next to the Time field can be set to prevent the key from being dragged in Track View. The value fields show the values for the selected track; the number of fields changes depending on the type of track that is selected.

The Bézier controller produces smooth animation curves.

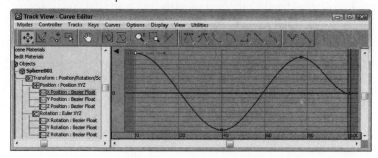

At the bottom of the Key Info (Basic) rollout are two flyout buttons for specifying the In and Out curves for the key. The arrows to the sides of these buttons move between the various In/Out curve types. The curve types include Smooth, Linear, Step, Slow, Fast, Custom, and Tangent Copy.

Cross-Reference

Chapter 37, "Working with the F-Curve Editor in the Track View," describes these various In/Out curve types. ■

The In and Out values in the Key Info (Advanced) rollout are enabled only when the Custom curve type is selected. These fields let you define the rate applied to each axis of the curve. The Lock button changes the two values by equal and opposite amounts. The Normalize Time button averages the positions of all keys. The Constant Velocity option interpolates the key between its neighboring keys to provide smoother motion.

Linear controller

 The Linear controller interpolates between two values to create a straight line by changing its value at a constant rate over time.

The Linear controller doesn't include any parameters and can be applied to time or values. Figure 22.10 shows the curves from the previous example after the Linear controller is assigned—all curves have been replaced with straight lines.

The Linear controller uses straight lines.

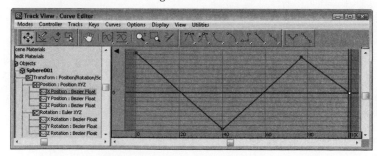

Noise controller

The Noise controller applies random variations in a track's values. In the Noise Controller dialog box, shown in Figure 22.11, the Seed value determines the randomness of the noise and the Frequency value determines how jagged the noise is. You also can set the Strength along each axis: The > (greater than) 0 option for each axis makes the noise values remain positive.

The Noise controller properties let you set the noise strength for each axis.

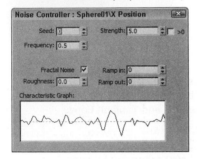

You also have an option to enable Fractal Noise with a Roughness setting.

The Ramp in and Ramp out values determine the length of time before or until the noise can reach full value. The Characteristic Graph gives a visual look at the noise over the range. Figure 22.12 shows the Noise controller assigned to the Position track. If you need to change any Noise properties, right-click the Noise track and select Properties from the pop-up menu.

The Noise controller lets you randomly alter track values.

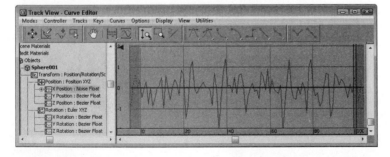

Spring controller

The Spring controller is similar in many ways to the Flex modifier in that it adds secondary motion associated with the wiggle of a spring after a force has been applied and then removed. When the Spring controller is applied, a panel with two rollouts appears. These rollouts, shown in Figure 22.13, let you control the physical properties of the spring and the forces that influence it.

FIGURE 22.13

The Spring controller rollouts can add additional springs and forces.

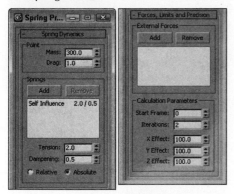

In the Spring Dynamics rollout, you can change the Mass and Drag values. Higher mass values result in greater secondary motion as the object is moved, and the Drag value controls how quickly the bouncing motion stops. You can add multiple springs, each with its own Tension and Damping values to be applied Relative or Absolute.

The Forces, Limits, and Precision rollout lets you add forces that affect the spring motion. The Add button lets you identify these forces, which are typically Space Warps, and you can limit the effect to specific axes.

Tutorial: Wagging a tail with the Spring controller

One of the best uses of the Spring controller is to gain the secondary motion associated with an existing motion. For example, if a character moves, then an appendage such as a tail can easily follow if you apply a Spring controller to it.

To wag a row of spheres using the Spring controller, follow these steps:

1. Open the Dog wagging tail.max file from the Chap 22 directory on the CD.

   This file contains a linked row of spheres with the head sphere animated rotating back and forth.

2. Select the smallest sphere, and choose the Animation ⇨ Position Controllers ⇨ Spring menu command. This moves the sphere to its parent. Choose the Select and Move button (or press the W key), and return the sphere to its original position.

3. Repeat Step 2 for the remaining spheres, moving from smallest to largest.

4. Click the Play Animation button (or press the / key) to see the resulting motion.

Figure 22.14 shows a frame of the final motion. Notice that the spheres aren't lined up exactly. The smallest sphere is moving the greatest distance because all the springs are adding their effect.

FIGURE 22.14

The Spring controller adds secondary motion to the existing motion of the largest sphere.

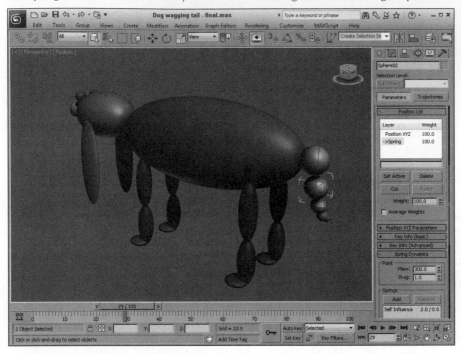

Position XYZ controller

The Position XYZ controller splits position transforms into three separate tracks, one for each axis. Each axis has a Bézier controller applied to it, but each component track can be assigned a different controller. The Position XYZ Parameters rollout lets you switch between the component axes.

The Rotation tracks use a variety of controllers, many of them common to the Position track. This section lists the controllers that can be used only with the Rotation track.

Scale XYZ controller

Max has one controller that you can use only in Scale tracks. The Scale XYZ controller breaks scale transforms into three separate tracks, one for each axis. This feature enables you to precisely control the scaling of an object along separate axes. It is a better alternative to using Select and Non-Uniform Scale from the main toolbar because it is independent of the object geometry.

The Scale XYZ Parameters rollout lets you select which axis to work with. This controller works the same way as the other position and rotation XYZ controllers.

Summary

Using the Animation ⇨ Constraints menu, you can apply constraints to objects. This menu also lets you select a target object. You can use the various constraints to limit the motion of objects, which is helpful as you begin to animate. If you're an animator, you should thank your lucky stars for controllers. Controllers offer power flexibility for animating objects—and just think of all those keys that you don't have to set by hand.

This chapter covered the basics of using the Expression controller. Using mathematical formulas to control the animation of an object's transformation and parameters offers lots of power. You also can use the values of one object to control another object.

In this chapter, you accomplished the following:

- Constrained an object to the surface of another object using the Attachment and Surface constraints
- Forced an object to travel along a path with the Path constraint
- Controlled the position and orientation of objects with weighted Position and Orientation constraints
- Shifted between two different controlling objects using the Link constraint
- Followed objects with the LookAt constraint
- Learned about the various controller types
- Discovered how to assign controllers using the Motion panel and the Track View
- Saw a few examples of using controllers

In the next chapter, you learn to final render a scene so you can have some output to hang on Mom's fridge.

Rendering a Scene and Enabling Quicksilver

After hours of long, hard work, the next step—rendering—is where the "rubber hits the road" and you get to see what you've worked on so hard. After modeling, applying materials, positioning lights and cameras, and animating your scene, you're finally ready to render the final output. Rendering deals with outputting the objects that make up a scene at various levels of detail.

Max includes a Scanline Renderer that is optimized to speed up this process, and several settings exist that you can use to make this process even faster. Understanding the Render Scene dialog box and its functions can save you many headaches and computer cycles. However, other rendering options are available.

The need for all these different rendering engines comes about because of a trade-off between speed and quality. For example, the renderer used to display objects in the viewports is optimized for speed, but the renderer used to output final images leans toward quality. Each renderer includes many settings that you can use to speed the rendering process or improve the quality of the results.

Render Parameters

Commands and settings for rendering an image are contained within the Render Scene dialog box. This dialog box includes several tabbed panels.

After you're comfortable with the scene file and you're ready to render a file, you need to open the Render Scene dialog box, shown in Figure 23.1, by means of the Rendering ⇨ Render Setup menu command (F10) or by clicking the Render Scene button on the main toolbar. This dialog box has several panels: Common, Renderer, Render Elements, Raytracer, and Advanced Lighting. The Common panel includes commands that are common for all renderers, but the Renderer panel includes specific settings for the selected renderer.

Cross-Reference

The Common and Renderer panels for the Default Scanline Renderer are covered in this chapter. The Raytracer and Renderer panel for the mental ray renderer are covered in Chapter 47, "Rendering with mental ray and iray"; the Render Elements panel is covered in Chapter 49, "Compositing with Render Elements and the Video Post Interface"; and the Advanced Lighting panel is covered in Chapter 45, "Working with Advanced Lighting, Light Tracing, and Radiosity." ■

FIGURE 23.1

You use the Render Scene dialog box to render the final output.

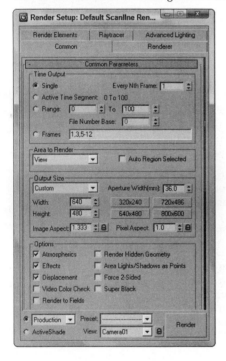

Initiating a render job

At the bottom of the Render Scene dialog box are several controls that are visible for all panels; these controls let you initiate a render job. The render modes are Production, Iterative (a selection in the drop-down list), and ActiveShade. Each of these modes can use a different renderer with different render settings as defined using the Assign Renderer rollout.

Note

If any objects in the rendered scene are missing mapping coordinates, then a dialog box appears as you try to render the scene with options to Continue or Cancel. A similar dialog box appears for any missing external files or any missing XRefs with options to continue, cancel, or browse from the missing file. ■

Iterative rendering mode is different from production in that it doesn't save the render to a file, use network rendering, or render multiple frames. Using this mode, you can leave the settings in the Render Scene dialog boxes unchanged while still getting a test render out quickly. This makes it a good mode to use for quickly getting test renders.

The Preset option lets you save and load a saved preset of renderer settings. When saving or loading a preset, the Select Preset Categories dialog box, shown in Figure 23.2, opens (after you select a preset file in a file dialog box). In this dialog box, you can select which panels of settings to include in the preset. The panels listed will depend on the selected renderer. All presets are saved with the .rps file extension.

FIGURE 23.2

The Select Preset Categories dialog box lets you choose which settings to include in the preset.

The Viewport drop-down list includes all the available viewports. When the Render Scene dialog box opens, the currently active viewport appears in the Viewport drop-down list. The one selected is the one that gets rendered when you click the Render button (or when you press Shift+Q). The Render button starts the rendering process. You can click the Render button without changing any settings, and the default parameters are used.

Tip

The little lock icon next to the viewport indicates that the selected viewport is always rendered when the Render button is clicked, regardless of the active viewport. ■

When you click the Render button, the Rendering dialog box appears. This dialog box, shown in Figure 23.3, displays all the settings for the current render job and tracks its progress. The Rendering dialog box also includes Pause and Cancel buttons for halting the rendering process. If the rendering is stopped, the Rendering dialog box disappears, but the Rendered Frame Window stays open.

Caution

If you close the Rendered Frame Window, the render job still continues. To cancel the rendering, click the Pause or Cancel button, or press the Esc key on your keyboard. ■

FIGURE 23.3

The Rendering dialog box displays the current render settings and progress of the render job.

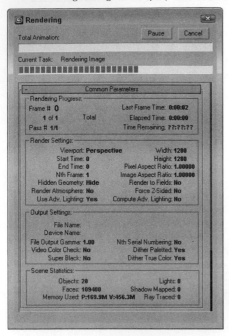

Tip

After you've set up the render settings for an image, you can re-render an image without opening the Render Scene dialog box by clicking the Quick Render button on the main toolbar, by selecting the Rendering ↔ Render menu command, by using the Shift+Q keyboard shortcut, or by selecting a render option from the Render Shortcuts toolbar. The F9 shortcut renders the last viewport again. ■

Common parameters

The Common Parameters rollout in the Render Scene dialog box includes the same controls regardless of the renderer being used.

Specifying range and size

The Time Output section defines which animation frames to include in the output. The Single option renders the current frame specified by the Time Slider. The Active Time Segment option renders the complete range of frames. The Range option lets you set a unique range of frames to render by entering the beginning and ending frame numbers. The last option is Frames, where you can enter individual frames and ranges using commas and hyphens. For example, entering "1, 6, 8-12" renders frames 1, 6, and 8 through 12. The Every Nth Frame value is active for the Active Time Segment and Range options. It renders every nth frame in the active segment. For example, entering 3 would cause every third frame to be rendered. This option is useful for sped-up animations. The File Number Base is the number to add to or subtract from the current frame number for the reference numbers attached to the end of each image file. For example, a File Number Base value of 10 for a Range value of 1–10 would label the files as image0011, image0012, and so on.

Tip

Don't render long animation sequences using the .avi, .mpeg, or .mov formats. If the rendering has trouble, the entire file will be corrupt. Instead, choose to render the frames as individual images. These individual images can then be reassembled into a video format using Max's RAM Player, the Video Post interface, or an external package like Adobe's Premiere. ∎

The Output Size section defines the resolution of the rendered images or animation. The drop-down list includes a list of standard film and video resolutions, including various 35mm and 70mm options, Anamorphic, Panavision, IMAX, VistaVision, NTSC (National Television Standards Committee), PAL (Phase Alternate Line), and HDTV standards. A Custom option allows you to select your own resolution.

Tip

Setting up the aspect ratio of the final rendering at the start of the project is helpful. Once an aspect ratio is established, you can use the Safe Frames panel in the Viewport Configuration dialog box to display the borders of the render region in the viewport. ∎

Aperture Width is a property of cameras that defines the relationship between the lens and the field of view. The resolutions listed in the Aperture Width drop-down list alter this value without changing the view by modifying the Lens value in the scene.

For each resolution, you can change the Width and Height values. Each resolution also has six preset buttons for setting these values.

Tip

You can set the resolutions of any of the preset buttons by right-clicking the button that you want to change. The Configure Preset dialog box opens, where you can set the button's Width, Height, and Pixel Aspect values. ∎

The Image Aspect is the ratio of the image width to its height. You can also set the Pixel Aspect ratio to correct rendering on different devices. Both of these values have lock icons to their left that lock the aspect ratio for the set resolution. Locking the aspect ratio automatically changes the Width dimension whenever the Height value is changed and vice versa. The Aperture Width, Image Aspect, and Pixel Aspect values can be set only when Custom is selected in the drop-down list.

Render options

The Options section includes the following options:

- **Atmospherics:** Renders any atmospheric effects that are set up in the Environment dialog box.
- **Effects:** Enables any Render Effects that have been set up.
- **Displacement:** Enables any surface displacement caused by an applied displacement map.
- **Video Color Check:** Displays any colors that cannot be displayed in the HSV (hue, saturation, and value) color space used by television in black.

- **Render to Fields:** Enables animations to be rendered as fields. Fields are used by video formats. Video animations include one field with every odd scan line and one field with every even scan line. These fields are composited when displayed.

- **Render Hidden Geometry:** Renders all objects in the scene, including hidden objects. Using this option, you can hide objects for quick viewport updates and include them in the final rendering.

- **Area Lights/Shadows as Points:** Rendering area lights and shadows can be time-consuming, but point lights render much more quickly. By enabling this option, you can speed the rendering process.

- **Force 2-Sided:** Renders both sides of every face. This option essentially doubles the render time and should be used only if singular faces or the inside of an object are visible.

- **Super Black:** Enables Super Black, which is used for video compositing. Rendered images with black backgrounds have trouble in some video formats. The Super Black option prevents these problems.

The Advanced Lighting section offers options to use Advanced Lighting or Compute Advanced Lighting when Required. Advanced lighting can take a long time to compute, so these two options give you the ability to turn advanced lighting on or off.

Cross-Reference

Advanced lighting is covered in more detail in Chapter 45, "Working with Advanced Lighting, Light Tracing, and Radiosity." ■

Bitmap Proxies

The Bitmap Proxies section includes a Setup button to enable a feature that can downscale all maps for the current scene. Clicking the Setup button opens the Global Settings and Defaults for Bitmap Proxies dialog box, shown in Figure 23.4.

FIGURE 23.4

The Bitmap Proxies dialog box lets you replace all texture maps with proxy images.

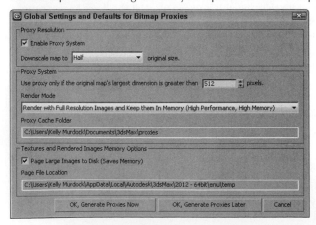

The Downscale map option lets you select to downscale all maps to Half, Third, Quarter, or Eighth, or to their current size. This lets you create your scene with high-quality maps and quickly reduce their sizes as needed without having to open and scale each individual map. The Proxy System lets you select to use a proxy image if the current map is larger than a specified size in pixels.

This dialog box also lets you set the Render Mode to be optimized for performance or memory. The options include Render with Proxies, Render with Full Resolution and Keep them [image maps] In Memory, and Render with Full Resolution and Free up the Memory once Rendered. If you enable the Page Large Images to Disk, large textures and rendered images are split into pages, which frees up memory, but it can make the update of the scene slower when a new page has to be recalled. The page file location can be specified.

Choosing a Render Output option

The Render Output section enables you to output the image or animations to a file, a device, or the Rendered Frame Window. To save the output to a file, click the Files button and select a location in the Render Output File dialog box. Supported formats include AVI, BMP, DDS, Postscript (EPS), JPEG, Kodak Cineon (CIN), Open EXR, Radiance Image File (HDRI), QuickTime (MOV), PNG, RLA, RPF, SGI's Format (RGB), Targa (TGA), and TIF. The Device button can output to a device such as a video recorder. If the Rendered Frame Window option is selected, then both the Files and Devices buttons are disabled. (The Rendered Frame Window is discussed later in this chapter.)

Tip

Each of these output formats has its advantages. For example, Targa files are good for compositing because they have an alpha channel. TIF and EPS files are good for files to be printed. JPEG, PNG, and GIF files are used for web images. DDS images are used in many game engines. ■

You also have an option to Put Image File List in Output Path, which creates a list of image files in the same location as the rendered file. You also have the choice of choosing Max's IFL standard or the Autodesk ME Image Sequence File (IMSQ). The Create Now button creates an image list instantly.

Cross-Reference

More on using Image File Lists is covered in Chapter 21, "Understanding Animation and Keyframes." ■

The Net Render option enables network rendering. The Skip Existing Images option doesn't replace any images with the same filename, a feature that you can use to continue a rendering job that has been canceled.

Cross-Reference

For more information on network rendering, see Chapter 48, "Batch and Network Rendering." ■

E-mail notifications

The process of rendering an animation (or even a single frame) can be brief or it can take several days, depending on the complexity of the scene. For complex scenes that will take a while to render, you can configure Max to send you an e-mail message when your rendering is complete or if it fails. These options are in the Email Notifications rollout, shown in Figure 23.5.

In addition to the options, you can enter whom the e-mail is from, whom it is to, and an SMTP Server.

The Email Notifications rollout includes options for sending an e-mail message to report on rendering status.

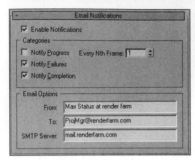

Adding pre-render and post-render scripts

The Scripts rollout includes File buttons for adding pre-render and post-render scripts. The scripts must be .ms scripts and are executed before and after the rendering of each file. These scripts can be used to compile information about the render or to do some post-processing work. Above each script file button is an Execute Now button that can be used to check the script before rendering.

Assigning renderers

Max performs rendering operations in several different places: The Render Scene dialog box renders to the Render Frame Window or to files; the sample slots in the Material Editor also are rendered; and the ActiveShade windows show another level of rendering.

The plug-in nature of Max enables you to select the renderer to use to output images. To change the default renderer, look in the Assign Renderers rollout in the Common panel of the Render Scene dialog box (F10). You can select different renderers for the Production, Material Editor, and ActiveShade modes. For each, you can select from the Default Scanline Renderer, the mental ray Renderer, Quicksilver Hardware Renderer, and the VUE File Renderer.

Note

The VUE File Renderer is used to create a VUE file, which is an editable text file that holds all the details of the scene. ■

The lock next to the Material Editor option indicates that the same renderer is used for both Production and Material Editor.

Scanline A-Buffer renderer

The Default Scanline Renderer rollout, found in the Renderer panel and shown in Figure 23.6, is the default renderer rollout that appears in the Render Scene dialog box. If a different renderer is loaded, then a different rollout for that renderer is displayed in the Renderer panel.

You can use the Options section at the top of the Default Scanline Renderer rollout to quickly disable various render options for quicker results. These options include Mapping, Shadows, Auto-Reflect/

Refract and Mirrors, and Force Wireframe. For the Force Wireframe option, you can define a Wire Thickness value in pixels. The Enabled SSE option uses Streaming SIMD (Single Instruction, Multiple Data) Extensions to speed up the rendering process by processing more data per instruction.

FIGURE 23.6

The Default Scanline Renderer rollout includes settings unique to this renderer.

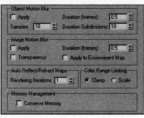

Tip

Intel Pentium III and later processors include the SSE instructions and can benefit from enabling this option. ■

Anti-alias filters

Another way to speed up rendering is to disable the Anti-aliasing and Filter Maps features. Anti-aliasing smoothes jagged edges that appear where colors change. The Filter Maps option allows you to disable the computationally expensive process of filtering material maps. The Filter drop-down list lets you select image filters that are applied at the pixel level during rendering. Below the drop-down list is a description of the current filter. The Filter Size value applies only to the Soften filter. Available filters include the following:

- **Area:** Does an anti-aliasing sweep using the designated area specified by the Filter Size value.
- **Blackman:** Sharpens the image within a 25-pixel area; provides no edge enhancement.
- **Blend:** Somewhere between a sharp and a coarse Soften filter; includes Filter Size and Blend values.
- **Catmull-Rom:** Sharpens with a 25-pixel filter and includes edge enhancement.
- **Cook Variable:** Can produce sharp results for small Filter Size values and blurred images for larger values.
- **Cubic:** Based on cubic-spline curves; produces a blurring effect.
- **Mitchell-Netravali:** Includes Blur and Ringing parameters.
- **Plate Match/MAX R2:** Matches mapped objects against background plates as used in Max R2.
- **Quadratic:** Based on a quadratic spline; produces blurring within a 9-pixel area.
- **Sharp Quadratic:** Produces sharp effects from a 9-pixel area.

619

- **Soften:** Causes mild blurring and includes a Filter Size value.
- **Video:** Blurs the image using a 25-pixel filter optimized for NTSC and PAL video.

SuperSampling

Global SuperSampling is an additional anti-aliasing process that you can apply to materials. This process can improve image quality, but it can take a long time to render; you can disable it using the Disable all Samplers option. SuperSampling can be enabled in the Material Editor for specific materials, but the SuperSampling rollout in the Material Editor also includes an option to Use Global Settings. The Global Settings are defined in the Default Scanline Renderer rollout.

Max includes anti-aliasing filters as part of the rendering process. You have several SuperSampling methods from which to choose.

SuperSampling is disabled if the Antialiasing option is disabled. Global SuperSampling can be enabled using the Enable Global SuperSampler option.

In a SuperSampling pass, the colors at different points around the center of a pixel are sampled. These samples are then used to compute the final color of each pixel. Max has four available SuperSampling methods: Max 2.5 Star, Hammersley, Adaptive Halton, and Adaptive Uniform.

Cross-Reference
You can find more information on each of these sampling methods in Chapter 16, "Creating and Applying Standard Materials." ■

Motion Blur

The Default Scanline Renderer rollout also offers two different types of motion blur: Object Motion Blur and Image Motion Blur. You can enable either of these using the Apply options.

Object Motion Blur is set in the Properties dialog box for each object. The renderer completes this blur by rendering the object over several frames. The movement of the camera doesn't affect this type of blur. The Duration value determines how long the object is blurred between frames. The Samples value specifies how many Duration units are sampled. The Duration Subdivision value is the number of copies rendered within each Duration segment. All these values can have a maximum setting of 16. The smoothest blurs occur when the Duration and Samples values are equal.

Image Motion Blur is also set in the Properties dialog box for each object. This type of blur is affected by the movement of the camera and is applied after the image has been rendered. You achieve this blur by smearing the image in proportion to the movement of the various objects. The Duration value determines the time length of the blur between frames. The Apply to Environment Map option lets you apply the blurring effect to the background as well as the objects. The Work with Transparency option blurs transparent objects without affecting their transparent regions. Using this option adds time to the rendering process.

Cross-Reference
You can add two additional blur effects to a scene: the Blur Render Effect, found in the Rendering Effects dialog box (covered in Chapter 46, "Using Atmospheric and Render Effects") and the Scene Motion Blur effect, available through the Video Post dialog box (covered in Chapter 49, "Compositing with Render Elements and the Video Post Interface"). ■

Other options

The Auto Reflect/Refract Maps section lets you specify a Rendering Iterations value for reflection maps within the scene. The higher the value, the more objects are included in the reflection computations and the longer the rendering time.

Color Range Limiting offers two methods for correcting over-brightness caused by applying filters. The Clamp method lowers any value above a relative ceiling of 1 to 1 and raises any values below 0 to 0. The Scale method scales all colors between the maximum and minimum values.

The Conserve Memory option optimizes the rendering process to use the least amount of memory possible. If you plan on using Max (or some other program) while it is rendering, you should enable this option.

Quicksilver Hardware Renderer

The Quicksilver Hardware Renderer takes advantage of the advanced graphics processing capabilities found in modern video cards. The advantage of this rendering option is speed. The Quicksilver Hardware Renderer can render scenes much faster than mental ray and at a better quality than the Scanline Renderer.

Caution

Some Max features don't work with Quicksilver including Exclude/Include for lights, Visibility in the Object Properties dialog box, Vertex Colors, multiple layers of transparency, and several map types including cellular, flat mirror, particle age, particle mblur, thin wall refraction, and non-regular noise. ■

The Quicksilver Hardware Renderer is available only if your video card supports Shader Model 3.0. If you select Help ⇨ Diagnose Video Hardware, Max runs a utility that checks and reports the capabilities of your current graphics card. Look for the GPU Shader Model Support to be SM3.0 or later.

When the Quicksilver Hardware Renderer is enabled, the Renderer panel displays the options available for this renderer, as shown in Figure 23.7. This renderer supports many of the options found in the more advanced mental ray Renderer, including the mental ray materials and lights. If you use any hardware shaders in the scene, you can specify their directory in the Hardware Shaders Cache Folder located at the bottom of the panel.

FIGURE 23.7

Many of the options for the Quicksilver Hardware Renderer are similar to the other renderers.

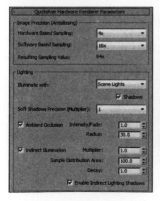

Part V: Animation and Rendering Basics

Cross-Reference

You can learn more about the mental ray rendering options in Chapter 47, "Rendering with mental ray and iray." ∎

Rendering Preferences

In addition to the settings available in the Render Scene dialog box, the Rendering panel in the Preference Settings dialog box includes many global rendering settings. The Preference Settings dialog box can be opened using the Customize ⇨ Preferences menu command. Figure 23.8 shows this panel.

The Rendering panel in the Preference Settings dialog box lets you set global rendering settings.

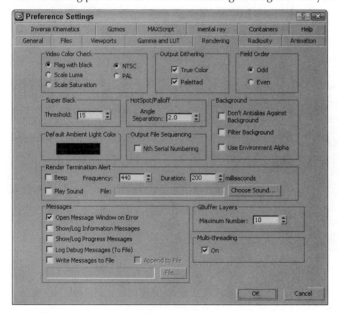

The Video Color Check options specify how unsafe video colors are flagged or corrected. The Flag with black option shows the unsafe colors, and the Scale Luma and Scale Saturation options correct them by scaling either the luminance or the saturation until they are in range. You can also choose to check NTSC or PAL formats.

Caution

Be aware that the Scale options can discolor some objects. ∎

Output Dithering options can enable or disable dithering of colors. The options include True Color for 24-bit images and Paletted for 8-bit images.

The Field Order options let you select which field is rendered first. Some video devices use even first, and others use odd first. Check your specific device to see which setting is correct.

The Super Black Threshold setting is the level below which black is displayed as Super Black.

The Angle Separation value sets the angle between the Hotspot and Falloff cones of a light. If the Hotspot angle equals the Falloff angle, then alias artifacts will appear.

The Don't Anti-alias Against Background option should be enabled if you plan on using a rendered object as part of a composite image. The Filter Background option includes the background image in the anti-aliasing calculations. The Use Environment Alpha option combines the background image's alpha channel with the scene object's alpha channel.

The Default Ambient Light Color is the darkest color for rendered shadows in the scene. Selecting a color other than black brightens the shadows.

You can set the Output File Sequencing option to list the frames in order if the Nth Serial Numbering option is enabled. If the Nth Serial Numbering option is disabled, the sequence uses the actual frame numbers.

In the Render Termination Alert section, you can elect to have a beep triggered when a rendering job is finished. The Frequency value changes the pitch of the sound, and the Duration value changes its length. You can also choose to load and play a different sound. The Choose Sound button opens a File dialog box where you can select the sound file to play.

You also can specify whether error messages are displayed and which messages are added to the log file. Log files by default are written to the renderassets folder, but you select a different path.

The GBuffer Layers value is the maximum number of graphics buffers to allow during rendering. This value can range between 1 and 1000. The value you can use depends on the memory of your system.

The Multi-threading option enables the renderer to complete different rendering tasks as separate threads. Threads use the available processor cycles more efficiently by subdividing tasks. This option should be enabled, especially if you're rendering on a multiprocessor computer.

Using the Rendered Frame Window

The Rendered Frame Window is a temporary window that holds any rendered images. Often when developing a scene, you want to test-render an image to view certain materials or transparency not visible in the viewports. The Rendered Frame Window, shown in Figure 23.9, enables you to view these test renderings without saving any data to the network or hard drive.

This buffer opens when you select the Rendered Frame Window option and click the Render button in the Render Scene dialog box. You can also view images from a local hard drive or a network drive in the Rendered Frame Window using the File ⇨ View Image File menu command.

To zoom in on the buffer, hold down the Ctrl key and click the window. Right-click while holding down the Ctrl key to zoom out. The Shift key enables you to pan the buffer image. You can also use the mouse wheel (if you have a scrolling mouse) to zoom and pan within the frame buffer.

Tip
You can zoom and pan the image while it is rendering. ∎

FIGURE 23.9

The Rendered Frame Window displays rendered images without saving them to a file.

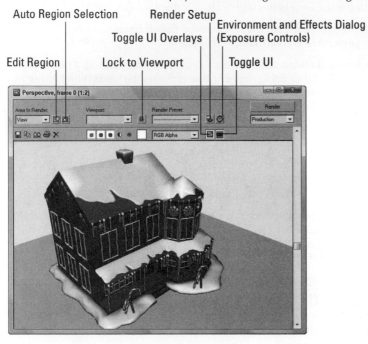

Using the Render Types

From the top of the Rendered Frame Window, the Area to Render drop-down list enables you to render subsections of the scene. The default setting is View. After you pick a selection from the list, click the Render button to begin the rendering. The available Render Types are described in Table 23.1.

TABLE 23.1

Render Type Options

Render Type	Description
View	Renders the entire view as shown in the active viewport.
Selected	Renders only the selected objects in the active viewport.
Region	Places a frame of dotted lines with handles in the active viewport. This frame lets you define a region to render. You can resize the frame by dragging the handles. When you have defined the region, click OK in the lower-right corner of the active viewport.
Crop	Similar to Region in that it uses a frame to define a region, but the Crop setting doesn't include the areas outside the defined frame.
Blowup	Takes the defined region and increases its size to fill the render window. The frame for Blowup is constrained to the aspect ratio of the final resolution.

At the top of the frame buffer window are several controls and icon buttons.

 The Edit Region button is activated when the Region option is selected. It lets you drag the center of the area to move it around or drag the edge and corner handles of the region to resize the render area. This option lets you precisely define the area that is rendered.

 The Auto Region Selected option automatically sets the render region to the current selection in the viewports.

 The Lock to Viewport causes all renders to be done used the specified viewport, regardless of which viewport is active. Using this option you can lock the renders to the Perspective viewport even if you're using a different viewport.

 The Render Setup button opens the Render Scene dialog box.

 The Environment and Effects Dialog button opens this dialog box, which includes the Exposure Control settings.

 The first is the Save Bitmap button, which enables you to save the current frame buffer image.

 The Copy Bitmap button copies the image in the Rendered Frame Window to the Windows clipboard where you can paste it into another application like Photoshop.

 The Clone Rendered Frame Window button creates another frame buffer dialog box. Any new rendering is rendered to this new dialog box, which is useful for comparing two images.

 The Print Image button sends the rendered image to the default printer.

 The Clear button erases the image from the window.

The next five buttons enable the red, green, blue, alpha, and monochrome channels. The alpha channel holds any transparency information for the image. The alpha channel is a grayscale map, with black showing the transparent areas and white showing the opaque areas. Next to the Display Alpha Channel button is the Monochrome button, which displays the image as a grayscale image.

The Channel Display drop-down list lets you select the channel to display. The color swatch at the right shows the color of the currently selected pixel. You can select new pixels by right-clicking and holding on the image. This temporarily displays a small dialog box with the image dimensions and the RGB value of the pixel directly under the cursor. The color in the color swatch can then be dragged and dropped in other dialog boxes such as the Material Editor.

 The Toggle UI Overlays button causes the frame that marks the region area to be visible when rendered.

 The Toggle UI button hides the top selection of controls in the Rendered Frame Window.

Previewing with ActiveShade

The ActiveShade window gives a quick semi-rendered look at the current scene. You can open an ActiveShade display within a viewport by clicking the viewport label in the upper-left corner of each viewport and choosing Views ⇨ ActiveShade from the pop-up menu.

Note

The ActiveShade window used to be quite valuable, but now that Max can render lights and shadows in the viewport, the ActiveShade window isn't as helpful. ∎

Only one ActiveShade viewport can be open at a time. If you try to open more than one window, a warning dialog box lets you know that opening it will close the previous window.

Tip

You can drag materials from the Material Editor and drop them directly on the ActiveShade window. ∎

Using the RAM Player

Just as you can use the Rendered Frame Window to view and compare rendered images, the RAM Player enables you to view rendered animations in memory. With animations loaded in memory, you can selectively change the frame rates. Figure 23.10 shows the RAM Player interface, which you open by choosing Rendering ⇨ RAM Player. You see two images of the rendered gingerbread house placed on top of each other with half of each showing. One was rendered using its default materials and the other was rendered using Ink 'n' Paint materials.

The RAM Player interface lets you load two different images or animations for comparison.

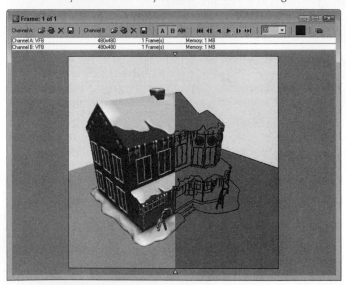

The buttons at the top of the RAM Player interface window, shown in Table 23.2, enable you to load an image to two different channels named A and B. The two Open Channel buttons open a file dialog box where you can select the file to load. Notice that the image on the right side of the RAM Player is a different frame from the left side.

TABLE 23.2

RAM Player Interface Buttons

Button	Description
	Open Channel
	Open Last Rendered Image
	Close Channel
	Save Channel
A|B	Horizontal/Vertical Screen Split
	Double Buffer

The Open Last Rendered Image button in the RAM Player interface window provides quick access to the last rendered image. The Close Channel button clears the channel. The Save Channel button opens a file dialog box for saving the current file.

Caution

All files that load into the RAM Player are converted to 24-bit images. ■

The Channel A and Channel B (toggle) buttons enable either channel or both. The Horizontal/Vertical Screen Split button switches the dividing line between the two channels to a horizontal or vertical line. When the images are aligned one on top of the other, two small triangles mark where one channel leaves off and the other begins. You can drag these triangles to alter the space for each channel.

The frame controls let you move between the frames. You can move to the first, previous, next, or last frame and play the animation forward or in reverse. The drop-down list to the right of the frame controls displays the current frame rate setting.

You can capture the color of any pixel in the image by holding down the Ctrl key while clicking the image with the right mouse button. This puts the selected color in the color swatch. The RGB value for this pixel is displayed in the blue title bar.

The Double Buffer button synchronizes the frames of the two channels.

Tip

You can use the arrow keys and Page Up and Page Down keys to move through the frames of the animation. The A and B keys are used to enable the two channels. ■

Tutorial: Using the RAM Player to combine rendered images into a video file

Not only can the RAM Player be used to load and compare images, but also it can handle animation files. It also can load in multiple frames of an animation that were saved as individual image files and save them back out as an animated file.

To combine multiple rendered image files into a video file using the RAM Player, follow these steps:

1. Select the Rendering ⇨ RAM Player menu command to open the RAM Player. Then click on the Open Channel A button and locate the Exploding Planet - frame 10.tif file from the Chap 23 directory on the CD.

    This file is the first rendered frame of a ten-frame animation.

2. The Image File List Control dialog box opens. Using this dialog box, you can specify the Start and End Frames to load. You also can select to load every nth frame. Select 0 as the Start Frame and 9 as the End Frame and click OK.

3. The RAM Player Configuration dialog box loads next, letting you set the Resolution and Memory Usage for the loaded files. Click OK to accept the default values.

    All of the image files that share the same base name as the selected file are loaded into the RAM Player sequentially. Press the Play button to see the loaded animation.

4. Click on the Save Channel A button to access the file dialog box, where you can save the loaded animation using the AVI, MPEG, or MOV video formats.

Figure 23.11 shows one frame of the loaded animation files.

FIGURE 23.11

This rendered image is just one of a series of rendered animation frames that can be viewed in the RAM Player.

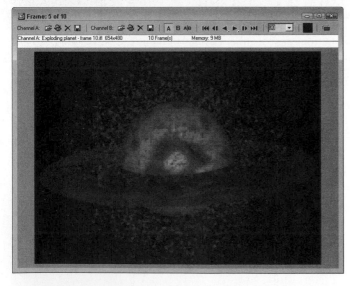

This space battle scene was created by Dragos Jieanu and is titled simply, "Battlefield." Dragos effectively uses many different effects to show the chaos of battle, including smoke trails, lightning, and glowing afterburners. Be sure to check out Dragos' website at www.jieanu.com.

Inspired by M.C. Escher, this work created by Jose Maria Andres Martin adds a new twist with projected lights, reflective surfaces, and glowing surfaces. Jose has titled this image "Impossible Cube," but don't look for this cube among the primitive objects in Max. More of Jose's work is located on his website at www.alzhem.com.

Using Command-Line Rendering

Within the default installation directory is a file named 3dsmaxcmd.exe. This file lets you initiate the rendering of files using a command-line interface. This feature enables you to create batch files that can be used to start Max, load several scenes, and render them automatically during the night while you sleep. You can find a command prompt interface in Windows XP using Start ⇨ All Programs ⇨ Accessories ⇨ Command Prompt.

Cross-Reference
If you're not comfortable with executing commands using the command line, you can set up batch rendering using the Batch Render feature covered in Chapter 48, "Batch and Network Rendering." ■

If you type **3dsmaxcmd -?**, the command line returns a list of available parameters that you can use. Typing **3dsmaxcmd –x** returns several sample commands. The simplest command to render a scene called coolstuff.max would be **3dsmaxcmd coolstuff.max**.

Using the various command-line flags, you can specify an image size and format, use Render Preset files to control the renderer settings, and even submit a job for network rendering.

Creating Panoramic Images

The Panorama Exporter tool (found in the Rendering menu and in the Utilities panel) can be used to create a panoramic scene consisting of images rendering in all six directions from the current camera and stitched together.

A camera needs to be added to the scene at the center of the panoramic view, and the camera needs to be selected. You can quickly create a camera using the Perspective view with the Views ⇨ Create Camera From View (Ctrl+C) command. Then click the Render button in the Panorama Exporter roll-out. This opens a Render Scene dialog box where you can specify the size of the images and the rest of the Render parameters. Click the Render button to render the panoramic scene.

Once rendered, the panoramic scene is opened within a Viewer, as shown in Figure 23.12, where you can move about the scene using the mouse. Dragging with the left mouse button spins the scene about its center point. Dragging with the middle mouse button zooms in and out of the scene. Dragging with the right mouse button pans the scene. The Viewer interface includes a File menu that can be used to open or export the scene file. Export options include a Cylinder, Sphere, and QuickTime VR.

FIGURE 23.12

The Panoramic Viewer lets you zoom, pan, and spin the scene about its center location.

Getting Printer Help

Printing still images from Max has always been a problem because you never knew quite what you would get. To solve this problem, Max now includes a Print Size Assistant located in the Rendering menu. This menu command opens the Print Size Wizard, as shown in Figure 23.13. This wizard sizes the output of the rendered image to one of the many paper sizes.

Note

Although the Print Size Wizard can size the rendered image, it cannot print rendered images. ■

FIGURE 23.13

The Print Size Wizard lets you set the image dimensions based on paper size and DPI (dots per inch) settings.

Using this Print Size Wizard, you can select a Paper Size and orientation, and a DPI setting and the Image dimensions are computed automatically. You can then click the Render Setup button to open the Render Scene dialog box with these dimensions. You also can select a filename using the Files button and click the Render button to render an image using the specified dimensions. The only available image format is TIFF.

Creating an Environment

Whether it's a beautiful landscape or just clouds drifting by, the environment behind the scene can do much to make the scene more believable. In this section, you learn to define an environment using the Rendering ⇨ Environment (8) menu command.

Environment maps are used as background for the scene and can also be used as images reflected off shiny objects. Environment maps are displayed only in the final rendering and not in the viewports, but you can add a background to any viewport and even set the environment map to be displayed as the viewport backdrop.

Cross-Reference

Chapter 2, "Controlling and Configuring the Viewports," covers adding a background image to a viewport. ∎

But there is more to an environment than just a background. It also involves altering the global lighting, controlling exposure, and introducing atmosphere effects.

Defining the rendered environment

You create environments in the Environment and Effects dialog box, shown in Figure 23.14, which you can open by choosing Rendering ⇨ Environment (or by pressing the 8 key). Several settings make up an environment, including a background color or image, global lighting, exposure control, and atmospheric effects.

FIGURE 23.14

The Environment and Effects dialog box lets you select a background color or image, define global lighting, control exposure, and work with atmospheric effects.

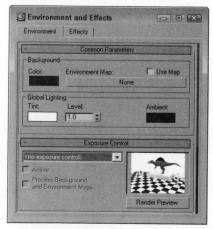

Setting a background color

The first color swatch in the Environment panel lets you specify a background color. This color appears by default if no environment map is specified or if the Use Map option is disabled (and is black by default). The background color is animatable, so you can set the background color to start black and slowly fade to white.

Using a background image

To select a background image to be used as an environment map, click the Environment Map button in the Environment panel to open the Material/Map browser. If you want to load a bitmap image as the background image, double-click the Bitmap selection to open the Select Bitmap Image dialog box. Locate the bitmap to use, and click OK. The bitmap name appears on the Environment Map button.

Tip

If the environment map that you want to use is already displayed in one of the Material Editor sample slots, you can drag it directly from the Material Editor and drop it on the Map button in the Environment panel. ■

To change any of the environment map parameters (such as the mapping coordinates), you need to load the environment map into the Material Editor. You can do so by dragging the map button from the Environment panel onto one of the sample slots in the Material Editor. After releasing the material, the Instance (Copy) Map dialog box asks whether you want to create an Instance or a Copy. If you select Instance, any parameter changes that you make to the material automatically update the map in the Environment panel.

Once in the Material Editor, you can use the Environment Map to create a Spherical Environment map that is used to reflect off objects in the scene.

Cross-Reference

For more information about the types of available mapping parameters, see Chapter 17, "Adding Material Details with Maps." ■

The background image doesn't need to be an image: You can also load animations. Supported formats include AVI, MPEG, MOV, and IFL files.

Figure 23.15 shows a scene with an image of the Golden Gate Bridge loaded as the environment map. Viewpoint Datalabs created the airplane model.

Setting global lighting

The Tint color swatch in the Global Lighting section of the Environment panel specifies a color used to tint all lights. The Level value increases or decreases the overall lighting level for all lights in the scene. The Ambient color swatch sets the color for the ambient light in the scene, which is the darkest color that any shadows in the scene can be. You can animate all these settings.

FIGURE 23.15

The results of a background image loaded into the Environment panel

Summary

This chapter covered the basics of producing output using the Render Scene dialog box. Although rendering a scene can take a long time to complete, Max includes many settings that can speed up the process and helpful tools such as the Rendered Frame Window and the RAM Player.

In this chapter, you accomplished the following:

- Discovering how to control the various render parameters
- Configuring the global rendering preferences
- Switching to a different renderer
- Learning about the command-line rendering interface
- Using the Rendered Frame Window and the RAM Player
- Understanding the different render types
- Exploring the Panoramic Exporter and Print Size Wizard tools
- Using the Environment panel to change the background color and image

The next chapter covers the ability to render the scene to one of the stylized options that Nitrous makes available such as Ink, Charcoal, or Acrylic.

CHAPTER

24

Rendering Non-Photorealistic Effects

For many years, the goal of 3D graphics has been to make scenes as realistic as possible, but other types of art emphasize style over realism. These stylistic approaches give us the cubes of Picasso, the points of Seurat, and the surreal landscapes of Dali. Although no software title has a button to magically turn your scene into a classic piece of art, the new Nitrous display drivers found in Max allow you to display your scene as if it were drawn using acrylic, ink, or pastels.

IN THIS CHAPTER

Displaying stylized scenes in the viewport

Rendering non-photorealistic scenes

Viewing Stylized Scenes

Stylized non-photorealistic effects often are not as computationally complex as realistic renderings, and as such, they can be enabled and displayed within the viewports as well as rendered images. Although you probably would want to work in one of these stylized display modes, you can use the Viewport title Rendering label to access a menu of available stylized display options.

New Feature

The Stylized display options available in the viewports are new to 3ds Max 2012. ∎

The available stylized display options are all located in the Stylized submenu under the Viewport Rendering Label menu in the upper-left corner of each viewport. The options include Graphite, Colored Pencil, Ink, Colored Ink, Acrylic, Pastel, and Tech. Figure 24.1 shows the gingerbread house model with the Colored Ink option.

FIGURE 24.1

The Gingerbread house scene is displayed using the Colored Ink display style.

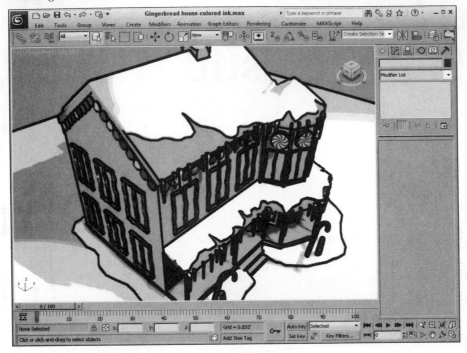

The various stylized display options also can be set in the Visual Style & Appearance panel in the Viewport Configuration dialog box.

Rendering Stylized Scenes

The same stylized display options that are available in the viewports also are available as render options using the Quicksilver rendering engine. To switch to the Quicksilver renderer, click the three dots to the right of the Production renderer in the Assign Renderer rollout of the Common panel in the Render Setup dialog box and choose the Quicksilver option.

Cross Reference

You can learn more about the Quicksilver renderer in Chapter 23, "Rendering a Scene and Enabling Quicksilver." ■

After Quicksilver is enabled, you can select one of the stylized render options from the Rendering Level drop-down list in the Visual Style & Appearance panel, shown in Figure 24.2.

When a stylized non-photorealistic rendering option is selected, clicking the Render button renders the scene in the Rendered Frame Window, as shown in Figure 24.3.

FIGURE 24.2

The Visual Style & Appearance panel includes all the stylized non-photorealistic rendering options.

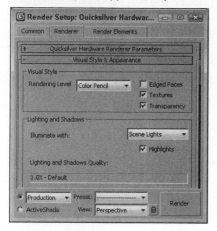

FIGURE 24.3

Non-photorealistic rendering methods can be specified in the Render Scene dialog box using the Quicksilver renderer.

Summary

This chapter covered the stylized non-photorealistic display options made available by the Nitrous display driver and showed how they could be rendered.

In this chapter, you accomplished the following:

- Viewing stylized scenes using ink, pastels, graphite, acrylic, and colored pencil
- Rendering non-photorealistic scenes using the Quicksilver renderer

The next chapter covers the ability to combine external objects and scenes into the current scene using Containers and XRefs.

Part VI

Advanced Modeling

Building Complex Scenes with Containers, XRefs, and the Schematic View

U sing containers and external references (XRefs), you can pull multiple scenes, objects, materials, and controllers together into a single scene. Both of these features allow a diverse team to work on separate parts of a scene at the same time. They also provide a great way to reuse existing resources.

A valuable tool for selecting, linking, and organizing scene objects is the Schematic View window. This window offers a 1,000-foot view of the objects in your scene. From this whole scene perspective, you can find the exact item you seek.

The Schematic View window shows all objects as simple nodes and uses arrows to show relationships between objects. This structure makes the Schematic View window the easiest place to establish links and to wire parameters. You also can use this view to quickly see all the instances of an object.

Working with Containers

Containers provide a great way to group several objects together, but containers have several additional features that extend beyond simply grouping objects together. For example, a container can be saved as an external file, which makes them easy to reuse in other scenes. Containers also can be unloaded from a scene to make the rest of the scene load quicker and to improve performance. Containers also can be locked, and the creator can set edit permissions for others.

Creating and filling containers

Containers are created using the Create ➪ Helpers ➪ Container menu and dragging in the scene to create the Container icon, which looks like an open box, as shown in Figure 25.1. When a container is created, it is initially empty, but you can easily add objects to the container by clicking the Add button in the Local Content rollout of the Modify panel. This opens an Object Selection list where you can choose the objects to add to the container.

FIGURE 25.1

Containers are displayed as simple open boxes.

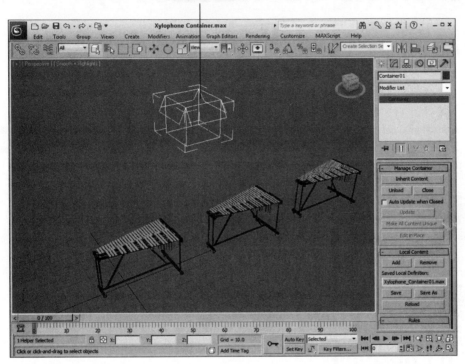

Container icon

You can also create a container and automatically add the selected objects using the Tools ⇨ Container ⇨ Create Container from Selection menu command. Container objects can be removed using the Remove button, which also opens an Object Selection list.

Another way to add and remove contents from a container is with the Containers toolbar, shown in Figure 25.2. You can access this toolbar by selecting it from the pop-up menu that appears by right-clicking the main toolbar away from the buttons. The Containers toolbar buttons are described in Table 25.1.

Note

These same commands for working with containers are available in the Tools ⇨ Containers menu. ∎

FIGURE 25.2

The Containers toolbar

TABLE 25.1

Containers Toolbar Buttons

Toolbar Button	Name	Description
	Inherit Container	Opens a file dialog box where a source container is loaded into the current scene
	Create Container from Selection	Creates a new container and adds the current selection to the container
	Add Selected to Container	Opens an object dialog box where you can select which objects to add to the current container
	Remove Selected from Container	Opens an object dialog box where you can select which objects to remove from the current container
	Load Container	Loads and displays the current container's objects in the scene
	Unload Container	Saves the current container and removes the display of its objects
	Open Container	Allows the container's objects to be edited
	Close Container	Saves the container and makes its objects so they can't be edited
	Save Container	Saves the current container
	Update Container	Reloads the saved container with any new edits
	Reload Container	Throws away any recent edits and reloads the saved container
	Make All Content Unique	Converts all displayed container objects including nested containers to a unique container
	Merge Container Source	Loads the most recent saved container without opening its nested containers
	Edit Container	Allows the current container to be opened and edited
	Override Object Properties	Uses the display settings for the container object instead of the display settings for the individual objects
	Override All Locks	Temporarily overrides the locks for the current local container

Note

The various container commands can be accessed from within the Scene Explorer by enabling the Containers toolbar. ■

When a container is created, you can move, rotate, scale, and change the display properties of all the objects contained within the container by simply selecting the container icon first.

Closing and saving containers

When a container is first created, it is open by default. The icon for an open container displays an open box. When you select the command to close a container, then the icon changes to display a closed box. The first time this happens, a file dialog box opens, where you can save and name the container. Max container files are saved using the .maxc file extension.

Note

Within the file dialog box, you can use the Save as Type drop-down list to save the container as a Max 2012 Container or as a Max 2010 Container. ■

Closed containers cannot be edited by anyone except their creator. Closing a container also causes its objects to be removed from the scene, but their display is still visible because the objects are referenced from the saved file.

Updating and reloading containers

When a container is loaded into a scene from a saved container file using the Inherit Content button, it is inherited into the current scene. The inherited file maintains a link to the original container, and if the original container is edited, you can use the Update button to get the most recently saved changes.

If the container is open and allows edits, the Edit in Place button may be clicked to allow the current user to make edits to the container contents. This locks the container from all other users while the Edit in Place button is enabled. Once released, the edits are saved and made available for other users.

If you make edits that you'd like to ignore, you can use the Reload command to throw away any changes that have occurred since the last save. You also can break the link to the container with the Make All Content Unique button.

Setting container rules

Before a container is closed, you can set rules for defining exactly what content can be edited by other users. These rules are found in the Rules rollout, shown in Figure 25.3. The options include No Access, which is applied when a container is closed; Only Edit in Place, which gives anyone that opens the container full rights to edit the container's contents; Only Add New Objects, which gives the user that opens the container the right to add new objects to the container, but not to edit any of the existing content; and Anything Unlocked, which gives the user that opens the container access to edit anything that is unlocked. Using the four toggle buttons at the bottom of the Rules rollout, you can select to lock all modifiers, materials, transforms, and objects. Clicking the Edit button opens the Track View where you can choose tracks to lock.

The Rules rollout lets you define precisely what in the container can be edited.

Lock All Objects

Lock All Transforms

Lock All Materials

Lock All Modifiers

Using container proxies

As an alternative to unloading a container from memory, you can specify a proxy container to take the place of the current container with the Proxies rollout, shown in Figure 25.4. The drop-down list can hold multiple proxy containers, allowing you to quickly change between different resolutions. Click the Modify List button to add proxy containers to the list.

The Proxies rollout lets you substitute proxy containers for the current one.

Modify List

Setting global container preferences

Within the Preference Settings dialog box is a panel for setting the global container preferences, shown in Figure 25.5. Using these settings you can define which rules are used when saving to the Max 2010 container format. You also can set how often containers are refreshed and whether to display the status of the scene containers.

FIGURE 25.5

The Containers panel of the Preference Settings dialog box holds the global container settings.

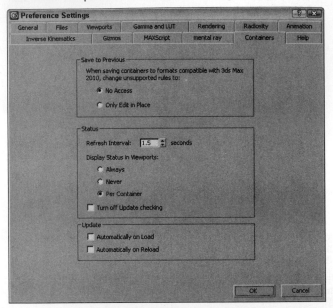

Referencing External Objects

No man is an island, and if Autodesk has its way, no Max user will be an island, either. XRefs (which stands for eXternal References) make it easy for creative teams to collaborate on a project without having to wait for another group member to finish his or her respective production task. External references are objects and scenes contained in separate Max files and made available for reference during a Max session. This arrangement enables several artists on a team to work on separate sections of a project without interfering with one another or altering each other's work.

Max includes two different types of XRefs: XRef scenes and XRef objects. You also can use XRef for materials, modifiers, and controllers.

Note
Although XRefs are helpful and maintained for backward compatibility, in many ways using containers is the preferred method for loading in external files. ■

Using XRef scenes

An externally referenced scene is one that appears in the current Max session, but that is not accessible for editing or changing. The scene can be positioned and transformed when linked to a parent object and can be set to update automatically as changes are made to the source file.

As an example of how XRef scenes facilitate a project, let's say that a design team is in the midst of creating an environment for a project while the animator is animating a character model. The animator can access the in-production environment as an XRef scene in order to help him move the character correctly about the environment. The design team members are happy because the animator didn't modify any of their lights, terrain models, maps, and props. The animator is happy because he won't have to wait for the design team members to finish all their tweaking before he can get started. The end result is one large, happy production team (if they can meet their deadlines).

Choose Application Button ➪ References ➪ XRef Scenes to open the XRef Scenes dialog box, shown in Figure 25.6, which you use to load XRef scenes into a file.

The XRef Scenes dialog box lets you specify which scenes to load as external references.

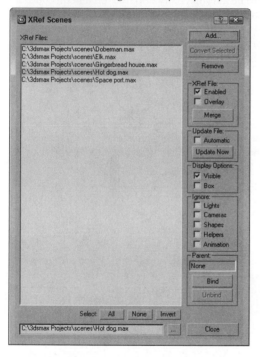

XRef scene options

In the XRef Scenes dialog box are several options for controlling the appearance of the scene objects, how often the scene is updated, and to which object the scene is bound. This dialog box is modeless, and you can open and change the options in this dialog box at any time.

The pane on the left lists all XRef scenes in the current scene. These scenes are displayed using their full path unless the Convert Local File Paths to Relative option in the Files panel of the Preference Settings dialog box is enabled. To the right are the settings, which can be different for each XRef scene in the list. To view or apply a setting, you first need to select the scene from the list. You can remove any scene by selecting it from the list and clicking the Remove button.

Caution

If an XRef scene in the list is displayed in red, then the scene could not be loaded. If the path or name is incorrect, you can change it in the Path field at the bottom of the list. ■

The Convert Selected button converts any selected objects in the current scene to XRef objects by saving them as a separate file. This button opens a dialog box to let you name and save the new file. If no objects are selected in the current scene, then this option is disabled.

Use the Enabled option to enable or disable all XRef scenes. Disabled scenes are displayed in gray. The Merge button lets you insert the current XRef scene into the current scene. This button removes the scene from the list and acts the same way as the Application Button ⇨ Import ⇨ Merge command.

Updating an external scene

Automatic is a key option that can set any XRef scene to be automatically updated. Enable this option by selecting a scene from the list and checking the Automatic option box; thereafter, the scene is updated anytime the source file is updated. This option can slow the system if the external scene is updated frequently, but the benefit is that you can work with the latest update.

The Update Now button is for manually updating the XRef scene. Click this button to update the external scene to the latest saved version.

External scene appearance

Other options let you decide how the scene is displayed in the viewports. You can choose to make the external scene invisible or to display it as a box. Making an external scene invisible removes it from the viewports, but the scene is still included in the rendered output. To remove a scene from the rendered output, deselect the Enabled option.

The Ignore section lists objects such as lights, cameras, shapes, helpers, and animation; selecting them causes them to be ignored and to have no effect in the scene. If an external scene's animation is ignored, then the scene appears as it does in frame 0.

Positioning an external scene

Positioning an external scene is accomplished by binding the scene to an object in the current scene (a dummy object, for example). The XRef Scenes dialog box is modeless, so you can select the object to bind to without closing the dialog box. After a binding object is selected, the external scene transforms to the binding object's pivot point. The name of the parent object is also displayed in the XRef Scenes dialog box.

Transforming the object to which the scene is bound can control how the external scene is repositioned. To unbind an object, click the Unbind button in the XRef Scenes dialog box. Unbound scenes are positioned at the World origin for the current scene.

Specifying an XRef as an overlay

The Overlay option in the XRef Scenes dialog box makes the XRef visible to the current scene, but not to any other scenes that XRef the scene including the overlay. This provides a way to hide XRef content from more than one level. Overlay XRefs also make it possible to avoid circular dependencies. For example, in previous Max versions, Max wouldn't allow two designers to XRef one another's scenes, but if one of the scenes is an overlay, then this can be done.

Working with XRef scenes

You can't edit XRef scenes in the current scene. Their objects are not visible in the Select by Name dialog box or in the Track and Schematic Views. You also cannot access the Modifier Stack of external scenes' objects. However, you can make use of external scene objects in other ways. For example, you can change a viewport to show the view from any camera or light in the external scene. External scene objects are included in the Summary Info dialog box.

Tip

Another way to use XRef scenes is to create a scene with lights and/or cameras positioned at regular intervals around the scene. You can then use the XRef Scenes dialog box to turn these lights on and off or to select from a number of different views without creating new cameras. ■

You also can nest XRef scenes within each other, so you can have one XRef scene for the distant mountains that includes another XRef for a castle.

Note

If a Max file is loaded with XRef files that cannot be located, a warning dialog box appears, enabling you to browse to the file's new location. If you click OK or Cancel, the scene still loads, but the external scenes are missing. ■

Tutorial: Adding an XRef scene

As an example of a project that would benefit from XRefs, I've created a maze environment. I open a new Max file and animate a simple mouse moving through this maze that is opened as an XRef scene.

To set up an XRef scene, follow these steps:

1. Create a new Max file by choosing Application Button ➪ New.
2. Choose Application Button ➪ References ➪ XRef Scenes to open the XRef Scenes dialog box.
3. Click the Add button, locate the Maze.max file from the Chap 25 directory on the CD, and click Open to add it to the XRef Scene dialog box list, but don't close the dialog box just yet.

Tip

You can add several XRef scenes by clicking the Add button again. You also can add a scene to the XRef Scene dialog box by dragging a .max file from Windows Explorer or from the Asset Manager window. ■

4. Select Create ➪ Helpers ➪ Dummy, and drag in the Perspective viewport to create a new Dummy object.
5. In the XRef Scenes dialog box, click the Bind button and select the dummy object.
   This enables you to reposition the XRef scene as needed.
6. Select the Automatic update option, and then click Close to exit the XRef Scene dialog box.
7. Now animate objects moving through the maze.

Figure 25.7 shows the Maze.max scene included in the current Max file as an XRef.

Tip

With the simple mouse animated, you can replace it at a later time with a detailed model of a furry mouse using the Application Button ➪ Import ➪ Replace command. ■

FIGURE 25.7

The maze.max file loaded into the current file as an XRef scene

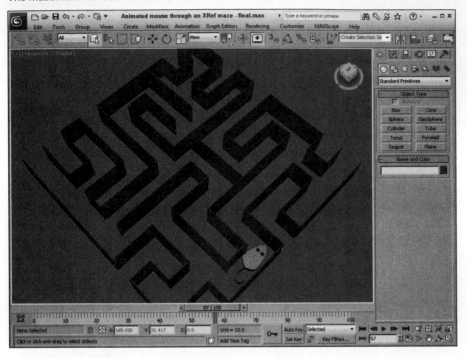

Using XRef objects

XRef objects are slightly different from XRef scenes. XRef objects appear in a scene and can be transformed and animated, but the original object's structure and Modifier Stack cannot be changed.

An innovative way to use this feature would be to create a library of objects that you could load on the fly as needed. For example, if you had a furniture library, you could load several different styles until you got just the look you wanted.

You also can use XRef objects to load low-resolution proxies of complex models in order to lighten the system load during a Max session. This method increases the viewport refresh rate.

Many of the options in the XRef Objects dialog box, shown in Figure 25.8, are the same as in the XRef Scenes dialog box.

The interface buttons for the XRef Objects dialog box are listed in Table 25.2.

FIGURE 25.8

The XRef Objects dialog box lets you choose which files to look in for external objects.

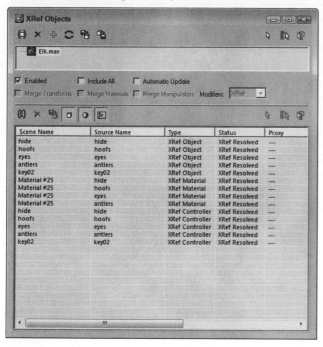

TABLE 25.2

XRef Objects Dialog Box

Button	Name	Description
	Create XRef Record from File	Opens the XRef Merge dialog box where you can select the XRef source file.
	Remove XRef Record	Deletes the selected XRef record.
	Combine XRef Record	Allows two or more selected XRef records pointing to the same file to be combined into a single record.
	Update	Updates the content of all XRefs.
	Merge in Scene	Makes all XRefs for the selected record part of the scene file. This also removes the XRef record from the dialog box.

continued

TABLE 25.2	(continued)	
Button	**Name**	**Description**
	Convert Selected Objects to XRefs	Opens a save dialog box and saves the selected scene objects as a separate scene file, which is an XRef in the current scene.
	Select	Selects the objects that are part of the selected XRef record.
	Select by Name	Opens the Select Objects dialog box listing all objects that are part of the selected XRef record.
	Highlight Selected Object's XRef Records	Highlights the XRef record that contains the objects selected in the viewport.
	Add Objects	Opens the XRef Merge dialog box where additional objects from the selected XRef record can be loaded.
	Delete XRef Entity	Deletes the current object from the XRef record.
	Merge in Scene	Merges the selected object to the current scene and removes its XRef.
	List Objects	Filters the display to show the XRef objects.
	List Materials	Filters the display to show the XRef materials.
	List Controllers	Filters the display to show the XRef controllers.

The XRef Objects dialog box is divided into two sections. The top section displays the externally refer-enced source files (or records), and the lower section displays the objects, materials, or controllers selected from the source file. If multiple files are referenced, then a file needs to be selected in the top pane in order for its objects and materials to be displayed in the lower pane.

The Convert Selected button works the same as in the XRef Scenes dialog box. It enables you to save the selected objects in the current scene to a separate file just like the Application Button ⇨ Save As ⇨ Save Selected command and to have them instantly made into XRefs.

In the XRef Objects dialog box, you can choose to automatically update the external referenced objects or use the Update button or you can enable the Automatic Update option. You also can enable or disable all objects in a file with the Enabled option. The Include All option skips the XRef Merge dialog box and automatically includes all objects in the source file.

If the Merge Transforms, Merge Materials, and Merge Manipulators options are enabled before an XRef file is added, all transforms, materials, and manipulators are automatically combined with the current scene instead of being referenced. When merged, the link between the source file is broken so that changes to the source file aren't propagated.

Using material XRefs

When a source file is loaded into the XRef Objects dialog box, both its objects and materials are loaded and included. If the Merge Materials option is selected before the source file is loaded, then the materials are included with the objects, but if the Merge Materials option isn't enabled, then the objects and the materials appear as separate entities. You can use the List Objects and the List Materials buttons to list just one type of entity.

Materials also can be referenced from directly within the Material Editor. If you used a material in a previous scene that would be perfect in your current scene, you can just select the XRef Material from the Material/Map Browser. This material type includes fields where you can browse to an external scene file and select a specific object. The selected material is added automatically to the XRef Objects dialog box.

Cross-Reference

You can learn more about applying materials and using the Material Editor in Chapter 15, "Using the Slate Material Editor." ■

Merging modifiers

If the Merge Manipulators option is enabled before loading the XRef file, then any manipulator that is part of the XRef object is merged and loaded along with the object. You also can specify how modifiers are included with XRef objects, but you must select the option from the Modifier drop-down list before the file is selected. The XRef option loads all modifiers with the XRef object, but hides them from being edited. New modifiers can be added to the object. The Merge option adds all modifiers to the XRef object and makes these modifiers accessible via the Modifier Stack. The Ignore option strips all modifiers from the XRef object.

XRef objects appear and act like any other object in the scene. You may see a slight difference if you open the Modifier Stack. The Stack displays "XRef Object" as its only entry.

Using proxies

When an XRef object is selected in the viewport, all details concerning the XRef object—including its source filename, Object Name, and status—are listed in the Modify panel. The Modify panel also includes a Proxy Object rollout, where you can select a separate object in a separate file as a proxy object. The File or Object Name buttons open a file dialog box where you can select a low-resolution proxy object in place of a more complex object. This feature saves memory by not requiring the more complex object to be kept in memory. You also can select to enable or disable the proxy or use the proxy in rendering.

Tip

The real benefit of using proxies is to replace complex referenced objects with simpler objects that update quickly. When creating a complex object, remember to also create a low-resolution version to use as a proxy. ■

Controller XRefs

In addition to objects, materials, and modifiers, controllers also can be externally referenced. This means that you can borrow the controller motions of an object in a separate scene and save some animation time. To reference an external controller, select the Transform track and choose the XRef Controller option. This opens a File dialog box followed by a Select Object dialog box where you can choose with the controller the object that you want to reference. XRef controllers also appear as records in the XRef Objects dialog box.

Cross-Reference

You can learn more about applying and using controllers in Chapter 22, "Animating with Constraints and Simple Controllers." ■

Configuring XRef paths

The Configure Paths dialog box includes an XRefs tab for setting the paths for XRef scenes and objects, shown in Figure 25.9. Choose Customize ⇨ Configure User Paths to open the XRefs panel.

FIGURE 25.9

The XRefs panel in the Configure User Paths dialog box lets you specify paths to be searched when an XRef cannot be located.

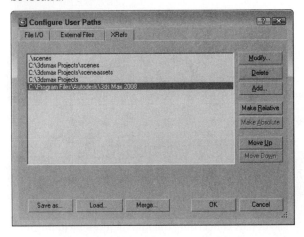

Max keeps track of the path of any XRefs used in a scene, but if it cannot find them, it looks at the paths designated in the XRefs panel of the Configure Paths dialog box. For projects that use lots of XRefs, populating this list with potential paths is a good idea. Paths are scanned in the order they are listed, so place the most likely paths at the top of the list.

To add a new path to the panel, click the Add button. You also can modify or delete paths in this panel with the Modify and Delete buttons.

Using the Schematic View Window

A great way to organize and select objects is to use the Schematic View window. Every object in the Schematic View is displayed as a labeled rectangular box. These boxes (or nodes) are connected to show the relationships among them. You can rearrange them and save the customized views for later access.

 You access the Schematic View window via the Graph Editors menu command or by clicking its button on the main toolbar. When the window opens, it floats on top of the Max interface and can be moved by dragging its title bar. You also can resize the window by dragging on its borders. The window is modeless and lets you access the viewports and buttons in the interface beneath it.

The Graph Editors menu options

The Schematic View menu options enable you to manage several different views. The Graph Editors ⇨ New Schematic View command opens the Schematic View window, shown in Figure 25.10. If you enter a name in the View Name field at the top of the window, you can name and save the current view. This name then appears in the Graph Editors ⇨ Saved Schematic Views submenu and also in the title bar when the saved view is open.

Every time the Graph Editors ⇨ New Schematic View menu command is used, a new view name is created and another view is added to the Saved Schematic Views submenu. The Schematic View ⇨ Delete Schematic View command opens a dialog box in which you can select the view you want to delete.

Tip

You can open any saved Schematic View window (or a new Schematic View window) within a viewport by right-clicking the viewport title, choosing Views ⇨ Schematic, and clicking the view name in the pop-up menu. ■

FIGURE 25.10

The Schematic View window displays all objects as nodes.

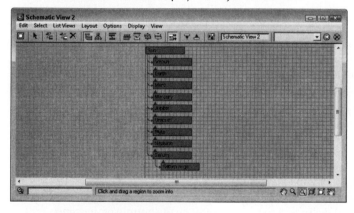

The Schematic View interface

The Schematic View window includes several common interface elements, including menus, toolbar buttons, and a right-click quadmenu. Just like the main interface, you can access the commands in many ways.

Using the Schematic View menus

The Schematic View window includes menus at the top of its interface, including Edit, Select, List Views, Layout, Options, Display, and View.

The Edit menu includes commands to Connect (C) and Unlink Selected object nodes. It also includes a Delete command, which deletes an object from the viewports as well as from the object node. The Edit menu includes commands to Assign Controllers, Wire Parameters, and open the Object Properties dialog box.

Note

Many of the keyboard shortcuts for the Schematic View window are the same as those in the main interface. If you enable the Keyboard Shortcut Override Toggle, you can use the Schematic View keyboard shortcuts. ∎

The Select menu includes commands for accessing the Select tool (S or Q); selecting All (Ctrl+A), None (Ctrl+D), and Invert (Ctrl+I); selecting (Ctrl+C) and deselecting children; and commands to sync the selected nodes in the Schematic View with the scene (Select from Scene) and vice versa (Select to Scene).

The List Views menu determines what is shown in the Schematic View. Options include All Relationships, Selected Relationships, All Instances, Selected Instances, Show Occurrences, and All Animated Controllers. Many of these options are available in the Display Floater as well.

The Layout menu includes various options for controlling how the nodes are arranged. The Align submenu lets you align selected nodes to the Left, Right, Top, Bottom, Center Horizontal, or Center Vertical. You can also Arrange Children or Arrange Selected. The Free Selected (Alt+S) and Free All (Alt+F) commands keep nodes from being auto arranged. With the Layout menu, you also can Shrink Selected, Unshrink Selected, Unshrink All, and Toggle Shrink (Ctrl+S).

The Options menu lets you select the Always Arrange option and view mode (either Hierarchy or Reference mode). You also can select the Move Children (Alt+C) option and open the Schematic View Preferences (P) dialog box.

The Display menu provides access to the Display Floater. The Display Floater (D) command opens the Display floater, which can be used to select the types of nodes to display. You also can hide and unhide nodes and expand or collapse the selected node.

The View menu includes commands for selecting the Pan (Ctrl+P), Zoom (Alt+Z), and Zoom Region (Ctrl+W) tools. You also can access the Zoom Extents (Alt+Ctrl+Z), Zoom Extents Selected (Z), and Pan to Selected commands. The View menu also includes options to Show/Hide Grid (G), Show/Hide Background, and Refresh View (Ctrl+U).

Learning the toolbar buttons

You can select most of these commands from the toolbar. Many of the toolbar buttons are toggle switches that enable and disable certain viewing modes. The background of these toggle buttons is highlighted yellow when selected. You'll also find some buttons along the bottom of the window. All Schematic View icon buttons are shown in Table 25.3 and are described in the following sections.

Note

The Schematic View toolbar buttons are permanently docked to the interface and cannot be removed. ∎

As you navigate the Schematic View window, you can save specific views as bookmarks by typing an identifying name in the Bookmark drop-down list. To recall these views later, select them from the drop-down list and click the Go to Bookmark icon in the Schematic View toolbar. Bookmarks can be deleted with the Delete Bookmark button.

Note

Most of the menu commands and toolbar buttons are available in a pop-up menu that you can access by right-clicking in the Schematic View window. ∎

TABLE 25.3

Schematic View Toolbar Buttons

Toolbar Button	Name	Description
	Display Floater	Opens the Display Floater, where you can toggle which items are displayed or hidden.
	Select (S)	Toggles selection mode on, where nodes can be selected by clicking.
	Connect (C)	Enables you to create links between objects in the Schematic View window; also used to copy modifiers and materials between objects.
	Unlink Selected	Destroys the link between the selected object and its parent.
	Delete Objects	Deletes the selected object in both the Schematic View and the viewports.
	Hierarchy Mode	Displays all child objects indented under their parent objects.
	References Mode	Displays all object references and instances and all materials and modifiers associated with the objects.
	Always Arrange	Causes all nodes to be automatically arranged in a hierarchy or in references mode, and disables moving of individual nodes.
	Arrange Children	Automatically rearranges the children of the selected object nodes.
	Arrange Selected	Automatically rearranges the selected object nodes.
	Free All	Allows all objects to be freely moved without being automatically arranged.
	Free Selected	Allows selected objects to be freely moved without being automatically arranged.
	Move Children	Causes children to move along with their parent node.
	Expand Selected	Reveals all nodes below the selected node.
	Collapse Selected	Rolls up all nodes below the selected node.
	Preferences	Opens the Schematic View Preferences dialog box.

continued

TABLE 25.3 *(continued)*

Toolbar Button	Name	Description
My Saved View	View Name field	Allows you to name the current display; named displays show up under the Graph Editors ⇨ Saved Schematic View submenu.
My Bookmark ▼	Bookmark Name	Marks a selection of nodes to which you can return later.
⊙	Go to Bookmark	Zooms and pans to the selected bookmarked objects.
⊗	Delete Bookmark	Removes the bookmark from the Bookmark selection list.

Navigating the Schematic View window

As the number of nodes increases, it can become tricky to locate and see the correct node to work with. Along the bottom edge of the Schematic View window are several navigation buttons that work similarly to the Viewport Navigation Control buttons. Using these buttons, you can pan, zoom, and zoom to the extents of all nodes. These buttons are described in Table 25.4.

TABLE 25.4

Schematic View Navigation Buttons

Toolbar Button	Name	Description
🔍	Zoom Selected Viewport Object	Zooms in on the nodes that correspond to the selected viewport objects.
Search	Search Name field	Locates an object node when you type its name.
✋	Pan	Moves the node view when you drag in the window.
🔍	Zoom	Zooms when you drag the mouse in the window.
🔍	Region Zoom	Zooms to an area selected when you drag an outline.
▢	Zoom Extents	Increases the window view until all nodes are visible.
▢	Zoom Extents Selected	Increases the window view until all selected nodes are visible.
✋	Pan to Selected	Moves the node view at the current zoom level to the selected objects.

The Schematic View navigation buttons also can be accessed from within the View menu. These menu commands include Pan Tool (Ctrl+P), Zoom Tool (Alt+Z), Zoom Region tool (Ctrl+W), Zoom Extents (Alt+Ctrl+Z), Zoom Extents Selected (Z), and Pan to Selected.

Tip

You also can navigate the Schematic View window using the mouse and its scroll wheel. Scrubbing the mouse wheel zooms in and out of the window in steps. Holding down the Ctrl key and dragging with the scroll wheel button zooms smoothly in and out of the window. Dragging the scroll wheel pans within the window. ■

Working with Schematic View nodes

Every object displayed in the scene has a *node*—a simple rectangular box that represents the object or attribute. Each node contains a label, and the color of the node depends on the node type.

Node colors

Nodes have a color scheme to help identify them. The colors of various nodes are listed in Table 25.5.

TABLE 25.5

Schematic View Node Colors

Color	Name
White	Selected node
Blue	Geometry Object node
Cyan	Shape Object node
Yellow	Light Object node
Dark Blue	Camera Object node
Green	Helper Object node
Purple	Space Warp Object node
Goldenrod	Modifier node
Dark Yellow	Base Object node
Brown	Material node
Dark Green	Map node
Salmon	Controller node
Magenta	Parameter Wires

Note

If you don't like any of these colors, you can set the colors used in the Schematic View using the Colors panel of the Customize ⇨ Customize User Interface dialog box. ■

Selecting nodes

When you click the Select (S) button, you enter select mode, which lets you select nodes within the Schematic View window by clicking the object node. You can select multiple objects by dragging an outline over them. Holding down the Ctrl key while clicking an object node selects or deselects it. Selected nodes are shown in white.

The Select menu includes several selection commands that enable you to quickly select (or deselect) many nodes, including Select All (Ctrl+A), Select None (Ctrl+D), Select Invert (Ctlr+I), Select Children (Ctrl+C), and Deselect Children.

If the Select ➪ Sync Selection option in the Select menu is enabled, then the node of any object that is selected in the viewports is also selected in the Schematic View window, and vice versa. If you disable the Sync Selection option, you can select different objects in the viewports and in the Schematic View at the same time. The node of the object selected in the viewports is outlined in white, and the interior of selected nodes is white. To select all the objects in the viewports that match the selected nodes without the Sync Selection option enabled, just use Select ➪ Select to Scene.

Tip

All animated objects have their node border drawn in red. ∎

Rearranging nodes

The Schematic View includes several options for arranging nodes. In the Options menu, you can toggle between Hierarchy and Reference modes. Hierarchy mode displays the nodes vertically with child objects indented under their parent. Reference mode displays the nodes horizontally, allowing for plenty of room to display all the various reference nodes under each parent node. Figure 25.11 shows these modes side by side.

FIGURE 25.11

The Schematic View window can automatically arrange nodes in two different modes: Hierarchy and Reference.

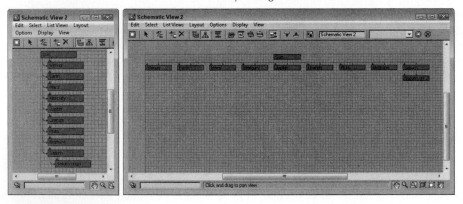

You can move nodes and rearrange them in any order. To move a node, simply click and drag it to a new location. When a node is dragged, all selected nodes move together, and any links follow the node movement. If a child node is moved, all remaining child nodes collapse together to maintain the specified arrangement mode. The moved node then becomes free, which is designated by an open rectangle on the left edge of the node. Figure 25.12 shows two nodes that were moved and thereby became free. The other children automatically moved closer together to close the gaps made by the moving nodes.

FIGURE 25.12

Free nodes are moved independent of the arranging mode.

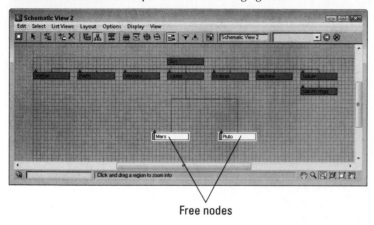

Free nodes

Using the Layout ⇨ Free Selected (Alt+S) and Free All (Alt+F) menu commands, you can free the selected nodes or all nodes. You also can auto arrange all the children of a node with the Layout ⇨ Arrange Children menu command or arrange just the selected nodes (Layout ⇨ Arrange Selected). The Options ⇨ Move Children (Alt+C) command causes all children to be moved along with their parent when the parent is moved. This causes free and non-free nodes to move with their parent.

If the Options ⇨ Always Arrange option is enabled, Max automatically arranges all the nodes using either the Hierarchy mode or Reference mode, but you cannot move any of the nodes while this option is enabled. If you move any nodes when the Always Arrange option is selected, a dialog box appears telling you that your custom layout will be lost. If the Always Arrange option is enabled, the Arrange Children, Free All (Alt+F), Free Selected (Alt+S), Move Children (Alt+C), and all the Align options are all disabled. If two or more nodes are selected, you can align them using the Layout ⇨ Align menu. The options include Left, Right, Top, Bottom, Center Horizontal, and Center Vertical.

Hiding, shrinking, and deleting nodes

If your Schematic View window starts to get cluttered, you can always hide nodes to simplify the view. To hide a node, select the nodes to hide and use the Display ⇨ Hide Selected menu command. The Display ⇨ Unhide All menu command can be used to make the hidden nodes visible again.

Note

If you hide a parent object, its children nodes are hidden also. ■

Another useful way to reduce clutter in the Schematic View window is with the Layout ➪ Shrink Selected command. This command replaces the rectangular node with a simple dot, but all hierarchical lines to the node are kept intact. Figure 25.13 shows a Schematic View with several shrunk nodes. Shrunk nodes can be unshrunk with the Layout ➪ Unshrink Selected and Unshrink All menu commands.

Note

The Shrink commands work only when Layout ➪ Toggle Shrink (Ctrl+S) is enabled. With this command, you can turn on and turn off the visibility of shrunken nodes. ■

FIGURE 25.13

Shrunken nodes appear as simple dots in the Schematic View.

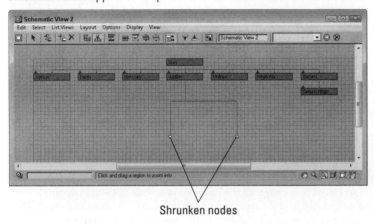

Shrunken nodes

To delete a node, select the node and click the Delete Objects button on the Schematic View toolbar or press the Delete key. If several nodes are selected, they are all deleted. This deletes the object in the viewports also.

Renaming objects

In the Schematic View window, you can rename objects quickly and conveniently. To rename an object, click a selected node and click again to highlight the text. When the text is highlighted, you can type the new name for the object. This works only for nodes that have a name, which includes materials.

Tutorial: Rearranging the solar system

To practice moving nodes around, you'll order the solar system model. When Max places nodes in the Schematic View, it really doesn't follow any specific order, but you can move them as needed by hand.

To rearrange the solar system nodes, follow these steps:

1. Open the Ordered solar system.max file from the Chap 25 directory on the CD.

   This file includes several named spheres representing the solar system.

2. Select Graph Editors ➪ New Schematic View to open the Schematic View window.

   All planets are displayed as blue nodes under the Sun object.

3. Select Options ⇨ Reference Mode (if it is not already selected) to position all the nodes horizontally. Click the Select tool on the main toolbar, or press the S key.

4. Make sure the Options ⇨ Always Arrange option is disabled. Then click and drag the Mercury node to the left, and place it in front of the Venus node.

5. Select the Options ⇨ Move Children (Alt+C) menu command, and drag and drop the Saturn node between the Jupiter and Uranus nodes.

   With the Move Children option enabled, the Saturn rings node moves with its parent.

6. Drag and drop the Pluto node beyond the Neptune node.

7. Select all the planet nodes, and choose Layout ⇨ Align ⇨ Top to align all the nodes together.

Note

Although astronomers no longer classify Pluto as a planet, I doubt that this book is required reading for astronomers. I think we can get away with calling Pluto a planet. ■

Figure 25.14 shows the rearranged hierarchy with all the planets lined up in order.

FIGURE 25.14

After rearranging nodes to the correct order, the planets are easy to locate.

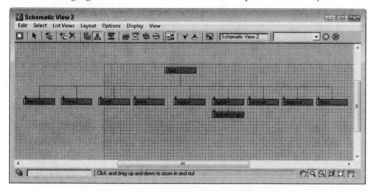

Working with Hierarchies

Another key benefit of the Schematic View is to see the relationships between different objects. With the Schematic View open, you can quickly tell which objects are children and which are parents. You also can see which objects have modifiers and which have materials applied. You can get a wealth of knowledge from the Schematic View.

Using the Display floater

With all relationships enabled, the Schematic View becomes a mess. Luckily, you can control which Relationships and which Entities are displayed using the Display floater, shown in Figure 25.15.

FIGURE 25.15

The Display floater can turn nodes and lines on and off in the Schematic View.

The top section of the Display floater shows or hides relationships between nodes, which are displayed as lines. The relationships that you can control include Constraints, Controllers, Parameter Wires, Light Inclusion, and Modifiers. If you hold the mouse over these relationship lines, the details of the relationship are shown in the tooltip that appears.

Tip

For some relationships, you can double-click the relationship line to open a dialog box where you can edit the relationship. For example, double-clicking a Parameter Wire relationship line opens the Parameter Wiring dialog box. ■

The lower section of the Display floater lets you show or hide entities that are displayed as nodes, including Base Objects, Modifier Stack, Materials, and Controllers. The P, R, and S buttons let you turn on Positional, Rotational, and Scale controllers. When a node has a relationship with another node, the right end of the node displays an arrow. Clicking this arrow toggles the relationship lines on and off.

The Expand button shows the actual nodes when enabled but only an arrow that can be clicked to access the nodes if disabled. The Focus button shows all related objects as colored nodes, and all other nodes are unshaded.

Figure 25.16 shows a Schematic View with the Base Objects and Controllers Entities selected in the Display floater. The Expand button also is disabled. This makes up and down arrows appear above each node. Clicking the up arrow collapses the node, rolling it up into its parent. Clicking the down arrow expands the node and displays the Base Object and Controller nodes for the node that you clicked, such as the Earth node in Figure 25.14. You also can expand and collapse nodes with the Display ⇨ Expand Selected and Collapse Selected menu commands.

Hierarchical relationships are shown as lines that connect the nodes. Even if the nodes are moved, the lines follow as needed to show the relationship between the nodes.

FIGURE 25.16

Schematic View nodes can be collapsed or expanded by clicking the up and down arrows.

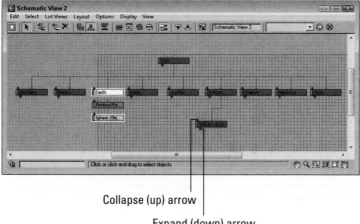

Collapse (up) arrow

Expand (down) arrow

Connecting nodes

To create a hierarchy, use the Edit ⇨ Connect menu command, or press the C shortcut, or click the Connect button on the Schematic View toolbar. This enters Connect mode, which lets you link objects together; copy modifiers, materials, or controllers between nodes; or even wire parameters.

For linking nodes, the Connect button works the same way here as it does on the main toolbar— selecting the child node and dragging a line from the child node to its parent. You can even select multiple nodes and link them all at once.

The Edit ⇨ Unlink Selected menu command (and toolbar button) destroys the link between any object and its immediate parent. Remember that every child object can have only one parent.

Copying modifiers and materials between nodes

Before you can copy materials or modifiers between nodes, you need to make sure they are visible. Material nodes and modifier nodes show up only if they are enabled in the Display floater. You can access this floater by clicking the Display floater button (or by pressing the D key).

To copy a material or modifier, select the material node for one object, click the Connect (C) button, and drag the material to another object node.

Note

In the Schematic View, materials can be copied only between objects; you cannot apply new materials from the Material Editor to Schematic View nodes. ∎

When modifiers are copied between nodes, a dialog box appears, giving you the chance to Copy, Move, or Instance the modifier. You also can use the Schematic View window to reorder the Modifier

Stack. Using the Connect tool, just drag the modifier node to the modifier node that you want to be beneath and the stack is reordered.

Cross-Reference

You can learn more about applying modifiers and the Modifier Stack in Chapter 11, "Introducing Modifiers and Using the Modifier Stack." ∎

Assigning controllers and wiring parameters

If controller nodes are visible, you can copy them to another node using the same technique used for materials and modifiers using the Connect (C) button. You also can assign a controller to an object node that doesn't have a controller using the Edit ⇨ Assign Controller menu command. This opens the Assign Controller dialog box, shown in Figure 25.17, where you can select the controller to apply.

FIGURE 25.17

Controllers can be assigned using the Schematic View window.

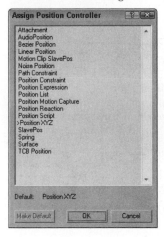

Nodes can be wired using the Schematic View window. To wire parameters, select the node you want to wire and select Edit ⇨ Wire Parameters. A pop-up menu of wire parameters appears that works the same as in the viewports. All parameter wiring relationships are shown in magenta.

Cross-Reference

You can learn more about parameter wiring in Chapter 21, "Understanding Animation and Keyframes." ∎

Tutorial: Linking a character with the Schematic View

Perhaps one of the greatest benefits of the Schematic View is its ability to link objects. This can be tricky in the viewports because some objects are small and hidden behind other items. The Schematic View with its nodes that are all the same size makes it easy, but only if the objects are named correctly.

To link a character model using the Schematic View, follow these steps:

1. Open the Futuristic man.max file from the Chap 25 directory on the CD.

   This file includes a simplified version of a futuristic man created by Viewpoint Datalabs with no links between the various parts.

2. Select Graph Editors ⇨ New Schematic View to open a Schematic View window, and name the view **Linked character**. Click the Region Zoom button in the lower-right corner, and drag over the nodes at the left end of the Schematic View.

   For this model, you want the pelvis to be the parent node.

3. Click the Connect button on the toolbar (or press the C key), and drag from the handr node to the armr node to link the two nodes. Continue linking by connecting the following nodes: handl to arml, head to neck, pupil to eyes, bootr to legr, bootl to legl, and torso to pelvis.

4. Select the eyes, mask, patch, and hair nodes, and drag them all to the head node.

5. Finally, grab the armr, arml, neck, and katana nodes, and drag them to the torso node and the legr and legl nodes to the pelvis node.

   This completes the hierarchy.

Note

Typically, when rigging characters, you want the pelvis to be the parent object because it is the center of most of the character movement. ■

Figure 25.18 shows the final geometry object nodes of the linked character. If you move the pelvis part in the viewports, all the parts move together.

FIGURE 25.18

All character parts are now linked to the man's pelvis part.

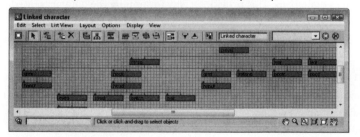

Setting Schematic View Preferences

The Preferences button (or the Options ⇨ Preferences command) opens the Schematic View Preferences dialog box, shown in Figure 25.19, where you can set which items are displayed or hidden, set up grids and background images, and specify how the Schematic View window looks.

FIGURE 25.19

The Schematic View Preferences dialog box lets you customize many aspects of the Schematic View window.

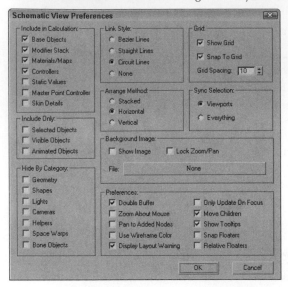

Limiting nodes

When the Schematic View window is opened, Max traverses the entire hierarchy looking for objects and features that can be presented as nodes. If you have a complex scene and don't intend to use the Schematic View to see materials or modifiers, you can disable them in the Include in Calculation section of the Schematic View Preferences dialog box. This provides a way to simplify the data presented. With less data, locating and manipulating what you are looking for becomes easier.

The Include in Calculation section includes options for limiting the following:

- **Base Objects:** The geometry type that makes up a node. The node is the named object, such as Earth; the Base Object is its primitive, such as Sphere (Object).
- **Modifier Stack:** Identifies all nodes with modifiers applied.
- **Materials/Maps:** Identifies all nodes with materials and maps applied.
- **Controllers:** Identifies all nodes that have controllers applied.
- **Static Values:** Displays unanimated parameter values.
- **Master Point Controller:** Displays nodes for any subobject selections that include controllers.
- **Skin Details:** Displays nodes for the modifiers and controllers that are used when the Skin modifier is applied to a bones system.

You also can limit the number of nodes by using the Include Only options. The Selected Objects option shows only the objects selected in the viewports. The nodes change as new objects are selected in the viewports. The Visible Objects option displays only the nodes for those objects that are not hidden in the viewports, and the Animated Objects option displays only the nodes of the objects that are animated.

Object categories that can be hidden include Geometry, Shapes, Lights, Cameras, Helpers, Space Warps, and Bone Objects. Figure 25.20 shows a single sphere object in the Schematic View window with all the Include in Calculation options selected.

FIGURE 25.20

Without limiting nodes, the Schematic View window can get very busy.

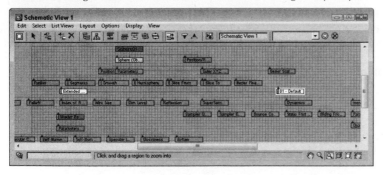

Working with grids and backgrounds

The Schematic View Preferences dialog box includes settings to Show Grid, Snap to Grid, and set Grid Spacing. The keyboard shortcut for toggling the grid on and off is G. Enabling the Snap to Grid option makes the nodes snap to the closest grid intersection. This helps keep the nodes aligned and looking neat.

The Background Image section of the Schematic View Preferences dialog box includes a File button that opens a file dialog box when clicked. Selecting an image file opens and displays the image as a background image. This is helpful as you arrange nodes. You need to select the Show Image option to see the background image; the Lock Zoom/Pan option locks the nodes to the background image so zooming in on a set of nodes also zooms in on the background image.

Tip

One of the easiest ways to get a background image of a model to use in the Schematic View is to render a single frame and save it from the Rendered Frame Window to a location where you can reopen it as the Schematic View background. If you want to print the hierarchy, you can do a screen capture of the Schematic View window, but it would be nice to have a print feature added to the window. ■

Display preferences

In the Schematic View Preferences dialog box, you can select the style to use for relationship lines. The options include Bezier, Straight, Circuit, and None. When the Always Arrange, Arrange Children, or Arrange Selected options are used, you can select to have the nodes arranged Stacked, Horizontal, or Vertical. The Sync Selection options enable you to synch the selection between the Schematic View and the Viewports or between Everything. If the Everything option is selected, not only are geometry objects in the viewports selected, but if a material is selected in the Schematic View, the material is selected in the Material Editor also. Sync Selection Everything also affects the Modifier Stack, the Controller pane in the Display panel, and the Wiring Parameters dialog box.

The Schematic View Preferences dialog box also includes a Preferences section. These preference settings include Double Buffer, which enables a double-buffer display and helps improve the viewport update performance. The Zoom About Mouse preference enables zooming by using the scroll wheel on your mouse or by pressing the middle mouse button while holding down the Ctrl key. The Move Children option causes children nodes to move along with their parent. The Pan to Added Nodes preference automatically resizes and moves the nodes to enable you to view any additional nodes that have been added.

The Use Wireframe Color option changes the node colors to be the same as the viewport object color. The Display Layout Warning preference lets you disable the warning that appears every time you use the Always Arrange feature. The Only Update On Focus option causes the Schematic View to update only when the window is selected. Until then, any changes are not propagated to the window. This can be a timesaver when complex scenes require redraws.

The Show Tooltips option allows you to disable tooltips if you desire. Tooltips show in the Schematic View window when you hover the cursor over the top of a node. Tooltips can be handy if you've zoomed out so far that you can't read the node labels; just move the cursor over a node, and its label appears. The Snap Floater option allows the Display and List floaters to be snapped to the edge of the window for easy access, and the Relative Floaters option moves and resizes the floaters along with the Schematic View window.

Tutorial: Adding a background image to the Schematic View

You can position nodes anywhere within the Schematic View window. For example, you can position the nodes to look something like the shape of the model that you're linking. When positioning the different objects, having a background image is really handy.

To add a background image for the Schematic View, follow these steps:

1. Open the Futuristic man with background.max file in the Chap 25 directory on the CD.

   This file uses the same futuristic man model used in the preceding example.

2. With the Perspective viewport maximized, select Tools ⇨ Grab Viewport. Give the viewport the name of **futuristic man–front view**, and click the Grab button.

   The viewport image opens the Rendered Frame Window.

3. Click the Save Bitmap button in the upper-left corner. Save the image as **Futuristic man–front view**. Then close the Rendered Frame Window.

4. Select Graph Editors ⇨ New Schematic View to open a Schematic View window, and name the view **Background**. Click the Preferences button on the Schematic View toolbar, and click the File button in the Background Image section.

5. Locate the saved image, and open it. Select the Show Image option in the Schematic View Preferences dialog box, and click OK.

   You can perform this step using the image file saved in the Chap 25 directory on the CD, if you so choose.

6. Select the View ⇨ Show Grid menu command (or press the G key) to turn off the grid. Drag the corner of the Schematic View interface to increase the size of the window so the whole background image is visible.

7. Before moving any of the nodes, enable the Lock Zoom/Pan option in the Schematic View Preferences dialog box so the image resizes with the nodes. Then select each of the nodes, and drag them so they are roughly positioned on top of the part they represent. Start by moving the parent objects first, and then work to their children.

Figure 25.21 shows all the nodes aligned over their respective parts. From this arrangement, you can clearly see how the links are organized.

FIGURE 25.21

Using a background image, you can see how the links relate to the model.

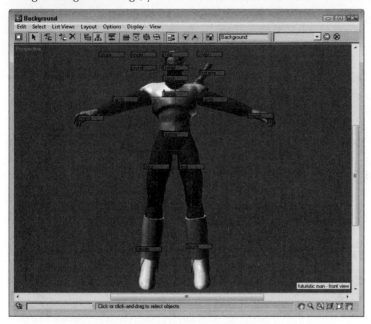

Using List Views

One of the last uses of the Schematic View is to list all nodes that have things in common. Using the List Views menu, you can select to see All Relationships, Selected Relationships, All Instances, Selected Instances, Show Occurrences, and All Animated Controllers.

The List Views ⇨ All Relationships menu command displays a separate dialog box, shown in Figure 25.22, containing a list of nodes and their relationships. The Selected Relationships menu command limits the list to only selected objects with relationships. The List Views dialog box also includes a Detach button to remove the relationships if desired. Double-clicking a relationship in the list opens its dialog box, where you can edit the relationship.

Tip
You can click each column head to sort the entries. ∎

The List Views ⇨ All Instances menu command displays all the instances found in the scene. This includes all types of instances, including geometry, modifiers, controllers, and so on. For the Instances list view, the Detach button is replaced with a Make Unique button.

FIGURE 25.22

The List Views dialog box includes a list of nodes with relationships.

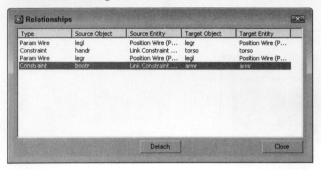

Note

Another way to identify instances is to look for bold text in the node. All label text for all instanced nodes is displayed in bold. ■

If a node is selected and you want to see all other nodes that share the same type of relationship or share a property, the List Views ⇨ Show Occurrences menu command displays them. The final list view shows All Animated Controllers.

Summary

Working with containers and XRefs lets you combine the work of several users and creatively collaborate across teams. Some tasks in the viewport, such as linking objects into a hierarchy, can be difficult. The Schematic View represents all data as simple rectangular nodes. These nodes make easy work of accomplishing a variety of tasks.

This chapter covered the following topics:

- Using containers and externally referenced scenes and objects to work on the same project at the same time as your fellow team members without interfering with their work (or they with yours)
- Configuring XRef paths to help Max track your XRef Scenes and Objects
- Viewing all objects as nodes using the Schematic View window
- Learning the Schematic View interface
- Using the Schematic View window to select, delete, and copy objects, materials, and modifiers
- Using the Schematic View to assign controllers and wire parameters
- Setting preferences for the Schematic View window
- Listing views of nodes with common properties

In the next chapter, you learn more about features that enable deforming meshes, including the Paint Deformation tool and various modifiers that may be applied to mesh objects.

#### CHAPTER 26

Deforming Surfaces and Using the Mesh Modifiers

When an Editable Poly object is selected, three specific deformation brushes may be selected in the Paint Deformation rollout. Using these brushes, you can deform the surface of an object by dragging over the surface with the selected brush.

In addition to the editing features available for Editable Mesh and Editable Poly objects and the Paint Deformation brushes, you also can modify mesh geometries using modifiers. The Modifiers menu includes a submenu of modifiers that are specific to mesh (and poly) objects. These modifiers are found in the Mesh Editing submenu and can be used to enhance the features available for these objects.

Another set of modifiers that apply specifically to mesh objects are the Subdivision Surface modifiers. These modifiers are also covered in this chapter.

The Basics of Deformation Painting

The first thing to remember about the Paint Deformation feature is that it is available only for Editable Poly objects (or objects with the Edit Poly modifier applied). When an Editable Poly object is selected, the Paint Deformation rollout appears at the very bottom of the Modify panel in the Command Panel.

Painting deformations

At the top of the Paint Deformation rollout are three buttons used to select the type of deformation brush to use. These three brushes are the Push/Pull brush, the Relax brush, and the Revert brush.

When one of these brushes is selected, the mouse cursor changes to a circular brush, shown in Figure 26.1, that follows the surface of the object as you move the mouse over the object. A single line points outward from the center of the circle in the direction of the surface normal. Dragging the mouse affects the surface in a certain manner, depending on the brush that is selected.

Dragging the Paint Deformation brush over the object surface deforms the surface by moving the vertices within the brush's area. The direction that the vertices are moved follows the surface normals by default, or you can have the deformation follow a deformed normal or along a specified transform axis. For example, if you select to deform vertices along the X-axis, then all vertices underneath the brush are moved along the X-axis as the brush is dragged over the surface.

FIGURE 26.1

The Paint Deformation brush looks like a circle that follows the surface.

Paint Deformation brush

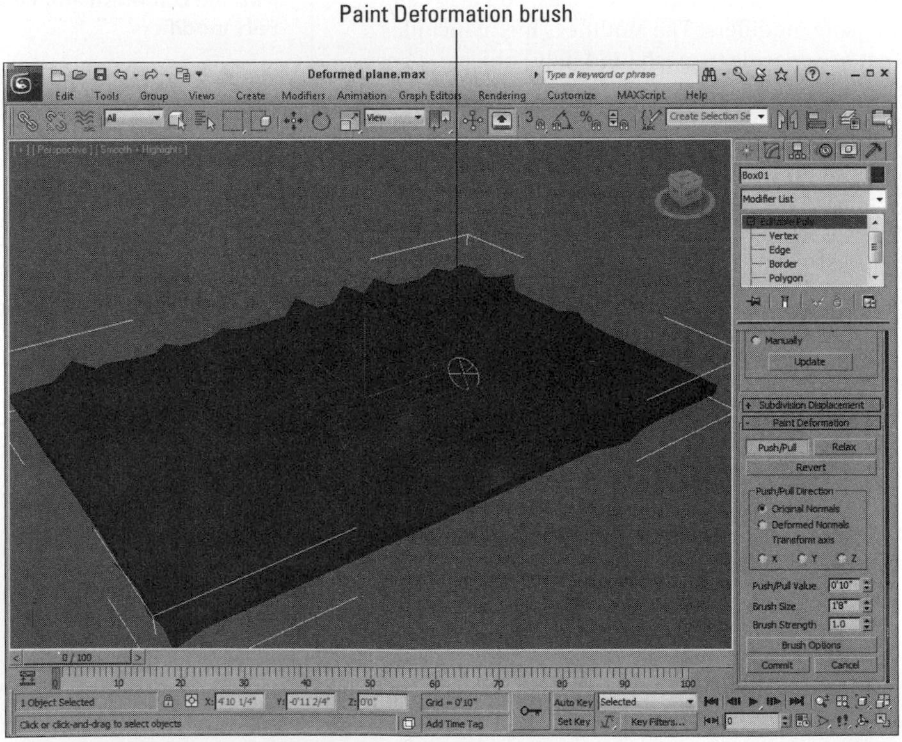

Note

Deformations created using the Paint Deformation brushes cannot be animated. For objects with the Edit Poly modifier applied, the Paint Deformation brushes are disabled when in Animate mode. ■

The Push/Pull value determines the distance that the vertices are moved, thereby setting the amount of the deformation. The Brush Size sets the size (or radius) of the brush and determines the area that is deformed. The Brush Strength value sets the rate at which the vertices are moved. For example, if the Push/Pull Value is set to 100 mm, then a Brush Strength value of 1.0 causes the vertices directly under the brush center to move 100 mm; a Brush Strength value of 0.4 causes the same vertices to move only 40 mm.

Tip

Holding down the Shift and Alt keys while dragging in the viewports lets you interactively change the Brush Strength value. ■

Accessing brush presets

If you right-click the main toolbar away from any of the buttons, you can access the Brush Presets toolbar, shown in Figure 26.2, from the pop-up menu.

FIGURE 26.2

The Brush Presets toolbar lets you quickly select from a selection of predefined brushes.

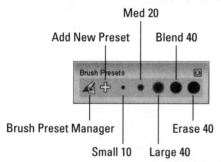

The first toolbar button opens the Brush Preset Manager, shown in Figure 26.3. From this interface, you can choose to create preset brushes for each of the different features that use brushes—Vertex Paint, Paint Deformation, Paint Soft Selection, Viewport Canvas, and Paint Skin Weights. The Add button works the same as the Add New Preset toolbar button. It opens a dialog box where you can name the new preset. The new preset is then added to the list of presets.

Note

The brushes in the Brush Presets toolbar become active only when one of the features that use brushes is selected. ■

FIGURE 26.3

The Brush Preset Manager lets you create new preset brushes.

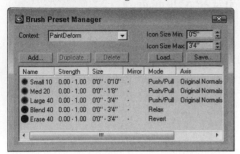

When a brush preset is selected on the Brush Presets toolbar, you can change its attributes using the Painter Options dialog box. The Paint Deformation rollout also includes a button for accessing the Painter Options dialog box. Any changes to the brush attributes are automatically updated in the Brush Preset Manager. The Load and Save buttons in the Brush Preset Manager dialog box let you save and load brush preset sets. The brush options are covered later in this chapter.

Using the Deformation Brushes

The Push/Pull brush may be used to pull vertices away from the object surface or to indent the surface by moving the surface toward the object's center. The difference is determined by the Push/Pull value. Positive values pull vertices, and negative values push vertices.

Tip

Holding down the Alt key while dragging reverses the direction of the Push/Pull brush, causing a pull brush to push and vice versa. ∎

Controlling the deformation direction

By default, dragging over vertices with the Push/Pull brush causes the affected vertices to be moved inward or outward along their normals. If you drag over the same vertices several times, they are still deformed using the original face normals.

The Deformed Normals option causes the vertices to be moved in the direction of the normal as the normals are deformed. Using the Original Normals option causes the deformed area to rise from the surface like a hill with a gradual increasing height. The Deformed Normals option causes the deformed area to bubble out from the surface.

The Transform Axis option causes the vertices to be moved in the direction of the selected transform axis. This option is useful if you want to skew or shift the deformed area.

Limiting the deformation

If a subobject selection exists, then the vertices that are moved are limited to the subobject area that is selected. You can use this to your advantage if you want to make sure that only a certain area is deformed.

Committing any changes

After you make some deformation changes, the Commit and Cancel buttons become active. Pressing the Commit button makes the changes permanent, which means that you can no longer return the vertices to their original location with the Revert brush. The Cancel button rejects all the recent deformation changes.

Using the Relax and Revert brushes

The Relax brush provides a much more subtle change. It moves vertices that are too close together farther apart, causing a general smoothing of any sharp points. It works the same way as the Relax feature for the Editable Poly object and the Relax modifier.

The Revert brush is used to return to their original position any vertices that have moved. For example, if you pushed and pulled several vertices, the Revert brush can undo all of these changes for the area under the brush cursor.

Tip
Holding down the Ctrl key while dragging with the Push/Pull brush lets you temporarily access the Revert brush. ∎

Tutorial: Adding veins to a forearm

The Paint Deformation feature is very useful in adding surface details to organic objects such as the veins of a forearm.

To add veins to a forearm object, follow these steps:

1. Open the Forearm with veins.max file from the Chap 26 directory on the CD.

    The polygons that make up the forearm object have been selected and tessellated to increase its resolution.

2. With the forearm object selected, open the Modify panel and in the Paint Deformation rollout, click the Relax button. Set the Brush Size to **1.0**, and drag over the entire forearm.

    This smoothes out some of the vertical lines that run along the forearm.

3. Click the Push/Pull button, and set the Push/Pull Value to **0.15**, the Brush Size to **0.08**, and the Brush Strength to **0.5**. Then draw in some veins extending from the elbow toward the hand.

4. Lower the Brush Strength value to **0.25**, and extend the vein farther down the arm. Then drop the Brush Strength to **0.1**, and finish the veins.

5. With the Push/Pull brush still selected, hold down the Alt key and drag near the wrist to indent the surface around the area where the hand tendons are located.

Figure 26.4 shows the resulting forearm.

FIGURE 26.4

The Paint Deformation brushes are helpful in painting on raised and indented surface features.

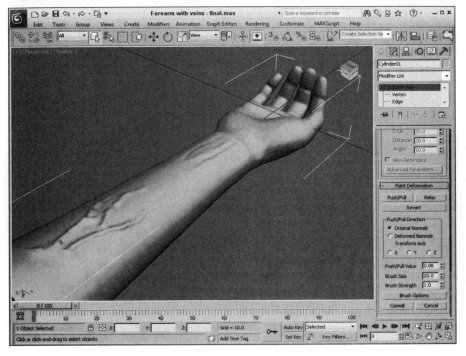

Setting Painter Options

At the bottom of the Paint Deformation rollout is a button labeled Brush Options. Clicking this button opens the Painter Options dialog box, shown in Figure 26.5. Using this dialog box, you can set several customized brush options, including the sensitivity of the brush.

Cross-Reference

The Painter Options dialog box is also used by the brushes to paint vertex colors for the Vertex Paint modifier and to paint skin weights as part of the Skin modifier. The Vertex Paint modifier is covered in Chapter 34, "Creating Baked Textures and Normal Maps," and the Skin modifier is covered in Chapter 40, "Skinning Characters." ■

FIGURE 26.5

The Painter Options dialog box includes a graph for defining the minimum and maximum brush strengths and sizes.

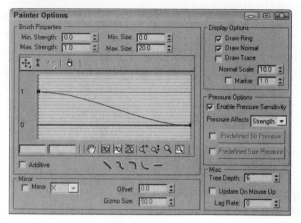

The Min/Max Strength and Min/Max Size values determine the minimum and maximum weight values and paint gizmo sizes. You can define the brush falloff using the curve. This keeps the weights from making an abrupt change (muscles tend to look funny when this happens). Under the curve are several buttons for quickly defining the shape of the falloff curve, including Linear, Smooth, Slow, Fast, and Flat.

The Display Options section includes options that determine the look of the painting gizmo. The Draw Ring, Draw Normal, and Draw Trace options make a ring; the surface normal or an arrow showing the trace direction appears. The Normal can be scaled, and the Marker option displays a small circular marker at the end of the normal.

The Pressure Options let you paint using a graphics tablet with the pressure applied to affect the Strength, Size, or a combination. You can enable Pressure Sensitivity for the brush gizmo. The options include None, Strength, Size, and Both. Using the graph, you can predefine Strength and Size pressure curves and then select to use them.

The Mirror option paints symmetrically on the opposite side of the gizmo across the specified axis. You can also set an Offset and the Gizmo Size. This is handy for muscles that you want to deform symmetrically.

In the Miscellaneous section, the Tree Depth, Update on Mouse Up, and Lag Rate options control how often the scene and the painted strokes are updated.

Primitive Maintenance Modifiers

Included among the Mesh Editing modifiers are two unique modifiers that can be applied to primitive objects, allowing them to maintain their parametric nature.

Note
Using the Edit Mesh or Edit Poly modifiers increases the file size and memory required to work with the object. You can reduce the overhead by collapsing the modifier stack. ∎

Edit Mesh modifier

All mesh objects are by default Editable Mesh objects. This modifier enables objects to be modified using the Editable Mesh features while maintaining their basic creation parameters.

When an object is converted to an Editable Mesh, its parametric nature is eliminated. However, if you use the Edit Mesh modifier, you can still retain the same object type and its parametric nature while having access to all the Editable Mesh features. For example, if you create a sphere and apply the Edit Mesh modifier and then extrude several faces, you can still change the radius of the sphere by selecting the Sphere object in the Modifier Stack and changing the Radius value in the Parameters rollout.

If the Sphere base object is selected after a modifier has been applied, the Topology Dependence warning dialog box appears. This dialog box doesn't prevent you from making any changes to the base object parameters, but it reminds you that changes you make to the base object's parameters may disrupt the changes to the surface accomplished by the modifiers. The warning dialog box also includes a Hold button to load the current scene in a buffer in case you don't like the results.

Caution
One drawback of the Edit Mesh modifier is that its subobjects cannot be animated. ∎

Edit Poly modifier

The Edit Poly modifier lets you work with primitive objects using the operators found in the Editable Poly rollouts. A huge benefit of this modifier is that you can remove it at any time if the changes don't work out.

The Edit Poly modifier includes two separate modes: Model and Animate. You can select these modes in the Edit Poly Mode rollout, shown in Figure 26.6.

Model mode lets you access the same features available for Editable Poly objects. Animate mode lets you animate subobject changes made with the features used to edit the object. To animate these subobject changes, you use the Auto Key or Set Key buttons to set the keys.

FIGURE 26.6

The Edit Poly Mode rollout lets you switch between Model and Animate modes.

The Commit button lets you freeze the changes and set the keyframe for the current change. The current change is listed directly above the Commit button. The Settings button lets you access the dialog box used to make the changes. The Cancel button cancels the last change, and the Show Cage option displays an orange cage around the object; you can change the color of the cage using the color swatch. The cage is useful when using the MeshSmooth modifier to see the original shape of the object before being smoothed.

The differences between the features available for the Edit Poly modifier and the Editable Poly object are subtle. In the Selection rollout is a Get Stack Selection button. Clicking this button passes the subobject selection up from the stack. Also, the Edit Poly modifier doesn't include the Subdivision Surfaces rollout, but you can use the MeshSmooth modifier to get this functionality.

Edit Geometry Modifiers

Most of the Mesh Editing modifiers are used to change the geometry of objects. Some of these modifiers, such as Extrude and Tessellate, perform the same operation as buttons available for the Editable Mesh or Editable Poly objects. Applying them as modifiers separates the operation from the base geometry.

Cross-Reference
You can find a more general explanation of modifiers in Chapter 11, "Introducing Modifiers and Using the Modifier Stack." ∎

Cap Holes modifier

The Cap Holes modifier patches any holes found in a geometry object. Sometimes when objects are imported, they are missing faces. This modifier can detect and eliminate these holes by creating a face along open edges.

For example, if a spline is extruded and you don't specify Caps, then the extruded spline has holes at its end. The Cap Holes modifier detects these holes and creates a Cap. Cap Holes parameters include Smooth New Faces, Smooth with Old Faces, and Triangulate Cap. Smooth with Old Faces applies the same smoothing group as that used on the bordering faces.

Delete Mesh modifier

You can use the Delete Mesh modifier to delete mesh subobjects. Subobjects that you can delete include Vertices, Edges, Faces, and Objects. The nice part about the Delete Mesh modifier is that it remains in the Modifier Stack and can be removed to reinstate the deleted subobjects.

The Delete Mesh modifier deletes the current selection as defined by the Mesh Select (or Poly Select) modifier. It can be used to delete a selection of Vertices, Edges, Faces, Polygons, or even the entire mesh if no subobject selection exists. The Delete Mesh modifier has no parameters.

Note
Even if the entire mesh is deleted using the Delete Mesh modifier, the object still remains. To completely delete an object, use the Delete key. ∎

Extrude modifier

The Extrude modifier can be applied only to spline or shape objects, but the resulting extrusion can be a Patch, Mesh, or NURBS object. This modifier copies the spline, moves it a given distance, and connects the two splines to form a 3D shape. Parameters for this modifier include an Amount value, which is the distance to extrude, and the number of segments to use to define the height. The Capping options let you select a Start Cap and/or an End Cap using either a Morph or Grid option. The Morph option divides the caps into long, thin polygons suitable for morph targets, and the Grid option divides the caps into a tight grid of polygons suitable for deformation operations. The Cap fills the spline area and can be made as a Patch, Mesh, or NURBS object. Only closed splines that are extruded can be capped. You can also have mapping coordinates and Material IDs generated automatically. The Smooth option smoothes the extrusion.

Cross-Reference
Chapter 12, "Drawing and Editing 2D Splines and Shapes," includes a good example of the Extrude modifier. ∎

Face Extrude modifier

The Face Extrude modifier extrudes the selected faces in the same direction as their normals. Face Extrude parameters include Amount and Scale values and an option to Extrude From Center. Figure 26.7 shows a mesh object with several extruded faces. The Mesh Select modifier was used to select the faces, and the extrude Amount was set to **30**.

FIGURE 26.7

Extruded faces are moved in the direction of the face normal.

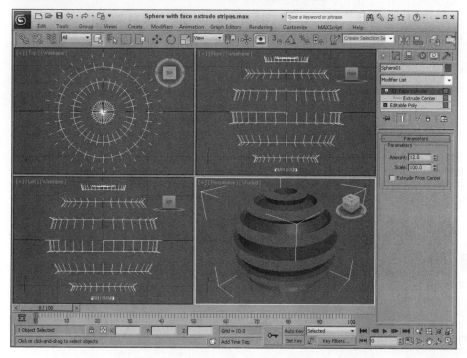

Tutorial: Extruding a bullet

As a simple example that uses a couple of Mesh modifiers, you'll create a single bullet using a hemisphere object. You can create this simple object in other ways, but this offers some good practice.

To create a bullet using the Face Extrude modifier, follow these steps:

1. Select Create ➪ Standard Primitives ➪ Sphere, and drag in the Top viewport to create a sphere object. Set the Radius value to **60** and the Hemisphere value to **0.5** to create half a sphere.

2. Right-click on the sphere object, and select Convert To ➪ Editable Poly in the pop-up quadmenu to convert the hemisphere to an Editable Poly object.

3. Select the Top viewport, right-click on the viewport name, and select Views ➪ Bottom from the pop-up menu (or press the B key) to switch to the Bottom view.

4. In the Selection rollout, click the Vertex button to enter Vertex subobject mode and enable the Ignore Backfacing option. Then select the single vertex in the center of the hemisphere, and press the Delete key.

5. In the Selection rollout, click the Border button to enter Border subobject mode, and then click the edge of the hemisphere in the Front viewport to select the border of the hole that was created by deleting the center vertex. Then click the Cap button in the Edit Borders rollout.

6. Select the Polygon button in the Selection rollout to enter Polygon subobject mode and select the bottom polygon subobject in the Perspective viewport after rotating the object around. Then select Modifiers ➪ Mesh Editing ➪ Face Extrude to apply the Face Extrude modifier to the selected polygon face. Set the Amount value to **200**.

7. Select Create ➪ Standard Primitives ➪ Cylinder, and drag in the Bottom viewport to create a thin Cylinder object that is just wider than the extruded hemisphere. Then move the new Cylinder object until it is positioned at the end of the bullet object.

Figure 26.8 shows the completed simple bullet.

FIGURE 26.8

A simple bullet can be created by extruding one face of a hemisphere.

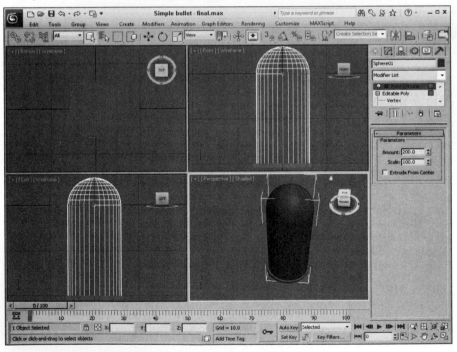

ProOptimizer modifier

Although the latest game consoles are getting much better at handling lots of polygons, sometimes you'll want to reduce a high-resolution model. For example, if you have a high-res statue in your scene, you might want the same statue to be lower-res when used as part of the background. Max offers an excellent modifier that enables you to reduce the total number of polygons in a model while maintaining its shape.

New Feature

The ProOptimizer modifier has been improved in 3ds Max 2012. The modifier is now faster and isn't as likely to flip faces. ■

When first applied, the ProOptimizer modifier doesn't do anything. To use it, you need to select the settings first and then click the Calculate button. The settings found in the Optimization Options rollouts let you define which vertices can be removed. For example, you can set the optimization to Crunch Borders, Protect Borders, or Exclude Borders. A border is an edge connected to a single face. The Crunch Borders option makes the borders fair game for being optimized. This can yield the greatest amount of reduction but also can change the surface of the model. The Protect Borders option minimizes the amount of reduction at the borders, and the Exclude Borders option removes any border faces from being considered for reduction. The last choice limits the amount of reduction that is possible, but rigidly maintains the surface.

Other settings let you specify the Material Boundaries, Textures, and/or UV Boundaries off-limits. Additional settings protect any applied Vertex Colors and Normals. The Merge tools cause all vertices and/or faces within a given Threshold to be merged before optimizing the mesh. This helps to eliminate any extra vertices or co-planar faces that could cause problems. Finally, the Sub-Object Selection setting lets you preserve a given selection of vertices and makes it possible to optimize only a portion of the model.

The Symmetry options cause the modifier to equally reduce polygons on either side of a designated axis to maintain visual symmetry. There is also a Tolerance value for looking for symmetrical edges. Within the Advanced Options rollout, the Favor Compact Faces resists eliminating a face if it causes sharp pointed faces as a result. You can also select to Prevent Flipped Normals and the Lock Vertex Position option prevents any of the remaining vertices from being moved from their original locations, thus maintaining the model's shape.

After all the settings have been configured, click the Calculate button to run the optimization pass. The Statistics panel (located under the Calculate button) shows the number of points and faces in the model. By dialing down the Vertex % value, you can interactively reduce the total number of faces.

Figure 26.9 shows an alligator model that has been optimized using the ProOptimizer modifier. Notice the dramatic reduction in the number of faces from the left to the right. Viewpoint Datalabs, known for producing high-resolution models, created this model. In the Modify panel, you can see that the number of faces has been reduced from 34,404 to 6,937 faces. (I guess that would make the gator on the right "lean and mean.")

Note
The Optimize and MultiRes modifiers are older versions of the ProOptimizer modifier and are maintained for compatibility with older files. ∎

If you have an entire folder full of models that you want to optimize, you can use the Batch ProOptimizer utility. This utility is available from the Utilities panel and opens a dialog box where you can specify the source files to optimize, all the optimization settings, and the out filenames and locations. Once configured, you can simply click the Ok button to optimize several model files in a batch process.

Tutorial: Creating a low-res hand
You can use the ProOptimizer modifier to dynamically dial down the resolution to exactly what you want. In this example, you use the ProOptimizer modifier on a high-res hand model created by Viewpoint Datalabs. The hand weighs in at 2,906 polygons, which is a little heavy for any game engine.

FIGURE 26.9

You can use the ProOptimizer modifier to reduce the complexity of the alligator model.

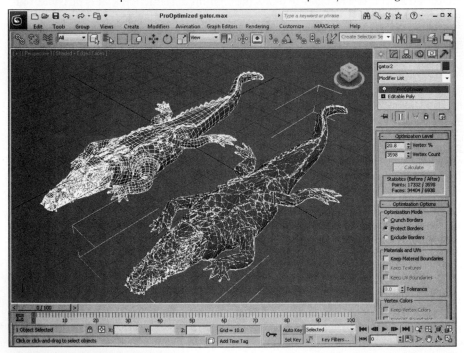

To create a MultiRes hand, follow these steps:

1. Open the ProOptimizer hand.max file from the Chap 26 directory on the CD.

   This file contains a simple hand model.

2. With the hand selected, choose ProOptimizer from the Modifier List to apply the modifier to the hand model.

3. In the Optimization Options rollout, enable the Protect Borders option, the Merge Vertices option with the Threshold to **0.05**, and the Merge Faces option with the Threshold set to 0.5. Then click the Calculate button.

4. Create a copy of the hand by holding down the Shift key and dragging the hand to the right. In the Clone Options dialog box that appears, select Copy, name the clone **Hand – Lo**, and click OK.

5. With the cloned hand selected, set the Vertex % to **10**.

   Notice that the number of faces has dropped from over 2,906 to 286.

Figure 26.10 shows the results of the MultiRes modifier. If you look closely, you can see that the hand on the right isn't as smooth, but it still looks pretty good and the game engine won't complain.

Caution

Reducing mesh density on the fly should not be done with animated objects such as characters because the mesh can become chaotic and dirty, resulting in poor deformations. However, the ProOptimizer modifier does work very well with static background objects. ∎

Quadify Mesh modifier

If you look at the individual shape of polygons in most models, you find either a triangle with three sides or a rectangle with four sides. Rectangle polygons are called quads, and they generally are nice to work with because they line up neatly into equal rows and columns. Triangles, on the other hand, flip back and forth even when lined up, making them more difficult to work with.

You can convert quads into triangles in many ways. This can be done in Max using a Triangulate command or modifier. This command simply divides the quads in half, but moving from triangles to quads isn't as easy and takes some clever calculating. But Max has figured it out and made it a feature with the Quadify Mesh modifier.

The single parameter for this modifier is the Quad Size %. Larger values result in bigger and fewer quads, and smaller values increase the number of quads. Figure 26.11 shows a simple shelf that has been quadified.

FIGURE 26.10

You can use the ProOptimizer modifier to dynamically dial back the complexity of a mesh.

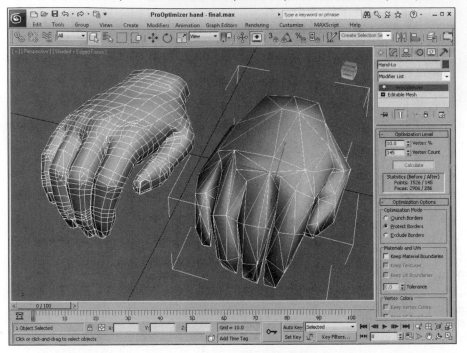

Tip

The Quadify Mesh modifier works well with shapes that have been extruded. ■

Smooth modifier

You can use the Smooth modifier to auto-smooth an object. This automates the creation of different smoothing groups based on the angular threshold. Smooth parameters include options for Auto Smooth and Prevent Indirect Smoothing along with a Threshold value. The Parameters rollout also includes a set of 32 Smoothing Groups buttons labeled 1 through 32. These same Smoothing Groups are available as options for the Polygon and Element subobjects.

Symmetry modifier

The Symmetry modifier allows you to mirror a mesh object across a single axis. You can also select to Slice Along Mirror and weld along the seam with a defined Threshold. The gizmo for this modifier is a plane, which matches the selected axis and the arrow vector that extends from the plane.

FIGURE 26.11

The Quadify Mesh modifier converts the model into regular-shaped quad faces.

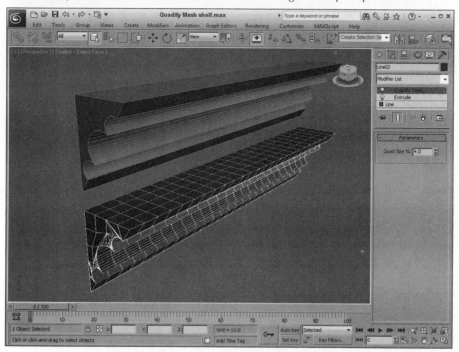

Tutorial: Creating symmetrical antlers

Using symmetry, you can create one half of a model and then use the mirror tool to create the other half. If you need to see the changes as you make them, you can use the Symmetry modifier. In this example, I've taken the antlers off an elk model so you can practice putting them back on.

To create a set of symmetrical antlers, follow these steps:

1. Open the Elk with short antlers.max file from the Chap 26 directory on the CD.

    This file contains an elk model created by Viewpoint Datalabs with its antlers removed.

2. With the elk object selected, select the Modifiers ➪ Mesh Editing ➪ Symmetry menu command to apply the Symmetry modifier. Its default setting has the X-axis selected, which places a plane running down the center of the elk model, but you need to enable the Flip option so the symmetry goes the right way.

3. In the Modifier Stack, select the Editable Poly object and enable the Polygon subobject mode. Then rotate the view until you're looking at the elk from behind its head. Select a polygon on the left side of the elk where the antler should be located.

4. In the Edit Polygons rollout, click the option dialog box button for the Bevel tool. Set the Height value to **2.0**, the Outline Amount to **-0.15**, and click OK.

5. With the polygon still selected, move the beveled polygon outward away from the elk's head.

6. Disable the polygon subobject mode and click on the Symmetry modifier in the Modifier Stack to see the symmetrical antler.

Tip

If you toggle the Show End Result button in the Modifier Stack, then you can see the results of the Symmetry modifier in real time. ■

Figure 26.12 shows the results of the Symmetry modifier.

FIGURE 26.12

When you use the Symmetry modifier, you have to model certain objects only once.

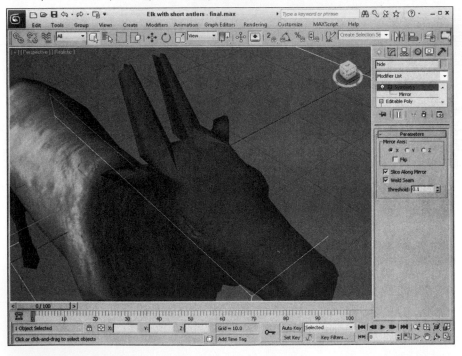

Tessellate modifier

You use the Tessellate modifier to subdivide the selected faces for higher-resolution models. You can apply tessellation to either Triangle or Polygonal faces. The Edge option creates new faces by dividing the face from the face center to the middle of the edges. The Face-Center option divides each face from the face center to the corners of the face. The Tension setting determines whether the faces are convex or concave. The Iterations setting is the number of times the modifier is applied.

Caution

Applying the Tessellate modifier to an object with a high Iterations value produces objects with many times the original number of faces. ■

Vertex Weld modifier

The Vertex Weld modifier is a simple modifier that welds all vertices within a certain Threshold value. This is a convenient modifier for cleaning up mesh objects.

Miscellaneous Modifiers

Several of the Mesh Editing modifiers are unique, special-purpose modifiers. The Edit Normals modifier, for example, lets you change the direction of face normals, which doesn't really change the geometry, but it can have a big impact on how the object is smoothed and shaded.

Edit Normals

The Edit Normals modifier enables you to select and move normals. Normals appear as blue lines that extend from the vertex of each face. The Edit Normal modifier includes a Normals subobject that you can select and change its direction. To move (or rotate) a normal, you can use the transform tools on the main toolbar. If your viewport has shading enabled, you can see the effect of moving the normals.

Tip

The Edit Normals modifier can be used to create the illusion of surface geometry. For example, by selecting and flipping specific localized normals, you can create what look like dents in a metal plate. ■

You can select normals by Normal, Edge, Vertex, or Face. Selecting normals by Face, for example, selects all normals attached to a face when you click on a face. Moving a normal then moves all selected normals together.

You also have options to Ignore Backfacing and to Show Handles. Handles appear as small squares at the top of the normal vector. The Display Length value defines the length of the normals displayed in the viewports. Figure 26.13 shows all the normals extending from a simple Sphere object.

FIGURE 26.13

The Edit Normals parameters let you work with normals.

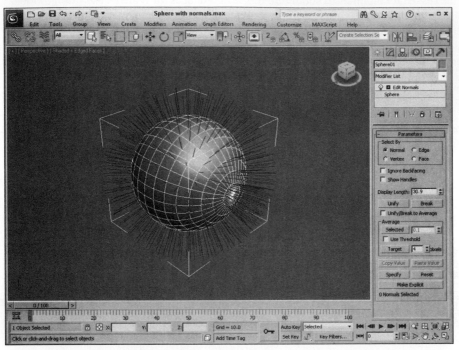

The modifier also includes buttons to Unify and to Break selected normals. Unify causes all selected normals to be combined to a single normal, and Break splits unified normals into their separate components again. The direction of the unified normal is an average of the surface points when unified or an average of the normals if the Unify/Break to Average option is enabled.

The Selected button in the Average section averages all selected normals that are within the specified value if the Use Threshold value is enabled. If it is not enabled, then all selected normals are averaged. The Average Target button lets you interactively select a normal and then click on another normal to average. The Target normal must be within the specified Target value.

The direction of selected normals can be copied and pasted between normals. The Specify button marks a normal as a Specified normal. These normals appear cyan in the viewport and ignore any smoothing group information associated with the vertex. Explicit normals are green in the viewport, which denotes a normal that has deviated from its regular position. The Make Explicit button can be used to make normals explicit, thereby removing them from the normal computation task. The Reset button returns a normal to its regular type and position. At the bottom of the Parameters rollout is an information line that displays which normal is selected or how many normals are selected.

Normal modifier

The Normal modifier is the precursor to the Edit Normals modifier. It enables object normals to be flipped or unified. When some objects are imported, their normals can become erratic, producing holes in the geometry. By unifying and flipping the normals, you can restore an object's consistency. This modifier includes only two options: Unify Normals and Flip Normals.

STL Check modifier

The STL Check modifier checks a model in preparation for exporting it to the Stereo-Lithography (STL) format. STL files require a closed surface: Geometry with holes or gaps can cause problems. Any problems are reported in the Status area of the Parameters rollout.

This modifier can check for several common errors, including Open Edge, Double Face, Spike, or Multiple Edge. Spikes are island faces with only one connected edge. You can select any or all of these options. If found, you can have the modifier select the problem Edges or Faces, or neither, or you can change the Material ID of the problem area.

Subdivision Surface Modifiers

The Modifiers menu also includes a submenu of modifiers for subdividing surfaces. These include the MeshSmooth and HSDS Modifiers. You can use these modifiers to smooth and subdivide the surface of an object. Subdividing a surface increases the resolution of the object, allowing for more detailed modeling.

MeshSmooth modifier

The MeshSmooth modifier smoothes the entire surface of an object by applying a chamfer function to both vertices and edges at the same time. This modifier has the greatest effect on sharp corners and edges. With this modifier, you can create a NURMS object. NURMS stands for Non-Uniform Rational MeshSmooth. NURMS can weight each control point. The Parameters rollout includes three MeshSmooth types: Classic, NURMS, and Quad Output. You can set it to operate on triangular or polygonal faces. Smoothing parameters include Strength and Relax values.

Settings for the number of Subdivision Iterations to run and controls for weighting selected control points are also available. Update Options can be set to Always, When Rendering, and Manually using the Update button. You can also select and work with either Vertex or Edge subobjects. These subobjects give you local control over the MeshSmooth object. Included within the Local Control rollout is a Crease value, which is available in Edge subobject mode. Selecting an Edge subobject and applying a 1.0 value causes a hard edge to be retained while the rest of the object is smoothed. The MeshSmooth modifier also makes the Soft Selection rollout available. The Reset rollout is included to quickly reset any crease and weight values.

TurboSmooth modifier

The TurboSmooth modifier works just like the MeshSmooth modifier, except that it is much faster and doesn't require as much memory.

Tutorial: Smoothing a birdbath

One effective way to model is to block out the details of a model using the Editable Poly features and then smooth the resulting model using the TurboSmooth modifier. This gives the model a polished look and increases the resolution.

To create a smoothed birdbath object, follow these steps:

1. Open the Birdbath.max file from the Chap 26 directory on the CD.

   This file includes a simple birdbath created by selecting and scaling rows of cylinder vertices. The water is simply an inverted cone.

2. Select and clone the existing birdbath as an instance by pressing the Shift key and moving the birdbath.

3. Select the cloned birdbath, and apply the TurboSmooth modifier with the Modifiers ⇨ Subdivision Surfaces ⇨ TurboSmooth menu.

4. In the TurboSmooth rollout, set the Iterations value to **2**.

   Notice that the entire birdbath is smooth and the resolution is greatly increased, as shown in Figure 26.14.

HSDS modifier

You use the HSDS (Hierarchical SubDivision Surfaces) modifier to increase the resolution and smoothing of a localized area. It works like the Tessellate modifier, except that it can work with small subobject sections instead of the entire object surface. The HSDS modifier lets you work with Vertex, Edge, Polygon, and Element subobjects. After a subobject area is selected, you can click the Subdivide button to subdivide the area. Each time you press the Subdivide button, the selected subobjects are subdivided again, and each subdivision level appears in the list above the Subdivide button.

Using the subdivision list, you can move back and forth between the various subdivision hierarchy levels. When edges are selected, you can specify a Crease value to maintain sharp edges. In the Advanced Options rollout, you can select to Smooth Result, Hide, or Delete Polygon. The Adaptive Subdivision button opens the Adaptive Subdivision dialog box, in which you can specify the detail parameters. This modifier also includes a Soft Selection rollout.

FIGURE 26.14

The TurboSmooth modifier can make a model flow better.

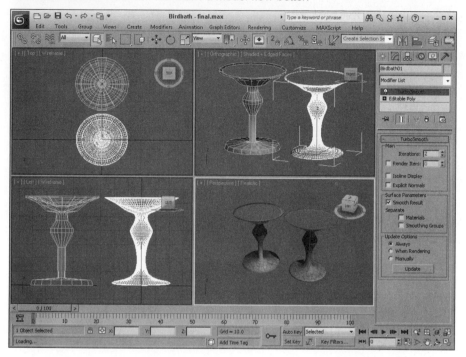

Summary

The Paint Deformation feature is a welcome addition, allowing you to add surface details using an intuitive and easy-to-use interface. Max includes several unique modifiers that apply specifically to mesh objects. This chapter covered these topics:

- Using the various Paint Deformation brushes
- Setting brush options with the Painter Options dialog box
- How the Edit Mesh and Edit Poly modifiers can be used to edit a primitive object using the Editable Mesh and Editable Poly features while maintaining its parametric nature
- How several mesh modifiers are used to edit surface geometry
- How to edit normals and what the effects are
- Working with the Subdivision Surface modifiers to smooth mesh objects

The next chapter focuses on working with a miscellaneous group of mutant objects called compound objects. These objects are unique and used for special purposes.

Working with Compound Objects

So far, I have covered a variety of modeling types, including shapes, meshes, and polys. The Compound Objects subcategory includes several additional modeling types that don't seem to fit anywhere else. As you will see in this chapter, these modeling types provide several new and unique ways to model objects, such as working with Boolean objects, scattering objects across the surface of another object, or lofting a cross section along a spline path.

Understanding Compound Object Types

The Compound Objects subcategory includes several unique object types. You can access these object types with the Create ⇨ Compound menu or by clicking the Geometry category button in the Create panel and selecting Compound Objects in the subcategory drop-down list. All the object types included in the Compound Objects subcategory are displayed as buttons at the top of the Create panel. They include the following:

- **Morph:** Consists of two or more objects with the same number of vertices. The vertices are interpolated from one object to the other over several frames.

- **Scatter:** Randomly scatters a source object about the scene. You can also select a Distribution object that defines the volume or surface where the objects scatter.

- **Conform:** Wraps the vertices of one object onto another. You can use this option to simulate a morph between objects with different numbers of vertices.

- **Connect:** Connects two objects with open faces by joining the holes with additional faces.
- **BlobMesh:** Creates a metaball object that flows from one object to the next like water.
- **ShapeMerge:** Lets you embed a spline into a mesh object or subtract the area of a spline from a mesh object.
- **Boolean:** Created by performing Boolean operations on two or more overlapping objects. The operations include Union, Subtraction, Intersection, and Cut.
- **Terrain:** Creates terrains from the elevation contour lines like those found on topographical maps.
- **Loft:** Sweeps a cross-section shape along a spline path.
- **Mesher:** Creates an object that converts particle systems into mesh objects as the frames progress. This makes assigning modifiers to particle systems possible.
- **ProBoolean:** Replaces the original Boolean compound object with the ability to perform Boolean operations on multiple objects at a time.
- **ProCutter:** Cuts a single stock object into multiple objects using several cutter objects.

Note

When two or more objects are combined into a single compound object, they use a single object material. The Multi/Sub-Object Material type can be used to apply different materials to the various parts. ∎

Morphing Objects

Morph objects are used to create a Morph animation by interpolating the vertices in one object to the vertex positions of a second object. The original object is called the *Base object,* and the second object is called the *Target object.* The Base and Target objects must have the same number of vertices. One Base object can be morphed into several targets.

Caution

To ensure that the Base and Target objects have the same number of vertices, create a copy of one object and modify it to be a target. Be sure to avoid such modifiers as Tessellate and Optimize, which change the number of vertices. ∎

To morph a Base object into a Target, select the Base object and select Create ⇨ Compound ⇨ Morph. Then click the Pick Target button in the Pick Targets rollout, shown in Figure 27.1, and select a Target object in the viewport. The cursor changes to a plus sign when it is over an acceptable object. Unavailable objects (that have a different number of vertices) cannot be selected. Pick Target options include Copy, Instance, Reference, and Move. (The Move option deletes the original object that is selected.) The Target object appears under the Current Targets rollout in the Morph Targets list.

Each Morph object can have several Target objects. You can use the Pick Target button to select several targets, and the order in which these targets appear in the list is the order in which they are morphed. To delete a Target object, select it from the list and click the Delete Morph Target button. Beneath the list is a Name field where you can change the name of the selected Target object.

FIGURE 27.1

A Morph rollout lets you pick targets and create morph keys.

Creating Morph keys

With a Target object name selected in the Morph Targets list, you can drag the Time Slider to a frame and set a Morph key by clicking the Create Morph Key button found at the bottom of the rollout. This option sets the number of frames used to interpolate among the different morph states.

Note

If the Morph object changes dramatically, set the Morph Keys to include enough frames to interpolate smoothly. ■

If a frame other than 0 is selected when a Target object is picked, a Morph Key is automatically created.

Morph objects versus the Morph modifier

Max includes two different ways to morph an object. You can create a Morph object or apply the Morph modifier to an existing object. The Morph object is different from the Morph modifier, but the results are the same; however, some subtle differences exist between these two.

A Morph object can include multiple Morph targets, but it can be created only once. Each target can have several Morph keys, which makes it easy to control. For example, you could set an object to morph to a different shape and return to its original form with only two Morph keys.

The Morph modifier, on the other hand, can be applied multiple times and works well with other modifiers, but the control for each modifier is buried in the Stack. The Parameters rollout options available for the Morph modifier are much more extensive than for the Morph object, and they include channels and support for a Morph material.

Cross-Reference

You can find more information on the Morph modifier in Chapter 21, "Understanding Animation and Keyframes." ∎

For the best of both worlds, apply the Morph modifier to a Morph object.

Tutorial: Morphing a woman's face

Although this example is fairly simple, it demonstrates a powerful technique that can be very helpful as you begin to animate characters. One of the key uses of morphing is to copy a character and move it about to create a new pose. You can then morph between the different poses to create smooth actions, gestures, or face motions.

To morph a woman's face, follow these steps:

1. Open the Greek woman head morph.max file from the Chap 27 directory on the CD.

   This file includes a woman's head. All objects have been attached to the face object to make working with it easy.

2. Select the head object, and hold down the Shift key while dragging to the right in the Top viewport. In the Clone Options dialog box that opens, select Copy and set the Number of Copies to **2**. Name one copy **frown face** and the other **smiling face**.

3. Select the object named "smiling face," and open the Modify panel. Zoom in around the mouth area, and enable Vertex subobject mode. Enable the Ignore Backfacing option in the Selection rollout, and turn on the Use Soft Selection option in the Soft Selection rollout with a Falloff value of **1.4**. Then select the vertex at the corner of the mouth, and drag it upward in the Front viewport to make the woman smile. Repeat this action for the vertex on the opposite side of the mouth. Click the Vertex subobject button again to exit subobject mode.

4. Select the original head object, and choose Create ➪ Compound ➪ Morph to make this object into a morph object. In the Pick Targets rollout, select the Copy option and click the Pick Target button. Then click the "frown face" object, or press the H key, and select it from the Select Objects dialog box. (Actually, it is the only object that you can select.) Then click the "smiling face" object. Both targets are now added to the list. Click the Pick Target button again to disable pick mode.

5. In the Morph Targets list, select the "frown face" object and click the Create Morph Key button. Then drag the Time Slider (below the viewports) to frame 50, select the "smiling face" object in the Morph Targets list, and press the Create Morph Key button again.

6. Click the Play button (in the Time Controls section at the bottom of the Max window) to see the morph. The woman's head object morphs when you move the Time Slider between frames 0 and 50. Figure 27.2 shows different stages of the morph object.

FIGURE 27.2

A woman's face being morphed to a smile

Creating Conform Objects

Conform compound objects mold one object over the surface of another. This compound object is useful for adding geometric details to objects, such as stitches to a baseball or a quilt.

The object that is modified is called the *Wrapper object.* The other object is the *Wrap-To object.* These objects need to be either mesh objects or objects that you can convert to mesh objects.

Cross-Reference

Another way to mold one object over the surface of another is with the Conform Space Warp. Find out more about this Space Warp in Chapter 42, "Using Space Warps." ■

To create a Conform object, select an object to be the Wrapper object and select Create ➪ Compound ➪ Conform. To select the Wrap-To object, click the Pick Wrap-To Object button in the Pick Wrap-To Object rollout and choose one of the options below the button (Reference, Move, Copy, or Instance).

Caution

Shapes and splines cannot be used as either the Wrapper or Wrap-To objects, even if they are renderable. ■

In the Parameters rollout, shown in Figure 27.3, the Objects section lists both the Wrapper and Wrap-To objects. Name fields are also available for changing the names of both objects.

FIGURE 27.3

The Parameters rollout of the Conform object lets you define how the object is wrapped.

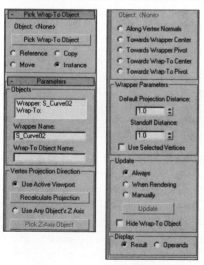

The Wrapper Parameters section includes two adjustable values: Default Projection Distance, which is the distance that the Wrapper moves if it doesn't intersect with the Wrap-To object, and Standoff Distance, which is the distance between the Wrapper and the Wrap-To object. The Use Selected Vertices option causes only the selected vertices passed up the Stack to be moved.

Setting a vertex projection direction

The Parameters rollout also includes controls for specifying the Vertex Projection Direction settings. You can select to project the vertices based on the current active viewport with the Use Active Viewport option. If the view changes, you can use the Recalculate Projection button to compute the new projection direction.

You can also use the local Z-axis of any object in the scene as the projection direction. The Pick Z-Axis Object button lets you select the object to use. After you have selected it, rotating this object can alter the projection direction. The name of the object is displayed below the Pick Z-Axis Object button.

Other projection options include Along Vertex Normals, Towards Wrapper Center, Towards Wrapper Pivot, Towards Wrap-To Center, and Towards Wrap-To Pivot. The Along Vertex Normals option sets the projection direction opposite the Wrapper's normals. The other options set the direction toward the center or pivot of the Wrapper or Wrap-To objects.

Tutorial: Placing a facial scar

As an example of the Conform object, you'll add a gruesome scar to the face of a character. Using the Conform compound object, details like this scar can be a mesh object and still perfectly match the contour of the face object.

To create a facial scar using the Conform object, follow these steps:

1. Open the Facial scar.max file from the Chap 27 directory on the CD.

   This file includes a face mesh with a mesh scar placed to its side. The face mesh was created by Viewpoint Datalabs.

2. Click the Select and Move button on the main toolbar, and select and move the scar to position it in front of the face mesh in the Front and Top viewports.

3. With the scar selected, choose the Create ⇨ Compound ⇨ Conform menu command.

4. Under the Parameters rollout, select the Use Active Viewport option and make sure that the Front viewport is active. In the Wrapper Parameters section, set the Standoff Distance value to **3.0**.

5. Click the Pick Wrap-To Object button, and click the face mesh. Select the Instance option.

6. The mesh gets the default object color, but you can see the original materials if you select the Display Operands option at the bottom of the Parameters rollout.

Tip

After using the Conform compound object, the object type is set to Conform, but if you collapse the stack to an Editable Poly, you'll be able to edit the resulting object. ■

Figure 27.4 shows a close-up of the surgery in the maximized Perspective view.

FIGURE 27.4

A patch grid being conformed to the front of a face object

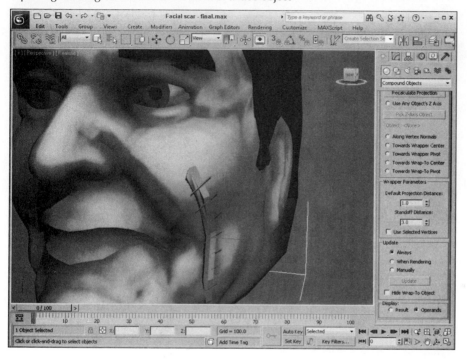

Creating a ShapeMerge Object

The ShapeMerge compound object enables you to use a spline shape as a cookie cutter to extract a portion of a mesh object. This button is enabled only if a mesh object and a spline exist in the scene. To use this object, select a mesh object and click the Pick Shape button in the Pick Operand rollout, and then select a spline shape. The shape can be a Reference, Move, Instance, or Copy.

The spline shape is always projected toward its negative Z-axis. By rotating and positioning the spline before selecting it, you can apply it to different sides of an object. You can apply multiple shapes to the same mesh object.

Caution

If you're using the Nitrous display driver, you may need to convert the ShapeMerge object to an Editable Poly object before it displays correctly in the viewports. ■

The Parameters rollout, shown in Figure 27.5, displays each mesh and shape object in a list. You can also rename either object using the Name field. The Extract Operand button lets you separate either object as an Instance or a Copy.

FIGURE 27.5

Use the Parameters rollout for the ShapeMerge compound object to cut or merge a shape.

Cookie Cutter and Merge options

The Operations group includes options for cutting the mesh, including Cookie Cutter and Merge. The Cookie Cutter option cuts the shape out of the mesh surface, and the Merge option combines the spline with the mesh. You can also Invert the operation to remove the inside or outside of the selected area.

Like the Boolean Subtraction operations, the Cookie Cutter option can remove sections of the mesh, but it uses the area defined by a spline instead of a volume defined by a mesh object. The Merge option is useful for marking an area for selection. Figure 27.6 shows a ShapeMerge object with the Cookie Cutter option selected.

Note
You can use the Merge option to create a precise face object that can be used with the Connect object. ■

The Output Sub-Mesh Selection option lets you pass the selection up the Stack for additional modifiers. Options include None, Face, Edge, and Vertex.

Note
To see the backsides of the faces, right-click the object, select Properties from the pop-up menu, and disable the Backface Cull option. ■

Tutorial: Using the ShapeMerge compound object

When outlined text is imported into Max, it typically contains letters that have shapes within shapes. For example, the letter *p*, when outlined, includes the outline of the letter *p* and a circle shape to denote the interior section of the letter. When outline text like this is converted to a mesh object, both the letter outline and its interior section are covered, making the text illegible. You can use the ShapeMerge compound object to remedy this tricky situation.

You can practice handling this situation using the logo for the fictional Box It Up company. Before this logo can be extruded, you need to do some work involving the ShapeMerge object.

A ShapeMerge object using the Cookie Cutter option

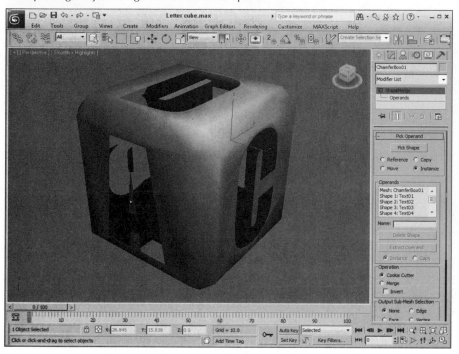

To use the ShapeMerge object to remove the center area from an extrusion, follow these steps:

1. Open the Box It Up Co logo.max file from the Chap 27 directory on the CD.

2. Select all the letters in the logo, press the Alt key, and deselect the interior shapes in the B, O, and P letters. Then apply the Modifiers ⇨ Mesh Editing ⇨ Extrude modifier with an Amount value of 0.010 feet.

3. Select the letter B shape again. Then select the Create ⇨ Compound ⇨ ShapeMerge menu command.

4. Set the Operation to Cookie Cutter, and click the Pick Shape button in the Pick Operand roll-out with the Copy option. Select the two interior shapes for the letter B. Then click the Select Object button on the main toolbar again to exit ShapeMerge mode. Then repeat this step for the letters O and P.

5. If the interior of the ShapeMerge letters is still visible, select each and convert it to an Editable Poly object by right-clicking its type in the Modifier Stack and selecting Editable Poly.

Figure 27.7 shows the finished logo. Notice that the letters have the interior sections removed.

FIGURE 27.7

The logo with the interior centers removed from extruded letters using the ShapeMerge object

Creating a Terrain Object

The Terrain object is a great object that enables you to create terrains from splines representing elevation contours. These contour splines can be created in Max or imported using a format like AutoCAD's DWG. If the splines are created in Max, make sure that each contour spline is a separate object. The splines all must be closed splines. If all the splines have an equal number of vertices, then the resulting terrain object is much cleaner. You can ensure this by copying and scaling the base spline.

To create a terrain, create splines at varying elevations, select all the splines, and click the Terrain button. The Terrain button is available only if closed splines are selected. You can use the Pick Operand button in the Pick Operand rollout to select additional splines to add to the Terrain object. All splines in the object become operands and are displayed in the Operands list.

The Form group includes three options that determine how the terrain is formed: Graded Surface, Graded Solid, and Layered Solid. The Graded Surface option displays a surface grid over the contour splines; the Graded Solid adds a bottom to the object; and the Layered Solid displays each contour as a flat, terraced area. The Stitch Border option causes polygons to be created to close open splines by creating a single edge that closes the spline. The Retriangulate option optimizes how the polygons are divided to better represent the contours.

The Display group includes options to display the Terrain mesh, the Contour lines, or Both. You can also specify how you want to update the terrain.

The Simplification rollout lets you alter the resolution of the terrain by selecting how many vertical and horizontal points and lines to use. Options include using all points (no simplification), half of the points, a quarter of the points, twice the points, or four times the points.

Coloring elevations

The Color by Elevation rollout, shown in Figure 27.8, displays as reference the Maximum and Minimum Elevations. Between these is a Reference Elevation value, which is the location where the landmass meets the water. Entering a Reference Elevation and clicking the Create Defaults button automatically creates several separate color zones. You can add, modify, or delete zones using the Add, Modify, or Delete Zone buttons.

FIGURE 27.8

The Color by Elevation rollout lets you change the color for different elevations.

You can access each color zone from a list. To change a zone's color, select it and click the color swatch. You can set colors to Blend to the Color Above or to be Solid to Top of Zone.

Tutorial: Creating an island with the Terrain compound object

In this tutorial, you create a simple island. The Color by Elevation rollout makes distinguishing the water from the land easy.

To create an island using the Terrain object, follow these steps:

1. Select Create ➪ Shapes ➪ Ellipse, and drag in the Top view to create several ellipses of various sizes representing the contours of the island.

   The first ellipse you create should be the largest, and the ellipses should get progressively smaller.

2. In the Left view, select and move the ellipses up and down so that the largest one is on the bottom and the smallest one is on top. You can create two smaller hills by including two ellipses at the same level.

Note

If you create the ellipses in the proper order from largest to smallest, then you can use the Select All command. If not, then select the splines in the order that they'll be connected from top to bottom before clicking on the Terrain button. ∎

3. Use the Edit ➪ Select All (Ctrl+A) menu command to select all the ellipses, and select Create ➪ Compound ➪ Terrain.

   The ellipses automatically join together. Joining all the ellipses forms the island.

4. In the Color by Elevation rollout, select a Reference Elevation of **5** and click the Create Defaults button.

   This automatically creates color zones for the island. The elevation values for each zone are displayed in a list within the Color by Elevation rollout. Selecting an elevation value in the list displays its color in the color swatch.

5. Select each elevation value individually, and set all Zones to Blend to the Color Above option for all zones, except for the Zone with the lightest blue.

   This creates a distinct break between the sea and the land of the island.

Figure 27.9 shows the final terrain. In an example later in this chapter, you'll use the Scatter compound object to add trees to the small terrain island.

Using the Mesher Object

You can use the Mesher compound object to convert objects to mesh objects on the fly as an animation progresses. This feature is useful for objects such as particle systems. After you convert the object to a mesh object, you can apply modifiers that weren't possible before, such as Optimize, UVW Map, and others.

Another benefit of the Mesher object is that you can apply several complex modifiers to a single Mesher object and load it to a particle system rather than applying the modifiers to all the pieces that make up a particle system.

The Parameters rollout of the Mesher object includes a Pick Object button. Click this button, and select an object in the viewport to make the selected object an instance of the Mesher object. This action does not delete the original object, and the Mesher instance is oriented to the Mesher object's coordinate system. The object name then appears on the button. You can change the object by clicking the button again and selecting a new object.

Caution

Do not delete the original object, or the Mesher instance also disappears. If you want to render only the Mesher instance, then select the original object and hide it using the Tools ➪ Display Floater command. ∎

The Time Offset is the number of the frames ahead (values can be negative) or behind the original object that the animation should progress. If the Build Only at Render Time option is set, then the Mesher instance is not visible in the viewports but shows up in the final rendered image. You can use the Update button to manually force an update of the Mesher instance after the settings for the original object have been modified.

FIGURE 27.9

A Terrain island created with the Terrain compound object

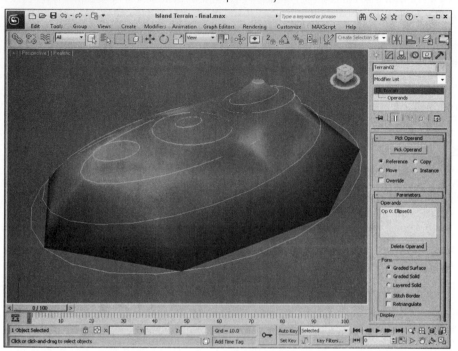

When you use the Mesher object to create an instance of a particle system, the bounding box of the particle system as it streams the particles becomes long and thin over time. This long, thin bounding box can potentially cause problems with certain modifiers. You can prevent these problems by selecting an alternative bounding box that doesn't change over time. To select a new bounding box, select the Custom Bounding Box option, click the Pick Bounding Box button, and click an object in the viewport. You can select the original object as the new bounding box. With the Mesher object selected, the bounding box is shown in orange wherever it is located. The corner coordinates of the custom bounding box are displayed under the Pick Bounding Box button. Mesher objects can also be used as Particle Flow events, using the Add and Remove buttons at the bottom of the Parameters rollout.

Cross-Reference

Chapter 41, "Creating Particles and Particle Flow," provides more information on working with particle systems. ■

Working with BlobMesh Objects

BlobMesh objects are simple spheres. If you have only one of them, they aren't interesting at all, but if you get them together, they run into each other much like the metal mercury. This makes them an ideal choice for modeling flowing liquids and soft organic shapes.

BlobMesh objects are used as sets of objects rather than as individual objects. If you click the BlobMesh button in the Compound Objects subcategory and then create a BlobMesh in the viewports, it appears as a sphere with the radius set using the Size parameter. The real benefit comes from clicking the Pick or Add buttons below the Blob Objects list and selecting an object in the scene.

Note
The Pick, Add, and Remove buttons become enabled only in the Modify panel. ∎

The object that is picked is added to the Blob Objects list, and each vertex of the object gets a BlobMesh added to it. If the BlobMesh objects are large enough to overlap, then the entire object is covered with these objects, and they run together to form a flowing mass of particles.

Setting BlobMesh parameters

The Size value sets the radius of the BlobMesh object. Larger sizes result in more overlapping of surrounding objects. For particle systems, the Size is discounted, and the size of the particles determines the size of the BlobMesh objects. The Tension value sets how loose or tight the surface of the BlobMesh object is. Small tension values result in looser objects that more readily flow together.

The Evaluation Coarseness value sets how dense the BlobMesh objects will be. By enabling the Relative Coarseness option, the density of the objects changes as the size of the objects changes. The Coarseness values can be different for the viewport and the Render engine.

When a BlobMesh object is selected and applied to the picked object, each vertex has an object attached to it, but if you apply a selection modifier, such as the Mesh Select modifier, to the picked object, then only the selected subobjects get a BlobMesh object. You also can use the Soft Selection option to select those subobjects adjacent to the selected subobjects. The Minimum Size value is the smallest-sized BlobMesh object that is used when Soft Selection is enabled.

The Large Data Optimization option is a quicker, more efficient way of rendering a huge set of BlobMesh objects. The benefit from this method comes when more than 2,000 BlobMesh objects need to be rendered. If the viewport updates are slow because of the number of BlobMesh objects, you can select to turn them Off in Viewport.

Cross-Reference
When BlobMesh objects are applied to a particle system, they can be used as part of a Particle Flow workflow. The Particle Flow Parameters rollout includes a list of events to apply to the BlobMesh objects. Particle Flow is covered in detail in Chapter 41, "Creating Particles and Particle Flow." ∎

Tutorial: Creating icy geometry with BlobMesh

The BlobMesh object can be combined with a geometry object to create the effect of an object that has been frozen in ice. Using the BlobMesh's Pick feature, you can select a geometry object, and a BlobMesh is placed at each vertex of the object. I suggest using an object with a fairly limited number of vertices.

To create the effect of an object covered in ice, follow these steps:

1. Open the Icy sled.max file from the Chap 27 directory on the CD.

   This file includes a sled model created by Viewpoint Datalabs.

2. With the sled selected, choose Create ➪ Compound ➪ BlobMesh, and create a simple BlobMesh by simply clicking in the Top viewport. Set the Size value to **6.0**. Then right-click to exit BlobMesh mode, click the Pick button in the Parameters rollout, and select the Sled object.

3. Press the M key to open the Material Editor, and select the first sample slot. Change the Diffuse color to a light blue, and set the Opacity to **20**. Then increase the Specular Level to **90** and the Glossiness to **40**, and apply the material to the BlobMesh object.

4. Render the Perspective View window to see the final result. The sled is embedded in ice.

Figure 27.10 shows the resulting sled, all ready to be defrosted.

FIGURE 27.10

BlobMesh objects can be used to cover objects in ice.

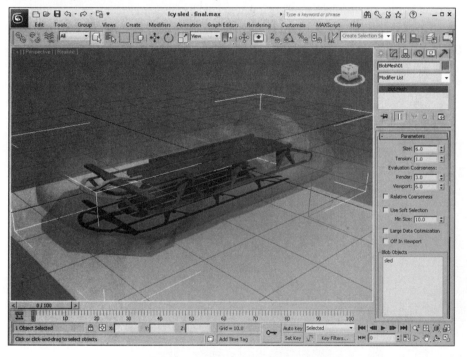

Creating a Scatter Object

A Scatter object spreads multiple copies of the object about the scene or within a defined area. The object that is scattered is called the *Source object,* and the area where the scatter objects can be placed is defined by a *Distribution object.*

Cross-Reference

Particle systems, which are discussed in Chapter 41, "Creating Particles and Particle Flow," can also create many duplicate objects, but you have more control over the placement of objects with a Scatter object. ∎

To create a Scatter object, choose an object that will be scattered over the surface and select the Create ⇨ Compound ⇨ Scatter menu command. The selected object becomes the Source object. A roll-out then opens, in which you can select the Distribution object or use defined transforms.

Under the Scatter Objects rollout, the Objects section lists the Source and Distribution objects. Name fields are also available for changing the name of either object. The Extract Operand button is available only in the Modify panel; it lets you select an operand from the list and make a copy or instance of it.

Note

The placement of the Source object on the distribution object is determined by the Source object's pivot point. ∎

Working with Source objects

The Source object is the object that is to be duplicated. Figure 27.11 shows a Cylinder primitive scattered over a spherical Distribution object with 500 duplicates. The Perpendicular and Distribute Using Even options are set.

FIGURE 27.11

A Scatter object made of a Cylinder spread over an area defined by a sphere

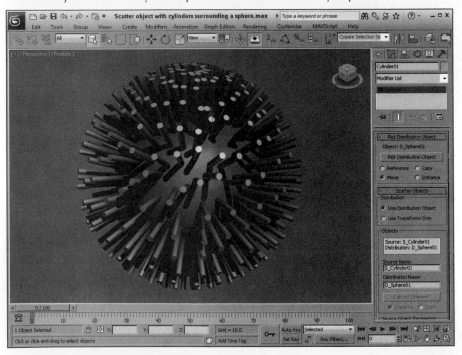

In the Scatter Objects rollout are several parameters for controlling the Source object. In the Source Object Parameters section, the Duplicates value specifies how many objects to scatter. You can also specify a Base Scale and the Vertex Chaos values. The Base Scale is the value that the object is scaled to before being scattered. All new objects are scaled equally to this value. The Vertex Chaos button randomly distributes the object vertices.

The Animation Offset defines the number of frames between a new duplicate and the previous one.

Note
If you look closely at a Scatter object, you'll notice that both the Source and Distribution objects have the same object color. To color them differently, use the Multi/Sub-Object Material. ■

Working with Distribution objects

To select a Distribution object, click the Pick Distribution Object button and select an object in the viewport. (Make sure that the Use Distribution Object option is selected in the Scatter Objects rollout.) You can specify the Distribution object as a Copy, Instance, Reference, or Move.

Under the Distribution Object Parameters section are several options for controlling the Distribution object. The Perpendicular option causes the Source objects to be aligned perpendicular to the Distribution object. If the Perpendicular option is disabled, the orientation remains the same as that of the default Source object. Figure 27.12 shows the same Scatter object as in the preceding figure, but with several different options.

A Scatter object with different options: Base Scale at 20%, Vertex Chaos at 2.0, Perpendicular option disabled, and Duplicates at 100

The Use Selected Faces Only option enables you to select the faces over which the duplicates are positioned. The Selected Faces are those passed up the Stack by the Mesh Select modifier.

Other Distribution object parameter options include Area, Even, Skip N, Random Faces, Along Edges, All Vertices, All Edge Midpoints, All Face Centers, and Volume. The Area option evenly distributes the objects over the surface area, and the Even option places duplicates over every other face. The Skip N option lets you specify how many faces to skip before placing an object. The Random Faces and Along Edges options randomly distribute the duplicates around the Distribution object. The All Vertices, All Edge Midpoints, and All Face Centers options ignore the Duplicates value (which specifies the number of duplicates) and place a duplicate at every vertex, edge midpoint, and face. Figure 27.13 shows several of these options.

FIGURE 27.13

A Scatter object with different distribution options: Area, Skip N where N=7, Random Faces, All Vertices, and All Face Centers

All the options described thus far place the duplicates on the surface of the object, but the Volume option scatters the duplicates inside the Distribution object's volume.

Setting Transforms

The Transforms rollout is used to specify the individual transformation limits of the duplicate objects. For example, if the Z-axis value is set to 90, then each new duplicate is randomly rotated about its local Z-axis at a distance somewhere between –90 and 90.

You can use these transformations with a Distribution object or by themselves if the Use Transforms Only option is selected under the Scatter Objects rollout. The Use Maximum Range option causes all three axes to adopt the same value. The Lock Aspect Ratio option maintains the relative dimensions of the Source object to ensure uniform scaling.

Speeding updates with a proxy

Working with a large number of duplicates can slow the viewport updates to a crawl. To speed these updates, select the Proxy option in the Display rollout. This option replaces each duplicate with a wedge-shaped object. For example, if you used the Scatter object to place people on a sidewalk, you can use the Proxy option to display simple cylinders in the viewports instead of the details of the person mesh.

Another way to speed the viewport updates is to use the Display spinner. Using this spinner, you can select a percentage of the total number of duplicates to display in the viewport. The rendered image still uses the actual number specified.

The Hide Distribution Object option lets you make the Distribution object visible or invisible. The Seed value is used to determine the randomness of the objects.

Loading and saving presets

With all the various parameters, the Load/Save Presets rollout enables you to Save, Load, or Delete various presets. You can use saved presets with another Source object.

Tutorial: Covering the island with trees

You can combine several different types of compound objects to create interesting effects. In this tutorial, you use the Scatter object to add trees to the Terrain object island created earlier in this chapter.

To add trees to the island with the Scatter object, follow these steps:

1. Open the Island terrain with trees.max file from the Chap 27 directory on the CD.

   This file is the same island terrain example that you completed earlier in this chapter, but it also has a simple tree added to it.

2. With the tree object selected, select the Create ⇨ Compound ⇨ Scatter menu command.

3. Click the Pick Distribution Object button, and select the island terrain. Set the number of Duplicates to **100,** and disable the Perpendicular option.

   All the trees now stand upright.

4. Select the Random Faces option.

   The trees become denser around the hills where there are more faces.

Figure 27.14 shows the island with the trees.

Using the Scatter object, you can add trees to your island terrain.

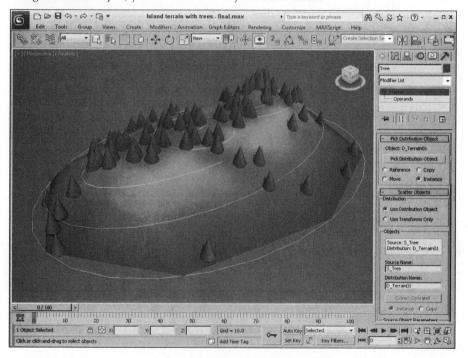

Creating Connect Objects

A Connect object is useful for building a connecting bridge between two separate objects. Each object must have an open face or hole that specifies where the two objects are to be connected.

To use this object, delete a face on two Editable Mesh objects and then position the holes across from each other. Select one of the objects, and choose the Create ⇨ Compound ⇨ Connect menu command. Then, click the Pick Operand button, and select the second object. The Connect object builds the additional faces required to connect the two holes.

Filling object holes

If multiple holes exist between the objects, the Connect object attempts to patch them all. You can also use the button several times to connect a single object to multiple objects.

Caution
The Connect object doesn't work well with NURBS (Non-Uniform Rational B-Splines) objects. ■

The Parameters rollout includes a list of all the operands or objects involved in the connection. You can delete any of these with the Delete Operand button. The Extract Operand button lets you separate the Operand object from the Connect object.

In the Interpolation section, the Segments value is the number of segments used to create the bridge section, and the Tension value is the amount of curvature to use in an attempt to smooth the connected bridge.

The Bridge Smoothing option smoothes the faces of the bridge, and the Ends option smoothes where the bridge and the original objects connect.

Tutorial: Creating a park bench

The Connect object is best used between two symmetrical copies of an object that need to be attached, as with a table or bridge. For this tutorial, you use the Connect object to create a park bench between two end pieces.

Note
Although the Connect compound object works fine, it requires that both holes have the same number of vertices. A more robust solution is the Editable Poly's Bridge feature. ■

To connect two ends of a park bench, follow these steps:

1. Open the Park bench.max file from the Chap 27 directory on the CD.

   This file includes symmetrical ends of the park bench. One end was created by extruding a spline shape and using the ShapeMerge tool to cut matching holes on the inner-facing surfaces. The Mirror tool was then used to create and rotate the symmetrical clone.

2. Select one end of the park bench, and select the Create ⇨ Compound ⇨ Connect menu command.

3. In the Pick Operand rollout, click the Pick Operand button, select the Move option, and click on the opposite side of the park bench.

   The two end pieces connect.

4. In the Parameters rollout, select the Smoothing: Bridge option to smooth the seat of the bench.

Figure 27.15 shows the resulting park bench.

FIGURE 27.15

A Connect compound object can join two open holes in separate objects.

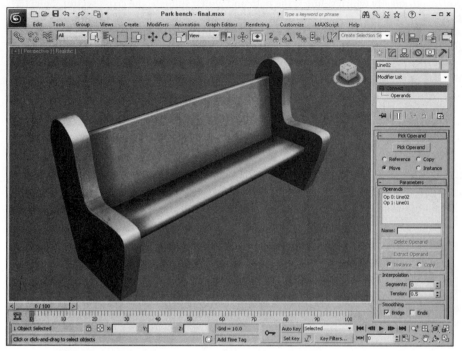

Creating a Loft Object

Lofting is a term that comes from the shipbuilding industry. It describes a method for building ships that creates and positions the cross sections and then attaches a surface or skin along the length of the cross sections.

To create a Loft object, you need to have at least two spline shapes: one shape that defines the path of the Loft and another shape that defines its cross section. After the shapes are created, select the Create ⇨ Compound menu command. A Loft button is enabled if two or more splines are present in the viewport.

Tip

Be aware of the orientation of the cross-section shape and the loft path before the loft is applied. The cross section's local Z-axis is always aligned with the path's local Y-axis. By making the correct orientations before applying the loft, you can save some headache. If the orientations aren't correct, you can edit the pivot on either object. ■

Using the Get Shape and Get Path buttons

After you click the Loft button, the Creation Method rollout displays the Get Path and Get Shape buttons, which you use to specify which spline is the path and which spline is the cross section. Select a spline, and then click either the Get Path button or the Get Shape button. If you click the Get Shape button, the selected spline is the path, and the next spline shape you select is the cross section. If you click the Get Path button, the selected spline is the shape, and the next spline shape you select is the path.

Note

After you click the Get Path or Get Shape button, although the cursor changes when you're over a valid spline, not all spline shapes can be used to create Loft objects. For example, you cannot use a spline created with the Donut button as a path. ■

When creating a Loft object with the Get Shape and Get Path buttons, you can specify either to Move the spline shape or to create a Copy or an Instance of it. The Move option replaces both splines with a Loft object. The Copy option leaves both splines in the viewport and creates a new Loft object. The Instance option maintains a link between the spline and the Loft object. This link enables you to modify the original spline. The Loft object is updated automatically.

The vertex order of the path spline is important. The Loft object is created starting at the vertex numbered 1.

Note

You can tell which vertex is the first by enabling Vertex Numbering in the Selection rollout of an editable spline. The first vertex is also identified with a yellow box. ■

Controlling surface parameters

All Loft objects include the Surface Parameters rollout. Using this rollout, you can set the smoothing of the Loft object with two different options: Smooth Length and Smooth Width. You can use the Mapping options to control the mapping of textures by setting values for the number of times the map repeats over the Length or Width of the Loft. The Normalize option applies the map to the surface evenly or proportionately according to the shape's vertex spacing. You can set the Loft object to automatically generate Material and Shape IDs, and you can specify the output of the Loft to be either a Patch or Mesh.

Changing path parameters

The Path Parameters rollout, shown in Figure 27.16, lets you position several different cross-sectional shapes at different positions along the Loft path. The Path value indicates either the Distance or Percentage along the path where this new shape should be located. The Snap option, if turned on, enables you to snap to consistent distances along the path. The Path Steps option enables you to place new shapes at steps along the path where the vertices are located. Each path will have a different number of steps, depending on its complexity.

FIGURE 27.16

The Loft compound object rollouts

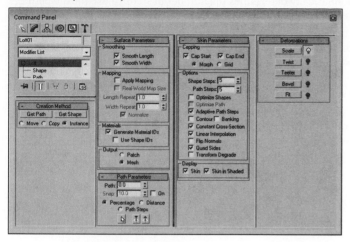

The viewport displays a small yellow X at the location where the new cross-sectional shape will be inserted. At the bottom of the rollout are three buttons, which are illustrated and described in Table 27.1.

TABLE 27.1

Path Rollout Buttons

Toolbar Button	Name	Description
	Pick Shape	Selects a new cross-section spline to be inserted at the specified location
	Previous Shape	Moves to the previous cross-section shape along the Loft path
	Next Shape	Moves to the next cross-section shape along the Loft path

Setting skin parameters

The Skin Parameters rollout includes many options for determining the complexity of the Loft skin. You can specify whether to cap either end of the Loft using the Cap Start and/or Cap End options. The caps can be either Morph or Grid type.

This rollout also includes the following options for controlling the look of the skin:

- **Shape and Path Steps:** Sets the number of segments that appear in each spline's cross-sectional shape and between each division along the path. The straight segments are ignored if the Optimize Path option is selected.

719

- **Optimize Shapes and Paths:** Reduces the Loft's complexity by deleting any unneeded edges or vertices.
- **Adaptive Path Steps:** Automatically determines the number of steps to use for the path in order to maintain a smooth curve.
- **Contour:** Determines how the cross-sectional shapes line up with the path. If this option is enabled, the cross section is aligned to be perpendicular to the path at all times. If disabled, this option causes the cross-sectional shapes to maintain their orientation as the path is traversed.
- **Banking:** Causes the cross-section shape to rotate as the path bends.
- **Constant Cross-Section:** Scales the cross-sectional shapes in order to maintain a uniform width along the path. Turning off this option causes the cross sections to pinch at any sharp angles along the path.
- **Linear Interpolation:** Causes straight linear edges to appear between different cross-sectional shapes. Turning off this option causes smooth curves to connect various shapes.
- **Flip Normals:** Used to correct difficulties that would appear with the normals. Often the normals are flipped accidentally when the Loft is created.
- **Quad Sides:** Creates four-sided polygons to connect to adjacent cross-section shapes with the same number of sides.
- **Transform Degrade:** Makes the Loft skin disappear when subobjects are transformed. This feature can help you better visualize the cross-sectional area while it is being moved.

The Display options at the bottom of the Skin Parameters rollout give you the choice of displaying the skin in all viewports or displaying the Loft skin only in the viewports with shading turned on.

Tutorial: Designing a slip-proof hanger

As an example of creating a Loft object with different cross-sectional shapes, you'll design a new hanger that includes some rough edges along its bottom section to keep slacks from sliding off.

To design a hanger Loft object with different cross sections, follow these steps:

1. Open the Lofted slip-proof hanger.max file from the Chap 27 directory on the CD.

   This file includes a spline outline of a hanger and two simple shapes.

2. Select the hanger spline, and choose the Create ⇨ Compound ⇨ Loft menu command.

3. In the Creation Method rollout, click the Get Shape button and then click the small circle shape (make sure that the Copy option is selected).

   This lofts the entire hanger with a circular cross section.

4. In the Path Parameters rollout, select the Path Steps option. A dialog box appears warning that this may change the relocate shapes. Click Yes to continue. Increment the Path value until the yellow X marker in the viewport is positioned at the beginning of the hanger's bottom bar (at Step 53 for this tutorial). Click the Get Shape button again, and click the small circular shape again.

   This extends the circular cross section from the start at Step 0 to Step 53.

5. Increment the Path value by 1 to Step 54, click the Get Shape button, and select the star shape. This makes the remainder of the hanger use a star-shaped cross section. Increment the Path value again to the end of the hanger's bottom bar (at Step 60), click the Get Shape button, and select the star shape again to end the star cross section.

Note

If you forget to start and end a section with the same cross section, the loft blends between the two different cross sections. ∎

6. In the Path Parameters rollout, increment the Path value a final time to Step 61, click the Get Shape button, and click the circular shape. Click the Pick Shape icon button at the bottom of the Path Parameters dialog box to change the cross section of the hanger to the end of the path. Right-click in the viewport to exit Get Shape mode.

Figure 27.17 shows the finished designer hanger.

FIGURE 27.17

A lofted hanger created with two different cross-sectional shapes

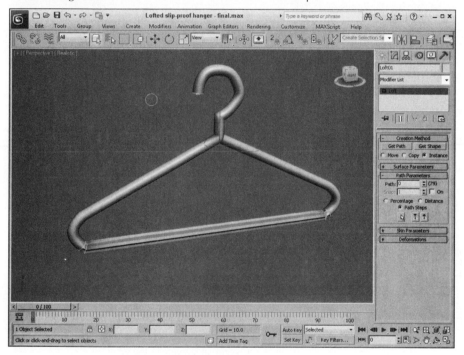

Deforming Loft objects

When you select a Loft object and open the Modify panel, the Deformation rollout appears. This rollout includes five buttons that let you Scale, Twist, Teeter, Bevel, and Fit the cross-section shapes along the path. All five buttons open similar graph windows that include control points and a line that represents the amount of the effect to apply. Next to each button is a toggle button with a light switch on it. This button enables or disables the respective effect.

The Deformation window interface

All five deformation options use the same basic window and controls. The vertical lines within the window represent the placement of vertices on the loft path. As an example of the Deformation window interface, Figure 27.18 shows the Scale Deformation window.

FIGURE 27.18

The Deformation dialog box interface lets you control the cross section over the length of the path.

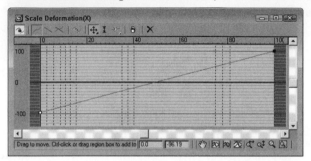

Dragging the curve directly can modify the deformation curve. You can also insert control points at any location along the curve. These control points can be one of three different types: Corner, Bézier Corner, or Bézier Smooth. Bézier type points have handles for controlling the curvature at the point. To change the point type, select the point and right-click. Then make your selection from the pop-up menu. The end points must always be either Corner or Bézier Corner type.

To move a control point, select and drag it or enter a horizontal and/or vertical value in the fields at the bottom of the window.

Table 27.2 describes the buttons at the top of the Deformation window.

TABLE 27.2

Deformation Dialog Box Buttons

Toolbar Button	Name	Description
	Make Symmetrical	Links the two curves so that changes made to one curve are also made to the other
	Display X-Axis	Makes the line controlling the X-axis visible
	Display Y-Axis	Makes the line controlling the Y-axis visible
	Display XY axes	Makes both lines visible
	Swap Deform Curves	Switches the lines
	Move Control Point	Enables you to move control points, and includes flyouts for horizontal and vertical movements

Toolbar Button	Name	Description
	Scale Control Point	Scales the selected control point
	Insert Corner Point, Insert Bézier Point	Inserts new points on a deformation curve
	Delete Control Point	Deletes the current control point
	Reset Curve	Returns the original curve
	Pan	Pans the curve as the mouse is dragged
	Zoom Extents	Zooms to display the entire curve
	Zoom Horizontal Extents	Zooms to display the entire horizontal curve range
	Zoom Vertical Extents	Zooms to display the entire vertical curve range
	Zoom Horizontally	Zooms on the horizontal curve range
	Zoom Vertically	Zooms on the vertical curve range
	Zoom	Zooms in and out as the mouse is dragged
	Zoom Region	Zooms to the region specified by the mouse

Note

Several buttons are disabled on the Twist and Bevel Deformation windows because these dialog boxes have only one deformation curve. ■

At the bottom of the Deformation dialog boxes are two value fields. The value fields display the X and Y coordinate values for the currently selected point. The navigation buttons enable you to pan and zoom within the dialog box.

Figures 27.19 and 27.20 show the various deformation options applied to a lofted column.

FIGURE 27.19

The Loft compound object deformation options: Scale, Twist, and Teeter

FIGURE 27.20

The Loft compound object deformation options: Bevel and Fit

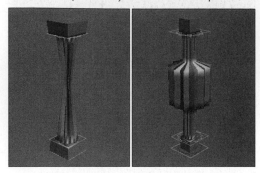

Scale Deformation

The Scale Deformation window can alter the relative scale of the Loft object at any point along its path. This window includes two lines: one red and one green. The red line displays the X-axis scale, and the green line displays the Y-axis scale. By default, both lines are positioned equally at the 100 percent value. Specifying a value greater than 100 percent increases the scale, and specifying a value less than 100 percent has the opposite effect.

Twist Deformation

The Twist Deformation rotates one cross section relative to the others along the shape's local Z-axis and can be used to create an object that spirals along its path. This option is similar to the Banking option, which can also produce rotations about the path.

The Twist Deformation window includes only one red line representing the rotation value. By default, this line is set to a 0-degree rotation value. Positive values result in counterclockwise rotations, and negative values have the opposite effect.

Teeter Deformation

Teeter Deformation rotates a cross section so that its outer edges move closer to the path. This is done by rotating the cross section about its local X-axis or Y-axis. The result is similar to that produced by the Contour option.

The Teeter Deformation window includes two lines: one red and one green. The red line displays the X-axis rotation, and the green line displays the Y-axis rotation. By default, both lines are positioned equally at the 0-degree value. Positive values result in counterclockwise rotations, and negative values have the opposite effect.

Bevel Deformation

Bevel Deformation bevels the cross-section shapes. To bevel an edge is to round the edge so it is smooth by adding more parallel edges. The Bevel Deformation window includes only one red line representing the amount of bevel applied. By default, this line is set to a 0 value. Positive values increase the bevel amount, which equals a reduction in the shape area, and negative values have the opposite effect.

You can also use the Bevel Deformation window to select three different types of beveling: Normal, Adaptive Linear, and Adaptive Cubic. Table 27.3 shows and describes the buttons for these three beveling types. You can select them from a flyout at the right end of the window.

TABLE 27.3

Bevel Deformation Buttons

Toolbar Button	Name	Description
	Normal Bevel	Produces a normal bevel with parallel edges, regardless of the path angle
	Adaptive (Linear)	Alters the bevel linearly, based on the path angle
	Adaptive (Cubic)	Alters the bevel using a cubic spline, based on the path angle

Fit Deformation

The Fit Deformation window, shown in Figure 27.21, lets you specify a profile for the outer edges of the cross-section shapes to follow. This window includes two lines: one red and one green. The red line displays the X-axis scale, and the green line displays the Y-axis scale. By default, both lines are positioned equally at the 100 percent value. Specifying a value that is greater than 100 percent increases the scale, and specifying a value less than 100 percent has the opposite effect.

Note

When using the Fit deformation, you cannot make the surface go backward on the path. ∎

FIGURE 27.21

A Loft object with Fit Deformation applied

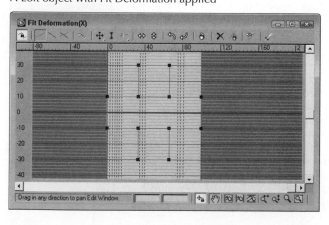

The Fit Deformation window includes ten buttons unique to it that are used to control the profile curves. These buttons are illustrated and described in Table 27.4.

TABLE 27.4

Fit Deformation Dialog Box Buttons

Toolbar Button	Name	Description
	Mirror Horizontally	Mirrors the selection horizontally
	Mirror Vertically	Mirrors the selection vertically
	Rotate 90 degrees CCW	Rotates the selection 90 degrees counterclockwise
	Rotate 90 degrees CW	Rotates the selection 90 degrees clockwise
	Delete Control Point	Deletes the selected control point
	Reset Curve	Returns the curve to its original form
	Delete Curve	Deletes the selected curve
	Get Shape	Selects a separate spline to use as a profile
	Generate Path	Replaces the current path with a straight line
	Lock Aspect	Maintains the relationship between height and width

Modifying Loft subobjects

When you select a Loft object, you can work with its subobjects in the Modify panel. The subobjects for a Loft include Path and Shape. The Path subobject opens the Path Commands rollout. This rollout has only a single button—Put—for creating a copy of the Loft path. If you click this button, the Put To Scene dialog box appears, enabling you to give the path a name and select to create it as a Copy or an Instance.

If your path is created as an Instance, you can edit it to control the Loft path.

Tip

Scaling or transforming a cross section has no effect on the Loft because there isn't any way to access the shape transform. If you add an XForm modifier on the cross section, then you can control its transform after it is lofted. ∎

The Shape subobject opens the Shape Commands rollout. This rollout also includes a Put button along with some additional controls. The Path Level value adjusts the shape's position on the path. The Compare button opens the Compare dialog box, which is discussed in the following section. The Reset button returns the shape to its former state before any rotation or scaling has taken place, and the Delete button deletes the shape entirely.

Note

You cannot delete a shape if it is the only shape in the Loft object. ∎

The Shape Commands rollout also includes six Align buttons for aligning the shape to the Center, Default, Left, Right, Top, and Bottom. For the Loft object local coordinates, Left and Right move the shape along the X-axis, and Top and Bottom move it along the Y-axis.

Comparing shapes

The Compare dialog box superimposes selected cross-sectional shapes included in a Loft object on top of one another to check their center alignment. The button in the upper-left corner is the Pick Shape button. This button lets you select which shapes to display in the dialog box. The button to its right is the Reset button, for removing a shape from the dialog box. Figure 27.22 shows the Compare dialog box with the two shapes from the pillar example selected. Notice that the first vertices on these two shapes are in different locations. This causes the strange twisting at both the top and bottom of the pillar.

FIGURE 27.22

You can use the Compare dialog box to align shapes included in a Loft.

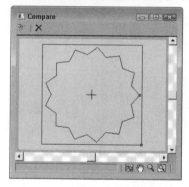

Note

You can align these two vertices by subdividing the square shape in Edit Spline mode and selecting a new first vertex with the Make First button. ∎

While the Compare dialog box is open, the Align buttons in the Shape Commands rollout are still active, and you can use them to move and position the shapes. The first vertex on each shape is shown as a small square. If these vertices aren't correctly aligned on top of one another, then the resulting Loft object will have skewed edges. The lower-right corner of the dialog box includes buttons to View Extents, Pan, Zoom, and Zoom Region.

Editing Loft paths

The original shapes that were used to create the Loft object can be edited at any time. These updates also modify the Loft object. The shapes, if not visible, can be selected using the Select by Name button. The shapes maintain their base parameters, or they can be converted to an Editable Spline.

Tutorial: Creating drapes

Modeling home interiors is a task commonly performed by professional architects and interior designers, and creating the drapes can be tricky. In this tutorial, you create some simple drapes using a Loft object.

To create drapes using a Loft object, follow these steps:

1. Open the Lofted drapes.max file from the Chap 27 directory on the CD.

   This file contains two splines that can be used to create the loft.

2. Select the straight line spline, and select the Create⇨Compound⇨Loft menu command. In the Creation Method rollout, click the Get Shape button and then click the cross-section spline.

3. Open the Modify panel, and under the Skin Parameters rollout, turn off the Contour and Banking options.

4. In the Deformations rollout, click the Scale button. In the Scale Deformation dialog box that opens, use the Insert Corner Point button to create a new point at roughly 75. Switch to the Move Control Point button and drag the new point downward to create an effect such as tying them together, as shown in Figure 27.23.

FIGURE 27.23

Drapes that have been modeled using a Loft object

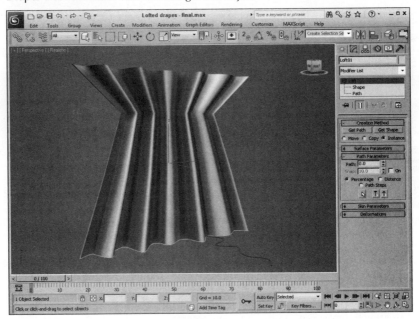

Loft objects versus surface tools

You can create compound Loft objects completely from 2D shape splines: One open spline is typically used as the Loft path, and other, closed splines are used as the cross sections. You can have several different cross sections, and these can change as you travel the path. Loft cross sections aren't required to have the same number of vertices, and you can modify the scale and rotation of the cross sections with the Deformation options.

Cross-Reference

See Bonus Chapter 5 on the CD, "Working with NURBS," for more detail on the surface tools. ∎

The surface tools, which include the CrossSection and Surface modifiers, provide another way to model that is similar to lofting. The CrossSection modifier takes several cross-section shapes and connects their vertices with additional splines to create a spline framework. You can then use the Surface modifier to cover this framework with a skin.

Although similar in nature, Loft objects and the surface tools have different subtleties and strengths.

One difference is that the CrossSection modifier connects spline cross sections according to their order. This can cause strange results if the order is incorrect. A Loft always follows a path, so the cross-section order isn't a problem.

Another difference is that surface tools give you more control over the surface of a created object. Because the underlying structure is a series of splines, you can add new branches and objects without much difficulty. This can be hard to do with Loft objects.

As a general guideline, Loft objects are better suited to modeling rigid objects with relatively uniform cross sections, whereas the surface tools are better for modeling more organic model types.

Working with ProBoolean and ProCutter Objects

The original Boolean compound object worked well enough for combining, subtracting, and intersecting objects, but it had some limitations that have been overcome with the ProBoolean and ProCutter compound objects. The original Boolean could combine only two operands together, but the ProBoolean object can perform multiple Boolean operations simultaneously. ProBoolean also can subdivide the result into quad faces. The results of the ProBoolean and ProCutter objects are much cleaner and more accurate than the original Boolean object.

The original Boolean compound object still is available for backward compatibility, but if you perform a new Boolean operation, you really should use the ProBoolean object.

Using ProBoolean

When two objects overlap, you can perform different Boolean operations on them to create a unique object. The ProBoolean operations include Union, Intersection, Subtraction, Merge, Attach, and Insert. Two additional options are available: Imprint and Cookie.

The Union operation combines two objects into one. The Intersection operation retains only the overlapping sections of two objects. The Subtraction operation subtracts the overlapping portions of one object from another. The Merge operation combines objects without removing the interior faces and adds new edges where the objects overlap. Figure 27.24 shows the original object and the first four possible Boolean operators.

Note

Unlike many CAD packages that deal with solid objects, Max's Booleans are applied to surfaces, so if the surfaces of the two objects don't overlap, all Boolean operations (except for Union) will have no effect. ∎

FIGURE 27.24

Object before any operations and with Boolean operations: Union, Intersection, Subtraction, and Merge with the Imprint option enabled

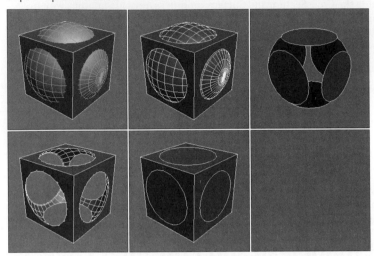

The Attach operation combines the objects like Union but keeps them as separate elements of the same compound object. For example, if you were to look inside a compound object created with Union, you would not see the interior polygons of the combined object, but with Attach, the interior polygons would still be there.

The Insert operation subtracts the second object from the first and then combines the two objects into one. If the subtracted volume makes a dent or hole into the first object, then that hole remains after the two are combined, but if the second surface has access to the first object through a hole, then the first surface covers the subtracted volume. In Figure 27.25, two tube objects have been overlapped with a box object. The left tube is capped at the bottom, forming a closed volume, but the right tube is open at the bottom. When made into a ProBoolean object with the Insert operations, the closed volume is subtracted, but the open volume is not.

The Cookie option causes the operation to cut the original object without adding any of the faces from the picked object to the original object. The Imprint option causes the outline of the operation to appear on the original object.

All Boolean operations are added in the order in which they are applied to a list in the Parameters rollout. You can select any of the operations in the list at any time and change the operation. For example, if you select the Subtraction operation from the list and then change the operation type to Union and click the Change Operation button, the Subtraction changes to a Union. With an operation selected in the list, the Extract Selected button restores the original object. When using this button, you can choose to Remove, Copy, or Instance the operation.

The order in which the operations are applied affects the result. You can reorder the operations in the list by selecting an operation, choosing its position in the list, and clicking the Reorder Ops button.

FIGURE 27.25

The Insert operation only maintains closed volumes when subtracted.

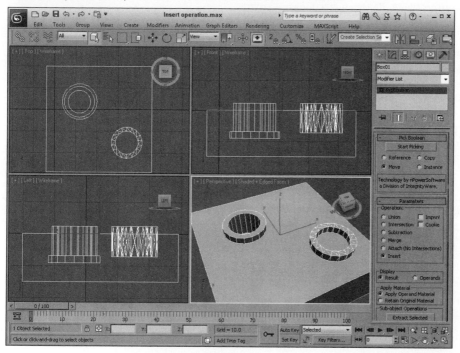

Cross-Reference

You also can apply Boolean operations to shapes using the Boolean operators available for Editable Meshes in the Geometry rollout. Chapter 12, "Drawing and Editing 2D Splines and Shapes," covers these 2D Boolean operators. ■

The materials that get applied to a ProBoolean result can be set to use the Operand Material or to retain the Original Material. If you use the Operand Material with the subtraction operation, then the surface that touches the picked object retains the removed object's material, and the rest of the object has the original object's material. If the Retain Original Material option is selected, then the entire result gets the original object's material.

In the Advanced Options rollout are options for updating the scene and for reducing the complexity of the object. The Decimation value is the percentage of edges to remove from the result. If you plan on smoothing the object or converting it to an Editable Poly object, then you want to enable the Make Quadrilaterals option, which causes the polygon reduction to avoid triangles in favor of quads. You also can set the Quad Size, and you can select how planar edges are handled.

Note

If you plan to deform the mesh as part of a skinned object or a cloth simulation, the resulting mesh has to be clean or the deformation will have problems. ■

Tutorial: Creating a keyhole

What was it that Alice saw when she looked through the keyhole? The ProBoolean feature is the perfect tool for cutting a keyhole through a doorknob plate.

To use the ProBoolean object to create a keyhole, follow these steps:

1. Open the Doorknob.max file from the Chap 27 directory on the CD.
2. Select the doorknob plate object positioned where the keyhole is, and choose the Create ⇨ Compound ⇨ ProBoolean menu command. In the Parameters rollout, select the Subtraction option.
3. In the Pick Boolean rollout, click the Start Picking button and select the Box and Cylinder objects positioned where the keyhole should be.

Figure 27.26 shows the finished keyhole.

FIGURE 27.26

A keyhole built using the ProBoolean object

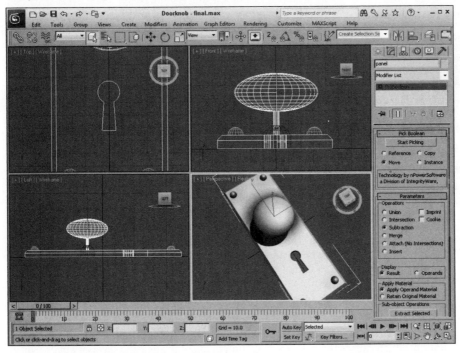

Using ProCutter

The original Boolean compound object included a Cut option. This feature has been replaced with ProCutter, which offers many more features than the original option. ProCutter allows you to cut a single object (known as the Stock object) with multiple cutter objects.

You can pick both the Stock and Cutter objects using the buttons found in the Cutter Picking Parameters rollout. You have four options with each selection: Reference, Move, Copy, or Instance. The Auto Extract Mesh option automatically replaces the selected stock object with the extracted result. The Explode by Elements option works only when the Auto Extract Mesh option is enabled. It separates each cut element into an object.

Within the Cutter Parameters rollout, you can select from three Cutting Options. The Stock Outside Cutter option keeps the portion of the stock object that is on the outside of the cutter. The Stock Inside Cutter option is the opposite, keeping the stock portion inside the cutters. The Cutters Outside Stock option maintains those portions of the cutters that are outside of the stock.

All selected cutters and stock objects are added to a list in the Cutter Parameters. Using the Extract Selected button, you can restore any cutter or stock object that has been operated on as a Copy or Instance. Materials and Decimation also work the same as for ProBoolean objects.

Tip

The ProCutter features are helpful for dividing an object that will be animated exploding into pieces. ∎

Tutorial: Creating a jigsaw puzzle

The ProCutter is useful for creating destructive scenes such as shattering glass to pieces and breaking down buildings, but it also can be used for constructive cutting such as creating a jigsaw puzzle.

To use the ProCutter compound object to divide an object into a jigsaw puzzle, follow these steps:

1. Open the ProCutter puzzle.max file from the Chap 27 directory on the CD. This file includes a simple box mapped with a scenic image and several extruded lines that mark the jigsaw puzzle's edges.
2. Select one of the extruded lines that mark where the cuts should be (known as a cutter), and choose the Create ➪ Compound ➪ ProCutter menu command.
3. Then click the Pick Cutter Objects button and select all of the remaining cutter objects. In the Cutter Parameters rollout, enable the Stock Outside Cutter along with the Stock Inside Cutter options. Select the Retain Original Material option also.
4. In the Cutter Picking Parameters rollout, enable the Auto Extract Mesh and Explode By Elements options; then select the Pick Stock Objects button and choose the Box object in the viewport.
5. Open the Material Editor and drag the image material onto each puzzle piece.

Note

If you don't want to see the cutter lines, you can select and hide them. ∎

Figure 27.27 shows the final puzzle with one piece moved away from the others.

FIGURE 27.27

A puzzle cut using the ProCutter compound object

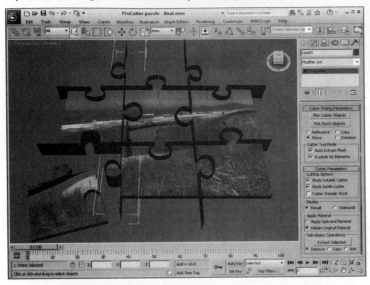

Summary

Compound objects add several additional modeling types to your bulging modeling toolkit. From morph objects to complex deformed lofts, you can use these special-purpose types to model many different objects. This chapter covered these topics:

- The various compound object types
- Morphing objects with the same number of vertices
- Creating a Conform object with differing numbers of vertices
- Using splines and mesh objects to create a ShapeMerge object
- Creating a Terrain object using splines
- The Mesher object
- Using the BlobMesh object to simulate water
- Creating a Scatter object
- Creating a Connect object to join two objects
- Creating a Loft object
- How to control Loft parameters
- Using Loft deformations
- Modifying Loft subobjects
- Comparing the strengths of Loft objects versus surface tools
- Modeling with the ProBoolean and ProCutter objects

Max generally uses polygons and meshes as its default modeling type, but CAD packages generally work with solids. The Body Object is the answer for working between solids and meshes, and it is covered next.

Working with Solids and Body Objects

Okay, here's a trick for you. Take a Max primitive object, and place it completely inside another Max primitive object, such as a cube inside a larger cube. Then use the ProBoolean feature to subtract the inner cube from the outer cube. The result is nothing. That's because Max objects deal with surfaces, and if the surfaces don't overlap, then no operation is performed.

The CAD world, on the other hand, deals with volumes, also known as solids, and such an operation is common. Because much of Autodesk's efforts are directed toward the CAD and architectural markets, working with volumes becomes important. It also provides a way to bridge the CAD and Max worlds.

To address this issue, Max has introduced a way to work with volumes and solids, which in Max are known as Body Objects. Objects that are imported from a CAD package appear in Max as Body Objects, and you also can convert Max objects to this Body Object type and export the results to a CAD package. Max also includes a way to perform Boolean operations on Body Objects, so you can finally remove that inner cube.

Importing CAD Objects

If you've spent lots of time working in a CAD package to get your design to look just right and now you need to take it to Max to add some animation for an upcoming presentation, you start by importing your objects into Max using the ACIS SAT import file type. Max can also import WIRE files from Autodesk Alias Studio.

New Feature

The ability to import WIRE files in new to 3ds Max 2012. ■

During the import, you get a SAT Import dialog box, as shown in Figure 28.1, full of options for the import. The Standard - No Welding option is the default and should be used in most cases. It imports all objects as separate objects, allowing you to select them independently.

The SAT Import dialog box includes options for importing CAD objects.

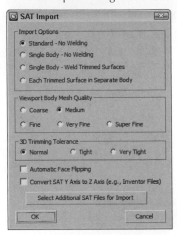

The Single Body options let you import all objects together as a single object in Max. If all objects are not welded together, you can select and move them independently in Element subobject mode. If they are welded, they act as a single object. This may be desirable if you are loading in a background or some terrain data. The final option imports each trimmed surface as a separate body object.

The Viewport Body Mesh Quality setting is used to set the density of the mesh displayed in the viewport. The 3D Trimming Tolerance option lets you set how accurately the imported objects are trimmed. It is best to start with a lower tolerance and increase it as you see import problems such as missing faces.

Caution

SAT files can be large, and selecting any of the Fine settings results in huge Max files. ∎

Enabling the Automatic Face Flipping option causes the importer to attempt to correct any normals that are pointing the wrong way. Most CAD formats have a different coordinate system with the Z axis pointing up instead of the Y axis. Enabling the Convert SAT Y Axis to Z Axis option fixes this for the imported objects.

The Select Additional SAT Files for Import button opens a file dialog box where you can select more files to import using the current settings. Importing SAT files takes a long time, so selecting and importing several files at once is a good idea.

Converting Max Objects to Body Objects

Objects that are imported from the SAT or WIRE formats appear in Max as Body Object types in the Modify panel. Max objects can be converted to the Body Object type using the Body Object button found in the Create panel by opening the Body Objects subcategory. Simply select the object to convert, and press the Body Object button.

The conversion works best when used on only the most basic primitive objects. If a more complex mesh object needs to be converted, try converting it to a NURBS object first and then to a Body Object.

Note

Max objects that are converted into Body Objects are still only shells and not solids. ■

If you have multiple objects that you want to convert to Body Objects, you can use the Body Utility button, also found in the Create panel. This button is also useful for changing the properties of multiple Body Objects at once.

Working with Body Objects

If you open a Body Object in the Modify panel, you can work with three subobjects: Edge, Face, and Element. Within the Modifier Stack is another subobject mode, Operand, which lets you work with the pieces resulting from a Boolean operation.

The notion of subobjects is unique to Body Objects. For example, the face subobject selected in Figure 28.2 wraps most of the way around the torus object. This is common for CAD object faces. You'll also notice, when subobjects are selected, that the transform tools are disabled.

FIGURE 28.2

The subobjects for Body Objects are unique from other modeling types.

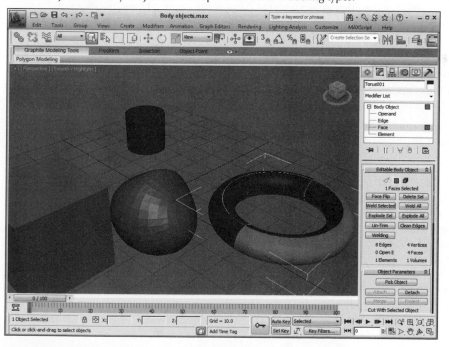

737

Editing Body Objects

Body Object edges are different from polygon edges in that they typically only show the profile of the object. When one Body Object is cut into another, an open edge is created. Open edges are not welded to the surface and are colored blue. Open edges also mark the borders where holes in the object are located. Edges are welded to the surface using the Weld Selected or the Weld All buttons. There is also a Welding button that opens a rollout with options for selecting and welding specific edges. Welded edges are displayed as white, and selected edges are red.

The opposite of welding edges and combining faces is to explode them apart. There are buttons for exploding the selected face or exploding all faces together. The Face Flip button provides a way to switch the normal for the surface using the Face Flipping/Visibility rollout.

Applying modifiers to Body Objects

One of the benefits that Max has over CAD packages is its lengthy list of modifiers. These modifiers can alter objects quickly without changing the parametric nature of the object, but not all modifiers preserve the default object type.

Using Boolean operations with Body Objects

Within the Object Parameters rollout is a Pick Object button. Using this button, you can select other Body Objects that are outside the current selection and then use the other buttons below the Pick Object button to define how the two objects are combined. The options include the following:

- **Attach:** Combines the other object as an element to the selected object and welds it edges.
- **Detach:** Removes the selected subobject from the current object and saves it as its own Body Object. Edges also are not welded.
- **Merge:** Combines the other object with the current selection, making one element.
- **Project:** Projects the curve of a single face onto the other object along the face's normal, creating new edges.
- **3-D Cut:** Creates new edges on the current object by tracing the overlapping volume of the picked object.
- **View Cut:** Cuts into the current Body Object using a projected profile from the picked object. If the Cut Selected Only option is enabled, then the cut affects only the selected subobject.

Figure 28.3 shows a cube Body Object that has been cut using the 3-D Cut and View Cut methods. For the 3-D Cut option, the torus object was used and then moved to reveal the remaining circle where the torus overlapped the cube. The View Cut option projected the edges from the cylinder onto the cube.

Using the Join Bodies and Body Cutter features

If two or more objects are selected, you can use the Join Bodies button found in the Body Objects subcategory of the Create panel to convert the objects into Body Objects and combine them. Within the Conversion Parameters rollout, you can select how the objects are combined. The options including weld only the edges, weld into solid, weld edges to surfaces, do nothing, intersect + merge faces, and Boolean union.

Body Objects can be cut using the 3-D Cut or View Cut operations.

3-D Cut   View Cut

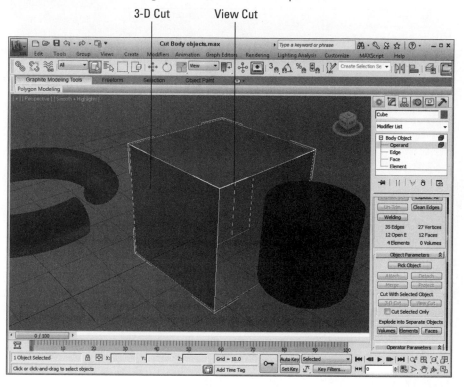

Note

The Join Bodies button doesn't require that one of the objects is already a Body Object. ■

The resulting object is a Join Bodies object type that allows you to revisit the Operands as subobjects and in the Operator Parameters rollout. If you're happy with the result, you can use the Body Objects button in the Create panel to convert the resulting object into a Body Object.

The Body Cutter works like the ProCutter tool and lets you cut away part of an overlapping volume. This begins by selecting an object; it doesn't need to be a Body Object. Then click the Body Cutter button in the Create panel. This creates a Body Cutter object and presents several rollouts of options. The Body Cutter object is a cutter, and you can choose the Pick Stocks button in the Body Cutter Parameters rollout to select the base object. You also can choose additional cutter objects with the Pick Cutters button.

Once cut, you can select which portion to display with the Cutting Options. The options include Stock Outside Cutters, Stock Inside Cutters, and Cutter Outside Stocks. Figure 28.4 shows a cylinder cut from a cube object.

FIGURE 28.4

The Body Cutter feature works like the ProCutter tool.

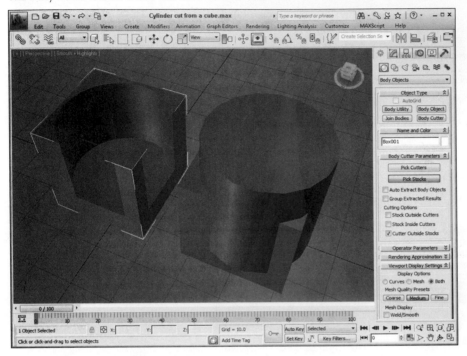

Setting display and rendering properties

Although Body Objects display and work in the Max world, you have control over how refined the objects are when being displayed in the viewport and when rendered. The Rendering Approximation rollout lets you define how the Body Object is treated when rendered. The simple method is to use the Draft, Good, and Production presets depending on how much time you have to wait for the rendering to finish. For each, you can get more specific in defining how the face, edges, and chords are approximated.

Many of the same values, along with three quality settings, also are available in the Viewport Display Settings rollout. These affect how the object appears within the viewports.

Exporting Body Objects

If you want to move the Body Objects back to a CAD package, you can use the File ⇨ Export menu and choose the ASIC format. This opens the SAT Export dialog box, shown in Figure 28.5. When exporting, you have the option of switching back to the standard CAD axis with the Z axis as up. You also need to specify the type of object being exported. It could be a simple primitive, a NURBS object, or a Mesh object.

If you are exporting an object that has modifiers applied to it, you want to use the Export Mesh Objects option and be aware that the stack will be collapsed during the export.

FIGURE 28.5

The SAT Export dialog box lets you specify what type of object is being exported.

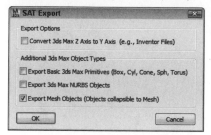

Summary

Body Objects provide a critical bridge between CAD objects and Max. Body Objects can be imported using the SAT format or Max objects can be converted to the Body Object type. Body Objects can be combined using several Boolean features and can be exported back to the CAD package. This chapter covered the following topics:

- Importing CAD objects
- Converting Max objects to Body Objects
- Applying modifiers to Body Objects
- Using the Join Bodies and Body Cutter tools
- Exporting Body Objects

The next chapter is really hairy. In fact, it is all about adding hair, fur, and cloth to your models.

Adding and Styling Hair and Fur, and Using Cloth

I want to start this chapter with a bold statement, "Bald Is Beautiful." I make this statement because I have a brother who, upon discovering his hair had started thinning, decided that bald was the way to go. But, after seeing far too many 3D models that were bald because of the unavailability of a decent hair plug-in in Max, I can also declare that "Bald Is Boring."

Now that Max has hair and fur, I expect to see the level of realism for a number of Max artists, including myself, take a quantum leap forward.

Creating cloth isn't that difficult. In fact, with a plane primitive, you can easily create a perfectly straight blanket, towel, or flag. However, animating cloth that drapes realistically over a character is very difficult and best left to dynamic engines like reactor.

Although you can still animate cloth collections using reactor, Max also has a separate stand-alone cloth simulation system aptly named Cloth that you can use to create deformable cloth and to animate it as well.

Cross-Reference

The hair and cloth systems in Max are dynamic, meaning that they are affected by forces in the scene such as wind and gravity. The dynamic nature of hair and cloth is covered in Chapter 44, "Animating Hair and Cloth." ■

Understanding Hair

Although a section titled "Understanding Hair" sounds like it would be taken from a beauty salon guide, the way Max deals with hair is unique and needs some explanation. Hair, like particle systems, deals with thousands of small items that can bring even the most powerful computer screeching to a halt if not managed.

In Max, hair doesn't exist as geometry but is applied to scene objects as a separate modifier. This level of separation keeps the hair solution independent of the geometry and makes removing or turning off the hair solution as needed easy. It also keeps the viewport display from bogging down. The Hair and Fur modifier is a World Space Modifier (WSM), meaning that it is applied using the World Space coordinates instead of local ones.

The other half of the Hair and Fur solution is a render effect that allows the hair to be rendered. This render effect is applied and configured automatically when the Hair and Fur modifier is applied to an object. This causes the scene with hair to be rendered in two passes. The geometry is rendered first, followed by the hair.

Note
Hair can be rendered only when a Perspective or Camera view is selected. Hair cannot be rendered in any of the orthogonal views. ■

Another similarity to particle systems is that the hair follicles can be replaced by instanced geometry, so you can create a matchstick head character by replacing hairs with an instance of a matchstick.

Tip
Using instanced geometry with a fur system is a great way to create and position plants and ground cover. ■

The materials that are used on hair are defined in the Material Parameters rollout in the Modify panel instead of in the Material Editor. Many of the hair parameters have a square button to their right that lets you apply a map to the parameter.

When the Hair and Fur modifier is added to an object in the scene, a Hair and Fur render element becomes available that you can use to render out just the hair for compositing.

Working with Hair

Applying hair to an object is as easy as selecting an object and choosing the Hair and Fur WSM modifier, which is found in the Modifiers ⇨ Hair and Fur ⇨ Hair and Fur WSM. After hair is applied to an object, you can use the parameters in the Modify panel to change the hair's properties.

Growing hair

Hair can be grown on any geometry surface, including splines, by simply applying the Hair and Fur WSM to the selected object. When the Hair and Fur modifier is first applied to an object, it is applied to the entire surface of the selected object, and when it is applied to a set of splines, the hair appears between the first and last spline.

If you want to localize the hair growth to a specific area of the object, you can make a subobject selection using the controls in the Selection rollout. The available subobjects include Face, Polygon, Element, and Guides. After making a subobject selection, click the Update Selection to display the guide hairs only in the selected area in the viewports. Figure 29.1 shows hair grown on a man's face to create a beard.

Tip

After taking the time to make a subobject selection, create a selection set for the hair area for quick recall. ■

FIGURE 29.1

By making a subobject selection, you can control precisely where hair is grown.

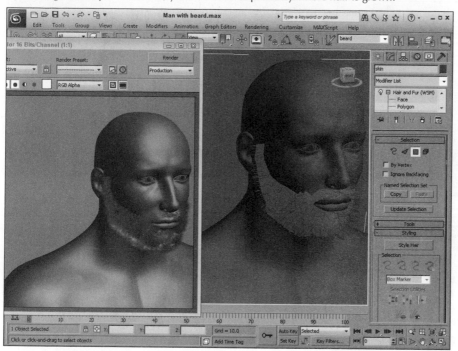

Applying hair to a single spline doesn't create any hair, but if multiple splines are included as part of the same Editable Spline object, then the hair is interpolated between the various splines in the order they are attached following the spline's curvature. This provides a great way to add special features like a ringlet to an existing set of hair.

Setting hair properties

Several rollouts of properties can be used to change the look of the hair. The General Parameters roll-out, shown in Figure 29.2, includes settings for the overall Hair Count, the number of Hair Segments between adjacent splines, the number of Hair Passes, Density, Scale, Cut Length, Random Scale, Root and Tip Thickness, and Displacement. The Hair Count value sets the total number of hairs for the given geometry. Higher values take longer to render but produce more realistic hair. The Hair Passes sets the number of render passes to use for determining hair transparency. The higher the Hair Passes value, the wispier the hair looks. The Rand Scale value provides a random amount of scaling for a percentage of hairs to look more natural. The Displacement value sets how far from the source object the hairs grow and can be a negative value.

Caution

Although the Hair Count value can accept huge numbers, adding a large number of hairs takes a long time to render and can really slow your system. ■

FIGURE 29.2

Hair properties can be altered using the General and Material Parameters rollouts.

Map button

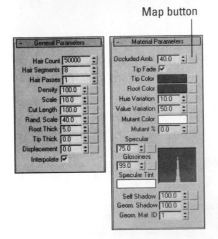

The buttons to the right of most of the parameters in the General Parameters rollout let you add a map to control the property with a grayscale bitmap. Figure 29.3 shows a simple plane object mapped with a bitmap used to control the hair density. The black areas of the bitmap have no hair growth, but the white areas have maximum growth. This provides a way to create patchy hair on a character or creature.

The Material Parameters rollout, also shown in Figure 29.2, includes settings for the Occluded Ambient value, controlling the tip and root colors, Hue and Value Variations, the addition of mutant hairs, percentage to include, and specular and glossiness settings. The Occluded Ambient value sets the contrast for the hair lighting. Smaller values have a stronger contrast, and higher values appear more washed out. The Hue and Value Variation values define a percentage that the hair color can deviate from the specified color to give the hair a more natural coloring. The Mutant percentage defines the percentage and color of hairs that are discolored, such as white hairs.

Note

The Occluded Ambient property is applied as an effect, so it is actually a fake global illumination pass. ■

The Tip Fade option causes the hair to be more transparent toward the tip. The Specular Tint color changes the color of specular highlights. The Tip Fade and Specular Tint options apply only to hairs rendered with mental ray. The Self Shadow value sets how much the individual hairs cast shadows on other hairs, and the Geometry Shadow settings determine how much shadow is contributed by other geometry objects. The Geometry Material ID is used to assign a material to geometry-rendered hair.

Many of the properties in the Material Parameters rollout also can be controlled using map buttons located to the right.

FIGURE 29.3

Many of the hair properties can be defined using maps.

Caution

Map colors are multiplied with the base color value, so set the base color to white before using a map. ■

In addition to the general and material parameters, rollouts also are available for controlling the amount of Frizz and Kink, and for the Multi-Strand nature of hair. Frizz causes the hair to curl at its tip or root. Kink parameters cause the hair to be zigzagged in shape; the Multi-Strand parameters cause hair to separate into groups like grass does. Figure 29.4 shows four areas with different hair properties applied, including normal straight hair with no frizz or kink, a section with Frizz, one with Kink, and Multi-Strand.

FIGURE 29.4

Changing hair properties can drastically alter the hair's look from normal to frizz, kink, and multi-strand.

Tutorial: Adding a spline fringe to a quilt

Quilts are designed to make you feel all warm and fuzzy, and what could be fuzzier than some soft fringe surrounding a quilt? Fringe makes grabbing the quilt easy.

To add hairy fringe to a quilt using splines, follow these steps:

1. Open the Patch quilt.max file from the Chap 29 directory on the CD.
2. Select the Create ➪ Shapes ➪ Line menu command, and draw a couple of simple splines that extend at right angles from every corner of the quilt in the Top view. These splines will be used to designate the start and end splines for the quilt fringe. Hair strands will be placed between these two simple splines. Start at one corner, and proceed in turn clockwise around each of the corners. Add a second line on top of the first line to complete the set of splines.
3. Select the first spline, and convert it to an Editable Spline object using the right-click quad-menu. Then click the Attach button, and select the splines in the order they were created.
4. With all the splines selected, choose the Modifiers ➪ Hair and Fur ➪ Hair and Fur WSM menu command to apply the Hair and Fur modifier to the splines.
5. Open the Modify panel, and in the General Parameters rollout, set the Hair Count to **2500**, the Random Scale value to **10**, and the Tip and Root Thickness to **5.0**. Then open the Material Parameters rollout, and change the Tip and Root colors to white.

Figure 29.5 shows the resulting quilt with its fringe, all warm and fuzzy.

FIGURE 29.5

Hair or fringe can be added to a subobject selection or to the entire object.

Styling Hair

The Display rollout (located way at the bottom of the rollouts) includes settings for controlling how many hairs are displayed in the viewports. To see all the hairs, you need to render the scene. You can select to display Guide Hairs and actual hairs and set a color for each. The Override option causes the color specified in the color swatch to be used instead of the render color. You also can select a Percentage value of the total hairs to display in the viewport up to the number in the Max Hairs value. Enabling the As Geometry option causes the hairs to appear as geometry objects instead of lines.

Guide hairs control the position of all adjacent hairs. Guide hairs extend from each vertex in the attached object. Guide hairs are yellow by default, and viewport hairs are red, but you can change the color for each in the Display rollout.

Guide hairs provide a simple way to style, comb, and brush hair. By positioning the guide hairs, you can control what the rest of the hair looks like.

Note

No guide hairs are available when the Hair and Fur modifier is applied to a selection of splines because the splines act as guides. ■

Using the Style interface

In addition to the hair properties, you can change the look of hair by using the various hair styling features. These features are found in the Styling rollout. The Style Hair button activates an interactive styling mode in the viewport where you can brush, comb, and manipulate the individual hairs. The Style Hair button is activated automatically when the Guides subobject mode is selected.

Within the Styling rollouts are several icon buttons. These buttons are described in Table 29.1. The brush size can be interactively set by holding down the Ctrl and Shift keys while dragging the mouse when in Brush mode, or you can change the brush size using the slider located under the Ignore Back Hairs option. The Distance Fade option causes the brushing effect to fade as it gets closer to the edge, resulting in a softer effect at the hair tips.

TABLE 29.1

Hair Styling Buttons

Toolbar Button	Name	Description
	Select by Hair Ends (Ctrl+1)	Selects the end vertex when you drag over hairs.
	Select the Whole Guide (Ctrl+2)	Selects all vertices in the whole strand when you drag over hairs.
	Select Guide Vertices (Ctrl+3)	Selects specific vertices when you drag over hairs.
	Select Guide by Root (Ctrl+4)	Selects the entire hair by selecting only the root vertex when you drag over hairs.
Box Marker ▼	Marker Style drop-down list	Choose the style to mark the selected vertices. Options include Box, Plus, X, and Dot.

continued

TABLE 29.1   *(continued)*

Toolbar Button	Name	Description
	Invert Selection (Shift+Ctrl+N)	Deselects the current selection, and selects all hairs not currently selected.
	Rotate Selection (Shift+Ctrl+R)	Rotates the current selection.
	Expand Selection (Shift+Ctrl+E)	Adds to the current selection set by increasing the selection area.
	Hide Selected (Shift+Ctrl+H)	Hides the selected vertices.
	Show Hidden (Shift+Ctrl+W)	Unhides all hidden vertices.
	Hair Brush (Ctrl+B)	Moves all selected vertices in the direction of the brush. Press Escape to exit this mode.
	Hair Cut (Ctrl+C)	Cuts the hair in length.
	Select (Ctrl+S)	Enters selection mode where you can select hairs by dragging over them.
☑ Distance Fade	Distance Fade (Shift+Ctrl+F)	Causes the brush effect to fade with distance. Available only in Hair Brush mode.
☑ Ignore Back Hairs	Ignore Back Hairs (Shift+Ctrl+B)	Causes only hairs facing the camera to be affected.
	Brush Size slider (Ctrl+Shift+mouse drag)	Changes the size of the brush.
	Translate (Shift+Ctrl+1, Ctrl+T)	Moves the selected guides in the direction of the brush when you drag.
	Stand (Shift+Ctrl+2, Ctrl+N)	Stands the selected guides up straight.
	Puff Roots (Shift+Ctrl+3, Ctrl+P)	Causes small deviations to appear at the root of each selected guide.
	Clump (Shift+Ctrl+4, Ctrl+M)	Pulls the selected guides together to the center of the brush.
	Rotate (Shift+Ctrl+5, Ctrl+R)	Rotates and spins the selected guides about the center of the brush.
	Scale (Shift+Ctrl+6, Ctrl+E)	Scales the selected guides when you drag with the brush.
	Attenuate (Shift+Ctrl+A)	Scales the hairs based on the size of the polygon.
	Pop Selected (Shift+Ctrl+P)	Lengthens the selected hairs along the surface normal.

Toolbar Button	Name	Description
	Pop Zero Sized (Shift+Ctrl+Z)	Lengthens any zero length hairs along the surface normal.
	Recomb (Shift+Ctrl+M)	Combs the hair from the top downward.
	Reset Rest (Shift+Ctrl+T)	Relaxes the hair by averaging the position of hairs.
	Toggle Collisions (Shift+Ctrl+C)	Turns collisions of hairs on and off.
	Toggle Hair (Shift+Ctrl+I)	Toggles the display of hairs on and off.
	Lock (Shift+Ctrl+L)	Locks the selected vertices so they cannot be moved by other tools.
	Unlock (Shift+Ctrl+U)	Unlocks any locked vertices.
	Undo (Ctrl+Z)	Undoes the last command.
	Split Selected Hair Groups (Shift+Ctrl+-)	Separates the selected hairs into separate groups.
	Merge Selected Hair Groups (Shift+Ctrl+=)	Combines the selected hairs into groups.

When you're finished styling, click the Finish Styling button in the Styling rollout to exit styling mode.

Tutorial: Creating a set of fuzzy dice

Fuzzy dice. What could be cooler?

To style the fur applied to a set of fuzzy dice, follow these steps:

1. Open the Fuzzy dice.max file from the Chap 29 directory on the CD.

2. Select one of the dice, and choose the Modifiers ⇨ Hair and Fur ⇨ Hair and Fur (WSM) menu command to apply hair to the selected die.

3. Open the General Parameters rollout, and set the Hair Count to **20000** and the Scale value to **50**. Then open the Material Parameters rollout, and change the Tip Color to white and the Root Color to Red. Then open the Frizz Parameters rollout, and set the Frizz Root and Frizz Tip values to **0**. This makes the hair strands straight and red.

4. Open the Styling rollout, and click the Style Hair button. In the Utilities section, click the Pop Selected button to make all the hair stand out. Then select the Hair Brush icon, and drag downward in the viewport near the guides at each of the top corners. Click the Finish Styling button when completed.

5. Drag the Hair and Fur (WSM) modifier from the Modifier Stack, and drop it on the unselected die.

Figure 29.6 shows the resulting pair of dice.

FIGURE 29.6

Hair can be styled by changing the position and orientation of the guide hairs.

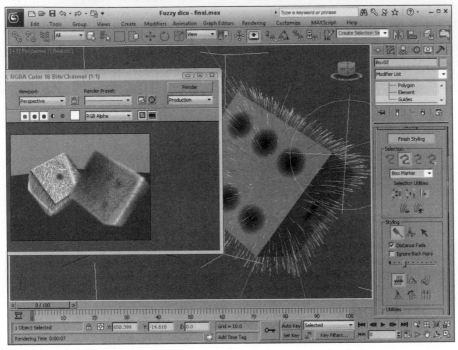

Using hair presets

If you have a specific set of parameters that create a unique hair look that you're happy with, you can save it using the Save presets button in the Tools rollout. Hair preset files are rendered on the spot and added to the Hair and Fur Presets dialog box, shown in Figure 29.7. To add a preset configuration to the current object, simply double-click it.

FIGURE 29.7

The Hair and Fur presets dialog box shows rendered thumbnails of the available presets.

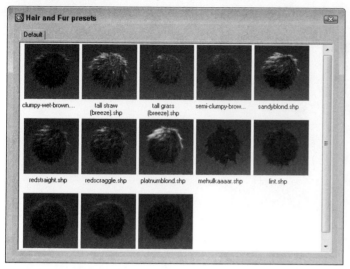

In addition to presets, hairdos—created by styling the hair—also can be copied and pasted onto other hair selections.

Tip

If you ever get into trouble styling hair, you can click the Regrow Hair button in the Tools rollout to reset all the styling to its original state. ■

Using hair instances

Although the default hair looks great, if you ever wanted to replace the hair splines with an instanced geometry, you can do so by using the Pick Instance Node in the Tools rollout. The X button to the right of the Instance Node Pick button is used to remove the instance. Figure 29.8 shows a funny head created using a matchstick for a hair instance.

Tip

Be sure to adjust the Hair Count value before selecting an instanced object. Complex instanced objects should be used only with manageable numbers. ■

FIGURE 29.8

Mr. Matchstick head has all his hair replaced with matchsticks, an instance.

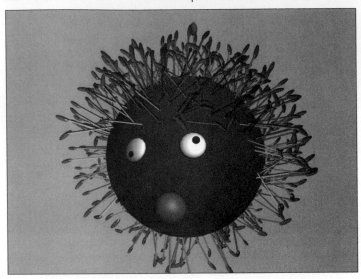

Rendering Hair

You can change the hair render settings by opening the Effects panel using the Rendering ⇨ Effects menu. The Render Settings button in the Tools rollout provides quick access to the Effects panel. The Hair and Fur rollout includes settings for the Hairs and Lighting rendering methods.

Hairs can be rendered using three options. The Buffer method renders each hair individually and combines the effect. It uses minimal memory requirements. When the buffer method is selected, you can choose the Raytrace Reflections/Refractions option for better quality. The Geometry method converts each hair into a geometry object that is rendered. The mr Prim method renders hair using the mental ray renderer. For this option, you can set the Voxel Resolution used to render hairs.

Cross-Reference

More on mental ray is covered in Chapter 47, "Rendering with mental ray and iray." ■

Motion Blur can be enabled to make hairs that are moving fast appear blurred. The Oversampling setting adds an anti-aliasing pass to the rendering. The options include Draft, Low, Medium, High, and Maximum. The Composite Method option depends on the rendering method that is selected. A list of occlusion objects and a setting for Shadow Density also are available.

By default, all lights (except for direct lights and daylight systems) are used to light hair, but if a spotlight is added to the scene, you can select the spotlight and click the Add Hair Properties button at the bottom of the Hair and Fur rollout. This adds a Hair Light Attributes rollout to the Modify panel for the selected spotlight where you can set the Resolution and Fuzz of the shadow map for the hair object cast by the light.

Understanding Cloth

If you drop a shirt over a chair, how does it land? It folds and bunches as it drapes over the solid object. Also notice how different types of cloth drape differently. Compare how silk reacts versus a terry cloth towel. Being able to accurately simulate how cloth reacts to scene objects and forces is yet another critical element that can really make a difference in your final scenes.

Cloth in Max is created using a modifier. This modifier can be applied to any object to make it a cloth object, or you can specifically create a set of clothes using the Garment Maker modifier. During the process of making an object into a cloth object, the object is divided into multiple faces using one of several subdivision methods. This provides the mesh with enough resolution to be deformed accurately.

Cloth objects are endowed with characteristics that let them respond to external forces within the scene including gravity, wind, and collisions with other scene objects. After all the scene objects, forces, and cloth objects are added to the scene, you can start a simulation that defines how the cloth moves within the scene under the effect of the other scene objects and forces.

Cross-Reference

This chapter focuses on creating and defining cloth objects. The dynamic nature of cloth is covered in Chapter 44, "Animating Hair and Cloth." ∎

Creating Cloth

When you start to model a cloth object, keep in mind that the model must have enough resolution so that it can accurately fold over itself several times. If the resolution isn't defined enough, then the bending of the cloth is not believable.

Note

Although dynamic cloth can be deformed under the effect of forces applied to it, cloth cannot apply a force back against the deforming object. This is a scenario that reactor can handle because it deals with all objects in the scene. A trampoline, for example, is a good example of a deformable cloth surface that can apply a force back on the deforming object using reactor. ∎

You can increase the resolution of a model in several ways. The Garment Maker modifier includes parameters that can increase the resolution of a mesh, or you can use the HSDS (for Hierarchical SubDivision Surfaces) modifier to increase an object's resolution.

Tip

When making cloth objects, use a single-sided Plane object instead of a Box object. Using a Box object needlessly doubles the number of polygons to be included in the simulation. ∎

Using Garment Maker to define cloth

Clothes can be added to models using a method that is similar to the way real clothes are made. Each section of cloth, called a panel, is outlined using lines and splines in the Top viewport. Clothes patterns also can be imported and used. Include a break at each corner of the panel, or the modifier will round the corner. After you have all the various panels created, convert one of the panels to an Editable Spline object and attach all the panels into a single object. You can apply the Modifiers ⇨ Cloth ⇨ Garment Maker to the set of panels.

Tip

The easiest way to create cloth panels is to draw the entire cloth panel and then use the Break Vertex command in Vertex subobject mode to break each corner. ■

When the Garment Maker modifier is first applied, the panel outlines are made into mesh objects and subdivided using the Delaunay algorithm, as shown in Figure 29.9. This algorithm uses random triangulation and divides the triangles into roughly equal shapes. This helps keep the cloth from folding along common lines caused by regular patterns. You can alter the number of polygons in the subdivided mesh using the Density value. If the Auto Mesh option is disabled, then you can update the density change using the Mesh It button. The Preserve option maintains the 3D shape of the object. If Preserve is disabled, then the panel is made flat.

FIGURE 29.9

The Garment Maker modifier uses the Delaunay algorithm for subdividing cloth meshes.

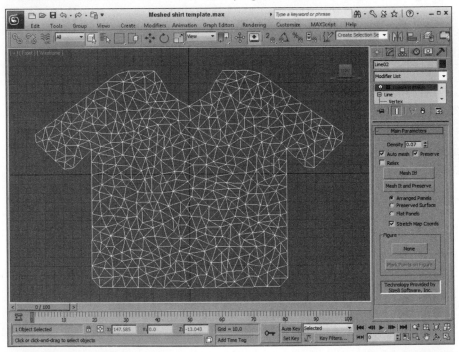

The next step is to position the panels so they surround the model that they will be draped over. The subject that is to receive the clothes can be selected by clicking the Figure button in the Main Parameters rollout. After an object is selected, clicking the Mark Points on Figure button makes a small figure outline appear in the upper-left corner of the viewport. This figure outline has markers corresponding to the chest, neck, pelvis, shoulder, and wrists. Dragging over the body of the character lets you mark corresponding locations on the character.

After body parts are marked, you can select a cloth panel and use the Panel Position buttons in the Panel rollout to position the various cloth panels around the body. The Panel Position buttons include Front Center, Front Right, Back Center, Right Arm, and so on. You also can position the panels manually.

The Garment Maker modifier has three subobjects: Curves, Panels, and Seams. With the panels in place, you can stitch seams between the panels using the Curves subobject mode for flat drawn panels or with the Seams subobject mode for panels that are positioned about a model. Each seam edge should be relatively the same length. The Seam Tolerance value sets how far apart the two edges can deviate. For each seam, you can set a Crease Angle and Strength. The Sewing Stiffness value determines the strength that the seams are pulled together.

After the seams are defined, you can apply the Modifiers ⇨ Cloth ⇨ Cloth modifier to pull the panels together and simulate the cloth's motion.

Creating cloth from geometry objects

Any geometry object can be made into a cloth object using the Cloth modifier available by selecting the Modifiers ⇨ Cloth ⇨ Cloth menu command. Although the modifier is added to the object, it is set to Inactive by default. To activate the cloth, you need to open the Object Properties dialog box, shown in Figure 29.10.

The list at the left holds all the objects that are involved in the cloth simulation. New objects can be added to the list using the Add Objects button. Each object can be set to Inactive, Cloth, or Collision Object, and properties can be set for each type. For cloth, the properties include Bend, Stretch, Shear, Density, Thickness, Friction, and Scale values. Defined cloth settings can be saved and recalled. Cloth property files are saved using the .sti file extension. Max also includes a sizable list of presets in a drop-down list, including Burlap, Cashmere, Cotton, Flannel, Rubber, Satin, Silk, Terrycloth, and Wool, among others.

In addition to objects added to the scene, a cloth simulation also can include forces. The Cloth Forces button opens a dialog box where you can select which forces in the scene can be added to the cloth simulation. Gravity is added by default automatically to the simulation. You can set the Gravity value in the Simulation Parameters rollout along with several other parameters, including the Start and End Frames.

With all the objects and forces added, click the Simulate Local button to set the initial state of the cloth simulation. This drapes the cloth over the scene objects and pulls all defined seams from the Garment Maker modifier together. Sometimes the Simulate Local button moves the cloth panels together too fast, so you can use the Simulate Local (damped) button to add lots of damping to the scene to prevent problems from panels moving too fast.

FIGURE 29.10

The Object Properties dialog box includes all the parameters for the cloth and collision objects.

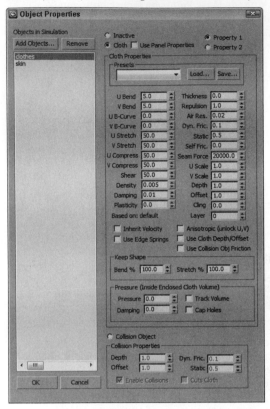

Tutorial: Clothing a 3D model

If you've ever wanted to design and outfit a set of models with a custom-made line of clothing, here's your chance. Using Garment Maker and the Cloth modifiers, you outfit the 3D model with a set of clothes. Watch for this new line next spring at your local retailers. This excellent female character was supplied by Zygote Media.

To create and apply a set of clothes to a 3D character, follow these steps:

1. Open the Zygote woman with clothes.max file from the Chap 29 directory on the CD.
2. Select the Create ⇨ Shapes ⇨ Line menu command, and draw in the Top viewport the front outline of a simple tank top and a simple skirt. Make sure the panels are closed splines. Then right-click in the viewport to exit Line mode.
3. Select the Tools ⇨ Mirror menu command, and create mirrored copies of the clothes for the back side. Then convert one of the panels to an Editable Spline, and attach all the other panels together into a single object. In Vertex subobject mode, select all the corner vertices in all panels and click the Break button.
4. With the clothes selected, choose the Modifiers ⇨ Cloth ⇨ Garment Maker modifier. This automatically subdivides all the cloth panels into multiple polygons.

5. In the Main Parameters rollout, click the Figure button and select the female character. Then click the Mark Points on Figure button. A small figure appears in the upper-left corner of each viewport with the upper chest area marked in red. Drag the cursor over the character until the matching upper chest area is located, and click. Repeat for all the marked positions. When all points are marked, click the Mark Points on Figure button again to exit marking mode.

6. In the Modify panel, select the Panels subobject mode and choose the tank top's front panel. Select the Top at Neck level, and click the Front Center button. This places the tank top's front in front of the character. Repeat the placement for the other panels. If the placement isn't correct, manually move the panels until they are in front of and behind the character, as shown in Figure 29.11.

FIGURE 29.11

Using figure markers, you can approximate where the clothes are positioned on a character.

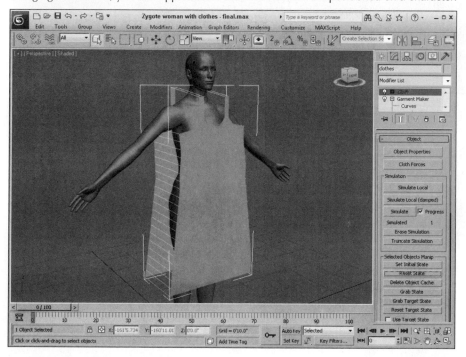

7. In the Modify panel, select the Seams subobject mode. In the Front viewport, select two edges that should be connected and click the Create Seam button. Repeat this for all seams including the sides of the skirt and shirt and the top of the shirt. Connecting lines are drawn between both sides of the seam. If the seam boundaries are crossed, then click the Reverse Seam button.

8. With the seams defined, select Modifiers ⇨ Cloth ⇨ Cloth to apply the Cloth modifier. In the Object rollout, click the Object Properties button. In the Object Properties dialog box, select the clothes object and enable the Cloth option. Then click the Add Objects button, select the character mesh, and mark it as a Collision Object. Set the Offset value for the clothes to **0.3**, and click Ok in the Object Properties dialog box.

9. Click the Simulate Local button. The cloth seams are pulled together, and the clothes are draped over the character.

Figure 29.12 shows the female character in a simple gown.

FIGURE 29.12

The Simulate Local button causes the clothes to be draped over the body.

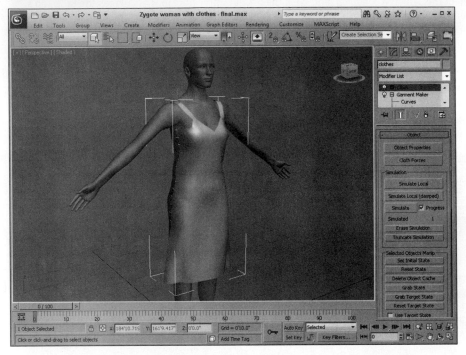

Summary

The Hair and Fur modifier allows you to add hair to scene objects. Using the parameters found in the various rollouts, you can define the type of hair that is created. The Cloth modifier enables a cloth dynamic system that can simulate the complex motion of cloth as it interacts with objects and forces in the scene.

Specifically, this chapter covered the following topics:

- Growing hair and setting hair parameters
- Styling hair and using the hair presets
- Understanding how cloth systems work
- Using the Garment Maker modifier
- Creating cloth objects from geometry objects using the Cloth modifier

Part VII, "Advanced Materials," is next. The first chapter in this part shows off all the cool specialized material types.

Part VII

Advanced Materials

Using Specialized Material Types

Y ou probably noticed back in the chapter on compound materials that a number of intriguing material types listed in the Material/Map Browser were not discussed. These material types are important, but they can't be classified as compound materials.

These specialized materials are sort of like your waffle iron. They're meant to be pulled out of your arsenal when you have a specific need. You wouldn't cook eggs on a waffle iron, would you?

The specialized materials include the Matte/Shadow material, the Ink 'n' Paint material, the Architectural materials, and the DirectX Shader material. These materials let you hide things in the scene, render the scene as a cartoon, use building materials, and view objects as they'll be seen in a game.

Even more special material types are listed after you enable the mental ray renderer. These materials are so specialized that they require a change in the rendering engine. These mental ray materials include an updated set of architectural materials, a Car Paint material, and several subsurface scattering materials.

With these specialized materials, you can create some really advanced, realistic results. Unfortunately, they don't make waffles.

Using the Matte/Shadow Material

You can apply matte/shadow materials to objects to make portions of the model invisible. This lets any objects behind the object or in the background show through. This material is also helpful for compositing 3D objects into a photographic background. Objects with matte/shadow materials applied can also cast and receive shadows. The effect of these materials is visible only when the object is rendered.

Note

The Matte/Shadow material type is unavailable if the mental ray renderer is enabled. ∎

Matte/Shadow Basic Parameters rollout

You can apply a matte/shadow material by double-clicking Matte/Shadow from the Material/Map Browser. Matte/shadow materials include only a single rollout: the Matte/Shadow Basic Parameters.

The Opaque Alpha option causes the matte material to appear in an alpha channel. This essentially is a switch for turning Matte objects on and off.

You can apply atmospheric effects such as fog and volume light to Matte materials. The At Background Depth option applies the fog to the background image. The At Object Depth option applies the fog as if the object were rendered.

Cross-Reference

Find out about Atmospheric effects in Chapter 46, "Using Atmospheric and Render Effects." ∎

The Receive Shadows section enables shadows to be cast on a Matte object. You can also specify the Shadow Brightness and color. Increasing Shadow Brightness values makes the shadow more transparent. The Affect Alpha option makes the shadows part of the alpha channel.

Matte objects can also have reflections. The Amount spinner controls how much reflection is used, and the Map button opens the Material/Map Browser.

Tutorial: Adding 3D objects to a scene

A common use of the Matte/Shadow map is to add 3D objects to a background image. For example, if you add a Plane object that is aligned with the ground plane in the background image that has a matte/shadow material applied to it, then the Plane object can capture the shadows of the 3D objects, but the matte/shadow material allows the background to be seen through the Plane object. The result is that the 3D object appears added to the background image scene.

To use a matte/shadow material to add an object to a background image, follow these steps:

1. Open the Xylophone on shadow matte.max file from the Chap 30 directory on the **CD.**

   This file contains a background image of a cow statue taken in front of the Boston Convention Center. The scene also includes a xylophone positioned on the Plane object. The Plane object has a Scale multiplier of 4 to make a complete ground plane when the scene is rendered.

2. Open the Slate Material Editor by pressing the M keyboard shortcut. Double-click the Matte/Shadow option in the Material/Map Browser. Name the material **Shadow plane**, and apply it to the Plane object in the Perspective viewport.

3. Select the Create ⇨ Lights ⇨ Standard Lights ⇨ Omni menu and click in the Top viewport to create a light. In the General Parameters rollout, enable the Shadows option. Then in the Shadow Parameters rollout, click the Color swatch. In the Color Selector that opens, select the Sample Screen Color eyedropper tool, and click the cow's shadow color to select it. Then adjust the Density setting to 0.7 to make the shadow slightly transparent.

4. Right-click the Perspective viewport's rendering label in the upper-left corner of the viewport and select the Lighting and Shadows ⇨ Enable Hardware Shading. Then select the Lighting and Shadows ⇨ Shadows option.

   This makes the shadows appear in the viewport on the Plane object.

5. Move the Omni light in the Left and Top views until the shadows are projected along the same path as the cow's shadows.

Tip

One way to help align the shadows is to make the shadows of parallel geometry objects, like the xylophone's vertical leg and the cow's leg, parallel. ■

6. To see the final result, you need to render the image. To do this, select Rendering ⇨ Render (or press F10) to open the Render Scene dialog box. Click the Render button at the bottom of the dialog box, and the image is rendered in the Rendered Frame Window, or press the F9 key.

Figure 30.1 shows the resulting rendered image.

FIGURE 30.1

A rendered xylophone fits into the scene because its shadows are cast on an object with a matte/shadow material applied.

Using the Ink 'n' Paint Material

Although it may seem silly, many different production houses use Max to create 2D line-drawn cartoons. This is accomplished using the Ink 'n' Paint material. Traditionally, cartoons have been drawn by hand using a paper and pen. Then animation houses found that, using computers, you can fill in a cartoon feature easily, but using a 3D program like Max with its ability to animate using keyframes simplifies the animation task even further. The difference is in how the objects are rendered; the Ink 'n' Paint material controls this.

With the Ink 'n' Paint material selected, several rollouts appear, including the Basic Material Extensions. This rollout includes options for making the material 2-Sided, enabling a Face Map, and making the material Faceted. Other options cause the background to be foggy when not painting and make the alpha channel opaque. Maps are available for Bump and Displacement.

Controlling paint and ink

The Paint Controls rollout includes settings for how the paint (or colors inside the ink outline) is applied. You can specify colors for the Lighted, Shaded, and Highlight colors. The Lighted color is used for sections of the material that face the scene lights, the Shaded color is used for sections that are in the shadows, and the Highlight color is for the specular highlights. For each color, you also can select a map with an amount value. The Paint Levels value sets the number of colors that are used to color the material. The Glossiness value determines the size of the highlight. Figure 30.2 shows materials with Paint Level values of 2–6.

FIGURE 30.2

Use the Paint Level value to set the number of colors used in the material.

The Ink Controls rollout includes an Ink option that you can use to turn off the outlining ink completely. You also can set the Ink Quality to values between 1 and 3. The higher-quality values trace the edges better, but require more time to complete. The width of the ink strokes can be set to Variable Width or a Clamped width. For each option, you can select a Minimum ink width, and if Variable Width is enabled, you can choose a Maximum ink width. For the Variable Width option, the stroke changes so that the minimum setting is used in lighted areas and the maximum width is used in shaded areas. This helps to accentuate the lighting. You can also apply the ink width as a map. Figure 30.3 shows the Ink 'n' Paint material applied to a cube. The first image shows a standard material; the second image has the Ink option disabled. The last three images have Width values of 1, 10, and 30.

Tip

Placing a noise map on the Ink Width property is a great way to give the ink outline a hand-drawn look. ■

FIGURE 30.3

The Paint Level value sets the number of colors used in the material.

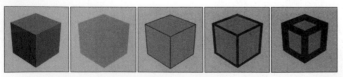

The rest of the options in the Ink Controls rollout are enabled to control where the ink is applied to the object. Options include Outline, Overlap, Underlap, Smoothing Group, and Material ID. For each of these options (except for Smoothing Group), you can alter a Bias value that can adjust intersecting edges. Each of these options can be applied as a map.

Tutorial: Cartooning a turtle

As an example of the Ink 'n' Paint material, you'll render a cartoonish turtle model created by Zygote Media as a cartoon that is fit for the Sunday papers.

To apply the Ink 'n' Paint material to a turtle model, follow these steps:

1. Open the Cartoon turtle.max file from the Chap 30 directory on the CD.

   This file includes a simple turtle model.

2. With the turtle model selected, open the Material Editor by choosing the Rendering ⇨ Material Editor ⇨ Slate Material Editor menu command (or by pressing the M key).

3. In the Utility panel, select the Color Clipboard button, and in the Color Clipboard rollout, click the New Floater button. A palette of colors opens. Drag the Diffuse colors from the Material Editor for each current material to the Color Clipboard. Max asks if you want to Swap, Copy, or Cancel the material. Select the Copy option. Leave the Color Clipboard window open.

4. Select the first sample slot, and click on the Material Type button to open the Material/Map Browser. Double-click the Ink 'n' Paint material type from the list. Then drag the corresponding color from the Color Clipboard and copy it in the Lighted color swatch of the Paint Controls rollout. Repeat this for each of the five materials.

5. Open and render the Perspective viewport using the Render Scene dialog box.

Figure 30.4 shows the resulting cartoon.

Cartooning made easy with the Ink 'n' Paint material

Using Architectural Materials

If you look in the Material/Map Browser, you'll notice an Architectural material. This material is specifically designed for creating realistic materials that can be applied to buildings and interiors. The Architectural material uses predefined templates to create almost any type of material that you'd find in a building, including ceramic, fabric, metal, glass, stone, wood, and water. The real benefit of using the Architectural materials is how they interact with real-world lights. Using Photometric lights and Radiosity produces realistic results.

Note

If you've selected the mental ray renderer, then the Arch & Design material and the various ProMaterials become available. These materials are a more powerful and extensive set of architectural materials. You can learn more about this and other mental ray materials later in this chapter. ■

Figure 30.5 shows a house that uses several of these architectural materials. Notice how the shingles on the roof are consistent.

FIGURE 30.5

Architectural materials make adding textures to a building easy.

Using the DirectX and MetaSL Shader Material

The Material Editor includes support for DirectX 9 and 10 shaders using the DirectX Shader material. These shaders are saved as .fx files and are available only if the Direct3D display driver is enabled. FX files are text files created using the Higher-Level Shader Language (HLSL). The DirectX Shader also can load in NVidia CgFX files and mental image's MetaSL shaders, saved with the .XMSL extension.

Note

The DirectX Shader material is available only if you are using the DirectX display driver. ■

In the maps/fx directory where Max is installed are several example DirectX shaders. You can load these example shaders using the button in the DirectX Shader rollout. The available parameters are different for each shader. Figure 30.6 shows several rifles with various FX shaders applied.

FIGURE 30.6

The Direct X Shader material lets you view game assets in the viewport.

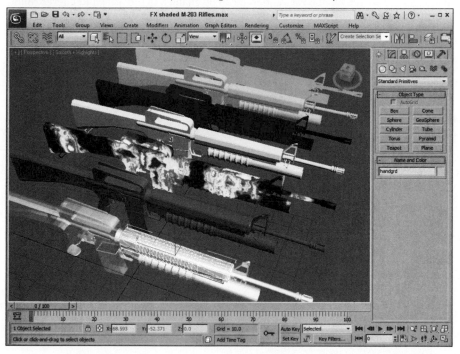

FX shaders are commonly used in games, and applying an FX shader to an object displays the shader in the viewport. This display looks the same as if the object were rendered in the game engine. However, if you render an object with an FX shader applied, it will appear as default gray unless you specify a material to appear using the Software Render Style rollout.

If the Quicksilver Hardware or mental ray renderers are enabled, you can also make MetaSL shader tree materials visible in the viewports. The Material/Map Browser includes several MetaSL shaders in the Maps/MetaSL rollout. Because these shaders are represented as maps in the Material Editor, you need to use the Map to Material Conversion material node to make the shaders visible in the viewports. You also need to enable hardware shading to view these shaders in the viewport. MetaSL materials also can be exported using the Material ⇨ Export As XMSL File menu command in the Slate Material Editor.

Note

MetaSL shaders can be created using mental mill, Artist Edition, which is available for download on the Autodesk site. ■

Using mental ray Materials and Shaders

If the mental ray, iray, or the Quicksilver Hardware renderer is enabled, you can open the Material/Map Browser in the Material Editor and be greeted with many additional material and map types and also the Autodesk Material Library, which includes hundreds of preset materials organized by category, as shown in Figure 30.7. The mental ray rendered can be enabled in the Assign Renderer rollout located at the bottom of the Common panel of the Render Scene dialog box.

Note

If you enable the Show Incompatible option in the Material/Map Browser pop-up menu, then you can view the list of mental ray materials even if the mental ray renderer isn't enabled. ■

Cross-Reference

You can learn more about enabling the mental ray renderer in Chapter 47, "Rendering with mental ray and iray." ■

FIGURE 30.7

The Material/Map Browser includes many additional mental ray materials from the Autodesk Material Library.

Understanding shaders

A *shader* is an algorithm that defines the surface color for all pixels in the scene. Surface Shaders come to this conclusion by factoring in such details as texture files, reflection, refraction, and atmospheric effects. Atmospheric Shaders change the light properties as they move through a volume. Shaders can be programmed and applied to objects and scenes, and renderers like mental ray render the scene based on these shaders.

Accessing mental ray materials and shaders

With the mental ray (or Quicksilver) renderer selected, all non–mental ray materials include an additional rollout labeled mental ray Connection. This rollout, shown in Figure 30.8, is available only if the mental ray extensions are enabled in the mental ray panel of the Preference Settings dialog box. They let you override the existing shaders used by the Scanline renderer and enable additional shaders that the mental ray renderer will use.

The mental ray Connection rollout in the Material Editor lets you override the default shaders.

The lock icons to the right of the shader buttons are the default shaders used by the Scanline renderer. To select a new shader, simply unlock these shaders by clicking the lock button. If a material is opaque, you can speed up the rendering process by flagging the material as Opaque, using the option at the bottom of the rollout.

If you want to get direct access to the shaders used by mental ray, use the mental ray material type, which presents all the shaders listed in the mental ray Connection rollout.

Using the Autodesk Material Library and the Arch & Design materials

The Autodesk Material Library and the Arch & Design materials are a set of advanced mental ray materials designed for architects to add to buildings and surfaces found in architecture renderings. All of these materials are based on physical properties that are typically found in environments lighted with global illumination. For example, the Satin Varnished Wood template includes slightly blurred reflections and a high glossiness to give it a realistic look.

The materials contained in the Autodesk Material Library are categorized into groups and subgroups. Each material has several parameters allowing you to change the color, glossiness, reflectivity, and so on. The available parameters change based on the selected material.

Many of the Arch & Design materials are already defined and available in the Templates rollout. The available presets include Pearl Finish, Satin Varnished Wood, Glazed Ceramic, Glossy Plastic, Masonry, Leather, Frosted Glass, Translucent Plastic Film, Brushed Metal, and Patterned Copper.

For each template, several rollouts of parameters are available for defining the Diffuse, Reflection, Refraction, Translucency, Anisotropy, Fresnel Reflections, Bumps, and Self-Illumination properties along with a full selection of maps. Figure 30.9 shows a sampling of the available materials.

FIGURE 30.9

The materials in the mental ray Arch & Design collection include a broad set of physical properties.

Within the Special Effects rollout are two specialized options that add to the render realism. Ambient Occlusion lights the scene based on how accessible ambient light is to scene objects. It is a material shader solution and is not based on lights. Areas that face a wall or are blocked by other objects are recessed in shadow. Areas facing the lights are highlighted more. Using the Samples and Max Distance, you can control the contrast of the resulting image. By default, ambient occlusion uses black and gray tones to show occluded areas, but if you enable the Use Color From Other Materials (Exact AO), then the object's diffuse color is reflected into the occluded areas. Figure 30.10 shows an example of Ambient Occlusion.

Note

The Nitrous display drivers make ambient occlusion effects visible in the viewports.

The other useful special effect option is Round Corners. When you apply this option to a mechanical object, the object's edge is rounded so the light source highlights the edge, but no change is made to the object's geometry. This creates a realistic soft edge without the time or extra polygons to create it using geometry.

Using the Self Illumination (Glow) rollout, you can make a material act as a light source to the scene. This rollout includes presets for photometric properties based on real-world values such as degrees Kelvin.

FIGURE 30.10

Ambient Occlusion lets you light the scene by controlling the ambient light that gets bounced around the scene.

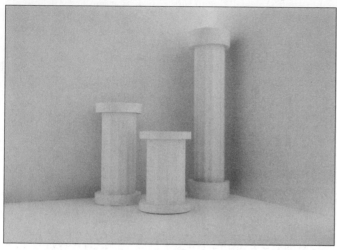

Using the Car Paint material

When cars are painted in the factory, the paint is composed of two layers that give the car its unique look. The undercoat is called the flake layer, and it shines through the top layer. The mental ray Car Paint material includes settings for defining both of these layers. Figure 30.11 shows a car painted with this material.

FIGURE 30.11

Cars rendered with the mental ray Car Paint shader use multiple layers, just like real cars.

Combining bump and displacement maps

When mental ray is enabled, you can also take advantage of the Utility Bump and Displace Combiner materials. These materials let you combine up to three different bump or displacement maps into a single material. Each map has its own multiplier that is used to set its intensity.

Using the Subsurface Scattering materials

The four mental ray materials that begin with "SSS" are Subsurface Scattering materials used to shade human skin. Skin has an interesting property that allows it to become slightly translucent when it is placed in front of a strong light source. The ears in particular are a good example of this because they allow light to penetrate and highlight their features. Most organic objects including leaves, rubber, milk, and skin can benefit from these materials.

Cross-Reference

If you want more information on mental ray, check out Chapter 47, "Rendering with mental ray and iray." ■

Summary

This chapter covered an assortment of specialized materials that enable specific types of effects. These specialized materials include matte/shadow, Ink 'n' Paint, DirectX Shader, and the various mental ray materials including the Arch & Design, Car Paint, and Subsurface Scattering materials.

In this chapter, you've learned about the following:

- Using the matte/shadow material to hide objects
- Creating a cartoon rendering with the Ink 'n' Paint materials
- Viewing game assets with the DirectX Shader
- Using the Arch & Design and ProMaterials materials
- Applying a multilayer car paint material
- Using the Subsurface Scattering materials

In the next chapter, you discover how the viewport can be made into a Canvas for painting directly on scene objects. The ability to render surface maps also is presented.

Working with Procedural Substance Textures

Substance materials are made possible using a Substance map type found in the Material Editor. Although using these Substance materials tends to produce materials that look the same as other material types, the procedural aspect of these materials makes them unique. Most materials with this level of detail require a bitmap texture, and the larger the bitmap, the better the detail. These bitmaps, even when saved using a compressed format, can easily run several megabytes in size. Procedural textures, however, are created using a code, and the result is file sizes that are usually measured in kilobytes instead of megabytes.

So the benefit to using procedural textures is that you can get the detail of an amazing material without the cost in file size. Another huge advantage is that you can easily make changes to the textures by inputting different values into the code. This gives you lots of variety without having to duplicate, reload, and save in memory several different bitmaps. For certain conditions, such as 3d for the Web or for games, these advantages are huge.

Selecting and Applying Substance Textures

The Substance textures feature isn't a whole new way of creating textures with its own interface and rendering engine. Substance textures work with the existing materials in the Material Editor, and unless you were looking for them, you might miss them. Substance textures are available in the Material/Map Browser under the Maps category and can be used with the normal set of default materials.

w Feature

tance procedural textures are new to 3ds Max 2012. ■

The Substance map node includes output nodes for Diffuse, Specular, Normal, Bump, Displacement, Height, and Glossiness attributes. The material tree, shown in Figure 31.1, uses a Substance map to control the Diffuse and Normal channels of a Standard material.

FIGURE 31.1

Substance materials are made possible using the Substance map node.

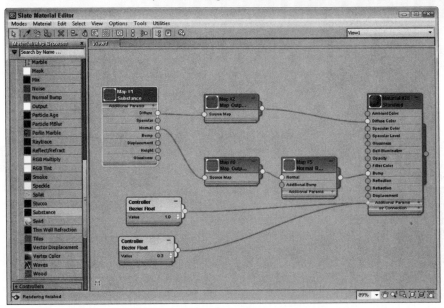

After it's correctly linked, the resulting material is applied to an object in the viewport as usual by selecting the object and clicking the Assign Material to Selection button in the Material Editor or by simply dragging the output for the Standard material node to the object. The applied material is then rendered using the default rendering methods. Figure 31.2 shows the resulting Old Painted Planks Substance material applied to a cube.

Loading Substance textures

The available Substance textures are limited to the included set that ships with Max, but within the Substance Package Browser rollout is a button to Get Substance From Marketplace. This button opens a web browser to the Allegorithmic website where you can browse and purchase additional texture sets. Allegorithmic is the company that created the Substance textures.

3ds Max includes more than 80 preinstalled Substance textures. To choose from the installed texture sets, simply click the Load Substance button in the Substance Package Browser rollout of the Material Editor. This opens to the Maps/Substance folder where Max is installed. The available textures are divided into two folders: Noises and Textures.

FIGURE 31.2

Substance materials have lots of detail despite their small file size.

Linking Substance maps

Because Substance textures are available only as map nodes in the Material Editor, you need to link them to a base material in order to apply them to objects. To do this, simply create a Substance node by selecting and double-clicking it in the Material/Map Browser. A base material node, such as Standard, also must be added to the Slate Material Editor view pane.

After a Substance node is in the Material Editor's view window, select it and use the Load Substance button in the Substance Package Browser rollout to load a specific texture type. Then drag from the Substance node's Diffuse channel to the Diffuse channel on the Standard node. A Map Output node is automatically added to the material tree between the Substance and Standard nodes.

The other channels—Normal, Bump, and Displacement on the Substance node—also can be mapped to the Standard node. If you link the Normal map to the Standard node, you need to go through a Normal Bump map before linking to the Standard node's Bump channel.

Any Substance textures that have a Displacement channel can link directly to the Displacement channel on the Standard material node. The Height channel in Substance textures also can be linked to the Standard node's Displacement channel. The Height channel combines the Bump and Displacement information into a single channel. If a Substance texture is linked to both the Bump and Displacement channels, you can use the Relief Balance setting in the Parameters rollout to change the weighting between these two channels.

Some Substance textures such as Fencing have an Opacity channel. Connecting this channel to the Opacity channel on the Standard node causes the area between the fence links to show what is behind them. The Autumn Leaves texture has an Opacity channel also. Figure 31.3 shows an autumn leaves texture on top of a grass texture.

FIGURE 31.3

Some textures use the Opacity channel to allow textures beneath to show through.

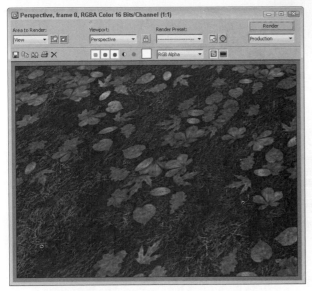

Several other Substance textures have an Emissive channel. This can be connected to the Self-Illumination channel to create a glow.

After the Substance map node is linked in, you can apply it to a scene object and render to see its results.

Randomizing Substance textures

Although the Substance node has several different rollouts available, including Texture Size, Coordinates, and Noise, each specific texture has its own set of parameters with several options for randomizing the texture. For example, Crumpled Paper has a Crumpled Paper Parameters rollout with settings for Crumple, Dirt, Paper Color, and so on.

Almost every Substance texture also has a Random Seed setting that controls the randomness of the texture. By changing this value, you can create a uniquely different texture, even though all the other settings are identical. Also, two textures with the same Random Seed value have the same results. Figure 31.4 shows the Cracked Plaster texture with identical settings except for the Random Seed value.

FIGURE 31.4

Substance textures can be made to appear different by changing the Random Seed value.

Tutorial: Applying Substance textures to a scene

The Substance textures are especially good at creating worn, old-looking textures. It is easy to add the randomness of rust and corrosion to surfaces, so we use several Substance textures to create an abandoned city scene.

To create a scene using Substance textures, follow these steps:

1. Open the Wall and crates.max file from the Chap 31 directory on the CD.

    This file contains several primitive shapes positioned to create a simple scene.

2. Select the plane object in front that represents the ground, and open the Slate Material Editor by choosing Rendering ⇨ Material Editor ⇨ Slate Material Editor (or by pressing the M key).

3. Double-click the Standard material in the Material/Map Browser, and then locate and double-click the Substance and Normal Bump maps in the Maps folder. Double-click the Substance node in the Node View pane, and click the Load Substance button. Select and load the Dry Ground 02 option from the file dialog box.

4. Connect the Diffuse channels from the Substance node to the Standard node, and then connect the Normal channel of the Substance node to the Normal Bump map and the output of the Normal Bump map node to the Bump mode of the Standard node. Between nodes, a Map Output node is automatically created. Double-click the Standard material node in the Node View, and click the Assign Material to Selection button in the Material Editor to apply the selected material.

5. Select the background wall object in the viewport, and repeat Steps 3 and 4, applying the Brick Wall 03 Substance texture.

6. Select the top crate object, and repeat Steps 3 and 4 to apply the Aircraft Metal Substance texture.

7. Select all the crate objects in the viewport, and apply the Aircraft Metal Substance texture to it using the method in Steps 3 and 4.

Figure 31.5 shows the resulting scene.

FIGURE 31.5

Substance textures can add lots of detail to a scene.

Summary

This chapter covered the basics of using the Substance map node to create highly detailed textures without the file size overhead. Textures created with Substance can be exported to a game engine using a plug-in tool that is available from Allegorithmic.

In this chapter, you accomplished the following:

- Selecting and applying Substance materials to objects
- Randomizing Substance textures using the Parameter values

The next chapter covers the Viewport Canvas, which lets you paint directly on objects. It also presents a feature for rendering surface maps.

Painting in the Viewport Canvas and Rendering Surface Maps

M ax is a 3D tool, and creating scenes with Max is quite a bit different from the traditional painting programs. Sometimes when you're working on a scene, especially when applying textures, you'll ache to return to those simple, older painting programs of yesteryear. Happily, Max includes a mode that lets you simply throw paint around just like those old paint programs.

This paint mode is called the Viewport Canvas, and it turns the entire active viewport into a 2D surface; even better, when you are finished painting, your masterpiece is automatically transferred to the current object as a texture map.

If the ability to paint directly in the viewport doesn't interest you, then you'll be happy to know that you can use Max to render out a surface map that you can load into Photoshop or your favorite image-editing package and use as a template for your textures.

Using the Viewport Canvas

The Viewport Canvas lets you easily apply a painted texture to the selected object. It also has a feature that lets you choose the type of brush you paint with. The Canvas also includes a standard paint brush that is configurable and a Clone brush for copying anything viewed in the active viewport, along with several other brushes.

To activate the Viewport Canvas, simply select the Tools ⇨ Viewport Canvas menu command, and the Viewport Canvas panel appears, as shown in Figure 32.1.

Tip

The Viewport Canvas palette can be docked to the left or right side of the interface by right-clicking the palette's title bar and selecting the dock location from the pop-up menu. ∎

FIGURE 32.1

The Viewport Canvas panel turns the viewport into a 2D painting canvas.

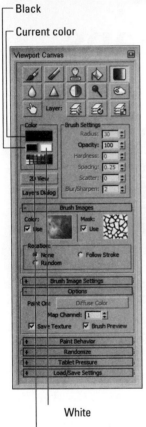

- Black
- Current color
- White
- Open Color Palette

Setting up an object for painting

The Canvas requires some setup before you can use it. The Viewport Canvas can be used on any object that has mapping coordinates. Mapping coordinates are applied to a primitive object by enabling the Generate Mapping Coordinates option in the Command Panel, or by adding the UVW Mapping or UVW Unwrap modifier to an object.

With an object selected, select one of the brushes in the Canvas palette; if the object has a material with a bitmap applied, you can begin painting right away. If the object doesn't have a material or a texture applied, then the Assign Material dialog box appears, as shown in Figure 32.2.

FIGURE 32.2

The Assign Material dialog box lets you choose the channel to paint on.

The Assign Standard Material button pops up a list of available channels where the texture may be applied using the Standard material. The Browse Material to Assign button opens the Material/Map Browser, where you can choose the type of material to use. The list of available channels includes Ambient Color, Diffuse Color, Specular Color, Specular Level, Glossiness, Self-Illumination, Opacity, Filter Color, Bump, Reflection, Refraction, and Displacement. After choosing a texture channel, the Create Texture dialog box appears, as shown in Figure 32.3, where you can set the size of the texture map and specify where the texture is saved, or you can select an existing texture. If a new texture is created, you need to specify a path and name for the new texture file. The texture is automatically mapped to the selected channel for the object's material. The Color setting is used for the texture's initial background color.

FIGURE 32.3

The Create Texture dialog box automates the process of applying a material with a texture.

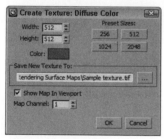

Using the Canvas brushes

After the texture is set up, you can begin painting by clicking the Paint brush icon and dragging in the viewport over the selected object. Using the settings under the brush icons, you can set the Color, Radius, Opacity, Hardness, Spacing, Scatter, and Blur/Sharpen values. The available settings change depending on the brush selected.

When a brush is selected, it is highlighted in the Viewport Canvas palette and remains active until another brush is selected or until you right-click in the viewport. Table 32.1 lists the available brushes and layer tools.

TABLE 32.1

Viewport Canvas Brush Icons

Palette Icon	Name	Description
	Paint	Applies paint using the selected color or image.
	Erase	Removes paint applied from any of the brushes on the selected layer, but not from the background layer.
	Clone	Copies paint from another part of the current texture. Click with the Alt key held down to set the copy point. A green dot marks the copy location. Within the Paint Behavior rollout, you can select the Clone Source to be the Current Layer, All Layers, the Viewport, or the Screen.
	Fill	Fills the entire texture with paint. If you're painting with an image, you can set the image to Tile or to 3D Wrap using the options in the Paint Behavior rollout.
	Gradient	Lets you drag to extend a gradient across the surface of the object. Full color (or image) is painted where you first click and full transparency is painted where you stop dragging. The orientation of the gradient is aligned to the direction that you drag.
	Blur	Blurs the area under the brush.
	Sharper	Sharpens the area under the brush.
	Contrast	Increases the contrast of the area under the brush.
	Dodge	Lightens the area under the brush.
	Burn	Darkens the area under the brush.
	Smudge	Distorts and smudges the area under the brush.
	Move Layer	Allows the current layer to be moved.
	Rotate Layer	Allows the current layer to be rotated about the texture's center.
	Scale Layer	Allows the current layer to be scaled about the texture's center.

New Feature

The ability to clone texture from anywhere on the screen in new to 3ds Max 2012. ∎

Caution

The Background layer cannot be moved, rotated, or scaled. ∎

If the Paint brush is selected, you can immediately switch to the Erase brush by holding down the Shift key. Holding down the Ctrl key lets you click to select a different color from the current texture. Pressing the Spacebar causes a straight line to be drawn from the last painted location to the current cursor location. The Spacebar shortcut also works with the Eraser brush.

With any of the standard brushes, you can hold down the Ctrl+Shift keys to drag and change the brush radius. The Alt+Shift keys change the brush Opacity, and the Ctrl+Alt keys change the brush's Hardness value.

Clicking the Color swatch opens a Color Selector dialog box where you can choose a new color. You also can load a custom color palette using the Open Color Palette button or quickly switch between black and white colors, which is helpful for painting value maps.

At any time while painting, you are free in the viewport to rotate the model around to paint in a different location.

If you don't like the results after the painted texture has been applied to the object, click the Undo/Redo button to remove the last set of changes. Clicking the Undo/Redo button again reapplies the recent changes.

Painting with images

In the Brush Images rollout are two swatches for selecting an image and a mask to paint with. Clicking the swatches opens a palette of presets, as shown in Figure 32.4. Clicking the Browse Custom Maps Directory button opens Windows Explorer to the Viewport Canvas folder where Max is installed. Within this folder are all the custom images and masks that are included in the palette.

FIGURE 32.4

Custom images and masks can be added to the available presets in the Viewport Canvas.

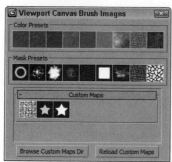

Placing a new image or an image with an alpha channel (for masks) in this folder makes them appear in the presets palette and allows you to select and paint with them. The Reload Custom Maps button reloads any images placed in the folder so they can be seen.

To use an image or a mask, simply enable the Use option next to each. You also have several Rotation options including None, Random, and Follow Stroke. Figure 32.5 shows examples of each painting with stars. The left eye shows the None option, and all stars are oriented exactly the same. The right eye shows the Random option with each star oriented differently; the lower line shows the Follow Stroke option with the stars aligned in the direction of the brush stroke.

The image rotation options determine how the stars are oriented.

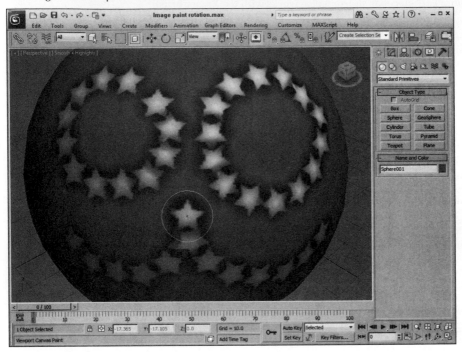

Within the Brush Image Settings rollout are some options for setting how the image is projected onto the object. The options include Hit Normal and From Screen. The Hit Normal option applies the image as if projected down onto the normal of the object. The From Screen option applies the texture as if projected from the screen position onto the object. Other options make the image fit within the brush size and offer tiling options of None, Tile, and Across Screen.

Using paint layers

The Viewport Canvas palette lets you paint on layers just like you can in Photoshop. To access the layers, click the Layers Dialog button in the Viewport Canvas dialog box. The Layers palette, shown in Figure 32.6, shows the current layers in a stack. Each layer can be named, and the layers are placed on the object with the top layers appearing on top of the lower layers. You also can select a blend method and an Opacity value. The buttons at the bottom of the Layers palette let you create new layers, duplicate the current layer, or delete a layer. The small light bulb icon to the left of the layer name lets you turn a layer on or off.

When a layer other than the Background layer is selected, you can use the Layer tool icons located at the top of the Viewport Canvas palette. These Layer tools let you move, rotate, and/or scale the current layer.

FIGURE 32.6

The Layers palette lets you work with layers for the current texture.

Blend method

Duplicate Layer

Add New Layer

Delete Layer

Caution

Be aware that you cannot erase any paint applied to the Background layer using the Erase tool. ■

The Layers palette includes some menus that have many of the same commands found in Photoshop. For example, you can use the Layer menu to add layer masks, merge a layer down, flip a layer either horizontally or vertically, or flatten all visible layers.

The Adjust menu includes options for changing the Brightness, Contrast, Hue, Saturation, Levels, or Color Balance. You also have an Auto Levels option. The Filter menu includes filters for blurring, sharpening, finding edges, median, threshold, high pass, and distort.

Within the File menu are options for pasting from the clipboard, loading a bitmap into the current layer, saving the current bitmap (as a flattened file), or saving the image with all layers to a PSD file that can be reopened in Photoshop.

Tip

If you want to maintain the various layers after you're finished painting, be sure to save your texture using an image format that supports layers, such as PSD. ■

If you've added any layers to your texture and you exit the Canvas, the Save Texture Layers dialog box, shown in Figure 32.7, opens. Using this dialog box, you can choose to continue painting, save the file as a PSD file, which maintains the various layers, flatten all layers and save the texture, save and replace, save, flatten and then save again, or simply discard. If you plan to revisit the layers of your texture, save it as a PSD file, but if you're happy with the results, you can flatten and save the texture.

FIGURE 32.7

The Save Texture Layers dialog box lets you maintain the various texture layers.

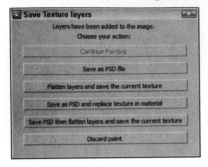

Painting in 2D

Painting directly on a 3D object has its advantages, but when painting over a random surface, the results can be irregular. The Viewport Canvas dialog box includes a 2D painting mode that displays the current texture in a rectangular window and lets you paint directly on the texture. This is helpful for textures that need to be projected onto an object such as those with text.

To access the 2D painting mode, simply click the 2D View button under the colors and the current texture is opened in a window, as shown in Figure 32.8. The buttons at the top of this window let you see the UV wireframes, fit the texture in the view, or view the image at its actual size. Any changes made to the texture in 2D painting mode are immediately reflected on the selected object in the viewports.

Clicking the 2D View button again toggles the 2D painting mode off, and the 2D Paint window closes.

Using the paint options

When the Viewport Canvas palette is open, several additional rollouts hold the options that affect the various brushes and texture. Within the Options rollout, you can select which map type and channel to paint on. There is also an option to Save Texture. If this option is disabled, any paint applied to the texture isn't saved. This lets you try a different look without saving it. You can also do this by painting on a new layer that could be deleted. The Brush Preview option shows the outline and size of the brush as you paint.

Within the Paint Behavior rollout are options to have the paint affect any areas of the object within the brush's spherical radius or to apply the paint through the entire object with the Depth option. The Mirroring options let you mirror all paint strokes across the X, Y, or Z axes.

The Randomize rollout, shown in Figure 32.9, lets you set the minimum and maximum values for several different settings including Brush Radius, Opacity, Spacing, Scatter, and Color.

Using the Table Pressure rollout, you can select which attributes are affected by an increase in the tablet pressure. The options include Brush Radius, Opacity, Hardness, and Scatter.

The Load/Save Settings rollout includes buttons for saving and loading the Viewpoint Canvas settings. Settings are saved using a simple text file. There is also a button for saving the current settings as the default.

FIGURE 32.8

2D painting mode lets you paint directly on the texture without any perspective distortion.

Toggle UV Wireframe

Fit Texture to View

Actual Size

FIGURE 32.9

Using the Randomize rollout, you can add variety to the texture.

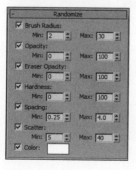

Tutorial: Face painting

To show off the Viewport Canvas, we do some face painting on a women's head model. This model was created by Zygote Media and is a good example of a high-res model.

To paint on a character's face using the Viewport Canvas, follow these steps:

1. Open the Face painting.max file from the Chap 32 directory on the CD.

    This file includes a women's head mesh created by Zygote Media.

2. Rotate the head model so the cheek is clearly visible, apply the UVW Map modifier to make sure the object has mapping coordinates with the Planar map, and click the View Align button.

3. Open the Viewport Canvas panel with the Tools ⇨ Viewport Canvas menu command.

4. Select the model, and click the Paint Brush icon in the Viewport Canvas panel, then select the Diffuse Color option in the pop-up menu. In the Create Texture dialog box that pops up next, select the 512 × 512 preset and click the file button next to the Save New Texture field to open the file dialog box. Save the file as Face Painting texture.tif, and click the Ok button.

5. Set the brush Radius to **32**, the blending mode to **Normal**, and the Opacity to **100,** and choose a bright red color. Then click the Brush icon, and draw a heart on the women's cheek. Then click the Paint icon again to apply the texture to the model.

Figure 32.10 shows the resulting applied texture.

FIGURE 32.10

The Viewport Canvas painting mode can be used to apply paint directly to a model.

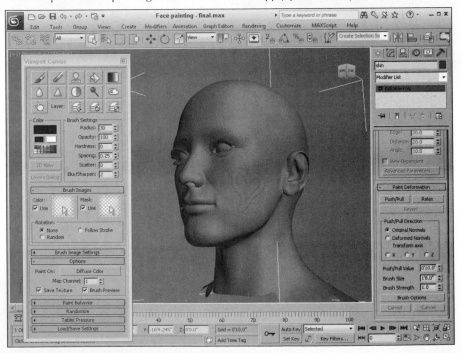

Using Vertex Colors

Another similar feature to the Viewport Canvas is the Vertex Paint modifier. This modifier lets you apply colors to a model without the weight of a texture. When creating models for games, the size of the texture map can be prohibitive. I mean, what model that weighs in at 16KB or less wants to carry around a 2MB texture map? The solution that much of the gaming world relies on is to apply a single color to a vertex. Having each vertex remember its color (or even several colors) requires very little additional information for the mesh and can create some good shading. Colors are then interpolated across the face of the polygon between two different colors on adjacent vertices.

The results aren't as clean and detailed as texture maps, but for their size, vertex colors are worth the price.

Assigning vertex colors

Vertex colors can be assigned in the Surface Properties rollout for Editable Mesh and Editable Patch objects, and in the Vertex and Polygon Properties rollouts for Editable Poly objects. They also can be assigned in Face, Polygon, and Element subobject modes using a little rollout section called Edit Vertex Colors. Within this section are two color swatches for selecting Color and Illumination values. The Alpha value sets the alpha transparency value for the vertex.

Painting vertices with the Vertex Paint modifier

Another, more interactive way to color vertices is with the Vertex Paint modifier. This modifier lets you paint on an object by specifying a color for each vertex. If adjacent vertices have different colors assigned, a gradient is created across the face. The benefit of this coloring option is that it is very efficient and requires almost no memory.

The Vertex Paint modifier lets you specify a color and paint directly on the surface of an object by painting the vertices. The color is applied with a paintbrush-shaped cursor. The modifier can be applied multiple times to an object, giving you the ability to blend several layers of vertex paints together. You can find this modifier in the Modifiers ⇨ Mesh Editing submenu.

Note

After the Vertex Paint modifier has been applied to an object, the Paintbox automatically reappears whenever the object is reselected. ■

Applying this modifier opens a Vertex Paint dialog box called the Paintbox, shown in Figure 32.11. At the top of the Paintbox are four icons that can be used to show the visible results of the painting in the viewports. The options include Vertex Color Display–Unshaded, Vertex Color Display–Shaded, Disable Vertex Color Display, and Toggle Texture Display On/Off.

The Vertex Color icon flyout lets you work on the Vertex Color, Illumination, Alpha, or any one of the 99 available map channels. The lock icon locks the display to the selected channel, or you could be looking at a different channel from the one you are painting.

The large Paint and Erase buttons let you add or remove vertex colors using the color specified in the color swatch. You also can select colors from objects in the viewports using the eyedropper tool and then set the Opacity.

FIGURE 32.11

The Paintbox palette for the Vertex Paint modifier includes a wealth of features.

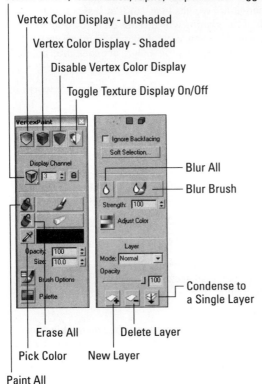

Vertex Colors, Illumination, Alpha, Map Channel Toggle

Vertex Color Display - Unshaded

Vertex Color Display - Shaded

Disable Vertex Color Display

Toggle Texture Display On/Off

Blur All

Blur Brush

Condense to a Single Layer

Erase All

Delete Layer

Pick Color

New Layer

Paint All

The Size value determines the size of the brush used to paint. Max supports pressure-sensitive devices such as a graphics tablet, and you can set the brush options using the Brush Options dialog box. When painting on the surface of an object, a blue normal line appears. This line guides you as you paint so you know you're on the correct surface.

Cross-Reference

The Painter Options dialog box also is used by the Skin modifier and the Paint Deformation tool. It is described in detail in Chapter 13, "Modeling with Polygons." ∎

Beneath the Brush Options button is a Palette button that opens the Color Palette interface, shown in Figure 32.12. The Color Palette holds custom colors and lets you copy and paste colors between the different swatches. Collections of colors can be saved by right-clicking the Color Palette and selecting the Save As command. Color palettes are saved as Color Clipboard files with the .ccb extension.

FIGURE 32.12

The Color Palette can display colors as a list or as swatches.

Copy

Delete | Paste

New | Color Picker

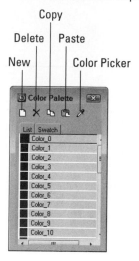

The Paintbox also includes three subobject selection icons. These icons can be used to select certain Vertices, Faces, or Elements to be painted. This limits the painting to the selected subobjects only. You also can select to Ignore Backfacing and use Soft Selection.

The Blur brush button lets you blur colors across polygons using a brush that works just like the Paint and Erase brushes.

The Adjust Color dialog box lets you change all the painted colors applied to an object using HSV or RGB color sliders. The Preview option makes the color adjustment visible in the viewports if selected. Below the Adjust Color icon is the Blur Selected icon that blurs together all the vertex colors based on the designated Amount value.

Colors can be mixed between layers using the various blending modes. Clicking the New Layer button adds a new instance of the Vertex Paint modifier to the Modifier Stack; the Delete Layer button does the opposite. Click the Condense to a Single Layer button to merge all the consecutive Vertex Paint modifiers to a single instance using the selected blending mode.

Tutorial: Marking heart tension

As an example of using the Vertex Paint modifier, imagine a doctor who has a 3D model of the human heart. While discussing the results of the latest test with a patient, the doctor can color parts of the heart model to illustrate the various points.

To color on a human heart using the Vertex Paint modifier, follow these steps:

1. Open the Vertex paint on the heart.max file from the Chap 32 directory on the CD.

    This file includes a heart mesh created by Viewpoint Datalabs.

2. Select a portion of the heart model, and choose Modifiers ➪ Mesh Editing ➪ Vertex Paint to apply the Vertex Paint modifier.

3. In the Paintbox that opens, choose the Vertex Color Display–Shaded button at the top of the Vertex Paint dialog box, select the red color, and click the Paint button. Then drag the mouse over the surface of the Perspective view.

Figure 32.13 shows the resulting color.

FIGURE 32.13

The Vertex Paint modifier can apply color to an object by assigning a color to its vertices.

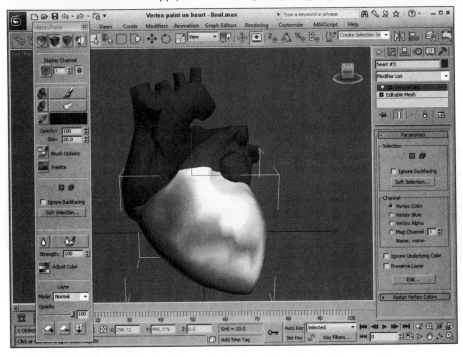

The Assign Vertex Color utility

The Assign Vertex Color utility works a little differently. It converts any existing material colors to vertex colors. To use this utility, select the utility from the Utilities list that opens when you click the More button in the Utility panel, select an object, choose a Channel, choose a Light Model (Lighting + Diffuse, Lighting Only, or Diffuse Only), and click the Assign to Selected button.

Rendering Surface Maps

Max can be used to create some useful maps based on the geometry of the object. For example, a Cavity map is generated by looking at the concavity of the model. This appears as a grayscale map where the convex portions are white and the concave portions are black. Such a map can then be reused as a diffuse dirt submaterial map for showing those areas that are tight and indented. These tightly concave areas are the likely areas for non-specular highlights and for dirt to appear on old and weathered models.

Max can use the Render Surface Map feature to render several types of surface maps, including the following:

- **Cavity map:** The Cavity map creates a grayscale map that highlights convex areas in white and concave areas in black. The Contrast value defines the difference between black and white values.

- **Density map:** The Density map option creates a map that shows the areas where the vertices are closest together as white and farther apart as black.

- **Dust map:** The Dust map option creates a grayscale map that identifies the areas that face upward as white and the underneath areas as black, as if the dust were to settle from above and land on all the white areas.

- **SubSurface map:** The SubSurface map is used to identify those areas of the mesh that are thickest as black and the thinnest areas of the mesh as white. This map type is used to show how likely light would pass through a given area. The Blur value is used to blur those areas between black and white.

- **Selection to Bitmap:** This map is used to identify a specific subobject selection. Each selected vertex is displayed as a white dot.

- **Texture Wrap:** The Texture Wrap feature lets you load in a texture that is wrapped about the object in a way to eliminate all seams. This texture could be a simple skin or hide texture. The Tile value is the number of times the texture is repeated end to end to cover the surface.

- **Bitmap Select:** This feature allows you to select specific subobject selections based on the color of the applied bitmap. For example, if you load a bitmap with white lines running through it, all polygon faces that touch those lines are selected.

To access the Render Surface Map panel, shown in Figure 32.14, select the Rendering ⇨ Render Surface Map. This feature works only on Editable Poly objects that have mapping coordinates. If any of these conditions are missing, a warning dialog box appears when you click one of the mapping buttons.

FIGURE 32.14

The Render Surface Map panel can create several different types of maps.

The Width and Height values set the resolution of the rendered bitmap. The Size button has several presets. You also can set the Map Channel and the Seam Bleed values. When you click the map type, the map is generated and displayed in the Rendered Frame Window. Figure 32.15 shows the Cavity map for the crocodile model. The jagged fins are all white because they stick out.

FIGURE 32.15

The Cavity map shows areas that are convex and concave.

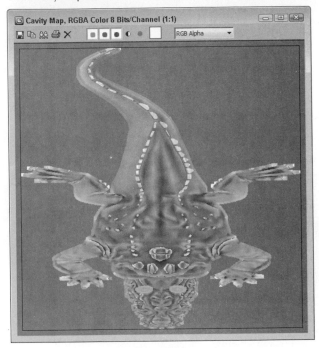

Summary

This chapter covered a couple of key features for applying materials. The Viewport Canvas lets you paint directly in the viewport and have the results transferred to the selected object. Surface maps can be rendered to provide a map that gives information about the surface of the object.

In this chapter, you learned about the following:

- Painting on objects with the Viewport Canvas
- Using Vertex Colors to paint models
- Rendering a variety of surface maps

In the next chapter, you learn how the Unwrap UVW modifier can be used to customize the mapping coordinates for an object. You also explore one specific type of mapping a little closer. The Pelt mapping method lets you split and unwrap complicated models by using seams.

Unwrapping UVs and Mapping Textures

Throughout the modeling chapter, as you created objects, the Generate Mapping Coordinates option appeared for almost all objects. Now you find out what mapping coordinates are and how to use them.

Mapping coordinates define how a texture map is aligned to an object. These coordinates are expressed using U, V, and W dimensions. U is a horizontal direction, V is a vertical direction, and W is depth.

When you enable the Generate Mapping Coordinates option for new objects, Max takes its best guess at where these coordinates should be located. For example, a Box primitive applies a texture map to each face. This works well in some cases, but you won't have to wait long until you'll want to change the coordinates.

Control over the mapping coordinates is accomplished using many different modifiers, including the granddaddy of them all—UVW Unwrap.

Peel and Pelt mapping are two additional mapping methods available within the Unwrap UVW modifier that let you stretch and smooth out mesh polygons onto a flat surface. You can access both from the Peel rollout.

Mapping Modifiers

Among the many modifiers found in the Modifiers menu are several that are specific to material maps. These modifiers are mainly found in the UV Coordinates submenu and are used to define the coordinates for positioning material maps. These modifiers include the UVW Map, UVW Mapping Add, UVW Mapping Clear, UVW XForm, MapScaler (WSM), Projection, Unwrap UVW, Camera Map (WSM), and Camera Map.

Cross-Reference

The Projection modifier is used to create normal maps and is covered in Chapter 34, "Creating Baked Textures and Normal Maps." ∎

UVW Map modifier

The UVW Map modifier lets you specify the mapping coordinates for an object. Primitives, Loft Objects, and NURBS can generate their own mapping coordinates, but you need to use this modifier to apply mapping coordinates to mesh objects and patches.

Note

Objects that create their own mapping coordinates apply them to Map Channel 1. If you apply the UVW Map modifier to Map Channel 1 of an object that already has mapping coordinates, then the applied coordinates overwrite the existing ones. ∎

You can apply the UVW Map modifier to different map channels. Applying this modifier places a map gizmo on the object. You can move, scale, or rotate this gizmo. To transform a UVW Map gizmo, you must select it from the subobject list. Gizmos that are scaled smaller than the object can be tiled.

Many different types of mappings exist, and the parameter rollout for this modifier lets you select which one to use. The Length, Width, and Height values are the dimensions for the UVW Map gizmo. You can also set tiling values in all directions.

Note

It is better to adjust the tiling within the UVW Map modifier than in the Material Editor because changes in the Material Editor affect all objects that have that material applied, but changes to a modifier affect only the object. ∎

The Alignment section offers eight buttons for controlling the alignment of the gizmo. The Fit button fits the gizmo to the edges of the object. The Center button aligns the gizmo center with the object's center. The Bitmap Fit button opens a File dialog box where you can align the gizmo to the resolution of the selected bitmaps. The Normal Align button lets you drag on the surface of the object, and when you release the mouse button, the gizmo origin is aligned with the normal. The View Align button aligns the gizmo to match the current viewport. The Region Fit button lets you drag a region in the viewport and match the gizmo to this region. The Reset button moves the gizmo to its original location. The Acquire button aligns the gizmo with the same coordinates as another object.

Figure 33.1 displays a brick map applied to an umbrella using spherical mapping.

Tutorial: Using the UVW Map modifier to apply decals

After mapping coordinates have been applied either automatically or with the UVW Map modifier, you can use the UVW XForm modifier to move, rotate, and scale the mapping coordinates.

Most objects can automatically generate mapping coordinates—with the exception of meshes. For meshes, you need to use the UVW Map modifier. The UVW Map modifier includes seven different mapping options. Each mapping option wraps the map in a different way. The options include Planar, Cylindrical, Spherical, Shrink Wrap, Box, Face, and XYZ to UVW.

FIGURE 33.1

The UVW Map modifier lets you specify various mapping coordinates for material maps.

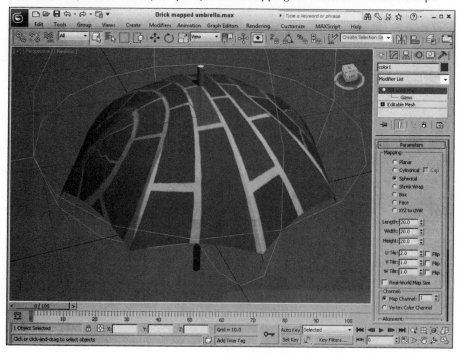

In this tutorial, you use the UVW Map modifier to apply a decal to a rocket model. Zygote Media created the rocket model.

To use the UVW Map modifier, follow these steps:

1. Open the Nasa decal on rocket.max file from the Chap 33 directory on the CD.

    This file includes a model of a rocket with the appropriate materials applied. The Chap 33 directory on the CD also includes a 300 × 600 image of the word NASA in black capital letters on a white background. The background color of this image was set to be transparent, and the image was saved as a .gif.

Note

The GIF format, typically used for Web pages, can easily make areas of the image transparent. These transparent areas become the alpha channel when loaded into Max. ∎

2. Open the Material Editor (or press the M key), and double-click on the Standard material in the Material/Map Browser. Name the material **NASA Logo**. Click the Diffuse color swatch, and select a white color. Then double-click on the Bitmap map button in the Material/Map Browser. Locate the NASA image from the Chap 33 directory on the CD, and click Open, then connect the Bitmap node to the Diffuse channel of the Standard material. The bitmap image loads, double-click the new node to view the Bitmap parameters display in the rollouts. In the Coordinates rollout, enter a value of **–90** in the W Angle field. The letters rotate vertically. Then, in the Bitmap Parameters rollout, select the Image Alpha option.

3. Select the lower white section of the rocket in the viewport, and open the Modify panel. At the top of the Modify panel, click the Modifier List and select the UVW Map modifier. Select the Cylindrical Mapping option, but don't select the Cap option in the Parameters rollout.

4. With the cylinder section selected, open the Material Editor again, select the logo material, and click the Assign Material to Selection button or drag from the material's output socket to the rocket cylinder. To see the applied logo, make sure the Views ⇨ Show Materials in Viewport As ⇨ Shaded Materials with Maps or the Realistic Materials with Maps menus are enabled.

Tip
When a bitmap is applied to an object using the UVW Map modifier, you can change the length, width, and tiling of the bitmap by using the UVW Map manipulator. If you enable the Select and Manipulate button on the main toolbar, the manipulator appears as green lines. When you move the mouse over the top of these green lines, they turn red, and you can drag them to alter the map dimensions. Use the small green circles at the edges of the map to change the tiling values. As you use the manipulator, the map is updated in real time within the viewports if you have enabled the Show Map in Viewport option in the Material Editor. ∎

Figure 33.2 shows the resulting rendered image.

FIGURE 33.2

You can use the UVW Map modifier to apply decals to objects.

UVW Mapping Add and Clear modifiers
The UVW Mapping Add and the UVW Mapping Clear modifiers are added to the Modifier Stack when you add or clear a channel using the Channel Info utility. More on this utility is covered in Chapter 34, "Creating Baked Textures and Normal Maps."

UVW XForm modifier

The UVW XForm modifier enables you to adjust mapping coordinates. It can be applied to mapping coordinates that are automatically created or to mapping coordinates created with the UVW Map modifier. The parameter rollout includes values for the UVW Tile and UVW Offsets. You can also select the Map Channel to use.

Map Scaler modifier

The Map Scaler modifier is available as both an Object-Space modifier and a World-Space modifier. The World-Space version of this modifier maintains the size of all maps applied to an object if the object itself is resized. The Object-Space version ties the map to the object, so the map scales along with the object. The Wrap Texture option wraps the texture around the object by placing it end to end until the whole object is covered.

Camera Map modifier

The Camera Map modifier creates planar mapping coordinates based on the camera's position. It comes in two flavors—one applied using Object-Space and another applied using World-Space.

The single parameter for this modifier is Pick Camera. To use this modifier, click the Pick Camera button and select a camera. The mapping coordinates are applied to the selected object.

Using the Unwrap UVW Modifier

The Unwrap UVW modifier lets you control how a map is applied to a subobject selection. It also can be used to unwrap the existing mapping coordinates of an object. You then can edit these coordinates as needed. This is accomplished by applying a texture map to an object. By selecting each face of the object, you then use the UVW Editor to move and orient the polygon in UVW space to determine how the polygon is set over the applied texture map. For example, imagine a bitmap texture that shows all the different sides of a die. In the UVW Editor, you could select and manipulate each face's UVs to align to the die sides included in the bitmap.

New Feature

The UVW Editor has been overhauled in 3ds Max 2012. Most of the common menu commands are now icon buttons, and several new features—such as the Peel toolset and the Grouping tools—are new. ■

You also can use the Unwrap UVW modifier to apply multiple planar maps to an object. You accomplish this task by creating planar maps for various sides of an object and then editing the mapping coordinates in the Edit UVWs interface.

Selecting UVW subobjects

The Unwrap UVW modifier lets you control precisely how a map is applied to an object. The Unwrap UVW modifier has Vertex, Edge, and Face subobject modes. In subobject mode, you can select a subobject, and the same selection is displayed in the Edit UVWs interface and vice versa. This synchronization between the Edit UVW window and the viewports helps to ensure that you're working on the same subobjects all the time.

The Selection rollout, shown in Figure 33.3, includes a button with a plus sign and one with a minus sign. These buttons grow or shrink the current selected subobject selection. When Edge subobjects are selected, the Ring and Loop buttons and the Point-to-Point Edge Selection button become active. The Point-to-Point Edge Selection button is a great way to create seams. When you select two points, all the edges connecting those two points are selected.

In Face subobject mode, the Select by Material ID and Select by Smoothing Group buttons are active. The Select by Element button selects all the subobjects in the current element, which is an easier way to quickly select all subobjects of a defined element. You also can select to Ignore Backfacing and Select by Planar Angle.

FIGURE 33.3

The Selection panel for the UVW Unwrap modifier lets you work with Vertex, Edge, and Face subobjects.

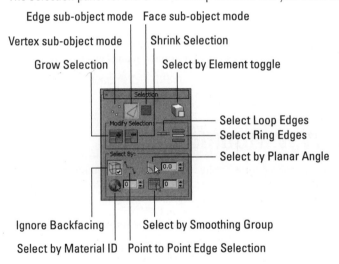

The Select menu commands let you convert selections between vertices, edges, and faces. Additional options in the Select menu let you select all inverted and overlapped faces, allowing you to find potential problem areas.

Accessing the Edit UVWs interface

The Edit UVs rollout includes a button named Open UV Editor. This button opens the Edit UVWs interface. Within the UVW Editor, you have complete control over the various UVs, and the subobject selected in the viewport also is selected within the UVW Editor. The UVW Editor also can select and display the applied texture bitmap; the mapped bitmap also is shown in the viewport.

Tweaking vertices in the viewport

The Edit UVs rollout also includes a Tweak in View button. When this button is enabled, you can drag a single vertex in the viewports to move the texture mapping. This doesn't cause the vertex's actual position in the scene to move, only the mapping. The effects of this mode are apparent only in the viewport when the texture is visible. Texture maps can be made visible in the viewports using the Views ➪ Show Materials in Viewports As ➪ Shaded Materials with Maps or Realistic Materials with Maps.

Using the Quick Planar Map

One of the easiest ways to isolate mapping surfaces is with the Quick Planar Map button found in the Edit UVs rollout under the Tweak in View button. If you select a set of faces either in the viewports or in the Edit UVW window and click this button, a planar map based on the X, Y, Z or an Averaged Normals is separated and the selected area is marked with a map seam. A button to Display Quick Planar Map shows the orientation of the mapping plan when enabled. Quick Planar Maps are one of the easiest ways to select, orient, and group mapping areas together.

Saving and loading mapping coordinates

You also can load and save the edited mapping coordinates using the Save and Load buttons in the Channel rollout, and the Reset UVWs button resets all the mapped coordinates. Saved mapping coordinate files have the .uvw extension and can be loaded for use on another object in another scene. For example, suppose you have a game level with multiple crates. If you create a texture that has all the different sides and correctly map the texture for one cube object, then all other crates in the scene could be correctly mapped by simply saving the mapping coordinates for the completed one and loading them into the others.

Each map can hold up to 99 mapping channels, and the Map Channel value lets you tell them apart. If a single object has multiple instances of the Unwrap UVW modifier applied, then each instance can have a different Map Channel value. Video game objects use these map channels to add wear and tear to a character as the game progresses. Also, the map channel can be a vertex color channel by enabling the Vertex Color Channel option.

The Configure rollout lets you set how the seams of the planar maps are displayed. The options include Map Seams, Peel Seams, and either Thick or Thin. Map seams show up as green lines, and peel seams show up as blue lines. By making the seams visible, you can easily tell where the textures don't match the object's creases.

Using the Edit UVWs Interface

Although several features for working with UVs are available in the various panels in the main interface, the main work is accomplished in the Edit UVWs interface. All changes made in the Edit UVWs window, shown in Figure 33.4, are automatically reflected in the viewports.

The Edit UVWs dialog box has multiple icons surrounding the main window. Along the top edge are buttons for selecting and transforming the selected subobjects. Table 33.1 shows and describes the buttons along the top edge.

FIGURE 33.4

The Edit UVWs interface lets you control how different planar maps line up with the model.

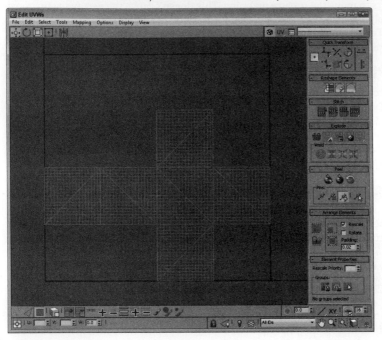

TABLE 33.1

Top Edit UVW Interface Buttons

Buttons	Name	Description
	Move, Move Horizontal, Move Vertical	Moves the selected vertices when dragged.
	Rotate	Rotates the selected vertices when dragged.
	Scale, Scale Horizontal, Scale Vertical	Scales the selected vertices when dragged.
	Freeform Modea	Displays a gizmo that you can use to transform the subobject selection.
	Mirror Horizontal, Mirror Vertical, Flip Horizontal, Flip Vertical	Mirrors or flips the selected vertices about the center of the selection.
	Show Map	Toggles the display of the map in the dialog box.

Buttons	Name	Description
UU	Coordinates	Displays the vertices for the UV, UW, and WU axes.
	Show Options	Opens the Options dialog box.
MAP # 1 (CELLULAR)	Pick Texture drop-down list	Displays a drop-down list of all the maps applied to this object. You can display new maps by using the Pick Texture option.

The gizmo is simply a rectangle gizmo that surrounds the current selection. Move the selection by clicking in the gizmo and dragging; Shift+dragging constrains the selection to move horizontally or vertically. The plus sign in the center marks the rotation and scale center point. Scale the selection by dragging one of its handles. Ctrl+dragging a handle maintains the aspect ratio of the selection. Click+dragging the middle handles rotates the selection. Ctrl+dragging snaps to 5-degree positions, and Alt+dragging snaps to 1-degree positions.

Within the Pick Texture drop-down list is a Checker Pattern option. This option applies a checker map to the mesh without having to assign a material. The checker pattern makes easy work of looking for stretching on the model. The drop-down list also includes any textures that are applied to the object. The selected texture appears in the background of the window.

Selecting subobjects within the dialog box

Under the main window in the Edit UVWs dialog box is a toolbar of icons for selecting different sub-objects. Table 33.2 shows and describes these buttons.

TABLE 33.2

Selection Buttons

Buttons	Name	Description
	Vertex Subobject mode	Allows Vertex UV selection
	Edge Subobject mode	Allows Edge UV selection
	Polygon Subobject mode	Allows Polygon UV selection
	Select by Element toggle	Selects all subobjects within the selected element
	Grow Selection	Adds adjacent subobjects to the current selection
	Shrink Selection	Subtracts adjacent subobjects from the current selection

continued

TABLE 33.2 *(continued)*

Buttons	Name	Description
	Loop	Selects a loop of edges placed end to end
	Grow Loop	Adds to the selected edge loop
	Shrink Loop	Subtracts from the selected edge loop
	Ring	Selects a ring of edges parallel to each other
	Grow Ring	Adds to the selected edge ring
	Shrink Ring	Subtracts from the selected edge ring
	Paint Selection	Allows selection by painting over the subobjects
	Enlarge Brush Size	Increases the radius of the selection brush
	Shrink Brush Size	Decreases the radius of the selection brush

Within the Selection toolbar are the Selection modes with buttons for selecting Vertex, Edge, and Face subobjects. Selected subobjects in the Edit UVW interface are highlighted red. Using the + (plus) and – (minus) buttons, you can expand or contract the current selection. The paintbrush icon button is used to Paint Select subobjects, and the Expand and Shrink Brush buttons to its immediate right allow you to increase and decrease the brush size. The Select Element option selects all subobjects in the given cluster. This happens only when the Select Face subobject mode is enabled.

The Loop button automatically selects all edges that form a loop with the current selected edges. Edge loops are edges that run end to end. You also can use the Ring button to select adjacent edges that are parallel to each other. The Grow and Shrink buttons next to the Loop and Ring buttons are used to select the adjacent edges on either side of the current selection in the loop or ring direction.

Tip
The Loop and Ring buttons also can be used on vertices and faces if two or more are selected. ■

To the right of the selection buttons located under the main view in the Edit UVWs dialog box are several buttons for enabling and configuring soft selections. Table 33.3 shows and describes these buttons.

Using these controls, you can enable Soft Selection with a specified Falloff value. The UV and XY options let you switch between texture coordinates and object coordinates for the falloff. The Edge Distance lets you specify the Soft Selection falloff in terms of the number of edges from the selection instead of a falloff value. You also can choose the falloff profile as Smooth, Linear, Slow Out, or Fast Out.

TABLE 33.3

Soft Selection Buttons

Buttons	Name	Description
	Enable Soft Selection	Toggles Soft Selection on and off
0.0	Soft Selection Falloff value	Sets the amount of falloff for soft selection
	Linear Falloff, Smooth Falloff, Slow Out Falloff, Fast Out Falloff	Changes the falloff type
XY UV	Soft Selection Falloff Space	Switches falloff coordinates between XY and UV space
	Limit Soft Selection by Edges	Limits falloff to a specified number of edges
16	Edge Limit value	Sets the number of edges to include in the falloff

Navigating the main view

Along the bottom edge of the Edit UVWs dialog box are several more buttons for viewing the coordinate values, changing the display options and navigating the main view. Table 33.4 shows and describes these buttons.

TABLE 33.4

Lower Toolbar Buttons

Buttons	Name	Description
	Absolute/Relative Toggle	Lets you enter U, V, and W values as absolute values or relative offsets.
U: 0.0 V: 0.0 W: 0.0	U, V, W values	Displays the coordinates of the selected vertex. You can use these values to move a vertex.
	Lock Selected Subobjects	Locks the selected components and prevents additional ones from being selected.
	Display Only Selected Faces	Displays vertices for only the selected faces.
	Hide/Unhide Selected Subobjects	Allows selected subobjects to be hidden and unhidden.
	Freeze/Unfreeze Selected Subobjects	Allows selected subobjects to be frozen and unfrozen.

continued

TABLE 33.4	(continued)	
Buttons	**Name**	**Description**
All IDs ▼	All IDs drop-down list	Filters selected material IDs.
🖐	Pan View	Lets you drag to pan the view.
🔍±	Zoom View	Lets you drag to zoom in on the view.
🔍	Zoom to Region	Lets you drag to zoom in a specific region.
📦📦📦	Zoom View Extents, Zoom to Selection, Zoom to Subobject Selection	Lets you zoom to include all the mapping coordinates, just the current selection, or any elements with a selected subobject.
🔲🔲	Snap to Pixel, Snap to Grid	Snaps to the closest pixel corner or to the closest grid intersection.

The buttons in the lower-right corner of the Edit UVWs dialog box work just like the Viewport Navigation buttons described in earlier chapters, including buttons to snap to grid and snap to pixel. You also can navigate about the Edit UVW window using the scroll wheel to zoom in and out of the window and dragging the scroll wheel to pan the view.

Using the Quick Transform buttons

One of the first tasks when unwrapping an object is to select and separate off different areas of polygons that have unique UVs. Each unique set of faces in the Edit UVW dialog box is called a cluster. For example, if you have a car with a matching texture, then the same texture can be mapped for each of the wheel hubs by placing each of the clusters for the wheel hub on top of each other over the bitmap section that shows the hub details. The same can be done for the side panels on the car, but one of the sides must be flipped horizontally. This is where the Quick Transform functions come in. They allow you to select and manipulate the different clusters.

The Quick Transform rollout, shown in Figure 33.5, in the Edit UVWs dialog box includes buttons for aligning, rotating, and spacing subobjects.

The Set Pivot button includes options as flyouts to set the pivot at the center or at any of the four corners of the selection. You also can move the pivot to a precise location by dragging it when the Freeform Mode button on the top toolbar is selected. The pivot is marked by an orange set of crosshairs, and it is the point about which the selection is rotated and scaled.

The Align feature includes buttons to align the selected vertices or edges to the current pivot or to an average of the selected subobjects. The Align to Pivot option is the default, and the average align is available as a flyout. If you press and hold the Shift key, the entire edge loop is aligned. When used on an edge ring, all the individual edges are oriented to be perfectly parallel. The Linear Align button aligns the vertices or edges to a straight line that stretches between the two endpoints. The Align to Edge button is available only in Edge subobject mode. It rotates the entire cluster until the selected edge is either vertically or horizontally aligned.

The Quick Transform rollout includes buttons for aligning, rotating, and spacing subobjects.

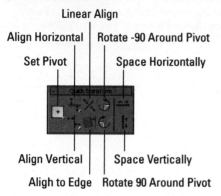

Linear Align

Align Horizontal   Rotate -90 Around Pivot

Set Pivot   Space Horizontally

Align Vertical   Space Vertically

Aligh to Edge   Rotate 90 Around Pivot

Caution

The align features are to be used only on vertices and edges, but you can select and use them on faces. However, this only collapses the faces to a single line because it acts to align all vertices in the selection. ■

The Rotate +90 and Rotate –90 buttons rotate the selected subobjects 90 degrees in the Edit UVW interface. The rotation is about the set pivot. The Space Horizontal and Space Vertical buttons are used to equally space all the selected vertices or edges. The Shift key applies this to the entire edge loop.

New Feature

The Set Pivot, Align to Pivot, Linear Align, and Align to Edge buttons in the Quick Transform rollout of the Edit UVW dialog box are all new to 3ds Max 2012. ■

Straightening and Relaxing UV clusters

Within the Reshape Elements rollout are three buttons for reshaping the selected cluster of UVs. The Straighten Selection button is available only in Face subobject mode. It realigns the selected polygons into a rectangular grid with all polygons oriented vertically and horizontally.

If your mapping coordinates are too tight, and you're having a tough time moving them, you can use the Relax feature to space the vertices equally. The second button is Relax Until Flat. It causes all vertices within the cluster to move in order to remove any tension from the cluster. It also tries to make all faces in the cluster roughly the same size. Relaxing a cluster removes stretching that occurs across the surface of the area.

New Feature

The Straighten Selection and Relax Until Flat buttons in the Reshape rollout of the Edit UVW dialog box are new to 3ds Max 2012. ■

If the Relax Until Flat option pushes the cluster too far, the third button allows you to apply a custom set of relax settings. You can access the Relax Tool dialog box using the flyout button under the Relax:Custom button or using the Tools ➪ Relax menu command. This tool works like the Relax modifier, pushing close vertices away and pulling far vertices closer together. Selecting this menu option opens the Relax Tool dialog box, shown in Figure 33.6, which offers three relax methods: Relax by Face Angles, Relax by Edge Angles, and Relax by Centers. The Iterations value is the number of times to apply the relax algorithm. The Amount value is how aggressive the movements of the vertices are, and the Stretch value controls how much vertices are allowed to move. You also have options to Keep Boundary Points Fixed and Save Outer Corners.

FIGURE 33.6

The Relax Tool dialog box includes custom settings for the Relax feature.

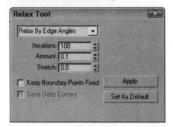

Stitching and welding

If you select some faces within the Edit UVWs dialog box and drag them away from the other faces, you notice that some edges connecting the selected faces with the non-selected faces remain. You can use the buttons in the Stitch and Explode rollouts, shown in Figure 33.7, to break these remaining edges and to stitch broken clusters back together again.

The Stitch button is used in Vertex mode to match the selected vertices along a border to their corresponding vertices. Clicking one of the Stitch buttons moves both faces to a new location, depending on the button you use. The Stitch to Target moves the selected subobjects to the location of their matching subobject. The Stitch to Average moves both to a location midway between each, and the Stitch to Source moves the matching subobjects to the location of the selected subobjects.

If you enable the Display ⇨ Show Shared Sub-Objects menu command, the shared edges of the selected vertices are shown as blue lines. This indicates where the subobject face would be moved to when stitched.

The Stitch Custom button moves the subobjects based on the Stitch Settings dialog box's configuration. You can access the Stitch Settings dialog box, shown in Figure 33.8, using the flyout button under the Stitch Custom button or using the Tools ⇨ Stitch Selected menu command. The Stitch Tool dialog box includes options to align and scale the moved cluster, and the Bias value determines how close the selection moves to or away from the target subobject. A value of 0 moves the target to the source, and a value of 1 moves the source to the target.

The Break button in the Explode rollout breaks the selected subobjects from their surrounding faces so they can be moved without stretching out the edges of the adjacent faces. This works best if the Break tool is used before moving the selected faces. When the Break tool is used on vertices or edges, two vertices or edges are created. This allows the independent vertices or edges to be moved away from each other. When Break is used on faces, a new cluster is created.

FIGURE 33.7

The Stitch and Explode rollouts include buttons for breaking, welding and stitching vertices.

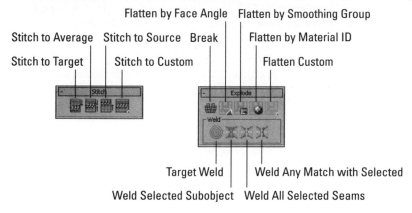

FIGURE 33.8

The Stitch Tool dialog box includes a Bias value to determine how far the selected subobjects move.

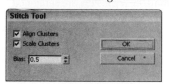

The opposite of Break is Weld, and the Explode rollout includes several ways to weld subobjects together. The Target Weld button enables a mode that lets you drag vertices or edges and drop them on their matching separated subobject. The cursor changes to a bold set of crosshairs when a matching subobject is under the cursor.

The Weld Selected Subobject button welds selected subobjects only if they are located within the Threshold value, which is found in the Unwrap Options dialog box. You can open the Unwrap Options dialog box using the Options ⇨ Preferences menu command.

If an edge is selected, its shared edge is highlighted in blue. Click the Weld All Selected Seams button once to automatically select the blue shared edges. If both shared edges are selected, then clicking the Weld All Selected Seams button again welds the two edges by moving both to an average location. The Weld Any Match with Selected button welds the selected subobject without requiring that both shared edges are selected, and it can be used on all vertices, edges, and faces.

The Edit menu also includes Copy, Paste, and Paste Weld commands. The Copy and Paste commands let you copy a mapping and paste it to another set of faces. The Paste Weld command welds vertices as it pastes the mapping.

Separating into clusters using flattening methods

The Explode rollout also includes several methods for automatically separating the object into clusters. This process is called flattening. The Flatten by Face Angle breaks the faces up using an angle threshold of 60 degrees. Any adjacent faces that have normals greater than this threshold are split along the edge they share. This breaks up a cube object into six separate faces.

You also can split up the UVs based on Smoothing Group values and Material IDs. Both of these are helpful if you've already applied smoothing groups or materials to the object. The Flatten Custom breaks the UVs into clusters based on the Flatten Mapping dialog box, which is accessed using the flyout button under the Flatten: Custom button or with the Mapping ⇨ Flatten Mapping menu.

New Feature

The Flatten by Smoothing Group and the Weld Any Match with Selected buttons are both new to 3ds Max 2012. ■

The Flatten Mapping dialog box, shown in Figure 33.9, lets you break the mesh into clusters based on the angle between adjacent faces. This option is good for objects that have sharp angles like a robot or a machine. The Spacing value sets the distance between adjacent clusters.

FIGURE 33.9

The Flatten Mapping dialog box includes a Face Angle Threshold value for determining how clusters are separated.

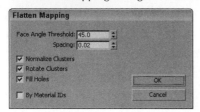

Figure 33.10 shows the UVs for a backhoe bucket that was separated into clusters using the Flatten Mapping method. All the clusters have been automatically aligned within the square texture area, and some smaller pieces have been placed within the holes created by the larger pieces. This makes the most of the available texture space.

In addition to the flattening options in the Explode rollout, the Mapping menu includes two additional auto-mapping options: Normal and Unfold Mapping.

The Normal Mapping option lets you select to map a mesh using only specific views, including Top/Bottom, Front/Back, Left/Right, Box, Box No Top, and Diamond. These views are based on the direction of the normals from the faces of the mesh. It is helpful for thin models like butterfly wings or coins.

FIGURE 33.10

The Flatten Mapping method was used to break this backhoe bucket object into several clusters.

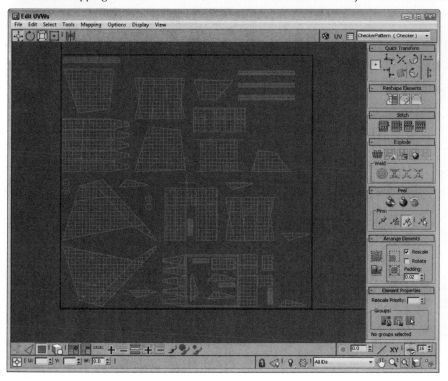

The Unfold Mapping option is unique because it starts at one face and slowly unwraps all the adjacent faces into a single segment if possible. Figure 33.11 shows a simple cylinder that has been unwrapped using this method. The advantage of this mapping is that it results in a map with no distortions. It includes two options: Walk to Closest Face and Walk to Farthest Face. You almost always want to use the Walk to Closest Face option.

Note

Within a single mesh, multiple different mapping methods can be used. For example, a car's wheel uses cylindrical mapping, but its hood might use planar mapping. Even a subobject selection can use different mapping methods. ■

FIGURE 33.11

The Unfold Mapping option splits the model and unfolds it by adjacent faces into a single segment.

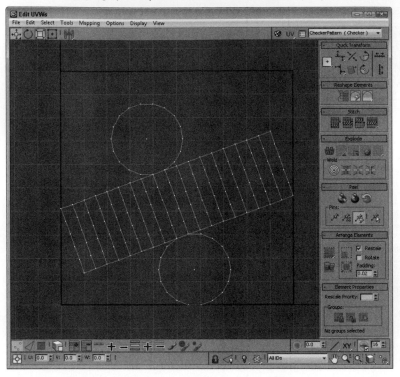

Arranging and grouping clusters

Within the Edit UVW dialog box is a square area that represents the texture bitmap. The goal is to use as much of this texture space as possible to ensure that the maximum amount of detail from the texture is used on the model. The various buttons in the Arrange Elements rollout help with this task.

After all the various clusters are separated from each other, the Pack Custom button packs all the clusters to fit within the texture space using the settings in the Pack dialog box, shown in Figure 33.12. This dialog box is accessed using the flyout under the Pack Custom button or using the Tools ⇨ Pack UVs menu command.

The Pack UVs menu command lets you combine UVs into a smaller space. Packed UVs are easy to move and work with because they use a smaller resolution bitmap. Two packing algorithms are available in the Pack dialog box. The Linear Packing method is fast but not very efficient, and the Recursive Packing option is more efficient, although it takes longer. Within the Pack dialog box, the Spacing value sets the amount of space between each segment, and the Normalize Clusters option fits all clusters into the given space. The Rotate Clusters option allows segments to be rotated to fit better, and the Fill Holes option places smaller segments within open larger segments.

FIGURE 33.12

The Pack dialog box includes settings for crunching all clusters within the given texture space.

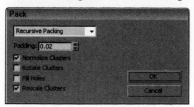

The Arrange Elements rollout also includes a Rescale Elements button that scales all clusters relative to each other. The Pack Together button fits all clusters within the texture space without normalizing. The Pack Normalize fits all clusters and allows scaling while fitting. You can select to enable or disable rescaling and rotating, and the padding value is the space between the clusters.

Within the Element Properties rollout are buttons to create, destroy, and select groups. For each group, you can set a Rescale Priority that determines which groups are rescaled during packing. To create a group of clusters, select two or more clusters using the Face subobject mode and click the Group Selected button. The Selected Groups label identifies each group with a number when selected.

New Feature

The ability to group clusters together is new to 3ds Max 2012. ∎

Accessing the Unwrap Options

The Options ⇨ Preferences menu command (Ctrl+O) opens the Unwrap Options dialog box, shown in Figure 33.13, and lets you set the Line and Selection Colors as well as the preferences for the Edit UVWs dialog box. You can load and tile background images at a specified map resolution or use the Use Custom Bitmap Size option. It also has a setting for the Weld Threshold and options to constantly update, show selected vertices in the viewport, and snap to the center pixel.

The Bitmap Options section lets you specify the exact size of the loaded bitmap. This only affects how the bitmap is displayed in the interface and doesn't change the actual bitmap file dimensions. The Tile Bitmap option places the bitmap end to end for the specified number of tiles. The Constant Update option causes the viewport to update along with the texture map. The Show Hidden Edges option lets you make the hidden edges visible or invisible. The Center Pixel Snap causes the Pixel Snap button at the bottom right of the interface to snap to the center of the background pixels instead of to its edges.

Tutorial: Controlling the mapping of a covered wagon

The covered wagon model created by Viewpoint Datalabs is strong enough to carry the pioneers across the plains, but you can add a motivating slogan to the wagon using the Unwrap UVW modifier. In this tutorial, you add and edit the mapping coordinates for the covered wagon using the Unwrap UVW modifier.

FIGURE 33.13

In the Unwrap Options dialog box, you can set the preferences for the Edit UVWs dialog box.

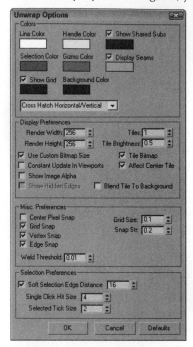

To control how planar maps are applied to the side of a covered wagon, follow these steps:

1. Open the Covered wagon.max file from the Chap 33 directory on the CD.

   This file includes a covered wagon model. The Chap 33 directory also includes a 256 × 256 image, created in Photoshop, of the paint that you want to apply to its side. The file is saved as Oregon or bust.tif. (Note that the spelling in the image is rough.)

2. With the covered section selected, choose Modifiers ⇨ UV Coordinates ⇨ Unwrap UVW. In the Parameters rollout, click the Edit button.

   The Edit UVWs interface opens. In the Modifier Stack, select the Polygon subobject mode.

3. In the Edit UVWs interface, choose Mapping ⇨ Normal Mapping. In the Normal Mapping dialog box, select the Left/Right Mapping option from the drop-down list and click OK.

   The left and right views of the wagon's top are displayed in the Edit UVWs interface.

4. From the drop-down list at the top of the interface, select the Pick Texture option. The Material/Map Browser opens. Double-click on the Bitmap option, and select the Oregon or bust.tif image from the Chap 33 directory on the CD.

   The texture appears in the window.

5. Drag the mouse over all the faces for the lower half of the wagon's cover, and select the Tools ⇨ Flip Horizontal menu command to flip the UVs so they match the top unselected UVs. Then drag and place the selected UVs on top of the unselected ones.

By matching these two UV sections together, you can apply the same texture to both sides of the covering.

6. Select all the UV faces, and with the Move tool, drag them to the center of the Edit UVWs window. Click and hold over the Scale tool, and select the Vertical Scale tool. Then drag in the window to vertically scale the vertices until they fit over the texture. Then horizontally scale the vertices slightly until the background texture is positioned within the wagon's top. When you're finished, click the X button in the upper-right corner to close the Edit UVW window.

Figure 33.14 shows the covered wagon with the mapped bitmap.

FIGURE 33.14

The Edit UVWs interface lets you transform the mapping coordinates by moving vertices.

7. Open the Compact Material Editor. Click on the mapping button next to the Diffuse color, and double-click on the Bitmap type in the Material/Map Browser. Then select the Oregon or bust.tif file from the Chap 33 directory on the CD. Apply this material to the covered wagon top. Click the Show Map in Viewport button (the small checkerboard cube icon) to see the map on the covered wagon.

Figure 33.15 shows the results of the new mapping coordinates.

FIGURE 33.15

The position of the covered wagon's texture map has been set using the Unwrap UVW modifier.

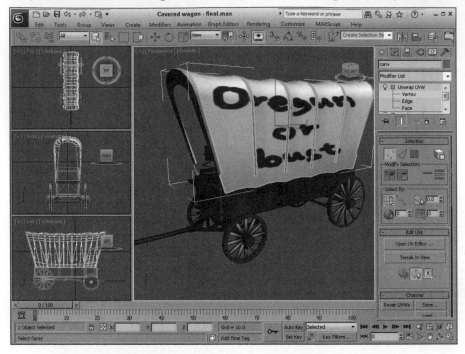

Rendering UV templates

After all the UV coordinates are mapped onto a model, you can paint the desired textures in an external paint program like Photoshop and load the texture back into the Edit UVWs window, where they can be aligned to the correct UVs. Using the Tools ⇨ Render UVs menu command, you can create a template that can be saved and loaded into Photoshop, showing you exactly where the UV boundaries are.

The Tools ⇨ Render UVW Template menu command opens the Render UVs dialog box, shown in Figure 33.16. This dialog box lets you set the template's dimensions, set the template's Fill and Edges colors, and show overlaps and seams. The Fill mode can be set to None, Solid, Normals, and Shaded, providing more information about the object.

Clicking the Render UV Template button renders the template into the Render Frame Buffer window where it can be saved to the needed image format. Then within Photoshop, you can make the template layer a background layer that you can turn on and off to show the lines that you need to stay within when creating a texture.

FIGURE 33.16

The Render UVs dialog box lets you render and save a template for painting textures.

Mapping multiple objects

If your model is divided into several different pieces, you're in luck because Max allows you to apply the Unwrap UVW modifier to several pieces at once. When loaded into the Edit UVW window, the wireframe for each piece is displayed using its object color, which makes identifying the various separate pieces easy.

Tutorial: Creating a mapping for a fighter plane

As a final example of unwrapping, you add a Navy logo to a P-28 Trojan fighter plane. This plane was created by Viewpoint Datalabs. The logo was created and saved as a PNG file, which allowed the background to be saved as transparent. This allows the shiny metallic material to show through the applied logo.

For this tutorial, you add the logo to one of the wings. The tricky part of this tutorial, which you didn't have for the earlier rocket tutorial, is that the wing's ailerons are separated from the wing. This makes it possible to animate the ailerons.

Note

I realize that all you military aircraft enthusiasts out there know that the logo actually belongs on the fuselage and not on the wing, but the fuselage isn't divided into separate parts like the wing, so I'm taking creative license for the sake of the tutorial. ∎

To add a texture map to several pieces of an airplane, follow these steps:

1. Open the T-28 Trojan plane.max file from the Chap 33 directory on the CD.
2. In the Perspective view, select the wing and the aileron and flaps. Don't select the molding between the wing and the ailerons.

3. Select the Modifiers ⇨ UV Coordinates ⇨ Unwrap UVW menu to apply the modifier to all the selected pieces. Then click the Edit button in the Parameters rollout to open the Edit UVWs window.

4. From the drop-down list at the top right of the Edit UVWs interface, select the Pick Texture option. The Material/Map Browser opens. In the Search by Name field, type **Bitmap** and double-click the Bitmap option, and select the T-28 Trojan logo.png image from the Chap 33 directory on the CD. To focus the bitmap, disable the Tile Bitmap option in the Options panel of the Edit UVWs window.

   The texture appears in the window.

5. Select Face subobject mode in the Modifier Stack and click in the viewport on the center of the right wing. Then click the Expand Selection button (the one with the plus sign) at the bottom of the Edit UVWs window to grow the selection. Keep clicking the Expand Selection button until the entire right half of the wing is selected. Then select the Tools ⇨ Break command. Then zoom out in the Edit UVWs window, and move the separated wing to the top of the window so it doesn't overlap any other sections.

   The selected wing UVs are separated from the rest of the wing object, which includes both wings.

Tip

Another way to select the faces is to use the Planar Angle value, which selects all the polygons on one side of the wing. ■

6. Select the center of one of the right ailerons, and click the Expand Selection button until the entire part is selected. Then click the Planar button in the Projection rollout in the Command Panel to orient the part to match the wing. Then move the aileron up to the top of the Edit UVWs window near the wing UVs. Repeat this step for the other right aileron.

7. Enable the Select Element option at the bottom of the Edit UVWs window so you can select the entire part by clicking it. Then use the Freeform mode button to move and scale the ailerons to fit next to the wing.

Tip

If you need to seamlessly fit two separate parts together, you can use the Welding feature in Vertex subobject mode to weld the vertices on each part. ■

8. Select all the remaining UVs, and move them to the bottom of the window where they don't overlap the logo. Then select the positioned wing and ailerons, and click the Rot -90 button to rotate the wing to align with the logo. Then scale and position the UVs over the logo, as shown in Figure 33.17. Then close the Edit UVWs window.

9. Press the M key to open the Material Editor. Click the mapping button next to the Diffuse color, and double-click the Bitmap type in the Material/Map Browser. Then select the T-28 Trojan logo.png file from the Chap 33 directory on the CD. Apply this material to the selected wing and ailerons. Click the Show Map in Viewport button (the small checkerboard cube icon) to see the map on the plane.

FIGURE 33.17

The UVs are positioned to match the loaded bitmap.

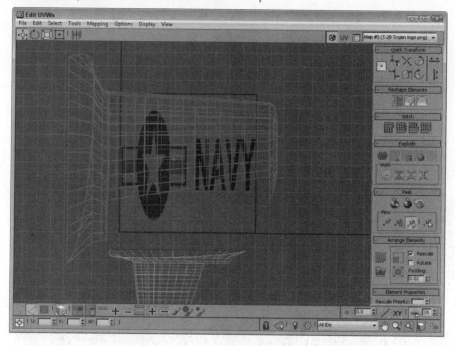

Figure 33.18 shows the results of the plane mapping. After the map is applied to the plane and visible in the viewports, you can open the Edit UVWs window again and tweak the mapping coordinates.

Using the Spline mapping

Spline mapping uses a spline and its cross sections to define the mapping coordinates. Tubular objects created with the Loft compound object or with the Sweep modifier are typically very difficult to correctly map given they don't fit in any of the existing mapping constructs. They can be unwrapped, but these objects usually have a lot of polygons, and this makes it difficult to unwrap or to pelt map.

The answer to this tricky object type is to use the Spline mapping method. With this mapping method, you can select to align the map to circular or planar cross sections. You can also add different cross sections if the lofted object uses different cross sections. Spline mapping is selected from the Wrap rollout in the Command Panel.

Tutorial: Spline mapping a snake

Spline mapping works well for objects like tentacles, arms, and ropes that have strong bends that cause mapping to be distorted. It also works well for simple snakes coiled and ready to strike.

FIGURE 33.18

The logo map is positioned on the wing and spreads over to the ailerons also, even though they are separate parts.

To add a texture map to a snake so it follows its length, follow these steps:

1. Open the Snake.max file from the Chap 33 directory on the CD. This object was created using the Sweep modifier and includes a lot of polygons. Before converting to an Editable Poly and forming the head, I cloned the path used to create the snake, so a spline that runs along the snake's midline is also in the scene.

2. With the snake objects selected, choose the Modifiers ⇨ UV Coordinates ⇨ Unwrap UVW menu to apply the modifier to the snake. Notice how the checkerboard texture is stretched along the snake's neck and head.

3. In the Modify panel, select the Face subobject and drag over all the polygons in the viewport or use the Ctrl+A shortcut to select them all. Then click the Spline mapping button in the Wrap rollout. This opens a simple panel where you can choose the Pick Spline button. Then choose the midline spline in the viewport. Notice how the mapping is immediately updated and aligned to run along the length of the snake, as shown in Figure 33.19.

FIGURE 33.19

Spline mapping lets you align the mapped textures to follow the length of a selected spline.

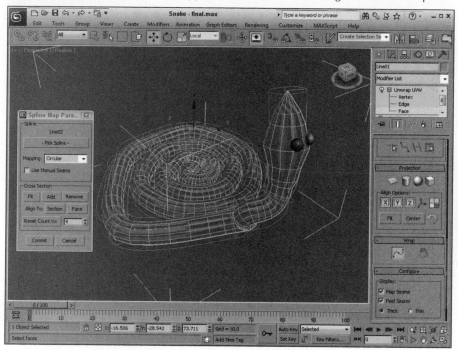

Unfolding a loop strip

Another handy tool in the Wrap rollout is the Unfold Strip from Loop. This feature is enabled when Edge subobject mode is enabled and is best used with an edgeloop. Once an edgeloop is selected, clicking this button will separate the polygons adjacent to the selected edgeloop and stretch them out into a long straight set of rows, which makes it easy to paint a texture.

Note

When the Unfold Strip from Loop command is used, the scale of the strip will be made extra large. Use can use the Pack tool to fit the strip back in scale with the other UVs. ∎

Figure 33.20 shows an edgeloop selected from the snake mesh in the previous example. Then with the Unfold Strip from Loop command, the polygons that run along the entire length of the snake have been pulled away as a separate strip.

FIGURE 33.20

Loop strips are easily separated from the rest of the mesh with the Unfold Strip from Loop button.

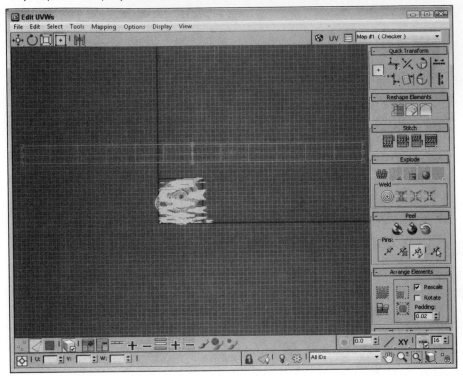

Using Peel and Pelt Mapping

In addition to the flatten, normal, and unfold mapping methods, the Unwrap UVW modifier includes nifty mapping methods for automatically unwrapping the UVs called Peel and Pelt mapping. But, before we dive into these methods, we need to understand and divide the mesh using seams. Seams are the borders between the various UV clusters. They can appear along smoothing groups, material boundaries, and hard edges.

Creating seams

Seams should be located in areas of the model that aren't clearly visible. For example, if you are unwrapping a head model, the back and top of the head are good choices because they probably will be covered with hair that will hide the seam. Locating a seam on the midline up the front of the face is a terrible choice, because lining up face details like the lips and the nose on opposite ends of the map is difficult. You also can define seam edges yourself using the buttons found in the bottom of the Peel rollout in the Command Panel.

Some seams are available when the Unwrap UVW modifier is first applied. These default seams follow the boundaries of the elements that make up the mesh. Seams are identified in the viewports as thick green lines. You can edit seams using the Edit Seams button in the Peel rollout. You also can create new seams using the Point to Point Seams and the Convert Edge Selections to Seams buttons.

Note

All open borders are automatically made into seams. ■

The Edit Seams button, at the bottom of the Peel rollout, lets you click edges to highlight them as seams. Press and hold the Alt key, and click an edge to remove it from the seam. This method can be time-consuming if you have a complex mesh. The Point to Point Seam button lets you click a starting point; a rubber band line then appears that lets you extend to an ending point. A seam is created between these two points using the shortest possible route. After an ending point is selected, the rubber band remains, letting you add to the seam. Right-click to exit the rubber band and to choose a new starting point. Figure 33.21 shows the seams added to the head model.

Tip

When placing pelt mapping seams, try to position the seams where they aren't readily visible, such as under the arms and legs or down the middle of the back. ■

FIGURE 33.21

Seams define where the mesh can be split.

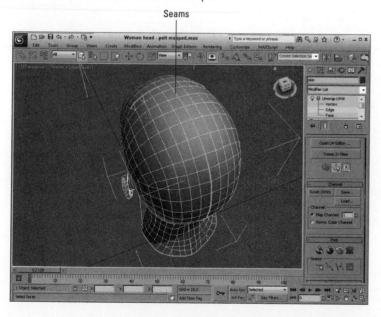

The Convert Edge Selection to Seams button converts an existing edge selection to a pelt seam, and the Expand Face Selection to Seams button selects all faces that are next to the seams. This is an easy way to select all faces within a cluster.

The Configure rollout contains options to display Map and Peel Seams. If either of these options is enabled, the seams are clearly shown. You also can set the size of the seams to thin or thick.

Using the Peel tools

The Peel tools are a new method of unwrapping UVs based on the LSCM (Least Square Conformal Maps) algorithm. They provide a way to select and expand different areas of a cluster by pulling its vertices away from the center. The results are like stretching out some clay and having all the vertices stretch around the movement.

New Feature

The Peel tools are new to 3ds Max 2012. ■

It is best to define the seams to use before using the Peel tools, but you also can break, weld, and work with the cluster while toggling Peel mode on and off. After a cluster that you want to work with is selected using the Faces subobject mode, select all the faces in the cluster using the Expand Face Selection to Seams button in the Peel rollout of the main interface or by enabling the Select by Element toggle in the Edit UVW dialog box.

Then either click the Quick Peel Map button or enable the Peel mode button in the Peel rollout. The Quick Peel Map button makes its best guess and unwraps the cluster, but Peel mode lets you select and drag individual vertices around to spread out the cluster after you switch to Vertex subobject mode. Figure 33.22 shows the UVs of a lion toy's face after using the Quick Peel Map button.

FIGURE 33.22

The lion toy face cluster is displayed after using the Quick Peel Map.

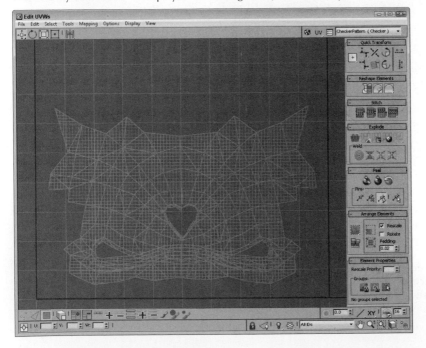

When the Quick Peel Map button gets fairly close, enable the Peel mode button, switch to the Vertex subobject mode, and then select and drag the vertices toward the top of the cluster away from the center to spread out the vertices. As you move each vertex, the rest of the cluster moves with it.

After the moved vertices are in place, you can pin them so they stay put. This allows the rest of the cluster to stretch out as other vertices are moved. Within the Peel rollout in the Edit UVWs window are several buttons for pinning the selected vertex, removing a pin, automatically pinning any moved vertices, and selecting all pinned vertices. Figure 33.23 shows the same cluster after pulling and pinning several vertices. Notice how the cluster makes much better use of the available texture space and how crowded areas have opened up.

FIGURE 33.23

The lion toy face cluster is displayed after moving and pinning vertices.

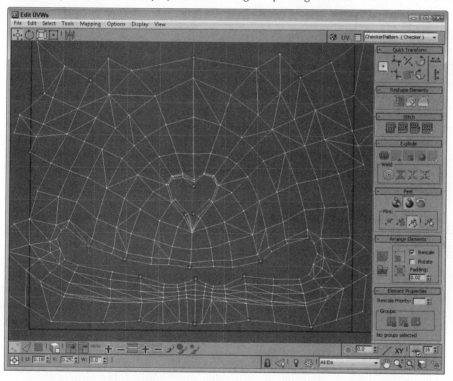

If you find that moving the vertices isn't helping, you can always click the Reset Peel button to start over. This automatically removes all pins and resets the cluster layout.

Using Pelt mapping

Pelts remind me of early turn-of-the-century explorers and trappers who captured and skinned critters such as foxes and wolves and preserved their fur pelts on a circular rack. These furs were valuable commodities that could be traded for whatever the trapper needed. The market for such furs has diminished significantly, but the concept works well for the virtual world as a mapping method for applying textures to 3D objects.

Another automatic mapping method available in the Peel rollout of the Command Panel is Pelt mapping. Consider mapping a complex mesh like the human head. Using traditional mapping methods, you would divide the head into sections based on planar projections like those in Figure 33.24. The UVs for this head include planar views of the front and back of the head. These provide good UV coordinates for features that are straight on with the projection, but the ears and the sides of the nose are all wrong using this method. You could divide the mesh into more projections, including one for each side of the head and for under the chin, but then you need to deal with matching the seams between the different parts, which is a tough challenge.

FIGURE 33.24

Planar mapping isn't a good solution for a complex head mesh.

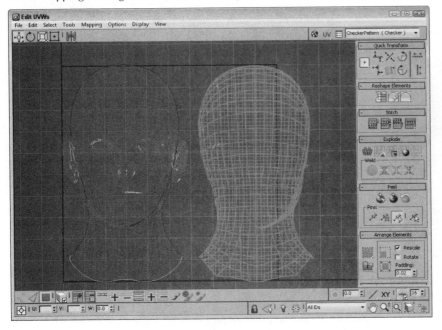

Pelt mapping overcomes these difficulties by allowing the user to define the seams for the mesh. These seams can be located along material boundaries or along mesh borders. The vertices along these defined seams are then positioned around the edges of a circle called the Stretcher and pulled until the mesh UVs are pulled flat. This results in clearly displaying and flattening all the UVs for the selected part, allowing you to easily paint and apply a texture map.

After the seams are defined, select all the faces that are to be mapped and click the Pelt button in the Peel rollout in the Command Panel. This opens the Edit UVW window along with the Pelt Map panel, shown in Figure 33.25.

FIGURE 33.25

The Pelt Map dialog box includes commands for stretching the pelt mapping.

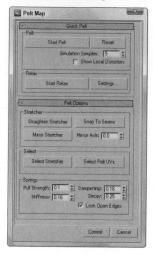

The Edit UVWs window opens with the front projection displayed, and all seam points are positioned in a circle around the selected faces, as shown in Figure 33.26. The circle of seam points is called the Stretcher, and the lines connecting the Stretcher points to the selected faces are springs.

FIGURE 33.26

Pelt mapping positions all seam points in a circle around the selected faces.

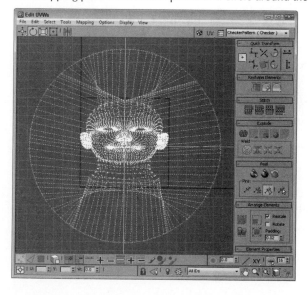

The Start Pelt button causes the springs to pull at the selected UV faces, causing them to stretch toward the Stretcher using the defined spring properties. The stretching continues until you click the Stop Pelt button. If you enable the Show Local Distortion option, all UVs that are severely distorted appear in red. Figure 33.27 shows the UV faces after being stretched.

After being stretched, the UV faces are lined up quite well.

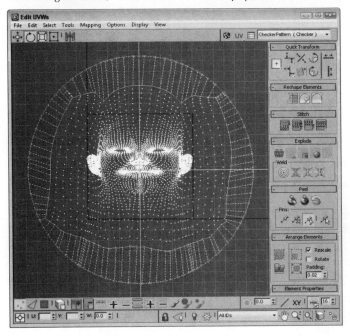

In the Pelt Options rollout are settings for altering the stretcher locations. The Select Stretcher and Select Pelt UVs buttons let you select and manipulate both the selected faces and the Stretcher points. You also can straighten and mirror the stretcher or have the UVs snap to seams. The Snap to Seams button is especially helpful if you have an object like a hand that curves back in on itself. If you Snap to Seams before stretching, the stretcher assumes the shape of the seams.

If you get confused, the Reset Stretcher button returns the mapping to its starting positions. The Relax buttons can be used to further move the UVs to eliminate any tension in the mapping.

Tip
To create an efficient pelt map, you should rotate the stretcher so the spring distance is at a minimum. ■

Tutorial: Using pelt mapping

Pelt mapping is especially helpful on characters because they have irregular seams and surfaces. The Pelt mapping method works well for smoothing out character textures.

To use pelt mapping on a character's face, follow these steps:

1. Open the Lion toy face.max file from the Chap 33 directory on the CD.

   This file includes just the face of a lion toy model.

2. With the face mesh selected, choose Modifiers ⇨ UV Coordinates ⇨ Unwrap UVW. Choose the Face subobject mode, and select all the face subobjects in the face mesh.

3. In the Peel rollout, click the Pelt Map button.

   A planar gizmo appears in the center of the viewport. Rotate and move the gizmo so it's parallel to the face mesh and in front of it (or press the Align Y button).

4. The Edit UVWs dialog box appears with each seam positioned along the Stretcher. Select all the stretcher points with the Select Stretcher button and rotate the Stretcher points about 10 degrees clockwise so the pelt is stretched out straight. Then click the Start Pelt button until the face is stretched out, as shown in Figure 33.28.

FIGURE 33.28

Using pelt mapping, you can stretch the UVs for a mesh object.

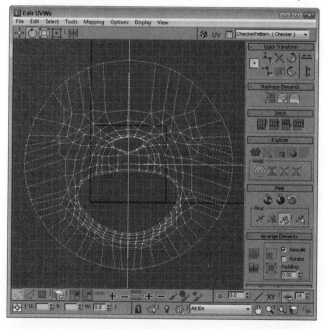

Summary

I covered lots of ground in this chapter because there are lots of different maps. Learning to use these maps will make a big difference in the realism of your materials.

In this chapter, you learned about the following:

- Understanding the basics of mapping coordinates
- Using mapping modifiers
- Applying labels with the UVW Map modifier
- Controlling mapping coordinates with the Unwrap UVW modifier
- Rendering a UV template
- Editing seams
- Using the Peel and Pelt mapping methods

In the next chapter, you learn how to use the Render to Texture interface to bake textures into an object. Creating normal maps is also covered.

Creating Baked Textures and Normal Maps

3D games pose an interesting dilemma—creating interactive scenes that are displayed in real time with the highest quality graphics. To achieve this, game developers use a number of tricks designed to speed up the rendering time. One of these tricks is pre-rendering textures that include all the lighting information and applying these pre-rendered textures as texture maps. This allows advanced lighting solutions such as global illumination to be included within a game without requiring extra time to render such a complex solution. The process of applying pre-rendered textures as maps is called *baking* a texture.

Rendering textures is a significant part of the rendering process, and baking a texture doesn't remove this step; it simply completes the step beforehand, so that the game engine doesn't need to do the texture calculations.

Another common efficiency trick is to use normal maps. Normal maps calculate the lighting results used to light small details that stick out from the surface of an object. These details are then re-created using a normal map that is applied back onto a simplified version of the object. The normal map allows these details to be simulated without the extra polygons used to create them. By allowing simple base objects to have details such as bolts and rivets without the extra polygons, the objects can be redrawn quickly without losing their visual quality.

This chapter covers some of the features found in Max that enable the amazing graphics that are found in the latest real-time games.

Using Channels

When 3D models are used in games, the color and material data for the models is stored in channels. The game engine then knows that if it wants to change the color of a group of vertices because of an explosion that has happened, it just looks in the preset channel, finds the vertices it needs, changes the color, and then goes on with the game.

Working with channels is a very efficient way to interface with the gaming engine, but a sloppy game developer can introduce a model to the game engine with all sorts of unneeded or exaggerated channels. If this happens, the game engine can ignore the extra channels and get the wrong information, which can cause your hero to march off into battle without a weapon. Worse, it can crash the system.

To prevent problems and to streamline the number of channels that are included with game models, Max includes a Map Channel Info editor that you can use to manipulate the various channel data. This editor, shown in Figure 34.1, can be opened using the Tools ⇨ Channel Info menu command.

FIGURE 34.1

The Map Channel Info dialog box lets you edit channel data.

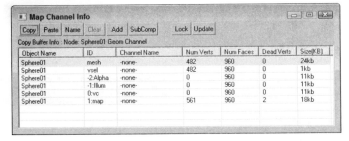

Using the Map Channel Info dialog box

The Map Channel Info dialog box shows lots of information, including the Object Name; its ID; its Channel Name; the number of Vertices, Faces, and Dead Vertices (unattached vertices); and its Size. With this information, you can quickly determine which channels are taking up the most space and eliminate them.

All objects include some default channels for mesh, which holds the geometry; vsel, which holds the selected vertices; -2:Alpha, which holds the alpha channel information; -1:Illum, which holds illumination values; and channel 0:vc, which holds vertex color information. Objects also include at least one default map channel (even if it is empty). These channels cannot be deleted.

Cross-Reference

Vertex colors are covered along with painting on objects in Chapter 18, "Creating Compound Materials and Using Material Modifiers." ■

The interface lets you Copy and Paste selected channels. You can give each channel a name with the Name button. Beneath the Copy button, text appears that lists the information currently copied in the Copy Buffer. Selected channels can be copied only between channels that have the same number of vertices.

The Clear button clears out the selected channels, but you cannot clear a map channel if there is another map channel above it. The Add button adds a new map channel to the object. Objects can hold as many as 99 map channels. The Clear and Add buttons also apply UVW Mapping Clear or UVW Mapping Add modifiers to the Modifier Stack. The Paste command also adds a modifier. These modifiers are convenient because they can easily be removed or reordered in the Stack. If changes have been made in the Modifier Stack, the Update button reflects these changes in the Map Channel Info dialog box.

The SubComp button shows the channel components if they exist. For example, map channels can be broken into X, Y, and Z components, and other channels such as Alpha have R, G, and B components. The Lock button holds the current channels even if another object is selected.

Select by Channel modifier

After new channels have been created, you can recall them at any time using the Select by Channel modifier. This modifier is found in the Modifiers ⇨ Selection ⇨ Select by Channel menu command. Using this modifier, you can choose to Replace, Add, or Subtract a given channel from the selection. The available channels for the selection are listed by their channel name in a drop-down list.

Rendering to a Texture

When working with a game engine, game designers are always looking for ways to increase the speed and detail of objects in the game. One common way to speed game calculations is to pre-render the textures used in a game and then to save these textures as texture maps. The texture map takes more memory to save but can greatly speed the rendering time required by the game engine. This process of pre-rendering a texture is called *texture baking*.

Caution

If you bake a texture into an object and then render it with the rest of the scene, the object gets a double dose of light. ■

Texture baking can be accomplished in Max using the Rendering ⇨ Render to Texture menu command (or by pressing the 0 key). This opens the Render to Texture dialog box. In several ways, the Render to Texture dialog box, shown in Figure 34.2, resembles the Render Scene dialog box, including a Render button at the bottom edge of the interface.

FIGURE 34.2

The General Settings rollout of the Render to Textures panel includes settings for all objects.

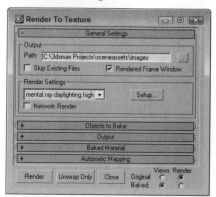

To create a baked texture, select a Texture Element from the Output rollout and click the Render button. Clicking the Render button creates the baked texture for the selected object and saves it in the directory specified in the General Settings rollout. It also applies an Automatic Flatten UVs modifier to the

Modifier Stack and applies a Shell material to the object. The Shell material contains the object's original material along with the new baked material. You can select which material is displayed in the viewport and which is rendered using the options to the bottom right of the Render to Texture dialog box.

Note

You also can select Use an Existing Channel for mapping coordinates. This is a good choice because the Auto Unwrap option doesn't have the control over the UV coordinates that you may want, and sometimes it does a poor job of unwrapping the mesh. ■

The interface also includes an Unwrap Only button. This button can be used to flatten the UVW Coordinates for the selected objects and to automatically create a map channel.

General Settings

The General Settings rollout includes an output path where the baked texture is saved. The file is saved by default using the Targa file format. The Skip Existing Files option renders only those elements that don't already exist in the designated directory. The Rendered Frame Window option displays the resulting map in the Rendered Frame Window along with saving the image as a file. For the render pass, you can select which rendering settings to use, including the mental ray rendering engine. The Setup button opens the Render Scene panel, where you can change the render settings.

Selecting objects to bake

In the Objects to Bake rollout, shown in Figure 34.3, a list displays exactly which objects, subobjects, and channels will be included in the rendered texture. The Padding value defines the overlap in pixels of the texture. The Objects to Bake rollout also includes a Presets list that lets you save and reload defined settings.

FIGURE 34.3

The Objects to Bake rollout of the Render to Textures panel lets you specify which objects are baked into the texture map.

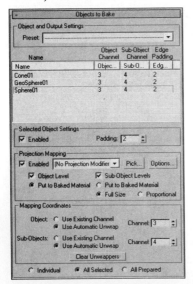

The Projection Mapping section lets you enable the creation of a normal map using a Projection modifier. These settings are covered in detail in the "Creating Normal Maps" section that appears later in this chapter.

The Mapping Coordinates section lets you choose to use the mapping coordinates of the Object or the Subobject selection contained within a specified channel, or you can select to use the Use Automatic Unwrap feature, which automatically flattens the mapping coordinates. If the Use Automatic Unwrap option is selected, you can set the mapping options in the Automatic Mapping rollout. By default, unwrap mapping uses channel 3, but you can change this channel if you wish. If a different mapping uses channel 3 and you don't change this, the new mapping replaces the old one. The Clear Unwrappers button removes any existing Unwrap UVW modifiers from the object's stack.

You can select to bake an Individual object, All Selected objects, or All Prepared objects, which are all objects with at least one texture element.

Output settings

The Output rollout, shown in Figure 34.4, lists the texture elements that are included in the texture map. The Enable option can be used to disable the selected texture element, or elements can be deleted with the Delete button.

The Output rollout of the Render to Textures panel lets you choose which texture elements are baked.

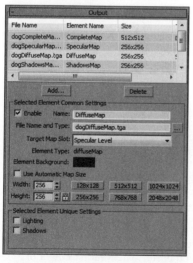

Clicking the Add button lets you select the type of texture elements that you can render. You'll want to use different maps depending on the purpose of the map, and you may want to render several at a time. The available types are CompleteMap, SpecularMap, DiffuseMap, ShadowsMap, LightingMap, NormalsMap, BlendMap, AlphaMap, and HeightMap. You can also change the map size or use the Automatic Map Size option, which bases the map size on the object size. Some map elements present a list of components to include in the map. These components appear below the size settings.

Tip
If the mental ray renderer is selected, then Ambient Occlusion is added to the list of available texture elements. The Ambient Occlusion option creates a map that re-creates effects created by limited light bounces resulting from surrounding objects. ∎

Baked Material and Automatic Mapping settings

The Baked Material and Automatic Mapping rollouts, shown in Figure 34.5, provide a way to keep the existing object material using the Shell material. The Clear Shell Materials button removes the Shell materials for the baked objects and restores their original materials.

<hr>

FIGURE 34.5

The final two rollouts of the Render to Textures panel include settings for handling the baked material and how the texture is mapped.

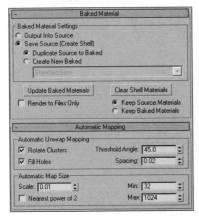

In the Automatic Mapping rollout, you can set how the mapping is applied. If the Use Automatic Unwrap option in the Objects to Bake rollout is enabled, then the object to be baked has the Automatic Flatten UVs modifier applied. For this type, you can set the Threshold Angle (which is the difference between the normals of adjacent faces; if the angular value is greater than the Threshold Angle value, then a hard edge is created between the faces), the Spacing (which is the amount of space between different map pieces), and whether map pieces can be rotated and used to fill in holes of larger map pieces.

The size of the texture map depends on the size of the object, but you can set a Scale value for greater resolution and set Min and Max values to keep the maps within reason. By default, maps are saved to the /images directory, but you can select a different directory if you prefer. The Nearest Power of 2 option causes the map to be optimized for use in memory to a square pixel size that is a power of 2, such as 8×8, 16×16, 32×32, or 64×64.

Note
Most game engines require square texture maps because they are efficiently loaded into memory. Main characters can use texture maps that are 1024×1024 or even 2048×2048, but background characters and props usually only have textures maps that are 256×256 or 512×512, so clustering is important to get as much into the textures as you can. ∎

Tutorial: Baking the textures for a dog model

To practice baking textures, you'll bake a complete map of just the dog's head.

To bake a dog's head texture, follow these steps:

1. Open the Doberman.max file from the Chap 34 directory on the CD.

   This file includes a dog model created by Viewpoint Datalabs.

2. Select Rendering ⇨ Render to Texture (or press the 0 key) to open the Render to Textures dialog box.

3. Select the dog's body object. In the Render to Textures dialog box, set the Threshold Angle to **75** in the Automatic Mapping rollout, and make sure that the Rendered Frame Window option in the General Settings rollout is set. In the Output rollout, click the Add button and double-click the CompleteMap option. Set the Map Size to **512**, select the Diffuse Color option as the Target Map Slot, and click the Render button.

Figure 34.6 shows the resulting texture map. If you look in the Modify panel, you'll see that the Automatic Flatten UVs modifier has been applied to the object. If you look at the material applied to the object, you'll see that it consists of a Shell material.

FIGURE 34.6

A texture map created with the Render to Textures panel

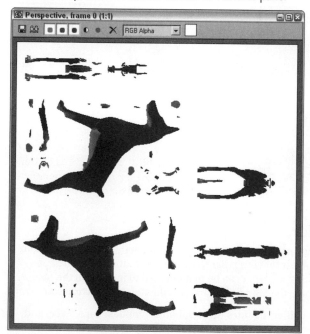

Creating Normal Maps

Normal maps are becoming more common in games because they offer a way to increase the bump details of a model by mapping high-detail bump information onto a low-resolution model. Normal maps are created using the Render to Texture interface and applied to an object using the Normal Bump map type found in the Material Editor.

The Normal Bump map type is typically applied as a bump map in the Maps rollout and includes a separate button, shown in Figure 34.7, to apply an additional bump map.

Caution

Normal maps can be displayed in the viewports only if the DirectX display driver is selected. ■

Although normal maps are created using the Render to Texture dialog box, they are applied using the Material Editor.

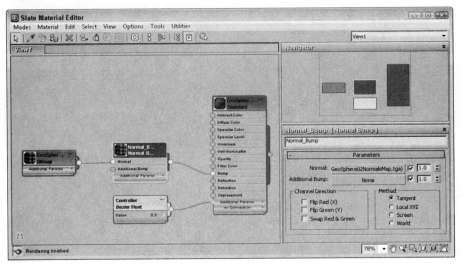

Using the Projection modifier

The Projection modifier is used to create a normal map. It works by being applied to a low-resolution object, and then you pick a high-resolution object that is similar to the low-resolution one. The Projection modifier surrounds the object with a cage that can be manipulated to include all the object details. The Projection modifier is applied using the Modifiers ⇨ UV Coordinates ⇨ Projection command.

Within the Modifier Stack, the Projection modifier includes three subobject modes: Cage, Face, and Element. The Geometry Selection rollout includes a list of objects, a Pick button, and a Pick List for selecting the high-resolution object to be used.

The Cage rollout includes settings for displaying and pushing the cage out from the surface of the object. A Tolerance setting is used for wrapping the cage about the surface. The Selection Check rollout informs you if the Material IDs or Geometry faces are overlapping.

Setting Projection Mapping options

With a Projection modifier applied to a selected object, the Projection Mapping option can be enabled in the Objects to Bake rollout of the Render to Texture dialog box. The object can actually include several Projection modifiers, so a drop-down list lets you select the one to use, or you can use the Pick button to select a target object in the viewports.

The Options button in the Render to Texture dialog box opens the Projection Options dialog box, shown in Figure 34.8. Using this dialog box, you can set the projection method, determine how to resolve how vertices get projected, and define the Map Space.

FIGURE 34.8

The Projection Options dialog box lets you specify how the projection values are determined.

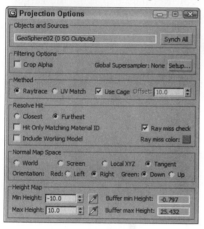

At the top of the Projection Options dialog box is the Source object. The Synch All button causes each object to use its active source for the projection. The two projection methods are Raytrace, which traces each normal line from its source to its target, and UV Match, which works by matching the UV coordinates between the source and the target objects.

For transparent objects, two projection rays may hit the same point. The Resolve Hit options let you set which one is selected, either the Closest or the Furthest. Most projections use the Tangent Map Space, but you can select to use the World, Screen, or Local Map Spaces also.

Note

Before the Projection modifier is applied, you need to have the high-res object and the low-res object positioned at the same place. ∎

Tutorial: Creating a normal map for an optimized gator

For this example, we reuse the optimized gator created earlier when mesh modifiers were covered. The ProOptimizer modifier was used to reduce this high-res gator model from 34,000 faces to fewer than 1,000. This kind of reduction represents a huge step down for the quality of the model, but it enables it to be lightning fast when used in a game. The normal map makes it possible to use the lower poly model while recovering much of the display quality.

To create a normal map for the optimized gator model, follow these steps:

1. Open the ProOptimized gator.max file from the Chap 34 directory on the CD.

2. Select and move the low-res gator model over the top of the high-res gator model in the Top viewport.

3. With the low-res gator model selected, choose the Rendering ⇨ Render to Texture menu command (or press the 0 key) to open the Render to Texture dialog box. In the General Settings rollout, select the Scanline renderer, no advanced lighting option as the Render Settings. In the Select Preset Categories dialog box that appears, click the Load button.

4. In the Objects to Bake rollout, click the Pick button, select the gator1 object (the high-res gator model) in the Select Targets dialog box that appears, and click the Add button. Then enable Projection Mapping.

5. In the Output rollout, click on the Add button and select the Normals map. From the Target Map Slot drop-down list, select the Bump option. Click the 512 button to set the map size, and enable the Output into Normal Bump option.

6. Click the Render button at the bottom of the Render to Texture dialog box.

7. Drag the low-res gator model away from the high-res model.

8. To see the normal map when rendered, open the Material Editor and use the Material ⇨ Get All Scene Materials menu. This loads all the material nodes including the normal map. There are separate materials for the skin, eyes, and claws. Locate and select the green material node. The normal map is connected to this material's Bump map. Locate the Bump map in the Maps rollout of the Parameter Editor rollout and increase the Bump Amount to 100, and then drag the green material's output socket and drop it on the low-res gator's skin.

9. Render the two gators side by side.

Figure 34.9 shows the resulting normal map rendered on the right gator.

FIGURE 34.9

The normal map for the gator can be applied as a bump map to reclaim the high-res details.

Summary

If you're working with games, then you'll want to use these features to help keep your models small and fleet. This chapter covers the following topics:

- Discovering what channels the models have
- Learning how to bake textures
- Creating normal maps using the Projection modifier

The next part takes up the topic of animation again, starting with animation modifiers.

Part VIII

Advanced Animation Techniques

Using Animation Layers, Modifiers, and Complex Controllers

J ust as layers can be used to organize a scene by placing unique objects on different layers, you also can separate the various animation motions into different layers. This gives you great control over how motions are organized and blended together.

If you've worked to animate some Max object and are pleased with the result, you can save the animation clip and reuse it. Several animation clips can be mixed together to create an entirely new animation sequence.

Modifiers can be used to deform and otherwise alter the geometry of objects, but they also can be used to affect other aspects of an object, including animated changes. One such important animation modifier is the Point Cache modifier. This modifier lets the movement of each vertex in the scene be saved to a cached file for immediate recall and for animating multiple objects simultaneously.

The Modifiers menu also includes an Animation submenu that contains many such modifiers. These modifiers are unique in that each of them changes with time. They can be useful as an alternate to controllers, but their resulting effects are very specific. Included with this submenu are modifiers such as Morpher, which allows an object to move through several different preset shapes, and Flex, which is used to add soft-body dynamics to your scene. Other animation modifiers include Melt and PathDeform.

This chapter also discusses all those miscellaneous Controllers that weren't covered earlier. These Controllers are more complex and enable a wide range of unique motions.

Using the Animation Layers Toolbar

Behind the scenes, animation layers add several new controller tracks to objects that are visible in the Motion panel and in the Track View interface, but the front end is accessible through a simple toolbar. The Animation Layers toolbar, shown in Figure 35.1, is similar in many ways to the Layers toolbar.

Cross-Reference

The Layers toolbar is covered in Chapter 6, "Selecting Objects and Setting Object Properties." ■

FIGURE 35.1

The Animation Layers toolbar includes icons for defining and merging layers.

You can open the Animation Layers toolbar by right-clicking the main toolbar away from the buttons and selecting Animation Layers from the pop-up menu. Each of the toolbar buttons is labeled and explained in Table 35.1.

TABLE 35.1

Animation Layers Toolbar Controls

Toolbar Button	Name	Description
	Enable Animation Layers	Turns the animation layers system on
	Select Active Layer Objects	Selects the objects in the viewport that are on the active animation layer
	Layer Selection drop-down list	Presents a selection list of all the available animation layers
	Animation Layer Weight	Displays the weight value for the current animation layer
	Animation Layer Properties	Opens the Animation Layer Properties dialog box
	Add Animation Layer	Adds another animation layer
	Delete Animation Layer	Deletes the current animation layer
	Copy Animation Layer	Copies the current animation layer
	Paste Active Animation Layer	Pastes the keys from the current animation layer to the selected object
	Paste New Layer	Pastes the copied animation layer keys to a new layer
	Collapse Animation Layer	Combines and deletes the current animation layer with the layer above it
	Disable Animation Layer	Turns the current animation layer off

When a new animation layer is created using the Add Animation Layer button, a new entry is added to the Animation Layer Selection List. This list displays the default name of the animation layer as AnimLayer with a number. The original layer is named Base Layer. To the left of the animation layer name is a small light bulb icon that indicates whether the animation layer is enabled or disabled.

Caution

You cannot rename animation layer names. ∎

Each layer can have a weight assigned to it. These weight values control how much influence the current animation layer has. The weight value also can be animated. For example, if a car is animated moving forward 100 meters over 50 frames, then weighting the animation layer to 30 causes the car to move forward only 30 meters over the 50 frames.

Working with Animation Layers

Animation layers are good for organizing motions into sets that can be easily turned on and off, but you also can use them to blend between motions to create an entirely new set of motions.

Note

Animations can be divided into primary motions, which are the major motions, and secondary motions, which are derivative motions that depend on the animation of other parts. Using animation layers, you can separate primary motions, like foot placement, from secondary motions, like a swinging arm, and adjust them independently. ∎

Enabling animation layers

The first button on the Animation Layers toolbar is the Enable Animation Layers button. Clicking this button opens a dialog box, shown in Figure 35.2, where you can filter the type of keys to include in the animation layer.

The Enable Animation Layers dialog box lets you limit which type of keys are included.

The base animation layer can be disabled using the Disable Animation Layer button. This button is available only when you collapse all its layers. This changes the light bulb icon on the Selection list to indicate that the layer is disabled.

Note

If Animation Layers are enabled for an object whose animation is loaded into the Motion Mixer, then a dialog box automatically appears, asking if you want to create a new map file for the animation. ∎

Setting animation layers properties

The button to the right of the Weight value opens the Layer Properties dialog box, shown in Figure 35.3. This dialog box lets you specify the type of controller to which the layers are collapsed. The options include Bézier (for Position and Scale tracks) or Euler (for Rotation tracks), Linear or TCB, and Default. You also can specify a range to collapse.

FIGURE 35.3

The Layer Properties dialog box lets you set the controller type to collapse to.

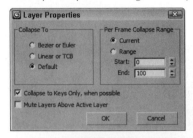

Collapsing animation layers

By collapsing layers, you combine the animation keys on each layer into a single set of keys that includes all the various motions. Be careful when collapsing; the results can be unexpected. Collapsing animation layers is accomplished with the Collapse Animation Layers button.

Tutorial: Using animation layers for a plane takeoff

Have you ever been to a small airport and watched the commuter planes take off? Sometimes they leave the ground and then return to the ground and then finally take off. It's like they need to get a good bounce to overcome gravity. This is a good example of when animation layers come in handy.

To animate a jet's takeoff using animation layers, follow these steps:

1. Open the Mig take-off.max file from the Chap 35 directory on the CD.

   This file includes a detailed Mig-29 jet model created by Viewpoint Datalabs.

2. With the jet selected, open the Animation Layers toolbar by right-clicking the main toolbar away from the buttons and choosing Animation Layers from the pop-up menu.

3. Click the Enable Animation Layers button, and enable the Position track, then click Ok to close the pop-up dialog box. This adds a Base Layer to the Selection list.

4. Click the Auto Key, drag the Time Slider to frame 100, and move the jet to the far end of the runway. Then disable the Auto Key button. Set the Weight value for this layer to **0**.

5. In the Animation Layer toolbar, click the Add Animation Layer button to add a new layer. In the Create New Animation Layer dialog box that appears, select the Duplicate the Active Controller Type option and click OK. A new layer labeled AnimLayer01 is added to the Selection list.

6. Click the Auto Key button again, drag the Time Slider to frame 100, and move the jet upward away from the runway. Then disable the Auto Key button again.

7. Select the Base Layer from the Selection list in the Animation Layers toolbar and set its Weight value to **100**. Then drag the Time Slider, and notice that the jet moves up at an angle over the 100 frames.

8. Click the Auto Key button again, drag the Time Slider to frame 0, and set the Weight value for AnimLayer01 to **0**; drag the Time Slider to frame 30, and set the Weight to **60**; drag the Time Slider to frame 50, and set the Weight back to **0**; and finally drag the Time Slider to frame 80, and set the Weight to **80**. Then disable the Auto Key button again.

Dragging the Time Slider shows the jet bounce down the runway before taking off, as shown in Figure 35.4.

FIGURE 35.4

The Animation Layers feature provides a single parameter for controlling the plane's height.

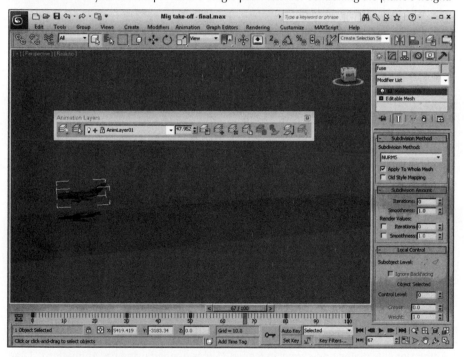

Saving Animation Files

Before an animation sequence can be mixed in the Motion Mixer, it must be saved. The Motion Mixer easily can load any existing animation sequence in the current opened Max file, but saving a sequence to the local hard disk makes it accessible for other Max scenes. The Motion Mixer can be accessed using the Graph Editors ⇨ Motion Mixer menu command. More on the Motion Mixer is presented as a bonus chapter on the book's CD.

Saving general animations

The animation of objects can be saved using the XML Animation File (XAF) format. To save the animation for the selected object, open the Save XML Animation File dialog box, shown in Figure 35.5, using the Animation ⇨ Save Animation.

FIGURE 35.5

The Save XML Animation File dialog box is used to save animations of the selected object.

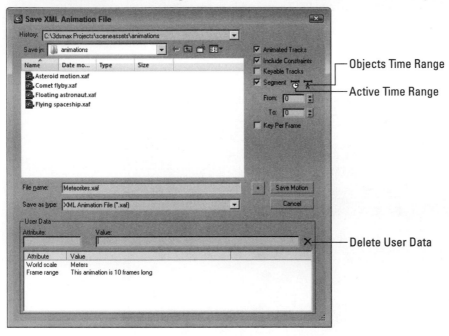

For general animations, you can select to include tracks, constraints, only keyable tracks, and a specific range. The User Data fields let you enter notes or specific data used by plug-ins about the animation sequence.

Loading Animation Sequences

The Load XML Animation File dialog box, shown in Figure 35.6, is opened using the Animation ⇨ Load Animation menu command. It looks like a normal file dialog box, but it has some additional features.

Caution

Within the Character Assembly rollout for Character objects is a button to Save Animation. This button saves character animations using the ANM file format, which cannot be opened using the Animation ⇨ Load Animation menu command. ■

The Relative and Absolute options determine whether the animation is loaded relative to the object's current location or whether it is loaded into the frames where it was saved. The Replace and Insert options let the new keys overwrite the existing ones or move them out to insert the loaded keys. You can even select the frame where the new keys are loaded. The Load Motion button lets you load an existing mapping file named the same as the animation file if one exists or lets you create a new one.

Note
The Animation ➪ Load Animation and Animation ➪ Save Animation menu commands are active only when an object is selected. ■

FIGURE 35.6

The Load XML Animation File dialog box lets you load animation files from one scene and apply them to another.

Mapping files are listed in the drop-down list for easy selection, or you can use the Get Mapping button to select a different mapping file to load. Mapping files are saved with the .xmm file extension. The Edit Mapping button is active when a mapping associated with the file in the Load Animation dialog box opens the Map Animation dialog box, where you can define the mapping between objects in the two scenes.

Mapping animated objects
Mapping files define a relationship between objects in the saved animation file and objects in the current Max file. These relationships allow the animation keys to be transferred from one scene object to another.

Using the Map Animation dialog box

The Map Animation dialog box, shown in Figure 35.7, includes several rollouts. The Motion Mapping Parameters rollout includes options for allowing Max to make its best guess at mapping objects. If the scenes are fairly similar, then this option may be just the ticket. The Exact Names, Closest Names, and Hierarchy buttons allow Max to attempt the mapping on its own. This works especially well on bipeds that use the default naming conventions. You also can select to have Max look at the various controllers that are used when trying to match up objects.

The Map Animation dialog box lets you map objects to receive animation.

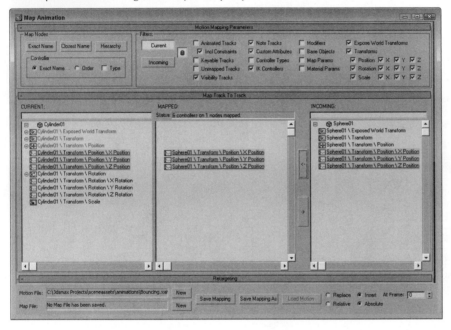

The Filters section lets you filter out the tracks that you don't want to see. The Lock button applies the selected filters to both the Current and Incoming lists.

The Map Track to Track rollout consists of three lists. The left list contains all the tracks for the current scene objects, the middle list contains all the mapped tracks, and the right list contains all the tracks from the incoming animation file. Select tracks and click the button with the left-pointing arrow to add tracks to the Mapped list; click the other arrow button to remove them.

At the bottom of the Map Animation dialog box are buttons for saving the current mapping file.

Retargeting animations

The Retargeting rollout, shown in Figure 35.8, lets you specify how the scale changes between certain mapped objects. Scale values can be entered for the mapped nodes as Absolute or Derived Scale values for each axis. Derived scale values can be obtained from a specific origin object. After the settings are right, the Set button applies the scaling to the selected mapping.

FIGURE 35.8

Use the Retargeting rollout to specify how the scale changes between mapped objects.

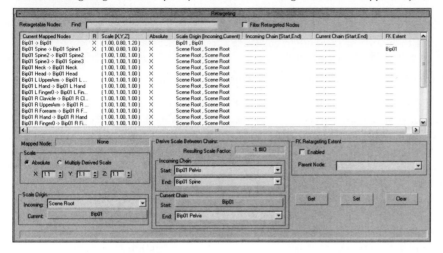

Baking Animation Keys with the Point Cache Modifier

When you add keys to an object to control its animation using modifiers, the modifiers remain with the object and can be revisited and altered as needed. However, if you have multiple objects that follow the same set of keys, such as for a crowd scene, then including a set of modifiers for each object can increase the overhead many times over. A simple solution is to bake all the keys into the object, allowing all the keys to be pulled from an external file. This frees the resources required to animate multiple objects and makes the animated keys portable. The Point Cache modifier makes this possible.

You also can use the Point Cache modifier when playback in the viewport is too slow because Max needs to compute the vertex positions of a huge number of vertices. Reading their position from a separate file increases the playback speed. You also can use the file on a cloned object to control its motion at a different speed.

The Point Cache modifier records the movement of every vertex of an object to a file. Point Cache files have the .xml extension, but they can also be saved using the older .pc2 extension. To create a Point Cache file, click the New button and name a new file on the hard drive. Then set the range of the animation to capture and click the Record button. Once recorded, the total number of points along with the sample rate and range are displayed for the active cache.

Caution

Point Cache files can be loaded and used only on objects with the same number of vertices as the original used to record the file. ■

If you select the Disable Modifiers Below option, then all modifiers below the Point Cache in the Modifier Stack are disabled. You can enable the Relative Offset option and set the Strength value to cause the cached animation to be exaggerated or even reversed. In the Playback Type section, you can control the range of the animation.

Tutorial: Trees in a hurricane

As an example of using the Point Cache modifier, you'll use a tree that is bending under violent forces such as a hurricane and duplicate it many times.

To create a forest of trees in a hurricane, follow these steps:

1. Open the Bending tree.max file from the Chap 35 directory on the CD.

   This file includes an animated tree swaying back and forth using the Bend modifier.

2. Select the tree and choose the Modifiers ⇨ Cache Tools ⇨ Point Cache menu to apply the Point Cache modifier to the tree.

3. In the Parameters rollout, click the New button, create a file named "Bending tree.xml," and click the Save button to create the animation file. Then click the Record button to save all the animation data to the file.

4. Select the tree and delete its Bend modifier. Then use the Tools ⇨ Array dialog box to create several rows of trees. Be sure to create the trees as copies and not instances.

5. Select several random trees and change the Playback Type to **Custom Start** in the Parameters rollout and change the Start Frame to **−2** to cause some random motion.

6. Press the Play Animation button to see the results.

Figure 35.9 shows several of the trees being moved about by the storm.

FIGURE 35.9

Using the Point Cache modifier, you can animate a whole forest of trees.

Using the Animation Modifiers

Animation is more than just moving an object from here to there. All objects move not only with major transformations but with lots of secondary motions also. When a human character walks, the motions of his arms and legs are major, but the secondary motions of his swinging hips and bobbing shoulders make the walk realistic. Many of the animation modifiers enable these key secondary motions.

All the animation modifiers presented in this chapter are located in the Modifiers ⇨ Animation submenu.

Cross-Reference

Also included among the Animation modifiers are several Skin modifiers, which are used to make an object move by attaching it to an underlying skeleton. The Skin modifiers are covered in Chapter 40, "Skinning Characters." ■

Morpher modifier

The Morpher modifier lets you change a shape from one form into another. You can apply this modifier only to objects with the same number of vertices.

Cross-Reference

In many ways, the Morpher modifier is similar to the Morph compound object, which is covered in Chapter 27, "Working with Compound Objects." ■

The Morpher modifier can be very useful for creating facial expressions and character lip-synching. You can also use it to morph materials. Max makes 100 separate channels available for morph targets, and channels can be mixed. You can use the Morpher modifier in conjunction with the Morph material. For example, you could use the Morph material to blush a character for an embarrassed expression.

Tip

When it comes to making facial expressions, a mirror and your own face can be the biggest help. Coworkers may look at you funny, but your facial expressions will benefit from the exercise. ■

The first task before using this modifier is to create all the different morph targets. Because the morph targets need to contain the same number of vertices as the base object, make a copy of the base object for each morph target that you are going to create. As you create these targets, be careful not to add or delete any vertices from the object.

Note

Because morph targets deal with each vertex independently, you cannot mirror morph targets, so if you want a morph target for raising the left eyebrow and a morph target for raising the right eyebrow, you need to create each morph target by hand. ■

After all your morph targets are created, select a channel in the Channel Parameters rollout, shown in Figure 35.10, and use the Pick Object from Scene button to select the morph target for that channel. Another option for picking is to use Capture Current State. After a morph target has been added to a channel, you can view it in the Channel List rollout.

FIGURE 35.10

The Morpher modifier's rollouts

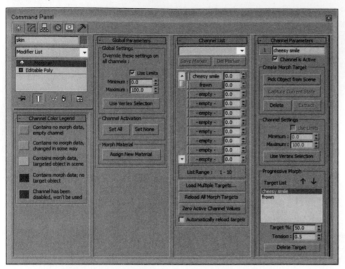

As you animate, you can specify the amount of each morph target to include in the frame using the value to the right of the channel name in the Channel List rollout. The slim color bar to the left of the channel name designates the status of the channel. You can find information on what each color represents in the Channel Color Legend rollout.

The Channel Parameters rollout also includes a Progressive Morph section. This feature lets you define an intermediate step for how the morph is to progress, with the final step being the morph target. Using these intermediate steps, you can control how the object morphs.

Tutorial: Morphing facial expressions

The Morpher modifier is very helpful when you're trying to morph facial expressions, such as those to make a character talk. With the various sounds added to the different channels, you can quickly morph between them. In this example, you use the Morpher modifier to change the facial expressions of the general character.

Tip

When creating facial expressions, be sure to enable the Soft Selection features, which make modifying the face meshes much easier. ■

To change facial expressions using the Morpher modifier, follow these steps:

1. Open the Morphing facial expressions.max file from the Chap 35 directory on the CD.

   This file includes a head model created by Viewpoint Datalabs. The model has been copied twice, and the morph targets have already been created by modifying the subobjects around the mouth.

2. Select the face on the left, and select the Modifiers ⇨ Animation Modifiers ⇨ Morpher menu command to apply the Morpher modifier.

3. In the Channel List rollout, select channel 1, click the Pick Object from Scene button, and select the middle face object. Then select the second empty channel from the Channel List rollout; in the Channel Parameters rollout, again click the Pick Object from Scene button and select the face on the right.

   If you look in the Channel List rollout, you'll see "cheesy smile" in Channel 1 and "frown" in Channel 2.

4. Click the Auto Key button (or press the N key), drag the Time Slider to frame 50, and then increase the "cheesy smile" channel in the Channel List rollout to **50**. Drag the Time Slider to frame 100, and increase the "frown" channel to **100** and the "cheesy smile" channel to **0**. Then return the Time Slider to **50**, and set the "frown" channel to **0**.

5. Click the Play Animation button in the Time Controls to see the resulting animation.

Figure 35.11 shows the three facial expressions. The Morpher modifier is applied to the left face.

Tip

Be sure to keep the morph target objects around. You can hide them in the scene or select them and save them to a separate file with the File ⇨ Save Selected menu command. ∎

FIGURE 35.11

Using the Morpher modifier, you can morph one facial expression into another.

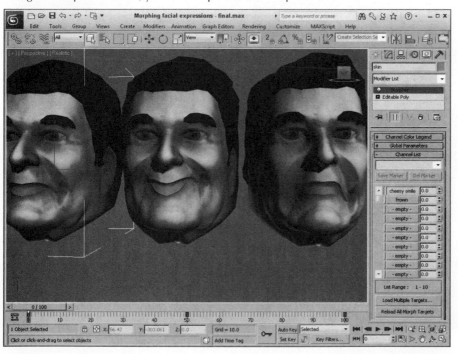

Using the Flex modifier

The Flex modifier can add soft body dynamic characteristics to an object. The characteristic of a *soft body* is one that moves freely under a force. Examples of soft body objects are clothes, hair, and balloons. The opposite of soft body dynamics is *rigid body* dynamics. Think of a statue in the park. When the wind blows, it doesn't move. The statue is an example of a rigid body. On the other hand, the flag flying over the library moves all over when the wind blows. The flag is an example of a soft body.

Cross-Reference

Soft body objects can also be defined and simulated using reactor, which is covered in Chapter 43, "Simulating Physics-Based Motion with MassFX." ∎

Another way to think of soft bodies is to think of things that can flex. Objects such as a clothesline flex under very little stress, but other objects like a CD flex only a little when you apply a significant force. The settings of the Flex modifier make it possible to represent all kinds of soft body objects.

Figure 35.12 shows many of the rollouts available for the Flex modifier.

FIGURE 35.12

The Flex modifier rollout lets you control the flex settings.

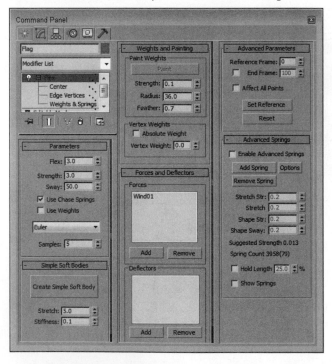

Flex subobjects

In the Modifier Stack, the Flex modifier has three subobjects that you can access: Center, Edge Vertices, and Weights and Springs. The Center subobject is a simple box gizmo that marks the center of the flex effect. Portions of the object that are farther from the center move a greater distance. The Edge Vertices subobject can be selected to control the direction and falloff of the flex effect. The Weights and Springs rollout controls the Weights and Springs subobject.

Setting flex strength

The Parameters rollout includes a Flex value, which controls the amount of bending the object does; a Strength value, which controls the rigidity of the object; and a Sway value, which controls how long the flexing object moves back and forth before coming to a stop. An antenna on a car is an example of an object that has fairly high Flex and Sway values and a low Strength value.

Chase Springs cause an object to return to its original position when the force is removed. A twig on a tree is an example of an object with Chase Springs. The Use Chase Springs option lets you disable these springs. A piece of cloth is an example of when you would want Chase Springs disabled.

Selecting the Weights and Springs subobject lets you apply weights to certain selected springs. You can disable these weights using the Use Weights option. If you disable these weights, the entire object acts together.

The Flex modifier offers three solution methods to compute the motions of objects. These are presented in a drop-down list. The Euler solution is the simplest method, but it typically requires five samples to complete an accurate solution. The Midpoint and Runge-Kutta4 solutions are more accurate and require fewer samples, but they require more computational time. Setting the Samples value higher produces a more accurate solution.

Creating simple soft bodies

In the Simple Soft Bodies rollout, use the Create Simple Soft Body button to automatically set the springs for the selected object to act like a soft body. You can also set the amount of Stretch and Stiffness the object has. For cloth, you want to use a high Stretch value and a low Stiffness value, but a racquetball would have both high Stretch and Stiffness values.

Tip
You can manually set the spring settings for the object using the Advanced Springs rollout. ■

Painting weights

When you select the Weights and Springs subobject mode, the spring vertices are displayed on the object. The vertices are colored to reflect their weight. By default, the vertices that are farthest from the object's pivot point have the lowest weight value. Vertices with the greatest weight value (closest to 1) are colored red, and spring vertices with the lowest weight value (closest to –1) are blue. Vertices in between these two values are orange and yellow. The lower-weighted vertices move the greatest distance, and the higher-weighted vertices move the least.

Selecting the Weights and Springs subobject also enables the Paint button in the Weights and Springs rollout. Clicking this button puts you in Paint mode, where you can change the weight of the spring vertices by dragging a paint gizmo over the top of the object in the viewports. As you paint the spring vertices, they change color to reflect their new weights.

The Strength value sets the amount of weight applied to the vertices. This value can be negative. The Radius and Feather settings change the size and softness of the Paint brush. Figure 35.13 shows a dinosaur model with the Flex modifier applied. The dinosaur has had some weights painted so its tail, arms, and neck move under the influence of the Flex modifier. The blue vertices are the weights that don't move as much.

FIGURE 35.13

Use the Paint button to change the weight of the spring vertices.

The weights applied using the Paint button are relative to the existing vertex weight. If you select the Absolute Weight option, then the Vertex Weight value is applied to the selected vertices.

Adding Forces and Deflectors

To see the effect of the Flex modifier, you need to add some motion to the scene. The flex object flexes only when it is moving. One of the easiest ways to add motion to the scene is with Space Warps.

The Forces and Deflectors rollout includes two lists: one for Forces and one for Deflectors. Below each are Add and Remove buttons. Using these buttons, you can add and remove Space Warps from the list. The Forces list can use any of the Space Warps in the Forces subcategory (except for Path Follow). The Deflector list can include any of the Space Warps in the Defectors subcategory.

Tip

When you add Space Warps to the Forces and Deflectors list for the Flex modifier, they do not need to be bound to the object. ∎

Manually creating springs

The final two rollouts for the Flex modifier are Advanced Parameters and Advanced Springs. The Advanced Parameters rollout includes settings for controlling the Start and End frames where the Flex modifier has an effect. The Affect All Points option ignores any subobject selections and applies the modifier to the entire object. The Set Reference button updates all viewports, and the Reset button resets all the vertices' weights to their default values.

You can use the Advanced Springs rollout to manually add and configure springs to the object. Clicking the Options button opens a dialog box where you can select the type of spring to add to the selected vertices, including Edge and Shape springs. Edge springs are applied to vertices at the edges of an object, and Shape springs are applied between vertices. For these advanced springs, you can set the Stretch Strength, Stretch Sway, Shape Strength, and Shape Sway.

Melt modifier

The Melt modifier simulates an object melting by sagging and spreading edges over time. Melt parameters include Amount and Spread values, Solidity (which can be Ice, Glass, Jelly, or Plastic), and a Melt Axis.

Figure 35.14 shows the Melt modifier applied to the snowman model (it was inevitable).

FIGURE 35.14

The Melt modifier slowly deforms objects to a flat plane.

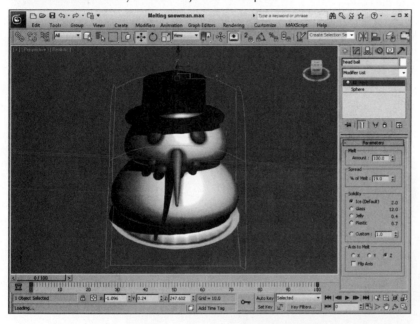

PatchDeform and SurfDeform modifiers

Among the animation modifiers are several that are similar in function but that work on different types of objects. The PatchDeform modifier uses patches, and the SurfDeform modifier deforms an object according to a NURBS surface.

In the Parameters rollout for each of these modifiers is a Pick Patch (or Surface) button that lets you select an object to use in the deformation process. After the object is selected, you can enter the Percent and Stretch values for the U and V directions, along with a Rotation value.

Note

The PatchDeform modifier is also available as a World Space Modifier (WSM). WSMs are similar to the normal Object Space Modifiers (OSM), except that they use World Space coordinates instead of Object Space coordinates. The most noticeable differences are that WSMs don't use gizmos and that the OSM moves the patch to the object, while the WSM causes the object to move to the patch. ■

Tutorial: Deforming a car going over a hill

Have you seen those commercials that use rubber cars to follow the curvature of the road as they drive? In this tutorial, you use the PatchDeform modifier to bend a car over a hill made from a patch.

To deform a car according to a patch surface, follow these steps:

1. Open the Car bending over a hill.max file from the Chap 35 directory on the CD.

    This file contains a simple hill made from patch objects and a car model created by Viewpoint Datalabs.

2. Select the car model, and choose Modifiers ⇨ Animation Modifiers ⇨ PatchDeform (WSM). Then click the Pick Patch button in the Parameters rollout, and select the hill object.

    This applies the World Space PatchDeform modifier (WSM) to the car object and moves the car to align with the hill.

3. Set the V Percent value to **0** in the Parameters rollout. Then, click the Auto Key button (or press the N key) to enable key mode, and drag the Time Slider to frame 100. Then set the V Percent value to **–50**, and click the Auto Key button again to disable key mode.

4. Click the Play button (or press the / key) to see the car deform over the hill.

Figure 35.15 shows the results of this tutorial.

FIGURE 35.15

The car model hugs the road, thanks to the PatchDeform modifier.

PathDeform modifier

The PathDeform modifier uses a spline path to deform an object. The Pick Path button lets you select a spline to use in the deformation process. You can select either an open or closed spline. The Parameters rollout also includes spinners for controlling the Percent, Stretch, Rotation, and Twist of the object. The Percent value is the distance the object moves along the path.

Note

If you use the PathDeform modifier, you can benefit from using the Follow/Bank utility, which gives you control over how the object follows and banks along the path. ∎

Figure 35.16 shows some text wrapped around a spline path.

FIGURE 35.16

The text in this example has been deformed around a spline path using the PathDeform modifier.

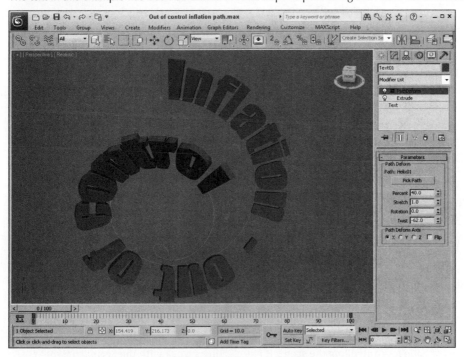

Linked XForm modifier

The Linked XForm modifier passes all transformations of one object onto another, but not vice versa. The object that controls the transformation is designated as the Control Object and is selected via the Pick Control Object button (which is the only control in the Parameters rollout for this modifier). After the Control object is selected, the Control Object controls the selected object's transforms, but the object that is being controlled can move independently of the control object without affecting the control object.

SplineIK Control modifier

The SplineIK Control modifier can be applied only to spline objects. In the Spline IK Control Parameters rollout, you can click the Create Helpers button, which adds a dummy object to every vertex on the spline. These dummy objects make it much easier to control the spline without having to enter vertex subobject mode. You can also specify how the dummy objects are linked and how they are displayed.

Attribute Holder modifier

The Attribute Holder modifier displays all custom defined attributes in their own rollout. Creating custom attributes and wiring attributes is discussed in Chapter 36, "Animating with the Expression Controller and Wiring Parameters."

Examining Complex Controllers

Now that you are somewhat familiar with controllers and how they work, let's look at some more complex controllers. Max includes a vast assortment of controllers, and you can add more controllers as plug-ins.

Transform controllers

Multi-track transform controllers work with the Position, Rotation, and Scale tracks all at the same time. You access them by selecting the Transform track in the Motion panel and then clicking the Assign Controller button or by choosing the Animation ➪ Transform Controllers menu command.

Note

Each of the available constraints is listed again in the appropriate controller submenu. ∎

Position/Rotation/Scale Transform controller

The Position/Rotation/Scale Transform controller is the default controller for all transforms. This controller includes a Bézier controller for the Position and Scale tracks and a Euler XYZ controller for the Rotation track.

The PRS Parameters rollout, shown in Figure 35.17, lets you create and delete keys for Position, Rotation, and Scale transforms. The Position, Rotation, and Scale buttons control the fields that appear in the Key Info rollouts positioned below the PRS Parameters rollout.

Script controller

The Script controller is similar to the Expression controller, except that it can work with the MAXScript lines of code for controlling the scene. Right-clicking a track with the Script controller assigned and selecting Properties opens the Script Controller dialog box. Script controllers are available for all transform tracks including Transform, Position, Rotation, and Scale. The flexibility of the Script controller is quite robust. The Script controller is covered in more detail at the end of this chapter, as is the Expression controller.

FIGURE 35.17

The PRS Parameters rollout is the default transform controller.

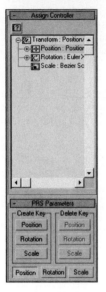

On the CD-ROM

For more information on MAXScript, Bonus Chapter 21, "Automating with MAXScript," on the CD. ■

XRef controller

If you have a defined motion used by an object in another file that you want to access, you can use the XRef controller. This controller can be assigned only to the Transform track. When this controller is assigned, a file dialog box opens where you can select the XRef file; then in the Merge Object dialog box, you can select a specific object that has the controller and motion you want to use.

 In the Parameters rollout for the XRef controller is a button to open the XRef Object dialog box with the XRef Record highlighted. The Parameters rollout also lists the XRef file, object, and status.

Cross-Reference

XRefs are covered in detail in Chapter 3, "Working with Files, Importing, and Exporting." ■

Position track controllers

Position track controller types include some of the common default controllers and can be assigned to the Position track. They typically work with three unique values representing the X-, Y-, and Z-axes. These controllers can be assigned from the Animation ➪ Position Controllers menu. Many of the controllers found in this menu also are found in the Rotation and Scale Controllers menu.

Audio controller

 The Audio controller can control an object's transform, color, or parameter value in response to the amplitude of a sound file. The Audio Controller dialog box, shown in Figure 35.18, includes Choose Sound and Remove Sound buttons for loading or removing sound files. You can access the Audio Controller dialog box by right-clicking on the track where the Audio Controller is assigned and selecting the Properties menu from the pop-up menu, or simply double-click on the track.

FIGURE 35.18

The Audio Controller dialog box lets you change values based on the amplitude of a sound file.

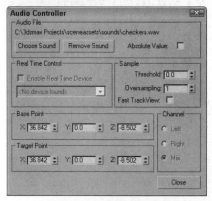

The Real Time Control drop-down list lets you specify a device to control the system. To control the sound input, you can specify a Sample Threshold and Oversampling rate. You also can set Base Point and Target Point values for each axis. The Channel options let you specify which channel to use: Left, Right, or Mix.

Motion Clip Slave controller

The Motion Clip Slave controller lets a linked motion clip that is loaded and defined in the Motion Mixer control the object's transform.

Motion Capture controller

 The Motion Capture controller allows you to control an object's transforms using an external device such as a mouse, keyboard, joystick, or MIDI device. This controller works with the Motion Capture utility to capture motion data.

After you assign the Motion Capture controller to a track, right-click the track and select Properties from the pop-up menu to open the Motion Capture panel, shown in Figure 35.19. This dialog box lets you select the devices to use to control the motion of the track values. Options include Keyboard, Mouse, Joystick, and MIDI devices.

FIGURE 35.19

The Motion Capture controller lets you control track values using external devices.

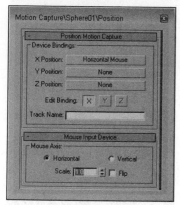

For the Keyboard control, the Keyboard Input Device rollout appears, as shown in Figure 35.20. The Assign button lets you select a keyboard key to track. The other settings control the Envelope Graph, which defines how quickly key presses are tracked.

FIGURE 35.20

The Keyboard Input Device rollout lets you select which key press is captured.

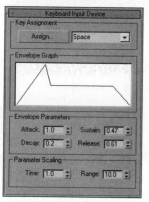

The Motion Capture dialog box defines only which device controls which values. The actual capturing of data is accomplished using the Motion Capture utility. Selecting the Motion Capture utility in the Utility panel displays the Motion Capture rollout. This rollout includes buttons to Start, Stop, and Test the data-capturing process.

Before you can use the Start, Stop, and Test buttons, you need to select the tracks to capture from the Tracks list. The Record Range section lets you set the Preroll, In, and Out values, which are the frame numbers to include. You also can set the number of Samples Per Frame. The Reduce Keys option removes any unnecessary keys, if enabled.

Tutorial: Drawing with a pencil with the Motion Capture controller

Some motions, such as drawing with a pencil, are natural motions for our hands, but they become very difficult when you're trying to animate using keyframes. This tutorial uses the Motion Capture controller and utility to animate the natural motion of drawing with a pencil.

To animate a pencil drawing on paper, follow these steps:

1. Open the Drawing with a pencil.max file from the Chap 35 directory on the CD.

   This file has a pencil object positioned on a piece of paper.

2. Select the pencil object, open the Motion panel, and select the Position track for the pencil object. Then click the Assign Controller button, and double-click the Position Motion Capture selection.

   The Motion Capture dialog box opens.

3. Click the X Position button, and double-click the Mouse Input Device selection. Then click the Y Position button, and double-click the Mouse Input Device selection again. In the Mouse Input Device rollout, select the Vertical option. This sets the X Position to the Horizontal Mouse movement and the Y Position to the Vertical Mouse movement. Close the Motion Capture dialog box.

4. Open the Utilities panel, and click the Motion Capture button. In the Motion Capture rollout, select the Position track, and get the mouse ready to move. Then click the Start button in the Record Controls section, and move the mouse as if you were drawing with the mouse. The pencil object moves in the viewport along with your mouse movements.

   The Motion Capture utility creates a key for each frame. It quits capturing the motion when it reaches frame 100.

5. Click the Play Animation button (or press the / key) to see the results.

Figure 35.21 shows the scene after the Motion Capture controller has computed all the frames.

Quaternion (TCB) controller

 The Quaternion (TCB) controller produces curved animation paths similar to the Bézier controller, but it uses the values for Tension, Continuity, and Bias to define their curvature. The benefit of this controller is that it enables objects to be rotated without having the problem of Gimbal lock, which can happen when the Euler XYZ controller is used. Gimbal lock can occur when two of the rotation axes become aligned, causing the object to lose one of its degrees of freedom.

The parameters for this controller are displayed in a single Key Info rollout. Like the Bézier controller rollouts, the Quaternion (TCB) controller rollout includes arrows and Key, Time, and Value fields. It also includes a graph of the TCB values; the red plus sign represents the current key's position, while the rest of the graph shows the regular increments of time as black plus signs. Changing the Tension, Continuity, and Bias values in the fields below the graph changes its shape. Right-clicking the track and selecting Properties from the pop-up menu opens the TCB graph dialog box, shown in Figure 35.22.

FIGURE 35.21

The Motion Capture controller and utility let you animate with a mouse, keyboard, joystick, or MIDI device.

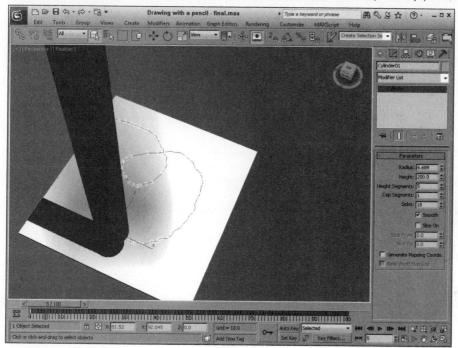

FIGURE 35.22

This dialog box shows, and lets you control, a curve defined by the Tension, Continuity, and Bias values.

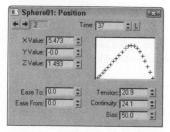

The Tension value controls the amount of curvature: High Tension values produce a straight line leading into and away from the key, and low Tension values produce a round curve. The Continuity value controls how continuous, or smooth, the curve is around the key: The default value of 25 produces the smoothest curves, whereas high and low Continuity values produce sharp peaks from the top or bottom. The Bias value controls how the curve comes into and leaves the key point, with high Bias values causing a bump to the right of the key and low Bias values causing a bump to the left.

The Ease To and Ease From values control how quickly the key is approached or left.

Note
Enabling the trajectory path by clicking the Trajectory button in the Motion panel lets you see the changes to the path as they are made in the Key Info rollout. ■

Figure 35.23 shows three TCB curves assigned to the Position track of an object.

Note
Some controllers are assigned through the Animation menu and others through the Assign Controller dialog box. Look to both if you cannot find a specific controller. ■

FIGURE 35.23

The TCB controller offers a different way to work with curves.

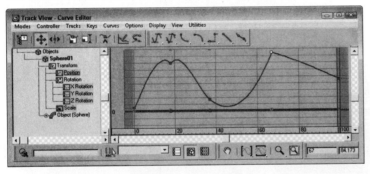

Reaction controller

The Reaction controller changes its values as a reaction to another controller. This controller is different from the Attachment controller in that the motions don't need to be in the same direction. For example, you can have one object rise as another object moves to the side.

Cross-Reference
Don't confuse the Reaction controller with the reactor plug-in, which computes motion based on physical dynamics. The reactor plug-in is covered in Chapter 43, "Simulating Physics-Based Motion with MassFX." ■

After the Reaction controller is assigned to a track, you can define the reactions using the Reaction Manager dialog box, shown in Figure 35.24. Selecting and right-clicking the track with this controller assigned and selecting Properties from the pop-up menu opens this dialog box. You also can open the Reaction Manager dialog box using the Animation ➪ Reaction Manager menu.

The Reaction Manager is made up of two lists and a graph of function curves. The top list holds all the object values that are involved in reactions. These are listed in a hierarchy with the master object listed above the slave object. A single master object can control several slave parameters.

The buttons above the Reactions list let you add new masters, slaves, and selected objects to the list. The cursor changes after you click any of these buttons, allowing you to click an object in the viewport and select a value from a pop-up menu.

FIGURE 35.24

The Reaction Manager dialog box lets you set the parameters of a reaction.

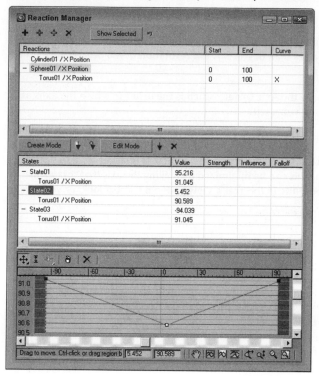

For the slave objects selected in the Reactions list, you can set states using the buttons above the States list. To set a state, click the Create Mode button, drag the Time Slider to the appropriate frame, and change the slave object's value. Then click the Create State button to create the target object state. Several unique states can be defined for each slave object.

State values can be changed by accessing the Edit Mode button or by editing the curves displayed at the bottom of the Reaction Manager dialog box.

Rotation and Scale track controllers

The Rotation and Scale track controller types include some of the common default controllers and can be assigned to the Rotation and Scale tracks. They typically work with three unique values representing the X-, Y-, and Z-axes. These controllers can be assigned from the Animation ⇨ Rotation (Scale) Controllers menu. Many of the controllers found in this menu also are found in the Position Controllers menu. Only the controllers unique to the Rotation and Scale tracks are covered here.

Euler XYZ Rotation controller

The Euler XYZ Rotation controller lets you control the rotation angle along the X-, Y-, and Z-axes based on a single float value for each frame. Euler rotation is different from Max's default rotation method (which is quaternion rotation and not as smooth).

The main difference is that Euler rotation gives you access to the function curves. Using these curves, you can smoothly define the rotation motion of the object.

Note

Euler XYZ Rotation values are in radians instead of degrees. If using these as part of an expression, be sure to use radians and not degrees. Radians are much smaller values than degrees. A full revolution is 360 degrees or 2 times Pi radians, so 1 degree equals about 0.0174 radians. ■

The Euler Parameters rollout lets you choose the Axis Order, which is the order in which the axes are calculated. You also can choose which axis to work with.

Caution

The Euler XYZ controller is susceptible to Gimbal lock, which occurs when two of the three axes align to each other, causing the object to lose a degree of freedom. This can be minimized by making the axis that rotates the least the middle axis. You also can use the Euler Filter utility in the Track View to avoid Gimbal lock, or you can use the Quaternion controller instead.

Smooth Rotation controller

The Smooth Rotation controller automatically produces a smooth rotation. This controller doesn't add any new keys; it simply changes the timing of the existing keys to produce a smooth rotation. It does not have any parameters.

Parameter controllers

Other controllers are used to affect the animated changes of parameters whether they are float, Point3, or other parameter types. Many of these controllers combine several controllers into one, such as the List and Block controllers. Others include separate interfaces, such as the Waveform controller for defining the controller's functions.

Most of these special-purpose controllers can be assigned only by using the Track View window. The Motion panel contains only the tracks for transformations.

Boolean controller

The Boolean controller, like the On/Off controller, can hold one of two states: 0 for off and 1 for on. But, unlike the On/Off controller, the Boolean controller changes only when a different state is encountered.

Limit controller

The Limit controller sets limits for the motion or parameters of the selected controller. It is applied on top of the existing controller and opens the Limit Controller dialog box, shown in Figure 35.25, when applied.

The upper limit is the maximum value to which the controller can be set, and the lower limit is the minimum value that the controller uses. Controller values may exceed the upper and lower limit values, but the object's motion stops at the limit values when the Limit controller is enabled. The Smoothing Buffer value provides a range that gradually alters the value as it approaches the limit value.

FIGURE 35.25

The Limit controller dialog box lets you set upper and lower limits for the current controller value.

After a Limit controller is applied to an object, you can quickly change its upper and lower limit values by right-clicking the object in the Track View and accessing the Limit Controller option in the quadmenu.

Tip

You can disable all limits at once using the Animation⇨Toggle Limits menu command. ∎

List controller

You can use the List controller to apply several controllers at once. This feature enables you to produce smaller, subtler deviations, such as adding some noise to a normal Path controller.

When the List controller is applied, the default track appears as a subtrack along with another subtrack labeled Available. By selecting the Available subtrack and clicking the Assign Controller button, you can assign additional controllers to the current track.

All subtrack controllers are included in the List rollout of the Motion panel. You also can access this list by right-clicking the track and selecting Properties from the pop-up menu. The order of the list is important because it defines which controllers are computed first.

The Set Active button lets you specify which controller you can interactively control in the viewport; the active controller is marked with an arrow, which is displayed to the left of the name. You also can cut and paste controllers from and to the list. Because you can use the same controller type multiple times, you can distinguish each one by entering a name in the Name field.

On/Off controller

The On/Off controller works on tracks that hold a binary value, such as the Visibility track; you can use it to turn the track on and off or to enable and disable options. In the Track View, each On section is displayed in blue, with keys alternating between on and off. No parameters exist for this controller. Figure 35.26 shows a Visibility track that has been added to a sphere object. This track was added using the Tracks⇨Visibility Track⇨Add menu command. You can add keys with the Add Keys button. Each new key toggles the track on and off.

Note

You also can add a Visibility track by changing the Visibility value in the Object Properties dialog box. ∎

FIGURE 35.26

The On/Off controller lets you make objects appear and disappear.

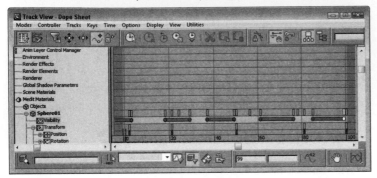

Waveform controller

 The Waveform controller can produce regular periodic waveforms, such as a sinusoidal wave. Several different waveform types can make up a complete waveform. The Waveform Controller dialog box, shown in Figure 35.27, includes a list of all the combined waveforms. To add a waveform to this list, click the Add button.

When you select a waveform in the list, you can give it a name and edit its shape using the buttons and values. Preset waveform shapes include Sine, Square, Triangle, Sawtooth, and Half Sine. You also can invert and flip these shapes.

FIGURE 35.27

The Waveform Controller dialog box lets you produce sinusoidal motions.

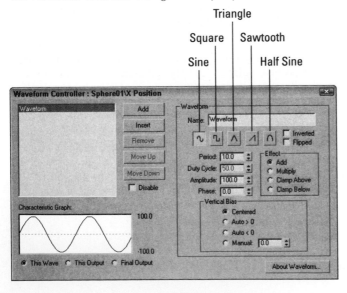

The Period value defines the number of frames required to complete one full pattern. The Amplitude value sets the height of the wave, and the Phase value determines its location at the start of the cycle. The Duty Cycle value is used only for the square wave to define how long it stays enabled.

You can use the Vertical Bias options to set the values range for the waveform. Options include Centered, which sets the center of the waveform at 0; Auto > 0, which causes all values to be positive; Auto < 0, which causes all values to be negative; and Manual, which lets you set a value for the center of the waveform.

The Effect option determines how different waveforms in the list are combined. They can be added, multiplied, clamped above, or clamped below. The Add option simply adds the waveform values together, and the Multiply option multiplies the separate values. The Clamp Above and Clamp Below options force the values of one curve to its maximum or minimum while not exceeding the values of the other curve. The Characteristic Graph shows the selected waveform, the output, or the final resulting curve. Figure 35.28 shows the Characteristic Graph for each Effect option when a sine wave and a square wave are combined.

FIGURE 35.28

Combining sine and square waves with the Add, Multiply, Clamp Above, and Clamp Below Effect options

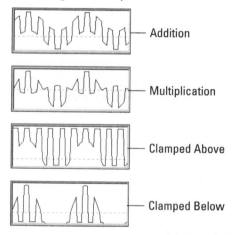

— Addition

— Multiplication

— Clamped Above

— Clamped Below

Color RGB controller

You can use the Color RGB controller to animate colors. Color values are different from regular float values in that they include three values that represent the amounts of red, green, and blue (referred to as RGB values) present in the color. This data value type is known as Point3.

The Color RGB controller splits a track with color information into its component RGB tracks. You can use this controller to apply a different controller to each color component and also to animate any color swatch in Max.

Cubic Morph controller

You can assign the Cubic Morph controller to a morph compound object. You can find the track for this object under the Objects track. A subtrack of the morph object is the Morph track, which holds the morph keys.

The Cubic Morph controller uses Tension, Continuity, and Bias values to control how targets blend with one another. You can access these TCB values in the Key Info dialog box by right-clicking any morph key or by right-clicking the Morph track and selecting Properties from the pop-up menu.

Note
You also can access the TCB values by right-clicking the keys in the Track Bar. ■

Barycentric Morph controller
The Barycentric Morph controller is automatically applied when a morph compound object is created. Keys are created for this controller based on the morph targets set in the Modify panel under the Current Targets rollout for the morph compound object. You can edit these keys using the Barycentric controller Key Info dialog box, which you can open by right-clicking a morph key in the Track View or in the Track Bar.

The main difference between the Cubic Morph controller and the Barycentric Morph controller is that the latter can have weights applied to the various morph keys.

The Barycentric Morph controller Key Info dialog box includes a list of morph targets. If a target is selected, its Percentage value sets the influence of the target. The Time value is the frame where this key is located. The TCB values and displayed curve control the Tension, Continuity, and Bias parameters for this controller. The Constrain to 100% option causes all weights to equal 100 percent; changing one value changes the other values proportionally if this option is selected.

Block controller
 The Block controller combines several tracks into one block so you can handle them all together. This controller is located in the Global Tracks track. If a track is added to a Block controller, a Slave controller is placed in the track's original location.

To add a Block controller, select the Available track under the Block Control track under the Global Tracks track, and click the Assign Controller button. From the Assign Constant Controller dialog box that opens, select Master Block and click OK. Right-click the Master Block track and select Properties to open the Master Block Parameters dialog box, shown in Figure 35.29.

FIGURE 35.29
The Master Block Parameters dialog box lists all the tracks applied to a Block controller.

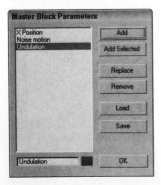

In the Master Block Parameters dialog box, you can add a track to the Block controller with the Add button. All tracks added are displayed in the list on the left. You can give each track a name by using the Name field. You also can use the Add Selected button to add any selected tracks. The Replace button lets you select a new controller to replace the currently selected track. The Load and Save buttons enable you to load or save blocks as separate files.

The Add button opens the Track View Pick dialog box, shown in Figure 35.30. This dialog box displays all valid tracks in a darker color to make them easier to see, while graying out invalid tracks.

FIGURE 35.30

The Track View Pick dialog box lets you select the tracks you want to include in the Block controller.

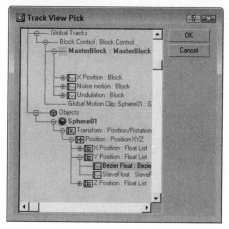

Select the tracks that you want to include, and click OK. The Block Parameters dialog box opens, shown in Figure 35.31, in which you can name the block, specify Start and End frames, and choose a color. Click OK when you're finished with this dialog box.

FIGURE 35.31

The Block Parameters dialog box lets you name a block.

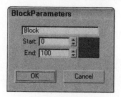

Back in the Master Block Parameters dialog box, click the Load button to open a file dialog box where you can load a saved block of animation parameters. The saved block files have the .blk extension. After the parameters have loaded, the Attach Controls dialog box opens, as shown in Figure 35.32. This dialog box includes two panes. The Incoming Controls pane on the left lists all motions in the saved block. By clicking the Add button, you can add tracks from the current scene, to which you can copy the saved block motions.

FIGURE 35.32

The Attach Controls dialog box lets you attach saved tracks to the Block controller.

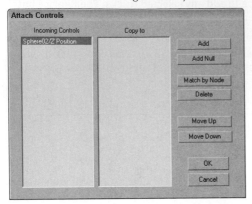

Because the saved motions in the Incoming Controls pane will match up with the Copy to entries in the right pane, the Add Null button adds a space in place of a specific track if you don't want a motion to be copied. The Match by Node button matches tracks by means of the Track View Pick dialog box.

IK controller

The IK controller works on a bones system for controlling the bone objects of an IK (inverse kinematics) system. The IK controller includes many different rollouts for defining joint constraints and other parameters.

Cross-Reference

Find out more about the IK controller in Chapter 38, "Understanding Rigging, Kinematics and Working with Bones." ∎

Master Point controller

 The Master Point controller controls the transforms of any point or vertex subobject selections. The Master Point controller is a controller that you can select and add, but instead it gets added as a track to an object whose subobjects are transformed. Subtracks under this track are listed for each subobject. The keys in the Master track are colored green.

Right-clicking a green master key opens the Master Track Key Info dialog box, shown in Figure 35.33. This dialog box shows the Key number with arrows for selecting the previous or next key, a Time field that displays the current frame number, and a list of all the vertices. Selecting a vertex from the list displays its parameters at the bottom of the dialog box.

Summary

The Animation Layers feature provides a simple way to organize animated motions into an easy-to-manage method. The Animation Layers toolbar includes all the tools you need to manage these unique layers. Animation clips for standard objects can be added and mixed in the Motion Mixer. The File ⇨ Load Animation option, along with its mapping and retargeting features, lets you reuse saved animations by applying them to other scenes. This chapter also introduced all the available animation modifiers and showed you how to use several of them. Finally, the chapter covered several complex controllers.

FIGURE 35.33

The Master Track Key Info dialog box lets you change the key values for each vertex.

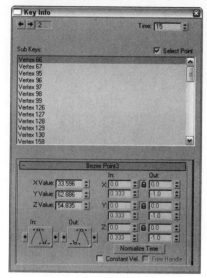

In this chapter, you learned about the following:

- Using the Animation Layers toolbar
- Creating new layers and using weights
- Collapsing animation layers
- Loading saved XML animation files
- Remapping animation tracks between objects
- Retargeting to adjust for a change in scale
- Using the Point Cache modifier
- Using the Morpher modifier to deform a face
- Using the Flex modifier and the other deformation modifiers
- Using the various miscellaneous animation modifiers
- Examining the various controllers in several different categories

The next chapter takes a close look at the Expression Controller that gives you·the ability to script the controller's behavior. It also covers wiring parameters so that one parameter can control another, and creating custom parameters.

Animating with the Expression Controller and Wiring Parameters

E xpressions are looks that you make in the mirror when you're trying to wake up, but in Max they are a series of equations that define how an object acts. Max expressions can be as simple as adding two numbers together or as complex as several lines of MAXScript. But expressions enable you to create customized animated reactions.

Although Max expressions can be used with any Max spinner, they are mainly used within MAXScript scripts or in the Expression controller. The Expression controller is a specialized controller that lets you control the object's behavior using scripted expressions.

This chapter then looks at a unique way to drive animations based on object parameters. Parameters of one object can be wired to parameters of another object so that when one parameter changes, the wired parameter changes with it. For example, you can wire the On/Off parameter of a light to the movement of a switch. All parameters that can be animated can be wired.

As long as you are working with parameters, Max includes several helpful tools for viewing and working with the available parameters including the Parameter Collector. If the Parameter Collector doesn't gather the exact parameters that you need, you can create your own custom parameters also.

Working with Expressions in Spinners

Although much of this chapter focuses on using the Expression controller, the Expression Controller Interface isn't the only place where you can play with expressions. Expressions can also be entered into spinner controls using the Numerical Expression Evaluator, shown in Figure 36.1. This simple dialog box is accessed by selecting a spinner and pressing Ctrl+N.

Note

Another place that commonly uses expressions is the Parameter Wiring dialog box, which is covered later in this chapter. ∎

FIGURE 36.1

The Numerical Expression Evaluator dialog box lets you enter expressions for a spinner.

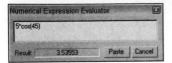

To use this evaluator, just type the expression in the field; the result is displayed in the result field. The result field is updated as you type the expression. If you make a mistake, the Result is blanked out. The Paste button places the result value in the spinner, and the Cancel button closes the dialog box without a change.

Tip

You can enter a relative value in a spinner by typing the letter R and a value. For example, if the Segments value of a sphere object is 32, then typing R20 changes the value to 52, and R-20 changes the value to 12. ∎

Understanding the Expression Controller Interface

The term *expression* refers to a mathematical expression or simple formula that computes a value based on other values. These expressions can be simple, as with moving a bicycle based on the rotation of the pedals, or they can be complex, as with computing the sinusoidal translation of a boat on the sea as a function of the waves beneath it.

You can use almost any value as a variable in an expression, from object coordinates and modifier parameters to light and material settings. The results of the expression are computed for every frame and used to affect various parameters in the scene. You can include the number of frames and time variables in the expression to cause the animation results to repeat for the entire sequence.

Note

Although it is not as powerful as the Script controller, the Expression controller is much faster than the Script controller because it doesn't require any compile time. ∎

Of all the controllers that are available, the Expression controller has limitless possibilities that could fill an entire book. This section covers the basics of building expressions and includes several examples.

The Expression controller is just one of the many controllers that are available for automating animations. This controller enables you to define how the object is transformed by means of a mathematical formula or expression, which you can apply to any of the object's tracks. It shows up in the controller list, based on the type of track to which it is assigned, as a Position Expression, Rotation Expression, Scale Expression, Float Expression, or Point3 Expression controller.

Before you can use the Expression controller on a track, you must assign it to a track. You can assign controllers to the Position, Rotation, and Scale tracks using the Motion panel or the Track View or you can apply a controller by right-clicking on a track in the Track View and selecting the Assign Controller option. After you assign a controller, the Expression Controller dialog box immediately opens, or you can access this dialog box at any time by right-clicking the track and selecting Properties from the pop-up menu. For example, select an object in your scene, open the Motion panel, and select the Position track. Then click the Assign Controller button at the top of the Assign Controller rollout, and select Position Expression from the list of Controllers. This causes the Expression Controller dialog box to appear.

You can use this dialog box to define variables and write expressions. The dialog box, shown in Figure 36.2, includes four separate panes used to display a list of Scalar and Vector variables, build an expression, and enter a description of the expression.

FIGURE 36.2

You can use the Expression controller to build expressions and define their results.

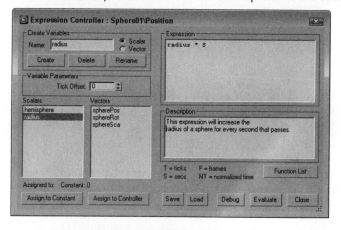

Defining variables

Variables are placeholders for different values. For example, creating a variable for a sphere's radius called "r" would simplify an expression for doubling its size from "take the sphere's radius and multiply it by two," to simply "r times 2."

To add variables to the list panes in the Expression Controller dialog box, type a name in the Name field, select the Scalar or Vector option type, and click the Create button; the new variable appears in the Scalars or Vectors list. To delete a variable, select it from the list and click the Delete button. The Tick Offset value is the time added to the current time and can be used to delay variables.

You can assign any new variable either to a constant or to a controller. Assigning a variable to a constant does the same thing as typing the constant's value in the expression. Constant variables are simply for convenience in writing expressions. The Assign to Controller button opens the Track View Pick dialog box, shown in Figure 36.3, where you can select the specific controller track for the variable, such as the position of an object.

FIGURE 36.3

The Track View Pick dialog box displays all the tracks for the scene. Tracks that you can select are displayed in black.

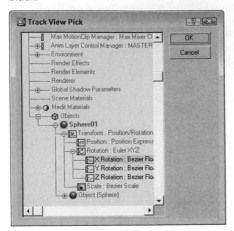

Assigning a variable to a controller enables you to animate the selected object based on other objects in the scene. To do this, create a variable and assign it to an animated track of another object. For example, if you create a Vector variable named boxPos and assign it to the Position track for a box object, then within the expression you can use this variable to base the motion of the assigned object on the box's position.

Building expressions

You can type expressions directly into the Expression pane of the Expression Controller dialog box. To use a named variable from one of the variable lists (Scalars or Vectors), type its name in the Expression pane. Predefined variables (presented later in the chapter) such as F and NT do not need to be defined in the variable panes. The Function List button opens a list of functions, shown in Figure 36.4, where you can view the functions that can be included in the expression. This list is for display only; you still need to type the function in the Expression pane.

Tip

One way to learn the syntax for different expressions is to enable the MacroRecorder in the MAXScript Listener window and look in the upper pane while performing a task in the viewports. ■

Note

The Expression pane ignores any white space, so you can use line returns and spaces to make the expression easier to see and read. ■

Debugging and evaluating expressions

After typing an expression in the Expression pane, you can check the values of all variables at any frame by clicking the Debug button. This opens the Expression Debug window, shown in Figure 36.5. This window displays the values for all variables, as well as the return value. The values are automatically updated as you move the Time Slider.

FIGURE 36.4

The Function List dialog box lets you view all the available functions that you can use in an expression.

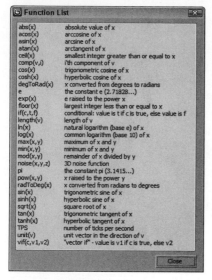

FIGURE 36.5

The Expression Debug window offers a way to test the expression before applying it.

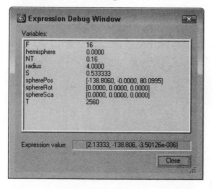

The Evaluate button in the Expression Controller dialog box commits the results of the expression to the current frame segment. If the expression contains an error, an alert dialog box warns you of the error. Replacing the controller with a different one can erase the animation resulting from an Expression controller.

Managing expressions

You can use the Save and Load button to save and recall expressions. Saved expressions are saved as files with an .xpr extension. Expression files do not save variable definitions.

Caution

If you load a saved expression into the Expression Controller dialog box, you need to reassign all variables before you can use the loaded expression. ∎

Tutorial: Creating following eyes

As a quick example, you'll start with a simple expression. The Expression controller is very useful for setting the eye pupil objects to move along with the ball's motion. This same functionality can be accomplished using a manipulator and wiring the parameter, but you show it with the Float Expression controller.

To make eye pupil objects follow a moving ball object, follow these steps:

1. Open the Following eyes.max file from the Chap 36 directory on the CD.

   This file includes a face taken from a Greek model made by Viewpoint Datalabs, along with a ball that is animated to move back and forth.

2. Select the left eye pupil object named "pupil_l" (the right pupil has been linked to move with the left pupil), and open the Motion panel. Select the Position track, and click the Assign Controller button. Select the Position Expression controller, and click OK.

   The Expression Controller dialog box opens.

3. Create a new vector variable named **ballPos** by typing its name in the Name field, selecting the Vector option, and clicking the Create button.

4. With the ballPos variable selected, click the Assign to Controller button. In the Track View Pick dialog box, locate and select Objects and click the "+" to the left. Then choose Sphere01 and click the "+" to its left. Finally, choose the Position: Position XYZ, as shown in Figure 36.6, and click OK.

FIGURE 36.6

Select the Position track for the Sphere01 object in the Track View Pick dialog box.

5. In the Expression pane, erase the existing expression and type the following:

```
[ -3.1 + ballPos.x/20, -2.9, 41.0 ]
```

Then click the Debug button. The Expression Debug window appears, in which you can see the variable values change as items in the scene change. With the expression complete, you can drag the Time Slider back and forth and watch the pupil follow the ball from side to side. If you're happy with the motion, click the Evaluate button and then the Close button to exit the interface.

This is a simple example, but it demonstrates what is possible. Figure 36.7 shows the resulting face.

FIGURE 36.7

The Expression controller was used to animate the eyes following the ball in this example.

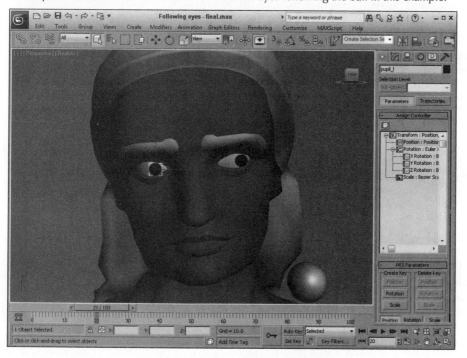

Using Expression Controllers

You can use expressions to control the transforms of objects. You can access these transforms from the Track View or from the Motion panel. You can also use expressions to control object parameters such as a box's length or material properties such as the amount of illumination applied to a material. You can access all these parameters from the Track View.

Animating transforms with the Expression controller

After you assign a controller to a transform track, the Expression pane in the Expression Controller dialog box includes the current values of the selected object. Position transforms display the X, Y, and

Z coordinates of the object; Rotation transforms display the rotation value in radians; and Scale transforms display values describing the relative scaling values for each axis.

Note

Radians are another way to measure angles. A full revolution equals 360 degrees, which equates to 2 × pi radians. The Expression dialog box includes the `degToRad` and `radToDeg` functions to convert back and forth between these two measurement systems. ∎

Animating parameters with the Float Expression controller

To assign the Float Expression controller, select an object with a parameter or Modifier applied and open the Track View. Find the track for the parameter that you want to change, and click the Assign Controller button. Select the Float Controller from the list, and click OK.

Note

The actual controller type depends on the parameter selected. Many parameters use float expressions, but some use Transform controllers. ∎

After you assign the Expression controller, the Expression Controller dialog box opens, or you can open it by right-clicking the track and selecting Properties from the pop-up menu to load the dialog box. Within this dialog box, the Expression pane includes the current value of the selected parameter.

Tutorial: Inflating a balloon

The Push Modifier mimics filling a balloon with air by pushing all its vertices outward. In this tutorial, you'll use a balloon model created by Zygote Media to see how you can use the Float Expression controller to control the parameters of a modifier.

To inflate a balloon using the Float Expression controller, follow these steps:

1. Open the Balloon and pump.max file from the Chap 36 directory on the CD.

   This file includes a pump created from primitives and the balloon model with the Push modifier applied.

2. Next, open the Track View by choosing Graph Editors ⇨ Track View ⇨ Curve Editor. Select the balloon and navigate the balloon object's tracks until you find the Push Value track (found under Objects ⇨ b3 ⇨ Modified Object ⇨ Push ⇨ Push Value). Select the Push Value track, and click the Assign Controller button (or select it from the right-click pop-up menu). From the list of controllers, select Float Expression and click OK.

   The Expression Controller dialog box opens.

3. In the Expression pane, you should see a single scalar value of 0. Modify the expression to read like this:

   ```
   2 * NT
   ```

   Click the Debug button to see the value results. With the Expression Debug window open, drag the Time Slider and notice that the balloon inflates.

Note

If you use a parameter such as Radius as part of an Expression, then the parameter is unavailable in the Modify panel if you try to change it by hand. ∎

Figure 36.8 shows the balloon as it is being inflated.

FIGURE 36.8

A balloon being inflated using an Expression controller to control the Push modifier

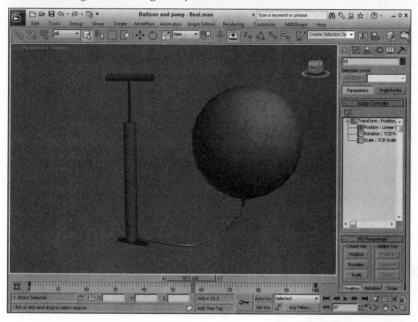

Animating materials with the Expression controller

You can locate the material's parameter in the Track View and assign the Expression controller to it to control material parameters. Some of these parameters are scalar values, but any material parameter set with a color swatch has a Point3 return type.

When using material parameters and color values, be sure not to combine them in expressions with vector values.

Wiring Parameters

When parameters are wired together, the value of one parameter controls the value of the parameter to which it is wired. This is a powerful animation technique that lets a change in one part of the scene control another aspect of the scene. Another way to use wired parameters is to create custom animation controls such as a slider that dims a light source that animators can use as needed.

Using the Parameter Wiring dialog box

You can access the Parameter Wiring dialog box in several places. The Animation ⇨ Wire Parameters ⇨ Wire Parameters (Ctrl+5) menu makes a pop-up menu of parameters appear. Selecting a parameter from the menu changes the cursor to a dotted line (like the one used when linking objects). Click the object that you want to wire to, and another pop-up menu lets you choose the parameter to wire to. The Parameter Wiring dialog box appears with the parameter for each object selected from a hierarchy tree.

You can also wire parameters by right-clicking the quadmenu and selecting Wire Parameters. The Wire Parameters option is disabled if multiple objects are selected.

The Parameter Wiring dialog box (Alt+5), shown in Figure 36.9, displays two tree lists containing all the available parameters. This tree list looks very similar to the Track View and lets you connect parameters in either direction or to each other. If you used the Wire Parameters feature to open the Parameter Wiring dialog box, then the parameter for each object is already selected and highlighted in yellow.

FIGURE 36.9

The Parameter Wiring dialog box can work with expressions.

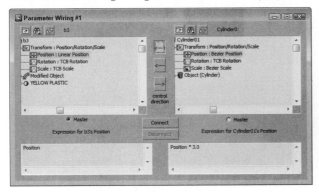

The three arrow buttons between the two tree lists let you specify the connection direction. These buttons connect the parameter in one pane to the selected parameter in the opposite pane. The direction determines whether the parameter in the left pane controls the parameter in the right pane, or vice versa. You can also select the top bidirectional button to make the parameters mutually affect each other. Below each tree list is a text area where you can enter an expression. An *expression* is a mathematical statement that follows a specific syntax for defining how one parameter controls the other. These expressions can be any valid expression that is accepted in the Animation Controller dialog box or in MAXScript.

Cross-Reference

You can learn more about creating and using expressions in Chapter 22, "Animating with Constraints and Simple Controllers." ■

After an expression is entered, click the Connect button to complete the wiring. Based on the connection direction, the Master radio button indicates which object controls the other. You can also use this dialog box to disconnect existing wired parameters. You can use the icon buttons at the top of the dialog box, shown in Table 36.1, to Show All Tracks, to find the next wired parameter, and to refresh the tree view.

TABLE 36.1	

Parameter Wiring Dialog Box Icons

Button	Description
	Show All Tracks
	Next Wired Parameter
	Refresh Tree View

After the wiring is completed, the Parameter Wiring dialog box remains open. You can try out the wiring by moving the master object. If the results aren't what you wanted, you can edit the expression and click the Update button (the Connect button changes to an Update button).

Note

When you select objects to be wired, the order in which the objects are selected doesn't matter because in the Parameter Wiring dialog box you can select the direction of control. ■

After you've made a connection in the Parameter Wiring dialog box, the track name for the controlling object turns green, and the track name of the object being controlled turns red. If you make a bidirectional connection, then both tracks turn green.

Manipulator helpers

To create general-use controls that can be wired to control various properties, Max includes three manipulator helpers. These helpers are Cone Angle, Plane Angle, and Slider. They are available as a subcategory under the Helpers category of the Create panel or in the Create ⇨ Helpers ⇨ Manipulators menu.

For the Cone Angle helper, you can set the Angle, Distance, and Aspect settings. The default cone is a circle, but you can make it a square. The Plane Angle helper includes settings for Angle, Distance, and Size.

You can name the Slider helper. This name appears in the viewports above the slider object. You can also set a default value along with maximum and minimum values. To position the object, you can set the X Position, Y Position, and Width settings. You can also set a snap value for the slider.

Once created, you can use these manipulator helpers when the Select and Manipulate button on the main toolbar is enabled (this button must be disabled before the manipulator helpers can be created). The advantage of these helpers is in wiring parameters to be controlled using the helpers.

Tutorial: Controlling a crocodile's bite

One way to use manipulator helpers and wired parameters is to control within limits certain parameters that can be animated. This gives your animation team controls they can use to quickly build animation sequences. In this example, you use a slider to control a crocodile's jaw movement.

To create a slider to control a crocodile's bite, follow these steps:

1. Open the Biting crocodile.max file from the Chap 36 directory on the CD.

    This file includes a crocodile model created by Viewpoint Datalabs. For this model, the head, eyes, and upper teeth have been joined into a single object, and the pivot point for this object has been moved to where the jaw hinges.

893

2. Select Create ⇨ Helpers ⇨ Manipulators ⇨ Slider, and click in the Perspective view above the crocodile. Name the slider **Croc Bite**, and set the Maximum value to **60**.

3. With the Slider selected, choose Animation ⇨ Wire Parameter ⇨ Wire Parameter (or press the Ctrl+5) to access the pop-up menu. Choose Object (Slider) ⇨ value option, drag the dotted line to the crocodile's head object, and click. Choose Transform ⇨ Rotation ⇨ Y Rotation.

   The Parameter Wiring dialog box appears.

4. In the Parameter Wiring dialog box, click the direction arrow that points from the Slider to the head so that the slider is set to control the head. Then click the Connect button and drag the Slider.

Note

Before you can drag the slider, you need to enable the Select and Manipulate button in the main toolbar. ∎

The crocodile's jaw spins around erratically. This happens because the rotation values are in radians and you need them in degrees.

5. In the expression text area under the head object, enter the expression **degToRad(value)** and click the Update button. Then drag the Slider again.

   Now the values are in degrees, and the range is correct, but the croc's upper jaw rotates unrealistically through the bottom jaw. This can be fixed by multiplying by a negative 1.

6. In the expression text area under the head object, update the expression to be `-1*degToRad(value)` and click the Update button.

7. Click the Select and Manipulate button on the main toolbar, and drag the slider to the right.

   The crocodile's mouth opens.

Figure 36.10 shows the crocodile biting using the slider control.

FIGURE 36.10

A slider control is wired to open the crocodile's mouth.

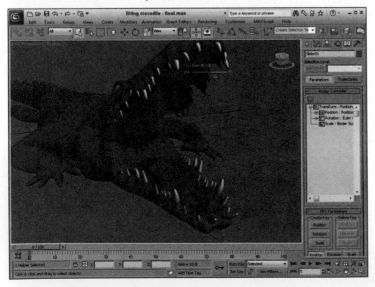

Collecting Parameters

To help in organizing the various parameters that you use to animate a scene, you can use the Parameter Collector to gather all custom and animated parameters used in the scene. The Parameter Editor can be used to create custom attributes and parameters, but the custom attributes are attached to the specific object or element that was selected when the attribute was created. This can make finding the custom attributes difficult, but Max includes another tool that you can use to collect all these custom attributes into a single location—the Parameter Collector.

Open the Parameter Collector dialog box, shown in Figure 36.11, with the Animation ⇨ Parameter Collector (Alt+2) menu command. This dialog box lets you gather a set of parameters into a custom rollout that can be opened and accessed from anywhere. This provides a convenient way to compile and look at only the parameters that you need to animate a certain task. Under the menus are several toolbar buttons, explained in Table 36.2.

FIGURE 36.11

The Parameter Collector dialog box is used to gather several different parameters into a custom rollout.

Select parameter marker   Select rollout marker   Properties

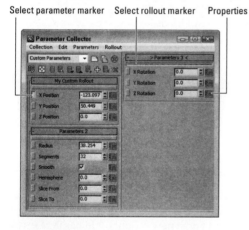

TABLE 36.2

Parameter Collector Toolbar Buttons

Toolbar Button	Name	Description
Sphere Collection ▼	Collection Name	Enters a name for the current collection or selects an existing collection.
▢	New Collection	Creates a new collection of parameters.
▣	Duplicate Collection	Creates a copy of the existing collection.
⊗	Delete Collection	Deletes the current collection.

continued

TABLE 36.2	(continued)	
Toolbar Button	**Name**	**Description**
	Multiple Edits	Toggle button that allows multiple parameters to be changed at once when enabled.
	Absolute/Relative	Toggle button that maintains the current value in Absolute mode and resets the value to 0 when the mouse is released in Relative mode.
	Key Selected	Creates a key for the selected parameters when the Auto Key mode is enabled.
	Reset Selected	Sets the selected parameter values to 0.
	Move Parameters Down	Moves the selected parameters downward in the rollout order.
	Move Parameters Up	Moves the selected parameters upward in the rollout order.
	Add to Selected Rollout	Opens a Track View Pick dialog box where you can select the parameter to add to the selected rollout.
	Add to New Rollout	Opens a Track View Pick dialog box where you can select the parameter to add to a new rollout.
	Delete Selected	Deletes the selected parameters.
	Delete All	Deletes all parameters in the current collection.
	Properties	Opens the Key Info dialog box for the selected parameter if a key is set. This button is found to the right of a parameter.

Within the Parameter Collection dialog box, you can create and name new rollouts, add parameters to these rollouts using a Track View Pick dialog box, and save multiple rollouts into collections that can be recalled.

Collections are named by typing a new name in the drop-down list located in the upper-left corner of the interface. This drop-down list holds all available collections. The Collection menu (or the toolbar buttons) may be used to create, rename, duplicate, or delete a collection.

A Parameter Collection can include multiple rollouts. The current active rollout is marked with a yellow bar directly under the rollout title and with brackets that surround the rollout name. Using the Rollout menu (or the toolbar buttons) you can create a new rollout, or rename, reorder, or delete existing rollouts.

Parameters are added to the rollouts using the Parameters ⇨ Add to Selected and the Parameters ⇨ Add to New Rollout menu commands. Both of these commands open a Track View Pick dialog box where you can select the specific parameter to add to the current rollout. To the left of each parameter is a small box that you can use to select the parameter. You can also select parameters using the Edit menu commands.

If multiple parameters are selected, then you can change the values for all selected parameters at the same time by enabling the Edit ⇨ Multiple Edits option. With the Multiple Edits option enabled, changing any parameter value also changes all other selected parameters.

Caution

Multiple parameters' values can be changed together only if they are of the same type. ∎

At the bottom of the Edit menu is the Edit Notes menu command. Using this menu command, you can change the parameter's name, link it to a URL, and type some notes about how this parameter works.

The Parameter Collector dialog box can also be used to create animation keys. To create a key for the selected parameters, you'll need to enable the Auto Key button and then select the Parameters ⇨ Key Selected or Parameters ⇨ Key All menu commands. If a key exists for the selected parameter, the Properties button to the right of the parameter becomes active and displays the Key Info dialog box when clicked.

Using the Collection ⇨ Show Selected Keys in Track Bar menu command, you can see the keys for the selected parameters regardless of whether the objects are selected in the viewports.

Adding Custom Parameters

Another useful way to expand the number of parameters is to create custom parameters. These custom parameters can define some aspect of the scene that makes sense to you. For example, if you create a model of a bicycle, you can define a custom parameter for the pedal rotation. You can add your own custom parameters using the Parameter Editor dialog box, shown in Figure 36.12. You can open this modeless panel by choosing Animation ⇨ Parameter Editor (or by pressing the Alt+1 keys).

The Add to Type drop-down list at the top of the Attribute rollout in the Parameter Editor dialog box lets you select where the custom attribute shows up. Custom attributes can be created for an object, for the selected modifier, for the object's material, or for any track found in the Track View. The Pick Explicit Track button opens a dialog box where you can select a specific track.

The Add button creates the custom attribute and adds it to a rollout named Custom Attributes for the specified element. If the specified element is selected, you can click the Edit/Delete button to open the Edit Attributes/Parameters dialog box, shown in Figure 36.13. All custom attributes associated with the selected element are displayed.

Note

Custom attributes show up in a rollout named Custom Attributes positioned beneath all the other rollouts, but if you add the Attribute Holder modifier to the object before creating the new attribute, then the Custom Attributes rollout appears under the Attribute Holder modifier. ∎

FIGURE 36.12

You can use the Parameter Editor dialog box to create custom parameters.

Pick Explicit Track

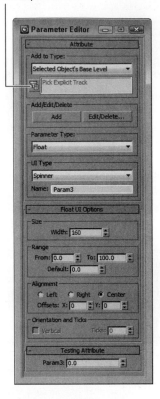

FIGURE 36.13

The Edit Attributes/Parameters dialog box lets you edit or delete custom attributes.

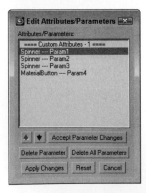

The Edit Attributes/Parameters dialog box lets you select and reorder the custom attributes within their rollout. Selecting a custom attribute also loads its settings into the Parameter Editor where they can be changed.

The Parameter Type drop-down list lets you choose the parameter format. Possibilities include Angle, Array, Boolean (true or false), Color, Float (a decimal point number), fRGBA, Integer, Material, Node, Percent, String, TextureMap, and WorldUnits. The UI Type drop-down list defines how the parameter is displayed in the rollout. How the parameter looks depends on the type of parameter. Float and integer values can be spinners or sliders, Boolean values can be check boxes or radio buttons, array values are drop-down lists, nodes are pick buttons (allowing you to select an object in the viewports), color and RGB values are color pickers, and texture maps are map buttons. You can also name the parameter.

The Options rollout changes depending on which parameter type was selected. These rollouts contain settings for the interface's Width, value ranges, default values, Alignment (left, right, or center), and list items.

The Testing Attribute rollout shows what the interface element will look like and lets you change the attribute to see how the custom parameter works.

The value of custom attributes becomes apparent when you start wiring parameters.

Summary

This chapter covered the basics of using the Expression controller. Using mathematical formulas to control the animation of an object's transformation and parameters offers lots of power. You also can use the values of one object to control another object.

Along with the Expression controller, the ability to wire parameters together in the Parameter Wire dialog box opens up a whole new way to control objects. This chapter also covered how you can create new parameters with the Parameter Collector dialog box. All of these tools give you lots of control over the scene using parameters and expressions. In this chapter, you accomplished the following:

- Practiced building expressions in the Expression Controller dialog box
- Learned about expressions and what they can do
- Reviewed the available operators, variables, and functions
- Tried out examples of controlling object transformations and parameters
- Created and wired parameters
- Gathered and edited several parameters at once with the Parameter Collector
- Created custom parameters with the Parameter Editor

In the next chapter, you learn to use the Track View to display and manage all the details of the current scene.

Working with the F-Curve Editor in the Track View

As you move objects around in a viewport, you often find yourself eyeballing the precise location of an object in the scene. If you've ever found yourself wishing that you could precisely see all the values behind the scene, then you need to find the Track View. The Track View can be viewed using three different layouts: Curve Editor, Dope Sheet, and Track Bar. Each of these interfaces offers a unique view into the details of the scene.

These Track View layouts can display all the details of the current scene, including all the parameters and keys. This view lets you manage and control all these parameters and keys without having to look in several different places.

The Track View also includes additional features that enable you to edit key ranges, add and synchronize sound to your scene, and work with animation controllers using function curves.

Learning the Track View Interface

Although the Track View can be viewed using different layouts, the basic interface elements are the same. They all have menus, toolbars, a Controller pane, a Key pane, and a Time Ruler. Figure 37.1 shows these interface elements. You can hide any of these interface elements using the Show UI Elements option in the pop-up menu that appears when you right-click the title bar. Also, you can quickly hide the Controller pane by clicking the triangle icon in the upper-left corner of the Key pane.

New Feature

The Show/Hide Controller pane button is new to 3ds Max 2012. ■

FIGURE 37.1

The Track View interface offers a complete hierarchical look at your scene.

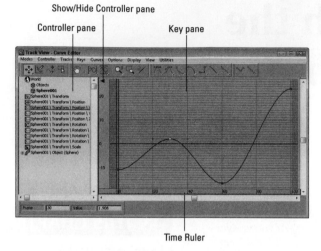

The Track View layouts

The Track View includes three different layouts: a Curve Editor, a Dope Sheet, and the Track Bar. The Curve Editor layout displays all parameter and motion changes as graphs that change over time. You manipulate these curves just like normal splines. You can use the Dope Sheet layout to coordinate key ranges between the different parameter tracks. And the Track Bar layout offers a way to quickly view the Track View within the viewports.

You can open the Curve Editor and Dope Sheet layouts using the Graph Editors menu. You can open the Curve Editor window by choosing Graph Editors ⇨ Track View–Curve Editor or by clicking the Curve Editor button on the main toolbar. You open the Dope Sheet interface in a similar manner by choosing Graph Editors ⇨ Track View–Dope Sheet.

Cross-Reference

You also use the Graph Editors menu to access the Schematic View interface. For more on the Schematic View interface, see Chapter 25, "Building Complex Scenes with Containers, XRefs, and the Schematic View." ■

After the Track View opens, you can give it a unique name using the Track View–Curve Editor field found on the Name: Track View toolbar. If the Name toolbar isn't visible, right-click the title bar and select Show Toolbars ⇨ Name: Track View from the pop-up menu. These named views are then listed in the Graph Editors ⇨ Saved Track Views menu. Any saved Track Views that are named are saved along with the scene file.

To open the Track Bar layout in the viewports, expand the Track Bar using the Open Mini Curve Editor button at the left end of the Timeline. Close the Track Bar layout by clicking the Close button on the toolbar. Figure 37.2 shows this Track View.

After you open a Track View, you can switch between the Curve Editor and the Dope Sheet using the Modes menu or by right-clicking the menu bar or toolbar (away from the buttons) and selecting a new layout from the Load Layout menu. You can also save customized layouts using the Save Layout or Save Layout As menu commands.

FIGURE 37.2

The Track Bar offers quick access to the Track View.

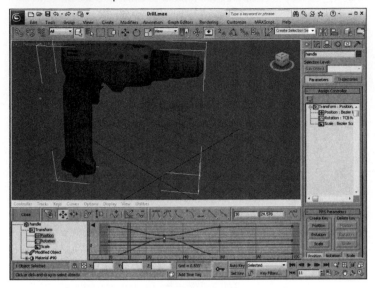

Track View menus and toolbars

In many cases, the menus and the toolbars provide access to the same functionality. One difference is the Modes menu, which lets you switch the current interface between the Curve Editor and the Dope Sheet layouts. The Curve Editor menus include Modes, Controller, Tracks, Keys, Curves, Options, Display, View, and Utilities. The Dope Sheet menu loses the Curves menus and adds a Time menu in its place. The Track Bar menus are the same as the Curve Editor menus, except that the Modes menu is absent.

The Track View consists of several toolbars. You can open these toolbars by right-clicking the toolbar (away from the buttons) and selecting the Show Toolbars submenu. The available toolbars depend on the layout (Function Curve Layout, Function Curve Layout [Classic], or Dope Sheet). The default Function Curve toolbars are the Key Controls, Navigation, Key Tangents, Tangent Actions, and Key Entry. For the Track View–Dope Sheet, the default toolbars at the top of the interface include the Keys, Time, Display, and Name toolbars. All these toolbars can be docked, floated, and hidden. You also can add and delete new toolbars using the right-click pop-up menu.

New Feature

The Key Controls, Key Entry, and Tangent Actions toolbars are all new to 3ds Max 2012. ■

Cross-Reference

You can learn more about docking and floating toolbars in Chapter 1, "Exploring the Max Interface." ■

For the Function Curve Editor, these toolbars are a reduced set that includes the main functions. The older toolbars are still available and can be selected using the Load Layout➪ Function Curve Layout (Classic) menu command in the toolbar right-click pop-up menu.

Note

Depending on the size of the Track View window, you may need to drag the toolbar to the left to see the buttons at the right end of the toolbar. ∎

Key Controls toolbar

The Key Controls toolbar is the first of the default toolbars for the Function Curve Editor. Table 37.1 describes these buttons.

TABLE 37.1

Key Controls Toolbar Buttons

Toolbar Button	Name	Description
	Move Keys, Move Keys Horizontal, Move Keys Vertical	Enables you to move the selected keys or limit their movement to horizontal or vertical
	Draw Curves	Creates a function curve by dragging the mouse; Curve Editor layout only
	Insert Keys	Enables you to add new keys to a track
	Region tool	Lets you drag to select move and/or scale multiple keys at once

Navigation toolbar

The Navigation toolbar for the Curve Editor lets you pan and zoom to focus on a specific area of the Track View window. Table 37.2 describes these buttons. This same toolbar is available in the Dope Sheet.

TABLE 37.2

Navigation Toolbar Buttons

Status Bar Button	Name	Description
	Pan	Pans the view
	Zoom Horizontal Extents, Zoom Horizontal Extents Keys	Displays the entire horizontal track or keys
	Zoom Value Extents	Displays the entire vertical track
	Zoom, Zoom Time, Zoom Values	Zooms in and out of the view
	Zoom Region	Zooms within a region selected by dragging the mouse
	Isolate Curve	Temporarily hides all function curves except for those with selected keys

New Feature

The Region tool and Isolate Curve tool are both new to 3ds Max 2012. ∎

Key Tangents toolbar

The Key Tangents toolbar is another of the default Curve Editor toolbars. It is used to set the In and Out curve types. This toolbar also is available in the Dope Sheet layout. Table 37.3 describes these buttons.

TABLE 37.3

Key Tangents Toolbar Buttons

Toolbar Button	Name	Description
	Set Tangents to Auto, Set In Tangents to Auto, Set Out Tangents to Auto	Sets curve to approach and leave the key in an automatic manner
	Set Tangents to Spline, Set In Tangents to Spline, Set Out Tangents to Spline	Sets curve to approach and leave the key in a custom manner defined by the handle positions
	Set Tangents to Fast, Set In Tangents to Fast, Set Out Tangents to Fast	Sets curve to approach and leave the key in an ascending manner
	Set Tangents to Slow, Set In Tangents to Slow, Set Out Tangents to Slow	Sets curve to approach and leave the key in a descending manner
	Set Tangents to Step, Set In Tangents to Step, Set Out Tangents to Step	Sets curve to approach and leave the key in a stepping manner
	Set Tangents to Linear, Set In Tangents to Linear, Set Out Tangents to Linear	Sets curve to approach and leave the key in a linear manner
	Set Tangents to Smooth, Set In Tangents to Smooth, Set Out Tangents to Smooth	Sets curve to approach and leave the key in a smooth manner

Tangent Actions toolbar

The Tangent Actions toolbar is another of the default toolbars in the Curve Editor. It is used to quickly break and unify tangent handles. Table 37.4 describes these buttons.

TABLE 37.4

Tangent Actions Toolbar Buttons

Toolbar Button	Name	Description
	Break Tangents	Allows the tangent handles on either side of the key to move independently
	Unify Tangents	Moves the tangent handles so they form a straight line

New Feature
Both the Break and Unify Tangents tools are new to 3ds Max 2012. ■

Key Entry toolbar
The Key Entry toolbar in the Curve Editor displays the current frame and value for the selected key. If multiple keys are selected, only the frame value is displayed. You also can enter values in these fields to change the current frame and/or value for the selected key or keys. This is a huge timesaver if you want to change multiple keys to the same value.

The same frame and value fields are available in the Dope Sheet in the Key Stats toolbar.

Key Tangents toolbar
The Key Tangents toolbar is the first of the default toolbars in the Dope Sheet. Table 37.5 describes these buttons.

TABLE 37.5

Key Tangents Toolbar Buttons

Toolbar Button	Name	Description
	Edit Keys	Enables edit keys mode
	Edit Ranges	Enables edit ranges mode
	Filters	Opens the Filter dialog box, where you can specify which tracks will appear
	Move Keys, Move Keys Horizontal, Move Keys Vertical	Enables you to move the selected keys or limit their movement to horizontal or vertical
	Slide Keys	Enables you to slide the selected keys
	Insert Keys	Enables you to add new keys to a track
	Scale Keys	Enables you to scale the selected keys

Time toolbar
The Time toolbar is another of the default toolbars for the Dope Sheet. It is used to work with time ranges. Table 37.6 describes these buttons.

TABLE 37.6

Time Toolbar Buttons

Toolbar Button	Name	Description
	Select Time	Enables you to select a block of time by clicking and dragging
	Delete Time	Deletes the selected block of time
	Reverse Time	Reverses the order of the selected time block
	Scale Time	Scales the current time block
	Insert Time	Inserts an additional amount of time
	Cut Time	Deletes the selected block of time and places it on the clipboard for pasting
	Copy Time	Makes a copy of the selected block of time and places it on the clipboard for pasting
	Paste Time	Inserts the current clipboard time selection

Display toolbar

The Display toolbar is another of the default toolbars for the Dope Sheet. Table 37.7 describes these buttons.

TABLE 37.7

Display Toolbar Buttons

Toolbar Button	Name	Description
	Lock Selection	Prevents any changes to the current selection
	Snap Frames	Causes moved tracks to snap to the nearest frame
	Show Keyable Icons	Displays a key icon next to all tracks that can be animated
	Modify Subtree	Causes changes to a parent to affect all tracks beneath the parent in the hierarchy; Dope Sheet layout only
	Modify Child Keys	Causes changes to child keys when parent keys are changed; Dope Sheet layout only

Track Selection toolbar

At the bottom edge of the Dope Sheet window are three toolbars that appear by default. These toolbars are the Track Selection, Key Stats, and Navigation. Using these toolbars, you can locate specific tracks, see information on the various keys, and navigate the interface.

In the Track Selection toolbar is the Zoom Selected Object button and the Select by Name field, in which you can type a name to locate any tracks with that name.

Note

In the Select by Name field, you also can use wildcard characters such as * (asterisk) and ? (question mark) to find several tracks. ■

The Key Stats toolbar includes Key Time and Value Display fields that display the current time and value. You can enter values in these fields to change the value for the current time. You also can enter an expression in these fields in which the variable *n* equals the key time or value. For example, to specify a key value that is 20 frames from the current frame, enter *n*+20 (where you supply the current value in place of *n*). You also can include any function valid for the Expression controller, such as sin( ) or log( ). Click the Show Selected Key Stats button to display the key value in the Key pane.

Cross-Reference

Chapter 22, "Animating with Constraints and Simple Controllers," presents the functions that are part of the Expression controller. ■

Table 37.8 describes the buttons found in the Track Selection and Key Stats toolbars.

TABLE 37.8

Track Selection and Key Stats Toolbar Buttons

Toolbar Button	Name	Description
	Zoom Selected Object	Places current selection at the top of the hierarchy
	Edit Track Set	Opens a dialog box where selected sets of tracks can be edited
	Filter Selected Tracks	Toggles to show only the selected tracks in the Controller pane
	Filter Selected Objects	Toggles to show the tracks for the selected objects in the Controller pane
	Filter Animated Tracks	Toggles to show only the animated tracks in the Controller pane
	Filter Unlocked Attributes	Toggles to show only the tracks with unlocked attributes in the Controller pane
	Show Selected Key Statistics	Displays the frame number and values next to each key

Other toolbars

The other toolbars provide access to features that also are available through the menus. These toolbars are hidden by default, but they can be made visible using the Show Toolbars menu command in the right-click pop-up menu.

Controller and Key panes

Below the menus (and below the topped docked toolbars) are two panes. The left pane, called the Controller pane, presents a hierarchical list of all the tracks. The right pane is called the Key pane, and it displays the time range, keys, or function curves, depending on the layout. You can pan the Controller pane by clicking and dragging on a blank section of the pane: The cursor changes to a hand to indicate when you can pan the pane.

Tip

Using the triangle icon in the upper-left corner of the Key pane, you can quickly hide the Controller pane. ■

Each track can include several subtracks. To display these subtracks, click the plus sign (+) to the left of the track name. To collapse a track, click the minus sign (–). You can also use the Settings menu to Auto Expand a selected hierarchy. Under the Options ⇨ Auto Expand menu are options for Selected Objects Only, Transforms, XYZ Components, Limits, Keyable, Animated, Base Objects, Modifiers, Materials, and Children. For example, if the Auto Expand ⇨ Transforms option is enabled, then the Transform tracks for all objects is automatically expanded in the Track View. Using these settings can enable you to quickly find the track you're looking for.

The Options ⇨ Auto Select ⇨ Animated toggle automatically selects all tracks that are animated. You can also auto select Position, Rotation, and/or Scale tracks. The Options ⇨ Auto Scroll menu command can be set for Selected and/or Objects tracks. This command automatically moves either the Selected tracks or the Objects track to the top of the Controller pane.

Note

You can also select, expand, and collapse tracks using the right-click pop-up quadmenu. ■

The Controller pane includes many different types of tracks. By default, every scene includes the following tracks: World, Sound, Video Post, Global Tracks, SME, Anim Layer Control Manager, Environment, Render Effects, Render Elements, Renderer, Global Shadow Parameters, Scene Materials, Medit Materials (for materials in the Material Editor), and Objects, as shown in Figure 37.3.

FIGURE 37.3

Several tracks are available by default.

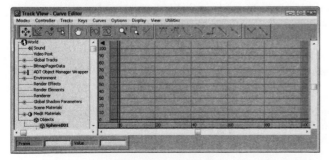

The Shift, Ctrl, and Alt keys make selecting and deselecting multiple tracks possible. To select a contiguous range of tracks, select a single track and then select another track while holding down the Shift key. This selects the two tracks and all tracks in between. Hold down the Ctrl key while selecting tracks to select multiple tracks that are not contiguous. The Alt key removes selected items from the selection set.

Below the right pane is the Time Ruler, which displays the current time as specified in the Time Configuration dialog box. The current frame is marked with a light blue time bar. This time bar is linked to the Time Slider, and moving one updates the other automatically.

At the top right of the Key pane (above the vertical scroll bar) is a split tab that you can use to split the Controller and Key pane into two separate views, as shown in Figure 37.4. Using this feature, you can look at two different sections of the tree at the same time. This makes it easy to copy and paste keys between different tracks.

Tip

You can drag the Time Ruler vertically in the right pane. ∎

FIGURE 37.4

Drag the tab above the vertical scroll tab to split the Track View into two views.

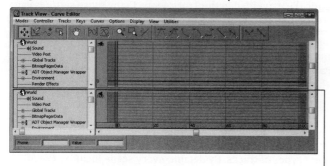

Split tab

Working with Keys

Keys define the main animation points in an animation. Max interpolates all the positions and values between the key points to generate the animation. Using the Track View, you can edit these animation keys with precision. Keys can be edited in either layout but are probably easiest to edit in the Dope Sheet layout with the Edit Keys button enabled.

Cross-Reference

Chapter 21, "Understanding Animation and Keyframes," covers key creation in more detail. ∎

In the Curve Editor, keys are shown as small squares positioned along the curve. In the Dope Sheet, keys are shown as colored lines that extend across the applicable tracks, as shown in Figure 37.5. The keys for the Position track are red, the Rotation track keys are green, the Scale track keys are blue, and the Parameter tracks (all non-transformation keys) are gray. Parent tracks (such as an object's name) are colored gray. Selecting a parent key selects all its children keys. Any selected keys appear white. A track title that includes a key is highlighted yellow.

Caution

If the Key pane is not wide enough, then a key is shown as a thick, black line. ∎

FIGURE 37.5

In the Dope Sheet, Position keys are red, Rotation keys are green, Scale keys are blue, and Parameter keys are gray.

Red Position key   Green Rotation key

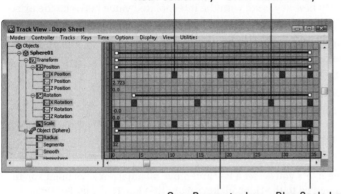

Gray Parameter key   Blue Scale key

Selecting keys

Before you can move and edit keys, you need to be able to select them. Just like selecting keys on the Track Bar, you select keys by clicking them. Selected keys turn white. To select multiple keys, hold down the Ctrl key while clicking several keys, or drag an outline over several keys to select them. Click away from the keys to deselect all the selected keys.

With a key or multiple keys selected, you can lock the selection with the Lock Selection button. The space-bar is the keyboard shortcut for this button. With the selection locked, you cannot select any new keys.

Tip

If you want to access a specific parameter in the Track View, you can right-click the parameter and select the Show in Track View command from the pop-up menu, and the Track View loads with the parameter visible. ∎

Using soft selection

The Keys menu also includes a Use Soft Select option. This feature is similar to the soft selection found in the Modify panel when working on a subobject, except that it works with keys causing adjacent keys to move along with the selected keys, but not as much. The Keys ⇨ Soft Select Settings menu command opens a simple toolbar where you can enable soft selection and set the Range and Falloff values.

When enabled, all keys within a specified range are also selected and moved to a lesser degree than the selected key. When enabled, the function curve is displayed with a gradient for the Curve Editor layout and as a gradient across the key markers in the Dope Sheet layout. This shows the range and falloff for the curve.

The Keys ➪ Soft Select Settings menu opens a hidden toolbar that lets you enable and disable the soft selection feature with a single button labeled Soft. The Range value sets how many frames the soft selection covers. This toolbar may be docked to the edge of the window.

Adding and deleting keys

You can add a key by clicking the Insert Keys button (or pressing the A key) and clicking the location where the new key should appear. Each new key is set with the interpolated value between the existing keys. This can be done whether the Auto Key button at the bottom of the Max interface is on or off.

To delete keys, select the keys and press the Delete key on the keyboard. If a key is deleted, the function curve changes to account for the missing key.

Moving, sliding, and scaling keys

The Move Keys button (keyboard shortcut M) lets you select and move a key to a new location. You can clone keys by pressing and holding the Shift key while moving a key. Using the flyout buttons, you can select to restrict the movement horizontally or vertically. You also can move the selected key to the cursor's location (the current frame) with the Keys ➪ Align to Cursor menu command.

The Slide Keys button in the Dope Sheet lets you select a key and move all adjacent keys in unison to the left or right. If the selected key is moved to the right, all keys from that key to the end of the animation slide to the right. If the key is moved to the left, then all keys to the beginning of the animation slide to the left.

The Scale Keys button, also in the Dope Sheet, lets you move a group of keys closer together or farther apart. The scale center is the current frame. You can use the Shift key to clone keys while dragging.

If the Dope Sheet's Snap Frames button (keyboard shortcut S) is enabled, the selected key snaps to the nearest key as it is moved. This makes aligning keys to the same frame easy.

Using the Region tool

Within the Curve Editor, the Region tool is used to move, slide, and scale a set of selected keys. To use this tool, simply drag in the Key pane over the keys you want to select. A box is displayed around all the selected keys with handles at each edge, as shown in Figure 37.6. The selected keys can be moved to a different location by clicking within the region and dragging to a new location. You can drag the selected keys up or down to change their values or left and right to change their frame.

New Feature

The Region tool is new to 3ds Max 2012. ■

FIGURE 37.6

The Region tool places handles around each side of the selected keys for sliding and scaling keys.

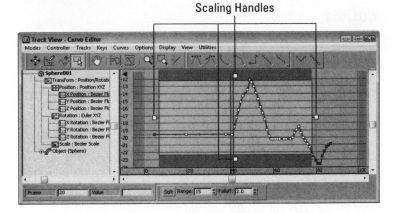

Dragging on either of the side handles scales the range of the selected keys, and dragging on the top or bottom handles scales their values. The side of the selected handle is the side of the region that moves during a scale operation, but if you press and hold the Shift key, the region is scaled equally from both sides. If you scale the region over any non-selected keys, those non-selected keys are simply deleted. The Region tool remains active until another tool, such as the Move tool is selected. If you click and drag outside of the selected region, a new region is selected.

Editing keys

To edit the key parameters for any controller, right-click the key in the Curve Editor or click the Properties button in the Dope Sheet; this opens the Key Info dialog box for most controllers. You also can access this dialog box by right-clicking a track and selecting Properties from the pop-up menu. These commands also can be used when multiple keys on the same or on different tracks are selected.

Using the Randomize Keys utility

The Randomize Keys utility lets you generate random time or key positions with an offset value. To access this utility, select the track of keys that you want to randomize and choose Utilities ⇨ Track View Utilities to open the Track View Utilities dialog box. From this dialog box, select Randomize Keys from the list of utilities and click OK; the Randomize Keys utility dialog box opens, as shown in Figure 37.7.

FIGURE 37.7

Use the Randomize Keys utility to create random key positions and values.

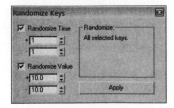

In this dialog box, you can specify positive and negative shift values for both Time and Value. Click the Apply button to apply the randomization process.

Using the Euler Filter utility

Euler rotations are easy to understand and use. They provide rotations about each of the three axes or can be thought of as yaw, pitch, and roll, but they have an inherit flaw—they are susceptible to Gimbal flipping and Gimbal lock. Gimbal flipping can occur when the rotation is directed straight up or straight down. This causes the object to instantly flip 180 degrees to continue its rotation. Gimbal lock can occur when two Euler rotation angles are aligned, causing the object to lose a degree of freedom.

To counter these problems, Max has the ability to use Quaternions instead of Euler angles. Quaternions are vector-based instead of angle-based, so they aren't susceptible to the Gimbal flipping and lock problems, but many animators find Quaternions difficult to understand and use, so they stick to Euler rotations and are watchful for potential problems.

The Track View has a utility that can help if you're dealing with Euler rotations. The Euler Filter utility analyzes the current frame range and corrects any Gimbal flipping that it detects. Selecting this utility from the Track View Utilities dialog box opens a simple dialog box where you can set the range to analyze. You also have an option to Insert Keys if Needed.

Displaying keyable icons

If you're not careful, you could animate a track that you didn't mean to (especially with the Auto Key mode enabled). By marking a track as non-keyable or keyable, you can control which tracks can be animated. To do this, choose the Display ➪ Keyable Icons menu. This places a small red key icon to the left of each track that can be animated. You can then click the icon to change it to a non-keyable track. Figure 37.8 shows the Curve Editor with this feature enabled.

FIGURE 37.8

The Keyable Icons feature displays an icon next to all tracks that can be keyed.

Keyable track

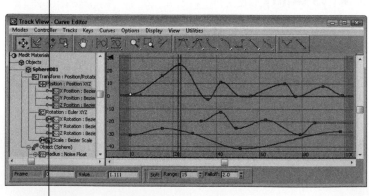

Non-keyable track

Editing Time

In some cases, directly working with keys isn't what you want to do. For example, if you need to change the animation length from six seconds to five seconds, you want to work in the Dope Sheet's Edit Ranges mode. To switch to this mode, click the Edit Ranges button on the Key Tangents toolbar. In this mode, the key ranges are displayed as black lines with square markers on either end, as shown in Figure 37.9.

Click the Edit Ranges button to display the key ranges in the Key pane.

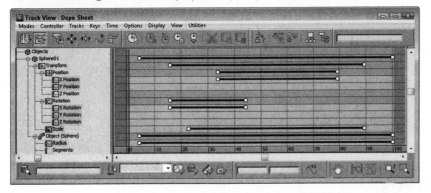

Selecting time and the Select Keys by Time utility

Before you can scale, cut, copy, or paste time, you need to select a track and then select a time block. To select a section of time, click the Select Time button and drag the mouse over the time block.

The Select Keys by Time utility lets you select all the keys within a given time block by entering the frame or time values. To use this utility, click the Track View Utilities button or select the Utilities ⇨ Track View Utilities menu command to open the Track View Utilities dialog box, and choose the Select Keys by Time utility from the list. Then in the Select Keys by Time dialog box, enter the Start and End values to complete the selection.

Deleting, cutting, copying, and pasting time

After you select a block of time, you can delete it by clicking the Delete Time button. Another way to delete a block of time is to use the Cut Time button, which removes the selected time block but places a copy of it on the clipboard for pasting. The Copy Time button also adds the time block to the clipboard for pasting, but it leaves the selected time in the track.

After you copy a time block to the clipboard, you can paste it to a different location within the Track View. The track where you paste it must be of the same type as the one from which you copied it.

All keys within the time block are also pasted, and you can select whether they are pasted relatively or absolutely. *Absolute* pasting adds keys with the exact values as the ones on the clipboard. *Relative* pasting adds the key value to the current initial value at the place where the key is pasted.

You can enable the Exclude Left End Point and Exclude Right End Point buttons on the Extras toolbar when pasting multiple sections next to each other. By excluding either end point, the time block loops seamlessly.

Reversing, inserting, and scaling time

The Reverse Time button flips the keys within the selected time block.

The Insert Time button lets you insert a section of time anywhere within the current track. To insert time, click and drag to specify the amount of time to insert; all keys beyond the current insertion point slide to accommodate the inserted time.

The Scale Time button scales the selected time block. This feature causes all keys to be pushed closer together or farther apart. The scaling takes place around the current frame.

Setting ranges

The Position Ranges button on the Ranges toolbar enables you to move ranges without moving keys. In this mode, you can move and scale a range bar independently of its keys, ignoring any keys that are out of range. For example, this button, when enabled, lets you remove the first several frames of an animation without moving the keys. The Recouple Ranges button can be used to line up the keys with the range again. The left end of the range aligns with the first key, and the right end aligns with the last key.

Editing Curves

When an object is moving through the scene, estimating the exact point where its position changes direction can sometimes be difficult. Function curves provide this information by presenting a controller's value as a function of time. The slope of the function curve shows the value's rate of change. Steep curves show quick movements. Shallow lines are slow-moving values. Each key is a vertex in the curve. Function curves are visible only in the Curve Editor and the Track Bar layout.

Function curves mode lets you edit and work with these curves for complete control over the animation parameters. Figure 37.10 shows the Position curves for a sphere that moves about the scene.

FIGURE 37.10

Function curves display keys as square markers along the curve.

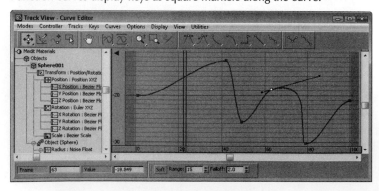

Inserting new keys and moving keys

Function curves with only two keys have slow in and out tangents, making the animation start slow, speed up, and then slow down. You can add more curvature to the line with the addition of another key. To add another key, click the Insert Keys button, and then click the curve where you want to place the key.

Tip

Keep the total number of keys to a minimum. More keys make editing more difficult. ■

If the curve contains multiple curves, such as a curve for the Position or RGB color values, then a point is added to each curve. The Move Keys button enables you to move individual keys by dragging them. It also includes flyouts for constraining the key movement to a horizontal or vertical direction.

To scale keys, use the Region tool; you also could use the Keys ⇨ Scale Keys–Time command to move the selected keys toward or away from the current time. The keys move only horizontally. The Keys ⇨ Scale Values command is used to move the selected keys toward or away from the zero value. The keys move only vertically.

Tutorial: Animating a monorail

As an example of working with function curves, you'll animate a monorail that moves around its track, changing speeds, and stopping for passengers.

To animate the monorail using function curves, follow these steps:

1. Open the Monorail.max file from the Chap 37 directory on the CD.

   This file contains a simple monorail setup made from primitives.

2. Click the Play button, and watch the train move around the track.

   As a default, the Path Constraint's Percent track has a Linear controller that causes the train to move at a constant speed. To refine the animation, you need to change it.

3. Open the Track View–Curve Editor by first selecting the train object in the scene and then right-clicking and choosing Curve Edit from the pop-up quadmenu. The Track View-Curve Editor window opens and shows the controls related to the object in the scene you have selected. Click the Assign Controller button or right-click and select Assign Controller from the pop-up menu to open the Assign Float Controller dialog box. Select the Bézier Float controller, and click OK.

Note

If the Objects track isn't visible, open the Filter Tracks dialog box and make sure the Objects option is enabled. ■

4. Click the Play button. The train starts slowly (represented by the flattish part of the curve), accelerates (the steeper part of the curve), and slows down again (another flattish part).

Tip

When "reading" function curves, remember that a steep curve produces fast animation, a shallow curve produces slow animation, a horizontal curve produces no movement or value change, and a straight curve produces a constant animation. ■

5. You need the train to stop for passengers at the station, so click the Insert Keys button (or right-click and choose Insert Keys) and add a key somewhere around frame 115 when the train is near the dock.

6. Select the newly created key, and choose the Move Keys Horizontal button from the Move Keys flyout. Hold down the Shift key, and drag right to copy the key to frame 135.

   The curve is flat, so the train stops at the station.

7. To adjust the actual position where the train stops, choose the Move Keys Vertical button from the Move Keys flyout, select both keys, and move them up or down until the train's position at the station is correct.

   Because the default in and out tangent types cause the curve to flatten out at the keys, the train slows as it reaches the station and then starts out slow and picks up speed as it leaves the station. Anyone who has ever ridden on a train knows that stopping and starting are not always smooth operations. Next, you add a few more keys to make the train shudder to a stop and lurch as it starts out again.

8. Click the Insert Keys button (or right-click and choose Insert Keys), and insert keys somewhere around frames 105, 109, 113, 142, and 150. Use Zoom Region to zoom in on the keys where the train pulls into the station to stop.

9. Change the Move Keys Vertical button back to Move Keys by selecting it from the flyout, and move the keys slightly up or down to send the train backward and forward along the path.

10. As you can see, a little movement goes a long way, so the keys need only to be offset a very small amount. Use the Zoom Values button from the Zoom flyout and the Pan button to help in making the small changes to the animation.

11. Repeat for the keys where the train leaves the station.

    The train also needs to slow down to look at one of the famous buildings in "Primitive Town," the Tubular "building" on the far side of the track.

12. Add a couple more keys somewhere around frames 18 and 50. Lower the second of the new keys until the curve is shallower but not horizontal. Again, adjust the train's position on the track (Percent along the path) by raising or lowering the two new keys.

13. Adjust the Out tangent handle of the very first key and the In tangent handle of the very last key to produce a smooth looping animation.

Figure 37.11 shows the final curve after you've completed the editing, and Figure 37.12 shows the monorail along its path.

FIGURE 37.11

The finished Percent curve for the train's position along the path

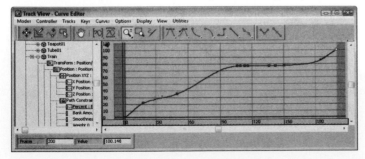

Drawing curves

If you know what the curve you want is supposed to look like, you can actually draw it in the Key pane with the Draw Curves button enabled. This mode adds a key for every change in the curve. You may want to use the Reduce Keys optimization after drawing a curve.

Tip

If you make a mistake, you can just draw over the top of the existing curve to make corrections. ∎

Figure 37.13 shows a curve that was created with the Draw Curves feature.

FIGURE 37.12

The monorail and "Primitive Town"

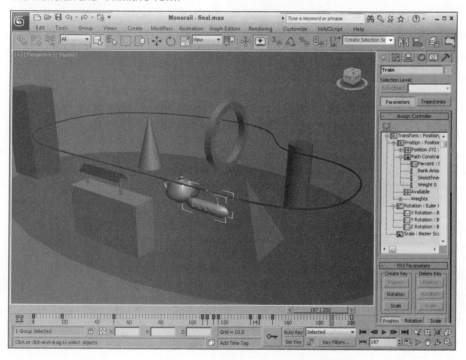

FIGURE 37.13

Drawing curves results in numerous keys.

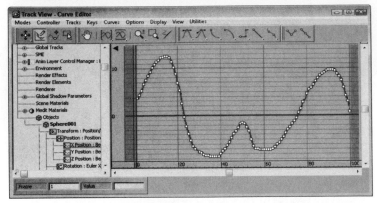

Reducing keys

The Keys ➪ Reduce Keys menu command enables you to optimize the number of keys used in an animation. Certain IK (inverse kinematics) methods and the Dynamics utility calculate keys for every frame in the scene, which can increase your file size greatly. By optimizing with the Reduce Keys command, you can reduce the file size and complexity of your animations.

Using the Reduce Keys command opens the Reduce Keys dialog box. The threshold value determines how close to the actual position the solution must be to eliminate the key. Figure 37.14 shows the same curve created with the Draw Curves feature after it has been optimized with a Threshold value of 0.5 using the Reduce Keys feature.

FIGURE 37.14

The Reduce Keys feature optimizes the curve by reducing keys.

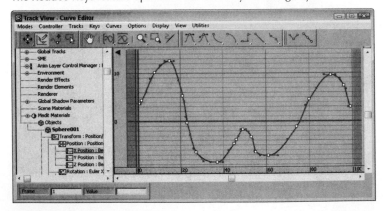

Working with tangents

Function curves for the Bézier controller have tangents associated with every key. To view and edit these tangents, select the Display ⇨ All Tangents menu command. These tangents are lines that extend from the key point with a handle on each end. By moving these handles, you can alter the curvature of the curve around the key.

You can select the type of tangent from the Key Tangents toolbar. These can be different for the In and Out portion of the curve. You can also select them using the Key dialog box. The default tangent type for all new keys is set using the button to the left of the Key Filters button at the bottom of the Max interface. Using this button, you can quickly select from any of the available tangent types.

You open the Key dialog box, shown in Figure 37.15, by selecting a key and right-clicking the key. It lets you specify two different types of tangent points: Continuous and Discontinuous. *Continuous* tangents are points with two handles on the same line. The curvature for continuous tangents is always smooth. *Discontinuous* tangents have any angle between the two handle lines. These tangents form a sharp point.

By default, all tangents are continuous and move together, but you can break them apart to be discontinuous by clicking the Break Tangents button in the Tangent Actions toolbar. This lets each handle be moved independently. Broken tangents can be locked together again with the Unify Tangents button, so they move together. This unifies the tangent handles even if they don't form a straight line.

New Feature

The Break and Unify Tangents buttons are new to 3ds Max 2012. ∎

Tip

Holding down the Shift key while dragging a handle lets you drag the handle independently of the other handle. ∎

FIGURE 37.15

The Key dialog box lets you change the key's Time, Value, or In and Out tangent curves.

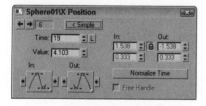

The Lock Tangents button in the Key Info dialog box lets you change the handles of several keys at the same time. If this button is disabled, adjusting a tangent handle affects only the key of that handle.

Tutorial: Animating a flowing river

The default auto-tangent types create a function curve that has ease-in and ease-out built into the curve. This causes the animation to start slowly, speed up, and then slow to a stop. While this may be a good starting point for many animations, it won't work for those that should have a constant speed. This example shows how to create a river with a material animated to a constant speed.

To create a flowing river, follow these steps:

1. Open the River.max file from the Chap 37 directory on the CD.

   This file contains a river surface made from a loft. The V Offset for the River Water material's diffuse channel has been animated to simulate flowing water (yes, this river has a checkered past . . .).

2. Click the Play button.

   The river flow starts out slow, speeds up, and then slows to a stop.

Note
The river flows using a checker texture map. Make sure to select a viewport with textures enabled to see the flowing effect. ∎

3. Open the Track View–Curve Editor, and locate and select the V Offset track for the river's material. (You can find this track under the Scene Materials ⇨ River Water ⇨ Maps ⇨ Diffuse Color: Map #2 (Checker) ⇨ Coordinates ⇨ V Offset menu command.)

4. You have two easy options for creating an animation with a constant speed. The first changes the entire controller type; the second changes the individual key's tangent types.

   Option 1: Right-click over the V Offset track and choose Assign Controller or choose Assign from Controller on the menu bar to open the Assign Float Controller dialog box. Select Linear Float, and click OK.

   or

   Option 2: Select both keys by clicking one key, holding down the Ctrl button, and clicking the other, or by dragging an outline around both keys. Click the Set Tangents to Linear button.

   Whichever method you use, the line between the two keys is now straight.

5. Click the Play button.

   The river now flows at a constant speed.

6. To increase the speed of the flow, select Move Keys Vertical from the Move Keys button flyout, and select and move the end key higher in the graph.

   The river flows faster.

Figure 37.16 shows the river as it flows along.

Applying out-of-range, ease, and multiplier curves

Out-of-range curves define what the curve should do when it is beyond the range of specified keys. For example, you could tell the curve to loop or repeat its previous range of keys. To apply these curves, select a track and select the Out-of-Range menu command from the Controller menu. This opens a dialog box, shown in Figure 37.17, where you can select from the available curve types.

FIGURE 37.16

The Checkered River flows evenly.

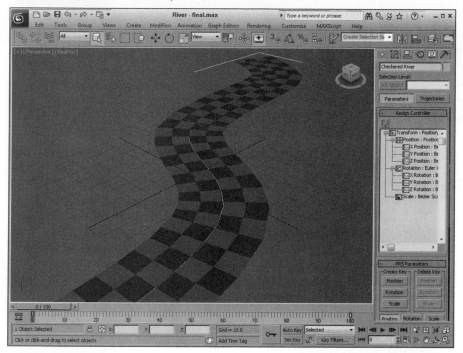

FIGURE 37.17

The Param Curve Out-of-Range Types dialog box lets you select the type of out-of-range curve to use.

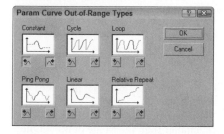

Note

You can also apply an out-of-range curve to a select range of frames using the **Create Out-of-Range Keys** utility. This utility is available via the Track View Utilities menu. ■

By clicking the buttons below the types, you can specify a curve for the beginning and end. This Out-of-Range dialog box includes six options:

- **Constant:** Holds the value constant for all out-of-range frames
- **Cycle:** Repeats the track values as soon as the range ends
- **Loop:** Repeats the range values, like the Cycle option, except that the beginning and end points are interpolated to provide a smooth transition
- **Ping Pong:** Repeats the range values in reverse order after the range end is reached
- **Linear:** Projects the range values in a linear manner when out of range
- **Relative Repeat:** Repeats the range values offset by the distance between the start and end values

You can apply ease curves (choose Curves ⇨ Apply Ease Curve, or press Ctrl+E) to smooth the timing of a function curve. You can apply multiplier curves (Curves ⇨ Apply Multiplier Curve, Ctrl+M) to alter the scaling of a function curve. You can use ease and multiplier curves to automatically smooth or scale an animation's motion. Each of these buttons adds a new track and function curve to the selected controller track.

Ease and Multiplier curves add another layer of control on top of the existing animation and allow you to edit the existing animation curves without changing the original animation keys. For example, if you have a standard walk cycle, you can use an ease curve to add a limp to the walk cycle or you can reuse the walk cycle for a taller character by adding a multiplier curve.

Note

Not all controllers can have an ease or multiplier curve applied. ■

You can delete these tracks and curves using the Curves ⇨ Remove menu command. You also can enable or disable these curves with the Curves ⇨ Enable Ease/Multiplier Curve Toggle menu command.

After you apply an ease or multiplier curve, you can assign the type of curve to use with the Ease Curve Out-of-Range Types button. This button opens the Ease Curve Out-of-Range Types dialog box, which includes the same curve types as the Out-of-Range curves, except for the addition of an Identity curve type.

Note

In the Ease Curve Out-of-Range Types dialog box is an Identity option that isn't present in the Parameter Curve Out-of-Range Types dialog box. The Identity option begins or ends the curve with a linear slope that produces a gradual, constant rate increase. ■

When editing ranges, you can make the range of a selected track smaller than the range of the whole animation. These tracks then go out of range at some point during the animation. The Ease/Multiplier Curve Out-of-Range Types buttons are used to tell the track how to handle its out-of-range time.

Tutorial: Animating a wind-up teapot

As an example of working with multiplier curves, you'll create a wind-up teapot that vibrates its way across a surface.

To animate the vibrations in the Track View, follow these steps:

1. Open the Wind-up teapot.max file from the Chap 37 directory on the CD.

   This file contains a teapot with legs.

2. Click the Play button.

   The teapot's key winds up to about frame 40 and then runs down again as the teapot moves around a bit. To add the random movement and rotation to make the vibrations, you use Noise controllers and Multiplier curves to limit the noise.

3. Open the Track View–Curve Editor, and navigate down to the Wind-up Key's X Rotation track, located at Objects, Teapot Group, Key, Rotation: Euler XYZ, X Rotation. Take a moment to observe the shape of the curve, shown in Figure 37.18.

   The key is "wound up" in short spurts and then runs down, slowing until it stops. The vibration, then, should start midway and then taper off as the key runs down.

FIGURE 37.18

The rotation of the Wind-up Key object

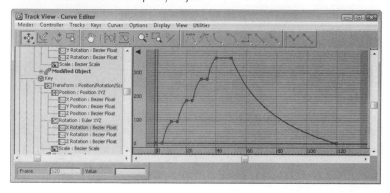

4. Click the teapot in the viewport to have the curves for its transforms selected and centered in the Track View.

   When adding the Noise controller, you should assign a List controller first to retain the ability to transform the object independently of the Noise.

Note

Assigning controllers through the Animation menu automatically creates a List controller first. ■

5. Select the teapot's Position track, and click the C key to access the Assign Controller dialog box. Choose Position List. Under the Position track are now the X, Y, and Z Position tracks and an Available track. Select the Available track, access the Assign Controller dialog box again, and choose Noise Position. The default controller should remain the Position XYZ controller, so close the List Controller dialog box. Click Play.

Note

Remember that the C keyboard shortcut works only if the Keyboard Shortcut Override Toggle button on the main toolbar is enabled. ∎

The teapot vibrates the entire animation. You add a multiplier curve to correct the situation.

6. Select the Noise Position track, and choose Curves ⇨ Apply-Multiplier Curve. Select the Multiplier curve track. Assign the first key a value of **0**. Change its Out tangent to Stepped so it holds its value until the next key. Click the Insert Keys button, and add a key at frame 50 with a value of **1**. Move the last key to frame 120, and set a value of **0**. The Multiplier curve should now look like the curve in Figure 37.19. Select the Noise Position track.

The noise curve now conforms to the multiplier track.

FIGURE 37.19

The Multiplier curve keeps the Noise track in check.

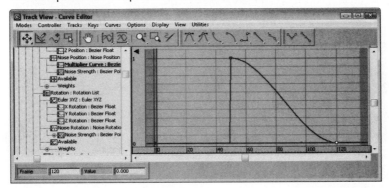

---

7. With the Noise Position track still selected, right-click and choose Properties. In the Noise Position dialog box, set the X and Y Strength to **30**, set the Z strength to **20**, and check the >0 check box to keep the teapot from going through the floor. Close the dialog box, and click Play.

The animation is much better. Next, you add some noise to the Rotation track.

8. Select the Rotation track, right-click, and choose Assign controller or click the C key to bring up the Assign Controller dialog box. Select Rotation List, and click OK. Select the Available track, access the Assign Controller dialog box again, and choose Noise Rotation.

Click Play. Again, the noise is out of control.

9. This time, select the Noise Strength track and add a multiplier curve.

You already have a perfectly good multiplier curve, so you can instance it into the new track.

10. Select the position multiplier track, right-click, and choose Copy. Now select the rotation Noise Strength multiplier track, right-click, and choose Paste. Choose Instance, and close the dialog box.

11. Click the Play button, and watch the Teapot wind up and then vibrate itself along until it winds down.

Figure 37.20 shows the teapot as it dances about, compliments of a controlled noise controller.

FIGURE 37.20

FIGURE 37.20

The wind-up teapot moves about the scene.

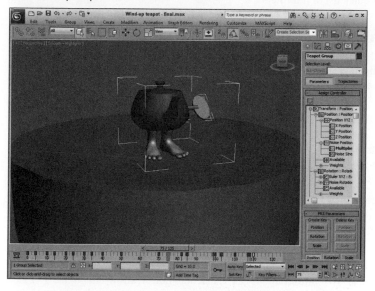

Filtering Tracks and Creating Track Sets

With all the information included in the Track View, finding the exact tracks you need can be difficult. The Filters button on the Key Tangents toolbar (or in the Display menu) can help. Clicking this button (or pressing the Q keyboard shortcut) opens the Filters dialog box, shown in Figure 37.21.

FIGURE 37.21

The Filters dialog box lets you focus on the specific tracks.

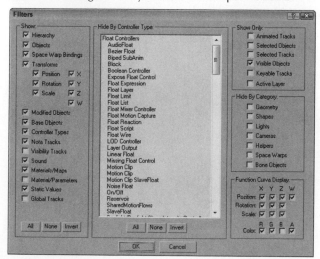

Tip
Right-clicking the Filters button reveals a quick list of filter items. ■

Using the Filters dialog box

Using this dialog box, you can limit the number of tracks that are displayed in the Track View. The Show section contains many display options. The Hide by Controller Type pane lists all the available controllers. Any controller types selected from this list do not show up in the Track View. You can also elect to not display objects by making selections from the check boxes in the Hide By Category section.

The Show Only group includes options for displaying only the Animated Tracks, Selected Objects, Selected Tracks, Visible Objects, Keyable Tracks, Active Layer, or any combination of these. For example, if you wanted to see the animation track for a selected object, select the Animated Tracks option and click OK; then open the Filters dialog box again, choose Selected Objects, and click OK.

You can also specify whether the function curve display includes the Position, Rotation, and Scale components for each axis or the RGB color components.

Creating a track set

A selection of tracks can be saved into a track set by clicking the Edit Track Set button located at the bottom of the Track View interface. This button opens the Track Sets Editor, shown in Figure 37.22. Clicking the Create a New Track Set button in the Track Sets Editor creates a new track set containing all the currently selected tracks and lists it in the editor window. Selected tracks can be added, removed, and selected using the other editor buttons.

FIGURE 37.22

The Track Sets Editor dialog box lets you name track selections for easy recall.

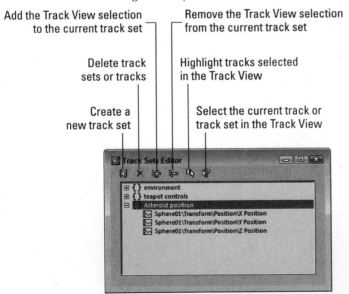

Add the Track View selection to the current track set

Remove the Track View selection from the current track set

Delete track sets or tracks

Highlight tracks selected in the Track View

Create a new track set

Select the current track or track set in the Track View

After a track set is created, its tracks can be instantly selected by choosing the track set's name from the drop-down list located next to the Edit Track Set button at the bottom of the Track View window.

Working with Controllers

Controllers offer an alternative to positioning keys manually. Each controller can automatically control a key's position or a parameter's value. The Controller menu includes several commands for working with controllers. The Copy Controller and Paste Controller commands let you move existing controllers between different tracks, and the Assign Controller command lets you add a new controller to a track.

Cross-Reference
Chapter 22, "Animating with Constraints and Simple Controllers," covers all the various controllers used to auto- mate animated sequences. ■

Although the commands are named Copy Controller and Paste Controller, they can be used to copy different tracks. Tracks can be copied and pasted only if they are of the same type. You can copy only one track at a time, but that single controller can be pasted to multiple tracks. A pasted track can be a copy or an instance, and you have the option to replace all instances. For example, if you have several objects that move together, using the Replace All Instances option when modifying the track for one object modifies the tracks for all objects that share the same motion.

All instanced copies of a track change when any instance of that track is modified. To break the link- ing between instances, you can use the Controller⇨Make Unique menu command.

Selecting the Controller⇨Assign Controller menu command opens the Assign Controller dialog box, where you can select the controller to apply. If the controller types are similar, the keys are main- tained, but a completely different controller replaces any existing keys in the track.

Using visibility tracks

When an object track is selected, you can add a visibility track using the Tracks⇨Visibility Track⇨ Add menu command or the Object Properties dialog box. This track enables you to make the object visible or invisible. The selected track is automatically assigned the Bézier controller, but you can change it to an On/Off controller if you want that type of control. You can use function curves mode to edit the visibility track.

Adding note tracks

You can add note tracks to any track and use them to attach information about the track. The Tracks⇨Note Track⇨Add menu command is used to add a note track, which is marked with a yel- low triangle and cannot be animated.

After you've added a note track in the Controller pane, use the Insert Keys button to position a note key in the Key pane by clicking in the note track. This adds a small note icon. Right-clicking the note icon opens the Notes dialog box, where you can enter the notes, as shown in Figure 37.23. Each note track can include several note keys.

The Notes dialog box includes arrow controls that you can use to move between the various notes. The field to the right of the arrows displays the current note key number. The Time value displays the frame where a selected note is located, and the Lock Key option locks the note to the frame so it can't be moved or scaled.

You can use the Tracks ⇨ Note Track ⇨ Remove menu command to delete a selected note track.

FIGURE 37.23

The Notes dialog box lets you enter notes and position them next to keys.

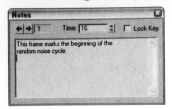

Tutorial: Animating a hazard light

As an example of working with the Track View, you'll animate a flashing hazard light in this tutorial.

To animate a flashing hazard light using function curves, follow these steps:

1. Open the Hazard.max file from the Chap 37 directory on the CD.

   This file contains a hazard barrier with a light.

2. Select Omni01, open the Track View–Curve Editor, and locate the Omni light's Multiplier track. (You can find this track under the Objects ⇨ Omni01 ⇨ Object(Omni Light) ⇨ Multiplier menu command.) Click the Insert Keys button (or press the A key), and create a key on the dotted line (its current multiplier value) at frame 0 and at frame 15. Set the end key to a value of **1.2**.

3. Select the first key and set its position to 0 by moving the key down or by typing **0** in the value display field. Click the Zoom Value Extends button to better see the shape of the curve. Click the Play button.

   The light comes on slowly. It should be either on or off, so you need to change the tangent types to Stepped.

4. Select both keys, and click the Set Tangents to Stepped button. Click the Play button.

   The light turns on at frame 15.

5. Select the first key, and choose the Move Keys Horizontal button from the Move Keys flyout. Hold down the Shift key and drag right to copy the key at frame 30.

   The light now turns off at frame 30. You can continue to make the rest of the keys in that fashion, but using the Parameter Out of Range feature to complete the animation is easier.

6. With the Multiplier curve selected, click the Parameter Curves Out-of-Range Types button or Choose Out-of-Range Types from the Controller menu item. The Out-of-Range Types dialog box appears. Choose Cycle, and click OK.

   Figure 37.24 shows the Stepped tangents.

7. Click Play.

   The light flashes off and on. The animation would be more convincing if the light lens object appeared to turn off and on as well. Next, you animate the self-illumination of the lens material.

FIGURE 37.24

The curve with Stepped in and out tangents and a Cycle Parameter Out-of-Range type

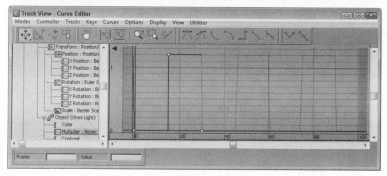

8. With the Omni light's multiplier track still selected, right-click over the track in the controller pane and choose Copy. Locate and select the Light Lens material's Self-Illumination track. (You can find this track under the Scene Materials ⇨ Lens (Standard) ⇨ Shader Basic Parameters ⇨ Self-Illumination menu command.) Right-click, choose Paste, and paste as Copy.

9. Because the Self-Illumination should top out at 100 percent, not 120 percent, select the second key and change its value to **100**. Click the Play button.

    The Omni light and lens flash off and on together.

    Figure 37.25 shows the hazard light as it repeatedly blinks on and off.

FIGURE 37.25

The hazard light flashing on

Tutorial: Animating a checkers move

As an example of working with function curves, you'll animate a checkers move in this tutorial. It is often easiest to block in the animation using keyframing and then to refine the animation in the Track View.

To animate a white checker making its moves, follow these steps:

1. Open the Checkers.max file from the Chap 37 directory on the CD.

   This file contains a simple checkerboard with one white piece and three red pieces.

   The white checker is on the wrong-colored square to start, so first you move it into place and then to each successive position.

2. Turn on Auto Key. Move the time slider to frame 25, and move the white checker to the square with the "1" text object (visible in the Top viewport). Move the time slider to 50, and move the white piece to the "2" position. At frame 75, move it to the "3" position, and at 100, move it to the "4" position. Turn off Auto Key.

3. Right-click over the white piece, and choose Curve Editor to open the Track View–Curve Editor. The white piece's X, Y, and Z Position tracks should be highlighted, and you should be able to see the function curves in the graph editor. If not, find them by choosing Objects ⇨ White Piece ⇨ Transform ⇨ Position ⇨ X, Y and Z Position.

   Keeping in mind that RGB (red, green, blue) = XYZ, you can see the white checker's movement across the board. From 0 to 25, it moves only in the X direction. From 25 to 100, it moves diagonally across the board as indicated by the slope of both the X and Y curves. Note that when the object goes back the other way in the X direction at frame 75, the curve goes in the opposite direction, as shown in Figure 37.26.

FIGURE 37.26

The blocked-in animation curves for the white piece

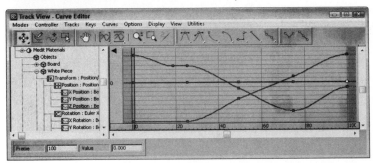

4. Click the Play button.

   The white piece slides sloppily around the board. Next, you create keys to make it hop over the red pieces.

5. Click the Insert Keys button, or select Insert Keys from the right-click menu. Click to insert keys on the Z-position track between the second, third, fourth, and fifth keys.

6. Select Move Keys Vertical from the Move Keys flyout, and select the three new keys. Move them up about 50 units, as shown in Figure 37.27.

FIGURE 37.27

The new keys are moved up.

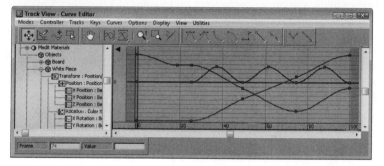

The white piece hops over the red pieces, but the motion is not correct. The In and Out tangents should be fast so the piece does not spend much time on the board.

7. With the new keys still selected, hold the Shift key down, and move the handles on the keys to make them discontinuous tangent types, as shown in Figure 37.28.

FIGURE 37.28

The In and Out tangents corrected for the new keys

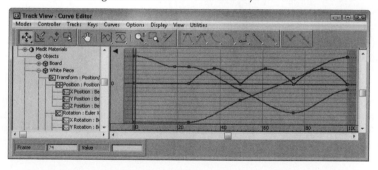

The hopping looks better, but the sliding motion would look better with a slight pause before hopping over the first red piece.

8. Select Move Keys Horizontal from the Move Keys flyout, and choose the second X-position track key. Hold down the Shift key, and move the key a few frames to the left to make a copy of the original key. Click the play button.

   The red pieces should disappear as the white piece hops over them.

9. Scroll down the Controller pane on the left, and select the three red pieces. Under Tracks on the menu bar, choose Visibility ⇨ Add.

   A visibility track has been added to each of the red pieces, directly below the root name.

   With visibility, a value of 0 is invisible, and a value of 1 is visible. You could change the tangent types to Stepped to turn the red pieces invisible from one frame to the next, but changing the entire track to an On/Off controller helps to visualize what is happening.

10. Select the visibility track for Red Piece 01. Right-click, and choose Assign Controller. Choose On/Off.

    Nothing seems to have happened. The Off/On controller is best used in Dope Sheet mode.

11. Choose Dope Sheet from the Modes menu. The On/Off controller track is represented with a blue bar. Blue indicates "on" or visible. Click the Insert Keys button, and click to add a key at frame 50. The blue bar stops at the key at frame 50. Click Play.

    The first red piece disappears at frame 50. You can copy and paste tracks to save yourself a bit of work.

12. Select Red Piece 01's visibility track in the Controller pane. Right-click, and choose Copy. Select the visibility tracks for Red Piece 02 and Red Piece 03 (hold down the Ctrl key to add to the selection). Right-click, and choose Paste.

    Paste as a Copy because the other pieces should disappear at different times.

13. Move Red Piece 02's key to 75 and Red Piece 03's key to 100. Click Play.

    Things are looking pretty good, but the animation would look better if the whole thing were faster.

14. Click the Edit Ranges button and the Modify Subtree button. A World track bar appears at the top of the Key Pane. Click and drag the rightmost end of the range bar to frame 75 to scale all the tracks at one time. Click Play.

    The animation is quite respectable as the white piece slides into the correct square and then hops over and captures the three red pieces.

Figure 37.29 shows the checkerboard.

Using the ProSound dialog box, you can load and arrange multiple sound files. ProSound supports loading in WAV and AVI sound files. For the selected sound file, you can view its Length, Format, and Statistics. You also can set the sound's Start and End frame. Multiple other options are available for controlling how the audio file plays and how it interacts with other sounds.

The ProSound dialog box also includes some Metronome settings for keeping a defined beat. For a metronome, you can specify the beats per minute and the beats per measure. The first option sets how often the beats occur, and the second option determines how often a different tone is played. This dialog box also contains an Active option for turning the metronome on and off.

FIGURE 37.29

The checker pieces on the checkerboard

Using the ProSound Plug-in

Max includes an audio plug-in called ProSound for adding multiple audio tracks to a scene. You need to initialize the plug-in before you start, using the Animation panel in the Preference Settings dialog box. You can access this dialog box with the Customize ➪ Preferences menu.

To select the ProSound plug-in, click the Assign button and select the ProSound option. Once enabled, you can access ProSound by right-clicking the Sound track in the Track View and choosing the Properties menu. This opens the ProSound dialog box, as shown in Figure 37.30.

The ProSound dialog box lets you configure sounds to play during the animation.

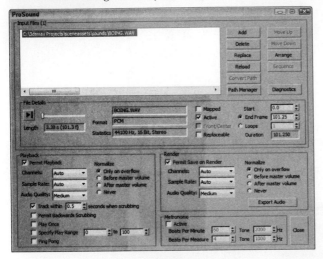

Tutorial: Adding sound to an animation

As an example of adding sound to an animation, you'll work with a hyper pogo stick and synchronize its animation to a sound clip.

To synchronize an animation to a sound clip, follow these steps:

1. Open the Hyper pogo stick with sound.max file from the Chap 37 directory on the CD.

2. In the Track View–Dope Sheet window, right-click the Sound track and select Properties from the pop-up menu to open the ProSound dialog box. In this dialog box, click the Add button. Then locate the boing.wav file from the Chap 37 directory on the CD, and click OK. Make sure the Permit Playback option is selected.

   The sound file appears as a waveform in the Track View, as shown in Figure 37.31.

FIGURE 37.31

Sounds loaded into the sound track appear as waveforms.

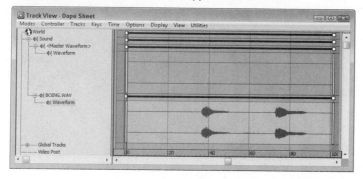

Note

The ProSound dialog box includes a play button that lets you play the sound before loading it. ∎

3. Enter a Start frame value of **2** for the audio file to align with the pogo stick's upward motion.
4. Click the Play Animation button, and the sound file plays with the animation.

Figure 37.32 shows the sound track under the Track Bar for this example.

FIGURE 37.32

To help synchronize sound, the audio track can be made visible under the Track Bar.

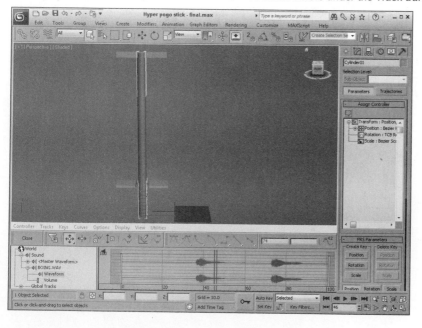

Summary

Using the Track View, you have access to all the keys, parameters, and objects in a scene in one convenient location. Different features are available in the different layouts. In this chapter, you accomplished the following:

- Learned the Track View interface elements
- Learned about the different Track View layouts, including the Curve Editor, Dope Sheet, and Track Bar
- Discovered how to work with keys, times, and ranges
- Controlled and adjusted function curves
- Selected specific tracks using the Filter dialog box
- Assigned controllers
- Explored the different out-of-range types
- Added notes to a track
- Added multi-track audio with ProSound

The next chapter dives into working with characters, rigging, and bones.

Part IX

Working with Characters

Understanding Rigging, Kinematics, and Working with Bones

W hat does a graveyard have in common with animated characters? The answer is bones. Bones are used as an underlying structure attached to a character that is to be animated. By using a bones structure, you can produce complex character motions by simply animating the bones and not having to move all the vertices associated with a high-resolution character.

Although Max includes a prebuilt skeleton with its Biped and CAT systems, at times you may want to build a custom bones system because not all characters stand on two feet. Have you ever seen a sci-fi movie in which the alien was less than humanlike? If your character can't be created by modifying a biped, then you need to use the traditional manual methods of rigging.

This chapter focuses on the process of manually rigging a character that, depending on the complexity of your character, could end up being even easier than working with bipeds. It also gives you a clear idea of concepts of rigging.

This chapter also presents the idea of kinematics. *Kinematics* is a branch of mechanics that deals with the motions of a system of objects, so *inverse kinematics* is its evil twin brother that deals with the non-motion of a system of objects, right? Well, not exactly.

In Max, a system of objects is a bunch of objects that are linked together. After a system is built and the parameters of the links are defined, the motions of all the pieces below the parent object can be determined as the parent moves, using kinematics formulas.

Inverse kinematics (IK) is similar, except that it determines all the motions of objects in a system when the last object in the hierarchy chain is moved. The position of the last object, such as a finger or a foot, is typically the one you're concerned with. With IK, you can use these solutions to animate the system of objects by moving the last object in the system.

IN THIS CHAPTER

Creating a rigging workflow

Understanding forward and inverse kinematics

Using interactive and applied IK methods

Setting thresholds in the Inverse Kinematics panel of the Preference Settings dialog box

Learning to work with the HI, HD, and IK Limb solvers

Building a bones system

Setting bone parameters and IK Solvers

Making linked objects into a bones system

Creating a Rigging Workflow

A rigged character starts with a linked hierarchy. A linked hierarchy attaches, or links, one object to another and makes it possible to transform the attached object by moving the one to which it is linked. The arm is a classic example of a linked hierarchy: When the shoulder rotates, so do the elbow, wrist, and fingers. Establishing linked hierarchies can make moving, positioning, and animating many objects easy.

A bones system is a unique case of a linked hierarchy that has a specific structure. You can create a structure of bones from an existing hierarchy, or you can create a bones system and attach objects to it. A key advantage of a bones system is that you can use IK (inverse kinematics) Solvers to manipulate and animate the structure. These IK Solvers enable the parents to rotate when the children are moved. In this way, the IK Solver maintains the chain integrity. Another advantage of a bones structure is that you can constrain the motion of bones so the motion is forced to be realistic, just like a real character.

After the bone structure is created, it needs to be edited to fit the skin mesh that it will control. You also need to define the limits of each bone and joint. This helps prevent the skeleton from moving in unrealistic ways. Applying IK systems is another way to control the motion of the bones and joints. This process of creating a skeleton structure and defining its limits is called *rigging*.

After you've edited a system of bones, you can cover the bones with objects that have the Skin modifier applied. This modifier lets the covering object move and bend with the bones structure underneath. The process of attaching a model to a bones system is called *skinning*.

Cross-Reference

The Skin modifier is covered, along with other aspects of skinning a character, in Chapter 40, "Skinning Characters." ∎

After a character is rigged and skinned, the character is ready to be animated.

Building a Bones System

In some instances, establishing a hierarchy of objects before linking objects is easier. By building the hierarchy first, you can be sure of the links between objects. One way to build this hierarchy is to use a *bones system*. A bones system consists of many bone objects that are linked together. These bone objects are normally not rendered, but you can set them to be renderable, like splines. You can also assign an IK Solver to the bones system for controlling their motion.

To create a bones system, select Create ⇨ Systems ⇨ Bones IK Chain, click in a viewport to create a root bone, click a short distance away to create another bone, and repeat this a few more times. Each subsequent click creates another bone linked to the previous one. When you're finished adding bones, right-click to exit bone creation mode. In this manner, you can create a long chain of bone objects all linked together.

These bones are actually linked joints. Moving one bone pulls its neighbors in the chain along with it. Bones can also be rotated, scaled, and stretched. Scaling a bones system affects the distance between the bones.

Caution

Bones should never be scaled without the XForm modifier applied, or all animation keys will behave erratically. ■

To branch the hierarchy of bones, simply click the bone where you want the branch to start while still in bone creation mode. A new branching bone is created automatically. Click the Bones button again to create a new bone. Then continue to click to add new bones to the branch.

Figure 38.1 shows the rollouts that are available for creating bones.

FIGURE 38.1

The Bone rollouts let you specify which bones get assigned an IK Controller.

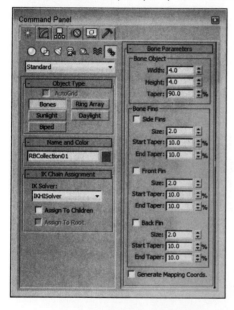

Assigning an IK Solver

When you first create a bone chain in the IK Chain Assignment rollout of the Create panel, you can select from four IK Solvers: History Dependent, IKHISolver, IKLimb, and SplineIK Solver. You can assign each of these solver types to children and to the root bone using the available options. You need to select both the Assign to Children and the Assign to Root options to assign the IK Controller to all bones in the system. If the Assign to Children option is deselected, then the Assign to Root option is disabled.

Note

Each of these IK Solvers is presented later in this chapter. ■

Setting bone parameters

The Bone Parameters rollout (also in the Modify panel) includes parameters for setting the size of each individual bone, including its Width and Height. You can also set the percentage of Taper applied to the bone.

Tip

Because bones are simple geometry objects, you can apply an Edit Poly modifier to it and edit the bone shape to be whatever you'd like. Custom bone geometry doesn't always work with the Bone Tools. ■

Fins can be displayed on the front, back, and/or sides of each bone. For each fin, you can specify its size and start and end taper values. Including fins on your bones makes correctly positioning and rotating the bone objects easier. Figure 38.2 shows a simple bones system containing two bones. The first bone has fins.

FIGURE 38.2

This bone includes fins that make understanding its orientation easier.

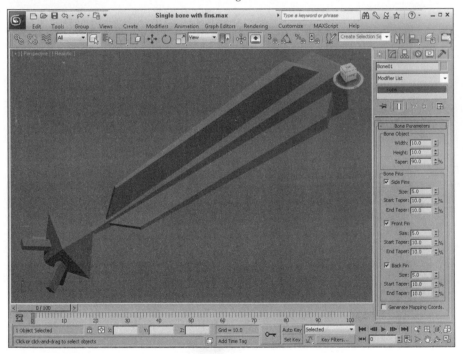

At the bottom of the Bone Parameters rollout is an option to Generate Mapping Coordinates. Bones are renderable objects, so this option lets you apply texture maps to them.

Tutorial: Creating a bones system for an alligator

To practice creating a bones system, you'll take a trip to the Deep South to gator country. The main movement for this gator is going to be in its tail, so you need the most bones there. The front legs are smaller and can be controlled with only two simple bones. You also won't worry about fingers.

To create a bones system for an alligator, follow these steps:

1. Open the Alligator bones.max file from the Chap 38 directory on the CD.

    This file includes an alligator model created by Viewpoint Datalabs.

2. Select Create ⇨ Systems ⇨ Bones IK Chain, and in the IK Chain Assignment rollout, select IK Limb from the IK Solver drop-down list. Then set the Width and Height values to **10** and enable all the bone fins and set their Size to **5**.

3. In the Top viewport, click once at the pelvis and then again at the mid-abdomen, the base of the neck, and the end of the nose. Then right-click to end the bones chain.

4. While still in Bones mode, click below the pelvis and create an additional five bones to define the tail. Then right-click to end the chain. Select the first bone in the tail chain and link it to the first joint with the Select and Link tool that moves from the pelvis to the nose, which is the root joint.

Tip
If you can't see the bones to make the link, then hide the body so the bones are clearly visible. ∎

5. Click on the Bones button in the Create panel, select the bone just in front of the legs in the Top viewport (the cursor changes to a cross-hair when it is over a bone), and drag to the top to form the left shoulder, left upper-arm and left lower-arm bones. Right-click to end the chain. Repeat to create bones for the left leg.

6. Select the Animation ⇨ Bone Tools menu command to open the Bone Tools dialog box. Select all the bones in the left arm and leg and click the Mirror button. In the Bone Mirror dialog box, select the Y-axis and click OK.

7. Click the Select Objects button on the main toolbar to exit Bones mode, and select and name each bone object so it can be easily identified later.

Tip
The Schematic View window is a good interface for quickly labeling bones. ∎

Figure 38.3 shows the completed bones system for the alligator.

FIGURE 38.3

This bones system for an alligator was easy to create.

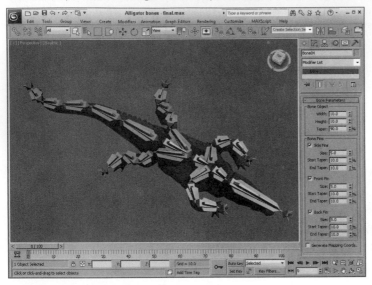

Using the Bone Tools

After you've created a bones system, you can use the Bone Tools to edit and work with the bones system. You access these tools from a panel that is opened using the Animation ⇨ Bone Tools menu command. Figure 38.4 shows this panel of tools, which includes three separate rollouts: Bone Editing Tools, Fin Adjustment Tools, and Object Properties.

FIGURE 38.4

The Bone Tools palette includes several buttons for working with bones systems.

Reordering bones

You can use the transform buttons on the main toolbar to move, rotate, and scale a bone along with all its children, but if you want to transform the parent without affecting any of the children, you need to open the Bone Tools panel using the Animation ⇨ Bone Tools menu command. Bone Edit Mode lets you move and realign a bone without affecting its children.

Clicking the Remove Bone button removes the selected bone and reconnects the bone chain by stretching the child bone. If you hold down the Shift key while removing a bone, the parent is stretched. Clicking the Delete Bone button deletes the selected bone and adds an End bone to the last child.

Caution

Using the Delete key to delete a bone does not add an End bone, and the bone chain does not work correctly with an IK Solver. ■

If a bone exists that isn't connected to another bone, you can add an End bone to the bone using the Create End button. The bone chain must end with an End bone in order to be used by an IK Solver.

The Connect Bones button lets you connect the selected bone with another bone. After clicking this button, you can drag a line from the selected bone to another bone to connect the two bones.

Use the Reassign Root button to reverse the chain and move the End bone from the parent to the last child.

Refining and mirroring bones

As you start to work with a bones system that you've created, you may discover that the one long bone for the backbone of your monster is too long to allow the monster to move like you want. If this happens, you can refine individual bones using the Refine button. This button appears at the bottom of the Bone Tools section of the Bone Editing Tools rollout.

Clicking the Refine button enables you to select bones in the viewport. Every bone that you select is divided into two bones at the location where you click. Click on the Refine button again to exit Refine mode.

The Mirror button lets you create a mirror copy of the selected bones. This button makes the Bone Mirror dialog box appear, where you can select the Mirror Axis and the Bone Axis to Flip. You also can specify an Offset value. In the previous example, you created arms and legs manually, but you could have created one of them and used the Mirror button to create its opposite.

Coloring bones

Bones, like any other objects, are assigned a default object color, and materials can be applied from the Material Editor. For each separate bone, its object color can be changed in the Modify panel or in the Bone Tools panel.

You can also apply a gradient to a bone chain using the Bone Tools palette. This option is available only if two or more bones are selected. The Start Color is applied to the chain's head, and the End Color is applied to the last selected child. The colors are applied or updated when the Apply Gradient button is clicked. Figure 38.5 shows a long, spiral bone chain with a white-to-black gradient applied.

FIGURE 38.5

A white-to-black gradient was applied to this spiral bone chain.

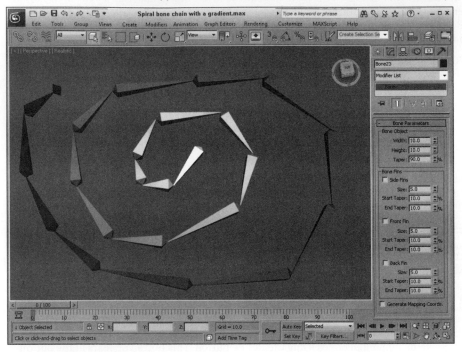

Adjusting fins

The Fin Adjustment Tools rollout includes the same parameters as those found in the Bone Parameters rollout. You can specify the dimensions and taper of a bone and its fins. But you can also specify that the parameters are applied using Absolute or Relative values. Relative values are based on the parameters of the bone that is above the current bone in the chain.

This rollout also includes Copy and Paste buttons that you can use to copy the bone parameters from one bone to another.

Making objects into bones

You can make any object act like a bone. To make an object into a bone, you need to open the Object Properties rollout in the Bone Tools panel. The Object Properties rollout includes a setting for Bone On. If enabled, the object acts like a bone. When the Bone On/Off option is enabled, the remaining Bone controls become available. The Auto-Align option causes the pivot points of adjacent bones to be aligned automatically. The Freeze Length option causes a bone to keep its length as the bones system is moved. If the Freeze Length is disabled, you can specify a Stretch type. None prevents any stretching from occurring, and Scale changes the size along one axis, but Squash causes the bone to get wider as its length is decreased and thinner as it is elongated. You can also select to stretch an axis and choose whether to Flip the axis.

You can use the Realign button to realign a bone: click the Reset Stretch button to normalize the stretch value to its current value.

Forward Kinematics versus Inverse Kinematics

Before you can understand IK, you need to realize that another type of kinematics exists: forward kinematics. Kinematics solutions work only on a kinematics chain, which you can create by linking children objects to their parents.

Cross-Reference

Chapter 9, "Grouping, Linking, and Parenting Objects," covers linking objects and creating kinematics chains. ■

Forward kinematics causes objects at the bottom of a linked structure to move along with their parents. For example, consider the linked structure of an arm, where the upper arm is connected to a forearm, which is connected to a hand, and finally connected to some fingers. Using forward kinematics, the lower arm, hand, and fingers all move when the upper arm is moved.

Having the linked children move with their parent is what you would expect and want, but suppose the actual object that you wanted to place is the hand. IK enables child objects to control their parent objects. So, using IK, you can drag the hand to the exact position you want, and all other parts in the system follow.

Forward kinematics in Max involves simply transforming linked hierarchies. When you move, rotate, or scale a linked hierarchy, the children move with the parent, but the child object also can be transformed independent of its parent.

Creating an Inverse Kinematics System

Before you can animate an IK system, you need to build and link the system, define joints by positioning pivot points, and define any joint constraints you want.

Building and linking a system

The first step in creating an IK system is to create and link several objects together. You can create links using the Link button on the main toolbar.

With the linked system created, position the child object's pivot point at the center of the joint between it and its parent. For example, the joint between an upper and lower arm would be at the elbow, so this is where the pivot point for the lower arm should be located.

Cross-Reference

Chapter 9, "Grouping, Linking, and Parenting Objects," covers creating linked systems, and Chapter 7, "Transforming Objects, Pivoting, Aligning, and Snapping," covers moving pivot points. ■

While creating the linked system, you can select the IK Solver in the Create panel, and later after correctly positioning your pivot points, you can access the IK parameters in the Hierarchy panel by clicking the IK button. Several rollouts open that let you control the IK system, including the Object Parameters rollout shown in Figure 38.6.

FIGURE 38.6

The IK rollouts let you control the binding of an IK system.

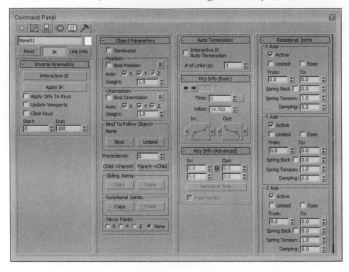

Selecting a terminator

Because child objects in an IK system can cause their parents to move, moving a child could cause unwanted movements all the way up the system to the root object. For example, pulling on the little finger of a human model could actually move the head. To prevent this, you can select an object in the system to be a terminator.

A *terminator* is the last object in the IK system that is affected by the child's movement. Making the upper arm a terminator prevents the finger's movement from affecting any objects above the arm.

To set a terminator, select an object and enable the Terminator option in the Object Parameters rollout.

For Interactive IK mode, you also can enable the Auto Termination option included in the Auto Termination rollout. The Number (#) of Links Up value sets the terminator a specified number of links above the current selection.

Defining joint constraints

The next step is to define the joint constraints, which you specify in the Sliding Joints and Rotational Joints rollouts. The availability of these limits depends on the selected IK Solver and its options. By default, each joint has six degrees of freedom, meaning that the two objects that make up the joint can each move or rotate along the X-, Y-, or Z-axis. The axis settings for all other sliding and rotational joints are identical. Defining joint constraints enables you to constrain these motions to prevent unnatural motions, such as an elbow bending backward. To constrain an axis, select the object that includes the pivot point for the joint, locate in the appropriate rollout the section for the axis that you want to restrict, and deselect the Active option. If an axis's Active option is deselected, the axis is constrained. You also can limit the motion of joints by selecting the Limited option.

When the Limited option is selected, the object can move only within the bounds set by the From and To values. The Ease option causes the motion of the object to slow as it approaches either limit. The Spring Back option lets you set a rest position for the object; the object returns to this position when pulled away. The Spring Tension sets the amount of force that the object uses to resist being moved from its rest position. The Damping value sets the friction in the joint, which is the value with which the object resists any motion.

Note

As you enter values in the From and To fields, the object moves to that value to show visually the location specified. You also can press and hold the left mouse button on the From and To values to cause the object to move temporally to its limits. These settings are based on the current Reference Coordinate system. ■

Copying, pasting, and mirroring joints

Defining joint constraints can be lots of work—work that you wouldn't want to have to duplicate if you didn't have to. The Copy and Paste buttons in the Object Parameters rollout enable you to copy Sliding Joints or Rotational Joints constraints from one IK joint to another.

To use these buttons, select an IK system and click the Copy button; then select each of the joints to be constrained in a similar manner, and click the Paste button. You also have an option to mirror the joints about an axis. It is useful for duplicating an IK system for opposite arms or legs of a human or animal model.

Binding objects

When using applied IK, you need to bind an object in the IK system to a follow object. The IK joint that is bound to the follow object then follows the follow object around the scene. The bind controls are located in the Hierarchy panel under the Object Parameters rollout. To bind an object to a follow object, click the Bind button in the Object Parameters rollout and select the follow object.

In addition to binding to a follow object, IK joints also can be bound to the world for each axis by position and orientation. This causes the object to be locked in its current position so it won't move or rotate along the axis that is selected. You also can assign a Weight value. When the IK computations determine that two objects need to move in opposite directions, the solution favors the object with the largest Weight value.

The Unbind button eliminates the binding.

Understanding precedence

When Max computes an IK solution, the order in which the joints are solved determines the end result. The Precedence value (located in the Object Parameters rollout) lets you set the order in which joints are solved. To set the precedence for an object, select the object and enter a value in the Precedence value setting. Max computes the object with a higher precedence value first.

The default joint precedence for all objects is 0. This assumes that the objects farthest down the linkage move the most. The Object Parameters rollout also includes two default precedence settings. The Child to Parent button sets the precedence value for the root object to 0 and increments the precedence of each level under the root by 10. The Parent to Child button sets the opposite precedence, with the root object having a value of 0 and the precedence value of each successive object decreasing by 10.

Tutorial: Controlling a backhoe

As an example of a kinematics system, you start with a backhoe, which is a simple linkage system with tracks that can move forward, a chair housing that can rotate independently, and an arm and bucket that can rotate about a pivot. When you're finished with this tutorial, you can take the backhoe out and dig a hole for a swimming pool. I think you deserve it.

To create an inverse kinematics system for a backhoe, follow these steps:

1. Open the Backhoe.max file from the Chap 38 directory on the CD.
2. Open the Schematic View window with the Graph Editors ➪ New Schematic View menu. Click the Connect button, and connect the tracks to the base plate, the base plate and the housing to the base cylinder, the bucket to the arm, and the arm to the housing. The connections should look like those in Figure 38.7.

Cross-Reference

You can learn more about the Schematic View window in Chapter 25, "Building Complex Scenes with Containers, XRefs, and the Schematic View." ■

FIGURE 38.7

The Schematic View window is helpful for linking hierarchies.

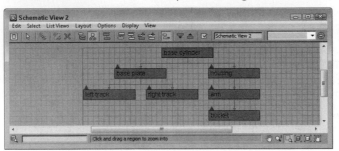

3. Next, you need to define the pivots for the objects that can rotate. Select the housing, and notice that its pivot is already located in the center of the base cylinder where it should be. Then select the arm, open the Hierarchy panel, and click the Pivot button. Click the Affect Pivot Only button, and move the pivot to the center of the cylinder that connects it to the housing. Then do the same for the bucket. Click the Affect Pivot Only button again to exit pivot-editing mode.
4. The next step is to define the joint constraints for the system. Open the Hierarchy panel, and click the IK button. In the Object Parameters rollout, select the base cylinder and enable the Terminator, Bind Position, and Bind Orientation options; doing so prevents the base cylinder from moving anywhere. In the Rotational Joint rollout, deactivate all the axes.
5. Select the housing object, and enable the Bind Position axes and the X and Y Orientation axes. Then disable the X and Y Rotation axes. Select the arm object, and enable all the Bind Position axes and the X and Z Orientation axes. Then disable the X and Z Rotational axes. Click the Copy button for the Rotational joint type in the Object Parameters rollout, select the bucket object, and click the Paste button. This copies the joint constraints from the arm object to the bucket object.

6. To test the system, select the Interactive IK button in the Inverse Kinematics rollout and select and move the bucket.

As the bucket is moved, the arm rotates and the housing spins about its axis, just as you'd expect.

Figure 38.8 shows the bucket moving. With the Interactive IK mode disabled, any object can be moved and/or rotated, and only the links are enforced.

The objects in this scene are part of an inverse kinematics system.

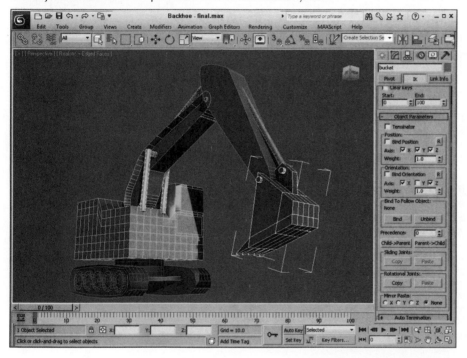

Using the Various Inverse Kinematics Methods

After you create a linked hierarchy chain, you need to apply an IK method to the chain before you can animate it. Max includes several methods for animating using IK. The traditional methods of Interactive and Applied IK are now joined with IK solvers. The Interactive and Applied IK methods are applied using the Hierarchy panel; the IK solvers can be applied to a bones system, or you can use the Animation ⇨ IK Solvers menu.

An IK solver is a specialized controller that computes an IK solution. This solution is used to automatically set all the required keys needed for the animation. Max offers four IK solvers: History Dependent (HD) IK, History Independent (HI) IK, IK Limb, and Spline IK solvers.

Interactive IK

Interactive IK is the method that lets you position a linked hierarchy of objects at different frames. Max then interpolates all the keyframes between the various keys. This method isn't as precise, but it uses a minimum number of keys and is useful for an animation sequence involving many frames. Interactive IK interpolates positions between the two different keys, whereas Applied IK computes positions for every key. Because the motions are simple interpolations between two keys, the result may not be accurate, but the motion is smooth.

Caution

Be aware that Interactive IK is not available for all IK Solvers. ■

After your IK system is established, animating using the Interactive IK method is simple. First, you need to enable the Auto Key button and select the Interactive IK button in the IK rollout of the Hierarchy panel. Enabling this button places you in Interactive IK mode, causing the system to move together as a hierarchy. Then reposition the system in a different frame; Max automatically interpolates between the two positions and creates the animation keys. To exit Interactive IK mode, simply click the Interactive IK button again.

The IK rollout includes several options. The Apply Only to Keys option forces Max to solve IK positions for only those frames that currently have keys. The Update Viewports option shows the animation solutions in the viewports as it progresses, and the Clear Keys option removes any existing keys as the solution is calculated. The Start and End values mark the frames to include in the solution.

IK Preference settings

The required accuracy of the IK solution can be set using the Inverse Kinematics panel in the Preference Settings dialog box, shown in Figure 38.9. You can open this dialog box by choosing Customize ⇨ Preferences. For the Interactive and Applied IK methods, you can set Position and Rotation Thresholds. These Threshold values determine how close the moving object must be to the defined position for the solution to be valid.

FIGURE 38.9

The Inverse Kinematics panel of the Preference Settings dialog box lets you set the global Threshold values.

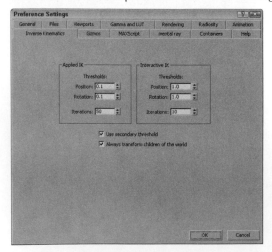

You also can set an Iterations limit for both methods. The Iterations value is the maximum number of times the calculations are performed. This value limits the time that Max spends looking for a valid solution. The Iterations settings control the speed and accuracy of each IK solution.

Note

If the Iterations value is reached without a valid solution, Max uses the last calculated iteration. ■

The Use Secondary Threshold option provides a backup method for determining whether Max should continue to look for a valid solution. This method should be used if you want Max to bail out of a particularly difficult situation rather than to continue to look for a solution. If you are working with very small thresholds, you want to enable this option.

The Always Transform Children of the World option enables you to move the root object when it is selected by itself, but constrains its movement when any of its children are moved.

Tutorial: Animating a simple IK propeller system

Machines are good examples of kinematics systems. In this example, you animate a simple gear-and-propeller system using the Applied IK method.

To animate an inverse kinematics system with a propeller, follow these steps:

1. Open the Gear and prop.max file from the Chap 38 directory on the CD.

   This file includes a simple handle-and-prop system.

2. To accomplish the first task—linking the model—click the Select and Link button on the main toolbar, and drag from each child object to its parent. Connect the propeller to the shaft, the shaft to the gear, and the gear to the handle.

3. Open the Hierarchy panel, and click the IK button. Constrain the motions of the parts by selecting the handle object. All Sliding Joints can be deactivated, and only the Z Axis Rotational Joint needs to be activated. To do this, make sure that a check mark is next to the Active option. When this is set for the handle object, click the Copy button for both joint types, select the gear object, and click Paste to copy these constraints. Then select the shaft object, click both Paste buttons again, and repeat this process for the propeller.

4. Enable the Auto Key button (or press the N key), drag the Time Slider to frame 100 (or press the End key), and click the Interactive IK button in the Inverse Kinematics rollout of the Hierarchy panel. Select the Select and Rotate button (or press E), and drag in the Left viewport to rotate the handle about its Z-axis.

Figure 38.10 shows the propeller system.

Applied IK

Applied IK applies a solution over a range of frames, computing the keys for every frame. This task is accomplished by binding the IK system to an object that it follows. This method is more precise than the interactive IK method, but it creates lots of keys. Because keys are set for every object and every transform, this solution sets lots of keys, which increases the size and complexity of the scene. Each frame has its own set of keys, which could result in jerky, non-smooth results.

FIGURE 38.10

The propeller rotates by turning the handle and using IK.

To animate using the Applied IK method, you need to bind one or more parts of the system to a follow object, which can be a dummy object or an object in the scene. You do so by clicking the Bind button in the Object Parameters rollout of the Hierarchy panel and selecting an object in one of the viewports. After the system has a bound follow object, select an object in the system. Open the Hierarchy panel; in the Inverse Kinematics rollout, click the Apply IK button. Max computes the keys for every frame between the Start and End frames specified in the rollout. Click the Apply IK button to start the computation process that sets all the animation keys for the range of frames indicated.

History Independent IK solver

The History Independent (HI) IK solver looks at each keyframe independently when making its solution. You can animate linked chains with this IK solver applied by positioning the goal object; the solver then inserts a keyframe at the pivot point of the last object in the chain to match the goal object.

You can apply IK solvers to any hierarchy of objects. IK solvers are applied automatically to a bones system when you create the system. You also can choose Animation ➪ IK Solvers to select an IK solver.

When you choose Animation ➪ IK Solver, a dotted line appears from the selected object. You can drag this line within a viewport and click another object within the hierarchy to be the end joint. A white line is drawn between the beginning and ending joints. The pivot point of the end joint is the goal for the IK solver. It is known as the end effector. The end effector of the IK solver is marked by a blue cross. Several rollouts within the Motion panel also appear. These rollouts let you set the parameters for the IK solver.

The first rollout, after the Assign Controller rollout, is the IK Solver rollout, shown in Figure 38.11. Using this rollout, you can select to switch between the HI IK solver and the IK Limb solver. The Enabled button lets you disable the solver. By disabling the solver, you can use forward kinematics to move the objects. To return to the IK solution, simply click the Enabled button again. The IK for FK Pose option enables IK control even if the IK solver is disabled. This lets you manipulate the hierarchy of objects using forward kinematics while still working with the IK solution. If both the IK for FK Pose and the Enabled buttons are disabled, then the goal can move without affecting the hierarchy of objects.

FIGURE 38.11

The IK Solver rollout lets you enable or disable the IK solver.

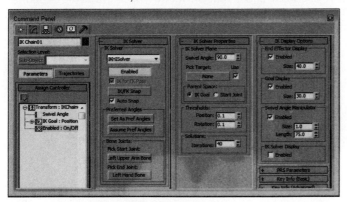

If the goal ever gets moved away from the end link, clicking the IK/FK Snap button automatically moves the goal to match the end links position. Auto Snap automatically keeps the goal and the end link together. The Set as Preferred Angle button remembers the angles for the IK system. These angles can be recalled at any time using the Assume Preferred Angle button.

When you choose Animation ⇨ IK Solvers ⇨ HI Solver, the start joint is the selected object, and the end joint is the object to which you drag the dotted line. If you want to change these objects, you can click the Pick Start Joint or Pick End Joint buttons.

Tip
The best way to select an object using the Pick Start Joint and Pick End Joint buttons is to open the Select by Name dialog box by pressing the H key. Using this dialog box, you can select an exact object without missing selecting it in a complex viewport. ■

Caution
If you select a child as the start joint and an object above the child as the end joint, then moving the goal has no effect on the IK chain. ■

Defining a swivel angle

The IK Solver Properties rollout includes the Swivel Angle value. The swivel angle defines the plane that includes the joint objects and the line that connects the starting and ending joints. This plane is key because it defines the direction that the joint moves when bent.

The Swivel Angle value can change during an animation. Using the Pick Target button, you also can select a Target object to control the swivel angle. The Use button turns the target on and off. The Parent Space group defines whether the IK Goal's parent object or the Start Joint's parent object is used to define the plane. Having an option lets you select two different parent objects that control the swivel plane if two or more IK solvers are applied to a single IK chain.

You also can change the Swivel Angle value by using a manipulator. To view the manipulator, click the Select and Manipulate button on the main toolbar. This manipulator is a green line with a square on the end of it. Dragging this manipulator in the viewports causes the swivel angle to change.

To understand the swivel angle, consider the two puppet bones systems displayed in Figure 38.12. The HI solver has been applied to the right arms of both puppets with the upper arm as the beginning joint and the hand as the end joint. The swivel angle for the left bones system is 90 degrees, and the swivel angle for the right bones system is 180. You can see the manipulators for both bones systems. The left one is pointing upward, and the right one is pointing straight out from the puppet's head. Notice that the swivel angle determines the direction the elbow joint is pointing. The left bones system's elbow is pointing up and away from the spine, and the right bones system's elbow is pointing painfully out in front of the puppet in the direction of the manipulator.

FIGURE 38.12

The swivel angle defines the plane along which the joint moves.

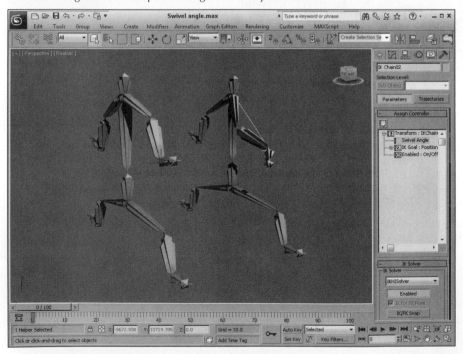

The IK Solver Properties rollout also includes Threshold values. These values determine how close the end joint and the goal must be before the solution is pronounced valid. You can set thresholds for Position and Rotation. The Iterations value sets the number of times the solution is tried.

Tip

Setting the Iterations value to a higher number produces smoother (less jerky) results, but it increases the time required to find a solution. ■

Displaying IK controls

The IK Display Options rollouts can enable, disable, and set the size of the gizmos used when working with IK solvers. Using this rollout, you can Enable the End Effector, the Goal, the Swivel Angle Manipulator, and the IK solver (which is the line connecting the start and end joints).

Tutorial: Animating a puppet with the HI IK solver

The HI solver is probably the best solver to use for animating characters. This fine fellow made of bones makes a good candidate for trying out the HI solver.

To animate a puppet with the HI IK solver, follow these steps:

1. Open the Dancing puppet.max file from the Chap 38 directory on the CD.

   This file is the same file that was created using the bones system.

2. Apply the HI solver to the arm chains by selecting the left upper arm and choosing Animation ⇨ IK Solvers ⇨ HI Solver. A dotted line appears in the viewports extending from the selected object. Move the cursor over the left hand object, and click.

3. Repeat Step 2 for the right arm and both leg chains.

4. Click the Auto Key button, and drag the Time Slider to frame 20. Select the goal for the left leg IK chain, click the Select and Move button on the main toolbar (or press the W key), and move the left leg goal upward.

5. Repeat Step 4 for frames 40, 60, 80, and 100, moving the various IK chains in different directions.

6. Move the Time Slider to frame 50, and select all objects by choosing Edit ⇨ Select All (or by pressing Ctrl+A). Drag all the objects upward a short distance. Drag the Time Slider to frame 100 (or press the End key), and drag all the objects back down again.

7. Click the Play Animation button (or press /) to see the resulting dance.

Figure 38.13 shows one frame of the dancing puppet.

FIGURE 38.13

Moving the goal for each IK chain makes animating a character easy.

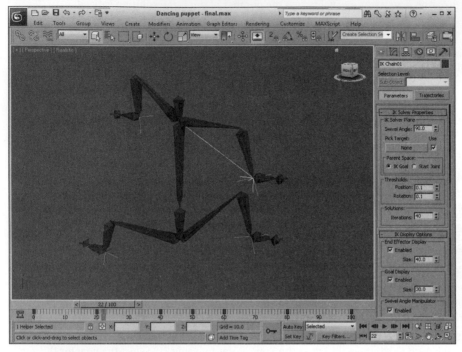

History Dependent IK solver

The History Dependent (HD) IK solver takes into account the previous keyframes as it makes a solution. This solver makes having very smooth motion possible, but the cost of time to compute the solution is increased significantly. You also can assign this IK solver to a bones system by specifying the History Dependent solver in the IK Chain Assignment rollout or by choosing Animation ⇨ IK Solvers ⇨ HD Solver.

This IK solver shows up as a controller in the Motion panel when the IK chain is selected. The settings are contained in a rollout named IK Controller Parameters, which is visible in the Motion panel if you select one of the end effector gizmos. The end effector gizmo is the object that you move to control the IK chain. It is displayed as a set of crossing axes.

You can access the IK Controller Parameters rollout, shown in Figure 38.14, in the Motion panel. Any parameter changes affect all bones in the current structure. In the Thresholds section, the Position and Rotation values set how close the end effector must be to its destination before the solution is complete. In the Solution section, the Iterations value determines the maximum number of times the solution is attempted. These Thresholds and Iterations values are the same as those in the Preference Settings dialog box, except that they affect only the current linkage. The Start Time and End Time values set the frame range for the IK solution.

FIGURE 38.14

The IK Controller Parameters rollout sets the boundaries of the IK solution.

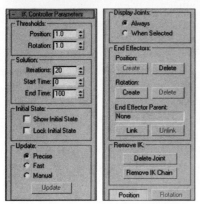

The Show Initial State option displays the initial state of the linkage and enables you to move it by dragging the end effector object. The Lock Initial State option prevents any linkage other than the end effector from moving.

The Update section enables you to set how the IK solution is updated with Precise, Fast, and Manual options. The Precise option solves for every frame, Fast solves for only the current frame, and Manual solves only when the Update button is clicked. The Display Joints options determine whether joints are Always displayed or only When Selected.

When you first create a bones system, an end effector is set to the last joint automatically. In the End Effectors section, at the bottom of the IK Controller Parameters rollout, you can set any joint to be a Positional or Rotational end effector. To make a bone an end effector, select the bone and click the Create button. If the bone is already an end effector, then the Delete button is active. You also can link the bone to another parent object outside of the linkage with the Link button. The linked object then inherits the transformations of this new parent.

Click the Delete Joint button in the Remove IK section to delete a joint. If a bone is set to be an end effector, the Position or Rotation button displays the Key Info parameters for the selected bone.

Tutorial: Animating a spyglass with the HD IK solver

A telescoping spyglass is a good example of a kinematics system that you can use to show off the HD solver. The modeling of this example is easy because it consists of a bunch of cylinders that gradually get smaller.

To animate a spyglass with the HD IK solver, follow these steps:

1. Open the Spyglass.max file from the Chap 38 directory on the CD.

   This file includes a simple spyglass made from primitive objects. The pieces of the spyglass are linked from the smallest section to the largest section. At the end of the spyglass is a dummy object linked to the last tube object.

2. To define the joint properties, select the largest tube object, open the Hierarchy panel, and click the IK button. In the Object Parameters rollout, select the Terminator, Bind Position, and Bind Orientation options to keep this joint from moving.

3. With the largest tube section selected, make the Z Axis option active in the Sliding Joints rollout, and disable all the axes in the Rotational Joints rollout. Click the Copy button for both Sliding Joints and Rotational Joints in the Object Properties rollout.

4. Select each remaining tube object individually, and click the Paste buttons for both the Sliding Joints and Rotational Joints.

   This enables the local Z-axis sliding motion for all tube objects.

5. Select the largest tube section again, and choose Animation ⇨ IK Solvers ⇨ HD Solver. Then drag the dotted line to the dummy object at the end of the spyglass.

6. Select the second largest tube object, and for the Sliding Joint Z Axis, select the Limited option with values from **0.0** to **−80**. Click the Copy button for the Sliding Joints in the Object Parameters rollout. Select tubes 3 through 6 individually, and click the Paste button for the Sliding Joints to apply these same limits to the other tube objects.

7. Click the Auto Key button (or press N), drag the Time Slider to frame 100 (or press End), select the Select and Move button on the main toolbar (or press W), and drag the dummy object away from the largest tube object.

Figure 38.15 shows the end tube segment collapsing within the spyglass.

FIGURE 38.15

The HD IK solver is used to control the spyglass.

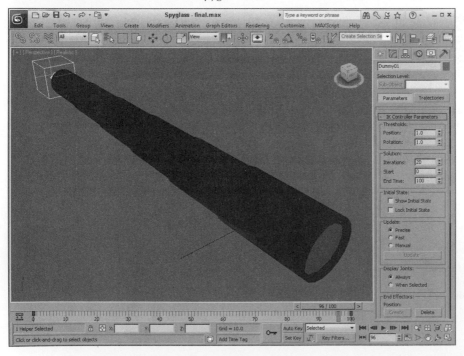

IK Limb solver

The IK Limb solver was specifically created to work with limbs. It is used on chains of three bones such as a hip, upper leg, and lower leg. Only two of the bones in the chain actually move. The goal for these three joints is located at the pivot point for the third bone. This solver is ideal for game character rigging.

This solver works by considering the first joint as a spherical joint that can rotate along three different axes, such as a hip or shoulder joint. The second joint can bend only in one direction, such as an elbow or knee joint.

The rollouts and controls for the IK Limb solver are exactly the same as those used for the HI solver covered earlier in this chapter.

Tutorial: Animating a spider's leg with the IK Limb solver

As an example of the IK Limb solver, you should probably animate a limb, so I created a simple spider skeleton with not two limbs, but eight. I created this skeleton fairly quickly using four bones for the abdomen; then I created one limb and cloned it three times. Then I used the Bone Tools to connect the leg bones to the abdomen bones, and finally I selected and mirrored the bones on all four legs to get the opposite legs. The hardest part was naming all the bones.

To animate a spider skeleton's leg using the IK Limb solver, follow these steps:

1. Open the Spider skeleton.max file from the Chap 38 directory on the CD.
2. Click the Select by Name button on the main toolbar (or press the H key) to open the Select Objects dialog box. Double-click the RUpperlegBone0l object to select the upper leg bone object.
3. With the upper leg bone selected, choose Animation⇨IK Solvers⇨IK Limb Solver. A dotted line appears in the viewport. Press the H key again to open the Pick Object dialog box, and double-click the RFootBone0l object to select it.

   This bone corresponds to the foot bone, which is the end of the limb hierarchy.
4. With the IK Chain01 object selected, click the Auto Key button (or press the N key) and drag the Time Slider to frame 100 (or press End). With the Select and Move button (or by pressing the W key), move the IK chain in the viewport.

   The leg chain bends as you move the end effector.

Figure 38.16 shows the spider's leg being moved via the IK Limb solver. The IK Limb solver provides a simple and quick way to add an effector to the end of a limb, giving you good control for animating the spider's walk cycles.

FIGURE 38.16

You can use the IK Limb solver to control limbs such as legs and arms.

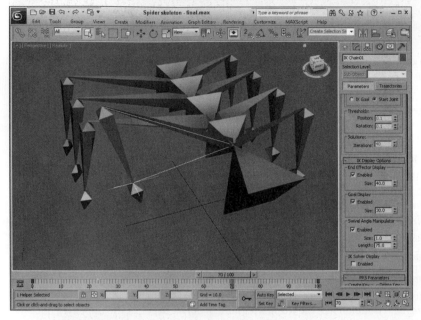

Spline IK solver

The IK Limb solver works well for arms and legs that have a joint in the middle, but it doesn't work well for tails. Tails are unique because they require multiple bones to deform correctly. The Spline IK solver works well for tails, but it also works well for rigging tentacles, chains, and rope.

To use the Spline IK solver, you need to create a chain of bones and a spline path. By selecting the first and last bone and then selecting the spline, the bone chain moves to the spline. Each control point on the spline has a dummy object associated with it. By moving these dummy objects, you can control the position of the bones. At either end of the spline are manipulators that you can use to twist and rotate the bones.

The easiest way to use this IK solver is to select SplineIKSolver from the drop-down list in the IK Chain Assignment rollout while you're creating the bone structure. After the bone structure is complete, the Spline IK Solver dialog box appears. With this dialog box, you can select a name for the IK chain, specify the curve type, and set the number of spline knots. The curve type options include Bézier, NURBS Point, and NURBS CV. You also can select to Create Helpers and to display several options.

Another way to use this IK solver is with an existing bone structure. To do this, you need a spline curve in the scene that matches how you want the bone chain to look. Select the first bone where you want the solver to be applied, and choose Animation ➪ IK Solvers ➪ Spline IK. In the viewports, a dragging line appears; move the line to the last bone that you want to include, and then drag a second time to the spline that you want to use.

The bone structure then assumes the shape of the spline curve. A helper object is positioned at the location of each curve vertex. These helper objects let you refine the shape of the curve.

Tutorial: Building an IK Spline alligator

The IK Spline solver is perfect for creating long, winding objects like snakes or an alligator's tail. For this example, you take an existing bone structure and, using the Spline IK solver, make it match a spline.

To create a bone structure for an alligator that follows a spline using the IK Spline solver, follow these steps:

1. Open the Alligator spline IK.max file from the Chap 38 directory on the CD.

    This file includes an alligator model created by Viewpoint Datalabs, a simple bone chain, the Skin modifier, and a spline.

Tip

If you're having trouble seeing the bones located inside the alligator, you can enable the See Through option in the Object Properties dialog box or press the Alt+X keyboard shortcut. ■

2. With the first bone in the tail chain selected, choose Animation ⇨ IK Solvers ⇨ SplineIK Solver.

    A dragging line appears in the viewport extending from the first bone.
3. Drag and click the cursor on the last bone in the bone tail chain.
4. Another dragging line appears; drag and click the spline, and the bone structure moves to match the spline's curve.

Figure 38.17 shows the bone structure for the gator's tail. You can now control the gator's tail by moving the dummy objects along the spline.

FIGURE 38.17

The IK Spline solver is perfect for creating objects such as snakes and animal tails.

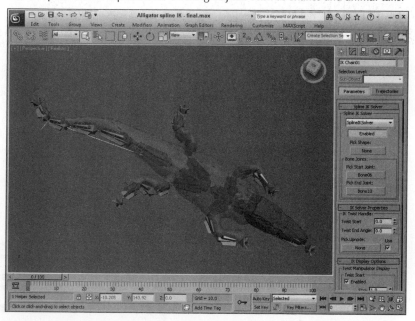

Summary

Understanding the benefits of a bones system helps if you ever need to customize a rig or create a new rig from scratch. Inverse kinematics (IK) provides a unique way to control and animate hierarchical structures by transforming the child node. In this chapter, you learned how to create and work with bones systems and the Bone Tools. This chapter covered the following topics:

- Creating bones systems
- Setting bone parameters and the IK Solver
- Using the Bone Tools
- Making objects into bones systems
- The basic concepts behind IK
- Exploring the difference between interactive and applied IK methods
- Creating and animating an IK system
- Using the IK settings in the Preference Settings dialog box
- Learning how to use IK solvers

Now that you've learned the process for rigging a character and using IK, we look at using the Character Animation Toolkit (CAT) next and discover the benefits of using a pre-rigged skeleton.

Animating Characters with CAT

Max has always had a great way to create and animate characters, but in early versions of Max, it was available only as a separate plug-in known as Character Studio. Happily, Character Studio has been integrated into Max to the point that it isn't distinguishable as a separate package. Character Studio was a good first step, and it still exists in Max, but it has lots of shortcomings that make it difficult to work with.

Another plug-in package known as Character Animation Toolkit, or CAT for short, has been embraced by many Max animators, and now CAT is embedded within 3ds Max. CAT offers a simple interface that gets great results whether you're building your own custom rig or animating an existing preset rig.

Although Max includes other features for rigging characters, if you plan on animating a character, then CAT is definitely the way to go. It's an incredible time-saver.

Character Creation Workflow

A typical workflow for creating characters in Max involves first creating a skin mesh object. After the skin mesh is complete, you can create a skeletal rig to drive its animation. The skeleton consists of a pre-rigged set of bones that provide an underlying structure to the character. Animating these bones provides an easy way to give life to the character.

With a skeletal rig created, position the rig within the skin mesh and match the bone links to the relative size and position inside the skin mesh. The bones do not need to be completely within the skin mesh, but the closer they are to the skin mesh, the more accurate the movements of the character are.

After the rig is sized and matched to the skin mesh, use the Skin modifier to attach the skin mesh to the rig. This automatically sets all the envelopes that govern which skin parts move with which bones. You can also use the Skin modifier settings to deform the skin at certain bone angles, such as bulging a muscle when the arm is raised.

Note

The original Character Studio package used the Physique modifier to bind the mesh skin to the biped. Although this modifier still exists and can be used, the Skin modifier includes many new features and is the preferred method for binding a mesh skin to the biped. ■

The next step is to animate the rig using its animation tools, which can include walk, run, and jump cycles using keys. Along the way, you can save, load, and reuse animation sequences, including motion capture files. Animated sequences can be combined and mixed together to form a smooth-flowing animation using the Motion Mixer.

Creating a CAT Rig

Creating a hierarchical skeleton that is used to control the animation of the mesh skin that is draped over it is quite easy using CAT. The skeleton can be set to be invisible in the final render and exists only to make the process of animating easier. Although Max includes a robust set of tools that can be used to create a skeleton of bones, CAT features automate this entire process and even include a number of prebuilt skeletons.

Cross-Reference

For some characters, modifying a prebuilt skeleton is more work than building a custom skeleton. For these occasions, you can manually create a skeleton structure. Building a rig system by hand is covered in Chapter 38, "Understanding Rigging, Kinematics, and Working with Bones." ■

Using prebuilt CAT rigs

To add a prebuilt CAT rig to the scene, simply open the Create panel and select the Helpers category. When you choose the CAT Objects subcategory, you have three options: CAT Parent, CAT Muscle, and Muscle Strand. Click the CAT Parent button and drag in the viewport to place the CAT Parent object. This parent is simply an icon used to control the global position of the rig and is not rendered.

Tip

It is best to place the CAT Parent object at the origin of the scene. ■

While the CAT Parent object is selected, you can choose a preset rig from the list in the CAT Rig Load Save rollout in the Modify panel or you can select a preset before creating a CAT parent to make the specified preset. The size of the rig is determined by how far you drag in the viewport, or you can set the size using the CATUnits Ratio value in the Command Panel. These custom rigs include a variety of human-shaped and animal-shaped rigs, such as the Alien rig shown in Figure 39.1.

FIGURE 39.1

CAT includes several default preset rigs such as this alien character.

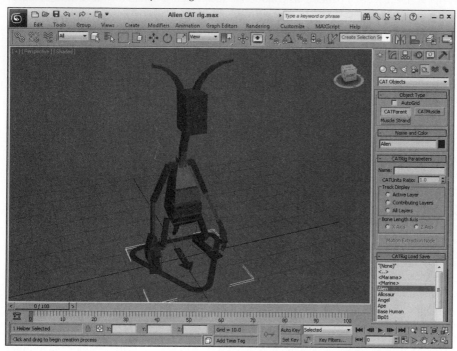

One key advantage of CAT rigs over the rigs available in Character Studio and Biped is that they aren't limited in their structure. Although the available CAT rig presets includes a Base Human and even a Bip01 rig that are used for animating human characters, some of the other presets are dragon, horse, lizard, spider, and centipede. These different rigs have multiple legs, arms, and wings and all are easily controlled.

Modifying prebuilt CAT rigs

With a prebuilt rig added to the scene, you can use the Transform tools to select and move the bones to match the skin mesh. The arms are automatically set up as a Forward Kinematics (FK) chain, so rotating the upper arm bone automatically rotates the rest of the arm bones with it. The legs are set up with an Inverse Kinematics (IK) chain, so you can position the legs by dragging the feet, and the rest of the leg bones follow. By default, all CAT prebuilt rigs have stretchy bones, so if you select and move a bone, the selected and attached bones stretch to maintain the joint connection.

Tip

If you double-click a bone, the bone and all its children are selected. For example, double-clicking a collar bone selects the entire arm, making it easy to move the whole arm into place. ■

A CAT rig keeps track of the different types of body parts and presents the appropriate set of parameters depending on which bone is selected. For example, if you select any part of the arm, the Limb Setup rollouts appear in the Modify panel. This rollout has specific parameters for the arms and legs, as shown in Figure 39.2. CAT also recognizes spines, tails, palms, digits (fingers and toes), hubs (head and pelvis), and generic bones.

The Limb Setup rollout appears when any arm bone is selected.

Copy Limb Settings

Paste Limb Settings

Paste/Mirror Limb Settings

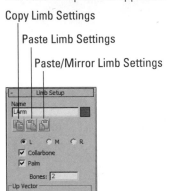

Using these settings, you can specify whether the selected arm is the left, middle, or right arm. You also can choose whether this arm has a collarbone or a palm. The Bones value determines the number of bones that make up the arm. The default is 2, but you can change this to be any whole number from 1 to 20. Because arms can be above or below the head, the Up Vector lets you determine which bone points up.

Beneath the Name are three icons used to copy the settings between two bones. The Copy and Paste Settings buttons let you transfer the settings and orientation of one bone to another. The Paste/Mirror Settings mirror the position of one bone to the opposite side. This lets you set up one arm just right and then quickly copy the settings to the opposite arm.

For spines, you can set the number of bones in the chain, the length and size of the spine bones, and the spine curvature using a simple graph. Tails have these same parameters, plus a height and taper value. For palms and ankles, you can specify the length, width, height, and number of digits.

Individual bones that make up the arms and legs also have a Segments value that you can set. Within the Limb Setup is a value for setting the number of bones in the limb, but you can use the Segments value to set the number of segments for each individual bone. This allows you to change a long bone, like the thigh bone, into a series of segments that can rotate independent of each other. This allows for twisting bones, as shown for the forearm in Figure 39.3. You also can set the weight curve for bones with many segments.

FIGURE 39.3

Increasing the number of bone segments allows the bone to twist like this forearm.

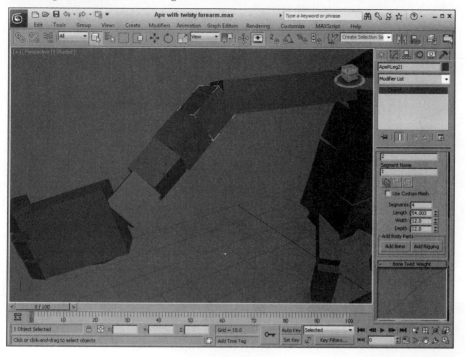

If you want to save the preset rig after you've made some changes, simply select the CAT Parent object and click the Save Preset Rig button in the CAT Rig Load Save rollout. Rigs are saved by default to the CATRigs folder using the .rg3 extension. Once saved, the rigs appear in the list with the other CAT rig presets for easy recall.

Rigs also are easy to delete. Simply select the CAT Parent object and press the Delete key.

Using custom meshes

The bones that make up a CAT rig by default are simple box objects. This allows them to move quickly with a minimum amount of lag, but the bones don't need to be overly simple. The power of modern computers allows complex scenes to be animated without any lag. If you select a bone and enable the Use Custom Mesh option in the Setup rollout, you can access and modify the existing bone to be more representative of the mesh.

To edit an existing bone, simply apply a modifier to the bone object or an Edit Poly modifier and edit the bone as you wish. You also can attach another mesh to the Edit Poly modifier. Once editing is done, simply collapse the changes to the base bone object, and then you can switch back and forth between normal box bones and the custom mesh using the Use Custom Mesh option. Figure 39.4 shows the preset for a gnou.

Tip

If you've gone to all the trouble of building a skin mesh, then you can quickly use the same skin mesh as the skeleton by stripping down its details and using it as a custom mesh. ■

FIGURE 39.4

Simplified meshes can be used as custom rig bones like this gnou preset.

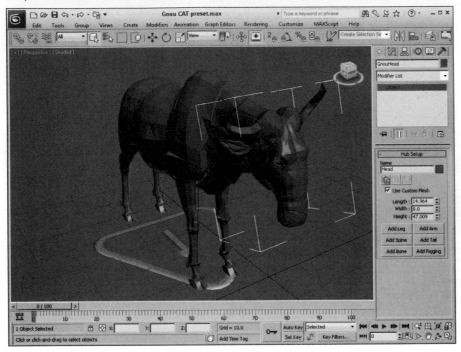

Tutorial: Editing the head bone

Starting with the alien preset CAT rig, this example edits the alien's head bone to show more character and to demonstrate how custom meshes can be used.

To edit the head bone on a CAT rig, follow these steps:

1. Open the Custom alien head bone.max file from the Chap 39 directory on the CD. This file includes the Alien CAT preset rig.

2. Select the head bone and open the Modify panel. Enable the Use Custom Mesh option in the Hub Setup rollout.

3. Apply the TurboSmooth modifier from the Modifier list and scale the head object up to match the other bones.

4. Open the Create panel and select the Sphere button. Enable the AutoGrid option at the top of the Object Type rollout and drag on the surface of the head to create two eyes and a nose.

5. Open the Modify panel again, select the head bone, and apply the Edit Poly modifier to the object. Then click the Attach button and pick the two eyes and nose objects to combine them to the head object.

6. Right-click in the Modifier Stack, select the Collapse All option from the pop-up menu, and click Yes in the warning dialog box that appears.

Figure 39.5 shows the custom alien head bone. You can switch back to the default box bone by disabling the Use Custom Mesh option.

FIGURE 39.5

Bones can be replaced with custom mesh objects.

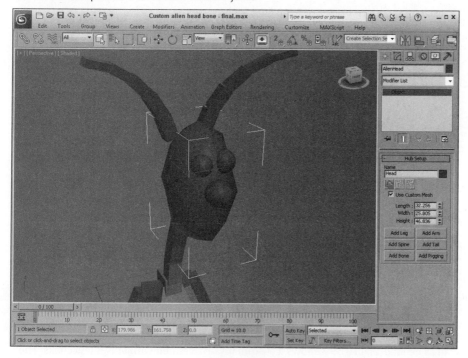

Building a custom CAT rig

When building a custom CAT rig, start with the CAT Parent object, but make sure the None option is selected in the CAT Rig Load Save rollout. Then, right-click in the viewport to exit CAT Parent creation mode. This creates the parent without any rig. Position the CAT Parent object so both feet of the skin mesh are contained within the parent's outline.

Tip

If you make the skin mesh object frozen and enable the See-Through option in the Object Properties dialog box, you can easily place the rig bones where they need to be. ∎

The first step in creating a custom CAT rig is to create the pelvis using the Create Pelvis button beneath the list of presets. The pelvis object appears as a simple box object above the CAT Parent object. You can then use the Transform tools to move, scale, and rotate the pelvis into place to match the skin mesh.

With the pelvis object in place and selected, you then have options in the Hub Setup rollout, shown in Figure 39.6, to add legs, arms, and a spine or a tail if you want. The Add Leg button adds to the pelvis a leg with two bones that extends to the floor and an ankle. You can position the leg bones by dragging the foot into position. When one of the legs is in position, you can select the pelvis again and click the Add Leg button again to create the opposite leg. The opposite leg is created using the same settings and position as the first.

The Hub Setup rollout includes buttons for creating connected legs, arms, and spine.

With the pelvis selected again, click the Add Spine button. This adds a set of spine bones with another hub object on top. The top hub object is used to connect the arms and the neck. The neck is simply another set of spine bones with a hub object on top for the head.

Note

For creatures with multiple arms and legs, the difference between the limbs is that a leg extends from the hub to the ground, and the arm hangs loosely. ■

You can then select the pelvis, shoulder, or head hub objects and use the Add Tail button to add a tail, wings, or ponytail as needed. Figure 39.7 shows a custom CAT rig created with only a few clicks. The rig includes IK chains on both legs and FK chains on the arms. Fingers and toes could be added easily by selecting the palm or ankle objects and specifying the number of digits.

Naming CAT bones

When bones are added to a CAT rig, they are automatically named using the text entered into the Name field. The default name of the entire rig is taken from the name entered into the Name field when the CAT Parent is selected, and names for each body part are associated with the various object parts such as RLeg and LArm. Each bone within a chain is given a default number, so the upper arm object is labeled as 1 and the lower arm is 2.

FIGURE 39.7

Custom CAT rigs are easily created using the CAT tools.

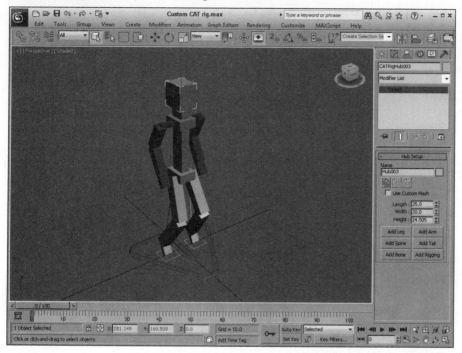

If you change the name field, all bone names that are affected by the name change are automatically updated, so changing the Name field in the CAT Parent to Reuben automatically changes all bones to start with this name. This makes keeping track of all the various bones much easier and intuitive. It also helps when you start to animate the rig.

Tutorial: Building a custom CAT rig to match a skin mesh

For this example, we use the CAT tools to create a custom rig that matches a mesh skin. The chosen mesh skin is none other than Marvin Moose.

To create a custom CAT rig, follow these steps:

1. Open the Marvin Moose.max file from the Chap 39 directory on the CD. This file includes the Marvin Moose skin mesh positioned at the origin.
2. Select and right-click the moose skin mesh object, and select the Object Properties option from the quadmenu. Enable the See-Through and Freeze options in the Object Properties dialog box.

Tip

The keyboard shortcut for making an object see-through is Alt+X. ■

3. Click the Helpers category, open the CAT Objects subcategory in the Create panel, click the CAT Parent button, and drag in the viewport to create the object. Make the CAT Parent just big enough to contain the moose's feet.

4. With the CAT Parent object selected, open the Modify panel and click the Create Pelvis button. Then select and resize the pelvis object and position it to match the skin mesh.

5. With the pelvis object selected, click the Add Leg button to create the left leg. Select and rotate the ankle so the foot is flat against the ground. Scale the foot to roughly match the skin mesh's foot.

6. Select the pelvis, and click Add Leg to create the opposite leg; then click the Add Spine button to create the spine and an object for the shoulders. Position and scale the shoulder hub object. Select the shoulder hub object, and click the Add Arm button. Position the arm bones to match the skin mesh.

7. Select the shoulder hub object, and click Add Arm to create the opposite arm; then click the Add Spine button to create another spine and an object for the head. Select one of the new spine bones, and change the name to **Neck** and the number of bones to **2**. Then scale the head bone to match the moose's head and horns, and name the head bone **Head**.

Figure 39.8 shows the completed custom CAT rig ready to be skinned and animated.

FIGURE 39.8

The moose's skin has been rigged using the CAT tools.

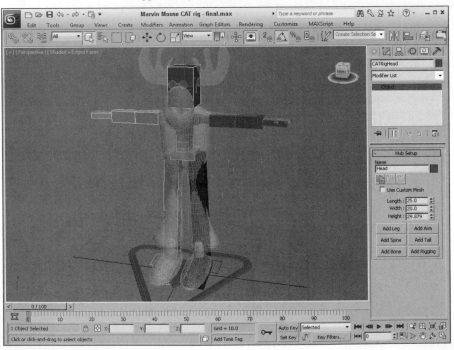

Animating a CAT Rig

The best rig in the world doesn't do you much good if you can't animate it well. Luckily, CAT's animation tools are excellent, just like its rigging tools. CAT uses the concept of animation layers to hold its animation keys. This allows you to blend between different motions.

Cross-Reference

Animation layers are also discussed in Chapter 35, "Using Animation Layers, Modifiers, and Complex Controllers." ∎

All the animation controls for CAT rigs are found in the Motion panel whenever any of the rig's bones are selected. Within the Layer Manager rollout, shown in Figure 39.9, is a list of the available animation layers. To create a new animation layer, select from four different types, using the Add Layer drop-down list at the bottom right of the list. The four animation layer types include the following:

- **Absolute Layer:** Holds animation key data that defines full motions
- **Local Adjustment Layer:** Holds relative key data relative to the local coordinate system of the above layer
- **World Adjustment Layer:** Applies relative motion in world space that is independent of the previous layers
- **CAT Motion Layer:** Creates procedural-based looping motion such as walk cycles

After an animation layer is added and selected, you need to press the Setup/Animation Mode toggle button to begin adding keys to the selected animation layer. You do this using the Auto or Set Key modes to create the keys like normal. Any time a new animation is added, it is automatically placed above the currently selected animation layer.

Tip

If you're animating some of the rig bones using Auto Key and the keys don't appear on the Track Bar, check to make sure you have clicked the Setup/Animation Mode toggle button to enable animation. ∎

The selected animation layer can be removed from the list using the Delete Layer button. You also can copy and paste layers between different rigs using the Copy and Paste Layer buttons. The Move Layer Up and Move Layer Down buttons are used to reorder the selected layer. Each layer can be given a unique name using the Name field.

The Ignore option disables the selected animation layer, and the Solo option disables all animation layers except for the current selection.

Blending absolute animation layers

When several absolute animation layers are added, the layers are evaluated according to their order in the Layer Manager list from top to bottom. Each layer can have a Global Weight value that determines how much of the animation layer is blended.

For example, if the top absolute animation layer contains keys for a character raising an arm, and a second absolute animation layer is added that has keys of the character waving its hand, these two can be blended to create the combined motion of the character raising its hand and waving by setting the Global Weight for the second absolute animation layer to 50 percent, as shown in Figure 39.10. If the second layer is set to 0 percent, the character simply raises its arm; if the Global Weight of the second layer is set to 100 percent, the layer takes over the entire animation and the character waves its hand without raising its arm.

FIGURE 39.9

The Layer Manager rollout holds the various animation layers.

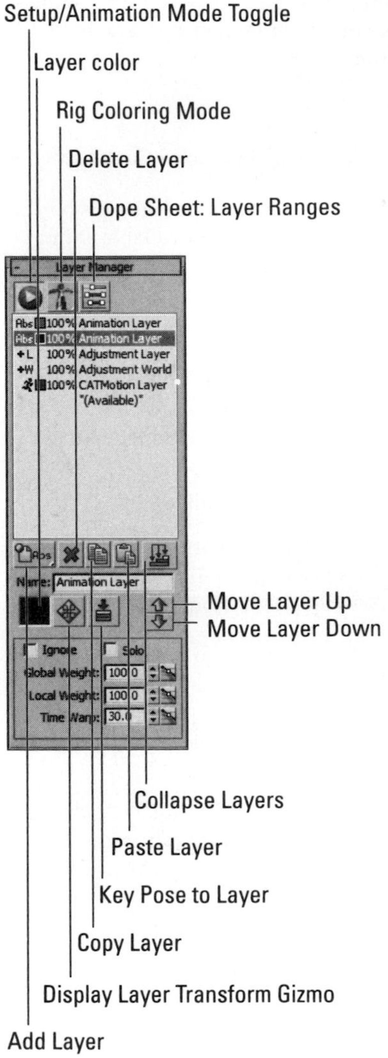

Setup/Animation Mode Toggle

Layer color

Rig Coloring Mode

Delete Layer

Dope Sheet: Layer Ranges

Move Layer Up
Move Layer Down

Collapse Layers

Paste Layer

Key Pose to Layer

Copy Layer

Display Layer Transform Gizmo

Add Layer

In addition to the Global Weight value, which affects all parts of the rig, you can also set a Local Weight value for specific bones. For example, if an absolute animation layer is set that moves the rig to a specific pose, you select the left collar bone and set its Local Weight to be a percentage of the final pose. The Local Weight setting lets you control individual bones and limbs differently from the global animation layer.

FIGURE 39.10

If the Layer Manager contains multiple animation layers, you can blend between them using the Global Weight values.

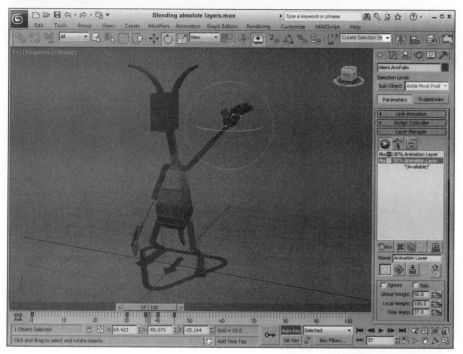

Another helpful tool as you begin to animate your rig is the Rig Coloring Mode option located to the right of the Set/Animation Mode toggle button. If you switch the Rig Coloring Mode to display Layer Colors, then the color of the rig matches the color of the animation layer; if two layers are blended together, then the color of the rig also is mixed. If a specific bone is given a different Local Weight, then that bone is colored the same as the animation layer that is controlling it.

Tip

If you plan to blend layers, setting each layer to use a primary color makes it easier to see where layers are blended when the Layer Colors option is enabled. ■

Clicking the Dope Sheet: Layer Ranges button opens the Dope Sheet with the ranges of the various animation layers displayed. This provides an easy way to modify the ranges for the different animation layers. You also can access the Curve Editor for each of the Global and Local Weights using the button to the right of the respective weight values.

You can use the Display Layer Transform Gizmo button for each layer. This creates a simple helper object that is linked to the character. It can be moved and rotated to control the entire rig. The gizmo is normally placed at floor level between the rig's feet, but if you hold down the Ctrl key while clicking this button, the gizmo is placed at the current bone; if you hold down the Alt key, the gizmo is placed at the world origin. This gizmo is available only for absolute animation layers.

Using adjustment animation layers

If you have your animation layers working just right with the motion you like, but your animation needs a little more exaggeration or a hand needs to reach just a little farther to grab a doorknob, then you can return to the base absolute layer and make the change, or you can apply an adjustment layer.

There are two different adjustment layer types: local and world. The difference is in how they are affected by the previous animation layer. Local adjustment layers add the adjustment layers changes onto the above layer's motion, so if a local adjustment layer has a hand reach forward a little more, the motion is added to the existing motion.

World adjustment layers work in world space and cause the hand to reach to a specific location in the world. This still blends with the previous layer's motion, but it also moves the selected object to a global position.

Creating a walk cycle with a CAT motion layer

Keyframing absolute animation layers is okay, but it can be tedious. The CAT Motion layer is where the fun really begins. Adding a CAT Motion layer to the list automatically applies a walk cycle to the rig. This is done without having to create any keys; just press the Play button, and you see the default walk cycle.

When a CAT Motion layer is selected in the Layer Manager rollout, the CAT Motion Editor button appears to the right of the layer color swatch. This button opens the CAT Motion dialog box, shown in Figure 39.11. Using this dialog box, you can adjust the parameters of the walk cycle.

FIGURE 39.11

The CAT Motion dialog box lets you alter the walk cycle parameters.

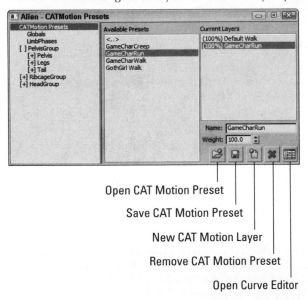

Open CAT Motion Preset

Save CAT Motion Preset

New CAT Motion Layer

Remove CAT Motion Preset

Open Curve Editor

The first panel of the CAT Motion dialog box presents a list of available presets. The buttons at the lower-right corner of the dialog box let you open saved presets. You also can name and save custom presets. The CAT Motion dialog box has its own set of animation layers that are listed in the rightmost pane. Double-clicking a preset opens a simple dialog box with options to load the preset into a new layer or into the existing layer.

The layers work just like those in the Layer Manager rollout with weights assigned to each layer. For example, if you add the default walk cycle and then a new run cycle set to 50 percent, the run cycle is blended with the walk cycle, creating a slower run cycle. You also can open the Curve Editor to change the shape of the weight curves.

Setting global parameters

Clicking the Globals option in the leftmost pane of the CAT Motion dialog box opens a panel of global CAT motion parameters, shown in Figure 39.12. At the top of the global parameters are settings for changing the start and end frame of the walk cycle. Note that these settings are different from the start and end time settings in the Time Configuration dialog box, and they affect only the CAT rig motion.

FIGURE 39.12

The Globals panel of the CAT Motion dialog box lets you change the walk tempo, speed, and direction.

Curve Editor

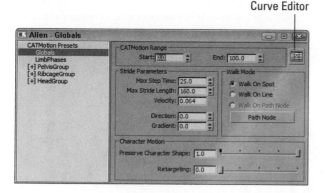

The Max Step Time defines how quickly each step is taken. Low values make the character walk crazy fast, and higher values make a slower, more casual walk. The Max Stride Length sets the distance of each step. These two values together determine the Velocity, but you can't alter the Velocity setting.

The character by default is pointing in the direction indicated on the CAT Parent object, but you can alter the direction that the character is walking by altering the Direction value. A setting of 0 makes the character walk in the direction he is pointing, a value of 90 makes the character shuffle to his right, a value of 180 makes the character walk backward, and a value of 270 makes the character shuffle to the left. The Gradient setting controls the angle that the character is pointing. Negative values make the character point forward as if walking down a hill, and large, positive values make the character walk as if going up a hill.

Walking along a path

The default is to have the character walk in place, but if you select the Walk On Line option, then the character walks forward in a straight line. When the range of frames is reached, the character returns to its starting position and walks the line again. If the Direction value is changed, the character moves straight in the specified direction.

If you click the Path Node button, you can choose a scene object that the character will follow. For example, if you make the Path Node a dummy object, then the character is positioned and walks on top of the dummy object. You can then animate the movement of the dummy object in the scene, and the character follows it.

To make the character walk along a path, you simply need to create a path using the Line tool. Then select the dummy object and use the Animation ⇨ Path Constraint menu to attach the dummy object to the path. If you enable the Follow option in the Motion panel after making the link, the character turns to stay on the path.

When having a character follow a path with tight corners, the character may become distorted as it attempts to stay on the path. The Preserve Character Shape setting lets you minimize the distortion. A setting of 0 allows the distortion caused by tight corners.

Controlling footsteps and limbs

The Limb Phases panel of the CAT Motion dialog box, shown in Figure 39.13, controls the placement of footsteps and the swing of each leg and arm. The footprints that appear when a character is walking are tied to the rig, so altering the footsteps also alters the rig. If the footsteps don't appear when you select a walk cycle, you can use the Create button to make them appear. You also can delete them with the Delete button. If you move or rotate any of the footsteps, you can use the Reset button to remove any changes for All footsteps or for just the selected footsteps.

FIGURE 39.13

The Limb Phases panel lets you set how the arms and legs swing relative to each other.

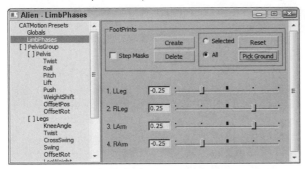

The sliders for each leg and arm at the bottom of the Limb Phases panel let you alter how the arms and legs swing relative to each other. By default, the opposite leg and arm swing together, but you can alter these sliders to give the walk cycle a different look.

Matching footsteps to the ground

After footsteps appear, you can select them and use the Pick Ground button. This lets you select a ground plane object. This ground object needs to be a single object, but once selected, the footsteps are moved vertically to align to the ground plane, causing the character to walk along the surface of the ground.

Controlling secondary motions

The remaining panels in the CAT Motion dialog box are used to control the motions of the other rig groups, such as the pelvis, head, and ribcage. If you open the Pelvis group, you see several parameters that you can access including Twist, Roll, Pitch, Lift, Push, Weight Shift, and positional and rotation offsets. Each of these parameters shows an animation curve that you can use to exaggerate or calm the selected motion, such as the Twist parameter shown in Figure 39.14.

FIGURE 39.14

Using the parameter curves in the CAT Motion dialog box, you can control motions such as the twisting of the pelvis.

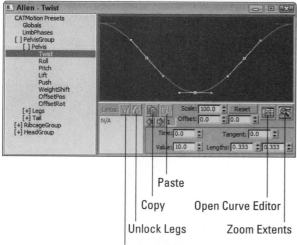

Paste

Copy   Open Curve Editor

Unlock Legs   Zoom Extents

Toggle Independent Leg Settings

Tutorial: Animating a character walking along a path

In this example, you take the default alien character rig and make it walk along a drawn path.

To animate a character walking along a path, follow these steps:

1. Open the Wandering alien.max file from the Chap 39 directory on the CD. This file includes the default CAT alien rig and a random path.

2. With the alien rig's parent object selected, open the Motion panel and add a CAT Motion animation layer to the Layer Manager list. Then click the Animation Mode button. If you click the Play button, you can see the alien walk in place.

3. Click the Helpers category, and create a dummy object.

4. Select any part of the rig again, and click the CAT Motion Editor button in the Motion panel. Select the Globals panel, and click the Path Node button. Then select the dummy object in the scene.

5. With the dummy object selected, move and rotate the character so it's facing the starting end of the path. Then select the Animation ⇨ Path Constraint menu, and click the path. Open the Motion panel, and enable the Follow option in the Path Parameters rollout. You need to rotate the dummy object to align the character with the path again.

6. Click the Play button; the character walks along the path, and footsteps mark each step the character takes.

7. Select the File ⇨ Import ⇨ Merge menu command, and merge the object in the Hilly surface. max file into the current scene. This curvy surface appears as a ground plane. Select the character rig and in the Limb Phases panel of the CAT Motion dialog box, click the Pick Ground button and select the ground plane. The footsteps rise to match the ground plane, as shown in Figure 39.15.

FIGURE 39.15

Constraining the path node to a path makes the character walk along the path.

Working with Muscles

Bones are great for controlling rigid motion, but they don't help much when it comes to creating muscle bulges or the fluid motion of skin moving over muscles. CAT has solutions for these cases also in the form of two different types of muscles. Muscle strands are composed of a set of spheres that squash and stretch when their end points are linked to bones. The second muscle type is a series of rectangular panels that flow and move together.

Both muscle strands and CAT muscle objects are created using their respective buttons in the CAT Objects subcategory of the Helpers panel in the Command Panel.

Note

Generally, muscle strands are used on the arms and legs, and CAT muscles are used for the abdomen, chest, and shoulders. ■

Using muscle strands

Muscle strand objects are created by clicking in the viewport to place control handles. A single muscle strand has four unique handles, divided into two sets. Click and drag to create the first set and repeat to create the second set. The first and last handles mark the end points of the muscle strand, and the middle two handles can be moved to affect the position of the center line of the muscle. The handles can be made visible or hidden, or you can change their size using the settings in the Muscle Strand rollout.

Using the options in the Muscle Strand rollout, you can set the muscle to replace an existing bone in the rig with the Bones option, or you can include the muscle strand with the bone and use the Skin Wrap modifier to drape the skin mesh over the muscle with the Mesh option.

The Muscle Strand rollout also includes buttons for copying and pasting properties between muscles and for setting the muscle as a left, middle, or right side of the body. You also can set a mirror axis for the muscle.

The shape of the muscle is determined by the number of spheres that gradually get larger and then smaller again as you traverse the muscle length. You can change the number of spheres included in the muscle or set the size of each individual muscle sphere. The Show Profile Curve button displays the profile curve for the muscle in a window that you can edit.

Once the muscle is in place, you can link its end points to the nearby bones using the standard Link tool found on the main toolbar. Within linked end points, the muscle compresses and stretches as the bones are moved. You also can enable the Squash/Stretch feature in the Muscle Strand rollout to add this behavior to the muscle. The midpoint for the squash and stretch is set using the Set Relaxed State button.

Figure 39.16 shows the Ape rig preset with two muscle strands inserts for the rig's upper arm bones. Notice how the right arm bulges when the forearm is brought forward.

FIGURE 39.16

Muscle strands provide the bulging effect of muscles.

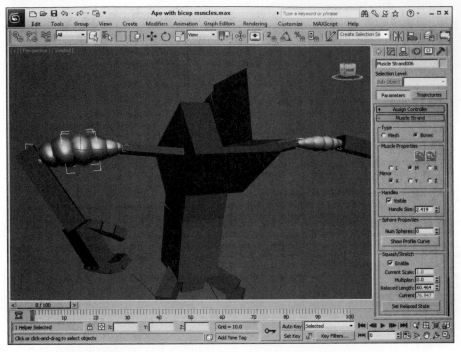

Using CAT muscles

CAT muscle objects are composed of sheets of rectangles that move and slide relative to each other. They are created by dragging out a rectangle area much like a plane object. Each corner of the CAT muscle has a handle, and several interior handles are also available for deforming the muscle. You can hide the corner handles or the middle handles, or you can set their size using the settings in the Command Panel.

Just like muscle strands, you can specify that the CAT muscles are either Bones or Mesh objects. The resolution of the muscle plane is set using the U and V Segs, which can be increased for greater resolution. Once the CAT muscle is in place, you can link its corners to the rig bones, and the plane deforms as the attached bones are moved.

CAT muscles include another really nice feature: collision detection. This lets you place objects underneath the CAT muscle and add them to a list of objects for collision detection. The result is that the muscle is molded to fit the underlying object. The collision object can be any standard object or even a muscle strand object. Figure 39.17 shows a CAT muscle that is being molded by an elongated sphere. For each collision object, you also can set the Hardness and Distortion values.

FIGURE 39.17

FIGURE 39.17

CAT muscles provide a way to simulate flatter rows of muscles.

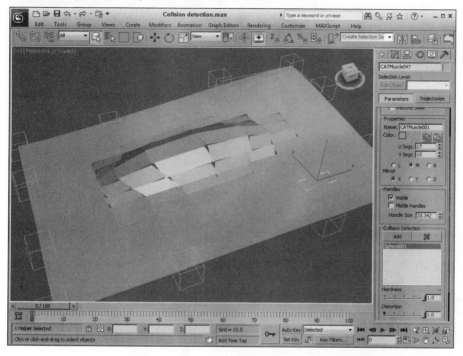

Tutorial: Adding muscles to a rig

In this example, you take the default human character rig and add a CAT muscle to the front for the chest and stomach definition.

To add muscles to a rig, follow these steps:

1. Open the Human char with muscles.max file from the Chap 39 directory on the CD. This file includes the default CAT human rig.

2. Open the Create panel and choose the Helpers category and the CAT Objects subcategory. Click the CAT Muscle button and drag in the Front viewport to create a CAT muscle that runs from the collar bone to the pelvis on the left side. Then move the muscle plane into position in front of the ribcage bone.

3. Open the Modify panel and set the U and V Segs values to 15. Select and move the outer corners and their adjacent handles to make the muscles bend around the side of the body.

4. Select Create ⇨ Extended Primitives ⇨ Chamfer Box menu and drag to create a box with rounded corners. Then create and elongate a sphere object with the Create ⇨ Standard Primitives ⇨ Sphere menu. Position the rounded box at the location of the pectoral muscle. Position and clone the sphere to show three rows of stomach muscles.

5. Select the CAT muscle object, and in the Modify panel click the Add button for the Collision Detection section, and select the rounded box and sphere objects. Then move the collision objects to create the desired muscle look in the CAT muscle.

6. Select each of the collision objects, right-click, and choose the Hide Selected option from the pop-up quadmenu.

Figure 39.18 shows the CAT muscle with some deformation for the pec and stomach muscles.

FIGURE 39.18

The CAT muscles can be used to create muscle deformations.

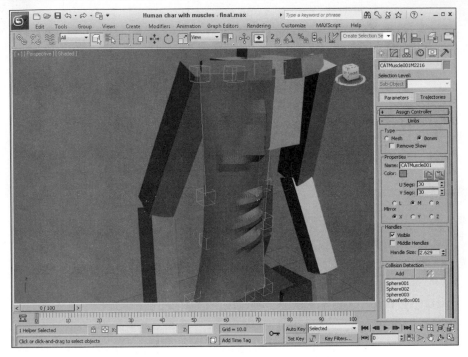

Summary

This chapter serves as an introduction to CAT and covers all aspects of working with CAT rigs, including its presets, custom rigs, and animation. The following topics were covered:

- Learning the basic workflow for creating characters
- Creating and editing CAT rigs
- Creating a custom CAT rig
- Animating CAT rigs
- Creating walk cycles with the CAT Motion dialog box
- Using muscle strands and muscle planes

Whether you're using a custom rig or a CAT rig, the next step is to begin the skinning process, which is covered next. Skinning surrounds the skeleton with a mesh skin and matches the way the skin aligns and moves with the underlying rig.

Skinning Characters

In the taxidermy world, skinning an animal usually involves removing its skin, but in the Max world, skinning a character involves adding a skin mesh to a group of controlling bones. Skinning a character also involves defining how the skin deforms as the bones are moved.

A character skin created in Max can be any type of object and is attached to a biped or a bones skeleton using the Skin modifier. The Skin modifier isn't alone. Max includes other modifiers like the Skin Wrap and Skin Morph modifiers that make your skin portable. This chapter covers how the various Skin modifiers are attached to a skeleton and used to aid in animating your character.

Understanding Your Character

What are the main aspects of your character? Is it strong and upright, or does it hunch over and move with slow, twisted jerks? Before you begin modeling a character, you need to understand the character. It is helpful to sketch the character before you begin. This step gives you a design that you can return to as needed.

Tip

The sketched design also can be loaded and planar mapped to a plane object to provide a guide to modeling. ∎

You have an infinite number of reference characters available to you (just walk down a city street if you can't think of anything new). If you don't know where to start, then try starting with a human figure. The nice thing about modeling a human is that an example is close by (try looking in the mirror).

We all know the basic structure of humans: two arms, two legs, one head, and no tail. If your character is human, then starting with a human character and changing elements as needed is the easiest way to go. As you begin to model human figures, being familiar with anatomy is helpful. Understanding the structure of muscles and skeletal systems helps explain the funny bumps you see in your elbow and why muscles bulge in certain ways.

Tip
If you don't have the model physique, then a copy of Gray's Anatomy can help. With its detailed pictures of the underlying muscular and skeletal systems, you'll have all the details you need without having to pull your own skin back. ■

The curse and blessing of symmetry

The other benefit of the human body is that it is symmetrical. You can use this to your benefit as you build your characters, but be aware that unless you're creating a band of killer robots, it is often the imperfections in the characters that give them, well, character. Positioning an eye a little off normal might give your character that menacing look you need.

Dealing with details

When you start to model a human figure, you quickly realize that the body includes lots of detail, but before you start naming an object "toenail lint on left foot," look for details you won't need. For example, modeling toes is pointless if your character will be wearing shoes and won't be taking them off. (In fact, I think shoes were invented so that animators wouldn't have to model toes.)

At the same time, details in the right places add to your character. Look for the right details to help give your character life—a pirate with an earring, a clown with a big, red nose, a tiger with claws, a robot with rivets, and so on.

Figure 40.1 shows two good examples. The ninja warrior on the left doesn't need the details of a mouth or teeth because they are hidden behind his mask. In fact, if you were to remove his mask, it would leave a large gaping hole. The Greek woman statue model on the right includes many necessary details including fingernails, toes, a bellybutton, and, uh, well, uh, other details.

Note
You can actually find these two character models on the CD at the back of the book, compliments of Viewpoint Datalabs. ■

FIGURE 40.1

These two characters have details modeled where needed.

Animated Skin Modifiers

Of all the animation modifiers, several specifically are used to deal with skin. The Skin modifier is a key modifier for enabling character animation. The Skin Morph modifier lets you deform a skin object and create a morph target. It is designed to help fix problem areas, such as shoulders and hips, that have trouble with the standard Skin modifier. The Skin Wrap offers a way to animate a low-res proxy and then apply the same animation to a high-res wrapped object.

Note

A Physique modifier left over from the Character Studio suite of tools has been integrated into Max. The Physique modifier also is used to bind skin meshes to skeletons, but the Skin modifier is easier to use and more powerful. The Physique modifier remains for backward compatibility. ∎

Understanding the skinning process

Unless you like animating using only a skeleton or a biped by itself, a bones system will have a skin attached to it. Any mesh can be made into a skin using the Skin modifier. The Skin modifier is used to bind a skin mesh to a bones system and to define the associations between the skin vertices and the bones. The first step is to bind the skin mesh to the skeleton object. With a skin attached to a bones system, you can move the bones system and the skin follows, but just how well it follows the skeleton's motion depends on a process called skinning.

Cross-Reference

Creating a bones system is covered in more detail in Chapter 37, "Understanding Rigging, Kinematics, and Working with Bones." Bipeds are covered in Chapter 39, "Animating Characters with CAT." ∎

Skinning is where you tell which parts of the skin mesh to move with which bones. Obviously, you'd want all the skin vertices in the hand to move with the hand bone, but the skin vertices around the waist and shoulders are trickier.

Each skin area that surrounds a bone gets encompassed by a capsule-shaped envelope. All vertices within this envelope move along with the bone. When two of these envelopes overlap, their surfaces blend together like skin around a bone joint. Most of the skinning process involves getting the skin vertices into the right envelope. The Skin modifier includes several tools to help make this easier, including the Skin Weight table and a painting weights feature.

Binding to a skeleton

After you have both a skeleton and a skin mesh, you need to bind the skin to the skeleton before you can edit the influence envelopes. The binding process is fairly easy: Simply select the skin mesh, and apply the Skin modifier to it using the Modifiers ⇨ Animation ⇨ Skin menu command.

Tip

Before binding a skeleton to a skin mesh, take some time to match the size and dimensions of the bones close to the skin mesh. The skin mesh is bound to the skeleton, and the envelopes are created automatically. If the bones match the skin, then the new envelopes are pretty close to what they need to be. ∎

In the Parameters rollout, click the Add button above the bones list. This opens a Select Bones dialog box where you can select the bones to use to animate this skin. The selected bones appear in the bones list. The text field directly under the bones list lets you locate specific bones in the list by typing the name. Only one bone at a time may be selected from the list. The Remove button removes the selected bone from the bone list.

Tutorial: Attaching skin to a CAT rig

For human figures, using a biped skeleton saves lots of time. For this example, because he's human in form, you'll bind a biped skeleton to the Future man model.

To bind the skin of a model to a biped skeleton, follow these steps:

1. Open the Marvin Moose CAT rig - final.max file from the Chap 40 directory on the CD.

   This file includes the CAT rig built in Chapter 39 for the Marvin Moose character.

2. With the CAT rig aligned to the skin mesh, select Unfreeze All from the right-click quadmenu and disable the See-Through option in the Object Properties dialog box. Select the moose model, and choose Modifiers ➪ Animation Modifiers ➪ Skin to apply the Skin modifier.

3. In the Parameters rollout, click the Add button. The Select Bones dialog box opens. Click the All button to select all the bones, and click Select. Don't include the Footsteps, Character001, or the Leg Platform objects.

4. In the Parameters rollout, select each of the bones in the list and click the Edit Envelopes button. Zoom in on the highlighted bone (which is the left shin bone), select the cross-section handles for this bone, and set the Radius values to **0.15** near the body and **0.1** for the other end. Figure 40.2 shows the moose skin with all the CAT rig bones added.

FIGURE 40.2

Bone references are added to the skin modifier.

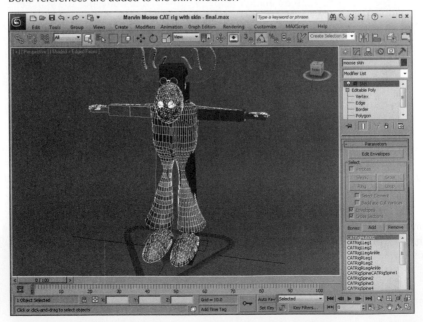

After the Skin modifier is applied and bound to the skin mesh, every bone includes an area of influence called an envelope that defines the skin vertices that it controls. If any of the skin mesh vertices
are outside of the bone's envelope or are included in an envelope for the wrong bone, then the vertices are left behind when the bone is moved. This causes an odd stretching of the skin that is easy to
identify.

To check the envelopes, select and rotate several of the skeleton's key bones. If any envelope problems exist, they are easy to spot, as shown in Figure 40.3. The incorrect stretching of the vertices for
the boot simply means that the envelopes need to be adjusted.

FIGURE 40.3

If the envelopes are off for any of the skin vertices, the skin stretches incorrectly.

Editing envelopes

When the Skin modifier is selected, the Parameters rollout includes an Edit Envelopes button that
places you in a special mode that lets you edit the envelope for the selected bone in the bone list. This
mode is also enabled by selecting the Envelope subobject under the Skin modifier at the top of the
Modifier Stack.

When the Edit Envelopes mode is enabled, the entire skin mesh is colored with a gradient of colors to
visually show the influence of the envelope. Areas of red are completely inside the envelope's influence, areas of green are somewhat affected by the bone, and areas of gray are completely outside the
envelope's influence.

Figure 40.4 shows a simple loft object surrounding three bone objects with a Skin modifier applied. The Add Bone button was used to include the three bones within the Skin modifier list. The skin has been set to See Through in the Properties dialog box, so the bones are visible. The first bone was selected in the bone list, and the Edit Envelope button was clicked, revealing the envelope for the first bone.

FIGURE 40.4

Envelopes define which Skin vertices move with the underlying bone.

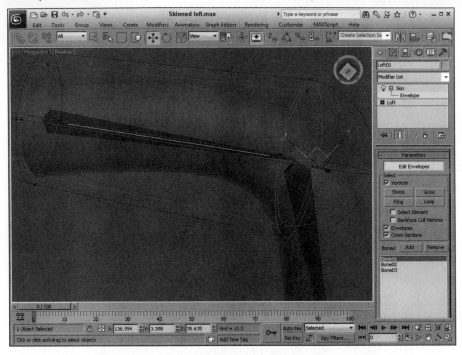

An envelope consists of two capsule-shaped volumes within each other called the Inner and Outer Envelopes. Any vertices within the inner envelope are controlled exclusively by that bone. Any vertices positioned between the inner and outer envelopes are controlled by a falloff where the influence is shared between bones.

At either end of these envelopes are four small handles that can be dragged to change the cross-section radius. The cross-section area changes to pink when selected. The radius of the selected cross section is displayed in the Radius field within the Envelope Properties section of the Parameters rollout. The Squash value determines the amount of squash applied to the object for bones that can stretch. You can change an envelope's size by changing its Radius value or by dragging the cross-section handles. Within the Select section of the Parameters rollout, you can choose to select and edit Vertices, Envelopes, and/or Cross Sections. If you choose the Vertices option, selected vertices are shown as small squares, and the Shrink, Grow, Ring, and Loop buttons become active. These buttons allow you to select a desired set of vertices easily. If the Select Element option is enabled, then all vertices in the element are selected, and the Backface Cull Vertices option prevents vertices on the backside of the object from being selected.

If a cross section is selected, you can add a different cross-section shape using the Add button. This button lets you select a cross-section shape within the viewports. The Remove Cross Section button removes an added cross section from the envelope.

Note

The orientation of the envelope spline is set by the longest dimension of the bone. This works well for arm and leg bones, but the pelvis or clavicle may end up with the wrong orientation. ■

The Envelope Properties section of the Parameters rollout (just below the Radius and Squash buttons) includes five icon buttons, shown in Table 40.1. The first toggles between Absolute and Relative. All vertices that fall within the outer envelope are fully weighted when the Absolute toggle is set, but only those within both envelopes are fully weighted when the Relative toggle is selected.

TABLE 40.1

Envelope Properties

Button	Name	Description
A	Absolute/Relative	Toggles between Absolute and Relative
	Envelope Visibility	Makes envelopes remain visible when another bone is selected
	Falloff Linear, Falloff Sinual, Falloff Fast Out, Falloff Slow Out	Sets Falloff curve shape
	Copy Envelope	Copies envelope settings to a temporary buffer
	Paste Envelope, Paste to All Bones, Paste to Multiple Bones	Pastes envelope settings to the selected bone, to all bones, or to multiple bones chosen from a dialog box

The second icon button enables envelopes to be visible even when not selected. This helps you see how adjacent bones overlap. The third icon button sets the Falloff curve for the envelopes. The options within this flyout are Linear, Sinual, Fast Out, and Slow Out. The last two icon buttons can be used to Copy and Paste envelope settings to other bones. The flyout options for the Paste button include Paste (to a single bone), Paste to All Bones, and Paste to Multiple Bones (which opens a selection dialog box).

Working with weights

For a selection of vertices, you can set its influence value (called its Weight value) between 0 for no influence and 1.0 for maximum influence. This provides a way to blend the motion of vertices between two or more bones. For example, the vertices on the top of a character's shoulder could have a weight value of 1.0 for the shoulder bone, a weight value of 0.5 for the upper arm bone, and a weight value of 0 for all other bones. This lets the shoulder skin area move completely when the shoulder bone moves and only halfway when the upper arm moves.

Note

The shading in the viewport changes as vertices are weighted between 0 and 1. Weight values around 0.125 are colored blue, weight values around 0.25 are colored green, weight values around 0.5 are colored yellow, and weight values around 0.75 are colored orange. ∎

The Absolute Effect field lets you specify a weight value for the selected vertices. The Rigid option makes the selected vertices move only with a single bone. The Rigid Handles causes the handles of the selected vertices for a patch object to move only with a single bone. This is important if the character is wearing a hard item such as armor plates. By enabling this option, you can be sure that the armor plate doesn't deform. The Normalize option requires that all the weights assigned to the selected vertices add up to 1.0.

The other buttons found in the Weight Properties section of the Parameters rollout are defined in Table 40.2. Include Vertices and Exclude Vertices buttons let you remove the selected vertices from those being affected by the selected bone. The Select Exclude Verts button selects all excluded vertices.

TABLE 40.2

Envelope Properties

Button	Name	Description
	Exclude Selected Vertices	Excludes the selected vertices from the influence of the current bone.
	Include Selected Vertices	Includes all selected vertices in the bone's influence.
	Select Excluded Vertices	Selects all excluded vertices.
	Bake Selected Verts	Bakes the vertex weights into the model so they aren't changed with the envelope. Baked vertices can be changed using the Weight Table or the Absolute Effect value.
	Weight Tool	Opens the Weight Tool interface.

Using the Weight Tool

The Weight Tool button in the Parameters rollout opens the Weight Tool dialog box, shown in Figure 40.5. The Shrink, Grow, Ring, and Loop buttons work the same as those in the Select section, and they let you quickly select precise groups of vertices. The value buttons on the second row allow you to change weight values with a click of the button or by adding or subtracting from the current value.

The Copy, Paste, and Paste Position buttons let you copy weights between vertices quickly. The Paste Position button pastes the given weight to the surrounding vertices based on the Tolerance value. The Blend button quickly blends all the surrounding vertices from the current weight value to 0, creating a smooth blend weight. The Weight Tool dialog box also lists the number of vertices in the copy buffer and currently selected. The list at the bottom of the dialog box lists the weight and bone for the selected vertices.

FIGURE 40.5

The Weight Tool dialog box includes buttons for quickly altering weight values and for blending the weights of adjacent vertices.

Using the Weight Table

The Weight Table button opens the Weight Table interface, shown in Figure 40.6. This table displays all the vertices for the skinned object by ID in a column on the left side of the interface. All bones are listed in a row along the top. For each vertex and bone, you can set a weight.

FIGURE 40.6

The Weight Table lets you specify weight values for each vertex and for each bone.

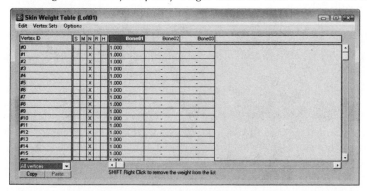

The Edit menu includes commands to Copy and Paste weights. It also includes commands to Select All, Invert, and None. A selection of vertices can be combined into a Vertex Set and named. The Vertex Sets menu lets you create and delete these sets.

The Options menu lets you flip the interface so that bones are displayed in the first column and the vertex IDs are along the top row. The Update On Mouse Up option limits the updates until the mouse is released. Several options for showing and hiding interface elements are included. The Show

Affected Bones option lists only the bones that are affected. The Show Attributes option displays a column of attributes labeled S, M, N, R, and H. The Show Exclusions option makes a check box available in each cell. When checked, the vertex is excluded. The Show Global option makes a drop-down list available that enables you to set an attribute for all vertices. The Show Locks option (like the Show Exclusions option) makes a check box available for each cell. Enabling this check box (the left one) locks the weight so it can't change. The Set Sets UI makes available two buttons for creating and deleting vertex sets.

The S attribute is marked if a vertex is selected, the M attribute marks a vertex weight that has been modified, the N attribute marks a normalized weight, the R attribute marks rigid vertices, and an H attribute marks a vertex with rigid handles.

To set a weight, just locate the vertex for the bone, click in the cell, and type the new value. If you click a cell and drag to the left or right, the weight value changes. Weight values can be dragged between cells. Right-clicking a cell sets its value to 0, and right-clicking with the Ctrl key held down sets its value to 1.0.

After the vertex weights are set, you can click the Bake Selected Vertices to lock down the weight values. Changes to envelopes do not affect baked vertices.

Painting weights

Using the Paint Weights button, you can paint with a brush over the surface of the skin object. The Paint Strength value sets the value of each brush stroke. This value can be positive (up to 1.0) for vertices that will move with the bone or negative (to –1.0) for vertices that will not move with the bone.

To the right of the Paint Weights button is the Painter Options button (it has three dots on it), which opens the Painter Options dialog box.

Cross-Reference
The Painter Options dialog box also is used by the Vertex Paint modifier and the Paint Deformation tool. It is described in detail in Chapter 13, "Modeling with Polygons." ■

Tutorial: Applying skin weights

In this example, you change the skin weights of the future man character in an attempt to fix the problem you saw with his boots.

To apply the skin weights to a character, follow these steps:

1. Open the Future man with skin final.max file from the Chap 40 directory on the CD.
2. With the mesh skin selected, open the Modify panel and choose the Bip01 L Foot bone in the bone list. Then click the Edit Envelopes button at the top of the Parameters rollout. This displays the envelopes around the foot object. Zoom in on the foot object, and change the display option to Realistic or press the F3 key, so you can see the weight shading.
3. Make sure the Cross Sections option in the Select section of the Parameters rollout is selected. Then select the cross-section handles on the outer envelope and pull them in toward the foot. Rotate the side to make sure that the toe and heel of the boot are still covered.
4. Click the Vertices option in the Parameters rollout, and disable the Backface Cull Vertices option. Drag over all the vertices that are contained in the lower part of the boot, and enable the Rigid option. Then select the vertices above the boot in the shin. You can use the Loop button to select all vertices about the upper part of the boot and press and hold the Alt key to remove any vertices that are part of the lower boot.

5. In the Weight Properties section of the Parameters rollout, click the Weight Tool button. In the Weight Tool dialog box, click the .25 button. This changes the weight of the selected vertices. Then click the Blend button to smooth the transition areas.

6. Click the Edit Envelopes button to exit Edit Envelopes mode. Then select and rotate the upper leg to see whether the problem has been fixed. As I rotated my model, I noticed that some vertices on the back of the boot were left behind, which means that they aren't being influenced by the foot bone.

Caution

Be sure to undo the upper leg rotation before making changes to the envelopes, or the envelopes will move along with the rotation. ■

7. Enter Edit Envelopes mode again, and click the Paint Weights button. The cursor changes to a round brush. Click the Brush Options button (which is next to the Paint Weights button with three dots). This opens the Brush Options dialog box. Set the Max Strength value to **1.0**, and close the dialog box. Then paint in the viewport over the vertices on the back of the boot heel, including those areas that aren't shaded red. Figure 40.7 shows the correct boot with its envelopes.

8. Exit Edit Envelopes mode again, and check the changes by rotating the upper leg bone.

FIGURE 40.7

Vertices' weights can be fixed with the Weight Tool and by Painting Weights.

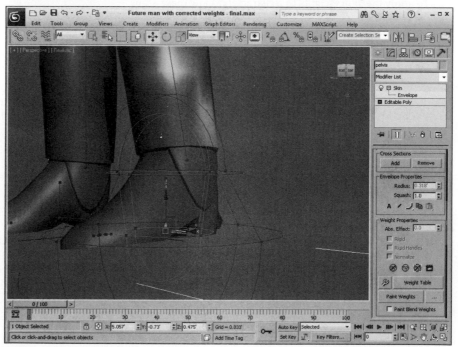

Mirror settings

Most characters have a natural symmetry, and you can use this symmetry to mirror envelopes and vertex weights between different sides of a model. You can use this feature by clicking the Mirror Mode button in the Mirror Parameters rollout. This button is active only when the Edit Envelope button is active.

In Mirror Mode, you see an orange plane gizmo that marks the symmetrical line for the model. You can move and orient this plane using the Mirror Offset and Mirror Plane controls. Once oriented, Max computes the matching vertices based on the volumes from the mirror plane. All vertices on one half of the character appear blue, and all the matching vertices appear green. All vertices that cannot be matched appear red.

If you drag over bones or vertices in the viewports, you can select them. Clicking the Mirror Paste button pastes the envelopes and vertex weights of the selected vertices to their matches. Or you can select the Paste Green to Blue Bones button or one of its neighbors to copy all the green bones or vertices to their matches, or vice versa.

The Display Projection drop-down list projects the position of the selected vertices onto the Mirror Plane so you can compare their locations relative to each other. With lots of vertices in your skin, you want to enable the Manual Update, or the viewport refreshes become slow.

Tutorial: Mirroring skin weights

Now that you have spent the time correcting the skin weights for the left boot, you use the Mirror Weights feature to apply the same weights to the opposite foot.

To apply the skin weights to a character, follow these steps:

1. Open the Future man with corrected weights - final.max file from the Chap 40 directory on the CD.
2. With envelope mode turned on, select the Bip01 L Foot bone from the list in the Parameters rollout, and click the Mirror Mode button in the Mirror Parameters rollout. An orange gizmo is added to the viewport that divides the model, as shown in Figure 40.8.
3. Drag over all the vertices that make up the left boot, and then click the Paste Blue to Green Verts button. All the vertex weights on the left side of the model are copied to the right side. The pasted vertices turn yellow once pasted.

Display and Advanced settings

The Display rollout controls which features are visible within the viewports. Options include Show Colored Vertices, Show Colored Faces, Color All Weights, Show All Envelopes, Show All Vertices, Show All Gizmos, Show No Envelopes, Show Hidden Vertices, Draw On Top Cross Sections, and Draw On Top Envelopes.

With these display options, you can turn on and off the weight color shading on vertices and faces. You can also select to show all envelopes, vertices, and gizmos. The Color All Weights option is unique. It assigns every bone a different color and shows how the weights blend together between bones.

FIGURE 40.8

In Mirror mode, matched bones and vertices appear green and blue.

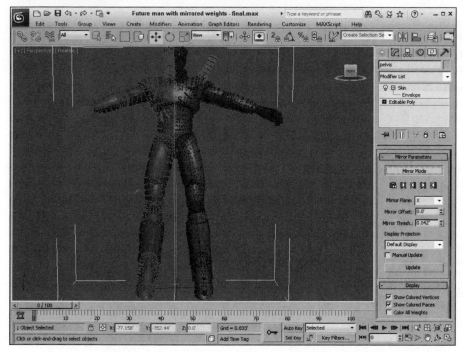

The Advanced Parameters rollout includes an option to Back Transform Vertices. This option avoids applying transform keys to the skin because the bones control the motion. The Rigid Vertices and Rigid Patch Handles options set the vertices so that they are controlled by only one bone. This rollout also includes buttons to Reset Selected Vertices, Reset Selected Bones, and Reset All Bones. This is handy if you really mess up a skinning job, because it gives you a chance to start over. It also includes buttons for saving and loading envelopes. The envelopes are saved as files with the .env extension.

The Animatable Envelopes option lets you create keys for envelopes. Weight All Vertices is a useful option that automatically applies a weight to the nearest bone of all vertices that have no weight. The Remove Zero Weights button removes the vertex weight of any vertex that has a value lower than the Zero Limit. This can be used to remove lots of unnecessary data from your model if you need to put it on a diet.

Using deformers

Below the Advanced Parameters rollout is the Gizmos rollout. You use this rollout to apply deformers to selected skin object vertices. Three deformers are available in the Gizmos rollout: a Joint Angle Deformer, a Bulge Angle Deformer, and a Morph Angle Deformer.

Each of these deformers is unique. They include the following features:

- **Joint Angle Deformer:** Deforms the vertices around the joint between two bones where the skin can bunch up and cause problems. This deformer moves vertices on both the parent and child bones.
- **Bulge Angle Deformer:** Moves vertices away from the bone to simulate a bulging muscle. This deformer works only on the parent bone.
- **Morph Angle Deformer:** Can be used on vertices for both the parent and child bones to move the vertices to a morph position.

All deformers added to a skin object are listed in the Gizmo rollout. You can add deformers to and remove deformers from this list using the Add and Remove Gizmo buttons. You can also Copy and Paste the deformers to other sets of vertices. Before a deformer gizmo can be applied, you need to select vertices within the skin object. To select vertices, enable the Vertices check box of the Parameters rollout and drag over the vertices in the viewport to select the vertices.

The parameters for the deformer selected in the Gizmo rollout's list appear when the deformer is selected in the Deformer Parameters rollout. This rollout lists the Parent and Child bones for the selected vertices and the Angle between them. This rollout changes depending on the type of deformer selected.

For the Joint and Bulge Angle Deformers, a new rollout labeled Gizmo Parameters or Deformer Parameters appears. The Gizmo Parameters rollout includes buttons to edit the control Lattice and to edit the deformer Key Curves. The Edit Lattice button lets you move the lattice control points in the viewports. The Edit Angle Keys Curves opens a Graph window that displays the transformation curves for the deformation.

Using the Skin Wrap modifiers

If you've created a high-resolution model that you want to animate as a skin object, but the mesh is too complex to move around, then the Skin Wrap modifier might be just what you need. The Skin Wrap modifier may be applied to a high-resolution mesh, and with the Parameters rollout you can select a low-resolution control object. Any movements made by the low-resolution control object automatically are applied to high-resolution mesh.

Tip

Skin Wrap is also very useful for animating clothes on a character. ■

The Skin Wrap modifier has two available Deformation Engines: Face Deformation and Vertex Deformation. Each vertex contained with the control object acts as a control vertex. The Vertex Deformation option moves the vertices closest to each control vertex when the control vertex is moved, and the Face Deformation option moves the faces that are closest.

For each deformation mode, you can set a Falloff value, which moves vertices farther from the moved control vertex to a lesser extent to ensure a smoother surface. For the Vertex Deformation mode, you can also set a Distance Influence value and Face Limit values to increase the extent of influence for a control vertex.

The Reset button can be used to reset the control object to the high-resolution mesh object. This is useful if you need to realign the control object to the Skin Wrap object. When you're finished animating the control object, the Convert to Skin button may be used to transfer the animation keys to the high-resolution objects.

The Advanced Parameters rollout includes a button for mirroring the selected vertices to the opposite side of the control object.

The Modifiers menu also includes a Skin Wrap Patch modifier, which works the same as the Skin Wrap modifier, but it allows the control object to be a patch.

Tutorial: Making a simple squirt bottle walk

Creating a bones structure and applying a Skin modifier works well for characters with structure, but to animate the motion of an amorphous object such as a squirt bottle, the Skin Wrap modifier works much better than bones.

To animate a squirt bottle object walking using the Skin Wrap modifier, follow these steps:

1. Open the Walking squirt bottle.max file from the Chap 40 directory on the CD.

   This file includes a squirt bottle model with all its parts attached together. The file also includes a simple box object that is roughly the same shape as the squirt bottle. The box object has been animated walking forward.

2. With the squirt bottle object selected, choose the Modifiers ⇨ Animation ⇨ Skin Wrap menu command to apply the Skin Wrap modifier.

3. In the Parameters rollout, click the Add button and select the Box object. The Box object is added to the Skin Wrap list in the Parameters rollout.

4. Select the Box object and hide it in the scene.

5. Click the Play Animation button, and the hi-res bottle follows the same animation as the box object.

Figure 40.9 shows the squirt bottle as it moves through the scene.

FIGURE 40.9

Not all animated objects need a bone structure.

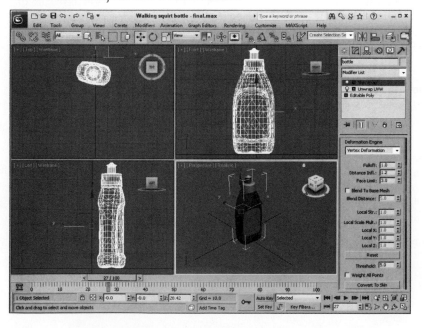

Using the Skin Morph modifier

Using the deformation options found in the Skin modifier, you can deform any part of the skin, but this feature relies on using gizmos found in an already complex envelope-editing mode. Skin Morph offers another way to deform a skin object using the underlying bones. The Skin Morph modifier is applied on top of a Skin modifier and lets you pick which bones to use in the deformation. For example, for bulging muscles, the forearm bone is rotated and should be added to the list in the Parameters rollout.

After selecting a bone from the Parameters rollout list, select the frame where the deformation is at a maximum. Then click the Create Morph button in the Local Properties rollout to create the morph target. Morph targets can be given names to make them easy to select later. The Edit button in the Local Properties rollout then lets you move the vertices for the deformation.

Tutorial: Bulging arm muscles

Perhaps the most common bulging deformation for characters is making the bicep muscle bulge as the forearm is raised. This effect can be simplified using the Skin Morph modifier.

To bulge an arm muscle using the Skin Morph modifier, follow these steps:

1. Open the Bulging bicep.max file from the Chap 40 directory on the CD.

   This file includes a rough arm model with a Skin modifier applied attached to a four-bone chain.

2. With the arm skin selected, choose the Modifiers ⇨ Animation ⇨ Skin Morph menu command to apply the Skin Morph modifier on top of the Skin modifier.

3. In the Parameters rollout, click the Add Bone button and select the forearm bone object.

   The bone object is added to the Skin Morph list in the Parameters rollout.

4. Select and rotate the forearm bone to the location where the deformation is at its maximum. Then select the bone object from the list in the Parameters rollout, and click the Create Morph button in the Local Properties rollout. In the Morph Name window name the morph **Bulging bicep**.

Tip
The forearm bone can be hard to see under the skin, but you can always select the bone using the Select by Name dialog box, which is opened by pressing H. ■

5. In the Local Properties rollout, click the Edit button. This enables the Points subobject mode. Then enable the Edge Limit option in the Selection rollout, so the vertices on the forearm aren't accidentally selected. Drag over the points on the front of the bicep muscle in the Left viewport, and enable the Use Soft Selection option in the Selection rollout. Set the Radius value to **0.5**, and scale the points to the right in the Left viewport to form a bulge. Click the Edit button again to exit Edit mode.

6. Select and rotate the forearm bone to see the bulging bicep muscle.

Figure 40.10 shows the arm muscle as it bulges along with the rotating forearm.

FIGURE 40.10

Using the Skin Morph, you can set a muscle to bulge as the forearm is rotated.

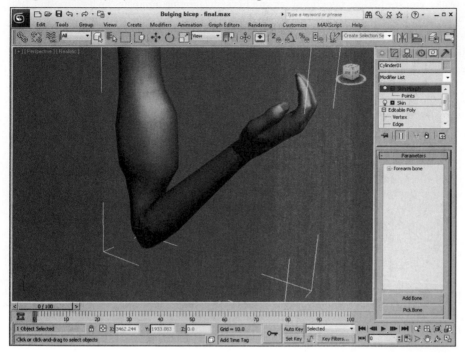

Using Character Animation Techniques

When it comes to character animation, several techniques can really help. Keeping these points in mind as you animate characters can make a difference:

- **Use Biped:** Manual rigging is useful for those cases where Biped won't work, but the tools and features found in Biped make it silly to look elsewhere for human characters.

- **Use dynamics:** Dynamic packages like reactor can provide incredibly realistic motion based on physical properties. Learning to use this powerful tool for even the most basic animation sequences is worth the effort.

- **Learn by example:** If you're working on a cartoon character, then by all means, watch cartoons. Traditional cartoons understand and invented the language of cartoon motion, including squash and stretch, exaggerated motion, or scaling eyes large to indicate surprise. If your character motion is more realistic, find the motion, videotape it, and watch it over and over to catch the subtle secondary motion.

- **Use background animations:** The Viewport Background can load animation clips, which can make positioning characters to match real motion easy. This is a poor man's motion capture system.

- **Include secondary motion:** The primary motion of a character is often the main focus, but you can enhance the animation by looking for secondary motion. For example, when a person walks, you see his legs take the steps and his arms moving opposite the legs' motion, but secondary motion includes his hair swishing back and forth and shoelaces flopping about.

- **Use the Flex modifier:** The Flex modifier gives soft bodies, such as tails, hair, ears, and clothing, the realistic secondary motion needed to make them believable.

- **Use the Morph modifier:** The Morph modifier can be used to morph a character between two poses or to morph its face between the different phonemes as the character talks.

- **Use IK:** The next chapter covers this in detail, but here's a quick tip: Having a character move by positioning its foot or hand is often much easier than pushing it into position.

- **Use the Spring Controller:** Another good way to get secondary motion is to use the Spring Controller. This controller works well with limbs.

- **Add randomness with the Noise Controller:** Often, perfect animation sequences don't look realistic, and using the Noise Controller can help to make a sequence look more realistic, whether the Noise Controller is applied to a walking sequence or to the subtle movement of the eyes.

- **Use manipulators:** Manipulators can be created and wired to give you control over the animation values of a single motion, such as opening and closing the character's eyes.

Summary

Characters are becoming more and more important in the Max world and can be saved as separate files just like Max scene files. Combining a detailed skin mesh with a skeletal biped lets you take advantage of Character Studio's unique animation features. This chapter covered the following topics:

- Designing your character before building
- Working with the Skin modifier
- Reusing animations with Skin Wrap
- Bulging muscles with Skin Morph

In Part X, "Dynamic Animation," you'll examine the dynamic animation features, starting with particle systems.

Part X

Dynamic Animation

Creating Particles and Particle Flow

E very object that you add to the scene slows down Max to a small
degree because Max needs to keep track of every object. If you add
thousands of objects to a scene, not only does Max slow down noticeably, but also the objects become difficult to identify. For example, if you had
to create thousands of simple snowflakes for a snowstorm scene, the system
would become unwieldy, and the number wouldn't get very high before you
ran out of memory.

Particle systems are specialized groups of objects that are managed as a single entity. By grouping all the particle objects into a single controllable system, you can easily make modifications to all the objects with a single
parameter. This chapter discusses using these special systems to produce
rain and snow effects, fireworks sparks, sparkling butterfly wings, and even
fire-breathing dragons.

Understanding the Various Particle Systems

A *particle* is a small, simple object that is duplicated en masse, like snow,
rain, or dust. Just as in real life, Max includes many different types of particles that can vary in size, shape, texture, color, and motion. These different
particle types are included in various particle systems.

When a particle system is created, all you can see in the viewport is a single
gizmo known as an *emitter icon*. An emitter icon is the object (typically a
gizmo, but it can be a scene object) where the particles originate. Selecting a
particle system gizmo makes the parameters for the particle system appear
in the Modify panel.

Max includes the following particle systems:

- **Particle Flow Source:** Particles that can be defined using the Particle Flow window and controlled using actions and events.
- **Spray:** Simulates drops of water. These drops can be Drops, Dots, or Ticks. The particles travel in a straight line from the emitter's surface after they are created.
- **Snow:** Similar to the Spray system, with the addition of some fields to make the particles Tumble as they fall. You also can render the particles as Six Pointed shapes that look like snowflakes.
- **Blizzard:** An advanced version of the Snow system that can use the same mesh object types as the Super Spray system. Binding the system to the Wind Space Warp can create storms.
- **PArray:** Can use a separate distribution object as the source for the particles. For this system, you can set the particle type to Fragment and bind it to the PBomb Space Warp to create explosions.
- **PCloud:** Confines all generated particles to a certain volume. A good use of this system is to reproduce bubbles in a glass or cars on the road.
- **Super Spray:** An advanced version of the Spray system that can use different mesh objects, closely packed particles called MetaParticles, or an instanced object as its particles. Super Spray is useful for rain and fountains. Binding it to the Path Follow Space Warp can create waterfalls.

Creating a Particle System

You can find all the various particle systems under the Create panel and also in the Create menu. To access these systems, click the Geometry category and select the Particle Systems subcategory from the drop-down list. All the particle systems then appear as buttons. Or you can select the Create ⇨ Particles menu.

With the Particle Systems subcategory selected, click the button for the type of particle system that you want to use, and then click in a viewport to create the particle system emitter icon. The emitter icon is a gizmo that looks like a plane or a sphere and that defines the location in the system where the particles all originate. Attached to the icon is a single line that indicates the direction in which the particles move when generated. This line points by default toward the construction grid's negative Z-axis when first created. Figure 41.1 shows the emitter icons for each particle system type including, from left to right, Particle Flow Source; Super Spray; Spray, Snow, and Blizzard (which all have the same emitter icon); PArray; and PCloud.

FIGURE 41.1

The emitter icons for each particle system type

You can transform these icons using the standard transform buttons on the main toolbar. Rotating an emitter changes the direction in which the particles initially move.

After an icon is created, you can set the number, shape, and size of the particles and define their motion in the Parameter rollouts. To apply a material to the particles, simply apply the material to the system's icon. This material is applied to all particles included in the system.

Note

Be aware that the particles are displayed as simple objects such as ticks or dots in the viewports. To see the actual resulting particles, you need to render the scene file. ■

You can set the parameters for the Max particle systems in the Create panel when they are first created or in the Modify panel at any time. The simpler systems, Spray and Snow, have a single Parameters rollout, but the advanced systems—Particle Flow Source, Super Spray, and Blizzard—include multiple Parameters rollouts. The PArray and PCloud systems have similar multiple rollouts, with a few subtle differences, and the Particle Flow system includes several rollouts, but most of the action is with the Particle Flow window. The following sections describe how to use these rollouts to set the parameters for the various particle systems.

Using the Spray and Snow Particle Systems

All I can say about the Spray and Snow particle systems is that when it rains, it pours. The Spray Parameters rollout includes values for the number of particles to be included in the system. These values can be different for the viewport and the renderer. By limiting the number of particles displayed in the viewport, you can make the viewport updates quicker. You also can specify the drop size, initial speed, and variation. The Variation value alters the spread of the particles' initial speed and direction. A Variation value of 0 makes the particles travel in a straight line away from the emitter.

Spray particles can be Drops, Dots, or Ticks, which affect how the particles look only in the viewport. Drops appear as streaks, Dots are simple points, and Ticks are small plus signs. You also can set how the particles are rendered—as Tetrahedron objects or as Facing objects (square faces that always face the viewer).

Note

The Facing option is visible only in the Perspective view but can be rendered using any viewport, including a camera viewport. ■

The Timing values determine when the particles appear and how long the particles stay around. The Start Frame is the first frame where particles begin to appear, and the Life value determines the number of frames in which the particles are visible. When a particle's lifetime is up, it disappears. The Birth Rate value lets you set how many new particles appear in each frame; you can use this setting or select the Constant option. The Constant option determines the Birth Rate value by dividing the total number of particles by the number of frames.

The emitter dimensions specify the width and height of the emitter gizmo. You also can hide the emitter with the Hide option.

Note

The Hide option hides the emitter only in the viewports. Emitters are never rendered. ■

The parameters for the Snow particle system are similar to the Spray particle system, except for a few unique settings. Snow can be set with a Tumble and Tumble Rate. The Tumble value can range from 0 to 1, with 1 causing a maximum amount of rotation. The Tumble Rate determines the speed of the rotation.

The Render options are also different for the Snow particle system. The three options are Six Point, Triangle, and Facing. The Six Point option renders the particle as a six-pointed star. Triangles and Facing objects are single faces.

Tutorial: Creating rain showers

One of the simplest uses for particle systems is to simulate rain or snow. In this tutorial, you use the Spray system to create rain and then learn how to use the Snow system to create snow.

To create a scene with rain using the Spray particle system, follow these steps:

1. Open the Simple rain.max file from the Chap 41 directory on the CD.

    This file includes an umbrella model created by Zygote Media.

2. Select the Create ⇨ Particles ⇨ Spray menu command, and drag the icon in the Top viewport to cover the entire scene. Position the icon above the objects, and make sure that the vector is pointing down toward the scene objects.

3. Open the Modify panel, and in the Parameters rollout, set the Render Count to **1000** and the Drop Size to **2**. Keep the default speed of **10**, and select the **Drops** option; these settings make the particles appear as streaks. Select the Tetrahedron Render method, and set the Start and Life values to **0** and **100**, respectively.

Note

To cover the entire scene with an average downpour, set the number of particles to 1000 for a 100-frame animation. ∎

4. Open the Material Editor (by pressing the M key), and drag a light blue–colored material to the particle system icon.

Figure 41.2 shows the results of this tutorial.

FIGURE 41.2

Rain created with the Spray particle system

Tutorial: Creating a snowstorm

Creating a snowstorm is very similar to what you did in the preceding tutorial. To create a snowstorm, use the Snow particle system with the same number of particles and apply a white material to the particle system.

To create a scene with snow using the Snow particle system, follow these steps:

1. Open the Snowman in snowstorm.max file from the Chap 41 directory on the CD.

   This file includes a snowman created using primitive objects.

2. Select the Create ⇨ Particles ⇨ Snow menu command, and drag the icon in the Top viewport to cover the entire scene. Position the icon above the objects, and make sure that the vector is pointing down toward the scene objects.

3. Open the Modify panel, and in the Parameters rollout, set the Render Count to **1000** and the Flake Size to **6**, and use the Six Point Render option. Set the Start and Life values to **0** and **100**, respectively.

4. Open the Material Editor (by pressing the M key), and drag a white-colored material with some self-illumination added to the particle system gizmo.

Figure 41.3 shows the results of this tutorial.

FIGURE 41.3

A simple snowstorm created with the Snow particle system

Using the Super Spray Particle System

If you think of the Spray particle system as a light summer rain shower, then the Super Spray particle system is like a fire hose. The Super Spray particle system is considerably more complex than its Spray and Snow counterparts. With this complexity comes a host of features that make this one of the most robust effects creation tools in Max.

Unlike the Spray and Snow particle systems, the Super Spray particle system includes several rollouts.

Super Spray Basic Parameters rollout

The Super Spray particle system emits all particles from the center of the emitter icon. The emitter icon is a simple cylinder and an arrow that points in the direction in which the particles will travel. In the Basic Parameters rollout, shown in Figure 41.4, the Off Axis value sets how far away from the icon's arrow the stream of particles will travel. A value of 0 lines up the particle stream with the icon's arrow, and a value of 180 emits particles in the opposite direction. The Spread value can range from 0 to 180 degrees and fans the particles equally about the specified axis. The Off Plane value spins the particles about its center axis, and the Spread value sets the distance from this center axis that particles can be created. If all these values are left at 0, then the particle system emits a single, straight stream of particles, and if all values are 180, then particles go in all directions from the center of the emitter icon.

FIGURE 41.4

The Basic Parameters rollout lets you specify where and how the particles appear in the viewports.

The icon size can be set or the icon can be hidden in the viewport. You also can set the particles to be displayed in the viewport as Dots, Ticks, Meshes, or Bounding Boxes. The Percentage value is the number of the total particles that are visible in the viewport and should be kept low to ensure rapid viewport updates.

Particle Generation rollout

The Particle Generation rollout, shown in Figure 41.5, is where you set the number of particles to include in a system as either a Rate or Total value. The Rate value is the number of particles per frame that are generated. The Total value is the number of particles generated over the total number of frames. Use the Rate value if you want the animation to have a steady stream of particles throughout the animation; use the Total value if you want to set the total number of particles that will appear throughout the entire range of frames.

FIGURE 41.5

The Particle Generation rollout lets you control the particle motion.

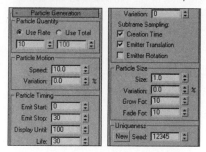

In the Particle Motion group, the Speed value determines the initial speed and direction of particles. The Variation value alters this initial speed as a percentage of the Speed value. A high Variation value results in particles with all sorts of different speeds.

Note

Be sure to use the Variation values liberally to get more realistic particle behavior. ■

In the Particle Timing group, you can set when the emitting process starts and stops. Using the Display Until value, you also can cause the particles to continue displaying after the emitting has stopped. The Life value is how long particles stay around, which can vary based on another Variation setting.

When an emitter is animated (such as moving back and forth), the particles can clump together where the system changes direction. This clumping effect is called *puffing*. The Subframe Sampling options help reduce this effect. The three options are Creation Time (which controls emitting particles over time), Emitter Translation (which controls emitting particles as the emitter is moved), and Emitter Rotation (which controls emitting particles as the emitter is rotated). All three options can be enabled, but each one that is enabled adds the computation time required to the render.

Note

The Subframe Sampling options increase the rendering time and should be used only if necessary. ■

You can specify the particle size along with a Variation value. You also can cause the particles to grow and fade for a certain number of frames.

The Seed value helps determine the randomness of the particles. Clicking the New button automatically generates a new Seed value.

Note

If you clone a particle system and each system has the same Seed value, then the two systems will be exactly the same. Two cloned particle systems with different Seed values will be unique. ■

Particle Type rollout

The Particle Type rollout, shown in Figure 41.6, lets you define the look of the particles. At the top of the rollout are three Particle Type options: Standard Particles, MetaParticles, and Instanced Geometry.

FIGURE 41.6

The Particle Type rollout (shown in four parts) lets you define how the particles look.

If you select Standard Particles as the particle type, you can select which geometric shape you want to use from the Standard Particles section. The options are Triangle, Special, Constant, SixPoint, Cube, Facing, Tetra, and Sphere.

The Special type consists of three intersecting planes, which are useful if you apply maps to them. The Facing type is also useful with maps; it creates a simple square face that always faces the viewer. The Constant type maintains the same pixel size, regardless of the distance from the camera or viewer. The Six Point option renders each particle as a 2D six-pointed star. All other types are common geometric objects.

Tutorial: Creating a fireworks fountain

For an example of the Super Spray particle system, you create a fireworks fountain. Fireworks are essentially just lots of particles with a short life span and a high amount of self-illumination. (Tell yourself that the next time you watch a fireworks display.)

Cross-Reference

The ready-made material for this example uses the Glow Render effect to make the particles glow. You can learn more about render effects in Chapter 46, "Using Atmospheric and Render Effects." ■

To create a fireworks fountain using a particle system, follow these steps:

1. Open the Fireworks fountain.max file from the Chap 41 directory on the CD.

   This file includes a simple fountain base and the Gravity space warp to cause the particles to curve back toward the ground.

Tip

Some of the most amazing special effects are made possible by combining particle systems with Space Warps. ■

2. Select the Create ⇨ Particles ⇨ Super Spray menu command, drag in the Top view, and position the system at the top of the cylinder with the direction arrow pointing toward the sky.

3. Open the Modify panel, and set the Off Axis Spread to **45** and the Off Plane Spread to **90**. In the Particle Generation rollout, set the Total of particles to **2000** with a Speed of **20** and a Variation of **100**. Set the Emit Start to **0** and the Emit Stop to **100**. Set the Display Until to **100** and the Life to **25** with a Variation of **20**. The Size of the particles should be **5**.

4. Open the Material Editor (by pressing the M key), and select the first sample slot. This slot includes a material named Spark. Drag the material from the Material Editor to the particle system's icon.

5. Select the Super Spray icon, right-click it to open the pop-up menu, and select the Properties menu option. In the Object Properties dialog box, select the Object Motion Blur option.

Caution

When viewing the animation, maximize a single viewport. If Max tries to update all four viewports at once with this many particle objects, the update is slow. The shortcut to maximize the viewport is Alt+W. ■

Figure 41.7 shows sparks emitting from the fireworks fountain.

FIGURE 41.7

The Super Spray particle system is used to create fireworks sparks.

Tutorial: Adding spray to a spray can

The Super Spray particle system is complex enough to warrant another example. What good is a spray can without any spray? In this tutorial, you create a spray can model and then use the Super Spray particle system to create the spray coming from it.

To create a stream of spray for a spray can, follow these steps:

1. Open the Spray can.max file from the Chap 41 directory on the CD.

   This file includes a simple spray can object created using a cylinder for the can base and the nozzle and a lathed spline for the top of the can.

2. Select the Particle Systems subcategory button from the drop-down list, and click the Super Spray button. Drag in the Top viewport to create the Super Spray icon, and position it at the mouth of the nozzle.

3. In the Basic Parameters rollout, set the Off Axis Spread to **20** and the Off Plane Spread to **90**. In the Particle Generation rollout, set the Emit Rate to **1000**, the Speed to **20**, and the Life to **30**. Set the Size of the particles to **5**.

4. Open the Material Editor (by pressing M), and select the material named Spray Mist. Then drag this material onto the Super Spray icon to apply this material to the Super Spray particle system.

Figure 41.8 shows the fine spray from an aerosol can.

FIGURE 41.8

Using a mostly transparent material, you can create a fine mist spray.

Using the MetaParticles option

The MetaParticles option in the Particle Type rollout makes the particle system release Metaball objects. *Metaballs* are viscous spheres that, like mercury, flow into each other when close. These particles take a little longer to render but are effective for simulating water and liquids. The MetaParticles type is available for the Super Spray, Blizzard, PArray, and PCloud particle systems.

Selecting the MetaParticles option in the Particle Types section enables the MetaParticle Parameters group. In this group are options for controlling how the MetaParticles behave. The Tension value determines how easily objects blend together. MetaParticles with a high tension resist merging with other particles. You can vary the amount of tension with the Variation value. The Tension value can range between 0.1 and 10, and the Variation can range from 0 to 100 percent.

Because MetaParticles can take a long time to render, the Evaluation Coarseness settings enable you to set how computationally intensive the rendering process is. This can be set differently for the viewport and the renderer—the higher the value, the quicker the results. You also can set this to Automatic Coarseness, which automatically controls the coarseness settings based on the speed and ability of the renderer. The One Connected Blob option speeds the rendering process by ignoring all particles that aren't connected.

Tutorial: Spilling soda from a can

MetaParticles are a good option to use to create drops of liquid, like those from a soda can.

To create liquid flowing from a can, follow these steps:

1. Open the MetaParticles from a soda can.max file from the Chap 41 directory on the CD.

   This file includes a soda can model created by Zygote Media positioned so the can is on its side.

2. Select the Create ⇨ Particles ⇨ Super Spray menu command, and drag the icon in the Front viewport. Position the icon so that its origin is at the opening of the can and the directional vector is pointing outward.

3. With the Super Spray icon selected, open the Modify panel, and in the Basic Parameters roll-out, set the Off Axis and Off Plane Spread values to **40**.

4. In the Particle Generation rollout, keep the default Rate and Speed values, but set the Speed Variation to **50** to alter the speed of the various particles. Set the Particle Size to **20**.

5. In the Particle Type rollout, select the MetaParticles option, set the Tension value to **1**, and make sure that the Automatic Coarseness option is selected.

6. Open the Material Editor (by pressing the M key), and drag the Purple Soda material to the particle system icon.

Figure 41.9 shows a rendered image of the MetaParticles spilling from a soda can at frame 25.

FIGURE 41.9

MetaParticles emitting from the opening of a soda can

Instanced Geometry

Using the Particle Type rollout, you can select an object to use as the particle. If the Instanced Geometry option is selected as the particle type, you can select an object to use as the particle. To choose an object to use as a particle, click the Pick Object button and then select an object from the viewport. If the Use Subtree Also option is selected, then all child objects are also included.

Caution

Using complicated objects as particles can slow down a system and increase the rendering time. ■

The Animation Offset Keying option determines how an animated object that is selected as the particle is animated. The None option animates all objects the same, regardless of when they are born. The Birth option starts the animation for each object when it is created, and the Random option offsets the timing randomly based on the Frame Offset value. For example, if you have selected an animated bee that flaps its wings as the particle, and you select None as the Animation Offset Keying option, all the bees flap their wings in concert. Selecting the Birth option instead starts them flapping their wings when they are born, and selecting Random offsets each instance differently.

For materials, the Time and Distance values determine the number of frames or the distance traveled before a particle is completely mapped. You can apply materials to the icon that appears when the particle system is created. The Get Material From button lets you select the object from which to get the material. The options include the icon and the Instanced Geometry.

Rotation and Collision rollout

In the Rotation and Collision rollout is an option to enable interparticle collisions. This option causes objects to bounce away from one another when their object boundaries overlap.

The Rotation and Collision rollout, shown in Figure 41.10, contains several controls to alter the rotation of individual particles. The Spin Time is the number of frames required to rotate a full revolution. The Phase value is the initial rotation of the particle. You can vary both of these values with Variation values.

Note

The Rotation and Collision rollout options also can increase the rendering time of a scene. ■

You also can set the axis about which the particles rotate. Options include Random, Direction of Travel/MBlur, and User Defined. The Stretch value under the Direction of Travel option causes the object to elongate in the direction of travel. The User Defined option lets you specify the degrees of rotation about each axis.

Interparticle collisions are computationally intensive and can easily be enabled or disabled with the Enable option. You also can set how often the collisions are calculated. The Bounce value determines the speed of particles after collisions as a percentage of their collision speed. You can vary the amount of Bounce with the Variation value.

FIGURE 41.10

The Rotation and Collision rollout options can control how objects collide with one another.

Tutorial: Basketball shooting practice

When an entire team is warming up before a basketball game, the space around the basketball hoop is quite chaotic—with basketballs flying in all directions. In this tutorial, you use a basketball object as a particle and spread it around a hoop. (Watch out for flying basketballs!)

To use a basketball object as a particle, follow these steps:

1. Open the Basketballs at a hoop.max file from the Chap 41 directory on the CD.

   This file includes basketball and basketball hoop models created by Zygote Media.

2. Select the Create ⇨ Particles ⇨ Super Spray menu command, and drag the icon in the viewport. Position the icon in the Front view so that its origin is above and slightly in front of the hoop and the directional vector is pointing down. (You need to rotate the emitter icon.)

3. Open the Modify panel, and in the Basic Parameters rollout, set the Off Axis Spread value to **90** and the Off Plane Spread value to **40**; this randomly spreads the basketballs around the hoop. In the Viewport Display group of the Basic Parameters rollout, select the Mesh option. Set the Percentage of Particles to **100** percent to see the position of each basketball object in the viewport.

Caution

Because the basketball is a fairly complex model, using the Mesh option severely slows down the viewport update. You can speed the viewport display using the Bbox (Bounding Box) option, but you'll need to choose it after selecting the Instanced Geometry option. ■

4. In the Particle Generation rollout, select the Use Total option, and enter **30** for the value. (This number is reasonable and not uncommon during warm-ups.) Set the Speed value to **0.2** and the Life value to **100** because you don't want basketballs to disappear. Because of the low number of particles, you can disable the Subframe Sampling options. Set the Grow For and Fade For values to **0**.

5. In the Particle Type rollout, select the Instanced Geometry option and click the Pick Object button. Make sure that the Use Subtree Also option is selected to get the entire group, and then select the basketball group in the viewport. At the bottom of this rollout, select the Instanced Geometry option and click the Get Material From button to give all the particles the same material as the original object.

6. In the Rotation and Collision rollout, set the Spin Time to **100** to make the basketballs spin as they move about the scene. Set the Spin Axis Control to Random. Also enable the Interparticle Collisions option, and set the Calculation Interval to **1** and the Bounce value to **100**.

   With the Collisions option enabled, the basketballs are prevented from overlapping one another.

7. At the floor of the basketball hoop is a Deflector Space Warp. Click the Bind to Space Warp button on the main toolbar, and drag from this floor deflector to the Super Spray icon.

   This makes the basketballs bounce off the floor.

Figure 41.11 shows a rendered image of the scene at frame 30 with several basketballs bouncing chaotically around a hoop.

FIGURE 41.11

Multiple basketball particles flying around a hoop

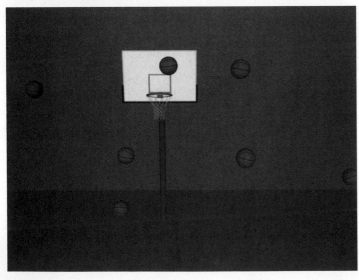

Object Motion Inheritance rollout

The settings on the Object Motion Inheritance rollout, shown in Figure 41.12, determine how the particles move when the emitter is moving. The Influence value defines how closely the particles follow the emitter's motion; a value of 100 has particles follow exactly, and a value of 0 means they don't follow at all.

FIGURE 41.12

The Object Motion Inheritance rollout sets how the particles inherit the motion of their emitter, and the Bubble Motion rollout defines how particles act like bubbles.

The Multiplier value can exaggerate or diminish the effect of the emitter's motion. Particles with a high multiplier can actually precede the emitter.

Bubble Motion rollout

The Bubble Motion rollout, also shown in Figure 41.12, simulates the wobbling motion of bubbles as they rise in a liquid. Three values define this motion, each with variation values. Amplitude is the distance that the particle moves from side to side. Period is the time that it takes to complete one side-to-side motion cycle. Phase defines where the particle starts along the amplitude curve.

Particle Spawn rollout

The Particle Spawn rollout, shown in Figure 41.13, sets options for spawning new particles when a particle dies or collides with another particle. If the setting is None, colliding particles bounce off one another and dying particles simply disappear. The Die After Collision option causes a particle to disappear after it collides. The Persist value sets how long the particle stays around before disappearing. The Variation value causes the Persist value to vary by a defined percentage.

FIGURE 41.13

The Particle Spawn rollout (shown in two parts) can cause particles to spawn new particles.

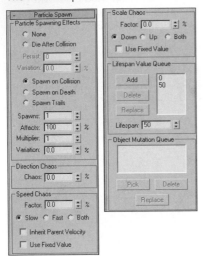

The Spawn on Collision, Spawn on Death, and Spawn Trails options all enable the spawn controls and define when particles spawn new particles. The Spawns value is the number of times a particle can spawn other particles. The Affects value is the percentage of particles that can spawn new particles; lowering this value creates some duds that do not spawn. The Multiplier value determines the number of new particles created.

Note

The Spawn Trails option causes every particle to spawn a new particle at every frame. This option can quickly create an enormous number of particles and should be used with caution. ■

The Chaos settings define the direction and speed of the spawned particles. A Direction Chaos value of 100 gives the spawned particles the freedom to travel in any direction, whereas a setting of 0 moves them in the same direction as their originator.

The Chaos Speed Factor is the difference in speed between the spawned particle and its originator. This factor can be faster or slower than the original. Selecting the Both option speeds up some particles and slows others randomly. You also can choose to have spawned particles use their parent's velocity or use the factor value as a fixed value.

The Scale Chaos Factor works similarly to the Chaos Speed Factor, except that it scales particles to be larger or smaller than their originator.

The Lifespan Value Queue lets you define different lifespan levels. Original particles have a lifespan equal to the first entry in the queue. The particles that are spawned from those spawned particles last as long as the second value, and so on. To add a value to the list, enter the value in the Lifespan spinner and click the Add button. The Delete button removes values from the list, and the Replace button switches value positions.

If Instanced Geometry is the selected particle type, you can fill the Object Mutation Queue with additional objects to use at each spawn level. These objects appear after a particle is spawned. To pick a new object to add to the queue, use the Pick button. You can select several objects, and they are used in the order in which they are listed.

Load/Save Presets rollout

You can save and load each particle configuration using the Load/Save Presets rollout, shown in Figure 41.14. To save a configuration, type a name in the Preset Name field and click the Save button. All saved presets are displayed in the list. To use one of these preset configurations, select it and click the Load button.

FIGURE 41.14

The Load/Save Presets rollout enables you to save different parameter settings.

Note

A saved preset is valid only for the type of particle system used to save it. For example, you cannot save a Super Spray preset and load it for a Blizzard system. ∎

Max includes several default presets that can be used as you get started. These presets include Bubbles, Fireworks, Hose, Shockwave, Trail, Welding Sparks, and Default (which produces a straight line of particles).

Using the Blizzard Particle System

The Blizzard particle system uses the same rollouts as the Super Spray system, with some slightly different options. The Blizzard emitter icon is a plane with a line pointing in the direction of the particles (similar to the Spray and Snow particle systems). Particles are emitted across the entire plane surface.

The differences between the Blizzard and Super Spray parameters include dimensions for the Blizzard icon. In the Particle Generation rollout, you'll find values for Tumble and Tumble Rate. Another difference is the Emitter Fit Planar option under the Material Mapping group of the Particle Type rollout. This option sets particles to be mapped at birth, depending on where they appear on the emitter. The other big difference is that the Blizzard particle system has no Bubble Motion rollout, because snowflakes don't make very good bubbles. Finally, you'll find a different set of presets in the Load/Save Presets rollout, including Blizzard, Rain, Mist, and Snowfall.

Using the PArray Particle System

The PArray particle system is a unique particle system. It emits particles from the surface of a selected object. These particles can be emitted from the object's surface, edges, or vertices. The particles are emitted from an object separate from the emitter icon.

The PArray particle system includes many of the same rollouts as the Super Spray particle system. The PArray particle system's emitter icon is a cube with three tetrahedron objects inside it. This system has some interesting parameter differences, starting with the Basic Parameters rollout, shown in Figure 41.15.

FIGURE 41.15

The Basic Parameters rollout for the PArray particle system lets you select the location where the particles form.

In the PArray system, you can select separate objects as emitters with the Pick Object button. You also can select the location on the object where the particles are formed. Options include Over Entire Surface, Along Visible Edges, At All Vertices, At Distinct Points, and At Face Centers. For the At Distinct Points option, you can select the number of points to use.

The Use Selected SubObject option forms particles in the locations selected with the Pick Object button, but only within the subobject selection passed up the Stack. This is useful if you want to emit particles only from a certain selection of a mesh, such as a dragon's mouth or the end of a fire hose. The other options in the PArray system's Basic Parameters rollout are the same as in the other systems.

The Particle Generation rollout includes a Divergence value. This value is the angular variation of the velocity of each particle from the emitter's normal.

Splitting an object into fragments

The Particle Type rollout for the PArray system contains a unique particle type: Object Fragments. This type breaks the selected object into several fragments. Object Fragment settings include a Thickness value. This value gives each fragment a depth. If the value is set to 0, the fragments are all single-sided polygons.

Also in the Particle Type rollout, the All Faces option separates each individual triangular face into a separate fragment. An alternative to this option is to use the Number of Chunks option, which enables you to divide the object into chunks and define how many chunks to use. A third option splits up an object based on the smoothing angle, which can be specified.

In the Material section of the Particle Type rollout, you can select material IDs to use for the fragment's inside, outside, and backside.

The Load/Save Presets rollout includes a host of interesting presets, including the likes of Blast, Disintegrate, Geyser, and Comet.

Tutorial: Creating rising steam

In this tutorial, you create the effect of steam rising from a street vent. Using the PArray particle system, you can control the precise location of the steam.

To create the effect of steam rising from a vent, follow these steps:

1. Open the Street vent.max file from the Chap 41 directory on the CD.

   This file includes a street scene with a vent. The car model was created by Viewpoint Datalabs.

2. Select the Create ➪ Particles ➪ PArray menu command, and drag in the Front viewport to create the system.

3. In the Basic Parameters rollout, click the Pick Object button and select the Quadpatch object that is positioned directly beneath the vent object. Set the Particle Formation option to Over Entire Surface.

   Because the Plane object only has a single face, the particles travel in the direction of the Plane's normal.

4. In the Particle Generation rollout, set the Emit Stop value to **100** and the Life value to **60** with a Variation of **50**. Set the Particle Size value to **5.0** with a Variation of **30**.

5. In the Particle Type rollout, select the Standard Particles and the Constant options.

6. Open the Material Editor (by selecting the M key), and name the selected sample slot **steam**. Click the map button to the right of the Opacity value, and double-click the Mask map type from the Material/Map Browser. In the Mask Parameters rollout, click the map button and select the Noise map type. Then click the Go to Parent button to return to the Mask map, click the Mask button, and select the Gradient map type. For the Gradient material, drag the black color swatch to the white color swatch, select Swap in the dialog box that appears, and enable the Radial option. Finally, drag the steam material to the PArray icon.

Figure 41.16 shows the steam vent at frame 60.

FIGURE 41.16

A Plane object positioned beneath the vent is an emitter for the particle system.

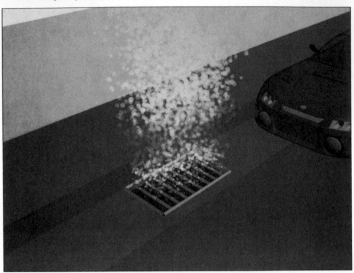

Using the PCloud Particle System

The PCloud particle system keeps all emitted particles within a selected volume. This volume can be a box, sphere, cylinder, or a selected object. The emitter icon is shaped as the selected volume. This particle system includes the same rollouts as the Super Spray system, with some subtle differences.

The options on the Basic Parameters rollout are unique to this system. This system can use a separate mesh object as an emitter. To select this emitter object, click the Pick Object button and select the object to use. Other options include Box, Sphere, and Cylinder Emitter. For these emitters, the Rad/Len, Width, and Height values are active for defining its dimensions.

In addition to these differences in the Basic Parameters rollout, several Particle Motion options in the Particle Generation rollout are different for the PCloud system as well. Particle Motion can be set to a random direction, a specified vector, or in the direction of a reference object's Z-axis.

The only two presets for this particle system in the Load/Save Presets rollout are Cloud/Smoke and Default.

Using Particle System Maps

Using material maps on particles is another way to add detail to a particle system without increasing its geometric complexity. You can apply all materials and maps available in the Material Editor to particle systems. To apply them, select the particle system icon and click the Assign Material to Selection button in the Material Editor.

Cross-Reference

For more details on using maps, see Chapter 17, "Adding Material Details with Maps." ∎

Two map types are specifically designed to work with particle systems: Particle Age and Particle MBlur. You can find these maps in the Material/Map Browser. You can access the Material/Map Browser using the Rendering ⇨ Material Map Browser menu command or from the Material Editor by clicking the Get Material button.

Using the Particle Age map

The Particle Age map parameters include three different colors that can be applied at different times, depending on the Life value of the particles. Each color includes a color swatch, a map button, an Enable check box, and an Age value for when this color should appear.

This map typically is applied as a Diffuse map because it affects the color.

Using the Particle MBlur map

The Particle MBlur map changes the opacity of the front and back of a particle, depending on the color values and sharpness specified in its parameters rollout. This results in an effect of blurred motion if applied as an Opacity map.

Note

MBlur does not work with the Constant, Facing, MetaParticles, or PArray object fragments. ∎

Tutorial: Creating jet engine flames

The Particle Age and MBlur maps work well for adding opacity and colors that change over time, such as hot jets of flames, to a particle system.

To create jet engine flames, follow these steps:

1. Open the Jet airplane flames.max file from the Chap 41 directory on the CD.

   This file includes an A-10 airplane model created by Viewpoint Datalabs.

2. Select the Create ⇨ Particles ⇨ Super Spray menu command, and drag the icon in the viewport. Rotate and position the emitter icon so that its origin is right in the jet's exhaust port and the directional vector is pointing outward, away from the jet.

3. Open the Modify panel, and in the Basic Parameters rollout, set the Off Axis Spread value to **20** and the Off Plane Spread value to **90**.

   These settings focus the flames shooting from the jet's exhaust.

4. In the Particle Generation rollout, set the Emit Stop to **100**, the Life value to **30**, and the Particle Size to **5.0**.

5. In the Particle Type rollout, select the Standard Particles option and select the Sphere type.

6. Open the Material Editor by pressing the M key, and select the first sample slot. Name this material **Jet's Exhaust**, and click the map button to the right of the Diffuse color.

7. From the Material/Map Browser that opens, select the Particle Age map. In the Particle Age Parameters rollout, select dark red, dark yellow, and black as colors for the ages 0, 50, and 100.

   You should use darker colors because the scene is lighted.

8. Click the Go to Parent button to access the Jet's Exhaust material again, and then click the map button to the right of the Opacity setting. Select the Particle MBlur map.

9. In the Particle MBlur Parameters rollout, make Color #1 white and Color #2 black with a Sharpness value of **0.1**. Then drag this material from its sample slot onto the particle system's icon to apply the material (or click the Assign Material to Selection button if the emitter icon is still selected).

10. With the Shift key held down, drag the Super Spray icon in the Front viewport to the other exhaust port. Make the new Super Spray an instance of the original.

Figure 41.17 shows the jet at frame 30 with its fiery exhaust.

FIGURE 41.17

Realistic jet flames created using the Particle Age and MBlur maps

Controlling Particles with Particle Flow

Particle systems like Super Spray are great for certain applications, but they suffer from an inflexibility. Each system has lots of parameters, but once the parameters are set, the particles follow the set parameters without changing. The Particle Flow system is an event-driven system that constantly tests its particles for certain criteria and alters its actions based on these defined criteria. This gives you the ability to program the particles to react in unique and different ways not possible with the other systems.

The Particle Flow Source option in the Create ⇨ Particles menu is more than just a new particle system: It is a whole new interface and paradigm that you can use to control particles throughout their life. This is accomplished using the Particle View window, where you can visually program the flow of particles.

The Particle View window

The Particle View window, shown in Figure 41.18, is opened by clicking the Particle View button in the Setup rollout when a Particle Flow Source icon is selected or by pressing the keyboard shortcut, 6. Pressing 6 opens the Particle View window even if its icon isn't selected.

FIGURE 41.18

The Particle View window lets you program the flow of particles using a visual editor.

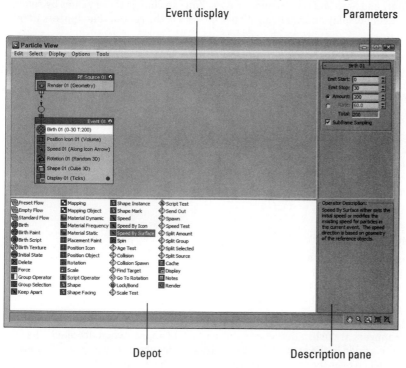

Event display   Parameters

Depot   Description pane

The Particle View window is divided into four panes. The Event display contains all the event nodes. These nodes contain individual actions, and nodes can be wired to one another to define the flow. The Parameter pane in the upper-right corner displays the parameters in rollouts for the action selected in the Event display. The Depot pane is below the Event display pane and contains all the possible actions that can work with particles. In the lower right is a Description pane that offers a brief description of the action that is selected in the Depot pane. Except for the Event display pane, you can turn off the other panes using the Display menu.

In the lower-right corner of the window are several display tools. These tools can be used to navigate the Event display. The Display tools include Pan, Zoom, Region Zoom, Zoom Extents, and No Zoom. The No Zoom button eliminates all zooming and displays the nodes at their normal size.

Tip
With the Particle View window open, you can Pan the Event display by dragging the scroll wheel on the mouse. ∎

The Standard Flow

When the Particle Flow (PF) Source icon is created and the Particle View window is first opened, two nodes appear in the Event display. These nodes are called a Standard Flow. These two nodes identify the Particle Flow Source and are wired to an event node containing a Birth action. The Birth action defines when particles Start and Stop and the Amount or Rate. You can change these values by selecting the Birth event in the Event display and changing its parameters in the rollout that appears in the Parameters pane.

Several other default events appear in this default event node, including Position Icon, Speed, Rotation, Shape, and Display. Each of these events has parameters that you can alter that appear in the Parameters pane when the action is selected, and each event and action is identified with a number (such as 01) that appears next to its name. Each new event or action gets an incremented number. You also can rename any of these events if you right-click the event and select Rename from the pop-up menu.

A new Standard Flow can be created using the Edit ⇨ New ⇨ Particle System ⇨ Standard Flow menu command. An Empty Flow includes only the PF Source node. When a new Standard Flow (or Empty Flow) is created in the Particle Flow window, a PF Source icon is added to the viewports. And if the PF Source icon is deleted in the viewports, the associated event nodes are also deleted in the Particle Flow window.

Working with actions

The Depot pane includes all the different actions that can affect particles. These actions can be categorized into Birth actions (identified with green icons), Operator actions (identified with blue icons), Test actions (identified with yellow icons), and Miscellaneous actions (which are also blue). Each of these categories also can be found in the Edit ⇨ New menu.

New events can be dragged from the Depot pane to the Event display. If you place them within an existing node, a blue line appears at the location where the action will appear when dropped. The particles are affected within a node in the order, from top to bottom, in which they appear. If a new action from the Depot is dragged over the top of an existing action in the Event display, a red line appears on top of the existing action. When you drop the new action, it replaces the existing action.

Actions also can be dropped away from an event node, making it a new event node. If an event is a new node, then you can wire certain actions that are tested as true. For example, if you have a set of particles with a random speed assigned, then you could use a Test event to determine which particles are moving faster than a certain speed and wire those particles to change size using the new event node.

Clicking the action's icon disables the action.

Tutorial: Creating an avalanche

One of the cautions that come with particles is that if you're not careful, you can quickly spawn enough particles to bring any system to its knees. Using the particle spawn feature is one of the worst offenders. For this tutorial, you use a Collision Spawn action to create an avalanche, but you must be sure to keep the number of spawned particles in check.

To use Particle Flow to make an avalanche effect, follow these steps:

1. Open the Avalanche.max file from the Chap 41 directory on the CD.

    This file includes a simple hillside covered with snow.

2. Select Create ⇨ Space Warps ⇨ Deflectors ⇨ SOmniFlect, and drag in the Top viewport to create a spherical deflector that covers the entire hill. Click the Select and Scale tool, and in the Z-axis, scale the SOmniFlect sphere down in the Left viewport until it is roughly the same thickness as the hill object. Then rotate the SOmniFlect until it is aligned parallel to the hill. This deflector is going to keep the snowball particles on top of the hill.

3. Select Create ⇨ Particles ⇨ Particle Flow Source, and drag in the Top viewport to create the emitter icon. Scale and rotate the emitter icon so it is positioned inside the SOmniFlect object on the uphill side pointing downhill. The emitter can be fairly small so it fits inside the deflector.

4. With the Particle Flow Source still selected, click the Particle View button in the Modify panel of the Command Panel to open the Particle View window (or press 6). In the Event 01 box, select the Shape01 action, and in the rollout that appears to the right, set the Shape to Sphere and the Size to **5.0**. Select the Speed01 action, and set the Speed value to **100**. Click the colored dot to the right of the Display01 action, and select white as the new color.

5. Select the Collision Spawn action from the Depot pane, and drop it in Event01 beneath the Display01 action. Then select the Collision Spawn action, click the By List button in the Parameters pane, and select the SOmniFlect object. Then disable the Test True for Parent and Spawn Particles option, enable the Spawn On Each Collision option, and set the Offspring value to **10**.

Figure 41.19 shows an avalanche of snowballs as it rages down a snowy hillside.

Using the Collision Spawn and a well-placed deflector, you can create an avalanche effect.

Using Particle Flow helpers

In addition to the Standard Flow event, several other actions create icons in the viewports that are controlled using the action parameters. One of these helpers appears when the Find Target action is added to an event node. This helper is a simple sphere, but all particles in the scene are attracted to it. It also can be animated.

The Speed By Icon action creates an icon that forces particles to follow its trajectory path.

Wiring events

Each new event node that is created has an input that extends from the upper-left corner of the node, and each Test event that is added has an output that extends to the left of its icon, as shown in Figure 41.20. Test action outputs can be wired to event inputs by dragging from one to the other. The cursor changes when it is over each.

FIGURE 41.20

Event outputs can be wired to event inputs.

Event output

Event input

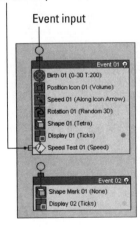

Once wired, all particles that are tested to be true are transferred to the new event node and are subject to the actions in the wired event node.

Tutorial: Moths chasing a light

Another cool feature that the Particle Flow interface makes available is the ability to have particles chase a target object. In this example, you use the Target event to make some annoying bugs follow a lantern's light.

To use Particle Flow to make several bugs chase a light, follow these steps:

1. Open the Moths chasing light.max file from the Chap 41 directory on the CD.

   This file includes a simple lantern created from primitives that is suspended from a chain and animated rocking back and forth. The file also includes a simple moth.

2. Select Create ⇨ Particles ⇨ Particle Flow Source, and drag in the Front viewport to create the emitter icon. Click the Particle View button to open the Particle View interface.

3. In the Event01 node, select the Birth01 action and set the Emit Stop to **100** with an Amount of **50**.

4. Drag the Position Object action from the Depot pane, and drop it on top of the Position Icon action to replace it. Select the new Position Object action, click the By List button under the Emitter Objects list in the Parameters pane, and select the Sphere01 object.

   This sphere surrounds the lantern and is the source of the moths. It has a material with an Opacity setting of 0 applied so that it is not visible in the scene.

5. Select the Rotation action in the Event01 node, and change the Orientation Matrix option to Speed Space Follow.

   This rotates the moths as they follow the swinging lantern.

6. Drag the Shape Instance action from the Depot pane, and drop it on top of the Shape action to replace it. Select the new Shape Instance action, click the Particle Geometry Object button in the Parameters pane, and select the moth object in the viewports.

7. Drag the Find Target action from the Depot pane, and drop it at the bottom of the Event01 node. This adds a new Find Target icon to the viewports. Select the Find Target icon in the viewports, and move it to the lantern flame's position. Select Group ⇨ Attach, and click the lantern object to add the Find Target icon to the lantern group. This makes the target move with the lantern. Enable the Use Cruise Speed option, and then set the Speed to **1000** with a Variation of **50** and the Accel Limit to **5000** with an Ease % of **50**. You also need to enable the Follow Target Animation option.

8. Drag the Material Dynamic from the Depot pane to the Event Display pane, and drop it outside the Event01 node to create a new node called Event02. In the Parameters pane, enable the Assign Material button and click the material button. Select the Flash material from the Material/Map Browser (select the Material Editor option to see the sample slot materials). Then drag a wire from Event01 to Event02.

9. Drag the Age Test action from the Depot pane, and drop it below the Material Dynamic action. Then select Event Age from the drop-down list in the Parameters pane, and set the Test Value to **2**.

10. Finally, drag the Delete action from the Depot pane, and drop it away from the other events. Then wire Event02 to the new event node, and select the Selected Particles Only option in the Parameters pane.

Figure 41.21 shows several moths eagerly pursuing the swinging lantern.

FIGURE 41.21

All the moths in this scene are particles and are following a target linked to the lantern.

Debugging test actions

Any test action can be made to return a True or False value if you click the left (for True) or right (for False) side of the test action's icon in the Particle View interface. This lets you debug the particle flow. Tests set to be true show an icon with a green light, and tests set to be false show a red light icon.

Tutorial: Firing at a fleeing spaceship

Well, it is about time for a space scene, and we all know that lots of particles float around out in space—stars, asteroids, comets, and so forth. It's all great stuff to animate. For this scene, you use the Particle Flow feature to fire laser blasts on a fleeing spaceship.

To use Particle Flow to fire on a fleeing spaceship, follow these steps:

1. Open the Fleeing spaceship.max file from the Chap 41 directory on the CD.

   This file includes a spaceship model created by Viewpoint Datalabs that has been animated as if it were fleeing.

2. Select Create ⇨ Particles ⇨ Particle Flow Source, and drag in the Front viewport to create the emitter. With the Select and Move (W) button selected, move the emitter until it is aligned with the end of the laser gun. Then click the Select and Link button, and drag from the emitter to the gun object to bind the emitter to the gun.

   The emitter now moves with the animated laser gun.

3. With the Particle Flow Source icon selected, open the Modify panel and click the Particle View button in the Setup rollout (or press the 6 key) to open the Particle View interface.

4. In the Event01 node, select the Birth 03 event; in the Parameters panel, set the Emit Stop to **100** and the Amount to **50**. This produces a laser blast every two frames. Click the blue dot in the lower-right corner of the Event node, and select a red color from the Color Selector that appears.

5. Select Create ⇨ Standard Primitives ⇨ Cylinder, and drag in the Front viewport to create a Cylinder object. In the Hierarchy panel, select the Affect Pivot Only button and rotate the Cylinder's Pivot Point until its Y-axis points at the spaceship. Then in the Particle View window, drag the Shape Instance event from the depot and drop it on top of the Shape event in the Event 01 node. This replaces the Shape event with a Shape Instance event. In the Parameters rollout, click the Particle Geometry Object button and select the Cylinder object. Select the Rotation event, and delete it with the Delete key.

6. Select Create ⇨ Space Warps ⇨ Deflectors ⇨ SOmniFlect, and drag in the Top viewport to create a spherical deflector that encompasses the spaceship. Click the Select and Non-Uniform Scale button, and scale the X- and Z-axes until the deflector just fits around the spaceship. Then link the deflector Space Warp to the spaceship.

7. In the Particle View window, drag the Collision event from the depot to the bottom of the Event 01 node. In the rollout, below the Deflectors list, click the Add button and select the SOmniFlect01 object surrounding the spaceship.

8. Drag a Spawn event from the depot to the event display, and then connect the Collision event by dragging from its output to the input of the new Spawn event. Then click the color for the new event particles, and change it to orange. Select the Spawn 01 event, enable the Delete Parent option, and set the Offspring to **200** and the Variation % to **20**. Then set the Inherited % to **50** with a Variation of **30**.

9. Drag the Delete event to the bottom of the Event 02 node, select the By Particle Age option, and set the Life Span to **20** and the Variation to **30**. Drag a Shape event to the Event 02 node, and set the Shape to Sphere and the Size to **0.5**.

10. Finally, click the Play button to see the resulting animation.

Figure 41.22 shows the final Particle View flow, and Figure 41.23 shows a frame of the animation in the viewport. You can still do several things to improve this animation, such as adding a Glow Render Effect to the laser blasts and using the Particle Age material with some transparency to improve the explosion's look.

FIGURE 41.22

The Particle View window shows the flow of the particles in the animation.

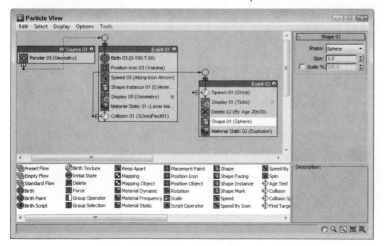

FIGURE 41.23

The spaceship is trying to outrun the laser blasts.

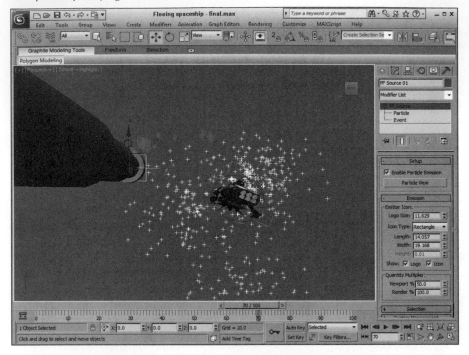

Summary

This chapter presented particle systems and showed how you can use them. The chapter also took a close look at each system, including Spray, Snow, Super Spray, Blizzard, PArray, PCloud, and Particle Flow. This chapter covered these topics:

- Learning about the various particle systems
- Creating a particle system for producing rain and snow
- Using the Super Spray particle system
- Working with MetaParticles
- Specifying an object to use as a particle and an object to use as an emitter
- Using the PArray and PCloud particle systems
- Using the Particle Age and Particle MBlur maps on particles
- Controlling and programming the flow of particles with the Particle Flow window

The next chapter explains working with Space Warps to add forces to a scene. These forces can be used to control the motion of objects in the scene.

Using Space Warps

IN THIS CHAPTER

Creating and binding Space Warps to objects

Understanding the various Space Warp types

Working with Space Warps and particle systems

S pace Warps sound like a special effect from a science fiction movie, but actually they are nonrenderable objects that let you affect another object in many unique ways to create special effects.

You can think of Space Warps as the unseen forces that control the movement of objects in the scene such as gravity, wind, and waves. Several Space Warps, such as Push and Motor, deal with dynamic simulations and can define forces in real-world units. Some Space Warps can deform an object's surface; others provide the same functionality as certain modifiers.

Space Warps are particularly useful when combined with particle systems. This chapter includes some examples of Space Warps that have been combined with particle systems.

Creating and Binding Space Warps

Space Warps are a way to add forces to the scene that can act on an object. Space Warps are not renderable and must be bound to an object to have an effect. A single Space Warp can be bound to several objects, and a single object can be bound to several Space Warps.

In many ways, Space Warps are similar to modifiers, but modifiers typically apply to individual objects, whereas Space Warps can be applied to many objects at the same time and are applied using World Space Coordinates. This ability to work with multiple objects makes Space Warps the preferred way to alter particle systems and to add forces to dynamic hair and cloth systems.

Creating a Space Warp

Space Warps are found in the Create ⇨ Space Warps menu, which opens the Space Warps category (the icon is three wavy lines) in the Create panel.

From the subcategory drop-down list, you can select from several different subcategories. Each subcategory has buttons to enable several different Space Warps, or you can select them using the Create ⇨ Space Warps menu command. To create a Space Warp, click a button or select a menu option and then click and drag in a viewport.

When a Space Warp is created, a gizmo is placed in the scene. This gizmo can be transformed as other objects can: by using the standard transformation buttons. The size and position of the Space Warp gizmo often affect its results. After a Space Warp is created, it affects only the objects to which it is bound.

Binding a Space Warp to an object

 A Space Warp's influence is felt only by its bound objects, so you can selectively apply gravity only to certain objects. The Bind to Space Warp button is on the main toolbar next to the Unlink button. After clicking the Bind to Space Warp button, drag from the Space Warp to the object to which you want to link it or vice versa.

All Space Warp bindings appear in the Modifier Stack. You can use the Edit Modifier Stack dialog box to copy and paste Space Warps between objects.

Some Space Warps can be bound only to certain types of objects. Each Space Warp has a Supports Objects of Type rollout that lists the supported objects. If you're having trouble binding a Space Warp to an object, check this rollout to see whether the object is supported.

Understanding Space Warp Types

Just as many different types of forces exist in nature, many different Space Warp types exist. These appear in several different subcategories, based on their function. The subcategories are Forces, Deflectors, Geometric/Deformable, Modifier-Based, and Particles & Dynamics.

Note

The Particles & Dynamics subcategory includes a Vector Field button that is used with biped crowds, discussed in Bonus Chapter 8, "Creating Character Crowds." ∎

Force Space Warps

The Forces subcategory of Space Warps is mainly used with particle systems and dynamic simulations. Space Warps in this subcategory include Motor, Vortex, Path Follow, Displace, Wind, Push, Drag, PBomb, and Gravity. Figure 42.1 shows the gizmos for these Space Warps.

Motor

The Motor Space Warp applies a rotational torque to objects. This force accelerates objects radially instead of linearly. The Basic Torque value is a measurement of torque in newton-meters, foot-pounds, or inch-pounds.

The On Time and Off Time options set the frames where the force is applied and disabled, respectively. Many of the Space Warps have these same values.

FIGURE 42.1

The Force Space Warps: Motor, Vortex, Path Follow, Displace, Wind, Push, Drag, PBomb, and Gravity

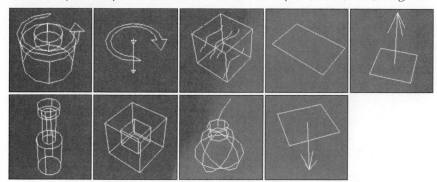

The Feedback On option causes the force to change as the object's speed changes. When this option is off, the force stays constant. You can also set Target Revolution units in revolutions per hour (RPH), revolutions per minute (RPM), or revolutions per second (RPS), which is the speed at which the force begins to change if the Feedback option is enabled. The Reversible option causes the force to change directions if the Target Speed is reached, and the Gain value is how quickly the force adjusts.

The motor force can also be adjusted with Periodic Variations, which cause the motor force to increase and then decrease in a regular pattern. You can define two different sets of Periodic Variation parameters: Period 1, Amplitude 1, Phase 1; and Period 2, Amplitude 2, Phase 2.

For particle systems, you can enable and set a Range value. The Motor Space Warp doesn't affect particles outside this distance. At the bottom of the Parameters rollout, you can set the size of the gizmo icon. You can find this same value for all Space Warps.

Figure 42.2 shows the Motor Space Warp twisting the particles being emitted from the Super Spray particle system in the direction of the icon's arrow.

Push

The Push Space Warp accelerates objects in the direction of the Space Warp's icon from the large cylinder to the small cylinder. Many of the parameters for the Push Space Warp are similar to those for the Motor Space Warp. Using the Parameters rollout, you can specify the force Strength in units of newtons or pounds.

The Feedback On option causes the force to change as the object's speed changes, except that it deals with Target Speed instead of Target Revolution like the Motor Space Warp does.

The push force can also be set to include Periodic Variations that are the same as with the Motor Space Warp. Figure 42.3 shows the Push Space Warp pushing the particles being emitted from the Super Spray particle system.

FIGURE 42.2

You can use the Motor Space Warp to apply a twisting force to particles and dynamic objects.

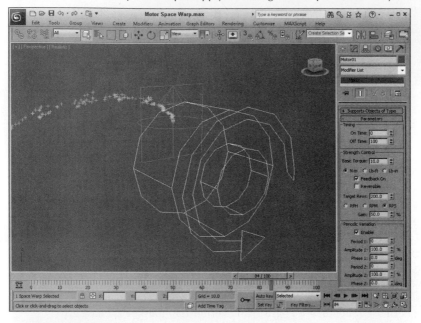

FIGURE 42.3

You can use the Push Space Warp to apply a controlled force to particles and dynamic objects.

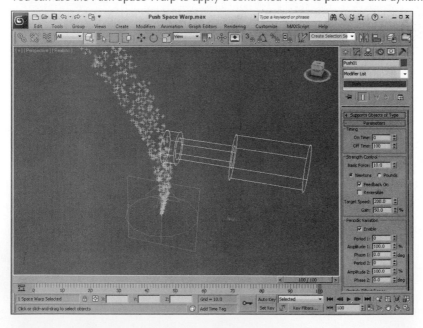

Vortex

You can use the Vortex Space Warp on particle systems to make particles spin around in a spiral like going down a whirlpool. You can use the Timing settings to set the beginning and ending frames where the effect takes place.

You can also specify Taper Length and Taper values, which determine the shape of the vortex. Lower Taper Length values wind the vortex tighter, and the Taper Curve values can range between 1.0 and 4.0 and control the ratio between the spiral diameter at the top of the vortex versus the bottom of the vortex.

The Axial Drop value specifies how far each turn of the spiral is from the adjacent turn. The Damping value sets how quickly the Axial Drop value takes effect. The Orbital Speed is how fast the particles rotate away from the center. The Radial Pull value is the distance from the center of each spiral path that the particles can rotate. If the Unlimited Range option is disabled, then Range and Falloff values are included for each setting. You can also specify whether the vortex spins clockwise or counterclockwise.

Figure 42.4 shows a Vortex Space Warp being bound to a particle system.

FIGURE 42.4

You can use the Vortex Space Warp to force a particle system into a spiral like a whirlpool.

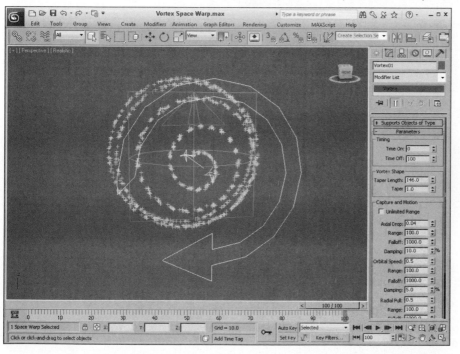

Drag

Drag is another common force that can be simulated with a Space Warp. The Drag Space Warp can be Linear, Spherical, or Cylindrical. This Space Warp causes particle velocity to be decreased, such as when simulating air resistance or fluid viscosity. Use the Time On and Time Off options to set the frame where the Space Warp is in effect.

For each of the Damping shape types—Linear, Spherical, and Cylindrical—you can set the drag, which can be along each axis for the Linear shape or in the Radial, Tangential, and Axial direction for the Spherical and Cylindrical shapes. If the Unlimited Range option is not selected, then the Range and Falloff values are available.

Figure 42.5 shows a Drag Space Warp surrounding a particle system. Notice how the particles are slowed and moved to the side as they pass through the Drag space warp.

FIGURE 42.5

You can use the Drag Space Warp to slow the velocity of particles.

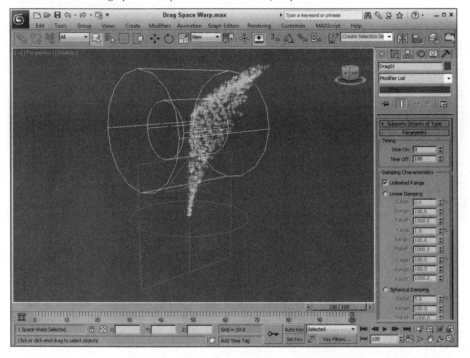

PBomb

The PBomb (particle bomb) Space Warp was designed specifically for the PArray particle system, but it can be used with any particle system. To blow up an object with the PBomb Space Warp, create an object, make it a PArray emitter, and then bind the PBomb Space Warp to the PArray.

Cross-Reference

You can find more information on the PArray particle system in Chapter 41, "Creating Particles and Particle Flow." ∎

Basic parameters for this Space Warp include three blast symmetry types: Spherical, Cylindrical, and Planar. You can also set the Chaos value as a percentage.

In the Explosion Parameters section, the Start Time is the frame where the explosion takes place, and the Duration defines how long the explosion forces are applied. The Strength value is the power of the explosion.

A Range value can be set to determine the extent of the explosion. It is measured from the center of the Space Warp icon. If the Unlimited Range option is selected, the Range value is disabled. The Linear and Exponential options change how the explosion forces die out. The Range Indicator option displays the effective blast range of the PBomb.

Figure 42.6 shows a box selected as an emitter for a PArray. The PBomb is bound to the PArray and not to the box object. The Speed value for the PArray has been set to 0, and the Particle Type is set to Fragments. Notice that the PBomb's icon determines the center of the blast.

FIGURE 42.6

You can use the PBomb Space Warp with the PArray particle system to create explosions.

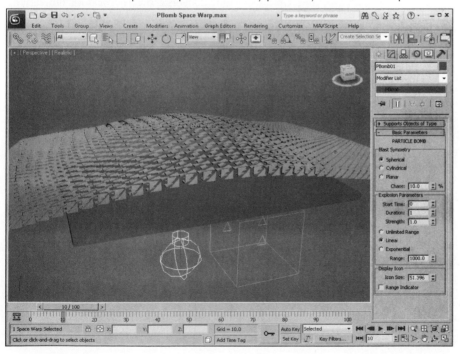

Path Follow

The Path Follow Space Warp causes particles to follow a path defined by a spline. The Basic Parameters rollout for this Space Warp includes a Pick Shape Object button for selecting the spline path to use. You can also specify a Range value or the Unlimited Range option. The Range distance is measured from the path to the particle.

Cross-Reference

The Path Follow Space Warp is similar to the Path Constraint, which is discussed in Chapter 22, "Animating with Constraints and Simple Controllers." ■

In the Motion Timing section, the Start Frame value is the frame where the particles start following the path, the Travel Time is the number of frames required to travel the entire path, and the Last Frame is where the particles no longer follow the path. There is also a Variation value to add some randomness to the movement of the particles.

The Basic Parameters rollout also includes a Particle Motion section with two options for controlling how the particles proceed down the path: Along Offset Splines and Along Parallel Splines. The first causes the particles to move along splines that are offset from the original, and the second moves all particles from their initial location along parallel path splines. The Constant Speed option makes all particles move at the same speed.

Also in the Particle Motion section is the Stream Taper value. This value is the amount by which the particles move away from the path over time. Options include Converge, Diverge, or Both. Converging streams move all particles closer to the path, and diverging streams do the opposite. The Stream value is the number of spiral turns that the particles take along the path. This swirling motion can be Clockwise, Counterclockwise, or Bidirectional. The Seed value determines the randomness of the stream settings.

Figure 42.7 shows a Path Follow Space Warp bound to a Super Spray particle system. A Helix shape has been selected as the path.

Gravity

The Gravity Space Warp adds the effect of gravity to a scene. This causes objects to accelerate in the direction specified by the Gravity Space Warp, like the Wind Space Warp. The Parameters rollout includes Strength and Decay values. Additional options make the gravity planar or spherical. You can turn on the Range Indicators to display a plane or sphere where the gravity is half its maximum value.

Wind

The Wind Space Warp causes objects to accelerate. The Parameters rollout includes Strength and Decay values. Additional options make the gravity planar or spherical. The Turbulence value randomly moves the objects in different directions, and the Frequency value controls how often these random turbulent changes occur. Larger Scale values cause turbulence to affect larger areas, but smaller values are wilder and more chaotic.

You can turn on the Range Indicators just like the Gravity Space Warp. Figure 42.8 shows the Wind Space Warp pushing the particles being emitted from a Super Spray particle system.

FIGURE 42.7

A Path Follow Space Warp bound to an emitter from the Super Spray particle system and following a Helix path

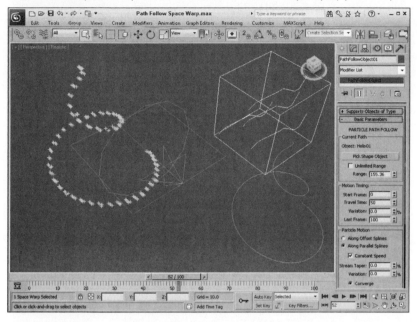

FIGURE 42.8

You can use the Wind Space Warp to blow particles and dynamic objects.

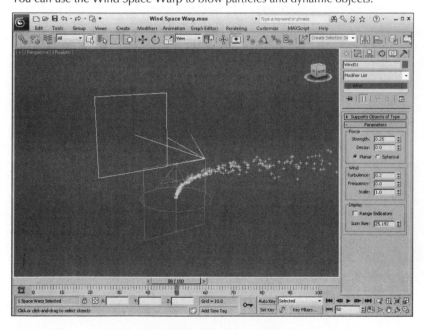

Displace

The Displace Space Warp is like a force field: It pushes objects and is useful when applied to a particle system. It can also work on any deformable object in addition to particle systems. The strength of the displacement can be defined with Strength and Decay values or with a grayscale bitmap.

The Strength value is the distance that the geometry is displaced and can be positive or negative. The Decay value causes the displacement to decrease as the distance increases. The Luminance Center is the grayscale point where no displacement occurs; any color darker than this center value is moved away, and any brighter areas move closer.

The Bitmap and Map buttons let you load images to use as a displacement map; the amount of displacement corresponds with the brightness of the image. A Blur setting blurs the image. You can apply these maps with different mapping options, including Planar, Cylindrical, Spherical, and Shrink Wrap. You can also adjust the Length, Width, and Height dimensions and the U, V, and W Tile values.

Cross-Reference

The Displace Space Warp is similar in function to the Displace modifier. The Displace modifier is discussed in Chapter 17, "Adding Material Details with Maps." ■

Figure 42.9 shows two Displace Space Warps with opposite Strength values.

FIGURE 42.9

The Displace Space Warp can raise or indent the surface of a patch grid.

Deflector Space Warps

The Deflectors subcategory of Space Warps includes POmniFlect, SOmniFlect, UOmniFlect, Deflector, SDeflector, and UDeflector. You use them all with particle systems. This category includes several different types of deflectors starting with P, S, and U. The difference between these types is their shape. P-type (planar) deflectors are box shaped, S-type (spherical) deflectors are spherical, and U-type (universal) deflectors include a Pick Object button that you can use to select any object as a deflector.

Figure 42.10 shows the icons for each of these Space Warps. All the P-type deflectors are in the first column, the S-type deflectors are in the second column, and the U-type deflectors are in the third column.

Tip

When you use deflector objects, the number of polygons makes a big difference. The deflector object uses the normal to calculate the bounce direction, so if the deflector object includes lots of polygon faces, then the system slows way down. A solution to this, especially if you're using a simple plane deflector, because all its polygon normals are the same, anyway, is to use a simplified proxy object as the deflector and hide it so the particles look like they are hitting the complex object. ■

FIGURE 42.10

The Deflector Space Warps: POmniFlect, SOmniFlect, UOmniFlect, UDeflector, SDeflector, and Deflector

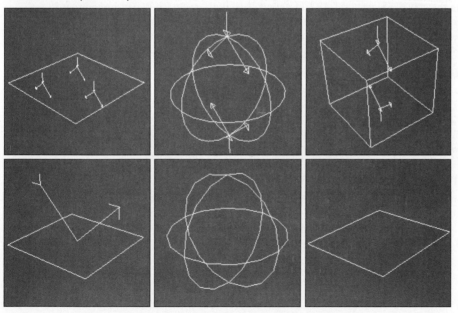

POmniFlect, SOmniFlect, and UOmniFlect

The POmniFlect Space Warp is a planar deflector that defines how particles reflect and bounce off other objects. The SOmniFlect Space Warp is just like the POmniFlect Space Warp, except that it is spherical in shape. The UOmniFlect Space Warp is another deflector, but this one can assume the shape of another object using the Pick Object button in the Parameters rollout. Its Parameters rollout includes a Timing section with Time On and Time Off values and a Reflection section.

The difference between this type of Space Warp and the other deflector Space Warps is the addition of refraction. Particles bound to this Space Warp can be refracted through an object. The values entered in the Refraction section of the Parameters rollout change the velocity and direction of a particle. The Refracts value is the percentage of particles that are refracted. The Pass Vel (velocity) is the amount that the particle speed changes when entering the object; a value of 100 maintains the same speed. The Distortion value affects the angle of refraction; a value of 0 maintains the same angle, and a value of 100 causes the particle to move along the surface of the struck object. The Diffusion value spreads the particles throughout the struck object. You can vary each of these values by using its respective Variation value.

Note

If the Refracts value is set to 100 percent, no particles are available to be refracted. ∎

You can also specify Friction and Inherit Velocity values. In the Spawn Effects Only section, the Spawns and Pass Velocity values control how many particle spawns are available and their velocity upon entering the struck object. Figure 42.11 shows each of these Space Warps bound to a Super Spray particle system. The Reflect percentage for each of the Space Warps is set to 50, and the remaining particles are refracted through the Space Warp's plane. Notice that the particles are also reflecting off the opposite side of the refracting object.

Deflector, SDeflector, and UDeflector

The Deflector and SDeflector Space Warps are simplified versions of the POmniFlect and SOmniFlect Space Warps. Their parameters include values for Bounce, Variation, Chaos, Friction, and Inherit Velocity. The UDeflector Space Warp is a simplified version of the UOmniFlect Space Warp. It has a Pick Object button for selecting the object to act as the deflector and all the same parameters as the SDeflector Space Warp.

Geometric/Deformable Space Warps

You use Geometric/Deformable Space Warps to deform the geometry of an object. Space Warps in this subcategory include FFD (Box), FFD (Cyl), Wave, Ripple, Displace, Conform, and Bomb. These Space Warps can be applied to any deformable object. Figure 42.12 shows the icons for each of these Space Warps.

FIGURE 42.11

The POmniFlect, SOmniFlect, and UOmniFlect Space Warps reflecting and refracting particles emitted from the Super Spray particle system

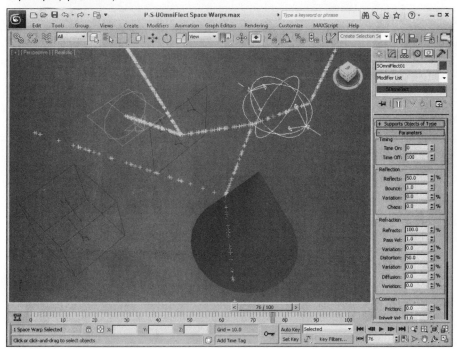

FIGURE 42.12

The Geometric/Deformable Space Warps: FFD (Box), FFD (Cyl), Wave, Ripple, Displace, Conform, and Bomb

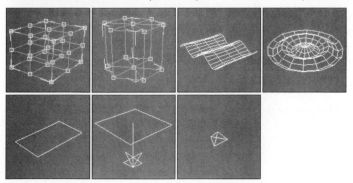

FFD (Box) and FFD (Cyl)

The FFD (Box) and FFD (Cyl) Space Warps show up as a lattice of control points in the shape of a box and a cylinder; you can select and move the control points that make up the Space Warp to deform an object that is bound to the Space Warp. The object is deformed only if the bound object is within the volume of the Space Warp.

These Space Warps have the same parameters as the modifiers with the same name found in the Modifiers ⇨ Free Form Deformers menu. The difference is that the Space Warps act in World coordinates and aren't tied to a specific object. This allows a single FFD Space Warp to affect multiple objects.

Cross-Reference

To learn about the FFD (Box) and FFD (Cyl) modifiers, see Chapter 11, "Introducing Modifiers and Using the Modifier Stack." ∎

To move the control points, select the Space Warp object, open the Modify panel, and select the Control Points subobject, which lets you alter the control points individually.

FFD Select modifier

The FFD Select modifier is another unique selection modifier. It enables you to select a group of control point subobjects for the FFD (Box) or the FFD (Cyl) Space Warps and apply additional modifiers to the selection. When an FFD Space Warp is applied to an object, you can select the Control Points subobjects and apply modifiers to the selection. The FFD Select modifier lets you select a different set of control points for a different modifier.

Wave and Ripple

The Wave and Ripple Space Warps create linear and radial waves in the objects to which they are bound. Parameters in the rollout help define the shape of the wave. Amplitude 1 is the wave's height along the X-axis, and Amplitude 2 is the wave's height along its Y-axis. The Wave Length value defines how long each wave is. The Phase value determines how the wave starts at its origin. The Decay value sets how quickly the wave dies out. A Decay value of 0 maintains the same amplitude for the entire wave.

The Sides (Circles) and Segments values determine the number of segments for the X- and Y-axes. The Division value changes the icon's size without altering the wave effect. Figure 42.13 shows a Wave Space Warp applied to a simple Box primitive. Notice that the Space Warp icon is smaller than the box, yet it affects the entire object.

Note

Be sure to include enough segments in the bound object, or the effect won't be visible. ∎

FIGURE 42.13

The Wave and Ripple Space Warps applied to a patch grid object

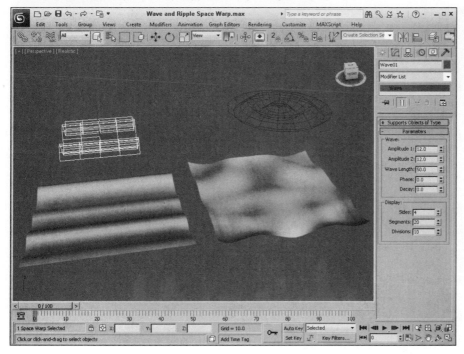

Tutorial: Creating pond ripples

For this tutorial, you position a patch object so it aligns with a background image and apply the Ripple Space Warp to it.

To add ripples to a pond, follow these steps:

1. Open the Pond ripple.max file from the Chap 42 directory on the CD.

   This file includes a background image of a bridge matched to a patch grid where the pond is located with a reflective material assigned to it.

Tip
If you're having trouble locating the patch grid, press F3 to switch to Wireframe mode. ■

2. Select the Create ➪ Space Warps ➪ Geometric/Deformable ➪ Ripple menu command. Drag in the Perspective view to create a Space Warp object. In the Parameters rollout, set the Amplitudes to **2** and the Wave Length to **30**.

3. Click the Bind to Space Warp button, and drag from the patch object to the Space Warp.

Figure 42.14 shows the resulting image.

FIGURE 42.14

A ripple in a pond produced using the Ripple Space Warp

Conform

The Conform Space Warp pushes all object vertices until they hit another target object called the Wrap To Object, or until they've moved a preset amount. The Conform Parameters rollout includes a Pick Object button that lets you pick the Wrap To Object. The object vertices move no farther than this Wrap To Object.

You can also specify a Default Projection Distance and a Standoff Distance. The Default Projection Distance is the maximum distance that the vertices move if they don't intersect with the Wrap To Object. The Standoff Distance is the separation amount maintained between the Wrap To Object and the moved vertices. Another option, Use Selected Vertices, moves only a subobject selection.

Cross-Reference

The Conform Space Warp is similar in function to the Conform compound object that is covered in Chapter 27, "Working with Compound Objects." ∎

Figure 42.15 shows some text being deformed with the Conform Space Warp. A warped quad patch has been selected as the Wrap To object.

FIGURE 42.15

The Conform Space Warp wraps the surface of one object around another object.

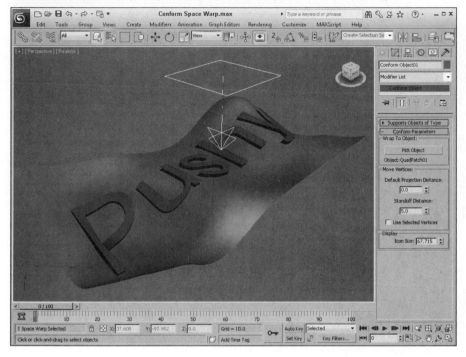

Bomb

The Bomb Space Warp causes an object to explode from its individual faces. The Strength value is the power of the bomb and determines how far objects travel when exploded. The Spin value is the rate at which the individual pieces rotate. The Falloff value defines the boundaries of faces affected by the bomb. Object faces beyond this distance remain unaffected. You must select Falloff On for the Falloff value to work.

The Min and Max Fragment Size values set the minimum and maximum number of faces caused by the explosion.

The Gravity value determines the strength of gravity and can be positive or negative. Gravity always points toward the world's Z-axis. The Chaos value can range between 0 and 10 to add variety to the explosion. The Detonation value is the number of the frame where the explosion should take place, and the Seed value alters the randomness of the event. Figure 42.16 shows a frame of an explosion produced by the Bomb Space Warp.

FIGURE 42.16

The Bomb Space Warp causes an object to explode.

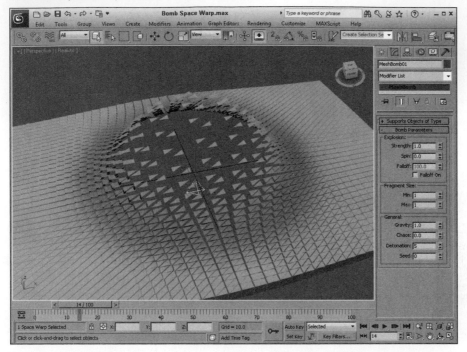

Note

The Bomb Space Warp is seen over time. At frame 0, the object shows no effect. ∎

Tutorial: Blowing a dandelion puff

You can use Space Warps with other types of objects besides particle systems. The Scatter object, for example, can quickly create many unique objects that can be controlled by a Space Warp. In this tutorial, you create a simple dandelion puff that can blow away in the wind.

To create and blow away a dandelion puff, follow these steps:

1. Open the Dandelion puff.max file from the Chap 42 directory on the CD.

   This file includes a sphere covered with a Scatter compound object representing the seeds of a dandelion.

2. Select the Create ⇨ Space Warps ⇨ Geometric/Deformable ⇨ Bomb menu command. Click in the Front viewport, and position the Bomb icon to the left and slightly below the dandelion object. In the Bomb Parameters rollout, set the Strength to **10**, the Spin to **0.5**, the Min and Max Fragment Size values to **24**, the Gravity to **0.2**, and the Chaos to **2.0**.

   This is the total number of faces included in the dandelion object.

3. Click the Bind to Space Warp button on the main toolbar, and drag from the dandelion object to the Space Warp. Then press the Play button to see the animation.

Figure 42.17 shows one frame of the dandelion puff being blown away.

You can use Space Warps on Scatter objects as well as particle systems.

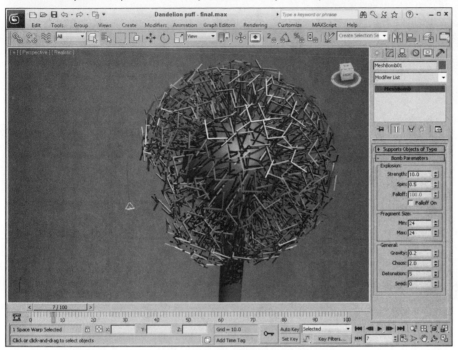

Modifier-Based Space Warps

Modifier-Based Space Warps produce the same effects as many of the standard modifiers, but because they are Space Warps, they can be applied to many objects simultaneously. Space Warps in this subcategory include Bend, Noise, Skew, Taper, Twist, and Stretch, as shown in Figure 42.18. All Modifier-Based Space Warp gizmos are simple box shapes. The parameters for all Modifier-Based Space Warps are identical to the modifiers (found in the Parametric Deformers category) of the same name. These Space Warps don't include a Supports Objects of Type rollout because they can be applied to all objects.

Cross-Reference

For details on the Bend, Noise, Skew, Taper, Twist, and Stretch modifiers and their parameters, see Chapter 11, "Introducing Modifiers and Using the Modifier Stack." ■

FIGURE 42.18

The Modifier-Based Space Warps: Bend, Noise, Skew, Taper, Twist, and Stretch

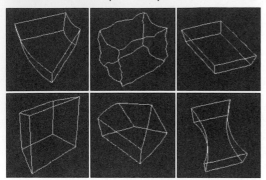

These Space Warps include a Gizmo Parameters rollout with values for the Length, Width, and Height of the gizmo. You can also specify the deformation decay. The Decay value causes the Space Warp's effect to diminish with distance from the bound object.

You can reposition the Modifier-Based Space Warp's gizmo as a separate object, but the normal modifiers require that you select the gizmo subobject to reposition it. Unlike modifiers, Space Warps don't have any subobjects.

Combining Particle Systems with Space Warps

To conclude this chapter, you'll look at some examples that use Space Warps along with particle systems. With all these Space Warps and their various parameters combined with particle systems, the possibilities are endless. These examples are only a small representation of what is possible.

Tutorial: Shattering glass

When glass shatters, it is very chaotic, sending pieces in every direction. For this tutorial, you shatter a glass mirror on a wall. The wall keeps the pieces from flying off, and most pieces fall straight to the floor.

To shatter glass, follow these steps:

1. Open the Shattering glass.max file from the Chap 42 directory on the CD.

   This file includes a simple mirror created from patch grid objects. The file also includes a simple sphere that is animated striking the mirror.

2. Select the Create ⇨ Particles ⇨ PArray menu command. Then drag in the Front viewport to create the PArray icon. In the Basic Parameters rollout, click the Pick Object button and select the first patch object. In the Viewport Display section, select the Mesh option. In the Particle Generation rollout, set the Speed and Divergence to **0**. Also set the Emit Start to **30** and the Life value to **100**, so it matches the last frame. In the Particle Type rollout, select the Object Fragments option, and set the Thickness to **1.0**. Then in the Object Fragment Controls section, select the Number of Chunks option with a Minimum value of **30**. In the Rotation and Collision rollout, set the Spin Time to **100** and the Variation to **50**.

   These settings cause the patch to emit 30 object fragments with a slow, gradual rotation.

3. Select the Space Warps category button, and choose the Forces subcategory from the drop-down list. Click the PBomb button, and create a PBomb Space Warp in the Top view; then center it above the Mirror patch. In the Modify panel, set the Blast Symmetry option to Spherical with a Chaos value of **50** percent. Set the Start Time to **30** with a Strength value of **0.2**. Then click the Bind to Space Warp button, and drag from the PBomb Space Warp to the PArray icon.

4. Select the Create ⇨ Space Warps ⇨ Forces ⇨ Gravity menu command, and drag in the Front viewport to create a Gravity Space Warp. Position the Gravity Space Warp so that the icon arrow is pointing down in the Front viewport. In the Modify panel, set the Strength value to **0.1**. Then bind this Space Warp to the PArray icon.

5. Select the Create ⇨ Space Warps ⇨ Deflectors ⇨ POmniFlect menu command. Drag this Space Warp in the Top view, and make it wide enough to be completely under the mirror object. Rotate the POmniFlect Space Warp so that its arrows are pointing up at the mirror. Position it so that it lies in the same plane as the plane object that makes up the floor. In the Modify panel, set the Reflects value to **100** percent and the Bounce value to **0**. Bind this Space Warp to the PArray as well; this keeps the pieces from falling through the floor. Press Play to see the results.

Figure 42.19 shows the mirror immediately after being struck by a ball.

FIGURE 42.19

A shattering mirror

Tutorial: Making water flow down a trough

That should be enough destruction for a while. In this final example, you'll make some water particles flow down a trough. You accomplish this using the Path Follow Space Warp.

To make water flow down a trough, follow these steps:

1. Open the Water flowing down a trough.max file from the Chap 42 directory on the CD.

   This file includes a simple trough made from primitives and a spline path that the water will follow.

2. Select Particle Systems from the subcategory drop-down list, and click the Super Spray button. Create a Super Spray object in the Front viewport and position its pointer where you want the particles to first appear. In the Viewport Display section, select the Ticks particles option. In the Particle Generation rollout, set the Speed to **10** and the Variation to **100**. Then set the Emit Start to **0** and the Display Until and Life values to **100**. In the Particle Type rollout, select MetaParticles and enable the Automatic Coarseness option.

3. Select the Space Warps category button, and choose Forces from the subcategory drop-down list. Click the Path Follow button, and create a Path Follow object; then click the Bind to Space Warp button on the main toolbar, and drag from the Path Follow icon to the first Super Spray icon. Open the Modify panel, select the Path Follow icon, click the Pick Shape Object button, and select the path in the viewports. Set the Start Frame to **0** and the Travel Time to **100**.

Figure 42.20 shows the rendered result.

FIGURE 42.20

Water flowing down a trough using the Path Follow Space Warp

Summary

Space Warps are useful for adding forces and effects to objects in the scene. Max has several different types of Space Warps, and most of them can be applied only to certain object types. In this chapter, you learned the following:

- How to create Space Warps
- How to bind Space Warps to objects
- How to use all the various Space Warps in several subcategories
- How to combine Space Warps with particle systems to shatter glass and explode a planet

You can have Max dynamically compute all the animation frames in a scene using the physics-based MassFX engine, which is covered in the next chapter.

Simulating Physics-Based Motion with MassFX

When you speak of MassFX in Max, you really are speaking of physics. Physics is one of the coolest arms of science because it deals with the science of matter and energy and includes laws that govern the motions and interactions between objects. For animators, this is great news because what you are trying to do is to animate the motions and interactions between objects.

So, should all animators study physics? The answer is absolutely. Understanding these laws through study and experience will sharpen your animating skills. But you can also take advantage of the work that other animators have done in understanding the laws of physics and turning them into a product that ships with Max. The other animators are the PhysX group at NVIDIA, and the product is MassFX.

The MassFX physics engine included in Max is the same engine commonly used in games to simulate game-world physics.

Using MassFX, you can simulate many physical properties like density, mass, and friction and automatically capture keyframes as the objects interact. It's like getting a physics degree for free.

The MassFX tools include everything you need to access the MassFX physics simulation engine. After physical properties are defined, you can define physical forces to act on these objects and simulate the resulting animation. Not only does MassFX make difficult physical motions realistic, but it also is fun to play with.

Understanding Dynamics

Dynamics is a branch of physics that deals with forces and the motions they cause, and regardless of your experience in school, physics is your friend—especially in the world of 3D. Dynamics in Max can automate the creation of animation keys by calculating the position, rotation, and collisions between objects based on physics equations.

Consider the motion of a simple yo-yo. Animating this motion with keys is fairly simple: Set rotation and position keys halfway through the animation and again at the end, and you're finished.

Now think of the forces controlling the yo-yo. Gravity causes the yo-yo to accelerate toward the ground, causing the string to unwind, which makes the yo-yo spin about its axis. When it reaches the end of the string, the rotation reverses and the yo-yo rises. Using Gravity and Motor Space Warps, you can simulate this motion, but setting the keys manually is probably easier for these few objects.

But before you write off dynamics, think of the motion of popcorn popping. With all the pieces involved, setting all the position and rotation keys would take a long time. For this system, using dynamics makes sense.

Dynamic tools let you specify objects to include in a simulation, the forces they interact with, and the objects to be involved in collisions. After the system is defined, the Dynamics utility automatically calculates the movement and collisions of these objects according to the forces involved, and then it sets the keys for you.

New Feature

The MassFX system is new to 3ds Max 2012. ∎

Note

MassFX isn't the first physic-based system available in Max. Early versions of Max had a Dynamics utility, and recently dynamics were possible using Max's reactor system. These early systems have been replaced by MassFX, which is easier to use and much more robust than earlier versions. ∎

Using MassFX

The MassFX plug-in was developed by a company named PhysX, which is now part of NVIDIA. MassFX is a complex piece of software with a huge assortment of features that enable you to define physical properties and forces and have the scene automatically generate the resulting animation keys as the objects interact while following the laws of physics.

The MassFX plug-in interface can be accessed from a simple toolbar that's opened using the right-click pop-up menu on any toolbar. The toolbar is named MassFX, shown in Figure 43.1, and it is surprisingly simple, consisting of only five buttons. With the MassFX toolbar, you can open the MassFX Tools dialog box, define objects and constraints to include in the simulation, and control the simulation. The toolbar also includes several flyout tools that are described in Table 43.1.

FIGURE 43.1

Use the MassFX toolbar to open the MassFX Tools dialog box and define and control simulations.

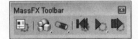

TABLE 43.1

MassFX Toolbar Buttons

Toolbar Button	Name	Description
	Display MassFX Tools Dialog	Opens the MassFX Tools dialog box
	Set Selected as Dynamic Rigid Body, Set Selected as Kinematic Rigid Body, Set Selected as Static Rigid Body	Sets the object type for the selected object to dynamic, kinematic, or static
	Create Rigid Constraint, Create Slide Constraint, Create Hinge Constraint, Create Twist Constraint, Create Universal Constraint, Create Ball & Socket Constraint	Adds a constraint to the scene the limits the motions of specific objects.
	Reset Simulation	Resets the scene to a state as before the simulation started
	Start Simulation, Start Simulation without Animation	Begins the simulation
	Step Simulation	Moves the simulation forward one frame

The MassFX commands also are available as menu options in the Animation ⇨ Simulation–MassFX menu.

The MassFX process

Before getting into the details of MassFX, I want to briefly explain the process involved in using this feature. MassFX works with geometry that is defined with certain physical properties. After these properties are defined, the MassFX engine can take over and determine how all the various objects interact with one another.

The first step is to assign each object to be included in the simulation an object type. These can be either Dynamic, Kinematic, or Static. Dynamic objects are ones that are included in the simulation, Kinematic objects apply forces to the simulation and can be changed to a Dynamic object to interact with other objects, but Static objects don't move and provide the walls and floor for the objects to crash against.

In addition to the object type, you can specify values for the object's Density, Mass, Friction, and Bounciness using the MassFX Tools dialog box. More on these values is presented later in this chapter.

When an object is assigned a type, it automatically assumes a proxy shape that surrounds the object that is used to calculate any collisions. To keep the simulation calculations simple, this default proxy shape is usually a simple box or sphere. MassFX allows you to use a more complex collision mesh, but doing so compounds the simulation calculations and should be used sparingly. Within the Edit panel of the MassFX Tools dialog box are several options for defining the collision mesh, including a tool to generate a custom collision mesh based on the object's geometry.

Establishing the simulation properties

The MassFX Tools dialog box, shown in Figure 43.2, is opened using the first button in the MassFX toolbar. The MassFX Tools dialog box holds the settings for the World values. These World values are the global settings for the simulation. The global values defined in the World panel apply to all objects included in the simulation, but these global values can be changed for each individual object using the settings in the Edit panel.

FIGURE 43.2

The MassFX Tools dialog box includes World settings.

By default, the ground plane acts as a static object, and gravity is enabled. You can change the value of gravity and even make it a positive value so objects float upward using the settings in the World panel.

The number of Substeps determines the amount of calculations that the simulation goes through. Generally, the higher the Substeps value, the more accurate the simulation collisions and the longer it takes to complete. This is also impacted by the Solver Iterations. More Solver Iterations are needed for simulations involving a lot of constraints and collisions, but a value larger than 30 is overkill.

The Collision Overlap value is the amount of overlap between collision meshes that is allowed. If this is set to 0, the objects can jitter about erratically, but values too high will allow the objects to penetrate each other noticeably.

If you know that some objects, such as a projectile, will travel very fast, you can enable the Use High Velocity Collisions option. This option uses a different algorithm that prevents gross overlapping of surfaces for high velocity objects.

Within the Advanced Settings rollout, you can set the minimum speed and spin values for the Sleep, High Velocity, and Bounce settings. These settings are global for all objects in the simulation unless overwritten by a setting for the individual object.

The Simulation Settings rollout includes several options that define what to do when the last frame of the animation is reached. The options are to simply continue the simulation. Be aware that any motion beyond the last frame will not be captured if you bake the motion down into keyframes. You can also choose to stop the simulation, loop the animation by resetting it or continuing it.

Finally, the Engine rollout includes an option for enabling multithreading if your system includes multiple cores. The Hardware Acceleration option can be used for Nvidia cards to speed the simulation calculations.

Starting and stopping the simulation

After the world and object properties are set, you can click the Start Simulation button in the MassFX toolbar and the results are immediately calculated and displayed within the viewport. The MassFX toolbar also includes a button to reset the simulation and another button to step through the simulation one frame at a time.

As a flyout option under the Start Simulation button is an option to Start the Simulation with Animation. This runs the simulation without changing the current frame on the Track Bar.

Tutorial: Filling a glass bowl

Imagine trying to animate a bunch of marbles falling into a glass bowl. If you were using keyframes, determining whether an object overlaps another would be difficult, but with this quick example you see the power of MassFX.

To animate marbles falling into a glass bowl, follow these steps:

1. Open the Glass bowl of marbles.max file from the Chap 43 directory on the CD.

   This file includes a glass bowl and several marbles positioned above its opening.

2. Right-click the main toolbar, and select MassFX Toolbar. Then select all the marbles located above the bowl, and click the Set Selected as Dynamic Rigid Body button.

3. Select the tabletop object, and click the Set Selected as Static Rigid Body button. This button is a flyout under the Set Selected as Dynamic Rigid Body button. Then click the Start Simulation button in the MassFX toolbar, and notice how the marbles all fall and spread out on the tabletop.

4. Select the bowl object, and set it as a static object by repeating Step 3. This time, the marbles all fall into the bowl.

Figure 43.3 shows the bowl full of marbles positioned using MassFX.

FIGURE 43.3

MassFX can compute all the collisions between all these marbles.

Setting Object Properties

One of the first steps in creating with a simulation is defining the object properties. For example, a simple sphere object in Max could represent a bowling ball, an orange, or a tennis ball. Each of these objects responds very differently when being animated to drop on the floor.

Setting the object type

All objects involved in a MassFX simulation must be assigned one of three object types. The available object types are:

- **Dynamic:** These objects move when they collide with other objects. Dynamic objects also are affected by gravity.

- **Kinematic:** These objects impact other dynamic objects in the scene, but they don't move when they collide with dynamic objects. They can be animated and often provide the force to the simulation. Kinematic objects are not affected by gravity.

- **Static:** These objects have an infinite mass and don't move when they collide with other objects. They frequently are used for ground and walls. They also are not affected by gravity.

These object types are available as buttons in the MassFX toolbar. To specify an object as one of these types, simply select the object and click the object type button in the toolbar. Any object with a defined object type is automatically added to the simulation. Any scene object without an object type is simply ignored.

Kinematic objects can be animated using standard keyframe animation and then be changed to a dynamic object at a given frame using the Until Frame value located in the Rigid Body Properties rollout. This provides a way to add forces to the simulation such as a marble that is animated being shot at a group of marbles. Just before colliding, you can set the shot marble to become dynamic so it continues its motion and then interacts with the other marbles based on the physics.

When one of the object types is assigned to an object, it appears as a modifier in the Modifier Stack. If you remove this modifier, the object is removed from the simulation and returned to its original state.

When an object's type is defined as a dynamic, kinematic, or static, the system automatically assigns some rough physical properties based on the object's size in the scene. Static objects, for example, are given a large mass, which essentially makes them immovable, and small dynamic objects are given very small mass values.

The Rigid Body Properties rollout also includes options for disabling gravity and collisions and computing for high-velocity objects.

When dynamic objects are placed in the scene, it is often difficult to get them positioned exactly on top of one another. Actually, it is better to have a small gap between objects so they don't overlap. Overlapping objects will repel one another when the simulation first starts causing motion before you want it. Within the Rigid Body Properties rollout is the Start in Sleep Mode option that causes all dynamic objects to freeze in their initial positions until hit by another object. Enabling this option helps prevent the initial movement of stacked objects when the simulation starts due to gravity.

Regardless of the object type and its default values, you can set the actual physical properties for the selected object using the settings in the Physical Material rollout in the Command Panel when the object is selected. You can access these same properties in the Edit panel of the MassFX Tools dialog box, shown in Figure 43.4. You also can select and set the properties for multiple selected objects at the same time.

Tip

Although the Command Panel and the MassFX Tools dialog box have mostly the same settings, the MassFX Tools dialog box lets you set values for multiple selections at once. ■

FIGURE 43.4

The Edit panel of the MassFX Tools dialog box includes physical property values for the selected object.

Density, mass, friction, and elasticity

Although many different physical properties are available, the MassFX system is mainly concerned with collisions between rigid body objects, which can be computed using a short list of physical properties including Density, Mass, Static Friction, Dynamic Friction, and Bounciness.

The Density property is the amount of mass per volume, so it's related to mass. The Mass property defines how heavy the object is. For example, a bowling ball has a higher mass value than a Ping-Pong ball, and a Ping-Pong ball is not as dense (or heavy) as a golf ball, even though they are roughly the same size.

Friction is the force of contact between two touching objects. It defines how resistant the object is to rolling or sliding along the floor. For example, when you slide an air-hockey puck over an air-hockey table, the friction is very low because of the jets of air, but moving a piece of sandpaper across a piece of wood has a very high value of friction that resists the movement.

Friction is actually defined by two properties. Static friction is the initial force required to start an object sliding across another, and dynamic friction is the amount of force required to keep the object sliding over the top of the other. Both of these properties are available in the MassFX system.

Note

A rigid body with a Mass value of 0 causes problems for all calculations, so the system automatically sets the Density or Mass value to 0.01 when you try to set it to 0.

Creating presets

If you've done some research and figured out the exact physical properties for a specific object, you can use the Create Preset button in the Physical Material rollout of the MassFX Tools dialog box to save and name the physical values for the selected object. All defined presets are populated in the drop-down list. This provides a great way to reuse values that you know are right. The eyedropper tool lets you quickly pick the properties from another object in the scene.

When a preset is used, all its properties are automatically locked, but you can unlock and change them using the Lock icon in the upper-left corner of the Physical Material Properties rollout of the MassFX Tools dialog box in the Edit panel.

Defining collision boundaries

Another common property that you can set pertains to how the object deals with collision detection. You can select the volume to use to determine when two objects collide with each other. If this sounds a bit funny because any collision volume that doesn't use the actual mesh would be inaccurate, then you need to realize that a complex simulation with lots of collisions of complex objects could take a long time to compute. If MassFX has only to compute collisions based on the object's bounding box instead of the actual mesh object, the simulation runs much more quickly, and the inaccuracies aren't even noticeable.

Before deciding on the collision boundary to use, you need to determine whether an object is convex or concave. A *convex* object is one that you can penetrate with a ray and cross its mesh boundary only twice. *Concave* objects require more than two crossings with an imaginary ray. In other words, concave meshes have surface areas that bend inward like a doughnut and convex meshes don't, like a normal sphere. Convex meshes are much easier to use when calculating collisions than concave meshes.

Using convex meshes

A convex object can use several of the options found in the Physical Meshes rollout, including Sphere, Box, Capsule, and Convex. Use the shape that best fits the mesh you are working with.

The properties for the mesh types are listed in the Physical Mesh Parameters rollout. When an object type is applied to an object, the Convex mesh type is applied by default, because it generally works for all objects. The Convex mesh type is created from a Geosphere object represented by 32 vertices. If you reduce the number of vertices—or switch to a Sphere, Box, or Capsule mesh type—you can speed up the simulation calculations.

Using the Inflation value, you can increase or decrease the size of the collision mesh. Additional settings are available in the Physical Mesh Parameters rollout for each type. For example, the Sphere mesh type has a Radius value and the Box mesh type has Length, Height, and Width values. If you make changes to the Convex mesh type that don't work, you can always regenerate the mesh using the Regenerate from Original button.

If the collision mesh shape is right, but its position is off, then you can choose the Mesh Transform subobject mode in the Modifier Stack and change the mesh's position and orientation.

Using concave meshes

If you have a concave object that you want to use in the simulation, you should first try to use a convex collision mesh if possible, but if you can't (such as with the bowl in the preceding example), the best option is the Composite mesh type. For example, a doughnut-shaped object bouncing in a scene could easily use a flat sphere shaped convex collision mesh because it isn't likely that a smaller object will go through the doughnut's center. However, if you are dealing with a basketball rim, then enabling a convex mesh won't work because objects will be going through the rim's center, so a concave collision mesh is required.

This Composite option lets you specify the number of vertices and several other settings and includes a Generate button to automatically create the collision mesh based on the object's geometry. Once generated, the number hulls and vertices included in the collision mesh are displayed. If these numbers are still too high, you can change the Max Vertices, Split Levels, or Size Difference values and try the Generate button again. Remember that more vertices means better accuracy in the simulation, but also more time to complete.

The Original option works well for concave objects that are set to static and won't move during the simulation. It uses the actual mesh as the collision mesh.

The Custom option lets you create a collision mesh based on selected piece of geometry in the scene. It includes buttons for picking the source object and extracting a mesh from the source object. The proxy mesh should be a low-resolution version of an object used here for collision detection.

Caution

Custom collision meshes are limited to objects with 256 vertices or less. ∎

Setting initial motion

Every dynamic object has an initial motion setting that you can control to start the object in motion. This works whether gravity is enabled or disabled. The Initial Motion values are located in the Advanced rollout and can be set to an Absolute or Relative value. If a kinematic object is in motion when it is converted to a dynamic object using the Until Frame setting and it has an initial motion value, then the Absolute setting uses only the initial motion value and the Relative option adds the initial motion value to the existing keyframed motion that the object already has. The X, Y, and Z value denote a direction, and Speed sets how fast the object is moving. A setting for the initial spin of the object is available as well.

The Damping values are used to slow down the motion (Linear) and the rotation (Angular) of objects in motion with higher values causing the objects to rapidly decrease their speed.

Under the MassFX Rigid Body modifier that is applied to the selected object, you can select the Initial Velocity and Initial Spin subobject modes, and an arrow shows the current direction of the initial movement or spin. While either of these subobject modes is selected, you can use the Rotate tool to change them in the viewport. This is easier than having to enter values in the rollout.

The modifier also includes an option for changing the Center of Mass location and for moving and manipulating the collision mesh's transform.

Displaying interactions

The Display panel of the MassFX Tools dialog box has a number of options that you turn on and off to see the simulation properties. The Display Physical Meshes option shows the collision mesh for all objects or only for the selected objects if the Selected Objects Only option is enabled.

If you turn on the Enable Visualizer option, then a whole range of different properties are made visible as the simulation proceeds including arrows showing object speed, contact points between objects and collision meshes.

Tutorial: Knocking over milk cans

You can add motion to the simulation objects in two ways. One is to use the initial motion values in the Advanced rollout of the Edit panel of the MassFX Tools dialog box. The other is to set an object as a Kinematic object that is animated using standard keyframes and then switched to a Dynamic object at a given frame with the Until Frame option in the Rigid Body Properties rollout of the MassFX Tools dialog box.

To animate the milk can tipping carnival game, follow these steps:

1. Open the Tipping milk cans.max file from the Chap 43 directory on the CD.

   This file includes several milk cans positioned on a cylinder along with three balls.

2. Right-click the main toolbar, and select MassFX Toolbar. Then select all the milk cans located above the cylinder, and click the Set Selected as Dynamic Rigid Body button. Then click the Display MassFX Tools Dialog button on the MassFX toolbar and in the Edit panel, set the Density value to 10 for all the milk cans.

4. Select the cylinder and the floor objects, and click the Set Selected as Static Rigid Body button.

5. Select the smallest ball object, and click the Set Selected as Dynamic Rigid Body button. Then open the Advanced rollout and set the X Initial Velocity value to -1 and the Speed value to 2500. Then click the Start Simulation button in the MassFX toolbar, and notice how the first ball falls a little short. Click the Reset Simulation button in the MassFX toolbar.

6. Locate and click the Time Configuration button beneath the Play button at the bottom of the interface and in the Time Configuration dialog box, set the End Time to 300.

7. Select the second ball object, and click the Set Selected as Kinematic Rigid Body button. Then enable the Until Frame option in the Rigid Body Properties rollout to 100. Then set the Density to 3, the X Initial Velocity value to -1 and the Speed value to 2500. Then click the Start Simulation button in the MassFX toolbar, and notice how the second ball knocks them all down.

Figure 43.5 shows the large ball striking the milk cans.

FIGURE 43.5

Kinematic objects can be made to start at a later frame.

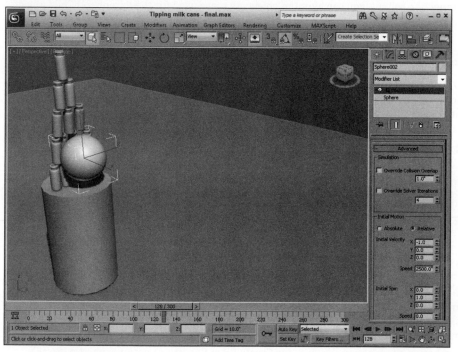

Using Constraints

Constraints are ways to limit the amount of motion that an object can do. Using constraints can help control objects in the scene as they interact with other objects. Perhaps the simplest constraint isn't a constraint at all. If you set an object to be Static, it won't move.

Other constraints found in the MassFX toolbar include Rigid Constraint, Slide Constraint, Hinge Constraint, Twist Constraint, Universal Constraint, and Ball & Socket Constraint. To apply a constraint, you need two objects, and they both must be selected. The first object you select becomes the parent object and the second the child.

Note
You can also select a single object and apply a constraint and then pick the parent object later using the button in the Modify panel. ■

After the constraint is selected, a helper object titled UConstraint is added to the scene, and you can drag out the helper object to show the range of the applied constraint. When the helper constraint object is selected, the parameters for the constraint are displayed in the Command Panel.

Constraints can be made Breakable, and you can set the Max Force and/or Torque required to break the constraint. Once a constraint is broken, it no longer has any affect on the simulation.

Within the Connection rollout, you can alter the objects that are used for the Parent and Child objects. Additional rollouts define the available translation, swing, twist, and spring properties for each type of constraint. For each, you can set the constraint to be Locked, Limited, or Free about each axis. If the Limited option is enabled, then you can set the limits using the values such as Limit Radius, Bounce, Spring, and Damping.

Although you can move the constraint helper to wherever it needs to be, it is often easier to define the constraint's location by positioning the object's pivot. In the Advanced rollout are buttons for moving the constraint helper to the parent or child's pivot location.

Tutorial: Opening a door
Each of the constraints enables different types of motion and some situations require multiple constraints, such as the hinge on a door.

To use constraints to restrict the motion of a door, follow these steps:

1. Open the Door with a hinge.max file from the Chap 43 directory on the CD.

   This file includes a simple door between two walls.

2. Open the MassFX toolbar. Then select all the objects except the floor and click the Set Selected to Dynamic Rigid Body button. Select the floor object and set it to **Static**.

3. Select the far wall object and then the door object and click the Create Hinge Constraint from the MassFX toolbar. Then drag in the viewport to set the constraint's size. Move the constraint so it is positioned at the point between the wall and the door and rotate it so it allows the door to swing away from the ball.

4. Select both wall objects and choose the Create Rigid Constraint option from the MassFX toolbar. This prevents the walls from moving.

Caution
Static objects cannot be used as a parent or child for a constraint. ■

5. Select the ball object and set its Density to 20, the X Initial Velocity value to -1, and the Speed value to 5000. This should be enough to give the door a good kick.

6. Click the Start Simulation button in the MassFX toolbar.

Figure 43.6 shows the door flying open.

FIGURE 43.6

Using the hinge constraint controls the motion of this door.

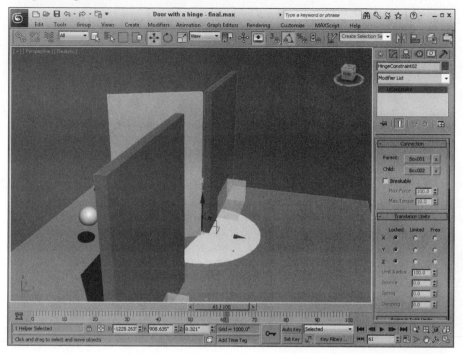

Capturing the Simulation Motion as Keys

Once you're happy with the motion created by the simulation, you can capture the motion as keys using the Bake command. There is a Bake button in the Rigid Body Properties rollout of the Edit panel in the MassFX Tools dialog box. There are also several different bake options in the Tools panel including options to Bake All, Bake Selected, Unbake All, and Unbake Selected.

Once the motion is baked, the keys for each object in the simulation show up on the Track Bar and the animation can be manipulated and edited using the animation tools and the Track View.

The Tools panel also includes another helpful button. The Capture Transforms button causes the current state of the selected objects to be reset as its new initial position. If the Reset Simulation button is then used, this new initial position is used instead of the object's original location. This is great because it give you a chance to let the objects settle at the start simulation and then reset them in this location before starting the simulation.

Within the Utilities rollout of the Tools panel, the Explore Scene button opens the Scene Explorer where it shows all the objects included in the simulation and their respective simulation properties including SimType, SimMode, SimEnabled, and SimBaked. From this scene, you can quickly enable and disable multiple objects or change their object type.

The Validate Scene button runs a quick check on the simulation looking for potential problems that might be encountered when the scene is exported, as shown in Figure 43.7. It looks for issues such as non-uniform scaling and skewed objects. The Export Scene button opens a dialog box where you can set the export options. Simulations can be exported to the XML, binary, or Collada formats.

FIGURE 43.7

Scenes can be validated before exporting to look for potential problems.

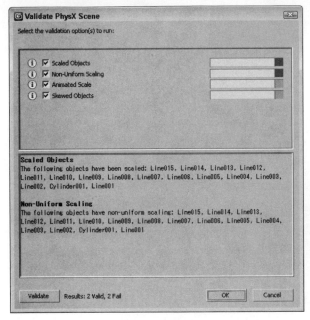

Tutorial: Dropping a plate of donuts

All the great books have an element of tragedy, so consider a policeman carrying a dozen donuts on a plate when he stumbles and drops the plate. Donuts everywhere, how tragic! This animation sequence would be difficult or at least time-consuming if it were not for MassFX.

To use MassFX to animate a falling plate of donuts, follow these steps:

1. Open the Falling plate of donuts.max file from the Chap 43 directory on the CD.

   This file includes a simple plate of donuts created from primitives.

2. Open the MassFX toolbar. Then select all the donuts and the plate, and click the Set Selected to Dynamic Rigid Body button.

3. Because the floor object is aligned to the ground plane, just make sure that the Use Ground Plane and the Gravity Enabled options are enabled in the World panel of the MassFX Tools dialog box.

4. Click the Start Simulation button in the MassFX toolbar.

5. After the simulation is complete and looks fine, click the Bake All button in the Tools panel of the MassFX Tools dialog box, and the keys for the animation are added to the Track Bar.

6. When it completes, press the Play Animation button (or press the / key) to see the results.

Figure 43.8 shows the upturned plate of donuts. Oh, the tragedy, the horror, the creamy fillings.

FIGURE 43.8

Animating these falling donuts was easy with MassFX.

Summary

This chapter covered the basics of animating a dynamic simulation using MassFX. In this chapter, you accomplished the following:

- Understanding the principles of dynamics
- Accessing the MassFX tools
- Defining object types and properties
- Setting the collision mesh type
- Setting initial motion
- Working with constraints
- Baking animation keys

The next chapter covers the dynamic abilities of Max's hair and cloth systems.

Animating Hair and Cloth

The specialized hair and cloth systems can create believable, realistic hair, but the real benefit to making hair and cloth come alive is found in the dynamic abilities of both.

In this chapter, you'll look at the dynamic abilities of both the hair and cloth systems. Using these systems, you can simulate hair blown by the wind and cloth that drapes over and around underlying objects.

Cross-Reference

Creating and defining both the Hair and Cloth systems is covered in Chapter 29, "Adding and Styling Hair and Fur, and Using Cloth." ∎

Using Hair Dynamics

Being able to style hair is great, but have you ever left the barbershop and had the wind do its own styling job on your hair? The Dynamics rollout for Hair and Fur lets you define specific forces and let the hair fall where it may.

Tip

Be conservative with the forces that are applied to a hair system. Too many forces or too extreme forces can easily destroy any styling that you've created. ∎

Making hair live

The Dynamics rollout is available only if the Hair and Fur (WSM) modifier has been applied to an object. At the top of the Dynamics rollout are three modes: None, Live, and Precomputed. If you select the Live mode, then the hair around the growth object immediately becomes subject to gravity and other forces in real time, causing the hair to droop about the growth object.

Moreover, if you move the object within the viewport, the hair flows about the object as if you were moving a real object with hair attached. Figure 44.1 shows a simple mouse with hair attached. The image on the left shows the hair particles with the None mode enabled, and the image on the right shows the hair after the Live mode is enabled. Notice how the hair particles fall around the mouse object.

FIGURE 44.1

The Live dynamic mode makes the hair react in real time to the scene forces.

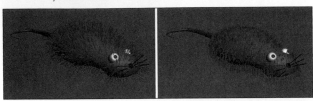

If you press the Escape key while in Live mode, a dialog box appears, giving you the option to Freeze, Stop, or Continue. If you click the Freeze button, then the hair stays in its current position.

The Precomputed mode is available only after you've specified a Stat File name. This mode lets you save the hair motions into a separate stat file.

Setting properties

Only a few properties need to be defined to enable hair dynamics. In the Dynamics rollout, you find values for Gravity, Stiffness, Root Hold, and Dampen. These properties control how the hair behaves in response to the environment forces. The Gravity value can be negative if you want the hair to rise instead of fall. You can simulate space environments by setting the gravity to 0. The Stiffness value eliminates all dynamic movement if set to 1.0. If you want the hair to move only slightly as the object moves, then a Stiffness value close to 1.0 should work. The Root Hold value is like stiffness but applies only to the root. The Dampen value causes motions to die out quickly.

All dynamic properties except Gravity can be controlled using a grayscale map, using the small button to the right of the value field.

Enabling collisions

The first type of dynamic force to address is to enable collisions between the hair and the other scene objects. To enable collisions between the growth object and its hair, simply enable the Use Growth Object option. This option is only enabled when Sphere or Polygon Collisions are enabled first. In addition to the growth object, other scene objects can be added to the list with which the hair will collide. To add other objects, click the Add button and pick the object to add in the viewport. Each collision object can use either a boundary Sphere to define its collision volume or a Polygon, which bases collisions on the actual surface geometry. The latter takes longer to compute, but it's more accurate.

Enabling forces

In addition to the ubiquitous gravity, you can enable collisions between the hairs and the growth object and any other scene objects. To add another scene object to the collision calculations, click the Add button and select the new collision object. The External Forces list lets you add Space Warps for additional forces such as Wind.

Running a simulation

The Precomputed mode lets you save the hair dynamics to a separate stat file. If you want to capture the dynamic simulation, you first must specify a stat file by clicking the button to the right of the Stat File section. With a stat file specified, click the Run button in the Simulation section to calculate the dynamic solution. The Start and End fields let you enter the range for the simulation. A separate stat file is generated for every frame of the animation.

If you enable the Precomputed mode option before you render, then the stat file is read and used during the rendering process. You can delete all stat files quickly with the scarily named Delete all files button.

Tutorial: Simulating hair dynamics

Dynamic hair moves and flows around the other objects in the scene that are animated. As an example of this, you'll move a female character's head back and forth and simulate how the hair moves. I selected the Mohawk hairstyle because I'm hip and cool, a real rebel. Actually, the Mohawk is a simple style and gives you a chance to play with the Stiffness property.

To simulate the dynamics of a hair system, follow these steps:

1. Open the Female head with mohawk.max file from the Chap 44 directory on the CD.

   This file includes the head from a female character model created by Zygote Media. The hair modifier already has been added to this character and styled.

2. Click the Auto Key button, drag the Time Slider to frame 5, and move the character to the right in the Top viewport. Then drag the Time Slider to frame 10, and move the character back to the left. This simple motion should be enough to bend the hair over. Then disable the Auto Key mode.

3. With the head selected, open the Dynamics rollout and set the Stiffness value to **0.8**. This should keep the hair standing straight up. To check this, enable the Live mode and watch how the hair reacts.

4. Set the Simulation to run from 0 to 10 frames, and then open and specify a stat file location. The path of the stat file location is displayed. Then click the Run button to start the simulation. The precomputed values are saved to stat files.

5. Select the Precomputed mode option and drag through the animation frames to see how the hair reacts.

Figure 44.2 shows the hair bending to one side as the female head moves.

FIGURE 44.2

Using precomputed hair can save you a bundle of time when rendering.

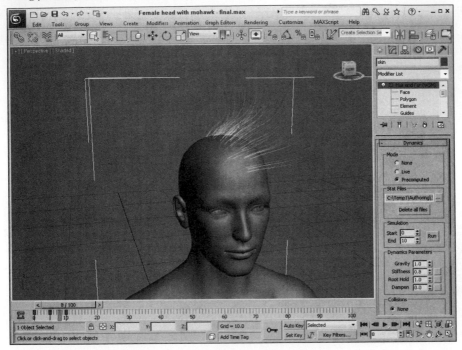

Simulating Cloth Dynamics

Hair isn't the only system that has the benefit of dynamic motion. Cloth also can benefit from dynamic simulations. The steps for setting up a dynamic cloth simulation are similar to those for hair. First, apply the cloth modifier and define the cloth properties and the environmental forces acting on the cloth. Then run the simulation.

Defining cloth properties and forces

To add objects (both cloth and collision objects) to the simulation, click the Object Properties button in the Object rollout. This opens the Object Properties dialog box, shown in Figure 44.3. Clicking the Add Objects button lets you select scene objects to add to the simulation. Only objects added to the scene are included in the simulation. If an object isn't added, it's ignored. All objects added to the simulation are added to the list at the left. Selected objects in the list can be specified as Inactive, Cloth, or Collision Object. For Cloth and Collision Objects, you can set properties. You also can load and save cloth presets. Cloth presets are saved using the .sti extension.

Tip

If the cloth tends to pass through objects, then you can increase the Offset value for the collision object. ∎

FIGURE 44.3

The Object Properties dialog box lets you define the properties of cloth and collision objects.

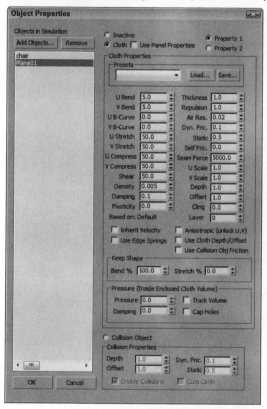

After all the objects involved in the simulation are included and defined, you can set the simulation range in the Simulation Parameters rollout. The initial state for the object to be draped may be set using the Set Initial State button, which is located in the Object rollout. The Cloth Forces button, in the Object rollout, opens a simple dialog box where you can select to add additional forces to the simulation. Gravity is added by default, but you can change its value in the Simulation Parameters rollout.

Creating a cloth simulation

After completing the initial setup, clicking the Simulate button starts the simulation process. The objects are updated in the viewport as each frame is calculated. After every frame is calculated, you can see the entire dynamic simulation by dragging the Time Slider or clicking the Play Animation button. If you want to drape the cloth without running it over several frames, you can use the Simulate Local button. The Simulate Local (damped) button causes the simulation to run local with a large amount of damping, which is useful if the cloth tends to drape too fast. If you want to remove the current simulation because some properties have changed, click the Erase Simulation button, or you can remove all frames after the current simulation frame with the Truncate Simulation button.

Tip
If the simulation is taking too long to compute, you can cancel the simulation by pressing the Escape button. ∎

If you need to change a cloth or force property, click Erase Simulation, make the change, and run the simulation again. Simulation motions can be saved as keys with the Create Keys button. Figure 44.4 shows a simple plane object that has been draped over a chair over the course of 100 frames.

FIGURE 44.4

After you've defined cloth and force properties, an executed simulation drapes the cloth over a chair.

Viewing cloth tension

For cloth objects created using the Garment Maker modifier, you can view the tension in the cloth using the Tension option in the Simulation Parameters rollout. This option shows the areas of greatest tension in shaded colors. Figure 44.5 shows the tension in the dress draped over the female model from Chapter 29, "Adding and Styling Hair and Fur, and Using Cloth." You can also select a seam to tear when enough force is applied to it.

FIGURE 44.5

You can view the tension for cloth created with the Garment Maker modifier.

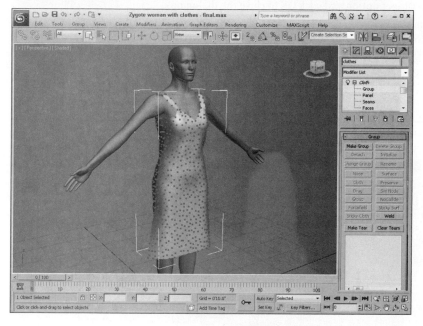

Tutorial: Draping cloth over a jet

For a larger example of a cloth system, you'll drape a drop cloth over a jet.

To simulate the dynamics of a cloth object, follow these steps:

1. Open the Sheet over Mig jet.max file from the Chap 44 directory on the CD.

    This file includes a Mig-29 jet model created by Viewpoint Datalabs.

2. Choose the Create ➪ Standard Primitives ➪ Plane menu command, and drag in the Top view-port to create a plane object that covers the jet. Set the Length and Width values to **150** and the Length and Width Segment values to **100** to make the sufficient resolution for the cloth, and drag the plane object upward in the Front viewport, so it sits above the jet.

Note

You also can create the cloth from a rectangular spline that has the Garment Maker modifier applied to it. This approach uses the Delaunay tessellation, which is better for simulating cloth than the rectangular sections in the Plane object. ■

3. With the plane object selected, choose the Modifiers ➪ Cloth ➪ Cloth menu command to apply the Cloth modifier to the object.

4. Open the Modifier panel, and click the Object Properties button in the Object rollout to open the Object Properties dialog box. Select the Plane01 object in the left list, and choose the Cloth option. Then select the Silk option from the Presets drop-down list, and set the Thickness to **0.5**.

5. With the Object Properties dialog box still open, click the Add Objects button, click the Select All button, and click the Add button. With all added properties in the left list selected, choose the Collision Object option and click OK to close the dialog box.

6. In the Simulation Parameters rollout, enable the End Frame option and set the end frame to **100**. Then click the Simulate button in the Object rollout. The plane object descends and covers the jet being draped as it falls.

Figure 44.6 shows the sheet draped over the jet.

FIGURE 44.6

Computing the dynamics of a cloth object is possible with a cloth system.

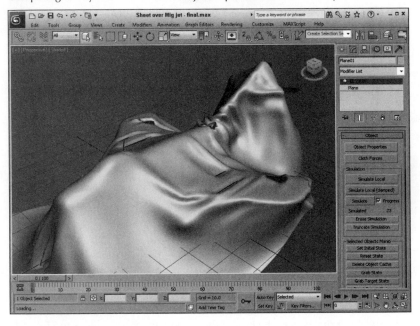

Summary

Using dynamic simulations, you can control and compute the motions of hair, fur, and cloth. These motions take into account the various forces and collision objects included in the scene.

Specifically, this chapter covered the following topics:

- Enabling hair dynamics
- Simulating cloth dynamic motion by initiating a simulation process

Part XI, "Advanced Lighting and Rendering," is up next. It includes coverage of several advanced topics beginning with the advanced lighting options.

Part XI

Advanced Lighting and Rendering

Working with Advanced Lighting, Light Tracing, and Radiosity

I f you were to walk into a dark room and reach for the light switch, you would be confused if you found a separate switch that controlled the advanced lighting. But in Max the advanced lighting controls are worth the trouble. They enable you to take your lighting solution to the next level.

The advanced lighting controls in Max enable you to light scenes using two separate global illumination techniques known as light tracing and radiosity. Both solutions deal with the effect of light bouncing off objects and being reflected to the environment.

Light tracing is typically used for outdoor scenes where the light consists of a single powerful light source at a far distance from the scene. Light tracing includes support for color bleeding between surfaces. Another aspect of light tracing is that the shadows are softer.

Radiosity computes lighting solutions that are much more realistic than using standard lights. As you learn to use radiosity, you quickly discover that it is a complex system that takes lots of tweaking to get just right.

Selecting Advanced Lighting

You control the advanced lighting settings for the scene in the Advanced Lighting panel, which is part of the Render Scene dialog box. You can access this panel by selecting Rendering ⇨ Light Tracer or Rendering ⇨ Radiosity (or by pressing the 9 key). The Advanced Lighting panel includes a rollout with a single drop-down list where you can select the lighting plug-in to use. The options are None, Light Tracer, and Radiosity.

Note

The Light Tracer and Radiosity options aren't available if the mental ray renderer is enabled. ∎

Light Tracer and Radiosity are two different techniques for applying advanced lighting to a scene. Although they are fundamentally different, they both simulate a critical piece of the lighting puzzle that adds dramatically to the realism of the lights in the scene—light bouncing. When light strikes a surface in real life, a portion of the light bounces off the surface and illuminates other surfaces. Traditionally, Max hasn't worried about this, which required that users add more lights to the scene to account for this additional lighting. Both the Light Tracer and the Radiosity solutions include light bouncing in their calculations.

How light tracing works

The Light Tracer is a Global Illumination (GI) system that is similar to raytracing, but it focuses more on calculating how light bounces off surfaces in the scene. The results are fairly realistic without being computationally expensive, and its solutions are rendered much quicker than a radiosity solution.

Cross-Reference

The Light Tracer is similar in many ways to raytracing. Chapter 47, "Rendering with mental ray and iray," presents more information on raytracing. ∎

The Light Tracer works by dividing the scene into sample points. These sample points are more heavily concentrated along the edges of objects in the scene. An imaginary light ray is then shot at each sample point, and the light intensity at the location of contact is recorded; then it is computed where the light ray would bounce to, and a reduced intensity value is recorded. One of the settings is how many times the light rays will bounce within the scene, and this value increases the amount of time required to compute the solution. When all the rays and light bounces have been computed, the total light intensity value for each sample point is totaled and averaged.

Caution

Transparent objects split each ray in two. One ray bounces, and the second ray is projected through the transparent object. Transparent objects in the scene quickly double the amount of time required to compute a solution. ∎

The end result of a light tracing solution is that objects that are typically hidden in the shadows become much easier to see. Figure 45.1 shows a house model that was rendered using the standard lighting solution with raytraced shadows and then again using the Light Tracer opened side by side in the RAM Player. Notice that many of the details hidden in the shadows of one figure are visible in the other.

FIGURE 45.1

A house scene rendered using standard lighting (left) and light tracing (right)

Enabling light tracing

To enable light tracing in a scene, select Rendering ⇨ Light Tracer to open the Advanced Lighting panel in the Render Scene dialog box, as shown in Figure 45.2.

FIGURE 45.2

The Light Tracer Parameters rollout sets values for GI lighting.

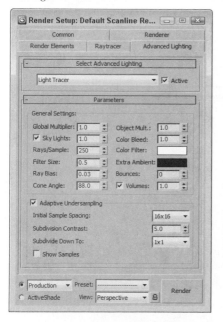

The Global Multiplier value increases the overall effect of the Light Tracer, much like increasing the multiplier of a light. The net result is to brighten the scene. You also can increase the multiplier of skylights with the Sky Lights values. The Object Multiplier sets the amount of light energy that bounces off the objects.

Color bleeding

Another characteristic of global illumination is color bleeding. As a light ray strikes the surface of an object and bounces, it carries the color of the object that is struck with it to the next object. The result of this is that colors from one object bleed onto adjacent objects. You can control this effect using the Color Bleed setting. You can greatly exaggerate the amount of color bleeding by increasing the Object Multiplier along with the Color Bleed value. You also can select colors to use for a color filter and for extra ambient light.

Note
The color bleeding effect doesn't happen unless the Bounce value is set to 2 or greater. ■

When using color bleeding, you also want to enable the Exposure Control to the scene. Exposure Control is found in the Environment panel (keyboard shortcut, 8), which can be opened with the Rendering⇨Environment menu command.

Tip
When changing the Exposure Control settings, you can get a quick preview of the scene by clicking the Render Preview button in the Exposure Control rollout of the Environments and Effects dialog box. ■

Cross-Reference
The Exposure Control features are discussed in Chapter 23, "Rendering a Scene and Enabling Quicksilver." ■

Figure 45.3 shows an example of color bleeding with several colored cylinders projecting from a gray Box object. The Object Multiplier value was set to 4.0, and the Color Bleed was set a maximum value of 25.0 with a Bounce value of 3. Using the Exposure Control settings, you can isolate the color bleed.

FIGURE 45.3

Color bleeding spreads color about the scene. Exposure Control can highlight it with Automatic (left) and Logarithmic (right).

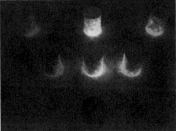

Quality versus speed

The big trade-off of global illumination is between quality and render time. The more rays per sample that you specify, the better the quality and the longer the render time. This is controlled with the Rays/Sample setting. The Rays/Sample setting and the number of Bounces dramatically increase the rendering time. The Ray Bias setting biases rays toward object edges versus flat areas.

Tip

If you want to see a preview of your scene using light tracing, set the Rays/Sample value to around 10 percent of its normal value and render the scene. The resulting image is grainy, but it shows a rough approximation of the scene lighting without having to change the Bounce value. ■

If you don't include enough rays in the scene, then noise patterns appear within the scene. The Filter Size can help control the amount of noise that appears in the scene.

The number of Bounces value specifies the number of times the ray bounces before being dropped from the solution. A setting of 0 is the same as disabling the Light Tracer, and the maximum value of 10 requires a long time to compute. The Cone Angle defines the cone region within which the rays are projected. The Volumes option is a multiplier for the Volume Light and Volume Fog atmosphere effects.

Adaptive undersampling

With the Adaptive Undersampling option enabled, the Light Tracer focuses on the areas of most contrast, which usually occur along the edges of objects. When this option is enabled, you can specify the spacing of the samples and how finely the samples get subdivided. The Initial Sample Spacing options range from 1×1 to a very dense 32×32. The Subdivision Contrast affects the density for contrast edges between objects and shadows. This value is a minimum amount of contrast that is allowed. If the amount of contrast is greater than this value, then the area is further subdivided into more samples. These high-contrast areas use the Subdivide Down To setting. The Show Samples option displays each sample as a red dot on the rendered image.

Tutorial: Viewing color bleeding

One of the easiest effects of the Light Tracer to see is color bleeding. Although this is often undesirable, it is a telltale sign of global illumination.

To compare the differences between a regular rendering and the Light Tracer, follow these steps:

1. Open the Hotplate.max file from the Chap 45 directory on the CD.

   This file includes a simple model of a hotplate.

2. Open the Advanced Lighting panel by selecting Rendering ⇨ Light Tracer (or press the 9 key). In the Parameters rollout, set the Object Multiplier to **10**, the Color Bleed to **25**, and the Bounces to **1**.

3. Select the Rendering ⇨ Environment (8) menu command to open the Environment and Effects panel. In the Exposure Control rollout, select the Linear Exposure Control option and enable the Process Background and Environment Maps option. In the Linear Exposure Control Parameters rollout, adjust the Brightness to **40** and click the Render Preview button to see a quick preview of the results in the Exposure Control rollout.

4. In the Render Scene dialog box, click the Render button.

   This renders the scene in the Rendered Frame Window.

Caution

Remember that selecting an advanced lighting option greatly increases the render time. ■

Figure 45.4 shows the scene rendered with advanced lighting.

Color bleeding happens only when global illumination is enabled.

Using Local Advanced Lighting Settings

You can set advanced lighting settings locally for specific objects using the Object Properties dialog box, as shown in Figure 45.5.

At the top of the Advanced Lighting panel in the Object Properties dialog box is the number of selected objects and lights. The Object Properties dialog box is opened using Edit ⇨ Object Properties. This dialog box lets you specify whether this object should be excluded from the advanced lighting calculations. The properties can be set By Object or By Layer. If included, you can select whether the object casts shadows, whether it receives illumination, and how it handles radiosity. The Number Regathering Rays Multiplier option sets the number of rays cast by the selected object. For large, smooth surfaces, reducing artifacts by increasing this value can be helpful. The remaining settings in this panel deal with radiosity.

Use the Advanced Lighting panel in the Object Properties dialog box to disable advanced lighting.

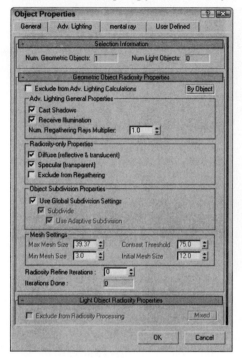

Tutorial: Excluding Objects from Light Tracing

Using the Object Properties dialog box, you can exclude certain objects from the light tracing calculations.

To exclude objects from the Light Tracer, follow these steps:

1. Open the Hotplate.max file from the Chap 45 directory on the CD.

   This file includes a simple model of a hotplate.

2. Open the Advanced Lighting panel by selecting Rendering ⇨ Light Tracer (or press the 9 key). In the Parameters rollout, set the Bounces value to **2**.

3. In the Front viewport, select the plug, cord, and floor objects, and then select Edit ⇨ Object Properties to open the Properties dialog box for these objects. In the Object Properties dialog box, open the Advanced Lighting panel and enable the Exclude from Advanced Lighting Calculations option. Then click OK.

4. In the Render Scene dialog box, click the Render button.

   This renders the scene in the Rendered Frame Window.

Figure 45.6 shows the scene rendered with advanced lighting that excludes certain objects.

FIGURE 45.6

Color bleeding becomes much stronger with a higher Bounce value.

Understanding Radiosity

Imagine a scene that includes an umbrella with a light source directly overhead. If you rendered the scene, the object caught in the umbrella's shadow would be too dark for you to see clearly. To fix this situation, you would need to add some extra lights under the umbrella and set them to not cast shadows. Although this workaround provides the solution you want, it is interesting to note that this isn't the case in real life.

The difference between the workaround and real life has to do with the effect of light energy being reflected (or bounced) off the lit objects. It is this phenomenon that allows me to look down the hall and see whether my children's light is still on past bedtime. Even though I can't see the light directly, I know it is on because of the light that reflects off the other walls.

Radiosity is a lighting algorithm that is based on how heat or energy transfers across surfaces. Every time a bit of light energy, called a photon, strikes a surface, the light energy is reduced, but the light energy is bounced onto the surrounding faces. The greater the number of bounces that are computed, the more realistic the lighting solution, but the longer it takes to compute. So, using radiosity, the objects under the umbrella are visible even if they are in the shadows. Because of the way the light is computed, radiosity solutions are not capable of generating direct specular highlights.

Radiosity is mostly used to light indoor scenes because that is where the effect of light bouncing is most evident. Radiosity, along with light tracing, is another method for computing global illumination. Figure 45.7 shows the dinosaur exhibit in a museum with and without radiosity. Notice how dark the shadows are in the normal lighting image.

FIGURE 45.7

This scene is lighted using normal lighting (left) and radiosity lighting (right).

Lighting for radiosity

The Advanced Lighting panel in Max includes Light Tracing and Radiosity options. You can choose either option from the Advanced Lighting panel in the Render Scene dialog box. You can open this panel with the Radiosity option selected using the Rendering ⇨ Radiosity menu command. Pressing the 9 key opens the Render Scene dialog box with the Advanced Lighting panel open.

Radiosity lighting is not displayed until you have Max compute it by clicking the Start button in the Radiosity Processing Parameters rollout. After a radiosity solution is calculated, the results are saved as light maps. These maps are easy to apply to a scene and can be viewed within the viewports. However, when the geometry or lights of the scene change, you need to recalculate the lighting solution.

The Radiosity Processing Parameters rollout, shown in Figure 45.8, lets you set the quality of the radiosity solution. You also can specify the number of iterations to use for the scene and for the selected objects. These are different steps in the radiosity computation. The Initial Quality defines the accuracy of the rays that are bounced around the scene. This stage sets the brightness for the scene. The Refine Iterations improves the general quality of the lighting solution for each iteration. You can refine iterations only for the selected object. This lets you target the iterations instead of computing them for the entire scene.

The Interactive Tools section lets you specify a Filtering value. A greater Filtering value eliminates noise between adjacent surfaces by averaging the lighting coming from all surrounding surfaces. The Setup button offers access to the Exposure Control rollout in the Environment panel. You also can turn off radiosity in the viewports.

Cross-Reference

Chapter 23, "Rendering a Scene and Enabling Quicksilver," includes coverage of the Exposure Control rollout. ■

Subdividing a mesh for radiosity

As you begin to play with radiosity, you'll quickly find that to get accurate results, you need to have good, clean models. If any models have long, thin faces, then the results are unpredictable.

The Radiosity Meshing Parameters rollout includes an option to enable meshing and a Meshing Size value. This setting is the same as the Size value parameter for the Subdivide modifier, except that it is applied globally.

FIGURE 45.8

The Radiosity Processing Parameters rollout includes buttons for computing a solution.

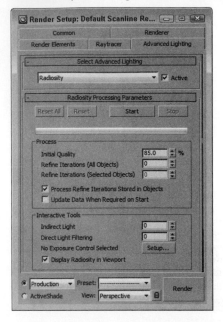

Tip

If you're creating an indoor room using the Box object, be aware that Box objects have only one external face sur-face with normals, so the interior of a Box object will not have the correct lighting. You can easily fix this by applying the Shell modifier to the Box object. This adds an interior set of faces to the Box object.

Using the Subdivide modifier

The Modifiers menu includes a submenu for Radiosity modifiers. This submenu includes only the Subdivide modifier and a World-Space version of the Subdivide modifier. This modifier accomplishes a simple task—creating a mesh that has regular, equally shaped triangular faces that work well when computing a radiosity solution.

Tip

Although this modifier was created to help with radiosity solutions, it also helps with other commands that require regular mesh faces, such as the Boolean and Terrain compound objects. ■

The Parameters rollout includes a Size value that determines the density of the mesh. The lower the value, the denser the mesh and the better the resulting radiosity solution, but the longer the solution takes. This same Subdivision Size setting also can be found (and set globally) in the Radiosity Meshing

Parameters rollout of the Advanced Lighting panel. It is also found in the Advanced Lighting panel of the Object Properties dialog box. Figure 45.9 shows a simple cube with the Subdivide modifier applied and the Size value set to (from left to right) 50, 30, 25, 20, and 12.

Tip
If you drag the Size value, you'll probably want to set the Update option to Manual or you'll find yourself waiting while Max computes some seriously dense mesh, or you can just disable the Display Subdivision option. ∎

FIGURE 45.9

The Subdivide modifier changes all mesh faces into regularly shaped triangular faces.

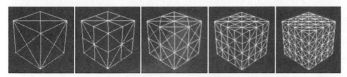

Tutorial: Preparing a mesh for radiosity

When it comes to meshes that have long, thin, and irregular faces, you don't have to look any further than Boolean compound objects. These objects typically are divided along strange angles, producing ugly meshes. The good news is that these meshes are easy to subdivide.

To subdivide an irregular mesh in preparation for a radiosity solution, follow these steps:

1. Open the Boolean object.max file from the Chap 45 directory on the CD.

   This file includes two copies of a Box object with an arch shape Boolean subtracted from it.

2. Select the top object, and choose the Modifiers ⇨ Radiosity Modifiers ⇨ Subdivide menu command.

   This applies the Subdivide modifier to the object.

3. In the Parameters rollout, select the Manual update option, set the Size value to **5.0**, and click Update Now.

   If the Display Subdivision option is enabled, then the changes are visible in the viewport.

4. Open the Advanced Lighting panel with the Rendering ⇨ Radiosity menu command (or press the 9 key). Select Radiosity from the drop-down menu.

Figure 45.10 shows the two objects with and without the Subdivide modifier applied. The top object is ready for a radiosity solution.

FIGURE 45.10

Subdividing an irregular mesh prepares it for radiosity lighting.

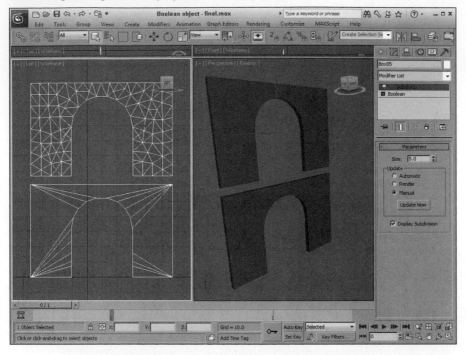

Painting with light

The Light Painting rollout (found in the Advanced Lighting panel of the Render Scene dialog box), shown in Figure 45.11, includes buttons for Adding Illumination, Subtracting Illumination, and Picking an Illumination value from the scene. Using these tools, you can paint lighting on the objects in the scene. The Clear button removes all the changes you've made using the Light Painting tool.

FIGURE 45.11

Because lighting is saved as a light map, you can add or subtract light from the scene using a brush tool.

Rendering parameters and statistics

Settings in the Rendering Parameters rollout (shown in Figure 45.12) are used during the rendering process. The Re-Use and Render Direct Illumination options give you the chance to reuse the existing radiosity solution when rendering or to recalculate it as part of the rendering process. This can save some time during rendering.

FIGURE 45.12

The Rendering Parameters and Statistics rollouts offer rendering options and statistics for radiosity solutions.

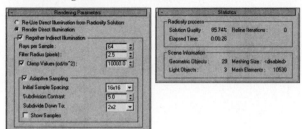

The Regather Indirect Illumination option enables a Light-Tracer-like step along with the radiosity solution and produces an image that has the best of both solutions. The regathering options are the same as those defined for the light tracer.

The Statistics rollout includes information about the radiosity process. Using this information, you can judge whether the settings are too high or too low.

Tutorial: Lighting a house interior with radiosity

Radiosity works best in indoor scenes or scenes that are mostly interior. The only light source for this scene is a Daylight system and a single Omni light in the front hallway.

To light a house interior with radiosity, follow these steps:

1. Open the House interior.max file from the Chap 45 directory on the CD.
2. Open the Advanced Lighting panel with the Rendering ⇨ Radiosity menu command (or press the 9 key). Select Radiosity from the drop-down list in the Select Advanced Lighting rollout.
3. In the Radiosity Processing Parameters rollout, set the Refine Iterations value to 2 and click the Start button to have Max compute the radiosity solution.
4. In the Rendering Parameters rollout, enable the Render Direct Illumination, the Regather Indirect Illumination, and the Adaptive Sampling options. Then click the Render button to begin the rendering process.

Figure 45.13 shows the finished rendered house interior. Notice that all surfaces are well lit even though the scene has a limited number of lights.

Cross-Reference

This same house interior is rendered with mental ray in Chapter 47, "Rendering with mental ray and iray." ■

FIGURE 45.13

The radiosity solution for this scene adds to the lighting levels for the entire room.

Using Local and Global Advanced Lighting Settings

Just like with the Light Tracer, you can set advanced lighting settings locally for specific objects using the Object Properties dialog box, opened with the Edit ➪ Object Properties menu command. This dialog box includes an Advanced Lighting panel, and several of the settings are specific to radiosity.

For the selected objects, you can specify whether they Cast Shadows and Receive Illumination. For a radiosity solution, you also can select to enable or disable Diffuse, Specular, Exclude from Regathering, and Subdividing. The Radiosity Refine Iterations value lets you set the number of iterations for the current selection. Think of Refine Iterations as the quality setting. You can set it for all objects or just for the selected object. It works by comparing the variance between adjacent faces.

If any light objects are selected, you can select to exclude them from radiosity processing or to store the illumination values with the mesh.

The Preference Settings dialog box also includes a Radiosity panel. Using this panel, shown in Figure 45.14, you can set the advanced lighting settings that apply to all objects globally.

In the Radiosity panel of the Preference Settings dialog box is an option to Display Reflectance & Transmittance Information. If this option is enabled, this information (average and maximum percent values) appears directly below the sample slots. You also can select to have the radiosity solution displayed in the viewports and to automatically process any refine iterations noted in the Object Properties dialog box for a given object. Radiosity processing includes a couple of warning dialog boxes that appear—one when the current solution is reset, and another to update the solution when the Start button is clicked. You can disable both of these warnings. The final option is to save the radiosity solution with the Max file. This slightly increases the file size, but it doesn't require that you recalculate the radiosity solution when the file is opened again.

FIGURE 45.14

FIGURE 45.14

Use the Radiosity panel of the Preference Settings dialog box to set global parameters.

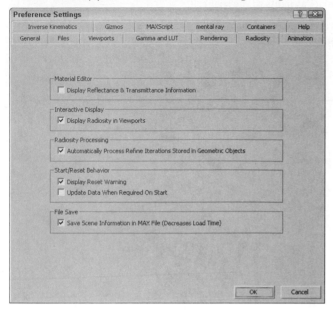

Working with Advanced Lighting Materials

Applying an advanced lighting solution can have a direct impact on the materials in the scene. The Material Editor includes two materials that are useful for working with advanced lighting: Advanced Lighting Override and Lightscape materials.

Advanced Lighting Override

The Advanced Lighting Override material type includes material parameters that override the global Advanced Lighting solution. These parameters let you set the amount of Reflectance, Color Bleed, Transmittance, Luminance, and Bump Map Scale that the material uses. This offers a way to make a specific material have its own defined lighting parameters.

Note

The Advanced Lighting Override material does not need to be applied to all objects that are to receive advanced lighting. It is used only to override the existing scene settings for certain materials. ∎

As an example of how this material can be used, consider the hot plate example. Rather than excluding objects from the Advanced Lighting calculations, you can instead use the Light Tracer panel to set the global settings for the scene and apply the Advanced Lighting Override material to the hot plate coils with a higher Color Bleed value. This causes the coils to bleed, but not the rest of the scene.

Another common use for this material is to use the Luminance Scale value to cause self-illuminating materials to add light energy to the global illumination calculations. In other words, increasing this value makes self-illuminating materials act as lights to the scene.

The Advanced Lighting Override material parameters, shown in Figure 45.15, let you set the amount of Reflectance, Color Bleed, Transmittance, Luminance, and Indirect Light Bump Scale that the material uses.

FIGURE 45.15

The Advanced Lighting Override Material rollout defines how light interacts with the material.

Lightscape material

The Lightscape material type lets you apply a material to objects that are imported from Lightscape. They are used to control how the radiosity is mapped to objects. The Basic Parameters rollout includes values for Brightness, Contrast, Ambient Light, and Bump Amount. You also can enable Daylight and Exterior Scene options. These values are applied in addition to the base material.

Using Lighting Analysis

To get information about the current lighting solution, you can use the Lighting Analysis Assistant. The scene must include a lighting solution before this tool is available. You can access this tool by selecting the Lighting Analysis menu command. This opens the Lighting Analysis Assistant dialog box, shown in Figure 45.16.

Note

This feature is available only in 3ds Max 2012 Design. ■

FIGURE 45.16

The Lighting Analysis Assistant dialog box displays the light values at the specified location.

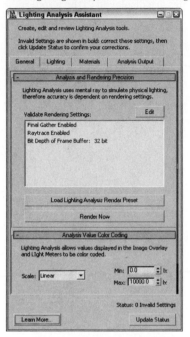

In order for the Lighting Analysis Assistant tools to work, you need to have a lighting solution for the current scene, and you need to have mental ray enabled using real-world parameters and photometric lights. If any of these conditions isn't met, it is indicated in the General panel and listed in bold. After making changes, you can press the Update Status button to recheck the settings. The General panel also includes a color spectrum that will be overlaid over the scene to show lighting values in different colors. This helps you identify places where the light isn't sufficient or where lights are too bright.

The Lighting panel shows the current lights applied to the scene and lets you edit their parameters from a single location. If any of the lights are invalid, then they will be identified in the Lighting panel. If you click the Select Invalid Light button, then any invalid lights are selected, and you can turn them on in the Modify panel.

The Lighting Analysis tools also require that all scene materials are physically correct using the mental ray architecture materials or the ProMaterials. Invalid materials are identified in the Materials panel, which can be a large number if you have a complex scene. The Materials panel includes a button to Assign Generic Valid Material to Selected Objects that can be used to quickly reassign any invalid materials.

The Analysis Output panel includes a button for creating Light Meters that can measure the light intensity at placed locations in the scene. Light Meters also can be created and placed using the Create ⇨ Helpers ⇨ LightMeter menu command. When you press the Calculate All Light Meters Now button in the Lighting Analysis Assistant dialog box, the scene is rendered and the light values are displayed within the viewports. This information also can be exported to a CSV file. Light Meters can be set to measure Total Illuminance, Direct Illuminance, Indirect Illuminance, or Daylight Factor.

The Lighting Output panel in the Lighting Analysis Assistant dialog box includes a feature to Create Image Overlay Render Effect. This button adds a render effect to the scene that displays the lighting levels for the entire scene. When the scene is rendered, lighting values are displayed in the Rendered Frame Window, as shown in Figure 45.17.

The Lighting Analysis Assistant renders the scene with lighting values shown.

Summary

Advanced lighting offers a new way to shine lights on your scenes. With these features, many new lighting options are available. Advanced lighting enables two global illumination methods: light tracing and radiosity. In this chapter, you accomplished the following:

- Enabled advanced lighting
- Discovered light tracing
- Set local advanced lighting settings
- Discovered radiosity
- Used the Subdivide modifier
- Set local and global advanced lighting settings
- Used advanced lighting materials and the Lighting Analysis Assistant

The next chapter deals with fire and smoke and other Atmospheric effects. It also deals with the various Render Effects that Max can generate.

Using Atmospheric and Render Effects

In the real world, an environment of some kind surrounds all objects. The environment does much to set the ambiance of the scene. For example, an animation set at night in the woods has a very different environment than one set at the horse races during the middle of the day. Max includes dialog boxes for setting the color, background images, and lighting environment; these features can help define your scene.

This chapter covers Exposure Controls, atmospheric effects, including the likes of clouds, fog, and fire. These effects can be seen only when the scene is rendered.

Max also has a class of effects that you can interactively render to the Rendered Frame window without using any post-production features, such as the Video Post dialog box. These effects are called *render effects*. Render effects can save you lots of time that you would normally spend rendering an image, touching it up, and repeating the process again and again.

Using Exposure Controls

The Exposure Control rollout of the Environment panel lets you control output levels and color rendering ranges. You can access the Environment panel from the Rendering ⇨ Environment menu command or by pressing the 8 key. Controlling the exposure of film is a common procedure when working with film and can result in a different look for your scene. Enabling the Exposure Controls can add dynamic range to your rendered images that is more comparable to what the eyes actually see. If you've worked with a Histogram in Photoshop, then you'll understand the impact that the Exposure Controls can have. The default selection is Automatic Exposure Control.

The Active option lets you turn this feature on and off. The Process Background and Environment Maps option causes the exposure settings to affect the background and environment images. When this option is disabled, only the scene objects are affected by the exposure control settings. The Exposure Control rollout also includes a Render Preview button that displays the rendered scene in a tiny pane. The preview pane is small, but for most types of exposure control settings it is enough. When you click the Render Preview button, the scene is rendered. This preview is then automatically updated whenever a setting is changed.

Automatic, Linear, and Logarithmic Exposure Control

Selecting Automatic Exposure Control from the drop-down list automatically adjusts your rendered output to be closer to what your eyes can detect. Monitors are notoriously bad at reducing the dynamic range of the colors in your rendered image. This setting provides the needed adjustments to match the expanded dynamic range of your eyes.

When the Automatic Exposure Control option is selected, a new rollout appears in the Environment panel. This rollout includes settings for Brightness, Contrast, Exposure Value, and Physical Scale. You also can enable Color Correction, select a color, and select an option to Desaturate Low Levels. The Contrast and Brightness settings can range from 0 to 100. A Contrast value of 0 displays all scene objects with the same flat, gray color, and a Brightness value of 100 displays all scene objects with the same flat, white color. The Exposure Value can range from –5 to 5 and determines the amount of light allowed in the scene.

Another exposure control option is Linear Exposure Control. Although this option presents the same settings as the Automatic Exposure Control, the differences between the minimum and maximum values are a straight line across the light spectrum.

Tip

The tricky part is to know when to use which Exposure Control. For still images, the Automatic Exposure Control is your best bet, but for animations, you should use the Logarithmic Exposure Control. Automatic is also a good choice for any scenes that use many lighting effects. Using any of the exposure controls besides the Logarithmic Exposure Control when animating can lead to flickering. The Linear Exposure Control should be used for low dynamic range scenes such as nighttime or cloudy scenes. ■

The Logarithmic Exposure Control option replaces the Exposure Value setting with a Mid Tones setting. This setting controls the colors between the lowest and highest values. This exposure control option also includes options to Affect Indirect Only and Exterior Daylight. You should enable the Affect Indirect Only option if you use only standard lights in the scene, but if your scene includes an IES Sun light, then enable the Exterior Daylight option to tone down the intensity of the light.

Cross-Reference

You should always use the Logarithmic Exposure Control setting when enabling the advanced lighting features because it works well with low-level light. You can learn more about the advanced lighting radiosity features in Chapter 45, "Working with Advanced Lighting, Light Tracing, and Radiosity." ■

Pseudo Color Exposure Control

As you work with advanced lighting solutions and with radiosity, determining whether interior spaces and objects have too much light or not enough light can be difficult, especially when comparing objects on opposite sides of the scene. This is where the Pseudo Color Exposure Control option comes in handy.

This exposure control option projects a band of colors (or grayscale) in place of the material and object colors that represent the illumination or luminance values for the scene. With these pseudo-colors, you can quickly determine where all the lighting is consistent and where it needs to be addressed.

In the Pseudo Color Exposure Control rollout, shown in Figure 46.1, you can select to apply the colors to show Illumination or Luminance. You also can select to use a Colored or Grayscale style and to make the Scale Linear or Logarithmic. The Min and Max settings let you control the ranges of the colors, and a Physical Scale setting is included. The color (or grayscale) band is shown across the bottom of the rollout with the values for each color underneath.

FIGURE 46.1

The Pseudo Color Exposure Control rollout can display illumination and luminance values as colors.

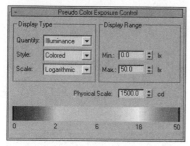

When this exposure control is used, the associated render element is automatically set in the Render Elements rollout of the Render Scene dialog box. If the scene is rendered, then the appropriate (Illumination or Luminance) render element is also rendered.

Cross-Reference

See Chapter 49, "Compositing with Render Elements and the Video Post Interface," for more on render elements. ■

Photographic Exposure Control

If you're comfortable working with camera settings such as Shutter Speed, Aperture, and Film Speed, then the Photographic Exposure Control puts these settings at your fingertips using real-world values. Even if you're not familiar with camera settings, you can use one of the available presets from the list at the top of the rollout, shown in Figure 46.2.

Note

The Photographic Exposure Control is available only for the mental ray render engine. ■

Tutorial: Using the Logarithmic Exposure Control

As you start to use the new photometric lights, you may find it difficult to get the settings just right. The results are oversaturation or undersaturation, but luckily the Logarithmic Exposure Control can quickly fix any problems that appear.

FIGURE 46.2

The Photographic Exposure Control rollout works with real-world camera settings.

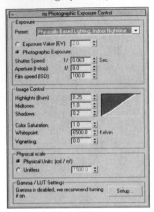

To adjust the effect of a photometric light using the Logarithmic Exposure Control, follow these steps:

1. Open the Array of chrome spheres.max file from the Chap 46 directory on the CD.

    This file contains lots and lots of chrome mapped spheres with advanced lighting enabled.

2. Choose Rendering ⇨ Render (or press the F10 key) to open the Render Scene dialog box, and click the Render button.

    It takes a while to render, but notice the results, shown on the left in Figure 46.3.

3. Choose Rendering ⇨ Environment (or press the 8 key) to open the Environment & Effects dialog box. In the Exposure Control rollout, select Logarithmic Exposure Control from the drop-down list, and enable the Active and Process Background and Environment Maps options. Then click the Render Preview button.

4. In the Logarithmic Exposure Control rollout, set the Brightness value to **60**, set the Contrast value to **100**, and enable the Desaturate Low Levels option.

5. In the Render Scene dialog box, click the Render button again to see the updated rendering.

The image on the right in Figure 46.3 shows the rendered image with exposure control enabled.

FIGURE 46.3

This rendered image shows an image before and after exposure control was enabled.

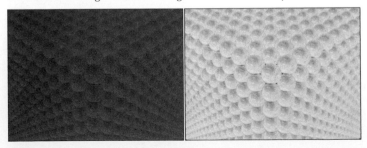

Creating Atmospheric Effects

The Environment and Effects dialog box (keyboard shortcut, 8) contains rollouts for adding atmospheric effects to your scene, but the first question is where. Atmospheric effects are placed within a container called an Atmospheric Apparatus gizmo, which tells the effect where it should be located. However, only the Fire and the Volume Fog effects need Atmospheric Apparatus gizmos. To create an Atmospheric Apparatus gizmo, select Create ⇨ Helpers ⇨ Atmospherics and choose the apparatus type.

The three different Atmospheric Apparatus gizmos are BoxGizmo, SphereGizmo, and CylGizmo. Each has a different shape similar to the primitives.

Working with the Atmospheric Apparatus

Selecting a gizmo and opening the Modify panel reveal two different rollouts: one for defining the basic parameters such as the gizmo dimensions, and another labeled Atmospheres & Effects, which you can use to Add or Delete an Environment Effect to the gizmo. Each gizmo parameters rollout also includes a Seed value and a New Seed button. The Seed value sets a random number used to compute the atmospheric effect, and the New Seed button automatically generates a random seed. Two gizmos with the same seed values have nearly identical results.

Adding effects to a scene

The Add button opens the Add Atmosphere dialog box, where you can select an atmospheric effect. The selected effect is then included in a list in the Atmospheres & Effects rollout. You can delete these atmospheres by selecting them from the list and clicking the Delete button. The Setup button is active if an effect is selected in the list. It opens the Environment and Effects dialog box. Adding Atmospheric Effects in the Modify panel is purely for convenience. They can also be added using the Environment and Effects dialog box.

In addition to the Modify panel, you can add atmospheric effects to the scene using the Atmosphere rollout in the Environment and Effects dialog box, shown in Figure 46.4. This rollout is pretty boring until you add an effect to it. You can add an effect by clicking on the Add button. This opens the Add Atmospheric Effect dialog box, which includes by default four atmospheric effects: Fire Effect, Fog, Volume Fog, and Volume Light. With plug-ins, you can increase the number of effects in this list. The selected effect is added to the Effects list in the Atmosphere rollout.

FIGURE 46.4

The Environment and Effects dialog box lets you select atmospheric effects.

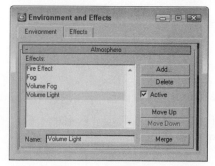

You can delete an effect from the current Effects list in the Environment and Effects dialog box by selecting the effect and clicking the Delete button. The effects are applied in the order in which they are listed, so the effects at the bottom of the list are layered on top of all other effects. To the right of the Effects pane are the Move Up and Move Down buttons, used to position the effects in the list. Below the Effects pane is a Name field where you can type a new name for any effect in this field. This enables you to use the same effect multiple times. The Merge button opens the Merge Atmospheric Effects dialog box, where you can select a separate Max file. You can then select and load any render effects from the other file.

Using the Fire Effect

To add the Fire effect to the scene, select the Rendering ➪ Environment (8) menu command and open the Environment panel; then click the Add button and select the Fire Effect selection. This opens the Fire Effect Parameters rollout, shown in Figure 46.5. At the top of the Fire Effect Parameters rollout is the Pick Gizmo button; clicking this button lets you select a gizmo in the scene. The selected gizmo appears in the drop-down list to the right. You can select multiple gizmos. To remove a gizmo from the list, select it and click the Remove Gizmo button.

FIGURE 46.5

The Fire Effect Parameters rollout lets you define the look of the effect.

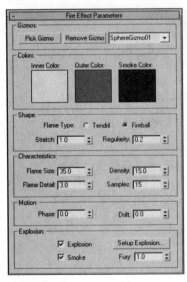

Note
The Fire effect renders only in nonorthographic views such as Perspective or a camera view. ■

The three color swatches define the color of the fire effect and include an Inner Color, an Outer Color, and a Smoke Color. The Smoke Color is used only when the Explosion option is set. The default red and yellow colors make fairly realistic fire.

The Shape section includes two Flame Type options: Tendril and Fireball. The Tendril shape produces veins of flames, and the Fireball shape is rounder and puffier. Figure 46.6 shows four fire effects. The left two have the Tendril shape, and the two on the right are set to Fireball. The difference is in the Density and Flame Detail settings.

FIGURE 46.6

The Fire atmospheric effect can be either Tendril or Fireball shaped.

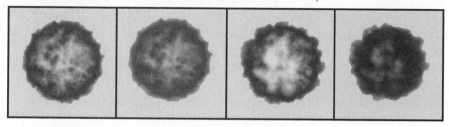

The Stretch value elongates the individual flames along the gizmo's Z-axis. Figure 46.7 shows the results of using the Stretch value. The Stretch values for these gizmos, from left to right, are 0.1, 1.0, 5.0, and 50.

FIGURE 46.7

The Stretch value can elongate flames.

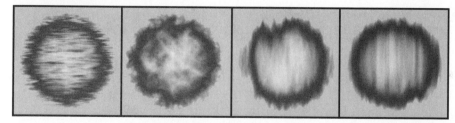

The Regularity value determines how much of the Atmospheric Apparatus is filled. The spherical gizmos in the previous figures were all set to 0.2, so the entire sphere shape wasn't filled. A setting of 1.0 adds a spherical look to the Fire effect because the entire gizmo is filled. For a more random shape, use a small Regularity value.

The Flame Size value affects the overall size of each individual flame (though this is dependent on the gizmo size as well). The Flame Detail value controls the edge sharpness of each flame and can range from 1 to 10. Lower values produce fuzzy, smooth flames, but higher values result in sharper, more distinct flames.

The Density value determines the thickness of each flame in its center; higher Density values result in flames that are brighter at the center, while lower values produce thinner, wispy flames. Figure 46.8 shows the difference caused by Density values of, from left to right, 10, 20, 50, and 100.

FIGURE 46.8

The Fire effect brightness is tied closely to the flame's Density value.

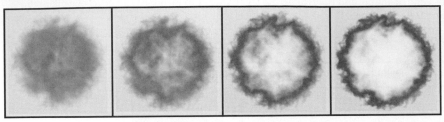

The Samples value sets the rate at which the effect is sampled. Higher sample values are required for more detail, but they increase the render time.

The Motion section includes options for setting the Phase and Drift of a fire effect. The Phase value determines how wildly the fire burns. For a wild, out-of-control fire, animate the Phase value to change rapidly. For a constant, steady fire, keep the value constant throughout the frames. The Drift value sets the height of the flames. High Drift values produce high, hot-burning flames.

When the Explosion check box is selected, the fire is set to explode. The Start and End Times for the explosion are set in the Setup Explosion Phase Curve dialog box that opens when the Setup Explosion button is clicked. If the Smoke option is checked, then the fire colors change to the smoke color for Phase values between 100 and 200. The Fury value varies the churning of the flames. Values greater than 1.0 cause faster churning, and values lower than 1.0 cause slower churning.

Tutorial: Creating the sun

You can use the Fire effect to create a realistic sun. The modeling part is easy—all it requires is a simple sphere—but the real effects come from the materials and the Fire effect.

To create a sun, follow these steps:

1. Open the Sun.max file from the Chap 46 directory on the CD.

   This file contains a simple sphere with a bright yellow material applied to it.

2. Select Create ⇨ Helpers ⇨ Atmospherics ⇨ Sphere Gizmo, and drag a sphere in the Front viewport that encompasses the "sun" sphere.

3. With the SphereGizmo still selected, open the Modify panel and click the Add button in the Atmospheres & Effects rollout or you can use the Add button located in the Atmosphere rollout in the Environment and Effects dialog box, which is opened using the Rendering ⇨ Environment menu command or by pressing the 8 key. Select Fire Effect from the Add Atmosphere dialog box, and click OK. Then select the Fire effect, and click the Setup button.

   The Environment and Effects dialog box opens.

4. In the Fire Effects Parameters rollout, leave the default colors as they are—Inner Color yellow, Outer Color red, and Smoke Color black. For the Flame Type, select Tendril with Stretch and Regularity values of 1. Set the Flame Size to **30**, the Density to **15**, the Flame Detail to **10**, and the Samples to **15**.

Figure 46.9 shows the resulting sun after it's been rendered.

FIGURE 46.9

A sun image created with a simple sphere, a material with a Noise Bump map, and the Fire effect

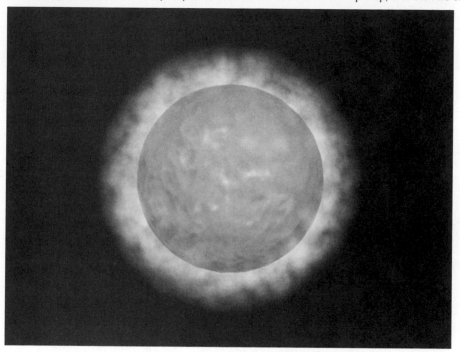

Tutorial: Creating clouds

Sky images are fairly easy to find, or you can just take your camera outside and capture your own. The trick comes when you are trying to weave an object in and out of clouds. Although you can do this with a Shadow/Matte mask, it would be easier if the clouds were actual 3D objects. In this tutorial, you'll create some simple clouds using the Fire effect.

To create some clouds for a sky backdrop, follow these steps:

1. Open the Clouds.max file from the Chap 46 directory on the CD.

   This file includes several hemispherical-shaped Atmospheric Apparatus gizmos.

2. Choose Rendering ➪ Environment (or press the 8 key) to open the Environment and Effects dialog box. Click the Background Color swatch, and select a light blue color. In the Atmosphere section, click the Add button, select Fire Effect from the Add Atmospheric Effect list, and click OK.

3. Name the effect **Clouds**, click the Pick Gizmo button, select each of the Sphere Gizmo objects in the viewports, and then click on each of the color swatches. Change the Inner Color to a dark gray, the Outer Color to a light gray, and the Smoke Color to white. Set the Shape to Fireball with a Stretch of **1** and a Regularity of **0.2**. Set the Flame Size to 35, the Flame Detail to **3**, the Density to **15**, and the Samples to **15**.

Tip

If you want to add some motion to the clouds, click the Animate button, drag the Time Slider to the last frame, and change the Phase value to 45 and the Drift value to 30. The clouds slowly drift through the sky. Disable the Animate button when you're finished. ■

4. In the Fire Effect Parameters rollout, click the Pick Gizmo button and then click one of the gizmos in the viewports. Repeat this step until you've selected all the gizmos.

Figure 46.10 shows the resulting sky backdrop. By altering the Fire parameters, you can create different types of clouds.

FIGURE 46.10

You can use the Fire atmospheric effect to create clouds.

Using the Fog Effect

Fog is an atmospheric effect that obscures objects or backgrounds by introducing a hazy layer; objects farther from view are less visible. The normal Fog effect is used without an Atmospheric Apparatus gizmo and appears between the camera's environment range values. The camera's Near and Far Range settings set these values.

In the Environment and Effects dialog box, the Fog Parameters rollout appears when the Fog effect is added to the Effects list. This rollout, shown in Figure 46.11, includes a color swatch for setting the fog color. It also includes an Environment Color Map button for loading a map. If a map is selected, the Use Map option turns it on or off. You can also select a map for the Environment Opacity, which affects the fog density.

The Fog Background option applies fog to the background image. The Type options include Standard and Layered fog. Selecting one of these fog background options enables its corresponding parameters.

FIGURE 46.11

The Fog Parameters rollout lets you use either Standard fog or Layered fog.

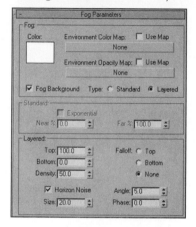

The Standard parameters include an Exponential option for increasing density as a function of distance. If this option is disabled, the density is linear with distance. The Near and Far values are used to set the range densities.

Layered fog simulates layers of fog that move from dense areas to light areas. The Top and Bottom values set the limits of the fog, and the Density value sets its thickness. The Falloff option lets you set where the fog density goes to 0. The Horizon Noise option adds noise to the layer of fog at the horizon as determined by the Size, Angle, and Phase values.

Figure 46.12 shows several different fog options. The upper-left image shows the scene with no fog, the upper-right image uses the Standard option, and the lower-left image uses the Layered option with a Density of 50. The lower-right image has the Horizon Noise option enabled.

Using the Volume Fog effect

You can add the Volume Fog effect to a scene by clicking the Add button and selecting the Volume Fog selection. This effect is different from the Fog effect in that it gives you more control over the exact position of the fog. This position is set by an Atmospheric Apparatus gizmo. The Volume Fog Parameters rollout, shown in Figure 46.13, lets you select a gizmo to use with the Pick Gizmo button. The selected gizmo is included in the drop-down list to the right of the buttons. Multiple gizmos can be selected. The Remove Gizmo button removes the selected gizmo from the list.

FIGURE 46.12

A rendered image with several different Fog effect options applied

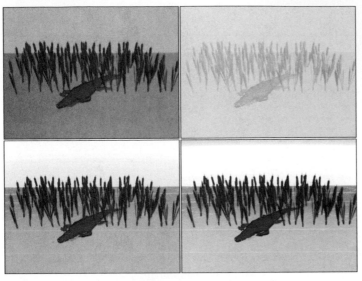

Note

The Atmospheric Apparatus gizmo contains only a portion of the total Volume Fog effect. If the gizmo is moved or scaled it displays a different cropped portion of fog. ∎

FIGURE 46.13

The Volume Fog Parameters rollout includes parameters for controlling the fog density and type.

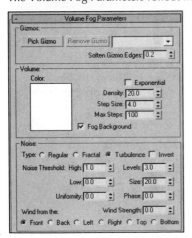

The Soften Gizmo Edges value feathers the fog effect at each edge. This value can range from 0 to 1.

Many of the settings for Volume Fog are the same as those for the Fog effect, but Volume Fog has several settings that are unique to it. These settings help set the patchy nature of Volume Fog. Step Size determines how small the patches of fog are. The Max Steps value limits the sampling of these small steps to keep the render time in check.

The Noise section settings also help determine the randomness of Volume Fog. Noise types include Regular, Fractal, Turbulence, and Invert. The Noise Threshold limits the effect of noise. Wind settings include direction and strength. The Phase value determines how the fog moves.

Tutorial: Creating a swamp scene

When I think of fog, I think of swamps. In this tutorial, you model a swamp scene. To use the Volume Fog effect to create the scene, follow these steps:

1. Open the Dragonfly in a foggy swamp.max file from the Chap 46 directory on the CD.

   This file includes several cattail plants and a dragonfly positioned on top of one of the cattails.

2. Select Create ⇨ Helpers ⇨ Atmospherics ⇨ Box Gizmo, and drag a box that covers the lower half of the cattails in the Top viewport.

3. Choose Rendering ⇨ Environment (or press the 8 key) to open the Environment and Effects dialog box. Click the Add button to open the Add Atmospheric Effect dialog box, and then select Volume Fog. Click OK. In the Volume Fog Parameters rollout, click the Pick Gizmo button and select the BoxGizmo in a viewport.

4. Set the Density to **0.5**, enable the Exponential option and select the Noise Type Turbulence. Then set the Uniformity to **1.0** and the Wind Strength to **10** from the Left.

Figure 46.14 shows the finished image. Using Atmospheric Apparatus gizmos, you can position the fog in the exact place where you want it.

FIGURE 46.14

A rendered image that uses the Volume Fog effect

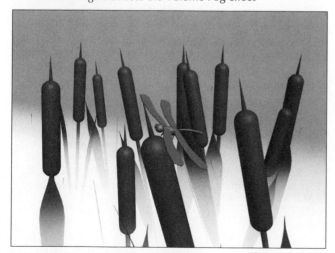

Using the Volume Light effect

The final choice in the Environment and Effects dialog box is the Volume Light effect. This effect shares many of the same parameters as the other atmospheric effects. Although this is one of the atmospheric effects, it deals with lights and fits better in that section.

Cross-Reference

To learn about the Volume Light atmospheric effect, see Chapter 20, "Using Lights and Basic Lighting Techniques." ■

Adding Render Effects

In many cases, rendering a scene is only the start of the work to produce some final output. The post-production process is often used to add lots of different effects, as you'll see when I discuss the Video Post interface. But just because you can add it in post-production doesn't mean you have to add it in post-production. Render effects let you apply certain effects as part of the rendering process.

You can set up all render effects from the Rendering Effects panel, which you open by choosing Rendering ⇨ Effects. Figure 46.15 shows this dialog box.

FIGURE 46.15

The Effects panel lets you apply interactive post-production effects to an image.

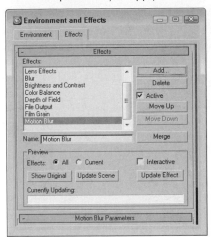

The Effects pane displays all the effects that are included in the current scene. To add a new effect, click the Add button to open the Add Effect dialog box, in which you can select from a default list of nine effects: Hair and Fur, Lens Effects, Blur, Brightness and Contrast, Color Balance, Depth of Field, File Output, Film Grain, and Motion Blur. You can delete an effect from the current list by selecting that effect and clicking the Delete button.

Below the Effects pane is a Name field. You can type a new name for any effect in this field; doing so enables you to use the same effect multiple times. The effects are applied in the order in which they are listed in the Effects pane. To the right of the Effects pane are the Move Up and Move Down buttons, which you use to reposition the effects in the list. The effects are added to the scene in the order that they are listed.

Caution

It is possible for one effect to cover another effect. Rearranging the order can help resolve this problem. ∎

The Merge button opens the Merge Effect dialog box, where you can select a separate Max file. If you select a Max file and click Open, the Merge Rendering Effects dialog box presents you with a list of render effects used in the opened Max file. You can then select and load any of these render effects into the current scene.

The Preview section holds the controls for interactively viewing the various effects. Previews are displayed in the Rendered Frame Window and can be set to view All the effects or only the Current one. The Show Original button displays the scene before any effects are applied, and the Update Scene button updates the rendered image if any changes have been made to the scene.

Note

If the Rendered Frame Window isn't open, any of these buttons opens it and renders the scene with the current settings in the Render Scene dialog box. ∎

The Interactive option automatically updates the image whenever an effect parameter or scene object is changed. If this option is disabled, you can use the Update Effect button to manually update the image.

Caution

If the Interactive option is enabled and the Rendering Effects panel is open, the image is re-rendered in the Rendered Frame Window every time a change is made to the scene. This can slow down the system dramatically. ∎

The Currently Updating bar shows the progress of the rendering update.

The remainder of the Rendering Effects panel contains global parameters and rollouts for the selected render effect. These rollouts are covered in this chapter, along with their corresponding effects.

Cross-Reference

The Hair and Fur render effect offers the ability to add hair and fur to models. The Hair and Fur features—including the render effect—are covered in Chapter 29, "Adding and Styling Hair and Fur, and Using Cloth." ∎

Creating Lens Effects

Of the eight available render effects, the first one on the list will be used perhaps more often than all the others combined. The Lens Effects option includes several different effects itself, ranging from glows and rings to streaks and stars.

Lens Effects simulate the types of lighting effects that are possible with actual camera lenses and filters. When the Lens Effects selection is added to the Effects list and selected, several different effects become available in the Lens Effects Parameters rollout, including Glow, Ring, Ray, Auto Secondary, Manual Secondary, Star, and Streak. When one of these effects is included in a scene, rollouts and parameters for that effect are added to the panel as well.

Several of these Lens Effects can be used simultaneously. To include an effect, open the Environment and Effects dialog box with the Rendering⇨Effects menu command, click the Add button, and select Lens Effect from the available effects. Then go to the Lens Effects Parameters rollout, select the desired effect from the list on the left, and click the arrow button pointing to the right. The pane on the right lists the included effects. Use the left-pointing arrow button to remove effects from the list.

Global Lens Effects Parameters

Under the Lens Effects Parameters rollout in the Rendering Effects panel is the Lens Effects Globals rollout. All effects available in Lens Effects use the two common tabbed panels in this rollout: Parameters and Scene. These two tabbed panels are shown side by side in Figure 46.16.

FIGURE 46.16

The Parameters tabbed panel of the Lens Effects Globals rollout lets you load and save parameter settings. The Scene tabbed panel lets you set the effect's Size and Intensity.

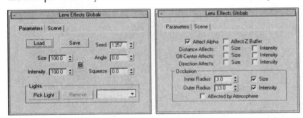

The Global Parameters tabbed panel

The Parameters panel of the Lens Effects Globals rollout includes Load and Save buttons for loading and saving parameter settings specified in the various rollouts. These settings are saved as LZV files.

The Size value determines the overall size of the effect as a percentage of the rendered image. Figure 46.17 shows the center of the Star Lens Effects with an Intensity value of 500 and Size values of 5, 10, 20, 50, and 100. The Size value increases the entire effect diameter and also the width of each radial line.

FIGURE 46.17

These Star Lens Effects vary in size.

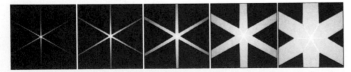

The Intensity value controls the brightness and opacity of the effect. Large values are brighter and more opaque, and small values are dimmer and more transparent. The Size and Intensity values can be locked together. Intensity and Size values can range from 0 to 500. Figure 46.18 shows a glow effect with Intensity values of (from left to right) 50, 100, 200, 350, and 500.

FIGURE 46.18

Lens Effects also can vary in intensity, like these glows.

The Seed value provides the randomness of the effect. Changing the Seed value changes the effect's look. The Angle value spins the effect about the camera's axis. The Squeeze value lengthens the horizontal axis for positive values and lengthens the vertical axis for negative values. Squeeze values can range from –100 to 100. Figure 46.19 shows a Ring effect with Squeeze values of (from left to right) –30, –15, 0, 10, and 20.

FIGURE 46.19

These Ring effects vary in Stretch values.

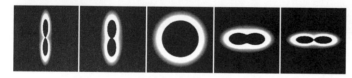

All effects are applied to light sources, and the Pick Light button lets you select a light in the viewport to apply the effect to. Each selected light is displayed in a drop-down list. You can remove any of these lights with the Remove Light button.

The Global Scene tabbed panel

The second Lens Effects Globals tabbed panel common to all effects is the Scene panel. This rollout includes an Affect Alpha option that lets the effect work with the image's alpha channel. The alpha channel holds the transparency information for the rendered objects and for effects if this option is enabled. If you plan on using the effect in a composite image, then enable this option.

Tip

Click the Display Alpha Channel button in the Rendered Frame Window to view the alpha channel. ■

The Affect Z Buffer option stores the effect information in the Z Buffer, which is used to determine the depth of objects from the camera's viewpoint.

The Distance Affects option alters the effect's Size and/or Intensity based on its distance from the camera. The Off-Center Affects option is similar, except that it affects the effect's size and intensity based on its Off-Center distance. The Direction Affects options can affect the size and intensity of an effect based on the direction in which a spotlight is pointing.

The Occlusion settings can be used to cause an effect to be hidden by an object that lies between the effect and the camera. The Inner Radius value defines the area that an object must block in order to hide the effect. The Outer Radius value defines where the effect begins to be occluded. You can also set the Size and Intensity options for the effect. The Affected by Atmospheres option allows effects to be occluded by atmospheric effects.

Glow

The Glow Element rollout, shown in Figure 46.20, includes parameters for controlling the look of the Glow Lens Effect. This rollout has two tabbed panels: Parameters and Options.

FIGURE 46.20

The Glow Element rollout lets you set the parameters for the Glow effect.

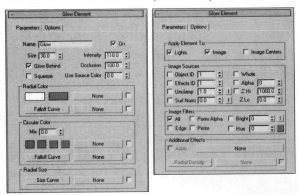

The Glow Element Parameters tabbed panel

In the Parameters tabbed panel of the Glow Element rollout, there is a Name field. Several glow effects can be added to a scene, and each one can have a different name. The On option turns each glow on and off.

The Parameters panel also includes Size and Intensity values. These work with the Global settings to determine the size of the glow and can be set to any positive value. The Occlusion and Use Source Color values are percentages. The Occlusion value determines how much of the occlusion set in the Scene panel of the Lens Effects Globals rollout is to be used. If the Use Source Color is at 100 percent, then the glow color is determined by the light color; if it is set to any value below 100, then the colors specified in the Source and Circular Color sections are combined with the light's color.

This panel also includes Glow Behind and Squeeze options. Glow Behind makes the glow effect visible behind objects. Squeeze enables any squeeze settings specified in the Parameters panel.

If the Use Source Color value is set to 0 percent, only the Radial Color swatches determine the glow colors. Radial colors proceed from the center of the glow circle to the outer edge. The first swatch is the inner color, and the second is the outer color. The Falloff Curve button opens the Radial Falloff function curve dialog box, shown in Figure 46.21, where you can use a curve to set how quickly or slowly the colors change.

The Radial Falloff dialog box lets you control how the inner radial color changes to the outer radial color.

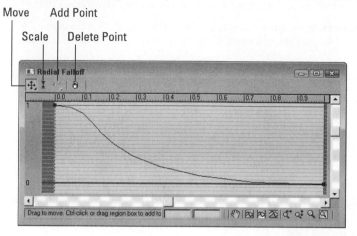

The Circular Color swatches specify the glow color around the glow circle starting from the top point and proceeding clockwise. The Mix value is the percentage to mix the Circular colors with the Radial Colors; a value of 0 displays only the Radial colors, and a value of 100 displays only the Circular colors. You can also access the Falloff Curve dialog box for the Circular Color Falloff curve.

You can also control the Radial Size using a curve by clicking the Size Curve button. Clicking the Size Curve button accesses the Radial Size dialog box. Figure 46.22 shows several glow effects where the radial size curve has been altered. The curves are, from left to right, roughly a descending linear curve, a v-shaped curve, a wide u-shaped curve, an m-shaped curve, and a sine curve.

These glow effects are distorted using the Radial Size function curves.

All these colors and function curves have map buttons (initially labeled None) that enable you to load maps. Useful maps to use include Falloff, Gradient and Gradient Ramp, Noise, and Swirl. You can enable a map by using the check box to its immediate right.

The Glow Element Options tabbed panel

The Options panel of the Glow Element rollout defines where to apply the glow effect. In the Apply Element To section, the first option is to apply a glow to the Lights. These lights are selected in the Lights section of the Lens Effects Globals rollout using the Pick Light button. The other two options—Image and Image Centers—apply glows using settings contained in the Options panel.

In the Image Sources section, you can apply glows to specific objects using the Object ID option and settings. Object IDs are set for objects in the Object Properties dialog box. If the corresponding Object ID is selected and enabled in the Options panel, the object is endowed with the Glow Lens Effect.

The Effects ID option and settings work in a manner similar to Object IDs, except that they are assigned to materials in the Material Editor. You can use Effects IDs to make a subobject selection glow.

The Unclamp option and settings enable colors to be brighter than pure white. Pure White is a value of 1. The Unclamp value is the lowest value that glows. The Surf Norm (Surface Normal) option and value let you set object areas to glow based on the angle between the surface normal and the camera. The "I" button to the right inverts the value.

Figure 46.23 shows an array of spheres with the Surf Norm glow enabled. Because the glows multiply, a value of only 2 was applied. Notice that the spheres in the center have a stronger glow.

FIGURE 46.23

The Surf Norm option causes objects to glow, based on the angle between their surface normals and the camera.

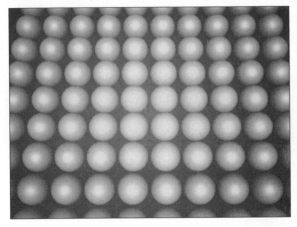

In the Image Sources section, options enable these glows to be applied to the Whole scene, the Alpha channel, or the Z buffer with specified Hi and Lo values.

The Image Filters section can further refine which objects to apply the glow effect to. Options include All, Edge, Perim (Perimeter) Alpha, Perim, Brightness, and Hue. The All option applies the effect to all pixels that are part of the source. The Edge, Perim Alpha, and Perim options apply the effect only to the edges, perimeter of the alpha channel, or perimeter of the source. The Brightness option includes a value and an "I" invert button. This applies the effect only to areas with a brightness greater than the specified value. The Hue option also includes a value and a color swatch for setting the hue, which receives the effect.

The Additional Effects section lets you apply a map to the Glow Lens Effect with an Apply option and a map button. You can also control the Radial Density function curve or add a map for the Radial Density.

Tutorial: Creating shocking electricity from a plug outlet

In addition to the light objects, lighting in a scene can be provided by self-illuminating an object and using a Glow render effect. Self-illuminating an object is accomplished by applying a material with a

Self-Illumination value greater than 0 or a color other than black. You can create glows by using the Render Effects dialog box or the Video Post dialog box.

Cross-Reference

For more information on applying glows using the Video Post interface, see Chapter 49, "Compositing with Render Elements and the Video Post Interface." ■

Working with a faulty electrical outlet can be a shocking experience. In this tutorial, you create an electric arc that runs from an outlet to a plug. To create the effect of electricity, you can use a renderable spline with several vertices and apply the Noise modifier to make it dance around. You can set the light by using a self-illuminating material and a Glow render effect.

To create an electric arc that runs between an outlet and a plug, follow these steps:

1. Open the Electricity.max file from the Chap 46 directory on the CD.

   This file includes an outlet and an electric plug. A spline runs between the outline and the plug with a Noise modifier applied to it, which will be our electric arc.

2. Open the Material Editor by pressing the M key, and select the first sample slot. Select a yellow Diffuse color and an equally bright yellow for the Self-Illumination color. Set the Material Effects Channel to 1 by clicking the Material Effects ID button and holding it down until a pop-up array of numbers appears, and then drag to the number 1 and release the mouse. Drag this new material to the electric arc and close the Material Editor.

3. Open the Render Effects dialog box by choosing Rendering ⇨ Effects. Click the Add button, select the Lens Effects option, and click OK. Then select Lens Effects from the list, and double-click Glow in the Lens Effects Parameters rollout. Select Glow from the list; in the Glow Element rollout, set the Size to **1** and the Intensity value to **50**. Then open the Options panel, set the Material ID to **1**, and enable it.

Figure 46.24 shows the resulting electric arc.

FIGURE 46.24

You can create electricity using a simple spline, the Noise modifier, and the Glow render effect.

Tutorial: Creating neon

You can also use the Glow render effect to create neon signs. The letters for these signs can be simple renderable splines, as this tutorial shows.

To create a neon sign, follow these steps:

1. Open the Blues neon.max file from the Chap 46 directory on the CD.

   This file includes a simple sign that reads "Blues."

2. Open the Material Editor with the M key, select the first sample slot, and name it **Blue Neon**. Set its Diffuse color to blue and its Self-Illumination color to dark blue. Set the Material Effects Channel to **1**, and apply the material to the sign.

3. Open the Rendering Effects panel, and click the Add button. Double-click the Lens Effects option to add it to the Effects list. In the Lens Effects rollout, double-click the Glow option and select it in the list to enable its rollouts. In the Lens Effects Globals rollout, set the Size and Intensity values to **1**. In the Glow Element rollout, set the Size to **10** and the Intensity to **100**, and make sure that the Glow Behind option is selected. For the neon color, set the Use Source Color to **100**. Finally, open the Options panel, set the Material ID to **1**, and enable it.

Note

As an alternative to using the source color, you could set the Use Source Color value to 0 and set the Radial Color swatch to blue. This gives you more control over the glow color. ■

Figure 46.25 shows the rendered neon effect.

FIGURE 46.25

The glow of neon lights, easily created with render effects

Ring

The Ring Lens Effect is also circular and includes all the same controls and settings as the Glow Lens Effect. The only additional values are the Plane and Thickness values. The Plane value positions the Ring center relative to the center of the screen, and the Thickness value determines the width of the Ring's band.

Figure 46.26 shows several Ring effects with various Thickness values (from left to right): 1, 3, 6, 12, and 24.

FIGURE 46.26

Ring effects can vary in thickness.

Ray

The Ray Lens Effect emits bright, semitransparent rays in all directions from the source. It also uses the same settings as the Glow effect, except for the Num (Number) and Sharp values. The Num value is the number of rays, and the Sharp value can range from 0 to 10 and determines how blurry the rays are.

Figure 46.27 shows the Ray effect applied to a simple Omni light with increasing Num values: 6, 12, 50, 100, and 200. Notice that the rays aren't symmetrical and are randomly placed.

FIGURE 46.27

The Ray effect extends a given number of rays out from the effect center.

Star

The Star Lens Effect radiates semitransparent bands of light at regular intervals from the center of the effect. It uses the same controls as the Glow effect, with the addition of Width, Taper, Qty (Quantity), and Sharp values. The Width sets the width of each band. The Taper value determines how quickly the width angles to a point. The Qty value is the number of bands, and the Sharp value determines how blurry the bands are.

Figure 46.28 shows several Star effects with (from left to right) 3, 4, 5, 6, and 12 bands.

FIGURE 46.28

The Star effect lets you set the number of bands emitting from the center.

Streak

The Streak Lens Effect adds a horizontal band through the center of the selected object. It is similar to the Star effect, except it has only two bands that extend in opposite directions.

Figure 46.29 shows several Streak effects angled at 45 degrees with Width values of (from left to right) 2, 4, 10, 15, and 20.

FIGURE 46.29

The Streak effect enables you to create horizontal bands.

Auto Secondary

When a camera is moved past a bright light, several small circles appear lined up in a row proceeding from the center of the light. These secondary lens flares are caused by light refracting off the lens. You can simulate this effect by using the Auto Secondary Lens Effect.

Many of the settings in the Auto Secondary Element rollout are the same as in the Glow effect rollout described previously, but the Auto Secondary Element rollout has several unique values. Figure 46.30 shows this rollout.

The Min and Max values define the minimum and maximum size of the flares. The Axis is the length of the axis along which the flares are positioned. Larger values spread the flares out more than smaller values. The actual angle of the flares depends on the angle between the camera and the effect object.

The Quantity value is the number of flares to include. The Sides drop-down list lets you select a Circular flare or flares with three to eight sides. Below the Sides drop-down list are several preset options in another drop-down list. These include options such as Brown Ring, Blue Circle, and Green Rainbow, among others.

You can also use four Radial Colors to define the flares. The color swatches from left to right define the colors from the inside out. The spinners below each color swatch indicate where the color should end.

Figure 46.31 shows the Auto Secondary Effect with the Rainbow preset and the Intensity increased to 50.

FIGURE 46.30

The Auto Secondary Element rollout sets the parameters for this effect.

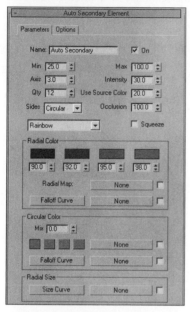

FIGURE 46.31

The Auto Secondary Effect displays several flares extending at an angle from the center of the effect.

Manual Secondary

In addition to the Auto Secondary Lens Effect, you can add a Manual Secondary Lens Effect to add some more flares with a different size and look. This effect includes a Plane value that places the flare in front of (positive value) or behind (negative value) the flare source.

Figure 46.32 shows the same flares from the previous figure with an additional Manual Secondary Effect added.

FIGURE 46.32

The Manual Secondary Effect can add some randomness to a flare lineup.

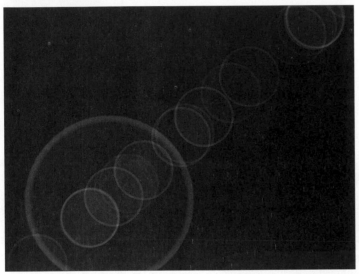

Tutorial: Making an airplane sparkle

When shiny metal planes fly through the sky, they often give off sparkling light effects. Adding some Lens Effects to an airplane scene can simulate this effect.

To make an object bright and shiny using Lens Effects, follow these steps:

1. Open the Spruce Goose.max file from the Chap 46 directory on the CD.

   This file includes an airplane model of the famous Spruce Goose created by Viewpoint Datalabs.

2. Open the Create panel, and click the Lights category button. Create several Omni lights, and position them around the scene to provide adequate lighting. Position a single light close to the plane's surface where you want the highlight to be located—make it near the surface, and set the Multiplier value to **0.5**.

3. Open the Rendering Effects panel by choosing Rendering ➪ Effects (or press the 8 key). Click the Add button, and select Lens Effects. Then, in the Lens Effects Parameters rollout, select the Glow effect in the left pane and click the button pointing to the right pane.

4. In the Parameters panel, click the Pick Light button and select the light close to the surface. Set the Size around **30** and the Intensity at **100**. Go to the Glow Element rollout, and in the Parameters panel, set the Use Source Color to **0**. Then, in the Radial Color section, click the second Radial Color swatch, and in the Color Selector dialog box, select a color like yellow and click the Close button.

5. Back in the Lens Effects Parameters rollout, select Star, and add it to the list of effects. It automatically uses the same light specified for the Glow effect. In the Star Element rollout, set the Quantity (Qty) value to **6**, the Size to **200**, and the Intensity to **100**.

Figure 46.33 shows the resulting airplane with a nice shine.

FIGURE 46.33

The Spruce Goose has had a sparkle added to it using the Glow and Star Lens Effects.

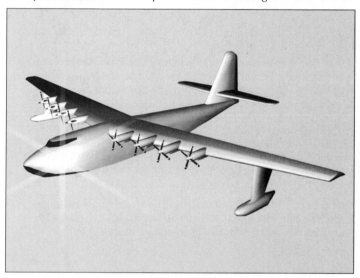

Using Other Render Effects

Now that I've covered the big brother of the render effects, let's return to the Add Effect dialog box, where six other render effects are available. If these selections aren't enough, Max also enables you to add even more options to this list via plug-ins.

Blur render effect

The Blur render effect displays three different blurring methods in the Blur Type panel: Uniform, Directional, and Radial. You can find these options in the Blur Type tabbed panel in the Blur Parameters rollout, shown in Figure 46.34.

FIGURE 46.34

The Blur Parameters rollout lets you select a Uniform, Directional, or Radial blur type.

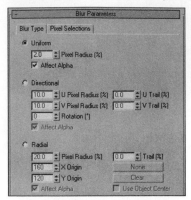

The Uniform blur method applies the blur evenly across the whole image. The Pixel Radius value defines the amount of the blur. The Directional blur method can be used to blur the image along a certain direction. The U Pixel Radius and U Trail values define the blur in the horizontal direction, and the V Pixel Radius and V Trail values blur in a vertical direction. The Rotation value rotates the axis of the blur.

The Radial blur method creates concentric blurred rings determined by the Radius and Trail values. When the Use Object Center option is selected, the None and Clear buttons become active. Clicking the None button lets you select an object about which you want to center the radial blur. The Clear button clears this selection.

Figure 46.35 shows a dinosaur model created by Viewpoint Datalabs. The actual rendered image shows the sharp edges of the polygons. The Blur effect can help this by softening all the hard edges. The left image is the original dinosaur, and the right image has a Directional blur applied.

FIGURE 46.35

The Blur effect can soften an otherwise hard model.

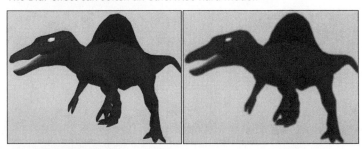

The Blur Parameters rollout also includes a Pixel Selections tabbed panel, shown in Figure 46.36, that contains parameters for specifying which parts of the image get blurred. Options include the Whole Image, Non-Background, Luminance, Map Mask, Object ID, and Material ID.

The Pixel Selections tabbed panel (shown in two parts) of the Blur Parameters rollout lets you select the parts of the image that get the Blur effect.

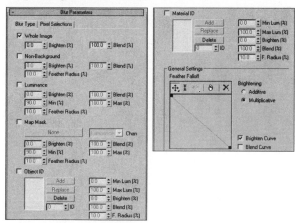

You can use the Feather Falloff curve at the bottom of the Blur Parameters rollout to define the Brighten and Blend curves. The buttons above this curve are for adding points, scaling the points, and moving them within the curve interface.

Brightness and Contrast render effect

The Brightness and Contrast render effect can alter these amounts in the image. The Brightness and Contrast Parameters rollout is a simple rollout with values for both the brightness and contrast that can range from 0 to 1. It also contains an Ignore Background option.

Color Balance render effect

The Color Balance effect enables you to tint the image using separate Cyan/Red, Magenta/Green, and Yellow/Blue channels. To change the color balance, drag the sliders in the Color Balance Parameters rollout. Other options include Preserve Luminosity and Ignore Background. The Preserve Luminosity option tints the image while maintaining the luminosity of the image, and the Ignore Background option tints the rendered objects but not the background image.

File Output render effect

The File Output render effect enables you to save the rendered file to a File or to a Device at any point during the render effect's post-processing. Figure 46.37 shows the File Output Parameters rollout.

FIGURE 46.37

The File Output Parameters rollout lets you save a rendered image before a render effect is applied.

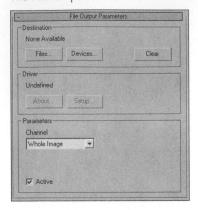

Using the Channel drop-down list in the Parameters section, you can save out Whole Images, as well as grayscale Luminance, Depth, and Alpha images.

Film Grain render effect

The Film Grain effect gives an image a grained look, which hardens the overall look of the image. You can also use this effect to match rendered objects to the grain of the background image. This helps the objects blend into the scene better. Figure 46.38 shows the effect.

The Grain value can range from 0 to 1. The Ignore Background option applies the grain effect only to the objects in the scene and not to the background.

FIGURE 46.38

The Film Grain render effect applies a noise filter to the rendered image.

Motion Blur render effect

The Motion Blur effect applies a simple image motion blur to the rendered output. The Motion Blur Parameters rollout includes settings for working with Transparency and a value for the Duration of the blur. Objects that move rapidly within the scene are blurred.

Depth of Field render effect

The Depth of Field effect enhances the sense of depth by blurring objects close to or far from the camera. The Pick Cam button in the Depth of Field Parameters rollout, shown in Figure 46.39, lets you select a camera in the viewport to use for this effect. Multiple cameras can be selected, and all selected cameras are displayed in the drop-down list. A Remove button lets you remove cameras.

The Depth of Field Parameters rollout lets you select a camera or a Focal Point to apply the effect to.

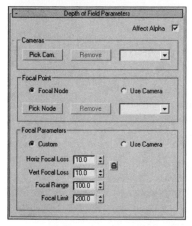

In the Focal Point section, the Pick Node button lets you select an object to use as the focal point. This object is where the camera focuses. Objects far from this object are blurred. These nodes are also listed in a drop-down list. You can remove objects from the list by selecting them and clicking the Remove button. The Use Camera option uses the camera's own settings to determine the focal point.

In the Focal Parameters section, if you select the Custom option, then you can specify values for the Horizontal and Vertical Focal Loss, the Focal Range, and the Focal Limit. The Loss values indicate how much blur occurs. The Focal Range is where the image starts to blur, and the Focal Limit is where the image stops blurring.

Figure 46.40 shows a beach scene created by Viewpoint Datalabs. For this figure, I applied the Depth of Field effect using the Pick Node button and selecting some leaves on the tree. Then I set the Focal Range to 100, the Focal Limit to 200, and the Focal Loss values to 10 for both the Horizontal and Vertical.

Cross-Reference

The Depth of Field and Motion Blur effects can also be applied using a Multi-Pass camera, as discussed in Chapter 19, "Configuring and Aiming Cameras." ■

FIGURE 46.40

The Depth of Field effect focuses a camera on an object in the middle and blurs objects closer or farther away.

Summary

Creating the right environment can add lots of realism to any rendered scene. Using the Environment and Effects dialog box, you can work with atmospheric effects. Atmospheric effects include Fire, Fog, Volume Fog, and Volume Light.

Render effects are useful because they enable you to create effects and update them interactively. This gives a level of control that was previously unavailable. This chapter explained how to use render elements and render effects and described the various types.

This chapter covered these topics:

- Creating Atmospheric Apparatus gizmos for positioning atmospheric effects
- Working with the Fire atmospheric effects
- Creating fog and volume fog effects
- Applying render effects
- Using the Lens Effects to create glows, rays, and stars
- Working with the remaining render effects to control brightness and contrast, film grain, blurs, and more
- Learning how exposure controls can work

The next chapter delves into the amazing mental ray rendering engine.

Rendering with mental ray and iray

M ax includes a plug-in architecture that lets you replace or extend any part of the software including the rendering engine. Mental ray is a plug-in rendering engine that offers many advanced features. This engine takes the rendering in Max to a new level, enabling you to render your scenes with amazing accuracy. It also includes a host of advanced rendering features including caustics and global illumination that are physically realistic.

Although the mental ray renderer is awesome, it can take lots of tweaking to get results to look just right. This is where iray comes in. iray lets you start a render, and it automatically adjusts the settings to give you great results based on the amount of time you give it. In other words, iray is mental ray for dummies.

Enabling mental ray and iray

If you're accustomed to using the Default Scanline Renderer and you're wondering if the mental ray or iray rendering engines are worth using, the answer is yes. Actually, you should try a couple of test renderings first and play with the different settings, but in working with mental ray I've been amazed at its results. One of the chief benefits of mental ray is its speed. It can render a fully raytraced scene in a fraction of the time without sacrificing quality.

Note

If you need even more speed and don't mind sacrificing a little quality, then try the Quicksilver Hardware renderer. It works with most of the mental ray materials, lights, and settings. ∎

Note

mental ray is an external rendering engine that plugs into 3ds Max. It was developed by a company named mental images, so its development is separate from Max. Versions of the mental ray rendering engine also can be found in Maya and Softimage as well as a stand-alone version. ■

mental ray and iray also include support for global illumination without your having to enable the Advanced Lighting settings. In addition, mental ray can use all of Max's existing materials without having to use a limited specialized material like the raytrace material. Each material has a new rollout that lets you specialize mental ray settings. However, iray requires that you use only a specific set of materials, including the Arch & Design and those materials in the Autodesk Material Library.

Note

mental ray can't use the Advanced Lighting settings. mental ray has its own lighting solution that is independent of Advance Lighting. ■

Cross-Reference

Many of the available mental ray materials are covered in Chapter 30, "Using Specialized Material Types." ■

mental ray also includes native support for Area Lights, Shaders, Depth of Field, and Motion Blur. It also includes some specialized lights that offer functionality, such as caustics, that are unavailable in the Scanline Renderer.

To choose mental ray or iray as the renderer for your scene, simply select it from the list of available renderers in the Assign Renderer rollout of the Common panel of the Render Scene dialog box. You can set a different renderer for Production, the Material Editor, and the ActiveShade viewer. To make mental ray your default renderer, click the Save as Defaults button in this rollout.

Once selected as your Production renderer, you don't need to modify any other settings for the renderer to work. The mental ray settings in the Material Editor, Lights category, and Object Properties dialog box enable additional features that mental ray can take advantage of, but they aren't required to render the scene. The current mental ray version is 3.9.

Note

You may have noticed the Raytracer rollout in the Render Setup dialog box when the Scanline Renderer is enabled. There is also a Raytrace material in the Standard set of the materials. These settings and materials are used to enable and configure raytracing in the Default Scanline Renderer, but the mental ray results are much better than these raytrace options, so the focus is to learn mental ray instead of the older raytrace options. ■

Working with iray

After iray is enabled, you'll notice that the number of panels for configuring it in the Render Setup dialog box has been greatly reduced. The whole idea behind iray is to make the process of configuring the renderer easier. The single configuration panel for iray is the Renderer panel, shown in Figure 47.1.

FIGURE 47.1

The iray renderer has only a single panel of options in the Render Setup dialog box.

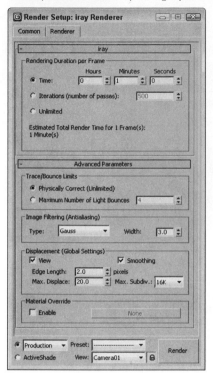

Within iray's Renderer panel, you can set the time for the render to take, choose the number of iterations, or make simply set enable the Unlimited option. The iray renderer then renders and continually
refines the given scene. As it renders, the results are shown in the Rendered Frame Window, and the
render can be stopped and saved at any time.

The Advanced Parameters rollout includes options for limiting the number of light bounces, options
for picking the anti-aliasing filter to use (Box, Gauss, or Triangle), and global settings for handling displacement maps. The Material Override option lets you replace all applied materials with a single
designated material that is selected using the button to the right. This lets you see the lighting and
shadow effects quickly or get a result if unsupported materials are used in the scene.

One "gotcha" when working with iray is that if a material or map is used that it doesn't support, the
object is rendered as flat gray. The supported iray materials are those that have information on how
the light interacts with it. For Max, the Arch & Design materials, the Autodesk Material Library
(except for the Metallic Paint material, which isn't supported), Bitmaps, Mix, Noise, Normal Bump,
RGB Multiply, and mr Physical Sky are supported. Also, iray supports only Photometric lights.

Figure 47.2 shows a sample scene rendered with iray. The image on the left shows the scene after only a few seconds, and the one on the right shows the scene after a longer render time.

FIGURE 47.2

The iray renderer progressively refines the image for as long as you let it run.

Tutorial: Starting iray

Once you get the hang of using iray, you'll find it is great to start the renderer with the unlimited setting before running off to lunch and check out the results when you get back.

To use the iray renderer to render a scene, follow these steps:

1. Open the Plant in corner.max file from the Chap 47 directory on the CD.

   This file includes several simple objects and a plant. The scene already has materials applied from the Autodesk Material Library.

2. Open the Render Scene dialog box (F10), and switch the Production Renderer in the Assign Renderer rollout of the Common panel to the iray renderer.

3. In the Renderer panel of the Render Setup dialog box, enable the Unlimited option and click the Render button.

4. Let the scene render for a while and when it looks good enough, click the Cancel button in the Rendering dialog box. The rendered results are displayed in the Rendered Frame Window where you can save the image if you desire.

Figure 47.3 shows the scene rendered with iray.

FIGURE 47.3

Using the Unlimited option lets the iray renderer keep running as long as it can.

Accessing mental ray Preferences

In the Preference Settings dialog box is a panel of global mental ray settings, shown in Figure 47.4. In this panel, you can select to Enable mental ray Extensions. These extensions add some additional controls to several of the various mental ray panels.

When the Scanline Renderer renders a scene, it progresses one line of pixels at a time down the image, but mental ray renders the image by breaking it up into blocks and rendering a block at a time. The Show Brackets on Current Buckets option displays white brackets around the current block as the image renders.

FIGURE 47.4

The Preference Settings dialog box includes a panel of mental ray settings.

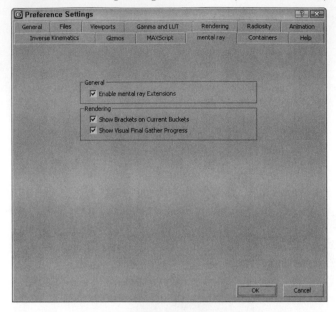

Note

Multiple white brackets may be visible if you're rendering across a network or using a computer with multiple processors. ■

The Show Visual Final Gather Progress option displays a rough approximation of the render scene as it is being rendered before waiting for a Final Gather solution. This gives you a quick look at the scene before it computes a Final Gather solution. You can also select to clear the frame before rendering.

The Messages section lets you specify which messages are displayed as the file renders. Options include Errors, Log Information, Log Progress, Debug Messages, and whether to write this information to a file.

Using mental ray Lights and Shadows

If you look in the Lights category of the Create ⇨ Lights ⇨ Standard Lights menu, you'll see two mental ray specific lights: mental ray Area Omni and mental ray Area Spot. These area lights spread light from a defined area in the Area Light Parameters rollout. By default, all mental lights use the Global Settings for their illumination values, but by using the mental ray Indirect Illumination rollout, shown in Figure 47.5, found in the Modify panel, you can override the global settings for the selected light.

The mental ray Indirect Illumination rollout lets you define the light settings for individual lights.

Enabling mental ray Shadow Maps

In the Shadows drop-down list of the Shadow Parameters rollout is an option to enable mental ray Shadow Maps. These shadow maps are more accurate than normal shadow maps.

Using mental ray Sun & Sky

If you want to quickly create an outdoor scene and render it using mental ray, then the Daylight system that uses the mr Sun and Sky is an easy quality solution. Before adding the Daylight system to your scene, switch the renderer to mental ray in the Render Setup dialog box. Then add the Daylight system to the scene, and in the Modify panel, select mr Sun in the Sunlight drop-down list and mr Sky in the Skylight drop-down list. When you first select the Daylight system, a dialog box appears recommending that you use the mr Photographic Exposure Control. Click the Yes button to enable this control. When you select the mr Sky option, another dialog box appears, asking if you want to enable the mr Physical Sky environment map. Click Yes to this also.

If you look in the Environment panel, you can see the mr Physical Sky material applied. This material defines how the sky and ground planes look. The default settings look pretty good.

The Daylight system includes controls for positioning the sun in the sky based on a physical location, day of the year, and time of the day. By changing these controls, you can manipulate the sun's position in the sky relative to the scene objects. If the sun appears in the viewport, it is rendered with lens flares, as shown in Figure 47.6.

FIGURE 47.6

The Daylight can be endowed with mr Sun and mr Sky.

When a Sky & Sun system is in place, you can ensure that it displays within the viewport if you open the Views ⇨ Viewport Background ⇨ Viewport Background dialog box (Alt+B) and enable the Use Environment Background settings. Make sure also that the Display Background option is set. Using this method makes the Sun & Sky system visible even if the Viewport Shading option is set to Off.

Selecting the sun light object and moving it about the scene or changing the Time and Date parameters automatically updates the background and the scene. This provides a good way to precisely position the sun where you want it, as shown in Figure 47.7. For best results, select the Enable Hardware Shading option in the Lighting and Shadows menu for the viewport shading label.

Using mental ray Sky Portal

If you look closely at the Photometric light category, you'll notice another light type sandwiched between the mr Sky and mr Sun lights. The mr Sky Portal provides a way to focus light streaming into an interior space from an external source using a designated portal. This can be thought of as a sky light that causes all Final Gather light rays to be focused on a specific area. It results in a better Final Gather result with fewer light rays. The Sky Portal is direct light giving you one bounce for free if Final Gather is disabled.

To use a Sky Portal, you must have mental ray enabled, include a skylight or a Sun & Sky system, and have Final Gather turned on. Then simply drag over the area where the window is located, and all light rays entering the interior space are focused on those areas defined by the Sky Portal. The gizmo for the Sky Portal is a simple rectangular box with an arrow pointing in the direction of the light rays. If the light rays are pointing outward, you can use the Flip Light Flux Direction option to change their direction.

FIGURE 47.7

The Sun & Sky system can be viewed and interactively updated in the viewport.

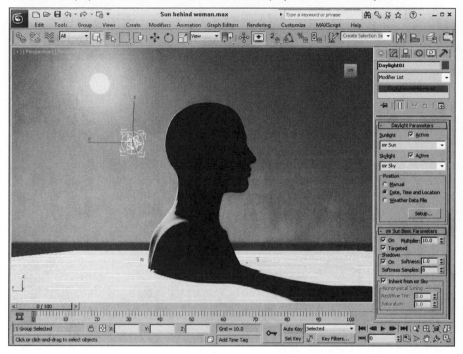

Tip

For better results for interior scenes using exterior lighting, enable the mr Photographic Exposure Control and use the Physically Based Lighting, Indoor Daylight preset. ∎

Within the mr Skylight Portal Parameters rollout, you can enable or disable the Sky Portal. A Multiplier value and a Filter Color work just like other lights. If the image appears grainy, you can increase the Shadow Samples value to remove any splotchy effect on the walls, but this increases the render time. Within the Advanced Parameters rollout, the Visible to Renderer makes the Sky Portal visible in the rendered image, causing exterior objects to be blotted out.

You also can set the Color Source to Use the Scene Environment if you want light to be pulled from the environment map. Sky Portals also support HDRI maps as lighting sources. Figure 47.8 shows a house interior lighted using mental ray, Final Gather, and two Sky Portals.

FIGURE 47.8

Sky Portals can focus all rays coming from an external light source to speed up Final Gather passes.

Understanding Caustics and Photons

Light properties for the mental ray renderer include four unique properties: Energy, Decay, Caustic Photons, and Global Illumination (GI) Photons. You can find the settings for these properties in the mental ray Indirect Illumination rollout. Before learning about these properties, you need to understand what caustics and photons are.

Caustics are those strange glowing lines that you see at the bottom of an indoor swimming pool caused by the light refracting through the water. Caustics are common in nature, and now with mental ray you can add these effects to your scenes. *Photons* are small bundles of light energy, and like the raytracing rays, they are emitted from a light source with a given amount of energy. This energy is lost as the photon travels and as it hits objects in the scene.

The Energy value is the amount of light energy that each photon starts out with, and the Decay value specifies how quickly that energy dissipates. The number of Caustic and GI Photons determines the resulting accuracy of the lighting. More photons yield a better solution, but the greater number also increases the render time substantially. The Multiplier and color swatch lets you set the intensity and color of the caustics.

Figure 47.9 shows a swimming pool with caustics glowing on the side of the wall. The left image shows the pool scene with caustics disabled, and the right image shows them enabled.

To get caustics to work in your scene, you need to add a Raytrace, Flat Mirror, or Reflect/Refract map to the Reflection map channel for the material that you want to generate caustics.

FIGURE 47.9

This indoor swimming pool scene is rendered without caustics (left) and with caustics (right).

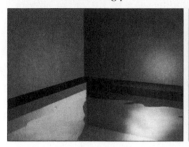 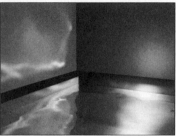

Tutorial: Using Caustic Photons to create a disco ball

When using the mental ray renderer, you can see the caustic photons as they are reflected around the room to help you determine the correct settings you need, but these photons themselves can be used to make a good disco ball effect.

Tip

A common way to get a good, crisp caustic effect is to use significantly more photons than you would need for global illumination—on the order of millions of photons—for good results. ■

To create a disco ball effect using caustic photons, follow these steps:

1. Open the Disco ball.max file from the Chap 47 directory on the CD.

   This file includes a simple room.

2. Open the Render Scene dialog box (F10), and switch the Production Renderer in the Assign Renderer rollout of the Common panel to the mental ray renderer.

3. Select Create ⇨ Standard Primitives ⇨ Sphere, and click in the Top viewport to create a sphere positioned toward the top of the room.

4. Press the M key to open the Slate Material Editor, double-click on the Standard material in the Material/Map Browser, and then double-click on the Raytrace map type in the Material/Map Browser. Then drag on the output socket for the Raytrace map and drop on the Reflection parameter. Then double-click the Standard material node to make its parameters appear, enable the Faceted option in the Shader Basic Parameters rollout; set the Opacity to **50**, the Specular Level to **95**, and the Glossiness to **30**; and drag the standard material's output socket to the sphere object.

5. Select Create Lights ⇨ Standard Lights ⇨ mr Area Omni, and click in the Top viewport to create four lights that surround the sphere object. From the main menu, select the Tools ⇨ Light Lister option where you can quickly change the Multiplier value for each of the lights to **0.3**. Then, using the Move tool, offset each light vertically from the others.

6. Select and right-click on each of the lights and open the Object Properties dialog box from the pop-up quadmenu. Open the mental ray panel in the Object Properties dialog box and enable the Generate Caustics option for each light.

7. Open the Render Scene dialog box (F10). In the Indirect Illumination panel, locate the Caustics section. Enable the Caustics option, set the Multiplier to **10**, enable the Maximum Sampling Radius option, and set the Maximum Sampling Radius value to **1.0**. At the bottom or the Caustics and Global Illumination (GI) rollout, enable the All Objects Generate and Receive GI & Caustics option. Then click the Render button.

Note
If the caustics aren't visible, make sure the Use Advanced Lighting option in the Render Setup dialog box is enabled. ∎

Figure 47.10 shows the resulting disco scene with thousands of lights visible on the walls.

FIGURE 47.10
This disco ball simply reflects the caustic photons around the room.

Enabling caustics and global illumination for objects

Another "gotcha" when dealing with caustics and global illumination is that each object can be specified to generate and/or receive caustics and global illumination. These settings are found in the mental ray panel of the Object Properties dialog box, shown in Figure 47.11. This dialog box can be opened using the Edit ⇨ Properties menu command. If your scene isn't generating caustics and you can't figure out why, check this dialog box, because the Generate Caustics option is disabled by default. There is also an option to exclude the object from caustics and from GI.

The mental ray panel in the Object Properties dialog box also includes settings so that you can configure how the object is treated during the Final Gather pass. Using the Return Black or Pass Through options, you can make the object unshaded or invisible to the final gather.

FIGURE 47.11

The Object Properties dialog box includes options for generating and receiving caustics and global illumination.

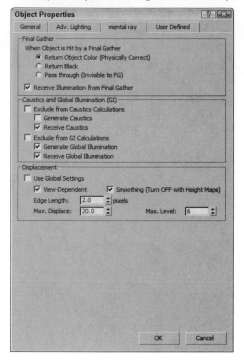

Tip

The Indirect Illumination panel of the Render Scene dialog box includes an option that can be used to cause All Objects to Generate and Receive Caustics and GI. Enabling this option enables these options for all objects regardless of their Object Properties settings. ■

Controlling Indirect Illumination

In addition to the light settings, you can set many of the properties that control how caustics, global illumination, and Final Gather are computed in two rollouts of the Indirect Illumination panel of the Render Scene dialog box, shown in Figure 47.12. These two rollouts are the Final Gather rollout and the Caustics and Global Illumination (GI) rollout.

FIGURE 47.12

The Indirect Illumination panel includes settings for caustics, GI, and Final Gather.

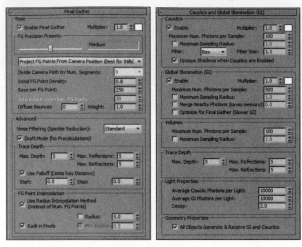

The Final Gather rollout is split into two parts. The top part features a set of Basic settings with several Presets that take the guesswork out of the settings. Simply choose one of the presets from the drop-down list, and all the key settings are automatically made for you. The preset options include Draft, Low, Medium, High, and Very High. The Multiplier and color swatch changes the intensity and color of the indirect light. The Weight value sets how much indirect light affects the Final Gather solution.

For caustics and for global illumination, the Maximum Number of Photons per Sample value determines how the caustic photons are blended. A higher value results in more blending and softer edges. The Maximum Sampling Radius value sets the size of each photon. This value is set automatically depending on the size of the scene. However, you can enable the Radius value and enter a new value manually.

The Volumes setting is used by Volume material shaders to set the photon's size. The Trace Depth settings determine the maximum number of reflections and refractions that a photon can take before it is ignored.

Photon and Final Gather maps can take a while to generate for a complicated scene, but once computed, they can be saved and reloaded. These files are saved using the .pmap and .fgm extensions. To generate a photon map, click the Generate Photon Map Now, or to generate a final gather map, click the Generate Final Gather Map Now button.

Final Gather sends out rays to a scene that has computed caustics and global illumination already and computes the light at that location. All these rays are then combined to produce a total lighting picture of the scene and then blended to help fix any lighting abnormalities that may exist in the scene. The Samples value determines how many rays are cast into the scene. The Final Gather lighting pass can then be saved to a file after it is computed.

Rendering control

The core rendering settings for the mental ray renderer are contained within the Renderer panel of the Render Scene dialog box, shown in Figure 47.13. Using these settings, you can increase the speed of the renderer (at the expense of image quality).

The Renderer panel includes several rollouts of settings for controlling the mental ray renderer.

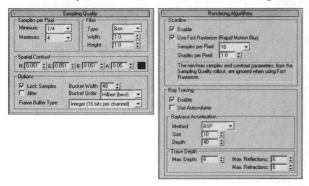

The Sampling settings are used to apply an anti-aliasing pass to the rendered image. These samples can be filtered, and you can control the details of the contrast between the samples. The Bucket Width is the size of the blocks that are identified and rendered. Smaller buckets do not take as long to render and provide quicker feedback in the Render window.

The mental ray renderer uses several different algorithms, and you can specify which ones to ignore in order to speed up the rendering cycle in the Rendering Algorithms rollout. If a needed algorithm is disabled, the features that rely on that algorithm are skipped. You can also set the Trace Depth for Reflections and Refractions and control the Raytrace Acceleration values.

When a preview render is rendered in the Rendered Frame Window while mental ray is enabled, an additional panel of options appears below the window as shown in Figure 47.14. The options on this panel let you quickly adjust the precision value for the Antialiasing, Soft Shadows, Final Gather Precision, Reflection, and Refraction settings. You also can speed the re-render by reusing the Geometry and Final Gather solutions if they haven't changed. The Render button lets you re-render the scene immediately.

Advanced mental ray

The mental ray renderer also includes many additional features that you can take advantage of, including Depth of Field, Motion Blur, Contours, Displacement, and Camera Shaders. The settings for these additional features are located in rollouts at the bottom of the Renderer panel. For example, if you add the Glare map to the Output map in the Camera Shader section, then you can get a strong glare from light in the scene, as shown for the house interior in Figure 47.15.

FIGURE 47.14

When mental ray is rendered in the Render Frame Window, a panel of options appears below for tweaking the image.

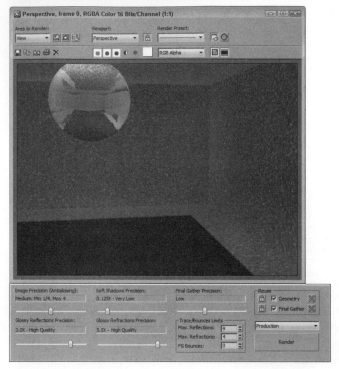

FIGURE 47.15

Placing the Glare map in the Output Camera Shader, you can get a strong glare from the light in the window.

Using mental ray proxies

Complex scenes can have hundreds of objects and when rendered in mental ray, single frames can take several hours to render. This can make it tough to get previews to test lighting and atmospheric effects. If you know that the objects look fine, then you can use the mental ray proxy object to replace multiple objects or a single high-resolution object with a proxy.

To use a mental ray proxy object, add a mr proxy object to the scene using the Create ⇨ mental ray ⇨ mr Proxy menu command. Select the Modify panel and click on the Source Object button, then select the object that you want to replace with the proxy.

Note

You can only select the source object in the Modify panel. ∎

When the source object is selected, you can save the object to a file. Source objects are saved as .mib files. The object is then displayed within the scene as a point cloud or as a bounding box, and a preview of the source object is displayed in the Parameters rollout. You also can change the number of vertices that are displayed in the viewports.

When the scene is rendered, the source object file is read in and used for the render.

Summary

If you're looking for a rendering option that perfectly calculates reflections, refractions, and transparencies, then the mental ray renderer is what you need. iray is another option for rendering when you aren't sure how to configure mental ray.

In this chapter, you accomplished the following:

- Learned to enable the mental ray and iray renderers
- Used the iray renderer to progressively render complex scenes
- Created mental ray lights
- Worked with caustics and photons
- Used mental ray proxies

Now that I've told you how to overload the rendering engine, the next chapter offers a way to get some help by batch rendering and rendering over the network.

Batch and Network Rendering

M ax can help you create some incredible images and animations, but that power comes at a significant price—time. Modeling scenes and animation sequences takes enough time on its own, but after you're finished, you still have to wait for the rendering to take place, which for a final rendering at the highest detail settings can literally take days. Because the time rendering takes is directly proportional to the amount of processing power you have access to, Max lets you use network rendering to add more hardware to the equation and speed up those painfully slow jobs.

This chapter shows you how to set up Max to distribute the rendering workload across an entire network of computers, helping you finish big rendering jobs in record time.

Batch Rendering Scenes

If you work all day modeling, texturing, and animating sequences, only to find that most of your day is shot waiting for a sequence to be rendered, then happily you have several solutions. You can get a second system and use it for rendering while you work on the first system, you can use the network rendering feature to render over the network, or you have a third possibility: you can use the Batch Render tool.

Unless you are working around the clock (which is common for many game productions), you can set up a batch rendering queue before you leave for the evening, using the Batch Render tool. This queue runs through the night, giving you a set of takes to review in the morning.

Using the Batch Render tool

The Batch Render window, shown in Figure 48.1, is accessed from the Rendering menu. Render tasks can be added to the list by clicking the Add button. Render tasks can be disabled by selecting the check box to the left of the task name.

The Batch Render window lets you define render tasks to be run as a batch process.

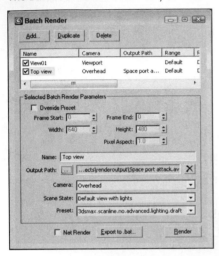

For each task, you can set the task's Name, Output Path, Camera, and render Preset. The Scene State drop-down list lets you select any scene states that are defined using the Tools ⇨ Manage Scene States command.

Each new task added to the Batch Render window uses the default render parameters for its frame range, dimensions, and pixel aspect, but if you enable the Override Preset option, then you can customize each of these parameters for the selected task.

The Batch Render queue can be rendered over the network by enabling the Net Render option at the bottom of the Batch Render window.

Managing scene states

A single scene file may have many different settings that you'd like to try as different renderings. For example, you can set up a scene with different light settings, with different camera properties, or with unique materials. Scene states let you define different sets of properties that can be recalled prior to a batch rendering. Each of these scene states can be part of a single Max file.

When the Tools ⇨ Manage Scene States menu command is selected, the Manage Scene States dialog box appears, as shown in Figure 48.2, which lets you Save, Restore, Rename, and Delete the existing list of scene states. Clicking the Save button opens the Save Scene State dialog box, also shown in Figure 48.2. In the Save Scene State dialog box, you can enter the name for the scene state and select which group of settings to use. The options include Light Properties, Light Transforms, Object Properties, Camera Transforms, Camera Properties, Layer Properties, Layer Assignment, Materials, Environment, and Anim Layer Properties.

FIGURE 48.2

The Manage Scene States and Save Scene State dialog boxes let you define which properties to save as a state that can be recalled for a batch render task.

Creating a stand-alone executable

After a batch render queue is established, you can click the Export to .bat button to open the Batch Render Export to Batch File dialog box, where you can save the batch file as a .bat file. This saved file can be executed from the command line or by using an agent.

Understanding Network Rendering

When you use network rendering to render your animation, Max divides the work among several machines connected via a network, with each machine rendering some of the frames. The increase in speed depends on how many machines you can devote to rendering frames: Add just one computer, and you double the rate at which you can render. Add seven or eight machines, and instead of missing that important deadline by a week, you can get done early and take an extra day off.

Machines connected to handle network rendering are often referred to collectively as a *rendering farm*. The basic process during a network rendering goes like this: One machine manages the entire process and distributes the work among all the computers in the farm. Each machine signals the managing computer when it is ready to work on another frame. The manager then sends or "farms out" a new frame, which gets worked on by a computer in the rendering farm, and the finished frame gets saved in whatever format you've chosen.

The software in Max that makes network rendering possible is called Backburner. You may have noticed that it was installed when Max was installed. Max has several features to make the network rendering process easier. If one of the computers in your rendering farm crashes or loses its connection with the manager, the manager reclaims the frame that was assigned to the down computer and farms it out to a different machine. You can monitor the status of any rendering job you have running, and you can even have Max e-mail you when a job is complete.

Note

One additional caveat to using network rendering is that you have no guarantee that the frames of your animation will be rendered in order. Each participating computer renders frames as quickly as possible and saves them as separate files, so you cannot use network rendering to create .avi or .mov files. Instead, you have to render the scene with each frame saved as a separate bitmap file, and then use the RAM Player, Video Post, or a third-party program (such as Adobe Premiere) to combine them into an animation file format such as .avi. ∎

Note

A licensed version of Max is required to do network rendering, but the good news is that only one machine in your farm needs to have an authorized copy of Max installed. No authorization whatsoever is needed on machines used for network rendering only. Simply install Max, and each network rendering machine gets its authorization from the computer that launched the render job. ∎

Setting Up a Network Rendering System

Before getting into the details of setting up Max for network rendering, it's important to understand the different parts of the network rendering system. This list shows the major players involved:

- **Manager:** The *manager* is a program (manager.exe) that acts as the network manager. It's the network manager's job to coordinate the efforts of all the other computers in your rendering farm. Only one machine on your network needs to be running the manager, and that same machine can also be used to render.

- **Server:** A rendering server is any computer on your network used to render frames of your animation. When you run the server program (server.exe), it contacts the network manager and informs it that this particular computer is available to render. The server starts up Max when the manager sends a frame to be rendered.

- **3ds Max:** At least one computer in your rendering farm must have an authorized copy of Max running, although it does not need to be the same computer that is running the manager. It is from this machine that you initiate a rendering job.

- **Monitor:** The Monitor (monitor.exe) is a special program that lets you monitor your rendering farm. You can use it to check the current state of jobs that are running or that have been queued. You can also use it to schedule network rendering times. The Monitor is completely independent from the actual rendering process, so you can use it on one of the machines in your rendering farm, or you can use it to remotely check the status of things by connecting over the network.

Starting the Network Rendering System

Now that you know all the pieces involved, you'll need to set up your network and install a copy of Max on all the network machines that you plan on using. When installing Max on a network machine, you can use the Compact option so that Max installs only the minimum number of files it needs to be able to render. You also need to choose a destination directory where you want Max to be installed. If possible, just accept the displayed default destination and click Next.

Tip

Installing 3ds Max in the same directory on every computer can save you some maintenance headaches later on. Managing bitmap and plug-in directories is much easier if each machine has the same directory layout. ∎

You also need to set up several shared directories on the network where the scenes and materials can be accessed from and where the rendered scenes can be saved. Once you have these shared folders in place, you are ready to start up your network rendering system.

Tutorial: Initializing the network rendering system

The very first time you start your rendering farm, you need to help Max do a little initialization.

To initialize the network rendering system, follow these steps:

1. Start the network manager on one machine in your rendering farm. This program, Manager. exe, is in the Backburner directory. You can start the manager by selecting it and pressing Enter in Windows Explorer. After it starts up, you first see the Backburner Manager General Properties dialog box. This dialog box appears only the first time you run the Manager.exe program or if you choose Edit ➪ General Settings. I cover its settings later in the chapter. After setting these properties, click OK, and the Manager window, shown in Figure 48.3, runs.

FIGURE 48.3

Starting the network manager

2. Now start a network server on each computer that you plan to use for rendering. To do this, find and start the Server.exe program just like you did with Manager.exe. When you start this program for the first time, the Backburner Server General Properties dialog box appears. This dialog box is covered later in the chapter. Click OK, and the Network Server window appears, as shown in Figure 48.4.

FIGURE 48.4

Starting a network server. Notice that the server is already looking for the manager.

When the server finds the manager, it displays a message that the registration is accepted. The Network Manager window also shows a similar message.

If the server had trouble connecting to the manager, you need to follow these two additional steps:

1. If automatic detection of the manager fails, the server keeps trying until it times out. If it times out, or if you just get tired of waiting, choose Edit ➪ General Settings to open the Backburner Server General Properties dialog box, shown in Figure 48.5. In this dialog box, uncheck the Automatic Search box and type in the name or IP address of the computer that is running the network manager. In this case, the server tried but couldn't quite find the manager, so it had to be told that the manager was running on the computer whose IP address is 150.150.150.150.

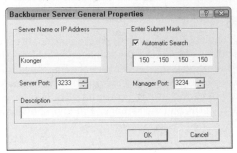

FIGURE 48.5

Manually choosing the manager's IP address

2. Click OK to close the Backburner Server General Properties dialog box, and then click Close to shut down the server (doing so forces the server to save the changes you've made). Restart the server the same way you did before, and now the server and manager are able to find each other.

Note
The network manager does not need to have a computer all to itself, so you can also run a network server on the same computer and use it to participate in the rendering. ■

Tutorial: Completing your first network rendering job

Your rendering farm is up and running and just dying to render something, so let's put those machines to work.

To start a network rendering job, follow these steps:

1. Start Max, and create a simple animation scene.

   This should be as simple as possible because all you're doing here is verifying that the rendering farm is functional.

2. In Max, choose Rendering ➪ Render (F10) to bring up the Render Setup dialog box. In the Time Output section of this dialog box, be sure that Range is selected so that you really do render multiple frames instead of the default single frame.

3. In the Render Output section of the Render Setup dialog box, click Files to open the Render Output File dialog box. In the Save In section, choose the output drive that can be accessed over the network and directory that you created earlier.

4. In the File name section of the Render Output File dialog box, type the name of the first frame. Max automatically numbers each frame for you. Choose a bitmap format from the Save as type list (remember, an animation format will not work).

5. Click Save to close the Render Output File dialog box. (Some file formats might ask you for additional information for your files; if so, just click OK to accept the default options.) Back in the Render Scene dialog box, Max displays the full path to the output directory.

6. In the Render Output section of the Render Scene dialog box, check the Net Render option, as shown in Figure 48.6. Change any other settings you want, such as selecting a viewport, and then click Render.

FIGURE 48.6

The Net Render option must be enabled to start a network rendering job.

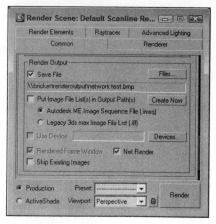

A Network Job Assignment dialog box opens, like the one shown in Figure 48.7.

FIGURE 48.7

Use the Network Job Assignment dialog box to locate the manager to handle the rendering job.

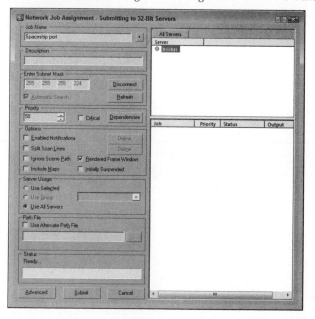

7. In the Enter Subnet section of the Network Job Assignment dialog box, click Connect if the Automatic Search box is checked. If it isn't checked, or if your servers had trouble finding the manager in the "Initializing the network rendering system" tutorial earlier in this chapter, type the IP address of the machine running the manager and then click Connect.

8. Max then searches for any available rendering servers, connects with it, and adds its name to the list of available servers. Click the server name once, and click Submit.

Tip

If you try to submit the same job again (after either a failed or a successful attempt at rendering), Max complains because that job already exists in the job queue. You can remove the job using the Monitor, or you can click the + button on the Network Job Assignment dialog box, and Max adds a number to the job name to make it unique. ■

After you've submitted your job, notices appear on the manager and the servers (like the ones shown in Figures 48.8 and 48.9) that the job has been received. Soon Max starts up on each server, and you see a Rendering dialog box showing the progress of the rendering task. As you can see, this displays useful information such as what frame is being rendered and how long the job is taking. When the entire animation has been rendered, you can go to your output directory to get the bitmap files that Max generated. The render servers and the render manager keep running, ready for the next job request to come in.

FIGURE 48.8

The network manager detects the new job.

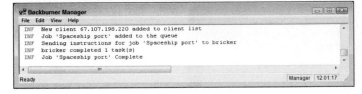

FIGURE 48.9

One of the network servers receives the command to start a new job.

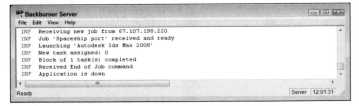

Job assignment options

The Network Job Assignment dialog box, shown previously in Figure 48.7, has an important section that you didn't use for your first simple render job; it's called Options.

The Options section has the following settings:

- **Enabled Notifications:** This option lets you tell Max when to notify you that certain events have occurred. If you check the Enable Notifications option, the Define button becomes active. The Define button opens a Notifications dialog box, shown in Figure 48.10.

FIGURE 48.10

The Notifications dialog box lets you specify which type of notifications to receive.

- **Split Scan Lines:** This option breaks a rendered image into strips that can be rendered separately. The Define button lets you specify the Strip Height, Number of Strips, and any Overlap.

- **Ignore Scene Path:** Use this option to force the servers to retrieve the scene file via TCP/IP. If disabled, the manager copies the scene file to the server.

- **Rendered Frame Window:** Use this option if you want to be able to see the image on the server as it gets rendered.

- **Include Maps:** Checking this box makes Max compress everything that it needs to render the scene (including the maps) into a single file and send it to each server. This option is useful if you're setting up a rendering farm over the Internet, although it takes more time and network bandwidth to send all that extra information.

- **Initially Suspended:** This option pauses the rendering before it starts so that you can manually start it when the network is ready.

- **Use Selected/Use Group/Use All Servers:** The Server Usage option makes the selected server, a group of servers, or all servers listed in the Server panel fair game for rendering.

- **Use Alternate Path File:** This option lets you specify an alternate path for map and other files, which is entered in the text field below the check box.

Configuring the Network Manager and Servers

You can configure both the manager and servers using their respective General Properties dialog boxes. You open these dialog boxes by choosing Edit ➪ General Settings.

The network manager settings

The rendering manager has some options that let you modify how it behaves. You specify these options in the Network Manager General Properties dialog box, shown in Figure 48.11. To open this dialog box, select Edit➪ General Settings in the Manager window.

The Backburner Manager General Properties dialog box

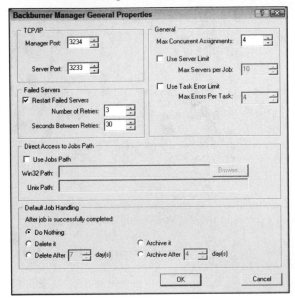

This dialog box includes the following sections:

- **TCP/IP:** Here you can change the communications ports used by the manager and the servers. In general, leaving these alone is a good idea. If some other program is using one of these ports, however, Max won't be able to render via the network, so you need to change them. If you change the Server Port number, be sure to change it to the same number on all your rendering servers. If you change the Manager Port number, you also need to change two files on your hard drive to match: queueman.ini (in your 3dsmax directory) and client.ini (in your 3dsmax\network directory). Both have lines for the Manager Port, and you can edit these files with any text editor or word processor.

- **General:** The Max Concurrent Assignments field is used to specify how many jobs the rendering manager sends out at a time. If you make this number too high, the manager might send out jobs faster than the servers can handle them. The default value here is fine for most cases.

Note

The network manager can automatically attempt to restart servers that failed, giving your rendering farm much more stability. ∎

- **Failed Servers:** Usually, Max doesn't send more frames to a server that previously failed. If you check the Restarts Failed Servers box, Max tries to give the server another chance. The Number of Retries field tells Max how many times it should try to restart a server before giving up on the particular server for good, and the Minutes Between Retries field tells Max the number of minutes it should wait before trying to give the failing server another job.

Note

The rendering manager writes the configuration settings to a file on the disk that gets read when the manager loads. If you make changes to any of the settings, shutting down the manager and starting it up again to guarantee that the changes take effect is best. ■

- **Direct Access to Jobs Path:** This setting lets you specify a different path that exists anywhere on the network, regardless of where the manager is running. Separate fields are available for Win32 paths and Unix paths. If the Use Jobs Path option is selected, then the specified path is used.
- **Default Job Handling:** This section lets you tell the Manager what to do after the rendering job is finished. The options include Do Nothing, Delete or Archive, and Delete or Archive after a specified number of days. This option gives you a way to clean out your queue.

The network servers settings

As you may have guessed, the Properties button on the Network Server window serves a similar purpose as the one on the Network Manager window: It enables you to specify the behavior of the network server. Clicking this button displays the Backburner Server General Properties dialog box.

This dialog box has the following section:

- **TCP/IP:** The port numbers serve the same function as they do for the rendering manager, described in the previous section. If you change them in the manager properties, change them here. If you change them here, change them in the manager properties.

Note

The Manager Name or IP Address setting lets you override automatic detection of the rendering manager and specify its exact location on the network. Generally, letting Max attempt to find the manager itself is best; if it fails, override the automatic detection by clearing the Automatic check box. If you happen to be running multiple managers on the same network, the servers connect to the first one they find. In this case, you have to manually choose the correct server. ■

Keep in mind that the server properties aren't shared among your servers, so if you want something to change on all your servers, you have to make that change on each machine.

Note

As with the rendering manager settings, if you change anything in the Network Servers Properties dialog box, be sure to shut down the server and restart it. ■

Logging Errors

Both the Network Manager and Network Server windows have a Logging button that you can click to access the Logging Properties dialog box, where you can configure how log information gets handled. This dialog box, shown in Figure 48.12, looks the same for managers and servers. You can access this dialog box with the Edit ⇨ Log Settings command.

The logging options for managers and servers let you tell Max where to report what.

Max generates the following types of messages:

- **Error:** Anything that goes wrong and is serious enough to halt the rendering of a frame.
- **Warning:** A problem that Max can still work around. If a server fails, for example, a warning is generated, but Max continues the rendering job by using other servers.
- **Info:** A general information message, such as notification that a job has arrived or that a frame is complete.
- **Debug:** A lower-level message that provides information to help debug problems with the rendering farm.
- **Debug Extended:** The same as the Debug option with more details.

Max displays the type of message and the message itself in two locations: in the list window and in a log file (in your 3dsmax\network directory). The Logging Properties dialog box lets you choose whether each type of message gets reported to the screen, the log file, both places, or neither place. You can also use the Clear buttons to get rid of old messages.

Using the Monitor

The Monitor is a powerful utility that helps you manage your rendering farm and all the jobs in it. If you use network rendering frequently, then the Monitor quickly becomes your best friend. You start it the same way that you start a rendering server or manager: Go to the 3dsmax directory, find QueueManager.exe, and double-click it. Every computer that has Max installed on it also has a copy of the Monitor, so you can use it from any machine on your network. The main screen is shown in Figure 48.13.

FIGURE 48.13

The Monitor makes managing a rendering farm quick and easy.

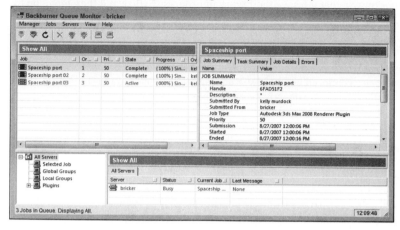

When the Monitor starts up, it automatically searches for the rendering manager and connects to it. (If you have more than one manager running, you have to choose which one to connect to.)

The main screen is divided into three panes. The top-left pane shows the job queue and their Priority and Status, and the top-right pane shows information about whatever you have selected in the left pane. You can use the tabs at the top of this pane to select the information that you want to view. The information tabs include Job Summary, Frames Summary, Advanced (which shows the rendering parameters), Render Elements, and Log.

The bottom pane lists all the available servers. Next to each server in the left pane is an icon that reflects its current status. Green icons mean that the job or server is active and hard at work. Yellow means the server is idle. Red means that something has gone wrong, and gray means that a job has been inactivated or that a server is assigned to a job but is absent. When a job is complete, it can be deleted from the queue.

Jobs

If you choose a job in the top-left pane, the top-right pane displays information about the selected job. The panels in the top-right pane are as follows:

- **Job Summary:** Lists some of the rendering options you chose before you submitted the job. Among other things, the example in the figure shows that the job was rendered to 640 × 480 pixels.

- **Frames Summary:** Lists the details of rendering each frame in the animation, including the time required to render and the server used.

- **Advanced:** Lists advanced settings from the Render Scene dialog box and gives limited information about the scene itself.

- **Render Elements:** Lists the details of each render element included as part of the job.

- **Log:** Displays important messages from the job log. Whereas the log file on each server lists events for a particular server, this pane lets you see all the messages relating to a particular job.

When you point at a job in the top-left pane and right-click, a small pop-up menu appears. On this menu, you can delete a job from the queue or you can choose to activate or deactivate it. If you deactivate a job, all the servers working on that job save their work in progress to disk and then move on to the next job in the queue. This feature is very useful when you have a lower-priority job that you run when no other jobs are waiting; when something more important comes along, you deactivate the job so that you can later activate it when the servers are free again.

One last useful feature for jobs is that you can reorder them by dragging a job above or below other jobs. Jobs higher on the screen are rendered before lower ones, which enables you to "bump up" the priority of a particular job without having to deactivate other ones.

Note

A file with a Critical priority is rendered immediately. ∎

Servers

If you right-click a server and select Properties from the pop-up menu, the Server Properties dialog box, shown in Figure 48.14, opens. This dialog box contains information about the selected server.

FIGURE 48.14

The Server Properties dialog box displays information about the server.

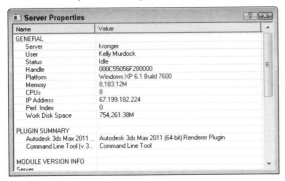

Many other features are available in the right-click pop-up menu. Using this pop-up menu, you can assign the server to a selected job, remove the server from its selected job, display specific server information, create a server group, or view the Week Schedule, as shown in Figure 48.15. Using the Week Schedule dialog box, you can set the active rendering period for a server.

The Week Schedule dialog box lets you decide when a particular machine is available for rendering. (For example, you can have your coworker's computer automatically become available for rendering after he or she goes home for the night.)

Click and drag with your mouse over different hours to select a group of times. Alternatively, you can click a day of the week to select the entire day or click a time to select that time for every day. In the example shown in Figure 48.15, the server is scheduled to render in the evenings and on the weekends.

After you've selected a group of times, click Allow to make the server available for rendering during that time or click Disallow to prevent rendering. When you're finished, click OK to close the Server Properties dialog box and return to the Monitor dialog box.

FIGURE 48.15

The Week Schedule dialog box can set the time during the week when a server is available for rendering.

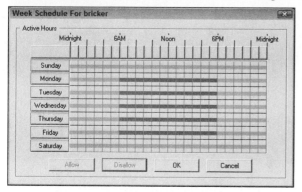

If you have several jobs going at once but suddenly need to get one finished quickly, you can take servers off one job and put them on another. To remove a server, right-click its name in the left pane of the Monitor dialog box and choose Delete Server (Ctrl+Enter) from the pop-up menu. The icon next to the server turns black, indicating that it has been unassigned. To assign this server to another job, right-click the server name in the list of servers for the job you want to assign it to, and choose Assign to Selected Jobs.

Summary

If your goal is to spend more time modeling and less time waiting for rendering jobs to complete, then the network rendering services provided by 3ds Max can help you take a step in the right direction. After the initial complexities of setting up a rendering farm are out of the way, network rendering can be a great asset in helping you reach important deadlines, and it lets you enjoy your finished work sooner. Even if you can afford to add only one or two computers to your current setup, you'll see a tremendous increase in productivity—an increase that you can't truly appreciate until you've completed a job in a fraction of the time it used to take!

In this chapter, you accomplished the following:

- Used the Batch Render window to create a batch render queue
- Used the rendering manager and servers to carry out rendering jobs
- Used the Monitor to control job priority
- Made Max notify you when problems occur or when jobs finish
- Performed batch rendering even if you don't have a network

Compositing with Render Elements and the Video Post Interface

After you've completed your scene and rendered it, you're finished, right? Well, not exactly. You still have post-production to complete: That's where you work with the final rendered images to add some additional effects. This phase of production typically takes place in another package, such as Photoshop, Autodesk's Composite, or Adobe's After Effects, and understanding how to interact with these packages can be a lifesaver when your client wants some last-minute changes (and they always do).

You can set Max to render any part in the rendering pipeline individually. These settings are called *render elements*. By rendering out just the Specular layer or just the shadow, you have more control over these elements in your compositor.

If you don't have access to a compositing package, or even if you do, Max includes a simple interface that can be used to add some post-production effects. This interface is the Video Post interface.

You can use the Video Post window to composite the final rendered image with several other images and filters. These filters let you add lens effects like glows and flares, and other effects like blur and fade, to the final output. The Video Post window provides a post-processing environment within the Max interface.

Note

Many of the post-processing effects, such as glows and blurs, also are available as render effects, but the Video Post window is capable of much more. Render effects are covered in Chapter 46, "Using Atmospheric and Render Effects." ∎

Using External Compositing Packages

Before delving into the Video Post interface, let's take a quick look at some of the available compositing packages. Several of these packages have direct links into Max that can be used to give you a jump on the post-production process.

Compositing with Photoshop

Perhaps the most common tool for compositing images is Photoshop. Photoshop can bring multiple images together in a single file and position them relative to one another. Working with layers makes applying simple filters and effects to the various element pieces easy.

Figure 49.1 shows Photoshop with several separate pieces, each on a different layer.

FIGURE 49.1

Photoshop is an important compositing tool for static images.

To composite images in Photoshop, you need to load all the separate images into Photoshop and then select the portions of the images that you want to combine. When saving image files in Max, be sure to include an alpha channel. You can see the alpha channel in the Rendered Frame window if you click the Display Alpha Channel button, as shown in Figure 49.2.

FIGURE 49.2

The Rendered Frame window can display an image's alpha channel.

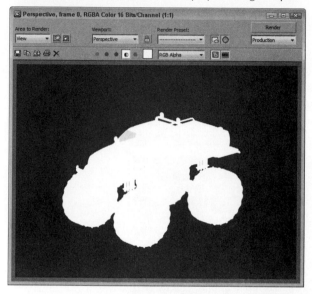

In Photoshop, you can see an image's alpha channel if you select the Channels panel in the Layers palette. Selecting the alpha channel and using the Magic Wand tool makes selecting the rendered object easy. After it's selected, you can copy and paste the rendered image onto your background image as a new layer.

Note

Not all image file formats support an alpha channel. When rendering images to be composited, be sure to use an alpha channel format such as RLA, RPF, PNG, or TGA. ■

After all your images have been positioned on the background image, you can apply a filter, such as a Gaussian Blur, to smooth the edges between the composite images.

Video editing with Premiere

Photoshop works with still images, but if you work with animations, then Adobe has Premiere to help with your video editing needs. The editing that Premiere makes possible includes patching several animation clips together, adding sound, color-correcting the frames, and adding transitions between animation clips.

Within Premiere, various animation clips can be imported (or dragged directly from Windows Explorer) into the Project panel. From here, the clips can be dropped onto the Timeline in the desired order. The Monitor panel shows the current animation or individual animation clips.

Sound clips can be dropped in the Timeline in the Audio track. The Title menu also can be used to add text to the animation. Another common activity in Premiere is to add transition effects between clips.

This is done by clicking the Effects tab in the Project panel, selecting a transition effect, dragging the effect to the Timeline, and dropping it between two animation clips.

When the entire sequence is completed, you can render it using the Sequence ⇨ Render Work Area menu command. The completed animation file then can be saved using the File ⇨ Export menu command.

Figure 49.3 shows the Premiere interface with the animation clips loaded and positioned in the Timeline panel.

FIGURE 49.3

Premiere can be used to combine several animation sequences together.

Video compositing with After Effects

If you need to add a little more to your animations than just transitions, you should look into Adobe's After Effects. After Effects lets you composite 2D and 3D clips into a single image or animation. You can paint directly on the animation frames, add lights and cameras, and create visual effects such as Distort, Shatter, and Warp.

After Effects includes a library of resources much like those found in Premiere. These resources can be positioned on a Composition pane. Effects applied to the loaded animation clip are listed in the Effects panel along with all the effects settings.

After Effects includes many of the same tools used in Photoshop and Illustrator. These tools let you paint and select portions of the animation clip as if it were a still image, but the results can be added or removed over time.

Tutorial: Adding animation effects using After Effects

Some effects are much easier to add using a package like After Effects than to create in Max. A good example is adding a blurry look and the waves coming from a heat source to the melting snowman animation created in Chapter 22.

To add video effects using After Effects, follow these steps:

1. Open After Effects, and drag the Melting snowman.avi file from the Chap 49 directory to the Project panel.

2. Select Composition ⇨ New Composition, select the NTSC, 640 × 480 option from the Preset list, and click OK.

3. Drag the Melting snowman.avi file from the Project panel, and drop it on the Composition pane.

4. With the animation selected in the Composition pane, select Effect ⇨ Distort ⇨ Wave Warp. The Wave Warp effect appears in a panel. Set the Wave Height to **4**, the Wave Width to **30**, the Direction to **Vertical**, and the Wave Speed to **1**. This adds a heat wave effect to the entire animation.

5. Select Effect ⇨ Blur & Sharpen ⇨ Gaussian Blur, and set the Blurriness value to **3.0**.

6. In the Timeline panel, drag the Work Area End icon so that it coincides with the end of the animation.

7. Select Composition ⇨ Make Movie. In the Render Queue dialog box that opens, click the Render button to render the animation with its effects.

Figure 49.4 shows the After Effects interface with the animation clip loaded.

FIGURE 49.4

After Effects can add special effects to an animation sequence.

Introducing Composite

Autodesk offers an end-to-end solution for production houses to complete their work, and Max now ships with its own compositing tool called Composite, shown in Figure 49.5. Composite is a different animal from Max, but its array of weapons is just as deadly in a slightly different arena. The biggest difference between Composite and Photoshop is that Composite can handle animations and Photoshop can work only with static images.

Composite is a full-featured compositing tool that ships with Max.

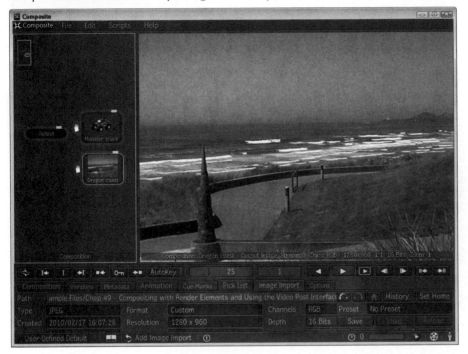

Composite enables motion graphics, compositing, and visual effects, which doesn't sound too different from what Max does, except for that funny word—*compositing*. If you think of the final rendered image produced using Max as just an image that needs to be combined with other elements such as text, logos, other images, or even a DVD menu, then you're starting to see what post-production teams know. Compositing is the process of combining several different elements into a finished product. Positioning these elements can even be done in 3D by placing images behind or in front of other images or in time by working with animations.

But wait, you say: This is a book about Max, not about Composite. Yes, but Composite is integrated with Max very nicely, and that is what I want to show. Several key integration points include Composite maps and Render Elements.

Using Render Elements

If your production group includes a strong post-processing team that does compositing, there may be times when you just want to render certain elements of the scene, such as the alpha information or a specific atmospheric effect. Applying individual elements to a composite image gives you better control over the elements. For example, you can reposition or lighten a shadow without having to re-render the entire scene.

Using the Render Elements panel of the Render Setup dialog box, shown in Figure 49.6, you can render a single effect and save it as an image.

FIGURE 49.6

You can use the Render Elements rollout to render specific effects.

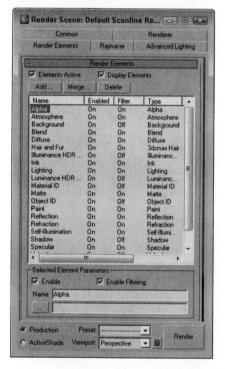

You can select and render several render elements at the same time. The available render elements include Alpha, Atmosphere, Background, Blend, Diffuse, Hair and Fur, Illuminance HDR Data, Ink, Lighting, Luminance HDR Data, Material ID, Matte, Object ID, Paint, Reflection, Refraction, Self-Illumination, Shadow, Specular, Velocity, and Z Depth.

If the mental ray rendering engine is enabled, then many more Render Elements are also available, including all the parameters that are included as part of the Arch&Design materials, along with a mental ray Shader Element and the mental ray Labeled Render Element.

The Render Elements rollout can render several elements at once. The Add button opens the Render Elements dialog box, where you can select the elements to include. The Merge button lets you merge the elements from another Max scene, and the Delete button lets you delete elements from the list. To be included in the rendered image, the Elements Active option must be checked. The Display Elements option causes the results to be rendered separately and displayed in the Rendered Frame Window.

The Enable check box can turn off individual elements; Enable Filtering enables the anti-aliasing filtering as specified in the Max Default Scanline A-Buffer rollout. A separate Rendered Frame Window is opened for each render element that is enabled.

Clicking the Browse button opens a file dialog box where you can give the rendered element a name. Max automatically appends an underscore and the name of the element on the end of the filename. For example, if you name the file **myScene** and select to render the Alpha element, the filename for this element is **myScene_alpha**.

When you select the Blend and Z Depth render elements, an additional rollout of parameters appears. You can use the Blend render element to combine several separate elements together. The Blend Element Parameters rollout includes check boxes for each render element type. The Z Depth render element includes parameters for setting Min and Max depth values.

Figure 49.7 shows the resulting image in the Rendered Frame Window for the Alpha render element.

FIGURE 49.7

The Alpha render element shown in the Rendered Frame Window

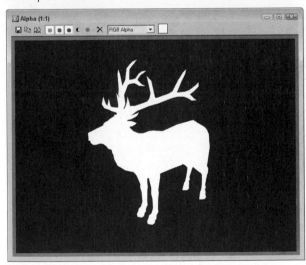

The Render Elements rollout can also output files that Autodesk's Composite product can use. These files have the .cws extension. Composite is a compositing product that can work with individual elements to increase the highlights, change color hues, darken and blur shadows, and do many other things without having to re-render the scene.

Completing Post-Production with the Video Post Interface

Post-production is the work that comes after the scene is rendered. It is the time when you add effects, such as glows and highlights, as well as add transitional effects to an animation. For example, if you want to include a logo in the lower-right corner of your animation, you can create and render the logo and composite several rendered images into one during post-production.

Video Post interface is the post-processing interface within Max that you can use to combine the current scene with different images, effects, and image-processing filters. Compositing is the process of combining several different images into a single image. Each element of the composite is included as a separate event. These events are lined up in a queue and processed in the order in which they appear in the queue. The queue can also include looping events.

The Video Post interface, like the Render Scene dialog box (covered in Chapter 23, "Rendering a Scene and Enabling Quicksilver"), provides another way to produce final output. You can think of the Video Post process as an artistic assembly line. As the image moves down the line, each item in the queue adds an image, drops a rendered image on the stack, or applies a filter effect. This process continues until the final output event is reached.

The Video Post interface, shown in Figure 49.8, includes a toolbar, a pane of events and ranges, and a status bar. You can open it by choosing Rendering ⇨ Video Post.

FIGURE 49.8

The Video Post interface lets you composite images with your final rendering.

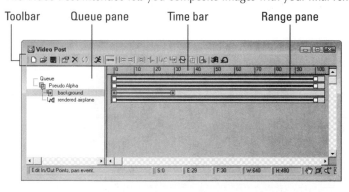

Toolbar   Queue pane   Time bar   Range pane

In many ways, the Video Post interface is similar to the Track View interfaces. Each event is displayed as a track in the Queue pane to the left. To the right is the Range pane, where the range for each track is displayed as lines with square boxes at each end. You can edit these ranges by dragging the squares on either end. The time bar, above the Range pane, displays the frames for the current sequence, and the status bar at the bottom of the interface includes information and view buttons.

The Video Post toolbar

At the top of the Video Post interface is a toolbar with several buttons for managing the Video Post features. Table 49.1 shows and explains these buttons.

TABLE 49.1

Video Post Toolbar Buttons

Toolbar Button	Name	Description
	New Sequence	Creates a new sequence
	Open Sequence	Opens an existing sequence
	Save Sequence	Saves the current sequence
	Edit Current Event	Opens the Edit Current Event dialog box where you can edit events
	Delete Current Event	Removes the current event from the sequence
	Swap Events	Changes the position in the queue of two selected events
	Execute Sequence	Runs the current sequence
	Edit Range Bar	Enables you to edit the event ranges
	Align Selected Left	Aligns the left ranges of the selected events
	Align Selected Right	Aligns the right ranges of the selected events
	Make Selected Same Size	Makes the ranges for the selected events the same size
	Abut Selected	Places event ranges end-to-end
	Add Scene Event	Adds a rendered scene to the queue
	Add Image Input Event	Adds an image to the queue
	Add Image Filter Event	Adds an image filter to the queue
	Add Image Layer Event	Adds a compositing plug-in to the queue when two events are selected
	Add Image Output Event	Sends the final composited image to a file or device
	Add External Event	Adds an external image-processing event to the queue
	Add Loop Event	Causes other events to loop

The Video Post Queue and Range panes

Below the toolbar are the Video Post Queue and Range panes. The Queue pane is on the left; it lists all the events to be included in the post-processing sequence in the order in which they are processed. You can rearrange the order of the events by dragging an event in the queue to its new location.

You can select multiple events by holding down the Ctrl key and clicking the event names, or you can select one event, hold down the Shift key, and click another event to select all events between the two.

Each event has a corresponding range that appears in the Range pane to the right. Each range is shown as a line with a square on each end. The left square marks the first frame of the event, and the right square marks the last frame of the event. You can expand or contract these ranges by dragging the square on either end of the range line.

If you click the line between two squares, you can drag the entire range. If you drag a range beyond the given number of frames, then additional frames are added.

The time bar is at the top of the Range pane. This bar shows the number of total frames included in the animation. You can also slide the time bar up or down to move it closer to a specific track by dragging it.

The Video Post status bar

The status bar includes a prompt line, several value fields, and some navigation buttons. The fields to the right of the prompt line include Start, End, Current Frames, and the Width and Height of the image. The navigation buttons include (in order from left to right) Pan, Zoom Extents, Zoom Time, and Zoom Region.

Working with Sequences

All the events that are added to the Queue pane make up a *sequence.* You can save these sequences and open them at a later time. The Execute Sequence button (Ctrl+R), found on the toolbar, starts the compositing process.

Note

The keyboard shortcuts for the Video Post interface work only if the Keyboard Shortcut Override Toggle on the main toolbar is enabled. ■

To save a sequence, click the Save button on the toolbar to open the Save Sequence dialog box, where you can save the queue sequence. Sequences are saved along with the Max file when the scene is saved, but they can also be saved independently of the scene. By default, these files are saved with the .vpx extension in the vpost directory.

Note

Saving a sequence as a VPX file maintains the elements of the queue, but it resets all parameter settings. Saving the file as a Max file maintains the queue order along with the parameter settings. ■

You can open saved sequences using the Open Sequence button on the toolbar. When a saved sequence is opened, all the current events are deleted. Clicking the New Sequence button also deletes any current events.

The Execute Sequence toolbar button opens the Execute Video Post interface, shown in Figure 49.9. The controls in this dialog box work exactly the way those in the Render Scene dialog box work.

Note

The time and resolution settings in the Execute Video Post dialog box are unique from those in the Render Scene dialog box. ■

FIGURE 49.9

The Execute Video Post interface includes the controls for producing the queue output.

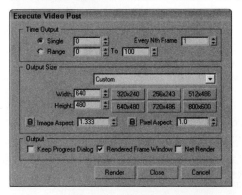

The Time Output section enables you to specify which frames to render, and the Output Size section lets you specify the size of the output. The Custom selection lets you enter Width and Height values, or you can use one of the presets in the drop-down list or one of the preset resolution buttons. This dialog box also includes controls for entering the Image Aspect and Pixel Aspect ratios.

The Output options let you select to keep the Progress dialog box open, to render to the Rendered Frame Window, and/or to use network rendering. When you're ready to render the queue, click the Render button.

Adding and Editing Events

The seven event types that you can add to the queue are Image Input, Scene, Image Filter, Image Layer, Loop, External, and Image Output. If no events are selected, then adding an event positions the event at the bottom of the list. If an event is selected, the added event becomes a subevent under the selected event.

Every event dialog box, such as the Add Image Input Event dialog box shown in Figure 49.10, includes a Label field where you can name the event. This name shows up in the queue window and is used to identify the event.

The Add Image Input Event dialog box lets you load an image to add to the queue.

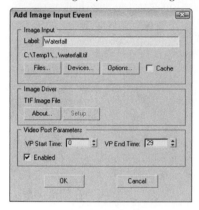

Each event dialog box includes a Video Post Parameters section. This section contains VP Start Time and VP End Time values for defining precisely the length of the Video Post range. It also includes an Enabled option for enabling or disabling an event. Disabled events are grayed out in the queue.

To edit an event, you simply need to double-click its name in the Queue pane (or press Ctrl+E) to open an Edit Event dialog box.

Note

Remember that you need to enable the Keyboard Shortcut Override button on the main toolbar before you can use any keyboard shortcuts in the Video Post interface. ■

Adding an image input event

The Add Image Input Event dialog box lets you add a simple image to the queue. For example, you can add a background image using this dialog box rather than the Environment dialog box. To open the Add Image Input Event dialog box, click the Add Image Input Event button (Ctrl+I) on the toolbar.

Tip

If you don't name the image event, then the filename appears in the Queue pane as the name for the event. ■

The Files button in this dialog box opens the Select Image File for Video Post Input dialog box, where you can locate an image file to load from the hard disk or network. Supported image types include AVI, BMP, MPEG, Kodak Cineon, Combustion, FLC, GIF, IFL, JPEG, PIC, PNG, PSD, MOV, SGI Image, RLA, RPF, TGA, TIF, and YUV. The Devices button lets you access an external device such as a video recorder. The Options button becomes enabled when you load an image. The Cache option causes the image to be loaded into memory, which can speed up the Video Post process by not requiring the image to be loaded for every frame.

The Image Driver section of the Add Image Input Event dialog box lets you specify the settings for the image driver, such as the compression settings for an AVI file. Clicking the Setup button opens a dialog box of options available for the selected format, but note that the Setup button is not active for all formats.

The Image Input Options dialog box, shown in Figure 49.11, lets you set the alignment, size, and frames where the image appears. The Alignment section of the Image Input Options dialog box includes nine presets for aligning the image. Preset options include top-left corner, top centered, top-right corner, left centered, centered, right centered, bottom-left corner, bottom centered, and bottom-right corner. You can also use the Coordinates option to specify in pixels the image's upper-left corner.

FIGURE 49.11

The Image Input Options dialog box lets you align and set the size of the image.

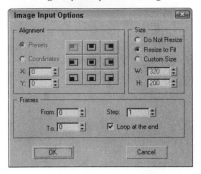

In the Size section of this dialog box, you can control the size of the image, using the Do Not Resize, Resize to Fit, or Custom Size options. The Custom Size option lets you enter Width and Height values.

The Frames section applies only to animation files. The From and To values define which frames of the animation to play. The Step value lets you play every nth frame as specified. The Loop at the End value causes the animation to loop back to the beginning when finished.

Adding scene events

A scene event is the rendered scene that you've built in Max. When you click the Add Scene Event button on the toolbar, the Add Scene Event dialog box shown in Figure 49.12 opens. This dialog box lets you specify the scene ranges and define the render options.

Below the Label field where you can name the event is a drop-down list that lets you select which viewport to use to render your scene. The active viewport is selected by default. The Render Options button opens the Render Scene panel, where the Render button has been replaced with OK and Cancel buttons because the rendering is initiated with the Execute Sequence button.

Cross-Reference

For more information about the Render Scene panel, see Chapter 23, "Rendering a Scene and Enabling Quicksilver." ∎

The Scene Options section of the Add Scene Event dialog box also includes an option for enabling Scene Motion Blur. This motion blur type is different from the object motion blur that is set in the Object Properties dialog box. Scene motion blur is applied to the entire image and is useful for blurring objects that are moving fast. The Duration (frames) value sets how long the blur effect is computed per frame. The Duration Subdivisions value is how many computations are done for each duration. The Dither % value sets the amount of dithering to use for blurred sections.

FIGURE 49.12

The Add Scene Event dialog box lets you specify which viewport to use to render your scene.

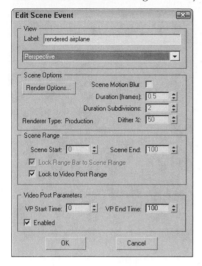

Cross-Reference

You can find more information on object motion blur in Chapter 6, "Selecting Objects and Setting Object Properties." ■

In the Scene Range section, the Scene Start and Scene End values let you define the range for the rendered scene. The Lock Range Bar to Scene Range option maintains the range length as defined in the Time Slider, though you can still reposition the start of the rendered scene. The Lock to Video Post Range option sets the range equal to the Video Post range.

Adding image filter events

The Add Image Filter Event button (Ctrl+F) on the toolbar opens the Add Image Filter Event dialog box, shown in Figure 49.13, where you can select from many filter types. The available filters are included in a drop-down list under the Label field.

Below the filter drop-down list are two buttons: About and Setup. The About button gives some details about the creator of the filter. The Setup button opens a separate dialog box that controls the filter. The dialog box that appears depends on the type of filter that you selected in the drop-down list.

Several, but not all, filters require a mask such as the Image Alpha filter. To open a bitmap image to use as the mask, click the Files button in the Mask section and select the file in the Select Mask Image dialog box that opens. A drop-down list lets you select the channel to use. Possible channels include Red, Green, Blue, Alpha, Luminance, Z Buffer, Material Effects, and Object. The mask can be Enabled or Inverted. The Options button opens the Image Input Options dialog box for aligning and sizing the mask.

Note

Several Lens Effects filters are also included in the drop-down list. These filters use an advanced dialog box with many options, which is covered in the "Working with Lens Effects Filters" section later in the chapter. ■

FIGURE 49.13

The Add Image Filter Event dialog box lets you select from many filter types.

Contrast filter

You use the Contrast filter to adjust the brightness and contrast. Selecting this filter and clicking the Setup button opens the Image Contrast Control dialog box. This simple dialog box includes values for Contrast and Brightness. Both values can be set from 0 to 1. The Absolute option computes the center gray value based on the highest color value. The Derived option uses an average value of the components of all three colors (red, green, and blue).

Fade filter

You can use the Fade filter to fade out the image over time. You can select it from the drop-down list. Clicking the Setup button opens the Fade Image Control dialog box where you select to fade either In or Out. The fade takes place over the length of the range set in the Range pane.

Image Alpha filter

The Image Alpha filter sets the alpha channel as specified by the mask. This filter doesn't have a setup dialog box.

Negative filter

The Negative filter inverts all the colors, as in the negative of a photograph. The Negative Filter dialog box includes a simple Blend value.

Pseudo Alpha filter

The Pseudo Alpha filter sets the alpha channel based on the pixel located in the upper-left corner of the image. This filter can make an unrendered background transparent. When this filter is selected, the Setup button is disabled because it doesn't have a setup dialog box.

Simple Wipe filter

The Simple Wipe filter removes the image by replacing it with a black background. The length of the wipe is determined by the event's time range. The Simple Wipe Control dialog box, shown in Figure 49.14, lets you wipe from the left to the right or from the right to the left. You can also set the mode to Push, which displays the image, or to Pop, which erases it.

FIGURE 49.14

The Simple Wipe Control dialog box lets you select which direction to wipe the image.

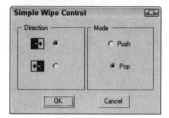

Starfield filter

The Starfield filter creates a starfield image. By using a camera, you can motion blur the stars. The Stars Control dialog box, shown in Figure 49.15, includes a Source Camera drop-down list that you can use to select a camera.

FIGURE 49.15

The Stars Control dialog box lets you load a custom database of stars.

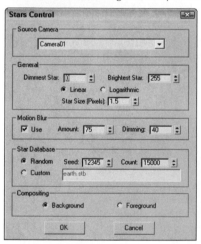

The General section sets the brightness and size of the stars. You can specify brightness values for the Dimmest Star and the Brightest Star. The Linear and Logarithmic options use two different algorithms to compute the brightness values of the stars as a function of distance. The Star Size value sets the size of the stars in pixels. Size values can range from 0.001 to 100.

The Motion Blur settings let you enable motion blurring, set the blur Amount, and specify a Dimming value.

The Star Database section includes settings for defining how the stars are to appear. The Random option displays stars based on the Count value, and the random Seed determines the randomness of the star's positions. The Custom option reads a star database specified in the Database field.

Note
Max includes a starfield database named earth.stb that includes the stars as seen from Earth. ∎

You can also specify whether the stars are composited in the background or foreground.

Tutorial: Creating space backdrops
Space backgrounds are popular backdrops, and Max includes a special Video Post filter for creating starfield backgrounds. You would typically want to use the Video Post interface to render the starfield along with any animation that you've created, but in this tutorial, you render a starfield for a single planet that you've created and outfitted with a planet material.

To create a starfield background, follow these steps:

1. Open the Planet with starfield background.max file from the Chap 49 directory on the CD.

   This file includes a simple space scene with a camera because the Starfield filter requires a camera.

2. Choose Rendering ⇨ Video Post to open the Video Post interface. A Scene Event must be added to the queue in order for the render job to be executed. Click the Add Scene Event button, type **planet scene** in the Label field, Select Camera01 as the Source Camera, and click OK.

   This adds the event to the Queue pane.

3. Click the Add Image Filter Event button (or press Ctrl+F) to open the Add Image Filter Event dialog box, and in the Label field type the name **starfield bg**. Select Starfield from the drop-down list, and click the Setup button to open the Stars Control dialog box, set the Star Size to **3.0** and the Count to **150,000**, and click OK.

4. Click the Execute Sequence button (or press Ctrl+R), select the Single output time option and an Output Size, and click the Render button.

Figure 49.16 shows the resulting space scene.

Adding image layer events
In addition to the standard filters that can be applied to a single image, several more filters, called *layer events*, can be applied to two or more images or rendered scenes. The Add Layer Event button (Ctrl+L) is available on the toolbar only when two image events are selected in the Queue pane. The first image (which is the selected image highest in the queue) becomes the source image, and the second image is the compositor. Both image events become subevents under the layer event.

Note
If the layer event is deleted, the two subevent images remain. ∎

The dialog box for the Add Image Layer Event is the same as the Add Image Filter Event dialog box shown earlier, except that the drop-down list includes filters that work with two images.

Adobe Premiere Transition filter
When it comes to transitions, Adobe Premiere already has created so many cool transitions that it makes sense to just use theirs. In Max, you can access these filters through the Adobe Premiere Transition Filter Setup dialog box.

This dialog box includes an Add path button to tell Max where to look for filters. All available filters are displayed in the Filter Selection list. You can access the filter interface with the Custom Parameters button. The two preview windows to the right display the filter effects. You also have options to Swap Input (which switches the source image) and Use Stand-In (which lets you specify a sample image to preview the effect).

A space scene with a background, compliments of the Video Post interface

Simple Wipe compositor

The Simple Wipe compositor is similar to the Simple Wipe filter, except that it slides the image in or out instead of erasing it. Its setup dialog box looks just like that of the Simple Wipe Control dialog box.

Other layer filters

The remaining layer filters include simple methods for compositing images and some simple transitions. None of these other filters has a Setup dialog box.

You can use the Alpha compositor to composite two images, using the alpha channel of the foreground image. The Cross Fade Transition compositor fades one image out as it fades another image in. You can use the Pseudo Alpha compositor to combine two images if one doesn't have an alpha channel. This compositor uses the upper-left pixel to designate the transparent color for the image. The Simple Additive Compositor combines two images based on the intensity of the second image.

Adding external events

The Add External Event button on the toolbar lets you use an external image-processing program to edit the image. This button is available only when an image event is selected, and the image event becomes a sub-event under the external event. The Add External Event dialog box, shown in Figure 49.17, includes a Browse button for locating the external program. It also includes a Command Line Options field for entering text commands for the external program. Many external programs use the clipboard to do their processing, so the Write image to clipboard and Read image from clipboard options make this possible.

FIGURE 49.17

The Add External Event dialog box lets you access an external program to edit images.

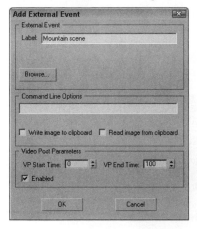

Using loop events

The Add Loop Event button is enabled on the Video Post toolbar when any single event is selected. This button enables an event to be repeated a specified number of times or throughout the Video Post range. The Add Loop Event dialog box, shown in Figure 49.18, includes a value field for the Number of Times to repeat the event, along with Loop and Ping Pong options. The Loop option repeats from beginning to end until the Number of Times value is reached. The Ping Pong option alternates playing the event forward and in reverse. You can name Loop events using the Label field.

Adding an image output event

If you've added all the events you need and configured them correctly, and you click the Execute Sequence button and nothing happens, then chances are good that you've forgotten to add an Image Output event. This event adds the surface that all the events use to output to and should appear last in the queue.

The Add Image Output Event dialog box (Ctrl+O) looks the same as the Add Image Input Event dialog box shown earlier. The output can be saved to a file or to a device using any of the standard file types.

Note

If you don't give the output event a name, the filename automatically becomes the event name. ■

FIGURE 49.18

The Add Loop Event dialog box lets you play an event numerous times.

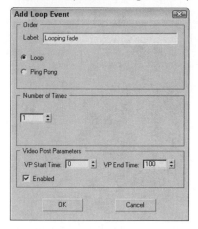

Working with Ranges

The Range pane in the Video Post interface is found to the right of the Queue pane. It displays the ranges for each event. These turn red when selected. The beginning and end points of the range are marked with squares. You can move these points by dragging the squares. This moves the beginning and end points for all selected events.

Note

Before you can move the ranges or drag the end points of a range, you need to select the Edit Range Bar button from the toolbar. The button is highlighted yellow when active. ∎

When two or more events are selected, several additional buttons on the toolbar become enabled, including Swap Events, Align Selected Left, Align Selected Right, Make Selected Same Size, and Abut Selected. (These buttons were shown earlier in Table 49.1.)

The Swap Events button is enabled only if two events are selected. When clicked, it changes the position of the two events. Because the order of the events is important, this can alter the final output.

The Align Selected Left and Align Selected Right buttons move the beginning or end points of every selected track until they line up with the first or last points of the top selected event.

The Make Selected Same Size button resizes any bottom events to be the same size as the top selected event. The Abut Selected button moves each selected event under the top event until its first point lines up with the last point of the selected event above it.

Figure 49.19 shows four image events that have been placed end-to-end using the Abut Selected button. Notice that the queue range spans the entire distance.

You can use the Abut Selected button to position several events end-to-end.

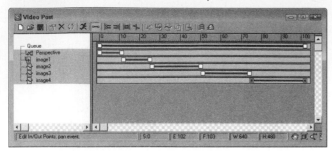

Working with Lens Effects Filters

The Add Image Filter Event dialog box's drop-down list has several Lens Effects filters. These filters include Lens Effects Flare, Focus, Glow, and Highlight. Each of these filters is displayed and discussed in the sections that follow, but several parameters are common to all of them. You can access the Lens Effects dialog boxes by clicking the Setup button in the Add Image Filter Event dialog box.

Many lens effects parameters in the various Lens Effects setup dialog boxes can be animated, such as Size, Hue, Angle, and Intensity. These are identified in the dialog boxes by green arrow buttons to the right of the parameter fields. These buttons work the way the Animate button in the main interface works. To animate a parameter, just click the corresponding arrow button, move the Time Slider to a new frame, and change the parameter. Figure 49.20 shows how these buttons look in the Lens Effects Flare dialog box.

Green arrow buttons in the Lens Effects Flare dialog box identify the parameters that can be animated for this effect.

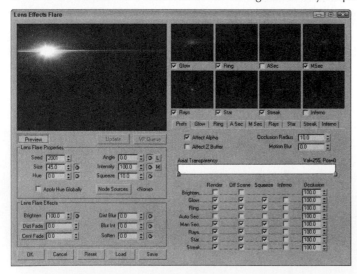

Each Lens Effects dialog box also includes a preview pane in the upper-left corner with three buttons underneath. Clicking the Preview button renders all enabled lens effects in the preview pane. The VP Queue button renders the current Video Post queue. Using the preview pane, you can get an idea of how the final output should look. With the Preview button enabled, any parameter changes in the dialog box are automatically updated in the preview pane. The Update button enables you to manually update the preview. You can right-click the Preview pane to change its resolution for faster updates at lower resolutions.

Tip

If the VP Queue button is enabled, then a default Lens Effects image is displayed. Using this image, you can play around with the various settings while the Preview mode is enabled to gain an idea of what the various settings do. ■

You can save the settings in each Lens Effect dialog box as a separate file that can be recalled at any time. These saved files have an .lzf extension and can be saved and loaded with the Save and Load buttons at the bottom left of the dialog box.

Adding flares

The Lens Effects Flare dialog box includes controls for adding flares of various types to an image. This dialog box includes a main preview pane and several smaller preview panes for each individual effect. The check boxes below these smaller preview panes let you enable or disable these smaller panes.

Under the main preview pane are several global commands, and to their right is a series of tabbed panels that contain the settings for each individual effect type. The first panel is labeled Prefs and sets which effects are rendered (on and off scene), which are squeezed, which have the Inferno noise filter applied, and which have an Occlusion setting.

The settings for the individual flare types are included in the subsequent tabbed panels. They include Glow, Ring, A Sec, M Sec, Rays, Star, Streak, and Inferno. These tabbed panels include gradient color bars for defining the Radial Color, Radial Transparency, Circular Color, Circular Transparency, and Radial Size. Each of these tabbed panels has different settings, but Figure 49.21 shows the tabbed panels for the Glow and Ring effects.

FIGURE 49.21

The Glow and Ring tabbed panels are representative of all the different lens effect settings.

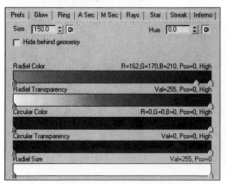
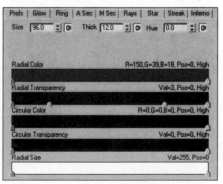

The gradient colors found in these tabbed panels are controlled by flags that appear under the gradient band. Double-clicking a flag opens a Color Selector dialog box where you can select a new color. Dragging these flags moves the gradient color. You can add a new flag to the band by clicking under the gradient away from the existing flags. The active flag is colored green. To delete flags, select them and press the Delete key. By right-clicking the gradient band, you can access a pop-up menu of options that let you access several options for the selected gradient color. You can even load and save gradients. Gradients are saved as files with the .dgr extension.

The rightmost tabbed panel, shown in Figure 49.22, is labeled Inferno and provides a way to add noise to any of the effects. The Prefs tabbed panel includes a check box for enabling the Inferno settings for each effect. Inferno noise can be set to three different states: Gaseous, Fiery, and Electric. If your effect is looking too perfect, you can add some randomness to it with the Inferno option.

FIGURE 49.22

The Inferno tabbed panel includes options for enabling noise for the various flare effects.

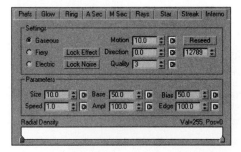

Adding focus

The Lens Effects Focus dialog box, shown in Figure 49.23, includes options for adding Scene Blur, Radial Blur, and Focal Node effects. If you click the Select button, the Select Focal Object dialog box opens and lets you choose an object to act as the focal point for the scene.

You can also set values for the Horizontal Focal Loss and Vertical Focal Loss or enable the Lock button to lock these two parameters together. The Focal Range and Focal Limit values determine the distance from the focal point where the blurring begins or reaches full strength. You can also set the blurring to affect the Alpha channel.

Adding glow

The Lens Effects Glow dialog box, shown in Figure 49.24, enables you to apply glows to the entire scene or to specific objects based on the Object ID or Effects ID. Other Source options include Unclamped, Surf Norm (Surface Normals), Mask, Alpha, Z High, and Z Lo. This dialog box also enables you to filter the glow using options such as All, Edge, Perimeter Alpha, Perimeter, Bright, and Hue.

Additional tabbed panels under the preview pane let you control the Preferences, Gradients, and Inferno settings. In the Preferences tabbed panel, you can set the color of the glow to be based on the Gradient tabbed panel–defined gradients, based on Pixel or a User-defined color. You also can set the Intensity in the Preference tabbed panel.

FIGURE 49.23

You can use the Lens Effects Focus dialog box to blur an image.

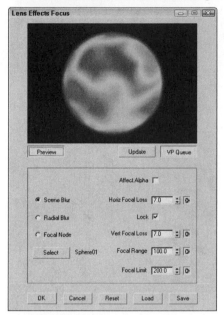

FIGURE 49.24

Use the Lens Effects Glow dialog box to make objects and scenes glow.

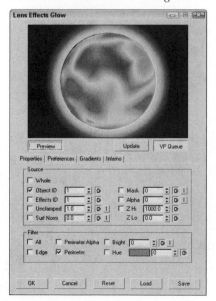

Adding highlights

The Lens Effects Highlight dialog box, shown in Figure 49.25, includes the same Properties, Preferences, and Gradient tabbed panels as the Glow dialog box, except that the effects it produces are highlights instead of glows. The Geometry tabbed panel includes options for setting the Size and Angle of the highlights and how they rotate away from the highlighted object.

Use the Lens Effects Highlight dialog box to add highlights to scene objects.

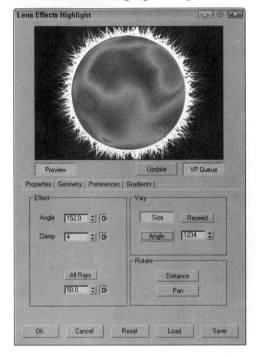

Tutorial: Making a halo shine

When it comes to glowing objects, I think of radioactive materials, celestial objects like comets and meteors, and heavenly objects like angels. In this tutorial, I'm leaning toward heaven in an attempt to create some glory. But because I couldn't locate an angel, you'll use a simple halo.

To add highlights to a halo using the Video Post interface, follow these steps:

1. Open the Glowing halo.max file from the Chap 49 directory on the CD.

   This file contains a head model and a halo. The halo object has been set to the G-Buffer Object Channel of 1 in its Object Properties dialog box.

2. Choose Rendering ⇨ Video Post to open the Video Post interface. Click the Add Scene Event button on the toolbar.

   The Add Scene Event dialog box appears.

3. Type a name for the event in the Label text field, and click OK.

   The event is added to the Queue pane.

4. Select the halo object in the viewport and click the Add Image Filter Event button on the toolbar (or press Ctrl+F) to open the associated dialog box. Select Lens Effects Highlight from the drop-down list, and click the Setup button.

   The Lens Effects Highlight dialog box appears.

5. Click the VP Queue button followed by the Preview button to see the rendered scene. In the Properties tabbed panel, select the Object ID option and set the Object ID to **1** to match the G-Buffer channel for the halo object. In the Filter section, enable the All option. In the Preferences tabbed panel, set the Size to **3.0**, Points to **4**, the Color option to **Pixel**, and Intensity to **100**. Then click OK.

6. Click the Execute Sequence button on the toolbar (or press Ctrl+R), and then click Render in the Execute Video Post dialog box.

Figure 49.26 shows the completed halo in all its shining glory.

FIGURE 49.26

Using the Lens Effects Highlight dialog box, you can add shining highlights to objects like this halo.

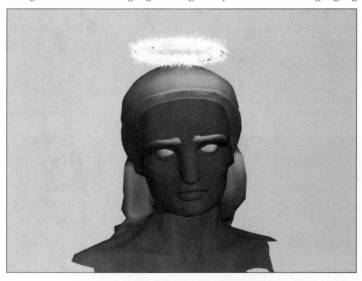

Adding backgrounds and filters using Video Post

As an example of the Video Post interface in action, you'll composite a background image of a waterfall with a rendered scene of an airplane model created by Viewpoint Datalabs. You'll then add some filter effects.

To composite an image with the Video Post interface, follow these steps:

1. Open the Airplane over waterfall.max file from the Chap 49 directory on the CD.

   This file includes an airplane model. The directory also includes an image called waterfall.tif that is used later.

2. Open the Video Post interface by choosing Rendering ⇨ Video Post.

3. Add a background image to the queue by clicking the Add Image Input Event button (or press Ctrl+I). Click the Files button. Locate the waterfall.tif image from the Chap 49 directory on the CD, and click Open. Then click OK again to exit the Add Image Input Event dialog box.

4. Next add the rendered image by clicking the Add Scene Event button and selecting the Perspective view. Name the event **rendered airplane**. Click the Render Setup button to open the Render Setup dialog box and select the Renderer panel. Disable the Anti-Aliasing option in the MAX Default Scanline Renderer rollout in the Renderer panel, and click OK. Click OK again to exit the Edit Scene Event dialog box.

5. Select both the background (waterfall.tif) and rendered airplane (Perspective) events, and click the Add Image Layer Event button (or press Ctrl+L). Select the Alpha Compositor option, and click OK.

   This composites the background image and the rendered image together by removing all the green background from the rendered scene.

6. To run the processing, click the Execute Sequence button on the toolbar (or press Ctrl+R) to open the Execute Video Post interface, select the Single output range option, click the 640 × 480 size button, and click Render.

Figure 49.27 shows the final composited image.

FIGURE 49.27

The airplane in this image is rendered, and the background is composited.

Summary

Post-production is an important, often overlooked, part of the production pipeline. Using compositing packages, as simple as Photoshop and Premiere or as advanced as Composite and After Effects, enables you to make necessary edits after rendering.

Max's render elements enable you to pick apart the rendering details of your scene. Rendering using render elements allows you to have more control over individual scene elements in the compositing tool.

Using the Video Post interface, you can composite several images, filters, and effects together. All these compositing elements are listed as events in a queue. The Video Post interface provides, along with the Render Scene dialog box, another way to create output. In this chapter, you learned about the following:

- The post-production process
- How Photoshop can be used to composite images
- How Premiere and After Effects can be used to composite animations
- The Composite interface
- How to use render elements
- The Video Post interface
- How to work with sequences
- The various filter types
- How to add and edit events and manipulate their ranges
- The Lens Effects filters

This concludes the Advanced Lighting and Rendering part of the book. The next part, "Extending Max," presents ways to extend the functionality of Max using plug-ins and by customizing the interface. You'll have the means to extend the software even further so the party never ends.

What's New with 3ds Max 2012

With each revision of Max, I'm always amazed at the new features that are included. Max is a large and complex piece of software, and just when I think it can't hold anything more, a new revision with a host of new features appears. Max 2012 is no different.

You can find in-depth coverage of the new features in the various chapters, but this appendix provides a quick overview of these new features, along with references on where to learn more about them. Throughout the book, the New Feature icon identifies the features that are new to 3ds Max 2012.

Note

If Max needs some improvements that haven't made it into the latest release, you can join Autodesk's Customer Involvement Program using the Help⇨Customer Involvement Program menu command. This program lets you provide feedback and suggestions to the Max team. ∎

Major Improvements

3ds Max 2012 includes lots of new improvements. Some are considered major because they likely will affect every user's workflow, and others are minor because they are smaller in scale. However, an improvement listed as minor may be the one you've been waiting for.

Note

Within the Introduction section of the Max Help file is a What's New in 3ds Max 2012 page. You also can access the What's New link in the Help menu. ∎

Nitrous viewports

The way that the viewports are rendered has been completely overhauled in this latest version of Max. The new rendering method is called Nitrous, and it has several improvements that make the viewports redraw faster and with better quality. This requires fewer test renders, which helps you get to the final results more quickly. Nitrous takes advantage of the latest advances in GPU-based video cards. It also threads each viewport separately, so it is even faster on multi-core and multi-processor computers.

These improvements allow more details to be displayed in the viewports, including soft shadows, ambient occlusion, and transparency. More on the Nitrous viewport features is covered in Chapter 2, "Controlling and Configuring the Viewports."

Non-photorealistic rendering

Another benefit of Nitrous is the ability to render the viewports or the final render using a non-photorealistic render style. The available options include pencil, acrylic, ink, colored pencil, colored ink, graphite, pastel, and technical drawing. These various render styles are covered in more detail in Chapter 24, "Rendering Non-Photorealistic Effects."

New Graphite Modeling tools

The Graphite Modeling tools found in Max have several new tools, including the Conform Brush. This new brush lets you sculpt polygons to conform to an underlying object by moving, rotating, scaling, and relaxing vertices. Other new tools include Shift Rotate, Shift Scale, and Constrain to Spline. You can learn more about these new tools and other improvements to the Graphite Modeling tools in Chapter 14, "Using the Graphite Modeling Tools and Painting with Objects."

Substance procedural textures

Max's Material Editor now includes a new library of procedural textures. These textures, called Substance textures, were developed by Allegorithmic, and they provide detailed textures created using procedural code rather than a bitmap. The Substance textures are created using a file that is many times smaller than comparable bitmaps, and they can easily be randomized to add variety to your scene. The available Substance textures are presented in Chapter 31, "Working with Procedural Substance Textures."

Improved UVW Editor interface

The UV Editor interface has been completely redesigned. The new interface is streamlined and includes many icons for accomplishing things that were only in the menus previously. The new interface also includes a new set of Peel tools for unwrapping and several new grouping tools for working UV clusters. You can learn all the new UV editor secrets in Chapter 33, "Unwrapping UVs and Mapping Textures."

Improved F-Curve Editor

Max's new F-Curve Editor is the same editor used in Maya, Softimage, and MotionBuilder. The improvements have taken the best features from each product and made those features common to all programs. The new editor offers better control over curves and the ability to work with multiple points at a time. The improved F-Curve editor is presented in Chapter 37, "Working with the F-Curve Editor in the Track View."

MassFX physics

The new MassFX tools in Max provide rigid-body dynamics directly within the viewport. The system is based on NVIDIA's PhysX engine, and it lets you quickly define solid rigid-body objects along with several different types of constraints. The system also can be used to quickly populate a scene, such as an avalanche of rocks. MassFX is covered in Chapter 43, "Simulating Physics-Based Motion with MassFX."

iray renderer

Rendering with mental ray can create amazing details, but with so many different settings, it can be a long game of trial and error to get the results you want. The iray rendering engine removes the guesswork. It progressively renders the scene, and you can stop it whenever the results get close to what you want. The iray renderer is covered in Chapter 47, "Rendering with mental ray and iray."

Minor Improvements

In addition to the major improvements, many minor improvements make working with objects, materials, and other facets of Max easier. Minor improvements found in version 2012 include the following:

- **Darker default theme:** Max has adopted as default the darker interface theme, which is easier on your eyes in low light.
- **Online help files:** The Max help files are opened in a web browser loaded from Autodesk. com when accessed using the Help menu. This ensures the latest and most up-to-date version of the help files.
- **Faster start-up time:** Max 2012 starts up more quickly and requires less memory than previous versions. This is accomplished by loading only the tools needed.
- **mental ray 3.9:** Max 2012 includes the latest version of mental ray 3.9.
- **Undo feature in Slate Material Editor:** The Slate Material Editor now allows undo and redo commands.
- **Vector displacement maps:** Vector displacement maps exported from Mudbox are now supported within Max.
- **Screen Clone feature:** The Viewport Canvas has a new feature that lets you clone an image from anywhere on the computer screen, including Photoshop if it is open.
- **ProOptimizer improvements:** The ProOptimizer modifier has been improved to yield better, faster results. You also can interpolate the optimized mesh by UVs and normals.
- **Single-step transfer to other Autodesk products:** Max's File menu includes a Send To option for sending the current scene to Softimage, Mudbox, or MotionBuilder automatically.
- **Support for WIRE files:** 3ds Max 2012 allows WIRE files from Autodesk Alias Design to be imported into Max as Body objects.

What's on the CD-ROM

T hroughout this book, you'll find many tutorials that help you understand the principles being discussed. All the example files used to create these tutorials are included on the CD that comes with this book.
In addition to these files, you'll find sample 3D models and an electronic version of the book.

This appendix provides you with information on the contents of the CD. For
the latest and greatest information, please refer to the Readme file located at
the root of the CD.

System Requirements

Make sure that your computer meets the minimum system requirements
listed in this section. If your computer doesn't match up to most of these
requirements, you may have a problem using the contents of the CD.

**For Windows 7 (recommended), Windows Vista, Windows XP
Professional SP2, or Windows XP Home Edition SP2:**

- Intel® Pentium® III or AMD® processor, 500 MHz or higher
  (dual Intel)
- Xeon® or dual AMD Athlon® or Opteron® (32-bit system
  recommended)
- 512MB RAM (1GB recommended)
- 500MB swap space (2GB recommended)
- Graphics card supporting 1024 × 768 × 16-bit color with 64MB
  RAM (OpenGL® and Direct3D® hardware acceleration supported;
  3D graphics accelerator 1280 × 1024 × 32-bit color with 256MB
  RAM recommended)

- Microsoft® Windows®–compliant pointing device (optimized for Microsoft IntelliMouse®)
- Microsoft Internet Explorer 6
- A CD drive

Using the CD with Windows

To install the items from the CD to your hard drive, follow these steps:

1. Insert the CD into your computer's CD drive. The license agreement appears.

Note

The interface won't launch if you have autorun disabled. In that case, click Start⇨ Run. In the dialog box that appears, type D:\start.exe. (Replace D with the proper letter if your CD drive uses a different letter. If you don't know the letter, see how your CD drive is listed under My Computer.) Click OK. ■

2. Read through the license agreement, and then click the Accept button if you want to use the CD. After you click Accept, the License Agreement window won't appear again.

    The CD interface appears. The interface allows you to install the programs and run the demos with just a click of a button (or two).

What's on the CD

The following sections provide a summary of the software and other materials you'll find on the CD.

Note

Some of the files provided on the CD are in zip compressed format. To work with these files you need an unzipping utility such as WinZip (www.winzip.com). ■

Author-created materials

The example files used in the tutorials throughout the book are included in the "Chapter Example Files" directory. Within this directory are separate subdirectories for each chapter. Supplemental files such as models and images are also included in these directories. Animated scenes include a rendered AVI file of the animation. For each tutorial, the resulting example after all steps are completed has the word "final" in the filename. Using these final examples, you can compare the results to your own work.

Applications

The following applications are on the CD:

- **Adobe Reader:** A freeware application for viewing files in the Adobe Portable Document Format

Shareware programs are fully functional, free, trial versions of copyrighted programs. If you like particular programs, register with their authors for a nominal fee and receive licenses, enhanced versions, and technical support.

Freeware programs are free, copyrighted games, applications, and utilities. You can copy them to as many PCs as you like—for free—but they offer no technical support.

GNU software is governed by its own license, which is included inside the folder of the GNU software. There are no restrictions on distribution of GNU software. See the GNU license at the root of the CD for more details.

Trial, demo, or *evaluation* versions of software are usually limited either in terms of the time you can use them or the functionality they offer (such as not letting you save a project after you create it).

3D models

Viewpoint Datalabs and Zygote Media have provided sample 3D models. Many of these models were used in the tutorials, and you can find the complete set of models in the "3D Models" directory.

Troubleshooting

If you have difficulty installing or using any of the materials on the companion CD, try the following solutions:

- **Turn off any anti-virus software that you may have running.** Installers sometimes mimic virus activity and can make your computer incorrectly believe that it is being infected by a virus. (Be sure to turn the anti-virus software back on later.)
- **Close all running programs.** The more programs you're running, the less memory is available to other programs. Installers also typically update files and programs; if you keep other programs running, installation may not work properly.
- **See the ReadMe file.** Please refer to the ReadMe file located at the root of the CD for the latest product information at the time of publication.

Customer Care

If you still have trouble with the CD, please call the Wiley Product Technical Support telephone number: (800) 762-2974. Outside the United States, call 1 (317) 572-3994. You can also contact Wiley Product Technical Support at `http://support.wiley.com`. John Wiley & Sons will provide technical support only for installation and other general quality control items. For technical support on the applications themselves, consult the program's vendor or author.

To place additional orders or to request information about other Wiley products, please call (800) 225-5945.

Index

Symbols and Numerics

Index

Index

B

Index

Index

Index

Index

H

Index

Index

Index

Index

Index

Index

Index

Index

Index

Index

Index

John Wiley & Sons, Inc.
End-User License Agreement

READ THIS. You should carefully read these terms and conditions before opening the software packet(s) included with this book "Book". This is a license agreement "Agreement" between you and John Wiley & Sons, Inc. "Wiley". By opening the accompanying software packet(s), you acknowledge that you have read and accept the following terms and conditions. If you do not agree and do not want to be bound by such terms and conditions, promptly return the Book and the unopened software packet(s) to the place you obtained them for a full refund.

1. **License Grant.** Wiley grants to you (either an individual or entity) a nonexclusive license to use one copy of the enclosed software program(s) (collectively, the "Software") solely for your own personal or business purposes on a single computer (whether a standard computer or a workstation component of a multi-user network). The Software is in use on a computer when it is loaded into temporary memory (RAM) or installed into permanent memory (hard disk, CD-ROM, or other storage device). Wiley reserves all rights not expressly granted herein.

2. **Ownership.** Wiley is the owner of all right, title, and interest, including copyright, in and to the compilation of the Software recorded on the disk(s) or CD-ROM "Software Media". Copyright to the individual programs recorded on the Software Media is owned by the author or other authorized copyright owner of each program. Ownership of the Software and all proprietary rights relating thereto remain with Wiley and its licensers.

3. **Restrictions On Use and Transfer.**

    (a) You may only (i) make one copy of the Software for backup or archival purposes, or (ii) transfer the Software to a single hard disk, provided that you keep the original for backup or archival purposes. You may not (i) rent or lease the Software, (ii) copy or reproduce the Software through a LAN or other network system or through any computer subscriber system or bulletin-board system, or (iii) modify, adapt, or create derivative works based on the Software.

    (b) You may not reverse engineer, decompile, or disassemble the Software. You may transfer the Software and user documentation on a permanent basis, provided that the transferee agrees to accept the terms and conditions of this Agreement and you retain no copies. If the Software is an update or has been updated, any transfer must include the most recent update and all prior versions.

4. **Restrictions on Use of Individual Programs.** You must follow the individual requirements and restrictions detailed for each individual program in the "What's on the CD-ROM" appendix of this Book. These limitations are also contained in the individual license agreements recorded on the Software Media. These limitations may include a requirement that after using the program for a specified period of time, the user must pay a registration fee or discontinue use. By opening the Software packet(s), you will be agreeing to abide by the licenses and restrictions for these individual programs that are detailed in the "What's on the CD-ROM" appendix and on the Software Media. None of the material on this Software Media or listed in this Book may ever be redistributed, in original or modified form, for commercial purposes.

5. **Limited Warranty.**

    (a) Wiley warrants that the Software and Software Media are free from defects in materials and workmanship under normal use for a period of sixty (60) days from the date of purchase of this Book. If Wiley receives notification within the warranty period of defects in materials or workmanship, Wiley will replace the defective Software Media.

(b) **WILEY AND THE AUTHOR OF THE BOOK DISCLAIM ALL OTHER WARRANTIES, EXPRESS OR IMPLIED, INCLUDING WITHOUT LIMITATION IMPLIED WARRANTIES OF MERCHANTABILITY AND FITNESS FOR A PARTICULAR PURPOSE, WITH RESPECT TO THE SOFTWARE, THE PROGRAMS, THE SOURCE CODE CONTAINED THEREIN, AND/OR THE TECHNIQUES DESCRIBED IN THIS BOOK. WILEY DOES NOT WARRANT THAT THE FUNCTIONS CONTAINED IN THE SOFTWARE WILL MEET YOUR REQUIREMENTS OR THAT THE OPERATION OF THE SOFTWARE WILL BE ERROR FREE.**

(c) This limited warranty gives you specific legal rights, and you may have other rights that vary from jurisdiction to jurisdiction.

6. **Remedies.**

(a) Wiley's entire liability and your exclusive remedy for defects in materials and workmanship shall be limited to replacement of the Software Media, which may be returned to Wiley with a copy of your receipt at the following address: Software Media Fulfillment Department, Attn.: *3ds Max 2012 Bible,* John Wiley & Sons, Inc., 10475 Crosspoint Blvd., Indianapolis, IN 46256, or call 1-877-762-2974. Please allow four to six weeks for delivery. This Limited Warranty is void if failure of the Software Media has resulted from accident, abuse, or misapplication. Any replacement Software Media will be warranted for the remainder of the original warranty period or thirty (30) days, whichever is longer.

(b) In no event shall Wiley or the author be liable for any damages whatsoever (including without limitation damages for loss of business profits, business interruption, loss of business information, or any other pecuniary loss) arising from the use of or inability to use the Book or the Software, even if Wiley has been advised of the possibility of such damages.

(c) Because some jurisdictions do not allow the exclusion or limitation of liability for consequential or incidental damages, the above limitation or exclusion may not apply to you.

7. **U.S. Government Restricted Rights.** Use, duplication, or disclosure of the Software for or on behalf of the United States of America, its agencies and/or instrumentalities "U.S. Government" is subject to restrictions as stated in paragraph (c)(1)(ii) of the Rights in Technical Data and Computer Software clause of DFARS 252.227-7013, or subparagraphs (c) (1) and (2) of the Commercial Computer Software - Restricted Rights clause at FAR 52.227-19, and in similar clauses in the NASA FAR supplement, as applicable.

8. **General.** This Agreement constitutes the entire understanding of the parties and revokes and supersedes all prior agreements, oral or written, between them and may not be modified or amended except in a writing signed by both parties hereto that specifically refers to this Agreement. This Agreement shall take precedence over any other documents that may be in conflict herewith. If any one or more provisions contained in this Agreement are held by any court or tribunal to be invalid, illegal, or otherwise unenforceable, each and every other provision shall remain in full force and effect.